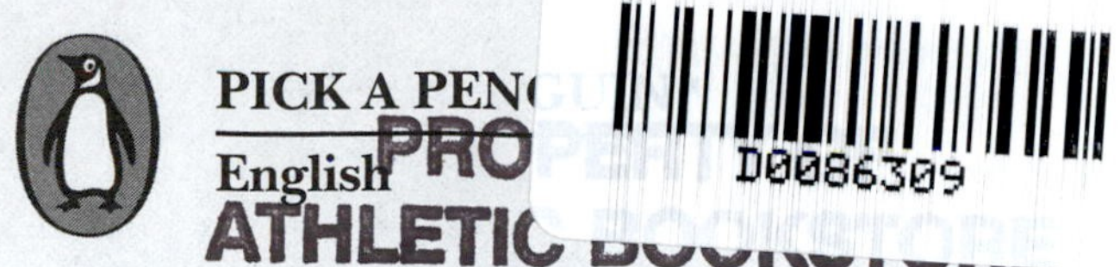

Package up to two of the following Penguin titles at no additional cost with this anthology:

- Nathaniel Hawthorne, *The Scarlet Letter*
- Frederick Douglass, *Narrative of the Life of Frederick Douglass*
- Edith Wharton, *Ethan Frome*
- Willa Cather, *My Antonia*
- Kate Chopin, *The Awakening*

We also offer select Penguin Putnam titles at a substantial discount to your students when you request a special package of one or more Penguin titles with this text. Among the many additional American Literature titles available from Penguin Putnam are:

- Stephen Crane, *The Red Badge of Courage*
- John Steinbeck, *The Grapes of Wrath*
- Toni Morrison, *The Bluest Eye*
- Paul Auster, *Leviathan*
- August Wilson, *The Piano Lesson*
- Lorraine Hansberry, *A Raisin in the Sun*
- Tennessee Williams, *A Streetcar Named Desire*
- Ken Kesey, *One Flew over the Cuckoo's Nest*
- Ralph Ketcham, *The Antifederalist Papers*

Don't see what you are looking for? No problem! We can still package many more Penguin titles at a discount. Just visit www.penguinputnam.com and contact your Prentice Hall sales representative with the author, title, and ISBN.

***For college adoptions only.**

www.prenhall.com/english

PICK A PENGUIN*

English

- Ralph Ellison, [illegible]

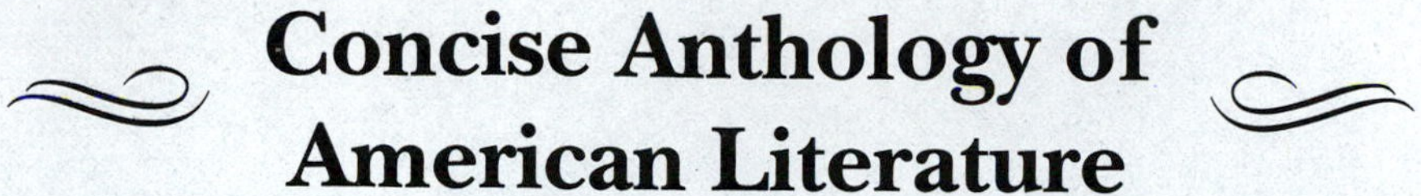

Concise Anthology of American Literature

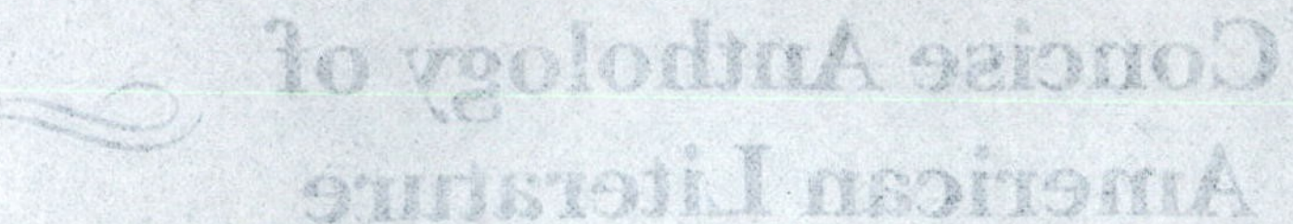

Concise Anthology of American Literature

Sixth Edition

George McMichael

California State University, Hayward

James S. Leonard

The Citadel

Upper Saddle River, New Jersey 07458

Library of Congress Cataloging-in-Publication Data

Concise anthology of American literature/[compiled by] George McMichael, James S. Leonard.—6th ed.

p. cm.

Includes bibliographical references and index.

ISBN 0-13-193792-8

1. American literature. 2. United States—Literary collections. I. McMichael, George L. II. Leonard, J. S. (James S.)

PS507.C56 2006

810.8—dc22

2005030019

Editorial Director: Leah Jewell
Acquisitions Editor: Vivian Garcia
Editorial Assistant: Christina Volpe
Director of Marketing: Brandy Dawson
Assistant Marketing Manager: Andrea Messineo
Marketing Assistant: Jennifer Lang
Prepress and Manufacturing Buyer: Christina Helder
Cover Art Director: Jayne Conte
Cover Design: Maureen Eide
Cover Art: Flag Quilt designed by Connie Kuntz, Dawn Denman, Julie Waldman, and Lisa Hacker using EQ5 software from The Electric Quilt Company, www.electricquilt.com
Composition/Full-Service Project Management: Kari Callaghan Mazzola and John P. Mazzola
Printer/Binder: Courier Companies, Inc.
Cover Printer: Phoenix Color Corp.

This book was set in 10/11 New Baskerville.

Grateful acknowledgment is made to the copyright holders on pages 2320–2326, which are hereby a continuation of this copyright page.

Pearson Education LTD.
Pearson Education Singapore, Pte. Ltd
Pearson Education, Canada, Ltd
Pearson Education–Japan
Pearson Education Australia PTY, Limited
Pearson Education North Asia Ltd
Pearson Educación de Mexico, S.A. de C.V.
Pearson Education Malaysia, Pte. Ltd
Pearson Education, Upper Saddle River, NJ

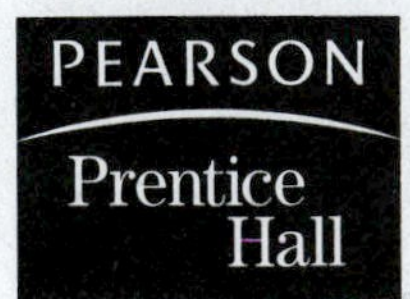

10 9 8 7 6 5 4 3
ISBN 0-13-193792-8

Contents

Preface

For more than three decades, students and instructors have complemented their introductory American literature studies with *Anthology of American Literature*. The McMichael anthology, in both its two-volume and concise editions, has secured its reputation with a solid core of writers and works, and it has now enhanced that reputation with four helpful supplements: the Pick-A-Penguin Program, the American Literature Database, the text specific Companion Website™, and the Research Navigator™ (each described below).

In preparing this sixth concise edition the editors have continued to follow the principles of selection that have made the previous concise editions so successful, and have:

- selected works primarily for their literary significance;
- represented authors with extended selections of their works;
- included various longer works in their entirety;
- provided clear, concise, and informative introductions and headnotes that are suited to student readers;
- explained unfamiliar terms and allusions with full footnotes and references;
- presented author bibliographies that are selective and current.

Authors and works in the anthology follow a generally chronological order. In selecting a text from among the various editions available, we have chosen, whenever possible, that edition most respected by modern scholars. The text reprinted is identified at the end of the headnote for each author. Spelling and punctuation are, in some instances, regularized and modernized to correct obvious errors and to suit the reader's convenience. An editorial excision of one paragraph is indicated by an ellipsis (. . .); excisions of a paragraph or more are indicated by a centered ellipsis, thus:

. . .

New to the Sixth Concise Edition

We have updated and revised the introductions to each period, and have added new selections from the works of the following authors previously included in the concise edition of *Anthology of American Literature*:

Sherwood Anderson
Willa Cather

Kate Chopin
Hart Crane
E. E. Cummings
Emily Dickinson
Theodore Dreiser
F. Scott Fitzgerald
Robert Frost
Ernest Hemingway
Zora Neale Hurston
W. S. Merwin
Joyce Carol Oates
Katherine Anne Porter
Wallace Stevens

And we have added the following authors new to the concise edition of *Anthology of American Literature*:

Ambrose Bierce
Judy Budnitz
Charles Waddell Chesnutt
W. E. B. Du Bois
Hannah Webster Foster
Charlotte Perkins Gilman
Tina Howe
Zora Neale Hurston
Harriet Ann Jacobs
June Jordan
Jack London
Frank Norris
Amy Tan
Jean Toomer
Alice Walker
Tennessee Williams

The *Concise Anthology of American Literature* also offers design features that make it easily accessible to students. The typeface for the headnotes and literary selections is easy to read. A chronological chart with a time-line offers students at-a-glance information about the lives of authors and their works, as well as key historical, political, technological, and cultural contexts.

A Complete American Literature Resource

The McMichael *Concise Anthology of American Literature* offers four helpful supplements to students and instructors of American literature courses:

Pick-a-Penguin Program

Prentice Hall is proud to announce an agreement with Penguin Putnam that allows us to package—at substantial discounts—the most popular American Literature trade paperbacks with the McMichael *Concise Anthology of American Literature.* Ask your Prentice Hall sales representative for details and for a listing of available American Literature titles.

American Literature Database

Now instructors can customize course material with the Pearson Custom Library of American Literature. A database featuring more than 1,700 literary works, the Pearson Custom Library of American Literature gives instructors the flexibility to choose other selections they might want to use along with the McMichael anthology. For details, visit <http://www.pearsoncustom.com/database/americanlit>, or contact your Prentice Hall sales representative.

American Literature Online

The expanded Companion Website™ at <www.prenhall.com/mcmichael> offers an interactive experience for students and instructors. Weblinks, interactive timelines, author profiles, essay questions, and general resources all make the McMichael Website an excellent resource for in-class discussions and out-of-class research.

Research Navigator™

Research Navigator™ is an ideal tool for instructors and students who need more resources for research. Available free for qualified adopters, Research Navigator™ offers coverage of the research writing process with three databases of source material, including EBSCO's *ContentSelect™*, *The New York Times* Search-by-Subject Archive, and a Literature Link Library. Take a tour on the Web at <http://www.researchnavigator.com>.

To obtain other supplements, including the Instructor's Manual, please contact your Prentice Hall sales representative.

Acknowledgments

We would like to thank the countless instructors, students, and editorial and production teams who have contributed their time and ideas to the sixth concise edition of *Anthology of American Literature*. Our special thanks are extended to J. Michael Duvall of Georgia State University, Linda Smoak Schwartz of Coastal Carolina University, Margaret Murphy of Monroe Community College, and Reginald Watson of East Carolina University.

We would also like to express our gratitude to the Prentice Hall publishing team—Leah Jewell, Vivian Garcia, Christina Volpe, and Ann Marie McCarthy—and to Kari Callaghan Mazzola of Big Sky Composition.

George McMichael
James S. Leonard

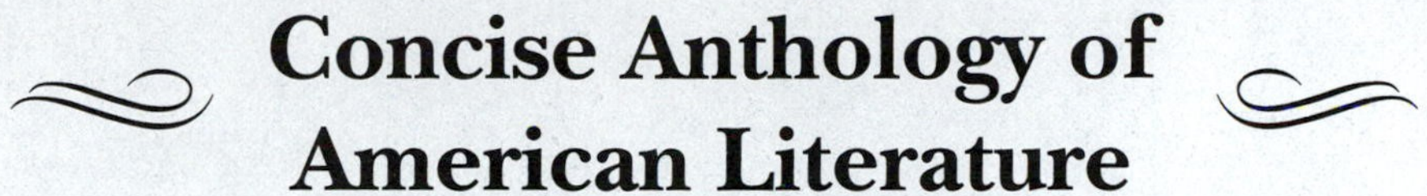

Concise Anthology of American Literature

The Literature of Colonial America

The United States of America grew out of religious controversy; out of the desire of monarchs to expand their empires; out of the human longing for land, adventure, and "glysteringe gold"; even out of nations' efforts to rid themselves of surplus populations: "valiant youths rusting and hurtful by lack of employment," as well as thieves, murderers, paupers, and runaways—the "scums of the land." The growth of colonial America into the United States is recorded in a literature that began as reports of exploration and colonization. European explorers, traders, and settlers wrote of their hopes, rare triumphs, and frequent disasters—and thereby created a literature that is large, various, and amazingly rich.

Early colonial writers did not think of themselves or their writings as American. English settlers in the New World did not regularly call themselves Americans until the 1760s, when they were well on their way to creating the national identity that finally emerged during the American Revolution. Before that time the colonists thought of themselves as Europeans. They worshiped as European Christians, built European houses, spoke European languages. Even when they came to identify themselves as Connecticut or Carolina men and women, they remained European in their ways of thought.

Frenchmen settled along the St. Lawrence River, Swedes along the Delaware, Dutch along the Hudson, Germans and Scotch-Irish in New York and Pennsylvania, and Spaniards in Florida. There were African Negroes in New England, the Middle Colonies, and throughout the South. And American Indians were everywhere. All contributed to the forming of the American civilization, but the colonies that became the first United States were for the most part English, sustained by English traditions, ruled by English laws, supported by English commerce, and named after English monarchs and English lands: Georgia, Carolina, Virginia, Maryland, New York, New Hampshire, New England.

Beyond the thin line of English settlement on the Atlantic Coast a vast wilderness stretched to the distant Pacific. The immensity of the new land exceeded the wildest dreams of the first explorers. North America alone was more than a hundred times the size of England, more than three times the size of all Europe. Deep in the interior of that American wilderness lived some 2 million American Indians and a few settlers from Spain and France. But they had little impact on the culture of the first English colonists on the Atlantic Coast.

The Indians of North America had widely differing cultures. They spoke a thousand different tongues, each so distinct that the speakers of one could not understand the speakers of another. And they had no written languages. As a result, the Indians lacked the kind of unified cultural tradition that could be readily absorbed by English-speaking men and women living in small, isolated colonies on the Atlantic Coast.

Nor did the culture of Spain and Spanish America have a strong influence on the early settlers of English North America. Spain had established an outpost in Florida, at St. Augustine, in 1565, the first permanent European settlement in lands that later became the United States. But Spanish civilization in North America was a dominating force only in distant Mexico and on the Pacific Coast—far from the English colonies in Virginia and New England.

French colonial power in the New World remained always feeble. As a result, the impact of French culture on the English colonists was slight. In all the boundless and remote colonies of French North America, settlers numbered no more than 80,000 by the middle of the eighteenth century; by that time the English colonies had a population of almost 2 million. Even as late as 1763, after more than a century and a half of French rule, no newspaper or book had ever been published in New France, but in that same period, more than 12,000 separate works had been published in the English colonies of North America.

The wilderness, the mountains, great distances, and great differences blocked cultural exchange. Not until the eighteenth and nineteenth centuries, when Americans made their great migration westward from the Atlantic Coast, did large numbers of English-speaking people come under the strong influence of other cultures on far-distant frontiers.

Exploration and Colonization

European expansion into the New World had begun with the Spanish Conquest of the lands they called "Las Indias." As a result of the Conquest, plundered wealth from the Americas—dazzling streams of gold, silver, and precious jewels—glutted Spain in the sixteenth century. Tales of looted Indian palaces, of vast silver mines, of the gleaming walls of golden cities fired the envy of other European nations, rousing them to colonizing efforts of their own. Yet the English moved slowly. England was small and poor, and the English government was beset by troubles at home—by rebellion and turmoil in Scotland, Wales, and Ireland. And neither English monarchs nor English nobles were willing to risk large sums in schemes for "Western Planting," projects for settling colonists in the English lands far across the Atlantic.

England's claim to North America had been established early. In 1497, King Henry VII of England sent John Cabot to discover "regions or provinces of the heathen and infidel, whatsoever they be." Cabot sought what Columbus had hoped to find, a sea route to the Orient and the "land of the Great Khan." Cabot discovered, instead, North America, and he claimed it for England and King Henry. But the English failed to exploit Cabot's discovery. For almost a century they made no attempts to colonize their "remote and heathen lands" in North America. Finally, Sir Walter Raleigh organized two English expeditions that sailed in 1584 and 1585 to Virginia, the land named in honor of Elizabeth, England's Virgin Queen. Raleigh's attempts to plant colonies in the New World were rashly planned and ill-organized, and they failed completely. Nevertheless, within a century, large numbers of Englishmen had poured into North America, and they established themselves so firmly along the Atlantic Coast that the culture of the first colonies that were to become the United States was solidly fixed as English.

The first permanent English settlement in North America was established at Jamestown, Virginia, in 1607. Among the members of the small band of Jamestown settlers was Captain John Smith, an English soldier of fortune. His reports of exploration and settlement, published in the early 1600s, have been described as the first distinctly American literature to be written in English. Smith filled his descriptions of America with themes, myths, images, scenes, characters, and events that were a foundation for the nation's literature. He portrayed English North America as a land of endless bounty, a land of nourishment and redemption. His vision of a new and abundant world helped lure to America the Pilgrims and the Puritans who saw themselves as people elected by God to flee from the Old World to a new Promised Land in the America that John Smith had described as a "Paradice."

Smith's stirring vision of America as a land of promise and opportunity is reflected in the works of writers of the Southern and Middle Colonies who followed him. Their great contribution to American literature came in the eighteenth century, in the Age of Reason and Revolution. Then appeared such literary aristocrats as William Byrd II and such political philosophers as Thomas Jefferson. Until that time, literature developed slowly, especially in the South. Towns were few, and farms were widely separated. The urban audience for books and newspapers was scant. And there was little of the spiritual ferment and zeal that caused a tide of religious literature to flow from Puritan New England.

Until the 1620s the settlement of New England had lagged behind that of colonies to the south. An attempt to plant settlers on the coast of Maine, in 1607, had failed because they were ill-supplied and unprepared for the bitter cold of a New England winter. Outposts for fishing and Indian trading had long existed on the Atlantic Coast, but they were temporary, operating only during the summer as depots for furs and fish awaiting shipment to Europe. No permanent colonies were planted in New England until the Pilgrim settlement of Plymouth (1620) and the Puritan "Great Migration" to the Massachusetts Bay Colony (1628–1643).

The Renaissance and Reformation

The Pilgrims of Plymouth and the Puritans of Massachusetts Bay were products of the Renaissance and Reformation. Few men or women understood such terms or realized they lived in times that one day would bear such lofty titles. Nonetheless, their lives had been transformed by the rebirth of classical learning in the Renaissance and by the Protestant separation from Roman Catholicism that took place during the Reformation.

The Renaissance, which began in Italy in the fourteenth and fifteen centuries, soon spread through western Europe, bringing the end of the Middle Ages and the beginning of modern civilization. With the Renaissance came advances in the arts, government, philosophy, and science—discoveries about the world, the universe, and man. The arts ceased to be primarily religious, concerned with the heavenly world. Artists and their patrons began to display a growing interest in earthly nature and in earthly man—and woman.

The most important music was now heard outside rather than inside the churches, and the great builders of the age now more frequently constructed palaces and town halls than cathedrals and monasteries. And just as philosophers began to emphasize the pagan Greek maxim "man is the measure of all things," so sculptors began to portray the human form larger than life, dominating its surroundings. Painters began to depict the human face and form more realistically. They painted fewer pictures of eternity, heaven, and angels—more pictures of the earth and the people on it. The art of biography grew beyond the mere recording of the lives of saints and martyrs. Drama and poetry flourished, and great literary figures emerged: Erasmus, Shakespeare, Cervantes.

The two greatest and most destructive technical achievements of the age—gunpowder and the printing press—rapidly spread "truth" and "heresy," Christianity and paganism. Cannons and books broke down castle walls and social barriers. Firearms destroyed the effectiveness of body armor and broke the military power of feudal knighthood. Books weakened the authority of kings and priests by giving men and women new power to form their own ideas and to defend them with learned arguments.

Thinkers and philosophers turned more and more from the religious concerns of the Middle Ages to the study of what was ancient and pagan, as well as what was modern and scientific. They speculated. They questioned. They argued with authorities and with tradition. After Copernicus published *On the Revolution of the Celestial Spheres* (1543), large numbers of educated people finally ceased to believe that the earth was the center of the universe. "Scientists" had yet to appear (the word *scientist* was not even coined until 1840), but the invention of scientific instruments such as the microscope (1590) and the telescope (1606) quickly inspired a new spirit of scientific enquiry.

New machinery, powered by waterwheels and windmills, ground and drilled, sawed wood and crushed ore. A sixteenth-century Englishman invented a knitting machine that was ten times faster than human hands. Ordinary men and women slowly began to escape from the ordeal of back-breaking and repetitious labor. Man now seemed better able to understand and control his environment, better able to shape his own life, even his destiny. Religion too underwent great changes. Renewed study of ancient Greek and Hebrew literature inspired a new and critical interest in the Bible and close scrutiny of its text. A new concern with humankind arose, an interest in the achievements of living men and women. The new Humanism and the critical spirit of the Renaissance in turn gave impetus to the Reformation, the religious revolution that dominated western Europe in the sixteenth century, bringing the rise of Protestantism and the end of medieval Christianity.

Since its beginning, movements to reform Christianity had risen often and succeeded seldom. But early in the sixteenth century religious reformers began new efforts to correct the flagrant abuses that had stained the medieval Christian Church. The reformers believed that the Church had departed fatally from the true path, that it had grown relaxed, worldly, and corrupt. Reformers protested against the authority of its spiritual leader, the pope, for whom they found no justification in the Bible. They protested against the power of its priests, many of whom they saw as ignorant and rank with corruption. Because of the reformers' relentless protests against church doctrines, their protests against the power of priests, their protests against the commands of bishops and popes, they came to be called Protestants.

The revolutionary changes that accompanied the Protestant Reformation struck all aspects of society. The unity of Christendom in western Europe was broken. The possibility of a single church, a single religion for all Christians, now seemed gone forever. Old religious and social patterns were changed permanently, utterly. New churches were established with new forms of worship. New political forces emerged. New social classes rose to power.

Puritans and Pilgrims

Among the new Protestant Christians were the Puritans and Pilgrims who came to North America. By law they were members of the Protestant Church of England, obliged to attend its services and obey its rules. Formed in 1534 by King Henry VIII, the Church of England had been established as a national church, controlled by Englishmen and free of the pope and Roman Catholicism. Henry had sought to create religious independence and religious unity in the lands he ruled. But his Church of England was torn by discord stirred up by radical reformers who continued the disputes that had originally marked the Reformation.

The Puritans and Pilgrims who settled in New England were extreme reformers. They believed that the Church of England's break from Rome had not gone far enough. They wanted to purify their English church still further, to purge from it any "Romishe taint" that yet remained. They yearned to break their religion free from what they believed were the encrusted errors of a thousand years. They hoped to restore church worship to the "pure and unspotted" condition of its earliest days, to recover what William Bradford described as Christianity's "primative order, libertie and bewtie."

Puritans and Pilgrims opposed the elaborate pageantry of the Church of England. They opposed church rituals that remained similar to those of Roman Catholicism. They objected to required forms of prayer, to the veneration of images and relics. They objected to the choirs, bells, and organ music that ornamented English church services; to the decorated vestments, "robes of Rome," that ornamented English priests. Puritans even objected to the crosses and stained-glass windows that ornamented English church buildings. Such "signs and daubs," they thought, only served to seduce the eye and entice the mind away from the preacher's sermon, away from the word of God.

And the English radicals objected not only to the doctrines and practices of their church, they also objected to its organization. The Church of England was controlled by the English monarch and a hierarchy of priests and bishops. That organization, the Puritans and Pilgrims believed, had no sanction in the Bible. It served only to rob the people of their right to practice their "true" religion. Angered by "corrupt" priests forced on them by distant authorities, congregations of English reformers drew up public lists of the most notorious: "ale house haunters" who "diced and danced"; "Dumme Doggs" too ignorant to preach; "Destroying Drones" fit only to mumble set prayers taken from a book; "dunghill knaves" who played at cards; a "Rousey, Ragged Rabblement of Rakehells" who fathered bastard children and would not repent. All such things the reformers saw as signs of corruption at the heart of their English Church, signs of its departure from the commands of the Bible.

The Pilgrims and Puritans were "People of the Book." They believed that the Bible, all of it, was the revealed word of God. Therefore the Bible, not kings, not popes, not bishops, should rule the lives of men and women. Devout Pilgrims and Puritans of every social class read and reread the Bible. They argued about its meaning, used it as a guide to religion, civil government, business and commerce. The Bible showed them how to live and how to die. It gave them rules for courtship, marriage, and warfare. It told them what to do at births, how to cure the sick, how to curse the wicked, how to bury the dead. It even furnished rules for dress and table etiquette.

Their Bible was the Geneva Bible, the work of English scholars who lived in Geneva, Switzerland, the center of Protestant learning and theology in Europe. First published in 1560, the Geneva Bible was the most widely read and the most accurate English translation of its time. And it became the Bible of English-speaking Protestants throughout Europe and the colonies of the New World.

The Geneva Bible came to America with the Pilgrims, who established themselves at Plymouth in New England in 1620. That small band of religious dissenters had fled first from their homes in England to Holland in 1608. They had wanted to break completely away from the Church of England, to end all ties with a church they believed to be fatally mired in "Romanism" and corrupt beyond redemption. Their fervid desire to separate entirely from "that masse of old and stinkinge workes," their English church, brought them the name "Separatists." And their pious refusal to bend to the will of their English king and the laws of his English church stirred the religious and civil persecution that finally drove them from their English homeland.

Holland had long been a haven for religious refugees, and when the English Separatists arrived, the Dutch welcomed them as devout and hardworking people. But the Separatists soon grew dissatisfied with their life in "Dutch exile." Sinking in poverty, fearing they would lose their identity and be swallowed up in the dominant Dutch culture, they decided to leave Holland on a pilgrimage to America.

When the Separatists—who now thought of themselves as "Pilgrims"—came to the New World, they were sorely tested. The colony they established at Plymouth was small and weak. Half of the original 102 settlers died of starvation and sickness in the first year. Their leaders were largely uneducated and unfamiliar with the harsh life of a wilderness frontier. The winters were unexpectedly cold. Food was scarce: the colonists knew little of growing crops in America; they brought no draft animals, had no plows, and their farmland was poor—covered with thin and rocky soil. Because they lacked experience with firearms, they were inept as hunters. Of fishing they knew even less: in their first month they caught only one cod although the sea around Cape Cod teemed with them.

Plymouth failed to become a profitable seaport for shipping and traders: its harbor was too shallow for large, seagoing vessels, and no river gave easy access into the interior and the lucrative Indian trade. But most important, the Pilgrims' deliberate separation from the English church and government deprived them of spiritual and financial help from their English homeland. As a result, the Plymouth Colony, although it was the oldest, remained one of the poorest of the New England colonies. And finally, in 1691, it was absorbed by the large and prosperous Massachusetts Bay Colony that had been established at Boston, some thirty-five miles to the north.

Like the Separatists at Plymouth, the Massachusetts Bay Puritans believed that the Church of England retained too many Roman Catholic creeds and rituals, that English priests and bishops had too much authority and too little respect for the teachings of the Bible. And like the Separatists at Plymouth, the Puritans came to New England to establish a colony based on Bible law. But unlike the Separatists, the Puritans of Massachusetts Bay believed that the English Church was not wholly beyond reform. They believed that it could be purified of its errors, and thus, when they migrated to the New World, the Puritans came not as Separatists but as official members of the Church of England.

Religion was the primary but not the sole concern of the Puritans. They were a worldly people. They did not practice a cloistered devotion, a pious withdrawal from human society and its sins. Instead, they made a conscious effort to apply God's rules in the everyday world. They wanted to bring religion out of the church and the monastery and into life on the farm and in the town. Nor were their lives devoid of worldly pleasures. They wore gaily-colored clothes. They heartily enjoyed games, celebrations, and feasts with "strong waters." And even though they were isolated colonists living in a wilderness, they had a surpassing esthetic sense that still shines forth in their architecture.

Yet their strict piety and their literal application of the Bible to all aspects of life won them the reputation of being gloomy and solemn, indifferent to beauty and fun, devoted only to rabid dissent and militant zeal. Their enemies said they hated joy, that they were "drunk on religion" and "intoxicated with God." Because of their ceaseless efforts to "purify" the English Church, to purge it of each "taint and relic" of corruption, they earned the name "Puritans." And for their attacks on the church hierarchy, at whose head stood their king, they suffered the royal hatred and government persecution that drove them to seek a haven, a New Jerusalem, on the barren coast of New England.

The religious doctrines of the Puritans and Separatists had been strongly shaped by the teachings of two great religious leaders, the "precious, shining lights" of the Reformation: Martin Luther (1483–1546), a German monk who was a professor of theology at the University of Wittenberg; and John Calvin (1509–1564), a French theologian who lived and taught at Geneva, Switzerland. Luther and Calvin asserted that all men have the right and the obligation to read and study the Bible, for it alone is the word of God. Luther's doctrine of the "priesthood of all believers" argued that priests should not be considered a privileged class, separate and more holy than ordinary men and women. All true believers are equally endowed with grace. And although ministers should be men great in learning, men who can teach the true meaning of the Scriptures, they are no more divine than any other devout man or woman.

From Calvin's great work, *The Institutes of the Christian Religion* (1536–1559), the New England colonists derived their basic theological doctrines: of *total depravity*, that the disobedience of Adam and Eve, the original sin, had stained all mankind, even unborn generations, leaving them "corrupt and prone to evil"; of *limited atonement*, that Jesus' sacrifice had earned God's forgiveness, or grace, but only for a limited few, the elect; of *irresistible grace*, that salvation is given only by God, that it can not be earned by even the most pious believer, nor can it be spurned by the vilest sinner; of *perseverance of the saints*, that those chosen by God will remain in a state of grace, among the elect, to the end of their lives, when they will be taken to heaven; and of *predestination,* that God at the beginning of time had predestined all events and had chosen all to be saved in heaven, all to be lost in hell.

To modern eyes, such doctrines may seem harsh, even cruel. And John Calvin has been described as a man whose intellect was locked in ice while his heart burned with vindictive fires. Yet, his teachings were received with joy and comfort by the English Puritans and Separatists. John Cotton, the famous New England preacher, recorded that before going to bed at night he would customarily "sweeten his mouth with a bit of Calvin," for Calvinism, although stern and unrelenting in its logic, was nonetheless heartening and optimistic to its believers.

Calvinism affirmed that the universe is controlled by neither satanic evil nor absurd chance. The universe, however it might seem to mortals, is stable and divinely just, for it is controlled wholly by God. All things originate with God. He is everywhere. He causes every birth, every death, bountiful harvests, storms at sea, the falling of a single leaf, the movement of the smallest mote of dust. The entire universe and all events within it testify to God's existence and His power. All is for the best, all is just, and all men and women, rich or poor, are equal in God's sight. Special privileges that could be bought by the rich, the pardons and indulgences sold to give remission of sins and to ensure salvation, are worthless, for God alone can forgive the sins of man. Even kings, with all their power and wealth, have no greater chance for heaven than the most miserable pauper—indeed, the worldly lust of kings for pomp and glory suggests that they have less chance than those who are simple paupers but true believers.

God's Chosen People

In the rigor of its beliefs and in the tenacity of its believers, Puritanism was akin to Judaism. The idea of that kinship was wonderfully appealing to devout New Englanders. It helped confirm their conviction that they, like the Israelites in the Old Testament, were a chosen people, a people specially favored by God. That self-exalting belief the New Englanders justified, in part, by finding strong likenesses between the Israelites and themselves. Like the Old Testament Jews, the New World Puritans were certain that they worshiped the one true God; like the Jews, the Puritans had fled from oppression and had suffered for their religious ideals. And just as Moses had led the Israelites from slavery in Egypt, Puritan leaders had brought their followers out of bondage in the Old World. Therefore the journey to the New World was not just a migration. It was a new Exodus, ordained by God and foretold in the Bible, just as the Bible promised the creation of a New Jerusalem, in America. There, surely, God's people would be delivered from evil; there, at long last, God's will would be done on earth, as it is in heaven.

Central to a belief that they were a special people was the New Englander's "covenant theology." Like many pious Christians, they believed that when God created the earth and all creatures, He made an agreement, a covenant, with Adam. That first agreement was a Covenant of Works. It provided that Adam would enjoy eternal life in the Garden of Eden. In return,

Adam was to be obedient, to do "good works." When Adam disobeyed, when he committed that original sin, he broke the Covenant of Works. And for that most terrible act, Adam was cast out of Eden and condemned, with all his descendants, to live first in a world of labor and misery and then to suffer death and eternal damnation in hell.

Pilgrims and Puritans literally believed that all humankind was stained by Adam's fall and drenched in sin. They rhymed it for their children's schoolbooks:

In Adam's fall,
We sinned all.

But they also believed that after condemning Adam and all his descendants, God had later relented. He had made another agreement, this time a Covenant of Grace with Abraham. Under that Covenant of Grace a special few, the "seed of Abraham," were chosen to escape eternal damnation and be taken to heaven. And the Puritans believed that they were among that special few, the elect, that they were, as Edward Taylor put it, "Encoached for heaven" with hearts "Enfired with holy flame!"

The certainty that they were a special people in covenant with God created great cohesion among Puritans and Separatists. As men and women "covenanted to cleave together in the service of God," they took a vital interest in each other's spiritual and public lives. And they found great strength in community, in what a later age would call "togetherness." Their solidarity was most evident at their religious services, where they joined together to listen to sermons. And they remained a close-knit people in their everyday lives. They worked and played together. They stood and voted together at town meetings. Families ate from a common bowl at meal tables, where they sat close together on benches—individual chairs did not become common until the eighteenth century. They even slept together, entire households in a single room—servants, masters, children—two, three, even four to a bed.

The Puritans' strong sense of unity and their religious ideas were not new. Christians had long emphasized their dependence upon one another, their duties to one another, just as they had long believed in the omnipotence of a single God and in His direct intervention in the lives of all humankind. The great Puritan achievement was not the creating of a new religion or a new way of life, for Puritans were not innovators but conservatives who wanted to return the church to its original forms, to its early simplicity. Instead, the Puritans' contributions to religion came from the example of their unrelenting quest for religious independence, from the strength of their faith, and from their devotion to preaching, to hearing the word of God expounded by their ministers.

Puritans set an example to the Christian world by their absolute dedication to their religion. They withstood persecution of all kinds: They suffered the seizure of their worldly goods; they underwent torture, burning, hanging, mutilation; and still they kept their faith—indeed, their suffering only made their faith stronger. In withstanding persecution, in rejecting the authority of popes, kings, and bishops, the Puritans fostered a tradition of independent congregations, of men and women free to choose their own ministers and set their own doctrines. And that Puritan dedication to self-determination helped establish the independence and freedom that Americans have long cherished as their greatest possessions. Puritans also established a strong tradition of preaching, a tradition whose abiding force is unmistakable in modern America, where sermonizing evangelists who can stir the generosity of audiences have taken revivalism out of the narrow world of canvas tents and sawdust floors and brought it into the vast and moneyed universe of television.

Preaching and Sermons

The importance of the sermon in early New England is still evident in New England's two greatest artistic achievements: its literature and its church architecture. Sermons were by far the most popular literary form of the time. Of all the books published in the entire history of colonial New England, nearly half dealt with religion, and most of those were collections of sermons. That dominating interest in sermons is also visible in the design of early churches—New Englanders called them "meetinghouses." They had no lengthy naves, no long aisles for grand religious processions. Neither were they decorated for ornate rituals that would capture the eye and fire the emotions.

New England meetinghouses were built as simple lecture halls. Their interiors were starkly plain. They had conspicuous pulpits closely surrounded by pews and benches for the congregations. The center of attention was not the altar but the pulpit, not the priest and his rituals but the preacher and his sermon. Pews and pulpits were placed so the preacher could be seen and heard. And where preachers could preach and congregations could hear the powerful word of God, what need was there for elaborate altars, or statues, or stained-glass windows? Such "artifacts of the devil" would only cloud the mind and block the light of God's truth.

Listening to sermons was considered an essential Christian act. Calvin had declared that "true preaching and reverent hearing of the gospel" were indispensable for a "true church." Devout Puritans believed that a sermon was "the chariot on which salvation came riding into the hearts of men." In no better way could the soul be prepared to receive grace and qualify for heaven. Therefore, ardent worshippers came to sermons at every opportunity, traveling from distant farms and villages, through storms and bitter weather, trudging for hours in "Holy Walking" to hear words that would make their souls "tender for God."

Ministers strove to rouse men and women from doubt and apathy and to "Shake Hell" with forceful preaching directed to the human intellect. As a result, their sermons were lengthy exercises in logic, more like legal documents than works of literary art. Ministers were advised not to "pinch" their congregations with scanty preaching, and the ministers complied. They seldom spoke for less than two hours. They preached regularly on Sunday and Thursday, and on all special occasions: at notable deaths and births, on election days and at army musters, when criminals were hanged, when crops failed, when storms rose and ships sank. Sermons were fundamental religious exercises and much more. In that day before newspapers and the electronic news media, sermons were a public forum, a source of news and informed opinion.

The Ideals of Literacy and Learning

Because they were devoted to sermons and to Bible study, the Massachusetts Bay colonists placed great emphasis on education. They wanted to maintain a learned clergy, and they wanted congregations that could understand both their preachers and their Bible. As a result, New England Puritans were remarkably bookish and literate, and the Massachusetts Bay Colony soon became the cultural center of the English colonies in the New World. The first college in English North America, Harvard, was founded at Cambridge in 1636. The first colonial press was established in 1638, also at Cambridge, where the first American book to be published in English was printed in 1640. The first colonial newspaper appeared in Boston in 1690. It lasted only one issue, but in 1704, the first continuing newspaper, *The Boston News-Letter*, appeared and marked the real beginning of journalism in the colonies.

The written expression of religious ideas became New England's great contribution to American literature. Sermons and numerous biographies of New England's worthies were created to serve as moral lessons, to encourage piety and holiness. Diaries emphasized the importance of the individual's spiritual health and the need for constant self-examination. Poems by poets as distinct as Anne Bradstreet and Edward Taylor were filled with expressions of devotion and faith. Even gory tales of Indian captivity, such as Mary Rowlandson's *Narrative*, were read as lessons that showed how true Christians could be delivered from red-skinned agents of satanic evil.

Religious ideas were expressed in a biblical style of writing. It was meant to be simple and useful, like New England churches scoured free of needless decoration. All "silken language" was to be shunned, as were long Greek and Latin quotations. Writing was to be as clear as fine glass, free of distortions, free of the "quiddities" and "quirkes" of dull scholars. Preachers were warned not to "shoot over the heads" of their congregations but to compose sermons with an "admirable plainesse" so that the minds and hearts of even the ignorant and the skeptical could be pierced by divine truth. Preachers who used "swelling words," who provided spiritual meals with "more sauce than meat," were rebuked for offering a mere "blubber-lipt ministry."

Devotion to the simple style is apparent in the stark lessons of the *New England Primer*. Plain and simple language brightens the ungarnished diaries of Puritan stalwarts such as John Winthrop and Samuel Sewall. The Pilgrim William Bradford declared that he would write the history of Plymouth Plantation in "a plain style, with singular regard unto the simple truth in all things." And the creators of the *Bay Psalm Book* defended their unpolished translation of the Psalms by announcing:

> If therefore the verses are not always so smooth and elegant as some may desire or expect, let them consider that God's altar needs not our polishings . . . for we have respected rather a plain translation than to smooth our verses with the sweetness of any paraphrase and so have attended conscience rather than elegance. . . .

To such Puritans, the human desire for rich, artistic embellishment found easy expression only privately—as in the metaphysical poetry of Edward Taylor—or publicly in complex theological disputes and in the death's heads, ornate symbols of human mortality, that they carved upon their gravestones.

The Decline of the Puritan Ideal

For all its lofty fervor and sense of divine mission, American Puritanism often showed the same intolerance its believers had fled England to escape. Puritan New England never developed the open-mindedness and lenient traditions found in colonies to the south. The modern age has come to see the actions of the Puritans as harsh and cruel—to the Native Americans whom they displaced and to fellow Christians who rejected their beliefs and suffered from their vengeance. But what the modern age sees as intolerance, the Puritans saw as a necessary defense against the intrusion of false belief and paganism. Puritans objected not so much to different religions as they did to the practice of different religions in their midst, in the New Jerusalem they had struggled so hard to build for themselves in New England. In warring against nonconformity and change, the Puritans struck at religious and social deviants of all kinds, at Anglicans, Roman Catholics, Baptists, and Quakers, at dancing masters and wigmakers, at whores, actors, profiteers, and radical democrats. But it was all to no avail. For change was unavoidable and came relentlessly.

Well before the end of the colonial period, the power and the unity of New England Puritanism had greatly declined. Puritanism had attacked the authority of kings and priests; it had shattered ancient laws and social traditions. Now Puritanism in turn was beset by dissenters who attacked its authority and upset its laws. Political radicals agitated successfully against the power of the Puritan upper class. New and divisive religious sects sprouted in the New England soil, and their members would not be silenced. New religious leaders spoke out against strict Calvinism in favor of a milder, a more congenial Christianity—evident in the writings of Roger Williams and John Woolman.

Besieged by change, the Puritan ministers of New England lost the political power they once had used so effectively. Dissension went unchecked. By 1700, only seventy years after the founding of the Massachusetts Bay Colony, the civil government ceased to require religious conformity from unwilling citizens; once-powerful church authorities could no longer force men and women to submit to church rules. Yet, Puritanism declined not only because its enemies grew strong but because its defenders grew weak and divided.

As the first generation of Puritan "saints" died off, their piety and faith died with them. Their children and grandchildren were not content to sacrifice everything to preserve old dreams of a Bible commonwealth, old faith in a divine mission. Preachers spoke out bitterly against the decline of religious fervor and the rise of vanity, disobedience, and false belief. They spoke against the wearing of luxurious clothes and elaborate wigs, against young fops who wore hats in church, against good-for-nothings who defied their betters, against the growing tendency of Christians to return to the pagan celebration of Christmas.

But preachers could no longer command from New Englanders a religious fidelity like that of the Puritan "First Comers." Religious and social unity steadily gave way to diversity. The American tradition of pluralism, of contending factions, rose as a tide, and Puritanism more and more came to resemble a small island sinking in a turbulent sea of change. Even the efforts of Jonathan Edwards, whose writings were the last great statement of the Puritan ideal in America, could not halt that change and regenerate the faith.

But if Puritanism waned as a religious and social force, it remained hard impressed on the American mind. Puritanism had spoken for the preeminence of the individual, for freedom from oppressive distant governments, and for the value of learning and education. It led Americans to examine their beliefs, their world, and each other. It gave ordinary men and women a sense of purpose. It encouraged them to scrutinize issues in religion and in government and to speak out. It helped to create in Americans a sense of duty to their God, their nation, and their fellow men and women. It taught them to labor to be good and to judge others by their lives, not their birth. At its height, Puritanism served as the dominant force in the creation of American literature. And even in its decline, the ideas of Puritanism profoundly shaped the way Americans thought, helping to bring the revolutionary glories of the American Enlightenment and the artistic triumphs of the Age of American Romanticism.

Christopher Columbus 1451–1506

Although he made his discoveries in the name of Ferdinand and Isabella, the Spanish king and queen, Christofero Columbo (his name in Italian) remained all his life a citizen of Genoa, Italy, where he was born and where he spent his early years. As a boy, Columbus worked as a weaver, his father's trade, but as he grew older, he followed the custom of other young men of Genoa and shipped out as a seaman on Mediterranean merchant ships. In his early twenties he went to Lisbon, Portugal, then the center of Atlantic merchant shipping and explorations by sea, where his brother had established himself as a maker of maps and nautical charts. Columbus worked briefly at mapmaking, and he sailed as a seaman on trading vessels to the Portuguese islands of the Azores and Madeira. He sailed north to England and perhaps as far west as Iceland. By the 1480s, when he was in his thirties, he had risen to the rank of captain in the merchant service of Portugal.

Like other seamen of his day, Columbus heard tales of lands to the west, far across the Atlantic, and, like the vast majority of educated people of the time, he believed the world was round and that by sailing west, ships could reach the Indies, the rich lands of the Orient. As Columbus grew skilled in seamanship and expert in navigation, he developed a burning determination to lead what he called an "enterprise of the Indies," an expedition of ships to sail west from the Atlantic coast of Europe to the Orient, to establish lucrative trading posts in China, Japan, and the Spice Islands.

Columbus first sought money for his "enterprise of the Indies" from the Portuguese king, but his proposals were rejected. He then went to Spain where, for eight years, he directed appeals and petitions to the Spanish monarchs and their advisers. Ferdinand and Isabella were eager to expand their empire and fill their treasury with riches gained from trade with the Indies, but a commission appointed by Queen Isabella to study Columbus's proposal recommended against him because it deemed the voyage impossible, the distance too far, the dangers too great, and because "God would never have allowed any uninhabited land of real value to be concealed from His people for so many centuries." Yet the king and queen did not completely reject Columbus's ideas. They awarded him a small pension that permitted him to remain in Spain, and they continued to listen to his theories and study his plans. Finally, in April 1492, when they learned that other monarchs were planning to send expeditions to the west in search of a new trade route to China, Ferdinand and Isabella granted Columbus the authority and the financial support to undertake his "enterprise of the Indies."

On August 3, 1492, he sailed from Palos, Spain with some ninety men and boys in a fleet of three small ships, the Santa Maria, the Niña, and the Pinta. Columbus first sailed to the Canary Islands, where he completed his preparations, and then he began his voyage into the unknown. Thirty-three days later, on October 12, 1492, he made his first landing in the New World, on a small Caribbean island that he named San Salvador. From there he continued westward, exploring other islands, including Cuba and Hispaniola. Columbus did not know that he had found a new world. He believed instead that he had landed on islands off the coast of China, a belief he retained throughout his life. When he returned to Spain he proclaimed that he had found rich lands of the exotic east, near Cathay (China) and Cipangu (Japan), lands that he had rightfully claimed for Spain in the name of Ferdinand and Isabella. He told of opportunities to extract gems and gold from the land and from the natives, whom he described as now in heathen darkness and ready for conversion to Christianity for the greater glory of Spain and its monarchs. For his achievements, Ferdinand and Isabella gave Columbus the title of Admiral of the

Ocean Sea and they appointed him Governor General of all lands that he had discovered or would discover in the future.

Columbus now had little trouble in getting funds for another voyage, and in 1493 he sailed a second time to the New World, with a fleet of seventeen ships and 1,500 settlers. In the next three years of colonizing and exploration, he established a permanent colony on Hispaniola, the first European settlement in the New World since the coming of the Northmen to North America centuries before. He made voyages of discovery to the Leeward Islands, Puerto Rico, and Jamaica, where he was shipwrecked and marooned for a year. He also made further explorations of Cuba, which he believed was a province of China and where he first saw people of the New World "drinking" tobacco smoke.

On his third voyage (1498–1500), Columbus discovered Trinidad, where he expected but failed to find "Chinese Mandarins." And on Sunday, August 5, 1498, he made his first landing on the continent of the New World, on the coast of present-day Venezuela, a land that seemed so marvelous that he named it "The Gardens." In his report of his third voyage, he described it as the place "in which I am assured in my heart that the earthly paradise is," the Garden of Eden of the Bible, where the Lord had placed the tree of life. But it was soon apparent that he had not found earthly paradise, nor was he successful in his efforts to establish and to regulate colonies. Although he was a great navigator, Columbus was inept as a colonial governor. Officials whom he appointed to office betrayed him through greed for gold. Under his rule, the Indians of Hispaniola and other islands were brutally exploited, beaten, murdered, their goods plundered, their homes destroyed—and the Indians responded with murderous fury, slaughtering the colonists, a grim sequence that would be reenacted again and again in the following centuries as Europeans settled on the lands of the New World. Riches were scarce, colonists' deaths were many, conversions of the natives to Christianity were few and lasted only briefly. What had begun as a great mercantile and colonizing enterprise was becoming a great mercantile and colonizing disaster.

Reports sent back to Spain by Columbus's detractors, and they were many, described him as vain, grasping, uncaring, incompetent. They complained of his mistreatment of the Europeans as well as the natives, pointing out that he had failed to put down insurrections, to subdue gangs of brigands with voracious and lethal appetites for plunder. Finally, in 1500, a royal official was sent from Spain to inquire into charges that Columbus had criminally misgoverned Hispaniola. After only a brief attempt to establish the facts, the royal official had Columbus arrested, placed in chains, and returned to Spain for trial.

When Columbus reached Spain, in October 1500, authorities promptly released him from his chains, but his reputation was badly stained by the failures of the colony of Hispaniola and by charges made against him. His undeviating self-assurance, his unwillingness to bend to the desires of others—the very qualities that had made him a great navigator and sea captain—had brought his downfall as a colonial leader. Columbus was stripped of his powers as governor, but he remained Admiral of the Ocean Sea. And he was outfitted for a fourth voyage, not to establish colonies but to find a passage through the islands he had discovered, to the mainland of China. In 1502 he left Spain, full of hope, on a voyage that was to last until 1505, but again he failed. His path was blocked by a continent of an enormity he could never grasp. When he returned from his fourth voyage he was fifty-three years old, an aged man by the standards of the day. Now, with his reputation in ruins, even his most loyal supporters abandoned him. He could gather neither the energy nor the popular support needed to organize another voyage. Two years later he died, disdained, neglected, still believing that he had sailed to the Indies, still unaware that he had brought a New World to the Old.

Columbus was not the first European to discover the continent of America. Vikings had reached the mainland of North America as early as the tenth century. Yet Viking settlement was only temporary, and the Vikings' achievement was preserved largely in fantasies, myths, and sagas. It was Columbus who united Europe and America. He was the greatest of navigators in the greatest age of navigators. No one in history had discovered so much territory unknown to Europeans and had so stirred their imaginations. Columbus laid the basis for Spanish land claims and for the spread of Spanish culture from the Caribbean and Florida across the Pacific to the Philippines. He changed forever the way the world saw itself. And in his reports he first confirmed the age-old dream that there was indeed an idyllic land of beauty and opportunity, a new land, the great hope of earth, that would, for more than 500 years, draw the people of the world to its shores.

FURTHER READING: W. Irving, *A History of the Life and Voyages of Christopher Columbus,* 4 vols., 1828; D. Sargent, *Christopher Columbus,* 1941; S. Morison, *Christopher Columbus, Mariner,* 1955; E. Bradford, *Christopher Columbus,* 1973; S. Morison, *The European Discovery of America,* 2 vols., 1971, 1974; *First Images of America,* 2 vols., ed. F. Chiappelli, 1976; T. Todorov, *The Conquest of America,* 1984; *In the Wake of Columbus,* ed. J. Parker and L. De Vorsey, 1985; J. Hart, *Columbus, Shakespeare, and the Interpretation of the New World,* 2003; T. Bowden, *The Enemies of Christopher Columbus,* 2003; G. Symcox and B. Sullivan, *Christopher Columbus and the Enterprise of the Indies,* 2005; M. Dugard, *The Last Voyage of Columbus,* 2005.

TEXTS: "Columbus's Letter Describing His First Voyage," is from *Select Documents Illustrating the Four Voyages of Columbus,* ed. C. Jane, 1930. Columbus's journal entries for October 11 and October 14, 1492, are from *The Diario of Christopher Columbus's First Voyage to America, 1492–1493,* trans. O. Dunn and J. Kelley, 1988.

COLUMBUS'S LETTER DESCRIBING HIS FIRST VOYAGE[1]

SIR,[2] As I know that you will be pleased at the great victory with which Our Lord has crowned my voyage, I write this to you, from which you will learn how in thirty-three days, I passed from the Canary Islands[3] to the Indies[4] with the fleet which the most illustrious king and queen, our sovereigns, gave to me. And there I found very many islands filled with people innumerable, and

[1]The earliest report by Columbus of his voyage to what he believed were the Indies. Printed first in Spanish then in Latin in 1493, the letter was soon translated into the major languages of Europe.

[2]First printed versions of Columbus's letter (the original has been lost) were addressed to either Raphael (Gabriel) Sanchez or to Luis de Santangel. Both men were officials in the court of Ferdinand and Isabella. Historians have speculated that Columbus sent the letter to Sanchez or to Santangel (or copies to both) in order to ensure its prompt and proper transmission to the king and queen.

[3]Columbus sailed from Spain first to the Canary Islands, where he completed preparations for his voyage.

[4]In Columbus's day the name "Indies" was used for lands east of India, including the Malay Peninsula, China, Japan, and Indonesia.

of them all I have taken possession for their highnesses, by proclamation made and with the royal standard unfurled, and no opposition was offered to me. To the first island which I found, I gave the name *San Salvador,*[5] in remembrance of the Divine Majesty, Who has marvellously bestowed all this; the Indians call it 'Guanahani'. To the second, I gave the name *Isla de Santa María de Concepción;* to the third, *Fernandina;* to the fourth, *Isabella;* to the fifth, *Isla Juana,*[6] and so to each one I gave a new name.

When I reached Juana, I followed its coast to the westward, and I found it to be so extensive that I thought that it must be the mainland, the province of Catayo.[7] And since there were neither towns nor villages on the seashore, but only small hamlets, with the people of which I could not have speech, because they all fled immediately, I went forward on the same course, thinking that I should not fail to find great cities and towns. And, at the end of many leagues,[8] seeing that there was no change and that the coast was bearing me northwards, which I wished to avoid, since winter was already beginning and I proposed to make from it to the south, and as moreover the wind was carrying me forward, I determined not to wait for a change in the weather and retraced my path as far as a certain harbour known to me. And from that point, I sent two men inland to learn if there were a king or great cities. They travelled three days' journey and found an infinity of small hamlets and people without number, but nothing of importance. For this reason, they returned.

I understood sufficiently from other Indians, whom I had already taken, that this land was nothing but an island. And therefore I followed its coast eastwards for one hundred and seven leagues to the point where it ended. And from that cape, I saw another island, distant eighteen leagues from the former, to the east, to which I at once gave the name "Española".[9] And I went there and followed its northern coast, as I had in the case of Juana, to the eastward for one hundred and eighty-eight great leagues in a straight line. This island and all the others are very fertile to a limitless degree, and this island is extremely so. In it there are many harbours on the coast of the sea, beyond comparison with others which I know in Christendom, and many rivers, good and large, which is marvellous. Its lands are high, and there are in it very many sierras and very lofty mountains, beyond comparison with the island of Teneriffe.[10] All are most beautiful, of a thousand shapes, and all are accessible and filled with trees of a thousand kinds and tall, and they seem to touch the sky. And I am told that they never lose their foliage, as I can understand, for I saw them as green and as lovely as they are in Spain in May, and some of them were flowering, some bearing fruit, and some in another stage, according to their nature. And the nightingale was singing[11] and other birds of a thousand kinds in the month of November there where I went. There are six or eight kinds of palm, which are a wonder

[5]Spanish: Holy Savior. Watlings Island in the Bahamas has traditionally been accepted as the island on which Columbus first landed, but the actual identity of the island is not known with certainty and remains a subject of historical dispute.

[6]Of the four islands named by Columbus, only Juana (Cuba) has been identified with certainty.

[7]Cathay (China). [8]Approximately $3\frac{1}{2}$ miles each.

[9]Now known as Hispaniola, the location of the Dominican Republic and Haiti.

[10]Largest of the Canary Islands.

[11]Columbus mistook a New World thrush for the European nightingale. Nightingales did not appear in the New World until they were imported by bird lovers, centuries later.

to behold on account of their beautiful variety, but so are the other trees and fruits and plants. In it are marvellous pine groves, and there are very large tracts of cultivatable lands, and there is honey, and there are birds of many kinds and fruits in great diversity. In the interior are mines of metals, and the population is without number.[12] Española is a marvel.

The sierras and mountains, the plains and arable lands and pastures, are so lovely and rich for planting and sowing, for breeding cattle of every kind, for building towns and villages. The harbours of the sea here are such as cannot be believed to exist unless they have been seen, and so with the rivers, many and great, and good waters, the majority of which contain gold.[13] In the trees and fruits and plants, there is a great difference from those of Juana. In this island, there are many spices and great mines of gold and of other metals.

The people of this island, and of all the other islands which I have found and of which I have information, all go naked, men and women, as their mothers bore them, although some women cover a single place with the leaf of a plant or with a net of cotton which they make for the purpose. They have no iron or steel or weapons, nor are they fitted to use them, not because they are not well built men and of handsome stature, but because they are very marvellously timorous. They have no other arms than weapons made of canes, cut in seeding time, to the ends of which they fix a small sharpened stick. And they do not dare to make use of these, for many times it has happened that I have sent ashore two or three men to some town to have speech, and countless people have come out to them, and as soon as they have seen my men approaching they have fled, even a father not waiting for his son. And this, not because ill has been done to anyone; on the contrary, at every point where I have been and have been able to have speech, I have given to them of all that I had, such as cloth and many other things, without receiving anything for it; but so they are, incurably timid. It is true that, after they have been reassured and have lost their fear, they are so guileless and so generous with all they possess, that no one would believe it who has not seen it. They never refuse anything which they possess, if it be asked of them; on the contrary, they invite anyone to share it, and display as much love as if they would give their hearts, and whether the thing be of value or whether it be of small price, at once with whatever trifle of whatever kind it may be that is given to them, with that they are content. I forbade that they should be given things so worthless as fragments of broken crockery and scraps of broken glass, and ends of straps, although when they were able to get them, they fancied that they possessed the best jewel in the world. So it was found that a sailor for a strap received gold to the weight of two and a half *castellanos,*[14] and others much more for other things which were worth much less. As for new *blancas,*[15] for them they would give everything which they had, although it might be two or three *castellanos'* weight of gold or an *arroba*[16] or two of spun cotton. They took even the pieces of the broken hoops of the wine barrels and, like savages, gave what they had, so that it seemed to me to be wrong and I forbade

[12]Earliest fifteenth-century estimates placed the population of Hispaniola at three or four million. The true number was probably less than 200,000.

[13]The first of many unsubstantiated conjectures made by Columbus and subsequent New World explorers about the abundance of gold.

[14]Small, fifteenth-century Spanish gold coin.

[15]Small, copper Spanish coins of low value.

[16]A roll of cloth weighing about 25 pounds.

it. And I gave a thousand handsome good things, which I had brought, in order that they might conceive affection, and more than that, might become Christians and be inclined to the love and service of their highnesses and of the whole Castilian[17] nation, and strive to aid us and to give us of the things which they have in abundance and which are necessary to us. And they do not know any creed and are not idolaters;[18] only they all believe that power and good are in the heavens, and they are very firmly convinced that I, with these ships and men, came from the heavens, and in this belief they everywhere received me, after they had overcome their fear. And this does not come because they are ignorant; on the contrary, they are of a very acute intelligence and are men who navigate all those seas, so that it is amazing how good an account they give of everything, but it is because they have never seen people clothed or ships of such a kind.

And as soon as I arrived in the Indies, in the first island which I found, I took by force some of them,[19] in order that they might learn and give me information of that which there is in those parts, and so it was that they soon understood us, and we them, either by speech or signs, and they have been very serviceable. I still take them with me, and they are always assured that I come from Heaven, for all the intercourse which they have had with me; and they were the first to announce this wherever I went, and the others went running from house to house and to the neighbouring towns, with loud cries of, 'Come! Come to see the people of Heaven!' So all, men and women alike, when their minds were set at rest concerning us, came, so that not one, great or small, remained behind, and all brought something to eat and drink, which they gave with extraordinary affection.

. . .

In conclusion, to speak only of that which has been accomplished on this voyage, which was so hasty, their highnesses can see that I will give them as much gold as they may need, if their highnesses will render me very slight assistance; moreover, spice and cotton, as much as their highnesses shall command; and mastic, as much as they shall order to be shipped and which, up to now, has been found only in Greece, in the island of Chios, and the Seignory[20] sells it for what it pleases; and aloe wood, as much as they shall order to be shipped, and slaves, as many as they shall order to be shipped and who will be from the idolaters.[21] And I believe that I have found rhubarb and cinamon, and I shall find a thousand other things of value, which the people whom I have left there will have discovered, for I have not delayed at any point, so far as the wind allowed me to sail, except in the town of Navidad,[22]

[17]Spanish. [18]Idol worshipers, thought by fifteenth-century Christians to be disciples of Satan.

[19]Historians have sometimes identified this as the first instance of the European enslavement of Indians. The practice was not unique to New World explorers, for it had long been customary for European discoverers to bring home trophies, among them living human beings, as evidence of their explorations.

[20]Italian officials in control of the trade in mastic (an aromatic resin from mastic trees) on the Greek island of Chios in the eastern Mediterranean.

[21]I.e., only those natives who failed to convert to Christianity would be enslaved.

[22]Villa de la Navidad (Spanish: Town of the Nativity), a fortified camp on the island of Hispaniola where Columbus left 21 men (during his first voyage) to trade with the Indians and explore for gold. When Columbus returned on his second voyage, he discovered that the natives had murdered all the Europeans and destroyed the camp.

in order to leave it secured and well established, and in truth, I should have done much more, if the ships had served me, as reason demanded.

This is enough . . . and the eternal God, our Lord, Who gives to all those who walk in His way triumph over things which appear to be impossible, and this was notably one; for, although men have talked or have written of these lands, all was conjectural, without suggestion of ocular evidence, but amounted only to this, that those who heard for the most part listened and judged it to be rather a fable than as having any vestige of truth. So that, since Our Redeemer has given this victory to our most illustrious king and queen, and to their renowned kingdoms, in so great a matter, for this all Christendom ought to feel delight and make great feasts and give solemn thanks to the Holy Trinity with many solemn prayers for the great exaltation which they shall have, in the turning of so many peoples to our holy faith, and afterwards for temporal benefits, for not only Spain but all Christians will have hence refreshment and gain.

. . .

1493 1493

from *THE DIARIO OF CHRISTOPHER COLUMBUS'S FIRST VOYAGE TO AMERICA*[1]

THURSDAY 11 OCTOBER 1492[2]

He steered west-southwest. They took much water aboard, more than they had taken in the whole voyage. They saw petrels[3] and a green bulrush near the ship. The men of the caravel[4] *Pinta* saw a cane and a stick, and took on board another small stick that appeared to have been worked with iron, and a piece of cane, and other vegetation originating on land, and a small plank. The men of the caravel *Niña* also saw other signs of land and a small stick loaded with barnacles. With these signs everyone breathed more easily and cheered up. On this day, up to sunset, they made 27 leagues.

After sunset he steered on his former course to the west. They made about 12 miles each hour and, until two hours after midnight, made about 90 miles, which is twenty-two leagues and a half. And because the caravel *Pinta* was a better sailer and went ahead of the Admiral it found land and made the signals that the Admiral had ordered. A sailor named Rodrigo de Triana saw this land first, although the Admiral, at the tenth hour of the night, while he was on the sterncastle,[5] saw a light, although it was something so faint that

[1]Columbus presented the original diary (or journal) of his first voyage to America, to Ferdinand and Isabella and had a personal copy made for himself. Both have been lost. The only version of the diary known to exist is a copy made by Bartolomé de las Casas in the 1530s. Las Casas in part copied and in part summarized Columbus's personal copy of the original journal.

[2]The journal entry for October 11 includes the report of the first sighting of land on October 12.

[3]A seabird that flies long distances from land.

[4]A small, maneuverable sailing vessel. Both the *Niña* and the *Pinta* were caravels. The *Santa Maria,* flagship for Columbus (the "Admiral"), was a nao, a larger sailing vessel designed to haul cargo.

[5]Elevated deck at the rear of the ship.

he did not wish to affirm that it was land. But he called Pero Gutiérrez, the steward of the king's dais,[6] and told him that there seemed to be a light, and for him to look: and thus he did and saw it. He also told Rodrigo Sánchez de Segovia, whom the king and queen were sending as *veedor*[7] of the fleet, who saw nothing because he was not in a place where he could see it. After the Admiral said it, it was seen once or twice; and it was like a small wax candle that rose and lifted up, which to few seemed to be an indication of land. But the Admiral was certain that they were near land, because of which when they recited the *Salve*,[8] which sailors in their own way are accustomed to recite and sing, all being present, the Admiral entreated and admonished them to keep a good lookout on the forecastle and to watch carefully for land; and that to the man who first told him that he saw land he would later give a silk jacket in addition to the other rewards that the sovereigns had promised, which were ten thousand *maravedís*[9] as an annuity to whoever should see it first.

At two hours after midnight [October 12] the land appeared, from which they were about two leagues distant. They hauled down all the sails and kept only the *treo,* which is the mainsail without bonnets,[10] and jogged on and off,[11] passing time until daylight Friday, when they reached an islet of the Lucayas, which was called Guanahani in the language of the Indians. Soon they saw naked people; and the Admiral went ashore in the armed launch, and Martín Alonso Pinzón and his brother Vicente Anes, who was captain of the *Niña.* The Admiral brought out the royal banner and the captains two flags with the green cross, which the Admiral carried on all the ships as a standard, with an F and a Y, and over each letter a crown, one on one side of the ✝ and the other on the other. Thus put ashore they saw very green trees and many ponds and fruits of various kinds. The Admiral called to the two captains and to the others who had jumped ashore and to Rodrigo Descobedo, the *escrivano*[12] of the whole fleet, and to Rodrigo Sánchez de Segovia; and he said that they should be witnesses that, in the presence of all, he would take, as in fact he did take, possession of the said island for the king and for the queen his lords, making the declarations that were required, and which at more length are contained in the testimonials made there in writing. Soon many people of the island gathered there. What follows are the very words of the Admiral in his book about his first voyage to, and discovery of, these Indies. I, he says, in order that they would be friendly to us—because I recognized that they were people who would be better freed [from error] and converted to our Holy Faith by love than by force—to some of them I gave red caps, and glass beads which they put on

[6]An official of the king's household.

[7]A royal official responsible for recording (to protect against theft) all jewels, gold, and other valuables gathered during the voyage.

[8]"Salve Regina," a hymn to the Virgin Mary, asking for mercy, sung at the close of day.

[9]Copper coins.

[10]Smaller sails attached to the foremast.

[11]Tacked back and forth to avoid approaching land and possibly dangerous shoals in the dark.

[12]The fleet's purser (business manager), a high ranking officer in charge of accounting records and financial affairs.

their chests, and many other things of small value, in which they took so much pleasure and became so much our friends that it was a marvel. Later they came swimming to the ships' launches where we were and brought us parrots and cotton thread in balls and javelins and many other things, and they traded them to us for other things which we gave them, such as small glass beads and bells. In sum, they took everything and gave of what they had very willingly. But it seemed to me that they were a people very poor in everything. All of them go around as naked as their mothers bore them; and the women also, although I did not see more than one quite young girl. And all those that I saw were young people, for none did I see of more than 30 years of age. They are very well formed, with handsome bodies and good faces. Their hair [is] coarse—almost like the tail of a horse—and short. They wear their hair down over their eyebrows except for a little in the back which they wear long and never cut. Some of them paint themselves with black, and they are of the color of the Canarians,[13] neither black nor white; and some of them paint themselves with white, and some of them with red, and some of them with whatever they find. And some of them paint their faces, and some of them the whole body, and some of them only the eyes, and some of them only the nose. They do not carry arms nor are they acquainted with them, because I showed them swords and they took them by the edge and through ignorance cut themselves. They have no iron. Their javelins are shafts without iron and some of them have at the end a fish tooth and others of other things. All of them alike are of good-sized stature and carry themselves well. I saw some who had marks of wounds on their bodies and I made signs to them asking what they were; and they showed me how people from other islands nearby came there and tried to take them, and how they defended themselves; and I believed and believe that they come here from *tierra firme*[14] to take them captive. They should be good and intelligent servants, for I see that they say very quickly everything that is said to them; and I believe that they would become Christians very easily, for it seemed to me that they had no religion. Our Lord pleasing, at the time of my departure I will take six of them from here to Your Highnesses in order that they may learn to speak. No animal of any kind did I see on this island except parrots. All are the Admiral's words.

SUNDAY 14 OCTOBER 1492

As soon as it dawned I ordered the ship's boat and the launches of the caravels made ready and went north-northeast along the island in order to see what there was in the other part, which was the eastern part. And also to see the villages, and I soon saw two or three, as well as people, who all came to the beach calling to us and giving thanks to God. Some of them brought us water; others, other things to eat; others, when they saw that I did not care to go ashore, threw themselves into the sea swimming and came to us, and we understood that they were asking us if we had come from the heavens.

[13]Inhabitants of the Canary Islands.

[14]The mainland.

And one old man got into the ship's boat, and others in loud voices called to all the men and women: Come see the men who came from the heavens. Bring them something to eat and drink. Many men came, and many women, each one with something, giving thanks to God, throwing themselves on the ground; and they raised their hands to heaven, and afterward they called to us in loud voices to come ashore. But I was afraid, seeing a big stone reef that encircled that island all around. And in between the reef and shore there was depth and harbor for as many ships as there are in the whole of Christendom, and the entrance to it is very narrow. It is true that inside of this belt of stone there are some shallows, but the sea is no more disturbed than inside a well. And I bestirred myself this morning to see all of this, so that I could give an account of everything to Your Highnesses, and also to see where a fort could be made. And I saw a piece of land formed like an island, although it was not one, on which there were six houses. This piece of land might in two days be cut off to make an island, although I do not see this to be necessary since these people are very naive about weapons, as Your Highnesses will see from seven that I caused to be taken in order to carry them away to you and to learn our language and to return them. Except that, whenever Your Highnesses may command, all of them can be taken to Castile or held captive in this same island; because with 50 men all of them could be held in subjection and can be made to do whatever one might wish. And later [I noticed], near the said islet, groves of trees, the most beautiful that I saw and with their leaves as green as those of Castile in the months of April and May, and lots of water. I looked over the whole of that harbor and afterward returned to the ship and set sail, and I saw so many islands that I did not know how to decide which one I would go to first. And those men whom I had taken told me by signs that they were so very many that they were numberless. And they named by their names more than a hundred. Finally I looked for the largest and to that one I decided to go and so I am doing. It is about five leagues distant from this island of San Salvador, and the others of them some more, some less. All are very flat without mountains and very fertile and all populated and they make war on one another, even though these men are very simple and very handsome in body.

1492 1825

Captain John Smith 1580–1631

In 1606 King James I of England granted a royal charter allowing two companies of "Knights, Gentlemen, Merchants, and other Adventurers" to plant colonies in England's North American territories. The next year, three shiploads of settlers landed in Virginia and founded Jamestown, the first permanent English colony in the New World.

They came full of hope for a land the English poet Michael Drayton had called "Earth's only paradise,"

Where nature hath in store
Fowl, venison and fish,
And the fruitfullest soil,
Without your toil,
Three harvests more,
All greater than you wish.

But from the start the settlers faced disaster. Jamestown was laid out on swampy, unhealthy ground. The colony lacked steadfast leaders. Too many of the 105 settlers were headstrong gentlemen-idlers or work-shy ne'er-do-wells, the "offscourings" of English society. They neglected to build houses or fortifications. They wasted time in searching for gold or a waterway to the Orient. Having failed to plant a crop, they were soon without food. During their first winter, more than half of them died from Indian arrows, sickness, or starvation.

Fortunately for the colony, Captain John Smith was among the survivors. Born in England of poor farmers, he had run away as a youth to become a mercenary soldier in the wars of Europe and the Near East. There he had learned courage, guile, and doggedness. There also he had achieved, or so he later claimed, a series of fantastic conquests—both military and amorous.

In Jamestown he soon emerged as the leader who could save the colony from ruin. He forced "lie-abeds" to build defenses and plant crops. He traded for food with the Indians, learned their customs and language. In 1608 he was named president of the colony, and by 1609, when he returned to England, he had started Jamestown on its way to survival.

Five years later, Smith again sailed to America, to New England, sent by merchant investors to search for gold, collect furs, and kill whales for oil. From April to July 1614 he sailed the New England coast, fishing and trading with the Indians and making the first accurate charts of the coastline from Maine to Cape Cod.

But the voyage was a financial failure. And none of Smith's future attempts to carry out new explorations or to plant new settlements was to succeed. He offered himself to the Pilgrims, but they, like other colonizers, found it "better cheap" to buy his maps and reports than to hire him as their leader. As a result, Smith never returned to the New World. Most of his remaining years he spent in London, writing and rewriting his histories and reports while vainly seeking to promote new expeditions.

Smith's first published work was a letter he sent from Virginia to a friend in England, where it was printed in 1608 as A True Relation of Occurrences and Accidents in Virginia. *It was the first English book written in America. In 1616 Smith published* A Description of New England, *based on his voyage of 1614. In 1624 he published* The General History of Virginia, *his longest and most influential work.*

Smith's General History of Virginia, *like his other histories, was written not merely to record the settlement of North America but also to serve as propaganda, as an advertisement for the lands he had explored. Its descriptions of New World riches and wilderness delights confirmed the European dream of America as a place of freedom, joy, and abundance. It was the delectable vision that lured investors and brought thousands of settlers to America, among them the Pilgrims and Puritans who used Smith's maps and reports to seek a new Eden in that portion of America he had named "New England."*

The story of his most famous adventure, his capture in Virginia by the Indians under Powhatan, first appeared in A True Relation *in 1608 and made no mention of his rescue by Pocahontas. The full details of that story were not published until 1624, seven years after Pocahontas's death. Thus some historians have questioned Smith's honesty, calling him a vain braggart, a teller of tall tales. But none can doubt that his story of capture and rescue has become an authentic American legend, a national fable that has filled the popular imagination with exotic visions of deliverance in the arms of a dusky princess of the forest.*

John Smith's writings remain the chief source of what little we know about the Virginia Indians before they were destroyed by European guns, disease, and rum. His books helped set the form of the exploration reports that inspired men to move westward to America and across the continent. His account of capture and escape from the Indians is one of the earliest examples of the "Indian captivity narrative," once a vastly popular literary genre that fascinated readers with vivid accounts of savage life.

As an explorer and colonizer, Smith has been enshrined as a national hero, as "that pink of gallantry, that flower of chivalry," the "founder of Virginia/And the pride of the Southern land!" His experiences have become a part of the epic of the American frontier. And they have given shape and substance to a New World allegory that shows Americans as a chosen people, led through trial and woe to the promised land where, as Cotton Mather proclaimed and wise men came to believe, "Divine providence hath irradiated an Indian wilderness."

FURTHER READING: *The Complete Works of Captain John Smith,* 3 vols., ed. P. Barbour, 1986; P. Barbour, *The Three Worlds of Captain John Smith,* 1964; B. Smith, *Captain John Smith: His Life and Legend,* 1953; *The Jamestown Voyages Under the First Charter, 1606–1609,* 2 vols., ed. P. Barbour, 1969; P. Barbour, *Pocahontas and Her World,* 1970; E. Emerson, *Captain John Smith,* 1971, 1993; A. Vaughan, *American Genesis, Captain John Smith and the Founding of Virginia,* 1975, 1997; F. Mossiker, *Pocahontas, the Life and the Legend,* 1976; N. Gerson, *Glorious Scoundrel, A Biography of Captain John Smith,* 1978; J. Lemay, *The American Dream of Captain John Smith,* 1991; K. Hayes, *Captain John Smith, A Reference Guide,* 1991; D. Price, *Love and Hate in Jamestown,* 2003.

TEXT: *Travels and Works of Captain John Smith,* ed. E. Arber, 1884, reprinted with an introduction by A. Bradley, 2 vols., 1910. Spelling, punctuation, and usage have been changed to conform more nearly to modern practice.

from *THE GENERAL HISTORY OF VIRGINIA*

THE THIRD BOOK

CHAPTER I

It might well be thought a country so fair (as Virginia is) and a people so tractable [as the Indians are] would long ere this have been quietly possessed, to the satisfaction of the adventurers[1] and the eternizing[2] of the

[1]I.e., peacefully settled, to the satisfaction of the English investors who had "ventured" their money to finance the colony.

[2]Perpetuating, glorifying.

memory of those that effected it. But because all the world does see a defailment,[3] this following treatise shall give satisfaction to all indifferent[4] readers [by showing] how the business has been carried [out] whereby no doubt they will easily understand an answer to their question, how it came to pass there was no better speed and success in those proceedings.

Captain Bartholomew Gosnold, one of the first movers of this plantation, having many years solicited many of his friends but [having] found small assistance, at last prevailed with some gentlemen, [such] as Captain John Smith,[5] Master Edward Maria Wingfield, Master Robert Hunt, and divers others, who depended[6] a year upon his projects; but nothing could be effected till by their great charge[7] and industry it came to be apprehended[8] by certain of the nobility, gentry, and merchants, so that his Majesty by his letters patent[9] gave commission for establishing councils to direct here [in London], and to govern and to execute there [in Virginia].[10] To effect this, was spent another year, and by that [time], three ships were provided, one of 100 tons, another of 40, and a pinnace of 20.[11] The transportation of the company was committed to Captain Christopher Newport, a mariner well practiced for the western parts of America.[12] But their orders for government were put in a box not to be opened nor [the identity of] the governors known until they arrived in Virginia.

On the 19th of December, 1606 we set sail from Blackwall[13] but by unprosperous winds were kept six weeks in the sight of England, all which time Master Hunt, our Preacher, was so weak and sick that few expected his recovery. Yet, although he was but twenty miles from his habitation (the time we were in the Downs)[14] and notwithstanding the stormy weather nor the scandalous imputations (of some few, little better than atheists, of the greatest rank amongst us) suggested against him, all this could never force from him so much as a seeming desire to leave the business, but [he] preferred the service of God, in so good a voyage, before any affection to contest with his godless foes whose disastrous designs (could they have prevailed) had even then overthrown the business, so many discontents did then arise, had he not with the water of patience and his godly exhortations (but chiefly by his true, devoted examples) quenched those flames of envy and dissension.

[3]Failure. [4]Unbiased.

[5]Smith freely used extracts from works by other authors who had earlier referred to Smith in the third person. When later compiling his own histories, Smith often continued to refer to himself in the third person.

[6]Waited. [7]Expense. [8]Understood, appreciated.

[9]The royal charter granted in April 1606 by King James I.

[10]King James established a ruling council in London whose orders were to be carried out by a subordinate council of governors in Virginia.

[11]The *Susan Constant, Godspeed,* and *Discovery* (the pinnace, a light, two-masted sailing ship). Their size, expressed in marine tons, represents carrying capacity in tuns, large barrels that held about 250 gallons each.

[12]I.e., the coast of North America, which is far to the west of the easternmost coast of South America.

[13]On the Thames River below London.

[14]Protected anchorage for ships in the English Channel, off the coast of Kent, England. There ships waited for good weather before entering the open sea.

We watered at the Canaries;[15] we traded with the savages at Dominica; three weeks we spent in refreshing ourselves amongst these West India isles; in Guadeloupe we found a bath so hot as in it we boiled pork as well as over the fire. And at a little isle called Monito, we took from the bushes with our hands nearly two hogsheads full of birds in three or four hours. In Nevis, Mona, and the Virgin Isles[16] we spent some time where, with a loathsome beast like a crocodile, called an iguana, tortoises, pelicans, parrots, and fishes, we daily feasted.

Gone from thence in search of Virginia, the company was not a little discomforted seeing the mariners had three days passed their reckoning[17] and found no land, so that Captain Ratcliffe (Captain of the pinnace) rather desired to bear up the helm to return for England than make further search. But God the guider of all good actions, forcing them by an extreme storm to hull[18] all night, did drive them by His providence to their desired port, beyond all their expectations, for never any of them had seen that coast.

The first land they made they called Cape Henry,[19] where thirty of them recreating themselves on shore were assaulted by five savages, who hurt two of the English very dangerously. That night was the box opened and the orders [sent by the London Council] read, in which Bartholomew Gosnold, John Smith, Edward Wingfield, Christopher Newport, John Ratcliffe, John Martin, and George Kendall were named to be the Council and [directed] to choose a President amongst them for a year who with the Council should govern. Matters of moment[20] were to be examined by a jury but determined[21] by the major part of the Council, in which the President had two voices.[22] Until the 13th of May they sought a place to plant in; then the Council was sworn [into office]; Master Wingfield was chosen President and an oration made [to explain] why Captain Smith was not admitted to the Council as the rest.[23]

Now falls every man to work, the Council contrive the fort, the rest cut down trees to make place to pitch their tents, some provide clapboard to reload the ships, some make gardens, some nets, &c. The savages often visited us kindly.[24] The President's overweening jealousy[25] would admit no exercise at arms or fortification but the boughs of trees cast together in the form of a half moon by the extraordinary pains and diligence of Captain Kendall.

Newport, Smith, and twenty others were sent to discover the head of the [James] river. By divers small habitations they passed; in six days they arrived at a town called Powhatan, consisting of some twelve houses pleasantly

[15]Canary Islands, off the coast of Africa.

[16]Dominica, Guadeloupe, Monito, Nevis, Mona, and the Virgin Isles: islands in the Caribbean.

[17]Estimated time of arrival.

[18]To ride before the wind with sails furled.

[19]Point of land ("cape") near present-day Norfolk, Virginia, at the entrance to Chesapeake Bay. It was named for Henry, Prince of Wales, son of the reigning English King, James I.

[20]Importance. [21]Judged. [22]Votes.

[23]Smith had been charged with mutiny and imprisoned during the voyage. Thus he was denied membership in the local Virginia Council, which thereby disregarded the orders of the higher London Council.

[24]I.e., in a civil, friendly manner.

[25]Extreme caution. The London Council had ordered the colonists not to offend the Indians by making a military display.

seated on a hill, before it three fertile isles, about it many of their cornfields; the place is very pleasant and strong by nature; of this place the Prince is called Powhatan and his people Powhatans. To this place the river is navigable; but higher, within a mile, by reason of the rocks and isles, there is not passage for a small boat; this they call the Falls. The people in all parts kindly entreated them, till being returned within twenty miles of Jamestown, they [the Indians] gave just cause of jealousy,[26] but had God not blessed the discoverers[27] otherwise than those at the fort, there had then been an end of that plantation, for at the fort, where they arrived the next day, they found seventeen men hurt and a boy slain by the savages, and had it not chanced a cross-bar shot[28] from the ships struck down a bough from a tree amongst them [the Indians], that caused them to retire, our men had all been slain, being securely all at work and their arms in dry vats.[29]

Hereupon the President was contented the fort should be palisaded,[30] the ordnance[31] mounted, his men armed and exercised,[32] for many were the assaults and ambuscades of the savages, and our men by their disorderly straggling were often hurt, when the savages by the nimbleness of their heels well escaped.

What toil we had, with so small a power to guard our workmen by day, watch all night, resist our enemies, and effect our business to reload the ships, cut down trees, and prepare the ground to plant our corn,[33] &c, I refer to the reader's consideration. Six weeks being spent in this manner, Captain Newport (who was hired only for our transportation) was to return with the ships. Now Captain Smith, . . . all this time from their departure from the Canaries, was restrained as a prisoner upon the scandalous suggestions of some of the chief [colonists] (envying his repute) who feigned [that] he intended to usurp the government, murder the Council, and make himself king, that his confederates were dispersed in all the three ships, and that divers of his confederates that revealed it would affirm it; for this he was committed as a prisoner.

Thirteen weeks he remained thus suspected, and by that time [when] the ships should return they [authorities at Jamestown] pretended out of their commiserations to refer him to the Council in England to receive a check,[34] rather than by particulating[35] his designs [and thereby] make him so odious to the world as to touch his life or utterly overthrow his reputation. But he so much scorned their charity and publicly defied the uttermost of their cruelty [that] he wisely prevented their policies, though he could not suppress their envies; yet so well he demeaned himself in this business as all the company did see his innocence and his adversaries' malice; and those suborned to accuse him, accused his accusers of subornation; many untruths were alleged against him, but being so apparently disproved, [the false charges] begot a general hatred in the hearts of the company against such unjust commanders, [and for] that the President was adjudged to give him £200[36] so

[26]Fury, mistrust. [27]Explorers.
[28]Cannonball with bars projecting from two sides, for use against an enemy ship's ropes and sails.
[29]Storage cases.
[30]Protected with wooden timbers set upright as a fence. [31]Cannon. [32]Drilled.
[33]Wheat and other European grains. [34]Punishment or reprimand. [35]Specifying.
[36]The Council in Virginia ordered Wingfield to pay £200 damages to Smith for falsely charging him with mutiny.

that all he [President Wingfield] had was seized upon in part of satisfaction, which Smith presently returned to the [communal] store[house] for the general use of the Colony.

Many were the mischiefs that daily sprung from their ignorant (yet ambitious) spirits, but the good doctrine and exhortation of our Preacher, Master Hunt, reconciled them and caused Captain Smith to be admitted to the Council. The next day all received the Communion; the day following, the savages voluntarily desired peace, and Captain Newport returned for England with news, leaving in Virginia 100 [men], the 15th of June, 1607.

By this observe:

Good men did ne'er their country's ruin bring.
But when evil men shall injuries begin,
Not caring to corrupt and violate
The judgements-seats for their own lucre's sake,
Then look that country cannot long have peace,
Though for the present it have rest and ease.[37]

. . .

CHAPTER II

WHAT HAPPENED TILL THE FIRST SUPPLY

Being thus left to our fortunes, it fortuned that within ten days, scarce ten amongst us could either go or well stand, such extreme weakness and sickness oppressed us. And thereat none need marvel if they consider the cause and reason which was this: While the ships stayed, our allowance was somewhat bettered by a daily proportion of biscuit, which the sailors would pilfer to sell, give, or exchange with us for money, sassafras,[38] furs, or love. But when they departed, there remained neither tavern, beer house, nor place of relief but the common kettle.[39] Had we been as free from all sins as [we were free from] gluttony and drunkenness, we might have been canonized for saints; but our President would never had been admitted [to sainthood], for [he was guilty of] engrossing to his private,[40] oatmeal, sack,[41] oil, aqua vitae,[42] beef, eggs, or what not but the kettle; that indeed he allowed equally to be distributed, and that was half a pint of wheat and as much barley boiled with water for a man a day, and this, having fried some twenty-six weeks in the ship's hold, contained as many worms as grains so that we might truly call it rather so much bran than corn; our drink was water,[43] our lodgings castles in the air.

With this lodging and diet, our extreme toil in bearing and planting palisades so strained and bruised us, and our continual labor in the extremity of the heat had so weakened us, as were cause sufficient to have made us as

[37]A quotation from the *Maxims* of the Greek poet Theognis of Megara (fl. 550 B.C.).
[38]A tree whose bark and roots were thought to have great curative powers.
[39]I.e., jointly shared provisions.
[40]I.e., taking for his private use.
[41]Dry white wine.
[42]Distilled alcoholic spirits, such as brandy.
[43]The colonists preferred wine or beer. Water was thought to be unwholesome.

miserable in our native country or any other place in the world. From May to September, those that escaped [death] lived upon sturgeon and sea crabs. Fifty in this time we buried; the rest [of us] seeing the President's projects to escape these miseries in our pinnace by flight (who all this time had neither felt want nor sickness) so moved our dead spirits as we deposed him and established Ratcliffe in his place (Gosnold being dead), Kendall [having been] deposed.[44] Smith [being] newly recovered, Martin and Ratcliffe were by his care preserved and relieved, and the most of the soldiers recovered with the skillful diligence of Master Thomas Wotton our surgeon general. But now was all our provision spent, the sturgeon gone, all helps abandoned, each hour expecting the fury of the savages, when God, the patron of all good endeavors, in that desperate extremity so changed the heart of the savages that they brought such plenty of their fruits and provision as no man wanted.

And now where some affirmed it was ill done of the [London] Council to send forth men so badly provided, this incontradictable reason will show them plainly they are too ill advised to nourish such ill conceits: First, the fault of our going was our own; what could be thought fitting or necessary we had, but [of] what we should find, or want, or where we should be, we were all ignorant; and supposing to make our passage in two months, with victual to live and the advantage of the spring to work, we were at sea five months, where we both spent our victual and lost the opportunity of the time and season to plant, by the unskillful presumption of our ignorant transporters[45] that understood not at all what they undertook.

Such actions have ever since the world's beginning been subject to such accidents, and everything of worth is found full of difficulties, but nothing [is] so difficult as to establish a commonwealth so far remote from men and means and where men's minds are so untoward[46] as neither do well themselves nor suffer others. But to proceed.

The new President [Ratcliffe] and Martin, being little beloved, of weak judgment in dangers, and less industry in peace, committed the managing of all things abroad[47] to Captain Smith, who, by his own example, good words, and fair promises, set some to mow, others to bind thatch, some to build houses, others to thatch them, himself always bearing the greatest task for his own share, so that in short time he provided most of them lodgings, neglecting any for himself. This done, seeing the savages' superfluity[48] begin to decrease, [Smith] (with some of his workmen) shipped himself in the shallop[49] to search the country for trade. The want of the language, [the want of] knowledge to manage his boat without sailors, the want of a sufficient power (knowing the multitude of the savages), [the want of] apparel for his men, and [the want of] other necessaries were infinite impediments yet no discouragement.

Being but six or seven in company he went down the river to Kecoughtan,[50] where at first they [the Indians] scorned him as a famished

[44]Wingfield was removed from the presidency and the council for misconduct. Gosnold, who would normally have succeeded Wingfield as president, had died the previous month. Kendall had also been deposed and was later executed for mutiny.

[45]Ships' captains and crews. [46]Perverse, unreasonable. [47]Outdoors.

[48]Excess food supply. [49]Open sailboat for use in shallow waters.

[50]Indian village and tribe, near the mouth of the James River, whose chief was Powhatan's son.

man and would in derision offer him a handful of corn, a piece of bread, for their [the Englishmen's] swords and muskets, and such like proportions also for their apparel. But seeing by trade and courtesy there was nothing to be had, he made bold to try such conclusions[51] as necessity enforced; though contrary to his commission, [he] let fly[52] his muskets [and] ran his boat on shore; whereat they all fled into the woods.

So marching towards their houses, they might see great heaps of corn; much ado he had to restrain his hungry soldiers from present taking of it, expecting as it happened that the savages would assault them, as not long after they did with a most hideous noise. Sixty or seventy of them, some black, some red, some white, some parti-colored, came in a square order, singing and dancing out of the woods with their Okee (which was an idol made of skins, stuffed with moss, all painted and hung with chains and copper) borne before them; and in this manner, being well armed with clubs, targets,[53] bows, and arrows, they charged the English that so kindly[54] received them with their muskets loaded with pistol shot that down fell their god, and divers [Indians] lay sprawling on the ground; the rest fled again to the woods and ere long sent one of their Quiyoughcosucks[55] to offer peace and redeem their Okee.

Smith told them if only six of them would come unarmed and load his boat, he would not only be their friend but restore them their Okee and give them beads, copper, and hatchets besides, which on both sides was to their contents performed, and then they brought him venison, turkeys, wild fowl, bread, and what they had, singing and dancing in sign of friendship till they departed. In his return he discovered the town and country of Warraskoyack.[56]

Thus God unboundless by his power,
Made them thus kind, would us devour.[57]

Smith, perceiving (notwithstanding their late misery) not any regarded but from hand to mouth (the company being well recovered), caused the pinnace to be provided with things fitting to get provision for the year following, but in the interim he made three or four journeys and discovered the people of Chickahominy,[58] yet what he carefully provided the rest carelessly spent.

. . .

The Spaniard never more greedily desired gold than he [Smith] victual, nor his soldiers more to abandon the country than he to keep it. But . . . [he found] plenty of corn in the river of Chickahominy, where hundreds of savages in divers places stood with baskets expecting his coming. And now [with] the winter approaching, the rivers became so covered with swans, geese, ducks, and cranes that we daily feasted with good bread, Virginia

[51]Decisive acts, stratagems. [52]Fire. [53]Shields. [54]Properly. [55]Priests.
[56]Village and tribe on the James River, subject to Powhatan.
[57]One of two verses in the *General History* written, perhaps, by Smith himself.
[58]Village and tribe on the Chickahominy River.

peas, pumpkins, and persimmons, fish, fowl, and divers sorts of wild beasts as fat as we could eat them, so that none of our tuftaffaty humorists[59] desired to go for England.

But our comedies never endured long without a tragedy; some idle exceptions[60] being muttered against Captain Smith for not discovering the head of [the] Chickahominy river and [being] taxed by the Council to be too slow in so worthy an attempt,[61] the next voyage he proceeded so far that with much labor by cutting of trees asunder he made his passage; but when his barge could pass no farther, he left her in a broad bay out of danger of shot, commanding [that] none should go ashore till his return; himself with two English and two savages went up higher in a canoe, but he was not long absent but his men [in the barge] went ashore, whose want of government[62] gave both occasion and opportunity to the savages to surprise one George Cassen, whom they slew, and [they] much failed not to have cut off the boat and all the rest.

Smith little dreaming of that accident, being got to the marshes at the river's head twenty miles in the desert,[63] had his two men[64] slain (as is supposed) sleeping by the canoe, while himself by fowling sought them victual, who finding he was beset with 200 savages, two of them he slew, still defending himself with the aid of a savage his guide, whom he bound to his arm with his garters[65] and used him as a buckler,[66] yet he [Smith] was shot in his thigh a little, and had many arrows that stuck in his clothes but no great hurt, till at last they took him prisoner. . . .

The manner how they used and delivered him is as follows:

The savages having drawn from George Cassen whither Captain Smith was gone, prosecuting that opportunity they followed him with 300 bowmen, conducted by the King of Pamunkey,[67] who in divisions searching the turnings of the river found Robinson and Emry by the fireside; those they shot full of arrows and slew. Then finding the Captain, as is said, who used the savage that was his guide as his shield (three of them being slain and divers others so galled) all the rest would not come near him. Thinking thus to have returned to his boat, regarding them, as he marched, more than his way, [he] slipped up to the middle in an oozy creek and his savage with him, yet dared they not come to him till being near dead with cold he threw away his arms. Then according to their composition[68] they drew him forth and led him to the fire where his men were slain. Diligently they chafed his benumbed limbs.

He demanding for their captain, they showed him Opechancanough, King of Pamunkey, to whom he gave a round ivory double compass dial. Much they marveled at the playing of the fly[69] and needle, which they could see so plainly and yet not touch it because of the glass that covered them. But when he demonstrated by that globe-like jewel the roundness of the

[59]I.e., Headstrong dandies (wearing tufted taffeta clothes). [60]Complaints.

[61]I.e., so important a task. [62]Lack of discipline, disobedience. [63]Wilderness.

[64]Jehu Robinson, a "gentleman," and Thomas Emry, a "carpenter."

[65]Straps and laces used (instead of buttons) to secure clothing. [66]Shield.

[67]Opechancanough, half-brother to the great chief Powhatan and chief of the Pamunkeys, a subtribe of the Powhatan alliance.

[68]Agreement with Smith. [69]Compass card showing points of direction.

earth and skies, the sphere of the sun, moon, and stars, and how the sun did chase the night round about the world continually, the greatness of the land and sea, the diversity of nations, variety of complexions, and how we were to them antipodes,[70] and many other such like matters, they all stood as amazed with admiration. Notwithstanding, within an hour after, they tied him to a tree, and as many as could stand about him prepared to shoot him, but [seeing] the King holding up the compass in his hand, they all laid down their bows and arrows and in a triumphant manner led him to Orapaks,[71] where he was after their manner kindly feasted and well used.

Their order in conducting him was thus: Drawing themselves all in file, the King in the midst had all their pieces and swords borne before him. Captain Smith was led after him by three great savages holding him fast by each arm, and on each side six went in file with their arrows nocked.[72] But arriving at the town (which was but only thirty or forty hunting houses made of mats, which they remove as they please, as we our tents), all the women and children staring to behold him, the soldiers first all in file performed the form of a bissom[73] so well as could be, and on each flank, officers as sergeants to see them keep their orders. A good time they continued this exercise and then cast themselves in a ring, dancing in such several postures and singing and yelling out such hellish notes and screeches; being strangely painted, every one [had] his quiver of arrows and at his back a club, on his arm a fox or an otter's skin or some such matter for his vambrace;[74] their heads and shoulders [were] painted red with oil and pocones[75] mingled together, which scarlet-like color made an exceeding handsome show; [each had] his bow in his hand and the skin of a bird with her wings [spread] abroad, dried, tied on his head, [with] a piece of copper, a white shell, a long feather with a small rattle growing at the tails of their snakes tied to it, or some such like toy.

All this while, Smith and the King stood in the midst, guarded as before is said, and after three dances they all departed. Smith they conducted to a long house where thirty or forty tall fellows did guard him, and ere long more bread and venison was brought him than would have served twenty men. I think his stomach at that time was not very good; what he left they put in baskets and tied over his head. About midnight they set the meat again before him; all this time not one of them would eat a bit with him, till the next morning [when] they brought him as much more, and then did they eat all the old and reserved the new as they had done the other, which made him think they would fat him to eat him. Yet in this desperate estate, to defend him from the cold, one Maocassater brought him his gown in requital of some beads and toys Smith had given him at his first arrival in Virginia.

[70]I.e., from the opposite side of the world.

[71]Indian village, with a temple and residence for Powhatan, located near the head of the Chickahominy River.

[72]I.e., with bowstrings set in the arrows' notch, ready to shoot.

[73]Military parade maneuver in which a file of troops marches back and forth in a winding, snake-like line—from Italian *biscione,* "great snake."

[74]Armor for the forearm.

[75]Plants with roots that yield a red pigment.

Two days after, a man would have slain him (but that the guard prevented it) for the death of his son, to whom they conducted him [Smith] to recover the poor man then breathing his last. Smith told them that at Jamestown he had a water [that] would do it, if they would let him fetch it, but they would not permit that, but [they] made all the preparations they could to assault Jamestown, craving his advice, and for recompense he should have life, liberty, land, and women. In part of a table book[76] he wrote his mind to them at the fort, what was intended, how they should follow that direction to affright the messengers, and without fail send him such things as he wrote for, and an inventory with them. The difficulty and danger he told the savages of, the mines, great guns, and other engines,[77] exceedingly affrighted them, yet according to his request they went to Jamestown in as bitter weather as could be of frost and snow, and within three days returned with an answer.

But when they came to Jamestown, seeing men sally out as he had told them they would, they fled, yet in the night they came again to the same place where he had told them they should receive an answer and such things as he had promised them, which they found accordingly and with which they returned with no small expedition,[78] to the wonder of them all that heard it, that he could either divine[79] or the paper could speak. Then they led him to the Youghtanunds, the Mattapanients, the Payankatanks, the Nantaughtacunds, and Onawmanients[80] upon the rivers of Rappahannock and Potomac, over all those rivers and back again by divers other several nations[81] to the King's habitation at Pamunkey, where they entertained him with most strange and fearful conjurations;[82]

As if near led to hell,
Amongst the devils to dwell.[83]

Not long after, early in a morning, a great fire was made in a long house and a mat spread on the one side as on the other; on the one they caused him to sit, and all the guard went out of the house, and presently came skipping in a great grim fellow all painted over with [char]coal mingled with oil, and many snakes' and weasels' skins stuffed with moss, and all their tails tied together so as they met on the crown of his head in a tassel, and round about the tassel was as a coronet of feathers, the skins hanging round about his head, back, and shoulders and in a manner covered his face, with a hellish voice, and a rattle in his hand. With most strange gestures and passions he began his invocation and environed the fire with a circle of meal; which done, three more such like devils came rushing in with the like antic tricks, painted half black, half red, but all their eyes were painted white and some red strokes like mustaches along their cheeks. Round about him those fiends danced a pretty while, and then came in three more as ugly as the rest, with red eyes and white strokes over their black faces; at last they all sat right opposite him, three of them on the one hand of the chief priest and three on the other. Then all with rattles began a song; which ended, the

[76]Tablet, notebook. [77]Devices. [78]Speed. [79]Make magic.
[80]Five tribes subject to Powhatan. [81]Tribes. [82]Rituals.
[83]Smith quotes the Latin poet Lucius Annaeus Seneca (c. 4 B.C.–A.D. 65).

chief priest laid down five wheat corns;[84] then, straining his arms and hands with such violence that he sweat and his veins swelled, he began a short oration; at the conclusion they all gave a short groan and then laid down three grains more. After that [they] began their song again and then another oration, ever laying down so many corns as before till they had twice encircled the fire; that done, they took a bunch of little sticks prepared for that purpose, continuing still their devotion, and at the end of every song and oration they laid down a stick betwixt the divisions of corn. Till night, neither he nor they did either eat or drink, and then they feasted merrily with the best provisions they could make.

Three days they used this ceremony; the meaning whereof, they told him, was to know if he intended them well or no. The circle of meal signified their country, the circles of corn the bounds of the sea, and the sticks his country. They imagined the world to be flat and round, like a trencher,[85] and they in the midst. After this they brought him a bag of gunpowder, which they carefully preserved till the next spring, to plant as they did their corn, because they would be acquainted with the nature of that seed. Opitchapam,[86] the King's brother, invited him to his house, where, with as many platters of bread, fowl, and wild beasts as did environ him, he bid him welcome, but not any of them would eat a bit with him but put up all the remainder in baskets. At his return to Opechancanough's, all the King's women and their children flocked about him for their parts,[87] as a due by custom, to be merry with such fragments.

> But his waking mind in hideous dreams did
> oft see wondrous shapes
> Of bodies strange, and huge in growth, and
> of stupendous makes.[88]

At last they brought him to Werowocomoco,[89] where was Powhatan, their Emperor. Here more than two hundred of those grim courtiers stood wondering at him, as [if] he had been a monster, till Powhatan and his train had put themselves in their greatest braveries.[90] Before a fire, upon a seat like a bedstead, he sat covered with a great robe made of raccoon skins and all the tails hanging by. On either hand did sit a young wench of sixteen or eighteen years and along on each side [of] the house, two rows of men and behind them as many women, with all their heads and shoulders painted red, many of their heads bedecked with the white down of birds, but every one with something, and a great chain of white beads about their necks.

[84]Grains, or kernels, of Indian corn. [85]Platter.
[86]Indian chief, heir and half-brother to Powhatan.
[87]Portions or gifts.
[88]A quotation from the Roman poet Titus Lucretius Carus (c. 94–55 B.C.).
[89]Chief's Town—on the York River, twelve miles from Jamestown. It was the residence of Powhatan, the great chief of the Powhatans and ruler of some thirty Indian tribes.
[90]Costumes.

At his entrance before the King, all the people gave a great shout. The Queen of Appomattoc[91] was appointed to bring him water to wash his hands, and another brought him a bunch of feathers, instead of a towel, to dry them. Having feasted him after their best barbarous manner they could, a long consultation was held, but the conclusion was, two great stones were brought before Powhatan; then as many as could laid hands on him [Smith], dragged him to them, and thereon laid his head, and being ready with their clubs to beat out his brains, Pocahontas, the King's dearest daughter, when no entreaty could prevail, got his head in her arms and laid her own upon his to save him from death, whereat the Emperor was contented he should live to make him hatchets, and her bells, beads, and copper, for they thought him as well [capable] of all occupations as themselves. For the King himself will make his own robes, shoes, bows, arrows, pots; plant; hunt; or do anything so well as the rest.

They say he bore a pleasant show,
But sure his heart was sad.
For who can pleasant be, and rest,
That lives in fear and dread:
And having life suspected, doth
It still suspected lead.[92]

Two days after, Powhatan, having disguised himself in the most fearfulest manner he could, caused Captain Smith to be brought forth to a great house in the woods and there upon a mat by the fire to be left alone. Not long after, from behind a mat that divided the house, was made the most dolefulest noise he ever heard; then Powhatan, more like a devil than a man, with some two hundred more as black as himself, came unto him and told him now they were friends, and presently he should go to Jamestown to send him two great guns and a grindstone for which he would give him the country of Capahowasic[93] and forever esteem him as his son Nantaquond.

So to Jamestown with twelve guides Powhatan sent him. That night they quartered in the woods, he still expecting (as he had done all this long time of his imprisonment) every hour to be put to one death or other, for all their feasting. But almighty God (by His divine providence) had mollified the hearts of those stern barbarians with compassion. The next morning betimes[94] they came to the fort, where Smith having used the savages with what kindness he could, he showed Rawhunt, Powhatan's trusty servant, two demiculverins[95] and a millstone to carry [to] Powhatan; they found them somewhat too heavy, but when they did see him discharge them, being loaded with stones, among the boughs of a great tree loaded with icicles, the ice and branches came so tumbling down that the poor savages ran away half dead with fear. But at last we regained some conference with them and gave them such toys and sent to Powhatan, his women, and children such presents as gave them in general full content.

[91]Powhatan tribe on the James River near the mouth of the Appomattox River.
[92]A quotation from the Greek dramatist Euripides (c. 480–406 B.C.).
[93]Neighboring tribe and village. [94]Early.
[95]Cannon nine feet long, each weighing about two tons.

POWHATAN'S DISCOURSE OF PEACE AND WAR[1]

Captain Smith, you may understand that I having seen the death of all my people thrice, and not anyone [is] living of those three generations but myself; I know the difference of peace and war better than any in my country. But now I am old and ere long must die; my brethren, namely Opitchapam, Opechancanough, and Kecoughtan, my two sisters, and their two daughters, are distinctly each other's successors. I wish their experience [with you to be] no less than mine, and your love to them no less than mine to you. But this bruit[2] from Nandsamund,[3] that you are come to destroy my country, so much affrighteth all my people as they dare not visit you. What will it avail you to take that by force [which] you may quickly have by love, or to destroy them that provide you [with] food? What can you get by war, when we can hide our provisions and fly to the woods whereby you must famish[4] by wronging us your friends? And why are you thus jealous[5] of our love, seeing us unarmed, and [we] both do and are willing still to feed you with that [which] you cannot get but by our labors? Think you I am so simple [as] not to know it is better to eat good meat, lie well and sleep quietly with my women and children, laugh and be merry with you, have copper, hatchets, or what I want, being your friend, than be forced to fly from all, to lie cold in the woods, feed upon acorns, roots, and such trash, and be so hunted by you that I can neither rest, eat, nor sleep, but my tired men must watch, and if a twig but break, everyone cryeth, here commeth Captain Smith. Then I must fly I know not whither and thus, with miserable fear, end my miserable life, leaving my pleasures to such youths as you [are], who through your rash unadvisedness may quickly as miserably end [your own life] for lack of that [grain and meat] which you never know where to find. Let this therefore assure you of our love, and every year our friendly trade shall furnish you with corn, and [I would give you corn] now also, if you would come in [a] friendly manner to see us, and not [come] thus with your guns and swords as [if you intended] to invade your foes.

1624

[1]Late in 1608 Powhatan invited Smith to Werowocomoco to trade guns, swords, copper, and beads for the Indians' grain. Smith was warned by a friendly Indian chief, and by Pocahontas herself, that at Werowocomoco Powhatan planned first to beguile the Jamestown traders with expressions of friendship, then to gain possession of their weapons and murder them. When Smith and his men arrived, Powhatan urged them to give up their swords and guns, "for here they are needless, we being all friends." He then spoke his "Discourse of Peace and War," which Smith recorded, translating it into the language of seventeenth-century Englishmen. Unmoved by Powhatan's eloquence, Smith continued to believe that Powhatan did "but trifle the time to cut his throat." Thus he and his men kept their weapons, and their lives.

[2]Report.

[3]Chief of a tribe and village near Jamestown, subordinate to Powhatan. Nandsamund had failed to provide 400 baskets of grain promised to the colonists at Jamestown, who were threatened with starvation. Shortly before Smith's trading expedition to Powhatan, an armed force from Jamestown raided the Nandsamund village and seized the grain. Nandsamund's report of the raid preceded Smith to Werowocomoco.

[4]Starve.

[5]Suspicious.

Native American Voices I

The earliest Americans arrived from Asia as early as 30,000 B.C., perhaps even earlier. They came across a land bridge that reached from the Old World to the New, across the Bering Sea between present-day Siberia and Alaska. They were immigrants, the first of a succession of people who came to America bringing with them their languages, their customs, beliefs, and visions. They came in waves, over thousands of years, moving down through North America to the southern reaches of South America.

By the time Columbus arrived in 1492, Native Americans had developed hundreds of different cultures and languages. Theirs was an oral culture, their traditions and religions preserved in oral tales and myths. Spoken literature was handed down from generation to generation, to speakers and talkers, who memorized the stories, shaping and adapting them to meet the changes they experienced.

Like the people of all cultures, they developed myths and legends that explained their origins and the origin of the worlds they lived in. Stories, poems, and orations were part of their daily lives, essential to their cohesion as a people and as guides to life—and to death.

Until the twentieth century the literature of Native Americans in the United States was overshadowed by the culture and the literature of the European settlers who had come to the New Eden across the Atlantic. The stories, poems, biographies, and speeches of Native Americans had remained largely the concern of anthropologists, ethnologists, and cultural historians who were interested in recording the varieties of native culture before they were completely engulfed by the dominating civilization of the intruding Europeans.

But the last half of the twentieth century has seen a rebirth of interest in the culture, the art, the literature of Native Americans. Just as all Americans have come more fully to understand and to emulate the Native Americans' profound interest in preserving the land and its animals, so modern-day Americans of all cultural varieties are beginning to understand and to value more fully the verbal and written art of America's first immigrants.

FURTHER READING: A. Day, *The Sky Clears, The Poetry of the American Indians,* 1951, 1964; M. Astrov, *American Indian Prose and Poetry,* 1962; *Native American Testimony,* ed. P. Nabakov, 1978, 1991; G. Hobson, *The Remembered Earth, An Anthology of Contemporary Native American Literature,* 1979, 1981; *Literature of the American Indian,* ed. T. Sanders and W. Peek, 1973; K. Lincoln, *Native American Renaissance,* 1983; A. Ruoff, *American Indian Literatures, An Introduction,* 1990; *Redefining American Literary History,* ed. A. Ruoff and J. Ward, 1990; *Early Images of the Americas,* ed. J. Williams and R. Lewis, 1993; J. Moffitt and S. Sebastián, *O Brave New People,* 1996; *Early Native American Writing,* ed. H. Jakoski, 1996; J. Porter and K. Roemer, *The Cambridge Companion to Native American Literature,* 2005.

TEXTS: "How the World Began," *Seneca Myths and Folk Tales,* ed. A. Parker, 1923; "How the World Was Made," *Nineteenth Annual Report of the Bureau of American Ethnology, 1897–98,* ed. J. Powell, 1900; "The Beginning of Summer and Winter," *Indian Legends from the Northern Rockies,* ed. E. Clark, 1966; "The Gift of the Sacred Pipe," *The Sacred Pipe, Black Elk's Account of the Seven Rites of the Oglala Sioux,* ed. J. Brown, 1953; "Thunder, Dizzying Liquid, and Cups that Do Not Grow," *The Menominee Indians,* ed. W. Hoffman, 1897.

MYTHS AND TALES

HOW THE WORLD BEGAN[1]

Beyond the dome we call the sky there is another world. There in the most ancient of times was a fair country where lived the great chief of the up-above-world and his people, the celestial beings. This chief had a wife who was very aged in body, having survived many seasons.

In that upper world there were many things of which men of today know nothing. This world floated like a great cloud and journeyed where the great chief wished it to go. The crust of that world was not thick, but none of these men beings knew what was under the crust.

In the center of that world there grew a great tree which bore flowers and fruits and all the people lived from the fruits of the tree and were satisfied. Now, moreover, the tree bore a great blossom at its top, and it was luminous and lighted the world above, and wonderful perfume filled the air which the people breathed. The rarest perfume of all was that which resembled the smoke of sacred tobacco and this was the incense greatly loved by the great chief. It grew from the leaves that sprouted from the roots of the tree.

The roots of the tree were white and ran in four directions. Far through the earth they ran, giving firm support to the tree. Around this tree the people gathered daily, for here the great chief had his lodge where he dwelt. Now, in a dream he was given a desire to take as his wife a certain maiden who was very fair to look upon. So, he took her as his wife for when he had embraced her he found her most pleasing. When he had eaten the marriage bread he took her to his lodge, and to his surprise found that she was with child. This caused him great anger and he felt himself deceived, but the woman loved the child, which had been conceived by the potent breath of her lover when he had embraced her. He was greatly distressed, for this fair Awehai was of the noblest family. It is she who is customarily called Iagetci.

He, the Ancient One, fell into a troubled sleep and a dream commanded him to have the celestial tree uprooted as a punishment to his wife, and as a relief of his troubled spirit. So on the morrow he announced to his wife that he had a dream and could not be satisfied until it had been divined.[2] Thereupon she "discovered his word," and it was that the tree should be uprooted. "Truly you have spoken," said Ancient One, "and now my mind shall be satisfied." And the woman, his wife, saw that there was trouble ahead for the sky world, but she too found pleasure in the uprooting of the tree, wishing to know what was beneath it. Yet did she know that to uproot the tree meant disaster for her, through the anger of Ancient One against her.

It so happened that the chief called all his people together and they endeavored to uproot the tree, it being deep-rooted and firm. Then did the chief grow even more angry for Iagetci had cried out that calamity threatened and nobody would avert it. Then did the chief, himself embrace the tree and with a mighty effort uprooted it, throwing it far away. His effort was tremendous, and in uprooting the tree he shook down fruits and leaves. Thereafter he went into his lodge and entered into the apartment where his

[1]A myth of the Seneca Indians of western New York. [2]Explained.

wife, Iagetci, lay moaning that she too must be satisfied by a look into the hole. So the chief led her to the hole made by uprooting the tree.

He caused her to seat herself on the edge of the hole and peer downward. Again his anger returned against her, for she said nothing to indicate that she had been satisfied. Long she sat looking into the hole until the chief in rage drew her blanket over her head and pushed her with his foot, seeking to thrust her into the hole, and be rid of her. As he did this she grasped the earth at her side and gathered in her fingers all manner of seeds that had fallen from the shaken tree. In her right hand she held the leaves of the plant that smelled like burning tobacco, for it grew from a root that had been broken off. Again the chief pushed the woman, whose curiosity had caused the destruction of the greatest blessing of the up-above-world. It was a mighty push, and despite her hold upon the plant and upon the ground, she fell into the hole.

Now, this hole had penetrated the crust of the upper world and when Iagetci fell she went far down out of sight and the chief could not see her in the depths of the darkness below. As she fell she beheld a beast that emitted fire from its head whom she called Gaasiondietha (Gahashondietoh). It is said that as she passed by him he took out a small pot, a corn mortar, a pestle, a marrow bone and an ear of corn and presented them to her, saying, "Because thou hast thus done, thou shalt eat by these things, for there is nothing below, and all who eat shall see me once and it will be the last."

Now it is difficult to know how this Fire Beast can be seen for he is of the color of the wind and is of the color of anything that surrounds it, though some say he is pure white.

Hovering over the troubled waters below were other creatures, some like and some unlike those that were created afterward. It is said by the old people that in those times lived the spirit of Gaha and of Shagodiiowegowa, of Hino and of Deiodasondaiko (The Wind, the Defending Face, the Thunder and the Heavy Night). There were also what seemed to be ducks upon the water and these also saw the descending figure.

The creature-beings knew that a new body was coming to them and that here below there was no abiding place for her. They took council together and sought to devise a way to provide for her.

It was agreed that the duck-creatures should receive her on their interknit wings and lower her gently to the surface below. The great turtle from the under-world was to arise and make his broad back a resting-place. It was as has been agreed and the woman came down upon the floating island.

Then did the creatures seek to make a world for the woman, and one by one they dove to the bottom of the water seeking to find earth to plant upon the turtle's back. A duck dived but went so far that it breathed the water and came up dead. A pickerel went down and came back dead. Many creatures sought to find the bottom of the water but could not. At last the creature called muskrat made the attempt and only succeeded in touching the bottom with his nose but this was sufficient for he was enabled to smear it upon the shell and the earth immediately grew, and as the earth-substance increased so did the size of the turtle.

After a time the woman, who lay prone, aroused herself and released what was in her hands, dropping many seeds into the folds of her garment. Likewise she spread out the earth from the heaven world which she had grasped and thus caused the seeds to spring into germination as they dropped from her dress.

The root of the tree which she had grasped she sunk into the soil where she had fallen and this too began to grow until it formed a tree with all manner of fruits and flowers and bore a luminous orb at its top by which the new world became illuminated.

Now in due season the Sky Woman lay beneath the tree and to her a daughter was born. She was then happy for she had a companion. Rapidly the girl child grew until very soon she could run about. It was then the custom of Ancient One to say: "My daughter, run about the island and return telling me what you have seen."

Day by day the girl ran around the island and each time it became larger, making her trips longer and longer. She observed that the earth was carpeted with grass and that shrubs and trees were springing up everywhere. This she reported to her mother, who sat beneath the centrally situated great tree.

In one part of the island there was a tree on which grew a long vine and upon this vine the girl was accustomed to swing for amusement, and her body moved to and fro giving her great delight. Then did her mother say, "My daughter, you laugh as if being embraced by a lover. Have you seen a man?"

"I have seen no one but you, my mother," answered the girl, "but when I swing I know someone is close to me, and I feel my body embraced as if with strong arms. I feel thrilled and I tingle, which causes me to laugh."

Then did the Sky Woman look sad, and she said, "My daughter, I know not now what will befall us. You are married to Gaha, and he will be the father of your children. There will be two boys."

In due season the voices of two boys were heard speaking, eiadagon, and the words of one were kind and he gave no trouble, but the words of the other were harsh and he desired to kill his mother. His skin was covered with warts and boils and he was inclined to cause great pain.

When the two boys were born, Elder One made his mother happy but when Warty One was born he pierced her through the arm pit and stood upon her dead body. So did the mother perish, and because of this the Sky Woman wept.

The boys required little care but instantly became able to care for themselves. After the mother's body had been arranged for burial, the Sky Woman saw the Elder One whom she called Good Mind, approach, and he said, "Grandmother, I wish to help you prepare the grave." So he helped his grandmother, who continually wept, and deposited the body of his mother in a grave. Thereupon did the grandmother speak to her daughter:

"Oh, my daughter," she said. "You have departed and made the first path to the world from which I came bringing your life. When you reach that homeland make ready to receive many beings from this place below, for I think the path will be trodden by many."

Good Mind watched at the grave of his mother and watered the earth above it until the grass grew. He continued to watch until he saw strange buds coming out of the ground.

Where the feet were the earth sprouted with a plant that became the stringed-potato, (onennodaowe) where her fingers lay sprang the beans, where her abdomen lay sprang the squash, where her breasts lay sprang the corn plant, and from the spot above her forehead sprang the tobacco plant.

Now the warty one was named Evil Mind, and he neglected his mother's grave and spent his time tearing up the land and seeking to do evil.

When the grandmother saw the plants springing from the grave of her daughter and cared for by Good Mind she was thankful and said, "By these things we shall hereafter live, and they shall be cooked in pots with fire, and the corn shall be your milk and sustain you. You shall make the corn grow in hills like breasts, for from the corn shall flow our living."

Then the Grandmother, the Sky Woman, took Good Mind about the island and instructed him how to produce plants and trees. So he spoke to the earth and said, "Let a willow here come forth," and it came. In a like manner he made the oak, the chestnut, the beech, the hemlock, the spruce, the pine, the maple, the button-ball, the tulip, the elm and many other trees that should become useful.

With a jealous stomach the Evil Mind followed behind and sought to destroy the good things but could not, so he spoke to the earth and said: "Briars come forth," and they came forth. Likewise he created poisonous plants and thorns upon bushes.

Upon a certain occasion Good Mind made inquiries of his Grandmother, asking where his father dwelt. Then did the Sky Woman say: "You shall now seek your father. He lives to the uttermost east and you shall go to the far eastern end of the island and go over the water until you behold a mountain rising from the sea. You shall walk up the mountain and there you will find your father seated upon the top."

Good Mind made the pilgrimage and came to the mountain. At the foot of the mountain he looked upward and called, "My father, where art thou?" And a great voice sounded the word: "A son of mine shall cast the cliff from the mountain's edge to the summit of this peak." Good Mind grasped the cliff and with a mighty effort flung it to the mountain top. Again he cried, "My father, where art thou?" The answer came, "A son of mine shall swim the cataract from the pool below to the top." Good Mind leaped into the falls and swam upward to the top where the water poured over. He stood there and cried again, "My father, where art thou?" The voice answered, "A son of mine shall wrestle with the wind." So, there at the edge of a terrifying precipice Good Mind grappled with Wind and the two wrestled, each endeavoring to throw the other over. It was a terrible battle and Wind tore great rocks from the mountain side and lashed the water below, but Good Mind overcame Wind, and he departed moaning in defeat. Once more Good Mind called, "My father, where art thou?" In awesome tones the voice replied, "A son of mine shall endure the flame," and immediately a flame sprang out of the mountain side and enveloped Good Mind. It blinded him and tortured him with its cruel heat, but he threw aside its entwining arms and ran to the mountain top where he beheld a being sitting in the midst of a blaze of light.

"I am thy father," said the voice. "Thou art my son."

"I have come to receive power," said the son. "I wish to rule all things on the earth."

"You have power," answered the father. "You have conquered. I give to you the bags of life, the containers of living creatures that will bless the earth."

Thus did the father and son counsel together and the son learned many things that he should do. He learned how to avoid the attractive path that descended to the place of the cave where Hanisheono dwells.

Now the father said, "How did you come to find me, seeing I am secluded by many elements?"

The Good Mind answered, "When I was about to start my journey Sky Woman, my grandmother, gave me a flute and I blew upon it, making music. Now, when the music ceased the flute spoke to me, saying, 'This way shalt thou go,' and I continued to make music and the voice of the flute spoke to me."

Then did the father say, "Make music by the flute and listen, then shalt thou continue to know the right direction."

In course of time Good Mind went down the mountain and he waded the sea, taking with him the bags with which he had been presented. As he drew near the shore he became curious to know what was within, and he pinched one bag hoping to feel its contents. He felt a movement inside which increased until it became violent. The bag began to roll about on his back until he could scarcely hold it and a portion of the mouth of the bag slipped from his hand. Immediately the things inside began to jump out and fall into the water with a great splash, and they were water animals of different kinds. The other bag began to roll around on his back but he held on tightly until he could do so no more, when a portion of the mouth slipped and out flew many kinds of birds, some flying seaward and others inland toward the trees. Then as before the third bag began to roll about but he held on very tight, but it slipped and fell into the water and many kinds of swimming creatures rushed forth, fishes, crabs and eels. The fourth bag then began to roll about, but he held on until he reached the land when he threw it down, and out rushed all the good land animals, of kinds he did not know. From the bird bag had come good insects, and from the fish bag had also come little turtles and clams.

When Good Mind came to his grandmother beneath the tree she asked what he had brought, for she heard music in the trees and saw creatures scampering about. Thereupon Good Mind related what had happened, and Sky Woman said, "We must now call all the animals and discover their names, and moreover we must so treat them that they will have fat."

So then she spoke, "Cavity be in the ground and be filled with oil." The pool of oil came, for Sky Woman had the power of creating what she desired.

Good Mind then caught the animals one by one and brought them to his grandmother. She took a large furry animal and cast it into the pool and it swam very slowly across, licking up much oil. "This animal shall hereafter be known as niagwaih, (bear) and you shall be very fat." Next came another animal with much fur and it swam across and licked up the oil, and it was named degiiago, (buffalo). So in turn were named the elk, the moose, the badger, the woodchuck, and the raccoon, and all received much fat. Then came the beaver (naganiago), the porcupine and the skunk. Now Good Mind wished the deer to enter but it was shy and bounded away, whereupon he took a small arrow and pierced its front leg, his aim being good. Then the deer came and swam across the pool and oil entered the wound and healed it. This oil of the deer's leg is a medicine for wounds to this day and if the eyes are anointed with it one may shoot straight.

Again other animals came and one by one they were named weasel, mink, otter, fisher, panther, lynx, wild cat, fox, wolf, big wolf, squirrel, chipmunk, mole, and many others.

And many animals that were not desired plunged into the pool of oil, and these Good Mind seized as they came out and he stripped them of their fat and pulled out their bodies long. So he did to the otter, fisher, weasel and mink. So he did to the panther, wolf, big wolf, and fox, the lynx and the wild-cat. Of these the fat to this day is not good tasting. But after a time Evil Mind secured a bag of creatures from the road to the cave and unloosed it, and evil things crawled into the pool and grew fat. So did the rattlesnake and great bugs and loathly worms.

Thus did Evil Mind secure many evil monsters and insects, and he enticed good animals into his traps and perverted them and gave them appetites for men-beings. He was delighted to see how fierce he could make the animals, and set them to quarreling.

He roamed about visiting the streams of pure water made by Good Mind and filling them with mud and slime, and he kicked rocks in the rivers and creeks to make passage difficult, and he planted nettles and thorns in the paths. Thus did he do to cause annoyance.

Now Good Mind sat with his grandmother beneath the tree of light and he spoke to her of the world and how he might improve it. "Alas," said she, "I believe that only one more task awaits me and then I shall go upon my path and follow your mother back to the world beyond the sky. It remains for me to call into being certain lights in the blackness above where Heavy Night presides."

So saying she threw the contents of a bag into the sky and it quickly became sprinkled with stars. And thus there came into being constellations (haditgwada), and of these we see the bear chase, the dancing brothers, the seated woman, the beaver skin, the belt, and many others.

Now it seems that Good Mind knew that there should be a luminous orb and, so it is said, he took his mother's face and flung it skyward and made the sun, and took his mother's breast and flinging it into the sky made the moon. So it is said, but there are other accounts of the creation of these lights. It is said that the first beings made them by going into the sky.

Shortly after the creation of the stars (gadjisoda), the Grandmother said unto Good Mind, "I believe that the time has come when I should depart, for nearly all is finished here. There is a road from my feet, and I have a song which I shall sing by which I shall know the path. There is one more matter that troubles me for I see that your brother is jealous and will seek to kill you. Use great care that you overcome him, and when you have done so confine him in the cave and send with him the evil spirit beasts, lest they injure men."

When morning came the Sky Woman had departed and her journey was toward the sky world.

Good Mind felt lonely and believed that his own mission was about at end. He had been in conflict with his brother, Evil Mind, and had sought, moreover, to overcome and to teach the Whirlwind and Wind, and the Fire Beast.

Soon Evil Mind came proposing a hunting trip and Good Mind went with him on the journey. When they had gone a certain distance the Evil Mind said, "My elder brother, I perceive that you are about to call forth men-beings who shall live on the island that we here have inhabited. I propose to afflict them with disease and to make life difficult, for this is not their world but mine, and I shall do as I please to spoil it."

Then did Good Mind answer and say, "Verily, I am about to make men-beings who shall live here when I depart, for I am going to follow the road skyward made first by my mother."

"This is good news," answered Evil Mind. "I propose that you then reveal unto me the word that has power over your life, that I may possess it and have power when you are gone."

Good Mind now saw that his brother wished to destroy him, and so he said, "It may happen that you will employ the cat-tail flag, whose sharp leaves will pierce me."

Good Mind then lay down and slumbered, but soon was awakened by Evil Mind who was lashing him with cat-tail flags, and yelling loudly, "Thou shalt die." Good Mind arose and asked his brother what he meant by lashing him and he answered, "I was seeking to awaken you from a dream, for you were speaking."

So, soon again the brother, Evil Mind, asked, "My brother, I wish to know the word that has power over you." And Good Mind perceiving his intention answered, "It may be that deer-horns will have power over me, they are sharp and hard."

Soon Good Mind slept again and was awakened by Evil Mind beating him with deer-horns, seeking to destroy him. They rushed inland to the foot of the tree and fought each other about it. Evil Mind was very fierce and rushed at his brother thrusting the horns at him and trying to pierce his chest, his face or tear his abdomen. Finally, Good Mind disarmed him, saying, "Look what you have done to the tree where Ancient One was wont to care for us, and whose branches have supplied us with food. See how you have torn this tree and stripped it of its valuable products. This tree was designed to support the life of men-beings and now you have injured it. I must banish you to the region of the great cave, and you shall have the name of Destroyer."

So saying he used his good power to overcome Evil Mind's otgont (evil power) and thrust him into the mouth of the cave, and with him all manner of enchanted beasts. There he placed the white buffalo, the poison beaver, the poison otter, snakes and many bewitched things that were otgont. So there to this day abides Evil Mind seeking to emerge, and his voice is heard giving orders.

Then Good Mind went back to the tree and soon saw a being walking about. He walked over to the place where the being was pacing to and fro. He saw that it was Shagodiiwegowa, who was a giant with a grotesque face. "I am master of the earth," roared this being (called also Great Defender), for he was the whirlwind. "If you are master," said Good Mind, "prove your power."

Defender said, "What shall be our test?"

"Let this be the test," said Good Mind, "that the mountain yonder shall approach us at your bidding."

So Defender spoke saying, "Mountain, come hither." And they turned their backs that they might not see it coming until it stood at their backs. Soon they turned about again and the mountain had not moved.

"So now, I shall command," said Good Mind, and he spoke saying, "Mountain, come hither," and they turned their backs. There was a rushing of air and Defender turned to see what was behind him and fell against the onrushing mountain, and it bent his nose and twisted his mouth, and from this he never recovered.

Then did Defender say, "I do now acknowledge you to be master. Command me and I will obey."

"Since you love to wander," said Good Mind, "it shall be your duty to move about over the earth and stir up things. You shall abandon your evil intentions and seek to overcome your otgont nature, changing it to be of benefit to man-beings, whom I am about to create."

"Then," said Defender, "shall man-beings offer incense tobacco to me and make a song that is pleasing to me, and they shall carve my likeness from the substance of trees, and my orenda will enter the likeness of my face and it shall be a help to men-beings and they shall use the face as I shall direct. Then shall all the diseases that I may cause depart and I shall be satisfied."

Again Good Mind wandered, being melancholy. Looking up he saw another being approaching.

"I am Thunder," said the being.

"What can you do to be a help to me?" asked Good Mind.

"I can wash the earth and make drink for the trees and grass," said Thunder.

"What can you do to be a benefit to the men-beings I am about to create?" asked Good Mind.

"I shall slay evil monsters when they escape from the under-world," said Thunder. "I shall have scouts who will notify me and I shall shoot all otgont beings."

Then was Good Mind satisfied, and he pulled up a tree and saw the water fill the cavity where the roots had been. Long he gazed into the water until he saw a reflection of his own image. "Like unto that will I make men-beings," he thought. So then he took clay and molded it into small images of men and women. These he placed on the ground and when they were dry he spoke to them and they sprang up and lived.

When he saw them he said unto them, "All this world I give unto you. It is from me that you shall say you are descended and you are the children of the first-born of earth, and you shall say that you are the flesh of Iagetci, she the Ancient Bodied One.

When he had acquainted them with the other first beings, and shown them how to hunt and fish and to eat of the fruits of the land, he told them that they should seek to live together as friends and brothers and that they should treat each other well.

He told them how to give incense of tobacco, for Awehai, Ancient Bodied One, had stripped the heaven world of tobacco when she fell, and thus its incense should be a pleasing one into which men-beings might speak their words when addressing him hereafter. These and many other things did he tell them.

Soon he vanished from the sight of created men beings, and he took all the first beings with him upon the sky road.

Soon men-beings began to increase and they covered the earth, and from them we are descended. Many things have happened since those days, so much that all can never be told.

1923

HOW THE WORLD WAS MADE[1]

The earth is a great island floating in a sea of water, and suspended at each of the four cardinal points by a cord hanging down from the sky vault, which is of solid rock. When the world grows old and worn out, the people will die and the cords will break and let the earth sink down into the ocean, and all will be water again. The Indians are afraid of this.

When all was water, the animals were above in Galunlati, beyond the arch; but it was very much crowded, and they were wanting more room. They wondered what was below the water, and at last Dayunisi, "Beaver's Grandchild," the little Water-beetle, offered to go and see if it could learn. It darted in every direction over the surface of the water, but could find no firm place to rest. Then it dived to the bottom and came up with some soft mud, which began to grow and spread on every side until it became the island which we call the earth. It was afterward fastened to the sky with four cords, but no one remembers who did this.

At first the earth was flat and very soft and wet. The animals were anxious to get down, and sent out different birds to see if it was yet dry, but they found no place to alight and came back again to Galunlati. At last it seemed to be time, and they sent out the Buzzard and told him to go and make ready for them. This was the Great Buzzard, the father of all the buzzards we see now. He flew all over the earth, low down near the ground, and it was still soft. When he reached the Cherokee country, he was very tired, and his wings began to flap and strike the ground, and wherever they struck the earth there was a valley, and where they turned up again there was a mountain. When the animals above saw this, they were afraid that the whole world would be mountains, so they called him back, but the Cherokee country remains full of mountains to this day.

When the earth was dry and the animals came down, it was still dark, so they got the sun and set it in a track to go every day across the island from east to west, just overhead. It was too hot this way, and Tsiskagili, the Red Crawfish, had his shell scorched a bright red, so that his meat was spoiled: and the Cherokee do not eat it. The conjurers put the sun another handbreadth higher in the air, but it was still too hot. They raised it another time, and another, until it was seven handbreadths high and just under the sky arch. Then it was right, and they left it so. This is why the conjurers call the highest place Gulkwagine Digalunlatiyun, "the seventh height," because it is seven hand-breadths above the earth. Every day the sun goes along under this arch, and returns at night on the upper side to the starting place.

There is another world under this, and it is like ours in everything—animals, plants, and people—save that the seasons are different. The streams that come down from the mountains are the trails by which we reach this underworld, and the springs at their heads are the doorways by which we enter it, but to do this one must fast and go to water and have one of the underground people for a guide. We know that the seasons in the underworld are different from ours, because the water in the springs is always warmer in winter and cooler in summer than the outer air.

[1]A myth of the Cherokee Indians of North Carolina.

When the animals and plants were first made—we do not know by whom—they were told to watch and keep awake for seven nights, just as young men now fast and keep awake when they pray to their medicine.[2] They tried to do this, and nearly all were awake through the first night, but the next night several dropped off to sleep, and the third night others were asleep, and then others, until, on the seventh night, of all the animals only the owl, the panther, and one or two more were still awake. To these were given the power to see and to go about in the dark, and to make prey of the birds and animals which must sleep at night. Of the trees only the cedar, the pine, the spruce, the holly, and the laurel were awake to the end, and to them it was given to be always green and to be greatest for medicine, but to the others it was said: "Because you have not endured to the end you shall lose your hair every winter."

Men came after the animals and plants. At first there were only a brother and sister until he struck her with a fish and told her to multiply, and so it was. In seven days a child was born to her, and thereafter every seven days another, and they increased very fast until there was danger that the world could not keep them. Then it was made that woman should have only one child in a year, and it has been so ever since.

1900

THE BEGINNING OF SUMMER AND WINTER[1]

Long ago, when the world was young and people had not come out yet, there lived in the warm southland a family of five brothers and their sister. They were surrounded by sunshine and flowers and the music of birds. The brothers, who were hunters, were always successful. They never went hunting without bringing back some meat.

Their sister stayed at home, mending their clothes and preparing their meals. She was always nicely dressed in buckskin that she had ornamented with elks' teeth and had painted with yellow powder.

In the northland there lived a family of five brothers and their sister. They lived in the midst of ice and snow. These brothers also were hunters, but they had so little success that they were often hungry. One time when their food supply was almost gone, the brothers said to their sister, "You will have to go to the five brothers in the southland. When you reach them, you will say, 'We are all very hungry. My brothers have sent me to ask for food from you.'"

At first the girl refused to go, but her brothers insisted. After many persuasive words from them, she started south, carrying in her hands some large icicles. Her brothers used icicles as spears. As she approached the southland, traveling in the form of a large black cloud, the five southern brothers saw her. The oldest said to their sister, "Paint yourself gorgeously with yellow powder, and sprinkle over your dress the perfumes of flowers. When the girl

[2]Magic powers.

[1]A myth of the Yakima Indians of the Pacific Northwest.

from the north comes close, go out and meet her. When you get to her, shake yourself."

"Yes, my brother," she replied.

When she was ready, the girl of the south walked out to meet the girl from the north. The black cloud made the air chilly and uncomfortable. The girl of the south smiled gently and shook her dress. From it flew fine dry powder and the sweet fragrance of summer flowers. Instantly the icicles which the northern girl planned to use as weapons fell to the ground. The black cloud scattered. Soon the particles of what remained were lost to sight.

How the girl returned home is not known, but when she told her brothers what had happened, they were angry. "Let us challenge the southern brothers to wrestle with us," they said to each other.

They sent their challenge, and the five southern brothers accepted it. When it was almost autumn, the two families met halfway between their homes. The sister in each group took with her five buckets. In the buckets of the southern girl was hot water; in the buckets of the northern girl were ice and cold water. Each planned to throw the contents of her buckets at the feet of the wrestlers.

When everything was ready, the oldest northern brother wrestled with the oldest southern brother. They were so evenly matched that for a long time neither was able to throw the other. Suddenly both heard the sound of rushing water. The northern girl emptied one of her buckets, and the cold water made the northern man fight harder. Then the girl from the south threw hot water at the feet of the wrestlers. The ice melted, and immediately the southern man overcame his rival. The oldest brother from the north lay on the ground dead.

At once the next oldest from the northern family ran up to the victor and began to wrestle with him. In a short but fierce struggle he overcame the southern brother. The oldest brother from the southland also lay on the ground dead. One by one the brothers from each tribe wrestled with a brother from the other tribe. After a while, only the youngest in each family was left alive.

For five days these two wrestled, neither of them able to overcome the other. On the sixth day the southern boy got tired and almost fell, but in some unknown way he regained his feet. Then they decided to stop for a while. The southern boy went to his home and stayed there for five moons.

At the end of that time he traveled north and met the northern brother at the place where they had fought before. This time the southern boy easily defeated the northern boy and drove him far back into the cold land. For about six moons the southern brother had possession of the lands of the northern family. At the end of six moons the northern boy returned, and the two wrestled for one whole moon. This time the southern boy was defeated and driven home.

Even today the two continue to wrestle for mastery of the land. When the southern wrestler defeats the northern one, we have summer. When the northern wrestler defeats the southern one, we have winter. Two battles are waged every year. Just before spring, the southern boy conquers the northern boy; in the autumn, the northern boy conquers the southern boy. Each rules the land for a few months.

1966

THE GIFT OF THE SACRED PIPE[1]

Early one morning, very many winters ago, two Lakota were out hunting with their bows and arrows, and as they were standing on a hill looking for game, they saw in the distance something coming towards them in a very strange and wonderful manner. When this mysterious thing came nearer to them, they saw that it was a very beautiful woman, dressed in white buckskin, and bearing a bundle on her back. Now this woman was so good to look at that one of the Lakota had bad intentions and told his friend of his desire, but this good man said that he must not have such thoughts, for surely this is a *wakan*[2] woman. The mysterious person was now very close to the men, and then putting down her bundle, she asked the one with bad intentions to come over to her. As the young man approached the mysterious woman, they were both covered by a great cloud, and soon when it lifted the sacred woman was standing there, and at her feet was the man with the bad thoughts who was now nothing but bones, and terrible snakes were eating him.

"Behold what you see!" the strange woman said to the good man. "I am coming to your people and wish to talk with your chief *Hehlokecha Najin* [Standing Hollow Horn]. Return to him, and tell him to prepare a large tipi in which he should gather all his people, and make ready for my coming. I wish to tell you something of great importance!"

The young man then returned to the tipi of his chief, and told him all that had happened: that this *wakan* woman was coming to visit them and that they must all prepare. The chief, Standing Hollow Horn, then had several tipis taken down, and from them a great lodge was made as the sacred woman had instructed. He sent out a crier to tell the people to put on their best buckskin clothes and to gather immediately in the lodge. The people were, of course, all very excited as they waited in the great lodge for the coming of the holy woman, and everybody was wondering where this mysterious woman came from and what it was that she wished to say.

Soon the young men who were watching for the coming of the *wakan* person announced that they saw something in the distance approaching them in a beautiful manner, and then suddenly she entered the lodge, walked around sun-wise,[3] and stood in front of Standing Hollow Horn. She took from her back the bundle, and holding it with both hands in front of the chief, said: "Behold this and always love it! It is *lela wakan* [very sacred], and you must treat it as such. No impure man should ever be allowed to see it, for within this bundle there is a sacred pipe. With this you will, during the winters to come, send your voices to *Wakan-Tanka*, your Father and Grandfather."

After the mysterious woman said this, she took from the bundle a pipe, and also a small round stone which she placed upon the ground. Holding the pipe up with its stem to the heavens, she said: "With this sacred pipe you will walk upon the Earth; for the Earth is your Grandmother and Mother, and She is sacred. Every step that is taken upon Her should be as a prayer. The bowl of this pipe is of red stone; it is the Earth. Carved in the stone and

[1]A myth of the Oglala Sioux. [2]Sacred. [3]Clockwise.

facing the center is this buffalo calf who represents all the four-leggeds who live upon your Mother. The stem of the pipe is of wood, and this represents all that grows upon the Earth. And these twelve feathers which hang here where the stem fits into the bowl are from *Wanbli Galeshka*, the Spotted Eagle, and they represent the eagle and all the wingeds of the air. All these peoples, and all the things of the universe, are joined to you who smoke the pipe—all send their voices to *Wakan-Tanka*, the Great Spirit. When you pray with this pipe, you pray for and with everything."

The *wakan* woman then touched the foot of the pipe to the round stone which lay upon the ground, and said: "With this pipe you will be bound to all your relatives; your Grandfather and Father, your Grandmother and Mother. This round rock, which is made of the same red stone as the bowl of the pipe, your Father *Wakan-Tanka* has also given to you. It is the Earth, your Grandmother and Mother, and it is where you will live and increase. This Earth which he has given to you is red, and the two-leggeds who live upon the Earth are red; and the Great Spirit has also given to you a red day, and a red road.[4] All of this is sacred and so do not forget! Every dawn as it comes is a holy event, and every day is holy, for the light comes from your Father *Wakan-Tanka*; and also you must always remember that the two-leggeds and all the other peoples who stand upon this earth are sacred and should be treated as such.

"From this time on, the holy pipe will stand upon this red Earth, and the two-leggeds will take the pipe and will send their voices to *Wakan-Tanka*. These seven circles which you see on the stone have much meaning, for they represent the seven rites in which the pipe will be used. The first large circle represents the first rite which I shall give to you, and the other six circles represent the rites which will in time be revealed to you directly. Standing Hollow Horn, be good to these gifts and to your people, for they are *wakan*! With this pipe the two-leggeds will increase, and there will come to them all that is good. From above *Wakan-Tanka* has given to you this sacred pipe, so that through it you may have knowledge. For this great gift you should always be grateful! But now before I leave I wish to give to you instructions for the first rite in which your people will use this pipe.

"It should be for you a sacred day when one of your people dies. You must then keep his soul as I shall teach you, and through this you will gain much power; for if this soul is kept, it will increase in you your concern and love for your neighbor. So long as the person, in his soul, is kept with your people, through him you will be able to send your voice to *Wakan-Tanka*.

"It should also be a sacred day when a soul is released and returns to its home, *Wakan-Tanka*, for on this day four women will be made holy, and they will in time bear children who will walk the path of life in a sacred manner, setting an example to your people. Behold Me, for it is I that they will take in their mouths, and it is through this that they will become *wakan*.

"He who keeps the soul of a person must be a good and pure man, and he should use the pipe so that all the people, with the soul, will together send their voices to *Wakan-Tanka*. The fruit of your Mother the Earth and the fruit of all that bears will be blessed in this manner, and your people will then

[4]The "red road" is that which runs north and south and is the good or straight way.

walk the path of life in a sacred way. Do not forget that *Wakan-Tanka* has given you seven days in which to send your voices to Him. So long as you remember this you will live; the rest you will know from *Wakan-Tanka* directly."

The sacred woman then started to leave the lodge, but turning again to Standing Hollow Horn, she said: "Behold this pipe! Always remember how sacred it is, and treat it as such, for it will take you to the end. Remember, in me there are four ages. I am leaving now, but I shall look back upon your people in every age, and at the end I shall return."

Moving around the lodge in a sun-wise manner, the mysterious woman left, but after walking a short distance she looked back towards the people and sat down. When she rose the people were amazed to see that she had become a young red and brown buffalo calf. Then this calf walked farther, lay down, and rolled, looking back at the people, and when she got up she was a white buffalo. Again the white buffalo walked farther and rolled on the ground, becoming now a black buffalo. This buffalo then walked farther away from the people, stopped, and after bowing to each of the four quarters of the universe, disappeared over the hill.

1953

THUNDER, DIZZYING LIQUID, AND CUPS THAT DO NOT GROW

When the Menominee[1] lived on the shore of the sea,[2] they one day were looking out across the water and observed some large vessels, which were near to them and wonderful to behold. Suddenly there was a terrific explosion, as of thunder, which startled the people greatly.

When the vessels approached the shore, men with light-colored skin landed. Most of them had hair on their faces, and they carried on their shoulders heavy sticks ornamented with shining metal. As the strangers came toward the Indians, the latter believed the leader to be a great manido [spirit], with his companions.

It is customary, when offering tobacco to a manido, to throw it into the fire, that the fumes may ascend to him and that he may be inclined to grant their request; but as this light-skin manido came in person, the chief took some tobacco and rubbed it on his forehead. The strangers appeared desirous of making friends with the Indians, and all sat on the ground and smoked. Then some of the strangers brought from the vessel some parcels which contained a liquid, of which they drank, finally offering some to the Menominee. The Indians, however, were afraid to drink such a pungent liquor indiscriminately, fearing it would kill them; therefore four useless old men were selected to drink the liquor, and thus to be experimented on, that it might be found whether the liquid would kill them or not.

The men drank the liquid, and although they had previously been very silent and gloomy, they now began to talk and to grow amused. Their speech

[1]Indians of the Great Lakes region. [2]Probably a reference to Lake Michigan.

flowed more and more freely, while the remainder of the Indians said, "See, now it is beginning to take effect!" Presently the four old men arose, and while walking about seemed very dizzy, when the Indians said, "See, now they are surely dying!" Presently the men dropped down and became unconscious; then the Indians said to one another, "Now they are dead; see what we escaped by not drinking the liquid!" There were sullen looks directed toward the strangers, and murmurings of destroying them for the supposed treachery were heard.

Before things came to a dangerous pass, however, the four old men got up, rubbed their eyes, and approached their kindred, saying, "The liquor is good, and we have felt very happy; you must try it, too." Notwithstanding the rest of the tribe were afraid to drink it then, they recalled the strangers, who were about to return to their boats.

The chief of the strangers next gave the Indians some flour, but they did not know what to do with it. The white chief then showed the Indians some biscuits, and told them how they were baked. When that was over, one of the white men presented to an Indian a gun, after firing it to show how far away anything could be killed. The Indian was afraid to shoot it, fearing the gun would knock him over, but the stranger showed the Indian how to hold it and to point it at a mark; then pulling the trigger, it made a terrific noise, but did not harm the Indian at all, as he had expected. Some of the Indians then accepted guns from the white strangers.

Next the white chief brought out some kettles and showed the Indians how to boil water in them. But the kettles were too large and too heavy to carry about, so the Indians asked that they be given small ones—cups as large as a clenched fist, for they believed they would grow to be large ones by and by.

The Indians received some small cups, as they desired, when the strangers took their departure. But the cups never grew to be kettles.

1897

William Bradford 1590–1657

When he was twelve, William Bradford left the Church of England for the "forward" services of a nonconformist congregation near his home in Yorkshire, England. He was the orphaned son of a yeoman farmer, a sickly but intelligent boy who was a devoted reader of the Bible. In 1606, disregarding the "scoff" of his neighbors, he joined an outlawed group of religious separatists that met secretly in the nearby village of Scrooby.

In 1607 the Scrooby group decided to move to the Low Countries "where they heard was freedom of religion for all men." Bradford went with them, first to Amsterdam in 1608 and then to Leyden the following year. In Leyden, Bradford became a weaver; he learned Dutch, French, and some Latin, Greek, and Hebrew. And he continued to study the Bible, whose stories he absorbed and whose words were to echo through his history of Plymouth Plantation.

In 1617, troubled by poverty and fearful that they would be absorbed by the Dutch, the Separatists decided to leave Holland on a pilgrimage to the New World. In 1620 they obtained a charter from England granting them the right to settle on land in America owned by the Virginia Company of London, and in that same year a group of English investors, "Merchant Adventurers," agreed to finance the Pilgrims' trip to the New World. In return, the Pilgrims agreed to repay their backers with shipments of furs, fish, and mineral riches.

Bradford was in the first group to leave Leyden for England, where 102 men, women, and children crowded on the Mayflower *and, after many delays, began their passage to Virginia. Only a minority of the passengers were Separatists, or "Saints," as they called themselves. The majority were "Strangers," Church of England members who hoped to build a new life in America.*

They left England in September 1620. Sixty-five days later they sighted land at Cape Cod, Massachusetts. Weakened by exposure and sickness, and fearful of sailing over the winter Atlantic south to Virginia, the Pilgrims decided to remain in New England. To halt arguments that their rules for government were void because their charter applied only in Virginia, the Pilgrims created the Mayflower Compact. It was the first effort to establish formal self-government in the New World.

Bradford was one of the signers of the Compact. He was one of the leaders sent to explore the coast and harbor where, according to legend, the Pilgrims landed on Plymouth Rock. And when the Pilgrim governor, John Carver, died, Bradford was chosen to succeed him in office, a position to which Bradford was elected thirty times, serving almost continuously from 1621 to 1656.

He began writing his history of Plymouth Plantation in 1630. He described it as merely "scribled writings" that he "peeced up at times of leisure." His history covered the experiences of the Separatists, from their beginnings at Scrooby to the year 1647 at Plymouth. The history was not published in Bradford's lifetime, and after his death the manuscript passed down through his family. Later it was deposited in the Library of the Old South Church in Boston. During the Revolution and the occupation of Boston by the British, the manuscript disappeared. In the mid-nineteenth century it was discovered in England, in the library of the Bishop of London. Finally, in 1856, two centuries after it was written, the full text of Bradford's history of the Pilgrims was published for the first time.

He had witnessed stirring events that he had helped to shape, but he was himself shaped by a faith that gave him a narrow, partisan view. He was tolerant in all things but religion. He saw the Separatists as God's elect. He believed that Quakers, the "darkness of popery," and Indians were all instruments of the Antichrist. He believed in providences—divine interventions in the affairs of men—just as he believed that a man's salvation or even his worldly success was the "special work and hand of God." Bradford saw the "root and rise" of the Plymouth Colony as a divine repetition of the trials of the Children of Israel, for the Pilgrims, too, were a chosen people, beset by cruel enemies in a wilderness. To Bradford all such truths were absolute; all were revealed in the Bible, the book to which he devoted his life and from which he drew his strength.

Throughout his life, Bradford remained a humble man. He sought neither personal glory nor riches. When he died at sixty-seven he owned little more than some land, his house in Plymouth, and a few personal possessions, including a "red Turkey suit" and a "great beer bowle." He had lived to see the weakening of the Pilgrim ideal. Piety declined. "Wickedness did grow and break forth." New sects arose. Many original church members died or moved away, and newcomers began to question the divine authority of Plymouth's religious leaders. But Bradford held fast to his faith in the divine mission of his people. And his faith still shines forth clearly in his history of the Pilgrims, a book that has become part of the nation's heritage and stands as one of the great works of colonial America.

FURTHER READING: *William Bradford, The Collected Verse,* ed. M. Runyan, 1974; G. Willison, *Saints and Strangers,* 1945; B. Smith, *Bradford of Plymouth,* 1951; E. Morgan, *Visible Saints,* 1963; G. Langdon, *Pilgrim Colony,* 1966; J. Demos, *A Little Commonwealth,* 1970; K. Caffrey, *The Mayflower,* 1974; P. Westbrook, *William Bradford,* 1978; F. Ogburn, *Style as Structure and Meaning, William Bradford's Of Plymouth Plantation,* 1981; A. Kemp, *The Estrangment of the Past,* 1990; J. Pafford, *How Firm a Foundation, William Bradford and Plymouth,* 2001; D. Anderson, *William Bradford's Books,* 2003.

TEXT: *History of Plymouth Plantation, 1620–1646,* ed. W. Davis, 1901. Spelling, punctuation, and usage have been changed to conform more nearly to modern practice.

from *OF PLYMOUTH PLANTATION*

And first of the occasion and inducements thereunto; the which, that I may truly unfold, I must begin at the very root and rise of the same. The which I shall endeavour to manifest in a plain style, with singular regard unto the simple truth in all things; at least as near as my slender judgment can attain the same.

Chapter I
[BRADFORD ON THE RISE OF PROTESTANTISM]

It is well known unto the godly and judicious, how ever since the first breaking out of the light of the gospel in our honourable nation of England, (which was the first of nations whom the Lord adorned therewith after the gross darkness of popery which had covered and overspread the Christian world), what wars and oppositions ever since, Satan hath raised, maintained and continued against the Saints,[1] from time to time, in one sort or other. Sometimes by bloody death and cruel torments; other whiles imprisonments, banishments and other hard usages; as being loath his kingdom should go down, the truth prevail and the churches of God revert to their ancient purity and recover their primitive order, liberty and beauty. But when he could not prevail by these means against the main truths of the gospel, but that they began to take rooting in many places, being watered with the blood of the martyrs and blessed from heaven with a gracious increase; he then began to take him to his ancient stratagems, used of old against the first Christians. That when by the bloody and barbarous persecutions of the heathen emperors he could not stop and subvert the course of the gospel, but that it speedily overspread, with a wonderful celerity, the then best known parts of the world; he then began to sow errors, heresies and wonderful dissensions amongst the professors[2] themselves, working upon their pride and ambition,

[1]Bradford uses the word "Saint" to mean a church member (and therefore one of the elect), not a person canonized by the Roman Catholic or other Christian church.

[2]I.e., those who professed to be Christians.

with other corrupt passions incident to all mortal men, yea to the Saints themselves in some measure, by which woeful effects followed. As not only bitter contentions and heartburnings, schisms, with other horrible confusions, but Satan took occasion and advantage thereby to foist in a number of vile ceremonies, with many unprofitable canons[3] and decrees, which have since been as snares to many poor and peaceable souls even to this day.

. . .

So many, therefore, of these professors as saw the evil of these things in these parts, and whose hearts the Lord had touched with heavenly zeal for His truth, they shook off this yoke of antichristian bondage, and as the Lord's free people joined themselves (by a covenant of the Lord) into a church estate, in the fellowship of the gospel, to walk in all His ways made known, or to be made known unto them, according to their best endeavours, whatsoever it should cost them, the Lord assisting them.[4] And that it cost them something this ensuing history will declare.

. . .

They could not long continue in any peaceable condition, but were hunted and persecuted on every side, so as their former afflictions were but as flea-bitings in comparison of these which now came upon them. For some were taken and clapped up in prison, others had their houses beset and watched night and day, and hardly escaped their hands; and the most were fain to flee and leave their houses and habitations, and the means of their livelihood. Yet these and many other sharper things which afterward befell them were no other than [what] they looked for, and therefore [they] were the better prepared to bear them by the assistance of God's grace and Spirit. Yet seeing themselves thus molested, and that there was no hope of their continuance there, by a joint consent they resolved to go into the Low Countries, where they heard was freedom of religion for all men.

Chapter III
Of Their Settling in Holland, and Their Manner of Living, and Entertainment There

Being now come into the Low Countries, they saw many goodly and fortified cities, strongly walled and guarded with troops of armed men. Also, they heard a strange and uncouth language, and beheld the different manners and customs of the people, with their strange fashions and attires; all so far differing from that of their plain country villages (wherein they were bred and had so long lived) as it seemed they were come into a new world. But these were not the things they much looked on, or long took up their thoughts, for they had other work in hand and another kind of war to wage and maintain. For though they saw fair and beautiful cities, flowing with abundance of all sorts of wealth and riches, yet it was not long before they

[3]Church regulations.

[4]Bradford paraphrases the words of the covenant made by those who formed the Separatist (Congregational) church.

saw the grim and grisly face of poverty coming upon them like an armed man,[1] with whom they must buckle[2] and encounter, and from whom they could not fly. But they were armed with faith and patience against him and all his encounters; and though they were sometimes foiled, yet by God's assistance they prevailed and got the victory.

. . .

And when they had lived at Amsterdam about a year, Mr. Robinson their pastor[3] and some others of best discerning, seeing how Mr. John Smith[4] and his company was already fallen into contention with the church that was there before them, and no means they could use would do any good to cure the same, and also that the flames of contention were like to break in that ancient church itself (as afterwards lamentably came to pass); which things they prudently foreseeing thought it was best to remove before they were any way engaged with the same, though they well knew it would be much to the prejudice of their outward estates, both at present and in likelihood in the future; as indeed it proved to be.

Their Removal to Leyden

For these and some other reasons they removed to Leyden,[5] a fair and beautiful city and of a sweet situation, but made more famous by the university wherewith it is adorned, in which of late had been so many learned men.[6] But wanting that traffic by sea which Amsterdam enjoys, it was not so beneficial for their outward means of living and estate. But being now here pitch[ed], they fell to such trades and employments as they best could, valuing peace and their spiritual comfort above any other riches whatsoever. And at length they came to raise a competent and comfortable living, but with hard and continual labour. . . .

Chapter IV

Showing the Reasons and Causes of Their Removal

After they had lived in this city[1] about some eleven or twelve years (which is the more observable being the whole time of that famous truce between that state and the Spaniards)[2] and sundry of them were taken away by

[1]"So shall thy poverty come as one that travelleth; and thy want as an armed man." Proverbs 24:34.

[2]Grapple.

[3]John Robinson (c. 1575–1625). A graduate of Cambridge, he joined the Scrooby group in 1606 and became their pastor in 1609. When the small group of Pilgrims left for America in 1620, he remained in Leyden with the majority of his Separatist congregation.

[4]John Smith (d. 1612), a graduate of Cambridge and pastor of the Separatist church at Gainsborough (near Scrooby). In 1608 he emigrated to Amsterdam with his congregation. His often changing theological views bred dissension among his followers, who eventually broke into factions and merged with other congregations.

[5]By May 1609 the Separatists (numbering about one hundred) had moved to Leyden, twenty-five miles southwest of Amsterdam.

[6]The University of Leyden, founded in 1575, had become the most renowned Protestant university in Europe.

[1]Leyden.

[2]The Dutch war for independence from Spain was halted during the Twelve-Years' Truce (1609–1621). The Separatists feared that renewal of the war might bring victory for Spain and the return of the Inquisition with its persecution of Protestants.

death and many others began to be well stricken in years (the grave mistress Experience having taught them many things), those prudent governors with sundry of the sagest members began both deeply to apprehend their present dangers and wisely to foresee the future and think of timely remedy. In the agitation of their thoughts, and much discourse of things hereabout, at length they began to incline to this conclusion: of removal to some other place. Not out of any newfangledness, or other such like giddy humor, by which men are oftentimes transported to their great hurt and danger, but for sundry weighty and solid reasons, some of the chief of which I will here briefly touch.

And first, they saw and found by experience the hardness of the place and country to be such as few in comparison would come to them, and fewer that would bide it out and continue with them. For many that came to them, and many more that desired to be with them, could not endure that great labour and hard fare, with other inconveniences which they underwent and were contented with. But though they loved their persons, approved their cause and honoured their sufferings, yet they left them as it were weeping, as Orpah did her mother-in-law Naomi,[3] or as those Romans did Cato in Utica[4] who desired to be excused and borne with, though they could not all be Catos. For many, though they desired to enjoy the ordinances of God in their purity and the liberty of the gospel with them, yet (alas) they admitted of bondage, with danger of conscience, rather than to endure these hardships. Yea, some preferred and chose the prisons in England rather than this liberty in Holland, with these afflictions. But it was thought that if a better and easier place of living could be had, it would draw many and take away these discouragements. Yea, their pastor would often say that many of those who both wrote and preached now against them, if they were in a place where they might have liberty and live comfortably, they would then practice as they did.

Secondly. They saw that though the people generally bore all these difficulties very cheerfully and with a resolute courage, being in the best and strength of their years; yet old age began to steal on many of them; and their great and continual labours, with other crosses and sorrows, hastened it before the time. So as it was not only probably thought, but apparently seen, that within a few years more they would be in danger to scatter, by necessities pressing them, or sink under their burdens, or both. And therefore according to the divine proverb, that a wise man seeth the plague when it cometh, and hideth himself, Proverbs 22:3, so they like skillful and beaten[5] soldiers were fearful either to be entrapped or surrounded by their enemies so as they should neither be able to fight nor fly. And therefore thought it better to dislodge betimes to some place of better advantage and less danger, if any such could be found.

[3]The weeping of Orpah, when she was forced to part from her mother-in-law, Naomi, is described in Ruth 1.

[4]Cato of Utica (95–46 B.C.), a Roman general who committed suicide rather than surrender to his enemy, Julius Caesar.

[5]Hardened, experienced.

Thirdly. As necessity was a taskmaster over them, so they were forced to be such, not only to their servants but in a sort to their dearest children, the which as it did not a little wound the tender hearts of many a loving father and mother, so it produced likewise sundry sad and sorrowful effects. For many of their children that were of best dispositions and gracious inclinations, having learned to bear the yoke in their youth[6] and willing to bear part of their parents' burden, were oftentimes so oppressed with their heavy labours that though their minds were free and willing, yet their bodies bowed under the weight of the same, and became decrepit in their early youth, the vigour of nature being consumed in the very bud as it were. But that which was more lamentable, and of all sorrows most heavy to be borne, was that many of their children, by these occasions and the great licentiousness of youth in that country, and the manifold temptations of the place, were drawn away by evil examples into extravagant and dangerous courses, getting the reins off their necks and departing from their parents. Some became soldiers, others took upon them far voyages by sea, and others some worse courses tending to dissoluteness and the danger of their souls, to the great grief of their parents and dishonour of God. So that they saw their posterity would be in danger to degenerate and be corrupted.

Lastly (and which was not least), a great hope and inward zeal they had to laying some good foundation, or at least to make some way thereunto, for the propagating and advancing the gospel of the kingdom of Christ in those remote parts of the world; yea, though they should be but even as stepping-stones unto others for the performing of so great a work.

These and some other like reasons moved them to undertake this resolution of their removal; the which they afterward prosecuted with so great difficulties, as by the sequel will appear.

The place they had thoughts on was some of those vast and unpeopled countries of America, which are fruitful and fit for habitation, being devoid of all civil inhabitants, where there are only savage and brutish men which range up and down, little otherwise than the wild beasts of the same. . . .

Chapter VII
OF THEIR DEPARTURE FROM LEYDEN, AND OTHER THINGS THEREABOUT; WITH THEIR ARRIVAL AT SOUTHAMPTON, WHERE THEY ALL MET TOGETHER AND TOOK IN THEIR PROVISIONS

At length, after much travel and these debates, all things were got ready and provided. A small ship[1] was bought and fitted in Holland, which was intended as to serve to help to transport them, so to stay in the country and attend upon fishing and such other affairs as might be for the good and benefit of the colony when they came there. Another was hired at London, of burthen about 9 score,[2] and all other things got in readiness.

[6]"It is good for a man that he bear the yoke in his youth." Lamentations 3:27.
[1]"Of some 60 ton."—Bradford's note. He refers to the *Speedwell*.
[2]The *Mayflower*, of 180 tons.

So being ready to depart, they had a day of solemn humiliation, their pastor taking his text from Ezra 8:21, "And there at the river, by Ahava, I proclaimed a fast, that we might humble ourselves before our God, and seek of him a right way for us, and for our children, and for all substance."[3] Upon which he spent a good part of the day very profitably and suitable to their present occasion; the rest of the time was spent in pouring out prayers to the Lord with great fervency, mixed with abundance of tears. And the time being come that they must depart, they were accompanied with most of their brethren out of the city, unto a town sundry miles off called Delftshaven,[4] where the ship lay ready to receive them. So they left that goodly and pleasant city which had been their resting place near twelve years; but they knew they were pilgrims,[5] and looked not much on those things, but lifted up their eyes to the heavens, their dearest country, and quieted their spirits.

When they came to the place they found the ship and all things ready, and such of their friends as could not come with them followed after them, and sundry also came from Amsterdam to see them shipped and to take their leave of them. That night was spent with little sleep by the most, but with friendly entertainment and Christian discourse and other real expressions of true Christian love. The next day, the wind being fair, they went aboard and their friends with them, where truly doleful was the sight of that sad and mournful parting, to see what sighs and sobs and prayers did sound amongst them, what tears did gush from every eye, and pithy speeches pierced each heart; that sundry of the Dutch strangers that stood on the quay as spectators could not refrain from tears. Yet comfortable and sweet it was to see such lively and true expressions of dear and unfeigned love. But the tide (which stays for no man) calling them away that were thus loath to depart, their reverend pastor falling down on his knees (and they all with him) with watery cheeks commended them with most fervent prayers to the Lord and His blessing. And then with mutual embraces and many tears they took their leaves one of another which proved to be the last leave to many of them.

Thus hoisting sail,[6] with a prosperous wind they came in short time to Southampton,[7] where they found the bigger ship come from London, lying ready, with all the rest of their company.

. . .

[3]Here, as throughout, Bradford quotes from the Geneva Bible of 1560. Published by Calvinist English refugees in Geneva, it was preferred by Puritans over the Authorized King James Version of 1611. Ahava was a settlement near the Tigris River, where Ezra assembled the Jews for their journey from Babylonian captivity back to Jerusalem.

[4]Dutch harbor at the mouth of the Maas River, near Rotterdam.

[5]"Hebrews 11:13–16."—Bradford's note. It was from this reference that the Plymouth Separatists later came to be called "Pilgrims."

[6]"This was about 22 of July [1620]."—Bradford's note.

[7]Seaport on the English Channel.

Chapter IX

Of Their Voyage, and How They Passed the Sea; and of Their Safe Arrival at Cape Cod

September 6 [1620]. These troubles being blown over,[1] and now all being compact together in one ship, they put to sea again with a prosperous wind, which continued divers days together, which was some encouragement unto them; yet, according to the usual manner, many were afflicted with seasickness. And I may not omit here a special work of God's providence. There was a proud and very profane young man, one of the seamen, of a lusty,[2] able body, which made him the more haughty; he would always be contemning the poor people in their sickness and cursing them daily with grievous execrations; and did not let[3] to tell them that he hoped to help to cast half of them overboard before they came to their journey's end, and to make merry with what they had; and if he were by any gently reproved, he would curse and swear most bitterly. But it pleased God before they came half seas over, to smite this young man with a grievous disease, of which he died in a desperate manner, and so was himself the first that was thrown overboard. Thus his curses lit on his own head, and it was an astonishment to all his fellows for they noted it to be the just hand of God upon him.

After they had enjoyed fair winds and weather for a season, they were encountered many times with cross winds and met with many fierce storms with which the ship was shroudly[4] shaken, and her upper works made very leaky; and one of the main beams in the midships was bowed and cracked, which put them in some fear that the ship could not be able to perform the voyage. So some of the chief of the company, perceiving the mariners to fear the insufficiency of the ship as appeared by their mutterings, they entered into serious consultation with the master[5] and other officers of the ship, to consider in time of the danger, and rather to return than to cast themselves into a desperate and inevitable peril. And truly there was great distraction and difference of opinion amongst the mariners themselves; fain would they do what could be done for their wages' sake (being now near half the seas over) and on the other hand they were loath to hazard their lives too desperately. But in examining of all opinions, the master and others affirmed they knew the ship to be strong and firm under water; and for the buckling of the main beam, there was a great iron screw[6] the passengers brought out of Holland, which would raise the beam into his place; the which being

[1]The Separatists first sailed from Southampton, England, in the *Speedwell* and the *Mayflower* in August 1620. The *Speedwell* soon proved unseaworthy. Both ships then returned to Plymouth, where passengers and stores were transferred to the *Mayflower,* which sailed for America in September 1620. The dates cited by Bradford follow the Old Style (Julian) calendar and are ten days earlier than those of the present New Style (Gregorian) calendar. Dates in the text and the footnotes are given in both Old and New Style.

[2]Robust, energetic.

[3]Hesitate.

[4]Wickedly, severely.

[5]Ship captain.

[6]A lifting screw (jack) used for raising heavy weights.

done, the carpenter and master affirmed that with a post put under it, set firm in the lower deck and otherways bound, he would make it sufficient. And as for the decks and upper works, they would caulk them as well as they could, and though with the working[7] of the ship they would not long keep staunch,[8] yet there would otherwise be no great danger, if they did not overpress her with sails. So they committed themselves to the will of God and resolved to proceed.

In sundry of these storms the winds were so fierce and the seas so high, as they could not bear a knot of sail,[9] but were forced to hull[10] for divers days together. And in one of them, as they thus lay at hull in a mighty storm, a lusty young man called John Howland, coming upon some occasion above the gratings[11] was, with a seele[12] of the ship, thrown into sea; but it pleased God that he caught hold of the topsail halyards[13] which hung overboard and ran out at length. Yet he held his hold (though he was sundry fathoms under water) till he was hauled up by the same rope to the brim of the water, and then with a boat hook and other means got into the ship again and his life saved. And though he was something ill with it, yet he lived many years after and became a profitable member both in church and commonwealth. In all this voyage there died but one of the passengers, which was William Butten, a youth, servant to Samuel Fuller, when they drew near the coast.

But to omit other things (that I may be brief) after long beating[14] at sea they fell with that land which is called Cape Cod;[15] the which being made and certainly known to be it, they were not a little joyful. After some deliberation had amongst themselves and with the master of the ship, they tacked about and resolved to stand for the southward (the wind and weather being fair) to find some place about Hudson's River for their habitation. But after they had sailed that course about half the day, they fell amongst dangerous shoals and roaring breakers, and they were so far entangled therewith as they conceived themselves in great danger; and the wind shrinking[16] upon them withal, they resolved to bear up again for the Cape and thought themselves happy to get out of those dangers before night overtook them, as by God's good providence they did. And the next day[17] they got into the Cape Harbor[18] where they rode[19] in safety. . . .

Being thus arrived in a good harbor, and brought safe to land, they fell upon their knees and blessed the God of Heaven who had brought them over the vast and furious ocean, and delivered them from all the perils and

[7]The twisting of a ship's planking, thus opening the hull and causing leaks.
[8]Watertight.
[9]I.e., the area of sail required to move the ship at the speed of one nautical mile (1.15 land miles) per hour.
[10]Shorten sail, turn the bow toward the storm, and drift with the wind.
[11]Wooden grids that cover openings in the deck.
[12]Roll.
[13]Ropes used to raise and lower sails.
[14]Sailing back and forth against the wind.
[15]The Pilgrims first sighted the coast of Cape Cod at dawn 9/19 November 1620.
[16]With the wind lessening, the *Mayflower* was in danger of drifting uncontrollably onto the shoals south of Cape Cod.
[17]November 11/21, 1620.
[18]Now Provincetown Harbor.
[19]Anchored.

miseries thereof, again to set their feet on the firm and stable earth, their proper element. And no marvel if they were thus joyful, seeing wise Seneca was so affected with sailing a few miles on the coast of his own Italy, as he affirmed, that he had rather remain twenty years on his way by land than pass by sea to any place in a short time, so tedious and dreadful was the same unto him.[20]

But here I cannot but stay and make a pause, and stand half amazed at this poor people's present condition; and so I think will the reader, too, when he well considers the same. Being thus passed the vast ocean, and a sea of troubles before in their preparation (as may be remembered by that which went before), they had now no friends to welcome them nor inns to entertain or refresh their weatherbeaten bodies; no houses or much less towns to repair to, to seek for succour. It is recorded in scripture[21] as a mercy to the Apostle and his shipwrecked company, that the barbarians showed them no small kindness in refreshing them, but these savage barbarians, when they met with them (as after will appear) were readier to fill their sides full of arrows than otherwise. And for the season it was winter, and they that know the winters of that country know them to be sharp and violent, and subject to cruel and fierce storms, dangerous to travel to known places, much more to search an unknown coast. Besides, what could they see but a hideous and desolate wilderness, full of wild beasts and wild men—and what multitudes there might be of them they knew not. Neither could they, as it were, go up to the top of Pisgah to view from this wilderness a more goodly country to feed their hopes;[22] for which way soever they turned their eyes (save upward to the heavens) they could have little solace or content in respect of any outward objects. For summer being done, all things stand upon them with a weatherbeaten face, and the whole country, full of woods and thickets, represented a wild and savage hue. If they looked behind them, there was the mighty ocean which they had passed and was now as a main bar and gulf to separate them from all civil parts of the world. If it be said they had a ship to succour them, it is true; but what heard they daily from the master and company? But that with speed they should look out a place (with their shallop[23]) where they would be, at some near distance; for the season was such as he would not stir from thence till a safe harbor was discovered by them, where they would be, and he might go without danger; and that victuals[24] consumed apace but he must and would keep sufficient for themselves and their return. Yea, it was muttered by some that if they got not a place in time, they would turn them and their goods ashore and leave them. Let it also be considered what weak hopes of supply and succour they left behind them, that might bear up their minds in this sad condition and trials they were under; and they could not but be very small. It is true, indeed, the affections and love of their brethren at Leyden[25] was

[20]"Epistle 53."—Bradford's note. He refers to the *Epistles* of the Roman statesman and philosopher Seneca (4 B.C.–A.D. 65).

[21]"Acts 28."—Bradford's note. He refers to verse 2, where Paul, shipwrecked on his way to Rome, is helped by "the barbarous people [who] shewed us no little kindness. . . ."

[22]On Mount Pisgah, the Lord showed Moses the Promised Land. Deuteronomy 34:1–4.

[23]Open sailboat used in shallow waters.

[24]Food.

[25]The majority of the Separatists had remained in the Netherlands.

cordial and entire towards them, but they had little power to help them or themselves; and how the case stood between them and the merchants[26] at their coming away hath already been declared.

What could now sustain them but the Spirit of God and His grace? May not and ought not the children of these fathers rightly say: "Our fathers were Englishmen which came over this great ocean, and were ready to perish in this wilderness; but they cried unto the Lord, and He heard their voice and looked on their adversity,"[27] etc. "Let them therefore praise the Lord, because He is good: and His mercies endure forever." "Yea, let them which have been redeemed of the Lord, shew how He hath delivered them from the hand of the oppressor. When they wandered in the desert wilderness out of the way, and found no city to dwell in, both hungry and thirsty, their soul was overwhelmed in them. Let them confess before the Lord His loving kindness and His wonderful works before the sons of men."[28]

Chapter X
Showing How They Sought Out a Place of Habitation, and What Befell Them Thereabout

Being thus arrived at Cape Cod the 11th of November, and necessity called them to look out a place for habitation (as well as the master's and mariners' importunity); they having brought a large shallop with them out of England, stowed in quarters in the ship, they now got her out and set their carpenters to work to trim her up; but being much bruised and shattered in the ship with foul weather, they saw she would be long in mending. Whereupon a few of them tendered themselves to go by land and discover those nearest places, whilst the shallop was in mending; and the rather because as they went into that harbor there seemed to be an opening some two or three leagues off, which the master judged to be a river. It was conceived there might be some danger in the attempt, yet seeing them resolute, they were permitted to go, being sixteen of them well armed under the conduct of Captain Standish,[1] having such instructions given them as was thought meet.

They set forth the 15th of November; and when they had marched about the space of a mile by the seaside, they espied five or six persons with a dog coming towards them, who were savages; but they fled from them and ran up into the woods, and the English followed them, partly to see if they could speak with them, and partly to discover if there might not be more of them lying in ambush. But the Indians seeing themselves thus followed, they again forsook the woods and ran away on the sands as hard as they could, so as they could not come near them but followed them by the track of their feet sundry miles and saw that they had come the same way. So, night coming on, they made their rendezvous and set out their sentinels, and rested in quiet that night; and the next morning followed their track till they had headed a great creek and so left the sands, and turned another

[26] I.e., the merchants who had financed the Pilgrims.

[27] "Deuteronomy 26:5, 7."—Bradford's note. He refers to the deliverance of the Israelites from Egyptian bondage.

[28] "Psalm 107:1, 2, 4, 5, 8."—Bradford's note.

[1] Myles Standish (1584?–1656), military leader of the Pilgrims.

way into the woods. But they still followed them by guess, hoping to find their dwellings; but they soon lost both them and themselves, falling into such thickets as were ready to tear their clothes and armor in pieces; but were most distressed for want of drink. But at length they found water and refreshed themselves, being the first New England water they drunk of, and was now in great thirst as pleasant unto them as wine or beer had been in foretimes.

Afterwards they directed their course to come to the other shore, for they knew it was a neck of land they were to cross over, and so at length got to the seaside and marched to this supposed river, and by the way found a pond of clear, fresh water, and shortly after a good quantity of clear ground where the Indians had formerly set corn, and some of their graves. And proceeding further they saw new stubble where corn had been set the same year; also they found where lately a house had been, where some planks and a great kettle was remaining, and heaps of sand newly paddled with their hands. Which, they digging up, found in them divers fair Indian baskets filled with corn, and some in ears, fair and good, of divers colours, which seemed to them a very goodly sight (having never seen any such before). This was near the place of that supposed river they came to seek, unto which they went and found it to open itself into two arms with a high cliff of sand in the entrance but more like to be creeks of salt water than any fresh, for aught they saw; and that there was good harborage for their shallop, leaving it further to be discovered by their shallop, when she was ready. So, their time limited them being expired, they returned to the ship lest they should be in fear of their safety; and took with them part of the corn and buried up the rest. And so, like the men from Eshcol, carried with them the fruits of the land and showed their brethren;[2] of which, and their return, they were marvelously glad and their hearts encouraged.

After this, the shallop being got ready, they set out again for the better discovery of this place, and the master of the ship desired to go himself. So there went some thirty men but found it to be no harbor for ships but only for boats. There was also found two of their houses covered with mats, and sundry of their implements in them, but the people were run away and could not be seen. Also there was found more of their corn and of their beans of various colours; the corn and beans they brought away, purposing to give them full satisfaction when they should meet with any of them as, about some six months afterward they did, to their good content.

And here is to be noted a special providence of God, and a great mercy to this poor people, that here they got seed to plant them corn the next year, or else they might have starved, for they had none nor any likelihood to get any till the season had been past, as the sequel did manifest. Neither it is likely they had had this, if the first voyage had not been made, for the ground was now all covered with snow and hard frozen; but the Lord is never wanting unto His in their greatest needs; let His holy name have all the praise.

. . .

[2]Scouts sent by Moses to the Valley of Eshcol brought back a cluster of grapes so heavy that two men were required to carry it. Numbers 13:23–26. The Pilgrims later repaid the Indians for the stolen corn, giving them "full satisfaction."

On Monday [December 11/21] they sounded[3] the harbor and found it fit for shipping, and marched into the land and found divers cornfields and little running brooks, a place (as they supposed) fit for situation.[4] At least it was the best they could find, and the season and their present necessity made them glad to accept of it. So they returned to their ship again with this news to the rest of their people, which did much comfort their hearts.

On the 15th of December they weighed anchor to go to the place they had discovered, and came within two leagues of it, but were fain to bear up again; but the 16th day, the wind came fair, and they arrived safe in this harbor.[5] And afterwards took better view of the place, and resolved where to pitch their dwelling; and the 25th day began to erect the first house for common use to receive them and their goods.

[Chapter XI]

The Remainder of Anno 1620
[The Mayflower Contract][1]

I shall a little return back, and begin with a combination[2] made by them before they came ashore, being the first foundation of their government in this place [and being] occasioned partly by the discontented and mutinous speeches that some of the Strangers[3] amongst them had let fall from them in the ship: That when they came ashore they would use their own liberty, for none had power to command them, the patent they had being for Virginia and not for New England, which belonged to another government, with which the Virginia Company had nothing to do. And partly that such an act by them done, this their condition considered, might be as firm as any patent,[4] and in some respects more sure.

The form was as followeth:

In the Name of God, Amen.

We whose names are underwritten, the loyal subjects of our dread Sovereign Lord King James, by the Grace of God of Great Britain, France, and Ireland King, Defender of the Faith, etc.

[3]I.e., measured the depth of.

[4]Settlement.

[5]Explorations of Plymouth Harbor had been carried out in a shallop while the *Mayflower* itself remained in Provincetown Harbor, at the tip of Cape Cod.

[1]The Pilgrims' charter from the Virginia Company of London did not authorize colonization north of 41° (near present-day New York City). Because the Pilgrims lacked a valid title to any land in New England, some disgruntled passengers could argue that the rules for government were also invalid. The Mayflower Compact was therefore drawn up to create a government through a binding social contract. It was the first effort to establish a direct popular government in the New World and the first of many such "plantation covenants" created by settlers who had migrated far beyond the authority of their home governments. The Mayflower Compact was signed 11/21 November 1620. In June 1621 the newly formed Council for New England granted to the Pilgrim colonists a patent that finally established their legal right to the lands they had settled.

[2]Agreement.

[3]The majority of the *Mayflower* passengers were "Strangers," non-church members who migrated not for religion but for adventure and profit.

[4]A binding, legal document signed or authorized by the king.

Having undertaken, for the Glory of God and advancement of the Christian Faith and Honour of our King and Country, a Voyage to plant the First Colony in the Northern Parts of Virginia,[5] do by these presents[6] solemnly and mutually in the presence of God and one of another, Covenant and Combine ourselves together into a Civil Body Politic, for our better ordering and preservation and furtherance of the ends aforesaid; and by virtue hereof to enact, constitute and frame such just and equal Laws, Ordinances, Acts, Constitutions and Offices, from time to time, as shall be thought most meet and convenient for the general good of the Colony, unto which we promise all due submission and obedience. In witness whereof we have hereunder subscribed our names at Cape Cod, the 11th of November, in the year of the reign of our Sovereign Lord King James, of England, France and Ireland the eighteenth, and of Scotland the fifty-fourth. Anno Domini 1620.

After this they chose, or rather confirmed, Mr. John Carver[7] (a man godly and well approved amongst them) their Governor for that year. And after they had provided a place for their goods, or common store (which were long in unlading[8] for want of boats, foulness of the winter weather and sickness of divers[9]) and begun some small cottages for their habitation; as time would admit, they met and consulted of laws and orders, both for their civil and military government as the necessity of their condition did require, still adding thereunto as urgent occasion in several times, and as cases did require.

In these hard and difficult beginnings they found some discontents and murmurings arise amongst some, and mutinous speeches and carriages[10] in others; but they were soon quelled and overcome by the wisdom, patience, and just and equal carriage of things, by the Governor and better part, which clave[11] faithfully together in the main.

[Disease, Starvation, and Death]

But that which was most sad and lamentable was, that in two or three months' time half of their company died, especially in January and February, being the depth of winter, and wanting houses and other comforts; being infected with the scurvy[12] and other diseases which this long voyage and their inaccommodate[13] condition had brought upon them. So as there died

[5]I.e., New England. The term *Virginia* was generally used as the name for all English territories from present-day Maine to the Carolinas. The term *New England,* though widely known, was not formally recognized until the Council for New England was organized November 1620, more than a month after the Pilgrims had sailed from England.

[6]I.e., the provisions of this legal document.

[7]John Carver (1575?–1621) had been appointed governor before the Pilgrims left England. The election after the signing of the Mayflower Compact formally confirmed his previous appointment. Carver thereby became the first governor in the history of English colonizing to be popularly elected.

[8]Unloading.

[9]I.e., of various persons.

[10]Behavior, deportment.

[11]Cleaved, stuck.

[12]A severe disease caused by a deficiency of vitamin C.

[13]Unsuitable.

sometimes two or three of a day in the foresaid time, that of 100 and odd persons, scarce fifty remained.[14] And of these, in the time of most distress, there was but six or seven sound persons who to their great commendations, be it spoken, spared no pains night nor day, but with abundance of toil and hazard of their own health, fetched them wood, made them fires, dressed them meat, made their beds, washed their loathsome clothes, clothed and unclothed them. In a word, did all the homely[15] and necessary offices[16] for them which dainty and queasy stomachs cannot endure to hear named; and all this willingly and cheerfully, without any grudging in the least, showing herein their true love unto their friends and brethren; a rare example and worthy to be remembered. Two of these were Mr. William Brewster, their reverend Elder,[17] and Myles Standish, their Captain and military commander, unto whom myself and many others were much beholden in our low and sick condition. And yet the Lord so upheld these persons as in this general calamity they were not at all infected either with sickness or lameness. And what I have said of these I may say of many others who died in this general visitation,[18] and others yet living; that whilst they had health, yea, or any strength continuing, they were not wanting[19] to any that had need of them. And I doubt not but their recompense is with the Lord.

But I may not here pass by another remarkable passage not to be forgotten. As this calamity fell among the passengers that were to be left here to plant, and were hasted ashore and made to drink water that the seamen might have the more beer, and one[20] in his sickness desiring but a small can of beer, it was answered that if he were their own father he should have none. The disease began to fall amongst them[21] also, so as almost half of their company died before they went away, and many of their officers and lustiest men, [such] as the boatswain, gunner, three quartermasters, the cook and others. At which the Master[22] was something strucken and sent to the sick ashore and told the Governor he should send for beer for them that had need of it, though he drunk water homeward bound.

But now amongst his company there was far another kind of carriage in this misery than amongst the passengers. For they that before had been boon companions in drinking and jollity in the time of their health and welfare, began now to desert one another in this calamity, saying they would

[14]Of the 102 passengers on the *Mayflower,* 50 had died (including most of the women) by the summer of 1621.

[15]Personal, intimate.

[16]Tasks.

[17]The Separatists, like other Puritans, called the chief officers of their church "Elders." Brewster (1567–1644), a Pilgrim leader, was the senior Elder of the Separatist church at Plymouth. In the absence of an ordained minister, he could, like any layman, conduct church services and preach. But not being an ordained minister, he could not administer the only two sacraments recognized by the Separatists and Puritans: baptism and the sacrament of the Lord's Supper (Communion).

[18]Epidemic.

[19]Lacking in kindness.

[20]"Which was the author himself."—Bradford's note.

[21]I.e., the ship's crew. The last of the *Mayflower* passengers did not go ashore until March 1621. The ship and its crew left Plymouth for England on 5/15 April 1621.

[22]Christopher Jones, captain of the *Mayflower.*

not hazard their lives for them, they should be infected by coming to help them in their cabins; and so, after they came to lie by it,[23] would do little or nothing for them but, "if they died, let them die." But such of the passengers as were yet aboard showed them what mercy they could, which made some of their hearts relent, as the boatswain (and some others) who was a proud young man and would often curse and scoff at the passengers. But when he grew weak, they had compassion on him and helped him; then he confessed he did not deserve it at their hands, he had abused them in word and deed. "Oh!" (said he) "you, I now see, show your love like Christians indeed one to another, but we let one another lie and die like dogs." Another lay cursing his wife, saying if it had not been for her he had never come to this unlucky voyage, and anon cursing his fellows, saying he had done this and that for some of them; he had spent so much and so much amongst them, and they were now weary of him and did not help him, having need. Another gave his companion all he had, if he died, to help him in his weakness; he went and got a little spice and made him a mess of meat once or twice. And because he died not so soon as he expected, he went amongst his fellows and swore the rogue would cozen[24] him, he would see him choked before he made him any more meat; and yet the poor fellow died before morning.

. . .

[Chapter XII
THE NARRAGANSETT THREAT]

That great people of the Narragansetts,[1] in a braving[2] manner, sent a messenger unto them with a bundle of arrows tied about with a great snakeskin, which their interpreters told them was a threatening and a challenge. Upon which the Governor, with the advice of others, sent them a round[3] answer that if they had rather have war than peace, they might begin when they would; they had done them no wrong, neither did they fear them or should they find them unprovided. And by another messenger sent the snakeskin back with bullets in it. But they would not receive it, but sent it back again. . . .[4]

This made them the more carefully to look to themselves, so as they agreed to enclose their dwellings with a good strong pale,[5] and make flankers[6] in convenient places with gates to shut, which were every night locked, and a watch kept; and when need required, there was also warding[7] in the daytime. And the company was by the Captain's and the Governor's

[23]I.e., after sickness forced them to lie in bed.
[24]Cheat.
[1]Indians of the Algonquian family and the most powerful tribe in southern New England.
[2]Arrogant, hostile.
[3]Blunt, unrestrained.
[4]Canonicus, chief of the Narragansetts, sent the challenge. Squanto, the Indian friendly to the Pilgrims, was the interpreter. The event occurred in January 1622. Perhaps because of the Pilgrims' threatening response, the Indians chose not to go to war.
[5]Palisade, defensive wall.
[6]Projections from the defensive walls. From such flankers the defenders could enfilade (shoot down the line, or flank, of) attackers.
[7]I.e., posting of guards.

advice divided into four squadrons, and everyone had their quarter appointed them unto which they were to repair upon any sudden alarm. And if there should be any cry of fire, a company were appointed for a guard, with muskets, whilst others quenched the same, to prevent Indian treachery. This was accomplished very cheerfully, and the town impaled round[8] by the beginning of March, in which every family had a pretty garden plot secured.

And herewith I shall end this year [1621]. Only I shall remember one passage more, rather of mirth than of weight. On the day called Christmas Day,[9] the Governor called them out to work as was used.[10] But the most of this new company excused themselves and said it went against their consciences to work on that day. So the Governor told them that if they made it [a] matter of conscience, he would spare them till they were better informed; so he led away the rest and left them. But when they came home at noon from their work, he found them in the street at play, openly; some pitching the bar, and some at stool-ball[11] and such like sports. So he went to them and took away their implements and told them that was against his conscience, that they should play and others work. If they made the keeping of it [a] matter of devotion, let them keep [to] their houses; but there should be no gaming or reveling in the streets. Since which time nothing hath been attempted that way, at least openly.

[Chapter XIV]

Anno Dom:1623 [Ending the "Common Course and Condition"]

They began to think how they might raise as much corn as they could, and obtain a better crop than they had done, that they might not still thus languish in misery.[1] At length, after much debate of things, the Governor (with the advice of the chiefest amongst them) gave way that they should set corn every man for his own particular, and in that regard trust to themselves; in all other things to go on in the general way as before.[2] And so [the Governor] assigned to every family a parcel of land, according to the proportion of their number, for that end, only for present use (but made no division for inheritance) and ranged all boys and youth under some family.[3] This had

[8]The palisade enclosing Plymouth was about ten feet high and more than half a mile around.

[9]The Plymouth Separatists did not celebrate Christmas, arguing that December 25 was not the correct date of the birth of Christ. Many of the Plymouth "New Company," those who had arrived after the *Mayflower* Pilgrims, were "Strangers" and still observed the traditional celebration day.

[10]Customary, usual.

[11]Pitching the bar is javelin throwing. In stool ball, a game like baseball, players bat a ball from stool to stool.

[1]By the spring of 1623, it was clear to the Pilgrims that the colony, already on half rations, would not survive another year of poor harvests.

[2]The merchant investors had insisted that the colony operate on a communal basis. Except for some personal belongings, all property, including land, houses, and cattle, was held communally. All settlers, regardless of their contributions, received equal portions of food and other products. Any surplus or profit was to be sent as debt payment to the merchant investors in England. Because that system bred "much confusion and discontent," Bradford, in 1623, agreed to allocate to each family a plot of land for private cultivation. For a time all other assets continued to be held in common. Beginning in 1627, most of the remaining assets were divided among the colonists and became private property, thus effectively ending the "Common Course and Condition."

[3]I.e., under the control of some family.

very good success, for it made all hands very industrious, so as much more corn was planted than otherwise would have been by any means the Governor or any other could use, and saved him a great deal of trouble, and gave far better content. The women now went willingly into the field, and took their little ones with them to set corn; which before would allege weakness and inability; whom to have compelled would have been thought great tyranny and oppression.

The experience that was had in this common course and condition, tried sundry years and that amongst godly and sober men, may well evince the vanity of that conceit of Plato's and other ancients applauded by some of later times; that the taking away of property and bringing in community[4] into a commonwealth would make them happy and flourishing; as if they were wiser than God.[5] For this community (so far as it was) was found to breed much confusion and discontent and retard much employment that would have been to their benefit and comfort. For the young men, that were most able and fit for labour and service, did repine[6] that they should spend their time and strength to work for other men's wives and children without any recompense. The strong, or man of parts, had no more in division of victuals and clothes than he that was weak and not able to do a quarter the other could; this was thought injustice. The aged and graver[7] men to be ranked and equalized in labours and victuals, clothes, etc., with the meaner[8] and younger sort, thought it some indignity and disrespect unto them. And for man's wives to be commanded to do service for other men, as dressing their meat, washing their clothes, etc., they deemed it a kind of slavery, neither could many husbands well brook it. Upon the point all being to have alike, and all to do alike, they thought themselves in the like condition,[9] and one as good as another; and so, if it did not cut off those relations that God hath set amongst men, yet it did at least much diminish and take off the mutual respects that should be preserved amongst them. And [it] would have been worse if they had been men of another condition. Let none object this is men's corruption, and nothing to the course itself. I answer, seeing all men have this corruption in them, God in His wisdom saw another course fitter for them.

[Chapter XXVIII]

ANNO DOM:1637 [WAR WITH THE PEQUOTS]

In the fore part of this year, the Pequots[1] fell openly upon the English at Connecticut, in the lower parts of the river,[2] and slew sundry of them as they were at work in the fields, both men and women, to the great terrour of the rest, and went away in great pride and triumph, with many high threats. They

[4]Joint ownership of property.

[5]In his *Republic,* the Greek philosopher Plato (427?–347 B.C.) argued that the holding of private property damages human relationships and thus weakens the unity of the state.

[6]Grumble.

[7]Dignified, important.

[8]Lowly, common.

[9]Social position or rank.

[1]A warlike Algonquian Indian tribe of Connecticut, where their quarrels with the English colonists led to the Pequot War of 1637.

[2]The Connecticut River.

also assaulted a fort at the river's mouth, though strong and well defended; and though they did not there prevail, yet it struck them with much fear and astonishment to see their bold attempts in the face of danger. Which made them in all places to stand upon their ground and to prepare for resistance, and earnestly to solicit their friends and confederates in the Bay of Massachusetts to send them speedy aid, for they looked for more forcible assaults. Mr. Vane,[3] being the Governor, writ from their General Court to them here to join with them in this war, to which they were cordially willing.[4]

. . .

The Court here agreed forthwith to send fifty men at their own charge; and with as much speed as possibly they could, got them armed and had made them ready under sufficient leaders, and provided a bark[5] to carry them provisions and tend upon them for all occasions. But when they were ready to march, with a supply from the Bay, they had word to stay; for the enemy was as good as vanquished and there would be no need.

I shall not take upon me exactly to describe their proceedings in these things, because I expect it will be fully done by themselves who best know the carriage[6] and circumstances of things. I shall therefore but touch them in general. From Connecticut, who were most sensible of the hurt sustained and the present danger, they sent out a party of men, and another party met them from the Bay, at Narragansetts', who were to join with them. The Narragansetts were earnest to be gone before the English were well rested and refreshed, especially some of them which came last. It should seem their desire was to come upon the enemy suddenly and undiscovered. There was a bark of this place, newly put in there, which was come from Connecticut, who did encourage them to lay hold of the Indians' forwardness, and to show as great forwardness as they, for it would encourage them, and expedition might prove to their great advantage. So they went on, and so ordered their march as the Indians brought them to a fort of the enemy's[7] (in which most of their chief men were) before day. They approached the same with great silence and surrounded it both with English and Indians, that they might not break out; and so assaulted them with great courage, shooting amongst them, and entered the fort with all speed. And those that first entered found sharp resistance from the enemy who both shot at and grappled with them; others ran into their houses and brought out fire and set them on fire, which soon took in their mat;[8] and standing close together, with the wind all was quickly on a flame, and thereby more were burnt to death than was otherwise slain; it burnt their bowstrings and made them unserviceable; those that scraped the fire were slain with the sword, some hewed to pieces, others run through with their rapiers, so as they were quickly dispatched and very few escaped. It was

[3]Henry Vane (1613–1662), governor of the Massachusetts Bay Colony.

[4]I.e., the General Court (a legislative body made up of the governor and his assistants) of the Massachusetts Bay Colony wrote to the General Court of the Plymouth Colony, asking for aid against the Pequots.

[5]A small sailing vessel.

[6]Events.

[7]Mystic Fort, on the Mystic River in Connecticut.

[8]I.e., the woven matting used for walls and floors soon caught fire.

conceived they thus destroyed about 400 at this time. It was a fearful sight to see them thus frying in the fire and the streams of blood quenching the same, and horrible was the stink and scent thereof; but the victory seemed a sweet sacrifice,[9] and they gave the praise thereof to God, who had wrought so wonderfully for them, thus to enclose their enemies in their hands and give them so speedy a victory over so proud and insulting an enemy.

[Chapter XXXVI]

ANNO DOM:1646 [WINSLOW ABANDONS THE PLYMOUTH COLONY]

This year Mr. Edward Winslow[1] went into England, upon this occasion: some discontented persons under the government of the Massachusetts sought to trouble their peace and disturb, if not innovate,[2] their government by laying many scandals upon them, and intended to prosecute against them in England by petitioning and complaining to the Parliament. . . . So as they made choice of Mr. Winslow to be their agent to make their defense, and gave him commission and instructions for that end. In which he so carried himself as did well answer their ends and cleared them from any blame or dishonour, to the shame of their adversaries. But by reason of the great alterations in the State,[3] he was detained longer than was expected, and afterwards fell into other employments there; so as he hath now been absent this four years, which hath been much to the weakening of this government, without whose consent he took these employments upon him.

Anno·1647·~~~~And Anno·1648[4]

1630–1650 1856

[9]"The Priest shall burn the memorial . . . upon the altar, to be an offering made by fire, of a sweet savour unto the Lord." Leviticus 2:2.

[1]Edward Winslow (1595–1655), governor of the Plymouth Colony in 1633, 1636, and 1644. One of the original passengers on the *Mayflower,* he had gone to England at the request of the Massachusetts Bay Colony, to defend it against charges that it had deprived members of the Church of England of their religious and civil rights. After successfully answering the charges, Winslow elected to abandon Plymouth and remain in England, now ruled by the Puritans. He never returned to New England.

[2]Change, disrupt.

[3]While Winslow was in England, the Puritan Revolution occurred, King Charles was deposed and executed, and a Puritan republic was established under Oliver Cromwell as Lord Protector.

[4]Bradford's final entry. Thereafter he added only an appendix listing the *Mayflower* passengers and their descendants.

John Winthrop 1588–1649

In 1630 a fleet of ships landed on the Massachusetts shore, bringing 2,000 men, women, and children to establish a Bible commonwealth in New England. It was the start of the Great Migration of Puritans that eventually brought 20,000 settlers to the Massachusetts Bay Colony.

Their leader was John Winthrop. Born to a family of rich merchants and landed gentry, he was educated at Cambridge University. He studied the law and then became a justice of the peace, a successful London lawyer, and the squire of Groton Manor in Suffolk. As a staunch Puritan, he was troubled by the English government's oppression of English Calvinists. And in 1629, persuaded that "God will bring some heavy affliction upon this land, and that speedily," he joined in organizing the Massachusetts Bay Company to establish a Christian colony in New England.

Winthrop was elected governor of the colony, and in 1630 he set sail to the New World on the Arbella, *with the first contingent of settlers. Shortly after arriving, he established the center of government at Boston, where he served as Governor or Deputy Governor of the Colony for all but seven of the remaining years of his life—directing land distribution, establishing church and civil government, and meeting the crises caused by Indians, heretical Quakers, and such troublers as Roger Williams and Anne Hutchinson.*

Winthrop began writing his Journal *in 1630, during his voyage to America, and he continued his record of events until his death in 1649. The* Journal's *measured and judicial style reflects the ordered mind of its author and his desire to tell the plain truth, even against himself. It reveals Puritan attitudes toward women and the world of commerce. It shows the Puritans' need to find divine sanction for their acts and shows their craving for evidence of a divine purpose in even the trivial events of their daily lives. The* Journal *is an unpolished chronicle rather than a finished history, but like Bradford's* Of Plymouth Plantation, *it has the virtue of being written by someone at the center of events. Winthrop knew well the sharp disputes between the Puritans in America and the royal authorities in England. And he lived amid intense religious quarrels that threatened to scatter the Bay Colony into jarring sects.*

Winthrop's political creed was based on the Calvinist axiom that all mankind was corrupted by the original sin of Adam. Winthrop had no faith in democracy, believing there was "no such government in Israel." He was convinced that America was a land where God's vice-regents on earth were divinely appointed to maintain law. Because of his political views, Winthrop's enemies saw him as harsh and autocratic—Thomas Morton called him "King Winthrop." But his supporters saw him as the Moses of his colony, the protector of orthodoxy. And in his Journal, *he is revealed as a humane and devoted leader, one wholly committed to the building of a Christian society in the New World.*

Like other Puritan leaders, Winthrop found his guiding principles in the Scriptures and in the teachings of Puritanism. But with the decline of the Puritan state, Americans began to find their guiding principles elsewhere: in egalitarianism, in radical individualism, and in capitalism. Yet the Puritan principles of hard work, independence, and moral strength, shown by men like John Winthrop, survived the passing of the New England Way. Such ideals were major forces in shaping the American Revolution and in the growth of the new nation. Today they remain dominant elements in the cultural heritage of the American people.

FURTHER READING: *The Winthrop Papers,* ed. A. Forbes, 5 vols., 1929–1947; *The Journal of John Winthrop,* ed. R. Dunn and L. Yeandle, 1996; R. Winthrop, *Life and Letters of John Winthrop,* 1864–1867; S. Morison, *Builders of the Bay Colony,* 1930; L. Mayo, *The Winthrop Family in America,* 1948; E. Morgan, *The Puritan Dilemma,* 1958; R. Dunn, *Puritans and*

Yankees, 1962; D. Rutman, *Winthrop's Boston,* 1965; R. Black, *The Younger John Winthrop,* 1966; L. Schweninger, *John Winthrop,* 1990; J. Moseley, *John Winthrop's World,* 1992; M. Winship, *Making Heretics, Militant Protestantism and Free Grace in Massachusetts, 1636–1641,* 2002; F. Bremer, *John Winthrop, America's Forgotten Founding Father,* 2003.

TEXT: *The History of New England,* ed. J. Savage, 2 vols., 1853. Spelling, punctuation, and usage have been changed to conform more nearly to modern practice.

from *THE JOURNAL*[1] *OF JOHN WINTHROP*

[June 14, 1631] At this court [session] one Philip Ratcliff, a servant of Mr. Cradock, being convicted, ore tenus,[2] of most foul, scandalous invectives against our churches and government, was censured to be whipped, lose his ears, and be banished [from] the plantation, which was presently executed.

[July 5, 1632] At Watertown there was (in the view of divers witnesses) a great combat between a mouse and a snake; and, after a long fight, the mouse prevailed and killed the snake. The pastor of Boston, Mr. Wilson,[3] a very sincere, holy man, hearing of it, gave this interpretation: That the snake was the devil; the mouse was a poor contemptible people, which God had brought hither, which should overcome Satan here, and dispossess him of his kingdom.

. . .

[November 1633] A great mortality among the Indians. Chickatabot, the sagamore[4] of Naponsett,[5] died, and many of his people. The disease was the small pox. Some of them were cured by such means as they had from us; many of their children escaped and were kept by the English.

. . .

[December 5, 1633] John Sagamore died of the small pox, and almost all his people (above thirty buried by Mr. Maverick of Winesemett[6] in one day). The towns in the bay took away many of the children; but most of them died soon after.

James Sagamore of Sagus[7] died also, and most of his folks. John Sagamore desired to be brought among the English, (so he was) and promised (if he recovered) to live with the English and serve their God. He left one son, which he disposed to Mr. Wilson, the pastor of Boston, to be brought up by him. He gave to the governor a good quantity of wampompeague,[8] and to divers others of the English he gave gifts and took order for the payment of his own debts and his men's. He died in a persuasion that he should go to the Englishmen's God. Divers of them, in their sickness, confessed that the Englishmen's God was a good God and that, if they recovered, they would serve him.

It wrought[9] much with them, that when their own people forsook them, yet the English came daily and ministered to them; and yet few, only two

[1]Sometimes entitled *The History of New England,* the *Journal* was largely limited to events in Massachusetts. It was first published in complete form in 1826.
[2]Latin: orally. Ratcliff had spoken, rather than written, his "invectives."
[3]John Wilson (1588–1667), pastor of the Boston Church.
[4]Algonquian: subchief, local chief. [5]On the nearby Neponset River, south of Boston.
[6]Present-day Chelsea, Massachusetts. [7]Present-day Lynn, Massachusetts.
[8]Wampum. Strands of polished shells, used by the Indians as money. [9]Counted, weighed.

families, took any infection by it. Among others, Mr. Maverick of Winesemett is worthy of a perpetual remembrance. Himself, his wife, and servants, went daily to them, ministered to their necessities, and buried their dead, and took home many of their children. So did other of the neighbors.

. . .

[January 1636] The governor[10] and assistants met at Boston to consider about Mr. Williams,[11] for that they were credibly informed, that, notwithstanding the injunction laid upon him (upon the liberty granted him to stay till the spring) not to go about to draw others to his opinions, he did use to entertain company in his house, and to preach to them, even of such points as he had been censured for; and it was agreed to send him into England by a ship then ready to depart. The reason was, because he had drawn above twenty persons to his opinion, and they were intended to erect a plantation[12] about the Narranganset Bay,[13] from whence the infection would easily spread into these churches (the people being, many of them, much taken with the apprehension of his godliness). Whereupon a warrant was sent to him to come presently to Boston, to be shipped [to England], etc. He returned answer (and divers of Salem came with it) that he could not come without hazard of his life, etc. Whereupon a pinnace was sent with commission to Capt. Underhill, etc., to apprehend him, and carry him aboard the ship (which then rode at Nantasket) but, when they came at his house, they found he had been gone three days before; but whither they could not learn.

He had so far prevailed at Salem, as many there (especially of devout women) did embrace his opinions, and separated from the churches.

. . .

[October 21, 1636] About the middle of this month, John Tilley, master of a bark, coming down [the] Connecticut River, went on shore in a canoe, three miles above the fort, to kill fowl; and having shot off his piece, many Indians arose out the covert[14] and took him and killed one other who was in the canoe. This Tilley was a very stout[15] man, and of great understanding. They cut off his hands . . . and afterwards cut off his feet. He lived three days after his hands were cut off; and [the Indians] themselves confessed that he was a stout man because he cried not in his torture.

. . .

One Mrs. Hutchinson,[16] a member of the church of Boston, a woman of a ready wit and bold spirit, brought over with her two dangerous errors: 1. That the person of the Holy Ghost dwells in a justified[17] person. 2. That no

[10]John Haynes (1594–1654). Winthrop was re-elected governor in 1637.

[11]Roger Williams. [12]I.e., settle a colony. [13]The Providence Plantation in Rhode Island.

[14]Underbrush. [15]Courageous.

[16]Anne Hutchinson (1591–1643) came to Boston with her husband and eleven children in 1634 and settled in a house across the street from Winthrop. The disputed religious services she held in her home caused a crisis in the colony, for she taught the doctrine of the Inner Light, that the elect were in direct communication with God and need not heed the laws of the church or the teaching of clergymen, who might themselves be lacking in grace. Her antinomianism (opposition to divine laws) and her verbal assaults on clergymen and magistrates were seen as a threat to civil and religious harmony and brought her banishment and excommunication.

[17]Cleansed of sin and made worthy of salvation.

sanctification[18] can help to evidence to us our justification.—From these two [errors] grew many branches.

. . .

[November 1, 1637] There was great hope that the late general assembly would have had some good effect in pacifying the troubles and dissensions about matters of religion; but it fell out otherwise. . . .

The court . . . sent for Mrs. Hutchinson, and charged her with divers matters, as her keeping two public lectures every week in her house, whereto sixty or eighty persons did usually resort, and for reproaching most of the ministers (viz., all except Mr. Cotton[19]) for not preaching a covenant of free grace,[20] and that they had not the seal of the spirit, nor were able ministers of the New Testament; which were clearly proved against her, though she sought to shift it off.[21] And, after many speeches to and fro, at last she was so full as she could not contain, but vented her revelations;[22] amongst which this was one, that she had it revealed to her, that she should come into New England, and should here be persecuted, and that God would ruin us and our posterity, and the whole state, for the same. So the court proceeded and banished her; but, because it was winter, they committed her to a private house, where she was well provided, and her own friends and the elders permitted to go to her, but none else.

.

[March 1638] While Mrs. Hutchinson continued at Roxbury,[23] divers of the elders and others resorted to her, and finding her to persist in maintaining those gross errors beforementioned, and many others, to the number of thirty or thereabout, some of them wrote to the church at Boston, offering to make proof of the same before the church, etc. . . . whereupon she was called (the magistrates being desired to give her license to come), and the lecture was appointed to begin at ten. . . . When she appeared, the errors were read to her . . . but yet she held her own; so as the church (all but two of her sons) agreed she should be admonished,[24] and because her sons would not agree to it, they were admonished also.

Mr. Cotton pronounced the sentence of admonition with great solemnity, and with much zeal and detestation of her errors and pride of spirit. The assembly continued till eight at night, and all did acknowledge the special presence of God's spirit therein; and she was appointed to appear again the next lecture day.

. . .

[March 22, 1638] Mrs. Hutchinson appeared again (she had been licensed by the court, in regard she had given hope of her repentance, to be at Mr. Cotton's house, that both he and Mr. Davenport[25] might have the

[18]The good moral conduct that shows justification. Orthodox Puritans held that proper social behavior was one sign that a Christian had received God's grace.

[19]John Cotton (1584–1652), a minister of the Boston Church.

[20]I.e., that grace was a gift of God and could not be earned by good deeds. Anne Hutchinson argued that most ministers, other than Cotton, taught that individuals could earn God's grace by good conduct, a belief that conflicted with the doctrine that God's gift of grace was wholly free.

[21]Avoid responsibility.

[22]She claimed to receive special revelations directly from God.

[23]Before deportation, she was temporarily held at Roxbury, Massachusetts.

[24]A lesser punishment than excommunication.

[25]John Davenport (1597–1670), Puritan minister.

more opportunity to deal with her); and the articles being again read to her, and her answer required, she delivered it in writing, wherein she made a retractation of near all, but with such explanations and circumstances as gave no satisfaction to the church, so as she was required to speak further to them. Then she declared that it was just with God to leave her to herself, as he had done, for her slighting his ordinances both magistracy and ministry;[26] and confessed that what she had spoken against the magistrates at the court (by way of revelation) was rash and ungrounded, and desired the church to pray for her. This gave the church good hope of her repentance; but when she was examined about some particulars, as that she had denied inherent righteousness,[27] etc., she affirmed that it was never her judgment; and though it was proved by many testimonies that she had been of that judgment, and so had persisted, and maintained it by argument against divers, yet she impudently persisted in her affirmation, to the astonishment of all the assembly. So that, after much time and many arguments had been spent to bring her to see her sin, but all in vain, the church, with one consent, cast her out. Some moved to have her admonished once more; but, it being for manifest evil in matter of conversation, it was agreed otherwise; and for that reason also the sentence was denounced[28] by the pastor, matter of manners[29] belonging properly to his place.

After she was excommunicated,[30] her spirits, which seemed before to be somewhat dejected, revived again, and she gloried in her sufferings, saying that it was the greatest happiness, next to Christ, that ever befell her. Indeed, it was a happy day to the churches of Christ here, and to many poor souls, who had been seduced by her, who, by what they heard and saw that day, were (through the grace of God) brought off quite from her errors, and settled again in the truth.

. . .

[September 1638] Mrs. Hutchinson, being removed to the Isle of Aquidneck,[31] in the Narragansett Bay, after her time was fulfilled, that she expected deliverance of a child, was delivered of a monstrous birth, which, being diversely related in the country (and in the open assembly at Boston, upon a lecture day), [was] declared by Mr. Cotton to be twenty-seven several lumps of man's seed, without any alteration or mixture of anything from the woman, and thereupon gathered that it might signify her error in denying inherent righteousness but [insisting] that all was Christ in us.

. . .

[26]Her teachings were considered a violation of both civil and church laws.

[27]I.e., she denied that righteousness was inherent in humankind, arguing that righteousness existed only in Christ.

[28]Proclaimed.

[29]Because Anne Hutchinson was judged guilty of speaking untruths, a violation of moral behavior ("manners"), her sentence of excommunication was proclaimed not by a civil magistrate but by the pastor of the Boston Church, John Wilson.

[30]She was first banished from the colony by civil authorities, then excommunicated from the church by ecclesiastical authorities.

[31]After her banishment, Anne Hutchinson moved to the island of Aquidneck, now Rhode Island. In 1642 she moved to Long Island, New York, where one year later she was killed in an Indian massacre.

[December 13, 1638] At Providence, also, the devil was not idle. For whereas, at their first coming thither, Mr. Williams and the rest did make an order that no man should be molested for his conscience, now men's wives, and children, and servants claimed liberty hereby to go to all religious meetings, though never [before] so often, or though private, upon the week days; and because one Verin refused to let his wife go to Mr. Williams so oft as she was called for, they required to have him censured.

. . .

[November 1639] At a general court held at Boston, great complaint was made of the oppression used in the county in sale of foreign commodities; and Mr. Robert Keayne, who kept a shop in Boston, was notoriously above others observed and complained of; and, being convented,[32] he was charged with many particulars; in some, for taking above six-pence in the shilling profit; in some above eight-pence; and, in some small things, above two for one; and being hereof convicted, (as appears by the records) he was fined £200. . . . After the court had censured him, the church of Boston called him also in question, where (as before he had done in the court) he did, with tears, acknowledge and bewail his covetous and corrupt heart, yet making some excuse for many of the particulars, which were charged upon him, as partly by pretence of ignorance of the true price of some wares, and chiefly by being misled by some false principles. . . . These things gave occasion to Mr. Cotton, in his public exercise the next lecture day, to lay open the error of such false principles, and to give some rules of direction in the case.

Some false principles were these:

1. That a man might sell as dear as he can, and buy as cheap as he can.
2. If a man lose by casualty[33] of sea, etc., in some of his commodities, he may raise the price of the rest.
3. That he may sell as he bought, though he paid too dear, etc., and though the commodity be fallen [in price], etc.
4. That, as a man may take the advantage of his own skill or ability, so he may of another's ignorance or necessity.
5. Where one gives time for payment, he is to take like recompense of one as of another.

The rules for trading were these:

1. A man may not sell above the current price, i.e., such a price as is usual in the time and place, and as another (who knows the worth of the commodity) would give for it, if he had occasion to use it; as that is called current money, which every man will take, etc.
2. When a man loseth in his commodity for want of skill, etc., he must look at it as his own fault or cross, and therefore must not lay it upon another.

[32]Summoned before the court. [33]Accident.

3. Where a man loseth by casualty of sea, or, etc., it is a loss cast upon himself by providence, and he may not ease himself of it by casting it upon another; for so a man should seem to provide against all providences, etc., that he should never lose; but where there is a scarcity of the commodity, there men may raise their price; for now it is a hand of God upon the commodity, and not the person.

4. A man may not ask any more for his commodity than his selling price; as Ephron to Abraham,[34] the land is worth thus much.

The cause being debated by the church, some were earnest to have him excommunicated; but the most thought an admonition would be sufficient. . . . In the end, the church consented to an admonition.

. . .

[December 15, 1640] About this time there fell out a thing worthy of observation. Mr. Winthrop the younger,[35] one of the magistrates, having many books in a chamber where there was corn of divers sorts, had among them one wherein the Greek testament, the psalms and the common prayer[36] were bound together. He found the common prayer eaten with mice, every leaf of it, and not any of the two other touched, nor any other of his books, though there were above a thousand.

. . .

[April 13, 1641] A negro maid, servant to Mr. Stoughton of Dorchester, being well approved by divers years' experience, for sound knowledge and true godliness, was received into the church and baptized.

. . .

[June 21, 1641] There arose a question in court about the punishment of single fornication, because, by the law of God, the [guilty] man was only [required] to marry the maid, or pay a sum of money to her father;[37] but the case falling out[38] between two servants, they were whipped for the wrong offered to the master in abusing his house.

. . .

Mrs. Hutchinson and those of Aquidneck Island broached new heresies every year. Divers of them turned professed anabaptists, and would not wear any arms, and denied all magistracy[39] among Christians, and maintained that there were no churches since those founded by the apostles and evangelists,

[34]Ephron offered to give Abraham, without cost, a cave for the burial of the dead. Abraham insisted on paying full price. Genesis 23.

[35]John Winthrop's son.

[36]The Book of Common Prayer of the Church of England.

[37]Deuteronomy 22:28–29.

[38]Occurring.

[39]Anabaptists objected to infant baptism, urged separation of church and state, refused to bear arms, and denied the jurisdiction of civil authorities in religious matters.

nor could any be, nor any pastors ordained, nor seals[40] administered but by such, and that the church was to want[41] these all the time she[42] continued in the wilderness, as yet she was.

. . .

[September 22, 1642] The court, with advice of the elders, ordered a general fast. The occasions were, 1. The ill news we had out of England concerning the breach between the king and parliament. 2. The danger of the Indians. 3. The unseasonable weather, the rain having continued so long, viz.[43] near a fortnight together, scarce one fair day, and much corn[44] and hay spoiled, though indeed it proved a blessing to us, for it being with warm easterly winds, it brought the Indian corn to maturity, which otherwise would not have been ripe, and it pleased God, that so soon as the fast was agreed upon, the weather changed, and proved fair after.

. . .

The sudden fall[45] of land and cattle, and the scarcity of foreign commodities, and money, etc., with the thin access of people from England, put many into an unsettled frame of spirit, so as they concluded there would be no subsisting here, and accordingly they began to hasten away, some to the West Indies, others to the Dutch, at Long Island, etc. (for the governor there invited them by fair offers), and others back for England.

. . .

Much disputation there was about liberty of removing for outward advantages, and all ways were sought for an open door to get out at; but it is to be feared many crept out at a broken wall. For such as come together into a wilderness, where are nothing but wild beasts and beastlike men, and there confederate together in civil and church estate, whereby they do, implicitly at least, bind themselves to support each other, and all of them that society, whether civil or sacred, whereof they are members. How they can break from this without free consent is hard to find, so as may satisfy a tender or good conscience in time of trial. Ask thy conscience, if thou wouldst have plucked up thy stakes, and brought thy family 3000 miles, if thou hadst expected that all, or most, would have forsaken thee there. Ask again, what liberty thou hast towards others, which thou likest not to allow others towards thyself; for if one may go, another may, and so the greater part, and so church and commonwealth may be left destitute in a wilderness, exposed to misery and reproach, and all for thy ease and pleasure, whereas these all, being now thy brethren, as near to thee as the Israelites were to Moses, it were much safer for thee, after his example, to choose rather to suffer affliction with thy brethren, than to enlarge thy ease and pleasure by furthering the occasion of their ruin.

. . .

[40] Baptism and the Lord's Supper, the two sacraments of the Puritan church. [41] Lack.
[42] I.e., the church. [43] Latin: namely.
[44] Wheat and similar grains. [45] In value.

[April 13, 1645] Mr. Hopkins,[46] the governor of Hartford upon Connecticut, came to Boston, and brought his wife with him, (a godly young woman, and of special parts) who was fallen into a sad infirmity, the loss of her understanding and reason, which had been growing upon her divers years, by occasion of her giving herself wholly to reading and writing, and had written many books. Her husband, being very loving and tender of her, was loath to grieve her; but he saw his error when it was too late. For if she had attended her household affairs and such things as belong to women, and not gone out of her way and calling to meddle in such things as are proper for men, whose minds are stronger, etc., she had kept her wits and might have improved them usefully and honorably in the place God had set her.

. . .

[Speech to the General Court[47]]

[July 3, 1645] I suppose something may be expected from me, upon this charge that is befallen me, which moves me to speak now to you; yet I intend not to intermeddle in the proceedings of the court, or with any of the persons concerned therein. Only I bless God, that I see an issue of this troublesome business. I also acknowledge the justice of the court, and, for mine own part, I am well satisfied, I was publicly charged, and I am publicly and legally acquitted, which is all I did expect or desire. And though this be sufficient for my justification before men, yet not so before the God, who hath seen so much amiss in my dispensations (and even in this affair) as calls me to be humble. For to be publicly and criminally charged in this court, is matter of humiliation, (and I desire to make a right use of it) notwithstanding I be thus acquitted. If her father had spit in her face (saith the Lord concerning Miriam), should she not have been ashamed seven days?[48] Shame had lain upon her, whatever the occasion had been. I am unwilling to stay you from your urgent affairs, yet give me leave (upon this special occasion) to speak a little more to this assembly. It may be of some good use, to inform and rectify the judgments of some of the people, and may prevent such distempers[49] as have arisen amongst us. The great questions that have troubled the country are about the authority of the magistrates and the liberty of the people. It is yourselves who have called us to this office, and being called by you, we have our authority from God, in way of an ordinance, such as hath the image of God eminently stamped upon it, the contempt and violation whereof hath been vindicated with examples of divine vengeance. I entreat you to consider, that when you choose magistrates, you take them from among yourselves, men subject to like passions as you are. Therefore when you see infirmities in us, you should reflect

[46]Edward Hopkins (1600–1657).

[47]In 1645, Winthrop was charged with exceeding his authority as a magistrate. Following a trial and exoneration, he addressed the General Court (legislature) on the Puritan ideals of liberty, the duties of magistrates, and the duty of the people to submit to the authority of magistrates (God's lieutenants) and their interpretations of God's ordinances.

[48]And the Lord said unto Moses, "If her father had but spit in her face, should she not be ashamed seven days?" Numbers 12:14.

[49]Disturbances.

upon your own, and that would make you bear the more with us, and not be severe censurers of the failings of your magistrates, when you have continual experience of the like infirmities in yourselves and others. We account him a good servant, who breaks not his covenant. The covenant between you and us is the oath you have taken of us, which is to this purpose, that we shall govern you and judge your causes by the rules of God's laws and our own, according to our best skill. When you agree with a workman to build you a ship or house, etc., he undertakes as well for his skill as for his faithfulness, for it is his profession, and you pay him for both. But when you call one to be a magistrate, he doth not profess nor undertake to have sufficient skill for that office, nor can you furnish him with gifts, etc., therefore you must run the hazard of his skill and ability. But if he fail in faithfulness, which by his oath he is bound unto, that he must answer for. If it fall out that the case be clear to common apprehension, and the rule clear also, if he transgress here, the error is not in the skill, but in the evil of the will: it must be required of him. But if the case be doubtful, or the rule doubtful, to men of such understanding and parts as your magistrates are, if your magistrates should err here, yourselves must bear it.

For the other point concerning liberty, I observe a great mistake in the country about that. There is a twofold liberty, natural (I mean as our nature is now corrupt) and civil or federal. The first is common to man with beasts and other creatures. By this, man, as he stands in relation to man simply, hath liberty to do what he lists; it is a liberty to evil as well as to good. This liberty is incompatible and inconsistent with authority, and cannot endure the least restraint of the most just authority. The exercise and maintaining of this liberty makes men grow more evil, and in time to be worse than brute beasts: *omnes sumus licentia deteriores.*[50] This is that great enemy of truth and peace, that wild beast, which all the ordinances of God are bent against, to restrain and subdue it. The other kind of liberty I call civil or federal, it may also be termed moral, in reference to the covenant between God and man, in the moral law, and the politic covenants and constitutions, amongst men themselves. This liberty is the proper end and object of authority, and cannot subsist without it; and it is a liberty to that only which is good, just, and honest. This liberty you are to stand for, with the hazard (not only of your goods, but) of your lives, if need be. Whatsoever crosses this, is not authority, but a distemper thereof. This liberty is maintained and exercised in a way of subjection to authority; it is of the same kind of liberty wherewith Christ has made us free. The woman's own choice makes such a man her husband; yet being so chosen, he is her lord, and she is to be subject to him, yet in a way of liberty, not of bondage; and a true wife accounts her subjection her honor and freedom, and would not think her condition safe and free, but in her subjection to her husband's authority. Such is the liberty of the church under the authority of Christ, her king and husband; his yoke is so easy and sweet to her as a bride's ornaments; and if through forwardness or wantonness, etc., she shake it off, at any time, she is at no rest in her spirit, until she take it up again; and whether

[50]Latin: "all are weakened by excess liberty," a quotation derived from *Heauton Timorumenos (The Self-Tormentor),* line 483, by the Roman poet Terence (c. 190–159 B.C.).

her lord smiles upon her, and embraces her in his arms, or whether he frowns, or rebukes, or smites her, she apprehends the sweetness of his love in all, and is refreshed, supported, and instructed by every such dispensation of his authority over her. On the other side, ye know who they are that complain of this yoke and say, let us break their bands, etc., we will not have this man to rule over us. Even so, brethren, it will be between you and your magistrates. If you stand for your natural corrupt liberties, and will do what is good in your own eyes, you will not endure the least weight of authority, but will murmur, and oppose, and be always striving to shake off that yoke; but if you will be satisfied to enjoy such civil and lawful liberties, such as Christ allows you, then will you quietly and cheerfully submit unto that authority which is set over you, in all the administrations of it, for your good. Wherein, if we fail at any time, we hope we shall be willing (by God's assistance) to hearken to good advice from any of you, or in any other way of God; so shall your liberties be preserved, in upholding the honor and power of authority amongst you.

. . .

[June 4, 1648] At this court one Margaret Jones of Charlestown was indicted and found guilty of witchcraft and hanged for it. The evidence against her was: 1, that she was found to have such a malignant touch, as many persons (men, women, and children) whom she stroked or touched with any affection or displeasure or etc. were taken with deafness, or vomiting, or other violent pains or sickness; 2, she practising physic,[51] and her medicines being such things as (by her own confession) were harmless, [such] as aniseed, liquors, and etc., yet [they] had extraordinary violent effects; 3, she would use to tell such [persons] as would not make use of her physic that they would never be healed, and accordingly their diseases and hurts continued, with relapses against the ordinary course[52] and beyond the apprehension of all physicians and surgeons; 4, some things which she foretold came to pass accordingly; other things she could tell of (such as secret speeches, etc.), which she had no ordinary means to come to the knowledge of; 5, she had (upon search) an apparent[53] teat in her secret parts as fresh as if it had been newly sucked, and after it had been scanned, upon a forced search, that [teat] was withered and another began on the opposite side;[54] 6, in the prison, in the clear daylight, there was seen in her arms, she sitting on the floor and her clothes up, etc., a little child, which ran from her into another room, and the officer following it, it was vanished. The like child was seen in two other places, to which she had relation; and one maid that saw it, fell sick upon it, and was cured by the said Margaret, who used means to be employed to that end. Her behaviour at her trial was very intemperate, lying notoriously, and railing upon the jury

[51]Medicine.

[52]Unusual, unexpected relapses.

[53]Visible.

[54]Such growths were thought to be used to suckle demons; hence they were considered evidence of witchcraft.

and witnesses, etc., and in the like distemper she died. The same day and hour she was executed, there was a very great tempest at Connecticut, which blew down many trees, etc.

. . .

[August 15, 1648] The synod[55] met at Cambridge. . . . Mr. Allen of Dedham preached out of Acts 15, a very godly, learned, and particular handling of near all the doctrines and applications concerning that subject with a clear discovery and refutation of such errors, objections, and scruples as had been raised about it by some young heads in the country.

It fell out, about the midst of his sermon, there came a snake into the seat,[56] where many of the elders sat behind the preacher. It came in at the door where people stood thick upon the stairs. Divers of the elders shifted from it, but Mr. Thomson, one of the elders of Braintree (a man of much faith), trod upon the head of it, and so held it with his foot and staff with a small pair of grains,[57] until it was killed. This being so remarkable, and nothing falling out but by divine providence, it is out of doubt [that] the Lord discovered[58] somewhat of his mind in it. The serpent is the devil; the synod, the representative of the churches of Christ in New England. The devil had formerly and lately attempted their disturbance and dissolution; but their faith in the seed of the woman[59] overcame him and crushed his head.

1630–1649 1826

The Bay Psalm Book 1640

The Whole Book of Psalms Faithfully Translated into English Meter, *commonly known as* The Bay Psalm book, *was the first book in English to be printed in America. It provided a metrical version of the Psalms that could be sung by all the congregation at Puritan church services. Its creators, a group of worthies drawn from among the "chief divines" of the Massachusetts Bay Colony, were faced with the task of making a translation of the Hebrew Psalms that met the demand for close adherence to the Word and at the same time fit the tunes that New England settlers knew.*

In recent years, readers who looked at the words and forgot the tunes described the Bay Psalms as "rhythmic and syntactic wreckage" with "sentences wrenched about, end for end, clauses heaved up and abandoned in chaos," the cankered verse of men

[55]A meeting for discussion of church doctrine.
[56]Church area, near the pulpit, where dignitaries sat.
[57]A fish spear with two "grains" (prongs).
[58]Revealed.
[59]Genesis 3:15.

whose piety transcended their poetry. Yet the intent of the translators was not beauty but utility and accuracy, aims they defended in their Preface: *"If therefore the verses are not always so smooth and elegant as some may desire or expect, let them consider that God's altar needs not our polishings . . . for we have respected rather a plain translation, than to smooth our verses with the sweetness of any paraphrase, and so have attended conscience rather than elegance, fidelity rather than poetry. . . ."*

The Bay Psalm Book *was America's first bestseller and the first published expression of the Bay Colony's Calvinism, revealing Puritan devotion to the Bible and a belief in the need to adapt the forms of literature to the service of religion, subordinating art to spiritual and social purpose.*

FURTHER READING: H. Foote, *Three Centuries of American Hymnody,* 1940; Z. Haraszti, *The Enigma of the Bay Psalm Book,* 1956; *The Bay Psalm Book,* ed. Z. Haraszti, 1956; I. Lowens, *Music and Musicians in Early America,* 1964.

TEXT: *The Whole Book of Psalms,* 1640. Punctuation, spelling, and usage have been changed to conform more nearly to modern practice.

from *THE BAY PSALM BOOK*

PSALM 6

To the chief musician on Neginoth upon Sheminith, a psalm of David

Lord in Thy wrath rebuke me not,
nor in Thy hot wrath chasten me.
Pity me Lord, for I am weak;
Lord heal me, for my bones vexed be.
Also my soul is troubled sore;
how long Lord wilt Thou me forsake?
Return O Lord, my soul release;
O save me for Thy mercy's sake.
In death no mem'ry is of Thee,
and who shall pray Thee in the grave?
I faint with groans; all night my bed
swims; I with tears my couch washed have.
Mine eye with grief is dim and old
because of all mine enemies.
But now depart away from me,
all ye that work iniquities;
For Jehovah ev'n now hath heard
the voice of these my weeping tears.
Jehovah hear my humble suit;
Jehovah doth receive my prayers.
Let all mine enemies be ashamed
and greatly troubled let them be;
Yea let them be returned back,
and be ashaméd suddenly.

PSALM 23

A Psalm of David

The Lord to me a shepherd is,
want therefore shall not I.
He in the folds of tender grass,
doth cause me down to lie.
To waters calm me gently leads;
restore my soul doth He;
He doth in paths of righteousness
for His name's sake lead me.
Yea though in valley of death's shade
I walk, none ill I'll fear,
Because Thou art with me; Thy rod
and staff my comfort are.
For me a table Thou has spread,
in presence of my foes.
Thou dost anoint my head with oil;
my cup it overflows.
Goodness and mercy surely shall
all my days follow me;
And in the Lord's house I shall dwell
so long as days shall be.

PSALM 100

A Psalm of Praise

Make ye a joyful sounding noise
Jehovah all the earth;
Serve ye Jehovah with gladness;
before him come with mirth.
Know, that Jehovah He is God,
who hath us formed it is He,
And not ourselves; His own people
and sheep of His pasture are we.
Enter into His gates with praise,
into His courts with thankfulness;
Make ye confession unto Him,
and His name reverently bless,
Because Jehovah He is good,
forevermore is His mercy;
And unto generations all
continue doth His verity.

ANOTHER OF THE SAME

Make ye a joyful noise unto
Jehovah all the earth;
Serve ye Jehovah with gladness:
before Him come with mirth.
Know, that Jehovah He is God,
not we ourselves, but He
Hath made us. His people, and sheep
of His pasture are we.
O enter ye into His gates
with praise, and thankfulness
Into His courts; confess to Him,
and His name do ye bless.
Because Jehovah He is good,
His bounteous mercy
Is everlasting; and His truth
is to eternity.

PSALM 137

The rivers on of Babylon
there when we did sit down,
Yea even then we mourned, when
we remembered Zion.
Our harps we did hang it amid,
upon the willow tree,
Because there they that us away
led in captivity,
Required of us a song, and thus
asked mirth, us waste who laid;
Sing us among a Zion's song,
unto us then they said.
The Lord's song sing can we? being
in stranger's land. Then let
Lose her skill my right hand, if I
Jerusalem forget.
Let cleave my tongue my palate on,
if mind thee do not I,
If chief joys o'er I prize not more
Jerusalem my joy.

Remember Lord, Edom's sons'[1] word,
 unto the ground said they,
It raze, it raze, when as it was
 Jerusalem her day.
Blessed shall he be, that payeth thee,
 daughter of Babylon,
Who must be waste, that which thou hast
 rewarded us upon.
O happy he shall surely be
 that taketh up, that eke
Thy little ones against the stones
 doth into pieces break.

1640

The New England Primer c. 1683

The New England Primer *was a small textbook filled with short verses, hymns, prayers, and rhyming alphabets. It was designed to provide "Spiritual Milk for American Babes" and to teach them to read so they might understand the Bible, free from the "wiles of Popish priests" and the snares of "that old deluder Satan." The* Primer *was first published at Boston, in the Massachusetts Bay Colony. Its author and the exact date of the first edition are unknown, but it was clearly an expression of a communal faith in the virtues of literacy and in the need to convert "young vipers" into obedient and pious adults, devoted to the Puritan creed. The* Primer *was the most widely used schoolbook of early America. The reported 5 million published copies helped engrave Puritan ideals on the American mind, and they established a national tradition of schools and schoolbooks that celebrated both literacy and Protestant dogma in teaching "millions to read, and not one to sin."*

FURTHER READING: C. Heartman, *The New-England Primer Issued Prior to 1830,* 1934; C. Butterworth, *The English Primers,* 1953; J. Nietz, *Old Textbooks,* 1961; *The New England Primer,* ed. P. Ford, 1897, 1962; P. Crain, *The Story of A, The Alphabetization of America from the New England Primer to the Scarlett Letter,* 2002.

TEXT: *The New England Primer,* 1727.

[1]The Edomites opposed the Israelites on their route from Egypt.

from *THE NEW ENGLAND PRIMER*[1]

A In *Adam's* Fall
We Sinned all.

B Thy Life to Mend
This *Book* Attend.

C The *Cat* doth play
And after ſlay.

D A *Dog* will bite
A Thief at night.

E An *Eagle's* flight
Is out of ſight.

F The Idle *Fool*
Is whipt at School.

G As runs the *Glaſs*
Mans life doth paſs.

H My *Book* and *Heart*
Shall never part.

J *Job* feels the Rod
Yet bleſſes GOD.

K Our *KING* the good
No man of blood.

L The *Lion* bold
The *Lamb* doth hold.

M The *Moon* gives light
In time of night.

N *Nightengales* ſing
In Time of Spring.

O The *Royal Oak*
it was the Tree
That ſav'd His
Royal Majeſtie.

P *Peter* denies
His Lord and cries

Q Queen *Eſther* comes
in Royal State
To Save the JEWS
from diſmal Fate

R *Rachel* doth mourn
For her fiſt born.

S *Samuel* anoints
Whom God appoints.

T *Time* cuts down all
Both great and ſmall.

U *Uriah's* beauteous Wife
Made David ſeek his
Life.

W *Whales* in the Sea
God's Voice obey.

X *Xerxes* the great did
die,
And ſo muſt you & I.

Y *Youth* forward ſlips
Death ſooneſt nips.

Z *Zacheus* he
Did climb the Tree
His Lord to ſee,

[1]The poems "Verses" and "Again" (pages 91–92) appeared on pages of the 1727 edition that no longer exist, and therefore the texts of the poems as they appeared in later editions of the *Primer* have been used here.

Now the Child being entred in his Letters and Spelling, let him learn these and such like Sentences by Heart, whereby he will be both instructed in his Duty, and encouraged in his Learning.

THE DUTIFUL CHILD'S PROMISES,

I Will fear GOD, and honour the KING.

I will honour my Father & Mother.
I will Obey my Superiours.
I will Submit to my Elders,
I will Love my Friends.
I will hate no Man.
I will forgive my Enemies, and pray to
God for them.
I will as much as in me lies keep all God's
Holy Commandments.
I will learn my Catechism.
I will keep the Lord's Day Holy.
I will Reverence God's Sanctuary,
For our GOD is a consuming Fire.

VERSES.

I in the Burying Place may see
Graves shorter there than I;
From Death's Arrest no Age is free,
Young Children too may die;
My God, may such an awful Sight,
Awakening be to me!
Oh! that by early Grace I might
For Death prepared be.

AGAIN.

First in the Morning when thou doft awake,
To God for his Grace thy Petition make,
Some Heavenly Petition ufe daily to fay,
That the God of Heaven may blefs thee alway.

. . .

Good Children muft,
Fear God all Day, Love Chrift
alway,
Parents obey, In Secret Pray,
No falfe thing fay, Mind little Play,
By no Sin ftray, Make no delay,
In doing Good.
Awake, arife, behold thou haft
Thy Life a Leaf, thy Breath a Blaft;
At Night lye down prepar'd to have
Thy fleep, thy death, thy bed, thy
grave.

1683?

THE SHORTER CATECHISM

AGREED UPON BY THE REVEREND

*ASS*EMBLY OF DIVINES *at Weftminfter*[1]

Queft WHat is the chief End of Man?

Anfw. Man's chief End is to Glorify God, and to Enjoy Him for ever.

Q. *What Rule hath God given to direct us how we may glorify and enjoy Him?*

A. The Word of God which is contained in the Scriptures of the Old

[1]In 1647, an assembly of Puritan clergymen (divines) meeting in Westminster Abbey drew up the "Larger" and the "Smaller" or (Shorter) catechisms for use in instructing the faithful. The "Shorter Catechism," devised for children and for such adults "as are of weaker capacity," was widely reprinted in schoolbooks. Its 107 questions and answers covered matters of faith, the Lord's Prayer, and the Ten Commandments.

and New Teſtament, is the only Rule to direct us how we may glorify and enjoy him.

· ·

Q. *How doth God execute his Decrees?*

A. God executeth his Decrees in the Works of Creation & Providence.

Q. *What is the Work of Creation?*

A. The Work of Creation is God's Making all things of Nothing, by the Word of his Power.

Q. *What are God's Works of Providence?*

A. God's Works of Providence are his moſt holy, wiſe & powerful preſerving & governing all his Creatures and all their Actions.

Q. *What ſpecial Act of Providence did God exerciſe towards Man in the Eſtate wherein he was created?*

A. When God had created Man, He entred into a Covenant of Life with him, upon condition of perfect Obedience, forbidding him to Eat of the Tree of knowledge of good and evil upon pain of Death.

Q. *Did our firſt Parents continue in the eſtate wherein they were created?*

A. Our firſt Parents being left to the freedom of their own Will, fell from the eſtate wherein they were created, by ſinning against God.

· · ·

Q. *Did all Mankind fall in Adam's firſt tranſgreſſion?*

A. The Covenant being made with *Adam,* not only for himſelf but for his Posterity, all Mankind descending from him by ordinary Generation, sinned in him, & fell with him in his first transgression.

. . .

Q. *What is the Misery of that estate whereinto Man fell?*

A. All Mankind by their fall, lost Communion with God, are under his Wrath & Curse, and so made liable to all Miseries in this Life, to Death it self, and to the pains of Hell for ever.

Q. *Did God leave all Mankind to perish in the estate of Sin & Misery?*

A. God having out of his meer good pleasure from all Eternity, Elected some to everlasting Life, did enter into a Covenant of Grace, to deliver them out of the state of Sin & Misery, and to being them into a state of Salvation by a Redeemer,

Q. *Who is the Redeemer of God's Elect?*

A. The only Redeemer of God's Elect, is the Lord Jesus Christ, who being the eternal Son of God, became Man, and so was, and continues to be God and Man in two distinct Natures, and one Person for ever.

. . .

Q. *What is effectual Calling?*

A. Effectual Calling is the Work of God's Spirit, whereby convincing us of our Sin & Misery, enlightning our Minds in the Knowledge of Christ, & renewing our Wills, he doth perswade & enable us to embrace Jesus Christ, freely offered to us in the Gospel.

Q. *What Benefits do they that are effectually called partake of in this Life?*

A. They that are Effectually called, do in this Life partake of Juſtification, Adoption, Sanctification, & the ſeveral Benefits which in this Life do either accompany or flow from them.

Q. *What is Juſtification ?*

A. Juſtification is an act of God's free Grace, wherein he pardoneth all our Sins, and accepteth us as righteous in his ſight, only for the righteouſneſs of Chriſt imputed to us, and received by Faith alone.

Q. *What is Adoption?*

A. Adoption is an Act of God's Free Grace, whereby we are received into the Number, and have Right to all the Priviledges of the Sons of God.

Q. *What is Sanctification ?*

A. Sanctification is the Work of God's free Grace, whereby we are renewed in the whole Man, after the Image of God, & are enabled more & more to die unto Sin, & live unto Righteouſneſs.

Q. *What are the Benefits which in this life do accompany or flow from Juſtification, Adoption & Sanctification?*

A. The Benefits which in this Life do accompany or flow from Juſtification, Adoption or Sanctification, are aſſurance of God's love, peace of Conſcience, joy in the Holy Ghoſt, increaſe of Grace, & perſeverance therein to the end.

Q. *What benefits do Believers receive from Chrift at their Death ?*

A. The Souls of Believers are at their Death made perfect in Holinefs, & do immediately pafs into Glory, & their Bodies being ftill united to Chrift, do reft in their Graves till the Refurrecton.

. . .

Q. *What are the outward & ordinary means whereby Chrift communicateth to us the benefits of Redemption?*

A. The outward and ordinary means whereby Chrift communicateth to us the benefits of Redemption are his Ordinances, efpecially the Word, Sacraments & Prayer; all which are made effectual to the Elect for Salvation.

Q. *How is the word made effectual to Salvation ?*

A. The Spirit of God maketh the Reading, but efpecially the Preaching of the Word an effectual Means of Convincing & Converting Sinners, and of building them up in Holinefs & Comfort, through Faith unto Salvation.

Anne Bradstreet 1612–1672

Anne Bradstreet was the first notable poet in the English-speaking lands of the New World—an authentic Puritan voice with a simplicity and force rarely found in her contemporaries. She was born in England, and raised in comparative luxury on the estate of the Earl of Lincoln, where her father, Thomas Dudley, was steward (manager of business affairs). She had a childhood common to Puritan children seized by the force of Calvinist doctrine, but Thomas Dudley saw to it that his high-spirited young daughter was educated beyond the simple household skills and the lessons in submission often given to women of her time and station.

At sixteen, she married Simon Bradstreet, a sturdy Puritan and a graduate of Cambridge University. Two years later, in 1630, she left England with her husband and her parents on the ship Arbella, *sailing to the Massachusetts Bay Colony. In Massachusetts her father became one of the Colony's leaders and succeeded John Winthrop as Governor. Anne and her husband settled on a farm near the frontier village of Andover, on the Merrimac River. There she confronted a primitive life at which her heart rebelled until she "was convinced it was the way of God" and "submitted." She became a dutiful housewife, raised eight children, and, in the midst of her household tasks, stole time to read and write poetry. Versifiers were common enough in colonial New England, but few were women. Anne Bradstreet recognized that a Puritan community frowned on writing as unseemly behavior for a woman, especially the daughter of the Governor:*

I am obnoxious to each carping tongue
Who says my hand a needle better fits.

In 1647 her brother-in-law, John Woodbridge, pastor of the Andover church, sailed to England taking copies of her poems with him. There, in 1650, and without her knowledge, they were published under the title The Tenth Muse Lately Sprung Up in America or Several Poems, Compiled With a Great Variety of Wit and Learning, Full of Delight . . . By a Gentlewoman of Those Parts. *It was the first published volume of poetry written by a settler in the English colonies.*

The poems in The Tenth Muse *were obviously imitative, filled with well-worn poetic stock. In laboring and tedious couplets they dwelt on the vanity of worldly pleasures, the brevity of life, and resignation to God's will. Her poetry reflected the influence of the Bible and the translations of the French poet Guillaume du Bartas (1544–1590), who had decorated his scriptural epics with an overabundance of strained metaphors and conceits. When Anne Bradstreet saw her poetry in print, she was dismayed; she called it an "ill-formed offspring," "my rambling brat in print," but in London her volume of poems was a success and soon was listed among "the most vendable books" of the age.*

Little is known of the remaining years of her life except that in the midst of her daily routine of caring for her family in an isolated frontier village she revised her early work and composed new poems. Published posthumously in 1678, they were her best work, showing in greater depth the spiritual struggles of a Christian "on earth perplexed," confronting doubt and skepticism. She had moved from a concern with historical events, philosophical lore, and fantastic literary devices borrowed from Quarles, Herbert, and du Bartas, and she had achieved a simpler, more lyrical poetry expressing a mind whose emotionalism struggled with the Puritan conscience it had inherited.

In the eighteenth century her poetry was considered, as Cotton Mather noted, a "grateful entertainment unto the ingenious." In the nineteenth century it was dismissed as merely quaint and curious, a "relic of the earliest literature of our country." Today her work stands with that of Edward Taylor as part of the true poetry of seventeenth-century New England. She was one of the first women in America to speak in her own behalf, and her lyrics remained unsurpassed by any American woman writer for 200 years, until the nineteenth century and the coming of Emily Dickinson.

FURTHER READING: *The Works of Anne Bradstreet,* ed. J. Ellis, 1867, 1962; H. Campbell, *Anne Bradstreet and Her Time,* 1891; J. Berryman, *Homage to Mistress Bradstreet,* 1955; *The Tenth Muse* (1650), ed. J. Piercy, 1965; J. Piercy, *Anne Bradstreet,* 1965; *Poems of Anne Bradstreet,* ed. R. Hutchinson, 1969; E. White, *Anne Bradstreet, "The Tenth Muse,"* 1971; A. Stanford, *Anne Bradstreet, The Worldly Pilgrim,* 1974; *The Complete Works of Anne Bradstreet,* ed. J. McElrath and A. Robb, 1981; *Critical Essays on Anne Bradstreet,* ed. P. Cowell and A. Stanford, 1983; W. Martin, *An American Triptych: Anne Bradstreet, Emily Dickinson, Adrienne Rich,* 1984; R. Dolle, *Anne Bradstreet, A Reference Guide,* 1990; R. Rosenmeier, *Anne Bradstreet Revisited,* 1991; T. Nicolay, *Gender Roles, Literary Authority, and Three American Women Writers,* 1996; R. Craig, *A Concordance to the Complete Works of Anne Bradstreet,* 2000; *Essays on Anne Bradstreet, Edward Taylor, Nathaniel Hawthorne . . .,* ed. M. Schuldiner, 2001; D. Wilson and G. Grant, *Beyond the Stateliest Marble, The Passionate Femininity of Anne Bradstreet,* 2001.

TEXT: *The Works of Anne Bradstreet,* ed. J. Hensley, 1967, 1981. Spelling, punctuation, and usage have been changed to conform more nearly to modern practice.

THE PROLOGUE[1]

1

To sing of wars, of captains, and of kings,
Of cities founded, commonwealths begun,
For my mean pen are too superior things:
Or how they all, or each their dates have run
Let poets and historians set these forth,
My obscure lines shall not so dim their worth.

2

But when my wond'ring eyes and envious heart
Great Bartas'[2] sugared lines do but read o'er,
Fool I do grudge the Muses[3] did not part
'Twixt him and me that overfluent store:
A Bartas can do what a Bartas will
But simple I, according to my skill.

3

From schoolboy's tongue no rhet'ric we expect,
Nor yet a sweet consort[4] from broken strings,
Nor perfect beauty where's a main defect:
My foolish, broken, blemished Muse so sings,
And this to mend, alas, no art is able,
'Cause nature made it so irreparable.

[1]First published in *The Tenth Muse* (1650), "The Prologue" introduced a series of poems on the history of civilization.

[2]Guillaume du Bartas (1544–1590), a French poet whose ornate epic on the creation of the world, *The Divine Weeks and Works* (1578–1584), was translated into English (1592–1599) by Joshua Sylvester.

[3]The nine Greek goddesses of literature and the arts.

[4]Harmony.

4

Nor can I, like that fluent sweet tongued Greek,[5]
Who lisped at first, in future times speak plain.
By art he gladly found what he did seek,
A full requital of his striving pain.
Art can do much, but this maxim's most sure:
A weak or wounded brain admits no cure.

5

I am obnoxious to each carping tongue
Who says my hand a needle better fits,
A poet's pen all scorn I should thus wrong,
For such despite[6] they cast on female wits:
If what I do prove well, it won't advance,
They'll say it's stol'n, or else it was by chance.

6

But sure the antique Greeks were far more mild,
Else of our sex, why feigned[7] they those nine
And poesy made Calliope's[8] own child;
So 'mongst the rest they placed the arts divine:
But this weak knot they will full soon untie,
The Greeks did nought, but play the fools and lie.

7

Let Greeks be Greeks, and women what they are,
Men have precedency and still excel,
It is but vain unjustly to wage war;
Men can do best, and women know it well.
Preeminence in all and each is yours;
Yet grant some small acknowledgement of ours.

8

And oh ye high flown quills[9] that soar the skies,
And ever with your prey still catch your praise,
If e'er you deign these lowly lines your eyes,
Give thyme or parsley wreath, I ask no bays;[10]
This mean and unrefined ore of mine
Will make your glist'ring gold but more to shine.

1650

[5]Demosthenes (c. 383–322 B.C.), who conquered a speech defect and became a famous Athenian orator.

[6]Scorn, contempt.

[7]Invented, conceived.

[8]Greek Muse of all poetic inspiration.

[9]Quill pens.

[10]Laurel, the traditional garland of honor.

CONTEMPLATIONS

1

Some time now past in the autumnal tide,
When Phoebus[1] wanted but one hour to bed,
The trees all richly clad, yet void of pride,
Were gilded o'er by his rich golden head.
Their leaves and fruits seemed painted, but was true,
Of green, of red, of yellow, mixed hue;
Rapt[2] were my senses at this delectable view.

2

I wist[3] not what to wish, yet sure thought I,
If so much excellence abide below,
How excellent is He that dwells on high,
Whose power and beauty by his works we know?
Sure he is goodness, wisdom, glory, light,
That hath this under world so richly dight;[4]
More heaven than earth was here, no winter and no night.

3

Then on a stately oak I cast mine eye,
Whose ruffling top the clouds seemed to aspire;
How long since thou wast in thine infancy?
Thy strength, and stature, more thy years admire,
Hath hundred winters past since thou wast born?
Or thousand since thou breakest thy shell of horn?[5]
If so, see these as nought, eternity doth scorn.

4

Then higher on the glistering Sun I gazed,
Whose beams was shaded by the leavie[6] tree;
The more I looked, the more I grew amazed,
And softly said, "What glory's like to thee?"
Soul of this world, this universe's eye,
No wonder some made thee a deity;
Had I not better known, alas, the same had I.

[1]Personification of the sun in Greek myth.
[2]Lifted by divine force.
[3]Knew.
[4]Dressed.
[5]The acorn.
[6]Leafy.

5

Thou as a bridegroom from thy chamber rushes,
And as a strong man, joys to run a race;[7]
The morn doth usher thee with smiles and blushes;
The Earth reflects her glances in thy face.
Birds, insects, animals with vegative,[8]
Thy heat from death and dullness doth revive,
And in the darksome womb of fruitful nature dive.

6

Thy swift annual and diurnal[9] course,
Thy daily straight and yearly oblique path,
Thy pleasing fervor and thy scorching force,
All mortals here the feeling knowledge hath.
Thy presence makes it day, thy absence night,
Quaternal[10] seasons caused by thy might;
Hail creature, full of sweetness, beauty, and delight.

7

Art thou so full of glory that no eye
Hath strength thy shining rays once to behold?
And is thy splendid throne erect so high,
As to approach it, can no earthly mould?
How full of glory then must thy Creator be,
Who gave this bright light luster unto thee?
Admired, adored for ever, be that Majesty.

8

Silent alone, where none or saw, or heard,
In pathless paths I led my wand'ring feet,
My humble eyes to lofty skies I reared
To sing some song, my mazed[11] Muse thought meet.[12]
My great Creator I would magnify,
That nature had thus decked liberally;
But Ah, and Ah, again, my imbecility!

[7]The sun "is a bridegroom coming out of his chamber, and rejoiceth as a strong man to run a race." Psalm 19:4–5.

[8]Plants.

[9]Daily.

[10]Four.

[11]Bewildered.

[12]Suitable.

9

I heard the merry grasshopper then sing.
The black-clad cricket bear a second part;
They kept one tune and played on the same string,
Seeming to glory in their little art.
Shall creatures abject thus their voices raise
And in their kind resound their Maker's praise,
Whilst I, as mute, can warble forth no higher lays?

10

When present times look back to ages past,
And men in being fancy those are dead,
It makes things gone perpetually to last,
And calls back months and years that long since fled.
It makes a man more aged in conceit[13]
Than was Methuselah, or's grandsire great,[14]
While of their persons and their acts his mind doth treat.

11

Sometimes in Eden fair he seems to be,
Sees glorious Adam there made lord of all,
Fancies the apple, dangle on the tree,
That turned his sovereign to a naked thrall.[15]
Who like a miscreant's driven from that place,
To get his bread with pain and sweat of face,
A penalty imposed on his backsliding race.[16]

12

Here sits our grandame[17] in retired place,
And in her lap her bloody Cain new-born;
The weeping imp oft looks her in the face,
Bewails his unknown hap[18] and fate forlorn;
His mother sighs to think of Paradise,
And how she lost her bliss to be more wise,
Believing him that was, and is, father of lies.[19]

[13]Conception, thought.

[14]Methuselah was reported to have lived 969 years; his grandfather Jared, 962 years. Genesis 5:18–27.

[15]Slave.

[16]References to the expulsion of Adam and Eve from Eden, their sufferings, and the murder of Abel by Cain are drawn from Genesis 3 and 4.

[17]Eve.

[18]Fortune.

[19]Satan.

13

Here Cain and Abel come to sacrifice,
Fruits of the earth and fatlings[20] each do bring,
On Abel's gift the fire descends from skies,
But no such sign on false Cain's offering;
With sullen hateful looks he goes his ways,
Hath thousand thoughts to end his brother's days,
Upon whose blood his future good he hopes to raise.

14

There Abel keeps his sheep, no ill he thinks;
His brother comes, then acts his fratricide;
The virgin Earth of blood her first draught drinks,
But since that time she often hath been cloyed.
The wretch with ghastly face and dreadful mind
Thinks each he sees will serve him in his kind,
Though none on earth but kindred near then could he find.

15

Who fancies not his looks now at the bar,[21]
His face like death, his heart with horror fraught,
Nor malefactor ever felt like war,
When deep despair with wish of life hath fought,
Branded with guilt and crushed with treble woes,
A vagabond to Land of Nod[22] he goes.
A city builds, that walls might him secure from foes.

16

Who thinks not oft upon the fathers' ages,
Their long descent, how nephews' sons they saw,
The starry observations of those sages,
And how their precepts to their sons were law,
How Adam sighed to see his progeny,
Clothed all in his black sinful livery,
Who neither guilt nor yet the punishment could fly.

17

Our life compare we with their length of days
Who to the tenth of theirs doth now arrive?
And though thus short, we shorten many ways,
Living so little while we are alive;
In eating, drinking, sleeping, vain delight.
So unawares comes on perpetual night,
And puts all pleasures vain into eternal flight.

[20]Animals fattened for slaughter. [21]The place of trial and judgment.
[22]The land east of Eden to which Cain was banished to wander after slaying Abel. Genesis 4:16.

18

When I behold the heavens as in their prime,
And then the earth (though old) still clad in green,
The stones and trees, insensible of time,
Nor age nor wrinkle on their front are seen;
If winter come and greenness then do fade,
A spring returns, and they more youthful made;
But man grows old, lies down, remains where once he's laid.

19

By birth more noble than those creatures all,
Yet seems by nature and by custom cursed,
No sooner born, but grief and care makes fall
That state obliterate he had at first:
Nor youth, nor strength, nor wisdom spring again,
Nor habitations long their names retain,
But in oblivion to the final day remain.

20

Shall I then praise the heavens, the trees, the earth
Because their beauty and their strength last longer?
Shall I wish there, or never to had birth,
Because they're bigger, and their bodies stronger?
Nay, they shall darken, perish, fade and die,
And when unmade, so ever shall they lie,
But man was made for endless immortality.

21

Under the cooling shadow of a stately elm
Close sat I by a goodly river's side,
Where gliding streams the rocks did overwhelm,
A lonely place, with pleasures dignified.
I once that loved the shady woods so well,
Now thought the rivers did the trees excel,
And if the sun would ever shine, there would I dwell.

22

While on the stealing stream I fixt mine eye,
Which to the longed-for ocean held its course,
I marked, nor crooks, nor rubs[23] that there did lie
Could hinder ought,[24] but still augment its force.
"O happy flood," quoth I, "that holds thy race
Till thou arrive at thy beloved place,
Nor is it rocks or shoals that can obstruct thy pace;

[23]I.e., neither bends nor barriers.
[24]Anything.

23

Nor is't enough, that thou alone mayst slide,
But hundred brooks in thy clear waves do meet,
So hand in hand along with thee they glide
To Thetis'[25] house, where all embrace and greet.
Thou emblem true of what I count the best,
O could I lead my rivulets to rest,
So may we press to that vast mansion, ever blest."

24

Ye fish, which in this liquid region 'bide,
That for each season have your habitation,
Now salt, now fresh where you think best to glide
To unknown coasts to give a visitation,
In lakes and ponds you leave your numerous fry;
So nature taught, and yet you know not why,
You wat'ry folk that know not your felicity.

25

Look how the wantons frisk to taste the air,
Then to the colder bottom straight they dive;
Eftsoon[26] to Neptune's[27] glassy hall repair
To see what trade they great ones there do drive,
Who forage o'er the spacious sea-green field,
And take the trembling prey before it yield,
Whose armour is their scales, their spreading fins their shield.

26

While musing thus with contemplation fed,
And thousand fancies buzzing in my brain,
The sweet-tongued Philomel[28] perched o'er my head
And chanted forth a most melodious strain
Which rapt me so with wonder and delight,
I judged my hearing better than my sight,
And wished me wings with her a while to take my flight.

27

"O merry Bird," said I, "that fears no snares,
That neither toils nor hoards up in thy barn,
Feels no sad thoughts nor cruciating[29] cares
To gain more good or shun what might thee harm.
Thy clothes ne'er wear, thy meat is everywhere,
Thy bed a bough, thy drink the water clear,
Reminds[30] not what is past, nor what's to come dost fear."

[25]A nymph, in Greek mythology, who lived in the sea. [26]Soon afterward.
[27]Roman god of the sea. [28]The nightingale. [29]Excruciating, tormenting. [30]Recalls.

28

"The dawning morn with songs thou dost prevent,[31]
Sets hundred notes unto thy feathered crew,
So each one tunes his pretty instrument,
And warbling out the old, begin anew,
And thus they pass their youth in summer season,
Then follow thee into a better region,
Where winter's never felt by that sweet airy legion."

29

Man at the best a creature frail and vain,
In knowledge ignorant, in strength but weak,
Subject to sorrows, losses, sickness, pain,
Each storm his state, his mind, his body break,
From some of these he never finds cessation,
But day or night, within, without, vexation,
Troubles from foes, from friend, from dearest, near'st relation.

30

And yet this sinful creature, frail and vain,
This lump of wretchedness, of sin and sorrow,
This weatherbeaten vessel wracked with pain,
Joys not in hope of an eternal morrow;
Nor all his losses, crosses, and vexation,
In weight, in frequency and long duration
Can make him deeply groan in that divine translation.[32]

31

The mariner that on smooth waves doth glide
Sings merrily and steers his bark with ease,
As if he had command of wind and tide,
And now become great master of the seas:
But suddenly a storm spoils all the sport,
And makes him long for a more quiet port,
Which 'gainst all adverse winds may serve for fort.

32

So he that saileth in this world of pleasure,
Feeding on sweets, that never bit of th' sour,
That's full of friends, of honour, and of treasure,
Fond fool, he takes this earth ev'n for heav'n's bower.
But sad affliction comes and makes him see
Here's neither honour, wealth, nor safety;
Only above is found all with security.

[31]Come before, precede.
[32]I.e., transformation to immortality.

33

O Time the fatal wrack of mortal things,
That draws oblivion's curtains over kings;
Their sumptuous monuments, men know them not,
Their names without a record are forgot,
Their parts, their ports, their pomp's all laid in th' dust,
Nor wit nor gold, nor buildings scape time's rust;
But he whose name is graved in the white stone[33]
Shall last and shine when all of these are gone.

1664–1665? 1678

THE FLESH AND THE SPIRIT

In secret place where once I stood
Close by the banks of Lacrim flood,[1]
I heard two sisters reason on
Things that are past and things to come;
One Flesh was called, who had her eye
On worldly wealth and vanity;
The other Spirit, who did rear
Her thoughts unto a higher sphere:
Sister, quoth Flesh, what liv'st thou on,
Nothing but meditation?
Doth contemplation feed thee so
Regardlessly to let earth go?
Can speculation satisfy
Notion[2] without reality?
Dost dream of things beyond the moon,
And dost thou hope to dwell there soon?
Hast treasures there laid up in store
That all in th' world thou count'st but poor?
Art fancy sick, or turned a sot
To catch at shadows which are not?
Come, come, I'll show unto thy sense,
Industry hath its recompense.
What canst desire, but thou may'st see
True substance in variety?
Dost honour like? Acquire the same,
As some to their immortal fame,
And trophies to thy name erect
Which wearing time shall ne'er deject.

[33]"To him that overcometh will I give . . . a white stone, and in the stone a new name written. . . ." Revelation 2:17.

[1]The river of tears: from Latin *lacrima,* tear.

[2]The mind or intellect.

For riches dost thou long full sore?
Behold enough of precious store.
Earth hath more silver, pearls, and gold,
Than eyes can see or hands can hold.
Affect'st[3] thou pleasure? Take thy fill,
Earth hath enough of what you will.
Then let not go, what thou may'st find
For things unknown, only in mind.

Spirit: Be still, thou unregenerate part,
Disturb no more my settled heart,
For I have vowed (and so will do)
Thee as a foe still to pursue.
And combat with thee will and must,
Until I see thee laid in th' dust.
Sisters we are, yea, twins we be,
Yet deadly feud 'twixt thee and me;
For from one father are we not,
Thou by old Adam wast begot,
But my arise is from above,
Whence my dear Father I do love.
Thou speak'st me fair, but hat'st me sore,
Thy flatt'ring shows I'll trust no more.
How oft thy slave, hast thou me made,
When I believed what thou hast said,
And never had more cause of woe
Than when I did what thou bad'st do.
I'll stop mine ears at these thy charms,
And count them for my deadly harms.
Thy sinful pleasures I do hate,
Thy riches are to me no bait,
Thine honours do, nor will I love;
For my ambition lies above.
My greatest honour it shall be
When I am victor over thee,
And triumph shall with laurel head,
When thou my captive shalt be led,
How I do live, thou need'st not scoff,
For I have meat thou know'st not of;[4]
The hidden manna[5] I do eat,
The word of life it is my meat.

[3]Seek.
[4]A paraphrase of Jesus' words to His disciples. John 4:32.
[5]Divine spiritual food, a reference to the words of Jesus: "To him that overcometh will I give to eat of the hidden manna." Revelation 2:17.

My thoughts do yield me more content
Than can thy hours in pleasure spent.
Nor are they shadows which I catch,
Nor fancies vain at which I snatch,
But reach at things that are so high,
Beyond thy dull capacity;
Eternal substance I do see,
With which enriched I would be.
Mine eye doth pierce the heavens and see
What is invisible to thee.
My garments are not silk nor gold,
Nor such like trash which earth doth hold,
But royal robes I shall have on,
More glorious than the glist'ring sun;
My crown not diamonds, pearls, and gold,
But such as angels' heads enfold.
The city[6] where I hope to dwell,
There's none on earth can parallel;
The stately walls both high and strong,
Are made of precious jasper stone;
The gates of pearl, both rich and clear,
And angels are for porters there;
The streets thereof transparent gold,
Such as no eye did e'er behold;
A crystal river there doth run,
Which doth proceed from the Lamb's throne.
Of life, there are the waters sure,
Which shall remain forever pure,
Nor sun, nor moon, they have no need,
For glory doth from God proceed.
No candle there, nor yet torchlight,
For there shall be no darksome night.
From sickness and infirmity
For evermore they shall be free;
Nor withering age shall e'er come there,
But beauty shall be bright and clear;
This city pure is not for thee,
For things unclean there shall not be.
If I of heaven may have my fill,
Take thou the world and all that will.
1660–1670? 1678

[6]Lines 85 to 107 are based on descriptions of the holy city of God in Revelation 21 and 22.

THE AUTHOR TO HER BOOK[1]

Thou ill-formed offspring of my feeble brain,
Who after birth didst by my side remain,
Till snatched from thence by friends, less wise than true,
Who thee abroad, exposed to public view,
Made thee in rags, halting to th' press to trudge,
Where errors were not lessened (all may judge).
At thy return my blushing was not small,
My rambling brat (in print) should mother call,
I cast thee by as one unfit for light,
Thy visage was so irksome in my sight;
Yet being mine own, at length affection would
Thy blemishes amend, if so I could:
I washed thy face, but more defects I saw,
And rubbing off a spot still made a flaw.
I stretched thy joints to make thee even feet,[2]
Yet still thou run'st more hobbling than is meet;
In better dress to trim thee was my mind,
But nought save homespun cloth i' th' house I find.
In this array 'mongst vulgars[3] may'st thou roam.
In critics' hands beware thou dost not come,
And take thy way where yet thou art not known;
If for thy father asked, say thou hadst none;
And for thy mother, she alas is poor,
Which caused her thus to send thee out of door.
1650–1670? 1678

BEFORE THE BIRTH OF ONE OF HER CHILDREN

All things within this fading world hath end,
Adversity doth still our joys attend;
No ties so strong, no friends so dear and sweet,
But with death's parting blow is sure to meet.
The sentence past is most irrevocable,
A common thing, yet oh, inevitable.
How soon, my Dear, death may my steps attend,
How soon't may be thy lot to lose thy friend,
We both are ignorant, yet love bids me
These farewell lines to recommend to thee,
That when that knot's untied that made us one,
I may seem thine, who in effect am none.

[1] *The Tenth Muse,* published in London, 1650, without her knowledge. Her corrections, and this poem, appeared in the second edition, published in Boston in 1678.
[2] I.e., regular meter (metrical feet). [3] Ignorant, insensitive readers.

And if I see not half my days that's due,[1]
What nature would, God grant to yours and you;
The many faults that well you know I have
Let be interred in my oblivious grave;
If any worth or virtue were in me,
Let that live freshly in thy memory
And when thou feel'st no grief, as I no harms,
Yet love thy dead, who long lay in thine arms.
And when thy loss shall be repaid with gains
Look to my little babes, my dear remains.
And if thou love thyself, or loved'st me,
These O protect from step-dame's[2] injury.
And if chance to thine eyes shall bring this verse,
With some sad sighs honour my absent hearse;[3]
And kiss this paper for thy love's dear sake,
Who with salt tears this last farewell did take.
1640–1652? 1678

TO MY DEAR AND LOVING HUSBAND

If ever two were one, then surely we.
If ever man were loved by wife, then thee;
If ever wife was happy in a man,
Compare with me, ye women, if you can.
I prize thy love more than whole mines of gold
Or all the riches that the East doth hold.
My love is such that rivers cannot quench,
Nor ought[1] but love from thee, give recompense.
Thy love is such I can no way repay,
The heavens reward thee manifold, I pray.
Then while we live, in love let's so persevere[2]
That when we live no more, we may live ever.
1641–1643? 1678

A LETTER TO HER HUSBAND ABSENT UPON PUBLIC EMPLOYMENT

My head, my heart, mine eyes, my life, nay, more,
My joy, my magazine[1] of earthly store,
If two be one, as surely thou and I,

[1]Thirty-five years. "The days of our years are threescore years and ten." Psalm 90:10.
[2]Stepmother's. [3]Body, corpse.
[1]Anything. [2]Pronounced "per sévер" in the seventeenth century.
[1]Storehouse.

How stayest thou there, whilst I at Ipswich lie?[2]
So many steps, head from the heart to sever,
If but a neck, soon should we be together.
I, like the Earth this season, mourn in black,
My Sun is gone so far in's zodiac,
Whom whilst I 'joyed, nor storms, nor frost I felt,
His warmth such frigid cold did cause to melt.
My chilled limbs now numbed lie forlorn;
Return, return, sweet Sol, from Capricorn;[3]
In this dead time, alas, what can I more
Than view those fruits which through thy heat I bore?
Which sweet contentment yield me for a space,
True living pictures of their father's face.
O strange effect! now thou art southward gone,
I weary grow the tedious day so long;
But when thou northward to me shalt return,
I wish my Sun may never set, but burn
Within the Cancer[4] of my glowing breast,
The welcome house of him my dearest guest.
Where ever, ever stay, and go not thence,
Till nature's sad decree shall call thee hence;
Flesh of thy flesh, bone of thy bone,[5]
I here, thou there, yet both but one.
1641–1643? 1678

IN REFERENCE TO HER CHILDREN, 23 JUNE, 1659

I had eight birds hatched in one nest,
Four cocks there were, and hens the rest.
I nursed them up with pain and care,
Nor cost, nor labour did I spare,
Till at the last they felt their wing,
Mounted the trees, and learned to sing;
Chief of the brood then took his flight[1]
To regions far and left me quite.
My mournful chirps I after send,
Till he return, or I do end:

[2]The Bradstreets lived in Ipswich, Massachusetts from c. 1635 to c. 1645, when they moved to Andover.

[3]Tenth sign of the zodiac, here signifying winter.

[4]Fourth sign of the zodiac, signifying summer.

[5]When Eve was created from Adam's rib, he said, "This is now bone of my bones, and flesh of my flesh: she shall be called Woman because she was taken out of Man." Genesis 2:23.

[1]Samuel spent four years in England, 1657–1661.

Leave not thy nest, thy dam and sire,
Fly back and sing amidst this choir.
My second bird[2] did take her flight,
And with her mate flew out of sight;
Southward they both their course did bend,
And seasons twain they there did spend,
Till after blown by southern gales,
They norward steered with filled sails.
A prettier bird was no where seen,
Along the beach among the treen.[3]
I have a third[4] of colour white,
On whom I placed no small delight;
Coupled with mate loving and true,
Hath also bid her dam adieu;
And where Aurora[5] first appears,
She now hath perched to spend her years.
One to the academy[6] flew
To chat among that learned crew;
Ambition moves still in his breast
That he might chant above the rest,
Striving for more than to do well,
That nightingales he might excel.
My fifth, whose down is yet scarce gone,[7]
Is 'mongst the shrubs and bushes flown,
And as his wings increase in strength,
On higher boughs he'll perch at length.
My other three still with me nest,[8]
Until they're grown, then as the rest,
Or here or there they'll take their flight,
As is ordained, so shall they light.
If birds could weep, then would my tears
Let others know what are my fears
Lest this my brood some harm should catch,
And be surprised for want of watch,
Whilst pecking corn and void of care,
They fall un'wares in fowler's snare,
Or whilst on trees they sit and sing,
Some untoward boy at them do fling,
Or whilst allured with bell and glass,
The net be spread, and caught, alas.
Or lest by lime-twigs they be foiled,[9]

[2]Dorothy married, lived briefly in Connecticut, and then moved to New Hampshire.
[3]Trees. [4]Sarah married and moved to Ipswich, fifteen miles to the east of Andover.
[5]Roman goddess of the dawn. [6]Simon attended Harvard College.
[7]Probably a heedless reference to her seventh child, Dudley. Her fifth and sixth were daughters.
[8]Hannah, Mercy, and John still lived at home at the time of the writing of the poem.
[9]Sticky bird-lime was smeared on tree limbs to catch birds.

Or by some greedy hawks be spoiled.
O would my young, ye saw my breast,
And knew what thoughts there sadly rest,
Great was my pain when I you bred,
Great was my care when you I fed,
Long did I keep you soft and warm,
And with my wings kept off all harm,
My cares are more and fears than ever,
My throbs such now as 'fore were never.
Alas, my birds, you wisdom want,
Of perils you are ignorant;
Oft times in grass, on trees, in flight,
Sore accidents on you may light.
O to your safety have an eye,
So happy may you live and die.
Meanwhile my days in tunes I'll spend,
Till my weak lays with me shall end.
In shady woods I'll sit and sing,
And things that past to mind I'll bring.
Once young and pleasant, as are you,
But former toys (no joys) adieu.
My age I will not once lament,
But sing, my time so near is spent.
And from the top bough take my flight
Into a country beyond sight,
Where old ones instantly grow young,
And there with seraphims[10] set song;
No seasons cold, nor storms they see;
But spring lasts to eternity.
When each of you shall in your nest
Among your young ones take your rest,
In chirping language, oft them tell,
You had a dam that loved you well,
That did what could be done for young,
And nursed you up till you were strong,
And 'fore she once would let you fly,
She showed you joy and misery;
Taught what was good, and what was ill,
What would save life, and what would kill.
Thus gone, amongst you I may live,
And dead, yet speak, and counsel give:
Farewell, my birds, farewell adieu,
I happy am, if well with you.

1659 1678

[10]Angels.

IN MEMORY OF MY DEAR GRANDCHILD ELIZABETH BRADSTREET, WHO DECEASED AUGUST, 1665, BEING A YEAR AND HALF OLD

Farewell dear babe, my heart's too much content,
Farewell sweet babe, the pleasure of mine eye,
Farewell fair flower that for a space was lent,
Then ta'en away unto eternity.
Blest babe, why should I once bewail thy fate,
Or sigh thy days so soon were terminate,
Sith[1] thou art settled in an everlasting state.

2

By nature trees do rot when they are grown,
And plums and apples thoroughly ripe do fall,
And corn and grass are in their season mown,
And time brings down what is both strong and tall.
But plants new set to be eradicate,
And buds new blown to have so short a date,
Is by His hand alone that guides nature and fate.

1665 1678

ON MY DEAR GRANDCHILD SIMON BRADSTREET, WHO DIED ON 16 NOVEMBER, 1669, BEING BUT A MONTH, AND ONE DAY OLD

No sooner came, but gone, and fall'n asleep,
Acquaintance short, yet parting caused us weep;
Three flowers, two scarcely blown, the last i' th' bud,
Cropt by th' Almighty's hand; yet is He good.
With dreadful awe before Him let's be mute,
Such was His will, but why, let's not dispute,
With humble hearts and mouths put in the dust,
Let's say He's merciful as well as just.
He will return and make up all our losses,
And smile again after our bitter crosses
Go pretty babe, go rest with sisters twain;
Among the blest in endless joys remain.

1678

[1]Since.

[ON DELIVERANCE] FROM ANOTHER SORE FIT

In my distress I sought the Lord
When naught on earth could comfort give,
And when my soul these things abhorred,
Then, Lord, Thou said'st unto me, "Live."

Thou knowest the sorrows that I felt;
My plaints and groans were heard of Thee,
And how in sweat I seemed to melt
Thou help'st and Thou regardest me.

My wasted flesh Thou didst restore,
My feeble loins didst gird with strength,[1]
Yea, when I was most low and poor,
I said I shall praise Thee at length.

What shall I render to my God
For all His bounty showed to me?
Even for His mercies in His rod,
Where pity most of all I see.

My heart I wholly give to Thee;
O make it fruitful, faithful Lord.
My life shall dedicated be
To praise in thought, in deed, in word.

Thou know'st no life I did require
Longer than still Thy name to praise,
Nor ought on earth worthy desire,
In drawing out these wretched days.

Thy name and praise to celebrate,
O Lord, for aye is my request.
O grant I do it in this state,
And then with Thee, which is the best.

1867

UPON THE BURNING OF OUR HOUSE, JULY 10TH, 1666[1]

In silent night when rest I took
For sorrow near I did not look
I wakened was with thund'ring noise

[1]"She girdeth her loins with strength, and she strengtheneth her arms." Proverbs 31:17.
[1]The stanza breaks of the version printed in 1867 are preserved here.

And piteous shrieks of dreadful voice.
That fearful sound of "Fire!" and "Fire!"
Let no man know is my desire.

I, starting up, the light did spy,
And to my God my heart did cry
To strengthen me in my distress
And not to leave me succorless.
Then, coming out, beheld a space
The flame consume my dwelling place.

And when I could no longer look,
I blest His name that gave and took,[2]
That laid my goods now in the dust.
Yea, so it was, and so 'twas just.
It was His own, it was not mine,
Far be it that I should repine;

He might of all justly bereft
But yet sufficient for us left.
When by the ruins oft I past
My sorrowing eyes aside did cast,
And here and there the places spy
Where oft I sat and long did lie:

Here stood that trunk, and there that chest,
There lay that store I counted best.
My pleasant things in ashes lie,
And them behold no more shall I.
Under thy roof no guest shall sit,
Nor at thy table eat a bit.

No pleasant tale shall e'er be told,
Nor things recounted done of old.
No candle e'er shall shine in thee,
Nor bridegroom's voice e'er heard shall be.[3]
In silence ever shall thou lie,
Adieu, Adieu, all's vanity.[4]

Then straight I 'gin my heart to chide,
And did thy wealth on earth abide?
Didst fix thy hope on mold'ring dust?
The arm of flesh didst make thy trust?
Raise up thy thoughts above the sky
That dunghill mists away may fly.

[2]"The Lord gave, and the Lord hath taken away; blessed be the name of the Lord." Job 1:21.

[3]"And the light of a candle shall shine no more at all in thee; and the voice of the bridegroom and of the bride shall be heard no more at all in thee." Revelations 18:23.

[4]"Vanity of vanities, saith the Preacher, vanity of vanities; all is vanity." Ecclesiastes 1:2.

Thou hast an house on high erect,
Framed by that mighty Architect,
With glory richly furnished,
Stands permanent though this be fled.
It's purchased and paid for too
By Him who hath enough to do.

A price so vast as is unknown
Yet by His gift is made thine own;
There's wealth enough, I need no more,
Farewell, my pelf,[5] farewell my store.
The world no longer let me love,
My hope and treasure lies above.

1666 1867

AS WEARY PILGRIM

As weary pilgrim, now at rest,
 Hugs with delight his silent nest,
His wasted limbs now lie full soft
 That mirey steps have trodden oft,
Blesses himself to think upon
 His dangers past, and travails done.
The burning sun no more shall heat,
 Nor stormy rains on him shall beat.
The briars and thorns no more shall scratch,
 Nor hungry wolves at him shall catch.
He erring paths no more shall tread,
 Nor wild fruits eat instead of bread.
For waters cold he doth not long
 For thirst no more shall parch his tongue.
No rugged stones his feet shall gall,
 Nor stumps nor rocks cause him to fall.
All cares and fears he bids farewell
 And means in safety now to dwell.
A pilgrim I, on earth perplexed
 With Sins, with cares and sorrows vext,
By age and pains brought to decay,
 And my clay house mold'ring away.
Oh, how I long to be at rest
 And soar on high among the blest.
This body shall in silence sleep,
 Mine eyes no more shall ever weep,
No fainting fits shall me assail,
 Nor grinding pains my body frail,

[5]Riches.

With cares and fears ne'er cumb'red be
　　Nor losses know, nor sorrows see.
What though my flesh shall there consume,
　　It is the bed Christ did perfume,
And when a few years shall be gone,
　　This mortal shall be clothed upon.
A corrupt carcass down it lies,
　　A glorious body it shall rise.
In weakness and dishonour sown,
　　In power 'tis raised by Christ alone.
Then soul and body shall unite
　　And of their Maker have the sight.
Such lasting joys shall there behold
　　As ear ne'er heard nor tongue e'er told.
Lord make me ready for that day,
　　Then come, dear Bridegroom, come away.

1669　　　1867

from *MEDITATIONS DIVINE AND MORAL*

1

There is no object that we see, no action that we do, no good that we enjoy, no evil that we feel or fear, but we may make some spiritual advantage of all; and he that makes such improvement is wise as well as pious.

2

Many can speak well, but few can do well. We are better scholars in the theory than the practice part, but he is a true Christian that is a proficient in both.

5

It is reported of the peacock that, priding himself in his gay feathers, he ruffles them up, but spying his black feet, he soon lets fall his plumes; so he that glories in his gifts and adornings should look upon his corruptions, and that will damp his high thoughts.

8

Downy beds make drowsy persons, but hard lodging keeps the eyes open; a prosperous state makes a secure Christian, but adversity makes him consider.

9

Sweet words are like honey: a little may refresh, but too much gluts the stomach.

10

Diverse children have their different natures: some are like flesh which nothing but salt will keep from putrefaction, some again like tender fruits that are best preserved with sugar. Those parents are wise that can fit their nurture according to their nature.

16

That house which is not often swept makes the cleanly inhabitant soon loath it, and that heart which is not continually purifying itself is no fit temple for the spirit of God to dwell in.

19

Corn, till it have past through the mill and been ground to powder, is not fit for bread. God so deals with his servants: he grinds them with grief and pain till they turn to dust, and then are they fit manchet[1] for his mansion.

23

The skillful fisher hath his several baits for several fish, but there is a hook under all; Satan, that great Angler, hath his sundry baits for sundry tempers of men, which they all catch greedily at, but few perceive the hook till it be too late.

31

Iron, till it be thoroughly heat, is uncapable to be wrought; so God sees good to cast some men into the furnace of affliction and then beats them on His anvil into what frame he pleases.

34

Dim eyes are the concomitants of old age, and shortsightedness in those that are eyes of a republic fortells a declining state.

36

Sore labourers have hard hands and old sinners have brawny consciences.

38

Some children are hardly weaned;[2] although the teat be rubbed with wormwood or mustard, they will either wipe it off, or else suck down sweet and bitter together. So is it with some Christians: let God embitter all the sweets of this life, that so they might feed upon more substantial food, yet they are so childishly sottish that they are still hugging and sucking these empty breasts that God is forced to hedge up their way with thorns or lay affliction on their loins that so they might shake hands with the world, before it bid them farewell.

40

The spring is a lively emblem of the resurrection: after a long winter we see the leafless trees and dry stocks (at the approach of the sun) to resume their former vigor and beauty in a more ample manner than what they lost in the

[1]Bread. [2]I.e., hard to wean.

autumn; so shall it be at that great day after a long vacation, when the Sun of righteousness shall appear; those dry bones shall arise in far more glory than that which they lost at their creation, and in this transcend the spring that their leaf shall never fail nor their sap decline.

45

We often see stones hang with drops not from any innate moisture, but from a thick air about them; so may we sometime see marble-hearted sinners seem full of contrition, but it is not from any dew of grace within but from some black clouds that impend them, which produce these sweating effects.

60

He that would be content with a mean condition must not cast his eye upon one that is in a far better estate than himself, but let him look upon him that is lower than he is, and if he see that such a one bears poverty comfortably, it will help to quiet him, but if that will not do, let him look on his own unworthiness and that will make him say with Jacob: I am less than the least of Thy mercies.[3]

67

All the works and doings of God are wonderful, but none more awful than His great work of election and reprobation; when we consider how many good parents have had bad children, and again how many bad parents have had pious children, it should make us adore the sovereignty of God, who will not be tied to time nor place, nor yet to persons, but takes and chooses, when and where and whom He pleases; it should also teach the children of godly parents to walk with fear and trembling, lest they through unbelief fall short of a promise; it may also be a support to such as have or had wicked parents, that if they abide not in unbelief, God is able to gaff[4] them in. The upshot of all should make us with the apostle to admire the justice and mercy of God and say how unsearchable are His ways and His footsteps past finding out.

77

God hath by his providence so ordered that no one country hath all commodities within itself, but what it wants another shall supply that so there may be a mutual commerce through the world. As it is with countries so it is with men; there was never yet any one man that had all excellences, let his parts natural and acquired, spiritual and moral, be never so large, yet he stands in need of something which another man hath (perhaps meaner than himself) which shows us perfection is not below, as also that God will have us beholden one to another.

1664 1867

[3]"I am not worthy of the least of all the mercies, and of all the truth, which thou has shewed unto they servant." Genesis 32:10.

[4]Hook.

Edward Taylor c. 1642–1729

Little in the outward life of Edward Taylor suggests his achievement as a poet. He was an orthodox, even conservative, Puritan minister. He believed in the sinfulness and damnation of man. He believed in the salvation of an elect few who would be exalted in heaven. He believed in the redeeming grace of an omnipotent God. He wanted a church purified of the embellishments of the Roman Catholic and Anglican liturgies. And, with other educated men of his time, he accepted the existence of evil spirits, devils, and witches. A godly and obscure frontier parson in western Massachusetts, he devoted his life to a vain struggle against the weakening of church discipline and the decline of the Puritan Way.

Taylor was born in England and grew up during the Puritan Commonwealth and the Protectorate of Oliver Cromwell. It is possible that he attended Cambridge University for a short time and served as a schoolmaster. In his twenties, he left England and emigrated to Massachusetts, where he entered Harvard College to prepare himself for the ministry. After graduating in 1671, he accepted a call to serve as pastor of the church at Westfield, a trading post and frontier farming village 100 miles west of Boston. There, on the edge of a "vast and roaring" wilderness, he spent the remaining fifty-eight years of his life, serving both as minister and as town physician.

His poetry was largely unknown to his contemporaries. Only a fragment of a single poem was printed in his lifetime. Perhaps because he feared his poems would be considered too sensual for a clergyman, Taylor never published the remainder of his writings. As a result, his poetry was forgotten until his manuscripts were rediscovered in the Yale University Library and finally published in the 1930s.

The appearance of his poems, two centuries after his death, revealed a mind radically different from that commonly ascribed to Puritan preachers. Their religious views were thought to be stern and sober. Their few artistic efforts seemed to smother in didactic purpose. But Taylor had written in the tradition of such metaphysical poets as Donne and Herbert, expressing divine and elevated ideas in unrelated, homely terms that were sometimes erotic, even scatological. He had created elaborate conceits and metaphors that used spinning wheels, bowling balls, excrement, and insects to give ingenious and often grotesque expression to his intense emotions.

Taylor thought his poems were "ragged rhymes," the product of a "tattered fancy." Some critics have since judged them a botch of needless archaisms, jigging meter, and clashing images. Others have found them a frivolous union of lofty themes and earthy diction that reveal an extravagant sense of sin and display a self-indulgent emotionalism. Taylor's best work was not intended as public art but as a record of his private efforts to confirm a mystical union with God, and at their best his poems have a tension, richness, and daring beyond any other colonial American poetry. With their mystical, even occult, intensity, with their detonating metaphors, and with their expression of unity in divine diversity, they anticipate the poetic art of Emily Dickinson and Walt Whitman, and they stand with the finest literature of early America.

FURTHER READING: *The Poetical Works of Edward Taylor,* ed. T. Johnson, 1939; *The Unpublished Writings of Edward Taylor,* ed. T. Davis and V. Davis, 3 vols., 1981; N. Grabo, *Edward Taylor,* 1962, 1988; *The Diary of Edward Taylor,* ed. F. Murphy, 1964; D. Stanford, *Edward Taylor,* 1965; W. Scheick, *The Will and the Word, Conversion in the Poetry of Edward Taylor,* 1974; K. Rowe, *Saint and Singer, Edward Taylor's Typology and the Poetics of Meditation,* 1986; J. Gatta, *Gracious Laughter, The Meditative Wit of Edward Taylor,* 1989; T. Davis, *A Reading of Edward Taylor,* 1992; J. Hammond, *Edward Taylor, Fifty Years of Scholarship and Criticism,* 1993; D. Miller, *The Word Made Flesh Made Word,* 1995; *The Tayloring Shop,* ed. M. Schuldiner, 1997; R. Clark, *The Marriage of Heaven and Earth,* 2000.

TEXT: *The Poems of Edward Taylor,* ed. D. Stanford, 1960. Spelling, punctuation, and usage have been changed to conform more nearly to modern practice.

PROLOGUE[1]

Lord, can a crumb of dust the earth outweigh,
 Outmatch all mountains, nay the crystal sky?
Embosom in't designs that shall display
 And trace into the boundless Deity?
 Yea hand[2] a pen whose moisture doth guild o'er
 Eternal glory with a glorious glore.[3]

If it its pen had of an angel's quill,
 And sharpened on a precious stone ground tight,[4]
And dipped in liquid gold, and moved by skill
 In crystal leaves[5] should golden letters write,
 It would but blot and blur, yea, jag and jar,
 Unless Thou mak'st the pen, and scrivener.

I am this crumb of dust which is designed
 To make my pen unto Thy praise alone,
And my dull fancy[6] I would gladly grind
 Unto an edge on Zion's precious stone[7]
 And write in liquid gold upon[8] Thy name
 My letters till Thy glory forth doth flame.

Let not th' attempts break down my dust I pray,
 Nor laugh Thou them to scorn but pardon give.
Inspire this crumb of dust till it display
 Thy glory through't, and then Thy dust shall live.
 Its failings then Thou'lt overlook I trust,
 They being slips slipped from Thy crumb of dust.

Thy crumb of dust breathes two words from its breast,
 That Thou wilt guide its pen to write aright
To prove Thou art, and that Thou art the best,
 And show Thy properties[9] to shine most bright.
 And then Thy works will shine as flowers on stems
 Or as in jewellary[10] shops, do gems.

c. 1682 1937

[1]The "Prologue" was intended as an introduction to Taylor's *Preparatory Meditations,* more than two hundred poems divided into two series which he wrote at intervals over forty-three years. The poems were usually based on biblical passages that Taylor used in sermons preached to celebrate the sacrament of the Lord's Supper.

[2]Manipulate. [3]Scottish dialect for "glory." [4]Quickly, vigorously.

[5]Book pages. [6]Imagination.

[7]"Thus saith the Lord God, Behold, I lay in Zion for a foundation a stone, a tried stone, a precious corner stone of sure foundation." Isaiah 28:16. Christians have traditionally identified Christ as the divine "corner stone of sure foundation."

[8]About. [9]Qualities, characteristics.

[10]Taylor's spelling of "jewelry" to preserve the four-syllable pronunciation required by the meter.

from *PREPARATORY MEDITATIONS*

THE REFLEXION

Lord, art Thou at the table head above
  Meat, med'cine, sweetness, sparkling beauties, to
Enamor souls with flaming flakes of love,
  And not my trencher,[1] nor my cup o'erflow?
  Be n't I a bidden guest? Oh! sweat mine eye;
  O'erflow with tears; Oh! draw thy fountains dry.

Shall I not smell Thy sweet, oh! Sharon's rose?[2]
  Shall not mine eye salute Thy beauty? Why?
Shall Thy sweet leaves their beauteous sweets upclose?
  As half ashamed my sight should on them lie?
  Woe's me! For this my sighs shall be in grain[3]
  Offered on sorrow's altar for the same.

Had not my soul's, Thy conduit, pipes stopped been
  With mud, what ravishment would'st Thou convey?
Let grace's golden spade dig till the spring
  Of tears arise, and clear this filth away.
  Lord, let Thy spirit raise my sighings till
  These pipes my soul do with Thy sweetness fill.

Earth once was paradise of heaven below
  Till inkfaced sin had it with poison stocked,
And chased this paradise away into
  Heav'ns upmost loft, and it in glory locked.
  But Thou, sweet Lord, hast with Thy golden key
  Unlocked the door, and made a golden day.

Once at Thy feast,[4] I saw Thee pearl-like stand
  'Tween heaven and earth, where heaven's bright glory all
In streams fell on Thee, as a floodgate and,
  Like sunbeams through Thee on the world to fall.
  Oh! sugar sweet then! My dear sweet Lord, I see
  Saints' heavens-lost happiness restored by Thee.

[1]A flat, wooden plate.

[2]A reference to Canticles (Song of Solomon) 2:1, "I am the rose of Sharon." The rose was often interpreted as symbolic of Christ and of God's grace. Sharon, part of the coastal plain of Palestine, was renowned for its fertility.

[3]Thoroughly, completely.

[4]The sacrament of The Lord's Supper, or the Eucharist, wherein believers achieve communion with Christ.

Shall heaven and earth's bright glory all up lie
Like sunbeams bundled in the sun, in Thee?
Dost Thou sit rose at table head, where I
Do sit, and carv'st no morsel sweet for me?
So much before, so little now! Sprindge,[5] Lord,
Thy rosy leaves, and me their glee afford.

Shall not Thy rose my garden fresh perfume?
Shall not Thy beauty my dull heart assail?
Shall not Thy golden gleams run through this gloom?
Shall my black velvet mask Thy fair face veil?
Pass o'er my faults; shine forth, bright sun; arise,
Enthrone Thy rosy-self within mine eyes.

1683 1937

MEDITATION 6 (FIRST SERIES)

Am I Thy gold? Or purse, Lord, for Thy wealth;
Whether in mine or mint refined for Thee?
I'm counted so, but count me o'er Thyself,
Lest gold-washed[1] face and brass in heart I be.
I fear my touchstone[2] touches when I try[3]
Me and my counted gold too overly.

Am I new minted by Thy stamp[4] indeed?
Mine eyes are dim; I cannot clearly see.
Be Thou my spectacles that I may read
Thine image and inscription stamped on me.
If Thy bright image do upon me stand
I am a golden angel[5] in Thy hand.

Lord, make my soul Thy plate. Thine image bright
Within the circle of the same enfoil.[6]
And on its brims in golden letters write
Thy superscription[7] in a holy style.
Then I shall be Thy money, Thou my hoard.
Let me Thy angel be, be Thou my Lord.

1683? 1939

[5]Spread.

[1]Covered with a thin wash (layer) of gold.

[2]A dark stone against which gold or silver alloys are scraped. From the color of the resulting streak, experts judge the proportion of precious metal and hence the value of the alloy.

[3]Test, examine. [4]The die used to impress designs on coins.

[5]An English gold coin circulated in the seventeenth century. On it was stamped the figure of the archangel Michael.

[6]Decorate with gold or silver foil. [7]Name, signature.

MEDITATION 8 (FIRST SERIES)

John 6:51: I am the living bread.[1]

I kenning[2] through astronomy divine
The world's bright battlement, wherein I spy
A golden path my pencil cannot line
From that bright throne unto my threshold lie.
And while my puzzled thoughts about it pour,
I find the bread of life in't at my door.

When that this bird of paradise[3] put in
This wicker cage (my corpse) to tweedle[4] praise
Had pecked the fruit forbad, and so did fling
Away its food, and lost its golden days,
It fell into celestial famine sore,
And never could attain a morsel more.

Alas! Alas! Poor bird, what wilt thou do?
The creatures' field[5] no food for souls e'er gave;
And if thou knock at angels' doors, they show
An empty barrel; they no soul bread have.
Alas! Poor bird, the world's white loaf is done,
And cannot yield thee here the smallest crumb.

In this sad state, God's tender bowels[6] run
Out streams of grace; and He to end all strife
The purest wheat in heaven, His dear-dear Son,
Grinds and kneads up into this bread of life,
Which bread of life from heaven down came and stands
Dished on thy table up by angels' hands.

Did God mold up this bread in heaven, and bake,
Which from His table came, and to thine goeth?
Doth He bespeak thee thus, "This soul bread take;
Come, eat thy fill of this, thy God's white loaf!
It's food too fine for angels, yet come, take
And eat thy fill. It's heaven's sugar cake."

[1]The complete verse reads: "I am the living bread which came down from heaven: if any man eat of this bread, he shall live forever: and the bread that I will give is my flesh, which I will give for the life of the world."
[2]Discovering, knowing.
[3]The human soul.
[4]Sing, warble.
[5]I.e., the world of man.
[6]From ancient times considered the center and source of compassion.

What grace is this knead in this loaf? This thing
  Souls are but petty things it to admire.
Ye angels, help; this fill would to the brim
  Heav'ns whelmed-down[7] crystal meal bowl, yea and higher.
  This bread of life dropped in my mouth doth cry:
  "Eat, eat me, soul, and thou shalt never die."

1684 1937

MEDITATION 38 (FIRST SERIES)

1 John 2:1: An advocate with the father.[1]

Oh! What a thing is man? Lord, who am I?
  That thou shouldst give him law[2] (Oh! golden line)
To regulate his thoughts, words, life thereby.
  And judge him wilt thereby too in Thy time.
  A court of justice Thou in heaven holdst
  To try his case while he's here housed on mold.[3]

How do Thy angels lay before Thine eye
  My deeds both white and black I daily do?
How doth Thy court Thou panelest[4] there them try?
  But flesh complains. What right for this? Let's know.
  For right or wrong I can't appear unto't.
  And shall a sentence pass on such a suit?

Soft; blemish not this golden bench or place.
  Here is no bribe nor colorings[5] to hide,
Nor pettifogger[6] to befog the case,
  But justice hath her glory here well tried.
  Her spotless law all spotted cases tends,
  Without respect or disrespect them ends.

God's judge Himself; and Christ attorney is;
  The Holy Ghost registerer[7] is found.
Angels the sergeants[8] are; all creatures kiss
  The book, and do as evidences[9] abound.
  All cases pass according to pure law,
  And in the sentence is no fret[10] or flaw.

[7]Inverted.

[1]The verse reads: "If any man sin, we have an advocate with the Father, Jesus Christ the righteous." [2]The laws set forth in the Bible. [3]The earth. [4]Impanel, as a jury. [5]Disguises, misrepresentations. [6]Disreputable lawyer. [7]Registrar, record keeper. [8]Officers who keep order in the court. [9]Witnesses. [10]Cause for distress.

What sayest, my soul? Here all thy deeds are tried.
Is Christ thy advocate to plead thy cause?
Art thou his client? Such shall never slide.[11]
He never lost his case; he pleads such laws
As carry do the same, nor doth refuse
The vilest sinner's case that doth him choose.

This is his honor, nor dishonor; nay
No *habeas-corpus*[12] 'gainst his clients came;
For all their fines his purse doth make down pay.
He non-suits[13] Satan's suit or casts[14] the same.
He'll plead thy case and not accept a fee.
He'll plead *sub forma pauperis*[15] for thee.

My case is bad. Lord, be my advocate.
My sin is red; I'm under God's arrest.
Thou hast the hint[16] of pleading; plead my state.
Although it's bad thy plea will make it best.
If thou wilt plead my case before the king,
I'll wagon loads of love and glory bring.
1690 1937

MEDITATION 39 (FIRST SERIES)

1 John 2:1: If any man sin, we have an advocate.

My sin! My sin, my God, these cursed dregs,
Green, yellow, blue streaked poison, hellish, rank,
Bubs[1] hatched in nature's nest on serpents' eggs,
Yelp, chirp and cry; they set my soul acramp.
I frown, chide, strike and fight them, mourn and cry
To conquer them, but cannot them destroy.

I cannot kill nor coop them up; my curb
'S less than a snaffle[2] in their mouth; my reins
They as a twine thread, snap; by hell they're spurred
And load my soul with swagging[3] loads of pains.
Black imps, young devils, snap, bite, drag to bring
And pitch me headlong hell's dread whirlpool in.

[11]Slide into hell.
[12]Latin: You shall have the body. The first words of a legal document used to summon a person before a court of judgment.
[13]Gains dismissal of a law suit, usually by showing that the opposition lacks sufficient evidence.
[14]Defeats.
[15]Latin: In the form of a poor person. A legal plea requesting exemption from court costs because of poverty.
[16]Opportunity.
[1]Pustules. [2]A bridle-bit. [3]Heavily sagging.

Lord, hold Thy hand, for handle me Thou may'st
In wrath; but, oh, a twinkling ray of hope
Methinks I spy Thou graciously display'st.
There is an advocate; a door is ope.
Sin's poison swell my heart would till it burst,
Did not a hope hence creep in't thus, and nurse't.

Joy, joy, God's Son's the sinner's advocate
Doth plead the sinner guiltless, and a saint.
But yet attorneys' pleas spring from the state
The case is in; if bad it's bad in plaint.[4]
My papers do contain no pleas that do
Secure me from, but knock me down to, woe.

I have no plea mine advocate to give;
What now? He'll anvil arguments great store
Out of His flesh and blood to make thee live.
Oh! dear bought arguments; good pleas therefore.
Nails made of heavenly steel, more choice than gold,
Drove home, well clinched,[5] eternally will hold.

Oh! dear bought plea, dear Lord, what buy't so dear?
What with Thy blood purchase Thy plea for me?
Take argument out of Thy grave t'appear
And plead my case with, me from guilt to free.
These maul both sins and devils, and amaze
Both saints and angels; Wreathe their mouths with praise.

What shall I do, my Lord? What do, that I
May have Thee plead my case? I fee[6] thee will
With faith, repentance, and obediently
Thy service 'gainst satanic sins fulfill.
I'll fight Thy fields while live I do, although
I should be hacked in pieces by Thy foe.

Make me Thy friend, Lord, be my surety. I
will be thy client; be my advocate;
My sins make Thine; Thy pleas make mine hereby.
Thou wilt me save; I will Thee celebrate.
Thou'lt kill my sins that cut my heart within;
And my rough feet[7] shall Thy smooth praises sing.

1690 1954

[4]A written complaint in law.
[5]Fastened securely by bending over the exposed points of driven nails.
[6]Pay.
[7]Metrical units of verse.

MEDITATION 150 (SECOND SERIES)

Canticles 7:3: Thy two breasts are like two young roes[1] that are twins.[2]

My blessed Lord, how doth Thy beauteous spouse
  In stately stature rise in comeliness?
With her two breasts like two little roes that browse
  Among the lilies in their shining dress
  Like stately milk pails ever full and flow
  With spiritual milk to make her babes to grow.

Celestial nectar wealthier far than wine
  Wrought in the spirit's brew house and up tund[3]
Within these vessels which are trussed up fine,
  Liken'd to two pretty neat twin roes that run'd
  Most pleasantly by their dam's sides like cades[4]
  And suckle with their milk Christ's spiritual babes.

Lord put these nipples then my mouth into
  And suckle me therewith I humbly pray;
Then with this milk Thy spiritual babe I'dst grow,
  And these two milk pails shall themselves display
  Like to these pretty twins in pairs round neat
  And shall sing forth Thy praise over this meat.[5]

1719 1960

from *GOD'S DETERMINATIONS*

THE PREFACE[1]

  Infinity, when all things it beheld
In nothing, and of nothing all did build,
Upon what base was fixed the lathe, wherein
He turned this globe, and riggaled[2] it so trim?

[1]Small deer.

[2]The Canticles (Song of Solomon) consist of a series of love and marriage poems celebrating the union of bride and groom. The poems have traditionally been interpreted by Christians as a representation of the union of Christ with the faithful. Here Taylor portrays the bride, God's "spouse," as the source of spiritual nourishment.

[3]Put up in a barrel (tun). [4]Pets.

[5]The food (host) symbolic of Christ's flesh in the sacrament of the Lord's Supper.

[1]Around 1685, Taylor began a series of thirty-five poems entitled *God's Determinations Touching His Elect: and the Elects' Combat in their Conversion and Coming Up to Christ.* . . . It was a collection of lyrics and versified sermons celebrating the transcendent power of God and describing the soul's struggle to achieve assurance of grace.

[2]Grooved.

Who blew the bellows of his furnace vast?
Or held the mold wherein the world was cast?
Who laid its corner stone? Or whose command?[3]
Where stand the pillars upon which it stands?
Who laced and filleted[4] the earth so fine,
With rivers like green ribbons smaragdine?[5]
Who made the seas its selvage,[6] and it locks
Like a quilt[7] ball within a silver box?
Who spread its canopy? Or curtains spun?
Who in this bowling alley bowled the sun?
Who made it always when it rises set
To go at once both down, and up to get?
Who th'curtain rods made for this tapestry?
Who hung the twinkling lanterns in the sky?
Who? Who did this? Or who is he? Why, know
It's only might almighty this did do.
His hand hath made this noble work which stands
His glorious handiwork not made by hands.
Who spoke all things from nothing, and with ease
Can speak all things to nothing, if He please.
Whose little finger at His pleasure can
Out mete[8] ten thousand worlds with half a span;
Whose might almighty can by half a looks
Root up the rocks and rock the hills by th'roots.
Can take this mighty world up in His hand,
And shake it like a squitchen[9] or a wand.
Whose single frown will make the heavens shake
Like as an aspen leaf the wind makes quake.
Oh! what a might is this whose single frown
Doth shake the world as it would shake it down?
Which all from nothing fet,[10] from nothing, all;
Hath all on nothing set, lets nothing fall;
Gave all to nothing man indeed, whereby
Through nothing man all might Him glorify.
In nothing then embossed the brightest gem
More precious than all preciousness in them.
But nothing man did throw down all by sin,
And darkenéd that lightsome gem in him.
    That now His brightest diamond is grown
    Darker by far than any coalpit stone.

c. 1685 1939

[3]I.e., Who commanded the creation of the universe?
[4]I.e., adorned with ribbons or bands.
[5]Emerald green.
[6]Border.
[7]Multicolored as a quilt.
[8]Measure.
[9]A switch or stick.
[10]Fetched (made).

THE JOY OF CHURCH FELLOWSHIP RIGHTLY ATTENDED[1]

In heaven soaring up, I dropped an ear
  On earth; and oh! sweet melody:
And listening, found it was the saints[2] who were
  Encoached for heaven that sang for joy.
  For in Christ's coach[3] they sweetly sing,
  As they to glory ride therein.

Oh! joyous hearts! Enfired with holy flame!
  Is speech thus tasseled[4] with praise?
Will not your inward fire of joy contain,
  That it in open flames doth blaze?
  For in Christ's coach saints sweetly sing,
  As they to glory ride therein.

And if a string do slip, by chance, they soon
  Do screw it up again,[5] whereby
They set it in a more melodious tune
  And a diviner harmony.
  For in Christ's coach they sweetly sing,
  As they to glory ride therein.

In all their acts, public, and private, nay
  And secret too, they praise impart.
But in their acts divine and worship, they
  With hymns do offer up their heart.
  Thus in Christ's coach they sweetly sing,
  As they to glory ride therein.

Some few not in;[6] and some whose time and place
  Block up this coach's way,[7] do go
As travelers afoot, and so do trace
  The road that gives them right thereto;
  While in this coach these sweetly sing
  As they to glory ride therein.

c. 1685 1937

[1]In this final poem of *God's Determinations,* Taylor completes the cycle, having moved from celebration of God's absolute power, in "The Preface," to this description of the souls of the elect as they journey to heaven.

[2]"Visible" saints, living church members.

[3]The church, as vehicle for the rise to heaven of the elect.

[4]Decorated, embellished.

[5]The string of a musical instrument, tightened and made harmonious.

[6]The few who chose to remain outside the church but are nonetheless among the elect.

[7]The many who lived before Christ or in heathen lands but are nevertheless among the elect.

UPON A SPIDER CATCHING A FLY[1]

Thou sorrow, venom elf.
Is this thy play,
To spin a web out of thyself
To catch a fly?
For why?

I saw a pettish[2] wasp
Fall foul therein,
Whom yet thy whorl pins[3] did not clasp
Lest he should fling
His sting.

But as afraid, remote
Didst stand hereat
And with thy little fingers stroke
And gently tap
His back.

Thus gently him didst treat
Lest he should pet,[4]
And in a froppish[5] waspish heat
Should greatly fret
Thy net.

Whereas the silly fly,
Caught by its leg,
Thou by the throat took'st hastily,
And 'hind the head
Bite dead.

This goes to pot,[6] that not
Nature doth call.
Strive not above what strength hath got,
Lest in the brawl
Thou fall.

This fray seems thus to us:
Hell's spider gets
His entrails spun to whipcords[7] thus,
And wove to nets
And sets,[8]

[1]This and the poems that follow belong to no specific sequence and have been collected as "Miscellaneous Poems" by Taylor's editors.
[2]Angry. [3]Whirling pins on a spinning wheel that catch and hold the thread.
[4]Grow angry. [5]Peevish. [6]Ruin, destruction. [7]Strong cords. [8]Traps, snares.

To tangle Adam's race
  In's stratagems
To their destructions, spoiled, made base
  By venom things,
    Damned sins.

But mighty, gracious Lord,
  Communicate
Thy grace to break the cord; afford
  Us glory's gate
    And state.

We'll Nightingale sing like,
  When perched on high
In glory's cage, Thy glory, bright,
  And thankfully,
    For joy.

c. 1685 1939

HUSWIFERY

Make me, O Lord, Thy spinning wheel complete.
  Thy holy word my distaff[1] make for me.
Make mine affections[2] Thy swift flyers neat,
  And make my soul Thy holy spool to be.
  My conversation make to be Thy reel,
  And reel the yarn thereon spun of Thy wheel.

Make me Thy loom then, knit therein this twine;
  And make Thy holy spirit, Lord, wind quills;[3]
Then weave the web Thyself. The yarn is fine.
  Thine ordinances make my fulling mills.[4]
  Then dye the same in heavenly colors choice,
  All pinked[5] with varnished[6] flowers of paradise.

Then clothe therewith mine understanding, will,
  Affections, judgment, conscience, memory,
My words and actions, that their shine may fill
  My ways with glory and Thee glorify.
  Then mine apparel shall display before Ye
  That I am clothed in holy robes for glory.

c. 1685 1937

[1]On a spinning wheel, the distaff holds the fibers of wool to be spun; the revolving flyers twist them into thread or yarn, which is then wound on the spool or reel.
[2]Religious emotions or passions. [3]Spindles or bobbins to hold the thread.
[4]Mills in which cloth is cleaned and stiffened. [5]Decorated. [6]Shining, glistening.

THE EBB AND FLOW

When first thou on me, Lord, wrought'st Thy sweet print,
My heart was made Thy tinder[1] box.
My 'ffections were Thy tinder in't,
Where fell Thy sparks by drops.
Those holy sparks of heavenly fire that came
Did ever catch and often out would flame.

But now my heart is made Thy censer[2] trim,
Full of Thy golden altar's fire,
To offer up sweet incense in
Unto Thyself entire;
I find my tinder scarce Thy sparks can feel
That drop out from Thy holy flint and steel.

Hence doubts out bud for fear Thy fire in me
'S a mocking *ignis fatuus*,[3]
Or lest Thine altar's fire out be,
It's hid in ashes thus.
Yet when the bellows of Thy spirit blow
Away mine ashes, then Thy fire doth glow.

1937

A FIG FOR THEE OH! DEATH

Thou king of terrors with thy ghastly eyes,
With butter teeth,[1] bare bones, grim looks likewise,
And grizzly hide, and clawing talons, fell,[2]
Op'ning to sinners vile, trap door of hell,
That on in sin impenitently trip,
The downfall[3] art of the infernal pit;
Thou struckst thy teeth deep in my Lord's bless'd side,
Who dashed it out, and all its venom 'stroyed
That now thy pounderall[4] shall only dash
My flesh and bones to bits, and cask[5] shall clash.[6]
Thou'rt not so frightful now to me, thy knocks
Do crack my shell. Its heavenly kernel's box
Abides most safe. Thy blows do break its shell,
Thy teeth its nut. Cracks are that on it fell.

[1]Flammable material, used for starting a fire with flint and steel.
[2]A vessel for burning incense.
[3]Latin: foolish fire; a term used for natural, phosphorescent, swamp lights that mislead travelers; hence, a misleading influence or thing; the will o' the wisp.

[1]Large, protruding front teeth. [2]Deadly, cruel. [3]Precipice.
[4]Pounder or pestle. [5]Human body. [6]Strike.

Thence out its kernel fair and nut, by worms
Once vitiated out, new formed forth turns,
And on the wings of some bright angel flies
Out to bright glory of God's blissful joys.
Hence thou to me with all thy ghastly face
Art not so dreadful unto me through grace.
I am resolved to fight thee, and ne'er yield,
Blood up to th'ears, and in the battlefield
Chasing thee hence: But not for this my flesh,
My body, my vile harlot, it's thy mess,[7]
Laboring to drown me into sin, disguise
By eating and by drinking such evil joys
Though grace preservéd me that I ne'er have
Surprised been nor tumbled in such grave.
Hence for my strumpet I'll ne'er draw my sword
Nor thee restrain at all by iron curb[8]
Nor for her safety will I 'gainst thee strive
But let thy frozen grips take her captive
And her imprison in thy dungeon cave
And grind to powder in thy mill the grave,
Which powder in thy van[9] thou'st safely keep
Till she hath slept out quite her fatal sleep.
When the last cock shall crow the last day[10] in
And the archangel's trumpet sound shall ring
Then th'eye omniscient seek shall all there round
Each dust death's mill had very finely ground,
Which in death's smoky furnace well refined
And each to'ts fellow hath exactly joined,
Is raised up anew and made all bright
And crystallized, all topfull of delight,
And entertains its soul again in bliss,
And holy angels waiting all on this,
The soul and body now, as two true lovers,
E'ry night how do they hug and kiss each other.
And going hand in hand thus through the skies
Up to eternal glory glorious rise.
Is this the worst thy terrors then canst? Why
Then should this grimace at me terrify?
Why cam'st thou then so slowly? Mend[11] thy pace.
Thy slowness me detains from Christ's bright face.
Although thy terrors rise to th'highest degree,
I still am where I was, a fig for thee.

1960

[7]Meal.
[8]A restraining device, like a horse's bit.
[9]Tomb, grave.
[10]Judgment Day, when all the virtuous are to be rewarded and the sinful punished.
[11]Correct.

Samuel Sewall 1652–1730

Until the late nineteenth century, Samuel Sewall was chiefly known as a judge in the Salem witchcraft trials—the ardent Puritan who, in the words of the poet Whittier, "spoke the word that gave the witch's neck to the cord." But since the publication of The Diary of Samuel Sewall *(1878–1882), a century and a half after Sewall's death, he has come to stand as more than "the Judge of the old Theocracy." He is now seen as an index to the times, an exemplar of all those convinced Puritans who kept their settled Christian vision through an age of rising secularism.*

He was born in England and came to Massachusetts with his parents on the Prudent Mary *in 1661, when he was nine. He was educated as a gentleman. At Harvard, where he was the roommate of the poet Edward Taylor, Sewall developed a fondness for theological dispute. For his prudence and rectitude, he was made Keeper of the college library, and after receiving his B.A. in 1671, he was appointed a college tutor. Three years later, having written a thesis on original sin, he received his M.A. Life and training had prepared him for the church, and all but three of his Harvard classmates entered the ministry, but Sewall saw that advantage (a word he frequently used) lay not in the pulpit but in public service and the countinghouse.*

In 1676 he married Hannah Hull, the daughter of John Hull, one of the wealthiest men in Massachusetts. Enriched with a wedding dowry of 10,000 shillings, Sewall embarked on a prosperous career as a merchant and banker, a dealer in oil, tobacco, grain, wood, and pickled fish. He soon rose to membership in Boston's plutocracy and became a member of the Colonial Governor's Council. In 1683 he was elected to the Massachusetts General Court (legislature). Although he lacked formal training in law, he was appointed a judge, eventually becoming Chief Justice of the highest court in the Colony. In 1692 he served as one of seven magistrates selected to conduct the Salem witch trials, which sent twenty victims to their deaths. Five years later Sewall acknowledged his misdoing in a confession that was read out to his church congregation as he stood before it with bowed head. He was the only one of the Salem judges publicly to admit his great error and repent.

Late in 1673 Sewall began his diary. For the next fifty-six years, he recorded his private and public life, with observations on religion, politics, sickness, dreams, disasters, and triumphs. The diary reveals the doubts that could assault a man driven by lofty ethics and worldly desires. It shows the radical Puritan antagonism toward Anglicans and Quakers ("devil worshippers"), Christmas and crucifixes, Sabbath breaking and Bible oaths, foppish wigs and powdered dandies. Sewall had little sympathy for change. He saw himself as a steward of society, a rock of Israel in a New Jerusalem. He sought truth eternal in the great world and in the small. Like his Puritan forebears he searched trivial events for revelations of divine intent and found them, reading God's will in the fears of his children, the feeding of his chickens, and the robbery of his house.

Sewall's diary also reveals a worldly, mercenary man, conventional, honorable, and stern. With equal intensity he could record his devotion to Calvin and, following the death of his wife of forty-one years, describe his calculating pursuit of eligible widows whom he hoped to attract with gifts of sermons, shoebuckles, and raisins "with proportionable almonds."

In his lifetime, Sewall was the author of numerous essays, poems, and funeral elegies that earned him the title of "Our Israel's judge and singer sweet." His most notable short piece of writing was The Selling of Joseph *(1700), one of the first antislavery tracts printed in America. But it is* The Diary of Samuel Sewall*, showing* *second- and third-generation New England Puritans confronting a world of change, that has provided a store of information to historians and has given Sewall his place among the monuments of colonial America.*

FURTHER READING: *Samuel Sewall's Diary,* ed. M. Van Doren, 1927; *The Diary of Samuel Sewall,* ed. H. Wish, 1967; *The Diary of Samuel Sewall, 1674–1729,* 2 vols., ed. M. Thomas, 1973; N. Chamberlain, *Samuel Sewall and the World He Lived In,* 1897, 1980; O. Winslow, *Samuel Sewall of Boston,* 1964; T. Strandness, *Samuel Sewall, A Puritan Portrait,* 1967; J. Graham, *Puritan Family Life, The Diary of Samuel Sewall,* 2000.

TEXT: *Diary of Samuel Sewall, 1674–1729,* 1878–1882. Spelling, punctuation, and usage have been changed to conform more nearly to modern practice.

from *THE DIARY OF SAMUEL SEWALL*

January 13, 1677. Giving my chickens meat,[1] it came to mind that I gave them nothing save Indian corn and water, and yet they eat it and thrived very well, and that that food was necessary for them, how mean soever, which much affected me and convinced [me] what need I stood in of spiritual food and that I should not nauseate[2] daily duties of prayer, etc.

July 8, 1677. New Meeting House. *Mane:*[3] In sermon time there came in a female Quaker in a canvas frock, her hair disheveled and loose like a periwig,[4] her face as black as ink, led by two other Quakers, and two others followed. It occasioned the greatest and most amazing uproar that I ever saw. Isaiah 1:12, 14.[5]

Wednesday, June 17th [1685]. A Quaker or two go to the Governor and ask leave to enclose the ground [on the Boston Common] the hanged Quakers are buried in, under or near the gallows, with pales.[6] Governor proposed it to the Council[7] who unanimously denied it as very inconvenient[8] for persons so dead and buried in the place to have any monument.[9]

Saturday [June 20, 1685], P.M. Carried my wife to Dorchester to eat cherries, raspberries, chiefly to ride and take the air. The time my wife and Mrs. Flint spent in the orchard, I spent in Mr. Flint's study, reading Calvin on the Psalms etc. . . .

Thursday, November 12 [1685]. The ministers of this town come to the Court and complain against a dancing master who seeks to set up here and have mixed dances, and his time of meeting is lecture day;[10] and 'tis reported he should say that by one play[11] he could teach more divinity than Mr.

[1]Feed [2]Loathe, avoid. [3]Latin: Morning. [4]Wig.

[5]"When ye come to appear before me, who hath required this at your hand, to tread my courts." "Your new moons and your appointed feasts my soul hateth: they are a trouble unto me, I am weary to bear them." To show their disregard for Puritan orthodoxy, zealous Quakers purposely disrupted Puritan church services.

[6]Fencing. [7]The Council of advisers to the Governor. Sewall was a member. [8]Unsuitable.

[9]Four Quakers, hanged for heresy and sedition (1659–1661), had been buried in the Common.

[10]The mid-week day (usually Thursday) devoted to Bible exposition by the minister.

[11]Dramatic performances were banned in Boston.

Willard[12] or the Old Testament. Mr. Moodey[13] said 'twas not a time for New England to dance. Mr. Mather[14] struck at the root, speaking against mixed dances. . . .[15]

April 11th, 1692. Went to Salem, where, in the meetinghouse, the persons accused of witchcraft were examined;[16] was a very great assembly; 'twas awful to see how the afflicted persons[17] were agitated. . . .

August 19th, 1692. This day George Burrough, John Willard, John Proctor, Martha Carrier, and George Jacobs were executed at Salem, a very great number of spectators being present. . . . All of them said they were innocent, Carrier and all. Mr. Mather[18] says they all died by a righteous sentence. Mr. Burrough by his speech, prayer, protestation of his innocence, did much move unthinking persons, which occasions their speaking hardly[19] concerning his being executed.

Monday, September 19, 1692. About noon, at Salem, Giles Corey was pressed to death for standing mute;[20] much pains was used with him two days, one after another, by the Court and Captain Gardner of Nantucket, who had been of his acquaintance, but all in vain.

September 21 [1692]. A petition is sent to town in behalf of Dorcas Hoar, who now confesses. Accordingly an order is sent to the Sheriff to forbear her execution, notwithstanding her being in the warrant to die tomorrow.[21] This is the first condemned person who has confessed.

November 6 [1692]. Joseph threw a knob of brass and hit his sister Betty[22] on the forehead so as to make it bleed and swell; upon which, and for his playing at prayer time, and eating when return thanks,[23] I whipped him pretty smartly. When I first went in (called by his grandmother), he sought to shadow and hide himself from me behind the head of the cradle, which gave me the sorrowful remembrance of Adam's carriage.[24]

Second day, January 6th, 1696. Kept a Day of Fasting with Prayer for the Conversion of my Son, and his settlement in a Trade that might be good for Soul and body. . . . Read Epistles to Timothy, Titus, Philemon, Hebrews. Sung the 143, 51, and 130 Psalms. I had hope that seeing God pardon'd all Israel's Iniquities, He would pardon mine, as being part of Israel.

January 13, 1696. When I came in, past seven at night, my wife met me in the entry and told me Betty had surprised them. I was surprised with the

[12]Samuel Willard (1640–1707), Sewall's minister at the Old South Church, Boston.

[13]Joshua Moodey, minister of the First Church, Boston. [14]Increase Mather.

[15]By the next July, the dancing master, Francis Stepney, was forced to flee Boston.

[16]Sewall's first mention of Salem witchcraft. In the margin of the entry he wrote, "Woe, Woe, Woe, Witchcraft." Beginning the next June, 1692, Sewall served as one of the seven magistrates who tried those accused of witchcraft at Salem.

[17]Those thought to be bewitched. [18]Cotton Mather. [19]Harshly, critically.

[20]Corey, eighty-one years old, remained silent, either in defiance or in the belief that his property would be confiscated and his family impoverished if he were to plead innocent and then be found guilty. Because he refused to speak, English law required that he be "pressed," laid flat on the ground and buried under heavy stones until he spoke or died.

[21]By law, confession of guilt secured those accused of witchcraft from trial, imprisonment, or execution.

[22]Joseph and Elizabeth, two of Sewall's fourteen children. In 1692 Elizabeth was eleven years old; Joseph was four.

[23]I.e., eating while grace was being said. Joseph was four years old at the time.

[24]Adam's posture. After eating the forbidden fruit, Adam and Eve cowered in hiding from the Lord. Genesis 3:8.

abruptness of the relation. It seems Betty Sewall had given some signs of dejection and sorrow, but a little after dinner she burst out into an amazing cry, which caused all the family to cry too. Her mother asked the reason; she gave none; at last said she was afraid she should go to hell, her sins were not pardoned. She was first wounded by my reading a sermon of Mr. Norton's,[25] about the 5th of January. Text John 7:34, "Ye shall seek me and shall not find me." And those words in the sermon, John 8:21, "Ye shall seek me, and shall die in your sins," ran in her mind and terrified her greatly. . . .

[*January 15, 1697*]. Copy of the bill[26] I put up on the fast day,[27] giving it to Mr. Willard as he passed by, and standing up at the reading of it, and bowing when finished, in the afternoon.

"Samuel Sewall, sensible of the reiterated strokes of God upon himself and family,[28] and being sensible that, as to the guilt contracted upon the opening of the late Commission of Oyer and Terminer[29] at Salem (to which the order for this day relates), he is, upon many accounts, more concerned than any that he knows of, desires to take the blame and shame of it, asking pardon of men and especially desiring prayers that God, who has an unlimited authority, would pardon that sin and all his other sins, personal and relative, and according to His infinite benignity and sovereignty not visit the sin of him, or of any other, upon himself or any of his, nor upon the land, but that He would powerfully defend him against all temptations to sin, for the future, and vouchsafe him the efficacious, saying conduct of His word and spirit."

Fourth Day, June 19, 1700. Having been long and much dissatisfied with the trade of fetching Negroes from Guinea,[30] at last I had a strong inclination to write something about it, but it wore off. At last reading Baynes's *Ephesians*[31] about servants, who mentions blackamoors,[32] I began to be uneasy that I had so long neglected doing anything. When I was thus thinking, in came Brother Belknap to show me a petition he intended to present to the General Court for the freeing [of] a Negro and his wife who were unjustly held in bondage. And there is a motion by a Boston committee to get a law that all importers of Negroes shall pay forty shillings per head, to discourage the bringing of them. And Mr. C. Mather resolves to publish a sheet to exhort masters to labor [for] their conversion,[33] which makes me hope that I was called of God to write this apology[34] for them; let His blessing accompany the same.

Tuesday, June 10th [1701]. Having last night heard that Josiah Willard[35] had cut off his hair (a very full head of hair) and put on a wig, I went to him this morning. Told his mother what I came about, and she called him. I inquired

[25]The Rev. John Norton of Hingham, Massachusetts, one of Sewall's Harvard classmates.

[26]Announcement.

[27]The Colony observed January 14, 1697, as a fast day, to atone for the execution of the Salem witches. Sewall's "bill" was a public confession of error for his part in the witchcraft trials.

[28]Several of Sewall's children had recently died.

[29]The court commissioned "to hear and to determine" the guilt of those accused of witchcraft.

[30]West Africa. Slavery existed in all thirteen original colonies. Massachusetts, the first English colony to legalize slavery (in 1641), did not abolish it until 1783.

[31]Paul Baynes, *Commentary on the First Chapter of the Epistle of St. Paul, Written to the Ephesians,* 1618.

[32]Negroes. [33]To Christianity.

[34]In June 1700, Sewall published *The Selling of Joseph,* one of the first antislavery tracts in America.

[35]The son of Sewall's pastor, Samuel Willard.

of him what extremity had forced him to put off his own hair and put on a wig? He answered, "None at all." But said that his hair was straight and that it parted behind. Seemed to argue that men might as well shave their hair off their head as off their face. I answered men were men before they had hair on their faces (half of mankind have never any). God seems to have ordained our hair as a test, to see whether we can bring our minds to be content to be at his finding or whether we would be our own carvers, lords, and come no more to Him. . . .

December 8 [1702]. Mr. Robert Gibbs dies, one of our Select men, a very good man and much Lamented; died suddenly of the Small Pocks. His death, and the death of John Adams, the Master, Isaac Loring, and Peybody, is a great stroke to our church and congregation. The Lord vouchsafe to dwell with us, and Not break up Housekeeping among us!

March 27th [1706]. I walk in the Meetinghouse. Set out homeward, lodg'd at Cushing's. *Note.* I pray'd not with my Servant, being weary. [Seeing no Chamberpot call'd for one; A little before day I us'd it in the Bed, and the bottom came out, and all the water run upon me. I was amaz'd, not knowing the bottom was out till I felt it in the Bed. The Trouble and Disgrace of it did afflict me. As soon as it was Light, I call'd up my man and he made fire and warm'd me a clean Shirt, and [I] put it on and was comfortable.][36] How unexpectedly a man may be expos'd! There's no security but in God, who is to be sought by Prayer.

Lord's Day, June 15th [1707]. I felt myself dull and heavy and listless as to spiritual good; carnal, lifeless. I sighed to God that he would quicken[37] me.

June 16 [1707]. My house was broken open in two places and about twenty pounds worth of plate stolen away, and some linen. My spoon, and knife, and neckcloth were taken. I said, "Is not this an answer of prayer?" Jane[38] came up and gave us the alarm betime[39] in the morn. I was helped to submit to Christ's stroke and say, "Welcome CHRIST!"

April 3 [1711]. I dine with the Court [legislature]. . . . Spoke much of Negroes; I mentioned the problem, whether [they] should be white after the Resurrection. Mr. Bolt took it up as absurd because the body should be void of all color, spoke as if it should be a spirit. I objected what Christ said to His Disciples after the Resurrection.[40] He said 'twas not so after His ascension.

October 15 [1717]. My wife[41] got some relapse by a new cold and grew very bad. . . .

Friday, October 18 [1717]. My wife grows worse and exceedingly restless. Prayed God to look upon her. . . .

Seventh Day, October 19 [1717]. Called Dr. C. Mather to pray, which he did excellently in the dining room, having suggested good thoughts to my wife before he went down. After, Mr. Wadsworth prayed in the chamber when 'twas supposed my wife took little notice. About a quarter of an hour past four, my dear wife expired in the afternoon, whereby the chamber was filled

[36]The passage in brackets was removed from the 1878–1882 edition as being indecent. It was restored from the original manuscript by later editors.

[37]Enliven. [38]Jane Hirst, Sewall's granddaughter. [39]Early.

[40]"Behold my hands and my feet, that it is I myself: handle me, and see; for a spirit hath not flesh and bones, as ye see me have." Luke 24:39.

[41]Hannah, his first wife. She was fifty-nine and had been married to Sewall for forty-one years.

with a flood of tears. God is teaching me a new lesson, to live a widower's life. Lord help me to learn, and be a sun and shield to me, now so much of my comfort and defense are taken away.

October 21 [1717]. Monday, my dear wife is embowelled[42] and put in cerecloth,[43] the weather being more than ordinarily hot.

Midweek, October 23 [1717]. My dear wife is interred. Bearers, Lieutenant Governor Dummer, Major General Winthrop, Colonel Elisha Hutchinson, Colonel Townsend, Andrew Belcher Esq., and Simeon Stoddard Esq. I intended Colonel Taylor for a bearer, but he was [away] from home. Had very comfortable weather. Brother Gerrish prayed with us when returned from the tomb. I went into it. Governor had a scarf and ring, and the bearers. . . .[44]

February 6 [1718]. This morning wondering in my mind whether to live a single or a married life. I had a sweet and very affectionate meditation concerning the Lord Jesus. . . .

March 14 [1718]. Deacon Marion comes to me, sits with me a great while in the evening. After a great deal of discourse about his courtship, he told [me] the Olivers said they wished I would court their aunt.[45] I said little, but said 'twas not five months since I buried my dear wife. Had said before 'twas hard to know whether best to marry again or no. . . .

June 17 [1718]. Went to Roxbury[46] lecture, visited Mr. Walter. Mr. Webb preached. Visited Governor Dudley, Mrs. Denison;[47] gave her Dr. Mather's sermons very well bound; told her we were in it invited to a wedding. She gave me very good curds.

July 25 [1718]. I go in the hackney coach to Roxbury. Call at Mr. Walter's who is not at home, nor Governor Dudley, nor his lady. Visit Mrs. Denison. She invites me to eat. I give her two cases with a knife and fork in each, one turtle shell tackling,[48] the other long, with ivory handles, squared, cost 4^{s}6^d;[49] [and a] pound of raisins with proportionable almonds. . . .

Wednesday, October 15 [1718]. Visit Mrs. Denison on horseback; present her with a pair of shoe buckles, cost 5^{s}6^d. . . .

Seventh Day, November 1 [1718]. My son from Brookline[50] being here, I took his horse and visited Mrs. Denison. Sat in the chamber next Major Bowls.[51] I told her 'twas time now to finish our business. Asked her what I should allow her. She not speaking, I told her I was willing to give her two [hundred] and fifty pounds per annum during her life if it should please God to take me out of the world before her. She answered she had better keep as she was, than give a certainty for an uncertainty. She should pay dear for dwelling at Boston. I desired her to make proposals, but she made none.[52] I had

[42]Eviscerated, prepared for burial. [43]A waxed shroud.

[44]Funeral custom required the giving of gifts to distinguished guests and coffin bearers.

[45]The widow Katherine Winthrop (1664–1725). She was fifty-six and Sewall sixty-nine when their courtship began.

[46]Roxbury, Massachusetts, three miles from Boston.

[47]The widow Dorothy Denison. She spurned Sewall and married Samuel Williams on 28 April 1720.

[48]Decoration. [49]Four shillings, sixpence.

[50]Samuel Sewall Jr. of Brookline, Massachusetts, four miles from Boston.

[51]John Bowles, the son of one of Sewall's Harvard classmates.

[52]Sewall courted rich widows. Thus financial settlements were a prime part of his marriage negotiations.

thoughts of publishment[53] next Thursday the 6th. But I now seem to be far from it. May God, Who has the pity of a father, direct and help me!

Friday, November 28, 1718. Having consulted with Mr. Walter after lecture, he advised me to go and speak with Mrs. Denison. I went this day in the coach, had a fire made in the chamber where I spoke with her before, November the first. I inquired how she had done these three or four weeks. Afterwards I told her our conversation had been such when I was with her last that it seemed to be a direction in providence not to proceed any further. She said it must be what I pleased, or to that purpose. . . . My bowels[54] yearn towards Mrs. Denison, but I think God directs me in His providence to desist. . . .

September 2 [1719]. Visit Mrs. Tilley[55] and speak with her in her chamber, ask her to come and dwell at my house. She expresses her unworthiness of such a thing with much respect. . . .

September 16 [1719]. After the meeting I visited Mrs. Tilley.

September 18 [1719]. Ditto.

September 21 [1719]. I gave Mrs. Tilley a little book entitled *Ornaments for the Daughters of Sion.*[56] I gave it to my dear wife, August 28, 1702.

[October] *26 or 27* [1719]. I visited Dr. I. Mather, designing to ask him to marry me. I asked him whether it was convenient to marry on the evening after the Thanksgiving. He made me no answer. I asked again. He said Mr. Prince had been with him to marry him,[57] but he told him he could not go abroad in the evening. Then I thought 'twas in vain to proceed any further, for Mrs. Tilley's preparations were such that I could not defer it any longer. . . .

October 29 [1719]. Thanksgiving day. Between six and seven, Brother Moodey and I went to Mrs. Tilley's and, about seven or eight, were married by Mr. J. Sewall,[58] in the best room below stairs. . . . Mrs. Armitage introduced me into my bride's chamber after she was abed. I thanked her that she had left her room in that chamber to make way for me and prayed God to provide for her a better lodging. So none saw us after I went to bed. Quickly after our being abed, my bride grew so very bad she was fain to sit up in her bed. I rose to get her petty coats about her. I was exceedingly amazed, fearing lest she should have died. Through the favor of God she recovered in some considerable time of her fit of the tissick,[59] spitting partly blood. She herself was under great consternation.

[December] *29, Wednesday* [1719]. My wife had a very bad night, thought she should have died, had such a shaking ague fit. But through mercy, all went over well.

May 26 [1720]. Went to bed after ten. About eleven or before, my dear wife was oppressed with a rising of flegm that obstructed her breathing. . . . About midnight my dear wife expired to our great astonishment, especially mine. May the sovereign Lord pardon my sin and sanctify to me this very extraordinary awful dispensation. . . .

[53]Announcement of proposed marriage. [54]Emotions, heart. [55]The widow Abigail Tilley.

[56]By Cotton Mather. Printed 1692.

[57]Prince had asked Mather to officiate at Prince's marriage.

[58]Sewall's son Joseph (1688–1769), minister at the Old South Church, Boston.

[59]Phthisic. An asthmatic seizure.

October 1 [1720]. Saturday, I dine at Mr. Stoddard's. From thence I went to Madam Winthrop's[60] just at three. Spoke to her, saying my loving wife died so soon and suddenly, 'twas hardly convenient for me to think of marrying again. However, I came to this resolution, that I would not make my court to any person without first consulting with her. . . .

October 3 [1720]. Waited on Madam Winthrop again; 'twas a little while before she came in. Her daughter Noyes[61] being there alone with me, I said I hoped my waiting on her mother would not be disagreeable to her. . . . At last Madam Winthrop came in. After a considerable time, I went up to her and said, if it might not be inconvenient I desired to speak with her. . . . I prayed that Katherine might be the person assigned for me. She instantly took it up in the way of denial, as if she had catched at an opportunity to do it, saying she could not do it before she was asked. Said that was her mind unless she should change it, which she believed she should not; could not leave her children. . . .

October 6th [1720]. A little after 6 P.M. I went to Madam Winthrop's. . . . Madam seemed to harp upon the same string. Must take care of her children, could not leave that house and neighborhood where she had dwelt so long. I told her she might do her children as much or more good by bestowing what she laid out in housekeeping, upon them. Said her son would be of age the 7th of August. I said it might be inconvenient for her to dwell with her daughter-in-law, who must be mistress of the house. I gave her a piece of Mr. Belcher's cake and gingerbread[62] wrapped up in a clean sheet of paper. . . .

October 12th [1720]. At Madam Winthrop's. . . . Mrs. Anne Cotton came to door ('twas before eight), said Madam Winthrop was within, directed me into the little room where she was full of work behind a stand. Mrs. Cotton came in and stood. Madam Winthrop pointed to her to set me a chair. Madam Winthrop's countenance was much changed from what 'twas on Monday, looked dark and lowering. At last, the work (black stuff or silk) was taken away; I got my chair in place, had some converse, but very cold and indifferent to what 'twas before. Asked her to acquit me of rudeness if I drew off her glove. Inquiring the reason, I told her 'twas great odds between handling a dead goat and a living lady. Got it off. I told her I had one petition to ask of her, that was that she would take off the negative she laid on me the third of October. She readily answered she could not and enlarged upon it. She told me of it so soon as she could; could not leave her house, children, neighbors, business. . . . I gave her Dr. Preston, *The Church's Marriage and the Church's Carriage,*[63] which cost me 6^s at the sale. The door standing open, Mr. Ayers[64] came in, hung up his hat, and sat down. After a while, Madam

[60]The widow Katherine Winthrop (1664–1725). She remained single. Sewall was a pallbearer at her funeral.

[61]Mrs. Katherine Noyes.

[62]Jonathan Belcher (1682–1757), a rich Boston merchant, governor of Massachusetts (1730–1741). He had given Sewall the cake and gingerbread (leftovers from a party) the day before.

[63]John Preston (1587–1628), English theologian, whose works, popular among Puritans, included *The Golden Scepter Held Forth to the Humble, With the Church's Dignity by Her Marriage, And the Church's Duty in Her Carriage,* 1638, a large and expensive book.

[64]Obadiah Ayers, chaplain of Castle William, the fortified island at the entrance to Boston harbor.

Winthrop moving, he went out. John Eyre[65] looked in; I said, "How do ye," or "Your servant, Mr. Eyre," but heard no word from him. Sarah filled a glass of wine. She drank to me, I to her. She sent Juno[66] home with me with a good lantern. I gave her 6^{d} and bid her thank her mistress. . . .

October 17 [1720]. In the evening I visited Madam Winthrop, who treated me courteously, but not in clean linen as sometimes. . . . Juno came home with me.

October 19 [1720]. Midweek, visited Madam Winthrop; Sarah told me she was at Mr. Walley's, would not come home till late. . . . I went and found her there with Mr. Walley and his wife[67] in the little room below. At seven o'-clock I mentioned going home. At eight I put on my coat and quickly waited on her home. She found occasion to speak loud to the servant as if she had a mind to be known. Was courteous to me but took occasion to speak pretty earnestly about my keeping a coach. I said 'twould cost £100 per annum. She said 'twould cost but £40. . . .

October 21 [1720]. Friday, my son, the minister, came to me P.M. by appointment, and we pray one for another in the old chamber, more especially respecting my courtship. About six o'clock I go to Madam Winthrop's. Sarah told me her mistress was gone out but did not tell me whither she went. She presently ordered me a fire, so I went in, having Dr. Sibbes's *Bowels*[68] with me to read. . . . A while after, I heard Madam Winthrop's voice inquiring something about John. After a good while and clapping the garden door twice or thrice, she came in. I mentioned something of the lateness. She bantered me and said I was later. She received me courteously. I asked when our proceedings should be made public. She said they were like to be no more public than they were already. Offered me no wine that I remember. I rose up at eleven o'clock to come away, saying I would put on my coat. She offered not to help me. I prayed her that Juno might light me home. She opened the shutter and said 'twas pretty light abroad, Juno was weary and gone to bed. So I came home by star light as well as I could. . . .

October 24 [1720]. I went in the hackney coach[69] through the Common. Stopped at Madam Winthrop's (had told her I would take my departure from thence). Sarah came to the door with Katie[70] in her arms, but I did not think to take notice of the child. Called her mistress. I told her . . . I was come to inquire whether she could find it in her heart to leave that house and neighborhood and go and dwell with me at the south end.[71] I think she said softly, "Not yet." I told her it did not lie in my lands to keep a coach. If I should, I should be in danger to be brought to keep company with her neighbor Brooker (he was a little before sent to prison for debt). Told her I had an antipathy against those who would pretend to give themselves, but [give] nothing of their estate. I would [give] a proportion of my estate with myself. And I supposed she would do so. As to a periwig,[72] my best and

[65]Madam Winthrop's son by an earlier marriage. [66]Sarah and Juno were servants.

[67]Madam Winthrop's daughter, Bethiah Walley.

[68]Richard Sibbes (1577–1635), a Puritan divine and author of *Bowels Opened, or a Discovery of the Near and Dear Love . . . Between Christ and the Church,* 1639.

[69]Hired, public coach. [70]Madam Winthrop's granddaughter, Katherine Walley.

[71]Of Boston.

[72]Sewall wore a velvet cap to cover his baldness. Madam Winthrop had urged him to wear a wig.

greatest Friend, I could not possibly have a greater, began to find me with hair before I was born and had continued to do so ever since; and I could not find in my heart to go to another. She commended the book I gave her, Dr. Preston, *The Church's Marriage,* quoted him saying 'twas inconvenient keeping out of a fashion commonly used. I said the time and tide did circumscribe my visit. She gave me a dram of black-cherry brandy and gave me a lump of the sugar that was in it. She wished me a good journey. I prayed God to keep her and came away. Had a very pleasant journey to Salem.

November 2 [1720]. Midweek, went again [to Madam Winthrop's] and found Mrs. Alden there, who quickly went out. Gave her[73] about one half pound of sugar almonds, cost 3^{s} per pound. Carried them on Monday. She seemed pleased with them, asked what they cost. Spoke of giving her a hundred pounds per annum if I died before her. Asked her what sum she would give me if she should die first? Said I would give her time to consider of it. . . . Gave me a glass or two of canary.[74]

November 4th [1720]. Friday, went again about seven o'clock, found there Mr. John Walley and his wife. . . . About nine they went away. I asked Madam what fashioned necklace I should present her with. She said, "None at all." I asked her whereabout we left off last time, mentioned what I had offered to give her, asked her what she would give me. She said she could not change her condition; she had said so from the beginning, could not be so far from her children, the lecture. [She] quoted the Apostle Paul affirming that a single life was better than a married. . . .[75]

Monday, November 7th [1720]. I went to Madam Winthrop, found her rocking her little Katie in the cradle. I excused my coming so late (near eight). She set me an arm chair and cushion, and so the cradle was between her arm chair and mine. Gave her the remnant of my almonds. She did not eat of them as before but laid them away. I said I came to inquire whether she had altered her mind since Friday or remained of the same mind still. She said, "Thereabouts." I told her I loved her and was so fond as to think that she loved me. She said [she] had a great respect for me. I told her I had made her an offer without asking any advice; she had so many to advise with, that 'twas a hindrance. The fire was come to one short brand besides the block, which brand was set up in end; at last it fell to pieces, and no recruit[76] was made. She gave me a glass of wine. . . . Took leave of her. . . . I did not bid her draw off her glove as sometime I had done. Her dress was not so clean as sometime it had been. Jehovah jireh![77]

Midweek, November 9th [1720]. Dine at Brother Stoddard's.[78] Were so kind as to inquire of me if they should invite Madam Winthrop. I answered, "No.". . .

Saturday, July 15 [1721]. Call and sit awhile with Madam Ruggles. She tells me they had been up all night; her daughter, Joseph Ruggles's wife, was brought to bed of a daughter. I showed my willingness to renew my old acquaintance [as suitor]. She expressed her inability to be serviceable. Gave me cider to drink. I came home.

[73]Madam Winthrop. [74]Wine from the Canary Islands.

[75]"I say therefore to the unmarried and widows, It is good for them if they abide ever as I." 1 Corinthians 7:8.

[76]Replenishment. [77]"The Lord will provide." Genesis 22:14.

[78]Simeon Stoddard, like Sewall, a member of the Royal Council. His wife, Mehitable, was the mother, by a previous marriage, of the Reverend William Cooper, the husband of Sewall's daughter Judith.

Copy of a Letter to Mrs. Mary Gibbs, Widow, at Newton, January 12th, 1722.[79]

"Madam, your removal out of town and the severity of the winter are the reasons of my making you this epistolary visit. In times past (as I remember) you were minded that I should marry you, by giving you to your desirable bridegroom.[80] Some sense of this intended respect abides with me still and puts me upon inquiring whether you be willing that I should marry you now, by becoming your husband. Aged, and feeble and exhausted as I am, your favorable answer to this inquiry, in a few lines, the candor of it will much oblige, Madam, your humble servant, S.S."

Friday, January 26 [1722]. I rode to Newton in the coach and visited Mrs. Gibbs. . . .

March 29th [1722]. Samuel Sewall and Mrs. Mary Gibbs were joined together in marriage by the Reverend Mr. William Cooper. . . .

Midweek, January 2, 1723. His Honour the Lieutenant Governor [*William Dummer*] takes the Oaths in council, as to the Acts relating to Trade and of his Office. After Mr. Checkley had pray'd, the Lieutenant Governor sent for the Deputies in and made his Speech. When the Representatives were return'd to their own Chamber, I stood up and said, "If your Honour and this honourable Board please to give me leave, I would speak a Word or two upon this solemn Occasion.—Although the unerring Providence of GOD has brought you to the Chair of Government in a cloudy and Tempestuous Time; yet you have this for your Encouragement, that the People you Have to do with, are a part of the Israel of GOD, and you may expect to have of the Prudence and Patience of Moses communicated to you for your conduct. It is evident that our Almighty Saviour Counselled the First Planters to remove hither, and Settle here; and they dutifully followed his Advice; and therefore He will never leave nor forsake them, nor Theirs: so that your Honour must needs be happy in sincerely seeking their Interest and Wellfare; which your Birth and Education will incline you to do. *Difficilia quae pulchra!*[81]

Lord's Day, December 17 [1727]. I was surprised to hear Mr. Thacher[82] of Milton, my old friend, prayed for as dangerously sick. Next day, December 18, 1727, I am informed by Mr. Gerrish[83] that my dear friend died last night. . . .

Friday, December 22 [1727]. The day after the fast, [Thacher] was interred. . . . having a pair of gloves sent me,[84] I determined to go to the funeral, if the weather proved favorable, which it did. . . . It was sad to see [that I had] triumphed over my dear friend! I rode in my coach to the burying place, not being able to get nearer by reason of the many horses. . . . Now I can go to no more funerals of my classmates, nor none at mine, for the survivors, the Reverend Mr. Samuel Mather at Windsor and the Reverend Mr. Taylor[85] at Westfield [are] one hundred miles off and are entirely enfeebled. I humbly pray that Christ may be

[79]Sewall's courtship of his third wife was largely through letters, the text of this one being entered in Sewall's diary.

[80]I.e., that she had wanted Sewall to officiate at her marriage (in 1692) to her first husband, Robert Gibbs.

[81]Latin: The best things are the most difficult to obtain.

[82]Reverend Peter Thacher (1651–1727), minister at Milton, Massachusetts and one of Sewall's Harvard classmates.

[83]Samuel Gerrish, husband of Sewall's daughter Mary and town clerk of Boston.

[84]Custom required the sending of gloves to those honored guests invited to a funeral.

[85]Edward Taylor, the poet.

graciously present with us all three both in life and in death, and then we shall safely and comfortably walk through the shady valley that leads to glory.

At Boston upon the *Lord's Day August 11th,* 1728, about 6. P.M. a Noble *Rainbow* was seen in the Cloud, after great Thundering, and Darkness, and Rain: One foot thereof stood upon Dorchester Neck, the Eastern end of it; and the other foot stood upon the Town. It was very bright, and the Reflection of it caused another faint Rainbow to the westward of it. For the entire Compleatness of it, throughout the whole Arch, and for its duration, the like has been rarely seen. It lasted about a quarter of an hour. The middle parts were discontinued for a while; but the former Integrity and Splendor were quickly Recovered. I hope this is a sure Token that CHRIST Remembers his Covenant for his beloved *Jews* under their Captivity and Dispersion; and that He will make haste to prepare for them a City that has foundations, whose Builder and Maker is GOD.

1674–1729 1878–1882

Mary Rowlandson c. 1637–1711

At sunrise, on February 20, 1676, a band of Indians attacked the frontier village of Lancaster, Massachusetts, butchering many of the inhabitants and carrying off survivors. It was one of many Indian attacks on white, frontier settlements during the years of King Philip's War (1675–1678), the bloodiest war in American colonial history.

Among the hostages taken at Lancaster was Mary Rowlandson, mother of four and wife of Joseph Rowlandson, minister of the Lancaster church. For almost three months, until early May 1676, she lived as a captive of the "atheistical, proud, wild, cruel, barbarous, bruitish" Indians as they fled through the wilderness before the pursuing colonial militia. When she was ransomed for £20, money gathered in a public subscription among the women of Boston, she returned to her home and set forth the story of her ordeal.

In simple, artless prose she recorded the harrowing experiences of each journey, or "remove": the murder of her friends, the death of her child, her starvation, the oppression of her spirits. Her words show the colonial dread of the wilderness. She saw the Indians as fiends, "roaring lions and savage bears," for her Puritan vision was not colored by the later, romantic concept of the Indian as a noble savage. Like other zealous Christians she came to see her fate in symbolic religious terms: the Indians were instruments of Satan come to test her faith; she, a pious believer, was tormented to show God's mysterious will to bring pain as well as joy; and her final escape was a lesson to "make us the more to acknowledge His hand and to see that our help is always in Him."

Mary Rowlandson's story was among the first of the Indian Captivity Narratives, seventeenth-century adventure thrillers set in the colonial frontier. Such tales of attack, capture, and escape were enormously popular. They told of bravery and guile, of strange places and exotic people. They showed the triumph of the godly over harsh wilderness and pagan evil. And they set the stage for the American cowboy tales and the pioneer epics that have captivated the popular imagination and translated America's frontier experience to the world.

FURTHER READING: R. Van Der Beets, *The Indian Captivity Narrative, An American Genre,* 1984; M. Breitwieser, *American Puritanism and the Defense of Mourning: Religion, Grief, and Ethnology in Mary White Rowlandson's Captivity Narrative,* 1990; K. Derounian-Stodola and J. Lavernier, *The Indian Captivity Narrative 1550–1900,* 1993; J. Namias, *White Captives, Gender and Ethnicity on the American Frontier,* 1993; G. Ebersole, *Captured Texts, Puritan to Postmodern Images of Indian Captivity,* 1995; M. Burnham, *Captivity and Sentiment,* 1997.

TEXT: *Narratives of the Indian Wars,* ed. H. Lincoln, 1913. Some spelling, punctuation, and usage have been changed to avoid ambiguities and to correct obvious errors.

from *A NARRATIVE OF THE CAPTIVITY AND RESTAURATION OF MRS. MARY ROWLANDSON*

On the tenth of February 1675,[1] Came the Indians with great numbers upon Lancaster:[2] Their first coming was about Sun-rising; hearing the noise of some Guns, we looked out; several Houses were burning, and the Smoke ascending to Heaven. There were five persons taken in one house; the Father, and the Mother and a sucking[3] Child, they knockt on the head; the other two they took and carried away alive. Their were two others, who being out of their Garrison[4] upon some occasion were set upon; one was knockt on the head, the other escaped: Another there was who running along was shot and wounded, and fell down; he begged of them his life, promising them Money (as they told me) but they would not hearken to him but knockt him in head, and stript him naked, and split open his Bowels. Another seeing many of the Indians about his Barn, ventured and went out, but was quickly shot down. There were three others belonging to the same Garrison who were killed; the Indians getting up upon the roof of the Barn, had advantage to shoot down upon them over their Fortification. Thus these murtherous wretches went on, burning and destroying before them.

At length they came and beset our own house, and quickly it was the dolefullest day that ever mine eyes saw. The House stood upon the edge of a hill; some of the Indians got behind the hill, others into the Barn, and others behind any thing that could shelter them; from all which places they shot against the House, so that the Bullets seemed to fly like hail; and quickly they wounded one man among us, then another, and then a third. About two hours (according to my observation, in that amazing time) they had been about the house before they prevailed to fire it (which they did with Flax and Hemp, which they brought out of the Barn, and there being no defence

[1]February 20, 1676, by the present-day Gregorian Calendar, which replaced the Julian Calendar in England's North America colonies in 1752.

[2]Lancaster, Massachusetts, thirty miles west of Boston, one of many frontier villages attacked by Indians during King Philip's War (1676–1678).

[3]Nursing.

[4]In expectation of attack, Lancaster villagers had fortified six houses, including the Rowlandson house, which sheltered thirty-seven people.

about the House, only two Flankers[5] at two opposite corners and one of them not finished) they fired it once and one ventured out and quenched it, but they quickly fired it again, and that took. Now is the dreadfull hour come, that I have often heard of (in time of War, as it was the case of others) but now mine eyes see it. Some in our house were fighting for their lives, others wallowing in their blood, the House on fire over our heads, and the bloody Heathen ready to knock us on the head, if we stirred out. Now might we hear Mothers and Children crying out for themselves, and one another, Lord, What shall we do? Then I took my Children[6] (and one of my sisters, hers) to go forth and leave the house: but as soon as we came to the door and appeared, the Indians shot so thick that the bulletts rattled against the House, as if one had taken an handfull of stones and threw them, so that we were fain to give back.[7] We had six stout Dogs belonging to our Garrison, but none of them would stir, though another time, if any Indian had come to the door, they were ready to fly upon him and tear him down. The Lord hereby would make us the more to acknowledge his hand, and to see that our help is always in him.[8] But out we must go, the fire increasing, and coming along behind us, roaring, and the Indians gaping[9] before us with their Guns, Spears and Hatchets to devour us. No sooner were we out of the House, but my Brother in Law (being before wounded, in defending the house, in or near the throat) fell down dead, whereat the Indians scornfully shouted, and hallowed, and were presently upon him, stripping off his cloaths, the bulletts flying thick, one went through my side, and the same (as would seem) through the bowels and hand of my dear Child in my arms.[10] One of my elder Sister's Children, named William, had then his Leg broken, which the Indians perceiving, they knockt him on head. Thus were we butchered by those merciless Heathen, standing amazed, with the blood running down to our heels. My eldest Sister being yet in the House, and seeing those woefull sights, the Infidels hauling Mothers one way, and Children another, and some wallowing in their blood, and her elder Son telling her that her Son William was dead, and my self was wounded, she said, And, Lord, let me die with them; which was no sooner said, but she was struck with a Bullet, and fell down dead over the threshold. I hope she is reaping the fruit of her good labours, being faithfull to the service of God in her place. In her younger years she lay under much trouble upon spiritual accounts, till it pleased God to make that precious Scripture take hold of her heart, 2 Corinthians 12:9, *And he said unto me, my Grace is sufficient for thee.* More than twenty years after I have heard her tell how sweet and comfortable that place was to her. But to return: The Indians laid hold of us, pulling me one way, and the Children another, and said, Come go along with us; I told them they would kill me: they answered, If I were willing to go along with them, they would not hurt me.

Oh the doleful sight that now was to behold at this House! *Come, behold the works of the Lord, what desolations he has made in the Earth.*[11] Of thirty seven persons who were in this one House, none escaped either present death, or a

[5]Structures (bastions) projecting from the corners of the fortified houses, from which defenders could fire at the flank of (enfilade) attackers.

[6]Joseph, Mary, and Sarah Rowlandson. [7]I.e., forced to turn back. [8]I.e., only from God.

[9]Gesturing. [10]Her younger daughter, Sarah, six years old. [11]Psalm 46:8.

bitter captivity, save only one,[12] who might say as he, Job 1:15, *And I only am escaped alone to tell the News.* There were twelve killed, some shot, some stab'd with their Spears, some knock'd down with their Hatchets. When we are in prosperity, Oh the little that we think of such dreadfull sights, and to see our dear Friends, and Relations lie bleeding out their heart-blood upon the ground. There was one who was chopt into the head with a Hatchet, and stript naked, and yet was crawling up and down. It is a solemn sight to see so many Christians lying in their blood, some here, and some there, like a company of Sheep torn by Wolves, All of them stript naked by a company of hell-hounds, roaring, singing, ranting and insulting, as if they would have torn our very hearts out; yet the Lord by his Almighty power preserved a number of us from death, for there were twenty-four of us taken alive and carried Captive.

I had often before this said, that if the Indians should come, I should chuse rather to be killed by them than taken alive but when it came to the trial my mind changed; their glittering weapons so daunted my spirit, that I chose rather to go along with those (as I may say) ravenous Beasts, than that moment to end my days; and that I may the better declare what happened to me during that grievous Captivity, I shall particularly speak of the severall Removes[13] we had up and down the Wilderness.

The first Remove

Now away we must go with those Barbarous Creatures, with our bodies wounded and bleeding, and our hearts no less than our bodies. About a mile we went that night, up upon a hill within sight of the Town[14] where they intended to lodge. There was hard by a vacant house (deserted by the English before, for fear of the Indians). I asked them whether I might not lodge in the house that night to which they answered, what will you love English men still? This was the dolefullest night that ever my eyes saw. Oh the roaring, and singing and dancing, and yelling of those black creatures in the night, which made the place a lively resemblance of hell. And as miserable was the waste that was there made, of Horses, Cattle, Sheep, Swine, Calves, Lambs, Roasting Pigs, and Fowl (which they had plundered in the Town) some roasting, some lying and burning, and some boiling to feed our merciless Enemies; who were joyful enough though we were disconsolate. To add to the dolefulness of the former day, and the dismalness of the present night, my thoughts ran upon my losses and sad bereaved condition. All was gone, my Husband gone (at least separated from me, he being in the Bay;[15] and to add to my grief, the Indians told me they would kill him as he came homeward) my Children gone, my Relations and Friends gone, our House and home and all our comforts within door, and without, all was gone, (except my life) and I knew not but the next moment that might go too. There remained nothing to me but one poor wounded Babe, and it seemed at present worse than death that it was in such a pitiful condition, bespeaking Compassion, and I had no refreshing[16] for it, nor suitable things to revive it. Little do many

[12]Her neighbor Ephraim Roper. Rowlandson was unaware that three children of the Kettle family also escaped.

[13]Journeys—to escape the pursuing colonial military forces. After each move, the group remained encamped for several days. Rowlandson's journey took her northwest, across Massachusetts, into present-day New Hampshire and Vermont, and back again to Lancaster and Boston.

[14]Encampment. [15]I.e., in or near Boston. [16]Food and resting place.

think what is the savageness and bruitishness of this barbarous Enemy, aye even those that seem to profess more than others among them,[17] when the English have fallen into their hands.

Those seven that were killed at Lancaster the summer before upon a Sabbath day, and the one that was afterward killed upon a week day, were slain and mangled in a barbarous manner, by one-ey'd John, and Marlborough's Praying Indians, which Capt. Mosely brought to Boston, as the Indians told me.[18]

The second Remove[19]

But now, the next morning, I must turn my back upon the Town, and travel with them into the vast and desolate Wilderness, I knew not whither. It is not my tongue, or pen can express the sorrows of my heart, and bitterness of my spirit, that I had at this departure; but God was with me, in a wonderfull manner, carrying me along, and bearing up my spirit, [so] that it did not quite fail. One of the Indians carried my poor wounded Babe upon a horse; it went moaning all along, I shall die, I shall die. I went on foot after it, with sorrow that cannot be exprest. At length I took it off the horse, and carried it in my armes till my strength failed, and I fell down with it: Then they set me upon a horse with my wounded Child in my lap, and there being no furniture[20] upon the horse back, as we were going down a steep hill, we both fell over the horse's head, at which they like inhumane creatures laught, and rejoiced to see it, though I thought we should there have ended our days, as overcome with so many difficulties. But the Lord renewed my strength still, and carried me along, [so] that I might see more of his Power, yea, so much that I could never have thought of, had I not experienced it.

After this it quickly began to snow, and when night came on, they stopt; and now down I must sit in the snow, by a little fire, and a few boughs behind me, with my sick Child in my lap; and calling much for water, being now (through the wound) fallen into a violent Fever. My own wound also growing so stiff, that I could scarce sit down or rise up; yet so it must be, that I must sit all this cold winter night upon the cold snowy ground, with my sick Child in my arms, looking that every hour would be the last of its life, and having no Christian friend near me, either to comfort or help me. Oh, I may see the wonderfull power of God, that my Spirit did not utterly sink under my affliction; still the Lord upheld me with his gracious and mercifull Spirit, and we were both alive to see the light of the next morning.

The third Remove[21]

The morning being come, they prepared to go on their way. One of the Indians got up upon a horse, and they set me up behind him, with my poor sick Babe in my lap. A very wearisome and tedious day I had of it; what with my own wound, and my Child's being so exceeding sick, and in a lamentable

[17]I.e., even the Christian Indians who most profess their faith.

[18]On August 30, 1675, a colonial military force under Captain Samuel Mosely invaded the community of Christian (Praying) Indians near Marlborough, Massachusetts. Fifteen of the Indians were bound together by the neck and forcibly marched to Boston to answer charges that Marlborough Indians had joined in the raid on the village of Lancaster on August 22, 1675.

[19]To Princeton, Massachusetts. [20]Saddle.

[21]To an Indian village on the Ware River near New Braintree, Massachusetts.

condition with her wound. It may be easily judged what a poor feeble condition we were in, there being not the least crumb of refreshing that came within either of our mouths, from Wednesday night to Saturday night, except only a little cold water. This day in the afternoon, about an hour by Sun, we came to the place where they intended, *viz.*[22] an Indian Town, called Wenimesset, Northward of Quabaug. When we were come, Oh the number of Pagans (now merciless enemies) that there came about me, that I may say as David, Psalms 27:13, *I had fainted, unless I had believed,* etc. The next day was the Sabbath: I then remembered how careless I had been of God's holy time, how many Sabbaths I had lost and mispent, and how evily I had walked in God's sight, which lay so close unto my spirit, that it was easie for me to see how righteous it was with God to cut off the thread of my life and cast me out of his presence for ever. Yet the Lord still showed mercy to me, and upheld me; and as he wounded me with one hand, so he healed me with the other. This day there came to me one Robbert Pepper (a man belonging to Roxbury) who was taken in Captain Beers his Fight,[23] and had been now a considerable time with the Indians; and [he went] up with them almost as far as Albany,[24] to see king Philip, as he told me, and was now very lately come into these parts. Hearing, I say, that I was in this Indian Town, he obtained leave to come and see me. He told me, he himself was wounded in the leg at Captain Beers his Fight, and was not able some time to go, but as they carried him, and as he took Oaken leaves and laid to his wound, and through the blessing of God he was able to travel again. Then I took Oaken leaves and laid to my side, and with the blessing of God it cured me also; yet before the cure was wrought, I may say, as it is in Psalms 38:5,6, *My wounds stink and are corrupt, I am troubled, I am bowed down greatly, I go mourning all the day long.* I sat much alone with a poor wounded Child in my lap, which moaned night and day, having nothing to revive the body, or cheer the spirits of her, but in stead of that, sometimes one Indian would come and tell me one hour, that your Master[25] will knock your Child in the head, and then a second, and then a third, your Master will quickly knock your Child in the head.

This was the comfort I had from them, miserable comforters are ye all, as he said.[26] Thus nine days I sat upon my knees, with my Babe in my lap, till my flesh was raw again; my Child being even ready to depart this sorrowfull world, they bade me carry it out to another Wigwam (I suppose because they would not be troubled with such spectacles) Whither I went with a very heavy heart, and down I sat with the picture of death in my lap. About two hours in the night, my sweet Babe like a Lamb departed this life, on Feb. 18, 1675. It being about six years, and five months old. It was nine days from the first wounding, in this miserable condition, without any refreshing of one nature or other, except a little cold water. I cannot, but take notice, how at another time I could not bear to be in the room where any dead person was, but now the case is changed; I must and could lie down by my dead Babe, side by side all the night after. I have thought since of the wonderfull goodness of God to me, in preserving me

[22]Latin: namely.

[23]On September 4, 1675, in one of the battles of King Philip's War, a military force led by Captain Richard Beers was attacked by Indians near Deerfield, Massachusetts. Beers and nineteen others were killed.

[24]King Philip's winter encampment, twenty miles north of Albany, New York.

[25]Her Indian captor and owner. [26]Job, in Job 16:2.

in the use of my reason and senses, in that distressed time, that I did not use wicked and violent means to end my own miserable life.

. . .

Now the Indians began to talk of removing from this place, some one way, and some another. There were now besides my self nine English Captives in this place (all of them Children, except one Woman). I got an opportunity to go and take my leave of them; they being to go one way, and I another. I asked them whether they were earnest with God for deliverance; they told me, they did as they were able, and it was some comfort to me, that the Lord stirred up Children to look to him. The Woman *viz.* Goodwife Joslin told me she should never see me again, and that she could find in her heart to run away; I wisht her not to run away by any means, for we were near thirty miles from any English Town, and she very big with Child, and had but one week to reckon,[27] and another Child in her Arms, two years old, and bad Rivers there were to go over, and we were feeble, with our poor and coarse entertainment.[28] I had my Bible with me, I pulled it out, and asked her whether she would read; we opened the Bible and lighted on Psalms 27, in which Psalm we especially took notice of that, *ver. ult.*,[29] *Wait on the Lord, Be of good courage, and he shall strengthen thine Heart, wait I say on the Lord.*

The fourth Remove[30]

And now I must part with that little Company I had. Here I parted from my Daughter Mary, (whom I never saw again till I saw her in Dorchester,[31] returned from Captivity), and from four little Cousins and Neighbours, some of which I never saw afterward; the Lord only knows the end of them. Amongst them also was that poor Woman before mentioned, who came to a sad end, as some of the company told me in my travel: She having much grief upon her Spirit, about her miserable condition, being so near her time,[32] she would be often asking the Indians to let her go home; they not being willing to that, and yet vexed with her importunity, gathered a great company together about her, and stript her naked, and set her in the midst of them; and when they had sung and danced about her (in their hellish manner) as long as they pleased, they knockt her on head, and the child in her arms with her: when they had done that, they made a fire and put them both into it, and told the other Children that were with them, that if they attempted to go home, they would serve them in like manner: The Children said, she did not shed one tear, but prayed all the while. But to return to my own Journey; we travelled about half a day or little more, and came to a desolate place in the Wilderness, where there were no Wigwams or Inhabitants before; we came about the middle of the afternoon to this place, cold and wet, and snowy, and hungry, and weary, and no refreshing for man, but the cold ground to sit on, and our poor Indian cheer.[33]

Heart-aching thoughts here I had about my poor Children, who were scattered up and down among the wild beasts of the forrest: My head was light and dizzey (either through hunger or hard lodging, or trouble or altogether) my knees feeble, my body raw by sitting double[34] night and day, that I cannot

[27]I.e., one week before giving birth. [28]Food and housing. [29]Latin: last verse.
[30]To an Indian encampment at present-day Petersham, Massachusetts. [31]Near Boston.
[32]I.e., near the end of her pregnancy. [33]Food and drink.
[34]Riding behind the first rider, on horseback.

express to man the affliction that lay upon my Spirit, but the Lord helped me at that time to express it to himself. I opened my Bible to read, and the Lord brought that precious Scripture to me, Jeremiah 31:16, *Thus saith the Lord, refrain thy voice from weeping, and thine eyes from tears, for thy work shall be rewarded, and they shall come again from the land of the Enemy.* This was a sweet Cordial[35] to me, when I was ready to faint, many and many a time have I sat down, and wept sweetly over this Scripture. At this place we continued about four days.

The fifth Remove[36]

The occasion (as I thought) of their moving at this time, was, the English Army,[37] it being near and following them: For they went, as if they had gone for their lives, for some considerable way, and then they made a stop, and chose some of their stoutest men, and sent them back to hold the English Army in play[38] whilst the rest escaped. . . .

The first week of my being among them, I hardly ate any thing; the second week, I found my stomach grow very faint for want of something; and yet it was very hard to get down their filthy trash; but the third week, though I could think how formerly my stomach would turn against this or that, and I could starve and die before I could eat such things, yet they were sweet and savoury to my taste. I was at this time knitting a pair of white cotton stockings for my mistress; and had not yet wrought upon a Sabbath day; when the Sabbath came they bade me go to work; I told them it was the Sabbath-day, and desired them to let me rest, and told them I would do as much more to morrow; to which they answered me, they would break my face. And here I cannot but take notice of the strange providence of God in preserving the heathen: They were many hundreds, old and young, some sick, and some lame, many had Papooses at their backs, the greatest number at this time with us were Squaws, and they travelled with all they had, bag and baggage, and yet they got over this River aforesaid; and on Monday they set their Wigwams on fire, and away they went: On that very day came the English Army after them to this River, and saw the smoke of their Wigwams, and yet this River put a stop to them. God did not give them courage or activity to go over after us; we were not ready for so great a mercy as victory and deliverance; if we had been, God would have found out a way for the English to have passed this River, as well as for the Indians with their Squaws and Children, and all their Luggage. *Oh that my People had hearkened to me, and Israel had walked in my ways, I should soon have subdued their Enemies, and turned my hand against their Adversaries,* Psalms 81:13–14.

The sixth Remove[39]

On Monday (as I said) they set their Wigwams on fire, and went away. It was a cold morning, and before us there was a great Brook with ice on it; some waded through it, up to the knees and higher, but others went till they came to a Beaver-dam, and I amongst them, where through the good providence of God, I did not wet my foot. I went along that day mourning and

[35]An aromatic, stimulating medicine or liquor.

[36]Across Miller's (Baquaug) River at Orange, Massachusetts.

[37]The colonial military force created during King Philip's War. The unit pursuing Rowlandson's captors was composed of militia men from Massachusetts and Connecticut.

[38]Engaged in battle. [39]To encampment near Northfield, Massachusetts.

lamenting, leaving farther my own Country, and travelling into the vast and howling Wilderness, and I understood something of Lot's Wife's Temptation, when she looked back:[40] we came that day to a great Swamp, by the side of which we took up our lodging that night. When I came to the brow of the hill, that looked toward the Swamp, I thought we had been come to a great Indian Town (though there were none but our own Company). The Indians were as thick as the trees: it seemed as if there had been a thousand Hatchets going at once: if one looked before one, there was nothing but Indians, and behind one, nothing but Indians, and so on either hand, I my self in the midst, and no Christian soul near me, and yet how hath the Lord preserved me in safety? Oh the experience that I have had of the goodness of God, to me and mine!

The seventh Remove[41]

After a restless and hungry night there, we had a wearisome time of it the next day. The Swamp by which we lay, was, as it were, a deep Dungeon, and an exceeding high and steep hill before it. Before I got to the top of the hill, I thought my heart and legs and all would have broken, and failed me. What through faintness, and soreness of body, it was a grievous day of travel to me. As we went along, I saw a place where English Cattle had been; that was comfort to me, such as it was: Quickly after that we came to an English Path, which so took with me, that I thought I could have freely lain down and died. That day, a little after noon, we came to Squaukheag, where the Indians quickly spread themselves over the deserted English Fields, gleaning what they could find; some pickt up ears of Wheat that were crickled[42] down, some found ears of Indian Corn, some found Ground-nuts,[43] and others sheaves of Wheat that were frozen together in the shock, and went to threshing of them out. My self got two ears of Indian Corn, and whilst I did but turn my back, one of them was stolen from me, which much troubled me. There came an Indian to them at that time, with a basket of Horse-liver. I asked him to give me a piece: What, says he, can you eat Horse-liver? I told him, I would try, if he would give a piece, which he did, and I laid it on the coals to roast; but before it was half ready they got half of it away from me, so that I was fain to take the rest and eat it as it was, with the blood about my mouth, and yet a savoury bit it was to me: *For to the hungry Soul every bitter thing is sweet.*[44] A solemn sight methought it was, to see Fields of wheat and Indian Corn forsaken and spoiled; and the remainders of them to be food for our merciless Enemies. That night we had a mess of wheat for our Supper.

The eighth Remove[45]

On the morrow morning we must go over the River, *i.e.* Connecticut, to meet with King Philip;[46] two Canoes full, they had carried over, the next Turn I my self was to go; but as my foot was upon the Canoe to step in, there

[40]As Lot and his wife fled the condemned city of Sodom, Lot's wife, in violation of the command of the Lord, looked backward at the city and was turned into a pillar of salt. Genesis 19:26.

[41]To Squakeag, near Northfield, Massachusetts. [42]Trampled.

[43]A flowering legume with an edible tuber, also known as potato bean. [44]Proverbs 27:7.

[45]To South Vernon, Vermont.

[46]Metacomet, son of Massasoit and chief of the Wampanoag. He was leader of the Indian tribes in King Philip's War against the New England Colonies. Colonists had named him "King Philip" for his proud manner. He was killed in August 1676.

was a sudden out-cry among them, and I must step back; and instead of going over the River, I must go four or five miles up the River farther Northward. Some of the Indians ran one way, and some another. The cause of this rout was, as I thought, their espying some English Scouts, who were thereabout. In this travel up the River, about noon the Company made a stop, and sat down; some to eat, and others to rest them. As I sat amongst them, musing of things past, my Son Joseph unexpectedly came to me: we asked of each other's welfare, bemoaning our dolefull condition, and the change that had come upon us. We had Husband and Father, and Children, and Sisters, and Friends, and Relations, and House, and Home, and many Comforts of this Life: but now we may say, as Job, *Naked came I out of my Mother's Womb, and naked shall I return: The Lord gave, and the Lord hath taken away, Blessed be the Name of the Lord*. . . .[47] We travelled on till night; and in the morning, we must go over the River to Philip's Crew. When I was in the Canoe, I could not but be amazed at the numerous crew of Pagans that were on the Bank on the other side. When I came ashore, they gathered all about me, I sitting alone in the midst: I observed they asked one another questions, and laughed, and rejoiced over their Gains and Victories. Then my heart began to fail; and I fell a weeping which was the first time, to my remembrance, that I wept before them. Although I had met with so much Affliction, and my heart was many times ready to break, yet could I not shed one tear in their sight, but rather had been all this while in a maze, and like one astonished; but now I may say as, Psalms 137:1, *By the Rivers of Babylon, there we sat down: yea, we wept when we remembered Zion*. There one of them asked me, why I wept, I could hardly tell what to say; yet I answered, they would kill me: No, said he, none will hurt you. Then came one of them and gave me two spoon-fulls of Meal to comfort me, and another gave me half a pint of Peas, which was more worth than many Bushels at another time. Then I went to see King Philip; he bade me come in and sit down, and asked me whether I would smoke it (a usual Complement nowadays amongst Saints and Sinners) but this no way suited me. For though I had formerly used Tobacco, yet I had left it ever since I was first taken. It seems to be a Bait, the Devil lays to make men loose their precious time: I remember with shame, how formerly, when I had taken two or three pipes, I was presently ready for another, such a bewitching thing it is: But I thank God, he has now given me power over it; surely there are many who may be better employed than to lie sucking a stinking Tobacco-pipe.

. . .

The twelfth Remove[48]

It was upon a Sabbath-day-morning, that they prepared for their Travel. This morning I asked my master whether he would sell me to my Husband; he answered me *Nux*,[49] which did much to rejoice my spirit. My mistress, before we went, was gone to the burial of a Papoos, and returning, she found me sitting and reading in my Bible; she snatched it hastily out of my hand, and threw it out of doors; I ran out and catcht it up, and put it into my pocket, and never let her see it afterward. Then they packed up their things to be gone, and gave me my load: I complained it was too heavy, whereupon she gave me a slap in the face, and bade me go; I lifted up my heart to God,

[47]Job 1:21. [48]From encampment near Chesterfield, New Hampshire. [49]"Yes."

hoping the Redemption was not far off, and the rather because their insolency grew worse and worse.

But the thoughts of my going homeward (for so we bent our course) much cheered my Spirit, and made my burden seem light, and almost nothing at all. . . .

The thirteenth Remove[50]

Instead of going toward the Bay, which was that I desired, I must go with them five or six miles down the River into a mighty Thicket of Brush, where we abode almost a fortnight. Here one asked me to make a shirt for her Papoos,[51] for which she gave me a mess of Broth, which was thickened with meal made of the Bark of a Tree, and to make it the better, she had put into it about a handfull of Peas and a few roasted Ground-nuts. I had not seen my son a pretty while, and here was an Indian of whom I made inquiry after him, and asked him when he saw him: He answered me, that [at] such a time his master roasted him, and that himself did eat a piece of him, as big as his two fingers, and that he was very good meat: But the Lord upheld my Spirit, under this discouragement; and I considered their horrible addictedness to lying, and that there is not one of them that makes the least conscience of speaking of truth. In this place, on a cold night, as I lay by the fire, I removed a stick that kept the heat from me, a Squaw moved it down again, at which I lookt up, and she threw a handfull of ashes in mine eyes; I thought I should have been quite blinded, and [should] have never seen more; but lying down, the water run out of my eyes, and carried the dirt with it, [so] that by morning, I recovered my sight again. Yet upon this, and the like occasions, I hope it is not too much to say with Job, *Have pitty upon me, have pitty upon me, O ye my Friends, for the Hand of the Lord has touched me.*[52]

. . .

Then my Son came to see me, and I asked his master to let him stay a while with me, that I might comb his head, and look over him, for he was almost overcome with lice. He told me, when I had done, that he was very hungry, but I had nothing to relieve him but bid him go into the Wigwams as he went along, and see if he could get any thing among them. Which he did, and it seemes tarried a little too long; for his Master was angry with him, and beat him, and then sold him. Then he came running to tell me he had a new Master, and that he had given him some Groundnuts already. Then I went along with him to his new Master who told me he loved him, and he should not want. So his Master carried him away, and I never saw him afterward, till I saw him at Pascataqua in Portsmouth.[53]

. . .

[50]To Hinsdale, New Hampshire, near the Connecticut River.

[51]Before the coming of European explorers and traders, North American Indians lacked woven cloth, and as late as the 17th century they largely remained unskilled in weaving and sewing. Thus Rowlandson's ability to sew and knit was highly valued.

[52]Job 19:21. [53]Indian village near Portsmouth, New Hampshire.

The fourteenth Remove[54]

Now must we pack up and be gone from this Thicket, bending our course toward the Bay-towns, I having nothing to eat by the way this day, but a few crumbs of Cake, that an Indian gave my girl the same day we were taken. She gave it me, and I put it in my pocket; there it lay, till it was so mouldy (for want of good baking) that one could not tell what it was made of; it fell all to crumbs, and grew so dry and hard, that it was like little flints; and this refreshed me many times, when I was ready to faint. It was in my thoughts when I put it into my mouth, that if ever I returned, I would tell the World what a blessing the Lord gave to such mean food. As we went along, they killed a Deer, with a young one in her; they gave me a piece of the Fawn, and it was so young and tender, that one might eat the bones as well as the flesh, and yet I thought it very good. When night came on we sat down; it rained, but they quickly got up a Bark Wigwam, where I lay dry that night. I looked out in the morning, and many of them had lain in the rain all night, I saw by their Reeking.[55] Thus the Lord dealt mercifully with me many times, and I fared better than many of them. In the morning they took the blood of the Deer, and put it into the Paunch,[56] and so boiled it; I could eat nothing of that, though they ate it sweetly. And yet they were so nice[57] in other things, that when I had fetcht water, and had put the Dish I dipt the water with, into the Kettle of water which I brought, they would say, they would knock me down; for they said it was a sluttish trick.

The fifteenth Remove

We went on our Travel. I having got one handfull of Ground-nuts, for my support that day, they gave me my load, and I went on cheerfully (with the thoughts of going homeward) having my burden more on my back than my spirit: We came to Baquaug River again that day, near which we abode a few days. Sometimes one of them would give me a Pipe, another a little Tobacco, another a little Salt: which I would change for a little Victuals. I cannot but think what a Wolvish appetite persons have in a starving condition; for many times when they gave me that which was hot, I was so greedy, that I would burn my mouth, [so] that it would trouble me hours after, and yet I would quickly do the same again. And after I was thoroughly hungry, I was never again satisfied. For though sometimes it fell out, that I got enough, and did eat till I could eat no more, yet I was as unsatisfied as I was when I began. And now could I see that Scripture verified (there being many Scriptures which we do not take notice of, or understand till, we are afflicted) Micah 6:14, *Thou shalt eat and not be satisfied.* Now might I see more than ever before, the miseries that sin hath brought upon us: Many times I should be ready to run out against the Heathen, but the Scripture would quiet me again, Amos 3:6, *Shall there be evil in the City, and the Lord hath not done it?* The Lord help me to make a right improvment of His Word, and that I might learn that great lesson, Micah, 6:8–9, *He hath showed thee (Oh Man) what is good, and what doth the Lord require of thee, but to do justly, and love mercy, and walk humbly with thy God? Hear ye the rod, and who hath appointed it.*

[54]On removes fourteen to twenty, the captives generally retraced their route, ending at an encampment at Wachusett Lake, Princeton, Massachusetts, where Mary Rowlandson was ransomed. Subsequently, she was reunited with the surviving members of her family.

[55]Giving off vapor, steaming. [56]Stomach. [57]Fastidious.

The sixteenth Remove

We began this Remove with wading over Baquag River: The water was up to the knees, and the stream very swift, and so cold that I thought it would have cut me in sunder. I was so weak and feeble, that I reeled as I went along, and thought there I must end my days at last, after my bearing and getting through so many difficulties; the Indians stood laughing to see me staggering along: But in my distress the Lord gave me experience of the truth and goodness of that promise, Isaiah 43:2, *When thou passest through the Waters, I will be with thee, and through the Rivers, they shall not overflow thee.* Then I sat down to put on my stockings and shoes, with the teares running down mine eyes, and many sorrowfull thoughts in my heart, but I got up to go along with them. Quickly there came up to us an Indian, who informed them, that I must go to Wachusit to my master, for there was a Letter come from the Council to the Sagamores, about redeeming[58] the Captives, and that there would be another in fourteen days, and that I must be there ready. My heart was so heavy before that I could scarce speak or go in the path, and yet now so light, that I could run. My strength seemed to come again, and recruit[59] my feeble knees, and aching heart: yet it pleased them to go but one mile that night, and there we stayed two days. In that time came a company of Indians to us, near thirty, all on horseback. My heart skipt within me, thinking they had been English-men at the first sight of them, for they were dressed in English Apparel, with Hats, white Neckcloths, and Sashes about their waists, and Ribbons upon their shoulders; but when they came near, their was a vast difference between the lovely faces of Christians and the foul looks of those Heathens, which much damped my spirit again.

The eighteenth Remove

We took up our packs and along we went, but a wearisome day I had of it. As we went along I saw an English-man stript naked and lying dead upon the ground, but knew not who it was. Then we came to another Indian Town, where we stayed all night. In this Town there were four English Children, Captives; and one of them my own Sister's [child]. I went to see how she did, and she was well, considering her Captive-condition. I would have tarried that night with her, but they that owned her would not suffer it. Then I went into another Wigwam, where they were boiling Corn and Beans, which was a lovely sight to see, but I could not get a taste thereof. Then I went to another Wigwam, where there were two of the English Children; the Squaw was boiling Horse's feet; then she cut me off a little piece, and gave one of the English Children a piece also. Being very hungry I had quickly eat up mine, but the Child could not bite it, it was so tough and sinewy, but lay sucking, gnawing, chewing and slabbering of it in the mouth and hand; then I took it of the Child, and eat it my self, and savoury it was to my taste. Then I may say as Job, 6:7, *The things that my soul refused to touch, are as my sorrowfull meat.* Thus the Lord made that pleasant refreshing, which another time would have been an abomination. Then I went home to my mistress's Wigwam; and they told me I disgraced my master with begging, and if I did so any more, they would knock me in head: I told them, they had as good knock me in head as starve me to death.

[58]Ransoming. [59]Refresh, restore.

The nineteenth Remove

They said, when we went out, that we must travel to Wachuset this day. But a bitter weary day I had of it, travelling now three days together, without resting any day between. At last, after many weary steps, I saw Wachuset hills, but many miles off. Then we came to a great Swamp; through which we travelled, up to the knees in mud and water, which was heavy going to one tired before. Being almost spent, I thought I should have sunk down at last, and never got out; but I may say, as in Psalms 94:18, *When my foot slipped, thy mercy, O Lord, held me up.* Going along, having indeed my life, but little spirit, Philip, who was in the Company, came up and took me by the hand, and said, Two weeks more and you shall be Mistress again. I asked him, if he spoke true? He answered, Yes, and quickly you shall come to your master again, who had been gone from us three weeks. After many weary steps we came to Wachuset, where he was; and glad I was to see him. He asked me, When I washt me? I told him not this month, then he fetcht me some water himself, and bid me wash, and gave me the Glass to see how I lookt, and bid his Squaw give me something to eat; so she gave me a mess of Beans and meat, and a little Ground-nut Cake. I was wonderfully revived with this favour showed me, Psalms 106:46. *He made them also to be pittied, of all those that carried them Captives.*

My master had three Squaws, living sometimes with one, and sometimes with another one, this old Squaw, at whose Wigwam I was, and with whom my Master had been those three weeks. Another was Weetamoo with whom I had lived and served all this while: A severe and proud Dame she was, bestowing every day in dressing her self neat as much time as any of the Gentry of the land, powdering her hair, and painting her face, going with Neck-laces, with Jewels in her ears, and Bracelets upon her hands: When she had dressed her self, her work was to make Girdles of Wampum and Beads. The third Squaw was a younger one, by whom he had two Papooses. By that time I was refresht by the old Squaw, with whom my master was, Weetamoo's Maid came to call me home, at which I fell a weeping. Then the old Squaw told me, to encourage me, that if I wanted victuals, I should come to her, and that I should lie there in her Wigwam. Then I went with the maid, and quickly came again and lodged there. The Squaw laid a Mat under me, and a good Rugg over me; the first time I had any such kindness showed me. I understood that Weetamoo thought, that if she should let me go and serve with the old Squaw, she would be in danger to lose, not only my service, but the redemption-pay also. And I was not a little glad to hear this, being by it raised in my hopes that in God's due time there would be an end of this sorrowfull hour. Then came an Indian, and asked me to knit him three pair of Stockings, for which I had a Hat, and a silk Handkerchief. Then another asked me to make her a shift,[60] for which she gave me an Apron.

Then came Tom and Peter,[61] with the second Letter from the Council, about the Captives. Though they were Indians, I got them by the hand, and burst out into tears; my heart was so full that I could not speak to them; but recovering my self, I asked them how my husband did, and all my friends and acquaintances? They said, They are all very well but melancholy. They brought me two Biskets, and a pound of Tobacco. The Tobacco I quickly

[60]Undergarment, slip.

[61]Tom Dublet and Peter Conway, Christian Indians who negotiated for the release of the captives.

gave away; when it was all gone, one asked me to give him a pipe of Tobacco. I told him it was all gone; then began he to rant and threaten. I told him when my Husband came I would give him some: Hang him [as a] Rogue (says he) I will knock out his brains, if he comes here. And then again, in the same breath they would say that if there should come an hundred without Guns, they would do them no hurt. So unstable and like mad men they were. So that fearing the worst, I durst not send to my Husband, though there were some thoughts of his coming to Redeem and fetch me, not knowing what might follow. For there was little more trust to them than to the master they served. When the Letter was come, the Sagamores met to consult about the Captives, and called me to them to enquire how much my husband would give to redeem me, when I came I sat down among them, as I was wont to do, as their manner is: Then they bade me stand up, and said, they were the General Court.[62] They bade me speak what I thought he would give. Now knowing that all we had was destroyed by the Indians, I was in a great strait: I thought if I should speak of but a little, it would be slighted, and hinder the matter; if of a great sum, I knew not where it would be procured; yet at a venture, I said Twenty pounds, yet desired them to take less; but they would not hear of that, but sent that message to Boston, that for Twenty pounds I should be redeemed. It was a Praying-Indian that wrote their Letter for them. There was another Praying Indian, who told me, that he had a brother that would not eat Horse, his conscience was so tender and scrupulous (though as large as hell, for the destruction of poor Christians). Then he said, he read that Scripture to him, 2 Kings 6:25, *There was a famine in Samaria, and behold they besieged it, untill an ass's head was sold for fourscore pieces of silver, and the fourth part of a kab of dove's dung, for five pieces of silver.* He expounded this place to his brother, and showed him that it was lawfull to eat that in a Famine which is not at another time. And now, says he, he will eat Horse with any Indian of them all. . . .

The twentieth Remove

It was their usual manner to remove, when they had done any mischief, lest they should be found out; and so they did at this time. We went about three or four miles, and there they built a great Wigwam, big enough to hold an hundred Indians, which they did in preparation to a great day of Dancing. . . . My Sister being not far from the place where we now were, and hearing that I was here, desired her master to let her come and see me, and he was willing to it, and would go with her; but she being ready before him, told him she would go before, and was come within a Mile or two of the place. Then he overtook her, and began to rant as if he had been mad, and made her go back again in the Rain, so that I never saw her till I saw her in Charlestown. But the Lord requited many of their ill doings, for this Indian, her Master, was hanged afterward at Boston. The Indians now began to come from all quarters, against[63] their merry dancing day. Among some of them came one Goodwife Kettle: I told her my heart was so heavy that it was ready to break:

[62]I.e., the Indian counterpart of the General Assembly (legislature) of the Massachusetts Bay Colony.

[63]To prepare for.

so is mine too said she, but yet said, I hope we shall hear some good news shortly. I could hear how earnestly my Sister desired to see me, and I as earnestly desired to see her; and yet neither of us could get an opportunity. My Daughter was also now about a mile off, and I had not seen her in nine or ten weeks, as I had not seen my Sister since our first taking. I earnestly desired them to let me go and see them: Yea, I intreated, begged, and perswaded them but to let me see my Daughter; and yet so hard hearted were they, that they would not suffer it. They made use of their tyrannical power whilst they had it; but through the Lord's wonderfull mercy, their time was now but short.

On a Sabbath day, the Sun being about an hour high in the afternoon, came Mr. John Hoar (the Council permitting him, and his own foreward[64] spirit inclining him) together with the two forementioned Indians, Tom and Peter, with their third Letter from the Council. When they came near, I was abroad; though I saw them not, they presently called me in and bade me sit down and not stir. Then they catched up their Guns, and away they ran, as if an Enemy had been at hand; and the Guns went off apace. I manifested some great trouble, and they asked me what was the matter? I told them, I thought they had killed the English-man (for they had in the mean time informed me that an English-man was come); they said, No; They shot over his Horse and under, and before his Horse; and they pusht him this way and that way, at their pleasure: showing what they could do: Then they let them come to their Wigwams. I begged of them to let me see the English-man, but they would not. But there was I fain to sit their pleasure. When they had talked their fill with him, they suffered me to go to him. We asked each other of our welfare, and how my Husband did, and all my Friends? He told me they were all well, and would be glad to see me. Amongst other things which my Husband sent me, there came a pound of Tobacco: which I sold for nine shillings in Money: for many of the Indians for want of Tobacco, smoked Hemlock, and Ground-Ivy. It was a great mistake in any, who thought I sent for Tobacco, for through the favour of God, that desire was overcome. I now asked them, whether I should go home with Mr. Hoar? They answered No, one and another of them, and it being night, we lay down with that answer; in the morning, Mr Hoar invited the Sagamores[65] to Dinner; but when we went to get it ready, we found that they had stollen the greatest part of the Provision Mr. Hoar had brought, out of his Bags, in the night. And we may see the wonderfull power of God, in that one passage, in that when there was such a great number of the Indians together, and so greedy of a little good food, and no English there but Mr. Hoar and my self, that there they did not knock us in the head, and take what we had, there being not only some Provision but also Trading-cloth, a part of the twenty pounds agreed upon: But instead of doing us any mischief, they seemed to be ashamed of the fact, and said, it were some Matchit[66] Indian that did it. Oh, that we could believe that there is no thing too hard for God! God showed his Power over the Heathen in this, as he did over the hungry Lions when Daniel was cast into the Den. . . .[67]

[64]Zealous. He came to bargain for Rowlandson's release. [65]Indian leaders. [66]Bad.
[67]The story of Daniel in the lion's den is told in Daniel 6:1–29.

On Tuesday morning they called their General Court (as they call it) to consult and determine, whether I should go home or no: And they all as one man did seemingly consent to it, that I should go home; except Philip, who would not come among them.

. . .

And now God hath granted me my desire. O the wonderfull power of God that I have seen, and the experience that I have had: I have been in the midst of those roaring Lions, and Savage Bears, that feared neither God, nor Man, nor the Devil, by night and day, alone and in company, sleeping all sorts together, and yet not one of them ever offered me the least abuse of unchastity to me, in word or action. Though some[68] are ready to say [that] I speak it for my own credit; But I speak it in the presence of God, and to his Glory. God's Power is as great now, and as sufficient to save, as when he preserved Daniel in the Lions' Den; or the three Children in the fiery Furnace.[69] I may well say as his Psalms 107:1, *Oh give thanks unto the Lord for he is good, for his mercy endureth for ever.* Let the Redeemed of the Lord say so, whom he hath redeemed from the hand of the Enemy, especially that I should come away in the midst of so many hundreds of Enemies quietly and peaceably, and not a Dog moving his tongue. So I took my leave of them, and in coming along my heart melted into tears, more than all the while I was with them, and I was almost swallowed up with the thoughts that ever I should go home again. About the Sun going down, Mr. Hoar, and my self, and the two Indians came to Lancaster, and a solemn sight it was to me. There had I lived many comfortable years amongst my Relations and Neighbours, and now not one Christian to be seen, nor one house left standing. We went [farther] on to a Farm house that was yet standing, where we lay all night; and a comfortable lodging we had, though nothing but straw to lie on. The Lord preserved us in safety that night, and raised us up again in the morning, and carried us along, [so] that before noon we came to Concord. Now was I full of joy, and yet not without sorrow; joy to see such a lovely sight, so many Christians together, and some of them my Neighbours: There I met with my Brother, and my Brother in Law, who asked me, if I knew where his Wife was? Poor heart! He had helped to bury her, and knew it not. She, being shot down by the house, was partly burnt, so that those who were at Boston at [the time of] the desolation of the Town, and came back afterward, and buried the dead, did not know her. Yet I was not without sorrow, to think how many were looking and longing, and my own Children amongst the rest, to enjoy that deliverance that I had now received, and I did not know whether ever I should see them again. Being recruited[70] with food and raiment we went to Boston that day, where I met with my dear Husband, but the thoughts of our dear Children, one being dead, and the other we could not tell where, abated our comfort each to other. I was not before so much hem'd in with the merciless and cruel Heathen, but now as

[68]I.e., those who believed that Indians sexually abused female captives.

[69]Shadrach, Meshach, and Abednego, in Daniel 3:13–30.

[70]Refreshed.

much with pittiful, tender-hearted and compassionate Christians. In that poor, and distressed, and beggerly condition I was received in, I was kindly entertained in severall Houses; so much love I received from several (some of whom I knew, and others I knew not) that I am not capable to declare it. But the Lord knows them all by name: The Lord reward them seven fold into their bosoms of his spirituals, for their temporals.[71]

. . .

I have seen the extreme vanity of this World: One hour I have been in health, and wealth, wanting nothing: But the next hour in sickness and wounds, and death, having nothing but sorrow and affliction.

Before I knew what affliction meant, I was ready sometimes to wish for it. When I lived in prosperity, having the comforts of the World about me, my relations by me, my Heart cheerfull, and taking little care for any thing; and yet seeing many, whom I preferred before my self, under many trials and afflictions, in sickness, weakness, poverty, losses, crosses, and cares of the World, I should be sometimes jealous lest I should not have my portion in this life, and that Scripture would come to my mind, Hebrews 12:6, *For whom the Lord loveth he chasteneth, and scourgeth every Son whom he receiveth.* But now I see the Lord had his time to scourge and chasten me. The portion of some is to have their afflictions by drops, now one drop and then another; but the dregs of the Cup, the Wine of astonishment, like a sweeping rain that leaveth no food,[72] did the Lord prepare to be my portion. Affliction I wanted, and affliction I had, full measure (I thought) pressed down and running over;[73] yet I see, when God calls a Person to any thing, and through ever so many difficulties, yet he is fully able to carry them through, and make them see, and say they have been gainers thereby. And I hope I can say in some measure, As David did, *It is good for me that I have been afflicted.*[74] The Lord hath showed me the vanity of these outward things. That they are the Vanity of vanities, and vexation of spirit; that they are but a shadow, a blast, a bubble, and things of no continuance. That we must rely on God himself, and our whole dependence must be upon him. If trouble from smaller matters begin to arise in me, I have something at hand to check my self with, and say, why am I troubled? It was but the other day that if I had had the world, I would have given it for my freedom, or to have been a Servant to a Christian. I have learned to look beyond present and smaller troubles, and to be quieted under them, as Moses said, Exodus 14:13, *Stand still and see the salvation of the Lord.*

1677 1682

[71]I.e., reward their acts of temporal (worldly) goodness with spiritual (divine) blessings.

[72]Quotations from Isaiah 51:17, Psalms 60:3, and Proverbs 28:3.

[73]A quotation from Luke 6:38.

[74]Psalms 119:17.

William Byrd II 1674–1744

William Byrd II has been described as one who "could never resist an old book, a young girl, or a fresh idea." He was an American plantation aristocrat, an ornamental English gentleman, an amateur explorer and scientist, and he was a literary dilettante who wrote some of the most urbane and witty prose of colonial America.

Half his life was spent abroad, yet it ended where it began, on a Virginia plantation near the site of Jamestown, the first permanent English settlement in America. In 1681 his father, a colonial aristocrat grown rich on tobacco and the Indian trade, sent his seven-year-old son to England for a public school education. Young Byrd later studied law at London's Inns of Court. He then traveled to Holland to learn principles of trade and commerce, and he served in England as the official colonial agent for Virginia. His interests in science brought him election to Britain's Royal Society. His wealth and polished manners allowed him to live the life of a London gallant. He filled his days and nights with wenching and gambling, and he cultivated friendships with nobles and such literary wits as the playwrights Congreve and Wycherley.

During his years in Virginia, Byrd was one of the Colony's ruling class, a member of the House of Burgesses and the Council of State. He founded the cities of Richmond and Petersburg. He supervised a vast plantation that grew to more than 179,000 acres. And he rebuilt his plantation home, Westover, into one of the country's finest Georgian manor houses. It still stands today as a monument to his artistic taste and to the elegance possible in eighteenth-century America.

Byrd's reputation as a man of letters rests on a scattering of literary works: satirical verse and character sketches, translations of the classics, and journals of his experiences in London and America. In 1709 he began a secret diary, written in a shorthand code. In it he recorded the squalor and richness of the eighteenth century. The diary reports the intimate details of his private life: his business deals; his eating, drinking, and tree planting; his political maneuverings; his trials with his spoiled and temperamental wife; his passions and infidelities; and his promptly broken vows of repentance and reformation.

Little of his writing was printed in his lifetime. The secret diaries were not decoded and published until the 1940s. Most of his neoclassic verses and character sketches were circulated only in manuscript among his friends, as was his History of the Dividing Line (1841), *the narrative of a 1728 expedition that traveled westward from the sea, over hills, rivers, and through the Great Dismal Swamp to survey the boundary line between Virginia and North Carolina.*

Byrd was a man of sophisticated taste and learning rare among the colonists. He read Greek, Hebrew, Latin, Italian, Dutch, and French, and his library of 3,600 volumes was, next to that of Cotton Mather in Boston, the largest in the American Colonies. His faith was a mingling of rationalism and religion in a mind free of the strained Calvinism of his New England contemporaries. He was an early example of the Enlightenment in America, a jovial man who tolerated the flaws of others just as he found the cause for his own failings not in original sin but in his "combustible nature." When he died in 1744, he was buried at Westover, where his epitaph records his honors rather than his piety. Byrd was a man of this world who was more regular in his rituals of classical reading and calisthenics than he was in his prayers. He found the models for his beliefs and his art not in the Bible but in Pope and Swift and in such pagan classical writers as Horace. And it was from Horace that he took his guide to life and the aptly ambiguous motto of his coat-of-arms: "No Guilt to Make One Pale."

FURTHER READING: R. Beatty, *William Byrd of Westover,* 1932, 1970; P. Marambaud, *William Byrd of Westover, 1674–1744,* 1971; *The London Diary (1717–1721) and Other Writings,* ed. L. Wright and M. Tinling, 1958; *The Correspondence of the Three William Byrds of Westover, Virginia, 1684–1776,* M. Tinling, 2 vols., 1977; K. Lockridge, *The Diary and Life of William Byrd II of Virginia,* 1987; R. Miller, *William Byrd II, 1674–1744,* 1988; R. Wenger, *The English Travels of Sir John Percival and William Byrd II,* 1989; *The Commonplace Book of William Byrd II,* ed. K. Berland, J. Gilliam, and K. Lockridge, 2001.

TEXTS: *The Secret Diary of William Byrd of Westover, 1709–1712,* ed. L. Wright and M. Tinling, 1941; *Another Secret Diary of William Byrd of Westover, 1739–1741,* ed. M. Woodfin and M. Tinling, 1942. Spelling, punctuation, and usage have been changed to conform more nearly to modern practice.

from *THE SECRET DIARY OF WILLIAM BYRD OF WESTOVER, 1709–1712*

[1709]

[February] 22. I rose at 7 o'clock and read a chapter in Hebrew and 200 verses in Homer's *Odyssey.* I said my prayers, and ate milk for breakfast. I threatened Anaka[1] with a whipping if she did not confess the intrigue between Daniel[2] and Nurse, but she prevented by a confession. I chided Nurse severely about it, but she denied, with an impudent face, protesting that Daniel only lay on the bed for the sake of the child. I ate nothing but beef for dinner. The Doctor went to Mr. Dick Cocke who was very dangerously sick. I said my prayers. I had good health, good thoughts, and good humor, thanks be to God Almighty.

[May] 21. I rose at 5 o'clock and read a chapter in Hebrew and some Greek in Josephus.[3] I said my prayers and ate milk for breakfast. I danced my dance.[4] About 12 o'clock Mr. Bland came from Williamsburg and brought me some letters from England and an account from Mr. Perry[5] of £7 a hogshead. He gave me the comfort that the skins and 350 hogsheads of tobacco were saved out of the *Perry and Lane* and some tobacco out of the other ships that were lost in the storm that happened in January last in England. The [hatter] brought some [hats] from Appomattox.[6] They both dined with us. I ate mutton and sallet[7] for dinner. In the afternoon we played at billiards. In the evening they went away and I took a walk about the plantation. I was out of humor at my wife's climbing over the pales[8] of the garden, now she is with child. I recommended my all to God. I had good health, good thoughts, and good humor, thanks be to God Almighty.

[1]A Negro houseservant.
[2]Daniel Wilkinson, Byrd's secretary.
[3]Flavius Josephus (c. 37–100), Jewish statesman and historian.
[4]Byrd's term for his daily calisthenics.
[5]Micajah Perry, a London merchant.
[6]A plantation on the nearby Appomattox River.
[7]Salad. [8]Fencing.

[October] 6. I rose at 6 o'clock and said my prayers and ate milk for breakfast. Then I proceeded to Williamsburg,[9] where I found all well. I went to the capitol where I sent for the wench to clean my room and when I came I kissed her and felt her, for which God forgive me. Then I went to see the President,[10] whom I found indisposed in his ears, I dined with him on beef on beef [*sic*]. Then we went to his house and played at piquet[11] where Mr. Clayton[12] came to us. We had much to do to get a bottle of French wine. About 10 o'clock I went to my lodgings. I had good health but wicked thoughts, God forgive me.

[October] 19. I rose at 6 o'clock and could not say my prayers because Colonel Bassett and Colonel Duke[13] came to see me. For the same reason I could read nothing. I ate milk for breakfast. About ten o'clock we went to court where a man was tried for ravishing a very homely woman. There were abundance of women in the gallery. I recommended myself to God before I went into court. About one o'clock I went to my chambers for a little refreshment. The court rose about 4 o'clock and I dined with the Council. I ate boiled beef for dinner. I gave myself the liberty to talk very lewdly, for which God forgive me. I said my prayers and had good health, good thoughts, and good humor, thanks be to God Almighty.

[October] 28. I rose at 6 o'clock but read nothing because Colonel Randolph[14] came to see me in the morning. I neglected to say my prayers but I ate milk for breakfast. . . . We went to court but much time was taken up in reading our letters and not much business was done. About 3 we rose and had a meeting of the College[15] in which it was agreed to turn Mr. Blackamore[16] out from being master of the school for being so great a sot. I ate boiled beef for dinner and in the evening went home after walking with Colonel Bassett. I said my prayers and had good health, good thoughts, and good humor, thanks be to God Almighty.

[October] 29. I rose at 6 o'clock and read nothing because the governors of the College were to meet again. However I said my prayers and ate milk for breakfast. When we met, Mr. Blackamore presented a petition in which he set forth that if the governors of the College would forgive him what was past, he would for the time to come mend his conduct. On which the governors at last agreed to keep him on, on trial, some time longer. . . .[17]

[November] 2. I rose at 6 o'clock and read a chapter in Hebrew and some Greek in Lucian. I said my prayers and ate milk for breakfast, and settled some accounts, and then went to court where we made an end of the business. We went to dinner about 4 o'clock and I ate boiled beef again. In the

[9]The colonial capital of Virginia. [10]Of the Council of State.

[11]A card game [12]John Clayton, attorney-general for Virginia.

[13]William Bassett and Henry Duke, members of the Council of State. [14]William Randolph.

[15]The College of William and Mary at Williamsburg. Byrd was one of its Overseers.

[16]The Reverend Arthur Blackamore, headmaster of the grammar school of William and Mary College, 1706–1716.

[17]After seven years of abstinence, frequently broken by drunken relapses, Blackamore was finally removed as master in 1716.

evening I went to Dr. [Barret's][18] where my wife came this afternoon. Here I found Mrs. Chiswell, my sister Custis,[19] and other ladies. We sat and talked till about 11 o'clock and then retired to our chambers. I played at [r-m][20] with Mrs. Chiswell and kissed her on the bed till she was angry and my wife also was uneasy about it, and cried as soon as the company was gone. I neglected to say my prayers, which I should not have done, because I ought to beg pardon for the lust I had for another man's wife. However I had good health, good thoughts, and good humor, thanks be to God Almighty.

[1710]

[February] 26. I rose at 8 o'clock and read nothing because of my company. I neglected to say my prayers, for which God forgive me. . . . In the afternoon we saw a good battle between a stallion and Robin[21] about the mare, but at last the stallion had the advantage and covered the mare three times. . . . My wife was out of humor with us for going to see so filthy a sight as the horse to cover the mare. In the evening we drank a bottle of wine and were very merry till 9 o'clock. I neglected to say my prayers but had good health, good thoughts, and good humor, thanks be to God Almighty.

[March] 31. I rose at 7 o'clock and read some Greek in bed. I said my prayers and ate milk for breakfast. Then about 8 o'clock we got a-horseback and rode to Mr. Harrison's[22] and found him very ill but sensible.[23] Here I met Mr. Bland,[24] who brought me several letters from England and among the rest two from Colonel Blakiston[25] who had endeavored to procure the government of Virginia for me at the price of £1,000 of my Lady Orkney[26] and that my Lord [agreed] but the Duke of Marlborough declared that no one but soldiers should have the government of a plantation, so I was disappointed. God's will be done. . . .

[July] 15. I rose at 5 o'clock and read two chapters in Hebrew and some Greek in Thucydides.[27] I said my prayers and ate milk and pears for breakfast. About 7 o'clock the negro boy [*or* Betty] that ran away was brought home. My wife against my will called little Jenny[28] to be burned with a hot iron, for which I quarreled with her. . . .

[July] 30. I rose at 5 o'clock. . . . I read two chapters in Hebrew and some Greek in Thucydides. I said my prayers and ate boiled milk for breakfast. I danced my dance. I read a sermon in Dr. Tillotson[29] and then took a little [nap]. I ate fish for dinner. In the afternoon my wife and I had a little quarrel which I reconciled with a flourish. Then she read a sermon in Dr.

[18]Possibly Charles Barret.

[19]Wife of Charles Chiswell, clerk of the General Court. Frances Custis, Byrd's sister-in-law.

[20]Byrd's original shorthand entry, the meaning of which remains unknown.

[21]The servant who tended Byrd's livestock. [22]Benjamin Harrison, Byrd's neighbor.

[23]Clearheaded. [24]Richard Bland, Byrd's neighbor

[25]Nathaniel Blakiston, Virginia's agent in England.

[26]Wife of George Hamilton, Earl of Orkney and Governor of Virginia (1704–1737). He remained in England, appointing lieutenant governors to rule in Virginia. On July 23, 1710, Alexander Spotswood received the appointment sought by Byrd.

[27]Greek historian (c. 460–400 B.C.). [28]A houseservant.

[29]John Tillotson (1630–1694), Archbishop of Canterbury and popular author of sermons.

Tillotson to me. It is to be observed that the flourish was performed on the billiard table. I read a little Latin. In the evening we took a walk about the plantation. I neglected to say my prayers but had good health, good thoughts, and good humor, thanks be to God. . . .

[December] 31. Some night this month I dreamed that I saw a flaming sword in the sky and called some company to see it but before they could come it was disappeared and about a week after my wife and I were walking and we discovered in the clouds a shining cloud exactly in the shape of a dart and seemed to be over my plantation but it soon disappeared likewise. Both these appearances seemed to foretell some misfortune to me which afterwards came to pass in the death of several of my negroes after a very unusual manner. My wife about two months since dreamed she saw an angel in the shape of a big woman who told her the time was altered and the seasons were changed and that several calamities would follow that confusion. God avert his judgment from this poor country.

[1711]

[February] 5. I rose about 8 o'clock and found my cold still worse. I said my prayers and ate milk and potatoes for breakfast. My wife and I quarreled about her pulling her brows.[30] She threatened she would not go to Williamsburg if she might not pull them; I refused, however, and got the better of her, and maintained my authority. . . .

[October] 21. I rose about 6 o'clock and we began to pack up our baggage in order to return. We drank chocolate with the Governor and about 10 o'-clock we took leave of the Nottoway town[31] and the Indian boys went away with us that were designed[32] for the College. The Governor made three proposals to the Tuscaroras:[33] that they would join with the English to cut off those Indians that had killed the people of Carolina, that they should have 40 shillings for every head they brought in of those guilty Indians and be paid the price of a slave for all they brought in alive, and that they should send one of the chief men's sons out of every town to the College. . . . About 4 we dined and I ate some boiled beef. My man's horse was lame for which he was let blood. At night I asked a negro girl to kiss me, and when I went to bed I was very cold because I pulled off my clothes after lying in them so long. I neglected to say my prayers but had good health, good thoughts, and good humor, thank God Almighty.

[1712]

[February] 5. I rose about 8 o'clock, my wife kept me so long in bed where I rogered her. I read nothing because I put my matters in order. I neglected to say my prayers but ate boiled milk for breakfast. My wife caused several of

[30]I.e., plucking her eyebrows.

[31]Of the Nottaway Indians in southeast Virginia.

[32]Selected.

[33]In the Tuscarora War (1711–1713) white settlements in North Carolina were attacked by southern tribes of Tuscaroras who were eventually defeated by an alliance of colonists and northern Tuscaroras.

the people to be whipped for their laziness. I settled accounts and put several matters in order till dinner. I ate some boiled beef. . . . At night I read some Latin. I said my prayers and had good health, good thoughts, and good humor, thank God Almighty. I rogered my wife again.

[May] 22. I rose about 6 o'clock and read two chapters in Hebrew and some Greek in Lucian. I said my prayers and ate boiled milk for breakfast. I danced my dance. It rained a little this morning. My wife caused Prue[34] to be whipped violently notwithstanding I desired not, which provoked me to have Anaka whipped likewise who had deserved it much more, on which my wife flew into such a passion that she hoped she would be revenged of me. I was moved very much at this but only thanked her for the present lest I should say things foolish in my passion. I wrote more accounts to go to England. My wife was sorry for what she had said and came to ask my pardon and I forgave her in my heart but seemed to resent, that she might be the more sorry for her folly. She ate no dinner nor appeared the whole day. I ate some bacon for dinner. In the afternoon I wrote two more accounts till the evening and then took a walk in the garden. I said my prayers and was reconciled to my wife and gave her a flourish in token of it. I had good health, good thoughts, but was a little out of humor, for which God forgive me.

Jonathan Edwards 1703–1758

Jonathan Edwards suffers notoriety today as the stereotype of the searing preacher of the American Great Awakening. He is pictured as a sulphurous theologian who taught complacent New Englanders to tremble at a wrathful God. Edwards' writings and his life fascinate poets, historians, and theologians, who find in him a convergence of the opposing doctrines of his time: on the one hand the Puritan ideas that man was sinful and God unknowable, and on the other hand the new rationalism of Locke and Newton who taught that man could be brought to goodness and could understand the mysteries of the universe.

Edwards was born in Connecticut in 1703, the only son in a family of eleven children. He was a brilliant and precocious child, educated at home by his minister father and strong-minded mother. In 1716, when he was thirteen, he entered Yale, and it was during his college years that he underwent the experience of religious conversion. After graduating from college, he briefly served as minister to a Presbyterian congregation in New York City, and for three years he worked as a tutor at Yale.

[34]A houseservant.

In 1727 he was appointed assistant minister to his grandfather, Solomon Stoddard, the renowned minister of the church at Northampton, Massachusetts. Two years later, when Stoddard died, Edwards became chief minister to the congregation, a position he filled for more than twenty years. At Northampton, he stirred his congregation into a series of intense religious "awakenings," revivals that achieved a climax during the Great Awakening, the eighteenth-century religious wildfire that burned the length of the Colonies, from New England to Georgia.

Stunned by the violence of the "awakening," Edwards warned against the excesses of emotion-torn congregations. He attacked the "beastly brayings" of revival preachers who stirred their listeners into shrieking mobs. But he also welcomed the Great Awakening as a way to lift religion out of the cool formalism into which Puritanism had declined. He sought to teach men and women their utter dependence on God and to arouse their yearning for an inner sense of God's spirit. Sermons like his "Sinners in the Hands of an Angry God" terrorized his listeners with visions of unregenerate men helplessly dangled over the pit of hell by a wrathful God, but Edwards intended not to dismay his listeners; rather he wanted to awaken in them a true sense of their sins and to prepare them to receive God's grace.

Edwards' preaching brought him renown throughout New England as the "greatest pillar in this part of Zion's building." "Sinners in the Hands of an Angry God" became the most famous (even notorious) sermon in American history. But the Great Awakening eventually collapsed from its own excesses and from the exhaustion of its believers. Doctrinal disputes arose from its ruins. At Northampton, arguments over church membership and public resentment of Edwards' indictments of backsliders created a furor that led to his dismissal.

In 1751 he left his congregation to become minister in Stockbridge, Massachusetts, an Indian mission village on the western frontier. There, retired from the controversies of Northampton (though new exasperations beset him in Stockbridge), he wrote his greatest and most complex philosophical works, including Freedom of the Will *(1754),* The Doctrine of Original Sin Defended *(1758), and* The Nature of True Virtue *(1765). They were strenuous efforts to show the relations between religious emotions and virtue, and they attempted to resolve the question of the existence of free will in a predestined universe. Publication of his great works brought Edwards renown far beyond the limits of New England. In 1758, he became the president of Princeton, but after less than two months in office, and while he was at the peak of his powers as a theologian, the "arrows of death" flew "unseen at noon," and he died abruptly from a smallpox inoculation that went bad.*

At Edwards' death, more than a thousand sermons, notebooks (including Images or Shadows of Divine Things*), and fragments of longer works still remained unpublished. But in his lifetime he had published nine major works and numerous sermons, written in close-textured, precise prose that qualifies him as the most sensitive stylist of American Puritanism. He became, aside from Benjamin Franklin, the most influential of all colonial American writers.*

Edwards was the country's greatest theologian, one of the most penetrating minds ever produced in America. His faith was both mystical and logical. He taught that the world was moving toward a millennium that would begin in America. He preached the power of God and the depravity of man, and he argued that God's grace might be recognized by the mystical, inward "supernatural sense" that God gave to regenerate believers.

Edwards was a brilliant anachronism who refurbished Calvinism, he thought, for a new life. But he demanded faith in divine omnipotence and in human limitation at a time when Americans were moving toward other beliefs. With the onset of the Enlightenment and the age of romanticism, the exaltation of man and the worship of nature became articles of faith. The power of Edwards' teaching declined. His words filled the shelves of libraries but no longer the minds of the people he had yearned to save. For his knowledge of the new science and the new psychology, for his awareness of a world lighted by Newton and revealed by Locke, Edwards has been called the first modern American. But as a relic of Puritanism, oppressed by the thunderbolts of God, he remains America's last great medieval man.

FURTHER READING: *The Works of Jonathan Edwards,* ed. J. Smith et al., 23 vols. to date, 1994; *Jonathan Edwards' Scientific and Philosophical Writing,* ed. W. Anderson, 1980; C. Cherry, *The Theology of Jonathan Edwards,* 1990; G. McDermott, *One Holy and Happy Society, The Public Theology of Jonathan Edwards,* 1992; S. Yarbrough and J. Adams, *Delightful Conviction, Jonathon Edwards and the Rhetoric of Conversion,* 1993; S. Daniel, *The Philosophy of Jonathan Edwards,* 1994; *A Jonathan Edwards Reader,* ed. J. Smith and H. Stout, 1995; J. Conforti, *Jonathan Edwards, Religious Tradition, and American Culture,* 1996; L. Chai, *Jonathan Edwards and the Limits of Enlightenment Philosophy,* 1998; G. McDermott, *Jonathan Edwards Confronts the Gods,* 2000; S. Nichols, *Jonathan Edwards, A Guided Tour of His Life and Thought,* 2001; R. Brown, *Jonathan Edwards and the Bible,* 2002; G. Marsden, *Jonathan Edwards, A Life,* 2003.

TEXT: *Images or Shadows of Divine Things,* ed. P. Miller, 1948. Other texts are from *The Works of President Edwards,* ed. S. Dwight, 10 vols., 1829–1830. Spelling, punctuation, and usage have been changed to conform more nearly to modern practice.

SARAH PIERREPONT[1]

They say there is a young lady [in New Haven] who is loved of that Great Being, who made and rules the world; and that there are certain seasons in which this Great Being, in some way or other invisible, comes to her and fills her mind with exceeding sweet delight; and that she hardly cares for anything, except to meditate on Him; that she expects after a while to be received up where He is, to be raised up out of the world and caught up into heaven, being assured that He loves her too well to let her remain at a distance from Him always. There she is to dwell with Him, and to be ravished with His love and delight forever. Therefore, if you present all the world before her, with the richest of its treasures, she disregards it, and cares not for it, and is unmindful of any pain or affliction. She has a strange sweetness in her mind and singular purity in her affections; is most just and conscientious in all her conduct; and you could not persuade her to do anything wrong or sinful, if you would give her all the world, lest she should offend this Great Being. She is of a wonderful sweetness, calmness, and universal benevolence of mind, especially after this Great God has manifested Himself to her mind. She will sometimes go about from place to place, singing sweetly; and seems to be always full of joy and pleasure; and no one knows for what. She loves to be alone, walking in the fields and groves, and seems to have someone invisible always conversing with her.

1723 1829

[1]Edwards' future wife. At the time he wrote this brief tribute, Edwards was twenty and Sarah Pierrepont thirteen. They married four years later (1727).

SINNERS IN THE HANDS OF AN ANGRY GOD[1]

Deuteronomy 32:35.—*Their foot shall slide in due time.*[2]

In this verse is threatened the vengeance of God on the wicked unbelieving Israelites, that were God's visible people, and lived under means of grace;[3] and that—not withstanding all God's wonderful works that He had wrought towards that people—yet remained, as is expressed [in] verse 28,[4] void of counsel, having no understanding in them; and that, under all the cultivations of heaven, brought forth bitter and poisonous fruit, as [seen] in the two verses next preceding the text.[5]

The expression that I have chosen for my text, *their foot shall slide in due time,* seems to imply the following things relating to the punishment and destruction that these wicked Israelites were exposed to.

1. That they are always exposed to *destruction,* as one that stands or walks in slippery places is always exposed to fall. This is implied in the manner of their destruction's coming upon them, being represented by their foot's sliding. The same is expressed, Psalm 73:18: "Surely thou didst set them in slippery places: thou castedst them down into destruction."

2. It implies that they were always exposed to sudden, unexpected destruction. As he that walks in slippery places is every moment liable to fall, he cannot foresee one moment whether he shall stand or fall the next; and when he does fall, he falls at once, without warning, which is also expressed in that Psalm 73:18–19: "Surely thou didst set them in slippery places: thou castedst them down into destruction. How are they brought into desolation as in a moment."

3. Another thing implied is that they are liable to fall of *themselves,* without being thrown down by the hand of another, as he that stands or walks on slippery ground needs nothing but his own weight to throw him down.

4. That the reason why they are not fallen already, and do not fall now, is only that God's appointed time is not come. For it is said that when that due time or appointed time comes, *their foot shall slide.* Then they shall be left to fall, as they are inclined by their own weight. God will not hold them up in

[1]In 1741, in the midst of the Great Awakening, Edwards delivered this, his most famous sermon. His description of the impending and awesome wrath of an inscrutable and arbitrary God and the exquisite tortures to be suffered by men and women was meant to destroy the religious complacency of his audience, the "loose and indolent" congregation at Enfield, Connecticut. Witnesses recorded that his words, spoken with dramatic calmness and restraint, brought comfort to some of his listeners but roused others to shrieks, groans, and writhing and left them "bowed down with awful conviction of their sin and danger."

[2]The complete verse from which Edwards took the brief "text" for his sermon reads: "To me belongeth vengeance, and recompence; their foot shall slide in due time: for the day of their calamity is at hand, and the things that shall come upon them make haste." Edwards' references to Deuteronomy are drawn from Chapter 32 in which Moses speaks God's words of warning to the Israelites and exhorts them to obey God's commands lest He forsake and destroy them.

[3]The Decalogue, or Ten Commandments, under which the Israelites were to live and thereby remain God's chosen people.

[4]"They are a nation void of counsel, neither is there any understanding in them."

[5]"For their vine is the vine of Sodom and of the fields of Gomorrah: their grapes are grapes of gall, their clusters are bitter: Their wine is the poison of dragons, and the cruel venom of asps. Is not this laid up in stores with me, and sealed up among my treasures?" Deuteronomy 32:32–34.

these slippery places any longer but will let them go; and then, at that very instant, they shall fall into destruction; as he that stands on such slippery declining ground on the edge of a pit that he cannot stand alone, when he is let go he immediately falls and is lost.

The observation from the words that I would now insist upon is this.

There is nothing that keeps wicked men at any one moment out of hell, but the mere pleasure of God.

By the *mere* pleasure of God, I mean His *sovereign* pleasure, His arbitrary will, restrained by no obligation, hindered by no manner of difficulty, any more than if nothing else but God's mere will had in the least degree, or in any respect whatsoever, any hand in the preservation of wicked men one moment.

The truth of this observation may appear by the following considerations.

1. There is no want of *power* in God to cast wicked men into hell at any moment. Men's hands cannot be strong when God rises up: the strongest have no power to resist Him, nor can any deliver[6] out of His hands.

He is not only able to cast wicked men into hell, but He can most easily do it. Sometimes an earthly prince meets with a great deal of difficulty to subdue a rebel that has found means to fortify himself and has made himself strong by the number of his followers. But it is not so with God. There is no fortress that is any defense against the power of God. Though hand join in hand, and vast multitudes of God's enemies combine and associate themselves, they are easily broken in pieces; they are as great heaps of light chaff before the whirlwind, or large quantities of dry stubble before devouring flames. We find it easy to tread on and crush a worm that we see crawling on the earth; so it is easy for us to cut or singe a slender thread that anything hangs by; thus easy is it for God, when He pleases, to cast his enemies down to hell. What are we that we should think to stand before Him, at whose rebuke the earth trembles and before Whom the rocks are thrown down![7]

2. They *deserve* to be cast into hell; so that divine justice never stands in the way, it makes no objection against God's using His power at any moment to destroy them. Yea, on the contrary, justice calls aloud for an infinite punishment of their sins. Divine justice says of the tree that brings forth such grapes of Sodom, "Cut it down, why cumbereth it the ground?" Luke 13:7. The sword of divine justice is every moment brandished over their heads, and it is nothing but the hand of arbitrary mercy, and God's mere will, that holds it back.

3. They are already under a sentence of *condemnation* to hell. They do not only justly deserve to be cast down thither, but the sentence of the law of God, that eternal and immutable rule of righteousness that God has fixed between Him and mankind, is gone out against them and stands against them, so that they are bound over already to hell: John 3:18, "He that believeth not is condemned already." So that every unconverted man properly belongs to hell; that is his place; from thence he is: John 8:23, "Ye are from beneath," and thither he is bound; it is the place that justice, and God's word, and the sentence of his unchangeable law, assign to him.

[6]I.e., rescue others.

[7]"The mountains quake at him, and the hills melt, and the earth is burned at his presence, yea, the world, and all that dwell therein. Who can stand before this indignation? and who can abide in the fierceness of his anger? his fury is poured out like fire, and the rocks are thrown down by him." Nahum 1:5–6.

4. They are now the objects of that very same *anger* and wrath of God that is expressed in the torments of hell; and the reason why they do not go down to hell at each moment, is not because God, in whose power they are, is not then very angry with them, as angry as He is with many of those miserable creatures that He is now tormenting in hell, and do there feel and bear the fierceness of His wrath. Yea, God is a great deal more angry with great numbers that are now on earth, yea, doubtless, with many that are now in this congregation, that, it may be, are at ease and quiet, than He is with many of those that are now in the flames of hell.

So that it is not because God is unmindful of their wickedness, and does not resent it, that He does not let loose his hand and cut them off. God is not altogether such a one as themselves, though they may imagine Him to be so. The wrath of God burns against them; their damnation does not slumber; the pit is prepared; the fire is made ready; the furnace is now hot, ready to receive them; the flames do now rage and glow. The glittering sword is whet,[8] and held over them, and the pit hath opened its mouth under them.

5. The *devil* stands ready to fall upon them, and seize them as his own, at what moment God shall permit him. They belong to him; he has their souls in his possession, and under his dominion. The Scripture represents them as his goods, Luke 11:21.[9] The devils watch them; they are ever by them, at their right hand; they stand waiting for them, like greedy hungry lions that see their prey, and expect to have it, but are for the present kept back; if God should withdraw His hand, by which they are restrained, they would in one moment fly upon their poor souls. The old serpent is gaping for them; hell opens its mouth wide to receive them; and if God should permit it, they would be hastily swallowed up and lost.

6. There are in the souls of wicked men those hellish *principles* reigning that would presently kindle and flame out into hell-fire if it were not for God's restraints. There is laid in the very nature of carnal men a foundation for the torments of hell; there are those corrupt principles, in reigning power in them, and in full possession of them, that are the beginnings of hell-fire. These principles are active and powerful, exceeding violent in their nature, and if it were not for the restraining hand of God upon them, they would soon break out; they would flame out after the same manner as the same corruptions, the same enmity does in the hearts of damned souls, and would beget the same torments in them as they do in them. The souls of the wicked are in Scripture compared to the troubled sea, Isaiah 57:20.[10] For the present, God restrains their wickedness by His mighty power, as He does the raging waves of the troubled sea, saying, "Hitherto shalt thou come, but no further;"[11] but if God should withdraw that restraining power, it would soon carry all before it. Sin is the ruin and misery of the soul; it is destructive in its nature; and if God should leave it without restraint, there would need nothing else to make the soul perfectly miserable. The corruption of the heart of man is a thing that is immoderate and boundless in its fury; and while wicked men live here, it is like fire pent up by God's restraints; whereas if it were let

[8]Sharpened. [9]"When a strong man armed keepeth his palace, his goods are in peace."
[10]"But the wicked are like the troubled sea, when it cannot rest, whose waters cast up mire and dirt."
[11]Job 38:11.

loose, it would set on fire the course of nature; and as the heart is now a sink of sin, so, if sin was not restrained, it would immediately turn the soul into a fiery oven or a furnace of fire and brimstone.

7. It is no security to wicked men for one moment that there are no visible means of death at hand. It is no security to a natural[12] man that he is now in health, and that he does not see which way he should now immediately go out of the world by any accident, and that there is no visible danger in any respect in his circumstances. The manifold and continual experience of the world in all ages shows that this is no evidence that a man is not on the very brink of eternity and that the next step will not be into another world. The unseen, unthought of ways and means of persons going suddenly out of the world are innumerable and inconceivable. Unconverted men walk over the pit of hell on a rotten covering, and there are innumerable places in this covering so weak that they will not bear their weight, and these places are not seen. The arrows of death fly unseen at noonday;[13] the sharpest sight cannot discern them. God has so many different, unsearchable ways of taking wicked men out of the world and sending them to hell that there is nothing to make it appear that God had need to be at the expense of a miracle, or go out of the ordinary course of His providence, to destroy any wicked man, at any moment. All the means that there are of sinners going out of the world are so in God's hands and so absolutely subject to His power and determination, that it does not depend at all less on the mere will of God, whether sinners shall at any moment go to hell, than if means were never made use of or at all concerned in the case.

8. Natural men's *prudence* and *care* to preserve their own lives, or the care of others to preserve them, do not secure them a moment. This, divine providence and universal experience do also bear testimony to. There is this clear evidence that men's own wisdom is no security to them from death, that if it were otherwise we should see some difference between the wise and politic men of the world and others, with regard to their liableness to early and unexpected death; but how is it in fact? Ecclesiastes 2:16, "How dieth the wise man? As the fool."

9. All wicked men's *pains* and *contrivance* they use to escape hell, while they continue to reject Christ and so remain wicked men, do not secure them from hell one moment. Almost every natural man that hears of hell flatters himself that he shall escape it; he depends upon himself for his own security; he flatters himself in what he has done, in what he is now doing, or what he intends to do; everyone lays out matters in his own mind how he shall avoid damnation and flatters himself that he contrives well for himself, and that his schemes will not fail. They hear indeed that there are but few saved and that the bigger part of men that have died heretofore are gone to hell; but each one imagines that he lays out matters better for his own escape than others have done; he does not intend to come to that place of torment; he says within himself that he intends to take care that shall be effectual[14] and to order matters so for himself as not to fail.

[12]Unredeemed by religion, unsaved, lacking supernatural grace.

[13]Cf. "Thou shalt not be afraid for the terror by night; nor for the arrow that flieth by day." Psalm 91:5.

[14]Effective.

But the foolish children of men do miserably delude themselves in their own schemes and in their confidence in their own strength and wisdom; they trust to nothing but a shadow. The greater part of those that heretofore have lived under the same means of grace, and are now dead, are undoubtedly gone to hell; and it was not because they were not as wise as those that are now alive; it was not because they did not lay out matters as well for themselves to secure their own escape. If it were so that we could come to speak with them, and could inquire of them, one by one, whether they expected, when alive, and when they used to hear about hell, ever to be subjects of that misery, we doubtless should hear one and another reply, "No, I never intended to come here; I had laid out matters otherwise in my mind; I thought I should contrive well for myself; I thought my scheme good; I intended to take effectual care; but it came upon me unexpectedly; I did not look for it at that time, and in that manner; it came as a thief; death outwitted me; God's wrath was too quick for me; O my cursed foolishness! I was flattering myself and pleasing myself with vain dreams of what I would do hereafter; and when I was saying, peace and safety, then sudden destruction came upon me."

10. God has laid Himself under *no obligation,* by any promise, to keep any natural man out of hell one moment; God certainly has made no promises either of eternal life, or of any deliverance or preservation from eternal death, but what are contained in the covenant of grace,[15] the promises that are given in Christ, in whom all the promises are yea and amen. But surely they have no interest in the promises of the covenant of grace that are not the children of the covenant, and that do not believe in any of the promises of the covenant, and have no interest in the Mediator[16] of the covenant.

So that, whatever some have imagined and pretended[17] about promises made to natural men's earnest seeking and knocking,[18] it is plain and manifest that whatever pains a natural man takes in religion, whatever prayers he makes, till he believes in Christ, God is under no manner of obligation to keep him a moment from eternal destruction.

So that thus it is, that natural men are held in the hand of God, over the pit of hell; they have deserved the fiery pit and are already sentenced to it; and God is dreadfully provoked; His anger is as great towards them as to those that are actually suffering the executions of the fierceness of His wrath in hell, and they have done nothing in the least to appease or abate that anger; neither is God in the least bound by any promise to hold them up one moment; the devil is waiting for them; hell is gaping for them; the flames gather and flash about them, and would fain lay hold on them and swallow them up; the fire pent up in their own hearts is struggling to break out; and they have no interest in any Mediator; there are no means within reach that can be any security to them. In short, they have no refuge, nothing to take hold of; all that preserves them every moment is the mere arbitrary will and uncovenanted, unobliged forbearance of an incensed God.

[15]The covenant, or agreement, by which God, because of Jesus' atonement, restored the possibility of grace, or salvation, that had previously been lost to mankind by the fall of Adam.

[16]Christ, mediator between God and man.

[17]Asserted, claimed.

[18]I.e., knocking to gain admittance to salvation.

Application

The use of this awful[19] subject may be of awakening unconverted persons in this congregation. This that you have heard is the case of everyone of you that are out of Christ. That world of misery, that lake of burning brimstone, is extended abroad under you. There is the dreadful pit of the glowing flames of the wrath of God; there is hell's wide gaping mouth open; and you have nothing to stand upon, nor anything to take hold of. There is nothing between you and hell but the air; it is only the power and mere pleasure of God that holds you up.

You probably are not sensible[20] of this; you find you are kept out of hell but do not see the hand of God in it; but look at other things, [such] as the good state of your bodily constitution, your care of your own life, and the means you use for your own preservation. But indeed these things are nothing; if God should withdraw His hand, they would avail no more to keep you from falling than the thin air to hold up a person that is suspended in it.

Your wickedness makes you, as it were, heavy as lead and to tend downwards with great weight and pressure towards hell; and if God should let you go, you would immediately sink and swiftly descend and plunge into the bottomless gulf, and your healthy constitution, and your own care and prudence, and best contrivance, and all your righteousness, would have no more influence to uphold you and keep you out of hell than a spider's web would have to stop a falling rock. Were it not that so is the sovereign pleasure of God, the earth would not bear you one moment; for you are a burden to it; the creation groans with you; the creature[21] is made subject to the bondage of your corruption, not willingly; the sun does not willingly shine upon you to give you light to serve sin and Satan; the earth does not willingly yield her increase to satisfy your lusts; nor is it willingly a stage for your wickedness to be acted upon; the air does not willingly serve you for breath to maintain the flame of life in your vitals while you spend your life in the service of God's enemies. God's creatures are good, and were made for men to serve God with, and do not willingly subserve to any other purpose, and groan when they are abused to purposes so directly contrary to their nature and end. And the world would spew you out, were it not for the sovereign hand of Him who hath subjected it in hope. There are the black clouds of God's wrath now hanging directly over your heads, full of the dreadful storm and big with thunder; and were it not for the restraining hand of God, it would immediately burst forth upon you. The sovereign pleasure of God, for the present, stays His rough wind; otherwise it would come with fury, and your destruction would come like a whirlwind, and you would be like the chaff of the summer threshing floor.

The wrath of God is like great waters that are dammed for the present; they increase more and more, and rise higher and higher, till an outlet is given; and the longer the stream is stopped, the more rapid and mighty is its course when once it is let loose. It is true that judgment against your evil works has not been executed hitherto; the floods of God's vengeance have been withheld; but your guilt in the meantime is constantly increasing, and

[19]Awesome. [20]Aware. [21]Body, flesh.

you are every day treasuring up more wrath; the waters are continually rising and waxing more and more mighty; and there is nothing but the mere pleasure of God that holds the waters back that are unwilling to be stopped and press hard to go forward. If God should only withdraw His hand from the floodgate, it would immediately fly open, and the fiery floods of the fierceness and wrath of God would rush forth with inconceivable fury and would come upon you with omnipotent power; and if your strength were ten thousand times greater than it is, yea, ten thousand times greater than the strength of the stoutest, sturdiest devil in hell, it would be nothing to withstand or endure it.

The bow of God's wrath is bent, and the arrow made ready on the string, and justice bends the arrow at your heart and strains the bow, and it is nothing but the mere pleasure of God, and that of an angry God, without any promise or obligation at all, that keeps the arrow one moment from being made drunk with your blood.

Thus are all you that never passed under a great change of heart, by the mighty power of the Spirit of God upon your souls; all that were never born again, and made new creatures, and raised from being dead in sin, to a state of new, and before altogether unexperienced light and life (however you may have reformed your life in many things, and may have had religious affections,[22] and may keep up a form of religion in your families, and closets,[23] and in the houses of God, and may be strict in it), you are thus in the hands of an angry God; it is nothing but His mere pleasure that keeps you from being this moment swallowed up in everlasting destruction.

However unconvinced you may now be of the truth of what you hear, by and by you will be fully convinced of it. Those that are gone from being in the like circumstances with you, see that it was so with them; for destruction came suddenly upon most of them, when they expected nothing of it and while they were saying, "Peace and safety"; now they see that those things that they depended on for peace and safety were nothing but thin air and empty shadows.

The God that holds you over the pit of hell, much as one holds a spider or some loathsome insect over the fire, abhors you and is dreadfully provoked; His wrath towards you burns like fire; He looks upon you as worthy of nothing else but to be cast into the fire; He is of purer eyes than to bear to have you in His sight; you are ten thousand times more abominable in His eyes than the most hateful and venomous serpent is in ours. You have offended Him infinitely more than ever a stubborn rebel did his prince; and yet it is nothing but His hand that holds you from falling into the fire every moment; it is to be ascribed to nothing else that you did not go to hell the last night, that you were suffered[24] to awake again in this world, after you closed your eyes to sleep; and there is no other reason to be given, why you have not dropped into hell since you arose in the morning, but that God's hand has held you up; there is no other reason to be given why you have not gone to hell, since you have sat here in the house of God, provoking His pure eyes by your sinful, wicked manner of attending His solemn worship; yea, there is nothing else that is to be given as a reason why you do not this very moment drop down into hell.

[22]Feelings. [23]Private rooms used for prayer and meditation. [24]Permitted.

O sinner! consider the fearful danger you are in; it is a great furnace of wrath, a wide and bottomless pit, full of the fire of wrath, that you are held over in the hand of that God, whose wrath is provoked and incensed as much against you, as against many of the damned in hell; you hang by a slender thread, with the flames of divine wrath flashing about it and ready every moment to singe it and burn it asunder; and you have no interest in any Mediator and nothing to lay hold of to save yourself, nothing to keep off the flames of wrath, nothing of your own, nothing that you ever have done, nothing that you can do to induce God to spare you one moment.

And consider here more particularly several things concerning that wrath that you are in such danger of.

1. *Whose* wrath it is. It is the wrath of the infinite God. If it were only the wrath of man, though it were of the most potent prince, it would be comparatively little to be regarded. The wrath of kings is very much dreaded, especially of absolute monarchs that have the possessions and lives of their subjects wholly in their power, to be disposed of at their mere will. Proverbs 20:2, "The fear of a king is as the roaring of a lion: whoso provoketh him to anger sinneth against his own soul." The subject that very much enrages an arbitrary prince is liable to suffer the most extreme torments that human art can invent or human power can inflict. But the greatest earthly potentates, in their greatest majesty and strength, and when clothed in their greatest terrors, are but feeble, despicable worms of the dust, in comparison of the great and almighty Creator and King of heaven and earth; it is but little that they can do, when most enraged and when they have exerted the utmost of their fury. All the kings of the earth, before God, are as grasshoppers; they are nothing and less than nothing; both their love and their hatred is to be despised. The wrath of the great King of kings is as much more terrible than theirs, as His majesty is greater. Luke 12:4–5, "And I say unto you, my friends, Be not afraid of them that kill the body, and after that, have no more that they can do. But I will forewarn you whom ye shall fear: Fear him, which after he hath killed, hath power to cast into hell; yea, I say unto you, Fear him."

2. It is the *fierceness* of His wrath that you are exposed to. We often read of the fury of God; as in Isaiah 59:18: "According to their deeds, accordingly he will repay fury to his adversaries." So Isaiah 66:15, "For behold, the Lord will come with fire, and with his chariots like a whirlwind, to render his anger with fury, and his rebuke with flames of fire." And so in many other places. So Revelation 19:15.[25] There we read of "the winepress of the fierceness and wrath of Almighty God." The words are exceedingly terrible; if it had only been said, "the wrath of God," the words would have implied that which is infinitely dreadful; but it is not only said so, but "the fierceness and wrath of God," the fury of God! the fierceness of Jehovah! Oh how dreadful must that be! Who can utter or conceive what such expressions carry in them! But it is also "the fierceness and wrath of Almighty God." As though there would be a very great manifestation of His almighty power in what the fierceness of His wrath should inflict, as though omnipotence should be, as it were, enraged and exerted, as men are wont to exert their strength in the fierceness of their wrath. Oh! then, what will be the consequence! What will become of the

[25]"He treadeth the winepress of the fierceness and wrath of Almighty God."

poor worm that shall suffer it! Whose hands can be strong! And whose heart endure! To what a dreadful, inexpressible, inconceivable depth of misery must the poor creature be sunk who shall be the subject of this!

Consider this, you that are here present, that yet remain in an unregenerate state. That God will execute the fierceness of His anger implies that He will inflict wrath without any pity; when God beholds the ineffable extremity of your case, and sees your torment so vastly disproportioned to your strength and sees how your poor soul is crushed and sinks down, as it were, into an infinite gloom, He will have no compassion upon you; He will not forbear the executions of his wrath or in the least lighten His hand; there shall be no moderation or mercy, nor will God then at all stay His rough wind; He will have no regard to your welfare, nor be at all careful lest you should suffer too much in any other sense, than only that you should not suffer beyond what strict justice requires; nothing shall be withheld because it is so hard for you to bear. Ezekiel 8:18, "Therefore will I also deal in fury: mine eye shall not spare, neither will I have pity: and though they cry in mine ears with a loud voice, yet will I not hear them." Now God stands ready to pity you; this is a day of mercy; you may cry now with some encouragement of obtaining mercy; but when once the day of mercy is past, your most lamentable and dolorous cries and shrieks will be in vain; you will be wholly lost and thrown away of God, as to any regard to your welfare; God will have no other use to put you to but to suffer misery; you shall be continued in being to no other end; for you will be a vessel of wrath fitted to destruction; and there will be no other use of this vessel but to be filled full of wrath; God will be so far from pitying you when you cry to him, that it is said he will only "laugh and mock," Proverbs 1:25–26,[26] &c.

How awful are those words, Isaiah 63:3, which are the words of the great God: "I will tread them in mine anger, and trample them in my fury; and their blood shall be sprinkled upon my garments, and I will stain all my raiment." It is perhaps impossible to conceive of words that carry in them greater manifestations of these three things, viz., contempt, and hatred, and fierceness of indignation. If you cry to God to pity you, He will be so far from pitying you in your doleful case, or showing you the least regard or favor, that instead of that He will only tread you under foot; and though He will know that you cannot bear the weight of omnipotence treading upon you, He will not regard that, but He will crush you under His feet without mercy; He will crush out your blood and make it fly, and it shall be sprinkled on His garments, so as to stain all His raiment. He will not only hate you, but He will have you in the utmost contempt; no place shall be thought fit for you but under His feet, to be trodden down as the mire in the streets.

3. The *misery* you are exposed to is that which God will inflict to that end, [so] that He might show what that wrath of Jehovah is. God hath had it on His heart to show to angels and men both how excellent His love is and also how terrible His wrath is. Sometimes earthly kings have a mind to show how terrible their wrath is, by the extreme punishments they would execute on those that provoke them. Nebuchadnezzar, that mighty and haughty monarch of the Chaldean empire, was willing to show his wrath

[26]"But ye have set at nought all my counsel, and would none of my reproof: I also will laugh at your calamity; I will mock you when your fear cometh."

when enraged with Shadrach, Meshech, and Abednego[27] and accordingly gave order that the burning fiery furnace should be heated seven times hotter than it was before; doubtless, it was raised to the utmost degree of fierceness that human art could raise it; but the great God is also willing to show His wrath and magnify His awful majesty and mighty power in the extreme sufferings of His enemies. Romans 9:22, "What if God, willing to show his wrath, and to make his power known, endured with much long-suffering, the vessels of wrath fitted to destruction?" And seeing this is His design, and what He has determined, to show how terrible the unmixed, unrestrained wrath, the fury, and fierceness of Jehovah is, He will do it to effect. There will be something accomplished and brought to pass that will be dreadful with a witness. When the great and angry God hath risen up and executed His awful vengeance on the poor sinner and the wretch is actually suffering the infinite weight and power of His indignation, then will God call upon the whole universe to behold that awful majesty and mighty power that is to be seen in it. Isaiah 33:12–14, "And the people shall be as the burnings of lime: as thorns cut up shall they be burnt in the fire. Hear, ye that are afar off, what I have done; and ye that are near, acknowledge my might. The sinners in Zion are afraid; fearfulness hath surprised the hypocrites," &c.

Thus it will be with you that are in an unconverted state, if you continue in it; the infinite might, and majesty, and terribleness of the omnipotent God shall be magnified upon you in the ineffable strength of your torments; you shall be tormented in the presence of holy angels, and in the presence of the Lamb; and when you shall be in this state of suffering, the glorious inhabitants of heaven shall go forth and look on the awful spectacle, that they may see what the wrath and fierceness of the Almighty is; and when they have seen it, they will fall down and adore that great power and majesty. Isaiah 66:23–24, "And it shall come to pass, that from one new moon to another, and from one Sabbath to another, shall all flesh come to worship before me, saith the Lord. And they shall go forth and look upon the carcasses of the men that have transgressed against me; for their worm[28] shall not die, neither shall their fire be quenched; and they shall be an abhorring unto all flesh."

4. It is *everlasting* wrath. It would be dreadful to suffer this fierceness and wrath of almighty God one moment; but you must suffer it to all eternity; there will be no end to this exquisite, horrible misery; when you look forward, you shall see a long forever, a boundless duration before you which will swallow up your thoughts and amaze your soul; and you will absolutely despair of ever having any deliverance, any end, any mitigation, any rest at all; you will know certainly that you must wear out long ages, millions of millions of ages, in wrestling and conflicting with this almighty, merciless vengeance; and then when you have so done, when so many ages have actually been spent by you in this manner, you will know that all is but a point to what remains. So that your punishment will indeed be infinite. Oh, who can express what the state of a soul in such circumstances is! All that we can possibly say about it, gives but a very feeble, faint representation of it; it is inexpressible and inconceivable; for "who knows the power of God's anger?"[29]

[27]Described in Daniel 3:1–30. [28]That eternally gnaws at their bodies.

[29]"Who knoweth the power of thine anger? even according to thy fear, so is thy wrath." Psalm 90:11.

How dreadful is the state of those that are daily and hourly in danger of this great wrath and infinite misery! But this is the dismal case of every soul in this congregation that has not been born again, however moral and strict, sober and religious, they may otherwise be. Oh that you would consider it, whether you be young or old! There is reason to think that there are many in this congregation now hearing this discourse, that will actually be the subjects of this very misery to all eternity. We know not who they are, or in what seats they sit, or what thoughts they now have. It may be they are now at ease, and hear all these things without much disturbance, and are now flattering themselves that they are not the persons, promising themselves that they shall escape. If we knew that there was one person, and but one, in the whole congregation that was to be the subject of this misery, what an awful thing it would be to think of! If we knew who it was, what an awful sight would it be to see such a person! How might all the rest of the congregation lift up a lamentable and bitter cry over him! But alas! Instead of one, how many is it likely will remember this discourse in hell! And it would be a wonder if some that are now present should not be in hell in a very short time, even before this year is out. And it would be no wonder if some persons, that now sit here in some seats of this meeting-house, in health, and quiet and secure, should be there before tomorrow morning. Those of you that finally continue in a natural condition, that shall keep out of hell longest, will be there in a little time! Your damnation does not slumber; it will come swiftly and, in all probability, very suddenly upon many of you. You have reason to wonder that you are not already in hell. It is doubtless the case of some whom you have seen and known, that never deserved hell more than you, and that heretofore appeared as likely to have been now alive as you. Their case is past all hope; they are crying in extreme misery and perfect despair; but here you are in the land of the living and in the house of God, and have an opportunity to obtain salvation. What would not those poor damned hopeless souls give for one day's opportunity such as you now enjoy!

And now you have an extraordinary opportunity, a day wherein Christ has thrown the door of mercy wide open and stands in, calling and crying with a loud voice to poor sinners, a day wherein many are flocking to Him and pressing into the kingdom of God. Many are daily coming from the east, west, north and south; many that were very lately in the same miserable condition that you are in, are now in a happy state, with their hearts filled with love to Him who has loved them and washed them from their sins in His own blood, and rejoicing in hope of the glory of God. How awful it is to be left behind at such a day! To see so many others feasting, while you are pining and perishing! To see so many rejoicing and singing for joy of heart, while you have cause to mourn for sorrow of heart and howl for vexation of spirit! How can you rest one moment in such a condition? Are not your souls as precious as the souls of the people at Suffield,[30] where they are flocking from day to day to Christ?

Are there not many here who have lived long in the world, and are not to this day born again? and so are aliens from the commonwealth of Israel,[31]

[30]"A town in the neighborhood."—Edwards' note.

[31]I.e., not one of the Chosen People, not one of the elect.

and have done nothing ever since they have lived, but treasure up wrath against the day of wrath? Oh, sirs, your case, in an especial manner, is extremely dangerous. Your guilt and hardness of heart is extremely great. Do you not see how generally persons of your years are passed over and left, in the present remarkable and wonderful dispensation of God's mercy? You had need to consider yourselves and awake thoroughly out of sleep. You cannot bear the fierceness and wrath of the infinite God. And you, young men and young women, will you neglect this precious season which you now enjoy, when so many others of your age are renouncing all youthful vanities and flocking to Christ? You especially have now an extraordinary opportunity; but if you neglect it, it will soon be with you as with those persons who spent all the precious days of youth in sin and are now come to such a dreadful pass in blindness and hardness. And you children who are unconverted, do not you know that you are going down to hell, to bear the dreadful wrath of that God who is now angry with you every day and every night? Will you be content to be the children of the devil, when so many other children in the land are converted and are become the holy and happy children of the King of kings?

And let every one that is yet of Christ, and hanging over the pit of hell, whether they be old men and women, or middle-aged, or young people, or little children, now hearken to the loud calls of God's word and providence. This acceptable year of the Lord, a day of such great favors to some, will doubtless be a day of as remarkable vengeance to others. Men's hearts harden, and their guilt increases apace at such a day as this, if they neglect their souls; and never was there so great a danger of such persons being given up to hardness of heart and blindness of mind. God seems now to be hastily gathering in His elect in all parts of the land; and probably the greater part of adult persons that ever shall be saved will be brought in now in a little time and that it will be as it was on the great out-pouring of the Spirit upon the Jews in the apostles' days; the election will obtain, and the rest will be blinded. If this should be the case with you, you will eternally curse this day, and will curse the day that ever you were born to see such a season of the pouring out of God's Spirit, and will wish that you had died and gone to hell before you had seen it. Now undoubtedly it is, as it was in the days of John the Baptist, the axe is in an extraordinary manner laid at the root of the trees, that every tree which brings not forth good fruit may be hewn down and cast into the fire.[32]

Therefore, let every one that is out of Christ, now awake and fly from the wrath to come. The wrath of almighty God is now undoubtedly hanging over a great part of this congregation: Let every one fly out of Sodom: "Haste and escape for your lives, look not behind you, escape to the mountain, lest you be consumed."[33]

1741 1741

[32]An adaptation of Matthew 3:10.
[33]Genesis 19:17.

from *IMAGES OR SHADOWS OF DIVINE THINGS*[1]

1. Death temporal is a shadow of eternal death. The agonies, the pains, the groans and gasps of death, the pale, horrid, ghastly appearance of the corpse, its being laid in the dark and silent grave, there putrifying and rotting and become exceeding loathsome and being eaten with worms (Isaiah 66:24[2]), is an image of the misery of hell. And the body's continuing in the grave, and never rising more in this world, is to shadow forth the eternity of the misery of hell.

3. Roses grow upon briars, which is to signify that all temporal sweets are mixed with bitter. But what seems more especially to be meant by it is that pure happiness, the crown of glory, is to be come at in no other way than by bearing Christ's cross, by a life of mortification, self-denial, and labor, and bearing all things for Christ. The rose, that is chief of all flowers, is the last thing that comes out. The briary, prickly bush grows before that; the end and crown of all is the beautiful and fragrant rose.

4. The heavens' being filled with glorious, luminous bodies is to signify the glory and happiness of the heavenly inhabitants, and amongst these the sun signifies Christ and the moon the church.

5. Marriage signifies the spiritual union and communion of Christ and the church, and especially the glorification of the church in the perfection of this union and communion forever. . . .

8. Again it is apparent and allowed that there is a great and remarkable analogy in God's works. There is a wonderful resemblance in the effects which God produces, and consentaneity[3] in His manner of working in one thing and another throughout all nature. It is very observable in the visible world; therefore it is allowed that God does purposely make and order one thing to be in agreeableness and harmony with another. And if so, why should not we suppose that He makes the inferior in imitation of the superior, the material of the spiritual, on purpose to have a resemblance and shadow of them? We see that even in the material world, God makes one part of it strangely to agree with another, and why is it not reasonable to suppose He makes the whole as a shadow of the spiritual world? . . .

[1]Also entitled "The Language and Lessons of Nature," a collection of 212 unpublished notes jotted down by Edwards over the years to record similarities between the spiritual and visible worlds. His observations followed the earlier Puritan tradition of typology, the recognizing of events in the Old Testament (types) as prophetic rehearsals for events in the New Testament (anti-types). To Puritans, such biblical correspondences stood as emblems of the predicament of man and a confirmation of the Puritan ideal of a moral and regulated universe. Edwards' extension of typology beyond the strict limits of Bible events to include the general world of nature was itself a prophetic rehearsal of the use of nature symbolism in nineteenth-century American romanticism and by the transcendentalists.

[2]"And they shall go forth, and look upon the carcasses of the men that have transgressed against me: for their worm shall not die, neither shall their fire be quenched; and they shall be an abhorring unto all flesh."

[3]Agreement, harmony.

10. Children's coming into the world naked and filthy and in their blood, and crying and impotent, is to signify the spiritual nakedness and pollution of nature and wretchedness of condition with which they are born.

11. The serpents' charming of birds and other animals into their mouths, and the spider's taking and sucking the blood of the fly in his snare are lively representations of the Devil's catching our souls by his temptations.

25. There are many things in the constitution of the world that are not properly shadows and images of divine things that yet are significations of them, as children's being born crying is a signification of their being born to sorrow. A man's coming into the world after the same manner as the beasts is a signification of the ignorance and brutishness of man, and his agreement in many things with the beasts.

33. The extreme fierceness and extraordinary power of the heat of lighting is an intimation of the exceeding power and terribleness of the wrath of God.

35. The silk-worm is a remarkable type of Christ, which when it dies yields us that of which we make such glorious clothing. Christ became a worm for our sakes, and by His death kindled that righteousness with which believers are clothed, and thereby procured that we should be clothed with robes of glory. . . .

41. Children's coming to their inheritance by the death of their parents and by their will and testament, which becomes of force by their death, is a designed type and shadow of believers receiving their inheritance by the free and sovereign disposal and gift of God in His Word, which is His testament or declaration of His will with respect to the disposal of His goods or the blessings He has in store for men. And believers come to the possession thereof by the spirit of Christ. . . .

43. It is a great argument with me that God, in the creation and disposal of the world and the state and course of things in it, had great respect to a showing forth and resembling spiritual things, because God in some instances seems to have gone quite beside the ordinary laws of nature in order to it, particularly that in serpents charming birds and squirrels and such animals. The material world, and all things pertaining to it, is by the creator wholly subordinated to the spiritual and moral world. To show this, God, in some things in providence, has set aside the ordinary course of things in the material world to subserve to the purposes of the moral and spiritual, as in miracles. And to show that all things in heaven and earth, the whole universe, is wholly subservient, the greater parts of it as well as the smaller, God has once or twice interrupted the course of the greater wheels of the machine, as when the sun stood still in Joshua's time.[4] So, to show how much He regards things in the spiritual world, there are some

[4]"The sun stood still, and the moon stayed, until the people had avenged themselves upon their enemies." Joshua 10:13.

things in the ordinary course of things that fall out in a manner quite diverse and alien from the ordinary laws of nature in other things, to hold forth and represent spiritual things.

54. As the sun, by rising out of darkness and from under the earth, raises the whole world with him, raises mankind out of their beds, and by his light, as it were, renews all things and fetches them up out of darkness, so Christ, rising from the grave and from a state of death, He, as the first begotten from the dead, raises all His church with him, Christ the first fruits and afterwards they that are Christ's at His coming. And as all the world is enlightened and brought out of darkness by the rising of the sun, so by Christ's rising we are begotten again to a lively hope, and all our happiness and life and light and glory and the restitution of all things is from Christ rising from the dead, and is by His resurrection.

60. That of so vast and innumerable a multitude of blossoms that appear on a tree, so few come to ripe fruit, and that so few of so vast a multitude of seeds as are yearly produced, so few come to be a plant, and that there is so great a waste of the seed of both plants and animals, but one in a great multitude ever bringing forth anything, seem to be lively types how few are saved out of the mass of mankind, and particularly how few are sincere, of professing Christians, that never wither away but endure to the end, and how of the many that are called few are chosen.

61. Ravens, that with delight feed on carrion, seem to be remarkable types of devils, who with delight prey upon the souls of the dead. A dead, filthy, rotten carcass is a lively image of the soul of a wicked man, that is spiritually and exceedingly filthy and abominable. Their spiritual corruption is of a far more loathsome savour than the stench of a putrefying carcass. Such souls the Devil delights in; they are his proper food. Again, dead corpses are types of the departed souls of the dead and are so used. (Isaiah 66:24.[5]) Ravens don't prey on the bodies of animals till they are dead; so the Devil has not the souls of wicked men delivered into his tormenting hands and devouring jaws till they are dead. Again, the body in such circumstances being dead and in loathsome putrefaction is a lively image of a soul in the dismal state it is in under eternal death. . . . Ravens are birds of the air that are expressly used by Christ as types of the Devil in the parable of the sower and the seed.[6] The Devil is the prince of the power of the air, as he is called; devils are spirits of the air. The raven by its blackness represents the prince of darkness. Sin and sorrow and death are all in Scripture represented by darkness or the color black, but the Devil is the father of sin, a most foul and wicked spirit, and the prince of death and misery.

[5]See note 2, page 186.

[6]"A sower went out to sow his seed: and as he sowed, some fell by the wayside . . . and the fowls of the air devoured it. . . . Now the parable is this: The seed is the word of God. Those by the wayside are that they hear; then cometh the devil and taketh away the word out of their hearts, lest they should believe and be saved." Luke 8:5–12.

63. In the manner in which birds and squirrels that are charmed by serpents, go into their mouths, and are destroyed by them is a lively representation of the manner in which sinners under the Gospel are very often charmed and destroyed by the Devil. The animal that is charmed by the serpent seems to be in great exercise and fear, screams and makes ado, but yet doesn't flee away. It comes nearer to the serpent, and then seems to have its distress increased, and goes a little back again, but then comes still nearer than ever, and then appears as if greatly affrighted, and runs or flies back again a little way, but yet doesn't flee quite away, and soon comes a little nearer and a little nearer with seeming fear and distress that drives it a little back between whiles, until at length, it comes so [near] that the serpent can lay hold of it and it becomes the prey. Just thus often times sinners under the Gospel are bewitched by their lusts. They have considerable fears of destruction and remorse of conscience that makes them hang back, and they have a great deal of exercise between while, and some partial reformations, but yet they don't flee away. They will not wholly forsake their beloved lusts but return to them again. And so, whatever warnings they have and whatever checks of conscience that may exercise them and make them go back a little and stand off for a while, yet they will keep their beloved sin in sight and won't utterly break off from it and forsake [it], but will return to it again and again and go a little further and a little further, until Satan remedilessly makes a prey of them. But if any one comes and kills the serpent, the animal immediately escapes. So the way in which our souls are delivered from the snare of the Devil is by Christ's coming and bruising the serpent's head.

73. The way of a cat with a mouse that it has taken captive is a lively emblem of the way of the Devil with many wicked men. A mouse is a foul, unclean creature, a fit type of a wicked man, Leviticus 11:29: These also shall be unclean, the weasel and the mouse; Isaiah 66:17: Eating swine's flesh and the abomination and the mouse. The cat makes a play and sport of the poor mouse; so the Devil does, as it were, make himself sport with a wicked man. The cat lets the mouse go, and it seems to have escaped; it hopes it is delivered, but [it] is suddenly catched up again before it can get clear. And so time after time, the mouse makes many vain attempts, thinks itself free when it is still a captive, is taken up again by the jaws and into the jaws of its devourer as if it were just going to be destroyed, but then is let go again, but never quite escapes, till at last it yields its life to its enemy, and is crushed between his teeth and totally devoured. So, many wicked men, especially false professors of religion and sinners under Gospel light, are led captive by Satan at his will, are under the power and dominion of their lusts, and though they have many struggles of conscience about their sins, yet [they] never wholly escape them. When they seem to escape, they fall into them again, and so again and again, till at length they are totally and utterly devoured by Satan.

104. There is the tongue and another member of the body that have a natural bridle, which is to signify to us the peculiar need we have to bridle and restrain those two members.

115. Man's inwards are full of dung and filthiness, which is to denote that the inner man, which is often represented by various parts of his inwards, sometimes the heart, sometimes the bowels, sometimes the belly, sometimes the veins, is full of spiritual corruption and abomination. So, as there are many foldings and turnings in the bowels, it denotes the great and manifold intricacies, secret windings and turnings, shifts, wiles, and deceits that are in their hearts. . . .

116. This world is all over dirty. Everywhere it is covered with that which tends to defile the feet of the traveler. Our streets are dirty and muddy, intimating that the world is full of that which tends to defile the soul, that worldly objects and worldly concerns and worldly company tend to pollute us.

117. The water, as I have observed elsewhere, is a type of sin or the corruption of man and of the state of misery that is the consequence of it. It is like sin in its flattering discoveries. How smooth and harmless does the water oftentimes appear, and as if it had paradise and heaven in its bosom. Thus when we stand on the banks of a lake or river, how flattering and pleasing does it oftentimes appear, as though under more pleasant and delightful groves and bowers and even heaven itself in its clearness wrought to tempt one unacquainted with its nature to descend thither. But indeed it is all a cheat; if we should descend into it, instead of finding pleasant, delightful groves and a garden of pleasure and heaven in its clearness, we should meet with nothing but death, a land of darkness, or darkness itself. . . .

146. The late invention of telescopes, whereby heavenly objects are brought so much nearer and made so much plainer to sight and such wonderful discoveries have been made in the heavens, is a type and forerunner of the great increase in the knowledge of heavenly things that shall be in the approaching glorious times of the Christian church.

147. The changing of the course of trade and the supplying of the world with its treasures from America is a type and forerunner of what is approaching in spiritual things, when the world shall be supplied with spiritual treasures from America.

1948

The Literature of Reason and Revolution

The eighteenth century in America is known from its dominating ideas as the Age of Reason, the Age of Neoclassicism, and the Age of the Enlightenment. It was a time of new scientists, religious rationalists, and political philosophers; a time of worldly men and women, cool toward organized religion and critical of governments. Their ideas were rooted in the classical worlds of Greece and Rome, in the Renaissance, and in the Protestant Reformation that shattered the unity of Christendom. They placed their faith in the achievements of a new science, and in hopeful visions of a stable world, free of drift and uncertainty.

The Age of Reason developed first in seventeenth-century England, spread to France and Europe, and finally came to the English colonies in America in the eighteenth century. Its precepts were apparent in the philosophy of Descartes (1596–1650) and his rejection of medieval authoritarianism; they were evident in the writing of Voltaire (1694–1778) and his attack on dogma; and they led to the founding of the Royal Society of London in 1662, "For the Improvement of Natural Knowledge."

It was an age of great discoverers, and the greatest of all was Isaac Newton (1642–1727). His *Principia Mathematica* (1687), or *Mathematical Principles of Natural Philosophy,* revealed that the universe is not a mystery moving at the whim of an inscrutable God but a mechanism operating by a rational formula that can be understood by any intelligent person. Humanity could at last escape uncertainty, for Newton offered a single mathematical law that accounted for the movements of the tides, the earth, even the stars. It was the beginning of modern science, weakening man's faith in miracles, in holy books, and in the divinity of kings and priests. In their place science now offered the idea of a changeless, intelligible universe—an idea that would dominate scientific thought for two hundred years.

People of the Age of Reason sought order everywhere in the natural world—and found it, not in religion but in the new science. Educated amateurs studied astronomy and mathematics as their forebears had studied the Scriptures. Kings, who once expounded theology, now collected fossils; princes studied botany; courtly ladies and gentlemen devoted themselves to their microscopes as ardently as to their scandals. Science intruded into philosophy and ethics. The English philosopher John Locke (1632–1704) concluded that "morality is capable of demonstration, as well as mathematics." Benjamin Franklin advocated the "reasonable science of virtue." Tom Paine, in *The Age of Reason* (1794–1796), attacked the "irrationality" of traditional Christianity. He encouraged people to believe that "miracles" could be logically explained, and to doubt the divinity of Jesus. And Paine declared that proof of God is found not in the Bible but in nature, that perfect expression of God's omnipotent goodness. Bible fundamentalism and the fiery excitements of religion continued to attract the mass of men and women, but the dominating idea of hell faded from the thought of the educated. The gentler God of natural philosophy replaced the Puritan and Calvinist God of wrath and dismissed the belief that most mortals were drenched in sin. Humanitarianism and service to man became the social ideal. Theology became rational; religion became deistic.

Deism was an informal, unorganized religious movement among the upper classes and intellectuals. It was a body of commonly held ideas, a faith without church or churchmen. It was validated not by revelation but by mathematics, scientific observation, and logic. Its followers believed in a God who was the "First Cause" of Newton's universe. Hellfire revivalists raged that deism was a menace beyond even popery itself, but Franklin, Jefferson, Paine, and other "Reasoning Unbelievers" continued to doubt miracles and scriptural revelation. They dethroned saints and relics, enthroning reason in their place. Men and women turned from theism—the belief in the all-present God of the Puritans—to belief in a deistic God who appeared to have designed the universe according to scientific laws and had then withdrawn from direct intervention in human affairs. Newtonian science suggested that the universe is just a superlative machine created by God, a universal clock. And as the existence of a clock argued for the existence of a clockmaker, so the ordered machine of the universe argued for the existence of God, the great cosmic mechanic.

The Ideals of Progress and Social Contract

Faith in a Newtonian universe and in a deistic God led men and women of reason to believe that human society must also operate by natural laws. By discovering and applying such laws, mankind could achieve almost infinite improvement. The idea of progress became one of the dominant concepts of the age. And as the idea of progress converged with Christian sentiments, there arose movements for social betterment, for humanitarianism: charities; prison reform; sympathy for the Indian, the slave, the poor, the oppressed.

John Locke wrote his *Treatises of Civil Government* (1690) to argue that governments were not based on divinely ordained hierarchies extending from God through kings to the people. Governments were the result of agreements between people, "social contracts" in which individuals surrendered some freedoms to protect their natural rights to life, liberty, and property. Thus, liberties once surrendered were not forever lost, and governments that violated natural rights and oppressed the weak deserved to be overthrown. In the Age of Reason such beliefs evolved into a celebration of political change. Where believers had once sought salvation through their churches, they now sought salvation through rebellion. It became an age of political dissent, an age of revolution.

The Calvinist view of mankind as innately evil, stained by original sin, came under increasing attack. In his *Essay Concerning Human Understanding* (1690), Locke held that predestination and total depravity were religious fictions; the human mind at birth was a *tabula rasa*, a blank sheet of paper; therefore human beings were born neither good nor bad; all was the result of experience. It was an environmentalist view, asserting that the making of good men and women required only the making of good societies. It was the view of the "American Farmer" Crèvecoeur, who declared that "men are like plants," their goodness "proceeds from the particular soil . . . in which they grow." By the end of the eighteenth century, optimistic faith in the perfectibility of humankind had reached its ultimate form in the writings of the Swiss philosopher Jean-Jacques Rousseau (1712–1778), who declared that men and women are not merely free of evil; they are naturally good.

With the rise of humanitarianism, environmentalism, and faith in human goodness and the dignity of man, there came increasing demands for human liberties. Tom Paine spoke out for the rights of individuals, Jefferson for "life, liberty, and the pursuit of happiness"; the poet Freneau demanded "From Reason's source, a bold reform," and the members of Franklin's benevolent society, the Junto, stood for the abolition of slavery and promised to love mankind. By the end of the eighteenth century, Americans asserted, and many believed, that it was now "the Age of Philanthropy and America is the empire of reason."

The New Classicism and Its Aftermath

Artists, living in an age that had rejected medieval doctrines as guides to life and art, took renewed interest in the classical, pagan thought of the Renaissance. They felt a desire to recreate in America not a New Jerusalem or a New Eden, but a New Athens, a New Rome. Writers dedicated to the new classicism (or neoclassicism), took their literary models and their critical maxims from Greek and Roman literary works whose durability had made them "classics." The ancient ideals of clarity, decorum, and regularity became the measures of eighteenth-century art. Such principles were evident in the balanced proportions of neoclassic architecture, in the symmetry of neoclassic music, and in the geometric regularity of neoclassic landscape gardening. Devotion to restraint and rationalism gave strong support to the "rule" that literature was to avoid the ornate, the extravagant, the bombastic. Writing was to exhibit "clear sense" and "mathematical plainness." Prose should approach the rhythm of cultivated speech; poetry should be written in the measured cadences of the heroic couplet; and drama should no longer deal with the impossible, the supernatural, or the miraculous, but should observe the "unities of time, place, and action," should have but one plot, and should occur in a single day and in a single place, for that was "reasonable" and "true to life." In England, John Dryden (1631–1700) stood as the "glorious founder" and Alexander Pope (1688–1744) as the "splendid high priest" of a neoclassic age. Its literature reaffirmed the artistic doctrines of classicism and focused on man's society, not on God's mysteries. Pope announced the new secular theology in his *Essay on Man:*

> Know then thyself, presume not God to scan,
> The proper study of mankind is man.

But Newton's fundamental law of motion—"to every action there is an equal and opposite reaction"—applied even to art itself, and toward the last of the eighteenth century, a reaction set in against the artistic formality and restraint of neoclassicism. Believers in the emerging ideas of romanticism objected to the "mere mechanic art" of the followers of Pope and Dryden. The neoclassic emphasis on traditional forms and structures had seemed to "freeze" art into rigid modes of expression. Writers now began to set greater value on what they felt were the spontaneous and therefore truer expressions of human emotions, without regard to classical precedent. The optimism and deism of the Age of Enlightenment had argued that men and women are naturally good, that their natural emotions are divine. Now the age that had perfected upholstered furniture and carriage springs discovered the still greater comforts of sentimentalism and extravagant feelings—even the emotional pleasures of "divine despair."

Philosophers and artists began to glorify humble and rural life, wilderness nature, the intuitive and nonrational virtues of the child and primitive man. The idea of the "Noble Savage" (a phrase first used by Dryden) became one of the great clichés of all time. Poets and novelists began to find inspiration in the picturesque, the irregular, and what came to be called the sublime—powerful ideas and overwhelming scenes that aroused the passions and "ravished the soul." Writers sought to create turbulent effects in literature, just as the political pamphleteers of the age had sought to create the violent crises of revolution.

In America, the beliefs and traditions of the seventeenth century had prepared men and women to receive the new ideas of the Age of Reason and the enlightenment. A native sense that Americans were sojourners in a New Israel coincided with the European idealization of the New World as a land of virtue and beauty. Seventeenth-century theological concern with natural phenomena—the storms, earthquakes, and meteors that believers had searched for evidence of God's providences—prepared the way for acceptance of the new science. And even Puritan intellectualism created a tradition of learning and education that readied men and women for new and rational theologies.

The secular ideals of the American Enlightenment were exemplified in the life and career of Benjamin Franklin, who instructed his countrymen as a printer, not a priest. He was a humanist, concerned with this world and the people in it. He was a scientist; a master of diplomacy; a humanitarian who helped establish hospitals, schools, and libraries. He was a believer in the possibilities of human progress and the comforts of material success; and he was a prose stylist whose writing reflected the neoclassic ideals of clarity, restraint, simplicity, and balance. Franklin seemed to represent the age in his paradoxical faith in both social order and in natural rights, in love of stability and devotion to revolutionary change. He was symbolic even in his success in the printing trade, for the eighteenth century in America was a time of an immense expansion of publishing that fed a growing and increasingly literate colonial population.

The Growth of an American Literature

In 1700, the settlers in British North America numbered little more than 250,000. By 1800, the population of the new United States exceeded 5 million. At the beginning of the century, the Colonies had only one newspaper. By 1800, the number had risen to around 200. Franklin began America's first significant magazine, the *General Magazine*, in Philadelphia in 1741. By 1800, ninety-one magazines had been established in the colonies. Most were short-lived, but they reflected the rapid growth of a reading public and the American desire to throw off English dominance in literature just as Americans had thrown off English dominance in government.

In 1783, the year the United States achieved its independence, Noah Webster declared, "America must be as independent in literature as she is in politics, as famous for the arts as for arms." The beginnings of literary independence were evident in such celebrations of the American scene as Crèvecoeur's *Letters from an American Farmer* (1782), Jefferson's *Notes on the State of Virginia* (1785), and Bartram's *Travels* (1791). Yet American literature throughout the century was largely patterned on the writing of eighteenth-century Englishmen. The most important poets of the period derived their power and style, their sentiments and regular couplets from English models. Franklin shaped his writing after the *Spectator Papers* (1711–1712) of the English essayists Addison and Steele. An ever growing and largely feminine reading audience created a rising demand for novels that was met by the importation of large numbers of English books. The first American novel, William Hill Brown's *The Power of Sympathy*, did not appear until 1789. The first popular American novel,

Susanna Rowson's *Charlotte Temple* (1791), was first published in England although it was eventually reprinted more than 200 times in America. Both were based vaguely on American events, but they followed closely the tradition established by the English novelist Samuel Richardson, whose *Pamela* (1740) set a standard for didactic sentimentalism that long dominated American fiction.

The moral temper of the colonies discouraged development of the drama. A Pennsylvania law of 1700 prohibited stage plays and other "rude and riotous sports." Colonists, especially in the Middle and New England Colonies, often considered the public performance of plays, like the services of dancing masters, to be indecent and corrupting. The theater was considered "dangerous to the souls of men" and filled with "lewd and filthy jests." Professional actors were thought to spread sickness, immorality, and lice. The first American play to appear on the American stage, Thomas Godfrey's *The Prince of Parthia*, was not presented until 1767 (and not revived until 1915). Royall Tyler's *The Contrast*, the first American drama on a native theme and the first American comedy, appeared in 1787. It helped introduce the American "Jonathan," the "stage Yankee" who became one of the stock characters in the American drama of the next century. Its prologue announced boldly:

> Exult each patriot heart!—this night is shown
> A piece, which we may fairly call our own.

Neither Godfrey nor Tyler nor their imitators departed significantly from the conventions of English drama that dominated the American theater until the late nineteenth century. But, while imaginative literature in America remained derivative and dependent, the heroic and revolutionary ambitions of the age were creating great political pamphleteering and state papers. Essayists and journalists had shaped the nation's beliefs with reason dressed in clear and forceful prose. Out of the tumult of the age came the inspired writing of Jefferson in the Declaration of Independence, of Tom Paine in *The Crisis* (1776), and of *The Federalist* (1787–1788), which stirred the world and helped form the American republic.

Although the eighteenth century was an age of enlightenment and reason, it was not wholly an enlightened age. The mass of men and women did not pause to examine theoretical arguments justifying a revolution that could free them from their debts and foreign masters. And once the Revolution was over, the citizens of the new nation did not unite in striving to fulfill the philosophical ideals of rationalism and benevolence. Merchants and the rising industrialists, no longer restrained by British laws, took advantage of unregulated commerce, exploited workers, and piled up ever greater fortunes. White settlers, hungry for land and riches, began thrusting relentlessly westward, uprooting native cultures, ruthlessly seizing Indian lands no longer protected by British authority.

Slavery, which had existed in each of the thirteen original colonies, continued to exist in each of the new thirteen states. In the South, slavery became more deeply entrenched, and in the North, although abolition of slavery began, the institution of slavery was not legally and completely abolished until the middle decades of the nineteenth century. The Age of Reason and Revolution failed to achieve its professed goals of good sense, justice, and benevolence. Nevertheless, it implanted ideals in the American mind that continued to grow and that flourish today, in the national dedication to pragmatism, in the vision of a unique and glorious American destiny, and in the belief that justice, liberty, and equality are the natural rights of all mankind.

Benjamin Franklin 1706–1790

Benjamin Franklin is fixed in the American mind in a series of images: as the runaway apprentice munching a roll while walking the streets of Philadelphia; as "Poor Richard" or "Father Abraham" preaching the virtues of thrift, prudence, and a reasonable degree of chastity; as the scientific wizard who flew a kite in a thunderstorm and "snatched the lightning from the sky"; as the rustic ambassador to Europe who spoke out against British imperialism and beguiled France into joining the American War for Independence. Benjamin Franklin is the model of the self-made man, a culture-hero whose life exemplifies the American dream of the poor boy who makes good.

He was born in Boston, the fifteenth child of a poor candlemaker. As a youth, he was apprenticed to his brother, a Boston printer. At twelve, Franklin published his first works: two ballads on the drowning of a lighthouse keeper and on the capture of Blackbeard the pirate. By the time he was sixteen he was writing for his brother's newspaper, using the pen name "Silence Dogood" to make satirical comments on Boston society, politics, and religion.

When Franklin was seventeen he ran off to Philadelphia, where he became a thriving printer. In 1732, under the name "Richard Saunders," he began publishing Poor Richard's Almanack, *a calendar filled with advertisements, weather forecasts, recipes, jokes, and a swarm of proverbs that entered the American mind and stuck: "A rolling stone gathers no moss." "Honesty is the best policy." "A penny saved is a penny earned." The* Almanack *became one of the most influential publications in American history, a delight to generations of readers gratified by preachments on the virtues of hard work, thrift, and success.*

When Franklin was forty-two, wealthy, and famous, he retired from business to devote himself to science and public service. He helped organize the American Philosophical Society, the University of Pennsylvania, and the first charity hospital in the Colonies. He studied the Gulf Stream, fossils, and earthquakes; invented bifocal spectacles and the lightning rod (long called the "Franklin Rod"); and made fundamental discoveries about the character of electricity.

Between 1757 and 1775 he represented the Colonies in England, where his propagandizing roused an angry British government to brand him the "inventor and first planner" of colonial discord. On the eve of the Revolution, he returned to Philadelphia. There he was named a delegate to the Second Continental Congress and a member of the committee chosen to write the Declaration of Independence. In 1776 Congress sent him once again to Europe, as Minister to France, to seek aid for the faltering Revolution. At the French court the seventy-year-old Franklin purposely played the role of a noble rustic. He dressed in plain clothes, wore a frontiersman's fur cap instead of a powdered wig, and he carried a formidable staff of apple wood. Dressed as the virtuous New World man he confirmed romantic European notions of natural American goodness, an impression he deliberately fostered to dramatize the natural justice of the American cause.

In Paris he negotiated the treaty of alliance of 1778 that joined France with America in the war against England. Five years later he signed the peace treaty that confirmed the American victory in the Revolution and established the nation's independence. When he returned to America for the last time, he was named a delegate to the Constitutional Convention in Philadelphia, and there he spent the last energies of his life, working to reconcile conflicts between states and to gain ratification of the Constitution.

As a homespun sage, as a statesman, and as a pamphleteer in the cause of liberty, Franklin shaped the character of the nation. He was the only American to sign the four documents that created the republic: the Declaration of Independence, the treaty of alliance with France, the treaty of peace with England, and the Constitution. At the time of his death, his countrymen considered him, more than Washington, to be the father of his country.

Franklin was a primary figure in the rise of American pragmatism. He helped create the cult of self-reliance that ripened into the wonders of Emersonian transcendentalism and into the gaudy excesses of American industrial society. His life and popular writings became instruments of instruction used by parents to teach wayward offspring that public virtue and pluck are keys to the kingdom of worldly success. He came to be invoked as the patron of businessmen and bankers, of boosters and rugged individualists who wanted to believe that, as Franklin had written, "God helps them that help themselves."

By the middle of the nineteenth century the inevitable reaction had set in. Franklin was derided as the shallow philosopher of the full belly and tight purse, the capitalist saint. His detractors took the remarks of his literary characters to be Franklin's total thought. They blamed him for faults they found in his ethical heirs and in the excesses of American capitalism. Critics mistook his subtleties and ironies for simple-minded pieties. They scoffed at him as the originator of simplistic rags-to-riches tales, such as the Horatio Alger success stories the world found so peculiarly American. By the last of the nineteenth century his place in the pantheon of American heroes had been taken by Washington and Lincoln.

But to the Age of Enlightenment, Franklin was the nation's "greatest man and ornament." Europeans thought he was greater than Voltaire, wiser than Rousseau. More than any other patriot, he had created the American republic. He was a master of the periodical essay, of satire, and of political journalism. He helped establish a tradition in American writing of the simple, utilitarian style, and with his Autobiography *he set the form for autobiography as a genre. Franklin was the greatest literary artist of eighteenth-century America. He created America's first great book. And he remains today the most widely read and influential of all American writers.*

FURTHER READING: *Benjamin Franklin, Writings,* ed. J. Lemay, 1987; A. Aldridge, *Benjamin Franklin, Philosopher and Man,* 1965; T. Fleming, *The Man Who Dared the Lightning,* 1971; C. Bowen, *The Most Dangerous Man in America,* 1974; C. Lopez and E. Herbert, *The Private Franklin,* 1975; B. Granger, *Benjamin Franklin,* 1976; *The Oldest Revolutionary,* ed. J. Lemay, 1976; D. Schoenbrun, *Triumph in Paris, The Exploits of Benjamin Franklin,* 1976; D. Hawke, *Franklin,* 1976; A. Tourtellot, *Benjamin Franklin . . . the Boston Years,* 1977; R. Clark, *Benjamin Franklin,* 1983; E. Wright, *Franklin of Philadelphia,* 1986; O. Seavey, *Becoming Benjamin Franklin, The Autobiography and the Life,* 1988; C. Tanford, *Ben Franklin Stilled the Waves,* 1989; P. Zall, *Franklin's Autobiography, A Model Life,* 1989; B. Cohen, *Benjamin Franklin's Science,* 1990; R. Middlekauff, *Benjamin Franklin and His Enemies,* 1996; D. Morgan, *The Devious Dr. Franklin, Colonial Agent,* 1996; D. Anderson, *The Radical Enlightenment of Benjamin Franklin,* 1997; H. Brands, *The First American, The Life and Times of Benjamin Franklin,* 2000; E. Morgan, *Benjamin Franklin,* 2002; W. Isaacson, *Benjamin Franklin, An American Life,* 2003; G. Wood, *The Americanization of Benjamin Franklin,* 2003; S. Schiff, *A Great Improvisation, Franklin, France, and the Birth of America,* 2005.

TEXTS: *The Autobiography of Benjamin Franklin,* ed. L. Labaree et al., 1964; *The Autobiography of Benjamin Franklin,* ed. M. Farrand, 1949.

from *THE AUTOBIOGRAPHY*[1]

PART ONE

Twyford,[2] at the Bishop of St. Asaph's, 1771.

Dear Son,[3]

I have ever had a Pleasure in obtaining any little Anecdotes of my Ancestors. You may remember the Enquiries I made among the Remains of my Relations when you were with me in England; and the Journey I took for that purpose.[4] Now imagining it may be equally agreable to you to know the Circumstances of *my* Life, many of which you are yet unacquainted with; and expecting a Week's uninterrupted Leisure in my present Country Retirement, I sit down to write them for you. To which I have besides some other Inducements. Having emerg'd from the Poverty and Obscurity in which I was born and bred, to a State of Affluence and some Degree of Reputation in the World, and having gone so far thro' Life with a considerable Share of Felicity, the conducing Means I made use of, which, with the Blessing of God, so well succeeded, my Posterity may like to know, as they may find some of them suitable to their own Situations, and therefore fit to be imitated. That Felicity, when I reflected on it, has induc'd me sometimes to say, that were it offer'd to my Choice, I should have no Objection to a Repetition of the same Life from its Beginning, only asking the Advantage Authors have in a second Edition to correct some Faults of the first. So would I if I might, besides corr[ectin]g the Faults, change some sinister Accidents and Events of it for others more favourable, but tho' this were deny'd, I should still accept the Offer. However, since such a Repetition is not to be expected, the next Thing most like living one's Life over again, seems to be a *Recollection* of that Life; and to make that Recollection as durable as possible, the putting it down in Writing. Hereby, too, I shall indulge the Inclination so natural in old Men, to be talking of themselves and their own past Actions, and I shall indulge it, without being troublesome to others who thro' respect to Age might think themselves oblig'd to give me a Hearing, since this may be read or not as any one pleases. And lastly, (I may as well confess it, since my Denial of it will be believ'd by no body) perhaps I shall a good deal gratify my own *Vanity*. Indeed I scarce ever heard or saw the introductory Words, *Without Vanity I may say*, &c. but some vain thing immediately follow'd. Most People dislike Vanity in others whatever Share they have of it themselves, but I give it fair Quarter[5] wherever I meet with it, being persuaded that it is often productive of Good to the Possessor and to others that are within his Sphere of Action: And

[1]Franklin began his *Autobiography* (he called it his *Memoirs*) at the age of sixty-five while vacationing in England at the home of Bishop Jonathan Shipley. The first section, addressed to Franklin's son William, was written in 1771. The remaining three sections, written over the next nineteen years, were not completed until the final year of Franklin's life. The account stops in 1758, before his greatest achievements as a diplomat and public servant. Thus it is not a true indication of the depth of his mind or the breadth of his accomplishments; nevertheless, it remains a masterpiece of autobiography and one of America's literary monuments.

[2]A village near Winchester, about fifty miles from London, and the name of the home of Jonathan Shipley, the Bishop of St. Asaph.

[3]William Franklin (1731–1813). Named royal governor of New Jersey in 1763, he remained a loyalist during the Revolution and was estranged from his father. They were partially reconciled in 1784, after the Revolution.

[4]Franklin and his son had toured England in 1758, visiting the homes of their ancestors.

[5]Respect, consideration.

therefore in many Cases it would not be quite absurd if a Man were to thank God for his Vanity among the other Comforts of Life.

And now I speak of thanking God, I desire with all Humility to acknowledge, that I owe the mention'd Happiness of my past Life to his kind Providence, which led me to the Means I us'd and gave them Success. My Belief of this, induces me to *hope,* tho' I must not *presume,* that the same Goodness will still be exercis'd towards me in continuing that Happiness, or in enabling me to bear a fatal Reverse, which I may experience as others have done, the Complexion of my future Fortune being known to him only: and in whose Power it is to bless to us even our Afflictions.

The Notes one of my Uncles (who had the same kind of Curiosity in collecting Family Anecdotes) once put into my Hands, furnish'd me with several Particulars relating to our Ancestors. From these Notes I learnt that the Family had liv'd in the same Village, Ecton[6] in Northamptonshire, for 300 Years, and how much longer he knew not (perhaps from the Time when the Name *Franklin* that before was the Name of an Order of People,[7] was assum'd by them for a Surname, when others took Surnames all over the Kingdom). (Here a Note)[8] on a Freehold[9] of about 30 Acres, aided by the Smith's Business which had continued in the Family till his Time, the eldest Son being always bred to that Business. A Custom which he and my Father both followed as to their eldest Sons. When I search'd the Register at Ecton, I found an Account of their Births, Marriages and Burials, from the Year 1555 only, there being no Register kept in that Parish at any time preceding. By that Register I perceiv'd that I was the youngest Son of the youngest Son for 5 Generations back.

My Grandfather Thomas, who was born in 1598, lived at Ecton till he grew too old to follow Business longer, when he went to live with his Son John, a Dyer[10] at Banbury in Oxfordshire, with whom my Father serv'd an Apprenticeship. There my Grandfather died and lies buried. We saw his Gravestone in 1758. His eldest Son Thomas liv'd in the House at Ecton, and left it with the Land to his only Child, a Daughter, who with her Husband, one Fisher of Wellingborough sold it to Mr. Isted, now Lord of the Manor there. My Grandfather had 4 Sons that grew up, viz.[11] Thomas, John, Benjamin and Josiah. I will give you what Account I can of them at this distance from my Papers,[12] and if they are not lost in my Absence, you will among them find many more Particulars. Thomas was bred a Smith under his Father, but being ingenious, and encourag'd in Learning (as all his Brothers like wise were) by an Esquire Palmer then the principal Gentleman in that Parish, he qualify'd for the Business of Scrivener,[13] became a considerable Man in the County Affairs, was a chief Mover of all publick Spirited Undertakings, for the County, or Town of Northampton and his own Village, of which many Instances were told us at Ecton and he was much taken Notice of and patroniz'd by the then Lord Halifax. He died in 1702, Jan. 6, old Stile, just 4 Years a Day before I was born.[14] The Account we receiv'd of his Life and Character

[6]A village about 50 miles north of London.

[7]In medieval England the word *franklin* was used to describe a middle-class landowner.

[8]Franklin omitted the note he offered to insert here.

[9]Land held free of other claims of ownership. [10]One who dyes cloth. [11]Namely.

[12]Franklin's personal papers, kept in Philadelphia.

[13]A professional writer of legal documents.

[14]In 1752 the Gregorian ("New Style") calendar replaced the Julian ("Old Style") calendar in England and the British North American colonies. The change advanced the calendar by eleven days. Thus Franklin's birthday (January 6, Old Style) became January 17, 1706, New Style.

from some old People at Ecton, I remember struck you as something extraordinary from its Similarity to what you knew of mine. Had he died on the same Day, you said one might have suppos'd a Transmigration.[15]

John was bred a Dyer, I believe of Woollens. Benjamin, was bred a Silk Dyer, serving an Apprenticeship at London. He was an ingenious Man, I remember him well, for when I was a Boy he came over to my Father in Boston, and lived in the House with us some Years. He lived to a great Age. His Grandson Samuel Franklin now lives in Boston. He left behind him two Quarto Volumes, M.S. of his own Poetry, consisting of little occasional Pieces address'd to his Friends and Relations, of which the following sent to me, is a Specimen. (Here insert it.)[16] He had form'd a Shorthand of his own, which he taught me, but never practising it I have now forgot it. I was nam'd after this Uncle, there being a particular Affection between him and my Father. He was very pious, a great Attender of Sermons of the best Preachers, which he took down in his Shorthand and had with him many Volumes of them. He was also much of a Politician, too much perhaps for his Station. There fell lately into my Hands in London a Collection he had made of all the principal Pamphlets relating to Publick affairs from 1641 to 1717. Many of the Volumes are wanting, as appears by the Numbering, but there still remains 8 Vols. Folio, and 24 in 4to and 8vo.[17] A Dealer in old Books met with them, and knowing me by my sometimes buying of him, he brought them to me. It seems my Uncle must have left them here when he went to America, which was above 50 Years since. There are many of his Notes in the Margins.

This obscure Family of ours was early in the Reformation, and continu'd Protestants thro' the Reign of Queen Mary, when they were sometimes in Danger of Trouble on Account of their Zeal against Popery.[18] They had got an English Bible,[19] and to conceal and secure it, it was fastned open with Tapes under and within the Frame of a Joint Stool.[20] When my Great Great Grandfather read in it to his Family, he turn'd up the Joint Stool upon his Knees, turning over the Leaves then under the Tapes. One of the Children stood at the Door to give Notice if he saw the Apparitor coming, who was an Officer of the Spiritual Court.[21] In that Case the Stool was turn'd down again upon its feet, when the Bible remain'd conceal'd under it as before. This Anecdote I had from my Uncle Benjamin. The Family continu'd all of the Church of England till about the End of Charles the 2ds Reign,[22] when some of the Ministers that had been outed for Nonconformity,[23] holding Conventicles[24] in Northamptonshire, Benjamin and Josiah adher'd to

[15]The passing of a soul to another body after death.

[16]The specimen was omitted from Franklin's manuscript.

[17]"Folio," "quarto" ("4to"), and "octavo" ("8vo") are designations of books sized from large to small and made from sheets with two, four, or eight pages printed on each side.

[18]Queen Mary reigned from 1553 to 1558 and attempted to reimpose Roman Catholicism on Protestant England. For her persecution of Protestants, she earned the name "Bloody Mary."

[19]Probably the English "Great Bible" (1539–1540). During Queen Mary's reign, Bibles in English were not officially prohibited, but many copies were seized and destroyed in an effort to root out the sources of Protestantism.

[20]A four-legged stool that is "joined" by a furniture maker rather than nailed together by rough carpentry. The horizontal stretcher (frame) that braces the upper legs also obscures the underside of the seat.

[21]An ecclesiastical court established to root out heresy.

[22]Charles II reigned from 1660 to 1685.

[23]Ousted from the Church of England for failure to conform to required religious practices.

[24]The secret and illegal meetings of religious nonconformists.

them, and so continu'd all their Lives. The rest of the Family remain'd with the Episcopal Church.[25]

Josiah, my Father, married young, and carried his Wife with three Children unto New England, about 1682.[26] The Conventicles having been forbidden by Law, and frequently disturbed, induced some considerable Men of his Acquaintance to remove to that Country, and he was prevail'd with to accompany them thither, where they expected to enjoy their Mode of Religion with Freedom. By the same Wife he had 4 Children more born there, and by a second Wife ten more, in all 17, of which I remember 13 sitting at one time at his Table, who all grew up to be Men and Women, and married. I was the youngest Son and the youngest Child but two, and was born in Boston, N. England.

My Mother the 2d Wife was Abiah Folger, a Daughter of Peter Folger, one of the first Settlers of New England, of whom honourable mention is made by Cotton Mather, in his Church History of that Country, (entitled Magnalia Christi Americana) as a *godly learned Englishman,* if I remember the words rightly. I have heard that he wrote sundry small occasional Pieces, but only one of them was printed which I saw now many Years since. It was written in 1675, in the homespun Verse of that Time and People, and address'd to those then concern'd in the Government there.[27] It was in favour of Liberty of Conscience, and in behalf of the Baptists, Quakers, and other Sectaries, that had been under Persecution; ascribing the Indian Wars and other Distresses, that had befallen the Country to that Persecution, as so many Judgments of God, to punish so heinous an Offence; and exhorting a Repeal of those uncharitable Laws. The whole appear'd to me as written with a good deal of Decent Plainness and manly Freedom. The six last concluding Lines I remember, tho' I have forgotten the two first of the Stanza, but the Purport of them was that his Censures proceeded from *Goodwill,* and there he would be known as the Author,

> because to be a Libeller, (says he)
> I hate it with my Heart.
> From Sherburne Town[28] where now I dwell,
> My Name I do put here,
> Without Offence, your real Friend,
> It is Peter Folgier.

My elder Brothers were all put Apprentices to different Trades. I was put to the Grammar School at Eight Years of Age, my Father intending to devote me as the Tithe[29] of his Sons to the Service of the Church. My early Readiness in learning to read (which must have been very early, as I do not remember when I could not read) and the Opinion of all his Friends that I should certainly make a good Scholar, encourag'd him in this Purpose of his. My Uncle Benjamin too approv'd of it, and propos'd to give me all his Shorthand Volumes of Sermons I suppose as a Stock to set up with, if I would learn his Character.[30] I continu'd however at the Grammar School not quite one

[25]The Episcopal Church of England. [26]Actually 1683.

[27]Peter Folger's *A Looking Glass for the Times,* written in 1676, was not published until 1725.

[28]"In the Island of Nantucket."—Franklin's note. [29]Tenth.

[30]Shorthand system.

Year, tho' in that time I had risen gradually from the Middle of the Class of that Year to be the Head of it, and farther was remov'd into the next Class above it, in order to go with that into the third at the End of the Year. But my Father in the mean time, from a View of the Expence of a College Education which, having so large a Family, he could not well afford, and the mean Living many so educated were afterwards able to obtain, Reasons that he gave to his Friends in my Hearing, altered his first Intention, took me from the Grammar School, and set me to a School for Writing and Arithmetic kept by a then famous Man, Mr. Geo. Brownell, very successful in his Profession generally, and that by mild encouraging Methods. Under him I acquired fair Writing pretty soon, but I fail'd in the Arithmetic, and made no Progress in it.

At Ten Years old, I was taken home to assist my Father in his Business, which was that of a Tallow Chandler and Sope-Boiler.[31] A Business he was not bred to, but had assumed on his Arrival in New England and on finding his Dying Trade would not maintain his Family, being in little Request. Accordingly I was employed in cutting Wick for the Candles, filling the Dipping Mold, and the Molds for cast Candles, attending the Shop, going of Errands, &c. I dislik'd the Trade and had a strong Inclination for the Sea; but my Father declar'd against it; however, living near the Water, I was much in and about it, learnt early to swim well, and to manage Boats, and when in a Boat or Canoe with other Boys I was commonly allow'd to govern,[32] especially in any case of Difficulty; and upon other Occasions I was generally a Leader among the Boys, and sometimes led them into Scrapes, of which I will mention one Instance, as it shows an early projecting public Spirit, tho' not then justly conducted. There was a Salt Marsh that bounded part of the Mill Pond, on the Edge of which at Highwater, we us'd to stand to fish for Minews.[33] By much Trampling, we had made it a mere Quagmire. My Proposal was to build a Wharf there fit for us to stand upon, and I show'd my Comrades a large Heap of Stones which were intended for a new House near the Marsh, and which would very well suit our Purpose. Accordingly in the Evening when the Workmen were gone, I assembled a Number of my Playfellows, and working with them diligently like so many Emmets,[34] sometimes two or three to a Stone, we brought them all away and built our little Wharff. The next Morning the Workmen were surpriz'd at Missing the Stones; which were found in our Wharff; Enquiry was made after the Removers; we were discovered and complain'd of; several of us were corrected by our Fathers; and tho' I pleaded the Usefulness of the Work, mine convinc'd me that nothing was useful which was not honest.

I think you may like to know Something of his Person and Character. He had an excellent Constitution of Body, was of middle Stature, but well set and very strong. He was ingenious, could draw prettily, was skill'd a little in Music and had a clear pleasing Voice, so that when he play'd Psalm Tunes on his Violin and sung withal as he sometimes did in an Evening after the Business of the Day was over, it was extreamly agreable to hear. He had a mechanical Genius too, and on occasion was very handy in the Use of other Tradesmen's Tools. But his great Excellence lay in a sound Understanding, and solid Judgment in prudential Matters, both in private and publick Affairs. In the latter indeed he was never employed, the numerous Family he

[31]A maker of candles and soap.
[32]Steer. [33]Minnows. [34]Ants.

had to educate and the straitness of his Circumstances, keeping him close to his Trade, but I remember well his being frequently visited by leading People, who consulted him for his Opinion in Affairs of the Town or of the Church he belong'd to and show'd a good deal of Respect for his Judgment and Advice. He was also much consulted by private Persons about their Affairs when any Difficulty occur'd, and frequently chosen an Arbitrator between contending Parties. At his Table he lik'd to have as often as he could, some sensible Friend or Neighbour, to converse with, and always took care to start some ingenious or useful Topic for Discourse, which might tend to improve the Minds of his Children. By this means he turn'd our Attention to what was good, just, and prudent in the Conduct of Life; and little or no Notice was ever taken of what related to the Victuals on the Table, whether it was well or ill drest, in or out of season, of good or bad flavour, preferable or inferior to this or that other thing of the kind; so that I was bro't up in such a perfect Inattention to those Matters as to be quite Indifferent what kind of Food was set before me; and so unobservant of it, that to this Day, if I am ask'd I can scarce tell, a few Hours after Dinner, what I din'd upon. This has been a Convenience to me in travelling, where my Companions have been sometimes very unhappy for want of a suitable Gratification of their more delicate because better instructed Tastes and Appetites.

My Mother had likewise an excellent Constitution. She suckled all her 10 Children. I never knew either my Father or Mother to have any Sickness but that of which they dy'd, he at 89 and she at 85 Years of age. They lie buried together at Boston, where I some Years since plac'd a Marble stone over their Grave with this Inscription

Josiah Franklin
And Abiah his Wife
Lie here interred.
They lived lovingly together in Wedlock
Fifty-five Years.
Without an Estate or any gainful Employment,[35]
By constant labour and Industry,
With God's Blessing,
They maintained a large Family
Comfortably;
And brought up thirteen Children,
And seven Grand Children
Reputably.
From this Instance, Reader,
Be encouraged to Diligence in thy Calling,
And distrust not Providence.
He was a pious & prudent Man,
She a discreet and virtuous Woman.
Their youngest Son,
In filial Regard to their Memory,
Places this Stone.
J.F. born 1655—Died 1744. Ætat[36] 89
A.F. born 1667—died 1752–85

[35]I.e., without an inheritance or profitable appointment. [36]Latin: aged.

By my rambling Digressions I perceive my self to be grown old. I us'd to write more methodically. But one does not dress for private Company as for a publick Ball. 'Tis perhaps only Negligence.

To return, I continu'd thus employ'd in my Father's Business for two Years, that is till I was 12 Years old; and my Brother John,[37] who was bred to that Business having left my Father, married and set up for himself at Rhodeisland, there was all Appearance that I was destin'd to supply his Place and be a Tallow Chandler. But my Dislike to the Trade continuing, my Father was under Apprehensions that if he did not find one for me more agreable, I should break away and get to Sea, as his Son Josiah had done to his great Vexation. He therefore sometimes took me to walk with him, and see Joiners, Bricklayers, Turners, Braziers,[38] &c. at their Work, that he might observe my Inclination, and endeavour to fix it on some Trade or other on Land. It has ever since been a Pleasure to me to see good Workmen handle their Tools; and it has been useful to me, having learnt so much by it, as to be able to do little Jobs my self in my House, when a Workman could not readily be got; and to construct little Machines for my Experiments while the Intention of making the Experiment was fresh and warm in my Mind. My Father at last fix'd upon the Cutler's Trade, and my Uncle Benjamin's Son Samuel who was bred to that Business in London being about that time establish'd in Boston, I was sent to be with him some time on liking. But his Expectations of a Fee with me displeasing my Father, I was taken home again.

From a Child I was fond of Reading, and all the little Money that came into my Hands was ever laid out in Books. Pleas'd with the Pilgrim's Progress, my first Collection was of John Bunyan's Works, in separate little Volumes.[39] I afterwards sold them to enable me to buy R. Burton's Historical Collections; they were small Chapmen's books and cheap 40 or 50 in all.[40] My Father's little Library consisted chiefly of Books in polemic Divinity, most of which I read, and have since often regretted, that at a time when I had such a Thirst for Knowledge, more proper Books had not fallen in my Way, since it was now resolv'd I should not be a Clergyman. Plutarch's Lives there was, in which I read abundantly, and I still think that time spent to great Advantage.[41] There was also a Book of Defoe's, called an Essay on Projects, and another of Dr. Mather's, call'd Essays to do Good which perhaps gave me a Turn of Thinking that had an Influence on some of the principal future Events of my Life.[42]

This Bookish Inclination at length determin'd my Father to make me a Printer, tho' he had already one Son, (James) of that Profession. In 1717 my

[37]John Franklin (1690–1756), Benjamin's favorite brother, later postmaster of Boston.

[38]Woodworkers, bricklayers, latheworkers, brassworkers.

[39]John Bunyan (1628–1688), Puritan preacher, author of *The Pilgrim's Progress* (1678).

[40]Nathaniel Crouch, who wrote as either Robert or Richard Burton, "melted down the best of our English histories into twelve-penny books, which are filled with wonders, rareties, and curiosities." Chapmen's books: peddler's books.

[41]The widely read *Parallel Lives* of the Greek writer Plutarch (A.D. 46–120) is a series of forty-six biographies, mostly in pairs, coupling a noted Greek and a noted Roman who were similar in activity or personal quality.

[42]Daniel Defoe's *Essay upon Projects* (1697), proposing numerous schemes for civic and economic improvement, and Cotton Mather's *Bonifacius. An Essay Upon the Good, that is to be Devised and Designed, by those Who Desire . . . to Do Good While they Live* (1710). The Mather essay was an inspiration to Franklin in forming the Junto, and to some extent he modeled his club on the neighborhood benefit societies Mather had organized in Boston.

Brother James return'd from England with a Press and Letters[43] to set up his Business in Boston. I lik'd it much better than that of my Father, but still had a Hankering for the Sea. To prevent the apprehended Effect of such an Inclination, my Father was impatient to have me bound[44] to my Brother. I stood out some time, but at last was persuaded and signed the Indentures,[45] when I was yet but 12 Years old.[46] I was to serve as an Apprentice till I was 21 Years of Age, only I was to be allow'd Journeyman's Wages[47] during the last Year. In a little time I made great Proficiency in the Business, and became a useful Hand to my Brother. I now had Access to better Books. An Acquaintance with the Apprentices of Booksellers, enabled me sometimes to borrow a small one, which I was careful to return soon and clean. Often I sat up in my Room reading the greatest Part of the Night, when the Book was borrow'd in the Evening and to be return'd early in the Morning lest it should be miss'd or wanted. And after some time an ingenious Tradesman Mr. Matthew Adams who had a pretty Collection of Books, and who frequented our Printing House, took Notice of me, invited me to his Library, and very kindly lent me such Books as I chose to read. I now took a Fancy to Poetry, and made some little Pieces. My Brother, thinking it might turn to account encourag'd me, and put me on composing two occasional Ballads. One was called the *Light House Tragedy,* and contain'd an Account of the drowning of Capt. Worthilake with his Two Daughters; the other was a Sailor Song on the Taking of *Teach* or Blackbeard the Pirate.[48] They were wretched Stuff, in the Grubstreet Ballad Stile,[49] and when they were printed he sent me about the Town to sell them. The first sold wonderfully, the Event being recent, having made a great Noise. This flatter'd my Vanity. But my Father discourag'd me, by ridiculing my Performances, and telling me Versemakers were generally Beggars; so I escap'd being a Poet, most probably a very bad one. But as Prose Writing has been of great Use to me in the Course of my Life, and was a principal Means of my Advancement, I shall tell you how in such a Situation I acquir'd what little Ability I have in that Way.

There was another Bookish Lad in the Town, John Collins by Name, with whom I was intimately acquainted. We sometimes disputed, and very fond we were of Argument, and very desirous of confuting one another. Which disputacious Turn, by the way, is apt to become a very bad Habit, making People often extreamly disagreable in Company, by the Contradiction that is necessary to bring it into Practice, and thence, besides souring and spoiling the Conversation, is productive of Disgusts and perhaps Enmities where you may have occasion for Friendship. I had caught it by reading my Father's Books of Dispute about Religion. Persons of good Sense, I have since observ'd, seldom fall into it, except Lawyers, University Men, and Men of all Sorts that have been bred at Edinborough. A Question was once some how or other started between Collins and me, of the Propriety of educating the Female Sex in Learning, and their Abilities for Study. He was of Opinion

[43]Type. [44]Apprenticed. [45]Contract.

[46]James Franklin was nine years older than Benjamin. This difference helps account for the friction that developed between the two.

[47]Daily wages.

[48]The full texts of these two ballads have not survived. George Worthylake, keeper of the light on Beacon Island, Boston Harbor, his wife, and one daughter were drowned November 3, 1718. The pirate Blackbeard, Edward Teach, was killed November 22, 1718.

[49]I.e., written in the style of those literary hacks who lived in London's Grub Street.

that it was improper; and that they were naturally unequal to it. I took the contrary Side, perhaps a little for Dispute sake. He was naturally more eloquent, had a ready Plenty of Words, and sometimes as I thought bore me down more by his Fluency than by the Strength of his Reasons. As we parted without settling the Point, and were not to see one another again for some time, I sat down to put my Arguments in Writing, which I copied fair and sent to him. He answer'd and I reply'd. Three or four Letters of a Side had pass'd, when my Father happen'd to find my Papers, and read them. Without entering into the Discussion, he took occasion to talk to me about the Manner of my Writing, observ'd that tho' I had the Advantage of my Antagonist in correct Spelling and pointing (which I ow'd to the Printing House)[50] I fell far short in elegance of Expression, in Method and in Perspicuity, of which he convinc'd me by several Instances. I saw the Justice of his Remarks, and thence grew more attentive to the *Manner* in Writing, and determin'd to endeavour at Improvement.

About this time I met with an odd Volume of the Spectator.[51] It was the third. I had never before seen any of them. I bought it, read it over and over, and was much delighted with it. I thought the Writing excellent, and wish'd if possible to imitate it. With that View, I took some of the Papers, and making short Hints of the Sentiment in each Sentence, laid them by a few Days, and then without looking at the Book, try'd to compleat the Papers again, by expressing each hinted Sentiment at length and as fully as it had been express'd before, in any suitable Words, that should come to hand.

Then I compar'd my Spectator with the Original, discover'd some of my Faults and corrected them. But I found I wanted a Stock of Words or a Readiness in recollecting and using them, which I thought I should have acquir'd before that time, if I had gone on making Verses, since the continual Occasion for Words of the same Import but of different Length, to suit the Measure,[52] or of different Sound for the Rhyme, would have laid me under a constant Necessity of searching for Variety, and also have tended to fix that Variety in my Mind, and make me Master of it. Therefore I took some of the Tales and turn'd them into Verse: And after a time, when I had pretty well forgotten the Prose, turn'd them back again. I also sometimes jumbled my Collections of Hints into Confusion, and after some Weeks, endeavour'd to reduce them into the best Order, before I began to form the full Sentences, and compleat the Paper. This was to teach me Method in the Arrangement of Thoughts. By comparing my work afterwards with the original, I discover'd many faults and amended them; but I sometimes had the Pleasure of Fancying that in certain Particulars of small Import, I had been lucky enough to improve the Method or the Language and this encourag'd me to think I might possibly in time come to be a tolerable English Writer, of which I was extreamly ambitious.

[50]Even among the well educated, spelling and punctuation ("pointing") were not standardized. As the text of Franklin's *Autobiography* reveals, he was generally, but not entirely, consistent in his spelling and punctuation.

[51]*The Spectator* was a paper issued daily between March 1, 1711, and December 6, 1712, containing essays of which Joseph Addison wrote nearly half and Richard Steele most of the rest. The style, which Samuel Johnson called "familiar, but not coarse, and elegant but not ostentatious," greatly influenced English prose writing. A set of bound volumes of the papers was kept in James Franklin's printing office.

[52]Meter.

My Time for these Exercises and for Reading, was at Night, after Work or before Work began in the Morning; or on Sundays, when I contrived to be in the Printing house alone, evading as much as I could the common Attendance on publick Worship, which my Father used to exact of me when I was under his Care: And which indeed I still thought a Duty; tho' I could not, as it seemed to me, afford the Time to practise it.

When about 16 Years of Age, I happen'd to meet with a Book, written by one Tryon, recommending a Vegetable Diet.[53] I determined to go into it. My Brother being yet unmarried, did not keep House, but boarded himself and his Apprentices in another Family. My refusing to eat Flesh occasioned an Inconveniency, and I was frequently chid[54] for my singularity. I made my self acquainted with Tryon's Manner of preparing some of his Dishes, such as Boiling Potatoes or Rice, making Hasty Pudding,[55] and a few others, and then propos'd to my Brother, that if he would give me Weekly half the Money he paid for my Board I would board my self. He instantly agreed to it, and I presently found that I could save half what he paid me. This was an additional Fund for buying Books: But I had another Advantage in it. My Brother and the rest going from the Printing House to their Meals, I remain'd there alone, and dispatching presently my light Repast, (which often was no more than a Bisket or a Slice of Bread, a Handful of Raisins or a Tart from the Pastry Cook's, and a Glass of Water) had the rest of the Time till their Return, for Study, in which I made the greater Progress from that greater Clearness of Head and quicker Apprehension which usually attend Temperance in Eating and Drinking. And now it was that being on some Occasion made asham'd of my Ignorance in Figures, which I had twice failed in learning when at School, I took Cocker's Book of Arithmetick,[56] and went thro' the whole by my self with great Ease. I also read Seller's and Sturmy's Books of Navigation,[57] and became acquainted with the little Geometry they contain, but never proceeded far in that Science. And I read about this Time Locke on Human Understanding, and the Art of Thinking by Messrs. du Port Royal.[58]

While I was intent on improving my Language, I met with an English Grammar (I think it was Greenwood's)[59] at the End of which there were two little Sketches of the Arts of Rhetoric and Logic, the latter finishing with a Specimen of a Dispute in the Socratic Method. And soon after I procur'd Xenophon's Memorable Things of Socrates,[60] wherein there are many Instances of the same Method. I was charm'd with it, adopted it, dropt my abrupt Contradiction, and positive Argumentation, and put on the humble Enquirer and Doubter. And being then, from reading Shaftsbury and

[53]Thomas Tryon, *The Way to Health, Long Life and Happiness, or a Discourse of Temperance* (1683).

[54]Ridiculed, teased. [55]Boiled cornmeal.

[56]Edward Cocker (1631–1675) was the author of several arithmetical works; which one Franklin used is not known.

[57]John Seller, *An Epitome of the Art of Navigation* (1681), and Samuel Sturmy, *The Mariner's Magazine; or, Sturmy's Mathematical and Practical Arts* (1669).

[58]John Locke's *Essay Concerning Human Understanding* (1690). Antoine Arnauld and Pierre Nicole, of Port-Royal (near Paris), *Logic: or the Art of Thinking,* English translation (1685) of the Latin work of 1662. This was one of the most influential logic texts of the age; James Franklin's printing office had a copy.

[59]James Greenwood, *An Essay towards a Practical English Grammar* (1711). Franklin recommended this book in 1749 for the academy he proposed in Pennsylvania.

[60]Xenophon, *The Memorable Things of Socrates,* translated by Edward Bysshe (1712).

Collins,[61] become a real Doubter in many Points of our Religious Doctrine, I found this Method safest for my self and very embarassing to those against whom I used it, therefore I took a Delight in it, practis'd it continually and grew very artful and expert in drawing People even of superior Knowledge into concessions the Consequences of which they did not foresee, entangling them in Difficulties out of which they could not extricate themselves, and so obtaining Victories that neither my self nor my Cause always deserved.

I continu'd this Method some few Years, but gradually left it, retaining only the Habit of expressing my self in Terms of modest Diffidence, never using when I advance any thing that may possibly be disputed, the Words, *Certainly, undoubtedly,* or any others that give the Air of Positiveness to an Opinion; but rather say, I conceive, or I apprehend a Thing to be so or so, It appears to me, or I should think it so or so for such and such Reasons, or I imagine it to be so, or it is so if I am not mistaken. This Habit I believe has been of great Advantage to me, when I have had occasion to inculcate my Opinions and persuade Men into Measures that I have been from time to time engag'd in promoting. And as the chief Ends of Conversation are to *inform,* or to be *informed,* to *please* or to *persuade,* I wish wellmeaning sensible Men would not lessen their Power of doing Good by a Positive assuming Manner that seldom fails to disgust, tends to create Opposition, and to defeat every one of those Purposes for which Speech was given us, to wit, giving or receiving Information, or Pleasure: For if you would *inform,* a positive dogmatical Manner in advancing your Sentiments, may provoke Contradiction and prevent a candid Attention. If you wish Information and Improvement from the Knowledge of others and yet at the same time express your self as firmly fix'd in your present Opinions, modest sensible Men, who do not love Disputation, will probably leave you undisturb'd in the Possession of your Error; and by such a Manner you can seldom hope to recommend your self in *pleasing* your Hearers, or to persuade those whose Concurrence you desire. Pope says, judiciously,

Men should be taught as if you taught them not,
And things unknown propos'd as things forgot,[62]

farther recommending it to us,

To speak tho' sure, with seeming Diffidence.[63]

And he might have coupled with this Line that which he has coupled with another, I think less properly,

For Want of Modesty is Want of Sense.

[61]Anthony Ashley Cooper, third Earl of Shaftesbury (1671–1713), a religious skeptic, and Anthony Collins (1676–1729), a deist.

[62]Alexander Pope, *An Essay on Criticism* (1711), lines 574–575. Franklin is quoting inaccurately from memory. The first line should read, "Men must be taught as if you taught them not."

[63]*An Essay on Criticism,* line 567. The line should read, "And speak, tho' sure, with seeming diffidence."

If you ask why, *less properly,* I must repeat the Lines;

> Immodest Words admit of *no* Defence;
> *For* Want of Modesty is Want of Sense.[64]

Now is not *Want of Sense* (where a Man is so unfortunate as to want it) some Apology for his *Want of Modesty?* and would not the Lines stand more justly thus?

> Immodest Words admit *but this* Defence,
> That Want of Modesty is Want of Sense.

This however I should submit to better Judgments.

My Brother had in 1720 or 21, begun to print a Newspaper. It was the second that appear'd in America, and was called *The New England Courant.* The only one before it, was *the Boston News Letter.*[65] I remember his being dissuaded by some of his Friends from the Undertaking, as not likely to succeed, one newspaper being in their Judgment enough for America. At this time 1771 there are not less than five and twenty. He went on however with the Undertaking, and after having work'd in composing the Types and printing off the Sheets I was employ'd to carry the Papers thro' the Streets to the Customers. He had some ingenious Men among his Friends who amus'd themselves by writing little Pieces for this Paper, which gain'd it Credit, and made it more in Demand; and these Gentlemen often visited us. Hearing their Conversations, and their Accounts of the Approbation their Papers were receiv'd with, I was excited to try my Hand among them. But being still a Boy, and suspecting that my Brother would object to printing any Thing of mine in his Paper if he knew it to be mine, I contriv'd to disguise my Hand, and writing an anonymous Paper[66] I put it in at Night under the Door of the Printing House. It was found in the Morning and communicated to his Writing Friends when they call'd in as usual. They read it, commented on it in my Hearing, and I had the exquisite Pleasure, of finding it met with their Approbation, and that in their different Guesses at the Author none were named but Men of some Character among us for Learning and Ingenuity.

I suppose now that I was rather lucky in my Judges: And that perhaps they were not really so very good ones as I then esteem'd them. Encourag'd however by this, I wrote and convey'd in the same Way to the Press several more Papers, which were equally approv'd, and I kept my Secret till my small Fund of Sense for such Performances was pretty well exhausted, and then I

[64]Often attributed to Pope, the couplet is actually by Wentworth Dillon, Earl of Roscommon, from his *Essay on Translated Verse* (1684), lines 113–114. The second line should read, "For want of decency is want of sense."

[65]The first newspaper in the Colonies was Boston's *Public Occurrences* which appeared on September 25, 1690, and had but a single issue. *The Boston Newsletter,* established April 24, 1704, was the second; *The Boston Gazette,* December 21, 1719, was the third; *The American Weekly Mercury,* Philadelphia, December 22, 1719, was the fourth, and James Franklin's *New-England Courant,* August 7, 1721, was the fifth. Earlier, James had briefly been printer for the *Gazette,* which may account for Franklin's faulty recollection.

[66]The first of the fourteen "Silence Dogood" letters, published in the *Courant,* April 12–October 8, 1722.

discovered[67] it; when I began to be considered a little more by my Brother's Acquaintance, and in a manner that did not quite please him, as he thought, probably with reason, that it tended to make me too vain. And perhaps this might be one Occasion of the Differences that we frequently had about this Time. Tho' a Brother, he considered himself as my Master, and me as his Apprentice; and accordingly expected the same Services from me as he would from another; while I thought he demean'd me too much in some he requir'd of me, who from a Brother expected more Indulgence. Our Disputes were often brought before our Father, and I fancy I was either generally in the right, or else a better Pleader, because the Judgment was generally in my favour: But my Brother was passionate and had often beaten me, which I took extreamly amiss; and thinking my Apprenticeship very tedious, I was continually wishing for some Opportunity of shortening it, which at length offered in a manner unexpected.[68]

One of the Pieces in our News-Paper, on some political Point which I have now forgotten, gave Offence to the Assembly.[69] He was taken up, censur'd and imprison'd for a Month by the Speaker's Warrant, I suppose because he would not discover his Author. I too was taken up and examin'd before the Council; but tho' I did not give them any Satisfaction, they contented themselves with admonishing me, and dismiss'd me; considering me perhaps as an Apprentice who was bound to keep his Master's Secrets. During my Brother's Confinement, which I resented a good deal, notwithstanding our private Differences, I had the Management of the Paper, and I made bold to give our Rulers some Rubs in it, which my Brother took very kindly, while others began to consider me in an unfavourable Light, as a young Genius that had a Turn for Libelling and Satyr.[70] My Brother's Discharge was accompany'd with an Order of the House, (a very odd one) *that James Franklin should no longer print the Paper called the New England Courant.* There was a Consultation held in our Printing House among his Friends what he should do in this Case. Some propos'd to evade the Order by changing the Name of the paper; but my Brother seeing Inconveniences in that, it was finally concluded on as a better Way, to let it be printed for the future under the Name of *Benjamin Franklin.* And to avoid the Censure of the Assembly that might fall on him, as still printing it by his Apprentice, the Contrivance was, that my old Indenture should be return'd to me with a full Discharge on the Back of it, to be shown on Occasion; but to secure to him the Benefit of my Service I was to sign new Indentures for the Remainder of the Term, which were to be kept private. A very flimsy Scheme it was, but however it was immediately executed, and the Paper went on accordingly under my Name for several Months.[71] At length a fresh Difference arising between my Brother and me, I took upon me to assert my Freedom, presuming that he would not venture to produce the new

[67]Revealed.

[68]"I fancy his harsh and tyrannical Treatment of me, might be a means of impressing me with that Aversion to arbitrary Power that has stuck to me thro' my whole Life."—Franklin's note.

[69]One of the two Houses of the Massachusetts legislature. [70]Satire.

[71]On June 11, 1722, James Franklin insinuated in the *Courant* that the government was lax in suppressing piracy. As a result, he was jailed for a month. Later the government moved to forbid him to publish his paper without prior censorship. Since the censorship rule applied only to James, the paper was issued over Benjamin's name. On May 7, 1723, James was cleared by a grand jury, but the *Courant* continued to appear over Benjamin's name until at least 1726, nearly three years after he had left Boston. The *Courant* ceased publication by early 1727.

Indentures. It was not fair in me to take this Advantage, and this I therefore reckon one of the first Errata[72] of my Life: But the Unfairness of it weigh'd little with me, when under the Impression of Resentment, for the Blows his Passion too often urg'd him to bestow upon me. Tho' he was otherwise not an ill-natur'd Man: Perhaps I was too saucy and provoking.

When he found I would leave him, he took care to prevent my getting Employment in any other Printing-House of the Town, by going round and speaking to every Master, who accordingly refus'd to give me Work. I then thought of going to New York as the nearest Place where there was a Printer: and I was the rather inclin'd to leave Boston, when I reflected that I had already made myself a little obnoxious to the governing Party; and from the arbitrary Proceedings of the Assembly in my Brother's Case it was likely I might if I stay'd soon bring myself into Scrapes; and farther that my indiscrete Disputations about Religion began to make me pointed at with Horror by good People, as an Infidel or Atheist. I determin'd on the Point: but my Father now siding with my Brother, I was sensible that If I attempted to go openly, Means would be used to prevent me. My Friend Collins therefore undertook to manage a little for me. He agreed with the Captain of a New York Sloop for my Passage, under the Notion of my being a young Acquaintance of his that had got a naughty Girl with Child, whose Friends would compel me to marry her, and therefore I could not appear or come away publickly. So I sold some of my Books to raise a little Money, Was taken on board privately, and as we had a fair Wind in three Days I found my self in New York near 300 Miles from home, a Boy of but 17, without the least Recommendation to or Knowledge of any Person in the Place, and with very little Money in my Pocket.

My Inclinations for the Sea, were by this time worne out, or I might now have gratify'd them. But having a Trade, and supposing my self a pretty good Workman, I offer'd my Service to the Printer of the Place, old Mr. Wm. Bradford,[73] (who had been the first Printer in Pensilvania, but remov'd from thence upon the Quarrel of Geo. Keith[74]). He could give me no Employment, having little to do, and Help enough already. But, says he, my Son at Philadelphia has lately lost his principal Hand, Aquila Rose, by Death. If you got thither I believe he may employ you. Philadelphia was 100 Miles farther. I set out, however, in a Boat for Amboy,[75] leaving my Chest and Things to follow me round by Sea. In crossing the Bay we met with a Squall that tore our rotten Sails to pieces, prevented our getting into the Kill,[76] and drove us upon Long Island. In our Way a drunken Dutchman, who was a Passenger too, fell over board; when he was sinking I reach'd thro' the Water to his shock Pate[77] and drew him up so that we got him in again. His Ducking sober'd him a little, and he went to sleep, taking first out of his Pocket a Book which he desir'd I would dry for him. It prov'd to be my old favourite Author Bunyan's Pilgrim's Progress in Dutch, finely printed on good Paper with copper Cuts,[78] a Dress better than I had ever seen it wear in its own

[72]A printer's term for "errors."
[73]William Bradford (1663–1752), a pioneer American printer and father of Franklin's competitor, Andrew Bradford (1686–1742).
[74]George Keith (1638–1716), a Quaker leader who quarreled with other Quakers and was "disowned."
[75]Perth Amboy, New Jersey.
[76]Narrow channel separating Staten Island, New York, from New Jersey.
[77]Bushy hair. [78]Illustrations printed from engraved copper plates.

Language. I have since found that it has been translated into most of the Languages of Europe, and suppose it has been more generally read than any other Book except perhaps the Bible. Honest John was the first that I know of who mix'd Narration and Dialogue, a Method of Writing very engaging to the Reader, who in the most interesting Parts finds himself as it were brought into the Company, and present at the Discourse. Defoe in his Cruso, his Moll Flanders, Religious Courtship, Family Instructor, and other Pieces, has imitated it with Success. And Richardson has done the same in his Pamela, &c.[79]

When we drew near the Island we found it was at a Place where there could be no Landing, there being a great Surf on the stony Beach. So we dropt Anchor and swung round towards the Shore. Some People came down to the Water Edge and hallow'd to us, as we did to them. But the Wind was so high and the Surf so loud, that we could not hear so as to understand each other. There were Canoes on the Shore, and we made Signs and hallow'd that they should fetch us, but they either did not understand us, or thought it impracticable. So they went away, and Night coming on, we had no Remedy but to wait till the Wind should abate, and in the mean time the Boatman and I concluded to sleep if we could, and so crouded into the Scuttle[80] with the Dutchman who was still wet, and the Spray beating over the Head of our Boat, leak'd thro' to us, so that we were soon almost as wet as he. In this Manner we lay all Night with very little Rest. But the Wind abating the next Day, we made a Shift to reach Amboy before Night, having been 30 Hours on the Water without Victuals, or any Drink but a Bottle of filthy Rum: The Water we sail'd on being salt.

In the evening I found my self very feverish, and went in to Bed. But having read somewhere that cold Water drank plentifully was good for a Fever, I follow'd the prescription, sweat plentifully most of the Night, my Fever left me, and in the Morning crossing the Ferry, I proceeded on my Journey, on foot, having 50 Miles to Burlington,[81] where I was told I should find Boats that would carry me the rest of the Way to Philadelphia.

It rain'd very hard all the Day, I was thoroughly soak'd and by Noon a good deal tir'd, so I stopt at a poor Inn, where I staid all Night, beginning now to wish I had never left home. I cut so miserable a Figure too, that I found by the Questions ask'd me I was suspected to be some runaway Servant, and in danger of being taken up on that Suspicion. However I proceeded the next Day, and got in the Evening to an Inn within 8 or 10 Miles of Burlington, kept by one Dr. Brown.[82]

He entered into Conversation with me while I took some Refreshment, and finding I had read a little, became very sociable and friendly. Our Acquaintance continu'd as long as he liv'd. He had been, I imagine, an itinerant Doctor, for there was no Town in England, or Country in Europe, of which he could not give a very particular Account. He had some Letters,[83]

[79]Daniel Defoe wrote *Robinson Crusoe* (1719), *Moll Flanders* (1722), *Religious Courtship* (1722), *The Family Instructor* (1715–18). Samuel Richardson wrote *Pamela, or Virtue Rewarded* (1740). Franklin became the first to publish a novel in the Colonies when he reprinted *Pamela* in 1744.

[80]An opening in a ship's deck, covered by a movable lid (hatch).

[81]In western New Jersey, about eighteen miles up the Delaware River from Philadelphia.

[82]John Browne (c. 1667–1737), a religious skeptic, physician, and innkeeper in Burlington, New Jersey.

[83]Learning or education.

and was ingenious, but much of an Unbeliever, and wickedly undertook some Years after to travesty the Bible in doggrel Verse as Cotton had done Virgil.[84] By this means he set many of the Facts in a very ridiculous Light, and might have hurt weak minds if his Work had been publish'd: but it never was. At his House I lay that Night, and the next Morning reach'd Burlington. But had the Mortification to find that the regular Boats were gone, a little before my coming, and no other expected to go till Tuesday, this being Saturday. Wherefore I return'd to an old Woman in the Town of whom I had bought Gingerbread to eat on the Water, and ask'd her Advice; she invited me to lodge at her House till a Passage by Water should offer: and being tired with my foot Travelling, I accepted the Invitation. She understanding I was a Printer, would have had me stay at that Town and follow my Business, being ignorant of the Stock necessary to begin with. She was very hospitable, gave me a Dinner of Ox Cheek with great Goodwill, accepting only of a Pot of Ale in return. And I tho't my self fix'd till Tuesday should come. However walking in the Evening by the Side of the River a Boat came by, which I found was going towards Philadelphia, with several People in her. They took me in, and as there was no Wind, we row'd all the Way; and about Midnight not having yet seen the City, some of the Company were confident we must have pass'd it, and would row no farther, the others knew not where we were, so we put towards the Shore, got into a Creek, landed near an old Fence with the Rails of which we made a Fire, the Night being cold, in October, and there we remain'd till Daylight. Then one of the Company knew the Place to be Cooper's Creek a little above Philadelphia, which we saw as soon as we got out of the Creek, and arriv'd there about 8 or 9 a Clock, on the Sunday morning, and landed at the Market street Wharff.[85]

I have been the more particular in this Description of my Journey, and shall be so of my first Entry into that City, that you may in your Mind compare such unlikely Beginnings with the Figure I have since made there. I was in my Working Dress, my best Cloaths being to come round by Sea. I was dirty from my Journey; my Pockets were stuff'd out with Shirts and Stockings; I knew no Soul, nor where to look for Lodging. I was fatigu'd with Traveling, Rowing and Want of Rest. I was very hungry, and my whole Stock of Cash consisted of a Dutch Dollar and about a Shilling in Copper. The latter I gave the People of the Boat for my Passage, who at first refus'd it on Account of my Rowing; but I insisted on their taking it, a Man being sometimes more generous when he has but a little Money than when he has plenty, perhaps thro' Fear of being thought to have but little.

Then I walk'd up the Street, gazing about, till near the Market House I met a Boy with Bread. I had made many a Meal on Bread, and inquiring where he got it, I went immediately to the Baker's he directed me to in second Street; and ask'd for Bisket, intending such as we had in Boston, but they it seems were not made in Philadelphia, then I ask'd for a threepenny Loaf, and was told they had none such: so not considering or knowing the Difference of Money and the greater Cheapness nor the Names of his Bread, I bad him give me three penny worth of any sort. He gave me accordingly

[84]Charles Cotton (1630–1687), who wrote the burlesque poem, *Scarronides, or the First Book of Virgil Travestied* (1664).
[85]October 6, 1723.

three great Puffy Rolls. I was surpriz'd at the Quantity, but took it, and having no room in my Pockets, walk'd off, with a Roll under each Arm, and eating the other. Thus I went up Market Street as far as fourth Street, passing by the Door of Mr. Read, my future Wife's Father, when she standing at the Door saw me, and thought I made as I certainly did a most awkward ridiculous Appearance. Then I turn'd and went down Chestnut Street and part of Walnut Street, eating my Roll all the Way, and coming round found my self again at Market Street Wharff, near the Boat I came in, to which I went for a Draught of the River Water, and being fill'd with one of my Rolls, gave the other two to a Woman and her Child that came down the River in the Boat with us and were waiting to go farther. Thus refresh'd I walk'd again up the Street, which by this time had many clean dress'd People in it who were all walking the same Way; I join'd them, and thereby was led into the great Meeting house of the Quakers near the Market. I sat down among them, and after looking round a while and hearing nothing said,[86] being very drowsy thro' Labour and want of Rest the preceding Night, I fell fast asleep, and continu'd so till the Meeting broke up, when one was kind enough to rouse me. This was therefore the first House I was in or slept in, in Philadelphia.

Walking again down towards the River, and looking in the Faces of People, I met a young Quaker Man whose Countenance I lik'd, and accosting him requested he would tell me where a Stranger could get Lodging. We were then near the Sign of the Three Mariners. Here, says he, is one Place that entertains Strangers, but it is not a reputable House; if thee wilt walk with me, I'll show thee a better. He brought me to the Crooked Billet in Water-Street.[87] Here I got a Dinner. And while I was eating it, several sly Questions were ask'd me, as it seem'd to be suspected from my youth and Appearance, that I might be some Runaway. After Dinner my Sleepiness return'd: and being shown to a Bed, I lay down without undressing, and slept till Six in the Evening; was call'd to Supper; went to Bed again very early and slept soundly till the next Morning. Then I made my self as tidy as I could, and went to Andrew Bradford the Printer's. I found in the Shop the old Man his Father, whom I had seen at New York, and who travelling on horse back had got to Philadelphia before me. He introduc'd me to his Son, who receiv'd me civilly, gave me a Breakfast, but told me he did not at present want a Hand, being lately supply'd with one. But there was another Printer in town lately set up, one Keimer,[88] who perhaps might employ me; if not, I should be welcome to lodge at his House, and he would give me a little Work to do now and then till fuller Business should offer.

The old Gentleman said, he would go with me to the new Printer: And when we found him, Neighbour, says Bradford, I have brought to see you a young Man of your Business, perhaps you may want such a One. He ask'd me a few Questions, put a Composing Stick in my Hand to see how I work'd, and then said he would employ me soon, tho' he had just then nothing for me to do. And taking old Bradford whom he had never seen before, to be one of the Towns People that had a Good Will for him, enter'd into a Conversation

[86]Franklin refers to the Quaker practice of remaining silent in religious services until one of the congregation is moved to speak out.

[87]The Crooked Billet Tavern.

[88]Samuel Keimer (c. 1688–1742). He had arrived from London the year before. Unsuccessful as a printer, he left Philadelphia in 1730.

on his present Undertaking and Prospects; while Bradford not discovering[89] that he was the other Printer's Father, on Keimer's saying he expected soon to get the greatest Part of the Business into his own Hands, drew him on by artful Questions and starting little Doubts, to explain all his Views, what Interest he rely'd on, and in what manner he intended to proceed. I who stood by and heard all, saw immediately that one of them was a crafty old Sophister,[90] and the other a mere Novice. Bradford left me with Keimer, who was greatly surpriz'd when I told him who the old Man was.

Keimer's Printing House I found, consisted of an old shatter'd Press, and one small worn-out Fount of English,[91] which he was then using himself, composing in it an Elegy on Aquila Rose before-mentioned, an ingenious young Man of excellent Character much respected in the Town, Clerk of the Assembly, and a pretty Poet. Keimer made Verses, too, but very indifferently. He could not be said to write them, for his Manner was to compose them in the Types directly out of his Head; so there being no Copy, but one Pair of Cases,[92] and the Elegy likely to require all the Letter, no one could help him. I endeavour'd to put his Press (which he had not yet us'd, and of which he understood nothing) into Order fit to be work'd with; and promising to come and print off his Elegy as soon as he should have got it ready, I return'd to Bradford's who gave me a little Job to do for the present, and there I lodged and dieted.[93] A few Days after Keimer sent for me to print off the Elegy. And now he had got another Pair of Cases,[94] and a Pamphlet to reprint, on which he set me to work.

These two Printers I found poorly qualified for their Business. Bradford had not been bred to it, and was very illiterate; and Keimer tho' something of a Scholar, was a mere Compositor, knowing nothing of Presswork. He had been one of the French Prophets and could act their enthusiastic Agitations.[95] At this time he did not profess any particular Religion, but something of all on occasion; was very ignorant of the World, and had, as I afterwards found, a good deal of the Knave in his Composition. He did not like my Lodging at Bradford's while I work'd with him. He had a House indeed, but without Furniture, so he could not lodge me: But he got me a Lodging at Mr. Read's before-mentioned, who was the Owner of his House. And my Chest and Clothes being come by this time, I made rather a more respectable Appearance in the Eyes of Miss Read, than I had done when she first happen'd to see me eating my Roll in the Street.

I began now to have some Acquaintance among the young People of the Town, that were Lovers of Reading with whom I spent my Evenings very pleasantly and gaining Money by my Industry and Frugality, I lived very agreably, forgetting Boston as much as I could, and not desiring that any there should know where I resided, except my Friend Collins who was in my Secret, and kept it when I wrote to him. At length an Incident happened that sent me back again much sooner than I had intended.

[89]Revealing. [90]Trickster. [91]Oversized type, and thus unsuitable.

[92]Boxes of type containing uppercase and lowercase letters.

[93]Boarded.

[94]I.e., he had got enough type to fill two cases, the compartmented trays in which type is distributed.

[95]French Protestant refugees who fled to England in 1706. They were given to trances, accompanied by jerking movements, during which they received revelations about a Messianic kingdom soon to come.

I had a Brother-in-law, Robert Holmes,[96] Master of a Sloop, that traded between Boston and Delaware. He being at New Castle 40 Miles below Philadelphia, heard there of me, and wrote me a Letter, mentioning the Concern of my Friends in Boston at my abrupt Departure, assuring me of their Goodwill to me, and that every thing would be accommodated to my Mind if I would return, to which he exhorted me very earnestly. I wrote an Answer to his Letter, thank'd him for his Advice, but stated my Reasons for quitting Boston fully, and in such a Light as to convince him I was not so wrong as he had apprehended.

Sir William Keith[97] Governor of the Province, was then at New Castle, and Capt. Holmes happening to be in Company with him when my Letter came to hand, spoke to him of me, and show'd him the Letter. The Governor read it, and seem'd surpriz'd when he was told my Age. He said I appear'd a young Man of promising Parts, and therefore should be encouraged: The Printers of Philadelphia were wretched ones, and if I would set up there, he made no doubt I should succeed; for his Part, he would procure me the publick Business, and do me every other Service in his Power. This my Brother-in-Law afterwards told me in Boston. But I knew as yet nothing of it; when one Day Keimer and I being at Work together near the Window, we saw the Governor and another Gentleman (which prov'd to be Col. French, of New Castle) finely dress'd, come directly across the Street to our House, and heard them at the Door. Keimer ran down immediately, thinking it a Visit to him. But the Governor enquir'd for me, came up, and with a Condescension and Politeness I had been quite unus'd to, made me many Compliments, desired to be acquainted with me, blam'd me kindly for not having made my self known to him when I first came to the Place, and would have me away with him to the Tavern where he was going with Col. French to taste as he said some excellent Madeira. I was not a little surpriz'd, and Keimer star'd like a Pig poison'd. I went however with the Governor and Col. French, to a Tavern the Corner of Third Street, and over the Madeira he propos'd my Setting up my Business, laid before me the Probabilities of Success, and both he and Col. French assur'd me I should have their Interest and Influence in procuring the Publick Business of both Governments. On my doubting whether my Father would assist me in it, Sir William said he would give me a Letter to him, in which he would state the Advantages, and he did not doubt of prevailing with him. So it was concluded I should return to Boston in the first Vessel with the Governor's Letter recommending me to my Father. In the mean time the Intention was to be kept secret, and I went on working with Keimer as usual, the Governor sending for me now and then to dine with him, a very great Honour I thought it, and conversing with me in the most affable, familiar, and friendly manner imaginable.

About the End of April 1724, a little Vessel offer'd for Boston. I took Leave of Keimer as going to see my Friends. The Governor gave me an ample Letter, saying many flattering things of me to my Father, and strongly recommending the Project of my setting up at Philadelphia, as a Thing that must make my Fortune. We struck on a Shoal in going down the Bay and sprung a

[96]Robert Holmes (d. before 1743), husband of Franklin's sister Mary, ship's captain in the coastal trade.

[97]Sir William Keith (1680–1749), governor of Pennsylvania 1717–1726.

Leak, we had a blustering time at Sea, and were oblig'd to pump almost continually, at which I took my Turn. We arriv'd safe however at Boston in about a Fortnight. I had been absent Seven Months and my Friends had heard nothing of me; for my Br. Holmes was not yet return'd; and had not written about me. My unexpected Appearance surpriz'd the Family; all were however very glad to see me and made me Welcome, except my Brother. I went to see him at his Printing-House: I was better dress'd than ever while in his Service, having a genteel new Suit from Head to foot, a Watch, and my Pockets lin'd with near Five Pounds Sterling in Silver. He receiv'd me not very frankly, look'd me all over, and turn'd to his Work again. The Journey-Men were inquisitive where I had been, what sort of a Country it was, and how I lik'd it? I prais'd it much, and the happy Life I led in it; expressing strongly my Intention of returning to it; and one of them asking what kind of Money we had there, I produc'd a handful of Silver and spread it before them, which was a kind of Raree-Show[98] they had not been us'd to, Paper being the Money of Boston. Then I took an Opportunity of letting them see my Watch: and lastly, (my Brother still grum and sullen) I gave them a Piece of Eight to drink[99] and took my Leave. This visit of mine offended him extreamly. For when my Mother some time after spoke to him of a Reconciliation, and of her Wishes to see us on good Terms together, and that we might live for the future as Brothers, he said, I had insulted him in such a Manner before his People that he could never forget or forgive it. In this however he was mistaken.

My Father receiv'd the Governor's Letter with some apparent Surprize; but said little of it to me for some Days; when Capt. Holmes returning, he show'd it to him, ask'd if he knew Keith, and What kind of a Man he was: Adding his Opinion that he must be of small Direction, to think of setting a Boy up in Business who wanted yet 3 Years of Being at Man's Estate. Holmes said what he could in favour of the Project; but my Father was clear in the Impropriety of it; and at last gave a flat Denial to it. Then he wrote a civil Letter to Sir William thanking him for the Patronage he had so kindly offered me, but declining to assist me as yet in Setting up, I being in his Opinion too young to be trusted with the Management of a Business so important, and for which the Preparation must be so expensive.

My Friend and Companion Collins, who was a Clerk at the Post-Office, pleas'd with the Account I gave him of my new Country, determin'd to go thither also: And while I waited for my Fathers Determination,[100] he set out before me by Land to Rhodeisland, leaving his Books which were a pretty Collection of Mathematicks and Natural Philosophy,[101] to come with mine and me to New York where he propos'd to wait for me. My Father, tho' he did not approve Sir William's Proposition was yet pleas'd that I had been able to obtain so advantageous a Character from a Person of such Note where I had resided, and that I had been so industrious and careful as to equip my self so handsomely in so short a time: therefore seeing no Prospect of an Accommodation between my Brother and me, he gave his Consent to my Returning again to Philadelphia, advis'd me to behave respectfully to the People there, endeavour to obtain the general Esteem, and avoid lampooning and libelling to which he thought I had too much Inclination; telling me,

[98]A peepshow set up on the street.
[99]I.e., he gave a Spanish dollar for drinks. [100]Decision. [101]Natural sciences.

that by steady Industry and a prudent Parsimony, I might save enough by the time I was One and Twenty to set me up, and that if I came near the Matter he would help me out with the rest. This was all I could obtain, except some small Gifts as Tokens of his and my Mother's Love, when I embark'd again for New York, now with their Approbation and their Blessing.

The Sloop putting in at Newport, Rhodeisland, I visited my Brother John, who had been married and settled there some Years. He received me very affectionately, for he always lov'd me. A Friend of his, one Vernon, having some Money due to him in Pensilvania, about 35 Pounds Currency, desired I would receive it for him, and keep it till I had his Directions what to remit it in. Accordingly he gave me an Order. This afterwards occasion'd me a good deal of Uneasiness. At Newport we took in a Number of Passengers for New York: Among which were two young Women, Companions, and a grave, sensible Matron-like Quaker-Woman with her Attendants. I had shown an obliging readiness to do her some little Services which impress'd her I suppose with a degree of Good-will towards me. Therefore when she saw a daily growing Familiarity between me and the two Young Women, which they appear'd to encourage, she took me aside and said, Young Man, I am concern'd for thee, as thou has no Friend with thee, and seems not to know much of the World, or of the Snares Youth is expos'd to; depend upon it those are very bad Women, I can see it in all their Actions, and if thee art not upon thy Guard, they will draw thee into some Danger: they are Strangers to thee, and I advise thee in a friendly Concern for thy Welfare, to have no Acquaintance with them. As I seem'd at first not to think so ill of them as she did, she mention'd some Things she had observ'd and heard that had escap'd my Notice; but now convinc'd me she was right. I thank'd her for her kind Advice, and promis'd to follow it. When we arriv'd at New York, they told me where they liv'd, and invited me to come and see them: but I avoided it. And it was well I did: For the next Day, the Captain miss'd a Silver Spoon and some other Things that had been taken out of his Cabbin, and knowing that these were a Couple of Strumpets, he got a Warrant to search their Lodgings, found the stolen Goods, and had the Thieves punish'd. So tho' we had escap'd a sunken Rock which we scrap'd upon in the Passage, I thought this Escape of rather more Importance to me.

At New York I found my Friend Collins, who had arriv'd there some Time before me. We had been intimate from Children,[102] and had read the same Books together. But he had the Advantage of more time for reading, and Studying and a wonderful Genius for Mathematical Learning in which he far outstript me. While I liv'd in Boston most of my Hours of Leisure for Conversation were spent with him, and he continu'd a sober as well as an industrious Lad; was much respected for his Learning by several of the Clergy and other Gentlemen, and seem'd to promise making a good Figure in Life: but during my Absence he had acquir'd a Habit of Sotting[103] with Brandy; and I found by his own Account and what I heard from others, that he had been drunk every day since his Arrival at New York, and behav'd very oddly. He had gam'd too and lost his Money, so that I was oblig'd to discharge[104] his Lodgings, and defray his Expenses to and at Philadelphia: Which prov'd extreamly inconvenient to me. The then Governor of N[ew] York, Burnet,[105] Son of Bishop Burnet

[102]Since childhood. [103]Getting drunk. [104]Pay for.

[105]William Burnet (1688–1729), governor of New York and New Jersey (1720–1728), son of the Bishop of Salisbury.

hearing from the Captain that a young Man, one of his Passengers, had a great many Books, desired he would bring me to see him. I waited upon him accordingly, and should have taken Collins with me but that he was not sober. The Governor treated me with great Civility, show'd me his Library, which was a very large one, and we had a good deal of Conversation about Books and Authors. This was the second Governor who had done me the Honor to take Notice of me, which to a poor Boy like me was very pleasing.

We proceeded to Philadelphia. I received on the Way Vernon's Money, without which we could hardly have finish'd our Journey. Collins wish'd to be employ'd in some Counting House; but whether they discover'd his Dramming by his Breath, or by his Behaviour, tho' he had some Recommendations, he met with no Success in any Application, and continu'd Lodging and Boarding at the same House with me and at my Expense. Knowing I had that Money of Vernon's he was continually borrowing of me, still promising Repayment as soon as he should be in Business. At length he had got so much of it, that I was distress'd to think what I should do, in case of being call'd on to remit it. His Drinking continu'd about which we sometimes quarrel'd, for when a little intoxicated he was very fractious. Once in a Boat on the Delaware with some other young Men, he refused to row in his Turn: I will be row'd home, says he. We will not row you, says I. You must or stay all Night on the Water, says he, just as you please. The others said, Let us row; what signifies it? But my Mind being soured with his other Conduct, I continu'd to refuse. So he swore he would make me row, or throw me overboard; and coming along stepping on the Thwarts[106] towards me, when he came up and struck at me and I clapt my Hand under his Crutch,[107] and rising pitch'd him head-foremost into the River. I knew he was a good Swimmer, and so was under little Concern about him; but before he could get round to lay hold of the Boat, we had with a few Strokes pull'd her out of his Reach. And ever when he drew near the Boat, we ask'd if he would row, striking a few Strokes to slide her away from him. He was ready to die with Vexation, and obstinately would not promise to row; however seeing him at last beginning to tire, we lifted him in; and brought him home dripping wet in the Evening. We hardly exchang'd a civil Word afterwards; and a West India Captain who had a Commission to procure a Tutor for the Sons of a Gentleman at Barbadoes,[108] happening to meet with him, agreed to carry him thither. He left me then, promising to remit me the first Money he should receive in order to discharge the Debt. But I never heard of him after.

The Breaking into this Money of Vernon's was one of the first great Errata of my Life. And this Affair show'd that my Father was not much out in his Judgment when he suppos'd me too young to manage Business of Importance. But Sir William, on reading his Letter, said he was too prudent. There was great Difference in Persons, and Discretion did not always accompany Years, nor was Youth always without it. And since he will not set you up, says he, I will do it myself. Give me an Inventory of the Things necessary to be had from England, and I will send for them. You shall repay me when you are able; I am resolv'd to have a good Printer here, and I am sure you must succeed. This was spoken with such an Appearance of Cordiality, that I had

[106]Cross seats in an open boat.
[107]Crotch.
[108]Island in the British West Indies.

not the least doubt of his meaning what he said. I had hitherto kept the Proposition of my Setting up a Secret in Philadelphia, and I still kept it. Had it been known that I depended on the Governor, probably some Friend that knew him better would have advis'd me not to rely on him, as I afterwards heard it as his known Character to be liberal of Promises which he never meant to keep. Yet unsolicited as he was by me, how could I think his generous Offers insincere? I believ'd him one of the best Men in the World.

I presented him an Inventory of a little Printing House, amounting by my Computation to about £100 Sterling. He lik'd it, but ask'd me if my being on the Spot in England to chuse the Types and see that every thing was good of the kind, might not be of some Advantage. Then, says he, when there, you may make Acquaintances and establish Correspondencies in the Bookselling and Stationary Way. I agreed that this might be advantageous. Then says he, get yourself ready to go with Annis;[109] which was the annual Ship, and the only one at that Time usually passing between London and Philadelphia. But it would be some Months before Annis sail'd, so I continu'd working with Keimer, fretting about the Money Collins had got from me, and in daily Apprehensions of being call'd upon by Vernon, which however did not happen for some Years after.

I believe I have omitted mentioning that in my first Voyage from Boston, being becalm'd off Block Island,[110] our People set about catching Cod and hawl'd up a great many. Hitherto I had stuck to my Resolution of not eating animal Food; and on this Occasion, I consider'd with my Master Tryon, the taking every Fish as a kind of unprovok'd Murder, since none of them had or ever could do us any Injury that might justify the Slaughter. All this seem'd very reasonable. But I had formerly been a great Lover of Fish, and when this came hot out of the Frying Pan, it smelt admirably well. I balanc'd some time between Principle and Inclination: till I recollected, that when the Fish were opened, I saw smaller Fish taken out of their Stomachs: Then thought I, if you eat one another, I don't see why we mayn't eat you. So I din'd upon Cod very heartily and continu'd to eat with other People, returning only now and then occasionally to a vegetable Diet. So convenient a thing it is to be a *reasonable Creature*, since it enables one to find or make a Reason for every thing one has a mind to do.

Keimer and I liv'd on a pretty good familiar Footing and agreed tolerably well: for he suspected nothing of my Setting up. He retain'd a great deal of his old Enthusiasms, and lov'd Argumentation. We therefore had many Disputations. I us'd to work him so with my Socratic Method, and had trapann'd[111] him so often by Questions apparently so distant from any Point we had in hand, and yet by degrees led to the Point, and brought him into Difficulties and Contradictions that at last he grew ridiculously cautious, and would hardly answer me the most common Question, without asking first, *What do you intend to infer from that?* However it gave him so high an Opinion of my Abilities in the Confuting Way, that he seriously propos'd my being his Colleague in a Project he had of setting up a new Sect. He was to preach the Doctrines, and I was to confound all Opponents. When he came to explain with me upon the Doctrines, I found several Conundrums[112] which I objected to unless I might have my Way a little too, and introduce some of mine. Keimer

[109]Thomas Annis, captain of the "annual Ship" that sailed between England and Philadelphia.
[110]Ten miles off the coast of Rhode Island. [111]Trapped. [112]Puzzling questions.

wore his Beard at full Length, because somewhere in the Mosaic Law it is said, *thou shalt not mar the Corners of thy Beard.*[113] He likewise kept the seventh day Sabbath; and these two Points were Essentials with him. I dislik'd both, but agreed to admit them upon Condition of his adopting the Doctrine of using no animal Food. I doubt, says he, my Constitution will not bear that. I assur'd him it would, and that he would be the better for it. He was usually a great Glutton, and I promised my self some Diversion in half-starving him. He agreed to try the Practice if I would keep him Company. I did so and we held it for three Months. We had our Victuals dress'd and brought to us regularly by a Woman in the Neighbourhood, who had from me a List of 40 Dishes to be prepar'd for us at different times, in all which there was neither Fish Flesh nor Fowl, and the whim suited me the better at this time from the Cheapness of it, not costing us about 18*d.*[114] Sterling each, per Week. I have since kept several Lents most strictly, Leaving the common Diet for that, and that for the common, abruptly, without the least Inconvenience: So that I think there is little in the Advice of making those Changes by easy Gradations, I went on pleasantly, but poor Keimer suffer'd grievously, tir'd of the Project, long'd for the Flesh Pots of Egypt,[115] and order'd a roast Pig. He invited me and two Women Friends to dine with him, but it being brought too soon upon table, he could not resist the Temptation, and ate it all up before we came.

I had made some Courtship during this time to Miss Read. I had a great Respect and Affection for her, and had some Reason to believe she had the same for me: but as I was about to take a long Voyage, and we were both very young, only a little above 18, it was thought most prudent by her Mother to prevent our going too far at present, as a Marriage if it was to take place would be more convenient after my Return, when I should be as I expected set up in my Business. Perhaps too she thought my Expectations not so well-founded as I imagined them to be.

My chief Acquaintances at this time were, Charles Osborne, Joseph Watson, and James Ralph;[116] All Lovers of Reading. The two first were Clerks to an eminent Scrivener or Conveyancer[117] in the Town, Charles Brogden;[118] the other was Clerk to a Merchant. Watson was a pious sensible young Man, of great Integrity. The others rather more lax in their Principles of Religion, particularly Ralph, who as well as Collins had been unsettled by me, for which they both made me suffer. Osborne was sensible, candid, frank, sincere, and affectionate to his Friends; but in litterary Matters too fond of Criticising. Ralph, was ingenious, genteel in his Manners, and extremely eloquent; I think I never knew a prettier Talker. Both of them great Admirers of Poetry, and began to try their Hands in little Pieces. Many pleasant Walks we four had together on Sundays into the Woods near Skuylkill,[119] where we read to one another and conferr'd on what we read.

[113]"Ye shall not round the corners of your heads, neither shall thou mar the corners of thy beard." Leviticus 19:27. [114]Eighteen pence.

[115]"And the whole congregation of the children of Israel murmured against Moses and Aaron in the wilderness: and the children of Israel said unto them, Would to God that we had died by the hands of the Lord in the land of Egypt, when we sat by the flesh pots, and when we did eat bread to the full." Exodus 16:2,3.

[116]James Ralph (d. 1762). His attempts at verse failed, but he became an effective political writer in England. When Franklin returned to London in 1757, Ralph helped him in propagandizing for the Colonies. [117]One who draws up leases and deeds to property.

[118]Charles Brockden (1683–1769). [119]Schuylkill River in Philadelphia.

Ralph was inclin'd to pursue the Study of Poetry, not doubting but he might become eminent in it and make his Fortune by it, alledging that the best Poets must when they first begin to write, make as many Faults as he did. Osborne dissuaded him, assur'd him he had no Genius for Poetry, and advis'd him to think of nothing beyond the Business he was bred to; that in the mercantile way tho' he had no Stock, he might by his Diligence and Punctuality recommend himself to Employment as a Factor,[120] and in time acquire wherewith to trade on his own Account. I approv'd the amusing one's self with Poetry now and then, so far as to improve one's Language, but no farther. On this it was propos'd that we should each of us at our next Meeting produce a Piece of our own Composing, in order to improve by our mutual Observations, Criticisms and Corrections. As Language and Expression was what we had in View, we excluded all Considerations of Invention, by agreeing that the Task should be a version of the 18th Psalm, which describes the Descent of a Deity. When the Time of our Meeting drew nigh, Ralph call'd on me first, and let me know his Piece was ready. I told him I had been busy, and having little Inclination had done nothing. He then show'd me his Piece for my Opinion; and I much approv'd it, as it appear'd to me to have great Merit. Now, says he, Osborne never will allow the least Merit in any thing of mine, but makes 1000 Criticisms out of mere Envy. He is not so jealous of you. I wish therefore you would take this Piece, and produce it as yours. I will pretend not to have had time, and so produce nothing: We shall then see what he will say to it. It was agreed, and I immediately transcrib'd it that it might appear in my own hand. We met. Watson's Performance was read: there were some Beauties in it: but many Defects. Osborne's was read: It was much better. Ralph did it Justice, remark'd some Faults, but applauded the Beauties. He himself had nothing to produce. I was backward, seem'd desirous of being excus'd, had not had sufficient Time to correct; &c. but no Excuse could be admitted, produce I must. It was read and repeated; Watson and Osborne gave up the Contest; and join'd in applauding it immoderately. Ralph only made some Criticisms and propos'd some Amendments, but I defended my Text. Osborne was against Ralph, and told him he was no better a Critic than Poet; so he dropt the Argument. As they two went home together, Osborne express'd himself still more strongly in favour of what he thought my Production, having restrain'd himself before as he said, lest I should think it Flattery. But who would have imagin'd, says he, that Franklin had been capable of such a Performance; such Painting, such Force! such Fire! he has even improv'd the Original! In his common Conversation, he seems to have no Choice of Words; he hesitates and blunders; and yet, good God, how he writes! When we next met, Ralph discover'd the Trick, we had plaid him, and Osborne was a little laught at. This Transaction fix'd Ralph in his Resolution of becoming a Poet. I did all I could to dissuade him from it, but He continued scribbling Verses, till Pope cur'd him.[121] He became however a pretty good Prose Writer. More of him thereafter.

But as I may not have occasion again to mention the other two, I shall just remark here, that Watson died in my Arms a few Years after, much lamented,

[120]Business agent.

[121]Ralph defended some writers attacked by Alexander Pope in the first edition of the *Dunciad* (1728). Pope then added a couplet in later editions:

"Silence, ye Wolves! while Ralph to Cynthia howls,
And makes Night hideous—Answer him ye Owls." III, 159–60.

being the best of our Set. Osborne went to the West Indies, where he became an eminent Lawyer and made Money, but died young. He and I had made a serious Agreement, that the one who happen'd first to die, should if possible make a friendly Visit to the other, and acquaint him how he found things in that Separate State. But he never fulfill'd his Promise.

The Governor, seeming to like my Company, had me frequently to his House; and his Setting me up was always mention'd as a fix'd thing. I was to take with me Letters recommendatory to a Number of his Friends, besides the Letter of Credit to furnish me with the necessary Money for purchasing the Press and Types, Paper, &c. For these Letters I was appointed to call at different times, when they were to be ready, but a future time was still[122] named. Thus we went on till the ship whose Departure too had been several times postponed was on the Point of sailing. Then when I call'd to take my Leave and Receive the Letters, his Secretary, Dr. Bard,[123] came out to me and said the Governor was extreamly busy, in writing, but would be down at Newcastle[124] before the Ship, and there the Letters would be delivered to me.

Ralph, tho' married and having one Child, had determined to accompany me in this Voyage. It was thought he intended to establish a Correspondence, and obtain Goods to sell on Commission. But I found afterwards, that thro' some Discontent with his Wifes Relations, he purposed to leave her on their Hands, and never return again. Having taken leave of my Friends, and interchang'd some Promises with Miss Read, I left Philadelphia in the Ship, which anchor'd at Newcastle. The Governor was there. But when I went to his Lodging, the Secretary came to me from him with the civillest Message in the World, that he could not then see me being engag'd in Business of the utmost Importance; but should send the Letters to me on board, wish'd me heartily a good Voyage and a speedy Return, &c. I return'd on board, a little puzzled, but still not doubting.

Mr. Andrew Hamilton,[125] a famous Lawyer of Philadelphia, had taken Passage in the same Ship for himself and Son: and with Mr. Denham a Quaker Merchant, and Messrs. Onion and Russel Masters of an Iron Work in Maryland, had engag'd the Great Cabin; so that Ralph and I were forc'd to take up with a Birth in the Steerage:[126] And none on board knowing us, were considered as ordinary Persons. But Mr. Hamilton and his Son (it was James, since Governor[127]) return'd from New Castle to Philadelphia, the Father being recall'd by a great Fee to plead for a seized Ship. And just before we sail'd Col. French coming on board, and showing me great Respect, I was more taken Notice of, and with my Friend Ralph invited by the other Gentlemen to come into the Cabin, there being now Room. Accordingly we remov'd thither.

Understanding that Col. French had brought on board the Governor's Dispatches, I ask'd the Captain for those Letters that were to be under my Care. He said all were put into the Bag together; and he could not then come at them; but before we landed in England, I should have an Opportunity of picking them out. So I was satisfy'd for the present, and we proceeded on our Voyage. We had a sociable Company in the Cabin, and lived uncommonly

[122]Always. [123]Patrick Baird, a surgeon. [124]Delaware.

[125]Andrew Hamilton (c. 1678–1741), defender of John Peter Zenger at his trial for seditious libel in 1735.

[126]I.e., share a berth in the least costly part of the ship, near the rudder.

[127]James Hamilton (c. 1710–1783), four times governor of Pennsylvania between 1748 and 1773.

well, having the Addition of all Mr. Hamilton's Stores, who had laid in plentifully. In this Passage Mr. Denham contracted a Friendship for me that continued during his life.[128] The Voyage was otherwise not a pleasant one, as we had a great deal of bad Weather.

When we came into the Channel, the Captain kept his Word with me, and gave me an Opportunity of examining the Bag for the Governor's Letters. I found none upon which my Name was put, as under my Care; I pick'd out 6 or 7 that by the Hand writing I thought might be the promis'd Letters, especially as one of them was directed to Basket the King's Printer,[129] and another to some Stationer. We arriv'd in London the 24th of December, 1724. I waited upon the stationer who came first in my Way, delivering the Letter as from Gov. Keith. I don't know such a Person, says he: but opening the Letter, O, this is from Riddlesden;[130] I have lately found him to be a compleat Rascal, and I will have nothing to do with him, nor receive any Letters from him. So putting the Letter into my Hand, he turn'd on his Heel and left me to serve some Customer. I was surprized to find these were not the Governor's Letters. And after recollecting and comparing Circumstances, I began to doubt his Sincerity. I found my Friend Denham, and opened the whole Affair to him. He let me into Keith's Character, told me there was not the least Probability that he had written any Letters for me, that no one who knew him had the smallest Dependance on him, and he laught at the Notion of the Governor's giving me a Letter of Credit, having as he said no Credit to give. On my expressing some Concern about what I should do: He advis'd me to endeavour getting some Employment in the Way of my Business. Among the Printers here, says he, you will improve yourself; and when you return to America, you will set up to greater Advantage.

We both of us happen'd to know, as well as the Stationer, that Riddlesden the Attorney, was a very Knave. He had half ruin'd Miss Read's Father by drawing him in to be bound for him.[131] By his Letter it appear'd, there was a secret Scheme on the foot to the Prejudice of Hamilton, (Suppos'd to be then coming over with us,) and that Keith was concern'd in it with Riddlesden. Denham, who was a Friend of Hamilton's, thought he ought to be acquainted with it. So when he arriv'd in England, which was soon after, partly from Resentment and Ill-Will to Keith and Riddlesden, and partly from Good Will to him: I waited on him, and gave him the Letter. He thank'd me cordially, the Information being of Importance to him. And from that time he became my Friend, greatly to my Advantage afterwards on many Occasions.

But what shall we think of a Governor's playing such pitiful Tricks, and imposing so grossly on a poor ignorant Boy! It was a Habit he had acquired. He wish'd to please every body; and having little to give, he gave Expectations. He was otherwise an ingenious sensible Man, a pretty good Writer, and a good Governor for the People, tho' not for his Constituents the Proprietaries,[132] whose Instructions he sometimes disregarded. Several of our best Laws were of his Planning, and pass'd during his Administration.

[128]Thomas Denham (d. 1728), Philadelphia merchant, Franklin's later benefactor.

[129]John Baskett (d. 1742).

[130]William Riddlesden (d. before 1733), a swindler described by the Maryland government as "a Person of matchless Character in Infamy."

[131]I.e., Read was victimized by being led into accepting legal responsibility for the actions and debts of Riddlesden.

[132]The Penn family, Proprietors of Pennsylvania.

Ralph and I were inseparable Companions. We took Lodgings together in Little Britain[133] at *3s. 6d.*[134] per Week, as much as we could then afford. He found some Relations, but they were poor and unable to assist him. He now let me know his Intentions of remaining in London, and that he never meant to return to Philadelphia. He had brought no Money with him, the whole he could muster having been expended in paying his Passage. I had 15 Pistoles:[135] So he borrowed occasionally of me, to subsist while he was looking out for Business. He first endeavoured to get into the Playhouse, believing himself qualify'd for an Actor; but Wilkes,[136] to whom he apply'd, advis'd him candidly not to think of that Employment, as it was impossible he should succeed in it. Then he propos'd to Roberts, a Publisher in Pasternoster Row,[137] to write for him a Weekly Paper like the Spectator, on certain Conditions, which Roberts did not approve. Then he endeavor'd to get Employment as a Hackney Writer[138] to copy for the Stationers[139] and Lawyers about the Temple:[140] but could find no Vacancy.

I immediately got into Work at Palmer's then a famous Printing House in Bartholomew Close;[141] and here I continu'd near a Year. I was pretty diligent; but spent with Ralph a good deal of my Earnings in going to Plays and other Places of Amusement. We had together consum'd all my Pistoles, and now just rubb'd on from hand to mouth. He seem'd quite to forget his Wife and Child, and I by degrees my Engagements with Miss Read, to whom I never wrote more than one Letter, and that was to let her know I was not likely soon to return. This was another of the great Errata of my Life, which I should wish to correct if I were to live it over again. In fact, by our Expences, I was constantly kept unable to pay my Passage.

At Palmer's I was employ'd in composing for the second Edition of Woollaston's Religion of Nature.[142] Some of his Reasonings not appearing to me well-founded, I wrote a little metaphysical Piece, in which I made Remarks on them, It was entitled, *A Dissertation on Liberty and Necessity, Pleasure and Pain.* I inscrib'd it to my Friend Ralph. I printed a small Number. It occasion'd my being more consider'd by Mr. Palmer, as a young Man of some Ingenuity, tho' he seriously expostulated with me upon the Principles of my Pamphlet which to him appear'd abominable. My printing this Pamphlet was another Erratum.[143]

While I lodg'd in Little Britain I made an Acquaintance with one Wilcox a Bookseller, whose shop was at the next Door. He had an immense Collection of second-hand Books. Circulating Libraries were not then in Use; but we

[133]A short London street near St. Paul's Cathedral. [134]Three shillings, sixpence.

[135]Spanish gold coins, each worth about eighteen English shillings.

[136]Robert Wilks (1665?–1732), London actor.

[137]A street near St. Paul's Cathedral and a center of the printing business.

[138]A hired copyist who rode from job to job and did his work in a horse-drawn cab, or hackney; hence "hack writer" and "hack."

[139]Printers and sellers of legal forms and documents.

[140]The Inner and the Middle Temples were two of the four Inns of Court, four sets of buildings that were London's center for the legal profession.

[141]A small square in London, a center for printers.

[142]Actually a third edition (1725) of *The Religion of Nature Delineated* (1722), a treatise on rational morality by William Wollaston, an Anglican clergyman and schoolmaster.

[143]The pamphlet (1725) denied the existence of vice and virtue and thus exposed Franklin to charges of atheism. He later burned all but one of the copies he had retained. Four copies are known to have survived.

agreed that on certain reasonable Terms which I have now forgotten, I might take, read and return any of his Books. This I esteem'd a great Advantage, and I made as much use of it as I could.

My Pamphlet by some means falling into the Hands of one Lyons, a Surgeon, Author of a Book intituled *The Infallibility of Human Judgment,* it occasioned an Acquaintance between us; he took great Notice of me, call'd on me often, to converse on those Subjects, carried me to the Horns a pale Ale-House in [blank] Lane, Cheapside, and introduc'd me to Dr. Mandeville, Author of the Fable of the Bees[144] who had a Club there, of which he was the Soul, being a most facetious entertaining Companion. Lyons too introduc'd me, to Dr. Pemberton, at Batson's Coffee House,[145] who promis'd to give me an Opportunity some time or other of seeing Sir Isaac Newton, of which I was extremely desirous; but this never happened.

I had brought over a few Curiosities among which the principal was a Purse made of the Asbestos, which purifies by Fire. Sir Hans Sloane[146] heard of it, came to see me, and invited me to his House in Bloomsbury Square, where he show'd me all his Curiosities, and persuaded me to let him add to the Number, for which he paid me handsomely.

In our House there lodg'd a young Woman; a Millener, who I think had a Shop in the Cloisters.[147] She had been genteelly bred, was sensible and lively, and of most pleasing Conversation. Ralph read Plays to her in the Evenings, they grew intimate, she took another Lodging, and he follow'd her. They liv'd together some time, but he being still out of Business, and her Income not sufficient to maintain them with her Child, he took a Resolution of going from London, to try for a Country School, which he thought himself well qualify'd to undertake, as he wrote an excellent Hand, and was a Master of Arithmetic and Accounts. This however he deem'd a Business below him, and confident of future better Fortune when he should be unwilling to have it known that he once was so meanly employ'd, he chang'd his Name, and did me the Honour to assume mine. For I soon after had a Letter from him, acquainting me, that he was settled in a small Village in Berkshire, I think it was, where he taught reading and writing to 10 or a dozen Boys at 6 pence each per Week, recommending Mrs. T. to my Care, and desiring me to write to him directing for Mr. Franklin Schoolmaster at such a Place. He continu'd to write frequently, sending me large Specimens of an Epic Poem, which he was then composing, and desiring my Remarks and Corrections. These I gave him from time to time, but endeavour'd rather to discourage his Proceeding. One of Young's Satires was then just publish'd. I copy'd and sent him a great Part of it, which set in a strong Light the Folly of pursuing the Muses with any Hope of Advancement by them.[148] All was in vain. Sheets of the Poem continu'd to come by every Post. In the mean time Mrs. T. having on his Account lost her Friends and Business, was often in Distress, and us'd to send

[144]First published, 1705, as *The Grumbling Hive, or Knaves Turned Honest,* Bernard Mandeville's doggerel poem was republished in 1714 as *The Fable of the Bees, or Private Vices Public Benefits.* Moralists denounced its cynicism, but it was widely read and went through many editions.

[145]Batson's, in Cornhill near the Royal Exchange, was a favorite meeting place of physicians.

[146]Hans Sloane (1660–1753), physician and scientist.

[147]Possibly a reference to buildings located near St. Bartholomew's Church.

[148]Probably Satire IV in *Love of Fame, The Universal Passion* (1725–1728) by Edward Young (1683–1765).

for me, and borrow what I could spare to help her out of them. I grew fond of her Company, and being at this time under no Religious Restraints, and presuming on my Importance to her, I attempted Familiarities (another Erratum) which she repuls'd with a proper Resentment, and acquainted him with my Behaviour. This made a Breach between us, and when he return'd again to London, he let me know he thought I had cancel'd all the Obligations he had been under to me. So I found I was never to expect his Repaying me what I lent to him or advance'd for him. This was however not then of much Consequence, as he was totally unable. And in the Loss of his Friendship I found my self reliev'd from a Burthen. I now began to think of getting a little Money beforehand; and expecting better Work, I left Palmer's to work at Watts's[149] near Lincoln's Inn Fields, a still greater Printing House. Here I continu'd all the rest of my Stay in London.

At my first Admission into this Printing House, I took to working at Press, imagining I felt a Want of the Bodily Exercise I had been us'd to in America, where Presswork is mix'd with Composing. I drank only Water; the other Workmen, nearly 50 in Number, were great Guzzlers of Beer. On occasion I carried up and down Stairs a large Form of Types[150] in each hand, when others carried but one in both Hands. They wonder'd to see from this and several Instances that the Water-American as they call'd me was *stronger* than themselves who drank *strong* Beer. We had an Alehouse Boy who attended always in the House to supply the Workmen. My Companion at the Press, drank every day a Pint before Breakfast, a Pint at Breakfast with his Bread and Cheese; a Pint between Breakfast and Dinner; a Pint at Dinner; a Pint in the Afternoon about Six o'Clock, and another when he had done his Day's-Work. I thought it a detestable Custom. But it was necessary, he suppos'd, to drink *strong* Beer that he might be *strong* to labour. I endeavour'd to convince him that the Bodily Strength afforded by Beer could only be in proportion to the Grain or Flour of the Barley dissolved in the Water of which it was made; that there was more Flour in a Penny-worth of Bread, and therefore if he would eat that with a Pint of Water, it would give him more Strength than a Quart of Beer. He drank on however, and had 4 or 5 Shillings to pay out of his Wages every Saturday Night for that muddling Liquor; an Expence I was free from. And thus these poor Devils keep themselves always under.

Watts after some Weeks desiring to have me in the Composing Room, I left the Pressmen. A new *Bienvenu*[151] or sum for drink being 5*s.*,[152] was demanded of me by the Compositors. I thought it an Imposition, as I had paid below. The Master thought so too, and forbad my Paying it. I stood out two or three Weeks, was accordingly considered as an Excommunicate, and had so many little Pieces of private Mischief done me, by mixing my sorts,[153] transposing my Pages, breaking my Matter,[154] &c. &c. if I were ever so little out of the Room, and all ascrib'd to the Chapel Ghost, which they said ever haunted those not regularly admitted, that notwithstanding the Master's Protection, I found myself oblig'd to comply and pay the Money; convinc'd of the Folly of being on ill Terms with those one is to live with continually. I was now on a fair Footing with them, and soon acquir'd considerable influence. I propos'd

[149]John Watts (c. 1678–1763). [150]A body of type, set and locked in a metal frame.
[151]French: Welcome. [152]Five shillings. [153]Type characters or letters.
[154]Type set up for printing.

some reasonable Alterations in their Chapel[155] Laws, and carried them against all Opposition. From my Example a great Part of them, left their muddling Breakfast of Beer and Bread and Cheese, finding they could with me be supply'd from a neighbouring House with a large Porringer of hot Water-gruel, sprinkled with Pepper, crumb'd with Bread, and a Bit of Butter in it, for the Price of a Pint of Beer, viz, three halfpence. This was a more comfortable as well as cheaper Breakfast, and kept their Heads clearer. Those who continu'd sotting with Beer all day, were often, by not paying, out of Credit at the Alehouse, and us'd to make Interest with me to get Beer, *their Light,* as they phras'd it, *being out.* I watch'd the Pay table on Saturday Night, and collected what I stood engag'd for them, having to pay some times near Thirty Shillings a Week on their Accounts. This, and my being esteem'd a pretty good Riggite, that is a jocular verbal Satyrist, supported my Consequence in the Society. My constant Attendance, (I never making a St. Monday),[156] recommended me to the Master; and my uncommon Quickness at Composing, occasion'd my being put upon all Work of Dispatch which was generally better paid. So I went on now very agreably.

My Lodging in Little Britain being too remote, I found another in Duke-street opposite to the Romish Chapel.[157] It was two pair of Stairs backwards at an Italian Warehouse. A Widow Lady kept the House; she had a Daughter and a Maid Servant, and a Journeyman who attended the Warehouse, but lodg'd abroad. After sending to enquire my Character at the House where I last lodg'd, she agreed to take me in at the same Rate, 3*s.* 6*d.* per Week, cheaper as she said from the Protection she expected in having a Man lodge in the House. She was a Widow, an elderly Woman, had been bred a Protestant, being a Clergyman's Daughter, but was converted to the Catholic Religion by her Husband, whose Memory she much revered, had lived much among People of Distinction, and knew a 1000 Anecdotes of them as far back as the Times of Charles the Second. She was lame in her Knees with the Gout, and therefore seldom stirr'd out of her Room, so sometimes wanted Company; and hers was so highly amusing to me; that I was sure to spend an Evening with her whenever she desired it. Our Supper was only half an Anchovy each, on a very little Strip of Bread and Butter, and half a Pint of Ale between us. But the Entertainment was in her Conversation. My always keeping good Hours, and giving little Trouble in the Family, made her unwilling to part with me; so that when I talk'd of a lodging I had heard of, nearer my Business, for 2*s.* a Week, which intent as I now was on saving Money, made some Difference; she bid me not think of it, for she would abate me two Shillings a Week for the future, so I remain'd with her at 1*s.* 6*d.* as long as I staid in London.

In a Garret of her House there lived a Maiden Lady of 70 in the most retired Manner, of whom my Landlady gave me this Account, that she was a Roman Catholic, had been sent abroad when young and lodg'd in a Nunnery with an Intent of becoming a Nun: but the Country not agreeing with her, she return'd to England, where there being no Nunnery, she had vow'd to lead the Life of a Nun as near as might be done in those Circumstances: Accordingly she had given all her Estate to charitable Uses, reserving only Twelve Pounds a Year to live on, and out of this Sum she still gave a great deal in

[155]"A Printing House is always called a Chappel by the Workmen."—Franklin's note.

[156]I.e., never missed work on a Monday with the excuse of having observed a saint's day.

[157]The Roman Catholic Chapel of Saints Anselm and Cecilia.

Charity, living her self on Water-gruel only, and using no Fire but to boil it. She had lived many Years in that Garret, being permitted to remain there gratis by successive Catholic Tenants of the House below, as they deem'd it a Blessing to have her there. A Priest visited her, to confess her every Day. I have ask'd her, says my Landlady, how she, as she liv'd, could possibly find so much Employment for a Confessor? O, says she, it is impossible to avoid *vain Thoughts.* I was permitted once to visit her: She was chearful and polite, and convers'd pleasantly. The Room was clean, but had no other Furniture than a Matras, a Table with a Crucifix and Book, a Stool which she gave me to sit on, and a Picture over the Chimney of St. Veronica, displaying her Handkerchief with the miraculous Figure of Christ's bleeding Face on it, which she explain'd to me with great Seriousness. She look'd pale, but was never sick, and I give it as another Instance on how small an Income Life and Health may be supported.

At Watts's Printinghouse I contracted an Acquaintance with an ingenious young Man, one Wygate, who having wealthy Relations, had been better educated than most Printers, was a tolerable Latinist, spoke French, and lov'd Reading. I taught him, and a Friend of his, to swim, at twice going into the River, and they soon became good Swimmers. They introduc'd me to some Gentlemen from the Country who went to Chelsea by Water to see the College[158] and Don Saltero's Curiosities.[159] In our Return, at the Request of the Company, whose Curiosity Wygate had excited, I stript and leapt into the River, and swam from near Chelsea to Blackfryars,[160] performing on the Way many Feats of Activity both upon and under Water, that surpriz'd and pleas'd those to whom they were Novelties. I had from a Child been ever delighted with this Exercise, had studied and practis'd all Thevenot's Motions and Positions,[161] added some of my own, aiming at the graceful and easy, as well as the Useful. All these I took this Occasion of exhibiting to the Company, and was much flatter'd by their Admiration. And Wygate, who was desirous of becoming a Master, grew more and more attach'd to me, on that account, as well as from the Similarity of our Studies. He at length propos'd to me travelling all over Europe together, supporting ourselves everywhere by working at our Business. I was once inclin'd to it. But mentioning it to my good Friend Mr. Denham, with whom I often spent an Hour, when I had Leisure. He dissuaded me from it, advising me to think only of returning to Pensilvania, which he was now about to do.

I must record one Trait of this good Man's Character. He had formerly been in Business at Bristol, but fail'd in Debt to a Number of People, compounded[162] and went to America. There, by a close Application to Business as a Merchant, he acquir'd a plentiful Fortune in a few Years. Returning to England in the Ship with me, He invited his old Creditors to an Entertainment, at which he thank'd them for the easy Composition[163] they had favor'd him with, and when they expected nothing but the Treat, every Man at the first Remove,[164] found under his Plate an Order on a Banker for the full Amount of the unpaid Remainder with Interest.

[158]Probably Chelsea Hospital, erected in 1682 on the site of the former Chelsea College.

[159]James Salter ran a coffeehouse and museum in Chelsea where he exhibited various curiosities of doubtful authenticity, including the word of William the Conqueror and the tears of Job.

[160]About three and one half miles.

[161]Melchisédec de Thévenot, *The Art of Swimming* (1699). [162]Partially settled his debts.

[163]Settlement. [164]Removal of the meal's first course.

He now told me he was about to return to Philadelphia, and should carry over a great quantity of Goods in order to open a Store there: He propos'd to take me over as his Clerk, to keep his Books (in which he would instruct me) copy his Letters, and attend the Store. He added, that as soon as I should be acquainted with mercantile Business he would promote me by sending me with a Cargo of Flour and Bread &c. to the West Indies, and procure me Commissions from others; which would be profitable, and if I manag'd well, would establish me handsomely. The Thing pleas'd me, for I was grown tired of London, remember'd with Pleasure the happy Months I had spent in Pennsylvania, and wish'd again to see it. Therefore I immediately agreed, on the Terms of Fifty Pounds a Year, Pennsylvania Money; less indeed than my present Gettings as a Compostor,[165] but affording a better Prospect.

I now took Leave of Printing, as I thought for ever, and was daily employ'd in my new Business; going about with Mr. Denham among the Tradesmen, to purchase various Articles, and seeing them pack'd up, doing Errands, calling upon Workmen to dispatch, &c. and when all was on board, I had a few Days Leisure. On one of these Days I was to my Surprize sent for by a great Man I knew only by Name, a Sir William Wyndham[166] and I waited upon him. He had heard by some means or other of my Swimming from Chelsey to Blackfryars, and of my teaching Wygate and another young Man to swim in a few Hours. He had two Sons about to set out on their Travels; he wish'd to have them first taught Swimming; and propos'd to gratify me handsomely if I would teach them. They were not yet come to Town and my Stay was uncertain, so I could not undertake it. But from this Incident I thought it likely, that if I were to remain in England and open a Swimming School, I might get a good deal of Money. And it struck me so strongly, that had the Overture been sooner made me, probably I should not so soon have returned to America. After many Years, you and I had something of more Importance to do with one of these Sons of Sir William Wyndham, become Earl of Egremont, which I shall mention in its Place.[167]

Thus I spent about 18 months in London. Most Part of the Time, I work'd hard at my Business, and spent but little upon my self except in seeing Plays and in Books. My friend Ralph had kept me poor. He owed me about 27 Pounds; which I was now never likely to receive; a great Sum out of my small Earnings. I lov'd him notwithstanding, for he had many amiable Qualities. Tho' I had by no means improv'd my Fortune. But I had pick'd up some very ingenious Acquaintance whose Conversation was of great Advantage to me, and I had read considerably.

We sail'd from Gravesend on the 23rd of July 1726. For the Incidents of the Voyage, I refer you to my Journal, where you will find them all minutely related. Perhaps the most important Part of that Journal is the *Plan* to be found in it which I formed at Sea, for regulating my future Conduct in Life.[168] It is the more remarkable, as being form'd when I was so young, and yet being pretty faithfully adhered to quite thro' to old Age. We landed in Philadelphia the 11th of October, where I found sundry Alterations. Keith

[165]Compositor, typesetter.
[166]Sir William Wyndham (1687–1740), prominent English politician.
[167]Franklin failed to do so. [168]The full text of the "Plan" is lost.

was no longer Governor, being superceded by Major Gordon:[169] I met him walking the Streets as a common Citizen. He seem'd a little asham'd at seeing me, but pass'd without saying any thing. I should have been as much asham'd at seeing Miss Read, had not her Friends, despairing with Reason of my Return, after the Receipt of my Letter, persuaded her to marry another, one Rogers, a Potter, which was done in my Absence. With him however she was never happy, and soon parted from him, refusing to cohabit with him, or bear his Name, It being now said that he had another Wife. He was a worthless Fellow tho' an excellent Workman which was the Temptation to her Friends. He got into Debt, and ran away in 1727 or 28, Went to the West Indies, and died there. Keimer had got a better House, a Shop well supply'd with Stationary, plenty of new Types, a number of Hands tho' none good, and seem'd to have a great deal of Business.

Mr. Denham took a Store in Water Street, where we open'd our Goods. I attended the Business diligently, studied Accounts, and grew in a little Time expert at selling. We lodg'd and boarded together, he counsell'd me as a Father, having a sincere Regard for me: I respected and lov'd him: and we might have gone on together very happily: But in the Beginning of Feby. 1726/7 when I had just pass'd my 21st Year, we both were taken ill. My Distemper was a Pleurisy,[170] which very nearly carried me off: I suffered a good deal, gave up the Point[171] in my own mind, and was rather disappointed when I found my Self recovering; regretting in some degree that I must now some time or other have all that disagreable Work to do over again. I forget what his Distemper was. It held him a long time, and at length carried him off. He left me a small Legacy in a noncupative Will,[172] as a Token of his Kindness for me, and he left me once more to the wide World. For the Store was taken into the Care of his Executors, and my Employment under him ended: My Brother-in-law Holmes, being now at Philadelphia, advis'd my Return to my Business. And Keimer tempted me with an Offer of large Wages by the Year to come and take the Management of his Printing-House, that he might better attend his Stationer's Shop. I had heard a bad Character of him in London, from his Wife and her Friends, and was not fond of having any more to do with him. I try'd for farther Employment as a Merchant's Clerk; but not readily meeting with any, I clos'd[173] again with Keimer.

I found in *his* House these Hands; Hugh Meredith[174] a Welsh-Pensilvanian, 30 Years of Age, bred to Country Work: honest, sensible, had a great deal of solid Observation, was something of a Reader, but given to drink: Stephen Potts,[175] a young Country Man of full Age, bred to the Same: of uncommon natural Parts,[176] and great Wit and Humour, but a little idle. These he had agreed with at extream low Wages, per Week, to be rais'd a Shilling every 3 Months, as they would deserve by improving in their Business, and the Expectation of these high Wages to come on hereafter was what he had drawn them in with. Meredith was to work at Press, Potts at Bookbinding, which he by Agreement, was to teach them, tho' he knew neither one nor t'other.

[169]Patrick Gordon (1644–1736), Governor of Pennsylvania from 1726 to 1736.

[170]A respiratory disease. [171]Will to live.

[172]An oral, not a written, will. [173]Made an agreement.

[174]Hugh Meredith (c. 1696–c. 1749), later Franklin's business partner.

[175]Stephen Potts (d. 1758), later a bookseller and tavern keeper. [176]Talents, ability.

John—a wild Irishman brought up to no Business, whose Service for 4 Years Keimer had purchas'd[177] from the Captain of a Ship. He too was to be made a Pressman. George Webb,[178] an Oxford Scholar, whose Time for 4 Years he had likewise bought, intending him for a Compositor: of whom more presently. And David Harry,[179] a Country Boy, whom he had taken Apprentice. I soon perceiv'd that the Intention of engaging me at Wages so much higher than he had been us'd to give, was to have these raw cheap Hands form'd thro' me, and as soon as I had instructed them, then, they being all articled to him,[180] he should be able to do without me. I went on however, very chearfully; put his Printing House in Order, which had been in great Confusion, and brought his Hands by degrees to mind their Business and to do it better.

It was an odd Thing to find an Oxford Scholar in the Situation of a bought Servant. He was not more than 18 Years of Age, and gave me this Account of himself; that he was born in Gloucester, educated at a Grammar School there, had been distinguish'd among the Scholars for some apparent Superiority in performing his Part when they exhibited Plays; belong'd to the Witty Club there, and had written some Pieces in Prose and Verse which were printed in the Gloucester Newspapers. Thence he was sent to Oxford; there he continu'd about a Year, but not well-satisfy'd, wishing of all things to see London and become a Player. At length receiving his Quarterly allowance of 15 Guineas,[181] instead of discharging his Debts, he walk'd out of Town, hid his Gown in a Furz Bush,[182] and footed it to London, where having no Friend to advise him, he fell into bad Company, soon spent his Guineas, found no means of being introduc'd among the Players, grew necessitous, pawn'd his Cloaths and wanted Bread. Walking the Street very hungry, and not knowing what to do with himself, a Crimp's Bill[183] was put into his Hand, offering immediate Entertainment and Encouragement to such as would bind themselves to serve in America. He went directly, sign'd the Indentures, was put into the Ship and came over; never writing a Line to acquaint his Friends what was become of him. He was lively, witty, goodnatur'd, and a pleasant Companion, but idle, thoughtless and imprudent to the last Degree.

John the Irishman soon ran away. With the rest I began to live very agreeably; for they all respected me, the more as they found Keimer incapable of instructing them, and that from me they learnt something daily. We never work'd on a Saturday, that being Keimer's Sabbath. So I had two Days for Reading. My Acquaintance with Ingenious People in the Town increased. Keimer himself treated me with great Civility, and apparent Regard; and nothing now made me uneasy but my Debt to Vernon, which I was yet unable to pay being hitherto but a poor Oeconomist. He however kindly made no Demand of it.

Our Printing-House often wanted Sorts,[184] and there was no Letter Founder in America. I had seen Types cast at James's in London,[185] but without much Attention to the Manner: However I now contriv'd a Mould, made

[177]By paying for his passage. [178]George Webb (born c. 1709).

[179]David Harry (1708–1760). [180]Bound by a contract to work only for him.

[181]A coin worth one pound plus one shilling.

[182]I.e., hid his academic robes in an evergreen bush. [183]A recruiter's advertisement.

[184]I.e., lacked letters or characters in a set of type. A printer who lacked the necessary type was "out of sorts," and thus angry; hence the familiar expression.

[185]Thomas James's type foundry, the largest in London.

use of the Letters we had, as Puncheons,[186] struck the Matrices[187] in Lead, and thus supply'd in a pretty tolerable way all Deficiencies. I also engrav'd several Things on occasion. I made the Ink, I was Warehouse-man and every thing, in short quite a Factotum.[188]

But however serviceable I might be, I found that my Services became every Day of less Importance, as the other Hands improv'd in the Business. And when Keimer paid my second Quarter's Wages, he let me know that he felt them too heavy, and thought I should make an Abatement. He grew by degrees less civil, put on more of the Master, frequently found Fault, was captious and seem'd ready for an Out-breaking. I went on nevertheless with a good deal of Patience, thinking that his incumber'd Circumstances were partly the Cause. At length a Trifle snapt our Connexion. For a great Noise happening near the Courthouse, I put my Head out of the Window to see what was the Matter. Keimer being in the Street look'd up and saw me, call'd out to me in a loud Voice and angry Tone to mind my Business, adding some reproachful Words, that nettled me the more for their Publicity, all the Neighbours who were looking out on the same Occasion being Witnesses how I was treated. He came up immediately into the Printing-House, continu'd the Quarrel, high Words pass'd on both Sides, he gave me the Quarter's Warning we had stipulated, expressing a Wish that he had not been oblig'd to so long a Warning: I told him his Wish was unnecessary for I would leave him that Instant; and so taking my Hat walk'd out of Doors; desiring Meredith[189] whom I saw below to take care of some Things I left, and bring them to my Lodging.

Meredith came accordingly in the Evening, when we talk'd my Affair over. He had conceiv'd a great Regard for me, and was very unwilling that I should leave the House while he remain'd in it. He dissuaded me from returning to my native Country which I began to think of. He reminded me that Keimer was in debt for all he possess'd, that his Creditors began to be uneasy, that he kept his Shop miserably, sold often without Profit for ready Money, and often trusted without keeping Accounts. That he must therefore fail; which would make a Vacancy I might profit of. I objected my Want of Money. He then let me know, that his Father had a high Opinion of me, and from some Discourse that had pass'd between them, he was sure would advance Money to set us up, if I would enter into Partnership with him. My Time, says he, will be out with Keimer in the Spring. By that time we may have our Press and Types in from London: I am sensible I am no Workman. If you like it, Your Skill in the Business shall be set against the Stock I furnish; and we will share the Profits equally. The Proposal was agreable, and I consented. His Father was in Town, and approv'd of it, the more as he saw I had great Influence with his Son, had prevail'd on him to abstain long from Dramdrinking,[190] and he hop'd might break him of that wretched Habit entirely, when we came to be so closely connected. I gave an Inventory to the Father, who carry'd it to a Merchant; the Things were sent for; the Secret was to be kept till

[186]Stamping tools. [187]Molds for casting type

[188]One who "does everything," a jack-of-all-trades.

[189]Simon Meredith (d. 1745?), father of Hugh Meredith (c. 1697–1749), one of the original members of Franklin's Junto.

[190]Drinking drams (small measures) of alcoholic beverages.

they should arrive, and in the mean time I was to get work if I could at the other Printing House. But I found no Vacancy there, and so remain'd idle a few Days, when Keimer, on a Prospect of being employ'd to print some Paper-money, in New Jersey, which would require Cuts and various Types that I only could supply, and apprehending Bradford might engage me and get the Jobb from him, sent me a very civil Message, that old Friends should not part for a few Words, the Effect of sudden Passion, and wishing me to return. Meredith persuaded me to comply, as it would give more Opportunity for his Improvement under my daily Instructions. So I return'd, and we went on more smoothly than from some time before. The New Jersey Jobb was obtain'd. I contriv'd a Copper-Plate Press for it, the first that had been seen in the Country. I cut several Ornaments and Checks for the Bills. We went together to Burlington,[191] where I executed the Whole to Satisfaction, and he received so large a Sum for the Work, as to be enabled thereby to keep his Head much longer above Water.

At Burlington I made an Acquaintance with many principal People of the Province. Several of them had been appointed by the Assembly a Committee to attend the Press, and take Care that no more Bills were printed than the Law directed. They were therefore by Turns constantly with us, and generally he who attended brought with him a Friend or two for company. My Mind having been much more improv'd by Reading than Keimer's, I suppose it was for that Reason my Conversation seem'd to be more valu'd. They had me to their Houses, introduc'd me to their Friends and show'd me much Civility, while he, tho' the Master, was a little neglected. In truth he was an odd Fish, ignorant of common Life, fond of rudely opposing receiv'd Opinions, slovenly to extream dirtiness, enthusiastic[192] in some Points of Religion, and a little Knavish withal. We continu'd there near 3 Months, and by that time I could reckon among my acquired Friends, Judge Allen, Samuel Bustill, the Secretary of the Province, Isaac Pearson, Joseph Cooper and several of the Smiths, Members of Assembly, and Isaac Decow the Surveyor General. The latter was a shrewd sagacious old Man, who told me that he began for himself when young by wheeling Clay for the Brickmakers, learnt to write after he was of Age, carry'd the Chain for Surveyors, who taught him Surveying, and he had now by his Industry acquir'd a good Estate; and says he, I foresee, that you will soon work this Man out of his Business and make a Fortune in it at Philadelphia. He had not then the least Intimation of my Intention to set up there or any where. These Friends were afterwards of great Use to me, as I occasionally was to some of them. They all continued their Regard for me as long as they lived.

Before I enter upon my public Appearance in Business it may be well to let you know the then State of my Mind, with regard to my Principles and Morals, that you may see how far those influenc'd the future Events of my Life. My Parents had early given me religious Impressions, and brought me through my Childhood piously in the Dissenting Way.[193] But I was scarce 15 when, after doubting by turns of several Points as I found them disputed in

[191]Burlington, New Jersey. [192]Overemotional.
[193]As one, such as a Congregationalist, who dissents from the doctrines of the Church of England.

the different Books I read, I began to doubt of Revelation it self. Some Books against Deism fell into my Hands; they were said to be the Substance of Sermons preached at Boyle's Lectures.[194] It happened that they wrought an Effect on me quite contrary to what was intended by them: For the arguments of the Deists which were quoted to be refuted, appeared to me much stronger than the Refutations. In short I soon became a thorough Deist. My Arguments perverted some others, particularly Collins and Ralph: but each of them having afterwards wrong'd me greatly without the least Compunction and recollecting Keith's Conduct towards me, (who was another Freethinker) and my own towards Vernon and Miss Read which at Times gave me great Trouble, I began to suspect that this Doctrine tho' it might be true, was not very useful. My London Pamphlet, which had for its Motto those Lines of Dryden

> *—Whatever is, is right—*
> *Tho' purblind Man.*
> *Sees but a Part of the Chain, the nearest Link,*
> *His Eyes not carrying to the equal Beam,*
> *That poizes all, above.*[195]

And from the Attributes of God, his infinite Wisdom, Goodness and Power concluded that nothing could possibly be wrong in the World, and that Vice and Virtue were empty Distinctions, no such Things existing: appear'd now not so clever a Performance as I once thought it; and I doubted whether some Error had not insinuated itself unperceiv'd into my Argument, so as to infect all that follow'd, as is common in metaphysical Reasonings. I grew convinc'd that *Truth, Sincerity and Integrity* in Dealings between Man and Man, were of the utmost Importance to the Felicity of Life, and I form'd written Resolutions, (which still remain in my Journal Book) to practice them ever while I lived. Revelation had indeed no weight with me as such; but I entertain'd an Opinion, that tho' certain Actions might not be bad *because* they were forbidden by it, or good *because* it commanded them; yet probably those Actions might be forbidden *because* they were bad for us, or commanded *because* they were beneficial to us, in their own Natures, all the Circumstances of things considered. And this Persuasion, with the kind hand of Providence, or some guardian Angel, or accidental favourable Circumstances and Situations, or all together, preserved me (thro' this dangerous Time of Youth and the hazardous Situations I was sometimes in among Strangers, remote from the Eye and Advice of my Father) without any *wilful* gross Immorality or Injustice that might have been expected from my Want of Religion. I say *wilful,* because the Instances I have mentioned, had something of *Necessity* in them, from my Youth, Inexperience, and the Knavery of others. I had therefore a tolerable Character to begin the World with, I valued it properly, and determin'd to preserve it.

[194]The chemist Robert Boyle (1627–1691) had established a series of lectures to defend Christianity against skeptics.

[195]The first line is not from John Dryden but from Pope's *Essay on Man* (1733), Epistle I, line 294. The remainder is an approximate quotation from Dryden's *Oedipus,* Act III, Scene i, lines 244–248.

We had not been long return'd to Philadelphia, before the New Types arriv'd from London. We settled with Keimer, and left him by his Consent before he heard of it. We found a House to hire near the Market, and took it. To lessen the Rent, (which was then but £24 a Year tho' I have since known it let for 70) We took in Tho' Godfrey a Glazier[196] and his Family, who were to pay a considerable Part of it to us, and we to board with them. We had scarce opened our Letters and put our Press in Order, before George House, an Acquaintance of Mine, brought a Country-man to us; whom he had met in the Street enquiring for a Printer. All our Cash was now expended in the Variety of Particulars we had been obliged to procure and this Countryman's Five Shillings being our first Fruits, and coming so seasonably, gave me more Pleasure than any Crown[197] I have since earn'd; and from the Gratitude I felt towards House, has made me often more ready than perhaps I should otherwise have been to assist young Beginners.

There are Croakers in every Country always boding its Ruin. Such a one then lived in Philadelphia, a Person of Note, an elderly Man, with a wise Look, and very grave Manner of speaking. His Name was Samuel Mickle. This Gentleman, a Stranger to me, stopt one Day at my Door, and asked me if I was the young Man who had lately opened a new Printing House: Being answer'd in the Affirmative; he said he was sorry for me, because it was an expensive Undertaking and the Expence would be lost; for Philadelphia was a sinking[198] Place, the People already half Bankrupts or near being so; all Appearances of the contrary, such as new Buildings and the Rise of Rents being to his certain Knowledge fallacious, for they were in fact among the Things that would soon ruin us. And he gave me such a Detail of Misfortunes, now existing or that were soon to exist, that he left me half-melancholy. Had I known him before I engag'd in this Business, probably I never should have done it. This Man continu'd to live in this decaying Place; and to declaim in the same Strain, refusing for many Years to buy a House there, because all was going to Destruction, and at last I had the Pleasure of seeing him give five times as much for one as he might have bought it for when he first began his Croaking.

I should have mention'd before, that in the Autumn of the preceding Year I had form'd most of my ingenious Acquaintance into a Club for mutual Improvement, which we call'd the Junto.[199] We met on Friday Evenings. The Rules I drew up requir'd that every Member in his Turn should produce one or more Queries on any Point of Morals, Politics or Natural Philosophy, to be discuss'd by the Company, and once in three Months produce and read an Essay of his own Writing on any Subject he pleased. Our Debates were to be under the Direction of a President, and to be conducted in the sincere Spirit of Enquiry after Truth, without Fondness for Dispute, or Desire of Victory; and to prevent Warmth all Expressions of Positiveness in Opinion, or of direct Contradiction, were after some time made contraband and prohibited under small pecuniary Penalties. The first Members were Joseph Brientnal, A Copyer of Deeds for the Scriveners; a good-natur'd friendly middle-ag'd Man, a great Lover of Poetry, reading all he could meet with, and writing

[196]One who sets glass, as windowpanes. [197]A five-shilling coin. [198]Failing.
[199]A Spanish word meaning "joined," used to describe a small, private, or secret group.

some that was tolerable; very ingenious in many little Nicknackeries, and of sensible Conversation. Thomas Godfrey, a self-taught Mathematician, great in his Way, and afterwards Inventor of what is now call'd Hadley's Quadrant. But he knew little out of his way, and was not a pleasing Companion, as like most Great Mathematicians I have met with, he expected unusual Precision in every thing said, or was forever denying or distinguishing upon Trifles, to the Disturbance of all Conversation. He soon left us. Nicholas Scull, a Surveyor, afterwards Surveyor-General, Who lov'd Books, and sometimes made a few Verses. William Parsons, bred a Shoemaker, but loving Reading, had acquir'd a considerable Share of Mathematics, which he first studied with a View to Astrology that he afterwards laught at. He also became Surveyor General. William Maugridge, a Joiner, a most exquisite Mechanic and a solid sensible Man. Hugh Meredith, Stephen Potts, and George Webb, I have Characteris'd before. Robert Grace, a young Gentleman of some Fortune, generous, lively and witty, a Lover of Punning and of his Friends. And William Coleman, then a Merchant's Clerk, about my Age, who had the coolest clearest Head, the best Heart, and the exactest Morals, of almost any Man I ever met with. He became afterwards a Merchant of Great Note, and one of our Provincial Judges: Our Friendship continued without Interruption to his Death upwards of 40 Years.

And the club continu'd almost as long and was the best School of Philosophy, Morals and Politics that then existed in the Province; for our Queries which were read the Week preceding their Discussion, put us on Reading with Attention upon the several Subjects, that we might speak more to the purpose: and here too we acquired better Habits of Conversation, every thing being studied in our Rules which might prevent our disgusting each other. From hence the long Continuance of the Club, which I shall have frequent Occasion to speak farther of hereafter; But my giving this Account of it here, is to show something of the Interest I had, every one of these exerting themselves in recommending Business to us. Brientnal particularly procur'd us from the Quakers, the Printing 40 Sheets of their History, the rest being to be done by Keimer: and upon this we work'd exceeding hard, for the Price was low. It was a Folio, Pro Patria Size, in Pica[200] with Long Primer[201] Notes. I compos'd of it a Sheet a Day, and Meredith work'd it off at Press. It was often 11 at Night and sometimes later, before I had finish'd my Distribution[202] for the next days Work: For the little Jobbs sent in by our other Friends now and then put us back. But so determin'd I was to continue doing a Sheet a Day of the Folio, that one Night when having impos'd my Forms,[203] I thought my Days Work over, one of them by accident was broken and two Pages reduc'd to Pie,[204] I immediately distributed and compos'd it over again before I went to bed. And this Industry visible to our Neighbours began to give us Character and Credit; particularly I was told, that mention being made of the new Printing Office at the Merchants every-night-Club, the general Opinion was that it must fail, there being already two Printers in the Place, Keimer and Bradford; but Doctor Baird (whom you and I saw many Years after at his native Place, St. Andrews in Scotland) gave a contrary Opinion; for the Industry

[200]A large volume, set in 12-point type. [201]10-point type.
[202]I.e., placing each piece of type in its place in the typecase.
[203]Locked the type into its form, ready for printing. [204]A jumble.

of that Franklin, says he, is superior to any thing I ever saw of the kind: I see him still at work when I go home from Club; and he is at Work again before his Neighbours are out of bed. This struck the rest, and we soon after had Offers from one of them to Supply us with Stationary. But as yet we did not chuse to engage in Shop Business.

I mention this Industry the more particularly and the more freely, tho' it seems to be talking in my own Praise, that those of my Posterity who shall read it, may know the Use of that Virtue, when they see its Effects in my Favour throughout this Relation.

George Webb, who had found a Female Friend that lent him wherewith to purchase his Time of Keimer, now came to offer himself as a Journeyman to us. We could not then imploy him, but I foolishly let him know, as a Secret, that I soon intended to begin a Newspaper, and might then have Work for him. My Hopes of Success as I told him were founded on this, that the then only Newspaper,[205] printed by Bradford was a paltry thing, wretchedly manag'd, and no way entertaining; and yet was profitable to him. I therefore thought a good Paper could scarcely fail of good Encouragement. I requested Webb not to mention it, but he told it to Keimer, who immediately, to be beforehand with me, published Proposals for Printing one himself, on which Webb was to be employ'd. I resented this, and to counteract them, as I could not yet begin our Paper, I wrote several Pieces of Entertainment for Bradford's Paper, under the Title of the Busy Body which Brientnal continu'd some Months.[206] By this means the Attention of the Publick was fix'd on that Paper, and Keimers Proposals which we burlesqu'd and ridicul'd, were disregarded. He began his Paper however, and after carrying it on three Quarters of a Year, with at most only 90 Subscribers, he offer'd it to me for a Trifle, and I having been ready some time to go on with it, took it in hand directly, and it prov'd in a few Years extreamly profitably to me.[207]

I perceive that I am apt to speak in the singular Number, though our Partnership still continu'd. The Reason may be, that in fact the whole Management of the Business lay upon me. Meredith was no Compositor, a poor Pressman, and seldom sober. My friends lamented my Connection with him, but I was to make the best of it.

Our first Papers made a quite different Appearance from any before in the Province, a better Type and better printed: but some spirited Remarks of my Writing on the Dispute then going on between Govr. Burnet and the Massachusetts Assembly,[208] struck the principal People, occasion'd by the Paper and the Manager of it to be much talk'd of, and in a few Weeks brought them all to be our Subscribers. Their Example was follow'd by many, and our Number went on growing continually. This was one of the first good Effects of my having learnt a little to scribble. Another was, that the leading Men, seeing a News Paper now in the hands of one who could also handle a Pen,

[205] *The American Weekly Mercury,* established December 22, 1719.

[206] Franklin wrote all of four and part of two essays in this series.

[207] Keimer began *The Universal Instructor in All Arts and Sciences: and Pennsylvania Gazette* on December 24, 1728. Franklin took it over in October 1729, shortened the title to *The Pennsylvania Gazette,* and made it one of the best papers in the Colonies.

[208] William Burnet (1688–1729), Governor of Massachusetts. The dispute rose over his demands for a salary of £1,000 per year. The Assembly offered less. Franklin sided with the Assembly, writing in the *Pennsylvania Gazette,* October 9, 1729.

thought it convenient to oblige and encourage me. Bradford still printed the Votes and Laws and other Publick Business. He had printed an Address of the House[209] to the Governor in a coarse blundering manner; We reprinted it elegantly and correctly, and sent one to every Member. They were sensible of the Difference, it strengthen'd the Hands of our Friends in the House, and they voted us their Printers for the Year ensuing.

Among my Friends in the House I must not forget Mr. Hamilton before mentioned, who was now returned from England and had a Seat in it.[210] He interested himself[211] for me strongly in that Instance, as he did in many others afterwards, continuing his Patronage till his Death. Mr. Vernon about this time put me in mind of the Debt I ow'd him: but did not press me. I wrote him an ingenuous Letter of Acknowledgments, crav'd his Forbearance a little longer which he allow'd me, and as soon as I was able I paid the Principal with Interest and many Thanks. So that *Erratum* was in some degree corrected.

But now another Difficulty came upon me, which I had never the least Reason to expect. Mr. Meredith's Father, who was to have paid for our Printing House according to the Expectations given me, was able to advance only one Hundred Pounds, Currency, which had been paid, and a Hundred more was due to the Merchant; who grew impatient and su'd us all. We gave Bail, but saw that if the Money could not be rais'd in time, the Suit must come to a Judgment and Execution,[212] and our hopeful Prospects must with us be ruined, as the Press and Letters must be sold for Payment, perhaps at half Price. In this Distress two true Friends whose Kindness I have never forgotten nor ever shall forget while I can remember any thing, came to me separately unknown to each other, and without any Application from me, offering each of them to advance me all the Money that should be necessary to enable me to take the whole Business upon my self if that should be practicable, but they did not like my continuing the Partnership with Meredith, who as they said was often seen drunk in the Streets, and playing at low Games in Alehouses, much to our Discredit. These two Friends were William Coleman and Robert Grace.[213] I told them I could not propose a Separation while any Prospect remain'd of the Merediths fulfilling their Part of our Agreement. Because I thought myself under great Obligations to them for what they had done and would do if they could. But if they finally fail'd in their Performance, and our Partnership must be dissolv'd, I should then think myself at Liberty to accept the Assistance of my Friends.

Thus the matter rested for some time. When I said to my Partner, perhaps your Father is dissatisfied at the Part you have undertaken in this Affair of ours, and is unwilling to advance for you and me what he would for you alone: If that is the Case, tell me, and I will resign the whole to you and go about my Business. No says he, my Father has really been disappointed and is really unable; and I am unwilling to distress him farther. I see this is a Business I am not fit for. I was bred a Farmer, and it was a Folly in me to come to

[209]Assembly. [210]Andrew Hamilton, Speaker of the Assembly in various sessions.

[211]"I got his Son once £500."—Franklin's note.

[212]A court judgment ordering seizure and sale of property.

[213]William Coleman (1704–1769), Robert Grace (1709–1766), original members of Franklin's Junto. Grace's ironworks manufactured Franklin's "fireplace."

Town and put my Self at 30 Years of Age an Apprentice to learn a new Trade. Many of our Welsh People are going to settle in North Carolina where Land is cheap: I am inclin'd to go with them, and follow my old Employment. You may find Friends to assist you. If you will take the Debts of the Company upon you, return to my Father the hundred Pound he has advanc'd, pay my little personal Debts, and give me Thirty Pounds and a new Saddle, I will relinquish the Partnership and leave the whole in your Hands. I agreed to this Proposal. It was drawn up in Writing, sign'd and seal'd immediately. I gave him what he demanded and he went soon after to Carolina; from whence he sent me next Year two long Letters, containing the best Account that had been given of that Country, the Climate, Soil, Husbandry, &c. for in those Matters he was very judicious. I printed them in the Papers,[214] and they gave grate Satisfaction to the Publick.

As soon as he was gone, I recurr'd to my two Friends; and because I would not give an unkind Preference to either, I took half what each had offered and I wanted, of one, and half of the other; paid off the Company Debts, and went on with the Business in my own Name, advertising that the Partnership was dissolved. I think this was in or about the Year 1729.[215]

About this Time there was a Cry among the People for more Paper-Money, only £15,000 being extant in the Province and that soon to be sunk.[216] The wealthy Inhabitants oppos'd any Addition, being against all Paper Currency, from an Apprehension that it would depreciate as it had done in New England to the Prejudice of all Creditors. We had discuss'd this Point in our Junto, where I was on the Side of Addition, being persuaded that the first small Sum struck in 1723 had done much good, by increasing the Trade Employment, and Number of Inhabitants in the Province, since I now saw all the old Houses inhabited, and many new ones building, where as I remember'd well, that when I first walk'd about the Streets of Philadelphia, eating my Roll, I saw most of the Houses in Walnut street between Second and Front streets with Bills[217] on their Doors, to be let; and many likewise in Chestnut Street, and other Streets; which made me then think the Inhabitants of the City were one after another deserting it. Our Debates possess'd me so fully of the Subject, that I wrote and printed an anonymous Pamphlet on it, entitled, *The Nature and Necessity of a Paper Currency.*[218] It was well receiv'd by the common People in general; but the Rich Men dislik'd it; for it increas'd and strengthen'd the Clamour for more Money; and they happening to have no Writers among them that were able to answer it, their Opposition slacken'd, and the Point was carried by a Majority in the House. My Friends there, who conceiv'd I had been of some Service, thought fit to reward me, by employing me in printing the Money, a very profitable Jobb, and a great Help to me.[219] This was another Advantage gain'd by my being able to write. The Utility of this Currency became by Time and Experience so evident, as never afterwards to be much disputed, so that it grew soon to £55,000 and in 1739 to £80,000 since which it arose during War to upwards of £350,000. Trade,

[214]*Pennsylvania Gazette,* May 6 and 13, 1731. [215]Actually July 14, 1730.
[216]Removed from circulation. [217]Signs.
[218]*A Modest Inquiry into the Nature and Necessity of a Paper-Currency* (1729).
[219]The 1729 contract to print £20,000 was actually given to Andrew Bradford. Franklin received the 1731 contract to print £40,000. He was paid £100 plus the cost of the paper.

Building and Inhabitants all the while increasing. Tho' I now think there are Limits beyond which the Quantity may be hurtful.

I soon after obtain'd, thro' my Friend Hamilton, the Printing of the New Castle Paper Money,[220] another profitable Jobb, as I then thought it; small Things appearing great to those in small Circumstances. And these to me were really great Advantages, as they were great Encouragements. He procured me also the Printing of the Laws and Votes of that Government which continu'd in my Hands as long as I follow'd the Business.

I now open'd a little Stationer's Shop.[221] I had in it Blanks of all Sorts the correctest that ever appear'd among us, being assisted in that by my Friend Brientnal; I had also Paper, Parchment, Chapmen's Books, &c. One Whitemash a Compositor I had known in London, an excellent Workman now came to me and work'd with me constantly and diligently, and I took an Apprentice the Son of Aquila Rose. I began now gradually to pay off the Debt I was under for the Printing-House. In order to secure my Credit and Character as a Tradesman, I took care not only to be in *Reality* Industrious and frugal, but to avoid all *Appearances* of the Contrary. I drest plainly; I was seen at no Places of idle Diversion; I never went out a-fishing or shooting; a Book, indeed, sometimes debauch'd me from my Work; but that was seldom, snug, and gave no Scandal: and to show that I was not above my Business, I sometimes brought home the Paper I purchas'd at the Stores, thro' the Streets on a Wheelbarrow. Thus being esteem'd an industrious thriving young Man, and paying duly for what I bought, the Merchants who imported Stationary solicited my Custom, others propos'd supplying me with Books, and I went on swimmingly. In the mean time Keimer's Credit and Business declining daily, he was at last forc'd to sell his Printinghouse to satisfy his Creditors. He went to Barbadoes, and there lived some Years, in very poor Circumstances.

His Apprentice David Harry, whom I had instructed while I work'd with him, set up in his Place at Philadelphia, having bought his Materials. I was at first apprehensive of a powerful Rival in Harry, as his Friends were very able, and had a good deal of Interest. I therefore propos'd a Partnership to him; which he, fortunately for me, rejected with Scorn. He was very proud, dress'd like a Gentleman, liv'd expensively, took much Diversion and Pleasure abroad, ran in debt, and neglected his Business, upon which all Business left him; and finding nothing to do, he follow'd Keimer to Barbadoes; taking the Printinghouse with him. There this Apprentice employ'd his former Master as a Journeyman. They quarrel'd often. Harry went continually behindhand, and at length was forc'd to sell his Types, and return to his Country Work in Pensilvania. The Person that bought them, employ'd Keimer to use them, but in a few years he died. Their remain'd now no Competitor with me at Philadelphia, but the old one, Bradford, who was rich and easy, did a little Printing now and then by straggling Hands, but was not very anxious about the Business. However, as he kept the Post Office, it was imagined he had better Opportunities of obtaining News, his

[220]The counties of New-Castle, Kent, and Sussex (now Delaware) had the same proprietary governor as Pennsylvania but a separate legislature. Andrew Hamilton was Speaker of both Assemblies.

[221]Franklin's earliest surviving account books suggest that he opened his shop about July 1730.

Paper was thought a better Distributer of Advertisements than mine, and therefore had many more, which was a profitable thing to him and a Disadvantage to me. For tho' I did indeed receive and send Papers by Post, yet the publick Opinion was otherwise; for what I did send was by Bribing the Riders who took them privately: Bradford being unkind enough to forbid it: which ocasion'd some Resentment on my Part; and I thought so meanly of him for it, that when I afterwards came into his Situation,[222] I took care never to imitate it.

I had hitherto continu'd to board with Godfrey who lived in Part of my House with his Wife and Children, and had one Side of the Shop for his Glazier's Business, tho' he work'd little, being always absorb'd in his Mathematics. Mrs. Godfrey projected a Match for me with a Relation's Daughter, took Opportunities of bringing us often together, till a serious Courtship on my Part ensu'd, the Girl being in herself very deserving. The old Folks encourag'd me by continual Invitations to Supper, and by leaving us together, till at length it was time to explain. Mrs. Godfrey manag'd our little Treaty. I let her know that I expected as much Money with their Daughter as would pay off my Remaining Debt for the Printing-house, which I believe was not then above a Hundred Pounds. She brought me Word they had no such Sum to spare. I said they might mortgage their House in the Loan Office. The Answer to this after some Days was that they did not approve the Match; that on Enquiry of Bradford they had been inform'd the Printing Business was not a profitable one, the Types would soon be worn out and more wanted, that S. Keimer and D. Harry had fail'd one after the other, and I should probably soon follow them; and therefore I was forbidden the House, and the Daughter shut up. Whether this was a real Change of Sentiment, or only Artifice, on a Supposition of our being too far engag'd in Affection to retract, and therefore that we should steal a Marriage, which would leave them at Liberty to give or withold what they pleas'd, I know not: But I suspected the latter, resented it, and went no more. Mrs. Godfrey brought me afterwards some more favourable Accounts of their Disposition, and would have drawn me on again: but I declared absolutely my Resolution to have nothing more to do with that Family.[223] This was resented by the Godfreys, we differ'd, and they removed, leaving me the whole House, and I resolved to take no more Inmates.

But this Affair having turn'd my Thoughts to Marriage, I looks round me, and made Overtures of Acquaintance in other Places; but soon found that the Business of a Printer being generally thought a poor one, I was not to expect Money with a Wife unless with such a one, as I should not otherwise think agreable. In the mean time, that hard-to-be-govern'd Passion of Youth, had hurried me frequently into Intrigues with low Women that fell in my Way, which were attended with some Expence and great Inconvenience, besides a continual Risque to my Health by a Distemper[224] which of all Things I dreaded, tho' by great good Luck I escaped it.

[222]Franklin became Deputy Postmaster-General for the Colonies in 1753.

[223]In an age where most marriages were arranged with financial considerations in mind, Franklin's dowry expectations were not unusual.

[224]Syphilis.

A friendly Correspondence as Neighbours and old Acquaintances, had continued between me and Mrs. Read's Family, who all had a Regard for me from the time of my first Lodging in their House. I was often invited there and consulted in their Affairs, wherein I sometimes was of service. I pity'd poor Miss Read's unfortunate Situation, who was generally dejected, seldom chearful, and avoided Company. I consider'd my Giddiness and Inconstancy when in London as in a great degree the Cause of her Unhappiness; tho' the Mother was good enough to think the Fault more her own than mine, as she had prevented our Marrying before I went thither, and persuaded the other Match in my Absence. Our mutual Affection was revived, but there were now great Objections to our Union. That Match was indeed look'd upon as invalid, a preceding Wife being said to be living in England; but this could not easily be prov'd, because of the Distance. And tho' there was a Report of his Death, it was not certain. Then tho' it should be true, he had left many Debts which his Successor might be call'd on to pay. We ventured however, over all these Difficulties, and I [took] her to Wife Sept. 1, 1730.[225] None of the Inconveniences happened that we had apprehended, she prov'd a good and faithful Helpmate, assisted me much by attending the Shop, we throve together, and have ever mutually endeavour'd to make each other happy. Thus I corrected that great *Erratum* as well as I could.

About this Time our Club meeting, not at a Tavern, but in a little Room of Mr. Grace's set apart for that Purpose; a Proposition was made by me that since our Books were often referr'd to in our Disquisitions upon the Queries, it might be convenient to us to have them all together where we met, that upon Occasion they might be consulted; and by thus clubbing our Books to a common Library, we should, while we lik'd to keep them together, have each of us the Advantage of using the Books of all the other Members, which would be nearly as beneficial as if each owned the whole. It was lik'd and agreed to, and we fill'd one End of the Room with such Books as we could best spare. The Number was not so great as we expected; and tho' they had been of great Use, yet some Inconveniencies occurring for want of due Care of them, the Collection after almost a Year was separated, and each took his Books home again.

And now I set on foot my first Project of a public Nature, that for a Subscription Library. I drew up the Proposals, got them put into Form by our great Scrivener Brockden, and by the help of my Friends in the Junto, procur'd Fifty Subscribers of 40*s.* each to begin with and 10*s.* a Year for 50 Years, the Term our Company was to continue. We afterwards obtain'd a Charter, the Company being increas'd to 100. This was the Mother of all the N American Subscription Libraries now so numerous.[226] It is become a great thing itself, and continually increasing. These Libraries have improv'd the

[225]Without proof that Deborah's first husband, the missing John Rogers, was now dead or that he had been a bigamist, Deborah was technically still his wife and could not officially remarry. Thus Franklin and Deborah entered into an informal "common law" marriage without a civil or church ceremony. Their "Match" was considered legally valid and their children were regarded as legitimate. The absence of laws allowing divorce or annulment made such arrangements relatively common. Deborah died in Philadelphia in 1774 while Franklin was in England, serving as agent for Pennsylvania.

[226]Although the Library Company of Philadelphia (1731) was the first *subscription* library, various public and semipublic book collections existed in North America before 1731.

general Conversation of the Americans, made the common Tradesmen and Farmers as intelligent as most Gentlemen from other Countries, and perhaps have contributed in some degree to the Stand so generally made throughout the Colonies in Defence of their Privileges.

Two Letters

Memo.

Thus far was written with the Intention express'd in the Beginning and therefore contains several little family Anecdotes of no Importance to others. What follows was written many Years after in compliance with the Advice contain'd in these Letters, and accordingly intended for the Publick. The Affairs of the Revolution occasion'd the Interruption.

Letter from Mr. Abel James[227] with Notes of my Life, to be here inserted. Also

Letter from Mr. Vaughan to the same purpose[228]

My Dear and honored Friend.

I have often been desirous of writing to thee, but could not be reconciled to the Thoughts that the Letter might fall into the Hands of the British,[229] lest some Printer or busy Body should publish some Part of the Contents and give our Friends Pain and myself Censure.

Some Time since there fell into my Hands to my great Joy about 23 Sheets in thy own hand-writing containing an Account of the Parentage and Life of thyself, directed to thy Son ending in the Year 1730 with which there were Notes likewise in thy writing,[230] a Copy of which I inclose in Hopes it may be a means if thou continuedst it up to a later period, that the first and latter part may be put together, and if it is not yet continued, I hope thou wilt not delay it, Life is uncertain as the Preacher tells us, and what will the World say if kind, humane and benevolent Ben Franklin should leave his Friends and the World deprived of so pleasing and profitable a Work, a Work which would be useful and entertaining not only to a few, but to millions.

The Influence Writings under that Class have on the Minds of Youth is very great, and has no where appeared so plain as in our public Friend's Journal. It almost insensibly leads the Youth into the Resolution of endeavouring to become as good and as eminent as the Journalist. Should thine for Instance when published, and I think it could not fail of it, lead the Youth to equal the Industry and Temperance of thy early Youth, what a Blessing with that Class would such a Work be. I know of no Character living nor many of them put together, who has so much in his Power as Thyself to promote a greater Spirit of Industry and early Attention to Business, Frugality and Temperance with the American Youth. Not that I think the Work would have no other Merit and Use in the World, far from it, but the first is of such vast Importance, that I know nothing that can equal it. . . . ABEL JAMES

[227]Abel James (c. 1726–1790), Philadelphia Quaker merchant.

[228]Benjamin Vaughan (1751–1835), English diplomat. He edited the first general collection of Franklin's works, 1779.

[229]The letter was written to Franklin in Paris in 1782 while Britain was still at war with the Colonies.

[230]Franklin drew up an outline for his autobiography soon after he began to write in 1771. It reveals various topics he intended, but failed, to cover.

The foregoing letter and the minutes accompanying it being shewn to a friend, I received from him the following:

Paris, January 31, 1783.

My dearest sir,

When I had read over your sheets of minutes of the principal incidents of your life, recovered for you by your Quaker acquaintance; I told you I would send you a letter expressing my reasons why I thought it would be useful to complete and publish it as he desired. Various concerns have for some time past prevented this letter being written, and I do not know whether it was worth any expectation: happening to be at leisure however at present, I shall by writing at least interest and instruct myself; but as the terms I am inclined to use may tend to offend a person of your manners, I shall only tell you how I would address any other person, who was as good and as great as yourself, but less diffident. I would say to him, Sir, I *solicit* the history of your life from the following motives.

Your history is so remarkable, that if you do not give it, somebody else will certainly give it; and perhaps so as nearly to do as much harm, as your own management of the thing might do good.

It will moreover present a table of the internal circumstances of your country, which will very much tend to invite to it settlers of virtuous and manly minds. And considering the eagerness with which such information is sought by them, and the extent of your reputation, I do not know of a more efficacious advertisement than your Biography would give.

All that has happened to you is also connected with the detail of the manners and situation of a *rising* people; and in this respect I do not think that the writings of Caesar and Tacitus can be more interesting to a true judge of human nature and society.

But these, Sir, are small reasons in my opinion, compared with the chance which your life will give for the forming of future great men; and in conjunction with your Art of Virtue, (which you design to publish) of improving the features of private character, and consequently of aiding all happiness both public and domestic.

The two works I allude to, Sir, will in particular give a noble rule and example of *self-education*. School and other education constantly proceed upon false principles, and shew a clumsy apparatus pointed at a false mark; but your apparatus is simple, and the mark a true one; and while parents and young persons are left destitute of other just means of estimating and becoming prepared for a reasonable course in life, your discovery that the thing is in many a man's private power, will be invaluable!

Influence upon the private character late in life, is not only an influence late in life, but a weak influence. It is in *youth* that we plant our chief habits and prejudices; it is in youth that we take our party[231] as to profession, pursuits, and matrimony. In youth therefore the turn is given; in youth the education even of the next generation is given; in youth the private and public character is determined; and the term of life extending but from youth to age, life ought to begin well from youth; and more especially *before* we take our party as to our principal objects.

[231]Make our decisions.

But your Biography will not merely teach self-education, but the education of *a wise man;* and the wisest man will receive lights and improve his progress, by seeing detailed the conduct of another wise man. And why are weaker men to be deprived of such helps, when we see our race has been blundering on in the dark, almost without a guide in this particular, from the farthest trace of time? Shew then, Sir, how much is to be done, *both to sons and fathers;* and invite all wise men to become like yourself; and other men to become wise.

When we see how cruel statesmen and warriors can be to the humble race, and how absurd distinguished men can be to their acquaintance, it will be instructive to observe the instances multiply of pacific acquiescing manners; and to find how compatible it is to be great and *domestic,* enviable and yet *good-humored.*

The little private incidents which you will also have to relate, will have considerable use, as we want above all things, *rules of prudence in ordinary affairs;* and it will be curious to see how you have acted in these. It will be so far a sort of key to life, and explain many things that all men ought to have once explained to them, to give them a chance of becoming wise by foresight.

The nearest thing to having experience of one's own, is to have other people's affairs brought before us in a shape that is interesting; this is sure to happen from your pen. Your affairs and management will have an air of simplicity or importance that will not fail to strike; and I am convinced you have conducted them with as much originality as if you had been conducting discussions in politics or philosophy; and what more worthy of experiments and system, (its importance and its errors considered) than human life!

Some men have been virtuous blindly, others have speculated fantastically, and others have been shrewd to bad purposes; but you, Sir, I am sure, will give under your hand, nothing but what is at the same moment, wise, practical, and good.

Your account of yourself (for I suppose the parallel I am drawing for Dr. Franklin, will hold not only in point of character but of private history), will shew that you are ashamed of no origin; a thing the more important, as you prove how little necessary all origin is to happiness, virtue, or greatness.

As no end likewise happens without a means, so we shall find, Sir, that even you yourself framed a plan by which you became considerable; but at the same time we may see that though the event is flattering, the means are as simple as wisdom could make them; that is, depending upon nature, virtue, thought, and habit.

Another thing demonstrated will be the propriety of every man's waiting for his time for appearing upon the stage of the world. Our sensations being very much fixed to the moment, we are apt to forget that more moments are to follow the first, and consequently that man should arrange his conduct so as to suit the *whole* of a life. Your attribution appears to have been applied to your *life,* and the passing moments of it have been enlivened with content and enjoyment, instead of being tormented with foolish impatience or regrets. Such a conduct is easy for those who make virtue and themselves their standard, and who try to keep themselves in countenance by examples of other truly great men, of whom patience is so often the characteristic.

Your Quaker correspondent, Sir, (for here again I will suppose the subject of my letter resembling Dr. Franklin,) praised your frugality, diligence, and temperance, which he considered as a pattern for all youth; but it is singular that he should have forgotten your modesty, and your disinterestedness, without which you never could have waited for your advancement, or found your situation in the mean time comfortable; which is a strong lesson to shew the poverty of glory, and the importance of regulating our minds.

If this correspondent had known the nature of your reputation as well as I do, he would have said; your former writings and measures would secure attention to your Biography and Art of Virtue; and your Biography and Art of Virtue, in return, would secure attention to them. This is an advantage attendant upon a various character, and which brings all that belongs to it into greater play; and it is the more useful, as perhaps more persons are at a loss for the *means* of improving their minds and characters, than they are for the time or the inclination to do it.

But there is one concluding reflection, Sir, that will shew the use of your life as a mere piece of biography. This style of writing seems a little gone out of vogue, and yet it is a very useful one; and your specimen of it may be particularly serviceable, as it will make a subject of comparison with the lives of various public cutthroats and intriguers, and with absurd monastic self-tormentors, or vain literary triflers. If it encourages more writings of the same kind with your own, and induces more men to spend lives fit to be written; it will be worth all Plutarch's Lives put together.

But being tired of figuring to myself a character of which every feature suits only one man in the world, without giving him the praise of it; I shall end my letter, my dear Dr. Franklin, with a personal application to your proper self.

I am earnestly desirous then, my dear Sir, that you should let the world into the traits of your genuine character, as civil broils may otherwise tend to disguise or traduce it. Considering your great age, the caution of your character, and your peculiar style of thinking, it is not likely that any one besides yourself can be sufficiently master of the facts of your life, or the intentions of your mind.

Besides all this, the immense revolution of the present period, will necessarily turn our attention towards the author of it; and when virtuous principles have been pretended in it, it will be highly important to shew that such have really influenced; and, as your own character will be the principal one to receive a scrutiny, it is proper (even for its effects upon your vast and rising country, as well as upon England and upon Europe), that it should stand respectable and eternal. For the furtherance of human happiness, I have always maintained that it is necessary to prove that man is not even at present a vicious and detestable animal; and still more to prove that good management may greatly amend him; and it is for much the same reason, that I am anxious to see the opinion established, that there are fair characters existing among the individuals of the race; for the moment that all men, without exception, shall be conceived abandoned, good people will cease efforts deemed to be hopeless, and perhaps think of taking their share in the scramble of life, or at least of making it comfortable principally for themselves.

Take then, my dear Sir, this work most speedily into hand: shew yourself good as you are good, temperate as you are temperate; and above all things, prove yourself as one who from your infancy have loved justice, liberty, and concord, in a way that has made it natural and consistent for you to have acted, as we have seen you act in the last seventeen years of your life. Let Englishmen be made not only to respect, but even to love you. When they think well of individuals in your native country, they will go nearer to thinking well of your country; and when your countrymen see themselves well thought of by Englishmen, they will go nearer to thinking well of England. Extend your views even further; do not stop at those who speak the English tongue, but after having settled so many points in nature and politics, think of bettering the whole race of men.

As I have not read any part of the life in question, but know only the character that lived it, I write somewhat at hazard. I am sure however, that the life, and the treatise I allude to (on the Art of Virtue), will necessarily fulfil the chief of my expectations; and still more so if you take up the measure of suiting these performances to the several views above stated. Should they even prove unsuccessful in all that a sanguine admirer of yours hopes from them, you will at least have framed pieces to interest the human mind; and whoever gives a feeling of pleasure that is innocent to man, has added so much to the fair side of a life otherwise too much darkened by anxiety, and too much injured by pain.

In the hope therefore that you will listen to the prayer addressed to you in this letter, I beg to subscribe myself, my dearest Sir, &c. &c.

BENJ. VAUGHAN.

PART TWO

CONTINUATION OF THE ACCOUNT OF MY LIFE

BEGUN AT PASSY[1] 1784

It is some time since I receiv'd the above Letters, but I have been too busy till now to think of complying with the Request they contain. It might too be much better done if I were at home among my Papers, which would aid my Memory and help to ascertain Dates. But my Return being uncertain, and having just now a little Leisure,[2] I will endeavour to recollect and write what I can; if I live to get home, it may there be corrected and improv'd.

Not having any Copy here of what is already written, I know not whether an Account is given of the means I used to establish the Philadelphia publick Library, which from a small Beginning is now become so considerable, though I remember to have come down to near the Time of that Transaction, 1730. I will therefore begin here, with an Account of it, which may be struck out if found to have been already given.

At the time I establish'd my self in Pennsylvania, there was not a good Bookseller's Shop in any of the Colonies to the Southward of Boston. In New-York and Philadelphia the Printers were indeed Stationers, they sold only Paper, &c., Almanacks, Ballads, and a few common School Books. Those who lov'd Reading were oblig'd to send for their Books from England. The Members of the Junto had each a few. We had left the Alehouse where we

[1]A suburb of Paris, France, where Franklin lived while negotiating the Treaty of Paris (1783), ending the war between the American colonies and Great Britain.

[2]The Treaty of Peace with Britain was signed in Paris, September 3, 1783. Franklin asked Congress for permission to return home, but he remained as Minister until Thomas Jefferson succeeded him in May 1785. He left Paris for America that July. At the time he wrote this part of his autobiography, he was seventy-eight years old.

first met, and hired a Room to hold our Club in. I propos'd that we should all of us bring our Books to that Room, where they would not only be ready to consult in our Conferences, but become a common Benefit, each of us being at Liberty to borrow such as he wish'd to read at home. This was accordingly done, and for some time contented us. Finding the Advantage of this little Collection, I propos'd to render the Benefit from Books more common by commencing a Public Subscription Library. I drew a Sketch of the Plan and Rules that would be necessary, and got a skillful Conveyancer, Mr. Charles Brockden to put the whole in Form of Articles of Agreement to be subscribed; by which each Subscriber engag'd to pay a certain Sum down for the first Purchase of Books and an annual Contribution for encreasing them. So few were the Readers at that time in Philadelphia, and the Majority of us so poor, that I was not able with great Industry to find more than Fifty Persons, mostly young Tradesmen, willing to pay down for this purpose Forty shillings each, and Ten Shillings per Annum. On this little Fund we began. The Books were imported. The Library was open one Day in the Week for lending them to the Subscribers, on their Promisory Notes to pay Double the Value if not duly returned. The Institution soon manifested its Utility, was imitated by other Towns and in other Provinces, the Librarys were augmented by Donations, Reading became fashionable, and our People having no publick Amusements to divert their Attention from Study became better acquainted with Books, and in a few Years were observ'd by Strangers to be better instructed and more intelligent than People of the same Rank generally are in other Countries.

When we were about to sign the above-mentioned Articles, which were to be binding on us, our Heirs, &c. for fifty Years, Mr. Brockden, the Scrivener, said to us, "You are young Men, but it is scarce probable that any of you will live to see the Expiration of the Term fix'd in this Instrument." A Number of us, however, are yet living: But the Instrument was after a few Years rendered null by a Charter that incorporated and gave Perpetuity to the Company.

The Objections, and Reluctances I met with in Soliciting the Subscriptions, made me soon feel the Impropriety of presenting one's self as the Proposer of any useful Project that might be suppos'd to raise one's Reputation in the smallest degree above that of one's Neighbours, when one has need of their Assistance to accomplish that Project. I therefore put my self as much as I could out of sight, and stated it as a Scheme of a *Number of Friends*, who had requested me to go about and propose it to such as they thought Lovers of Reading. In this way my Affair went on more smoothly, and I ever after practis'd it on such Occasions; and from my frequent Successes, can heartily recommend it. The present little Sacrifice of your Vanity will afterwards be amply repaid. If it remains a while uncertain to whom the Merit belongs, some one more vain than yourself will be encourag'd to claim it, and then even Envy will be dispos'd to do you Justice, by plucking those assum'd Feathers, and restoring them to their right Owner.

This Library afforded me the means of Improvement by constant Study, for which I set apart an Hour or two each Day; and thus repair'd in some Degree the Loss of the Learned Education my Father once intended for me. Reading was the only Amusement I allow'd my self. I spent no time in Taverns, Games, or Frolicks of any kind. And my Industry in my Business continu'd as indefatigable as it was necessary. I was in debt for my Printing-house, I had a young Family coming on to be educated,[3] and I had to contend with for Business two Printers who were establish'd in the Place before me. My Circumstances however grew daily easier: my original Habits of Frugality continuing. And my Father having among his Instructions to me when a Boy, frequently repeated a Proverb of Solomon, "*Seest thou a Man diligent in his Calling, he shall stand before Kings, he shall not stand before mean Men.*"[4] I from thence consider'd Industry as a Means of obtaining Wealth and Distinction, which encourag'd me, tho' I did not think that I should ever literally stand before Kings, which however has since happened.—for I have stood before five, and even had the honor of sitting down with one, the King of Denmark, to Dinner.[5]

We have an English Proverb that says,

He that would thrive
Must ask his Wife;

it was lucky for me that I had one as much dispos'd to Industry and Frugality as my self. She assisted me chearfully in my Business, folding and stitching Pamphlets, tending Shop, purchasing old Linen Rags for the Paper-makers, &c. &c. We kept no idle Servants, our Table was plain and simple, our furniture of the cheapest. For instance my Breakfast was a long time Bread and Milk, (no Tea) and I ate it out of a twopenny earthen Porringer[6] with a Pewter Spoon. But mark how Luxury will enter Families, and make a Progress, in Spite of Principle. Being call'd one Morning to Breakfast, I found it in a China Bowl with a Spoon of Silver. They had been bought for me without my Knowledge by my Wife, and had cost her the enormous Sum of three and twenty Shillings, for which she had no other Excuse or Apology to make, but that she thought *her* Husband deserv'd a Silver Spoon and China Bowl as well as any of his Neighbours. This was the first Appearance of Plate[7] and China in our House, which afterwards in a Course of Years as our Wealth encreas'd augmented gradually to several Hundred Pounds in Value.

I had been religiously educated as a Presbyterian; and tho' some of the Dogmas of that Persuasion, such as the Eternal Decrees of God, Election, Reprobation, &c. appear'd to me unintelligible, others doubtful, I early absented myself from the Public Assemblies of the Sect, Sunday being my Studying-Day, I never was without some religious Principles; I never doubted, for instance, the Existance of the Deity, that he made the World, and govern'd it by his Providence; that the most acceptable Service of God was the doing Good to Man; that our Souls are immortal; and that all Crime will be punished and Virtue rewarded either here or hereafter; these I esteem'd the Essentials of every Religion, and being to be found in all the Religions we had in our Country I respected them all, tho' with different degrees of Respect as I found them more or less mix'd with other Articles which without any Tendency to inspire, promote or confirm Morality, serv'd principally to

[3]Franklin's children were William, born about 1731; Francis, born 1732; and Sarah, born 1743.

[4]Proverbs 22:29.

[5]Louis XV and Louis XVI of France, George II and George III of England, and Christian VI of Denmark.

[6]Porridge bowl. [7]Utensils and dishes plated with silver.

divide us and make us unfriendly to one another. This Respect to all, with an Opinion that the worst had some good Effects, induc'd me to avoid all Discourse that might tend to lessen the good Opinion another might have of his own Religion; and as our Province increas'd in People and new Places of worship were continually wanted, and generally erected by voluntary Contribution, my Mite[8] for such purpose, whatever might be the Sect, was never refused.[9]

Tho' I seldom attended any Public Worship, I had still an Opinion of its Propriety, and of its Utility when rightly conducted, and I regularly paid my annual Subscription for the Support of the only Presbyterian Minister or Meeting we had in Philadelphia. He us'd to visit me sometimes as a Friend, and admonish me to attend his Administrations, and I was now and then prevail'd on to do so, once for five Sundays successively. Had he been, *in my Opinion,* a good Preacher perhaps I might have continued, notwithstanding the occasion I had for the Sunday's Leisure in my Course of Study: But his Discourses were chiefly either polemic Arguments, or Explications of the peculiar Doctrines of our Sect, and were all to me very dry, uninteresting and unedifying, since not a single moral Principle was inculcated or enforc'd, their Aim seeming to be rather to make us Presbyterians than good Citizens. At length he took for his Text that Verse of the 4th Chapter of Philippians, *Finally, Brethren, Whatsoever Things are true, honest, just, pure, lovely, or of good report, if there be any virtue, or any praise, think on these Things;*[10] and I imagin'd in a Sermon on such a Text, we could not miss of having some Morality: But he confin'd himself to five Points only as meant by the Apostle, viz. 1. Keeping holy the Sabbath Day. 2. Being diligent in Reading the Holy Scriptures. 3. Attending duly the Publick Worship. 4. Partaking of the Sacrament. 5. Paying a due Respect to God's Ministers. These might be all good Things, but as they were not the kind of good Things that I expected from that Text, I despaired of ever meeting with them from any other, was disgusted, and attended his Preaching no more. I had some Years before compos'd a little Liturgy or Form of Prayer for my own private Use, viz, in 1728, entitled, *Articles of Belief and Acts of Religion.* I return'd to the Use of this, and went no more to the public Assemblies. My Conduct might be blameable, but I leave it without attempting farther to excuse it, my present purpose being to relate Facts, and not to make Apologies for them.

It was about this time that I conceiv'd the bold and arduous Project of arriving at moral Perfection. I wish'd to live without committing any Fault at any time; I would conquer all that either Natural Inclination, Custom, or Company might lead me into. As I knew, or thought I knew, what was right and wrong, I did not see why I might not *always* do the one and avoid the other. But I soon found I had undertaken a Task of more Difficulty than I had imagined. While my *Attention was taken up* in guarding against one Fault, I was often surpriz'd by another. Habit took the Advantage of Inattention. Inclination was sometimes too strong for Reason. I concluded at length, that the mere speculative Conviction that it was our Interest to be

[8]Small contribution.

[9]In 1788 Franklin was one of the largest contributors to the building of a synagogue for a Jewish congregation in Philadelphia.

[10]Philippians 4:8.

compleatly virtuous, was not sufficient to prevent our Slipping, and that the contrary Habits must be broken and good ones acquired and established, before we can have any Dependance on a steady uniform Rectitude of Conduct. For this purpose I therefore contriv'd the following Method.

In the various Enumerations of the moral Virtues I had met with in my Reading, I found the Catalogue more or less numerous, as different Writers included more or fewer Ideas under the same Name. Temperance, for Example, was by some confin'd to Eating and Drinking, while by others it was extended to mean the moderating every other Pleasure, Appetite, Inclination or Passion, bodily or mental, even to our Avarice and Ambition. I propos'd to myself, for the sake of Clearness, to use rather more Names with fewer Ideas annex'd to each, than a few Names with more Ideas; and I included under Thirteen Names of Virtues all that at that time occurr'd to me as necessary or desirable, and annex'd to each a short Precept, which fully express'd the Extent I gave to its Meaning.

These Names of Virtues with their Precepts were

1. Temperance.

Eat not to Dulness.
Drink not to Elevation.

2. Silence.

Speak not but what may benefit others or yourself. Avoid trifling Conversation.

3. Order.

Let all your Things have their Places. Let each Part of your Business have its Time.

4. Resolution.

Resolve to perform what you ought. Perform without fail what you resolve.

5. Frugality.

Make no Expence but to do good to others or yourself: i.e., Waste nothing.

6. Industry.

Lose no Time. Be always employ'd in something useful. Cut off all unnecessary Actions.

7. Sincerity.

Use no hurtful Deceit.
Think innocently and justly; and, if you speak, speak accordingly.

8. Justice.

Wrong none, by doing Injuries or omitting the Benefits that are your Duty.

9. Moderation.

Avoid Extreams. Forbear resenting Injuries so much as you think they deserve.

10. CLEANLINESS.

Tolerate no Uncleanness in Body, Cloaths or Habitation.

11. TRANQUILITY.

Be not disturbed at Trifles, or at Accidents common or unavoidable.

12. CHASTITY.

Rarely use Venery but for Health or Offspring; Never to Dulness, Weakness, or the Injury of your own or another's Peace or Reputation.

13. HUMILITY.

Imitate Jesus and Socrates.

My Intention being to acquire the *Habitude* of all these Virtues, I judg'd it would be well not to distract my Attention by attempting the whole at once, but to fix it on one of them at a time, and when I should be Master of that, then to proceed to another, and so on till I should have gone thro' the thirteen. And as the previous Acquisition of some might facilitate the Acquisition of certain others, I arrang'd them with that View as they stand above. *Temperance* first, as it tends to produce that Coolness and Clearness of Head, which is so necessary where constant Vigilance was to be kept up, and Guard maintained, against the unremitting Attraction of ancient Habits, and the Force of perpetual Temptations. This being acquir'd and establish'd, *Silence* would be more easy, and my Desire being to gain Knowledge at the same time that I improv'd in Virtue, and considering that in Conversation it was obtain'd rather by use of the Ears than of the Tongue, and therefore wishing to break a Habit I was getting into of Prattling, Punning and Joking, which only made me acceptable to trifling Company, I gave *Silence* the second Place. This, and the next, *Order,* I expected would allow me more Time for attending to my Project and my Studies; RESOLUTION, once become habitual, would keep me firm in my Endeavours to obtain all the subsequent Virtues; *Frugality* and *Industry,* by freeing me from my remaining Debt, and producing Affluence and Independance, would make more easy the Practice of *Sincerity* and *Justice,* &c. &c. Conceiving then that agreable to the Advice of Pythagoras in his Golden Verses[11] daily Examination would be necessary, I contriv'd the following Method for conducting that Examination.

I made a little Book in which I allotted a Page for each of the Virtues. I rul'd each Page with red Ink, so as to have seven Columns, one for each Day of the Week, marking each Column with a Letter for the Day. I cross'd these Columns with thirteen red Lines, marking the Beginning of each Line with the first Letter of one of the Virtues, on which Line and in its proper Column I might mark by a little black Spot every Fault I found upon Examination to have been committed respecting that Virtue upon that Day.

I determined to give a Week's strict Attention to each of the Virtues successively. Thus in the first Week my great Guard was to avoid every the least

[11]Pythagoras (b. 580 B.C.?), an ascetic Greek philosopher and mathematician. A note in Franklin's manuscript provided for insertion of verses translated: "Let sleep not close your eyes till you have thrice examined the transactions of the day: where have I strayed, what have I done, what good have I omitted?"

Offence against Temperance, leaving the other Virtues to their ordinary Chance, only marking every Evening the Faults of the Day. Thus if in the first Week I could keep my first Line marked T clear of Spots, I suppos'd the Habit of that Virtue so much strengthen'd and its opposite weaken'd, that I might venture extending my Attention to include the next, and for the following Week keep both Lines clear of Spots. Proceeding thus to the last, I could go thro' a Course compleat in Thirteen Weeks, and four Courses in a year. And like him who having a Garden to weed, does not attempt to eradicate all the bad Herbs at once, which would exceed his Reach and his Strength, but works on one of the Beds at a time, and having accomplish'd the first proceeds to a Second; so I should have, (I hoped) the encouraging Pleasure of seeing on my Pages the Progress I made in Virtue, by clearing successively my Lines of their Spots, till in the End by a Number of Courses, I should be happy in viewing a clean Book after a thirteen Weeks daily Examination.

Form of the Pages

Temperance.							
Eat not to Dulness. Drink not to Elevation.							
	S	M	T	W	T	F	S
T							
S	••	•		•		•	
O	•	•	•		•	•	•
R			•			•	
F		•			•		
I			•	•			
S							
J							
M							
Cl.							
T							
Ch.							
H							

This my little Book had for its Motto these Lines from Addison's *Cato:*

Here will I hold: If there is a Pow'r above us,
(And that there is, all Nature cries aloud
Thro' all her Works) he must delight in Virtue,
And that which he delights in must be happy.[12]

Another from Cicero.

O Vitæ Philosophia Dux! O Virtutum indagatrix, expultrixque vitiorum! Unus dies bene, et ex preceptis tuis actus, peccanti immortalitati est anteponendus.[13]

[12]Joseph Addison, *Cato, A Tragedy* (1713), Act V, Scene i, lines 15–18.

[13]Marcus Tullius Cicero (106–43 B.C.), Roman philosopher and orator. The quotation is from *Tusculan Disputations,* Act V, Scene ii, line 5. Several lines are omitted after *vitiorum.* "Oh philosophy, guide of life! Oh searcher out of virtues and expeller of vices! . . . One day lived well and according to thy precepts is to be preferred to an eternity of sin."

Another from the Proverbs of Solomon speaking of Wisdom or Virtue;

Length of Days is in her right hand, and in her Left Hand Riches and Honours; Her Ways are Ways of Pleasantness, and all her Paths are Peace. III, 16, 17.

And conceiving God to be the Fountain of Wisdom, I thought it right and necessary to solicit his Assistance for obtaining it; to this End I form'd the following little Prayer, which was prefix'd to my Tables of Examination; for daily Use.

O Powerful Goodness! bountiful Father! merciful Guide! Increase in me that Wisdom which discovers my truest Interests; Strengthen my Resolutions to perform what that Wisdom dictates. Accept my kind Offices to thy other Children, as the only Return in my Power for thy continual Favours to me.

I us'd also sometimes a little Prayer which I took from Thomson's Poems. viz

Father of Light and Life, thou Good supreme,
O teach me what is good, teach me thy self!
Save me from Folly, Vanity and Vice,
From every low Pursuit, and fill my Soul
With Knowledge, conscious Peace, and Virtue pure,
Sacred, substantial, neverfading Bliss![14]

The Precept of *Order* requiring that *every Part of my Business should have its allotted Time,* one Page in my little Book contain'd the following Scheme of Employment for the Twenty-four Hours of a natural Day.

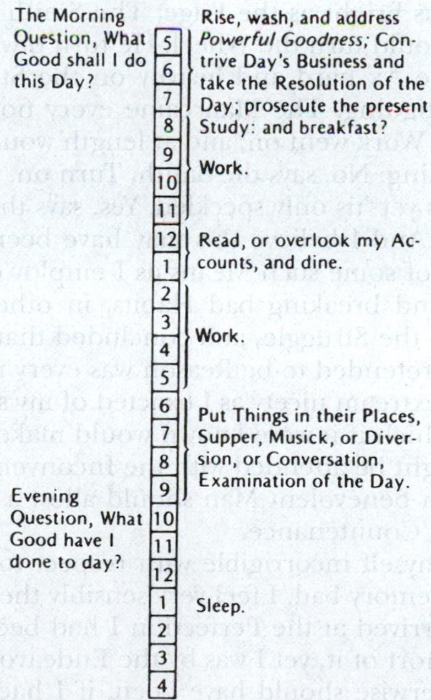

The Morning Question, What Good shall I do this Day?
5
6
7
8
Rise, wash, and address *Powerful Goodness;* Contrive Day's Business and take the Resolution of the Day; prosecute the present Study: and breakfast?
9
10
11
Work.
12
1
Read, or overlook my Accounts, and dine.
2
3
4
5
Work.
6
7
8
9
Put Things in their Places, Supper, Musick, or Diversion, or Conversation, Examination of the Day.
Evening Question, What Good have I done to day?
10
11
12
1
2
3
4
Sleep.

[14]From James Thomson (1700–1748), *The Seasons,* "Winter" (1726), lines 218–23.

I enter'd upon the Execution of this Plan for Self-Examination, and continu'd it with occasional Intermissions for some time. I was surpriz'd to find myself so much fuller of Faults than I had imagined, but I had the Satisfaction of seeing them diminish. To avoid the Trouble of renewing now and then my little Book, which by scraping out the Marks on the Paper of old Faults to make room for new Ones in a new Course, became full of Holes: I transferr'd my Tables and Precepts to the Ivory Leaves of a Memorandum Book, on which the Lines were drawn with red Ink that made a durable Stain, and on those Lines I mark'd my Faults with a black Lead Pencil, which Marks I could easily wipe out with a wet Sponge. After a while I went thro' one Course only in a Year, and afterwards only one in several years, till at length I omitted them entirely, being employ'd in Voyages and Business abroad with a Multiplicity of Affairs, that interfered, but I always carried my little Book with me.

My scheme of ORDER, gave me the most Trouble, and I found, that tho' it might be practicable where a Man's Business was such as to leave him the Disposition of his Time, that of a Journey-man Printer for instance, it was not possible to be exactly observ'd by a Master, who must mix with the World, and often receive People of Business at their own Hours. *Order* too, with regard to Places for Things, Papers, &c. I found extreamly difficult to acquire. I had not been early accustomed to *Method*, and having an exceeding good Memory, I was not so sensible of the Inconvenience attending Want of Method. This Article therefore cost me so much painful Attention and my Faults in it vex'd me so much, and I made so little Progress in Amendment, and had such frequent Relapses, that I was almost ready to give up the Attempt, and content my self with a faulty Character in that respect. Like the Man who in buying an Ax of a Smith my neighbour, desired to have the whole of its Surface as bright as the Edge; The Smith consented to grind it bright for him if he would turn the Wheel. He turn'd while the Smith press'd the broad Face of the Ax hard and heavily on the Stone, which made the Turning of it very fatiguing. The Man came every now and then from the Wheel to see how the Work went on; and at length would take his Ax as it was without farther Grinding. No, says the Smith, Turn on, turn on; we shall have it bright by and by; as yet 'tis only speckled. Yes, says the Man; but—*I think I like a speckled Ax best.* And I believe this may have been the Case with many who having for want of some such Means as I employ'd found the Difficulty of obtaining good, and breaking bad Habits, in other Points of Vice and Virtue, have given up the Struggle, and concluded that *a speckled Ax was best.* For something that pretended to be Reason was every now and then suggesting to me, that such extream nicety as I exacted of my self might be a kind of Foppery in Morals, which if it were known would make me ridiculous; that a perfect Character might be attended with the Inconvenience of being envied and hated; and that a benevolent Man should allow a few Faults in himself, to keep his Friends in Countenance.

In Truth I found myself incorrigible with respect to *Order;* and now I am grown old, and my Memory bad, I feel very sensibly the want of it. But on the whole, tho' I never arrived at the Perfection I had been so ambitious of obtaining, but fell far short of it, yet I was by the Endeavour a better and a happier Man than I otherwise should have been, if I had not attempted it; As those who aim at perfect Writing by imitating the engraved Copies, tho' they never reach the wish'd for Excellence of those Copies, their Hand is mended by the Endeavour, and is tolerable while it continues fair and legible.

And it may be well my Posterity should be informed, that to this little Artifice, with the Blessing of God, their Ancestor ow'd the constant Felicity of his Life down to his 79th Year in which this is written. What Reserves may attend the Remainder is in the Hand of Providence: But if they arrive the Reflection on past Happiness enjoy'd ought to help his Bearing them with more Resignation. To *Temperance* he ascribes his long-continu'd Health, and what is still left to him of a good Constitution. To *Industry* and *Frugality* the early Easiness of his Circumstances, and Acquisition of his Fortune, with all that Knowledge which enabled him to be an useful Citizen, and obtain'd for him some Degree of Reputation among the Learned. To *Sincerity* and *Justice* the Confidence of his Country, and the honourable Employs it conferr'd upon him. And to the joint Influence of the whole Mass of the Virtues, even in the imperfect State he was able to acquire them, all that Evenness of Temper, and that Chearfulness in Conversation which makes his Company still sought for, and agreable even to his younger Acquaintance. I hope therefore that some of my Descendants may follow the Example and reap the Benefit.

It will be remark'd that, tho' my Scheme was not wholly without Religion there was in it no Mark of any of the distinguishing Tenets of any particular Sect. I had purposely avoided them; for being fully persuaded of the Utility and Excellency of my Method, and that it might be serviceable to People in all Religions, and intending some time or other to publish it, I would not have any thing in it that should prejudice any one of any Sect against it. I purposed writing a little Comment on each Virtue, in which I would have shown the Advantages of possessing it, and the Mischiefs attending its opposite Vice; and I should have called my Book the ART of *Virtue,* because it would have shown the *Means and Manner* of obtaining Virtue, which would have distinguish'd it from the mere Exhortation to be good, that does not instruct and indicate the Means; but is like the Apostle's Man of verbal Charity, who only, without showing to the Naked and the Hungry *how* or where they might get Cloaths or Victuals, exhorted them to be fed and clothed. *James* II, 15, 16.[15]

But it so happened that my Intention of writing and publishing this Comment was never fulfilled. I did indeed, from time to time put down short Hints of the Sentiments, Reasonings, &c. to be made use of in it; some of which I have still by me: But the necessary close Attention to private Business in the earlier part of Life, and public Business since, have occasioned my postponing it. For it being connected in my Mind with a *great and extensive Project* that required the whole Man to execute, and which an unforeseen Succession of Employs prevented my attending to, it has hitherto remain'd unfinish'd.

In this Piece it was my Design to explain and enforce this Doctrine, that vicious Actions are not hurtful because they are forbidden, but forbidden because they are hurtful, the Nature of Man alone consider'd: That it was

[15]"If a brother or sister be naked, and destitute of daily food. And one of you say unto them, Depart in peace, be ye warmed and filled; notwithstanding ye give them not those things which are needful to the body; what doth it profit?"

therefore every one's Interest to be virtuous, who wish'd to be happy even in this World. And I should from this Circumstance, there being always in the World a Number of rich Merchants, Nobility, States and Princes, who have need of honest Instruments for the Management of their Affairs, and such being so rare have endeavoured to convince young Persons, that no Qualities were so likely to make a poor Man's Fortune as those of Probity and Integrity.

My List of Virtues contain'd at first but twelve: But a Quaker Friend having kindly inform'd me that I was generally thought proud; that my Pride show'd itself frequently in Conversation; that I was not content with being in the right when discussing any Point, but was overbearing and rather insolent; of which he convinc'd me by mentioning several Instances; I determined endeavouring to cure myself if I could of this Vice or Folly among the rest, and I added *Humility* to my List, giving an extensive Meaning to the Word. I cannot boast of much Success in acquiring the *Reality* of this Virtue; but I had a good deal with regard to the *Appearance* of it. I made it a Rule to forbear all direct Contradiction to the Sentiments of others, and all positive Assertion of my own. I even forbid myself agreable to the old Laws of our Junto, the Use of every Word or Expression in the Language that imported[16] a fix'd Opinion; such as *certainly, undoubtedly,* &c. and I adopted instead of them, *I conceive, I apprehend,* or *I imagine* a thing to be so or so, or it so appears to me at present. When another asserted something, that I thought an Error, I deny'd my self the Pleasure of contradicting him abruptly, and of showing immediately some Absurdity in his Proposition; and in answering I began by observing that in certain Cases or Circumstances his Opinion would be right, but that in the present case there *appear'd* or *seem'd* to me some Difference, &c. I soon found the Advantage of this Change in my Manners. The Conversations I engag'd in went on more pleasantly. The modest way in which I propos'd my Opinions, procur'd them a readier Reception and less Contradiction; I had less Mortification when I was found to be in the wrong, and I more easily prevail'd with others to give up their Mistakes and join with me when I happen'd to be in the right. And this Mode, which I at first put on, with some violence to natural Inclination, became at length so easy and so habitual to me, that perhaps for these Fifty Years past no one has ever heard a dogmatical Expression escape me. And to this Habit (after my Character of Integrity) I think it principally owing, that I had early so much Weight with my Fellow Citizens, when I proposed new Institutions, or Alterations in the old; and so much Influence in public Councils when I became a Member. For I was but a bad Speaker, never eloquent, subject to much Hesitation in my choice of Words, hardly correct in Language, and yet I generally carried my Points.

In reality there is perhaps no one of our natural Passions so hard to subdue as *Pride*. Disguise it, struggle with it, beat it down, stifle it, mortify it as much as one pleases, it is still alive, and will every now and then peep out and show itself. You will see it perhaps often in this History. For even if I could conceive that I had compleatly overcome it, I should probably by [be] proud of my Humility.

Thus far written at Passy 1784

1771–1790 1791, 1828, 1868

[16]Suggested.

Michel-Guillaume-Jean de Crèvecoeur 1735–1813

Crèvecoeur was born in France, the son of a minor nobleman. He attended a Jesuit college, and in 1754 traveled to England to complete his education. The next year, after a disappointing love affair, he sailed to America, arriving in New France at the beginning of the French and Indian War (1756–1763). In Canada he enlisted in the French Colonial Militia and was commissioned an officer, but in 1758 he was captured in the defeat of the French forces at Quebec. Resigning his commission Crèvecoeur migrated to New York, where he changed his name to J. Hector St. John. He worked as a surveyor and an Indian trader, and he traveled the length and breadth of the English Colonies. In 1765 he became a naturalized citizen of New York. Four years later he married, purchased 120 acres of farmland 60 miles northeast of New York City, and settled down to become an American farmer.

Around 1774 Crèvecoeur began to write a series of essays on American life and manners, but before they were completed, the American Revolution had begun, and Crèvecoeur, a British sympathizer, found himself living in the midst of hostile revolutionaries. In 1778 he applied for permission to return to Europe, giving as his reason a wish to re-establish his claim to his ancestral property in France. In 1780, after long delays and three months' imprisonment by the British in New York City (who suspected that he was a spy), Crèvecoeur sailed for Britain. In London he placed the manuscript of his essays on American life with a publisher, and in 1781, after an absence of twenty-seven years, he returned to France.

In 1782, Crèvecoeur's essays, now revised into epistolary form, were published in London as Letters from an American Farmer. *They were soon reprinted in Germany, Holland, and Ireland. While living in France, Crèvecoeur began rewriting and translating his essays for a French edition, but, before it could be published, he was appointed French consul to America and returned to New York. In America his success as a French diplomat was so great that he was elected to the American Philosophical Society; various American cities gave him honorary citizenship, and the Vermont Legislature named the town of St. Johnsbury in his honor. In 1785 he returned on leave to France and discovered that the French version of his* Letters from an American Farmer, *published in his absence the previous year, had made him a literary celebrity, famous as the "Cultivateur Américain." Crèvecoeur returned to America in 1787 to resume his duties as consul, but shortly after the French Revolution began in 1789, he was obliged to return once again to Paris, leaving his adopted home, never to return.*

With the outbreak of the Reign of Terror in 1793, Crèvecoeur fled Paris for the safety of his family home in Normandy, and there he set to work on yet another book on America. It was published in 1801 as Journey into Northern Pennsylvania and the State of New York. *But the French, now swollen with the glory of the European triumphs of Napoleon, showed little interest in another book on America, and Crèvecoeur spent the remaining twelve years of his life living as an obscure Frenchman amid the turmoil of the French European wars.*

From their first appearance, Crèvecoeur's writings served as a major contribution to the European interpretation of American society. His essay "What Is an American?" published as one of the "letters," became one of the most influential single reports on America ever written. Many Americans found Crèvecoeur's views, as George Washington did, "embellished" and "rather too flattering," and Crèvecoeur's exuberant praise of the new nation as "the most perfect society now existing in the world," often led his readers to ignore the harsh realities of colonial life. But Crèvecoeur's essays confirmed the hopes of a revolutionary generation yearning for a Jeffersonian Eden, a place of serenity and plenty that could be a haven from the disillusionments of history. His writing appeared at a time when the European imagination was warmly receptive to the paradoxical notion of America as a land of both innocence and progress, a comforting idea that remained an article of faith for Europeans and Americans alike, until the twentieth century.

FURTHER READING: *Letters from an American Farmer,* ed. L. Lewisohn, 1904; *Letters from an American Farmer,* ed. A. Stone, 1963; *More Letters from the American Farmer,* ed. D. Moore, 1995; *Sketches of 18th-Century America,* ed. H. Bourdin, R. Gabriel, and S. Williams, 1925; *Crèvecoeur's 18th-Century Travels in Pennsylvania and New York,* ed. P. Adams, 1962; *Journey into Northern Pennsylvania and the State of New York,* ed. C. Bostelmann, 1964; J. Mitchell, *St. Jean de Crèvecoeur,* 1916; T. Philbrick, *St. John de Crèvecoeur,* 1970; G. Allen and R. Asselineau, *St. John de Crèvecoeur,* 1987.

TEXT: J. Hector St. John, *Letters from an American Farmer,* London, 1782. Spelling and punctuation have been changed to conform more nearly to modern practice.

from *LETTERS FROM AN AMERICAN FARMER*

LETTER III[1]

WHAT IS AN AMERICAN?

I wish I could be acquainted with the feelings and thoughts which must agitate the heart and present themselves to the mind of an enlightened Englishman, when he first lands on this continent. He must greatly rejoice that he lived at a time to see this fair country discovered[2] and settled; he must necessarily feel a share of national pride when he views the chain of settlements which embellishes these extended shores. When he says to himself, this is the work of my countrymen, who, when convulsed by factions,[3] afflicted by a variety of miseries and wants, restless and impatient, took refuge here. They brought along with them their national genius,[4] to which they principally owe what liberty they enjoy and what substance they possess. Here he sees the industry of his native country displayed in a new manner and traces in their works the embryos of all the arts, sciences, and ingenuity which flourish in Europe. Here he beholds fair cities, substantial villages, extensive fields, an immense country filled with decent houses, good roads, orchards, meadows, and bridges, where an hundred years ago all was wild, woody, and uncultivated! What a train of pleasing ideas this fair spectacle must suggest; it is a prospect which must inspire a good citizen with the most

[1]In twelve essays, or "letters," Crèvecoeur sketched the range of American life in the last of the eighteenth century. Letter III, his most famous essay, shows the promises of American life contrasted with the decadence of Europe. Letter IX reveals Crèvecoeur's emotional confrontation with one of the "desolating consequences" of the American civilization he had praised.

[2]Explored. [3]Contentious groups, cliques. [4]Distinctive character.

heartfelt pleasure. The difficulty consists in the manner of viewing so extensive a scene. He is arrived on a new continent; a modern society offers itself to his contemplation, different from what he had hitherto seen. It is not composed, as in Europe, of great lords who possess everything, and of a herd of people who have nothing. Here are no aristocratical families, no courts, no kings, no bishops, no ecclesiastical dominion, no invisible power giving to a few a very visible one, no great manufacturers employing thousands, no great refinements of luxury. The rich and the poor are not so far removed from each other as they are in Europe. Some few towns excepted, we are all tillers of the earth, from Nova Scotia to West Florida. We are a people of cultivators, scattered over an immense territory, communicating with each other by means of good roads and navigable rivers, united by the silken bands of mild government, all respecting the laws without dreading their power, because they are equitable. We are all animated with the spirit of an industry which is unfettered and unrestrained because each person works for himself. If he travels through our rural districts he views not the hostile castle and the haughty mansion, contrasted with the clay-built hut and miserable cabin where cattle and men help to keep each other warm and dwell in meanness, smoke and indigence. A pleasing uniformity of decent competence appears throughout our habitations. The meanest of our loghouses is a dry and comfortable habitation. Lawyer or merchant are the fairest titles our towns afford; that of a farmer is the only appellation of the rural inhabitants of our country. It must take some time ere he can reconcile himself to our dictionary, which is but short in words of dignity and names of honor. There, on a Sunday, he sees a congregation of respectable farmers and their wives, all clad in neat homespun, well mounted, or riding in their own humble wagons. There is not among them an esquire,[5] saving[6] the unlettered magistrate. There he sees a parson as simple as his flock, a farmer who does not riot[7] on the labor of others. We have no princes, for whom we toil, starve, and bleed; we are the most perfect society now existing in the world. Here man is free as he ought to be; nor is this pleasing equality so transitory as many others are. Many ages will not see the shores of our great lakes replenished with inland nations, nor the unknown bounds of North America entirely peopled. Who can tell how far it extends? Who can tell the millions of men whom it will feed and contain? for no European foot has yet travelled half the extent of this mighty continent!

. . .

In this great American asylum, the poor of Europe have by some means met together and in consequence of various causes; to what purpose should they ask one another what countrymen they are? Alas, two thirds of them had no country. Can a wretch who wanders about, who works and starves, whose life is a continual scene of sore affliction or pinching penury, can that man call England or any other kingdom his country? A country that had no bread for him, whose fields procured him no harvest, who met with nothing but the frowns of the rich, the severity of the laws, with jails and punishments; who owned not a single foot of the extensive surface of this planet? No! urged by a variety of motives, here they came. Everything has tended to

[5]Member of the gentry, the upper class. [6]Except. [7]Live extravagantly.

regenerate them: new laws, a new mode of living, a new social system; here they are become men; in Europe they were as so many useless plants, wanting vegetative mold[8] and refreshing showers; they withered and were mowed down by want, hunger, and war; but now by the power of transplantation, like all other plants they have taken root and flourished! Formerly they were not numbered in any civil lists[9] of their country, except in those of the poor; here they rank as citizens. By what invisible power has this surprising metamorphosis been performed? By that of the laws and that of their industry. The laws, the indulgent laws, protect them as they arrive, stamping on them the symbol of adoption; they receive ample rewards for their labors; these accumulated rewards procure them lands; those lands confer on them the title of freemen, and to that title every benefit is affixed which men can possibly require. This is the great operation daily performed by our laws. From whence proceed these laws? From our government. Whence the government? It is derived from the original genius and strong desire of the people ratified and confirmed by the crown.[10] This is the great chain which links us all. . . .

What attachment can a poor European emigrant have for a country where he had nothing? The knowledge of the language, the love of a few kindred as poor as himself were the only cords that tied him; his country is now that which gives him land, bread, protection, and consequence; *Ubi panis ibi patria,*[11] is the motto of all emigrants. What then is the American, this new man? He is either an European or the descendant of an European, hence that strange mixture of blood, which you will find in no other country. I could point out to you a family whose grandfather was an Englishman, whose wife was Dutch, whose son married a French woman, and whose present four sons have now four wives of different nations. *He* is an American who, leaving behind him all his ancient prejudices and manners, receives new ones from the new mode of life he has embraced, the new government he obeys, and the new rank he holds. He becomes an American by being received in the broad lap of our great *Alma Mater.*[12] Here individuals of all nations are melted into a new race whose labors and posterity will one day cause great changes in the world. Americans are the western pilgrims who are carrying along with them that great mass of arts, sciences, vigor, and industry which began long since in the east; they will finish the great circle. The Americans were once scattered all over Europe; here they are incorporated into one of the finest systems of population which has ever appeared and which will hereafter become distinct by the power of the different climates they inhabit. The American ought therefore to love this country much better than that wherein either he or his forefathers were born. Here the rewards of his industry follow with equal steps the progress of his labor; his labor is founded on the basis of nature, *self-interest;* can it want a stronger allurement? Wives and children, who before in vain demanded of him a morsel of bread, now, fat and frolicsome, gladly help their father to clear those fields whence exuberant crops are to arise to feed and to clothe them all, without any part being claimed, either by a despotic prince, a

[8]Fertilizer.

[9]Lists of government employees.

[10]Crèvecoeur, a British sympathizer during the American Revolution, saw the British government and monarchy as protectors of stability and just government.

[11]Latin: Where one gets bread, there is one's fatherland.

[12]Latin: Fostering Mother, i.e., America.

rich abbot, or a mighty lord. Here religion demands but little of him, a small voluntary salary to the minister, and gratitude to God; can he refuse these? The American is a new man, who acts upon new principles; he must therefore entertain new ideas and form new opinions. From involuntary idleness, servile dependence, penury, and useless labor, he has passed to toils of a very different nature, rewarded by ample subsistence.—This is an American.

Men are like plants; the goodness and flavor of the fruit proceeds from the peculiar soil and exposition in which they grow. We are nothing but what we derive from the air we breathe, the climate we inhabit, the government we obey, the system of religion we profess, and the nature of our employment. Here you will find but few crimes; these have acquired as yet no root among us. I wish I were able to trace all my ideas; if my ignorance prevents me from describing them properly, I hope I shall be able to delineate a few of the outlines, which are all I propose.

Those who live near the sea feed more on fish than on flesh, and often encounter that boisterous element. This renders them more bold and enterprising; this leads them to neglect the confined occupations of the land. They see and converse with a variety of people; their intercourse with mankind becomes extensive. The sea inspires them with a love of traffic, a desire of transporting produce from one place to another; and leads them to a variety of resources which supply the place of labor. Those who inhabit the middle settlements, by far the most numerous, must be very different; the simple cultivation of the earth purifies them, but the indulgences of the government, the soft remonstrances of religion, the rank of independent freeholders, must necessarily inspire them with sentiments very little known in Europe among people of the same class. What do I say? Europe has no such class of men; the early knowledge they acquire, the early bargains they make, give them a great degree of sagacity. As freemen they will be litigious;[13] pride and obstinacy are often the cause of law suits; the nature of our laws and governments may be another. As citizens it is easy to imagine that they will carefully read the newspapers, enter into every political disquisition, freely blame or censure governors and others. As farmers they will be careful and anxious to get as much as they can because what they get is their own. As northern men they will love the cheerful cup. As Christians, religion curbs them not in their opinions; the general indulgence leaves every one to think for themselves in spiritual matters; the laws inspect our actions, our thoughts are left to God. Industry, good living, selfishness, litigiousness, country politics, the pride of freemen, religious indifference, are their characteristics. If you recede still farther from the sea, you will come into more modern[14] settlements; they exhibit the same strong lineaments in a ruder appearance. Religion seems to have still less influence, and their manners are less improved.

Now we arrive near the great woods, near the last inhabited districts;[15] there men seem to be placed still farther beyond the reach of government, which in some measure leaves them to themselves. How can it pervade every corner; as

[13]Prone to engage in lawsuits. [14]More recent.

[15]In the 1770s the frontier line of settlement lay between the Appalachian Mountains and the Mississippi River.

they were driven there by misfortunes, necessity of beginnings, desire of acquiring large tracts of land, idleness, frequent want of economy,[16] ancient debts, the reunion of such people does not afford a very pleasing spectacle. When discord, want of unity and friendship, when either drunkenness or idleness prevail in such remote districts, contention, inactivity, and wretchedness must ensue. There are not the same remedies to these evils as in a long established community. The few magistrates they have are in general little better than the rest; they are often in a perfect state of war; that of man against man, sometimes decided by blows, sometimes by means of the law; that of man against every wild inhabitant of these venerable woods, of which they are come to dispossess them. There men appear to be no better than carnivorous animals of a superior rank, living on the flesh of wild animals when they can catch them, and when they are not able, they subsist on grain. He who would wish to see America in its proper light, and have a true idea of its feeble beginnings and barbarous rudiments, must visit our extended line of frontiers where the last[17] settlers dwell and where he may see the first labors of settlement, the mode of clearing the earth, in all their different appearances; where men are wholly left dependent on their native tempers and on the spur of uncertain industry, which often fails when not sanctified by the efficacy of a few moral rules. There, remote from the power of example and check[18] of shame, many families exhibit the most hideous parts of our society. They are a kind of forlorn hope, preceding by ten or twelve years the most respectable army of veterans which come after them. In that space, prosperity will polish some, vice and the law will drive off the rest, who uniting again with others like themselves will recede still farther, making room for more industrious people who will finish their improvements, convert the loghouse into a convenient habitation, and, rejoicing that the first heavy labors are finished, will change in a few years that hitherto barbarous country into a fine, fertile, well regulated district. Such is our progress, such is the march of the Europeans toward the interior parts of this continent. . . .

As I have endeavored to show you how Europeans become Americans, it may not be disagreeable to show you likewise how the various Christian sects introduced, wear out, and how religious indifference becomes prevalent. When any considerable number of a particular sect happen to dwell contiguous to each other, they immediately erect a temple and there worship the Divinity agreeably to their own peculiar ideas. Nobody disturbs them. If any new sect springs up in Europe, it may happen that many of its professors will come and settle in America. As they bring their zeal with them, they are at liberty to make proselytes if they can, and to build a meeting[19] and to follow the dictates of their consciences, for neither the government nor any other power interferes. If they are peaceable subjects and are industrious, what is it to their neighbors how and in what manner they think fit to address their prayers to the Supreme Being? But if the sectaries are not settled close together, if they are mixed with other denominations, their zeal will cool for want of fuel and will be extinguished in a little time. Then the Americans become as to religion, what they are as to country, allied to all. In them the name of Englishman, Frenchman, and European is lost, and in like manner, the strict modes of Christianity as practised in Europe are lost

[16]Lack of thrift. [17]Latest, most recent. [18]Restraint. [19]Congregation.

also. This effect will extend itself still farther hereafter, and though this may appear to you as a strange idea, yet it is a very true one. I shall be able perhaps hereafter to explain myself better; in the meanwhile, let the following example serve as my first justification.

Let us suppose you and I to be travelling; we observe that in this house, to the right, lives a Catholic who prays to God as he has been taught and believes in transubstantiation;[20] he works and raises wheat, he has a large family of children, all hale and robust; his belief, his prayers, offend nobody. About one mile farther on the same road, his next neighbor may be a good honest plodding German Lutheran, who addresses himself to the same God, the God of all, agreeably to the modes he has been educated in, and believes in consubstantiation;[21] by so doing he scandalizes nobody; he also works in his fields, embellishes the earth, clears swamps, &c. What has the world to do with his Lutheran principles? He persecutes nobody, and nobody persecutes him; he visits his neighbors, and his neighbors visit him. Next to him lives a seceder,[22] the most enthusiastic of all sectaries;[23] his zeal is hot and fiery, but separated as he is from others of the same complexion, he has no congregation of his own to resort to, where he might cabal[24] and mingle religious pride with worldly obstinacy. He likewise raises good crops, his house is handsomely painted, his orchard is one of the fairest in the neighborhood. How does it concern the welfare of the country or of the province at large, what this man's religious sentiments are or really whether he has any at all? He is a good farmer, he is a sober, peaceable, good citizen; William Penn[25] himself would not wish for more. This is the visible character, the invisible one is only guessed at, and is nobody's business. . . . Each of these people instruct their children as well as they can, but these instructions are feeble compared to those which are given to the youth of the poorest class in Europe. Their children will therefore grow up less zealous and more indifferent in matters of religion than their parents. The foolish vanity, or rather the fury of making proselytes, is unknown here; they have no time, the seasons call for all their attention, and thus in a few years, this mixed neighborhood will exhibit a strange religious medley that will be neither pure Catholicism nor pure Calvinism. . . . Thus all sects are mixed as well as all nations; thus religious indifference is imperceptibly disseminated from one end of the continent to the other, which is at present one of the strongest characteristics of the Americans. Where this will reach no one can tell; perhaps it may leave a vacuum fit to receive other systems. Persecution, religious pride, the love of contradiction, are the food of what the world commonly calls religion. These motives have ceased here; zeal in Europe is confined, here it evaporates in the great distance it has to travel; there it is a grain of powder enclosed,[26] here it burns away in the open air, and consumes[27] without effect.

[20]The Roman Catholic doctrine that during the Eucharist, bread and wine are changed into the actual body and blood of Christ.

[21]The Lutheran doctrine that during the Eucharist the substance of the bread and wine remains and is not changed into the body and blood of Christ.

[22]A name often given to members of Presbyterian and other reformed Protestant sects that withdrew (seceded) from established churches.

[23]Narrow, zealous dissenters. [24]Plot. [25]English Quaker, founder of Pennsylvania.

[26]Gunpowder enclosed, as in a bomb casing, and hence more powerfully destructive when exploded.

[27]Is used up, expended.

But to return to our back settlers. I must tell you that there is something in the proximity of the woods which is very singular. It is with men as it is with the plants and animals that grow and live in the forests; they are entirely different from those that live in the plains. I will candidly tell you all my thoughts, but you are not to expect that I shall advance any reasons. By living in or near the woods, their actions are regulated by the wildness of the neighborhood. The deer often come to eat their grain, the wolves to destroy their sheep, the bears to kill their hogs, the foxes to catch their poultry. This surrounding hostility immediately puts the gun into their hands; they watch these animals; they kill some, and thus by defending their property, they soon become professed hunters; this is the progress; once hunters, farewell to the plow. The chase renders them ferocious, gloomy, and unsociable; a hunter wants no neighbor; he rather hates them because he dreads the competition. In a little time their success in the woods makes them neglect their tillage. They trust to the natural fecundity of the earth, and therefore do little; carelessness in fencing often exposes what little they sow to destruction; they are not at home to watch; in order therefore to make up the deficiency, they go oftener to the woods. That new mode of life brings along with it a new set of manners, which I cannot easily describe. These new manners being grafted on the old stock produce a strange sort of lawless profligacy, the impressions of which are indelible. The manners of the Indian natives are respectable, compared with this European medley. Their wives and children live in sloth and inactivity; and having no proper pursuits, you may judge what education the latter receive. Their tender minds have nothing else to contemplate but the example of their parents; like them they grow up a mongrel breed, half civilized, half savage, except nature stamps on them some constitutional propensities. That rich, that voluptuous sentiment is gone that struck them so forcibly; the possession of their freeholds[28] no longer conveys to their minds the same pleasure and pride. To all these reasons you must add their lonely situation, and you cannot imagine what an effect on manners the great distances they live from each other has! Consider one of the last settlements in its first view; of what is it composed? Europeans who have not that sufficient share of knowledge they ought to have in order to prosper, people who have suddenly passed from oppression, dread of government, and fear of laws, into the unlimited freedom of the woods. This sudden change must have a very great effect on most men, and on that class particularly. Eating of wild meat, whatever you may think, tends to alter their temper, though all the proof I can adduce, is, that I have seen it; and having no place of worship to resort to, what little society this might afford is denied them. The Sunday meetings, exclusive of religious benefits, were the only social bonds that might have inspired them with some degree of emulation in neatness. Is it then surprising to see men thus situated, immersed in great and heavy labors, degenerate a little? It is rather a wonder the effect is not more diffusive. The Moravians[29] and the Quakers are the only instances in exception to what I have advanced. The first never settle singly; it is a colony of the society which emigrates; they carry with them their forms, worship,

[28]Lands and property fully owned.

[29]A Protestant Christian sect whose members, refugees from religious persecution in Europe, came to Pennsylvania in 1740.

rules, and decency; the others never begin so hard; they are always able to buy improvements,[30] in which there is a great advantage, for by that time the country is recovered from its first barbarity. Thus our bad people are those who are half cultivators and half hunters; and the worst of them are those who have degenerated altogether into the hunting state. As old plowmen and new men of the woods, as Europeans and new made Indians, they contract the vices of both; they adopt the moroseness and ferocity of a native without his mildness or even his industry at home. If manners are not refined, at least they are rendered simple and inoffensive by tilling the earth; all our wants are supplied by it; our time is divided between labor and rest and leaves none for the commission of great misdeeds. As hunters it is divided between the toil of the chase, the idleness of repose, or the indulgence of inebriation. Hunting is but a licentious idle life, and if it does not always pervert good dispositions yet, when it is united with bad luck, it leads to want; want stimulates that propensity to rapacity and injustice, too natural to needy men, which is the fatal gradation. After this explanation of the effects which follow by living in the woods, shall we yet vainly flatter ourselves with the hope of converting the Indians? We should rather begin with converting our backsettlers; and now if I dare mention the name of religion, its sweet accents would be lost in the immensity of these woods. Men thus placed, are not fit either to receive or remember its mild instructions; they want temples[31] and ministers, but as soon as men cease to remain at home and begin to lead an erratic life, let them be either tawny or white, they cease to be its disciples.

A European, when he first arrives, seems limited in his intentions as well as in his views, but he very suddenly alters his scale; two hundred miles formerly appeared a very great distance; it is now but a trifle; he no sooner breathes our air than he forms schemes and embarks in designs he never would have thought of in his own country. There the plentitude of society confines many useful ideas and often extinguishes the most laudable schemes which here ripen into maturity. Thus Europeans become Americans.

But how is this accomplished in that crowd of low, indigent people who flock here every year from all parts of Europe? I will tell you; they no sooner arrive than they immediately feel the good effects of that plenty of provisions we possess; they fare on our best food and are kindly entertained; their talents, character, and peculiar industry are immediately inquired into; they find countrymen everywhere disseminated, let them come from whatever part of Europe. Let me select one as an epitome of the rest; he is hired, he goes to work, and works moderately; instead of being employed by a haughty person, he finds himself with his equal, placed at the substantial table of the farmer or else at an inferior one as good; his wages are high, his bed is not like that bed of sorrow on which he used to lie; if he behaves with propriety and is faithful, he is caressed and becomes as it were a member of the family. He begins to feel the effects of a sort of resurrection; hitherto he had not lived but simply vegetated; he now feels himself a man because he is treated as such; the laws of his own country had overlooked him in his insignificancy; the laws of this cover him with their mantle. Judge what an alteration there

[30]Land that has been cleared and developed.
[31]Lack church buildings.

must arise in the mind and thoughts of this man; he begins to forget his former servitude and dependence; his heart involuntarily swells and glows; this first swell inspires him with those new thoughts which constitute an American. What love can he entertain for a country where his existence was a burden to him; if he is a generous good man, the love of this new adoptive parent will sink deep into his heart. He looks around and sees many a prosperous person who but a few years before was as poor as himself. This encourages him much; he begins to form some little scheme, the first, alas, he ever formed in his life. If he is wise he thus spends two or three years, in which time he acquires knowledge, the use of tools, the modes of working the lands, felling trees, &c. This prepares the foundation of a good name, the most useful acquisition he can make. He is encouraged; he has gained friends; he is advised and directed; he feels bold; he purchases some land; he gives all the money he has brought over, as well as what he has earned, and trusts to the God of harvests for the discharge of the rest. His good name procures him credit. He is now possessed of the deed, conveying to him and his posterity the fee simple[32] and absolute property of two hundred acres of land, situated on such a river. What an epoch in this man's life! He is become a freeholder, from perhaps a German boor[33]—he is now an American, a Pennsylvanian, an English subject. He is naturalized, his name is enrolled with those of the other citizens of the province. Instead of being a vagrant, he has a place of residence; he is called the inhabitant of such a country or of such a district, and for the first time in his life counts for something; for hitherto he has been a cipher. I only repeat what I have heard many say, and no wonder their hearts should glow and be agitated with a multitude of feelings not easy to describe. From nothing to start into being; from a servant to the rank of a master; from being the slave of some despotic prince to become a free man invested with lands to which every municipal blessing is annexed! What a change indeed! It is in consequence of that change that he becomes an American. This great metamorphosis has a double effect; it extinguishes all his European prejudices, he forgets that mechanism of subordination, that servility of disposition which poverty had taught him; and sometimes he is apt to forget too much, often passing from one extreme to the other. If he is a good man, he forms schemes of future prosperity; he proposes to educate his children better than he has been educated himself; he thinks of future modes of conduct, feels an ardor to labor he never felt before. Pride steps in and leads him to everything that the laws do not forbid; he respects them; with a heartfelt gratitude he looks toward the east, toward that insular government from whose wisdom all his new felicity is derived and under whose wings and protection he now lives. These reflections constitute him the good man and the good subject. Ye poor Europeans, ye who sweat and work for the great—ye who are obliged to give so many sheaves[34] to the church, so many to your lords, so many to your government, and have hardly any left for yourselves—ye who are held in less estimation than favorite hunters[35] or useless lapdogs—ye who only breathe the air of nature, because it cannot be withheld from you; it is here that ye can conceive the possibility of those feelings I have been describing; it is here the laws of naturalization

[32]Total legal possession. [33]Peasant.
[34]Stalks of grain (such as wheat) gathered in bundles. [35]Horses used for hunting.

invite everyone to partake of our great labors and felicity, to till unrented, untaxed lands! Many, corrupted beyond the power of amendment, have brought with them all their vices and, disregarding the advantages held to them, have gone on in their former career of iniquity until they have been overtaken and punished by our laws. It is not every emigrant who succeeds; no, it is only the sober, the honest, and industrious; happy those to whom this transition has served as a powerful spur to labor, to prosperity, and to the good establishment of children, born in the days of their poverty, and who had no other portion to expect but the rags of their parents, had it not been for their happy emigration. . . .

After a foreigner from any part of Europe is arrived, and become a citizen, let him devoutly listen to the voice of our great parent which says to him, "Welcome to my shores, distressed European; bless the hour in which thou didst see my verdant fields, my fair navigable rivers, and my green mountains! If thou wilt work, I have bread for thee; if thou wilt be honest, sober, and industrious, I have greater rewards to confer on thee—ease and independence. I will give thee fields to feed and clothe thee, a comfortable fireside to sit by and tell thy children by what means thou hast prospered, and a decent bed to repose on. I shall endow thee beside with the immunities of a freeman. If thou wilt carefully educate thy children, teach them gratitude to God, and reverence to that government, that philanthropic government which has collected here so many men and made them happy, I will also provide for thy progeny; and to every good man this ought to be the most holy, the most powerful, the most earnest wish he can possibly form, as well as the most consolatory prospect when he dies. Go thou and work and till; thou shalt prosper, provided thou be just, grateful, and industrious."

LETTER IX[1]

DESCRIPTION OF CHARLESTON; THOUGHTS ON SLAVERY; ON PHYSICAL EVIL; A MELANCHOLY SCENE

Charleston is, in the north, what Lima[2] is in the south; both are capitals of the richest provinces of their respective hemispheres: you may therefore conjecture, that both cities must exhibit the appearances necessarily resulting from riches. Peru abounding in gold, Lima is filled with inhabitants who enjoy all those gradations of pleasure, refinement, and luxury which proceed from wealth. Carolina produces commodities more valuable perhaps than gold because they are gained by greater industry; it exhibits also on our northern stage a display of riches and luxury inferior indeed to the former but far superior to what are to be seen in our northern towns. Its situation is admirable, being built at the confluence of two large rivers which receive in

[1]Crèvecoeur's description of Charleston and slavery exhibits his thesis that the corruptions and brutalities of civilized society can exceed even those of life in the wilderness.
[2]Charleston, South Carolina; Lima, Peru.

their course a great number of inferior streams, all navigable in the spring, for flat boats. Here the produce of this extensive territory concenters; here therefore is the seat of the most valuable exportation; their wharfs, their docks, their magazines,[3] are extremely convenient to facilitate this great commercial business. The inhabitants are the gayest in America; it is called the center of our beau monde,[4] and is always filled with the richest planters of the province, who resort hither in quest of health and pleasure. . . .

While all is joy, festivity, and happiness in Charleston, would you imagine that scenes of misery overspread in the country? Their ears by habit are become deaf; their hearts are hardened; they neither see, hear, nor feel for the woes of their poor slaves from whose painful labors all their wealth proceeds. Here the horrors of slavery, the hardship of incessant toils, are unseen, and no one thinks with compassion of those showers of sweat and of tears which from the bodies of Africans daily drop and moisten the ground they till. The cracks of the whip urging these miserable beings to excessive labor are far too distant from the gay capital to be heard. The chosen race eat, drink, and live happy, while the unfortunate one grubs up the ground, raises indigo, or husks the rice, exposed to a sun full as scorching as their native one, without the support of good food, without the cordials of any cheering liquor.[5] This great contrast has often afforded me subjects of the most afflicting meditation. On the one side, behold a people enjoying all that life affords most bewitching and pleasurable, without labor, without fatigue, hardly subjected to the trouble of wishing. With gold, dug from Peruvian mountains, they order vessels to the coasts of Guinea;[6] by virtue of that gold, wars, murders, and devastations are committed in some harmless, peaceable African neighborhood where dwelt innocent people who even knew not but that all men were black. The daughter torn from her weeping mother, the child from the wretched parents, the wife from the loving husband, whole families swept away and brought through storms and tempests to this rich metropolis! There, arranged like horses at a fair, they are branded like cattle and then driven to toil, to starve, and to languish for a few years on the different plantations of these citizens. And for whom must they work? For persons they know not and who have no other power over them than that of violence, no other right than what this accursed metal has given them! Strange order of things! Oh, Nature, where are thou?—Are not these blacks thy children as well as we? On the other side, nothing is to be seen but the most diffusive misery and wretchedness, unrelieved even in thought or wish! Day after day they drudge on without any prospect of ever reaping for themselves; they are obliged to devote their lives, their limbs, their will, and every vital exertion to swell the wealth of masters who look not upon them with half the kindness and affection with which they consider their dogs and horses. Kindness and affection are not the portion of those who till the earth, who carry the burdens, who convert the logs into useful boards. This reward, simple and natural as one would conceive it, would border on humanity, and planters must have none of it!

[3]Warehouses.
[4]French: high society.
[5]I.e., without the benefits of any cheering beverage.
[6]West Africa.

. . .

Were I to be possessed of a plantation and my slaves treated as in general they are here, never could I rest in peace; my sleep would be perpetually disturbed by a retrospect of the frauds committed in Africa in order to entrap them, frauds surpassing in enormity everything which a common mind can possibly conceive. I should be thinking of the barbarous treatment they meet with on shipboard, of their anguish, of the despair necessarily inspired by their situation when torn from their friends and relations, when delivered into the hands of a people differently colored whom they cannot understand, carried in a strange machine over an ever agitated element which they had never seen before, and finally delivered over to the severities of the whippers and the excessive labors of the field. Can it be possible that the force of custom should ever make me deaf to all these reflections, and as insensible to the injustice of that trade, and to their miseries, as the rich inhabitants of this town seem to be? What then is man, this being who boasts so much of the excellence and dignity of his nature among that variety of unscrutable mysteries, of unsolvable problems, with which he is surrounded? . . .

But is it really true, as I have heard it asserted here, that those blacks are incapable of feeling the spurs of emulation and the cheerful sound of encouragement? By no means; there are a thousand proofs existing of their gratitude and fidelity; those hearts in which such noble dispositions can grow are then like ours; they are susceptible of every generous sentiment, of every useful motive of action; they are capable of receiving lights,[7] of imbibing ideas that would greatly alleviate the weight of their miseries. But what methods have in general been made use of to obtain so desirable an end? None; the day in which they arrive and are sold, is the first of their labors, labors which from that hour admit of no respite; for though indulged by law with relaxation on Sundays, they are obliged to employ that time which is intended for rest, to till their little plantations. What can be expected from wretches in such circumstances? Forced from their native country, cruelly treated when on board and not less so on the plantations to which they are driven; is there any thing in this treatment but what must kindle all the passions, sow the seeds of inveterate resentment, and nourish a wish of perpetual revenge? They are left to the irresistible effects of those strong and natural propensities; the blows they receive, are they conducive to extinguish them or to win their affections? They are neither soothed by the hopes that their slavery will ever terminate but with their lives not yet encouraged by the goodness of their food or the mildness of their treatment. The very hopes held out to mankind by religion, that consolatory system so useful to the miserable, are never presented to them; neither moral nor physical means are made use of to soften their chains; they are left in their original and untutored state, that very state where in the natural propensities of revenge and warm passions are so soon kindled. Cheered by no one single motive that can impel the will, or excite

[7]I.e., capable of intellectual or spiritual understanding.

their efforts, nothing but terrors and punishments are presented to them; death is denounced[8] if they run away; horrid dilaceration[9] if they speak with their native freedom; perpetually awed by the terrible cracks of whips or by the fear of capital punishments, while even those punishments often fail of their purpose.

. . .

Everywhere one part of the human species are taught the art of shedding the blood of the other, of setting fire to their dwellings, of leveling the works of their industry, half of the existence of nations regularly employed in destroying other nations. What little political felicity is to be met with here and there, has cost oceans of blood to purchase, as if good was never to be the portion of unhappy man. Republics, kingdoms, monarchies, founded either on fraud or successful violence, increase by pursuing the steps of the same policy until they are destroyed in their turn, either by the influence of their own crimes or by more successful but equally criminal enemies.

If from this general review of human nature, we descend to the examination of what is called civilized society; there the combination of every natural and artificial want makes us pay very dear for what little share of political felicity we enjoy. It is a strange heterogeneous assemblage of vices, and virtues, and of a variety of other principles, forever at war, forever jarring, forever producing some dangerous, some distressing extreme. Where do you conceive then that nature intended we should be happy? Would you prefer the state of men in the woods to that of men in a more improved situation? Evil preponderates in both; in the first they often eat each other for want of food, and in the other they often starve each other for want of room. For my part, I think the vices and miseries to be found in the latter exceed those of the former, in which real evil is more scarce, more supportable, and less enormous. Yet we wish to see the earth peopled, to accomplish the happiness of kingdoms, which is said to consist in numbers. Gracious God! to what end is the introduction of so many beings into a mode of existence in which they must grope amidst as many errors, commit as many crimes, and meet with as many diseases, wants, and sufferings!

The following scene will I hope account for these melancholy reflections and apologize for the gloomy thoughts with which I have filled this letter; my mind is, and always has been, oppressed since I became a witness to it. I was not long since invited to dine with a planter who lived three miles from—,[10] where he then resided. In order to avoid the heat of the sun, I resolved to go on foot, sheltered in a small path leading through a pleasant wood. I was leisurely traveling along, attentively examining some peculiar

[8]I.e., sentence of death is pronounced.
[9]Tearing to pieces.
[10]Crèvecoeur omitted the name.

plants which I had collected, when all at once I felt the air strongly agitated, though the day was perfectly calm and sultry. I immediately cast my eyes toward the cleared ground, from which I was but at a small distance, in order to see whether it was not occasioned by a sudden shower, when at that instant a sound resembling a deep rough voice, uttered, as I thought, a few inarticulate monosyllables. Alarmed and surprised, I precipitately looked all round, when I perceived at about six rods distance something resembling a cage, suspended to the limbs of a tree, all the branches of which appeared covered with large birds of prey fluttering about and anxiously endeavouring to perch on the cage. Actuated by an involuntary motion of my hands, more than by any design of my mind, I fired at them; they all flew to a short distance, with a most hideous noise, when, horrid to think and painful to repeat, I perceived a Negro, suspended in the cage and left there to expire! I shudder when I recollect that the birds had already picked out his eyes, his cheek bones were bare, his arms had been attacked in several places, and his body seemed covered with a multitude of wounds. From the edges of the hollow sockets and from the lacerations with which he was disfigured, the blood slowly dropped and tinged the ground beneath. No sooner were the birds flown, than swarms of insects covered the whole body of this unfortunate wretch, eager to feed on his mangled flesh and to drink his blood. I found myself suddenly arrested by the power of affright and terror; my nerves were convulsed; I trembled; I stood motionless, involuntarily contemplating the fate of this Negro, in all its dismal latitude. The living specter, though deprived of his eyes, could still distinctly hear, and in his uncouth dialect begged me to give him some water to allay his thirst. Humanity herself would have recoiled back with horror; she would have balanced whether to lessen such reliefless distress or mercifully with one blow to end this dreadful scene of agonizing torture! Had I had a ball in my gun, I certainly should have despatched him; but finding myself unable to perform so kind an office, I sought, though trembling, to relieve him as well as I could. A shell ready fixed to a pole, which had been used by some Negroes, presented itself to me; I filled it with water, and with trembling hands I guided it to the quivering lips of the wretched sufferer. Urged by the irresistible power of thirst, he endeavoured to meet it, as he instinctively guessed its approach by the noise it made in passing through the bars of the cage. "Tankè, you whitè man, tankè you, putè somè poison and givè me." How long have you been hanging there? I asked him. "Two days, and me no die; the birds, the birds; aaah me!" Oppressed with the reflections which this shocking spectacle afforded me, I mustered strength enough to walk away and soon reached the house at which I intended to dine. There I heard that the reason for this slave being thus punished, was on account of his having killed the overseer of the plantation. They told me that the laws of self-preservation rendered such executions necessary and supported the doctrine of slavery with the arguments generally made use of to justify the practice, with the repetition of which I shall not trouble you at present.

1774–1781 1782

Thomas Paine 1737–1809

When he first came to America in 1774, Tom Paine was an impoverished Englishman whose life had been a series of failures. Two years later he was the most famous and powerful voice of revolution in America. He was born the son of a Quaker farmer and corset maker in Thetford, England. After attending grammar school he worked briefly for his father as a staymaker and then served as a sailor, schoolteacher, and government tax collector. By the time he was thirty-seven he had failed at a variety of professions, had been dismissed from his government post as a troublemaker, and had been declared a bankrupt.

In London he met Benjamin Franklin. Shortly afterward, Paine left for America with a letter of introduction from Franklin, recommending him as "an ingenious worthy young man." On arriving in Philadelphia, he began to write for the newly established Pennsylvania Magazine. *It was a time of great political and social ferment: England had issued a proclamation declaring a state of rebellion in the Colonies; the Battles of Lexington and Bunker Hill had been fought; and the Second Continental Congress had convened in Philadelphia to prosecute the war. Stirred by the ideas of revolution that surrounded him, Paine published* Common Sense *in January 1776, declaring that the turmoil could not be solved by submission to authority and laws. The answer now lay in man's instincts, in common sense.*

Paine's small book was filled with the rhetoric of revolution. It was written in a forceful style that the average man could quickly understand. It appealed to resentment at British atrocities, urged pity for the oppressed, and painted a picture of the glories possible if the Colonies would strive for complete independence from the "fraud" of monarchy. Such arguments had been presented elsewhere, but never before with such success. Within a few months, 100,000 copies were distributed throughout the thinly populated Colonies.

Common Sense *helped to create the national mood that inspired the Declaration of Independence six months later, but it was not the last of Paine's rhetorical triumphs in the Colonies. At one of the darkest moments of the Revolution, after Washington's defeat in New York and his desperate retreat across New Jersey toward Philadelphia, Paine brought out the first of his* Crisis *papers (December 1776). It roused the colonists with the famous words, "These are the times that try men's souls" and with its denunciation of "the summer soldier and the sunshine patriot." Washington had* Crisis I *read aloud to his soldiers before they crossed the Delaware to defeat the Hessians at Trenton, and Paine was later voted a salary of $800 a year by Congress to enable him to continue "informing the people and rousing them to action." Fifteen more* Crisis *papers appeared over the next seven years. They argued for revolution and independence and opposed each new scheme for reconciliation with Britain. When the final paper appeared in 1783, it announced that the Revolution was "gloriously and happily accomplished" and urged that Americans form "confederated states" to make "the whole secure."*

After the Revolution, Paine devoted himself to designs for a radically new, single-span iron bridge. In 1787 he sailed to Europe in search of financial backers. While in France he witnessed the early events of the French Revolution and was honored by Lafayette, who gave him the key to the Bastille for presentation to George Washington. In England, Paine read Edmund Burke's Reflections on the French Revolution *(1790) and quickly set to work on a reply. Burke had defended the institution of monarchy and condemned revolutions that would displace legal kings. Paine's answer,* The Rights of Man *(1791–1792), defended revolution and insisted that man was bound to no hereditary rulers.*

For his defense of the overthrow of kings, the British government charged Paine with sedition and ordered him to trial. He then fled to France where he was given French citizenship and a seat in the National Assembly. Soon, however, his outspoken opposition to the execution of Louis XVI angered extremist Jacobins, and in 1793 Paine was arrested and imprisoned for ten months. Finally, James Monroe, American ambassador to France, gained Paine's release on the grounds that he was an American citizen.

In Paris, while recuperating from the effects of his imprisonment, Paine completed The Age of Reason *(1794–1796). It was an attack on the irrationality of religion, the source of "the most detestable wickedness, the most horrid cruelties, that have afflicted the human race." It was a crude but forceful statement of the doctrines of deism. It advocated reason rather than divine revelation as the proper guide for man, and it raised a storm of protest. Although he insisted on his belief in God, Paine was charged with atheism. Conservatives in England and America pictured Paine as a fiend, masterminding a plot to undermine all Christian morality. He was vilified in pulpits and journals as a man devoted more to the destruction of governments, laws, and religions than to the building of democracy and justice.*

With the end of the Reign of Terror, Paine resumed his seat in the French Assembly, but his service was brief and ineffective. In 1802 he returned to America, broken in health and impoverished. In America he grew embittered by the treatment he received in the new republic that had the greatest cause to honor him. He had aroused the masses against their government; now he saw the religious fury of the masses aroused against him, and his illusions about man's natural goodness were shattered. He had outlived his time. The Age of Revolution had ended; its prophets were now without honor. When he died, in 1809, his request for a grave in a Quaker cemetery was refused, and he was buried on his farm in New Rochelle, New York. Ten years later, his remains were exhumed and taken to England, where they were lost. The final resting place of America's greatest propagandist for revolution is unknown.

Paine was not a systematic philosopher but a man who felt and responded. He preached the doctrines of natural rights, the equality of men, and the social contract. But he shaped these ideas according to his own humanitarian impulses. His success had come from the simplicity of his arguments, from the force and passion of his writing, and from events that created an audience ready to hear his words. He was an inspired agitator whom history had obeyed, and his opposition to tyranny and injustice still serve as an inspiration to men and women of good hope throughout the world.

FURTHER READING: *Thomas Paine, Representative Selections,* ed. H. Clark, 1944, 1961; *The Crisis Papers,* ed. C. Norman, 1990; *Thomas Paine, Collected Writings,* ed. E. Foner, 1995; M. Conway, *The Life of Thomas Paine,* 2 vols., 1892; S. Berthold, *Thomas Paine, America's First Liberal,* 1938; A. Aldridge, *Man of Reason, The Life of Thomas Paine,* 1959; A. Williamson, *Tom Paine,* 1973; D. Hawke, *Tom Paine,* 1974; E. Foner, *Tom Paine and Revolutionary America,* 1976, 2001; J. Wilson and W. Ricketson, *Thomas Paine,* 1978, 1989; A. Aldridge, *Thomas Paine's American Ideology,* 1985; D. Powell, *Tom Paine, The Greatest Exile,* 1985; A. Ayer, *Thomas Paine,* 1988; J. Keane, *Tom Paine, A Political Life,* 1995; J. Fruchtman, *Thomas Paine, Apostle of Freedom,* 1995.

TEXT: *The Writings of Thomas Paine,* ed. M. Conway, 4 vols., 1894–1896. Spelling and punctuation have been changed to conform more nearly to modern practice.

from *COMMON SENSE*

ON THE ORIGIN AND DESIGN OF GOVERNMENT IN GENERAL

Some writers have so confounded[1] society with government, as to leave little or no distinction between them; whereas they are not only different, but have different origins. Society is produced by our wants, and government by our wickedness; the former promotes our happiness *positively* by uniting our affections, the latter *negatively* by restraining our vices. The one encourages intercourse, the other creates distinctions. The first is a patron, the last a punisher.

Society in every state is a blessing, but Government, even in its best state, is but a necessary evil; in its worst state an intolerable one: for when we suffer, or are exposed to the same miseries *by a Government,* which we might expect in a country *without Government,* our calamity is heightened by reflecting that we furnish the means by which we suffer. Government, like dress, is the badge of lost innocence; the palaces of kings are built upon the ruins of the bowers of paradise. For were the impulses of conscience clear, uniform and irresistibly obeyed, man would need no other lawgiver; but that not being the case, he finds it necessary to surrender up a part of his property to furnish means for the protection of the rest; and this he is induced to do by the same prudence which in every other case advises him, out of two evils to choose the least. Wherefore, security being the true design and end of government, it unanswerably follows that whatever form thereof appears most likely to ensure it to us, with the least expense and greatest benefit, is preferable to all others.

In order to gain a clear and just idea of the design and end of government, let us suppose a small number of persons settled in some sequestered part of the earth, unconnected with the rest; they will then represent the first peopling of any country, or of the world. In this state of natural liberty, society will be their first thought. A thousand motives will excite them thereto; the strength of one man is so unequal to his wants, and his mind so unfitted for perpetual solitude, that he is soon obliged to seek assistance and relief of another, who in his turn requires the same. Four or five united would be able to raise a tolerable dwelling in the midst of a wilderness, but one man might labor out the common period of life without accomplishing any thing; when he had felled his timber he could not remove it, nor erect it after it was removed; hunger in the mean time would urge him to quit his work, and every different want would call him a different way. Disease, nay even misfortune, would be death; for though neither might be mortal, yet either would disable him from living, and reduce him to a state in which he might rather be said to perish than to die.

Thus necessity, like a gravitating power, would soon form our newly arrived emigrants into society, the reciprocal blessings of which would supersede, and render the obligations of law and government unnecessary while they remained perfectly just to each other; but as nothing but Heaven is impregnable to vice, it will unavoidably happen that in proportion as they surmount the first difficulties of emigration, which bound them together in a common cause, they will begin to relax in their duty and attachment to each other:

[1]Mixed, joined.

and this remissness will point out the necessity of establishing some form of government to supply the defect of moral virtue.

Some convenient tree will afford them a State House, under the branches of which the whole Colony may assemble to deliberate on public matters. It is more than probable that their first laws will have the title only of Regulations and be enforced by no other penalty than public disesteem. In this first parliament every man by natural right will have a seat.

But as the Colony increases, the public concerns will increase likewise, and the distance at which the members may be separated, will render it too inconvenient for all of them to meet on every occasion as at first, when their number was small, their habitations near, and the public concerns few and trifling. This will point out the convenience of their consenting to leave the legislative part to be managed by a select number chosen from the whole body, who are supposed to have the same concerns at stake which those have who appointed them, and who will act in the same manner as the whole body would act were they present. If the colony continue increasing, it will become necessary to augment the number of representatives, and so that the interest of every part of the colony may be attended to, it will be found best to divide the whole into convenient parts, each part sending its proper number: and so that the *elected* might never form to themselves an interest separate from the *electors,* prudence will point out the propriety of having elections often: because as the *elected* might by that means return and mix again with the general body of the *electors* in a few months, their fidelity to the public will be secured by the prudent reflection of not making a rod for themselves.[2] And as this frequent interchange will establish a common interest with every part of the community, they will mutually and naturally support each other, and on this, (not on the unmeaning name of king,) depends the *strength of government, and the happiness of the governed.*

Here then is the origin and rise of government; namely, a mode rendered necessary by the inability of moral virtue to govern the world; here too is the design and end of government, viz. Freedom and security. And however our eyes may be dazzled with show, or our ears deceived by sound; however prejudice may wrap our wills, or interest darken our understanding, the simple voice of nature and reason will say, 'tis right.

. . .

1776

from *THE AMERICAN CRISIS*[1]

NUMBER 1

These are the times that try men's souls. The summer soldier and the sunshine patriot will, in this crisis, shrink from the service of their country; but he that stands it *now,* deserves the love and thanks of man and woman.

[2]I.e., not causing their own punishments.

[1]Originally published in the *Pennsylvania Journal,* December 19, 1776, subsequently issued in many pamphlet editions, of which that dated December 23, 1776 is reprinted here.

Tyranny, like hell, is not easily conquered; yet we have this consolation with us, that the harder the conflict, the more glorious the triumph. What we obtain too cheap, we esteem too lightly: it is dearness only that gives every thing its value. Heaven knows how to put a proper price upon its goods; and it would be strange indeed if so celestial an article as FREEDOM should not be highly rated. Britain, with an army to enforce her tyranny, has declared that she has a right (*not only to* TAX) but "to BIND *us in* ALL CASES WHATSOEVER,"[2] and if being *bound in that manner,* is not slavery, then is there not such a thing as slavery upon earth. Even the expression is impious; for so unlimited a power can belong only to God.

Whether the independence of the continent was declared too soon, or delayed too long,[3] I will not now enter into as an argument; my own simple opinion is, that had it been eight months earlier, it would have been much better. We did not make a proper use of last winter, neither could we, while we were in a dependent state. However, the fault, if it were one, was all our own;[4] we have none to blame but ourselves. But no great deal is lost yet. All that Howe[5] has been doing for this month past, is rather a ravage than a conquest, which the spirit of the Jerseys,[6] a year ago, would have quickly repulsed, and which time and a little resolution will soon recover.

I have as little superstition in me as any man living, but my secret opinion has ever been, and still is, that God Almighty will not give up a people to military destruction, or leave them unsupportedly to perish, who have so earnestly and so repeatedly sought to avoid the calamities of war, by every decent method which wisdom could invent. Neither have I so much of the infidel in me, as to suppose that He has relinquished the government of the world, and given us up to the care of devils; and as I do not, I cannot see on what grounds the king of Britain can look up to heaven for help against us: a common murderer, a highwayman, or a house-breaker, has as good a pretense as he.

'Tis surprising to see how rapidly a panic will sometimes run through a country. All nations and ages have been subject to them: Britain has trembled like an ague[7] at the report of a French fleet of flat bottomed boats; and in the fourteenth century[8] the whole English army, after ravaging the kingdom of France, was driven back like men petrified with fear; and this brave exploit was performed by a few broken forces collected and headed by a woman, Joan of Arc. Would that heaven might inspire some Jersey maid to spirit up her countrymen, and save her fair fellow sufferers from ravage and

[2]Paine quotes the Declaratory Act of Parliament (February 1766) that asserted Britain's complete authority over the American Colonies.

[3]The American Revolution began in April 1775. The Declaration of Independence was not adopted until July 1776.

[4]"The present winter is worth an age, if rightly employed; but if lost or neglected, the whole continent will partake of the evil; and there is no punishment that man does not deserve, be he who, or what, or where he will, that may be the means of sacrificing a season so precious and useful."—Paine's note, a quotation from *Common Sense.*

[5]Lord William Howe (1729–1814), commander of British forces in America from 1775 to 1778.

[6]Colonial New Jersey, having been divided into East Jersey and West Jersey from 1676 to 1702, was often referred to as the Jerseys.

[7]I.e., as though it had an ague, a chill.

[8]Paine mistakenly places Joan of Arc (1412–1431), and the defeat of the English in France, in the fourteenth instead of the fifteenth century.

ravishment! Yet panics, in some cases, have their uses; they produce as much good as hurt. Their duration is always short; the mind soon grows through them, and acquires a firmer habit than before. But their peculiar advantage is, that they are the touchstones of sincerity and hypocrisy, and bring things and men to light, which might otherwise have lain forever undiscovered. In fact, they have the same effect on secret traitors, which an imaginary apparition would have upon a private murderer. They sift out the hidden thoughts of man, and hold them up in public to the world. Many a disguised Tory[9] has lately shown his head, that shall penitentially solemnize with curses the day on which Howe arrived upon the Delaware.

As I was with the troops at Fort Lee, and marched with them to the edge of Pennsylvania, I am well acquainted with many circumstances, which those who live at a distance know but little or nothing of.[10] Our situation there was exceedingly cramped, the place being a narrow neck of land between the North River[11] and the Hackensack. Our force was inconsiderable, being not one fourth so great as Howe could bring against us. We had no army at hand to have relieved the garrison, had we shut ourselves up and stood on our defence. Our ammunition, light artillery, and the best part of our stores, had been removed, on the apprehension that Howe would endeavor to penetrate the Jerseys, in which case Fort Lee could be of no use to us; for it must occur to every thinking man, whether in the army or not, that these kinds of field forts are only for temporary purposes, and last in use no longer than the enemy directs his force against the particular object, which such forts are raised to defend. Such was our situation and condition at Fort Lee on the morning of the 20th of November, when an officer arrived with information that the enemy with 200 boats had landed about seven miles above: Major General Green,[12] who commanded the garrison, immediately ordered them under arms, and sent express to General Washington at the town of Hackensack, distant by the way of the ferry, six miles. Our first object was to secure the bridge over the Hackensack, which laid up the river between the enemy and us, about six miles from us, and three from them. General Washington arrived in about three quarters of an hour, and marched at the head of the troops towards the bridge, which place I expected we should have a brush[13] for; however, they did not choose to dispute it with us, and the greatest part of our troops went over the bridge, the rest over the ferry, except some which passed at a mill on a small creek, between the bridge and the ferry, and made their way through some marshy grounds up to the town of Hackensack, and there passed the river. We brought off as much baggage as the wagons could contain, the rest was lost. The simple object was to bring off the garrison, and march them on till they could be strengthened by the Jersey or Pennsylvania

[9]Derisive term used to describe an American who favored the British cause during the American Revolution.

[10]Paine underplays American losses. With the capture of Forts Lee and Washington on opposite sides of the Hudson River, the British general Howe took nearly 3,000 prisoners and large quantities of military supplies, inflicting one of the most costly American defeats of the war on American forces. Washington's army was reduced to fewer than 3,000 men. It was while serving with the American army during its retreat through New Jersey that Paine wrote *Crisis I.*

[11]Hudson River.

[12]Nathanael Green (1742–1786). Paine served as his aide-de-camp.

[13]Fight, skirmish.

militia, so as to be enabled to make a stand. We stayed four days at Newark, collected our out-posts with some of the Jersey militia, and marched out twice to meet the enemy, on being informed that they were advancing, though our numbers were greatly inferior to theirs. Howe, in my little opinion, committed a great error in generalship in not throwing a body of forces off from Staten Island through Amboy,[14] by which means he might have seized all our stores at Brunswick,[15] and intercepted our march into Pennsylvania; but if we believe the power of hell to be limited, we must likewise believe that their agents are under some providential control.

I shall not now attempt to give all the particulars of our retreat to the Delaware; suffice it for the present to say, that both officers and men, though greatly harassed and fatigued, frequently without rest, covering, or provision, the inevitable consequences of a long retreat, bore it with a manly and martial spirit. All their wishes centered in one, which was, that the country would turn out and help them to drive the enemy back. Voltaire has remarked that king William[16] never appeared to full advantage but in difficulties and in action; the same remark may be made on General Washington, for the character fits him. There is a natural firmness in some minds which cannot be unlocked by trifles, but which, when unlocked, discovers a cabinet[17] of fortitude; and I reckon it among those kinds of public blessings, which we do not immediately see, that God hath blessed him with uninterrupted health, and given him a mind that can even flourish upon care.

I shall conclude this paper with some miscellaneous remarks on the state of our affairs; and shall begin with asking the following question, Why is it that the enemy have left the New-England provinces, and made these middle ones the seat of war? The answer is easy: New-England is not infested with Tories, and we are. I have been tender in raising the cry against these men, and used numberless arguments to show them their danger, but it will not do to sacrifice a world either to their folly or their baseness. The period is now arrived, in which either they or we must change our sentiments, or one or both must fall. And what is a Tory? Good God! what is he? I should not be afraid to go with a hundred Whigs[18] against a thousand Tories, were they to attempt to get into arms. Every Tory is a coward; for servile, slavish, self-interested fear is the foundation of Toryism; and a man under such influence, though he may be cruel, never can be brave.

But, before the line of irrecoverable separation be drawn between us, let us reason the matter together: Your conduct is an invitation to the enemy, yet not one in a thousand of you has heart enough to join him. Howe is as much deceived by you as the American cause is injured by you. He expects you will all take up arms, and flock to his standard, with muskets on your shoulders. Your opinions are of no use to him, unless you support him personally, for 'tis soldiers, and not Tories, that he wants.

I once felt all that kind of anger, which a man ought to feel, against the mean principles that are held by the Tories: a noted one, who kept a tavern

[14]Perth Amboy, New Jersey.

[15]New Brunswick, New Jersey.

[16]François Arouet, called Voltaire (1694–1778), French philosopher and writer. William III (1650–1702), king of England from 1689 to 1702.

[17]Storehouse.

[18]Members of the political party that opposed the Tories and supported the American Revolution.

at Amboy,[19] was standing at his door, with as pretty a child in his hand, about eight or nine years old, as I ever saw, and after speaking his mind as freely as he thought was prudent, finished with this unfatherly expression, *"Well! give me peace in my day."*[20] Not a man lives on the continent but fully believes that a separation must some time or other finally take place, and a generous parent should have said, *"If there must be trouble, let it be in my day, that my child may have peace";* and this single reflection, well applied, is sufficient to awaken every man to duty. Not a place upon earth might be so happy as America. Her situation is remote from all the wrangling world, and she has nothing to do but to trade with them. A man can distinguish himself between temper and principle, and I am as confident, as I am that God governs the world, that America will never be happy till she gets clear of foreign dominion. Wars, without ceasing, will break out till that period arrives, and the continent must in the end be conqueror; for though the flame of liberty may sometimes cease to shine, the coal can never expire.

America did not, nor does not want force; but she wanted a proper application of that force. Wisdom is not the purchase of a day, and it is no wonder that we should err at the first setting off. From an excess of tenderness, we were unwilling to raise an army, and trusted our cause to the temporary defence of a well-meaning militia. A summer's experience has now taught us better; yet with those troops, while they were collected, we were able to set bounds to the progress of the enemy, and, thank God! they are again assembling. I always considered militia as the best troops in the world for a sudden exertion, but they will not do for a long campaign. Howe, it is probable, will make an attempt on this city;[21] should he fail on this side the Delaware, he is ruined: if he succeeds, our cause is not ruined. He stakes all on his side against a part on ours; admitting he succeeds, the consequence will be, that armies from both ends of the continent will march to assist their suffering friends in the middle states; for he cannot go everywhere, it is impossible. I consider Howe as the greatest enemy the Tories have; he is bringing a war into their country, which, had it not been for him and partly for themselves, they had been clear of. Should he now be expelled, I wish with all the devotion of a Christian, that the names of Whig and Tory may never more be mentioned; but should the Tories give him encouragement to come, or assistance if he come, I as sincerely wish that our next year's arms may expel them from the continent, and the congress appropriate their possessions to the relief of those who have suffered in well-doing. A single successful battle next year will settle the whole. America could carry on a two years war by the confiscation of the property of disaffected persons, and be made happy by their expulsion. Say not that this is revenge, call it rather the soft resentment of a suffering people, who, having no object in view but the *good* of *all,* have staked their *own all* upon a seemingly doubtful event. Yet it is folly to argue against determined hardness; eloquence may strike the

[19]In August 1776 Paine had enlisted in the Continental Army and was stationed at Perth Amboy, New Jersey.

[20]"There shall be peace and truth in my days." Isaiah 39:8.

[21]After the retreat through New Jersey, Paine went to Philadelphia to prepare *Crisis I* for publication. The British eventually occupied Philadelphia September 26, 1777.

ear, and the language of sorrow draw forth the tear of compassion, but nothing can reach the heart that is steeled with prejudice.

Quitting this class of men, I turn with the warm ardor of a friend to those who have nobly stood, and are yet determined to stand the matter out: I call not upon a few, but upon all: not on *this* state, but on *every* state: up and help us; lay your shoulders to the wheel; better have too much force than too little, when so great an object is at stake. Let it be told to the future world, that in the depth of winter, when nothing but hope and virtue could survive, that the city and the country, alarmed at one common danger, came forth to meet and to repulse it. Say not that thousands are gone, turn out your tens of thousands;[22] throw not the burden of the day upon Providence, but *"show your faith by your works,"*[23] that God may bless you. It matters not where you live, or what rank of life you hold, the evil or the blessing will reach you all. The far and the near, the home counties and the back,[24] the rich and the poor, will suffer or rejoice alike. The heart that feels not now, is dead: the blood of his children will curse his cowardice, who shrinks back at a time when a little might have saved the whole, and made *them* happy. I love the man that can smile in trouble, that can gather strength from distress, and grow brave by reflection. 'Tis the business of little minds to shrink; but he whose heart is firm, and whose conscience approves his conduct, will pursue his principles unto death. My own line of reasoning is to myself as straight and clear as a ray of light. Not all the treasures of the world, so far as I believe, could have induced me to support an offensive war, for I think it murder; but if a thief breaks into my house, burns and destroys my property, and kills or threatens to kill me, or those that are in it, and to *"bind me in all cases whatsoever"*[25] to his absolute will, am I to suffer it? What signifies it to me, whether he who does it is a king or a common man; my countryman or not my countryman; whether it be done by an individual villain, or an army of them? If we reason to the root of things we shall find no difference; neither can any just cause be assigned why we should punish in the one case and pardon in the other. Let them call me rebel, and welcome, I feel no concern from it; but I should suffer the misery of devils, were I to make a whore of my soul by swearing allegiance to one whose character is that of a sottish, stupid, stubborn, worthless, brutish man. I conceive likewise a horrid idea in receiving mercy from a being, who at the last day shall be shrieking to the rocks and mountains to cover him, and fleeing with terror from the orphan, the widow, and the slain of America.

There are cases which cannot be overdone by language, and this is one. There are persons, too, who see not the full extent of the evil which threatens them; they solace themselves with hopes that the enemy, if he succeed, will be merciful. It is the madness of folly, to expect mercy from those who have refused to do justice; and even mercy, where conquest is the object, is only a trick of war; the cunning of the fox is as murderous as the violence of the wolf, and we ought to guard equally against both. Howe's first object is, partly by threats and partly by promises, to terrify or seduce the people to

[22]"Saul hath slain his thousands, and David his ten thousands." I Samuel 18:7.
[23]An adaptation of James 2:18.
[24]Home (eastern) counties, and western (backwoods) counties.
[25]Paine quotes the British Declaratory Act of 1766.

deliver up their arms and receive mercy. The ministry[26] recommended the same plan to Gage,[27] and this is what the Tories call making their peace, *"a peace which passeth all understanding" indeed!*[28] A peace which would be the immediate forerunner of a worse ruin than any we have yet thought of. Ye men of Pennsylvania, do reason upon these things! Were the back counties to give up their arms, they would fall an easy prey to the Indians, who are all armed: this perhaps is what some Tories would not be sorry for. Were the home counties to deliver up their arms, they would be exposed to the resentment of the back counties, who would then have it in their power to chastise their defection at pleasure. And were any one state to give up its arms, *that* state must be garrisoned by all Howe's army of Britons and Hessians[29] to preserve it from the anger of the rest. Mutual fear is the principal link in the chain of mutual love, and woe be to that state that breaks the compact. Howe is mercifully inviting you to barbarous destruction, and men must be either rogues or fools that will not see it. I dwell not upon the vapors of imagination; I bring reason to your ears, and, in language as plain as A, B, C, hold up truth to your eyes.

I thank God, that I fear not. I see no real cause for fear. I know our situation well, and can see the way out of it. While our army was collected, Howe dared not risk a battle; and it is no credit to him that he decamped from the White Plains,[30] and waited a mean opportunity to ravage the defenceless Jerseys; but it is great credit to us, that, with a handful of men, we sustained an orderly retreat for near an hundred miles, brought off our ammunition, all our field pieces, the greatest part of our stores, and had four rivers to pass. None can say that our retreat was precipitate, for we were near three weeks in performing it, that the country[31] might have time to come in. Twice we marched back to meet the enemy, and remained out till dark. The sign of fear was not seen in our camp, and had not some of the cowardly and disaffected inhabitants spread false alarms through the country, the Jerseys had never been ravaged. Once more we are again collected and collecting; our new army at both ends of the continent is recruiting fast, and we shall be able to open the next campaign with sixty thousand men, well armed and clothed. This is our situation, and who will may know it. By perseverance and fortitude we have the prospect of a glorious issue; by cowardice and submission, the sad choice of a variety of evils—a ravaged country—a depopulated city—habitations without safety, and slavery without hope—our homes turned into barracks and bawdyhouses for Hessians, and a future race to provide for, whose fathers we shall doubt of. Look on this picture and weep over it! and if there yet remains one thoughtless wretch who believes it not, let him suffer it unlamented.

—Common Sense
1776

[26]I.e., the British government.
[27]General Thomas Gage commanded British forces in America from 1763 to 1775.
[28]"And the peace of God, which passeth all understanding, shall keep your hearts and minds through Christ Jesus." Philippians 4:7.
[29]German mercenaries, from the state of Hesse, fighting for the British.
[30]The Battle of White Plains, north of New York City, October 28, 1776.
[31]I.e., volunteers from throughout the countryside.

Thomas Jefferson 1743–1826

Jefferson was the kind of man the eighteenth century liked to call a polymath, a man of encyclopedic knowledge and accomplishment. He was a politician, statesman, artist, scientist, inventor, patron of education, literary stylist, and servant of the Republic. He served as a member of the Continental Congress (1775–1776), Governor of Virginia (1779–1781), American minister to France (1784–1789), Secretary of State (1790–1793), Vice President (1797–1801), and President of the United States (1801–1809).

He shaped our public schools and proposed the decimal system of American pennies, dimes, and dollars. He commissioned the Lewis and Clark Expedition; he founded the University of Virginia and what became the modern Democratic party. As president, his greatest triumph was the Louisiana Purchase (1803), which doubled the size of the United States and gave it control of the Mississippi River. In his lifetime he worked to establish religious freedom, to end slavery, to weaken the power of entrenched aristocracy, and to assert the idea of man's inalienable rights.

Jefferson was born in central Virginia. When he was seventeen, he was sent to the College of William and Mary at Williamsburg, where he began to collect a library that ultimately grew to more than 10,000 volumes and formed the basis of the Library of Congress. Before he was twenty, he was one of the best-read men in the colony. After graduation he studied law, and in 1769 he was elected to the Virginia colonial legislature, the House of Burgesses. In 1774 he wrote A Summary View of the Rights of British America, *which attacked the colonial authority of Parliament; when the American Revolution began, he was sent with the delegation from Virginia to the Second Continental Congress in Philadelphia.*

Members of the Continental Congress chose Jefferson to draft the Declaration of Independence, in recognition of his wide knowledge of political philosophy and because, as John Adams pointed out, "You write ten times better than I do." Jefferson's aim was to "place before mankind the common sense of the subject, in terms so plain and firm as to command their assent." The Declaration carried the famous pronouncement: "that all men are created equal, that they are endowed by their creator with certain unalienable Rights, that among these are Life, Liberty and the pursuit of Happiness."

Jefferson was an egalitarian who opposed the frigid ceremonies surrounding high office. As president he wore shoes with laces because he considered the more stylish shoebuckles to be undemocratic and dandified. He forbade the national celebration of his birthday and refused to permit the use of his face on coins. He was devoted to the ideal of aristocracy—the "rule of the best"—but he meant an aristocracy of virtue and talent rather than an aristocracy of wealth and family. He was a poor military leader and no orator, yet he ranks with Lincoln among the masters of American political prose. His philosophy and his style are evident throughout his writing and in the architecture with which he sought to express the ideals of the new nation. His neoclassical designs for the Virginia State House; for his home, Monticello; and for the University of Virginia helped give historic, rational, and monumental form to republican building.

Among his other monuments are the eloquent arguments for democracy set forth in his two inaugural addresses and in his voluminous correspondence, over 18,000 letters that are the "richest political correspondence in American history." His Notes on the State of Virginia *(1785) has been judged the most important American political and scientific book of the age. It grew out of answers to inquiries made in 1780 by a French diplomat gathering data on America. His questions were sent to Jefferson, who was serving as wartime Governor of Virginia. Jefferson's reply began as a statistical survey and became an encyclopedic commentary on American life and the ideals of the*

American Enlightenment. It reveals Jefferson's major beliefs, his ideas on art and education, his attitudes toward slavery, his devotion to science and nature, and it sets forth the Jeffersonian democratic faith in the small farmer, the conviction that "those who labor in the earth are the chosen people of God."

After completing his reply in 1781, Jefferson revised the manuscript for publication, partly as a patriotic response to criticism by the famous French naturalist Buffon, who had suggested that, contrary to the hopes of Enlightenment believers, all species, including man, tended to degenerate in the New World. Jefferson's reply in his Notes on the State of Virginia *won an apology from Buffon, but Jefferson's political opponents used the book and his speculation on the age of the earth and the development of man to assert that he had cast doubt on the Christian truth of the Bible and now stood revealed as a "confirmed infidel," a "howling atheist." The very range of Jefferson's accomplishments allowed his enemies to treat him as a satanic villain, a sophisticated humbug.*

In the twentieth century Jefferson has been described as a racist hypocrite, for while he spoke and wrote against slavery and for freedom and equality, he was himself a slaveholder. And recent study of the genetic inheritance of Jefferson's decendents has led to the charge that he fathered a child by one of his slaves. In response, Jefferson's defenders argue that freeing his slaves would not have advanced the struggle against slavery. Instead it would have brought destitution to the freed slaves, left idle and threatened in a land of legalized slavery where former slaves who lacked employment could be reenslaved, by force if necessary. And to the charge that Jefferson fathered a slave child, his defenders answer that the evidence actually proves only that the father was one out of a group that included Jefferson and more than two dozen of his close male relatives.

The debate over the real and imagined contradictions in Jefferson's life and in the lives of other slave-holding early patriots, including George Washington and Patrick Henry, will certainly continue. Nevertheless, for his political genius, for his stand on human freedom, and for the literary power with which he expressed his ideas, Jefferson remains one of the great figures in the history of America.

Jefferson died on July 4, 1826, exactly fifty years after the adoption of the Declaration of Independence. For his tombstone he had ordered an inscription that would record the achievements for which he wanted most to be remembered: "Author of the Declaration of American Independence, of the Statute of Virginia for religious freedom, and Father of the University of Virginia." But a more fitting epitaph was provided by John Adams, who lay dying on that same Fourth of July and who uttered for his last words: "Thomas Jefferson still survives."

FURTHER READING: C. Becker, *The Declaration of Independence,* 1942; D. Malone, *Jefferson and His Time,* 6 vols., 1948–1981; T. Fleming, *The Man from Monticello,* 1969; M. Peterson, *Thomas Jefferson and the New Nation,* 1970; J. Miller, *Thomas Jefferson and Slavery,* 1977; N. Cunningham, *In Pursuit of Reason, The Life of Thomas Jefferson,* 1987; H. Hellenbrand, *The Unfinished Revolution, Education and Politics in the Thought of Thomas Jefferson,* 1990; C. O'Brien, *The Long Affair, Thomas Jefferson and the French Revolution,* 1996; E. Gaustad, *Sworn on the Altar of God, A Religious Biography of Thomas Jefferson,* 1996; J. Ellis, *American Sphinx, The Character of Thomas Jefferson,* 1996; A. Jayne, *Jefferson's Declaration of Independence,* 1998; M. Beran, *Jefferson's Demons,* 2003; R. Bernstein, *Thomas Jefferson,* 2003; C. Hitchens, *Thomas Jefferson, Author of America,* 2005.

TEXTS: *Notes on the State of Virginia,* ed. W. Peden, 1955. Letter to John Adams is from *The Writings of Thomas Jefferson,* ed. P. Ford, 10 vols., 1892–1899. All other selections are from *The Papers of Thomas Jefferson,* ed. J. Boyd et al., 24 vols., 1950–1991. Some spelling and punctuation have been changed to conform more nearly to modern practice.

THE DECLARATION OF INDEPENDENCE[1] AS ADOPTED BY CONGRESS

In Congress, July 4, 1776.

THE UNANIMOUS DECLARATION OF THE THIRTEEN UNITED STATES OF AMERICA,

When in the Course of human events, it becomes necessary for one people to dissolve the political bands which have connected them with another, and to assume among the powers of the earth, the separate and equal station to which the Laws of Nature and of Nature's God entitle them, a decent respect to the opinions of mankind requires that they should declare the causes which impel them to the separation. We hold these truths to be self-evident, that all men are created equal, that they are endowed by their Creator with certain unalienable Rights, that among these are Life, Liberty and the pursuit of Happiness.[2] That to secure these rights, Governments are instituted among Men, deriving their just powers from the consent of the governed, That whenever any Form of Government becomes destructive of these ends, it is the Right of the People to alter or to abolish it, and to institute new Government, laying its foundation on such principles and organizing its powers in such form, as to them shall seem most likely to effect their Safety and Happiness. Prudence, indeed, will dictate that Governments long established should not be changed for light and transient causes; and accordingly all experience hath shewn, that mankind are more disposed to suffer, while evils are sufferable, than to right themselves by abolishing the forms to which they are accustomed. But when a long train of abuses and usurpations, pursuing invariably the same Object evinces a design to reduce them under absolute Despotism, it is their right, it is their duty, to throw off such Government, and to provide New Guards for their future security. Such has been the patient sufferance of these Colonies; and such is now the necessity which constrains them to alter their former Systems of Government. The history of the present King of Great Britain[3] is a history of repeated injuries and usurpations, all having in direct object the establishment of an absolute Tyranny over these States. To prove this, let Facts be submitted to a candid world. He has refused his Assent to Laws, the most wholesome and necessary for the public good. He has forbidden his Governors to pass Laws of immediate and pressing importance, unless suspended in their operation till his Assent should be obtained; and when so suspended, he has utterly neglected to attend to them. He has refused to pass other Laws for the accommodation of large districts of people, unless these people would relinquish the right of Representation in the Legislature, a

[1]The committee to draft the Declaration of Independence began its work on June 11. On June 28 it presented the draft to the Congress. The document was primarily the work of Jefferson with revisions recommended by other members of the committee, especially Franklin and John Adams. The final version, reprinted here, had undergone further revision before it was adopted by the Congress.

[2]John Locke's *Treatises of Civil Government* (1690) had asserted that human rights include life, liberty, and property.

[3]George III (reigned 1760–1820).

right inestimable to them and formidable to tyrants only. He has called together legislative bodies at places unusual, uncomfortable, and distant from the depository of their public Records, for the sole purpose of fatiguing them into compliance with his measures. He has dissolved Representative Houses repeatedly, for opposing with manly firmness his invasions on the rights of the people. He has refused for a long time, after such dissolutions, to cause others to be elected; whereby the Legislative powers, incapable of Annihilation, have returned to the People at large for their exercise; the State remaining in the mean time exposed to all the dangers of invasion from without, and convulsions within. He has endeavoured to prevent the population of these States; for that purpose obstructing the Laws for Naturalization of Foreigners; refusing to pass others to encourage their migrations hither, and raising the conditions of new Appropriations of Lands. He has obstructed the Administration of Justice, by refusing his Assent to Laws for establishing Judiciary powers. He has made Judges dependent on his Will alone, for the tenure of their offices, and the amount and payment of their salaries. He has erected a multitude of New Offices, and sent hither swarms of Officers to harass our people, and eat out their substance. He has kept among us, in times of peace, standing Armies without the Consent of our legislatures. He has affected to render the Military independent of and superior to the Civil power. He has combined with others[4] to subject us to a jurisdiction foreign to our constitution, and unacknowledged by our laws; giving his Assent to their Acts of pretended Legislation: For Quartering large bodies of armed troops among us: For protecting them, by a mock Trial, from punishment for any Murders which they should commit on the Inhabitants of these States: For cutting off our Trade with all parts of the world: For imposing Taxes on us without our Consent: For depriving us in many cases of the benefits of Trial by Jury: For transporting us beyond Seas to be tried for pretended offences: For abolishing the free System of English Laws in a neighbouring Province,[5] establishing therein an Arbitrary government, and enlarging its Boundaries so as to render it at once an example and fit instrument for introducing the same absolute rule into these Colonies: For taking away our Charters, abolishing our most valuable Laws, and altering fundamentally the Forms of our Governments: For suspending our own Legislatures, and declaring themselves invested with power to legislate for us in all cases whatsoever. He has abdicated Government here, by declaring us out of his Protection and waging War against us. He has plundered our seas, ravaged our Coasts, burnt our towns, and destroyed the Lives of our people. He is at this time transporting large Armies of foreign Mercenaries[6] to compleat the works of death, desolation and tyranny, already begun with circumstances of Cruelty & perfidy scarcely paralleled in the most barbarous ages, and totally unworthy the Head of a civilized nation. He has constrained our fellow Citizens taken Captive on the high Seas to bear Arms against their Country, to become the executioners of their friends and Brethren, or to fall themselves by their Hands. He has excited domestic insurrections amongst us,

[4]The British Parliament.

[5]The Quebec Act (1774) recognized the Roman Catholic religion in Quebec and extended the province's boundaries to the Ohio River. New England colonists considered it one of the anticolonial "Intolerable Acts" of 1774.

[6]German soldiers, mostly Hessians, hired by the British.

and has endeavoured to bring on the inhabitants of our frontiers, the merciless Indian Savages, whose known rule of warfare, is an undistinguished destruction of all ages, sexes and conditions. In every stage of these Oppressions We have Petitioned for Redress in the most humble terms: Our repeated Petitions have been answered only by repeated injury. A Prince, whose character is thus marked by every act which may define a Tyrant, is unfit to be the ruler of a free people. Nor have We been wanting in attentions to our British brethren. We have warned them from time to time of attempts by their legislature to extend an unwarrantable jurisdiction over us. We have reminded them of the circumstances of our emigration and settlement here. We have appealed to their native justice and magnanimity, and we have conjured them by the ties of our common kindred to disavow these usurpations, which, would inevitably interrupt our connections and correspondence. They too have been deaf to the voice of justice and of consanguinity. We must, therefore, acquiesce in the necessity, which denounces[7] our Separation, and hold them, as we hold the rest of mankind, Enemies in War, in Peace Friends.

We, therefore, the Representatives of the United States of America, in General Congress, Assembled, appealing to the Supreme Judge of the world for the rectitude of our intentions, do, in the Name, and by Authority of the good People of these Colonies, solemnly publish and declare, That these United Colonies are, and of right ought to be Free and Independent States; that they are Absolved from all Allegiance to the British Crown, and that all political connection between them and the State of Great Britain, is and ought to be totally dissolved; and that as Free and Independent States, they have full Power to levy War, conclude Peace, contract Alliances, establish Commerce, and to do all other Acts and Things which Independent States may of right do. And for the support of this Declaration, with a firm reliance on the protection of divine Providence, we mutually pledge to each other our Lives, our Fortunes and our sacred Honor.

from *NOTES ON THE STATE OF VIRGINIA*

from QUERY V:[1] CASCADES

The *Natural Bridge*,[2] the most sublime of Nature's works, though not comprehended under the present head,[3] must not be pretermitted.[4] It is on the ascent of a hill, which seems to have been cloven through its length by some great convulsion. The fissure, just at the bridge, is, by some admeasurements,

[7]Announces.

[1]Jefferson's *Notes on the State of Virginia* was a response to a series of "Queries" by the French government regarding the geography, resources, inhabitants, and civilization of America. Using the form of responses to the "Queries," Jefferson described Virginia and its inhabitants and presented his views of government, slavery, and the "Jeffersonian" agrarian ideal, and he gave a detailed rebuttal to the assertion of European naturalists that the environment of the New World caused all species to degenerate.

[2]The Natural Bridge stands on property Jefferson owned near Lexington, Virginia.

[3]I.e., though not covered by the present heading, "Cascades." [4]Omitted.

270 feet deep, by others only 205. It is about 45 feet wide at the bottom, and 90 feet at the top; this of course determines the length of the bridge, and its height from the water. Its breadth in the middle, is about 60 feet, but more at the ends, and the thickness of the mass at the summit of the arch, about 40 feet. A part of this thickness is constituted by a coat of earth, which gives growth to many large trees. The residue, with the hill on both sides, is one solid rock of limestone. The arch approaches the semi-elliptical form; but the larger axis of the ellipsis, which would be the cord of the arch, is many times longer than the semi-axis which gives its height. Though the sides of this bridge are provided in some parts with a parapet of fixed rocks, yet few men have resolution to walk to them and look over into the abyss. You involuntarily fall on your hands and feet, creep to the parapet and peep over it. Looking down from this height about a minute, gave me a violent head ache. This painful sensation is relieved by a short, but pleasing view of the Blue ridge along the fissure downwards, and upwards by that of the Short hills, which, with the Purgatory mountain is a divergence from the North ridge; and, descending then to the valley below, the sensation becomes delightful in the extreme. It is impossible for the emotions, arising from the sublime, to be felt beyond what they are here: so beautiful an arch, so elevated, so light, and springing, as it were, up to heaven, the rapture of the spectator is really indescribable! The fissure continues deep and narrow and, following the margin of the stream upwards about three eights of a mile you arrive at a limestone cavern, less remarkable, however, for height and extent than those before described. Its entrance into the hill is but a few feet above the bed of the stream. This bridge is in the county of Rockbridge, to which it has given name, and affords a public and commodious passage over a valley, which cannot be crossed elsewhere for a considerable distance. The stream passing under it is called Cedar creek. It is a water[5] of James river, and sufficient in the driest seasons to turn a grist-mill, though its fountain[6] is not more than two miles above.

from QUERY VI: PRODUCTIONS MINERAL, VEGETABLE AND ANIMAL

The opinion advanced by the Count de Buffon,[1] is 1. That the animals common both the old and new world, are smaller in the latter. 2. That those peculiar to the new, are on a smaller scale. 3. That those which have been domesticated in both, have degenerated in America: and 4. That on the whole it exhibits fewer species. . . .

Hitherto I have considered this hypothesis as applied to brute animals only, and not in its extension to the man of America, whether aboriginal or transplanted. It is the opinion of Mons. de Buffon that the former furnishes no exception to it: "Although the savage of the new world is about the same

[5]Tributary. [6]Source, origin.

[1]Georges-Louis Leclerc de Buffon (1707–1788), French naturalist who advanced the idea of the degeneration of New World species, in his 44-volume *Natural History* (1749–1804), the most widely read scientific work of the century. Jefferson sent Buffon a copy of *Notes on the State of Virginia* together with the skin of a panther and the "skin, the skeleton, and horns of a moose," to convince Buffon of the fallacy of his theories. Buffon was convinced.

height as man in our world, this does not suffice for him to constitute an exception to the general fact that all living nature has become smaller on that continent. The savage is feeble, and has small organs of generation; he has neither hair nor beard, and no ardor whatever for his female; although swifter than the European because he is better accustomed to running, he is, on the other hand, less strong in body; he is also less sensitive, and yet more timid and cowardly; he has no vivacity, no activity of mind; the activity of his body is less an exercise, a voluntary motion, than a necessary action caused by want; relieve him of hunger and thirst, and you deprive him of the active principle of all his movements; he will rest stupidly upon his legs or lying down entire days. There is no need for seeking further the cause of the isolated mode of life of these savages and their repugnance for society; the most precious spark of the fire of nature has been refused to them; they lack ardor for their females, and consequently have no love for their fellow men; not knowing this strongest and most tender of all affections, their other feelings are also cold and languid; they love their parents and children but little; the most intimate of all ties, the family connection, binds them therefore but loosely together; between family and family there is no tie at all; hence they have no communion, no commonwealth, no state of society. Physical love constitutes their only morality; their heart is icy, their society cold, and their rule harsh. They look upon their wives only as servants for all work, or as beasts of burden, which they load without consideration with the burden of their hunting, and which they compel without mercy, without gratitude, to perform tasks which are often beyond their strength. They have only few children, and they take little care of them. Everywhere the original defect appears: they are indifferent because they have little sexual capacity, and this indifference to the other sex is the fundamental defect which weakens their nature, prevents its development, and—destroying the very germs of life—uproots society at the same time. Man is here no exception to the general rule. Nature, by refusing him the power of love, has treated him worse and lowered him deeper than any animal." An afflicting picture indeed, which, for the honor of human nature, I am glad to believe has no original. Of the Indian of South America I know nothing; for I would not honor with the appelation of knowledge, what I derive from the fables published of them. These I believe to be just as true as the fables of Aesop. This belief is founded on what I have seen of man, white, red, and black, and what has been written of him by authors, enlightened themselves, and writing amidst an enlightened people. The Indian of North America being more within our reach, I can speak of him somewhat from my own knowledge, but more from the information of others better acquainted with him, and on whose truth and judgment I can rely.[2] From these sources I am able to say, in contradiction to this representation, that he is neither defective in ardor, nor more impotent with his female, than the white reduced to the same diet and exercise; that he is brave, when an enterprize depends on bravery; education with him making the point of honor consist in the destruction of an enemy

[2]As a boy, growing up on the frontier in Virginia, Jefferson had become "very familiar" with the Indians.

by stratagem, and in the preservation of his own person free from injury; or perhaps this is nature; while it is education which teaches us to honor force more than finesse; that he will defend himself against an host of enemies, always choosing to be killed, rather than to surrender, though it be to the whites, who he knows will treat him well; that in other situations also he meets death with more deliberation, and endures tortures with a firmness unknown almost to religious enthusiasm with us; that he is affectionate to his children, careful of them, and indulgent in the extreme; that his affections comprehend his other connections, weakening, as with us, from circle to circle, as they recede from the center; that his friendships are strong and faithful to the uttermost extremity; that his sensibility is keen, even the warriors weeping most bitterly on the loss of their children, though in general they endeavor to appear superior to human events; that his vivacity and activity of mind is equal to ours in the same situation, hence his eagerness for hunting, and for games of chance. The women are submitted to unjust drudgery. This I believe is the case with every barbarous people. With such, force is law. The stronger sex therefore imposes on the weaker. It is civilization alone which replaces women in the enjoyment of their natural equality. That first teaches us to subdue the selfish passions and to respect those rights in others which we value in ourselves. Were we in equal barbarism, our females would be equal drudges. The man with them is less strong than with us, but their woman stronger than ours; and both for the same obvious reason: because our man and their woman is habituated to labour, and formed by it. With both races the sex which is indulged with ease is least athletic. An Indian man is small in the hand and wrist for the same reason for which a sailor is large and strong in the arms and shoulders, and a porter in the legs and thighs. They raise fewer children than we do. The causes of this are to be found, not in a difference of nature but of circumstance. The women very frequently attending the men in their parties of war and of hunting, child-bearing becomes extremely inconvenient to them. It is said, therefore, that they have learnt the practice of procuring abortion by the use of some vegetable and that it even extends to prevent conception for a considerable time after. During these parties they are exposed to numerous hazards, to excessive exertions, to the greatest extremities of hunger. Even at their homes the nation depends for food, through a certain part of every year, on the gleanings of the forest; that is, they experience a famine once in every year. With all animals, if the female be badly fed, or not fed at all, her young perish; and if both male and female be reduced to like want, generation becomes less active, less productive. To the obstacles then of want and hazard, which nature has opposed to the multiplication of wild animals for the purpose of restraining their numbers within certain bounds, those of labour and of voluntary abortion are added with the Indian. No wonder then if they multiply less than we do. Where food is regularly supplied, a single farm will show more of cattle, than a whole country of forests can of buffaloes. The same Indian women, when married to white traders, who feed them and their children plentifully and regularly, who exempt them from excessive drudgery, who keep them stationary and unexposed to accident, produce and raise as many children as the white women.

. . .

Before we condemn the Indians of this continent as wanting genius,[3] we must consider that letters have not yet been introduced among them. Were we to compare them in their present state with the Europeans north of the Alps, when the Roman arms and arts first crossed those mountains, the comparison would be unequal, because, at that time, those parts of Europe were swarming with numbers; because numbers produce emulation, and multiply the chances of improvement, and one improvement begets another. Yet I may safely ask, How many good poets, how many able mathematicians, how many great inventors in arts or sciences, had Europe north of the Alps then produced? And it was sixteen centuries after this before a Newton could be formed. I do not mean to deny, that there are varieties in the race of man, distinguished by their powers both of body and mind. I believe there are, as I see to be the case in the races of other animals. I only mean to suggest a doubt, whether the bulk and faculties of animals depend on the side of the Atlantic on which their food happens to grow, or which furnishes the elements of which they are compounded? Whether nature has enlisted herself as a Cis[4] or Trans-Atlantic partisan? I am induced to suspect, there has been more eloquence than sound reasoning displayed in support of this theory, that it is one of those cases where the judgment has been seduced by a glowing pen; and whilst I render every tribute of honor and esteem to the celebrated zoologist, who has added, and is still adding, so many precious things to the treasures of science, I must doubt whether in this instance he has not cherished error also, by lending her for a moment his vivid imagination and bewitching language.

So far the Count de Buffon has carried this new theory of the tendency of nature to belittle her productions on this side of the Atlantic. Its application to the race of whites, transplanted from Europe, remained for the Abbé Raynal.[5] "One must be astonished (he says) that America has not yet produced one good poet, one able mathematician, one man of genius in a single art or a single science." "America has not yet produced one good poet." When we shall have existed as a people as long as the Greeks did before they produced a Homer, the Romans a Virgil, the French a Racine and Voltaire, the English a Shakespeare and Milton, should this reproach be still true, we will enquire from what unfriendly causes it has proceeded that the other countries of Europe and quarters of the earth shall not have inscribed any name in the roll of poets. But neither has America produced "one able mathematician, one man of genius in a single art or a single science." In war we have produced a Washington, whose memory will be adored while liberty shall have votaries, whose name will triumph over time, and will in future ages assume its just station among the most celebrated worthies of the world, when that wretched philosophy shall be forgotten which would have arranged him among the degeneracies of nature. In physics we have produced a Franklin, than whom no one of the present age has made more important discoveries, nor has enriched philosophy with more, or more ingenious solutions of the phenomena of nature. We have

[3]Mental ability.
[4]"On this side," i.e., European.
[5]Guillaume Thomas François Raynal (1713–1796), French writer and historian.

supposed Mr. Rittenhouse[6] second to no astronomer living; that in genius he must be the first, because he is self-taught. As an artist he has exhibited as great a proof of mechanical genius as the world has ever produced. He has not indeed made a world; but he has by imitation approached nearer its Maker than any man who has lived from the creation to this day.[7] As in philosophy and war, so in government, in oratory, in painting, in the plastic art, we might show that America, though but a child of yesterday, has already given hopeful proofs of genius, as well of the nobler kinds, which arouse the best feelings of man, which call him into action, which substantiate his freedom, and conduct him to happiness, as of the subordinate, which serve to amuse him only. We therefore suppose, that this reproach is as unjust as it is unkind; and that, of the geniuses which adorn the present age, America contributes its full share. For comparing it with those countries, where genius is most cultivated, where are the most excellent models for art, and scaffoldings for the attainment of science, as France and England for instance, we calculate thus. The United States contain three millions of inhabitants; France twenty millions; and the British islands ten. We produce a Washington, a Franklin, a Rittenhouse. France then should have half a dozen in each of these lines, and Great-Britain half that number, equally eminent. It may be true, that France has; we are but just becoming acquainted with her, and our acquaintance so far gives us high ideas of the genius of her inhabitants. It would be injuring too many of them to name particularly a Voltaire, a Buffon, the constellation of Encyclopedists,[8] the Abbé Raynal himself, &c. &c. We therefore have reason to believe she can produce her full quota of genius. The present war having so long cut off all communication with Great Britain, we are not able to make a fair estimate of the state of science in that country. The spirit in which she wages war is the only sample before our eyes, and that does not seem the legitimate offspring either of science or of civilization. The sun of her glory is fast descending to the horizon. Her philosophy has crossed the Channel, her freedom the Atlantic, and herself seems passing to that awful dissolution, whose issue is not given human foresight to scan.

. . .

from QUERY XVII: RELIGION

The first settlers in this country were emigrants from England, of the English church, just at a point of time when it was flushed with complete victory over the religious of all other persuasions. Possessed, as they became, of the powers of making, administering, and executing the laws, they showed equal intolerance in this country with their Presbyterian brethren,[1] who had emigrated to the northern government. . . . The Anglicans[2] retained full

[6]David Rittenhouse (1732–1796), American scientist and builder of mathematical instruments.

[7]Rittenhouse built orreries, planetarium models showing the positions and movements of bodies in the solar system.

[8]The contributors to the French *Encyclopedia* (1751–1772), which purported to embody all enlightened thought of the age.

[1]The Puritans of New England. [2]Members of the Church of England.

possession of the country about a century. Other opinions began then to creep in, and the great care of the government to support their own church, having begotten an equal degree of indolence in its clergy, two-thirds of the people had become dissenters at the commencement of the present revolution.[3] The laws indeed were still oppressive on them, but the spirit of the one party had subsided into moderation, and of the other had risen to a degree of determination which commanded respect.

The present state of our laws on the subject of religion is this. The convention of May 1776,[4] in their declaration of rights, declared it to be a truth, and a natural right, that the exercise of religion should be free. . . . The same convention . . . repealed all *acts of parliament* which had rendered criminal the maintaining any opinions in matters of religion, the forbearing to repair to church,[5] and the exercising any mode of worship; and suspended the laws giving salaries to the clergy, which suspension was made perpetual in October 1779. Statutory oppressions in religion being thus wiped away, we remain at present under those only imposed by the common law, or by our own acts of assembly. . . . The legitimate powers of government extend to such acts only as are injurious to others. But it does me no injury for my neighbour to say there are twenty gods, or no god. It neither picks my pocket nor breaks my leg. If it be said, his testimony in a court of justice cannot be relied on, reject it then, and be the stigma on him. Constraint may make him worse by making him a hypocrite, but it will never make him a truer man. It may fix him obstinately in his errors, but will not cure them. Reason and free enquiry are the only effectual agents against error. Give a loose to them, they will support the true religion, by bringing every false one to their tribunal, to the test of their investigation. They are the natural enemies of error, and of error only. Had not the Roman government permitted free enquiry, Christianity could never have been introduced. Had not free enquiry been indulged, at the era of the Reformation, the corruptions of Christianity could not have been purged away. If it be restrained now, the present corruptions will be protected, and new ones encouraged. Was the government to prescribe to us our medicine and diet, our bodies would be in such keeping as our souls are now. Thus in France the emetic was once forbidden as a medicine, and the potato as an article of food. Government is just as infallible too when it fixes systems in physics. Galileo[6] was sent to the Inquisition for affirming that the earth was a sphere: the government had declared it to be as flat as a trencher,[7] and Galileo was obliged to abjure[8] his error. This error however at length prevailed, the earth became a globe, and Descartes[9] declared it was whirled round its axis by a vortex. The government in which he lived was wise enough to see that this was no question of civil jurisdiction, or we should all have been involved by authority in vortices. In fact, the vortices have been exploded, and the Newtonian principle of gravitation is now more firmly established, on the basis of reason, than it would be were the government to step in, and to

[3]The American Revolution (1775–1783).

[4]The Virginia Convention of 1776, assembled to prepare a state constitution, adopted (June 12) the Virginia Declaration of Rights, establishing freedom of religion.

[5]I.e., failure to attend church.

[6]Italian astronomer (1564–1642). In 1633 he was tried in Rome by the Inquisition for his heretical scientific assertions.

[7]Platter. [8]Renounce, retract. [9]French mathematician and philosopher (1596–1650).

make it an article of necessary faith. Reason and experiment have been indulged, and error has fled before them. It is error alone which needs the support of government. Truth can stand by itself. Subject opinion to coercion: whom will you make your inquisitors? Fallible men; men governed by bad passions, by private as well as public reasons. And why subject it to coercion? To produce uniformity. But is uniformity of opinion desireable? No more than of face and stature. Introduce the bed of Procrustes[10] then, and as there is danger that the large men may beat the small, make us all of a size, by lopping the former and stretching the latter. Difference of opinion is advantageous in religion. The several sects perform the office of a censor morum[11] over each other. Is uniformity attainable? Millions of innocent men, women, and children, since the introduction of Christianity, have been burnt, tortured, fined, imprisoned; yet we have not advanced one inch towards uniformity. What has been the effect of coercion? To make one half the world fools, and the other half hypocrites. To support roguery and error all over the earth. Let us reflect that it is inhabited by a thousand millions of people. That these profess probably a thousand different systems of religion. That ours is but one of that thousand. That if there be but one right, and ours that one, we should wish to see the 999 wandering sects gathered into the fold of truth. But against such a majority we cannot effect this by force. Reason and persuasion are the only practicable instruments. To make way for these, free enquiry must be indulged; and how can we wish others to indulge it while we refuse it ourselves. But every state, says an inquisitor, has established some religion. No two, say I, have established the same. Is this a proof of the infallibility of establishments? Our sister states of Pennsylvania and New York, however, have long subsisted without any establishment at all. The experiment was new and doubtful when they made it. It has answered beyond conception. They flourish infinitely. Religion is well supported; of various kinds, indeed, but all good enough; all sufficient to preserve peace and order: or if a sect arises, whose tenets would subvert morals, good sense has fair play, and reasons and laughs it out of doors, without suffering the state to be troubled with it. They do not hang more malefactors than we do. They are not more disturbed with religious dissensions. On the contrary, their harmony is unparalleled, and can be ascribed to nothing but their unbounded tolerance, because there is no other circumstance in which they differ from every nation on earth. They have made the happy discovery, that the way to silence religious disputes, is to take no notice of them. Let us too give this experiment fair play, and get rid, while we may, of these tyrannical laws. It is true, we are as yet secured against them by the spirit of the times. I doubt whether the people of this country would suffer an execution for heresy, or a three years imprisonment for not comprehending the mysteries of the Trinity. But is the spirit of the people an infallible, a permanent reliance? Is it government? Is this the kind of protection we receive in return for the rights we give up? Besides, the spirit of the times may alter, will alter. Our rules will become corrupt, our people careless. A single zealot may commence persecutor, and better men be his victims. It can never be too often repeated,

[10]In Greek myth, Procrustes amputated or stretched the legs of his victims so they would fit his iron bed.

[11]Censor of morals.

that the time for fixing every essential right on a legal basis is while our rulers are honest, and ourselves united. From the conclusion of this war we shall be going down hill. It will not then be necessary to resort every moment to the people for support. They will be forgotten, therefore, and their rights disregarded. They will forget themselves, but in the sole faculty of making money, and will never think of uniting to effect a due respect for their rights. The shackles, therefore, which shall not be knocked off at the conclusion of this war, will remain on us long, will be made heavier and heavier, till our rights shall revive or expire in a convulsion.

from QUERY XVIII: MANNERS

It is difficult to determine on the standard by which the manners of a nation may be tried, whether *catholic,*[1] or *particular.* It is more difficult for a native to bring to that standard the manners of his own nation, familiarized to him by habit. There must doubtless be an unhappy influence on the manners of our people produced by the existence of slavery among us. The whole commerce between master and slave is a perpetual exercise of the most boisterous passions, the most unremitting despotism on the one part, and degrading submissions on the other. Our children see this, and learn to imitate it; for man is an imitative animal. This quality is the germ of all education in him. From his cradle to his grave he is learning to do what he sees others do. If a parent could find no motive either in his philanthrophy or his self-love, for restraining the intemperance of passion towards his slave, it should always be a sufficient one that his child is present. But generally it is not sufficient. The parent storms, the child looks on, catches the lineaments of wrath, puts on the same airs in the circle of smaller slaves, gives a loose to his worst of passions, and thus nursed, educated, and daily exercised in tyranny, cannot but be stamped by it with odious peculiarities. The man must be a prodigy who can retain his manners and morals undepraved by such circumstances. And with what execration should the statesman be loaded, who permitting one half the citizens thus to trample on the rights of the other, transforms those into despots, and these into enemies, destroys the morals of the one part, and the *amor patriæ*[2] of the other. For if a slave can have a country in this world, it must be any other in preference to that in which he is born to live and labour for another; in which he must lock up the faculties of his nature, contribute as far as depends on his individual endeavours to the evanishment[3] of the human race, or entail[4] his own miserable condition on the endless generations proceeding from him. With the morals of the people, their industry also is destroyed. For in a warm climate, no man will labour for himself who can make another labour for him. This is so true, that of the proprietors of slaves a very small proportion indeed are ever seen to labour. And can the liberties of a nation be thought secure when we have removed their only firm basis, a conviction in the minds of the people that these liberties are of the gift of God? That they are not to be violated but with his wrath? Indeed I tremble for my country when I reflect

[1]Universal, general. [2]Latin: patriotism, love of country. [3]Death. [4]Impose.

that God is just; that his justice cannot sleep for ever; that considering numbers, nature and natural means only, a revolution of the wheel of fortune, an exchange of situation, is among possible events; that it may become probable by supernatural interference! The Almighty has no attribute which can take side with us in such a contest. But it is impossible to be temperate and to pursue this subject through the various considerations of policy, of morals, of history natural and civil. We must be contented to hope they will force their way into every one's mind. I think a change already perceptible, since the origin of the present revolution. The spirit of the master is abating, that of the slave rising from the dust, his condition mollifying, the way I hope preparing, under the auspices of heaven, for a total emancipation, and that this is disposed, in the order of events, to be with the consent of the masters, rather than by their extirpation.

from QUERY XIX: MANUFACTURES

The political economists of Europe have established it as a principle that every state should endeavour to manufacture for itself; and this principle, like many others, we transfer to America, without calculating the difference of circumstance which should often produce a difference of result. In Europe the lands are either cultivated or locked up against the cultivator. Manufacture must therefore be resorted to of necessity not of choice, to support the surplus of their people. But we have an immensity of land courting the industry of the husbandman.[1] Is it best then that all our citizens should be employed in its improvement, or that one half should be called off from that to exercise manufactures and handicraft arts for the other? Those who labour in the earth are the chosen people of God, if ever he had a chosen people, whose breasts he has made his peculiar deposit for substantial and genuine virtue. It is the focus in which he keeps alive that sacred fire, which otherwise might escape from the face of the earth. Corruption of morals in the mass of cultivators is a phenomenon of which no age nor nation has furnished an example. It is the mark set on those, who not looking up to heaven, to their own soil and industry, as does the husbandman, for their subsistance, depend for it on the casualties and caprice of customers. Dependence begets subservience and venality, suffocates the germ of virtue, and prepares fit tools for the designs of ambition. This, the natural progress and consequence of the arts, has sometimes perhaps been retarded by accidental circumstances: but, generally speaking, the proportion which the aggregate of the other classes of citizens bears in any state to that of its husbandmen, is the proportion of its unsound to its healthy parts, and is a good-enough barometer whereby to measure its degree of corruption. While we have land to labour then, let us never wish to see our citizens occupied at a work-bench, or twirling a distaff.[2] Carpenters, masons, smiths, are wanting[3] in husbandry; but, for the general operations of manufacture, let our work-shops remain in Europe. It is better to carry provisions and materials to workmen there, than bring them to the provisions and materials, and with them their

[1]Farmer. [2]The stick on which wool or cotton is wound in spinning thread. [3]Needed.

manners and principles. The loss by the transportation of commodities across the Atlantic will be made up in happiness and permanence of government. The mobs of great cities add just so much to the support of pure government, as sores do to the strength of the human body. It is the manners and spirit of a people which preserve a republic in vigour. A degeneracy in these is a canker which soon eats to the heart of its laws and constitution.

1780–1785 1785

TO JAMES MADISON

DEAR SIR Paris Dec. 20. 1787.

. . . The season admitting only of operations in the Cabinet,[1] and these being in a great measure secret, I have little to fill a letter. I will therefore make up the deficiency by adding a few words on the Constitution proposed by our Convention.[2] I like much the general idea of framing a government which should go on of itself peaceably, without needing continual recurrence to the state legislatures. I like the organization of the government into Legislative, Judiciary and Executive. I like the power given the Legislature to levy taxes; and for that reason solely approve of the greater house being chosen by the people directly.[3] For tho' I think a house chosen by them will be very illy qualified to legislate for the Union, for foreign nations &c. yet this evil does not weigh against the good of preserving inviolate the fundamental principle that the people are not to be taxed but by representatives chosen immediately by themselves. I am captivated by the compromise of the opposite claims of the great and little states, of the latter to equal, and the former to proportional influence.[4] I am much pleased too with the substitution of the method of voting by persons, instead of that of voting by states; and I like the negative given to the Executive with a third of either house,[5] though I should have liked it better had the Judiciary been associated for that purpose, or invested with a similar and separate power. There are other good things of less moment. I will now add what I do not like. First the omission of a bill of rights[6] providing clearly and without the aid of sophisms[7] for freedom of religion, freedom of the press, protection against standing armies, restriction against monopolies, the eternal and unremitting force of the habeas

[1]The French government. Jefferson was serving in Paris as American minister to France (1785–1789) and corresponding with Madison in America.

[2]The Constitutional Convention that met in Philadelphia, May–September 1787.

[3]Article I of the Constitution gave the House of Representatives the sole right to introduce tax bills. Members of the Senate were to be chosen by state legislatures; members of the House by the direct vote of the people. The selection of Senators was changed in 1913 by the 17th Amendment.

[4]The "Great Compromise," in which it was agreed that the number of Representatives in the House was to be based on population, the number of Senators to be two from each state.

[5]Article I of the Constitution gave the president power to veto legislation and the Congress power to override such a veto with a two-thirds majority vote.

[6]The Bill of Rights, the first ten amendments to the Constitution, was not ratified by the states and made part of the Constitution until 1791.

[7]Specious arguments.

corpus laws, and trials by jury in all matters of fact triable by the laws of the land and not by the law of Nations. To say, as Mr. Wilson[8] does, that a bill of rights was not necessary because all is reserved in the case of the general government which is not given, while in the particular ones all is given which is not reserved might do for the audience to whom it was addressed, but is surely *gratis dictum,*[9] opposed by strong inferences from the body of the instrument, as well as from the omission of the clause of our present confederation which had declared that in express terms. It was a hard conclusion to say because there has been no uniformity among the states as to the cases triable by jury, because some have been so incautious as to abandon this mode of trial, therefore the more prudent states shall be reduced to the same level of calamity. It would have been much more just and wise to have concluded the other way that as most of the states had judiciously preserved this palladium,[10] those who had wandered should be brought back to it, and to have established general right instead of general wrong. Let me add that a bill of rights is what the people are entitled to against every government on earth, general or particular, and what no just government should refuse, or rest on inference. The second feature I dislike, and greatly dislike, is the abandonment in every instance of the necessity of rotation in office, and most particularly in the case of the President. Experience concurs with reason in concluding that the first magistrate will always be re-elected if the constitution permits it. He is then an officer for life. This once observed it becomes of so much consequence to certain nations to have a friend or a foe at the head of our affairs that they will interfere with money and with arms. A Galloman or an Angloman[11] will be supported by the nation he befriends. If once elected, and at a second or third election outvoted by one or two votes, he will pretend false votes, foul play, hold possession of the reins of government, be supported by the states voting for him, especially if they are the central ones lying in a compact body themselves and separating their opponents; and they will be aided by one nation of Europe, while the majority are aided by another. The election of a President of America some years hence will be much more interesting to certain nations of Europe than ever the election of a king of Poland was. Reflect on all the instances in history ancient and modern, of elective monarchies, and say if they do not give foundation for my fears, the Roman emperors, the popes, while they were of any importance, the German emperors till they became hereditary in practice, the kings of Poland, the Deys of the Ottoman dependencies.[12] It may be said that if elections are to be attended with these disorders, the seldomer they are renewed the better. But experience shows that the only way to prevent disorder is to render them uninteresting by frequent changes. An incapacity to be elected a second time would have been the only effectual preventative. The power of removing him every fourth year by the vote of the people is a power which will not be exercised. The king of Poland is removable every day by the Diet,[13] yet he is never removed. Smaller objections are the appeal in fact as

[8]James Wilson (1742–1798), Congressman and delegate to the Constitutional Convention. He was a member of the committee chosen to draft the Constitution.

[9]Latin: a gratuitous remark. [10]Safeguard. [11]Frenchman or Englishman.

[12]Governors of Turkish territories. [13]Legislature.

well as law, and the binding all persons Legislative, Executive and Judiciary by oath to maintain that constitution. I do not pretend to decide what would be the best method of procuring the establishment of the manifold good things in this constitution, and of getting rid of the bad. Whether by adopting it in hopes of future amendment, or, after it has been duly weighted and canvassed by the people, after seeing the parts they generally dislike, and those they generally approve, to say to them "We see now what you wish. Send together your deputies again, let them frame a constitution for you omitting what you have condemned, and establishing the powers you approve. Even these will be a great addition to the energy of your government." At all events I hope you will not be discouraged from other trials, if the present one should fail of its full effect. I have thus told you freely what I like and dislike, merely as a matter of curiosity, for I know your own judgment has been formed on all these points after having heard every thing which could be urged on them. I own I am not a friend to a very energetic government. It is always oppressive. The late rebellion in Massachusetts[14] has given more alarm than I think it should have done. Calculate that one rebellion in 13 states in the course of 11 years is but one for each state in a century and a half. No country should be so long without one. Nor will any degree of power in the hands of government prevent insurrections. France with all its despotism, and two or three hundred thousand men always in arms, has had three insurrections in the three years I have been here in every one of which greater numbers were engaged than in Massachusetts and a great deal more blood was spilt. In Turkey, which Montesquieu[15] supposes more despotic, insurrections are the events of every day. In England, where the hand of power is lighter than here[16] but heavier than with us, they happen every half dozen years. Compare again the ferocious depredations of their insurgents with the order, the moderation and the almost self extinguishment of ours. After all, it is my principle that the will of the Majority should always prevail. If they approve the proposed Convention in all its parts, I shall concur in it cheerfully, in hopes that they will amend it whenever they shall find it work wrong. I think our governments will remain virtuous for many centuries, as long as they are chiefly agricultural; and this will be as long as there shall be vacant lands in any part of America. When they get piled upon one another in large cities, as in Europe, they will become corrupt as in Europe. Above all things I hope the education of the common people will be attended to, convinced that on their good sense we may rely with the most security for the preservation of a due degree of liberty. I have tired you by this time with my disquisitions and will therefore only add assurances of the sincerity of those sentiments of esteem and attachment with which I am Dear Sir your affectionate friend & servant,

TH: JEFFERSON

[14]Shays' Rebellion (1786), an uprising of Massachusetts farmers and debtors, put down by the state militia. The inability of the Congress to raise an army to suppress the rebellion revealed the weakness of the Articles of Confederation under which the federal government operated and helped lead to the calling of the Constitutional Convention.

[15]Charles Louis de Secondat, baron de Montesquieu (1689–1755), French political philosopher.

[16]Jefferson is writing from Paris.

P.S. The instability of our laws is really an immense evil. I think it would be well to provide in our constitutions that there shall always be a twelvemonth between the ingrossing[17] a bill and passing it; that it should then be offered to its passage without changing a word; and that if circumstances should be thought to require a speedier passage, it should take two thirds of both houses instead of a bare majority.

TO JOHN ADAMS

MONTICELLO OCTOBER 28, 1813.

DEAR SIR,—According to the reservation between us, of taking up one of the subjects of our correspondence at a time,[1] I turn to your letters of August the 16th and September the 2d.

. . .

I agree with you that there is a natural aristocracy among men. The grounds of this are virtue and talents. Formerly, bodily powers gave place among the *aristoi.*[2] But since the invention of gunpowder has armed the weak as well as the strong with missile death, bodily strength, like beauty, good humor, politeness and other accomplishments, has become but an auxiliary ground for distinction. There is also an artificial aristocracy, founded on wealth and birth, without either virtue or talents; for with these it would belong to the first class. The natural aristocracy I consider as the most precious gift of nature, for the instruction, the trusts, and government of society. And indeed, it would have been inconsistent in creation to have formed man for the social state, and not to have provided virtue and wisdom enough to manage the concerns of the society. May we not even say that that form of government is the best which provides the most effectually for a pure selection of these natural *aristoi* into the offices of government? The artificial aristocracy is a mischievous ingredient in government, and provision should be made to prevent its ascendency. On the question, what is the best provision, you and I differ; but we differ as rational friends, using the free exercise of our own reason, and mutually indulging its errors. You think it best to put the *pseudo-aristoi*[3] into a separate chamber of legislation, where they may be hindered from doing mischief by their co-ordinate branches, and where, also, they may be a protection to wealth against the agrarian and plundering enterprises of the majority of the people. I think that to give them power in order to prevent them from doing mischief, is arming them for it, and increasing instead of remedying the evil. For if the co-ordinate branches can arrest their action,

[17]Writing or submitting.

[1]In 1812, John Adams and Jefferson, who had been bitter political enemies, renewed their friendship and their correspondence, which lasted for the remaining fourteen years of their lives. As Adams explained, "You and I ought not to die, before we have explained ourselves to each other." They remained fundamentally apart on one point: aristocracy. Jefferson argued for a distinction between genuine and artificial aristocracy. Adams insisted that they were ultimately, even unfortunately, one and the same.

[2]The aristocracy. Greek: the best.

[3]"False aristocracy."

so may they that of the co-ordinates. Mischief may be done negatively as well as positively. Of this, a cabal[4] in the Senate of the United States has furnished many proofs. Nor do I believe them necessary to protect the wealthy; because enough of these will find their way into every branch of the legislation, to protect themselves. From fifteen to twenty legislatures of our own, in action for thirty years past, have proved that no fears of an equalization of property are to be apprehended from them. I think the best remedy is exactly that provided by all our constitutions, to leave to the citizens the free election and separation of the *aristoi* from the *pseudo-aristoi,* of the wheat from the chaff.[5] In general they will elect the really good and wise. In some instances, wealth may corrupt, and birth blind them, but not in sufficient degree to endanger the society.

. . .

At the first session of our legislature after the Declaration of Independence, we passed a law abolishing entails.[6] And this was followed by one abolishing the privilege of primogeniture,[7] and dividing the lands of intestates[8] equally among all their children, or other representatives. These laws, drawn by myself, laid the ax to the foot of pseudo-aristocracy. And had another which I prepared been adopted by the legislature, our work would have been complete. It was a bill for the more general diffusion of learning. This proposed to divide every county into wards of five or six miles square, like your townships; to establish in each ward a free school for reading, writing and common arithmetic; to provide for the annual selection of the best subjects from these schools, who might receive, at the public expense, a higher degree of education at a district school; and from these district schools to select a certain number of the most promising subjects, to be completed at a university, where all the useful sciences should be taught. Worth and genius would thus have been sought out from every condition of life, and completely prepared by education for defeating the competition of wealth and birth for public trusts. My proposition had, for a further object, to impart to these wards those portions of self-government for which they are best qualified, by confiding to them the care of their poor, their roads, police, elections, the nomination of jurors, administration of justice in small cases, elementary exercises of militia; in short, to have made them little republics, with a warden at the head of each, for all those concerns which, being under their eye, they would better manage than the larger republics of the county or State. A general call of ward meetings by their wardens on the same day through the State, would at any time produce the genuine sense of the people on any required point, and would enable the State to act in mass, as your people have so often done, and with so much effect by their town meetings. The law for religious freedom, which made a part of this system, having put down the aristocracy of the clergy, and restored to the citizen the freedom of

[4]Group of plotters. [5]Husks.

[6]The right to entail property permitted the original owner to limit the line of inheritance, thus ensuring the survival of large estates and the power of landed wealth.

[7]Limiting inheritance to the first-born child, thus keeping the estate intact. Jefferson objected to primogeniture and entail because he believed they sustain a false aristocracy of birth and wealth.

[8]Persons who die without leaving wills.

the mind, and those of entails and descents nurturing an equality of condition among them, this on education would have raised the mass of the people to the high ground of moral respectability necessary to their own safety, and to orderly government. . . .

With respect to aristocracy, we should further consider, that before the establishment of the American States, nothing was known to history but the man of the old world, crowded within limits either small or overcharged, and steeped in the vices which that situation generates. A government adapted to such men would be one thing; but a very different one, that for the man of these States. Here every one may have land to labor for himself, if he chooses; or, preferring the exercise of any other industry, may exact for it such compensation as not only to afford a comfortable subsistence, but wherewith to provide for a cessation from labor in old age. Every one, by his property, or by his satisfactory situation, is interested in the support of law and order. And such men may safely and advantageously reserve to themselves a wholesome control over their public affairs, and a degree of freedom, which, in the hands of the *canaille*[9] of the cities of Europe, would be instantly perverted to the demolition and destruction of everything public and private. The history of the last twenty-five years of France,[10] and of the last forty years in America, nay of its last two hundred years, proves the truth of both parts of this observation.

But even in Europe a change has sensibly taken place in the mind of man. Science had liberated the ideas of those who read and reflect, and the American example had kindled feelings of right in the people. An insurrection has consequently begun, of science, talents, and courage, against rank and birth, which have fallen into contempt. It has failed in its first effort, because the mobs of the cities, the instrument used for its accomplishment, debased by ignorance, poverty, and vice, could not be restrained to rational action. But the world will recover from the panic of this first catastrophe. Science is progressive, and talents and enterprise on the alert. Resort may be had to the people of the country, a more governable power from their principles and subordination; and rank, and birth, and tinsel-aristocracy will finally shrink into insignificance, even there. This, however, we have no right to meddle with. It suffices for us, if the moral and physical condition of our own citizens qualifies them to select the able and good for the direction of their government, with a recurrence of elections at such short periods as will enable them to displace an unfaithful servant, before the mischief he mediates may be irremediable.

I have thus stated my opinion on a point on which we differ, not with a view to controversy, for we are both too old to change opinions which are the result of a long life of inquiry and reflection, but on the suggestions of a former letter of yours, that we ought not to die before we have explained ourselves to each other. We acted in perfect harmony, through a long and perilous contest for our liberty and independence. A constitution has been acquired, which, though neither of us thinks perfect, yet both consider as competent to render our fellow citizens the happiest and the securest on whom the sun has ever shone. If we do not think exactly alike as to its imperfections, it matters little

[9]Rabble.

[10]I.e., since the French Revolution, 1789.

to our country, which, after devoting to it long lives of disinterested labor, we have delivered over to our successors in life, who will be able to take care of it and of themselves. . . .

THOMAS JEFFERSON

The Federalist 1787–1788

In the spring of 1787 the Constitutional Convention met in Philadelphia to amend the Articles of Confederation, the frame of government under which the United States had struggled to operate since 1781. Once in session, the Convention quickly abandoned attempts to revise the Articles of Confederation. Instead, the delegates set out to create a totally new federal constitution. In mid-September the Constitution was adopted by the Convention and sent to the states for ratification.

Not all Americans approved of the new Constitution. Its opponents (the anti-Federalists) argued that it gave too much power to a centralized, federal government, that it lacked a bill of rights to protect citizens against the coercive powers of the state. Others objected to its "glittering generalities." Southerners opposed provisions that ended the slave trade. Backcountry farmers felt that the new document favored Eastern urban centers over rural interests. But ultimately the widespread desire for a stable federal government and the promise of the prompt addition of a bill of rights brought ratification from the required majority of states.

In New York, ratification came largely through the propaganda efforts of the pro-Constitution Federalists, led by Alexander Hamilton (1757–1804). A conservative New Yorker, a lawyer and statesman, Hamilton had served under Washington in the Revolutionary War and as a delegate to the Continental Congress. In the fall of 1787, shortly after the new Constitution had been presented to the states, Hamilton recognized that widespread opposition in New York might block ratification and exclude New York from union with the new United States. He then decided to write a series of articles for publication in New York newspapers.

Hamilton wanted to generate popular support for ratification and to present the Federalist arguments for the need for a strong central government to guard against the "heats and ferments" of extreme democracy. Shortly afterward, John Jay (1745–1829) and James Madison (1751–1836) agreed to collaborate. Jay was a New York jurist who had served as president of the Continental Congress and was to become the first Chief Justice of the U.S. Supreme Court. Madison was a Virginian who later became the fourth president of the United States (1809–1817). His efforts at the Constitutional Convention in Philadelphia won him the title Father of the Constitution. In 1787–1788 he was a member of the Congress, which met in New York City.

The first seventy-seven essays appeared in New York newspapers three or four times a week from October 1787 to April 1788. In May 1788 eight additional essays were added, and the total of eighty-five was published as The Federalist. *Jay, who became ill early in the venture, wrote only five. The remainder were written by Hamilton and Madison. The original purpose of* The Federalist *was political propaganda, to convince the citizens of New York that it was in their best interest to adopt the Constitution. But the eighty-five essays of* The Federalist *have come to be considered the best critical evaluation ever made of the U.S. Constitution. The arguments reflect, as does the Constitution itself, the ideas of John Locke and the concepts of "social contract" and of the natural rights of man. The essays exhibited the eighteenth-century ideal of stability and "domestic tranquillity," and they remain a significant part of the continuing debate over the conflicting ideals of authority and of individualism.*

Hamilton recognized that the effect of the hasty preparation of the essays and the repetition of ideas required by publication in newspapers could not "but displease a critical reader." But his aim had been to promote what he saw as "the cause of truth" and the "interests of the community," and although the essays lack the grace and polish of the political writing of Jefferson, they nonetheless came to be recognized even by the anti-Federalist Jefferson himself as the "best commentary on the principles of government which ever was written."

FURTHER READING: *The Federalist,* ed. E. Earle, 1937; *The Federalist,* ed. B. Wright, 1961; B. Mitchell, *Alexander Hamilton, Youth to Maturity, 1755–1788,* 1957, and *Alexander Hamilton, The National Adventure, 1788–1804,* 1962; I. Brant, *James Madison, Father of the Constitution,* 1950; F. Monaghan, *John Jay, Defender of Liberty,* 1935; S. Livermore, *The Twilight of Federalism,* 1969; L. Kerber, *Federalists in Dissent,* 1970; G. Wills, *Explaining America, The Federalist,* 1981, 2000; A. Furtwangler, *The Authority of Publius, A Reading of the Federalist Papers,* 1984; R. Mathews, *If Men Were Angels, James Madison and the Heartless Empire of Reason,* 1995; L. Ball, *The Federalist–Anti-Federalist Debate over States' Rights,* 2004.

TEXT: *The Federalist,* 1788. Some spelling and punctuation have been changed to conform more nearly to modern practice.

THE FEDERALIST NO. 10[1]

JAMES MADISON

November 22, 1787

To the People of the State of New York.

Among the numerous advantages promised by a well constructed union, none deserves to be more accurately developed than its tendency to break and control the violence of faction. The friend of popular[2] governments, never finds himself so much alarmed for their character and fate, as when he contemplates their propensity to this dangerous vice. He will not fail therefore to set a due value on any plan which, without violating the principles to which he is attached, provides a proper cure for it. The instability, injustice and confusion introduced into the public councils, have in truth been the mortal diseases under which popular governments have everywhere perished, as they continue to be the favorite and fruitful topics from which the adversaries to liberty derive their most specious[3] declamations. The valuable improvements made by the American Constitutions on the popular models, both ancient and modern, cannot certainly be too much admired; but it would be an unwarrantable partiality, to contend that they have as effectually

[1]Madison's first essay and the most famous of the *Federalist* papers. It discusses the need of governments to protect themselves from the "convulsions" of internal enemies. Madison's suggestions for controlling "the violence of faction" are a classic argument for the need of large and strong central governments for the preservation of liberty from attacks by special interest groups and from the evils of unrestrained rule by the majority.

[2]Democratic. [3]Deceptive, misleading.

obviated the danger on this side as was wished and expected. Complaints are every where heard from our most considerate and virtuous citizens, equally the friends of public and private faith, and of public and personal liberty; that our governments are too unstable; that the public good is disregarded in the conflicts of rival parties; and that measures are too often decided not according to the rules of justice and the rights of the minor party, but by the superior force of an interested and over-bearing majority. However anxiously we may wish that these complaints had no foundation, the evidence of known facts will not permit us to deny that they are in some degree true. It will be found indeed, on a candid review of our situation, that some of the distresses under which we labor, have been erroneously charged on the operation of our governments; but it will be found, at the same time, that other causes will not alone account for many of our heaviest misfortunes, and particularly for that prevailing and increasing distrust of public engagements, and alarm for private rights, which are echoed from one end of the continent to the other. These must be chiefly, if not wholly, effects of the unsteadiness and injustice with which a factious spirit has tainted our public administrations.

By a faction I understand a number of citizens, whether amounting to a majority or minority of the whole, who are united and actuated by some common impulse of passion, or of interest, adverse to the rights of other citizens or to the permanent and aggregate interests of the community.

There are two methods of curing the mischiefs of faction: the one, by removing its causes; the other, by controlling its effects.

There are again two methods of removing the causes of faction: the one by destroying the liberty which is essential to its existence; the other, by giving to every citizen the same opinions, the same passions, and the same interests.

It could never be more truly said than of the first remedy, that it is worse than the disease. Liberty is to faction what air is to fire, an aliment[4] without which it instantly expires. But it could not be a less folly to abolish liberty, which is essential to political life, because it nourishes faction, than it would be to wish the annihilation of air, which is essential to animal life, because it imparts to fire its destructive agency.

The second expedient is as impracticable, as the first would be unwise. As long as the reason of man continues fallible and he is at liberty to exercise it, different opinions will be formed. As long as the connection subsists between his reason and his self-love, his opinions and his passions will have a reciprocal influence on each other; and the former will be objects to which the latter will attach themselves. The diversity in the faculties of men from which the rights of property originate, is not less an insuperable obstacle to a uniformity of interests. The protection of these faculties is the first object of government. From the protection of different and unequal faculties of acquiring property, the possession of different degrees and kinds of property immediately results; and from the influence of these on the sentiments and views of the respective proprietors, ensues a division of the society into different interests and parties.

The latent causes of faction are thus sown in the nature of man; and we see them every where brought into different degrees of activity, according to the different circumstances of civil society. A zeal for different opinions concerning

[4]Sustenance.

religion, concerning government and many other points, as well of speculation as of practice; an attachment to different leaders ambitiously contending for preeminence and power; or to persons of other descriptions whose fortunes have been interesting to the human passions, have in turn divided mankind into parties,[5] inflamed them with mutual animosity, and rendered them much more disposed to vex and oppress each other, than to co-operate for their common good. So strong is this propensity of mankind to fall into mutual animosities, that where no substantial occasion presents itself, the most frivolous and fanciful distinctions have been sufficient to kindle their unfriendly passions and excite their most violent conflicts. But the most common and durable source of factions has been the various and unequal distribution of property. Those who hold and those who are without property have ever formed distinct interests in society. Those who are creditors and those who are debtors fall under a like discrimination. A landed interest, a manufacturing interest, a mercantile interest, a monied interest, with many lesser interests, grow up of necessity in civilized nations and divide them into different classes, actuated by different sentiments and views. The regulation of these various and interfering interests forms the principal task of modern legislation and involves the spirit of party and faction in the necessary and ordinary operations of government.

No man is allowed to be a judge in his own cause because his interest would certainly bias his judgment and, not improbably, corrupt his integrity. With equal, nay with greater reason, a body of men are unfit to be both judges and parties at the same time; yet, what are many of the most important acts of legislation but so many judicial determinations, not indeed concerning the right of single persons but concerning the rights of large bodies of citizens; and what are the different classes of legislators but advocates and parties to the causes which they determine? Is a law proposed concerning private debts? It is a question to which the creditors are parties on one side and the debtors on the other. Justice ought to hold the balance between them. Yet the parties are and must be themselves the judges; and the most numerous party, or, in other words, the most powerful faction must be expected to prevail. Shall domestic manufactures be encouraged, and in what degree, by restrictions on foreign manufactures? are questions which would be differently decided by the landed and the manufacturing classes, and probably by neither with a sole regard to justice and the public good. The apportionment of taxes on the various descriptions of property is an act which seems to require the most exact impartiality; yet, there is perhaps no legislative act in which greater opportunity and temptation are given to a predominant party, to trample on the rules of justice. Every shilling with which they over-burden the inferior number is a shilling saved to their own pockets.

It is in vain to say that enlightened statesmen will be able to adjust these clashing interests and render them all subservient to the public good. Enlightened statesmen will not always be at the helm; Nor, in many cases, can such an adjustment be made at all, without taking into view indirect and remote considerations, which will rarely prevail over the immediate interest which one party may find in disregarding the rights of another, or the good of the whole.

[5]Factions, contending groups.

The inference to which we are brought, is, that the *causes* of faction cannot be removed and that relief is only to be sought in the means of controlling its *effects*.

If a faction consists of less than a majority, relief is supplied by the republican principle, which enables the majority to defeat its sinister views by regular vote. It may clog the administration, it may convulse the society; but it will be unable to execute and mask its violence under the forms of the Constitution. When a majority is included in a faction, the form of popular government on the other hand enables it to sacrifice to its ruling passion or interest, both the public good and the rights of other citizens. To secure the public good, and private rights, against the danger of such a faction, and at the same time to preserve the spirit and the form of popular government, is then the great object to which our enquiries are directed. Let me add that it is the great desideratum,[6] by which alone this form of government can be rescued from the opprobrium under which it has so long labored, and be recommended to the esteem and adoption of mankind.

By what means is this object attainable? Evidently by one of two only. Either the existence of the same passion or interest in a majority at the same time, must be prevented; or the majority, having such co-existent passion or interest, must be rendered, by their number and local situation, unable to concert and carry into effect schemes of oppression. If the impulse and the opportunity be suffered to coincide, we well know that neither moral nor religious motives can be relied on as an adequate control. They are not found to be such on the injustice and violence of individuals and lose their efficacy in proportion to the number combined together, that is, in proportion as their efficacy becomes needful.

From this view of the subject, it may be concluded that a pure democracy, by which I mean a society consisting of a small number of citizens who assemble and administer the government in person, can admit of no cure for the mischiefs of faction. A common passion or interest will, in almost every case, be felt by a majority of the whole; a communication and concert[7] results from the form of government itself; and there is nothing to check the inducements to sacrifice the weaker party or an obnoxious[8] individual. Hence it is that such democracies have ever been spectacles of turbulence and contention, have ever been found incompatible with personal security or the rights of property, and have in general been as short in their lives as they have been violent in their deaths. Theoretic politicians, who have patronized this species of government have erroneously supposed that by reducing mankind to a perfect equality in their political rights, they would at the same time be perfectly equalized and assimilated in their possessions, their opinions, and their passions.

A republic, by which I mean a government in which the scheme of representation takes place, opens a different prospect and promises the cure for which we are seeking. Let us examine the points in which it varies from pure democracy, and we shall comprehend both the nature of the cure and the efficacy which it must derive from the union.

[6]Essential thing. [7]Joining together. [8]Here used in its older sense to mean vulnerable.

The two great points of difference between a democracy and a republic are first, the delegation of the government, in the latter, to a small number of citizens elected by the rest; secondly, the greater number of citizens and greater sphere of country over which the latter may be extended.

The effect of the first difference is, on the one hand, to refine and enlarge the public views by passing them through the medium of a chosen body of citizens whose wisdom may best discern the true interest of their country and whose patriotism and love of justice will be least likely to sacrifice it to temporary or partial considerations. Under such a regulation, it may well happen that the public voice pronounced by the representatives of the people will be more consonant to the public good than if pronounced by the people themselves convened for the purpose. On the other hand, the effect may be inverted. Men of factious tempers, of local prejudices, or of sinister designs, may by intrigue, by corruption or by other means, first obtain the suffrages[9] and then betray the interests of the people. The question resulting is, whether small or extensive republics are most favorable to the election of proper guardians of the public weal;[10] and it is clearly decided in favor of the latter by two obvious considerations.

In the first place it is to be remarked that however small the republic may be, the representatives must be raised to a certain number in order to guard against the cabals[11] of a few, and that however large it may be, they must be limited to a certain number in order to guard against the confusion of a multitude. Hence the number of representatives in the two cases, not being in proportion to that of the constituents, and being proportionally greatest in the small republic, it follows that if the proportion of fit characters[12] be not less in the large than in the small republic, the former will present a greater option and consequently a greater probability of a fit choice.

In the next place, as each representative will be chosen by a greater number of citizens in the large than in the small republic, it will be more difficult for unworthy candidates to practise with success the vicious arts by which elections are too often carried, and the suffrages of the people being more free, will be more likely to center on men who possess the most attractive merit and the most diffusive and established characters.

It must be confessed that in this, as in most other cases, there is a mean, on both sides of which inconveniencies will be found to lie. By enlarging too much the number of electors, you render the representative too little acquainted with all their local circumstances and lesser interests; as by reducing it too much, you render him unduly attached to these, and too little fit to comprehend and pursue great and national objects. The Federal Constitution forms a happy combination in this respect; the great and aggregate interests being referred to the national, the local and particular to the state legislatures.

The other point of difference is, the greater number of citizens and extent of territory which may be brought within the compass of republican, than of democratic government; and it is this circumstance principally which renders factious combinations less to be dreaded in the former, than in the latter.

[9]Votes. [10]Well-being. [11]Plots. [12]Reputations.

The smaller the society, the fewer probably will be the distinct parties and interests composing it; the fewer the distinct parties and interests, the more frequently will a majority be found of the same party; and the smaller the number of individuals composing a majority, and the smaller the compass within which they are placed, the more easily will they concert and execute their plans of oppression. Extend the sphere, and you take in a greater variety of parties and interests; you make it less probable that a majority of the whole will have a common motive to invade the rights of other citizens; or if such a common motive exists, it will be more difficult for all who feel it to discover their own strength and to act in unison with each other. Besides other impediments, it may be remarked that where there is a consciousness of unjust or dishonorable purposes, communication is always checked by distrust, in proportion to the number whose concurrence is necessary.

Hence it clearly appears that the same advantage which a republic has over a democracy, in controlling the effects of faction, is enjoyed by a large over a small republic—is enjoyed by the union over the states composing it. Does this advantage consist in the substitution of representatives whose enlightened views and virtuous sentiments render them superior to local prejudices and to schemes of injustice? It will not be denied that the representation of the union will be most likely to possess these requisite endowments. Does it consist in the greater security afforded by a greater variety of parties, against the event of any one party being able to outnumber and oppress the rest? In an equal degree does the increased variety of parties, comprised within the union, increase this security. Does it, in fine,[13] consist in the greater obstacles opposed to the concert and accomplishment of the secret wishes of an unjust and interested majority? Here, again, the extent of the union gives it the most palpable advantage.

The influence of factious leaders may kindle a flame within their particular states, but will be unable to spread a general conflagration through the other states; a religious sect, may degenerate into a political faction in a part of the confederacy; but the variety of sects dispersed over the entire face of it, must secure the national councils against any danger from that source; a rage for paper money, for an abolition of debts, for an equal division of property, or for any other improper or wicked project, will be less apt to pervade the whole body of the union than a particular member of it; in the same proportion as such a malady is more likely to taint a particular county or district, than an entire state.

In the extent and proper structure of the union, therefore, we behold a republican remedy for the diseases most incident[14] to republican government. And according to the degree of pleasure and pride, we feel in being republicans, ought to be our zeal in cherishing the spirit, and supporting the character of Federalists.

PUBLIUS[15]

[13] In sum, finally.

[14] Related.

[15] The pseudonym adopted by Hamilton, Jay, and Madison, in the custom of political journalism in the eighteenth century. The true and multiple identity of "Publius" was widely known.

THE FEDERALIST NO. 51[1]

JAMES MADISON[2]

February 6, 1788

To the People of the State of New York.

To what expedient then shall we finally resort for maintaining in practice the necessary partition of power among the several departments, as laid down in the Constitution? The only answer that can be given is that as all these exterior provisions are found to be inadequate, the defect must be supplied[3] by so contriving the interior structure of the government as that its several constituent parts may, by their mutual relations, be the means of keeping each other in their proper places. Without presuming to undertake a full development of this important idea, I will hazard a few general observations which may perhaps place it in a clearer light and enable us to form a more correct judgment of the principles and structure of the government planned by the convention.

In order to lay a due foundation for that separate and distinct exercise of the different powers of government, which to a certain extent is admitted on all hands to be essential to the preservation of liberty, it is evident that each department should have a will of its own and consequently should be so constituted, that the members of each should have as little agency as possible in the appointment of the members of the others. Were this principle rigorously adhered to, it would require that all the appointments for the supreme executive, legislative, and judiciary magistracies, should be drawn from the same fountain of authority, the people, through channels, having no communication whatever with one another. Perhaps such a plan of constructing the several departments would be less difficult in practice than it may in contemplation appear. Some difficulties however, and some additional expense, would attend the execution of it. Some deviations therefore from the principle must be admitted. In the constitution of the judiciary department in particular, it might be inexpedient to insist rigorously on the principle; first, because peculiar[4] qualifications being essential in the members, the primary consideration ought to be to select that mode of choice which best secures these qualifications; secondly, because the permanent tenure by which the appointments are held in that department must soon destroy all sense of dependence on the authority conferring them.

It is equally evident that the members of each department should be as little dependent as possible on those of the others, for the emoluments annexed to[5] their offices. Were the executive magistrate, or the judges, not

[1]In the original newspaper versions of the essays, Nos. 32 and 33 were printed as a single essay. Subsequent editions separated the two and assigned No. 51 to this essay, although it originally appeared in the newspapers as No. 50.

[2]The authorship of 15 of the essays has been disputed. No. 51 has sometimes been attributed to Hamilton, but the best evidence indicates that the author was Madison.

[3]Remedied, corrected.

[4]Distinctive, special.

[5]I.e., fees or salaries allowed for.

independent of the legislature in this particular, their independence in every other would be merely nominal.

But the great security against a gradual concentration of the several powers in the same department consists in giving to those who administer each department the necessary constitutional means, and personal motives, to resist encroachments of the others. The provision for defense must in this, as in all other cases, be made commensurate to the danger of attack. Ambition must be made to counteract ambition. The interest of the man must be connected with the constitutional rights of the place. It may be a reflection on human nature that such devices should be necessary to control the abuses of government. But what is government itself but the greatest of all reflections on human nature? If men were angels, no government would be necessary. If angels were to govern men, neither external nor internal controls on government would be necessary. In framing a government which is to be administered by men over men, the great difficulty lies in this: You must first enable the government to control the governed; and in the next place, oblige it to control itself. A dependence on the people is no doubt the primary control on the government; but experience has taught mankind the necessity of auxiliary precautions.

This policy of supplying by opposite and rival interests, the defect[6] of better motives, might be traced through the whole system of human affairs, private as well as public. We see it particularly displayed in all the subordinate distributions of power, where the constant aim is to divide and arrange the several offices in such a manner as that each may be a check on the other, that the private interest of every individual, may be a sentinel over the public rights. These inventions of prudence cannot be less requisite in the distribution of the supreme powers of the state.

But it is not possible to give to each department an equal power of self defense. In republican government the legislative authority, necessarily, predominates. The remedy for this inconveniency is, to divide the legislature into different branches and to render them by different modes of election, and different principles of action, as little connected with each other as the nature of their common functions and their common dependence on the society will admit. It may even be necessary to guard against dangerous encroachments by still further precautions. As the weight of the legislative authority requires that it should be thus divided, the weakness of the executive may require, on the other hand, that it should be fortified. An absolute negative, on the legislature, appears at first view to be the natural defense with which the executive magistrate should be armed. But perhaps it would be neither altogether safe, nor alone sufficient. On ordinary occasions, it might not be exerted with the requisite firmness; and on extraordinary occasions, it might be perfidiously abused. May not this defect of an absolute negative be supplied by some qualified connection between this weaker department, and the weaker branch of the stronger department, by which the latter may be led to support the constitutional rights of the former without being too much detached from the rights of its own department?

If the principles on which these observations are founded be just, as I persuade myself they are, and they be applied as a criterion to the several state

[6]Lack.

constitutions and to the federal constitution, it will be found that if the latter does not perfectly correspond with them the former are infinitely less able to bear such a test.

There are moreover two considerations particularly applicable to the federal system of America, which place that system in a very interesting point of view.

First. In a single republic, all the power surrendered by the people is submitted to the administration of a single government; and usurpations are guarded against by a division of the government into distinct and separate departments. In the compound republic of America, the power surrendered by the people is first divided between two distinct governments, and then the portion allotted to each, subdivided among distinct and separate departments. Hence a double security arises to the rights of the people. The different governments will control each other at the same time that each will be controlled by itself.

Second. It is of great importance in a republic not only to guard the society against the oppression of its rulers but to guard one part of the society against the injustice of the other part. Different interests necessarily exist in different classes of citizens. If a majority be united by a common interest, the rights of the minority will be insecure. There are but two methods of providing against this evil: The one by creating a will in the community independent of the majority, that is, of the society itself; the other by comprehending[7] in the society so many separate descriptions of citizens, as will render an unjust combination of a majority of the whole very improbable, if not impracticable. The first method prevails in all governments possessing an hereditary or self appointed authority. This at best is but a precarious security because a power independent of the society may as well espouse the unjust views of the major, as the rightful interests of the minor party, and may possibly be turned against both parties. The second method will be exemplified in the federal republic of the United States. Whilst all authority in it will be derived from and dependent on the society, the society itself will be broken into so many parts, interests and classes of citizens, that the rights of individuals or of the minority will be in little danger from interested combinations of the majority. In a free government, the security for civil rights must be the same as for religious rights. It consists in the one case in the multiplicity of interests, and in the other, in the multiplicity of sects. The degree of security in both cases will depend on the number of interests and sects; and this may be presumed to depend on the extent of country and number of people comprehended under the same government. This view of the subject must particularly recommend a proper federal system to all the sincere and considerate friends of republican government. Since it shows that in exact proportion as the territory of the union may be formed into more circumscribed confederacies or states, oppressive combinations of a majority will be facilitated, the best security under the republican form, for the rights of every class of citizens, will be diminished; and consequently, the stability and independence of some member of the government, the only other security, must be proportionally increased. Justice is the end[8] of government. It is

[7]Including. [8]Aim, goal.

the end of civil society. It ever has been and ever will be pursued until it be obtained or until liberty be lost in the pursuit. In a society under the forms of which the stronger faction can readily unite and oppress the weaker, anarchy may as truly be said to reign, as in a state of nature where the weaker individual is not secured against the violence of the stronger. And as in the latter state even the stronger individuals are prompted by the uncertainty of their condition, to submit to a government which may protect the weak as well as themselves, so in the former state, will the more powerful factions or parties be gradually induced by a like motive, to wish for a government which will protect all parties, the weaker as well as the more powerful. It can be little doubted that if the state of Rhode Island was separated from the confederacy[9] and left to itself, the insecurity of rights under the popular form of government within such narrow limits would be displayed by such reiterated oppressions of factious majorities that some power altogether independent of the people would soon be called for by the voice of the very factions whose misrule had proved the necessity of it. In the extended republic of the United States, and among the great variety of interests, parties and sects which it embraces, a coalition of a majority of the whole society could seldom take place on any other principles than those of justice and the general good; and there being thus less danger to a minor from the will of the major party, there must be less pretext also, to provide for the security of the former, by introducing into the government a will not dependent on the latter, or in other words, a will independent of the society itself. It is no less certain than it is important, notwithstanding the contrary opinions which have been entertained, that the larger the society, provided it lie within a practicable sphere, the more duly capable it will be of self government. And happily for the *republican cause,* the practicable sphere may be carried to a very great extent by a judicious modification and mixture of the *federal principle.*

PUBLIUS

Phillis Wheatley 1754?–1784

In 1761 Phillis Wheatley was taken from her home by African slave traders and brought to America, where she was sold in the Boston slave market. Because she was "shedding her front teeth," she was judged to be about seven years old. She was bought as a house servant for Susannah Wheatley, the wife of John Wheatley, a Boston tailor. Given the name Phillis Wheatley, she was kindly treated in the Wheatley home, and under the tutoring of the Wheatleys' daughter, Phillis quickly learned to read the Bible and to write. When she was about thirteen, she began to show a precocious talent for versifying. The Wheatleys encouraged her to study astronomy, geography, and history.

[9]The union, or confederation, of the American States under the Articles of Confederation, by which the nation was governed 1781–1789.

She learned to read classical writers, both in translation and in the original. She learned Latin to be able to read Horace, Virgil, and Ovid. She read the Roman Terence because he too was born in Africa.

In Boston the achievements of "the sooty prodigy" attracted much attention, and she was often called upon to write public poems recording the events of the day. Her first published poem appeared in 1767, when she was little more than thirteen, and thereafter many of her occasional poems appeared in popular broadside sheets to be sold on the streets of Boston. In 1773 she accompanied one of the Wheatleys on a trip to England. In London a collection of thirty-nine of her poems was published as Poems on Various Subjects, Religious and Moral *(1773). It was probably the first book ever published by a black American.*

Phillis Wheatley's work received favorable notice from British critics, and she became the rage of London as the "Sable Muse." Benjamin Franklin, America's colonial agent in Britain, came to visit her. The Lord Mayor of London presented her with a copy of Paradise Lost, *and even Voltaire read her poems and praised them as "very good English verse." Shortly afterward she returned to America, where she gained her freedom, left the Wheatleys, and married John Peters, another free African American. Her last years, however, were marred by illness, family disruptions, and the deaths of her children. She died in Boston in obscure poverty when she was around thirty.*

Phillis Wheatley's poetic subjects were derived from the Bible, from celebrated public events, and from the religion she had absorbed from her pious owners. She dealt with the conventional themes of neoclassicism and styled her poetic couplets after the Augustan English poets—Pope's translation of Homer was her favorite secular English book. But, though her work was derivative and limited, and though it relied on a repeated store of classical allusions, it was remarkable in the eighteenth century when few women in the colonies could read and write, and it was astonishing for a slave with no formal education.

Phillis Wheatley was the first important African-American poet, but only rarely does her poetry reveal an awareness of the problems of blackness. Her apparent concern was not for freedom from slavery but for abstract liberty, the patriotic theme of the years before the Revolution. She had firmly adopted the devout religion of New England and thanked Christians for bringing her from "the heathen shore," the "dark abodes" of her native Africa, a "land of errors, and Egyptian gloom." It was the conventional wisdom of the day in a New England society comforted by the glib assumption that slavery brought the blessings of Christianity to pagans. Later, in the nineteenth century, her work was reprinted. And during the rise of the abolition movement in New England of the 1830s and 1840s, her poems were used as strong evidence to bolster the emerging philanthropic creed that blacks possessed "intellectual powers by no means inferior to any other portion of mankind," just as she herself had written:

> *Remember,* Christians, Negroes, *black as* Cain,
> *May be refin'd and join th' angelic train.*

FURTHER READING: *The Collected Works of Phillis Wheatley,* ed. J. Shields, 1988; M. Richmond, *Bid the Vassal Soar,* 1974; W. Robinson, *Phillis Wheatley,* 1975; W. Robinson, *Phillis Wheatley, A Bio-Bibliography,* 1980; *Critical Essays on Phillis Wheatley,* ed. W. Robinson, 1982; *Phillis Wheatley and Her Writings,* ed. W. Robinson, 1984; H. Gates, *The Trials of Phillis Wheatley,* 2003.

TEXT: *The Poems of Phillis Wheatley,* ed. J. Mason, 1966, 1989. Spelling and punctuation have been changed to conform more nearly to modern practice.

ON VIRTUE

O thou bright jewel in my aim I strive
To comprehend thee. Thine own words declare
Wisdom is higher than a fool can reach.
I cease to wonder, and no more attempt
Thine height t'explore, or fathom thy profound.
But, O my soul, sink not into despair,
Virtue is near thee, and with gentle hand
Would now embrace thee, hovers o'er thine head.
Fain[1] would the heav'n-born soul with her converse,
Then seek, then court her for her promis'd bliss.

Auspicious queen, thine heav'nly pinions spread,
And lead celestial *Chastity* along;
Lo! now her sacred retinue descends,
Array'd in glory from the orbs above.
Attend me, *Virtue,* thro' my youthful years!
O leave me not to the false joys of time!
But guide my steps to endless life and bliss.
Greatness, or *Goodness,* say what I shall call thee,
To give an higher appellation still,
Teach me a better strain, a nobler lay,
O Thou, enthron'd with Cherubs in the realms of day!

1766 1773

TO THE UNIVERSITY OF CAMBRIDGE,[1] IN NEW ENGLAND

While an intrinsic ardor prompts to write,
The muses promise to assist my pen;
'Twas not long since I left my native shore
The land of errors,[2] and *Egyptian* gloom:[3]
Father of mercy, 'twas thy gracious hand
Brought me in safety from those dark abodes.

Students, to you 'tis giv'n to scan the heights
Above, to traverse the etheral space,
And mark the systems of revolving worlds.

[1]Willingly, happily.

[1]Harvard.

[2]Religious errors, because Africa was non-Christian.

[3]How the Lord punished the land of Egypt with darkness is told in Exodus 10:20–23.

Still more, ye sons of science,[4] ye receive
The blissful news by messengers from heav'n
How *Jesus'* blood for your redemption flows.
See Him with hands outstretched upon the cross;
Immense compassion in His bosom glows;
He hears revilers, nor resents their scorn;
What matchless mercy in the Son of God!
When the whole human race by sin had fall'n,
He deign'd to die that they might rise again,
And share with Him in the sublimest skies,
Life without death, and glory without end.

Improve your privileges while they stay,
Ye pupils, and each hour redeem, that bears
Or good or bad report of you to heav'n.
Let sin, that baneful evil to the soul,
By you be shunned, nor once remit your guard;
Suppress the deadly serpent in its egg.
Ye blooming plants of human race divine,
An *Ethiop*[5] tells you 'tis your greatest foe;
Its transient sweetness turns to endless pain,
And in immense perdition sinks the soul.
1767 1773

ON BEING BROUGHT FROM AFRICA TO AMERICA

'Twas mercy brought me from my *Pagan* land,
Taught my benighted soul to understand
That there's a God, that there's a *Saviour* too:
Once I redemption neither sought nor knew.
Some view our sable[1] race with scornful eye,
"Their colour is a diabolic dye."
Remember, *Christians, Negroes,* black as *Cain,*[2]
May be refin'd, and join th' angelic train.
1768 1773

[4]Knowledge.
[5]Ethiopian.
[1]Black.
[2]The slayer of Abel. See Genesis 4:1–15. The "mark" set upon Cain by the Lord was sometimes taken as the origin of the Negro.

ON IMAGINATION

Thy various works, imperial queen, we see,
How bright their forms! how decked with pomp by thee!
Thy wond'rous acts in beauteous order stand,
And all attest how potent is thine hand.

From *Helicon's*[1] refulgent heights attend,
Ye sacred choir, and my attempts befriend:
To tell her glories with a faithful tongue.
Ye blooming graces, triumph in my song.

Now here, now there, the roving *Fancy* flies,
Till some loved object strikes her wand'ring eyes,
Whose silken fetters all the senses bind,
And soft captivity involves the mind.

Imagination! who can sing thy force?
Or who describe the swiftness of thy course?
Soaring through air to find the bright abode,
Th' empyreal[2] palace of the thund'ring God,
We on thy pinions can surpass the wind,
And leave the rolling universe behind:
From star to star the mental optics rove,
Measure the skies, and range the realms above.
There in one view we grasp the mighty whole,
Or with new worlds amaze th' unbounded soul.

Though *Winter* frowns to *Fancy's* raptured eyes
The fields may flourish, and gay scenes arise;
The frozen deeps may break their iron bands,
And bid their waters murmur o'er the sands.
Fair *Flora*[3] may resume her fragrant reign,
And with her flow'ry riches deck the plain;
Sylvanus[4] may diffuse his honours round,
And all the forest may with leaves be crowned:
Show'rs may descend, and dews their gems disclose,
And nectar sparkle on the blooming rose.
Such is thy pow'r, nor are thine orders vain,

O thou the leader of the mental train:
In full perfection all thy works are wrought,
And thine the sceptre o'er the realms of thought.
Before thy throne the subject-passions bow,
Of subject-passions sov'reign ruler Thou,
At thy command joy rushes on the heart,
And through the glowing veins the spirits dart.

[1]Mt. Helicon in Greece, the legendary home of the Muses. [2]Celestial.
[3]Roman goddess of fertility and flowers. [4]Roman god of the woods.

Fancy might now her silken pinions try
To rise from earth, and sweep th' expanse on high;
From *Tithon's*[5] bed now might *Aurora* rise,
Her cheeks all glowing with celestial dyes,
While a pure stream of light o'er flows the skies.
The monarch of the day I might behold,
And all the mountains tipt with radiant gold,
But I reluctant leave the pleasing views,
Which *Fancy* dresses to delight the *Muse;*
Winter austere forbids me to aspire,

And northern tempests damp the rising fire;
They chill the tides of *Fancy's* flowing sea,
Cease then, my song, cease the unequal lay.[6]

1773

TO S. M.[1] A YOUNG AFRICAN PAINTER, ON SEEING HIS WORKS

To show the lab'ring bosom's deep intent,
And thought in living characters to paint,
When first thy pencil did those beauties give,
And breathing figures learnt from thee to live,
How did those prospects give my soul delight,
A new creation rushing on my sight?
Still, wound'rous youth! each noble path pursue,
On deathless glories fix thine ardent view;
Still may the painter's and the poet's fire
To aid thy pencil, and thy verse conspire!
And may the charms of each seraphic theme
Conduct thy footsteps to immortal fame!
High to the blissful wonders of the skies
Elate thy soul, and raise thy wishful eyes.
Thrice happy, when exalted to survey
That splendid city, crowned with endless day,
Whose twice six gates[2] on radiant hinges ring:
Celestial *Salem*[3] blooms in endless spring.

Calm and serene thy moments glide along,
And may the music inspire each future song!
Still, with the sweets of contemplation bless'd,
May peace with balmy wings your soul invest!

[5]In Greek myth, Tithonus was loved by Eos, goddess of the dawn (Aurora in Roman myth).
[6]I.e., the inadequate ballad.
[1]Scipio Moorhead, a slave in Boston.
[2]Revelation 21:12 describes the walls of the heavenly Jerusalem as twelve-gated.
[3]Jerusalem, i.e., "Heaven."

But when these shades of time are chased away,
And darkness ends in everlasting day,
On what seraphic pinions shall we move,
And view the landscapes in the realms above?
There shall thy tongue in heav'nly murmurs flow.
And there my muse with heav'nly transport glow:
No more to tell of *Damon's*[4] tender sighs,
Or rising radiance of *Aurora's* eyes,
For nobler themes demand a nobler strain,
And purer language on th' ethereal plain.
Cease, gentle muse! the solemn gloom of night
Now seals the fair creation from my sight.

1773

RECOLLECTION

To Miss A——M——, Humbly Inscribed by the Authoress.

Mneme,[1] begin; inspire, ye sacred Nine!
Your vent'rous[2] *Afric* in the deep design.
Do ye rekindle the celestial fire,
Ye god-like powers! the glowing thoughts inspire,
Immortal Pow'r! I trace thy sacred spring,
Assist my strains, while I *thy* glories sing.
By *thee,* past acts of many thousand years,
Rang'd in due order, to the mind appears;
The *long-forgot* thy gentle hand conveys,
Returns, and soft upon the fancy plays.
Calm, in the visions of the night he pours
Th' exhaustless treasures of his secret stores.
Swift from above he wings his downy flight
Thro' *Phoebe's*[3] realm, fair regent of the night.
Thence to the raptured poet gives his aid,
Dwells in his heart, or hovers round his head;
To give instruction to the lab'ring mind,
Diffusing light celestial and refin'd.

[4]A shepherd singer in the *Eclogues* of the Roman poet Virgil.
[1]Mnemosyne, mother of the Greek Muses and a personification of memory or recollection.
[2]Adventurous.
[3]The moon.

Still he pursues, unwearied in the race,
And wraps his senses in the pleasing maze.
The Heav'nly Phantom *points* the actions done
In the past world, and tribes beneath the sun.
He, from his throne in ev'ry human breast,
Has *vice* condemn'd, and ev'ry *virtue* blessed.
Sweet are the sounds in which thy words we hear,
Celestial music to the ravished ear.
We hear thy voice, resounding o'er the plains,
Excelling Maro's[4] sweet Menellian[5] strains.
But awful *Thou!* to that perfidious race,
Who scorn thy warnings, nor the good embrace;
By *Thee* unveil'd, the horrid crime appears,
Thy mighty hand redoubled fury bears;
The time mis-spent augments their hell of woes,
While through each breast the dire contagion flows.
Now turn and leave the rude ungraceful scene,
And paint fair Virtue in immortal green.
For ever flourish in the glowing veins,
For ever flourish in poetic strains.
Be *Thy* employ to guide my early days,
And *Thine* the tribute of my youthful lays.
Now *eighteen years*[6] their destined course have run,
In due succession, round the central sun;
How did each folly unregarded pass!
But sure 'tis graven on eternal brass!
To *recollect,* inglorious I return;
'Tis mine past follies and past crimes to mourn.
The *virtue,* ah! unequal to the *vice,*
Will scarce afford small reason to rejoice.
Such, RECOLLECTION! is thy pow'r, high-throned
In ev'ry breast of mortals, ever own'd.
The wretch, who dared the vengeance of the skies,
At last awakes with horror and surprise.
By *Thee* alarm'd, he sees impending fate,
He howls in anguish, and repents too late.
But oft *thy* kindness moves with timely fear
The furious rebel in his mad career.
Thrice bless'd the man, who in *thy* sacred shrine
Improves the REFUGE from the wrath divine.

1773

[4]The family name of the Roman poet Virgil.

[5]"Arcadian," from Maenalus, a mountain in Arcadia, Greece, sacred to Pan, the god of shepherds.

[6]Phillis Wheatley was eighteen.

TO HIS EXCELLENCY GENERAL WASHINGTON

SIR.

I Have taken the freedom to address your Excellency in the enclosed poem, and entreat your acceptance, though I am not insensible of its inaccuracies. Your being appointed by the Grand Continental Congress to be Generalissimo of the armies of North America, together with the frame of your virtues, excite sensations not easy to suppress. Your generosity, therefore, I presume, will pardon the attempt. Wishing your Excellency all possible success in the great cause you are so generously engaged in. I am,

Your Excellency's most obedient humble servant,

PHILLIS WHEATLEY.

Providence, Oct. 26, 1775.
His Excellency Gen. Washington.

Celestial choir! enthron'd in realms of light,
  Columbia's[1] scenes of glorious toils I write.
While freedom's cause her anxious breast alarms,
She flashes dreadful in refulgent arms.
See mother earth her offspring's fate bemoan,
And nations gaze at scenes before unknown!
See the bright beams of heaven's revolving light
Involved in sorrows and the veil of night!
  The goddess comes, she moves divinely fair,
Olive and laurel bind her golden hair;
Wherever shines this native of the skies,
Unnumber'd charms and recent graces rise.
  Muse! bow propitious while my pen relates
How pour her armies through a thousand gates,
As when Eolus[2] heaven's fair face deforms,
Enwrapp'd in tempest and a night of storms;
Astonish'd ocean feels the wild uproar,
The refluent surges beat the sounding shore;
Or thick as leaves in Autumn's golden reign,
Such, and so many, moves the warrior's train.
In bright array they seek the work of war,
Where high unfurl'd the ensign[3] waves in air.
Shall I to Washington their praise recite?
Enough thou know'st them in the fields of fight.

[1]Poetic term for "America."
[2]God of the winds in classical myth.
[3]Flag.

Thee, first in peace and honours,—we demand
The grace and glory of thy martial band.
Fam'd for thy valour, for thy virtues more,
Hear every tongue thy guardian aid implore!
 One century scarce perform'd its destined round,
When Gallic powers Columbia's fury found;[4]
And so may you, whoever dares disgrace
The land of freedom's heaven-defended race!
Fix'd are the eyes of nations on the scales,
For in their hopes Columbia's arm prevails.
Anon Britannia[5] droops the pensive head,
While round increase the rising hills of dead.
Ah! cruel blindness to Columbia's state!
Lament thy thirst of boundless power too late.
 Proceed, great chief, with virtue on thy side,
Thy ev'ry action let the goddess guide.
A crown, a mansion, and a throne that shine,
With gold unfading, WASHINGTON! be thine.
1775 1776

Philip Freneau 1752–1832

Thomas Jefferson described Freneau as the man who "saved our constitution which was fast galloping into monarchy." But to George Washington and the Federalists, he was "that rascal Freneau," a "wretched and insolent dog." He was born in New York to a prosperous family whose ancestors came to America as Protestant refugees from seventeenth-century France. At the age of sixteen Freneau entered Princeton, where he was a classmate of James Madison and the future novelist H. H. Brackenridge. While an undergraduate, Freneau wrote "The Power of Fancy," his first important poem, and he collaborated with Brackenridge on a patriotic, visionary poem, "The Rising Glory of America," read at the commencement ceremonies in 1771.

After graduation Freneau worked briefly and unsuccessfully as a schoolmaster. In the summer of 1775, at the start of the American Revolution, he was in New York, where he wrote a series of stinging, patriotic satires such as "A Political Litany," his

[4]A reference to the warfare between French and British colonial forces in North America, which broke out periodically in the first half of the eighteenth century and culminated in the British victory in the French and Indian War (1754–1763).

[5]Personification of Great Britain.

mock-prayer for deliverance from British colonial oppression. In 1776 he traveled to the West Indies. There he wrote "The House of Night," a poem lush with images of tropical nature, and he saw the horrors of slavery that he later attacked in "To Sir Toby." Two years later Freneau returned to North America, where he enlisted in the colonial militia and then became a seaman on a blockade-runner. In 1780 he was captured by British naval forces and imprisoned for six weeks on The Scorpion, *a British prison-ship in New York Harbor. Imprisonment increased his hatred for the British and all coercive government. When he was released in an exchange of prisoners, he made his way to Philadelphia, where he began to write for the* Freeman's Journal *and won the title Poet of the American Revolution for his ardent patriotic verse and for his scathing satire of the British and of royalist sympathizers.*

With the end of the Revolution, Freneau returned to the sea for his livelihood, serving between 1784 and 1790 as master of a merchant ship. In 1786 his first volume of poems was published, and in 1790 he resumed his career as a journalist. A year later, with the aid of Thomas Jefferson, Secretary of State under Washington, Freneau was appointed a translator in the State Department, and he established the National Gazette, *a semiweekly newspaper that became the voice of liberal democracy in American politics. For the next two years, Freneau joined in a series of vicious political battles against the Federalist supporters of Washington's government. With his own strident satires, lampoons, and exposés, and with learned essays on government written by Madison and Brackenridge, Freneau vilified the politics of the Federalists. Washington branded the attacks as "outrages to common decency" and protested to Jefferson for employing "that rascal Freneau," that "barking cur," in the very government he so impudently attacked.*

In 1793, Jefferson retired as Washington's Secretary of State. With his patron out of office and with the circulation of his newspaper dwindling, Freneau closed the Gazette *and retired to his family farm in New Jersey. In 1803 he was forced to return to the sea to earn his living as a ship's captain. Four years later he returned once more to his New Jersey farm and worked the last years of his life as an occasional laborer and wandering tinker. In 1832, when he was eighty, he became lost in a snowstorm on his way home from a tavern and died of exposure.*

Freneau's political journalism in behalf of democracy had won him fame and helped lead to the rise of Jacksonism and the "Age of the Common Man" in America. But since the mid-nineteenth century, his journalistic triumphs have been overshadowed by his growing reputation as the most significant poet of the eighteenth century in America, the Father of American Poetry.

Freneau's literary work is a fusion of neoclassicism and romanticism. His patriotic and political poems, even when "full of invective and loaded with spleen," used the diction, poetic forms, landscapes, mythologies, and deistic thought of the eighteenth century. Yet his poetry also exhibits the lyric qualities, the sensuous images, and the adulation of nature and primitivism that became the conventions of American romanticism in the next century. "The House of Night," though uneven and crude, is one of the first distinctly romantic poems in American literature. It is filled with demonic and luxuriant images that anticipate the gothic horrors and the obsession with death evident in the poetry of Poe and his disciples a half century later. Freneau's deistic celebration of nature, in such poems as "The Wild Honey Suckle," anticipated the nineteenth-century romantic use of simple nature imagery. And his poem "The Indian Burying Ground" anticipated romantic primitivism and the celebration of the "Noble Savage."

The work of Freneau's last years marked a return to the concepts of deism, to arguments for faith in the transcendent workings of the universe. Nonetheless, most of his poetry—from his early, moralizing satire through what he named his "Poems of Romantic Imagination"—reflected the themes and images, even the resignation and nihilism, that were later evident in the work of Bryant, Emerson, Cooper, Poe, and Melville and became dominating characteristics of literature in the age of American romanticism.

FURTHER READING: *The Last Poems of Philip Freneau,* ed. L. Leary, 1945; *The Newspaper Verse of Philip Freneau,* ed. J. Hiltner, 1988; L. Leary, *That Rascal Freneau,* 1941, 1964; N. Adkins, *Philip Freneau and the Cosmic Enigma,* 1949, 1971; P. Axelrad, *Philip Freneau, Poet and Journalist,* 1967; P. Marsh, *The Works of Philip Freneau, A Critical Study,* 1968; M. Bowden, *Philip Freneau,* 1976; R. Vitzhum, *Land and Sea, the Lyric Poetry of Philip Freneau,* 1978; M. Austin, *Philip Freneau, Poet of the Revolution,* 1993.

TEXTS: "On Mr. Paine's Rights of Man" and "On the Universality and Other Attributes of the God of Nature" are from *Poems of Freneau,* ed. H. Clark, 1929. All others are from *The Poems of Philip Freneau,* ed. F. Pattee, 3 vols., 1902–1907, 1963. Spelling and punctuation have been changed to conform more nearly to modern practice.

THE POWER OF FANCY[1]

Wakeful, vagrant, restless thing,
Ever wandering on the wing,
Who thy wondrous source can find,
Fancy, regent of the mind;
A spark from Jove's[2] resplendent throne,
But thy nature all unknown.
This spark of bright, celestial flame,
From Jove's seraphic altar came,
And hence alone in man we trace,
Resemblance to the immortal race.
Ah! what is all this mighty whole,
These suns and stars that round us roll!
What are they all, where'er they shine,
But Fancies of the Power Divine!
What is this globe, these lands, and seas,
And heat, and cold, and flowers, and trees,
And life, and death, and beast, and man,
And time—that with the sun began—
But thoughts on reason's scale combin'd,
Ideas of the Almighty mind!
On the surface of the brain
Night after night she walks unseen,

[1]Written when Freneau was an undergraduate at Princeton. It reveals the influence of the classics in its form and allusions and gives early evidence of his romantic tendencies in poetry.
[2]Chief Roman god.

Noble fabrics doth she raise
In the woods or on the seas,
On some high, steep, pointed rock,
Where the billows loudly knock
And the dreary tempests sweep
Clouds along the uncivil deep.
　　Lo! she walks upon the moon,
Listens to the chimy tune
Of the bright, harmonious spheres,[3]
And the song of angels hears;
Sees this earth a distant star,[4]
Pendant, floating in the air;
Leads me to some lonely dome,
Where Religion loves to come,
Where the bride of Jesus[5] dwells,
And the deep ton'd organ swells
In notes with lofty anthems join'd,
Notes that half distract the mind.
　　Now like lightning she descends
To the prison of the fiends,
Hears the rattling of their chains,
Feels their never ceasing pains—
But, O never may she tell
Half the frightfulness of hell.
　　Now she views Arcadian[6] rocks,
Where the shepherds guard their flocks,
And, while yet her wings she spreads,
Sees chrystal streams and coral beds,
Wanders to some desert deep,
Or some dark, enchanted steep,
By the full moonlight doth shew
Forests of a dusky blue,
Where, upon some mossy bed,
Innocence reclines her head.
　　Swift, she stretches o'er the seas
To the far off Hebrides,[7]
Canvas on the lofty mast
Could not travel half so fast—
Swifter than the eagle's flight
Or instantaneous rays of light!

[3]In ancient astronomy, the sun, planets, and stars were thought to be contained in a series of layered, transparent spheres. As they revolved, their friction produced a harmonious "music of the spheres."

[4]"Milton's *Paradise Lost,* B. II, v. 1052."—Freneau's note.

[5]In the New Testament, the "bride of Jesus" is identified with the community of believers in Christ (Ephesians 5:22–27) and with the heavenly city (Revelation 21:9–10).

[6]Arcadia, in Greece, a mountainous area used as a pastoral setting by ancient poets to exemplify rustic delights and simple contentment.

[7]Islands off the western coast of Scotland.

Lo! contemplative she stands
On Norwegia's[8] rocky lands—
Fickle Goddess, set me down
Where the rugged winters frown
Upon Orca's[9] howling steep,
Nodding o'er the northern deep,
Where the winds tumultuous roar,
Vext that Ossian[10] sings no more.
Fancy, to that land repair,
Sweetest Ossian slumbers there;
Waft me far to southern isles
Where the soften'd winter smiles,
To Bermuda's orange shades,
Or Demarara's[11] lovely glades;
Bear me o'er the sounding cape,
Painting death in every shape,
Where daring Anson[12] spread the sail
Shatter'd by the stormy gale—
Lo! she leads me wild and far,
Sense can never follow her—
Shape thy course o'er land and sea,
Help me to keep pace with thee,
Lead me to yon' chalky cliff,
Over rock and over reef,
Into Britain's fertile land,
Stretching far her proud command.
Look back and view, thro' many a year,
Cæsar, Julius Cæsar, there.[13]
    Now to Tempe's[14] verdant wood,
Over the mid-ocean flood
Lo! the islands of the sea—
Sappho,[15] Lesbos mourns for thee:
Greece, arouse thy humbled head,[16]
Where are all thy mighty dead,
Who states to endless ruin hurl'd
And carried vengeance through the world?—
Troy, thy vanish'd pomp resume,
Or, weeping at thy Hector's[17] tomb,
Yet those faded scenes renew,
Whose memory is to Homer due.

[8]Norway's. [9]The Orkney Islands, off the northern coast of Scotland.
[10]A legendary Gaelic hero and poet. [11]Area in British Guiana.
[12]George Anson (1697–1762), British naval explorer of the Pacific.
[13]Caesar landed in Britain in 55 B.C.
[14]Valley in Thessaly, Greece, considered sacred to Apollo.
[15]Sappho (seventh century B.C.), the most famous of Greek women poets, lived on Lesbos (present-day Mytilene) in the Aegean off the coast of Turkey.
[16]Conquered by Turkey in the mid-fifteenth century, Greece did not achieve complete independence until 1829.
[17]In Homer's *Iliad,* a Trojan prince killed by Achilles.

Fancy, lead me wandering still
Up to Ida's[18] cloud-topt hill;
Not a laurel there doth grow
But in vision thou shalt show,—
Every sprig on Virgil's[19] tomb
Shall in livelier colours bloom,
And every triumph Rome has seen
Flourish on the years between.
    Now she bears me far away
In the east to meet the day,
Leads me over Ganges'[20] streams,
Mother of the morning beams—
O'er the ocean hath she ran,
Places me on Tinian;[21]
Farther, farther in the east,
Till it almost meets the west,
Let us wandering both be lost,
On Tahiti's[22] sea-beat coast,
Bear me from that distant strand,
Over ocean, over land,
To California's golden shore—
Fancy, stop, and rove no more.
    Now, tho' late, returning home,
Lead me to Belinda's[23] tomb;
Let me glide as well as you
Through the shroud and coffin too,
And behold, a moment, there,
All that once was good and fair—
Who doth here so soundly sleep?
Shall we break this prison deep?—
Thunders cannot wake the maid,
Lightnings cannot pierce the shade,
And tho' wintry tempests roar,
Tempests shall disturb no more.
    Yet must those eyes in darkness stay,
That once were rivals to the day?—
Like heaven's bright lamp beneath the main
They are but set to rise again.
    Fancy, thou the muses' pride,
In thy painted realms reside
Endless images of things,
Fluttering each on golden wings,
Ideal objects, such a store,
The universe could hold no more:

[18]Mountain near Troy. From its summit, Zeus watched the Trojan War.
[19]Roman poet (70–19 B.C.), author of the *Aeneid*.
[20]River in India. [21]Island in the Pacific. [22]Island in the Pacific.
[23]Idealized and imaginary woman, often invoked in neoclassic literature.

Fancy, to thy power I owe
Half my happiness below;
By thee Elysian[24] groves were made,
Thine were the notes that Orpheus play'd;
By thee was Pluto[25] charm'd so well
While rapture seiz'd the sons of hell—
Come, O come—perceiv'd by none,
You and I will walk alone.
1770 1786

THE HURRICANE[1]

Happy the man who, safe on shore,
Now trims, at home, his evening fire;
Unmov'd, he hears the tempests roar,
That on the tufted groves expire:
Alas! on us they doubly fall,
Our feeble barque[2] must bear them all.

Now to their haunts the birds retreat,
The squirrel seeks his hollow tree,
Wolves in their shaded caverns meet,
All, all are blest but wretched we—
Foredoomed a stranger to repose,
No rest the unsettled ocean knows.

While o'er the dark abyss[3] we roam,
Perhaps, with last departing gleam,
We saw the sun descend in gloom,
No more to see his morning beam;
But buried low, by far too deep,
On coral beds, unpitied, sleep!

But what a strange, uncoasted strand
Is that, where fate permits no day—
No charts have we to mark that land,
No compass to direct that way—
What Pilot shall explore that realm,
What new Columbus take the helm!

[24]Elysium. In Greek myth, the home of the blessed dead.

[25]Orpheus, son of Apollo, famous in Greek legend as a poet and musician. He secured the release of his wife, Eurydice, from Hades by charming Pluto and all the underworld with his music.

[1]Written as a result of Freneau's experiencing a hurricane at sea on a voyage to Jamaica in 1784.

[2]Bark. A three-masted sailing vessel.

[3]"Near the east end of Jamaica, July 30, 1784."—Freneau's note.

While death and darkness both surround,
And tempests rage with lawless power,
Of friendship's voice I hear no sound,
No comfort in this dreadful hour—
What friendship can in tempests be,
What comfort on this raging sea?

The barque, accustomed to obey,
No more the trembling pilots guide:
Alone she gropes her trackless way,
While mountains burst on either side—
Thus, skill and science both must fall;
And ruin is the lot of all.
1784 1785, 1795

TO SIR TOBY

A Sugar Planter in the interior parts of Jamaica,
near the City of San Jago de la Vega,
(Spanish town) 1784

"The motions of his spirit are black as night,
And his affections dark as Erebus."
—SHAKESPEARE.[1]

If there exists a hell—the case is clear—
Sir Toby's slaves enjoy that portion here:
Here are no blazing brimstone lakes—'tis true;
But kindled Rum too often burns as blue;
In which some fiend, whom nature must detest,
Steeps Toby's brand, and marks poor Cudjoe's breast.[2]
Here whips on whips excite perpetual fears,
And mingled howlings vibrate on my ears:
Here nature's plagues abound, to fret and tease,
Snakes, scorpions, despots, lizards, centipees[3]—
No art, no care escapes the busy lash;
All have their dues—and all are paid in cash—
The eternal driver keeps a steady eye
On a black herd, who would his vengeance fly.
But chained, imprisoned, on a burning soil,
For the mean avarice of a tyrant, toil!

[1] *The Merchant of Venice,* Act V., Scene i, line 79. Freneau changed "dull as night" to "black as night."

[2] "This passage has a reference to the West India custom (sanctioned by law) of branding a newly imported slave on the breast, with a red-hot iron, as an evidence of the purchaser's property."—Freneau's note. "Cudjoe," an African day-name meaning Monday, was a common name for male slaves.

[3] Centipedes.

The lengthy cart-whip guards this monster's reign—
And cracks, like pistols, from the fields of cane.
    Ye powers! who formed these wretched tribes, relate,
What had they done, to merit such a fate!
Why were they brought from Eboe's[4] sultry waste,
To see that plenty which they must not taste—
Food, which they cannot buy, and dare not steal;
Yams and potatoes—many a scanty meal!—
    One, with a gibbet[5] wakes his Negro's fears,
One to the windmill nails him by the ears;
One keeps his slave in darkened dens, unfed,
One puts the wretch in pickle ere he's dead:
This, from a tree suspends him by the thumbs,
That, from his table grudges even the crumbs!
    O'er yond' rough hills a tribe of females go,
Each with her gourd,[6] her infant, and her hoe;
Scorched by a sun that has no mercy here,
Driven by a devil, whom men call overseer—
In chains, twelve wretches to their labors haste;
Twice twelve I saw, with iron collars graced!—
    Are such the fruits that spring from vast domains?
Is wealth, thus got, Sir Toby, worth your pains!—
Who would your wealth on terms, like these, possess,
Where all we see is pregnant with distress—
Angola's[7] natives scourged by ruffian hands,
And toil's hard product shipp'd to foreign lands.
    Talk not of blossoms, and your endless spring;
What joy, what smile, can scenes of misery bring?—
Though Nature, here, has every blessing spread,
Poor is the laborer—and how meanly fed!—
    Here Stygian[8] paintings light and shade renew,
Pictures of hell, that Virgil's[9] pencil drew:
Here, surly Charons[10] make their annual trip,
And ghosts arrive in every Guinea ship,[11]
To find what beasts these western isles afford,
Plutonian[12] scourges, and despotic lords:—
    Here, they, of stuff determined to be free,
Must climb the rude cliffs of the Liguanee;[13]
Beyond the clouds, in skulking haste repair,
And hardly safe from brother traitors[14] there.—
1784   1792, 1795, 1809

[4]"A small Negro kingdom near the river Senegal."—Freneau's note. [5]Gallows.
[6]Water gourd. [7]Portuguese colony in West Africa. [8]Hellish.
[9]The Roman poet Virgil described Hades in Book VI of his *Aeneid*.
[10]Charon, the ferryman in Greek myth, carried the dead over the river Styx to Hades.
[11]Slave ships from Guinea, West Africa. [12]Pluto was ruler of Hades.
[13]"The mountains northward of Kingston."—Freneau's note.
[14]"Alluding to the *Independent* Negroes in the blue mountains, who for a stipulated reward, deliver up every fugitive that falls into their hands, to the English Government."—Freneau's note.

THE WILD HONEY SUCKLE

Fair flower, that dost so comely grow,
Hid in this silent, dull retreat,
Untouched thy honied blossoms blow,[1]
Unseen thy little branches greet:
No roving foot shall crush thee here,
No busy hand provoke a tear.

By Nature's self in white arrayed,
She bade thee shun the vulgar eye,
And planted here the guardian shade,
And sent soft waters murmuring by;
Thus quietly thy summer goes,
Thy days declining to repose.

Smit with those charms, that must decay,
I grieve to see your future doom;
They died—nor were those flowers more gay,
The flowers that did in Eden bloom;
Unpitying frosts, and Autumn's power
Shall leave no vestige of this flower.

From morning suns and evening dews
At first thy little being came:
If nothing once, you nothing lose,
For when you die you are the same;
The space between, is but an hour,
The frail duration of a flower.

1786 1786, 1788, 1795

THE INDIAN BURYING GROUND

In spite of all the learned have said,
I still my old opinion keep;
The posture, that we give the dead,
Points out the soul's eternal sleep.

Not so the ancients of these lands—
The Indian, when from life released,
Again is seated with his friends,
And shares again the joyous feast.[1]

[1]Bloom.

[1]"The North American Indians bury their dead in a sitting posture; decorating the corpse with wampum, the images of birds, quadrupeds, &c: And (if that of a warrior) with bows, arrows, tomahawks, and other military weapons."—Freneau's note.

His imaged birds, and painted bowl,
And venison, for a journey dressed,
Bespeak the nature of the soul,
Activity, that knows no rest.

His bow, for action ready bent,
And arrows, with a head of stone,
Can only mean that life is spent,
And not the old ideas gone.

Thou, stranger, that shalt come this way,
No fraud upon the dead commit—
Observe the swelling turf, and say
They do not lie, but here they sit.

Here still a lofty rock remains,
On which the curious eye may trace
(Now wasted, half, by wearing rains)
The fancies of a ruder race.

Here still an aged elm aspires,
Beneath whose far-projecting shade
(And which the shepherd still admires)
The children of the forest played!

There oft a restless Indian queen
(Pale Shebah,[2] with her braided hair)
And many a barbarous form is seen
To chide the man that lingers there.

By midnight moons, o'er moistening dews;
In habit for the chase arrayed,
The hunter still the deer pursues,
The hunter and the deer, a shade![3]

And long shall timorous fancy see
The painted chief, and pointed spear,
And Reason's self shall bow the knee
To shadows and delusions here.

1787, 1795

[2]The Queen of Sheba, renowned for her beauty. See I Kings 10.
[3]Ghost, spirit.

ON THE UNIVERSALITY AND OTHER ATTRIBUTES OF THE GOD OF NATURE

All that we see, about, abroad,
What is it all, but nature's God?
In meaner works discover'd here
No less than in the starry sphere.

In seas, on earth, this God is seen;
All that exist, upon him lean;
He lives in all, and never stray'd
A moment from the works he made:

His system fix'd on general laws
Bespeaks a wise creating cause;
Impartially he rules mankind
And all that on this globe we find.

Unchanged in all that seems to change,
Unbounded space is his great range;
To one vast purpose always true,
No time, with him, is old or new.

In all the attributes divine
Unlimited perfectings shine;
In these enwrapt, in these complete,
All virtues in that centre meet.

This power who doth all powers transcend,
To all intelligence a friend,
Exists, the *greatest and the best*[1]
Throughout all worlds, to make them blest.

All that he did he first approved
He all things into *being* loved;
O'er all he made he still presides,
For them in life, or death provides.

1815

[1]"Jupiter, optimus, maximus.—Cicero."—Freneau's note.

Hannah Webster Foster 1758–1840

On August 5, 1797, a Boston newspaper announced, "Just Published, (In 1 vol. neatly bound and lettered, price One Dollar) . . . The Coquette; or, The History of Eliza Wharton, a Novel; Founded on Fact by a Lady of Massachusetts.*" Its author, thirty-nine-year-old Hannah Webster Foster, was the daughter of a respectable Massachusetts merchant and the wife of the well-known minister John Foster. She had chosen to be the anonymous "Lady of Massachusetts" because she knew that for genteel ladies of the eighteenth century, reading novels might be permissible (except of course on Sundays), but writing them was not—especially not if one were a mature gentlewomen and the wife of a minister of the gospel.*

Moralists of the age had charged that novels and novelists taught only folly and immorality, that the virtuous woman should direct her attention "to the cradle, the stove, and the washtub" rather than to the reading of a novel lest its,

> *. . . high-wrought whim, the tender strain*
> *Elate her mind and turn her brain.*

To overcome objections that fiction perverted innocent and vulnerable minds, Hannah Foster larded The Coquette *with moralizing lessons to teach that "virtue alone, independent of the trappings of wealth, the parade of equipage, and the adulation of gallantry, can secure lasting felicity." And to answer objections that fiction was false and therefore treacherous, she announced that her novel was "founded on fact." She had drawn on the notorious adventures of Elizabeth Whitman, a distant relative and a lady of social distinction who had spurned marriage and "having coquetted till past her prime, fell into criminal indulgences." She was then seduced and ruined by a heartless rake who abandoned her to a dreadful but well-publicized and therefore edifying fate.*

Changing her heroine's name to Eliza Wharton, Hannah Foster set forth her adventures in seventy-four letters written by Eliza and those who knew her. The novel followed in the tradition of sentimental epistolary novels of seduction that had begun with Samuel Richardson's Pamela *(1740), and like Richardson's novel,* The Coquette *was a great success. A best-seller, it was frequently reprinted in the nineteenth century, and it remains in print today, almost two hundred years after it was written.*

The popularity of The Coquette *came in part because the "American Fair" were seized by its descriptions of social intrigues, of illicit passion, of seduction and its consequences. It showed the wicked falsities of dashing gallants, the menace of seducers driven by pride and lust, and the folly of women who are flirtatious, coquettish, and attracted to "the dissipating amusements of the gay world." But Hannah Foster's novel rose above the common stream of sentimental stories of seduction, the innumerable "woe fraught tales" that ended with domestic tranquility restored, passions sanitized, thwarted libertines reformed, and imperiled virtue preserved.*

Despite its lengthy moralizing and sanctimonious lamentations, the story of the temptation, submission, and doom of Eliza Wharton is the most subtle of the early American sentimental novels. It avoids the extremes of "greasy combustible" emotions presented in most tales of sensibility, the passionate excesses that were so easily parodied by the satirists of the day. Its characters are complex. Its rakish hero, torn by his obsessive love for Eliza, is far more than a simple villain intent on the gratification of his lust. And the heroine is more than a foolish victim of her own indulgences. She yearns to be independent, to escape the social conventions that require her submission to a life of dull respectability. And unlike most of the popular sentimental novels of the day,

The Coquette *is told primarily from the point of view of women, not dominating men, and therefore it speaks distinctly to readers of the twentieth century who are concerned with the fate of all vulnerable women and men who confront the engulfing and stultifying powers of emotion and authority.*

FURTHER READING: *The Coquette,* ed. C. Davidson, 1987; C. Bolton, *The Elizabeth Whitman Mystery,* 1912; H. Brown, *The Sentimental Novel in America, 1798–1869, 1940*; C. Davidson, *Revolution and the Word, The Rise of the Novel in America,* 1986; J. Stern, *The Plight of Feeling,* 1997; B. Burgett, *Sentimental Bodies,* 1998; D. Bontatibus, *The Seduction Novel of the Early Nation,* 1999; K. Boudreau, *Sympathy in American Literature,* 2002.

TEXT: *The Coquette,* 1797. Some spelling and punctuation have been changed to conform more nearly to modern practice.

from *THE COQUETTE; OR, THE HISTORY OF ELIZA WHARTON; A NOVEL; FOUNDED ON FACT*

Letter LXV

To Mr. Charles Deighton.

Hartford.

Good news, Charles, good news! I have arrived to the utmost bounds of my wishes; the full possession of my adorable Eliza! I have heard a quotation from a certain book; but what book it was I have forgotten, if I ever knew. No matter for that; the quotation is that "stolen waters are sweet, and bread eaten in secret is pleasant."[1] If it has reference to the pleasures which I have enjoyed with Eliza, I like it hugely, as Tristram Shandy's father said of Yorick's sermon;[2] and I think it fully verified.

I had a long and tedious siege. Every method which love could suggest, or art invent, was adopted. I was sometimes ready to despair, under an idea that her resolution was unconquerable, her virtue impregnable. Indeed, I should have given over the pursuit long ago but for the hopes of success I entertained from her parleying with me, and in reliance upon her own strength, endeavoring to combat and counteract my designs. Whenever this has been the case, Charles, I have never yet been defeated in my plan. If a lady will consent to enter the lists[3] against the antagonist of her honor, she may be sure of losing the prize. Besides, were her delicacy genuine, she would banish the man at once, who presumed to doubt, which he certainly does, who attempts to vanquish it!

But far be it from me to criticize the pretensions of the sex. If I gain the rich reward of my dissimulation and gallantry, that you know is all I want.

To return then to the point. An unlucky, but not a miraculous accident, has taken place, which must soon expose our amour. What can be done? At the first discovery, absolute distraction seized the soul of Eliza, which has

[1] Proverbs 9:17.

[2] In *The Life and Opinions of Tristram Shandy* (1760) by the English novelist Laurence Sterne (1713–1768).

[3] I.e., enter the fields of combat.

since terminated in a fixed melancholy. Her health too is much impaired. She thinks herself rapidly declining; and I tremble when I see her emaciated form!

My wife has been reduced very low, of late. She brought me a boy a few weeks past, a dead one though.

These circumstances give me neither pain nor pleasure. I am too much engrossed by my divinity to take an interest in anything else. True, I have lately suffered myself to be somewhat engaged here and there by a few jovial lads, who assist me in dispelling the anxious thoughts which my perplexed situation excites. I must, however, seek some means to relieve Eliza's distress. My finances are low; but the last fraction shall be expended in her service, if she need it.

Julia Granby is expected at Mrs. Wharton's every hour. I fear that her inquisitorial eye will soon detect our intrigue and obstruct its continuation. Now there's a girl, Charles, I should never attempt to seduce; yet she is a most alluring object, I assure you. But the dignity of her manners forbids all assaults upon her virtue. Why, the very expression of her eye blasts in the bud every thought derogatory to her honor and tells you plainly that the first insinuation of the kind would be punished with eternal banishment and displeasure! Of her there is no danger! But I can write no more, except that I am, &c.

PETER SANFORD.

Letter LXVI

To Mrs. Lucy Sumner.

Hartford.

Oh, my friend! I have a tale to unfold, a tale which will rend every nerve of sympathizing pity, which will rack the breast of sensibility and unspeakably distress your benevolent heart! Eliza—Oh the ruined, lost Eliza!

I want words to express the emotions of indignation and grief which oppress me! But I will endeavor to compose myself and relate the circumstances as they came to my knowledge.

After my last letter, Eliza remained in much the same gloomy situation as I found her. She refused to go, agreeably to her promise,[1] to visit your mama and under one pretext or another has constantly declined accompanying me anywhere else, since my arrival.

Till last Thursday night she slept in the same bed with me, when she excused herself, by saying she was restless and should disturb my repose. I yielded to her humor of taking a different apartment, little suspecting the real cause! She frequently walked out; and though I sometimes followed, I very seldom found her. Two or three times, when I happened to be awake, I heard her go down stairs; and on inquiry in the morning, she told me that she was very thirsty and went down for water. I observed a degree of hesitancy in her answers, for which I could not account. But last night, the dreadful mystery was developed![2] A little before day I heard the front door opened with great caution. I sprang from my bed and, running to the window, saw by the light of the moon a man going from the house. Soon after, I perceived a footstep upon the stairs, which carefully approached and entered Eliza's chamber.

[1]I.e., in compliance with her promise. [2]Revealed, uncovered.

Judge of my astonishment, my surprise, my feelings, upon this occasion! I doubted not but Major Sanford was the person I had seen; and the discovery of Eliza's guilt in this infamous intrigue almost deprived me of thought and recollection! My blood thrilled with horror at this sacrifice of virtue! After a while I recovered myself and put on my clothes. But what to do, I knew not; whether to go directly to her chamber, and let her know that she was detected, or to wait another opportunity.

I resolved on the first. The day had now dawned. I tapped at her door; and she bid me come in. She was sitting in an easy chair by the side of her bed. As I entered she withdrew her handkerchief from her face and, looking earnestly at me, said, what procures me the favor of a visit, at this early hour, Miss Granby? I was disturbed, said I, and wished not to return to my bed. But what breaks your rest and calls you up so unseasonably, Eliza? Remorse, and despair, answered she, weeping. After what I have witnessed, this morning, rejoined I, I cannot wonder at it! Was it not Major Sanford whom I saw go from the house some time ago? She was silent, but tears flowed abundantly. It is too late, continued I, to deny or evade. Answer my question sincerely; for believe me, Eliza, it is not malice but concern for you which prompts it. I will answer you, Julia, said she. You have discovered a secret which harrows up my very soul! A secret which I wished you to know but could not exert resolution to reveal! Yes! It was Major Sanford, the man who has robbed me of my peace, who has triumphed in my destruction, and who will cause my sun to set at noon![3]

I shudder, said I, at your confession! Wretched, deluded girl! Is this a return for your parent's love and assiduous care, for your friends' solicitude and premonitory advice? You are ruined, you say! You have sacrificed your virtue to an abandoned, despicable profligate! And you live to acknowledge and bear your infamy! I do, said she; but not long shall I support this burden! See you not, Julia, my decaying frame, my faded cheek and tottering limbs? Soon shall I be insensible to censure and reproach! So shall I be sequestered in that mansion, "where the wicked cease from troubling, and where the weary are at rest!"[4] Rest! said I, can you expect to find rest either in this world, or another, with such a weight of guilt on your head? She exclaimed, with great emotion, add not to the upbraidings of a wounded spirit! Have pity upon me, Oh! my friend, have pity upon me!

Could you know what I suffer, you would think me sufficiently punished! I wish you no other punishment, said I, than what may effect your repentance and reformation. But your mother, Eliza! She cannot long be ignorant of your fall; and I tremble to think of her distress! It will break her widowed heart! How has she loved; how has she doted upon you! Dreadful is the requital which you have made! My mother, rejoined she—Oh, name her not! The very sound is distraction to me! Oh, my Julia, if your heart be not shut against mercy and compassion towards me, aid me through this trying scene! Let my situation call forth your pity, and induce[5] you, undeserving as I am, to exert it in my behalf!

During this time, I had walked the chamber. My spirits had been raised above their natural key and were exhausted. I sat down but thought I should

[3]God threatened to punish wayward Israelites and "cause the sun to go down at noon." Amos 8:9.
[4]Job 3:17. [5]Lead, encourage.

have fainted, till a copious flood of tears gave me relief. Eliza was extremely affected. The appearance of calamity which she exhibited would have softened the most obdurate anger. Indeed, I feared some immediate and fatal effect. I therefore seated myself beside her; and assuming an air of kindness, compose yourself, Eliza, said I; I repeat what I told you before; it is the purest friendship which thus interests me in your concerns. This, under the direction of charity, induces me again to offer you my hand. Yet you have erred against knowledge and reason, against warning and counsel. You have forfeited the favor of your friends; and reluctant will be their forgiveness. I plead guilty, said she, to all your charges. From the general voice I expect no clemency. If I can make my peace with my mother, it is all I seek or wish on this side of the grave.

In your benevolence I confide for this. In you I hope to find an intercessor. By the remembrance of our former affection and happiness, I conjure[6] you, refuse me not. At present, I entreat you to conceal from her this distressing tale. A short reprieve is all I ask. Why, said I, should you defer it? When the painful task is over, you may find relief in her lenient kindness. After she knows my condition, I cannot see her, resumed she, till I am assured of her forgiveness. I have not strength to support the appearance of her anger and grief. I will write to her what I cannot speak. You must bear the melancholy message and plead for me that her displeasure may not follow me to the grave, whither I am rapidly hastening. Be assured, replied I, that I will keep your secret as long as prudence requires. But I must leave you now; your mama will wonder at our being thus closetted together. When opportunity presents, we will converse further on the subject. In the meantime, keep yourself as composed as possible, if you would avoid suspicion. She raised her clasped hands and, with a piteous look, threw her handkerchief over her face and reclined in her chair, without speaking a word. I returned to my chamber and endeavored to dissipate every idea which might tend to disorder my countenance and break the silence I wished to observe, relative to what had happened.

When I went down, Mrs. Wharton desired me to step up and inform Eliza that breakfast was ready. She told me she could not yet compose herself sufficiently to see her mama and begged me to excuse her absence as I thought proper. I accordingly returned for answer to Mrs. Wharton, that Eliza had rested but indifferently and being somewhat indisposed, would not come down but wished me to bring her a bowl of chocolate, when we had breakfasted. I was obliged studiously to suppress even my thoughts concerning her, lest the emotions they excited might be observed. Mrs. Wharton conversed much of her daughter and expressed great concern about her health and state of mind. Her return to this state of dejection, after having recovered her spirits and cheerfulness, in a great degree was owing, she feared, to some cause unknown to her; and she entreated me to extract the secret, if possible. I assured her of my best endeavors and doubted not, I told her, but I should be able in a few days to effect what she wished.

Eliza came down and walked in the garden before dinner, at which she commanded herself much better than I expected. She said that a little ride might, she imagined, be of service to her and asked me if I would accompany

[6]Urge.

her a few miles in the afternoon. Her mama was much pleased with the proposition, and the chaise was accordingly ordered.

I observed to Eliza, as we rode, that with her natural and acquired abilities, with her advantages of education, with her opportunities of knowing the world and of tracing the virtues and vices of mankind to their origin, I was surprised at her becoming the prey of an insidious libertine, with whose character she was well acquainted and whose principles she was fully apprised would prompt him to deceive and betray her. Your surprise is very natural, said she. The same will doubtless be felt and expressed by everyone to whom my sad story is related. But the cause may be found in that unrestrained levity of disposition, that fondness for dissipation and coquetry which alienated the affections of Mr. Boyer from me. This event fatally depressed and enfeebled my mind. I embraced with avidity the consoling power of friendship, ensnaringly offered by my seducer, vainly inferring from his marriage with a virtuous woman that he had seen the error of his ways and forsaken his licentious practices, as he affirmed, and I, fool that I was, believed it!

It is needless for me to rehearse the perfidious arts by which he insinuated himself into my affections and gained my confidence. Suffice it to say, he effected his purpose! But not long did I continue in the delusive dream of sensual gratification. I soon awoke to a most poignant sense of his baseness and of my own crime and misery. I would have fled from him; I would have renounced him forever and, by a life of sincere humility and repentance, endeavored to make my peace with heaven and to obliterate, by the rectitude of my future conduct, the guilt I had incurred; but I found it too late! My circumstances called for attention; and I had no one to participate[7] my cares, to witness my distress, and to alleviate my sorrows, but him. I could not therefore prevail on myself, wholly to renounce his society. At times I have admitted his visits, always meeting him in the garden or grove adjoining, till of late the weather, and my ill health, induced me to comply with his solicitations and receive him into the parlor.

Not long, however, shall I be subject to these embarrassments. Grief has undermined my constitution. My health has fallen a sacrifice to a disordered mind. But I regret not its departure! I have not a single wish to live. Nothing which the world affords can restore my former serenity and happiness.

The little innocent I bear, will quickly disclose its mother's shame! God Almighty grant it may not live as a monument of my guilt and a partaker of the infamy and sorrow, which is all I have to bequeath it! Should it be continued in life, it will never know the tenderness of a parent; and, perhaps, want and disgrace may be its wretched portion! The greatest consolation I can have will be to carry it with me to a state of eternal rest; which, vile as I am, I hope to obtain, through the infinite mercy of heaven, as revealed in the gospel of Christ.

I must see Major Sanford again. It is necessary to converse further with him, in order to carry my plan of operation into execution. What is this plan of operation, Eliza? said I. I am on the rack of anxiety for your safety. Be patient, continued she, and you shall soon be informed. Tomorrow I shall write my dreadful story to my mother. She will be acquainted with my future

[7]Share.

intentions; and you shall know, at the same time, the destination of your lost friend. I hope, said I, that you have formed no resolution against your own life. God forbid, rejoined she. My breath is in his hands; let him do what seemeth good in his sight! Keep my secret one day longer, and I will never more impose so painful a silence upon you.

By this time we had reached home. She drank tea with composure and soon retired to rest. Mrs. Wharton eagerly inquired whether I had found out the cause of Eliza's melancholy. I have urged her, said I, on the subject; but she alleges that she has particular reasons for present concealment. She has, notwithstanding, promised to let me know the day after tomorrow. Oh, said she, I shall not rest till the period arrives. Dear, good woman, said I to myself, I fear you will never rest afterwards!

This is our present situation. Think what a scene rises to the view of your Julia! She must share the distresses of others, though her own feelings, on this unhappy occasion, are too keen to admit a moment's serenity! My greatest relief is in writing to you, which I shall do again by the next post. In the meantime, I must beg leave to subscribe myself, sincerely yours,

JULIA GRANBY.

Letter LXVII

To the Same.

Hartford.

All is now lost; lost, indeed! She is gone! Yes, my dear friend, our beloved Eliza is gone! Never more shall we behold this once amiable companion, this once innocent and happy girl. She has forsaken and, as she says, bid an everlasting adieu to her home, her afflicted parent, and her friends! But I will take up my melancholy story where I left it in my last.

She went, as she told me she expected, into the garden and met her detestable paramour. In about an hour she returned and went directly to her chamber. At one o'clock I went up and found her writing and weeping. I begged her to compose herself and go down to dinner. No; she said, she could not eat and was not fit to appear before anybody. I remonstrated against her immoderate grief, represented[1] the injury she must sustain by the indulgence of it, and conjured her to suppress the violence of its emotions.

She entreated me to excuse her to her mama, said she was writing to her and found it a task too painful to be performed with any degree of composure; that she was almost ready to sink under the weight of her affliction but hoped and prayed for support, both in this and another trying scene, which awaited her. In compliance with her desire, I now left her and told her mama that she was very busy in writing, wished not to be interrupted at the present, but would take some refreshment an hour or two hence. I visited her again, about four o'clock, when she appeared more calm and tranquil.

It is finished, said she, as I entered her apartment, it is finished. What, said I, is finished? No matter, replied she; you will know all tomorrow, Julia. She complained of excessive fatigue and expressed an inclination to lie down, in which I assisted her and then retired. Some time after, her mama went up and found her still on the bed. She rose, however, and accompanied her down stairs. I met her at the door of the parlor and, taking her by the hand,

[1]Pointed out.

inquired how she did. Oh, Julia, miserably indeed, said she. How severely does my mother's kindness reproach me! How insupportably it increases my self-condemnation! She wept; she wrung her hands and walked the room in the greatest agony! Mrs. Wharton was exceedingly distressed by her appearance. Tell me, Eliza, said she, tell me the cause of your trouble! Oh, kill me not by your mysterious concealment! My dear child, let me, by sharing, alleviate your affliction! Ask me not, madam, said she; O my mother, I conjure you not to insist on my divulging tonight the fatal secret which engrosses and distracts my mind! Tomorrow I will hide nothing from you. I will press you no further, rejoined her mama. Choose your own time, my dear; but remember, I must participate your grief, though I know not the cause.

Supper was brought in, and we endeavored to prevail on Eliza to eat, but in vain. She sat down, in compliance with our united importunities; but neither of us tasted food. It was removed untouched. For a while Mrs. Wharton and I gazed in silent anguish upon the spectacle of woe before us! At length Eliza rose to retire. Julia, said she, will you call at my chamber as you pass to your own? I assented. She then approached her mama, fell upon her knees before her, and clasping her hand, said in broken accents, Oh madam! Can you forgive a wretch who has forfeited your love, your kindness, and your compassion? Surely, Eliza, said she, you are not that being! No, it is impossible. But however great your transgression, be assured of my forgiveness, my compassion, and my continued love! Saying this, she threw her arms about her daughter's neck and affectionately kissed her. Eliza struggled from her embrace and, looking at her with wild despair, exclaimed, this is too much! Oh, this unmerited goodness is more than I can bear! She then rushed precipitately out of the room and left us overwhelmed in sympathy and astonishment.

When Mrs. Wharton had recovered herself a little, she observed that Eliza's brain was evidently disordered. Nothing else, continued she, could impel her to act in this extraordinary manner. At first she was resolved to follow her; but I dissuaded her from it, alleging that as she had desired me to come into her chamber, I thought it better for me to go alone. She acquiesced but said she should not think of going to bed but would, however, retire to her chamber and seek consolation there. I bade her good night and went up to Eliza, who took me by the hand and let me to the toilet,[2] upon which she laid the two enclosed letters, the one to her mama and the other to me. These, said she, contain what I had not resolution to express. Promise me, Julia, that they shall not be opened till tomorrow morning. I will, said I. I have thought and wept, continued she, till I have almost exhausted my strength and my reason. I would now obtain a little respite, that I may prepare my mind for the account I am one day to give at a higher tribunal than that of earthly friends. For this purpose, what I have written, and what I shall yet say to you, must close the account between you and me. I have certainly no balance against you, said I. In my breast you are fully acquitted. Your penitential tears have obliterated your guilt and blotted out your errors with your Julia. Henceforth, be they all forgotten. Live, and be happy. Talk not, said she, of life. It would be a vain hope though I cherished it myself.

[2]Toilet table, dressing table.

"That I must die is my only comfort;
Death is the privilege of human nature;
And life without it were not worth our taking.
Thither the poor, the prisoner, and the mourner
Fly for relief and lay their burdens down!"

You have forgiven me, Julia; my mother has assured me of her forgiveness, and what have I more to wish? My heart is much lightened by these kind assurances; they will be a great support to me in the dreadful hour which awaits me! What mean you, Eliza? said I. I fear some desperate purpose labors in your mind. Oh, no, she replied; you may be assured your fear is groundless. I know not what I say: my brain is on fire; I am all confusion! Leave me, Julia; when I have had a little rest, I shall be composed. These letters have almost distracted me; but they are written, and I am comparatively easy. I will not leave you, Eliza, said I, unless you will go directly to bed and endeavor to rest. I will, said she, and the sooner the better. I tenderly embraced her and retired, though not to bed. About an hour after, I returned to her chamber and, opening the door very softly, found her apparently asleep. I acquainted Mrs. Wharton with her situation, which was a great consolation to us both, and encouraged us to go to bed. Having suffered much in my mind, and being much fatigued, I soon fell asleep, but the rattling of a carriage, which appeared to stop at a little distance from the house, awoke me. I listened a moment and heard the door turn slowly on its hinges. I sprang from my bed and reached the window just in time to see a female handed into a chaise by a man who hastily followed her and drove furiously away! I at once concluded they could be no other than Eliza and Major Sanford. Under this impression I made no delay but ran immediately to her chamber. A candle was burning on the table; but Eliza was not there! I thought it best to acquaint her mama with the melancholy discovery and, stepping to her apartment for the purpose, found her rising. She had heard me walk and was anxious to know the cause. What is the matter, Julia? said she. What is the matter? Dear Madam, said I, arm yourself with fortitude! What new occurrence demands it? rejoined she. Eliza has left us! Left us! What mean you? She is just gone! I saw her handed into a chaise, which instantly disappeared!

At this intelligence she gave a shriek and fell back on her bed! I alarmed the family and by their assistance soon recovered her. She desired me to inform her of every particular, relative to her elopement, which I did, and then delivered her the letter which Eliza had left for her. I suspect, said she, as she took it; I have long suspected what I dared not believe! The anguish of my mind has been known only to myself and my God! I could not answer her and therefore withdrew. When I had read Eliza's letter to me and wept over the sad fall and, as I fear, the total loss of this once amiable and accomplished girl, I returned to Mrs. Wharton. She was sitting in her easy chair and still held the fatal letter in her hand. When I entered, she fixed her streaming eyes upon me and exclaimed, O Julia, this is more than the bitterness of death! True, madam, said I, your affliction must be great; yet that all-gracious Being, who controls every event, is able and, I trust, disposed to support you! To Him, replied she, I desire humbly to resign myself; but I think I could have borne almost any other calamity with greater resignation and composure than this. With how much comparative ease could I have followed her to the grave, at any period since her birth! Oh, my child, my child! Dear, very dear hast thou been to my fond heart! Little did I think it possible for you to prepare so dreadful a cup of sorrow for your widowed mother! But where, continued she, where can the poor fugitive have fled? Where can she find that protection and tenderness which, notwithstanding her great apostacy, I should never have withheld? From whom can she receive those kind attentions which her situation demands?

The agitation of her mind had exhausted her strength; and I prevailed on her to refresh and endeavor to compose herself to rest; assuring her of my utmost exertions to find out Eliza's retreat and restore her to a mother's arms.

I am obliged to suppress my own emotions and to bend all my thoughts towards the alleviation of Mrs. Wharton's anxiety and grief.

Major Sanford is from home, as I expected; and I am determined, if he return, to see him myself and extort from him the place of Eliza's concealment. Her flight, in her present state of health, is inexpressibly distressing to her mother; and, unless we find her soon, I dread the effects!

I shall not close this till I have seen or heard from the vile miscreant who has involved a worthy family in wretchedness!

Friday Morning—Two days have elapsed without affording us much relief. Last evening I was told that Major Sanford was at home. I immediately wrote him a billet,[3] entreating and conjuring him to let me know where the hapless Eliza had fled. He returned me the following answer.

"Miss Granby need be under no apprehensions respecting the situation of our beloved Eliza. She is well provided for, conveniently accommodated, and has everything to make her happy which love or affluence can give.

Major Sanford has solemnly sworn not to discover[4] her retreat. She wishes to avoid the accusations of her friends, till she is better able to bear them.

Her mother may rest assured of immediate information should any danger threaten her amiable daughter and also of having seasonable notice of her safety."

Although little dependence can be placed upon this man, yet these assurances have, in a great degree, calmed our minds. We are, however, contriving means to explore[5] the refuge of the wanderer and hope, by tracing his steps, to accomplish our purpose. This we have engaged a friend to do.

I know, my dear Mrs. Sumner, the kind interest you will take in this disastrous affair. I tremble to think what the event may be! To relieve your suspense, however, I shall write you every circumstance, as it occurs. But at present, I shall only enclose Eliza's letters to her mama and me, and subscribe myself your sincere and obliged friend.

JULIA GRANBY.

Letter LXVIII
To Mrs. M. Wharton.

Tuesday.

My Honored and Dear Mama,

In what words, in what language shall I address you? What shall I say on a subject which deprives me of the power of expression? Would to God I had been totally deprived of that power before so fatal a subject required its

[3]Letter. [4]Reveal. [5]Search out.

exertion! Repentance comes too late, when it cannot prevent the evil lamented. For your kindness, your more than maternal affection towards me, from my infancy to the present moment, a long life of filial duty and unerring rectitude could hardly compensate. How greatly deficient in gratitude must I appear then, while I confess that precept and example, counsel and advice, instruction and admonition, have been all lost upon me!

Your kind endeavors to promote my happiness have been repaid by the inexcusable folly of sacrificing it. The various emotions of shame and remorse, penitence and regret, which torture and distract my guilty breast, exceed description. Yes, madam, your Eliza has fallen; fallen, indeed! She has become the victim of her own indiscretion and of the intrigue and artifice of a designing libertine who is the husband of another! She is polluted, and no more worthy of her parentage! She flies from you, not to conceal her guilt, that she humbly and penitently owns, but to avoid what she has never experienced and feels herself unable to support, a mother's frown; to escape the heart-rending sight of a parent's grief, occasioned by the crimes of her guilty child!

I have become a reproach and disgrace to my friends. The consciousness of having forfeited their favor and incurred their disapprobation and resentment, induces me to conceal from them the place of my retirement; but, lest your benevolence should render you anxious for my comfort in my present situation, I take the liberty to assure you that I am amply provided for.

I have no claim even upon your pity; but from my long experience of your tenderness, I presume to hope it will be extended to me. Oh, my mother, if you knew what the state of my mind is, and has been, for months past, you would surely compassionate[1] my case. Could tears efface the stain, which I have brought upon my family, it would long since have been washed away! But, alas, tears are vain; and vain is my bitter repentance! It cannot obliterate my crime nor restore me to innocence and peace! In this life I have no ideas of happiness. These I have wholly resigned! The only hope which affords me any solace is that of your forgiveness. If the deepest contrition can make an atonement, if the severest pains, both of body and mind, can restore me to your charity, you will not be inexorable! Oh, let my sufferings be deemed a sufficient punishment; and add not the insupportable weight of a parent's wrath! At present I cannot see you. The effect of my crime is too obvious to be longer concealed, to elude the invidious eye of curiosity. This night, therefore, I leave your hospitable mansion! This night I become a wretched wanderer from thy paternal roof! Oh, that the grave were this night to be my lodging. Then should I lie down and be at rest! Trusting in the mercy of God, through the mediation of his son, I think I could meet my heavenly father with more composure and confidence, than my earthly parent!

Let not the faults and misfortunes of your daughter oppress your mind. Rather let the conviction of having faithfully discharged your duty to your lost child support and console you in this trying scene.

Since I wrote the above, you have kindly granted me your forgiveness, though you knew not how great, how aggravated, was my offence! You forgive me, you say: Oh, the harmonious, the transporting sound! It has revived my drooping spirits and will enable me to encounter, with resolution, the trials before me!

[1]Pity.

Farewell, my dear mama! Pity and pray for your ruined child; and be assured that affection and gratitude will be the last sentiments which expire in the breast of your repenting daughter.

ELIZA WHARTON.

Letter LXIX

To Miss Julia Granby.

Tuesday.

My Dear Friend,

By that endearing title you permit me still to address you and such you have always proved yourself, by a participation of my distresses as well as by the consoling voice of pity and forgiveness. What destiny Providence designs for me, I know not; but I have my forebodings that this is the last time I shall ever accost you! Nor does this apprehension arise merely from a disturbed imagination. I have reason to think myself in a confirmed consumption,[1] which commonly proves fatal to persons in my situation. I have carefully concealed every complaint of the kind from my mama, for fear of distressing her; yet I have never been insensible of their probable issue, and have bidden a sincere welcome to them, as the harbingers of my speedy release from a life of guilt and woe!

I am going from you, Julia. This night separates us, perhaps, forever! I have not resolution to encounter the tears of my friends and therefore seek shelter among strangers, where none knows, or is interested in, my melancholy story. The place of my seclusion I studiously conceal; yet I shall take measures that you may be apprized of my fate.

Should it please God to spare and restore me to health, I shall return and endeavor, by a life of penitence and rectitude, to expiate my past offences. But should I be called from this scene of action and leave behind me a helpless babe, the innocent sufferer of its mother's shame, Oh, Julia, let your friendship for me extend to the little stranger! Intercede with my mother to take it under her protection and transfer to it all her affection for me, to train it up in the ways of piety and virtue that it may compensate her for the afflictions which I have occasioned!

One thing more I have to request. Plead for me with my two best friends, Mrs. Richman and Mrs. Sumner. I ask you not to palliate my faults, that cannot be done, but to obtain, if possible, their forgiveness. I cannot write all my full mind suggests on this subject. You know the purport and can better express it for me.

And now, my dear Julia, recommending myself again to your benevolence, to your charity, and (may I add?) to your affection, and entreating that the fatal consequences of my folly, now fallen upon my devoted head, may suffice for my punishment, let me conjure you to bury my crimes in the grave with me and to preserve the remembrance of my former virtues, which engaged your love and confidence, more especially of that ardent esteem for you, which will glow till the last expiring breath of your despairing

ELIZA WHARTON.

[1]A wasting disease, such as tuberculosis.

Letter LXX

To Mr. Charles Deighton.

Hartford.

I have, at last, accomplished the removal of my darling girl, from a place where she thought every eye accused, and every heart condemned her.

She has become quite romantic in her notions. She would not permit me to accompany her, lest it should be reported that we had eloped together. I provided amply for her future exigencies and conveyed her by night to the distance of ten or twelve miles, where we met the stage, in which I had previously secured her a seat. The agony of her grief at being thus obliged to leave her mother's house baffles all description.

It very sensibly affected me, I know. I was almost a penitent. I am sure I acted like one, whether I were sincere or not. She chose to go where she was totally unknown. She would leave the stage, she said, before it reached Boston, and take passage in a more private carriage to Salem, or its vicinity, where she would fix her abode; chalking the initials of my name over the door, as a signal to me of her residence.

She is exceedingly depressed and says she neither expects nor wishes to survive her lying in.[1] Insanity, for aught I know, must be my lot, if she should die. But I will not harbor the idea. I hope, one time or other, to have the power to make her amends, even by marriage. My wife may be provoked, I imagine, to sue for a divorce. If she should, she would find no difficulty in obtaining it; and then I would take Eliza in her stead. Though I confess that the idea of being thus connected with a woman whom I have been able to dishonor would be rather hard to surmount. It would hurt even my delicacy, little as you may think me to possess, to have a wife whom I know to be seducible. And, on this account, I cannot be positive that even Eliza would retain my love.

My Nancy and I have lived a pretty uncomfortable life, of late. She has been very suspicious of my amour with Eliza and now and then expressed her jealous sentiments a little more warmly than my patience would bear. But the news of Eliza's circumstances and retirement, being publicly talked of, have reached her ears and rendered her quite outrageous. She tells me she will no longer brook my indifference and infidelity, intends soon to return to her father's house and extricate herself from me entirely. My general reply to all this is that she knew my character before we married and could reasonably expect nothing less than what has happened. I shall not oppose her leaving me, as it may conduce to the execution of the plan I have hinted above.

Tomorrow I shall set out to visit my disconsolate fair one. From my very soul I pity her and wish I could have preserved her virtue consistently with the indulgence of my passion. To her I lay not the principal blame, as in like cases I do to the sex in general. My finesse was too well planned for detection and my snares too deeply laid for anyone to escape who had the least warmth in her constitution or affection in her heart. I shall, therefore, be the less whimsical about a future connection and the more solicitous to make her reparation, should it ever be in my power.

[1] I.e., confinement for childbirth.

Her friends are all in arms about her. I dare say I have the imprecations of the whole fraternity. They may thank themselves in part, for I always swore revenge for their dislike and coldness towards me. Had they been politic, they would have conducted [themselves] more like the aborigines of the country, who are said to worship the devil out of fear.

I am afraid I shall be obliged to remove my quarters, for Eliza was so great a favorite in town that I am looked upon with an evil eye. I pled with her before we parted last, to forgive my seducing her, alleged[2] my ardent love and my inability to possess her in any other way. How, said she, can that be love which destroys its object? But granting what you say, you have frustrated your own purpose. You have deprived yourself of my society, which might have been innocently enjoyed. You have cut me off from life in the midst of my days.[3] You have rendered me the reproach of my friends, the disgrace of my family, and a dishonor to virtue and my sex! But I forgive you, added she. Yes, Sanford, I forgive you and sincerely pray for your repentance and reformation. I hope to be the last wretched female sacrificed by you to the arts of falsehood and seduction!

May my unhappy story serve as a beacon to warn the American fair of the dangerous tendency and destructive consequences of associating with men of your character, of destroying their time, and risking their reputation by the practice of coquetry and its attendant follies! But for these, I might have been honorably connected and capable, at this moment, of diffusing and receiving happiness! But for your arts, I might have remained a blessing to society as well as the delight and comfort of my friends!

Your being a married man unspeakably aggravates both your guilt and mine. This circumstance annexes indelible shame to our crime! You have rent asunder the tenderest ties of nature! You have broken the bonds of conjugal love, which ought ever to be kept sacred and inviolate! You have filled with grief and discontent the heart of your amiable wife, whom gratitude, if no other principle, should have induced you to cherish with tenderness; and I, wretch that I am, have been your accomplice!

But I cease to reproach you. You have acted but too consistently with the character which I was sufficiently apprised you sustained. The blame then may be retorted on myself for disregarding the counsels, warnings, and admonitions of my best friends. You have prided yourself in the character of a libertine. Glory no longer in your shame! You have accomplished your designs, your dreadful designs against me! Let this suffice. Add not to the number of those deluded creatures who will one day rise up in judgment against you and condemn you.

By this time we had nearly reached the inn and were soon to part. I seized her hand and exclaimed, you must not leave me, Eliza, with that awful anathema on your lips! Oh, say that you will forget my past faults. That, said she, I shall soon do; for in the grave there is no remembrance! This to my mind was a harsher sentence than the other and almost threw me into despair. Never was I so wrought upon before! I knew not what to say or do! She saw my distress and kindly softened her manner. If I am severe, said she, it is because I wish to impress your mind with such a sense of your offences against

[2]Declared.

[3]"I said, O my God, take me not away in the midst of my days." Psalm 102:24.

your Maker, your friends, and society in general, as may effect your repentance and amendment. I wish not to be your accuser but your reformer. On several accounts I view my own crime in a more aggravated light than yours; but my conscience is awakened to a conviction of my guilt. Yours, I fear, is not. Let me conjure you to return home and endeavor, by your future kindness and fidelity to your wife, to make her all the amends in your power. By a life of virtue and religion you may yet become a valuable member of society and secure happiness both here and hereafter.

I begged leave to visit her retirement next week, not in continuation of our amour but as a friend, solicitous, to know her situation and welfare. Unable to speak, she only bowed assent. The stage being now ready, I whispered some tender things in her ear and, kissing her cheek, which was all she would permit, suffered her to depart.

My body remains behind; but my soul, if I have any, went with her!

This was a horrid lecture, Charles! She brought every charge against me which a fruitful and gloomy imagination could suggest! But I hope, when she recovers, she will resume her former cheerfulness and become as kind and agreeable as ever. My anxiety for her safety is very great. I trust, however, it will soon be removed and peace and pleasure be restored to your humble servant,

PETER SANFORD.

Letter LXXI

To Mrs. Lucy Sumner.

Hartford.

The drama is now closed! A tragical one indeed it has proved!

How sincerely, my dear Mrs. Sumner, must the friends of our departed Eliza sympathize with each other and with her afflicted, bereaved parent!

You have doubtless seen the account, in the public papers, which gave us the melancholy intelligence. But I will give you a detail of circumstances.

A few days after my last was written, we heard that Major Sanford's property was attached and he a prisoner in his own house. He was the last man to whom we wished to apply for information respecting the forlorn wanderer; yet we had no other resource. And after waiting a fortnight in the most cruel suspense, we wrote a billet, entreating him, if possible, to give some intelligence concerning her. He replied that he was unhappily deprived of all means of knowing himself but hoped soon to relieve his own and our anxiety about her.

In this situation we continued, till a neighbor (purposely, we since concluded) sent us a Boston paper. Mrs. Wharton took it and, unconscious of its contents, observed that the perusal might divert her a few moments. She read for some time when it suddenly dropped upon the floor. She clasped her hands together and, raising her streaming eyes to heaven, exclaimed, It is the Lord; let him do what he will! Be still, O my soul, and know that he is God!

What, madam, said I, can be the matter? She answered not; but with inexpressible anguish depicted in her countenance, pointed to the paper. I took it up and soon found the fatal paragraph. I shall not attempt to paint our heart-felt grief and lamentation upon this occasion; for we had no doubt of Eliza's being the person described as a stranger who died at Danvers last July.

Her delivery of a child, her dejected state of mind, the marks upon her linen, indeed every circumstance in the advertisement[1] convinced us beyond dispute that it could be no other. Mrs. Wharton retired immediately to her chamber, where she continued overwhelmed with sorrow that night and the following day. Such, in fact, has been her habitual frame ever since, though the endeavors of her friends, who have sought to console her, have rendered her somewhat more conversable. My testimony of Eliza's penitence, before her departure, is a source of comfort to this disconsolate parent. She fondly cherished the idea that, having expiated her offence by sincere repentance and amendment, her deluded child finally made a happy exchange of worlds. But the desperate resolution, which she formed and executed, of becoming a fugitive, of deserting her mother's house and protection, and of wandering and dying among strangers, is a most distressing reflection to her friends, especially to her mother, in whose breast so many painful ideas arise that she finds it extremely difficult to compose herself to that resignation, which she evidently strives to exemplify.

Eliza's brother has been to visit her last retreat and to learn the particulars of her melancholy exit. He relates that she was well accommodated and had every attention and assistance which her situation required. The people where she resided appear to have a lively sense of her merit and misfortunes. They testify her modest deportment, her fortitude under the sufferings to which she was called, and the serenity and composure with which she bid a last adieu to the world. Mr. Wharton has brought back several scraps of her writing containing miscellaneous reflections on her situation, the death of her babe, and the absence of her friends. Some of these were written before, some after her confinement. These valuable testimonies of the affecting sense and calm expectation she entertained of her approaching dissolution are calculated to sooth and comfort the minds of mourning connections. They greatly alleviate the regret occasioned by her absence at this awful period.

Her elopement can be equaled only by the infatuation which caused her ruin.

> "But let no one reproach her memory.
> Her life has paid the forfeit of her folly.
> Let that suffice."

I am told that Major Sanford is quite frantic. Sure I am that he has reason to be. If the mischiefs he has brought upon others return upon his own head, dreadful indeed must be his portion! His wife has left him and returned to her parents. His estate, which has been long mortgaged, is taken from him; and poverty and disgrace await him! Heaven seldom leaves injured innocence unavenged! Wretch that he is, he ought forever to be banished from human society! I shall continue with Mrs. Wharton till the lenient hand of time has assuaged her sorrows, and then make my promised visit to you. I will bring Eliza's posthumous papers with me, when I come to Boston, as I have not time to copy them now.

[1]Public announcement.

I foresee, my dear Mrs. Sumner, that this disastrous affair will suspend your enjoyments as it has mine. But what are our feelings compared with the pangs which rend a parent's heart? This parent, I here behold, inhumanly stripped of the best solace of her declining years by the ensnaring machinations of a profligate debauchee! Not only the life but what was still dearer, the reputation and virtue of the unfortunate Eliza, have fallen victims at the shrine of *libertinism*! Detested be the epithet! Let it henceforth bear its true signature, and candor itself shall call it *lust* and *brutality*!

Execrable is the man, however arrayed in magnificence, crowned with wealth, or decorated with the external graces and accomplishments of fashionable life, who shall presume to display them at the expense of virtue and innocence! Sacred names! Attended with real blessings; blessings too useful and important to be trifled away! My resentment at the base arts which must have been employed to complete the seduction of Eliza, I cannot suppress. I wish them to be exposed and stamped with universal ignominy! Nor do I doubt but you will join with me in execrating the measures by which *we* have been robbed of so valuable a friend and *society*, of so ornamental a member. I am, &c.

JULIA GRANBY.

Letter LXXII

To Mr. Charles Deighton.

Hartford.

Confusion, horror, and despair are the portion of your wretched, unhappy friend! Oh, Deighton, I am undone! Misery irremediable is my future lot! She is gone; yes, she is gone forever! The darling of my soul, the center of all my wishes and enjoyments is no more! Cruel fate has snatched her from me; and she is irretrievably lost! I rave and then reflect! I reflect and then rave! I have not patience to bear this calamity nor power to remedy it! Where shall I fly from the upbraidings of my mind, which accuses me as the murderer of my Eliza? I would fly to death and seek a refuge in the grave; but the forebodings of a retribution to come, I cannot away with! Oh, that I had seen her, that I had once more asked her forgiveness! But even that privilege, that consolation was denied me! The day on which I meant to visit her, most of my property was attached, and to secure the rest, I was obliged to shut my doors and become a prisoner in my own house! High living and old debts, incurred by extravagance, had reduced the fortune of my wife to very little, and I could not satisfy the clamorous demands of my creditors.

I would have given millions, had I possessed them, to have been at liberty to see and to have had the power to preserve Eliza from death! But in vain was my anxiety; it could not relieve, it could not liberate me! When I first heard the dreadful tidings of her exit, I believe I acted like a madman! Indeed, I am little else now!

I have compounded[1] with my creditors and resigned the whole of my property.

Thus, that splendor and equipage, to secure which I have sacrificed a virtuous woman, is taken from me; that poverty, the dread of which prevented my

[1]I.e., reached an agreement.

forming an honorable connection with an amiable and accomplished girl, the only one I ever loved, has fallen with redoubled vengeance upon my guilty head; and I must become a vagabond in the earth![2]

I shall fly my country as soon as possible; I shall go from every object which reminds me of my departed Eliza! But never, never shall I eradicate from my bosom the idea of her excellence or the painful remembrance of the injuries I have done her! Her shade will perpetually haunt me! The image of her, as she appeared when mounting the carriage which conveyed her forever from my sight, she waved her hand in token of a last adieu, will always be present to my imagination! The solemn counsel she gave me before we parted, never more to meet, will not cease to resound in my ears!

While my being is prolonged, I must feel the disgraceful and torturing effects of my guilt in seducing her! How madly have I deprived her of happiness, of reputation, of life! Her friends, could they know the pangs of contrition, and the horror of conscience which attend me, would be amply revenged!

It is said she quitted the world with composure and peace. Well she might! She had not that insupportable weight of iniquity which sinks me to despair! She found consolation in that religion which I have ridiculed as priestcraft and hypocrisy! But whether it be true, or false, would to heaven I could now enjoy the comforts which its votaries evidently feel!

My wife has left me. As we lived together without love, we parted without regret.

Now, Charles, I am to bid you a long, perhaps a last, farewell. Where I shall roam in future, I neither know nor care; I shall go where the name of Sanford is unknown and his person and sorrows unnoticed.

In this happy clime I have nothing to induce my stay. I have not money to support me with my profligate companions; nor have I any relish, at present, for their society. By the virtuous part of the community I am shunned as the pest and bane of social enjoyment. In short I am debarred from every kind of happiness. If I look back, I recoil with horror from the black catalogue of vices which have stained my past life and reduced me to indigence and contempt. If I look forward, I shudder at the prospects which my foreboding mind presents to view, both in this and a coming world! This is a deplorable, yet just, picture of myself! How totally the reverse of what I once appeared!

Let it warn you, my friend, to shun the dangerous paths which I have trodden, that you may never be involved in the hopeless ignominy and wretchedness of

PETER SANFORD.

Letter LXXIII

To Mrs. Julia Granby.

Boston.

A melancholy tale have you unfolded, my dear Julia; and tragic indeed is the concluding scene!

Is she then gone! gone in this most distressing manner! Have I lost my once loved friend, lost her in a way which I could never have conceived to be possible!

[2]For his murder of Abel, Cain was cursed by God: "A fugitive and a vagabond shalt thou be in the earth." Genesis 4:12.

Our days of childhood were spent together in the same pursuits, in the same amusements. Our riper years increased our mutual affection, and maturer judgment most firmly cemented our friendship. Can I then calmly resign her to so severe a fate! Can I bear the idea of her being lost to honor, to fame, and to life! No; she shall still live in the heart of her faithful Lucy, whose experience of her numerous virtues and engaging qualities has imprinted her image too deeply on the memory to be obliterated. However she may have erred, her sincere repentance is sufficient to restore her to charity.

Your letter gave me the first information of this awful event. I had taken a short excursion into the country, where I had not seen the papers, or, if I had, paid little or no attention to them. By your directions I found the distressing narrative of her exit. The poignancy of my grief, and the unavailing lamentations which the intelligence excited, need no delineation. To scenes of this nature you have been habituated in the mansion of sorrow where you reside.

How sincerely I sympathize with the bereaved parent of the dear, deceased Eliza, I can feel, but have not power to express. Let it be her consolation that her child is at rest. The resolution which carried this deluded wanderer thus far from her friends, and supported her through her various trials, is astonishing. Happy would it have been had she exerted an equal degree of fortitude in repelling the first attacks upon her virtue. But she is no more, and Heaven forbid that I should accuse or reproach her.

Yet in what language shall I express my abhorrence of the monster whose detestable arts have blasted one of the fairest flowers in creation? I leave him to God and his own conscience. Already is he exposed in his true colors. Vengeance already begins to overtake him. His sordid mind must now suffer the deprivation of those sensual gratifications beyond which he is incapable of enjoyment.

Upon your reflecting and steady mind, my dear Julia, I need not inculcate the lessons which may be drawn from this woe-fraught tale; but for the sake of my sex in general, I wish it engraved upon every heart, that virtue alone, independent of the trappings of wealth, the parade of equipage, and the adulation of gallantry, can secure lasting felicity. From the melancholy story of Eliza Wharton let the American fair learn to reject with disdain every insinuation derogatory to their true dignity and honor. Let them despise and forever banish the man who can glory in the seduction of innocence and the ruin of reputation. To associate is to approve; to approve is to be betrayed. I am, &c.,

LUCY SUMNER.

Letter LXXIV
To Mrs. M. Wharton.

Boston.

Dear madam: We have paid the last tribute of respect to your beloved daughter. The day after my arrival, Mrs. Sumner proposed that we should visit the sad spot which contains the remains of our once amiable friend. "The grave of Eliza Wharton," said she, "shall not be unbedewed by the tears of friendship."

Yesterday we went accordingly, and were much pleased with the apparent sincerity of the people in their assurances that every thing in their power had been done to render her situation comfortable. The minutest circumstances were faithfully related; and, from the state of her mind in her last hours, I think much comfort may be derived to her afflicted friends.

We spent a mournful hour in the place where she is interred, and then returned to the inn, while Mrs. Sumner gave orders for a decent stone to be erected over her grave, with the following inscription:—

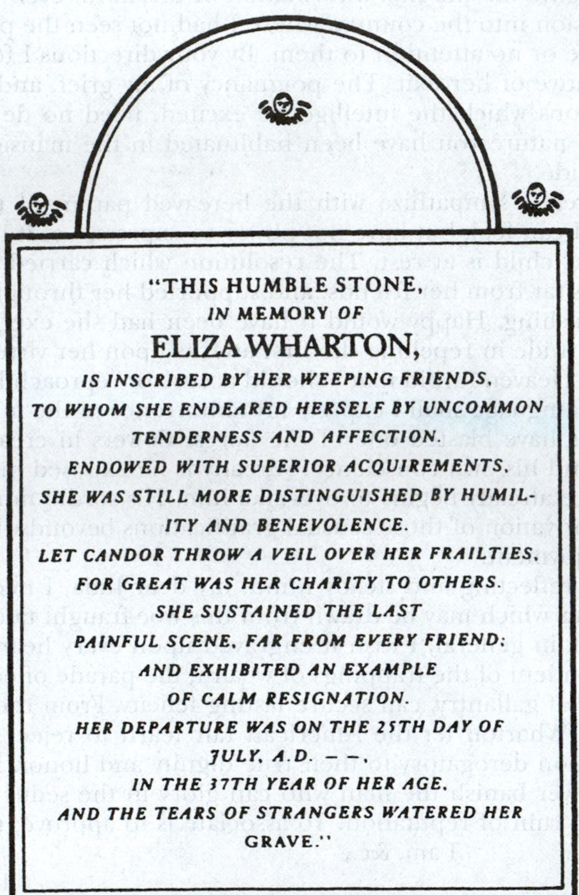

"THIS HUMBLE STONE,
IN MEMORY OF
ELIZA WHARTON,
IS INSCRIBED BY HER WEEPING FRIENDS,
TO WHOM SHE ENDEARED HERSELF BY UNCOMMON
TENDERNESS AND AFFECTION.
ENDOWED WITH SUPERIOR ACQUIREMENTS,
SHE WAS STILL MORE DISTINGUISHED BY HUMIL-
ITY AND BENEVOLENCE.
LET CANDOR THROW A VEIL OVER HER FRAILTIES,
FOR GREAT WAS HER CHARITY TO OTHERS.
SHE SUSTAINED THE LAST
PAINFUL SCENE, FAR FROM EVERY FRIEND;
AND EXHIBITED AN EXAMPLE
OF CALM RESIGNATION.
HER DEPARTURE WAS ON THE 25TH DAY OF
JULY, A.D. — —,
IN THE 37TH YEAR OF HER AGE,
AND THE TEARS OF STRANGERS WATERED HER
GRAVE."

I hope, madam, that you will derive satisfaction from these exertions of friendship, and that, united to the many other sources of consolation with which you are furnished, they may alleviate your grief, and, while they leave the pleasing remembrance of her virtues, add the supporting persuasion that your Eliza is happy. I am, &c.,

JULIA GRANBY.

1797

William Bartram 1739–1823

To the Seminole Indians, William Bartram was known as Puc Puggy, *the "Flower Hunter." To generations of nineteenth-century Europeans, he was a source of their visionary concept of the American wilderness. To literary historians, he stands as an example of the American transition from the Enlightenment to the age of romanticism.*

Bartram was born in Philadelphia and raised on the grounds of the renowned botanical gardens established in 1728 by his Quaker father, the famous naturalist John Bartram. William Bartram was strongly influenced by his father's Quakerism, and he absorbed his father's powers of observation, a deep appreciation of nature, and a talent for drawing and painting.

As a youth William accompanied his father on trips through rural Pennsylvania and New York to make sketches and gather specimens of seeds, plants, and animals for shipment to European naturalists. In 1757, when he was eighteen, William was apprenticed to a Philadelphia merchant, but in 1766 he gladly abandoned his merchant career to join a botanizing expedition through the wilds of Georgia and Florida with his father, who had recently been appointed Royal Botanist of the Floridas by King George III of England, who had won Florida from Spain in 1763.

The journal of the expedition, written by John Bartram and illustrated by his son William, brought wide attention and funds for further botanical expeditions. In 1773 William set out alone on a four-year journey through the Carolinas, Georgia, Florida, and westward to the Mississippi. He collected and drew specimens of plants and animals and recorded the life of the frontiersmen and Indians, among them the Seminoles who befriended Bartram and named him "Flower Hunter." In 1791, with the aid of a subscription supported by Jefferson, Washington, and Franklin, the journal of William Bartram's expedition was published as Travels Through North and South Carolina, Georgia, East and West Florida.

The book found a wide European audience eager to read of the wonders of the New World. Soon it was reprinted in London and Dublin and translated into German, Dutch, and French. Where John Bartram's reports had been written in the restrained, scientific language of neoclassicism, the journal of his son William revealed the mind of a poet and painter, strongly influenced by the new romanticism. Amid conventional passages of scientific report, William Bartram interposed rhapsodic descriptions of rare and exotic plants, primitive men, and terrifying animals, all living in a divine allegorical community. His writing was as rich and ornate as the plumage of the birds he had painted, and it exhibited a catalogue of themes and attitudes that were to become the romantic conventions of the next century: the sublimity of the wilderness, the regenerative power of untouched nature, the personification of plants and animals endowed with human virtues and emotions. William Bartram presented visions of a terrestrial paradise, and he celebrated the simple life and the primitive virtues of the "Noble Savage," who was blessed with innate goodness but colorfully debauched by civilization and the white man's rum.

Early reviewers objected that Bartram's Travels *violated neoclassic canons of decorum: His sympathies for the Indians were "extravagant," and his "rhapsodical effusions" were "too luxuriant and florid to merit the palm of chastity and correctness." But his* Travels *fired the imagination of the mass of readers, who found them blessed with a "rich vein of piety blended with purest morality."*

The English historian Carlyle praised the "wondrous kind of floundering eloquence" with which Bartram had perfumed his writing. English romantic poets such as Wordsworth, Coleridge, and Southey mined his labyrinthine imagery for themes and spectacles of the exotic and the sublime. The French romanticist Chateaubriand, who came to be called the "Revealer of America" for his accounts of the American scene and his tales of Indian life, adapted whole passages from The Travels, *presenting them as his own "exclamatory admiration" of lands he had not visited and Indians he had not seen.*

To eighteenth century readers, Bartram's writings seemed to confirm romantic dreams of an American wilderness where one could pursue the dazzling hope of perfectibility. To modern readers, discontented with urban life and the poisonous residue of industrialism, Bartram has become a naturalist hero, harmonizing with a green world of simplicity and celebrating the bountiful glories of life.

FURTHER READING: *The Travels of William Bartram,* ed. M. Van Doren, 1928; N. Fagin, *William Bartram, Interpreter of the American Landscape, 1933;* E. Earnest, *John and William Bartram, Botanists and Explorers,* 1940; *John and William Bartram's America,* ed. H. Cruickshank, 1957; P. Regis, *Describing Early America,* 1992; T. Slaughter, *The Natures of John and William Bartram,* 1996; E. Cashin, *William Bartram and the American Revolution on the Southern Frontier,* 2000; B. Sanders, *A Guide to William Bartram's Travels,* 2002; D. Ray, *The Flower Hunter, William Bartram, America's First Naturalist,* 2004.

TEXT: *The Travels of William Bartram,* ed. F. Harper, 1958. Some spelling and punctuation have been changed to conform more nearly to modern practice.

from *TRAVELS THROUGH NORTH AND SOUTH CAROLINA, GEORGIA, EAST AND WEST FLORIDA*

THE AUTHOR SETS SAIL FROM PHILADELPHIA, AND ARRIVES AT CHARLESTON, FROM WHENCE HE BEGINS HIS TRAVELS.

At the request of Dr. Fothergill, of London,[1] to search the Floridas, and the western parts of Carolina and Georgia, for the discovery of rare and useful productions of nature, chiefly in the vegetable kingdom; in April, 1773, I embarked for Charleston, South Carolina. . . .

There are few objects out at sea to attract the notice of the traveller, but what are sublime,[2] awful, and majestic: the seas themselves, in a tempest, exhibit a tremendous scene, where the winds assert their power, and, in furious conflict, seem to set the ocean on fire. On the other hand, nothing can be more sublime than the view of the encircling horizon, after the turbulent winds have taken their flight, and the lately agitated bosom of the deep has again become calm and pacific; the gentle moon rising in dignity from the east, attended by millions of glittering orbs; the luminous appearance of the seas at night, when all the waters seem transmuted into liquid silver; the prodigious bands of porpoises foreboding tempest, that appear to cover the

[1]John Fothergill (1712–1780), Quaker physician and botanist who subsidized Bartram's explorations in exchange for Bartram shipping Fothergill specimens and drawings of plants and animals.

[2]Here and in following passages, Bartram presents some of the earliest American literary expression of the idea of the sublime, an aesthetic concept of the classical age that re-emerged in the eighteenth century. During the high romanticism of the nineteenth century, use of the sublime became a stylistic convention. Numerous writers portrayed the tempestuous and overmastering sights of nature's grandeurs in an effort to rouse the passions and elevate the souls of readers and transport them to higher and nobler levels of imaginative understanding. In America it is evident in the nature writing of Jefferson, in the fiction of Cooper, and in the metaphysical writing of the transcendentalists. At its extreme, the concept decayed into the extravagances of gothic romances designed to evoke terror and woe in readers addicted to the mindless joys of excitement.

ocean; the mighty whale, sovereign of the watery realms, who cleaves the seas in his course; the sudden appearance of land from the sea, the strand stretching each way, beyond the utmost reach of sight; the alternate appearance and recess of the coast, whilst the far distant blue hills slowly retreat and disappear; or, as we approach the coast, the capes and promontories first strike our sight, emerging from the watery expanse, and, like mighty giants, elevating their crests towards the skies; the water suddenly alive with its scaly inhabitants; squadrons of sea-fowl sweeping through the air, impregnated with the breath of fragrant aromatic trees and flowers; the amplitude and magnificence of these scenes are great indeed, and may present to the imagination, an idea of the first appearance of the earth to man at the creation.

. . .

I arrived at St. Ille's[3] in the evening, where I lodged, and next morning having crossed over in a ferry boat, set forward for St. Mary's.[4] The situation of the territory, its soil and productions between these two last rivers, are nearly similar to those which I had passed over, except that the savannas[5] are more frequent and extensive.

It may be proper to observe, that I had now passed the utmost frontier of the white settlements on that border. It was drawing on towards the close of day, the skies serene and clam, the air temperately cool, and gentle zephyrs breathing through the fragrant pines; the prospect around enchantingly varied and beautiful; endless green savannas, checquered with coppices[6] of fragrant shrubs, filled the air with the richest perfume. The gaily attired plants which enamelled the green had begun to imbibe the pearly dew of evening; nature seemed silent, and nothing appeared to ruffle the happy moments of evening contemplation: when, on a sudden, an Indian appeared crossing the path, at a considerable distance before me. On perceiving that he was armed with a rifle, the first sight of him startled me, and I endeavoured to elude his sight, by stopping my pace, and keeping large trees between us; but he espied me, and turning short about, set spurs to his horse, and came up on full gallop. I never before this was afraid at the sight of an Indian, but at this time, I must own that my spirits were very much agitated; I saw at once, that being unarmed, I was in his power, and having now but a few moments to prepare, I resigned myself entirely to the will of the Almighty, trusting to his mercies for my preservation; my mind then became tranquil, and I resolved to meet the dreaded foe with resolution and cheerful confidence. The intrepid Seminole stopped suddenly, three or four yards before me, and silently viewed me, his countenance angry and fierce, shifting his rifle from shoulder to shoulder, and looking about instantly on all sides. I advanced towards him, and with an air of confidence offered him my hand, hailing him, brother; at this he hastily jerked back his arm, with a look of malice, rage and disdain, seeming every way disconcerted; when again looking at me more attentively, he instantly spurred up to me, and, with dignity in his look and action, gave me his hand. Possibly the silent language of his soul, during the moment of suspense (for I believe his design was to kill me when he first came up) was after this manner: "White man, thou art my enemy, and thou and thy

[3]The Satilla River in southeast Georgia.
[4]River forming part of the boundary between Georgia and Florida.
[5]Open grasslands. [6]Copses, thickets.

brethren may have killed mine; yet it may not be so, and even were that the case, thou art now alone, and in my power. Live; the Great Spirit forbids me to touch thy life; go to thy brethren, tell them thou sawest an Indian in the forests, who knew how to be humane and compassionate." In fine, we shook hands, and parted in a friendly manner, in the midst of a dreary wilderness; and he informed me of the course and distance to the trading-house, where I found he had been extremely ill treated the day before.

I now set forward again, and after eight or ten miles riding, arrived at the banks of St. Mary's, opposite the stores,[7] and got safe over before dark. The river is here about one hundred yards across, has ten feet water, and, following its course, about sixty miles to the sea, though but about twenty miles by land. The trading company here received and treated me with great civility. On relating my adventures on the road, particularly the last with the Indian, the chief replied, with a countenance that at once bespoke surprise and pleasure, "My friend, consider yourself a fortunate man; that fellow," said he, "is one of the greatest villains on earth, a noted murderer, and outlawed by his countrymen. Last evening he was here, we took his gun from him, broke it in pieces, and gave him a severe drubbing; he, however, made his escape, carrying off a new rifle gun, with which, he said, going off, he would kill the first white man he met."

On seriously contemplating the behaviour of this Indian towards me, so soon after his ill treatment, the following train of sentiments insensibly crowded in upon my mind.

Can it be denied, but that the moral principle, which directs the savages to virtuous and praiseworthy actions, is natural or innate? It is certain they have not the assistance of letters, or those means of education in the schools of philosophy, where the virtuous sentiments and actions of the most illustrious characters are recorded, and carefully laid before the youth of civilized nations: therefore this moral principle must be innate, or they must be under the immediate influence and guidance of a more divine and powerful preceptor, who, on these occasions, instantly inspires them, and as with a ray of divine light, points out to them at once the dignity, propriety, and beauty of virtue.

. . .

The river St. Mary has its source from a vast lake, or marsh, called Ouaquaphenogaw,[8] which lies between Flint and Oakmulge[9] rivers, and occupies a space of near three hundred miles in circuit. This vast accumulation of waters, in the wet season, appears as a lake, and contains some large islands or knolls, of rich high land; one of which the present generation of the Creeks[10] represent to be a most blissful spot of the earth: they say it is inhabited by a peculiar race of Indians, whose women are incomparably beautiful; they also tell you, that this terrestrial paradise has been seen by some of their enterprising hunters, when in pursuit of game, who being lost in inextricable swamps and bogs, and on the point of perishing, were unexpectedly relieved by a company of beautiful women, whom they call daughters of the sun, who

[7]Indian trading posts. [8]The Okefenokee Swamp in southeast Georgia. [9]Ocmulgee.
[10]Indian tribes of the Creek Confederation, including the Seminoles.

kindly gave them such provisions as they had with them, which were chiefly fruit, oranges, dates, &c. and some corn cakes, and then enjoined them to fly for safety to their own country, for that their husbands were fierce men, and cruel to strangers; they further say, that these hunters had a view of their settlements, situated on the elevated banks of an island, or promontory, in a beautiful lake; but that in their endeavours to approach it, they were involved in perpetual labyrinths, and, like enchanted land, still as they imagined they had just gained it, it seemed to fly before them, alternately appearing and disappearing. They resolved, at length, to leave the delusive pursuit, and to return; which, after a number of inexpressible difficulties, they effected. When they reported their adventures to their countrymen, their young warriors were enflamed with an irresistible desire to invade, and make a conquest of, so charming a country; but all their attempts have hitherto proved abortive, never having been able again to find that enchanting spot, nor even any road or pathway to it.

. . .

Having completed my Hortus Siccus,[11] and made up my collections of seeds and growing roots, the fruits of my late western tour, and sent them to Charleston, to be forwarded to Europe, I spent the remaining part of this season in botanical excursions to the low countries, between Carolina and East Florida, and collected seeds, roots, and specimens, making drawings of such curious subjects as could not be preserved in their native state of excellence.

During this recess from the high road of my travels, having obtained the use of a neat light cypress canoe, at Broughton Island,[12] a plantation, the property of the Hon. Henry Laurens, Esq.[13] where I stored myself with necessaries, for the voyage, and resolved upon a trip up the Alatamaha.

I ascended this beautiful river, on whose fruitful banks the generous and true sons of liberty securely dwell, fifty miles above the white settlements.

How gently flow thy peaceful floods, O Alatamaha! How sublimely rise to view, on thy elevated shores, yon Magnolian groves, from whose tops the surrounding expanse is perfumed, by clouds of incense, blended with the exhalating balm of the Liquid-amber,[14] and odours continually arising from circumambient aromatic groves of Illicium, Myrica, Laurus, and Bignonia.[15]

When wearied, with working my canoe against the impetuous current (which becomes stronger by reason of the mighty floods of the river, with collected force, pressing through the first hilly ascents, where the shores on each side the river present to view rocky cliffs rising above the surface of the water, in nearly flat horizontal masses, washed smooth by the descending floods, and which appear to be a composition, or concrete, of sandy lime-stone) I resigned my bark to the friendly current, reserving to myself

[11]Latin: Dry Garden; a collection of dried plants.

[12]Broton Island in the mouth of the Altamaha River in Georgia.

[13]Bartram's agent in Charleston, South Carolina, who shipped his collections to England.

[14]The sweet gum tree.

[15]Purple anis, wax myrtle, and plants of the genus Lauraceae (such as sassafras). Bignonia is a woody vine with large red flowers.

the control of the helm. My progress was rendered delightful by the sylvan elegance of the groves, cheerful meadows, and high distant forests, which in grand order presented themselves to view. The winding banks of the river, and the high projecting promontories, unfolded fresh scenes of grandeur and sublimity. The deep forests and distant hills re-echoed the cheering social lowings of domestic herds. The air was filled with the loud and shrill whooping of the wary sharp-sighted crane. Behold, on yon decayed, defoliated Cypress tree, the solitary wood-pelican, dejectedly perched upon its utmost elevated spire; he there, like an ancient venerable sage, sets himself up as a mark of derision, for the safety of his kindred tribes. The crying-bird, another faithful guardian, screaming in the gloomy thickets, warns the feathered tribes of approaching peril; and the plumage of the swift sailing squadrons of Spanish curlews (white as the immaculate robe of innocence) gleam in the cerulean skies.

Thus secure and tranquil, and meditating on the marvellous scenes of primitive nature, as yet unmodified by the hand of man, I gently descended the peaceful stream, on whose polished surface were depicted the mutable shadows from its pensile[16] banks; whilst myriads of finny inhabitants sported in its pellucid floods.

The glorious sovereign of day, cloathed in light refulgent, rolling on his gilded chariot, speeds to revisit the western realms. Gray pensive eve now admonishes us of gloomy night's hasty approach: I am roused by care to seek a place of secure repose, ere darkness comes on.

. . .

Nature now weary, I resigned myself to rest; the night passed over; the cool dews of the morning awake me; my fire burnt low; the blue smoke scarce rises above the moistened embers; all is gloomy: the late starry skies, now overcast by thick clouds, I am warned to rise and be going. The livid purple clouds thicken on the frowning brows of the morning; the tumultuous winds from the east now exert their power. O peaceful Alatamaha! gentle by nature! how thou art ruffled! thy wavy surface disfigures every object, presenting them obscurely to the sight, and they at length totally disappear, whilst the furious winds and sweeping rains bend the lofty groves, and prostate the quaking grass, driving the affrighted creatures to their dens and caverns.

The tempest now relaxes, its impetus is spent, and a calm serenity gradually takes place; by noon they break away, the blue sky appears, the fulgid[17] sunbeams spread abroad their animating light, and the steady western wind resumes his peaceful reign. The waters are purified, the waves subside, and the beautiful river regains its native calmness; so it is with the varied and mutable scenes of human events on the stream of life. The higher powers and affections of the soul are so blended and connected with the inferior passions, that the most painful feelings are excited in the mind when the latter are crossed; thus in the moral system, which we have planned for our

[16]Overhanging.
[17]Glittering.

conduct, as a ladder whereby to mount to the summit of terrestrial glory and happiness, and from whence we perhaps meditated our flight to heaven itself, at the very moment when we vainly imagine ourselves to have attained its point, some unforeseen accident intervenes, and surprises us; the chain is violently shaken, we quit our hold and fall; the well contrived system at once becomes a chaos; every idea of happiness recedes; the splendour of glory darkens, and at length totally disappears; every pleasing object is defaced; all is deranged, and the flattering scene passes quite away, a gloomy cloud pervades the understanding, and when we see our progress retarded, and our best intentions frustrated, we are apt to deviate from the admonitions and convictions of virtue, to shut our eyes upon our guide and protector, doubt of his power, and despair of his assistance. But let us wait and rely on our God, who in due time will shine forth in brightness, dissipate the envious cloud, and reveal to us how finite and circumscribed is human power, when assuming to itself independent wisdom.

. . .

Having rested myself a few days, and by ranging about the neighbouring plains and groves, surrounding this pleasant place,[18] pretty well recovered my strength and spirits, I began to think of planning my future excursions, at a distance round about this center.

. . .

About the middle of May, every thing being in readiness, to proceed up the river, we set sail. The traders with their goods in a large boat, went ahead, and myself in my little vessel followed them; and as their boat was large, and deeply laden, I found that I could easily keep up with them, and if I chose, out-sail them; but I preferred keeping them company, as well for the sake of collecting what I could from conversation, as on account of my safety in crossing the great lake,[19] expecting to return alone, and descend the river at my own leisure.

We had a pleasant day, the wind fair and moderate, and ran by Mount Hope,[20] so named by my father John Bartram, when he ascended this river, about fifteen years ago. It is a very high shelly bluff, upon the little lake. It was at that time a fine Orange grove, but now cleared and converted into a large Indigo plantation, the property of an English gentleman, under the care of an agent. In the evening we arrived at Mount Royal,[21] where we came to, and stayed all night: we were treated with great civility, by a gentleman whose name was——Kean,[22] and had been an Indian trader.

[18]Near present-day Jacksonville, Florida. Bartram here began his voyage up the St. John's River in northeastern Florida.

[19]Lake Beresford.

[20]At the outlet of Little Lake George, Florida.

[21]Site of an Indian ceremonial mound. Bartram had visited it previously with his father, in 1765–1766.

[22]Bartram left space for his host's first name.

From this place we enjoyed a most enchanting prospect of the great Lake George, through a grand avenue, if I may so term this narrow reach of the river, which widens gradually for about two miles, towards its entrance into the lake, so as to elude the exact rules of perspective and appears of an equal width.

At about fifty yards distance from the landing place, stands a magnificent Indian mount. About fifteen years ago I visited this place, at which time there were no settlements of white people, but all appeared wild and savage; yet in that uncultivated state, it possessed an almost inexpressible air of grandeur, which was not entirely changed. At that time there was a very considerable extent of old fields, round about the mount; there was also a large Orange grove, together with palms and Live Oaks, extending from near the mount, along the banks, downwards, all of which has since been cleared away to make room for planting ground. But what greatly contributed towards completing the magnificence of the scene, was a noble Indian highway, which led from the great mount, on a straight line, three quarters of a mile, first through a point or wing of the Orange grove, and continuing thence through an awful forest, of Live Oaks, it was terminated by Palms and Laurel Magnolias, on the verge of an oblong artificial lake, which was on the edge of an extensive green level savanna. This grand highway was about fifty yards wide, sunk a little below the common level, and the earth thrown up on each side, making a bank of about two feet high. Neither nature nor art, could any where present a more striking contrast, as you approach this savanna. The glittering water pond, plays on the sight, through the dark grove, like a brilliant diamond, on the bosom of the illumined savanna, bordered with various flowery shrubs and plants; and as we advance into the plain, the sight is agreeably relieved by a distant view of the forests, which partly environ the green expanse, on the left hand, whilst the imagination is still flattered and entertained by the far distant misty points of the surrounding forests, which project into the plain, alternately appearing and disappearing, making a grand sweep round on the right, to the distant banks of the great lake. But that venerable grove is now no more. All has been cleared away and planted with Indigo, Corn and Cotton, but since deserted; there was now scarcely five acres of ground under fence. It appeared like a desert, to a great extent, and terminated, on the land side, by frightful thickets and open Pine forests.

It appears however, that the late proprietor had some taste, as he has preserved the mount, and this little adjoining grove inviolate. The prospect from this station is so happily situated by nature, as to comprise at one view, the whole of the sublime and pleasing.

At the reanimating appearance of the rising sun, nature again revives; and I obey the cheerful summons of the gentle monitors of the meads and groves.

Yet vigilant and faithful servants of the Most High! ye who worship the Creator, morning, noon and eve, in simplicity of heart; I haste to join the universal anthem. My heart and voice unite with yours, in sincere homage to the great Creator, the universal sovereign.

O may I be permitted to approach the throne of mercy! may these my humble and penitent supplications, amidst the universal shouts of homage, from thy creatures, meet with thy acceptance.

And although, I am sensible, that my service, cannot increase, or diminish thy glory, yet it is pleasing to thy servant, to be permitted to sound thy praise; for O sovereign Lord! we know that thou alone art perfect, and worthy to be worshiped. O universal Father! look down upon us we beseech thee, with an eye of pity and compassion, and grant that universal peace and love, may prevail in the earth, even that divine harmony, which fills the heavens, thy glorious habitation.

And O sovereign Lord! since it has pleased thee to endue[23] man with power, and pre-eminence, here on earth, and establish his dominion over all creatures, may we look up to thee, that our understanding may be so illuminated with wisdom and our hearts warmed and animated, with a due sense of charity, that we may be enabled to do thy will, and perform our duty towards those submitted to our service, and protection, and be merciful to them even as we hope for mercy.

Thus may we be worthy of the dignity, and superiority of the high, and distinguished station, in which thou has placed us here on earth.

. . .

How supremely blessed were our hours at this time! plenty of delicious and healthful food, our stomachs keen, with contented minds; under no control, but what reason and ordinate passions dictated, far removed from the seats of strife.

Our situation was like that of the primitive state of man, peaceable, contented, and sociable. The simple and necessary calls of nature, being satisfied. We were altogether as brethren of one family, strangers to envy, malice and rapine.

The night being over we arose, and pursued our course up the river, and in the evening reached the trading-house, Spalding's upper store,[24] where I took up my quarters for several weeks.

On our arrival at the upper store, we found it occupied by a white trader, who had for a companion, a very handsome Seminole young woman. Her father, who was a prince, by the name of the White Captain, was an old chief of the Seminoles, and with part of his family, to the number of ten or twelve, were encamped in an Orange grove near the stores, having lately come in from a hunt.

This white trader, soon after our arrival, delivered up the goods and storehouses to my companion,[25] and joined his father-in-law's camp, and soon after went away into the forests on hunting and trading amongst the flying camps of Seminoles.

He is at this time, unhappy in his connections with his beautiful savage. It is but a few years since he came here, I think from North Carolina, a stout genteel well-bred man, active, and of a heroic and amiable disposition, and by his industry, honesty, and engaging manners, had gained the affections of the Indians, and soon made a little fortune by traffic with the Seminoles;

[23]Provide.

[24]A trading post on the St. John's River, about five miles above Lake George.

[25]Bartram was briefly joined in his expedition by an Indian whom he did not name.

when, unfortunately, meeting with this little charmer, they were married in the Indian manner. He loves her sincerely, as she possesses every perfection in her person to render a man happy. Her features are beautiful, and manners engaging. Innocence, modesty, and love, appear to a stranger in every action and movement; and these powerful graces she has so artfully played upon her beguiled and vanquished lover, and unhappy slave, as to have already drained him of all his possessions, which she dishonestly distributes amongst her savage relations. He is now poor, emaciated, and half distracted, often threatening to shoot her, and afterwards put an end to his own life; yet he has not resolution even to leave her; but now endeavours to drown and forget his sorrows, in deep draughts of brandy. Her father condemns her dishonest and cruel conduct.

These particulars were related to me by my old friend the trader, directly after a long conference which he had with the White Captain on the subject, his son-in-law being present. The scene was affecting; they both shed tears plentifully. My reasons for mentioning this affair, so foreign to my business, was to exhibit an instance of the power of beauty in a savage, and their art and finesse in improving it to their private ends. It is, however, but doing justice to the virtue and moral conduct of the Seminoles, and American Aborigines in general, to observe, that the character of this woman is condemned and detested by her own people, of both sexes; and if her husband should turn her away, according to the customs and usages of these people, she would not get a husband again, as a divorce seldom takes place but in consequence of a deliberate impartial trial, and public condemnation, and then she would be looked upon as a harlot.

Such is the virtue of these untutored savages; but I am afraid this is a common phrase epithet, having no meaning, or at least improperly applied; for these people are both well tutored and civil; and it is apparent to an impartial observer, who resides but a little time amongst them, that it is from the most delicate sense of the honour and reputation of their tribes and families, that their laws and customs receive their force and energy. This is the divine principle which influences their moral conduct, and solely preserves their constitution and civil government in that purity in which they are found to prevail amongst them.

. . .

Being desirous of continuing my travels and observations, higher up the river. . . .[26]

Provisions and all necessaries being procured, and the morning pleasant, we went on board and stood up the river. We passed for several miles on the left, by islands of high swamp land, exceedingly fertile, their banks for a good distance from the water, much higher than the interior part, and sufficiently so to build upon, and be out of the reach of inundations. They consist of a loose black mould, with a mixture of sand, shells and dissolved vegetables. The opposite Indian coast is a perpendicular bluff, ten or twelve feet high. . . .

[26]The St. John's River.

At the upper end of this bluff is a fine Orange grove. Here my Indian companion requested me to set him on shore, being already tired of rowing under a fervid sun, and having for some time intimated a dislike to his situation, I readily complied with his desire, knowing the impossibility of compelling an Indian against his own inclinations, or even prevailing upon him by reasonable arguments, when labour is in the question; before my vessel reached the shore, he sprang out of her and landed, when uttering a shrill and terrible whoop, he bounded off like a roebuck, and I lost sight of him. I at first apprehended that as he took his gun with him, he intended to hunt for some game and return to me in the evening. The day being excessively hot and sultry, I concluded to take up my quarters here until next morning.

The Indian not returning this morning, I set sail alone. . . .

The little lake, which is an expansion of the river, now appeared in view; on the East side are extensive marshes, and on the other high forests and Orange groves, and then a bay, lined with vast Cypress swamps, both coasts gradually approaching each other, to the opening of the river again, which is in this place about three hundred yards wide; evening now drawing on, I was anxious to reach some high bank of the river, where I intended to lodge, and agreeably to my wishes, I soon after discovered on the West shore, a little promontory, a the turning of the river, contracting it here to about one hundred and fifty yards in width. . . .

The evening was temperately cool and calm. The crocodiles began to roar and appear in uncommon numbers along the shores and in the river. I fixed my camp in an open plain, near the utmost projection of the promontory, under the shelter of a large Live Oak, which stood on the highest part of the ground and but a few yards from my boat. From this open, high situation, I had a free prospect of the river, which was a matter of no trivial consideration to me, having good reason to dread the subtle attacks of the alligators,[27] who were crowding about my harbour. Having collected a good quantity of wood for the purpose of keeping up a light and smoke during the night, I began to think of preparing my supper, when, upon examining my stores, I found but a scanty provision, I thereupon determined, as the most expeditious way of supplying my necessities, to take my bob[28] and try for some trout. About one hundred yards above my harbour, began a cove or bay of the river, out of which opened a large lagoon. The mouth or entrance from the river to it was narrow, but the waters soon after spread and formed a little lake, extending into the marshes, its entrance and shores within I observed to be verged with floating lawns of the Pistia and Nymphea[29] and other aquatic plants; these I knew were excellent haunts for trout.

The verges and islets of the lagoon were elegantly embellished with flowering plants and shrubs; the laughing coots[30] with wings half spread were tripping over the little coves and hiding themselves in the tufts of grass; young broods of the painted summer teal,[31] skimming the still surface of

[27]Bartram used the terms *crocodile* and *alligator* synonymously. He never traveled far enough south to see true crocodiles.

[28]Fishing tackle with a float. [29]Water lettuce and water chestnut. [30]Ducklike birds.

[31]Wood duck.

the waters, and following the watchful parent unconscious of danger, were frequently surprised by the voracious trout, and he in turn, as often by the subtle, greedy alligator. Behold him rushing forth from the flags and reeds. His enormous body swells. His plaited tail brandished high, floats upon the lake. The waters like a cataract descend from his opening jaws. Clouds of smoke issue from his dilated nostrils. The earth trembles with his thunder. When immediately from the opposite coast of the lagoon, emerges from the deep his rival champion. They suddenly dart upon each other. The boiling surface of the lake marks their rapid course, and a terrific conflict commences. They now sink to the bottom folded together in horrid wreaths. The water becomes thick and discoloured. Again they rise, their jaws clap together, re-echoing through the deep surrounding forests. Again they sink, when the contest ends at the muddy bottom of the lake, and the vanquished makes a hazardous escape, hiding himself in the muddy turbulent waters and sedge on a distant shore. The proud victor exulting returns to the place of action. The shores and forests resound his dreadful roar, together with the triumphing shouts of the plaited tribes around, witnesses of the horrid combat.

My apprehensions were highly alarmed after being a spectator of so dreadful a battle; it was obvious that every delay would but tend to increase my dangers and difficulties, as the sun was near setting, and the alligators gathered around my harbour from all quarters; from these considerations I concluded to be expeditious in my trip to the lagoon, in order to take some fish. Not thinking it prudent to take my fusee[32] with me, lest I might lose it overboard in case of a battle, which I had every reason to dread before my return, I therefore furnished myself with a club for my defence, went on board, and penetrating the first line of those which surrounded my harbour, they gave way; but being pursued by several very large ones, I kept strictly on the watch, and paddled with all my might towards the entrance of the lagoon, hoping to be sheltered there from the multitude of my assailants; but ere I had half-way reached the place, I was attacked on all sides, several endeavouring to overset the canoe. My situation now became precarious to the last degree: two very large ones attacked me closely, at the same instant, rushing up with their heads and part of their bodies above the water, roaring terribly and belching floods of water over me. They struck their jaws together so close to my ears, as almost to stun me, and I expected every moment to be dragged out of the boat and instantly devoured, but I applied my weapons so effectually about me, though at random, that I was so successful as to beat them off a little; when, finding that they designed to renew the battle, I made for the shore, as the only means left me for my preservation, for, by keeping close to it, I should have my enemies on one side of me only, whereas I was before surrounded by them, and there was a probability, if pushed to the last extremity of saving myself, by jumping out of the canoe on shore, as it is easy to outwalk them on land, although comparatively as swift as lightning in the water. I found this last expedient alone could fully answer my expectations, for as soon as I gained

[32]Flintlock gun.

the shore they drew off and kept aloof. This was a happy relief, as my confidence was, in some degree, recovered by it. . . . I soon caught more trout than I had present occasion for, and the air was too hot and sultry to admit of their being kept for many hours, even though salted or barbecued. I now prepared for my return to camp, which I succeeded in with but little trouble, by keeping close to the shore, yet I was opposed upon reentering the river out of the lagoon, and pursued near to my landing (though not closely attacked) particularly by an old daring one, about twelve feet in length, who kept close after me, and when I stepped on shore and turned about, in order to draw up my canoe, he rushed up near my feet and lay there for some time, looking me in the face, his head and shoulders out of water; I resolved he should pay for his temerity, and having a heavy load in my fusee, I ran to my camp, and returning with my piece,[33] found him with his foot on the gunwale of the boat, in search of fish, on my coming up he withdrew sullenly and slowly into the water, but soon returned and placed himself in his former position, looking at me and seeming neither fearful or any way disturbed. I soon dispatched him by lodging the contents of my gun in his head, and then proceeded to cleanse and prepare my fish for supper, and accordingly took them out of the boat, laid them down on the sand close to the water, and began to scale them, when, raising my head, I saw before me, through the clear water, the head and shoulders of a very large alligator, moving slowly towards me; I instantly stepped back, when, with a sweep of his tail, he brushed off several of my fish. It was certainly most providential that I looked up at that instant, as the monster would probably, in less than a minute, have seized and dragged me into the river. This incredible boldness of the animal disturbed me greatly, supposing there could now be no reasonable safety for me during the night, but by keeping continually on the watch; I therefore, as soon as I had prepared the fish, proceeded to secure myself and effects in the best manner I could. . . .

It was by this time dusk, and the alligators had nearly ceased their roar, when I was again alarmed by a tumultuous noise that seemed to be in my harbour, and therefore engaged my immediate attention. Returning to my camp I found it undisturbed, and then continued on to the extreme point of the promontory, where I saw a scene, new and surprising, which at first threw my senses into such a tumult, that it was some time before I could comprehend what was the matter; however, I soon accounted for the prodigious assemblage of crocodiles at this place, which exceeded every thing of the kind I had ever heard of.

How shall I express myself so as to convey an adequate idea of it to the reader, and at the same time avoid raising suspicions of my want of veracity. Should I say, that the river (in this place) from shore to shore, and perhaps near half a mile above and below me, appeared to be one solid bank of fish, of various kinds, pushing through this narrow pass of St. Juan's[34] into the little lake, on their return down the river, and that the alligators were in such incredible numbers, and so close together from shore to shore, that it would have been easy to have walked across on their heads, had the animals been

[33]Gun. [34]The St. John's River.

harmless. What expressions can sufficiently declare the shocking scene that for some minutes continued, whilst this mighty army of fish were forcing the pass? During this attempt, thousands, I may say hundreds of thousands of them were caught and swallowed by the devouring alligators. I have seen an alligator take up out of the water several great fish at a time, and just squeeze them betwixt his jaws, while the tails of the great trout flapped about his eyes and lips, ere he had swallowed them. The horrid noise of their closing jaws, their plunging amidst the broken banks of fish, and rising with their prey some feet upright above the water, the floods of water and blood rushing out of their mouths, and the clouds of vapour issuing from their wide nostrils, were truly frightful. This scene continued at intervals during the night, as the fish came to the pass. After this sight, shocking and tremendous as it was, I found myself somewhat easier and more reconciled to my situation, being convinced that their extraordinary assemblage here, was owing to this annual feast of fish, and that they were so well employed in their own element, that I had little occasion to fear their paying me a visit.

On my return to the store on St. Juan's the trading schooner was there, but as she was not to return to Georgia until the autumn, I found I had time to pursue my travels in Florida, and might at leisure plan my excursions to collect seeds and roots in boxes, &c.

At this time the talks (or messages between the Indians and white people) were perfectly peaceable and friendly, both with the Lower Creeks and the Nation or Upper Creeks; parties of Indians were coming in every day with their hunts; indeed the Muscogulges[35] or Upper Creeks very seldom disturb us. Bad talks from the Nation is always a very serious affair, and to the utmost degree alarming to the white inhabitants.

The Muscogulges are under a more strict government or regular civilization than the Indians in general. They lie near their potent and declared enemy, the Choctaws;[36] their country having a vast frontier, naturally accessible and open to the incursions of their enemies on all sides, they find themselves under the necessity of associating in large, populous towns, and these towns as near together as convenient that they may be enabled to succour and defend one another in case of sudden invasion; this consequently occasions deer and bear to be scarce and difficult to procure, which obliges them to be vigilant and industrious; this naturally begets care and serious attention, which we may suppose in some degree forms their natural disposition and manners, and gives them that air of dignified gravity, so strikingly characteristic in their aged people, and that steadiness, just and cheerful reverence in the middle aged and youth, which sits so easy upon them, and appears so natural; for however strange it may appear to us, the same moral duties which with us form the amiable, virtuous character, and is so difficult to maintain, there, without compulsion or visible restraint, operates like instinct, with a surprising harmony and natural ease, insomuch that it seems impossible for them to act out of the common highroad to virtue.

[35]Indian tribe of the Creek Confederation.
[36]Indians of southern Mississippi, Louisiana, and Alabama.

We will now take a view of the Lower Creeks or Seminoles, and the natural disposition which characterises this people, when, from the striking contrast, the philosopher may approve or disapprove, as he may think proper, from the judgment and opinion given by different men.

The Seminoles, but a weak people, with respect to numbers, all of them I suppose would not be sufficient to people one of the towns in the Muscogulge (for instance, the Uches[37] on the main branch of the Apalachucla river,[38] which alone contains near two thousand inhabitants.) Yet this handful of people possess a vast territory, all East Florida and the greatest part of West Florida, which being naturally cut and divided into thousands of islets, knolls and eminences, by the innumerable rivers, lakes, swamps, vast savannas and ponds, form so many secure retreats and temporary dwelling places, that effectually guard them from any sudden invasions or attacks from their enemies; and being such a swampy, hummocky[39] country, furnishes such a plenty and variety of supplies for the nourishment of varieties of animals, that I can venture to assert, that no part of the globe so abounds with wild game or creatures fit for the food of man.

Thus they enjoy a superabundance of the necessaries and conveniences of life, with the security of person and property, the two great concerns of mankind. The hides of deer, bears, tigers and wolves, together with honey, wax and other productions of the country, purchase their clothing, equipage and domestic utensils from the whites. They seem to be free from want or desires. No cruel enemy to dread; nothing to give them disquietude, but the gradual encroachments of the white people. Thus contented and undisturbed, they appear as blithe and free as the birds of the air, and like them as volatile and active, tuneful and vociferous. The visage, action and deportment of a Seminole, being the most striking picture of happiness in this life; joy, contentment, love and friendship, without guile or affectation, seem inherent in them, or predominant in their vital principle, for it leaves them but with the last breath of life. It even seems imposing a constraint upon their ancient chiefs and senators, to maintain a necessary decorum and solemnity, in their public councils; not even the debility and decrepitude of extreme old age, is sufficient to erase from their visages, this youthful, joyous simplicity; but like the grey eve of a serene and calm day, a gladdening, cheering blush remains on the Western horizon after the sun is set.

I doubt not but some of my countrymen who may read these accounts of the Indians, which I have endeavoured to relate according to truth, at least as they appeared to me, will charge me with partiality or prejudice in their favour.

I will, however, now endeavour to exhibit their vices, immoralities and imperfections, from my own observations and knowledge, as well as accounts from the white traders, who reside amongst them.

The Indians make war against, kill and destroy their own species, and their motives spring from the same erroneous source as it does in all other

[37]The Yuchi Indians of southern Alabama, southern Georgia, and northern Florida.

[38]The Apalachicola River in Florida.

[39]Marked by islets and low knolls.

nations of mankind; that is, the ambition of exhibiting to their fellows a superior character of personal and national valour, and thereby immortalize themselves, by transmitting their names with honour and luster to posterity; or in revenge of their enemy, for public or personal insults; or lastly, to extend the borders and boundaries of their territories; but I cannot find, upon the strictest enquiry, that their bloody contests at this day are marked with deeper stains of inhumanity or savage cruelty, than what may be observed amongst the most civilized nations; they do indeed scalp their slain enemy, but they do not kill the females or children of either sex; the most ancient traders, both in the Lower and Upper Creeks, assured me they never saw an instance of either burning or tormenting their male captives, though it is said they used to do it formerly. I saw in every town in the Nation and Seminoles that I visited, more or less male captives, some extremely aged, who were free and in good circumstances as their masters; and all slaves have their freedom when they may, which is permitted and encouraged, when they and their offspring, are every way upon an equality with their conquerors; they are given to adultery and fornication, but I suppose in no greater excess than other nations of men. They punish the delinquents, male and female, equally alike, by taking off their ears. This is the punishment for adultery. Infamy and disgrace is supposed to be a sufficient punishment for fornication, in either sex.

They are fond of games and gambling, and amuse themselves like children, in relating extravagant stories, to cause surprise and mirth.

They wage eternal war against deer and bear, to procure food and clothing, and other necessaries and conveniences; which is indeed carried to an unreasonable and perhaps criminal excess, since the white people have dazzled their senses with foreign superfluities.

. . .

At the trading-house I found a very large party of the Lower Creeks encamped in a grove, just without the pallisadoes;[40] this was a predatory band of the Seminoles, consisting of about forty warriors destined against the Choctaws of West Florida. They had just arrived here from St. Augustine, where they had been with a large troop of horses for sale, and furnished themselves with a very liberal supply of spirituous liquors, about twenty kegs, each containing five gallons.

These sons of Mars had the continence and fortitude to withstand the temptation of even tasting a drop of it until their arrival here, where they purposed to supply themselves with necessary articles to equip them for the expedition, and proceed on directly; but here meeting with our young traders and packhorse men, they were soon prevailed on to broach their beloved nectar; which in the end caused some disturbance, and the consumption of most of their liquor, for after they had once got a smack of it, they never were sober for ten days, and by that time there was but little left.

[40]Palisades, defensive walls.

In a few days this festival exhibited one of the most ludicrous bacchanalian scenes that is possible to be conceived, white and red men and women without distinction, passed the day merrily with these jovial, amorous topers,[41] and the nights in convivial songs, dances and sacrifices to Venus, as long as they could stand or move; for in these frolicks both sexes take those liberties with each other, and act, without constraint or shame, such scenes as they would abhor when sober or in their senses; and would endanger their ears and even their lives; but at last their liquor running low, and being most of them sick through intoxication, they became more sober, and now the dejected lifeless sots would pawn everything they were in possession of, for a mouthful of spirits to settle their stomachs, as they termed it. This was the time for the wenches to make their markets, as they had the fortitude and subtlety by dissimulation and artifice to save their share of the liquor during the frolick, and that by a very singular stratagem, for, at these riots, every fellow who joins in the club, has his own quart bottle of rum in his hand, holding it by the neck so sure that he never looses hold of it day or night, drunk or sober, as long as the frolick continues, and with this, his beloved friend, he roves about continually, singing, roaring and reeling to and fro, either alone or arm in arm with a brother toper, presenting his bottle to every one, offering a drink, and is sure to meet his beloved female if he can, whom he complaisantly begs to drink with him, but the modest fair, veiling her face in a mantle,[42] refuses (at the beginning of the frolick) but he presses and at last insists; she being furnished with an empty bottle, concealed in her mantle, at last consents, and taking a good day[43] draught, blushes, drops her pretty face on her bosom and artfully discharges the rum into her bottle, and by repeating this artifice soon fills it; this she privately conveys to her secret store, and then returns to the jovial game, and so on during the festival; and when the comic farce is over, the wench retails this precious cordial[44] to them at her own price. There were a few of the chiefs, particularly the Long Warrior[45] their leader, who had the prudence and fortitude to resist the alluring temptation during the whole farce; but though he was a powerful chief, a king and a very cunning man, he was not able to control these madmen, although he was acknowledged by the Indians to have communion with powerful invisible beings or spirits, and on that account esteemed worthy of homage and great respect.

. . .

1791

[41]Drunkards.
[42]Robe.
[43]Large.
[44]Liquor.
[45]Mico Clucco ("Long Warrior") was Chief of the Seminoles.

Native American Voices II

The literature of the North American Indian, written by a Native American and printed in English, made its first appearance in 1772, with the publication of A Sermon Preached at the Execution of Moses Paul, an Indian, *by Samson Occom. A Methodist preacher, Occom was a missionary to the Indians of New England. In his sermon he spoke of the destruction of Indian life and the ruinous effect on Native Americans of the culture and the temptations of white America. His sermon was a best-seller in its day, but through the early years of the nineteenth century, Native American literature of North America remained, as much of it remains today, unpublished, an oral literature preserved in the memories of the people who celebrate it and live by it. Some rituals and narratives were recorded in early pictographs by North American Indians who lived in lands that would become part of the United States, but many myths, rituals, narratives, poems and songs (the largest element in native American oral literature) resisted translation and publication: They were, and they remain today, best presented in oral performances rather than in the words of a European language written on the printed page. Furthermore, many myths, rituals, and narratives were considered to be too sacred to be written or repeated to translators. And of those translations that were made in the nineteenth century, many were marred by the attempts of white translators to inject European eloquence into the literature of the Indians, to reshape Indian literature according to the ideals of Western European culture.*

The tradition of published autobiography written by Native Americans did not begin until 1829, with the publication of A Son of the Forest *by William Apess. But as the century progressed, an increasing number of autobiographies, personal histories, speeches, and poems were printed and distributed to a growing audience in America and Europe. That published literature became more extensive and diverse through most of the nineteenth century, portraying the life of American Indians both as it had always been and as it was changing before the onrush of white European settlers into lands the Indians had once held as their own.*

In the last years of the nineteenth century and the early years of the twentieth century, broad popular interest in Indian culture and its literature waned as American Indians were set aside on reservations or assimilated in some measure into the dominant European culture of the United States. But in the last half of the twentieth century, interest in Native American life and literature has been reborn. And with it has come a vast expansion in the publication of the literature of American Indians. Modern editions of ancient myths and narratives have appeared, and out of the newly reprinted autobiographies, poems, and oratory of an older Native American tradition, writers of the 1990s are creating a new Native American literature that has become a vital part of the art and culture of the United States as it moves into the twenty-first century.

FURTHER READING: *Tales of the North American Indians,* ed. S. Thompson, 1922, 1929; A. Day, *The Sky Clears, The Poetry of the American Indians,* 1951, 1964; J. Melville, *The Content and Style of an Oral Literature,* 1959; M. Astrov, *American Indian Prose and Poetry,* 1962; *Native American Testimony,* ed. P. Nabakov, 1978, 1991; *Literature of the American Indian,* ed. T. Sanders and W. Peek, 1973; K. Lincoln, *Native American Renaissance,* 1983, 1985; *Critical Essays on Native American Literature,* ed. A. Wiget, 1985; A. Wiget, *Native American Literature,* 1985; *Recovering the Word, Essays on Native American Literature,* ed. B. Swann and A. Krupat, 1987; D. Brumble, *American Indian Autobiography,* 1988; A. Ruoff, *American Indian Literature, An Introduction,* 1990; *Redefining in American Literary History,* ed. A. Ruoff and J. Ward, 1990; H. Wyss, *Writing Indians,*

Literacy, Christianity, and Native Community in Early America, 2000; J. Porter and K. Roemer, *The Cambridge Companion to Native American Literature,* 2005.

TEXTS: *A Son of the Forest,* 1829; *Crashing Thunder, The Autobiography of an American Indian,* 1912; *Story of the Indian,* 1895; W. Matthews, "Legend of the Snake Order," *The Journal of American Folklore,* Vol. I, 1888; A. O'Bryan, *The Dîné: Origin Myths of the Navaho Indians,* 1956; P. Goddard, *Navajo Texts, Anthropological Papers of the American Museum of Natural History,* Vol. XXXIV, Part 1, 1933; *Pawnee Hero Stories and Folk Tales,* ed. G. Grinnell, 1889; F. Densmore, *Papago Music,* 1929; T. Jefferson, "The Speech of Logan," *Notes on the State of Virginia,* 1787; J. Hunter, "The Speech of Tecumseh," *Memoirs of a Captivity among the Indians of North America,* 1823; "Farewell to Blackhawk," *Indian Oratory,* ed. W. Vanderwerth, 1971; "The Speech of Chief Joseph," U.S. Congress, House Executive Document, 45th Congress, and Session, 1877–1878.

from *A SON OF THE FOREST*

CHAPTER I

William Apess, the author of the following narrative, was born in the town of Colrain, Massachusetts, on the thirty-first of January, in the year of our Lord seventeen hundred and ninety-eight. My grandfather was a white man and married a female attached to the royal family of Philip, king of the Pequot tribe of Indians,[1] so well known in that part of American history which relates to the wars between the whites and natives. My grandmother was, if I am not misinformed, the king's granddaughter and a fair and beautiful woman. This statement is given not with a view of appearing great in the estimation of others—what, I would ask, is *royal* blood?—the blood of a king is no better than that of the subject. We are in fact but one family; we are all the descendants of one great progenitor—Adam. I would not boast of my extraction, as I consider myself nothing more than a worm of the earth.

I have given the above account of my origin with the simple view of narrating the truth as I have received it, and under the settled conviction that I must render an account at the last day, to the sovereign Judge of all men, for every word contained in this little book.

As the story of King Philip is perhaps generally known, and consequently the history of the Pequot tribe, over whom he reigned, it will suffice to say that he was overcome by treachery, and the goodly heritage occupied by this once happy, powerful, yet peaceful people was possessed in the process of time by their avowed enemies, the whites, who had been welcomed to their land in that spirit of kindness so peculiar to the red men of the woods. But the violation of their inherent rights, by those to whom they had extended the hand of friendship, was not the only act of injustice which this oppressed and afflicted nation was called to suffer at the hands of their white neighbors—alas! They were subject to a more intense and heart-corroding affliction, that of having their daughters claimed by the conquerors, and however much subsequent efforts were made to soothe their sorrows, in this particular, they considered the glory of their nation as having departed.

[1]King Philip, Metacomet, was chief of the Wampanoag Indians. King Philip's war against the English settlers (1675–1676) was the most destructive war in the history of New England.

From what I have already stated, it will appear that my father was of mixed blood, his father being a white man and his mother a native or, in other words, a red woman. On attaining a sufficient age to act for himself, he joined the Pequot tribe, to which he was maternally connected. He was well received, and in a short time afterward married a female of the tribe, in whose veins a single drop of the white man's blood never flowed. Not long after his marriage, he removed to what was then called the back settlements, directing his course first to the west and afterward to the northeast, where he pitched his tent in the woods of a town called Colrain, near the Connecticut River, in the state of Massachusetts. In this, the place of my birth, he continued some time and afterward removed to Colchester, New London County, Connecticut. At the latter place, our little family lived for nearly three years in comparative comfort.

Circumstances, however, changed with us, as with many other people, in consequence of which I was taken together with my two brothers and sisters into my grandfather's family. One of my uncles dwelt in the same hut. Now my grandparents were not the best people in the world—like all others who are wedded to the beastly vice of intemperance, they would drink to excess whenever they could procure rum, and as usual in such cases, when under the influence of liquor, they would not only quarrel and fight with each other but would at times turn upon their unoffending grandchildren and beat them in a most cruel manner. It makes me shudder, even at this time, to think how frequent and how great have been our sufferings in consequence of the introduction of this "cursed stuff" into our family—and I could wish, in the sincerity of my soul, that it were banished from our land.

Our fare was of the poorest kind, and even of this we had not enough. Our clothing also was of the worst description: Literally speaking, we were clothed with rags, so far only as rags would suffice to cover our nakedness. We were always contented and happy to get a cold potato for our dinners—of this at times we were denied, and many a night have we gone supperless to rest, if stretching our limbs on a bundle of straw, without any covering against the weather, may be called rest. Truly, we were in a most deplorable condition—too young to obtain subsistence of ourselves, by the labor of our hands, and our wants almost totally disregarded by those who should have made every exertion to supply them. Some of our white neighbors, however, took pity on us and measurably administered to our wants, by bringing us frozen milk, with which we were glad to satisfy the calls of hunger. We lived in this way for some time, suffering both from cold and hunger. Once in particular, I remember that when it rained very hard my grandmother put us all down cellar, and when we complained of cold and hunger, she unfeelingly bid us dance and thereby warm ourselves—but we had no food of any kind; and one of my sisters almost died of hunger. Poor dear girl, she was quite overcome. Young as I was, my very heart bled for her. I merely relate this circumstance, without any embellishment or exaggeration, to show the reader how we were treated. The intensity of our sufferings I cannot tell. Happily, we did not continue in this very deplorable condition for a great length of time. Providence smiled on us, but in a particular manner.

Our parents quarreled, parted, and went off to a great distance, leaving their helpless children to the care of their grandparents. We lived at this time in an old house, divided into two apartments—one of which was occupied by my uncle. Shortly after my father left us, my grandmother, who had been out among the whites, returned in a state of intoxication and, without any provocation whatever on my part, began to belabor me most unmercifully with a club; she asked me if I hated her, and I very innocently answered in the affirmative as I did not then know what the word meant and thought all the while that I was answering aright; and so she continued asking me the same question, and I as often answered her in the same way, whereupon she continued beating me, by which means one of my arms was broken in three different places. I was then only four years of age and consequently could not take care of or defend myself—and I was equally unable to seek safety in flight. But my uncle who lived in the other part of the house, being alarmed for my safety, came down to take me away, when my grandfather made toward him with a firebrand, but very fortunately he succeeded in rescuing me and thus saved my life, for had he not come at the time he did, I would most certainly have been killed. My grandparents who acted in this unfeeling and cruel manner were by my mother's side—those by my father's side were Christians, lived and died happy in the love of God; and if I continue faithful in improving that measure of grace with which God hath blessed me, I expect to meet them in a world of unmingled and ceaseless joys. But to return:—

The next morning, when it was discovered that I had been most dangerously injured, my uncle determined to make the whites acquainted with my condition. He accordingly went to a Mr. Furman, the person who had occasionally furnished us with milk, and the good man came immediately to see me. He found me dreadfully beaten, and the other children in a state of absolute suffering; and as he was extremely anxious that something should be done for our relief, he applied to the selectmen of the town in our behalf, who after duly considering the application adjudged that we should be severally taken and bound out. Being entirely disabled in consequence of the wounds I had received, I was supported at the expense of the town for about twelve months.

When the selectmen were called in, they ordered me to be carried to Mr. Furman's—where I received the attention of two surgeons. Some considerable time elapsed before my arm was set, which was consequently very sore, and during this painful operation I scarcely murmured. Now this dear man and family were sad on my account. Mrs. Furman was a kind, benevolent, and tenderhearted lady—from her I received the best possible care: Had it been otherwise I believe that I could not have lived. It pleased God, however, to support me. The great patience that I manifested I attribute mainly to my improved situation. Before, I was almost always naked, or cold, or hungry—now, I was comfortable, with the exception of my wounds.

In view of this treatment, I presume that the reader will exclaim, "What savages your grandparents were to treat unoffending, helpless children in this cruel manner." But this cruel and unnatural conduct was the effect of some cause. I attribute it in a great measure to the whites, inasmuch as they introduced among my countrymen that bane of comfort and happiness, ardent spirits—seduced them into a love of it and, when under its unhappy influence, wronged them out of their lawful possessions—that land, where reposed the ashes of their sires; and not only so, but they committed violence of the most revolting kind upon the persons of the female portion of the tribe who, previous to the introduction among them of the arts, and vices, and debaucheries of the whites, were as unoffending and happy as they roamed over their goodly possessions as any people on whom the sun of heaven ever shone. The consequence was that they were scattered abroad. Now many of them were seen reeling about intoxicated with liquor, neglecting to provide for themselves and families, who before were assiduously engaged in supplying the necessities of those depending on them for support. I do not make this statement in order to justify those who had treated me so unkindly, but simply to show that, inasmuch as I was thus treated only when they were under the influence of spirituous liquor, that the whites were justly chargeable with at least some portion of my sufferings.

After I had been nursed for about twelve months, I had so far recovered that it was deemed expedient to bind me out, until I should attain the age of twenty-one years.[2] Mr. Furman, the person with whom the selectmen had placed me was a poor man, a cooper by trade, and obtained his living by the labor of his hands. As I was only five years old, he at first thought that his circumstances would not justify him in keeping me, as it would be some considerable time before I could render him much service. But such was the attachment of the family toward me that he came to the conclusion to keep me until I was of age, and he further agreed to give me so much instruction as would enable me to read and write. Accordingly, when I attained my sixth year, I was sent to school, and continued for six successive winters. During this time I learned to read and write, though not so well as I could have wished. This was all the instruction of the kind I ever received. Small and imperfect as was the amount of the knowledge I obtained, yet in view of the advantages I have thus derived, I bless God for it.

Chapter II

I believe that it is assumed as a fact among divines that the Spirit of Divine Truth, in the boundless diversity of its operations, visits the mind of every intelligent being born into the world—but the time when is only fully known to the Almighty and the soul which is the object of the Holy Spirit's enlightening influence. It is also conceded on all hands that the Spirit of Truth operates on different minds in a variety of ways—but always with the design of convincing man of sin and of a judgment to come. And, oh, that men would regard their real interests and yield to the illuminating influences of the Spirit of God—then wretchedness and misery would abound no longer, but everything of the kind give place to the pure principles of peace, godliness, brotherly kindness, meekness, charity, and love. These graces are spontaneously produced in the human heart and are exemplified in the Christian deportment of every soul under the mellowing and sanctifying influences of the Spirit of God. They are the peaceable fruits of a meek and quiet spirit.

The perverseness of man in this respect is one of the great and conclusive proofs of his apostasy, and of the rebellious inclination of his unsanctified heart to the will and wisdom of his Creator and his Judge.

I have heard a great deal said respecting infants feeling, as it were, the operations of the Holy Spirit on their minds, impressing them with a sense of their wickedness and the necessity of a preparation for a future state.

[2]Bound, contracted out as an indentured worker, in return for food, housing, and clothing.

Children at a very early age manifest in a strong degree two of the evil passions of our nature—*anger* and *pride.* We need not wonder, therefore, that persons in early life feel good impressions; indeed, it is a fact, too well established to admit of doubt or controversy, that many children have manifested a strength of intellect far above their years and have given ample evidence of a good work of grace manifest by the influence of the Spirit of God in their young and tender minds. But this is perhaps attributable to the care and attention bestowed upon them.

If constant and judicious means are used to impress upon their young and susceptible minds sentiments of truth, virtue, morality, and religion, and these efforts are sustained by a corresponding practice on the part of parents or those who strive to make these early impressions, we may rationally trust that as their young minds expand they will be led to act upon the wholesome principles they have received—and that at a very early period these good impressions will be more indelibly engraved on their hearts by the cooperating influences of that Spirit, who in the days of his glorious incarnation said, "Suffer little children to come unto me, and forbid them not, for of such is the kingdom of heaven."

But to my experience—and the reader knows full well that experience is the best schoolmaster, for what we have experienced, that we know, and all the world cannot possibly beat it out of us. I well remember the conversation that took place between Mrs. Furman and myself when I was about six years of age; she was attached to the Baptist church and was esteemed as a very pious woman. Of this I have not the shadow of a doubt, as her whole course of conduct was upright and exemplary. On this occasion, she spoke to me respecting a future state of existence and told me that I might die and enter upon it, to which I replied that I was too young—that old people only died. But she assured me that I was not too young, and in order to convince me of the truth of the observation, she referred me to the graveyard, where many younger and smaller persons than myself were laid to molder in the earth. I had of course nothing to say—but, notwithstanding, I could not fully comprehend the nature of death and the meaning of a future state. Yet I felt an indescribable sensation pass though my frame; I trembled and was sore afraid and for some time endeavored to hide myself from the destroying monster, but I could find no place of refuge. The conversation and pious admonitions of this good lady made a lasting impression upon my mind. At times, however, this impression appeared to be wearing away—then again I would become thoughtful, make serious inquiries, and seem anxious to know something more certain respecting myself and that state of existence beyond the grave, in which I was instructed to believe. About this time I was taken to meeting in order to hear the word of God and receive instruction in divine things. This was the first time I had ever entered a house of worship, and instead of attending to what the minister said, I was employed in gazing about the house or playing with the unruly boys with whom I was seated in the gallery. On my return home, Mr. Furman, who had been apprised of my conduct, told me that I had acted very wrong. He did not, however, stop here. He went on to tell me how I ought to behave in church, and to this very day I bless God for such wholesome and timely instruction. In this particular I was not slow to learn, as I do not remember that I have from that day to this misbehaved in the house of God.

It may not be improper to remark, in this place, that a vast proportion of the misconduct of young people in church is chargeable to their parents and guardians. It is to be feared that there are too many professing Christians who feel satisfied if their children or those under their care enter on a Sabbath day within the walls of the sanctuary, without reference to their conduct while there. I would have such persons seriously ask themselves whether they think they discharge the duties obligatory on them by the relation in which they stand to their Maker, as well as those committed to their care, by so much negligence on their part. The Christian feels it a duty imposed on him to conduct his children to the house of God. But he rests not here. He must have an eye over them and, if they act well, approve and encourage them; if otherwise, point out to them their error and persuade them to observe a discreet and exemplary course of conduct while in church.

After a while I became very fond of attending on the word of God—then again I would meet the enemy of my soul, who would strive to lead me away, and in many instances he was but too successful, and to this day I remember that nothing scarcely grieved me so much, when my mind has been thus petted, than to be called by a nickname. If I was spoken to in the spirit of kindness, I would be instantly disarmed of my stubbornness and ready to perform anything required of me. I know of nothing so trying to a child as to be repeatedly called by an improper name. I thought it disgraceful to be called an Indian; it was considered as a slur upon an oppressed and scattered nation, and I have often been led to inquire where the whites received this word, which they so often threw as an opprobrious epithet at the sons of the forest. I could not find it in the Bible and therefore concluded that it was a word imported for the special purpose of degrading us. At other times I thought it was derived from the term *in-gen-uity.* But the proper term which ought to be applied to our nation, to distinguish it from the rest of the human family, is that of *"Natives"*—and I humbly conceive that the natives of this country are the only people under heaven who have a just title to the name, inasmuch as we are the only people who retain the original complexion of our father Adam.[1] Notwithstanding my thoughts on this matter, so completely was I weaned from the interests and affections of my brethren that a mere threat of being sent away among the Indians into the dreary woods had a much better effect in making me obedient to the commands of my superiors than any corporal punishment that they ever inflicted. I had received a lesson in the unnatural treatment of my own relations, which could not be effaced, and I thought that, if those who should have loved and protected me treated me with such unkindness, surely I had not reason to expect mercy or favor at the hands of those who knew me in no other relation than that of a cast-off member of the tribe. A threat, of the kind alluded to, invariably produced obedience on my part, so far as I understood the nature of the command.

I cannot perhaps give a better idea of the dread which pervaded my mind on seeing any of my brethren of the forest than by relating the following occurrence. One day several of the family went into the woods to gather berries, taking me with them. We had not been out long before we fell in with a company of white females, on the same errand—their complexion

[1]Sometimes identified as one of the Ten Lost Tribes of Israel, the American Indians were hence thought to resemble Adam and Eve.

was, to say the least, as *dark* as that of the natives. This circumstance filled my mind with terror, and I broke from the party with my utmost speed, and I could not muster courage enough to look behind until I had reached home. By this time my imagination had pictured out a tale of blood, and as soon as I regained breath sufficient to answer the questions which my master asked, I informed him that we had met a body of the natives in the woods, but what had become of the party I could not tell. Notwithstanding the manifest incredibility of my tale of terror, Mr. Furman was agitated; my very appearance was sufficient to convince him that I had been terrified by something, and summoning the remainder of the family, he sallied out in quest of the absent party, whom he found searching for me among the bushes. The whole mystery was soon unraveled. It may be proper for me here to remark that the great fear I entertained of my brethren was occasioned by the many stories I had heard of their cruelty toward the whites—how they were in the habit of killing and scalping men, women, and children. But the whites did not tell me that they were in a great majority of instances the aggressors—that they had imbrued their hands in the lifeblood of my brethren, driven them from their once peaceful and happy homes—that they introduced among them the fatal and exterminating diseases of civilized life. If the whites had told me how cruel they had been to the "poor Indian," I should have apprehended as much harm from them.

Shortly after this occurrence I relapsed into my former bad habits—was fond of the company of boys—and in a short time lost in a great measure that spirit of obedience which had made me the favorite of my mistress. I was easily led astray, and, once in particular, I was induced by a boy (my senior by five or six years) to assist him in his depredations on a watermelon patch belonging to one of the neighbors. But we were found out, and my companion in wickedness led me deeper in sin by persuading me to deny the crime laid to our charge. I obeyed him to the very letter and, when accused, flatly denied knowing anything of the matter. The boasted courage of the boy, however, began to fail as soon as he saw danger thicken, and he confessed it as strongly as he had denied it. The man from whom we had pillaged the melons threatened to send us to Newgate,[2] but he relented. The story shortly afterward reached the ears of the good Mrs. Furman, who talked seriously to me about it. She told me that I could be sent to prison for it, that I had done wrong, and gave me a great deal of wholesome advice. This had a much better effect than forty floggings—it sunk so deep into my mind that the impression can never be effaced.

I now went on without difficulty for a few months, when I was assailed by fresh and unexpected troubles. One of the girls belonging to the house had taken some offense at me and declared she would be revenged. The better to effect this end, she told Mr. Furman that I had not only threatened to kill her but had actually pursued her with a knife, whereupon he came to the place where I was working and began to whip me severely. I could not tell for what. I told him I had done no harm, to which he replied, "I will learn you, you Indian dog, how to chase people with a knife." I told him I had not, but he would not believe me and continued to whip me for a long while. But the poor man soon found out his error, as *after* he had flogged me he undertook

[2]A prison in Connecticut.

to investigate the matter, when to his amazement he discovered it was nothing but fiction, as all the children assured him that I did no such thing. He regretted being so hasty—but I saw wherein the great difficulty consisted; if I had not denied the melon affair he would have believed me, but as I had uttered an untruth about that it was natural for him to think that the person who will tell one lie will not scruple at two. For a long while after this circumstance transpired, I did not associate with my companions.

1829

William Apess

from *CRASHING THUNDER, THE AUTOBIOGRAPHY OF AN AMERICAN INDIAN*

FASTING

At this stage of life I secretly got the desire to make myself pleasing to the opposite sex.

The Indians then lived in their old-fashioned lodges. Women, however, whenever they had their menses, were placed in special huts. There the young men would go to court them at night when their parents were asleep. I used to go along with the men on such occasions, for even although I did not enter any lodges but merely accompanied the older men, I enjoyed it.

My parents were greatly in fear of my coming into contact with menstruating women so therefore I went with these men secretly. My parents were even afraid of having me cross the path over which a menstruating woman had passed. They worried so much about it at that time, because I was to fast as soon as autumn came. They did not wish me to be near menstruating women, for were I to grow up in their midst I would assuredly be weak and of little account. Such was their reason.

Before long I started to fast again together with an older brother of mine, both day and night. It was during the fall moving, and several lodges of people were living near us. There it was that my elder brother and I fasted. Among the people of the other lodges were four girls whose duty it was to carry wood. Whenever these girls went out to get wood my older brother and I would play around with them a great deal. We did this even although we were fasting at the time. Of course we had to do it in secret. Whenever our parents found out we got a scolding and so did the girls. At home we were warned to keep away from menstruating women, but we ourselves always sought them.

After a while some of the people living in the lodges moved away and we were left alone. They moved far ahead of us. We ourselves were to move only a short distance at a time. My father and my brother-in-law went out hunting and killed seventy deer between them, so that we had plenty of meat.

When the girls with whom I used to play moved away I became very lonesome. In the evenings I used to cry. I longed for them greatly and they had moved far away!

Soon we got fairly well started on our way back. We moved to a place where all the leaders used to give their feasts. Near the place where we lived there were three lakes and a black-hawk's nest. Right near the tree where the nest was located, they built a lodge and our war-bundle[1] was placed in it. There my elder brother and myself were to pass the night. It was said that if any one fasted at such a place for four nights, he would be blessed with victory and the power to cure the sick. All the spirits would bless him.

We were told the following would happen to us. On the first night we would imagine ourselves surrounded by spirits whose whisperings we would hear outside of the lodge. The spirits would even whistle. I was told that I would be frightened and nervous and that if I still remained there, I would be molested by large monsters, fearful to look upon. Even the bravest man might well be frightened. Should I, however, manage to get through that night I would then on the following night be molested by ghosts whom I would hear speaking outside. These ghosts would say things that might well cause me to run away. Towards morning I was told these ghosts would even take my blanket away from me. They would grab hold of me and drive me out of the lodge and not stop until the sun rose. If I was able to endure a third night, then I would be addressed by the true spirits. They would bless me and say, "We bless you. We had really intended to turn you over to the monsters and bad spirits and that is why these approached you first, but you overcame them and now they will not be able to take you away. Now you may go home for we bless you with victory and long life; we bless you with the power of healing the sick. Nor shall you lack wealth. So go home and eat, for a large war-party is soon to fall upon you. As soon as the sun rises the war whoops will be given so that if you do not go home now you will be killed."

Thus the spirits would speak to me. I was told that if I did not care to do the bidding of one particular spirit, then some other would address me and repeat very much the same thing. So the spirits would speak alternately until the break of day. Then, just before sunrise, a man wearing a warrior's costume, would come and peep into the lodge. He would be a scout. I was told that when this happened, then I would surely believe that a war-party had come upon me. Soon another spirit would come and say, "Grandson, I have taken pity upon you and I will bless you with all the good things that the earth holds. Go home now for a war-party is about to rush upon you." If then I went home the war-whoops would be given just as the sun rose. The members of this war party would give the whoop all at the same time. They would rush upon me and capture me and after *coup* had been counted upon me (*i.e.,* after I had been struck) they would say, "Now, grandson, we have acted thus in order to teach you. Thus shall you act. You have completed your fasting."

Thus would the spirits talk to me, I was told. Now this war-party was really composed of spirits, spirits from the heaven and the earth. Indeed all the spirits that exist would be there. These would all bless me. I was also told that it would be a very difficult thing to obtain this particular blessing.

So there I fasted at the black-hawk's nest, where a lodge had been built for me. The first night I stayed there I wondered when something would happen. But nothing took place. The second night, rather late in the night, my father came and opened the war-bundle and then taking out a gourd, began

[1]A collection of tribal sacred relics with magic power to protect warriors in battle.

to sing. I stood beside him without any clothing except my breech-clout and, holding tobacco in each hand, I uttered my cry to the spirits:

"O spirits, here humble in heart I stand beseeching you."

My father sang war-bundle songs and wept as he sang. I also wept as I uttered my cry to the spirits.

1912

Sam Blowsnake

from *STORY OF THE INDIAN*

The first horses we ever saw came from west of the mountains. A band of the Piegans[1] were camped on Belly River, at a place that we call "Smash the Heads," where we jumped buffalo. They had been driving buffalo over the cliff here, so that they had plenty of meat.

There had come over the mountains to hunt buffalo a Kutenai who had some horses, and he was running buffalo; but for some reason he had no luck. He could kill nothing. He had seen from far off the Piegan camp, but he did not go near it, for the Piegans and the Kutenais were enemies.

This Kutenai could not kill anything, and he and his family had nothing to eat and were starving. At last he made up his mind that he would go into the camp of his enemies and give himself up, for he said, "I might as well be killed at once as die of hunger." So with his wife and children he rode away from his camp up in the mountains, leaving his lodge standing and his horses feeding about it, all except those which his woman and his three children were riding, and started for the camp of the Piegans.

They had just made a big drive, and had run a great lot of buffalo over the cliff. There were many dead in the pískun [corral] and the men were killing those that were left alive, when suddenly the Kutenai, on his horse, followed by his wife and children on theirs, rode over a hill nearby. When they saw him, all the Piegans were astonished and wondered what this could be. None of them had ever seen anything like it, and they were afraid. They thought it was something mysterious. The chief of the Piegans called out to his people: "This is something very strange. I have heard of wonderful things that have happened from the earliest times until now, but I never heard of anything like this. This thing must have come from above (i.e., from the sun), or else it must have come out of the hill (i.e., from the earth). Do not do anything to it; be still and wait. If we try to hurt it, may be it will ride into that hill again, or may be something bad will happen. Let us wait."

As it drew nearer, they could see that it was a man coming, and that he was on some strange animal. The Piegans wanted their chief to go toward him and speak to him. The chief did not wish to do this; he was afraid; but at last he started to go to meet the Kutenai, who was coming. When he got near to him, the Kutenai made signs that he was friendly, and patted his horse on his neck and made signs to the chief. "I give you this animal." The chief made

[1]One of three main tribes of the Blackfoot Indians (so called because of their black-colored moccasins) living in the northern Great Plains area of the United States and Canada.

signs that he was friendly, and the Kutenai rode into the camp and were received as friends, and food was given them and they ate, and their hunger was satisfied.

The Kutenai stayed with these Piegans for some time, and the Kutenai man told the chief that he had more horses at his camp up in the mountains, and that beyond the mountains there were plenty of horses. The Piegan said, "I have never heard of a man riding an animal like this." He asked the Kutenai to bring in the rest of his horses; and one night he started out, and the next day came back driving all his horses before him, and they came to the camp, and all the people saw them and looked at them and wondered. . . .

This young man . . . finally became head chief of the Piegans. His name at first was Dog, and afterward Sits-in-the-Middle, and at last Many Horses. He had so many horses he could not keep track of them all. After he had so many horses, he would select ten boys out of each band of the Piegans to care for his horses. Many Horses had more horses than all the rest of the tribe. Many Horses died a good many years ago. These were the first horses the Piegans saw.

When they first got horses, the people did not know what they fed on. They would offer the animals pieces of dried meat, or would take a piece of backfat and rub their noses with it, to try to get them to eat it. Then the horses would turn away and put down their heads, and begin to eat the grass of the prairie. . . .

White people had begun to come into this country, and Many Horses' young men wanted ropes and iron arrowpoints and saddle blankets, and the people were beginning to kill furs and skins to trade. Many Horses began to trade with his own people for these things. He would ask the young men of the tribe to kill skins for him, and they would bring them to him and he would give them a horse or two in exchange. Then he would send his relations in to the Hudson's Bay post to trade, but he would never go himself. The white men wanted to see him, and sent word to him to come in, but he would never do so.

At length, one winter, these white men packed their dog sledges with goods and started to see Many Horses. They took with them guns. The Piegans heard that the whites were coming, and Many Horses sent word to all the people to come together and meet him at a certain place, where the whites were coming. When these came to the camp, they asked where Many Horses' lodge was, and the people pointed out to them the Crow painted lodge. The whites went to this lodge and began to unpack their things—guns, clothing, knives, and goods of all kinds.

Many Horses sent two men to go in different directions through the camp and ask all the principal men, young and old, to come together to his lodge. They all came. Some went in and some sat outside. Then these white men began to distribute the guns, and with each gun they gave a bundle of powder and ball. At this same time, the young men received white blankets and the old men black coats. Then we first got knives, and the white men showed us how to use knives; to split down the legs and rip up the belly—to skin for trade.

1895

Wolf Calf

from *PAWNEE HERO STORIES*

I heard that long ago there was a time when there were no people in this country except Indians. After that, the people began to hear of men that had white skins; they had been seen far to the east. Before I was born, they came out to our country and visited us. The man who came was from the Government. He wanted to make a treaty with us, and to give us presents, blankets and guns, and flint and steel, and knives.

The Head Chief told him that we needed none of these things. He said, "We have our buffalo and our corn. These things the Ruler gave to us, and they are all that we need. See this robe. This keeps me warm in winter. I need no blanket."

The white men had with them some cattle, and the Pawnee Chief said, "Lead out a heifer here on the prairie." They led her out, and the Chief, stepping up to her, shot her through behind the shoulder with his arrow, and she fell down and died. Then the Chief said, "Will not my arrow kill? I do not need your guns." Then he took his stone knife and skinned the heifer, and cut off a piece of fat meat. When he had done this, he said, "Why should I take your knives? The Ruler has given me something to cut with."

Then taking the fire sticks, he kindled a fire to roast the meat, and while it was cooking, he spoke again and said, "You see, my brother, that the Ruler has given us all that we need; the buffalo for food and clothing; the corn to eat with our dried meat; bows, arrows, knives and hoes; all the implements which we need for killing meat, or for cultivating the ground. Now go back to the country from whence you came. We do not want your presents, and we do not want you to come into our country."

1889

Curly Chief

LEGEND OF THE SNAKE ORDER . . .[1] AS TOLD BY OUTSIDERS[2]

Many years ago, when the people were greatly scattered over the land, there lived in a house seven brothers, who were said to be the best of all men then living, for they did not of nights interfere with others, nor did they dwell with women. They were named Red-Corn, Blue-Corn, Yellow-Corn, White-Corn, Green-Corn, Spotted-Corn, and Black-Corn. None of them married until the youngest, Black-Corn, had attained the age of manhood. He was then told by his older brothers to take a wife. This displeased him, for among all the women of his tribe there was none he liked. He grew sad, and said he would go away, and not return until after he had found a wife. He started upon his journey, taking with him only four plume-sticks and a bag of sacred meal. After journeying many days, until nearly dead with hunger and thirst, he came to a large lake which lay to the west of his own house. He did not drink from this lake, but from a stream of water which issued from a hill at a little distance from the lake. Next day, when he awoke, he went down to the side of

[1]A legend of the Hopi Indians of the Southwest.

[2]I.e., those who are not members of the Snake Order of the Hopi Indians.

the water, and said to Daw-wa, the sun-chief: "Oh, Daw-wa! father! I have been sent from my home, and my heart is heavy. I am weary, father; give me rest, give me a home where my heart will once more be filled with the joyous song of the lark, and not with the sad song of the dove."

Daw-wa heard his prayer, and told him to tie his four sticks together and place them on the water, which done the sticks became great logs and the feathers a shade (after the manner of an umbrella). He was then directed to gather certain roots, after eating which he would not be hungry for a long while. He was told that in four days he was to sail away upon this raft, and after he started he was not to land until asked to come ashore by a snake, whose name was Wapa Tcua (Big Rattlesnake). On the fourth morning, before sunrise, he was awakened by the rocking motion of his raft, and after the sun had risen he looked around, but could see no land. He was afraid, but Oman comforted him, assuring him of safety. At sunset, one evening, after his voyage had continued several days, a buzzard came and told him that in two or three days he would see land, and cautioned him not to be frightened at anything he should see or hear. At the end of three days land came in view. He sailed two days in sight of land, and at sunset on the fourth day the raft was thrown upon the shore. It began to grow small, compelling him to get ashore. In the morning, Daw-wa told him to pick up his plume-sticks, which had now assumed their natural size. Daw-wa then directed him to travel to the south and west, telling him that he would be met by an old man, who would guide him to a running stream where the Big Snake kept watch, to whom he should give the plume-sticks and pouch of meal. He began his journey at noon, and night came on while he was climbing a mountain. He continued his journey in the early morning as soon as the star rose, and when the sun rose a very old man, leaning on a stick, came from behind a rock. This old man had eyes and ears, but had neither mouth nor nose; he could not speak, but with his stick, which was shaped like a crook, he seized the young man by the neck, and led him along, stopping at intervals to let his companion rest, for the old man almost ran, so fast was his gait. At sunset he stopped, and by signs told the young man that on the morrow his part of the journey would be done; that he had been a long time awaiting the young man's arrival. The old man said he was glad of his arrival, for now he (the old man) could go home and die in peace. While the old man was making signs, he was struck by a flash of lighting and rendered unconscious.

The young man's name was Kwe-teat-rï-yi, White-Corn. White-Corn was afraid, and started to run away, but the old man opened his eyes, and called him by name, telling him to get a piece of black rock, lying near, and with it cut the skin on his (the old man's) face, beginning at a point between the eyes, and cutting downward the length of one of the plume-sticks, then cutting across the face the same distance. White-Corn did as he was directed, and immediately the old man became a young man. In the morning they resumed their journey in high glee, singing and telling each other of their homes. At noon they stopped to rest, and the young old man dug a hole in the sand, and, placing one of White-Corn's plume-sticks in it, he began to sing and dance, and the hole filled with water, from which they drank, and then resumed their journey. At sunset they came to the top of a hill, from which White-Corn saw the long-expected stream; so, when he spoke of it, he turned to look at his companion, but the latter had vanished. During the night White-Corn was afraid. At daylight he resumed his march, and got to the stream before sunrise. He sprinkled meal upon the water, and, hearing a peculiar sound in the grass, he turned round and saw a tremendous snake coming toward him, with head raised several feet above ground, its skin shining like beautiful rocks [gems?]. The snake halted at a little distance from him, and began to talk, making inquiry as to where he came from and where he was going, but especially questioning to ascertain whether he was trustworthy. By the direction of the snake, he again threw his remaining plume-sticks into the stream, and, as before, they immediately became a raft. He was directed to get upon the raft, and remain until noon of the fourth day. After this four days' voyage he would reach a hill, which he was to climb, and would then receive further instructions. He accordingly got upon the raft, and it at once began to move rapidly off, much faster than a horse could run; he was frightened, and longed to jump off upon the river bank, but he feared injury: so he sat still and gazed in wonder until night, when he watched the stars. In this way he continued until noon of the fourth day.

He was startled on the fourth day by seeing an immense rock in front, blocking up the entire passage of the river. While he was yet thinking how he could save himself, his raft was suddenly lifted by the roaring water, and he and it were thrown high up on the hill, beside the rock. He lay there, bruised and trembling, for a long while, and pondering over what course to pursue, until he fell asleep. When he awoke in the morning the sun was well up, and he hastened to climb the hill, the summit of which he reached at sunset. He stood looking at a rock partly buried in the sand, and as he continued to observe it a snake's head protruded from beneath. He sprinkled sacred meal, and placed his plume-sticks before the snake, which coiled around them, and breathed upon each separate feather. The snake then returned beneath the rock, and directed him to proceed with certain ceremonies. As directed, White-Corn placed the plume-sticks in front of the snake, then sprinkled corn-meal in such a manner as to describe a circle, then in the area of this circle he sprinkled meal in three straight lines . . . . These three lines he named the points whence the rain and winds come.

The snake was well pleased with this conduct, and he concluded not to wait for morning, but to take White-Corn at once into the presence of the great snake-chief, and let him see what the young man did. The rock was suddenly lifted up, and a large opening was exposed. The snake told him to follow quickly, as it was growing dark and cold, and that, although the path was short, it was very rough, and in the dark would be attended by many falls. White-Corn immediately followed the snake, and in a little while after getting into this cavern a mighty noise like thunder was heard. The snake told him not to fear, as the noise was caused by rocks falling down to close up the entrance through which they had just come. This was to prevent any one gaining entrance except those selected, and to prevent the escape of those who had entered. They went on until they heard the sound of falling water and beautiful music, filling the heart full of dreams of beautiful women bathing in streams of liquid light. Suddenly his eyes were dazzled by a great light, which disclosed, standing against the sides of a spacious cavern, men and women, clad on their right with sunbeams, and on their left with moonbeams. In the centre were many maidens, dancing and tying each other with ribbons of fleecy clouds; these were clothed with the stolen rays of the stars and the spray of dashing waters. In the midst of the throng sat an old man, looking angrily at White-Corn.

While enjoying the scene, he was suddenly interrupted, and all of his happy thoughts spread like snow before the gale. The old man addressed him, saying that for many days he and his children had been watching in the east for the approach of him who was to break apart the rocks which held them from the sight of the sun and the beautiful world; for the approach of him who was to impart to them a new life, but who was to go through the ordeal of the Snake Order before being released or releasing others from the dark and lonely life. After many things had been told him, he was led by a snake up to the falling water; the snake then directed him to cast his clothing aside and bathe in it. After bathing, he was moving off from the water, but his foot was drawn back; then he noticed for the first time that all of the others had a peculiar skin, like a snake's skin, and that he himself was being enveloped with a similar covering. He was then brought before the old man again, and told to get something to eat, and to choose a maiden for a sweetheart. He was unable to make a choice, and asked the old man to select one for him. The old man, reaching back, took hold of a cloudy substance, and began pulling, when there emerged from it a beautiful girl called "Bright Eyes," who was given to White-Corn for his wife. As directed, he followed her and got food. It is unknown how long he stayed in this house, but it was long enough for him to learn all the songs and ceremonials pertaining to the Snake Order.

One day, while all the people were present before the old man, White-Corn told them that he had been with them for a long while, and the time had now come for him to return to his own people; that his people were calling for him; that, while he was enjoying plenty, his brothers were doubtless suffering: hence he proposed to take his wife and start for his home. The people all laughed at him, but he said, "Never mind; the same god that brought me will show me the return path." All the inhabitants of the cave were sad except White-Corn and the old man, who were together oftener than formerly, and were in very secret confidences. One day (how they distinguished day from night is not told) White-Corn was seen to take a bunch of feathers from a long rope hanging from the ceiling. He tied the feathers to a short stick. From a peg in the wall he took a stick with two feathers fastened to it. He gave the bunch of feathers to his wife. He bade good-bye to all the people, and the old man took him by a secret path to the earth's surface. The old man, wishing White-Corn a speedy journey, returned to his cave. White-Corn asked his wife if she could tell him the direction in which his home lay; she said that when the sun came up she would be able to tell, as one of the *Fits-ki,* or rays, pointed directly to the home of his people. Next day, at sunrise, she pointed to a large mound, and said that from the top of it the mountains that were near his home could be seen. He ran to the top of this mound, so glad was he to get away from the constant glare of the magical light, and to think that in a few days he would again see his brothers and friends. They travelled fast for four days; on the fifth day the road led through such rough hills they were forced to turn toward the south. They found a well-travelled trail leading to water, around which were houses and places to keep sheep or horses, —peculiar houses, too, almost round and very high, in which were found many strange vessels and other utensils made of clay and horn; also funnel-shaped baskets, designed to be carried on the back. They made but a short halt in these places, fearing that the people who built them might return and harm or kill them. So they kept going, until one morning, having ascended a very high mountain, the smoke of fires was seen in the valley. Telling his wife to keep a little way behind, White-Corn went towards the fires, the first of which he reached at sunset. He found there his uncle and cousin, who had been searching for him, but, deeming him lost forever, were now on their return home. White-Corn told his adventures, and brought his wife to them. After a few days' travel they all reached home.

At this time there was a great drought prevailing, and it was observed that whenever Tcua-wuti (White-Corn's wife) came before the altar and sprinkled meal rain was sure to follow. So they called upon her husband to give them soup, whereby they, too, might invoke the rain-god of his wife's country. But she said No: not until a son was born to her could the altar of her rain-god be raised in a strange land. After there had been a severe storm, it was observed that Tcua-wuti was with child, and this caused great rejoicing among the people, for they wished her to bear a boy who would become their rain-chief. When the time came for her to bear her child White-Corn went away with her to a high mesa on the west of the village. After an absence of seven days they returned to the villages, bringing with them her offspring, consisting of five snakes. This enraged the people so that they would have killed them all, but an old man, who was standing by, said, "No, I will be their father, come and live with me." He took them to his home, and that night the people were startled by loud and strange cries coming from the old man's house; a great smoke issued from the doorway and other rents, where people on the outside could look in. No one but the old man, his wife, and one son, beside White-Corn, knew what took place in that house during the night, for the next day the old man went off to the valley. In three days, Tcua-wuti took her snake children and the old man, and went into the valley. In the afternoon the old man came back alone, but Tcua-wuti has never been seen again.

1888

WHEN THE COYOTE MARRIED THE MAIDEN[1]

After the first loom was made the people lived peacefully for about half a century. Then these strange creatures that were born began to eat the people. There is a little hill called tqnts'i'se ko just across the Mancos Canyon, which used to be a house. It was the home of twelve brothers. (On the top of this hill you can see a ruin.) The brothers were great hunters and hunted all over the mesas. They had one sister. The girl grew to be a beautiful maiden, and the holy men came from far and wide to ask her to marry them.

The maiden's name was Ataed'diy ini. When her brothers were away hunting she stayed at home alone. Now the Coyote came to the brothers and called out: "Brothers-in-law." He wanted this maiden to become his wife. Ataed'diy ini told him "No," for only the one who killed the giant would become her

[1]A legend of the Navajo Indians of the Southwest.

husband. The Coyote sat there with his head down for a moment, then he said: "Very well." He left her and went to the home of the giant.

When he saw the giant he said: "Brother, why do people outrun you? Now if you want me to, I can make you run as fast as I can. I have no trouble getting meat. I know of herbs that will clean your system; and I will show you the medicine which I use on my legs to make me run fast."

Now this giant was very clumsy; he just walked along slowly and when people saw him they became so frightened that they were unable to run away. Because of this he could pick them up and put them in his big basket. The giant was, however, interested in the Coyote's plan.

The Coyote told the giant to build a sweat house; and while the giant was doing this the Coyote gathered the herbs. He also got a fresh leg of deer. When the sweat house was built and the hot stones placed inside they both entered it. Each took a good drink of the herb infusion the Coyote prepared. Now the drink made them nauseated and they vomited into the bowls each had taken in the sweat house. In the Coyote's bowl were found grasshoppers and lizards; the giant had vomited fat meat; but the Coyote hastily changed the bowls, and pulling aside the door covering and letting in the light, he showed them to the giant and said: "Look what you vomited. These things keep you from running swiftly". The giant said: "I see." They left the sweat house to get cool.

"Now," said the Coyote, "I will give you the medicine for your legs so that you will run swiftly." It was well with the giant. They returned to the sweat house; and the Coyote secretly took the deer's leg with him. The Coyote said: "Now comes the last step. This is very powerful medicine that I use." In the darkness he laid the deer's leg over his own leg and cut it in two. He put the giant's hand over the severed leg and showed him that it was indeed in two pieces. The giant said: "I see." The Coyote then quickly put the pieces of the deer's leg back of himself. He commenced spitting on his own leg and said: "Now get well, get well." After this he made the giant feel his perfect leg. The Coyote told the giant that now all the bad food was out of his stomach, and all the bad blood was out of his leg, and that he could outrun anything he saw. The giant said again, "I see."

After this the Coyote got out his knife and said that he would do the same thing for the giant's leg. He cut off one of them, and the giant groaned with great pain. The giant began to spit on the two parts. He tried to make them grow together. But the Coyote grabbed the giant's severed leg and ran away with it, saying: "I never heard of a bone growing together in a day."

The Coyote took the giant's leg to the maiden and told her that he had killed the giant. But the maiden said that before she would marry him she would have to kill him; and if he could return to life, then he could be her husband. The Coyote hung his head and covered his eyes with his hand for a moment. "Very well," he said, and he went away.

He went a short distance to the east side of the dwelling, and there he formed a little black mountain. He put a tunnel through the mountain, and he traveled still farther to the east. He then took out his lungs and heart and wrapped them in the Black Wind. He returned through the tunnel to the maiden's home. He said: "Now you can do as you wish with me." She got a club and killed him and threw his body on the ash dump. She went into her house, but he followed her. "Are you my wife now?" he asked her. But she said: "I have to kill you twice." So he left her and traveled to the south, and there he built a blue mountain, and he carved a tunnel through it. To the south he took out his heart and his lungs and he wrapped them in the Blue Wind. Only his body returned to the maiden's dwelling. He said: "Now do whatever you wish with me." So she killed him and cut him into pieces and threw them on the ash heap. But he followed her into her house and asked: "Are you my wife now?" But she said: "No, I must kill you three times." He left her and went out to the west, and there he built a yellow mountain; and he cut a tunnel through it; and in the west he left his heart and lungs wrapped in the Yellow Wind. He returned to the maiden and spoke to her as before. But again she killed him and ground the carcass with earth and threw it out. She returned to the house but he followed her. He said: "Are you my wife now?" But she answered: "No, four times I must kill you." This time the Coyote went to the north and built a white mountain. He cut a tunnel, as before. At its end he left his heart and lungs wrapped in the White Wind. His body returned to the maiden. "Now do with me whatever you wish," he said. This time, after she killed him, she cut him into pieces, ground the pieces with earth and threw it in all directions. Satisfied, she returned to her home; but after a little while the Coyote came in and said: "Now are you my wife?" The maiden asked him how he could do these things. He told her that after she became his wife he would show her his magic. She let the Coyote come. He became her husband and she became his wife. Then he took her to the east and showed her the mountain and the tunnel that he had made. And he took her to the south, and west, and north. She learned to do what the Coyote had done. He taught her his ways.

And now she was called Jikai'naazi'li, Tingling Maiden.

After a time they saw the brothers returning. The two were frightened and did not know what to do. The Coyote jumped over a pile of goods (blankets) and his wife covered him. When the brothers entered the house the fire was out, and the girl sat there looking strangely. She was not the same. The eldest brother asked in surprise: "Why is the fire out? Why is there nothing cooking? Why is the home not in order?"

The eldest brother told the others to get wood. The brothers did this and built a fire of cedar wood. When the fire was burning the odor of coyote was strong inside the house. The eldest brother told the others to throw out the wood and to bring fresh wood. A second fire was built of fresh wood, but still they smelled coyote. They threw the firewood out again and they gathered the branches of trees, but it did no good; they gathered the topmost branches, but still the odor of coyote was strong in the dwelling. The eldest brother then cursed the coyote. "The Coyote with his ugly odor is everywhere," he said. Just then the Coyote threw the cover off and came out, saying: "What is the trouble, my brothers-in-law?"

Now the brothers did not know what to say. They sat around the fire with their heads down. In a short time they went out and built themselves a little shelter, and they camped there that night. The house they left for the Coyote and his wife.

The following morning when the brothers went out to hunt, the Coyote said that he would go with them. The eldest brother told the others that from then on they could only expect trouble. "But it is our duty to hunt," he said, "and we must go and hunt today."

Now in those days all was sacred and holy. There was a rainbow, formed like a young man, lying by the canyon's edge. They threw him over the canyon and crossed on him. After the brothers had crossed the canyon they heard the Coyote calling far behind them. The eldest brother said: "I guess that we had better bring him across before he does something worse than howling." So they went back and brought him on the rainbow.

They were on a mesa north of the Mancos Canyon when the Coyote came chasing a big ram. (There were many mountain sheep there at that time.) One of the brothers pulled his bow and aimed his arrow at the ram. He shot the arrow and killed the ram. Now in those days the horn of the mountain sheep was filled with fat, delicious marrow; and all the hunters prized it as their favorite fat. Whoever killed a sheep, to him went the horns. When the Coyote saw that the ram he had been chasing had been killed by one of the brothers he claimed the horns. The brother spoke to the Coyote and told him to behave like a man once in a while. "There was a rule that whoever kills a sheep gets the horns." With this the brother began to cut the pair of horns. The Coyote stood to one side and whispered: "Turn to bone. Turn to bone." The brother cut and cut, but the horn had turned to solid bone. And where he had tried to cut it ridges formed. That is why there are rings on mountain sheep horns today.

The brothers dressed the sheep and rolled the meat into a little ball. They told the Coyote to take the meat to his wife and to tell her to have it ready for them when they returned. One of the brothers took the Coyote across the canyon. He warned him by no means to put the meat ball down on the way. But no sooner had the brother departed than he put down the meat ball. Immediately it turned into the big pile of meat. The Coyote thought that he could do what the brothers had done. He tried to roll it into a little ball again; but he could not do it. He walked over to the canyon's edge and he saw that way down in the bottom of the canyon a big game was going on. There were people in the canyon playing this game. They were the Swallow People or cliff dwellers. The Coyote called down to them; he said that they were certainly an ugly people—the men and their wives alike. He said that his wife was beautiful and light of skin.

All this made the cliff people very angry, and they decided to get rid of him, to kill him. While the Coyote sat up there calling out insults, two young spider men climbed up the wall of the canyon; and from the cliff's edge they spun a long, high fence strong as woven mats. It was very high and very strong, and it extended for a long way back of the Coyote. After the two young men had finished they returned to the bottom of the canyon. Then all the cliff people went after the Coyote who was still sitting there on the rim mocking them. He insulted them and he kicked at them and he said that not one in all that crowd could catch him. Just as they reached the rim of the canyon, away he went as fast as he could run. But he came up against the spider men's fence and it threw him back. He tried to jump over it but failed. Now the cliff people were very near. He tried and tried to jump over the fence, and the fourth time he fell back among the cliff people. They caught him and killed him. They cut his hide into strips and made headbands of the fur. That is why swallows have a little ring around their heads. They have worn these little light bands ever since they made them out of the Coyote's hide.

1956

THE CREATION OF THE HORSE[1]

Something was spread over it. It moved and became alive. It whimpered. Woman-who-changes began to sing: —

> Changing Woman I am, I hear.
> In the center of my house behind the fire, I hear.
> Sitting on jewels spread wide, I hear.
> In a jet basket, in a jet house, there now it lies.
> Vegetation with its dew in it, it lies.
> Over there,
> It increases, not hurting the house now with it it lies,
> inside it lies.

Its feet were made of mirage. They say that because a horse's feet have stripes. Its gait was a rainbow, its bridle of sun strings. Its heart was made of red stone. Its intestines were made of water of all kinds, its tail of black rain. Its mane was a cloud with a little rain. Distant lightning composed its ears. A big spreading twinkling star formed its eye and striped its face. Its lower legs were white. At night it gives light in front because its face was made of vegetation. Large beads formed its lips; white shell, its teeth, so they would not wear out quickly. A black flute was put into its mouth for a trumpet. Its belly was made of dawn, one side white, one side black. That is why it is called "half white."

A white-shell basket stood there. In it was the water of a mare's afterbirth. A turquoise basket stood there. It contained the water of the afterbirth. An abalone basket full of the eggs of various birds stood there. A jet basket with eggs stood there. The baskets stand for quadrupeds, the eggs for birds. Now as Changing-woman began to sing the animals came up to taste. The horse tasted twice; hence mares sometimes give birth to twins. One ran back without tasting. Four times, he ran up and back again. The last time he said, "Sh!" and did not taste. "She will not give birth. Long-ears (Mule) she will be called," said Changing-Woman. The others tasted the eggs from the different places. Hence there are many feathered people. Because they tasted the eggs in the abalone and jet baskets many are black.

1934

POEMS[1]

SONG WITH WHICH TWO BOYS KILLED THEIR GRANDMOTHER[2]

> Our grandmother says it will be all right that she dies,
> Because she has been alive a long time.
> That is why she does not mind dying,
> Because we can not keep up with the crowd.

[1]A legend of the Navajo Indians of the Southwest.

[1]Of the Papago Indians of the Pima tribes of Arizona and northern Mexico.

[2]A song sung by two boys, the singing of which was to cause the death of an old woman who could no longer keep up with the migrations of the tribe.

A WHITE WIND FROM THE WEST

From the west a white wind is coming out.
Stand there and look, it is not near,
It is beside the ocean, there you will see it.
By the reflected light of the sun you will see it.

THE SUNRISE[3]

The sun is rising
At either side a bow is lying,
Beside the bows are lion-babies,
The sky is pink,
    That is all.

The moon is setting,
At either side are bamboos for arrow-making,
Beside the bamboos are wild-cat babies,
They walk uncertainly
    That is all.

[A COMPANION SONG]

The sun is slowly departing,
It is slower in its setting,
Black bats will be swooping when the sun is gone,
    That is all.

The spirit children are beneath,
They are moving back and forth,
They roll in play among tufts of white eagle down,
    That is all.

SONGS OF OWL WOMAN[4]

BROWN OWLS

Brown owls come here in the blue evening,
They are hooting about,
They are shaking their wings and hooting.

IN THE BLUE NIGHT

How shall I begin my song
In the blue night that is settling?
I will sit here and begin my song.

[3]Songs used to treat sickness caused by the spirits of dead Apaches.

[4]Songs of Owl Woman, a Papago medicine woman, the first four of which she sang when beginning her treatment of the sick.

THE OWL FEATHER

The owl feather is rolling in this direction and beginning to sing.
The people listen and come to hear the owl feather
Rolling in this direction and beginning to sing.

THEY COME HOOTING

Early in the evening they come hooting about,
Some have small voices and some have large voices,
Some have voice of medium strength, hooting about.

HIS HEART IS ALMOST COVERED WITH NIGHT[5]

Poor old sister, you have cared for this man and you want to see him again, but now his heart is almost covered with night. There is just a little left.

WE WILL JOIN THEM[6]

Yonder are spirits laughing and talking as though drunk.
They do the same things that we do.
Now we will join them.

"THE CLOUDS ARE APPROACHING"[7]

(1)

Clouds are standing in the east, they are approaching,
It rains in the distance,
Now it is raining here and the thunder rolls.

(2)

Green rock mountains are thundering with clouds.
With this thunder the Akim village is shaking.
The water will come down the arroyo and I will float on the water.
Afterwards the corn will ripen in the fields.

(3)

Close to the west the great ocean is singing.
The waves are rolling toward me, covered with many clouds.
Even here I catch the sound.
The earth is shaking beneath me and I hear the deep rumbling.

[5]A song given a Papago woman by the spirit of her brother, who told her that a man she was going to visit was about to die.

[6]A song taught to Owl Woman by the spirit of a dead Papago man.

[7]Four songs sung at a ceremony to bring rain.

(4)

A cloud on top of Evergreen Trees Mountain is singing,
A cloud on top of Evergreen Trees Mountain is standing still,
It is raining and thundering up there,
It is raining here,
Under the mountain the corn tassels are shaking,
Under the mountain the horns[8] of the child corn are glistening.

ORATIONS

SPEECH OF LOGAN[1]

I appeal to any white to say, if ever he entered Logan's cabin hungry, and he gave him not meat; if ever he came cold and naked and he clothed him not. During the course of the last long bloody war, Logan remained idle in his cabin, an advocate for peace. Such was my love for the whites, that my countrymen pointed as they passed, and said, "Logan is the friend of white men." I had even thought to have lived with you, but for the injuries of one man. Col. Cresap[2] the last spring, in cold blood, and unprovoked, murdered all the relations of Logan, not sparing even my women and children. There runs not a drop of my blood in the veins of any living creature. This called on me for revenge. I have sought it. I have killed many. I have fully glutted my vengeance. For my country, I rejoice at the beams of peace. But do not harbor a thought that mine is the joy of fear. Logan never felt fear. He will not turn on his heel to save his life. Who is there to mourn for Logan?—Not one!

1774 1775, 1787

SPEECH OF TECUMSEH[1]

Brothers—We all belong to one family; we are all children of the Great Spirit; we walk in the same path; slake our thirst at the same spring; and now affairs of the greatest concern lead us to smoke the pipe around the same council fire!

Brothers—We are friends; we must assist each other to bear our burdens. The blood of many of our fathers and brothers has run like water on the ground, to satisfy the avarice of the white men. We, ourselves, are threatened with a great evil; nothing will pacify them but the destruction of all the red men.

[8]The pointed tops of young corn stalks.

[1]Mingo (Iroquois) orator (c. 1725–1780). His speech was sent to the Earl of Dunmore (1732–1809), royal governor of Virginia, after an army of colonial militia defeated the Indians in Lord Dunmore's War (April–November 1774).

[2]Michael Cresap (1742–1775), reputed leader of a massacre of Indians in April, 1774.

[1]Shawnee chief (1768–1813). In 1812 he addressed a group of Osage Indians, urging them to make war against white settlers who were encroaching upon Indian lands.

Brothers—When the white men first set foot on our grounds, they were hungry; they had no place on which to spread their blankets, or to kindle their fires. They were feeble; they could do nothing for themselves. Our fathers commiserated their distress, and shared freely with them whatever the Great Spirit had given his red children. They gave them food when hungry, medicine when sick, spread skins for them to sleep on, and gave them grounds, that they might hunt and raise corn. Brothers, the white people are like poisonous serpents: when chilled, they are feeble and harmless; but invigorate them with warmth, and they sting their benefactors to death.

The white people came among us feeble; and now we have made them strong, they wish to kill us, or drive us back, as they would wolves and panthers.

Brothers—The white men are not friends to the Indians, at first, they only asked for land sufficient for a wigwam; now, nothing will satisfy them but the whole of our hunting grounds, from the rising to the setting sun.

Brothers—The white men want more than our hunting grounds; they wish to kill our warriors; they would even kill our old men, women, and little ones.

Brothers—Many winters ago, there was no land; the sun did not rise and set: all was darkness. The Great Spirit made all things. He gave the white people a home beyond the great waters. He supplied these grounds with game, and gave them to his red children; and he gave them strength and courage to defend them.

Brothers—My people wish for peace: the red men all wish for peace, but where the white people are, there is no peace for them, except it be on the bosom of our mother.

Brothers—The white men despise and cheat the Indians; they abuse and insult them; they do not think the red men sufficiently good to live.

The red men have borne many and great injuries; they ought to suffer them no longer. My people will not; they are determined on vengeance; they have taken up the tomahawk; they will make it fat with blood; they will drink the blood of the white people.

Brothers—My people are brave and numerous; but the white people are too strong for them alone. I wish you to take up the tomahawk with them. If we all unite, we will cause the rivers to stain the great waters with their blood.

Brothers—If you do not unite with us, they will first destroy us, and then you will fall an easy prey to them. They have destroyed many nations of red men because they were not united, because they were not friends to each other.

Brothers—The white people send runners amongst us; they wish to make us enemies, that they may sweep over and desolate our hunting grounds, like devastating winds, or rushing waters.

Brothers—Our Great Father,[2] over the great waters, is angry with the white people, our enemies. He will send his brave warriors against them; he will send us rifles, and whatever else we want—he is our friend, and we are his children.

Brothers—Who are the white people that we should fear them? They cannot run fast, and are good marks to shoot at: they are only men; our fathers

[2]George III, King of England (1760–1820).

have killed many of them: we are not squaws, and we will stain the earth red with their blood.

Brothers—The Great Spirit is angry with our enemies; he speaks in thunder, and the earth swallows up villages, and drinks up the Mississippi. The great waters will cover their lowlands; their corn cannot grow; and the Great Spirit will sweep those who escape to the hills from the earth with his terrible breath.

Brothers—We must be united; we must smoke the same pipe; we must fight each other's battles; and more than all, we must love the Great Spirit: he is for us; he will destroy our enemies, and make all his red children happy.

1812? 1823

FAREWELL TO BLACK HAWK[1]

You have taken me prisoner, with all my warriors. I am much grieved; for I expected, if I did not defeat you, to hold out much longer, and give you more trouble before I surrendered. I tried hard to bring you into ambush, but your last general understood Indian fighting. I determined to rush upon you, and fight you face to face. I fought hard, but your guns were well aimed. The bullets flew like birds in the air, and whizzed by our ears like the wind through the trees in winter.

My warriors fell around me; it began to look dismal. I saw my evil day at hand. The sun rose dim on us in the morning, and at night it sank in a dark cloud, and looked like a ball of fire. That was the last sun that shone on Black Hawk. His heart is dead, and no longer beats quick in his bosom. He is now a prisoner to the white men; they will do with him as they wish. But he can stand torture, and is not afraid of death. He is no coward. Black Hawk is an Indian!

He has done nothing for which an Indian ought to be ashamed. He has fought for his countrymen, against the white men who came, year after year, to cheat them and take away their lands. You know the cause of our making war. It is known to all white men. They ought to be ashamed of it. The white men despise the Indians and drive them back from their homes. But the Indians are not deceitful. The white men speak bad of the Indian, and look at him spitefully. But the Indian does not tell lies. Indians do not steal. An Indian who is as bad as a white man could not live in our nation. He would be put to death and eaten by the wolves.

The white men are bad schoolmasters. They carry false looks and deal in false actions. They smile in the face of the poor Indian, to cheat him; they shake him by the hand to gain his confidence, to make him drunk, and to deceive him. We told them to let us alone, and keep away from us; but they followed on, and beset our paths, and they coiled themselves among us, like the snake. They poisoned us by their touch. We were not safe; we lived in danger. We were becoming like them, hypocrites and liars; all talkers and no workers.

We looked up to the Great Spirit. We went to our Father. We were encouraged. His great council gave us fair words and big promises; but we obtained

[1]Leader of the defeated Sauk and Fox Indians in the Black Hawk War of 1832.

no satisfaction. Things were growing worse. There were no deer in the forest. The opossum and the beaver were fled. The springs were drying up, and our people were without food to keep them from starving. We called a great council and built a big fire. The spirit of our fathers arose and spoke to us to avenge our wrongs or die. We set up the war whoop and dug up the tomahawk; our knives were ready, and the heart of Black Hawk swelled high in his bosom when he led his warriors to battle. He is satisfied. He will go to the world of spirits contented. He has done his duty. His father will meet him there and commend him. Black Hawk is a true Indian. He feels for his wife, his children, his friends, but he does not care for himself. He cares for the nation and for the Indians. They will suffer. He laments their fate.

The white men do not scalp the head, they do worse—they poison the heart. It is not pure with them. His countrymen will not be scalped, but will in a few years be like the white men, so you cannot trust them; and there must be in the white settlements as many officers as men, to take care of them and keep them in order.

Farewell, my nation! Black Hawk tried to save you, and avenge your wrongs. He drank the blood of some of the whites. He has been taken prisoner, and his plans are stopped. He can do no more! He is near his end. His sun is setting, and he will rise no more. Farewell to Black Hawk!

1832 1910

THE SPEECH OF CHIEF JOSEPH[1]

Tell General Howard[2] I know his heart. What he told me before, I have in my heart.

I am tired of fighting. Our chiefs are killed. Looking Glass is dead. Toohoolhoolzote is dead. The old men are all dead.

It is the young men who say yes and no. He who led on the young men is dead. It is cold and we have no blankets. The little children are freezing to death.

My people, some of them, have run away to the hills, and have no blankets, no food; no one knows where they are—perhaps freezing to death.

I want to have time to look for my children and see how many I can find. Maybe I shall find them among the dead.

Hear me, my chiefs. I am tired; my heart is sick and sad.

From where the sun now stands I will fight no more forever.

1877 1878

[1]Chief of the Nez Percé Indians, defeated and captured in 1877. [2]Chief Joseph's pursuer.

The Age of Romanticism

In 1810 the population of the seventeen United States totaled little more than 7 million. Fifty-one years later, at the beginning of the Civil War, the number of states had doubled, and the population had increased to more than 31 million. American pioneers had pushed the frontier line of settlement beyond the Mississippi to the Great Plains, and the nation's center of population had shifted westward from the eastern seaboard, across the Appalachians, to Ohio. The West had risen as a sectional power to challenge the political dominance of the East and the South. In 1828 the election of the frontier hero Andrew Jackson as the seventh President of the United States had brought an end to the "Virginia Dynasty" of American Presidents. By the 1840s the Age of the Common Man had arrived. Voting restrictions were eased. The Jeffersonian concept of a natural aristocracy had been replaced by the egalitarian belief that all white men are literally equal, and most are capable of political leadership. A new nationalism had emerged, proudly American and justified by "Manifest Destiny," the doctrine asserting that the new nation was spiritually supreme and its expansion was the will of God.

Industrialization and Social Change

Well before 1860 the United States had begun to change into an industrial and urban society. The word "technology" was coined in 1829. A form of automation had come with the construction of a one-man flour mill in Virginia; Americans had invented the cotton gin, the sewing machine, and the telegraph; the principles of assembly-line mass production had been established in 1800 when Eli Whitney built a factory in Whitneyville, Connecticut to make muskets for the United States Army. The fire and roar of newly perfected steam engines symbolized the beginning of a technology that would bring vast material benefits and cause overwhelming social disorders. In its first years the United States had been a republic of small landholders, without sharp contrasts of wealth. Now the nation became a land of contrasting riches and poverty. The numbers of "millionaires" multiplied, as did the number of paupers. Political corruption grew widespread: during Jackson's administration the New York Collector of the Customs, Samuel Swartwout, became the first public servant known in American history to steal a million dollars. In the first half of the nineteenth century the proportion of Americans who labored on farms declined as more and more men and women left the land to work in urban businesses and factories. New York became America's largest city, supplanting Boston and Philadelphia as the economic and cultural capital of the nation.

Through the first half of the century the pursuit of simplicity, utility, and perfection remained an American characteristic. Gentlemen ceased to wear ornate, powdered wigs, and they replaced their elegant knee breeches with drab stove-pipe trousers. High-fashioned ladies adopted simpler dress styles and spurned the elaborate use of cosmetics. Utopian communal societies flourished. Transcendentalists, Baptists, Presbyterians, Methodists, and visionaries who called themselves Millennialists, Universalists, Perfectionists, and Come-Outers, all offered new paths to God. A renewed interest in reform and humanitarianism appeared. Churches embarked on temperance crusades to save drunkards and to slay "demon rum." In 1817 the Society for the Prevention of Pauperism was formed, and in 1833 a national coalition of abolitionist groups established the American Anti-Slavery Society. The branding, mutilation, and whipping of convicts declined. Imprisonment for debt was abolished.

By mid-century the bread lines and soup kitchens of public aid societies had become a permanent part of life in America's big cities. The feminist movement blazed forth with a host of notable women battling for their rights and for social reform. Elizabeth Cady Stanton and Lucy Stone fought to establish women's right to vote and to hold property. Dorothea Lynde Dix led a movement to improve prisons and insane asylums. Amelia Jenks Bloomer worked to promote woman's education and left her name to the pantaloons she wore to foster the movement for dress reform. In 1837 the first college-level institution for women, Mount Holyoke Female Seminary, opened in Massachusetts to serve "the muslin sex."

The Growth of Publishing

By the 1850s the level of education and literacy had risen significantly. State legislatures had started to enact compulsory school attendance laws. More Americans began to read books, magazines, and newspapers. Improvements in the printing press and the expansion of the postal service made possible the rapid production and wide distribution of periodicals. George Washington had proclaimed that magazines were "easy vehicles of knowledge" that would "preserve the liberty, stimulate the industry, and meliorate the morals of an enlightened and free people." In 1794 five magazines were published in the United States; by 1825 there were 100; by 1860 more than 500. The mass circulation penny press began with the establishment of the New York *Herald* and the New York *Sun,* and such distinguished journals as the *North American Review, Graham's,* and the *Southern Literary Messenger* gained wide circulation.

The turn of the century continued to be an age of literary dilettantes and gentleman authors. Book royalties were few and meager. Compensation for magazine contributors was almost unknown until the 1820s, and long thereafter payment remained slight and uncertain. But by mid-century, magazines were paying Henry Wadsworth Longfellow $50 for a poem and James Fenimore Cooper $10 for a page of his prose. A swarm of professional "magazinists" appeared, "quill drivers" and "inkslingers," male and female, who strove to earn their living with a pen.

In the years preceding the Civil War relatively few works of imaginative literature were published in the United States. Most books were almanacs, schoolbooks, self-help manuals, or works on religion, medicine, or law. Fewer than a dozen volumes of poetry were published annually. Fiction was a prime component of ladies' magazines. Novels were increasingly popular, especially historical romances written by Europeans, most notably by "the monarch and master of modern fiction," Sir Walter Scott. But as the century progressed, native American writers won increasing national and international fame. Washington Irving's *Sketch Book* (1819–1820) became the first work by an American writer to win financial success on both sides of the Atlantic. By the 1830s Irving was judged the nation's greatest writer, a lofty position he later shared with James Fenimore Cooper and William Cullen Bryant. Soon a rich national literature had begun to emerge at the hands of Poe, Melville, Hawthorne, Thoreau, Emerson, and Whitman.

The attitudes of America's writers were shaped by their New World environment and an array of ideas inherited from the romantic traditions of Europe. A new romanticism had appeared in England in the last years of the eighteenth century. It spread to continental Europe and then came to America early in the nineteenth century. It was pluralistic; its manifestations were as varied, as individualistic, and as conflicting as the cultures and the intellects from which it sprang. Yet romantics frequently shared certain general characteristics: moral enthusiasm, faith in the value of individualism and intuitive perception, and a presumption that the natural world is a source of goodness and man's societies a source of corruption.

The Ideals of Romanticism

Romantic values were prominent in American politics, art, and philosophy until the Civil War. The romantic exaltation of the individual suited the nation's revolutionary heritage and its frontier egalitarianism. The romantic revolt against traditional art forms gratified those cramped by the strict limits of neoclassic literature, painting, and architecture. The romantic rejection of rationalism gladdened those who were opposed to cool, intellectual religions encrusted with the remnants of Calvinism. Increasing numbers of Americans turned to the fervid joys of camp-meeting revivalism or to the buoyant teachings of New England transcendentalism.

As a moral philosophy, transcendentalism was neither logical nor systematized. It exalted feeling over reason, individual expression over the restraints of law and custom. It appealed to those who disdained the harsh God of their Puritan ancestors, and it appealed to those who scorned the pale deity of New England Unitarianism. Transcendentalists took their ideas from the romantic literature of Europe, from neo-Platonism, from German idealistic philosophy, and from the revelations of Oriental mysticism. They spoke for cultural rejuvenation and against the materialism of American society. They believed in the transcendence of the "Oversoul," an all-pervading power for goodness from which all things come and of which all things are a part.

As a philosophical and literary movement, transcendentalism flourished in New England from the 1830s to the Civil War. Its doctrines found their greatest literary advocates in Emerson, who believed that man was a part of absolute good, and in Thoreau, who beheld divinity in the "unspotted innocence" of nature. To later generations, scarred by the horrors of the Civil War, the transcendentalist persuasion that humanity was godlike and that evil was nonexistent seemed to be an optimistic folly. Yet transcendentalism was a powerful expression of the intellectual mood of the age, and the ideas it represented have remained a strong influence on American writers from the days of Nathaniel Hawthorne and Walt Whitman to the present.

Cultural Nationalism

The growth of cultural nationalism aroused American artists to write patriotic songs, to paint vast panoramas of American scenes, and to design monumental buildings that would register the grandeur of the American people and their land. Yet, in the midst of expansion and change, most American music, except for black spirituals and work songs, remained derivative. Composers adapted European operatic forms to American legends and lore. Hymns and songs were set to European tunes: Francis Scott Key's "Star-Spangled Banner" borrowed the music of an English drinking song.

In the 1820s American painters began to turn away from the European conventions of eighteenth-century aristocratic portraiture. The Hudson River School of landscape painters emerged; artists roamed from the Catskills and the Hudson River to the Rockies in search of the "wild grandeur" of America's mountains, valleys, forests, and rivers. A reaction developed against the artificial elegance of neoclassic gardening. The uncluttered vistas and geometric hedgerows of well-tempered eighteenth-century domestic landscapes were rebuilt to display scenes of untamed nature. Well-to-do nineteenth-century Americans sometimes adorned their gardens with artificial ruins that tastefully suggested nature's triumph over the works of man. By the 1850s a growing interest in the asymmetrical art of the Middle Ages had generated a new taste for Gothic design and challenged the dominance of Greek Revival architecture. Gothic arches, towers, and ornamental details began to replace the Greek and Roman temple style in the design of the banks, courthouses, university buildings, mansions, cottages, and even the backyard privies of Americans.

Literature ceased to be primarily didactic, a servant of politics and religion. The great age of American political writing by the Founding Fathers had ended. Statesmen, such as Daniel Webster, now dominated American politics not with their prose but with the emotional force of their oratory. Novels, short stories, and poems replaced sermons and manifestoes as America's principal literary forms. The playhouse was no longer considered to be wholly a source of wickedness, but native playwrights still were few and their works second-rate. A small number of dramas based on native themes had appeared, but throughout the period a lack of effective copyright protection and the large-scale importation of English plays and actors gave little encouragement to the development of American drama. Yet the mass of men and women could find their yearning for entertainment satisfied in the revivalism of evangelical churches, in parades and patriotic festivals, in the freaks, trained fleas, and wild beasts exhibited by such showmen as Phineas T. Barnum, or in the gentler excitements of lecture-going.

Imaginative literature became intense, personal, and symbolic as more writers perceived themselves not as literary craftsmen following the ordered rules of neoclassic literature but as prophets and seers. Moved by calls for a national literature that would glorify the land, that would "breathe the spirit of our republican institutions," writers celebrated America's meadows, groves, and streams, its endless prairies, dense forests, and vast oceans. The wilderness came to function almost as a dramatic character that illustrated moral law. The desire for an escape from society and a return to nature became a permanent convention of American literature, evident in Cooper's *Leatherstocking Tales*, in Thoreau's *Walden*, and later in Mark Twain's *Huckleberry Finn* and in the twentieth-century writing of Ernest Hemingway and William Faulkner.

Romantic writers placed increasing value on the free expression of emotion and displayed increasing attention to the psychic states of their characters. Heroes and heroines exhibited extremes of sensitivity and excitement. The novel of terror became the profitable literary staple that it remains today. Writers of gothic terror novels sought to arouse in their readers a turbulent sense of the remote, the supernatural, and the terrifying by describing castles and landscapes illuminated by moonlight and haunted by specters. A preoccupation with the demonic and the mystery of evil marked the works of Poe, Hawthorne, Melville, and a host of lesser writers.

Nationalism stimulated a greater interest in America's language and its common people. In 1828 Noah Webster published *An American Dictionary of the English Language.* American character types speaking local dialects appeared in poetry and fiction with increasing frequency. Literature began to celebrate American farmers, the poor, the unlettered, children, and noble savages (red and white) untainted by society.

At mid-century a cultural reawakening brought a "flowering of New England." Led by Hawthorne, Emerson, and Thoreau, and stirred by the teachings of transcendentalism, writers of Boston and nearby towns and villages produced a New England literary renaissance. Bancroft, Prescott, Motley, and Parkman found literary fame in the writing of history; and the "Schoolroom Poets," Longfellow, Lowell, Holmes, and Whittier, interpreted the aspirations of the age to their countrymen and brought honor to the nation by achieving international fame.

America, from the early 1800s to the Civil War, was a land of paradoxes, a land stirred by spiritual dreams and shaped by the realities of a growing materialism. The age had rejected the ruined promise and stale wisdom it saw in eighteenth-century rationalism. Americans had sought new liberties and new ideas in life and art, but the excesses and conflicts of their society had brought a bloody Civil War. To the Age of Realism following that great national agony, the ideas of the romantic era often seemed to have produced not only a catastrophic war but also a national decline.

Political egalitarianism had brought a politics that was often ignorant, impulsive, and irrational, a rabid democracy that its patrician detractors described as rule by "King Mob." Intense individualism and soaring optimism had deteriorated into their natural consequences: selfishness, a crippling pessimism, and a frivolous addiction to the pleasures of despair and woe. Romanticism had encouraged the worship of outcasts and worthless chivalric ideals. In its efforts to capture the popular imagination and excite the public mind, it had senselessly generated phantoms and gothic bugaboos. The exaltation of nature had often decomposed into a sprawling pantheism and giddy worship of "each daisy in the leafy glen." The rejection of society and the exaltation of primitive men, "nurslings of nature without art and without schooling," was often a cranky rejection of the problems faced by humans obliged to live in complex societies.

Yet romanticism remained one of the glories of the age. It accelerated the spread of democracy to the downtrodden and the poor. It revitalized art and established new ways of perceiving humanity and the universe. And it remains evident today, in the resurgence of democratic radicalism, in the fascination with nature and the simple life, in the exaltation of love, in the renewed interest in folk-tales and balladry, in the popularity of novels and movies of heroic adventure and intense introspection, and in the social and sexual upheavals that have become a characteristic of American life.

Washington Irving 1783–1859

Washington Irving was the first American writer of imaginative literature to gain international fame. He became, in the words of the English novelist Thackeray, "the first Ambassador whom the New World of Letters sent to the Old." Irving was born the year the United States won its independence from Britain, and he was named after the new nation's greatest revolutionary general and first president. As the youngest of eleven children of a prosperous New York merchant, Irving enjoyed a pampered childhood. He became a precocious reader and wrote numerous juvenile poems, plays, and essays. When he was sixteen he ceased his formal education and began the study of law, but he had little relish for such a burdensome task; he was, as he later acknowledged, a "poor scholar—fond of roguery." He preferred instead to pass his time in desultory reading and in the society of the literary wits of New York City. At nineteen, using the name "Jonathan Oldstyle" and adopting the pose of an urbane cosmopolite rambling about the town, he began to contribute a series of sketches, or "letters," on society and the theater to the Morning Chronicle, *a New York newspaper.*

When he was twenty-one Irving went on a grand tour of Europe. Two years later he returned to New York to be admitted to the bar and to begin the leisurely life of a gentleman lawyer. He joined with his brother William and with James Kirke Paulding in publishing Salmagundi *(1807–1808), a short-lived periodical of social satire and lampoon, grandly intended to "correct the town and castigate the age." Shortly afterward, Irving started work on what was to be his first literary triumph, his* History of New York *(1809) by "Diedrich Knickerbocker." It was an irreverent spoof of historical scholarship, salted with off-color comments. The book satirized the complacent Dutch burghers of early New York and pointed at the political follies of nineteenth-century America. It also marked the beginning of the "Knickerbocker School" of New York literary satirists, including Paulding (1778–1860), Fitz-Greene Halleck (1790–1867), and Joseph Rodman Drake (1795–1820), who took their name and humorous tone from Irving's Knickerbocker History and flourished in New York in the first decades of the nineteenth century.*

At the end of the War of 1812, Irving was sent to England to supervise the Liverpool branch of the family firm, but in 1818, as a result of the war and bad management, the firm went bankrupt. Irving was left with a dislike for the "dirty soul-killing" world of business and a need to find a livelihood. His History of New York *had earned the magnificent sum of $3,000, so he turned to writing and began preparation of* The Sketch Book of Geoffrey Crayon, Gent *(1820). It was the first work by an American to receive wide international acclaim, and it made Irving a celebrity, praised alike in America and England. In it were the two tales that brought him his most enduring fame, "Rip Van Winkle" and "The Legend of Sleepy Hollow."*

With his new literary success, Irving gave up all thought of returning to America and the world of trade or law. He set out to become a professional man of letters. The Sketch Book *was soon followed by* Bracebridge Hall *(1822), a series of sketches on English country life. In 1824 he published* Tales of a Traveller, *his first volume of fiction, filled with yarns of the supernatural and clanking with the ghostly machinery of romantic gothicism. In 1826 his literary fame earned him appointment as an American diplomatic attaché in Spain, and there he gathered material for a biography of Christopher Columbus (1828). He wrote* A Chronicle of the Conquest of Granada *(1829) and* The Alhambra *(1832), a Spanish sketchbook that grew out of three months he had spent at the famous Moorish palace in Granada.*

Irving then returned to England, where he accepted appointment as an American diplomat in London. Three years later, when he was nearing fifty, he returned to the United States after an absence of seventeen years. He bought "Sunnyside," his famous home on the Hudson River at Tarrytown, and there, except for four years as U.S. minister to Spain (1842–1846), he lived as a country squire, writing a series of histories and biographies.

Irving was a transitional figure. His work reflected the shift in American literature from the rationalism of the eighteenth century to the sentimental romanticism of the nineteenth century. His early satirical writing had displayed a neoclassical pleasure in the comic qualities of life. His humor was often exaggerated, pun-ridden, and scornful of political liberalism. Yet his taste for satire was mingled with a love of melancholy, of a mawkish, even morbid, world of sentiment. Irving was, like most of his writing, amiable, civilized, and gentlemanly, interested in moods and emotions rather than in the metaphysical speculation that became a characteristic of American romanticism.

His writing was English as much as it was American, and it revealed a sense of the contrast between continental Europe and America that later was reflected in Hawthorne and Henry James. Irving tended to find value in the past and in the traditions of the Old World. He did not share the hopeful American vision of the New World as an Eden, free of the corrupt traditions of Europe. Much of Irving's popularity in England and America sprang from the very fact that, amid the rising materialism and commercialism of the times, he stood for the comforting values of an older civilization, for "well established principles," and for "reverend custom." He believed that "we are a young people . . . and must take our examples and models in a great degree, from the existing nations of Europe." A nativist literature that would clearly reflect the breadth of American life was yet to be written, and Irving is most clearly seen today as his friend Thackeray saw him: "a very nice bonhomious old gentleman," with "a pleasant chirping voice quite natural and unaffected—speaking English, however, not American."

FURTHER READING: *The Complete Works of Washington Irving,* ed. H. Pochmann, H. Kleineld, R. Rust, 28 vols., 1969–1989; S. Williams, *The Life of Washington Irving,* 2 vols., 1935; V. Brooks, *The World of Washington Irving,* 1944; E. Wagenknecht, *Washington Irving, Moderation Displayed,* 1962; L. Leary, *Washington Irving,* 1963; W. Hedges, *Washington Irving, An American Study,* 1965; J. Johnston, *The Heart That Would Not Hold, A Biography of Washington Irving,* 1971; *A Century of Commentary on the Works of Washington Irving,* ed. A. Myers, 1976; M. Roth, *Comedy and America, The Lost World of Washington Irving,* 1976; P. McFarland, *Sojourners,* 1979; M. Bowden, *Washington Irving,* 1981; *The Old and New World Romanticism of Washington Irving,* ed. S. Brodwin, 1986; J. Rubin-Dorsky, *Adrift in the Old World, The Psychological Pilgrimage of Washington Irving,* 1988; *Critical Essays on Washington Irving,* ed. R. Aderman, 1990; P. Antelyes, *Tales of Adventurous Enterprise,* 1990.

TEXT: *The Works of Washington Irving,* 21 vols., 1860–1861.

from *A HISTORY OF NEW YORK, BY DIEDRICH KNICKERBOCKER*[1]

BOOK III. IN WHICH IS RECORDED THE GOLDEN REIGN OF WOUTER VAN TWILLER[2]

Chapter IV

Containing Further Particulars of the Golden Age and What Constituted a Fine Lady and Gentleman in the Days of Walter the Doubter.

In this dulcet period of my history, when the beauteous island of Mannahata[3] presented a scene, the very counterpart of those glowing pictures drawn of the golden reign of Saturn,[4] there was, as I have before observed, a happy ignorance, an honest simplicity prevalent among its inhabitants, which, were I even able to depict, would be but little understood by the degenerate age for which I am doomed to write. Even the female sex, those arch innovators upon the tranquillity, the honesty, and gray-beard customs of society, seemed for a while to conduct themselves with incredible sobriety and comeliness.

Their hair, untortured by the abominations of art, was scrupulously pomatumed[5] back from their foreheads with a candle, and covered with a little cap of quilted calico, which fitted exactly to their heads. Their petticoats of linsey-woolsey[6] were striped with a variety of gorgeous dyes,—though I must confess these gallant garments were rather short, scarce reaching below the knee, but then they made up in the number, which generally equalled that of the gentleman's small-clothes;[7] and what is still more praiseworthy, they were all of their own manufacture,—of which circumstance, as may well be supposed, they were not a little vain.

These were the honest days in which every woman staid at home, read the Bible, and wore pockets,—ay, and that too of a goodly size, fashioned with patchwork into many curious devices, and ostentatiously worn on the outside. These, in fact, were convenient receptacles, where all good housewives

[1] Irving's history of New York began as a short parody of Samuel Mitchill's guidebook, *The Picture of New York* (1807), and soon was expanded into a mock history of the Dutch colony of New Netherland "from the Beginning of the World to the End of the Dutch Dynasty" in 1664, when the British conquered the colony and established New York. Irving's aim was to give "notices of the customs, manners, and institutions of the city; written in a serio-comic vein, and treating local errors, follies, and abuses with good-humored satire." The result was a mixture of historical fact and fancy, broad burlesque of the foibles of the Dutch settlers and their quixotic governors, and satirical comment on the political scene of the United States in Irving's day. Shortly before the book's appearance, Irving's fictional author, Diedrich Knickerbocker, "a small elderly gentleman," was reported in spurious newspaper advertisements to have left the manuscript in his New York lodgings and to have disappeared from the city, "not entirely in his right mind."

[2] "Walter the Doubter" (1580?–1656), Dutch Governor of New Netherlands, 1633–1637.

[3] Manhattan Island, the site of the Dutch village of New Amsterdam. It was named for the Manahata Indians. In 1626 the Dutchman Peter Minuit purchased the island from the Canarsie Indians for 60 guilders ($24) worth of trinkets.

[4] Saturn, god of agriculture, was thought to have been an early king at Rome. His reign was considered a Golden Age.

[5] Oiled, greased. [6] Coarse cloth of linen and wool. [7] Knee breeches.

carefully stored away such things as they wished to have at hand; by which means they often came to be incredibly crammed; and I remember there was a story current, when I was a boy, that the lady of Wouter Van Twiller once had occasion to empty her right pocket in search of a wooden ladle, when the contents filled a couple of corn-baskets, and the utensil was discovered lying among some rubbish in one corner;—but we must not give too much faith to all these stories, the anecdotes of those remote periods being very subject to exaggeration.

Besides these notable pockets, they likewise wore scissors and pin-cushions suspended from their girdles by red ribands,[8] or, among the more opulent and showy classes, by brass, and even silver chains,—indubitable tokens of thrifty housewives and industrious spinsters. I cannot say much in vindication of the shortness of the petticoats; it doubtless was introduced for the purpose of giving the stockings a chance to be seen, which were generally of blue worsted, with magnificent red clocks,[9]—or, perhaps, to display a well-turned ankle, and a neat, though serviceable foot, set off by a high-heeled leathern shoe, with a large and splendid silver buckle. Thus we find that the gentle sex in all ages have shown the same disposition to infringe a little upon the laws of decorum, in order to betray a lurking beauty, or gratify an innocent love of finery.

From the sketch here given, it will be seen that our good grandmothers differed considerably in their ideas of a fine figure from their scantily dressed descendants of the present day. A fine lady, in those times, waddled under more clothes, even on a fair summer's day, than would have clad the whole bevy of a modern ball-room. Nor were they the less admired by the gentlemen in consequence thereof. On the contrary, the greatness of a lover's passion seemed to increase in proportion to the magnitude of its object,—and a voluminous damsel, arrayed in a dozen of petticoats, was declared by a Low-Dutch sonneteer[10] of the province to be radiant as a sunflower, and luxuriant as a full-blown cabbage. Certain it is, that in those days the heart of a lover could not contain more than one lady at a time; whereas the heart of a modern gallant has often room enough to accommodate half a dozen. The reason of which I conclude to be, that either the hearts of the gentlemen have grown larger, or the persons of the ladies smaller: this, however, is a question for physiologists to determine.

But there was a secret charm in these petticoats, which, no doubt, entered into the consideration of the prudent gallants. The wardrobe of a lady was in those days her only fortune; and she who had a good stock of petticoats and stockings was as absolutely an heiress as is a Kamtchatka[11] damsel with a store of bearskins, or a Lapland[12] belle with a plenty of reindeer. The ladies, therefore, were very anxious to display these powerful attractions to the greatest advantage; and the best rooms in the house, instead of being adorned with caricatures of dame Nature, in water-colors and needle-work, were always hung round with abundance of homespun garments, the manufacture and

[8]Ribbons. [9]Ornamental designs.

[10]I.e., a sonneteer who wrote in Low Dutch, the language of Holland.

[11]Peninsula in Russian Asia, on the Bering Sea. [12]Arctic region north of Sweden.

the property of the females,—a piece of laudable ostentation that still prevails among the heiresses of our Dutch villages.

The gentlemen, in fact, who figured in the circles of the gay world in these ancient times, corresponded, in most particulars, with the beauteous damsels whose smiles they were ambitious to deserve. True it is, their merits would make but a very inconsiderable impression upon the heart of a modern fair:[13] they neither drove their curricles, nor sported their tandems,[14] for as yet those gaudy vehicles were not even dreamt of; neither did they distinguish themselves by their brilliancy at the table, and their consequent recontres[15] with watchmen, for our forefathers were of too pacific a disposition to need those guardians of the night, every soul throughout the town being sound asleep before nine o'clock. Neither did they establish their claims to gentility at the expense of their tailors, for as yet those offenders against the pockets of society, and the tranquility of all aspiring young gentlemen, were unknown in New Amsterdam;[16] every good housewife made the clothes of her husband and family, and even the goede vrouw[17] of Van Twiller himself thought it no disparagement to cut out her husband's linsey-woolsey galligaskins.[18]

Not but what there were some two or three youngsters who manifested the first dawning of what is called fire and spirit; who held all labor in contempt; shulked about docks and market-places; loitered in the sunshine; squandered what little money they could procure at hustlecap and chuck-farthing,[19] swore, boxed, fought cocks, and raced their neighbors' horses; in short, who promised to be the wonder, the talk, and abomination of the town, had not their stylish career been unfortunately cut short by an affair of honor with a whipping-post.

Far other, however, was the truly fashionable gentleman of those days: his dress, which served for both morning and evening, street and drawing-room, was a linsey-woolsey coat, made, perhaps, by the fair hands of the mistress of his affections, and gallantly bedecked with abundance of large brass buttons; half a score of breeches heightened the proportions of his figure; his shoes were decorated by enormous copper buckles; a low-crowned broad-rimmed hat overshadowed his burly visage; and his hair dangled down his back in a prodigious queue of eel-skin.[20]

Thus equipped, he would manfully sally forth, with pipe in mouth, to besiege some fair damsel's obdurate heart,—not such a pipe, good reader, as that which Acis did sweetly tune in praise of his Galatea,[21] but one of true Delft[22] manufacture, and furnished with a charge of fragrant tobacco. With

[13]I.e., a fair young maiden.

[14]Fashionable carriages. Curricles were drawn by two horses, abreast, tandems by two horses, one behind the other.

[15]Encounters.

[16]Dutch village, on lower Manhattan Island, which became the city of New York.

[17]Dutch: good wife. [18]Large, wide breeches.

[19]Games of chance where coins are shaken in a cap or tossed at a mark.

[20]Hair braided with an eel skin, a fashion of the day.

[21]A sea-nymph in classical legend, loved by Acis, a shepherd who played the pipes to win her affection.

[22]City in the Netherlands, renowned for its ceramic products.

this would he resolutely set himself down before the fortress, and rarely failed, in the process of time, to smoke the fair enemy into a surrender, upon honorable terms.

Such was the happy reign of Wouter Van Twiller, celebrated in many a long-forgotten song as the real golden age, the rest being nothing but counterfeit copper-washed[23] coin. In that delightful period, a sweet and holy calm reigned over the whole province. The burgomaster smoked his pipe in peace; the substantial solace of his domestic cares, after her daily toils were done, sat soberly at the door, with her arms crossed over her apron of snowy white, without being insulted with ribald street-walkers or vagabond boys,—those unlucky urchins who do so infest our streets, displaying, under the roses of youth, the thorns and briers of iniquity. Then it was that the lover with ten breeches, and the damsel with petticoats of half a score, indulged in all the innocent endearments of virtuous love, without fear and without reproach; for what had that virtue to fear, which was defended by a shield of good linsey-woolseys, equal at least to the seven bull-hides[24] of the invincible Ajax?

Ah, blissful and never to be forgotten age! when everything was better than it has ever been since, or ever will be again,—when Buttermilk Channel[25] was quite dry at low water,—when the shad in the Hudson were all salmon,—and when the moon shone with a pure and resplendent whiteness, instead of that melancholy yellow light which is the consequence of her sickening at the abominations she every night witnesses in this degenerate city!

Happy would it have been for New Amsterdam could it always have existed in this state of blissful ignorance and lowly simplicity; but, alas! the days of childhood are too sweet to last! Cities, like men, grow out of them in time, and are doomed alike to grow into the bustle, the cares, and miseries of the world. Let no man congratulate himself, when he beholds the child of his bosom or the city of his birth increasing in magnitude and importance,—let the history of his own life teach him the dangers of the one, and this excellent little history of Mannahata convince him of the calamities of the other.

BOOK IV. CONTAINING THE CHRONICLES OF THE REIGN OF WILLIAM THE TESTY[1]

Chapter I

Showing the Nature of History in General; Containing Farthermore the Universal Acquirements of William the Testy, and How a Man May Learn So Much As to Render Himself Good for Nothing.

When the lofty Thucydides[2] is about to enter upon his description of the plague that desolated Athens, one of his modern commentators assures the reader, that the history is now going to be exceeding solemn, serious, and

[23]I.e., covered with a thin layer (wash) of copper.

[24]The shield of Ajax, legendary Greek warrior at the siege of Troy, described in Homer's *Iliad.* The shield was made of hides stretched on a frame.

[25]Channel in New York harbor, separating Governor's Island from Brooklyn.

[1]William Kieft (1597–1647), an autocratic and imprudent Governor of New Netherland, 1637–1645. Irving, a Federalist partisan, used his description of Kieft to satirize Thomas Jefferson, portraying him as a pedant, a scientific dabbler, and a political ditherer.

[2]Greek historian (460?–400 B.C.), whose *History of the Peloponneisan War* described the great plague in Athens in 430 B.C.

pathetic, and hints, with that air of chuckling gratulation[3] with which a good dame draws forth a choice morsel from a cupboard to regale a favorite, that this plague will give his history a most agreeable variety.

In like manner did my heart leap within me, when I came to the dolorous dilemma of Fort Goed Hoop,[4] which I at once perceived to be the forerunner of a series of great events and entertaining disasters. Such are the true subjects for the historic pen. For what is history, in fact, but a kind of Newgate calendar,[5] a register of the crimes and miseries that man has inflicted on his fellow-man? It is a huge libel on human nature, to which we industriously add page after page, volume after volume, as if we were building up a monument to the honor, rather than the infamy of our species. If we turn over the pages of these chronicles that man has written of himself, what are the characters dignified by the appellation of great, and held up to the admiration of posterity? Tyrants, robbers, conquerors, renowned only for the magnitude of their misdeeds, and the stupendous wrongs and miseries they have inflicted on mankind,—warriors, who have hired themselves to the trade of blood, not from motives of virtuous patriotism, or to protect the injured and defenceless, but merely to gain the vaunted glory of being adroit and successful in massacring their fellow-beings? What are the great events that constitute a glorious era?—The fall of empires; the desolation of happy countries; splendid cities smoking in their ruins; the proudest works of art tumbled in the dust; the shrieks and groans of whole nations ascending unto heaven!

It is thus the historian may be said to thrive on the miseries of mankind, like birds of prey which hover over the field of battle to fatten on the mighty dead. It was observed by a great projector of inland lock-navigation,[6] that rivers, lakes, and oceans were only formed to feed canals. In like manner I am tempted to believe that plots, conspiracies, wars, victories, and massacres are ordained by Providence only as food for the historian.

It is a source of great delight to the philosopher, in studying the wonderful economy of nature, to trace the mutual dependencies of things, how they are created reciprocally for each other, and how the most noxious and apparently unnecessary animal has its uses. Thus those swarms of flies, which are so often execrated as useless vermin, are created for the sustenance of spiders; and spiders, on the other hand, are evidently made to devour flies. So those heroes, who have been such scourges to the world, were bounteously provided as themes for the poet and historian, while the poet and the historian were destined to record the achievements of heroes!

These, and many similar reflections, naturally arose in my mind as I took up my pen to commence the reign of William Kieft; for now the stream of our history, which hitherto has rolled in a tranquil current, is about to depart forever from its peaceful haunts, and brawl through many a turbulent and rugged scene.

[3]Joy.

[4]Fort Good Hope, a Dutch outpost on the Connecticut River. Built in 1633, in defiance of the protests of Massachusetts and Plymouth authorities, it was abandoned after 1639.

[5]A record of criminal court cases at Newgate prison in London.

[6]I.e., a speculator who proposes the building of inland waterways (with locks).

As some sleek ox, sunk in the rich repose of a clover-field, dozing and chewing the cud, will bear repeated blows before it raises itself, so the province of Nieuw Nederlandts, having waxed fat under the drowsy reign of the Doubter, needed cuffs and kicks to rouse it into action. The reader will now witness the manner in which a peaceful community advances towards a state of war; which is apt to be like the approach of a horse to a drum, with much prancing and little progress, and too often with the wrong end foremost.

Wilhelmus Kieft, who in 1634[7] ascended the gubernatorial chair, (to borrow a favorite though clumsy appellation of modern phraseologists,) was of a lofty descent, his father being inspector of windmills in the ancient town of Saardam;[8] and our hero, we are told, when a boy, made very curious investigations into the nature and operation of these machines,[9] which was one reason why he afterwards came to be so ingenious a governor. His name, according to the most authentic etymologists, was a corruption of Kyver, that is to say, a *wrangler* or *scolder,* and expressed the characteristic of his family, which, for nearly two centuries, had kept the windy town of Saardam in hot water, and produced more tartars and brimstones[10] than any ten families in the place; and so truly did he inherit this family peculiarity, that he had not been a year in the government of the province, before he was universally denominated William the Testy.[11] His appearance answered to his name. He was a brisk, wiry, waspish little old gentleman; such a one as may now and then be seen stumping about our city in a broad-skirted coat with huge buttons, a cocked hat stuck on the back of his head, and a cane as high as his chin. His face was broad, but his features were sharp; his cheeks were scorched into a dusky red[12] by two fiery little gray eyes, his nose turned up, and the corners of his mouth turned down, pretty much like the muzzle of an irritable pug-dog.

I have heard it observed by a profound adept in human physiology, that if a woman waxes fat with the progress of years, her tenure of life is somewhat precarious, but if haply she withers as she grows old, she lives forever. Such promised to be the case with William the Testy, who grew tough in proportion as he dried. He had withered, in fact, not through the process of years, but through the tropical fervor of his soul, which burnt like a vehement rushlight[13] in his bosom, inciting him to incessant broils and bickerings. Ancient traditions speak much of his learning, and of the gallant inroads he had made into the dead languages,[14] in which he had made captive a host of Greek nouns and Latin verbs, and brought off rich booty in ancient saws and apothegms, which he was wont to parade in his public harangues, as a

[7]Kieft was actually appointed Governor in 1637. He arrived in New Amsterdam in 1638.
[8]Zaandam, Holland, near Amsterdam.
[9]Irving alludes to Jefferson's lifelong interest in mechanical devices.
[10]I.e., persons of violent and fiery temper.
[11]Jefferson's political opponents often thought him testy and waspish.
[12]Jefferson was red-complexioned.
[13]Light from a candle made of a rush dipped in grease.
[14]Jefferson was renowned for his knowledge of classical and modern languages.

triumphant general of yore his *spolia opima.*[15] Of metaphysics he knew enough to confound all hearers and himself into the bargain. In logic, he knew the whole family of syllogisms and dilemmas, and was so proud of his skill that he never suffered even a self-evident fact to pass unargued.[16] It was observed, however, that he seldom got into an argument without getting into a perplexity, and then into a passion with his adversary for not being convinced gratis.

He had, moreover, skirmished smartly on the frontiers of several of the sciences, was fond of experimental philosophy, and prided himself upon inventions of all kinds. His abode, which he had fixed at a Bowerie or country-seat at a short distance from the city,[17] just at what is now called Dutch Street, soon abounded with proofs of his ingenuity: patent smoke-jacks[18] that required a horse to work them; Dutch ovens that roasted meat without fire; carts that went before the horses; weather-cocks that turned against the wind; and other wrong-headed contrivances that astonished and confounded all beholders. The house, too, was beset with paralytic cats and dogs, the subjects of his experimental philosophy;[19] and the yelling and yelping of the latter unhappy victims of science, while aiding in the pursuit of knowledge, soon gained for the place the name of "Dog's Misery," by which it continues to be known even at the present day.

It is in knowledge as in swimming: he who founders and splashes on the surface makes more noise, and attracts more attention, than the pearl-diver who quietly dives in quest of treasures to the bottom. The vast acquirements of the new governor were the theme of marvel among the simple burghers of New Amsterdam; he figured about the place as learned a man as a Bonze[20] at Pekin, who has mastered one half of the Chinese alphabet, and was unanimously pronounced a "universal genius!"[21]

I have known in my time many a genius of this stamp; but, to speak my mind freely, I never knew one who, for the ordinary purposes of life, was worth his weight in straw. In this respect, a little sound judgment and plain common sense is worth all the sparkling genius that ever wrote poetry or invented theories. . . .

1809

[15]Latin: Rich spoils of war displayed in a triumphal parade as symbols of victory.

[16]Irving alludes to Jefferson's displays of philosophical knowledge.

[17]Monticello, Jefferson's country home near Charlottesville, Virginia, was filled with ingenious mechanical devices, including a weather vane with its indicator built into the ceiling of his porch.

[18]A device for turning a roasting spit in a fireplace chimney.

[19]Jefferson's interest in natural science ("natural philosophy") led him to experiment with animals and to study their bones and fossils uncovered in excavations.

[20]Buddhist monk.

[21]A title given Jefferson by his supporters.

from *THE SKETCH-BOOK*[1] *OF GEOFFREY CRAYON, GENT.*

THE AUTHOR'S ACCOUNT OF HIMSELF

> *"I am of this mind with Homer, that as the snaile that crept out of her shel was turned eftsoons into a toad, and thereby was forced to make a stoole to sit on; so the traveller that stragleth from his owne country is in a short time transformed into so monstrous a shape, that he is faine to alter his mansion with his manners, and to live where he can, not where he would."*
>
> LYLY'S *Eupheus.*[2]

I was always fond of visiting new scenes, and observing strange characters and manners. Even when a mere child I began my travels, and made many tours of discovery into foreign parts and unknown regions of my native city, to the frequent alarm of my parents, and the emolument of the town-crier.[3] As I grew into boyhood, I extended the range of my observations. My holiday afternoons were spent in rambles about the surrounding country. I made myself familiar with all its places famous in history or fable. I knew every spot where a murder or robbery had been committed, or a ghost seen. I visited the neighboring villages, and added greatly to my stock of knowledge, by noting their habits and customs, and conversing with their sages and great men. I even journeyed one long summer's day to the summit of the most distant hill, whence I stretched my eye over many a mile of terra incognita,[4] and was astonished to find how vast a globe I inhabited.

This rambling propensity strengthened with my years. Books of voyages and travels became my passion, and in devouring their contents, I neglected the regular exercises of the school. How wistfully would I wander about the pier-heads in fine weather, and watch the parting ships, bound to distant climes—with what longing eyes would I gaze after their lessening sails, and waft myself in imagination to the ends of the earth!

Further reading and thinking, though they brought this vague inclination into more reasonable bounds, only served to make it more decided. I visited various parts of my own country; and had I been merely a lover of fine scenery, I should have felt little desire to seek elsewhere its gratification, for on no country have the charms of nature been more prodigally lavished. Her mighty lakes, like oceans of liquid silver; her mountains, with their bright aerial tints; her valleys, teeming with wild fertility; her tremendous cataracts, thundering in their solitudes; her boundless plains, waving with spontaneous verdure; her broad deep rivers, rolling in solemn silence to the ocean; her trackless forests, where vegetation puts forth all its magnificence; her skies,

[1]First published serially from 1819 to 1820. Irving later revised and expanded *The Sketch Book* to a total of 32 sketches and tales. The majority were on English life and manners, but the most famous, "Rip Van Winkle" and "The Legend of Sleepy Hollow," were set in America. Irving adopted the pseudonym Geoffrey Crayon, Gent. to pose as a gentle and shy spectator gracefully sketching the world through which he moves.

[2]John Lyly (1554?–1606), author of *Eupheus and His England* (1580), a prose romance whose hero had, like Geoffrey Crayon, a "rambling propensity."

[3]I.e., to the advantage of the town-crier, who was paid to announce that a boy was lost.

[4]Latin: unknown land.

kindling with the magic of summer clouds and glorious sunshine;—no, never need an American look beyond his own country for the sublime and beautiful of natural scenery.

But Europe held forth the charms of storied and poetical association. There were to be seen the masterpieces of art, the refinements of highly-cultivated society, the quaint peculiarities of ancient and local custom. My native country was full of youthful promise: Europe was rich in the accumulated treasures of age. Her very ruins told the history of times gone by, and every mouldering stone was a chronicle. I longed to wander over the scenes of renowned achievement—to tread, as it were, in the footsteps of antiquity—to loiter about the ruined castle—to meditate on the falling tower—to escape, in short, from the commonplace realities of the present, and lose myself among the shadowy grandeurs of the past.

I had, beside all this, an earnest desire to see the great men of the earth. We have, it is true, our great men in America: not a city but has an ample share of them. I have mingled among them in my time, and been almost withered by the shade into which they cast me; for there is nothing so baleful to a small man as the shade of a great one, particularly the great man of a city. But I was anxious to see the great men of Europe; for I had read in the works of various philosophers, that all animals degenerated in America, and man among the number.[5] A great man of Europe, thought I, must therefore be as superior to a great man of America, as a peak of the Alps to a highland of the Hudson; and in this idea I was confirmed, by observing the comparative importance and swelling magnitude of many English travellers among us, who, I was assured, were very little people in their own country. I will visit this land of wonders, thought I, and see the gigantic race from which I am degenerated.

It has been either my good or evil lot to have my roving passion gratified. I have wandered through different countries, and witnessed many of the shifting scenes of life. I cannot say that I have studied them with the eye of a philosopher; but rather with the sauntering gaze with which humble lovers of the picturesque stroll from the window of one print-shop to another; caught sometimes by the delineations of beauty, sometimes by the distortions of caricature, and sometimes by the loveliness of landscape. As it is the fashion for modern tourists to travel pencil in hand, and bring home their port-folios filled with sketches, I am disposed to get up a few for the entertainment of my friends. When, however, I look over the hints and memorandums I have taken down for the purpose, my heart almost fails me at finding how my idle humor has led me aside from the great objects studied by every regular traveller who would make a book. I fear I shall give equal disappointment with an unlucky landscape painter, who had travelled on the continent, but, following the bent of his vagrant inclination, had sketched in nooks, and corners, and by-places. His sketch-book was accordingly crowded with cottages, and landscapes, and obscure ruins; but he had neglected to paint St. Peter's,[6] or the Coliseum;[7] the cascade of Terni,[8] or the bay of Naples; and had not a single glacier or volcano in his whole collection.

1819

[5]The French naturalist Georges Louis Leclerc de Buffon (1707–1788) and his followers asserted that the environment of the New World caused all living species to degenerate.

[6]Church in Rome, the largest in the world, built 1506–1626.

[7]Amphitheater in Rome, built c. 75–80. [8]Waterfalls in northern Italy.

RIP VAN WINKLE[1]

A POSTHUMOUS WRITING OF DIEDRICH KNICKERBOCKER.

By Woden,[2] God of Saxons,
From whence comes Wensday, that is Wodensday,
Truth is a thing that ever I will keep
Unto thylke day in which I creep into
My sepulchre—

CARTWRIGHT[3]

[The following Tale was found among the papers of the late Diedrich Knickerbocker, an old gentleman of New York, who was very curious in the Dutch history of the province, and the manners of the descendants from its primitive settlers. His historical researches, however, did not lie so much among books as among men; for the former are lamentably scanty on his favorite topics; whereas he found the old burghers, and still more their wives, rich in that legendary lore, so invaluable to true history. Whenever, therefore, he happened upon a genuine Dutch family, snugly shut up in its low-roofed farmhouse, under a spreading sycamore, he looked upon it as a little clasped volume of black-letter,[4] and studied it with the zeal of a bookworm.

The result of all these researches was a history of the province during the reign of the Dutch governors, which he published some years since. There have been various opinions as to the literary character of his work, and, to tell the truth, it is not a whit better than it should be. Its chief merit is its scrupulous accuracy, which indeed was a little questioned on its first appearance, but has since been completely established; and it is now admitted into all historical collections, as a book of unquestionable authority.

The old gentleman died shortly after the publication of his work, and now that he is dead and gone, it cannot do much harm to his memory to say that his time might have been much better employed in weightier labors. He, however, was apt to ride his hobby his own way; and though it did now and then kick up the dust a little in the eyes of his neighbors, and grieve the spirit of some friends, for whom he felt the truest deference and affection; yet his errors and follies are remembered "more in sorrow than in anger,"[5] and it begins to be suspected, that he never intended to injure or offend. But however his memory may be appreciated by critics, it is still held dear by many folks, whose good opinion is well worth having; particularly by certain

[1]Irving took the plots for "Rip Van Winkle" and "The Legend of Sleepy Hollow" from German folk-legends. Both stories show the influence of his reading in German romantic literature and mark his turn from the neoclassicism of his earlier, satirical writing toward the sentimental romanticism of his later work.

[2]Teutonic god.

[3]William Cartwright (1611–1643), English playwright. The quotation is from *The Ordinary* (1651).

[4]A heavy-faced type, now called Gothic and Old English.

[5]*Hamlet*, Act I, Scene ii, line 232.

biscuit-bakers, who have gone so far as to imprint his likeness on their new-year cakes; and have thus given him a chance for immortality, almost equal to the being stamped on a Waterloo Medal, or a Queen Anne's Farthing.[6]]

Whoever has made a voyage up the Hudson must remember the Kaatskill[7] mountains. They are a dismembered branch of the great Appalachian family, and are seen away to the west of the river, swelling up to a noble height, and lording it over the surrounding country. Every change of season, every change of weather, indeed, every hour of the day, produces some change in the magical hues and shapes of these mountains, and they are regarded by all the good wives, far and near, as perfect barometers. When the weather is fair and settled, they are clothed in blue and purple, and print their bold outlines on the clear evening sky; but, sometimes, when the rest of the landscape is cloudless, they will gather a hood of gray vapors about their summits, which, in the last rays of the setting sun, will glow and light up like a crown of glory.

At the foot of these fairy mountains, the voyager may have descried the light smoke curling up from a village, whose shingle-roofs gleam among the trees, just where the blue tints of the upland melt away into the fresh green of the nearer landscape. It is a little village of great antiquity, having been founded by some of the Dutch colonists, in the early times of the province, just about the beginning of the government of the good Peter Stuyvesant,[8] (may he rest in peace!) and there were some of the houses of the original settlers standing within a few years, built of small yellow bricks brought from Holland, having latticed windows and gable fronts, surmounted with weather-cocks.

In that same village, and in one of these very houses (which, to tell the precise truth, was sadly time-worn and weather-beaten), there lived many years since, while the country was yet a province of Great Britain, a simple good-natured fellow of the name of Rip Van Winkle. He was a descendant of the Van Winkles who figured so gallantly in the chivalrous days of Peter Stuyvesant, and accompanied him to the siege of Fort Christina.[9] He inherited, however, but little of the martial character of his ancestors. I have observed that he was a simple good-natured man; he was, moreover, a kind neighbor, and an obedient hen-pecked husband. Indeed, to the latter circumstance might be owing that meekness of spirit which gained him such universal popularity; for those men are most apt to be obsequious and conciliating abroad, who are under the discipline of shrews at home. Their tempers, doubtless, are rendered pliant and malleable in the fiery furnace of domestic tribulation; and a curtain lecture[10] is worth all the sermons in the

[6]The Waterloo Medal commemorated the British victory over Napoleon in 1815. Farthings (small coins) minted in the reign of England's Queen Anne (1702–1714) bore her image.

[7]The Catskill Mountains in southeastern New York.

[8]Last Governor of New Netherland (1647–1664).

[9]In 1655, Dutch forces under Peter Stuyvesant defeated the colonists of New Sweden at Fort Christina, near present-day Wilmington, Delaware.

[10]An angry lecture given by a wife from her place in bed, behind the bed curtains.

world for teaching the virtues of patience and long-suffering. A termagant wife may, therefore, in some respects, be considered a tolerable blessing; and if so, Rip Van Winkle was thrice blessed.

Certain it is, that he was a great favorite among all the good wives of the village, who, as usual, with the amiable sex, took his part in all family squabbles; and never failed, whenever they talked those matters over in their evening gossipings, to lay all the blame on Dame Van Winkle. The children of the village, too, would shout with joy whenever he approached. He assisted at their sports, made their playthings, taught them to fly kites and shoot marbles, and told them long stories of ghosts, witches, and Indians. Whenever he went dodging about the village, he was surrounded by a troop of them, hanging on his skirts, clambering on his back, and playing a thousand tricks on him with impunity; and not a dog would bark at him throughout the neighborhood.

The great error in Rip's composition was an insuperable aversion to all kinds of profitable labor. It could not be from the want of assiduity or perseverance; for he would sit on a wet rock, with a rod as long and heavy as a Tartar's lance, and fish all day without a murmur, even though he should not be encouraged by a single nibble. He would carry a fowling-piece on his shoulder for hours together, trudging through woods and swamps, and up hill and down dale, to shoot a few squirrels or wild pigeons. He would never refuse to assist a neighbor even in the roughest toil, and was a foremost man at all country frolics for husking Indian corn, or building stone-fences; the women of the village, too, used to employ him to run their errands, and to do such little odd jobs as their less obliging husbands would not do for them. In a word Rip was ready to attend to anybody's business but his own; but as to doing family duty, and keeping his farm in order, he found it impossible.

In fact, he declared it was of no use to work on his farm; it was the most pestilent little piece of ground in the whole country; every thing about it went wrong, and would go wrong, in spite of him. His fences were continually falling to pieces; his cow would either go astray, or get among the cabbages; weeds were sure to grow quicker in his fields than anywhere else; the rain always made a point of setting in just as he had some out-door work to do; so that though his patrimonial estate had dwindled away under his management, acre by acre, until there was little more left than a mere patch of Indian corn and potatoes, yet it was the worst conditioned farm in the neighborhood.

His children, too, were as ragged and wild as if they belonged to nobody. His son Rip, an urchin begotten in his own likeness, promised to inherit the habits, with the old clothes of his father. He was generally seen trooping like a colt at his mother's heels, equipped in a pair of his father's cast-off galligaskins, which he had much ado to hold up with one hand, as a fine lady does her train in bad weather.

Rip Van Winkle, however, was one of those happy mortals, of foolish, well-oiled dispositions, who take the world easy, eat white bread or brown, whichever can be got with least thought or trouble, and would rather starve on a penny than work for a pound. If left to himself, he would have whistled life away in perfect contentment; but his wife kept continually dinning in his ears about his idleness, his carelessness, and the ruin he was bringing on his family. Morning, noon, and night, her tongue was incessantly going, and everything he said or did was sure to produce a torrent of household eloquence. Rip had but one way of replying to all lectures of the kind, and that, by frequent use, had grown into a habit. He shrugged his shoulders, shook his head, cast up his eyes, but said nothing. This, however, always provoked a fresh volley from his wife; so that he was fain to draw off his forces, and take to the outside of the house—the only side which, in truth, belongs to a henpecked husband.

Rip's sole domestic adherent was his dog Wolf, who was as much henpecked as his master; for Dame Van Winkle regarded them as companions in idleness, and even looked upon Wolf with an evil eye, as the cause of his master's going so often astray. True it is, in all points of spirit befitting an honorable dog, he was as courageous an animal as ever scoured the woods—but what courage can withstand the ever-during and all-besetting terrors of a woman's tongue? The moment Wolf entered the house his crest fell, his tail drooped to the ground, or curled between his legs, he sneaked about with a gallows air, casting many a sidelong glance at Dame Van Winkle, and at the least flourish of a broomstick or ladle, he would fly to the door with yelping precipitation.

Times grew worse and worse with Rip Van Winkle as years of matrimony rolled on; a tart temper never mellows with age, and a sharp tongue is the only edged tool that grows keener with constant use. For a long while he used to console himself, when driven from home, by frequenting a kind of perpetual club of the sages, philosophers, and other idle personages of the village; which held its sessions on a bench before a small inn, designated by a rubicund portrait of His Majesty George the Third. Here they used to sit in the shade through a long lazy summer's day, talking listlessly over village gossip, or telling endless sleepy stories about nothing. But it would have been worth any statesman's money to have heard the profound discussions that sometimes took place, when by chance an old newspaper fell into their hands from some passing traveller. How solemnly they would listen to the contents, as drawled out by Derrick Van Bummel, the schoolmaster, a dapper learned little man, who was not to be daunted by the most gigantic word in the dictionary; and how sagely they would deliberate upon public events some months after they had taken place.

The opinions of this junto[11] were completely controlled by Nicholas Vedder, a patriarch of the village, and landlord of the inn, at the door of which he took his seat from morning till night, just moving sufficiently to avoid the sun and keep in the shade of a large tree; so that the neighbors could tell the hour by his movements as accurately as by a sun-dial. It is true he was rarely heard to speak, but smoked his pipe incessantly. His adherents, however (for every great man has his adherents), perfectly understood him, and knew how to gather his opinions. When any thing that was read or related displeased him, he was observed to smoke his pipe vehemently, and to send forth short,

[11]Group.

frequent and angry puffs; but when pleased, he would inhale the smoke slowly and tranquilly, and emit it in light and placid clouds; and sometimes, taking the pipe from his mouth, and letting the fragrant vapor curl about his nose, would gravely nod his head in token of perfect approbation.

From even this stronghold the unlucky Rip was at length routed by his termagant wife, who would suddenly break in upon the tranquillity of the assemblage and call the members all to naught; nor was that august personage, Nicholas Vedder himself, sacred from the daring tongue of this terrible virago, who charged him outright with encouraging her husband in habits of idleness.

Poor Rip was at last reduced almost to despair; and his only alternative, to escape from the labor of the farm and clamor of his wife, was to take gun in hand and stroll away into the woods. Here he would sometimes seat himself at the foot of a tree, and share the contents of his wallet[12] with Wolf, with whom he sympathized as a fellow-sufferer in persecution. "Poor Wolf," he would say, "thy mistress leads thee a dog's life of it; but never mind, my lad, whilst I live thou shalt never want a friend to stand by thee!" Wolf would wag his tail, look wistfully in his master's face, and if dogs can feel pity I verily believe he reciprocated the sentiment with all his heart.

In a long ramble of the kind on a fine autumnal day, Rip had unconsciously scrambled to one of the highest parts of the Kaatskill mountains. He was after his favorite sport of squirrel shooting, and the still solitudes had echoed and reechoed with the reports of his gun. Panting and fatigued, he threw himself, late in the afternoon, on a green knoll, covered with mountain herbage, that crowned the brow of a precipice. From an opening between the trees he could overlook all the lower country for many a mile of rich woodland. He saw at a distance the lordly Hudson, far, far below him, moving on its silent but majestic course, with the reflection of a purple cloud, or the sail of a lagging bark, here and there sleeping on its glassy bosom, and at last losing itself in the blue highlands.

On the other side he looked down into a deep mountain glen, wild, lonely, and shagged, the bottom filled with fragments from the impending cliffs, and scarcely lighted by the reflected rays of the setting sun. For some time Rip lay musing on this scene; evening was gradually advancing; the mountains began to throw their long blue shadows over the valleys; he saw that it would be dark long before he could reach the village, and he heaved a heavy sigh when he thought of encountering the terrors of Dame Van Winkle.

As he was about to descend, he heard a voice from a distance, hallooing, "Rip Van Winkle! Rip Van Winkle!" He looked round, but could see nothing but a crow winging its solitary flight across the mountain. He thought his fancy must have deceived him, and turned again to descend, when he heard the same cry ring through the still evening air; "Rip Van Winkle! Rip Van Winkle!"—at the same time Wolf bristled up his back, and giving a low growl, skulked to his master's side, looking fearfully down into the glen. Rip now felt a vague apprehension stealing over him; he looked anxiously in the same

[12]Knapsack.

direction, and perceived a strange figure slowly toiling up the rocks, and bending under the weight of something he carried on his back. He was surprised to see any human being in this lonely and unfrequented place, but supposing it to be some one of the neighborhood in need of his assistance, he hastened down to yield it.

On nearer approach he was still more surprised at the singularity of the stranger's appearance. He was a short square-built old fellow, with thick bushy hair, and a grizzled beard. His dress was of the antique Dutch fashion—a cloth jerkin[13] strapped round the waist—several pair of breeches, the outer one of ample volume, decorated with rows of buttons down the sides, and bunches at the knees. He bore on his shoulder a stout keg, that seemed full of liquor, and made signs for Rip to approach and assist him with the load. Though rather shy and distrustful of this new acquaintance, Rip complied with his usual alacrity; and mutually relieving one another, they clambered up a narrow gully, apparently the dry bed of a mountain torrent. As they ascended, Rip every now and then heard long rolling peals, like distant thunder, that seemed to issue out of a deep ravine, or rather cleft, between lofty rocks, toward which their rugged path conducted. He paused for an instant, but supposing it to be the muttering of one of those transient thundershowers which often take place in mountain heights, he proceeded. Passing through the ravine, they came to a hollow, like a small amphitheatre, surrounded by perpendicular precipices, over the brinks of which impending trees shot their branches, so that you only caught glimpses of the azure sky and the bright evening cloud. During the whole time Rip and his companion had labored on in silence; for though the former marvelled greatly what could be the object of carrying a keg of liquor up this wild mountain, yet there was something strange and incomprehensible about the unknown, that inspired awe and checked familiarity.

On entering the amphitheatre, new objects of wonder presented themselves. On a level spot in the centre was a company of oddlooking personages playing at nine-pins. They were dressed in a quaint outlandish fashion; some wore short doublets,[14] others jerkins, with long knives in their belts, and most of them had enormous breeches, of similar style with that of the guide's. Their visages, too, were peculiar; one had a large beard, broad face, and small piggish eyes: the face of another seemed to consist entirely of nose, and was surmounted by a white sugar-loaf hat set off with a little red cock's tail. They all had beards, of various shapes and colors. There was one who seemed to be the commander. He was a stout old gentleman, with a weather-beaten countenance; he wore a laced doublet, broad belt and hanger,[15] high-crowned hat and feather, red stockings, and high-heeled shoes, with roses[16] in them. The whole group reminded Rip of the figures in an old Flemish painting, in the parlor of Dominie[17] Van Shaick, the village parson, and which had been brought over from Holland at the time of the settlement.

[13]Tight, hip-length, armless jacket.
[14]Close-fitting, waist-length jacket.
[15]Short sword hung at the side.
[16]I.e., rose designs.
[17]Pastor.

What seemed particularly odd to Rip was, that though these folks were evidently amusing themselves, yet they maintained the gravest faces, the most mysterious silence, and were, withal, the most melancholy party of pleasure he had ever witnessed. Nothing interrupted the stillness of the scene but the noise of the balls, which, whenever they were rolled, echoed along the mountains like rumbling peals of thunder.

As Rip and his companion approached them, they suddenly desisted from their play, and stared at him with such fixed statuelike gaze, and such strange, uncouth, lack-lustre countenances, that his heart turned within him, and his knees smote together. His companion now emptied the contents of the keg into large flagons,[18] and made signs to him to wait upon the company. He obeyed with fear and trembling; they quaffed the liquor in profound silence, and then returned to their game.

By degrees Rip's awe and apprehension subsided. He even ventured, when no eye was fixed upon him, to taste the beverage, which he found had much of the flavor of excellent Hollands.[19] He was naturally a thirsty soul, and was soon tempted to repeat the draught. One taste provoked another; and he reiterated his visits to the flagon so often that at length his senses were overpowered, his eyes swam in his head, his head gradually declined, and he fell into a deep sleep.

On waking, he found himself on the green knoll whence he had first seen the old man of the glen. He rubbed his eyes—it was a bright sunny morning. The birds were hopping and twittering among the bushes, and the eagle was wheeling aloft, and breasting the pure mountain breeze. "Surely," thought Rip, "I have not slept here all night." He recalled the occurrences before he fell asleep. The strange man with a keg of liquor—the mountain ravine—the wild retreat among the rocks—the woe-begone party at nine-pins—the flagon—"Oh! that flagon! that wicked flagon!" thought Rip—"what excuse shall I make to Dame Van Winkle!"

He looked round for his gun, but in place of the clean well-oiled fowling-piece, he found an old firelock lying by him, the barrel incrusted with rust, the lock falling off, and the stock worm-eaten. He now suspected that the grave roisterers of the mountain had put a track upon him,[20] and, having dosed him with liquor, had robbed him of his gun. Wolf, too, had disappeared, but he might have strayed away after a squirrel or partridge. He whistled after him and shouted his name, but all in vain; the echoes repeated his whistle and shout, but no dog was to be seen.

He determined to revisit the scene of the last evening's gambol, and if he met with any of the party, to demand his dog and gun. As he rose to walk, he found himself stiff in the joints, and wanting in his usual activity. "These mountain beds do not agree with me," thought Rip, "and if this frolic should lay me up with a fit of the rheumatism, I shall have a blessed time with Dame Van Winkle." With some difficulty he got down into the glen: he found the

[18]Bottles.
[19]Dutch gin.
[20]I.e., had followed him.

gully up which he and his companion had ascended the preceding evening; but to his astonishment a mountain stream was now foaming down it, leaping from rock to rock, and filling the glen with babbling murmurs. He, however, made shift to scramble up its sides, working his toilsome way through thickets of birch, sassafras, and witch-hazel, and sometimes tripped up or entangled by the wild grapevines that twisted their coils or tendrils from tree to tree, and spread a kind of network in his path.

At length he reached to where the ravine had opened through the cliffs to the amphitheatre; but no traces of such opening remained. The rocks presented a highly impenetrable wall over which the torrent came tumbling in a sheet of feathery foam, and fell into a broad deep basin, black from the shadows of the surrounding forest. Here, then, poor Rip was brought to a stand. He again called and whistled after his dog; he was only answered by the cawing of a flock of idle crows, sporting high in air about a dry tree that overhung a sunny precipice; and who, secure in their elevation, seemed to look down and scoff at the poor man's perplexities. What was to be done? the morning was passing away, and Rip felt famished for want of his breakfast. He grieved to give up his dog and gun; he dreaded to meet his wife; but it would not do to starve among the mountains. He shook his head, shouldered the rusty firelock, and, with a heart full of trouble and anxiety, turned his steps homeward.

As he approached the village he met a number of people, but none whom he knew, which somewhat surprised him, for he had thought himself acquainted with every one in the country round. Their dress, too, was of a different fashion from that to which he was accustomed. They all stared at him with equal marks of surprise, and whenever they cast their eyes upon him, invariably stroked their chins. The constant recurrence of this gesture induced Rip, involuntarily to do the same, when, to his astonishment, he found his beard had grown a foot long!

He had now entered the skirts of the village. A troop of strange children ran at his heels, hooting after him, and pointing at his gray beard. The dogs, too, not one of which he recognized for an old acquaintance, barked at him as he passed. The very village was altered; it was larger and more populous. There were rows of houses which he had never seen before, and those which had been his familiar haunts had disappeared. Strange names were over the doors—strange faces at the windows—every thing was strange. His mind now misgave him; he began to doubt whether both he and the world around him were not bewitched. Surely this was his native village, which he had left but the day before. There stood the Kaatskill mountains—there ran the silver Hudson at a distance—there was every hill and dale precisely as it had always been—Rip was sorely perplexed—"That flagon last night," thought he, "has addled my poor head sadly!"

It was with some difficulty that he found the way to his own house, which he approached with silent awe, expecting every moment to hear the shrill voice of Dame Van Winkle. He found the house gone to decay—the roof fallen in, the windows shattered, and the doors off the hinges. A half-starved dog that looked like Wolf was skulking about it. Rip called him by name, but the cur snarled, showed his teeth, and passed on. This was an unkind cut indeed—"My very dog," sighed poor Rip, "has forgotten me!"

He entered the house, which, to tell the truth, Dame Van Winkle had always kept in neat order. It was empty, forlorn, and apparently abandoned. This desolateness overcame all his connubial fears—he called loudly for his wife and children—the lonely chambers rang for a moment with his voice, and then all again was silence.

He now hurried forth, and hastened to his old resort, the village inn—but it too was gone. A large rickety wooden building stood in its place, with great gaping windows, some of them broken and mended with old hats and petticoats, and over the door was painted, "the Union Hotel, by Jonathan Doolittle." Instead of the great tree that used to shelter the quiet little Dutch inn of yore, there now was reared a tall naked pole, with something on the top that looked like a red night-cap,[21] and from it was fluttering a flag, on which was a singular assemblage of stars and stripes—all this was strange and incomprehensible. He recognized on the sign, however, the ruby face of King George, under which he had smoked so many a peaceful pipe; but even this was singularly metamorphosed. The red coat was changed for one of blue and buff,[22] a sword was held in the hand instead of a sceptre, the head was decorated with a cocked hat, and underneath was painted in large characters, GENERAL WASHINGTON.

There was, as usual, a crowd of folk about the door, but none that Rip recollected. The very character of the people seemed changed. There was a busy, bustling, disputatious tone about it, instead of the accustomed phlegm and drowsy tranquillity. He looked in vain for the sage Nicholas Vedder, with his broad face, double chin, and fair long pipe, uttering clouds of tobacco-smoke instead of idle speeches; or Van Bummel, the schoolmaster, doling forth the contents of an ancient newspaper. In place of these, a lean, bilious-looking fellow, with his pockets full of handbills, was haranguing vehemently about rights of citizens—elections—members of congress—liberty—Bunker's Hill—heroes of seventy-six—and other words, which were a perfect Babylonish jargon[23] to the bewildered Van Winkle.

The appearance of Rip, with his long grizzled beard, his rusty fowling-piece,[24] his uncouth dress, and an army of women and children at his heels, soon attracted the attention of the tavern politicians. They crowded round him, eyeing him from head to foot with great curiosity. The orator bustled up to him, and, drawing him partly aside, inquired "on which side

[21]The Liberty Pole and Liberty Cap, used as symbols of liberty in the American and French Revolutions.

[22]Colors of the uniforms of the Revolutionary Army.

[23]Gibberish. Referring to the "confusion of tongues" and the Tower of Babel in Genesis 11:1–9.

[24]Gun for killing birds, a shotgun.

he voted?" Rip stared in vacant stupidity. Another short but busy little fellow pulled him by the arm, and rising on tiptoe, inquired in his ear, "Whether he was Federal or Democrat?"[25] Rip was equally at a loss to comprehend the question; when a knowing, self-important old gentleman, in a sharp cocked hat, made his way through the crowd, putting them to the right and left with his elbows as he passed, and planting himself before Van Winkle, with one arm akimbo, the other resting on his cane, his keen eyes and sharp hat penetrating, as it were, into his very soul, demanded in an austere tone, "what brought him to the election with a gun on his shoulder, and a mob at his heels, and whether he meant to breed a riot in the village?"—"Alas! gentlemen," cried Rip, somewhat dismayed, "I am a poor quiet man, a native of the place, and a loyal subject of the king, God bless him!"

Here a general shout burst from the by-standers—"A tory! a tory! a spy! a refugee! hustle him! away with him!" It was with great difficulty that the self-important man in the cocked hat restored order; and, having assumed a tenfold austerity of brow, demanded again of the unknown culprit, what he came there for, and whom he was seeking? The poor man humbly assured him that he meant no harm, but merely came there in search of some of his neighbors, who used to keep about the tavern.

"Well—who are they?—name them."

Rip bethought himself a moment, and inquired, "Where's Nicholas Vedder?"

There was a silence for a little while, when an old man replied, in a thin piping voice, "Nicholas Vedder! why, he is dead and gone these eighteen years! There was a wooden tombstone in the churchyard that used to tell all about him, but that's rotten and gone too."

"Where's Brom Dutcher?"

"Oh, he went off to the army in the beginning of the war; some say he was killed at the storming of Stony Point[26]—others say he was drowned in a squall at the foot of Anthony's Nose.[27] I don't know—he never came back again."

"Where's Van Bummel, the schoolmaster?"

"He went off to the wars too, was a great militia general, and is now in congress."

Rip's heart died away at hearing of these sad changes in his home and friends, and finding himself thus alone in the world. Every answer puzzled him too, by treating of such enormous lapses of time, and of matters which he could not understand: war—congress—Stony Point;—he had

[25]A Federalist (conservative) or Democratic-Republican (liberal) in his politics.

[26]On the west bank of the Hudson River, below West Point. It was captured by General Anthony Wayne in the American Revolution.

[27]A mountain near West Point, on the Hudson River.

no courage to ask after any more friends, but cried out in despair, "Does nobody here know Rip Van Winkle?"

"Oh, Rip Van Winkle!" exclaimed two or three, "Oh, to be sure! that's Rip Van Winkle yonder, leaning against the tree."

Rip looked, and beheld a precise counterpart of himself, as he went up the mountain: apparently as lazy, and certainly as ragged. The poor fellow was now completely confounded. He doubted his own identity, and whether he was himself or another man. In the midst of his bewilderment, the man in the cocked hat demanded who he was, and what was his name?

"God knows," exclaimed he, at his wit's end; "I'm not myself—I'm somebody else—that's me yonder—no—that's somebody else got into my shoes—I was myself last night, but I fell asleep on the mountain, and they've changed my gun, and every thing's changed, and I'm changed, and I can't tell what's my name, or who I am!"

The by-standers began now to look at each other, nod, wink significantly, and tap their fingers against their foreheads. There was a whisper, also, about securing the gun, and keeping the old fellow from doing mischief, at the very suggestion of which the self-important man in the cocked hat retired with some precipitation. At this critical moment a fresh comely woman pressed through the throng to get a peep at the gray-bearded man. She had a chubby child in her arms, which, frightened at his looks, began to cry. "Hush, Rip," cried she, "hush, you little fool; the old man won't hurt you." The name of the child, the air of the mother, the tone of her voice, all awakened a train of recollections in his mind. "What is your name, my good woman?" asked he.

"Judith Gardenier."

"And your father's name?"

"Ah, poor man, Rip Van Winkle was his name, but it's twenty years since he went away from home with his gun, and never has been heard of since—his dog came home without him; but whether he shot himself, or was carried away by the Indians, nobody can tell. I was then but a little girl."

Rip had but one question more to ask; but he put it with a faltering voice:

"Where's your mother?"

"Oh, she too had died but a short time since; she broke a blood-vessel in a fit of passion at a New-England peddler."

There was a drop of comfort, at least, in this intelligence. The honest man could contain himself no longer. He caught his daughter and her child in his arms. "I am your father!" cried he—"Young Rip Van Winkle once—old Rip Van Winkle now!—Does nobody know poor Rip Van Winkle?"

All stood amazed, until an old woman, tottering out from among the crowd, put her hand to her brow, and peering under it in his face for a moment, exclaimed, "Sure enough! it is Rip Van Winkle—it is himself! Welcome home again, old neighbor—Why, where have you been these twenty long years?"

Rip's story was soon told, for the whole twenty years had been to him but as one night. The neighbors stared when they heard it; some were seen to wink at each other, and put their tongues in their cheeks: and the self-important man in the cocked hat, who, when the alarm was over, had returned to the field, screwed down the corners of his mouth, and shook his head—upon which there was a general shaking of the head throughout the assemblage.

It was determined, however, to take the opinion of old Peter Vanderdonk, who was seen slowly advancing up the road. He was a descendant of the historian of that name,[28] who wrote one of the earliest accounts of the province. Peter was the most ancient inhabitant of the village, and well versed in all the wonderful events and traditions of the neighborhood. He recollected Rip at once, and corroborated his story in the most satisfactory manner. He assured the company that it was a fact, handed down from his ancestor the historian, that the Kaatskill mountains had always been haunted by strange beings. That it was affirmed that the great Hendrick Hudson,[29] the first discoverer of the river and country, kept a kind of vigil there every twenty years, with his crew of the Half-moon; being permitted in this way to revisit the scenes of his enterprise, and keep a guardian eye upon the river, and the great city called by his name.[30] That his father had once seen them in their old Dutch dresses playing at nine-pins in a hollow of the mountain; and that he himself had heard, one summer afternoon, the sound of their balls, like distant peals of thunder.

To make a long story short, the company broke up, and returned to the more important concerns of the election. Rip's daughter took him home to live with her; she had a snug, well-furnished house, and a stout cheery farmer for a husband, whom Rip recollected for one of the urchins that used to climb upon his back. As to Rip's son and heir, who was the ditto of himself, seen leaning against the tree, he was employed to work on the farm; but evinced an hereditary disposition to attend to any thing else but his business.

Rip now resumed his old walks and habits; he soon found many of his former cronies, though all rather the worse for the wear and tear of time; and preferred making friends among the rising generation, with whom he soon grew into great favor.

Having nothing to do at home, and being arrived at that happy age when a man can be idle with impunity, he took his place once more on the bench at the inn door, and was reverenced as one of the patriarchs of the village, and a chronicle of the old times "before the war." It was some time before he could get into the regular track of gossip, or could be made to comprehend the strange events that had taken place during his torpor. How that there had been a revolutionary war—that the country had thrown off the yoke of old England—and that, instead of being a subject of his Majesty George the Third, he was now a free citizen of the United States. Rip, in fact, was no politician; the changes of states and empires made but little impression on him; but there was one species of despotism under which he had long groaned, and that was—petticoat government. Happily that was at an end;

[28]Adriaen Van der Donck (1620?–1655), author of a description of New Netherland published at Amsterdam in 1655.

[29]Henry Hudson (d. 1611), an English explorer. Hired by the Dutch, he was, in 1609, the first to ascend the river that now bears his name.

[30]The city of Hudson, on the Hudson River.

he had got his neck out of the yoke of matrimony, and could go in and out whenever he pleased, without dreading the tyranny of Dame Van Winkle. Whenever her name was mentioned, however, he shook his head, shrugged his shoulders, and cast up his eyes; which might pass either for an expression of resignation to his fate, or joy at his deliverance.

He used to tell his story to every stranger that arrived at Mr. Doolittle's hotel. He was observed, at first, to vary on some points every time he told it, which was, doubtless, owing to his having so recently awaked. It at last settled down precisely to the tale I have related, and not a man, woman, or child in the neighborhood, but knew it by heart. Some always pretended to doubt the reality of it, and insisted that Rip had been out of his head, and that this was one point on which he always remained flighty. The old Dutch inhabitants, however, almost universally gave it full credit. Even to this day they never hear a thunderstorm of a summer afternoon about the Kaatskill, but they say Hendrick Hudson and his crew are at their game of nine-pins; and it is a common wish of all henpecked husbands in the neighborhood, when life hangs heavy on their hands, that they might have a quieting draught out of Rip Van Winkle's flagon.

NOTE.—The foregoing tale, one would suspect, had been suggested to Mr. Knickerbocker by a little German superstition about the Emperor Frederick *der Rothbart* and the Kypphauser mountain;[31] the subjoined note, however, which he had appended to the tale, shows that it is an absolute fact, narrated with his usual fidelity:

"The story of Rip Van Winkle may seem incredible to many, but nevertheless I give it my full belief, for I know the vicinity of our old Dutch settlements to have been very subject to marvelous events and appearances. Indeed, I have heard many stranger stories than this, in the villages along the Hudson, all of which were too well authenticated to admit of a doubt. I have even talked with Rip Van Winkle myself, who, when last I saw him, was a very venerable old man, and so perfectly rational and consistent on every other point that I think no conscientious person could refuse to take this into the bargain; nay, I have seen a certificate on the subject taken before a country justice, and signed with a cross, in the justice's own handwriting. The story, therefore, is beyond the possibility of doubt." D.K.

POSTSCRIPT

The following are travelling notes from a memorandum book of Mr. Knickerbocker.

The Kaatsberg or Catskill mountains have always been a region full of fable. The Indians considered them the abode of spirits who influenced the weather, spreading sunshine or clouds over the landscape and sending good or bad hunting seasons. They were ruled by an old squaw spirit, said to be their mother. She dwelt on the highest peak of the Catskills and had charge of the doors of day and night to open and shut them at the proper hour. She

[31]Frederick I (1123–1190), Holy Roman emperor (1152–1190). Legend holds that he sleeps in a cavern in the Kyffhäuser mountain in Germany, waiting until his country's need shall bring him forth.

hung up the new moons in the skies and cut up the old ones into stars. In times of drought, if properly propitiated, she would spin light summer clouds out of cobwebs and morning dew, and send them off, from the crest of the mountain, flake after flake, like flakes of carded cotton to float in the air: until, dissolved by the heat of the sun, they would fall in gentle showers, causing the grass to spring, the fruits to ripen and the corn to grow an inch an hour. If displeased, however, she would brew up clouds black as ink, sitting in the midst of them like a bottle bellied spider in the midst of its web; and when these clouds broke—woe betide the valleys!

In old times say the Indian traditions, there was a kind of Manitou or Spirit, who kept about the wildest recesses of the Catskill mountains, and took a mischievous pleasure in wreaking all kinds of evils and vexations upon the red men. Sometimes he would assume the form of a bear or a panther or a deer, lead the bewildered hunter a weary chase through tangled forests and among rugged rocks; and then spring off with a loud ho! ho! leaving him aghast on the brink of a beetling precipice or raging torrent.

The favorite abode of this Manitou is still shown. It is a great rock or cliff in the loneliest part of the mountains, and, from the flowering vines which clamber about it, and the wild flowers which abound in its neighborhood, is known by the name of the Garden Rock. Near the foot of it is a small lake the haunt of the solitary bittern, with water snakes basking in the sun on the leaves of the pond lillies which lie on the surface. This place was held in great awe by the Indians, insomuch that the boldest hunter would not pursue his game within its precincts. Once upon a time, however, a hunter who had lost his way, penetrated to the garden rock where he beheld a number of gourds placed in the crotches of trees. One of these he seized and made off with it, but in the hurry of his retreat he let it fall among the rocks, when a great stream gushed forth which washed him away and swept him down precipices where he was dashed to pieces, and the stream made its way to the Hudson and continues to flow to the present day; being the identical stream known by the name of the Kaaters-kill.

1818 1819

THE LEGEND OF SLEEPY HOLLOW

Found Among the Papers of the Late Diedrich Knickerbocker

A pleasing land of drowsy head it was,
Of dreams that wave before the half-shut eye;
And of gay castles in the clouds that pass,
For ever flushing round a summer sky.

Castle of Indolence[1]

In the bosom of one of those spacious coves which indent the eastern shore of the Hudson, at that broad expansion of the river denominated by the ancient Dutch navigators the Tappan Zee,[2] and where they always prudently

[1]By the Scottish poet, James Thomson (1700–1748). It tells the enchantment of pilgrims in the castle of the Wizard of Indolence and of their liberation by the Knight of Art and Industry.
[2]A widening in the Hudson River near Tarrytown, above New York City.

shortened sail, and implored the protection of St. Nicholas when they crossed, there lies a small market-town or rural port, which by some is called Greensburgh, but which is more generally and properly known by the name of Tarry Town. This name was given, we are told, in former days, by the good housewives of the adjacent country, from the inveterate propensity of their husbands to linger about the village tavern on market days. Be that as it may, I do not vouch for the fact, but merely advert to it, for the sake of being precise and authentic. Not far from this village, perhaps about two miles, there is a little valley, or rather lap[3] of land, among high hills, which is one of the quietest places in the whole world. A small brook glides through it, with just murmur enough to lull one to repose; and the occasional whistle of a quail, or tapping of a woodpecker, is almost the only sound that ever breaks in upon the uniform tranquillity.

I recollect that, when a stripling, my first exploit in squirrel-shooting was in a grove of tall walnut-trees that shades one side of the valley. I had wandered into it at noon time, when all nature is peculiarly quiet, and was startled by the roar of my own gun, as it broke the Sabbath stillness around, and was prolonged and reverberated by the angry echoes. If ever I should wish for a retreat, whither I might steal from the world and its distractions, and dream quietly away the remnant of a troubled life, I know of none more promising than this little valley.

From the listless repose of the place, and the peculiar character of its inhabitants, who are descendants from the original Dutch settlers, this sequestered glen has long been known by the name of SLEEPY HOLLOW,[4] and its rustic lads are called the Sleepy Hollow Boys throughout all the neighboring country. A drowsy, dreamy influence seems to hang over the land, and to pervade the very atmosphere. Some say that the place was bewitched by a high German doctor,[5] during the early days of the settlement; others, that an old Indian chief, the prophet or wizard of his tribe, held his powwows there before the country was discovered[6] by Master Hendrick Hudson.[7] Certain it is, the place still continues under the sway of some witching power, that holds a spell over the minds of the good people, causing them to walk in a continual reverie. They are given to all kinds of marvellous beliefs; are subject to trances and visions; and frequently see strange sights, and hear music and voices in the air. The whole neighborhood abounds with local tales, haunted spots, and twilight superstitions; stars shoot and meteors glare oftener across the valley than in any other part of the country, and the nightmare, with her whole nine fold,[8] seems to make it the favorite scene of her gambols.

The dominant spirit, however, that haunts this enchanted region, and seems to be commander-in-chief of all the powers of the air, is the apparition of a figure on horseback without a head. It is said by some to be the ghost of

[3]Fold.
[4]At Tarrytown.
[5]I.e., a learned scholar from northern Germany.
[6]Explored.
[7]Henry Hudson.
[8]In folk-legend, the nightmare had nine foals or imps.

a Hessian[9] trooper, whose head had been carried away by a cannon-ball, in some nameless battle during the revolutionary war; and who is ever and anon seen by the country folk, hurrying along in the gloom of night, as if on the wings of the wind. His haunts are not confined to the valley, but extend at times to the adjacent roads, and especially to the vicinity of a church at no great distance. Indeed, certain of the most authentic historians of those parts, who have been careful in collecting and collating the floating facts concerning this spectre, allege that the body of the trooper, having been buried in the church-yard, the ghost rides forth to the scene of battle in nightly quest of his head; and that the rushing speed with which he sometimes passes along the Hollow, like a midnight blast, is owing to his being belated, and in a hurry to get back to the church-yard before daybreak.[10]

Such is the general purport of this legendary superstition, which has furnished materials for many a wild story in that region of shadows; and the spectre is known, at all the country firesides, by the name of the Headless Horseman of Sleepy Hollow.

It is remarkable that the visionary propensity I have mentioned is not confined to the native inhabitants of the valley, but is unconsciously imbibed by every one who resides there for a time. However wide awake they may have been before they entered that sleepy region, they are sure, in a little time, to inhale the witching influence of the air, and begin to grow imaginative—to dream dreams, and see apparitions.

I mention this peaceful spot with all possible laud; for it is in such little retired Dutch valleys, found here and there embosomed in the great State of New York, that population, manners, and customs, remain fixed; while the great torrent of migration and improvement, which is making such incessant changes in other parts of this restless country, sweeps by them unobserved. They are like those little nooks of still water which border a rapid stream; where we may see the straw and bubble riding quietly at anchor, or slowly revolving in their mimic harbor, undisturbed by the rush of the passing current. Though many years have elapsed since I trod the drowsy shades of Sleepy Hollow, yet I question whether I should not still find the same trees and the same families vegetating in its sheltered bosom.

In this by-place of nature, there abode, in a remote period of American history, that is to say, some thirty years since, a worthy wight of the name of Ichabod Crane; who sojourned, or, as he expressed it, "tarried," in Sleepy Hollow, for the purpose of instructing the children of the vicinity. He was a native of Connecticut; a State which supplies the Union with pioneers for the mind as well as for the forest, and sends forth yearly its legions of frontier woodsmen and country schoolmasters. The cognomen of Crane was not inapplicable to his person. He was tall, but exceedingly lank, with narrow shoulders, long arms and legs, hands that dangled a mile out of his sleeves, feet that might have served for shovels, and his whole frame most loosely hung together. His head was small, and flat at top, with huge ears, large

[9]German mercenary hired by the British to fight in the American Revolutionary War.

[10]Irving refers to the superstition that the spirits of the dead must return to their graves before dawn.

green glassy eyes, and a long snipe nose, so that it looked like a weather-cock, perched upon his spindle neck, to tell which way the wind blew. To see him striding along the profile of a hill on a windy day, with his clothes bagging and fluttering about him, one might have mistaken him for the genius[11] of famine descending upon the earth, or some scarecrow eloped from a cornfield.

His school-house was a low building of one large room, rudely constructed of logs; the windows partly glazed, and partly patched with leaves of old copy-books. It was most ingeniously secured at vacant hours, by a withe[12] twisted in the handle of the door, and stakes set against the window shutters; so that, though a thief might get in with perfect ease, he would find some embarrassment in getting out; an idea most probably borrowed by the architect, Yost Van Houten, from the mystery of an eel-pot.[13] The school-house stood in a rather lonely but pleasant situation, just at the foot of a woody hill, with a brook running close by, and a formidable birch tree growing at one end of it. From hence the low murmur of his pupils' voices, conning over their lessons, might be heard in a drowsy summer's day, like the hum of a bee-hive; interrupted now and then by the authoritative voice of the master, in the tone of menace or command; or, peradventure, by the appalling sound of the birch, as he urged some tardy loiterer along the flowery path of knowledge. Truth to say, he was a conscientious man, and ever bore in mind the golden maxim, "Spare the rod and spoil the child."[14]—Ichabod Crane's scholars certainly were not spoiled.

I would not have it imagined, however, that he was one of those cruel potentates of the school, who joy in the smart[15] of their subjects; on the contrary, he administered justice with discrimination rather than severity; taking the burthen off the backs of the weak, and laying it on those of the strong. Your mere puny stripling, that winced at the least flourish of the rod, was passed by the indulgence; but the claims of justice were satisfied by inflicting a double portion on some little, tough, wrong-headed, broad-skirted Dutch urchin, who sulked and swelled and grew dogged and sullen beneath the birch. All this he called "doing his duty by their parents;" and he never inflicted a chastisement without following it by the assurance, so consolatory to the smarting urchin, that "he would remember it, and thank him for it the longest day he had to live."

When school hours were over, he was even the companion and playmate of the larger boys; and on holiday afternoons would convoy some of the smaller ones home, who happened to have pretty sisters, or good housewives for mothers, noted for the comforts of the cupboard. Indeed it behooved him to keep on good terms with his pupils. The revenue arising from his school was small, and would have been scarcely sufficient to furnish him with daily bread, for he was a huge feeder, and though lank, had the dilating powers of an anaconda;[16] but to help out his maintenance, he was, according to country custom in those parts, boarded and lodged at the houses of the farmers, whose children he instructed. With these he lived successively a week at a

[11]Image. [12]A flexible branch. [13]An eel trap.
[14]From *Hudibras* (1664) by Samuel Butler (1612–1680). The saying derives from Proverbs 13:24, "He that spareth his rod, hateth his son."
[15]Pain. [16]A large snake that can stretch (dilate) to swallow large animals.

time; thus going the rounds of the neighborhood, with all his worldly effects tied up in a cotton handkerchief.

That all this might not be too onerous on the purses of his rustic patrons, who are apt to consider the costs of schooling a grievous burden, and schoolmasters as mere drones, he had various ways of rendering himself both useful and agreeable. He assisted the farmers occasionally in the lighter labors of their farms; helped to make hay; mended the fences; took the horses to water; drove the cows from pasture; and cut wood for the winter fire. He laid aside, too, all the dominant dignity and absolute sway with which he lorded it in his little empire, the school, and became wonderfully gentle and ingratiating. He found favor in the eyes of the mothers, by petting the children, particularly the youngest; and like the lion bold, which whilom[17] so magnanimously the lamb did hold,[18] he would sit with a child on one knee, and rock a cradle with his foot for whole hours together.

In addition to his other vocations, he was the singing-master of the neighborhood, and picked up many bright shillings by instructing the young folks in psalmody.[19] It was a matter of no little vanity to him, on Sundays, to take his station in front of the church gallery, with a band of chosen singers; where, in his own mind, he completely carried away the palm from the parson. Certain it is, his voice resounded far above all the rest of the congregation; and there are peculiar quavers still to be heard in that church, and which may even be heard half a mile off, quite to the opposite side of the mill-pond, on a still Sunday morning, which are said to be legitimately descended from the nose of Ichabod Crane. Thus, by divers little make-shifts in that ingenious way which is commonly denominated "by hook and by crook,"[20] the worthy pedagogue got on tolerably enough, and was thought, by all who understood nothing of the labor of headwork, to have a wonderfully easy life of it.

The schoolmaster is generally a man of some importance in the female circle of a rural neighborhood; being considered a kind of idle gentlemanlike personage, of vastly superior taste and accomplishments to the rough country swains, and, indeed, inferior in learning only to the parson. His appearance, therefore, is apt to occasion some little stir at the tea-table of a farmhouse, and the addition of a supernumerary dish of cakes or sweetmeats, or, peradventure, the parade of a silver tea-pot. Our man of letters, therefore, was peculiarly happy in the smiles of all the country damsels. How he would figure among them in the church-yard, between services on Sundays! gathering grapes for them from the wild vines that overrun the surrounding trees; reciting for their amusement all the epitaphs on the tombstones; or sauntering, with a whole bevy of them, along the banks of the adjacent mill-pond; while the more bashful country bumpkins hung sheepishly back, envying his superior elegance and address.

From his half itinerant life, also, he was a kind of travelling gazette, carrying the whole budget of local gossip from house to house; so that his

[17]Formerly.

[18]In the *New England Primer* the illustration for "L" showed a lion and lamb and read, "The Lion bold/The Lamb doth hold." It was derived from Isaiah 11:6–9.

[19]The singing of psalms.

[20]Irving quotes "Colyn Cloute" (1519?) by the English poet John Skelton (1460?–1529).

appearance was always greeted with satisfaction. He was, moreover, esteemed by the women as a man of great erudition, for he had read several books quite through, and was a perfect master of Cotton Mather's history of New England Witchcraft,[21] in which, by the way, he most firmly and potently believed.

He was, in fact, an odd mixture of small shrewdness and simple credulity. His appetite for the marvellous, and his powers of digesting it, were equally extraordinary; and both had been increased by his residence in this spell-bound region. No tale was too gross or monstrous for his capacious swallow. It was often his delight, after his school was dismissed in the afternoon, to stretch himself on the rich bed of clover, bordering the little brook that whimpered by his schoolhouse, and there con[22] over old Mather's direful tales, until the gathering dusk of the evening made the printed page a mere mist before his eyes. Then, as he wended his way, by swamp and stream and awful[23] woodland, to the farmhouse where he happened to be quartered, every sound of nature, at that witching hour, fluttered his excited imagination: the moan of the whip-poor-will[24] from the hill-side; the boding cry of the tree-toad, that harbinger of storm; the dreary hooting of the screech-owl, or the sudden rustling in the thicket of birds frightened from their roost. The fire-flies, too, which sparkled most vividly in the darkest places, now and then startled him, as one of uncommon brightness would stream across his path; and if, by chance, a huge blockhead of a beetle came winging his blundering flight against him, the poor varlet was ready to give up the ghost, with the idea that he was struck with a witch's token. His only resource on such occasions, either to drown thought, or drive away evil spirits, was to sing psalm tunes;—and the good people of Sleepy Hollow, as they sat by their doors of an evening, were often filled with awe, at hearing his nasal melody, "in linked sweetness long drawn out,"[25] floating from the distant hill, or along the dusky road.

Another of his sources of fearful pleasure was, to pass long winter evenings with the old Dutch wives, as they sat spinning by the fire, with a row of apples roasting and spluttering along the hearth, and listen to their marvellous tales of ghosts and goblins, and haunted fields, and haunted brooks, and haunted bridges, and haunted houses, and particularly of the headless horseman, or Galloping Hessian of the Hollow, as they sometimes called him. He would delight them equally by his anecdotes of witchcraft, and of the direful omens and portentous sights and sounds in the air, which prevailed in the earlier times of Connecticut; and would frighten them wofully with speculations upon comets and shooting stars; and with the alarming fact that the world did absolutely turn round, and that they were half the time topsy-turvy!

But if there was a pleasure in all this, while snugly cuddling in the chimney corner of a chamber that was all of a ruddy glow from the crackling wood fire, and where, of course, no spectre dared to show his face, it was dearly

[21]Cotton Mather wrote *Memorable Providences Relating to Witchcraft* (1689), and *The Wonders of the Invisible World* (1693).

[22]Read. [23]Awesome, frightening.

[24]"The whip-poor-will is a bird which is only heard at night. It receives its name from its note, which is thought to resemble those words."—Irving's note.

[25]From John Milton's "L'Allegro" (1632), line 140.

purchased by the terrors of his subsequent walk homewards. What fearful shapes and shadows beset his path amidst the dim and ghastly glare of a snowy night!—With what wistful look did he eye every trembling ray of light streaming across the waste fields from some distant window!—How often was he appalled by some shrub covered with snow, which, like a sheeted spectre, beset his very path!—How often did he shrink with curdling awe at the sound of his own steps on the frosty crust beneath his feet; and dread to look over his shoulder, lest he should behold some uncouth being tramping close behind him!—and how often was he thrown into complete dismay by some rushing blast, howling among the trees, in the idea that it was the Galloping Hessian on one of his nightly scourings!

All these, however, were mere terrors of the night, phantoms of the mind that walk in darkness; and though he had seen many spectres in his time, and been more than once beset by Satan in divers shapes, in his lonely perambulations, yet daylight put an end to all these evils; and he would have passed a pleasant life of it, in despite of the devil and all his works, if his path had not been crossed by a being that causes more perplexity to mortal man than ghosts, goblins, and the whole race of witches put together, and that was—a woman.

Among the musical disciples who assembled, one evening in each week, to receive his instructions in psalmody, was Katrina Van Tassel, the daughter and only child of a substantial Dutch farmer. She was a blooming lass of fresh eighteen; plump as a partridge; ripe and melting and rosy cheeked as one of her father's peaches, and universally famed, not merely for her beauty, but her vast expectations. She was withal a little of a coquette, as might be perceived even in her dress, which was a mixture of ancient and modern fashions, as most suited to set off her charms. She wore the ornaments of pure yellow gold, which her great-great-grandmother had brought over from Saardam; the tempting stomacher[26] of the olden time; and withal a provokingly short petticoat, to display the prettiest foot and ankle in the country round.

Ichabod Crane had a soft and foolish heart towards the sex;[27] and it is not to be wondered at, that so tempting a morsel soon found favor in his eyes; more especially after he had visited her in her paternal mansion. Old Baltus Van Tassel was a perfect picture of a thriving, contented, liberal-hearted farmer. He seldom, it is true, sent either his eyes or his thoughts beyond the boundaries of his own farm; but within those every thing was snug, happy, and well-conditioned. He was satisfied with his wealth, but not proud of it; and piqued himself upon the hearty abundance, rather than the style in which he lived. His stronghold was situated on the banks of the Hudson, in one of those green, sheltered, fertile nooks, in which the Dutch farmers are so fond of nestling. A great elmtree spread its broad branches over it; at the foot of which bubbled up a spring of the softest and sweetest water, in a little well, formed of a barrel; and then stole sparkling away through the grass, to a neighboring brook, that bubbled along among alders and dwarf willows. Hard by the farmhouse was a vast barn, that might have served for a church; every window and crevice of which seemed bursting forth with the treasures of the farm; the flail[28] was busily resounding within it from morning to night;

[26]A decorated garment worn over the stomach and chest. [27]Women.

[28]A long staff with a wooden bar or heavy stick flexibly attached, used to thresh grain.

swallows and martins skimmed twittering about the eaves; and rows of pigeons, some with one eye turned up, as if watching the weather, some with their heads under their wings, or buried in their bosoms, and others swelling, and cooing, and bowing about their dames, were enjoying the sunshine on the roof. Sleek unwieldy porkers were grunting in the repose and abundance of their pens; whence sallied forth, now and then, troops of sucking pigs, as if to snuff the air. A stately squadron of snowy geese were riding in an adjoining pond, convoying whole fleets of ducks; regiments of turkeys were gobbling through the farmyard and guinea fowls fretting about it, like ill-tempered housewives, with their peevish discontented cry. Before the barn door strutted the gallant cock, that pattern of a husband, a warrior, and a fine gentleman, clapping his burnished wings, and crowing in the pride and gladness of his heart—sometimes tearing up the earth with his feet, and then generously calling his ever-hungry family of wives and children to enjoy the rich morsel which he had discovered.

The pedagogue's mouth watered, as he looked upon this sumptuous promise of luxurious winter fare. In his devouring mind's eye, he pictured to himself every roasting-pig running about with a pudding in his belly, and an apple in his mouth; the pigeons were snugly put to bed in a comfortable pie, and tucked in with a coverlet of crust; the geese were swimming in their own gravy; and the ducks pairing cosily in dishes, like snug married couples, with a decent competency of onion sauce. In the porkers he saw carved out the future sleek side of bacon, and juicy relishing ham; not a turkey but he beheld daintily trussed up, with its gizzard under its wing, and, peradventure, a necklace of savory sausages; and even bright chanticleer[29] himself lay sprawling on his back, in a side-dish, with uplifted claws, as if craving that quarter[30] which his chivalrous spirit disdained to ask while living.

As the enraptured Ichabod fancied all this, and as he rolled his great green eyes over the fat meadow-lands, the rich fields of wheat, of rye, of buckwheat, and Indian corn, and the orchards burthened with ruddy fruit, which surrounded the warm tenement[31] of Van Tassel, his heart yearned after the damsel who was to inherit these domains, and his imagination expanded with the idea, how they might be readily turned into cash, and the money invested in immense tracts of wild land, and shingle palaces in the wilderness. Nay, his busy fancy already realized his hopes, and presented to him the blooming Katrina, with a whole family of children, mounted on the top of a wagon loaded with household trumpery, with pots and kettles dangling beneath; and he beheld himself bestriding a pacing mare, with a colt at her heels, setting out for Kentucky, Tennessee, or the Lord knows where.

When he entered the house the conquest of his heart was complete. It was one of those spacious farmhouses, with high-ridged, but lowly-sloping roofs, built in the style handed down from the first Dutch settlers; the low projecting eaves forming a piazza along the front, capable of being closed up in bad weather. Under this were hung flails, harness, various utensils of husbandry, and nets for fishing in the neighboring river. Benches were built along the sides for summer use; and a great spinning-wheel at one end, and a churn at the other, showed the various uses to which this important porch might be

[29]A rooster. [30]Clemency. [31]Residence.

devoted. From this piazza the wondering Ichabod entered the hall, which formed the centre of the mansion and the place of usual residence. Here, rows of resplendent pewter, ranged on a long dresser, dazzled his eyes. In one corner stood a huge bag of wool ready to be spun; in another a quantity of linsey-woolsey just from the loom; ears of Indian corn, and strings of dried apples and peaches, hung in gay festoons along the walls, mingled with the gaud[32] of red peppers; and a door left ajar gave him a peep into the best parlor, where the claw-footed chairs, and dark mahogany tables, shone like mirrors; andirons, with their accompanying shovel and tongs, glistened from their covert[33] of asparagus tops;[34] mock-oranges and conch-shells decorated the mantelpiece; strings of various colored birds' eggs were suspended above it: a great ostrich egg was hung from the centre of the room, and a corner cupboard, knowingly left open, displayed immense treasures of old silver and well-mended china.

From the moment Ichabod laid his eyes upon these regions of delight, the peace of his mind was at an end, and his only study was how to gain the affections of the peerless daughter of Van Tassel. In this enterprise, however, he had more real difficulties than generally fell to the lot of a knight-errant[35] of yore, who seldom had any thing but giants, enchanters, fiery dragons, and such like easily-conquered adversaries, to contend with; and had to make his way merely through gates of iron and brass, and walls of adamant,[36] to the castle keep,[37] where the lady of his heart was confined; all which he achieved as easily as a man would carve his way to the centre of a Christmas pie; and then the lady gave him her hand as a matter of course. Ichabod, on the contrary, had to win his way to the heart of a country coquette, beset with a labyrinth of whims and caprices, which were for ever presenting new difficulties and impediments; and he had to encounter a host of fearful adversaries of real flesh and blood, the numerous rustic admirers, who beset every portal to her heart; keeping a watchful and angry eye upon each other, but ready to fly out in the common cause against any new competitor.

Among these the most formidable was a burly, roaring, roistering blade, of the name of Abraham, or, according to the Dutch abbreviation, Brom Van Brunt, the hero of the country round, which rang with his feats of strength and hardihood. He was broad-shouldered and double-jointed, with short curly black hair, and a bluff, but not unpleasant countenance, having a mingled air of fun and arrogance. From his Herculean frame and great powers of limb, he had received the nickname of BROM BONES, by which he was universally known. He was famed for great knowledge and skill in horsemanship, being as dexterous on horseback as a Tartar.[38] He was foremost at all races and cock-fights; and, with the ascendency which bodily strength acquires in rustic life, was the umpire in all disputes, setting his hat on one side, and giving his decisions with an air and tone admitting of no gainsay or appeal. He was always ready for either a fight or a frolic; but had more mischief than ill-will in his composition; and, with all his overbearing roughness, there was a strong dash of waggish good humor at bottom. He had three or

[32]Ornamental display. [33]Hiding place.
[34]Arrayed in the fireplace as summertime decoration.
[35]A knight who wanders in search of adventure. [36]Stone of extreme hardness.
[37]The fortified part of a castle. [38]Fierce Asian warrior.

four boon companions, who regarded him as their model, and at the head of whom he scoured the country, attending every scene of feud or merriment for miles round. In cold weather he was distinguished by a fur cap, surmounted with a flaunting fox's tail; and when the folks at a country gathering descried this well-known crest at a distance, whisking about among a squad of hard riders, they always stood by for a squall. Sometimes his crew would be heard dashing along past the farmhouses at midnight, with whoop and halloo, like a troop of Don Cossacks;[39] and the old dames, startled out of their sleep, would listen for a moment till the hurry-scurry had clattered by, and then exclaim, "Ay, there goes Brom Bones and his gang!" The neighbors looked upon him with a mixture of awe, admiration, and good will; and when any madcap prank, or rustic brawl, occurred in the vicinity, always shook their heads, and warranted Brom Bones was at the bottom of it.

This rantipole[40] hero had for some time singled out the blooming Katrina for the object of his uncouth gallantries, and though his amorous toyings were something like the gentle caresses and endearments of a bear, yet it was whispered that she did not altogether discourage his hopes. Certain it is, his advances were signals for rival candidates to retire, who felt no inclination to cross a lion in his amours; insomuch, that when his horse was seen tied to Van Tassel's paling,[41] on a Sunday night, a sure sign that his master was courting, or, as it is termed, "sparking," within, all other suitors passed by in despair, and carried the war into other quarters.

Such was the formidable rival with whom Ichabod Crane had to contend, and, considering all things, a stouter man than he would have shrunk from the competition, and a wiser man would have despaired. He had, however, a happy mixture of pliability and perseverance in his nature; he was in form and spirit like a supplejack[42]—yielding, but tough; though he bent, he never broke; and though he bowed beneath the slightest pressure, yet, the moment it was away—jerk! he was as erect, and carried his head as high as ever.

To have taken the field openly against his rival would have been madness; for he was not a man to be thwarted in his amours, any more than that stormy lover, Achilles.[43] Ichabod, therefore, made his advances in a quiet and gently-insinuating manner. Under cover of his character of singing-master, he made frequent visits at the farmhouse; not that he had any thing to apprehend from the meddlesome interference of parents, which is so often a stumbling-block in the path of lovers. Balt Van Tassel was an easy indulgent soul; he loved his daughter better even than his pipe, and, like a reasonable man and an excellent father, let her have her way in every thing. His notable little wife, too, had enough to do to attend to her housekeeping and manage her poultry; for, as she sagely observed, ducks and geese are foolish things, and must be looked after, but girls can take care of themselves. Thus while the busy dame bustled about the house, or plied her spinning-wheel at one end of the piazza, honest Balt would sit smoking his evening pipe at the other, watching the achievements of a little wooden warrior,[44] who, armed

[39]Horsemen of the Don River area in Russia. [40]Reckless.

[41]Fence. [42]Strong, woody vine.

[43]In Homer's *Iliad,* Achilles became enraged when his love, Briseis, was taken from him by the Greek commander, Agamemnon.

[44]A whirligig, in the form of a soldier, whose whirling arms show the speed and direction of the wind.

with a sword in each hand, was most valiantly fighting the wind on the pinnacle of the barn. In the mean time, Ichabod would carry on his suit with the daughter by the side of the spring under the great elm, or sauntering along in the twilight, that hour so favorable to the lover's eloquence.

I profess not to know how women's hearts are wooed and won. To me they have always been matters of riddle and admiration. Some seem to have but one vulnerable point, or door of access; while others have a thousand avenues, and may be captured in a thousand different ways. It is a great triumph of skill to gain the former, but a still greater proof of generalship to maintain possession of the latter, for the man must battle for his fortress at every door and window. He who wins a thousand common hearts is therefore entitled to some renown; but he who keeps undisputed sway over the heart of a coquette, is indeed a hero. Certain it is, this was not the case with the redoubtable Brom Bones; and from the moment Ichabod Crane made his advances, the interests of the former evidently declined; his horse was no longer seen tied at the palings on Sunday nights, and a deadly feud gradually arose between him and the preceptor of Sleepy Hollow.

Brom, who had a degree of rough chivalry in his nature, would fain have carried matters to open warfare, and have settled their pretensions to the lady, according to the mode of those most concise and simple reasoners, the knights-errant of yore—by single combat; but Ichabod was too conscious of the superior might of his adversary to enter the lists against him: he had overheard a boast of Bones, that he would "double the schoolmaster up, and lay him on a shelf of his own school-house;" and he was too wary to give him an opportunity. There was something extremely provoking in this obstinately pacific system; it left Brom no alternative but to draw upon the funds of rustic waggery in his disposition, and to play off boorish practical jokes upon his rival. Ichabod became the object of whimsical persecution to Bones, and his gang of rough riders. They harried his hitherto peaceful domains; smoked out his singing school, by stopping up the chimney; broke into the schoolhouse at night, in spite of its formidable fastenings of withe and window stakes, and turned every thing topsy-turvy: so that the poor schoolmaster began to think all the witches in the country held their meetings there. But what was still more annoying, Brom took all opportunities of turning him into ridicule in presence of his mistress, and had a scoundrel dog whom he taught to whine in the most ludicrous manner, and introduced as a rival of Ichabod's to instruct her in psalmody.

In this way matters went on for some time, without producing any material effect on the relative situations of the contending powers. On a fine autumnal afternoon, Ichabod, in pensive mood, sat enthroned on the lofty stool whence he usually watched all the concerns of his little literary realm. In his hand he swayed a ferule, that sceptre of domestic power; the birth of justice reposed on three nails, behind the throne, a constant terror to evil doers; while on the desk before him might be seen sundry contraband articles and prohibited weapons, detected upon the persons of idle urchins; such as half-munched apples, popguns, whirligigs, fly-cages, and whole legions of rampant little paper gamecocks. Apparently there had been some appalling act of justice recently inflicted, for his scholars were all busily intent upon their books, or slyly whispering behind them with one eye kept upon the master; and a kind of buzzing stillness reigned throughout the school-room. It was suddenly interrupted by the appearance of a Negro, in tow-cloth jacket and trowsers, a round-crowned fragment of a hat, like the cap of Mercury,[45] and mounted on the back of a ragged wild, half-broken colt, which he managed with a rope by way of halter. He came clattering up to the school door with an invitation to Ichabod to attend a merrymaking or "quilting frolic," to be held that evening at Mynheer Van Tassel's; and having delivered his message with that air of importance, and effort at fine language, which a Negro is apt to display on petty embassies of the kind, he dashed over the brook, and was seen scampering away up the hollow, full of the importance and hurry of his mission.

All was now bustle and hubbub in the late quiet school-room. The scholars were hurried through their lessons, without stopping at trifles; those who were nimble skipped over half with impunity, and those who were tardy, had a smart application now and then in the rear, to quicken their speed, or help them over a tall word. Books were flung aside without being put away on the shelves, inkstands were overturned, benches thrown down, and the whole school was turned loose an hour before the usual time, bursting forth like a legion of young imps, yelping and racketing about the green, in joy at their early emancipation.

The gallant Ichabod now spent at least an extra hour at his toilet, brushing and furbishing up his best, and indeed only suit of rusty black, and arranging his looks by a bit of broken looking-glass, that hung up in the school-house. That he might make his appearance before his mistress in the true style of a cavalier, he borrowed a horse from the farmer with whom he was domiciliated, a choleric old Dutchman, of the name of Hans Van Ripper, and, thus gallantly mounted, issued forth, like a knight-errant in quest of adventures. But it is meet[46] I should, in the true spirit of romantic story, give some account of the looks and equipments of my hero and his steed. The animal he bestrode was a broken-down plough-horse, that had outlived almost every thing but his viciousness. He was gaunt and shagged, with a ewe neck and a head like a hammer; his rusty mane and tail were tangled and knotted with burrs; one eye had lost its pupil, and was glaring and spectral; but the other had the gleam of a genuine devil in it. Still he must have had fire and mettle in his day, if we may judge from the name he bore of Gunpowder. He had, in fact, been a favorite steed of his master's, the choleric Van Ripper, who was a furious rider, and had infused, very probably, some of his own spirit into the animal; for, old and broken-down as he looked, there was more of the lurking devil in him than in any young filly in the country.

Ichabod was a suitable figure for such a steed. He rode with short stirrups, which brought his knees nearly up to the pommel of the saddle; his sharp elbows stuck out like grasshoppers'; he carried his whip perpendicularly in his hand, like a sceptre, and, as his horse jogged on, the motion of his arms was not unlike the flapping of a pair of wings. A small wool hat rested on the top of his nose, for so his scanty strip of forehead might be called; and the skirts of his black coat fluttered out almost to the horse's tail. Such was the appearance of Ichabod and his steed, as they shambled out of the gate of Hans Van

[45]Mercury, Roman messenger of the gods, wore a winged hat. [46]Fitting, appropriate.

Ripper, and it was altogether such an apparition as is seldom to be met with in broad daylight.

It was, as I have said, a fine autumnal day, the sky was clear and serene, and nature wore that rich and golden livery which we always associate with the idea of abundance. The forests had put on their sober brown and yellow, while some trees of the tenderer kind had been nipped by the frosts into brilliant dyes of orange, purple, and scarlet. Streaming files of wild ducks began to make their appearance high in the air; the bark of the squirrel might be heard from the groves of beech and hickory nuts, and the pensive whistle of the quail at intervals from the neighboring stubble-field.

The small birds were taking their farewell banquets. In the fulness of their revelry, they fluttered, chirping and frolicking, from bush to bush, and tree to tree, capricious from the very profusion and variety around them. There was the honest cock-robin, the favorite game of stripling sportsmen, with its loud querulous note; and the twittering blackbirds flying in sable clouds; and the golden-winged woodpecker, with his crimson crest, his broad black gorget,[47] and splendid plumage; and the cedar bird, with its red-tipt wings and yellow-tipt tail, and its little monteiro cap of feathers;[48] and the blue-jay, that noisy coxcomb, in his gay light-blue coat and white under-clothes; screaming and chattering, nodding and bobbing and bowing, and pretending to be on good terms with every songster of the grove.

As Ichabod jogged slowly on his way, his eye, ever open to every symptom of culinary abundance, ranged with delight over the treasures of jolly autumn. On all sides he beheld vast store of apples; some hanging in oppressive opulence on the trees; some gathered into baskets and barrels for the market; others heaped up in rich piles for the cider-press. Farther on he beheld great fields of Indian corn, with its golden ears peeping from their leafy coverts, and holding out the promise of cakes and hasty pudding; and the yellow pumpkins lying beneath them, turning up their fair round bellies to the sun, and giving ample prospects of the most luxurious of pies; and anon he passed the fragrant buckwheat fields, breathing the odor of the bee-hive, and as he beheld them, soft anticipations stole over his mind of dainty slapjacks, well buttered, and garnished with honey or treacle,[49] by the delicate little dimpled hand of Katrina Van Tassel.

Thus feeding his mind with many sweet thoughts and "sugared suppositions," he journeyed along the sides of a range of hills which look out upon some of the goodliest scenes of the mighty Hudson. The sun gradually wheeled his broad disk down into the west. The wide bosom of the Tappan Zee lay motionless and glassy, excepting that here and there a gentle undulation waved and prolonged the blue shadow of the distant mountain. A few amber clouds floated in the sky, without a breath of air to move them. The horizon was a fine golden tint, changing gradually into a pure apple green, and from that into the deep blue of the mid-heaven. A slanting ray lingered on the woody crests of the precipices that overhung some parts of the river, giving greater depth of the dark-gray and purple of their rocky sides. A sloop was loitering in the distance, dropping slowly down with the tide, her sail

[47]Throat feathers. [48]I.e., feathered crest resembling a cap with flaps. [49]Molasses.

hanging uselessly against the mast; and as the reflection of the sky gleamed along the still water, it seemed as if the vessel was suspended in the air.

It was toward evening that Ichabod arrived at the castle of the Heer Van Tassel, which he found thronged with the pride and flower of the adjacent country. Old farmers, a spare leathern-faced race, in homespun coats and breeches, blue stockings, huge shoes, and magnificent pewter buckles. Their brisk withered little dames, in close crimped caps, long-waisted short-gowns, homespun petticoats, with scissors and pincushions, and gay calico pockets hanging on the outside. Buxom lasses, almost as antiquated as their mothers, excepting where a straw hat, a fine ribbon, or perhaps a white frock, gave symptoms of city innovation. The sons, in short square-skirted coats with rows of stupendous brass buttons; and their hair generally queued in the fashion of the times, especially if they could procure an eel-skin for the purpose, it being esteemed, throughout the country, as a potent nourisher and strengthener of the hair.

Brom Bones, however, was the hero of the scene, having come to the gathering on his favorite steed Daredevil, a creature, like himself, full of mettle and mischief, and which no one but himself could manage. He was, in fact, noted for preferring vicious animals, given to all kinds of tricks, which kept the rider in constant risk of his neck, for he held a tractable well-broken horse as unworthy of a lad of spirit.

Fain would I pause to dwell upon the world of charms that burst upon the enraptured gaze of my hero, as he entered the state parlor of Van Tassel's mansion. Not those of the bevy of buxom lasses, with their luxurious display of red and white; but the ample charms of a genuine Dutch country tea-table, in the sumptuous time of autumn. Such heaped-up platters of cakes of various and almost indescribable kinds, known only to experienced Dutch housewives! There was the doughty dough-nut, the tenderer oly koek,[50] and the crisp and crumbling cruller; sweet cakes and short cakes, ginger cakes and honey cakes, and the whole family of cakes. And then there were apple pies and peach pies and pumpkin pies; besides slices of ham and smoked beef; and moreover delectable dishes of preserved plums, and peaches, and pears, and quinces; not to mention broiled shad and roasted chickens; together with bowls of milk and cream, all mingled higgledy-piggledy, pretty much as I have enumerated them, with the motherly tea-pot sending up its clouds of vapor from the midst—Heaven bless the mark! I want[51] breath and time to discuss this banquet as it deserves, and am too eager to get on with my story. Happily, Ichabod Crane was not in so great a hurry as his historian, but did ample justice to every dainty.

He was a kind of thankful creature, whose heart dilated in proportion as his skin was filled with good cheer; and whose spirit rose with eating as some men's do with drink. He could not help, too, rolling his large eyes round him as he ate, and chuckling with the possibility that he might one day be lord of all this scene of almost unimaginable luxury and splendor. Then, he thought, how soon he'd turn his back upon the old school-house; snap his fingers in the face of Hans Van Ripper, and every other niggardly patron, and kick any itinerant pedagogue out of doors that should dare to call him comrade!

[50]"Oil cake." Pastry fried in deep fat. [51]Lack.

Old Baltus Van Tassel moved about among his guests with a face dilated with content and good humor, round and jolly as the harvest moon. His hospitable attentions were brief, but expressive, being confined to a shake of the hand, a slap on the shoulder, a loud laugh, and a pressing invitation to "fall to, and help themselves."

And now the sound of the music from the common room, or hall, summoned to the dance. The musician was an old grayheaded Negro, who had been the itinerant orchestra of the neighborhood for more than half a century. His instrument was as old and battered as himself. The greater part of the time he scraped on two or three strings, accompanying every movement of the bow with a motion of the head; bowing almost to the ground, and stamping with his foot whenever a fresh couple were to start.

Ichabod prided himself upon his dancing as much as upon his vocal powers. Not a limb, not a fibre about him was idle; and to have seen his loosely hung frame in full motion, and clattering about the room, you would have thought Saint Vitus[52] himself, that blessed patron of the dance, was figuring before you in person. He was the admiration of all the Negroes; who, having gathered, of all ages and sizes, from the farm and the neighborhood, stood forming a pyramid of shining black faces at every door and window, gazing with delight at the scene, rolling their white eye-balls, and showing grinning rows of ivory from ear to ear. How could the flogger of urchins be otherwise than animated and joyous? the lady of his heart was his partner in the dance, and smiling graciously in reply to all his amorous oglings; while Brom Bones, sorely smitten with love and jealousy, sat brooding by himself in one corner.

When the dance was at an end, Ichabod was attracted to a knot of the sager folks, who, with old Van Tassel, sat smoking at one end of the piazza, gossiping over former times, and drawling out long stories about the war.

This neighborhood, at the time of which I am speaking, was one of those highly-favored places which abound with chronicle and great men. The British and American line had run near it during the war; it had, therefore, been the scene of marauding, and infested with refugees, cow-boys,[53] and all kinds of border chivalry. Just sufficient time had elapsed to enable each story-teller to dress up his tale with a little becoming fiction, and, in the indistinctness of his recollection, to make himself the hero of every exploit.

There was the story of Doffue Martling, a large blue-bearded Dutchman, who had nearly taken a British frigate with an old iron nine-pounder[54] from a mud breast-work,[55] only that his gun burst at the sixth discharge. And there was an old gentleman who shall be nameless, being too rich a mynheer[56] to be lightly mentioned, who, in the battle of White-plains,[57] being an excellent master of defence, parried a musket ball with a small sword, insomuch that he absolutely felt it whiz round the blade, and glance off at the hilt: in proof of which, he was ready at any time to show the sword, with the hilt a little bent. There were several more that had been equally great in the field, not

[52]An early Christian martyr. He was invoked by those suffering from chorea, or "St. Vitus' Dance," a nervous disease producing involuntary jerking.

[53]Pro-British guerrillas active near New York City during the American Revolution.

[54]Cannon firing a ball weighing nine pounds. [55]Fortification built breast high.

[56]Dutch: gentleman. [57]Scene of a British victory near New York City in 1776.

one of whom but was persuaded that he had a considerable hand in bringing the war to a happy termination.

But all these were nothing to the tales of ghosts, and apparitions that succeeded. The neighborhood is rich in legendary treasures of the kind. Local tales and superstitions thrive best in these sheltered long-settled retreats; but are trampled under foot by the shifting throng that forms the population of most of our country places. Besides, there is no encouragement for ghosts in most of our villages, for they have scarcely had time to finish their first nap, and turn themselves in their graves, before their surviving friends have travelled away from the neighborhood; so that when they turn out at night to walk their rounds, they have no acquaintance left to call upon. This is perhaps the reason why we so seldom hear of ghosts except in our long-established Dutch communities.

The immediate cause, however, of the prevalence of supernatural stories in these parts, was doubtless owing to the vicinity of Sleepy Hollow. There was a contagion in the very air that blew from that haunted region; it breathed forth an atmosphere of dreams and fancies infecting all the land. Several of the Sleepy Hollow people were present at Van Tassel's, and, as usual, were doling out their wild and wonderful legends. Many dismal tales were told about funeral trains, and mournful cries and wailings heard and seen about the great tree where the unfortunate Major André[58] was taken, and which stood in the neighborhood. Some mention was made also of the woman in white, that haunted the dark glen at Raven Rock, and was often heard to shriek on winter nights before a storm, having perished there in the snow. The chief part of the stories, however, turned upon the favorite spectre of Sleepy Hollow, the headless horseman, who had been heard several times of late, patrolling the country; and, it was said, tethered his horse nightly among the graves in the church-yard.

The sequestered situation of this church seems always to have made it a favorite haunt of troubled spirits. It stands on a knoll, surrounded by locust-trees and lofty elms, from among which its decent whitewashed walls shine modestly forth, like Christian purity beaming through the shades of retirement. A gentle slope descends from it to a silver sheet of water, bordered by high trees, between which, peeps may be caught at the blue hills of the Hudson. To look upon its grass-grown yard, where the sunbeams seem to sleep so quietly, one would think that there at least the dead might rest in peace. On one side of the church extends a wide woody dell, along which raves a large brook among broken rocks and trunks of fallen trees. Over a deep black part of the stream, not far from the church, was formerly thrown a wooden bridge; the road that led to it, and the bridge itself, were thickly shaded by overhanging trees, which cast a gloom about it, even in the daytime; but occasioned a fearful darkness at night. This was one of the favorite haunts of the headless horseman; and the place where he was most frequently encountered. The tale was told of old Brouwer, a most heretical disbeliever in ghosts, how he met the horseman returning from his foray into Sleepy Hollow, and was obliged to get up behind him; how they galloped over bush and brake, over hill and swamp, until they reached the bridge;

[58]John André (1751–1780), a British spy captured and executed near Tarrytown.

when the horseman suddenly turned into a skeleton, threw old Brouwer into the brook, and sprang away over the tree-tops with a clap of thunder.

This story was immediately matched by a thrice marvellous adventure of Brom Bones, who made light of the Galloping Hessian as an arrant jockey.[59] He affirmed that, on returning one night from the neighboring village of Sing Sing,[60] he had been overtaken by this midnight trooper; that he had offered to race with him for a bowl of punch, and should have won it too, for Daredevil beat the goblin horse all hollow, but just as they came to the church bridge, the Hessian bolted, and vanished in a flash of fire.

All these tales, told in that drowsy undertone with which men talk in the dark, the countenances of the listeners only now and then receiving a casual gleam from the glare of a pipe, sank deep in the mind of Ichabod. He repaid them in kind with large extracts from his invaluable author, Cotton Mather, and added many marvellous events that had taken place in his native State of Connecticut, and fearful sights which he had seen in his nightly walks about Sleepy Hollow.

The revel now gradually broke up. The old farmers gathered together their families in their wagons, and were heard for some time rattling along the hollow roads, and over the distant hills. Some of the damsels mounted on pillions[61] behind their favorite swains, and their light-hearted laughter, mingling with the clatter of hoofs, echoed along the silent woodlands, sounding fainter and fainter until they gradually died away—and the late scene of noise and frolic was all silent and deserted. Ichabod only lingered behind according to the custom of country lovers, to have a tête-à-tête[62] with the heiress, fully convinced that he was now on the high road to success. What passed at this interview I will not pretend to say, for in fact I do not know. Something, however, I fear me, must have gone wrong, for he certainly sallied forth, after no very great interval, with an air quite desolate and chopfallen.[63]—Oh these women! these women! Could that girl have been playing off any of her coquettish tricks?—Was her encouragement of the poor pedagogue all a mere sham to secure her conquest of his rival?—Heaven only knows, not I!—Let it suffice to say, Ichabod stole forth with the air of one who had been sacking a hen-roost, rather than a fair lady's heart. Without looking to the right or left to notice the scene of rural wealth, on which he had so often gloated, he went straight to the stable, and with several hearty cuffs and kicks, roused his steed most uncourteously from the comfortable quarters in which he was soundly sleeping, dreaming of mountains of corn and oats, and whole valleys of timothy and clover.

It was the very witching time of night[64] that Ichabod, heavy-hearted and crest-fallen, pursued his travel homewards, along the sides of the lofty hills which rise above Tarry Town, and which he had traversed so cheerily in the afternoon. The hour was as dismal as himself. Far below him, the Tappan Zee spread its dusky and indistinct waste of waters, with here and there the tall mast of a sloop, riding quietly at anchor under the land. In the dead hush of

[59]Cheater. [60]Present-day Ossining.

[61]Small pad for an extra rider behind the regular horse saddle.

[62]Private conversation. [63]Slack-jawed, low in spirit.

[64]A reference to *Hamlet,* Act III, Scene ii, lines 406–408: "Tis now the very witching time of night,/When churchyards yawn, and hell itself breathes out/Contagion to this world."

midnight, he could even hear the barking of the watch dog from the opposite shore of the Hudson; but it was so vague and faint as only to give an idea of his distance from this faithful companion of man. Now and then, too, the long-drawn crowing of a cock, accidentally awakened, would sound far, far off, from some farmhouse away among the hills—but it was like a dreaming sound in his ear. No signs of life occurred near him, but occasionally the melancholy chirp of a cricket, or perhaps the guttural twang of a bull-frog, from a neighboring marsh, as if sleeping uncomfortably, and turning suddenly in his bed.

All the stories of ghosts and goblins that he had heard in the afternoon, now came crowding upon his recollection. The night grew darker and darker; the stars seemed to sink deeper in the sky, and driving clouds occasionally hid them from his sight. He had never felt so lonely and dismal. He was, moreover, approaching the very place where many of the scenes of the ghost stories had been laid. In the centre of the road stood an enormous tulip-tree, which towered like a giant above all the other trees of the neighborhood, and formed a kind of landmark. Its limbs were gnarled, and fantastic, large enough to form trunks for ordinary trees, twisting down almost to the earth, and rising again into the air. It was connected with the tragical story of the unfortunate André who had been taken prisoner hard by; and was universally known by the name of Major Andre's tree. The common people regarded it with a mixture of respect and superstition, partly out of sympathy for the fate of its ill-starred namesake, and partly from the tales of strange sights and doleful lamentations told concerning it.

As Ichabod approached this fearful tree, he began to whistle: he thought his whistle was answered—it was but a blast sweeping sharply through the dry branches. As he approached a little nearer, he thought he saw something white, hanging in the midst of the tree—he paused and ceased whistling; but on looking more narrowly, perceived that it was a place where the tree had been scathed by lightning, and the white wood laid bare. Suddenly he heard a groan—his teeth chattered and his knees smote against the saddle: it was but the rubbing of one huge bough upon another, as they were swayed about by the breeze. He passed the tree in safety, but new perils lay before him.

About two hundred yards from the tree a small brook crossed the road, and ran into a marshy and thickly-wooded glen, known by the name of Wiley's swamp. A few rough logs, laid side by side, served for a bridge over this stream. On that side of the road where the brook entered the wood, a group of oaks and chestnuts, matted thick with wild grapevines, threw a cavernous gloom over it. To pass this bridge was the severest trial. It was at this identical spot that the unfortunate André was captured, and under the covert of those chestnuts and vines were the sturdy yeomen concealed who surprised him. This has ever since been considered a haunted stream, and fearful are the feelings of the schoolboy who has to pass it alone after dark.

As he approached the stream his heart began to thump; he summoned up, however, all his resolution, gave his horse half a score of kicks in the ribs, and attempted to dash briskly across the bridge; but instead of starting forward, the perverse old animal made a lateral movement, and ran broadside against the fence. Ichabod, whose fears increased with the delay, jerked the reins on the other side, and kicked lustily with the contrary foot: it was all in vain; his steed started, it is true, but it was only to plunge to the opposite side of the road into a thicket of brambles and alder bushes. The schoolmaster now bestowed both whip and heel upon the starveling ribs of old Gunpowder, who dashed forward, snuffling and snorting, but came to a stand just by the bridge, with a suddenness that had nearly sent his rider sprawling over his head. Just at this moment a plashy tramp by the side of the bridge caught the sensitive ear of Ichabod. In the dark shadow of the grove, on the margin of the brook, he beheld something huge, misshapen, black and towering. It stirred not, but seemed gathered up in the gloom, like some gigantic monster ready to spring upon the traveller.

The hair of the affrighted pedagogue rose upon his head with terror. What was to be done? To turn and fly was now too late; and besides, what chance was there of escaping ghost or goblin, if such it was, which could ride upon the wings of the wind? Summoning up, therefore, a show of courage, he demanded in stammering accents—"Who are you?" He received no reply. He repeated his demand in a still more agitated voice. Still there was no answer. Once more he cudgelled the sides of the inflexible Gunpowder, and, shutting his eyes, broke forth with involuntary fervor into a psalm tune. Just then the shadowy object of alarm put itself in motion, and, with a scramble and a bound, stood at once in the middle of the road. Though the night was dark and dismal, yet the form of the unknown might now in some degree be ascertained. He appeared to be a horseman of large dimensions, and mounted on a black horse of powerful frame. He made no offer of molestation or sociability, but kept aloof on one side of the road, jogging along on the blind side of old Gunpowder, who had now got over his fright and waywardness.

Ichabod, who had no relish for this strange midnight companion, and bethought himself of the adventure of Brom Bones with the Galloping Hessian, now quickened his steed, in hopes of leaving him behind. The stranger, however, quickened his horse to an equal pace. Ichabod pulled up, and fell into a walk, thinking to lag behind—the other did the same. His heart began to sink within him; he endeavored to resume his psalm tune, but his parched tongue clove to the roof of his mouth, and he could not utter a stave.[65] There was something in the moody and dogged silence of this pertinacious companion, that was mysterious and appalling. It was soon fearfully accounted for. On mounting a rising ground, which brought the figure of his fellow-traveller in relief against the sky, gigantic in height, and muffled in a cloak, Ichabod was horror-struck, on perceiving that he was headless!—but his horror was still more increased, on observing that the head, which should have rested on his shoulders, was carried before him on the pommel of the saddle: his terror rose to desperation; he rained a shower of kicks and blows upon Gunpowder, hoping, by a sudden movement, to give his companion the slip—but the spectre started full jump with him. Away then they dashed, through thick and thin; stones flying, and sparks flashing at every bound. Ichabod's flimsy garments fluttered in the air, as he stretched his long lank body away over his horse's head, in the eagerness of his flight.

They had now reached the road which turns off to Sleepy Hollow; but Gunpowder, who seemed possessed with a demon, instead of keeping up it, made an opposite turn, and plunged headlong down hill to the left. This

[65]Stanza, verse.

road leads through a sandy hollow, shaded by trees for about a quarter of a mile, where it crosses the bridge famous in goblin story, and just beyond swells the green knoll on which stands the whitewashed church.

As yet the panic of the steed had given his unskillful rider an apparent advantage in the chase; but just as he had got half way through the hollow, the girths of the saddle gave way, and he felt it slipping from under him. He seized it by the pommel, and endeavored to hold it firm, but in vain; and had just time to save himself by clasping old Gunpowder round the neck, when the saddle fell to the earth, and he heard it trampled under foot by his pursuer. For a moment the terror of Hans Van Ripper's wrath passed across his mind—for it was his Sunday saddle; but this was no time for petty fears; the goblin was hard on his haunches; and (unskillful rider that he was!) he had much ado to maintain his seat; sometimes slipping on one side, sometimes on another, and sometimes jolted on the high ridge of his horse's back-bone, with a violence that he verily feared would cleave him asunder.

An opening in the trees now cheered him with the hopes that the church bridge was at hand. The wavering reflection of a silver star in the bosom of the brook told him that he was not mistaken. He saw the walls of the church dimly glaring under the trees beyond. He recollected the place where Brom Bones's ghostly competitor had disappeared. "If I can but reach that bridge," thought Ichabod, "I am safe."[66] Just then he heard the black steed panting and blowing close behind him; he even fancied that he felt his hot breath. Another convulsive kick in the ribs, and old Gunpowder sprang upon the bridge; he thundered over the resounding planks; he gained the opposite side; and now Ichabod cast a look behind to see if his pursuer should vanish, according to rule, in a flash of fire and brimstone. Just then he saw the goblin rising in his stirrups, and in the very act of hurling his head at him. Ichabod endeavored to dodge the horrible missile, but too late. It encountered his cranium with a tremendous crash—he was tumbled headlong into the dust, and Gunpowder, the black steed, and the goblin rider, passed by like a whirlwind.

The next morning the old horse was found without his saddle, and with the bridle under his feet, soberly cropping the grass at his master's gate. Ichabod did not make his appearance at breakfast—dinner-hour came, but no Ichabod. The boys assembled at the school-house, and strolled idly about the banks of the brook; but no schoolmaster. Hans Van Ripper now began to feel some uneasiness about the fate of poor Ichabod, and his saddle. An inquiry was set on foot, and after diligent investigation they came upon his traces. In one part of the road leading to the church was found the saddle trampled in the dirt; the tracks of horses' hoofs deeply dented in the road, and evidently at furious speed, were traced to the bridge, beyond which, on the bank of a broad part of the brook, where the water ran deep and black, was found the hat of the unfortunate Ichabod, and close beside it a shattered pumpkin.

The brook was searched, but the body of the schoolmaster was not to be discovered. Hans Van Ripper, as executor of his estate, examined the bundle which contained all his worldly effects. They consisted of two shirts and a half; two stocks[67] for the neck; a pair or two of worsted stockings; an old pair

[66]Evil spirits were thought to be unable to cross water.

[67]Scarves or neck bands.

of corduroy small-clothes; a rusty razor; a book of psalm tunes, full of dogs' ears;[68] and a broken pitchpipe. As to the books and furniture of the school-house, they belonged to the community, excepting Cotton Mather's History of Witchcraft, a New England Almanac, and a book of dreams and fortune-telling; in which last was a sheet of foolscap much scribbled and blotted in several fruitless attempts to make a copy of verses in honor of the heiress of Van Tassel. These magic books and the poetic scrawl were forthwith consigned to the flames by Hans Van Ripper; who from that time forward determined to send his children no more to school; observing, that he never knew any good come of this same reading and writing. Whatever money the school-master possessed, and he had received his quarter's pay but a day or two before, he must have had about his person at the time of his disappearance.

The mysterious event caused much speculation at the church on the following Sunday. Knots of gazers and gossips were collected in the churchyard, at the bridge, and at the spot where the hat and pumpkin had been found. The stories of Brouwer, of Bones, and a whole budget of others, were called to mind; and when they had diligently considered them all, and compared them with the symptoms of the present case, they shook their heads, and came to the conclusion that Ichabod had been carried off by the galloping Hessian. As he was a bachelor, and in nobody's debt, nobody troubled his head any more about him. The school was removed to a different quarter of the hollow, and another pedagogue reigned in his stead.

It is true, an old farmer, who had been down to New York on a visit several years after, and from whom this account of the ghostly adventure was received, brought home the intelligence that Ichabod Crane was still alive; that he had left the neighborhood, partly through fear of the goblin and Hans Van Ripper, and partly in mortification at having been suddenly dismissed by the heiress; that he had changed his quarters to a distant part of the country; had kept school and studied law at the same time, had been admitted to the bar, turned politician, electioneered, written for the newspapers, and finally had been made a justice of the Ten Pound Court.[69] Brom Bones too, who shortly after his rival's disappearance conducted the blooming Katrina in triumph to the altar, was observed to look exceedingly knowing whenever the story of Ichabod was related, and always burst into a hearty laugh at the mention of the pumpkin; which led some to suspect that he knew more about the matter than he chose to tell.

The old country wives, however, who are the best judges of these matters, maintain to this day that Ichabod was spirited away by supernatural means; and it is a favorite story often told about the neighborhood round the winter evening fire. The bridge became more than ever an object of superstitious awe, and that may be the reason why the road has been altered of late years, so as to approach the church by the border of the mill-pond. The school-house being deserted, soon fell to decay, and was reported to be haunted by the ghost of the unfortunate pedagogue; and the ploughboy,

[68]I.e., with many page corners bent over.

[69]Where cases involving small sums, no more than £10, were tried.

loitering homeward of a still summer evening, has often fancied his voice at a distance, chanting a melancholy psalm tune among the tranquil solitudes of Sleepy Hollow.

POSTSCRIPT

FOUND IN THE HANDWRITING OF MR. KNICKERBOCKER

THE preceding Tale is given, almost in the precise words in which I heard it related at a Corporation meeting of the ancient city of the Manhattoes,[70] at which were present many of its sagest and most illustrious burghers. The narrator was a pleasant, shabby, gentlemanly old fellow in pepper-and-salt[71] clothes, with a sadly humorous face; and one whom I strongly suspected of being poor—he made such efforts to be entertaining. When his story was concluded there was much laughter and approbation, particularly from two or three deputy aldermen, who had been asleep the greater part of the time. There was, however, one tall, dry-looking old gentleman, with beetling eyebrows, who maintained a grave and rather severe face throughout; now and then folding his arms, inclining his head, and looking down upon the floor, as if turning a doubt over in his mind. He was one of your wary men, who never laugh but upon good grounds—when they have reason and the law on their side. When the mirth of the rest of the company had subsided, and silence was restored, he leaned one arm on the elbow of his chair, and sticking the other akimbo, demanded, with a slight but exceedingly sage motion of the head and contraction of the brow, what was the moral of the story, and what it went to prove.

The story-teller, who was just putting a glass of wine to his lips, as a refreshment after his toils, paused for a moment, looked at his inquirer with an air of infinite deference, and lowering the glass slowly to the table, observed that the story was intended most logically to prove:

"That there is no situation in life but has its advantages and pleasures—provided we will but take a joke as we find it;

"That, therefore, he that runs races with goblin troopers is likely to have rough riding of it;

"Ergo, for a country schoolmaster to be refused the hand of a Dutch heiress is a certain step to high preferment in the State."

The cautious old gentleman knit his brows tenfold closer after this explanation, being sorely puzzled by the ratiocination of the syllogism; while, methought, the one in pepper-and-salt eyed him with something of a triumphant leer. At length he observed, that all this was very well, but still he thought the story a little on the extravagant—there were one or two points on which he had his doubts:

"Faith, sir," replied the story-teller, "as to that matter, I don't believe one-half of it myself."

D.K.

1819

[70]New York City. [71]Cloth woven of mixed black and white yarn.

James Fenimore Cooper 1789–1851

James Fenimore Cooper never saw the frontier. The advanced line of settlement that moved westward from the Atlantic had passed beyond Cooperstown, New York, before his birth, and throughout his life he never traveled farther west than Michigan. Yet his writing helped create a mythical West that transcended the reality of life on the frontier, and in his greatest character—Natty Bumppo, or "Leather-Stocking,"—Cooper created an archetypal Western hero whose many literary descendants range from the cowboys of the movies and popular fiction to the renegade heroes of Melville, Twain, and Faulkner.

James Cooper (he added his mother's name, Fenimore, when he was thirty-seven) was born in Burlington, New Jersey. When he was thirteen months old, he was taken with his family to a small wilderness settlement on Lake Otsego, 150 miles north of New York City. The village was named Cooperstown after his father, William Cooper, a rich member of the landed gentry who had acquired vast tracts of land in New York State following the American Revolution. James Cooper was raised in the rural luxury of the family "Manor House," and he roamed the edge of a wilderness that stretched a thousand miles to the Mississippi. Although he saw the white hunters and the numerous wagon trains of settlers that passed through Cooperstown on their way west, he saw little of the once-numerous redmen of the eastern forests. Later in life he acknowledged, "I was never among the Indians. All that I know of them is from reading, and from hearing my father speak of them."

When Cooper was fourteen he entered Yale, but in his junior year, after a series of undergraduate brawls and pranks, he was expelled and went to sea as a common sailor on an Atlantic merchant ship. In 1808 he became a midshipman in the U.S. Navy and served on Lake Ontario and later as a recruiting officer for the famous sloop Wasp, *under James Lawrence. In 1811, after the death of his father left him an inheritance of $50,000, Cooper resigned from the Navy. He then married, and began the free-spending life of a wealthy gentleman. By 1819 his inheritance was gone, and he was heavily in debt. To regain his fortunes he speculated in land, invested in a frontier store and a whaling ship, and in 1820 he began writing the fiction that eventually brought him wealth and world fame.*

According to tradition, he once tossed aside a popular sentimental novel with the comment that he could do better himself. When his family challenged him to fulfill his boast, he wrote a tale that he quickly recognized as a botch and destroyed. His second attempt was Precaution *(1820). A full-length novel of English life, written in imitation of Jane Austen and filled with the conventional sentimentality of the day's best-sellers,* Precaution *was dull, predictable, and a financial failure, but it brought Cooper recognition and helped prepare the way for his next work,* The Spy *(1821). A novel of the American Revolution,* The Spy *appealed to patriotic Americans hungry for exciting fiction that dealt with American scenes and events. It soon went through three editions; it was translated into several European languages and turned into a stage play. And it started Cooper on his career as the first eminent American novelist.*

Two years later Cooper published The Pioneers *(1823), a romance of the American frontier that was an immediate bestseller. It was the first of the "Leather-Stocking Tales," five novels of the life of Natty Bumppo. They include* The Last of the Mohicans *(1826),* The Prairie *(1827),* The Pathfinder *(1840), and* The Deerslayer *(1841). Following his success with* The Pioneers, *Cooper drew upon his own experiences and wrote* The Pilot *(1824), the first of eleven novels of the sea that he produced over a period of three decades.*

In 1826, with his financial burdens eased by the income from his writing, Cooper left America to live abroad, partly to escape his remaining debts and partly to experience what he saw as the richer context of European society. While living in Paris and London and touring the Continent, he completed seven more novels, and he received the adulation of a vast audience that read the numerous European translations of his works. In 1833, now financially independent, he returned to the United States and eventually settled in Cooperstown. There he continued his prolific writing of novels (he eventually wrote thirty-two), histories, and essays on society and politics. In his last years he entered into lengthy quarrels with the American press, which baited him for his unpopular elitist views, such as those he had presented in The American Democrat *(1838) and in two novels,* Homeward Bound *(1838) and* Home as Found *(1838). And critics increasingly complained of the deficiencies of his romances, especially his "Leather-Stocking Tales," which were criticized for their stilted dialogue, improbable plots, and flat, one-dimensional characters, particularly the sentimental heroines, whom the poet James Russell Lowell satirized in* A Fable for Critics *(1848):*

> *The women he draws from one model don't vary,*
> *All sappy as maples and flat as a prairie.*

But in spite of all his "literary offenses," which Mark Twain later attacked with merciless glee, Cooper was one of the great innovators of American literature. With The Pilot *he established a genre of accurate, detailed sea fiction.* The Spy, *with its portraits of Washington and other historical figures and events, was the beginning of the American historical novel. His frontier tales transplanted the chivalric romances of Europe to the forests of the New World and served as the forerunners of an endless series of American stagecoach and wagon-train epics.*

Patriotic, early critics honored Cooper for creating a literature out of native materials, and they hailed him as the American Scott—an apt but patronizing comparison that Cooper came to detest. His greatest achievement was his portrayal of the age-old theme of innocence struggling in a paradise lost, of frontier Americans striving in an Edenic American wilderness that, for all its nobility and grandeur, is being overwhelmed by the irresistible onrush of civilization. It was a theme embodied in the character and the actions of his archetypal hero, Natty Bumppo, whose flights from society and domesticity mark him as the first of the symbolic rebels in American writing and one of the most memorable characters in all of fiction.

FURTHER READING: An edition, *The Writings of James Fenimore Cooper,* ed. J. Beard et al., is now in preparation, of which 17 of the proposed 48 volumes have been published. *James Fenimore Cooper, Representative Selections,* ed. R. Spiller, 1936; *The Letters and Journals of James Fenimore Cooper,* ed. J. Beard, 6 vols., 1960–1968; D. Ringe, *James Fenimore Cooper,* 1962, 1988; W. Walker, *James Fenimore Cooper,* 1962; G. Dekker, *James Fenimore Cooper, The Novelist,* 1968; B. Nevius, *Cooper's Landscapes,* 1975; H. Peck, *A World by Itself, The Pastoral Moment in Cooper's Fiction,* 1977; S. Railton, *Fenimore Cooper,* 1978; A. Axelrad, *History and Utopia, a Study of the World View of James Fenimore Cooper,* 1978; W. Franklin, *The New World of James Fenimore Cooper,* 1982; *James Fenimore Cooper, New Critical Essays,* ed. R. Clark, 1985; J. Wallace, *Early Cooper and His Audience,* 1986; J. W. Motley, *The American Abraham, James Fenimore Cooper and the Frontier Patriarch,* 1987; R. Long, *James Fenimore Cooper,* 1990; C. Adams, *"The Guardian of the Law," Authority and Identity in James Fenimore Cooper,* 1990; G. Rans, *Cooper's Leather-Stocking Series, A Secular Reading,* 1991; D. Darnell, *James Fenimore Cooper, Novelist of Manners,* 1993; R. Newman, *The Gentleman in the Garden,* 2003.

TEXT: *The Works of James Fenimore Cooper,* 33 vols., 1895–1900. Some corrections have been made in spelling, punctuation, and usage.

PREFACE TO THE LEATHER-STOCKING TALES[1]

This series of Stories, which has obtained the name of "The Leather-Stocking Tales," has been written in a very desultory and inartificial manner. The order in which the several books appeared was essentially different from that in which they would have been presented to the world, had the regular course of their incidents been consulted. In "The Pioneers," the first of the series written, the Leather-Stocking is represented as already old, and driven from his early haunts in the forest, by the sound of the axe and the smoke of the settler. "The Last of the Mohicans," the next book in the order of publication, carried the readers back to a much earlier period in the history of our hero, representing him as middle-aged, and in the fullest vigor of manhood. In "The Prairie," his career terminates, and he is laid in his grave. There, it was originally the intention to leave him, in the expectation that, as in the case of the human mass, he would soon be forgotten. But a latent regard for this character induced the author to resuscitate him in "The Pathfinder," a book that was not long after succeeded by "The Deerslayer," thus completing the series as it now exists.

While the five books that have been written were originally published in the order just mentioned, that of the incidents insomuch as they are connected with the career of their principal character, is, as has been stated, very different. Taking the life of the Leather-Stocking as a guide, "The Deerslayer" should have been the opening book, for in that work he is seen just emerging into manhood; to be succeeded by "The Last of the Mohicans," "The Pathfinder," "The Pioneers," and "The Prairie." This arrangement embraces the order of events, though far from being that in which the books at first appeared. "The Pioneers" was published in 1822;[2] "The Deerslayer" in 1841; making the interval between them nineteen years. Whether these progressive years have had a tendency to lessen the value of the last-named book, by lessening the native fire of its author, or of adding somewhat in the way of improved taste and a more matured judgment, is for others to decide.

If anything from the pen of the writer of these romances is at all to outlive himself, it is, unquestionably, the series of "The Leather-Stocking Tales." To say this is not to predict a very lasting reputation for the series itself, but simply to express the belief it will outlast any, or all, of the works from the same hand.

It is undeniable that the desultory manner in which "The Leather-Stocking Tales" were written has, in a measure, impaired their harmony, and otherwise lessened their interest. This is proved by the fate of the two books last published, though probably the two most worthy an enlightened and cultivated reader's notice. If the facts could be ascertained, it is probable the result would show that of all those (in America, in particular) who have read the three first books of the series, not one in ten has a knowledge of the existence even of the two last. Several causes have tended to produce this result. The long interval of time between the appearance of "The Prairie" and that

[1]Written in 1850 for a new edition of the five "Leather-Stocking Tales," which Cooper had first published between 1823 and 1841.

[2]Actually, February 1823.

of "The Pathfinder" was itself a reason why the later books of the series should be overlooked. There was no longer novelty to attract attention, and the interest was materially impaired by the manner in which events were necessarily anticipated, in laying the last of the series first before the world. With the generation that is now coming on the stage this fault will be partially removed by the edition contained in the present work, in which the several tales will be arranged solely in reference to their connection with each other.

The author has often been asked if he had any original in his mind for the character of Leather-Stocking. In a physical sense, different individuals known to the writer in early life certainly presented themselves as models, through his recollections; but in a moral sense this man of the forest is purely a creation. The idea of delineating a character that possessed little of civilization but its highest principles as they are exhibited in the uneducated, and all of savage life that is not incompatible with these great rules of conduct, is perhaps natural to the situation in which Natty was placed. He is too proud of his origin to sink into the condition of the wild Indian, and too much a man of the woods not to imbibe as much as was at all desirable from his friends and companions. In a moral point of view it was the intention to illustrate the effect of seed scattered by the wayside. To use his own language, his "gifts" were "white gifts," and he was not disposed to bring on them discredit. On the other hand, removed from nearly all the temptations of civilized life, placed in the best associations of that which is deemed savage, and favorably disposed by nature to improve such advantages, it appeared to the writer that his hero was a fit subject to represent the better qualities of both conditions, without pushing either to extremes.

There was no violent stretch of the imagination, perhaps, in supposing one of civilized associations in childhood retaining many of his earliest lessons amid the scenes of the forest. Had these early impressions, however, not been sustained by continued though casual connection with men of his own color, if not of his own caste, all our information goes to show he would soon have lost every trace of his origin. It is believed that sufficient attention was paid to the particular circumstances in which this individual was placed, to justify the picture of his qualities that has been drawn. The Delawares early attracted the attention of the missionaries, and were a tribe unusually influenced by their precepts and example. In many instances they became Christians, and cases occurred in which their subsequent lives gave proof of the efficacy of the great moral changes that had taken place within them.

A leading character in a work of fiction has a fair right to the aid which can be obtained from a poetical view of the subject. It is in this view, rather than in one more strictly circumstantial, that Leather-Stocking has been drawn. The imagination has no great task in portraying to itself a being removed from the every-day inducements to err which abound in civilized life, while he retains the best and simplest of his early impressions; who sees God in the forest; hears him in the winds; bows to him in the firmament that o'ercanopies all; submits to his sway in a humble belief of his justice and mercy—in a word, a being who finds the impress of the Deity in all the works of nature, without any of the blots produced by the expedients, and passion, and mistakes of man. This is the most that has been attempted in the character of Leather-Stocking. Had this been done without any of the drawbacks of humanity, the picture would have been, in all probability, more pleasing than just. In order to preserve the *vraisemblable*,[3] therefore, traits derived from the prejudices, tastes, and even the weaknesses of his youth, have been mixed up with these higher qualities and longings, in a way, it is hoped, to represent a reasonable picture of human nature, without offering to the spectator a "monster of goodness."

It has been objected to these books that they give a more favorable picture of the red man than he deserves. The writer apprehends that much of this objection arises from the habits of those who have made it. One of his critics, on the appearance of the first work in which Indian character was portrayed, objected that its "characters were Indians of the school of Heckewelder,[4] rather than of the school of nature." These words quite probably contain the substance of the true answer to the objection. Heckewelder was an ardent, benevolent missionary, bent on the good of the red man, and seeing in him one who had the soul, reason, and characteristics of a fellow-being. The critic is understood to have been a very distinguished agent of the government, one very familiar with Indians, as they are seen at the councils to treat for the sale of their lands, where little or none of their domestic qualities come in play, and where, indeed, their evil passions are known to have the fullest scope. As just would it be to draw conclusions of the general state of American society from the scenes of the capitol, as to suppose that the negotiating of one of these treaties is a fair picture of Indian life.

It is the privilege of all writers of fiction, more particularly when their works aspire to the elevation of romances, to present the *beau-idéal*[5] of their characters to the reader. This it is which constitutes poetry, and to suppose that the red man is to be represented only in the squalid misery or in the degraded moral state that certainly more or less belongs to his condition, is, we apprehend, taking a very narrow view of an author's privileges. Such criticism would have deprived the world of even Homer.

1850 1850

from *THE DEERSLAYER*

from CHAPTER I

[YOUNG LEATHER-STOCKING][1]

The incidents of this tale occurred between the years 1740 and 1745, when the settled portions of the Colony of New York were confined to the four Atlantic counties, a narrow belt of country on each side of the Hudson,

[3]French: verisimilitude.

[4]John Gottlieb Heckewelder (1743–1823), a Moravian missionary to the Indians. His *Account of the History, Manners, and Customs of the Indian Nations Who Once Inhabited Pennsylvania and the Neighboring States* (1819) was Cooper's chief source of information on the Indians.

[5]French: ideal of beauty.

[1]Titles in brackets have been supplied by the editor.

extending from its mouth to the falls near its head, and to a few advanced "neighborhoods" on the Mohawk and the Schoharie. Broad belts of the virgin wilderness, not only reached the shores of the first river, but they even crossed it, stretching away into New England, and affording forest cover to the noiseless moccasin of the native warrior, as he trod the secret and bloody war-path. A bird's eye view of the whole region east of the Mississippi, must then have offered one vast expanse of woods, relieved by a comparatively narrow fringe of cultivation along the sea, dotted by the glittering surfaces of lakes, and intersected by the waving lines of rivers. In such a vast picture of solemn solitude, the district of country we design to paint, sinks into insignificance, though we feel encouraged to proceed by the conviction that, with slight and immaterial distinctions, he who succeeds in giving an accurate idea of any portion of this wild region, must necessarily convey a tolerably correct notion of the whole.

Whatever may be the changes produced by man, the eternal round of the seasons is unbroken. Summer and winter, seed time and harvest, return in their stated order, with a sublime precision, affording to man one of the noblest of all the occasions he enjoys of proving the high powers of his far reaching mind, in compassing the laws that control their exact uniformity, and in calculating their never ending revolutions. Centuries of summer suns had warmed the tops of the same noble oaks and pines, sending their heats even to the tenacious roots, when voices were heard calling to each other, in the depths of a forest, of which the leafy surface lay bathed in the brilliant light of a cloudless day in June, while the trunks of the trees rose in gloomy grandeur in the shades beneath. The calls were in different tones, evidently proceeding from two men who had lost their way, and were searching in different directions for their path. At length a shout proclaimed success, and presently a man of gigantic mould broke out of the tangled labyrinth of a small swamp, emerging into an opening that appeared to have been formed partly by the ravages of the wind, and partly by those of fire. This little area, which afforded a good view of the sky, although it was pretty well filled with dead trees, lay on the side of one of the high hills, or low mountains, into which nearly the whole surface of the adjacent country was broken.

"Here is room to breathe in!" exclaimed the liberated forester, as soon as he found himself under a clear sky, shaking his huge frame like a mastiff that has just escaped from a snow bank; "Hurrah! Deerslayer; here is day-light, at last, and yonder is the lake, itself."

These words were scarcely uttered when the second forester dashed aside the bushes of the swamp, and appeared in the area. After making a hurried adjustment of his arms and disordered dress, he joined his companion, who had already begun his dispositions for a halt.

"Do you know this spot?" demanded the one called Deerslayer, "or do you shout at the sight of the sun?"

"Both, lad, both; I know the spot, and am not sorry to see so useful a friend as the sun. Now we have got the p'ints of the compass in our minds, once more, and 'twill be our own faults if we let any thing turn them topsy turvy, ag'in, as has just happened. My name is not Hurry Harry, if this be not the very spot where the land-hunters 'camped the last summer, and passed a week. See, yonder are the dead bushes of their bower, and here is the spring. Much as I like the sun, boy, I've no occasion for it to tell me it is noon; this stomach of mine is as good a timepiece as is to be found in the colony, and it already p'ints to half past twelve. So open the wallet,[2] lad, and let us wind up for another six hours' run."

At this suggestion both set themselves about making the preparations necessary for their usual frugal, but hearty, meal. We will profit by this pause in the discourse to give the reader some idea of the appearance of the men, each of whom is destined to enact no insignificant part in our legend. It would not have been easy to find a more noble specimen of vigorous manhood, than was offered in the person of him who called himself Hurry Harry. His real name was Henry March, but the frontiermen having caught the practice of giving *sobriquets,*[3] from the Indians, the appellation of Hurry was far oftener applied to him than his proper designation, and not unfrequently he was termed Hurry Skurry, a nick-name he had obtained from a dashing, reckless, off-hand manner, and a physical restlessness that kept him so constantly on the move, as to cause him to be known along the whole line of scattered habitations that lay between the province and the Canadas. The stature of Hurry Harry exceeded six feet four, and being unusually well proportioned, his strength fully realized the idea created by his gigantic frame. The face did no discredit to the rest of the man, for it was both good-humoured and handsome. His air was free, and though his manner necessarily partook of the rudeness of a border life, the grandeur that pervaded so noble a physique prevented it from becoming altogether vulgar.

Deerslayer, as Hurry called his companion, was a very different person in appearance, as well as in character. In stature, he stood about six feet in his moccasins, but his frame was comparatively light and slender, showing muscles, however, that promised unusual agility, if not unusual strength. His face would have had little to recommend it except youth, were it not for an expression that seldom failed to win upon those who had leisure to examine it, and to yield to the feeling of confidence it created. This expression was simply that of guileless truth, sustained by an earnestness of purpose, and a sincerity of feeling, that rendered it remarkable. At times this air of integrity seemed to be so simple as to awaken the suspicion of a want of the usual means to discriminate between artifice and truth, but few came in serious contact with the man, without losing this distrust in respect for his opinions and motives.

Both these frontiermen were still young, Hurry having reached the age of six or eight and twenty, while Deerslayer was several years his junior. Their attire needs no particular description, though it may be well to add that it was composed in no small degree of dressed deer skin, and had the usual signs of belonging to those who passed their time between the skirts of civilized society and the boundless forests. There was, notwithstanding, some attention to smartness and the picturesque in the arrangements of Deerslayer's dress, more particularly to the part connected with his arms and accoutrements. His rifle was in perfect condition, the handle of his hunting knife was neatly carved, his powder horn was ornamented with suitable devices lightly cut into the material, and his shot-pouch was decorated with wampum. On the other hand, Hurry Harry, either from constitutional recklessness, or from a

[2]Bag, backpack. [3]Nicknames.

secret consciousness how little his appearance required artificial aids, wore every thing in a careless, slovenly manner, as if he felt a noble scorn for the trifling accessories of dress and ornaments. Perhaps the peculiar effect of his fine form and great stature was increased, rather than lessened, by this unstudied and disdainful air of indifference.

"Come, Deerslayer, fall to, and prove that you have a Delaware stomach, as you say you have had a Delaware edication,"[4] cried Hurry, setting the example, by opening his mouth to receive a slice of cold venison steak, that would have made an entire meal for a European peasant. "Fall to, lad, and prove your manhood, on this poor devil of a doe, with your teeth, as you've already done with your rifle."

"Nay—nay, Hurry, there's little manhood in killing a doe, and that, too, out of season; though there might be some, in bringing down a painter, or a catamount,"[5] returned the other disposing himself to comply. "The Delawares have given me my name, not so much on account of a bold heart, as on account of a quick eye, and an act*y*ve foot. There may not be any coward*y*ce, in overcoming a deer, but sartain it is, there's no great valour."

"The Delawares, themselves, are no heroes," muttered Hurry through his teeth, the mouth being too full to permit it to be fairly opened, "or, they would never have allowed them loping vagabonds, the Mingos,[6] to make them women."

"That matter is not rightly understood—has never been rightly explained," said Deerslayer earnestly, for he was as zealous a friend, as his companion was dangerous as an enemy. "The Mengwe[7] fill the woods with their lies, and misconstruct words and treaties. I have now lived ten years with the Delawares, and know them to be as manful as any other nation, when the proper time to strike comes."

"Harkee, Master Deerslayer, since we are on the subject, we may as well open our minds to each other in a man to man way; answer me one question; you have had so much luck among the game as to have gotten a title, it would seem, but did you ever hit any thing human, or intelligible: did you ever pull trigger on an inimy that was capable of pulling one upon you?"

This question produced a singular collision between mortification and correct feeling, in the bosom of the youth, that was easily to be traced in the workings of his ingenuous countenance. The struggle was short, however, uprightness of heart soon getting the better of false pride, and frontier boastfulness.

"To own the truth, I never did," answered Deerslayer, "seeing that a fitting occasion never offered. The Delawares have been peaceable since my sojourn with 'em, and I hold it to be onlawful to take the life of man, except in open and ginerous warfare."

[4]Natty Bumppo had lived among the Delaware Indians, who gave him the name Deerslayer. The Delawares, one of the Algonquian tribes, had been named by English colonists who confronted them first on the Delaware River.

[5]"A panther, or a mountain lion."

[6]An Algonquian word meaning "the treacherous ones," used by the Delawares to describe their enemies, the Iroquois.

[7]A variant of "Mingos."

"What!—Did you never find a fellow thieving among your traps and skins, and do the law on him, with your own hands, by way of saving the magistrates trouble, in the settlements, and the rogue himself the costs of the suit?"

"I am no trapper, Hurry," returned the young man proudly. "I live by the rifle, a we'pon at which I will not turn my back on any man of my years, atween the Hudson and the St. Lawrence. I never offer a skin, that has not a hole in its head, besides them which natur' made to see with, or to breathe through."

"Ay—ay—this is all very well, in the animal way, though it makes but a poor figure along side of scalps and and-bushes. Shooting an Indian from an and-bush is acting up to his own principles, and now we have what you call a lawful war, on our hands, the sooner you wipe that disgrace off your character, the sounder will be your sleep; if it only come from knowing there is one inimy the less prowling in the woods. I shall not frequent your society long, friend Natty, unless you look higher than four footed beasts to practyse your rifle on."

"Our journey is nearly ended you say, Master March, and we can part to-night, if you see occasion. I have a fri'nd waiting for me, who will think it no disgrace to consart with a fellow creatur' that has never yet slain his kind."

"I wish I knew what has brought that skulking Delaware into this part of the country, so early in the season"—muttered Hurry to himself, in a way to show equally distrust, and a recklessness of its betrayal. "Where did you say, the young chief was to give you the meeting?"

"At a small round rock, near the foot of the lake, where they tell me the tribes are given to resorting to make their treaties, and to bury their hatchets. This rock have I often heard the Delawares mention, though lake and rock are equally strangers to me. The country is claimed by both Mingos and Mohicans, and is a sort of common territory to fish and hunt through, in times of peace, though what it may become in wartime, the Lord only knows!"

"Common territory!" exclaimed Hurry, laughing aloud. "I should like to know what Floating Tom Hutter would say to that? He claims the lake as his own property, in vartue of fifteen years' possession, and will not be likely to give it up to either Mingo or Delaware, without a battle for it."

"And what will the Colony say to such a quarrel—all this country must have some owner, the gentry pushing their cravings into the wilderness, even where they never dare to ventur' in their own parsons to look at the land they own."

"That may do in other quarters of the colony, Deerslayer, but it will not do here. Not a human being, the Lord excepted, owns a foot of s'ile, in this part of the country. Pen was never put to paper, consarning either hill or valley, hereaway, as I've heard old Tom say, time and ag'in, and so he claims the best right to it of any man breathing; and what Tom claims, he'll be very likely to maintain."

"By what I've heard you say, Hurry, this Floating Tom must be an oncommon mortal; neither Mingo, Delaware, nor Pale Face. His possession, too, has been long, by your tell, and altogether beyond frontier endurance. What's the man's history and human natur'?"

"Why as to old Tom's human natur' it is not much like other men's human natur', but more like a muskrat's human natur', seeing that he takes more to the ways of that animal than to the ways of any other fellow creatur'. Some think he was a free liver on the salt-water in his youth, and a companion of a sartain Kidd, who was hanged for piracy, long afore you and I were born, or acquainted, and that he came up into these regions, thinking that the King's cruisers[8] could never cross the mountains, and that he might enjoy the plunder peaceably in the woods."

"There he was wrong, Hurry; very wrong. A man can enjoy plunder *peaceably* no where."

"That's much as his turn of mind may happen to be. I've known them that never could enjoy it at all, unless it was in the midst of a jollification, and them ag'in that enjoyed it best in a corner. Some men have no peace if they don't find plunder, and some if they do. Human natur' is crooked in these matters. Old Tom seems to belong to neither set, as he enjoys his, if plunder he has really got, with his darters, in a very quiet and comfortable way, and wishes for no more."

"Ay, he has darters, too; I've heard the Delawares, who've hunted this-a-way, tell their histories of these young women. Is there no mother, Hurry?"

"There was *once*, as in reason; but she has now been dead and sunk these two good years."

"Anan?"[9] said Deerslayer, looking up at his companion in a little surprise.

"Dead and sunk, I say, and I hope that's good English. The old fellow lowered his wife into the lake, by way of seeing the last of her, as I can testify, being an eye-witness of the ceremony; but whether Tom did it to save digging, which is no easy job among roots, or out of a consait that water washes away sin sooner than 'arth, is more than I can say."

"Was the poor woman oncommon wicked, that her husband should take so much pains with her body?"

"Not onreasonable; though she had her faults. I consider Judith Hutter to have been as graceful, and about as likely to make a good ind, as any woman who had lived so long beyond the sound of church bells, and I conclude old Tom sunk her as much by way of *saving* pains, as by way of *taking* it. There was a little steel in her temper, it's true, and as old Hutter is pretty much flint, they struck out sparks once and awhile, but, on the whole, they might be said to live amicable like. When they did kindle, the listeners got some such insights into their past lives, as one gets into the darker parts of the woods, when a stray gleam of sunshine finds its way down to the roots of the trees. But Judith I shall always esteem, as it's recommend enough to one woman to be the mother of such a creatur' as her darter, Judith Hutter!"

"Ay, Judith was the name the Delawares mentioned, though it was pronounced after a fashion of their own. From their discourse I do not think the girl would much please my fancy."

"Thy fancy!" exclaimed March, taking fire equally at the indifference and at the presumption of his companion, "what the devil have you to do with a fancy, and that too consarning one like Judith? You are but a boy—a sapling that has scarce got root—Judith has had *men* among her suitors, ever since she was fifteen; which is now near five years; and will not be apt to cast even a look upon a half grown creatur' like you!"

[8]Officers of the royal colonial government.
[9]"What?"

"It is June, and there is not a cloud atween us and the sun, Hurry, so all this heat is not wanted," answered the other, altogether undisturbed; "any one may have a fancy, and a squirrel has a right to make up his mind touching a catamount."

"Ay, but it might not be wise, always, to let the catamount know it," growled March. "But you're young and thoughtless, and I'll overlook your ignorance. Come, Deerslayer," he added, with a good-natured laugh, after pausing a moment to reflect, "come, Deerslayer, we are sworn fri'nds, and will not quarrel about a light-minded, jilting jade,[10] just because she happens to be handsome; more especially as you have never seen her. Judith is only for a man whose teeth show the full marks, and it's foolish to be afeard of a boy. What *did* the Delawares say of the hussy; for, an Indian, after all, has his notions of womankind, as well as a white man?"

"They said she was fair to look on, and pleasant of speech; but over-given to admirers, and light-minded."

"They are devils incarnate! After all, what schoolmaster is a match for an Indian, in looking into natur'? Some people think they are only good on a trail, or the war-path, but I say that they are philosophers, and understand a man, as well as they understand a beaver, and a woman as well as they understand either. Now that's Judith's character to a riband![11] To own the truth to you, Deerslayer, I should have married the gal two years since, if it had not been for two particular things, one of which was this very light-mindedness."

"And what may have been the other?" demanded the hunter, who continued to eat like one that took very little interest in the subject.

"T' other was an insartainty about her having *me.* The hussy is handsome, and she knows it. Boy, not a tree that is growing in these hills is straighter, or waves in the wind with an easier bend, nor did you ever see the doe that bounded with a more nat'ral motion. If that was all, every tongue would sound her praises; but she has such failings that I find it hard to overlook them, and sometimes I swear I'll never visit the lake ag'in."

"Which is the reason that you always come back? Nothing is ever made more sure by swearing about it."

"Ah, Deerslayer, you are a novelty in these partic'lars; keeping as true to edication as if you had never left the settlements. With me the case is different, and I never want to clinch an idee, that I do not feel a wish to swear about it. If you know'd all that I know consarning Judith, you'd find a justification for a little cussing. Now, the officers sometimes stray over to the lake, from the forts on the Mohawk, to fish and hunt, and then the creatur' seems beside herself! You can see it in the manner in which she wears her finery, and the airs she gives herself with the gallants."

"That is unseemly in a poor man's darter," returned Deerslayer gravely, "the officers are all gentry, and can only look on such as Judith with evil intentions."

"There's the unsartainty, and the damper! I have my misgivings about a particular captain, and Jude has no one to blame but her own folly, if I'm wrong. On the whole, I wish to look upon her as modest and becoming, and

[10]An ill-tempered woman, a shrew.
[11]Ribbon.

yet the clouds that drive among these hills are not more unsartain. Not a dozen white men have ever laid eyes upon her, since she was a child, and yet her airs, with two or three of these officers, are extinguishers!"

"I would think no more of such a woman, but turn my mind altogether to the forest; *that* will not deceive you, being ordered and ruled by a hand that never wavers."

"If you know'd Judith, you would see how much easier it is to say this, than it would be to do it. Could I bring my mind to be easy about the officers, I would carry the gal off to the Mohawk by force, make her marry me in spite of her whiffling, and leave old Tom to the care of Hetty, his other child, who, if she be not as handsome, or as quick-witted as her sister, is much the most dutiful."

"Is there another bird in the same nest?" asked Deerslayer, raising his eyes with a species of half-awakened curiosity—"The Delawares spoke to me only of one."

"That's nat'ral enough, when Judith Hutter and Hetty Hutter are in question. Hetty is only comely, while her sister, I tell thee, boy, is such another as is not to be found atween this and the sea; Judith is as full of wit, and talk, and cunning, as an old Indian orator, while poor Hetty, is at the best but 'compass meant us.'"[12]

"Anan?" inquired, again, the Deerslayer.

"Why, what the officers call, 'compass meant us,' which I understand to signify that she means always to go in the right direction, but sometimes does'nt know how. 'Compass' for the p'int, and 'meant us' for the intention. No, poor Hetty, is what I call on the varge of ignorance, and sometimes she stumbles on one side of the line, and sometimes on t'other."

"Them are beings that the Lord has in his 'special care," said Deerslayer, solemnly, "for he looks carefully to all who fall short of their proper share of reason. The Redskins honor and respect them who are so gifted, knowing that the Evil Spirit delights more to dwell in an artful body, than in one that has no cunning to work upon."

"I'll answer for it, then, that he will not remain long with poor Hetty—for the child is just 'compass meant us,' as I have told you. Old Tom has a feeling for the gal, and so has Judith, quick witted and glorious as she is herself; else would I not answer for her being altogether safe among the sort of men that sometimes meet on the lake shore."

"I thought this water an onknown and little frequented sheet," observed the Deerslayer, evidently uneasy at the idea of being too near the world.

"It's all that, lad, the eyes of twenty white men never having been laid on it; still, twenty true bred frontiermen—hunters, and trappers, and scouts, and the like,—can do a deal of mischief if they try. 'Twould be an awful thing to me, Deerslayer, did I find Judith married, after an absence of six months!"

"Have you the gal's faith, to incourage you to hope otherwise?"

"Not at all. I know not how it is—I'm good-looking, boy; that much I can see in any spring on which the sun shines—and yet I could never get the hussy to a promise, or even a cordial willing smile, though she will laugh by

[12]I.e., *non compos mentis,* Latin: "not having control of the mind."

the hour. If she *has* dared to marry in my absence, she'll be like to know the pleasures of widowhood, afore she is twenty!"

"You would not harm the man she had chosen, Hurry, simply because she found him more to her liking than yourself?"

"Why not? If an inimy crosses my path, will I not beat him out of it! Look at me—am I a man like to let any sneaking, crawling, skin-trader, get the better of me in a matter that touches me as near as the kindness of Judith Hutter? Besides, when we live beyond law, we must be our own judges and executioners. And if a man *should* be found dead in the woods, who is there to say who slew him, even admitting that the Colony took the matter in hand, and made a stir about it?"

"If that man should be Judith Hutter's husband, after what has passed, I might tell enough, at least, to put the Colony on the trail."

"You!—half-grown, venison hunting bantling![13] You, dare to think of informing against Hurry-Harry in so much as a matter touching a mink, or a woodchuck!"

"I would dare to speak truth, Hurry, consarning you, or any man that ever lived."

March looked at his companion, for a moment, in silent amazement; then seizing him by the throat, with both hands, he shook his comparatively slight frame, with a violence that menaced the dislocation of some of the bones. Nor was this done jocularly, for anger flashed from the giant's eyes, and there were certain signs, that seemed to threaten much more earnestness than the occasion would appear to call for. Whatever might be the real intention of March, and it is probable there was none settled in his mind, it is certain that he was unusually aroused, and most men who found themselves throttled by one of a mould so gigantic, in such a mood, and in a solitude so deep and helpless, would have felt intimidated, and tempted to yield even the right. Not so, however, with Deerslayer. His countenance remained unmoved; his hand did not shake, and his answer was given in a voice that did not resort to the artifice of louder tones, even, by way of proving its owner's resolution.

"You may shake, Hurry, until you bring down the mountain," he said quietly, "but nothing beside truth will you shake from me. It is probable that Judith Hutter has no husband to slay, and you may never have a chance to way lay one, else would I tell her of your threat, in the first conversation I held with the gal."

March released his gripe, and sat regarding the other, in silent astonishment.

"I thought we had been friends," he at length added—"but you've got the last secret of mine, that will ever enter your ears."

"I want none, if they are to be like this. I know we live in the woods, Hurry, and are thought to be beyond human laws—and perhaps we are so, in fact, whatever it may be in right—but there is a law, and a law maker, that rule across the whole continent. He that flies in the face of either, need not call me fri'nd."

[13]Babe, young child.

"Damme, Deerslayer, if I do not believe you are, at heart, a Moravian,[14] and no fair minded, plain dealing hunter, as you've pretended to be!"

"Fair minded or not, Hurry, you will find me as plain-dealing in deeds, as I am in words. But this giving way to sudden anger is foolish, and proves how little you have sojourned with the red men. Judith Hutter no doubt is still single, and you spoke but as the tongue ran, and not as the heart felt. There's my hand, and we will say and think no more about it."

Hurry seemed more surprised than ever; then he burst forth in a loud good-natured laugh, which brought tears to his eyes. After this, he accepted the offered hand, and the parties became friends.

"'Twould have been foolish to quarrel about an idee," March cried, as he resumed his meal, "and more like lawyers in the towns, than like sensible men in the woods. They tell me, Deerslayer, much ill blood grows out of idees, among the people in the lower counties, and that they sometimes get to extremities upon them."

"That do they—that do they, and about other matters that might better be left to take care of themselves. I have heard the Moravians say that there are lands in which men quarrel even consarning their religion, and if they can get their tempers up on such a subject, Hurry, the Lord have marcy on 'em. Howsever, there is no occasion for our following their example, and more especially about a husband that this Judith Hutter may never see, or never wish to see. For my part, I feel more cur'osity about the feeble-witted sister, than about your beauty. There's something that comes close to a man's feelin's, when he meets with a fellow creatur' that has all the outward show of an accountable mortal, and who fails of being what he seems, only through a lack of reason. This is bad enough in a man, but when it comes to a woman, and she a young, and may-be a winning creatur', it touches all the pitiful thoughts his natur' has. God knows, Hurry, that such poor things be defenceless enough with all their wits about 'em; but it's a cruel fortun' when that great protector and guide fails 'em."

"Harkee, Deerslayer, you know what the hunters, and trappers, and peltrymen in general be, and their best friends will not deny that they are headstrong and given to having their own way without much bethinking 'em of other people's rights, or feelin's, and yet I don't think the man is to be found, in all this region, who would harm Hetty Hutter, if he could; no, not even a red skin."

"Therein, fri'nd Hurry, you do the Delawares at least, and all their allied tribes only justice, for a red skin looks upon a being thus struck by God's power, as especially under his care. I rejoice to hear what you say, howsever, I rejoice to hear it, but as the sun is beginning to turn towards the a'ternoon's sky, had we not better strike the trail ag'in, and make forward that we may get an opportunity of seeing these wonderful sisters."

Harry March giving a cheerful assent, the remnants of the meal were soon collected; then the travellers shouldered their packs, resumed their arms, and quitting the little area of light, they again plunged into the deep shadows of the forest.

[14]Later in the novel, Natty Bumppo describes his early training by the Christian missionaries of the Moravian Church in America.

from CHAPTER VII

[DEERSLAYER KILLS A MINGO]

Deerslayer's attention was first given to the canoe ahead.[1] It was already quite near the point, and a very few strokes of the paddle sufficed to tell him that it must touch before he could possibly overtake it. Just at this moment, too, the wind inopportunely freshened, rendering the drift of the light craft much more rapid and certain. Feeling the impossibility of preventing a contact with the land, the young man wisely determined not to heat himself with unnecessary exertions, but, first looking to the priming of his piece, he proceeded slowly and warily towards the point, taking care to make a little circuit, that he might be exposed on only one side, as he approached.

The canoe adrift, being directed by no such intelligence, pursued its proper way, and grounded on a small sunken rock, at the distance of three or four yards from the shore. Just at that moment, Deerslayer had got abreast of the point, and turned the bows of his own boat to the land; first casting loose his tow, that his movements might be unencumbered. The canoe hung an instant on the rock, then it rose a hair's breadth on an almost imperceptible swell of the water, swung round, floated clear, and reached the strand. All this the young man noted, but it neither quickened his pulses, nor hastened his hand. If any one had been lying in wait for the arrival of the waif, he must be seen, and the utmost caution in approaching the shore became indispensable. If no one was in ambush, hurry was unnecessary. The point being nearly diagonally opposite to the Indian encampment, he hoped the last, though the former was not only possible, but probable; for the savages were prompt in adopting all the expedients of their particular modes of warfare, and quite likely had many scouts searching the shores for craft to carry them off to the castle. As a glance at the lake from any height, or projection, would expose the smallest object on its surface, there was little hope that either of the canoes could pass unseen, and Indian sagacity needed no instruction to tell which way a boat, or a log, would drift, when the direction of the wind was known.

As Deerslayer drew nearer and nearer to the land, the stroke of his paddle grew slower, his eye became more watchful, and his ears and nostrils almost dilated with the effort to detect any lurking danger. 'Twas a trying moment for a novice, nor was there the encouragement which even the timid sometimes feel, when conscious of being observed and commended. He was entirely alone, thrown on his own resources, and was cheered by no friendly eye, emboldened by no encouraging voice. Notwithstanding all these circumstances, the most experienced veteran in forest warfare could not have behaved better. Equally free from recklessness and hesitation, his advance was marked by a sort of philosophical prudence, that appeared to render

[1]Hurry Harry and Tom Hutter, while seeking to take Indian scalps for bounty money, have been captured by hostile Huron (Iroquois) Indians. Deerslayer has set out in a canoe to recover another canoe adrift on Lake Glimmerglass, hoping thereby to keep the Hurons from using it to attack Tom Hutter's "castle," a log blockhouse built on a shoal in the middle of the lake.

him superior to all motions but those which were best calculated to effect his purpose. Such was the commencement of a career in forest exploits, that afterwards rendered this man, in his way, and under the limits of his habits and opportunities, as renowned as many a hero whose name has adorned the pages of works more celebrated than legends simple as ours can ever become.

When about a hundred yards from the shore, Deerslayer rose in the canoe, gave three or four vigorous strokes with the paddle, sufficient of themselves to impel the bark to land, and then quickly laying aside the instrument of labor, he seized that of war. He was in the very act of raising the rifle, when a sharp report, was followed by the buzz of a bullet that passed so near his body, as to cause him involuntarily to start. The next instant Deerslayer staggered, and fell his whole length in the bottom of the canoe. A yell—it came from a single voice—followed, and an Indian leaped from the bushes, upon the open area of the point, bounding towards the canoe. This was the moment the young man desired. He rose on the instant, and levelled his own rifle, at his uncovered foe; but his finger hesitated about pulling the trigger on one whom he held at such a disadvantage. This little delay, probably saved the life of the Indian, who bounded back into the cover, as swiftly as he had broken out of it. In the mean time Deerslayer had been swiftly approaching the land, and his own canoe reached the point just as his enemy disappeared. As its movements had not been directed, it touched the shore a few yards from the other boat, and though the rifle of his foe had to be loaded, there was not time to secure his prize, and to carry it beyond danger, before he would be exposed to another shot. Under the circumstances, therefore, he did not pause an instant, but dashed into the woods and sought a cover.

On the immediate point there was a small open area, partly in native grass, and partly beach, but a dense fringe of bushes lined its upper side. This narrow belt of dwarf vegetation passed, one issued immediately into the high, and gloomy vaults of the forest. The land was tolerably level for a few hundred feet, and then it rose precipitously in a mountain side. The trees were tall, large, and so free from underbrush, that they resembled vast columns, irregularly scattered, upholding a dome of leaves. Although they stood tolerably close together, for their ages and size, the eye could penetrate to considerable distances, and bodies of men, even, might have engaged beneath their cover, with concert and intelligence.

Deerslayer knew that his adversary must be employed in reloading, unless he had fled. The former proved to be the case, for the young man had no sooner placed himself behind a tree, than he caught a glimpse of the arm of the Indian, his body being concealed by an oak, in the very act of forcing the leathered bullet home. Nothing would have been easier than to spring forward and decide the affair by a close assault on his unprepared foe, but every feeling of Deerslayer revolted at such a step, although his own life had just been attempted from a cover. He was as yet unpractised in the ruthless expedients of savage warfare, of which he knew nothing except by tradition and theory, and it struck him as an unfair advantage to assail an unarmed foe. His colour had heightened, his eye frowned, his lips were compressed, and all his energies were collected and ready, but, instead of advancing to fire, he dropped his rifle to the usual position of a sportsman in readiness to catch his aim, and muttered to himself, unconscious that he was speaking—

"No—no—that may be red-skin warfare, but it's not a christian's gifts. Let the miscreant charge, and then we'll take it out like men; for the canoe he *must* not and *shall* not have. No—no; let him have time to load, and then God will take care of the right!"

All this time the Indian had been so intent on his own movements, that he was even ignorant that his enemy was in the wood. His only apprehension was that the canoe would be recovered and carried away, before he might be in readiness to prevent it. He had sought the cover from habit, but was within a few feet of the fringe of bushes, and could be at the margin of the forest, in readiness to fire in a moment. The distance between him and his enemy was about fifty yards, and the trees were so arranged by nature that the line of sight was not interrupted, except by the particular tree behind which each party stood.

His rifle was no sooner loaded, than the savage glanced around him, and advanced, incautiously as regarded the real, but stealthily as respected the fancied position of his enemy, until he was fairly exposed. Then Deerslayer stepped from behind his own cover, and hailed him.

"This-a-way, red-skin; this-a-way, if you're looking for me," he called out. "I'm young in war, but not so young as to stand on an open beach to be shot down like an owl by day-light. It rests on yourself whether it's peace, or war, atween us, for my gifts are white gifts, and I'm not one of them that thinks it valiant to slay human mortals singly, in the woods."

The savage was a good deal startled by this sudden discovery of the danger he run. He had a little knowledge of English, however, and caught the drift of the other's meaning. He was also too well schooled to betray alarm, but dropping the butt of his rifle to the earth, with an air of confidence, he made a gesture of lofty courtesy. All this was done with the ease and self possession of one accustomed to consider no man his superior. In the midst of this consummate acting, however, the volcano that raged within, caused his eyes to glare, and his nostrils to dilate, like those of some wild beast, that is suddenly prevented from taking the fatal leap.

"Two canoe," he said, in the deep guttural tones of his race, holding up the number of fingers he mentioned, by way of preventing mistakes—"one for you—one for me."

"No—no—Mingo, that will never do. You own neither; and neither shall you have, as long as I can prevent it. I know it's war atween your people and mine, but that's no reason why human mortals should slay each other, like savage creatur's, that meet in the woods; go your way then, and leave me to go mine. The world is large enough for us both, and when we meet fairly in battle, why the Lord will order the fate of each of us."

"Good!" exclaimed the Indian—"My brother, missionary—great talk; all about Manitou."[2]

"Not so—not so, warrior. I'm not good enough for the Moravians, and am too good for most of the other vagabonds that preach about in the woods. No—no—I'm only a hunter as yet, though afore the peace is made, 'tis like enough there'll be occasion to strike a blow at some of your people. Still I

[2]The Great Spirit.

wish it to be done in fair fight, and not in a quarrel about the ownership of a miserable canoe."

"Good! My brother very young—but, he very wise. Little warrior, great talker. Chief, sometime, in council."

"I do'n't know this, nor do I say it, Injin," returned Deerslayer, colouring a little at the ill concealed sarcasm of the other's manner. "I look forward to a life in the woods, and I only hope it may be a peaceable one. All young men must go on the war path when there's occasion, but war is'n't needfully massacre. I've seen enough of the last, this very night, to know that providence frowns on it, and I now invite you to go your own way, while I go mine; and hope that we may part fri'nds."

"Good! My brother has two scalp—gray hair under t' other. Old wisdom, young tongue."

Here the savage advanced with confidence, his hand extended, his face smiling, and his whole bearing denoting amity and respect. Deerslayer met his offered friendship in a proper spirit, and they shook hands cordially, each endeavoring to assure the other of his sincerity and desire to be at peace.

"All have his own," said the Indian—"my canoe, mine; your canoe, your'n. Go look; if your'n, you keep; if mine, my keep."

"That's just, red-skin, though you must be wrong in thinking the canoe your property. Howsever, seein' is believin', and we'll go down to the shore, where you may look with your own eyes, for it's likely you'll object to trustin' altogether to mine."

The Indian uttered his favorite exclamation of "good!" and then they walked, side by side, towards the shore. There was no apparent distrust in the manner of either, the Indian moving in advance, as if he wished to show his companion that he did not fear turning his back to him. As they reached the open ground, the former pointed towards Deerslayer's boat, and said emphatically—

"No mine—Pale face canoe—*this* red man's. No want other man's canoe—want his own."

"You're wrong, red-skin, you're altogether wrong. This canoe was left in old Hutter's keeping, and is his'n according to all law, red or white, 'till its owner comes to claim it. Here's the seats and the stitching of the bark to speak for themselves—no man ever know'd an Injin to turn off such work."

"Good—my brother little ole, big wisdom. Injin no make him. White man's work."

"I'm glad you think so, for holding out to the contrary might have made ill blood atween us. Every one having a right to take possession of his own, I'll just shove the canoe out of reach of dispute, at once, as the quickest way of settling difficulties."

While Deerslayer was speaking he put a foot against the end of the light boat, and giving a vigorous shove, he sent it out into the lake, a hundred feet or more, where, taking the true current, it would necessarily float past the point, and be in no further danger of coming ashore. The savage started at this ready and decided expedient, and his companion saw that he cast a hurried and fierce glance at his own canoe, or that which contained the paddles. The change of manner, however, was but momentary, and then the Iroquois resumed his air of friendliness, and a smile of satisfaction.

"Good," he repeated with stronger emphasis than ever. "Young head, old mind. Know how to settle quarrel. Farewell, brother. He go to house in water—muskrat house—Injin go to camp; tell chief no find canoe."

Deerslayer was not sorry to hear this proposal, for he felt anxious to join the females, and he took the offered hand of the Indian very willingly. The parting words were friendly, and while the red man walked calmly towards the wood, with his rifle in the hollow of his arm, without once looking back in uneasiness or distrust, the white man moved towards the remaining canoe, carrying his piece in the same pacific manner it is true, but keeping his eyes fastened on the movements of the other. This distrust, however, seemed to be altogether uncalled for, and, as if ashamed to have entertained it, the young man averted his look, and stepped carelessly up to his boat. Here he began to push the canoe from the shore, and to make his other preparations for departing. He might have been thus employed a minute, when happening to turn his face towards the land, his quick and certain eye told him at a glance, the imminent jeopardy in which his life was placed. The black, ferocious eyes of the savage were glaring on him, like those of the crouching tiger, through a small opening in the bushes, and the muzzle of his rifle seemed already to be opening in a line with his own body.

Then, indeed, the long practice of Deerslayer as a hunter, did him good service. Accustomed to fire with the deer on the bound, and often when the precise position of the animal's body, had in a manner to be guessed at, he used the same expedients here. To cock and poise his rifle were the acts of a single moment, and a single motion; then, aiming almost without sighting, he fired into the bushes where he knew a body ought to be, in order to sustain the appalling countenance which alone was visible. There was not time to raise the piece any higher, or to take a more deliberate aim. So rapid were his movements that both parties discharged their pieces at the same instant, the concussions mingling in one report. The mountains, indeed, gave back but a single echo. Deerslayer dropped his piece, and stood, with head erect, steady as one of the pines in the calm of a June morning, watching the result; while the savage gave the yell that has become historical for its appalling influence, leaped through the bushes, and came bounding across the open ground, flourishing a tomahawk. Still, Deerslayer moved not, but stood with his unloaded rifle fallen against his shoulder, while with a hunter's habits, his hands were mechanically feeling for the powder horn and charger. When about forty feet from his enemy, the savage hurled his keen weapon, but it was with an eye so vacant, and a hand so unsteady and feeble, that the young man caught it by the handle, as it was flying past him. At that instant, the Indian staggered and fell, his whole length on the ground.

"I know'd it—I knowed it!" exclaimed Deerslayer, who was already preparing to force a fresh bullet into his rifle—"I know'd it must come to this, as soon as I had got the range from the creatur's eyes. A man sights suddenly, and fires quick, when his own life's in danger; yes, I know'd it would come to this. I was about the hundredth part of a second too quick for him, or it might have been bad for me! The riptyle's bullet has just grazed my side, but say what you will, for or ag'in 'em, a red-skin is by no means as sartain with powder and ball, as a white man. Their gifts do'n't seem to lie that-a-way.

Even Chingachgook,[3] great as he is in other matters, is not downright deadly with the rifle."

By this time the piece was reloaded, and Deerslayer, after tossing the tomahawk into the canoe, advanced to his victim, and stood over him, leaning on his rifle, in melancholy attention. It was the first instance in which he had seen a man fall in battle, it was the first fellow creature against whom he had ever seriously raised his own hand. The sensations were novel; and regret, with the freshness of our better feelings, mingled with his triumph. The Indian was not dead, though shot directly through the body. He lay on his back motionless, but his eyes, now full of consciousness, watched each action of his victor, as the fallen bird regards the fowler, jealous of every movement. The man probably expected the fatal blow, which was to precede the loss of his scalp; or, perhaps he anticipated that this latter act of cruelty would precede his death. Deerslayer read his thoughts, and he found a melancholy satisfaction in relieving the apprehensions of the helpless savage.

"No—no—red-skin," he said. "You've nothing more to fear from me. I am of a christian stock, and scalping is not of my gifts—I'll just make sartain of your rifle, and then come back and do you what sarvice I can. Though here I can't stay much longer, as the crack of three rifles will be apt to bring more of your devils upon me."

The close of this was said in a sort of a soliloquy, as the young man went in quest of the fallen rifle. The piece was found where its owner had dropped it, and was immediately put into the canoe. Laying his own rifle at its side, Deerslayer then returned and stood over the Indian, again.

"All inmity atween you and me's at an ind, red-skin," he said, "and you may set your heart at rest, on the score of the scalp, or any further injury. My gifts are white, as I've told you, and I hope my conduct will be white also."

Could looks have conveyed all they meant, it is probable Deerslayer's innocent vanity on the subject of colour, would have been rebuked a little, but he comprehended the gratitude that was expressed in the eyes of the dying savage, without, in the least, detecting the bitter sarcasm that struggled with the better feeling.

"Water—" ejaculated the thirsty and unfortunate creature—"give poor Injin water—"

"Ay, water you shall have, if you drink the lake dry. I'll just carry you down to it, that you may take your fill. This is the way, they tell me, with all wounded people—water is their greatest comfort and delight."

So saying, Deerslayer raised the Indian in his arms and carried him to the lake. Here he first helped him to take an attitude in which he could appease his burning thirst; after which he seated himself on a stone, and took the head of his wounded adversary in his own lap, and endeavored to soothe his anguish, in the best manner he could.

"It would be sinful in me to tell you your time had'n't come, warrior," he commenced, "and, therefore, I'll not say it. You're passed the middle age, already, and considerin' the sort of lives ye lead, your days have been pretty well filled. The principal thing now, is to look forward to what comes next. Neither red skin nor pale face, on the whole, calculates much on sleepin'

[3]Deerslayer's Delaware Indian companion.

forever, but both expect to live in another world. Each has his gifts, and will be judged by 'em, and I suppose you've thought these matters over enough, not to stand in need of sarmons when the trial comes. You'll find your happy hunting grounds, if you've been a just Injin, and if an onjust, you'll meet your desarts in another way. I've my own idees about these things, but you're too old and exper'enced to need any explanations from one as young as I."

"Good!" ejaculated the Indian, whose voice retained its depth, even as life ebbed away. "Young head—ole wisdom."

"It's sometimes a consolation when the mind comes to know that them we've harmed, or *tried* to harm, forgive us. I suppose natur' seeks this relief, by way of getting a pardon on 'arth, as we never can know whether *He* pardons, who is all in all, till judgment itself comes. It's soothing to know that *any* pardon, at such times, and that I conclude is the secret. Now, as for myself, I overlook altogether your designs ag'in my life; first, because no harm came of 'em; next, because it's your gifts, and natur' and trainin', and I ought not to have trusted you, at all; and, finally and chiefly, because I can bear no ill will to a dying man, whether heathen or christian. So put your heart at ease, so far as I'm consarned; you know best what other matters ought to trouble you, or what ought to give you satisfaction in so trying a moment."

It is probable that the Indian had some of the fearful glimpses of the unknown state of being, which God, in mercy, seems, at times, to afford to all the human race, but they were necessarily in conformity with his habits and prejudices. Like most of his people, and like too many of our own, he thought more of dying in a way to gain applause among those he left, than to secure a better state of existence, hereafter. While Deerslayer was speaking, his mind was a little bewildered, though he felt that the intention was good; and when he had done, a regret passed over his spirit that none of his own tribe were present to witness his stoicism, under extreme bodily suffering, and the firmness with which he met his end. With the high, innate courtesy that so often distinguishes the Indian warrior, before he becomes corrupted by too much intercourse with the worst class of the white men, he endeavored to express his thankfulness for the other's good intentions, and to let him understand that they were appreciated.

"Good!" he repeated, for this was an English word much used by savages—"good—young head; young *heart*, too. *Old* heart tough; no shed tear. Hear Indian when he die, and no want to lie—what he call him?"

"Deerslayer is the name I bear now, though the Delawares have said that when I get back from this war-path, I shall bear a more manly title, provided I can 'arn one."

"That good name for boy—poor name for warrior. Get better quick. No fear *there*—" the savage had strength sufficient, under the strong excitement he felt, to raise a hand and tap the young man on his breast—"eye, sartain—finger, lightening—aim, death. Great warrior, soon—No Deerslayer—Hawkeye—Hawkeye—Hawkeye—Shake hand."

Deerslayer—or Hawkeye as the youth was then first named, for in after years he bore the appellation throughout all that region[4]—Deerslayer took the hand of the savage, whose last breath was drawn in that attitude, gazing

[4]Natty Bumppo bore various names in the "Leather-Stocking Tales," including "Deerslayer," "Hawkeye," "Straight-tongue," "Pathfinder," and "Leather-Stocking."

in admiration at the countenance of a stranger, who had shewn so much readiness, skill and firmness, in a scene that was equally trying and novel. When the reader remembers it is the highest gratification an Indian can receive to see his enemy betray weakness, he will be better able to appreciate the conduct which had extorted so great a concession, at such a moment.

"His spirit has fled!" said Deerslayer, in a suppressed, melancholy, voice. "Ah's, me!—Well, to this we must all come, sooner or later; and he is happiest, let his skin be of what colour it may, who is best fitted to meet it. Here lies the body of, no doubt, a brave warrior, and the soul is already flying towards its heaven, or hell, whether that be a happy hunting ground, or a place scant of game, regions of glory according to Moravian doctrine, or flames of fire! So it happens, too, as regards other matters! Here have old Hutter and Hurry Harry got themselves into difficulty, if they have'n't got themselves into torment and death, and all for a bounty that luck offers to me in what many would think a lawful and suitable manner. But not a farthing of such money shall cross my hand. White I was born, and white will I die; clinging to colour to the last, even though the King's Majesty, his governors, and all his councils, both at home and in the colonies, forget from what they come, and where they hope to go, and all for a little advantage in warfare. No—no—warrior; hand of mine shall never molest your scalp, and so your soul may rest in peace on the p'int of making a decent appearance, when the body comes to join it, in your own land of spirits."

Deerslayer arose as soon as he had spoken. Then he placed the body of the dead man, in a sitting posture, with its back against the little rock, taking the necessary care to prevent it from falling, or in any way settling into an attitude that might be thought unseemly by the sensitive, though wild, notions of a savage. When this duty was performed, the young man stood gazing at the grim countenance of his fallen foe, in a sort of melancholy abstraction. As was his practice, however, a habit gained by living so much alone in the forest, he then began, to give utterance to his thoughts, and feelings aloud.

"I did'n't wish your life, red-skin," he said, "but you left me no choice atween killing, or being killed. Each party acted according to his gifts, I suppose, and blame can light on neither. You were treacherous, according to your natur' in war, and I was a little oversightful, as I'm apt to be in trusting others. Well, this is my first battle with a human mortal, though it's not likely to be the last. I have fou't most of the creatur's of the forest, such as bears, wolves, painters and catamounts, but this is the beginning with red-skins. If I was Injin born, now, I might tell of this, or carry in the scalp, and boast of the expl'ite afore the whole tribe; or, if my inimy had only been even a bear, 'twould have been nat'ral and proper to let every body know what had happened; but I do'n't well see how I'm to let even Chingachgook into this secret, so long as it can be done only by boasting with a white tongue. And why should I wish to boast of it, a'ter all? It's slaying a human, although he was a savage; and how do I know that he was a just Injin; and that he has not been taken away suddenly, to any thing but happy hunting grounds. When it's onsartain whether good, or evil, has been done, the wisest way is not to be boastful—still, I *should* like Chingachgook to know that I have'n't discredited the Delawares, or my training!"

1841

. . .

from *THE PIONEERS*

CHAPTER XXII

[THE SLAUGHTER OF THE PIGEONS]

From this time to the close of April, the weather continued to be a succession of great and rapid changes. One day, the soft airs of spring seemed to be stealing along the valley, and, in unison with an invigorating sun, attempting, covertly, to rouse the dormant powers of the vegetable world; while on the next, the surly blasts from the north would sweep across the lake, and erase every impression left by their gentle adversaries. The snow, however, finally disappeared, and the green wheat fields were seen in every direction, spotted with the dark and charred stumps that had, the preceding season, supported some of the proudest trees of the forest. Ploughs were in motion, wherever those useful implements could be used, and the smokes of the sugar-camps[1] were no longer seen issuing from the woods of maple. The lake had lost the beauty of a field of ice, but still a dark and gloomy covering concealed its waters, for the absence of currents left them yet hid under a porous crust, which, saturated with the fluid, barely retained enough strength to preserve the contiguity of its parts. Large flocks of wild geese were seen passing over the country, which hovered, for a time, around the hidden sheet of water, apparently searching for a resting-place; and then, on finding themselves excluded by the chill covering, would soar away to the north, filling the air with discordant screams, as if venting their complaints at the tardy operations of nature.

For a week, the dark covering of the Otsego was left to the undisturbed possession of two eagles, who alighted on the centre of its field, and sat eyeing their undisputed territory. During the presence of these monarchs of the air, the flocks of migrating birds avoided crossing the plain of ice, by turning into the hills, apparently seeking the protection of the forests, while the white and bald heads of the tenants of the lake were turned upward, with a look of contempt. But the time had come, when even these kings of birds were to be dispossessed. An opening had been gradually increasing, at the lower extremity of the lake, and around the dark spot where the current of the river prevented the formation of ice, during even the coldest weather; and the fresh southerly winds, that now breathed freely upon the valley, made an impression on the waters. Mimic waves begun to curl over the margin of the frozen field, which exhibited an outline of crystallizations, that slowly receded towards the north. At each step the power of the winds and the waves increased, until, after a struggle of a few hours, the turbulent little billows succeeded in setting the whole field in motion, when it was driven beyond the reach of the eye, with a rapidity, that was as magical as the change produced in the scene by this expulsion of the lingering remnant of winter. Just as the last sheet of agitated ice was disappearing in the distance, the eagles rose, and soared with a wide sweep above the clouds, while the waves tossed their little caps of snow into the air, as if rioting in their release from a thraldom of five months' duration.

[1]Where maple sugar is made.

The following morning Elizabeth was awakened by the exhilarating sounds of the martins, who were quarreling and chattering around the little boxes suspended above her windows, and the cries of Richard, who was calling, in tones animating as the signs of the season itself—

"Awake! awake! my fair lady! the gulls are hovering over the lake already, and the heavens are alive with pigeons. You may look an hour before you can find a hole, through which, to get a peep at the sun. Awake! awake! lazy ones! Benjamin[2] is overhauling the ammunition, and we only wait for our breakfasts, and away for the mountains and pigeon-shooting."

There was no resisting this animated appeal, and in a few minutes Miss Temple and her friend descended to the parlour. The doors of the hall were thrown open, and the mild, balmy air of a clear spring morning was ventilating the apartment, where the vigilance of the ex-steward had been so long maintaining an artificial heat, with such unremitted diligence. The gentlemen were impatiently waiting for their morning's repast, each equipt in the garb of a sportsman. Mr. Jones made many visits to the southern door, and would cry—

"See, cousin Bess! see, 'Duke![3] the pigeon-roosts of the south have broken up! They are growing more thick every instant. Here is a flock that the eye cannot see the end of. There is food enough in it to keep the army of Xerxes[4] for a month, and feathers enough to make beds for the whole country. Xerxes, Mr. Edwards, was a Grecian king, who—no, he was a Turk, or a Persian, who wanted to conquer Greece, just the same as these rascals will overrun our wheat-fields, when they come back in the fall.——Away! away! Bess; I long to pepper them."

In this wish both Marmaduke and young Edwards seemed equally to participate, for the sight was exhilarating to a sportsman; and the ladies soon dismissed the party, after a hasty breakfast.

If the heavens were alive with pigeons, the whole village seemed equally in motion, with men, women, and children. Every species of firearms, from the French duckinggun, with a barrel near six feet in length, to the common horseman's pistol, was to be seen in the hands of the men and boys; while bows and arrows, some made of the simple stick of a walnut sapling, and others in a rude imitation of the ancient cross-bows, were carried by many of the latter.

The houses, and the signs of life apparent in the village, drove the alarmed birds from the direct line of their flight, towards the mountains, along the sides and near the bases of which they were glancing in dense masses, equally wonderful by the rapidity of their motion, and their incredible numbers.

We have already said, that across the inclined plane which fell from the steep ascent of the mountain to the banks of the Susquehanna, ran the highway, on either side of which a clearing of many acres had been made, at a very early day. Over those clearings, and up the eastern mountain, and along the dangerous path that was cut into its side, the different individuals posted themselves, and in a few moments the attack commenced.

[2]Benjamin Pump, a Temple household servant.

[3]Judge Marmaduke Temple, father of Elizabeth.

[4]According to the ancient Greek historian Herodotus, the army of the Persian emperor Xerxes (c. 519 B.C.–465 B.C.) numbered 1,700,000.

Amongst the sportsmen was the tall, gaunt form of Leather-Stocking, walking over the field, with his rifle hanging on his arm, his dogs at his heels; the latter now scenting the dead or wounded birds, that were beginning to tumble from the flocks, and then crouching under the legs of their master, as if they participated in his feelings, at this wasteful and unsportsmanlike execution.

The reports of the firearms became rapid, whole volleys rising from the plain, as flocks of more than ordinary numbers darted over the opening, shadowing the field, like a cloud; and then the light smoke of a single piece would issue from among the leafless bushes on the mountain, as death was hurled on the retreat of the affrighted birds, who were rising from a volley, in a vain effort to escape. Arrows, and missiles of every kind, were in the midst of the flocks; and so numerous were the birds, and so low did they take their flight, that even long poles, in the hands of those on the sides of the mountain, were used to strike them to the earth.

During all this time, Mr. Jones, who disdained the humble and ordinary means of destruction used by his companions, was busily occupied, aided by Benjamin, in making arrangements for an assault of a more than ordinarily fatal character. Among the relics of the old military excursions, that occasionally are discovered throughout the different districts of the western part of New-York, there had been found in Templeton, at its settlement, a small swivel,[5] which would carry a ball of a pound weight. It was thought to have been deserted by a war-party of the whites, in one of their inroads into the Indian settlements, when, perhaps, convenience or their necessity induced them to leave such an encumbrance behind them in the woods. This miniature cannon had been released from the rust, and being mounted on little wheels, was now in a state for actual service. For several years, it was the sole organ for extraordinary rejoicings used in those mountains. On the mornings of the Fourths of July, it would be heard ringing among the hills, and even Captain Hollister, who was the highest authority in that part of the country on all such occasions, affirmed that, considering its dimensions, it was no despicable gun for a salute. It was somewhat the worse for the service it had performed, it is true, there being but a trifling difference in size between the touch-hole and the muzzle. Still, the grand conceptions of Richard had suggested the importance of such an instrument, in hurling death at his nimble enemies. The swivel was dragged by a horse into a part of the open space, that the Sheriff thought most eligible for planting a battery of the kind, and Mr. Pump proceeded to load it. Several handfuls of duck-shot were placed on top of the powder, and the Major-domo announced that his piece was ready for service.

The sight of such an implement collected all the idle spectators to the spot, who, being mostly boys, filled the air with cries of exultation and delight. The gun was pointed high, and Richard, holding a coal of fire in a pair of tongs, patiently took his seat on a stump, awaiting the appearance of a flock worthy of his notice.

So prodigious was the number of the birds, that the scattering fire of the guns, with the hurling of missiles, and the cries of the boys, had no other effect than to break off small flocks from the immense masses that continued

[5]A small cannon, fixed on a swivel so it can be fired vertically.

to dart along the valley, as if the whole of the feathered tribe were pouring through that one pass. None pretended to collect the game, which lay scattered over the fields in such profusion, as to cover the very ground with the fluttering victims.

Leather-Stocking was a silent, but uneasy spectator of all these proceedings, but was able to keep his sentiments to himself until he saw the introduction of the swivel into the sports.

"This comes of settling a country!" he said—"here have I known the pigeons to fly for forty long years, and, till you made your clearings, there was nobody to skear or to hurt them. I loved to see them come into the woods, for they were company to a body; hurting nothing; being, as it was, as harmless as a garter-snake. But now it gives me sore thoughts when I hear the frighty things whizzing through the air, for I know it's only a motion to bring out all the brats in the village. Well! the Lord won't see the waste of his creaters for nothing, and right will be done to the pigeons, as well as others, by-and-by.——There's Mr. Oliver, as bad as the rest of them, firing into the flocks as if he was shooting down nothing but Mingo warriors."

Among the sportsmen was Billy Kirby, who, armed with an old musket, was loading, and, without even looking into the air, was firing, and shouting as his victims fell even on his own person. He heard the speech of Natty, and took upon himself to reply—

"What! old Leather-Stocking," he cried, "grumbling at the loss of a few pigeons! If you had to sow your wheat twice, and three times, as I have done, you wouldn't be so massyfully[6] feeling'd to'ards the divils.—Hurrah, boys! scatter the feathers. This is better than shooting at a turkey's head and neck, old fellow."

"It's better for you, maybe, Billy Kirby," replied the indignant old hunter, "and all them that don't know how to put a ball down a rifle-barrel, or how to bring it up ag'in with a true aim; but it's wicked to be shooting into flocks in this wastey manner; and none do it, who know how to knock over a single bird. If a body has a craving for pigeon's flesh, why! it's made the same as all other creater's, for man's eating, but not to kill twenty and eat one. When I want such a thing, I go into the woods till I find one to my liking, and then I shoot him off the branches without touching a feather of another, though there might be a hundred on the same tree. You couldn't do such a thing, Billy Kirby—you couldn't do it if you tried."

"What's that, old corn-stalk! you sapless stub!" cried the wood-chopper. "You've grown wordy, since the affair of the turkey; but if you're for a single shot, here goes at that bird which comes on by himself."

The fire from the distant part of the field had driven a single pigeon below the flock to which it belonged, and, frightened with the constant reports of the muskets, it was approaching the spot where the disputants stood, darting first from one side, and then to the other, cutting the air with the swiftness of lightning, and making a noise with its wings, not unlike the rushing of a bullet. Unfortunately for the wood-chopper, notwithstanding his vaunt, he did not see this bird until it was too late to fire as it approached, and he pulled his trigger at the unlucky moment when it was darting immediately over his head. The bird continued its course with the usual velocity.

[6]Mercifully.

Natty lowered the rifle from his arm, when the challenge was made, and, waiting a moment, until the terrified victim had got in a line with his eye, and had dropped near the bank of the lake, he raised it again with uncommon rapidity, and fired. It might have been chance, or it might have been skill, that produced the result; it was probably a union of both; but the pigeon whirled over in the air, and fell into the lake, with a broken wing. At the sound of his rifle, both his dogs started from his feet, and in a few minutes the "slut"[7] brought out the bird, still alive.

The wonderful exploit of Leather-Stocking was noised through the field with great rapidity, and the sportsmen gathered in to learn the truth of the report.

"What," said young Edwards, "have you really killed a pigeon on the wing, Natty, with a single ball?"

"Haven't I killed loons before now, lad, that dive at the flash?" returned the hunter. "It's much better to kill only such as you want, without wasting your powder and lead, than to be firing into God's creaters in this wicked manner. But I come out for a bird, and you know the reason why I like small game, Mr. Oliver, and now I have got one I will go home, for I don't relish to see these wasty ways that you are all practysing, as if the least thing was not made for use, and not to destroy."

"Thou sayest well, Leather-Stocking," cried Marmaduke, "and I begin to think it time to put an end to this work of destruction."

"Put an ind, Judge, to your clearings. An't the woods his work as well as the pigeons? Use, but don't waste. Wasn't the woods made for the beasts and birds to harbour in? and when man wanted their flesh, their skins, or their feathers, there's the place to seek them. But I'll go to the hut with my own game, for I wouldn't touch one of the harmless things that kiver the ground here, looking up with their eyes on me, as if they only wanted tongues to say their thoughts."

With this sentiment in his mouth, Leather-Stocking threw his rifle over his arm, and, followed by his dogs, stepped across the clearing with great caution, taking care not to tread on one of the wounded birds in his path. He soon entered the bushes on the margin of the lake, and was hid from view.

Whatever impression the morality of Natty made on the Judge, it was utterly lost on Richard. He availed himself of the gathering of the sportsmen, to lay a plan for one "fell swoop" of destruction. The musketmen were drawn up in battle array, in a line extending on each side of his artillery, with orders to await the signal of firing from himself.

"Stand by, my lads," said Benjamin, who acted as an aide-de-camp, on this occasion, "stand by, my hearties, and when Squire Dickens[8] heaves out the signal to begin the firing, d'ye see, you may open upon them in a broadside. Take care and fire low, boys, and you'll be sure to hull the flock."

"Fire low!" shouted Kirby—"hear the old fool! If we fire low, we may hit the stumps, but not ruffle a pigeon."

"How should you know, you lubber?"[9] cried Benjamin, with a very unbecoming heat, for an officer on the eve of battle—"how should you know, you

[7]A female dog.
[8]Nickname of Sheriff Jones.
[9]Fool, oaf.

grampus?[10] Havn't I sailed aboard of the Boadishy for five years? and wasn't it a standing order to fire low, and to hull your enemy? Keep silence at your guns, boys, and mind the order that is passed."

The loud laughs of the musketmen were silenced by the more authoritative voice of Richard, who called for attention and obedience to his signals.

Some millions of pigeons were supposed to have already passed, that morning, over the valley of Templeton; but nothing like the flock that was now approaching had been seen before. It extended from mountain to mountain in one solid blue mass, and the eye looked in vain over the southern hills to find its termination. The front of this living column was distinctly marked by a line, but very slightly indented, so regular and even was the flight. Even Marmaduke forgot the morality of Leather-Stocking as it approached, and, in common with the rest, brought his musket to a poise.

"Fire!" cried the Sheriff, clapping a coal to the priming of the cannon. As half of Benjamin's charge escaped through the touch-hole, the whole volley of the musketry preceded the report of the swivel. On receiving this united discharge of small-arms, the front of the flock darted upward, while, at the same instant, myriads of those in the rear rushed with amazing rapidity into their places, so that when the column of white smoke gushed from the mouth of the little cannon, an accumulated mass of objects was gliding over its point of direction. The roar of the gun echoed along the mountains, and died away to the north, like distant thunder, while the whole flock of alarmed birds seemed, for a moment, thrown into one disorderly and agitated mass. The air was filled with their irregular flight, layer rising above layer, far above the tops of the highest pines, none daring to advance beyond the dangerous pass; when, suddenly, some of the leaders of the feathered tribe shot across the valley, taking their flight directly over the village, and hundreds of thousands in their rear followed the example, deserting the eastern side of the plain to their persecutors and the slain.

"Victory!" shouted Richard, "victory! we have driven the enemy from the field."

"Not so, Dickon," said Marmaduke; "the field is covered with them; and, like the Leather-Stocking, I see nothing but eyes, in every direction, as the innocent sufferers turn their heads in terror. Full one half of those that have fallen are yet alive: and I think it is time to end the sport; if sport it be."

"Sport!" cried the Sheriff; "it is princely sport. There are some thousands of the blue-coated boys on the ground, so that every old woman in the village may have a pot-pie for the asking."

"Well, we have happily frightened the birds from this side of the valley," said Marmaduke, "and the carnage must of necessity end, for the present.——Boys, I will give thee sixpence a hundred for the pigeons' heads only; so go to work, and bring them into the village."

This expedient produced the desired effect, for every urchin on the ground went industriously to work to wring the necks of the wounded birds. Judge Temple retired towards his dwelling with that kind of feeling, that many a man has experienced before him, who discovers, after the excitement of the moment has passed, that he has purchased pleasure at the price of misery to others. Horses were loaded with the dead; and, after this first

[10]A whale.

burst of sporting, the shooting of pigeons became a business, with a few idlers, for the remainder of the season. Richard, however, boasted for many a year, of his shot with the "cricket;"[11] and Benjamin gravely asserted, that he thought they killed nearly as many pigeons on that day, as there were Frenchmen destroyed on the memorable occasion of Rodney's victory.[12]

1823

William Cullen Bryant 1794–1878

When he was about eight years old, William Cullen Bryant "began to make verses, some of which," he later recalled, "were utter nonsense." But others revealed a genuine poetic talent, and they forecast the eventual fulfillment of Bryant's childhood prayers that he be given the "gift of poetic genius and write verses that might endure." He was descended from a line of New England ministers and raised amid the dominant Calvinist orthodoxies of his birthplace at Cummington, in rural Massachusetts. His earliest juvenile poems were devotional rhymes and versifications of Old Testament passages. They revealed a familiarity with the Bible and classical poetry, a knowledge of Shakespeare, Milton, and the poets of eighteenth-century England, and they reflected a devout high-mindedness that remained in Bryant throughout his life.

His first published poem appeared in a local Massachusetts newspaper in 1807. Bryant wrote the poem when he was nine and recited it at a school assembly, rhyming out the development of American education and exhorting his classmates to "tread, as lowly Jesus trod,/The path that leads the sinner to his God." From the age of five, Bryant had been an avid reader of conservative New England newspapers. With the aid of his father, a physician and a Federalist politician, he wrote a long poem that was modeled on the political satires of eighteenth-century England. The poem presented a malicious attack on President Thomas Jefferson, his administration, and other "pimps of France." It was published and hawked on the streets of Boston in 1808, and when a second edition was printed the following year, it contained a testament certifying that the poem's clever scurrility was indeed the work of a thirteen-year-old.

In 1810 Bryant entered Williams College, in Massachusetts, but in his sophomore year he left (after composing a rhymed satire on the college) and began the study of the law. In 1815 Bryant was admitted to the bar and began to practice in Great Barrington, Massachusetts. He considered abandoning poetry to concentrate on his profession, but in 1817 his poem "Thanatopsis" was published in The North American Review*—despite the editors' doubts that such notable poetry could be the work of an American—and Bryant decided to continue his efforts to write enduring verse.*

His early poetry had used the heroic couplets and commonplace artifices of Augustan English poetry. It had reflected the Calvinist religion of his New England upbringing, the classicism of his education, and the conservative politics of his family. But

[11]Small cannon.

[12]George Brydges, Baron Rodney (1719–1792), English admiral who defeated the French in a battle for Jamaica in 1782.

"Thanatopsis" was an announcement of change. Inspired by English "Graveyard" poets, Bryant celebrated death, immortality, and the emotions of bereavement. In "Thanatopsis" he rejected the prevailing Christian idea of the afterlife and displayed instead a pagan, stoic, and pantheistic faith in man's ultimate "communion with the visible forms of nature."

The poems that followed won increasing recognition for their gladdening treatment of the beauties of American nature. In 1821 Bryant published the first collected edition of his work, and in 1825 he turned from his life as a country lawyer and left Massachusetts for the literary and journalistic world of New York City. There, his literary reputation won him a position on the editorial staff of the New York Evening Post. *Eventually he became part-owner and editor-in-chief, a position he held for half a century.*

Editions of Bryant's poetry appeared throughout his life, along with books of travel and literary criticism, but the bulk of his best poetry had been written by the 1840s, and in his latter years he devoted his talents largely to crusading for political reform. His political ideals had moved from the conservative Federalism of his youth to a faith in political liberalism and the rights of the common man. As editor of the Post *he campaigned vigorously for the abolition of slavery, for the rights of organized labor, and for free trade, free speech, and a free press. In an effort to foster political reform, he helped found the Republican party and became a powerful supporter of Lincoln and the Union cause during the Civil War. By the end of his life he was a public institution, a national oracle, "the first citizen of New York." When he died, in 1878, the city's flags were lowered to half-mast and storefronts were draped in black.*

Bryant was the first native poet in the United States to gain worldwide fame. His best poetry had been written not of European nightingales and Roman or Greek landscapes but of American sparrows, and of American prairies, and of the trees and flowers and grass of New England. Like the romantic landscapes of his friend, the painter Thomas Cole, Bryant's nature often dissolved into a misty softness. That amiable nature is evident in the soothing wilderness described in his "Inscription for the Entrance to a Wood," and it is evident in "A Forest Hymn," which portrayed nature's groves as temples more noble than man's cathedrals.

Bryant's harmonious and ameliorating scenes conveyed little of the complex reaches into philosophy achieved by the best of the American romantics who followed him, and in his last years he turned once again toward the poetic and religious orthodoxies of his youth. Throughout his life, he had held the classical view that literature should aim at the moral perfection of its audience, and his greatest poetry retained a neoclassic restraint and serenity that led Lowell to describe him as a poet who was "as quiet, as cool, and as dignified,/As a smooth, silent iceberg, that never is ignified." Bryant's departures from the trotting regularity of Augustan poetry, and his treatment of death, the past, and American nature were essential contributions to the development of American literature. He was the first American romantic poet, the nation's first native bard. In the minds of his compatriots he filled the role of a patriarch, a prophet whose bearded portrait, looking down from the walls of the nation's schoolrooms, reflected the ideals, the certitude, and the aspirations of an age.

FURTHER READING: *The Life and Works of William Cullen Bryant*, ed. P. Godwin, 6 vols., 1883–1884; *Letters of William Cullen Bryant*, 6 vols., ed. W. Bryant and T. Voss, 1975–1992; *William Cullen Bryant, Representative Selections*, ed. T. McDowell, 1935; H. Peckham, *Gotham Yankee, A Biography of William Cullen Bryant*, 1950; C. Johnson, *Politics and a Bellyfull*, 1962; A. McLean, *William Cullen Bryant*, 1964, 1989; C. Brown, *William Cullen Bryant*, 1971; *William Cullen Bryant and His America*, ed. S. Brodwin and M. D'Innocenzo, 1983; N. Krapf, *Under Open Sky, Poets on William Cullen Bryant*, 1986.

TEXT: *The Poetical Works of William Cullen Bryant*, ed. P. Godwin, 2 vols., 1883.

THANATOPSIS[1]

To him who in the love of Nature holds
Communion with her visible forms, she speaks
A various language; for his gayer hours
She has a voice of gladness, and a smile
And eloquence of beauty, and she glides
Into his darker musings, with a mild
And healing sympathy, that steals away
Their sharpness, ere he is aware. When thoughts
Of the last bitter hour come like a blight
Over thy spirit, and sad images
Of the stern agony, and shroud, and pall,
And breathless darkness, and the narrow house,
Make thee to shudder, and grow sick at heart;—
Go forth, under the open sky, and list
To Nature's teachings, while from all around—
Earth and her waters, and the depths of air—
Comes a still voice.—

Yet a few days, and thee
The all-beholding sun shall see no more
In all his course; nor yet in the cold ground,
Where thy pale form was laid, with many tears,
Nor in the embrace of ocean, shall exist
Thy image. Earth, that nourished thee, shall claim
Thy growth, to be resolved to earth again,
And, lost each human trace, surrendering up
Thine individual being, shalt thou go
To mix for ever with the elements,
To be a brother to the insensible rock
And to the sluggish clod, which the rude swain
Turns with his share,[2] and treads upon. The oak
Shall send his roots abroad, and pierce thy mould.

Yet not to thine eternal resting-place
Shalt thou retire alone, nor couldst thou wish
Couch more magnificent. Thou shalt lie down
With patriarchs of the infant world—with kings,
The powerful of the earth—the wise, the good,
Fair forms, and hoary seers of ages past,
All in one mighty sepulchre. The hills
Rock-ribbed and ancient as the sun,—the vales
Stretching in pensive quietness between;

[1]Bryant's most famous poem, "Thanatopsis" (Greek for "meditation on death"), shows his rejection of Christian orthodoxy and his move toward the Unitarianism of his later life. The poem was written around 1815 and first published in 1817. Bryant later revised it (for publication in 1821), adding the introduction (lines 1–17) and the conclusion (lines 66–82).
[2]Plowshare.

The venerable woods—rivers that move
In majesty, and the complaining brooks
That make the meadows green; and, poured round all,
Old Ocean's gray and melancholy waste,—
Are but the solemn decorations all
Of the great tomb of man. The golden sun,
The planets, all the infinite host of heaven,
Are shining on the sad abodes of death,
Through the still lapse of ages. All that tread
The globe are but a handful to the tribes
That slumber in its bosom.—Take the wings
Of morning, pierce the Barcan wilderness,[3]
Or lose thyself in the continuous woods
Where rolls the Oregon,[4] and hears no sound,
Save his own dashings—yet the dead are there:
And millions in those solitudes, since first
The flight of years began, have laid them down
In their last sleep—the dead reign there alone.
So shalt thou rest, and what if thou withdraw
In silence from the living, and no friend
Take note of thy departure? All that breathe
Will share thy destiny. The gay will laugh
When thou art gone, the solemn brood of care
Plod on, and each one as before will chase
His favorite phantom; yet all these shall leave
Their mirth and their employments, and shall come
And make their bed as thee. As the long train
Of ages glides away, the sons of men,
The youth in life's fresh spring, and he who goes
In the full strength of years, matron and maid,
The speechless babe, and the gray-headed man—
Shall one by one be gathered to thy side,
By those, who in their turn shall follow them.

So live, that when thy summons comes to join
The innumerable caravan, which moves
To that mysterious realm, where each shall take
His chamber in the silent halls of death,
Thou go not, like the quarry-slave at night,
Scourged[5] to his dungeon, but, sustained and soothed
By an unfaltering trust, approach thy grave,
Like one who wraps the drapery of his couch
About him, and lies down to pleasant dreams.
1815 1817, 1821

[3]The desert region of Barca, or Bargah, in Libya, North Africa.
[4]An Indian name for the Columbia River.
[5]Whipped.

TO A WATERFOWL

Whither, midst falling dew,
While glow the heavens with the last steps of day,
Far, through their rosy depths, dost thou pursue
Thy solitary way?

Vainly the fowler's eye
Might mark thy distant flight to do thee wrong,
As, darkly painted on the crimson sky,
Thy figure floats along.

Seek'st thou the plashy[1] brink
Of weedy lake, or marge of river wide,
Or where the rocking billows rise and sink
On the chafed ocean-side?

There is a Power whose care
Teaches thy way along that pathless coast—
The desert and illimitable air—
Lone wandering, but not lost.

All day thy wings have fanned,
At that far height, the cold, thin atmosphere,
Yet stoop not, weary, to the welcome land,
Though the dark night is near.

And soon that toil shall end;
Soon shalt thou find a summer home, and rest,
And scream among thy fellows; reeds shall bend,
Soon, o'er thy sheltered nest.

Thou'rt gone, the abyss of heaven
Hath swallowed up thy form; yet, on my heart
Deeply has sunk the lesson thou hast given,
And shall not soon depart.

He who, from zone to zone,
Guides through the boundless sky thy certain flight,
In the long way that I must tread alone,
Will lead my steps aright.

1815 1818, 1821

[1]Marshy.

TO COLE, THE PAINTER, DEPARTING FOR EUROPE[1]

Thine eyes shall see the light of distant skies;
Yet, COLE! thy heart shall bear to Europe's strand
A living image of our own bright land,
Such as upon thy glorious canvas lies;
Lone lakes—savannas where the bison roves—
Rocks rich with summer garlands—solemn streams—
Skies, where the desert eagle wheels and screams—
Spring bloom and autumn blaze of boundless groves.
Fair scenes shall greet thee where thou goest—fair,
But different—everywhere the trace of men,
Paths, homes, graves, ruins, from the lowest glen
To where life shrinks from the fierce Alpine air.
Gaze on them, till the tears shall dim thy sight,
But keep that earlier, wilder image bright.

1829 1832

TO THE FRINGED GENTIAN

Thou blossom bright with autumn dew,
And colored with the heaven's own blue,
That openest when the quiet light
Succeeds the keen and frosty night.

Thou comest not when violets lean
O'er wandering brooks and springs unseen,
Or columbines, in purple dressed,
Nod o'er the ground-bird's hidden nest.

Thou waitest late and com'st alone,
When woods are bare and birds are flown,
And frosts and shortening days portend
The aged year is near his end.

Then doth thy sweet and quiet eye
Look through its fringes to the sky,
Blue—blue—as if that sky let fall
A flower from its cerulean wall.

I would that thus, when I shall see
The hour of death draw near to me,
Hope, blossoming within my heart,
May look to heaven as I depart.

1829 1832

[1]Thomas Cole (1801–1848), an English-born painter, was Bryant's close friend and shared his nationalistic and romantic love of unspoiled American nature. Cole's paintings of Hudson River scenes made him the first of the "Hudson River School," the name given a group of early nineteenth-century landscape painters who were famous for their panoramas of native American scenes. Their credo was "Go first to nature to learn to paint." In 1829, Cole left America to study in Italy.

THE PRAIRIES[1]

These are the gardens of the Desert,[2] these
The unshorn fields, boundless and beautiful,
For which the speech of England has no name—
The Prairies.[3] I behold them for the first,
And my heart swells, while the dilated sight
Takes in the encircling vastness. Lo! they stretch,
In airy undulations, far away,
As if the ocean, in his gentlest swell,
Stood still, with all his rounded billows fixed,
And motionless forever.—Motionless?—
No—they are all unchained again. The clouds
Sweep over with their shadows, and, beneath,
The surface rolls and fluctuates to the eye;
Dark hollows seem to glide along and chase
The sunny ridges. Breezes of the South!
Who toss the golden and the flame-like flowers,
And pass the prairie-hawk that, poised on high,
Flaps his broad wings, yet moves not—ye have played
Among the palms of Mexico and vines
Of Texas, and have crisped the limpid brooks
That from the fountains of Sonora[4] glide
Into the calm Pacific—have ye fanned
A nobler or a lovelier scene than this?
Man hath no part in all this glorious work:
The hand that built the firmament hath heaved
And smoothed these verdant swells, and sown their slopes
With herbage, planted them with island groves,
And hedged them round with forests. Fitting floor
For this magnificent temple of the sky—
With flowers whose glory and whose multitude
Rival the constellations! The great heavens
Seems to stoop down upon the scene in love,—
A nearer vault, and of a tenderer blue,
Than that which bends above our eastern hills.

As o'er the verdant waste I guide my steed,
Among the high rank grass that sweeps his sides
The hollow beating of his footsteps seems
A sacrilegious sound. I think of those
Upon whose rest he tramples. Are they here—
The dead of other days?—and did the dust
Of these fair solitudes once stir with life

[1]Written after a visit to the prairies of Illinois in 1832.
[2]Bryant viewed the prairies as the verdant border of the "Great American Desert," the early nineteenth-century name for the Great Plains of the American West.
[3]French for "meadows."
[4]A state in northwest Mexico.

And burn with passion? Let the mighty mounds[5]
That overlook the rivers, or that rise
In the dim forest crowded with old oaks,
Answer. A race, that long has passed away,
Built them;—a disciplined and populous race
Heaped, with long toil, the earth, while yet the Greek
Was hewing the Pentelicus[6] to forms
Of symmetry, and rearing on its rock
The glittering Parthenon. These ample fields
Nourished their harvests, here their herds were fed,
When haply by their stalls the bison lowed,[7]
And bowed his manèd shoulder to the yoke.
All day this desert murmured with their toils.
Till twilight blushed, and lovers walked, and wooed
In a forgotten language, and old tunes,
From instruments of unremembered form,
Gave the soft winds a voice. The red man came—
The roaming hunter tribes, warlike and fierce,
And the mound-builders vanished from the earth.
The solitude of centuries untold
Has settled where they dwelt. The prairie-wolf
Hunts in their meadows, and his fresh-dug den
Yawns by my path. The gopher mines the ground
Where stood their swarming cities. All is gone;
All—save the piles of earth that hold their bones.
The platforms where they worshipped unknown gods,
The barriers which they builded from the soil
To keep the foe at bay—till o'er the walls
The wild beleaguerers broke, and, one by one,
The strongholds of the plain were forced, and heaped
With corpses. The brown vultures of the wood
Flocked to those vast uncovered sepulchres,
And sat unscared and silent at their feast.
Haply some solitary fugitive,
Lurking in marsh and forest, till the sense
Of desolation and of fear became
Bitterer than death, yielded himself to die.
Man's better nature triumphed then. Kind words
Welcomed and soothed him; the rude conquerors
Seated the captive with their chiefs; he chose
A bride among their maidens, and at length
Seemed to forget—yet ne'er forgot—the wife
Of his first love, and her sweet little ones,
Butchered, amid their shrieks, with all his race.

[5]Earthworks, thought to have been built by a vanished race of "Mound Builders."
[6]Mount Pentelikon, near Athens, where Greeks quarried the marble for the Parthenon.
[7]Bryant mistakenly asserts that his romantic primitives, the "Mound Builders," had domesticated the American buffalo (bison).

Thus change the forms of being. Thus arise
Races of living things, glorious in strength,
And perish, as the quickening breath of God
Fills them, or is withdrawn. The red man, too,
Has left the blooming wilds he ranged so long,
And, nearer to the Rocky Mountains, sought
A wilder hunting-ground. The beaver builds
No longer by these streams, but far away,
On waters whose blue surface ne'er gave back
The white man's face—among Missouri's springs,
And pools whose issues swell the Oregon[8]—
He rears his little Venice.[9] In these plains
The bison feeds no more. Twice twenty leagues
Beyond the remotest smoke of hunter's camp,
Roams the majestic brute, in herds that shake
The earth with thundering steps—yet here I meet
His ancient footprints stamped beside the pool.

Still this great solitude is quick with life.
Myriads of insects, gaudy as the flowers
They flutter over, gentle quadrupeds,
And birds, that scarce have learned the fear of man,
Are here, and sliding reptiles of the ground,
Startlingly beautiful. The graceful deer
Bounds to the wood at my approach. The bee,
A more adventurous colonist than man,
With whom he came across the eastern deep,
Fills the savannas with his murmurings,
And hides his sweets, as in the golden age,
Within the hollow oak. I listen long
To his domestic hum, and think I hear
The sound of that advancing multitude
Which soon shall fill these deserts. From the ground
Comes up the laugh of children, the soft voice
Of maidens, and the sweet and solemn hymn
Of Sabbath worshippers. The low of herds
Blends with the rustling of the heavy grain
Over the dark brown furrows. All at once
A fresher wind sweeps by, and breaks my dream,
And I am in the wilderness alone.

1832 1833

[8]The Columbia River.
[9]The beaver's canals and dams.

ABRAHAM LINCOLN[1]

Oh, slow to smite and swift to spare,
Gentle and merciful and just!
Who, in the fear of God, didst bear
The sword of power, a nation's trust!

In sorrow by the bier we stand,
Amid the awe that hushes all,
And speak the anguish of a land
That shook with horror at thy fall.

Thy task is done; the bond[2] are free:
We bear thee to an honored grave,
Whose proudest monument shall be
The broken fetters[3] of the slave.

Pure was thy life; its bloody close
Hath placed thee with the sons of light,
Among the noble host of those
Who perished in the cause of Right.

1865 1865

Edgar Allan Poe 1809–1849

To a world fascinated by the bizarre and the macabre, Poe has often seemed an embodiment of the characters in his fiction, the archetype of the neurotic genius. He left no diaries and had few intimate friends to set straight the details of his life, and the vivid derangements portrayed in his writings and the tales of his own depravities (many of which he told himself for their shock effect) have created a portrait of the writer and the man that is tantalizing and mysterious.

He was born Edgar Poe, in Boston, the child of traveling actors. Before he reached the age of three, the youngster's father deserted the family, his mother died, and he was taken into the home of John Allan, a prosperous merchant of Richmond, Virginia. Allan treated his foster child with alternating leniency and harsh severity. He had Poe baptized with the middle name of Allan but failed to adopt him legally. In 1815 Allan moved to Europe on business, settling his family in England, where Poe was entered in school. Five years later, the Allans returned to Virginia, where Poe's schoolmaster judged him "not especially studious" but an "excellent classicist" and "the best reader of Latin verse."

When he was seventeen, Poe entered the University of Virginia, where he distinguished himself in Latin and French and soon gained a reputation as a self-proclaimed

[1]Written shortly after the assassination of Abraham Lincoln on April 14, 1865.
[2]Slaves. [3]Shackles, leg irons.

"aristocrat," a poet, and a wit as well as a gambler and a heavy drinker. The next year, after bitter quarrels with "Master Allan," who refused to pay Poe's gambling debts—he had lost $2,000 at cards—Poe left the university and ran off to Boston, where he enlisted in the U.S. Army.

While stationed in Boston, he arranged the publication of his first book of poetry, Tamerlane and Other Poems *(1827). Two years later, he gained his release from the army, and soon after, revised some of his earlier poems and added some new work to publish a second volume,* Al Aaraaf, Tamerlane, and Minor Poems. *Following the death of his foster mother, Poe was briefly reconciled with Allan, who helped him secure appointment to West Point. Poe entered the academy as a cadet, when he was twenty-one, but he remained only eight months. Galled by academy regulations and angered by a lack of support from his foster father (Poe knew the army was no career for a poor man with literary interests), he deliberately violated a series of minor regulations, cut classes, and disobeyed orders to attend church—all of which contributed to his dismissal in 1831. Just after he left West Point, Poe published his third volume of poetry, dedicating it to "the U.S. Corps of Cadets." He then moved to Baltimore, where he lived with his aunt and devoted himself to earning his way as a writer.*

In 1832, Poe earned a few dollars publishing stories in the Saturday Courier, *a Philadelphia literary weekly. A year later, he won first prize of $100 in a short story contest run by a Baltimore newspaper. But Poe didn't begin earning a regular paycheck until he returned to Richmond, where he was appointed editor—at a salary of $10 a week—of the* Southern Literary Messenger. *During his time there, Poe experienced good fortune in both career and personal prospects, publishing a series of stories, poems, and acid literary reviews for the* Messenger, *and marrying his thirteen-year-old cousin, Virginia Clemm. But Poe's temper and habits went unchanged, and four years later, he left the* Messenger *and Richmond after a bitter argument with the owner—an angry scene that Poe was to repeat throughout his career.*

In 1838 he published The Narrative of Arthur Gordon Pym, *a tale of voyage and discovery which was Poe's only full-length novel. The next year he became coeditor of* Burton's Gentleman's Magazine, *a Philadelphia literary monthly to which he contributed "The Fall of the House of Usher" (1839) and his sonnet "Silence" (1840). Late in 1839* Tales of the Grotesque and Arabesque *appeared, his first collection of short stories (it sold fewer than 750 copies). But within a few months he was again discharged after an argument with the magazine's publisher over the severity of Poe's critical reviews and his irresponsibility. Poe next became an editor of another Philadelphia monthly,* Graham's Magazine, *which printed (in April 1841) "The Murders in the Rue Morgue," one of the first prototypes for popular American detective stories.*

The next year Poe left Graham's *to eke out an impoverished living by editing, lecturing, and writing short stories, poems, and reviews. While living in New York, in 1844, he wrote "The Raven," his most famous work. The poem became an immediate success and was quickly reprinted and even anthologized in a school text. Yet Poe remained "as poor now as ever I was in my life." In 1845 he became editor of the* Broadway Journal, *a monthly magazine of New York. It was for the* Journal *that Poe wrote a series of five articles on the "plagiarisms" he perceived in Longfellow's work. His articles drew wide attention and began what came to be called "The Longfellow War," but they did little to raise the circulation of the magazine.*

The next year, Poe had to face the untimely death of his young wife. Assaulted by his loss, his extreme poverty, and his own instability, Poe nonetheless continued to write, saying "I have a great deal to do; and I have made up my mind not to die 'til it is done." He embarked on a series of unsuccessful publishing schemes and unfortunate romances with his female literary admirers. Hoping to improve his circumstances, Poe returned briefly to

Richmond, where he became engaged to a childhood sweetheart, and then he set out for Philadelphia for yet another editing job. On the way, he stopped in Baltimore, and there, on October 2, 1849, he was found unconscious on the street. Four days later, he died.

Poe's life had been a series of disasters, including psychologically crippling childhood deprivations, bitter literary squabbles, overwhelming poverty, failed publishing ventures, and a suicide attempt in 1848. More harmful still to his reputation was his treatment at the hands of his literary executor, Rufus Griswold, an editor and anthologizer whom Poe had taken for a friend. In a vicious obituary that appeared in the New York Tribune *two days after Poe's death, and in a biographical "memoir" written for a commemorative edition of Poe's* Works *issued in 1850, Griswold painted a picture of Poe as a demonic and depraved man. It was later discovered that Griswold had altered the text of Poe's private letters to lend support to his harsh portrait of Poe. Griswold's account aided the sale of Poe's books, but it completely destroyed Poe's personal reputation and helped to confuse the facts of his life with legends and half-truths. As a result, he has long lived in the popular mind either as a drug addict, the incarnation of one of his own mad narrators, or as a noble and sensitive man, a Byronic hero, haunted by his own genius and destroyed by a cruel society and false friends.*

Americans long judged Poe's writing according to the legends surrounding his life. Patriots seeking a national literature charged that he lacked an American vision. The literary realists of the next generations complained that his work ignored American themes. Contemporaries, like poet Ralph Waldo Emerson called him "the jingle man," and novelist Mark Twain pronounced that he would read him only "on salary." Throughout his lifetime, Poe, derided as "the tomahawk man," made a host of literary enemies, who complained that his reviews were savage, and that he demonstrated vituperative coarseness and false erudition.

As a writer, Poe found his inspiration in a world of disorder, perversity, and romantic emotion. He helped establish one of the world's most popular literary genres, the detective story. His writing influenced a variety of writers who range from A. Conan Doyle and Robert Louis Stevenson to William Faulkner, T. S. Eliot, and H. P. Lovecraft. He was among the first modern literary theorists of America, and his arguments against the didactic motive for literature and for the creation of beauty and intensity of emotion, although they ran counter to the prevailing literary ideals of his time, have had a profound effect on the writers and critics who followed him. And more than a century and a half after his death, Poe remains one of the foremost writers of America and one of the most popular authors in the world.

FURTHER READING: *The Works of Edgar A. Poe,* 10 vols., ed. E. Stedman and G. Woodberry, 1894–1895; *The Complete Poems and Stories of Edgar Allan Poe,* 2 vols., ed. A. Quinn and E. O'Neill, 1946; *The Poems of Edgar Allan Poe,* ed. F. Stovall, 1965; *The Short Fiction of Edgar Allan Poe, An Annotated Edition,* ed. S. Levine and S. Levine, 1976, 1990; *The Letters of Edgar Allan Poe,* 2 vols., ed. J. Ostrom, 1948, 1966; *Edgar Allan Poe, The Critical Heritage,* ed. I. Walker, 1986; *Edgar Allan Poe, The Design of Order,* ed. A. Lee, 1987; D. Thomas and D. Jackson, *The Poe Log: A Documentary Life,* 1987; J. Kennedy, *Poe, Death, and the Life of Writing,* 1987; K. Silverman, *Edgar Allan Poe,* 1991; *On Poe,* ed. L. Budd and E. Cady, 1992; J. Meyers, *Edgar Allan Poe, His Life and Legacy,* 1992; E. Carlson, *A Companion to Poe Studies,* 1996; F. Frank and A. Magistrale, *The Poe Encyclopedia,* 1997; S. Peeples, *Edgar Allan Poe Revisited,* 1998; J. Hammond, *An Edgar Allan Poe Chronology,* 1998; K. Hayes, *Poe and the Printed Word,* 2000; J. Kennedy, *A Historical Guide to Edgar Allan Poe,* 2001; *The Cambridge Companion to Edgar Allan Poe,* ed. K. Hayes, 2002.

TEXTS: Poems and fiction are from *Collected Works of Edgar Allan Poe,* 3 vols., ed. T. Mabbott, 1969–1978. Essays are from *The Complete Works of Edgar Allan Poe,* 17 vols., ed. J. A. Harrison, 1902.

SONNET—TO SCIENCE

Science! true daughter of Old Time thou art!
Who alterest all things with thy peering eyes.
Why preyest thou thus upon the poet's heart,
Vulture, whose wings are dull realities?
How should he love thee? or how deem thee wise,
Who wouldst not leave him in his wandering
To seek for treasure in the jewelled skies,
Albeit he soared with an undaunted wing?
Hast thou not dragged Diana[1] from her car?
And driven the Hamadryad[2] from the wood
To seek a shelter in some happier star?
Hast thou not torn the Naiad from her flood,
The Elfin[3] from the green grass, and from me
The summer dream beneath the tamarind[4] tree?

1829, 1843

TO HELEN[1]

Helen, thy beauty is to me
Like those Nicéan[2] barks of yore,
That gently, o'er a perfumed sea,
The weary, way-worn wanderer bore
To his own native shore.

On desperate seas long wont to roam,
Thy hyacinth[3] hair, thy classic face,
Thy Naiad[4] airs have brought me home
To the glory that was Greece,
And the grandeur that was Rome.

Lo! in yon brilliant window-niche
How statue-like I see thee stand,
The agate lamp within thy hand!
Ah, Psyche,[5] from the regions which
Are Holy-Land!

1831, 1845

[1]Roman goddess often identified with the moon, her "car."
[2]In Greek myth, nymphs (female spirits) of the trees were Hamadryads. Nymphs of rivers and lakes were Naiads. [3]Elf. [4]An aromatic tree of the Indies.

[1]One of Poe's most famous lyrics, inspired by Mrs. Jane Stith Stanard, the mother of a schoolmate of Poe, in Richmond, Virginia. Poe described the poem as "lines written, in my passionate boyhood, to the first, purely ideal love of my soul." The Helen of Greek myth was the beautiful daughter of Zeus. Her abduction by Paris caused the Trojan War, the subject of Homer's *Iliad.*
[2]The word means "victorious." Poe's meaning is unclear. He may have intended reference to the ancient city of Nicea (or Nicaea), in Turkey, which was associated with the god Dionysus, a wanderer. Although many different interpretations have been put forward, all agree on the musical quality of the term and its implications of classical antiquity.
[3]Curly. [4]Nymphs of more placid fresh water, contrasted to the "desperate seas" above.
[5]Greek: soul. In classical legend Psyche, the lover of Cupid, was a woman so beautiful that the goddess Venus was jealous of her.

THE CITY IN THE SEA[1]

Lo! Death has reared himself a throne
In a strange city lying alone
Far down within the dim West,
Where the good and the bad and the worst and the best
Have gone to their eternal rest.
There shrines and palaces and towers
(Time-eaten towers that tremble not!)
Resemble nothing that is ours.
Around, by lifting winds forgot,
Resignedly beneath the sky
The melancholy waters lie.

No rays from the holy heaven come down
On the long night-time of that town;
But light from out the lurid sea
Streams up the turrets silently—
Gleams up the pinnacles far and free
Up domes—up spires—up kingly halls—
Up fanes[2]—up Babylon-like walls[3]
Up shadowy long-forgotten bowers
Of sculptured ivy and stone flowers—
Up many and many a marvellous shrine
Whose wreathéd friezes intertwine
The viol, the violet, and the vine.

Resignedly beneath the sky
The melancholy waters lie.
So blend the turrets and shadows there
That all seem pendulous in air,
While from a proud tower in the town
Death looks gigantically down.

There open fanes and gaping graves
Yawn level with the luminous waves;
But not the riches there that lie
In each idol's diamond eye—
Not the gaily-jewelled dead
Tempt the waters from their bed;
For no ripples curl, alas!
Along that wilderness of glass—
No swellings tell that winds may be
Upon some far-off happier sea—
No heavings hint that winds have been
On seas less hideously serene.

[1]Earlier entitled "The Doomed City" (1831) and "The City of Sin" (1836). It derives from numerous legends of drowned and buried cities. [2]Temples.
[3]In the Bible, the wicked city of Babylon and its walls were doomed to destruction by the Lord. See Isaiah 14 and 21; Revelation 16–18.

But lo, a stir is in the air!
The wave—there is a movement there!
As if the towers had thrust aside,
In slightly sinking, the dull tide—
As if their tops had feebly given
A void within the filmy Heaven.
The waves have now a redder glow—
The hours are breathing faint and low—
And when, amid no earthly moans,
Down, down that town shall settle hence,
Hell, rising from a thousand thrones,[4]
Shall do it reverence.

1831, 1845

SONNET[1]—SILENCE

There are some qualities—some incorporate things,
  That have a double life, which thus is made
A type of that twin entity which springs
  From matter and light, evinced in solid and shade.
There is a two-fold *Silence*—sea and shore—
  Body and Soul. One dwells in lonely places,
  Newly with grass o'ergrown; some solemn graces,
Some human memories and tearful lore,
Render him terrorless: his name's "No more."
He is the corporate Silence: dread him not!
  No power hath he of evil in himself;
But should some urgent fate (untimely lot!)
  Bring thee to meet his shadow (nameless elf,
That haunteth the lone regions where hath trod
No foot of man,) commend thyself to God!

1840, 1845

LENORE

Ah, broken is the golden bowl![1]—the spirit flown forever!
Let the bell toll!—a saintly soul floats on the Stygian river:—
And, Guy De Vere,[2] hast *thou* no tear?—weep now or never more!
See! on yon drear and rigid bier low lies thy love, Lenore!

[4]"Hell . . . stirreth up the dead for thee, even all the chief ones of the earth; it hath raised up from their thrones all the kings of the nations." Isaiah 14:9.

[1]One of Poe's five sonnets; a deliberate 15-line variation from the conventional 14-line sonnet form.

[1]"Or ever the silver cord be loosed, or the golden bowl be broken. . . . Then shall the dust return to the earth as it was: and the spirit shall return unto God." Ecclesiastes 12:6–7.

[2]An "aristocratic" name (suggesting "true") that Poe probably took from the popular fiction of the day.

Come, let the burial rite be read—the funeral song be sung!—
An anthem for the queenliest dead that ever died so young—
A dirge for her the doubly dead in that she died so young.
"Wretches! ye loved her for her wealth and ye hated her for her pride;
And, when she fell in feeble health, ye blessed[3] her—that she died:—
How *shall* the ritual[4] then be read—the requiem[5] how be sung
By you—by yours, the evil eye—by yours the slanderous tongue
That did to death the innocence that died and died so young?"

Peccavimus.[6]—yet rave not thus! but let a Sabbath song
Go up to God so solemnly the dead may feel no wrong!
The sweet Lenore hath gone before, with Hope that flew beside,
Leaving thee wild for the dear child that should have been thy bride—
For her, the fair and debonair, that now so lowly lies,
The life upon her yellow hair, but not within her eyes—
The life still there upon her hair, the death upon her eyes.

"Avaunt![7]—avaunt! to friends from fiends the indigent ghost is riven—
From Hell unto a high estate within the utmost Heaven—
From moan and groan to a golden throne beside the King of Heaven:—
Let *no* bell toll, then, lest her soul, amid its hallowed mirth
Should catch the note as it doth float up from the damnéd Earth!
And I—tonight my heart is light:—no dirge will I upraise,
But waft the angel on her flight with a Pæan[8] of old days!"

1843, 1849

THE RAVEN

Once upon a midnight dreary, while I pondered, weak and weary,
Over many a quaint and curious volume of forgotten lore—
While I nodded, nearly napping, suddenly there came a tapping,
As of some one gently rapping, rapping at my chamber door—
" 'Tis some visiter," I muttered, "tapping at my chamber door—
Only this and nothing more."

Ah, distinctly I remember it was in the bleak December;
And each separate dying ember wrought its ghost upon the floor.
Eagerly I wished the morrow;—vainly I had sought to borrow
From my books surcease of sorrow—sorrow for the lost Lenore—
For the rare and radiant maiden whom the angels name Lenore—
Nameless *here*[1] for evermore.

[3]Used ironically to mean "cursed."
[4]Burial service.
[5]Hymn used in services for the dead.
[6]"We have sinned." From the Latin version of Psalm 106:6.
[7]Be gone!
[8]Joyful song.
[1]I.e., not named or spoken to in this world.

And the silken, sad, uncertain rustling of each purple curtain
Thrilled me—filled me with fantastic terrors never felt before;
So that now, to still the beating of my heart, I stood repeating
"'Tis some visiter entreating entrance at my chamber door—
Some late visiter entreating entrance at my chamber door;—
This it is and nothing more."

Presently my soul grew stronger; hesitating then no longer,
"Sir," said I, "or Madam, truly your forgiveness I implore;
But the fact is I was napping, and so gently you came rapping,
And so faintly you came tapping, tapping at my chamber door,
That I scarce was sure I heard you"—here I opened wide the door;—
Darkness there and nothing more.

Deep into that darkness peering, long I stood there wondering, fearing,
Doubting, dreaming dreams no mortal ever dared to dream before;
But the silence was unbroken, and the stillness gave no token,
And the only word there spoken was the whispered word, "Lenore!"
This I whispered, and an echo murmured back the word, "Lenore!"
Merely this and nothing more.

Back into the chamber turning, all my soul within me burning,
Soon again I heard a tapping somewhat louder than before.
"Surely," said I, "surely that is something at my window lattice;
Let me see, then, what thereat is, and this mystery explore—
Let my heart be still a moment and this mystery explore;—
'Tis the wind and nothing more!"

Open here I flung the shutter, when, with many a flirt[2] and flutter,
In there stepped a stately Raven of the saintly days of yore;
Not the least obeisance made he; not a minute stopped or stayed he;
But, with mien of lord or lady, perched above my chamber door—
Perched upon a bust of Pallas[3] just above my chamber door—
Perched, and sat, and nothing more.

Then this ebony bird beguiling my sad fancy into smiling,
By the grave and stern decorum of the countenance it wore,
"Though thy crest be shorn and shaven, thou," I said, "art sure no craven,
Ghastly grim and ancient Raven wandering from the Nightly shore—
Tell me what thy lordly name is on the Night's Plutonian[4] shore!"
Quoth the Raven "Nevermore."

Much I marvelled this ungainly fowl to hear discourse so plainly,
Though its answer little meaning—little relevancy bore;
For we cannot help agreeing that no living human being
Ever yet was blessed with seeing bird above his chamber door—
Bird or beast upon the sculptured bust above his chamber door,
With such name as "Nevermore."

[2]Erratic movement. [3]Pallas Athena, in Greek myth the patron goddess of Athens.
[4]In Roman myth, Pluto ruled in Hades, the abode of the dead.

But the Raven, sitting lonely on the placid bust, spoke only
That one word, as if his soul in that one word he did outpour.
Nothing farther then he uttered—not a feather then he fluttered—
Till I scarcely more than muttered "Other friends have flown before—
On the morrow *he* will leave me, as my Hopes have flown before."
Then the bird said "Nevermore."

Startled at the stillness broken by reply so aptly spoken,
"Doubtless," said I, "what it utters is its only stock and store
Caught from some unhappy master whom unmerciful Disaster
Followed fast and followed faster till his songs one burden bore—
Till the dirges of his Hope that melancholy burden bore—
Of 'Never—nevermore.' "

But the Raven still beguiling my sad fancy into smiling,
Straight I wheeled a cushioned seat in front of bird, and bust and door;
Then, upon the velvet sinking, I betook myself to linking
Fancy unto fancy, thinking what this ominous bird of yore—
What this grim, ungainly, ghastly, gaunt, and ominous bird of yore
Meant in croaking "Nevermore."

Thus I sat engaged in guessing, but no syllable expressing
To the fowl whose fiery eyes now burned into my bosom's core;
This and more I sat divining, with my head at ease reclining
On the cushion's velvet lining that the lamp-light gloated[5] o'er,
But whose velvet-violet lining with the lamp-light gloating o'er,
She shall press, ah, nevermore!

Then, methought, the air grew denser, perfumed from an unseen censer
Swung by seraphim[6] whose foot-falls tinkled[7] on the tufted floor.
"Wretch," I cried, "thy God hath lent thee—by these angels he hath sent thee
Respite—respite and nepenthe[8] from thy memories of Lenore;
Quaff, oh quaff this kind nepenthe and forget this lost Lenore!"
Quoth the Raven "Nevermore."

"Prophet!" said I, "thing of evil!—prophet still, if bird or devil!—
Whether Tempter sent, or whether tempest tossed thee here ashore,
Desolate yet all undaunted, on the desert land enchanted—
On this home by Horror haunted—tell me truly, I implore—
Is there—*is* there balm in Gilead?[9]—tell me—tell me, I implore!"
Quoth the Raven "Nevermore."

[5]Meaning both "to look down on with evil satisfaction" and "to refract or reflect light."
[6]Angels.
[7]A reference to the sound of the small bells traditionally worn on the ankles and skirt hems of dancers in the Near East.
[8]In classical myth, a drink that banishes sorrow.
[9]"Is there no balm in Gilead?" Jeremiah 8:22. The balm was a medicine made from the resin of trees that grew in Gilead, in Jordan.

"Prophet!" said I, "thing of evil!—prophet still, if bird or devil!
By that Heaven that bends above us—by that God we both adore—
Tell this soul with sorrow laden if, within the distant Aidenn,[10]
It shall clasp a sainted maiden whom the angels name Lenore—
Clasp a rare and radiant maiden whom the angels name Lenore."
Quoth the Raven "Nevermore."

"Be that word our sign of parting, bird or fiend!" I shrieked, upstarting—
"Get thee back into the tempest and the Night's Plutonian shore!
Leave no black plume as a token of that lie thy soul hath spoken!
Leave my loneliness unbroken!—quit the bust above my door!
Take thy beak from out my heart, and take thy form from off my door!"
Quoth the Raven "Nevermore."

And the Raven, never flitting, still is sitting, *still* is sitting
On the pallid bust of Pallas just above my chamber door;
And his eyes have all the seeming of a demon's that is dreaming,
And the lamp-light o'er him streaming throws his shadow on the floor;
And my soul from out that shadow that lies floating on the floor
Shall be lifted—nevermore!

1844 1845, 1849

ANNABEL LEE[1]

It was many and many a year ago,
In a kingdom by the sea,
That a maiden there lived whom you may know
By the name of Annabel Lee;—
And this maiden she lived with no other thought
Than to love and be loved by me.

She was a child and *I* was a child,
In this kingdom by the sea,
But we loved with a love that was more than love—
I and my Annabel Lee—
With a love that the wingéd seraphs of Heaven
Coveted her and me.

And this was the reason that, long ago,
In this kingdom by the sea,
A wind blew out of a cloud by night
Chilling my Annabel Lee;
So that her highborn kinsmen came
And bore her away from me,
To shut her up, in a sepulchre
In this kingdom by the sea.

[10]Arabic *Adn* meaning "Eden" or "heaven."

[1]Poe's last poem, first published on October 9, 1849, two days after his death. The text reprinted here includes Poe's last revisions, among them a change in the final line. Earlier versions read, "In her tomb by the sounding sea." The change, in the view of most critics, was unfortunate.

The angels, not half so happy in Heaven,
Went envying her and me:—
Yes! that was the reason (as all men know,
In this kingdom by the sea)
That the wind came out of the cloud, chilling
And killing my Annabel Lee.

But our love it was stronger by far than the love
Of those who were older than we—
Of many far wiser than we—
And neither the angels in Heaven above
Nor the demons down under the sea
Can ever dissever my soul from the soul
Of the beautiful Annabel Lee:—

For the moon never beams without bringing me dreams
Of the beautiful Annabel Lee;
And the stars never rise but I see the bright eyes
Of the beautiful Annabel Lee;
And so, all the night-tide, I lie down by the side
Of my darling, my darling, my life and my bride
In her sepulchre there by the sea—
In her tomb by the side of the sea.

1849 1849

LIGEIA[1]

And the will therein lieth, which dieth not. Who knoweth the mysteries of the will, with its vigor? For God is but a great will pervading all things by nature of its intentness. Man doth not yield himself to the angels, nor unto death utterly, save only through the weakness of his feeble will.

JOSEPH GLANVILL[2]

I cannot, for my soul, remember how, when, or even precisely where, I first became acquainted with the lady Ligeia. Long years have since elapsed, and my memory is feeble through much suffering. Or, perhaps, I cannot *now* bring these points to mind, because, in truth, the character of my beloved, her rare learning, her singular yet placid cast of beauty, and the thrilling and enthralling eloquence of her low musical language, made their way into my heart by paces so steadily and stealthily progressive that they have been unnoticed and unknown. Yet I believe that I met her first and most frequently in some large, old, decaying city near the Rhine. Of her family—I have surely heard her speak. That it is of a remotely ancient date cannot be doubted.

[1]A name derived perhaps from Greek *ligys,* meaning clear-sounding, shrill. Virgil used the name for a dryad in his *Georgics,* Book IV, line 336. In Milton's *Comus,* it is the name of a Siren (line 880).

[2]Joseph Glanvill (1636–1680), English philosopher and believer in spiritualism and the occult. The quotation has not been found in his writings. It was, perhaps, contrived by Poe.

Ligeia! Ligeia! Buried in studies of a nature more than all else adapted to deaden impressions of the outward world, it is by that sweet word alone—by Ligeia—that I bring before mine eyes in fancy the image of her who is no more. And now, while I write, a recollection flashes upon me that I have *never known* the paternal name of her who was my friend and my betrothed, and who became the partner of my studies, and finally the wife of my bosom. Was it a playful charge on the part of my Ligeia? or was it a test of my strength of affection, that I should institute no inquiries upon this point? or was it rather a caprice of my own—a wildly romantic offering on the shrine of the most passionate devotion? I but indistinctly recall the fact itself—what wonder that I have utterly forgotten the circumstances which originated or attended it? And, indeed, if ever that spirit which is entitled *Romance*—if ever she, the wan and the misty-winged *Ashtophet*[3] of idolatrous Egypt, presided, as they tell, over marriages ill-omened, then most surely she presided over mine.

There is one dear topic, however, on which my memory fails me not. It is the *person* of Ligeia. In stature she was tall, somewhat slender, and, in her latter days, even emaciated. I would in vain attempt to portray the majesty, the quiet ease of her demeanor, or the incomprehensible lightness and elasticity of her footfall. She came and departed as a shadow. I was never made aware of her entrance into my closed study save by the dear music of her low sweet voice, as she placed her marble hand upon my shoulder. In beauty of face no maiden ever equalled her. It was the radiance of an opium-dream—an airy and spirit-lifting vision more wildly divine than the fantasies which hovered about the slumbering souls of the daughters of Delos.[4] Yet her features were not of that regular mould which we have been falsely taught to worship in the classical labors of the heathen. "There is no exquisite beauty," says Bacon, Lord Verulam, speaking truly of all the forms and *genera* of beauty, "without some *strangeness* in the proportion.[5] Yet, although I saw that the features of Ligeia were not of a classic regularity—although I perceived that her loveliness was indeed "exquisite," and felt that there was much of "strangeness" pervading it, yet I have tried in vain to detect the irregularity and to trace home my own perception of "the strange." I examined the contour of the lofty and pale forehead—it was faultless—how cold indeed that word when applied to a majesty so divine!—the skin rivalling the purest ivory, the commanding extent and repose, the gentle prominence of the regions above the temples; and then the raven-black, the glossy, the luxuriant and naturally-curling tresses, setting forth the full force of the Homeric epithet, "hyacinthine!"[6] I looked at the delicate outlines of the nose—and nowhere but in the graceful medallions of the Hebrews[7] had I beheld a similar perfection.

[3]Goddess of love and fertility of the ancient Near East.

[4]Island in the Aegean, associated with many Greek myths, among them that of two maidens from beyond the north wind who came bringing offerings of the first fruits. Upon their death they were entombed, and in their honor the youth of Delos placed offerings of their hair on the tombs.

[5]From "Of Beauty," in the *Essays* (1625) of Francis Bacon, Baron Verulam (1561–1626). Poe substituted "exquisite" for Bacon's "excellent."

[6]The curly hair of Odysseus is compared to the hyacinth in Homer's *Odyssey*, Book VI, line 231.

[7]Perhaps a reference to medallions found, with other artifacts, in nineteenth-century archeological explorations of the Bible lands.

There were the same luxurious smoothness of surface, the same scarcely perceptible tendency to the aquiline,[8] the same harmoniously curved nostrils speaking the free spirit. I regarded the sweet mouth. Here was indeed the triumph of all things heavenly—the magnificent turn of the short upper lip—the soft, voluptuous slumber of the under—the dimples which sported, and the color which spoke—the teeth glancing back, with a brilliancy almost startling, every ray of the holy light which fell upon them in her serene and placid, yet most exultingly radiant of all smiles. I scrutinized the formation of the chin—and here, too, I found the gentleness of breadth, the softness and the majesty, the fullness and the spirituality, of the Greek—the contour which the god Apollo revealed but in a dream, to Cleomenes,[9] the son of the Athenian. And then I peered into the large eyes of Ligeia.

For eyes we have no models in the remotely antique. It might have been, too, that in these eyes of my beloved lay the secret to which Lord Verulam alludes. They were, I must believe, far larger than the ordinary eyes of our own race. They were even fuller than the fullest of the gazelle eyes of the tribe of the valley of Nourjahad.[10] Yet it was only at intervals—in moments of intense excitement—that this peculiarity became more than slightly noticeable in Ligeia. And at such moments was her beauty—in my heated fancy thus it appeared perhaps—the beauty of beings either above or apart from the earth—the beauty of the fabulous Houri of the Turk. The hue of the orbs was the most brilliant of black, and, far over them, hung jetty lashes of great length. The brows, slightly irregular in outline, had the same tint. The "strangeness," however, which I found in the eyes, was of a nature distinct from the formation, or the color, or the brilliancy of the features, and must, after all, be referred to the *expression*. Ah, word of no meaning! behind whose vast latitude of mere sound we intrench our ignorance of so much of the spiritual. The expression of the eyes of Ligeia! How for long hours have I pondered upon it! How have I, through the whole of a midsummer night, struggled to fathom it! What was it—that something more profound than the well of Democritus[11]—which lay far within the pupils of my beloved? What *was* it? I was possessed with a passion to discover. Those eyes! those large, those shining, those divine orbs! they became to me twin stars of Leda,[12] and I to them devoutest of astrologers.

There is no point, among the many incomprehensible anomalies of the science of mind, more thrillingly exciting than the fact—never, I believe, noticed in the schools—that, in our endeavors to recall to memory something long forgotten, we often find ourselves *upon the very verge* of remembrance, without being able, in the end, to remember. And thus how frequently, in my intense scrutiny of Ligeia's eyes, have I felt approaching the full knowledge of their expression—felt it approaching—yet not quite be mine—and so at length entirely depart! And (strange, oh strangest mystery of all!) I found, in

[8]Curved, like an eagle's beak.

[9]Greek sculptor of Athens, reputedly the creator of the third-century B.C. statue that was the original of the Medici Aphrodite.

[10]A land of beautiful women in the Oriental romance, *The History of Nourjahad* (1767), by Frances Sheridan (1724–1766), the mother of the playwright Richard Sheridan.

[11]Greek philosopher (fifth century B.C.) who remarked that "truth lies at the bottom of a well."

[12]Leda and Zeus had twin sons, Castor and Pollux. Upon their death, they were transformed by Zeus into stars of the constellation Gemini.

the commonest objects of the universe, a circle of analogies to that expression. I mean to say that, subsequently to the period when Ligeia's beauty passed into my spirit, there dwelling as in a shrine, I derived, from many existences in the material world, a sentiment such as I felt always aroused within me by her large and luminous orbs. Yet not the more could I define that sentiment, or analyze, or even steadily view it. I recognized it, let me repeat, sometimes in the survey of a rapidly-growing vine—in the contemplation of a moth, a butterfly, a chrysalis, a stream of running water. I have felt it in the ocean; in the falling of a meteor. I have felt it in the glances of unusually aged people. And there are one or two stars in heaven—(one especially, a star of the sixth magnitude, double and changeable, to be found near the large star in Lyra[13]) in a telescopic scrutiny of which I have been made aware of the feeling. I have been filled with it by certain sounds from stringed instruments, and not unfrequently by passages from books. Among innumerable other instances, I well remember something in a volume of Joseph Glanvill, which (perhaps merely from its quaintness—who shall say?) never failed to inspire me with the sentiment;—"And the will therein lieth, which dieth not. Who knoweth the mysteries of the will, with its vigor? For God is but a great will pervading all things by nature of its intentness. Man doth not yield him to the angels, nor unto death utterly, save only through the weakness of his feeble will."

Length of years, and subsequent reflections, have enabled me to trace, indeed, some remote connection between this passage in the English moralist and a portion of the character of Ligeia. An *intensity* in thought, action, or speech, was possibly, in her, a result, or at least an index, of that gigantic volition which, during our long intercourse, failed to give other and more immediate evidence of its existence. Of all the women whom I have ever known, she, the outwardly calm, the ever-placid Ligeia, was the most violently a prey to the tumultuous vultures of stern passion. And of such passion I could form no estimate, save by the miraculous expansion of those eyes which at once so delighted and appalled me—by the almost magical melody, modulation, distinctness, and placidity of her very low voice—and by the fierce energy (rendered doubly effective by contrast with her manner of utterance) of the wild words which she habitually uttered.

I have spoken of the learning of Ligeia; it was immense—such as I have never known in woman. In the classical tongues was she deeply proficient, and as far as my own acquaintance extended in regard to the modern dialects of Europe, I have never known her at fault. Indeed upon any theme of the most admired, because simply the most abstruse of the boasted erudition of the academy, have I *ever* found Ligeia at fault? How singularly—how thrillingly, this one point in the nature of my wife has forced itself, at this late period only, upon my attention! I said her knowledge was such as I have never known in woman—but where breathes the man who has traversed, and successfully, *all* the wide areas of moral, physical, and mathematical science? I saw not then what I now clearly perceive, that the acquisitions of Ligeia were gigantic, were astounding; yet I was sufficiently aware of her infinite supremacy to resign myself, with a childlike confidence, to her guidance through the chaotic world of metaphysical investigation at which I was most

[13]A constellation containing the bright star Vega.

busily occupied during the earlier years of our marriage. With how vast a triumph—with how vivid a delight—with how much of all that is ethereal in hope—did I *feel*, as she bent over me in studies but little sought—but less known—that delicious vista by slow degrees expanding before me, down whose long, gorgeous, and all untrodden path, I might at length pass onward to the goal of a wisdom too divinely precious not to be forbidden!

How poignant, then, must have been the grief with which, after some years, I beheld my well-grounded expectations take wings to themselves and fly away! Without Ligeia I was but as a child groping benighted. Her presence, her readings alone, rendered vividly luminous the many mysteries of the transcendentalism in which we were immersed. Wanting the radiant lustre of her eyes, letters, lambent and golden, grew duller than Saturnian[14] lead. And now those eyes shone less and less frequently upon the pages over which I pored. Ligeia grew ill. The wild eyes blazed with a too—too glorious effulgence; the pale fingers became of the transparent waxen hue of the grave, and the blue veins upon the lofty forehead swelled and sank impetuously with the tides of the most gentle emotion. I saw that she must die—and I struggled desperately in spirit with the grim Azrael.[15] And the struggles of the passionate wife were, to my astonishment, even more energetic than my own. There had been much in her stern nature to impress me with the belief that, to her, death would have come without its terrors;—but not so. Words are impotent to convey any just idea of the fierceness of resistance with which she wrestled with the Shadow.[16] I groaned in anguish at the pitiable spectacle. I would have soothed—I would have reasoned; but, in the intensity of her wild desire for life,—for life—*but* for life—solace and reason were alike the uttermost of folly. Yet not until the last instance, amid the most convulsive writhings of her fierce spirit, was shaken the external placidity of her demeanor. Her voice grew more gentle—grew more low—yet I would not wish to dwell upon the wild meaning of the quietly uttered words. My brain reeled as I harkened entranced, to a melody more than mortal—to assumptions and aspirations which mortality had never before known.

That she loved me I should not have doubted; and I might have been easily aware that, in a bosom such as hers, love would have reigned no ordinary passion. But in death only, was I fully impressed with the strength of her affection. For long hours, detaining my hand, would she pour out before me the overflowing of a heart whose more than passionate devotion amounted to idolatry. How had I deserved to be so blessed by such confessions?—how had I deserved to be so cursed with the removal of my beloved in the hour of her making them? But upon this subject I cannot bear to dilate. Let me say only, that in Ligeia's more than womanly abandonment to a love, alas! all unmerited, all unworthily bestowed, I at length recognized the principle of her longing with so wildly earnest a desire for the life which was now fleeing so rapidly away. It is this wild longing—it is this eager vehemence of desire for life—*but* for life—that I have no power to portray—no utterance capable of expressing.

[14]The astrological influence of Saturn was supposed to make one gloomy, dull.
[15]The Angel of Death in Muslim and Jewish legend.
[16]Death.

At high noon of the night in which she departed, beckoning me, peremptorily, to her side, she bade me repeat certain verses composed by herself not many days before. I obeyed her.—They were these:

Lo! 'tis a gala night
  Within the lonesome latter years!
An angel throng, bewinged, bedight[17]
  In veils, and drowned in tears,
Sit in a theatre, to see
  A play of hopes and fears,
While the orchestra breathes fitfully
  The music of the spheres.[18]

Mimes,[19] in the form of God on high,
  Mutter and mumble low,
And hither and thither fly—
  Mere puppets they, who come and go
At bidding of vast formless things
  That shift the scenery to and fro,
Flapping from out their Condor wings
  Invisible Wo!

That motley[20] drama!—oh, be sure
  It shall not be forgot!
With its Phantom chased forever more,
  By a crowd that seize it not,
Through a circle that ever returneth in
  To the self-same spot,
And much of Madness and more of Sin
  And Horror the soul of the plot.

But see, amid the mimic rout,
  A crawling shape intrude!
A blood-red thing that writhes from out
  The scenic solitude!
It writhes!—it writhes!—with mortal pangs
  The mimes become its food,
And the seraphs sob at vermin fangs
  In human gore imbued.

Out—out are the lights—out all!
  And over each quivering form,
The curtain, a funeral pall,
  Comes down with the rush of a storm,
And the angels, all pallid and wan,
  Uprising, unveiling, affirm
That the play is the tragedy, "Man,"
  And its hero the Conqueror Worm.

[17]Adorned.

[18]To ancient astronomers the stars and planets seemed to be set in concentric, revolving, transparent spheres. When they revolved, the resulting friction was thought to produce divine melodies, "the music of the spheres." [19]Mimics. [20]Incongruous, mixed.

"O God!" half shrieked Ligeia, leaping to her feet and extending her arms aloft with a spasmodic movement, as I made an end of those lines—"O God! O Divine Father!—shall these things be undeviatingly so?—shall this Conqueror be not once conquered? Are we not part and parcel in Thee? Who—who knoweth the mysteries of the will with its vigor? Man doth not yield him to the angels, *nor unto death utterly,* save only through the weakness of his feeble will."

And now, as if exhausted with emotion, she suffered her white arms to fall, and returned solemnly to her bed of death. And as she breathed her last sighs, there came mingled with them a low murmur from her lips. I bent to them my ear and distinguished, again, the concluding words of the passage in Glanvill— *"Man doth not yield him to the angels, nor unto death utterly, save only through the weakness of his feeble will."*

She died;—and I, crushed into the very dust with sorrow, could no longer endure the lonely desolation of my dwelling in the dim and decaying city by the Rhine. I had no lack of what the world calls wealth. Ligeia had brought me far more, very far more than ordinarily falls to the lot of mortals. After a few months, therefore, of weary and aimless wandering, I purchased, and put in some repair, an abbey,[21] which I shall not name, in one of the wildest and least frequented portions of fair England. The gloomy and dreary grandeur of the building, the almost savage aspect of the domain, the many melancholy and time-honored memories connected with both, had much in unison with the feelings of utter abandonment which had driven me into that remote and unsocial region of the country. Yet although the external abbey, with its verdant decay hanging about it, suffered but little alteration, I gave way, with a child-like perversity, and perchance with a faint hope of alleviating my sorrows, to a display of more than regal magnificence within.—For such follies, even in childhood, I had imbibed a taste, and now they came back to me as if in the dotage of grief. Alas, I feel how much even of incipient madness might have been discovered in the gorgeous and fantastic draperies, in the solemn carvings of Egypt, in the wild cornices and furniture, in the Bedlam[22] patterns of the carpets of tufted gold! I had become a bounden slave in the trammels[23] of opium, and my labors and my orders had taken a coloring from my dreams. But these absurdities I must not pause to detail. Let me speak only of that one chamber, ever accursed, whither in a moment of mental alienation, I led from the altar as my bride—as the successor of the unforgotten Ligeia—the fair-haired and blue-eyed Lady Rowena Trevanion, of Tremaine.

There is no individual portion of the architecture and decoration of that bridal chamber which is not now visibly before me. Where were the souls of the haughty family of the bride, when, through thirst of gold, they permitted to pass the threshold of an apartment *so* bedecked, a maiden and a daughter so beloved? I have said that I minutely remember the details of the chamber—yet I am sadly forgetful on topics of deep moment—and here there was no system, no keeping, in the fantastic display, to take hold upon the memory. The room lay in a high turret of the castellated[24] abbey, was pentagonal[25] in shape, and of capacious size. Occupying the whole southern

[21]A house for monks, governed by an abbot.
[22]Insane. "Bedlam" is a contraction of "Bethlehem Hospital," a lunatic asylum in London.
[23]Shackles. [24]I.e., with the slotted, fortified walls of a castle. [25]Five-sided.

face of the pentagon was the sole window—an immense sheet of unbroken glass from Venice—a single pane, and tinted of a leaden hue, so that the rays of either the sun or moon, passing through it fell with a ghastly lustre on the objects within. Over the upper portion of this huge window, extended the trellice-work of an aged vine, which clambered up the massy walls of the turret. The ceiling, of gloomy-looking oak, was excessively lofty, vaulted, and elaborately fretted[26] with the wildest and most grotesque specimens of a semi-Gothic, semi-Druidical[27] device. From out the most central recess of this melancholy vaulting, depended, by a single chain of gold with a long link, a huge censer [28] of the same metal, Saracenic[29] in pattern, and with many perforations so contrived that there writhed in and out of them, as if endued with a serpent vitality, a continual succession of parti-colored fires.

Some few ottomans and golden candelabra, of Eastern figure, were in various stations about—and there was the couch, too—the bridal couch—of an Indian model, and low, and sculptured of solid ebony, with a pall-like canopy above. In each of the angles of the chamber stood on end a gigantic sarcophagus[30] of black granite, from the tombs of the kings over against Luxor,[31] with their aged lids full of immemorial sculpture. But in the draping of the apartment lay, alas! the chief phantasy of all. The lofty walls, gigantic in height—even unproportionably so—were hung from summit to foot, in vast folds, with a heavy and massive-looking tapestry—tapestry of a material which was found alike as a carpet on the floor, as a covering for the ottomans and the ebony bed, as a canopy for the bed, and as the gorgeous volutes[32] of the curtains which partially shaded the window. The material was the richest cloth of gold. It was spotted all over, at irregular intervals, with arabesque[33] figures, about a foot in diameter, and wrought upon the cloth in patterns of the most jetty black. But these figures partook of the true character of the arabesque only when regarded from a single point of view. By a contrivance now common, and indeed traceable to a very remote period of antiquity, they were made changeable in aspect. To one entering the room, they bore the appearance of simple monstrosities; but upon further advance, this appearance gradually departed; and step by step, as the visitor moved his station in the chamber, he saw himself surrounded by an endless succession of the ghastly forms which belong to the superstition of the Norman,[34] or arise in the guilty slumbers of the monk. The phantasmagoric[35] effect was vastly heightened by the artificial introduction of a strong continual current of wind behind the draperies—giving a hideous and uneasy animation to the whole.

In halls such as these—in a bridal chamber such as this—I passed, with the Lady of Tremaine, the unhallowed hours of the first month of our marriage—passed them with but little disquietude. That my wife dreaded the fierce moodiness of my temper—that she shunned me and loved me

[26]Decorated with interlocking designs.
[27]Druids were pre-Christian sorcerers in ancient Britain. [28]A vessel for burning incense.
[29]Arabic. [30]Coffin. [31]Ancient Egyptian city. [32]Spirals.
[33]Complex interlacing, as in the designs of Arabic ornamental art.
[34]The Normans, or Northmen, were Viking marauders who settled in present-day northern France, hence "Normandy." Their preoccupation with monsters and fantastic beasts is evident in their sagas and in their art.
[35]Evoking a succession of disordered images that flash in the mind.

but little—I could not help perceiving; but it gave me rather pleasure than otherwise. I loathed her with a hatred belonging more to demon than to man. My memory flew back, (oh, with what intensity of regret!) to Ligeia, the beloved, the august, the beautiful, the entombed. I revelled in recollections of her purity, of her wisdom, of her lofty, her ethereal nature, of her passionate, her idolatrous love. Now, then, did my spirit fully and freely burn with more than all the fires of her own. In the excitement of my opium dreams (for I was habitually fettered in the shackles of the drug) I would call aloud upon her name, during the silence of the night, or among the sheltered recesses of the glens by day, as if, through the wild eagerness, the solemn passion, the consuming ardor of my longing for the departed, I could restore her to the pathway she had abandoned—ah, *could* it be forever?—upon the earth.

About the commencement of the second month of the marriage, the Lady Rowena was attacked with sudden illness, from which her recovery was slow. The fever which consumed her rendered her nights uneasy; and in her perturbed state of half-slumber, she spoke of sounds, and of motions, in and about the chamber of the turret, which I concluded had no origin save in the distemper of her fancy, or perhaps in the phantasmagoric influences of the chamber itself. She became at length convalescent—finally well. Yet but a brief period elapsed, ere a second more violent disorder again threw her upon a bed of suffering; and from this attack her frame, at all times feeble, never altogether recovered. Her illnesses were, after this epoch, of alarming character, and of more alarming recurrence, defying alike the knowledge and the great exertions of her physicians. With the increase of the chronic disease which had thus, apparently, taken too sure hold upon her constitution to be eradicated by human means, I could not fail to observe a similar increase in the nervous irritation of her temperament, and in her excitability by trivial causes of fear. She spoke again, and now more frequently and pertinaciously, of the sounds—of the slight sounds—and of the unusual motions among the tapestries, to which she had formerly alluded.

One night, near the closing in of September, she pressed this distressing subject with more than usual emphasis upon my attention. She had just awakened from an unquiet slumber, and I had been watching, with feelings half of anxiety, half of vague terror, the workings of her emaciated countenance. I sat by the side of her ebony bed, upon one of the ottomans of India. She partly arose, and spoke, in an earnest low whisper, of sounds which she *then* heard, but which I could not hear—of motions which she *then* saw, but which I could not perceive. The wind was rushing hurriedly behind the tapestries, and I wished to show her (what, let me confess, I could not *all* believe) that those almost inarticulate breathings, and those very gentle variations of the figures upon the wall, were but the natural effects of that customary rushing of the wind. But a deadly pallor, overspreading her face, had proved to me that my exertions to reassure her would be fruitless. She appeared to be fainting, and no attendants were within call. I remembered where was deposited a decanter of light wine which had been ordered by her physicians, and hastened across the chamber to procure it. But, as I stepped beneath the light of the censer, two circumstances of a startling nature attracted my attention. I had felt that some palpable although invisible object had passed lightly by my person; and I saw that there lay upon the golden carpet, in the very middle of the rich lustre thrown from the censer, a shadow—a faint, indefinite shadow of angelic aspect—such as might be fancied for the shadow of a shade. But I was wild with the excitement of an immoderate dose of opium, and heeded these things but little, nor spoke of them to Rowena. Having found the wine, I recrossed the chamber, and poured out a goblet-ful, which I held to the lips of the fainting lady. She had now partially recovered, however, and took the vessel herself, while I sank upon an ottoman near me, with my eyes fastened upon her person. It was then that I became distinctly aware of a gentle foot-fall upon the carpet, and near the couch; and in a second thereafter, as Rowena was in the act of raising the wine to her lips, I saw, or may have dreamed that I saw, fall within the goblet, as if from some invisible spring in the atmosphere of the room, three or four large drops of a brilliant and ruby colored fluid. If this I saw—not so Rowena. She swallowed the wine unhesitatingly, and I forbore to speak to her of a circumstance which must, after all, I considered, have been but the suggestion of a vivid imagination, rendered morbidly active by the terror of the lady, by the opium, and by the hour.

Yet I cannot conceal it from my own perception that, immediately subsequent to the fall of the ruby-drops, a rapid change for the worse took place in the disorder of my wife; so that, on the third subsequent night, the hands of her menials prepared her for the tomb, and on the fourth, I sat alone, with her shrouded body, in that fantastic chamber which had received her as my bride.—Wild visions, opium-engendered, flitted, shadow-like, before me. I gazed with unquiet eye upon the sarcophagi in the angles of the room, upon the varying figures of the drapery, and upon the writhing of the particolored fires in the censer overhead. My eyes then fell, as I called to mind the circumstances of a former night, to the spot beneath the glare of the censer where I had seen the faint traces of the shadow. It was there, however, no longer; and breathing with greater freedom, I turned my glances to the pallid and rigid figure upon the bed. Then rushed upon me a thousand memories of Ligeia—and then came back upon my heart, with the turbulent violence of a flood, the whole of that unutterable woe with which I had regarded *her* thus enshrouded. The night waned; and still, with a bosom full of bitter thoughts of the one only and supremely beloved, I remained gazing upon the body of Rowena.

It might have been midnight, or perhaps earlier, or later, for I had taken no note of time, when a sob, low, gentle, but very distinct, startled me from my revery.—I *felt* that it came from the bed of ebony—the bed of death. I listened in an agony of superstitious terror—but there was no repetition of the sound. I strained my vision to detect any motion in the corpse—but there was not the slightest perceptible. Yet I could not have been deceived. I *had* heard the noise, however faint, and my soul was awakened within me. I resolutely and perseveringly kept my attention riveted upon the body. Many minutes elapsed before any circumstances occurred tending to throw light upon the mystery. At length it became evident that a slight, a very feeble, and barely noticeable tinge of color had flushed up within the cheeks, and along the sunken small veins of the eyelids. Through a species of unutterable horror and awe, for which the language of mortality has no sufficiently energetic expression, I felt my heart cease to beat, my limbs grow rigid where I sat. Yet a sense of duty finally operated to restore my self-possession. I could no longer doubt that we had been precipitate in our preparations—that Rowena still lived. It was necessary that some immediate exertion be made; yet the turret was altogether apart from the portion of the abbey tenanted by the servants—there were none within call—I had no means of summoning them to my aid without leaving the room for many minutes—and this I could not venture to do. I therefore struggled alone in my endeavors to call back the spirit still hovering. In a short period it was certain, however, that a relapse had taken place; the color disappeared from both eyelid and cheek, leaving a wanness even more than that of marble; the lips became doubly shrivelled and pinched up in the ghastly expression of death; a repulsive clamminess and coldness overspread rapidly the surface of the body; and all the usual rigorous stiffness immediately supervened. I fell back with a shudder upon the couch from which I had been so startlingly aroused, and again gave myself up to passionate waking visions of Ligeia.

An hour thus elapsed when (could it be possible?) I was a second time aware of some vague sound issuing from the region of the bed. I listened—in extremity of horror. The sound came again—it was a sigh. Rushing to the corpse, I saw—distinctly saw—a tremor upon the lips. In a minute afterward they relaxed, disclosing a bright line of the pearly teeth. Amazement now struggled in my bosom with the profound awe which had hitherto reigned there alone. I felt that my vision grew dim, that my reason wandered; and it was only by a violent effort that I at length succeeded in nerving myself to the task which duty thus once more had pointed out. There was now a partial glow upon the forehead and upon the cheek and throat; a perceptible warmth pervaded the whole frame; there was even a slight pulsation at the heart. The lady *lived*; and with redoubled ardor I betook myself to the task of restoration. I chafed and bathed the temples and the hands, and used every exertion which experience, and no little medical reading, could suggest. But in vain. Suddenly, the color fled, the pulsation ceased, the lips resumed the expression of the dead, and, in an instant afterward, the whole body took upon itself the icy chilliness, the livid hue, the intense rigidity, the sunken outline, and all the loathsome peculiarities of that which has been, for many days, a tenant of the tomb.

And again I sunk into visions of Ligeia—and again, (what marvel that I shudder while I write?) *again* there reached my ears a low sob from the region of the ebony bed. But why shall I minutely detail the unspeakable horrors of that night? Why shall I pause to relate how, time after time, until near the period of the gray dawn, this hideous drama of revivification was repeated; how each terrific relapse was only into a sterner and apparently more irredeemable death; how each agony wore the aspect of a struggle with some invisible foe; and how each struggle was succeeded by I know not what of wild change in the personal appearance of the corpse? Let me hurry to a conclusion.

The greater part of the fearful night had worn away, and she who had been dead, once again stirred—and now more vigorously than hitherto, although arousing from a dissolution more appalling in its utter hopelessness than any. I had long ceased to struggle or to move, and remained sitting rigidly upon the ottoman, a helpless prey to a whirl of violent emotions, of which extreme awe was perhaps the least terrible, the least consuming. The corpse, I repeat, stirred, and now more vigorously than before. The hues of life flushed up with unwonted energy into the countenance—the limbs relaxed—and, save that the eyelids were yet pressed heavily together, and that the bandages and draperies of the grave still imparted their charnel[36] character to the figure, I might have dreamed that Rowena had indeed shaken off, utterly, the fetters of Death. But if this idea was not, even then, altogether adopted, I could at least doubt no longer, when, arising from the bed, tottering, with feeble steps, with closed eyes, and with the manner of one bewildered in a dream, the thing that was enshrouded advanced boldly and palpably into the middle of the apartment.

I trembled not—I stirred not—for a crowd of unutterable fancies connected with the air, the stature, the demeanor of the figure, rushing hurriedly through my brain, had paralyzed—had chilled me into stone. I stirred not—but gazed upon the apparition. There was a mad disorder in my thoughts—a tumult unappeasable. Could it, indeed, be the *living* Rowena who confronted me? Could it indeed be Rowena *at all*—the fair-haired, the blue-eyed Lady Rowena Trevanion of Tremaine? Why, *why* should I doubt it? The bandage lay heavily about the mouth—but then might it not be the mouth of the breathing Lady of Tremaine? And the cheeks—there were the roses as in her noon of life—yes, these might indeed be the fair cheeks of the living Lady of Tremaine. And the chin, with its dimples, as in health, might it not be hers?—but *had she then grown taller since her malady?* What inexpressible madness seized me with that thought? One bound, and I had reached her feet! Shrinking from my touch, she let fall from her head, unloosened, the ghastly cerements[37] which had confined it, and there streamed forth, into the rushing atmosphere of the chamber, huge masses of long and dishevelled hair; *it was blacker than the raven wings of the midnight!* And now slowly opened *the eyes* of the figure which stood before me. "Here then, at least," I shrieked aloud, "can I never—can I never be mistaken—these are the full, and the black, and the wild eyes—of my lost love—of the lady—of the LADY LIGEIA."

1838

THE FALL OF THE HOUSE OF USHER

Son cœur est un luth suspendu;
Sitôt qu'on le touche, il résonne.
DE BERANGER.[1]

During the whole of a dull, dark, and soundless day in the autumn of the year, when the clouds hung oppressively low in the heavens, I had been passing alone, on horseback, through a singularly dreary tract of country; and at length found myself, as the shades of the evening drew on, within view of the

[36]Gravelike. [37]Shrouds.

[1]"His heart is a tight-strung lute; as soon as one touches it, it resounds." The quotation is from "Le Refus" (1831) by Pierre-Jean de Béranger (1780–1857), a French poet. Poe substituted "his heart" for the original "my heart."

melancholy House of Usher. I know not how it was—but, with the first glimpse of the building, a sense of insufferable gloom pervaded my spirit. I say insufferable; for the feeling was unrelieved by any of that half-pleasurable, because poetic, sentiment, with which the mind usually receives even the sternest natural images of the desolate or terrible. I looked upon the scene before me—upon the mere house, and the simple landscape features of the domain—upon the bleak walls—upon the vacant eye-like windows—upon a few rank sedges—and upon a few white trunks of decayed trees—with an utter depression of soul which I can compare to no earthly sensation more properly than to the after-dream of the reveller upon opium—the bitter lapse into everyday life—the hideous dropping off of the veil. There was an iciness, a sinking, a sickening of the heart—and unredeemed dreariness of thought which no goading of the imagination could torture into aught of the sublime. What was it—I paused to think—what was it that so unnerved me in the contemplation of the House of Usher? It was a mystery all insoluble; nor could I grapple with the shadowy fancies that crowded upon me as I pondered. I was forced to fall back upon the unsatisfactory conclusion, that while, beyond doubt, there *are* combinations of very simple natural objects which have the power of thus affecting us, still the analysis of this power lies among considerations beyond our depth. It was possible, I reflected, that a mere different arrangement of the particulars of the scene, of the details of the picture, would be sufficient to modify, or perhaps to annihilate its capacity for sorrowful impression; and, acting upon this idea, I reined my horse to the precipitous brink of a black and lurid tarn that lay in unruffled lustre by the dwelling, and gazed down—but with a shudder even more thrilling than before—upon the remodeled and inverted images of the gray sedge, and the ghastly tree-stems, and the vacant and eye-like windows.

Nevertheless, in this mansion of gloom I now proposed to myself a sojourn of some weeks. Its proprietor, Roderick Usher, had been one of my boon companions in boyhood; but many years had elapsed since our last meeting. A letter, however, had lately reached me in a distant part of the country—a letter from him—which, in its wildly importunate nature, had admitted of no other than a personal reply. The MS. gave evidence of nervous agitation. The writer spoke of acute bodily illness—of a mental disorder which oppressed him—and of an earnest desire to see me, as his best, and indeed his only personal friend, with a view of attempting, by the cheerfulness of my society, some alleviation of his malady. It was the manner in which all this, and much more, was said—it was the apparent *heart* that went with his request—which allowed me no room for hesitation; and I accordingly obeyed forthwith what I still considered a very singular summons.

Although, as boys, we had been even intimate associates, yet I really knew little of my friend. His reserve had been always excessive and habitual. I was aware, however, that his very ancient family had been noted, time out of mind, for a peculiar sensibility of temperament, displaying itself, through long ages, in many works of exalted art, and manifested, of late, in repeated deeds of munificent yet unobtrusive charity, as well as in a passionate devotion to the intricacies, perhaps even more than to the orthodox and easily recognisable beauties, of musical science. I had learned, too, the very remarkable fact, that the stem of the Usher race, all time-honoured as it was, had put forth, at no period, any enduring branch; in other words, that the entire family lay in the direct line of descent, and had always, with very trifling and very temporary variation, so lain. It was this deficiency, I considered, while running over in thought the perfect keeping of the character of the premises with the accredited character of the people, and while speculating upon the possible influence which the one, in the long lapse of centuries, might have exercised upon the other—it was this deficiency, perhaps, of collateral issue, and the consequent undeviating transmission, from sire to son, of the patrimony with the name, which had, at length, so identified the two as to merge the original title of the estate in the quaint and equivocal appellation of the "House of Usher"—an appellation which seemed to include, in the minds of the peasantry who used it, both the family and the family mansion.

I have said that the sole effect of my somewhat childish experiment—that of looking down within the tarn—had been to deepen the first singular impression. There can be no doubt that the consciousness of the rapid increase of my superstition—for why should I not so term it?—served mainly to accelerate the increase itself. Such, I have long known, is the paradoxical law of all sentiments having terror as a basis. And it might have been for this reason only, that, when I again uplifted my eyes to the house itself, from its image in the pool, there grew in my mind a strange fancy—a fancy so ridiculous, indeed, that I but mention it to show the vivid force of the sensations which oppressed me. I had so worked upon my imagination as really to believe that about the whole mansion and domain there hung an atmosphere peculiar to themselves and their immediate vicinity—an atmosphere which had no affinity with the air of heaven, but which had reeked up from the decayed trees, and the gray wall, and the silent tarn—a pestilent and mystic vapour, dull, sluggish, faintly discernible, and leaden-hued.

Shaking off from my spirit what *must* have been a dream, I scanned more narrowly the real aspect of the building. Its principal feature seemed to be that of an excessive antiquity. The discoloration of ages had been great. Minute fungi overspread the whole exterior, hanging in a fine tangled webwork from the eaves. Yet all this was apart from any extraordinary dilapidation. No portion of the masonry had fallen; and there appeared to be a wild inconsistency between its still perfect adaptation of parts, and the crumbling condition of the individual stones. In this there was much that reminded me of the specious totality of old wood-work which has rotted for long years in some neglected vault, with no disturbance from the breath of the external air. Beyond this indication of extensive decay, however, the fabric gave little token of instability. Perhaps the eye of a scrutinising observer might have discovered a barely perceptible fissure, which, extending from the roof of the building in front, made its way down the wall in a zigzag direction, until it became lost in the sullen waters of the tarn.

Noticing these things, I rode over a short causeway to the house. A servant in waiting took my horse, and I entered the Gothic archway of the hall. A valet, of stealthy step, thence conducted me, in silence, through many dark and intricate passages in my progress to the *studio* of his master. Much that I encountered on the way contributed, I know not how, to heighten the vague sentiments of which I have already spoken. While the objects around me—while the carvings of the ceilings, the sombre tapestries of the walls, the ebon blackness of the floors, and the phantasmagoric armorial trophies which rattled as I strode, were but matters to which, or to such as which, I had been accustomed from my infancy—while I hesitated not to acknowledge how familiar was all this—I still wondered to find how unfamiliar were the fancies which ordinary images were stirring up. On one of the staircases, I met the physician of the family. His countenance, I thought, wore a mingled expression of low cunning and perplexity. He accosted me with trepidation and passed on. The valet now threw open a door and ushered me into the presence of his master.

The room in which I found myself was very large and lofty. The windows were long, narrow, and pointed, and at so vast a distance from the black oaken floor as to be altogether inaccessible from within. Feeble gleams of encrimsoned light made their way through the trellised panes, and served to render sufficiently distinct the more prominent objects around; the eye, however, struggled in vain to reach the remoter angles of the chamber, or the recesses of the vaulted and fretted ceiling. Dark draperies hung upon the walls. The general furniture was profuse, comfortless, antique, and tattered. Many books and musical instruments lay scattered about, but failed to give any vitality to the scene. I felt that I breathed an atmosphere of sorrow. An air of stern, deep, and irredeemable gloom hung over and pervaded all.

Upon my entrance, Usher arose from a sofa on which he had been lying at full length, and greeted me with a vivacious warmth which had much in it, I at first thought, of an overdone cordiality—of the constrained effort of the *ennuye*[2] man of the world. A glance, however, at his countenance, convinced me of his perfect sincerity. We sat down; and for some moments, while he spoke not, I gazed upon him with a feeling half of pity, half of awe. Surely, man had never before so terribly altered, in so brief a period, as had Roderick Usher! It was with difficulty that I could bring myself to admit the identity of the wan being before me with the companion of my early boyhood. Yet the character of his face had been at all times remarkable. A cadaverousness of complexion; an eye large, liquid, and luminous beyond comparison; lips somewhat thin and very pallid, but of a surpassingly beautiful curve; a nose of a delicate Hebrew model, but with a breadth of nostril unusual in similar formations; a finely moulded chin, speaking, in its want of prominence, of a want of moral energy; hair of a more than web-like softness and tenuity; these features, with an inordinate expansion above the regions of the temple, made up altogether a countenance not easily to be forgotten. And now in the mere exaggeration of the prevailing character of these features, and of the expression they were wont to convey, lay so much of change that I doubted to whom I spoke. The now ghastly pallor of the skin, and the now miraculous lustre of the eye, above all things startled and even awed me. The silken hair, too, had been suffered to grow all unheeded, and as, in its wild gossamer texture, it floated rather than fell about the face, I could not, even with effort, connect its Arabesque expression with any idea of simple humanity.

In the manner of my friend I was at once struck with an incoherence—an inconsistency; and I soon found this to arise from a series of feeble and futile struggles to overcome an habitual trepidancy—an excessive nervous

[2]French: bored.

agitation. For something of this nature I had indeed been prepared, no less by his letter, than by reminiscences of certain boyish traits, and by conclusions deduced from his peculiar physical conformation and temperament. His action was alternately vivacious and sullen. His voice varied rapidly from a tremulous indecision (when the animal spirits seemed utterly in abeyance) to that species of energetic concision—that abrupt, weighty, unhurried, and hollow-sounding enunciation—that leaden, self-balanced and perfectly modulated guttural utterance, which may be observed in the lost drunkard, or the irreclaimable eater of opium, during the periods of his most intense excitement.

It was thus that he spoke of the object of my visit, of his earnest desire to see me, and of the solace he expected me to afford him. He entered, at some length, into what he conceived to be the nature of his malady. It was, he said, a constitutional and a family evil, and one for which he despaired to find a remedy—a mere nervous affection, he immediately added, which would undoubtedly soon pass off. It displayed itself in a host of unnatural sensations. Some of these, as he detailed them, interested and bewildered me; although, perhaps, the terms, and the general manner of the narration had their weight. He suffered much from a morbid acuteness of the senses; the most insipid food was alone endurable; he could wear only garments of certain texture; the odours of all flowers were oppressive; his eyes were tortured by even a faint light; and there were but peculiar sounds, and these from stringed instruments, which did not inspire him with horror.

To an anomalous species of terror I found him a bounden slave. "I shall perish," said he, "I *must* perish in this deplorable folly. Thus, thus, and not otherwise, shall I be lost. I dread the events of the future, not in themselves, but in their results. I shudder at the thought of any, even the most trivial, incident, which may operate upon this intolerable agitation of soul. I have, indeed, no abhorrence of danger, except in its absolute effect—in terror. In this unnerved—in this pitiable condition—I feel that the period will sooner or later arrive when I must abandon life and reason together, in some struggle with the grim phantasm, FEAR.

I learned, moreover, at intervals, and through broken and equivocal hints, another singular feature of his mental condition. He was enchanted by certain superstitious impressions in regard to the dwelling which he tenanted, and whence, for many years, he had never ventured forth—in regard to an influence whose supposititious force was conveyed in terms too shadowy here to be restated—an influence which some peculiarities in the mere form and substance of his family mansion, had, by dint of long sufference, he said, obtained over his spirit—an effect which the *physique*[3] of the gray walls and turrets, and of the dim tarn into which they all looked down, had, at length, brought about upon the *morale*[4] of his existence.

He admitted, however, although with hesitation, that much of the peculiar gloom which thus afflicted him could be traced to a more natural and far more palpable origin—to the severe and long-continued illness—indeed to the evidently approaching dissolution—of a tenderly beloved sister—his sole companion for long years—his last and only relative on earth. "Her

[3]French: structure. [4]French: spirit.

decease," he said, with a bitterness which I can never forget, "would leave him (him the hopeless and the frail) the last of the ancient race of the Ushers." While he spoke, the lady Madeline (for so was she called) passed slowly through a remote portion of the apartment, and, without having noticed my presence, disappeared. I regarded her with an utter astonishment not unmingled with dread—and yet I found it impossible to account for such feelings. A sensation of stupor oppressed me, as my eyes followed her retreating steps. When a door, at length, closed upon her, my glance sought instinctively and eagerly the countenance of the brother—but he had buried his face in his hands, and I could only perceive that a far more than ordinary wanness had overspread the emaciated fingers through which trickled many passionate tears.

The disease of the lady Madeline had long baffled the skill of her physicians. A settled apathy, a gradual wasting away of the person, and frequent although transient affections of a partially cataleptical character,[5] were the unusual diagnosis. Hitherto she had steadily borne up against the pressure of her malady, and had not betaken herself finally to bed; but, on the closing in of the evening of my arrival at the house, she succumbed (as her brother told me at night with inexpressible agitation) to the prostrating power of the destroyer; and I learned that the glimpse I had obtained of her person would thus probably be the last I should obtain—that the lady, at least while living, would be seen by me no more.

For several days ensuing, her name was unmentioned by either Usher or myself; and during this period I was busied in earnest endeavours to alleviate the melancholy of my friend. We painted and read together; or I listened, as if in a dream, to the wild improvisations of his speaking guitar. And thus, as a closer and still closer intimacy admitted me more unreservedly into the recesses of his spirit, the more bitterly did I perceive the futility of all attempt at cheering a mind from which darkness, as if an inherent positive quality, poured forth upon all objects of the moral and physical universe, in one unceasing radiation of gloom.

I shall ever bear about me a memory of the many solemn hours I thus spent alone with the master of the House of Usher. Yet I should fail in any attempt to convey an idea of the exact character of the studies, or of the occupations, in which he involved me, or led me the way. An excited and highly distempered ideality threw a sulphureous lustre over all. His long improvised dirges will ring forever in my ears. Among other things, I hold painfully in mind a certain singular perversion and amplification of the wild air of the last waltz of Von Weber.[6] From the paintings over which his elaborate fancy brooded, and which grew, touch by touch, into vaguenesses at which I shuddered the more thrillingly, because I shuddered knowing not why;—from these paintings (vivid as their images now are before me) I would in vain endeavour to educe more than a small portion which should lie within the compass of merely written words. By the utter simplicity, by the nakedness of

[5]An emotional state in which the victim loses the will to move and suffers from muscular rigidity.

[6]"The Last Waltz of Von Weber" was written by Karl Gottlieb Reissiger (1798–1859) in honor of the German composer Karl Maria Von Weber (1786–1826), whose romantic music often attempted to evoke a sense of the supernatural.

his designs, he arrested and overawed attention. If ever mortal painted an idea, that mortal was Roderick Usher. For me at least—in the circumstances then surrounding me—there arose out of the pure abstractions which the hypochondriac contrived to throw upon his canvas, an intensity of intolerable awe, no shadow of which felt I ever yet in the contemplation of the certainly glowing yet too concrete reveries of Fuseli.[7]

One of the phantasmagoric conceptions of my friend, partaking not so rigidly of the spirit of abstraction, may be shadowed forth, although feebly, in words. A small picture presented the interior of an immensely long and rectangular vault or tunnel, with low walls, smooth, white, and without interruption or device. Certain accessory points of the design served well to convey the idea that this excavation lay at an exceeding depth below the surface of the earth. No outlet was observed in any portion of its vast extent, and no torch, or other artificial source of light was discernible; yet a flood of intense rays rolled throughout, and bathed the whole in a ghastly and inappropriate splendour.

I have just spoken of that morbid condition of the auditory nerve which rendered all music intolerable to the sufferer, with the exception of certain effects of stringed instruments. It was, perhaps, the narrow limits to which he thus confined himself upon the guitar, which gave birth, in great measure, to the fantastic character of his performances. But the fervid *facility* of his *impromptus* could not be so accounted for. They must have been, and were, in the notes, as well as in the words of his wild fantasias (for he not unfrequently accompanied himself with rhymed verbal improvisations), the result of that intense mental collectedness and concentration to which I have previously alluded as observable only in particular moments of the highest artificial excitement. The words of one of these rhapsodies I have easily remembered. I was, perhaps, the more forcibly impressed with it, as he gave it, because, in the under or mystic current of its meaning, I fancied that I perceived, and for the first time, a full consciousness on the part of Usher, of the tottering of his lofty reason upon her throne. The verses, which were entitled "The Haunted Palace," ran very nearly, if not accurately, thus:

I.

In the greenest of our valleys,
    By good angels tenanted,
Once a fair and stately palace—
    Radiant palace—reared its head.
In the monarch Thought's dominion—
    It stood there!
Never seraph spread in pinion
    Over fabric half so fair.

II.

Banners yellow, glorious, golden,
    On its roof did float and flow;

[7]John Henry Fuseli (1741–1825), Swiss-born English artist, described as "extreme in everything." His famous painting "The Nightmare" (1785–1790) was an example of the romantic interest in psychologically terrifying experiences.

(This—all this—was in the olden
 Time long ago)
And every gentle air that dallied,
 In that sweet day,
Along the ramparts plumed and pallid,
 A winged odour went away.

III.

Wanderers in that happy valley.
 Through two luminous windows saw
Spirits moving musically
 To a lute's well-tunèd law,
Round about a throne, where sitting
 (Porphyrogene![8])
In state his glory well befitting,
 The ruler of the realm was seen.

IV.

And all with pearl and ruby glowing
 Was the fair palace door,
Through which came flowing, flowing, flowing
 And sparkling evermore,
A troop of Echoes whose sweet duty
 Was but to sing,
In voices of surpassing beauty,
 The wit and wisdom of their king.

V.

But evil things, in robes of sorrow,
 Assailed the monarch's high estate;
(Ah, let us mourn, for never morrow
 Shall dawn upon him, desolate!)
And, round about his home, the glory
 That blushed and bloomed
Is but a dim-remembered story
 Of the old time entomed.

VI.

And travellers now within that valley,
 Through the red-litten[9] windows, see
Vast forms that move fantastically
 To a discordant melody;
While, like a rapid ghastly river,
 Through the pale door,
A hideous throng rush out forever,
 And laugh—but smile no more.

[8]Latin: born to the purple, i.e., of royal birth. [9]Lighted.

I well remember that suggestions arising from this ballad, led us into a train of thought wherein there became manifest an opinion of Usher's which I mention not so much on account of its novelty, (for other men[10] have thought thus,) as on account of the pertinacity with which he maintained it. This opinion, in its general form, was that of the sentience[11] of all vegetable things. But, in his disordered fancy, the idea had assumed a more daring character, and trespassed, under certain conditions, upon the kingdom of inorganization. I lack words to express the full extent, or the earnest *abandon* of his persuasion. The belief, however, was connected (as I have previously hinted) with the gray stones of the home of his forefathers. The conditions of the sentience had been here, he imagined, fulfilled in the method of collocation of these stones—in the order of their arrangement, as well as in that of the many *fungi* which overspread them, and of the decayed trees which stood around—above all, in the long undisturbed endurance of this arrangement, and in its reduplication in the still waters of the tarn. Its evidence—the evidence of the sentience—was to be seen, he said, (and I here started as he spoke,) in the gradual yet certain condensation of an atmosphere of their own about the waters and the walls. The result was discoverable, he added, in that silent, yet importunate and terrible influence which for centuries had moulded the destinies of his family, and which made *him* what I now saw him—what he was. Such opinions need no comment, and I will make none.

Our books—the books which, for years, had formed no small portion of the mental existence of the invalid—were, as might be supposed, in strict keeping with this character of phantasm. We pored together over such works as the Ververt et Chartreuse of Gresset;[12] the Belphegor of Machiavelli; the Heaven and Hell of Swedenborg; the Subterranean Voyage of Nicholas Klimm by Holberg; the Chiromancy of Robert Flud, of Jean D'Indaginé, and of De la Chambre; the Journey into the Blue Distance of Tieck; and the City of the Sun of Campanella. One favourite volume was a small octavo edition

[10]"Watson, Dr. Percival, Spallanzani, and especially the Bishop of Llandaff.—See 'Chemical Essays,' vol. v."—Poe's note. Richard Watson (1737–1816) was an English theologian, Bishop of Llandaff, and also a chemist and the author of *Chemical Essays*, 5 vols. (1781–1787). Thomas Percival (1740–1804) was an English scientist and author of an essay on the sense perceptions of vegetables (1785). Lazzaro Spallanzani (1729–1799), Italian naturalist and physiologist, wrote *Dissertations Relative to the Natural History of Animals and Vegetables* (1784).

[11]Perception, consciousness.

[12]The books of Usher's library are meant to suggest his preoccupation with the supernatural and the demonic. Louis Gresset (1709–1777), French playwright and poet, author of *Ver-Vert* and *La Chartreuse.* Niccolò Machiavelli (1469–1527), Italian political philosopher, author of *Belfagor or The Demon Who Took a Wife* (c. 1515), a novel of the supernatural. Emanuel Swedenborg (1688–1772), Swedish mystic, author of *Heaven and Hell* (1758), a philosophical treatise filled with grotesque visions. Ludwig Holberg (1684–1754), author of *Niels Klim's Underground Journey,* a satire, modeled on *Gulliver's Travels,* that deals with a return to life after death. Robert Fludd (1574–1637), Joannes Indagine, and Martin Cureau de la Chambre (1594–1669) were authors of fifteenth- and sixteenth-century books on fortune-telling or chiromancy (palm reading). *Das alte Buch und die Reise ins Blaue hinein,* by the German romanticist Ludwig Tieck (1773–1853), described a journey from one world to another. Tommaso Campanella (1568–1639), author of *The City of the Sun,* a utopian novel. Nicholas Eymeric de Girone (1320?–1399), author of *Directorium Inquisitorum,* a treatise on the tortures of the Inquisition. Pomponius Mela, Roman author of *Chorographia,* a geography of the ancient world with accounts of fabulous beasts.

of the *Directorium Inquisitorum,* by the Dominican Eymeric De Gironne; and there were passages in Pomponius Mela, about the old African Satyrs and Ægipans,[13] over which Usher would sit dreaming for hours. His chief delight, however, was found in the perusal of an exceedingly rare and curious book in quarto Gothic—the manual of a forgotten church—*the Vigiliæ Mortuorum secundum Chorum Ecclesiæ Maguntinæ.*[14]

I could not help thinking of the wild ritual of this work, and of its probable influence upon the hypochondriac, when, one evening, having informed me abruptly that the lady Madeline was no more, he stated his intention of preserving her corpse for a fortnight, (previously to its final interment,) in one of the numerous vaults within the main walls of the building. The worldly reason, however, assigned for this singular proceeding, was one which I did not feel at liberty to dispute. The brother had been led to his resolution (so he told me) by consideration of the unusual character of the malady of the deceased, of certain obtrusive and eager inquiries on the part of her medical men, and of the remote and exposed situation of the burial-ground of the family. I will not deny that when I called to mind the sinister countenance of the person whom I met upon the staircase, on the day of my arrival at the house, I had no desire to oppose what I regarded as at best a harmless, and by no means an unnatural, precaution.[15]

At the request of Usher, I personally aided him in the arrangements for the temporary entombment. The body having been encoffined, we two alone bore it to its rest. The vault in which we placed it (and which had been so long unopened that our torches, half smothered in its oppressive atmosphere, gave us little opportunity for investigation) was small, damp, and entirely without means of admission for light; lying, at great depth, immediately beneath that portion of the building in which was my own sleeping apartment. It had been used, apparently, in remote feudal times, for the worst purposes of a donjon-keep,[16] and, in later days, as a place of deposit for powder, or some other highly combustible substance, as a portion of its floor, and the whole interior of a long archway through which we reached it, were carefully sheathed with copper. The door, of massive iron, had been, also, similarly protected. Its immense weight caused an unusually sharp grating sound, as it moved upon its hinges.

Having deposited our mournful burden upon tressels within this region of horror, we partially turned aside the yet unscrewed lid of the coffin, and looked upon the face of the tenant. A striking similitude between the brother and sister now first arrested my attention; and Usher, divining, perhaps, my thoughts, murmured out some few words from which I learned that the deceased and himself had been twins, and that sympathies of a scarcely intelligible nature had always existed between them. Our glances, however, rested not long upon the dead—for we could not regard her unawed. The

[13]In classical myth, satyrs were woodland deities with the horns and hindquarters of a goat. Aegipan was the Greek name sometimes used for the goatish god Pan.

[14]"Vigils for the Dead according to the Choir of the Church of Mayence." The work is unknown, but many similar descriptions of penitential rituals in behalf of the dead were written in the Middle Ages.

[15]I.e., a precaution against the possibility that "medical men" would steal the body for dissection and study.

[16]Underground prison cell beneath a castle tower.

disease which had thus entombed the lady in the maturity of youth, had left, as usual in all maladies of a strictly cataleptical character, the mockery of a faint blush upon the bosom and the face, and that suspiciously lingering smile upon the lip which is so terrible in death. We replaced and screwed down the lid, and, having secured the door of iron, made our way, with toil, into the scarcely less gloomy apartments of the upper portion of the house.

And now, some days of bitter grief having elapsed, an observable change came over the features of the mental disorder of my friend. His ordinary manner had vanished. His ordinary occupations were neglected or forgotten. He roamed from chamber to chamber with hurried, unequal, and objectless step. The pallor of his countenance had assumed, if possible, a more ghastly hue—but the luminousness of his eye had utterly gone out. The once occasional huskiness of his tone was heard no more; and a tremulous quaver, as if of extreme terror, habitually characterized his utterance. There were times, indeed, when I thought his unceasingly agitated mind was labouring with some oppressive secret, to divulge which he struggled for the necessary courage. At times, again, I was obliged to resolve all into the mere inexplicable vagaries of madness, for I beheld him gazing upon vacancy for long hours, in an attitude of the profoundest attention, as if listening to some imaginary sound. It was no wonder that his condition terrified—that it infected me. I felt creeping upon me, by slow yet certain degrees, the wild influences of his own fantastic yet impressive superstitions.

It was, especially, upon retiring to bed late in the night of the seventh or eighth day after the placing of the lady Madeline within the donjon, that I experienced the full power of such feelings. Sleep came not near my couch—while the hours waned and waned away. I struggled to reason off the nervousness which had dominion over me. I endeavored to believe that much, if not all of what I felt, was due to the bewildering influence of the gloomy furniture of the room—of the dark and tattered draperies, which, tortured into motion by the breath of a rising tempest, swayed fitfully to and fro upon the walls, and rustled uneasily about the decorations of the bed. But my efforts were fruitless. An irrepressible tremour gradually pervaded my frame; and, at length, there sat upon my very heart an incubus[17] of utterly causeless alarm. Shaking this off with a gasp and a struggle, I uplifted myself upon the pillows, and, peering earnestly within the intense darkness of the chamber, hearkened—I know not why, except that an instinctive spirit prompted me—to certain low and indefinite sounds which came, through the pauses of the storm, at long intervals, I knew not whence. Overpowered by an intense sentiment of horror, unaccountable yet unendurable, I threw on my clothes with haste (for I felt that I should sleep no more during the night), and endeavoured to arouse myself from the pitiable condition into which I had fallen, by pacing rapidly to and fro through the apartment.

I had taken but few turns in this manner, when a light step on an adjoining staircase arrested my attention. I presently recognised it as that of Usher. In an instant afterward he rapped, with a gentle touch, at my door, and entered, bearing a lamp. His countenance was, as usual, cadaverously wan—but, moreover, there was a species of mad hilarity in his eyes—an evidently restrained *hysteria* in his whole demeanour. His air appalled me—but anything

[17]Evil spirit.

was preferable to the solitude which I had so long endured, and I even welcomed his presence as a relief.

"And you have not seen it?" he said abruptly, after having stared about him for some moments in silence—"you have not seen it?—but, stay! you shall." Thus speaking, and having carefully shaded his lamp, he hurried to one of the casements, and threw it freely open to the storm.

The impetuous fury of the entering gust nearly lifted us from our feet. It was, indeed, a tempestuous yet sternly beautiful night, and one wildly singular in its terror and its beauty. A whirlwind had apparently collected its force in our vicinity; for there were frequent and violent alterations in the direction of the wind; and the exceeding density of the clouds (which hung so low as to press upon the turrets of the house) did not prevent our perceiving the life-like velocity with which they flew careering from all points against each other, without passing away into the distance. I say that even their exceeding density did not prevent our perceiving this—yet we had no glimpse of the moon or stars—nor was there any flashing forth of the lightning. But the under surfaces of the huge masses of agitated vapour, as well as all terrestrial objects immediately around us, were glowing in the unnatural light of a faintly luminous and distinctly visible gaseous exhalation which hung about and enshrouded the mansion.

"You must not—you shall not behold this!" said I, shudderingly, to Usher, as I led him, with a gentle violence, from the window to a seat. "These appearances, which bewilder you, are merely electrical phenomena not uncommon—or it may be that they have their ghastly origin in the rank miasma of the tarn. Let us close this casement;—the air is chilling and dangerous to your frame. Here is one of your favourite romances. I will read, and you shall listen;—and so we will pass away this terrible night together."

The antique volume which I had taken up was the "Mad Trist" of Sir Launcelot Canning;[18] but I had called it a favourite of Usher's more in sad jest than in earnest; for, in truth, there is little in its uncouth and unimaginative prolixity which could have had interest for the lofty and spiritual ideality of my friend. It was, however, the only book immediately at hand; and I indulged a vague hope that the excitement which now agitated the hypochondriac might find relief (for the history of mental disorder is full of similar anomalies) even in the extremeness of the folly which I should read. Could I have judged, indeed, by the wild overstrained air of vivacity with which he hearkened, or apparently hearkened, to the words of the tale, I might well have congratulated myself upon the success of my design.

I had arrived at that well-known portion of the story where Ethelred, the hero of the Trist, having sought in vain for peaceable admission into the dwelling of the hermit, proceeds to make good an entrance by force. Here, it will be remembered, the words of the narrative run thus:

"And Ethelred, who was by nature of a doughty heart, and who was now mighty withal, on account of the powerfulness of the wine which he had drunken, waited no longer to hold parley with the hermit, who, in sooth, was of an obstinate and maliceful turn, but, feeling the rain upon his shoulders, and fearing the rising of the tempest, uplifted his mace outright, and, with

[18]The unidentified work and author are perhaps Poe's invention.

blows, made quickly room in the plankings of the door for his gauntleted hand; and now pulling therewith sturdily, he so cracked, and ripped, and tore all asunder, that the noise of the dry and hollow-sounding wood alarumed and reverberated throughout the forest."

At the termination of this sentence I started, and for a moment, paused; for it appeared to me (although I at once concluded that my excited fancy had deceived me)—it appeared to me that, from some very remote portion of the mansion, there came, indistinctly, to my ears, what might have been, in its exact similarity of character, the echo (but a stifled and dull one certainly) of the very cracking and ripping sound which Sir Launcelot had so particularly described. It was, beyond doubt, the coincidence alone which had arrested my attention; for, amid the rattling of the sashes of the casements and the ordinary commingled noises of the still increasing storm, the sound, in itself, had nothing, surely, which should have interested or disturbed me. I continued the story:

"But the good champion Ethelred, now entering within the door, was sore enraged and amazed to perceive no signal of the maliceful hermit; but, in the stead thereof, a dragon of a scaly and prodigious demeanour, and of a fiery tongue, which sate in guard before a palace of gold, with a floor of silver; and upon the wall there hung a shield of shining brass with this legend enwritten—

> Who entereth herein, a conqueror hath bin;
> Who slayeth the dragon, the shield he shall win;

And Ethelred uplifted his mace, and struck upon the head of the dragon, which fell before him, and gave up his pesty breath, with a shriek so horrid and harsh, and withal so piercing that Ethelred had fain to close his ears with his hands against the dreadful noise of it, the like whereof was never before heard."

Here again I paused abruptly, and now with a feeling of wild amazement—for there could be no doubt whatever that, in this instance, I did actually hear (although from what direction it proceeded I found it impossible to say) a low and apparently distant, but harsh, protracted, and most unusual screaming or grating sound—the exact counterpart of what my fancy had already conjured up for the dragon's unnatural shriek as described by the romancer.

Oppressed, as I certainly was, upon the occurrence of the second and most extraordinary coincidence, by a thousand conflicting sensations, in which wonder and extreme terror were predominant, I still retained sufficient presence of mind to avoid exciting, by any observation, the sensitive nervousness of my companion. I was by no means certain that he had noticed the sounds in question; although, assuredly, a strange alteration had, during the last few minutes, taken place in his demeanour. From a position fronting my own, he had gradually brought round his chair, so as to sit with his face to the door of the chamber; and thus I could but partially perceive his features, although I saw that his lips trembled as if he were murmuring inaudibly. His head had drooped upon his breast—yet I knew that he was not asleep, from the wide and rigid opening of the eye as I caught a glance of it in profile. The motion of his body, too, was at variance with this idea—for he rocked from side to side with a gentle yet constant and uniform sway. Having rapidly taken notice of all this, I resumed the narrative of Sir Launcelot, which thus proceeded:

"And now, the champion, having escaped from the terrible fury of the dragon, bethinking himself of the brazen shield, and of the breaking up of the enchantment which was upon it, removed the carcass from out of the way before him, and approached valorously over the silver pavement of the castle to where the shield was upon the wall; which in sooth tarried not for his full coming, but fell down at his feet upon the silver floor, with a mighty great and terrible ringing sound."

No sooner had these syllables passed my lips, than—as if a shield of brass had indeed, at the moment, fallen heavily upon a floor of silver—I became aware of a distinct, hollow, metallic, and clangorous, yet apparently muffled reverberation. Completely unnerved, I leaped to my feet; but the measured rocking movement of Usher was undisturbed. I rushed to the chair in which he sat. His eyes were bent fixedly before him, and throughout his whole countenance there reigned a stony rigidity. But, as I placed my hand upon his shoulder, there came a strong shudder over his whole person; a sickly smile quivered about his lips; and I saw that he spoke in a low, hurried, and gibbering murmur, as if unconscious of my presence. Bending closely over him, I at length drank in the hideous import of his words.

"Not hear it?—yes, I hear it, and *have* heard it. Long—long—long—many minutes, many hours, many days, have I heard it—yet I dared not—oh, pity me, miserable wretch that I am!—I dared not—I *dared* not speak! *We have put her living in the tomb!* Said I not that my senses were acute? I *now* tell you that I heard her first feeble movements in the hollow coffin. I heard them—many, many days ago—yet I dared not—*I dared not speak!* And now—to-night—Ethelred—ha! ha!—the breaking of the hermit's door, and the death-cry of the dragon, and the clangour of the shield!—say, rather, the rending of her coffin, and the grating of the iron hinges of her prison, and her struggles within the coppered archway of the vault! Oh whither shall I fly? Will she not be here anon? Is she not hurrying to upbraid me for my haste? Have I not heard her footstep on the stair? Do I not distinguish that heavy and horrible beating of her heart? MADMAN!" here he sprang furiously to his feet, and shrieked out his syllables, as if in the effort he were giving up his soul—"MADMAN! I TELL YOU THAT SHE NOW STANDS WITHOUT THE DOOR!"

As if in the superhuman energy of his utterance there had been found the potency of a spell—the huge antique panels to which the speaker pointed, threw slowly back, upon the instant, their ponderous and ebony jaws. It was the work of the rushing gust—but then without those doors there DID stand the lofty and enshrouded figure of the lady Madeline of Usher. There was blood upon her white robes, and the evidence of some bitter struggle upon every portion of her emaciated frame. For a moment she remained trembling and reeling to and fro upon the threshold, then, with a low-moaning cry, fell heavily inward upon the person of her brother, and in her violent and now final death agonies, bore him to the floor a corpse, and a victim to the terrors he had anticipated.

From that chamber, and from the mansion, I fled aghast. The storm was still abroad in all its wrath as I found myself crossing the old causeway. Suddenly there shot along the path a wild light, and I turned to see whence a gleam so unusual could have issued; for the vast house and its shadows were alone behind me. The radiance was that of the full, setting, and blood-red moon which now shone vividly through that once barely-discernible fissure of which I have before spoken as extending from the roof of the building, in a zigzag direction, to the base. While I gazed, this fissure rapidly widened—there came a fierce breath of the whirlwind—the entire orb of the satellite burst at once upon my sight—my brain reeled as I saw the mighty walls rushing asunder—there was a long tumultuous shouting sound like the voice of a thousand waters—and the deep and dark tarn at my feet closed sullenly and silently over the fragments of the "House of Usher."

1839

THE PURLOINED LETTER

Nil sapientiae odiosius acumine nimio.

Seneca.[1]

At Paris, just after dark one gusty evening in the autumn of 18—, I was enjoying the twofold luxury of meditation and a meerschaum,[2] in company with my friend C. August Dupin, in his little back library, or book-closet, *au troisième,*[3] *No. 33, Rue Dunôt, Faubourg St. Germain.* For one hour at least we had maintained a profound silence; while each, to any casual observer, might have seemed intently and exclusively occupied with the curling eddies of smoke that oppressed the atmosphere of the chamber. For myself, however, I was mentally discussing certain topics which had formed matter for conversation between us at an earlier period of the evening; I mean the affair of the Rue Morgue, and the mystery attending the murder of Marie Rogêt.[4] I looked upon it, therefore, as something of a coincidence, when the door of our apartment was thrown open and admitted our old acquaintance, Monsieur G——, the Prefect[5] of the Parisian police.

We gave him a hearty welcome; for there was nearly half as much of the entertaining as of the contemptible about the man, and we had not seen him for several years. We had been sitting in the dark, and Dupin now arose for the purpose of lighting a lamp, but sat down again, without doing so, upon G.'s saying that he had called to consult us, or rather to ask the opinion of my friend, about some official business which had occasioned a great deal of trouble.

[1]Latin: Nothing is more odious to good sense than too great cunning. Seneca (c. 4 B.C.–A.D. 65), Roman philosopher. The quotation has not been found in Seneca's works.

[2]A tobacco pipe.

[3]French: the third floor; i.e., the third floor above the ground floor—in the U.S. the fourth floor.

[4]Cases solved by Dupin in Poe's stories "The Murders in the Rue Morgue" and "The Mystery of Marie Rogêt."

[5]Commissioner.

"If it is any point requiring reflection," observed Dupin, as he forebore to enkindle the wick, "we shall examine it to better purpose in the dark."

"That is another of your odd notions," said the Prefect, who had a fashion of calling every thing "odd" that was beyond his comprehension, and thus lived amid an absolute legion of "oddities."

"Very true," said Dupin, as he supplied his visiter with a pipe, and rolled towards him a comfortable chair.

"And what is the difficulty now?" I asked. "Nothing more in the assassination way, I hope?"

"Oh no; nothing of that nature. The fact is, the business is *very* simple indeed, and I make no doubt that we can manage it sufficiently well ourselves; but then I thought Dupin would like to hear the details of it, because it is so excessively *odd*."

"Simple and odd," said Dupin.

"Why, yes; and not exactly that, either. The fact is, we have all been a good deal puzzled because the affair *is* so simple, and yet baffles us altogether."

"Perhaps it is the very simplicity of the thing which puts you at fault," said my friend.

"What nonsense you *do* talk!" replied the Prefect, laughing heartily.

"Perhaps the mystery is a little *too* plain," said Dupin.

"Oh, good heavens! who ever heard of such an idea?"

"A little *too* self-evident."

"Ha! ha! ha!—ha! ha! ha!—ho! ho! ho!"—roared our visiter, profoundly amused, "oh, Dupin, you will be the death of me yet!"

"And what, after all, *is* the matter on hand?" I asked.

"Why, I will tell you," replied the Prefect, as he gave a long, steady, and contemplative puff, and settled himself in his chair. "I will tell you in a few words; but, before I begin, let me caution you that this is an affair demanding the greatest secrecy, and that I should most probably lose the position I now hold, were it known that I confided it to any one."

"Proceed," said I.

"Or not," said Dupin.

"Well, then; I have received personal information, from a very high quarter, that a certain document of the last importance, has been purloined from the royal apartments. The individual who purloined it is known; this beyond a doubt; he was seen to take it. It is known, also, that it still remains in his possession."

"How is this known?" asked Dupin.

"It is clearly inferred," replied the Prefect, "from the nature of the document, and from the non-appearance of certain results which would at once arise from its passing *out* of the robber's possession;—that is to say, from his employing it as he must design in the end to employ it."

"Be a little more explicit," I said.

"Well, I may venture so far as to say that the paper gives its holder a certain power in a certain quarter where such power is immensely valuable." The Prefect was fond of the cant of diplomacy.

"Still I do not quite understand," said Dupin.

"No? Well; the disclosure of the document to a third person, who shall be nameless, would bring in question the honor of a personage of most exalted station; and this fact gives the holder of the document an ascendancy over the illustrious personage whose honor and peace are so jeopardized."

"But this ascendancy," I interposed, "would depend upon the robber's knowledge of the loser's knowledge of the robber. Who would dare—"

"The thief," said G., "is the Minister D——, who dares all things, those unbecoming as well as those becoming a man. The method of the theft was not less ingenious than bold. The document in question—a letter, to be frank—had been received by the personage robbed while alone in the royal *boudoir.* During its perusal she was suddenly interrupted by the entrance of the other exalted personage from whom especially it was her wish to conceal it. After a hurried and vain endeavor to thrust it in a drawer, she was forced to place it, open as it was, upon a table. The address, however, was uppermost, and, the contents thus unexposed, the letter escaped notice. At this juncture enters the Minister D——. His lynx eye immediately perceives the paper, recognises the handwriting of the address, observes the confusion of the personage addressed, and fathoms her secret. After some business transactions, hurried through in his ordinary manner, he produces a letter somewhat similar to the one in question, opens it, pretends to read it, and then places it in close juxtaposition to the other. Again he converses, for some fifteen minutes, upon the public affairs. At length, in taking leave, he takes also from the table the letter to which he had no claim. Its rightful owner saw, but, of course, dared not call attention to the act, in the presence of the third personage who stood at her elbow. The minister decamped; leaving his own letter—one of no importance—upon the table."

"Here, then," said Dupin to me, "you have precisely what you demand to make the ascendancy complete—the robber's knowledge of the loser's knowledge of the robber."

"Yes," replied the Prefect; "and the power thus attained has, for some months past, been wielded, for political purposes, to a very dangerous extent. The personage robbed is more thoroughly convinced, every day, of the necessity of reclaiming her letter. But this, of course, cannot be done openly. In fine, driven to despair, she has committed the matter to me."

"Than whom," said Dupin, amid a perfect whirlwind of smoke, "no more sagacious agent could, I suppose, be desired, or even imagined."

"You flatter me," replied the Prefect; "but it is possible that some such opinion may have been entertained."

"It is clear," said I, "as you observe, that the letter is still in possession of the minister; since it is this possession, and not any employment of the letter, which bestows the power. With the employment the power departs."

"True," said G.; "and upon this conviction I proceeded. My first care was to make thorough search of the minister's hotel;[6] and here my chief embarrassment lay in the necessity of searching without his knowledge. Beyond all things, I have been warned of the danger which would result from giving him reason to suspect our design."

"But," said I, "you are quite *au fait*[7] in these investigations. The Parisian police have done this thing often before."

[6]Mansion, townhouse. [7]French: expert.

"O yes; and for this reason I did not despair. The habits of the minister gave me, too, a great advantage. He is frequently absent from home all night. His servants are by no means numerous. They sleep at a distance from their master's apartment, and, being chiefly Neapolitans, are readily made drunk. I have keys, as you know, with which I can open any chamber or cabinet in Paris. For three months a night has not passed, during the greater part of which I have not been engaged, personally, in ransacking the D—— Hôtel. My honor is interested, and, to mention a great secret, the reward is enormous. So I did not abandon the search until I had become fully satisfied that the thief is a more astute man than myself. I fancy that I have investigated every nook and corner of the premises in which it's possible that the paper can be concealed."

"But is it not possible," I suggested, "that although the letter may be in possession of the minister, as it unquestionably is, he may have concealed it elsewhere than upon his own premises?"

"This is barely possible," said Dupin. "The present peculiar condition of affairs at court, and especially of those intrigues in which D—— is known to be involved, would render the instant availability of the document—its susceptibility of being produced at a moment's notice—a point of nearly equal importance with its possession."

"Its susceptibility of being produced?" said I.

"That is to say, of being *destroyed,*" said Dupin.

"True," I observed; "the paper is clearly then upon the premises. As for its being upon the person of the minister, we may consider that as out of the question."

"Entirely," said the Prefect. "He has been twice waylaid, as if by footpads,[8] and his person rigorously searched under my own inspection."

"You might have spared yourself this trouble," said Dupin. "D——, I presume, is not altogether a fool, and, if not, must have anticipated these waylayings, as a matter of course."

"Not *altogether* a fool," said G., "but then he's a poet, which I take to be only one remove from a fool."

"True," said Dupin, after a long and thoughtful whiff from his meerschaum, "although I have been guilty of certain doggerel myself."

"Suppose you detail," said I, "the particulars of your search."

"Why the fact is, we took our time, and we searched *every where.* I have had long experience in these affairs. I took the entire building, room by room; devoting the nights of a whole week to each. We examined, first, the furniture of each apartment. We opened every possible drawer; and I presume you know that, to a properly trained police agent, such a thing as a *secret* drawer is impossible. Any man is a dolt who permits a 'secret' drawer to escape him in a search of this kind. The thing is *so* plain. There is a certain amount of bulk—of space—to be accounted for in every cabinet. Then we have accurate rules. The fiftieth part of a line could not escape us. After the cabinets we took the chairs. The cushions we probed with the fine long needles you have seen me employ. From the tables we removed the tops."

"Why so?"

[8]Those who rob pedestrians.

"Sometimes the top of a table, or other similarly arranged piece of furniture, is removed by the person wishing to conceal an article; then the leg is excavated, the article deposited within the cavity, and the top replaced. The bottoms and tops of bed-posts are employed in the same way."

"But could not the cavity be detected by sounding?" I asked.

"By no means, if, when the article is deposited, a sufficient wadding of cotton be placed around it. Besides, in our case, we were obliged to proceed without noise."

"But you could not have removed—you could not have taken to pieces *all* articles of furniture in which it would have been possible to make a deposit in the manner you mention. A letter may be compressed into a thin spiral roll, not differing much in shape or bulk from a large knitting-needle, and in this form it might be inserted into the rung of a chair, for example. You did not take to pieces all the chairs?"

"Certainly not; but we did better—we examined the rungs of every chair in the hotel, and, indeed, the jointings of every description of furniture, by the aid of a most powerful microscope.[9] Had there been any traces of recent disturbance we should not have failed to detect it instantly. A single grain of gimlet-dust,[10] for example, would have been as obvious as an apple. And disorder in the glueing—any unusual gaping in the joints—would have sufficed to insure detection."

"I presume you looked to the mirrors, between the boards and the plates, and you probed the beds and the bed-clothes, as well as the curtains and carpets."

"That of course; and when we had absolutely completed every particle of the furniture in this way, then we examined the house itself. We divided its entire surface into compartments, which we numbered, so that none might be missed; then we scrutinized each individual square inch throughout the premises, including the two houses immediately adjoining, with the microscope, as before."

"The two houses adjoining!" I exclaimed; "you must have had a great deal of trouble."

"We had; but the reward offered is prodigious."

"You include the *grounds* about the houses?"

"All the grounds are paved with brick. They gave us comparatively little trouble. We examined the moss between the bricks, and found it undisturbed."

"You looked among D——'s papers, of course, and into the books of the library?"

"Certainly; we opened every package and parcel; we not only opened every book, but we turned over every leaf in each volume, not contenting ourselves with a mere shake, according to the fashion of some of our police officers. We also measured the thickness of every book-*cover,* with the most accurate admeasurement, and applied to each the most jealous scrutiny of the microscope. Had any of the bindings been recently meddled with, it would have been utterly impossible that the fact should have escaped observation. Some five or six volumes, just from the hands of the binder, we carefully probed, longitudinally, with the needles."

[9]Magnifying glass. [10]Wood particles produced by a gimlet, a small, handheld boring tool.

"You explored the floors beneath the carpets?"

"Beyond doubt. We removed every carpet, and examined the boards with the microscope."

"And the paper on the walls?"

"Yes."

"You looked into the cellars?"

"We did."

"Then," I said, "you have been making a miscalculation, and the letter is *not* upon the premises, as you suppose."

"I fear you are right there," said the Prefect. "And now, Dupin, what would you advise me to do?"

"To make a thorough re-search of the premises."

"That is absolutely needless," replied G——. "I am not more sure that I breathe than I am that the letter is not at the Hôtel."

"I have no better advice to give you," said Dupin. "You have, of course, an accurate description of the letter?"

"Oh yes!"—And here the Prefect, producing a memorandum-book, proceeded to read aloud a minute account of the internal, and especially of the external appearance of the missing document. Soon after finishing the perusal of this description, he took his departure, more entirely depressed in spirits than I had ever known the good gentleman before.

In about a month afterwards he paid us another visit, and found us occupied very nearly as before. He took a pipe and a chair and entered into some ordinary conversation. At length I said—

"Well, but G——, what of the purloined letter? I presume you have at last made up your mind that there is no such thing as over-reaching the Minister?"

"Confound him, say I—yes; I made the re-examination, however, as Dupin suggested—but it was all labor lost, as I knew it would be."

"How much was the reward offered, did you say?" asked Dupin.

"Why, a very great deal—a *very* liberal reward—I don't like to say how much, precisely; but one thing I *will* say, that I wouldn't mind giving my individual check for fifty thousand francs to any one who could obtain me that letter. The fact is, it is becoming of more and more importance every day; and the reward has been lately doubled. If it were trebled, however, I could do no more than I have done."

"Why, yes," said Dupin, drawlingly, between the whiffs of his meerschaum, "I really—think, G——, you have not exerted yourself—to the utmost in this matter. You might—do a little more, I think, eh?"

"How?—in what way?"

"Why—puff, puff—you might—puff, puff—employ counsel in the matter, eh?—puff, puff, puff. Do you remember the story they tell of Abernethy?"[11]

"No; hang Abernethy!"

"To be sure! hang him and welcome. But, once upon a time, a certain rich miser conceived the design of spunging upon this Abernethy for a medical opinion. Getting up, for this purpose, an ordinary conversation in a private company, he insinuated his case to the physician, as that of an imaginary individual.

[11]John Abernethy (1764–1831), English surgeon.

"'We will suppose,' said the miser, 'that his symptoms are such and such; now, doctor, what would *you* have directed him to take?'

"'Take!' said Abernethy, 'why take *advice,* to be sure.'"

"But," said the Prefect, a little discomposed, "I am *perfectly* willing to take advice, and to pay for it. I would *really* give fifty thousand francs to any one who would aid me in the matter."

"In that case," replied Dupin, opening a drawer, and producing a check-book, "you may as well fill me up a check for the amount mentioned. When you have signed it, I will hand you the letter."

I was astounded. The Prefect appeared absolutely thunder-stricken. For some minutes he remained speechless and motionless, looking incredulously at my friend with open mouth, and eyes that seemed starting from their sockets; then, apparently recovering himself in some measure, he seized a pen, and after several pauses and vacant stares, finally filled up and signed a check for fifty thousand francs, and handed it across the table to Dupin. The latter examined it carefully and deposited it in his pocket-book; then, unlocking an *escritoire,*[12] took thence a letter and gave it to the Prefect. This functionary grasped it in a perfect agony of joy, opened it with a trembling hand, cast a rapid glance at its contents, and then, scrambling and struggling to the door, rushed at length unceremoniously from the room and from the house, without having uttered a syllable since Dupin had requested him to fill up the check.

When he had gone, my friend entered into some explanations.

"The Parisian police," he said, "are exceedingly able in their way. They are persevering, ingenious, cunning, and thoroughly versed in the knowledge which their duties seem chiefly to demand. Thus, when G—— detailed to us his mode of searching the premises at the Hôtel D——, I felt entire confidence in his having made a satisfactory investigation—so far as his labors extended."

"So far as his labors extended?" said I.

"Yes," said Dupin. "The measures adopted were not only the best of their kind, but carried out to absolute perfection. Had the letter been deposited within the range of their search, these fellows would, beyond a question, have found it."

I merely laughed—but he seemed quite serious in all that he said.

"The measures, then," he continued, "were good in their kind, and well executed; but their defect lay in their being inapplicable to the case, and to the man. A certain set of highly ingenious resources are, with the Prefect, a sort of Procrustean bed,[13] to which he forcibly adapts his designs. But he perpetually errs by being too deep or too shallow, for the matter in hand; and many a schoolboy is a better reasoner than he. I knew one about eight years of age, whose success at guessing in the game of 'even and odd' attracted universal admiration. This game is simple; and is played with marbles. One player holds in his hand a number of these toys, and demands of another whether that number is even or odd. If the guess is right, the guesser wins one; if wrong, he loses one. The boy to whom I allude won all

[12]French: writing desk.

[13]I.e., an inflexible system. From the mythical Greek Procrustes, a robber who tied his victims to an iron bed. If they were too long, he cut off their limbs. If too short, he stretched them to fit.

the marbles of the school. Of course he had some principle of guessing; and this lay in mere observation and admeasurement of the astuteness of his opponents. For example, an arrant simpleton is his opponent, and, holding up his closed hand, asks, 'are they even or odd?' Our schoolboy replies, 'odd,' and loses; but upon the second trial he wins, for he then says to himself, 'the simpleton had them even upon the first trial, and his amount of cunning is just sufficient to make him have them odd upon the second; I will therefore guess odd;'—he guesses odd, and wins. Now, with a simpleton a degree above the first, he would have reasoned thus: 'This fellow finds that in the first instance I guessed odd, and, in the second, he will propose to himself upon the first impulse, a simple variation from even to odd, as did the first simpleton; but then a second thought will suggest that this is too simple a variation, and finally he will decide upon putting it even as before. I will therefore guess even;'—he guesses even, and wins. Now this mode of reasoning in the schoolboy, whom his fellows term 'lucky,'—what, in its last analysis, is it?"

"It is merely," I said, "an identification of the reasoner's intellect with that of his opponent."

"It is," said Dupin; "and, upon inquiring of the boy by what means he effected the *thorough* identification in which his success consisted, I received answer as follows: 'When I wish to find out how wise, or how stupid, or how good, or how wicked is any one, or what are his thoughts at the moment, I fashion the expression of my face, as accurately as possible, in accordance with the expression of his, and then wait to see what thoughts or sentiments arise in my mind or heart, as if to match or correspond with the expression.' This response of the schoolboy lies at the bottom of all the spurious profundity which has been attributed to Rochefoucauld, to La Bruyere, to Machiavelli, and to Campanella."[14]

"And the identification," I said, "of the reasoner's intellect with that of his opponent, depends, if I understand you aright, upon the accuracy with which the opponent's intellect is admeasured."

"For its practical value it depends upon this," replied Dupin; "and the Prefect and his cohort fail so frequently, first, by default of this identification, and, secondly, by ill-admeasurement, or rather through nonadmeasurement, of the intellect with which they are engaged. They consider only their *own* ideas of ingenuity; and, in searching for anything hidden, advert only to the modes in which *they* would have hidden it. They are right in this much—that their own ingenuity is a faithful representative of *the mass;* but when the cunning of the individual felon is diverse in character from their own, the felon foils them, of course. This always happens when it is above their own, and very usually when it is below. They have no variation of principle in their investigations; at best, when urged by some unusual emergency—by some extraordinary reward—they extend or exaggerate their old modes of *practice,* without touching their principles. What, for example, in this case of D——, has been done to vary the principle of action? What is all this boring, and probing, and sounding, and scrutinizing with

[14]La Rochefoucauld (1613–1680), La Bruyère (1645–1696), Machiavelli (1469–1527), Campanella (1568–1639)—French and Italian philosophers and moralists.

the microscope, and dividing the surface of the building into registered square inches—what is it all but an exaggeration *of the application* of the one principle or set of principles of search, which are based upon the one set of notions regarding human ingenuity, to which the Prefect, in the long routine of his duty, has been accustomed? Do you not see he has taken it for granted that *all* men proceed to conceal a letter,—not exactly in a gimlet-hole bored in a chair-leg—but, at least, in *some* out-of-the-way hole or corner suggested by the same tenor of thought which would urge a man to secrete a letter in a gimlet-hole bored in a chair-leg? And do you not see also, that such *recherchés*[15] nooks for concealment are adapted only for ordinary occasions, and would be adopted only by ordinary intellects; for, in all cases of concealment, a disposal of the article concealed—a disposal of it in this *recherché* manner,—is, in the very first instance, presumable and presumed; and thus its discovery depends, not at all upon the acumen, but altogether upon the mere care, patience, and determination of the seekers; and where the case is of importance—or, what amounts to the same thing in the political eyes, when the reward is of magnitude,—the qualities in question have *never* been known to fail. You will now understand what I meant in suggesting that, had the purloined letter been hidden any where within the limits of the Prefect's examination—in other words, had the principle of its concealment been comprehended within the principles of the Prefect—its discovery would have been a matter altogether beyond question. This functionary, however, has been thoroughly mystified; and the remote source of his defeat lies in the supposition that the Minister is a fool, because he has acquired renown as a poet. All fools are poets; this the Prefect *feels;* and he is merely guilty of a *non distributio medii*[16] in thence inferring that all poets are fools."

"But is this really the poet?" I asked. "There are two brothers, I know; and both have attained reputation in letters. The Minister I believe has written learnedly on the Differential Calculus. He is a mathematician, and no poet."

"You are mistaken; I know him well; he is both. As poet *and* mathematician, he would reason well; as mere mathematician, he could not have reasoned at all, and thus would have been at the mercy of the Prefect."

"You surprise me," I said, "by these opinions, which have been contradicted by the voice of the world. You do not mean to set at naught the well-digested idea of centuries. The mathematical reason has long been regarded as *the* reason *par excellence.*"

"'*Il y a à parier,*'" replied Dupin, quoting from Chamfort, "'*que toute idée publique, toute convention reçue, est une sottise, car elle a convenu au plus grand nombre.*'[17] The mathematicians, I grant you, have done their best to promulgate the popular error to which you allude, and which is none the less an error for its promulgation as truth. With an art worthy a better cause, for

[15]French: exotic, rare.

[16]Latin: undistributed middle. A flaw in logical reasoning that leads to an unwarranted conclusion.

[17]"It's a good bet that every popular idea, every accepted convention, is a stupidity, for it suited the majority." Sebastien Chamfort (1741–1794). French moralist and writer of maxims.

example, they have insinuated the term 'analysis' into application to algebra. The French are the originators of this particular deception; but if a term is of any importance—if words derive any value from applicability—then 'analysis' conveys 'algebra' about as much as, in Latin, *'ambitus'* implies 'ambition,' *'religio'* 'religion,' or *'homines honesti,'*[18] a set of *honorable* men."

"You have a quarrel on hand, I see," said I, "with some of the algebraists of Paris; but proceed."

"I dispute the availability, and thus the value, of that reason which is cultivated in any especial form other than the abstractly logical. I dispute, in particular, the reason educed by mathematical study. The mathematics are the science of form and quantity; mathematical reasoning is merely logic applied to observation upon form and quantity. The great error lies in supposing that even the truths of what is called *pure* algebra, are abstract or general truths. And this error is so egregious that I am confounded at the universality with which it has been received. Mathematical axioms are *not* axioms of general truth. What is true of *relation*—of form and quantity—is often grossly false in regard to morals, for example. In this latter science it is very usually *un*true that the aggregated parts are equal to the whole. In chemistry also the axiom fails. In the consideration of motive it fails; for two motives, each of a given value, have not, necessarily, a value when united, equal to the sum of their values apart. There are numerous other mathematical truths which are only truths within the limits of *relation.* But the mathematician argues, from his *finite truths,* through habit, as if they were of an absolutely general applicability—as the world indeed imagines them to be. Bryant, in his very learned 'Mythology,'[19] mentions an analogous source of error, when he says that 'although the Pagan fables are not believed, yet we forget ourselves continually, and make inferences from them as existing realities.' With the algebraists, however, who are Pagans themselves, the 'Pagan fables' *are* believed, and the inferences are made, not so much through lapse of memory, as through an unaccountable addling of the brains. In short, I never yet encountered the mere mathematician who could be trusted out of equal roots, or one who did not clandestinely hold it as a point of his faith that x^2+px was absolutely and unconditionally equal to q. Say to one of these gentlemen, by way of experiment, if you please, that you believe occasions may occur where x^2+px is *not* altogether equal to q, and, having made him understand what you mean, get out of his reach as speedily as convenient, for, beyond doubt, he will endeavor to knock you down.

"I mean to say," continued Dupin, while I merely laughed at his last observations, "that if the Minister had been no more than a mathematician, the Prefect would have been under no necessity of giving me this check. I

[18] *Ambitus:* going around; hence, office seeking. *Religio:* sometimes taken to mean superstition. *Homines honesti:* a term used by the Roman statesman and orator Cicero to indicate men of his own party.

[19] Jacob Bryant (1715–1804), English antiquarian and author of *A New System, or an Analysis of Mythology* (1774).

knew him, however, as both mathematician and poet, and my measures were adapted to his capacity, with reference to the circumstances by which he was surrounded. I knew him as a courtier, too, and as a bold *intriguant.*[20] Such a man, I considered, could not fail to be aware of the ordinary political modes of action. He could not have failed to anticipate—and events have proved that he did not fail to anticipate—the waylayings to which he was subjected. He must have foreseen, I reflected, the secret investigations of his premises. His frequent absences from home at night, which were hailed by the Prefect as certain aids to his success, I regarded only as *ruses,* to afford opportunity for thorough search to the police, and thus the sooner to impress them with the conviction to which G——, in fact, did finally arrive—the conviction that the letter was not upon the premises. I felt, also, that the whole train of thought, which I was at some pains in detailing to you just now, concerning the invariable principle of political action in searches for articles concealed—I felt that this whole train of thought would necessarily pass through the mind of the Minister. It would imperatively lead him to despise all the ordinary *nooks* of concealment. *He* could not, I reflected, be so weak as not to see that the most intricate and remote recess of his hotel would be as open as his commonest closets to the eyes, to the probes, to the gimlets, and to the microscopes of the Prefect. I saw, in fine, that he would be driven, as a matter of course, to *simplicity,* if not deliberately induced to it as a matter of choice. You will remember, perhaps, how desperately the Prefect laughed when I suggested, upon our first interview, that it was just possible this mystery troubled him so much on account of its being so *very* self-evident."

"Yes," said I, "I remember his merriment well. I really thought he would have fallen into convulsions."

"The material world," continued Dupin, "abounds with very strict analogies to the immaterial; and thus some color of truth has been given to the rhetorical dogma, that metaphor, or simile, may be made to strengthen an argument, as well as to embellish a description. The principle of the *vis inertiæ,*[21] for example, seems to be identical in physics and metaphysics. It is not more true in the former, that a large body is with more difficulty set in motion than a smaller one, and that its subsequent *momentum* is commensurate with this difficulty, than it is, in the latter, that intellects of the vaster capacity, while more forcible, more constant, and more eventful in their movements than those of inferior grade, are yet the less readily moved, and more embarrassed and full of hesitation in the first few steps of their progress. Again: have you ever noticed which of the street signs, over the shop doors, are the most attractive of attention?"

"I have never given the matter a thought," I said.

"There is a game of puzzles," he resumed, "which is played upon a map. One party playing requires another to find a given word—the name of town, river, state or empire—any word, in short, upon the motley and perplexed surface of the chart. A novice in the game generally seeks to

[20]French: schemer.
[21]Latin: force of inertia.

embarrass his opponents by giving them the most minutely lettered names; but the adept selects such words as stretch, in large characters, from one end of the chart to the other. These, like the over-largely lettered signs and placards of the street, escape observation by dint of being excessively obvious; and here the physical oversight is precisely analogous with the moral inapprehension by which the intellect suffers to pass unnoticed those considerations which are too obtrusively and too palpably self-evident. But this is a point, it appears, somewhat above or beneath the understanding of the Prefect. He never once thought it probable, or possible, that the Minister had deposited the letter immediately beneath the nose of the whole world, by way of best preventing any portion of that world from perceiving it.

"But the more I reflected upon the daring, dashing, and discriminating ingenuity of D——; upon the fact that the document must always have been *at hand,* if he intended to use it to good purpose; and upon the decisive evidence, obtained by the Prefect, that it was not hidden within the limits of that dignitary's ordinary search—the more satisfied I became that, to conceal this letter, the Minister had resorted to the comprehensive and sagacious expedient of not attempting to conceal it at all.

"Full of these ideas, I prepared myself with a pair of green spectacles, and called one fine morning, quite by accident, at the Ministerial hotel. I found D—— at home, yawning, lounging, and dawdling, as usual, and pretending to be in the last extremity of *ennui.* He is, perhaps, the most really energetic human being now alive—but that is only when nobody sees him.

"To be even with him, I complained of my weak eyes, and lamented the necessity of the spectacles, under cover of which I cautiously and thoroughly surveyed the apartment, while seemingly intent only upon the conversation of my host.

"I paid special attention to a large writing-table near which he sat, and upon which lay confusedly, some miscellaneous letters and other papers, with one or two musical instruments and a few books. Here, however, after a long and very deliberate scrutiny, I saw nothing to excite particular suspicion.

"At length my eyes, in going the circuit of the room, fell upon a trumpery[22] fillagree card-rack of paste-board, that hung dangling by a dirty blue ribbon, from a little brass knob just beneath the middle of the mantelpiece. In this rack, which had three or four compartments, were five or six visiting cards and a solitary letter. This last was much soiled and crumpled. It was torn nearly in two, across the middle—as if a design, in the first instance, to tear it entirely up as worthless, had been altered, or stayed, in the second. It had a large black seal, bearing the D—— cipher *very* conspicuously, and was addressed, in a diminutive female hand, to D——, the minister, himself. It was thrust carelessly, and even, as it seemed, contemptuously, into one of the upper divisions of the rack.

"No sooner had I glanced at this letter, than I concluded it to be that of which I was in search. To be sure, it was, to all appearance, radically different

[22]Tawdry.

from the one which the Prefect had read us so minute a description. Here the seal was large and black, with the D—— cipher; there it was small and red, with the ducal arms of the S—— family. Here, the address, to the Minister, was diminutive and feminine; there the superscription, to a certain royal personage, was markedly bold and decided; the size alone formed a point of correspondence. But, then, the *radicalness* of these differences, which was excessive; the dirt; the soiled and torn condition of the paper, so inconsistent with the *true* methodical habits of D——, and so suggestive of a design to delude the beholder into an idea of the worthlessness of the document; these things, together with the hyperobtrusive situation of this document, full in the view of every visitor, and thus exactly in accordance with the conclusions to which I had previously arrived; these things, I say, were strongly corroborative of suspicion, in one who came with the intention to suspect.

"I protracted my visit as long as possible, and, while I maintained a most animated discussion with the Minister, on a topic which I knew well had never failed to interest and excite him, I kept my attention really riveted upon the letter. In this examination, I committed to memory its external appearance and arrangement in the rack; and also fell, at length, upon a discovery which set at rest whatever trivial doubt I might have entertained. In scrutinizing the edges of the paper, I observed them to be more *chafed* than seemed necessary. They presented the *broken* appearance which is manifested when a stiff paper, having been once folded and pressed with a folder, is refolded in a reversed direction, in the same creases or edges which had formed the original fold. This discovery was sufficient. It was clear to me that the letter had been turned, as a glove, inside out, re-directed, and re-sealed. I bade the Minister good morning, and took my departure at once, leaving a gold snuff-box upon the table.

"The next morning I called for the snuff-box, when we resumed, quite eagerly, the conversation of the preceding day. While thus engaged, however, a loud report, as if of a pistol, was heard immediately beneath the windows of the hotel, and was succeeded by a series of fearful screams, and the shoutings of a mob. D—— rushed to a casement, threw it open, and looked out. In the meantime, I stepped to the card-rack, took the letter, put it in my pocket, and replaced it by a *fac-simile,* (so far as regards externals,) which I had carefully prepared at my lodgings; imitating the D—— cipher, very readily, by means of a seal formed of bread.

"The disturbance in the street had been occasioned by the frantic behavior of a man with a musket. He had fired it among a crowd of women and children. It proved, however, to have been without a ball, and the fellow was suffered to go his way as a lunatic or a drunkard. When he had gone, D——came from the window, whither I had followed him immediately upon securing the object in view. Soon afterwards I bade him farewell. The pretended lunatic was a man in my own pay."

"But what purpose had you," I asked, "in replacing the letter by a *fac-simile?* Would it not have been better, at the first visit, to have seized it openly, and departed?"

"D——," replied Dupin, "is a desperate man, and a man of nerve. His hotel, too, is not without attendants devoted to his interests. Had I made the wild attempt you suggest, I might never have left the Ministerial presence alive. The good people of Paris might have heard of me no more. But I had an object apart from these considerations. In this matter, I act as a partisan of the lady concerned. For eighteen months the Minister has had her in his power. She has now him in hers; since, being unaware that the letter is not in his possession, he will proceed with his exactions as if it was. Thus will he inevitably commit himself, at once, to his political destruction. His downfall, too, will not be more precipitate than awkward. It is all very well to talk about the *facilis descensus Averni;*[23] but in all kinds of climbing, as Catalini[24] said of singing, it is far more easy to get up than to come down. In the present instance I have no sympathy—at least no pity—for him who descends. He is that *monstrum horrendum,*[25] an unprincipled man of genius. I confess, however, that I should like very well to know the precise character of his thoughts, when, being defied by her whom the Prefect terms 'a certain personage,' he is reduced to opening the letter which I left for him in the card-rack."

"How? did you put any thing particular in it?"

"Why—it did not seem altogether right to leave the interior blank—that would have been insulting. D——, at Vienna once, did me an evil turn, which I told him, quite good-humoredly, that I should remember. So, as I knew he would feel some curiosity in regard to the identity of the person who had outwitted him, I thought it a pity not to give him a clue. He is well acquainted with my MS., and I just copied into the middle of the blank sheet the words—

—Un dessein si funeste,
S'il n'est digne d'Atrée, est digne de Thyeste.[26]

They are to be found in Crébillon's 'Atrée.'"[27]

1845

[23]Latin: "easy descent to Hades," a quotation from Virgil's *Aeneid,* Book VI, line 126.

[24]Angelica Catalani (1780–1849), Italian soprano.

[25] Latin: horrendous monster.

[26]French: "A scheme so deadly, if not worthy of Atreus, is worthy of Thyestes." In Greek myth, Thyestes seduced the wife of Atreus. In revenge, Atreus killed the sons of Thyestes and served them to Thyestes at a banquet.

[27]Prosper Crébillon (1674–1762), author of the French tragedy *Atrée et Thyeste* (1707).

from *"TWICE-TOLD TALES, BY NATHANIEL HAWTHORNE"*

[A REVIEW][1]

We said a few hurried words about Mr. Hawthorne in our last number, with the design of speaking more fully in the present. We are still, however, pressed for room, and must necessarily discuss his volumes more briefly and more at random than their high merits deserve.

The book professes to be a collection of *tales,* yet is, in two respects, misnamed. These pieces are now in their third publication, and, of course, are thrice-told.[2] Moreover, they are by no means *all* tales, either in the ordinary or in the legitimate understanding of the term. Many of them are pure essays; for example, "Sights from a Steeple," "Sunday at Home," "Little Annie's Ramble," "A Rill from the Town Pump," "The Toll-Gatherer's Day," "The Haunted Mind," "The Sister Years," "Snow-Flakes," "Night-Sketches," and "Foot-Prints on the Sea-Shore." We mention these matters chiefly on account of their discrepancy with that marked precision and finish by which the body of the work is distinguished.

Of the essays just named, we must be content to speak in brief. They are each and all beautiful, without being characterised by the polish and adaptation so visible in the tales proper. A painter would at once note their leading or predominant feature, and style it *repose.* There is no attempt at effect. All is quiet, thoughtful, subdued. Yet this repose may exist simultaneously with high originality of thought; and Mr. Hawthorne has demonstrated the fact. At every turn we meet with novel combinations; yet these combinations never surpass the limits of the quiet. We are soothed as we read; and withal is a calm astonishment that ideas so apparently obvious have never occurred or been presented to us before. Herein our author differs materially from Lamb or Hunt or Hazlitt[3]—who, with vivid originality of manner and expression, have less of the true novelty of thought than is generally supposed, and whose originality, at best, has an uneasy and meretricious quaintness, replete with startling effects unfounded in nature, and inducing trains of reflection which lead to no satisfactory result. The Essays of Hawthorne have much of the character of Irving,[4] with more of originality, and less of finish; while, compared with the Spectator,[5] they have a vast superiority at all points. The Spectator, Mr. Irving, and Mr. Hawthorne have in common that tranquil and subdued manner which we have chosen to denominate *repose;* but, in the case of the two former,

[1]In the April 1842 issue of *Graham's Magazine,* Poe published a brief notice of Hawthorne's *Tales.* The next issue, May 1842, contained the expanded review, from which the following selection is taken.

[2]Hawthorne's tales were first published in various magazines. In 1837 they were collected and republished in a single volume. In 1842 the 1837 edition was republished. Poe reviewed the 1842 (third) version.

[3]Charles Lamb (1775–1834), Leigh Hunt (1784–1859), and William Hazlitt (1778–1830), English essayists.

[4]Washington Irving. In his brief notice the previous month, Poe had compared Hawthorne's tales to Irving's *Tales of a Traveller* (1824).

[5]The eighteenth-century English periodical conducted by the essayists Richard Steele (1672–1729) and Joseph Addison (1672–1719).

this repose is attained rather by the absence of novel combination, or of originality, than otherwise, and consists chiefly in the calm, quiet, unostentatious expression of commonplace thoughts, in an unambitious, unadulterated Saxon. In them, by strong effort, we are made to conceive the absence of all. In the essays before us the absence of effort is too obvious to be mistaken, and a strong undercurrent of *suggestion* runs continuously beneath the upper stream of the tranquil thesis. In short, these effusions of Mr. Hawthorne are the product of a truly imaginative intellect, restrained, and in some measure repressed, by fastidiousness of taste, by constitutional melancholy and by indolence.

But it is of his tales that we desire principally to speak. The tale proper, in our opinion, affords unquestionably the fairest field for the exercise of the loftiest talent, which can be afforded by the wide domains of mere prose. Were we bidden to say how the highest genius could be most advantageously employed for the best display of its own powers, we should answer, without hesitation—in the composition of a rhymed poem, not to exceed in length what might be perused in an hour. Within this limit alone can the highest order of true poetry exist. We need only here say, upon this topic, that, in almost all classes of composition, the unity of effect or impression is a point of the greatest importance. It is clear, moreover, that this unity cannot be thoroughly preserved in productions whose perusal cannot be completed at one sitting. We may continue the reading of a prose composition, from the very nature of prose itself, much longer than we can persevere, to any good purpose, in the perusal of a poem. This latter, if truly fulfilling the demands of the poetic sentiment, induces an exaltation of the soul which cannot be long sustained. All high excitements are necessarily transient. Thus a long poem is a paradox. And, without unity of impression, the deepest effects cannot be brought about. Epics were the offspring of an imperfect sense of Art, and their reign is no more. A poem *too* brief may produce a vivid, but never an intense or enduring impression. Without a certain continuity of effort—without a certain duration or repetition of purpose—the soul is never deeply moved. There must be the dropping of the water upon the rock. De Béranger[6] has wrought brilliant things—pungent and spirit-stirring—but, like all immassive[7] bodies, they lack *momentum,* and thus fail to satisfy the Poetic Sentiment. They sparkle and excite, but, from want of continuity, fail deeply to impress. Extreme brevity will degenerate into epigrammatism; but the sin of extreme length is even more unpardonable. *In medio tutissimus ibis.*[8]

Were we called upon, however, to designate that class of composition which, next to such a poem as we have suggested, should best fulfil the demands of high genius—should offer it the most advantageous field of exertion—we should unhesitatingly speak of the prose tale, as Mr. Hawthorne has here exemplified it. We allude to the short prose narrative, requiring from a half-hour to one or two hours in its perusal. The ordinary novel is objectionable, from its length, for reasons already stated in substance. As it cannot be read at one sitting, it deprives itself, of course, of the immense force derivable from *totality.* Worldly interests intervening during the pauses

[6]Pierre-Jean de Béranger (1780–1857), French poet.

[7]Lacking mass.

[8]Latin: "You will go most safely in the middle way." From the *Metamorphoses* of the Latin poet Ovid (43 B.C.–A.D. 18).

of perusal, modify, annul, or counteract, in a greater or less degree, the impressions of the book. But simple cessation in reading, would, of itself, be sufficient to destroy the true unity. In the brief tale, however, the author is enabled to carry out the fulness of his intention, be it what it may. During the hour of perusal the soul of the reader is at the writer's control. There are no external or extrinsic influences—resulting from weariness or interruption.

A skilful literary artist has constructed a tale. If wise, he has not fashioned his thoughts to accommodate his incidents; but having conceived, with deliberate care, a certain unique or single *effect* to be wrought out, he then invents such incidents—he then combines such events as may best aid him in establishing this preconceived effect. If his very initial sentence tend not to the outbringing of this effect, then he has failed in his first step. In the whole composition there should be no word written, of which the tendency, direct or indirect, is not to the one pre-established design. And by such means, with such care and skill, a picture is at length painted which leaves in the mind of him who contemplates it with a kindred art, a sense of the fullest satisfaction. The idea of the tale has been presented unblemished, because undisturbed; and this is an end unattainable by the novel. Undue brevity is just as exceptionable here as in the poem; but undue length is yet more to be avoided.

We have said that the tale has a point of superiority even over the poem. In fact, while the *rhythm* of this latter is an essential aid in the development of the poet's highest idea—the idea of the Beautiful—the artificialities of this rhythm are an inseparable bar to the development of all points of thought or expression which have their basis in *Truth.* But Truth is often, and in very great degree, the aim of the tale. Some of the finest tales are tales of ratiocination.[9] Thus the field of this species of composition, if not in so elevated a region on the mountain of Mind, is a table-land of far vaster extent than the domain of the mere poem. Its products are never so rich, but infinitely more numerous, and more appreciable by the mass of mankind. The writer of the prose tale, in short, may bring to his theme a vast variety of modes or inflections of thought and expression—(the ratiocinative, for example, the sarcastic, or the humorous) which are not only antagonistical to the nature of the poem, but absolutely forbidden by one of its most peculiar and indispensable adjuncts; we allude, of course, to rhythm. It may be added here, *par parenthèse,*[10] that the author who aims at the purely beautiful in a prose tale is laboring at great disadvantage. For Beauty can be better treated in the poem. Not so with terror, or passion, or horror, or a multitude of such other points. And here it will be seen how full of prejudice are the usual animadversions[11] against those *tales of effect,* many fine examples of which were found in the earlier numbers of Blackwood.[12] The impressions produced were wrought in a legitimate sphere of action, and constituted a legitimate although sometimes an exaggerated interest. They were relished by every man of genius; although there were found many men of genius who condemned them without just ground. The true critic will but demand that the design intended be accomplished, to the fullest extent, by the means most advantageously applicable.

[9]Exact reasoning.

[10]French: parenthetically. [11]Hostile remarks.

[12]*Blackwood's Edinburgh Magazine,* a British monthly (founded 1817) noted for publishing tales of Gothic terror.

We have very few American tales of real merit—we may say, indeed, none, with the exception of "The Tales of a Traveller" of Washington Irving, and these "Twice-Told Tales" of Mr. Hawthorne. Some of the pieces of Mr. John Neal[13] abound in vigor and originality; but in general, his compositions of this class are excessively diffuse, extravagant, and indicative of an imperfect sentiment of Art. Articles at random are, now and then, met with in our periodicals which might be advantageously compared with the best effusions of the British Magazines; but, upon the whole, we are far behind our progenitors in this department of literature.

Of Mr. Hawthorne's Tales we would say, emphatically, that they belong to the highest region of Art—and Art subservient to genius of a very lofty order. We had supposed, with good reason for so supposing, that he had been thrust into his present position by one of the impudent *cliques* which beset our literature, and whose pretensions it is our full purpose to expose at the earliest opportunity; but we have been most agreeably mistaken. We know of few compositions which the critic can more honestly commend than these "Twice-Told Tales." As Americans, we felt proud of the book.

Mr. Hawthorne's distinctive trait is invention, creation, imagination, originality—a trait which, in the literature of fiction, is positively worth all the rest. But the nature of originality, so far as regards its manifestation in letters, is but imperfectly understood. The inventive or original mind as frequently displays itself in novelty of *tone* as in novelty of matter. Mr. Hawthorne is original at *all* points.

. . .

In the ways of objection we have scarcely a word to say of these tales. There is, perhaps, a somewhat too general or prevalent *tone*—a tone of melancholy and mysticism. The subjects are insufficiently varied. There is not so much of *versatility* evinced as we might well be warranted in expecting from the high powers of Mr. Hawthorne. But beyond these trivial exceptions we have really none to make. The style is purity itself. Force abounds. High imagination gleams from every page. Mr. Hawthorne is a man of the truest genius. We only regret that the limits of our Magazine will not permit us to pay him that full tribute of commendation, which, under other circumstances, we should be so eager to pay.

1842

THE PHILOSOPHY OF COMPOSITION[1]

Charles Dickens, in a note now lying before me, alluding to an examination I once made of the mechanism of "Barnaby Rudge,"[2] says—"By the way, are you aware that Godwin wrote his 'Caleb Williams' backwards?[3] He first involved his

[13]American writer (1793–1876).

[1]Whether Poe actually composed *The Raven* as described here is a literary mystery that remains unsolved. Poe's intention in "The Philosophy of Composition" was to show the importance of conscious effort, rather than intuitive inspiration, in the creation of a work of art.

[2]In 1841, when the early chapters of Dickens' novel *Barnaby Rudge* had been serialized, Poe wrote a review in which he demonstrated his analytic powers by forecasting the outcome of the novel and correctly identifying the murderer.

[3]William Godwin (1756–1836), English essayist and novelist, reported in the preface to his novel of crime and detection, *Caleb Williams* (1794), that first he conceived the ending of the novel and then wrote the beginning.

hero in a web of difficulties, forming the second volume, and then, for the first, cast about him for some mode of accounting for what had been done."

I cannot think this the *precise* mode of procedure on the part of Godwin—and indeed what he himself acknowledges, is not altogether in accordance with Mr. Dickens' idea—but the author of "Caleb Williams" was too good an artist not to perceive the advantage derivable from at least a somewhat similar process. Nothing is more clear than that every plot, worth the name, must be elaborated to its *dénouement*[4] before anything be attempted with the pen. It is only with the *dénouement* constantly in view that we can give a plot its indispensable air of consequence, or causation, by making the incidents, and especially the tone at all points, tend to the development of the intention.

There is a radical error, I think, in the usual mode of constructing a story. Either history affords a thesis—or one is suggested by an incident of the day—or, at best, the author sets himself to work in the combination of striking events to form merely the basis of his narrative—designing, generally, to fill in with description, dialogue, or autorial comment, whatever crevices of fact, or action, may, from page to page, render themselves apparent.

I prefer commencing with the consideration of an *effect*. Keeping originality *always* in view—for he is false to himself who ventures to dispense with so obvious and so easily attainable a source of interest—I say to myself, in the first place, "Of the innumerable effects, or impressions, of which the heart, the intellect, or (more generally) the soul is susceptible, what one shall I, on the present occasion, select?" Having chosen a novel, first, and secondly a vivid effect, I consider whether it can be best wrought by incident or tone—whether by ordinary incidents and peculiar tone, or the converse, or by peculiarity both of incident and tone—afterward looking about me (or rather within) for such combinations of event, or tone, as shall best aid me in the construction of the effect.

I have often thought how interesting a magazine paper might be written by any author who would—that is to say who could—detail, step by step, the processes by which any one of his compositions attained its ultimate point of completion. Why such a paper has never been given to the world, I am much at a loss to say—but, perhaps, the autorial vanity has had more to do with the omission than any one other cause. Most writers—poets in especial—prefer having it understood that they compose by a species of fine frenzy—an ecstatic intuition—and would positively shudder at letting the public take a peep behind the scenes, at the elaborate and vacillating crudities of thought—at the true purposes seized only at the last moment—at the innumerable glimpses of idea that arrived not at the maturity of full view—at the fully matured fancies discarded in despair as unmanageable—at the cautious selections and rejections—at the painful erasures and interpolations—in a word, at the wheels and pinions—the tackle for scene-shifting—the step-ladders and demon traps—the cock's feathers, the red paint and the black patches, which, in ninety-nine cases out of the hundred, constitute the properties of the literary *histrio*.[5]

[4]From the French, *dénouer,* to untie; hence, the final revelation which shows the outcome of the plot.

[5]Latin: performer.

I am aware, on the other hand, that the case is by no means common, in which an author is at all in condition to retrace the steps by which his conclusions have been attained. In general, suggestions, having arisen pell-mell, are pursued and forgotten in a similar manner.

For my own part, I have neither sympathy with the repugnance alluded to, nor, at any time the least difficulty in recalling to mind the progressive steps of any of my compositions; and, since the interest of an analysis, or reconstruction, such as I have considered a *desideratum,*[6] is quite independent of any real or fancied interest in the thing analyzed, it will not be regarded as a breach of decorum on my part to show the *modus operandi*[7] by which some one of my own works was put together. I select "The Raven," as most generally known. It is my design to render it manifest that no one point in its composition is referrible either to accident or intuition—that the work proceeded, step by step, to its completion with the precision and rigid consequence of a mathematical problem.

Let us dismiss, as irrelevant to the poem, *per se,*[8] the circumstance—or say the necessity—which, in the first place, gave rise to the intention of composing *a* poem that should suit at once the popular and the critical taste.

We commence, then, with this intention.

The initial consideration was that of extent. If any literary work is too long to be read at one sitting, we must be content to dispense with the immensely important effect derivable from unity of impression—for, if two sittings be required, the affairs of the world interfere, and every thing like totality is at once destroyed. But since, *ceteris paribus,*[9] no poet can afford to dispense with *any thing* that may advance his design, it but remains to be seen whether there is, in extent, any advantage to counterbalance the loss of unity which attends it. Here I say no, at once. What we term a long poem is, in fact, merely a succession of brief ones—that is to say, of brief poetical effects. It is needless to demonstrate that a poem is such, only inasmuch as it intensely excites, by elevating, the soul; and all intense excitements are, through a psychal[10] necessity, brief. For this reason, at least one half of the "Paradise Lost"[11] is essentially prose—a succession of poetical excitements interspersed, *inevitably,* with corresponding depressions—the whole being deprived, through the extremeness of its length, of the vastly important artistic element, totality, or unity, of effect.

It appears evident, then, that there is a distinct limit, as regards length, to all works of literary art—the limit of a single sitting—and that, although in certain classes of prose composition, such as "Robinson Crusoe,"[12] (demanding no unity,) this limit may be advantageously overpassed, it can never properly be overpassed in a poem. Within this limit, the extent of a poem may be made to bear mathematical relation to its merit—in other words, to the excitement or elevation—again in other words, to the degree

[6]Something desired as essential.
[7]Latin: mode of operating.
[8]Latin: by itself.
[9]Latin: other things being equal.
[10]Spiritual or psychological.
[11]John Milton's epic poem, published in twelve "books" and with 10,556 lines of poetry.
[12]Novel by Daniel Defoe.

of the true poetical effect which it is capable of inducing; for it is clear that the brevity must be in direct ratio of the intensity of the intended effect:—this, with one proviso—that a certain degree of duration is absolutely requisite for the production of any effect at all.

Holding in view these considerations, as well as that degree of excitement which I deemed not above the popular, while not below the critical, taste, I reached at once what I conceived the proper *length* for my intended poem—a length of about one hundred lines. It is, in fact, a hundred and eight.

My next thought concerned the choice of an impression, or effect, to be conveyed: and here I may as well observe that, throughout the construction, I kept steadily in view the design of rendering the work *universally* appreciable. I should be carried too far out of my immediate topic were I to demonstrate a point upon which I have repeatedly insisted, and which, with the poetical, stands not in the slightest need of demonstration—the point, I mean, that Beauty is the sole legitimate province of the poem. A few words, however, in elucidation of my real meaning, which some of my friends have evinced a disposition to misrepresent. That pleasure which is at once the most intense, the most elevating, and the most pure, is, I believe, found in the contemplation of the beautiful. When, indeed, men speak of Beauty, they mean, precisely, not a quality, as is supposed, but an effect—they refer, in short, just to that intense and pure elevation of *soul—not* of intellect, or of heart—upon which I have commented, and which is experienced in consequence of contemplating "the beautiful." Now I designate Beauty as the province of the poem, merely because it is an obvious rule of Art that effects should be made to spring from direct causes—that objects should be attained through means best adapted for their attainment—no one as yet having been weak enough to deny that the peculiar elevation alluded to is *most readily* attained in the poem. Now the object, Truth, or the satisfaction of the intellect, and the object Passion, or the excitement of the heart, are, although attainable, to a certain extent, in poetry, far more readily attainable in prose. Truth, in fact, demands a precision, and Passion a *homeliness* (the truly passionate will comprehend me) which are absolutely antagonistic to that Beauty which, I maintain, is the excitement, or pleasurable elevation, of the soul. It by no means follows from any thing here said, that passion, or even truth, may not be introduced, and even profitably introduced, into a poem—for they may serve in elucidation, or aid the general effect, as do discords in music, by contrast—but the true artist will always contrive, first, to tone them into proper subservience to the predominant aim, and, secondly, to enveil them, as far as possible, in that Beauty which is the atmosphere and the essence of the poem.

Regarding, then, Beauty as my province, my next question referred to the *tone* of its highest manifestation—and all experience has shown that this tone is one of *sadness.* Beauty of whatever kind, in its supreme development, invariably excites the sensitive soul to tears. Melancholy is thus the most legitimate of all the poetical tones.

The length, the province, and the tone, being thus determined, I betook myself to ordinary induction, with the view of obtaining some artistic piquancy which might serve me as a key-note in the construction of the poem—some pivot upon which the whole structure might turn. In carefully thinking over all the usual artistic effects—or more properly *points,* in the theatrical sense—I did not fail to perceive immediately that no one had been so universally employed as that of the *refrain.* The universality of its employment sufficed to assure me of its intrinsic value, and spared me the necessity of submitting it to analysis. I considered it, however, with regard to its susceptibility of improvement, and soon saw it to be in a primitive condition. As commonly used, the *refrain,* or burden, not only is limited to lyric verse, but depends for its impression upon the force of monotone—both in sound and thought. The pleasure is deduced solely from the sense of identity—of repetition. I resolved to diversify, and so heighten, the effect, by adhering, in general, to the monotone of sound, while I continually varied that of thought: that is to say, I determined to produce continuously novel effects, by the variation *of the application* of the *refrain*—the *refrain* itself remaining, for the most part, unvaried.

These points being settled, I next bethought me of the *nature* of my *refrain.* Since its application was to be repeatedly varied, it was clear that the *refrain* itself must be brief, for there would have been an insurmountable difficulty in frequent variations of application in any sentence of length. In proportion to the brevity of the sentence, would, of course, be the facility of the variation. This led me at once to a single word as the best *refrain.*

The question now arose as to the *character* of the word. Having made up my mind to a *refrain,* the division of the poem into stanzas was, of course, a corollary; the *refrain* forming the close of each stanza. That such a close, to have force, must be sonorous and susceptible of protracted emphasis, admitted no doubt: and these considerations inevitably led me to the long *o* as the most sonorous vowel, in connection with *r* as the most producible consonant.

The sound of the *refrain* being thus determined, it became necessary to select a word embodying this sound, and, at the same time in the fullest possible keeping with that melancholy which I had predetermined as the tone of the poem. In such a search it would have been absolutely impossible to overlook the word "Nevermore." In fact, it was the very first which presented itself.

The next *desideratum* was a pretext for the continuous use of the one word "nevermore." In observing the difficulty which I at once found in inventing a sufficiently plausible reason for its continuous repetition, I did not fail to perceive that this difficulty arose solely from the pre-assumption that the word was to be so continuously or monotonously spoken by *a human* being—I did not fail to perceive, in short, that the difficulty lay in the reconciliation of this monotony with the exercise of reason on the part of the creature repeating the word. Here, then, immediately arose the idea of a *non*-reasoning creature capable of speech; and, very naturally, a parrot, in the first instance, suggested itself, but was superseded forthwith by a Raven, as equally capable of speech, and infinitely more in keeping with the intended *tone.*

I had now gone so far as the conception of a Raven—the bird of ill omen—monotonously repeating the one word, "Nevermore," at the conclusion of each stanza, in a poem of melancholy tone, and in length about one hundred lines. Now, never losing sight of the object *supremeness,* or perfection, at all points, I asked myself—"Of all melancholy topics, what, according to the *universal* understanding of mankind, is the *most* melancholy?" Death—was the obvious reply. "And when," I said, "is this most melancholy of topics most poetical?" From what I have already explained at some length, the answer, here also, is obvious—"When it most closely allies itself to *Beauty:* the death, then, of a beautiful woman is, unquestionably, the most poetical topic in the world—and equally is it beyond doubt that the lips best suited for such topic are those of a bereaved lover."

I had now to combine the two ideas, of a lover lamenting his deceased mistress and a Raven continuously repeating the word "Nevermore."—I had to combine these, bearing in mind my design of varying, at every turn, the *application* of the word repeated; but the only intelligible mode of such combination is that of imagining the Raven employing the word in answer to the queries of the lover. And here it was that I saw at once the opportunity afforded for the effect on which I had been depending—that is to say, the effect of the *variation of application.* I saw that I could make the first query propounded by the lover—the first query to which the Raven should reply "Nevermore"—that I could make this first query a commonplace one—the second less so—the third still less, and so on—until at length the lover, startled from his original *nonchalance* by the melancholy character of the word itself—by its frequent repetition—and by a consideration of the ominous reputation of the fowl that uttered it—is at length excited to superstition, and wildly propounds queries of a far different character—queries whose solution he has passionately at heart—propounds them half in superstition and half in that species of despair which delights in self-torture—propounds them not altogether because he believes in the prophetic or demoniac character of the bird (which, reason assures him, is merely repeating a lesson learned by rote) but because he experiences a phrenzied pleasure in so modeling his questions as to receive from the *expected* "Nevermore" the most delicious because the most intolerable of sorrow. Perceiving the opportunity thus afforded me—or, more strictly, thus forced upon me in the progress of the construction—I first established in mind the climax, or concluding query to which "Nevermore" should be in the last place an answer—that in reply to which this word "Nevermore" should involve the utmost conceivable amount of sorrow and despair.

Here then the poem may be said to have its beginning—at the end, where all works of art should begin—for it was here, at this point of my preconsiderations, that I first put pen to paper in the composition of the stanza:

"Prophet," said I, "thing of evil!—prophet still if bird or devil!
By that heaven that bends above us—by that God we both adore—
Tell this soul with sorrow laden, if within the distant Aidenn,
It shall clasp a sainted maiden whom the angels name Lenore—
Clasp a rare and radiant maiden whom the angels name Lenore."
Quoth the raven "Nevermore."

I composed this stanza, at this point, first that, by establishing the climax, I might the better vary and graduate, as regards seriousness and importance, the preceding queries of the lover—and, secondly, that I might definitely settle the rhythm, the metre, and the length and general arrangement of the stanza—as well as graduate the stanzas which were to precede, so that none of them might surpass this in rhythmical effect. Had I been able, in the subsequent composition, to construct more vigorous stanzas, I should, without scruple, have purposely enfeebled them, so as not to interfere with the climacteric effect.

And here I may as well say a few words of the versification. My first object (as usual) was originality. The extent to which this has been neglected, in versification, is one of the most unaccountable things in the world. Admitting that there is little possibility of variety in mere *rhythm,* it is still clear that the possible varieties of metre and stanza are absolutely infinite—and yet, *for centuries, no man, in verse, has ever done, or ever seemed to think of doing, an original thing.* The fact is, that originality (unless in minds of very unusual force) is by no means a matter, as some suppose, of impulse or intuition. In general, to be found, it must be elaborately sought, and although a positive merit of the highest class, demands in its attainment less of invention than negation.

Of course, I pretend to no originality in either the rhythm or metre of the "Raven." The former is trochaic—the latter is octameter acatalectic,[13] alternating with heptameter catalectic repeated in the *refrain* of the fifth verse, and terminating with tetrameter catalectic. Less pedantically—the feet employed throughout (trochees) consist of a long syllable followed by a short: the first line of the stanza consists of eight of these feet—the second of seven and a half (in effect two-thirds)—the third of eight—the fourth of seven and a half—the fifth the same—the sixth three and a half. Now, each of these lines, taken individually, has been employed before, and what originality the "Raven" has, is in their *combination into stanza;* nothing even remotely approaching this combination has ever been attempted. The effect of this originality of combination is aided by other unusual, and some altogether novel effects, arising from an extension of the application of the principles of rhyme and alliteration.

The next point to be considered was the mode of bringing together the lover and the Raven—and the first branch of this consideration was the *locale.* For this the most natural suggestion might seem to be a forest, or the fields—but it has always appeared to me that a close *circumscription of space* is absolutely necessary to the effect of insulated incident:—it has the force of a frame to a picture. It has an indisputable moral power in keeping concentrated the attention, and, of course, must not be confounded with mere unity of place.

I determined, then, to place the lover in his chamber—in a chamber rendered sacred to him by memories of her who had frequented it. The room is represented as richly furnished—this in mere pursuance of the ideas I have already explained on the subject of Beauty, as the sole true poetical thesis.

The *locale* being thus determined, I had now to introduce the bird—and the thought of introducing him through the window, was inevitable. The idea of making the lover suppose, in the first instance, that the flapping of the wings of the bird against the shutter, is a "tapping" at the door, originated in a wish to increase, by prolonging, the reader's curiosity, and in a desire to admit the incidental effect arising from the lover's throwing open the door, finding all dark, and thence adopting the half-fancy that it was the spirit of his mistress that knocked.

[13]Poetic lines lacking a part of the final metric foot are catalectic. Those with a complete final metric foot are acatalectic.

I made the night tempestuous, first, to account for the Raven's seeking admission, and secondly, for the effect of contrast with the (physical) serenity within the chamber.

I made the bird alight on the bust of Pallas, also for the effect of contrast between the marble and the plumage—it being understood that the bust was absolutely *suggested* by the bird—the bust of *Pallas* being chosen, first, as most in keeping with the scholarship of the lover, and, secondly, for the sonorousness of the word, Pallas, itself.

About the middle of the poem, also, I have availed myself of the force of contrast, with a view of deepening the ultimate impression. For example, an air of the fantastic—approaching as nearly to the ludicrous as was admissible—is given to the Raven's entrance. He comes in "with many a flirt and flutter."

> Not the *least obeisance made he;* not a moment stopped or stayed he;
> *But, with mien of lord or lady,* perched above my chamber door—

In the two stanzas which follow, the design is more obviously carried out:—

> Then this ebony bird beguiling my sad fancy into smiling,
> By the *grave and stern decorum of the countenance it wore,*
> "Though thy *crest be shorn and shaven,* thou," I said, "art sure no craven,
> Ghastly grim and ancient Raven wandering from the nightly shore—
> Tell me what thy lordly name is on the Night's Plutonian shore!"
> Quoth the Raven "Nevermore."
>
> Much I marvelled *this ungainly fowl* to hear discourse so plainly
> Though its answer little meaning—little relevancy bore;
> For we cannot help agreeing that no living human being
>
> *Ever yet was blessed with seeing bird above his chamber door—*
> *Bird or beast upon the sculptured bust above his chamber door,*
> With such a name as "Nevermore."

The effect of the *dénouement* being thus provided for, I immediately drop the fantastic for a tone of the most profound seriousness:—this tone commencing in the stanza directly following the one last quoted, with the line,

> But the Raven, sitting lonely on that placid bust, spoke only, etc.

From this epoch[14] the lover no longer jests—no longer sees any thing even of the fantastic in the Raven's demeanor. He speaks of him as a "grim, ungainly, ghastly, gaunt, and ominous bird of yore," and feels the "fiery eyes" burning into his "bosom's core." This revolution of thought, or fancy, on the lover's part, is intended to induce a similar one on the part of the reader—

[14]Significant moment.

to bring the mind into a proper frame for the *dénouement*—which is now brought about as rapidly and as *directly* as possible.

With the *dénouement* proper—with the Raven's reply, "Nevermore," to the lover's final demand if he shall meet his mistress in another world—the poem, in its obvious phase, that of a simple narrative, may be said to have its completion. So far, every thing is within the limits of the accountable—of the real. A raven, having learned by rote the single word "Nevermore," and having escaped from the custody of its owner, is driven at midnight, through the violence of a storm, to seek admission at a window from which a light still gleams—the chamberwindow of a student, occupied half in poring over a volume, half in dreaming of a beloved mistress deceased. The casement being thrown open at the fluttering of the bird's wings, the bird itself perches on the most convenient seat out of the immediate reach of the student, who, amused by the incident and the oddity of the visitor's demeanor, demands of it, in jest and without looking for a reply, its name. The raven addressed, answers with its customary word, "Nevermore"—a word which finds immediate echo in the melancholy heart of the student, who, giving utterance aloud to certain thoughts suggested by the occasion, is again startled by the fowl's repetition of "Nevermore." The student now guesses the state of the case, but is impelled, as I have before explained, by the human thirst for self-torture, and in part by superstition, to propound such queries to the bird as will bring him, the lover, the most of the luxury of sorrow, through the anticipated answer "Nevermore." With the indulgence, to the extreme, of this self-torture, the narration, in what I have termed its first or obvious phase, has a natural termination, and so far there has been no overstepping of the limits of the real.

But in subjects so handled, however skillfully, or with however vivid an array of incident, there is always a certain hardness or nakedness, which repels the artistical eye. Two things are invariably required—first, some amount of complexity, or more properly, adaptation; and, secondly, some amount of suggestiveness—some under-current, however indefinite, of meaning. It is this latter, in especial, which imparts to a work of art so much of that *richness* (to borrow from colloquy a forcible term) which we are too fond of confounding with *the ideal*. It is the *excess* of the suggested meaning—it is the rendering this the upper instead of the under current of the theme—which turns into prose (and that of the very flattest kind) the so called poetry of the so called transcendentalists.

Holding these opinions, I added the two concluding stanzas of the poem—their suggestiveness being thus made to pervade all the narrative which has preceded them. The under-current of meaning is rendered first apparent in the lines—

> "Take thy beak from out *my* heart, and take thy form from off my door!"
> Quoth the Raven "Nevermore."

It will be observed that the words, "from out my heart," involve the first metaphorical expression in the poem. They, with the answer, "Nevermore," dispose the mind to seek a moral in all that has been previously narrated. The reader begins now to regard the Raven as emblematical—but it is not until the very last line of the very last stanza, that the intention of making him emblematical of *Mournful and Never-ending Remembrance* is permitted distinctly to be seen:

> And the Raven, never flitting, still is sitting, *still* is sitting,
> On the pallid bust of Pallas, just above my chamber door;
> And his eyes have all the seeming of a demon's that is dreaming,
> And the lamp-light o'er him streaming throws his shadow on the
> floor;
> And my soul *from out that shadow* that lies floating on the floor
> Shall be lifted—nevermore.

1846

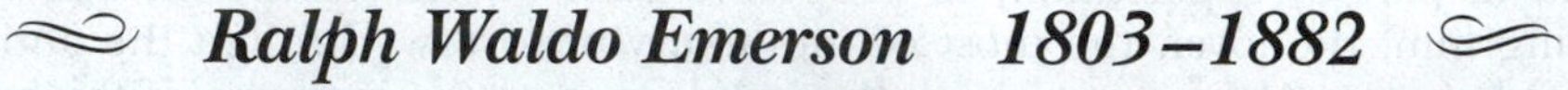

Ralph Waldo Emerson 1803–1882

Emerson was nineteenth-century America's most notable prophet and sage. He was an apostle of progress and optimism, and his dedication to self-reliant individualism inspired his fellow transcendentalist Bronson Alcott to observe, "Emerson's church consists of one member—himself. He waits for the world to agree with him." Emerson was born in Boston, the son of a Unitarian minister and the descendant of a long line of distinguished New England clergymen. He was educated at the Boston Latin School and at Harvard. After his graduation from college in 1821 Emerson taught in a Boston school for young ladies, daughters of the gentry. In 1825 he entered the Harvard Divinity School, where he absorbed the liberal, intellectualized Christianity of Unitarianism, which rejected the Calvinist ideas of predestination and total depravity, substituting instead a faith in the saving grace of divine love and a belief in the eventual brotherhood of man in a Kingdom of Heaven on earth.

In 1829 Emerson was ordained the Unitarian minister of the Second Church of Boston. He was a popular and successful preacher, but after three years he came to doubt the sacrament of the Lord's Supper, and his growing objections to even the remnants of Christian dogma that survived in early nineteenth-century Unitarianism led him to conclude that "to be a good minister it was necessary to leave the ministry."

After preaching his farewell sermon, Emerson went on a tour of Europe. There he met Samuel Taylor Coleridge, Thomas Carlyle, and William Wordsworth, and was strongly influenced by the ideas of European romanticism. On returning to America, he began his lifelong career as a public lecturer, a career that took him throughout much of the nation. He bought a house in Concord, Massachusetts, and there he associated with Henry David Thoreau, Nathaniel Hawthorne, Bronson Alcott, Margaret Fuller, and others who belonged to the informal Transcendentalist Club, organized for the "exchange of thought among those interested in the new views in philosophy, theology, and literature." Later on, Emerson's ideas would greatly influence the work of many of the club's members.

In Concord, Emerson became the intellectual leader of transcendentalism in America. His philosophy was a compound of Yankee Puritanism and Unitarianism merged with the teachings of European romanticism. The word "transcendental" had long been used in philosophy to describe truths that were beyond the reach of humans' limited senses, and as a transcendentalist, Emerson argued for intuition as a guide to universal truths that could not be reached by reason alone. He believed in an all-loving and all-pervading god whose presence in people made them divine and assured their salvation. Furthermore, Emerson believed in a correspondence between the world and the spirit, that nature is an image in which humans can perceive the divine.

Emerson's beliefs were a balance of skepticism and faith, stirred by moral fervor. To many of his readers, they have seemed neither coherent nor complete. Devout Christians rejected his early writings as "the latest form of infidelity." He has been called "St. Ralph, the Optimist" and charged with having a serene ignorance of the true nature of evil. His exaltation of intuition over reason has been dismissed as a justification of infantile enthusiasms; his celebration of individualism has been judged an argument for mindless self-assertiveness.

Emerson was a seer and poet, not a man of logic. In his letters, essays, and poems he sought to inspire a cultural rejuvenation, to transmit to his listeners and readers his own lofty perceptions. His appeal lay in his rejection of outworn traditions and in his faith in goodness and inevitable progress. His words both dazzled and puzzled his audience. Like his philosophy, his writing seemed to lack organization, but it swarmed with epigrams and memorable passages. His ideas influenced both his contemporaries and later authors, including E. A. Robinson, Robert Frost, Hart Crane, and Wallace Stevens.

Emerson's perceptions of people and nature as symbols of universal truth encouraged the development of the symbolist movement in American writing. His assertion that even the commonplaces of American life were worthy of the highest art helped to establish a national literature. His rejection of established traditions and institutions encouraged a literary revolution; his ideas, expressed in his own writing and in the works of others, have been taken as an intellectual foundation for movements of social change that have profoundly altered modern America. Emerson was no political revolutionary. He preached harmony in a discordant age, and he recognized the needs of human society as incompatible with unrestrained individualism. As he grew older, he became increasingly conservative, but he remained a firm advocate of self-reliant idealism, and in his writings and in the example of his life, Emerson has endured as a guide for those who would question conformity and escape blind submission to fate.

FURTHER READING: *The Collected Works of Ralph Waldo Emerson*, ed. A. Ferguson, et al., 1971–1983; G. Allen, *Waldo Emerson*, 1981; B. Packer, *Emerson's Fall*, 1982; D. Yannella, *Ralph Waldo Emerson*, 1982; J. McAleer, *Ralph Waldo Emerson, Days of Encounter*, 1984; J. Ellison, *Emerson's Romantic Style*, 1984; J. Michael, *Emerson and Skepticism*, 1987; M. Cayton, *Emerson's Emergence*, 1989; E. Barish, *Emerson, The Roots of Prophecy*, 1989; L Gougeon, *Virtue's Hero: Emerson, Antislavery, and Reform*, 1990; *Ralph Waldo Emerson*, ed. R. Poirier, 1990; M. Sealts, *Emerson on the Scholar*, 1992; D. Jacobson, *Emerson's Pragmatic Vision*, 1993; *Ralph Waldo Emerson, A Collection of Critical Essays*, ed. L. Buell, 1993; D. Robinson, *Emerson and the Conduct of Life*, 1993; R. Richardson, *Emerson, The Mind on Fire*, 1995; C. Baker, *Emerson Among the Eccentrics*, 1996; C. Newfield, *The Emerson Effect*, 1996; M. Lopez, *Emerson and Power*, 1996; J. Rowe, *At Emerson's Tomb*, 1996; *The Cambridge Companion to Ralph Waldo Emerson*, ed. J. Porte and S. Morris, 1999; J. Myerson, *A Historical Guide to Ralph Waldo Emerson*, 2000; P. Field, *Ralph Waldo Emerson, the Making of a Democratic Intellectual*, 2002.

TEXT: *The Complete Works of Ralph Waldo Emerson*, 12 vols., 1903–1904.

NATURE[1]

A subtle chain of countless rings
The next unto the farthest brings;
The eye reads omens where it goes,
And speaks all languages the rose;
And, striving to be man, the worm
Mounts through all the spires of form.[2]

INTRODUCTION

Our age is retrospective. It builds the sepulchres of the fathers. It writes biographies, histories, and criticism. The foregoing generations beheld God and nature face to face; we, through their eyes. Why should not we also enjoy an original relation to the universe? Why should not we have a poetry and philosophy of insight and not of tradition, and a religion by revelation to us, and not the history of theirs? Embosomed for a season in nature, whose floods of life stream around and through us, and invite us, by the powers they supply, to action proportioned to nature, why should we grope among the dry bones of the past, or put the living generation into masquerade out of its faded wardrobe? The sun shines to-day also. There is more wool and flax in the fields. There are new lands, new men, new thoughts. Let us demand our own works and laws and worship.

Undoubtedly we have no questions to ask which are unanswerable. We must trust the perfection of the creation so far as to believe that whatever curiosity the order of things has awakened in our minds, the order of things can satisfy. Every man's condition is a solution in hieroglyphic to those inquiries he would put. He acts it as life, before he apprehends it as truth. In like manner, nature is already, in its forms and tendencies, describing its own design. Let us interrogate the great apparition that shines so peacefully around us. Let us inquire, to what end is nature?

All science has one aim, namely, to find a theory of nature. We have theories of races and of functions, but scarcely yet a remote approach to an idea of creation. We are now so far from the road to truth, that religious teachers dispute and hate each other, and speculative men are esteemed unsound and frivolous. But to a sound judgment, the most abstract truth is the most practical. Whenever a true theory appears, it will be its own evidence. Its test is, that it will explain all phenomena. Now many are thought not only unexplained but inexplicable; as language, sleep, madness, dreams, beasts, sex.

Philosophically considered, the universe is composed of Nature and the Soul. Strictly speaking, therefore, all that is separate from us, all which

[1]*Nature,* published anonymously in 1836, was Emerson's first major work and has come to be called the manifesto of New England transcendentalism.

[2]The first edition had for its motto a quotation from the Roman philosopher Plotinus (205?–270 A.D.): "Nature is but an image or imitation of wisdom, the last thing of the soul; nature being a thing which doth only do, but not know." Emerson's poem on "Nature" was substituted in the edition of 1849.

Philosophy distinguishes as the NOT ME, that is, both nature and art, all other men and my own body, must be ranked under this name, NATURE. In enumerating the values of nature and casting up their sum, I shall use the word in both senses;—in its common and in its philosophical import. In inquiries so general as our present one, the inaccuracy is not material; no confusion of thought will occur. *Nature*, in the common sense, refers to essences unchanged by man; space, the air, the river, the leaf. *Art* is applied to the mixture of his will with the same things, as in a house, a canal, a statue, a picture. But his operations taken together are so insignificant, a little chipping, baking, patching, and washing, that in an impression so grand as that of the world on the human mind, they do not vary the result.

I
NATURE

To go into solitude, a man needs to retire as much from his chamber as from society. I am not solitary whilst I read and write, though nobody is with me. But if a man would be alone, let him look at the stars. The rays that come from those heavenly worlds will separate between him and what he touches. One might think the atmosphere was made transparent with this design, to give man, in the heavenly bodies, the perpetual presence of the sublime. Seen in the streets of cities, how great they are! If the stars should appear one night in a thousand years, how would men believe and adore; and preserve for many generations the remembrance of the city of God which had been shown! But every night come out these envoys of beauty, and light the universe with their admonishing smile.

The stars awaken a certain reverence, because though always present, they are inaccessible; but all natural objects make a kindred impression, when the mind is open to their influence. Nature never wears a mean appearance. Neither does the wisest man extort her secret, and lose his curiosity by finding out all her perfection. Nature never became a toy to a wise spirit. The flowers, the animals, the mountains, reflected the wisdom of his best hour, as much as they had delighted the simplicity of his childhood.

When we speak of nature in this manner, we have a distinct but most poetical sense in the mind. We mean the integrity of impression made by manifold natural objects. It is this which distinguishes the stick of timber of the woodcutter from the tree of the poet. The charming landscape which I saw this morning is indubitably made up of some twenty or thirty farms. Miller owns this field, Locke that, and Manning the woodland beyond. But none of them owns the landscape. There is a property in the horizon which no man has but he whose eye can integrate all the parts, that is, the poet. This is the best part of these men's farms, yet to this their warranty-deeds give no title.

To speak truly, few adult persons can see nature. Most persons do not see the sun. At least they have a very superficial seeing. The sun illuminates only the eye of the man, but shines into the eye and the heart of the child. The lover of nature is he whose inward and outward senses are still truly adjusted to each other; who has retained the spirit of infancy even into the era of manhood. His intercourse with heaven and earth becomes part of his daily food. In the presence of nature a wild delight runs through the man, in spite of real sorrows. Nature says,—he is my creature, and maugre[1] all his impertinent griefs, he shall be glad with me. Not the sun or the summer alone, but every hour and season yields its tribute of delight; for every hour and change corresponds to and authorizes a different state of the mind, from breathless noon to grimmest midnight. Nature is a setting that fits equally well a comic or a mourning piece. In good health, the air is a cordial of incredible virtue. Crossing a bare common, in snow puddles, at twilight, under a clouded sky, without having in my thoughts any occurrence of special good fortune, I have enjoyed a perfect exhilaration. I am glad to the brink of fear. In the woods, too, a man casts off his years, as the snake his slough, and at what period soever of life is always a child. In the woods is perpetual youth. Within these plantations of God, a decorum and sanctity reign, a perennial festival is dressed, and the guest sees not how he should tire of them in a thousand years. In the woods, we return to reason and faith. There I feel that nothing can befall me in life—no disgrace, no calamity (leaving me my eyes), which nature cannot repair. Standing on the bare ground,—my head bathed by the blithe air and uplifted into infinite space,—all mean egotism vanishes. I become a transparent eyeball; I am nothing; I see all; the currents of the Universal Being circulate through me; I am part or particle of God. The name of the nearest friend sounds then foreign and accidental; to be brothers, to be acquaintances, master or servant, is then a trifle and a disturbance. I am the lover of uncontained and immortal beauty. In the wilderness, I find something more dear and connate[2] than in streets or villages. In the tranquil landscape, and especially in the distant line of the horizon, man beholds somewhat as beautiful as his own nature.

The greatest delight which the fields and woods minister is the suggestion of an occult relation between man and the vegetable. I am not alone and unacknowledged. They nod to me, and I to them. The waving of the boughs in the storm is new to me and old. It takes me by surprise, and yet is not unknown. Its effect is like that of a higher thought or a better emotion coming over me, when I deemed I was thinking justly or doing right.

Yet it is certain that the power to produce this delight does not reside in nature, but in man, or in a harmony of both. It is necessary to use these pleasures with great temperance. For nature is not always tricked[3] in holiday attire, but the same scene which yesterday breathed perfume and glittered as for the frolic of the nymphs is overspread with melancholy to-day. Nature always wears the colors of the spirit. To a man laboring under calamity, the heat of his own fire hath sadness in it. Then there is a kind of contempt of the landscape felt by him who has just lost by death a dear friend. The sky is less grand as it shuts down over less worth in the population.

II
COMMODITY

Whoever considers the final cause of the world will discern a multitude of uses that enter as parts into that result. They all admit of being thrown into one of the following classes: Commodity; Beauty; Language; and Discipline.

[1]In spite of. [2]Related, congenial. [3]Dressed.

Under the general name of commodity, I rank all those advantages which our senses owe to nature. This, of course, is a benefit which is temporary and mediate,[1] not ultimate, like its service to the soul. Yet although low, it is perfect in its kind, and is the only use of nature which all men apprehend. The misery of man appears like childish petulance, when we explore the steady and prodigal provision that has been made for his support and delight on this green ball which floats him through the heavens. What angels invented these splendid ornaments, these rich conveniences, this ocean of air above, this ocean of water beneath, this firmament of earth between? this zodiac of lights, this tent of dropping clouds, this striped coat of climates, the fourfold year? Beasts, fire, water, stones, and corn serve him. The field is at once his floor, his work-yard, his play-ground, his garden, and his bed.

"More servants wait on men
Than he'll take notice of."[2]

Nature, in its ministry to man, is not only the material, but is also the process and the result. All the parts incessantly work into each other's hands for the profit of man. The wind sows the seed; the sun evaporates the sea; the wind blows the vapor to the field; the ice, on the other side of the planet, condenses rain on this; the rain feeds the plant; the plant feeds the animal; and thus the endless circulations of the divine charity nourish man.

The useful arts are reproductions or new combinations by the wit of man, of the same natural benefactors. He no longer waits for favoring gales, but by means of steam, he realizes the fable of Æolus's bag,[3] and carries the two and thirty winds in the boiler of his boat. To diminish friction, he paves the road with iron bars,[4] and, mounting a coach with a ship-load of men, animals, and merchandise behind him, he darts through the country, from town to town, like an eagle or a swallow through the air. By the aggregate of these aids, how is the face of the world changed, from the era of Noah to that of Napoleon! The private poor man hath cities, ships, canals, bridges, built for him. He goes to the post-office, and the human race run on his errands; to the book-shop, and the human race read and write of all that happens, for him; to the court-house, and nations repair his wrongs. He sets his house upon the road, and the human race go forth every morning, and shovel out the snow, and cut a path for him.

But there is no need of specifying particulars in this class of uses. The catalogue is endless, and the examples so obvious, that I shall leave them to the reader's reflection, with the general remark, that this mercenary benefit is one which has respect to a farther good. A man is fed, not that he may be fed, but that he may work.

[1]In the middle.
[2]From "Man" by the English poet George Herbert (1593–1633).
[3]In the *Odyssey* the god Aeolus gave a bag of winds to Odysseus to use to propel his boat on the journey home from Troy.
[4]Railroad tracks.

III
BEAUTY

A nobler want of man is served by nature, namely, the love of Beauty.

The ancient Greeks called the world κόσμος,[1] beauty. Such is the constitution of all things, or such the plastic power of the human eye, that the primary forms, as the sky, the mountain, the tree, the animal, give us a delight *in and for themselves*; a pleasure arising from outline, color, motion, and grouping. This seems partly owing to the eye itself. The eye is the best of artists. By the mutual action of its structure and of the laws of light, perspective is produced, which integrates every mass of objects, of what character soever, into a well colored and shaded globe, so that where the particular objects are mean and unaffecting, the landscape which they compose is round and symmetrical. And as the eye is the best composer, so light is the first of painters. There is no object so foul that intense light will not make beautiful. And the stimulus it affords to the sense, and a sort of infinitude which it hath, like space and time, make all matter gay. Even the corpse has its own beauty. But besides this general grace diffused over nature, almost all the individual forms are agreeable to the eye, as is proved by our endless imitations of some of them, as the acorn, the grape, the pine-cone, the wheat-ear, the egg, the wings and forms of most birds, the lion's claw, the serpent, the butterfly, sea-shells, flames, clouds, buds, leaves, and the forms of many trees, as the palm.

For better consideration, we may distribute the aspects of Beauty in a threefold manner.

1. First, the simple perception of natural forms is a delight. The influence of the forms and actions in nature is so needful to man, that, in its lowest functions, it seems to lie on the confines of commodity and beauty. To the body and mind which have been cramped by noxious work or company, nature is medicinal and restores their tone. The tradesman, the attorney comes out of the din and craft of the street and sees the sky and the woods, and is a man again. In their eternal calm, he finds himself. The health of the eye seems to demand a horizon. We are never tired, so long as we can see far enough.

But in other hours, Nature satisfies by its loveliness, and without any mixture of corporeal benefit. I see the spectacle of morning from the hilltop over against my house, from daybreak to sunrise, with emotions which an angel might share. The long slender bars of cloud float like fishes in the sea of crimson light. From the earth, as a shore, I look out into that silent sea. I seem to partake its rapid transformations; the active enchantment reaches my dust, and I dilate and conspire with the morning wind. How does Nature deify us with a few and cheap elements! Give me health and a day, and I will make the pomp of emperors ridiculous. The dawn is my Assyria;[2] the sunset and moonrise my Paphos,[3] and unimaginable realms of faerie; broad noon shall be my England of the senses and the understanding; the night shall be my Germany of mystic philosophy and dreams.

[1]Greek: *cosmos*, meaning order, harmony.
[2]Ancient Near Eastern empire, symbolic of splendor.
[3]Ancient city of Cyprus, seat of the worship of Aphrodite, goddess of love.

Not less excellent, except for our less susceptibility in the afternoon, was the charm, last evening, of a January sunset. The western clouds divided and subdivided themselves into pink flakes modulated with tints of unspeakable softness, and the air had so much life and sweetness that it was a pain to come within doors. What was it that nature would say? Was there no meaning in the live repose of the valley behind the mill, and which Homer or Shakespeare could not re-form for me in words? The leafless trees become spires of flame in the sunset, with the blue east for their background, and the stars of the dead calices[4] of flowers, and every withered stem and stubble rimed with frost, contribute something to the mute music.

The inhabitants of cities suppose that the country landscape is pleasant only half the year. I please myself with the graces of the winter scenery, and believe that we are as much touched by it as by the genial influences of summer. To the attentive eye, each moment of the year has its own beauty, and in the same field, it beholds, every hour, a picture which was never seen before, and which shall never be seen again. The heavens change every moment, and reflect their glory or gloom on the plains beneath. The state of the crop in the surrounding farms alters the expression of the earth from week to week. The succession of native plants in the pastures and roadsides, which makes the silent clock by which time tells the summer hours, will make even the divisions of the day sensible to a keen observer. The tribes of birds and insects, like the plants punctual to their time, follow each other, and the year has room for all. By water-courses, the variety is greater. In July, the blue pontederia or pickerel-weed blooms in large beds in the shallow parts of our pleasant river,[5] and swarms with yellow butterflies in continual motion. Art cannot rival this pomp of purple and gold. Indeed the river is perpetual gala, and boasts each month a new ornament.

But this beauty of Nature which is seen and felt as beauty, is the least part. The shows of day, the dewy morning, the rainbow, mountains, orchards in blossom, stars, moonlight, shadows in still water, and the like, if too eagerly hunted, become shows merely, and mock us with their unreality. Go out of the house to see the moon, and 'tis mere tinsel; it will not please as when its light shines upon your necessary journey. The beauty that shimmers in the yellow afternoons of October, who ever could clutch it? Go forth to find it, and it is gone; 'tis only a mirage as you look from the windows of diligence.

2. The presence of a higher, namely, of the spiritual element is essential to its perfection. The high and divine beauty which can be loved without effeminacy, is that which is found in combination with the human will. Beauty is the mark God sets upon virtue. Every natural action is graceful. Every heroic act is also decent, and causes the place and the bystanders to shine. We are taught by great actions that the universe is the property of every individual in it. Every rational creature has all nature for his dowry and estate. It is his, if he will. He may divest himself of it; he may creep into a corner, and abdicate his kingdom, as most men do, but he is entitled to the world by his constitution. In proportion to the energy of his thought and will, he takes up the world into himself. "All those things for which men plough, build, or sail,

[4]Calyxes, leaf-like outer coverings of flowers.
[5]The Concord River.

obey virtue;" said Sallust.[6] "The winds and waves" said Gibbon, "are always on the side of the ablest navigators."[7] So are the sun and moon and all the stars of heaven. When a noble act is done,—perchance in a scene of great natural beauty; when Leonidas[8] and his three hundred martyrs consume one day in dying, and the sun and moon come each and look at them once in the steep defile of Thermopylæ; when Arnold Winkelried,[9] in the high Alps, under the shadow of the avalanche, gathers in his side a sheaf of Austrian spears to break the line for his comrades; are not these heroes entitled to add the beauty of the scene to the beauty of the deed? When the bark of Columbus nears the shore of America;—before it the beach lined with savages, fleeing out of all their huts of cane; the sea behind; and the purple mountains of the Indian Archipelago around, can we separate the man from the living picture? Does not the New World clothe his form with her palm-groves and savannahs as fit drapery? Ever does natural beauty steal in like air, and envelope great actions. When Sir Harry Vane[10] was dragged up the Tower-hill,[11] sitting on a sled, to suffer death as the champion of the English laws, one of the multitude cried out to him, "You never sate on so glorious a seat!" Charles II, to intimidate the citizens of London, caused the patriot Lord Russell[12] to be drawn in an open coach through the principal streets of the city on his way to the scaffold. "But," his biographer says, "the multitude imagined they saw liberty and virtue sitting by his side." In private places, among sordid objects, an act of truth or heroism seems at once to draw to itself the sky as its temple, the sun as its candle. Nature stretches out her arms to embrace man, only let his thoughts be of equal greatness. Willingly does she follow his steps with the rose and the violet, and bend her lines of grandeur and grace to the decoration of her darling child. Only let his thoughts be of equal scope, and the frame will suit the picture. A virtuous man is in unison with her works, and makes the central figure of the visible sphere. Homer, Pindar,[13] Socrates, and Phocion,[14] associate themselves fitly in our memory with the geography and climate of Greece. The visible heavens and earth sympathize with Jesus. And in common life whosoever has seen a person of powerful character and happy genius will have remarked how easily he took all things along with him,—the persons, the opinions, and the day, and nature became ancillary to a man.

3. There is still another aspect under which the beauty of the world may be viewed, namely, as it becomes an object of the intellect. Beside the relation of things to virtue, they have a relation to thought. The intellect searches out the absolute order of things as they stand in the mind of God, and without the colors of affection.[15] The intellectual and the active powers

[6] *The Conspiracy of Catiline,* by Gaius Sallustius Crispus (86–35 B.C.), Roman historian.

[7] *The Decline and Fall of the Roman Empire* (1788), by Edward Gibbon, English historian (1737–1794).

[8] King of Sparta, killed in defending the pass at Thermophylae against the Persians (480 B.C.).

[9] Swiss hero in the Battle of Sempach (1386) against the Austrians. According to tradition he exposed himself as a target for the spears of the Austrians, who exhausted their supply and, thus disarmed, were defeated.

[10] English Puritan (1613–1662) executed for treason during the reign of Charles II.

[11] Hill, adjacent to the Tower of London, where traitors were executed.

[12] William Russell (1639–1683), executed for complicity in a plot to seize Charles II.

[13] Greek poet (522?–443 B.C.). [14] Athenian statesman (c. 402–318 B.C.). [15] Emotion.

seem to succeed each other, and the exclusive activity of the one generates the exclusive activity of the other. There is something unfriendly in each to the other, but they are like the alternate periods of feeding and working in animals; each prepares and will be followed by the other. Therefore does beauty, which, in relation to actions, as we have seen, comes unsought, and comes because it is unsought, remain for the apprehension and pursuit of the intellect; and then, again, in its turn, of the active power. Nothing divine dies. All good is eternally reproductive. The beauty of nature re-forms itself in the mind, and not for barren contemplation, but for new creation.

All men are in some degree impressed by the face of the world; some men even to delight. This love of beauty is Taste. Others have the same love in such excess, that, not content with admiring, they seek to embody it in new forms. The creation of beauty is Art.

The production of a work of art throws a light upon the mystery of humanity. A work of art is an abstract or epitome of the world. It is the result or expression of nature, in miniature. For although the works of nature are innumerable and all different, the result or the expression of them all is similar and single. Nature is a sea of forms radically alike and even unique. A leaf, a sunbeam, a landscape, the ocean, make an analogous impression on the mind. What is common to them all,—that perfectness and harmony, is beauty. The standard of beauty is the entire circuit of natural forms,—the total of nature; which the Italians expressed by defining beauty "il più nell' uno."[16] Nothing is quite beautiful alone; nothing but is beautiful in the whole. A single object is only so far beautiful as it suggests this universal grace. The poet, the painter, the sculptor, the musician, the architect, seek each to concentrate this radiance of the world on one point, and each in his several work to satisfy the love of beauty which stimulates him to produce. Thus is Art a nature passed through the alembic[17] of man. Thus in art does Nature work through the will of man filled with the beauty of her first works.

The world thus exists to the soul to satisfy the desire of beauty. This element I call an ultimate end. No reason can be asked or given why the soul seeks beauty. Beauty, in its largest and profoundest sense, is one expression for the universe. God is the all-fair. Truth, and goodness, and beauty, are but different faces of the same All. But beauty in nature is not ultimate. It is the herald of inward and eternal beauty, and is not alone a solid or satisfactory good. It must stand as a part, and not as yet the last or highest expression of the final cause of Nature.

IV
LANGUAGE

Language is the third use which Nature subserves to man. Nature is the vehicle of thought, and in a simple, double, and three-fold degree.

1. Words are signs of natural facts.
2. Particular natural facts are symbols of particular spiritual facts.
3. Nature is the symbol of spirit.

[16]Italian: the many in one. [17]A distilling apparatus.

1. Words are signs of natural facts. The use of natural history is to give us aid in super-natural history; the use of the outer creation, to give us language for the beings and changes of the inward creation. Every word which is used to express a moral or intellectual fact, if traced to its root, is found to be borrowed from some material appearance. *Right* means *straight; wrong* means *twisted. Spirit* primarily means *wind; transgression,* the crossing of a *line; supercilious,* the *raising of the eyebrow.* We say the *heart* to express *emotion,* the *head* to denote thought; and *thought* and *emotion* are words borrowed from sensible things, and now appropriated to spiritual nature. Most of the process by which this transformation is made, is hidden from us in the remote time when language was framed; but the same tendency may be daily observed in children. Children and savages use only nouns or names of things, which they convert into verbs, and apply to analogous mental acts.

2. But this origin of all words that convey spiritual import,—so conspicuous a fact in the history of language,—is our least debt to nature. It is not words only that are emblematic; it is things which are emblematic. Every natural fact is a symbol of some spiritual fact. Every appearance in nature corresponds to some state of the mind, and that state of the mind can only be described by presenting that natural appearance as its picture. An enraged man is a lion, a cunning man is a fox, a firm man is a rock, a learned man is a torch. A lamb is innocence; a snake is subtle spite; flowers express to us the delicate affections. Light and darkness are our familiar expression for knowledge and ignorance; and heat for love. Visible distance behind and before us, is respectively our image of memory and hope.

Who looks upon a river in a meditative hour and is not reminded of the flux of all things? Throw a stone into the stream, and the circles that propagate themselves are the beautiful type of all influence. Man is conscious of a universal soul within or behind his individual life, wherein, as in a firmament, the natures of Justice, Truth, Love, Freedom, arise and shine. This universal soul he calls Reason; it is not mine, or thine, or his, but we are its; we are its property and men. And the blue sky in which the private earth is buried, the sky with its eternal calm, and full of everlasting orbs, is the type of Reason. That which intellectually considered we call Reason, considered in relation to nature, we call Spirit. Spirit is the Creator. Spirit hath life in itself. And man in all ages and countries embodies it in his language as the FATHER.

It is easily seen that there is nothing lucky or capricious in these analogies, but that they are constant, and pervade nature. These are not the dreams of a few poets, here and there, but man is an analogist, and studies relations in all objects. He is placed in the centre of beings, and a ray of relation passes from every other being to him. And neither can man be understood without these objects, nor these objects without man. All the facts in natural history taken by themselves, have no value, but are barren, like a single sex. But marry it to human history, and it is full of life. Whole floras, all Linnæus' and Buffon's[1] volumes, are dry catalogues of facts; but the most trivial of these facts, the habit of a plant, the organs, or work, or noise of an insect, applied to the illustration of a fact in intellectual philosophy, or in any way associated to human nature, affects us in the most lively and agreeable manner. The

[1]Eighteenth-century European naturalists.

seed of a plant,—to what affecting analogies in the nature of man is that little fruit made use of, in all discourse, up to the voice of Paul, who calls the human corpse a seed,—"It is sown a natural body; it is raised a spiritual body."[2] The motion of the earth round its axis and round the sun, makes the day and the year. These are certain amounts of brute light and heat. But is there no intent of an analogy between man's life and the seasons? And do the seasons gain no grandeur or pathos from that analogy? The instincts of the ant are very unimportant considered as the ant's; but the moment a ray of relation is seen to extend from it to man, and the little drudge is seen to be a monitor, a little body with a mighty heart, then all its habit, even that said to be recently observed, that it never sleeps, becomes sublime.

Because of this radical correspondence between visible things and human thoughts, savages, who have only what is necessary, converse in figures. As we go back in history, language becomes more picturesque, until its infancy, when it is all poetry; or all spiritual facts are represented by natural symbols. The same symbols are found to make the original elements of all languages. It has moreover been observed, that the idioms of all languages approach each other in passages of the greatest eloquence and power. And as this is the first language, so is it the last. The immediate dependence of language upon nature, this conversion of an outward phenomenon into a type of somewhat in human life, never loses its power to affect us. It is this which gives that piquancy to the conversation of a strong-natured farmer or backwoodsman, which all men relish.

A man's power to connect his thought with its proper symbol, and so to utter it, depends on the simplicity of his character, that is, upon his love of truth and his desire to communicate it without loss. The corruption of man is followed by the corruption of language. When simplicity of character and the sovereignty of ideas is broken up by the prevalence of secondary desires,—the desire of riches, of pleasure, of power, and of praise,—and duplicity and falsehood take place of simplicity and truth, the power over nature as an interpreter of the will is in a degree lost; new imagery ceases to be created, and old words are perverted to stand for things which are not; a paper currency is employed, when there is no bullion in the vaults. In due time the fraud is manifest, and words lose all power to stimulate the understanding or the affections. Hundreds of writers may be found in every long-civilized nation who for a short time believe and make others believe that they see and utter truths, who do not of themselves clothe one thought in its natural garment, but who feed unconsciously on the language created by the primary writers of the country, those, namely, who hold primarily on nature.

But wise men pierce this rotten diction and fasten words again to visible things; so that picturesque language is at once a commanding certificate that he who employs it is a man in alliance with truth and God. The moment our discourse rises above the ground line of familiar facts and is inflamed with passion or exalted by thought, it clothes itself in images. A man conversing in earnest, if he watches his intellectual processes, will find that a material image more or less luminous arises in his mind, contemporaneous with every thought, which furnishes the vestment of the thought. Hence, good writing and brilliant discourse

[2]I Corinthians 15:44.

are perpetual allegories. This imagery is spontaneous. It is the blending of experience with the present action of the mind. It is proper creation. It is the working of the Original Cause through the instruments he has already made.

These facts may suggest the advantage which the country-life possesses, for a powerful mind, over the artificial and curtailed life of cities. We know more from nature than we can at will communicate. Its light flows into the mind evermore, and we forget its presence. The poet, the orator, bred in the woods, whose senses have been nourished by their fair and appeasing changes, year after year, without design and without heed,—shall not lose their lesson altogether, in the roar of cities or the broil of politics. Long hereafter, amidst agitation and terror in national councils,—in the hour of revolution,—these solemn images shall reappear in their morning lustre, as fit symbols and words of the thoughts which the passing events shall awaken. At the call of a noble sentiment, again the woods wave, the pines murmur, the river rolls and shines, and the cattle low upon the mountains, as he saw and heard them in his infancy. And with these forms, the spells of persuasion, the keys of power are put into his hands.

3. We are thus assisted by natural objects in the expression of particular meanings. But how great a language to convey such pepper-corn[3] informations! Did it need such noble races of creatures, this profusion of forms, this host of orbs in heaven, to furnish man with the dictionary and grammar of his municipal[4] speech? Whilst we use this grand cipher to expedite the affairs of our pot and kettle, we feel that we have not yet put it to its use neither are able. We are like travellers using the cinders of a volcano to roast their eggs. Whilst we see that it always stands ready to clothe what we would say, we cannot avoid the question whether the characters are not significant of themselves. Have mountains, and waves, and skies, no significance but what we consciously give them when we employ them as emblems of our thoughts? The world is emblematic. Parts of speech are metaphors, because the whole of nature is a metaphor of the human mind. The laws of moral nature answer to those of matter as face to face in a glass. "The visible world and the relation of its parts, is the dial plate of the invisible."[5] The axioms of physics translate the laws of ethics. Thus, "the whole is greater than its part;" "reaction is equal to action;" "the smallest weight may be made to lift the greatest, the difference of weight being compensated by time;" and many like propositions, which have an ethical as well as physical sense. These propositions have much more extensive and universal sense when applied to human life, than when confined to technical use.

In like manner, the memorable words of history and the proverbs of nations consist usually of a natural fact, selected as a picture or parable of a moral truth. Thus; A rolling stone gathers no moss; A bird in the hand is worth two in the bush; A cripple in the right way will beat a racer in the wrong; Make hay while the sun shines; 'Tis hard to carry a full cup even; Vinegar is the son of wine; The last ounce broke the camel's back; Long-lived trees made roots first;—and the like. In their primary sense these are trivial facts, but we repeat them for the value of their analogical import. What is true of proverbs, is true of all fables, parables, and allegories.

[3]Slight, as insignificant as a peppercorn. [4]Local.
[5]A quotation from the philosopher Emanuel Swedenborg (1688–1772).

This relation between the mind and matter is not fancied by some poet, but stands in the will of God, and so is free to be known by all men. It appears to men, or it does not appear. When in fortunate hours we ponder this miracle, the wise man doubts if at all other times he is not blind and deaf;

> "Can such things be,
> And overcome us like a summer's cloud,
> Without our special wonder?"[6]

for the universe becomes transparent, and the light of higher laws than its own shines through it. It is the standing problem which has exercised the wonder and the study of every fine genius since the world began; from the era of the Egyptians and the Brahmins to that of Pythagoras, of Plato, of Bacon, of Leibnitz,[7] of Swedenborg. There sits the Sphinx[8] at the road-side, and from age to age, as each prophet comes by, he tries his fortune at reading her riddle. There seems to be a necessity in spirit to manifest itself in material forms; and day and night, river and storm, beast and bird, acid and alkali, preëxist in necessary Ideas in the mind of God, and are what they are by virtue of preceding affections of the world of spirit. A Fact is the end or last issue of spirit. The visible creation is the terminus or the circumference of the invisible world. "Material objects," said a French philosopher,[9] "are necessarily kinds of *scoriæ*[10] of the substantial thoughts of the Creator, which must always preserve an exact relation to their first origin; in other words, visible nature must have a spiritual and moral side."

This doctrine is abstruse, and though the images of "garment," "scoriæ," "mirror," etc., may stimulate the fancy, we must summon the aid of subtler and more vital expositors to make it plain. "Every scripture is to be interpreted by the same spirit which gave it forth,"[11]—is the fundamental law of criticism. A life in harmony with Nature, the love of truth and of virtue, will purge the eyes to understand her text. By degrees we may come to know the primitive sense of the permanent objects of nature, so that the world shall be to us an open book, and every form significant of its hidden life and final cause.

A new interest surprises us, whilst, under the view now suggested, we contemplate the fearful extent and multitude of objects; since "every object rightly seen, unlocks a new faculty of the soul,"[12] That which was unconscious truth, becomes, when interpreted and defined in an object, a part of the domain of knowledge,—a new weapon in the magazine of power.

[6] *Macbeth*, Act III, Scene iv, lines 110–12.

[7] Gottfried Wilhelm von Leibnitz (1646–1716), German philosopher and mathematician.

[8] In classical myth the Sphinx (Greek: strangler) was a monster who killed all who failed to answer her riddle.

[9] Guillaume Oegger, in *The True Messiah* (1829).

[10] Refuse, leftovers.

[11] A quotation from the English Quaker George Fox (1624–1691).

[12] From *Aids to Reflection* (1825), a miscellany of philosophical and literary criticism by Samuel Taylor Coleridge (1772–1834).

V
DISCIPLINE

In view of the significance of nature, we arrive at once at a new fact, that nature is a discipline. This use of the world includes the preceding uses, as parts of itself.

Space, time, society, labor, climate, food, locomotion, the animals, the mechanical forces, give us sincerest lessons, day by day, whose meaning is unlimited. They educate both the Understanding and the Reason. Every property of matter is a school for the understanding,—its solidity or resistance, its inertia, its extension, its figure, its divisibility. The understanding adds, divides, combines, measures, and finds nutriment and room for its activity in this worthy scene. Meantime, Reason transfers all these lessons into its own world of thought, by perceiving the analogy that marries Matter and Mind.

1. Nature is a discipline of the understanding in intellectual truths. Our dealing with sensible objects is a constant exercise in the necessary lessons of difference, of likeness, of order, of being and seeming, of progressive arrangement; of ascent from particular to general; of combination to one end of manifold forces. Proportioned to the importance of the organ to be formed, is the extreme care with which its tuition[1] is provided,—a care pretermitted[2] in no single case. What tedious training, day after day, year after year, never ending, to form the common sense; what continual reproduction of annoyances, inconveniences, dilemmas; what rejoicing over us of little men; what disputing of prices, what reckonings of interest,—and all to form the Hand of the mind;—to instruct us that "good thoughts are no better than good dreams, unless they be executed!"[3]

The same good office is performed by Property and its filial systems of debt and credit. Debt, grinding debt, whose iron face the widow, the orphan, and the sons of genius fear and hate;—debt, which consumes so much time, which so cripples and disheartens a great spirit with cares that seem so base, is a preceptor whose lessons cannot be forgone, and is needed most by those who suffer from it most. Moreover, property, which has been well compared to snow,—"if it fall level to-day, it will be blown into drifts to-morrow,"—is the surface action of internal machinery, like the index of the face of a clock. Whilst now it is the gymnastics of the understanding, it is hiving, in the foresight of the spirit, experience in profounder laws.

The whole character and fortune of the individual are affected by the least inequalities in the culture of the understanding; for example, in the perception of differences. Therefore is Space, and therefore Time, that man may know that things are not huddled and lumped, but sundered and individual. A bell and a plough have each their use, and neither can do the office of the other. Water is good to drink, coal to burn, wool to wear; but wool cannot be drunk, nor water spun, nor coal eaten. The wise man shows his wisdom in separation, in gradation, and his scale of creatures and of merits is as wide as nature. The foolish have no range in their scale, but suppose every man is as every other man. What is not good they call the worst, and what is not hateful, they call the best.

[1]Guardianship. [2]Neglected.
[3]Paraphrased from "Of Great Place" in the *Essays* (1625) of Sir Francis Bacon.

In like manner, what good heed Nature forms in us! She pardons no mistakes. Her yea is yea, and her nay, nay.

The first steps in Agriculture, Astronomy, Zoölogy (those first steps which the farmer, the hunter, and the sailor take), teach that Nature's dice are always loaded; that in her heaps and rubbish are concealed sure and useful results.

How calmly and genially the mind apprehends one after another the laws of physics! What noble emotions dilate the mortal as he enters into the councils of the creation, and feels by knowledge the privilege to BE! His insight refines him. The beauty of nature shines in his own breast. Man is greater that he can see this, and the universe less, because Time and Space relations vanish as laws are known.

Here again we are impressed and even daunted by the immense Universe to be explored. "What we know is a point to what we do not know."[4] Open any recent journal of science, and weigh the problems suggested concerning Light, Heat, Electricity, Magnetism, Physiology, Geology, and judge whether the interest of natural science is likely to be soon exhausted.

Passing by many particulars of the discipline of nature, we must not omit to specify two.

The exercise of the Will, or the lesson of power, is taught in every event. From the child's successive possession of his several senses up to the hour when he saith, "Thy will be done!"[5] he is learning the secret that he can reduce under his will not only particular events but great classes, nay, the whole series of events, and so conform all facts to his character. Nature is thoroughly mediate. It is made to serve. It receives the dominion of man as meekly as the ass on which the Savior rode.[6] It offers all its kingdoms to man as the raw material which he may mould into what is useful. Man is never weary of working it up. He forges the subtile and delicate air into wise and melodious words, and gives them wing as angels of persuasion and command. One after another his victorious thought comes up with and reduces all things, until the world becomes at last only a realized will,—the double of the man.

2. Sensible objects conform to the premonitions of Reason and reflect the conscience. All things are moral; and in their boundless changes have an unceasing reference to spiritual nature. Therefore is nature glorious with form, color, and motion; that every globe in the remotest heaven, every chemical change from the rudest crystal up to the laws of life, every change of vegetation from the first principle of growth in the eye of a leaf, to the tropical forest and antediluvian coal-mine, every animal function from the sponge up to Hercules, shall hint or thunder to man the laws of right and wrong, and echo the Ten Commandments. Therefore is Nature ever the ally of Religion: lends all her pomp and riches to the religious sentiment. Prophet and priest, David, Isaiah, Jesus, have drawn deeply from this source. This ethical character so penetrates the bone and marrow of nature, as to seem the end for which it was made. Whatever private purpose is answered by any member or part, this is its public and universal function, and is never omitted. Nothing

[4]A quotation ascribed to Bishop Joseph Butler (1692–1752), English theologian and moralist.
[5]Matthew 6:10 and 26:42.
[6]"Behold, thy King cometh unto thee, meek, and sitting upon an ass." Matthew 21:5.

in nature is exhausted in its first use. When a thing has served an end to the uttermost, it is wholly new for an ulterior service. In God, every end is converted into a new means. Thus the use of commodity, regarded by itself, is mean and squalid. But it is to the mind an education in the doctrine of Use, namely, that a thing is good only so far as it serves; that a conspiring of parts and efforts to the production of an end is essential to any being. The first and gross manifestation of this truth is our inevitable and hated training in values and wants, in corn and meat.

It has already been illustrated, that every natural process is a version of a moral sentence. The moral law lies at the centre of nature and radiates to the circumference. It is the pith and marrow of every substance, every relation, and every process. All things with which we deal, preach to us. What is a farm but a mute gospel? The chaff and the wheat, weeds and plants, blight, rain, insects, sun,—it is a sacred emblem from the first furrow of spring to the last stack which the snow of winter overtakes in the fields. But the sailor, the shepherd, the miner, the merchant, in their several resorts, have each an experience precisely parallel, and leading to the same conclusion: because all organizations are radically alike. Nor can it be doubted that this moral sentiment which thus scents the air, grows in the grain, and impregnates the waters of the world, is caught by man and sinks into his soul. The moral influence of nature upon every individual is that amount of truth which it illustrates to him. Who can estimate this? Who can guess how much firmness the sea-beaten rock has taught the fisherman? how much tranquility has been reflected to man from the azure sky, over whose unspotted deeps the winds forevermore drive flocks of stormy clouds, and leave no wrinkle or stain? how much industry and providence and affection we have caught from the pantomime of brutes? What a searching preacher of self-command is the varying phenomenon of Health!

Herein is especially apprehended the unity of Nature,—the unity in variety,—which meets us everywhere. All the endless variety of things make an identical impression. Xenophanes[7] complained in his old age, that, look where he would, all things hastened back to Unity. He was weary of seeing the same entity in the tedious variety of forms. The fable of Proteus[8] has a cordial truth. A leaf, a drop, a crystal, a moment of time, is related to the whole, and partakes of the perfection of the whole. Each particle is a microcosm, and faithfully renders the likeness of the world.

Not only resemblances exist in things whose analogy is obvious, as when we detect the type of the human hand in the flipper of the fossil saurus,[9] but also in objects wherein there is great superficial unlikeness. Thus architecture is called "frozen music," by De Staël and Goethe.[10] Vitruvius[11] thought an architect should be a musician. "A Gothic church" said Coleridge, "is a petrified religion." Michael Angelo maintained, that, to an architect, a knowledge of anatomy is essential. In Haydn's oratorios,[12] the notes present

[7]Greek philosopher (570–480 B.C.).

[8]Mythic god who could assume various shapes. [9]Lizard.

[10]Anne Louise Germaine (1766–1817), Baronne de Staël, French writer; Johann Wolfgang von Goethe (1749–1832), German poet.

[11]Roman architect (first century B.C.).

[12]Choral music by Joseph Haydn (1732–1809), Austrian composer.

to the imagination not only motions, as of the snake, the stag, and the elephant, but colors also; as the green grass. The law of harmonic sounds reappears in the harmonic colors. The granite is differenced in its laws only by the more or less of heat from the river that wears it away. The river, as it flows, resembles the air that flows over it; the air resembles the light which traverses it with more subtile currents; the light resembles the heat which rides with it through Space. Each creature is only a modification of the other; the likeness in them is more than the difference, and their radical law is one and the same. A rule of one art, or a law of one organization, holds true throughout nature. So intimate is this Unity, that, it is easily seen, it lies under the undermost garment of Nature, and betrays its source in Universal Spirit. For it pervades Thought also. Every universal truth which we express in words, implies or supposes every other truth. *Omne verum vero consonat.*[13] It is like a great circle on a sphere, comprising all possible circles; which, however, may be drawn and comprise it in like manner. Every such truth is the absolute Ens[14] seen from one side. But it has innumerable sides.

The central Unity is still more conspicuous in actions. Words are finite organs of the infinite mind. They cannot cover the dimensions of what is in truth. They break, chop, and impoverish it. An action is the perfection and publication of thought. A right action seems to fill the eye, and to be related to all nature. "The wise man, in doing one thing, does all; or, in the one thing he does rightly, he sees the likeness of all which is done rightly."[15]

Words and actions are not the attributes of brute nature. They introduce us to the human form, of which all other organizations appear to be degradations. When this appears among so many that surround it, the spirit prefers it to all others. It says, "From such as this have I drawn joy and knowledge; in such as this I have found and beheld myself; I will speak to it; it can speak again; it can yield me thought already formed and alive." In fact, the eye,—the mind,—is always accompanied by these forms, male and female; and these are incomparably the richest informations of the power and order that lie at the heart of things. Unfortunately every one of them bears the marks as of some injury; is marred and superficially defective. Nevertheless, far different from the deaf and dumb nature around them, these all rest like fountain-pipes on the unfathomed sea of thought and virtue whereto they alone, of all organizations, are the entrances.

It were a pleasant inquiry to follow into detail their ministry to our education, but where would it stop? We are associated in adolescent and adult life with some friends, who, like skies and waters, are coextensive with our idea; who, answering each to a certain affection of the soul, satisfy our desire on that side; whom we lack power to put at such focal distance from us, that we can mend or even analyze them. We cannot choose but love them. When much intercourse with a friend has supplied us with a standard of excellence, and has increased our respect for the resources of God who thus sends a real person to outgo our ideal; when he has, moreover, become an object of thought, and, whilst his character retains all its unconscious effect, is converted in the mind into solid and sweet wisdom,—it is a sign to us that his office is closing, and he is commonly withdrawn from our sight in a short time.

[13]Latin: Every truth agrees with every other truth.
[14]Latin philosophical term for "abstract being."
[15]From Goethe's *Wilhelm Meister's Travels* (1821–1829).

VI
IDEALISM

Thus is the unspeakable but intelligible and practicable meaning of the world conveyed to man, the immortal pupil, in every object of sense. To this one end of Discipline, all parts of nature conspire.

A noble doubt perpetually suggests itself,—whether this end be not the Final Cause of the Universe; and whether nature outwardly exists. It is a sufficient account of that Appearance we call the World, that God will teach a human mind, and so makes it the receiver of a certain number of congruent sensations, which we call sun and moon, man and woman, house and trade. In my utter impotence to test the authenticity of the report of my senses, to know whether the impressions they make on me correspond with outlying objects, what difference does it make, whether Orion[1] is up there in heaven, or some god paints the image in the firmament of the soul? The relations of parts and the end of the whole remaining the same, what is the difference, whether land and sea interact, and worlds revolve and intermingle without number or end,—deep yawning under deep, and galaxy balancing galaxy, throughout absolute space,—or whether, without relations of time and space, the same appearances are inscribed in the constant faith of man? Whether nature enjoy a substantial existence without, or is only in the apocalypse[2] of the mind, it is alike useful and alike venerable to me. Be it what it may, it is ideal to me so long as I cannot try the accuracy of my senses.

The frivolous make themselves merry with the Ideal theory, as if its consequences were burlesque; as if it affected the stability of nature. It surely does not. God never jests with us, and will not compromise the end of nature by permitting any inconsequence in its procession. Any distrust of the permanence of laws would paralyze the faculties of man. Their permanence is sacredly respected, and his faith therein is perfect. The wheels and springs of man are all set to the hypothesis of the permanence of nature. We are not built like a ship to be tossed, but like a house to stand. It is a natural consequence of this structure, that so long as the active powers predominate over the reflective, we resist with indignation any hint that nature is more short-lived or mutable than spirit. The broker, the wheelwright, the carpenter, the tollman, are much displeased at the intimation.

But whilst we acquiesce entirely in the permanence of natural laws, the question of the absolute existence of nature still remains open. It is the uniform effect of culture on the human mind, not to shake our faith in the stability of particular phenomena, as of heat, water, azote;[3] but to lead us to regard nature as a phenomenon, not a substance; to attribute necessary existence to spirit; to esteem nature as an accident and an effect.

To the sense and the unrenewed understanding, belongs a sort of instinctive belief in the absolute existence of nature. In their view man and nature

[1]Constellation of stars.
[2]Prophecy, revelation.
[3]Nitrogen.

are indissolubly joined. Things are ultimates, and they never look beyond their sphere. The presence of Reason mars this faith. The first effort of thought tends to relax this despotism of the senses which binds us to nature as if we were a part of it, and shows us nature aloof, and, as it were, afloat. Until this higher agency intervened, the animal eye sees, with wonderful accuracy, sharp outlines and colored surfaces. When the eye of Reason opens, to outline and surface are at once added grace and expression. These proceed from imagination and affection, and abate somewhat of the angular distinctness of objects. If the Reason be stimulated to more earnest vision, outlines and surfaces become transparent, and are no longer seen; causes and spirits are seen through them. The best movements of life are these delicious awakenings of the higher powers, and the reverential withdrawing of nature before its God.

Let us proceed to indicate the effects of culture.

1. Our first institution in the Ideal philosophy is a hint from Nature herself.

Nature is made to conspire with spirit to emancipate us. Certain mechanical changes, a small alteration in our local position, apprizes us of a dualism. We are strangely affected by seeing the shore from a moving ship, from a balloon, or through the tints of an unusual sky. The least change in our point of view gives the whole world a pictorial air. A man who seldom rides, needs only to get into a coach and traverse his own town, to turn the street into a puppet-show. The men, the women,—talking, running, bartering, fighting, —the earnest mechanic, the lounger, the beggar, the boys, the dogs, are unrealized at once, or, at least, wholly detached from all relation to the observer, and seen as apparent, not substantial beings. What new thoughts are suggested by seeing a face of country quite familiar, in the rapid movement of the railroad car! Nay, the most wonted objects, (make a very slight change in the point of vision,) please us most. In a camera obscura,[4] the butcher's cart, and the figure of one of our own family amuse us. So a portrait of a well-known face gratifies us. Turn the eyes upside down, by looking at the landscape through your legs, and how agreeable is the picture, though you have seen it any time these twenty years!

In these cases, by mechanical means, is suggested the difference between the observer and the spectacle—between man and nature. Hence arises a pleasure mixed with awe; I may say, a low degree of the sublime is felt, from the fact, probably, that man is hereby apprized that whilst the world is a spectacle, something in himself is stable.

2. In a higher manner the poet communicates the same pleasure. By a few strokes he delineates, as on air, the sun, the mountain, the camp, the city, the hero, the maiden, not different from what we know them, but only lifted from the ground and afloat before the eye. He unfixes the land and the sea, makes them revolve around the axis of his primary thought, and disposes them anew. Possessed himself by a heroic passion, he uses matter as symbols of it. The sensual man conforms thoughts to things; the poet

[4]A room or a chamber into which an image is reflected and focused on a wall, a predecessor of the modern camera.

conforms things to his thoughts. The one esteems nature as rooted and fast; the other, as fluid, and impresses his being thereon. To him, the refractory world is ductile and flexible; he invests dust and stones with humanity, and makes them the words of the Reason. The Imagination may be defined to be the use which the Reason makes of the material world. Shakespeare possesses the power of subordinating nature for the purposes of expression, beyond all poets. His imperial muse tosses the creation like a bauble from hand to hand, and uses it to embody any caprice of thought that is uppermost in his mind. The remotest spaces of nature are visited, and the farthest sundered things are brought together, by a subtile spiritual connection. We are made aware that magnitude of material things is relative, and all objects shrink and expand to serve the passion of the poet. Thus in his sonnets, the lays of birds, the scents and dyes of flowers he finds to be the *shadow* of his beloved; time, which keeps her from his, is his *chest;* the suspicion she has awakened, is her *ornament;*

> The ornament of beauty is Suspect,
> A crow which flies in heaven's sweetest air.[5]

His passion is not the fruit of chance; it swells, as he speaks, to a city, or a state.

> No, it was builded far from accident;
> It suffers not in smiling pomp, nor falls
> Under the brow of thralling discontent;
> It fears not policy, that heretic,
> That works on leases of short numbered hours,
> But all alone stands hugely politic.[6]

In the strength of his constancy, the Pyramids seem to him recent and transitory. The freshness of youth and love dazzles him with its resemblance to morning;

> Take those lips away
> Which so sweetly were forsworn;
> And those eyes,—the break of day,
> Lights that do mislead the morn.[7]

The wild beauty of this hyperbole, I may say in passing, it would not be easy to match in literature.

This transfiguration which all material objects undergo through the passion of the poet,—this power which he exerts to dwarf the great, to magnify the small,—might be illustrated by a thousand examples from his Plays. I have before me the *Tempest,* and will cite only these few lines.

[5]Shakespeare, Sonnet 70. [6]Shakespeare, Sonnet 124.
[7]Shakespeare, *Measure for Measure,* Act IV, Scene i, lines 1–4.

ARIEL. The strong based promontory
Have I made shake, and by the spurs plucked up
The pine and cedar.

Prospero calls for music to soothe the frantic Alonzo, and his companions;

A solemn air, and the best comforter
To an unsettled fancy, cure thy brains
Now useless, boiled within thy skull.

Again;

The charm dissolves apace,
And, as the morning steals upon the night,
Melting the darkness, so their rising senses
Begin to chase the ignorant fumes that mantle
Their clearer reason.
Their understanding
Begins to swell: and the approaching tide
Will shortly fill the reasonable shores
That now lie foul and muddy.[8]

The perception of real affinities between events (that is to say, of *ideal* affinities, for those only are real), enables the poet thus to make free with the most imposing forms and phenomena of the world, and to assert the predominance of the soul.

3. Whilst thus the poet animates nature with his own thoughts, he differs from the philosopher only herein, that the one proposes Beauty as his main end; the other Truth. But the philosopher, not less than the poet, postpones the apparent order and relations of things to the empire of thought. "The problem of philosophy," according to Plato, "is, for all that exists conditionally, to find a ground unconditioned and absolute."[9] It proceeds on the faith that a law determines all phenomena, which being known, the phenomena can be predicted. That law, when in the mind, is an idea. Its beauty is infinite. The true philosopher and the true poet are one, and a beauty, which is truth, and a truth, which is beauty, is the aim of both. Is not the charm of one of Plato's or Aristotle's definitions strictly like that of the *Antigone* of Sophocles? It is, in both cases, that a spiritual life has been imparted to nature; that the solid seeming block of matter has been pervaded and dissolved by a thought; that this feeble human being has penetrated the vast

[8]Shakespeare, *The Tempest,* Act V, Scene i, lines 46–48, 58–60, 64–68, and 79–82. The opening lines are spoken by Prospero, not Ariel.

[9]From the *Republic,* Book V. Emerson quotes a shortened version from Coleridge's *The Friend* (1818).

masses of nature with an informing soul, and recognized itself in their harmony, that is, seized their law. In physics, when this is attained, the memory disburthens itself of its cumbrous catalogues of particulars, and carries centuries of observation in a single formula.

Thus even in physics, the material is degraded before the spiritual. The astronomer, the geometer, rely on their irrefragable analysis, and disdain the results of observation. The sublime remark of Euler[10] of his law of arches, "This will be found contrary to all experience, yet is true;" had already transferred nature into the mind, and left matter like an outcast corpse.

4. Intellectual science has been observed to beget invariably a doubt of the existence of matter. Turgot[11] said, "He that has never doubted the existence of matter, may be assured he has no aptitude for metaphysical inquiries." It fastens the attention upon immortal necessary uncreated natures, that is, upon Ideas; and in their presence we feel that the outward circumstance is a dream and a shade. Whilst we wait in this Olympus of gods, we think of nature as an appendix to the soul. We ascend into their region, and know that these are the thoughts of the Supreme Being. "These are they who were set up from everlasting, from the beginning, or ever the earth was. When he prepared the heavens, they were there; when he established the clouds above, when he strengthened the fountains of the deep. Then they were by him, as one brought up with him. Of them took he counsel."[12]

Their influence is proportionate. As objects of science they are accessible to few men. Yet all men are capable of being raised by piety or by passion, into their region. And no man touches these divine natures, without becoming, in some degree, himself divine. Like a new soul, they renew the body. We become physically nimble and lightsome; we tread on air; life is no longer irksome, and we think it will never be so. No man fears age or misfortune or death in their serene company, for he is transported out of the district of change. Whilst we behold unveiled the nature of Justice and Truth, we learn the difference between the absolute and the conditional or relative. We apprehend the absolute. As it were, for the first time, *we exist*. We become immortal, for we learn that time and space are relations of matter; that with a perception of truth or a virtuous will they have no affinity.

5. Finally, religion and ethics, which may be fitly called the practice of ideas, or the introduction of ideas into life, have an analogous effect with all lower culture, in degrading nature and suggesting its dependence on spirit. Ethics and religion differ herein; that the one is the system of human duties commencing from man; the other, from God. Religion includes the personality of God; Ethics does not. They are one to our present design. They both put nature under foot. The first and last lesson of religion is, "The things that are seen, are temporal; the things that are unseen, are eternal."[13] It puts an affront upon nature. It does that for the unschooled,

[10]Leonhard Euler (1707–1783), Swiss mathematician.
[11]Robert Jacques Turgot (1727–1781), French statesman and economist.
[12]Adapted from Proverbs 8:23, 27, 28, 30.
[13]II Corinthians 4:18.

which philosophy does for Berkeley and Viasa.[14] The uniform language that may be heard in the churches of the most ignorant sects is,—"Contemn the unsubstantial shows of the world; they are vanities, dreams, shadows, unrealities; seek the realities of religion." The devotee flouts nature. Some theosophists[15] have arrived at a certain hostility and indignation towards matter, as the Manichean[16] and Plotinus.[17] They distrusted in themselves any looking back to these flesh-pots of Egypt.[18] Plotinus was ashamed of his body. In short, they might all say of matter, which Michael Angelo said of external beauty, "It is the frail and weary weed,[19] in which God dresses the soul which he has called into time."[20]

It appears that motion, poetry, physical and intellectual science, and religion, all tend to affect our convictions of the reality of the external world. But I own there is something ungrateful in expanding too curiously the particulars of the general proposition, that all culture tends to imbue us with idealism. I have no hostility to nature, but a child's love to it. I expand and live in the warm day like corn and melons. Let us speak her fair. I do not wish to fling stones at my beautiful mother, nor soil my gentle nest. I only wish to indicate the true position of nature in regard to man, wherein to establish man all right education tends; as the ground which to attain is the object of human life, that is, of man's connection with nature. Culture inverts the vulgar views of nature, and brings the mind to call that apparent which it uses to call real, and that real which it uses to call visionary. Children, it is true, believe in the external world. The belief that it appears only, is an after-thought, but with culture this faith will as surely arise on the mind as did the first.

The advantage of the ideal theory over the popular faith is this, that it presents the world in precisely that view which is most desirable to the mind. It is, in fact, the view which Reason, both speculative and practical, that is, philosophy and virtue, take. For seen in the light of thought, the world always is phenomenal; and virtue subordinates it to the mind. Idealism sees the world in God. It beholds the whole circle of persons and things, of actions and events, of country and religion, not as painfully accumulated, atom after atom, act after act, in an aged creeping Past, but as one vast picture which God paints on the instant eternity for the contemplation of the soul. Therefore the soul holds itself off from a too trivial and microscopic study of the universal tablet. It respects the end too much to immerse itself in the means. It sees something more important in Christianity than the scandals of ecclesiastical history or the niceties of criticism; and, very incurious concerning persons or miracles, and not at all disturbed by chasms of historical evidence, it accepts from God the phenomenon, as it finds it, as

[14]George Berkeley (1685–1753), English philosophical idealist; Viasa, legendary Hindu philosopher.

[15]Religious believers whose faith is based on a mystical perception of God.

[16]Follower of Manes, third-century Christian mystic who taught the duality of good and evil.

[17]A Roman Neo-Platonist philosopher (205?–270?).

[18]The Israelites in the wilderness longed to return to the bountiful "flesh-pots" of Egypt. Exodus 16:2–3.

[19]Garment.

[20]Michelangelo, Sonnet 51.

the pure and awful form of religion in the world. It is not hot and passionate at the appearance of what it calls its own good or bad fortune, at the union or opposition of other persons. No man is its enemy. It accepts whatsoever befalls, as part of its lesson. It is a watcher more than a doer, and it is a doer, only that it may the better watch.

VII
SPIRIT

It is essential to a true theory of nature and of man, that it should contain[1] somewhat progressive. Uses that are exhausted or that may be, and facts that end in the statement, cannot be all that is true of this brave lodging wherein man is harbored, and wherein all his faculties find appropriate and endless exercise. And all the uses of nature admit of being summed in one, which yields the activity of man an infinite scope. Through all its kingdoms, to the suburbs and outskirts of things, it is faithful to the cause whence it had its origin. It always speaks of Spirit. It suggests the absolute. It is a perpetual effect. It is a great shadow pointing always to the sun behind us.

The aspect of Nature is devout. Like the figure of Jesus, she stands with bended head, and hands folded upon the breast. The happiest man is he who learns from nature the lesson of worship.

Of the ineffable essence which we call Spirit, he that thinks most, will say least. We can foresee God in the coarse, and, as it were, distant phenomena of matter; but when we try to define and describe himself, both language and thought desert us, and we are as helpless as fools and savages. That essence refuses to be recorded in propositions, but when man has worshipped him intellectually, the noblest ministry of nature is to stand as the apparition of God. It is the organ through which the universal spirit speaks to the individual, and strives to lead back the individual to it.

When we consider Spirit, we see that the views already presented do not include the whole circumference of man. We must add some related thoughts.

Three problems are put by nature to the mind: What is matter? Whence is it? and Whereto? The first of these questions only, the ideal theory answers. Idealism saith: matter is a phenomenon, not a substance. Idealism acquaints us with the total disparity between the evidence of our own being and the evidence of the world's being. The one is perfect; the other, incapable of any assurance; the mind is a part of the nature of things; the world is a divine dream, from which we may presently awake to the glories and certainties of day. Idealism is a hypothesis to account for nature by other principles than those of carpentry and chemistry. Yet if it only deny the existence of matter, it does not satisfy the demands of the spirit. It leaves God out of me. It leaves me in the splendid labyrinth of my perceptions, to wander without

[1]Remain, continue to be.

end. Then the heart resists it, because it balks the affections in denying substantive being to men and women. Nature is so pervaded with human life that there is something of humanity in all and in every particular. But this theory makes nature foreign to me, and does not account for that consanguinity which we acknowledge to it.

Let it stand then, in the present state of our knowledge, merely as a useful introductory hypothesis, serving to apprize us of the eternal distinction between the soul and the world.

But when, following the invisible steps of thought, we come to inquire, Whence is matter? and Whereto? many truths arise to us out of the recesses of consciousness. We learn that the highest is present to the soul of man; that the dread universal essence, which is not wisdom, or love, or beauty, or power, but all in one, and each entirely, is that for which all things exist, and that by which they are; that spirit creates; that behind nature, throughout nature, spirit is present; one and not compound it does not act upon us from without, that is, in space and time, but spiritually, or through ourselves: therefore, that spirit, that is, the Supreme Being, does not build up nature around us, but puts it forth through us, as the life of the tree puts forth new branches and leaves through the pores of the old. As a plant upon the earth, so a man rests upon the bosom of God; he is nourished by unfailing fountains, and draws at his need inexhaustible power. Who can set bounds to the possibilities of man? Once inhale the upper air, being admitted to behold the absolute natures of justice and truth, and we learn that man has access to the entire mind of the Creator, is himself the creator in the finite. This view, which admonished me where the sources of wisdom and power lie, and points to virtue as to

> "The golden key
> Which opes the palace of eternity,"[2]

carries upon its face the highest certificate of truth, because it animates me to create my own world through the purification of my soul.

The world proceeds from the same spirit as the body of man. It is a remoter and inferior incarnation of God, a projection of God in the unconscious. But it differs from the body in one important respect. It is not, like that, now subjected to the human will. Its serene order is inviolable by us. It is, therefore, to us, the present expositor of the divine mind. It is a fixed point whereby we may measure our departure. As we degenerate, the contrast between us and our house is more evident. We are as much strangers in nature as we are aliens from God. We do not understand the notes of birds. The fox and the deer run away from us; the bear and tiger rend us. We do not know the uses of more than a few plants, as corn and the apple, the potato and the vine. Is not the landscape, every glimpse of which hath a grandeur, a face of him? Yet this may show us what discord is between man and nature, for you cannot freely admire a noble landscape if laborers are

[2]Milton, *Comus*, lines 13–14.

digging in the field hard by. The poet finds something ridiculous in his delight until he is out of the sight of men.

VIII
PROSPECTS

In inquiries respecting the laws of the world and the frame of things, the highest reason is always the truest. That which seems faintly possible, it is so refined, is often faint and dim because it is deepest seated in the mind among the eternal verities. Empirical[1] science is apt to cloud the sight, and by the very knowledge of functions and processes to bereave the student of the manly contemplation of the whole. The savant[2] becomes unpoetic. But the best read naturalist who lends an entire and devout attention to truth, will see that there remains much to learn of his relation to the world, and that it is not to be learned by any addition or subtraction or other comparison of known quantities, but is arrived at by untaught sallies of the spirit, by a continued self-recovery, and by entire humility. He will perceive that there are far more excellent qualities in the student than preciseness and infallibility; that a guess is often more fruitful than an indisputable affirmation, and that a dream may let us deeper into the secret of nature than a hundred concerted experiments.

For the problems to be solved are precisely those which the physiologist and the naturalist omit to state. It is not so pertinent to man to know all the individuals of the animal kingdom, as it is to know whence and whereto is this tyrannizing unity in his constitution, which evermore separates and classifies things, endeavoring to reduce the most diverse to one form. When I behold a rich landscape, it is less to my purpose to recite correctly the order and superposition of the strata, than to know why all thought of multitude is lost in a tranquil sense of unity. I cannot greatly honor minuteness in details, so long as there is no hint to explain the relation between things and thoughts; no ray upon the *metaphysics* of conchology,[3] of botany, of the arts, to show the relation of the forms of flowers, shells, animals, architecture, to the mind and build science upon ideas. In a cabinet of natural history,[4] we become sensible of a certain occult recognition and sympathy in regard to the most unwieldy and eccentric forms of beast, fish, and insect. The American who has been confined, in his own country, to the sight of buildings designed after foreign models, is surprised on entering York Minster[5] or St. Peter's at Rome, by the feeling that these structures are imitations also,—fain copies of an invisible archetype. Nor has science sufficient humanity, so long as the naturalist overlooks

[1]Based on observation or experience rather than theory.
[2]Sage.
[3]The study of seashells.
[4]Display case of natural history specimens.
[5]Cathedral at York, England.

that wonderful congruity which subsists between man of the world; of which he is lord, not because he is the most subtile inhabitant, but because he is its head and heart, and finds something of himself in every great and small thing, in every mountain stratum, in every new law of color, fact of astronomy, or atmospheric influence which observation or analysis lays open. A perception of this mystery inspires the muse of George Herbert, the beautiful psalmist of the seventeenth century. The following lines are part of his little poem on Man.

> Man is all symmetry,
> Full of proportions, one limb to another,
> And all to all the world besides.
> Each part may call the farthest, brother;
> For head with foot hath private amity,
> And both with moons and tides.
>
> Nothing hath got so far
> But man hath caught and kept it as his prey;
> His eyes dismount the highest star:
> He is in little all the sphere.
> Herbs gladly cure our flesh, because that they
> Find their acquaintance there.
>
> For us, the winds, do blow,
> The earth doth rest, heaven move, and fountains flow;
> Nothing we see, but means our good,
> As our delight, or as our treasure;
> The whole is either our cupboard of food,
> Or cabinet of pleasure.
>
> The stars have us to bed:
> Night draws the curtain; which the sun withdraws.
> Music and light attend our head.
> All things unto our flesh are kind,
> In their descent and being; to our mind,
> In their ascent and cause.
>
> More servants wait on man
> Than he'll take notice of. In every path,
> He treads down that which doth befriend him
> When sickness makes him pale and wan.
> Oh mighty love! Man is one world, and hath
> Another to attend him.[6]

[6]The quotation is from stanzas 1, 2, 3, 4, and 6 of the poem "Man" (1633) by the English poet George Herbert (1593–1633).

The perception of this class of truths makes the attraction which draws men to science, but the end is lost sight of in attention to the means. In view of this half-sight of science, we accept the sentence of Plato, that "poetry comes nearer to vital truth than history."[7] Every surmise and vaticination[8] of the mind is entitled to a certain respect, and we learn to prefer imperfect theories, and sentences which contain glimpses of truth, to digested systems which have no one valuable suggestion. A wise writer will feel that the ends of study and composition are best answered by announcing undiscovered regions of thought, and so communicating, through hope, new activity to the torpid spirit.

I shall therefore conclude this essay with some traditions of man and nature, which a certain poet[9] sang to me; and which, as they have always been in the world, and perhaps reappear to every bard, may be both history and prophecy.

"The foundations of man are not in matter, but in spirit. But the element of spirit is eternity. To it, therefore, the longest series of events, the oldest chronologies are young and recent. In the cycle of the universal man, from whom the known individuals proceed, centuries are points, and all history is but the epoch of one degradation.

"We distrust and deny inwardly our sympathy with nature. We own and disown our relation to it, by turns. We are like Nebuchadnezzar, dethroned, bereft of reason, and eating grass like an ox.[10] But who can set limits to the remedial force of spirit?

"A man is a god in ruins. When men are innocent, life shall be longer, and shall pass into the immortal as gently as we awake from dreams. Now, the world would be insane and rabid, if these disorganizations should last for hundreds of years. It is kept in check by death and infancy. Infancy is the perpetual Messiah, which comes into the arms of fallen men, and pleads with them to return to paradise.

"Man is the dwarf of himself. Once he was permeated and dissolved by spirit. He filled nature with his overflowing currents. Out from him sprang the sun and moon; from man the sun, from woman the moon. The laws of his mind, the periods of his actions externized themselves into day and night, into the year and the seasons. But, having made for himself this huge shell, his waters retired; he no longer fills the veins and veinlets; he is shrunk to a drop. He sees that the structure still fits him, but fits him colossally. Say, rather, once it fitted him, now it corresponds to him from far and on high. He adores timidly his own work. Now is man the follower of the sun, and woman the follower of the moon. Yet sometimes he starts in his slumber, and wonders at himself and his house, and muses strangely at the resemblance betwixt him and it. He perceives that if his law is still paramount, if still he have elemental power, if his word is sterling yet in nature, it is not conscious power, it is not inferior but superior to his will. It is instinct." Thus my Orphic[11] poet sang.

[7]Emerson derived the quotation not from Plato but from Aristotle's *Poetics*, section 9.

[8]Prophecy.

[9]Possibly Emerson himself or Bronson Alcott (1799–1888), New England transcendentalist and author of *Orphic Sayings* (1840).

[10]Nebuchadnezzar lost his reason, "was driven from men, and did eat grass as oxen." Daniel 4:33.

[11]Mystic.

At present, man applies to nature but half his force. He works on the world with his understanding alone. He lives in it and masters it by a penny-wisdom; and he that works most in it is but a half-man, and whilst his arms are strong and his digestion good, his mind is embruted, and he is a selfish savage. His relation to nature, his power over it, is through the understanding, as by manure; the economic use of fire, wind, water, and the mariner's needle; steam, coal, chemical agriculture; the repairs of the human body by the dentist and the surgeon. This is such a resumption of power as if a banished king should buy his territories inch by inch, instead of vaulting at once into his throne. Meantime, in the thick darkness, there are not wanting gleams of a better light,—occasional examples of the action of man upon nature with his entire force,—with reason as well as understanding. Such examples are, the traditions of miracles in the earliest antiquity of all nations; the history of Jesus Christ; the achievements of a principle, as in religious and political revolutions, and in the abolition of the slave-trade; the miracles of enthusiasm,[12] as those reported of Swedenborg, Hohenlohe, and the Shakers;[13] many obscure and yet contested facts, now arranged under the name of Animal Magnetism;[14] prayer; eloquence; self-healing; and the wisdom of children. These are examples of Reason's momentary grasp of the sceptre; the exertions of a power which exists not in time or space, but an instantaneous in-streaming causing power. The difference between the actual and the ideal force of man is happily figured by the school-men, in saying, that the knowledge of man is an evening knowledge, *vespertina cognitio*, but that of God is a morning knowledge, *matutina cognitio*.

The problem of restoring to the world original and eternal beauty is solved by the redemption of the soul. The ruin or the blank that we see when we look at nature, is in our own eye. The axis of vision is not coincident with the axis of things, and so they appear not transparent but opaque. The reason why the world lacks unity, and lies broken and in heaps, is because man is disunited with himself. He cannot be a naturalist until he satisfies all the demands of the spirit. Love is as much its demand as perception. Indeed, neither can be perfect without the other. In the uttermost meaning of the words, thought is devout, and devotion is thought. Deep calls unto deep.[15] But in actual life, the marriage is not celebrated. There are innocent men who worship God after the tradition of their fathers, but their sense of duty has not yet extended to the use of all their faculties. And there are patient naturalists, but they freeze their subject under the wintry light of the understanding. Is not prayer also a study of truth,—a sally of the soul into the unfound infinite? No man ever prayed heartily without learning something. But when a faithful thinker, resolute to detach every object from personal relations and see it in the light of thought, shall, at the same time, kindle science with the fire of the holiest affections, then will God go forth anew into the creation.

[12]Divinely inspired frenzy.

[13]Leopold Emmerich, Prince of Hohenlohe-Waldenberg-Schillingfurst (1794–1849), German bishop and writer. Shakers were members of the Millennial Church, which originated in England in 1747 and won its popular name from its visionary enthusiasms and the shaking movements performed in its devotional services.

[14]Hypnotism. [15]Psalm 42:7.

It will not need, when the mind is prepared for study, to search for objects. The invariable mark of wisdom is to see the miraculous in the common. What is a day? What is a year? What is summer? What is woman? What is a child? What is sleep? To our blindness, these things seem unaffecting. We make fables to hide the baldness of the fact and conform it, as we say, to the higher law of the mind. But when the fact is seen under the light of an idea, the gaudy fable fades and shrivels. We behold the real higher law. To the wise, therefore, a fact is true poetry, and the most beautiful of fables. These wonders are brought to our own door. You also are a man. Man and woman and their social life, poverty, labor, sleep, fear, fortune, are known to you. Learn that none of these things is superficial, but that each phenomenon has its roots in the faculties and affections of the mind. Whilst the abstract question occupies your intellect, nature brings it in the concrete to be solved by your hands. It were a wise inquiry for the closet, to compare, point by point, especially at remarkable crises in life, our daily history with the rise and progress of ideas in the mind.

So shall we come to look at the world with new eyes. It shall answer the endless inquiry of the intellect,—What is truth? and of the affections,—What is good? by yielding itself passive to the educated Will. Then shall come to pass what my poet said: "Nature is not fixed but fluid. Spirit alters, moulds, makes it. The immobility or bruteness of nature is the absence of spirit; to pure spirit it is fluid, it is volatile, it is obedient. Every spirit builds itself a house, and beyond its house a world, and beyond its world a heaven. Know then that the world exists for you. For you is the phenomenon perfect. What we are, that only can we see. All that Adam had, all that Cæsar could, you have and can do. Adam called his house, heaven and earth; Cæsar called his house, Rome; you perhaps call yours, a cobbler's trade; a hundred acres of ploughed land; or a scholar's garret. Yet line for line and point for point your dominion is as great as theirs, though without fine names. Build therefore your own world. As fast as you conform your life to the pure idea in your mind, that will unfold its great proportions. A correspondent revolution in things will attend the influx of the spirit. So fast will disagreeable appearances, swine, spiders, snakes, pests, madhouses, prisons, enemies, vanish; they are temporary and shall be no more seen. The sordor[16] and filths of nature, the sun shall dry up and the wind exhale. As when the summer comes from the south the snow-banks melt and the face of the earth becomes green before it, so shall the advancing spirit create its ornaments along its path, and carry with it the beauty it visits and the song which enchants it; it shall draw beautiful faces, warm hearts, wise discourse, and heroic acts, around its way, until evil is no more seen. The kingdom of man over nature, which cometh not with observation,—a dominion such as now is beyond his dream of God,—he shall enter without more wonder than the blind man feels who is gradually restored to perfect sight."

1833–1836 1836, 1849

[16]Sordidness, foulness.

THE AMERICAN SCHOLAR

AN ORATION DELIVERED BEFORE THE
PHI BETA KAPPA SOCIETY,
AT CAMBRIDGE, AUGUST 31, 1837

Mr. President and Gentlemen:

I greet you on the recommencement of our literary year.[1] Our anniversary is one of hope, and, perhaps, not enough of labor. We do not meet for games of strength or skill, for the recitation of histories, tragedies, and odes, like the ancient Greeks; for parliaments of love and poesy, like the Troubadours;[2] nor for the advancement of science, like our contemporaries in the British and European capitals. Thus far, our holiday has been simply a friendly sign of the survival of the love of letters amongst a people too busy to give to letters any more. As such it is precious as the sign of an indestructible instinct. Perhaps the time is already come when it ought to be, and will be, something else; when the sluggard intellect of this continent will look from under its iron lids and fill the postponed expectation of the world with something better than the exertions of mechanical skill. Our day of dependence, our long apprenticeship to the learning of other lands, draws to a close. The millions that around us are rushing into life, cannot always be fed on the sere remains of foreign harvests. Events, actions arise, that must be sung, that will sing themselves. Who can doubt that poetry will revive and lead in a new age, as the star in the constellation Harp,[3] which now flames in our zenith, astronomers announce, shall one day be the pole-star[4] for a thousand years?

In this hope I accept the topic which not only usage but the nature of our association seem to prescribe to this day,—the AMERICAN SCHOLAR. Year by year we come up hither to read one more chapter of his biography. Let us inquire what light new days and events have thrown on his character and his hopes.

It is one of those fables which out of an unknown antiquity convey an unlooked-for wisdom, that the gods, in the beginning, divided Man into men, that he might be more helpful to himself; just as the hand was divided into fingers, the better to answer its end.

The old fable covers a doctrine ever new and sublime; that there is One Man,—present to all particular men only partially, or through one faculty; and that you must take the whole society to find the whole man. Man is not a farmer, or a professor, or an engineer, but he is all. Man is priest, and scholar, and statesman, and producer, and soldier. In the *divided* or social state these functions are parcelled out to individuals, each of whom aims to do his stint of the joint work, whilst each other performs his. The fable implies that the individual, to possess himself, must sometimes return from his own labor to embrace all the other laborers. But, unfortunately, this original unit, this fountain of power, has been so distributed to multitudes, has been so

[1]The academic year commencing in September.

[2]The musicians and poets of courtly love who flourished in southern France from the eleventh through the thirteenth centuries.

[3]The bright star Vega, in the constellation Lyra.

[4]The North Star, toward which the axis of the earth points.

minutely subdivided and peddled out, that it is spilled into drops, and cannot be gathered. The state of society is one in which the members have suffered amputation from the trunk, and strut about so many walking monsters,—a good finger, a neck, a stomach, an elbow, but never a man.

Man is thus metamorphosed into a thing, into many things. The planter, who is Man sent out into the field to gather food, is seldom cheered by any idea of the true dignity of his ministry. He sees his bushel and his cart, and nothing beyond, and sinks into the farmer, instead of Man on the farm. The tradesman scarcely ever gives an ideal worth to his work, but is ridden by the routine of his craft, and the soul is subject to dollars. The priest becomes a form; the attorney a statutebook; the mechanic a machine; the sailor a rope of the ship.

In this distribution of functions the scholar is the delegated intellect. In the right state he is *Man Thinking*. In the degenerate state, when the victim of society, he tends to become a mere thinker, or still worse, the parrot of other men's thinking.

In this view of him, as Man Thinking, the theory of his office[5] is contained. Him Nature solicits with all her placid, all her monitory pictures; him the past instructs; him the future invites. Is not indeed every man a student, and do not all things exist for the student's behoof? And, finally, is not the true scholar the only true master? But the old oracle said, "All things have two handles: beware of the wrong one." In life, too often, the scholar errs with mankind and forfeits his privilege. Let us see him in his school, and consider him in reference to the main influences he receives.

I. The first in time and the first in importance of the influences upon the mind is that of nature. Every day, the sun; and, after sunset, Night and her stars. Ever the winds blow; ever the grass grows. Every day, men and women, conversing—beholding and beholden. The scholar is he of all men whom this spectacle most engages. He must settle its value in his mind. What is nature to him? There is never a beginning, there is never an end, to the inexplicable continuity of this web of God, but always circular power returning into itself. Therein it resembles his own spirit, whose beginning, whose ending, he never can find,—so entire, so boundless. Far too as her splendors shine, system on system shooting like rays, upward, downward, without centre, without circumference,—in the mass and in the particle, Nature hastens to render account of herself to the mind. Classification begins. To the young mind every thing is individual, stands by itself. By and by it finds how to join two things and see in them one nature; then three, then three thousand; and so, tyrannized over by its own unifying instinct, it goes on tying things together, diminishing anomalies, discovering roots running under ground whereby contrary and remote things cohere and flower out from one stem. It presently learns that since the dawn of history there has been a constant accumulation and classifying of facts. But what is classification but the perceiving that these objects are not chaotic, and are not foreign, but have a law which is also a law of the human mind? The astronomer discovers that geometry, a pure abstraction of the human mind, is the measure of planetary motion. The chemist finds proportions and intelligible

[5]Function, duty.

method throughout matter; and science is nothing but the finding of analogy, identity, in the most remote parts. The ambitious soul sits down before each refractory fact; one after another reduces all strange constitutions, all new powers, to their class and their law, and goes on forever to animate the last fibre of organization, the outskirts of nature, by insight.

Thus to him, to this schoolboy under the bending dome of day, is suggested that he and it proceed from one root; one is leaf and one is flower; relation, sympathy, stirring in every vein. And what is that root? Is not that the soul of his soul? A thought too bold; a dream too wild. Yet when this spiritual light shall have revealed the law of more earthly natures,—when he has learned to worship the soul, and to see that the natural philosophy that now is, is only the first gropings of its gigantic hand, he shall look forward to an ever expanding knowledge as to a becoming creator. He shall see that nature is the opposite of the soul, answering to it part for part. One is seal and one is print. Its beauty is the beauty of his own mind. Its laws are the laws of his own mind. Nature then becomes to him the measure of his attainments. So much of nature as he is ignorant of, so much of his own mind does he not yet possess. And, in fine, the ancient precept, "Know thyself," and the modern precept, "Study nature," become at last one maxim.

II. The next great influence[6] into the spirit of the scholar is the mind of the Past,—in whatever form, whether of literature, of art, of institutions, that mind is inscribed. Books are the best type of influence of the past, and perhaps we shall get at the truth,—learn the amount of this influence more conveniently,—by considering their value alone.

The theory of books is noble. The scholar of the first age received into him the world around; brooded thereon; gave it the new arrangement of his own mind, and uttered it again. It came into him life; it went out from him truth. It came to him short-lived actions; it went out from him immortal thoughts. It came to him business; it went from him poetry. It was dead fact; now, it is quick[7] thought. It can stand, and it can go. It now endures, it now flies, it now inspires.[8] Precisely in proportion to the depth of mind from which it issued, so high does it soar, so long does it sing.

Or, I might say, it depends on how far the process had gone, of transmuting life into truth. In proportion to the completeness of the distillation, so will the purity and imperishableness of the product be. But none is quite perfect. As no air-pump can by any means make a perfect vacuum, so neither can any artist entirely exclude the conventional, the local, the perishable from his book, or write a book of pure thought, that shall be as efficient, in all respects, to a remote posterity, as to contemporaries, or rather to the second age. Each age, it is found, must write its own books; or rather, each generation for the next succeeding. The books of an older period will not fit this.

Yet hence arises a grave mischief. The sacredness which attaches to the act of creation, the act of thought, is transferred to the record. The poet chanting was felt to be a divine man: henceforth the chant is divine also. The writer was a just and wise spirit: henceforward it is settled the book is perfect; as love of the hero corrupts into worship of his statue. Instantly the

[6]Inflowing. [7]Living. [8]Breathes.

book becomes noxious: the guide is a tyrant. The sluggish and perverted mind of the multitude, slow to open to the incursions of Reason, having once so opened, having once received this book, stands upon it, and makes an outcry if it is disparaged. Colleges are built on it. Books are written on it by thinkers, not by Man Thinking; by men of talent, that is, who start wrong, who set out from accepted dogmas, not from their own sight of principles. Meek young men grow up in libraries, believing it their duty to accept the views which Cicero, which Locke, which Bacon, have given; forgetful that Cicero, Locke, and Bacon were only young men in libraries when they wrote these books.

Hence, instead of Man Thinking, we have the bookworm. Hence the book-learned class, who value books, as such; not as related to nature and the human constitution, but as making a sort of Third Estate[9] with the world and the soul. Hence the restorers of readings, the emendators,[10] the bibliomaniacs[11] of all degrees.

Books are the best of things, well used; abused, among the worst. What is the right use? What is the one end which all means go to effect? They are for nothing but to inspire. I had better never seen a book than to be warped by its attraction clean out of my own orbit, and made a satellite instead of a system. The one thing in the world, of value, is the active soul. This every man is entitled to; this every man contains within him, although in almost all men obstructed and as yet unborn. The soul active sees absolute truth and utters truth, or creates. In this action it is genius; not the privilege of here and there a favorite, but the sound estate of every man. In its essence it is progressive. The book, the college, the school of art, the institutions of any kind, stop with some past utterance of genius. This is good, say they,—let us hold by this. They pin me down. They look backward and not forward. But genius looks forward: the eyes of man are set in his forehead, not in his hindhead: man hopes: genius creates. Whatever talents may be, if the man create not, the pure efflux[12] of the Deity is not his;—cinders and smoke there may be, but not yet flame. There are creative manners, there are creative actions, and creative words; manners, actions, words, that is, indicative of no custom or authority, but springing spontaneous from the mind's own sense of good and fair.

On the other part, instead of being its own seer, let it receive from another mind its truth, though it were in torrents of light, without periods of solitude, inquest, and self-recovery, and a fatal disservice is done. Genius is always sufficiently the enemy of genius by over-influence. The literature of every nation bears me witness. The English dramatic poets have Shakspearized now for two hundred years.

Undoubtedly there is a right way of reading, so it be sternly subordinated. Man Thinking must not be subdued by his instruments. Books are for the scholar's idle times. When he can read God directly, the hour is too precious to be wasted in other men's transcripts of their readings. But when the intervals of darkness come, as come they must,—when the sun is hid and the stars withdraw their shining,—we repair to the lamps which were kindled by their

[9]Feudal Europe recognized three separate estates or classes: the clergy, the nobles, and the commons (middle class). Emerson thus implies a similar separation of the book learned from the world and the soul.

[10]Text editors—harmless drudges. [11]Those with a mania for books. [12]Outflowing.

ray, to guide our steps to the East again, where the dawn is. We hear, that we may speak. The Arabian proverb says, "A fig tree, looking on a fig tree, becometh fruitful."

It is remarkable, the character of the pleasure we derive from the best books. They impress us with the conviction that one nature wrote and the same reads. We read the verses of one of the great English poets, of Chaucer, of Marvell, of Dryden, with the most modern joy,—with a pleasure, I mean, which is in great part caused by the abstraction of all *time* from their verses. There is some awe mixed with the joy of our surprise, when this poet, who lived in some past world, two or three hundred years ago, says that which lies close to my own soul, that which I also had well-nigh thought and said. But for the evidence thence afforded to the philosophical doctrine of the identity of all minds, we should suppose some pre-ëstablished harmony, some foresight of souls that were to be, and some preparation of stores for their future wants, like the fact observed in insects, who lay up food before death for the young grub they shall never see.

I would not be hurried by any love of system, by any exaggeration of instincts, to underrate the Book. We all know, that as the human body can be nourished on any food, though it were boiled grass and the broth of shoes, so the human mind can be fed by any knowledge. And great and heroic men have existed who had almost no other information than by the printed page. I only would say that it needs a strong head to bear that diet. One must be an inventor to read well. As the proverb says, "He that would bring home the wealth of the Indies, must carry out the wealth of the Indies." There is then creative reading as well as creative writing. When the mind is braced by labor invention, the page of whatever book we read becomes luminous with manifold allusion. Every sentence is doubly significant, and the sense of our author is as broad as the world. We then see, what is always true, that as the seer's hour of vision is short and rare among heavy days and months, so is its record, perchance, the least part of his volume. The discerning will read, in his Plato or Shakespeare, only that least part,—only the authentic utterances of the oracle;—all the rest he rejects, were it never so many times Plato's and Shakespeare's.

Of course there is a portion of reading quite indispensable to a wise man. History and exact science he must learn by laborious reading. Colleges, in like manner, have their indispensable office,—to teach elements. But they can only highly serve us when they aim not to drill, but to create; when they gather from far every ray of various genius to their hospitable halls, and by the concentrated fires, set the hearts of their youth on flame. Thought and knowledge are natures in which apparatus and pretension avail nothing. Gowns[13] and pecuniary[14] foundations, though of towns of gold, can never contervail the least sentence or syllable of wit.[15] Forget this, and our American colleges will recede in their public importance, whilst they grow richer every year.

III. There goes in the world a notion that the scholar should be a recluse, a valetudinarian,[16]—as unfit for any handiwork or public labor as a penknife for an axe. The so-called "practical men" sneer at speculative men,

[13]Academic regalia. [14]Financial. [15]Wisdom. [16]Invalid.

as if, because they speculate[17] or *see,* they could do nothing. I have heard it said that the clergy,—who are always, more universally than any other class, the scholars of their day,—are addressed as women; that the rough, spontaneous conversation of men they do not hear, but only a mincing and diluted speech. They are often virtually disfranchised; and indeed there are advocates for their celibacy. As far as this is true of the studious classes, it is not just and wise. Action is with the scholar subordinate, but it is essential. Without it he is not yet man. Without it thought can never ripen into truth. Whilst the world hangs before the eye as a cloud of beauty, we cannot even see its beauty. Inaction is cowardice, but there can be no scholar without the heroic mind. The preamble of thought, the transition through which it passes from the unconscious to the conscious, is action. Only so much do I know, as I have lived. Instantly we know whose words are loaded with life, and whose not.

The world,—this shadow of the soul, or *other me,*—lies wide around. Its attractions are the keys which unlock my thoughts and make me acquainted with myself. I run eagerly into this resounding tumult. I grasp the hands of those next to me, and take my place in the ring to suffer and to work, taught by an instinct that so shall the dumb abyss be vocal with speech. I pierce its order; I dissipate its fear; I dispose of it within the circuit of my expanding life. So much only of life as I know by experience, so much of the wilderness have I vanquished and planted, or so far have I extended my being, my dominion. I do not see how any man can afford, for the sake of his nerves and his nap, to spare any action in which he can partake. It is pearls and rubies to his discourse. Drudgery, calamity, exasperation, want, are instructors in eloquence and wisdom. The true scholar grudges every opportunity of action past by, as a loss of power. It is the raw material out of which the intellect moulds her splendid products. A strange process too, this by which experience is converted into thought, as a mulberry leaf is converted into satin.[18] The manufacture goes forward at all hours.

The actions and events of our childhood and youth are now matters of calmest observation. They lie like fair pictures in the air. Not so with our recent actions,—with the business which we now have in hand. On this we are quite unable to speculate. Our affections as yet circulate through it. We no more feel or know it, than we feel the feet, or the hand, or the brain of our body. The new deed is yet a part of life,—remains for a time immersed in our unconscious life. In some contemplative hour, it detaches itself from the life like a ripe fruit, to become a thought of the mind. Instantly, it is raised, transfigured; the corruptible has put on incorruption.[19] Always now it is an object of beauty, however base its origin and neighborhood. Observe, too, the impossibility of antedating this act. In its grub state, it cannot fly, it cannot shine,—it is a dull grub. But suddenly, without observation, the selfsame thing unfurls beautiful wings, and is an angel of wisdom. So is there no fact, no event, in our private history, which shall not, sooner or later, lose its

[17]From Latin, observe.

[18]In Emerson's day satin was made only from silk, which is produced by worms that feed on mulberry leaves.

[19]"For this corruptible must put on incorruption, and this mortal must put on immortality." I Corinthians 15:53.

adhesive inert form, and astonish us by soaring from our body into the empyrean.[20] Cradle and infancy, school and playground, the fear of boys, and dogs, and ferules,[21] the love of little maids and berries, and many another fact that once filled the whole sky, are gone already; friend and relative, profession and party, town and country, nation and world, must also soar and sing.

Of course, he who has put forth his total strength in fit actions, has the richest return of wisdom. I will not shut myself out of this globe of action and transplant an oak into a flower pot, there to hunger and pine; nor trust the revenue of some single faculty, and exhaust one vein of thought, much like those Savoyards,[22] who, getting their livelihood by carving shepherds, shepherdesses, and smoking Dutchmen, for all Europe, went out one day to the mountain to find stock, and discovered that they had whittled up the last of their pine trees. Authors we have in numbers, who have written out their vein, and who, moved by a commendable prudence, sail for Greece or Palestine, follow the trapper into the prairie, or ramble round Algiers to replenish their merchantable stock.

If it were only for a vocabulary the scholar would be covetous of action. Life is our dictionary. Years are well spent in country labors; in town; in the insight into trades and manufactures; in frank intercourse with many men and women; in science; in art; to the one end of mastering in all their facts a language by which to illustrate and embody our perceptions. I learn immediately from any speaker how much he has already lived, through the poverty or the splendor of his speech. Life lies behind us as the quarry from whence we get tiles and copestones for the masonry of to-day. This is the way to learn grammar. Colleges and books only copy the language which the field and the work-yard made.

But the final value of action, like that of books, and better than books, is that it is a resource. That great principle of Undulation in nature, that shows itself in the inspiring and expiring of the breath; in desire and satiety; in the ebb and flow of the sea; in day and night; in heat and cold; and, as yet more deeply ingrained in every atom and every fluid, is known to us under the name of Polarity,—these "fits of easy transmission and reflection," as Newton[23] called them, are the law of nature because they are the law of spirit.

The mind now thinks, now acts, and each reproduces the other. When the artist has exhausted his materials, when the fancy no longer paints, when thoughts are no longer apprehended and books are a weariness,—he has always the resource *to live*. Character is higher than intellect. Thinking is the function. Living is the functionary. The stream retreats to its source. A great soul will be strong to live, as well as strong to think. Does he lack organ or medium to impart his truths? He can still fall back on this elemental force of living them. This is a total act. Thinking is a partial act. Let the grandeur of justice shine in his affairs. Let the beauty of affection cheer his lowly roof.

[20]Highest heavenly sphere. [21]Rods used for whipping.

[22]Inhabitants of Savoy, now a province of France, then a province of Italy.

[23]Isaac Newton (1642–1727), English scientist and philosopher. The quotation is from his *Optics* (1704).

Those "far from fame," who dwell and act with him, will feel the force of his constitution in the doings and passages of the day better than it can be measured by any public and designed display. Time shall teach him that the scholar loses no hour which the man lives. Herein he unfolds the sacred germ of his instinct, screened from influence. What is lost in seemliness is gained in strength. Not out of those on whom systems of education have exhausted their culture, comes the helpful giant to destroy the old or to build the new, but out of unhandselled[24] savage nature; out of terrible Druids[25] and Berserkers[26] come at last Alfred[27] and Shakespeare.

I hear therefore with joy whatever is beginning to be said of the dignity and necessity of labor to every citizen. There is virtue yet in the hoe and the spade, for learned as well as for unlearned hands. And labor is everywhere welcome; always we are invited to work; only be this limitation observed, that a man shall not for the sake of wider activity sacrifice any opinion to the popular judgments and modes of action.

I have now spoken of the education of the scholar by nature, by books, and by action. It remains to say somewhat of his duties.

They are such as become Man Thinking. They may all be comprised in self-trust. The office of the scholar is to cheer, to raise, and to guide men by showing them facts amidst appearances. He plies the slow, unhonored, and unpaid task of observation. Flamsteed and Herschel,[28] in their glazed observatories, may catalogue the stars with the praise of all men, and the results being splendid and useful, honor is sure. But he, in his private observatory, cataloguing obscure and nebulous stars of the human mind, which as yet no man has thought of as such,—watching days and months sometimes for a few facts; correcting still his old records;—must relinquish display and immediate fame. In the long period of his preparation he must betray often an ignorance and shiftlessness in popular arts, incurring the disdain of the able who shoulder him aside. Long he must stammer in his speech; often forgo the living for the dead. Worse yet, he must accept—how often!—poverty and solitude. For the ease and pleasure of treading the old road, accepting the fashions, the education, the religion of society, he takes the cross of making his own, and, of course, the self-accusation, the faint heart, the frequent uncertainty and loss of time, which are the nettles and tangling vines in the way of the self-relying and self-directed; and the state of virtual hostility in which he seems to stand to society, and especially to educated society. For all this loss and scorn, what offset? He is to find consolation in exercising the highest functions of human nature. He is one who raises himself from private considerations and breathes and lives on public and illustrious thoughts. He is the world's eye. He is the world's heart. He is to resist the vulgar prosperity that retrogrades ever to barbarism, by preserving and communicating heroic sentiments, noble biographies, melodious verse, and the conclusions of history. Whatsoever oracles the human heart, in all emergencies, in all

[24]Unappreciated. [25]Pagan Celtic priests. [26]Savage Norse warriors.

[27]Alfred (849–901), King of the West Saxons. He established English laws and promoted a national literature.

[28]John Flamsteed (1646–1719) and Sir William Herschel (1738–1822), pioneers in modern astronomy.

solemn hours, has uttered as its commentary on the world of actions,—these he shall receive and impart. And whatsoever new verdict Reason from her inviolable seat pronounces on the passing men and events of to-day,—this he shall hear and promulgate.

These being his functions, it becomes him to feel all confidence in himself, and to defer never to the popular cry. He and he only knows the world. The world of any moment is the merest appearance. Some great decorum,[29] some fetish of a government, some ephemeral trade, or war, or man, is cried up by half mankind and cried down by the other half, as if all depended on this particular up or down. The odds are that the whole question is not worth the poorest thought which the scholar has lost in listening to the controversy. Let him not quit his belief that a popgun is a popgun, though the ancient and honorable of the earth affirm it to be the crack of doom. In silence, in steadiness, in severe abstraction, let him hold by himself; add observation to observation, patient of neglect, patient of reproach, and bide his own time,—happy enough if he can satisfy himself alone that this day he has seen something truly. Success treads on every right step. For the instinct is sure, that prompts him to tell his brother what he thinks. He then learns that in going down into the secrets of his own mind he has descended into the secrets of all minds. He learns that he who has mastered any law in his private thoughts, is master to that extent of all men whose language he speaks, and of all into whose language his own can be translated. The poet, in utter solitude remembering his spontaneous thoughts and recording them, is found to have recorded that which men in crowded cities find true for them also. The orator distrusts at first the fitness of his frank confessions, his want of knowledge of the persons he addresses, until he finds that he is the complement of his hearers;—that they drink his words because he fulfils for them their own nature; the deeper he dives into his privatest, secretest presentiment, to his wonder he finds this is the most acceptable, most public, and universally true. The people delight in it; the better part of every man feels, This is my music; this is myself.

In self-trust all the virtues are comprehended. Free should the scholar be,—free and brave. Free even to the definition of freedom, "without any hindrance that does not arise out of his own constitution." Brave; for fear is a thing which a scholar by his very function puts behind him. Fear always springs from ignorance. It is a shame to him if his tranquillity, amid dangerous times, arise from the presumption that like children and women his is a protected class; or if he seek a temporary peace by the diversion of his thoughts from politics or vexed questions, hiding his head like an ostrich in the flowering bushes, peeping into microscopes, and turning rhymes, as a boy whistles to keep his courage up. So is the danger a danger still; so is the fear worse. Manlike let him turn and face it. Let him look into its eye and search its nature, inspect its origin,—see the whelping[30] of this lion,—which lies no great way back; he will then find in himself a perfect comprehension of its nature and extent; he will have made his hands meet on the other side, and can henceforth defy it and pass on superior. The world is his who can see through its pretension. What deafness, what stone-blind custom, what

[29]Standard or code. [30]Birth.

over-grown error you behold is there only by sufferance,—by your sufferance. See it to be a lie, and you have already dealt it its mortal blow.

Yes, we are the cowed,—we the trustless. It is a mischievous notion that we are come late into nature; that the world was finished a long time ago. As the world was plastic and fluid in the hands of God, so it is ever to so much of his attributes as we bring to it. To ignorance and sin, it is flint. They adapt themselves to it as they may; but in proportion as a man has any thing in him divine, the firmament flows before him and takes his signet[31] and form. Not he is great who can alter matter, but he who can alter my state of mind. They are the kings of the world who give the color of their present thought to all nature and all art, and persuade men by the cheerful serenity of their carrying the matter, that this thing which they do is the apple which the ages have desired to pluck, now at last ripe, and inviting nations to the harvest. The great man makes the great thing. Wherever Macdonald sits, there is the head of the table.[32] Linnæus makes botany the most alluring of studies, and wins it from the farmer and the herb-woman; Davy, chemistry, and Cuvier, fossils.[33] The day is always his who works in it with serenity and great aims. The unstable estimates of men crowd to him whose mind is filled with a truth, as the heaped waves of the Atlantic follow the moon.

For this self-trust, the reason is deeper than can be fathomed,—darker than can be enlightened. I might not carry with me the feeling of my audience in stating my own belief. But I have already shown the ground of my hope, in adverting to the doctrine that man is one. I believe man has been wronged; he has wronged himself. He has almost lost the light that can lead him back to his prerogatives. Men are become of no account. Men in history, men in the world of to-day, are bugs, are spawn, and are called "the mass" and "the herd." In a century, in a millennium, one or two men; that is to say, one or two approximations to the right state of every man. All the rest behold in the hero or the poet their own green and crude being,—ripened; yes, and are content to be less, so *that* may attain to its full stature. What a testimony, full of grandeur, full of pity, is borne to the demands of his own nature, by the poor clansman, the poor partisan, who rejoices in the glory of his chief. The poor and the low find some amends to their immense moral capacity, for their acquiescence in a political and social inferiority. They are content to be brushed like flies from the path of a great person, so that justice shall be done by him to that common nature which it is the dearest desire of all to see enlarged and glorified. They sun themselves in the great man's light, and feel it to be their own element. They cast the dignity of man from their down-trod selves upon the shoulders of a hero, and will perish to add one drop of blood to make that great heart beat, those giant sinews combat and conquer. He lives for us, and we live in him.

Men, such as they are, very naturally seek money or power; and power because it is as good as money,—the "spoils," so called, "of office." And why not? for they aspire to the highest, and this, in their sleep-walking, they dream is highest. Wake them and they shall quit the false good and leap to

[31]Seal.

[32]Emerson's adaptation of a contemporary proverb.

[33]Carolus Linnaeus (1707–1778), Swedish botanist; Sir Humphry Davy (1778–1829), English chemist; Georges Cuvier (1769–1832), French naturalist.

the true, and leave governments to clerks and desks. This revolution is to be wrought by the gradual domestication of the idea of Culture. The main enterprise of the world for splendor, for extent, is the upbuilding of a man. Here are the materials strewn along the ground. The private life of one man shall be a more illustrious monarchy, more formidable to its enemy, more sweet and serene in its influence to its friend, than any kingdom in history. For a man, rightly viewed, comprehendeth the particular natures of all men. Each philosopher, each bard, each actor has only done for me, as by a delegate, what one day I can do for myself. The books which once we valued more than the apple of the eye, we have quite exhausted. What is that but saying that we have come up with the point of view which the universal mind took through the eyes of one scribe; we have been that man, and have passed on. First, one, then another, we drain all cisterns, and waxing[34] greater by all these supplies, we crave a better and more abundant food. The man has never lived that can feed us ever. The human mind cannot be enshrined in a person who shall set a barrier on any one side to this unbounded, unboundable empire. It is one central fire, which, flaming now out of the lips of Etna,[35] lightens the capes of Sicily, and now out of the throat of Vesuvius,[36] illuminates the towers and vineyards of Naples. It is one light which beams out of a thousand stars. It is one soul which animates all men.

But I have dwelt perhaps tediously upon this abstraction of the Scholar. I ought not delay longer to add what I have to say of nearer reference to the time and to this country.

Historically, there is thought to be a difference in the ideas which predominate over successive epochs, and there are data for marking the genius of the Classic, of the Romantic, and now of Reflective or Philosophical age. With the views I have intimated of the oneness or the identity of the mind through all individuals, I do not much dwell on these differences. In fact, I believe each individual passes through all three. The boy is a Greek; the youth, romantic; the adult, reflective. I deny not, however, that a revolution in the leading idea may be distinctly enough traced.

Our age is bewailed as the age of Introversion. Must that needs be evil? We, it seems, are critical; we are embarrassed with second thoughts; we cannot enjoy any thing for hankering to know whereof the pleasure consists; we are lined with eyes; we see with our feet; the time is infected with Hamlet's unhappiness,—

> "Sicklied o'er with the pale cast of thought."[37]

Is it so bad then? Sight is the last thing to be pitied. Would we be blind? Do we fear lest we should outsee nature and God, and drink truth dry? I look upon the discontent of the literary class as a mere announcement of the fact that they find themselves not in the state of mind of their fathers, and regret the coming state as untried; as a boy dreads the water before he has learned that he can swim. If there is any period one would desire to be born in, is it not the age of Revolution; when the old and the new stand side by side and

[34]Growing. [35]Volcano in Sicily. [36]Volcano in Italy. [37]*Hamlet,* Act III, Scene i, line 85.

admit of being compared; when the energies of all men are searched by fear and by hope; when the historic glories of the old can be compensated by the rich possibilities of the new era? This time, like all times, is a very good one, if we but know what to do with it.

I read with some joy of the auspicious signs of the coming days, as they glimmer already through poetry and art, through philosophy and science, through church and state.

One of these signs is the fact that the same movement which effected the elevation of what was called the lowest class in the state, assumed in literature a very marked and as benign an aspect. Instead of the sublime and beautiful, the near, the low, the common, was explored and poetized. That which had been negligently trodden under foot by those who were harnessing and provisioning themselves for long journeys into far countries, is suddenly found to be richer than all foreign parts. The literature of the poor, the feelings of the child, the philosophy of the street, the meaning of household life, are the topics of the time. It is a great stride. It is a sign—is it not?—of new vigor when the extremities are made active, when currents of warm life run into the hands and the feet. I ask not for the great, the remote, the romantic; what is doing in Italy or Arabia; what is Greek art, or Provençal minstrelsy;[38] I embrace the common, I explore and sit at the feet of the familiar, the low. Give me insight into to-day, and you may have the antique and future worlds. What would we really know the meaning of? The meal in the firkin;[39] the milk in the pan; the ballad in the street; the news of the boat; the glance of the eye; the form and the gait of the body;—show me the ultimate reason of these matters; show me the sublime presence of the highest spiritual cause lurking, as always it does lurk, in these suburbs and extremities of nature; let me see every trifle bristling with the polarity that ranges it instantly on an eternal law; and the shop, the plough, and the ledger referred to the like cause by which light undulates and poets sing;—and the world lies no longer a dull miscellany and lumber-room,[40] but has form and order; there is no trifle, there is no puzzle, but one design unites and animates the farthest pinnacle and the lowest trench.

This idea has inspired the genius of Goldsmith, Burns, Cowper, and, in a newer time, of Goethe, Wordsworth, and Carlyle. This idea they have differently followed and with various success. In contrast with their writing, the style of Pope, of Johnson, of Gibbon, looks cold and pedantic. This writing is blood-warm. Man is surprised to find that things near are not less beautiful and wondrous than things remote. The near explains the far. The drop is a small ocean. A man is related to all nature. This perception of the worth of the vulgar is fruitful in discoveries. Goethe, in this very thing the most modern of the moderns, has shown us, as none ever did, the genius of the ancients.

[38]The singing and playing of the musical entertainers (minstrels) of medieval Provence, in southeast France.

[39]Small cask.

[40]Storeroom.

There is one man of genius who has done much for this philosophy of life, whose literary value has never yet been rightly estimated;—I mean Emanuel Swedenborg. The most imaginative of men, yet writing with the precision of a mathematician, he endeavored to engraft a purely philosophical Ethics on the popular Christianity of his time. Such an attempt of course must have difficulty which no genius could surmount. But he saw and showed the connection between nature and the affections of the soul. He pierced the emblematic or spiritual character of the visible, audible, tangible world. Especially did his shade-loving muse hover over and interpret the lower parts of nature; he showed the mysterious bond that allies moral evil to the foul material forms, and has given in epical parables a theory of insanity, of beasts, of unclean and fearful things.

Another sign of our times, also marked by an analogous political movement, is the new importance given to the single person. Every thing that tends to insulate the individual,—to surround him with barriers of natural respect, so that each man shall feel the world is his, and man shall treat with man as a sovereign state with a sovereign state,—tends to true union as well as greatness. "I learned," said the melancholy Pestalozzi,[41] "that no man in God's wide earth is either willing or able to help any other man." Help must come from the bosom alone. The scholar is that man who must take up into himself all the ability of the time, all the contributions of the past, all the hopes of the future. He must be an university of knowledges. If there be one lesson more than another which should pierce his ear, it is, The world is nothing, the man is all; in yourself is the law of all nature, and you know not yet how a globule of sap ascends; in yourself slumbers the whole of Reason; it is for you to know all; it is for you to dare all. Mr. President and Gentlemen, this confidence in the unsearched might of man belongs, by all motives, by all prophecy, by all preparation, to the American Scholar. We have listened too long to the courtly muses of Europe. The spirit of the American freeman is already suspected to be timid, imitative, tame. Public and private avarice make the air we breathe thick and fat. The scholar is decent, indolent, complaisant. See already the tragic consequence. The mind of this country, taught to aim at low objects, eats upon itself. There is no work for any but the decorous and the complaisant. Young men of the fairest promise, who begin life upon our shores, inflated by the mountain winds, shined upon by all the stars of God, find the earth below not in unison with these, but are hindered from action by the disgust which the principles on which business is managed inspire, and turn drudges, or die of disgust, some of them suicides. What is the remedy? They did not yet see, and thousands of young men as hopeful now crowding to the barriers for the career do not yet see, that if the single man plant himself indomitably on his instincts, and there abide, the huge world will come round to him. Patience,—patience; with the shades of all the good and great for company; and for solace the perspective of your own infinite life; and for work the study and the communication of

[41]Johann Heinrich Pestalozzi (1746–1827), Swiss educator.

principles, the making those instincts prevalent, the conversion of the world. Is it not the chief disgrace in the world, not to be an unit;—not to be reckoned one character;—not to yield that peculiar fruit which each man was created to bear, but to be reckoned in the gross, in the hundred, or the thousand, or the party, the section, to which we belong; and our opinion predicted geographically, as the north, or the south? Not so, brothers and friends—please God, ours shall not be so. We will walk on our own feet; we will work with our own hands; we will speak our own minds. The study of letters shall be no longer a name for pity, for doubt, and for sensual indulgence. The dread of man and the love of man shall be a wall of defence and a wreath of joy around all. A nation of men will for the first time exist, because each believes himself inspired by the Divine Soul which also inspires all men.

1837

SELF-RELIANCE

"Ne te quæsiveris extra."[1]

Man is his own star; and the soul that can
Render an honest and a perfect man,
Commands all light, all influence, all fate;
Nothing to him falls early or too late.
Our acts our angels are, or good or ill,
Our fatal shadows that walk by us still.

Epilogue to Beaumont and Fletcher's
Honest Man's Fortune[2]

Cast the bantling[3] *on the rocks,*
Suckle him with the she-wolf's teat;
Wintered with the hawk and fox,
Power and speed be hands and feet.[4]

I read the other day some verses written by an eminent painter[5] which were original and not conventional. The soul always hears an admonition in such lines, let the subject be what it may. The sentiment they instil is of more value than any thought they may contain. To believe your own thought, to believe that what is true for you in your private heart is true for all men,—that is genius. Speak your latent conviction, and it shall be the universal sense; for the

[1]Latin: "Look to no one outside yourself." Adapted from *Satires,* "Satira" I, line 7, by the Roman Stoic satirist Persius (34–62).

[2]Francis Beaumont (1584–1616) and John Fletcher (1579–1625), Elizabethan playwrights, authors of *The Honest Man's Fortune* (published 1647).

[3]Infant. [4]A quatrain composed by Emerson himself.

[5]The American painter-poet Washington Allston (1779–1843).

inmost in due time becomes the outmost, and our first thought is rendered back to us by the trumpets of the Last Judgment. Familiar as the voice of the mind is to each, the highest merit we ascribe to Moses, Plato and Milton is that they set at naught books and traditions, and spoke not what men, but what *they* thought. A man should learn to detect and watch that gleam of light which flashes across his mind from within, more than the lustre of the firmament of bards and sages. Yet he dismisses without notice his thought, because it is his. In every work of genius we recognize our own rejected thoughts; they come back to us with a certain alienated majesty. Great works of art have no more affecting lesson for us than this. They teach us to abide by our spontaneous impression with good-humored inflexibility then most when the whole cry of voices is on the other side. Else to-morrow a stranger will say with masterly good sense precisely what we have thought and felt all the time, and we shall be forced to take with shame our own opinion from another.

There is a time in every man's education when he arrives at the conviction that envy is ignorance; that imitation is suicide; that he must take himself for better for worse as his portion; that though the wide universe is full of good, no kernel of nourishing corn can come to him but through his toil bestowed on that plot of ground which is given to him to till. The power which resides in him is new in nature, and none but he knows what that is which he can do, nor does he know until he has tried. Not for nothing one face, one character, one fact, makes much impression on him, and another none. This sculpture in the memory is not without preëstablished harmony. The eye was placed where one ray should fall, that it might testify of that particular ray. We but half express ourselves, and are ashamed of that divine idea which each of us represents. It may be safely trusted as proportionate and of good issues, so it be faithfully imparted, but God will not have his work made manifest by cowards. A man is relieved and gay when he has put his heart into his work and done his best; but what he has said or done otherwise shall give him no peace. It is a deliverance which does not deliver. In the attempt his genius deserts him; no muse befriends; no invention, no hope.

Trust thyself: every heart vibrates to that iron string.[6] Accept the place the divine providence has found for you, the society of your contemporaries, the connection of events. Great men have always done so, and confided themselves childlike to the genius of their age, betraying their perception that the absolutely trustworthy was seated at their heart, working through their hands, predominating in all their being. And we are now men, and must accept in the highest mind the same transcendent destiny; and not minors and invalids in a protected corner, not cowards fleeing before a revolution, but guides, redeemers and benefactors, obeying the Almighty effort and advancing on Chaos and the Dark.

What pretty oracles nature yields us on this text in the face and behavior of children, babes, and even brutes! That divided and rebel mind, that distrust of a sentiment because our arithmetic has computed the strength and means opposed to our purpose, these have not. Their mind being whole, their eye is as yet unconquered, and when we look in their faces we

[6]Emerson used the words "iron" and "steel" interchangeably.

are disconcerted. Infancy conforms to nobody; all conform to it; so that one babe commonly makes four or five out of the adults who prattle and play to it. So God has armed youth and puberty and manhood no less with its own piquancy and charm, and made it enviable and gracious and its claims not to be put by, if it will stand by itself. Do not think the youth has no force, because he cannot speak to you and me. Hark! in the next room his voice is sufficiently clear and emphatic. It seems he knows how to speak to his contemporaries. Bashful or bold then, he will know how to make us seniors very unnecessary.

The nonchalance of boys who are sure of a dinner, and would disdain as much as a lord to do or say aught to conciliate one, is the healthy attitude of human nature. A boy is in the parlor what the pit[7] is in the playhouse; independent, irresponsible, looking out from his corner on such people and facts as pass by, he tries and sentences them on their merits, in the swift, summary way of boys, as good, bad, interesting, silly, eloquent, troublesome. He cumbers himself never about consequences, about interests; he gives an independent, genuine verdict. You must court him; he does not court you. But the man is as it were clapped into jail by his consciousness. As soon as he has once acted or spoken with *éclat*[8] he is a committed person, watched by the sympathy or the hatred of hundreds, whose affections must now enter into his account. There is no Lethe[9] for this. Ah, that he could pass again into his neutrality! Who can thus avoid all pledges and, having observed, observe again from the same unaffected, unbiased, unbribable, unaffrighted innocence,—must always be formidable. He would utter opinions on all passing affairs, which being seen to be not private but necessary, would sink like darts into the ear of men and put them in fear.

These are the voices which we hear in solitude, but they grow faint and inaudible as we enter into the world. Society everywhere is in conspiracy against the manhood of every one of its members. Society is a joint-stock company, in which the members agree, for the better securing of his bread to each shareholder, to surrender the liberty and culture of the eater. The virtue in most request is conformity. Self-reliance is its aversion. It loves not realities and creators, but names and customs.

Whoso would be a man, must be a nonconformist. He who would gather immortal palms[10] must not be hindered by the name of goodness, but must explore if it be goodness. Nothing is at last sacred but the integrity of your own mind. Absolve you to yourself, and you shall have the suffrage of the world. I remember an answer which when quite young I was prompted to make to a valued adviser who was wont to importune me with the dear old doctrines of the church. On my saying, "What have I to do with the sacredness of traditions, if I live wholly from within?" my friend suggested,—"But these impulses may be from below, not from above." I replied, "They do not seem to me to be such; but if I am the Devil's child, I will live then from the Devil." No law can be sacred to me but that of my nature. Good and bad are but names very readily transferable to that or this; the only right is what is after my constitution; the only wrong what is against it. A man is to carry himself in the presence of all opposition as if every thing were titular and

[7]Location of the cheapest seats in a theater; hence, a clamorous, uninhibited audience.
[8]Brilliance, ostentation. [9]River of forgetfulness in classical myth.
[10]Honors.

ephemeral but he. I am ashamed to think how easily we capitulate to badges and names, to large societies and dead institutions. Every decent and well-spoken individual affects and sways me more than is right. I ought to go upright and vital, and speak the rude truth in all ways. If malice and vanity wear the coat of philanthropy, shall that pass? If an angry bigot assumes this bountiful cause of Abolition, and comes to me with his last news from Barbadoes,[11] why should I not say to him, "Go love thy infant; love thy wood-chopper; be good-natured and modest; have that grace; and never varnish your hard, uncharitable ambition with this incredible tenderness for black folk a thousand miles off. Thy love afar is spite at home." Rough and graceless would be such greeting, but truth is handsomer than the affectation of love. Your goodness must have some edge to it,—else it is none. The doctrine of hatred must be preached, as the counteraction of the doctrine of love, when that pules and whines. I shun father and mother and wife and brother when my genius calls me. I would write on the lintels[12] of the door-post, *Whim*. I hope it is somewhat better than whim at last, but we cannot spend the day in explanation. Expect me not to show cause why I seek or why I exclude company. Then again, do not tell me, as a good man did today, of my obligation to put all poor men in good situations. Are they *my* poor? I tell thee, thou foolish philanthropist, that I grudge the dollar, the dime, the cent I give to such men as do not belong to me and to whom I do not belong. There is a class of persons to whom by all spiritual affinity I am bought and sold; for them I will go to prison if need be; but your miscellaneous popular charities; the education at college of fools; the building of meeting-houses to the vain end to which many now stand; alms to sots, and the thousand-fold Relief Societies;—though I confess with shame I sometimes succumb and give the dollar, it is a wicked dollar, which by and by I shall have the manhood to withhold.

Virtues are, in the popular estimate, rather the exception than the rule. There is the man *and* his virtues. Men do what is called a good action, as some piece of courage or charity, much as they would pay a fine in expiation of daily nonappearance on parade. Their works are done as an apology or extenuation of their living in the world,—as invalids and the insane pay a high board. Their virtues are penances. I do not wish to expiate, but to live. My life is for itself and not for a spectacle. I much prefer that it should be of a lower strain, so it be genuine and equal, than that it should be glittering and unsteady. I wish it to be sound and sweet, and not to need diet and bleeding. I ask primary evidence that you are a man, and refuse this appeal from the man to his actions. I know that for myself it makes no difference whether I do or forbear those actions which are reckoned excellent. I cannot consent to pay for a privilege where I have intrinsic right. Few and mean as my gifts may be, I actually am, and do not need for my own assurance or the assurance of my fellows any secondary testimony.

What I must do is all that concerns me, not what the people think. This rule, equally arduous in actual and in intellectual life, may serve for the whole distinction between greatness and meanness. It is the harder because

[11]British West Indian island where slavery was abolished in 1834.

[12]Horizontal piece that spans a doorway. Crosspiece in a door frame. Emerson refers to Deuteronomy 6:6–9.

you will always find those who think they know what is your duty better than you know it. It is easy in the world to live after the world's opinion; it is easy in solitude to live after our own; but the great man is he who in the midst of the crowd keeps with perfect sweetness the independence of solitude.

The objection to conforming to usages that have become dead to you is that it scatters your force. It loses your time and blurs the impression of your character. If you maintain a dead church, contribute to a dead Bible-society, vote with a great party either for the government or against it, spread your table like base housekeepers,—under all these screens I have difficulty to detect the precise man you are: and of course so much force is withdrawn from your proper life. But do your work, and I shall know you. Do your work, and you shall reinforce yourself. A man must consider what a blind-man's buff is this game of conformity. If I know your sect I anticipate your argument. I hear a preacher announce for his text and topic the expediency of one of the institutions of his church. Do I not know beforehand that not possibly can he say a new and spontaneous word? Do I not know that with all this ostentation of examining the grounds of the institution he will do no such thing? Do I not know that he is pledged to himself not to look but at one side, the permitted side, not as a man, but as a parish minister? He is a retained attorney, and these airs of the bench[13] are the emptiest affectation. Well, most men have bound their eyes with one or another handkerchief, and attached themselves to some one of these communities of opinion. This conformity makes them not false in a few particulars, authors of a few lies, but false in all particulars. Their every truth is not quite true. Their two is not the real two, their four not the real four; so that every word they say chagrins us and we know not where to begin to set them right. Meantime nature is not slow to equip us in the prison-uniform of the party to which we adhere. We come to wear one cut of face and figure, and acquire by degrees the gentlest asinine expression. There is a mortifying experience in particular, which does not fail to wreak itself also in the general history; I mean "the foolish face of praise,"[14] the forced smile which we put on in company where we do not feel at ease, in answer to conversation which does not interest us. The muscles, not spontaneously moved but moved by a low usurping wilfulness, grow tight about the outline of the face, with the most disagreeable sensation.

For nonconformity the world whips you with its displeasure. And therefore a man must know how to estimate a sour face. The bystanders look askance on him in the public street or in the friend's parlor. If this aversion had its origin in contempt and resistance like his own he might well go home with a sad countenance; but the sour faces of the multitude, like their sweet faces, have no deep cause, but are put on and off as the wind blows and a newspaper directs. Yet is the discontent of the multitude more formidable than that of the senate and the college. It is easy enough for a firm man who knows the world to brook the rage of the cultivated classes. Their rage is decorous and prudent, for they are timid, as being very vulnerable themselves. But when to their feminine rage the indignation of the people is added, when the ignorant and the poor are aroused, when the

[13]Where judges sit; hence, the demeanor or appearance of judicial impartiality.
[14]From Alexander Pope's satirical "Epistle to Dr. Arbuthnot," line 212.

unintelligent brute force that lies at the bottom of society is made to growl and mow,[15] it needs the habit of magnanimity and religion to treat it godlike as a trifle of no concernment.

The other terror that scares us from self-trust is our consistency; a reverence for our past act or word because the eyes of others have no other data for computing our orbit than our past acts, and we are loth to disappoint them.

But why should you keep your head over your shoulder? Why drag about this corpse of your memory, lest you contradict somewhat you have stated in this or that public place? Suppose you should contradict yourself; what then? It seems to be a rule of wisdom never to rely on your memory alone, scarcely even in acts of pure memory, but to bring the past for judgment into the thousand-eyed present, and live ever in a new day. In your metaphysics you have denied personality to the Deity, yet when the devout motions of the soul come, yield to them heart and life, though they should clothe God with shape and color. Leave your theory, as Joseph his coat in the hand of the harlot,[16] and flee.

A foolish consistency is the hobgoblin of little minds, adored by little statesmen and philosophers and divines. With consistency a great soul has simply nothing to do. He may as well concern himself with his shadow on the wall. Speak what you think now in hard words and to-morrow speak what to-morrow thinks in hard words again, though it contradict everything you said to-day.—"Ah, so you shall be sure to be misunderstood."—Is it so bad then to be misunderstood? Pythagoras[17] was misunderstood, and Socrates, and Jesus, and Luther, and Copernicus, and Galileo, and Newton, and every pure and wise spirit that ever took flesh. To be great is to be misunderstood.

I suppose no man can violate his nature. All the sallies of his will are rounded in by the law of his being, as the inequalities of Andes and Himmaleh[18] are insignificant in the curve of the sphere. Nor does it matter how you gauge and try him. A character is like an acrostic or Alexandrian stanza;[19]—read it forward, backward, or across, it still spells the same thing. In this pleasing contrite woodlife which God allows me, let me record day by day my honest thought without prospect or retrospect, and, I cannot doubt, it will be found symmetrical, though I mean it not and see it not. My book should smell of pines and resound with the hum of insects. The swallow over my window should interweave that thread or straw he carries in his bill into my web also. We pass for what we are. Character teaches above our wills. Men imagine that they communicate their virtue or vice only by overt actions, and do not see that virtue or vice emit a breath every moment.

There will be an agreement in whatever variety of actions, so they be each honest and natural in their hour. For of one will, the actions will be harmonious, however unlike they seem. These varieties are lost sight of at a little

[15]Grimace.

[16]Potiphar's wife caught Joseph, "by his garment, saying, Lie with me: and he left his garment in her hand, and fled." Genesis 39:12.

[17]Fifth century B.C. Greek philosopher who, like those whose names follow, roused enmity for his revolutionary ideas.

[18]Himalaya Mountains.

[19]A palindrome, a statement that reads the same forward and backward.

distance, at a little height of thought. One tendency unites them all. The voyage of the best ship is a zigzag line of a hundred tacks.[20] See the line from a sufficient distance, and it straightens itself to the average tendency. Your genuine action will explain itself and will explain your other genuine actions. Your conformity explains nothing. Act singly, and what you have already done singly will justify you now. Greatness appeals to the future. If I can be firm enough to-day to do right and scorn eyes, I must have done so much right before as to defend me now. Be it how it will, do right now. Always scorn appearances and you always may. The force of character is cumulative. All the foregone days of virtue work their health into this. What makes the majesty of the heroes of the senate and the field, which so fills the imagination? The consciousness of a train of great days and victories behind. They shed a united light on the advancing actor. He is attended as by a visible escort of angels. That is it which throws thunder into Chatham's[21] voice, and dignity into Washington's port,[22] and America into Adams's[23] eye. Honor is venerable to us because it is no ephemera. It is always ancient virtue. We worship it to-day because it is not of to-day. We love it and pay it homage because it is not a trap for our love and homage, but is self-dependent, self-derived, and therefore of an old immaculate pedigree, even if shown in a young person.

I hope in these days we have heard the last of conformity and consistency. Let the words be gazetted[24] and ridiculous henceforward. Instead of the gong for dinner, let us hear a whistle from the Spartan fife. Let us never bow and apologize more. A great man is coming to eat at my house. I do not wish to please him; I wish that he should wish to please me. I will stand here for humanity, and though I would make it kind, I would make it true. Let us affront and reprimand the smooth mediocrity and squalid contentment of the times, and hurl in the face of custom and trade and office, the fact which is the upshot of all history, that there is a great responsible Thinker and Actor working wherever a man works; that a true man belongs to no other time or place, but is the centre of things. Where he is, there is nature. He measures you and all men and all events. Ordinarily, every body in society reminds us of somewhat else, or of some other person. Character, reality, reminds you of nothing else; it takes place of the whole creation. The man must be so much that he must make all circumstances indifferent. Every true man is a cause, a country, and an age; requires infinite spaces and numbers and time fully to accomplish his design;—and posterity seem to follow his steps as a train of clients. A man Cæsar is born, and for ages after we have a Roman Empire. Christ is born, and millions of minds so grow and cleave to his genius that he is confounded with virtue and the possible of man. An institution is the lengthened shadow of one man, as, Monachism, of the Hermit Antony;[25] the

[20]Course changes.

[21]William Pitt (1708–1778), Earl of Chatham and renowned political orator.

[22]Bearing, demeanor.

[23]Samuel Adams (1722–1803), Revolutionary War patriot; or John Adams (1735–1826), second president of the United States; or John Quincy Adams (1767–1848), sixth president of the United States.

[24]Publicly dismissed.

[25]St. Anthony (c. 250–350), founder of Christian monachism (monasticism).

Reformation, of Luther; Quakerism, of Fox;[26] Methodism of Wesley;[27] Abolition, of Clarkson.[28] Scipio, Milton called "the height of Rome;"[29] and all history resolves itself very easily into the biography of a few stout and earnest persons.

Let a man then know his worth, and keep things under his feet. Let him not peep or steal, or skulk up and down with the air of a charity-boy, a bastard, or an interloper in the world which exists for him. But the man in the street, finding no worth in himself which corresponds to the force which built a tower or sculptured a marble god, feels poor when he looks on these. To him a palace, a statue, or a costly book have an alien and forbidding air, much like a gay equipage, and seem to say like that, "Who are you, Sir?" Yet they all are his, suitors for his notice, petitioners to his faculties that they will come out and take possession. The picture waits for my verdict; it is not to command me, but I am to settle its claims to praise. That popular fable of the sot who was picked up dead-drunk in the street, carried to the duke's house, washed and dressed and laid in the duke's bed, and, on his waking, treated with all obsequious ceremony like the duke, and assured that he had been insane,[30] owes its popularity to the fact that it symbolizes so well the state of man, who is in the world a sort of sot, but now and then wakes up, exercises his reason and finds himself a true prince.

Our reading is mendicant and sycophantic.[31] In history our imagination plays us false. Kingdom and lordship, power and estate, are a gaudier vocabulary than private John and Edward in a small house and common day's work; but the things of life are the same to both; the sum total of both is the same. Why all this deference to Alfred and Scanderbeg and Gustavus?[32] Suppose they were virtuous; did they wear out virtue? As great a stake depends on your private act to-day as followed their public and renowned steps. When private men shall act with original views, the lustre will be transferred from the actions of kings to those of gentlemen.

The world has been instructed by its kings, who have so magnetized the eyes of nations. It has been taught by this colossal symbol the mutual reverence that is due from man to man. The joyful loyalty with which men have everywhere suffered the king, the noble, or the great proprietor to walk among them by a law of his own, make his own scale of men and things and reverse theirs, pay for benefits not with money but with honor, and represent the law in his person, was the hieroglyphic by which they obscurely signified their consciousness of their own right and comeliness, the right of every man.

The magnetism which all original action exerts is explained when we inquire the reason of self-trust. Who is the Trustee? What is the aboriginal Self,

[26]George Fox (1624–1691), English founder of the Society of Friends.

[27]John Wesley (1703–1791), founder of Methodism.

[28]Thomas Clarkson (1760–1846), English abolitionist.

[29]Scipio was a Roman general (237–183 B.C.) who defeated Hannibal and destroyed Carthage. Milton praised him in *Paradise Lost,* Book IX, line 510.

[30]Shakespeare uses the fable in *The Taming of the Shrew,* Induction, Scene i, lines 34–68.

[31]Begging and parasitical.

[32]King Alfred of England (849–899); Scanderbeg (1403?–1468), Albanian patriot; Gustavus Adolphus (1594–1632), King of Sweden.

on which a universal reliance may be grounded? What is the nature and power of that science-baffling star, without parallax,[33] without calculable elements, which shoots a ray of beauty even into trivial and impure actions, if the least mark of independence appear? The inquiry leads us to that source, at once the essence of genius, of virtue, and of life, which we call Spontaneity or Instinct. We denote this primary wisdom as Intuition, whilst all later teachings are tuitions. In that deep force, the last fact behind which analysis cannot go, all things find their common origin. For the sense of being which in calm hours rises, we know not how, in the soul, is not diverse from things, from space, from light, from time, from man, but one with them and proceeds obviously from the same source whence their life and being also proceed. We first share the life by which things exist and afterwards see them as appearances in nature and forget that we have shared their cause. Here is the fountain of action and of thought. Here are the lungs of that inspiration which giveth man wisdom and which cannot be denied without impiety and atheism. We lie in the lap of immense intelligence, which makes us receivers of its truth and organs of its activity. When we discern justice, when we discern truth, we do nothing of ourselves, but allow a passage to its beams. If we ask whence this comes, if we seek to pry into the soul that causes, all philosophy is at fault. Its presence or its absence is all we can affirm. Every man discriminates between the voluntary acts of his mind and his involuntary perceptions, and knows that to his involuntary perceptions a perfect faith is due. He may err in the expression of them, but he knows that these things are so, like day and night, not to be disputed. My wilful actions and acquisitions are but roving;—the idlest reverie, the faintest native emotion, command my curiosity and respect. Thoughtless people contradict as readily the statement of perceptions as of opinions, or rather much more readily; for they do not distinguish between perception and notion. They fancy that I choose to see this or that thing. But perception is not whimsical, but fatal. If I see a trait, my children will see it after me, and in course of time all mankind,—although it may chance that no one has seen it before me. For my perception of it is as much a fact as the sun.

The relations of the soul to the divine spirit are so pure that it is profane to seek to interpose helps. It must be that when God speaketh he should communicate, not one thing, but all things; should fill the world with his voice; should scatter forth light, nature, time, souls, from the centre of the present thought; and new date and new create the whole. Whenever a mind is simple and receives a divine wisdom, old things pass away,—means, teachers, texts, temples fall; it lives now, and absorbs past and future into the present hour. All things are made sacred by relation to it,—one as much as another. All things are dissolved to their centre by their cause, and in the universal miracle petty and particular miracles disappear. If therefore a man claims to know and speak of God and carries you backward to the phraseology of some old mouldered nation in another country, in another world, believe him not. Is the acorn better than the oak which is its fulness and completion? Is the parent better than the child into whom he has cast his ripened being? Whence

[33]I.e., without the angular displacement of usual stars, when viewed from the earth's surface, hence immeasurable.

then this worship of the past? The centuries are conspirators against the sanity and authority of the soul. Time and space are but physiological colors which the eye makes, but the soul is light: where it is, is day; where it was, is night; and history is an impertinence and an injury if it be any thing more than a cheerful apologue or parable of my being and becoming.

Man is timid and apologetic; he is no longer upright; he dares not say "I think," "I am," but quotes some saint or sage. He is ashamed before the blade of grass or the blowing rose. These roses under my window make no reference to former roses or to better ones; they are for what they are; they exist with God to-day. There is no time to them. There is simply the rose; it is perfect in every moment of its existence. Before a leaf-bud has burst, its whole life acts; in the full-blown flower there is no more; in the leafless root there is no less. Its nature is satisfied and it satisfies nature in all moments alike. But man postpones or remembers; he does not live in the present, but with reverted eye laments the past, or, heedless of the riches that surround him, stands on tiptoe to foresee the future. He cannot be happy and strong until he too lives with nature in the present, above time.

This should be plain enough. Yet see what strong intellects dare not yet hear God himself unless he speak the phraseology of I know not what David, or Jeremiah, or Paul. We shall not always set so great a price on a few texts, on a few lives. We are like children who repeat by rote the sentences of grandames and tutors, and, as they grow older, of the men of talents and character they chance to see,—painfully recollecting the exact words they spoke; afterwards, when they come into the point of view which those had who uttered these sayings, they understand them and are willing to let the words go; for at any time they can use words as good when occasion comes. If we live truly, we shall see truly. It is as easy for the strong man to be strong, as it is for the weak to be weak. When we have new perception, we shall gladly disburden the memory of its hoarded treasures as old rubbish. When a man lives with God, his voice shall be as sweet as the murmur of the brook and the rustle of the corn.

And now at last the highest truth on this subject remains unsaid; probably cannot be said; for all that we say is the far-off remembering of the intuition. That thought by which I can now nearest approach to say it, is this. When good is near you, when you have life in yourself, it is not by any known or accustomed way; you shall not discern the footprints of any other; you shall not see the face of man; you shall not hear any name;—the way, the thought, the good, shall be wholly strange and new. It shall exclude example and experience. You take the way from man, not to man. All persons that ever existed are its forgotten ministers. Fear and hope are alike beneath it. There is somewhat low even in hope. In the hour of vision there is nothing that can be called gratitude, nor properly joy. The soul raised over passion beholds identity and eternal causation, perceives the self-existence of Truth and Right, and calms itself with knowing that all things go well. Vast spaces of nature, the Atlantic Ocean, the South Sea; long intervals of time, years, centuries, are of no account. This which I think and feel underlay every former state of life and circumstances, as it does underlie my present, and what is called life and what is called death.

Life only avails, not the having lived. Power ceases in the instant of repose; it resides in the moment of transition from a past to a new state, in the shooting of the gulf, in the darting to an aim. This one fact the world hates; that the soul *becomes;* for that forever degrades the past, turns all riches to poverty, all reputation to a shame, confounds the saint with the rogue, shoves Jesus and Judas equally aside. Why then do we prate of self-reliance? Inasmuch as the soul is present there will be power not confident but agent. To talk of reliance is a poor external way of speaking. Speak rather of that which relies because it works and is. Who has more obedience than I masters me, though he should not raise his finger. Round him I must revolve by the gravitation of spirits. We fancy it rhetoric when we speak of eminent virtue. We do not yet see that virtue is Height, and that a man or a company of men, plastic and permeable to principles, by the law of nature must overpower and ride all cities, nations, kings, rich men, poets, who are not.

This is the ultimate fact which we so quickly reach on this, as on every topic, the resolution of all into the ever-blessed ONE. Self-existence is the attribute of the Supreme Cause, and it constitutes the measure of good by the degree in which it enters into all lower forms. All things real are so by so much virtue as they contain. Commerce, husbandry, hunting, whaling, war, eloquence, personal weight, are somewhat, and engage my respect as examples of its presence and impure action. I see the same law working in nature for conservation and growth. Power is, in nature, the essential measure of right. Nature suffers nothing to remain in her kingdoms which cannot help itself. The genesis and maturation of a planet, its poise and orbit, the bended tree recovering itself from the strong wind, the vital resources of every animal and vegetable, are demonstrations of the self-sufficing and therefore self-relying soul.

Thus all concentrates: let us not rove; let us sit at home with the cause. Let us stun and astonish the intruding rabble of men and books and institutions by a simple declaration of the divine fact. Bid the invaders take the shoes from off their feet,[34] for God is here within. Let our simplicity judge them, and our docility to our own law demonstrate the poverty of nature and fortune beside our native riches.

But now we are a mob. Man does not stand in awe of man, nor is his genius admonished to stay at home, to put itself in communication with the internal ocean, but it goes abroad to beg a cup of water of the urns of other men. We must go alone. I like the silent church before the service begins, better than any preaching. How far off, how cool, how chaste the persons look, begirt each one with a precinct or sanctuary! So let us always sit. Why should we assume the faults of our friend, or wife, or father, or child, because they sit around our hearth, or are said to have the same blood? All men have my blood and I all men's. Not for that will I adopt their petulance or folly, even to the extent of being ashamed of it. But your isolation must not be mechanical, but spiritual, that is, must be elevation. At times the whole world seems to be in conspiracy to importune you with emphatic trifles. Friend, client, child, sickness, fear, want, charity, all knock at once at thy closet door and say,—"Come out unto us."[35] But keep thy state; come

[34]God said to Moses, "put off thy shoes from off thy feet, for the place whereon thou standest is holy ground." Exodus 3:5.

[35]"Make an agreement with me by a present, and come out to me." Isaiah 36:16.

not into their confusion. The power men possess to annoy me I give them by a weak curiosity. No man can come near me but through my act. "What we love that we have, but by desire we bereave ourselves of the love."[36]

If we cannot at once rise to the sanctities of obedience and faith, let us at least resist our temptations; let us enter into the state of war and wake Thor and Woden,[37] courage and constancy, in our Saxon breasts. This is to be done in our smooth times by speaking the truth. Check this lying hospitality and lying affection. Live no longer to the expectation of these deceived and deceiving people with whom we converse. Say to them, "O father, O mother, O wife, O brother, O friend, I have lived with you after appearances hitherto. Henceforward I am the truth's. Be it known unto you that henceforward I obey no law less than the eternal law. I will have no covenants but proximities. I shall endeavor to nourish my parents, to support my family, to be the chaste husband of one wife,—but these relations I must fill after a new and unprecedented way. I appeal from your customs. I must be myself. I cannot break myself any longer for you, or you. If you can love me for what I am, we shall be the happier. If you cannot, I will still seek to deserve that you should. I will not hide my tastes or aversions. I will so trust that what is deep is holy, that I will do strongly before the sun and moon whatever inly rejoices me and the heart appoints. If you are noble, I will love you; if you are not, I will not hurt you and myself by hypocritical attentions. If you are true, but not in the same truth with me, cleave to your companions; I will seek my own. I do this not selfishly but humbly and truly. It is alike your interest, and mine, and all men's, however long we have dwelt in lies, to live in truth. Does this sound harsh to-day? You will soon love what is dictated by your nature as well as mine, and if we follow the truth it will bring us out safe at last."—But so may you give these friends pain. Yes, but I cannot sell my liberty and my power, to save their sensibility. Besides, all persons have their moments of reason, when they look out into the region of absolute truth; then will they justify me and do the same thing.

The populace think that your rejection of popular standards is a rejection of all standard, and mere antinomianism,[38] and the bold sensualist will use the name of philosophy to gild his crimes. But the law of consciousness abides. There are two confessionals, in one or the other of which we must be shriven. You may fulfil your round of duties by clearing yourself in the *direct,* or in the *reflex* way. Consider whether you have satisfied your relations to father, mother, cousin, neighbor, town, cat and dog—whether any of these can upbraid you. But I may also neglect this reflex standard and absolve me to myself. I have my own stern claims and perfect circle. It denies the name of duty to many offices that are called duties. But if I can discharge its debts it enables me to dispense with the popular code. If any one imagines that this law is lax, let him keep its commandment one day.

And truly it demands something godlike in him who has cast off the common motives of humanity and has ventured to trust himself for a taskmaster. High be his heart, faithful his will, clear his sight, that he may in good

[36]Emerson's adaptation of an epigram by the German poet Friedrich Schiller (1759–1805).
[37]Thor: Norse god of thunder. Woden: Anglo-Saxon chief god.
[38]Opposition to moral laws, reliance on the power of faith.

earnest be doctrine, society, law, to himself, that a simple purpose may be to him as strong as iron necessity is to others!

If any man consider the present aspects of what is called by distinction *society,* he will see the need of these ethics. The sinew and heart of man seem to be drawn out, and we are become timorous, desponding whimperers. We are afraid of truth, afraid of fortune, afraid of death, and afraid of each other. Our age yields no great and perfect persons. We want men and women who shall renovate life and our social state, but we see that most natures are insolvent, cannot satisfy their own wants, have an ambition out of all proportion to their practical force and do lean and beg day and night continually. Our housekeeping is mendicant, our arts, our occupations, our marriages, our religion we have not chosen, but society has chosen for us. We are parlor soldiers. We shun the rugged battle of fate, where strength is born.

If our young men miscarry in their first enterprises they lose all heart. If the young merchant fails, men say he is *ruined.* If the finest genius studies at one of our colleges and is not installed in an office within one year afterwards in the cities or suburbs of Boston or New York, it seems to his friends and to himself that he is right in being disheartened and in complaining the rest of his life. A sturdy lad from New Hampshire or Vermont, who in turn tries all the professions, who *teams it, farms it, peddles,* keeps a school, preaches, edits a newspaper, goes to Congress, buys a township, and so forth, in successive years, and always like a cat falls on his feet, is worth a hundred of these city dolls. He walks abreast with his days and feels no shame in not "studying a profession," for he does not postpone his life, but lives already. He has not one chance, but a hundred chances. Let a Stoic[39] open the resources of man and tell men they are not leaning willows, but can and must detach themselves; that with the exercise of self-trust, new powers shall appear; that a man is the word made flesh,[40] born to shed healing to the nations;[41] that he should be ashamed of our compassion, and that the moment he acts from himself, tossing the laws, the books, idolatries and customs out of the window, we pity him no more but thank and revere him;—and that teacher shall restore the life of man to splendor and make his name dear to all history.

It is easy to see that a greater self-reliance must work a revolution in all the offices and relations of men; in their religion; in their education; in their pursuits; their modes of living; their association; in their property; in their speculative views.

1. In what prayers do men allow themselves! That which they call a holy office is not so much as brave and manly. Prayer looks abroad and asks for some foreign addition to come through some foreign virtue, and loses itself in endless mazes of natural and supernatural, and mediatorial and miraculous. Prayer that craves a particular commodity, anything less than all good, is vicious. Prayer is the contemplation of the facts of life from the highest point of view. It is the soliloquy of a beholding and jubilant soul. It is the spirit of God pronouncing his works good.[42] But prayer as a means to effect a private

[39]Stoic philosophers of ancient Greece taught that men should be passionless and independent.
[40]"The Word was made flesh and dwelt among us. . . ." John 1:14.
[41]". . . the leaves of the tree were for the healing of the nations." Revelation 22:2.
[42]"And God saw everything that he had made, and, behold, it was very good." Genesis 1:31.

end is meanness and theft. It supposes dualism and not unity in nature and consciousness. As soon as the man is at one with God, he will not beg. He will then see prayer in all action. The prayer of the farmer kneeling in his field to weed it, the prayer of the rower kneeling with the stroke of his oar, are true prayers heard throughout nature, though for cheap ends. Caratach, in Fletcher's "Bonduca,"[43] when admonished to inquire the mind of the god Audate, replies,—

> His hidden meaning lies in our endeavors;
> Our valors are our best gods.

Another sort of false prayers are our regrets. Discontent is the want of self-reliance: it is infirmity of will. Regret calamities if you can thereby help the sufferer; if not, attend your own work and already the evil begins to be repaired. Our sympathy is just as base. We come to them who weep foolishly and sit down and cry for company, instead of imparting to them truth and health in rough electric shocks, putting them once more in communication with their own reason. The secret of fortune is joy in our hands. Welcome evermore to gods and men is the self-helping man. For him all doors are flung wide; him all tongues greet, all honors crown, all eyes follow with desire. Our love goes out to him and embraces him because he did not need it. We solicitously and apologetically caress and celebrate him because he held on his way and scorned our disapprobation. The gods love him because men hated him. "To the persevering mortal," said Zoroaster,[44] "the blessed Immortals are swift."

As men's prayers are a disease of the will, so are their creeds a disease of the intellect. They say with those foolish Israelites, "Let not God speak to us, lest we die. Speak thou, speak any man with us, and we will obey."[45] Everywhere I am hindered of meeting God in my brother, because he has shut his own temple doors and recites fables merely of his brother's, or his brother's brother's God. Every new mind is a new classification. If it prove a mind of uncommon activity and power, a Locke, a Lavoisier, a Hutton, a Bentham, a Fourier,[46] it imposes its classification on other men, and lo! a new system. In proportion to the depth of the thought, and so to the number of the objects it touches and brings within reach of the pupil, is his complacency. But chiefly is this apparent in creeds and churches, which are also classifications of some powerful mind acting on the elemental thought of duty and man's relation to the Highest. Such is Calvinism, Quakerism, Swedenborgism. The pupil takes the same delight in subordinating every thing to the new terminology as a girl who has just learned botany in seeing a new earth and new seasons thereby. It will happen for a time that the pupil will find his intellectual power has grown by the study of his master's

[43]Elizabethan drama (c. 1614) by John Fletcher (1579–1625).

[44]Religious leader of ancient Persia. The quotation is from "The Chaldean Oracles of Zoroaster" (1832).

[45]The words said by the Israelites to Moses after he had spoken with God and had brought them the Ten Commandments. Exodus 20:1–19.

[46]John Locke (1632–1704), English philosopher; Antoine Lavoisier (1743–1794), French chemist; James Hutton (1726–1797), English geologist; Jeremy Bentham (1748–1832), English philosopher; François Fourier (1772–1837), French social reformer.

mind. But in all unbalanced minds the classification is idolized, passes for the end and not for a speedily exhaustible means, so that the walls of the system blend to their eye in the remote horizon with the walls of the universe; the luminaries of heaven seem to them hung on the arch their master built. They cannot imagine how you aliens have any right to see,—how you can see; "It must be somehow that you stole the light from us." They do not yet perceive that light, unsystematic, indomitable, will break into any cabin, even into theirs. Let them chirp awhile and call it their own. If they are honest and do well, presently their neat new pinfold[47] will be too strait and low, will crack, will lean, will rot and vanish, and the immortal light, all young and joyful, million-orbed, million-colored, will beam over the universe as on the first morning.

2. It is for want of self-culture that the superstition of Travelling, whose idols are Italy, England, Egypt, retains its fascination for all educated Americans. They who made England, Italy, or Greece venerable in the imagination, did so by sticking fast where they were, like an axis of the earth. In manly hours we feel that duty is our place. The soul is no traveller; the wise man stays at home, and when his necessities, his duties, on any occasion call him from his house, or into foreign lands, he is at home still and shall make men sensible by the expression of his countenance that he goes, the missionary of wisdom and virtue, and visits cities and men like a sovereign and not like an interloper or a valet.

I have no churlish objection to the circumnavigation of the globe for the purposes of art, of study, and benevolence, so that the man is first domesticated, or does not go abroad with the hope of finding somewhat greater than he knows. He who travels to be amused, or to get somewhat which he does not carry, travels away from himself, and grows old even in youth among old things. In Thebes, in Palmyra,[48] his will and mind have become old and dilapidated as they. He carries ruins to ruins.

Travelling is a fool's paradise. Our first journeys discover to us the indifference of places. At home I dream that at Naples, at Rome, I can be intoxicated with beauty and lose my sadness. I pack my trunk, embrace my friends, embark on the sea and at last wake up in Naples, and there beside me is the stern fact, the sad self, unrelenting, identical, that I fled from. I seek the Vatican and the palaces. I affect to be intoxicated with sights and suggestions, but I am not intoxicated. My giant goes with me wherever I go.

3. But the rage of travelling is a symptom of a deeper unsoundness affecting the whole intellectual action. The intellect is vagabond, and our system of education fosters restlessness. Our minds travel when our bodies are forced to stay at home. We initiate; and what is imitation but the travelling of the mind? Our houses are built with foreign taste; our shelves are garnished with foreign ornaments; our opinions, our tastes, our faculties, lean, and follow the Past and the Distant. The soul created the arts wherever they have flourished. It was in his own mind that the artist sought his model. It was an application of his own thought to the thing to be done and the conditions to be observed. And why need we copy the Doric or the Gothic model? Beauty,

[47]Animal pen.
[48]Ancient ruined cities in Egypt and Syria.

convenience, grandeur of thought and quaint expression are as near to us as to any, and if the American artist will study with hope and love the precise thing to be done by him, considering the climate, the soil, the length of the day, the wants of the people, the habit and form of the government, he will create a house in which all these will find themselves fitted, and taste and sentiment will be satisfied also.

Insist on yourself; never imitate. Your own gift you can present every moment with the cumulative force of a whole life's cultivation; but of the adopted talent of another you have only an extemporaneous half possession. That which each can do best, none but his Maker can teach him. No man yet knows what it is, nor can, till that person has exhibited it. Where is the master who could have taught Shakespeare? Where is the master who could have instructed Franklin, or Washington, or Bacon, or Newton? Every great man is a unique. The Scipionism of Scipio is precisely that part he could not borrow. Shakespeare will never be made by the study of Shakespeare. Do that which is assigned you, and you cannot hope too much or dare too much. There is at this moment for you an utterance brave and grand as that of the colossal chisel of Phidias,[49] or trowel of the Egyptians, or the pen of Moses or Dante, but different from all these. Not possibly will the soul, all rich, all eloquent, with thousand-cloven tongue,[50] deign to repeat itself; but if you can hear what these patriarchs say, surely you can reply to them in the same pitch of voice; for the ear and the tongue are two organs of one nature. Abide in the simple and noble regions of thy life, obey thy heart, and thou shalt reproduce the Foreworld again.

4. As our Religion, our Education, our Art look abroad, so does our spirit of society. All men plume themselves on the improvement of society, and no man improves.

Society never advances. It recedes as fast on one side as it gains on the other. It undergoes continual changes; it is barbarous, it is civilized, it is christianized, it is rich, it is scientific; but this change is not amelioration. For every thing that is given something is taken. Society acquires new arts and loses old instincts. What a contrast between the well-clad, reading, writing, thinking American, with a watch, a pencil and a bill of exchange in his pocket, and the naked New Zealander, whose property is a club, a spear, a mat and an undivided twentieth of a shed to sleep under! But compare the health of the two men and you shall see that the white man has lost his aboriginal strength. If the traveller tell us truly, strike the savage with a broad-axe and in a day or two the flesh will unite and heal as if you struck the blow into soft pitch, and the same blow shall send the white to his grave.

The civilized man has built a coach, but has lost the use of his feet. He is supported on crutches, but lacks so much support of muscle. He has a fine Geneva watch, but he fails of the skill to tell the hour by the sun. A Greenwich nautical almanac he has, and so being sure of the information when he

[49]Greek sculptor (fifth century B.C.).

[50]"And when the day of Pentecost was fully come, they were all with one accord in one place. . . . And they were all filled with the Holy Ghost, and began to speak with other tongues. . . ." Acts 2:1–4.

wants it, the man in the street does not know a star in the sky. The solstice he does not observe; the equinox he knows as little; and the whole bright calendar of the year is without a dial in his mind. His note-books impair his memory; his libraries overload his wit; the insurance-office increases the number of accidents; and it may be a question whether machinery does not encumber; whether we have not lost by refinement some energy, by a Christianity, entrenched in establishments and forms, some vigor of wild virtue. For every Stoic was a Stoic; but in Christendom where is the Christian?

There is no more deviation in the moral standard than in the standard of height or bulk. No greater men are now than ever were. A singular equality may be observed between the great men of the first and of the last ages; nor can all the science, art, religion, and philosophy of the nineteenth century avail to educate greater men than Plutarch's[51] heroes, three or four and twenty centuries ago. Not in time is the race progressive. Phocion,[52] Socrates, Anaxagoras, Diogenes,[53] are great men, but they leave no class. He who is really of their class will not be called by their name, but will be his own man, and in his turn the founder of a sect. The arts and inventions of each period are only its costume and do not invigorate men. The harm of the improved machinery may compensate its good. Hudson and Behring[54] accomplished so much in their fishing-boats as to astonish Parry and Franklin,[55] whose equipment exhausted the resources of science and art. Galileo,[56] with an opera-glass, discovered a more splendid series of celestial phenomena than any one since. Columbus found the New World in an undecked boat. It is curious to see the periodical disuse and perishing of means and machinery which were introduced with loud laudation a few years or centuries before. The great genius returns to essential man. We reckoned the improvements of the art of war among the triumphs of science, and yet Napoleon conquered Europe by the bivouac,[57] which consisted of falling back on naked valor and disencumbering it of all aids. The Emperor held it impossible to make a perfect army, says Las Cases,[58] "without abolishing our arms, magazines, commissaries and carriages, until, in imitation of the Roman custom, the soldier should receive his supply of corn, grind it in his hand-mill and bake his bread himself."

Society is a wave. The wave moves onward, but the water of which it is composed does not. The same particle does not rise from the valley to the ridge. Its unity is only phenomenal. The persons who make up a nation today, next year die, and their experience dies with them.

[51]Greek biographer (c. 46–c. 120) of noble Romans and Greeks.

[52]Greek statesman and military leader (402?–317 B.C.).

[53]Classical Greek philosophers.

[54]Henry Hudson (d. 1611), English explorer; Vitus Bering (1680–1741), Danish explorer.

[55]Sir William Edward Parry (1790–1855) and Sir John Franklin (1786–1847), English Arctic explorers.

[56]Italian physicist and astronomer (1564–1642), developer of the telescope.

[57]A temporary encampment with little shelter, hence a campaign conducted without the encumbrance of elaborate systems of supply.

[58]Comte Emmanuel Augustin de Las Cases (1766–1842), French historian, author of a book of Napoleon's comments.

And so, the reliance on Property, including the reliance on governments which protect it, is the want of self-reliance. Men have looked away from themselves and at things so long that they have come to esteem the religious, learned and civil institutions as guards of property, and they deprecate assaults on these, because they feel them to be assaults on property. They measure their esteem of each other by what each has, and not by what each is. But a cultivated man becomes ashamed of his property, out of new respect for his nature. Especially he hates what he has if he sees that it is accidental,—came to him by inheritance, or gift, or crime; then he feels that it is not having; it does not belong to him, has no root in him and merely lies there because no revolution or no robber takes it away. But that which a man is, does always by necessity acquire; and what the man acquires, is living property, which does not wait the beck of rulers, or mobs, or revolutions, or fire, or storm, or bankruptcies, but perpetually renews itself wherever the man breathes. "Thy lot or portion of life," said the Caliph Ali,[59] "is seeking after thee; therefore be at rest from seeking after it." Our dependence on these foreign goods leads us to our slavish respect for numbers. The political parties meet in numerous conventions; the greater the concourse and with each new uproar of announcement, The delegation from Essex![60] The Democrats from New Hampshire! The Whigs of Maine! the young patriot feels himself stronger than before by a new thousand of eyes and arms. In like manner the reformers summon conventions and vote and resolve in multitude. Not so, O friends! will the God deign to enter and inhabit you, but by a method precisely the reverse. It is only as a man puts off all foreign support and stands alone that I see him to be strong and to prevail. He is weaker by every recruit to his banner. Is not a man better than a town? Ask nothing of men, and, in the endless mutation, thou only firm column must presently appear the upholder of all that surrounds thee. He who knows that power is inborn, that he is weak because he has looked for good out of him and elsewhere, and, so perceiving, throws himself unhesitatingly on his thought, instantly rights himself, stands in the erect position, commands his limbs, works miracles; just as a man who stands on his feet is stronger than a man who stands on his head.

So use all that is called Fortune. Most men gamble with her, and gain all, and lose all, as her wheel rolls. But do thou leave as unlawful these winnings, and deal with Cause and Effect, the chancellors of God. In the Will work and acquire, and thou hast chained the wheel of Chance, and shall sit hereafter out of fear from her rotations. A political victory, a rise of rents, the recovery of your sick or the return of your absent friend, or some other favorable event raises your spirits, and you think good days are preparing for you. Do not believe it. Nothing can bring you peace but yourself. Nothing can bring you peace but the triumph of principles.

1832–1840 1841

[59]Ali ibn-abi-Talib (600?–661), fourth Muslim Caliph of Mecca.
[60]County in Massachusetts.

THE RHODORA:[1]

ON BEING ASKED, WHENCE IS THE FLOWER?

In May, when sea-winds pierced our solitudes,
I found the fresh Rhodora in the woods,
Spreading its leafless blooms in a damp nook,
To please the desert and the sluggish brook.
The purple petals, fallen in the pool,
Made the black water with their beauty gay;
Here might the red-bird come his plumes to cool,
And court the flower that cheapens his array.
Rhodora! if the sages ask thee why
This charm is wasted on the earth and sky,
Tell them, dear, that if eyes were made for seeing,
Then Beauty is its own excuse for being:
Why thou wert there, O rival of the rose!
I never thought to ask, I never knew:
But, in my simple ignorance, suppose
The self-same Power that brought me there brought you.
1834 1839

EACH AND ALL

Little thinks, in the field, yon red-cloaked clown[1]
Of thee from the hill-top looking down;
The heifer that lows in the upland farm,
Far-heard, lows not thine ear to charm;
The sexton, tolling his bell at noon,
Deems not that great Napoleon
Stops his horse, and lists with delight,
Whilst his files sweep round yon Alpine height;
Nor knowest thou what argument
Thy life to thy neighbor's creed has lent.
All are needed by each one;
Nothing is fair or good alone.
I thought the sparrow's note from heaven,
Singing at dawn on the alder bough;
I brought him home, in his nest, at even;
He sings the song, but it cheers not now,
For I did not bring home the river and sky;—
He sang to my ear,—they sang to my eye.
The delicate shells lay on the shore;
The bubbles of the latest wave
Fresh pearls to their enamel gave,
And the bellowing of the savage sea
Greeted their safe escape to me.

[1]A shrub, found in New England, related to the rhododendron.
[1]Used here in the sense of "peasant" or "rustic."

I wiped away the weeds and foam,
I fetched my sea-born treasures home;
But the poor, unsightly, noisome[2] things
Had left their beauty on the shore
With the sun and the sand and the wild uproar.
The lover watched his graceful maid,
As 'mid the virgin train she strayed,
Nor knew her beauty's best attire
Was woven still by the snow-white choir.
At last she came to this hermitage,
Like the bird from the woodlands to the cage;—
The gay enchantment was undone,
A gentle wife, but fairy none.
Then I said, "I covet truth;
Beauty is unripe childhood's cheat;
I leave it behind with the games of youth:"—
As I spoke, beneath my feet
The ground-pine curled its pretty wreath,
Running over the club-moss[3] burrs;
I inhaled the violet's breath;
Around me stood the oaks and firs;
Pine-cones and acorns lay on the ground;
Over me soared the eternal sky,
Full of light and of deity;
Again I saw, again I heard,
The rolling river, the morning bird;—
Beauty through my senses stole;
I yielded myself to the perfect whole.
1834? 1839

CONCORD HYMN

SUNG AT THE COMPLETION OF THE BATTLE MONUMENT, JULY 4, 1837[1]

By the rude bridge that arched the flood,
  Their flag to April's breeze unfurled,
Here once the embattled farmers stood
  And fired the shot heard round the world.

The foe long since in silence slept;
  Alike the conqueror silent sleeps;
And Time the ruined bridge has swept
  Down the dark stream which seaward creeps.

On this green bank, by this soft stream,
  We set to-day a votive stone;[2]

[2]Annoying. [3]Low-growing plants with evergreen leaves.

[1]A printed leaflet containing the poem was distributed at the dedication of the monument commemorating the Battles of Lexington and Concord (April 19, 1775).

[2]I.e., a stone monument built in fulfillment of a vow.

That memory may their deed redeem,
  When, like our sires, our sons are gone.

Spirit, that made those heroes dare
  To die, and leave their children free,
Bid Time and Nature gently spare
  The shaft we raise to them and thee.

1837 1837

THE PROBLEM

I like a church; I like a cowl;[1]
I love a prophet of the soul;
And on my heart monastic aisles
Fall like sweet strains, or pensive smiles;
Yet not for all his faith can see
Would I that cowlèd churchman be.

Why should the vest[2] on him allure,
Which I could not on me endure?

Not from a vain or shallow thought
His awful Jove young Phidias[3] brought;
Never from lips of cunning fell
The thrilling Delphic oracle;[4]
Out from the heart of nature rolled
The burdens of the Bible old;
The litanies of nations came,
Like the volcano's tongue of flame,
Up from the burning core below,—
The canticles of love and woe:
The hand that rounded Peter's dome
And groined the aisles of Christian Rome[5]
Wrought in a sad sincerity;
Himself from God he could not free;
He builded better than he knew;—
The conscious stone to beauty grew.

Know'st thou what wove yon woodbird's nest
Of leaves, and feathers from her breast?
Or how the fish outbuilt her shell,
Painting with morn each annual cell?
Or how the sacred pine-tree[6] adds
To her old leaves new myriads?
Such and so grew these holy piles,
Whilst love and terror laid the tiles.

[1]A monk's hood. [2]Vestment, ceremonial clothing.
[3]Athenian sculptor (fifth century B.C.). His masterpiece was a statue of Zeus (Jove).
[4]The divine prophecies uttered at the temple of Apollo at Delphi, Greece.
[5]Michelangelo designed the dome of St. Peter's and the vaulted ceilings of several Roman churches.
[6]The pine, symbol of creativity, was sacred to the Greek fertility god Dionysus.

Earth proudly wears the Parthenon,[7]
As the best gem upon her zone,[8]
And Morning opes with haste her lids
To gaze upon the Pyramids;
O'er England's abbeys bends the sky,
As on its friends, with kindred eye;
For out of Thought's interior sphere
These wonders rose to upper air;
And Nature gladly gave them place,
Adopted them into her race,
And granted them an equal date
With Andes and with Ararat.[9]

These temples grew as grows the grass;
Art might obey, but not surpass.
The passive Master[10] lent his hand
To the vast soul that o'er him planned;
And the same power that reared the shrine
Bestrode the tribes that knelt within.
Ever the fiery Pentecost[11]
Girds with one flame the countless host,
Trances the heart through chanting choirs,
And through the priest the mind inspires.
The word unto the prophet spoken
Was writ on tables yet unbroken[12]
The word by seers or sibyls told,
In groves of oak, or fanes[13] of gold,
Still floats upon the morning wind,
Still whispers to the willing mind.
One accent of the Holy Ghost
The heedless world hath never lost.
I know what say the fathers wise,—
The Book itself before me lies,
Old *Chrysostom,*[14] best Augustine,[15]
And he who blent both in his line,
The younger *Golden Lips* or mines,
Taylor,[16] the Shakespeare of divines.[17]
His words are music in my ear,
I see his cowlèd portrait dear;
And yet, for all his faith could see,
I would not the good bishop be.

1839 1840

[7]Temple of Athena, built on the Acropolis in Athens (447–438 B.C.). [8]Girdle, belt.

[9]Andes: mountain range in South America; Ararat: mountain in Turkey where Noah's Ark landed. Genesis 8:4. [10]Creative artist.

[11]On the Day of Pentecost, the Holy Spirit descended on the Apostles in "cloven tongues like as of fire," Acts 2:1–3.

[12]When Moses saw the Israelites worshipping the golden idol, he broke the stone tables or tablets on which God had written the Ten Commandments. Exodus 32:1–20. [13]Temples.

[14]St. John of Antioch (345?–407), named "Chrysostom" (Greek: Golden Lips) for his eloquence.

[15]St. Augustine (354–430), author of *The City of God* and *Confessions.*

[16]Jeremy Taylor (1613–1667), English theologian. [17]Clergymen, priests.

ODE

INSCRIBED TO W. H. CHANNING[1]

Though loath to grieve
The evil time's sole patriot,
I cannot leave
My honied thought
For the priest's cant,[2]
Or statesman's rant.

If I refuse
My study for their politique,
Which at best is trick,
The angry Muse
Puts confusion in my brain.

But who is he that prates
Of the culture of mankind,
Of better arts and life?
Go, blindworm, go,
Behold the famous States
Harrying Mexico
With rifle and with knife![3]

Or who, with accent bolder,
Dare praise the freedom-loving mountaineer?
I found by thee, O rushing Contoocook![4]
And in thy valleys, Agiochook![5]
The jackals of the negro-holder.[6]

The God who made New Hampshire
Taunted the lofty land
With little men;—
Small bat and wren
House in the oak:—
If earth-fire cleave
The upheaved land, and bury the folk,
The southern crocodile would grieve.
Virtue palters;[7] Right is hence;
Freedom praised, but hid;
Funeral eloquence
Rattles the coffin-lid.

[1]William Henry Channing (1810–1884), clergyman, abolitionist, and nephew of William Ellery Channing (1780–1842), Unitarian leader.

[2]Jargon; insincere, pious words.

[3]The Mexican War (1846–1848). Emerson opposed the war on grounds that it was an effort to extend slavery.

[4]River in New Hampshire.

[5]The White Mountains of New Hampshire.

[6]I.e., those who hunted escaped slaves for rewards offered by their owners (holders).

[7]Hesitates, acts insincerely.

What boots[8] thy zeal,
O glowing friend,
That would indignant rend
The northland from the south?
Wherefore? to what good end?
Boston Bay and Bunker Hill
Would serve things still;—Things are of the snake.

The horseman serves the horse,
The neatherd[9] serves the neat,
The merchant serves the purse,
The eater serves his meat;
'Tis the day of the chattel,
Web to weave, and corn to grind;
Things are in the saddle,
And ride mankind.

There are two laws discrete,[10]
Not reconciled,—
Law for man, and law for thing;
The last builds town and fleet,
But it runs wild,
And doth the man unking.

'Tis fit the forest fall,
The steep be graded,
The mountain tunnelled,
The sand shaded,
The orchard planted,
The glebe[11] tilled,
The prairie granted,
The steamer built.

Let man serve law for man;
Live for friendship, live for love,
For truth's and harmony's behoof;[12]
The state may follow how it can,
As Olympus follows Jove.[13]

Yet do not I implore
The wrinkled shopman to my sounding woods,
Nor bid the unwilling senator
Ask votes of thrushes in the solitudes.
Every one to his chosen work;—
Foolish hands may mix and mar;
Wise and sure the issues are.
Round they roll till dark is light,
Sex to sex, and even to odd;—

[8]Avails, profits. [9]The neat (cow) herder, the cowboy. [10]Distinct.
[11]Field. [12]Benefit.
[13]Zeus (Jove), chief diety of Greek myth and leader of the Olympian gods.

The over-god
Who marries Right to Might,
Who peoples, unpeoples,—
He who exterminates
Races by stronger races,
Black by white faces,—
Knows to bring honey
Out of the lion;[14]
Grafts gentlest scion
On pirate and Turk.

The Cossack eats Poland,[15]
Like stolen fruit;
Her last noble is ruined,
Her last poet mute:
Straight, into double band
The victors divide;
Half for freedom strike and stand;—
The astonished Muse finds thousands at her side.
1846 1847

HAMATREYA[1]

Bulkeley, Hunt, Willard, Hosmer, Meriam, Flint,[2]
Possessed the land which rendered to their toil
Hay, corn, roots, hemp, flax, apples, wool, and wood.
Each of these landlords walked amidst his farm,
Saying, " 'Tis mine, my children's and my name's.
How sweet the west wind sounds in my own trees!
How graceful climb those shadows on my hill!
I fancy these pure waters and the flags[3]
Know me, as does my dog: we sympathize;
And, I affirm, my actions smack of the soil."

Where are these men? Asleep beneath their grounds:
And strangers, fond[4] as they, their furrows plough.
Earth laughs in flowers, to see her boastful boys
Earth-proud, proud of the earth which is not theirs;
Who steer the plough, but cannot steer their feet
Clear of the grave.
They added ridge to valley, brook to pond,
And sighed for all that bounded their domain;

[14]Samson found "honey in the carcass of a lion." Judges 14:8.

[15]Reference to the repeated Russian attempts, in recent centuries, to subjugate Poland.

[1]In 1845, Emerson copied into his journal a passage from the sacred Hindu book *Vishnu Purana:* "Kings who with perishable frames have possessed this ever-enduring world, and who . . . have indulged the feeling that suggests 'This earth is mine. . . .' have all passed away. . . . Earth laughs. . . . I will repeat to you, Maitreya, the stanzas that were chanted by Earth." The title, "Hamatreya," is probably derived from "Maitreya," the Hindu god named in the *Vishnu Purana,* or possibly it comes from Greek words meaning "Earth-Mother."

[2]First settlers of Concord, Massachusetts. [3]Wild irises. [4]Foolish.

"This suits me for a pasture; that's my park;
We must have clay, lime, gravel, granite-ledge,
And misty lowland, where to go for peat.
The land is well,—lies fairly to the south.
'Tis good, when you have crossed the sea and back,
To find the sitfast acres where you left them."
Ah! the hot owner sees not Death, who adds
Him to his land, a lump of mould the more.
Hear what the Earth says;—

EARTH-SONG

'Mine and yours;
Mine, not yours.
Earth endures;
Stars abide—
Shine down in the old sea;
Old are the shores;
But where are the old men?
I who have seen much,
Such have I never seen.

'The lawyer's deed
Ran sure,
In tail,[5]
To them, and to their heirs
Who shall succeed,
Without fail,
Forevermore.

'Here is the land,
Shaggy with wood,
With its old valley,
Mound and flood.
But the heritors?—
Fled like the flood's foam.
The lawyer, and the laws,
And the kingdom,
Clean swept herefrom.

'They called me theirs,
Who so controlled me;
Yet every one
Wished to stay, and is gone.
How am I theirs,
If they cannot hold me,
But I hold them?'

When I heard the Earth-song,
I was no longer brave;
My avarice cooled
Like lust in the chill of the grave.

[5]Variant of "entail," the legal system of restricting inheritance.

GIVE ALL TO LOVE

Give all to love;
Obey thy heart;
Friends, kindred, days,
Estate, good-fame,
Plans, credit and the Muse,—
Nothing refuse.

'Tis a brave master;
Let it have scope:
Follow it utterly,
Hope beyond hope:
High and more high
It dives into noon,
With wing unspent,
Untold intent;
But it is a god,
Knows its own path
And the outlets of the sky.

It was never for the mean;
It requireth courage stout.
Souls above doubt,
Valor unbending,
It will reward,—
They shall return
More than they were,
And ever ascending.

Leave all for love;
Yet, hear me, yet,
One word more thy heart behoved,
One pulse more of firm endeavor,—
Keep thee to-day,
To-morrow, forever,
Free as an Arab
Of thy beloved.

Cling with life to the maid;
But when the surprise
First vague shadow of surmise
Flits across her bosom young,
Of a joy apart from thee,
Free be she, fancy-free;
Nor thou detain her vesture's hem,
Nor the palest rose she flung
From her summer diadem.

Though thou loved her as thyself,
As a self of purer clay,

Though her parting dims the day,
Stealing grave from all alive;
Heartily know,
When half-gods go,
The gods arrive.
1846 1847

DAYS

Daughters of Time, the hypocritic Days,
Muffled and dumb like barefoot dervishes,[1]
And marching single in an endless file,
Bring diadems and fagots[2] in their hands.
To each they offer gifts after his will,
Bread, kingdoms, stars, and sky that holds them all.
I, in my pleached[3] garden, watched the pomp,
Forgot my morning wishes, hastily
Took a few herbs and apples, and the Day
Turned and departed silent. I, too late,
Under her solemn fillet[4] saw the scorn.
1851 1857

BRAHMA[1]

If the red slayer[2] think he slays,
  Or if the slain think he is slain,
They know not well the subtle ways
  I keep, and pass, and turn again.

Far or forgot to me is near;
  Shadow and sunlight are the same;
The vanished gods to me appear;
  And one to me are shame and fame.

They reckon ill who leave me out;
  When me they fly, I am the wings;
I am the doubter and the doubt,
  And I the hymn the Brahmin sings.

The strong gods[3] pine for my abode,
  And pine in vain the sacred Seven,[4]
But thou, meek lover of the good!
  Find me, and turn thy back on heaven.
1856 1857

[1]Members of a Muslim religious order who have taken vows of poverty and live as wandering friars.
[2]I.e., bring jewelled crowns and bundles of sticks.
[3]Shaded with interlaced branches. [4]Headband.
[1]Brahma (or Brahman) is the supreme spirit in Hindu theology. [2]Death.
[3]Indra, god of the sky; Agni, god of fire; Yama, god of death. As secondary gods they, like mortals, seek reunion with the supreme god. [4]The highest saints of Hinduism.

Nathaniel Hawthorne 1804–1864 

When he was a young man, Nathaniel Hawthorne wrote, "I do not want to be a doctor and live by men's diseases, nor a minister to live by their sins, nor a lawyer and live by their quarrels. So, I don't see that there is anything left for me but to be an author." Yet Hawthorne, as an author, created tales and romances that probed deeply into the very diseases, sins, and quarrels he had once sought to avoid.

Hawthorne's literary imagination was strongly shaped by his early life in Salem, Massachusetts, where he was born on the fourth of July 1804. The history of Salem and American Puritanism provided a background against which he later presented his ideas about human nature, about sin and guilt, and about the perils of the intellect and the pleasures of the heart.

Hawthorne was himself the descendant of a line of Puritan worthies. His first ancestor in America, William Hathorne (the novelist himself later added the "w" to his family name), arrived in Salem in 1630. He became a colonial magistrate known for his persecution of Quakers. William's son John Hathorne won notoriety as one of the Puritan interrogators of those accused of witchcraft in Salem in 1692.

In the next century, Hawthorne's family, like Salem itself, declined from its early prominence and wealth. Nathaniel's father went to sea as a boy and rose to the rank of ship captain, but when Nathaniel was four years old, in 1808, his father died on a long voyage to the Caribbean. Nathaniel's widowed mother, with three children and little money, was forced to move her family into her brother's home, where she withdrew from life and spent her remaining years as a recluse. Her only son grew up as a solitary child who listened to stories of early Salem, read deeply in colonial history, and developed an intense awareness of his Puritan ancestors: "strong traits of their nature," he later observed, "have intertwined themselves with mine."

In 1821 he was sent to Bowdoin College in Brunswick, Maine. There he was a classmate of Longfellow and of Franklin Pierce, who later became the fourteenth President of the United States. After graduating in 1825, Hawthorne returned to Salem and a life of isolation and seclusion that lasted for twelve years. In 1837 he wrote to Longfellow, "I have been carried apart from the main current of life. . . . I have secluded myself from society. . . . I have made a captive of myself and put me into a dungeon; and now I cannot find the key to let me out. . . . "

In his third floor room of his uncle's house, Hawthorne spent hours in solitude, reading and making attempts at writing fiction. In 1828 he drew on his experiences as a student at Bowdoin to write an amateurish novel, Fanshawe, which he published anonymously at his own expense. It was a failure and Hawthorne later tried to destroy all remaining copies. In 1830 his first published tale appeared in the Salem Gazette, and he was soon writing stories that were published in magazines and in annual giftbooks printed in New York and Boston. For six months in 1836 he edited a Boston monthly, The American Magazine of Useful and Entertaining Knowledge, for which he wrote, with the help of his sister, almost the entire contents of each issue. When a disastrous fire brought the magazine to bankruptcy, Hawthorne resigned and wrote a children's history of the world that eventually sold over a million copies, but earned him a fee of only $100.

Hawthorne's first collection of short stores, Twice Told Tales (1837), brought him critical acclaim, but he was still unable to make his living as a writer. With the help of influential friends, he secured a government job as a measurer in the United States Customhouse in Boston. But after two years he quit, using his savings to buy a membership in Brook Farm, a rural Utopian commune just outside Boston. Brook Farm *had been established to join "intellectual and manual labor . . . to combine the thinker and the worker." For Hawthorne the experiment at communal living was a failure, and he withdrew after six months of too much manual labor and too little time to write. He then married and moved to Concord, Massachusetts, where he rented the "Old Manse," a house built by the grandfather of Ralph Waldo Emerson.*

In Concord, Hawthorne developed friendships with his neighbors Emerson, Thoreau, Ellery Channing, and Amos Bronson Alcott; and he turned once again to writing the sketches and tales he called "allegories of the heart." Another collection of his short stories, Mosses from an Old Manse, *was published in 1846, but it too earned him little money, and Hawthorne again called on politically powerful friends to help him obtain a government post. In 1846 he was appointed Surveyor of the United States Customhouse at Salem, but kept the position for only three years. In 1848 the election of Zachary Taylor to the presidency brought a different political party into power, and in 1849 Hawthorne, along with other appointees of the previous administration, was dismissed from office. He then began the novel that was to be his masterpiece,* The Scarlet Letter.

Hawthorne had judged that he was "the obscurest man of letters in America," but publication of The Scarlet Letter *(1850) brought him wide recognition. He was called "the greatest living American writer born in the present century." And even the critics who wanted to give him a "scorching rebuke," for daring to portray "unchaste crimes," acknowledged that he wrote with "all the fascination of genius, and all the charm of a highly polished style." With his literary reputation now clearly established and with sales of* The Scarlet Letter *easing his poverty, Hawthorne left Salem and moved his family to Lenox, in western Massachusetts. There Herman Melville, who was writing* Moby Dick, *was a neighbor and soon became a friend and frequent visitor.*

In Lenox, Hawthorne completed The House of Seven Gables *(1851). The next year* The Blithedale Romance, *a satirical dissection of the Brook Farm colony, appeared, and in the same year Hawthorne published* The Life of Franklin Pierce, *a presidential campaign biography of his college classmate. When Pierce was elected, Hawthorne was rewarded with appointment to the lucrative post of United States consul in Liverpool, England. He served as consul from 1853 to 1857. The next year he traveled to Italy, where he began* The Marble Faun *(1860), the novel of Americans in Europe that was his last completed work of fiction. Finally, in 1860, after seven years in Europe, Hawthorne returned to America and Concord, to live in the house he had purchased and named "The Wayside." Four years later, while on a vacation tour of New Hampshire with his old friend Franklin Pierce, Hawthorne died. On May 23, 1864, he was buried in Sleepy Hollow cemetery in Concord.*

Hawthorne had eventually prospered in the world and found fame. He had grown away from his early ways of solitude and become a man of his age, a literary laborer who could grind out popular history and potboiling magazine articles, children's stories, travel sketches, and gothic tales aimed at the markets of popular journalism. But his greatest achievement came from what Melville called his "great power of blackness," his portrayal of the dark landscape of the human mind. Hawthorne was a romantic whose short stories and novels (or "romances" as he called them) are marked by a concern with the American past, with the role of the imaginative artist in a materialistic society. He affirmed the virtues of the imagination and of human emotions and emphasized the perils of cold intellect. D. H. Lawrence called him a "blue-eyed darling" who knew "disagreeable things in his inner soul," but "was careful to send them out in disguise." Poe and Henry James scolded him for being too allegorical, a weakness

Hawthorne once acknowledged by saying, "I am not quite sure that I entirely comprehend my own meaning in some of these blasted allegories."

In his allegories of the mind and heart, Hawthorne used masks, veils, shadows, emblems, ironies, and ambiguities to portray the narrow separation between good and evil, to show humanity's foolish attempts to unlock the mysteries of nature. Hawthorne's moral and religious concerns were central to his literary art. His repeated portrayal of hidden sin and the individual's confrontation with evil led Melville to see in Hawthorne "That Calvinistic sense of Innate Depravity and Original Sin, from whose visitations, in some shape or other, no deeply thinking mind is always and wholly free."

Because Hawthorne wrote of the corrosive power of human isolation, biographers have portrayed him as a castaway from life, like the characters who filled his greatest stories. He has been called a writer haunted by ancestral ghosts and overburdened with a sense of gloom and guilt. He has also been identified as a novelist of social protest, as a novelist of the Christian tradition, and as a novelist of things "terrible, uncontrollable, and therefore demoralizing *in human nature." Yet his fiction displays a richness and a multiplicity of meanings that rise above the dogma of any single orthodoxy. "My writings," he once said, "do not appeal to the broadest class of sympathies," but the judgment of posterity is otherwise, for Hawthorne made his work contemporary and yet timeless, with insights into moral isolation and human emotion that give dramatic form to the ambiguities of life and the dilemmas of humankind.*

FURTHER READING: *The Centenary Edition of the Works of Nathaniel Hawthorne,* 22 vols., ed. W. Charvat, et al., 1962–1997; A. Turner, *Nathaniel Hawthorne, A Biography,* 1980; J. Mellow, *Nathaniel Hawthorne in His Times,* 1980; E. Miller, *Salem Is My Dwelling Place, A Life of Hawthorne,* 1992; C. Swann, *Nathaniel Hawthorne, Tradition and Revolution,* 1992; N. Whitelaw, *Nathaniel Hawthorne American Storyteller,* 1996; A. Easton, *The Making of the Hawthorne Subject,* 1996; L. Reynolds, *A Historical Guide to Nathaniel Hawthorne,* 2001; B. Wineapple, *Hawthorne, A Life,* 2004.

TEXT: *The Complete Works of Nathaniel Hawthorne,* 12 vols., ed. G. Lathrop, 1883.

YOUNG GOODMAN BROWN

Young Goodman[1] Brown came forth at sunset into the street at Salem village;[2] but put his head back, after crossing the threshold, to exchange a parting kiss with his young wife. And Faith, as the wife was aptly named, thrust her own pretty head into the street, letting the wind play with the pink ribbons of her cap while she called to Goodman Brown.

"Dearest heart," whispered she, softly and rather sadly, when her lips were close to his ear, "prithee put off your journey until sunrise and sleep in your own bed to-night. A lone woman is troubled with such dreams and such

[1]A form of address applied to persons of yeoman status, below the rank of gentleman.

[2]The village (now Danvers, a few miles north of Salem) where accusations of witchcraft led to the Salem trials and executions of 1692.

thoughts that she's afeard of herself sometimes. Pray tarry with me this night, dear husband, of all nights in the year."

"My love and my Faith," replied young Goodman Brown, "of all nights in the year, this one night must I tarry away from thee. My journey, as thou callest it, forth and back again, must needs be done 'twixt now and sunrise. What, my sweet, pretty wife, dost thou doubt me already, and we but three months married?"

"Then God bless you!" said Faith, with the pink ribbons; "and may you find all well when you come back."

"Amen!" cried Goodman Brown. "Say thy prayers, dear Faith, and go to bed at dusk, and no harm will come to thee."

So they parted; and the young man pursued his way until, being about to turn the corner by the meeting-house, he looked back and saw the head of Faith still peeping after him with a melancholy air, in spite of her pink ribbons.

"Poor little Faith!" thought he, for his heart smote him. "What a wretch am I to leave her on such an errand! She talks of dreams, too. Methought as she spoke there was trouble in her face, as if a dream had warned her what work is to be done to-night. But no, no; 'twould kill her to think it. Well, she's a blessed angel on earth; and after this one night I'll cling to her skirts and follow her to heaven."

With this excellent resolve for the future, Goodman Brown felt himself justified in making more haste on his present evil purpose. He had taken a dreary road, darkened by all the gloomiest trees of the forest, which barely stood aside to let the narrow path creep through, and closed immediately behind. It was all as lonely as could be; and there is this peculiarity in such a solitude, that the traveller knows not who may be concealed by the innumerable trunks and the thick boughs overhead; so that with lonely footsteps he may yet be passing through an unseen multitude.

"There may be a devilish Indian behind every tree," said Goodman Brown to himself; and he glanced fearfully behind him as he added, "What if the devil himself should be at my very elbow!"

His head being turned back, he passed a crook of the road, and, looking forward again, beheld the figure of a man, in grave and decent attire, seated at the foot of an old tree. He arose at Goodman Brown's approach and walked onward side by side with him.

"You are late, Goodman Brown," said he. "The clock of the Old South[3] was striking as I came through Boston, and that is full fifteen minutes agone."

"Faith kept me back a while," replied the young man, with a tremor in his voice, caused by the sudden appearance of his companion, though not wholly unexpected.

It was now deep dusk in the forest, and deepest in that part of it where these two were journeying. As nearly as could be discerned, the second traveller was about fifty years old, apparently in the same rank of life as Goodman Brown, and bearing a considerable resemblance to him, though perhaps more in expression than features. Still they might have been taken for father and son. And yet, though the elder person was as simply clad as the younger, and as simple in manner too, he had an indescribable air of one

[3]The Old South Church in Boston, first built in 1669, rebuilt in 1729.

who knew the world, and who would not have felt abashed at the governor's dinner table or in King William's[4] court, were it possible that his affairs should call him thither. But the only thing about him that could be fixed upon as remarkable was his staff, which bore the likeness of a great black snake, so curiously wrought that it might almost be seen to twist and wriggle itself like a living serpent. This, of course, must have been an ocular deception, assisted by the uncertain light.

"Come, Goodman Brown," cried his fellow-traveller, "this is a dull pace for the beginning of a journey. Take my staff, if you are so soon weary."

"Friend," said the other, exchanging his slow pace for a full stop, "having kept covenant by meeting thee here, it is my purpose now to return whence I came. I have scruples touching the matter thou wot'st[5] of."

"Sayest thou so?" replied he of the serpent, smiling apart. "Let us walk on, nevertheless, reasoning as we go; and if I convince thee not thou shalt turn back. We are but a little way in the forest yet."

"Too far! too far!" exclaimed the goodman, unconsciously resuming his walk. "My father never went into the woods on such an errand, nor his father before him. We have been a race of honest men and good Christians since the days of the martyrs;[6] and shall I be the first of the name of Brown that ever took this path and kept—"

"Such company, thou wouldst say," observed the elder person, interpreting his pause. "Well said, Goodman Brown! I have been as well acquainted with your family as with ever a one among the Puritans; and that's no trifle to say. I helped your grandfather, the constable, when he lashed the Quaker woman so smartly through the streets of Salem;[7] and it was I that brought your father a pitch-pine knot, kindled at my own hearth, to set fire to an Indian village, in King Philip's war.[8] They were my good friends, both; and many a pleasant walk have we had along this path, and returned merrily after midnight. I would fain be friends with you for their sake."

"If it be as thou sayest," replied Goodman Brown, "I marvel they never spoke of these matters; or, verily, I marvel not, seeing that the least rumor of the sort would have driven them from New England. We are a people of prayer, and good works to boot, and abide no such wickedness."

"Wickedness or not," said the traveller, with the twisted staff, "I have a very general acquaintance here in New England. The deacons of many a church have drunk the communion wine with me; the selectmen[9] of divers towns make me their chairman; and a majority of the Great and General Court[10] are firm supporters of my interest. The governor and I, too—But these are state secrets."

"Can this be so?" cried Goodman Brown, with a stare of amazement at his undisturbed companion. "Howbeit, I have nothing to do with the governor

[4]William III (1650–1702), King of England (1689–1702). [5]"Knowest."

[6]I.e., during the reign of Mary Tudor (1516–1558), Queen of England (1553–1558). She won the title "Bloody Mary" for her persecution of Protestants.

[7]A law of 1661 required that Quaker "rogues and vagabonds" who disobeyed the laws "be stripped naked from the middle upwards, and tied to a cart's tail, and whipped through the town. . . ."

[8]Uprising of New England Indians (1675–1676), led by the Indian chief Metacom, who was known as "King Philip."

[9]Town officers. [10]The ruling body or legislature of the Puritan Colony.

and council; they have their own ways, and are no rule for a simple husbandman[11] like me. But, were I to go on with thee, how should I meet the eye of that good old man, our minister, at Salem village? Oh, his voice would make me tremble both Sabbath day and lecture day."[12]

Thus far the elder traveller had listened with due gravity; but now burst into a fit of irrepressible mirth, shaking himself so violently that his snakelike staff actually seemed to wriggle in sympathy.

"Ha! ha! ha!" shouted he again and again; then composing himself, "Well, go on, Goodman Brown, go on; but, prithee, don't kill me with laughing."

"Well, then, to end the matter at once," said Goodman Brown, considerably nettled, "there is my wife, Faith. It would break her dear little heart; and I'd rather break my own."

"Nay, if that be the case," answered the other, "e'en go thy ways, Goodman Brown. I would not for twenty old women like the one hobbling before us that Faith should come to any harm."

As he spoke he pointed his staff at a female figure on the path, in whom Goodman Brown recognized a very pious and exemplary dame, who had taught him his catechism in youth, and was still his moral and spiritual adviser, jointly with the minister and Deacon Gookin.[13]

"A marvel, truly, that Goody[14] Cloyse should be so far in the wilderness at nightfall," said he. "But with your leave, friend, I shall take a cut through the woods until we have left this Christian woman behind. Being a stranger to you, she might ask whom I was consorting with and whither I was going."

"Be it so," said his fellow-traveller. "Betake you to the woods, and let me keep the path."

Accordingly the young man turned aside, but took care to watch his companion, who advanced softly along the road until he had come within a staff's length of the old dame. She, meanwhile, was making the best of her way; with singular speed for so aged a woman, and mumbling some indistinct words—a prayer, doubtless—as she went. The traveller put forth his staff and touched her withered neck with what seemed the serpent's tail.

"The devil!" screamed the pious old lady.

"Then Goody Cloyse knows her old friend?" observed the traveller, confronting her and leaning on his writhing stick.

"Ah, forsooth, and is it your worship indeed?" cried the good dame. "Yea, truly is it, and in the very image of my old gossip, Goodman Brown, the grandfather of the silly fellow that now is. But—would your worship believe it?—my broomstick hath strangely disappeared, stolen, as I suspect, by that unhanged witch, Goody Cory, and that, too, when I was all anointed with the juice of smallage and cinquefoil and wolf's bane"[15]—

[11]A term meaning "farmer," used here to suggest "man of modest station in life."

[12]A midweek lecture on the Scriptures, usually given on Thursday.

[13]Possibly Daniel Gookin (1612–1687), colonial Puritan magistrate and missionary to the Indians. He was never a Deacon at Salem. Hawthorne perhaps uses his name to evoke memories of a pious good man.

[14]A contraction of "Goodwife," the feminine equivalent of "Goodman." Goody Cloyse and Goody Cory (mentioned below) were among those sentenced to death in the Salem Witch Trials, 1692.

[15]Smallage: a wild celery; cinquefoil: a member of the rose family; wolf's bane: a poisonous herb; all plants thought to have magic powers.

"Mingled with fine wheat and the fat of a new-born babe," said the shape of old Goodman Brown.

"Ah, your worship knows the recipe," cried the old lady, cackling aloud. "So, as I was saying, being all ready for the meeting, and no horse to ride on, I made up my mind to foot it; for they tell me there is a nice young man to be taken into communion to-night. But now your good worship will lend me your arm, and we shall be there in a twinkling."

"That can hardly be," answered her friend. "I may not spare you my arm, Goody Cloyse; but here is my staff, if you will."

So saying, he threw it down at her feet, where, perhaps, it assumed life, being one of the rods which its owner had formerly lent to the Egyptian magi.[16] Of this fact, however, Goodman Brown could not take cognizance. He had cast up his eyes in astonishment, and, looking down again, beheld neither Goody Cloyse nor the serpentine staff, but his fellow-traveller alone, who waited for him as calmly as if nothing had happened.

"That old woman taught me my catechism," said the young man; and there was a world of meaning in this simple comment.

They continued to walk onward, while the elder traveller exhorted his companion to make good speed and persevere in the path, discoursing so aptly that his arguments seemed rather to spring up in the bosom of his auditor than to be suggested by himself. As they went, he plucked a branch of maple to serve for a walking stick, and began to strip it of the twigs and little boughs, which were wet with evening dew. The moment his fingers touched them they became strangely withered and dried up as with a week's sunshine. Thus the pair proceeded, at a good free pace, until suddenly, in a gloomy hollow of the road, Goodman Brown sat himself down on the stump of a tree and refused to go any farther.

"Friend," said he, stubbornly, "my mind is made up. Not another step will I budge on this errand. What if a wretched old woman do choose to go to the devil when I thought she was going to heaven: is that any reason why I should quit my dear Faith and go after her?"

"You will think better of this by and by," said his acquaintance, composedly. "Sit here and rest yourself a while; and when you feel like moving again, there is my staff to help you along."

Without more words, he threw his companion the maple stick, and was as speedily out of sight as if he had vanished into the deepening gloom. The young man sat a few moments by the roadside, applauding himself greatly, and thinking with how clear a conscience he should meet the minister in his morning walk, nor shrink from the eye of good old Deacon Gookin. And what calm sleep would be his that very night, which was to have been spent so wickedly, but so purely and sweetly now, in the arms of Faith! Amidst these pleasant and praiseworthy meditations, Goodman Brown heard the tramp of horses along the road, and deemed it advisable to conceal himself within the verge of the forest, conscious of the guilty purpose that had brought him thither, though now so happily turned from it.

[16]The magicians of Egypt and their rods that were turned into serpents are described in Exodus 7.

On came the hoof tramps and the voices of the riders, two grave old voices, conversing soberly as they drew near. These mingled sounds appeared to pass along the road, within a few yards of the young man's hiding-place; but, owing doubtless to the depth of the gloom at that particular spot, neither the travellers nor their steeds were visible. Though their figures brushed the small boughs by the wayside, it could not be seen that they intercepted, even for a moment, the faint gleam from the strip of bright sky athwart which they must have passed. Goodman Brown alternately crouched and stood on tiptoe, pulling aside the branches and thrusting forth his head as far as he durst without discerning so much as a shadow. It vexed him the more, because he could have sworn, were such a thing possible, that he recognized the voices of the minister and Deacon Gookin, jogging along quietly, as they were wont to do, when bound to some ordination or ecclesiastical council. While yet within hearing, one of the riders stopped to pluck a switch.

"Of the two, reverend sir," said the voice like the deacon's, "I had rather miss an ordination dinner[17] than to-night's meeting. They tell me that some of our community are to be here from Falmouth[18] and beyond, and others from Connecticut and Rhode Island, besides several of the Indian powwows,[19] who, after their fashion, know almost as much deviltry as the best of us. Moreover, there is a goodly young woman to be taken into communion."

"Mighty well, Deacon Gookin!" replied the solemn old tones of the minister. "Spur up, or we shall be late. Nothing can be done, you know, until I get on the ground."

The hoofs clattered again; and the voices, talking so strangely in the empty air, passed on through the forest, where no church had ever been gathered, nor solitary Christian prayed. Whither, then, could these holy men be journeying so deep into the heathen wilderness? Young Goodman Brown caught hold of a tree for support, being ready to sink down on the ground, faint and overburdened with the heavy sickness of his heart. He looked up to the sky, doubting whether there really was a heaven above him. Yet there was the blue arch, and the stars brightening in it.

"With heaven above and Faith below, I will yet stand firm against the devil!" cried Goodman Brown.

While he still gazed upward into the deep arch of the firmament and had lifted his hands to pray, a cloud, though no wind was stirring, hurried across the zenith and hid the brightening stars. The blue sky was still visible, except directly overhead, where this black mass of cloud was sweeping swiftly northward. Aloft in the air, as if from the depths of the cloud, came a confused and doubtful sound of voices. Once the listener fancied that he could distinguish the accents of towns-people of his own, men and women, both pious and ungodly, many of whom he had met at the communion table, and had seen others rioting at the tavern. The next moment, so indistinct were the sounds, he doubted whether he had heard aught but the murmur of the old forest, whispering without a wind. Then came a stronger swell of those familiar tones, heard daily in the sunshine at Salem village, but never until now from a cloud of night. There was one voice, of a young woman, uttering

[17]The celebration held when a Puritan minister was ordained.
[18]Village on Cape Cod, in southeastern Massachusetts. [19]Priests.

lamentations, yet with an uncertain sorrow, and entreating for some favor, which, perhaps, it would grieve her to obtain; and all the unseen multitude, both saints and sinners, seemed to encourage her onward.

"Faith!" shouted Goodman Brown, in a voice of agony and desperation; and the echoes of the forest mocked him, crying, "Faith! Faith!" as if bewildered wretches were seeking her all through the wilderness.

The cry of grief, rage, and terror was yet piercing the night, when the unhappy husband held his breath for a response. There was a scream, drowned immediately in a louder murmur of voices, fading into far-off laughter, as the dark cloud swept away, leaving the clear and silent sky above Goodman Brown. But something fluttered lightly down through the air and caught on the branch of a tree. The young man seized it, and beheld a pink ribbon.

"My Faith is gone!" cried he, after one stupefied moment. "There is no good on earth; and sin is but a name. Come, devil; for to thee is this world given."

And, maddened with despair, so that he laughed loud and long, did Goodman Brown grasp his staff and set forth again, at such a rate that he seemed to fly along the forest path rather than to walk or run. The road grew wilder and drearier and more faintly traced, and vanished at length, leaving him in the heart of the dark wilderness, still rushing onward with the instinct that guides mortal man to evil. The whole forest was peopled with frightful sounds—the creaking of the trees, the howling of wild beasts, and the yell of Indians; while sometimes the wind tolled like a distant church bell, and sometimes gave a broad roar around the traveller, as if all Nature were laughing him to scorn. But he was himself the chief horror of the scene, and shrank not from its other horrors.

"Ha! ha! ha!" roared Goodman Brown when the wind laughed at him. "Let us hear which will laugh loudest. Think not to frighten me with your deviltry. Come witch, come wizard, come Indian powwow, come devil himself, and here comes Goodman Brown. You may as well fear him as he fear you."

In truth, all through the haunted forest there could be nothing more frightful than the figure of Goodman Brown. On he flew among the black pines, brandishing his staff with frenzied gestures, now giving vent to an inspiration of horrid blasphemy, and now shouting forth such laughter as set all the echoes of the forest laughing like demons around him. The fiend in his own shape is less hideous than when he rages in the breast of man. Thus sped the demoniac on his course, until, quivering among the trees, he saw a red light before him, as when the felled trunks and branches of a clearing have been set on fire, and throw up their lurid blaze against the sky, at the hour of midnight. He paused, in a lull of the tempest that had driven him onward, and heard the swell of what seemed a hymn, rolling solemnly from a distance with the weight of many voices. He knew the tune; it was a familiar one in the choir of the village meetinghouse. The verse died heavily away, and was lengthened by a chorus, not of human voices, but of all the sounds of the benighted wilderness pealing in awful harmony together. Goodman Brown cried out, and his cry was lost to his own ear by its unison with the cry of the desert.

In the interval of silence he stole forward until the light glared full upon his eyes. At one extremity of an open space, hemmed in by the dark wall of the forest, arose a rock, bearing some rude, natural resemblance either to an altar or a pulpit, and surrounded by four blazing pines, their tops aflame, their stems untouched, like candles at an evening meeting. The mass of foliage that had overgrown the summit of the rock was all on fire, blazing high into the night and fitfully illuminating the whole field. Each pendent twig and leafy festoon was in a blaze. As the red light arose and fell, a numerous congregation alternately shone forth, then disappeared in shadow, and again grew, as it were, out of the darkness, peopling the heart of the solitary woods at once.

"A grave and dark-clad company," quoth Goodman Brown.

In truth they were such. Among them, quivering to and fro between gloom and splendor, appeared faces that would be seen next day at the council board of the province,[20] and others which, Sabbath after Sabbath, looked devoutly heavenward, and benignantly over the crowded pews, from the holiest pulpits in the land. Some affirm that the lady of the governor[21] was there. At least there were high dames well known to her, and wives of honored husbands, and widows, a great multitude, and ancient maidens, all of excellent repute, and fair young girls, who trembled lest their mothers should espy them. Either the sudden gleams of light flashing over the obscure field bedazzled Goodman Brown, or he recognized a score of the church members of Salem village famous for their especial sanctity. Good old Deacon Gookin had arrived, and waited at the skirts of that venerable saint, his revered pastor. But, irreverently consorting with these grave, reputable, and pious people, these elders of the church, these chaste dames and dewy virgins, there were men of dissolute lives and women of spotted fame, wretches given over to all mean and filthy vice, and suspected even of horrid crimes. It was strange to see that the good shrank not from the wicked, nor were the sinners abashed by the saints. Scattered also among their pale-faced enemies were the Indian priests, or powwows, who had often scared their native forest with more hideous incantations than any known to English witchcraft.

"But where is Faith?" thought Goodman Brown; and, as hope came into his heart, he trembled.

Another verse of the hymn arose, a slow and mournful strain, such as the pious love, but joined to words which expressed all that our nature can conceive of sin, and darkly hinted at far more. Unfathomable to mere mortals is the lore of fiends. Verse after verse was sung; and still the chorus of the desert swelled between like the deepest tone of a mighty organ; and with the final peal of that dreadful anthem there came a sound, as if the roaring wind, the rushing streams, the howling beasts, and every other voice of the unconverted wilderness were mingling and according with the voice of guilty man in homage to the prince of all. The four blazing pines threw up a loftier flame, and obscurely discovered shapes and visages of horror on the smoke wreaths above the impious assembly. At the same moment the fire on the rock shot redly forth and formed a glowing arch above its base, where now appeared a figure. With reverence be it spoken, the figure bore no slight

[20]The Governor's Council, consisting of "28 of the most considerable Gentlemen of the Country."

[21]Sir William Phips (1651–1695), royal Governor of Massachusetts (1692–1694). According to tradition, his wife was charged with but not tried for witchcraft at Salem in 1692.

similitude, both in garb and manner, to some grave divine of the New England churches.

"Bring forth the converts!" cried a voice that echoed through the field and rolled into the forest.

At the word, Goodman Brown stepped forth from the shadow of the trees and approached the congregation, with whom he felt a loathful brotherhood by the sympathy of all that was wicked in his heart. He could have well-nigh sworn that the shape of his own dead father beckoned him to advance, looking downward from a smoke wreath, while a woman, with dim features of despair, threw out her hand to warn him back. Was it his mother? But he had no power to retreat one step, nor to resist, even in thought, when the minister and good old Deacon Gookin seized his arms and led him to the blazing rock. Thither came also the slender form of a veiled female, led between Goody Cloyse, that pious teacher of the catechism, and Martha Carrier,[22] who had received the devil's promise to be queen of hell. A rampant hag was she. And there stood the proselytes beneath the canopy of fire.

"Welcome, my children," said the dark figure, "to the communion of your race! Ye have found thus young your nature and your destiny. My children, look behind you!"

They turned; and flashing forth, as it were, in a sheet of flame, the fiend worshippers were seen; the smile of welcome gleamed darkly on every visage.

"There," resumed the sable[23] form, "are all whom ye have reverenced from youth. Ye deemed them holier than yourselves, and shrank from your own sin, contrasting it with their lives of righteousness and prayerful aspirations heavenward. Yet here are they all in my worshipping assembly. This night it shall be granted you to know their secret deeds: how hoary-bearded elders of the church have whispered wanton words to the young maids of their households; how many a woman, eager for widow's weeds, has given her husband a drink at bedtime and let him sleep in her bosom; how beardless youths have made haste to inherit their fathers' wealth; and how fair damsels—blush not, sweet ones—have dug little graves in the garden, and bidden me, the sole guest, to an infant's funeral. By the sympathy of your human hearts for sin ye shall scent out all the places—whether in church, bed-chamber, street, field, or forest—where crime has been committed, and shall exult to behold the whole earth one stain of guilt, one mighty blood spot. Far more than this. It shall be yours to penetrate, in every bosom, the deep mystery of sin, the fountain of all wicked arts, and which inexhaustibly supplies more evil impulses than human power—than my power at its utmost—can make manifest in deeds. And now, my children, look upon each other."

They did so; and, by the blaze of the hell-kindled torches, the wretched man beheld his Faith, and the wife her husband, trembling before that unhallowed altar.

"Lo, there ye stand, my children," said the figure, in a deep and solemn tone, almost sad with its despairing awfulness, as if his once angelic nature could yet mourn for our miserable race. "Depending upon one another's

[22]Hanged as a witch at Salem, 1692. She had confessed that the devil had promised she would be "queen of hell."

[23]The term for "black" in heraldry.

hearts, ye had still hoped that virtue were not all a dream. Now are ye undeceived. Evil is the nature of mankind. Evil must be your only happiness. Welcome again, my children, to the communion of your race."

"Welcome," repeated the fiend worshippers, in one cry of despair and triumph.

And there they stood, the only pair, as it seemed, who were yet hesitating on the verge of wickedness in this dark world. A basin was hollowed, naturally, in the rock. Did it contain water, reddened by the lurid light? or was it blood? or, perchance, a liquid flame? Herein did the shape of evil dip his hand and prepare to lay the mark of baptism upon their foreheads, that they might be partakers of the mystery of sin, more conscious of the secret guilt of others, both in deed and thought, than they could now be of their own. The husband cast one look at his pale wife, and Faith at him. What polluted wretches would the next glance show them to each other, shuddering alike at what they disclosed and what they saw!

"Faith! Faith!" cried the husband, "look up to heaven, and resist the wicked one."

Whether Faith obeyed he knew not. Hardly had he spoken when he found himself amid calm night and solitude, listening to a roar of the wind which died heavily away through the forest. He staggered against the rock, and felt it chill and damp; while a hanging twig, that had been all on fire, besprinkled his cheek with the coldest dew.

The next morning young Goodman Brown came slowly into the street of Salem village, staring around him like a bewildered man. The good old minister was taking a walk along the graveyard to get an appetite for breakfast and meditate his sermon, and bestowed a blessing, as he passed, on Goodman Brown. He shrank from the venerable saint as if to avoid an anathema.[24] Old Deacon Gookin was at domestic worship, and the holy words of his prayer were heard through the open window. "What God doth the wizard pray to?" quoth Goodman Brown. Goody Cloyse, that excellent old Christian, stood in the early sunshine at her own lattice, catechizing a little girl who had brought her a pint of morning's milk. Goodman Brown snatched away the child as from the grasp of the fiend himself. Turning the corner by the meeting-house, he spied the head of Faith, with the pink ribbons, gazing anxiously forth, and bursting into such joy at sight of him that she skipped along the street and almost kissed her husband before the whole village. But Goodman Brown looked sternly and sadly into her face, and passed on without a greeting.

Had Goodman Brown fallen asleep in the forest and only dreamed a wild dream of a witch-meeting?

Be it so if you will; but, alas! it was a dream of evil omen for young Goodman Brown. A stern, a sad, a darkly meditative, a distrustful, if not a desperate man did he become from the night of that fearful dream. On the Sabbath day, when the congregation were singing a holy psalm, he could not listen because an anthem of sin rushed loudly upon his ear and drowned all the blessed strain. When the minister spoke from the pulpit with power and fervid eloquence, and, with his hand on the open Bible, of the sacred truths

[24]Curse.

of our religion, and of saint-like lives and triumphant deaths, and of future bliss or misery unutterable, then did Goodman Brown turn pale, dreading lest the roof should thunder down upon the gray blasphemer and his hearers. Often, awakening suddenly at midnight, he shrank from the bosom of Faith; and at morning or eventide, when the family knelt down at prayer, he scowled and muttered to himself, and gazed sternly at his wife, and turned away. And when he had lived long, and was borne to his grave a hoary corpse, followed by Faith, an aged woman, and children and grandchildren, a goodly procession, besides neighbors not a few, they carved no hopeful verse upon his tombstone, for his dying hour was gloom.

1828–1829 1835

THE MINISTER'S BLACK VEIL

A PARABLE[1]

The sexton stood in the porch of Milford[2] meeting-house, pulling busily at the bell-rope. The old people of the village came stooping along the street. Children, with bright faces, tripped merrily beside their parents, or mimicked a graver gait, in the conscious dignity of their Sunday clothes. Spruce bachelors looked sidelong at the pretty maidens, and fancied that the Sabbath sunshine made them prettier than on week days. When the throng had mostly streamed into the porch, the sexton began to toll the bell, keeping his eye on the Reverend Mr. Hooper's door. The first glimpse of the clergyman's figures was the signal for the bell to cease its summons.

"But what has good Parson Hooper got upon his face?" cried the sexton in astonishment.

All within hearing immediately turned about, and beheld the semblance of Mr. Hooper, pacing slowly his meditative way towards the meeting-house. With one accord they started, expressing more wonder than if some strange minister were coming to dust the cushions of Mr. Hooper's pulpit.

"Are you sure it is our parson?" inquired Goodman Gray of the sexton.

"Of a certainty it is good Mr. Hooper," replied the sexton. "He was to have exchanged pulpits with Parson Shute, of Westbury; but Parson Shute sent to excuse himself yesterday, being to preach a funeral sermon."

The cause of so much amazement may appear sufficiently slight. Mr. Hooper, a gentlemanly person, of about thirty, though still a bachelor, was dressed with due clerical neatness, as if a careful wife had starched his band,[3] and brushed the weekly dust from his Sunday's garb. There was but one thing remarkable in his appearance. Swathed about his forehead, and hanging down over his face, so low as to be shaken by his breath, Mr. Hooper had

[1]"Another clergyman in New England, Mr. Joseph Moody of York, Maine, who died about eighty years since, made himself remarkable by the same eccentricity that is here related of the Reverend Mr. Hooper. In this case, however, the symbol had a different import. In early life he had accidentally killed a beloved friend; and from that day till the hour of his own death, he hid his face from men."—Hawthorne's note.

[2]A town southwest of Boston. [3]Clerical collar.

on a black veil. On a nearer view it seemed to consist of two folds of crape, which entirely concealed his features, except the mouth and chin, but probably did not intercept his sight, further than to give a darkened aspect to all living and inanimate things. With this gloomy shade before him, good Mr. Hooper walked onward, at a slow and quiet pace, stooping somewhat, and looking on the ground, as is customary with abstracted men, yet nodding kindly to those of his parishioners who still waited on the meeting-house steps. But so wonder-struck were they that his greeting hardly met with a return.

"I can't really feel as if good Mr. Hooper's face was behind that piece of crape," said the sexton.

"I don't like it," muttered an old woman, as she hobbled into the meeting-house. "He has changed himself into something awful, only by hiding his face."

"Our parson has gone mad!" cried Goodman Gray, following him across the threshold.

A rumor of some unaccountable phenomenon had preceded Mr. Hooper into the meeting-house, and set all the congregation astir. Few could refrain from twisting their heads towards the door; many stood upright, and turned directly about; while several little boys clambered upon the seats, and came down again with a terrible racket. There was a general bustle, a rustling of the women's gowns and shuffling of the mens' feet, greatly at variance with that hushed repose which should attend the entrance of the minister. But Mr. Hooper appeared not to notice the perturbation of his people. He entered with an almost noiseless step, bent his head mildly to the pews on each side, and bowed as he passed his oldest parishioner, a white-haired great-grandsire, who occupied an arm-chair in the centre of the aisle. It was strange to observe how slowly this venerable man became conscious of something singular in the appearance of his pastor. He seemed not fully to partake of the prevailing wonder, till Mr. Hooper had ascended the stairs, and showed himself in the pulpit, face to face with his congregation, except for the black veil. That mysterious emblem was never once withdrawn. It shook with his measured breath, as he gave out the psalm; it threw its obscurity between him and the holy page, as he read the Scriptures; and while he prayed, the veil lay heavily on his uplifted countenance. Did he seek to hide it from the dread Being whom he was addressing?

Such was the effect of this simple piece of crape, that more than one woman of delicate nerves was forced to leave the meeting-house. Yet perhaps the pale-faced congregation was almost as fearful a sight to the minister, as his black veil to them.

Mr. Hooper had the reputation of a good preacher, but not an energetic one: he strove to win his people heavenward by mild, persuasive influences, rather than to drive them thither by the thunders of the Word. The sermon which he now delivered was marked by the same characteristics of style and manner as the general series of his pulpit oratory. But there was something, either in the sentiment of the discourse itself, or in the imagination of the auditors, which made it greatly the most powerful effort that they had ever heard from their pastor's lips. It was tinged, rather more darkly than usual, with the gentle gloom of Mr. Hooper's temperament. The subject had reference to secret sin, and those sad mysteries which we hide from our nearest and dearest, and would fain conceal from our own consciousness, even forgetting that the Omniscient can detect them. A subtle power was breathed into his words. Each member of the congregation, the most innocent girl, and the man of hardened breast, felt as if the preacher had crept upon them, behind his awful veil, and discovered their hoarded iniquity of deed or thought. Many spread their clasped hands on their bosoms. There was nothing terrible in what Mr. Hooper said, at least, no violence; and yet, with every tremor of his melancholy voice, the hearers quaked. An unsought pathos came hand in hand with awe. So sensible were the audience of some unwonted attribute in their minister, that they longed for a breath of wind to blow aside the veil, almost believing that a stranger's visage would be discovered, though the form, gesture, and voice were those of Mr. Hooper.

At the close of the services, the people hurried out with indecorous confusion, eager to communicate their pent-up amazement, and conscious of lighter spirits the moment they lost sight of the black veil. Some gathered in little circles, huddled closely together, with their mouths all whispering in the centre; some went homeward alone, wrapt in silent meditation; some talked loudly, and profaned the Sabbath day with ostentatious laughter. A few shook their sagacious heads, intimating that they could penetrate the mystery; while one or two affirmed that there was no mystery at all, but only that Mr. Hooper's eyes were so weakened by the midnight lamp, as to require a shade. After a brief interval, forth came good Mr. Hooper also, in the rear of his flock. Turning his veiled face from one group to another, he paid due reverence to the hoary heads, saluted the middle aged with kind dignity as their friend and spiritual guide, greeted the young with mingled authority and love, and laid his hands on the little children's heads to bless them. Such was always his custom on the Sabbath day. Strange and bewildered looks repaid him for his courtesy. None, as on former occasions, aspired to the honor of walking by their pastor's side. Old Squire Saunders, doubtless by an accidental lapse of memory, neglected to invite Mr. Hooper to his table, where the good clergyman had been wont to bless the food, almost every Sunday since his settlement. He returned, therefore, to the parsonage, and, at the moment of closing the door, was observed to look back upon the people, all of whom had their eyes fixed upon the minister. A sad smile gleamed faintly from beneath the black veil, and flickered about his mouth, glimmering as he disappeared.

"How strange," said a lady, "that a simple black veil, such as any woman might wear on her bonnet, should become such a terrible thing on Mr. Hooper's face!"

"Something must surely be amiss with Mr. Hooper's intellects," observed her husband, the physician of the village. "But the strangest part of the affair is the effect of this vagary, even on a sober-minded man like myself. The black veil, though it covers only our pastor's face, throws its influence over his whole person, and makes him ghostlike from head to foot. Do you not feel it so?"

"Truly do I," replied the lady; "and I would not be alone with him for the world. I wonder he is not afraid to be alone with himself!"

"Men sometimes are so," said her husband.

The afternoon service was attended with similar circumstances. At its conclusion, the bell tolled for the funeral of a young lady. The relatives and friends were assembled in the house, and the more distant acquaintances stood about the door, speaking of the good qualities of the decreased, when their talk was interrupted by the appearance of Mr. Hooper, still covered with his black veil. It was now an appropriate emblem. The clergyman stepped into the room where the corpse was laid, and bent over the coffin, to take a last farewell of his deceased parishioner. As he stooped, the veil hung straight down from his forehead, so that, if her eyelids had not been closed forever, the dead maiden might have seen his face. Could Mr. Hooper be fearful of her glance, that he so hastily caught back the black veil? A person who watched the interview between the dead and living, scrupled not to affirm, that, at the instant when the clergyman's features were disclosed, the corpse had slightly shuddered, rustling the shroud and muslin cap, though the countenance retained the composure of death. A superstitious old woman was the only witness of this prodigy. From the coffin Mr. Hooper passed into the chamber of the mourners, and thence to the head of the staircase, to make the funeral prayer. It was a tender and heart-dissolving prayer, full of sorrow, yet so imbued with celestial hopes, that the music of a heavenly harp, swept by the fingers of the dead, seemed faintly to be heard among the saddest accents of the minister. The people trembled, though they but darkly understood him when he prayed that they, and himself, and all of mortal race, might be ready, as he trusted this young maiden had been, for the dreadful hour that should snatch the veil from their faces. The bearers went heavily forth, and the mourners followed, saddening all the street, with the dead before them, and Mr. Hooper in his black veil behind.

"Why do you look back?" said one in the procession to his partner.

"I had a fancy," replied she, "that the minister and the maiden's spirit were walking hand in hand."

"And so had I, at the same moment," said the other.

That night, the handsomest couple in Milford village were to be joined in wedlock. Though reckoned a melancholy man, Mr. Hooper had a placid cheerfulness for such occasions, which often excited a sympathetic smile where livelier merriment would have been thrown away. There was no quality of his disposition which made him more beloved than this. The company at the wedding awaited his arrival with impatience, trusting that the strange awe, which had gathered over him throughout the day, would now be dispelled. But such was not the result. When Mr. Hooper came, the first thing that their eyes rested on was the same horrible black veil, which had added deeper gloom to the funeral, and could portend nothing but evil to the wedding. Such was its immediate effect on the guests that a cloud seemed to have rolled duskily from beneath the black crape, and dimmed the light of the candles. The bridal pair stood up before the minister. But the bride's cold fingers quivered in the tremulous hand of the bridegroom, and her deathlike paleness caused a whisper that the maiden who had been buried a few hours before was come from her grave to be married. If ever another wedding were so dismal, it was that famous one where they tolled the wedding knell. After performing the ceremony, Mr. Hooper raised a glass of wine to his lips, wishing happiness to the new-married couple in a strain of mild pleasantry that ought to have brightened the features of the guests, like a cheerful gleam from the hearth. At that instant, catching a glimpse of his figure in the looking-glass, the black veil involved his own spirit in the horror with which it overwhelmed all others. His frame shuddered, his lips grew white, he spilt the untasted wine upon the carpet, and rushed forth into the darkness. For the Earth, too, had on her Black Veil.

The next day, the whole village of Milford talked of little else than Parson Hooper's black veil. That, and the mystery concealed behind it, supplied a topic for discussion between acquaintances meeting in the street, and good women gossiping at their open windows. It was the first item of news that the tavernkeeper told to his guests. The children babbled of it on their way to school. One imitative little imp covered his face with an old black handkerchief, thereby so affrighting his playmates that the panic seized himself, and he well-nigh lost his wits by his own waggery.[4]

It was remarkable that of all the busybodies and impertinent people in the parish, not one ventured to put the plain question to Mr. Hooper, wherefore he did this thing. Hitherto, whenever there appeared the slightest call for such interference, he had never lacked advisers, nor shown himself averse to be guided by their judgment. If he erred at all, it was by so painful a degree of self-distrust, that even the mildest censure would lead him to consider an indifferent action as a crime. Yet, though so well acquainted with this amiable weakness, no individual among his parishioners chose to make the black veil a subject of friendly remonstrance. There was a feeling of dread, neither plainly confessed nor carefully concealed, which caused each to shift the responsibility upon another, till at length it was found expedient to send a deputation of the church, in order to deal with Mr. Hooper about the mystery, before it should grow into a scandal. Never did an embassy so ill discharge its duties. The minister received them with friendly courtesy, but became silent, after they were seated, leaving to his visitors the whole burden of introducing their important business. The topic, it might be supposed, was obvious enough. There was the black veil swathed round Mr. Hooper's forehead, and concealing every feature above his placid mouth, on which, at times, they could perceive the glimmering of a melancholy smile. But that piece of crape, to their imagination, seemed to hang down before his heart, the symbol of a fearful secret between him and them. Were the veil but cast aside, they might speak freely of it, but not till then. Thus they sat a considerable time, speechless, confused, and shrinking uneasily from Mr. Hooper's eye, which they felt to be fixed upon them with an invisible glance. Finally, the deputies returned abashed to their constituents, pronouncing the matter too weighty to be handled, except by a council of the churches, if, indeed, it might not require a general synod.[5]

But there was one person in the village unappalled by the awe with which the black veil had impressed all beside herself. When the deputies returned without an explanation, or even venturing to demand one, she, with the calm energy of her character, determined to chase away the strange cloud that appeared to be settling round Mr. Hooper, every moment more darkly than before. As his plighted[6] wife, it should be her privilege to know what the black veil concealed. At the minister's first visit, therefore, she entered upon the subject with a direct simplicity, which made the task easier both for him and her. After he had seated himself, she fixed her eyes steadfastly upon the veil, but could discern nothing of the dreadful gloom that had so overawed

[4]Mischievous joke. [5]An assembly of church officials. [6]Intended, promised.

the multitude: it was but a double fold of crape, hanging down from his forehead to his mouth, and slightly stirring with his breath.

"No," said she aloud, and smiling, "there is nothing terrible in this piece of crape, except that it hides a face which I am always glad to look upon. Come, good sir, let the sun shine from behind the cloud. First lay aside your black veil: then tell me why you put it on."

Mr. Hooper's smile glimmered faintly.

"There is an hour to come," said he, "when all of us shall cast aside our veils. Take it not amiss, beloved friend, if I wear this piece of crape till then."

"Your words are a mystery, too," returned the young lady. "Take away the veil from them, at least."

"Elizabeth, I will," said he, "so far as my vow may suffer me. Know, then, this veil is a type and a symbol, and I am bound to wear it ever, both in light and darkness, in solitude and before the gaze of multitudes, and as with strangers, so with my familiar friends. No mortal eye will see it withdrawn. This dismal shade must separate me from the world: even you, Elizabeth, can never come behind it!"

"What grievous affliction hath befallen you," she earnestly inquired, "that you should thus darken your eyes forever?"

"If it be a sign of mourning," replied Mr. Hooper, "I, perhaps, like most other mortals, have sorrows dark enough to be typified by a black veil."

"But what if the world will not believe that it is the type of an innocent sorrow?" urged Elizabeth. "Beloved and respected as you are, there may be whispers that you hide your face under the consciousness of secret sin. For the sake of your holy office, do away this scandal!"

The color rose into her cheeks as she intimated the nature of the rumors that were already abroad in the village. But Mr. Hooper's mildness did not forsake him. He even smiled again—that same sad smile, which always appeared like a faint glimmering of light, proceeding from the obscurity beneath of the veil.

"If I hide my face for sorrow, there is cause enough," he merely replied; "and if I cover it for secret sin, what mortal might not do the same?"

And with this gentle, but unconquerable obstinacy did he resist all her entreaties. At length Elizabeth sat silent. For a few moments she appeared lost in thought, considering, probably, what new methods might be tried to withdraw her lover from so dark a fantasy, which, if it had no other meaning, was perhaps a symptom of mental disease. Though of a firmer character than his own, the tears rolled down her cheeks. But, in an instant, as it were, a new feeling took the place of sorrow: her eyes were fixed insensibly on the black veil, when, like a sudden twilight in the air, its terrors fell around her. She arose, and stood trembling before him.

"And do you feel it then, at last?" said he mournfully.

She made no reply, but covered her eyes with her hand, and turned to leave the room. He rushed forward and caught her arm.

"Have patience with me, Elizabeth!" cried he, passionately. "Do not desert me, though this veil must be between us here on earth. Be mine, and hereafter there shall be no veil over my face, no darkness between our souls! It is but a mortal veil—it is not for eternity! O! you know not how lonely I am, and how frightened, to be alone behind my black veil. Do not leave me in this miserable obscurity forever!"

"Lift the veil but once, and look me in the face," said she.

"Never! It cannot be!" replied Mr. Hooper.

"Then farewell!" said Elizabeth.

She withdrew her arm from his grasp, and slowly departed, pausing at the door, to give one long shuddering gaze, that seemed almost to penetrate the mystery of the black veil. But, even amid his grief, Mr. Hooper smiled to think that only a material emblem had separated him from happiness, though the horrors, which it shadowed forth, must be drawn darkly between the fondest of lovers.

From that time no attempts were made to remove Mr. Hooper's black veil, or, by a direct appeal, to discover the secret which it was supposed to hide. By persons who claimed a superiority to popular prejudice, it was reckoned merely an eccentric whim, such as often mingles with the sober actions of men otherwise rational, and tinges them all with its own semblance of insanity. But with the multitude, good Mr. Hooper was irreparably a bugbear.[7] He could not walk the street with any peace of mind, so conscious was he that the gentle and timid would turn aside to avoid him, and that others would make it a point of hardihood to throw themselves in his way. The impertinence of the latter class compelled him to give up his customary walk at sunset to the burial ground; for when he leaned pensively over the gate, there would always be faces behind the gravestones, peeping at his black veil. A fable went the rounds that the stare of the dead people drove him thence. It grieved him, to the very depth of his kind heart, to observe how the children fled from his approach, breaking up their merriest sports, while his melancholy figure was yet afar off. Their instinctive dread caused him to feel more strongly than aught else, that a preternatural horror was interwoven with the threads of the black crape. In truth, his own antipathy to the veil was known to be so great, that he never willingly passed before a mirror, not stooped to drink at a still fountain, lest, in its peaceful bosom, he should be affrighted by himself. This was what gave plausibility to the whispers, that Mr. Hooper's conscience tortured him for some great crime too horrible to be entirely concealed, or otherwise than so obscurely intimated. Thus, from beneath the black veil, there rolled a cloud into the sunshine, an ambiguity of sin or sorrow, which enveloped the poor minister, so that love or sympathy could never reach him. It was said that ghost and fiend consorted with him there. With self-shudderings, and outward terrors, he walked continually in its shadow, groping darkly within his own soul, or gazing through a medium that saddened the whole world. Even the lawless wind, it was believed, respected his dreadful secret, and never blew aside the veil. But still good Mr. Hooper sadly smiled at the pale visages of the worldly throng as he passed by.

Among all its bad influences, the black veil had the one desirable effect, of making its wearer a very efficient clergyman. By the aid of his mysterious emblem—for there was no other apparent cause—he became a man of awful power over souls that were in agony for sin. His converts always regarded him with a dread peculiar to themselves, affirming, though but figuratively, that, before he brought them to celestial light, they had been with him behind that black veil. Its gloom, indeed, enabled him to sympathize with all dark affections. Dying sinners cried aloud for Mr. Hooper, and would not yield their breath till

[7]An object of fear and dread.

he appeared: though ever, as he stooped to whisper consolation, they shuddered at the veiled face so near their own. Such were the terrors of the black veil, even when Death had bared his visage! Strangers came long distances to attend service at his church, with the mere idle purpose of gazing at his figure, because it was forbidden them to behold his face. But many were made to quake ere they departed! Once, during Governor Belcher's administration,[8] Mr. Hooper was appointed to preach the election sermon.[9] Covered with his black veil, he stood before the chief magistrate, the council, and the representatives, and wrought so deep an impression, that the legislative measures of that year were characterized by all the gloom and piety of our earliest ancestral sway.

In this manner Mr. Hooper spent a long life, irreproachable in outward act, yet shrouded in dismal suspicions; kind and loving, though unloved, and dimly feared; a man apart from men, shunned in their health and joy, but ever summoned to their aid in mortal anguish. As years wore on, shedding their snows above his sable[10] veil, he acquired a name throughout the New England churches, and they called him Father Hooper. Nearly all his parishioners, who were of mature age when he was settled, had been borne away by many a funeral: he had one congregation in the church, and a more crowded one in the churchyard; and having wrought so late into the evening, and done his work so well, it was now good Father Hooper's turn to rest.

Several persons were visible by the shaded candlelight, in the death chamber of the old clergyman. Natural connections he had none. But there was the decorously grave, though unmoved physician, seeking only to mitigate the last pangs of the patient whom he could not save. There were the deacons, and other eminently pious members of his church. There, also, was the Reverend Mr. Clark, of Westbury, a young and zealous divine, who had ridden in haste to pray by the bedside of the expiring minister. There was the nurse, no hired handmaiden of death, but one whose calm affection had endured thus long in secrecy, in solitude, amid the chill of age, and would not perish, even at the dying hour. Who, but Elizabeth! And there lay the hoary head of good Father Hooper upon the death pillow, with the black veil still swathed about his brow, and reaching down over his face, so that each more difficult gasp of his faint breath caused it to stir. All through life that piece of crape had hung between him and the world: it had separated him from cheerful brotherhood and woman's love, and kept him in that saddest of all prisons, his own heart: and still it lay upon his face, as if to deepen the gloom of his darksome chamber, and shade him from the sunshine of eternity.

For some time previous, his mind had been confused, wavering doubtfully between the past and the present, and hovering forward, as it were, at intervals, into the indistinctness of the world to come. There had been feverish turns, which tossed him from side to side, and wore away what little strength he had. But in his most convulsive struggles, and in the wildest vagaries of his intellect, when no other thought retained its sober influence, he still showed an awful solicitude lest the black veil should slip aside. Even if his bewildered soul could have forgotten, there was a faithful woman at his pillow, who, with averted eyes, would have covered that aged face, which she had last beheld in

[8]Jonathan Belcher (1682–1757), royal Governor of Massachusetts (1730–1741).
[9]A special sermon delivered during the installation of the Colony's newly elected government officials. To be chosen to preach the sermon was a high distinction.
[10]Black.

the comeliness of manhood. At length the death-stricken old man lay quietly in the torpor of mental and bodily exhaustion, with an imperceptible pulse, and breath that grew fainter and fainter, except when a long, deep, and irregular inspiration seemed to preclude the flight of his spirit.

The minister of Westbury approached the bedside.

"Venerable Father Hooper," said he, "the moment of your release is at hand. Are you ready for the lifting of the veil that shuts in time from eternity?"

Father Hooper at first replied merely by a feeble motion of his head; then, apprehensive, perhaps, that his meaning might be doubtful, he exerted himself to speak.

"Yea," said he, in faint accents, "my soul hath a patient weariness until that veil be lifted."

"And is it fitting," resumed the Reverend Mr. Clark, "that a man so given to prayer, of such a blameless example, holy in deed and thought, so far as mortal judgment may pronounce; is it fitting that a father in the church should leave a shadow on his memory, that may seem to blacken a life so pure? I pray you, my venerable brother, let not this thing be! Suffer us to be gladdened by your triumphant aspect as you go to your reward. Before the veil of eternity be lifted, let me cast aside this black veil from your face!"

And thus speaking, the Reverend Mr. Clark bent forward to reveal the mystery of so many years. But, exerting a sudden energy, that made all the beholders stand aghast, Father Hooper snatched both his hands from beneath the bedclothes, and pressed them strongly on the black veil, resolute to struggle, if the minister of Westbury would contend with a dying man.

"Never!" cried the veiled clergyman. "On earth, never!"

"Dark old man!" exclaimed the affrighted minister, "with what horrible crime upon your soul are you now passing to the judgment?"

Father Hooper's breath heaved; it rattled in his throat; but, with a mighty effort, grasping forward with his hands, he caught hold of life, and held it back till he should speak. He even raised himself in bed; and there he sat, shivering with the arms of death around him, while the black veil hung down, awful, at that last moment, in the gathered terrors of a lifetime. And yet the faint, sad smile, so often there, now seemed to glimmer from its obscurity, and linger on Father Hooper's lips.

"Why do you tremble at me alone?" cried he, turning his veiled face round the circle of pale spectators. "Tremble also at each other! Have men avoided me, and women shown no pity, and children screamed and fled, only for my black veil? What, but the mystery which it obscurely typifies, has made this piece of crape so awful? When the friend shows his inmost heart to his friend; the lover to his best beloved; when man does not vainly shrink from the eye of his Creator, loathsomely treasuring up the secret of his sin; then deem me a monster for the symbol beneath which I have lived, and die! I look around me, and, lo! on every visage a Black Veil!"

While his auditors shrank from one another, in mutual affright, Father Hooper fell back upon his pillow, a veiled corpse, with a faint smile lingering on the lips. Still veiled, they laid him in his coffin, and a veiled corpse they bore him to the grave. The grass of many years has sprung up and withered on that grave, the burial stone is moss-grown, and good Mr. Hooper's face is dust; but awful is still the thought that it mouldered beneath the Black Veil!

1836 [1835]

THE BIRTH-MARK

In the latter part of the last century, there lived a man of science—an eminent proficient in every branch of natural philosophy—who, not long before our story opens, had made experience of a spiritual affinity, more attractive than any chemical one. He had left his laboratory to the care of an assistant, cleared his fine countenance from the furnace-smoke, washed the stain of acids from his fingers, and persuaded a beautiful woman to become his wife. In those days, when the comparatively recent discovery of electricity, and other kindred mysteries of nature, seemed to open paths into the region of miracle, it was not unusual for the love of science to rival the love of woman, in its depth and absorbing energy. The higher intellect, the imagination, the spirit, and even the heart, might all find their congenial aliment in pursuits which, as some of their ardent votaries believed, would ascend from one step of powerful intelligence to another, until the philosopher should lay his hand on the secret of creative force, and perhaps make new worlds for himself. We know not whether Aylmer possessed this degree of faith in man's ultimate control over nature. He had devoted himself, however, too unreservedly to scientific studies, ever to be weaned from them by any second passion. His love for his young wife might prove the stronger of the two; but it could only be by intertwining itself with his love of science, and uniting the strength of the latter to its own.

Such a union accordingly took place, and was attended with truly remarkable consequences, and a deeply impressive moral. One day, very soon after their marriage, Aylmer sat gazing at his wife, with a trouble in his countenance that grew stronger, until he spoke.

"Georgiana," said he, "has it never occurred to you that the mark upon your cheek might be removed?"

"No, indeed," said she, smiling; but perceiving the seriousness of his manner, she blushed deeply. "To tell you the truth, it has been so often called a charm, that I was simple enough to imagine it might be so."

"Ah, upon another face, perhaps it might," replied her husband. "But never on yours! No, dearest Georgiana, you came so nearly perfect from the hand of Nature, that this slightest possible defect—which we hesitate whether to term a defect or a beauty—shocks me, as being the visible mark of earthly imperfection."

"Shocks you, my husband!" cried Georgiana, deeply hurt; at first reddening with momentary anger, but then bursting into tears. "Then why did you take me from my mother's side? You cannot love what shocks you!"

To explain this conversation, it must be mentioned, that, in the centre of Georgiana's left cheek, there was a singular mark, deeply interwoven, as it were, with the texture and substance of her face. In the usual state of her complexion,—a healthy, though delicate bloom,—the mark wore a tint of deeper crimson, which imperfectly defined its shape amid the surrounding rosiness. When she blushed, it gradually became more indistinct, and finally vanished amid the triumphant rush of blood, that bathed the whole cheek with its brilliant glow. But, if any shifting emotion caused her to turn pale, there was the mark again, a crimson stain upon the snow, in what Aylmer sometimes deemed an almost fearful distinctness. Its shape bore not a little similarity to the human hand, though of the smallest pigmy size. Georgiana's lovers were wont to say, that some fairy, at her birth-hour, had laid her tiny hand upon the infant's cheek, and left this impress there, in token of the magic endowments that were to give her such sway over all hearts. Many a desperate swain would have risked life for the privilege of pressing his lips to the mysterious hand. It must not be concealed, however, that the impression wrought by this fairy sign-manual varied exceedingly, according to the difference of temperament in the beholders. Some fastidious persons—but they were exclusively of her own sex—affirmed that the Bloody Hand, as they chose to call it, quite destroyed the effect of Georgiana's beauty, and rendered her countenance even hideous. But it would be as reasonable to say, that one of those small blue stains, which sometimes occur in the purest statuary marble, would convert the Eve of Powers[1] to a monster. Masculine observers, if the birth-mark did not heighten their admiration, contented themselves with wishing it away, that the world might possess one living specimen of ideal loveliness, without the semblance of a flaw. After his marriage—for he thought little or nothing of the matter before—Aylmer discovered that this was the case with himself.

Had she been less beautiful—if Envy's self could have found aught else to sneer at—he might have felt his affection heightened by the prettiness of this mimic hand, now vaguely portrayed, now lost, now stealing forth again, and glimmering to-and-fro with every pulse of emotion that throbbed within her heart. But, seeing her otherwise so perfect, he found this one defect grow more and more intolerable, with every moment of their united lives. It was the fatal flaw of humanity, which Nature, in one shape or another, stamps ineffaceably on all her productions, either to imply that they are temporary and finite, or that their perfection must be wrought by toil and pain. The Crimson Hand expressed the ineludible gripe, in which mortality clutches the highest and purest of earthly mould, degrading them into kindred with the lowest, and even with the very brutes, like whom their visible frames return to dust. In this manner, selecting it as the symbol of his wife's liability to sin, sorrow, decay, and death, Alymer's sombre imagination was not long in rendering the birth-mark a frightful object, causing him more trouble and horror than ever Georgiana's beauty, whether of soul or sense, had given him delight.

At all the seasons which should have been their happiest, he invariably, and without intending it—nay, in spite of a purpose to the contrary—reverted to this one disastrous topic. Trifling as it at first appeared, it so connected itself with innumerable trains of thought, and modes of feeling, that it became the central point of all. With the morning twilight, Aylmer opened his eyes upon his wife's face, and recognized the symbol of imperfection; and when they sat together at the evening hearth, his eyes wandered stealthily to her cheek, and beheld, flickering with the blaze of the wood fire, the spectral Hand that wrote mortality, where he would fain have worshipped. Georgiana soon learned to shudder at his gaze. It needed but a glance, with the peculiar expression that his face often wore, to change the roses of her cheek into a deathlike paleness, amid which the Crimson Hand was brought strongly out, like a bas-relief of ruby on the whitest marble.

[1]"Eve before the Fall" (1839?), a statue by Hiram Powers (1805–1873), American sculptor famous for his idealized representations of feminine purity and innocence.

Late, one night, when the lights were growing dim, so as hardly to betray the stain on the poor wife's cheek, she herself, for the first time, voluntarily took up the subject.

"Do you remember, my dear Aylmer," said she, with a feeble attempt at a smile—"have you any recollection of a dream, last night, about this odious Hand?"

"None!—none whatever!" replied Aylmer, starting; but then he added in a dry, cold tone, affected for the sake of concealing the real depth of his emotion:—"I might well dream of it; for before I fell asleep, it had taken a pretty firm hold of my fancy."

"And you did dream of it," continued Georgiana, hastily; for she dreaded lest a gush of tears should interrupt what she had to say—"A terrible dream! I wonder that you can forget it. Is it possible to forget this one expression?—'It is in her heart now—we must have it out!'—Reflect, my husband; for by all means I would have you recall that dream."

The mind is in a sad note, when Sleep, the all-involving, cannot confine her spectres within the dim region of her sway, but suffers them to break forth, affrighting this actual life with secrets that perchance belong to a deeper one. Aylmer now remembered his dream. He had fancied himself, with his servant Aminadab, attempting an operation for the removal of the birth-mark. But the deeper went the knife, the deeper sank the Hand, until at length its tiny grasp appeared to have caught hold of Georgiana's heart; whence, however, her husband was inexorably resolved to cut or wrench it away.

When the dream had shaped itself perfectly in his memory, Aylmer sat in his wife's presence with a guilty feeling. Truth often finds its way to the mind close-muffled in robes of sleep, and then speaks with uncompromising directness of matters in regard to which we practise an unconscious self-deception, during our waking moments. Until now, he had not been aware of the tyrannizing influence acquired by one idea over his mind, and of the lengths which he might find in his heart to go, for the sake of giving himself peace.

"Aylmer," resumed Georgiana, solemnly, "I know not what may be the cost to both of us, to rid me of this fatal birth-mark. Perhaps its removal may cause cureless deformity. Or, it may be, the stain goes as deep as life itself. Again, do we know that there is a possibility, on any terms, of unclasping the firm gripe of this little Hand, which was laid upon me before I came into the world?"

"Dearest Georgiana, I have spent much thought upon the subject," hastily interrupted Aylmer—"I am convinced of the perfect practicability of its removal."

"If there be the remotest possibility of it," continued Georgiana, "let the attempt be made, at whatever risk. Danger is nothing to me; for life—which this hateful mark makes me the object of your horror and disgust—life is a burthen which I would fling down with joy. Either remove this dreadful Hand, or take my wretched life! You have deep science! All the world bears witness of it. You have achieved great wonders! Cannot you remove this little, little mark, which I cover with the tips of two small fingers? Is this beyond your power, for the sake of your own peace, and to save your poor wife from madness?"

"Noblest—dearest—tenderest wife!" cried Aylmer, rapturously. "Doubt not my power. I have already given this matter the deepest thought—thought which might almost have enlightened me to create a being less perfect than yourself. Georgiana, you have led me deeper than ever into the heart of science. I feel myself fully competent to render this dear cheek as faultless as its fellow; and then, most beloved, what will be my triumph, when I shall have corrected what Nature left imperfect, in her fairest work! Even Pygmalion,[2] when his sculptured woman assumed life, felt not greater ecstasy than mine will be."

"It is resolved, then," said Georgiana, faintly smiling,—"And, Aylmer, spare me not, though you should find the birth-mark take refuge in my heart at last."

Her husband tenderly kissed her cheek—her right cheek—not that which bore the impress of the Crimson Hand.

The next day, Aylmer apprized his wife of a plan that he had formed, whereby he might have opportunity for the intense thought and constant watchfulness, which the proposed operation would require; while Georgiana, likewise, would enjoy the perfect repose essential to its success. They were to seclude themselves in the extensive apartments occupied by Aylmer as a laboratory, and where, during his toilsome youth, he had made discoveries in the elemental powers of nature, that had roused the admiration of all the learned societies in Europe. Seated calmly in this laboratory, the pale philosopher had investigated the secrets of the highest cloud-region, and of the profoundest mines; he had satisfied himself of the causes that kindled and kept alive the fires of the volcano; and had explained the mystery of fountains, and how it is that they gush forth, some so bright and pure, and others with such rich medicinal virtues, from the dark bosom of the earth. Here, too, at an earlier period, he had studied the wonders of the human frame, and attempted to fathom the very process by which Nature assimilates all her precious influences from earth and air, and from the spiritual world, to create and foster Man, her masterpiece. The latter pursuit, however, Aylmer had long laid aside, in unwilling recognition of the truth, against which all seekers sooner or later stumble, that our great creative Mother, while she amuses us with apparently working in the broadest sunshine, is yet severely careful to keep her own secrets, and, in spite of her pretended openness, shows us nothing but results. She permits us indeed, to mar, but seldom to mend, and, like a jealous patentee, on no account to make. Now, however, Aylmer resumed these half-forgotten investigations; not, of course, with such hopes or wishes as first suggested them; but because they involved much physiological truth, and lay in the path of his proposed scheme for the treatment of Georgiana.

As he led her over the threshold of the laboratory, Georgiana was cold and tremulous. Aylmer looked cheerfully into her face, with intent to reassure her, but was so startled with the intense glow of the birth-mark upon the whiteness of her cheek, that he could not restrain a strong convulsive shudder. His wife fainted.

"Aminadab! Aminadab!" shouted Aylmer, stamping violently on the floor.

Forthwith, there issued from an inner apartment a man of low stature, but bulky frame, with shaggy hair hanging about his visage, which was grimed with the vapors of the furnace. This personage had been Aylmer's under-worker during his whole scientific career, and was admirably fitted for that office by his great mechanical readiness, and the skill with which, while incapable of comprehending a single principle, he executed all the practical details of his master's experiments. With his vast strength, his shaggy hair, his

[2]King of Cyprus, in Greek mythology, who fell in love with a statue he had sculpted. In answer to his prayers, Aphrodite, the goddess of love, brought the statue to life.

smoky aspect, and the indescribable earthiness that incrusted him, he seemed to represent man's physical nature; while Aylmer's slender figure, and pale, intellectual face, were no less apt a type of the spiritual element.

"Throw open the door of the boudoir, Aminadab," said Aylmer, "and burn a pastille."[3]

"Yes, master," answered Aminadab, looking intently at the lifeless form of Georgiana; and then he muttered to himself:—"If she were my wife, I'd never part with that birth-mark."

When Georgiana recovered consciousness, she found herself breathing an atmosphere of penetrating fragrance, the gentle potency of which had recalled her from her deathlike faintness. The scene around her looked like enchantment. Aylmer had converted those smoky, dingy, sombre rooms, where he had spent his brightest years in recondite pursuits, into a series of beautiful apartments, not unfit to be the secluded abode of a lovely woman. The walls were hung with gorgeous curtains, which imparted the combination of grandeur and grace, that no other species of adornment can achieve; and as they fell from the ceiling to the floor, their rich and ponderous folds, concealing all angles and straight lines, appeared to shut in the scene from infinite space. For aught Georgiana knew, it might be a pavilion among the clouds. And Aylmer, excluding the sunshine, which would have interfered with his chemical processes, had supplied its place with perfumed lamps, emitting flames of various hue, but all uniting in a soft, empurpled radiance. He now knelt by his wife's side, watching her earnestly, but without alarm; for he was confident in his science, and felt that he could draw a magic circle round her, within which no evil might intrude.

"Where am I?—Ah, I remember!" said Georgiana, faintly; and she placed her hand over her cheek, to hide the terrible mark from her husband's eyes.

"Fear not, dearest!" exclaimed he. "Do not shrink from me! Believe me, Georgiana, I even rejoice in this single imperfection, since it will be such rapture to remove it."

"Oh, spare me!" sadly replied his wife—"Pray do not look at it again. I never can forget that convulsive shudder."

In order to soothe Georgiana, and, as it were, to release her mind from the burthen of actual things, Aylmer now put in practice some of the light and playful secrets, which science had taught him among its profounder lore. Airy figures, absolutely bodiless ideas, and forms of unsubstantial beauty, came and danced before her, imprinting their momentary footsteps on beams of light. Though she had some indistinct idea of the method of these optical phenomena, still the illusion was almost perfect enough to warrant the belief that her husband possessed sway over the spiritual world. Then again, when she felt a wish to look forth from her seclusion, immediately, as if her thoughts were answered, the procession of external existence flitted across a screen. The scenery and the figures of actual life were perfectly represented, but with that bewitching, yet indescribable difference, which always makes a picture, an image, or a shadow, so much more attractive than the original. When wearied of this, Aylmer bade her cast her eyes upon a vessel, containing a quantity of earth. She did so, with little interest at first, but was soon startled, to perceive the germ of a plant, shooting upward from the soil.

[3]Incense.

Then came the slender stalk—the leaves gradually unfolded themselves—and amid them was a perfect and lovely flower.

"It is magical!" cried Georgiana, "I dare not touch it."

"Nay, pluck it," answered Aylmer, "pluck it, and inhale its brief perfume while you may. The flower will wither in a few moments, and leave nothing save its brown seed-vessels—but thence may be perpetuated a race as ephemeral as itself."

But Georgiana had no sooner touched the flower than the whole plant suffered a blight, its leaves turning coal-black, as if by the agency of fire.

"There was too powerful a stimulus," said Aylmer thoughtfully.

To make up for this abortive experiment, he proposed to take her portrait by a scientific process of his own invention. It was to be effected by rays of light striking upon a polished plate of metal. Georgiana assented—but, on looking at the result, was affrighted to find the features of the portrait blurred and indefinable; while the minute figure of a hand appeared where the cheek should have been. Aylmer snatched the metallic plate, and threw it into a jar of corrosive acid.

Soon, however, he forgot these mortifying failures. In the intervals of study and chemical experiment, he came to her, flushed and exhausted, but seemed invigorated by her presence, and spoke in glowing language of the resources of his art. He gave a history of the long dynasty of the Alchemists,[4] who spent so many ages in quest of the universal solvent, by which the Golden Principle might be elicited from all things vile and base. Aylmer appeared to believe, that, by the plainest scientific logic, it was altogether within the limits of possibility to discover this long-sought medium; but, he added, a philosopher who should go deep enough to acquire the power, would attain too lofty a wisdom to stoop to the exercise of it. Not less singular were his opinions in regard to the Elixir Vitae. He more than intimated, that it was his option to concoct a liquid that should prolong life for years—perhaps interminably—but that it would produce a discord in nature, which all the world, and chiefly the quaffer of the immortal nostrum, would find cause to curse.

"Aylmer, are you in earnest?" asked Georgiana, looking at him with amazement and fear; "it is terrible to possess such power, or even to dream of possessing it!"

"Oh, do not tremble, my love!" said her husband, "I would not wrong either you or myself by working such inharmonious effects upon our lives. But I would have you consider how trifling, in comparison, is the skill requisite to remove this little Hand."

At the mention of the birth-mark, Georgiana, as usual, shrank, as if a red-hot iron had touched her cheek.

Again, Aylmer applied himself to his labors. She could hear his voice in the distant furnace-room, giving directions to Aminadab, whose harsh, uncouth, misshapen tones were audible in response, more like the grunt or growl of a brute than human speech. After hours of absence, Aylmer reappeared, and proposed that she should now examine his cabinet of chemical products, and natural treasures of the earth. Among the former he showed her a small vial, in which, he remarked, was contained a gentle yet most

[4]Medieval scientists who sought to turn base metals into gold and create a compound (Elixir Vitae: elixir of life) that would prolong life indefinitely.

powerful fragrance, capable of impregnating all the breezes that blow across a kingdom. They were of inestimable value, the contents of that little vial; and, as he said so, he threw some of the perfume into the air, and filled the room with piercing and invigorating delight.

"And what is this?" asked Georgiana, pointing to a small crystal globe, containing a gold-colored liquid. "It is so beautiful to the eye, that I could imagine it the Elixir of Life."

"In one sense it is," replied Aylmer, "or rather the Elixir of Immortality. It is the most precious poison that ever was concocted in this world. By its aid, I could apportion the lifetime of any mortal at whom you might point your finger. The strength of the dose would determine whether he were to linger out years, or drop dead in the midst of a breath. No king, on his guarded throne, could keep his life, if I, in my private station, should deem that the welfare of millions justified me in depriving him of it."

"Why do you keep such a terrific drug?" inquired Georgiana in horror.

"Do not mistrust me, dearest!" said her husband, smiling; "its virtuous potency is yet greater than its harmful one. But, see! here is a powerful cosmetic. With a few drops of this, in a vase of water, freckles may be washed away as easily as the hands are cleansed. A stronger infusion would take the blood out of the cheek, and leave the rosiest beauty a pale ghost."

"Is it with this lotion that you intend to bathe my cheek?" asked Georgiana anxiously.

"Oh, no!" hastily replied her husband—"this is merely superficial. Your case demands a remedy that shall go deeper."

In his interviews with Georgiana, Aylmer generally made minute inquires as to her sensations, and whether the confinement of the rooms, and the temperature of the atmosphere, agreed with her. These questions had such a particular drift, that Georgiana began to conjecture that she was already subjected to certain physical influences, either breathed in with the fragrant air, or taken with her food. She fancied likewise—but it might be altogether fancy—that there was a stirring up of her system,—a strange indefinite sensation creeping through her veins, and tingling, half painfully, half pleasurably, at her heart. Still, whenever she dared to look into the mirror, there she beheld herself, pale as a white rose, and with the crimson birth-mark stamped upon her cheek. Not even Aylmer now hated it so much as she.

To dispel the tedium of the hours which her husband found it necessary to devote to the processes of combination and analysis, Georgiana turned over the volumes of his scientific library. In many dark old tomes, she met with chapters full of romance and poetry. They were the works of the philosophers of the middle ages, such as Albertus Magnus, Cornelius Agrippa, Paracelsus, and the famous friar who created the prophetic Brazen Head.[5] All these antique naturalists stood in advance of their centuries, yet were imbued with some of their credulity, and therefore were believed, and perhaps imagined themselves, to have acquired from the investigation of nature a power above nature, and from physics a sway over the spiritual world. Hardly less curious and imaginative were the early volumes of the Transactions of the Royal Society, in which the members, knowing little of the limits

[5]Friar Roger Bacon, English philosopher and scientist (1214?–1294?), was said to have created a brass head that could speak.

of natural possibility, were continually recording wonders, or proposing methods whereby wonders might be wrought.

But, to Georgiana, the most engrossing volume was a large folio from her husband's own hand, in which he had recorded every experiment of his scientific career, with its original aim, the methods adopted for its development, and its final success or failure, with the circumstances to which either event was attributable. The book, in truth, was both the history and emblem of his ardent, ambitious, imaginative, yet practical and laborious, life. He handled physical details, as if there were nothing beyond them; yet spiritualized them all, and redeemed himself from materialism, by his strong and eager aspiration towards the infinite. In his grasp, the veriest clod of earth assumed a soul. Georgiana, as she read, reverenced Aylmer, and loved him more profoundly than ever, but with a less entire dependence on his judgment than heretofore. Much as he had accomplished, she could not but observe that his most splendid successes were almost invariable failures, if compared with the ideal at which he aimed. His brightest diamonds were the merest pebbles, and felt to be so by himself, in comparison with the inestimable gems which lay hidden beyond his reach. The volume, rich with achievements that had won renown for its author, was yet as melancholy a record as ever mortal hand had penned. It was the sad confession, and continual exemplification, of the short-comings of the composite man—the spirit burthened with clay and working in matter—and of the despair that assails the higher nature, at finding itself so miserably thwarted by the earthly part. Perhaps every man of genius, in whatever sphere, might recognize the image of his own experience in Aylmer's journal.

So deeply did these reflections affect Georgiana, that she laid her face upon the open volume, and burst into tears. In this situation she was found by her husband.

"It is dangerous to read in a sorcerer's books," said he, with a smile, though his countenance was uneasy and displeased. "Georgiana, there are pages in that volume, which I can scarcely glance over and keep my senses. Take heed lest it prove as detrimental to you!"

"It has made me worship you more than ever," said she.

"Ah! wait for this one success," rejoined he, "then worship me if you will. I shall deem myself hardly unworthy of it. But, come! I have sought you for the luxury of your voice. Sing to me, dearest!"

So she poured out the liquid music of her voice to quench the thirst of his spirit. He then took his leave, with a boyish exuberance of gaiety, assuring her that her seclusion would endure but a little longer, and that the result was already certain. Scarcely had he departed, when Georgiana felt irresistibly impelled to follow him. She had forgotten to inform Aylmer of a symptom, which, for two or three hours past, had begun to excite her attention. It was a sensation in the fatal birth-mark, not painful, but which induced a restlessness throughout her system. Hastening after her husband, she intruded, for the first time, into the laboratory.

The first thing that struck her eye was the furnace, that hot and feverish worker, with the intense glow of its fire, which, by the quantities of soot clustered above it, seemed to have been burning for ages. There was a distilling apparatus in full operation. Around the room were retorts, tubes, cylinders, crucibles, and other apparatus of chemical research. An electrical machine stood ready for immediate use. The atmosphere felt oppressively close, and was tainted with gaseous odors, which had been tormented forth by the processes of science. The severe and homely simplicity of the apartment, with its naked walls and brick pavement, looked strange, accustomed as Georgiana had become to the fantastic elegance of her boudoir. But what chiefly, indeed almost solely, drew her attention, was the aspect of Aylmer himself.

He was pale as death, anxious, and absorbed, and hung over the furnace as if it depended upon his utmost watchfulness whether the liquid, which it was distilling, should be the draught of immortal happiness or misery. How different from the sanguine and joyous mien that he had assumed for Georgiana's encouragement!

"Carefully now, Aminadab! Carefully, thou human machine! Carefully, thou man of clay!" muttered Aylmer, more to himself than his assistant. "Now, if there be a thought too much or too little, it is all over!"

"Hoh! hoh!" mumbled Aminadab—"look, master, look!"

Aylmer raised his eyes hastily, and at first reddened, then grew paler than ever, on beholding Georgiana. He rushed towards her, and seized her arm with a gripe that left the print of his fingers upon it.

"Why do you come hither? Have you no trust in your husband?" cried he impetuously. "Would you throw the blight of that fatal birth-mark over my labors? It is not well done. Go, prying woman, go!"

"Nay, Aylmer," said Georgiana, with the firmness of which she possessed no stinted endowment, "it is not you that have a right to complain. You mistrust your wife! You have concealed the anxiety with which you watch the development of this experiment. Think not so unworthily of me, my husband! Tell me all the risk we run; and fear not that I shall shrink, for my share in it is far less than your own!"

"No, no, Georgiana!" said Aylmer impatiently, "it must not be."

"I submit," replied she calmly. "And, Aylmer, I shall quaff whatever draught you bring me; but it will be on the same principle that would induce me to take a dose of poison, if offered by your hand."

"My noble wife," said Aylmer, deeply moved, "I knew not the height and depth of your nature, until now. Nothing shall be concealed, Know, then, that this Crimson Hand, superficial as it seems, has clutched its grasp into your being, with a strength of which I had no previous conception. I have already administered agents powerful enough to do aught except to change your entire physical system. Only one thing remains to be tried. If that fail us, we are ruined!"

"Why did you hesitate to tell me this?" asked she.

"Because, Georgiana," said Aylmer, in a low voice, "there is danger!"

"Danger? There is but one danger—that this horrible stigma shall be left upon my cheek!" cried Georgiana. "Remove it! remove it!—whatever be the cost—or we shall both go mad!"

"Heaven knows, your words are too true," said Aylmer, sadly. "And now, dearest, return to your boudoir. In a little while, all will be tested."

He conducted her back, and took leave of her with a solemn tenderness, which spoke far more than his words how much was now at stake. After his departure, Georgiana became wrapt in musings. She considered the character of Aylmer, and did it completer justice than at any previous moment. Her heart exulted, while it trembled, at his honorable love, so pure and lofty that it would accept nothing less than perfection, nor miserably make itself contented with an earthlier nature than he had dreamed of. She felt how much more precious was such a sentiment, than that meaner kind which would have borne with the imperfection for her sake, and have been guilty of treason to holy love, by degrading its perfect idea to the level of the actual. And, with her whole spirit, she prayed, that, for a single moment, she might satisfy his highest and deepest conception. Longer than one moment, she well knew, it could not be; for his spirit was ever on the march—ever ascending—and each instant required something that was beyond the scope of the instant before.

The sound of her husband's footsteps aroused her. He bore a crystal goblet, containing a liquor colorless as water, but bright enough to be the draught of immortality. Aylmer was pale; but it seemed rather the consequence of a highly wrought state of mind, and tension of spirit, than of fear or doubt.

"The concoction of the draught has been perfect," said he, in answer to Georgiana's look. "Unless all my science have deceived me, it cannot fail."

"Save on your account, my dearest Aylmer," observed his wife, "I might wish to put off this birth-mark of mortality by relinquishing mortality itself, in preference to any other mode. Life is but a sad possession to those who have attained precisely the degree of moral advancement at which I stand. Were I weaker and blinder, it might be happiness. Were I stronger, it might be endured hopefully. But, being what I find myself, methinks I am of all mortals the most fit to die."

"You are fit for heaven without tasting death!" replied her husband. "But why do we speak of dying? The draught cannot fail. Behold its effect upon this plant!"

On the window-seat there stood a geranium, diseased with yellow blotches, which had overspread all its leaves. Aylmer poured a small quantity of the liquid upon the soil in which it grew. In a little time, when the roots of the plant had taken up the moisture, the unsightly blotches began to be extinguished in a living verdure.

"There needed no proof," said Georgiana, quietly. "Give me the goblet. I joyfully stake all upon your word."

"Drink, then, thou lofty creature!" exclaimed Aylmer, with fervid admiration. "There is no taint of imperfection on thy spirit. Thy sensible frame, too, shall be all perfect!"

She quaffed the liquid, and returned the goblet to his hand.

"It is grateful," said she, with a placid smile. "Methinks it is like water from a heavenly fountain; for it contains I know not what of unobtrusive fragrance and deliciousness. It allays a feverish thirst, that had parched me for many days. Now, dearest, let me sleep. My earthly senses are closing over my spirit, like the leaves round the heart of a rose, at sunset."

She spoke the last words with a gentle reluctance, as if it required almost more energy than she could command to pronounce the faint and lingering syllables. Scarcely had they loitered through her lips, ere she was lost in slumber. Aylmer sat by her side, watching her aspect with the emotions proper to a man, the whole value of whose existence was involved in the process now to be tested. Mingled with this mood, however, was the philosophic investigation, characteristic of the man of science. Not the minutest symptom escaped him. A heightened flush of the cheek—a slight irregularity of breath—a quiver of the eyelid—a hardly perceptible tremor through the frame—such were the details which, as the moments passed, he wrote down in his folio volume. Intense thought had set its stamp upon every previous page of that volume; but the thoughts of years were all concentrated upon the last.

While thus employed, he failed not to gaze often at the fatal Hand, and not without a shudder. Yet once, by a strange and unaccountable impulse, he pressed it with his lips. His spirit recoiled, however, in the very act, and Georgiana, out of the midst of her deep sleep, moved uneasily and murmured as if in remonstrance. Again, Aylmer resumed his watch. Nor was it without avail. The Crimson Hand, which at first had been strongly visible upon the marble paleness of Georgiana's cheek now grew more faintly outlined. She remained not less pale than ever; but the birth-mark, with every breath that came and went, lost somewhat of its former distinctness. Its presence had been awful; its departure was more awful still. Watch the stain of the rainbow fading out of the sky; and you will know how that mysterious symbol passed away.

"By Heaven, it is well nigh gone!" said Aylmer to himself, in almost irrepressible ecstasy. "I can scarcely trace it now. Success! Success! And now it is like the faintest rose-color. The slightest flush of blood across her cheek would overcome it. But she is so pale!"

He drew aside the window-curtain, and suffered the light of natural day to fall into the room, and rest upon her cheek. At the same time, he heard a gross, hoarse chuckle, which he had long known as his servant Aminadab's expression of delight.

"Ah, clod! Ah, earthly mass!" cried Aylmer, laughing in a sort of frenzy. "You have served me well! Matter and Spirit—Earth and Heaven—have both done their part in this! Laugh, thing of senses! You have earned the right to laugh."

These exclamations broke Georgiana's sleep. She slowly unclosed her eyes, and gazed into the mirror, which her husband had arranged for that purpose. A faint smile flitted over her lips, when she recognized how barely perceptible was now that Crimson Hand, which had once blazed forth with such disastrous brilliancy as to scare away all their happiness. But then her eyes sought Aylmer's face, with a trouble and anxiety that he could by no means account for.

"My poor Aylmer!" murmured she.

"Poor? Nay, richest! Happiest! Most favored!" exclaimed he. "My peerless bride, it is successful! You are perfect!"

"My poor Aylmer!" she repeated, with a more than human tenderness. "You have aimed loftily!—you have done nobly! Do not repent, that, with so high and pure a feeling, you have rejected the best that earth could offer. Aylmer—dearest Aylmer—I am dying!"

Alas, it was too true! The fatal Hand had grappled with the mystery of life, and was the bond by which an angelic spirit kept itself in union with a mortal frame. As the last crimson tint of the birth-mark—that sole token of human imperfection—faded from her cheek, the parting breath of the now perfect woman passed into the atmosphere, and her soul, lingering a moment near her husband, took its heavenward flight. Then a hoarse, chuckling laugh was heard again! Thus ever does the gross Fatality of Earth exult in its invariable triumph over the immortal essence, which, in this dim sphere of half-development, demands the completeness of a higher state.

Yet, had Aylmer reached a profounder wisdom, he need not thus have flung away the happiness, which would have woven his mortal life of the self-same texture with the celestial. The momentary circumstance was strong for him; he failed to look beyond the shadowy scope of Time, and living once for all in Eternity, to find the perfect Future in the present.

1843 1843

Herman Melville 1819–1891

In his lifetime, Herman Melville was known as the "man who lived among cannibals," a writer whose tales of island adventure in the Pacific had captured the popular imagination of mid-nineteenth-century readers eager for exotic yarns of the South Seas. Not until the "Melville Revival" of the 1920s and 1930s was he fully recognized for the breadth, penetration, and symbolic richness of his writing.

Melville was born into the security of the middle-class gentry of New York State, but when he was eleven, his father's import business failed. Two years later his father died, and Melville was forced to withdraw from school. He worked on a farm, as a messenger in a bank, and as a clerk in his brother's store. Two additional years of schooling qualified him for a period of elementary-school teaching, but when he was nineteen, his "roving disposition," and his hope to escape the boredom of the schoolroom, led him to sign on as a merchant seaman on a vessel bound for Liverpool, England.

Melville sailed for England in June 1839. Four months later he returned to America, where he took up school teaching once again. Then in the spring of 1840 he went west to visit relatives in Galena, Illinois, on the Mississippi River. Unable to find work in Illinois, Melville returned home the next fall, and in December of 1840 he signed on as an ordinary seaman on the Acushnet, *an American whaling ship bound for the South Pacific. Eighteen months later, when the whaler had rounded Cape Horn and crossed the Pacific to the Marquesas Islands, Melville deserted ship and was taken captive by the Typees, an island tribe noted for its cannibalism. After a month of captivity, Melville escaped and made his way to Tahiti, where he lived as a beachcomber. He then signed on as a harpooner on a whaling ship bound for the Hawaiian Islands. In Honolulu, Melville worked briefly as a store clerk, but the urge to return home led him to enlist as an ordinary seaman on the American naval frigate* United States. *Fourteen months later he arrived in Boston after an absence of almost four years.*

Melville had experienced the most exciting adventures of his life. He put them to use in becoming a writer, and the next five years were the period of his greatest popular literary successes. In 1846 he published his first book, Typee, A Peep at Polynesian Life, *an autobiographical novel of his adventures among the Marquesas cannibals that long remained his most popular work. In 1847 he published* Omoo, A Narrative of Adventures in the South Seas, *which drew upon his experiences in Tahiti. His next book,* Mardi *(1849), was a financial failure. His audience, expecting another exciting volume of South Seas perils and escapes, confronted instead a heavily symbolic quest novel written in an eccentric style and burdened with political allegory. Recognizing that as his writing grew profound his audience shrank, Melville returned to autobiographical adventure tales. He wrote* Redburn *(1849), a novel based on his youthful voyage to Liverpool, and* White-Jacket *(1850), which described the world of ruthless discipline he had experienced as a crewman on a United States man-of-war.*

In 1851 Melville moved to Pittsfield in western Massachusetts, six miles from the home of his friend Nathaniel Hawthorne, and there Melville worked on his great novel Moby Dick *(1851). It was begun as another autobiographical romance, but the story of the obsessive mania of its hero-villain, Captain Ahab, became an emblematic novel rich with symbolism.* Moby Dick *was completed when Melville was thirty-one. Its success was slight. Writing of the failures of human perception, the dangers of human isolation, and the nature of evil, he had created a masterpiece, but he failed to regain his popular audience.*

Melville then turned to work on Pierre *(1852), a melodramatic novel of a search for absolute morality. It was his greatest commercial failure. The first of his novels to be set on land rather than the sea,* Pierre *puzzled and shocked its readers with its portrayal of immorality and hints of incest. Critics called it a "bad book," "affected," "unnatural," "repulsive," its language "drunken and reeling." Scoffing reviewers advised Melville to return to "capital sea-pieces," the stories of sailors and ships that had first won him fame. Dismayed by the response to* Pierre, *Melville temporarily abandoned novels and turned to magazine journalism and the writing of articles and short stories.*

Piazza Tales, *a collection of his short stories that included "Bartleby the Scrivener" and "Benito Cereno," appeared in 1856. In the same year he completed his last novel,* The Confidence Man *(1857), a bitter portrait of the folly of hope and of the gullibility of men. Ill and debt-ridden at thirty-seven, he left America for an extended tour of the Holy Land, a trip financed by his wife's father. Upon his return, Melville tried for three years to earn his living as a lecturer, traveling through the South and Midwest. Finally, in 1866, he was appointed to the position of deputy inspector in the United States Customhouse in New York City, a position he held for almost twenty years.*

During his years of literary obscurity in New York City, Melville wrote several volumes of poetry, including Clarel: A Poem and Pilgrimage in the Holy Land, *his final long work. When it was published in 1876, it was ignored, and in his last years, Melville increasingly fell into a bitter irascibility over the public failure of his writing. Except for two small and unsuccessful volumes of poetry, he published nothing for the remainder of his life. When he died in 1891 he left in manuscript form a few poems and the short novel* Billy Budd, *on which he had worked during his last years.*

Melville's recurrent theme of the confrontation of innocence and evil, his pessimistic spirit, the morbidity and demonism he found central to the world, the agonies of self-discovery he portrayed, and his brooding doubts over the comforting nineteenth-century idea of progress all appealed less to his own age than to the twentieth century. Like many of his contemporaries he had developed an essential mistrust of the idea of unrestrained liberty. He conceived of man as radically imperfect, obliged to compromise between absolute good and worldly necessity. He saw a world filled with lost innocence and betrayed hope. He was, as Hawthorne observed, a man who could "neither believe nor be comfortable in his unbelief" and yet a man who was of "very high and noble nature, and better worth immortality than most of us."

FURTHER READING: *The Works of Herman Melville,* 16 vols., 1922–1924, 1963; *Complete Works of Herman Melville,* 7 vols. (of 14 projected), ed. H. Vincent, 1947–1969; *The Writings of Herman Melville,* 15 vols., ed. H. Hayford, et al., 1968–1993; *The Letters of Herman Melville,* ed. M. Davis and W. Gilman, 1960; R. Chase, *Herman Melville, A Critical Study,* 1949; N. Arvin, *Herman Melville,* 1950, 1957; J. Leyda, *The Melville Log,* 2 vols., 1951, 1969; L. Howard, *Herman Melville,* 1951, 1958, 1981; L. Robertson-Lorant, *Melville, A Biography,* 1996; H. Parker, *Herman Melville,* 1996, 2005; R. Fogle, *Melville's Shorter Tales,* 1960; J. Miller, *A Reader's Guide to Herman Melville,* 1962, 1973; J. Duban, *Melville's Major Fiction,* 1983; N. Tolchin, *Mourning, Gender, and Creativity in the Art of Herman Melville,* 1988; *A Companion to Melville Studies,* ed. John Bryant, 1986; L. Newman, *A Reader's Guide to the Short Stories of Herman Melville,* 1986; M. Bercaw, *Melville's Sources,* 1987; J. Samson, *White Lies, Melville's Narratives and Facts,* 1989; P. Bellis, *No Mysteries Out of Ourselves, Identity and Textural Form in the Novels of Herman Melville,* 1990; K. Kier, *A Melville Encyclopedia, The Novels,* 2 vols., 1990; C. Sten, *Savage Eye, Melville and the Visual Arts,* 1991; B. Short, *Cast by Means of Figures, Herman Melville's Rhetorical Development,* 1992; J. Bryant, *Melville and Repose,* 1993; *Melville, A Collection of Critical Essays,* ed. M. Jehlen, 1994; R. Gale, *A Herman Melville Encyclopedia,* 1995; J. Wenke, *Melville's Muse,* 1995; N. Fredericks, *Melville's Art of Democracy,* 1995; W. Kelley, *Melville's City,* 1996; C. Durer, *Herman Melville, Romantic and Prophet,* 1996; D. Robillard, *Melville and the Visual Arts,* 1997; *The Cambridge Companion to Herman Melville,* ed. R. Levine, 1998; S. Otter, *Melville's Anatomies,* 1999; H. Hayford, *Melville's Prisoners,* 2003; E. Dryden, *Monumental Melville,* 2004; C. Johnson, *Understanding Melville's Short Fiction,* 2005; G. Gunn, *A Historical Guide to Herman Melville,* 2005.

TEXTS: "The Paradise of Bachelors and the Tartarus of Maids," *Harper's New Monthly Magazine,* April 1855; "Bartleby, the Scrivener" and "Benito Cereno," *The Piazza Tales,* 1856. Poems are from *Battle-Pieces and Aspects of the War,* 1866; *John Marr and Other Sailors,* 1888, *Timoleon,* 1891.

BARTLEBY, THE SCRIVENER

A STORY OF WALL STREET[1]

I am a rather elderly man. The nature of my avocations, for the last thirty years, has brought me into more than ordinary contact with what would seem an interesting and somewhat singular set of men, of whom, as yet, nothing, that I know of, has ever been written—I mean, the law-copyists, or scriveners. I have known very many of them, professionally and privately, and, if I pleased, could relate divers histories, at which good-natured gentlemen might smile, and sentimental souls might weep. But I waive the biographies of all other scriveners, for a few passages in the life of Bartleby, who was a scrivener, the strangest I ever saw, or heard of. While, of other law-copyists, I might write the complete life, of Bartleby nothing of that sort can be done. I believe that no materials exist, for a full and satisfactory biography of this man. It is an irreparable loss to literature. Bartleby was one of those beings of whom nothing is ascertainable, except from the original sources, and, in his case, those are very small. What my own astonished eyes saw of Bartleby, *that* is all I know of him, except, indeed, one vague report, which will appear in the sequel.

[1]First published in *Putnam's Monthly Magazine,* 11 (November and December), 1853, from which the title and subtitle used here are taken.

Ere introducing the scrivener, as he first appeared to me, it is fit I make some mention of myself, my *employés*, my business, my chambers, and general surroundings; because some such description is indispensable to an adequate understanding of the chief character about to be presented. Imprimis:[2] I am a man who, from his youth upward, has been filled with a profound conviction that the easiest way of life is the best. Hence, though I belong to a profession proverbially energetic and nervous, even to turbulence, at times, yet nothing of that sort have I ever suffered to invade my peace. I am one of those unambitious lawyers who never addresses a jury, or in any way draws down public applause; but, in the cool tranquillity of a snug retreat, do a snug business among rich men's bonds, and mortgages, and title-deeds. All who know me, consider me an eminently *safe* man. The late John Jacob Astor,[3] a personage little given to poetic enthusiasm, had no hesitation in pronouncing my first grand point to be prudence; my next, method. I do not speak it in vanity, but simply record the fact, that I was not unemployed in my profession by the late John Jacob Astor; a name which, I admit, I love to repeat; for it hath a rounded and orbicular sound to it, and rings like unto bullion. I will freely add, that I was not insensible to the late John Jacob Astor's good opinion.

Some time prior to the period at which this little history begins, my avocations had been largely increased. The good old office, now extinct in the State of New York, of a Master in Chancery,[4] had been conferred upon me. It was not a very arduous office, but very pleasantly remunerative. I seldom lose my temper; much more seldom indulge in dangerous indignation at wrongs and outrages; but, I must be permitted to be rash here, and declare, that I consider the sudden and violent abrogation of the office of Master in Chancery, by the new Constitution,[5] as a——premature act; inasmuch as I had counted upon a life-lease of the profits, whereas I only received those of a few short years. But this is by the way.

My chambers were upstairs, at No.—Wall Street. At one end, they looked upon the white wall of the interior of a spacious skylight shaft, penetrating the building from top to bottom.

This view might have been considered rather tame than otherwise, deficient in what landscape painters call "life." But, if so, the view from the other end of my chambers offered, at least, a contrast, if nothing more. In that direction, my windows commanded an unobstructed view of a lofty brick wall, black by age and everlasting shade; which wall required no spy-glass to bring out its lurking beauties, but, for the benefit of all near-sighted spectators, was pushed up to within ten feet of my window panes. Owing to the great height of the surrounding buildings, and my chambers being on the second floor, the interval between this wall and mine not a little resembled a huge square cistern.

[2] In the first place.

[3] American millionaire (1763–1848), the richest of his era.

[4] Courts of Chancery dealt with equity law in which decisions were reached without the delays of a formal jury trial.

[5] The Office of Master of Chancery in New York State was abolished when a new state constitution was adopted in 1846.

At the period just preceding the advent of Bartleby, I had two persons as copyists in my employment, and a promising lad as an office-boy. First, Turkey; second, Nippers; third, Ginger Nut. These may seem names, the like of which are not usually found in the Directory.[6] In truth, they were nicknames, mutually conferred upon each other by my three clerks, and were deemed expressive of their respective persons or characters. Turkey was a short, pursy[7] Englishman, of about my own age—that is, somewhere not far from sixty. In the morning, one might say, his face was of a fine florid hue, but after twelve o'clock, meridian[8]—his dinner hour—it blazed like a grate full of Christmas coals;[9] and continued blazing—but, as it were, with a gradual wane—till six o'clock, P.M., or thereabouts; after which, I saw no more of the proprietor of the face, which, gaining its meridian with the sun, seemed to set with it, to rise, culminate, and decline the following day, with the like regularity and undiminished glory. There are many singular coincidences I have known in the course of my life, not the least among which was the fact, that, exactly when Turkey displayed his fullest beams from his red and radiant countenance, just then, too, at that critical moment, began the daily period when I considered his business capacities as seriously disturbed for the remainder of the twenty-four hours. Not that he was absolutely idle, or averse to business, then; far from it. The difficulty was, he was apt to be altogether too energetic. There was a strange, inflamed, flurried, flighty recklessness of activity about him. He would be incautious in dipping his pen into his inkstand. All his blots upon my documents were dropped there after twelve o'clock, meridian. Indeed, not only would he be reckless, and sadly given to making blots in the afternoon, but, some days, he went further, and was rather noisy. At such times, too, his face flamed with augmented blazonry, as if cannel coal had been heaped on anthracite.[10] He made an unpleasant racket with his chair; spilled his sand-box;[11] in mending his pens, impatiently split them all to pieces, and threw them on the floor in a sudden passion; stood up, and leaned over his table, boxing his papers about in a most indecorous manner, very sad to behold in an elderly man like him. Nevertheless, as he was in many ways a most valuable person to me, and all the time before twelve o'clock, meridian, was the quickest, steadiest creature, too, accomplishing a great deal of work in a style not easily to be matched—for these reasons, I was willing to overlook his eccentricities, though, indeed, occasionally, I remonstrated with him. I did this very gently, however, because, though the civilest, nay, the blandest and most reverential of men in the morning, yet, in the afternoon, he was disposed, upon provocation, to be slightly rash with his tongue—in fact, insolent. Now, valuing his morning services as I did, and resolved not to lose them—yet, at the same time, made uncomfortable by his inflamed way after twelve o'clock—and being a man of peace, unwilling by my admonitions to call forth unseemly retorts from him, I took upon me, one Saturday noon (he was always worse on Saturdays) to hint to him, very kindly, that, perhaps, now that he was growing old, it might be well to abridge his labours; in short, he need not come to my chambers

[6]The city directory, listing the names and addresses of the city's inhabitants. [7]Fat.
[8]Noon. [9]As in the festive fires of Christmas time.
[10]A fire of cannel (soft) coal mixed with anthracite (hard) coal emits great heat and light.
[11]Containing sand for blotting ink.

after twelve o'clock, but, dinner over, had best go home to his lodgings, and rest himself till tea-time. But no; he insisted upon his afternoon devotions. His countenance became intolerably fervid, as he oratorically assured me—gesticulating with a long ruler at the other end of the room—that if his services in the morning were useful, how indispensable, then, in the afternoon?

"With submission, sir," said Turkey, on this occasion, "I consider myself your right-hand man. In the morning I but marshal and deploy my columns; but in the afternoon I put myself at their head, and gallantly charge the foe, thus"—and he made a violent thrust with the ruler.

"But the blots, Turkey," intimated I.

"True; but, with submission, sir, behold these hairs! I am getting old. Surely, sir, a blot or two of a warm afternoon is not to be severely urged against gray hairs. Old age—even if it blot the page—is honourable. With submission, sir, we *both* are getting old."

This appeal to my fellow-feeling was hardly to be resisted At all events, I saw that go he would not. So, I made up my mind to let him stay, resolving, nevertheless, to see to it that, during the afternoon, he had to do with my less important papers.

Nippers, the second on my list, was a whiskered, sallow, and, upon the whole, rather piratical-looking young man, of about five-and-twenty. I always deemed him the victim of two evil powers—ambition and indigestion. The ambition was evinced by a certain impatience of the duties of a mere copyist, an unwarrantable usurpation of strictly professional affairs, such as the original drawing up of legal documents. The indigestion seemed betokened in an occasional nervous testiness and grinning irritability, causing the teeth to audibly grind together over mistakes committed in copying; unnecessary maledictions, hissed, rather than spoken, in the heat of business; and especially by a continual discontent with the height of the table where he worked. Though of a very ingenious mechanical turn, Nippers could never get this table to suit him. He put chips under it, blocks of various sorts, bits of pasteboard, and at last went so far as to attempt an exquisite adjustment, by final pieces of folded blotting-paper. But no invention would answer. If, for the sake of easing his back, he brought the table lid at a sharp angle well up toward his chin, and wrote there like a man using the steep roof of a Dutch house for his desk, then he declared that it stopped the circulation in his arms. If now he lowered the table to his waistbands, and stooped over it in writing, then there was a sore aching in his back. In short, the truth of the matter was, Nippers knew not what he wanted. Or, if he wanted anything, it was to be rid of a scrivener's table altogether. Among the manifestations of his diseased ambition was a fondness he had for receiving visits from certain ambiguous-looking fellows in seedy coats, whom he called his clients. Indeed, I was aware that not only was he, at times, considerable of a ward-politician, but he occasionally did a little business at the Justices' courts, and was not unknown on the steps of the Tombs.[12] I have good reason to believe, however, that one

[12]A prison in New York City. Begun in 1835, it was built in the Egyptian Revival style derived from Egyptian temples and tombs. Officially known as The Halls of Justice and House of Detention, it was a prison for petty criminals and debtors and those awaiting trial or execution. Politicians, lawyers, and hangers-on gathered on its steps, where they exchanged gossip and sought clients and political advancement.

individual who called upon him at my chambers, and who, with a grand air, he insisted was his client, was no other than a dun,[13] and the alleged title-deed, a bill. But, with all his failings, and the annoyances he caused me, Nippers, like his compatriot Turkey, was a very useful man to me; wrote a neat, swift hand; and, when he chose, was not deficient in a gentlemanly sort of deportment. Added to this, he always dressed in a gentlemanly sort of way; and so, incidentally, reflected credit upon my chambers. Whereas, with respect to Turkey, I had much ado to keep him from being a reproach to me. His clothes were apt to look oily, and smell of eating-houses. He wore his pantaloons very loose and baggy in summer. His coats were execrable; his hat not to be handled. But while the hat was a thing of indifference to me, inasmuch as his natural civility and deference, as a dependent Englishman, always led him to doff it the moment he entered the room, yet his coat was another matter. Concerning his coats, I reasoned with him; but with no effect. The truth was, I suppose, that a man with so small an income could not afford to sport such a lustrous face and a lustrous coat at one and the same time. As Nippers once observed, Turkey's money went chiefly for red ink. One winter day, I presented Turkey with a highly respectable-looking coat of my own—a padded gray coat, of a most comfortable warmth, and which buttoned straight up from the knee to the neck. I thought Turkey would appreciate the favour, and abate his rashness and obstreperousness of afternoons. But no; I verily believe that buttoning himself up in so downy and blanket-like a coat had a pernicious effect upon him—upon the same principle that too much oats are bad for horses. In fact, precisely as a rash, restive horse is said to feel his oats, so Turkey felt his coat. It made him insolent. He was a man whom prosperity harmed.

Though, concerning the self-indulgent habits of Turkey, I had my own private surmises, yet, touching Nippers, I was well persuaded that, whatever might be his faults in other respects, he was, at least, a temperate young man. But, indeed, nature herself seemed to have been his vintner, and, at his birth, charged him so thoroughly with an irritable, brandy-like disposition, that all subsequent potations were needless. When I consider how, amid the stillness of my chambers, Nippers would sometimes impatiently rise from his seat, and stooping over his table, spread his arms wide apart, seize the whole desk, and move it, and jerk it, with a grim, grinding motion on the floor, as if the table were a perverse voluntary agent, intent on thwarting and vexing him, I plainly perceive that, for Nippers, brandy-and-water were altogether superfluous.

It was fortunate for me that, owing to its peculiar cause—indigestion—the irritability and consequent nervousness of Nippers were mainly observable in the morning, while in the afternoon he was comparatively mild. So that, Turkey's paroxysms only coming on about twelve o'clock, I never had to do with their eccentricities at one time. Their fits relieved each other, like guards. When Nippers's was on, Turkey's was off; and *vice versa*. This was a good natural arrangement, under the circumstances.

Ginger Nut, the third on my list, was a lad, some twelve years old. His father was a carman,[14] ambitious of seeing his son on the bench instead of a

[13]Bill collector. [14]Wagon driver.

cart, before he died. So he sent him to my office, as student at law, errand-boy, cleaner and sweeper, at the rate of one dollar a week. He had a little desk to himself, but he did not use it much. Upon inspection, the drawer exhibited a great array of the shells of various sorts of nuts. Indeed, to this quick-witted youth, the whole noble science of the law was contained in a nutshell. Not the least among the employments of Ginger Nut, as well as one which he discharged with the most alacrity, was his duty as cake and apple purveyor for Turkey and Nippers. Copying law-papers being proverbially a dry, husky sort of business, my two scriveners were fain to moisten their mouths very often with Spitzenbergs,[15] to be had at the numerous stalls nigh the Custom House and Post Office. Also, they sent Ginger Nut very frequently for that peculiar cake—small, flat, round, and very spicy—after which he had been named by them. Of a cold morning, when business was but dull, Turkey would gobble up scores of these cakes, as if they were mere wafers—indeed, they sell them at the rate of six or eight for a penny—the scrape of his pen blending with the crunching of the crisp particles in his mouth. Of all the fiery afternoon blunders and flurried rashnesses of Turkey, was his once moistening a ginger-cake between his lips, and clapping it on to a mortgage, for a seal. I came within an ace of dismissing him then. But he mollified me by making an oriental bow, and saying—"With submission, sir, it was generous of me to find you in[16] stationery on my own account."

Now my original business—that of a conveyancer and title-hunter,[17] and drawer-up of recondite[18] documents of all sorts—was considerably increased by receiving the master's office. There was now great work for scriveners. Not only must I push the clerks already with me, but I must have additional help. In answer to my advertisement, a motionless young man one morning stood upon my office threshold, the door being open, for it was summer. I can see that figure now—pallidly neat, pitiably respectable, incurably forlorn! It was Bartleby.

After a few words touching his qualifications, I engaged him, glad to have among my corps of copyists a man of so singularly sedate an aspect, which I thought might operate beneficially upon the flighty temper of Turkey, and the fiery one of Nippers.

I should have stated before that ground-glass folding-doors divided my premises into two parts, one of which was occupied by my scriveners, the other by myself. According to my humour, I threw open these doors, or closed them. I resolved to assign Bartleby a corner by the folding-doors, but on my side of them, so as to have this quiet man within easy call, in case any trifling thing was to be done. I placed his desk close up to a small side-window in that part of the room, a window which originally had afforded a lateral view of certain grimy backyards and bricks, but which, owing to subsequent erections, commanded at present no view at all, though it gave some light. Within three feet of the panes was a wall, and the light came down from far above, between two lofty buildings, as from a very small opening in a dome. Still further to a satisfactory arrangement, I procured a high green

[15]A variety of apple. [16]I.e., supply you with.

[17]Conveyancer: one who writes legal documents that "convey" ownership of property from one person to another. Title-hunter: one who examines records to see if ownership (title) is clear.

[18]Complicated, understood by few.

folding-screen, which might entirely isolate Bartleby from my sight, though not remove him from my voice. And thus, in a manner, privacy and society were conjoined.

At first, Bartleby did an extraordinary quantity of writing. As if long famishing for something to copy, he seemed to gorge himself on my documents. There was no pause for digestion. He ran a day and night line, copying by sun-light and by candle-light. I should have been quite delighted with his application, had he been cheerfully industrious. But he wrote on silently, palely, mechanically.

It is, of course, an indispensable part of a scrivener's business to verify the accuracy of his copy, word by word. Where there are two or more scriveners in an office, they assist each other in this examination, one reading from the copy, the other holding the original. It is a very dull, wearisome, and lethargic affair. I can readily imagine that, to some sanguine temperaments, it would be altogether intolerable. For example, I cannot credit that the mettlesome poet, Byron, would have contentedly sat down with Bartleby to examine a law document of, say, five hundred pages, closely written in a crimpy hand.

Now and then, in the haste of business, it had been my habit to assist in comparing some brief document myself, calling Turkey or Nippers for this purpose. One object I had, in placing Bartleby so handy to me behind the screen, was, to avail myself of his services on such trivial occasions. It was on the third day, I think, of his being with me, and before any necessity had arisen for having his own writing examined, that, being much hurried to complete a small affair I had in hand, I abruptly called to Bartleby. In my haste and natural expectancy of instant compliance, I sat with my head bent over the original on my desk, and my right hand sideways, and somewhat nervously extended with the copy, so that, immediately upon emerging from his retreat, Bartleby might snatch it and proceed to business without the least delay.

In this very attitude did I sit when I called to him, rapidly stating what it was I wanted him to do—namely, to examine a small paper with me. Imagine my surprise, nay, my consternation, when, without moving from his privacy, Bartleby, in a singularly mild, firm voice, replied, "I would prefer not to."

I sat a while in perfect silence, rallying my stunned faculties. Immediately it occurred to me that my ears had deceived me, or Bartleby had entirely misunderstood my meaning. I repeated my request in the clearest tone I could assume; but in quite as clear a one came the previous reply, "I would prefer not to."

"Prefer not to," echoed I, rising in high excitement, and crossing the room with a stride. "What do you mean? Are you moon-struck?[19] I want you to help me compare this sheet here—take it," and I thrust it toward him.

"I would prefer not to," said he.

I looked at him steadfastly. His face was leanly composed; his gray eye dimly calm. Not a wrinkle of agitation rippled him. Had there been the least uneasiness, anger, impatience, or impertinence in his manner; in other

[19]Crazy, deranged.

words, had there been anything ordinarily human about him, doubtless I should have violently dismissed him from the premises. But as it was, I should have as soon thought of turning my pale plaster-of-paris bust of Cicero[20] out of doors. I stood gazing at him a while, as he went on with his own writing, and then reseated myself at my desk. This is very strange, thought I. What had one best do? But my business hurried me. I concluded to forget the matter for the present, reserving it for my future leisure. So calling Nippers from the other room, the paper was speedily examined.

A few days after this, Bartleby concluded four lengthy documents, being quadruplicates of a week's testimony taken before me in my High Court of Chancery. It became necessary to examine them. It was an important suit, and great accuracy was imperative. Having all things arranged, I called Turkey, Nippers, and Ginger Nut, from the next room, meaning to place the four copies in the hands of my four clerks, while I should read from the original. Accordingly, Turkey, Nippers, and Ginger Nut had taken their seats in a row, each with his document in his hand, when I called to Bartleby to join this interesting group.

"Bartleby! quick, I am waiting."

I heard a slow scrape of his chair legs on the uncarpeted floor, and soon he appeared standing at the entrance of his hermitage.

"What is wanted?" said he mildly.

"The copies, the copies," said I hurriedly. "We are going to examine them. There"—and I held toward him the fourth quadruplicate.

"I would prefer not to," he said, and gently disappeared behind the screen.

For a few moments I was turned into a pillar of salt,[21] standing at the head of my seated column of clerks. Recovering myself, I advanced toward the screen, and demanded the reason for such extraordinary conduct.

"*Why* do you refuse?"

"I would prefer not to."

With any other man I should have flown outright into a dreadful passion, scorned all further words, and thrust him ignominiously from my presence. But there was something about Bartleby that not only strangely disarmed me, but, in a wonderful manner, touched and disconcerted me. I began to reason with him.

"These are your own copies we are about to examine. It is labour saving to you, because one examination will answer for your four papers. It is common usage. Every copyist is bound to help examine his copy. Is it not so? Will you not speak? Answer!"

"I prefer not to," he replied in a flute-like tone. It seemed to me that, while I had been addressing him, he carefully revolved every statement that I made; fully comprehended the meaning; could not gainsay the irresistible conclusion; but, at the same time, some paramount consideration prevailed with him to reply as he did.

"You are decided, then, not to comply with my request—a request made according to common usage and common sense?"

He briefly gave me to understand, that on that point my judgment was sound. Yes: his decision was irreversible.

[20]Roman orator and statesman (106–43 B.C.), often taken as an ideal for lawyers.
[21]For punishment, Lot's wife was turned into a pillar of salt. Genesis 19:26.

It is not seldom the case that, when a man is browbeaten in some unprecedented and violently unreasonable way, he begins to stagger in his own plainest faith. He begins, as it were, vaguely to surmise that, wonderful as it may be, all the justice and all the reason is on the other side. Accordingly, if any disinterested persons are present, he turns to them for some reinforcement for his own faltering mind.

"Turkey," said I, "what do you think of this? Am I not right?"

"With submission, sir," said Turkey, in his blandest tone, "I think that you are."

"Nippers," said I, "what do *you* think of it?"

"I think I should kick him out of the office."

(The reader, of nice[22] perceptions, will here perceive that, it being morning, Turkey's answer is couched in polite and tranquil terms, but Nippers replies in ill-tempered ones. Or, to repeat a previous sentence, Nippers's ugly mood was on duty, and Turkey's off.)

"Ginger Nut," said I, willing to enlist the smallest suffrage[23] in my behalf, "what do *you* think of it?"

"I think, sir, he's a little *luny*," replied Ginger Nut, with a grin.

"You hear what they say," said I, turning toward the screen, "come forth and do your duty."

But he vouchsafed no reply. I pondered a moment in sore perplexity. But once more business hurried me. I determined again to postpone the consideration of this dilemma to my future leisure. With a little trouble we made out to examine the papers without Bartleby, though at every page or two Turkey deferentially dropped his opinion, that this proceeding was quite out of the common; while Nippers, twitching in his chair with a dyspeptic nervousness, ground out, between his set teeth, occasional hissing maledictions against the stubborn oaf behind the screen. And for his (Nippers's) part, this was the first and the last time he would do another man's business without pay.

Meanwhile Bartleby sat in his hermitage, oblivious to everything but his own peculiar business there.

Some days passed, the scrivener being employed upon another lengthy work. His late remarkable conduct led me to regard his ways narrowly. I observed that he never went to dinner; indeed, that he never went anywhere. As yet I had never, of my personal knowledge, known him to be outside of my office. He was a perpetual sentry in the corner. At about eleven o'clock though, in the morning, I noticed that Ginger Nut would advance toward the opening in Bartleby's screen, as if silently beckoned thither by a gesture invisible to me where I sat. The boy would then leave the office, jingling a few pence, and reappear with a handful of ginger-nuts, which he delivered in the hermitage, receiving two of the cakes for his trouble.

He lives, then, on ginger-nuts, thought I; never eats a dinner, properly speaking; he must be a vegetarian, then; but no; he never eats even vegetables, he eats nothing but ginger-nuts. My mind then ran on in reveries concerning the probable effects upon the human constitution of living entirely on ginger-nuts. Ginger-nuts are so called, because they contain ginger as

[22]Discriminating. [23]Support.

one of their peculiar constituents, and the final flavouring one. Now, what was ginger? A hot, spicy thing. Was Bartleby hot and spicy? Not at all. Ginger, then, had no effect upon Bartleby. Probably he preferred it should have none.

Nothing so aggravates an earnest person as a passive resistance. If the individual so resisted be of a not inhumane temper, and the resisting one perfectly harmless in his passivity, then, in the better moods of the former, he will endeavour charitably to construe to his imagination what proves impossible to be solved by his judgment. Even so, for the most part, I regarded Bartleby and his ways. Poor fellow! thought I, he means no mischief; it is plain he intends no insolence; his aspect sufficiently evinces that his eccentricities are involuntary. He is useful to me. I can get along with him. If I turn him away, the chances are he will fall in with some less-indulgent employer, and then he will be rudely treated, and perhaps driven forth miserably to starve. Yes. Here I can cheaply purchase a delicious self-approval. To befriend Bartleby; to humour him in his strange wilfulness, will cost me little or nothing, while I lay up in my soul what will eventually prove a sweet morsel for my conscience. But this mood was not invariable with me. The passiveness of Bartleby sometimes irritated me. I felt strangely goaded on to encounter him in new opposition—to elicit some angry spark from him answerable to my own. But, indeed, I might as well have essayed to strike fire with my knuckles against a bit of Windsor soap.[24] But one afternoon the evil impulse in me mastered me, and the following little scene ensued:—

"Bartleby," said I, "when those papers are all copied, I will compare them with you."

"I would prefer not to."

"How? Surely you do not mean to persist in that mulish vagary?"

No answer.

I threw open the folding-doors near by, and, turning upon Turkey and Nippers, exclaimed:

"Bartleby a second time says, he won't examine his papers. What do you think of it, Turkey?"

It was afternoon, be it remembered. Turkey sat glowing like a brass boiler; his bald head steaming; his hands reeling among his blotted papers.

"Think of it?" roared Turkey; "I think I'll just step behind his screen, and black his eyes for him!"

So saying, Turkey rose to his feet and threw his arms into a pugilistic position. He was hurrying away to make good his promise, when I detained him, alarmed at the effect of incautiously rousing Turkey's combativeness after dinner.

"Sit down, Turkey," said I, "and hear what Nippers has to say. What do you think of it, Nippers? Would I not be justified in immediately dismissing Bartleby?"

"Excuse me, that is for you to decide, sir. I think his conduct quite unusual, and, indeed, unjust, as regards Turkey and myself. But it may only be a passing whim."

"Ah," exclaimed I, "you have strangely changed your mind, then—you speak very gently of him now."

[24]A brand of toilet soap.

"All beer," cried Turkey; "gentleness is effects of beer—Nippers and I dined together to-day. You see how gentle *I* am, sir. Shall I go and black his eyes?"

"You refer to Bartleby, I suppose. No, not to-day, Turkey," I replied; "pray put up your fists."

I closed the doors, and again advanced toward Bartleby. I felt additional incentives tempting me to my fate. I burned to be rebelled against again. I remembered that Bartleby never left the office.

"Bartleby," said I, "Ginger Nut is away; just step around to the Post Office, won't you? (it was but a three minutes' walk), and see if there is anything for me."

"I would prefer not to."

"You *will* not?"

"I *prefer* not."

I staggered to my desk, and sat there in a deep study. My blind inveteracy returned. Was there any other thing in which I could procure myself to be ignominiously repulsed by this lean, penniless wight?—my hired clerk? What added thing is there, perfectly reasonable, that he will be sure to refuse to do?

"Bartleby!"

No answer.

"Bartleby," in a louder tone.

No answer.

"Bartleby," I roared.

Like a very ghost, agreeably to the laws of magical invocation, at the third summons, he appeared at the entrance of his hermitage.

"Go to the next room, and tell Nippers to come to me."

"I prefer not to," he respectfully and slowly said, and mildly disappeared.

"Very good, Bartleby," said I, in a quiet sort of serenely-severe self-possessed tone, intimating the unalterable purpose of some terrible retribution very close at hand. At the moment I half intended something of the kind. But upon the whole, as it was drawing toward my dinner-hour, I thought it best to put on my hat and walk home for the day, suffering much from perplexity and distress of mind.

Shall I acknowledge it? The conclusion of this whole business was, that it soon became a fixed fact of my chambers, that a pale young scrivener, by the name of Bartleby, had a desk there; that he copied for me at the usual rate of four cents a folio (one hundred words); but he was permanently exempt from examining the work done by him, that duty being transferred to Turkey and Nippers, out of compliment, doubtless to their superior acuteness; moreover, said Bartleby was never, on any account, to be dispatched on the most trivial errand of any sort; and that even if entreated to take upon him such a matter, it was generally understood that he would "prefer not to"—in other words, that he would refuse point-blank.

As days passed on, I became considerably reconciled to Bartleby. His steadiness, his freedom from all dissipation, his incessant industry (except when he chose to throw himself into a standing revery behind his screen), his great stillness, his unalterableness of demeanour under all circumstances, made him a valuable acquisition. One prime thing was this—*he was always there*—first in the morning, continually through the day, and the last at night. I had a singular confidence in his honesty. I felt my most precious papers perfectly safe in his hands. Sometimes, to be sure, I could not, for the very soul of me, avoid falling into sudden spasmodic passions with him. For it was exceedingly difficult to bear in mind all the time those strange peculiarities, privileges, and unheard-of exemptions, forming the tacit stipulations on Bartleby's part under which he remained in my office. Now and then, in the eagerness of dispatching pressing business, I would inadvertently summon Bartleby, in a short, rapid tone, to put his finger, say, on the incipient tie of a bit of red tape with which I was about compressing some papers. Of course, from behind the screen the usual answer, "I prefer not to," was sure to come; and then, how could a human creature, with the common infirmities of our nature, refrain from bitterly exclaiming upon such perverseness—such unreasonableness. However, every added repulse of this sort which I received only tended to lessen the probability of my repeating the inadvertence.

Here it must be said, that according to the custom of most legal gentlemen occupying chambers in densely populated law-buildings, there were several keys to my door. One was kept by a woman residing in the attic, which person weekly scrubbed and daily swept and dusted my apartments. Another was kept by Turkey for convenience sake. The third I sometimes carried in my own pocket. The fourth I knew not who had.

Now, one Sunday morning I happened to go to Trinity Church,[25] to hear a celebrated preacher, and finding myself rather early on the ground I thought I would walk round to my chambers for a while. Luckily I had my key with me; but upon applying it to the lock, I found it resisted by something inserted from the inside. Quite surprised, I called out; when to my consternation a key was turned from within; and thrusting his lean visage at me, and holding the door ajar, the apparition of Bartleby appeared, in his shirt-sleeves, and otherwise in a strangely tattered dishabille,[26] saying quietly that he was sorry, but he was deeply engaged just then, and—preferred not admitting me at present. In a brief word or two, he moreover added, that perhaps I had better walk round the block two or three times, and by that time he would probably have concluded his affairs.

Now, the utterly unsurmised appearance of Bartleby, tenanting my law-chambers of a Sunday morning, with his cadaverously gentlemanly nonchalance, yet withal firm and self-possessed, had such a strange effect upon me, that incontinently I slunk away from my own door, and did as desired. But not without sundry twinges of impotent rebellion against the mild effrontery of this unaccountable scrivener. Indeed, it was his wonderful mildness chiefly, which not only disarmed me, but unmanned me as it were. For I consider that one, for the time, is sort of unmanned when he tranquilly permits his hired clerk to dictate to him, and order him away from his own premises. Furthermore, I was full of uneasiness as to what Bartleby could possibly be doing in my office in his shirt-sleeves, and in an otherwise dismantled condition of a Sunday morning. Was anything amiss going on? Nay, that was out of the question. It was not to be thought of for a moment that Bartleby was an immoral person. But what could he be doing there?—copying? Nay again, whatever might be his eccentricities, Bartleby was an

[25]Episcopal Church in the Wall Street area of New York City.
[26]Careless dress, untidiness.

eminently decorous person. He would be the last man to sit down to his desk in any state approaching to nudity. Besides, it was Sunday; and there was something about Bartleby that forbade the supposition that he would by any secular occupation violate the properties of the day.

Nevertheless, my mind was not pacified; and full of a restless curiosity, at last I returned to the door. Without hindrance I inserted my key, opened it, and entered. Bartleby was not to be seen. I looked round anxiously, peeped behind his screen; but it was very plain that he was gone. Upon more closely examining the place, I surmised that for an indefinite period Bartleby must have ate, dressed, and slept in my office, and that, too, without plate, mirror, or bed. The cushioned seat of a rickety old sofa in one corner bore the faint impress of a lean, reclining form. Rolled away under his desk, I found a blanket, under the empty grate a blacking box and brush; on a chair, a tin basin, with soap and a ragged towel; in a newspaper a few crumbs of ginger-nuts and a morsel of cheese. Yes, thought I, it is evident that Bartleby has been making his home here, keeping bachelor's hall all by himself. Immediately then the thought came sweeping across me, what miserable friendlessness and loneliness are here revealed! His poverty is great; but his solitude, how horrible! Think of it. Of a Sunday, Wall Street is deserted as Petra;[27] and every night of every day it is an emptiness. This building, too, which of week-days hums with industry and life, at nightfall echoes with sheer vacancy, and all through Sunday is forlorn. And here Bartleby makes his home; sole spectator of a solitude which he has seen all-populous—a sort of innocent and transformed Marius brooding among the ruins of Carthage![28]

For the first time in my life a feeling of overpowering stinging melancholy seized me. Before, I had never experienced aught but a not unpleasing sadness. The bond of a common humanity now drew me irresistibly to gloom. A fraternal melancholy! For both I and Bartleby were sons of Adam. I remembered the bright silks and sparkling faces I had seen that day, in gala trim, swan-like sailing down the Mississippi of Broadway; and I contrasted them with the pallid copyist, and thought to myself, Ah, happiness courts the light, so we deem the world is gay; but misery hides aloof, so we deem that misery there is none. These sad fancyings—chimeras, doubtless of a sick and silly brain—led on to other and more special thoughts, concerning the eccentricities of Bartleby. Presentiments of strange discoveries hovered round me. The scrivener's pale form appeared to me laid out, among uncaring strangers, in its shivering winding-sheet.

Suddenly I was attracted by Bartleby's closed desk, the key in open sight left in the lock.

I mean no mischief, seek the gratification of no heartless curiosity, thought I; besides the desk is mine, and its contents, too, so I will make bold to look within. Everything was methodically arranged, the papers smoothly placed. The pigeon-holes were deep, and removing the files of documents, I groped

[27]Ancient city in Palestine. Its ruins were discovered in 1812.

[28]Caius Marius (c. 157–86 B.C.), a Roman general who was banished from Rome and fled to Africa, to the ruined city of Carthage, which he saw as symbolic of his own fallen glory. He was often portrayed in nineteenth-century art, most notably by the American painter John Vanderlyn (1775–1852) in the painting *Marius Amid the Ruins of Carthage* (1807).

into their recesses. Presently I felt something there, and dragged it out. It was an old bandanna handkerchief, heavy and knotted. I opened it, and saw it was a savings-bank.

I now recalled all the quiet mysteries which I had noted in the man. I remembered that he never spoke but to answer; that, though at intervals he had considerable time to himself, yet I had never seen him reading—no, not even a newspaper; that for long periods he would stand looking out, at his pale window behind the screen, upon the dead brick wall; I was quite sure he never visited any refectory or eating-house; while his pale face clearly indicated that he never drank beer like Turkey, or tea and coffee even, like other men; that he never went anywhere in particular that I could learn; never went out for a walk, unless, indeed, that was the case at present; that he had declined telling who he was, or whence he came, or whether he had any relatives in the world; that though so thin and pale, he never complained of ill health. And more than all, I remembered a certain unconscious air of pallid—how shall I call it?—of pallid haughtiness, say, or rather an austere reserve about him, which had positively awed me into my tame compliance with his eccentricities, when I had feared to ask him to do the slightest incidental thing for me, even though I might know, from his long-continued motionlessness, that behind his screen he must be standing in one of those dead-wall reveries of his.

Revolving all these things, and coupling them with the recently discovered fact, that he made my office his constant abiding-place and home, and not forgetful of his morbid moodiness; revolving all these things, a prudential feeling began to steal over me. My first emotions had been those of pure melancholy and sincerest pity; but just in proportion as the forlornness of Bartleby grew and grew to my imagination, did that same melancholy merge into fear, that pity into repulsion. So true it is, and so terrible, too, that up to a certain point the thought or sight of misery enlists our best affections; but, in certain special cases, beyond that point it does not. They err who would assert that invariably this is owing to the inherent selfishness of the human heart. It rather proceeds from a certain hopelessness of remedying excessive and organic ill. To a sensitive being, pity is not seldom pain. And when at last it is perceived that such pity cannot lead to effectual succour, common-sense bids the soul be rid of it. What I saw that morning persuaded me that the scrivener was the victim of innate and incurable disorder. I might give alms to his body; but his body did not pain him; it was his soul that suffered, and his soul I could not reach.

I did not accomplish the purpose of going to Trinity Church that morning. Somehow, the things I had seen disqualified me for the time for church-going. I walked homeward, thinking what I would do with Bartleby. Finally, I resolved upon this—I would put certain calm questions to him the next morning, touching his history, etc., and if he declined to answer them openly and unreservedly (and I supposed he would prefer not), then to give him a twenty-dollar bill over and above whatever I might owe him, and tell him his services were no longer required; but that if in any other way I could assist him, I would be happy to do so, especially if he desired to return to his native place, wherever that might be, I would willingly help to defray the expenses. Moreover, if, after reaching home, he found himself at any time in want of aid, a letter from him would be sure of a reply.

The next morning came.

"Bartleby," said I, gently calling to him behind his screen.

No reply.

"Bartleby," said I, in a still gentler tone, "come here; I am not going to ask you to do anything you would prefer not to do—I simply wish to speak to you."

Upon this he noiselessly slid into view.

"Will you tell me, Bartleby, where you were born?"

"I would prefer not to."

"Will you tell me *anything* about yourself?"

"I would prefer not to."

"But what reasonable objection can you have to speak to me? I feel friendly toward you."

He did not look at me while I spoke, but kept his glance fixed upon my bust of Cicero, which, as I then sat, was directly behind me, some six inches above my head.

"What is your answer, Bartleby?" said I, after waiting a considerable time for a reply, during which his countenance remained immovable, only there was the faintest conceivable tremor of the white attenuated mouth.

"At present I prefer to give no answer," he said, and retired into his hermitage.

It was rather weak in me, I confess, but his manner, on this occasion, nettled me. Not only did there seem to lurk in it a certain calm disdain, but his perverseness seemed ungrateful, considering the undeniable good usage and indulgence he had received from me.

Again I sat ruminating what I should do. Mortified as I was at his behaviour, and resolved as I had been to dismiss him when I entered my office, nevertheless I strangely felt something superstitious knocking at my heart, and forbidding me to carry out my purpose, and denouncing me for a villain if I dared to breathe one bitter word against this forlornest of mankind. At last, familiarly drawing my chair behind his screen, I sat down and said: "Bartleby, never mind, then, about revealing your history; but let me entreat you, as a friend, to comply as far as may be with the usages of this office. Say now, you will help to examine papers to-morrow or next day: in short, say now, that in a day or two you will begin to be a little reasonable:—say so, Bartleby."

"At present I would prefer not to be a little reasonable," was his mildly cadaverous reply.

Just then the folding-doors opened, and Nippers approached. He seemed suffering from an unusually bad night's rest, induced by severer indigestion than common. He overheard those final words of Bartleby.

"*Prefer not,* eh?" gritted Nippers—"I'd *prefer* him, if I were you, sir," addressing me—"I'd *prefer* him; I'd give him preferences, the stubborn mule! What is it, sir, pray, that he *prefers* not to do now?"

Bartleby moved not a limb.

"Mr. Nippers," said I, "I'd prefer that you would withdraw for the present."

Somehow, of late, I had got into the way of involuntarily using this word "prefer" upon all sorts of not exactly suitable occasions. And I trembled to think that my contact with the scrivener had already and seriously affected me in a mental way. And what further and deeper aberration might it not yet produce? This apprehension had not been without efficacy in determining me to summary measures.

As Nippers, looking very sour and sulky, was departing, Turkey blandly and deferentially approached.

"With submission, sir," said he, "yesterday I was thinking about Bartleby here, and I think that if he would but prefer to take a quart of good ale everyday, it would do much toward mending him, and enabling him to assist in examining his papers."

"So you have got the word too," said I, slightly excited.

"With submission, what word, sir," asked Turkey, respectfully crowding himself into the contracted space behind the screen, and by so doing, making me jostle the scrivener. "What word, sir?"

"I would prefer to be left alone here," said Bartleby, as if offended at being mobbed in his privacy.

"*That's* the word, Turkey," said I—"*that's* it."

"Oh, *prefer?* oh yes—queer word. I never use it myself. But, sir, as I was saying, if he would but prefer——"

"Turkey," interrupted I, "you will please withdraw."

"Oh certainly, sir, if you prefer that I should."

As he opened the folding-door to retire, Nippers at his desk caught a glimpse of me, and asked whether I would prefer to have a certain paper copied on blue paper or white. He did not in the least roguishly accent the word prefer. It was plain that it involuntarily rolled from his tongue. I thought to myself, surely I must get rid of a demented man, who already has in some degree turned the tongues, if not the heads of myself and clerks. But I thought it prudent not to break the dismission at once.

The next day I noticed that Bartleby did nothing but stand at his window in his dead-wall revery. Upon asking him why he did not write, he said that he had decided upon doing no more writing.

"Why, how now? what next?" exclaimed I, "do no more writing?"

"No more."

"And what is the reason?"

"Do you not see the reason for yourself?" he indifferently replied.

I looked steadfastly at him, and perceived that his eyes looked dull and glazed. Instantly it occurred to me, that his unexampled diligence in copying by his dim window for the first few weeks of his stay with me might have temporarily impaired his vision.

I was touched. I said something in condolence with him. I hinted that of course he did wisely in abstaining from writing for a while; and urged him to embrace that opportunity of taking wholesome exercise in the open air. This, however, he did not do. A few days after this, my other clerks being absent, and being in a great hurry to dispatch certain letters by the mail, I thought that having nothing else earthly to do, Bartleby would surely be less inflexible than usual, and carry these letters to the Post Office. But he blankly declined. So, much to my inconvenience, I went myself.

Still added days went by. Whether Bartleby's eyes improved or not, I could not say. To all appearance, I thought they did. But when I asked him if they did, he vouchsafed no answer. At all events, he would do no copying. At last, in reply to my urgings, he informed me that he had permanently given up copying.

"What!" exclaimed I; "suppose your eyes should get entirely well—better than ever before—would you not copy then?"

"I have given up copying," he answered, and slid aside.

He remained as ever, a fixture in my chamber. Nay—if that were possible—he became still more of a fixture than before. What was to be done? He would do nothing in the office; why should he stay there? In plain fact, he had now become a millstone[29] to me, not only useless as a necklace, but afflictive to bear. Yet I was sorry for him. I speak less than truth when I say that, on his own account, he occasioned me uneasiness. If he would but have named a single relative or friend, I would instantly have written, and urged their taking the poor fellow away to some convenient retreat. But he seemed alone, absolutely alone in the universe. A bit of wreck in the mid-Atlantic. At length, necessities connected with my business tyrannised over all other considerations. Decently as I could, I told Bartleby that in six days' time he must unconditionally leave the office. I warned him to take measures, in the interval, for procuring some other abode. I offered to assist him in this endeavour, if he himself would but take the first step toward a removal. "And when you finally quit me, Bartleby," added I, "I shall see that you go not away entirely unprovided. Six days from this hour, remember."

At the expiration of that period, I peeped behind the screen, and lo! Bartleby was there.

I buttoned up my coat, balanced myself; advanced slowly toward him, touched his shoulder, and said, "The time has come; you must quit this place; I am sorry for you; here is money; but you must go."

"I would prefer not," he replied, with his back still toward me.

"You *must.*"

He remained silent.

Now I had an unbounded confidence in this man's common honesty. He had frequently restored to me sixpences and shillings[30] carelessly dropped upon the floor, for I am apt to be very reckless in such shirt-button[31] affairs. The proceeding, then, which followed will not be deemed extraordinary.

"Bartleby," said I, "I owe you twelve dollars on account; here are thirty-two; the odd twenty are yours—Will you take it?" and I handed the bills toward him.

But he made no motion.

"I will leave them here, then," putting them under a weight on the table. Then taking my hat and cane and going to the door, I tranquilly turned and added—"After you have removed your things from these offices, Bartleby, you will of course lock the door—since everyone is now gone for the day but you—and if you please, slip your key underneath the mat, so that I may have it in the morning. I shall not see you again; so good-bye to you. If, hereafter, in your new place of abode, I can be of any service to you, do not fail to advise me by letter. Good-bye, Bartleby, and fare you well."

[29]"But whoso shall offend . . . it were better for him that a millstone were hanged about his neck, and that he were drowned in the depth of the sea." Matthew 18:6.

[30]English coins worth slightly more than eight cents and sixteen cents each. Although the United States began minting coins in 1793, foreign coins were circulated until 1857, when, by an act of Congress, foreign currency ceased to be legal tender.

[31]Slight, insignificant.

But he answered not a word; like the last column of some ruined temple, he remained standing mute and solitary in the middle of the otherwise deserted room.

As I walked home in a pensive mood, my vanity got the better of my pity. I could not but highly plume myself on my masterly management in getting rid of Bartleby. Masterly I call it, and such it must appear to any dispassionate thinker. The beauty of my procedure seemed to consist in its perfect quietness. There was no vulgar bullying, no bravado of any sort, no choleric hectoring, and striding to and fro across the apartment, jerking out vehement commands for Bartleby to bundle himself off with his beggarly traps. Nothing of the kind. Without loudly bidding Bartleby depart—as an inferior genius might have done—I *assumed* the ground that depart he must; and upon that assumption built all I had to say. The more I thought over my procedure, the more I was charmed with it. Nevertheless, next morning, upon awakening, I had my doubts—I had somehow slept off the fumes of vanity. One of the coolest and wisest hours a man has, is just after he awakes in the morning. My procedure seemed as sagacious as ever—but only in theory. How it would prove in practice—there was the rub. It was truly a beautiful thought to have assumed Bartleby's departure; but, after all, that assumption was simply my own, and none of Bartleby's. The great point was, not whether I had assumed that he would quit me, but whether he would prefer so to do. He was more a man of preferences than assumptions.

After breakfast, I walked down town, arguing the probabilities *pro* and *con*. One moment I thought it would prove a miserable failure, and Bartleby would be found all alive at my office as usual; the next moment it seemed certain that I should find his chair empty. And so I kept veering about. At the corner of Broadway and Canal Street, I saw quite an excited group of people standing in earnest conversation.

"I'll take odds he doesn't," said a voice as I passed.

"Doesn't go?—done!" said I; "put up your money."

I was instinctively putting my hand in my pocket to produce my own, when I remembered that this was an election day. The words I had overheard bore no reference to Bartleby, but to the success or non-success of some candidate for the mayoralty. In my intent frame of mind, I had, as it were, imagined that all Broadway shared in my excitement, and were debating the same question with me. I passed on, very thankful that the uproar of the street screened my momentary absent-mindedness.

As I had intended, I was earlier than usual at my office door. I stood listening for a moment. All was still. He must be gone. I tried the knob. The door was locked. Yes, my procedure had worked to a charm; he indeed must be vanished. Yet a certain melancholy mixed with this: I was almost sorry for my brilliant success. I was fumbling under the doormat for the key, which Bartleby was to have left there for me, when accidentally my knee knocked against a panel, producing a summoning sound, and in response a voice came to me from within—"Not yet; I am occupied."

It was Bartleby.

I was thunderstruck. For an instant I stood like the man who, pipe in mouth, was killed one cloudless afternoon long ago in Virginia, by summer lightning; at his own warm open window he was killed, and remained leaning out there upon the dreamy afternoon, till someone touched him, when he fell.

"Not gone!" I murmured at last. But again obeying that wondrous ascendency which the inscrutable scrivener had over me, and from which ascendency, for all my chafing, I could not completely escape, I slowly went downstairs and out into the street, and while walking round the block, considered what I should next do in this unheard-of perplexity. Turn the man out by an actual thrusting I could not; to drive him away by calling him hard names would not do; calling in the police was an unpleasant idea; and yet, permit him to enjoy his cadaverous triumph over me—this, too, I could not think of. What was to be done? or, if nothing could be done, was there anything further that I could *assume* in the matter? Yes, as before I had prospectively assumed that Bartleby would depart, so now I might retrospectively assume that departed he was. In the legitimate carrying out of this assumption, I might enter my office in a great hurry, and pretending not to see Bartleby at all, walk straight against him as if he were air. Such a proceeding would in a singular degree have the appearance of a home-thrust.[32] It was hardly possible that Bartleby could withstand such an application of the doctrine of assumptions. But upon second thoughts the success of the plan seemed rather dubious. I resolved to argue the matter over with him again.

"Bartleby," said I, entering the office, with a quietly severe expression, "I am seriously displeased. I am pained, Bartleby. I had thought better of you. I had imagined you of such a gentlemanly organisation, that in any delicate dilemma a slight hint would suffice—in short, an assumption. But it appears I am deceived. Why," I added, unaffectedly starting, "you have not even touched that money yet," pointing to it, just where I had left it the evening previous.

He answered nothing.

"Will you, or will you not, quit me?" I now demanded in a sudden passion, advancing close to him.

"I would prefer *not* to quit you," he replied, gently emphasizing the *not*.

"What earthly right have you to stay here? Do you pay any rent? Do you pay my taxes? Or is this property yours?"

He answered nothing.

"Are you ready to go on and write now? Are your eyes recovered? Could you copy a small paper for me this morning? or help examine a few lines? or step round to the Post Office? In a word, will you do anything at all, to give a colouring to your refusal to depart the premises?"

He silently retired into his hermitage.

I was not in such a state of nervous resentment that I thought it but prudent to check myself at present from further demonstrations. Bartleby and I were alone. I remembered the tragedy of the unfortunate Adams and the still more unfortunate Colt in the solitary office of the latter; and how poor Colt, being dreadfully incensed by Adams, and imprudently permitting himself to get wildly excited, was at unawares hurried into his fatal act—an act which certainly no man could possibly deplore more than the actor himself.[33] Often it had occurred to me in my ponderings upon the subject, that had that altercation taken place in the public street, or at a private residence, it would

[32]A thrust that hits home, a successful blow.

[33]A reference to the sensational murder of Samuel Adams by John C. Colt in 1841. Tried and found guilty, Colt committed suicide shortly before he was to be hanged.

not have terminated as it did. It was the circumstance of being alone in a solitary office, upstairs, of a building entirely unhallowed by humanising domestic associations—an uncarpeted office, doubtless, of a dusty, haggard sort of appearance—this it must have been, which greatly helped to enhance the irritable desperation of the hapless Colt.

But when this old Adam[34] of resentment rose in me and tempted me concerning Bartleby, I grappled him and threw him. How? Why, simply by recalling the divine injunction: "A new commandment give I unto you, that ye love one another."[35] Yes, this it was that saved me. Aside from higher considerations, charity often operates as a vastly wise and prudent principle—a great safeguard to its possessor. Men have committed murder for jealousy's sake, and anger's sake, and hatred's sake, and selfishness' sake, and spiritual pride's sake; but no man, that ever I heard of, ever committed a diabolical murder for sweet charity's sake. Mere self-interest, then, if no better motive can be enlisted should, especially with high-tempered men, prompt all beings to charity and philanthropy. At any rate, upon the occasion in question, I strove to drown my exasperated feelings toward the scrivener by benevolently construing his conduct. Poor fellow, poor fellow! thought I, he don't mean anything; and besides, he has seen hard times, and ought to be indulged.

I endeavoured, also, immediately to occupy myself, and at the same time to comfort my despondency. I tried to fancy, that in the course of the morning, at such time as might prove agreeable to him, Bartleby, of his own free accord, would emerge from his hermitage and take up some decided line of march in the direction of the door. But no. Half-past twelve o'clock came; Turkey began to glow in the face, overturn his ink-stand, and become generally obstreperous; Nippers abated down into quietude and courtesy; Ginger Nut munched his noon apple; and Bartleby remained standing at his window in one of his profoundest dead-wall reveries. Will it be credited? Ought I to acknowledge it? That afternoon I left the office without saying one further word to him.

Some days now passed, during which, at leisure intervals, I looked a little into "Edwards on the Will," and "Priestley on Necessity."[36] Under the circumstances, those books induced a salutary feeling. Gradually I slid into the persuasion that these troubles of mine, touching the scrivener, had been all predestinated from eternity, and Bartleby was billeted upon me for some mysterious purpose of an all-wise Providence, which it was not for a mere mortal like me to fathom. Yes, Bartleby, stay there behind your screen, thought I; I shall persecute you no more; you are harmless and noiseless as any of these old chairs; in short, I never feel so private as when I know you are here. At last I see it, I feel it; I penetrate to the predestinated purpose of my life. I am content. Others may have loftier parts to enact; but my mission in this world, Bartleby, is to furnish you with office-room for such period as you may see fit to remain.

[34]Demon. [35]Words spoken by Jesus to His disciples. John 13:34.

[36]Jonathan Edwards (1703–1758), American theologian. Joseph Priestley (1733–1804), English scientist. Both presented arguments that man's will is not free, that he must submit to the irresistible force of predestination and determinism.

I believe that this wise and blessed frame of mind would have continued with me, had it not been for the unsolicited and uncharitable remarks obtruded upon me by my professional friends who visited the rooms. But thus it often is, that the constant friction of illiberal minds wears out at last the best resolves of the more generous. Though to be sure, when I reflected upon it, it was not strange that people entering my office should be struck by the peculiar aspect of the unaccountable Bartleby, and so be tempted to throw out some sinister observations concerning him. Sometimes an attorney, having business with me, and calling at my office, and finding no one but the scrivener there, would undertake to obtain some sort of precise information from him touching my whereabouts; but without heeding his idle talk, Bartleby would remain standing immovable in the middle of the room. So after contemplating him in that position for a time, the attorney would depart, no wiser than he came.

Also, when a Reference[37] was going on, and the room full of lawyers and witnesses, and business driving fast, some deeply occupied legal gentleman present, seeing Bartleby wholly unemployed, would request him to run round to his (the legal gentleman's) office and fetch some papers for him. Thereupon, Bartleby would tranquilly decline, and yet remain idle as before. Then the lawyer would give a great stare, and turn to me. And what could I say? At last I was made aware that all through the circle of my professional acquaintance, a whisper of wonder was running round, having reference to the strange creature I kept at my office. This worried me very much. And as the idea came upon me of his possibly turning out a long-lived man, and keep occupying my chambers, and denying my authority; and perplexing my visitors; and scandalising my professional reputation; and casting a general gloom over the premises; keeping soul and body together to the last upon his savings (for doubtless he spent but half a dime a day), and in the end perhaps outlive me, and claim possession of my office by right of his perpetual occupancy: as all these dark anticipations crowded upon me more and more, and my friends continually intruded their relentless remarks upon the apparition in my room; a great change was wrought in me. I resolved to gather all faculties together, and forever rid me of this intolerable incubus.

Ere revolving any complicated project, however, adapted to this end, I first simply suggested to Bartleby the propriety of his permanent departure. In a calm and serious tone, I commended the idea to his careful and mature consideration. But, having taken three days to meditate upon it, he apprised me, that his original determination remained the same; in short, that he still preferred to abide with me.

What shall I do? I now said to myself, buttoning up my coat to the last button. What shall I do? what ought I to do? what does conscience say I *should* do with this man, or, rather, ghost? Rid myself of him, I must; go, he shall. But how? You will not thrust him, the poor, pale, passive mortal—you will not thrust such a helpless creature out of your door? you will not dishonour yourself by such cruelty? No, I will not, I cannot do that. Rather would I let him live and die here, and then mason up his remains in the wall. What,

[37]The proceedings of a chancery court to which a dispute has been referred.

then, will you do? For all your coaxing, he will not budge. Bribes he leaves under your own paperweight on your table; in short, it is quite plain that he prefers to cling to you.

Then something severe, something unusual must be done. What! surely you will not have him collared by a constable, and commit his innocent pallor to the common jail? And upon what ground could you procure such a thing to be done?—a vagrant, is he? What! he a vagrant, a wanderer, who refuses to budge? It is because he will *not* be a vagrant, then, that you seek to count him *as* a vagrant. That is too absurd. No visible means of support; there I have him. Wrong again: for indubitably he *does* support himself, and that is the only unanswerable proof that any man can show of his possessing the means so to do. No more, then. Since he will not quit me, I must quit him. I will change my offices; I will move elsewhere, and give him fair notice, that if I find him on my new premises I will then proceed against him as a common trespasser.

Acting accordingly, next day I thus addressed him: "I find these chambers too far from the City Hall; the air is unwholesome. In a word, I propose to remove my offices next week, and shall no longer require your services. I tell you this now, in order that you may seek another place."

He made no reply, and nothing more was said.

On the appointed day I engaged carts and men, proceeded to my chambers, and, having but little furniture, everything was removed in a few hours. Throughout, the scrivener remained standing behind the screen, which I directed to be removed the last thing. It was withdrawn; and, being folded up like a huge folio, left him the motionless occupant of a naked room. I stood in the entry watching him a moment, while something from within me upbraided me.

I re-entered, with my hand in my pocket—and—and my heart in my mouth.

"Good-bye, Bartleby; I am going—good-bye, and God some way bless you; and take that," slipping something in his hand. But it dropped upon the floor, and then—strange to say—I tore myself from him whom I had so longed to be rid of.

Established in my new quarters, for a day or two I kept the door locked, and started at every footfall in the passages. When I returned to my rooms, after any little absence, I would pause at the threshold for an instant, and attentively listen ere applying my key. But these fears were needless. Bartleby never came nigh me.

I thought all was going well, when a perturbed-looking stranger visited me, inquiring whether I was the person who had recently occupied rooms at No.—Wall Street.

Full of forebodings, I replied that I was.

"Then, sir," said the stranger, who proved a lawyer, "you are responsible for the man you left there. He refuses to do any copying; he refuses to do anything; he says he prefers not to; and he refuses to quit the premises."

"I am very sorry, sir," said I, with assumed tranquillity, but an inward tremor, "but, really, the man you allude to is nothing to me—he is no relation or apprentice of mine, that you should hold me responsible for him."

"In mercy's name, who is he?"

"I certainly cannot inform you. I know nothing about him. Formerly I employed him as a copyist; but he has done nothing for me now for some time past."

"I shall settle him, then—good morning, sir."

Several days passed, and I heard nothing more; and, though I often felt a charitable prompting to call at the place and see poor Bartleby, yet a certain squeamishness, of I know not what, withheld me.

All is over with him, by this time, thought I, at last, when, through another week, no further intelligence reached me. But, coming to my room the day after, I found several persons waiting at my door in a high state of nervous excitement.

"That's the man—here he comes," cried the foremost one, whom I recognised as the lawyer who had previously called upon me alone.

"You must take him away, sir, at once," cried a portly person among them, advancing upon me, and whom I knew to be the landlord of No.—Wall Street. "These gentlemen, my tenants, cannot stand it any longer; Mr. B——," pointing to the lawyer, "has turned him out of his room, and he now persists in haunting the building generally, sitting upon the banisters of the stairs by day, and sleeping in the entry by night. Everybody is concerned; clients are leaving the offices; some fears are entertained of a mob; something you must do, and that without delay."

Aghast at this torrent, I fell back before it, and would fain have locked myself in my new quarters. In vain I persisted that Bartleby was nothing to me—no more than to anyone else. In vain—I was the last person known to have anything to do with him, and they held me to the terrible account. Fearful, then, of being exposed in the papers (as one person present obscurely threatened), I considered the matter, and, at length, said, that if the lawyer would give me a confidential interview with the scrivener, in his (the lawyer's) own room, I would, that afternoon, strive my best to rid them of the nuisance they complained of.

Going upstairs to my old haunt, there was Bartleby silently sitting upon the banister at the landing.

"What are you doing here, Bartleby?" said I.

"Sitting upon the banister," he mildly replied.

I motioned him into the lawyer's room, who then left us.

"Bartleby," said I, "are you aware that you are the cause of great tribulation to me, by persisting in occupying the entry after being dismissed from the office?"

No answer.

"Now one of two things must take place. Either you must do something, or something must be done to you. Now what sort of business would you like to engage in? Would you like to re-engage in copying for someone?"

"No; I would prefer not to make any change."

"Would you like a clerkship in a dry-goods store?"

"There is too much confinement about that. No, I would not like a clerkship; but I am not particular."

"Too much confinement," I cried, "why, you keep yourself confined all the time!"

"I would prefer not to take a clerkship," he rejoined, as if to settle that little item at once.

"How would a bar-tender's business suit you? There is no trying of the eyesight in that."

"I would not like it at all; though, as I said before, I am not particular."

His unwonted wordiness inspirited me. I returned to the charge.

"Well, then, would you like to travel through the country collecting bills for the merchants? That would improve your health."

"No, I would prefer to be doing something else."

"How, then, would going as a companion to Europe, to entertain some young gentleman with your conversation—how would that suit you?"

"Not at all. It does not strike me that there is anything definite about that. I like to be stationary. But I am not particular."

"Stationary you shall be, then," I cried, now losing all patience, and, for the first time in all my exasperating connection with him, fairly flying into a passion. "If you do not go away from these premises before night, I shall feel bound—indeed, I *am* bound—to—to quit the premises myself!" I rather absurdly concluded, knowing not with what possible threat to try to frighten his immobility into compliance. Despairing of all further efforts, I was precipitately leaving him, when a final thought occurred to me—one which had not been wholly unindulged before.

"Bartleby," said I, in the kindest tone I could assume under such exciting circumstances, "will you go home with me now—not to my office, but my dwelling—and remain there till we can conclude upon some convenient arrangement for you at our leisure? Come, let us start now, right away."

"No; at present I would prefer not to make any change at all."

I answered nothing; but, effectually dodging everyone by the suddenness and rapidity of my flight, rushed from the building, ran up Wall Street toward Broadway, and, jumping into the first omnibus,[38] was soon removed from pursuit. As soon as tranquillity returned, I distinctly perceived that I had now done all that I possibly could, both in respect to the demands of the landlord and his tenants, and with regard to my own desire and sense of duty, to benefit Bartleby, and shield him from rude persecution. I now strove to be entirely carefree and quiescent; and my conscience justified me in the attempt; though, indeed, it was not so successful as I could have wished. So fearful was I of being again hunted out by the incensed landlord and his exasperated tenants, that, surrendering my business to Nippers, for a few days, I drove about the upper part of the town and through the suburbs, in my rockaway;[39] crossed over to Jersey City and Hoboken, and paid fugitive visits to Manhattanville and Astoria. In fact, I almost lived in my rockaway for the time.

When again I entered my office, lo, a note from the landlord lay upon the desk. I opened it with trembling hands. It informed me that the writer had sent to the police, and had Bartleby removed to the Tombs as a vagrant. Moreover, since I knew more about him than anyone else, he wished me to appear at that place, and make a suitable statement of the facts. These tidings had a conflicting effect upon me. At first I was indignant; but, at last, almost approved. The landlord's energetic, summary disposition had led him to adopt a procedure which I do not think I would have

[38]Bus. [39]A four-wheeled carriage with a top and open sides.

decided upon myself; and yet, as a last resort, under such peculiar circumstances, it seemed the only plan.

As I afterward learned, the poor scrivener, when told that he must be conducted to the Tombs, offered not the slightest obstacle, but, in his pale, unmoving way, silently acquiesced.

Some of the compassionate and curious bystanders joined the party; and headed by one of the constables arm in arm with Bartleby, the silent procession filed its way through all the noise, and heat, and joy of the roaring thoroughfares at noon.

The same day I received the note, I went to the Tombs, or, to speak more properly, the Halls of Justice. Seeking the right officer, I stated the purpose of my call, and was informed that the individual I described was, indeed, within. I then assured the functionary that Bartleby was a perfectly honest man, and greatly to be compassionated, however unaccountably eccentric. I narrated all I knew, and closed by suggesting the idea of letting him remain in as indulgent confinement as possible, till something less harsh might be done—though, indeed, I hardly knew what. At all events, if nothing else could be decided upon, the almshouse must receive him. I then begged to have an interview.

Being under no disgraceful charge, and quite serene and harmless in all his ways, they had permitted him freely to wander about the prison, and, especially, in the enclosed grass-platted yards thereof. And so I found him there, standing all alone in the quietest of the yards, his face toward a high wall, while all around, from the narrow slits of the jail windows, I thought I saw peering out upon him the eyes of murderers and thieves.

"Bartleby!"

"I know you," he said, without looking round—"and I want nothing to say to you."

"It was not I that brought you here, Bartleby," said I, keenly pained at his implied suspicion. "And to you, this should not be so vile a place. Nothing reproachful attaches to you by being here. And see, it is not so sad a place as one might think. Look, there is the sky, and here is the grass."

"I know where I am," he replied, but would say nothing more, and so I left him.

As I entered the corridor again, a broad meat-like man, in an apron, accosted me, and, jerking his thumb over his shoulder, said, "Is that your friend?"

"Yes."

"Does he want to starve? If he does, let him live on the prison fare, that's all."

"Who are you?" asked I, not knowing what to make of such an unofficially speaking person in such a place.

"I am the grub-man. Such gentlemen as have friends here, hire me to provide them with something good to eat."

"Is this so?" said I, turning to the turnkey.

He said it was.

"Well, then," said I, slipping some silver into the grub-man's hands (for so they called him), "I want you to give particular attention to my friend there; let him have the best dinner you can get. And you must be as polite to him as possible."

"Introduce me, will you?" said the grub-man, looking at me with an expression which seemed to say he was all impatience for an opportunity to give a specimen of his breeding.

Thinking it would prove of benefit to the scrivener, I acquiesced; and, asking the grub-man his name, went up with him to Bartleby.

"Bartleby, this is a friend; you will find him very useful to you."

"Your sarvant, sir, your sarvant," said the grub-man, making a low salutation behind his apron. "Hope you find it pleasant here, sir; nice grounds—cool apartments—hope you'll stay with us some time—try to make it agreeable. What will you have for dinner to-day?"

"I prefer not to dine to-day," said Bartleby, turning away. "It would disagree with me; I am unused to dinners." So saying, he slowly moved to the other side of the enclosure, and took up a position fronting the dead-wall.

"How's this?" said the grub-man, addressing me with a stare of astonishment. "He's odd, ain't he?"

"I think he is a little deranged," said I sadly.

"Deranged? deranged is it? Well, now, upon my word, I thought that friend of yourn was a gentleman forger; they are always pale and genteel-like, them forgers. I can't help pity 'em—can't help it, sir. Did you know Monroe Edwards?"[40] he added touchingly, and paused. Then, laying his hand piteously on my shoulder, sighed, "He died of consumption at Sing-Sing. So you weren't acquainted with Monroe?"

"No, I was never socially acquainted with any forgers. But I cannot stop longer. Look to my friend yonder. You will not lose by it. I will see you again."

Some few days after this, I again obtained admission to the Tombs, and went through the corridors in quest of Bartleby; but without finding him.

"I saw him coming from his cell not long ago," said a turnkey, "maybe he's gone to loiter in the yards."

So I went in that direction.

"Are you looking for the silent man?" said another turnkey, passing me. "Yonder he lies—sleeping in the yard there. 'Tis not twenty minutes since I saw him lie down."

The yard was entirely quiet. It was not accessible to the common prisoners. The surrounding walls, of amazing thickness, kept off all sounds behind them. The Egyptian character of the masonry weighed upon me with its gloom. But a soft imprisoned turf grew under foot. The heart of the eternal pyramids, it seemed, wherein, by some strange magic, through the clefts, grass-seed, dropped by birds, had sprung.

Strangely huddled at the base of the wall, his knees drawn up, and lying on his side, his head touching the cold stones, I saw the wasted Bartleby. But nothing stirred. I paused; then went close up to him; stooped over, and saw that his dim eyes were open; otherwise he seemed profoundly sleeping. Something prompted me to touch him. I felt his hand, when a tingling shiver ran up my arm and down my spine to my feet.

The round face of the grub-man peered upon me now. "His dinner is ready. Won't he dine to-day, either? Or does he live without dining?"

[40]A noted forger, he was first imprisoned in the Tombs and later, after his conviction in 1842, transferred to Sing-Sing Prison, at Ossining, New York, where he died.

"Lives without dining," said I, and closed the eyes.

"Eh!—He's asleep, ain't he?"

"With kings and counsellors,"[41] murmured I.

. . .

There would seem little need for proceeding further in this history. Imagination will readily supply the meagre recital of poor Bartleby's interment. But, ere parting with the reader, let me say, that if this little narrative has sufficiently interested him, to awaken curiosity as to who Bartleby was, and what manner of life he led prior to the present narrator's making his acquaintance, I can only reply, that in such curiosity I fully share, but am wholly unable to gratify it. Yet here I hardly know whether I should divulge one little item of rumour, which came to my ear a few months after the scrivener's decease. Upon what basis it rested I could never ascertain; and hence, how true it is I cannot now tell. But, inasmuch as this vague report has not been without a certain suggestive interest to me, however sad, it may prove the same with some others; and so I will briefly mention it. The report was this: that Bartleby had been a subordinate clerk in the Dead Letter[42] Office at Washington, from which he had been suddenly removed by a change in the administration. When I think over this rumour, hardly can I express the emotions which seize me. Dead letters! does it not sound like dead men? Conceive a man by nature and misfortune prone to a pallid hopelessness, can any business seem more fitted to heighten it than that of continually handling these dead letters, and assorting them for the flames? For by the cartload they are annually burned. Sometimes from out the folded paper the pale clerk takes a ring—the finger it was meant for, perhaps, moulders in the grave; a bank-note sent in swiftest charity—he whom it would relieve, nor eats nor hungers any more; pardon for those who died despairing; hope for those who died unhoping; good tidings for those who died stifled by unrelieved calamities. On errands of life, these letters speed to death.

Ah, Bartleby! Ah, humanity!

1853? 1853, 1856

BENITO CERENO[1]

In the year 1799, Captain Amasa Delano, of Duxbury, in Massachusetts, commanding a large sealer[2] and general trader, lay at anchor with a valuable cargo, in the harbor of St. Maria—a small, desert, uninhabited island toward

[41]Job, in the midst of his suffering, wished that he were dead and "at rest/with kings and counsellors of the earth." Job 3:13–14.

[42]A letter that, for lack of correct address, cannot be delivered.

[1]Written in the years preceding the American Civil War, "Benito Cereno" was based on Amasa Delano's *Narrative of Voyages and Travels* (1817), which recounted the events occurring aboard a Spanish ship near the coast of Chile in 1805. Melville changed the date of the events to 1799 and shaped Delano's account into a depiction of the tyrannies generated by oppression and the differences in human perceptions of reality.

[2]Seal-hunting ship.

the southern extremity of the long coast of Chili. There he had touched for water.

On the second day, not long after dawn, while lying in his berth, his mate came below, informing him that a strange sail was coming into the bay. Ships were then not so plenty in those waters as now. He rose, dressed, and went on deck.

The morning was one peculiar to that coast. Everything was mute and calm; everything gray. The sea, though undulated into long roods[3] of swells, seemed fixed, and was sleeked at the surface like waved lead that has cooled and set in the smelter's mould. The sky seemed a gray surtout.[4] Flights of troubled gray fowl, kith and kin with flights of troubled gray vapors among which they were mixed, skimmed low and fitfully over the waters, as swallows over meadows before storms. Shadows present, foreshadowing deeper shadows to come.

To Captain Delano's surprise, the stranger, viewed through the glass,[5] showed no colors; though to do so upon entering a haven, however uninhabited in its shores, where but a single other ship might be lying, was the custom among peaceful seamen of all nations. Considering the lawlessness and loneliness of the spot, and the sort of stories, at that day, associated with those seas, Captain Delano's surprise might have deepened into some uneasiness had he not been a person of a singularly undistrustful good nature, not liable, except on extraordinary and repeated incentives, and hardly then, to indulge in personal alarms, any way involving the imputation of malign evil in man. Whether, in view of what humanity is capable, such a trait implies, along with a benevolent heart, more than ordinary quickness and accuracy of intellectual perception, may be left to the wise to determine.

But whatever misgivings might have obtruded on first seeing the stranger, would almost, in any seaman's mind, have been dissipated by observing that, the ship, in navigating into the harbor, was drawing too near the land; a sunken reef making out[6] off her bow. This seemed to prove her a stranger, indeed, not only to the sealer, but the island; consequently, she could be no wonted freebooter[7] on that ocean. With no small interest, Captain Delano continued to watch her—a proceeding not much facilitated by the vapors partly mantling the hull, through which the far matin[8] light from her cabin streamed equivocally enough; much like the sun—by this time hemisphered on the rim of the horizon, and, apparently, in company with the strange ship entering the harbor—which wimpled[9] by the same low, creeping clouds, showed not unlike a Lima[10] intriguante's one sinister eye peering across the Plaza from the Indian loop-hole of her dusk[11] *saya-y-manta.*[12]

It might have been but a deception of the vapors, but, the longer the stranger was watched the more singular appeared her manœuvres. Ere long it seemed hard to decide whether she meant to come in or no—what she

[3]Rods, a measure of area equivalent to a quarter of an acre. [4]Overcoat.
[5]Spyglass, a small telescope. [6]Existing, lying.
[7]Knowledgeable pirate, one familiar with those seas and harbors.
[8]Morning. [9]Rippled. [10]Capital of Peru. [11]Shadowy, dark.
[12]Spanish: skirt and shawl; the name given a loose, hooded robe that could hide the identity of an "intriguante" (one involved in an illicit love affair).

wanted, or what she was about. The wind, which had breezed up a little during the night, was now extremely light and baffling,[13] which the more increased the apparent uncertainty of her movements.

Surmising, at last, that it might be a ship in distress, Captain Delano ordered his whale-boat[14] to be dropped, and, much to the wary opposition of his mate, prepared to board her, and, at the least, pilot her in. On the night previous, a fishing-party of the seamen had gone a long distance to some detached rocks out of sight from the sealer, and, an hour or two before daybreak, had returned, having met with no small success. Presuming that the stranger might have been long off soundings,[15] the good captain put several baskets of the fish, for presents, into his boat, and so pulled away. From her continuing too near the sunken reef, deeming her in danger, calling to his men, he made all haste to apprise those on board of their situation. But, some time ere the boat came up, the wind, light though it was, having shifted, had headed the vessel off, as well as partly broken the vapors from about her.

Upon gaining a less remote view, the ship, when made signally visible on the verge of the leaden-hued swells, with the shreds of fog here and there raggedly furring her, appeared like a white-washed monastery after a thunder-storm, seen perched upon some dun[16] cliff among the Pyrenees. But it was no purely fanciful resemblance which now, for a moment, almost led Captain Delano to think that nothing less than a ship-load of monks was before him. Peering over the bulwarks were what really seemed, in the hazy distance, throngs of dark cowls; while, fitfully revealed through the open port-holes, other dark moving figures were dimly descried, as of Black Friars[17] pacing the cloisters.

Upon a still nigher approach, this appearance was modified, and the true character of the vessel was plain—a Spanish merchantman of the first class, carrying negro slaves, amongst other valuable freight, from one colonial port to another. A very large, and, in its time, a very fine vessel, such as in those days were at intervals encountered along that main; sometimes superseded Acapulco treasure-ships,[18] or retired frigates of the Spanish king's navy, which, like super-annuated Italian palaces, still, under a decline of masters, preserved signs of former state.

As the whale-boat drew more and more nigh, the cause of the peculiar pipe-clayed[19] aspect of the stranger was seen in the slovenly neglect pervading her. The spars, ropes, and great part of the bulwarks, looked woolly, from long unacquaintance with the scraper, tar, and the brush. Her keel seemed laid, her ribs put together, and she launched, from Ezekiel's Valley of Dry Bones.[20]

[13]Diminishing.

[14]Long, narrow rowboat.

[15]I.e., long in the deep sea, far from shallow water.

[16]Dull brown.

[17]Dominican monks, called Black friars because they wore black hoods.

[18]Ships that carried gold and silver from America to Spain. Acapulco is a Mexican port on the Pacific Ocean.

[19]Whitened, as if with the white clay used to make tobacco pipes.

[20]"The Lord . . . set me down in the midst of the valley which was full of bones." Ezekiel 37:1.

In the present business in which she was engaged, the ship's general model and rig appeared to have undergone no material change from their original warlike and Froissart pattern.[21] However, no guns were seen.

The tops[22] were large, and were railed about with what had once been octagonal net-work, all now in sad disrepair. These tops hung overhead like three ruinous aviaries, in one of which was seen perched, on a ratlin,[23] a white noddy,[24] a strange fowl, so called from its lethargic, somnambulistic character, being frequently caught by hand at sea. Battered and mouldy, the castellated forecastle[25] seemed some ancient turret, long ago taken by assault, and then left to decay. Toward the stern, two high-raised quarter galleries[26]—the balustrades here and there covered with dry, tindery sea-moss—opening out from the unoccupied state-cabin,[27] whose dead-lights,[28] for all the mild weather, were hermetically closed and calked—these tenantless balconies hung over the sea as if it were the grand Venetian canal. But the principal relic of faded grandeur was the ample oval of the shield-like stern-piece, intricately carved with the arms of Castile and Leon,[29] medallioned about by groups of mythological or symbolical devices; uppermost and central of which was a dark satyr in a mask, holding his foot on the prostrate neck of a writhing figure, likewise masked.

Whether the ship had a figure-head, or only a plain beak,[30] was not quite certain, owing to canvas wrapped about that part, either to protect it while undergoing a re-furbishing, or else decently to hide its decay. Rudely painted or chalked, as in a sailor freak,[31] along the forward side of a sort of pedestal below the canvas, was the sentence, *"Seguid vuestro jefe,"* (follow your leader); while upon the tarnished headboards, near by, appeared, in stately capitals, once gilt, the ship's name, "SAN DOMINICK," each letter streakingly corroded with tricklings of copper-spike rust; while, like mourning weeds, dark festoons of sea-grass slimily swept to and fro over the name, with every hearse-like roll of the hull.

As, at last, the boat was hooked from the bow along toward the gangway[32] amidship, its keel, while yet some inches separated from the hull, harshly grated as on a sunken coral reef. It proved a huge bunch of conglobated[33] barnacles adhering below the water to the side like a wen[34]—a token of baffling airs[35] and long calms passed somewhere in those seas.

Climbing the side, the visitor was at once surrounded by a clamorous throng of whites and blacks, but the latter outnumbering the former more than could have been expected, negro transportation-ship as the stranger in port was. But, in one language, and as with one voice, all poured out a common tale of suffering; in which the negresses, of whom there were not a few,

[21]Jean Froissart (c. 1337–c. 1404) was a medieval French historian. Hence a ship of ancient design.

[22]Platforms on the masts. [23]Small lines forming the steps of a rope ladder.

[24]A small seagull. [25]Upper deck at the forward part of the ship.

[26]Balconies, walkways, attached to the sides of the ship's stern.

[27]A ship's best cabin. Usually reserved for the captain. [28]Shutters that close over portholes.

[29]The *San Dominick,* a Spanish ship, displayed the identifying arms of the Spanish kingdoms of Castile and Leon, a shield showing a castle (Castile) and a lion (Leon).

[30]I.e., a ship with or without a carved figure on its bow. [31]Prank, joke.

[32]I.e., when it reached the bow of the *San Dominick,* Delano's rowboat was towed to the gangway (steps) by which one climbed to the ship's deck.

[33]Ball-shaped. [34]Cyst. [35]Diminishing winds.

exceeded the others in their dolorous vehemence. The scurvy, together with the fever, had swept off a great part of their number, more especially the Spaniards. Off Cape Horn[36] they had narrowly escaped shipwreck; then, for days together, they had lain tranced without wind; their provisions were low; their water next to none; their lips that moment were baked.

While Captain Delano was thus made the mark of all eager tongues, his one eager glance took in all faces, with every other object about him.

Always upon first boarding a large and populous ship at sea, especially a foreign one, with a nondescript crew such as Lascars or Manilla[37] men, the impression varies in a peculiar way from that produced by first entering a strange house with strange inmates in a strange land. Both house and ship—the one by its walls and blinds, the other by its high bulwarks like ramparts—hoard from view their interiors till the last moment: but in the case of the ship there is this addition; that the living spectacle it contains, upon its sudden and complete disclosure, has, in contrast with the blank ocean which zones it, something of the effect of enchantment. The ship seems unreal; these strange costumes, gestures, and faces, but a shadowy tableau just emerged from the deep, which directly must receive back what it gave.

Perhaps it was some such influence, as above is attempted to be described, which, in Captain Delano's mind, heightened whatever, upon a staid scrutiny, might have seemed unusual; especially the conspicuous figures of four elderly grizzled negroes, their heads like black, doddered[38] willow tops, who, in venerable contrast to the tumult below them, were couched, sphynx-like, one on the starboard cat-head,[39] another on the larboard,[40] and the remaining pair face to face on the opposite bulwarks above the main-chains.[41] They each had bits of unstranded old junk[42] in their hands, and, with a sort of stoical self-content, were picking the junk into oakum,[43] a small heap of which lay by their sides. They accompanied the task with a continuous, low, monotonous chant; droning and druling[44] away like so many gray-headed bagpipers playing a funeral march.

The quarter-deck[45] rose into an ample elevated poop, upon the forward verge of which, lifted, like the oakum-pickers, some eight feet above the general throng, sat along in a row, separated by regular spaces, the cross-legged figures of six other blacks; each with a rusty hatchet in his hand, which, with a bit of brick and a rag, he was engaged like a scullion[46] in scouring; while between each two was a small stack of hatchets, their rusted edges turned forward awaiting a like operation. Though occasionally the four oakum-pickers would briefly address some person or persons in the crowd below, yet the six hatchet-polishers neither spoke to others, nor breathed a whisper among themselves, but sat intent upon their task, except at intervals, when, with the peculiar love in negroes of uniting industry with pastime, two and two they

[36]At the southern tip of South America.

[37]Sailors from East India or the Philippine Islands.

[38]Decayed, as if afflicted with dodder, a plant parasite.

[39]Projection near the vessel's starboard (right) bow, to which the anchor is hoisted.

[40]Left. [41]Supports for the rigging of the main mast. [42]Worn rope.

[43]Loose fibers for caulking ship seams. [44]Moaning.

[45]The section of a ship's main deck between the main mast and the elevated poop deck at the stern.

[46]Kitchen worker.

sideways clashed their hatchets together, like cymbals, with a barbarous din. All six, unlike the generality, had the raw aspect of unsophisticated Africans.

But that first comprehensive glance which took in those ten figures, with scores less conspicuous, rested but an instant upon them, as, impatient of the hubbub of voices, the visitor turned in quest of whomsoever it might be that commanded the ship.

But as if not unwilling to let nature make known her own case among his suffering charge, or else in despair of restraining it for the time, the Spanish captain, a gentlemanly, reserved-looking, and rather young man to a stranger's eye, dressed with singular richness, but bearing plain traces of recent sleepless cares and disquietudes, stood passively by, leaning against the main-mast, at one moment casting a dreary, spiritless look upon his excited people, at the next an unhappy glance toward his visitor. By his side stood a black of small stature, in whose rude face, as occasionally, like a shepherd's dog, he mutely turned it up into the Spaniard's, sorrow and affection were equally blended.

Struggling through the throng, the American advanced to the Spaniard, assuring him of his sympathies, and offering to render whatever assistance might be in his power. To which the Spaniard returned for the present but grave and ceremonious acknowledgments, his national formality dusked by the saturnine[47] mood of ill-health.

But losing no time in mere compliments, Captain Delano, returning to the gangway, had his baskets of fish brought up; and as the wind still continued light, so that some hours at least must elapse ere the ship could be brought to the anchorage, he bade his men return to the sealer, and fetch back as much water as the whale-boat could carry, with whatever soft bread the steward might have, all the remaining pumpkins on board, with a box of sugar, and a dozen of his private bottles of cider.

Not many minutes after the boat's pushing off, to the vexation of all, the wind entirely died away, and the tide turning, began drifting back the ship helplessly seaward. But trusting this would not long last, Captain Delano sought, with good hopes, to cheer up the strangers, feeling no small satisfaction that, with persons in their condition, he could—thanks to his frequent voyages along the Spanish main[48]—converse with some freedom in their native tongue.

While left alone with them, he was not long in observing some things tending to heighten his first impressions; but surprise was lost in pity, both for the Spaniards and blacks, alike evidently reduced from scarcity of water and provisions; while long-continued suffering seemed to have brought out the less good-natured qualities of the negroes, besides, at the same time, impairing the Spaniard's authority over them. But, under the circumstances, precisely this condition of things was to have been anticipated. In armies, navies, cities, or families, in nature herself, nothing more relaxes good order than misery. Still, Captain Delano was not without the idea, that had Benito Cereno been a man of greater energy, misrule would hardly have come to the present pass. But the debility, constitutional or induced by hardships, bodily and mental, of the Spanish captain, was too obvious to be overlooked. A prey to settled

[47]Gloomy, dull. [48]The mainland coast of Spanish America.

dejection, as if long mocked with hope he would not now indulge it, even when it had ceased to be a mock, the prospect of that day, or evening at furthest, lying at anchor, with plenty of water for his people, and a brother captain to counsel and befriend, seemed in no perceptible degree to encourage him. His mind appeared unstrung, if not still more seriously affected. Shut up in these oaken walls, chained to one dull round of command, whose unconditionality cloyed him, like some hypochondriac abbot he moved slowly about, at times suddenly pausing, starting, or staring, biting his lip, biting his finger-nail, flushing, paling, twitching his beard, with other symptoms of an absent or moody mind. This distempered spirit was lodged, as before hinted, in as distempered a frame. He was rather tall, but seemed never to have been robust, and now with nervous suffering was almost worn to skeleton. A tendency to some pulmonary complaint appeared to have been lately confirmed. His voice was like that of one with lungs half gone—hoarsely suppressed, a husky whisper. No wonder that, as in this state he tottered about, his private servant apprehensively followed him. Sometimes the negro gave his master his arm, or took his handkerchief out of his pocket for him; performing these and similar offices with that affectional zeal which transmutes into something filial or fraternal acts in themselves but menial; and which has gained for the negro the repute of making the most pleasing body-servant in the world; one, too, whom a master need be on no stiffly superior terms with, but may treat with familiar trust; less a servant than a devoted companion.

Marking the noisy indocility of the blacks in general, as well as what seemed the sullen inefficiency of the whites, it was not without humane satisfaction that Captain Delano witnessed the steady good conduct of Babo.

But the good conduct of Babo, hardly more than the ill-behavior of others, seemed to withdraw the half-lunatic Don[49] Benito from his cloudly langour. Not that such precisely was the impression made by the Spaniard on the mind of his visitor. The Spaniard's individual unrest was, for the present, but noted as a conspicuous feature in the ship's general affliction. Still, Captain Delano was not a little concerned at what he could not help taking for the time to be Don Benito's unfriendly indifference towards himself. The Spaniard's manner, too, conveyed a sort of sour and gloomy disdain, which he seemed at no pains to disguise. But this the American in charity ascribed to the harassing effects of sickness, since, in former instances, he had noted that there are peculiar natures on whom prolonged physical suffering seems to cancel every social instinct of kindness; as if, forced to black bread themselves, they deemed it but equity that each person coming nigh them should, indirectly, by some slight or affront, be made to partake of their fare.

But ere long Captain Delano bethought him that, indulgent as he was at the first, in judging the Spaniard, he might not, after all, have exercised charity enough. At bottom it was Don Benito's reserve which displeased him; but the same reserve was shown towards all but his faithful personal attendant. Even the formal reports which, according to sea-usage,[50] were, at stated times, made to him by some petty underling, either a white, mulatto or black,

[49]A title prefixed to the Christian name of a Spanish nobleman or gentleman.
[50]Customs of the sea.

he hardly had patience enough to listen to, without betraying contemptuous aversion. His manner upon such occasions was, in its degree, not unlike that which might be supposed to have been his imperial countryman's, Charles V.,[51] just previous to the anchoritish retirement of that monarch from the throne.

This splenetic disrelish of his place was evinced in almost every function pertaining to it. Proud as he was moody, he condescended to no personal mandate. Whatever special orders were necessary, their delivery was delegated to his body-servant, who in turn transferred them to their ultimate destination, through runners, alert Spanish boys or slave boys, like pages or pilot-fish[52] within easy call continually hovering round Don Benito. So that to have beheld this undemonstrative invalid gliding about, apathetic and mute, no landsman could have dreamed that in him was lodged a dictatorship beyond which, while at sea, there was no earthly appeal.

Thus, the Spaniard, regarded in his reserve, seemed the involuntary victim of mental disorder. But, in fact, his reserve might, in some degree, have proceeded from design. If so, then here was evinced the unhealthy climax of that icy though conscientious policy, more or less adopted by all commanders of large ships, which, except in signal emergencies, obliterates alike the manifestation of sway with every trace of sociality; transforming the man into a block, or rather into a loaded cannon, which, until there is call for thunder, has nothing to say.

Viewing him in this light, it seemed but a natural token of the perverse habit induced by a long course of such hard self-restraint, that, notwithstanding the present condition of his ship, the Spaniard should still persist in a demeanor, which, however harmless, or, it may be, appropriate, in a well-appointed vessel, such as the San Dominick might have been at the onset of the voyage, was anything but judicious now. But the Spaniard, perhaps thought that it was with captains as with gods: reserve, under all events, must still be their cue. But probably this appearance of slumbering dominion might have been but an attempted disguise to conscious imbecility—not deep policy, but shallow device. But be all this as it might, whether Don Benito's manner was designed or not, the more Captain Delano noted its pervading reserve, the less he felt uneasiness at any particular manifestation of that reserve towards himself.

Neither were his thoughts taken up by the captain alone. Wonted to the quiet orderliness of the sealer's comfortable family of a crew, the noisy confusion of the San Dominick's suffering host repeatedly challenged his eye. Some prominent breaches, not only of discipline but of decency, were observed. These Captain Delano could not but ascribe, in the main, to the absence of those subordinate deck-officers to whom, along with higher duties, is intrusted what may be styled the police department of a populous ship. True, the old oakum-pickers appeared at times to act the part of monitorial constables to their countrymen, the blacks; but though occasionally succeeding in allaying trifling outbreaks now and then between man and man, they could do little or nothing toward establishing general quiet. The San

[51]Charles V (1500–1558), King of Spain who became an anchorite (retiring from the world) and joined a monastery in 1556.

[52]Small fish that hover near sharks and seem to guide them.

Dominick was in the condition of a transatlantic emigrant ship, among whose multitude of living freight are some individuals, doubtless, as little troublesome as crates and bales; but the friendly remonstrances of such with their ruder companions are of not so much avail as the unfriendly arm of the mate. What the San Dominick wanted was, what the emigrant ship has, stern superior officers. But on these decks not so much as a fourth-mate was to be seen.

The visitor's curiosity was roused to learn the particulars of those mishaps which had brought such absenteeism, with its consequences; because, though deriving some inkling of the voyage from the wails which at the first moment had greeted him, yet of the details no clear understanding had been had. The best account would, doubtless, be given by the captain. Yet at first the visitor was loth to ask it, unwilling to provoke some distant rebuff. But plucking up courage, he at last accosted Don Benito, renewing the expression of his benevolent interest, adding, that did he (Captain Delano) but know the particulars of the ship's misfortunes, he would, perhaps, be better able in the end to relieve them. Would Don Benito favor him with the whole story.

Don Benito faltered; then, like some somnambulist suddenly interfered with, vacantly stared at his visitor, and ended by looking down on the deck. He maintained this posture so long, that Captain Delano, almost equally disconcerted, and involuntarily almost as rude, turned suddenly from him, walking forward to accost one of the Spanish seamen for the desired information. But he had hardly gone five paces, when, with a sort of eagerness, Don Benito invited him back, regretting his momentary absence of mind, and professing readiness to gratify him.

While most part of the story was being given, the two captains stood on the after part of the main-deck, a privileged spot, no one being near but the servant.

"It is now a hundred and ninety days," began the Spaniard, in his husky whisper, "that this ship, well officered and well manned, with several cabin passengers—some fifty Spaniards in all—sailed from Buenos Ayres bound to Lima, with a general cargo, hardware, Paraguay tea[53] and the like—and," pointing forward, "that parcel of negroes, now not more than a hundred fifty, as you see, but then numbering over three hundred souls. Off Cape Horn we had heavy gales. In one moment, by night, three of my best officers, with fifteen sailors, were lost, with the main-yard; the spar snapping under them in the slings,[54] as they sought, with heavers,[55] to beat down the icy sail. To lighten the hull, the heavier sacks of mata[56] were thrown into the sea, with most of the water-pipes[57] lashed on the deck at the time. And this last necessity it was, combined with the prolonged detentions afterwards experienced, which eventually brought about our chief causes of suffering. When—"

Here there was a sudden fainting attack of his cough, brought on, no doubt, by his mental distress. His servant sustained him, and drawing a cordial[58] from his pocket placed it to his lips. He a little revived. But unwilling to

[53]Dried leaves of the *Ilex paraguariensis,* a small shrub of the holly family, grown in Paraguay. From it is brewed a mild tea.

[54]Ropes that attach a yardarm to a mast.

[55]Rods or bars used as levers.

[56]Maté, Paraguay tea.

[57]Water casks.

[58]A container of medicine or liqueur.

leave him unsupported while yet imperfectly restored, the black with one arm still encircled his master, at the same time keeping his eye fixed on his face, as if to watch for the first sign of complete restoration, or relapse, as the event might prove.

The Spaniard proceeded, but brokenly and obscurely, as one in a dream.

—"Oh, my God! rather than pass through what I have, with joy I would have hailed the most terrible gales; but——"

His cough returned and with increased violence; this subsiding, with reddened lips and closed eyes he fell heavily against his supporter.

"His mind wanders. He was thinking of the plague that followed the gales," plaintively sighed the servant; "my poor, poor master!" wringing one hand, and with the other wiping the mouth. "But be patient, Señor," again turning to Captain Delano, "these fits do not last long; master will soon be himself."

Don Benito reviving, went on; but as this portion of the story was very brokenly delivered, the substance only will here be set down.

It appeared that after the ship had been many days tossed in storms off the Cape, the scurvy[59] broke out, carrying off numbers of the whites and blacks. When at last they had worked round into the Pacific, their spars and sails were so damaged, and so inadequately handled by the surviving mariners, most of whom were become invalids, that, unable to lay her northerly course by the wind, which was powerful, the unmanageable ship, for successive days and nights, was blown northwestward, where the breeze suddenly deserted her, in unknown waters, to sultry calms. The absence of the water-pipes now proved as fatal to life as before their presence had menaced it. Induced, or at least aggravated, by the more than scanty allowance of water, a malignant fever followed the scurvy; with the excessive heat of the lengthened calm, making such short work of it as to sweep away, as by billows, whole families of the Africans, and a yet larger number, proportionably, of the Spaniards, including, by a luckless fatality, every remaining officer on board. Consequently, in the smart west winds eventually following the calm, the already rent sails, having to be simply dropped, not furled, at need, had been gradually reduced to the beggars' rags they were now. To procure substitutes for his lost sailors, as well as supplies of water and sails, the captain, at the earliest opportunity, had made for Valdivia, the southernmost civilized port of Chili and South America; but upon nearing the coast the thick weather had prevented him from so much as sighting that harbor. Since which period, almost without a crew, and almost without canvas and almost without water, and, at intervals, giving its added dead to the sea, the San Dominick had been battle-dored[60] about by contrary winds, inveigled by currents, or grown weedy in calms. Like a man lost in woods, more than once she had doubled upon her own track.

"But throughout these calamities," huskily continued Don Benito, painfully turning in the half embrace of his servant. "I have to thank those negroes you see, who, though to your inexperienced eyes appearing unruly, have, indeed, conducted themselves with less of restlessness than even their owner could have thought possible under such circumstances."

[59]A wasting disease caused by lack of vitamin C.
[60]Batted, like the shuttlecock in badminton.

Here he again fell faintly back. Again his mind wandered; but he rallied, and less obscurely proceeded.

"Yes, their owner was quite right in assuring me that no fetters would be needed with his blacks; so that while, as is wont in this transportation, those negroes have always remained upon deck—not thrust below, as in the Guineamen[61]—they have, also, from the beginning, been freely permitted to range within given bounds at their pleasure."

Once more the faintness returned—his mind roved—but, recovering, he resumed:

"But it is Babo here to whom, under God, I owe not only my own preservation, but likewise to him, chiefly, the merit is due, of pacifying his more ignorant brethren, when at intervals tempted to murmurings."

"Ah, master," sighed the black, bowing his face, "don't speak of me; Babo is nothing; what Babo has done was but duty."

"Faithful fellow!" cried Captain Delano. "Don Benito, I envy you such a friend; slave I cannot call him."

As master and man stood before him, the black upholding the white, Captain Delano could not but bethink him of the beauty of that relationship which could present such a spectacle of fidelity on the one hand and confidence on the other. The scene was heightened by the contrast in dress, denoting their relative positions. The Spaniard wore a loose Chili jacket of dark velvet; white small-clothes and stockings, with silver buckles at the knee and instep; a high-crowned sombrero, of fine grass; a slender sword, silver mounted, hung from a knot in his sash—the last being an almost invariable adjunct, more for utility than ornament, of a South American gentleman's dress to this hour. Excepting when his occasional nervous contortions brought about disarray, there was a certain precision in his attire curiously at variance with the unsightly disorder around; especially in the belittered Ghetto, forward of the main-mast, wholly occupied by the blacks.

The servant wore nothing but wide trowsers, apparently, from their coarseness and patches, made out of some old topsail; they were clean, and confined at the waist by a bit of unstranded rope, which, with his composed, deprecatory air at times, made him look something like a begging friar of St. Francis.[62]

However unsuitable for the time and place, at least in the blunt-thinking American's eyes, and however strangely surviving in the midst of all his afflictions, the toilette of Don Benito might not, in fashion at least, have gone beyond the style of the day among South Americans of his class. Though on the present voyage sailing from Buenos Ayres, he had avowed himself a native and resident of Chili, whose inhabitants had not so generally adopted the plain coat and once plebian pantaloons; but, with a becoming modification, adhered to their provincial costume, picturesque as any in the world. Still, relatively to the pale history of the voyage, and his own pale face, there seemed something so incongruous in the Spaniard's apparel, as almost the image of an invalid courtier tottering about London streets in the time of the plague.

[61]Slave ships trading with Guinea in West Africa.
[62]A member of the Franciscan religious order.

The portion of the narrative which, perhaps, most excited interest, as well as some surprise, considering the latitudes in question, was the long calms spoken of, and more particularly the ship's so long drifting about. Without communicating the opinion, of course, the American could not but impute at least part of the detentions both to clumsy seamanship and faulty navigation. Eying Don Benito's small, yellow hands, he easily inferred that the young captain had not got into command at the hawse-hole,[63] but the cabin-window; and if so, why wonder at incompetence, in youth, sickness, and gentility united?

But drowning criticism in compassion, after a fresh repetition of his sympathies, Captain Delano, having heard out his story, not only engaged, as in the first place, to see Don Benito and his people supplied in their immediate bodily needs, but, also, now further promised to assist him in procuring a large permanent supply of water, as well as some sails and rigging; and, though it would involve no small embarrassment to himself, yet he would spare three of his best seamen for temporary deck officers; so that without delay the ship might proceed to Conception,[64] there to refit for Lima, her destined port.

Such generosity was not without its effect, even upon the invalid. His face lighted up; eager and hectic, he met the honest glance of his visitor. With gratitude he seemed overcome.

"This excitement is bad for master," whispered the servant, taking his arm, and with soothing words gently drawing him aside.

When Don Benito returned, the American was pained to observe that his hopefulness, like the sudden kindling in his cheek, was but febrile and transient.

Ere long, with a joyless mien, looking up towards the poop, the host invited his guest to accompany him there, for the benefit of what little breath of wind might be stirring.

As, during the telling of the story, Captain Delano had once or twice started at the occasional cymballing of the hatchet-polishers, wondering why such an interruption should be allowed, especially in that part of the ship, and in the ears of an invalid; and moreover, as the hatchets had anything but an attractive look, and the handlers of them still less so, it was, therefore, to tell the truth, not without some lurking reluctance, or even shrinking, it may be, that Captain Delano, with apparent complaisance, acquiesced in his host's invitation. The more so, since, with an untimely caprice of punctilio, rendered distressing by his cadaverous aspect, Don Benito, with Castilian[65] bows, solemnly insisted upon his guest's preceding him up the ladder leading to the elevation; where, one on each side of the last step, sat for armorial supporters and sentries two of the ominous file. Gingerly enough stepped good Captain Delano between them, and in the instant of leaving them behind, like one running the gauntlet,[66] he felt an apprehensive twitch in the calves of his legs.

[63]Hole for cables and chains in the ship's bow. Thus Melville implies that Don Benito had not risen from the ranks of the common sailors, and therefore he was inexperienced.

[64]Concepción, a seaport in Chile. [65]Courtly.

[66]Running between two files of men who strike at the runner with fists, whips, or clubs.

But when, facing about, he saw the whole file, like so many organ-grinders, still stupidly intent on their work, unmindful of everything beside, he could not but smile at his late fidgety panic.

Presently, while standing with his host, looking forward upon the decks below, he was struck by one of those instances of insubordination previously alluded to. Three black boys, with two Spanish boys, were sitting together on the hatches, scraping a rude wooden platter, in which some scanty mess had recently been cooked. Suddenly, one of the black boys, enraged at a word dropped by one of his white companions, seized a knife, and, though called to forbear by one of the oakum-pickers, struck the lad over the head, inflicting a gash from which blood flowed.

In amazement, Captain Delano inquired what this meant. To which the pale Don Benito dully muttered, that it was merely the sport of the lad.

"Pretty serious sport, truly," rejoined Captain Delano. "Had such a thing happened on board the Bachelor's Delight, instant punishment would have followed."

At these words the Spaniard turned upon the American one of his sudden, staring, half-lunatic looks; then, relapsing into his torpor, answered, "Doubtless, doubtless, Señor."

Is it, thought Captain Delano, that this hapless man is one of those paper captains I've known, who by policy wink at what by power they cannot put down? I know no sadder sight than a commander who has little of command but the name.

"I should think, Don Benito," he now said, glancing towards the oakum-picker who had sought to interfere with the boys, "that you would find it advantageous to keep all your blacks employed, especially the younger ones, no matter at what useless task, and no matter what happens to the ship. Why, even with my little band, I find such a course indispensable. I once kept a crew on my quarter-deck thrumming[67] mats for my cabin, when, for three days, I had given up my ship—mats, men, and all—for a speedy loss, owing to the violence of a gale, in which we could do nothing but helplessly drive before it."

"Doubtless, doubtless," muttered Don Benito.

"But," continued Captain Delano, again glancing upon the oakum-pickers and then at the hatchet-polishers, near by, "I see you keep some, at least, of your host employed."

"Yes," was again the vacant response.

"Those old men there, shaking their pows,[68] from their pulpits," continued Captain Delano, pointing to the oakum-pickers, "seem to act the part of old dominies[69] to the rest, little heeded as their admonitions are at times. Is this voluntary on their part, Don Benito, or have you appointed them shepherds to your flock of black sheep?"

"What posts they fill, I appointed them," rejoined the Spaniard, in an acrid tone, as if resenting some supposed satiric reflection.

"And these others, these Ashantee[70] conjurors here," continued Captain Delano, rather uneasily eying the brandished steel of the hatchet-polishers, where, in spots, it had been brought to a shine, "this seems a curious business they are at, Don Benito?"

[67]Weaving [68]Heads. [69]Clergyman or schoolmaster. [70]West African native.

"In the gales we met," answered the Spaniard, "what of our general cargo was not thrown overboard was much damaged by the brine. Since coming into calm weather, I have had several cases of knives and hatchets daily brought up for overhauling and cleaning."

"A prudent idea, Don Benito. You are part owner of ship and cargo, I presume; but none of the slaves, perhaps?"

"I am owner of all you see," impatiently returned Don Benito, "except the main company of blacks, who belonged to my late friend, Alexandro Aranda."

As he mentioned this name, his air was heart-broken; his knees shook; his servant supported him.

Thinking he divined the cause of such unusual emotion, to confirm his surmise, Captain Delano, after a pause, said: "And may I ask, Don Benito, whether—since awhile ago you spoke of some cabin passengers—the friend, whose loss so afflicts you, at the outset of the voyage accompanied his blacks?"

"Yes."

"But died of the fever?"

"Died of the fever. Oh, could I but—"

Again quivering, the Spaniard paused.

"Pardon me," said Captain Delano, lowly, "but I think that, by a sympathetic experience, I conjecture, Don Benito, what it is that gives the keener edge to your grief. It was once my hard fortune to lose, at sea, a dear friend, my own brother, then supercargo.[71] Assured of the welfare of his spirit, its departure I could have borne like a man; but that honest eye, that honest hand—both of which had so often met mine—and that warm heart; all, all—like scraps to the dogs—to throw all to the sharks! It was then I vowed never to have for fellow-voyager a man I loved, unless, unbeknown to him, I had provided every requisite, in case of a fatality, for embalming his mortal part for interment on shore. Were your friend's remains now on board this ship, Don Benito, not thus strangely would the mention of his name affect you."

"On board this ship?" echoed the Spaniard. Then, with horrified gestures, as directed against some spectre; he unconsciously fell into the ready arms of his attendant, who, with a silent appeal toward Captain Delano, seemed beseeching him not again to broach a theme so unspeakably distressing to his master.

This poor fellow now, thought the pained American, is the victim of that sad superstition which associates goblins with the deserted body of man, as ghosts with an abandoned house. How unlike are we made! What to me, in like case, would have been a solemn satisfaction, the bare suggestion, even, terrifies the Spaniard into this trance. Poor Alexandro Aranda! what would you say could you here see your friend—who, on former voyages, when you, for months, were left behind, has, I dare say, often longed, and longed, for one peep at you—now transported with terror at the least thought of having you anyway nigh him.

[71]Ship's officer in charge of business affairs.

At this moment, with a dreary grave-yard toll, betokening a flaw, the ship's forecastle bell, smote by one of the grizzled oakum-pickers, proclaimed ten o'clock, through the leaden calm; when Captain Delano's attention was caught by the moving figure of a gigantic black, emerging from the general crowd below, and slowly advancing towards the elevated poop. An iron collar was about his neck, from which depended a chain, thrice wound round his body; the terminating links padlocked together at a broad band of iron, his girdle.

"How like a mute Atufal moves," murmured the servant.

The black mounted the steps of the poop, and, like a brave prisoner, brought up to receive sentence, stood in unquailing muteness before Don Benito, now recovered from his attack.

At the first glimpse of his approach, Don Benito had started, a resentful shadow swept over his face; and, as with the sudden memory of bootless[72] rage, his white lips glued together.

This is some mulish mutineer, thought Captain Delano, surveying, not without a mixture of admiration, the colossal form of the negro.

"See, he waits your question, master," said the servant.

Thus reminded, Don Benito, nervously averting his glance, as if shunning, by anticipation, some rebellious response, in a disconcerted voice, thus spoke:—

"Atufal, will you ask my pardon, now?"

The black was silent.

"Again, master," murmured the servant, with bitter upbraiding eyeing his countryman, "Again, master; he will bend to master yet."

"Answer," said Don Benito, still averting his glance, "say but the one word, *pardon,* and your chains shall be off."

Upon this, the black, slowly raising both arms, let them lifelessly fall, his links clashing, his head bowed; as much as to say, "no, I am content."

"Go," said Don Benito, with inkept and unknown emotion.

Deliberately as he had come, the black obeyed.

"Excuse me, Don Benito," said Captain Delano, "but this scene surprises me; what means it, pray?"

"It means that that negro alone, of all the band, has given me peculiar cause of offense. I have put him in chains; I—"

Here he paused; his hand to his head, as if there were a swimming there, or a sudden bewilderment of memory had come over him; but meeting his servant's kindly glance seemed reassured, and proceeded:—

"I could not scourge such a form. But I told him he must ask my pardon. As yet he has not. At my command, every two hours he stands before me."

"And how long has this been?"

"Some sixty days."

"And obedient in all else? And respectful?"

"Yes."

"Upon my conscience, then," exclaimed Captain Delano, impulsively, "he has a royal spirit in him, this fellow."

"He may have some right to it," bitterly returned Don Benito, "he says he was king in his own land."

[72]Impotent.

"Yes," said the servant, entering a word, "those slits in Atufal's ears once held wedges of gold; but poor Babo here, in his own land, was only a poor slave; a black man's slave was Babo, who now is the white's."

Somewhat annoyed by these conversational familiarities, Captain Delano turned curiously upon the attendant, then glanced inquiringly at his master; but, as if long wonted to these little informalities, neither master nor man seemed to understand him.

"What, pray, was Atufal's offense, Don Benito?" asked Captain Delano; "if it was not something very serious, take a fool's advice, and, in view of his general docility, as well as in some natural respect for his spirit, remit him his penalty."

"No, no, master never will do that," here murmured the servant to himself, "proud Atufal must first ask master's pardon. The slave there carries the padlock, but master here carries the key."

His attention thus directed, Captain Delano now noticed for the first time, that, suspended by a slender silken cord, from Don Benito's neck, hung a key. At once, from the servant's muttered syllables, divining the key's purpose, he smiled and said:—"So, Don Benito—padlock and key—significant symbols, truly."

Biting his lip, Don Benito faltered.

Though the remark of Captain Delano, a man of such native simplicity as to be incapable of satire or irony, had been dropped in playful allusion to the Spaniard's singularly evidenced lordship over the black; yet the hypochondriac seemed some way to have taken it as a malicious reflection upon his confessed inability thus far to break down, at least, on a verbal summons, the entrenched will of the slave. Deploring this supposed misconception, yet despairing of correcting it, Captain Delano shifted the subject; but finding his companion more than ever withdrawn, as if still sourly digesting the lees[73] of the presumed affront above-mentioned, by-and-by Captain Delano likewise became less talkative, oppressed, against his own will, by what seemed the secret vindictiveness of the morbidly sensitive Spaniard. But the good sailor, himself of a quite contrary disposition, refrained, on his part, alike from the appearance as from the feeling of resentment, and if silent, was only so from contagion.

Presently the Spaniard, assisted by his servant somewhat discourteously crossed over from his guest; a procedure which, sensibly enough, might have been allowed to pass for idle caprice of ill-humor, had not master and man, lingering round the corner of the elevated skylight, begun whispering together in low voices. This was unpleasing. And more, the moody air of the Spaniard, which at times had not been without a sort of valetudinarian[74] stateliness, now seemed anything but dignified; while the menial familiarity of the servant lost its original charm of simple-hearted attachment.

In his embarrassment, the visitor turned his face to the other side of the ship. By so doing, his glance accidentally fell on a young Spanish sailor, a coil of rope in his hand, just stepped from the deck to the first round of the mizzen-rigging.[75] Perhaps the man would not have been particularly noticed, were it not that, during his ascent to one of the yards, he, with a sort of

[73]Dregs, leftovers. [74]Sickly, weak. [75]Rigging of the mast that is set nearest the stern.

covert intentness, kept his eye fixed on Captain Delano, from whom, presently, it passed, as if by a natural sequence, to the two whisperers.

His own attention thus redirected to that quarter, Captain Delano gave a slight start. From something in Don Benito's manner just then, it seemed as if the visitor had, at least partly, been the subject of the withdrawn consultation going on—a conjecture as little agreeable to the guest as it was little flattering to the host.

The singular alterations of courtesy and ill-breeding in the Spanish captain were unaccountable, except on one of two suppositions—innocent lunacy, or wicked imposture.

But the first idea, though it might naturally have occurred to an indifferent observer, and, in some respect, had not hitherto been wholly a stranger to Captain Delano's mind, yet, now that, in an incipient way, he began to regard the stranger's conduct something in the light of an intentional affront, of course the idea of lunacy was virtually vacated. But if not a lunatic, what then? Under the circumstances, would a gentleman, nay, any honest boor, act the part now acted by his host? The man was an imposter. Some low-born adventurer, masquerading as an oceanic grandee;[76] yet so ignorant of the first requisites of mere gentlemanhood as to be betrayed into the present remarkable indecorum. That strange ceremoniousness, too, at other times evinced, seemed not uncharacteristic of one playing a part above his real level. Don Benito Cereno—Don Benito Cereno—a sounding[77] name. One, too, at that period, not unknown, in the surname, to supercargoes and sea captains trading along the Spanish Main, as belonging to one of the most enterprising and extensive mercantile families in all those provinces; several members of it having titles; a sort of Castilian Rothschild,[78] with a noble brother, or cousin, in every great trading town of South America. The alleged Don Benito was in early manhood, about twenty-nine or thirty. To assume a sort of roving cadetship[79] in the maritime affairs of such a house, what more likely scheme for a young knave of talent and spirit? But the Spaniard was a pale invalid. Never mind. For even to the degree of simulating mortal disease, the craft of some tricksters has been known to attain. To think that, under the aspect of infantile weakness, the most savage energies might be couched—those velvets of the Spaniard but the silky paw to his fangs.

From no train of thought did these fancies come; not from within, but from without; suddenly, too, and in one throng, like hoar frost; yet as soon to vanish as the mild sun of Captain Delano's good-nature regained its meridian.

Glancing over once more towards his host—whose side-face, revealed above the skylight, was now turned towards him—he was struck by the profile, whose clearness of cut was refined by the thinness, incident to ill-health, as well as ennobled about the chin by the beard. Away with suspicion. He was a true off-shoot of a true hidalgo[80] Cereno.

[76]Spanish: nobleman of high rank. [77]High-sounding, sonorous.

[78]Family of bankers (originally German) that established commercial offices in various European cities.

[79]Apprenticeship. [80]Spanish: nobleman.

Relieved by these and other better thoughts, the visitor, lightly humming a tune, now began indifferently pacing the poop, so as not to betray to Don Benito that he had at all mistrusted incivility, much less duplicity; for such mistrust would yet be proved illusory, and by the event; though, for the present, the circumstance which had provoked that distrust remained unexplained. But when that little mystery should have been cleared up, Captain Delano thought he might extremely regret it, did he allow Don Benito to become aware that he had indulged in ungenerous surmises. In short, to the Spaniard's black-letter[81] text, it was best, for a while, to leave open margin.[82]

Presently, his pale face twitching and overcast, the Spaniard, still supported by his attendant, moved over towards his guest, when, with even more than his usual embarrassment, and a strange sort of intriguing intonation in his husky whisper, the following conversation began:—

"Señor, may I ask how long you have lain at this isle?"

"Oh, but a day or two, Don Benito."

"And from what port are you last?"

"Canton."[83]

"And there, Señor, you exchanged your sealskins for teas and silks, I think you said?"

"Yes. Silks, mostly."

"And the balance you took in specie,[84] perhaps?"

Captain Delano, fidgeting a little, answered—

"Yes; some silver; not a very great deal, though."

"Ah—well, May I ask how many men have you, Señor?"

Captain Delano slightly started, but answered—

"About five-and-twenty, all told."

"And at present, Señor, all on board, I suppose?"

"All on board, Don Benito," replied the Captain, now with satisfaction.

"And will be to-night, Señor?"

At this last question, following so many pertinacious ones, for the soul of him Captain Delano could not but look very earnestly at the questioner, who, instead of meeting the glance, with every token of craven discomposure dropped his eyes to the deck; presenting an unworthy contrast to his servant, who, just then, was kneeling at his feet, adjusting a loose shoe-buckle; his disengaged face meantime, with humble curiosity, turned openly up into his master's downcast one.

The Spaniard, still with a guilty shuffle, repeated his question:

"And—and will be to-night, Señor?"

"Yes, for aught I know," returned Captain Delano—"but nay," rallying himself into fearless truth, "some of them talked of going off on another fishing party about midnight."

"Your ships generally go—go more or less armed, I believe Señor?"

"Oh, a six-pounder or two, in case of emergency," was the intrepidly indifferent reply, "with a small stock of muskets, sealing-spears, and cutlasses, you know."

[81]Early design of printing type modeled on ornate manuscript writing and often difficult to read.

[82]I.e., to omit marginal comments; thus, without explanation.

[83]In China. [84]Coin, usually gold or silver.

As he thus responded, Captain Delano again glanced at Don Benito, but the latter's eyes were averted; while abruptly and awkwardly shifting the subject, he made some peevish allusion to the calm, and then, without apology, once more, with his attendant, withdrew to the opposite bulwarks, where the whispering was resumed.

At this moment, and ere Captain Delano could cast a cool thought upon what had just passed, the young Spanish sailor, before mentioned, was seen descending from the rigging. In act of stooping over to spring inboard to the deck, his voluminous, unconfined frock, or shirt, of coarse woolen, much spotted with tar, opened out far down the chest, revealing a soiled under garment of what seemed the finest line, edged, about the neck, with a narrow blue ribbon, sadly faded and worn. At this moment the young sailor's eye was again fixed on the whisperers, and Captain Delano thought he observed a lurking significance in it, as if silent signs, of some Freemason[85] sort, had that instant been interchanged.

This once more impelled his own glance in the direction of Don Benito, and, as before, he could not infer that himself formed the subject of the conference. He paused. The sound of the hatchet-polishing fell on his ears. He cast another swift side-look at the two. They had the air of conspirators. In connection with the late questionings, and the incident of the young sailor, these things now begat such return of involuntary suspicion, that the singular guilelessness of the American could not endure it. Plucking up a gay and humorous expression, he crossed over to the two rapidly, saying:—"Ha, Don Benito, your black here seems high in your trust; a sort of privy-counselor,[86] in fact."

Upon this, the servant looked up with a good-natured grin, but the master started as from a venomous bite. It was a moment or two before the Spaniard sufficiently recovered himself to reply; which he did, at last, with cold constraint:—"Yes, Señor, I have trust in Babo."

Here Babo, changing his previous grin of mere animal humor into an intelligent smile, not ungratefully eyed his master.

Finding that the Spaniard now stood silent and reserved, as if involuntarily, or purposely giving hint that his guest's proximity was inconvenient just then, Captain Delano, unwilling to appear uncivil even to incivility itself, made some trivial remark and moved off; again and again turning over in his mind the mysterious demeanor of Don Benito Cereno.

He had descended from the poop, and, wrapped in thought, was passing near a dark hatchway, leading down into the steerage,[87] when, perceiving motion there, he looked to see what moved. The same instant there was a sparkle in the shadowy hatchway, and he saw one of the Spanish sailors, prowling there, hurriedly placing his hand in the bosom of his frock, as if hiding something. Before the man could have been certain who it was that was passing, he slunk below out of sight. But enough was seen of him to make sure that he was the same young sailor before noticed in the rigging.

What was that which so sparkled? thought Captain Delano. It was no lamp—no match—no live coal. Could it have been a jewel? But how come sailors with jewels?—or with silk-trimmed undershirts either? Has he been

[85]Signals used by members of the secret fraternal society of Freemasons.
[86]Personal adviser. [87]Passenger area near the rudder.

robbing the trunks of the dead cabin-passengers? But if so, he would hardly wear one of the stolen articles on board ship here. Ah, ah—if, now, that was, indeed a secret sign I saw passing between this suspicious fellow and his captain awhile since; if I could only be certain that, in my uneasiness, my senses did not deceive me, then——

Here, passing from one suspicious thing to another, his mind revolved the strange questions put to him concerning his ship.

By a curious coincidence, as each point was recalled, the black wizards of Ashantee would strike up with their hatchets, as in ominous comment on the white stranger's thoughts. Pressed by such enigmas and portents, it would have been almost against nature, had not, even into the least distrustful heart, some ugly misgivings obtruded.

Observing the ship, now helplessly fallen into a current, with enchanted sails, drifting with increased rapidity seaward; and noting that, from a lately intercepted projection of the land, the sealer was hidden, the stout mariner began to quake at thoughts which he barely durst confess to himself. Above all, he began to feel a ghostly dread of Don Benito. And yet, when he roused himself, dilated his chest, felt himself strong on his legs, and coolly considered it—what did all these phantoms amount to?

Had the Spaniard any sinister scheme, it must have reference not so much to him (Captain Delano) as to his ship (the Bachelor's Delight). Hence the present drifting away of the one ship from the other, instead of favoring any such possible scheme, was, for the time, at least, opposed to it. Clearly any suspicion, combining such contradictions, must need be delusive. Beside, was it not absurd to think of a vessel in distress—a vessel by sickness almost dismanned of her crew—a vessel whose inmates were parched for water—was it not a thousand times absurd that such a craft should, at present, be of a piratical character; or her commander, either for himself or those under him, cherish any desire but for speedy relief and refreshment? But then, might not general distress, and thirst in particular, be affected? And might not that same undiminished Spanish crew, alleged to have perished off to a remnant, be at that very moment lurking in the hold? On heart-broken pretense of entreating a cup of cold water, fiends in human form had got into lonely dwellings, not retired until a dark deed had been done. And among the Malay pirates, it was no unusual thing to lure ships after them into their treacherous harbors, or entice boarders from a declared enemy at sea, by the spectacle of thinly manned or vacant decks, beneath which prowled a hundred spears with yellow arms ready to upthrust them through the mats. Not that Captain Delano had entirely credited such things. He had heard of them—and now, as stories, they recurred. The present destination of the ship was anchorage. There she would be near his own vessel. Upon gaining that vicinity, might not the San Dominick, like a slumbering volcano, suddenly let loose energies now hid?

He recalled the Spaniard's manner while telling his story. There was a gloomy hesitancy and subterfuge about it. It was just the manner of one making up his tale for evil purposes, as he goes. But if that story was not true, what was the truth? That the ship had unlawfully come into the Spaniard's possession? But in many of its details, especially in reference to the more calamitous parts, such as the fatalities among the seamen, the consequent prolonged beating about, the past sufferings from obstinate calms, and still continued suffering from thirst; in all these points, as well as others, Don Benito's story had corroborated not only the wailing ejaculations of the indiscriminate multitude, white and black, but likewise—what seemed impossible to be counterfeit—by the very expression and play of every human feature, which Captain Delano saw. If Don Benito's story was, throughout, an invention, then every soul on board, down to the youngest negress, was his carefully drilled recruit in the plot: an incredible inference. And yet, if there was ground for mistrusting his veracity, that inference was a legitimate one.

But those questions of the Spaniard. There, indeed, one might pause. Did they not seem put with much the same object with which the burglar or assassin, by day-time, reconnoitres the walls of a house? But, with ill purposes, to solicit such information openly of the chief person endangered, and so, in effect, setting him on his guard; how unlikely a procedure was that? Absurd, then, to suppose that those questions had been prompted by evil designs. Thus, the same conduct, which, in this instance, had raised the alarm, served to dispel it. In short, scarce any suspicion or uneasiness, however apparently reasonable at the time, which was not now, with equal apparent reason, dismissed.

At last he began to laugh at his former forebodings; and laugh at the strange ship for, in its aspect, someway siding with them, as it were; and laugh, too, at the odd-looking blacks, particularly those old scissors-grinders, the Ashantees; and those bed-ridden old knitting women, the oakum-pickers; and almost at the dark Spaniard himself, the central hobgoblin of all.

For the rest, whatever in a serious way seemed enigmatical, was now good-naturedly explained away by the thought that, for the most part, the poor invalid scarcely knew what he was about; either sulking in black vapors, or putting idle questions without sense or object. Evidently, for the present, the man was not fit to be entrusted with the ship. On some benevolent plea withdrawing the command from him, Captain Delano would yet have to send her to Conception, in charge of his second mate, a worthy person and good navigator—a plan not more convenient for the San Dominick than for Don Benito; for, relieved from all anxiety, keeping wholly to his cabin, the sick man, under the good nursing of his servant, would, probably, by the end of the passage, be in a measure restored to health, and with that he should also be restored to authority.

Such were the American's thoughts. They were tranquilizing. There was a difference between the idea of Don Benito's darkly preordaining Captain Delano's fate, and Captain Delano's lightly arranging Don Benito's. Nevertheless, it was not without something of relief that the good seaman presently perceived his whale-boat in the distance. Its absence had been prolonged by unexpected detention at the sealer's side, as well as its returning trip lengthened by the continual recession of the goal.

The advancing speck was observed by the blacks. Their shouts attracted the attention of Don Benito, who, with a return courtesy, approaching Captain Delano, expressed satisfaction at the coming of some supplies, slight and temporary as they must necessarily prove.

Captain Delano responded; but while doing so, his attention was drawn to something passing on the deck below: among the crowd climbing the landward bulwarks, anxiously watching the coming boat, two blacks, to all appearances accidentally incommoded by one of the sailors, violently pushed him aside, which the sailor somewhat resenting, they dashed him to the deck, despite the earnest cries of the oakum-pickers.

"Don Benito," said Captain Delano quickly, "do you see what is going on there? Look!"

But, seized by his cough, the Spaniard staggered, with both hands to his face, on the point of falling. Captain Delano would have supported him, but the servant was more alert, who, with one hand sustaining his master, with the other applied the cordial. Don Benito restored, the black withdrew his support, slipping aside a little, but dutifully remaining within call of a whisper. Such discretion was here evinced as quite wiped away, in the visitor's eyes, any blemish of impropriety which might have attached to the attendant, from the indecorous conferences before mentioned; showing, too, that if the servant were to blame, it might be more the master's fault than his own, since, when left to himself, he could conduct thus well.

His glance called away from the spectacle of disorder to the more pleasing one before him, Captain Delano could not avoid again congratulating his host upon possessing such a servant, who, though perhaps a little too forward now and then, must upon the whole be invaluable to one in the invalid's situation.

"Tell me, Don Benito," he added, with a smile—"I should like to have your man here, myself—what will you take for him? Would fifty doubloons[88] be any object?"

"Master wouldn't part with Babo for a thousand doubloons," murmured the black, overhearing the offer, and taking it in earnest, and, with the strange vanity of a faithful slave, appreciated by his master, scorning to hear so paltry a valuation put upon him by a stranger. But Don Benito, apparently hardly yet completely restored, and again interrupted by his cough, made but some broken reply.

Soon his physical distress became so great, affecting his mind, too, apparently, that, as if to screen the sad spectacle, the servant gently conducted his master below.

Left to himself, the American, to while away the time till his boat should arrive, would have pleasantly accosted some one of the few Spanish seamen he saw; but recalling something that Don Benito had said touching their ill conduct, he refrained; as a shipmaster indisposed to countenance cowardice or unfaithfulness in seamen.

While, with these thoughts, standing with eye directed forward towards that handful of sailors, suddenly he thought that one or two of them returned the glance and with a sort of meaning. He rubbed his eyes, and looked again; but again seemed to see the same thing. Under a new form, but more obscure than any previous one, the old suspicions recurred, but, in the absence of Don Benito, with less of panic than before. Despite the bad account given of the sailors, Captain Delano resolved forthwith to accost one of them. Descending the poop, he made his way through the blacks, his movement drawing a queer cry from the oakum-pickers, prompted by whom, the negroes, twitching each other aside, divided before him; but, as if curious to see what was the object of this deliberate visit to their Ghetto, closing in

[88]Spanish gold coins.

behind, in tolerable order, followed the white stranger up. His progress thus proclaimed as by mounted kings-at-arms,[89] and escorted as by a Caffre[90] guard of honor, Captain Delano, assuming a good-humored, off-handed air, continued to advance; now and then saying a blithe word to the negroes, and his eye curiously surveying the white faces, here and there sparsely mixed in the blacks, like stray white pawns venturously involved in the ranks of the chess-men opposed.

While thinking which of them to select for his purpose, he chanced to observe a sailor seated on the deck engaged in tarring the strap of a large block, a circle of blacks squatted round him inquisitively eyeing the process.

The mean employment of the man was in contrast with something superior in his figure. His hand, black with continually thrusting it into the tar-pot held for him by a negro, seemed not naturally allied to his face, a face which would have been a very fine one but for its haggardness. Whether this haggardness had aught to do with criminality, could not be determined; since, as intense heat and cold, though unlike, produce like sensations, so innocence and guilt, when, through casual association with mental pain, stamping any visible impress, use one seal—a hacked one.

Not again that this reflection occurred to Captain Delano at the time, charitable man as he was. Rather another idea. Because observing so singular a haggardness combined with a dark eye, averted as in trouble and shame, and then again recalling Don Benito's confessed ill opinion of his crew, insensibly he was operated upon by certain general notions which, while disconnecting pain and abashment from virtue, invariably link them with vice.

If, indeed, there be any wickedness on board the ship, thought Captain Delano, be sure that man there has fouled his hand in it, even as now he fouls it in the pitch. I don't like to accost him. I will speak to this other, this old Jack[91] here on the windlass.[92]

He advanced to an old Barcelona tar,[93] in ragged red breeches and dirty night-cap, cheeks trenched and bronzed, whiskers dense as thorn hedges. Seated between two sleepy-looking Africans, this mariner, like his younger shipmate, was employed upon some rigging—splicing a cable—the sleepy-looking blacks performing the inferior function of holding the outer parts of the ropes for him.

Upon Captain Delano's approach, the man at once hung his head below its previous level; the one necessary for business. It appeared as if he desired to be thought absorbed, with more than common fidelity, in his task. Being addressed, he glanced up, but with what seemed a furtive, diffident air, which sat strangely enough on his weather-beaten visage, much as if a grizzly bear, instead of growling and biting, should simper and cast sheep's eyes. He was asked several questions concerning the voyage—questions purposely referring to several particulars in Don Benito's narrative, not previously corroborated by those impulsive cries greeting the visitor on first coming on board. The questions were briefly answered, confirming all that remained to be confirmed of the story. The negroes about the windlass

[89]Heraldic officers. [90]Kaffir, a South African native.
[91]Sailor. [92]Drum, turned by a crank, upon which a line was wound, for hoisting.
[93]Sailor from Barcelona, Spain.

joined in with the old sailor; but, as they became talkative, he by degrees became mute, and at length quite glum, seemed morosely unwilling to answer more questions, and yet, all the while, this ursine[94] air was somehow mixed with his sheepish one.

Despairing of getting into unembarrassed talk with such a centaur,[95] Captain Delano, after glancing round for a more promising countenance, but seeing none, spoke pleasantly to the blacks to make way for him; and so, amid various grins and grimaces, returned to the poop, feeling a little strange at first, he could hardly tell why, but upon the whole with regained confidence in Benito Cereno.

How plainly, thought he, did that old whiskerando[96] yonder betray a consciousness of ill desert. No doubt, when he saw me coming, he dreaded lest I, apprised by his Captain of the crew's general misbehavior, came with sharp words for him, and so down with his head. And yet—and yet, now that I think of it, that very old fellow, if I err not, was one of those who seemed so earnestly eyeing me here awhile since. Ah, these currents spin one's head round almost as much as they do the ship. Ha, there now's a pleasant sort of sunny sight; quite sociable, too.

His attention had been drawn to a slumbering negress, partly disclosed through the lace-work of some rigging, lying, with youthful limbs carelessly disposed, under the lee of the bulwarks, like a doe in the shade of a woodland rock. Sprawling at her lapped breasts, was her wide-awake fawn, stark naked, its black little body half lifted from the deck, crosswise with its dam's; its hands, like two paws, clambering upon her; its mouth and nose ineffectually rooting to get at the mark; and meantime giving a vexatious half-grunt, blending with the composed snore of the negress.

The uncommon vigor of the child at length roused the mother. She started up, at a distance facing Captain Delano. But as if not at all concerned at the attitude in which she had been caught, delightedly she caught the child up, with maternal transports, covering it with kisses.

There's naked nature, now; pure tenderness and love, thought Captain Delano, well pleased.

This incident prompted him to remark the other negresses more particularly than before. He was gratified with their manners: like most uncivilized women, they seemed at once tender of heart and tough of constitution; equally ready to die for their infants or fight for them. Unsophisticated as leopardesses; loving as doves. Ah! thought Captain Delano, these, perhaps, are some of the very women whom Ledyard[97] saw in Africa, and gave such a noble account of.

These natural sights somehow insensibly deepened his confidence and ease. At last he looked to see how his boat was getting on; but it was still pretty remote. He turned to see if Don Benito had returned; but he had not.

To change the scene, as well as to please himself with a leisurely observation of the coming boat, stepping over into the mizzen-chains,[98] he clambered his way into the starboard quarter-gallery—one of those abandoned

[94]Bearish. [95]Wild animal of Greek myth, half-man, half-horse. [96]Heavily bearded man.
[97]John Ledyard (1751–1789), American traveler and author.
[98]Supports, built out from a ship's sides, for the rigging of the rear (mizzen) mast.

Venetian-looking water-balconies previously mentioned—retreats cut off from the deck. As his foot pressed the half-damp, half-dry sea-mosses matting the place, and a chance phantom cats-paw[99]—an islet of breeze, unheralded, unfollowed—as this ghostly cats-paw came fanning his cheek; as his glance fell upon the row of small, round dead-lights—all closed like coppered eyes of the coffined—and the state-cabin door, once connecting with the gallery, even as the dead-lights had once looked out upon it, but now calked fast like a sarcophagus lid; and to a purple-black tarred-over, panel, threshold, and post; and he bethought him of the time, when that state-cabin and this state-balcony had heard the voices of the Spanish king's officers, and the forms of the Lima viceroy's[100] daughters had perhaps leaned where he stood—as these and other images flitted through his mind, as the cats-paw through the calm, gradually he felt rising a dreamy inquietude, like that of one who alone on the prairie feels unrest from the repose of the noon.

He leaned against the carved balustrade, again looking off toward his boat; but found his eye falling upon the ribbon grass, trailing along the ship's waterline, straight as a border of green box; and parterres[101] of sea-weed, broad ovals and crescents, floating nigh and far, with what seemed long formal alleys between, crossing the terraces of swells, and sweeping round as if leading to the grottoes below. And overhanging all was the balustrade by his arm, which, partly stained with pitch and partly embossed with moss, seemed the charred ruin of some summer-house in a grand garden long running to waste.

Trying to break one charm, he was but becharmed anew. Though upon the wide sea, he seemed in some far inland country; prisoner in some deserted château, left to stare at empty grounds, and peer out at vague roads, where never wagon or wayfarer passed.

But these enchantments were a little disenchanted as his eye fell on the corroded main-chains.[102] Of an ancient style, massy and rusty in link, shackle and bolt, they seemed even more fit for the ship's present business than the one for which she had been built.

Presently he thought something moved nigh the chains. He rubbed his eyes, and looked hard. Groves of rigging were about the chains; and there, peering from behind a great stay,[103] like an Indian behind a hemlock, a Spanish sailor, a marlingspike[104] in his hand, was seen, who made what seemed an imperfect gesture towards the balcony, but immediately, as if alarmed by some advancing step along the deck within, vanished into the recesses of the hempen forest, like a poacher.

What meant this? Something the man had sought to communicate, unbeknown to any one, even to his captain. Did the secret involve aught unfavorable to his captain? Were those previous misgivings of Captain Delano's about to be verified? Or, in his haunted mood at the moment, had some random, unintentional motion of the man, while busy with the stay, as if repairing it, been mistaken for a significant beckoning?

[99]Light breeze that ruffles the water. [100]Spanish colonial governor.
[101]Flower beds, gardens. [102]Supports for the rigging of the middle (main) mast.
[103]Thick rope that supports (stays) a mast.
[104]Pointed iron tool used to separate strands in splicing rope.

Not unbewildered, again he gazed off for his boat. But it was temporarily hidden by a rocky spur of the isle. As with some eagerness he bent forward, watching for the first shooting view of its beak, the balustrade gave way before him like charcoal. Had he not clutched an outreaching rope he would have fallen into the sea. The crash, though feeble, and the fall, though hollow, of the rotten fragments, must have been overheard. He glanced up. With sober curiosity peering down upon him was one of the old oakum-pickers, slipped from his perch to an outside boom;[105] while below the old negro, and, invisible to him, reconnoitering from a port-hole like a fox from the mouth of its den, crouched the Spanish sailor again. From something suddenly suggested by the man's air, the mad idea now darted into Captain Delano's mind, that Don Benito's plea of indisposition, in withdrawing below, was but a pretense: that he was engaged there maturing his plot, of which the sailor, by some means gaining an inkling, had a mind to warn the stranger against; incited, it may be, by gratitude for a kind word on first boarding the ship. Was it from foreseeing some possible interference like this, that Don Benito had, beforehand, given such a bad character[106] of his sailors, while praising the negroes; though, indeed, the former seemed as docile as the latter the contrary? The whites, too, by nature, were the shrewder race. A man with some evil design, would he not be likely to speak well of that stupidity which was blind to his depravity, and malign that intelligence from which it might not be hidden? Not unlikely, perhaps. But if the whites had dark secrets concerning Don Benito, could then Don Benito be any way in complicity with the blacks? But they were too stupid. Besides, who ever heard of a white so far a renegade as to apostatize[107] from his very species almost, by leaguing in against it with negroes? These difficulties recalled former ones. Lost in their mazes, Captain Delano, who had now regained the deck, was uneasily advancing along it, when he observed a new face; an aged sailor seated cross-legged near the main hatchway. His skin was shrunk up with wrinkles like a pelican's empty pouch; his hair frosted; his countenance grave and composed. His hands were full of ropes, which he was working into a large knot. Some blacks were about him obligingly dipping the strands for him, here and there, as the exigencies of the operation demanded.

Captain Delano crossed over to him, and stood in silence surveying the knot; his mind, by a not uncongenial transition, passing from its own entanglements to those of the hemp. For intricacy, such a knot he had never seen in an American ship, nor indeed any other. The old man looked like an Egyptian priest, making Gordian[108] knots for the temple of Ammon.[109] The knot seemed a combination of double-bowline-knot, treble-crown-knot, back-handed-well-knot, knot-in-and-out-knot, and jamming-knot.

At last, puzzled to comprehend the meaning of such a knot, Captain Delano addressed the knotter:—

"What are you knotting there, my man?"

"The knot," was the brief reply, without looking up.

"So it seems; but what is it for?"

[105]Long spar. [106]Report. [107]To deny a pledge or renounce a religious oath.

[108]According to Greek legend, whoever could untie the intricate knot tied by King Gordius would rule Asia. Alexander the Great, unable to untie the knot, cut it with his sword and claimed that he had fulfilled the prophecy.

[109]Ancient Egyptian god.

"For some one else to undo," muttered back the old man, plying his fingers harder than ever, the knot being now nearly completed.

While Captain Delano stood watching him, suddenly the old man threw the knot towards him, saying in broken English—the first heard in the ship—something to this effect: "Undo it, cut it, quick." It was said lowly, but with such condensation of rapidity, that the long, slow words in Spanish, which had preceded and followed, almost operated as covers to the brief English between.

For a moment, knot in hand, and knot in head, Captain Delano stood mute; while, without further heeding him, the old man was now intent upon other ropes. Presently there was a slight stir behind Captain Delano. Turning, he saw the chained negro, Atufal, standing quietly there. The next moment the old sailor rose, muttering, and, followed by his subordinate negroes, removed to the forward part of the ship, where in the crowd he disappeared.

An elderly negro, in a clout[110] like an infant's, and with a pepper and salt head, and a kind of attorney air, now approached Captain Delano. In tolerable Spanish, and with a good-natured, knowing wink, he informed him that the old knotter was simple-witted, but harmless; often playing his odd tricks. The negro concluded by begging the knot, for of course the stranger would not care to be troubled with it. Unconsciously, it was handed to him. With a sort of congé,[111] the negro received it, and, turning his back, ferreted into it like a detective customhouse officer after smuggled laces. Soon, with some African word, equivalent to pshaw, he tossed the knot overboard.

All this is very queer now, thought Captain Delano, with a qualmish sort of emotion; but, as one feeling incipient sea-sickness, he strove, by ignoring the symptoms; to get rid of the malady. Once more he looked off for his boat. To his delight, it was now again in view, leaving the rocky spur astern.

The sensation here experienced, after at first relieving his uneasiness, with unforeseen efficacy soon began to remove it. The less distant sight of that well-known boat—showing it, not as before, half blended with the haze, but with outline defined, so that its individuality, like a man's, was manifest; that boat, Rover by name, which, though now in strange seas, had often pressed the beach of Captain Delano's home, and, brought to its threshold for repairs, had familiarly lain there, as a Newfoundland dog; the sight of that household boat evoked a thousand trustful associations, which, contrasted with previous suspicions, filled him not only with lightsome confidence, but somehow with half humorous self-reproaches at his former lack of it.

"What, I, Amasa Delano—Jack of the Beach, as they called me when a lad—I, Amasa; the same that, duck-satchel[112] in hand, used to paddle along the waterside to the school-house made from the old hulk—I, little Jack of the Beach, that used to go berrying with cousin Nat and the rest; I to be murdered here at the ends of the earth, on board a haunted pirate-ship by a horrible Spaniard? Too nonsensical to think of! Who would murder Amasa Delano? His conscience is clean. There is some one above. Fie, fie, Jack of the Beach! you are a child indeed; a child of the second childhood, old boy; you are beginning to dote and drule,[113] I'm afraid."

[110]Loin cloth. [111]Formal bow.
[112]Satchel made of duck (heavy cloth). [113]I.e., grow senile.

Light of heart and foot, he stepped aft, and there was met by Don Benito's servant, who, with a pleasing expression, responsive to his own present feelings, informed him that his master had recovered from the effects of his coughing fit, and had just ordered him to go present his compliments to his good guest, Don Amasa, and say that he (Don Benito) would soon have the happiness to rejoin him.

There now, do you mark that? again thought Captain Delano, walking the poop. What a donkey I was. This kind gentleman who here sends me his kind compliments, he, but ten minutes ago, dark-lantern in hand, was dodging round some old grind-stone in the hold, sharpening a hatchet for me, I thought. Well, well; these long calms have a morbid effect on the mind, I've often heard, though I never believed it before. Ha! glancing towards the boat; there's Rover; good dog; a white bone in her mouth.[114] A pretty big bone though, seems to me.—What? Yes, she has fallen afoul of the bubbling tide-rip there. It sets her the other way, too, for the time. Patience.

It was now about noon, though, from the grayness of everything, it seemed to be getting towards dusk.

The calm was confirmed. In the far distance, away from the influence of land, the leaden ocean seemed laid out and leaded up, its course finished, soul gone, defunct. But the current from landward, where the ship was, increased; silently sweeping her further and further towards the tranced waters beyond.

Still, from his knowledge of those latitudes, cherishing hopes of a breeze, and a fair and fresh one, at any moment, Captain Delano, despite present prospects, buoyantly counted upon bringing the San Dominick safely to anchor ere night. The distance swept over was nothing; since, with a good wind, ten minutes' sailing would retrace more than sixty minutes, drifting. Meantime, one moment turning to mark "Rover" fighting the tide-rip, and the next to See Don Benito approaching, he continued walking the poop.

Gradually he felt a vexation arising from the delay of his boat; this soon merged into uneasiness; and at last—his eye falling continually, as from a stagebox into the pit,[115] upon the strange crowd before and below him, and, by-and-by, recognizing there the face—now composed to indifference—of the Spanish sailor who had seemed to beckon from the main-chains—something of his old trepidations returned.

Ah, thought he—gravely enough—this is like the ague:[116] because it went off, it follows not that it won't come back.

Though ashamed of the relapse, he could not altogether subdue it; and so, exerting his good-nature to the utmost, insensibly he came to a compromise.

Yes, this is a strange craft; a strange history, too, and strange folks on board. But—nothing more.

By way of keeping his mind out of mischief till the boat should arrive, he tried to occupy it with turning over and over, in a purely speculative sort of way, some lesser peculiarities of the captain and crew. Among others, four curious points recurred:

First, the affair of the Spanish lad assailed with a knife by the slave boy; an act winked at by Don Benito. Second, the tyranny in Don Benito's treatment

[114]Said of a speeding vessel with white sea foam under the bow.
[115]I.e., as from the balcony to the orchestra pit. [116]Fever chills.

of Atufal, the black; as if a child should lead a bull of the Nile by the ring in his nose. Third, the trampling of the sailor by the two negroes; a piece of insolence passed over without so much as a reprimand. Fourth, the cringing submission to their master, of all the ship's underlings, mostly blacks; as if by the least inadvertence they feared to draw down his despotic displeasure.

Coupling these points, they seemed somewhat contradictory. But what then, thought Captain Delano, glancing towards his now nearing boat—what then? Why, Don Benito is a very capricious commander. But he is not the first of the sort I have seen; though it's true he rather exceeds any other. But as a nation—continued he in his reveries—these Spaniards are all an odd set; the very word Spaniard has a curious, conspirator, Guy-Fawkish[117] twang to it. And yet, I dare say, Spaniards in the main are as good folks as any in Duxbury, Massachusetts. Ah good! At last "Rover" has come.

As, with its welcome freight, the boat touches the side, the oakum-pickers, with venerable gestures, sought to restrain the blacks, who, at the sight of three gurried[118] water-casks in its bottom, and a pile of wilted pumpkins in its bow, hung over the bulwarks in disorderly raptures.

Don Benito, with his servant, now appeared; his coming, perhaps, hastened by hearing the noise. Of him Captain Delano sought permission to serve out the water, so that all might share alike, and none inure themselves by unfair excess. But sensible, and, on Don Benito's account, kind as this offer was, it was received with what seemed impatience; as if aware that he lacked energy as a commander, Don Benito, with the true jealousy of weakness, resented as an affront any interference. So, at least, Captain Delano inferred.

In another moment the casks were being hoisted in, when some of the eager negroes accidentally jostled Captain Delano, where he stood by the gangway; so that, unmindful of Don Benito, yielding to the impulse of the moment, with good-natured authority he bade the blacks stand back; to enforce his words making use of a half-mirthful, half-menacing gesture. Instantly the blacks paused, just where they were, each negro and negress suspended in his or her posture, exactly as the word had found them—for a few seconds continuing so—while, as between the responsive posts of a telegraph, an unknown syllable ran from man to man among the perched oakum-pickers. While the visitor's attention was fixed by this scene, suddenly the hatchet-polishers half rose, and a rapid cry came from Don Benito.

Thinking that at the signal of the Spaniard he was about to be massacred, Captain Delano would have sprung for his boat, but paused, as the oakum-pickers, dropping down into the crowd with earnest exclamations, forced every white and every negro back, at the same moment, with gestures friendly and familiar, almost jocose, bidding him, in substance, not be a fool. Simultaneously the hatchet-polishers resumed their seats, quietly as so many tailors, and at once, as if nothing had happened, the work of hoisting in the casks was resumed, whites and blacks singing at the tackle.

Captain Delano glanced towards Don Benito. As he saw his meagre form in the act of recovering itself from reclining in the servant's arms, into which the agitated invalid had fallen, he could not but marvel at the panic by which

[117]Guy Fawkes (1570–1606) was one of the conspirators in the Gunpowder Plot who tried to blow up the English House of Parliament in 1605.

[118]Fouled by fish guts.

himself had been surprised, on the darting supposition that such a commander, who, upon a legitimate occasion, so trivial, too, as it now appeared, could lose all self-command, was, with energetic iniquity, going to bring about his murder.

The casks being on deck, Captain Delano was handed a number of jars and cups by one of the steward's aids, who, in the name of his captain, entreated him to do as he had proposed—dole out the water. He complied, with republican impartiality as to this republican element, which always seeks one level, serving the oldest white no better than the youngest black; excepting, indeed, poor Don Benito, whose condition, if not rank, demanded an extra allowance. To him, in the first place, Captain Delano presented a fair pitcher of the fluid; but, thirsting as he was for it, the Spaniard quaffed not a drop until after several grave bows and salutes. A reciprocation of courtesies which the sight-loving Africans hailed with clapping of hands.

Two of the less wilted pumpkins being reserved for the cabin table, the residue were minced up on the spot for the general regalement. But the soft bread, sugar, and bottled cider, Captain Delano would have given the whites alone, and in chief Don Benito; but the latter objected; which disinterestedness not a little pleased the American; and so mouthfuls all around were given alike to whites and blacks; excepting one bottle of cider, which Babo insisted upon setting aside for his master.

Here it may be observed that as, on the first visit of the boat, the American had not permitted his men to board the ship, neither did he now; being unwilling to add to the confusion of the decks.

Not uninfluenced by the peculiar good-humor at present prevailing, and for the time oblivious of any but benevolent thoughts, Captain Delano, who, from recent indications, counted upon a breeze within an hour or two at furthest, dispatched the boat back to the sealer, with orders for all the hands that could be spared immediately to set about rafting casks to the watering-place and filling them. Likewise he bade word be carried to his chief officer, that if, against present expectation, the ship was not brought to anchor by sunset, he need be under no concern; for as there was to be a full moon that night, he (Captain Delano) would remain on board ready to play the pilot, come the wind soon or late.

As the two Captains stood together, observing the departing boat—the servant, as it happened, having just spied a spot on his master's velvet sleeve, and silently engaged rubbing it out—the American expressed his regrets that the San Dominick had no boats; none, at least, but the unseaworthy old hulk of the longboat, which, warped as a camel's skeleton in the desert, and almost as bleached, lay potwise inverted amidships, one side a little tipped, furnishing a subterraneous sort of den for family groups of the blacks, mostly women and small children; who, squatting on old mats below, or perched above in the dark dome, on the elevated seats, were descried, some distance within, like a social circle of bats, sheltering in some friendly cave; at intervals, ebon flights of naked boys and girls, three or four years old, darting in and out of the den's mouth.

"Had you three or four boats now, Don Benito," said Captain Delano, "I think that, by tugging at the oars, your negroes here might help along matters some. Did you sail from port without boats, Don Benito?"

"They were stove in the gales, Señor."

"That was bad. Many men, too, you lost then. Boats and men. Those must have been hard gales, Don Benito."

"Past all speech," cringed the Spaniard.

"Tell me, Don Benito," continued his companion with increased interest, "tell me, were these gales immediately off the pitch[119] of Cape Horn?"

"Cape Horn?—who spoke of Cape Horn?"

"Yourself did, when giving me an account of your voyage," answered Captain Delano, with almost equal astonishment at this eating of his own words, even as he ever seemed eating his own heart, on the part of the Spaniard. "You yourself, Don Benito, spoke of Cape Horn," he emphatically repeated.

The Spaniard turned, in a sort of stooping posture, pausing an instant, as one about to make a plunging exchange of elements, as from air to water.

At this moment a messenger-boy, a white, hurried by, in the regular performance of his function carrying the last expired half hour forward to the forecastle, from the cabin time-piece, to have it struck at the ship's large bell.[120]

"Master," said the servant, discontinuing his work on the coat sleeve, and addressing the rapt Spaniard with a sort of timid apprehensiveness, as one with a duty, the discharge of which, it was foreseen, would prove irksome to the very person who had imposed it, and for whose benefit it was intended, "master told me never mind where he was, or how engaged, always to remind him, to a minute, when shaving-time comes. Miguel has gone to strike the half-hour afternoon. It is *now* master. Will master go into the cuddy?"[121]

"Ah—yes," answered the Spaniard, starting, as from dreams into realities; then turning upon Captain Delano, he said that ere long he would resume the conversation.

"Then if master means to talk more to Don Amasa," said the servant, "why not let Don Amasa sit by master in the cuddy, and master can talk, and Don Amasa can listen, while Babo here lathers and strops."[122]

"Yes," said Captain Delano, not unpleased with this sociable plan, "yes, Don Benito, unless you had rather not, I will go with you."

"Be it so, Señor."

As the three passed aft, the American could not but think it another strange instance of his host's capriciousness, this being shaved with such uncommon punctuality in the middle of the day. But he deemed it more than likely that the servant's anxious fidelity had something to do with the matter; inasmuch as the timely interruption served to rally his master from the mood which had evidently been coming upon him.

The place called the cuddy was a light deck-cabin formed by the poop, a sort of attic to the large cabin below. Part of it had formerly been the quarters of the officers; but since their death all the partitionings had been thrown down, and the whole interior converted into one spacious and airy

[119]Tip.

[120]Until the early nineteenth century, time aboard ship was kept by a half-hour sand glass. It was the duty of a ship's boy to turn the glass each time it emptied and to signal for the ship's bell to be rung. When the sand glass was turned for the eighth time (at "the last expired half hour"), the ship's bell was struck eight times, marking the end of one four-hour watch and the beginning of the next.

[121]Small cabin.

[122]Sharpens the razor with a strap.

marine hall; for absence of fine furniture and picturesque disarray of odd appurtenances, somewhat answering to the wise, cluttered hall of some eccentric bachelor-squire in the country, who hangs his shooting-jacket and tobacco-pouch on deer antlers, and keeps his fishing-rod, tongs, and walking-stick in the same corner.

The similitude was heightened, if not originally suggested, by glimpses of the surrounding sea; since, in one aspect, the country and the ocean seem cousins-german.[123]

The floor of the cuddy was matted. Overhead, four or five old muskets were stuck into horizontal holes along the beams. On one side was a claw-footed old table lashed to the deck; a thumbed missal[124] on it, and over it a small, meagre crucifix attached to the bulk-head.[125] Under the table lay a dented cutlass or two, with a hacked harpoon, among some melancholy old rigging, like a heap of poor friars' girdles.[126] There were also two long, sharp-ribbed settees of Malacca cane, black with age, and uncomfortable to look at as inquisitors' racks, with a large, misshapen armchair, which, furnished with a rude barber's crotch[127] at the back, working with a screw, seemed some grotesque engine of torment. A flag locker was in one corner, open, exposing various colored bunting, some rolled up, others half unrolled, still others tumbled. Opposite was a cumbrous washstand, of black mahogany, all of one block, with a pedestal, like a font, and over it a railed shelf, containing combs, brushes and other implements of the toilet. A torn hammock of stained grass swung near; the sheets tossed, and the pillow wrinkled up like a brow, as if whoever slept here slept but illy, with alternate visitations of sad thoughts and bad dreams.

The further extremity of the cuddy, overhanging the ship's stern, was pierced with three openings, windows or port-holes, according as men or cannon might peer, socially or unsocially, out of them. At present neither men nor cannon were seen, though huge ring-bolts and other rusty iron fixtures of the woodwork hinted of twenty-four pounders.[128]

Glancing towards the hammock as he entered, Captain Delano said, "You sleep here, Don Benito?"

"Yes, Señor, since we got into mild weather."

"This seems a sort of dormitory, sitting-room, sail-lot, chapel, armory, and private closet all together, Don Benito," added Captain Delano, looking round.

"Yes, Señor; events have not been favorable to much order in my arrangements."

Here the servant, napkin on arm, made a motion as if waiting his master's good pleasure. Don Benito signified his readiness, when, seating him in the Malacca arm-chair, and for the guest's convenience drawing opposite one of the settees, the servant commenced operations by throwing back his master's collar and loosening his cravat.

There is something in the negro which, in a peculiar way, fits him for avocations about one's person. Most negroes are natural valets and hair-dressers;

[123]First cousins, close relatives. [124]Prayer book. [125]Partition wall.
[126]Rope belts. [127]The headrest on a barber's chair.
[128]Heavy cannon that fire a ball weighing twenty-four pounds.

taking to the comb and brush congenially as to the castinets, and flourishing them apparently with almost equal satisfaction. There is, too, a smooth tact about them in this employment, with a marvelous, noiseless, gliding briskness, not ungraceful in its way, singularly pleasing to behold, and still more so to be the manipulated subject of. And above all is the great gift of good-humor. Not the mere grin or laugh is here meant. Those were unsuitable. But a certain easy cheerfulness, harmonious in every glance and gesture; as though God had set the whole negro to some pleasant tune.

When to this is added the docility arising from the unaspiring contentment of a limited mind, and that susceptibility of bland attachment sometimes inhering in indisputable inferiors, one readily perceives why those hypochondriacs, Johnson and Byron—it may be, something like the hypochondriac Benito Cereno—took to their hearts, almost to the exclusion of the entire white race, their serving men, the negroes, Barber and Fletcher.[129] But if there be that in the negro which exempts him from the inflicted sourness of the morbid or cynical mind, how, in his most prepossessing aspects, must he appear to a benevolent one? When at ease with respect to exterior things, Captain Delano's nature was not only benign, but familiarly and humorously so. At home, he had often taken rare satisfaction in sitting in his door, watching some free man of color at his work or play. If on a voyage he chanced to have a black sailor, invariably he was on chatty and half-gamesome terms with him. In fact, like most men of a good, blithe heart, Captain Delano took to negroes, not philanthropically, but genially, just as other men to Newfoundland dogs.

Hitherto, the circumstances in which he found the San Dominick had repressed the tendency. But in the cuddy, relieved from his former uneasiness, and, for various reasons, more sociably inclined than at any previous period of the day, and seeing the colored servant, napkin on arm, so debonair about his master, in a business so familiar as that of shaving, too, all his old weakness for negroes returned.

Among other things, he was amused with an odd instance of the African love of bright colors and fine shows, in the black's informally taking from the flaglocker a great piece of bunting of all hues, and lavishly tucking it under his master's chin for an apron.

The mode of shaving among the Spaniards is a little different from what it is with other nations. They have a basin, specifically called a barber's basin, which on one side is scooped out, so as accurately to receive the chin, against which it is closely held in lathering; which is done, not with a brush, but with soap dipped in the water of the basin and rubbed on the face.

In the present instance salt-water was used for lack of better; and the parts lathered were only the upper lip, and low down under the throat, all the rest being cultivated beard.

The preliminaries being somewhat novel to Captain Delano, he sat curiously eying them, so that no conversation took place, nor, for the present, did Don Benito appear disposed to renew any.

[129]Francis Barber was the black servant of Samuel Johnson (1709–1784). William Fletcher, whom Melville mistakenly describes as a black, was the white English valet to George Gordon, Lord Byron (1788–1824).

Setting down his basin, the negro searched among the razors, as for the sharpest, and having found it, gave it an additional edge by expertly strapping it on the firm, smooth, oily skin of his open palm; he then made a gesture as if to begin, but midway stood suspended for an instant, one hand elevating the razor, the other professionally dabbling among the bubbling suds on the Spaniard's lank neck. Not unaffected by the close sight of the gleaming steel, Don Benito nervously shuddered; his usual ghastliness was heightened by the lather, which lather, again, was intensified in its hue by the contrasting sootiness of the negro's body. Altogether the scene was somewhat peculiar, at least to Captain Delano, nor, as he saw the two thus postured, could he resist the vagary, that in the black he saw a headsman,[130] and in the white a man at the block.[131] But this was one of those antic conceits, appearing and vanishing in a breath, from which, perhaps, the best regulated mind is not always free.

Meantime the agitation of the Spaniard had a little loosened the bunting from around him, so that one broad fold swept curtain-like over the chair-arm to the floor, revealing, amid a profusion of armorial bars and ground-colors—black, blue, and yellow—a closed castle in a blood-red field diagonal with a lion rampant in a white.

"The castle and the lion," exclaimed Captain Delano—"why, Don Benito, this is the flag of Spain you use here. It's well it's only I, and not the King, that sees this," he added, with a smile, "but"—turning towards the black—"it's all one, I suppose, so the colors be gay"; which playful remark did not fail somewhat to tickle the negro.

"Now, master," he said, readjusting the flag, and pressing the head gently further back into the crotch of the chair; "now, master," and the steel glanced nigh the throat.

Again Don Benito faintly shuddered.

"You must not shake so, master. See, Don Amasa, master always shakes when I shave him. And yet master knows I never yet have drawn blood, though it's true, if master will shake so, I may some of these times. Now master," he continued. "And now, Don Amasa, please go on with your talk about the gale, and all that; master can hear, and, between times, master can answer."

"Ah yes, these gales," said Captain Delano; "but the more I think of your voyage, Don Benito, the more I wonder, not at the gales, terrible as they must have been, but at the disastrous interval following them. For here, by your account, have you been these two months and more getting from Cape Horn[132] to St. Maria, a distance which I myself, with a good wind, have sailed in a few days. True, you had calms, and long ones, but to be becalmed for two months, that is, at least, unusual. Why, Don Benito, had almost any other gentleman told me such a story, I should have been half disposed to a little incredulity."

Here an involuntary expression came over the Spaniard, similar to that just before on the deck, and whether it was the start he gave, or a sudden gawky roll of the hull in the calm, or a momentary unsteadiness of the servant's hand, however it was, just then the razor drew blood, spots of which stained the creamy lather under the throat: immediately the black barber drew back his

[130]Executioner. [131]Chopping block. [132]At the southern tip of South America.

steel, and, remaining in his professional attitude, back to Captain Delano, and face to Don Benito, held up the trickling razor, saying, with a sort of half humorous sorrow, "See, master—you shook so—here's Babo's first blood."

No sword drawn before James the First of England,[133] no assassination in that timid King's presence, could have produced a more terrified aspect than was now presented by Don Benito.

Poor fellow, thought Captain Delano, so nervous he can't even bear the sight of barber's blood; and thus unstrung, sick man, is it credible that I should have imagined he meant to spill all my blood, who can't endure the sight of one little drop of his own? Surely, Amasa Delano, you have been beside yourself this day. Tell it not when you get home, sappy Amasa. Well, well, he looks like a murderer, doesn't he? More like as if himself were to be done for. Well, well, this day's experience shall be a good lesson.

Meantime, while these things were running through the honest seaman's mind, the servant had taken the napkin from his arm, and to Don Benito had said—"But answer Don Amasa, please, master, while I wipe this ugly stuff off the razor, and strop it again."

As he said the words, his face was turned half round, so as to be alike visible to the Spaniard and the American, and seemed, by its expression, to hint, that he was desirous, by getting his master to go on with the conversation, considerately to withdraw his attention from the recent annoying accident. As if glad to snatch the offered relief, Don Benito resumed, rehearsing to Captain Delano, that not only were the calms of unusual duration, but the ship had fallen in with obstinate currents; and other things he added, some of which were but repetitions of former statements, to explain how it came to pass that the passage from Cape Horn to St. Maria had been so exceedingly long; now and then mingling with his words, incidental praises, less qualified than before, to the blacks, for their general good conduct. These particulars were not given consecutively, the servant, at convenient times, using his razor, and so, between the intervals of shaving, the story and panegyric[134] went on with more than usual huskiness.

To Captain Delano's imagination, now again not wholly at rest, there was something so hollow in the Spaniard's manner, with apparently some reciprocal hollowness in the servant's dusky comment of silence, that the idea flashed across him, that possibly master and man, for some unknown purpose, were acting out, both in word and deed, nay, to the very tremor of Don Benito's limbs, some juggling play before him. Neither did the suspicion of collusion lack apparent support, from the fact of those whispered conferences before mentioned. But then, what could be the object of enacting this play of the barber before him? At last, regarding the notion as a whimsy, insensibly suggested, perhaps, by the theatrical aspect of Don Benito in his harlequin ensign,[135] Captain Delano speedily banished it.

The shaving over, the servant bestirred himself with a small bottle of scented waters, pouring a few drops on the head, and then diligently rubbing; the vehemence of the exercise causing the muscles of his face to twitch rather strangely.

[133]James (1566–1625), King of England (1603–1625), who feared assassination at the hands of Roman Catholic terrorists such as Guy Fawkes.

[134]Elaborate praise. [135]Many-colored flag.

His next operation was with comb, scissors, and brush; going round and round, smoothing a curl here, clipping an unruly whisker-hair there, giving a graceful sweep to the temple-lock, with other impromptu touches evincing the hand of a master; while, like any resigned gentleman in barber's hands, Don Benito bore all, much less uneasily, at least, than he had done the razoring; indeed, he sat so pale and rigid now, that the negro seemed a Nubian[136] sculptor finishing off a white statue-head.

All being over at last, the standard of Spain removed, tumbled up, and tossed back into the flag-locker, the negro's warm breath blowing away any stray which might have lodged down his master's neck; collar and cravat readjusted; a speck of lint whisked off the velvet lapel; all this being done; backing off a little space and pausing with an expression of subdued self-complacency, the servant for a moment surveyed his master, as, in toilet at least, the creature of his own tasteful hands.

Captain Delano playfully complimented him upon his achievement; at the same time congratulating Don Benito.

But neither sweet waters, nor shampooing, nor fidelity, nor sociality, delighted the Spaniard. Seeing him relapsing into forbidding gloom, and still remaining seated, Captain Delano, thinking that his presence was undesired just then, withdrew, on pretense of seeing whether, as he had prophesied, any signs of a breeze were visible.

Walking forward to the main-mast, he stood awhile thinking over the scene, and not without some undefined misgivings, when he heard a noise near the cuddy, and turning, saw the negro, his hand to his cheek. Advancing, Captain Delano perceived that the cheek was bleeding. He was about to ask the cause, when the negro's wailing soliloquy enlightened him.

"Ah, when will master get better from his sickness; only the sour heart that sour sickness breeds made him serve Babo so; cutting Babo with the razor, because, only by accident, Babo had given master one little scratch; and for the first time in so many a day, too. Ah, ah, ah," holding his hand to his face.

Is it possible, thought Captain Delano; was it to wreak in private his Spanish spite against this poor friend of his, that Don Benito, by his sullen manner, impelled me to withdraw? Ah, this slavery breeds ugly passions in man.—Poor fellow!

He was about to speak in sympathy to the negro, but with a timid reluctance he now re-entered the cuddy.

Presently master and man came forth; Don Benito leaning on his servant as if nothing had happened.

But a sort of love-quarrel, after all, thought Captain Delano.

He accosted Don Benito, and they slowly walked together. They had gone but a few paces, when the steward—a tall, rajah-looking mullato,[137] orientally set off with a pagoda turban formed by three or four Madras[138] handkerchiefs wound about his head, tier on tier—approaching with a salaam,[139] announced lunch in the cabin.

[136]Native of Nubia in East Africa.
[137]I.e., a person of mixed white and black ancestry who resembled a prince from India.
[138]Cotton cloth of a type originally produced in Madras, India.
[139]Muslim ceremonial greeting, meaning "peace."

On their way thither, the two captains were preceded by the mulatto, who, turning round as he advanced, with continual smiles and bows, ushered them on, a display of elegance which quite completed the insignificance of the small bare-headed Babo, who, as if not unconscious of inferiority, eyed askance the graceful steward. But in part, Captain Delano imputed his jealous watchfulness to that peculiar feeling which the full-blooded African entertains for the adulterated one. As for the steward, his manner, if not bespeaking much dignity or self-respect, yet evidences his extreme desire to please; which is doubly meritorious, as at once Christian and Chesterfieldian.[140]

Captain Delano observed with interest that while the complexion of the mulatto was hybrid, his physiognomy was European—classically so.

"Don Benito," whispered he, "I am glad to see this usher-of-the-golden-rod[141] of yours; the sight refutes an ugly remark once made to me by a Barbadoes[142] planter; that when a mulatto has a regular European face, look out for him; he is a devil. But see, your steward here has features more regular than King George's of England; and yet there he nods, and bows, and smiles; a king, indeed—the king of kind hearts and polite fellows. What a pleasant voice he has, too."

"He has, Señor."

"But tell me, has he not, so far as you have known him, always proved a good, worthy fellow?" said Captain Delano, pausing, while with a final genuflexion the steward disappeared into the cabin; "come, for the reason just mentioned, I am curious to know."

"Francesco is a good man," a sort of[143] sluggishly responded Don Benito, like a phlegmatic[144] appreciator, who would neither find fault nor flatter.

"Ah, I thought so. For it were strange, indeed, and not very creditable to us white-skins, if a little of our blood mixed with the African's, far from improving the latter's quality, have the sad effect of pouring vitriolic acid into black broth; improving the hue, perhaps, but not the wholesomeness."

"Doubtless, doubtless, Señor, but"—glancing at Babo—"not to speak of negroes, your planter's remark I have heard applied to the Spanish and Indian intermixtures in our provinces. But I know nothing about the matter," he listlessly added.

And here they entered the cabin.

The lunch was a frugal one. Some of Captain Delano's fresh fish and pumpkins, biscuit and salt beef, the reserved bottle of cider, and the San Dominick's last bottle of Canary.[145]

As they entered, Francesco, with two or three colored aids, was hovering over the table giving the last adjustments. Upon perceiving their master they withdrew, Francesco making a smiling congé, and the Spaniard, without

[140]Graceful and urbane. The cosmopolitan Philip Dormer Stanhope, Lord Chesterfield (1694–1773), gave his name to an overcoat, a couch, and a tradition of courtly good manners.

[141]The Usher of the Black Rod is one of the court officers of the English royal household. Melville uses "golden-rod" to pun upon the servant's European features.

[142]West Indian island.

[143]Melville's editors suggest "rather" for "a sort of" (a possible misprint).

[144]Of sluggish temperament, unemotional.

[145]Wine from the Canary Islands.

condescending to notice it, fastidiously remarking to his companion that he relished not superfluous attendance.

Without companions, host and guest sat down, like a childless married couple, at opposite ends of the table, Don Benito waving Captain Delano to his place, and, weak as he was, insisting upon that gentleman being seated before himself.

The negro placed a rug under Don Benito's feet, and cushion behind his back, and then stood behind, not his master's chair, but Captain Delano's. At first, this a little surprised the latter. But it was soon evident that, in taking his position, the black was still true to his master; since by facing him he could the more readily anticipate his slightest want.

"This is an uncommonly intelligent fellow of yours, Don Benito," whispered Captain Delano across the table.

"You say true, Señor."

During the repast, the guest again reverted to parts of Don Benito's story, begging further particulars here and there. He inquired how it was that the scurvy and fever should have committed such wholesale havoc upon the whites, while destroying less than half of the blacks. As if this question reproduced the whole scene of plague before the Spaniard's eyes, miserably reminding him of his solitude in a cabin where before he had had so many friends and officers round him, his hand shook, his face became hueless, broken words escaped; but directly the sane memory of the past seemed replaced by insane terrors of the present. With starting[146] eyes he stared before him at vacancy. For nothing was to be seen but the hand of his servant pushing the Canary over towards him. At length a few sips served partially to restore him. He made random reference to the different constitution of races, enabling one to offer more resistance to certain maladies than another. The thought was new to his companion.

Presently Captain Delano, intending to say something to his host concerning the pecuniary part of the business he had undertaken for him, especially—since he was strictly accountable to his owners—with reference to the new suit of sails, and other things of that sort; and naturally preferring to conduct such affairs in private, was desirous that the servant should withdraw; imagining that Don Benito for a few minutes could dispense with his attendance. He, however, waited awhile; thinking that, as the conversation proceeded, Don Benito, without being prompted, would perceive the propriety of the step.

But it was otherwise. At last catching his host's eye, Captain Delano, with a slight backward gesture of his thumb, whispered, "Don Benito, pardon me, but there is an interference with the full expression of what I have to say to you."

Upon this the Spaniard changed countenance; which was imputed to his resenting the hint, as in some way a reflection upon his servant. After a moment's pause, he assured his guest that the black's remaining with them could be of no disservice; because since losing his officers he had made Babo (whose original office, it now appeared, had been captain of the slaves) not only his constant attendant and companion, but in all things his confidant.

[146]Alarmed.

After this, nothing more could be said; though, indeed, Captain Delano could hardly avoid some little tinge of irritation upon being left ungratified in so inconsiderable a wish, by one, too, for whom he intended such solid services. But it is only his querulousness, thought he; and so filling his glass he proceeded to business.

The price of the sails and other matters was fixed upon. But while this was being done, the American observed that, though his original offer of assistance had been hailed with hectic animation, yet now when it was reduced to a business transaction, indifference and apathy were betrayed. Don Benito, in fact, appeared to submit to hearing the details more out of regard to common propriety, than from any impression that weighty benefit to himself and his voyage was involved.

Soon, his manner became still more reserved. The effort was vain to seek to draw him into social talk. Gnawed by his splenetic[147] mood, he sat twitching his beard, while to little purpose the hand of his servant, mute as that on the wall, slowly pushed over the Canary.

Lunch being over, they sat down on the cushioned transom;[148] the servant placing a pillow behind his master. The long continuance of the calm had now affected the atmosphere. Don Benito sighed heavily, as if for breath.

"Why not adjourn to the cuddy," said Captain Delano; "there is more air there." But the host sat silent and motionless.

Meantime his servant knelt before him, with a large fan of feathers. And Francesco coming in on tiptoes, handing the negro a little cup of aromatic waters, with which at intervals he chafed his master's brow; smoothing the hair along the temples as a nurse does a child's. He spoke no word. He only rested his eye on his master's, as if, amid all Don Benito's distress, a little to refresh his spirit by the silent sight of fidelity.

Presently the ship's bell sounded two-o'clock; and through the cabin windows a slight rippling of the sea was discerned; and from the desired direction.

"There," exclaimed Captain Delano, "I told you so, Don Benito, look!"

He had risen to his feet, speaking in a very animated tone, with a view the more to rouse his companion. But though the crimson curtain of the stern-window near him that moment fluttered against his pale cheek, Don Benito seemed to have even less welcome for the breeze than the calm.

Poor fellow, thought Captain Delano, bitter experience has taught him that one ripple does not make a wind, any more than one swallow a summer. But he is mistaken for once. I will get his ship in for him, and prove it.

Briefly alluding to his weak condition, he urged his host to remain quietly where he was, since he (Captain Delano) would with pleasure take upon himself the responsibility of making the best use of the wind.

Upon gaining the deck, Captain Delano started at the unexpected figure of Atufal, monumentally fixed at the threshold, like one of those sculptured porters of black marble guarding the porches of Egyptian tombs.

But this time the start was, perhaps, purely physical. Atufal's presence, singularly attesting docility even in sullenness, was contrasted with that of the hatchet-polishers, who in patience evinced their industry; while both

[147]Irritable. [148]Large crossbeam at the stern of a ship.

spectacles showed, that lax as Don Benito's general authority might be, still, whenever he chose to exert it, no man so savage or colossal but must, more or less, bow.

Snatching a trumpet which hung from the bulwarks, with a free step Captain Delano advanced to the forward edge of the poop, issuing his orders in his best Spanish. The few sailors and many negroes, all equally pleased, obediently set about heading the ship towards the harbor.

While giving some directions about setting a lower stu'n'-sail,[149] suddenly Captain Delano heard a voice faithfully repeating his orders. Turning, he saw Babo, now for the time acting, under the pilot, his original part of captain of the slaves. This assistance proved valuable. Tattered sails and warped yards were soon brought into some trim. And no brace or halyard was pulled but to the blithe songs of the inspirited negroes.

Good fellows, thought Captain Delano, a little training would make fine sailors of them. Why see, the very women pull and sing too. These must be some of those Ashantee negresses that make such capital soldiers, I've heard. But who's at the helm? I must have a good hand there.

He went to see.

The San Dominick steered with a cumbrous tiller, with large horizontal pullies attached. At each pulley-end stood a subordinate black, and between them, at the tiller-head, the responsible post, a Spanish seaman, whose countenance evinced his due share in the general hopefulness and confidence at the coming of the breeze.

He proved the same man who had behaved with so shame-faced an air on the windlass.

"Ah,—it is you, my man," exclaimed Captain Delano—"well, no more sheep's-eyes now;—look straight forward and keep the ship so. Good hand, I trust? And want to get into the harbor, don't you?"

The man assented with an inward chuckle, grasping the tiller-head firmly. Upon this, unperceived by the American, the two blacks eyed the sailor intently.

Finding all right at the helm, the pilot went forward to the forecastle,[150] to see how matters stood there.

The ship now had way enough to breast the current. With the approach of evening, the breeze would be sure to freshen.

Having done all that was needed for the present, Captain Delano, giving his last orders to the sailors, turned aft to report affairs to Don Benito in the cabin; perhaps additionally incited to rejoin him by the hope of snatching a moment's private chat while the servant was engaged upon deck.

From opposite sides, there were, beneath the poop, two approaches to the cabin; one further forward than the other, and consequently communicating with a longer passage. Marking the servant still above, Captain Delano, taking the nighest entrance—the one last named, and at whose porch Atufal still stood—hurried on his way, till, arrived at the cabin threshold, he paused an instant, a little to recover from his eagerness. Then, with the words of his intended business upon his lips, he entered. As he advanced toward the

[149]Small, auxiliary sail used in fine weather.
[150]The forward part of the ship, where the crew is quartered.

seated Spaniard, he heard another footstep, keeping time with his. From the opposite door, a salver in hand, the servant was likewise advancing.

"Confound the faithful fellow," thought Captain Delano; "what a vexatious coincidence."

Possibly, the vexation might have been something different, were it not for the brisk confidence inspired by the breeze. But even as it was, he felt a slight twinge, from a sudden indefinite association in his mind of Babo with Atufal.

"Don Benito," said he, "I give you joy; the breeze will hold, and will increase. By the way, your tall man and time-piece, Atufal, stands without. By your order, of course?"

Don Benito recoiled, as if at some bland satirical touch, delivered with such adroit garnish of apparent good breeding as to present no handle for retort.

He is like one flayed alive, thought Captain Delano; where may one touch him without causing a shrink?

The servant moved before his master, adjusting a cushion; recalled to civility, the Spaniard stiffly replied: "You are right. The slave appears where you saw him, according to my command; which is, that if at the given hour I am below, he must take his stand and abide my coming."

"Ah, now, pardon me, but that is treating the poor fellow like an ex-king indeed. Ah, Don Benito," smiling, "for all the license you permit in some things, I fear lest, at bottom, you are a bitter hard master."

Again Don Benito shrank; and this time, as the good sailor thought, from a genuine twinge of his conscience.

Again conversation became constrained. In vain Captain Delano called attention to the now perceptible motion of the keel gently cleaving the sea; with lack-lustre eye, Don Benito returned words few and reserved.

By-and-by, the wind having steadily risen, and still blowing right into the harbor, bore the San Dominick swiftly on. Rounding a point of land, the sealer at distance came into open view.

Meantime Captain Delano had again repaired to the deck, remaining there some time. Having at last altered the ship's course, so as to give the reef a wide berth, he returned for a few moments below.

I will cheer up my poor friend, this time, thought he.

"Better and better, Don Benito," he cried as he blithely reentered: "there will soon be an end to your cares, at least for awhile. For when, after a long, sad voyage, you know, the anchor drops into the haven, all its vast weight seems lifted from the captain's heart. We are getting on famously, Don Benito. My ship is in sight. Look through this side-light here; there she is; all a-taunt-o![151] The Bachelor's Delight, my good friend. Ah, how this wind braces one up. Come, you must take a cup of coffee with me this evening. My old steward will give you as fine a cup as ever any sultan tasted. What say you, Don Benito, will you?"

At first, the Spaniard glanced feverishly up, casting a longing look towards the sealer, while with mute concern his servant gazed into his face. Suddenly the old ague of coldness returned, and dropping back to his cushions he was silent.

[151]Full-rigged.

"You do not answer. Come, all day you have been my host; would you have hospitality all on one side?"

"I cannot go," was the response.

"What? it will not fatigue you. The ships will lie together as near as they can, without swinging foul. It will be little more than stepping from deck to deck; which is but from room to room. Come, come, you must not refuse me."

"I cannot go," decisively and repulsively repeated Benito.

Renouncing all but the last appearance of courtesy, with a sort of cadaverous sullenness, and biting his thin nails to the quick, he glanced, almost glared, at his guest, as if impatient that a stranger's presence should interfere with the full indulgence of his morbid hour. Meantime the sound of the parted waters came more and more gurglingly and merrily in at the windows; as reproaching him for his dark spleen; as telling him that, sulk as he might, and go mad with it, nature cared not a jot; since, whose fault was it, pray?

But the foul mood was now at its depth, as the fair wind at its height.

There was something in the man so far beyond any mere unsociality or sourness previously evinced, that even the forebearing good-nature of his guest could no longer endure it. Wholly at a loss to account for such demeanor, and deeming sickness with eccentricity, however extreme, no adequate excuse, well satisfied, too, that nothing in his own conduct could justify it, Captain Delano's pride began to be roused. Himself became reserved. But all seemed one to the Spaniard. Quitting him, therefore, Captain Delano once more went to the deck.

The ship was now within less than two miles of the sealer. The whale-boat was seen darting over the interval.

To be brief, the two vessels, thanks to the pilot's skill, ere long in the neighborly style lay anchored together.

Before returning to his own vessel, Captain Delano had intended communicating to Don Benito the smaller details of the proposed services to be rendered. But, as it was, unwilling anew to subject himself to rebuffs, he resolved, now that he had seen the San Dominick safely moored, immediately to quit her, without further allusion to hospitality or business. Indefinitely postponing his ulterior plans, he would regulate his future actions according to future circumstances. His boat was ready to receive him; but his host still tarried below. Well, thought Captain Delano, if he has little breeding, the more need to show mine. He descended to the cabin to bid a ceremonious, and, it may be, tacitly rebukeful adieu. But to his great satisfaction, Don Benito, as if he had begun to feel the weight of that treatment with which his slighted guest had, not indecorously, retaliated upon him, now supported by his servant, rose to his feet, and grasping Captain Delano's hand, stood tremulous; too much agitated to speak. But the good augury hence drawn was suddenly dashed, by his resuming all his previous reserve, with augmented gloom, as, with half-averted eyes, he silently reseated himself on his cushions. With a corresponding return of his own chilled feelings, Captain Delano bowed and withdrew.

He was hardly midway in the narrow corridor, dim as a tunnel, leading from the cabin to the stairs, when a sound, as of the tolling for execution in some jailyard, fell on his ears. It was the echo of the ship's flawed bell, striking the hour, drearily reverberated in this subterranean vault. Instantly, by a fatality not to be withstood, his mind, responsive to the portent, swarmed with superstitious suspicions. He paused. In images far swifter than these sentences, the minutest details of all his former distrusts swept through him.

Hitherto, credulous good-nature had been too ready to furnish excuses for reasonable fears. Why was the Spaniard, so superfluously punctilious at times, now heedless of common propriety in not accompanying to the side his departing guest? Did indisposition forbid? Indisposition had not forbidden more irksome exertion that day. His last equivocal demeanor recurred. He had risen to his feet, grasped his guest's hand, motioned toward his hat; then, in an instant, all was eclipsed in sinister muteness and gloom. Did this imply one brief, repentant relenting at the final moment, from some iniquitous plot, followed by remorseless return to it? His last glance seemed to express a calamitous, yet acquiescent farewell to Captain Delano forever. Why decline the invitation to visit the sealer that evening? Or was the Spaniard less hardened than the Jew, who refrained not from supping at the board of him whom the same night he meant to betray?[152] What imported all those day-long enigmas and contradictions, except they were intended to mystify, preliminary to some stealthy blow? Atufal, the pretended rebel, but punctual shadow, that moment lurked by the threshold without. He seemed a sentry, and more. Who, by his own confession, had stationed him there? Was the negro now lying in wait?

The Spaniard behind—his creature before: to rush from darkness to light was the involuntary choice.

The next moment, with clenched jaw and hand, he passed Atufal, and stood unharmed in the light. As he saw his trim ship lying peacefully at anchor, and almost within ordinary call; as he saw his household boat, with familiar faces in it, patiently rising and falling on the short waves by the San Dominick's side; and then, glancing about the decks where he stood, saw the oakum-pickers still gravely plying their fingers; and heard the low, buzzing whistle and industrious hum of the hatchet-polishers, still bestirring themselves over their endless occupation; and more than all, as he saw the benign aspect of nature, taking her innocent repose in the evening; the screened sun in the quiet camp of the west shining out like the mild light from Abraham's[153] tent; as charmed eye and ear took in all these, with the chained figure of the black, clenched jaw and hand relaxed. Once again he smiled at the phantoms which had mocked him, and felt something like a tinge of remorse, that, by harboring them even for a moment, he should, by implication, have betrayed an atheist doubt of the everwatchful Providence above.

There was a few minutes' delay, while, in obedience to his orders, the boat was being hooked along to the gangway. During this interval, a sort of saddened satisfaction stole over Captain Delano, at thinking of the kindly offices he had that day discharged for a stranger. Ah, thought he, after good actions one's conscience is never ungrateful, however much so the benefited party may be.

Presently, his foot, in the first act of descent into the boat, pressed the first round of the side-ladder, his face presented inward upon the deck. In the

[152]Judas Iscariot feasted with Jesus before betraying Him. Matthew 26.
[153]Old Testament patriarch. See Genesis 18.

same moment, he heard his name courteously sounded; and, to his pleased surprise, saw Don Benito advancing—an unwonted energy in his air, as if, at the last moment, intent upon making amends for his recent discourtesy. With instinctive good feeling, Captain Delano, withdrawing his foot, turned and reciprocally advanced. As he did so, the Spaniard's nervous eagerness increased, but his vital energy failed; so that, the better to support him, the servant, placing his master's hand on his naked shoulder, and gently holding it there, formed himself into a sort of crutch.

When the two captains met, the Spaniard again fervently took the hand of the American, at the same time casting an earnest glance into his eyes, but, as before, too much overcome to speak.

I have done him wrong, self-reproachfully thought Captain Delano; his apparent coldness has deceived me; in no instance has he meant to offend.

Meantime, as if fearful that the continuance of the scene might too much unstring his master, the servant seemed anxious to terminate it. And so, still presenting himself as a crutch, and walking between the two captains, he advanced with them towards the gangway; while still, as if full of kindly contrition, Don Benito would not let go the hand of Captain Delano, but retained it in his, across the black's body.

Soon they were standing by the side, looking over into the boat, whose crew turned up their curious eyes. Waiting a moment for the Spaniard to relinquish his hold, the now embarrassed Captain Delano lifted his foot, to overstep the threshold of the open gangway; but still Don Benito would not let go his hand. And yet, with an agitated tone, he said, "I can go no further; here I must bid you adieu. Adieu, my dear, dear Don Amasa. Go—go!" suddenly tearing his hand loose, "go, and God guard you better than me, my best friend."

Not unaffected, Captain Delano would now have lingered; but catching the meekly admonitory eye of the servant, with a hasty farewell he descended into his boat, followed by the continual adieus of Don Benito, standing rooted in the gangway.

Seating himself in the stern, Captain Delano, making a last salute, ordered the boat shoved off. The crew had their oars on end. The bowsmen pushed the boat a sufficient distance for the oars to be lengthwise dropped. The instant that was done, Don Benito sprang over the bulwarks, falling at the feet of Captain Delano; at the same time calling towards his ship, but in tones so frenzied, that none in the boat could understand him. But, as if not equally obtuse, three sailors, from three different and distant parts of the ship, splashed into the sea, swimming after their captain; as if intent upon his rescue.

The dismayed officer of the boat eagerly asked what this meant. To which, Captain Delano, turning a disdainful smile upon the unaccountable Spaniard, answered that, for his part, he neither knew nor cared; but it seemed as if Don Benito had taken it into his head to produce the impression among his people that the boat wanted to kidnap him. "Or else—give way[154] for your lives," he wildly added, starting at a clattering hubbub in the ship, above which rang the tocsin[155] of the hatchet-polishers; and seizing Don

[154]"Row!" "Get Moving!" [155]Alarm.

Benito by the throat he added, "this plotting pirate means murder!" Here, in apparent verification of the words, the servant, a dagger in his hand, was seen on the rail overhead, poised, in the act of leaping, as if with desperate fidelity to befriend his master to the last; while, seemingly to aid the black, the three white sailors were trying to clamber into the hampered bow. Meantime, the whole host of negroes, as if inflamed at the sight of their jeopardized captain, impended in one sooty avalanche over the bulwarks.

All this, with what preceded, and what followed, occurred with such involutions of rapidity, that past, present, and future seemed one.

Seeing the negro coming, Captain Delano had flung the Spaniard aside, almost in the very act of clutching him, and, by the unconscious recoil, shifting his place, with arms thrown up, so promptly grappled the servant in his descent, that with dagger presented at Captain Delano's heart, the black seemed of purpose to have leaped there as to his mark. But the weapon was wrenched away, and the assailant dashed down into the bottom of the boat, which now, with disentangled oars, began to speed through the sea.

At this juncture, the left hand of Captain Delano, on one side, again clutched the half-reclined Don Benito, heedless that he was in a speechless faint, while his right foot, on the other side, ground the prostrate negro; and his right arm pressed for added speed on the after oar, his eye bent forward, encouraging his men to their utmost.

But here, the officer of the boat, who had at last succeeded in beating off the towing sailors, and was now, with face turned aft, assisting the bowsman at his oar, suddenly called to Captain Delano, to see what the black was about; while a Portuguese oarsman shouted to him to give heed to what the Spaniard was saying.

Glancing down at his feet, Captain Delano saw the freed hand of the servant aiming with a second dagger—a small one, before concealed in his wool[156]—with this he was snakishly writhing up from the boat's bottom, at the heart of his master, his countenance lividly vindictive, expressing the centred purpose of his soul; while the Spaniard, half-choked, was vainly shrinking away, with husky words, incoherent to all but the Portuguese.

That moment, across the long-benighted mind of Captain Delano, a flash of revelation swept, illuminating, in unanticipated clearness, his host's whole mysterious demeanor, with every enigmatic event of the day, as well as the entire past voyage of the San Dominick. He smote Babo's hand down, but his own heart smote him harder. With infinite pity he withdrew his hold from Don Benito. Not Captain Delano, but Don Benito, the black, in leaping into the boat, had intended to stab.

Both the black's hands were held, as, glancing up toward the San Dominick, Captain Delano, now with scales dropped from his eyes, saw the negroes, not in misrule, not in tumult, not as if frantically concerned for Don Benito, but with mask torn away, flourishing hatchets and knives, in ferocious piratical revolt. Like delirious black dervishes,[157] the six Ashantees danced on the poop. Prevented by their foes from springing into the water, the Spanish boys were hurrying up to the topmost spars, while such of the few Spanish sailors, not already in the sea, less alert, were descried, helplessly mixed in, on deck, with the blacks.

[156]Hair. [157]Muslim holy men known for their dancing and whirling.

Meantime Captain Delano hailed his own vessel, ordering the ports up, and the guns run out. But by this time the cable of the San Dominick had been cut; and the fag-end, in lashing out, whipped away the canvas shroud about the beak, suddenly revealing, as the bleached hull swung round towards the open ocean, death for the figure-head, in a human skeleton; chalky comment on the chalked words below, *"Follow your leader."*

At the sight, Don Benito, covering his face, wailed out: "'Tis he, Aranda! my murdered, unburied friend!"

Upon reaching the sealer, calling for ropes, Captain Delano bound the negro, who made no resistance, and had him hoisted to the deck. He would then have assisted the now almost helpless Don Benito up the side; but Don Benito, wan as he was, refused to move, or be moved, until the negro should have been first put below out of view. When, presently assured that it was done, he no more shrank from the ascent.

The boat was immediately dispatched back to pick up the three swimming sailors. Meantime, the guns were in readiness, though, owing to the San Dominick having glided somewhat astern of the sealer, only the aftermost one could be brought to bear. With this, they fired six times; thinking to cripple the fugitive ship by bringing down her spars. But only a few inconsiderable ropes were shot away. Soon the ship was beyond the gun's range, steering broad out of the bay; the blacks thickly clustering round the bowsprit,[158] one moment with taunting cries towards the whites, the next with upthrown gestures hailing the now dusky moors of ocean—cawing crows escaped from the hand of the fowler.

The first impulse was to slip the cables and give chase. But, upon second thoughts, to pursue with whale-boat and yawl seemed more promising.

Upon inquiring of Don Benito what fire-arms they had on board the San Dominick, Captain Delano was answered that they had none that could be used; because, in the earlier stages of the mutiny, a cabin-passenger, since dead, had secretly put out of order the locks of what few muskets there were. But with all his remaining strength, Don Benito entreated the American not to give chase, either with ship or boat; for the negroes had already proved themselves such desperadoes, that, in case of a present assault, nothing but a total massacre of the whites could be looked for. But, regarding this warning as coming from one whose spirit had been crushed by misery the American did not give up his design.

The boats were got ready and armed. Captain Delano ordered his men into them. He was going himself when Don Benito grasped his arm.

"What! have you saved my life, Señor, and are you now going to throw away your own?"

The officers also, for reasons connected with their interests and those of the voyage, and a duty owing to the owners, strongly objected against their commander's going. Weighing their remonstrances a moment, Captain Delano felt bound to remain; appointing his chief-mate—an athletic and resolute man, who had been a privateer's-man[159]—to head the party. The more

[158]The large spar that extends up and forward from the front of a ship.

[159]I.e., had served on a privateer, a private ship given a government commission to serve as a naval vessel and seize the ships of the enemy.

to encourage the sailors, they were told, that the Spanish captain considered his ship good as lost; that she and her cargo, including some gold and silver, were worth more than a thousand doubloons. Take her, and no small part shall be theirs. The sailors replied with a shout.

The fugitives had now almost gained an offing.[160] It was nearly night; but the moon was rising. After hard, prolonged pulling, the boats came up on the ship's quarters, at a suitable distance laying upon their oars to discharge their muskets. Having no bullets to return, the negroes sent their yells. But, upon the second volley, Indian-like, they hurtled their hatchets. One took off a sailor's fingers. Another struck the whale-boat's bow, cutting off the rope there, and remaining stuck in the gunwale like a woodman's axe. Snatching it, quivering from its lodgment, the mate hurled it back. The returned gauntlet now stuck in the ship's broken quarter-gallery, and so remained.

The negroes giving too hot a reception, the whites kept a more respectful distance. Hovering now just out of reach of the hurtling hatchets, they, with a view to the close encounter which must soon come, sought to decoy the blacks into entirely disarming themselves of their most murderous weapons in a hand-to-hand fight, by foolishly flinging them, as missiles, short of the mark, into the sea. But, ere long, perceiving the strategem, the negroes desisted, though not before many of them had to replace their lost hatchets with hand-spikes; an exchange which, as counted upon, proved, in the end, favorable to the assailants.

Meantime, with a strong wind, the ship still clove the water; the boats alternately falling behind, and pulling up, to discharge fresh volleys.

The fire was mostly directed towards the stern, since there, chiefly, the negroes, at present, were clustering. But to kill or maim the negroes was not the object. To take them, with the ship, was the object. To do it, the ship must be boarded; which could not be done by boats while she was sailing so fast.

A thought now struck the mate. Observing the Spanish boys still aloft, high as they could get, he called to them to descend to the yards, and cut adrift the sails. It was done. About this time, owing to causes hereafter to be shown, two Spaniards, in the dress of sailors, and conspicuously showing themselves, were killed; not by volleys, but by deliberate marksman's shots; while, as it afterwards appeared, by one of the general discharges, Atufal, the black, and the Spaniard at the helm likewise were killed. What now, with the loss of the sails, and loss of leaders, the ship became unmanageable to the negroes.

With creaking masts, she came heavily round to the wind; the prow slowly swinging into view of the boats, its skeleton gleaming in the horizontal moonlight, and casting a gigantic ribbed shadow upon the water. One extended arm of the ghost seemed beckoning the whites to avenge it.

"Follow your leader!" cried the mate; and, one on each bow, the boats boarded. Sealing-spears[161] and cutlasses crossed hatchets and hand-spikes. Huddled upon the long-boat amidships, the negresses raised a wailing chant, whose chorus was the clash of the steel.

For a time, the attack wavered; the negroes wedging themselves to beat it back; the half-repelled sailors, as yet unable to gain a footing, fighting as

[160]Deep water offshore. [161]Spears used in killing seals.

troopers in the saddle, one leg sideways flung over the bulwarks, and one without, plying their cutlasses like carters' whips. But in vain. They were almost overborne, when, rallying themselves into a squad as one man, with a huzza, they sprang inboard, where, entangled, they involuntarily separated again. For a few breaths' space, there was a vague, muffled, inner sound, as of submerged sword-fish rushing hither and thither through shoals of black-fish. Soon, in a reunited band, and joined by the Spanish seamen, the whites came to the surface, irresistibly driving the negroes toward the stern. But a barricade of casks and sacks, from side to side, had been thrown up by the mainmast. Here the negroes faced about, and though scorning peace or truce, yet fain would have had respite. But, without pause, overleaping the barrier, the unflagging sailors again closed. Exhausted, the blacks now fought in despair. Their red tongues lolled, wolf-like, from their black mouths. But the pale sailors' teeth were set; not a word was spoken; and, in five minutes more, the ship was won.

Nearly a score of the negroes were killed. Exclusive of those by the balls,[162] many were mangled; their wounds—mostly inflicted by the long-edged sealing-spears, resembling those shaven ones of the English at Preston Pans,[163] made by the poled scythes[164] of the Highlanders. On the other side, none were killed, though several were wounded; some severely, including the mate. The surviving negroes were temporarily secured, and the ship, towed back into the harbor at midnight, once more lay anchored.

Omitting the incidents and arrangements ensuing, suffice it that, after two days spent in refitting, the ships sailed in company for Conception, in Chili, and thence for Lima, in Peru; where, before the vice-regal courts, the whole affair, from the beginning, underwent investigation.

Though, midway on the passage, the ill-fated Spaniard, relaxed from constraint, showed some signs of regaining health with free-will; yet, agreeably to his own foreboding, shortly before arriving at Lima, he relapsed, finally becoming so reduced as to be carried ashore in arms. Hearing of his story and plight, one of the many religious institutions of the City of Kings opened an hospitable refuge to him, where both physician and priest were his nurses, and a member of the order volunteered to be his one special guardian and consoler, by night and by day.

The following extracts, translated from one of the official Spanish documents, will, it is hoped, shed light on the preceding narrative, as well as, in the first place, reveal the true port of departure and true history of the San Dominick's voyage, down to the time of her touching at the island at St. Maria.

But, ere the extracts come, it may be well to preface them with a remark.

The document selected, from among many others, for partial translation, contains the deposition of Benito Cereno; the first taken in the case. Some disclosures therein were, at the time, held dubious for both learned and natural reasons. The tribunal inclined to the opinion that the deponent, not undisturbed in his mind by recent events, raved of some things which could never have happened. But subsequent depositions of the surviving sailors,

[162] I.e., those killed by musket balls.
[163] Battle site where Scottish Highlanders defeated the English in 1745.
[164] Scythes mounted on long shafts.

bearing out the revelations of their captain in several of the strangest particulars, gave credence to the rest. So that the tribunal, in its final decision, rested its capital sentences upon statements which, had they lacked confirmation, it would have deemed it but duty to reject.

—

I, DON JOSE DE ABOS AND PADILLA, His Majesty's Notary for the Royal Revenue, and Register of this Province, and Notary Public of the Holy Crusade of this Bishopric, etc.

Do certify and declare, as much as is requisite in law, that, in the criminal cause commenced the twenty-fourth of the month of September, in the year seventeen hundred and ninety-nine, against the negroes of the ship San Dominick, the following declaration before me was made:

Declaration of the first witness, DON BENITO CERENO.

The same day, and month, and year, His Honor, Doctor Juan Martinez de Rozas, Councilor of the Royal Audience of this Kingdom, and learned in the law of this Intendency,[165] ordered the captain of the ship San Dominick, Don Benito Cereno, to appear; which he did in his litter,[166] attended by the monk Infelez; of whom he received the oath, which he took by God, our Lord, and a sign of the Cross; under which he promised to tell the truth of whatever he should know and should be asked;—and being interrogated agreeably to the tenor of the act commencing the process, he said, that on the twentieth of May last, he set sail with his ship from the port of Valparaiso,[167] bound to that of Callao;[168] loaded with the produce of the country beside thirty cases of hardware and one hundred and sixty blacks, of both sexes, mostly belonging to Don Alexandro Aranda, gentleman, of the city of Mendoza;[169] that the crew of the ship consisted of thirty-six men, besides the persons who went as passengers; that the negroes were in part as follows:

[*Here, in the original, follows a list of some fifty names, descriptions, and ages, compiled from certain recovered documents of Aranda's, and also from recollections of the deponent, from which portions only are extracted.*][170]

—One, from about eighteen to nineteen years, named José, and this was the man that waited upon his master, Don Alexandro, and who speaks well the Spanish, having served him four or five years; *** a mulatto, named Francesco, the cabin steward, of a good person and voice, having sung in the Valparaiso churches, native of the province of Buenos Ayres, aged thirty-five years. *** A smart negro, named Dago, who had been for many years a gravedigger among the Spaniards, aged forty-six years. *** Four old negroes, born in Africa, from sixty to seventy, but sound, calkers by trade, whose names are as follows:—the first was named Muri, and he was killed (as was also his son named Diamelo); the second, Nacta; the third, Yola, likewise killed; the fourth, Ghofan; and six full-grown negroes, aged from thirty to forty-five, all

[165]A district ruled by an intendent (provincial officer). [166]Stretcher.
[167]Seaport in Chile. [168]Seaport in Peru. [169]City in western Argentina.
[170]The brackets, italics, and marks of ellipsis are Melville's insertions.

raw, and born among the Ashantees—Matiluqui, Yan, Lecbe, Mapenda, Yambaio, Akim; four of whom were killed; *** a powerful negro named Atufal, who being supposed to have been a chief in Africa, his owner set great store by him. *** And a small negro of Senegal,[171] but some years among the Spaniards, aged about thirty, which negro's name was Babo; *** that he does not remember the names of the others, but that still expecting the residue of Don Alexandro's papers will be found, will then take due account of them all, and remit to the court; *** and thirty-nine women and children of all ages.

[*The catalogue over, the deposition goes on.*]

*** That all the negroes slept upon deck, as is customary in this navigation, and none wore fetters, because the owner, his friend Aranda, told him that they were all tractable; *** that on the seventh day after leaving port, at three o'clock in the morning, all the Spaniards being asleep except the two officers on the watch, who were the boatswain,[172] Juan Robles, and the carpenter, Jaun Bautista Gayete, and the helmsman and his boy, the negroes revolted suddenly, wounded dangerously the boatswain and the carpenter, and successively killed eighteen men of those who were sleeping upon deck, some with hand-spikes and hatchets, and others by throwing them alive overboard, after tying them; that of the Spaniards upon deck, they left about seven, as he thinks, alive and tied, to manœuvre the ship, and three or four more, who hid themselves, remained also alive. Although in the act of revolt the negroes made themselves master of the hatchway, six or seven wounded went through it to the cockpit,[173] without any hindrance on their part; that during the act of revolt, the mate and another person, whose name he does not recollect, attempted to come up through the hatchway, but being quickly wounded, were obliged to return to the cabin; that the deponent resolved at break of day to come up the companion-way, where the negro Babo was, being the ringleader, and Atufal, who assisted him, and having spoken to them, exhorted them to cease committing such atrocities, asking them, at the same time, what they wanted and intended to do, offering, himself, to obey their commands; that notwithstanding this, they threw, in his presence, three men, alive and tied, overboard; that they told the deponent to come up, and that they would not kill him; which having done, the negro Babo asked him whether there were in those seas any negro countries where they might be carried, and he answered them, No; that the negro Babo afterwards told him to carry them to Senegal, or to the neighboring islands of St. Nicholas; and he answered, that this was impossible, on account of the great distance, the necessity involved of rounding Cape Horn, the bad condition of the vessel, the want of provisions, sails, and water; but that the negro Babo replied to him he must carry them in any way; that they would do and conform themselves to everything the deponent should require as to eating and drinking; that after a long conference, being absolutely compelled to please them, for they threatened to kill all the whites if they were not, at all events, carried to

[171]West African province. [172]Ship's officer in charge of the deck crew.
[173]Section of a ship where junior officers are quartered.

Senegal, he told them that what was most wanting for the voyage was water; that they would go near the coast to take it, and thence they would proceed on their course; that the negro Babo agreed to it; and the deponent steered towards the intermediate ports, hoping to meet some Spanish or foreign vessel that would save them; that within ten or eleven days they saw the land, and continued their course by it in the vicinity of Nasca;[174] that the deponent observed that the negroes were now restless and mutinous, because he did not effect the taking in of water, the negro Babo having required, with threats, that it should be done, without fail, the following day; he told him he saw plainly that the coast was steep, and the rivers designated in the maps were not to be found, with other reasons suitable to the circumstances; that the best way would be to go to the island of Santa Maria, where they might water easily, it being a solitary island, as the foreigners did; that the deponent did not go to Pisco,[175] that was near, nor make any other port of the coast, because the negro Babo had intimated to him several times, that he would kill all the whites the very moment he should perceive any city, town, or settlement of any kind on the shores to which they should be carried: that having determined to go to the island of Santa Maria, as the deponent had planned, for the purpose of trying whether, on the passage or near the island itself, they could find any vessel that should favor them, or whether he could escape from it in a boat to the neighboring coast of Arruco,[176] to adopt the necessary means he immediately changed his course, steering for the island; that the negroes Babo and Atufal held daily conferences, in which they discussed what was necessary for their design of returning to Senegal, whether they were to kill all the Spaniards, and particularly the deponent; that eight days after parting from the coast of Nasca, the deponent being on the watch a little after day-break, and soon after the negroes had their meeting, the negro Babo came to the place where the deponent was, and told him that he had determined to kill his master, Don Alexandro Aranda, both because he and his companions could not otherwise be sure of their liberty, and that to keep the seamen in subjection, he wanted to prepare a warning of what road they should be made to take did they or any of them oppose him; and that, by means of the death of Don Alexandro, that warning would best be given; but, that what this last meant, the deponent did not at the time comprehend, nor could not, further than the death of Don Alexandro was intended; and moreover the negro Babo proposed to the deponent to call the mate Raneds, who was sleeping in the cabin, before the thing was done, for fear, as the deponent understood it, that the mate, who was a good navigator, should be killed with Don Alexandro and the rest; that the deponent, who was the friend, from youth, of Don Alexandro, prayed and conjured, but all was useless; for the negro Babo answered him that the thing could not be prevented, and that all the Spaniards risked their death if they should attempt to frustrate his will in this matter, or any other; that, in this conflict, the deponent called the mate, Raneds, who was forced to go apart, and immediately the negro Babo commanded the Ashantee Martinqui and the Ashantee Lecbe to go and commit the murder; that those two went down with hatchets to the berth

[174]Nazca, city in west central Peru. [175]Seaport in Peru. [176]Arica, city in northern Chile.

of Don Alexandro; that, yet half alive and mangled, they dragged him on deck; that they were going to throw him overboard in that state, but the negro Babo stopped them, bidding the murder be completed on the deck before him, which was done, when, by his orders, the body was carried below, forward; that nothing more was seen of it by the deponent for three days; *** that Don Alonza Sidonia, an old man, long resident at Valparaiso, and lately appointed to a civil office in Peru, whither he had taken passage, was at the time sleeping in the berth opposite Don Alexandro's; that awakening at his cries, surprised by them, and at the sight of the negroes with their bloody hatchets in their hands, he threw himself into the sea through a window which was near him, and was drowned, without it being in the power of the deponent to assist or take him up; *** that a short time after killing Aranda, they brought upon deck his german-cousin, of middle-age, Don Francisco Masa, of Mendoza, and the young Don Joaquin, Marques de Aramboalaza, then lately from Spain, with his Spanish servant Ponce, and the three young clerks of Aranda, José Mozairi, Lorenzo Bargas, and Hermenegildo Gandix, all of Cadiz; that Don Joaquin and Hermenegildo Gandix, the negro Babo, for purposes hereafter to appear, preserved alive; but Don Francisco Masa, José Mozairi, and Lorenzo Bargas, with Ponce the servant, beside the boatswain, Juan Robles, the boatswain's mates, Manual Viscaya and Roderigo Hurta, and four of the sailors, the negro Babo ordered to be thrown alive into the sea, although they made no resistance, nor begged for anything else but mercy; that the boatswain, Jaun Robles, who knew how to swim, kept the longest above water, making acts of contrition, and, in the last words he uttered, charged this deponent to cause mass to be said for his soul to our Lady of Succor: *** that, during the three days which followed, the deponent, uncertain what fate had befallen the remains of Don Alexandro, frequently asked the negro Babo where they were, and if still on board, whether they were to be preserved for interment ashore, entreating him so to order it; that the negro Babo answered nothing till the fourth day, when at sunrise, the deponent coming on deck, the negro Babo showed him a skeleton, which had been substituted for the ship's proper figurehead—the image of Christopher Colon, the discoverer of the New World; that the negro Babo asked him whose skeleton that was, and whether, from its whiteness, he should not think it a white's; that, upon his covering his face, the negro Babo, coming close, said words to this effect: "Keep faith with the blacks from here to Senegal, or you shall in spirit, as now in body, follow your leader," pointing to the prow; *** that the same morning the negro Babo took by succession each Spaniard forward, and asked him whose skeleton that was, and whether, from its whiteness, he should not think it a white's; that each Spaniard covered his face; that then to each the negro Babo repeated the words in the first place said to the deponent; *** that they (the Spaniards), being then assembled aft, the negro Babo harangued them, saying that he had now done all; that the deponent (as navigator for the negroes) might pursue his course, warning him and all of them that they should, soul and body, go the way of Don Alexandro, if he saw them (the Spaniards) speak or plot anything against them (the negroes)—a threat which was repeated every day; that, before the events last mentioned, they had tied the cook to throw him overboard, for it is not known what thing they heard him speak, but finally the negro Babo spared his life, at the request of the deponent; that a few days after, the deponent, endeavoring not to omit any means to preserve the lives of the remaining whites, spoke to the negroes of peace and tranquillity, and agreed to draw up a paper, signed by the deponent and the sailors who could write, as also by the negro Babo, for himself and all the blacks, in which the deponent obliged himself to carry them to Senegal, and they not to kill any more, and he formally to make over to them the ship, with the cargo, with which they were for that time satisfied and quieted. *** But the next day, the more surely to guard against the sailors' escape, the negro Babo commanded all the boats to be destroyed but the long-boat, which was unseaworthy, and another, a cutter in good condition, which knowing it would yet be wanted for towing the water casks, he had it lowered down into the hold.

* * * * * * * * * * *

[*Various particulars of the prolonged and perplexed navigation ensuing here follow, with incidents of a calamitous calm, from which portion one passage is extracted, to wit:*]—That on the fifth day of the calm, all on board suffering much from the heat, and want of water, and five having died in fits, and mad, the negroes became irritable, and for a chance gesture, which they deemed suspicious—though it was harmless—made by the mate, Raneds, to the deponent in the act of handing a quadrant,[177] they killed him; but that for this they afterwards were sorry, the mate being the only remaining navigator on board, except the deponent.

* * * * * * * * * * *

—That omitting other events, which daily happened, and which can only serve uselessly to recall past misfortunes and conflicts, after seventy-three days' navigation, reckoned from the time they sailed from Nasca, during which they navigated under a scanty allowance of water, and were afflicted with the calms before mentioned, they at last arrived at the island of Santa Maria, on the seventeenth of the month of August, at about six o'clock in the afternoon, at which hour they cast anchor very near the American ship, Bachelor's Delight, which lay in the same bay, commanded by the generous Captain Amasa Delano; but at six o'clock in the morning, they had already descried the port, and the negroes became uneasy, as soon as at distance they saw the ship, not having expected to see one there; that the negro Babo pacified them, assuring them that no fear need be had; that straightway he ordered the figure on the bow to be covered with canvas, as for repairs, and had the decks a little set in order; that for a time the negro Babo and the negro Atufal conferred; that the negro Atufal was for sailing away, but the negro Babo would not, and, by himself, cast about what to do; that at last he came to the deponent, proposing to him to say and do all that the deponent declares to have said and done to the American captain;

* * * * * * * * * * *

that the negro Babo warned him that if he varied in the least, or uttered any word, or gave any look that should give the least intimation of the past events or present state, he would instantly kill him, with all his companions,

[177]Navigation instrument used to calculate latitude.

showing a dagger, which he carried hid, saying something which, as he understood it, meant that the dagger would be alert as his eye; that the negro Babo then announced the plan to all his companions, which pleased them; that he then, the better to disguise the truth, devised many expedients, in some of them uniting deceit and defense; that of this sort was the device of the six Ashantees before named, who were his bravoes;[178] that them he stationed on the break of the poop, as if to clean certain hatchets (in cases, which were part of the cargo), but in reality to use them, and distribute them at need, and at a given word he told them; that, among other devices, was the device of presenting Atufal, his right hand man, as chained, though in a moment the chains could be dropped; that in every particular he informed the deponent what part he was expected to enact in every device, and what story he was to tell on every occasion, always threatening him with instant death if he varied in the least; that, conscious that many of the negroes would be turbulent, the negro Babo appointed the four aged negroes, who were calkers, to keep what domestic order they could on the decks; that again and again he harangued the Spaniards and his companions, informing them of his intent, and of his devices, and of the invented story that this deponent was to tell; charging them lest any of them varied from that story; that these arrangements were made and matured during the interval of two or three hours, between their first sighting the ship and the arrival on board of Captain Amasa Delano; that this happened about half-past seven o'clock in the morning, Captain Amasa Delano coming in his boat, and all gladly receiving him; that the deponent, as well as he could force himself, acting then the part of principal owner, and a free captain of the ship, told Captain Amasa Delano, when called upon, that he came from Buenos Ayres, bound to Lima, with three hundred negroes; that off Cape Horn, and in a subsequent fever, many negroes had died; that also, by similar casualties, all the sea officers and the greatest part of the crew had died.

* * * * * * * * * * *

[*And so the deposition goes on, circumstantially recounting the fictitious story dictated to the deponent by Babo, and through the deponent imposed upon Captain Delano; and also recounting the friendly offers of Captain Delano, with other things, but all of which is here omitted. After the fictitious story, etc, the deposition proceeds:*]

* * * * * * * * * * *

—that the generous Captain Amasa Delano remained on board all the day, till he left the ship anchored at six o'clock in the evening, deponent speaking to him always of his pretended misfortunes, under the fore-mentioned principles, without having had it in his power to tell a single word, or give him the least hint, that he might know the truth and state of things; because the negro Babo, performing the office of an officious servant with all the appearance of submission of the humble slave, did not leave the deponent one moment; that this was in order to observe the deponent's actions and words, for the negro Babo understands well the Spanish; and besides, there were thereabout some others who were constantly on the watch, and

[178]Desperadoes, henchmen.

likewise understood the Spanish; *** that upon one occasion, while deponent was standing on the deck conversing with Amasa Delano, by a secret sign the negro Babo drew him (the deponent) aside, the act appearing as if originating with the deponent; that then, he being drawn aside, the negro Babo proposed to him to gain from Amasa Delano full particulars about his ship, and crew, and arms; that the deponent asked "For what?" that the negro Babo answered he might conceive; that, grieved at the prospect of what might overtake the generous Captain Amasa Delano, the deponent at first refused to ask the desired questions, and used every argument to induce the negro Babo to give up this new design; that the negro Babo showed the point of his dagger; that, after the information had been obtained the negro Babo again drew him aside, telling that that very night he (the deponent) would be captain of two ships, instead of one, for that, great part of the American's ship's crew being to be absent fishing, the six Ashantees, without any one else, would easily take it; that at this time he said other things to the same purpose; that no entreaties availed; that, before Amasa Delano's coming on board, no hint had been given touching the capture of the American ship: that to prevent this project the deponent was powerless; ***—that in some things his memory is confused, he cannot distinctly recall every event; ***—that as soon as they had cast anchor at six of the clock in the evening, as has before been stated, the American Captain took leave, to return to his vessel; that upon a sudden impulse, which the deponent believes to have come from God and his angels, he, after the farewell had been said, followed the generous Captain Amasa Delano as far as the gunwale,[179] where he stayed, under pretense of taking leave, until Amasa Delano should have been seated in his boat; that on shoving off the deponent sprang from the gunwale into the boat, and fell into it, he knows not how, God guarding him; that—

* * * * * * * * * * *

[*Here, in the original, follows the account of what further happened at the escape, and how the San Dominick was retaken, and of the passage to the coast; including in the recital many expressions of "eternal gratitude" to the "generous Captain Amasa Delano." The deposition then proceeds with recapitulatory remarks, and a partial renumeration of the negroes, making record of their individual part in the past events, with a view to furnishing, according to command of the court, the data whereon to found the criminal sentences to be pronounced. From this portion is the following:*]

—That he believes that all the negroes, though not in the first place knowing to the design of revolt, when it was accomplished, approved it. *** That the negro, José, eighteen years old, and in the personal service of Don Alexandro, was the one who communicated the information to the negro Babo, about the state of things in the cabin, before the revolt; that this is known, because, in the preceding midnight, he used to come from his berth,

[179]Upper part of a ship's side, the parapet of the uppermost deck, over which cannon were pointed on ancient ships.

which was under his master's, in the cabin, to the deck where the ringleader and his associates were, and had secret conversations with the negro Babo, in which he was several times seen by the mate; that, one night, the mate drove him away twice; *** that this same negro José was the one who, without being commanded to do so by the negro Babo, as Lecbe and Martinqui were, stabbed his master, Don Alexandro, after he had been dragged half-lifeless to the deck; *** that the mulatto steward, Francesco, was of the first band of revolters, that he was in all things, the creature and tool of the negro Babo; that, to make his court, he, just before a repast in the cabin, proposed, to the negro Babo, poisoning a dish for the generous Captain Amasa Delano; this is known and believed, because the negroes have said it; but that the negro Babo, having another design, forbade Francesco; *** that the Ashantee Lecbe was one of the worst of them; for that, on the day the ship was retaken, he assisted in the defense of her, with a hatchet in each hand, with one of which he wounded, in the breast, the chief mate of Amasa Delano, in the first act of boarding; this all knew; that, in sight of the deponent, Lecbe struck, with a hatchet, Don Francisco Masa, when, by the negro Babo's orders, he was carrying him to throw him overboard, alive; beside participating in the murder, before mentioned, of Don Alexandro Aranda, and others of the cabin-passengers; that, owing to the fury with which the Ashantees fought in the engagement with the boats, but this Lecbe and Yan survived; that Yan was bad as Lecbe; that Yan was the man who, by Babo's command, willingly prepared the skeleton of Don Alexandro, in a way the negroes afterwards told the deponent, but which he, so long as reason is left him, can never divulge; that Yan and Lecbe were the two who, in a calm by night, riveted the skeleton to the bow; this also the negroes told him; that the negro Babo was he who traced the inscription below it; that the negro Babo was the plotter from first to last; he ordered every murder, and was the helm and keel of the revolt; that Atufal was his lieutenant in all; but Atufal, with his hand, committed no murder, nor did the negro Babo; *** that Atufal was shot, being killed in the fight with the boats, ere boarding; *** that the negresses, of age, were knowing to the revolt, and testified themselves satisfied at the death of their master, Don Alexandro; that, had the negroes not restrained them, they would have tortured to death, instead of simply killing, the Spaniards slain by command of the negro Babo; that the negresses used their utmost influence to have the deponent made away with; that, in the various acts of murder, they sang songs and danced—not gaily, but solemnly; and before the engagement with the boats, as well as during the action, they sang melancholy songs to the negroes, and that this melancholy tone was more inflaming than a different one would have been, and was so intended; that all this is believed, because the negroes have said it.—that of the thirty-six men of the crew, exclusive of the passengers (all of whom are now dead), which the deponent had knowledge of, six only remained alive, with four cabin-boys and ship-boys, not included with the crew; ***—that the negroes broke an arm of one of the cabin-boys and gave him strokes with hatchets.

[*Then follow various random disclosures referring to various periods of time. The following are extracted:*]

—That during the presence of Captain Amasa Delano on board, some attempts were made by the sailors, and one by Hermenegildo Gandix, to convey hints to him of the true state of affairs; but that these attempts were ineffectual, owing to fear of incurring death, and, furthermore, owing to the devices which offered contradictions to the true state of affairs, as well as owing to the generosity and piety of Amasa Delano incapable of sounding such wickedness; *** that Luys Galgo, a sailor about sixty years of age, and formerly of the king's navy, was one of those who sought to convey tokens to Captain Amasa Delano; but his intent, though undiscovered, being suspected, he was, on a pretense, made to retire out of sight, and at last into the hold, and there was made away with. This the negroes have since said; *** that one of the ship-boys feeling, from Captain Amasa Delano's presence, some hopes of release, and not having enough prudence, dropped some chance-word respecting his expectations, which being overheard and understood by a slave-boy with whom he was eating at the time, the latter struck him on the head with a knife, inflicting a bad wound, but of which the boy is now healing; that likewise, not long before the ship was brought to anchor, one of the seamen, steering at the time, endangered himself by letting the blacks remark some expression in his countenance, arising from a cause similar to the above; but this sailor, by his heedful after conduct, escaped; *** that these statements are made to show the court that from the beginning to the end of the revolt, it was impossible for the deponent and his men to act otherwise than they did; ***—that the third clerk, Hermenegildo Gandix, who before had been forced to live among the seamen, wearing a seaman's habit, and in all respects appearing to be one for the time; he, Gandix, was killed by a musket ball fired through mistake from the boats before boarding; having in his fright run up the mizzen-rigging, calling to the boats—"don't board," lest upon their boarding the negroes should kill him; that this inducing the Americans to believe he some way favored the cause of the negroes, they fired two balls at him, so that he fell wounded from the rigging, and was drowned in the sea; ***—that the young Don Joaquin, Marquis de Aramboalaza, like Hermenegildo Gandix, the third clerk, was degraded to the office and appearance of a common seaman; that upon one occasion when Don Joaquin shrank, the negro Babo commanded the Ashantee Lecbe to take tar and heat it, and pour it upon Don Joaquin's hands; ***—that Don Joaquin was killed owing to another mistake of the Americans but one impossible to be avoided as upon the approach of the boats, Don Joaquin, with a hatchet tied edge out and upright to his hand, was made by the negroes to appear on the bulwarks; whereupon, seen with arms in his hand and in a questionable attitude, he was shot for a renegade seaman; ***—that on the person of Don Joaquin was found a secreted jewel, which, by papers that were discovered, proved to have been meant for the shrine of our Lady of Mercy in Lima; a votive offering, beforehand prepared and guarded, to attest his gratitude, when he should have landed in Peru, his last destination, for the safe conclusion of his entire voyage from Spain; ***—that the jewel, with the other effects of the late Don Joaquin, is in the custody of the brethren of the Hospital de Sacerdotes, awaiting the disposition of the honorable court; ***—that, owing to the condition of the deponent, as well as the haste in which the boats departed for the attack, the Americans were not forewarned that there were, among the apparent crew, a passenger and one of the clerks disguised by the negro Babo; ***—that, beside the negroes killed in the action, some were killed after the capture and re-anchoring at night, when shackled to the ring-bolts on deck; that these deaths were committed by the sailors, ere they could be prevented. That so soon as informed of it, Captain Amasa Delano used all his authority, and, in particular with his own hand, struck down Martinez Gola, who, having found a razor in the pocket of an old jacket of his; that the noble Captain Amasa Delano also wrenched from the hand of Bartholomew Barlo a dagger, secreted at the time of the massacre of the whites, with which he was in the act of stabbing a shackled negro, who, the same day, with another negro, had thrown him down and jumped upon him; ***—that, for all the events, befalling through so long a time, during which the ship was in the hands of the negro Babo, he cannot here give account; but that, what he has said is the most substantial of what occurs to him at present, and is the truth under the oath which he has taken; which declaration he affirmed and ratified, after hearing it read to him.

He said that he is twenty-nine years of age, and broken in body and mind; that when finally dismissed by the court, he shall not return home to Chili, but betake himself to the monastery on Mount Agonia without; and signed with his honor, and crossed himself, and, for the time, departed as he came, in his litter, with the monk Infelez, to the Hospital de Sacerdotes.

BENITO CERENO.

DOCTOR ROZAS

If the Deposition have served as the key to fit into the lock of the complications which precede it, then, as a vault whose door has been flung back, the San Dominick's hull lies open to-day.

Hitherto the nature of this narrative, besides rendering the intricacies in the beginning unavoidable, has more or less required that many things, instead of being set down in the order of occurrence, should be retrospectively, or irregularly given; this last is the case with the following passages, which will conclude the account:

During the long, mild voyage to Lima, there was, as before hinted, a period during which the sufferer a little recovered his health, or, at least in some degree, his tranquillity. Ere the decided relapse which came, the two captains had many cordial conversations—their fraternal unreserve in singular contrast with former withdrawments.

Again and again it was repeated how hard it had been to enact the part forced on the Spaniard by Babo.

"Ah, my dear friend," Don Benito once said, "at those very times when you thought me so morose and ungrateful, nay, when, as you now admit, you half thought me plotting your murder, at those very times my heart was frozen; I could not look at you, thinking of what, both on board this ship and your own, hung, from other hands, over my kind benefactor. And as God lives, Don Amasa, I know not whether desire for my own safety alone could have nerved me to that leap into your boat, had it not been for the thought that, did you, unenlightened, return to your ship, you, my friend, with all who might be with you, stolen upon, that night, in your hammocks, would never in this world have wakened again. Do but think how you walked this deck, how you sat in this cabin, every inch of ground mined into honey-combs under you. Had I dropped the least hint, made the least advance towards an understanding between us, death, explosive death—yours as mine—would have ended the scene."

"True, true," cried Captain Delano, starting, "you have saved my life, Don Benito, more than I yours; saved it, too, against my knowledge and will."

"Nay, my friend," rejoined the Spaniard, courteous even to the point of religion, "God charmed your life, but you saved mine. To think of some things you did—those smilings and chattings, rash pointings and gesturings. For less than these, they slew my mate, Raneds; but you had the Prince of Heaven's safe-conduct through all ambuscades."

"Yes, all is owing to Providence, I know: but the temper of my mind that morning was more than commonly pleasant, while the sight of so much suffering, more apparent than real, added to my good-nature, compassion, and charity, happily interweaving the three. Had it been otherwise, doubtless, as you hint, some of my interferences might have ended unhappily enough. Besides, those feelings I spoke of enabled me to get the better of momentary distrust, at times when acuteness might have cost me my life, without saving another's. Only at the end did my suspicions get the better of me, and you know how wide of the mark they then proved."

"Wide, indeed," said Don Benito, sadly; "you were with me all day; stood with me, sat with me, talked with me, looked at me, ate with me, drank with me; and yet, your last act was to clutch for a monster, not only an innocent man, but the most pitiable of all men. To such degree may malign machinations and deceptions impose. So far may even the best man err, in judging the conduct of one with the recesses of whose condition he is not acquainted. But you were forced to it; and you were in time undeceived. Would that, in both respects, it was so ever, and with all men."

"You generalize, Don Benito; and mournfully enough. But the past is passed; why moralize upon it? Forget it. See, yon bright sun has forgotten it all, and the blue sea, and the blue sky; these have turned over new leaves."

"Because they have no memory," he dejectedly replied; "because they are not human."

"But these mild trades[180] that now fan your cheek, do they not come with a human-like healing to you? Warm friends, steadfast friends are the trades."

"With their steadfastness they but waft me to my tomb, Señor," was the foreboding response.

"You are saved," cried Captain Delano, more and more astonished and pained; "you are saved: what has cast such a shadow upon you?"

"The negro."

There was silence, while the moody man sat, slowly and unconsciously gathering his mantle about him, as if it were a pall.

There was no more conversation that day.

But if the Spaniard's melancholy sometimes ended in muteness upon topics like the above, there were others upon which he never spoke at all; on which, indeed, all his old reserves were piled. Pass over the worst, and, only to elucidate, let an item or two of these be cited. The dress, so precise and costly, worn by him on the day whose events have been narrated, had not

[180]Trade winds.

willingly been put on. And that silver-mounted sword, apparent symbol of despotic command, was not, indeed, a sword, but the ghost of one. The scabbard, artificially stiffened, was empty.

As for the black—whose brain, not body, had schemed and led the revolt, with the plot—his slight frame, inadequate to that which it held, had at once yielded to the superior muscular strength of his captor, in the boat. Seeing all was over, he uttered no sound, and could not be forced to. His aspect seemed to say, since I cannot do deeds, I will not speak words. Put in irons in the hold, with the rest, he was carried to Lima. During the passage, Don Benito did not visit him. Nor then, nor at any time after, would he look at him. Before the tribunal he refused. When pressed by the judges he fainted. On the testimony of the sailors alone rested the legal identity of Babo.

Some months after, dragged to the gibbet at the tail of a mule, the black met his voiceless end. The body was burned to ashes; but for many days, the head, that hive of subtlety, fixed on a pole in the Plaza, met, unabashed, the gaze of the whites; and across the Plaza looked towards St. Bartholomew's church, in whose vaults slept then, as now, the recovered bones of Aranda: and across the Rimac bridge looked towards the monastery, on Mount Agonia without; where, three months after being dismissed by the court, Benito Cereno, borne on the bier, did, indeed, follow his leader.

1854–1855 1855, 1856

THE PARADISE OF BACHELORS AND THE TARTARUS[1] OF MAIDS

I. The Paradise of Bachelors

It lies not far from Temple-Bar.[2]

Going to it, by the usual way, is like stealing from a heated plain into some cool, deep glen, shady among harboring hills.

Sick with the din and soiled with the mud of Fleet Street—where the Benedick[3] tradesmen are hurrying by, with ledger-lines ruled along their brows, thinking upon rise of bread and fall of babies—you adroitly turn a mystic corner—not a street—glide down a dim, monastic way, flanked by dark, sedate, and solemn piles, and still wending on, give the whole careworn world the slip, and, disentangled, stand beneath the quiet cloisters[4] of the Paradise of Bachelors.

Sweet are the oases in Sahara; charming the isle-groves of August prairies; delectable pure faith amidst a thousand perfidies: but sweeter, still more charming, most delectable, the dreamy Paradise of Bachelors, found in the stony heart of stunning London.

[1]In Greek mythology the lower region of the underworld.

[2]Stone gateway that stood at the junction of Fleet Street and the Strand, a street along the bank of the Thames River, in London.

[3]Former bachelor, now married, named for the resolute bachelor in Shakespeare's play *Much Ado About Nothing* (1598–1599).

[4]London's Inn of Court, four groups of buildings (Inner Temple, Middle Temple, Lincoln's Inn, and Gray's Inn) occupied by lawyers and law students.

In mild meditation pace the cloisters; take your pleasure, sip your leisure, in the garden waterward; go linger in the ancient library; go worship in the sculptured chapel: but little have you seen, just nothing do you know, not the sweet kernel have you tasted, till you dine among the banded Bachelors, and see their convivial eyes and glasses sparkle. Not dine in bustling commons,[5] during term-time, in the hall; but tranquilly, by private hint, at a private table; some fine Templar's[6] hospitably invited guest.

Templar? That's a romantic name. Let me see. Brian de Bois Guilbert[7] was a Templar, I believe. Do we understand you to insinuate that those famous Templars still survive in modern London? May the ring of their armed heels be heard, and the rattle of their shields, as in mailed prayer the monk-knights kneel before the consecrated Host? Surely a monk-knight were a curious sight picking his way along the Strand, his gleaming corselet[8] and snowy surcoat[9] spattered by an omnibus. Long-bearded, too, according to his order's rule; his face fuzzy as a pard's,[10] how would the grim ghost look among the crop-haired, close-shaven citizens? We know indeed—sad history recounts it—that a moral blight tainted at last this sacred Brotherhood. Though no sworded foe might outskill them in the fence,[11] yet the worm of luxury crawled beneath their guard, gnawing the core of knightly troth,[12] nibbling the monastic vow, till at last the monk's austerity relaxed to wassailing,[13] and the sworn knights-bachelors grew to be but hypocrites and rakes.

But for all this, quite unprepared were we to learn that Knights-Templars (if at all in being) were so entirely secularized as to be reduced from carving out immortal fame in glorious battling for the Holy Land, to the carving of roast-mutton at a dinner-board. Like Anacreon,[14] do these degenerate Templars now think it sweeter far to fall in banquet than in war? Or, indeed, how can there be any survival of that famous order? Templars in modern London! Templars in their red-cross mantles[15] smoking cigars at the Divan![16] Templars crowded in a railway train, till, stacked with steel helmet, spear, and shield, the whole train looks like one elongated locomotive!

No. The genuine Templar is long since departed. Go view the wondrous tombs in the Temple Church;[17] see there the rigidly-haughty forms stretched out, with crossed arms upon their stilly hearts, in everlasting and undreaming rest.[18] Like the years before the flood,[19] the bold Knights-Templars are no

[5]A dining room.

[6]A member of the Knights Templar, the religious and military order established about 1118 to protect pilgrims in the Holy Land. The order grew corrupt and was suppressed in 1312. Its London headquarters became a legal center; lawyers and students living in or near the original buildings were called Templars.

[7]Brian de Bois-Guilbert, a villainous Knight Templar in the novel *Ivanhoe* (1819) by Sir Walter Scott (1771–1832).

[8]Body armor. [9]Outercoat worn over armor. [10]Leopard's. [11]Swordplay.

[12]I.e., the Templar's pledge to forgo worldly riches and luxury. [13]Carousing.

[14]Greek poet (563?–478? B.C.) whose poems celebrated wine and love. He is said to have died from choking on a grape seed.

[15]The Knights Templar wore cloaks (mantles) showing a red cross on a white background.

[16]Oriental royal court or council-chamber.

[17]The Church of St. Mary, built on the site of the original church of the Knights Templar in London.

[18]Stone effigies of knights, carved on church tombs.

[19]The Deluge of the days of Noah. Genesis 7.

more. Nevertheless, the name remains, and the nominal society, and the ancient grounds, and some of the ancient edifices. But the iron heel is changed to a boot of patent-leather; the long two-handed sword to a one-handed quill; the monk-giver of gratuitous ghostly counsel now counsels for a fee; the defender of the sarcophagus (if in good practice with his weapon) now has more than one case to defend; the vowed opener and clearer of all highways leading to the Holy Sepulchre,[20] now has it in particular charge to check, to clog, to hinder, and embarrass all the courts and avenues of Law; the knight-combatant of the Saracen,[21] breasting spear-points at Acre,[22] now fights law-points in Westminster Hall.[23] The helmet is a wig.[24] Struck by Time's enchanter's wand, the Templar is to-day a Lawyer.

But, like many others tumbled from proud glory's height—like the apple, hard on the bough but mellow on the ground—the Templar's fall has but made him all the finer fellow.

I dare say those old warrior-priests were but gruff and grouty at the best; cased in Birmingham hardware,[25] how could their crimped arms give yours or mine a hearty shake? Their proud, ambitious, monkish souls clasped shut, like horn-book missals;[26] their very faces clapped in bomb-shells;[27] what sort of genial men were these? But best of comrades, most affable of hosts, capital diner is the modern Templar. His wit and wine are both of sparkling brands.

The church and cloisters, courts and vaults,[28] lanes and passages, banquet-halls, refectories, libraries, terraces, gardens, broad walks, domicils, and dessert-rooms, covering a very large space of ground, and all grouped in central neighborhood, and quite sequestered from the old city's surrounding din; and every thing about the place being kept in most bachelor-like particularity, no part of London offers to a quiet wight so agreeable a refuge.

The Temple is, indeed, a city by itself. A city with all the best appurtenances, as the above enumeration shows. A city with a park to it, and flower-beds, and a river-wise—the Thames flowing by as openly, in one part, as by Eden's primal garden flowed the mild Euphrates. In what is now the Temple Garden the old Crusaders used to exercise their steeds and lances; the modern Templars now lounge on the benches beneath the trees, and, switching their patent-leather boots, in gay discourse exercise at repartee.

Long lines of stately portraits in the banquet-halls, show what great men of mark—famous nobles, judges, and Lord Chancellors—have in their time been Templars. But all Templars are not known to universal fame; though, if the having warm hearts and warmer welcomes, full minds and fuller cellars, and giving good advice and glorious dinners, spiced with rare divertisements

[20]The Roman Catholic church in Jerusalem, said to have been built on the site of the tomb of Jesus.

[21]Muslim.

[22]Seaport on the coast of Palestine. Its fortress, defended by the Knights Templar, was the last stronghold held by Christians in the Holy Land. It fell in 1291.

[23]London's Westminster Hall was used as a law court in the nineteenth century.

[24]English barristers (trial lawyers) wear wigs when appearing in court.

[25]English industrial city noted for its production of iron and steel.

[26]Devotional book pages mounted on a board and covered with a protective layer of transparent animal horn.

[27]A reference to the conical helmets worn by armored knights.

[28]Structure with an arched ceiling.

of fun and fancy, merit immortal mention, set down, ye muses, the names of R. F. C.[29] and his imperial brother.

Though to be a Templar, in the one true sense, you must needs be a lawyer, or a student at the law, and be ceremoniously enrolled as member of the order, yet as many such, though Templars, do not reside within the Temple's precincts, though they may have their offices there, just so, on the other hand, there are many residents of the hoary old domicils who are not admitted Templars. If being, say, a lounging gentleman and bachelor, or a quiet, unmarried, literary man, charmed with the soft seclusion of the spot, you much desire to pitch your shady tent among the rest in this serene encampment, then you must make some special friend among the order, and procure him to rent, in his name but at your charge, whatever vacant chamber you may find to suit.

Thus, I suppose, did Dr. Johnson,[30] that nominal Benedick and widower but virtual bachelor, when for a space he resided here. So, too, did that undoubted bachelor and rare good soul, Charles Lamb.[31] And hundreds more, of sterling spirits, Brethren of the Order of Celibacy, from time to time have dined, and slept, and tabernacled here. Indeed, the place is all a honeycomb of offices and domicils. Like any cheese, it is quite perforated through and through in all directions with the snug cells of bachelors. Dear, delightful spot! Ah! when I bethink me of the sweet hours there passed, enjoying such genial hospitalities beneath those time-honored roofs, my heart only finds due utterance through poetry; and, with a sigh, I softly sing, "Carry me back to old Virginny!"

Such then, at large, is the Paradise of Bachelors. And such I found it one pleasant afternoon in the smiling month of May, when, sallying from my hotel in Trafalgar Square,[32] I went to keep my dinner-appointment with that fine Barrister, Bachelor, and Bencher,[33] R. F. C. (he *is* the first and second, and *should be* the third; I hereby nominate him), whose card I kept fast pinched between my gloved forefinger and thumb, and every now and then snatched still another look at the pleasant address inscribed beneath the name, "No.—, Elm Court, Temple."

At the core he was a right bluff, care-free, right comfortable, and most companionable Englishman. If on a first acquaintance he seemed reserved, quite icy in his air—patience; this Champagne will thaw. And if it never do, better frozen Champagne than liquid vinegar.

There were nine gentlemen, all bachelors, at the dinner. One was from "No.—, King's Bench Walk, Temple;" a second, third, and fourth, and fifth, from various courts or passages christened with some similarly rich resounding syllables. It was indeed a sort of Senate of the Bachelors, sent to this dinner from widely-scattered districts, to represent the general celibacy of the Temple. Nay it was, by representation, a Grand Parliament of the best Bachelors in universal London; several of those present being from distant quarters of the town, noted immemorial seats of lawyers and unmarried men—Lincoln's Inn, Furnival's Inn;[34] and one gentleman, upon whom I looked

[29]Robert Francis Cooke, Melville's host at a bachelor dinner in London, December 1849.

[30]Samuel Johnson (1709–1784), English writer and dictionary maker.

[31]English essayist (1775–1834).

[32]Famous square in central London.

[33]One of the governors of an Inn of Court.

[34]One of the Inns of Chancery, attached to the Inns of Court, where legal professionals were trained but not qualified as trial lawyers.

with a sort of collateral awe, hailed from the spot where Lord Verulam[35] once abode a bachelor—Gray's Inn.

The apartment was well up toward heaven. I know not how many strange old stairs I climbed to get to it. But a good dinner, with famous company, should be well earned. No doubt our host had his dining-room so high with a view to secure the prior exercise necessary to the due relishing and digesting of it.

The furniture was wonderfully unpretending, old, and snug, No new shining mahogany, sticky with undried varnish; no uncomfortably luxurious ottomans, and sofas too fine to use, vexed you in this sedate apartment. It is a thing which every sensible American should learn from every sensible Englishman, that glare and glitter, gimcracks and gewgaws, are not indispensable to domestic solacement. The American Benedick snatches, down-town, a tough chop in a gilded show-box;[36] the English bachelor leisurely dines at home on that incomparable South Down[37] of his, off a plain deal board.[38]

The ceiling of the room was low. Who wants to dine under the dome of St. Peter's?[39] High ceilings! If that is your demand, and the higher the better, and you be so very tall, then go dine out with the topping giraffe in the open air.

In good time the nine gentlemen sat down to nine covers,[40] and soon were fairly under way.

If I remember right, ox-tail soup inaugurated the affair. Of a rich russet hue, its agreeable flavor dissipated my first confounding of its main ingredient with teamster's gads[41] and the raw-hides of ushers.[42] (By way of interlude, we here drank a little claret.) Neptune's was the next tribute rendered—turbot[43] coming second; snow-white, flaky, and just gelatinous enough, not too turtleish in its unctuousness.

(At this point we refreshed ourselves with a glass of sherry.) After these light skirmishers had vanished, the heavy artillery of the feast marched in, led by that well-known English generalissimo, roast beef. For aids-de-camp we had a saddle of mutton, a fat turkey, a chicken-pie, and endless other savory things; while for avant-couriers[44] came nine silver flagons of humming ale.[45] This heavy ordnance[46] having departed on the track of the light skirmishers, a picked brigade of game-fowl encamped upon the board, their camp-fires lit by the ruddiest of decanters.

Tarts and puddings followed, with innumerable niceties; then cheese and crackers. (By way of ceremony, simply, only to keep up good old fashions, we here each drank a glass of good old port.)

The cloth was now removed; and like Blucher's[47] army coming in at the death on the field of Waterloo, in marched a fresh detachment of bottles, dusty with their hurried march.

[35]Sir Francis Bacon (1561–1626), English philosopher, scientist, and writer.
[36]I.e., a fancy, overdecorated restaurant.
[37]Mutton, from the South Down breed of sheep.
[38]Wooden table.
[39]St. Peter's Church in Rome, the largest in the world. Its dome is 404 feet high.
[40]Table settings. [41]Goads, often made from oxtails.
[42]The ox-hide whips of teachers.
[43]Large flatfish. [44]The advanced guard of an army.
[45]Ale strong enough to cause a humming in the head. [46]Artillery, cannon.
[47]Gebhard Leberecht von Blucher (1742–1819), leader of Prussian forces in the defeat of Napoleon at Waterloo (1815).

All these manœvrings of the forces were superintended by a surprising old field-marshal (I can not school myself to call him by the inglorious name of waiter), with snowy hair and napkin, and a head like Socrates. Amidst all the hilarity of the feast, intent on important business, he disdained to smile. Venerable man!

I have above endeavored to give some slight schedule of the general plan of operations. But any one knows that a good, genial dinner is a sort of pell-mell, indiscriminate affair, quite baffling to detail in all particulars. Thus, I spoke of taking a glass of claret, and a glass of sherry, and a glass of port, and a mug of ale—all at certain specific periods and times. But those were merely the state bumpers,[48] so to speak. Innumerable impromptu glasses were drained between the periods of those grand imposing ones.

The nine bachelors seemed to have the most tender concern for each other's health. All the time, in flowing wine, they most earnestly expressed their sincerest wishes for the entire well-being and lasting hygiene of the gentlemen on the right and on the left. I noticed that when one of these kind bachelors desired a little more wine (just for his stomach's sake, like Timothy[49]), he would not help himself to it unless some other bachelor would join him. It seemed held something indelicate, selfish, and unfraternal, to be seen taking a lonely, unparticipated glass. Meantime, as the wine ran apace, the spirits of the company grew more and more to perfect genialness and unconstraint. They related all sorts of pleasant stories. Choice experiences in their private lives were now brought out, like choice brands of Moselle or Rhenish,[50] only kept for particular company. One told us how mellowly he lived when a student at Oxford; with various spicy anecdotes of most frank-hearted noble lords, his liberal companions. Another bachelor, a gray-headed man, with a sunny face, who, by his own account, embraced every opportunity of leisure to cross over into the Low Countries, on sudden tours of inspection of the fine old Flemish architecture there—this learned, white-haired, sunny-faced old bachelor, excelled in his descriptions of the elaborate splendors of those old guild-halls, town-halls, and stadthold-houses, to be seen in the land of the ancient Flemings. A third was a great frequenter of the British Museum, and knew all about scores of wonderful antiquities, of oriental manuscripts, and costly books without a duplicate. A fourth had lately returned from a trip to Old Granada,[51] and, of course, was full of Saracenic scenery. A fifth had a funny case in law to tell. A sixth was erudite in wines. A seventh had a strange characteristic anecdote of the private life of the Iron Duke,[52] never printed, and never before announced in any public or private company. An eighth had lately been amusing his evenings, now and then, with translating a comic poem of Pulci's.[53] He quoted for us the more amusing passages.

[48]Large drinking glasses filled to the brim.
[49]"Use a little wine for thy stomach's sake and thine often infirmities." I Timothy 5:23.
[50]Wines from the regions of the Moselle and the Rhine Rivers in Germany.
[51]Province of southern Spain, formerly a kingdom of the Muslim Moors.
[52]The Duke of Wellington (1769–1852), commander of British forces at Waterloo.
[53]Luigi Pulci (1432–1484), Florentine poet.

And so the evening slipped along, the hours told, not by a water-clock, like King Alfred's,[54] but a wind-chronometer. Meantime the table seemed a sort of Epsom Heath;[55] a regular ring, where the decanters galloped round. For fear one decanter should not with sufficient speed reach his destination, another was sent express after him to hurry him; and then a third to hurry the second; and so on with a fourth and fifth. And throughout all this nothing loud, nothing unmannerly, nothing turbulent. I am quite sure, from the scrupulous gravity and austerity of his air, that had Socrates, the field-marshal, perceived aught of indecorum in the company he served, he would have forthwith departed without giving warning. I afterward learned that, during the repast, an invalid bachelor in an adjoining chamber enjoyed his first sound refreshing slumber in three long, weary weeks.

It was the very perfection of quiet absorption of good living, good drinking, good feeling, and good talk. We were a band of brothers. Comfort—fraternal, household comfort, was the grand trait of the affair. Also, you could plainly see that these easy-hearted men had no wives or children to give an anxious thought. Almost all of them were travelers, too; for bachelors alone can travel freely, and without any twinges of their consciences touching desertion of the fire-side.

The thing called pain, the bugbear styled trouble—those two legends seemed preposterous to their bachelor imaginations. How could men of liberal sense, ripe scholarship in the world, and capacious philosophical and convivial understanding—how could they suffer themselves to be imposed upon by such monkish fables? Pain! Trouble! As well talk of Catholic miracles. No such thing.—Pass the sherry. Sir.—Pooh, pooh! Can't be!—The port, Sir, if you please. Nonsense; don't tell me so.—The decanter stops with you, Sir, I believe.

And so it went.

Not long after the cloth was drawn our host glanced significantly upon Socrates, who, solemnly stepping to a stand, returned with an immense convolved horn, a regular Jericho horn,[56] mounted with polished silver, and otherwise chased[57] and curiously enriched; not omitting two life-like goat's heads, with four more horns of solid silver, projecting from opposite sides of the mouth of the noble main horn.

Not having heard that our host was a performer on the bugle, I was surprised to see him lift this horn from the table, as if he were about to blow an inspiring blast. But I was relieved from this, and set quite right as touching the purposes of the horn, by his now inserting his thumb and forefinger into its mouth; whereupon a slight aroma was stirred up, and my nostrils were greeted with the smell of some choice Rappee.[58] It was a mull[59] of snuff. It went the rounds. Capital idea this, thought I, of taking snuff about this juncture. This goodly fashion must be introduced among my countrymen at home, further ruminated I.

[54]Alfred the Great (849–899), King of Wessex in England (871–899).
[55]Site of an English racetrack.
[56]The rams' horns that blasted the walls of Jericho. Joshua 6:2–20.
[57]Ornamented with hammered patterns. [58]Pungent snuff. [59]Small box.

The remarkable decorum of the nine bachelors—a decorum not to be affected by any quantity of wine—a decorum unassailable by any degree of mirthfulness—this was again set in a forcible light to me, by now observing that, though they took snuff very freely, yet not a man so far violated the properties, or so far molested the invalid bachelor in the adjoining room as to indulge himself in a sneeze. The snuff was snuffed silently, as if it had been some fine innoxious[60] powder brushed off the wings of butterflies.

But fine though they be, bachelors' dinners, like bachelors' lives, can not endure forever. The time came for breaking up. One by one the bachelors took their hats, and two by two, and arm-in-arm they descended, still conversing, to the flagging of the court; some going to their neighboring chambers to turn over the Decameron[61] ere retiring for the night; some to smoke a cigar, promenading in the garden on the cool river-side; some to make for the street, call a hack,[62] and be driven snugly to their distant lodgings.

I was the last lingerer.

"Well," said my smiling host, "what do you think of the Temple here, and the sort of life we bachelors make out to live in it?"

"Sir," said I, with a burst of admiring candor—"Sir, this is the very Paradise of Bachelors!"

II. The Tartarus of Maids

It lies not far from Woedolor Mountain in New England. Turning to the east, right out from among bright farms and sunny meadows, nodding in early June with odorous grasses, you enter ascendingly among bleak hills. These gradually close in upon a dusky pass, which, from the violent Gulf Stream of air unceasingly driving between its cloven walls of haggard rock, as well as from the tradition of a crazy spinster's hut having long ago stood somewhere hereabouts, is called the Mad Maid's Bellows'-pipe.

Winding along at the bottom of the gorge is a dangerously narrow wheel-road, occupying the bed of a former torrent. Following this road to its highest point, you stand as within a Dantean[1] gateway. From the steepness of the walls here, their strangely ebon hue, and the sudden contraction of the gorge, this particular point is called the Black Notch. The ravine now expandingly descends into a great, purple, hopper-shaped[2] hollow, far sunk among many Plutonian,[3] shaggy-wooded mountains. By the country people this hollow is called the Devil's Dungeon. Sounds of torrents fall on all sides upon the ear. These rapid waters unite at last in one turbid brick-colored stream, boiling through a flume among enormous boulders. They call this strange-colored torrent Blood River. Gaining a dark precipice it wheels suddenly to the west, and makes one maniac spring of sixty feet into the arms of a stunted wood of gray-haired pines, between which it thence eddies on its further way down to the invisible lowlands.

Conspicuously crowning a rocky bluff high to one side, at the cataract's verge, is the ruin of an old saw-mill, built in those primitive times when vast

[60]Harmless.
[61]Collection of romantic tales written by the Italian Giovanni Boccaccio (1313?–1375).
[62]Horse-drawn cab.
[1]In his *Inferno* the Italian poet Dante (1265–1321) described the entrance to Hell.
[2]Funnel-shaped. [3]Of the underworld, Hades, in Greek myth.

pines and hemlocks superabounded throughout the neighboring region. The black-mossed bulk of those immense, rough-hewn, and spike-knotted logs, here and there tumbled all together, in long abandonment and decay, or left in solitary, perilous projection over the cataract's gloomy brink, impart to this rude wooden ruin not only much of the aspect of one of rough-quarried stone, but also a sort of feudal, Rhineland, and Thurmberg[4] look, derived from the pinnacled wildness of the neighboring scenery.

Not far from the bottom of the Dungeon stands a large white-washed building, relieved, like some great whited sepulchre,[5] against the sullen background of mountain-side firs, and other hardy evergreens, inaccessibly rising in grim terraces for some two thousand feet.

The building is a paper-mill.

Having embarked on a large scale in the seedman's business (so extensively and broadcast, indeed, that at length my seeds were distributed through all the Eastern and Northern States, and even fell into the far soil of Missouri and the Carolinas), the demand for paper at my place became so great, that the expenditure soon amounted to a most important item in the general account. It need hardly be hinted how paper comes into use with seedsmen, as envelopes. These are mostly made of yellowish paper, folded square; and when filled, are all but flat, and being stamped, and superscribed with the nature of the seeds contained, assume not a little the appearance of business-letters ready for the mail. Of these small envelopes I used an incredible quantity—several hundreds of thousands in a year. For a time I had purchased my paper from the wholesale dealers in a neighboring town. For economy's sake, and partly for the adventure of the trip, I now resolved to cross the mountains, some sixty miles, and order my future paper at the Devil's Dungeon paper-mill.

The sleighing being uncommonly fine toward the end of January, and promising to hold so for no small period, in spite of the bitter cold I started one gray Friday noon in my pung,[6] well fitted with buffalo and wolf robes; and, spending one night on the road, next noon came in sight of Woedolor Mountain.

The far summit fairly smoked with frost; white vapors curled up from its white-wooded top, as from a chimney. The intense congelation made the whole country look like one petrifaction.[7] The steel shoes of my pung craunched and gritted over the vitreous, chippy snow, as if it had been broken glass. The forests here and there skirting the route, feeling the same all-stiffening influence, their inmost fibres penetrated with the cold, strangely groaned—not in the swaying branches merely, but likewise in the vertical trunk—as the fitful gusts remorselessly swept through them. Brittle with excessive frost, many colossal tough-grained maples, snapped in twain like pipe-stems, cumbered the unfeeling earth.

Flaked all over with frozen sweat, white as a milky ram, his nostrils at each breath sending forth two horn-shaped shoots of heated respiration, Black, my good horse, but six years old, started at a sudden turn, where, right across

[4]Valley and mountain wilderness.

[5]Matthew 23:27 describes "whited sepulchres" (tombs) that "appear beautiful outward, but are within full of dead men's bones, and of all uncleanness."

[6]A box-shaped sleigh with metal runners. [7]Stone creation.

the track—not ten minutes fallen—an old distorted hemlock lay, darkly undulatory as an anaconda.[8]

Gaining the Bellows'-pipe, the violent blast, dead from behind, all but shoved my high-backed pung up-hill. The gust shrieked through the shivered pass, as if laden with lost spirits bound to the unhappy world. Ere gaining the summit, Black, my horse, as if exasperated by the cutting wind, slung out with his strong hind legs, tore the light pung straight up-hill, and sweeping grazingly through the narrow notch, sped downward madly past the ruined saw-mill. Into the Devil's Dungeon horse and cataract rushed together.

With might and main, quitting my seat and robes, and standing backward, with one foot braced against the dash-board, I rasped and churned the bit, and stopped him just in time to avoid collision, at a turn, with the bleak nozzle of a rock, couchant[9] like a lion in the way—a road-side rock.

At first I could not discover the paper-mill.

The whole hollow gleamed with the white, except, here and there, where a pinnacle of granite showed one wind-swept angle bare. The mountains stood pinned in shrouds—a pass of Alpine corpses. Where stands the mill? Suddenly a whirling, humming sound broke upon my ear. I looked, and there, like an arrested avalanche, lay the large white-washed factory. It was subordinately surrounded by a cluster of other and smaller buildings, some of which, from their cheap, blank air, great length, gregarious windows, and comfortless expressions, no doubt were boarding-houses of the operatives.[10] A snow-white hamlet amidst the snows. Various rude, irregular squares and courts resulted from the somewhat picturesque clusterings of these buildings, owing to the broken, rocky nature of the ground, which forbade all method in their relative arrangement. Several narrow lanes and alleys, too, partly blocked with snow fallen from the roof, cut up the hamlet in all directions.

When, turning from the traveled highway, jingling with bells of numerous farmers—who, availing themselves of the fine sleighing, were dragging their wood to market—and frequently diversified with swift cutters dashing from inn to inn of the scattered villages—when, I say, turning from that bustling main-road, I by degrees wound into the Mad Maid's Bellows'-pipe, and saw the grim Black Notch beyond, then something latent, as well as something obvious in the time and scene, strangely brought back to my mind my first sight of dark and grimy Temple-Bar. And when Black, my horse, went darting through the Notch, perilously grazing its rocky wall, I remembered being in a runaway London omnibus, which in much the same sort of style, though by no means at an equal rate, dashed through the ancient arch of Wren.[11] Though the two objects did by no means completely correspond, yet this partial inadequacy but served to tinge the similitude not less with the vividness than the disorder of a dream. So that, when upon reining up at the protruding rock I at last caught sight of the quaint groupings of the factory-buildings, and with the traveled highway and the Notch behind, found myself all alone, silently and privily stealing through deep-cloven passages into this sequestered spot, and saw the long, high-gabled main factory edifice, with a

[8]Large South American snake that crushes its prey. [9]Crouching.
[10]Factory workers who operate machines.
[11]The Temple Bar, stone gateway that stood near the Inns of Court, designed by the English architect Sir Christopher Wren (1632–1723).

rude tower—for hoisting heavy boxes—at one end, standing among its crowded outbuildings and boarding-houses, as the Temple Church amidst the surrounding offices and dormitories, and when the marvelous retirement of this mysterious mountain nook fastened its whole spell upon me, then, what memory lacked, all tributary imagination furnished, and I said to myself, "This is the very counterpart of the Paradise of Bachelors, but snowed upon, and frost-painted to a sepulchre."

Dismounting, and warily picking my way down the dangerous declivity—horse and man both sliding now and then upon the icy ledges—at length I drove, or the blast drove me, into the largest square, before one side of the main edifice. Piercingly and shrilly the shotted blast blew by the corner; and redly and demoniacally boiled Blood River at one side. A long wood-pile, of many scores of cords, all glittering in mail of crusted ice, stood crosswise in the square. A row of horse-posts, their north sides plastered with adhesive snow, flanked the factory wall. The bleak frost packed and paved the square as with some ringing metal.

The inverted similitude recurred—"The sweet, tranquil Temple garden, with the Thames bordering its green beds," strangely meditated I.

But where are the gay bachelors?

Then, as I and my horse stood shivering in the wind-spray, a girl ran from a neighboring dormitory door, and throwing her thin apron over her bare head, made for the opposite building.

"One moment, my girl; is there no shed hereabouts which I may drive into?"

Pausing, she turned upon me a face pale with work, and blue with cold; an eye supernatural with related misery.

"Nay," faltered I, "I mistook you. Go on; I want nothing."

Leading my horse close to the door from which she had come, I knocked. Another pale, blue girl appeared, shivering in the doorway as, to prevent the blast, she jealously held the door ajar.

"Nay, I mistake again. In God's name shut the door. But hold, is there no man about?"

That moment a dark-complexioned well-wrapped personage passed, making for the factory door, and spying him coming, the girl rapidly closed the other one.

"Is there no horse-shed here, Sir?"

"Yonder to the wood-shed," he replied, and disappeared inside the factory.

With much ado I managed to wedge in horse and pung between the scattered piles of wood all sawn and split. Then, blanketing my horse, and piling my buffalo on the blanket's top, and tucking in its edges well around the breast-band and breeching, so that the wind might not strip him bare, I tied him fast, and ran lamely for the factory door, stiff with frost, and cumbered with my driver's dread-naught.[12]

Immediately I found myself standing in a spacious place, intolerably lighted by long rows of windows, focusing inward the snowy scene without.

At rows of blank-looking counters sat rows of blank-looking girls, with blank, white folders in their blank hands, all blankly folding blank paper.

[12]Heavy cloth coat.

In one corner stood some huge frame of ponderous iron, with a vertical thing like a piston periodically rising and falling upon a heavy wooden block. Before it—its tame minister—stood a tall girl, feeding the iron animal with half-quires[13] of rose-hued note paper, which, at every downward dab of the piston-like machine, received in the corner the impress of a wreath of roses. I looked from the rosy paper to the pallid cheek, but said nothing.

Seated before a long apparatus, strung with long, slender strings like any harp, another girl was feeding it with foolscap[14] sheets, which, so soon as they curiously traveled from her on the cords, were withdrawn at the opposite end of the machine by a second girl. They came to the first girl blank; they went to the second girl ruled.

I looked upon the first girl's brow, and saw it was young and fair; I looked upon the second girl's brow, and saw it was ruled and wrinkled. Then, as I still looked, the two—for some small variety to the monotony—changed places; and where had stood the young, fair brow, now stood the ruled and wrinkled one.

Perched high upon a narrow platform, and still higher upon a high stool crowning it, sat another figure serving some other iron animal; while below the platform sat her mate in some sort of reciprocal attendance.

Not a syllable was breathed. Nothing was heard but the low, steady, overruling hum of the iron animals. The human voice was banished from the spot. Machinery—that vaunted slave of humanity—here stood menially served by human beings, who served mutely and cringingly as the slave serves the Sultan. The girls did not so much seem accessory wheels to the general machinery as mere cogs to the wheels.

All this scene around me was instantaneously taken in at one sweeping glance—even before I had proceeded to unwind the heavy fur tippet[15] from around my neck. But as soon as this fell from me the dark-complexioned man, standing close by, raised a sudden cry, and seizing my arm, dragged me out into the open air, and without pausing for a word instantly caught up some congealed snow and began rubbing both my cheeks.

"Two white spots like the whites of your eyes," he said; "man, your cheeks are frozen."

"That may well be," muttered I; "'tis some wonder the frost of the Devil's Dungeon strikes in no deeper. Rub away."

Soon a horrible, tearing pain caught at my reviving cheeks. Two gaunt bloodhounds, one on each side, seemed mumbling[16] them. I seemed Actaeon.[17]

Presently, when all was over, I re-entered the factory, made known my business, concluded it satisfactorily, and then begged to be conducted throughout the place to view it.

"Cupid is the boy for that," said the dark-complexioned man. "Cupid!" and by this odd fancy-name calling a dimpled, red-cheeked, spirited-looking, forward little fellow, who was rather impudently, I thought, gliding about among the passive-looking girls—like a gold fish through hueless waves—yet doing

[13]Twelve sheets of paper.

[14]Paper sheets usually 16 × 13 inches, so-called from the conical fool's cap design often used as a watermark.

[15]Scarf, muffler. [16]Gnawing, chewing.

[17]Hunter in classical myth who was torn to pieces by his own dogs.

nothing in particular that I could see, the man bade him lead the stranger through the edifice.

"Come first and see the water-wheel," said this lively lad, with the air of boyishly-brisk importance.

Quitting the folding-room, we crossed some damp, cold boards, and stood beneath a great wet shed, incessantly showering with foam, like the green barnacled bow of some East Indiaman[18] in a gale. Round and round here went the enormous revolutions of the dark colossal water-wheel, grim with its one immutable purpose.

"This sets our whole machinery a-going, Sir; in every part of all these buildings; where the girls work and all."

I looked, and saw that the turbid waters of Blood River had not changed their hue by coming under the use of man.

"You make only blank paper; no printing of any sort, I suppose? All blank paper, don't you?"

"Certainly; what else should a paper-factory make?"

The lad here looked at me as if suspicious of my common-sense.

"Oh, to be sure!" said I, confused and stammering; "it only struck me as so strange that red waters should turn out pale chee—paper, I mean."

He took me up a wet and rickety stair to a great light room, furnished with no visible thing but rude, manger-like receptacles running all round its sides; and up to these mangers, like so many mares haltered to the rack, stood rows of girls. Before each was vertically thrust up a long, glittering scythe, immovably fixed at bottom to the manger-edge. The curve of the scythe, and its having no snath[19] to it, made it look exactly like a sword. To and fro, across the sharp edge, the girls forever dragged long strips of rags, washed white, picked from baskets at one side; thus ripping asunder every seam, and converting the tatters almost into lint. The air swam with the fine, poisonous particles, which from all sides darted, subtilely, as motes in sun-beams, into the lungs.

"This is the rag-room," coughed the boy.

"You find it rather stifling here," coughed I, in answer; "but the girls don't cough."

"Oh, they are used to it."

"Where do you get such hosts of rags?" picking up a handful from a basket.

"Some from the country round about; some from far over sea—Leghorn[20] and London."

"'Tis not unlikely, then," murmured I, "that among these heaps of rags there may be some old shirts, gathered from the dormitories of the Paradise of Bachelors. But the buttons are all dropped off. Pray, my lad, do you ever find any bachelor's buttons hereabouts?"

"None grow in this part of the country. The Devil's Dungeon is no place for flowers."

"Oh! you mean the *flowers* so called—the Bachelor's Buttons?"

"And was not that what you asked about? Or did you mean the gold bosom-buttons of our boss, Old Bach, as our whispering girls all call him?"

"The man, then, I saw below is a bachelor, is he?"

"Oh, yes, he's a Bach."

[18]Large sailing ship. [19]Scythe handle. [20]Italian seaport.

"The edges of those swords, they are turned outward from the girls, if I see right; but their rags and fingers fly so, I can not distinctly see."

"Turned outward."

Yes, murmured I to myself; I see it now; turned outward; and each erected sword is so borne, edge-outward, before each girl. If my reading fails me not, just so, of old, condemned state-prisoners went from the hall of judgment to their doom: an officer before, bearing a sword, its edge turned outward, in significance of their fatal sentence. So, through consumptive pallors[21] of this blank, raggy life, go these white girls to death.

"Those scythes look very sharp," again turning toward the boy.

"Yes; they have to keep them so. Look!"

That moment two of the girls, dropping their rags, plied each a whet-stone up and down the sword-blade. My unaccustomed blood curdled at the sharp shriek of the tormented steel.

Their own executioners; themselves whetting the very swords that slay them; meditated I.

"What makes those girls so sheet-white, my lad?"

"Why"—with a roguish twinkle, pure ignorant drollery, not knowing heartlessness—"I suppose the handling of such white bits of sheets all the time makes them so sheety."

"Let us leave the rag-room now, my lad."

More tragical and more inscrutably mysterious than any mystic sight, human or machine, throughout the factory, was the strange innocence of cruel-heartedness in this usage-hardened boy.

"And now," said he, cheerily, "I suppose you want to see our great machine, which cost us twelve thousand dollars only last autumn. That's the machine that makes the paper, too. This way, Sir."

Following him, I crossed a large, bespattered place, with two great round vats in it, full of a white, wet, woolly-looking stuff, not unlike the albuminous part of an egg, soft-boiled.

"There," said Cupid, tapping the vats carelessly, "these are the first beginnings of the paper; this white pulp you see. Look how it swims bubbling round and round, moved by the paddle here. From hence it pours from both vats into that one common channel yonder; and so goes, mixed up and leisurely, to the great machine. And now for that."

He led me into a room, stifling with a strange, blood-like, abdominal heat, as if here, true enough, were being finally developed the germinous particles lately seen.

Before me, rolled out like some long Eastern manuscript, lay stretched one continuous length of iron frame-work—multitudinous and mystical, with all sorts of rollers, wheels, and cylinders, in slowly-measured and unceasing motion.

"Here first comes the pulp now," said Cupid, pointing to the nighest end of the machine. "See; first it pours out and spreads itself upon this wide, sloping board; and then—look—slides, thin and quivering, beneath the first roller there. Follow on now, and see it as it slides from under that to the next

[21]The paleness that marks those suffering from consumption, tuberculosis.

cylinder. There; see how it has become just a very little less pulpy now. One step more, and it grows still more to some slight consistence. Still another cylinder, and it is so knitted—though as yet mere dragon-fly wing—that it forms an air-bridge here, like a suspended cobweb, between two more separated rollers; and flowing over the last one, and under again, and doubling about there out of sight for a minute among all those mixed cylinders you indistinctly see, it reappears here, looking now at last a little less like pulp and more like paper, but still quite delicate and defective yet awhile. But—a little further onward, Sir, if you please—here now, at this further point, it puts on something of a real look, as if it might turn out to be something you might possibly handle in the end. But it's not yet done, Sir. Good way to travel yet, and plenty more of cylinders must roll it."

"Bless my soul!" said I, amazed at the elongation, interminable convolutions, and deliberate slowness of the machine; "it must take a long time for the pulp to pass from end to end, and come out paper."

"Oh! not so long," smiled the precocious lad, with a superior and patronizing air; "only nine minutes. But look; you may try it for yourself. Have you a bit of paper? Ah! here's a bit on the floor. Now mark that with any word you please, and let me dab it on here, and we'll see how long before it comes out at the other end."

"Well, let me see," said I, taking out my pencil; "come, I'll mark it with your name."

Bidding me take out my watch, Cupid adroitly dropped the inscribed slip on an exposed part of the incipient mass.

Instantly my eye marked the second-hand on my dial-plate.

Slowly I followed the slip, inch by inch; sometimes pausing for full half a minute as it disappeared beneath inscrutable groups of the lower cylinders, but only gradually to emerge again; and so, on, and on, and on—inch by inch; now in open sight, sliding along like a freckle on the quivering sheet; and then again wholly vanished; and so, on, and on, and on—inch by inch; all the time the main sheet growing more and more to final firmness—when, suddenly, I saw a sort of paper-fall, not wholly unlike a water-fall; a scissory sound smote my ear, as of some cord being snapped; and down dropped an unfolded sheet of perfect foolscap, with my "Cupid" half faded out of it, and still moist and warm.

My travels were at an end, for here was the end of the machine.

"Well, how long was it?" said Cupid.

"Nine minutes to a second," replied I, watch in hand.

"I told you so."

For a moment a curious emotion filled me, not wholly unlike that which one might experience at the fulfillment of some mysterious prophecy. But how absurd, thought I again; the thing is a mere machine, the essence of which is unvarying punctuality and precision.

Previously absorbed by the wheels and cylinders, my attention was now directed to a sad-looking woman standing by.

"That is rather an elderly person so silently tending the machine-end here. She would not seem wholly used to it either."

"Oh," knowingly whispered Cupid, through the din, "she only came last week. She was a nurse formerly. But the business is poor in these parts, and she's left it. But look at the paper she is piling there."

"Ay, foolscap," handling the piles of moist, warm sheets, which continually were being delivered into the woman's waiting hands. "Don't you turn out any thing but foolscap at this machine?"

"Oh, sometimes, but not often, we turn out finer work—cream-laid and royal sheets, we call them. But foolscap being in chief demand, we turn out foolscap most."

It was very curious. Looking at that blank paper continually dropping, dropping, dropping, my mind ran on in wonderings of those strange uses to which those thousand sheets eventually would be put. All sorts of writings would be writ on those now vacant things—sermons, lawyers' briefs, physicians' prescriptions, love-letters, marriage certificates, bills of divorce, registers of births, death-warrants, and so on, without end. Then, recurring back to them as they here lay all blank, I could not but bethink me of that celebrated comparison of John Locke,[22] who, in demonstration of his theory that man had no innate ideas, compared the human mind at birth to a sheet of blank paper; something destined to be scribbled on, but what sort of characters no soul might tell.

Pacing slowly to and fro along the involved machine, still humming with its play, I was struck as well by the inevitability as the evolvement-power in all its motions.

"Does that thin cobweb there," said I, pointing to the sheet in its more imperfect stage, "does that never tear or break? It is marvelous fragile, and yet this machine it passes through is so mighty."

"It never is known to tear a hair's point."

"Does it never stop—get clogged?"

"No. It *must* go. The machinery makes it go just *so*; just that very way, and at that very pace you there plainly *see* it go. The pulp can't help going."

Something of awe now stole over me, as I gazed upon this inflexible iron animal. Always, more or less, machinery of this ponderous, elaborate sort strikes, in some moods, strange dread into the human heart, as some living, panting Behemoth might. But what made the thing I saw so specially terrible to me was the metallic necessity, the unbudging fatality which governed it. Though, here and there, I could not follow the thin, gauzy vail of pulp in the course of its more mysterious or entirely invisible advance, yet it was indubitable that, at those points where it eluded me, it still marched on in unvarying docility to the autocratic cunning of the machine. A fascination fastened on me. I stood spellbound and wandering in my soul. Before my eyes—there, passing in slow procession along the wheeling cylinders, I seemed to see, glued to the pallid incipience of the pulp, the yet more pallid faces of all the pallid girls I had eyed that heavy day. Slowly, mournfully, beseechingly, yet unresistingly, they gleamed along, their agony dimly outlined on the imperfect paper, like the print of the tormented face on the handkerchief of Saint Veronica.[23]

[22]English philosopher (1632–1704).

[23]According to legend the image of Christ appeared on the handkerchief given to him by St. Veronica to wipe his face as he carried the cross to his crucifixion.

"Halloa! the heat of the room is too much for you," cried Cupid, staring at me.

"No—I am rather chill, if any thing."

"Come out, Sir—out—out," and, with the protecting air of a careful father, the precocious lad hurried me outside.

In a few moments, feeling revived a little, I went into the folding-room—the first room I had entered, and where the desk for transacting business stood, surrounded by the blank counters and blank girls engaged at them.

"Cupid here has led me a strange tour," said I to the dark-complexioned man before mentioned, whom I had ere this discovered not only to be an old bachelor, but also the principal proprietor. "Yours is a most wonderful factory. Your great machine is a miracle of inscrutable intricacy."

"Yes, all our visitors think it so. But we don't have many. We are in a very out-of-the-way corner here. Few inhabitants, too. Most of our girls come from far-off villages."

"The girls," echoed I, glancing round at their silent forms. "Why is it, Sir, that in most factories, female operatives, of whatever age, are indiscriminately called girls, never women?"

"Oh! as to that—why, I suppose, the fact of their being generally unmarried—that's the reason, I should think. But it never struck me before. For our factory here, we will not have married women; they are apt to be off-and-on too much. We want none but steady workers: twelve hours to the day, day after day, through the three hundred and sixty-five days, excepting Sundays, Thanksgiving, and Fast-days. That's our rule. And so, having no married women, what females we have are rightly enough called girls."

"Then these are all maids," said I, while some pained homage to their pale virginity made me involuntarily bow.

"All maids."

Again the strange emotion filled me.

"Your cheeks look whitish yet, Sir," said the man, gazing at me narrowly. "You must be careful going home. Do they pain you at all now? It's a bad sign, if they do."

"No doubt, Sir," answered I, "when once I have got out of the Devil's Dungeon, I shall feel them mending."

"Ah, yes; the winter air in valleys, or gorges, or any sunken place, is far colder and more bitter than elsewhere. You would hardly believe it now, but it is colder here than at the top of Woedolor Mountain."

"I dare say it is, Sir. But time presses me; I must depart."

With that, remuffling myself in dread-naught and tippet, thrusting my hands into my huge seal-skin mittens, I sallied out into the nipping air, and found poor Black, my horse, all cringing and doubled up with the cold.

Soon, wrapped in furs and meditations, I ascended from the Devil's Dungeon.

At the Black Notch I paused, and once more bethought me of Temple-Bar. Then, shooting through the pass, all alone with inscrutable nature, I exclaimed—Oh! Paradise of Bachelors! and oh! Tartarus of Maids!

1853? 1855

THE PORTENT[1]

(1859)

Hanging from the beam,
  Slowly swaying (such the law),
Gaunt the shadow on your green,
  Shenandoah![2]
The cut is on the crown[3]
(Lo, John Brown),
And the stabs shall heal no more.

Hidden in the cap[4]
  Is the anguish none can draw;
So your future veils its face,
  Shenandoah!
But the streaming beard is shown[5]
(Weird[6] John Brown),
The meteor[7] of the war.
1859 1866

SHILOH[1]

A REQUIEM

(April 1862)

Skimming lightly, wheeling still,
  The swallows fly low
Over the field in clouded days,
  The forest-field of Shiloh—
Over the field where April rain
Solaced the parched ones stretched in pain

[1]An omen of evil to come. In October 1859, the abolitionist John Brown incited a slave rebellion and led an attack on the Federal Arsenal at Harpers Ferry, Virginia (now West Virginia). Captured and convicted of treason, he was hanged in 1859. His acts were widely seen as a portent of civil war.

[2]Brown was executed at Charlestown, in the Shenandoah Valley.

[3]Brown received a head wound when captured.

[4]Hood placed over the head of the condemned.

[5]Brown's beard extended below the execution hood.

[6]Extraordinary, fantastic.

[7]In folklore, meteors were taken as omens of plague, war, and disaster.

[1]Site of a bloody Civil War battle in western Tennessee, April 6–7, 1862.

Through the pause of night
That followed the Sunday fight
Around the church of Shiloh[2]—
The church so lone, the log-built one,
That echoed to many a parting groan
And natural prayer
Of dying foemen mingled there—
Foemen at morn, but friends at eve—
Fame or country least their care
(What like a bullet can undeceive!)
But now they lie low,
While over them the swallows skim,
And all is hushed at Shiloh.

1862 1866

MALVERN HILL[1]

(July 1862)

Ye elms that wave on Malvern Hill
In prime of morn and May,
Recall ye how McClellan's men
Here stood at bay?
While deep within yon forest dim
Our rigid comrades lay—
Some with the cartridge in their mouth,[2]
Others with fixed arms lifted South[3]—
Invoking so
The cypress glades? Ah wilds of woe!

The spires of Richmond, late beheld
Through rifts in musket-haze
Were closed from view in clouds of dust
On leaf-walled ways,

[2]The second day of battle centered around a log church.

[1]At Malvern Hill, Virginia, in the last action of the Seven Days' Battle (June 25–July 1, 1862), Union forces under General George McClellan repulsed the attacks of Confederate forces under General Robert E. Lee in one of the bloodiest battles of the American Civil War.

[2]Civil War muzzle-loading rifles used a paper-wrapped cartridge containing powder and ball. To load his weapon, a rifleman bit open the paper, emptied the powder into the barrel, and then rammed home the ball.

[3]Weapons readied and aimed toward the South.

Where streamed our wagons in caravan;
And the Seven Nights and Days
Of march and fast, retreat and fight,
Pinched our grimed faces to ghastly plight—
Does the elm wood
Recall the haggard beards of blood?

The battle-smoked flag, with stars eclipsed,
We followed (it never fell!)—
In silence husbanded our strength—
Received their yell;
Till on this slope we patient turned
With cannon ordered well;
Reverse we proved was not defeat;
But ah, the sod what thousands meet!—
Does Malvern Wood
Bethink itself, and muse and brood?

We elms of Malvern Hill
Remember every thing;
But sap the twig will fill:
Wag the world how it will,
Leaves must be green in Spring.

1862 1866

THE COLLEGE COLONEL[1]

He rides at their head;
A crutch[2] by his saddle just slants in view,
One slung arm is in splints, you see,
Yet he guides his strong steed—how coldly too.

He brings his regiment home—
Not as they filed two years before,
But a remnant half-tattered, and battered, and worn,
Like castaway sailors, who—stunned
By the surf's loud roar,
Their mates dragged back and seen no more—
Again and again breast the surge,
And at last crawl, spent, to shore.

[1]In 1863, when Melville was living in Pittsfield, Massachusetts, the town honored William Francis Bartlett, who had left Harvard, had enlisted in the Union Army, and had risen to the rank of colonel. In preparing the poem for publication in 1866, Melville added references to Bartlett's war experiences after 1863.

[2]Bartlett had lost a leg in battle.

A still rigidity and pale—
  An Indian aloofness lones his brow;
He has lived a thousand years
Compressed in battle's pains and prayers,
  Marches and watches slow.
There are welcome shouts, and flags;
  Old men off hat to the Boy,
Wreaths from gay balconies fall at his feet,
  But to *him*—there comes alloy.

It is not that a leg is lost,
  It is not that an arm is maimed,
It is not that the fever has racked—
  Self he has long disclaimed.

But all through the Seven Days' Fight,
  And deep in the Wilderness[3] grim,
And in the field-hospital tent.
  And Petersburg crater,[4] and dim
Lean brooding in Libby,[5] there came—
  Ah heaven!—what *truth* to him.

1866

THE ÆOLIAN HARP[1]

AT THE SURF INN

List the harp in window wailing
  Stirred by fitful gales from sea:
Shrieking up in mid crescendo—
  Dying down in plaintive key!

Listen: less a strain ideal
  Than Ariel's[2] rendering of the Real.
What that Real is, let hint
  A picture stamped in memory's mint.

[3]The Civil War Battle of the Wilderness, in Virginia, May 1864.

[4]Scene of the Battle of the Crater (July 1864), which followed the explosion of a gigantic mine under the Confederate lines during the siege of Petersburg, Virginia.

[5]Bartlett was captured in Petersburg and held in the Confederate Libby Prison at Richmond.

[1]Musical instrument that sounds when the wind strikes its strings.

[2]The airy spirit in Shakespeare's *The Tempest*.

Braced well up, with beams aslant,
Betwixt the continents sails the *Phocion*,
For Baltimore bound from Alicant.[3]
Blue breezy skies with fleeces fleck
Over the chill blue white-capped ocean:
From yard-arm comes—"Wreck ho, a wreck!"

Dismasted and adrift,
Long time a thing forsaken;
Overwashed by every wave
Like the slumbering kraken;[4]
Heedless if the billow roar,
Oblivious of the lull,
Leagues and leagues from shoal or shore,
It swims—a levelled hull:
Bulwarks gone—a shaven wreck,
Nameless, and a grass-green deck.
A lumberman: perchance, in hold
Prostrate pines with hemlocks rolled.

It has drifted, waterlogged,
Till by trailing weeds beclogged:
    Drifted, drifted, day by day,
    Pilotless on pathless way.
It has drifted till each plank
Is oozy as the oyster-bank:
    Drifted, drifted, night by night,
    Craft that never shows a light;
Nor ever, to prevent worse knell,
Tolls in fog the warning bell.
From collision never shrinking,
Drive what may through darksome smother;
Saturate, but never sinking,
Fatal only to the *other!*
    Deadlier than the sunken reef
Since still the snare it shifteth,
    Torpid in dumb ambuscade
Waylayingly it drifteth.

O, the sailors—O, the sails!
O, the lost crews never heard of!
Well the harp of Ariel wails
Thoughts that tongue can tell no word of!

1888

[3]Alicante, seaport in Spain.
[4]Legendary sea monster.

THE TUFT OF KELP[1]

All dripping in tangles green,
Cast up by a lonely sea,
If purer for that, O Weed,
Bitter, too, are ye?

1888

THE MALDIVE SHARK

About the Shark, phlegmatical one,
Pale sot[1] of the Maldive sea,[2]
The sleek little pilot-fish, azure and slim,
How alert in attendance be.
From his saw-pit of mouth, from his charnel of maw
They have nothing of harm to dread,
But liquidly glide on his ghastly flank
Or before his Gorgonian[3] head;
Or lurk in the port of serrated teeth
In white triple tiers of glittering gates,
And there find a haven when peril's abroad,
An asylum in jaws of the Fates!
They are friends; and friendly they guide him to prey,
Yet never partake of the treat—
Eyes and brains to the dotard lethargic and dull,
Pale ravener of horrible meat.

1888

THE BERG

A DREAM

I saw a ship of martial build
(Her standards[1] set, her brave apparel on)
Directed as by madness mere
Against a stolid iceberg steer,

[1]Seaweed.
[1]A lash or scourge—an instrument of punishment and torture.
[2]Off the Maldive Islands in the Indian Ocean.
[3]The Gorgons in Greek myth had hideous faces that petrified onlookers.
[1]Flags.

Nor budge it, though the infatuate[2] ship went down.
The impact made huge ice-cubes fall
Sullen, in tons that crashed the deck;
But that one avalanche was all—
No other movement save the foundering wreck.

Along the spurs of ridges pale,
Not any slenderest shaft and frail,
A prism over glass-green gorges lone,
Toppled; nor lace of traceries fine,
Nor pendant drops in grot[3] or mine
Were jarred, when the stunned ship went down.
Nor sole[4] the gulls in cloud that wheeled
Circling one snow-flanked peak afar,
But nearer fowl the floes that skimmed
And crystal beaches, felt no jar.
Nor thrill[5] transmitted stirred the lock
Of jack-straw needle-ice at base;
Towers undermined by waves—the block
Atilt impending—kept their place.
Seals, dozing sleek on sliddery[6] ledges
Slip never, when by loftier edges
Through very inertia overthrown,
The impetuous ship in bafflement went down.

Hard Berg (methought), so cold, so vast,
With mortal damps self-overcast;
Exhaling still thy darkish breath—
Adrift dissolving, bound for death;
Though lumpish thou, a lumbering one—
A lumbering lubbard[7] loitering slow,
Impingers rue thee and go down,
Sounding thy precipice below,
Nor stir the slimy slug that sprawls
Along thy dead indifference of walls.

1888

ART

In placid hours well-pleased we dream
Of many a brave unbodied scheme.
But form to lend, pulsed life create,
What unlike things must meet and mate:

[2]Foolish, confused. [3]Grotto. [4]Not only.
[5]Shudder, tremble. [6]Slippery. [7]A clumsy oaf.

A flame to melt—a wind to freeze;
Sad patience—joyous energies;
Humility—yet pride and scorn;
Instinct and study; love and hate;
Audacity—reverence. These must mate,
And fuse with Jacob's mystic heart,
To wrestle with the angel[1]—Art.

1891

GREEK ARCHITECTURE

Not magnitude, not lavishness,
But Form—the Site;
Not innovating wilfulness,
But reverence for the Archetype.

1891

Henry David Thoreau 1817–1862

During his lifetime, Henry David Thoreau published only two books, Walden *(1854) and* A Week on the Concord and Merrimack Rivers *(1849). Both sold poorly. In eight years* Walden *sold fewer than 2,000 copies. Sale of* A Week on the Concord and Merrimack Rivers *totaled little more than 200, and so many unsold volumes were returned to Thoreau (who had paid for their publication) that he was moved to write in his* Journal, *"I have now a library of nearly nine hundred volumes, over seven hundred of which I wrote myself."*

Thoreau's failures confirmed the views of many of his neighbors in Concord, Massachusetts, who considered him a loafer and a cranky eccentric. Yet Thoreau considered Concord, where he was born and spent most of his life, "the most estimable place in all the world." Thoreau's grandfather, a successful merchant, had moved his family to Concord from Boston in 1800, but his descendants failed to prosper. Thoreau's father, an unsuccessful storekeeper and later a pencilmaker, was amiable and meek, a passive little man who cherished peace and ease and had little in common with his strong-willed son Henry. Thoreau's mother was large and dynamic, a reform-minded woman who dominated her family. She encouraged her children to share her own deep interest

[1]Jacob wrestled with an angel and won a blessing. Genesis 32:24–30.

in nature and stirred in them ambitions to learn. In school, her son Henry was judged to be "an odd stick, not very studious," but his mother was determined that he would go to college, and when he was eleven he was enrolled in Concord Academy, a college preparatory school. Five years later he entered Harvard College.

In the 1830s, student life and the curriculum at Harvard were narrowly restricted, but Thoreau maintained his independent ways and his critical judgment: College regulations required students to wear black coats. Thoreau wore green. When later told by Emerson that Harvard taught most of the branches of learning, Thoreau replied, "all the branches and none of the roots." And of the parchment diplomas earned by Harvard graduates he once observed, "Let every sheep keep but his own skin, I say."

Thoreau was remembered as a student who displayed such "oddity in literary matters that his writings will never probably do him any justice." Many of his classmates thought him smug and filled with "Concord conceit," for Thoreau much preferred Concord to Cambridge or the busy world of Boston. And after graduating from Harvard in 1837 he returned to Concord, where he worked with his father in making and peddling pencils. From 1838 to 1841 he ran a private school, and he developed a friendship with Concord's most famous resident, Ralph Waldo Emerson. Thoreau readily absorbed Emerson's transcendentalist doctrines, becoming a member of the informal Transcendentalist Club that met in Emerson's home. For two years (1841–1843) he lived with the Emerson family, earning his room and board by working as a handyman.

In 1844 Emerson purchased some land on the shore of Walden Pond, just south of Concord Village. There, with Emerson's agreement, Thoreau began to build a cabin in March 1845. Four months later, on July 4, Independence Day, he moved in and "commenced housekeeping." For two years and two months Thoreau remained at Walden with the intention of living simply and cheaply while writing the description of a trip he had taken in 1839 on the Concord and Merrimack Rivers.

Thoreau left his cabin at Walden in September 1847, recalling later "I had several more lives to live and could not spare any more for that one," but it was at Walden Pond that he had begun his greatest work, Walden. *Portions of the manuscript were completed by early 1847. Thoreau hoped to publish it in 1849, but his first book,* A Week on the Concord and Merrimack Rivers, *had appeared and had failed, and no publisher would accept the new one. Thoreau then turned to revising* Walden. *He polished and expanded it for five more years, until it was finally published in 1854. It was also during Thoreau's stay at Walden that he was arrested and jailed for his refusal to pay his poll tax of $1.50. His imprisonment lasted only one night, but it inspired the writing of his most famous single essay, "Civil Disobedience."*

Much of Thoreau's work appeared in the transcendentalist journal, The Dial, *which he helped edit. Many of his essays were originally designed for delivery as lectures. Since 1838 he had frequently spoken before the Concord Lyceum, and he had traveled as far north as Portland, Maine, and as far south as Philadelphia to speak to similar groups. But he achieved little success on the lecture platform, for he was a poor speaker and often more interested in the sound of his own words than in the reactions of his audience. In* Walden *Thoreau announced, "I have traveled a good deal in Concord." He had also traveled as far west as Minnesota, but he remained a New Englander and spent most of his life within a few miles of Concord, where he was born and where he died when he was forty-five.*

For half a century after his death, Thoreau was largely consigned to obscurity as an insignificant eccentric among American writers. He was thought to be a "pale shadow" of Emerson, a mere woodsman and hermit whose nature writing was frequently marred by tedious moralizing. Lowell thought that Thoreau was provincial, lacked humor, and displayed "perversity of thought." Holmes called him a "nullifier of civilization," and Whittier thought that Thoreau's masterpiece, Walden, *was "wicked and heathenish." But since his death, Thoreau's reputation has steadily and, in recent years, dramatically risen. His writings, most of them gathered and published posthumously, have appeared in hundreds of editions and translations. He is now more widely read and vastly more influential than any other transcendentalist, including Emerson, whose mere disciple Thoreau was once thought to be.*

Thoreau's appeal to modern generations springs not only from his power with words but from the relevance of his ideas. His celebration of nature and his call to "simplify" have stirred countless readers who yearn to escape a society that is glutted with gadgetry and destroys nature in the name of progress. He has become a patron saint to those who feel that cause of conscience is more important than the laws devised by man. His "Civil Disobedience" has provided a philosophy and a handbook for movements of passive resistance throughout the world.

Thoreau himself objected to organized resistance as much as to organized institutions. He argued not for a change of governments but a change of individual lives. He was seldom a member of any formal group. He opposed slavery but was not an abolitionist, and with few exceptions he despised meddling reformers. Thoreau saw the futility at the core of most human endeavors; he had a poor opinion of his fellow men and avoided them when he could, which has inspired his detractors to judge him an eccentric collector of grievances against humanity and humanity's fabrications—civilization, religion, art. Walden *has been considered the work of an arrogant preacher, a pantheistic egotist, an antic stranger opposed to stability and order. Yet it remains a literary masterpiece, a great document of social dissent, and a spiritual testament that each year "seems to gain a little headway, as the world loses ground."*

FURTHER READING: *The Writings of Henry D. Thoreau,* 12 vols., ed. W. Harding, et al., 1971–1997; *The Journal of Henry D. Thoreau,* 2 vols., ed. B. Torrey and F. Allen, 1906, 1962; *Collected Poems of Henry Thoreau,* ed. C. Bode, 1943, 1964, 1974; R. Richardson, *Henry Thoreau, A Life of the Mind,* 1986; R. Schneider, *Henry David Thoreau,* 1987; R. Sattelmeyer, *Thoreau's Reading,* 1988; L. Neufeldt, *The Economist, Henry Thoreau and Enterprise,* 1989; H. Peck, *Thoreau's Morning Work,* 1990; G. Boudreau, *The Roots of Walden and the Tree of Life,* 1990; R. Borst, *The Thoreau Log, A Documentary Life,* 1992; *The Cambridge Companion to Henry David Thoreau,* ed. J. Myerson, 1995; B. Pepperman, *America's Bachelor Uncle, Thoreau and American Polity,* 1996; L. Owing, *Quest for Walden,* 1998; W. Cain, *A Historical Guide to Thoreau,* 2000; A. Hodder, *Thoreau's Ecstatic Witness,* 2001.

TEXT: *The Writings of Henry David Thoreau,* 20 vols., 1906.

CIVIL DISOBEDIENCE[1]

I heartily accept the motto, "That government is best which governs least;"[2] and I should like to see it acted up to more rapidly and systematically. Carried out, it finally amounts to this, which also I believe,—"That government

[1]First published as "Resistance to Civil Government," in a short-lived periodical, *Aesthetic Papers* (May 14, 1849), edited by the transcendentalist Elizabeth Peabody, Hawthorne's sister-in-law. Under its present title the essay was first published posthumously in *A Yankee in Canada* (1866).

[2]The idea expressed in the motto was a common one at the time. In his *First Inaugural Address* (1801), Jefferson advocated a government that would leave men "free to regulate their own pursuits." In *Politics* (1841) Emerson had written "The less government we have the better." Thoreau derived his motto from the words on the masthead of the *United States Magazine and Democratic Review,* a New York monthly.

is best which governs not at all;" and when men are prepared for it, that will be the kind of government which they will have. Government is at best but an expedient; but most governments are usually, and all governments are sometimes, inexpedient. The objections which have been brought against a standing army, and they are many and weighty, and deserve to prevail, may also at last be brought against a standing government. The standing army is only an arm of the standing government. The government itself, which is only the mode which the people have chosen to execute their will, is equally liable to be abused and perverted before the people can act through it. Witness the present Mexican war,[3] the work of comparatively a few individuals using the standing government as their tool; for, in the outset, the people would not have consented to this measure.

This American government,—what is it but a tradition, though a recent one, endeavoring to transmit itself unimpaired to posterity, but each instant losing some of its integrity? It has not the vitality and force of a single living man; for a single man can bend it to his will. It is a sort of wooden gun to the people themselves. But it is not the less necessary for this; for the people must have some complicated machinery or other, and hear its din, to satisfy that idea of government which they have. Governments show thus how successfully men can be imposed on, even impose on themselves, for their own advantage. It is excellent, we must all allow. Yet this government never of itself furthered any enterprise, but by the alacrity with which it got out of its way. *It* does not keep the country free. *It* does not settle the West. *It* does not educate. The character inherent in the American people has done all that has been accomplished; and it would have done somewhat more, if the government had not sometimes got in its way. For government is an expedient by which men would fain succeed in letting one another alone; and, as has been said, when it is most expedient, the governed are most let alone by it. Trade and commerce, if they were not made of India-rubber, would never manage to bounce over the obstacles which legislators are continually putting in their way; and, if one were to judge these men wholly by the effects of their actions and not partly by their intentions, they would deserve to be classed and punished with those mischievous persons who put obstructions on the railroads.

But, to speak practically and as a citizen, unlike those who call themselves no-government men, I ask for, not at once no government, but *at once* a better government. Let every man make known what kind of government would command his respect, and that will be one step toward obtaining it.

After all, the practical reason why, when the power is once in the hands of the people, a majority are permitted, and for a long period continue, to rule is not because they are most likely to be in the right, nor because this seems fairest to the minority, but because they are physically the strongest. But a government in which the majority rule in all cases cannot be based on justice, even as far as men understand it. Can there not be a government in which majorities do not virtually decide right and wrong, but conscience?—

[3]Thoreau wrote "Civil Disobedience" at the time of the Mexican War (1846–1848), a war which many New Englanders saw as a stratagem to aid the spread of Southern slavery. The essay was first presented as a lecture at the Concord Lyceum on January 26, 1848, under the title "The Rights and Duties of the Individual in Relation to Government."

in which majorities decide only those questions to which the rule of expediency is applicable? Must the citizen ever for a moment, or in the least degree, resign his conscience to the legislator? Why has every man a conscience, then? I think that we should be men first, and subjects afterward. It is not desirable to cultivate a respect for the law, so much as for the right. The only obligation which I have a right to assume is to do at any time what I think right. It is truly enough said that a corporation has no conscience; but a corporation of conscientious men is a corporation *with* a conscience. Law never made men a whit more just; and, by means of their respect for it, even the well-disposed are daily made the agents of injustice. A common and natural result of an undue respect for law is, that you may see a file of soldiers, colonel, captain, corporal, privates, powder-monkeys,[4] and all, marching in admirable order over hill and dale to the wars, against their wills, ay, against their common sense and consciences, which makes it very steep marching indeed, and produces a palpitation of the heart. They have no doubt that it is a damnable business in which they are concerned; they are all peaceably inclined. Now, what are they? Men at all? or small movable forts and magazines, at the service of some unscrupulous man in power? Visit the Navy-Yard,[5] and behold a marine, such a man as an American government can make, or such as it can make a man with its black arts,—a mere shadow and reminiscence of humanity, a man laid out alive and standing, and already, as one may say, buried under arms with funeral accompaniments, though it may be,—

> "Not a drum was heard, not a funeral note,
> As his corse[6] to the rampart we hurried;
> Not a soldier discharged his farewell shot
> O'er the grave where our hero we buried."[7]

The mass of men serve the state thus, not as men mainly, but as machines, with their bodies. They are the standing army, and the militia, jailers, constables, *posse comitatus*,[8] etc. In most cases there is no free exercise whatever of the judgment or of the moral sense; but they put themselves on a level with wood and earth and stones; and wooden men can perhaps be manufactured that will serve the purpose as well. Such command no more respect than men of straw or a lump of dirt. They have the same sort of worth only as horses and dogs. Yet such as these even are commonly esteemed good citizens. Others—as most legislators, politicians, lawyers, ministers, and office-holders—serve the state chiefly with their heads; and, as they rarely make any moral distinctions, they are as likely to serve the devil, without *intending* it, as God. A very few—as heroes, patriots, martyrs, reformers in the great sense, and *men*—serve the state with their consciences also, and so necessarily resist it for the most part; and they are commonly treated as enemies by it. A wise man will only be useful as a man, and will

[4]Boys who carried gunpowder to cannon.

[5]Presumably a reference to the U.S. Navy Yard in Boston, Massachusetts. [6]Corpse.

[7]From "The Burial of Sir John Moore at Corunna" (1817), by Charles Wolfe (1791–1823), Irish poet.

[8]Citizens authorized to help keep the peace—a sheriff's "posse."

not submit to be "clay," and "stop a hole to keep the wind away,"[9] but leave that office to his dust at least:—

> "I am too high-born to be propertied,
> To be a secondary at control,
> Or useful serving-man and instrument
> To any sovereign state throughout the world."[10]

He who gives himself entirely to his fellow-men appears to them useless and selfish; but he who gives himself partially to them is pronounced a benefactor and philanthropist.

How does it become a man to behave toward this American government to-day? I answer, that he cannot without disgrace be associated with it. I cannot for an instant recognize that political organization as *my* government which is the *slave's* government also.

All men recognize the right of revolution; that is, the right to refuse allegiance to, and to resist, the government, when its tyranny or its inefficiency are great and unendurable. But almost all say that such is not the case now. But such was the case, they think, in the Revolution of '75.[11] If one were to tell me that this was a bad government because it taxed certain foreign commodities brought to its ports, it is most probable that I should not make an ado about it, for I can do without them. All machines have their friction; and possibly this does enough good to counterbalance the evil. At any rate, it is a great evil to make a stir about it. But when the friction comes to have its machine, and oppression and robbery are organized, I say, let us not have such a machine any longer. In other words, when a sixth of the population of a nation which has undertaken to be the refuge of liberty are slaves, and a whole country[12] is unjustly overrun and conquered by a foreign army, and subjected to military law, I think that it is not too soon for honest men to rebel and revolutionize. What makes this duty the more urgent is the fact that the country so overrun is not our own, but ours is the invading army.

Paley,[13] a common authority with many on moral questions, in his chapter on the "Duty of Submission to Civil Government," resolves all civil obligation into expediency; and he proceeds to say that "so long as the interest of the whole society requires it, that is, so long as the established government cannot be resisted or changed without public inconveniency, it is the will of God . . . that the established government be obeyed,—and no longer. This principle being admitted, the justice of every particular case of resistance is reduced to a computation of the quantity of the danger and grievance on the one side, and of the probability and expense of redressing it on the other." Of this, he says, every man shall judge for himself. But Paley appears never to have contemplated those cases to which the rule of expediency does not apply, in which a people, as well as an individual, must do justice, cost what it

[9] "Imperious Caesar, dead and turn'd to clay, / Might stop a hole to keep the wind away." *Hamlet,* Act V, Scene i, lines 236–237.

[10] *King John,* Act V, Scene ii, lines 79–82.

[11] The American Revolution (1775–1783).

[12] Mexico.

[13] William Paley (1743–1805), English theologian, author of *Principles of Moral and Political Philosophy* (1785), which Thoreau quotes.

may. If I have unjustly wrested a plank from a drowning man, I must restore it to him though I drown myself. This, according to Paley, would be inconvenient. But he that would save his life, in such a case, shall lose it.[14] This people must cease to hold slaves, and to make war on Mexico, though it cost them their existence as a people.

In their practice, nations agree with Paley; but does any one think that Massachusetts does exactly what is right at the present crisis?

> "A drab of state, a cloth-o'-silver slut,
> To have her train borne up, and her soul trail in the dirt."[15]

Practically speaking, the opponents to a reform in Massachusetts are not a hundred thousand politicians at the South, but a hundred thousand merchants and farmers here, who are more interested in commerce and agriculture than they are in humanity, and are not prepared to do justice to the slave and to Mexico, *cost what it may.* I quarrel not with far-off foes, but with those who, near at home, coöperate with, and do the bidding of, those far away, and without whom the latter would be harmless. We are accustomed to say, that the mass of men are unprepared; but improvement is slow, because the few are not materially wiser or better than the many. It is not so important that many should be as good as you, as that there be some absolute goodness somewhere; for that will leaven the whole lump.[16] There are thousands who are *in opinion* opposed to slavery and to the war, who yet in effect do nothing to put an end to them; who, esteeming themselves children of Washington and Franklin, sit down with their hands in their pockets, and say that they know not what to do, and do nothing; who even postpone the question of freedom to the question of free trade, and quietly read the prices-current along with the latest advices[17] from Mexico, after dinner, and, it may be, fall asleep over them both. What is the price-current of an honest man and patriot to-day? They hesitate, and they regret, and sometimes they petition; but they do nothing in earnest and with effect. They will wait, well disposed, for others to remedy the evil, that they may no longer have it to regret. At most, they give only a cheap vote, and a feeble countenance and God-speed, to the right, as it goes by them. There are nine hundred and ninety-nine patrons of virtue to one virtuous man. But it is easier to deal with the real possessor of a thing than with the temporary guardian of it.

All voting is a sort of gaming, like checkers or backgammon, with a slight moral tinge to it, a playing with right and wrong, with moral questions; and betting naturally accompanies it. The character of the voters is not staked. I cast my vote, perchance, as I think right; but I am not vitally concerned that that right should prevail. I am willing to leave it to the majority. Its obligation, therefore, never exceeds that of expediency. Even voting *for the right* is *doing* nothing for it. It is only expressing to men feebly your desire that it should prevail. A wise man will not leave the right to the mercy of chance,

[14]Jesus said, "Whosoever will save his life shall lose it: but whosoever will lose his life for my sake, the same shall save it." Luke 9:24.

[15]Cyril Tourneur (1575?–1626), *The Revenger's Tragedy* (1607), Act IV, Scene iv, lines 70–72.

[16]"Know ye not that a little leaven leaveneth the whole lump?" I Corinthians 5:6.

[17]News.

nor wish it to prevail through the power of the majority. There is but little virtue in the action of masses of men. When the majority shall at length vote for the abolition of slavery, it will be because they are indifferent to slavery, or because there is but little slavery left to be abolished by their vote. *They* will then be the only slaves. Only *his* vote can hasten the abolition of slavery who asserts his own freedom by his vote.

I hear of a convention to be held at Baltimore,[18] or elsewhere, for the selection of a candidate for the Presidency, made up chiefly of editors, and men who are politicians by profession; but I think, what is it to any independent, intelligent, and respectable man what decision they may come to? Shall we not have the advantage of his wisdom and honesty, nevertheless? Can we not count upon some independent votes? Are there not many individuals in the country who do not attend conventions? But no: I find that the respectable man, so called, has immediately drifted from his position, and despairs of his country, when his country has more reason to despair of him. He forthwith adopts one of the candidates thus selected as the only *available* one, thus proving that he is himself *available* for any purposes of the demagogue. His vote is of no more worth than that of any unprincipled foreigner or hireling native, who may have been bought. O for a man who is a *man,* and, as my neighbor says, has a bone in his back which you cannot pass your hand through! Our statistics are at fault: the population has been returned too large. How many *men* are there to a square thousand miles in this country? Hardly one. Does not America offer any inducement for men to settle here? The American has dwindled into an Odd Fellow,[19]—one who may be known by the development of his organ of gregariousness,[20] and a manifest lack of intellect and cheerful self-reliance; whose first and chief concern, on coming into the world, is to see that the almshouses are in good repair; and, before yet he has lawfully donned the virile garb,[21] to collect a fund for the support of the widows and orphans that may be; who, in short, ventures to live only by the aid of the Mutual Insurance company, which has promised to bury him decently.

It is not a man's duty, as a matter of course, to devote himself to the eradication of any, even the most enormous, wrong; he may still properly have other concerns to engage him; but it is his duty, at least, to wash his hands of it, and, if he gives it no thought longer, not to give it practically his support. If I devote myself to other pursuits and contemplations, I must first see, at least, that I do not pursue them sitting upon another man's shoulders. I must get off him first, that he may pursue his contemplations too. See what gross inconsistency is tolerated. I have heard some of my townsmen say, "I should like to have them order me out to help put down an insurrection of the slaves, or to march to Mexico;—see if I would go;" and yet these very men have each, directly by their allegiance, and so indirectly, at least, by their money, furnished a substitute. The soldier is applauded who refuses to serve

[18]The Democratic Convention of 1848.

[19]The Independent Order of Odd Fellows (established 1819), a benevolent and mutual aid society that still exists.

[20]Phrenological terminology meaning one whose head shape indicates that he loves company.

[21]I.e., before he has become a man. Upon reaching manhood, Roman boys were permitted to wear the *toga virilis* (the adult male's outer garment of white wool).

in an unjust war by those who do not refuse to sustain the unjust government which makes the war; is applauded by those whose own act and authority he disregards and sets at naught; as if the state were penitent to that degree that it hired one to scourge it while it sinned, but not to that degree that it left off sinning for a moment. Thus, under the name of Order and Civil Government, we are all made at last to pay homage to and support our own meanness. After the first blush of sin comes its indifference; and from immoral it becomes, as it were, *un*moral, and not quite unnecessary to that life which we have made.

The broadest and most prevalent error requires the most disinterested virtue to sustain it. The slight reproach to which the virtue of patriotism is commonly liable, the noble are most likely to incur. Those who, while they disapprove of the character and measures of a government, yield to it their allegiance and support are undoubtedly its most conscientious supporters, and so frequently the most serious obstacles to reform. Some[22] are petitioning the State to dissolve the Union, to disregard the requisitions of the President.[23] Why do they not dissolve it themselves,—the union between themselves and the State,—and refuse to pay their quota into its treasury? Do not they stand in the same relation to the State that the State does to the Union? And have not the same reasons prevented the State from resisting the Union which have prevented them from resisting the State?

How can a man be satisfied to entertain an opinion merely, and enjoy *it*? Is there any enjoyment in it, if his opinion is that he is aggrieved? If you are cheated out of a single dollar by your neighbor, you do not rest satisfied with knowing that you are cheated, or with saying that you are cheated, or even with petitioning him to pay you your due; but you take effectual steps at once to obtain the full amount, and see that you are never cheated again. Action from principle, the perception and performance of right, changes things and relations; it is essentially revolutionary, and does not consist wholly with anything which was. It not only divides States and churches, it divides families; ay, it divides the *individual,* separating the diabolical in him from the divine.

Unjust laws exist: shall we be content to obey them, or shall we endeavor to amend them, and obey them until we have succeeded, or shall we transgress them at once? Men generally, under such a government as this, think that they ought to wait until they have persuaded the majority to alter them. They think that, if they should resist, the remedy would be worse than the evil. But it is the fault of the government itself that the remedy *is* worse than the evil. *It* makes it worse. Why is it not more apt to anticipate and provide for reform? Why does it not cherish its wise minority? Why does it cry and resist before it is hurt? Why does it not encourage its citizens to be on the alert to point out its faults, and *do* better than it would have them? Why does it always crucify Christ, and excommunicate Copernicus and Luther,[24] and pronounce Washington and Franklin rebels?

[22]Radical Massachusetts abolitionists who feared that the Mexican War would lead to the creation of new slave states.

[23]President James K. Polk's call for money and troops to fight Mexico.

[24]Nicolaus Copernicus, Polish astronomer (1473–1543) threatened with excommunication from the church for asserting that the Earth was not the center of the universe. Martin Luther (1483–1546), German monk and a founder of Protestantism.

One would think, that a deliberate and practical denial of its authority was the only offence never contemplated by government; else, why has it not assigned its definite, its suitable and proportionate, penalty? If a man who has no property refuses but once to earn nine shillings[25] for the State, he is put in prison for a period unlimited by any law that I know, and determined only by the discretion of those who placed him there; but if he should steal ninety times nine shillings from the State, he is soon permitted to go at large again.

If the injustice is part of the necessary friction of the machine of government, let it go, let it go: perchance it will wear smooth,—certainly the machine will wear out. If the injustice has a spring, or a pulley, or a rope, or a crank, exclusively, for itself, then perhaps you may consider whether the remedy will not be worse than the evil; but if it is of such a nature that it requires you to be the agent of injustice to another, then, I say, break the law. Let your life be a counter-friction[26] to stop the machine. What I have to do is to see, at any rate, that I do not lend myself to the wrong which I condemn.

As for adopting the ways which the State has provided for remedying the evil, I know not of such ways. They take too much time, and a man's life will be gone. I have other affairs to attend to. I came into this world, not chiefly to make this a good place to live in, but to live in it, be it good or bad. A man has not everything to do, but something; and because he cannot do *everything,* it is not necessary that he should do *something* wrong. It is not my business to be petitioning the Governor or the Legislature any more than it is theirs to petition me; and if they should not hear my petition, what should I do then? But in this case the State has provided no way: its very Constitution is the evil. This may seem to be harsh and stubborn and unconciliatory; but it is to treat with the utmost kindness and consideration the only spirit that can appreciate or deserves it. So is all change for the better, like birth and death which convulse the body.

I do not hesitate to say, that those who call themselves Abolitionists should at once effectually withdraw their support, both in person and property, from the government of Massachusetts, and not wait till they constitute a majority of one, before they suffer the right to prevail through them. I think that it is enough if they have God on their side, without waiting for that other one. Moreover, any man more right than his neighbors constitutes a majority of one already.

I meet this American government, or its representative, the State government, directly, and face to face, once a year—no more—in the person of its tax-gatherer; this is the only mode in which a man situated as I am necessarily meets it; and it then says distinctly, Recognize me; and the simplest, the most effectual, and, in the present posture of affairs, the indispensablest mode of treating with it on this head, of expressing your little satisfaction with and love for it, is to deny it then. My civil neighbor, the tax-gatherer, is the very man I have to deal with,—for it is, after all, with men and not with parchment that I quarrel,—and he has voluntarily chosen to be an agent of

[25] I.e., tax money totaling nine shillings ($1.50), which Thoreau refused to pay. Although there was no U.S. coin named "shilling," the term was used through the nineteenth century, especially in New England, to reckon sums at the rate of six shillings to the dollar.

[26] A device, like an automobile brake, that applies friction to slow or stop a moving part.

the government. How shall he ever know well what he is and does as an officer of the government, or as a man, until he is obliged to consider whether he shall treat me, his neighbor, for whom he has respect, as a neighbor and well-disposed man, or as a maniac and disturber of the peace, and see if he can get over this obstruction to his neighborliness without a ruder and more impetuous thought or speech corresponding with his action. I know this well, that if one thousand, if one hundred, if ten men whom I could name,—if ten *honest* men only,—ay, if *one* HONEST man, in this State of Massachusetts, *ceasing to hold slaves,* were actually to withdraw from this copartnership, and be locked up in the county jail therefor, it would be the abolition of slavery in America. For it matters not how small the beginning may seem to be: what is once well done is done forever. But we love better to talk about it: that we say is our mission. Reform keeps many scores of newspapers in its service, but not one man. If my esteemed neighbor, the State's ambassador,[27] who will devote his days to the settlement of the question of human rights in the Council Chamber, instead of being threatened with the prisons of Carolina, were to sit down the prisoner of Massachusetts, that State which is so anxious to foist the sin of slavery upon her sister,—though at present she can discover only an act of inhospitality to be the ground of a quarrel with her,—the Legislature would not wholly waive the subject the following winter.

Under a government which imprisons any unjustly, the true place for a just man is also a prison. The proper place to-day, the only place which Massachusetts has provided for her freer and less desponding spirits, is in her prisons, to be put out and locked out of the State by her own act, as they have already put themselves out by their principles. It is there that the fugitive slave, and the Mexican prisoner on parole, and the Indian come to plead the wrongs of his race should find them; on that separate, but more free and honorable, ground, where the State places those who are not *with* her, but *against* her,—the only house in a slave State in which a free man can abide with honor. If any think that their influence would be lost there, and their voices no longer afflict the ear of the State, that they would not be as an enemy within its walls, they do not know by how much truth is stronger than error, nor how much more eloquently and effectively he can combat injustice who has experienced a little in his own person. Cast your whole vote, not a strip of paper merely, but your whole influence. A minority is powerless while it conforms to the majority; it is not even a minority then; but it is irresistible when it clogs by its whole weight. If the alternative is to keep all just men in prison, or give up war and slavery, the State will not hesitate which to choose. If a thousand men were not to pay their tax-bills this year, that would not be a violent and bloody measure, as it would be to pay them, and enable the State to commit violence and shed innocent blood. This is, in fact, the definition of a peaceable revolution, if any such is possible. If the tax-gatherer, or any other public officer, asks me, as one has done, "But what shall I do?" my answer is, "If you really wish to do anything, resign

[27]Samuel Hoar (1778–1856), Massachusetts senator and Thoreau's neighbor at Concord, was sent to South Carolina in 1844 to protest the seizure of black seamen on Massachusetts ships in South Carolina ports. He was driven from South Carolina by threats and legal action.

your office." When the subject has refused allegiance, and the officer has resigned his office, then the revolution is accomplished. But even suppose blood should flow. Is there not a sort of blood shed when the conscience is wounded? Through this wound a man's real manhood and immortality flow out, and he bleeds to an everlasting death. I see this blood flowing now.

I have contemplated the imprisonment of the offender, rather than the seizure of his goods,—though both will serve the same purpose,—because they who assert the purest right, and consequently are most dangerous to a corrupt State, commonly have not spent much time in accumulating property. To such the State renders comparatively small service, and a slight tax is wont to appear exorbitant, particularly if they are obliged to earn it by special labor with their hands. If there were one who lived wholly without the use of money, the State itself would hesitate to demand it of him. But the rich man—not to make any invidious comparison—is always sold to the institution which makes him rich. Absolutely speaking, the more money, the less virtue; for money comes between a man and his objects, and obtains them for him; and it was certainly no great virtue to obtain it. It puts to rest many questions which he would otherwise be taxed to answer; while the only new question which it puts is the hard but superfluous one, how to spend it. Thus his moral ground is taken from under his feet. The opportunities of living are diminished in proportion as what are called the "means" are increased. The best thing a man can do for his culture when he is rich is to endeavor to carry out those schemes which he entertained when he was poor. Christ answered the Herodians according to their condition. "Show me the tribute-money," said he;—and one took a penny out of his pocket;—if you use money which has the image of Caesar on it, and which he has made current and valuable, that is, *if you are men of the State,* and gladly enjoy the advantages of Caesar's government, then pay him back some of his own when he demands it. "Render therefore to Caesar that which is Caesar's, and to God those things which are God's,"[28]—leaving them no wiser than before as to which was which; for they did not wish to know.

When I converse with the freest of my neighbors, I perceive that, whatever they may say about the magnitude and seriousness of the question, and their regard for the public tranquillity, the long and the short of the matter is, that they cannot spare the protection of the existing government, and they dread the consequences to their property and families of disobedience to it. For my own part, I should not like to think that I ever rely on the protection of the State. But, if I deny the authority of the State when it presents its tax-bill, it will soon take and waste all my property, and so harass me and my children without end. This is hard. This makes it impossible for a man to live honestly, and at the same time comfortably, in outward respects. It will not be worth the while to accumulate property; that would be sure to go again. You must hire[29] or squat somewhere, and raise but a small crop, and eat that soon. You must live within yourself, and depend upon yourself always tucked up and ready for a start, and not have many affairs. A man may grow rich in Turkey even, if he will be in all respects a good subject of the Turkish government.

[28]Matthew 22:16–22.
[29]Rent.

Confucius[30] said: "If a state is governed by the principles of reason, poverty and misery are subjects of shame; if a state is not governed by the principles of reason, riches and honors are the subjects of shame." No: until I want the protection of Massachusetts to be extended to me in some distant Southern port, where my liberty is endangered, or until I am bent solely on building up an estate at home by peaceful enterprise, I can afford to refuse allegiance to Massachusetts, and her right to my property and life. It costs me less in every sense to incur the penalty of disobedience to the State than it would to obey. I should feel as if I were worth less in that case.

Some years ago, the State met me in behalf of the Church, and commanded me to pay a certain sum toward the support of a clergyman whose preaching my father attended, but never I myself.[31] "Pay," it said, "or be locked up in the jail." I declined to pay. But, unfortunately, another man saw fit to pay it. I did not see why the schoolmaster should be taxed to support the priest, and not the priest the schoolmaster; for I was not the State's schoolmaster, but I supported myself by voluntary subscription. I did not see why the lyceum[32] should not present its tax-bill, and have the State to back its demand, as well as the Church. However, at the request of the selectmen,[33] I condescended to make some such statement as this in writing:—"Know all men by these presents, that I, Henry Thoreau, do not wish to be regarded as a member of any incorporated society which I have not joined." This I gave to the town clerk; and he has it. The State, having thus learned that I did not wish to be regarded as a member of that church, has never made a like demand of me since; though it said that it must adhere to its original presumption that time. If I had known how to name them, I should then have signed off in detail from all the societies which I never signed on to; but I did not know where to find a complete list.

I have paid no poll-tax for six years. I was put into a jail once on this account, for one night;[34] and, as I stood considering the walls of solid stone, two or three feet thick, the door of wood and iron, a foot thick, and the iron grating which strained the light, I could not help being struck with the foolishness of that institution which treated me as if I were mere flesh and blood and bones, to be locked up. I wondered that it should have concluded at length that this was the best use it could put me to, and had never thought to avail itself of my services in some way. I saw that, if there was a wall of stone between me and my townsmen, there was a still more difficult one to climb or break through before they could get to be as free as I was. I did not for a moment feel confined, and the walls seemed a great waste of stone and mortar. I felt as if I alone of all my townsmen had paid my tax. They plainly did

[30]Chinese philosopher (c. 551–479 B.C.). The quotation is from *The Analects,* chapter VIII, book 13.

[31]In nineteenth-century Massachusetts, church assessments were collected by town governments. Because Thoreau's parents were church members, Thoreau was listed on the church "tax" rolls and thus received bills (beginning in 1838) from the town treasurer.

[32]The Concord Lyceum, a voluntary educational society, sponsored an annual lecture series.

[33]Town officials.

[34]Thoreau was jailed July 23 or 24, 1846. Bronson Alcott had been arrested on the same charge three years before. Both Alcott and Thoreau refused to pay the poll tax (a general tax on all males between twenty and seventy) as a protest against Massachusetts' legal recognition of Southern slavery.

not know how to treat me, but behaved like persons who are underbred. In every threat and in every compliment there was a blunder; for they thought that my chief desire was to stand the other side of that stone wall. I could not but smile to see how industriously they locked the door on my meditations, which followed them out again without let or hindrance, and *they* were really all that was dangerous. As they could not reach me, they had resolved to punish my body; just as boys, if they cannot come at some person against whom they have a spite, will abuse his dog. I saw that the State was half-witted, that it was timid as a lone woman with her silver spoons, and that it did not know its friends from its foes, and I lost all my remaining respect for it, and pitied it.

Thus the State never intentionally confronts a man's sense, intellectual or moral, but only his body, his senses. It is not armed with superior wit or honesty, but with superior physical strength. I was not born to be forced. I will breathe after my own fashion. Let us see who is the strongest. What force has a multitude? They only can force me who obey a higher law than I. They force me to become like themselves. I do not hear of *men* being *forced* to live this way or that by masses of men. What sort of life were that to live? When I meet a government which says to me, "Your money or your life," why should I be in haste to give it my money? It may be in a great strait, and not know what to do: I cannot help that. It must help itself; do as I do. It is not worth the while to snivel about it. I am not responsible for the successful working of the machinery of society. I am not the son of the engineer. I perceive that, when an acorn and a chestnut fall side by side, the one does not remain inert to make way for the other, but both obey their own laws, and spring and grow and flourish as best they can, till one, perchance, overshadows and destroys the other. If a plant cannot live according to its nature, it dies; and so a man.

The night in prison was novel and interesting enough. The prisoners in their shirt-sleeves were enjoying a chat and the evening air in the doorway, when I entered. But the jailer[35] said, "Come, boys, it is time to lock up;" and so they dispersed, and I heard the sound of their steps returning into the hollow apartments.[36] My roommate was introduced to me by the jailer as "a first-rate fellow and a clever[37] man." When the door was locked, he showed me where to hang my hat, and how he managed matters there. The rooms were whitewashed once a month; and this one, at least, was the whitest, most simply furnished, and probably the neatest apartment in the town. He naturally wanted to know where I came from, and what brought me there; and, when I had told him, I asked him in my turn how he came there, presuming him to be an honest man, of course; and, as the world goes, I believe he was. "Why," said he, "they accuse me of burning a barn; but I never did it." As near as I could discover, he had probably gone to bed in a barn when drunk, and smoked his pipe there; and so a barn was burnt. He had the reputation of being a clever man, had been there some three months waiting for his trial to come on, and would have to wait as much longer; but he was quite domesticated and contented, since he got his board for nothing, and thought that he was well treated.

[35]Thoreau's personal friend Sam Staples. [36]Jail cells. [37]I.e., honest.

He occupied one window, and I the other; and I saw that if one stayed there long, his principal business would be to look out the window. I had soon read all the tracts that were left there, and examined where former prisoners had broken out, and where a grate had been sawed off, and heard the history of the various occupants of that room; for I found that even here there was a history and a gossip which never circulated beyond the walls of the jail. Probably this is the only house in town where verses are composed, which are afterward printed in a circular form, but not published. I was shown quite a long list of verses which were composed by some young men who had been detected in an attempt to escape, who avenged themselves by singing them.

I pumped my fellow-prisoner as dry as I could, for fear I should never see him again; but at length he showed me which was my bed, and left me to blow out the lamp.

It was like traveling into a far country, such as I had never expected to behold, to lie there for one night. It seemed to me that I never had heard the town clock strike before, nor the evening sounds of the village; for we slept with the windows open, which were inside the grating. It was to see my native village in the light of the Middle Ages, and our Concord was turned into a Rhine stream, and visions of knights and castles passed before me. They were the voices of old burghers that I heard in the streets. I was an involuntary spectator and auditor of whatever was done and said in the kitchen of the adjacent village inn,—a wholly new and rare experience to me. It was a closer view of my native town. I was fairly inside of it. I never had seen its institutions before. This is one of its peculiar institutions; for it is a shire town.[38] I began to comprehend what its inhabitants were about.

In the morning, our breakfasts were put through the hole in the door, in small oblong-square tin pans, made to fit, and holding a pint of chocolate, with brown bread, and an iron spoon. When they called for the vessels again, I was green enough to return what bread I had left; but my comrade seized it, and said that I should lay that up for lunch or dinner. Soon after he was let out to work at haying in a neighboring field, whither he went every day, and would not be back till noon; so he bade me good-day, saying that he doubted if he should see me again.

When I came out of prison,—for some one[39] interfered, and paid that tax,—I did not perceive that great changes had taken place on the common, such as he observed who went in a youth and emerged a tottering and gray-headed man; and yet a change had to my eyes come over the scene,—the town, and State, and country,—greater than any that mere time could effect. I saw yet more distinctly the State in which I lived. I saw to what extent the people among whom I lived could be trusted as good neighbors and friends; that their friendship was for summer weather only; that they did not greatly propose to do right; that they were a distinct race from me by their prejudices and superstitions, as the Chinamen and Malays are; that in their sacrifices to humanity they ran no risks, not even to their property; that after all they were not so noble but they treated the thief as he had

[38]A town where county (shire) offices, courts, and jails are located.
[39]Probably Thoreau's Aunt Maria Thoreau.

treated them, and hoped, by a certain outward observance and a few prayers, and by walking in a particular straight though useless path from time to time, to save their souls. This may be to judge my neighbors harshly; for I believe that many of them are not aware that they have such an institution as the jail in their village.

It was formerly the custom in our village, when a poor debtor came out of jail, for his acquaintances to salute him, looking through their fingers, which were crossed to represent the grating of a jail window, "How do ye do?" My neighbors did not thus salute me, but first looked at me, and then at one another, as if I had returned from a long journey. I was put into jail as I was going to the shoemaker's to get a shoe which was mended. When I was let out the next morning, I proceeded to finish my errand, and, having put on my mended shoe, joined a huckleberry party, who were impatient to put themselves under my conduct; and in half an hour,—for the horse was soon tackled,[40]—was in the midst of a huckleberry field, on one of our highest hills, two miles off, and then the State was nowhere to be seen.

This is the whole history of "My Prisons."[41]

I have never declined paying the highway tax, because I am as desirous of being a good neighbor as I am of being a bad subject; and as for supporting schools, I am doing my part to educate my fellow-countrymen now. It is for no particular item in the tax-bill that I refuse to pay it. I simply wish to refuse allegiance to the State, to withdraw and stand aloof from it effectually. I do not care to trace the course of my dollar, if I could, till it buys a man or a musket to shoot one with,—the dollar is innocent,—but I am concerned to trace the effects of my allegiance. In fact, I quietly declare war with the State, after my fashion, though I will still make what use and get what advantage of her I can, as is usual in such cases.

If others pay the tax which is demanded of me, from a sympathy with the State, they do but what they have already done in their own case, or rather they abet injustice to a greater extent than the State requires. If they pay the tax from a mistaken interest in the individual taxed, to save his property, or prevent his going to jail, it is because they have not considered wisely how far they let their private feelings interfere with the public good.

This, then, is my position at present. But one cannot be too much on his guard in such a case, lest his action be biased by obstinacy or an undue regard for the opinions of men. Let him see that he does only what belongs to himself and to the hour.

I think sometimes, Why, this people mean well, they are only ignorant; they would do better if they knew how: why give your neighbors this pain to treat you as they are not inclined to? But I think again, This is no reason why I should do as they do, or permit others to suffer much greater pain of a different kind. Again, I sometimes say to myself, When many millions of men, without heat, without ill will, without personal feeling of any kind, demand of you a few shillings only, without the possibility, such is their constitution,

[40]Harnessed.

[41]The title of a volume (1832) recounting the prison experiences of Silvio Pellico (1788–1854), Italian revolutionary patriot.

of retracting or altering their present demand, and without the possibility, on your side, of appeal to any other millions, why expose yourself to this overwhelming brute force? You do not resist cold and hunger, the winds and the waves, thus obstinately; you quietly submit to a thousand similar necessities. You do not put your head into the fire. But just in proportion as I regard this as not wholly a brute force, but partly a human force, and consider that I have relations to those millions as to so many millions of men, and not of mere brute or inanimate things, I see that appeal is possible, first and instantaneously, from them to themselves. But if I put my head deliberately into the fire, there is no appeal to fire or to the Maker of fire, and I have only myself to blame. If I could convince myself that I have any right to be satisfied with men as they are, and to treat them accordingly, and not according, in some respects, to my requisitions and expectations of what they and I ought to be, then, like a good Mussulman[42] and fatalist, I should endeavor to be satisfied with things as they are, and say it is the will of God. And, above all, there is this difference between resisting this and a purely brute or natural force, that I can resist this with some effect; but I cannot expect, like Orpheus,[43] to change the nature of the rocks and trees and beasts.

I do not wish to quarrel with any man or nation. I do not wish to split hairs, to make fine distinctions, or set myself up as better than my neighbors. I seek rather, I may say, even an excuse for conforming to the laws of the land. I am but too ready to conform to them. Indeed, I have reason to suspect myself on this head;[44] and each year, as the tax-gatherer comes round, I find myself disposed to review the acts and position of the general and State governments, and the spirit of the people, to discover a pretext for conformity.

> "We must affect our country as our parents,
> And if at any time we alienate
> Our love or industry from doing it honor,
> We must respect effects and teach the soul
> Matter of conscience and religion,
> And not desire of rule or benefit."[45]

I believe that the State will soon be able to take all my work of this sort out of my hands, and then I shall be no better a patriot than my fellow-countrymen. Seen from a lower point of view, the Constitution, with all its faults, is very good; the law and the courts are very respectable; even this State and this American government are, in many respects, very admirable, and rare things, to be thankful for, such as a great many have described them; but seen from a point of view a little higher, they are what I have described them; seen from a higher still, and the highest, who shall say what they are, or that they are worth looking at or thinking of at all?

[42]Muslim.

[43]In Greek legend, the music of Orpheus "charmed" gods, beasts, and even inanimate objects.

[44]Point.

[45]Adapted from *The Battle of Alcazar* (1594), Act II, Scene ii, lines 425–430, a drama by George Peele (1558?–1597?).

However, the government does not concern me much, and I shall bestow the fewest possible thoughts on it. It is not many moments that I live under a government, even in this world. If a man is thought-free, fancy-free, imagination-free, that which *is not* never for a long time appearing *to be* to him, unwise rulers or reformers cannot fatally interrupt him.

I know that most men think differently from myself; but those whose lives are by profession devoted to the study of these or kindred subjects content me as little as any. Statesmen and legislators, standing so completely within the institution, never distinctly and nakedly behold it. They speak of moving society, but have no resting-place without it. They may be men of a certain experience and discrimination, and have no doubt invented ingenious and even useful systems, for which we sincerely thank them; but all their wit and usefulness lie within certain not very wide limits. They are wont to forget that the world is not governed by policy and expediency. Webster[46] never goes behind government, and so cannot speak with authority about it. His words are wisdom to those legislators who contemplate no essential reform in the existing government; but for thinkers, and those who legislate for all time, he never once glances at the subject. I know of those whose serene and wise speculations on this theme would soon reveal the limits of his mind's range and hospitality. Yet, compared with the cheap professions of most reformers, and the still cheaper wisdom and eloquence of politicians in general, his are almost the only sensible and valuable words, and we thank Heaven for him. Comparatively, he is always strong, original, and above all, practical. Still, his quality is not wisdom, but prudence. The lawyer's truth is not Truth, but consistency or a consistent expediency. Truth is always in harmony with herself, and is not concerned chiefly to reveal the justice that may consist with wrong-doing. He well deserves to be called, as he has been called, the Defender of the Constitution. There are really no blows to be given by him but defensive ones. He is not a leader, but a follower. His leaders are the men of '87.[47] "I have never made an effort," he says, "and never propose to make an effort; I have never countenanced an effort, and never mean to countenance an effort, to disturb the arrangement as originally made, by which the various States came into the Union." Still thinking of the sanction which the Constitution gives to slavery, he says, "Because it was a part of the original compact,—let it stand." Notwithstanding his special acuteness and ability, he is unable to take a fact out of its merely political relations, and behold it as it lies absolutely to be disposed of by the intellect,—what, for instance, it behooves a man to do here in America to-day with regard to slavery,—but ventures, or is driven, to make some such desperate answer as the following, while professing to speak absolutely, and as a private man,—from which what new and singular code of social duties might be inferred? "The manner," says he, "in which the governments of those States where slavery exists are to regulate it, is for their own consideration, under their responsibility to their constituents, to the general laws of propriety, humanity, and justice, and to God. Associations formed elsewhere, springing from a feeling of humanity, or any

[46]Daniel Webster (1782–1852), Massachusetts senator and famous orator who angered abolitionists by supporting the Fugitive Slave Law, which assisted in the return of escaped slaves.

[47]Those who drafted the Constitution in 1787.

other cause, have nothing whatever to do with it. They have never received any encouragement from me, and they never will."[48]

They who know of no purer sources of truth, who have traced up its stream no higher, stand, and wisely stand, by the Bible and the Constitution, and drink at it there with reverence and humility; but they who behold where it comes trickling into this lake or that pool, gird up their loins once more, and continue their pilgrimage toward its fountain-head.

No man with a genius for legislation has appeared in America. They are rare in the history of the world. There are orators, politicians, and eloquent men, by the thousand; but the speaker has not yet opened his mouth to speak who is capable of settling the much-vexed questions of the day. We love eloquence for its own sake, and not for any truth which it may utter, or any heroism it may inspire. Our legislators have not yet learned the comparative value of free trade and of freedom, of union, and of rectitude, to a nation. They have no genius or talent for comparatively humble questions of taxation and finance, commerce and manufactures and agriculture. If we were left solely to the wordy wit of legislators in Congress for our guidance, uncorrected by the seasonable experience and the effectual complaints of the people, America would not long retain her rank among the nations. For eighteen hundred years, though perchance I have no right to say it, the New Testament has been written; yet where is the legislator who has wisdom and practical talent enough to avail himself of the light which it sheds on the science of legislation?

The authority of government, even such as I am willing to submit to,—for I will cheerfully obey those who know and can do better than I, and in many things even those who neither know nor can do so well,—is still an impure one: to be strictly just, it must have the sanction and consent of the governed. It can have no pure right over my person and property but what I concede to it. The progress from an absolute to a limited monarchy, from a limited monarchy to a democracy, is a progress toward a true respect for the individual. Even the Chinese philosopher[49] was wise enough to regard the individual as the basis of the empire. Is a democracy, such as we know it, the last improvement possible in government? Is it not possible to take a step further towards recognizing and organizing the rights of man? There will never be a really free and enlightened State until the State comes to recognize the individual as a higher and independent power, from which all its own power and authority are derived, and treats him accordingly. I please myself with imagining a State at last which can afford to be just to all men, and to treat the individual with respect as a neighbor; which even would not think it inconsistent with its own repose if a few were to live aloof from it, not meddling with it, nor embraced by it, who fulfilled all the duties of neighbors and fellow-men. A State which bore this kind of fruit, and suffered it to drop off as fast as it ripened, would prepare the way for a still more perfect and glorious State, which also I have imagined, but not yet anywhere seen.

1848 1849, 1866

[48]"These extracts have been inserted since the lecture was read."—Thoreau's note. He quotes from speeches by Webster in 1845 and 1848.

[49]Confucius.

from *WALDEN*

I
ECONOMY

When I wrote the following pages, or rather the bulk of them, I lived alone, in the woods, a mile from any neighbor, in a house which I had built myself, on the shore of Walden Pond, in Concord, Massachusetts, and earned my living by the labor of my hands only. I lived there two years and two months.[1] At present I am a sojourner in civilized life again.

I should not obtrude my affairs so much on the notice of my readers if very particular inquiries had not been made by my townsmen concerning my mode of life, which some would call impertinent, though they do not appear to me at all impertinent, but, considering the circumstances, very natural and pertinent. Some have asked what I got to eat; if I did not feel lonesome; if I was not afraid; and the like. Others have been curious to learn what portion of my income I devoted to charitable purposes; and some, who have large families, how many poor children I maintained. I will therefore ask those of my readers who feel no particular interest in me to pardon me if I undertake to answer some of these questions in this book. In most books, the *I*, or first person, is omitted; in this it will be retained; that, in respect to egotism, is the main difference. We commonly do not remember that it is, after all, always the first person that is speaking. I should not talk so much about myself if there were anybody else whom I knew as well. Unfortunately, I am confined to this theme by the narrowness of my experience. Moreover, I, on my side, require of every writer, first or last, a simple and sincere account of his own life, and not merely what he has heard of other men's lives; some such account as he would send to his kindred from a distant land; for if he has lived sincerely, it must have been in a distant land to me. Perhaps these pages are more particularly addressed to poor students. As for the rest of my readers, they will accept such portions as apply to them. I trust that none will stretch the seams in putting on the coat, for it may do good service to him whom it fits.

I would fain say something, not so much concerning the Chinese and Sandwich Islanders[2] as you who read these pages, who are said to live in New England; something about your condition, especially your outward condition or circumstances in this world, in this town, what it is, whether it is necessary that it be as bad as it is, whether it cannot be improved as well as not. I have travelled a good deal in Concord; and everywhere, in shops, and offices, and fields, the inhabitants have appeared to me to be doing penance in a thousand remarkable ways. What I have heard of Bramins[3] sitting exposed to four fires and looking in the face of the sun; or hanging suspended, with their heads downward, over flames; or looking at the heavens over their shoulders "until it becomes impossible for them to resume their natural position, while from the twist of the neck nothing but liquids can pass into the stomach"; or dwelling, chained for life, at the foot of a tree; or

[1]From July 4, 1845, to September 6, 1847. [2]Hawaiians.
[3]Members of the highest Hindu caste.

measuring with their bodies, like caterpillars, the breadth of vast empires; or standing on one leg on the top of pillars,—even these forms of conscious penance are hardly more incredible and astonishing than the scenes which I daily witness. The twelve labors of Hercules were trifling in comparison with those which my neighbors have undertaken; for they were only twelve, and had an end; but I could never see that these men slew or captured any monster or finished any labor. They have no friend Iolaus[4] to burn with a hot iron the root of the hydra's head, but as soon as one head is crushed, two spring up.

I see young men, my townsmen, whose misfortune it is to have inherited farms, houses, barns, cattle, and farming tools; for these are more easily acquired than got rid of. Better if they had been born in the open pasture and suckled by a wolf,[5] that they might have seen with clearer eyes what field they were called to labor in. Who made them serfs of the soil? Why should they eat their sixty acres, when man is condemned to eat only his peck of dirt?[6] Why should they begin digging their graves as soon as they are born? They have got to live a man's life, pushing all these things before them, and get on as well as they can. How many a poor immortal soul have I met well-nigh crushed and smothered under its load, creeping down the road of life, pushing before it a barn seventy-five feet by forty, its Augean stables[7] never cleansed, and one hundred acres of land, tillage, mowing, pasture, and wood-lot! The portionless, who struggle with no such unnecessary inherited encumbrances, find it labor enough to subdue and cultivate a few cubic feet of flesh.

But men labor under a mistake. The better part of the man is soon plowed into the soil for compost. By a seeming fate, commonly called necessity, they are employed, as it says in an old book, laying up treasures which moth and rust will corrupt and thieves break through and steal.[8] It is a fool's life, as they will find when they get to the end of it, if not before. It is said that Deucalion and Pyrrha[9] created men by throwing stones over their heads behind them:—

> Inde genus durum sumus, experiensque laborum,
> Et documenta damus quâ simus origine nati.[10]

Or, as Raleigh rhymes it in his sonorous way,—

> "From thence our kind hard-hearted is, enduring pain and care,
> Approving that our bodies of a stony nature are."[11]

[4]Of the twelve tasks Hercules had to perform to win freedom from slavery, one was to kill the monstrous nine-headed Hydra, which he accomplished with the aid of his servant Iolaus, who, as Hercules cut off each head, seared the neck, cauterizing it so new heads would not grow back.

[5]Romulus and Remus, the legendary founders of Rome, were said to have been suckled by a she-wolf.

[6]"Every man will eat a peck [two gallons] of dirt before he dies." A common adage in Thoreau's day.

[7]The fifth labor of Hercules was to clean the stables where King Augeas had kept 3,000 oxen for thirty years.

[8]The "old book" is the Bible. Thoreau paraphrases Matthew 6:19.

[9]In Greek myth, Deucalion and Pyrrha, like the biblical Noah, survived a great flood. To repopulate the earth they cast stones over their shoulders, and the stones turned into men and women.

[10]Ovid, *Metamorphoses,* Book I.

[11]Sir Walter Raleigh, *The History of the World* (1614).

So much for a blind obedience to a blundering oracle, throwing the stones over their heads behind them, and not seeing where they fell.

Most men, even in this comparatively free country, through mere ignorance and mistake, are so occupied with the factitious cares and superfluously coarse labors of life that its finer fruits cannot be plucked by them. Their fingers, from excessive toil, are too clumsy and tremble too much for that. Actually, the laboring man has no leisure for a true integrity day by day; he cannot afford to sustain the manliest relations to men; his labor would be depreciated in the market. He has no time to be anything but a machine. How can he remember well his ignorance—which his growth requires—who has so often to use his knowledge? We should feed and clothe him gratuitously sometimes, and recruit[12] him with our cordials,[13] before we judge of him. The finest qualities of our nature, like the bloom on fruits, can be preserved only by the most delicate handling. Yet we do not treat ourselves nor one another thus tenderly.

Some of you, we all know, are poor, find it hard to live, are sometimes, as it were, gasping for breath. I have no doubt that some of you who read this book are unable to pay for all the dinners which you have actually eaten, or for the coats and shoes which are fast wearing or are already worn out, and have come to this page to spend borrowed or stolen time, robbing your creditors of an hour. It is very evident what mean and sneaking lives many of you live, for my sight has been whetted by experience; always on the limits, trying to get into business and trying to get out of debt, a very ancient slough,[14] called by the Latins *aes alienum,* another's brass,[15] for some of their coins were made of brass; still living, and dying, and buried by this other's brass; always promising to pay, promising to pay, to-morrow, and dying today, insolvent; seeking to curry favor, to get custom,[16] by how many modes, only not stateprison offences; lying, flattering, voting, contracting yourselves into a nutshell of civility, or dilating into an atmosphere of thin and vaporous generosity, that you may persuade your neighbor to let you make his shoes, or his hat, or his coat, or his carriage, or import his groceries for him; making yourselves sick, that you may lay up something against a sick day, something to be tucked away in an old chest, or in a stocking behind the plastering, or, more safely, in the brick bank; no matter where, no matter how much or how little.

I sometimes wonder that we can be so frivolous, I may almost say, as to attend to the gross but somewhat foreign form of servitude called Negro Slavery, there are so many keen and subtle masters that enslave both North and South. It is hard to have a Southern overseer; it is worse to have a Northern one; but worst of all when you are the slave-driver of yourself. Talk of a divinity in man! Look at the teamster on the highway, wending to market by day or night; does any divinity stir within him? His highest duty to fodder and water his horses! What is his destiny to him compared with the shipping interests? Does not he drive for Squire Make-a-stir? How godlike, how immortal, is he? See how he cowers and sneaks, how vaguely all the day he fears, not being immortal nor divine, but the slave and prisoner of his own opinion of

[12]Refresh. [13]Medicines, liqueurs. [14]Mire.
[15]I.e., another's money. [16]Customers, business.

himself, a fame won by his own deeds. Public opinion is a weak tyrant compared with our own private opinion. What a man thinks of himself, that it is which determines, or rather indicates, his fate. Self-emancipation even in the West Indian provinces of the fancy and imagination,—what Wilberforce[17] is there to bring about? Think, also, of the ladies of the land weaving toilet[18] cushions against the last day, not to betray too green an interest in their fates! As if you could kill time without injuring eternity.

The mass of men lead lives of quiet desperation. What is called resignation is confirmed desperation. From the desperate city you go into the desperate country, and have to console yourself with the bravery of minks and muskrats. A stereotyped but unconscious despair is concealed even under what are called the games and amusements of mankind. There is no play in them, for this comes after work. But it is a characteristic of wisdom not to do desperate things.

When we consider what, to use the words of the catechism, is the chief end of man,[19] and what are the true necessaries and means of life, it appears as if men had deliberately chosen the common mode of living because they preferred it to any other. Yet they honestly think there is no choice left. But alert and healthy natures remember that the sun rose clear. It is never too late to give up our prejudices. No way of thinking or doing, however ancient, can be trusted without proof. What everybody echoes or in silence passes by as true to-day may turn out to be falsehood to-morrow, mere smoke of opinion, which some had trusted for a cloud that would sprinkle fertilizing rain on their fields. What old people say you cannot do, you try and find that you can. Old deeds for old people, and new deeds for new. Old people did not know enough once, perchance, to fetch fresh fuel to keep the fire a-going; new people put a little dry wood under a pot,[20] and are whirled round the globe with the speed of birds, in a way to kill old people, as the phrase is. Age is no better, hardly so well, qualified for an instructor as youth, for it has not profited so much as it has lost. One may almost doubt if the wisest man has learned anything of absolute value by living. Practically, the old have no very important advice to give the young, their own experience has been so partial, and their lives have been such miserable failures, for private reasons, as they must believe; and it may be that they have some faith left which belies that experience, and they are only less young than they were. I have lived some thirty years on this planet, and I have yet to hear the first syllable of valuable or even earnest advice from my seniors. They have told me nothing, and probably cannot tell me anything to the purpose. Here is life, an experiment to a great extent untried by me; but it does not avail me that they have tried it. If I have any experience which I think valuable, I am sure to reflect that this my Mentors[21] said nothing about.

[17]William Wilberforce (1759–1833), English abolitionist whose efforts helped bring about the abolition of slavery in the British Empire (1833).

[18]Dressing room.

[19]The catechism in the *New England Primer* taught that man's chief end is to "glorify God and to enjoy him forever."

[20]The boiler of a steam engine.

[21]Counselors, tutors.

One farmer says to me, "You cannot live on vegetable food solely, for it furnishes nothing to make bones with;" and so he religiously devotes a part of his day to supplying his system with the raw material of bones; walking all the while he talks behind his oxen, which, with vegetable-made bones, jerk him and his lumbering plow along in spite of every obstacle. Some things are really necessaries of life in some circles, the most helpless and diseased, which in others are luxuries merely, and in others still are entirely unknown.

The whole ground of human life seems to some to have been gone over by their predecessors, both the heights and the valleys, and all things to have been cared for. According to Evelyn,[22] "the wise Solomon prescribed ordinances for the very distances of trees; and the Roman praetors[23] have decided how often you may go into your neighbor's land to gather the acorns which fall on it without trespass, and what share belongs to that neighbor." Hippocrates[24] has even left directions how we should cut our nails; that is, even with the ends of the fingers, neither shorter nor longer. Undoubtedly the very tedium and ennui which presume to have exhausted the variety and the joys of life are as old as Adam. But man's capacities have never been measured; nor are we to judge of what he can do by any precedents, so little has been tried. Whatever have been thy failures hitherto, "be not afflicted, my child, for who shall assign to thee what thou hast left undone?"[25]

We might try our lives by a thousand simple tests; as, for instance, that the same sun which ripens my beans illumines at once a system of earths like ours. If I had remembered this it would have prevented some mistakes. This was not the light in which I hoed them. The stars are the apexes of what wonderful triangles! What distant and different beings in the various mansions of the universe are contemplating the same one at the same moment! Nature and human life are as various as our several constitutions. Who shall say what prospect life offers to another? Could a greater miracle take place than for us to look through each other's eyes for an instant? We should live in all the ages of the world in an hour; ay, in all the worlds of the ages. History, Poetry, Mythology!—I know of no reading of another's experience so startling and informing as this would be.

The greater part of what my neighbors call good I believe in my soul to be bad, and if I repent of anything, it is very likely to be my good behavior. What demon possessed me that I behaved so well? You may say the wisest thing you can, old man—you who have lived seventy years, not without honor of a kind,—I hear an irresistible voice which invites me away from all that. One generation abandons the enterprises of another like stranded vessels.

I think that we may safely trust a good deal more than we do. We may waive just so much care of ourselves as we honestly bestow elsewhere. Nature is as well adapted to our weakness as to our strength. The incessant anxiety and strain of some is a well-nigh incurable form of disease. We are made to exaggerate the importance of what work we do; and yet how much is not

[22]John Evelyn (1620–1706), English diarist who also wrote a book on tree-growing (*Sylva,* 1644).

[23]Magistrates.

[24]Greek physician (460?–377 B.C.).

[25]From the Hindu religious epic *Vishnu Purana.*

done by us! or, what if we had been taken sick? How vigilant we are! determined not to live by faith if we can avoid it; all the day long on the alert, at night we unwillingly say our prayers and commit ourselves to uncertainties. So thoroughly and sincerely are we compelled to live, reverencing our life, and denying the possibility of change. This is the only way, we say; but there are as many ways as there can be drawn radii from one centre. All change is a miracle to contemplate; but it is a miracle which is taking place every instant. Confucius[26] said, "To know that we know what we know, and that we do not know what we do not know, that is true knowledge." When one man has reduced a fact of the imagination to be a fact to his understanding, I foresee that all men will at length establish their lives on that basis.

Let us consider for a moment what most of the trouble and anxiety which I have referred to is about, and how much it is necessary that we be troubled, or at least careful. It would be some advantage to live a primitive and frontier life, though in the midst of an outward civilization, if only to learn what are the gross necessaries of life and what methods have been taken to obtain them; or even to look over the old day-books[27] of the merchants, to see what it was that men most commonly bought at the stores, what they stored, that is, what are the grossest groceries. For the improvements of ages have had but little influence on the essential laws of man's existence: as our skeletons, probably, are not to be distinguished from those of our ancestors.

By the words, *necessary of life,* I mean whatever, of all that man obtains by his own exertions, has been from the first, or from long use has become, so important to human life that few, if any, whether from savageness, or poverty, or philosophy, ever attempt to do without it. To many creatures there is in this sense but one necessary of life, Food. To the bison of the prairie it is a few inches of palatable grass, with water to drink; unless he seeks the Shelter of the forest or the mountain's shadow. None of the brute creation requires more than Food and Shelter. The necessaries of life for man in this climate may, accurately enough, be distributed under the several heads of Food, Shelter, Clothing, and Fuel; for not till we have secured these are we prepared to entertain the true problems of life with freedom and a prospect of success. Man has invented, not only houses, but clothes and cooked food; and possibly from the accidental discovery of the warmth of fire, and the consequent use of it, at first a luxury, arose the present necessity to sit by it. We observe cats and dogs acquiring the same second nature. By proper Shelter and Clothing we legitimately retain our own internal heat; but with an excess of these, or of Fuel, that is, with an external heat greater than our own internal, may not cookery properly be said to begin? Darwin, the naturalist, says of the inhabitants of Tierra del Fuego,[28] that while his own party, who were well clothed and sitting close to a fire, were far from too warm, these naked savages, who were farther off, were observed, to his great surprise, "to

[26]Chinese philosopher (c. 551–479 B.C.). The quotation is from *The Analects,* Book II, chapter 17.

[27]Account books.

[28]At the southern tip of South America. Charles Darwin (1809–1882) described the inhabitants in his *Journal of Researches* (1839).

be steaming with perspiration at undergoing such a roasting." So, we are told, the New Hollander[29] goes naked with impunity, while the European shivers in his clothes. Is it impossible to combine the hardiness of these savages with the intellectualness of the civilized man? According to Liebig,[30] man's body is a stove, and food the fuel which keeps up the internal combustion in the lungs. In cold weather we eat more, in warm less. The animal heat is the result of a slow combustion, and disease and death take place when this is too rapid; or for want of fuel, or from some defect in the draught, the fire goes out. Of course the vital heat is not to be confounded with fire; but so much for analogy. It appears, therefore, from the above list, that the expression, *animal life,* is nearly synonymous with the expression, *animal heat;* for while Food may be regarded as the Fuel which keeps up the fire within us,—and Fuel serves only to prepare that Food or to increase the warmth of our bodies by addition from without,—Shelter and Clothing also serve only to retain the *heat* thus generated and absorbed.

The grand necessity, then, for our bodies, is to keep warm, to keep the vital heat in us. What pains we accordingly take, not only with our Food, and Clothing, and Shelter, but with our beds, which are our night-clothes, robbing the nests and breasts of birds to prepare this shelter within a shelter, as the mole has its bed of grass and leaves at the end of its burrow! The poor man is wont to complain that this is a cold world; and to cold, no less physical than social, we refer directly a great part of our ails. The summer, in some climates, makes possible to man a sort of Elysian life.[31] Fuel, except to cook his Food, is then unnecessary; the sun is his fire, and many of the fruits are sufficiently cooked by its rays; while Food generally is more various, and more easily obtained, and Clothing and Shelter are wholly or half unnecessary. At the present day, and in this country, as I find by my own experience, a few implements, a knife, an axe, a spade, a wheelbarrow, etc., and for the studious, lamplight, stationery, and access to a few books, rank next to necessaries, and can all be obtained at a trifling cost. Yet some, not wise, go to the other side of the globe, to barbarous and unhealthy regions, and devote themselves to trade for ten or twenty years, in order that they may live,—that is, keep comfortably warm,—and die in New England at last. The luxuriously rich are not simply kept comfortably warm, but unnaturally hot;[32] as I implied before, they are cooked, of course *à la mode.*[33]

Most of the luxuries, and many of the so-called comforts of life, are not only not indispensable, but positive hindrances to the elevation of mankind. With respect to luxuries and comforts, the wisest have ever lived a more simple and meagre life than the poor. The ancient philosophers, Chinese, Hindoo, Persian, and Greek, were a class than which none has been poorer in outward riches, none so rich in inward. We know not much about them. It is remarkable that *we* know so much of them as we do. The same is true of the more modern reformers and benefactors of their race. None can be an impartial or wise observer of human life but from the vantage ground of what

[29]Aboriginal Australian. [30]Justus von Liebig (1803–1873), German chemist.
[31]Life in the Elysian Fields, home of the blessed dead in Greek myth.
[32]With central heating, a luxury in the nineteenth century.
[33]According to fashion, in a stylish way.

we should call voluntary poverty. Of a life of luxury the fruit is luxury, whether in agriculture, or commerce, or literature, or art. There are nowadays professors of philosophy, but not philosophers. Yet is is admirable to profess because it was once admirable to live. To be a philosopher is not merely to have subtle thoughts, nor even to found a school, but so to love wisdom as to live according to its dictates, a life of simplicity, independence, magnanimity, and trust. It is to solve some of the problems of life, not only theoretically, but practically. The success of great scholars and thinkers is commonly a courtier-like success, not kingly, not manly. They make shift to live merely by conformity, practically as their fathers did, and are in no sense the progenitors of a nobler race of men. But why do men degenerate ever? What makes families run out? What is the nature of the luxury which enervates and destroys nations? Are we sure that there is none of it in our own lives? The philosopher is in advance of his age even in the outward form of his life. He is not fed, sheltered, clothed, warmed, like his contemporaries. How can a man be a philosopher and not maintain his vital heat by better methods than other men?

When a man is warmed by the several modes which I have described, what does he want next? Surely not more warmth of the same kind, as more and richer food, larger and more splendid houses, finer and more abundant clothing, more numerous, incessant and hotter fires, and the like. When he has obtained those things which are necessary to life, there is another alternative than to obtain the superfluities; and that is, to adventure on life now, his vacation from humbler toil having commenced. The soil, it appears, is suited to the seed, for it has sent its radicle[34] downward, and it may now send its shoot upward also with confidence. Why has man rooted himself thus firmly in the earth, but that he may rise in the same proportion into the heavens above?—for the nobler plants are valued for the fruit they bear at last in the air and light, far from the ground, and are not treated like the humbler esculents,[35] which, though they may be biennials,[36] are cultivated only till they have perfected their root, and often cut down at top for this purpose, so that most would not know them in their flowering season.

I do not mean to prescribe rules to strong and valiant natures, who will mind their own affairs whether in heaven or hell, and perchance build more magnificently and spend more lavishly than the richest, without ever impoverishing themselves, not knowing how they live,—if, indeed, there are any such, as has been dreamed; nor to those who find their encouragement and inspiration in precisely the present condition of things, and cherish it with the fondness and enthusiasm of lovers,—and, to some extent, I reckon myself in this number; I do not speak to those who are well employed, in whatever circumstances, and they know whether they are well employed or not;—but mainly to the mass of men who are discontented, and idly complaining of the hardness of their lot or of the times, when they might improve them. There are some who complain most energetically and inconsolably of any, because they are, as they say, doing their duty. I also have in my mind that seemingly wealthy, but most terribly impoverished class of all,

[34]Root. [35]Edibles. [36]Plants that last only for two years.

who have accumulated dross,[37] but know not how to use it, or get rid of it, and thus have forged their own golden or silver fetters.[38]

If I should attempt to tell how I have desired to spend my life in years past, it would probably surprise those of my readers who are somewhat acquainted with its actual history; it would certainly astonish those who know nothing about it. I will only hint at some of the enterprises which I have cherished.

In any weather, at any hour of the day or night, I have been anxious to improve the nick of time,[39] and notch it on my stick[40] to stand on the meeting of two eternities, the past and future, which is precisely the present moment; to toe that line. You will pardon some obscurities, for there are more secrets in my trade than in most men's, and yet not voluntarily kept, but inseparable from its very nature. I would gladly tell all that I know about it, and never paint "No Admittance" on my gate.

I long ago lost a hound, a bay horse, and a turtle-dove, and am still on their trail. Many are the travellers I have spoken to concerning them, describing their tracks and what calls they answered to. I have met one or two who had heard the hound, and the tramp of the horse, and even seen the dove disappear behind a cloud, and they seemed as anxious to recover them as if they had lost them themselves.

To anticipate, not the sunrise and the dawn merely, but, if possible, Nature herself! How many mornings, summer and winter, before yet any neighbor was stirring about his business, have I been about mine! No doubt, many of my townsmen have met me returning from this enterprise, farmers starting for Boston in the twilight, or woodchoppers going to their work. It is true, I never assisted the sun materially in his rising, but, doubt not, it was of the last importance only to be present at it.

So many autumn, ay, and winter days, spent outside the town, trying to hear what was in the wind, to hear and carry it express! I well-nigh sunk all my capital in it, and lost my own breath into the bargain, running in the face of it. If it had concerned either of the political parties, depend upon it, it would have appeared in the Gazette[41] with the earliest intelligence.[42] At other times watching from the observatory of some cliff or tree, to telegraph any new arrival; or waiting at evening on the hill-tops for the sky to fall, that I might catch something, though I never caught much, and that, manna-wise, would dissolve again in the sun.[43]

For a long time I was reporter to a journal,[44] of no very wide circulation, whose editor has never yet seen fit to print the bulk of my contributions, and, as is too common with writers, I got only my labor for my pains. However, in this case my pains were their own reward.

For many years I was self-appointed inspector of snow-storms and rainstorms, and did my duty faithfully; surveyor, if not of highways, then of forest

[37]Impurities that form on the surface of molten metals, worthless possessions.
[38]Shackles. [39]The exact moment. [40]Record it.
[41]The Concord *Gazette,* a weekly newspaper. [42]News.
[43]Manna, the food miraculously given to the Israelites (Exodus 16), was said to melt in the sun.
[44]Probably Thoreau refers to his own journal (which he had kept since 1837) or to *The Dial,* a New England transcendentalist magazine that rejected his contributions.

paths and all across-lot routes, keeping them open, and ravines bridged and passable at all seasons, where the public heel had testified to their utility.

I have looked after the wild stock of the town, which give a faithful herdsman a good deal of trouble by leaping fences; and I have had an eye to the unfrequented nooks and corners of the farm; though I did not always know whether Jonas or Solomon worked in a particular field to-day; that was none of my business. I have watered the red huckleberry, the sand cherry and the nettle-tree, the red pine and the black ash, the white grape and the yellow violet, which might have withered else in dry seasons.

In short, I went on thus for a long time (I may say it without boasting), faithfully minding my business, till it became more and more evident that my townsmen would not after all admit me into the list of town officers, nor make my place a sinecure with a moderate allowance. My accounts, which I can swear to have kept faithfully, I have, indeed, never got audited, still less accepted, still less paid and settled. However, I have not set my heart on that.

Not long since, a strolling Indian went to sell baskets at the house of a well-known lawyer in my neighborhood. "Do you wish to buy any baskets?" he asked. "No, we do not want any," was the reply. "What!" exclaimed the Indian as he went out the gate, "do you mean to starve us?" Having seen his industrious white neighbors so well off,—that the lawyer had only to weave arguments, and, by some magic, wealth and standing followed,—he had said to himself: I will go into business; I will weave baskets; it is a thing which I can do. Thinking that when he had made the baskets he would have done his part, and then it would be the white man's to buy them. He had not discovered that it was necessary for him to make it worth the other's while to buy them, or at least make him think that it was so, or to make something else which it would be worth his while to buy. I too had woven a kind of basket of a delicate texture, but I had not made it worth any one's while to buy them. Yet not the less, in my case, did I think it worth my while to weave them, and instead of studying how to make it worth men's while to buy my baskets, I studied rather how to avoid the necessity of selling them. The life which men praise and regard as successful is but one kind. Why should we exaggerate any one kind at the expense of others?

Finding that my fellow-citizens were not likely to offer me any room in the court house, or any curacy or living[45] anywhere else, but I must shift for myself, I turned my face more exclusively than ever to the woods, where I was better known. I determined to go into business at once, and not wait to acquire the usual capital, using such slender means as I had already got. My purpose in going to Walden Pond was not to live cheaply nor to live dearly there, but to transact some private business[46] with the fewest obstacles; to be hindered from accomplishing which for want of a little common sense, a little enterprise and business talent, appeared not so sad as foolish.

I have always endeavored to acquire strict business habits; they are indispensable to every man. If your trade is with the Celestial Empire,[47] then some small counting house[48] on the coast, in some Salem harbor, will be fixture

[45]I.e., appointment as a clergyman, or income from a religious office.
[46]To write *A Week on the Concord and Merrimack Rivers* (1849).
[47]Nineteenth-century name for China. [48]Business office.

enough. You will export such articles as the country affords, purely native products, much ice and pine timber and a little granite, always in native bottoms.[49] These will be good ventures. To oversee all the details yourself in person; to be at once pilot and captain, and owner and underwriter; to buy and sell and keep the accounts; to read every letter received, and write or read every letter sent; to superintend the discharge of imports night and day; to be upon many parts of the coast almost at the same time,—often the richest freight will be discharged upon a Jersey shore;[50]—to be your own telegraph, unweariedly sweeping the horizon, speaking all passing vessels bound coastwise; to keep up a steady despatch of commodities, for the supply of such a distant and exorbitant market; to keep yourself informed of the state of the markets, prospects of war and peace everywhere, and anticipate the tendencies of trade and civilization,—taking advantage of the results of all exploring expeditions, using new passages and all improvements in navigation;—charts to be studied, the position of reefs and new lights and buoys to be ascertained, and ever, and ever, the logarithmic tables to be corrected, for by the error of some calculator the vessel often splits upon a rock that should have reached a friendly pier,—there is the untold fate of La Perouse;[51]—universal science to be kept pace with, studying the lives of all great discoverers and navigators, great adventurers and merchants, from Hanno and the Phœnicians[52] down to our day; in fine, account of stock to be taken from time to time, to know how you stand. It is a labor to task the faculties of a man,—such problems of profit and loss, of interest, of tare and tret,[53] and gauging of all kinds in it, as demand a universal knowledge.

I have thought that Walden Pond would be a good place for business, not solely on account of the railroad and the ice trade; it offers advantages which it may not be good policy to divulge; it is a good port and a good foundation. No Neva[54] marshes to be filled; though you must everywhere build on piles of your own driving. It is said that a flood-tide, with a westerly wind, and ice in the Neva, would sweep St. Petersburg from the face of the earth.

As this business was to be entered into without the usual capital, it may not be easy to conjecture where those means, that will still be indispensable to every such undertaking, were to be obtained. As for Clothing, to come at once to the practical part of the question, perhaps we are led oftener by the love of novelty and a regard for the opinions of men, in procuring it, than by a true utility. Let him who has work to do recollect that the object of clothing is, first, to retain the vital heat, and secondly, in this state of society, to cover nakedness, and he may judge how much of any necessary or important work may be accomplished without adding to his wardrobe. Kings and queens who wear a suit but once, though made by some tailor or dressmaker to their majesties, cannot know the comfort of wearing a suit that fits. They are no better than wooden horses[55] to hang the clean clothes on.

[49]Ships. [50]I.e., the coast of New Jersey.

[51]Jean François de Galaup, Count de la Pérouse (1741–1788?), French explorer who was shipwrecked and probably killed in the New Hebrides. The full details of his death remain unknown.

[52]The Carthaginian Hanno (fifth century B.C.) and the Phœnicians were noted ancient explorers.

[53]Commercial calculations of weight. [54]Russian river on which St. Petersburg was built.

[55]Frames.

Every day our garments become more assimilated to ourselves, receiving the impress of the wearer's character, until we hesitate to lay them aside; without such delay and medical appliances and some such solemnity even as our bodies. No man ever stood the lower in my estimation for having a patch in his clothes; yet I am sure that there is greater anxiety, commonly, to have fashionable, or at least clean and unpatched clothes, than to have a sound conscience. But even if the rent[56] is not mended, perhaps the worst vice betrayed is improvidence. I sometimes try my acquaintances by such tests as this,—Who could wear a patch, or two extra seams only, over the knee? Most behave as if they believed that their prospects for life would be ruined if they should do it. It would be easier for them to hobble to town with a broken leg than with a broken pantaloon. Often if an accident happens to a gentleman's legs, they can be mended; but if a similar accident happens to the legs of his pantaloons, there is no help for it; for he considers, not what is truly respectable, but what is respected. We know but few men, a great many coats and breeches. Dress a scarecrow in your last shift, you standing shiftless by, who would not soonest salute the scarecrow? Passing a cornfield the other day, close by a hat and coat on a stake, I recognized the owner of the farm. He was only a little more weatherbeaten than when I saw him last. I have heard of a dog that barked at every stranger who approached his master's premises with clothes on, but was easily quieted by a naked thief. It is an interesting question how far men would retain their relative rank if they were divested of their clothes. Could you, in such a case, tell surely of any company of civilized men which belonged to the most respected class? When Madam Pfeiffer,[57] in her adventurous travels round the world, from east to west, had got so near home as Asiatic Russia, she says that she felt the necessity of wearing other than a travelling dress, when she went to meet the authorities, for she "was now in a civilized country, where . . . people are judged of by their clothes." Even in our democratic New England towns the accidental possession of wealth, and its manifestation in dress and equipage alone, obtain for the possessor almost universal respect. But they who yield such respect, numerous as they are, are so far heathen, and need to have a missionary sent to them. Besides, clothes introduced sewing, a kind of work which you may call endless; a woman's dress, at least, is never done.

A man who has at length found something to do will not need to get a new suit to do it in; for him the old will do, that has lain dusty in the garret for an indeterminate period. Old shoes will serve a hero longer than they have served his valet,—if a hero ever has a valet,—bare feet are older than shoes, and he can make them do. Only they who go to soirées[58] and legislative halls must have new coats, coats to change as often as the man changes in them. But if my jacket and trousers, my hat and shoes, are fit to worship God in, they will do; will they not? Who ever saw his old clothes,—his old coat, actually worn out, resolved into its primitive elements, so that it was not a deed of charity to bestow it on some poor boy, by him perchance to be bestowed on some poorer still, or shall we say richer, who could do with less? I say, beware

[56]Rip.

[57]Ida Pfeiffer (1797–1858), Austrian author of travel books, including *A Woman's Journey Round the World* (1852).

[58]Evening parties.

of all enterprises that require new clothes, and not rather a new wearer of clothes. If there is not a new man, how can the new clothes be made to fit? If you have any enterprise before you, try it in your old clothes. All men want, not something to *do with,* but something to *do,* or rather something to *be.* Perhaps we should never procure a new suit, however ragged or dirty the old, until we have so conducted, so enterprised or sailed in some way, that we feel like new men in the old, and that to retain it would be like keeping new wine in old bottles.[59] Our moulting season, like that of the fowls, must be a crisis in our lives. The loon retires to solitary ponds to spend it. Thus also the snake casts its slough,[60] and the caterpillar its wormy coat, by an internal industry and expansion; for clothes are but our outmost cuticle and mortal coil. Otherwise we shall be found sailing under false colors, and be inevitably cashiered at last by our own opinion, as well as that of mankind.

We don garment after garment, as if we grew like exogenous plants[61] by addition without. Our outside and often thin and fanciful clothes are our epidemic, or false skin, which partakes not of our life, and may be stripped off here and there without fatal injury; our thicker garments, constantly worn, are our cellular integument, or cortex; but our shirts are our liber, or true bark, which cannot be removed without girdling and so destroying the man. I believe that all races at some seasons wear something equivalent to the shirt. It is desirable that a man be clad so simply that he can lay his hands on himself in the dark, and that he live in all respects so compactly and preparedly that, if an enemy take the town, he can, like the old philosopher, walk out the gate empty-handed without anxiety. While one thick garment is, for most purposes, as good as three thin ones, and cheap clothing can be obtained at prices really to suit customers; while a thick coat can be bought for five dollars, which will last as many years, thick pantaloons for two dollars, cowhide boots for a dollar and a half a pair, a summer hat for a quarter of a dollar, and a winter cap for sixty-two and a half cents, or a better be made at home at a nominal cost, where is he so poor that, clad in such a suit, *of his own earning,* there will not be found wise men to do him reverence?

When I ask for a garment of particular form, my tailoress tells me gravely, "They do not make them so now," not emphasizing the "They" at all, as if she quoted an authority as impersonal as the Fates,[62] and I find it difficult to get made what I want, simply because she cannot believe that I mean what I say, that I am so rash. When I hear this oracular sentence, I am for a moment absorbed in thought, emphasizing to myself each word separately that I may come at the meaning of it, that I may find out by what degree of consanguinity *They* are related to *me,* and what authority they may have in an affair which affects me so nearly; and, finally, I am inclined to answer her with equal mystery, and without any more emphasis of the "they,"—"It is true, they did not make them so recently, but they do now." Of what use this measuring of me if she does not measure my character, but only the breadth of my shoulders, as it were a peg to hang the coat on? We worship not the Graces,[63] nor the

[59]"Neither do men put new wine into old bottles; else the bottles break." Matthew 9:17.
[60]Sheds its skin.
[61]Plants that grow by adding external layers. [62]Three goddesses of destiny in Greek myth.
[63]Three Greek goddesses of brilliance, beauty, and joy.

Parcæ,[64] but Fashion. She spins and weaves and cuts with full authority. The head monkey[65] at Paris puts on a traveller's cap, and all the monkeys in America do the same. I sometimes despair of getting anything quite simple and honest done in this world by the help of men. They would have to be passed through a powerful press first, to squeeze their old notions out of them, so that they would not soon get upon their legs[66] again; and then there would be some one in the company with a maggot in his head, hatched from an egg deposited there nobody knows when, for not even fire kills these things, and you would have lost your labor. Nevertheless, we will not forget that some Egyptian wheat was handed down to us by a mummy.[67]

On the whole, I think that it cannot be maintained that dressing has in this or any country risen to the dignity of an art. At present men make shift to wear what they can get. Like shipwrecked sailors, they put on what they can find on the beach, and at a little distance, whether of space or time, laugh at each other's masquerade. Every generation laughs at the old fashions, but follows religiously the new. We are amused at beholding the costume of Henry VIII., or Queen Elizabeth,[68] as much as if it was that of the King and Queen of the Cannibal Islands. All costume off a man is pitiful or grotesque. It is only the serious eye peering from and the sincere life passed within it which restrain laughter and consecrate the costume of any people. Let Harlequin[69] be taken with a fit of the colic and his trappings will have to serve that mood too. When the soldier is hit by a cannon-ball, rags are as becoming as purple.[70]

The childish and savage taste of men and women for new patterns keeps how many shaking and squinting through kaleidoscopes that they may discover the particular figure which this generation requires to-day. The manufacturers have learned that this taste is merely whimsical. Of two patterns which differ only by a few threads more or less of a particular color, the one will be sold readily, the other lie on the shelf, though it frequently happens that after the lapse of a season the latter becomes the most fashionable. Comparatively, tattooing is not the hideous custom which it is called. It is not barbarous merely because the printing is skin-deep and unalterable.

I cannot believe that our factory system is the best mode by which men may get clothing. The condition of the operatives[71] is becoming every day more like that of the English; and it cannot be wondered at, since, as far as I have heard or observed, the principal object is, not that mankind may be well and honestly clad, but, unquestionably, that the corporations may be enriched. In the long run men hit only what they aim at. Therefore, though they should fail immediately, they had better aim at something high.

As for a Shelter, I will not deny that this is now a necessary of life, though there are instances of men having done without it for long periods in colder

[64]Three goddesses of destiny, in Roman myth, who spin the thread of life, decide its length, then cut it off.

[65]I.e., fashion leader. [66]I.e., speak out assertively.

[67]A reference to the mistaken nineteenth-century belief that wheat would grow from the seeds discovered in ancient Egyptian tombs.

[68]King of England (1509–1547); Queen of England (1558–1603).

[69]A character in comedy and pantomime, dressed in multicolored costume.

[70]The purple clothing of royalty. [71]Factory workers.

countries than this. Samuel Laing[72] says that "the Laplander in his skin dress, and in a skin bag which he puts over his head and shoulders, will sleep night after night on the snow . . . in a degree of cold which would extinguish the life of one exposed to it in any woollen clothing." He had seen them asleep thus. Yet he adds, "They are not hardier than other people." But, probably, man did not live long on the earth without discovering the convenience which there is in a house, the domestic comforts, which phrase may have originally signified the satisfactions of the house more than of the family; though these must be extremely partial and occasional in those climates where the house is associated in our thoughts with winter or the rainy season chiefly, and two thirds of the year, except for a parasol, is unnecessary. In our climate, in the summer, it was formerly almost solely a covering at night. In the Indian gazettes[73] a wigwam was the symbol of a day's march, and a row of them cut or painted on the bark of a tree signified that so many times they had camped. Man was not made so large limbed and robust but that he must seek to narrow his world, and wall in a space such as fitted him. He was at first bare and out of doors; but though this was pleasant enough in serene and warm weather, by daylight, the rainy season and the winter, to say nothing of the torrid sun, would perhaps have nipped his race in the bud if he had not made haste to clothe himself with the shelter of a house. Adam and Eve, according to the fable, wore the bower before other clothes. Man wanted a home, a place of warmth, or comfort, first of physical warmth, then the warmth of the affections.

We may imagine a time when, in the infancy of the human race, some enterprising mortal crept into a hollow in a rock for shelter. Every child begins the world again, to some extent, and loves to stay outdoors, even in wet and cold. It plays house, as well as horse, having an instinct for it. Who does not remember the interest with which, when young, he looked at shelving rocks, or any approach to a cave? It was the natural yearning of that portion of our most primitive ancestor which still survived in us. From the cave we have advanced to roofs of palm leaves, of bark and boughs, of linen woven and stretched, of grass and straw, of boards and shingles, of stones and tiles. At last, we know not what it is to live in the open air, and our lives are domestic in more senses than we think. From the hearth to the field is a great distance. It would be well, perhaps, if we were to spend more of our days and nights without any obstruction between us and the celestial bodies, if the poet did not speak so much from under a roof, or the same dwell there so long. Birds do not sing in caves, nor do doves cherish their innocence in dovecots.

However, if one designs to construct a dwelling-house, it behooves him to exercise a little Yankee shrewdness, lest after all he find himself in a workhouse, a labyrinth without a clue, a museum, an almshouse, a prison, or a splendid mausoleum instead. Consider first how slight a shelter is absolutely necessary. I have seen Penobscot Indians,[74] in this town, living in tents of thin cotton cloth, while the snow was nearly a foot deep around them, and I

[72]English writer (1780–1868), author of *Journal of a Residence in Norway* (1837).
[73]Idioms, sign languages.
[74]Of northern Maine. They traveled through Massachusetts selling their baskets.

thought that they would be glad to have it deeper to keep out the wind. Formerly, when how to get my living honestly, with freedom left for my proper pursuits, was a question which vexed me even more than it does now, for unfortunately I am become somewhat callous, I used to see a large box by the railroad, six feet long by three wide, in which the laborers locked up their tools at night; and it suggested to me that every man who was hard pushed might get such a one for a dollar, and having bored a few auger holes in it, to admit the air at least, get into it when it rained and at night, and hook down the lid, and so have freedom in his love, and in his soul be free. This did not appear the worst, nor by any means a despicable alternative. You could sit up as late as you pleased, and, whenever you got up, go abroad without any landlord or house-lord dogging you for rent. Many a man is harassed to death to pay the rent of a larger and more luxurious box who would not have frozen to death in such a box as this. I am far from jesting. Economy is a subject which admits of being treated with levity, but it cannot so be disposed of. A comfortable house for a rude and hardy race, that lived mostly out of doors, was once made here almost entirely of such materials as Nature furnished ready to their hands. Gookin,[75] who was superintendent of the Indians subject to the Massachusetts Colony, writing in 1674, says, "The best of their houses are covered very neatly, tight and warm, with barks of trees, slipped from their bodies at those seasons when the sap is up, and made into great flakes, with pressure of weighty timber, when they are green. . . . The meaner sort are covered with mats which they make of a kind of bulrush, and are also indifferently tight and warm, but not so good as the former. . . . Some I have seen, sixty or a hundred feet long and thirty feet broad. . . . I have often lodged in their wigwams, and found them as warm as the best English houses." He adds that they were commonly carpeted and lined within with well-wrought embroidered mats, and were furnished with various utensils. The Indians had advanced so far as to regulate the effect of the wind by a mat suspended over the hole in the roof and moved by a string. Such a lodge was in the first instance constructed in a day or two at most, and taken down and put up in a few hours; and every family owned one, or its apartment in one.

In the savage state every family owns a shelter as good as the best, and sufficient for its coarser and simpler wants; but I think that I speak within bounds when I say that, though the birds of the air have their nests, and the foxes their holes,[76] and the savages their wigwams, in modern civilized society not more than one half the families own a shelter. In the large towns and cities, where civilization especially prevails, the number of those who own a shelter is a very small fraction of the whole. The rest pay an annual tax for this outside garment of all, become indispensable summer and winter, which would buy a village of Indian wigwams, but now helps to keep them poor as long as they live. I do not mean to insist here on the disadvantage of hiring[77] compared

[75]Daniel Gookin (1612–1687), author of *Historical Collections of the Indians in New England* (1792).

[76]"The foxes have holes, and the birds of the air have nests; but the Son of man hath not where to lay his head." Matthew 8:20.

[77]Renting.

with owning, but it is evident that the savage owns his shelter because it costs so little, while the civilized man hires his commonly because he cannot afford to own it; nor can he, in the long run, any better afford to hire. But, answers one, by merely paying this tax the poor civilized man secures an abode which is a palace compared with the savage's. An annual rent of from twenty-five to a hundred dollars (these are the country rates) entitles him to the benefit of the improvements of centuries, spacious apartments, clean paint and paper, Rumford fireplace,[78] back plastering,[79] Venetian blinds, copper pump, spring lock, a commodious cellar, and many other things. But how happens it that he who is said to enjoy these things is so commonly a *poor* civilized man, while the savage, who has them not, is rich as a savage? If it is asserted that civilization is a real advance in the condition of man,—and I think that it is, though only the wise improve their advantages,—it must be shown that it has produced better dwellings without making them more costly; and the cost of a thing is the amount of what I will call life which is required to be exchanged for it, immediately or in the long run. An average house in this neighborhood costs perhaps eight hundred dollars, and to lay up this sum will take from ten to fifteen years of the laborer's life, even if he is not encumbered with a family,—estimating the pecuniary value of every man's labor at one dollar a day, for if some receive more, others receive less;—so that he must have spent more than half his life commonly before *his* wigwam will be earned. If we suppose him to pay a rent instead, this is but a doubtful choice of evils. Would the savage have been wise to exchange his wigwam for a palace on these terms?

It may be guessed that I reduce almost the whole advantage of holding this superfluous property as a fund in store against the future, so far as the individual is concerned, mainly to the defraying of funeral expenses. But perhaps a man is not required to bury himself. Nevertheless this points to an important distinction between the civilized man and the savage; and, no doubt, they have designs on us for our benefit, in making the life of a civilized people an *institution,* in which the life of the individual is to a great extent absorbed, in order to preserve and perfect that of the race. But I wish to show at what a sacrifice this advantage is at present obtained, and to suggest that we may possibly so live as to secure all the advantage without suffering any of the disadvantage. What mean ye by saying that the poor ye have always with you, or that the fathers have eaten sour grapes, and the children's teeth are set on edge?[80]

"As I live, saith the Lord God, ye shall not have occasion any more to use this proverb in Israel."

"Behold all souls are mine; as the soul of the father, so also the soul of the son is mine: the soul that sinneth it shall die."[81]

When I consider my neighbors, the farmers of Concord, who are at least as well off as the other classes, I find that for the most part they have been toiling twenty, thirty, or forty years, that they may become the real owners of their farms, which commonly they have inherited with encumbrances, or else bought with hired money,—and we may regard one third of that toil as the

[78]Smokeless stove perfected by Benjamin Thompson, Count Rumford (1753–1814).
[79]Insulation. [80]John 12:8 and Ezekiel 18:2. [81]Ezekiel 18:3–4.

cost of their houses,—but commonly they have not paid for them yet. It is true, the encumbrances sometimes outweigh the value of the farm, so that the farm itself becomes one great encumbrance, and still a man is found to inherit it, being well acquainted with it, as he says. On applying to the assessors, I am surprised to learn that they cannot at once name a dozen in the town who own their farms free and clear. If you would know the history of these homesteads, inquire at the bank where they are mortgaged. The man who has actually paid for his farm with labor on it is so rare that every neighbor can point to him. I doubt if there are three such men in Concord. What has been said of the merchants, that a very large majority, even ninety-seven in a hundred, are sure to fail, is equally true of the farmers. With regard to the merchants, however, one of them says pertinently that a great part of their failures are not genuine pecuniary failures, but merely failures to fulfil their engagements, because it is inconvenient; that is, it is the moral character that breaks down. But this puts an infinitely worse face on the matter, and suggests, beside, that probably not even the other three succeed in saving their souls, but are perchance bankrupt in a worse sense than they who fail honestly. Bankruptcy and repudiation are the springboards from which much of our civilization vaults and turns its somersets, but the savage stands on the unelastic plank of famine. Yet the Middlesex Cattle Show[82] goes off here with *éclat*[83] annually, as if all the joints of the agricultural machine were suent.[84]

The farmer is endeavoring to solve the problem of a livelihood by a formula more complicated than the problem itself. To get his shoestrings he speculates in herds of cattle. With consummate skill he has set his trap with a hair springe[85] to catch comfort and independence, and then, as he turned away, got his own leg into it. This is the reason he is poor; and for a similar reason we are all poor in respect to a thousand savage comforts, though surrounded by luxuries. As Chapman sings,—

> "the false society of men—
> —for earthly greatness
> All heavenly comforts rarefies to air."[86]

And when the farmer got his house, he may not be the richer but the poorer for it, and it be the house that has got him. As I understand it, that was a valid objection urged by Momus[87] against the house which Minerva[88] made, that she "had not made it movable, by which means a bad neighborhood might be avoided;" and it may still be urged, for our houses are such unwieldy property that we are often imprisoned rather than housed in them; and the bad neighborhood to be avoided is our own scurvy selves. I know one or two families, at least, in this town, who, for nearly a generation, have been wishing to sell their houses in the outskirts and move into the village, but have not been able to accomplish it, and only death will set them free.

[82]The Middlesex County agricultural fair held in Concord each September.
[83]With acclaim and approval. [84]In working order, smooth running.
[85]A snare with a noose of woven hair.
[86]George Chapman (1559?–1634), *Caesar and Pompey* (1631), Act V, Scene ii, lines 210 and 212–213.
[87]Critic and faultfinder in classical myth. [88]Goddess of handicrafts.

Granted that the *majority* are able at last either to own or hire the modern house with all its improvements. While civilization has been improving our houses, it has not equally improved the men who are to inhabit them. It has created palaces, but it was not so easy to create noblemen and kings. And *if the civilized man's pursuits are no worthier than the savage's, if he is employed the greater part of his life in obtaining gross necessaries and comforts merely, why should he have a better dwelling than the former?*

But how do the poor *minority* fare? Perhaps it will be found that just in proportion as some have been placed in outward circumstances above the savage, others have been degraded below him. The luxury of one class is counterbalanced by the indigence of another. On the one side is the palace, on the other are the almshouse and "silent poor."[89] The myriads who built the pyramids to be the tombs of the Pharaohs[90] were fed on garlic, and it may be were not decently buried themselves. The mason who finishes the cornice of the palace returns at night perchance to a hut not so good as a wigwam. It is a mistake to suppose that, in a country where the usual evidences of civilization exist, the condition of a very large body of the inhabitants may not be as degraded as that of savages. I refer to the degraded poor, not now to the degraded rich. To know this I should not need to look farther than to the shanties which everywhere border our railroads, that last improvement in civilization; where I see in my daily walks human beings living in sties, and all winter with an open door, for the sake of light, without any visible, often imaginable, wood-pile and the forms of both old and young are permanently contracted by the long habit of shrinking from cold and misery, and the development of all their limbs and faculties is checked. It certainly is fair to look at that class by whose labor the works which distinguish this generation are accomplished. Such too, to a greater or less extent, is the condition of the operatives of every denomination in England, which is the great workhouse of the world. Or I could refer you to Ireland, which is marked as one of the white or enlightened spots on the map. Contrast the physical condition of the Irish[91] with that of the North American Indian, or the South Sea Islander, or any other savage race before it was degraded by contact with the civilized man. Yet I have no doubt that that people's rulers are as wise as the average of civilized rulers. Their condition only proves what squalidness may consist[92] with civilization. I hardly need refer now to the laborers in our Southern States who produce the staple exports of this country, and are themselves a staple production of the South.[93] But to confine myself to those who are said to be in *moderate* circumstances.

Most men appear never to have considered what a house is, and are actually though needlessly poor all their lives because they think they must have such a one as their neighbors have. As if one were to wear any sort of coat which the tailor might cut out for him, or, gradually leaving off palm-leaf hat or cap of woodchuck skin, complain of hard times because he could not afford to buy such a crown! It is possible to invent a house still more convenient and luxurious than we have, which yet all would admit that man could

[89]I.e., those who hide their poverty. [90]Kings of ancient Egypt.
[91]In the 1840s the failure of the potato crop caused widespread starvation in Ireland.
[92]Exist. [93]I.e., a product of slave breeders.

not afford to pay for. Shall we always study to obtain more of these things, and not sometimes to be content with less? Shall the respectable citizen thus gravely teach, by precept and example, the necessity of the young man's providing a certain number of superfluous glow-shoes,[94] and umbrellas, and empty guest chambers for empty guests, before he dies? Why should not our furniture be as simple as the Arab's or the Indian's? When I think of the benefactors of the race, whom we have apotheosized as messengers from heaven, bearers of divine gifts to man, I do not see in my mind any retinue at their heels, any carload of fashionable furniture. Or what if I were to allow—would it not be a singular allowance?—that our furniture should be more complex than the Arab's, in proportion as we are morally and intellectually his superiors! At present our houses are cluttered and defiled with it, and a good housewife would sweep out the greater part into the dust hole, and not leave her morning's work undone. Morning work! By the blushes of Aurora[95] and the music of Memnon,[96] what should be man's *morning work* in this world? I had three pieces of limestone on my desk, but I was terrified to find that they required to be dusted daily, when the furniture of my mind was all undusted still, and I threw them out the window in disgust. How, then, could I have a furnished house? I would rather sit in the open air, for no dust gathers on the grass, unless where man has broken ground.

It is the luxurious and dissipated who set the fashions which the herd so diligently follow. The traveller who stops at the best houses, so called, soon discovers this, for the publicans presume him to be a Sardanapalus,[97] and if he resigned himself to their tender mercies he would soon be completely emasculated. I think that in the railroad car we are inclined to spend more on luxury than on safety and convenience, and it threatens without attaining these to become no better than a modern drawing-room, with its divans, and ottomans, and sun-shades, and a hundred other oriental things, which we are taking west with us, invented for the ladies of the harem and the effeminate natives of the Celestial Empire,[98] which Jonathan[99] should be ashamed to know the names of. I would rather sit on a pumpkin and have it all to myself than be crowded on a velvet cushion. I would rather ride on earth in an ox cart, with a free circulation, than go to heaven in the fancy car of an excursion train and breathe a *malaria* all the way.

The very simplicity and nakedness of man's life in the primitive ages imply this advantage, at least, that they left him still but a sojourner in nature. When he was refreshed with food and sleep, he contemplated his journey again. He dwelt, as it were, in a tent in this world, and was either threading the valleys, or crossing the plains, or climbing the mountain-tops. But lo! men have become the tools of their tools! The man who independently plucked the fruits when he was hungry is become a farmer; and he who stood under a tree for shelter, a housekeeper. We now no longer camp as for a night, but have settled down on earth and forgotten heaven. We have

[94]Galoshes. [95]Roman goddess of the dawn.

[96]Ancient Egyptian king whose giant statue was said to sound musically when struck by the morning sun.

[97]Last king of Assyria (ninth century B.C.), notorious for his effeminacy and his luxurious tastes.

[98]China. [99]Nickname for Americans.

adopted Christianity merely as an improved method of *agri*culture. We have built for this world a family mansion, and for the next a family tomb. The best works of art are the expression of man's struggle to free himself from this condition, but the effect of our art is merely to make this low state comfortable and that higher state to be forgotten. There is actually no place in this village for a work of *fine* art, if any had come down to us, to stand, for our lives, our houses and streets, furnish no proper pedestal for it. There is not a nail to hang a picture on, nor a shelf to receive the bust of a hero or a saint. When I consider how our houses are built and paid for, or not paid for, and their internal economy managed and sustained, I wonder that the floor does not give way under the visitor while he is admiring the gewgaws upon the mantel-piece, and let him through into the cellar, to some solid and honest though earthy foundation. I cannot but perceive that this so-called rich and refined life is a thing jumped at, and I do not get on in the enjoyment of the *fine* arts which adorn it, my attention being wholly occupied with the jump; for I remember that the greatest genuine leap, due to human muscles alone, on record, is that of certain wandering Arabs, who are said to have cleared twenty-five feet on level ground. Without factitious[100] support, man is sure to come to earth again beyond that distance. The first question which I am tempted to put to the proprietor of such great impropriety is, Who bolsters you? Are you one of the ninety-seven who fail, or the three who succeed? Answer me these questions, and then perhaps I may look at your baubles and find them ornamental. The cart before the horse is neither beautiful nor useful. Before we can adorn our houses with beautiful objects the walls must be stripped, and our lives must be stripped, and beautiful housekeeping and beautiful living be laid for a foundation: now, a taste for the beautiful is most cultivated out of doors, where there is no house and no housekeeper.

Old Johnson,[101] in his "Wonder-Working Providence," speaking of the first settlers of this town, with whom he was contemporary, tells us that "they burrow themselves in the earth for their first shelter under some hillside, and, casting the soil aloft upon timber, they make a smoky fire against the earth, at the highest side." They did not "provide them houses," says he, "till the earth, by the Lord's blessing, brought forth bread to feed them," and the first year's crop was so light that "they were forced to cut their bread very thin for a long season." The secretary of the Province of New Netherland,[102] writing in Dutch, in 1650, for the information of those who wished to take up land there, states more particularly that "those in New Netherland, and especially in New England, who have no means to build farmhouses at first according to their wishes, dig a square pit in the ground, cellar fashion, six or seven feet deep, as long and as broad as they think proper, case the earth inside with wood all round the wall, and line the wood with the bark of trees

[100]Artificial.

[101]Edward Johnson (1598–1672), Puritan historian, author of *Wonder-Working Providence of Sion's Saviour in New England* (1654), the first published general history of New England (from 1628 to 1652).

[102]Later the State of New York. Thoreau quotes from *Documents Relative to the Colonial History of the State of New York,* 4 vols. (1849–1851), ed. E. B. O'Callaghan, which reproduced the statement by the Provincial Secretary, Cornelius van Tienhoven, regarding settlement in the New Netherlands.

or something else to prevent the caving in of the earth; floor this cellar with plank, and wainscot it overhead for a ceiling, raise a roof of spars clear up, and cover the spars with bark or green sods, so that they can live dry and warm in these houses with their entire families for two, three, and four years, it being understood that partitions are run through those cellars which are adapted to the size of the family. The wealthy and principal men in New England, in the beginning of the colonies, commenced their first dwelling-houses in this fashion for two reasons: firstly, in order not to waste time in building, and not to want food the next season; secondly, in order not to discourage poor laboring people whom they brought over in numbers from Fatherland. In the course of three or four years, when the country became adapted to agriculture, they built themselves handsome houses, spending on them several thousands."

In this course which our ancestors took there was a show of prudence at least, as if their principle were to satisfy the more pressing wants first. But are the more pressing wants satisfied now? When I think of acquiring for myself one of our luxurious dwellings, I am deterred, for, so to speak, the country is not yet adapted to *human* culture, and we are still forced to cut our *spiritual* bread far thinner than our forefathers did their wheaten. Not that all architectural ornament is to be neglected even in the rudest periods; but let our houses first be lined with beauty, where they come in contact with our lives, like the tenement of the shell-fish, and not overlaid with it. But, alas! I have been inside one or two of them, and know what they are lined with.

Though we are not so degenerate but that we might possibly live in a cave or a wigwam or wear skins to-day, it certainly is better to accept the advantages, though so dearly bought, which the invention and industry of mankind offer. In such a neighborhood as this, boards and shingles, lime and bricks, are cheaper and more easily obtained than suitable caves, or whole logs, or bark in sufficient quantities, or even well-tempered clay or flat stones. I speak understandingly on this subject, for I have made myself acquainted with it both theoretically and practically. With a little more wit we might use these materials so as to become richer than the richest now are, and make our civilization a blessing. The civilized man is a more experienced and wiser savage. But to make haste to my own experiment.

Near the end of March, 1845, I borrowed an axe and went down to the woods by Walden Pond, nearest to where I intended to build my house, and began to cut down some tall, arrowy white pines, still in their youth, for timber. It is difficult to begin without borrowing, but perhaps it is the most generous course thus to permit your fellow-men to have an interest in your enterprise. The owner of the axe, as he released his hold on it, said that it was the apple of his eye; but I returned it sharper than I received it. It was a pleasant hillside where I worked, covered with pine woods, through which I looked out on the pond, and a small open field in the woods where pines and hickories were springing up. The ice in the pond was not yet dissolved, though there were some open spaces, and it was all dark-colored and saturated with water. There were some slight flurries of snow during the days that I worked there; but for the most part when I came out on to the railroad, on my way home, its yellow sand-heap stretched away gleaming in the hazy atmosphere, and the rails shone in the spring sun, and I heard the lark and pewee and other birds already come to commence another year with us. They were pleasant spring days, in which the winter of man's discontent[103] was thawing as well as the earth, and the life that had lain torpid began to stretch itself. One day, when my axe had come off[104] and I had cut a green hickory for a wedge, driving it with a stone, and had placed the whole to soak in a pond-hole in order to swell the wood, I saw a striped snake run into the water, and he lay on the bottom, apparently without inconvenience, as long as I stayed there, or more than a quarter of an hour; perhaps because he had not yet fairly come out of the torpid state. It appeared to me that for a like reason men remain in their present low and primitive condition; but if they should feel the influence of the spring of springs arousing them, they would of necessity rise to a higher and more ethereal life. I had previously seen the snakes in frosty mornings in my path with portions of their bodies still numb and inflexible, waiting for the sun to thaw them. On the 1st of April it rained and melted the ice, and in the early part of the day, which was very foggy, I heard a stray goose groping about over the pond and cackling as if lost, or like the spirit of the fog.

So I went on for some days cutting and hewing timber, and also studs and rafters, all with my narrow axe, not having many communicable or scholar-like thoughts, singing to myself,—

Men say they know many things;
But lo! they have taken wings,—
The arts and sciences,
And a thousand appliances;
The wind that blows
Is all that anybody knows.[105]

I hewed the main timbers six inches square, most of the studs on two sides only, and the rafters and floor timbers on one side, leaving the rest of the bark on, so that they were just as straight and much stronger than sawed ones. Each stick was carefully mortised or tenoned by its stump, for I had borrowed other tools by this time. My days in the woods were not very long ones; yet I usually carried my dinner of bread and butter, and read the newspaper in which it was wrapped, at noon, sitting amid the green pine boughs which I had cut off, and to my bread was imparted some of their fragrance, for my hands were covered with a thick coat of pitch. Before I had done I was more the friend than the foe of the pine tree, though I had cut down some of them, having become better acquainted with it. Sometimes a rambler in the wood was attracted by the sound of my axe, and we chatted pleasantly over the chips which I had made.

By the middle of April, for I made no haste in my work, but rather made the most of it, my house was framed and ready for the raising. I had already bought the shanty of James Collins, an Irishman who worked on the Fitchburg Railroad, for boards. James Collins' shanty was considered an uncommonly fine one. When I called to see it he was not at home. I walked about

[103]A phrase adapted from Shakespeare's *Richard III*, Act I, Scene i, line 1.
[104]I.e., when the axe head had come off the handle.
[105]Here and throughout, Thoreau omits quotation marks for his own verse.

the outside, at first unobserved from within, the window was so deep and high. It was of small dimensions, with a peaked cottage roof, and not much else to be seen, the dirt being raised five feet all around as if it were a compost heap. The roof was the soundest part, though a good deal warped and made brittle by the sun. Door-sill there was none, but a perennial passage for the hens under the door-board. Mrs. C. came to the door and asked me to view it from the inside. The hens were driven in by my approach. It was dark, and had a dirt floor for the most part, dank, clammy, and aguish, only here a board and there a board which would not bear removal. She lighted a lamp to show me the inside of the roofs and the walls, and also that the board floor extended under the bed, warning me not to step into the cellar, a sort of dust hole two feet deep. In her own words, they were "good boards overhead, good boards all around, and a good window,"—of two whole squares originally, only the cat had passed out that way lately. There was a stove, a bed, and a place to sit, an infant in the house where it was born, a silk parasol, gilt-framed looking-glass, and a patent new coffee-mill nailed to an oak sapling, all told. The bargain was soon concluded, for James had in the meanwhile returned. I to pay four dollars and twenty-five cents to-night, he to vacate at five to-morrow morning, selling to nobody else meanwhile: I to take possession at six. It were well, he said, to be there early, and anticipate certain indistinct but wholly unjust claims on the score of ground rent and fuel. This he assured me was the only encumbrance. At six I passed him and his family on the road. One large bundle held their all,—bed, coffee-mill, looking-glass, hens,—all but the cat; she took to the woods and became a wild cat, and, as I learned afterward, trod in a trap set for woodchucks, and so became a dead cat at last.

I took down this dwelling the same morning, drawing the nails, and removed it to the pond-side by small cartloads, spreading the boards on the grass there to bleach and warp back again in the sun. One early thrush gave me a note or two as I drove along the woodland path. I was informed treacherously by a young Patrick[106] that neighbor Seeley, an Irishman, in the intervals of the carting, transferred the still tolerable, straight, and drivable nails, staples, and spikes to his pocket, and then stood when I came back to pass the time of day, and look freshly up, unconcerned, with spring thoughts, at the devastation; there being a dearth of work, as he said. He was there to represent spectatordom, and help make this seeming insignificant event one with the removal of the gods of Troy.[107]

I dug my cellar in the side of a hill sloping to the south, where a woodchuck had formerly dug his burrow, down through sumach and blackberry roots, and the lowest stain of vegetation, six feet square by seven deep, to a fine sand where potatoes would not freeze in any winter. The sides were left shelving, and not stoned; but the sun having never shone on them, the sand still keeps its place. It was but two hours' work. I took particular pleasure in this breaking of ground, for in almost all latitudes men dig into the earth for an equable temperature. Under the most splendid house in the city is still to

[106]I.e., a young Irishman.

[107]Presumably a reference to the theft, by the Greeks, of the Palladium, the image of the goddess Pallas Athena kept in her temple at Troy. According to legend, Troy could not be conquered by the attacking Greeks as long as the image of the goddess remained in Troy.

be found the cellar where they store their roots as of old, and long after the superstructure has disappeared posterity remark its dent in the earth. The house is still but a sort of porch at the entrance of a burrow.

At length, in the beginning of May, with the help of some of my acquaintances, rather to improve so good an occasion for neighborliness than from any necessity, I set up the frame of my house. No man was ever more honored in the character of his raisers than I. They are destined, I trust, to assist at the raising of loftier structures one day. I began to occupy my house on the 4th of July, as soon as it was boarded and roofed, for the boards were carefully feather-edged and lapped,[108] so that it was perfectly impervious to rain, but before boarding I laid the foundation of a chimney at one end, bringing two cartloads of stones up the hill from the pond in my arms. I built the chimney after my hoeing in the fall, before a fire became necessary for warmth, doing my cooking in the meanwhile out of doors on the ground, early in the morning: which mode I still think is in some respects more convenient and agreeable than the usual one. When it stormed before my bread was baked, I fixed a few boards over the fire, and sat under them to watch my loaf, and passed some pleasant hours in that way. In those days, when my hands were much employed, I read but little, but the least scraps of paper which lay on the ground, my holder, or tablecloth, afforded me as much entertainment, in fact answered the same purpose as the Iliad.[109]

It would be worth the while to build still more deliberately than I did, considering, for instance, what foundation a door, a window, a cellar, a garret, have in the nature of man, and perchance never raising any superstructure until we found a better reason for it than our temporal necessities even. There is some of the same fitness in a man's building his own house that there is in a bird's building its own nest. Who knows but if men constructed their dwellings with their own hands, and provided food for themselves and families simply and honestly enough, the poetic faculty would be universally developed, as birds universally sing when they are so engaged? But alas! we do like cowbirds and cuckoos, which lay their eggs in nests which other birds have built, and cheer no traveller with their chattering and unmusical notes. Shall we forever resign the pleasure of construction to the carpenter? What does architecture amount to in the experience of the mass of men? I never in all my walks came across a man engaged in so simple and natural an occupation as building his house. We belong to the community. It is not the tailor alone who is the ninth part of a man;[110] it is as much the preacher, and the merchant, and the farmer. Where is this division of labor to end? and what objects does it finally serve? No doubt another *may* also think for me; but it is not therefore desirable that he should do so to the exclusion of my thinking for myself.

True, there are architects so called in this country, and I have heard of one at least possessed with the idea of making architectural ornaments have a core of truth, a necessity, and hence a beauty, as if it were a revelation to him. All very well perhaps from his point of view, but only a little better than the

[108]Cut with a thin edge so they overlapped and thus shed water.
[109]Homer's epic poem of the Greek conquest of Troy.
[110]"Nine tailors make a man," old English proverb.

common dilettantism. A sentimental reformer in architecture, he began at the cornice, not at the foundation. It was only how to put a core of truth within the ornaments, that every sugar-plum, in fact, might have an almond or caraway seed in it,—though I hold that almonds are most wholesome without the sugar,—and not how the inhabitant, the indweller, might build truly within and without, and let the ornaments take care of themselves. What reasonable man ever supposed that ornaments were something outward and in the skin merely,—that the tortoise got his spotted shell, or the shell-fish its mother-o'-pearl tints, by such a contract as the inhabitants of Broadway their Trinity Church?[111] But a man has no more to do with the style of architecture of his house than a tortoise with that of its shell: nor need the soldier be so idle as to try to paint the precise *color* of his virtue on his standard. The enemy will find it out. He may turn pale when the trial comes. This man seemed to me to lean over the cornice, and timidly whisper his half truth to the rude occupants who really knew it better than he. What of architectural beauty I now see, I know has gradually grown from within outward, out of the necessities and character of the indweller, who is the only builder,—out of some unconscious truthfulness, and nobleness, without ever a thought for the appearance; and whatever additional beauty of this kind is destined to be produced will be preceded by a like unconscious beauty of life. The most interesting dwellings in this country, as the painter knows, are the most unpretending, humble log huts and cottages of the poor commonly; it is the life of the inhabitants whose shells they are, and not any peculiarity in their surfaces merely, which makes them *picturesque;* and equally interesting will be the citizen's suburban box, when his life shall be as simple and as agreeable to the imagination, and there is as little straining after effect in the style of his dwelling. A great proportion of architectural ornaments are literally hollow, and a September gale would strip them off, like borrowed plumes, without injury to the substantials. They can do without *architecture* who have no olives nor wines in the cellar.[112] What if an equal ado were made about the ornaments of style in literature, and the architects of our bibles spent as much time about their cornices as the architects of our churches do? So are made the *belles-lettres* and the *beaux-arts*[113] and their professors. Much it concerns a man, forsooth, how a few sticks are slanted over him or under him, and what colors are daubed upon his box. It would signify somewhat, if, in any earnest sense, *he* slanted them and daubed it; but the spirit having departed out of the tenant, it is of a piece with constructing his own coffin,—the architecture of the grave, and "carpenter" is but another name for "coffin-maker." One man says, in his despair or indifference to life, take up a handful of the earth at your feet, and paint your house that color. Is he thinking of his last and narrow house?[114] Toss up a copper[115] for it as well. What an abundance of leisure he must have! Why do you take up a handful of dirt? Better paint your house your own complexion; let it turn pale or blush for you. An enterprise to improve the style of cottage architecture! When you have got my ornaments ready, I will wear them.

[111]Trinity Church in New York City, built (1839–1846) in an ornamented, Gothic style.
[112]I.e., those without goods to protect need no buildings in which to store them.
[113]French: fine letters (aesthetic literature); fine arts. [114]The grave.
[115]A coin. In Greek myth, Charon ferried the dead over the river Styx for payment of a coin.

Before winter I built a chimney, and shingled the sides of my house, which were already impervious to rain, with imperfect and sappy shingles made of the first slice of the log, whose edges I was obliged to straighten with a plane.

I have thus a tight shingled and plastered house, ten feet wide by fifteen long, and eight-feet posts, with a garret and a closet, a large window on each side, two trap-doors, one door at the end, and a brick fireplace opposite. The exact cost of my house, paying the usual price for such materials as I used, but not counting the work, all of which was done by myself, was as follows; and I give the details because very few are able to tell exactly what their houses cost and fewer still, if any, the separate cost of the various materials which compose them:—

Boards	\$8 03½,	mostly shanty boards.
Refuse shingles for roof and sides	4 00	
Laths	1 25	
Two second-hand windows with glass	2 43	
One thousand old brick	4 00	
Two casks of lime	2 40	That was high.
Hair	0 31	More than I needed.
Mantle-tree iron[116]	0 15	
Nails	3 90	
Hinges and screws	0 14	
Latch	0 10	
Chalk	0 01	
Transportation	1 40	I carried a good part on my back.
In all	\$28 12½	

These are all the materials, excepting the timber, stones, and sand, which I claimed by squatter's right. I have also a small woodshed adjoining, made chiefly by the stuff which was left after building the house.

I intend to build me a house which will surpass any on the main street in Concord in grandeur and luxury, as soon as it pleases me as much and will cost me no more than my present one.

I thus found that the student who wishes for a shelter can obtain one for a lifetime at an expense not greater than the rent which he now pays annually. If I seem to boast more than is becoming, my excuse is that I brag for humanity rather than for myself; and my shortcomings and inconsistencies do not affect the truth of my statement. Notwithstanding much cant and hypocrisy,—chaff which I find it difficult to separate from my wheat, but for which I am as sorry as any man,—I will breathe freely and stretch myself in this respect, it is such a relief to both the moral and physical system; and I am resolved that I will not through humility become the devil's attorney.[117] I will

[116] Iron support bar set in the facing of a chimney, over a fireplace.

[117] Roman Catholic official appointed to expose defects in persons proposed for sainthood, now generally called "devil's advocate."

endeavor to speak a good word for the truth. At Cambridge College[118] the mere rent of a student's room, which is only a little larger than my own, is thirty dollars each year, though the corporation had the advantage of building thirty-two side by side and under one roof, and the occupant suffers the inconvenience of many and noisy neighbors, and perhaps a residence in the fourth story. I cannot but think that if we had more true wisdom in these respects, not only less education would be needed, because, forsooth, more would already have been acquired, but the pecuniary expense of getting an education would in a great measure vanish. Those conveniences which the student requires at Cambridge or elsewhere cost him or somebody else ten times as great a sacrifice of life as they would with proper management on both sides. Those things for which the most money is demanded are never the things which the student most wants. Tuition, for instance, is an important item in the term bill, while for the far more valuable education which he gets by associating with the most cultivated of his contemporaries no charge is made. The mode of founding a college is, commonly, to get up a subscription of dollars and cents, and then, following blindly the principles of a division of labor to its extreme,—a principle which should never be followed but with circumspection,—to call in a contractor who makes this a subject of speculation, and he employes Irishmen or other operatives actually to lay the foundations, while the students that are to be are said to be fitting themselves for it; and for these oversights successive generations have to pay. I think that it would be *better than this,* for the students, or those who desire to be benefited by it, even to lay the foundation themselves. The student who secures his coveted leisure and retirement by systematically shirking any labor necessary to man obtains but an ignoble and unprofitable leisure, defrauding himself of the experience which alone can make leisure fruitful. "But," says one, "you do not mean that the students should go to work with their hands instead of their heads?" I do not mean that exactly, but I mean something which he might think a good deal like that; I mean that they should not *play* life, or *study* it merely, while the community supports them at this expensive game, but earnestly *live* it from beginning to end. How could youths better learn to live than by at once trying the experiment of living? Methinks this would exercise their minds as much as mathematics. If I wished a boy to know something about the arts and sciences, for instance, I would not pursue the common course, which is merely to send him into the neighborhood of some professor, where anything is professed and practised but the art of life;—to survey the world through a telescope or a microscope, and never with his natural eye; to study chemistry, and not learn how his bread is made, or mechanics, and not learn how it is earned; to discover new satellites to Neptune, and not detect the motes in his eyes, or to what vagabond he is a satellite himself; or to be devoured by the monsters that swarm all around him, while contemplating the monsters in a drop of vinegar. Which would have advanced the most at the end of a month,—the boy who had made his own jackknife from the ore which he had dug and smelted, reading as much as would be necessary for this—or the boy who had attended the lectures on metallurgy at the Institute in the meanwhile,

[118]Harvard College, in Cambridge, Massachusetts.

and had received a Rogers[119] penknife from his father? Which would be most likely to cut his fingers? . . . To my astonishment I was informed on leaving college that I had studied navigation!—why, if I had taken one turn down the harbor I should have known more about it. Even the *poor* student studies and is taught only *political* economy, while that economy of living which is synonymous with philosophy is not even sincerely professed in our colleges. The consequence is, that while he is reading Adam Smith, Ricardo, and Say,[120] he runs his father in debt irretrievably.

As with our colleges, so with a hundred "modern improvements;" there is an illusion about them; there is not always a positive advance. The devil goes on exacting compound interest to the last for his early share and numerous succeeding investments in them. Our inventions are wont to be pretty toys, which distract our attention from serious things. They are but improved means to an unimproved end, an end which it was already but too easy to arrive at; as railroads lead to Boston or New York. We are in great haste to construct a magnetic telegraph from Maine to Texas; but Maine and Texas, it may be, have nothing important to communicate. Either is in such a predicament as the man who was earnest to be introduced to a distinguished deaf woman, but when he was presented, and one end of her ear trumpet was put into his hand, had nothing to say. As if the main object were to talk fast and not to talk sensibly. We are eager to tunnel under the Atlantic and bring the Old World some weeks nearer to the New; but perchance the first news that will leak through into the broad, flapping American ear will be that the Princess Adelaide[121] has the whooping cough. After all, the man whose horse trots a mile in a minute does not carry the most important messages; he is not an evangelist, nor does he come round eating locusts and wild honey.[122] I doubt if Flying Childers[123] ever carried a peck of corn to mill.

One says to me, "I wonder that you do not lay up money; you love to travel; you might take the cars and go to Fitchburg[124] to-day and see the country." But I am wiser than that. I have learned that the swiftest traveller is he that goes afoot. I say to my friend, Suppose we try who will get there first. The distance is thirty miles; the fare ninety cents. That is almost a day's wages. I remember when wages were sixty cents a day for laborers on this very road. Well, I start now on foot, and get there before night; I have travelled at that rate by the week together. You will in the meanwhile have earned your fare, and arrive there some time to-morrow, or possibly this evening, if you are lucky enough to get a job in season. Instead of going to Fitchburg, you will be working here the greater part of the day. And so, if the railroad reached round the world, I think that I should keep ahead of you; and as for seeing the country and getting experience of that kind, I should have to cut your acquaintance together.

[119]Joseph Rodgers and Sons, English cutlery firm. [120]Eighteenth-century economists.

[121]Princess Adelaide of Orleans (1771–1847), sister of Louis-Philippe, King of France (reigned 1830–1848).

[122]While preaching in the wilderness, John the Baptist lived on locusts and wild honey. Matthew 3:40.

[123]Famous eighteenth-century race horse.

[124]Small town west of Concord and terminus of the Boston and Fitchburg Railroad that passed near Walden Pond.

Such is the universal law, which no man can ever outwit, and with regard to the railroad even we may say it is as broad as it is long. To make a railroad round the world available to all mankind is equivalent to grading the whole surface of the planet. Men have an indistinct notion that if they keep up this activity of joint stocks and spades[125] long enough all will at length ride somewhere, in next to no time, and for nothing; but though a crowd rushes to the depot, and the conductor shouts, "All aboard!" when the smoke is blown away and the vapor condensed, it will be perceived that a few are riding, but the rest are run over,—and it will be called, and will be, "A melancholy accident." No doubt they can ride at last who shall have earned their fare, that is, if they survive so long, but they will probably have lost their elasticity and desire to travel by that time. This spending of the best part of one's life earning money in order to enjoy a questionable liberty during the least valuable part of it reminds me of the Englishman who went to India to make a fortune first, in order that he might return to England and live the life of a poet. He should have gone up garret at once. "What!" exclaim a million Irishmen starting up from all the shanties in the land, "is not this railroad which we have built a good thing?" Yes, I answer, *comparatively* good, that is, you might have done worse; but I wish, as you are brothers of mine, that you could have spent your time better than digging in this dirt.

Before I finished my house, wishing to earn ten or twelve dollars by some honest and agreeable method, in order to meet my unusual expenses, I planted about two acres and a half of light and sandy soil near it chiefly with beans, but also a small part with potatoes, corn, peas, and turnips. The whole lot contains eleven acres, mostly growing up to pines and hickories, and was sold the preceding season for eight dollars and eight cents an acre. One farmer said that it was "good for nothing but to raise cheeping squirrels on." I put no manure whatever on this land, not being the owner, but merely a squatter, and not expecting to cultivate so much again, and I did not quite hoe it all once. I got out several cords of stumps in plowing, which supplied me with fuel for a long time, and left small circles of virgin mould, easily distinguishable through the summer by the greater luxuriance of the beans there. The dead and for the most part unmerchantable wood behind my house, and the driftwood from the pond, have supplied the remainder of my fuel. I was obliged to hire a team and a man for the plowing, though I held the plow myself. My farm outgoes for the first season were, for implements, seed, work, etc., \$14.72½. The seed corn was given me. This never costs anything to speak of, unless you plant more than enough. I got twelve bushels of beans, and eighteen bushels of potatoes, beside some peas and sweet corn. The yellow corn and turnips were too late to come to anything. My whole income from the farm was

	\$23 44.
Deducting the outgoes	14 72½
There are left	\$ 8 71½,

[125]Organizing joint stock companies (corporations) and digging railroad beds.

beside produce consumed and on hand at the time this estimate was made of the value of $4 50,—the amount on hand much more than balancing a little grass which I did not raise. All things considered, that is, considering the importance of a man's soul and of to-day, notwithstanding the short time occupied by my experiment, nay, partly even because of its transient character, I believe that that was doing better than any farmer in Concord did that year.

The next year I did better still, for I spaded up all the land which I required, about a third of an acre, and I learned from the experience of both years, not being in the least awed by many celebrated works on husbandry, Arthur Young[126] among the rest, that if one would live simply and eat only the crop which he raised, and raise no more than he ate, and not exchange it for an unsufficient quantity of more luxurious and expensive things, he would need to cultivate only a few rods of ground, and that it would be cheaper to spade up that than to use oxen to plow it, and to select a fresh spot from time to time than to manure the old, and he could do all his necessary farm work as it were with his left hand at odd hours in the summer; and thus he would not be tied to an ox, or horse, or cow, or pig, as at present. I desire to speak impartially on this point, and as one not interested in the success or failure of the present economical and social arrangements. I was more independent than any farmer in Concord, for I was not anchored to a house or farm, but could follow the bent of my genius, which is a very crooked one, every moment. Beside being better off than they already, if my house had been burned or my crops had failed, I should have been nearly as well off as before.

I am wont to think that men are not so much the keepers of herds as herds are the keepers of men, the former are so much the freer. Men and oxen exchange work; but if we consider necessary work only, the oxen will be seen to have greatly the advantage, their farm is so much the larger. Man does some of his part of the exchange work in his six weeks of haying, and it is no boy's play. Certainly no nation that lived simply in all respects, that is, no nation of philosophers, would commit so great a blunder as to use the labor of animals. True, there never was and is not likely soon to be a nation of philosophers, nor am I certain it is desirable that there should be. However, *I* should never have broken a horse or bull and taken him to board for any work he might do for me, for fear I should become a horse-man or a herds-man merely; and if society seems to be the gainer by so doing, are we certain that what is one man's gain is not another's loss, and that the stable-boy has equal cause with his master to be satisfied? Granted that some public works would not have been constructed without this aid, and let man share the glory of such with the ox and horse; does it follow that he could not have accomplished works yet more worthy of himself in that case? When men begin to do, not merely unnecessary or artistic, but luxurious and idle work, with their assistance, it is inevitable that a few do all the exchange work with the oxen, or, in other words, become the slaves of the strongest. Man thus not only works for the animal within him, but, for a symbol of this, he works for the

[126]English author (1741–1820) of *Farmer's Guide in Hiring and Stocking Farms* (1770).

animal without him. Though we have many substantial houses of brick and stone, the prosperity of the farmer is still measured by the degree to which the barn overshadows the house. This town is said to have the largest houses for oxen, cows, and horses hereabouts, and it is not behindhand in its public buildings; but there are very few halls for free worship or free speech in this country. It should not be by their architecture, but why not even by their power of abstract thought, that nations should seek to commemorate themselves? How much more admirable the Bhagvat-Geeta[127] than all the ruins of the East! Towers and temples are the luxury of princes. A simple and independent mind does not toil at the bidding of any prince. Genius is not a retainer to any emperor, nor is its material silver, or gold, or marble, except to a trifling extent. To what end, pray, is so much stone hammered? In Arcadia,[128] when I was there, I did not see any hammering stone. Nations are possessed with an insane ambition to perpetuate the memory of themselves by the amount of hammered stone they leave. What if equal pains were taken to smooth and polish their manners? One piece of good sense would be more memorable than a monument as high as the moon. I love better to see stones in place. The grandeur of Thebes[129] was a vulgar grandeur. More sensible is a rod[130] of stone wall that bounds an honest man's field than a hundred-gated Thebes that has wandered farther from the true end of life. The religion and civilization which are barbaric and heathenish build splendid temples but what you might call Christianity does not. Most of the stone a nation hammers goes toward its tomb only. It buries itself alive. As for the Pyramids, there is nothing to wonder at in them so much as the fact that so many men could be found degraded enough to spend their lives constructing a tomb for some ambitious booby, whom it would have been wiser and manlier to have drowned in the Nile, and then given his body to the dogs. I might possibly invent some excuse for them and him, but I have no time for it. As for the religion and love of art of the builders, it is much the same all the world over, whether the building be an Egyptian temple or the United States Bank. It costs more than it comes to.[131] The mainspring is vanity, assisted by the love of garlic and bread and butter. Mr. Balcom, a promising young architect, designs it on the back of his Vitruvius,[132] with hard pencil and ruler, and the job is let out to Dobson & Sons, stonecutters. When the thirty centuries begin to look down on it, mankind begin to look up at it. As for your high towers and monuments, there was a crazy fellow once in this town who undertook to dig through to China, and he got so far that, as he said, he heard the Chinese pots and kettles rattle; but I think that I shall not go out of my way to admire the hole which he made. Many are concerned about the monuments of the West and the East,—to know who built them. For my part, I should like to know who in those days did not build them,—who were above such trifling. But to proceed with my statistics.

[127]The *Bhagavad Gita,* Hindu religious scriptures.

[128]Area of ancient Greece, symbolic of simplicity and happiness. Thoreau was there only figuratively.

[129]Ancient Egyptian city. In the *Iliad* it is described as "hundred-gated."

[130]A unit of measurement equal to sixteen and a half feet.

[131]I.e., costs more than it is worth.

[132]The writings of Vitruvius, Roman architect (first century B.C.)

By surveying, carpentry, and day-labor of various other kinds in the village in the meanwhile, for I have as many trades as fingers, I had earned $13.34. The expense of food for eight months, namely, from July 4th to March 1st, the time when these estimates were made, though I lived there more than two years,—not counting potatoes, a little green corn, and some peas, which I had raised, nor considering the value of what was on hand at the last date,—was

Rice	$1 73½	
Molasses	1 73	Cheapest form of the saccharine.
Rye meal	1 04¾	
Indian meal	0 99¾	Cheaper than rye.
Pork	0 22	
Flour	0 88 }	Costs more than Indian meal, both money and trouble.
Sugar	0 80	
Lard	0 65	
Apples	0 25	
Dried apple	0 22	
Sweet potatoes	0 10	
One pumpkin	0 6	
One watermelon	0 2	
Salt	0 3	

(Pork through Salt: All experiments which failed.)

Yes, I did eat $8.74, all told; but I should not thus unblushingly publish my guilt, if I did not know that most of my readers were equally guilty with myself, and that their deeds would look no better in print. The next year I sometimes caught a mess of fish for my dinner, and once I went so far as to slaughter a woodchuck which ravaged my bean-field,—effect his transmigration, as a Tartar[133] would say,—and devour him, partly for experiment's sake; but though it afforded me a momentary enjoyment, notwithstanding a musky flavor, I saw that the longest use would not make that a good practice, however it might seem to have your woodchucks ready dressed by the village butcher.

Clothing and some incidental expenses within the same dates, though little can be inferred from this item, amounted to

	$8 40¾
Oil and some household utensils	2 00

So that all the pecuniary outgoes, excepting for washing and mending, which for the most part were done out of the house, and their bills have not yet been received,—and these are all and more than all the ways by which money necessarily goes out in this part of the world,—were

House	$28 12½
Farm one year	14 72½

[133]Tribesmen of Russian Asia who believed in the transmigration of souls after death.

Food eight months	8 74
Clothing, etc., eight months	8 40¾
Oil, etc., eight months	2 00
In all	$61 99¾

I address myself now to those of my readers who have a living to get. And to meet this I have for farm produce sold

	$23 44
Earned by day-labor	13 34
In all	$36 78,

which subtracted from the sum of the outgoes leaves a balance of $25.21¾ on the one side,—this being very nearly the means with which I started, and the measure of expenses to be incurred,—and on the other, beside the leisure and independence and health thus secured, a comfortable house for me as long as I choose to occupy it.

These statistics, however accidental and therefore uninstructive they may appear, as they have a certain completeness, have a certain value also. Nothing was given me of which I have not rendered some account. It appears from the above estimate, that my food alone cost me in money about twenty-seven cents a week. It was, for nearly two years after this, rye and Indian meal without yeast, potatoes, rice, a very little salt pork, molasses, and salt; and my drink, water. It was fit that I should live on rice, mainly, who loved so well the philosophy of India. To meet the objections of some inveterate cavillers, I may as well state, that if I dined out occasionally, as I always had done, and I trust shall have opportunities to do again, it was frequently to the detriment of my domestic arrangements. But the dining out, being, as I have stated, a constant element, does not in the least affect a comparative statement like this.

I learned from my two years' experience that it would cost incredibly little trouble to obtain one's necessary food, even in this latitude; that a man may use as simple a diet as the animals, and yet retain health and strength. I have made a satisfactory dinner, satisfactory on several accounts, simply off a dish of purslane *(Portulaca oleracea)* which I gathered in my cornfield, boiled and salted. I give the Latin on account of the savoriness of the trivial name. And pray what more can a reasonable man desire, in peaceful times, in ordinary noons, than a sufficient number of ears of green sweet corn boiled, with the addition of salt? Even the little variety which I used was a yielding to the demands of appetite, and not of health. Yet men have come to such a pass that they frequently starve, not for want of necessaries, but for want of luxuries; and I know a good woman who thinks that her son lost his life because he took to drinking water only.

The reader will perceive that I am treating the subject rather from an economic than a dietetic point of view, and he will venture to put my abstemiousness to the test unless he has a well-stocked larder.

Bread I at first made of pure Indian meal and salt, genuine hoecakes,[134] which I baked before my fire out of doors on a shingle or the end of a stick

[134]Thin cakes of cornmeal, originally baked on a hoe blade.

of timber sawed off in building my house; but it was wont to get smoked and to have a piny flavor. I tried flour also; but have at last found a mixture of rye and Indian meal most convenient and agreeable. In cold weather it was no little amusement to bake several small loaves of this in succession, tending and turning them as carefully as an Egyptian his hatching eggs.[135] They were a real cereal fruit which I ripened, and they had to my senses a fragrance like that of other noble fruits, which I kept in as long as possible by wrapping them in cloths. I made a study of the ancient and indispensable art of bread-making, consulting such authorities as offered, going back to the primitive days and first invention of the unleavened kind, when from the wildness of nuts and meats men first reached the mildness and refinement of this diet, and travelling gradually down in my studies through that accidental souring of the dough which, it is supposed, taught the leavening process, and through the various fermentations thereafter, till I came to "good, sweet, wholesome bread," the staff of life. Leaven, which some deem the soul of bread, the *spiritus*[136] which fills its cellular tissue, which is religiously preserved like the vestal fire,[137]—some precious bottleful, I suppose, first brought over in the Mayflower, did the business for America, and its influence is still rising, swelling, spreading, in cerealian[138] billows over the land,—this seed I regularly and faithfully procured from the village, till at length one morning I forgot the rules, and scalded my yeast; by which accident I discovered that even this was not indispensable,—for my discoveries were not by the synthetic but analytic process,—and I have gladly omitted it since, though most housewives earnestly assured me that safe and wholesome bread without yeast might not be, and elderly people prophesied a speedy decay of the vital forces. Yet I find it not to be an essential ingredient, and after going without it for a year am still in the land of the living; and I am glad to escape the trivialness of carrying a bottleful in my pocket, which would sometimes pop and discharge its contents to my discomfiture. It is simpler and more respectable to omit it. Man is an animal who more than any other can adapt himself to all climates and circumstances. Neither did I put any sal-soda, or other acid or alkali, into my bread. It would seem that I made it according to the recipe which Marcus Porcius Cato[139] gave about two centuries before Christ. "Panem depsticium sic facito. Manus mortariumque bene lavato. Farinam in mortarium indito, aquae paulatim addito, subigitoque pulchre. Ubi bene subegeris, defingito, coquitoque sub testu." Which I take to mean, "Make kneaded bread thus. Wash your hands and trough well. Put the meal into the trough, add water gradually, and knead it thoroughly. When you have kneaded it well, mould it, and bake it under a cover," that is, in a baking-kettle. Not a word about leaven. But I did not always use this staff of life. At one time, owing to the emptiness of my purse, I saw none of it for more than a month.

Every New Englander might easily raise all his own breadstuffs in this land of rye and Indian corn, and not depend on distant and fluctuating markets

[135]The ancient Egyptians hatched eggs artificially, through incubation.

[136]Latin: breath of life.

[137]Roman sacred fire.

[138]A pun on "cerulean," blue.

[139]Roman statesman (234–149 B.C.). Thoreau quotes from his *De Agricultura* (160? B.C.).

for them. Yet so far are we from simplicity and independence that, in Concord, fresh and sweet meal is rarely sold in the shops, and hominy and corn in a still coarser form are hardly used by any. For the most part the farmer gives to his cattle and hogs the grain of his own producing, and buys flour, which is at least no more wholesome, at a greater cost, at the store. I saw that I could easily raise my bushel or two of rye and Indian corn, for the former will grow on the poorest land, and the latter does not require the best, and grind them in a hand-mill, and so do without rice and pork; and if I must have some concentrated sweet, I found by experiment that I could make a very good molasses either of pumpkins or beets, and I knew that I needed only to set out a few maples to obtain it more easily still, and while these were growing I could use various substitutes beside those which I have named. "For," as the Forefathers sang,—

"we can make liquor to sweeten our lips
Of pumpkins and parsnips and walnut-tree chips."[140]

Finally, as for salt, that grossest of groceries, to obtain this might be a fit occasion for a visit to the seashore, or, if I did without it altogether, I should probably drink the less water. I do not learn that the Indians ever troubled themselves to go after it.

Thus I could avoid all trade and barter, so far as my food was concerned, and having a shelter already, it would only remain to get clothing and fuel. The pantaloons which I now wear were woven in a farmer's family—thank Heaven there is so much virtue still in man; for I think the fall from the farmer to the operative is great and memorable as that from the man to the farmer;—and in a new country, fuel is an encumbrance. As for a habitat, if I were not permitted still to squat, I might purchase one acre at the same price for which the land I cultivated was sold—namely, eight dollars and eight cents. But as it was, I considered that I enhanced the value of the land by squatting on it.

There is a certain class of unbelievers who sometimes ask me such questions as, if I think I can live on vegetable food alone; and to strike at the root of the matter at once,—for the root is faith,—I am accustomed to answer such, that I can live on board nails. If they cannot understand that, they cannot understand much that I have to say. For my part, I am glad to hear of experiments of this kind being tried; as that a young man tried for a fortnight to live on hard, raw corn on the ear, using his teeth for all mortar. The squirrel tribe tried the same and succeeded. The human race is interested in these experiments, though a few old women who are incapacitated for them, or who own their thirds in mills,[141] may be alarmed.

My furniture, part of which I made myself,—and the rest cost me nothing of which I have not rendered an account,—consisted of a bed, a table, a desk, three chairs, a looking-glass three inches in diameter, a pair of tongs

[140]From "The Forefathers Song," an anonymous colonial American poem.
[141]I.e., old women who lack teeth, or whose inheritance (the traditional one-third of a husband's estate) is invested in grinding or flour mills.

and andirons, a kettle, a skillet, and a frying-pan, a dipper, a wash-bowl, two knives and forks, three plates, one cup, one spoon, a jug for oil, a jug for molasses, and a japanned[142] lamp. None is so poor that he need sit on a pumpkin. That is shiftlessness. There is a plenty of such chairs as I like best in the village garrets to be had for taking them away. Furniture! Thank God, I can sit and I can stand without the aid of a furniture ware-house. What man but a philosopher would not be ashamed to see his furniture packed in a cart and going up country exposed to the light of heaven and the eyes of men, a beggarly account of empty boxes? That is Spaulding's furniture. I could never tell from inspecting such a load whether it belonged to a so-called rich man or a poor one; the owner always seemed poverty-stricken. Indeed, the more you have of such things the poorer you are. Each load looks as if it contained the contents of a dozen shanties; and if one shanty is poor, this is a dozen times as poor. Pray, for what we do *move* ever but to get rid of our furniture, our *exuviœ;*[143] at last to go from this world to another newly furnished, and leave this to be burned? It is the same as if all these traps were buckled to a man's belt, and he could not move over the rough country where our lines are cast without dragging them,—dragging his trap. He was a lucky fox that left his tail in the trap. The muskrat will gnaw his third leg off to be free. No wonder man has lost his elasticity. How often he is at a dead set![144] "Sir, if I may be so bold, what do you mean by a dead set?" If you are a seer, whenever you meet a man you will see all that he owns, ay, and much that he pretends to disown, behind him, even to his kitchen furniture and all the trumpery which he saves and will not burn, and he will appear to be harnessed to it and making what headway he can. I think that the man is at a dead set who has got through a knot-hole or gateway where his sledge load of furniture cannot follow him. I cannot but feel compassion when I hear some trig,[145] compact-looking man, seemingly free, all girded and ready, speak of his "furniture," as whether it is insured or not. "But what shall I do with my furniture?" My gay butterfly is entangled in a spider's web then. Even those who seem for a long while not to have any, if you inquire more narrowly you will find have some stored in somebody's barn. I look upon England to-day as an old gentleman who is travelling with a great deal of baggage, trumpery which has accumulated from long housekeeping, which he has not the courage to burn; great trunk, little trunk, bandbox and bundle. Throw away the first three at least. It would surpass the powers of a well man nowadays to take up his bed and walk,[146] and I should certainly advise a sick one to lay down his bed and run. When I have met an immigrant tottering under a bundle which contained his all,—looking like an enormous wen[147] which had grown out of the nape of his neck,—I have pitied him, not because that was his all, but because he had all *that* to carry. If I have got to drag my trap, I will take care that it be a light one and do not nip me in a vital part. But perchance it would be wisest never to put one's paw into it.

[142]Varnished. [143]Latin: castoffs. [144]Unable to move. [145]Trim.

[146]A reference to the man cured of palsy when Jesus said, "Arise, take up thy bed, and go unto thine house." Matthew 9:6.

[147]Cyst.

I would observe, by the way, that it costs me nothing for curtains, for I have no gazers to shut out but the sun and moon, and I am willing that they should look in. The moon will not sour milk nor taint meat of mine, nor will the sun injure my furniture or fade my carpet; and if he is sometimes too warm a friend, I find it still better economy to retreat behind some curtain which nature has provided, than to add a single item to the details of housekeeping. A lady once offered me a mat, but as I had no room to spare within the house, nor time to spare within or without it to shake it, I declined it, preferring to wipe my feet on the sod before my door. It is best to avoid the beginnings of evil.

Not long since I was present at the auction of a deacon's effects, for his life had not been ineffectual:—

"The evil that men do lives after them."[148]

As usual, a great proportion was trumpery which had begun to accumulate in his father's day. Among the rest was a dried tapeworm. And now, after lying half a century in his garret and other dust holes, these things were not burned; instead of a *bonfire,* or purifying destruction of them, there was an *auction,*[149] or increasing of them. The neighbors eagerly collected to view them, bought them all, and carefully transported them to their garrets and dust holes, to lie there till their estates are settled, when they will start again. When a man dies he kick the dust.

The customs of some savage nations might, perchance, be profitably imitated by us, for they at least go through the semblance of casting their slough annually; they have the idea of the thing, whether they have the reality or not. Would it not be well if we were to celebrate such a "busk," or "feast of first fruits," as Bartram[150] describes to have been the custom of the Mucclasse Indians? "When a town celebrates the busk," says he, "having previously provided themselves with new clothes, new pots, pans, and other household utensils and furniture, they collect all their worn out clothes and other despicable things, sweep and cleanse their houses, squares, and the whole town, of their filth, which with all the remaining grain and other old provisions they cast together into one common heap, and consume it with fire. After having taken medicine, and fasted for three days, all the fire in the town is extinguished. During this fast they abstain from the gratification of every appetite and passion whatever. A general amnesty is proclaimed; all malefactors may return to their town."

"On the fourth morning, the high priest, by rubbing dry wood together, produces new fire in the public square, from whence every habitation in the town is supplied with the new and pure flame."

They then feast on the new corn and fruits, and dance and sing for three days, "and the four following days they receive visits and rejoice with their friends from neighboring towns who have in the like manner purified and prepared themselves."

[148]*Julius Caesar,* Act III, Scene ii, line 81.
[149]From Latin *auctio,* an increasing; hence, modern "auction," to raise the price by bidding.
[150]William Bartram (1739–1823), American naturalist and explorer.

The Mexicans also practised a similar purification at the end of every fifty-two years, in the belief that it was time for the world to come to an end.

I have scarcely heard of a truer sacrament, that is, as the dictionary defines it, "outward and visible sign of an inward and spiritual grace," than this, and I have no doubt that they were originally inspired directly from Heaven to do thus, though they have no Biblical record of the revelation.

For more than five years I maintained myself thus solely by the labor of my hands, and I found that, by working about six weeks in a year, I could meet all the expenses of living. The whole of my winters, as well as most of my summers, I had free and clear for study. I have thoroughly tried school-keeping, and found that my expenses were in proportion, or rather out of proportion, to my income, for I was obliged to dress and train, not to say think and believe, accordingly, and I lost my time into the bargain. As I did not teach for the good of my fellow-men, but simply for a livelihood, this was a failure. I have tried trade; but I found that it would take ten years to get under way in that, and that then I should probably be on my way to the devil. I was actually afraid that I might by that time be doing what is called a good business. When formerly I was looking about to see what I could do for a living, some sad experience in conforming to the wishes of friends being fresh in my mind to tax my ingenuity, I thought often and seriously of picking huckleberries; that surely I could do, and its small profits might suffice,—for my greatest skill has been to want but little,—so little capital it required, so little distraction from my wonted moods, I foolishly thought. While my acquaintances went unhesitatingly into trade or the professions, I contemplated this occupation as most like theirs; ranging the hills all summer to pick the berries which came in my way, and thereafter carelessly dispose of them; so, to keep the flocks of Admetus.[151] I also dreamed that I might gather the wild herbs, or carry evergreens to such villages as loved to be reminded of the woods, even to the city, by hay-cart loads. But I have since learned that trade curses everything it handles; and though you trade in messages from heaven, the whole curse of trade attaches to the business.

As I preferred some things to others, and especially valued my freedom, as I could fare hard and yet succeed well, I did not wish to spend my time in earning rich carpets or other fine furniture, or delicate cookery, or a house in the Grecian or the Gothic style just yet. If there are any to whom it is no interruption to acquire these things, and who know how to use them when acquired, I relinquish to them the pursuit. Some are "industrious," and appear to love labor for its own sake, or perhaps because it keeps them out of worse mischief; to such I have at present nothing to say. Those who would not know what to do with more leisure than they now enjoy, I might advise to work twice as hard as they do,—work till they pay for themselves, and get their free papers.[152] For myself I found that the occupation of a day-laborer was the most independent of any, especially as it required only thirty or forty days in a year to support one. The laborer's days ends with the going down of

[151]In Greek myth, Apollo was banished from Olympus and forced to tend the flocks of Admetus.

[152]I.e., work off their debts as indentured servants.

the sun, and he is then free to devote himself to his chosen pursuit, independent of his labor, but his employer, who speculates from month to month, has no respite from one end of the year to the other.

In short, I am convinced, both by faith and experience, that to maintain one's self on this earth is not a hardship but a pastime, if we will live simply and wisely; as the pursuits of the simpler nations are still the sports of the more artificial. It is not necessary that a man should earn his living by the sweat of his brow, unless he sweats easier than I do.

One young man of my acquaintance, who has inherited some acres, told me that he thought he should live as I did, *if he had the means.* I would not have any one adopt *my* mode of living on any account; for, beside that before he has fairly learned it I may have found out another for myself, I desire that there may be as many different persons in the world as possible; but I would have each one be very careful to find out and pursue *his own* way, and not his father's or his mother's or his neighbor's instead. The youth may build or plant or sail, only let him not be hindered from doing that which he tells me he would like to do. It is by a mathematical point only that we are wise, as the sailor or the fugitive slave keeps the polestar[153] in his eye; but that is sufficient guidance for all our life. We may not arrive at our port within a calculable period, but we would preserve the true course.

Undoubtedly, in this case, what is true for one is truer for a thousand, as a large house is not proportionally more expensive than a small one, since one roof may cover, one cellar underlie, and one wall separate several apartments. But for my part, I preferred the solitary dwelling. Moreover, it will commonly be cheaper to build the whole yourself than to convince another of the advantage of the common wall; and when you have done this, the common partition, to be much cheaper, must be a thin one, and that other may prove a bad neighbor, and also not keep his side in repair. The only coöperation which is commonly possible is exceedingly partial and superficial; and what little true coöperation there is, is as if it were not, being a harmony inaudible to men. If a man has faith, he will coöperate with equal faith everywhere; if he has not faith, he will continue to live like the rest of the world, whatever company he is joined to. To coöperate in the highest as well as the lowest sense, means *to get our living together.* I heard it proposed lately that two young men should travel together over the world, the one without money, earning his means as he went, before the mast and behind the plow,[154] the other carrying a bill of exchange[155] in his pocket. It was easy to see that they could not long be companions or coöperate, since one would not *operate* at all. They would part at the first interesting crisis in their adventures. Above all, as I have implied, the man who goes alone can start to-day; but he who travels with another must wait till that other is ready, and it may be a long time before they get off.

But all this is very selfish, I have heard some of my townsmen say. I confess that I have hitherto indulged very little in philanthropic enterprises. I have made some sacrifices to a sense of duty, and among others have sacrificed

[153]The North Star, pointing to Canada. [154]I.e., as a sailor and as a farmer.
[155]I.e., traveler's checks.

this pleasure also. There are those who have used all their arts to persuade me to undertake the support of some poor family in the town; and if I had nothing to do—for the devil finds employment for the idle—I might try my hand at some such pastime as that. However, when I have thought to indulge myself in this respect, and lay their Heaven under an obligation by maintaining certain poor persons in all respects as comfortably as I maintain myself, and have even ventured so far as to make them the offer, they have one and all unhesitatingly preferred to remain poor. While my townsmen and women are devoted in so many ways to the good of their fellows, I trust that one at least may be spared to the other and less humane pursuits. You must have a genius for charity as well as for anything else. As for Doing-good, that is one of the professions which are full. Moreover, I have tried it fairly, and, strange as it may seem, am satisfied that it does not agree with my constitution. Probably I should not consciously and deliberately forsake my particular calling to do the good which society demands of me, to save the universe from annihilation; and I believe that a like but infinitely greater steadfastness elsewhere is all that now preserves it. But I would not stand between any man and his genius; and to him who does this work, which I decline, with his whole heart and soul and life, I would say, Persevere, even if the world call it doing evil, as it is most likely they will.

I am far from supposing that my case is a peculiar one; no doubt many of my readers would make a similar defence. At doing something,—I will not engage that my neighbors shall pronounce it good,—I do not hesitate to say that I should be a capital fellow to hire; but what that is, it is for my employer to find out. What *good* I do, in the common sense of that word, must be aside from my main path, and for the most part wholly unintended. Men say, practically, Begin where you are and such as you are, without aiming mainly to become of more worth, and with kindness aforethought go about doing good. If I were to preach at all in this strain, I should say rather, Set about being good. As if the sun should stop when he had kindled his fires up to the splendor of a moon or a star of the sixth magnitude, and go about like a Robin Goodfellow,[156] peeping in at every cottage window, inspiring lunatics, and tainting meats, and making darkness visible, instead of steadily increasing his genial heat and beneficence till he is of such brightness that no mortal can look him in the face, and then, and in the meanwhile too, going about the world in his own orbit, doing it good, or rather, as a truer philosophy has discovered, the world going about him getting good. When Phaëton,[157] wishing to prove his heavenly birth by his beneficence, had the sun's chariot but one day, and drove out of the beaten track, he burned several blocks of houses in the lower streets of heaven, and scorched the surface of the earth, and dried up every spring, and made the great desert of Sahara, till at length Jupiter hurled him headlong to the earth with a thunderbolt, and the sun, through grief at his death, did not shine for a year.

There is no odor so bad as that which arises from goodness tainted. It is human, it is divine, carrion. If I knew for a certainty that a man was coming to my house with the conscious design of doing me good, I should run for my life, as from that dry and parching wind of the African deserts called the

[156]A mischievous fairy in folklore. [157]Son of the Greek god of the sun, Apollo.

simoom, which fills the mouth and nose and ears and eyes with dust till you are suffocated, for fear that I should get some of his good done to me,—some of its virus mingled with my blood. No,—in this case I would rather suffer evil the natural way. A man is not a good *man* to me because he will feed me if I should be starving, or warm me if I should be freezing, or pull me out of a ditch if I should ever fall into one. I can find you a Newfoundland dog that will do as much. Philanthropy is not love for one's fellow-man in the broadest sense. Howard[158] was no doubt an exceedingly kind and worthy man in his way, and has his reward; but, comparatively speaking, what are a hundred Howards to *us*, if their philanthropy do not help *us* in our best estate, when we are most worthy to be helped? I never heard of a philanthropic meeting in which it was sincerely proposed to do any good to me, or the like of me.

The Jesuits[159] were quite balked by those Indians who, being burned at the stake, suggested new modes of torture to their tormentors. Being superior to physical suffering, it sometimes chanced that they were superior to any consolation which the missionaries could offer; and the law to do as you would be done by fell with less persuasiveness on the ears of those who, for their part, did not care how they were done by, who loved their enemies after a new fashion, and came very near freely forgiving them all they did.

Be sure that you give the poor the aid they most need, though it be your example which leaves them far behind. If you give money, spend yourself with it, and do not merely abandon it to them. We make curious mistakes sometimes. Often the poor man is not so cold and hungry as he is dirty and ragged and gross. It is partly his taste, and not merely his misfortune. If you give him money, he will perhaps buy more rags with it. I was wont to pity the clumsy Irish laborers who cut ice on the pond, in such mean and ragged clothes, while I shivered in my more tidy and somewhat more fashionable garments, till, one bitter cold day, one who had slipped into the water came to my house to warm him, and I saw him strip off three pairs of pants and two pairs of stockings ere he got down to the skin, though they were dirty and ragged enough, it is true, and that he could afford to refuse the *extra*[160] garments which I offered him, he had so many *intra*[161] ones. This ducking was the very thing he needed. Then I began to pity myself, and I saw that it would be a greater charity to bestow on me a flannel shirt than a whole slopshop[162] on him. There are a thousand hacking at the branches of evil to one who is striking at the root, and it may be that he who bestows the largest amount of time and money on the needy is doing the most by his mode of life to produce that misery which he strives in vain to relieve. It is the pious slavebreeder devoting the proceeds of every tenth slave[163] to buy a Sunday's liberty for the rest. Some show their kindness to the poor by employing them in their kitchens. Would they not be kinder if they employed themselves

[158]John Howard (1726?–1790), English philanthropist.

[159]Members of the Society of Jesus, a Roman Catholic religious order, who attempted to convert the Indians of the New World to Christianity.

[160]Latin: outer. [161]Latin: inner.

[162]A ship's store of clothing and supplies kept for sale to the crew during a voyage.

[163]An allusion to the custom of tithing, donating a tenth of one's income to the church.

there? You boast of spending a tenth part of your income in charity; maybe you should spend the nine tenths so, and done with it. Society recovers only a tenth part of the property then. Is this owing to the generosity of him in whose possession it is found, or to the remissness of the officers of justice?

Philanthropy is almost the only virtue which is sufficiently appreciated by mankind. Nay, it is greatly overrated; and it is our selfishness which overrates it. A robust poor man, one sunny day here in Concord, praised a fellow-townsman to me, because, as he said, he was kind to the poor; meaning himself. The kind uncles and aunts of the race are more esteemed than its true spiritual fathers and mothers. I once heard a reverend lecturer on England, a man of learning and intelligence, after enumerating her scientific, literary, and political worthies, Shakespeare, Bacon, Cromwell, Milton, Newton, and others, speak next of her Christian heroes, whom, as if his profession required it of him, he elevated to a place far above all the rest, as the greatest of the great. They were Penn, Howard, and Mrs. Fry.[164] Every one must feel the falsehood and cant of this. The last were not England's best men and women; only, perhaps, her best philanthropists.

I would not subtract anything from the praise that is due to philanthropy, but merely demand justice for all who by their lives and works are a blessing to mankind. I do not value chiefly a man's uprightness and benevolence, which are, as it were, his stem and leaves. Those plants of whose greenness withered we make herb tea for the sick serve but a humble use, and are most employed by quacks. I want the flower and fruit of a man; that some fragrance be wafted over from him to me, and some ripeness flavor our intercourse. His goodness must not be a partial and transitory act, but a constant superfluity, which costs him nothing and of which he is unconscious. This is a charity that hides a multitude of sins.[165] The philanthropist too often surrounds mankind with the remembrance of his own castoff griefs as an atmosphere, and calls it sympathy. We should impart our courage, and not our despair, our health and ease, and not our disease, and take care that this does not spread by contagion. From what southern plains[166] comes up the voice of wailing? Under what latitudes reside the heathen to whom we would send light? Who is that intemperate and brutal man whom we would redeem? If anything ail a man, so that he does not perform his functions, if he have a pain in his bowels even,—for that is the seat of sympathy,[167]—he forthwith sets about reforming—the world. Being a microcosm himself, he discovers—and it is a true discovery, and he is the man to make it—that the world has been eating green apples; to his eyes, in fact, the globe itself is a green apple, which there is danger awful to think of that the children of men will nibble before it is ripe; and straightway his drastic philanthropy seeks out the Esquimau[168] and the Patagonian[169] and embraces the populous Indian and Chinese villages; and thus, by a few years of philanthropic activity, the powers in the meanwhile using him for their own ends, no doubt, he cures himself of his dyspepsia, the globe acquires a faint blush on one or both of its cheeks, as if it were beginning to be ripe, and life loses its crudity and is once more

[164]William Penn (1644–1718) and Elizabeth Fry (1780–1845), Quaker reformers.
[165]"Charity shall cover the multitude of sins." I Peter 4:8.
[166]The slave states. [167]An ancient belief. [168]Eskimo.
[169]Inhabitant of Patagonia, the extreme southern part of South America.

sweet and wholesome to live. I never dreamed of any enormity greater than I have committed. I never knew, and never shall know, a worse man than myself.

I believe that what so saddens the reformer is not his sympathy with his fellows in distress, but, though he be the holiest son of God, is his private ail. Let this be righted, let the spring come to him, the morning rise over his couch, and he will forsake his generous companions without apology. My excuse for not lecturing against the use of tobacco is, that I never chewed it, that is a penalty which reformed tobacco-chewers have to pay; though there are things enough I have chewed which I could lecture against. If you should ever be betrayed into any of these philanthropies, do not let your left hand know what your right hand does,[170] for it is not worth knowing. Rescue the drowning and tie your shoestrings. Take your time, and set about some free labor.

Our manners have been corrupted by communication with the saints. Our hymn-books resound with a melodious cursing of God and enduring Him forever. One would say that even the prophets and redeemers had rather consoled the fears than confirmed the hopes of man. There is nowhere recorded a simple and irrepressible satisfaction with the gift of life, any memorable praise of God. All health and success does me good, however far off and withdrawn it may appear; all disease and failure helps to make me sad and does me evil, however much sympathy it may have with me or I with it. If, then, we would indeed restore mankind by truly Indian, botanic, magnetic, or natural means, let us first be as simple and well as Nature ourselves, dispel the clouds which hang over our own brows, and take up a little life into our pores. Do not stay to be an overseer of the poor, but endeavor to become one of the worthies of the world.

I read in the Gulistan, or Flower Garden, of Sheik Sadi of Shiraz,[171] that "they asked a wise man, saying: Of the many celebrated trees which the Most High God has created lofty and umbrageous, they call none azad, or free, excepting the cypress, which bears no fruit; what mystery is there in this? He replied: Each has its appropriate produce, and appointed season, during the continuance of which it is fresh and blooming, and during their absence dry and withered; to neither of which states is the cypress exposed, being always flourishing; and of this nature are the azads, or religious independents.—Fix not thy heart on that which is transitory; for the Dijlah, or Tigris, will continue to flow through Bagdad[172] after the race of caliphs is extinct; if thy hand has plenty, be liberal as the date tree; but if it affords nothing to give away, be an azad, or free man, like the cypress."

COMPLEMENTAL VERSES

THE PRETENSIONS OF POVERTY

"Thou dost presume too much, poor needy wretch,
To claim a station in the firmament
Because thy humble cottage, or thy tub,

[170]A quotation from Matthew 6:3.
[171]Thirteenth-century Persian poet, author of *Gulistan (Rose Garden)*, 1258.
[172]Baghdad, modern capital of Iraq. Situated on the Tigris (Dijlah) River.

Nurses some lazy or pedantic virtue
In the cheap sunshine or by shady springs,
With roots and pot-herbs; where thy right hand,
Tearing those humane passions from the mind,
Upon whose stocks fair blooming virtues flourish,
Degradeth nature, and benumbeth sense,
And, Gorgon-like,[173] turns active men to stone.
We not require the dull society
Of your necessitated temperance,
Or that unnatural stupidity
That knows nor joy nor sorrow; nor your forc'd
Falsely exalted passive fortitude
Above the active. This low abject brood,
That fix their seats in mediocrity,
Become your servile minds; but we advance
Such virtues only as admit excess,
Brave, bounteous acts, regal magnificence,
All-seeing prudence, magnanimity
That knows no bound, and that heroic virtue
For which antiquity hath left no name,
But patterns only, such as Hercules,
Achilles, Theseus. Back to thy loath'd cell;
And when thou seest the new enlightened sphere
Study to know but what those worthies were."

T. Carew[174]

II
WHERE I LIVED, AND WHAT I LIVED FOR

At a certain season of our life we are accustomed to consider every spot as the possible site of a house. I have thus surveyed the country on every side within a dozen miles of where I live. In imagination I have bought all the farms in succession, for all were to be bought, and I knew their price. I walked over each farmer's premises, tasted his wild apples, discoursed on husbandry with him, took his farm at his price, at any price, mortgaging it to him in my mind; even put a higher price on it,—took everything but a deed of it,—took his word for his deed, for I dearly love to talk,—cultivated it, and him too to some extent, I trust, and withdrew when I had enjoyed it long enough, leaving him to carry it on. This experience entitled me to be regarded as a sort of real-estate broker by my friends. Wherever I sat, there I might live, and the landscape radiated from me accordingly. What is a house but a *sedes,* a seat?—better if a country seat. I discovered many a site for a house not likely to be soon improved, which some might have thought too

[173]In Greek myth the three Gorgons were monsters so horrible that all who looked upon them were turned to stone.

[174]The poem, addressed to "Poverty," is taken from *Coelum Britannicum* (1661) by the English poet Thomas Carew (1595?–1645). Thoreau provided the title and modernized the spelling.

far from the village, but to my eyes the village was too far from it. Well, there I might live, I said; and there I did live, for an hour, a summer and a winter life; saw how I could let the years run off, buffet the winter through, and see the spring come in. The future inhabitants of this region, wherever they may place their houses, may be sure that they have been anticipated. An afternoon sufficed to lay out the land into orchard, wood-lot, and pasture, and to decide what fine oaks or pines should be left to stand before the door, and whence each blasted[1] tree could be seen to the best advantage; and then I let it lie, fallow perchance, for a man is rich in proportion to the number of things which he can afford to let alone.

My imagination carried me so far that I even had the refusal of several farms,—the refusal was all I wanted,—but I never got my fingers burned by actual possession. The nearest that I came to actual possession was when I bought the Hollowell Place,[2] and had begun to sort my seeds, and collected materials with which to make a wheelbarrow to carry it on or off with; but before the owner gave me a deed of it, his wife—every man has such a wife—changed her mind and wished to keep it, and he offered me ten dollars to release him. Now, to speak the truth, I had but ten cents in the world, and it surpassed my arithmetic to tell, if I was that man who had ten cents, or who had a farm, or ten dollars, or all together. However, I let him keep the ten dollars and the farm too, for I had carried it far enough; or rather, to be generous, I sold him the farm for just what I gave for it, and, as he was not a rich man, made him a present of ten dollars, and still had my ten cents, and seeds, and materials for a wheelbarrow left. I found thus that I had been a rich man without any damage to my poverty. But I retained the landscape, and I have since annually carried off what it yielded without a wheelbarrow. With respect to landscapes,—

> "I am monarch of all I *survey*,
> My right there is none to dispute."[3]

I have frequently seen a poet withdraw, having enjoyed the most valuable part of a farm, while the crusty farmer supposed that he had got a few wild apples only. Why, the owner does not know it for many years when a poet has put his farm in rhyme, the most admirable kind of invisible fence, has fairly impounded it, milked it, skimmed it, and got all the cream, and left the farmer only the skimmed milk.

The real attractions of the Hollowell farm, to me, were: its complete retirement, being about two miles from the village, half a mile from the nearest neighbor, and separated from the highway by a broad field; its bounding on the river, which the owner said protected it by its fogs from frosts in the spring, though that was nothing to me; the gray color and ruinous state of the house and barn, and the dilapidated fences, which put such an interval between me and the last occupant; the hollow and lichen-covered apple trees, gnawed by rabbits, showing what kind of neighbors I should have; but

[1]Withered, damaged by storm, battered. [2]An old farm near Concord.

[3]From "Verses Supposed to Be Written by Alexander Selkirk" by William Cowper (1731–1800). Thoreau italicized *survey* as a pun on his profession of surveyor.

above all, the recollection I had of it from my earliest voyages up the river, when the house was concealed behind a dense grove of red maples, through which I heard the house-dog bark. I was in haste to buy it, before the proprietor finished getting out some rocks, cutting down the hollow apple trees, and grubbing up some young birches which had sprung up in the pasture, or, in short, had made any more of his improvements. To enjoy these advantages I was ready to carry it on; like Atlas,[4] to take the world on my shoulders,—I never heard what compensation he received for that,—and do all those things which had no other motive or excuse but that I might pay for it and be unmolested in my possession of it; for I knew all the while that it would yield the most abundant crop of the kind I wanted, if I could only afford to let it alone. But it turned out as I have said.

All that I could say, then, with respect to farming on a large scale—I have always cultivated a garden—was, that I had had my seeds ready. Many think that seeds improve with age. I have no doubt that time discriminates between the good and the bad; and when at last I shall plant, I shall be less likely to be disappointed. But I would say to my fellows, once for all, As long as possible live free and uncommitted. It makes but little difference whether you are committed to a farm or the county jail.

Old Cato, whose "De Re Rusticâ"[5] is my "Cultivator," says,—and the only translation I have seen makes sheer nonsense of the passage,—"When you think of getting a farm turn it thus in your mind, not to buy greedily; nor spare your pains to look at it, and do not think it enough to go round it once. The oftener you go there the more it will please you, if it is good." I think I shall not buy greedily, but go round and round it as long as I live, and be buried in it first, that it may please me the more at last.

The present was my next experiment of this kind, which I purpose to describe more at length, for convenience putting the experience of two years into one.[6] As I have said, I do not propose to write an ode to dejection, but to brag as lustily as chanticleer[7] in the morning, standing on his roost, if only to wake my neighbors up.

When I first took up my abode in the woods, that is, began to spend my nights as well as days there, which, by accident, was on Independence Day, or the Fourth of July, 1845, my house was not finished for winter, but was merely a defence against the rain, without plastering or chimney, the walls being of rough, weather-stained boards, with wide chinks, which made it cool at night. The upright white hewn studs and freshly planed door and window casings gave it a clean and airy look, especially in the morning, when its timbers were saturated with dew, so that I fancied that by noon some sweet gum would exude from them. To my imagination it retained throughout the day more or less of this auroral[8] character, reminding me of a certain house on a mountain which I had visited a year before. This was an airy and unplastered cabin, fit to entertain a travelling god, and where a

[4]Greek god who carried the world and the sky on his shoulders.

[5]Marcus Porcius Cato (234–149 B.C.). His *De Agricultura* was sometimes known as *De Re Rustica.*

[6]To lend literary unity to *Walden,* Thoreau condensed his experiences over two years and two months into one year.

[7]The rooster. [8]Morning.

goddess might trail her garments. The winds which passed over my dwelling were such as sweep over the ridges of mountains, bearing the broken strains, or celestial parts only, of terrestrial music. The morning wind forever blows, the poem of creation is uninterrupted; but few are the ears that hear it. Olympus[9] is but the outside of the earth everywhere.

The only house I had been the owner of before, if I except a boat, was a tent, which I used occasionally when making excursions in the summer, and this is still rolled up in my garret; but the boat, after passing from hand to hand,[10] has gone down the stream of time. With this more substantial shelter about me, I had made some progress toward settling in the world. This frame, so slightly clad, was a sort of crystallization around me, and reacted on the builder. It was suggestive somewhat as a picture in outlines. I did not need to go outdoors to take the air, for the atmosphere within had lost none of its freshness. It was not so much within-doors as behind a door where I sat, even in the rainiest weather. The Harivansa[11] says, "An abode without birds is like a meat without seasoning." Such was not my abode, for I found myself suddenly neighbor to the birds; not by having imprisoned one, but having caged myself near them. I was not only nearer to some of those which commonly frequent the garden and the orchard, but to those wilder and more thrilling songsters of the forest which never, or rarely, serenade a villager,—the wood thrush, the veery, the scarlet tanager, the field sparrow, the whip-poor-will, and many others.

I was seated by the shore of a small pond, about a mile and a half south of the village of Concord and somewhat higher than it, in the midst of an extensive wood between that town and Lincoln, and about two miles south of that our only field known to fame, Concord Battle Ground;[12] but I was so low in the woods that the opposite shore, half a mile off, like the rest, covered with wood, was my most distant horizon. For the first week, whenever I looked out on the pond it impressed me like a tarn high up on the side of a mountain, its bottom far above the surface of other lakes, and, as the sun arose, I saw it throwing off its nightly clothing of mist, and here and there, by degrees, its soft ripples or its smooth reflecting surface was revealed, while the mists, like ghosts, were stealthily withdrawing in every direction into the woods, as at the breaking up of some nocturnal conventicle. The very dew seemed to hang upon the trees later into the day than usual, as on the sides of mountains.

This small lake was of most value as a neighbor in the intervals of a gentle rain-storm in August, when, both air and water being perfectly still, but the sky overcast, mid-afternoon had all the serenity of evening, and the wood thrush sang around, and was heard from shore to shore. A lake like this is never smoother than at such a time; and the clear portion of the air above it being shallow and darkened by clouds, the water, full of light and reflections, becomes a lower heaven itself so much the more important. From a hill-top near by, where the wood had been recently cut off, there was a pleasing vista

[9]Home of the gods in Greek myth.

[10]The boat, fifteen feet long, took Thoreau a week to build. In 1842 he sold it to Nathaniel Hawthorne for $7.00.

[11]Hindu religious epic (fifth century).

[12]Site of the Revolutionary War battle (April 19, 1775).

southward across the pond, through a wide indentation in the hills which form the shore there, where their opposite sides sloping toward each other suggested a stream flowing out in that direction through a wooded valley, but stream there was none. That way I looked between and over the near green hills to some distant and higher ones in the horizon, tinged with blue. Indeed, by standing on tiptoe I could catch a glimpse of some of the peaks of the still bluer and more distant mountain ranges in the northwest, those true-blue coins from heaven's own mint, and also of some portion of the village. But in other directions, even from this point, I could not see over or beyond the woods which surrounded me. It is well to have some water in your neighborhood, to give buoyancy to and float the earth. One value even of the smallest well is, that when you look into it you see that earth is not continent but insular. This is as important as that it keeps butter cool. When I looked across the pond from this peak toward the Sudbury meadows, which in time of flood I distinguished elevated perhaps by a mirage in their seething valley, like a coin in a basin, all the earth beyond the pond appeared like a thin crust insulated and floated even by this small sheet of intervening water, and I was reminded that this on which I dwelt was but *dry land.*

Though the view from my door was still more contracted, I did not feel crowded or confined in the least. There was pasture enough for my imagination. The low shrub oak plateau to which the opposite shore arose stretched away toward the prairies of the West and the steppes of Tartary,[13] affording ample room for all the roving families of men. "There are none happy in the world but beings who enjoy freely as vast horizon,"—said Damodara,[14] when his herds required new and larger pastures.

Both place and time were changed, and I dwelt nearer to those parts of the universe and to those eras in history which had most attracted me. Where I lived was as far off as many a region viewed nightly by astronomers. We are wont to imagine rare and delectable places in some remote and more celestial corner of the system, behind the constellation of Cassiopeia's Chair, far from noise and disturbance. I discovered that my house actually had its site in such a withdrawn, but forever new and unprofaned, part of the universe. If it were worth the while to settle in those parts near to the Pleiades or the Hyades, to Aldebaran or Altair,[15] then I was really there, or at an equal remoteness from the life which I had left behind, dwindled and twinkling with as fine a ray to my nearest neighbor, and to be seen only in moonless nights by him. Such was that part of creation where I had squatted;—

"There was a shepherd that did live,
And held his thoughts as high
As were the mounts whereon his flocks
Did hourly feed him by."[16]

What should we think of the shepherd's life if his flocks always wandered to higher pastures than his thoughts?

[13]The plains of Russian Asia. [14]One of the gods in the *Harivansa.*
[15]Constellations and stars.
[16]From "The Shepherd's Love for Philiday," an anonymous Jacobean poem that Thoreau probably found in *Old Ballads* (1810), ed. Thomas Evans.

Every morning was a cheerful invitation to make my life of equal simplicity, and I may say innocence, with Nature herself. I have been as sincere a worshipper of Aurora as the Greeks.[17] I got up early and bathed in the pond; that was a religious exercise, and one of the best things which I did. They say that characters were engraven on the bathing tub of King Tching-thang[18] to this effect: "Renew thyself completely each day; do it again, and again, and forever again." I can understand that. Morning brings back the heroic ages. I was as much affected by the faint hum of a mosquito making its invisible and unimaginable tour through my apartment at earliest dawn, when I was sitting with door and windows open, as I could be by any trumpet that ever sang of fame. It was Homer's requiem; itself an Iliad and Odyssey in the air, singing its own wrath and wanderings. There was something cosmical about it; a standing advertisement, till forbidden,[19] of the everlasting vigor and fertility of the world. The morning, which is the most memorable season of the day, is the awakening hour. Then there is least somnolence in us; and for an hour, at least, some part of us awakes which slumbers all the rest of the day and night. Little is to be expected of that day, if it can be called a day, to which we are not awakened by our Genius,[20] but by the mechanical nudgings of some servitor, are not awakened by our own newly acquired force and aspirations from within, accompanied by the undulations of celestial music, instead of factory bells, and fragrance filling the air—to a higher life than we fell asleep from; and thus the darkness bear its fruit, and prove itself to be good, no less than the light. That man who does not believe that each day contains an earlier, more sacred, and auroral hour than he has yet profaned, has despaired of life, and is pursuing a descending and darkening way. After a partial cessation of his sensuous life, the soul of man, or its organs rather, are reinvigorated each day, and his Genius tries again what noble life it can make. All memorable events, I should say, transpire in morning time and in a morning atmosphere. The Vedas[21] say, "All intelligences awake with the morning." Poetry and art, and the fairest and most memorable of the actions of men, date from such an hour. All poets and heroes, like Memnon,[22] are the children of Aurora, and emit their music at sunrise. To him whose elastic and vigorous thought keeps pace with the sun, the day is a perpetual morning. It matters not what the clocks say or the attitudes and labors of men. Morning is when I am awake and there is a dawn in me. Moral reform is the effort to throw off sleep. Why is it that men give so poor an account of their day if they have not been slumbering? They are not such poor calculators. If they had not been overcome with drowsiness, they would have performed something. The millions are awake enough for physical labor; but only one in a million is awake enough for effective intellectual exertion, only one in a hundred millions to a poetic or divine life. To be awake is to be alive. I have never yet met a man who was quite awake. How could I have looked him in the face?

[17]Aurora was the Roman goddess of the dawn. Her Greek counterpart was Eos.

[18]Chinese monarch, founder of the Shang dynasty (1766–1123 B.C.). The quotation is from a commentary on *The Great Learning* of Confucius.

[19]I.e., like a newspaper advertisement ordered to run until canceled.

[20]Guardian spirit.

[21]Ancient Hindu religious scriptures.

[22]See note 96, page 801.

We must learn to reawaken and keep ourselves awake, not by mechanical aids, but by an infinite expectation of the dawn, which does not forsake us in our soundest sleep. I know of no more encouraging fact than the unquestionable ability of man to elevate his life by a conscious endeavor. It is something to be able to paint a particular picture, or to carve a statue, and so to make a few objects beautiful; but it is far more glorious to carve and paint the very atmosphere and medium through which we look, which morally we can do. To affect the quality of the day, that is the highest of arts. Every man is tasked to make his life, even in its details, worthy of the contemplation of his most elevated and critical hour. If we refused, or rather used up, such paltry information as we get, the oracles would distinctly inform us how this might be done.

I went to the woods because I wished to live deliberately, to front only the essential facts of life, and see if I could not learn what it had to teach, and not, when I came to die, discover that I had not lived. I did not wish to live what was not life, living is so dear; nor did I wish to practise resignation, unless it was quite necessary. I wanted to live deep and suck out all the marrow of life, to live so sturdily and Spartan-like[23] as to put to rout all that was not life, to cut a broad swath and shave close, to drive life into a corner, and reduce it to its lowest terms, and, if it proved to be mean, why then to get the whole and genuine meanness of it, and publish its meanness to the world; or if it were sublime, to know it by experience, and be able to give a true account of it in my next excursion. For most men, it appears to me, are in a strange uncertainty about it, whether it is of the devil or of God, and have *somewhat hastily* concluded that it is the chief end of man here to "glorify God and enjoy him forever."

Still we live meanly, like ants; though the fable tells us that we were long ago changed into men,[24] like pygmies we fight with cranes;[25] it is error upon error, and clout upon clout,[26] and our best virtue has for its occasion a superfluous and enviable wretchedness. Our life is frittered away by detail. An honest man has hardly need to count more than his ten fingers, or in extreme cases he may add his ten toes, and lump the rest. Simplicity, simplicity, simplicity! I say, let your affairs be as two or three, and not a hundred or a thousand; instead of a million count half a dozen, and keep your accounts on your thumbnail. In the midst of this chopping sea of civilized life, such are the clouds and storms and quicksands and thousand-and-one items to be allowed for, that a man has to live, if he would not founder and go to the bottom and not make his port at all, by dead reckoning,[27] and he must be a great calculator indeed who succeeds. Simplify, simplify. Instead of three meals a day, if it be necessary eat but one; instead of a hundred dishes, five; and reduce other things in proportion. Our life is like a German Confederacy,[28] made up of petty states, with its boundary forever fluctuating, so that

[23]I.e., bravely and frugally.

[24]In Greek myth, Zeus changed ants into men to repeople a kingdom that had suffered a plague.

[25]In the *Iliad,* Book III, the Trojans are compared to cranes fighting with pygmies.

[26]Botch upon botch, mistake upon mistake.

[27]A method of estimating the position of a ship at sea by calculating the direction and distance traveled rather than by observing the sun and stars.

[28]Until unified (1871) by Bismarck, Germany was a patchwork of minor kingdoms.

even a German cannot tell you how it is bounded at any moment. The nation itself, with all its so-called internal improvements, which, by the way are all external and superficial, is just such an unwieldy and overgrown establishment, cluttered with furniture and tripped up by its own traps, ruined by luxury and heedless expense, by want of calculation and a worthy aim, as the million households in the land; and the only cure for it, as for them, is in a rigid economy, a stern and more than Spartan simplicity of life and elevation of purpose. It lives too fast. Men think that it is essential that the *Nation* have commerce, and export ice, and talk through a telegraph, and ride thirty miles an hour, without a doubt, whether *they* do or not; but whether we should live like baboons or like men, is a little uncertain. If we do not get out sleepers,[29] and forge rails, and devote days and nights to the work, but go to tinkering upon our *lives* to improve *them,* who will build railroads? And if railroads are not built, how shall we get to heaven in season? But if we stay at home and mind our business, who will want railroads? We do not ride on the railroad; it rides upon us. Did you ever think what those sleepers are that underlie the railroad? Each one is a man, an Irishman, or a Yankee man. The rails are laid on them, and they are covered with sand, and the cars run smoothly over them. They are sound sleepers, I assure you. And every few years a new lot is laid down and run over; so that, if some have the pleasure of riding on a rail, others have the misfortune to be ridden upon. And when they run over a man that is walking in his sleep, a supernumerary sleeper in the wrong position, and wake him up, they suddenly stop the cars, and make a hue and cry about it, as if this were an exception. I am glad to know that it takes a gang of men for every five miles to keep the sleepers down and level in their beds as it is, for this is a sign that they may sometime get up again.

Why should we live with such hurry and waste of life? We are determined to be starved before we are hungry. Men say that a stitch in time saves nine, and so they take a thousand stitches to-day to save nine to-morrow. As for *work,* we haven't any of any consequence. We have the Saint Vitus' dance,[30] and *cannot* possibly keep our heads still. If I should only give a few pulls at the parish bellrope, as for a fire, that is, without setting the bell,[31] there is hardly a man on his farm in the outskirts of Concord, notwithstanding that press of engagements which was his excuse so many times this morning, nor a boy, nor a woman, I might almost say, but would forsake all and follow that sound, not mainly to save property from the flames, but, if we will confess the truth, much more to see it burn, since burn it must, and we, be it known, did not set it on fire,—or to see it put out, and have a hand in it, if that is done as handsomely; yes, even if it were the parish church itself. Hardly a man takes a half-hour's nap after dinner, but when he wakes he holds up his head and asks, "What's the news?" as if the rest of mankind had stood his sentinels. Some give directions to be waked every half-hour, doubtless for no other purpose; and then, to pay for it, they tell what they have dreamed. After a night's sleep the news is as indispensable as the breakfast. "Pray tell me anything new that has happened to a man anywhere on this globe,"—and he reads it over his coffee and rolls, that a man has had his eyes gouged out this morning on

[29]Wooden railroad ties. [30]Nerve disease producing jerky movements.
[31]I.e., pulling the bell rope so hard that the bell stands inverted, mouth upward.

the Wachito River;[32] never dreaming the while that he lives in the dark unfathomed mammoth cave[33] of this world, and has but the rudiment of an eye himself.

For my part, I could easily do without the post-office. I think that there are very few important communications made through it. To speak critically, I never received more than one or two letters in my life—I wrote this some years ago—that were worth the postage. The penny-post is, commonly, an institution through which you seriously offer a man that penny for his thoughts which is so often safely offered in jest. And I am sure that I never read any memorable news in a newspaper. If we read of one man robbed, or murdered, or killed by accident, or one house burned, or one vessel wrecked, or one steamboat blown up, or one cow run over on the Western Railroad,[34] or one mad dog killed, or one lot of grasshoppers in the winter,—we never need read of another. One is enough. If you are acquainted with the principle, what do you care for a myriad instances and applications? To a philosopher all *news,* as it is called, is gossip, and they who edit and read it are old women over their tea. Yet not a few are greedy after this gossip. There was such a rush, as I hear, the other day at one of the offices to learn the foreign news by the last arrival, that several large squares of plate glass belonging to the establishment were broken by the pressure,—news which I seriously think a ready wit might write a twelvemonth, or twelve years, beforehand with sufficient accuracy. As for Spain, for instance, if you know how to throw in Don Carlos and the Infanta, and Don Pedro and Seville and Granada,[35] from time to time in the right proportions,—they may have changed the names a little since I saw the papers,—and serve up a bullfight when other entertainments fail, it will be true to the letter, and give us as good an idea of the exact state or ruin of things in Spain as the most succinct and lucid reports under this head in the newspapers: and as for England, almost the last significant scrap of news from that quarter was the revolution of 1649;[36] and if you have learned the history of her crops for an average year, you never need attend to that thing again, unless your speculations are of a merely pecuniary character. If one may judge who rarely looks into the newspapers, nothing new does ever happen in foreign parts, a French revolution not excepted.

What news! how much more important to know what that is which was never old! "Kieou-pe-yu (great dignitary of the state of Wei) sent a man to Khoungtseu[37] to know his news. Khoungtseu caused the messenger to be

[32]The Ouachita River in Arkansas.

[33]A reference to Mammoth Cave (Kentucky) and its waters in which blind fish had been found.

[34]Railroad that ran from Worcester, Massachusetts to Albany, New York.

[35]In 1833 the claim of the Infanta to the throne of Spain (as Queen Isabella II) was disputed by her uncle, Don Carlos. The resulting wars and political upheavals disrupted Spain for forty years. Pedro IV, king of Portugal, defeated reactionary revolutionary forces and established a constitutional monarchy in 1834. Seville and Granada, cities and provinces of southern Spain, were centers of political turmoil in the 1830s and 1840s.

[36]When the Puritan Commonwealth interrupted the monarchy.

[37]Confucius. The quotation that follows is from the *Analects,* Book XIV, chapter 26.

seated near him, and questioned him in these terms: What is your master doing? The messenger answered with respect: My master desires to diminish the number of his faults, but he cannot come to the end of them. The messenger being gone, the philosopher remarked: What a worthy messenger! What a worthy messenger!" The preacher, instead of vexing the ears of drowsy farmers on their day of rest at the end of the week,—for Sunday is the fit conclusion of an ill-spent week, and not the fresh and brave beginning of a new one,—with this one other draggle-tail of a sermon, should shout with thundering voice, "Pause! Avast! Why so seeming fast, but deadly slow?"

Shams and delusions are esteemed for soundest truths, while reality is fabulous. If men would steadily observe realities only, and not allow themselves to be deluded, life, to compare it with such things as we know, would be like a fairy tale and the Arabian Nights' Entertainments.[38] If we respected only what is inevitable and has a right to be, music and poetry would resound along the streets. When we are unhurried and wise, we perceive that only great and worthy things have any permanent and absolute existence, that petty fears and petty pleasures are but the shadow of the reality. This is always exhilarating and sublime. By closing the eyes and slumbering, and consenting to be deceived by shows, men establish and confirm their daily life of routine and habit everywhere, which still is built on purely illusory foundations. Children, who play life, discern its true law and relations more clearly than men, who fail to live it worthily, but who think that they are wiser by experience, that is, by failure. I have read in a Hindoo book, that "there was a king's son, who, being expelled in infancy from his native city, was brought up by a forester, and, growing up to maturity in that state, imagined himself to belong to the barbarous race with which he lived. One of his father's ministers having discovered him, revealed to him what he was, and the misconception of his character was removed, and he knew himself to be a prince. So soul," continues the Hindoo philosopher, "from the circumstances in which it is placed, mistakes its own character, until the truth is revealed to it by some holy teacher, and then it knows itself to be *Brahme*."[39] I perceive that we inhabitants of New England live this mean life that we do because our vision does not penetrate the surface of things. We think that that *is* which *appears* to be. If a man should walk through this town and see only the reality, where, think you, would the "Mill-dam"[40] go to? If he should give us an account of the realities he beheld there, we should not recognize the place in his description. Look at a meeting-house, or a court-house, or a jail, or a shop, or a dwelling-house, and say what that thing really is before a true gaze, and they would all go to pieces in your account of them. Men esteem truth remote, in the outskirts of the system, behind the farthest star, before Adam and after the last man. In eternity there is indeed something true and sublime. But all these times and places and occasions are now and here. God himself culminates in the

[38]The *Thousand and One Nights,* a collection of ancient tales from the Middle East and Orient.
[39]Brahma, the Hindu supreme soul and creator.
[40]Concord's main business street, closely lined with shops.

present moment, and will never be more divine in the lapse of all the ages. And we are enabled to apprehend at all what is sublime and noble only by the perpetual instilling and drenching of the reality that surrounds us. The universe constantly and obediently answers to our conceptions; whether we travel fast or slow, the track is laid for us. Let us spend our lives in conceiving then. The poet or the artist never yet had so fair and noble a design but some of his posterity at least could accomplish it.

Let us spend one day as deliberately as Nature, and not be thrown off the track by every nutshell and mosquito's wing that falls on the rails. Let us rise early and fast, or break fast, gently and without perturbation; let company come and let company go, let the bells ring and the children cry,—determined to make a day of it. Why should we knock under[41] and go with the stream? Let us not be upset and overwhelmed in that terrible rapid and whirlpool called a dinner, situated in the meridian shallows. Weather this danger and you are safe, for the rest of the way is downhill. With unrelaxed nerves, with morning vigor, sail by it, looking another way, tied to the mast like Ulysses.[42] If the engine whistles, let it whistle till it is hoarse for its pains. If the bell rings, why should we run? We will consider what kind of music they are like. Let us settle ourselves, and work and wedge our feet downward through the mud and slush of opinion, and prejudice, and tradition, and delusion, and appearance, that alluvion[43] which covers the globe, through Paris and London, through New York and Boston and Concord, through Church and State, through poetry and philosophy and religion, till we come to a hard bottom and rocks in place, which we can call *reality,* and say, This is, and no mistake; and then begin, having a *point d'appui,*[44] below freshet and frost and fire, a place where you might found a wall or a state, or set a lamp-post safely, or perhaps a gauge, not a Nilometer,[45] but a Realometer, that future ages might know how deep a freshet of shams and appearances had gathered from time to time. If you stand right fronting and face to face to a fact, you will see the sun glimmer on both its surfaces, as if it were a cimeter,[46] and feel its sweet edge dividing you through the heart and marrow, and so you will happily conclude your mortal career. Be it life or death, we crave only reality. If we are really dying, let us hear the rattle in our throats and feel cold in the extremities; if we are alive, let us go about our business.

Time is but the stream I go a-fishing in. I drink at it; but while I drink I see the sandy bottom and detect how shallow it is. Its thin current slides away, but eternity remains. I would drink deeper; fish in the sky, whose bottom is pebbly with stars. I cannot count one. I know not the first letter of the alphabet. I have always been regretting that I was not as wise as the day

[41]Knuckle under, submit.

[42]In the *Odyssey,* Ulysses had himself tied to the ship's mast so that he might hear the song of the Sirens but avoid their fatal attractions.

[43]Soil and debris deposited by a river or a flood.

[44]French: foundation point, support base.

[45]Markings in stone set on the bank of the Nile to show the river's rise and fall.

[46]Scimitar, a curve-bladed sword of bright steel.

I was born. The intellect is a cleaver; it discerns and rifts its way into the secret of things. I do not wish to be any more busy with my hands than is necessary. My head is hands and feet. I feel all my best faculties concentrated in it. My instinct tells me that my head is an organ for burrowing, as some creatures use their snout and fore paws, and with it I would mine and burrow my way through these hills. I think that the richest vein is somewhere hereabouts; so by the divining-rod[47] and thin rising vapors I judge; and here I will begin to mine.

IV
SOUNDS

But while we are confined to books, though the most select and classic, and read only particular written languages, which are themselves but dialects and provincial, we are in danger of forgetting the language which all things and events speak without metaphor, which alone is copious and standard. Much is published, but little printed. The rays which stream through the shutter will be no longer remembered when the shutter is wholly removed. No method nor discipline can supersede the necessity of being forever on the alert. What is a course of history or philosophy, or poetry, no matter how well selected, or the best society, or the most admirable routine of life, compared with the discipline of looking always at what is to be seen? Will you be a reader, a student merely, or a seer? Read your fate, see what is before you, and walk on into futurity.

I did not read books the first summer. I hoed beans. Nay, I often did better than this. There were times when I could not afford to sacrifice the bloom of the present moment to any work, whether of the head or hands. I love a broad margin to my life. Sometimes, in a summer morning, having taken my accustomed bath, I sat in my sunny doorway from sunrise till noon, rapt in a revery, amidst the pines and hickories and sumachs, in undisturbed solitude and stillness, while the birds sang around or flitted noiseless through the house, until by the sun falling in at my west window, or the noise of some traveller's wagon on the distant highway, I was reminded of the lapse of time. I grew in those seasons like corn in the night,[1] and they were far better than any work of the hands would have been. They were not time subtracted from my life, but so much over and above my usual allowance. I realized what the Orientals mean by contemplation and the forsaking of works. For the most part, I minded not how the hours went. The day advanced as if to light some work of mine; it was morning, and lo, now it is evening, and nothing memorable is accomplished. Instead of singing like the birds, I silently smiled at my incessant good fortune. As the sparrow had its trill, sitting on the hickory before my door, so had I my chuckle or suppressed warble which he might hear

[47]A dowsing rod, the forked stick used in searching for underground water or minerals.
[1]Abruptly and unseen.

out of my nest. My days were not days of the week, bearing the stamp of any heathen deity,[2] nor were they minced into hours and fretted by the ticking of a clock; for I lived like the Puri Indians,[3] of whom it is said that "for yesterday, to-day, and to-morrow they have only one word, and they express the variety of meaning by pointing backward for yesterday, forward for to-morrow, and overhead for the passing day." This was sheer idleness to my fellow-townsmen, no doubt; but if the birds and flowers had tried me by their standard, I should not have been found wanting. A man must find his occasions in himself, it is true. The natural day is very calm, and will hardly reprove his indolence.

I had this advantage, at least, in my mode of life, over those who were obliged to look abroad for amusement, to society and the theatre, that my life itself was become my amusement and never ceased to be novel. It was a drama of many scenes and without an end. If we were always, indeed, getting our living, and regulating our lives according to the last and best mode we had learned, we should never be troubled with ennui. Follow your genius closely enough, and it will not fail to show you a fresh prospect every hour. Housework was a pleasant pastime. When my floor was dirty, I rose early, and, setting all my furniture out of doors on the grass, bed and bedstead making but one budget,[4] dashed water on the floor, and sprinkled white sand from the pond on it, and then with a broom scrubbed it clean and white; and by the time the villagers had broken their fast the morning sun had dried my house sufficiently to allow me to move in again, and my meditations were almost uninterrupted. It was pleasant to see my whole household effects out on the grass, making a little pile like a gypsy's pack, and my three-legged table, from which I did not remove the books and pen and ink, standing amid the pines and hickories. They seemed glad to get out themselves, and as if unwilling to be brought in. I was sometimes tempted to stretch an awning over them and take my seat there. It was worth the while to see the sun shine on these things, and hear the free wind blow on them; so much more interesting most familiar objects look out of doors than in the house. A bird sits on the next bough, life-everlasting grows under the table, and blackberry vines run round its legs; pine cones, chestnut burs, and strawberry leaves are strewn about. It looked as if this was the way these forms came to be transferred to our furniture, to tables, chairs, and bedsteads,—because they once stood in their midst.

My house was on the side of a hill, immediately on the edge of the larger wood, in the midst of a young forest of pitch pines and hickories, and half a dozen rods from the pond, to which a narrow footpath led down the hill. In my front yard grew the strawberry, blackberry, and life-everlasting, johnswort and goldenrod, shrub oaks and sand cherry, blueberry and ground-nut. Near the end of May, the sand cherry *(Cerasus pumila)* adorned the sides of the path with its delicate flowers arranged in umbels cylindrically about its short stems, which last, in the fall, weighed down with good-sized and handsome cherries, fell over in wreaths like rays on every side. I tasted them out

[2]The weekday names, such as Wednesday (Woden's day) and Saturday (Saturn's day), derive from pagan Norse and Roman religions.

[3]Of Brazil. Thoreau's quotes Ida Pfeiffer's *Travels.*

[4]Parcel, grouping.

of compliment to Nature, though they were scarcely palatable. The sumach *(Rhus glabra)* grew luxuriantly about the house, pushing up through the embankment which I had made, and growing five or six feet the first season. Its broad pinnate tropical leaf was pleasant though strange to look on. The large buds, suddenly pushing out late in the spring from dry sticks which had seemed to be dead, developed themselves as by magic into graceful green and tender boughs, an inch in diameter; and sometimes, as I sat at my window, so heedlessly did they grow and tax their weak joints, I heard a fresh and tender bough suddenly fall like a fan to the ground, when there was not a breath of air stirring, broken off by its own weight. In August, the large masses of berries, which, when in flower, had attracted many wild bees, gradually assumed their bright velvety crimson hue, and by their weight again bent down and broke the tender limbs.

As I sit at my window this summer afternoon, hawks are circling about my clearing; the tantivy[5] of wild pigeons, flying by twos and threes athwart my view, or perching restless on the white pine boughs behind my house, gives a voice to the air; a fish hawk dimples the glassy surface of the pond and brings up a fish; a mink steals out of the marsh before my door and seizes a frog by the shore; the sedge is bending under the weight of the reed-birds flitting hither and thither; and for the last half-hour I have heard the rattle of railroad cars, now dying away and then reviving like the beat of a partridge, conveying travellers from Boston to the country. For I did not live so out of the world as that boy who, as I hear, was put out to a farmer in the east part of the town, but ere long run away and came home again, quite down at the heel and homesick. He had never seen such a dull and out-of-the-way place; the folks were all gone off; why, you couldn't even hear the whistle! I doubt if there is such a place in Massachusetts now:—

"In truth, our village has become a butt
For one of those fleet railroad shafts, and o'er
Our peaceful plain its soothing sound is—Concord."[6]

The Fitchburg Railroad touches the pond about a hundred rods south of where I dwell. I usually go to the village along its causeway, and am, as it were, related to society by this link. The men on the freight trains, who go over the whole length of the road, bow to me as to an old acquaintance, they pass me so often, and apparently they take me for an employee; and so I am. I too would fain be a track-repairer somewhere in the orbit of the earth.

The whistle of the locomotive penetrates my woods summer and winter, sounding like the scream of a hawk sailing over some farmer's yard, informing me that many restless city merchants are arriving within the circle of the town, or adventurous country traders from the other side. As they come under one horizon, they shout their warning to get off the track to the other, heard sometimes through the circles of two towns. Here come your groceries, country; your rations, countrymen! Nor is there any man so independent on his farm that he can say them nay. And here's your pay for them!

[5]Rush.
[6]From "Walden Spring," a poem by William Ellery Channing the younger (1818–1901).

screams the countryman's whistle; timber like long battering-rams going twenty miles an hour against the city's walls, and chairs enough to seat all the weary and heavy-laden that dwell within them. With such huge and lumbering civility the country hands a chair to the city. All the Indian huckleberry hills are stripped, all the cranberry meadows are raked into the city. Up comes the cotton, down goes the woven cloth; up comes the silk, down goes the woollen; up come the books, but down goes the wit that writes them.

When I meet the engine with its train of cars moving off with planetary motion,—or, rather, like a comet, for the beholder knows not if with that velocity and with that direction it will ever revisit this system, since its orbit does not look like a returning curve,—with its steam cloud like a banner streaming behind in golden and silver wreaths, like many a downy cloud which I have seen, high in the heavens, unfolding its masses to the light,—as if this travelling demigod, this cloud-compeller, would ere long take the sunset sky for the livery of his train; when I hear the iron horse make the hills echo with his snort like thunder, shaking the earth with his feet, and breathing fire and smoke from his nostrils (what kind of winged horse or fiery dragon they will put into the new Mythology I don't know), it seems as if the earth had got a race now worthy to inhabit it. If all were as it seems, and men made the elements their servants for noble ends! If the cloud that hangs over the engine were the perspiration of heroic deeds, or as beneficent as that which floats over the farmer's fields, then the elements and Nature herself would cheerfully accompany men on their errands and be their escort.

I watch the passage of the morning cars with the same feeling that I do the rising of the sun, which is hardly more regular. Their train of clouds stretching far behind and rising higher and higher, going to heaven while the cars are going to Boston, conceals the sun for a minute and casts my distant field into the shade, a celestial train beside which the petty train of cars which hugs the earth is but the barb of the spear. The stabler of the iron horse was up early this winter morning by the light of the stars amid the mountains, to fodder and harness his steed. Fire, too, was awakened thus early to put the vital heat in him and get him off. If the enterprise were as innocent as it is early! If the snow lies deep, they strap on his snowshoes, and, with the giant plow, plow a furrow from the mountains to the seaboard, in which the cars, like a following drill-barrow,[7] sprinkle all the restless men and floating merchandise in the country for seed. All day the fire-steed flies over the country, stopping only that his master may rest, and I am awakened by his tramp and defiant snort at midnight, when in some remote glen in the woods he fronts the elements incased in ice and snow; and he will reach his stall only with the morning star, to start once more on his travels without rest or slumber. Or perchance, at evening, I hear him in his stable blowing off the superfluous energy of the day, that he may calm his nerves and cool his liver and brain for a few hours of iron slumber. If the enterprise were as heroic and commanding as it is protracted and unwearied!

Far through unfrequented woods on the confines of towns, where once only the hunter penetrated by day, in the darkest night dart these bright saloons without the knowledge of their inhabitants; this moment stopping at

[7]Seed-planting machine.

some brilliant station-house in town or city, where a social crowd is gathered, the next in the Dismal Swamp,[8] scaring the owl and fox. The startings and arrivals of the cars are now the epochs in the village day. They go and come with such regularity and precision, and their whistle can be heard so far, that the farmers set their clocks by them, and thus one well-conducted institution regulates a whole country. Have not men improved somewhat in punctuality since the railroad was invented? Do they not talk and think faster in the depot than they did in the stage-office? There is something electrifying in the atmosphere of the former place. I have been astonished at the miracles it has wrought; that some of my neighbors, who, I should have prophesied, once for all, would never get to Boston by so prompt a conveyance, are on hand when the bell rings. To do things "railroad fashion" is now the byword; and it is worth the while to be warned so often and so sincerely by any power to get off its track. There is no stopping to read the riot act, no firing over the heads of the mob, in this case. We have constructed a fate, an *Atropos.*[9] (Let that be the name of your engine.) Men are advertised that at a certain hour and minute these bolts will be shot toward particular points of the compass; yet it interferes with no man's business, and the children go to school on the other track. We live the steadier for it. We are all educated thus to be sons of Tell.[10] The air is full of invisible bolts. Every path but your own is the path of fate. Keep on your own track, then.

What recommends commerce to me is its enterprise and bravery. It does not clasp its hands and pray to Jupiter. I see these men every day go about their business with more or less courage and content, doing more even than they suspect, and perchance better employed than they could have consciously devised. I am less affected by their heroism who stood up for half an hour in the front line at Buena Vista,[11] than by the steady and cheerful valor of the men who inhabit the snow-plow for their winter quarters; who have not merely the three-o'clock-in-the-morning courage, which Bonaparte[12] thought was the rarest, but whose courage does not go to rest so early, who go to sleep only when the storm sleeps or the sinews of their iron steed are frozen. On this morning of the Great Snow,[13] perchance, which is still raging and chilling men's blood, I hear the muffled tone of their engine bell from out the fog bank of their chilled breath, which announces that the cars *are coming,* without long delay, notwithstanding the veto of a New England northeast snowstorm, and I behold the plowmen covered with snow and rime,[14] their heads peering above the mould-board[15] which is turning down other than daisies and the nests of field mice, like bowlders of the Sierra Nevada,[16] that occupy an outside place in the universe.

Commerce is unexpectedly confident and serene, alert, adventurous, and unwearied. It is very natural in its methods withal, far more so than many

[8]Vast swamp in eastern Virginia and North Carolina.

[9]Greek: literally "No turn." It is the name of one of the Greek Fates. She controlled the human life-span.

[10]William Tell, legendary Swiss hero who shot an apple off his son's head.

[11]Battle (fought February 22–23, 1847) in which American forces defeated Mexican forces in the Mexican War (1846–1848).

[12]Napoleon Bonaparte (1769–1821), military general and Emperor of France (1804–1815).

[13]Presumably a reference to the great storm of February 1717.

[14]Frost.

[15]Snow plow.

[16]California mountain range.

fantastic enterprises and sentimental experiments, and hence its singular success. I am refreshed and expanded when the freight train rattles past me, and I smell the stores which go dispensing their odors all the way from Long Wharf[17] to Lake Champlain,[18] reminding me of foreign parts, of coral reefs, and Indian oceans, and tropical climes, and the extent of the globe. I feel more like a citizen of the world at the sight of the palm-leaf[19] which will cover so many flaxen New England heads the next summer, the Manilla hemp and cocoanut husks, the old junk, gunny bags, scrap iron, and rusty nails. This carload of torn sails is more legible and interesting now than if they should be wrought into paper and printed books. Who can write so graphically the history of the storms they have weathered as these rents have done? They are proof-sheets which need no correction. Here goes lumber from the Maine woods, which did not go out to sea in the last freshet, risen four dollars on the thousand because of what did go out or was split up; pine, spruce, cedar,—first, second, third and fourth qualities, so lately all of one quality, to wave over the bear, and moose, and caribou. Next rolls Thomaston[20] lime, a prime lot, which will get far among the hills before it gets slacked.[21] These rags in bales, of all hues and qualities, the lowest condition to which cotton and linen descend, the final result of dress,—of patterns which are now no longer cried up,[22] unless it be in Milwaukee, as those splendid articles, English, French, or American prints, ginghams, muslins, etc., gathered from all quarters both of fashion and poverty, going to become paper of one color or a few shades only, on which, forsooth, will be written tales of real life, high and low, and founded on fact! This closed car smells of salt fish, the strong New England and commercial scent, reminding me of the Grand Banks[23] and the fisheries. Who has not seen a salt fish, thoroughly cured for this world, so that nothing can spoil it, and putting the perseverance of the saints to the blush? with which you may sweep or pave the streets, and split your kindlings, and the teamster shelter himself and his landing against sun, wind, and rain behind it,—and the trader, as a Concord trader once did, hang it up by his door for a sign when he commences business, until at last his oldest customer cannot tell surely whether it be animal, vegetable, or mineral, and yet it shall be as pure as a snowflake, and if it be put into a pot and boiled, will come out an excellent dun fish[24] for a Saturday's dinner. Next Spanish hides, with the tails still preserving their twist and the angle of elevation they had when the oxen that wore them were careering over the pampas of the Spanish main,[25]—a type of all obstinacy, and evincing how almost hopeless and incurable are all constitutional vices. I confess, that practically speaking, when I have learned a man's real disposition, I have no hopes of changing it for the better or worse in this state of existence. As the Orientals say, "A cur's tail may be warmed, and pressed, and bound round with ligatures, and after a twelve years' labor bestowed upon it, still it will retain its natural form." The

[17]In Boston. [18]On the New York–Vermont border.

[19]I.e., woven into hats. [20]Town in Maine.

[21]Slaked, combined with water to produce hydrated lime for agricultural use.

[22]Prized, sought after. [23]Fishing banks off Newfoundland.

[24]Salted and dried, then aged to a light brown (dun) color in a hay stack or manure pile. A delicacy.

[25]I.e., running over the plains of the mainland of Spanish America.

only effectual cure for such inveteracies as these tails exhibit is to make glue of them, which I believe is what is usually done with them, and then they will stay put and stick. Here is a hogshead of molasses or of brandy directed to John Smith, Cuttingsville, Vermont, some trader among the Green Mountains, who imports for the farmers near his clearing, and now perchance stands over his bulkhead and thinks of the last arrivals on the coast, how they may affect the price for him, telling his customers this moment, as he has told them twenty times before this morning, that he expects some by the next train of prime quality. It is advertised in the Cuttingsville Times.

While these things go up other things come down. Warned by the whizzing sound, I look up from my book and see some tall pine, hewn on far northern hills, which has winged its way over the Green Mountains[26] and the Connecticut,[27] shot like an arrow through the township within ten minutes, and scarce another eye beholds it; going

"to be the mast
Of some great admiral."[28]

And hark! here comes the cattle-train bearing the cattle of a thousand hills, sheepcots, stables, and cow-yards in the air, drovers with their sticks, and shepherd boys in the midst of their flocks, all but the mountain pastures, whirled along like leaves blown from the mountains by the September gales. The air is filled with the bleating of calves and sheep, and the hustling of oxen, as if a pastoral valley were going by. When the old bell-wether[29] at the head rattles his bell, the mountains do indeed skip like rams and the little hills like lambs. A carload of drovers, too, in the midst, on a level with their droves now, their vocation gone, but still clinging to their useless sticks as their badge of office. But their dogs, where are they? It is a stampede to them; they are quite thrown out; they have lost the scent. Methinks I hear them barking behind the Peterboro' Hills,[30] or panting up the western slope of the Green Mountains. They will not be in at the death. Their vocation, too, is gone. Their fidelity and sagacity are below par now. They will slink back to their kennels in disgrace, or perchance run wild and strike a league with the wolf and the fox. So is your pastoral life whirled past and away. But the bell rings, and I must get off the track and let the cars go by;—

What's the railroad to me?
I never go to see
Where it ends.
It fills a few hollows,
And makes banks for the swallows,
It sets the sand a-blowing,
And the blackberries a-growing,

[26]Mountain range extending from Massachusetts to Canada.

[27]The Connecticut River.

[28]A ship that carries an admiral. The quotation is from Milton's *Paradise Lost,* Book I, lines 293–294.

[29]Male sheep, leader of the flock.

[30]In southern New Hampshire.

but I cross it like a cart-path in the woods. I will not have my eyes put out and my ears spoiled by its smoke and steam and hissing.

Now that the cars are gone by and all the restless world with them, and the fishes in the pond no longer feel their rumbling, I am more alone than ever. For the rest of the long afternoon, perhaps, my meditations are interrupted only by the faint rattle of a carriage or team along the distant highway.

Sometimes, on Sundays, I heard the bells, the Lincoln, Acton, Bedford,[31] or Concord bell, when the wind was favorable, a faint, sweet, and, as it were natural melody, worth importing into the wilderness. At a sufficient distance over the woods this sound acquires a certain vibratory hum, as if the pine needles in the horizon were the strings of a harp which it swept. All sound heard at the greatest possible distance produces one and the same effect, a vibration of the universal lyre, just as the intervening atmosphere makes a distant ridge of earth interesting to our eyes by the azure tint it imparts to it. There came to me in this case a melody which the air had strained, and which had conversed with every leaf and needle of the wood, that portion of the sound which the elements had taken up and modulated and echoed from vale to vale. The echo is, to some extent, an original sound, and therein is the magic and charm of it. It is not merely a repetition of what was worth repeating in the bell, but partly the voice of the wood; the same trivial words and notes sung by a wood-nymph.

At evening, the distant lowing of some cow in the horizon beyond the woods sounded sweet and melodious, and at first I would mistake it for the voices of certain minstrels by whom I was sometimes serenaded, who might be straying over hill and dale; but soon I was not unpleasantly disappointed when it was prolonged into the cheap and natural music of the cow. I do not mean to be satirical, but to express my appreciation of those youths' singing, when I state that I perceived clearly that it was akin to the music of the cow, and they were at length one articulation of Nature.

Regularly at half-past seven, in one part of the summer, after the evening train had gone by, the whip-poor-wills chanted their vespers for half an hour, sitting on a stump by my door, or upon the ridge-pole of the house. They would begin to sing almost with as much precision as a clock, within five minutes of a particular time, referred to the setting of the sun, every evening. I had a rare opportunity to become acquainted with their habits. Sometimes I heard four or five at once in different parts of the wood, by accident one a bar behind another, and so near me that I distinguished not only the cluck after each note, but often that singular buzzing sound like a fly in a spider's web, only proportionally louder. Sometimes one would circle round and round me in the woods a few feet distant as if tethered by a string, when probably I was near its eggs. They sang at intervals throughout the night, and were again as musical as ever just before and about dawn.

When other birds are still, the screech owls take up the strain, like mourning women their ancient u-lu-lu. Their dismal scream is truly Ben Jonsonian.[32] Wise midnight hags! It is no honest and blunt tu-whit tu-who of

[31] Villages near Concord.

[32] I.e., like the melancholy lyrics of Ben Johnson (1573–1637), Elizabethan playwright.

the poets, but, without jesting, a most solemn graveyard ditty, the mutual consolations of suicide lovers remembering the pangs and the delights of supernal love in the infernal groves. Yet I love to hear their wailing, their doleful responses, trilled along the woodside; reminding me sometimes of music and singing birds; as if it were the dark and tearful side of music, the regrets and sighs that would fain be sung. They are the spirits, the low spirits and melancholy forebodings, of fallen souls that once in human shape night-walked the earth and did the deeds of darkness, now expiating their sins with their wailing hymns or threnodies[33] in the scenery of their transgressions. They give me a new sense of the variety and capacity of that nature which is our common dwelling. *Oh-o-o-o-o that I never had been bor-r-r-r-n!* sighs one on this side of the pond, and circles with the restlessness of despair to some new perch on the gray oaks. Then—*that I never had been bor-r-r-r-n!* echoes another on the farther side with tremulous sincerity, and—*bor-r-r-r-n!* comes faintly from far in the Lincoln woods.

I was also serenaded by a hooting owl. Near at hand you could fancy it the most melancholy sound in Nature, as if she meant by this to stereotype and make permanent in her choir the dying moans of a human being,—some poor weak relic of mortality who has left hope behind, and howls like an animal, yet with human sobs, on entering the dark valley, made more awful by a certain gurgling melodiousness,—I find myself beginning with the letters *gl* when I try to imitate it,—expressive of a mind which has reached the gelatinous, mildewy stage in the mortification of all healthy and courageous thought. It reminded me of ghouls and idiots and insane howlings. But now one answers from far woods in a strain made really melodious by distance,—*Hoo, hoo, hoo, hoorer hoo;* and indeed for the most part it suggested only pleasing associations, whether heard by day or night, summer or winter.

I rejoice that there are owls. Let them do the idiotic and maniacal hooting for men. It is a sound admirably suited to swamps and twilight woods which no day illustrates, suggesting a vast and undeveloped nature which men have not recognized. They represent the stark twilight and unsatisfied thoughts which all have. All day the sun has shone on the surface of some savage swamp, where the single spruce stands hung with usnea lichens,[34] and small hawks circulate above, and the chickadee lisps amid the evergreens, and the partridge and rabbit skulk beneath; but now a more dismal and fitting day dawns, and a different race of creatures awakes to express the meaning of Nature there.

Late in the evening I heard the distant rumbling of wagons over bridges,—a sound heard farther than almost any other at night,—the baying of dogs, and sometimes again the lowing of some disconsolate cow in a distant barn-yard. In the meanwhile all the shore rang with the trump of bullfrogs, the sturdy spirits of ancient wine-bibbers and wassailers, still unrepentant, trying to sing a catch[35] in their Stygian lake,[36]—if the Walden

[33]Lamentations for the dead, elegies.

[34]Tree moss.

[35]A round song, in which the second singer seems to try to chase, or "catch," the words of the first singer.

[36]Like the River Styx in the underworld of Greek myth.

nymphs will pardon the comparison, for though there are almost no weeds, there are frogs there,—who would fain keep up the hilarious rules of their old festal tables, though their voices have waxed hoarse and solemnly grave, mocking at mirth, and the wine has lost its flavor, and become only liquor to distend their paunches, and sweet intoxication never comes to drown the memory of the past, but mere saturation and waterloggedness and distention. The most aldermanic,[37] with his chin upon a heart-leaf, which serves for a napkin to his drooling chaps, under this northern shore quaffs a deep draught of the once scorned water, and passes round the cup with the ejaculation *tr-r-r-oonk, tr-r-r-oonk, tr-r-r-oonk!* and straightway comes over the water from some distant cove the same password repeated, where the next in seniority and girth has gulped down to his mark;[38] and when this observance has made the circuit of the shores, then ejaculates the master of ceremonies, with satisfaction, *tr-r-r-oonk!* and each in his turn repeats the same down to the least distended, leakiest, and flabbiest paunched, that there be no mistake; and then the bowl goes round again and again, until the sun disperses the morning mist, and only the patriarch is not under the pond,[39] but vainly bellowing *troonk* from time to time, and pausing for a reply.

I am not sure that I ever heard the sound of cock-crowing from my clearing, and I thought that it might be worth the while to keep a cockerel for his music merely, as a singing bird. The note of this once wild Indian pheasant is certainly the most remarkable of any bird's, and if they could be naturalized without being domesticated, it would soon become the most famous sound in our woods, surpassing the clangor of the goose and the hooting of the owl; and then imagine the cackling of the hens to fill the pauses when their lords' clarions rested! No wonder that man added this bird to his tame stock,—to say nothing of the eggs and drumsticks. To walk in a winter morning in a wood where these birds abounded, their native woods, and hear the wild cockerels crow on the trees, clear and shrill for miles over the resounding earth, drowning the feebler notes of other birds,—think of it! It would put nations on the alert. Who would not be early to rise, and rise earlier and earlier, every successive day of his life, till he became unspeakably healthy, wealthy, and wise? This foreign bird's note is celebrated by the poets of all countries along with the notes of their native songsters. All climates agree with brave Chanticleer. He is more indigenous even than the natives. His health is ever good, his lungs are sound, his spirits never flag. Even the sailor on the Atlantic and Pacific is awakened by his voice;[40] but its shrill sound never roused me from my slumbers. I kept neither dog, cat, cow, pig, nor hens, so that you would have said there was a deficiency of domestic sounds; neither the churn, nor the spinning wheel, nor even the singing of the kettle, nor the hissing of the urn, nor children

[37]Portly, like a successful politician (alderman).

[38]Ancient drinking cups were sometimes marked to show each drinker's share.

[39]The bullfrog counterpart of "under the table," unconscious with drink.

[40]Nineteenth-century seagoing ships carried live chickens to supply fresh eggs and meat.

crying, to comfort one. An old-fashioned man would have lost his senses or died of ennui before this. Not even rats in the wall, for they were starved out, or rather were never baited in,—only squirrels on the roof and under the floor, a whip-poor-will on the ridge-pole, a blue jay screaming beneath the window, a hare or woodchuck under the house, a screech owl or a cat owl behind it, a flock of wild geese or a laughing loon on the pond, and a fox to bark in the night. Not even a lark or an oriole, those mild plantation birds, ever visited my clearing. No cockerels to crow nor hens to cackle in the yard. No yard! but unfenced nature reaching up to your very sills. A young forest growing under your windows, and wild sumachs and blackberry vines breaking through into your cellar; sturdy pitch pines rubbing and creaking against the shingles for want of room, their roots reaching quite under the house. Instead of a scuttle or a blind blown off in the gale,—a pine tree snapped off or torn up by the roots behind your house for fuel. Instead of no path to the front-yard gate in the Great Snow,—no gate—no front yard,—and no path to the civilized world.

XII
BRUTE NEIGHBORS

Sometimes I had a companion[1] in my fishing, who came through the village to my house from the other side of the town, and the catching of the dinner was as much a social exercise as the eating of it.

Hermit. I wonder what the world is doing now. I have not heard so much as a locust over the sweet-fern these three hours. The pigeons are all asleep upon their roosts,—no flutter from them. Was that a farmer's noon horn which sounded from beyond the woods just now? The hands are coming in to boiled salt beef and cider and Indian bread. Why will men worry themselves so? He that does not eat need not work. I wonder how much they have reaped. Who would live there where a body can never think for the barking of Bose?[2] And oh, the housekeeping! to keep bright the devil's doorknobs, and scour his tubs this bright day! Better not keep a house. Say, some hollow tree; and then for morning calls and dinner-parties! Only a woodpecker tapping. Oh, they swarm; the sun is too warm there; they are born too far into life for me. I have water from the spring, and a loaf of brown bread on the shelf.—Hark! I hear a rustling of the leaves. Is it some ill-fed village hound yielding to the instinct of the chase? or the lost pig which is said to be in these woods, whose tracks I saw after the rain? It comes on apace; my sumachs and sweetbriers tremble.—Eh, Mr. Poet, is it you? How do you like the world to-day?

[1]William Ellery Channing the younger, the "Poet" who talks to the "Hermit" (Thoreau) in the dialogue that follows.
[2]Common nineteenth-century name for a dog.

Poet. See those clouds; how they hang! That's the greatest thing I have seen to-day. There's nothing like it in old paintings, nothing like it in foreign lands,—unless when we were off the coast of Spain. That's a true Mediterranean sky. I thought, as I have my living to get, and have not eaten to-day, that I might go a-fishing. That's the true industry for poets. It is the only trade I have learned. Come, let's along.

Hermit. I cannot resist. My brown bread will soon be gone. I will go with you gladly soon, but I am just concluding a serious meditation. I think that I am near the end of it. Leave me alone, then, for a while. But that we may not be delayed, you shall be digging the bait meanwhile. Angleworms are rarely to be met with in these parts, where the soil was never fattened with manure; the race is nearly extinct. The sport of digging the bait is nearly equal to that of catching the fish, when one's appetite is not too keen; and this you may have all to yourself to-day. I would advise you to set in the spade down yonder among the groundnuts, where you see the johnswort waving. I think that I may warrant you one worm to every three sods you turn up, if you look well in among the roots of the grass, as if you were weeding. Or, if you choose to go farther, it will not be unwise, for I have found the increase of fair bait to be very nearly as the squares of the distances.

Hermit alone. Let me see; where was I? Methinks I was nearly in this frame of mind; the world lay about at this angle. Shall I go to heaven or a-fishing? If I should soon bring this meditation to an end, would another so sweet occasion be likely to offer? I was as near being resolved into the essence of things as ever I was in my life. I fear my thoughts will not come back to me. If it would do any good, I would whistle for them. When they make us an offer, it is wise to say, We will think of it. My thoughts have left no track, and I cannot find the path again. What was it that I was thinking of? It was a very hazy day. I will just try these three sentences of Confutsee;[3] they may fetch that state about again. I know not whether it was the dumps or a budding ecstasy. Mem.[4] There never is but one opportunity of a kind.

Poet. How now, Hermit, is it too soon? I have got just thirteen whole ones, beside several which are imperfect or undersized; but they will do for the smaller fry; they do not cover up the hook so much. Those village worms are quite too large; a shiner may make a meal off one without finding the skewer.

Hermit. Well, then, let's be off. Shall we to the Concord? There's good sport there if the water be not too high.

Why do precisely these objects which we behold make a world? Why has man just these species of animals for his neighbors; as if nothing but a mouse could have filled this crevice? I suspect that Pilpay & Co.[5] have put animals to their best use, for they are all beasts of burden, in a sense, made to carry some portion of our thoughts.

The mice which haunted my house were not the common ones, which are said to have been introduced into the country, but a wild native kind not

[3]Confucius.

[4]Memorandum.

[5]Fable tellers. Pilpay was the narrator of a collection of ancient Sanskrit animal fables.

found in the village. I sent one to a distinguished naturalist, and it interested him much. When I was building, one of these had its nest underneath the house, and before I had laid the second floor, and swept out the shavings, would come out regularly at lunch time and pick up the crumbs at my feet. It probably had never seen a man before; and it soon became quite familiar, and would run over my shoes and up my clothes. It could readily ascend the sides of the room by short impulses, like a squirrel, which it resembled in its motions. At length, as I leaned with my elbow on the bench one day, it ran up my clothes and along my sleeve, and round and round the paper which held my dinner, while I kept the latter close, and dodged and played at bopeep with it; and when at last I held still a piece of cheese between my thumb and finger, it came and nibbled it, sitting in my hand and afterward cleaned its face and paws, like a fly, and walked away.

A phœbe soon built in my shed, and a robin for protection in a pine which grew against the house. In June the partridge (*Tetrao umbellus*), which is so shy a bird, led her brood past my windows, from the woods in the rear to the front of my house, clucking and calling to them like a hen, and in all her behavior proving herself the hen of the woods. The young suddenly disperse on your approach, at a signal from the mother, as if a whirlwind had swept them away, and they so exactly resemble the dried leaves and twigs that many a traveller has placed his foot in the midst of a brood, and heard the whir of the old bird as she flew off, and her anxious calls and mewing, or seen her trail her wings to attract his attention, without suspecting their neighborhood. The parent will sometimes roll and spin round before you in such a dishabille, that you cannot, for a few moments, detect what kind of creature it is. The young squat still and flat, often running their heads under a leaf, and mind only their mother's directions given from a distance, nor will your approach make them run again and betray themselves. You may even tread on them, or have your eyes on them for a minute, without discovering them. I have held them in my open hand at such a time, and still their only care, obedient to their mother and their instinct, was to squat there without fear or trembling. So perfect is this instinct, that once, when I had lain them on the leaves again, and one accidentally fell on its side, it was found with the rest in exactly the same position ten minutes afterward. They are not callow like the young of most birds, but more perfectly developed and precocious even than chickens. The remarkably adult yet innocent expression of their open and serene eyes is very memorable. All intelligence seems reflected in them. They suggest not merely the purity of infancy, but a wisdom clarified by experience. Such an eye was not born when the bird was, but is coeval with the sky it reflects. The woods do not yield another such a gem. The traveller does not often look into such a limpid well. The ignorant or reckless sportsman often shoots the parent at such a time, and leaves these innocents to fall a prey to some prowling beast or bird, or gradually mingle with the decaying leaves which they so much resemble. It is said that when hatched by a hen they will directly disperse on some alarm, and so are lost, for they never hear the mother's call which gathers them again. These were my hens and chickens.

It is remarkable how many creatures live wild and free though secret in the woods, and still sustain themselves in the neighborhood of towns, suspected by hunters only. How retired the otter manages to live here! He grows to be four feet long, as big as a small boy, perhaps without any human being getting a glimpse of him. I formerly saw the raccoon in the woods behind where my house is built, and probably still heard their whinnering[6] at night. Commonly I rested an hour or two in the shade at noon, after planting, and ate my lunch, and read a little by a spring which was the source of a swamp and of a brook, oozing from under Brister's Hill, half a mile from my field. The approach to this was through a succession of descending grassy hollows, full of young pitch pines, into a larger wood about the swamp. There, in a very secluded and shaded spot, under a spreading white pine, there was yet a clean, firm sward to sit on. I had dug out the spring and made a well of clear gray water, where I could dip up a pailful without roiling it, and thither I went for this purpose almost every day in midsummer, when the pond was warmest. Thither, too, the woodcock led her brood to probe the mud for worms, flying but a foot above them down the bank, while they ran in a troop beneath; but at last, spying me, she would leave her young and circle round and round me, nearer and nearer till within four or five feet, pretending broken wings and legs, to attract my attention, and get off her young, who would already have taken up their march, with faint, wiry peep, single file through the swamp, as she directed. Or I heard the peep of the young when I could not see the parent bird. There too the turtle doves sat over the spring, or fluttered from bough to bough of the soft white pines over my head; or the red squirrel, coursing down the nearest bough, was particularly familiar and inquisitive. You only need sit still long enough in some attractive spot in the woods that all its inhabitants may exhibit themselves to you by turns.

I was witness to events of a less peaceful character. One day when I went out to my wood-pile, or rather my pile of stumps, I observed two large ants, the one red, the other much larger, nearly half an inch long, and black, fiercely contending with one another. Having once got hold they never let go, but struggled and wrestled and rolled on the chips incessantly. Looking farther, I was surprised to find that the chips were covered with such combatants, that it was not a *duellum*,[7] but a *bellum*, a war between two races of ants, the red always pitted against the black, and frequently two red ones to one black. The legions of these Myrmidons[8] covered all the hills and vales in my wood-yard, and the ground was already strewn with the dead and dying, both red and black. It was the only battle which I have ever witnessed, the only battle-field I ever trod while the battle was raging; internecine war; the red republicans on the one hand, and the black imperialists on the other. On every side they were engaged in deadly combat, yet without any noise that I could hear, and human soldiers never fought so resolutely. I watched a couple that were fast locked in each other's embraces, in a little sunny valley amid the chips, now at noonday prepared to fight till the sun went down, or life went out. The smaller red champion had fastened himself like a vise to his adversary's front, and through all the tumblings on that field never for an instant ceased to gnaw at one of his feelers near the root, having already caused the other to go by the board; while the stronger black one dashed him from side to side, and, as I saw on looking nearer, had already divested him of several

[6]Faint whining. [7]Latin: duel.
[8]Achilles' troops in the Trojan War of the *Iliad; Myrmex* is Greek for "ant."

of his members. They fought with more pertinacity than bulldogs. Neither manifested the least disposition to retreat. It was evident that their battle-cry was "Conquer or die." In the meanwhile there came along a single red ant on the hillside of this valley, evidently full of excitement, who either had despatched his foe, or had not yet taken part in the battle; probably the latter, for he had lost none of his limbs; whose mother had charged him to return with his shield or upon it.[9] Or perchance he was some Achilles, who had nourished his wrath apart, and had now come to avenge or rescue his Patroclus.[10] He saw this unequal combat from afar,—for the blacks were nearly twice the size of the red,—he drew near with rapid pace till he stood on his guard within half an inch of the combatants; then, watching his opportunity, he sprang upon the black warrior, and commenced his operations near the root of his right fore leg, leaving the foe to select among his own members; and so there were three united for life, as if a new kind of attraction had been invented which put all other locks and cements to shame. I should not have wondered by this time to find that they had their respective musical bands stationed on some eminent chip, and playing their national airs the while, to excite the slow and cheer the dying combatants. I was myself excited somewhat even as if they had been men. The more you think of it, the less the difference. And certainly there is not the fight recorded in Concord history, at least if in the history of America, that will bear a moment's comparison with this, whether for the numbers engaged in it, or for the patriotism and heroism displayed. For numbers and for carnage it was an Austerlitz or Dresden.[11] Concord Fight![12] Two killed on the patriots' side, and Luther Blanchard[13] wounded! Why here every ant was a Buttrick,—"Fire! for God's sake fire!"[14]—and thousands shared the fate of Davis and Hosmer.[15] There was not one hireling[16] there. I have no doubt that it was a principle they fought for, as much as our ancestors, and not to avoid a three-penny tax on their tea; and the results of this battle will be as important and memorable to those whom it concerns as those of the battle of Bunker Hill, at least.

I took up the chip on which the three I have particularly described were struggling, carried it into my house, and placed it under a tumbler on my window-sill, in order to see the issue. Holding a microscope[17] to the first-mentioned red ant, I saw that, though he was assiduously gnawing at the near fore leg of his enemy, having severed his remaining feeler, his own breast was all torn away, exposing what vitals he had there to the jaws of the black warrior, whose breastplate was apparently too thick for him to pierce; and the dark carbuncles of the sufferer's eyes shone with ferocity such as war only could excite. They struggled half an hour longer under the tumbler, and when I looked again the black soldier had severed the heads of his foes from

[9]The exhortation of Spartan mothers to their sons, reported in Plutarch's "Sayings of Spartan Women."

[10]In the *Iliad,* Achilles agreed to fight the Trojans only after he was angered by the death of his friend Patroclus.

[11]Battles of the Napoleonic Wars.

[12]The American Revolutionary War battle of April 1775.

[13]Blanchard, and others named here, took part in the Battle of Concord; Major John Butterick led the Minutemen.

[14]Battle cry at Concord.

[15]Two patriots killed in the battle at Concord.

[16]Mercenary.

[17]Magnifying glass.

their bodies, and the still living heads were hanging on either side of him like ghastly trophies at his saddle-bow, still apparently as firmly fastened as ever, and he was endeavoring with feeble struggles, being without feelers and with only the remnant of a leg, and I know not how many other wounds, to divest himself of them; which at length, after half an hour more, he accomplished. I raised the glass, and he went off over the windowsill in that crippled state. Whether he finally survived that combat, and spent the remainder of his days in some Hôtel des Invalides,[18] I do not know; but I thought that his industry would not be worth much thereafter. I never learned which party was victorious, nor the cause of the war; but I felt for the rest of that day as if I had my feelings excited and harrowed by witnessing the struggle, the ferocity and carnage, of a human battle before my door.

Kirby and Spence tell us that the battles of ants have long been celebrated and the date of them recorded, though they say that Huber[19] is the only modern author who appears to have witnessed them. "Æneas Sylvius,"[20] say they, "after giving a very circumstantial account of one contested with great obstinacy by a great and small species on the trunk of a pear tree," adds that "this action was fought in the pontificate of Eugenius the Fourth,[21] in the presence of Nicholas Pistoriensis, an eminent lawyer, who related the whole history of the battle with the greatest fidelity." A similar engagement between great and small ants is recorded by Olaus Magnus,[22] in which the small ones, being victorious, are said to have buried the bodies of their own soldiers, but left those of their giant enemies a prey to the birds. This event happened previous to the expulsion of the tyrant Christiern the Second[23] from Sweden." The battle which I witnessed took place in the Presidency of Polk, five years before the passage of Webster's Fugitive-Slave Bill.[24]

Many a village Bose, fit only to course[25] a mud-turtle in a victualling cellar, sported his heavy quarters in the woods, without the knowledge of his master, and ineffectually smelled at old fox burrows and woodchucks' holes; led perchance by some slight cur which nimbly threaded the wood, and might still inspire a natural terror in its denizens;—now far behind his guide, barking like a canine bull toward some small squirrel which had treed itself for scrutiny, then, cantering off, bending the bushes with his weight, imagining that he is on the track of some stray member of the gerbille[26] family. Once I was surprised to see a cat walking along the stony shore of the pond, for they rarely wander so far from home. The surprise was mutual. Nevertheless the most domestic cat, which has lain on a rug all her days, appears quite at home in the woods, and, by her sly and stealthy behavior, proves herself more native there than the regular inhabitants. Once, when berrying, I met with a cat with young kittens in the woods, quite wild, and they all, like their mother, had their backs up and were fiercely spitting at me. A few

[18]Soldiers' hospital in Paris.

[19]Pierre Huber (1777–1840), author of *The Natural History of Ants* (1810). His description of ant warfare was paraphrased by Kirby and Spence in their *Introduction to Entomology*.

[20]Pen name of Pope Pius II (1405–1464), theologian and historian.

[21]Pope from 1431 to 1447. [22]Swedish ecclesiastic and historian (1490–1557).

[23]Christian II (1481–1559), King of Denmark, Norway, and Sweden.

[24]James K. Polk was president from 1845 to 1849. Daniel Webster, senator from Massachusetts, supported the passage of the proslavery Fugitive Slave Law (1850).

[25]Pursue, harry. [26]Gerbil. Small mouse-like rodent.

years before I lived in the woods there was what was called a "winged cat" in one of the farmhouses in Lincoln nearest the pond, Mr. Gilian Baker's. When I called to see her in June, 1842, she was gone a-hunting in the woods, as was her wont (I am not sure whether it was a male or female, and so use the more common pronoun), but her mistress told me that she came into the neighborhood a little more than a year before, in April, and was finally taken into their house; that she was of a dark brownish-gray color, with a white spot on her throat, and white feet, and had a large bushy tail like a fox; that in the winter the fur grew thick and flatted out along her sides, forming strips ten or twelve inches long by two and a half wide, and under her chin like a muff, the upper side loose, the under matted like felt, and in the spring these appendages dropped off. They gave me a pair of her "wings," which I keep still. There is no appearance of a membrane about them. Some thought it was part flying squirrel or some other wild animal, which is not impossible, for, according to naturalists, prolific hybrids have been produced by the union of the marten and domestic cat. This would have been the right kind of cat for me to keep, if I had kept any; for why should not a poet's cat be winged as well as his horse?[27]

In the fall the loon (*Colymbus glacialis*) came, as usual, to moult and bathe in the pond, making the woods rings with his wild laughter before I had risen. At rumor of his arrival all the Mill-dam sportsmen are on the alert, in gigs[28] and on foot, two by two and three by three, with patent rifles and conical balls[29] and spyglasses. They come rustling through the woods like autumn leaves, at least ten men to one loon. Some station themselves on this side of the pond, some on that, for the poor bird cannot be omnipresent; if he dive here he must come up there. But now the kind October wind rises, rustling the leaves and rippling the surface of the water, so that no loon can be heard or seen, though his foes sweep the pond with spy-glasses, and make the woods resound with their discharges. The waves generously rise and dash angrily, taking sides with all water-fowl, and our sportsmen must beat a retreat to town and shop and unfinished jobs. But they were too often successful. When I went to get a pail of water early in the morning I frequently saw this stately bird sailing out of my cove within a few rods. If I endeavored to overtake him in a boat, in order to see how he would manœuvre, he would dive and be completely lost, so that I did not discover him again, sometimes, till the latter part of the day. But I was more than a match for him on the surface. He commonly went off in a rage.

As I was paddling along the north shore one very calm October afternoon, for such days especially they settle on to the lakes, like the milkweed down, having looked in vain over the pond for a loon, suddenly one, sailing out from the shore toward the middle a few rods in front of me, set up his wild laugh and betrayed himself. I pursued with a paddle and he dived, but when he came up I was nearer than before. He dived again, but I miscalculated the direction he would take, and we were fifty rods apart, when he came to the

[27]Pegasus, winged horse of Greek myth and the mount of poets.
[28]A light, two-wheeled carriage drawn by one horse.
[29]I.e., special rifles that fire the most modern conical-shaped bullets.

surface this time, for I had helped to widen the interval; and again he laughed long and loud, and with more reason than before. He manœuvred so cunningly that I could not get within half a dozen rods of him. Each time, when he came to the surface, turning his head this way and that, he coolly surveyed the water and the land, and apparently chose his course so that he might come up where there was the widest expanse of water and at the greatest distance from the boat. It was surprising how quickly he made up his mind and put his resolve into execution. He led me at once to the widest part of the pond, and could not be driven from it. While he was thinking one thing in his brain, I was endeavoring to divine his thought in mine. It was a pretty game, played on the smooth surface of the pond, a man against a loon. Suddenly your adversary's checker disappears beneath the board, and the problem is to place yours nearest to where his will appear again. Sometimes he would come up unexpectedly on the opposite side of me, having apparently passed directly under the boat. So long-winded was he and so unweariable, that when he had swum farthest he would immediately plunge again, nevertheless; and then no wit could divine where in the deep pond, beneath the smooth surface, he might be speeding his way like a fish, for he had time and ability to visit the bottom of the pond in its deepest part. It is said that loons have been caught in the New York lakes eighty feet beneath the surface, with hooks set for trout,—though Walden is deeper than that. How surprised must the fishes be to see this ungainly visitor from another sphere speeding his way amid their schools! Yet he appeared to know his course as surely under water as on the surface, and swam much faster there. Once or twice I saw a ripple where he approached the surface, just put his head out to reconnoitre, and instantly dived again. I found that it was as well for me to rest on my oars and wait his reappearing as to endeavor to calculate where he would rise; for again and again, when I was straining my eyes over the surface one way, I would suddenly be startled by his unearthly laugh behind me. But why, after displaying so much cunning, did he invariably betray himself the moment he came up by that loud laugh? Did not his white breast enough betray him? He was indeed a silly loon, I thought. I could commonly hear the plash of the water when he came up, and so also detected him. But after an hour he seemed as fresh as ever, dived as willingly, and swam yet farther than at first. It was surprising to see how serenely he sailed off with unruffled breast when he came to the surface, doing all the work with his webbed feet beneath. His usual note was this demoniac laughter, yet somehow like that of a water-fowl; but occasionally, when he had balked me most successfully and come up a long way off, he uttered a long-drawn unearthly howl, probably more like that of a wolf than any bird; as when a beast puts his muzzle to the ground and deliberately howls. This was his looning,—perhaps the wildest sound that is ever heard here, making the woods ring far and wide. I concluded that he laughed in derision of my efforts, confident of his own resources. Though the sky was by this time overcast, the pond was so smooth that I could see where he broke the surface when I did not hear him. His white breast, the stillness of the air, and the smoothness of the water were all against him. At length, having come up fifty rods off, he uttered one of those prolonged howls, as if calling on the god of loons to aid him, and immediately there came a wind from the east and rippled the surface, and filled the whole air with misty rain, and I was impressed as if it were the prayer of the loon answered, and his god was angry with me; and so I left him disappearing far away on the tumultuous surface.

For hours, in fall days, I watched the ducks cunningly tack and veer and hold the middle of the pond, far from the sportsman; tricks which they will have less need to practice in Louisiana bayous. When compelled to rise they would sometimes circle round and round and over the pond at a considerable height, from which they could easily see to other ponds and the river, like black motes in the sky; and, when I thought they had gone off thither long since, they would settle down by a slanting flight of a quarter mile to a distant part which was left free; but what beside safety they got by sailing in the middle of Walden I do not know, unless they love its water for the same reason that I do.

XVII
SPRING

The opening of large tracts by the ice-cutters commonly causes a pond to break up earlier; for the water, agitated by the wind, even in cold weather, wears away the surrounding ice. But such was not the effect on Walden that year, for she had soon got a thick new garment to take the place of the old. This pond never breaks up so soon as the others in this neighborhood on account both of its greater depth and its having no stream passing through it to melt or wear away the ice. I never knew it to open in the course of a winter, not excepting that of '52–3, which gave the ponds so severe a trial. It commonly opens about the first of April, a week or ten days later than Flint's Pond and Fair Haven, beginning to melt on the north side and in the shallower parts where it began to freeze. It indicates better than any water hereabouts the absolute progress of the season, being least affected by transient changes of temperature. A severe cold of a few days's duration in March may very much retard the opening of the former ponds, while the temperature of Walden increases almost uninterruptedly. A thermometer thrust into the middle of Walden on the 6th of March, 1847, stood at 32°, or freezing point; near the shore at 33°; in the middle of Flint's Pond, the same day, at 32½° at a dozen rods from the shore, in shallow water, under ice a foot thick, at 36°. This difference of three and a half degrees between the temperature of the deep water and the shallow in the latter pond, and the fact that a great proportion of it is comparatively shallow, show why it should break up so much sooner than Walden. The ice in the shallowest part was at this time several inches thinner than in the middle. In midwinter the middle had been the warmest and the ice thinnest there. So, also, every one who has waded about the shores of a pond in summer must have perceived how much warmer the water is close to the shore, where only three or four inches deep, than a little distance out, and on the surface where it is deep, than near the bottom. In spring the sun not only exerts an influence through the increased temperature of the air and earth, but its heat passes through ice a foot or more thick, and is reflected from the bottom in shallow water, and so also warms the water and melts the under side of the ice, at the same time that it is melting it more directly above, making it uneven, and causing the air bubbles which it contains to extend themselves upward and downward until it is completely honeycombed, and at last disappears suddenly in a single spring rain. Ice has its grain as well as wood, and when a cake begins to rot or "comb," that is, assume the appearance of a honeycomb, whatever may be its position, the air cells are at right angles with what was the water surface. Where there is a rock or a log rising near to the surface the ice over it is much thinner, and is frequently quite dissolved by this reflected heat; and I have been told that in the experiment at Cambridge to freeze water in a shallow wooden pond, though the cold air circulated underneath, and so had access to both sides, the reflection of the sun from the bottom more than counterbalanced this advantage. When a warm rain in the middle of winter melts off the snow ice from Walden, and leaves a hard dark or transparent ice on the middle, there will be a strip of rotten though thicker white ice, a rod or more wide, about the shores, created by this reflected heat. Also, as I have said, the bubbles themselves within the ice operate as burning-glasses to melt the ice beneath.

The phenomena of the year take place every day in a pond on a small scale. Every morning, generally speaking, the shallow water is being warmed more rapidly than the deep, though it may not be made so warm after all, and every evening it is being cooled more rapidly until the morning. The day is an epitome of the year. The night is the winter, the morning and evening are the spring and fall, and the noon is the summer. The cracking and booming of the ice indicate a change of temperature. One pleasant morning after a cold night, February 24th, 1850, having gone to Flint's Pond to spend the day, I noticed with surprise, that when I struck the ice with the head of my axe, it resounded like a gong for many rods around, or as if I had struck on a tight drum-head. The pond began to boom about an hour after sunrise, when it felt the influence of the sun's rays slanted up on it from over the hills; it stretched itself and yawned like a waking man with a gradually increasing tumult, which was kept up three or four hours. It took a short siesta at noon, and boomed once more toward night, as the sun was withdrawing his influence. In the right stage of the weather a pond fires its evening gun with great regularity. But in the middle of the day, being full of cracks, and the air also being less elastic, it had completely lost its resonance, and probably fishes and muskrats could not then have been stunned by a blow on it.[1] The fishermen say that the "thundering of the pond" scares the fishes and prevents their biting. The pond does not thunder every evening, and I cannot tell surely when to expect its thundering; but though I may perceive no difference in the weather, it does. Who would have suspected so large and cold and thickskinned a thing to be so sensitive? Yet it has its law to which it thunders obedience when it should as surely as the buds expand in the spring. The earth is all alive and covered with papillæ. The largest pond is as sensitive to atmospheric changes as the globule of mercury in its tube.

One attraction in coming to the woods to live was that I should have leisure and opportunity to see the Spring come in. The ice in the pond at length begins to be honeycombed, and I can set my heel in it as I walk. Fogs and rains and warmer suns are gradually melting the snow; the days have grown sensibly longer; and I see how I shall get through the winter without

[1]A reference to the winter fisherman's practice of giving the ice a hard blow, in an effort to stun the fish below and make them easy to catch.

adding to my woodpile, for large fires are no longer necessary. I am on the alert for the first signs of spring, to hear the chance note of some arriving bird, or the striped squirrel's chirp, for his stores must be now nearly exhausted, or see the woodchuck venture out of his winter quarters. On the 13th of March, after I had heard the bluebird, song sparrow, and red-wing, the ice was still nearly a foot thick. As the weather grew warmer it was not sensibly worn away by the water, nor broken up and floated off as in rivers, but, though it was completely melted for half a rod in width about the shore, the middle was merely honeycombed and saturated with water, so that you could put your foot through it when six inches thick; but by the next day evening, perhaps, after a warm rain followed by fog, it would have wholly disappeared, all gone off with the fog, spirited away. One year I went across the middle only five days before it disappeared entirely. In 1845 Walden was first completely open on the 1st of April; in '46, the 25th of March; in '47, the 8th of April; in '51, the 28th of March; in '52, the 18th of April; in '53, the 23rd of March; in '54 about the 7th of April.

Every incident connected with the breaking up of the rivers and ponds and the settling of the weather is particularly interesting to us who live in a climate of so great extremes. When the warmer days come, they who dwell near the river hear the ice crack at night with a startling whoop as loud as artillery, as if its icy fetters were rent from end to end, and within a few days see it rapidly going out. So the alligator comes out of the mud with the quakings of the earth. One old man, who has been a close observer of Nature, and seems as thoroughly wise in regard to all her operations as if she had been put upon the stocks when he was a boy, and he had helped to lay her keel,—who has come to his growth, and can hardly acquire more of natural lore if he should live to the age of Methuselah,[2]—told me—and I was surprised to hear him express wonder at any of Nature's operations, for I thought that there were no secrets between them—that one spring day he took his gun and boat, and thought that he would have a little sport with the ducks. There was ice still on the meadows, but it was all gone out of the river, and he dropped down without obstruction from Sudbury, where he lived, to Fair Haven Pond, which he found, unexpectedly, covered for the most part with a firm field of ice. It was a warm day, and he was surprised to see so great a body of ice remaining. Not seeing any ducks, he hid his boat on the north or back side of an island in the pond, and then concealed himself in the bushes on the south side, to await them. The ice was melted for three or four rods from the shore, and there was a smooth and warm sheet of water, with a muddy bottom, such as the ducks love, within, and he thought it likely that some would be along pretty soon. After he had lain still there about an hour he heard a low and seemingly very distant sound, but singularly grand and impressive, unlike anything he had ever heard, gradually swelling and increasing as if it would have a universal and memorable ending, a sullen rush and roar, which seemed to him all at once like the sound of a vast body of fowl coming in to settle there, and, seizing his gun, he started up in haste and excited; but he found, to his surprise, that the whole body of the ice had started while he lay there, and drifted in to the shore, and the sound he had

[2]969 years. Genesis 5:27.

heard was made by its edge grating on the shore,—at first gently nibbled and crumbled off, but at length heaving up and scattering its wrecks along the island to a considerable height before it came to a stand still.

At length the sun's ray have attained the right angle, and warm winds blow up mist and rain and melt the snowbanks, and the sun dispersing the mist smiles on a checkered landscape of russet and white smoking with incense, through which the traveller picks his way from islet to islet, cheered by the music of a thousand tinkling rills and rivulets whose veins are filled with the blood of winter which they are bearing off.

Few phenomena gave me more delight than to observe the forms which thawing sand and clay assume in flowing down the sides of a deep cut on the railroad through which I passed on my way to the village, a phenomenon not very common on so large a scale, though the number of freshly exposed banks of the right material must have been greatly multiplied since railroads were invented. The material was sand of every degree of fineness and of various rich colors, commonly mixed with a little clay. When the frost comes out in the spring, and even in a thawing day in the winter, the sand begins to flow down the slopes like lava, sometimes bursting out through the snow and overflowing it where no sand was to be seen before. Innumerable little streams overlap and interlace one with another, exhibiting a sort of hybrid product, which obeys half way the law of currents, and half way that of vegetation. As it flows it takes the forms of sappy leaves or vines, making heaps of pulpy sprays a foot or more in depth, and resembling, as you look down on them, the laciniated, lobed, and imbricated thalluses of some lichens;[3] or you are reminded of coral, of leopards' paws or birds' feet, of brains or lungs or bowels, and excrements of all kinds. It is a truly *grotesque* vegetation, whose forms and color we see imitated in bronze, a sort of architectural foliage more ancient and typical than acanthus, chicory, ivy, vine, or any vegetable leaves; destined perhaps, under some circumstances, to become a puzzle to future geologists. The whole cut impressed me as if it were a cave with its stalactites laid open to the light. The various shades of the sand are singularly rich and agreeable, embracing the different iron colors, brown, gray, yellowish, and reddish. When the flowing mass reaches the drain at the foot of the bank it spreads out flatter into *strands,* the separate streams losing their semi-cylindrical form and gradually becoming more flat and broad, running together as they are more moist, till they form an almost flat *sand,* still variously and beautifully shaded, but in which you can trace the original forms of vegetation; till at length, in the water itself, they are converted into *banks,* like those formed off the mouth of rivers, and the forms of vegetations are lost in the ripple-marks on the bottom.

The whole bank, which is from twenty to forty feet high, is sometimes overlaid with a mass of this kind of foliage, or sandy rupture, for a quarter of a mile on one side or both sides, the produce of one spring day. What makes this sand foliage remarkable is its springing into existence thus suddenly. When I see on the one side the inert bank,—for the sun acts on one side first,—and on the other this luxuriant foliage, the creation of an hour, I am affected as if in a peculiar sense I stood in the laboratory of the Artist who

[3]Mosslike plants with irregular, overlapping edges.

made the world and me,—and come to where he was still at work, sporting on this bank, and with excess of energy strewing his fresh designs about. I feel as if I were nearer to the vitals of the globe, for this sandy overflow is something such a foliaceous[4] mass as the vitals of the animal body. You find thus in the very sands an anticipation of the vegetable leaf. No wonder that the earth expresses itself outwardly in leaves, it so labors with the idea inwardly. The atoms have already learned this law, and are pregnant by it. The overhanging leaf sees here its prototype. *Internally,* whether in the globe or animal body, it is a moist thick *lobe,* a word especially applicable to the liver and lungs and the *leaves* of fat (*λείβω, labor, lapsus,* to flow or slip downward, a lapsing; *λοβος, globus,* lobe, globe; also lap, flap, and many other words); *externally,* a dry thin *leaf,* even as the *f* and *v* are pressed and dried *b.* The radicals of lobe are *lb,* the soft mass of the *b* (single-lobed, or B, double-lobed), with the liquid *l* behind it pressing it forward. In globe, *glb,* the guttural *g* adds to the meaning of the capacity of the throat. The feathers and wings of birds are still drier and thinner leaves. Thus, also, you pass from the lumpish grub in the earth to the airy and fluttering butterfly. The very globe continually transcends and translates itself, and becomes winged in its orbit. Even ice begins with delicate crystal leaves, as if it had flowed into moulds which the fronds of water-plants have impressed on the watery mirror. The whole tree itself is but one leaf, and rivers are still vaster leaves whose pulp is intervening earth, and towns and cities are the ova of insects in their axils.[5]

When the sun withdraws the sand ceases to flow, but in the morning the streams will start once more and branch and branch again into a myriad of others. You here see perchance how blood-vessels are formed. If you look closely you observe that first there pushes forward from the thawing mass a stream of softened sand with a drop-like point, like the ball of the finger, feeling its way slowly and blindly downward, until at last with more heat and moisture, as the sun gets higher, the most fluid portion, in its effort to obey the law to which the most inert also yields, separates from the latter and forms for itself a meandering channel or artery within that, in which is seen a little silvery stream glancing like lightning from one stage of pulpy leaves or branches to another, and ever and anon swallowed up in the sand. It is wonderful how rapidly yet perfectly the sand organizes itself as it flows, using the best material its mass affords to form the sharp edges of its channel. Such are the sources of rivers. In the silicious[6] matter which the water deposits is perhaps the bony system, and in the still finer soil and organic matter the fleshy fibre or cellular tissue. What is man but a mass of thawing clay? The ball of the human finger is but a drop congealed. The fingers and toes flow to their extent from the thawing mass of the body. Who knows what the human body would expand and flow out to under a more genial heaven? Is not the hand a spreading *palm* leaf with its lobes and veins? The ear may be regarded, fancifully, as a lichen, *umbilicaria,* on the side of the head, with its lobe or drop. The lip—*labium,* from *labor* (?)—laps or lapses from the sides of the cavernous mouth. The nose is a manifest congealed drop or stalactite. The chin is a still larger drop, the confluent dripping of the face. The cheeks are a slide from the brows into the valley of the face, opposed and diffused by the

[4]Resembling a leaf of foliage. [5]Angles or points where branches diverge. [6]Sandy.

cheek bones. Each rounded lobe of the vegetable leaf, too, is a thick and now loitering drop, larger or smaller; the lobes are the fingers of the leaf; and as many lobes as it has, in so many directions it tends to flow, and more heat or other genial influences would have caused it to flow yet farther.

Thus it seemed that this one hillside illustrated the principle of all the operations of Nature. The Maker of this earth but patented a leaf. What Champollion[7] will decipher this hieroglyphic for us, that we may turn over a new leaf at last? This phenomenon is more exhilarating to me that the luxuriance and fertility of vineyards. True, it is somewhat excrementitious in its character, and there is no end to the heaps of liver, lights,[8] and bowels, as if the globe were turned wrong side outward; but this suggests at least that Nature has some bowels, and there again is mother of humanity. This is the frost coming out of the ground; this is Spring. It precedes the green and flowery spring, as mythology precedes regular poetry. I know of nothing more purgative of winter fumes and indigestions. It convinces me that Earth is still in her swaddling-clothes, and stretches forth baby fingers on every side. Fresh curls spring from the baldest brow. There is nothing inorganic. These foliaceous heaps lie along the bank like the slag of a furnace, showing that Nature is "in full blast" within. The earth is not a mere fragment of dead history, stratum upon stratum like the leaves of a book, to be studied by geologists and antiquaries chiefly, but living poetry like the leaves of a tree, which precede flowers and fruit,—not a fossil earth, but a living earth; compared with whose great central life all animal and vegetable life is merely parasitic. Its throes will heave our exuviæ from their graves. You may melt your metals and cast them into the most beautiful moulds you can; they will never excite me like the forms which this molten earth flows out into. And not only it, but the institutions upon it are plastic like clay in the hands of the potter.

Ere long, not only on these banks, but on every hill and plain and in every hollow, the frost comes out of the ground like a dormant quadruped from its burrow, and seeks the sea with music, or migrates to other climes in clouds. Thaw with his gentle persuasion is more powerful than Thor with his hammer.[9] The one melts, the other but breaks in pieces.

When the ground was partially bare of snow, and a few warm days had dried its surface somewhat, it was pleasant to compare the first tender signs of the infant year just peeping forth with the stately beauty of the withered vegetation which had withstood the winter,—life-everlasting, goldenrods, pinweeds, and graceful wild grasses, more obvious and interesting frequently than in summer even, as if their beauty was not ripe till then; even cotton-grass, cat-tails, mulleins, johnswort, hardhack, meadow-sweet, and other strong-stemmed plants, those unexhausted granaries which entertain the earliest buds,—decent weeds,[10] at least, which widowed Nature wears. I am particularly attracted by the arching and sheaf-like top of the wool-grass; it brings back the summer to our winter memories, and is among the forms which art loves to copy, and which, in the vegetable kingdom, have the same relation to types already in the mind of man that astronomy has. It is an antique style, older than Greek or Egyptian. Many of the phenomena of Winter

[7]Jean François Champollion (1790–1832), French Egyptologist who deciphered the Rosetta Stone and made it possible to read the hieroglyphs of Egypt.

[8]Lungs. [9]Norse god of thunder. [10]Mourning clothing.

are suggestive of an inexpressible tenderness and fragile delicacy. We are accustomed to hear this king described as a rude and boisterous tyrant; but with the gentleness of a lover he adorns the tresses of Summer.

At the approach of spring the red squirrels got under my house, two at a time, directly under my feet as I sat reading or writing, and kept up the queerest chuckling and chirruping and vocal pirouetting and gurgling sounds that ever were heard; and when I stamped they only chirruped the louder, as if past all fear and respect in their mad pranks, defying humanity to stop them. No, you don't—chickaree—chickaree. They were wholly deaf to my arguments, or failed to perceive their force, and fell into a strain of invective that was irresistible.

The first sparrow of spring! The year beginning with younger hope than ever! The faint silvery warblings heard over the partially bare and moist fields from the bluebird, the song sparrow, and the red-wing, as if the last flakes of winter tinkled as they fell! What at such a time are histories, chronologies, traditions, and all written revelations? The brooks sing carols and glees to the spring. The marsh hawk, sailing low over the meadow, is already seeking the first slimy life that awakes. The sinking sound of melting snow is heard in all dells, and the ice dissolves apace in the ponds. The grass flames up on the hillsides like a spring,—"et primitus oritur herba imbribus primoribus evocata,"[11]—as if the earth sent forth an inward heat to greet the returning sun; not yellow but green is the color of its flame;—the symbol of perpetual youth, the grass-blade, like a long green ribbon, streams from the sod into the summer, checked indeed by the frost, but anon pushing on again, lifting its spear of the last year's hay with the fresh life below. It grows as steadily as the rill oozes out of the ground. It is almost identical with that, for in the growing days of June, when the rills are dry, the grass-blades are their channels, and from year to year the herds drink at this perennial green stream, and the mower draws from it betimes their winter supply. So our human life but dies down to its root, and still puts forth its green blade to eternity.

Walden is melting apace. There is a canal two rods wide along the northerly and westerly sides, and wider still at the east end. A great field of ice has cracked off from the main body. I hear a song sparrow singing from the bushes on the shore,—*olit, olit, olit,*—*chip, chip, chip, che char,*—*che wiss, wiss, wiss.* He too is helping to crack it. How handsome the great sweeping curves in the edge of the ice, answering somewhat to those of the shore, but more regular! It is unusually hard, owing to the recent severe but transient cold, and all watered or waved like a palace floor. But the wind slides eastward over its opaque surface in vain, till it reaches the living surface beyond. It is glorious to behold this ribbon of water sparkling in the sun, the bare face of the pond full of glee and youth, as if it spoke the joy of the fishes within it, and of the sands on its shore,—a silvery sheen as from the scales of a leuciscus,[12] as it were all one active fish. Such is the contrast between winter and spring. Walden was dead and is alive again. But this spring it broke up more steadily, as I have said.

[11]Latin: "and called forth by the first rains, the first grass begins to grow."
[12]Freshwater fish.

The change from storm and winter to serene and mild weather, from dark and sluggish hours to bright and elastic ones, is a memorable crisis which all things proclaim. It is seemingly instantaneous at last. Suddenly an influx of light filled my house, though the evening was at hand, and the clouds of winter still overhung it, and the eaves were dripping with sleety rain. I looked out the window, and lo! where yesterday was cold gray ice there lay the transparent pond already calm and full of hope as on a summer evening, reflecting a summer evening sky in its bosom, though none was visible overhead, as if it had intelligence with some remote horizon. I heard a robin in the distance, the first I had heard for many a thousand years, methought, whose note I shall not forget for many a thousand more,—the same sweet and powerful songs as of yore. O the evening robin, at the end of a New England summer day! If I could ever find the twig he sits upon! I mean *he;* I mean *the twig.* This at least is not the *Turdus migratorius.*[13] The pitch pines and shrub oaks about my house, which had so long drooped, suddenly resumed their several characters, looked brighter, greener, and more erect and alive, as if effectually cleansed and restored by the rain. I knew that it would not rain any more. You may tell by looking at any twig of the forest, ay, at your very wood-pile, whether its winter is past or not. As it grew darker, I was startled by the honking of geese flying low over the woods, like weary travellers getting in late from Southern lakes, and indulging at last in unrestrained complaint and mutual consolation. Standing at my door, I could hear the rush of their wings; when, driving toward my house, they suddenly spied my light, and with hushed clamor wheeled and settled in the pond. So I came in, and shut the door, and passed my first spring night in the woods.

In the morning I watched the geese from the door through the mist, sailing in the middle of the pond, fifty rods off, so large and tumultuous that Walden appeared like an artificial pond for their amusement. But when I stood on the shore they at once rose up with a great flapping of wings at the signal of their commander, and when they had got into rank circled about over my head, twenty-nine of them, and then steered straight to Canada, with a regular *honk* from the leader at intervals, trusting to break their fast in muddier pools. A "plump"[14] of duck rose at the same time and took the route to the north in the wake of their noisier cousins.

For a week I heard the circling, groping clangor of some solitary goose in the foggy mornings, seeking its companion, and still peopling the woods with the sound of larger life than they could sustain. In April the pigeons were seen again flying express in small flocks, and in due time I heard the martins twittering over my clearing, though it had not seemed that the township contained so many that it could afford me any, and I fancied that they were peculiarly of the ancient race that dwelt in hollow trees ere white men came. In almost all climes the tortoise and the frog are among the precursors and heralds of this season, and birds fly with song and glancing plumage, and plants spring and bloom, and winds flow, to correct this slight oscillation of the poles and preserve the equilibrium of nature.

As every season seems best to us in its turn, so the coming in of spring is like the creation of Cosmos out of Chaos and the realization of the golden Age.—

[13]American robin. [14]Flock.

"Eurus ad Auroram, Nabathæaque regna recessit,
Persidaque, et radiis juga subdita matutinis."

"The East-Wind withdrew to Aurora and the Nabathæan kingdom,
And the Persian, and the ridges placed under the morning rays.

. . .

Man was born. Whether that Artificer of things,
The origin of a better world, made him from the divine seed;
Or the earth, being recently and lately sundered from the high
Ether, retained some seeds of cognate heaven."[15]

A single gentle rain makes the grass many shades greener. So our prospects brighten on the influx of better thoughts. We should be blessed if we lived in the present always, and took advantage of every accident that befell us, like the grass which confesses the influence of the slightest dew that falls on it; and did not spend our time in atoning for the neglect of past opportunities, which we call doing our duty. We loiter in winter while it is already spring. In a pleasant spring morning all men's sins are forgiven. Such a day is a truce to vice. While such a sun holds out to burn, the vilest sinner may return. Through our own recovered innocence we discern the innocence of our neighbors. You may have known your neighbor yesterday for a thief, a drunkard, or a sensualist, and merely pitied or despised him, and despaired of the world; but the sun shines bright and warm this first spring morning, recreating the world, and you meet him at some serene work, and see how his exhausted and debauched veins expand with still joy and bless the new day, feel the spring influence with the innocence of infancy, and all his faults are forgotten. There is not only an atmosphere of good will about him, but even a savor of holiness groping for expression, blindly and ineffectually perhaps, like a new-born instinct, and for a short hour the south hillside echoes to no vulgar jest. You see some innocent fair shoots preparing to burst from his gnarled rind and try another year's life, tender and fresh, as the youngest plant. Even he has entered into the joy of his Lord. Why the jailer does not leave open his prison doors,—why the judge does not dismiss his case,—why the preacher does not dismiss his congregation! It is because they do not obey the hint which God gives them, nor accept the pardon which he freely offers to all.

"A return to goodness produced each day in the tranquil and beneficent breath of the morning, causes that in respect to the love of virtue and the hatred of vice, one approaches a little the primitive nature of man, as the sprouts of the forest which has been felled. In like manner the evil which one does in the interval of a day prevents the germs of virtues which began to spring up again from developing themselves and destroys them.

"After the germs of virtue have thus been prevented many times from developing themselves, then the beneficent breath of evening does not suffice to preserve them. As soon as the breath of evening does not suffice longer to

[15]From Ovid's *Metamorphoses,* Book I. Ellipses (. . .) here and following are Thoreau's own.

preserve them, then the nature of man does not differ much from that of the brute. Men seeing the nature of this man like that of the brute, think that he has never possessed the innate faculty of reason. Are those the true and natural sentiments of man?"[16]

> "The Golden Age was first created, which without any avenger
> Spontaneously without law cherished fidelity and rectitude.
> Punishment and fear were not; nor were threatening words read
> On suspended brass; nor did the suppliant crowd fear
> The words of their judge; but were safe without an avenger.
> Not yet the pine felled on its mountains had descended
> To the liquid waves that it might see a foreign world,
> And mortals knew no shores but their own.
>
> . . .
>
> There was eternal spring, and placid zephyrs with warm
> Blasts soothed the flowers born without seed."[17]

On the 29th of April, as I was fishing from the bank of the river near the Nine-Acre-Corner bridge, standing on the quaking grass[18] and willow roots, where the muskrats lurk, I heard a singular rattling sound, somewhat like that of the sticks which boys play with their fingers, when, looking up, I observed a very slight and graceful hawk, like a nighthawk, alternately soaring like a ripple and tumbling a rod or two over and over, showing the under side of its wings, which gleamed like a satin ribbon in the sun, or like the pearly inside of a shell. This sight reminded me of falconry and what nobleness and poetry are associated with that sport. The merlin it seemed to me it might be called: but I care not for its name. It was the most ethereal flight I had ever witnessed. It did not simply flutter like a butterfly, nor soar like the larger hawks, but it sported with proud reliance in the fields of air; mounting again and again with its strange chuckle, it repeated its free and beautiful fall, turning over and over like a kite, and then recovering from its lofty tumbling, as if it had never set its foot on *terra firma.* It appeared to have no companion in the universe,—sporting there alone,—and to need none but the morning and the ether with which it played. It was not lonely, but made all the earth lonely beneath it. Where was the parent which hatched it, its kindred, and its father in the heavens? The tenant of the air, it seemed related to the earth but by an egg hatched some time in the crevice of a crag;—or was its native nest made in the angle of a cloud, woven of the rainbow's trimmings and the sunset sky, and lined with some soft midsummer haze caught up from earth? Its eyry[19] now some cliffy cloud.

Besides this I got a rare mess of golden and silver and bright cupreous[20] fishes, which looked like a string of jewels. Ah! I have penetrated to those meadows on the morning of many a first spring day, jumping from hummock to hummock, from willow root to willow root, when the wild river valley and

[16]From the *Book of Mencius,* Book VI. [17]*Metamorphoses,* Book I.
[18]Grass (with a delicate, slender stalk) that appears to tremble when blown by a slight breeze.
[19]Bird's nest, now usually "aerie." [20]Copper-colored.

the woods were bathed in so pure and bright a light as would have waked the dead, if they had been slumbering in their graves, as some purpose. There needs no stronger proof of immortality. All things must live in such a light. O Death, where was thy sting? O Grave, where was thy victor,[21] then?

Our village life would stagnate if it were not for the unexplored forests and meadows which surround it. We need the tonic of wildness,—to wade sometimes in marshes where the bittern and the meadow-hen lurk, and hear the booming of the snipe; to smell the whispering sedge where only some wilder and more solitary fowl builds her nest, and the mink crawls with its belly close to the ground. At the same time that we are earnest to explore and learn all things, we require that all things be mysterious and unexplorable, that land and sea be infinitely wild, unsurveyed and unfathomed by us because unfathomable. We can never have enough of nature. We must be refreshed by the sight of inexhaustible vigor, vast and titanic features, the seacoast with its wrecks, the wilderness with its living and its decaying trees, the thundercloud, and the rain which lasts three weeks and produces freshets. We need to witness our own limits transgressed, and some life pasturing freely where we never wander. We are cheered when we observe the vulture feeding on the carrion which disgusts and disheartens us, and deriving health and strength from the repast. There was a dead horse in the hollow by the path to my house, which compelled me sometimes to go out of my way, especially in the night when the air was heavy, but the assurance it gave me of the strong appetite and inviolable health of Nature was my compensation for this. I love to see that Nature is so rife with life that myriads can be afforded to be sacrificed and suffered to prey on one another; that tender organizations can be so serenely squashed out of existence like pulp,—tadpoles which herons gobble up, and tortoises and toads run over in the road; and that sometimes it has rained flesh and blood! With the liability to accident, we must see how little account is to be made of it. The impression made on a wise man is that of universal innocence. Poison is not poisonous after all, nor are any wounds fatal. Compassion is a very untenable ground. It must be expeditious. Its pleadings will not bear to be stereotyped.

Early in May, the oaks, hickories, maples, and other trees, just putting out amidst the pine woods around the pond, imparted a brightness like sunshine to the landscape, especially in cloudy days, as if the sun were breaking through mists and shining faintly on the hillsides here and there. On the third or fourth of May I saw a loon in the pond, and during the first week of the month I heard the whip-poor-will, the brown thrasher, the veery, the wood pewee, the chewink, and other birds. I had heard the wood thrush long before. The phœbe had already come once more and looked in at my door and window, to see if my house was cavern-like enough for her, sustaining herself on humming wings with clinched talons, as if she held by the air, while she surveyed the premises. The sulphur-like pollen of the pitch pine soon covered the pond and the stones and rotten wood along the shore, so that you could have collected a barrelful. This is the "sulphur showers" we hear of. Even in Calidas' drama of Sacontala,[22] we read of "rills dyed yellow

[21]Adapted from Corinthians 15:55.

[22]Kalidasa (fifth century B.C.), Hindu poet and author of the Sanskrit drama *Sakuntala.*

with the golden dust of the lotus." And so the seasons went rolling on into summer, as one rambles into higher and higher grass.

Thus was my first year's life in the woods completed; and the second year was similar to it. I finally left Walden September 6th, 1847.

XVIII
CONCLUSION

To the sick the doctors wisely recommend a change of air and scenery. Thank Heaven, here is not all the world. The buckeye does not grow in New England, and the mockingbird is rarely heard here. The wild goose is more of a cosmopolite than we; he breaks his fast in Canada, takes a luncheon in the Ohio, and plumes himself for the night in a southern bayou. Even the bison, to some extent, keeps pace with the seasons, cropping the pastures of the Colorado only till a greener and sweeter grass awaits him by the Yellowstone. Yet we think that if rail fences are pulled down, and stone walls piled up on our farms, bounds are henceforth set to our lives and our fates decided. If you are chosen town clerk, forsooth, you cannot go to Tierra del Fuego[1] this summer: but you may go to the land of infernal fire nevertheless. The universe is wider than our views of it.

Yet we should oftener look over the tafferel[2] of our craft, like curious passengers, and not make the voyage like stupid sailors picking oakum.[3] The other side of the globe is but the home of our correspondent. Our voyaging is only great-circle sailing,[4] and the doctors prescribe for diseases of the skin merely. One hastens to southern Africa to chase the giraffe; but surely that is not the game he would be after. How long, pray, would a man hunt giraffes if he could? Snipes and woodcocks also may afford rare sport; but I trust it would be nobler game to shoot one's self.—

> "Direct your eye sight inward, and you'll find
> A thousand regions in your mind
> Yet undiscovered. Travel them and be
> Expert in home-cosmography."[5]

What does Africa,—what does the West stand for? Is not our own interior white on the chart?[6] black though it may prove, like the coast, when discovered? Is it the source of the Nile, or the Niger, or the Mississippi, or a Northwest Passage around this continent, that we would find? Are these the problems which most concern mankind? Is Franklin[7] the only man who is lost, that his wife should be so earnest to find him? Does Mr. Grinnell[8] know

[1]Spanish: Land of Fire. An archipelago at the southern tip of South America.
[2]Taffrail, a rail at the stern of a ship.
[3]The tedious labor of picking hemp rope apart to produce fibers for use as ship caulking.
[4]The most direct way.
[5]From "To My Honoured Friend, Sir Ed. P. Knight" by William Habington (1605–1654).
[6]I.e., an unexplored area.
[7]Sir John Franklin (1786–1847), Arctic explorer lost in searching for the Northwest Passage from the Atlantic to the Pacific.
[8]Henry Grinnell (1799–1874) financed a search for the lost Franklin.

where he himself is? Be rather the Mungo Park, the Lewis and Clark and Frobisher,[9] of your own streams and oceans; explore your own higher latitudes,—with shiploads of preserved meats to support you, if they be necessary; and pile the empty cans sky-high for a sign.[10] Were preserved meats invented to preserve meat merely? Nay, be a Columbus to whole new continents and worlds within you, opening new channels, not of trade, but of thought. Every man is the lord of a realm beside which the earthly empire of the Czar[11] is but a petty stake, a hummock left by the ice. Yet some can be patriotic who have no *self*-respect, and sacrifice the greater to the less. They love the soil which makes their graves, but have no sympathy with the spirit which may still animate their clay. Patriotism is a maggot in their heads. What was the meaning of that South-Sea Exploring Expedition,[12] with all its parade and expense, but an indirect recognition of the fact that there are continents and seas in the moral world to which every man is an isthmus or an inlet, yet unexplored by him, but that it is easier to sail many thousand miles through cold and storm and cannibals, in a government ship, with five hundred men and boys to assist one, than it is to explore the private sea, the Atlantic and Pacific Ocean of one's being alone.—

> "Erret, et extremos alter scrutetur Iberos.
> Plus habet hic vitae, plus habet ille viae."[13]
> Let them wander and scrutinize the outlandish Australians.
> I have more of God, they more of the road.

It is not worth the while to go round the world to count the cats in Zanzibar. Yet do this even till you can do better, and you may perhaps find some "Symmes' Hole"[14] by which to get at the inside at last. England and France, Spain and Portugal, Gold Coast and Slave Coast, all front on this private sea; but no bark from them has ventured out of sight of land, though it is without doubt the direct way to India. If you would learn to speak all tongues and conform to the customs of all nations, if you would travel farther than all travellers, be naturalized in all climes, and cause the Sphinx to dash her head against a stone,[15] even obey the precept of the old philosopher, and Explore thyself. Herein are demanded the eye and the nerve. Only the defeated and deserters go to the wars, cowards that run away and enlist. Start now on that farthest western way, which does not pause at the Mississippi or the Pacific, nor conduct toward a worn-out China or Japan, but leads on direct, a tangent to this sphere, summer and winter, day and night, sun down, moon down, and at last earth down too.

[9]Mungo Park (1771–1806), Scottish explorer of Africa; Lewis and Clark, explorers of the American Northwest; Sir Martin Frobisher (1535?–1594), English explorer of Canada.

[10]One of the few traces discovered of the vanished Franklin expedition was a pile of empty tin cans.

[11]Czarist Russia was the largest nation in Thoreau's day.

[12]U.S. Antarctic expedition (1838–1842).

[13]From the "Old Man of Verona" by the Roman poet Claudian. Thoreau changed the original "Spaniards" ("Iberos") to "Australians" and "of life" ("*vitae*") to "of God."

[14]John Symmes (1780–1829) theorized that the earth is hollow and open at both poles.

[15]The Sphinx killed herself when Oedipus solved her riddle.

It is said that Mirabeau[16] took to highway robbery "to ascertain what degree of resolution was necessary in order to place one's self in formal opposition to the most sacred laws of society." He declared that "a soldier who fights in the ranks does not require half so much courage as a foot-pad,"[17]—"that honor and religion have never stood in the way of a well-considered and a firm resolve." This was manly, as the world goes; and yet it was idle, if not desperate. A saner man would have found himself often enough "in formal opposition" to what are deemed "the most sacred laws of society," through obedience to yet more sacred laws, and so have tested his resolution without going out of his way. It is not for a man to put himself in such an attitude to society, but to maintain himself in whatever attitude he find himself through obedience to the laws of his being, which will never be one of opposition to a just government, if he should chance to meet with such.

I left the woods for as good a reason as I went there. Perhaps it seemed to me that I had several more lives to live, and could not spare any more time for that one. It is remarkable how easily and insensibly we fall into a particular route, and make a beaten track for ourselves. I had not lived there a week before my feet wore a path from my door to the pond-side; and though it is five or six years since I trod it, it is still quite distinct. It is true, I fear that others may have fallen into it, and so helped to keep it open. The surface of the earth is soft and impressible by the feet of men; and so with the paths which the mind travels. How worn and dusty, then, must be the highways of the world, how deep the ruts of tradition and conformity! I did not wish to take a cabin passage, but rather to go before the mast and on the deck of the world, for there I could best see the moonlight amid the mountains. I do not wish to go below now.

I learned this, at least, by my experiment; that if one advances confidently in the direction of his dreams, and endeavors to live the life which he has imagined, he will meet with a success unexpected in common hours. He will put some things behind, will pass an invisible boundary; new, universal, and more liberal laws will begin to establish themselves around and within him; or the old laws be expanded, and interpreted in his favor in a more liberal sense, and he will live with the license of a higher order of beings. In proportion as he simplifies his life, the laws of the universe will appear less complex, and solitude will not be solitude, nor poverty poverty, nor weakness weakness. If you have built castles in the air, your work need not be lost; that is where they should be. Now put the foundations under them.

It is a ridiculous demand which England and America make, that you shall speak so that they can understand you. Neither men nor toadstools grow so. As if that were important, and there were not enough to understand you without them. As if Nature could support but one order of understandings, could not sustain birds as well as quadrupeds, flying as well as creeping things, and *hush* and *who,*[18] which Bright can understand, were the best English. As if there were safety in stupidity alone, I fear chiefly lest my expression may not be *extravagant* enough, may not wander far enough

[16]Honoré Riqueti, Count de Mirabeau (1749–1791), French statesman.
[17]Thief.
[18]*Go* and *stop.* Terms used in driving an ox (a bright).

beyond the narrow limits of my daily experience, so as to be adequate to the truth of which I have been convinced. *Extra vagance!* it depends on how you are yarded. The migrating buffalo, which seeks new pastures in another latitude, is not extravagant like the cow which kicks over the pail, leaps the cow-yard fence, and runs after her calf, in milking time. I desire to speak somewhere *without* bonds; like a man in a waking moment, to men in their waking moments; for I am convinced that I cannot exaggerate enough even to lay the foundation of a true expression. Who that has heard a strain of music feared then lest he should speak extravagantly any more forever? In view of the future or possible, we should live quite laxly and undefined in front, our outlines dim and misty on that side; as our shadows reveal an insensible perspiration toward the sun. The volatile truth of our words should continually betray the inadequacy of the residual statement. Their truth is instantly *translated;* its literal monument alone remains. The words which express our faith and piety are not definite; yet they are significant and fragrant like frankincense to superior natures.

Why level downward to our dullest perception always, and praise that as common sense? The commonest sense is the sense of men asleep, which they express by snoring. Sometimes we are inclined to class those who are once-and-a-half-witted with the half-witted, because we appreciate only a third part of their wit. Some would find fault with the morning red, if they ever got up early enough. "They pretend," as I hear, "that the verses of Kabir[19] have four different senses; illusion, spirit, intellect, and the esoteric doctrine of the Vedas;" but in this part of the world is considered a ground for complaint if a man's writing admit of more than one interpretation. While England endeavors to cure the potato-rot, will not any endeavor to cure the brain-rot, which prevails so much more widely and fatally?

I do not suppose that I have attained to obscurity, but I should be proud if no more fatal fault were found with my pages on this score than was found with the Walden ice. Southern customers objected to its blue color, which is the evidence of its purity, as if it were muddy, and preferred the Cambridge ice, which is white, but tastes of weeds. The purity men love is like the mists which envelop the earth, and not like the azure ether beyond.

Some are dinning in our ears that we Americans and moderns generally, are intellectual dwarfs compared with the ancients, or even the Elizabethan men. But what is that to the purpose? A living dog is better than a dead lion.[20] Shall a man go hang himself because he belongs to the race of pygmies, and not be the biggest pygmy that he can? Let every one mind his own business, and endeavor to be what he was made.

Why should we be in such desperate haste to succeed and in such desperate enterprises? If a man does not keep pace with his companions, perhaps it is because he hears a different drummer. Let him step to the music which he hears, however measured or far away. It is not important that he should mature as soon as an apple tree or an oak. Shall he turn his spring into summer? If the condition of things which we were made for is not yet, what were any reality which we can substitute? We will not be shipwrecked on a vain

[19]Hindu mystic (1450?–1518).
[20]Ecclesiastes 9:4.

reality. Shall we with pains erect a heaven of blue glass over ourselves, though when it is done we shall be sure to gaze still at the true ethereal heaven far above, as if the former were not.

There was an artist in the city of Kouroo who was disposed to strive after perfection.[21] One day it came into his mind to make a staff. Having considered that in an imperfect work time is an ingredient, but in a perfect work time does not enter, he said to himself, It shall be perfect in all respects, though I should do nothing else in my life. He proceeded instantly to the forest for wood, being resolved that it should not be made of unsuitable material; and as he searched for and rejected stick after stick, his friends gradually deserted him, for they grew old in their works and died, but he grew not older by a moment. His singleness of purpose and resolution, and his elevated piety, endowed him, without his knowledge, with perennial youth. As he made no compromise with Time, Time kept out of his way, and only sighed at a distance because he could not overcome him. Before he had found a stick in all respects suitable the city of Kouroo was a hoary ruin, and he sat on one of its mounds to peel the stick. Before he had given it the proper shape the dynasty of the Candahars was at an end, and with the point of the stick he wrote the name of the last of that race in the sand, and then resumed his work. By the time he had smoothed and polished the staff Kalpa was no longer the polestar; and ere he had put on the ferule[22] and the head adorned with precious stones, Brahma had awoke and slumbered many times. But why do I stay to mention these things? When the finishing stroke was put to his work, it suddenly expanded before the eyes of the astonished artist into the fairest of all the creations of Brahma. He had made a new system in making a staff, a world with full and fair proportions; in which, though the old cities and dynasties had passed away, fairer and more glorious ones had taken their places. And now he saw by the heap of shavings still fresh at his feet, that, for him and his work, the former lapse of time had been an illusion, and that no more time had elapsed than is required for a single scintillation from the brain of Brahma to fall on and inflame the tinder of a mortal brain. The material was pure, and his art was pure; how could the result be other than wonderful?

No face which we can give to a matter will stead us so well at last as the truth. This alone wears well. For the most part, we are not where we are, but in a false position. Through an infirmity of our natures, we suppose a case, and put ourselves into it, and hence are in two cases at the same time, and it is doubly difficult to get out. In sane moments we regard only the facts, the case that is. Say what you have to say, not what you ought. Any truth is better than make-believe. Tom Hyde, the tinker, standing on the gallows, was asked if he had anything to say. "Tell the tailors," said he, "to remember to make a knot in their thread before they take the first stitch." His companion's prayer is forgotten.

[21]The source of the following legend is unknown. It is perhaps Thoreau's invention. The references to dynasties, stars, and the slumbers of Brahma are meant to indicate the passage of billions of years.

[22]Protective metal ring or cap.

However mean your life is, meet it and live it; do not shun it and call it hard names. It is not so bad as you are. It looks poorest when you are richest. The fault-finder will find faults even in paradise. Love your life, poor as it is. You may perhaps have some pleasant, thrilling, glorious hours, even in a poorhouse. The setting sun is reflected from the windows of the alms-house as brightly as from the rich man's abode; the snow melts before its door as early in the spring. I do not see but a quiet mind may live as contentedly there, and have as cheering thoughts, as in a palace. The town's poor seem to me often to live the most independent lives of any. Maybe they are simply great enough to receive without misgiving. Most think that they are above being supported by the town; but it oftener happens that they are not above supporting themselves by dishonest means, which should be more disreputable. Cultivate poverty like a garden herb, like sage. Do not trouble yourself much to get new things, whether clothes or friends. Turn the old; return to them. Things do not change; we change. Sell your clothes and keep your thoughts. God will see that you do not want society. If I were confined to a corner of a garret all my days, like a spider, the world would be just as large to me while I had my thoughts about me. The philosopher said: "From an army of three divisions one can take away its general, and put it in disorder: from the man the most abject and vulgar one cannot take away his thought." Do not seek so anxiously to be developed, to subject yourself to many influences to be played on; it is all dissipation. Humility like darkness reveals the heavenly lights. The shadows of poverty and meanness gather around us, "and lo! creation widens to our view."[23] We are often reminded that if there were bestowed on us the wealth of Crœsus,[24] our aims must still be the same, and our means essentially the same. Moreover, if you are restricted in your range by poverty, if you cannot buy books and newspapers, for instance, you are but confined to the most significant and vital experiences; you are compelled to deal with the material which yields the most sugar and the most starch. It is life near the bone where it is sweetest. You are defined from being a trifler. No man loses ever on a lower level by magnanimity on a higher. Superfluous wealth can buy superfluities only. Money is not required to buy one necessary of the soul.

I live in the angle of a leaden wall, into whose composition was poured a little alloy of bell-metal. Often, in the repose of my mid-day, there reaches my ears a confused *tintinnabulum*[25] from without. It is the noise of my contemporaries. My neighbors tell me of their adventures with famous gentlemen and ladies, what notabilities they met at the dinner-table; but I am no more interested in such things than in the contents of the Daily Times. The interest and the conversation are about costume and manners chiefly; but a goose is a goose still, dress it as you will. They tell me of California and Texas, of England and the Indies, of the Hon. Mr.——of Georgia or of Massachusetts, all transient and fleeting phenomena, till I am ready to leap from their courtyard like the Mameluke[26] bey. I delight to come to my bearings,—not walk in procession with pomp and parade, in a conspicuous place, but to walk even

[23]From "Sonnet to Night" (1828, 1838) by Joseph Blanco White (1775–1841).

[24]Ruler of ancient Lydia, renowned as the richest man of all time. [25]Ringing of bells.

[26]One of the Mamelukes, an Egyptian military caste, escaped a massacre in 1811 by leaping from the walls of the citadel at Cairo.

with the Builder of the universe, if I may,—not to live in this restless, nervous, bustling, trivial Nineteenth Century, but stand or sit thoughtfully while it goes by. What are men celebrating? They are all on a committee of arrangements, and hourly expect a speech from somebody. God is only the president of the day, and Webster[27] is his orator. I love to weigh, to settle, to gravitate toward that which most strongly and rightfully attracts me;—not hang by the beam of the scale and try to weigh less,—not suppose a case, but take the case that is; to travel the only path I can, and that on which no power can resist me. It affords me no satisfaction to commence to spring an arch before I have got a solid foundation. Let us not play at kittly-benders.[28] There is a solid bottom everywhere. We read that the traveller asked the boy if the swamp before him had a hard bottom. The boy replied that it had. But presently the traveller's horse sank in up to the girths, and he observed to the boy, "I thought you said that this bog had a hard bottom." "So it has," answered the latter, "but you have not got half way to it yet." So it is with the bogs and quicksands of society; but he is an old boy that knows it. Only what is thought, said, or done at a certain rare coincidence is good. I would not be one of those who will foolishly drive a nail into mere lath and plastering; such a deed would keep me awake nights. Give me a hammer, and let me feel for the furring.[29] Do not depend on the putty. Drive a nail home and clinch it so faithfully that you can wake up in the night and think of your work with satisfaction,—a work at which you would not be ashamed to invoke the muse. So will help you God, and so only. Every nail driven should be as another rivet in the machine of the universe, you carrying on the work.

Rather than love, than money, than fame, give me truth. I sat at a table where were rich food and wine in abundance, and obsequious attendance, but sincerity and truth were not; and I went away hungry from the inhospitable board. The hospitality was as cold as the ices. I thought that there was no need of ice to freeze them. They talked to me of the age of the wine and the fame of the vintage, but I thought of an older, a newer, and purer wine, of a more glorious vintage which they had not got, and could not buy. The style, the house and grounds and "entertainment" pass for nothing with me. I called on the king, but he made me wait in his hall, and conducted like a man incapacitated for hospitality. There was a man in my neighborhood who lived in a hollow tree. His manners were truly regal. I should have done better had I called on him.

How long shall we sit in our porticoes practising idle and musty virtues, which any work would make impertinent? As if one were to begin the day with long-suffering, and hire a man to hoe his potatoes; and in the afternoon go forth to practise Christian meekness and charity with goodness aforethought! Consider the China pride[30] and stagnant self-complacency of mankind. This generation inclines a little to congratulate itself on being the last of an illustrious line; and in Boston and London and Paris and Rome, thinking of its long descent, it speaks of its progress in art and science and literature with satisfaction. There are the records of the Philosophical Societies, and the public Eulogies of *Great Men!* It is the good Adam contemplating his own virtue. "Yes,

[27]Daniel Webster was the most famous American orator of the day.
[28]To skate or slide over thin ice; hence, to take a risk. [29]Wall studs.
[30]Extreme pride, thought to be characteristic of the Chinese.

we have done great deeds, and sung divine songs, which shall never die."—that is, as long as *we* can remember them. The learned societies and great men of Assyria,—where are they? What youthful philosophers and experimentalists we are! There is not one of my readers who has yet lived a whole human life. These may be but the spring months in the life of the race. If we have had the seven-years' itch, we have not seen the seventeen-year locust yet in Concord. We are acquainted with a mere pellicle[31] of the globe on which we live. Most have not delved six feet beneath the surface, nor leaped as many above it. We know not where we are. Beside, we are sound asleep nearly half our time. Yet we esteem ourselves wise, and have an established order on the surface. Truly, we are deep thinkers, we are ambitious spirits! As I stand over the insect crawling amid the pine needles on the forest floor, and endeavoring to conceal itself from my sight, and ask myself why it will cherish those humble thoughts, and hide its head from me who might, perhaps, be its benefactor, and impart to its race some cheering information, I am reminded of the greater Benefactor and Intelligence that stands over me the human insect.

There is an incessant influx of novelty into the world, and yet we tolerate incredible dulness. I need only suggest what kind of sermons are still listened to in the most enlightened countries. There are such words as joy and sorrow, but they are only the burden of a psalm, sung with a nasal twang, while we believe in the ordinary and mean. We think that we can change our clothes only. It is said that the British Empire is very large and respectable, and that the United States are a first-rate power. We do not believe that a tide rises and falls behind every man which can float the British Empire like a chip, if he should ever harbor it in his mind. Who knows what sort of seventeen-year locust will next come out of the ground? The government of the world I live in was not framed, like that of Britain, in after-dinner conversations over the wine.

The life in us is like the water in the river. It may rise this year higher than man has ever known it, and flood the parched uplands; even this may be the eventful year, which will drown out all our muskrats. It was not always dry land where we dwell. I see far inland the banks which the stream anciently washed before science began to record its freshets. Every one has heard the story which has gone the rounds of New England, of a strong and beautiful bug which came out of the dry leaf of an old table of apple-tree wood, which had stood in a farmer's kitchen for sixty years, first in Connecticut, and afterward in Massachusetts,—from an egg deposited in the living tree many years earlier still, as appeared by counting the annual layers beyond it; which was heard gnawing out for several weeks, hatched perchance by the heat of an urn. Who does not feel his faith in a resurrection and immortality strengthened by hearing of this? Who knows what beautiful and winged life, whose egg has been buried for ages under many concentric layers of woodenness in the dead dry life of society, deposited at first in the alburnum[32] of the green and living tree, which has been gradually converted into the semblance of its well-seasoned tomb,—heard perchance gnawing out now for years by the astonished family of man, as they sat round the festive board,—

[31]Skin. [32]Sapwood.

may unexpectedly come forth from amidst society's most trivial and handselled furniture,[33] to enjoy its perfect summer life at last!

I do not say that John or Jonathan[34] will realize all this; but such is the character of that morrow which mere lapse of time can never make to dawn. The light which puts out our eyes is darkness to us. Only that day dawns to which we are awake. There is more day to dawn. The sun is but a morning star.

1846 1854

Henry Wadsworth Longfellow 1807–1882 

Longfellow was one of America's literary Brahmins, a title derived from the highest, priestly caste of the Hindus and humorously applied to aristocratic New Englanders of the nineteenth century. Like his fellow Brahmins Lowell and Holmes, Longfellow was a professor at Harvard, and his life was rooted in Cambridge and Boston. His great fame began with the publication of his first volume of poems, Voices of the Night *(1839), which contained "A Psalm of Life," one of the nineteenth-century's best loved poems. His reputation continued to grow with the appearance of* Ballads *(1841), which included "The Village Blacksmith." Then came* Evangeline *(1847),* Hiawatha *(1855),* The Courtship of Miles Standish *(1858), and* Tales of a Wayside Inn *(1863).*

Poe disparaged Longfellow as a plagiarist who borrowed heavily from foreign literature, but Hawthorne placed him at "the head of our list of native poets," voicing the opinion of the vast number of readers who made Longfellow the most popular poet of his age. Hiawatha *sold 30,000 copies in six months. When* The Courtship of Miles Standish *was published, more than 15,000 copies were sold the first day. Longfellow became a national institution. His seventy-fifth birthday was celebrated by schoolchildren throughout the nation; people rose when he entered a room; gentlemen took off their hats in his presence. His poetry was translated throughout Europe; he was revered in England, where his popularity exceeded even that of Tennyson and Browning; and after his death his home became an American literary shrine.*

Longfellow transmitted European culture to his countrymen, popularized native American themes, and helped establish a national literature. His work was musical, mildly romantic, high-minded, and flavored with sentimental preachment. Yet the very qualities that brought excessive praise in his lifetime have since brought excessive critical reaction against him. His melodious measures are now condescendingly discounted as sing-song versification. He has been judged unduly didactic, passionless, and sweetly untouched by the social controversies of his time. As one of America's "schoolroom poets" Longfellow represented the ideals and aspirations of a young nation and a genteel tradition. He remains an index to a nineteenth-century culture whose ideals

[33]Furniture that has been "given away," hence: shabby, of little value.

[34]John Bull the Britisher and Brother Jonathan the American.

still survive, although its once-favorite poet has now been largely relegated to the elementary schoolroom. There his masterful storytelling verses are still cherished as guides to genteel morality and as rhymed introductions to the legends of American history.

FURTHER READING: *The Letters of Henry Wadsworth Longfellow,* vols. I–VI, 1967–1982; S. Longfellow, *Life of Henry Wadsworth Longfellow,* 3 vols., 1886, 1969; H. Gorman, *A Victorian American, Henry Wadsworth Longfellow,* 1926; L. Thompson, *Young Longfellow,* 1938, 1969; N. Arvin, *Longfellow,* 1963; C. Williams, *Henry Wadsworth Longfellow,* 1964; E. Wagenknecht, *Henry Wadsworth Longfellow,* 1966; E. Wagenknecht, *Henry Wadsworth Longfellow, His Poetry and Prose,* 1986; C. Calhoun, *Longfellow, A Rediscovered Life,* 2004.
TEXT: *The Complete Works of Henry Wadsworth Longfellow,* 11 vols., 1886.

A PSALM OF LIFE

WHAT THE HEART OF THE YOUNG MAN SAID TO THE PSALMIST

Tell me not, in mournful numbers,[1]
  Life is but an empty dream!—
For the soul is dead that slumbers,
  And things are not what they seem.

Life is real! Life is earnest!
  And the grave is not its goal;
Dust thou art, to dust returnest,[2]
  Was not spoken of the soul.

Not enjoyment, and not sorrow,
  Is our destined end or way;
But to act, that each to-morrow
  Find us farther than to-day.

Art is long, and Time is fleeting,[3]
  And our hearts, though stout and brave,
Still, like muffled drums, are beating
  Funeral marches to the grave.

In the world's broad field of battle,
  In the bivouac of Life,
Be not like dumb, driven cattle!
  Be a hero in the strife!

Trust no Future, howe'er pleasant!
  Let the dead Past bury its dead!
Act,—act in the living Present!
  Heart within, and God o'erhead!

[1]Poetic meters, rhythms. [2]"Dust thou art, and unto dust shalt thou return." Genesis 3:19.
[3]Adapted from the *Aphorisms* of Hippocrates (460?–377? B.C.), Greek physician.

Lives of great men all remind us
We can make our lives sublime,
And, departing, leave behind us
Footprints on the sands of time;

Footprints, that perhaps another,
Sailing o'er life's solemn main,
A forlorn and shipwrecked brother,
Seeing, shall take heart again.

Let us, then, be up and doing,
With a heart for any fate;
Still achieving, still pursuing,
Learn to labor and to wait.

1838 1838

THE ARSENAL AT SPRINGFIELD[1]

This is the Arsenal. From floor to ceiling,
Like a huge organ, rise the burnished arms;[2]
But from their silent pipes no anthem pealing
Startles the villages with strange alarms.

Ah! what a sound will rise, how wild and dreary,
When the death-angel touches those swift keys!
What loud lament and dismal Miserere[3]
Will mingle with their awful symphonies!

I hear even now the infinite fierce chorus,
The cries of agony, the endless groan,
Which, through the ages that have gone before us,
In long reverberations reach our own.

On helm and harness[4] rings the Saxon hammer,
Through Cimbric forest[5] roars the Norseman's song,
And loud, amid the universal clamor,
O'er distant deserts sounds the Tartar gong.[6]

[1]Longfellow visited the U.S. Arsenal at Springfield, Massachusetts, in 1843.
[2]I.e., gun barrels.
[3]Latin, from the prayer "Miserere mei, Domine" ("Have mercy on me, O Lord"). Psalm 51:1.
[4]Helmet and armor.
[5]Forest of the Cimbri, a Danish people who battled the Romans.
[6] Sounded to bring warriors to battle.

I hear the Florentine, who from his palace
Wheels out his battle-bell with dreadful din,[7]
And Aztec priests upon their teocallis[8]
Beat the wild war-drums made of serpent's skin;

The tumult of each sacked and burning village;
The shout that every prayer for mercy drowns;
The soldiers' revels in the midst of pillage;
The wail of famine in beleaguered towns;

The bursting shell, the gateway wrenched asunder,
The rattling musketry, the clashing blade;
And ever and anon, in tones of thunder
The diapason[9] of the cannonade.

Is it, O man, with such discordant noises,
With such accursed instruments as these,
Thou drownest Nature's sweet and kindly voices,
And jarrest the celestial harmonies?

Were half the power that fills the world with terror,
Were half the wealth bestowed on camps and courts,[10]
Given to redeem the human mind from error,
There were no need of arsenals or forts:

The warrior's name would be a name abhorrèd!
And every nation, that should lift again
Its hand against a brother, on its forehead
Would wear forevermore the curse of Cain![11]

Down the dark future, through long generations,
The echoing sounds grow fainter and then cease;
And like a bell, with solemn, sweet vibrations,
I hear once more the voice of Christ say, "Peace!"

Peace! and no longer from its brazen portals
The blast of War's great organ shakes the skies!
But beautiful as songs of the immortals,
The holy melodies of love arise.

1844 1844

[7]The city bell of medieval Florence, rung to summon the militia.
[8]Temples built on the top of pyramids.
[9]Musical tones.
[10]I.e., military camps and royal courts.
[11]"Whosoever slayeth Cain, vengeance shall be taken on him sevenfold. And the Lord set a mark upon Cain, lest any finding him should kill him." Genesis 4:15.

THE JEWISH CEMETERY AT NEWPORT[1]

How strange it seems! These Hebrews in their graves,
Close by the street of this fair seaport town,
Silent beside the never-silent waves,
At rest in all this moving up and down!

The trees are white with dust, that o'er their sleep
Wave their broad curtains in the south-wind's breath,
While underneath these leafy tents they keep
The long, mysterious Exodus[2] of Death.

And these sepulchral stones, so old and brown,
That pave with level flags[3] their burial-place,
Seem like the tablets of the Law, thrown down
And broken by Moses[4] at the mountain's base.

The very names recorded here are strange,
Of foreign accent, and of different climes;
Alvares and Rivera[5] interchange
With Abraham and Jacob of old times.

"Blessed be god, for he created Death!"
The mourners said, "and Death is rest and peace;"
Then added, in the certainty of faith,
"And giveth Life that nevermore shall cease."

Closed are the portals of their Synagogue,
No Psalms of David now the silence break,
No Rabbi reads the ancient Decalogue[6]
In the grand dialect[7] the Prophets spake.

Gone are the living,[8] but the dead remain,
And not neglected; for a hand unseen,
Scattering its bounty, like a summer rain,
Still keeps their graves and their remembrance green.

[1]Rhode Island seaport town.
[2]Journey, as in the book of Exodus, which tells of the migration of the Israelites from Egypt.
[3]Flagstones.
[4]When Moses saw the Israelites worshipping an idol, he broke the stone tablets containing the Ten Commandments. Exodus 32:1–19.
[5]Names of New England Jews of Portuguese and Spanish descent.
[6] The Ten Commandments.
[7]Hebrew.
[8]At the time of Longfellow's visit, no Jews remained in Newport.

How came they here? What burst of Christian hate,
  What persecution, merciless and blind,
Drove o'er the sea—that desert desolate—
  These Ishmaels and Hagars[9] of mankind?

They lived in narrow streets and lanes obscure,
  Ghetto and Judenstrass,[10] in mirk and mire;
Taught in the school of patience to endure
  The life of anguish and the death of fire.

All their lives long, with the unleavened bread
  And bitter herbs of exile and its fears,
The wasting famine of the heart they fed,
  And slaked its thirst with marah[11] of their tears.

Anathema maranatha![12] was the cry
  That rang from town to town, from street to street:
At every gate the accursed Mordecai[13]
  Was mocked and jeered, and spurned by Christian feet,

Pride and humiliation hand in hand
  Walked with them through the world where'er they went;
Trampled and beaten were they as the sand,
  And yet unshaken as the continent.

For in the background figures vague and vast
  Of patriarchs and of prophets rose sublime,
And all the great traditions of the Past
  They saw reflected in the coming time.

And thus forever with reverted look
  The mystic volume of the world they read,
Spelling it backward, like a Hebrew book,[14]
  Till life became a Legend of the Dead.

But ah! what once has been shall be no more!
  The groaning earth in travail and in pain
Brings forth its races, but does not restore,
  And the dead nations never rise again.

1852 1854

[9]Biblical wanderers and outcasts. Genesis 16 and 21.
[10]German: Street of Jews—a ghetto, or segregated area.
[11]Hebrew: bitterness.
[12]A biblical curse used against non-Christians. I Corinthians 16:22.
[13]Jewish leader mocked and cursed by the Persians. Esther 3–5.
[14]Hebrew is read from right to left.

MY LOST YOUTH

Often I think of the beautiful town[1]
That is seated by the sea;
Often in thought go up and down
The pleasant streets of that dear old town,
And my youth comes back to me.
And a verse of a Lapland song[2]
Is haunting my memory still:
"A boy's will is the wind's will,
And the thoughts of youth are long, long thoughts."

I can see the shadowy lines of its trees,
And catch, in the sudden gleams.
The sheen of the far-surrounding seas,
And islands that were the Hesperides[3]
Of all my boyish dreams.
And the burden of that old song,
It murmurs and whispers still:
"A boy's will is the wind's will,
And the thoughts of youth are long, long thoughts."

I remember the black wharves and the slips,
And the sea-tides tossing free;
And Spanish sailors with bearded lips,
And the beauty and mystery of the ships,
And the magic of the sea.
And the voice of that wayward song
Is singing and saying still:
"A boy's will is the wind's will,
And the thoughts of youth are long, long thoughts."

I remember the bulwarks by the shore,
And the fort upon the hill;
The sunrise gun, with its hollow roar,
The drum-beat repeated o'er and o'er,
And the bugle wild and shrill.
And the music of that old song
Throbs in my memory still:
"A boy's will is the wind's will,
And the thoughts of youth are long, long thoughts."

I remember the sea-fight[4] far away,
How it thundered o'er the tide!

[1]Portland, Maine, Longfellow's birthplace.

[2]A Lapland folksong translated by the German poet Johann Gottfried Von Herder (1744–1803).

[3]Distant western islands in classical legend.

[4]Naval battle off Portland, Maine, where the American ship *Enterprise* defeated the British *Boxer* in 1813. The ship captains, killed in the battle, were brought ashore for burial.

And the dead captains, as they lay
In their graves, o'erlooking the tranquil bay
Where they in battle died.
And the sound of that mournful song
Goes through me with a thrill:
"A boy's will is the wind's will,
And the thoughts of youth are long, long thoughts."

I can see the breezy dome of groves,
The shadows of Deering's Woods;[5]
And the friendships old and the early loves
Come back with a Sabbath sound, as of doves
In quiet neighborhoods.
And the verse of that sweet old song,
It flutters and murmurs still:
"A boy's will is the wind's will,
And the thoughts of youth are long, long thoughts."

I remember the gleams and glooms that dart
Across the school-boy's brain;
The song and the silence in the heart,
That in part are prophecies, and in part
Are longings wild and vain.
And the voice of that fitful song
Sings on, and is never still:
"A boy's will is the wind's will,
And the thoughts of youth are long, long thoughts."

There are things of which I may not speak;
There are dreams that cannot die;
There are thoughts that make the strong heart weak,
And bring a pallor into the cheek,
And a mist before the eye.
And the words of that fatal song
Come over me like a chill:
"A boy's will is the wind's will,
And the thoughts of youth are long, long thoughts."

Strange to me now are the forms I meet
When I visit the dear old town;
But the native air is pure and sweet,
And the trees that o'ershadow each well-known street,
And they balance up and down,
Are singing the beautiful song,
Are sighing and whispering still:
"A boy's will is the wind's will,
And the thoughts of youth are long, long thoughts."

[5]Forest near Portland.

And Deering's Woods are fresh and fair,
  And with joy that is almost pain
My heart goes back to wander there,
And among the dreams of the days that were,
  I find my lost youth again.
    And the strange and beautiful song,
    The groves are repeating it still:
    "A boy's will is the wind's will,
And the thoughts of youth are long, long thoughts."

1855 1855

AFTERMATH[1]

When the summer fields are mown,
When the birds are fledged and flown,
  And the dry leaves strew the path;
With the falling of the snow,
With the cawing of the crow,
Once again the fields we mow
  And gather in the aftermath.

Not the sweet, new grass with flowers
Is this harvesting of ours;
  Not the upland clover bloom;
But the rowen[2] mixed with weeds,
Tangled tufts from marsh and meads,
Where the poppy drops its seeds
  In the silence and the gloom.

1873

THE TIDE RISES, THE TIDE FALLS

The tide rises, the tide falls,
The twilight darkens, the curlew calls;
Along the sea-sands damp and brown
The traveller hastens toward the town,
  And the tide rises, the tide falls.

[1]In agriculture a term meaning second-growth crop.
[2]Synonym of "aftermath."

Darkness settles on roofs and walls,
But the sea, the sea in the darkness calls;
The little waves, with their soft, white hands,
Efface the footprints in the sands,
  And the tide rises, the tide falls.

The morning breaks; the steeds in their stalls
Stamp and neigh, as the hostler calls;
The day returns, but nevermore
Returns the traveller to the shore,
  And the tide rises, the tide falls.

1879 1880

James Russell Lowell 1819–1891

As a poet, essayist, editor, and public gentleman, James Russell Lowell reflected the taste of nineteenth-century America. Like Longfellow and Holmes he was one of the literary Brahmins who thought themselves to be the "untitled aristocracy" of Boston—and hence of all America. Lowell was born in Cambridge, Massachusetts, into an honored New England family. At Harvard he was the class poet, and not long after his graduation he published his first volume of poetry, A Year's Life *(1841). In a single year, 1848, he established himself firmly in New England's literary hierarchy by publishing four volumes that represented his most notable literary achievement:* Poems: Second Series; A Fable for Critics; The Biglow Papers; *and* The Vision of Sir Launfal, *a Christian parable in verse that became his most frequently reprinted work.*

As a young man Lowell was an ardent reformer; he crusaded for abolition, temperance, vegetarianism, and women's rights. But as he grew older he became a conservative spokesman for the dominant and comfortable society that honored him. For thirty years he was a professor of literature at Harvard, filling the position vacated by the poet Longfellow. He was the first editor of the Atlantic Monthly *and editor of the prestigious* North American Review. *He received honorary degrees from both Oxford and Cambridge. And for his political service to the Republican party he was made U.S. ambassador to Spain (1877–1880) and to England (1880–1885).*

Through his lifetime Lowell was a prolific writer of poems, essays, and literary criticism, and in his last years he was considered to be America's most distinguished man of letters. His poetry was fluent, cultivated, and facile; his dialect verse and his rhymed satire crackled with witty commentary on the follies of his age and on the character of his literary contemporaries, among them Poe, who was "three fifths of him genius and two fifths sheer fudge," and Thoreau, who "watched Nature like a detective." Yet Lowell's preference was for the mannered elegance of a poetry filled with "classic niceties." His life and his writings were detached from the human concerns of such writers as Whitman, whom Lowell thought a humbug. As a result, his own efforts to unite art and ethics produced a moralizing literature in many ways typical of New England's "schoolroom" poets, gentlemen who, once exalted in reputation, are today best understood as emblems of the orthodoxy and the genteel hopes of an age that has long since passed away.

FURTHER READING: *The Complete Poetical Works of James Russell Lowell,* ed. H. Scudder, 1897; *James Russell Lowell's The Biglow Papers* [*First Series*], ed. T. Wortham, 1977; R. C. Beatty, *James Russell Lowell,* 1942; L. Howard, *Victorian Knight-Errant, A Study of the Early Literary Career of James Russell Lowell,* 1952; M. Duberman, *James Russell Lowell,* 1966; C. McGlinchee, *James Russell Lowell,* 1967; E. Wagenknecht, *James Russell Lowell,* 1971; C. Heymann, *American Aristocracy,* 1980.

TEXT: *The Writings of James Russell Lowell,* 10 vols., 1890.

TO THE DANDELION

Dear common flower, that grow'st beside the way,
Fringing the dusty road with harmless gold,
First pledge of blithesome May,
Which children pluck, and full of pride uphold,
High-hearted buccaneers, o'erjoyed that they
An Eldorado[1] in the grass have found,
Which not the rich earth's ample round
May match in wealth, thou art more dear to me
Than all the prouder summer-blooms may be.

Gold such as thine ne'er drew the Spanish prow
Through the primeval hush of Indian seas,
Nor wrinkled the lean brow
Of age, to rob the lover's heart of ease;
'T is the Spring's largess, which she scatters now
To rich and poor alike, with lavish hand,
Though most hearts never understand
To take it at God's value, but pass by
The offered wealth with unrewarded eye.

[1]Legendary city of gold.

Thou art my tropics and mine Italy;
To look at thee unlocks a warmer clime;
The eyes thou givest me
Are in the heart, and heed not space or time:
Not in mid June the golden-cuirassed[2] bee
Feels a more summer-like warm ravishment
In the white lily's breezy tent,
His fragrant Sybaris,[3] than I, when first
From the dark green thy yellow circles burst.

Then think I of deep shadows on the grass,
Of meadows where in sun the cattle graze,
Where, as the breezes pass,
The gleaming rushes lean a thousand ways,
Of leaves that slumber in a cloudy mass,
Or whiten in the wind, of waters blue
That from the distance sparkle through
Some woodland gap, and of a sky above,
Where one white cloud like a stray lamb doth move.

My childhood's earliest thoughts are linked with thee;
The sight of thee calls back the robin's song,
Who, from the dark old tree
Beside the door, sang clearly all day long,
And I, secure in childish piety,
Listened as if I heard an angel sing
With news from heaven, which he could bring
Fresh every day to my untainted ears
When birds and flowers and I were happy peers.

How like a prodigal doth nature seem,
When thou, for all thy gold, so common art!
Thou teachest me to deem
More sacredly of every human heart,
Since each reflects in joy its scanty gleam
Of heaven, and could some wondrous secret show,
Did we but pay the love we owe,
And with a child's undoubting wisdom look
On all these living pages of God's book.

1845

[2]With gold coloring that resembles a cuirass (chest armor).
[3]Ancient Greek city renowned for its sensuous luxury.

from *THE BIGLOW PAPERS, FIRST SERIES*[1]

NO. I.

A LETTER

FROM MR. EZEKIEL BIGLOW OF JAALAM TO THE HON. JOSEPH T. BUCKINGHAM, EDITOR OF THE BOSTON COURIER, INCLOSING A POEM OF HIS SON, MR. HOSEA BIGLOW.

JAYLEM, june 1846.

MISTER EDDYTER:—Our Hosea wuz down to Boston last week, and he see a cruetin Sarjunt[2] a struttin round as popler[3] as a hen with 1 chicking, with 2 fellers a drummin and fifin arter him like all nater.[4] the sarjun he thout Hosea hedn't gut his i teeth cut cos he looked a kindo's though he'd jest com down,[5] so he cal'lated to hook him in, but Hosy woodn't take none o' his sarse[6] for all he hed much as 20 Rooster's tales stuck onto his hat and eenamost enuf brass a bobbin up and down on his shoulders and figureed onto his coat and trousis, let alone wut nater hed sot in his featers, to make a 6 pounder[7] out on.

wal, Hosea he com home considerabal riled, and arter I'd gone to bed I heern Him a thrashin round like a short-tailed Bull in flitime. The old Woman ses she to me ses she, Zekle, ses she, our Hosee's gut the chollery[8] or suthin anuther ses she, don't you Bee skeered, ses I, he's oney amaking pottery[9] ses i, he's ollers on hand at that ere busynes like Da & martin,[10] and shure enuf, cum mornin, Hosy he cum down stares full chizzle,[11] hare on eend and cote tales flyin, and sot rite of to go reed his varses to Parson Wilbur bein he haint aney grate shows o' book larnin himelf, bimeby he cum back and sed the parson wuz dreffle tickled with 'em as i hoop you will Be, and said they wuz True grit.

Hosea ses taint hardly fair to call 'em hisn now, cos the parson kind o' slicked off som o' the last varses but he told Hosee he didn't want to put his ore in to tetch to the Rest on 'em, bein they wuz verry well As thay wuz, and then Hosy ses he sed suthin a nuther about Simplex Mundishes[12] or sum

[1]Published anonymously (1846–1848), the first *Biglow Papers* were Lowell's protest against the Mexican War (1846–1847) and the spread of slavery. The *Papers* were presented as the work of a young New England Yankee farmer, Hosea Biglow. "H. W." was Hosea's parson, the Reverend Homer Wilbur, who "edited" Hosea's verses before their publication and whom Lowell created as a pedantic contrast to the versifying bumpkin, Hosea.

[2]Recruiting sergeant. To fight the Mexican War, the federal government sent out a nationwide call for volunteers. Massachusetts was asked to provide one regiment.

[3]Conceited. [4]Nature. [5]I.e., come down from the backcountry. [6]Sauce, insolence.

[7]A brass cannon that shoots a six-pound ball. [8]Choleric, out of humor.

[9]"*Aut insanit, aut versos facit.*—H. W."—Lowell's note. The Latin is Parson Wilbur's misquotation from the *Satires* (Book II, Satire vii, line 117) of the Roman poet Horace: "He is either insane or he is making verses."

[10]Day and Martin, shoe-polish makers who advertised in verse. [11]I.e., full speed.

[12]Parson Wilbur was quoting Horace (Book I, Ode v, line 5): "*simplex munditis,*" "simple elegance," i.e., unsophisticated.

sech feller, but I guess Hosea kind o' didn't hear him, for I never hearn o' nobody o' that name in this villadge, and I've lived here man and boy 76 year cum next tater diggin, and thair aint no wheres a kitting spryer'n I be.

If you print 'em I wish you'd jest let folks know who hosy's father is, cos my ant Keziah used to say it's nater to be curus ses she, she aint livin though and he's a likely kind o' lad.

EZEKIEL BIGLOW.

Thrash away, you'll *hev* to rattle
  On them kittle-drums o' yourn,—
'Taint a knowin' kind o' cattle
  Thet is ketched with mouldy corn;
Put in stiff, you fifer feller,
  Let folks see how spry you be,—
Guess you'll toot till you are yeller
  'Fore you git ahold o' me!

Thet air flag's a leetle rotten,
  Hope it ain't your Sunday's best;—
Fact! it takes a sight o' cotton
  To stuff out a soger's[13] chest:
Sense we farmers hev to pay fer't,
  Ef you mus wear humps like these,
S'posin' you should try salt hay fer't,
  It would du ez slick ez grease.

'T wouldn't suit them Southun fellers,
  They're a dreffle graspin' set,
We must ollers blow the bellers
  Wen they want their irons het;
May be it's all right ez preachin',
  But *my* narves it kind o' grates,
Wen I see the overreachin'
  O' them nigger-driven' States.

Them thet rule us, them slave-traders,
  Haint they cut a thunderin' swarth
(Helped by Yankee renegaders),
  Thru the vartu o' the North!
We begin to think it's nater
  To take sarse an' not be riled;—
Who'd expect to see a tater
  All on eend at bein' biled?

[13]Soldier's.

Ez fer war, I call it murder,—
 There you hev it plain an' flat;
I don't want to go no furder
 Than my Testyment fer that;
God hez sed so plump an' fairly,
 It's ez long ez it is broad,
An' you've gut to git up airly
 Ef you want to take in God.

'Taint your eppyletts[14] an' feathers
 Make the thing a grain more right;
'Taint afollerin' your bell-wethers[15]
 Will excuse ye in His sight;
Ef you take a sword an' dror it,
 An' go stick a feller thru,
Guf'ment ain't to answer for it,
 God'll send the bill to you.

Wut's the use o' meeting'-goin'
 Every Sabbath, wet or dry,
Ef it's right to go amowin'
 Feller-men like oats an' rye?
I dunno but wut it's pooty
 Trainin' round in bobtail coats,—
But it's curus Christian dooty
 This 'ere cuttin' folks's throats.

They may talk o' Freedom's airy[16]
 Tell they're pupple in the face,—
It's a grand gret cemetary
 Fer the barthrights of our race;
They jest want this Californy
 So's to lug new slave-states in[17]
To abuse ye, an' to scorn ye,
 An' to plunder ye like sin.

Aint it cute to see a Yankee
 Take sech everlastin' pains,
All to git the Devil's thankee
 Helpin' on 'em weld their chains?
Wy, it's jest ez clear ez figgers,
 Clear ez one an' one make two,
Chaps thet make black slaves o' niggers
 Want to make wite slaves o' you.

Tell ye jest the eend I've come to
 Arter cipherin' plaguy smart,

[14]Epaulets. [15]Male sheep that leads the flock. [16]Area.
[17]Abolitionists feared the admission of California would create another slave state.

An' it makes a handy sum, tu,
  Any gump[18] could larn by heart;
Laborin' man an' laborin' woman
  Hev one glory an' one shame,
Ev'y thin' thet's done inhuman
  Injers all on 'em the same.

'Taint by turnin' out to hack folks
  You're agoin' to git your right,
Nor by lookin' down on black folks
  Coz you're put upon by wite;
Slavery aint o' nary color,
  'Taint the hide thet makes it wus,
All it keers fer in a feller
  'S jest to make him fill its pus.[19]

Want to tackle *me* in, du ye?
  I expect you'll hev to wait;
Wen cold lead puts daylight thru ye
  You'll begin to kal'late;[20]
S'pose the crows wun't fall to pickin'
  All the carkiss from your bones,
Coz you helped to give a lickin'
  To them poor half-Spanish drones?[21]

Jest go home an' ask our Nancy
  Wether I'd be sech a goose
Ez to jine ye,—guess you'd fancy
  The etarnal bung[22] wuz loose!
She wants me fer home consumption,
  Let alone the hay's to mow,—
Ef you're arter folks o' gumption,
  You've a darned long row to hoe.

Take them editors thet's crowin'
  Like a cockerel three months old,—
Don't ketch any on 'em goin',
  Though they *be* so blasted bold;
Ain't they a prime lot o' fellers?
  'Fore they think on 't guess they'll sprout
(Like a peach thet's got the yellers),[23]
  With the meanness bustin' out.

Wal, go 'long to help 'em stealin'
  Bigger pens to cram with slaves,
Help the men thet's ollers dealin'
  Insults on your fathers' graves;

[18]Fool. [19]Purse. [20]Calculate. [21]The Mexicans. [22]I.e., the darned plug.
[23]A plant disease that causes yellowing of foliage.

Help the strong to grind the feeble,
  Help the many agin the few,
Help the men thet call your people
  Witewashed slaves[24] an' peddlin'[25] crew!

Massachusetts, God forgive her,
  She's akneelin' with the rest,[26]
She, thet ough' to ha' clung ferever
  In her grand old eagle-nest;
She thet ough' to stand so fearless
  W'ile the wracks[27] are round her hurled,
Holdin' up a beacon peerless
  To the oppressed of all the world!

Ha'n't they sold your colored seamen?
  Ha'n't they made your env'ys w'iz?[28]
Wut'll make ye act like freemen?
Wut'll git your dander riz?
Come, I'll tell ye wut I'm thinkin'
  Is our dooty in this fix,
They'd ha' done 't ez quick ez winkin'
  In the days o' seventy-six.

Clang the bells in every steeple,
  Call all true men to disown
The tradoocers of our people,
  The enslavers o' their own;
  Let our dear old Bay State proudly
  Put the trumpet to her mouth,
Let her ring his messidge loudly
  In the ears of all the South:—

"I'll return ye good fer evil
  Much ez we frail mortils can,
But I wun't go help the Devil
  Makin' man the cus o' man;
Call me coward, call me traiter,
  Jest ez suits your mean idees,—
  Here I stand a tyrant-hater,
  An' the friend o' God an' Peace!"

Ef I'd *my* way I hed ruther
  We should go to work an' part,[29]
They take one way, we take t' other,
  Guess it wouldn't break my heart;

[24]Defenders of Southern slavery had charged that Northern industrial workers were mere "white-washed wage slaves."

[25]Petty, insignificant.

[26]Massachusetts congressmen had voted for a declaration of war with Mexico. [27]Calamities.

[28]Envoys sent to the South to protest the seizure of free Negroes from Massachusetts were "made to whiz," i.e., made to flee.

[29]I.e., New England states should secede from their union with the slaveholding states.

Man hed ough' to put asunder
Them thet God has noways jined;[30]
An' I shouldn't gretly wonder
Ef there's thousand o' my mind.

1846

from *A FABLE FOR CRITICS*

Reader! walk up at once (it will soon be too late),
and buy at a perfectly ruinous rate

A FABLE FOR CRITICS:

OR, BETTER,

(I like, as a thing that the reader's first fancy may strike,
an old-fashioned title-page,
such as presents a tabular view of the volume's contents),

A GLANCE AT A FEW OF OUR LITERARY PROGENIES

(MRS. MALAPROP'S WORD)[1]

FROM THE TUB OF DIOGENES;[2]

A VOCAL AND MUSICAL MEDLEY,
THAT IS,

A SERIES OF JOKES

By A Wonderful Quiz,[3]

WHO ACCOMPANIES HIMSELF WITH A RUB-A-DUB-DUB, FULL OF SPIRIT
AND GRACE, ON THE TOP OF THE TUB.

Set forth in October, the 31st day,
In the year '48, G. P. Putnam, Broadway.

It being the commonest mode of procedure, I premise a few candid remarks

[30]"What therefore God hath joined together, let not man put asunder." Matthew 19:6.

[1]Mrs. Malaprop, a character in Sheridan's play *The Rivals* (1775), noted for her misuse of words, such as "progenies" for "prodigies."

[2]Greek philosopher and social critic who reputedly lived in a tub. [3]An eccentric person.

To the Reader:—

This trifle, begun to please only myself and my own private fancy, was laid on the shelf. But some friends, who had seen it, induced me, by dint of saying they liked it, to put it in print. That is, having come to that very conclusion, I asked their advice when 'twould make no confusion. For though (in the gentlest of ways) they had hinted it was scarce worth the while, I should doubtless have printed it.

I began it, intending a Fable, a frail, slender thing, rhyme-ywinged, with a sting in its tail. But, by addings and alterings not previously planned, digressions chance-hatched, like birds' eggs in the sand, and dawdlings to suit every whimsey's demand (always freeing the bird which I held in my hand, for the two perched, perhaps out of reach, in the tree),—it grew by degrees to the size which you see. I was like the old woman that carried the calf, and my neighbors, like hers, no doubt, wonder and laugh; and when, my strained arms with their grown burthen full, I call it my Fable, they call it a bull.[4]

Having scrawled at full gallop (as far as that goes) in a style that is neither good verse nor bad prose, and being a person whom nobody knows, some people will say I am rather more free with my readers than it is becoming to be, that I seem to expect them to wait on my leisure in following wherever I wander at pleasure, that, in short, I take more than a young author's lawful ease, and laugh in a queer way so like Mephistopheles,[5] that the Public will doubt, as they grope through my rhythm, if in truth I am making fun *of* them or *with* them.

So the excellent Public is hereby assured that the sale of my book is already secured. For there is not a poet throughout the whole land but will purchase a copy or two out of hand, in the fond expectation of being amused in it, by seeing his betters cut up and abused in it. Now, I find, by a pretty exact calculation, there are something like ten thousand bards in the nation, of that special variety whom the Review and Magazine critics call *lofty* and *true*, and about thirty thousand (*this* tribe is increasing) of the kinds who are termed *full of promise* and *pleasing*. The Public will see by a glance at this schedule, that they cannot expect me to be over-sedulous about courting *them*, since it seems I have got enough fuel made sure of for boiling my pot.

As for such of our poets as find not their names mentioned once in my pages, with praises or blames, let them SEND IN THEIR CARDS, without further DELAY, to my friend G. P. Putnam, Esquire, in Broadway, where a LIST will be kept with the strictest regard to the day and the hour of receiving the card. Then, taking them up as I chance to have time (that is, if their names can be twisted in rhyme), I will honestly give each his PROPER POSITION, at the rate of ONE AUTHOR to each NEW EDITION. Thus a PREMIUM is offered sufficiently HIGH (as the magazines say when they tell their best lie) to induce bards to CLUB their resources and buy the balance of every edition, until they have all of them fairly been run through the mill.

One word to such readers (judicious and wise) as read books with something behind the mere eyes, of whom in the country, perhaps, there are two, including myself, gentle reader, and you. All the characters sketched in this

[4] A term also meaning a jest or linguistic blunder. [5] I.e., with a devilish laugh.

slight *jeu d'esprit,*[6] though, it may be, they seem, here and there, rather free, and drawn from a somewhat too cynical standpoint, are *meant* to be faithful, for that is the grand point, and none but an owl would feel sore at a rub from a jester who tells you, without any subterfuge, that he sits in Diogenes' tub.

[EMERSON]

"There comes Emerson first, whose rich words, every one,
Are like gold nails in temples to hang trophies on,
Whose prose is grand verse, while his verse, the Lord knows,
Is some of it pr——No, 'tis not even prose;
I'm speaking of metres; some poems have welled
From those rare depths of soul that have ne'er been excelled;
They're not epics, but that doesn't matter a pin,
In creating, the only hard thing's to begin;
A grass-blade's no easier to make than an oak;
If you've once found the way, you've achieved the grand stroke;
In the worst of his poems are mines of rich matter,
But thrown in a heap with a crash and a clatter;
Now it is not one thing nor another alone
Makes a poem, but rather the general tone,
The something pervading, uniting the whole,
The before unconceived, unconceivable soul,
So that just in removing this trifle or that, you
Take away, as it were, a chief limb of the statue;
Roots, wood, bark, and leaves singly perfect may be,
But, clapt hodge-podge together, they don't make a tree.

"But, to come back to Emerson (whom, by the way,
I believe we left waiting),—his is, we may say,
A Greek head on right Yankee shoulders, whose range
Has Olympus for one pole, for t' other the Exchange;[7]
He seems, to my thinking (although I'm afraid
The comparison must, long ere this, have been made),
A Plotinus-Montaigne,[8] where the Egyptian's gold mist
And the Gascon's shrewd wit cheek-by-jowl coexist;
All admire, and yet scarcely six converts he's got
To I don't (nor they either) exactly know what;
For though he builds glorious temples, 't is odd
He leaves never a doorway to get in a god.
'T is refreshing to old-fashioned people like me
To meet such a primitive Pagan as he,
In whose mind all creation is duly respected
As parts of himself—just a little projected;
And who's willing to worship the stars and the sun,

[6]French: witticism.
[7]Olympus: the home of the gods in Greek myth; Exchange: the commercial stock exchange.
[8]Plotinus (205?–270?), a Greek idealistic philosopher born in Egypt. Montaigne (1533–1592), the skeptical essayist from Gascony, in France.

A convert to—nothing but Emerson.
So perfect a balance there is in his head,
That he talks of things sometimes as if they were dead;
Life, nature, love, God, and affairs of that sort,
He looks at as merely ideas; in short,
As if they were fossils stuck round in a cabinet,[9]
Of such vast extent that our earth's a mere dab in it;
Composed just as he is inclined to conjecture her,
Namely, one part pure earth, ninety-nine parts pure lecturer;
You are filled with delight at his clear demonstration,
Each figure, word, gesture, just fits the occasion,
With the quiet precision of science he'll sort 'em,
But you can't help suspecting the whole a *post mortem.*

. . .

"He has imitators in scores, who omit
No part of the man but his wisdom and wit,—
Who go carefully o'er the sky-blue of his brain,
And when he has skimmed it once, skim it again;
If at all they resemble him, you may be sure it is
Because their shoals mirror his mists and obscurities,
As a mud-puddle seems deep as heaven for a minute,
While a cloud that floats o'er is reflected within it.

. . .

[BRYANT]
"There is Bryant, as quiet, as cool, and as dignified,
As a smooth, silent iceberg, that never is ignified,
Save when by reflection 't is kindled o' nights
With a semblance of flame by the chill Northern Lights.
He may rank (Griswold[10] says so) first bard of your nation
(There's no doubt that he stands in supreme ice-olation),
Your topmost Parnassus[11] he may set his heel on,
But no warm applauses come, peal following peal on,—
He's too smooth and too polished to hang any zeal on;
Unqualified merits, I'll grant, if you choose, he has 'em,
But he lacks the one merit of kindling enthusiasm;
If he stir you at all, it is just, on my soul,
Like being stirred up with the very North Pole.

"He is very nice reading in summer, but *inter*
Nos,[12] we don't want *extra* freezing in winter;
Take him up in the depth of July, my advice is,
When you feel an Egyptian devotion to ices."[13]
But, deduct all you can, there's enough that's right good in him,
He has a true soul for field, river, and wood in him:

[9]Display case. [10]Rufus Griswold (1815–1857), American author and critic.
[11]Greek mountain sacred to the Muses. [12]Latin: between us.
[13]A pun on "Isis," the name of the Egyptian fertility goddess.

And his heart, in the midst of brick walls, or where'er it is,
Glows, softens, and thrills with the tenderest charities—
To you mortals that delve in this trade-ridden planet?
No, to old Berkshire's hills, with their limestone and granite.
If you're one who *in loco* (add *foco* here) *desipis*,[14]
You will get of his outermost heart (as I guess) a piece;
But you'd get deeper down if you came as a precipice,
And would break the last seal of its inwardest fountain,
If you only could palm yourself off for a mountain.
Mr. Quivis,[15] or somebody quite as discerning,
Some scholar who's hourly expecting his learning,
Calls B. the American Wordsworth; but Wordsworth
May be rated at more than your whole tuneful herd's worth.
No, don't be absurd, he's an excellent Bryant;
But, my friends, you'll endanger the life of your client,
By attempting to stretch him up into a giant:
If you choose to compare him, I think there are two per-
sons fit for a parallel—Thomson and Cowper;[16]
I don't mean exactly,—there's something of each,
There's T.'s love of nature, C.'s penchant to preach;
Just mix up their minds so that C.'s spice of craziness
Shall balance and neutralize T.'s turn for laziness,
And it gives you a brain cool, quite frictionless, quiet,
Whose internal police nips the buds of all riot,—
A brain like a permanent strait-jacket put on
The heart that strives vainly to burst off a button,—
A brain which, without being slow or mechanic,
Does more than a larger less drilled, more volcanic;
He's a Cowper condensed, with no craziness bitten,
And the advantage that Wordsworth before him had written.

"But, my dear little bardlings, don't prick up your ears
Nor suppose I would rank you and Bryant as peers;
If I call him an iceberg, I don't mean to say
There is nothing in that which is grand in its way;
He is almost the one of your poets that knows
How much grace, strength, and dignity lie in Repose;
If he sometimes fall short, he is too wise to mar
His thought's modest fulness by going too far;
'T would be well if your authors should all make a trial
Of what virtue there is in severe self-denial,

[14]A tortured pun on "*In loco desipis*" (Latin for "acts foolishly at times") and the Locofocos, a group of Democratic liberals in mid-nineteenth-century America.

[15]Latin: Mr. Whoever-he-is.

[16]"To demonstrate quickly and easily how per-
versely absurd 't is to sound his name *Cowper*,
As people in general call him, named *super*,
I remark that he rhymes it himself with horse-trooper."

——Lowell's note. James Thomson (1700–1748), English nature poet, author of *The Castle of Indolence* (1748); William Cowper (1731–1800), English nature poet who was periodically insane.

And measure their writings by Hesiod's staff,[17]
Which teaches that all has less value than half.

. . .

[Hawthorne]

"There is Hawthorne, with genius so shrinking and rare
That you hardly at first see the strength that is there;
A frame so robust, with a nature so sweet,
So earnest, so graceful, so lithe and so fleet,
Is worth a descent from Olympus to meet;
'T is as if a rough oak that for ages had stood,
With his gnarled bony branches like ribs of the wood,
Should bloom, after cycles of struggle and scathe,[18]
With a single anemone trembly and rathe;[19]
His strength is so tender, his wildness so meek,
That a suitable parallel sets one to seek,—
He's a John Bunyan Fouqué, a Puritan Tieck;[20]
When Nature was shaping him, clay was not granted
For making so full-sized a man as she wanted,
So, to fill out her model, a little she spared
From some finer-grained stuff for a woman prepared
And she could not have hit a more excellent plan
For making him fully and perfectly man.

. . .

[Cooper]

"Here's Cooper, who's written six volumes to show
He's as good as a lord: well, let's grant that he's so;
If a person prefer that description of praise,
Why, a coronet's[21] certainly cheaper than bays;[22]
But he need take no pains to convince us he's not
(As his enemies say) the American Scott.[23]
Choose any twelve men, and let C. read aloud
That one of his novels of which he's most proud,
And I'd lay any bet that, without ever quitting
Their box,[24] they'd be all, to a man, for acquitting.
He has drawn you one character, though, that is new,
One wildflower he's plucked that is wet with the dew
Of this fresh Western world, and, the thing not to mince,
He has done naught but copy it ill ever since;

[17]The staff, or poetic line, of Hesiod (eighth-century B.C. Greek poet) refers to line 40 of his *Works and Days:* "the half is better than the whole." I.e., moderation is better than excess.

[18]Misfortune. [19]Early in season.

[20]Lowell suggests that Hawthorne is both a Puritan and a romantic, that he is a combination of John Bunyan (1628–1688), Puritan author of *Pilgrim's Progress* (1678); Baron Fouqué (1777–1843), German romanticist; and a Puritanized Johann Ludwig Tieck (1773–1853), German romanticist.

[21]Small crown worn by nobles below the rank of king or queen.

[22]A garland or crown, usually laurel, given as a prize for excellence.

[23]Sir Walter Scott (1771–1832), British romantic Novelist. [24]Jury box.

His Indians, with proper respect be it said,
Are just Natty Bumppo,[25] daubed over with red,
And his very Long Toms[26] are the same useful Nat,
Rigged up in duck pants and a sou'wester hat
(Though once in a Coffin, a good chance was found
To have slipped the old fellow away underground).
All his other men-figures are clothes upon sticks,
The *derniére chemise*[27] of a man in a fix
(As a captain besieged, when his garrison's small,
Sets up caps upon poles to be seen o'er the wall);
And the women he draws from one model don't vary,
All sappy as maples and flat as a prairie.
When a character's wanted, he goes to the task
As a cooper would do in composing a cask;
He picks out the staves, of their qualities heedful,
Just hoops them together as tight as is needful,
And, if the best fortune should crown the attempt, he
Has made at the most something wooden and empty.

"Don't suppose I would underrate Cooper's abilities;
If I thought you'd do that, I should feel very ill at ease;
The men who have given to *one* character life
And objective existence are not very rife;
You may number them all, both prose-writers and singers,
Without overrunning the bounds of your fingers,
And Natty won't go to oblivion quicker
Than Adams the parson or Primrose the vicar.[28]

"There is one thing in Cooper I like, too, and that is
That on manners he lectures his countrymen gratis;
Not precisely so either, because, for a rarity,
He is paid for his tickets in unpopularity.
Now he may overcharge his American pictures,
But you'll grant there's a good deal of truth in his strictures;
And I honor the man who is willing to sink
Half his present repute for the freedom to think,
And, when he has thought, be his cause strong or weak,
Will risk t' other half for the freedom to speak,
Caring naught for what vengeance the mob has in store,
Let that mob be the upper ten thousand or lower.

. . .

[POE]
"There comes Poe, with his raven, like Barnaby Rudge,[29]
Three fifths of him genius and two fifths sheer fudge,

[25]The hero of Cooper's "Leather-Stocking Tales."
[26]Long Tom Coffin, a sailor in Cooper's novel *The Pilot* (1823). [27]French: last shirt.
[28]Parson Adams in Henry Fielding's *Joseph Andrews* (1742); Dr. Primrose in Oliver Goldsmith's *The Vicar of Wakefield* (1766).
[29]Title character of Charles Dickens's novel *Barnaby Rudge* (1841). He owned a raven.

Who talks like a book of iambs and pentameters,
In a way to make people of common sense damn metres,
Who has written some things quite the best of their kind,
But the heart somehow seems all squeezed out by the mind,
Who—But hey-day! What's this? Messieurs Mathews[30] and Poe,
You mustn't fling mud-balls at Longfellow so,
Does it make a man worse that his character's such
As to make his friends love him (as you think) too much?
Why, there is not a bard at this moment alive
More willing than he that his fellows should thrive;
While you are abusing him thus, even now
He would help either one of you out of a slough;
You may say that he's smooth and all that till you're hoarse,
But remember that elegance also is force;
After polishing granite as much as you will,
The heart keeps its tough old persistency still;
Deduct all you can, *that* still keeps you at bay;
Why, he'll live till men weary of Collins and Gray.[31]
I'm not over-fond of Greek metres in English,[32]
To me rhyme's a gain, so it be not too jinglish,
And your modern hexameter verses are no more
Like Greek ones than sleek Mr. Pope is like Homer;[33]
As the roar of the sea to the coo of a pigeon is,
So, compared to your moderns, sounds of old Melesigenes;[34]
I may be too partial, the reason, perhaps, o't is
That I've heard the old blind man[35] recite his own rhapsodies,
And my ear with that music impregnate may be,
Like the poor exiled shell with the soul of the sea,
Or as one can't bear Strauss[36] when his nature is cloven
To its deeps within deeps by the stroke of Beethoven;[37]
But, set aside, and 't is truth that I speak,
Had Theocritus[38] written in English, not Greek,
I believe that his exquisite sense would scarce change a line
In that rare, tender, virgin-like pastoral Evangeline.
That's not ancient nor modern, its place is apart
Where time has no sway, in the realm of pure Art,
'T is a shrine of retreat from Earth's hubbub and strife
As quiet and chaste as the author's own life.

. . .

[30]Cornelius Mathews (1817–1889), American critic who joined Poe in attacks on Longfellow's poetry.

[31]William Collins (1721–1759), English poet; Thomas Gray (1716–1771), English author of the famous "Elegy Written in a Country Churchyard" (1751).

[32]For his "Evangeline" Longfellow used the hexameters of Greek epic poetry.

[33]Alexander Pope (1688–1744) used eighteenth-century English heroic couplets for his translation of Homer.

[34]Homer. [35]Homer, who reputedly was blind.

[36]Johann Strauss (1804–1849), Viennese composer of waltzes.

[37]Ludwig van Beethoven (1770–1827), German composer of symphonies.

[38]Greek pastoral poet (third century B.C.).

[IRVING]

"What! Irving? thrice welcome, warm heart and fine brain,
You bring back the happiest spirit from Spain,[39]
And the gravest sweet humor, that ever were there
Since Cervantes[40] met death in his gentle despair;
Nay, don't be embarrassed, nor look so beseeching,
I sha'n't run directly against my own preaching,
And, having just laughed at their Raphaels and Dantes,
Go to setting you up beside matchless Cervantes;
But allow me to speak what I honestly feel,—
To a true poet-heart add the fun of Dick Steele,[41]
Throw in all of Addison,[42] *minus* the chill,
With the whole of that partnership's stock and good-will,
Mix well, and while stirring, hum o'er, as a spell,
The fine *old* English Gentleman,[43] simmer it well,
Sweeten just to your own private liking, then strain,
That only the finest and clearest remain,
Let it stand out of doors till a soul it receives
From the warm lazy sun loitering down through green leaves,
And you'll find a choice nature, not wholly deserving
A name either English or Yankee,—just Irving.

. . .

[LOWELL]

"There is Lowell, who's striving Parnassus to climb
With a whole bale of *isms* tied together with rhyme,
He might get on alone, spite of brambles and boulders,
But he can't with that bundle he has on his shoulders,
The top of the hill he will ne'er come nigh reaching
Till he learns the distinction 'twixt singing and preaching;
His lyre has some chords that would ring pretty well,
But he'd rather by half make a drum of the shell,
And rattle away till he's old as Methusalem,[44]
At the head of a march to the last new Jerusalem.

. . .

1848

[39]Washington Irving had written a history of Granada (1829) and *The Legends of the Alhambra* (1832).

[40]Miguel de Cervantes Saavedra (1547–1616), author of *Don Quixote* (1605, 1615).

[41]Richard Steele (1672–1729), English essayist.

[42]Joseph Addison (1672–1719), English essayist and collaborator with Steele on the eighteenth-century periodical *The Spectator*.

[43]"The English Country Gentleman" was an essay in Irving's *Bracebridge Hall* (1822).

[44]Methuselah is reported to have lived 969 years. Genesis 5:27.

Harriet Beecher Stowe 1811–1896

In 1862, when President Lincoln first met Harriet Beecher Stowe, he reportedly called her "the little lady who wrote the book that made this big war!" Lincoln expressed the view of many who have come to see her novel Uncle Tom's Cabin *(1852) as the greatest of all antislavery manifestoes, one that helped stir the North to embark on a military crusade against the slaveholding South.*

She also wrote a second antislavery novel, Dred; a Tale of the Great Dismal Swamp, *published in 1856, and intended as a complement to* Uncle Tom's Cabin. *In* Dred *she focused attention on the effects of slavery on the slave owners, and* Dred *is generally considered the better written of the two novels. Yet it was never as popular as* Uncle Tom's Cabin, *which was an immediate success; in its first year of publication more than 300,000 copies were sold, a phenomenal number for that time.*

Harriet Beecher Stowe was a shrewd businesswoman, far more successful in negotiating profitably with publishers than were Cooper, Melville, and Irving. In 1870 she made the then-daring proposal to her publisher that salesmen be sent into the South with an illustrated edition of Uncle Tom's Cabin. *"Books," she wrote her publisher, "to do anything here in these southern states must be sold by agents. . . . Yet there is money on hand even down to the colored families, and an attractive book would have a history."*

Harriet Beecher Stowe had been raised in New England, in a household dominated by her father, Lyman Beecher, one of America's most celebrated clergymen and the principal spokesman for Calvinism in nineteenth-century America. He was a passionate battler against infidels and backsliders, and his daughter, like her most famous brother, Henry Ward Beecher, was an evangelist for moralism and reform.

Her childhood was filled with spiritual exercises designed to fill her with the "iron of Calvinism" and to assist her to the blessings of religious conversion, a divine exultation she experienced twice. Educated in a female seminary, she read widely in Calvinist theology and New England history. When she was twenty-one she moved to Cincinnati, Ohio, where her father had become president of a theological seminary. Four years later she married one of the seminary professors, Calvin Stowe, and in 1850 she returned to New England when her husband was appointed to the faculty of Bowdoin College in Brunswick, Maine. It was there, while seated at the communion table in the Brunswick Congregational Church, that she received the inspiration for her most famous book, Uncle Tom's Cabin, *which she then wrote out at her kitchen table, under the divine direction (she later reported) of God.*

Harriet Beecher Stowe's literary models were the Bible and the works of Cooper, Scott, Dickens, and Defoe. She had also been influenced by her wide reading of antislavery literature, by stories of slavery she had heard from black freedmen and white travelers in the South, by her years in southern Ohio, where she saw the operation of the Underground Railroad, and by her visits to Kentucky plantations across the river from Cincinnati.

Uncle Tom's Cabin *has been called the "*Iliad *of the blacks," the "cornerstone of American protest fiction." The book's pathos, sensationalism, and timeliness made it enormously popular. Millions of copies were sold and it was translated throughout the world. It even inspired a literary genre: Anti-Uncle Tom novels written by opponents of abolition. It was abridged in religious tracts, versified, set to music, and dramatized by numerous barnstorming theatrical companies—called "Tom Shows"—whose melodramatic productions still appear in America.*

The historical significance of Uncle Tom's Cabin *has caused it to obscure its author's other literary achievements. Her earliest works were journalistic essays and sketches of New England scenes and characters such as those that appeared in her first book,* The Mayflower *(1843). After the enormous success of* Uncle Tom's Cabin *she eventually returned to writing New England local-color tales, among them* The Minister's Wooing *(1859),* The Pearl of Orr's Island *(1862), and* Oldtown Folks *(1869), a series of sketches loosely connected in novel form, which she called her masterpiece—"my resume of the whole spirit and body of New England."*

Harriet Beecher Stowe's collected works eventually totaled sixteen volumes. Like many literary ladies of the nineteenth century, she had turned to writing primarily to earn money; yet she succeeded in shaping the history and the social standards of her age. Just as her antislavery writing helped bring on the Civil War, the abundant morality of her fiction helped end nineteenth-century prejudices against novel reading and theatergoing—all seemingly in divine confirmation of her husband's pious observation, made when she first set out on her career: "God has written it in His book that you must be a literary woman, and who are we that we should contend against God?"

FURTHER READING: *The Writings of Harriet Beecher Stowe,* 16 vols., 1896; F. Wilson, *Crusader in Crinoline,* 1941; C. Foster, *The Rungless Ladder, Harriet Beecher Stowe and New England Puritanism,* 1954; J. Furnas, *Goodbye to Uncle Tom,* 1956; J. Adams, *Harriet Beecher Stowe,* 1963, 1989; J. Johnson, *Runaway to Heaven, The Story of Harriet Beecher Stowe,* 1963; E. Wagenknecht, *Harriet Beecher Stowe, The Known and the Unknown,* 1965; J. Hedrick, *Harriet Beecher Stowe, A Life,* 1994, 1995; A. Crozier, *The Novels of Harriet Beecher Stowe,* 1969; J. Fritz, *Harriet Beecher Stowe and the Beecher Preachers,* 1994, 1998; J. Hedrick, *Harriet Beecher Stowe, A Life,* 1994; J. Jordan-Lake, *White-Washing Uncle Tom's Cabin,* 2005.

TEXT: *Uncle Tom's Cabin,* 1852. Some corrections have been made in spelling and punctuation.

from *UNCLE TOM'S CABIN;*

OR,

LIFE AMONG THE LOWLY

CHAPTER I

IN WHICH THE READER IS INTRODUCED TO A MAN OF HUMANITY

Late in the afternoon of a chilly day in February, two gentlemen were sitting alone over their wine, in a well-furnished dining parlor, in the town of P——, in Kentucky. There were no servants present, and the gentlemen, with chairs closely approaching, seemed to be discussing some subject with great earnestness.

For convenience sake, we have said, hitherto, two *gentlemen*. One of the parties, however, when critically examined, did not seem, strictly speaking, to come under the species. He was a short, thick-set man, with coarse, commonplace features and that swaggering air of pretension which marks a low man who is trying to elbow his way upward in the world. He was much overdressed, in a gaudy vest of many colors, a blue neckerchief, bedropped gayly with yellow spots and arranged with a flaunting tie, quite in keeping with the general air of the man. His hands, large and coarse, were plentifully bedecked with rings; and he wore a heavy gold watch-chain, with a bundle of seals of portentous size, and a great variety of colors, attached to it,—which, in the ardor of conversation, he was in the habit of flourishing and jingling with evident satisfaction. His conversation was in free and easy defiance of Murray's Grammar,[1] and was garnished at convenient intervals with various profane expressions, which not even the desire to be graphic in our account shall induce us to transcribe.

His companion, Mr. Shelby, had the appearance of a gentleman; and the arrangements of the house, and the general air of the housekeeping, indicated easy, and even opulent circumstances. As we before stated, the two were in the midst of an earnest conversation.

"That is the way I should arrange the matter," said Mr. Shelby.

"I can't make trade that way—I positively can't, Mr. Shelby," said the other, holding up a glass of wine between his eye and the light.

"Why, the fact is, Haley, Tom is an uncommon fellow; he is certainly worth that sum anywhere,—steady, honest, capable, manages my whole farm like a clock."

"You mean honest, as niggers[2] go," said Haley, helping himself to a glass of brandy.

"No; I mean, really, Tom is a good, steady, sensible, pious fellow. He got religion at a camp-meeting,[3] four years ago; and I believe he really *did* get it. I 've trusted him, since then, with everything I have,—money, house, horses,—and let him come and go round the country; and I always found him true and square in everything."

"Some folks don't believe there is pious niggers, Shelby," said Haley, with a candid flourish of his hand, "but *I do*. I had a fellow, now, in this yer last lot I took to Orleans—'t was as good as a meetin',[4] now, really, to hear that critter pray; and he was quite gentle and quiet like. He fetched me a good sum, too, for I bought him cheap of a man that was 'bliged to sell out; so I realized six hundred on him. Yes, I consider religion a valeyable thing in a nigger, when it 's the genuine article, and no mistake."

"Well, Tom's got the real article, if ever a fellow had," rejoined the other. "Why, last fall, I let him go to Cincinnati alone, to do business for me, and bring home five hundred dollars. 'Tom,' says I to him, 'I trust you, because I think you 're a Christian—I know you would n't cheat.' Tom comes back,

[1]*English Grammar* (1795) by the American grammarian Lindley Murray (1745–1826).

[2]I.e., slaves. Now considered abusive, in pre–Civil-War America the word "nigger" (a variant pronunciation of "Negro") was found in the standard and respectable speech of whites and blacks alike.

[3]Evangelistic religious gatherings, held outdoors, to which those attending often traveled from afar and camped nearby.

[4]Religious service.

sure enough; I knew he would. Some low fellows, they say, said to him—'Tom, why don't you make tracks for Canada?' 'Ah, master trusted me, and I could n't,'—they told me about it. I am sorry to part with Tom, I must say. You ought to let him cover the whole balance of the debt; and you would, Haley, if you had any conscience."

"Well, I 've got just as much conscience as any man in business can afford to keep,—just a little, you know, to swear by, as 't were," said the trader, jocularly; "and, then, I 'm ready to do anything in reason to 'blige friends; but this yer, you see, is a leetle too hard on a fellow—a leetle too hard." The trader sighed contemplatively, and poured out some more brandy.

"Well, then, Haley, how will you trade?" said Mr. Shelby, after an uneasy interval of silence.

"Well, have n't you a boy or gal that you could throw in with Tom?"

"Hum!—none that I could well spare; to tell the truth, it 's only hard necessity makes me willing to sell at all. I don't like parting with any of my hands, that's a fact."

Here the door opened, and a small quadroon[5] boy, between four and five years of age, entered the room. There was something in his appearance remarkably beautiful and engaging. His black hair, fine as floss silk, hung in glossy curls about his round, dimpled face, while a pair of large dark eyes, full of fire and softness, looked out from beneath the rich, long lashes, as he peered curiously into the apartment. A gay robe of scarlet and yellow plaid, carefully made and neatly fitted, set off to advantage the dark and rich style of his beauty; and a certain comic air of assurance, blended with bashfulness, showed that he had been not unused to being petted and noticed by his master.

"Hulloa, Jim Crow!"[6] said Mr. Shelby, whistling, and snapping a bunch of raisins towards him, "pick that up, now!"

The child scampered, with all his little strength, after the prize, while his master laughed.

"Come here, Jim Crow," said he. The child came up, and the master patted the curly head, and chucked him under the chin.

"Now, Jim, show this gentleman how you can dance and sing." The boy commenced one of those wild, grotesque songs common among the negroes, in a rich, clear voice, accompanying his singing with many comic evolutions of the hands, feet, and whole body, all in perfect time to the music.

"Bravo!" said Haley, throwing him a quarter of an orange.

"Now, Jim, walk like old Uncle Cudjoe,[7] when he has the rheumatism," said his master.

Instantly the flexible limbs of the child assumed the appearance of deformity and distortion, as, with his back humped up, and his master's stick in his hand, he hobbled about the room, his childish face drawn into a doleful pucker, and spitting from right to left, in imitation of an old man.

Both gentlemen laughed uproariously.

[5]With one-fourth black ancestry.

[6]Name commonly used for blacks. It originated in the early nineteenth century and was popularized in a popular minstrel song of the 1830s. Use of the term "Jim Crow" to refer to segregation laws and customs began in the 1850s.

[7]An African "day-name," meaning Monday, given to black male slaves to show their day of birth.

"Now, Jim," said his master, "show us how old Elder Robbins leads the psalm." The boy drew his chubby face down to a formidable length, and commenced toning a psalm tune through his nose, with imperturbable gravity.

"Hurrah! bravo! what a young 'un!" said Haley; "that chap 's a case, I 'll promise. Tell you what," said he, suddenly clapping his hand on Mr. Shelby's shoulder, "fling in that chap, and I 'll settle the business—I will. Come, now, if that ain't doing the thing up about the rightest!"

At this moment, the door was pushed gently open, and a young quadroon woman, apparently about twenty-five, entered the room.

There needed only a glance from the child to her, to identify her as its mother. There was the same rich, full, dark eye, with its long lashes; the same ripples of silky black hair. The brown of her complexion gave way on the cheek to a perceptible flush, which deepened as she saw the gaze of the strange man fixed upon her in bold and undisguised admiration. Her dress was of the neatest possible fit, and set off to advantage her finely moulded shape;—a delicately formed hand and a trim foot and ankle were items of appearance that did not escape the quick eye of the trader, well used to run up at a glance the points of a fine female article.

"Well, Eliza?" said her master, as she stopped and looked hesitatingly at him.

"I was looking for Harry, please, sir;" and the boy bounded toward her, showing his spoils, which he had gathered in the skirt of his robe.

"Well, take him away, then," said Mr. Shelby; and hastily she withdrew, carrying the child on her arm.

"By Jupiter," said the trader, turning to him in admiration, "there 's an article, now! You might make your fortune on that ar gal in Orleans, any day. I 've seen over a thousand, in my day, paid down for gals not a bit handsomer."

"I don't want to make my fortune on her," said Mr. Shelby, dryly; and, seeking to turn the conversation, he uncorked a bottle of fresh wine, and asked his companion's opinion of it.

"Capital, sir—first chop!" said the trader; then turning, and slapping his hand familiarly on Shelby's shoulder, he added—

"Come, how will you trade about the gal?—what shall I say for her—what 'll you take?"

"Mr. Haley, she is not to be sold," said Shelby. "My wife would not part with her for her weight in gold."

"Ay, ay! women always say such things, cause they ha'nt no sort of calculation. Just show 'em how many watches, feathers, and trinkets, one's weight in gold would buy, and that alters the case, *I* reckon."

"I tell you, Haley, this must not be spoken of; I say no, and I mean no," said Shelby, decidedly.

"Well, you 'll let me have the boy, though," said the trader; "you must own I 've come down pretty handsomely for him."

"What on earth can you want with the child?" said Shelby.

"Why, I 've got a friend that 's going into this yer branch of the business—wants to buy up handsome boys to raise for the market. Fancy articles entirely—sell for waiters, and so on, to rich 'uns, that can pay for handsome 'uns. It sets off one of yer great places—a real handsome boy to open door, wait, and tend. They fetch a good sum; and this little devil is such a comical, musical concern, he's just the article."

"I would rather not sell him," said Mr. Shelby, thoughtfully; "the fact is, sir, I 'm a humane man, and I hate to take the boy from his mother, sir."

"O, you do?—La! yes—something of that ar natur. I understand, perfectly. It is mighty onpleasant getting on with women, sometimes. I al'ays hates these yer screachin', screamin' times. They are *mighty* onpleasant; but, as I manages business, I generally avoids 'em, sir. Now, what if you get the girl off for a day, or a week, or so; then the thing 's done quietly,—all over before she comes home. Your wife might get her some ear-rings, or a new gown, or some such truck, to make up with her."

"I 'm afraid not."

"Lor bless ye, yes! These critters an't like white folks, you know; they gets over things, only manage right. Now, they say," said Haley, assuming a candid and confidential air, "that this kind o' trade[8] is hardening to the feelings; but I never found it so. Fact is, I never could do things up the way some fellers manage the business. I 've seen 'em as would pull a woman's child out of her arms, and set him up to sell, and she screechin' like mad all the time;—very bad policy—damages the article—makes 'em quite unfit for service sometimes. I knew a real handsome gal once, in Orleans, as was entirely ruined by this sort o' handling. The fellow that was trading for her did n't want her baby; and she was one of your real high sort, when her blood was up. I tell you, she squeezed up her child in her arms, and talked, and went on real awful. It kinder makes my blood run cold to think on 't; and when they carried off the child, and locked her up, she jest went ravin' mad and died in a week. Clear waste, sir, of a thousand dollars, just for want of management,—there 's where 't is. It 's always best to do the humane thing, sir; that 's been *my* experience." And the trader leaned back in his chair, and folded his arm, with an air of virtuous decision, apparently considering himself a second Wilberforce.[9]

The subject appeared to interest the gentleman deeply; for while Mr. Shelby was thoughtfully peeling an orange, Haley broke out afresh, with becoming diffidence, but as if actually driven by the force of truth to say a few words more.

"It don 't look well, now, for a feller to be praisin' himself; but I say it jest because it 's the truth. I believe I 'm reckoned to bring in about the finest droves of niggers that is brought in,—at least, I 've been told so; if I have once, I reckon I have a hundred times,—all in good case,—fat and likely, and I lose as few as any man in the business. And I lays it all to my management, sir; and humanity, sir, I may say, is the great pillar of *my* management."

Mr. Shelby did not know what to say, and so he said, "Indeed!"

"Now, I 've been laughed at for my notions, sir, and I 've been talked to. They an't pop'lar, and they an't common; but I stuck to 'em, sir; I 've stuck to 'em, and realized well on 'em; yes, sir, they have paid their passage, I may say," and the trader laughed at his joke.

There was something so piquant and original in these elucidations of humanity, that Mr. Shelby could not help laughing in company. Perhaps you

[8]Buying and selling slaves.
[9]William Wilberforce (1759–1833), British statesman and philanthropist.

laugh too, dear reader; but you know humanity comes out in a variety of strange forms now-a-days, and there is no end to the odd things that humane people will say and do.

Mr. Shelby's laugh encouraged the trader to proceed.

"It 's strange now, but I never could beat this into people's heads. Now, there was Tom Loker, my old partner, down in Natchez;[10] he was a clever fellow, Tom was, only the very devil with niggers,—on principle 't was, you see, for a better hearted feller never broke bread; 't was his *system,* sir. I used to talk to Tom. 'Why, Tom,' I used to say, 'when your gals takes on and cry, what's the use o' crackin on 'em over the head, and knockin' on 'em round? It 's ridiculous,' says I, 'and don't do no sort o' good. Why, I don't see no harm in their cryin',' says I; 'it 's natur,' says I, 'and if natur can't blow off one way, it will another. Besides, Tom,' says I, 'it jest spiles your gals; they get sickly, and down in the mouth; and sometimes they gets ugly,—particular yallow[11] gals do,—and it 's the devil and all gettin' on 'em broke in. Now,' says I, 'why can't you kinder coax 'em up, and speak 'em fair? Depend on it, Tom, a little humanity, thrown in along, goes a heap further than all your jawin' and crackin'; and it pays better,' says I, 'depend on 't.' But Tom could n't get the hang on 't; and he spiled so many for me, that I had to break off with him, though he was a good-hearted fellow, and as fair a business hand as is goin'."

"And do you find your ways of managing do the business better than Tom's?" said Mr. Shelby.

"Why, yes, sir, I may say so. You see, when I any ways can, I takes a leetle care about the onpleasant parts like selling young uns and that,—get the gals out of the way—out of sight, out of mind, you know,—and when it 's clean done, and can't be helped, they naturally gets used to it. 'T an't, you know, as if it was white folks, that 's brought up in the way of 'spectin' to keep their children and wives, and all that. Niggers, you know, that 's fetched up properly, ha 'n't no kind of 'spectations of no kind; so all these things comes easier."

"I 'm afraid mine are not properly brought up, then," said Mr. Shelby.

"S'pose not; you Kentucky folks spile your niggers. You mean well by 'em, but 't an't no real kindness, arter all. Now, a nigger, you see, what 's got to be hacked and tumbled round the world, and sold to Tom, and Dick, and the Lord knows who, 't an't no kindness to be givin' on him notions and expectations, and bringin' on him up too well, for the rough and tumble comes all the harder on him arter. Now, I venture to say, your niggers would be quite chop-fallen[12] in a place where some of your plantation niggers would be singing and whooping like all possessed. Every man, you know, Mr. Shelby, naturally thinks well of his own ways; and I think I treat niggers just about as well as it 's ever worth while to treat 'em."

"It 's a happy thing to be satisfied," said Mr. Shelby, with a slight shrug, and some perceptible feelings of a disagreeable nature.

"Well," said Haley, after they had both silently picked their nuts[13] for a season, "what do you say?"

[10]Natchez, Mississippi. [11]Yellow, light-skinned; of mixed black and white ancestry.
[12]Jaw-fallen, dejected, gloomy. [13]Mused, pondered.

"I 'll think the matter over, and talk with my wife," said Mr. Shelby. "Meantime, Haley, if you want the matter carried on in the quiet way you speak of, you 'd best not let your business in this neighborhood be known. It will get out among my boys, and it will not be a particularly quiet business getting away any of my fellows, if they know it, I 'll promise you."

"O! certainly, by all means, mum! of course. But I 'll tell you, I 'm in a devil of a hurry, and shall want to know, as soon as possible, what I may depend on," said he, rising and putting on his overcoat.

"Well, call up this evening, between six and seven, and you shall have my answer," said Mr. Shelby, and the trader bowed himself out of the apartment.

"I 'd like to have been able to kick the fellow down the steps," said he to himself, as he saw the door fairly closed, "with his impudent assurance; but he knows how much he has me at advantage. If anybody had ever said to me that I should sell Tom down South[14] to one of those rascally traders, I should have said, 'Is thy servant a dog, that he should do this thing?'[15] And now it must come, for aught I see. And Eliza's child, too! I know that I shall have some fuss with wife about that; and, for that matter, about Tom, too. So much for being in debt,—heigho! The fellow sees his advantage, and means to push it."

. . .

CHAPTER IV

AN EVENING IN UNCLE TOM'S CABIN

The cabin of Uncle Tom was a small log building, close adjoining to "the house," as the negro *par excellence* designates his master's dwelling. In front it had a neat garden-patch, where, every summer, strawberries, raspberries, and a variety of fruits and vegetables, flourished under careful tending. The whole front of it was covered by a large scarlet bignonia and a native multiflora rose, which, entwisting and interlacing, left scarce a vestige of the rough logs to be seen. Here, also, in summer, various brilliant annuals, such as marigolds, petunias, four-o'clocks, found an indulgent corner in which to unfold their splendors, and were the delight and pride of Aunt Chloe's heart.

Let us enter the dwelling. The evening meal at the house is over, and Aunt Chloe, who presided over its preparation as head cook, has left to inferior officers in the kitchen the business of clearing away and washing dishes, and come out into her own snug territories, to "get her ole man's supper;" therefore, doubt not that it is her you see by the fire, presiding with anxious interest over certain frizzling items in a stew-pan, and anon with grave consideration lifting the cover of a bake-kettle, from whence steam forth indubitable intimations of "something good." A round, black, shining face is hers, so glossy as to suggest the idea that she might have been washed over with white

[14]I.e., send Tom to labor on one of the large plantations in the deep South.
[15]II Kings 8:13.

of eggs, like one of her own tea rusks.[1] Her whole plump countenance beams with satisfaction and contentment from under her well-starched checked turban, bearing on it, however, if we must confess it, a little of that tinge of self-consciousness which becomes the first cook of the neighborhood, as Aunt Chloe was universally held and acknowledged to be.

A cook she certainly was, in the very bone and centre of her soul. Not a chicken or turkey or duck in the barn-yard but looked grave when they saw her approaching, and seemed evidently to be reflecting on their latter end; and certain it was that she was always meditating on trussing, stuffing and roasting, to a degree that was calculated to inspire terror in any reflecting fowl living. Her corn-cake, in all its varieties of hoe-cake, dodgers, muffins, and other species too numerous to mention, was a sublime mystery to all less practised compounders; and she would shake her fat sides with honest pride and merriment, as she would narrate the fruitless efforts that one and another of her compeers had made to attain to her elevation.

The arrival of company at the house, the arranging of dinners and suppers "in style," awoke all the energies of her soul; and no sight was more welcome to her than a pile of travelling trunks launched on the verandah, for then she foresaw fresh efforts and fresh triumphs.

Just at present, however, Aunt Chloe is looking into the bake-pan; in which congenial operation we shall leave her till we finish our picture of the cottage.

In one corner of it stood a bed, covered neatly with a snowy spread; and by the side of it was a piece of carpeting, of some considerable size. On this piece of carpeting Aunt Chloe took her stand, as being decidedly in the upper walks of life; and it and the bed by which it lay, and the whole corner, in fact, were treated with distinguished consideration, and made, so far as possible, sacred from the marauding inroads and desecrations of little folks. In fact, that corner was the *drawing-room* of the establishment. In the other corner was a bed of much humbler pretensions, and evidently designed for *use.* The wall over the fireplace was adorned with some very brilliant scriptural prints, and a portrait of General Washington, drawn and colored in a manner which would certainly have astonished that hero, if ever he had happened to meet with its like.

On a rough bench in the corner, a couple of woolly-headed boys, with glistening black eyes and fat shining cheeks, were busy in superintending the first walking operations of the baby, which, as is usually the case, consisted in getting up on its feet, balancing a moment, and then tumbling down,—each successive failure being violently cheered, as something decidedly clever.

A table, somewhat rheumatic in its limbs, was drawn out in front of the fire, and covered with a cloth, displaying cups and saucers of a decidedly brilliant pattern, with other symptoms of an approaching meal. At this table was seated Uncle Tom, Mr. Shelby's best hand, who, as he is to be the hero of our story, we must daguerreotype[2] for our readers. He was a large, broad-chested, powerfully-made man, of a full glossy black, and a face whose truly African features were characterized by an expression of grave and steady good sense,

[1]Hard baked bread, often made sweet to serve as a dessert. When baked with a light covering of egg white, it has a glossy surface.

[2]I.e., portray realistically, photographically.

united with much kindliness and benevolence. There was something about his whole air self-respecting and dignified, yet united with a confiding and humble simplicity.

He was very busily intent at this moment on a slate lying before him, on which he was carefully and slowly endeavoring to accomplish a copy of some letters, in which operation he was overlooked by young Mas'r George, a smart, bright boy of thirteen, who appeared fully to realize the dignity of his position as instructor.

"Not that way, Uncle Tom,—not that way," said he, briskly, as Uncle Tom laboriously brought up the tail of his *g* the wrong side out; "that makes a *q*, you see."

"La sakes, now, does it?" said Uncle Tom, looking with a respectful, admiring air, as his young teacher flourishingly scrawled *q*'s and *g*'s innumerable for his edification; and then, taking the pencil in his big, heavy fingers, he patiently re-commenced.

"How easy white folks al'us does things!" said Aunt Chloe, pausing while she was greasing a griddle with a scrap of bacon on her fork, and regarding young Master George with pride. "The way he can write, now! and read, too! and then to come out here evenings and read his lessons to us,—it 's mighty interestin'!"

"But, Aunt Chloe, I 'm getting mighty hungry," said George. "Is n't that cake in the skillet almost done?"

"Mose done, Mas'r George," said Aunt Chloe, lifting the lid and peeping in,—"browning beautiful—a real lovely brown. Ah! let me alone for dat. Missis let Sally try to make some cake, t' other day, jes to *larn* her, she said. 'O, go way, Missis,' says I; 'it really hurts my feelin's, now, to see good vittles spiled dat ar way! Cake ris all to one side—no shape at all; no more than my shoe;—go way!"

And with this final expression of contempt for Sally's greenness, Aunt Chloe whipped the cover off the bake-kettle, and disclosed to view a neatly-baked pound-cake, of which no city confectioner need to have been ashamed. This being evidently the central point of the entertainment, Aunt Chloe began now to bustle about earnestly in the supper department.

"Here you, Mose and Pete! get out de way, you niggers! Get away, Polly, honey,—mammy 'll give her baby somefin, by and by. Now, Mas'r George, you jest take off dem books, and set down now with my old man, and I 'll take up de sausages, and have de first griddle full of cakes on your plates in less dan no time."

"They wanted me to come to supper in the house," said George; "but I knew what was what too well for that, Aunt Chloe."

"So you did—so you did, honey," said Aunt Chloe, heaping the smoking batter-cakes on his plate; "you know'd your old aunty 'd keep the best for you. O, let you alone for dat! Go way!" And, with that, aunty gave George a nudge with her finger, designed to be immensely facetious, and turned again to her griddle with great briskness.

"Now for the cake," said Mas'r George, when the activity of the griddle department had somewhat subsided; and, with that, the youngster flourished a large knife over the article in question.

"La bless you, Mas'r George!" said Aunt Chloe, with earnestness, catching his arm, "you would n't be for cuttin' it wid dat ar great heavy knife! Smash all down—spile all de pretty rise of it. Here, I 've got a thin old knife, I keeps sharp a purpose. Dar now, see! comes apart light as a feather! Now eat away—you won't get anything to beat dat ar."

"Tom Lincon says," said George, speaking with his mouth full, "that their Jinny is a better cook than you."

"Dem Lincons an't much count, no way!" said Aunt Chloe, contemptuously; "I mean, set along side *our* folks. They 's 'spectable folks enough in a kinder plain way; but, as to gettin' up anything in style, they don't begin to have a notion on 't. Set Mas'r Lincon, now, alongside Mas'r Shelby! Good Lor! and Missis Lincon,—can she kinder sweep it into a room like my missis,—so kinder splendid, yer know! O, go way! don't tell me nothin' of dem Lincons!"—and Aunt Chloe tossed her head as one who hoped she did know something of the world.

"Well, though, I 've heard you say," said George, "that Jinny was a pretty fair cook."

"So I did," said Aunt Chloe,—"I may say dat. Good, plain, common cookin', Jinny 'll do;—make a good pone o' bread,—bile her taters *far,*—her corn cakes is n't extra, not extra now, Jinny's corn cakes is n't, but then they's far,—but, Lor, come to de higher branches, and what *can* she do? Why, she makes pies—sartin she does; but what kinder crust? Can she make your real flecky paste, as melts in your mouth, and lies all up like a puff? Now, I went over thar when Miss Mary was gwine to be married, and Jinny she jest showed me de weddin' pies. Jinny and I is good friends, ye know. I never said nothin'; but go long, Mas'r George! Why, I should n't sleep a wink for a week, if I had a batch of pies like dem ar. Why, dey wan't no 'count 't all."

"I suppose Jinny thought they were ever so nice," said George.

"Thought so!—did n't she? Thar she was, showing 'em, as innocent—ye see, it 's jest here, Jinny *don't know.* Lor, the family an't nothing! She can't be spected to know! 'Ta'nt no fault o' hern. Ah, Mas'r George, you does n't know half your privileges in yer family and bringin' up!" Here Aunt Chloe sighed, and rolled up her eyes with emotion.

"I'm sure, Aunt Chloe, I understand all my pie and pudding privileges," said George. "Ask Tom Lincon if I don't crow over him, every time I meet him."

Aunt Chloe sat back in her chair, and indulged in a hearty guffaw of laughter, at this witticism of young Mas'r's, laughing till the tears rolled down her black, shining cheeks, and varying the exercise with playfully slapping and poking Mas'r Georgey, and telling him to go way, and that he was a case—that he was fit to kill her, and that he sartin would kill her, one of these days; and, between each of these sanguinary predictions, going off into a laugh, each longer and stronger than the other, till George really began to think that he was a very dangerously witty fellow, and that it became him to be careful how he talked "as funny as he could."

"And so ye telled Tom, did ye? O, Lor! what young uns will be up ter! Ye crowed over Tom? O, Lor! Mas'r George, if ye would n't make a hornbug laugh!"

"Yes," said George, "I says to him, 'Tom, you ought to see some of Aunt Chloe's pies; they 're the right sort,' says I."

"Pity, now, Tom could n't," said Aunt Chloe, on whose benevolent heart the idea of Tom's benighted condition seemed to make a strong impression.

"Ye oughter just ask him here to dinner, some o' these times, Mas'r George," she added; "it would look quite pretty of ye. Ye know, Mas'r George, ye oughtenter feel 'bove nobody, on 'count yer privileges, 'cause all our privileges is gi'n to us; we ought al'ays to 'member that," said Aunt Chloe, looking quite serious.

"Well, I mean to ask Tom here, some day next week," said George; "and you do your prettiest, Aunt Chloe, and we 'll make him stare. Won't we make him eat so he won't get over it for a fortnight?"

"Yes, yes—sartin," said Aunt Chloe, delighted; "you 'll see. Lor! to think of some of our dinners! Yer mind dat ar great chicken pie I made when we guv de dinner to General Knox? I and Missis, we come pretty near quarrelling about dat ar crust. What does get into ladies sometimes, I don't know; but, sometimes, when a body has de heaviest kind o' 'sponsibility on 'em, as ye may say, and is all kinder *'seris'* and taken up, dey takes dat ar time to be hangin' round and kinder interferin'! Now, Missis, she wanted me to do dis way, and she wanted me to do dat way; and, finally, I got kinder sarcy, and, says I, 'Now, Missis, do jist look at dem beautiful white hands o' yourn, with long fingers, and all a sparkling with rings, like my white lilies when de dew 's on 'em; and look at my great black stumpin hands. Now, don't ye think dat de Lord must have meant *me* to make de pie-crust, and you to stay in de parlor?' Dar! I was jist so sarcy, Mas'r George."

"And what did mother say?" said George.

"Say?—why, she kinder larfed in her eyes—dem great handsome eyes o' hern; and, says she, 'Well, Aunt Chloe, I think you are about in the right on 't,' says she; and she went off in de parlor. She oughter cracked me over de head for bein' so sarcy; but dar 's whar 't is—I can't do nothin' with ladies in de kitchen!"

"Well, you made out well with that dinner.—I remember everybody said so," said George.

"Did n't I? And wan't I behind de dinin'-room door dat bery day? and did n't I see de General pass his plate three times for some more dat bery pie?—and, says he, 'You must have an uncommon cook, Mrs. Shelby.' Lor! I was fit to split myself.

"And de Gineral, he knows what cookin' is," said Aunt Chloe, drawing herself up with an air. "Bery nice man, de Gineral! He comes of one of de bery *fustest* families in Old Virginny! He knows what 's what, now, as well as I do—de Gineral. Ye see, there's *pints* in all pies, Mas'r George; but tan't everybody knows what they is, or orter be. But the Gineral, he knows; I knew by his 'marks he made. Yes, he knows what de pints is!"

By this time, Master George had arrived at that pass to which even a boy can come (under uncommon circumstances,) when he really could not eat another morsel and, therefore, he was at leisure to notice the pile of woolly heads and glistening eyes which were regarding their operations hungrily from the opposite corner.

"Here, you Mose, Pete," he said, breaking off liberal bits, and throwing it at them; "you want some, don't you? Come, Aunt Chloe, bake them some cakes."

And George and Tom moved to a comfortable seat in the chimney-corner, while Aunt Chloe, after baking a goodly pile of cakes, took her baby on her lap, and began alternately filling its mouth and her own, and distributing to

Mose and Pete, who seemed rather to prefer eating theirs as they rolled about on the floor under the table, tickling each other, and occasionally pulling the baby's toes.

"O! go long, will ye?" said the mother, giving now and then a kick, in a kind of general way, under the table, when the movement became too obstreperous. "Can't ye be decent when white folks comes to see ye? Stop dat ar, now, will ye? Better mind yerselves, or I 'll take ye down a button-hole lower, when Mas'r George is gone!"

What meaning was couched under this terrible threat, it is difficult to say; but certain it is that its awful indistinctness seemed to produce very little impression on the young sinners addressed.

"La, now!" said Uncle Tom, "they are so full of tickle all the while, they can't behave theirselves."

Here the boys emerged from under the table, and, with hands and faces well plastered with molasses, began a vigorous kissing of the baby.

"Get along wid ye!" said the mother, pushing away their woolly heads. "Ye 'll all stick together, and never get clar, if ye do dat fashion. Go long to de spring and wash yerselves!" she said, seconding her exhortations by a slap, which resounded very formidably, but which seemed only to knock out so much more laugh from the young ones, as they tumbled precipitately over each other out of doors, where they fairly screamed with merriment.

"Did ye ever see such aggravating young uns?" said Aunt Chloe, rather complacently, as, producing an old towel, kept for such emergencies, she poured a little water out of the cracked tea-pot on it, and began rubbing off the molasses from the baby's face and hands; and, having polished her till she shone, she set her down in Tom's lap, while she busied herself in clearing away supper. The baby employed the intervals in pulling Tom's nose, scratching his face, and burying her fat hands in his woolly hair, which last operation seemed to afford her special content.

"Aint she a peart young un?" said Tom, holding her from him to take a full-length view; then, getting up, he set her on his broad shoulder, and began capering and dancing with her, while Mas'r George snapped at her with his pocket-handkerchief, and Mose and Pete, now returned again, roared after her like bears, till Aunt Chloe declared that they "fairly took her head off" with their noise. As, according to her own statement, this surgical operation was a matter of daily occurrence in the cabin, the declaration no whit abated the merriment, till every one had roared and tumbled and danced themselves down to a state of composure.

"Well, now, I hopes you 're done," said Aunt Chloe, who had been busy in pulling out a rude box of a trundle-bed;[3] "and now, you Mose and you Pete, get into thar; for we 's goin' to have the meetin'."

"O mother, we don't wanter. We wants to sit up to meetin',—meetin's is so curis. We likes 'em."

"La, Aunt Chloe, shove it under, and let 'em sit up," said Mas'r George, decisively, giving a push to the rude machine.

Aunt Chloe, having thus saved appearances, seemed highly delighted to push the thing under, saying, as she did so, "Well, mebbe 't will do 'em some good."

[3]A space-saving, low bed that can be rolled (trundled) under another bed when not in use.

The house now resolved itself into a committee of the whole, to consider the accommodations and arrangements for the meeting.

"What we 's to do for cheers, now, *I* declar I don't know," said Aunt Chloe. As the meeting had been held at Uncle Tom's, weekly, for an indefinite length of time, without any more "cheers," there seemed some encouragement to hope that a way would be discovered at present.

"Old Uncle Peter sung both de legs out of dat oldest cheer, last week," suggested Mose.

"You go long! I 'll boun' you pulled 'em out; some o' your shines," said Aunt Chloe.

"Well, it 'll stand, if it only keeps jam up agin de wall!" said Mose.

"Den Uncle Peter mus'n't sit in it, cause he al'ays hitches when he gets a singing. He hitched pretty nigh across de room, t' other night," said Pete.

"Good Lor! get him in it, then," said Mose, "and den he 'd begin, 'Come saints and sinners, hear me tell,' and den down he 'd go,"—and Mose imitated precisely the nasal tones of the old man, tumbling on the floor, to illustrate the supposed catastrophe.

"Come now, be decent, can't ye?" said Aunt Chloe; "an't yer shamed?"

Mas'r George, however, joined the offender in the laugh, and declared decidedly that Mose was a "buster." So the maternal admonition seemed rather to fail of effect.

"Well, ole man," said Aunt Chloe, "you 'll have to tote in them ar bar'ls."

"Mother's bar'ls is like dat ar widder's,[4] Mas'r George was reading 'bout, in de good book,—dey never fails," said Mose, aside to Pete.

"I 'm sure one on 'em caved in last week," said Pete, "and let 'em all down in de middle of de singin'; dat ar was failin', warnt it?"

During this aside between Mose and Pete, two empty casks had been rolled into the cabin, and being secured from rolling, by stones on each side, boards were laid across them, which arrangement, together with the turning down of certain tubs and pails, and the disposing of the rickety chairs, at last completed the preparation.

"Mas'r George is such a beautiful reader, now, I know he 'll stay to read for us," said Aunt Chloe; "'pears like 't will be so much more interestin'."

George very readily consented, for your boy is always ready for anything that makes him of importance.

The room was soon filled with a motley assemblage, from the old gray-headed patriarch of eighty, to the young girl and lad of fifteen. A little harmless gossip ensued on various themes, such as where old Aunt Sally got her new red head-kerchief, and how "Missis was a going to give Lizzy that spotted muslin gown, when she 'd got her new berage[5] made up;" and how Mas'r Shelby was thinking of buying a new sorrel colt that was going to prove an addition to the glories of the place. A few of the worshippers belonged to families hard by,[6] who had got permission to attend, and who brought in various choice scraps of information, about the sayings and doings at the house and on the place, which circulated as freely as the same sort of small change does in higher circles.

After a while the singing commenced, to the evident delight of all present. Not even all the disadvantage of nasal intonation could prevent the effect of

[4]The story of a poor widow's meal barrel, filled by the Lord, is told in I Kings 17:12–16.
[5]Clothing. [6]I.e., families living nearby.

the naturally fine voices, in airs at once wild and spirited. The words were sometimes the well-known and common hymns sung in the churches about, and sometimes of a wilder, more indefinite character, picked up at camp-meetings.

The chorus of one of them, which ran as follows, was sung with great energy and unction:

"Die on the field of battle,
Die on the field of battle,
Glory in my soul."

Another special favorite had oft repeated the words—

"O, I 'm going to glory,—won't you come along with me?
Don't you see the angels beck'ning, and a calling me away?
Don't you see the golden city and the everlasting day?"

There were others, which made incessant mention of "Jordan's banks," and "Canaan's fields," and the "New Jerusalem;" for the negro mind, impassioned and imaginative, always attaches itself to hymns and expressions of a vivid and pictorial nature; and, as they sung, some laughed, and some cried, and some clapped hands, or shook hands rejoicingly with each other, as if they had fairly gained the other side of the river.

Various exhortations, or relations of experience, followed, and intermingled with the singing. One old gray-headed woman, long past work, but much revered as a sort of chronicle of the past, rose, and leaning on her staff, said—

"Well, chil'en! Well, I 'm mighty glad to hear ye all and see ye all once more, 'cause I don't know when I 'll be gone to glory; but I 've done got ready, chil'en; 'pears like I 'd got my little bundle all tied up, and my bonnet on, jest a waitin' for the stage to come along and take me home; sometimes, in the night, I think I hear the wheels a rattlin', and I 'm lookin' out all the time; now, you jest be ready too, for I tell ye all, chil'en," she said, striking her staff hard on the floor, "dat ar *glory* is a mighty thing! It 's a mighty thing, chil'en,—you don'no nothing about it,—it 's *wonderful*." And the old creature sat down, with streaming tears, as wholly overcome, while the whole circle struck up—

"O Canaan, bright Canaan,
I 'm bound for the land of Canaan."

Mas'r George, by request, read the last chapters of Revelation, often interrupted by such exclamations as "The *sakes* now!" "Only hear that!" "Jest think on 't!" "Is all that a comin' sure enough?"

George, who was a bright boy, and well trained in religious things by his mother, finding himself an object of general admiration, threw in expositions of his own, from time to time, with a commendable seriousness and gravity, for which he was admired by the young and blessed by the old; and it was agreed, on all hands, that "a minister could n't lay it off better than he did;" that " 't was reely 'mazin'!"

Uncle Tom was a sort of patriarch in religious matters, in the neighborhood. Having, naturally, an organization in which the *morale* was strongly predominant, together with a greater breadth and cultivation of mind than obtained among his companions, he was looked up to with great respect, as a sort of minister among them; and the simple, hearty, sincere style of his exhortations might have edified even better educated persons. But it was in prayer that he especially excelled. Nothing could exceed the touching simplicity, the child-like earnestness, of his prayer, enriched with the language of Scripture, which seemed so entirely to have wrought itself into his being, as to have become a part of himself, and to drop from his lips unconsciously; in the language of a pious old negro, he "prayed right up." And so much did his prayer always work on the devotional feelings of his audiences, that there seemed often a danger that it would be lost altogether in the abundance of the responses which broke out everywhere around him.

While this scene was passing in the cabin of the man, one quite otherwise passed in the halls of the master.

The trader and Mr. Shelby were seated together in the dining room aforenamed, at a table covered with papers and writing utensils.

Mr. Shelby was busy in counting some bundles of bills, which, as they were counted, he pushed over to the trader, who counted them likewise.

"All fair," said the trader; "and now for signing these yer."

Mr. Shelby hastily drew the bills of sale towards him, and signed them, like a man that hurries over some disagreeable business, and then pushed them over with the money. Haley produced, from a well-worn valise, a parchment, which, after looking over it a moment, he handed to Mr. Shelby, who took it with a gesture of suppressed eagerness.

"Wal, now, the thing 's *done!*" said the trader, getting up.

"It 's *done!*" said Mr. Shelby, in a musing tone; and, fetching a long breath, he repeated, *"It 's done!"*

"Yer don't seem to feel much pleased with it, 'pears to me," said the trader.

"Haley," said Mr. Shelby, "I hope you 'll remember that you promised, on your honor, you would n't sell Tom, without knowing what sort of hands he 's going into."

"Why, you 've just done it, sir," said the trader.

"Circumstances, you well know, *obliged* me," said Shelby, haughtily.

"Wal, you know, they may 'blige *me*, too," said the trader. "Howsomever, I 'll do the very best I can in gettin' Tom a good berth; as to my treatin' on him bad, you need n't be a grain afeard. If there 's anything that I thank the Lord for, it is that I 'm never noways cruel."

After the expositions which the trader had previously given of his humane principles, Mr. Shelby did not feel particularly reässured by these declarations; but, as they were the best comfort the case admitted of, he allowed the trader to depart in silence, and betook himself to a solitary cigar.

CHAPTER V

SHOWING THE FEELINGS OF LIVING PROPERTY ON CHANGING OWNERS

Mr. and Mrs. Shelby had retired to their apartment for the night. He was lounging in a large easy-chair, looking over some letters that had come in the afternoon mail, and she was standing before her mirror, brushing out the complicated braids and curls in which Eliza had arranged her hair; for, noticing her pale cheeks and haggard eyes, she had excused her attendance that night, and ordered her to bed. The employment, naturally enough, suggested her conversation with the girl in the morning; and, turning to her husband, she said, carelessly,

"By the by, Arthur, who was that low-bred fellow that you lugged in to our dinner-table to-day?"

"Haley is his name," said Shelby, turning himself rather uneasily in his chair, and continuing with his eyes fixed on a letter.

"Haley! Who is he, and what may be his business here, pray?"

"Well, he 's a man that I transacted some business with, last time I was at Natchez," said Mr. Shelby.

"And he presumed on it to make himself quite at home, and call and dine here, ay?"

"Why, I invited him; I had some accounts with him," said Shelby.

"Is he a negro-trader?" said Mrs. Shelby, noticing a certain embarrassment in her husband's manner.

"Why, my dear, what put that into your head?" said Shelby, looking up.

"Nothing,—only Eliza came in here, after dinner, in a great worry, crying and taking on, and said you were talking with a trader, and that she heard him make an offer for her boy—the ridiculous little goose!"

"She did, hey?" said Mr. Shelby, returning to his paper, which he seemed for a few moments quite intent upon, not perceiving that he was holding it bottom upwards.

"It will have to come out," said he, mentally; "as well now as ever."

"I told Eliza," said Mrs. Shelby, as she continued brushing her hair, "that she was a little fool for her pains, and that you never had anything to do with that sort of persons. Of course, I knew you never meant to sell any of our people,—least of all, to such a fellow."

"Well, Emily," said her husband, "so I have always felt and said; but the fact is that my business lies so that I cannot get on without. I shall have to sell some of my hands."

"To that creature? Impossible! Mr. Shelby, you cannot be serious."

"I 'm sorry to say that I am," said Mr. Shelby. "I 've agreed to sell Tom."

"What! our Tom?—that good, faithful creature!—been your faithful servant from a boy! O, Mr. Shelby!—and you have promised him his freedom, too,—you and I have spoken to him a hundred times of it. Well, I can believe anything now,—I can believe *now* that you could sell little Harry, poor Eliza's only child!" said Mrs. Shelby, in a tone between grief and indignation.

"Well, since you must know all, it is so. I have agreed to sell Tom and Harry both; and I don't know why I am to be rated,[1] as if I were a monster, for doing what every one does every day."

"But why, of all others, choose these?" said Mrs. Shelby. "Why sell them, of all on the place, if you must sell at all?"

"Because they will bring the highest sum of any,—that 's why. I could choose another, if you say so. The fellow made me a high bid on Eliza, if that would suit you any better," said Mr. Shelby.

"The wretch!" said Mrs. Shelby, vehemently.

"Well, I did n't listen to it, a moment,—out of regard to your feelings, I would n't;—so give me some credit."

"My dear," said Mrs. Shelby, recollecting herself, "forgive me. I have been hasty. I was surprised, and entirely unprepared for this;—but surely you will allow me to intercede for these poor creatures. Tom is a noble-hearted, faithful fellow, if he is black. I do believe, Mr. Shelby, that if he were put to it, he would lay down his life for you."

"I know it,—I dare say;—but what 's the use of all this?—I can't help myself."

"Why not make a pecuniary sacrifice? I 'm willing to bear my part of the inconvenience. O, Mr. Shelby, I have tried—tried most faithfully, as a Christian woman should—to do my duty to these poor, simple, dependent creatures. I have cared for them, instructed them, watched over them, and known all their little cares and joys, for years; and how can I ever hold up my head again among them, if, for the sake of a little paltry gain, we sell such a faithful, excellent, confiding creature as poor Tom, and tear from him in a moment all we have taught him to love and value? I have taught them the duties of the family, of parent and child, and husband and wife; and how can I bear to have this open acknowledgment that we care for no tie, no duty, no relation, however sacred, compared with money? I have talked with Eliza about her boy—her duty to him as a Christian mother, to watch over him, pray for him, and bring him up in a Christian way; and now what can I say, if you tear him away, and sell him, soul and body, to a profane, unprincipled man, just to save a little money? I have told her that one soul is worth more than all the money in the world; and how will she believe me when she sees us turn round and sell her child?—sell him, perhaps, to certain ruin of body and soul!"

"I 'm sorry you feel so about it, Emily,—indeed I am," said Mr. Shelby; "and I respect your feelings, too, though I don't pretend to share them to their full extent; but I tell you now, solemnly, it 's of no use—I can't help myself. I did n't mean to tell you this, Emily; but, in plain words, there is no choice between selling these two and selling everything. Either they must go, or *all* must. Haley has come into possession of a mortgage, which, if I don't clear off with him directly, will take everything before it. I 've raked, and scraped, and borrowed, and all but begged,—and the price of these two was needed to make up the balance, and I had to give them up. Haley fancied the child; he agreed to settle the matter that way, and no other. I was in his

[1]Rebuked.

power, and *had* to do it. If you feel so to have them sold, would it be any better to have *all* sold?"

Mrs. Shelby stood like one stricken. Finally, turning to her toilet,[2] she rested her face in her hands, and gave a sort of groan.

"This is God's curse on slavery!—a bitter, bitter, most accursed thing!—a curse to the master and a curse to the slave! I was a fool to think I could make anything good out of such a deadly evil. It is a sin to hold a slave under laws like ours,—I always felt it was,—I always thought so when I was a girl,—I thought so still more after I joined the church; but I thought I could gild it over,—I thought, by kindness, and care, and instruction, I could make the condition of mine better than freedom—fool that I was!"

"Why, wife, you are getting to be an abolitionist,[3] quite."

"Abolitionist! if they knew all I know about slavery, they *might* talk! We don't need them to tell us; you know I never thought that slavery was right—never felt willing to own slaves."

"Well, therein you differ from many wise and pious men," said Mr. Shelby. "You remember Mr. B.'s sermon, the other Sunday?"

"I don't want to hear such sermons; I never wish to hear Mr. B. in our church again. Ministers can't help the evil, perhaps,—can't cure it, any more than we can,—but defend it!—it always went against my common sense. And I think you did n't think much of that sermon, either."

"Well," said Shelby, "I must say these ministers sometimes carry matters further than we poor sinners would exactly dare to do. We men of the world must wink pretty hard at various things, and get used to a deal that is n't the exact thing. But we don't quite fancy, when women and ministers come out broad and square, and go beyond us in matters of either modesty or morals, that 's a fact. But now, my dear, I trust you see the necessity of the thing, and you see that I have done the very best that circumstances would allow."

"O yes, yes!" said Mrs. Shelby, hurriedly and abstractedly fingering her gold watch,—"I have n't any jewelry of any amount," she added, thoughtfully; "but would not this watch do something?—it was an expensive one, when it was bought. If I could only at least save Eliza's child, I would sacrifice anything I have."

"I 'm sorry, very sorry, Emily," said Mr. Shelby, "I 'm sorry this takes hold of you so; but it will do no good. The fact is, Emily, the thing 's done; the bills of sale are already signed, and in Haley's hands; and you must be thankful it is no worse. That man has had it in his power to ruin us all,—and now he is fairly off. If you knew the man as I do, you 'd think that we had had a narrow escape."

"Is he so hard, then?"

"Why, not a cruel man, exactly, but a man of leather,—a man alive to nothing but trade and profit,—cool, and unhesitating, and unrelenting, as death and the grave. He 'd sell his own mother at a good per centage—not wishing the old woman any harm, either."

"And this wretch owns that good, faithful Tom, and Eliza's child!"

"Well, my dear, the fact is that this goes rather hard with me; it 's a thing I hate to think of. Haley wants to drive matters, and take possession to-morrow.

[2]Dressing table. [3]One who favored the abolition of slavery.

I 'm going to get out my horse bright and early, and be off. I can't see Tom, that 's a fact; and you had better arrange a drive somewhere, and carry Eliza off. Let the thing be done when she is out of sight."

"No, no," said Mrs. Shelby; "I 'll be in no sense accomplice or help in this cruel business. I 'll go and see poor old Tom, God help him, in his distress! They shall see, at any rate, that their mistress can feel for and with them. As to Eliza, I dare not think about it. The Lord forgive us! What have we done, that this cruel necessity should come on us?"

There was one listener to this conversation whom Mr. and Mrs. Shelby little suspected.

Communicating with their apartment was a large closet, opening by a door into the outer passage. When Mrs. Shelby had dismissed Eliza for the night, her feverish and excited mind had suggested the idea of this closet; and she had hidden herself there and, with her ear pressed close against the crack of the door, had lost not a word of the conversation.

When the voices died into silence, she rose and crept stealthily away. Pale, shivering, and rigid features and compressed lips, she looked an entirely altered being from the soft and timid creature she had been hitherto. She moved cautiously along the entry, paused one moment at her mistress' door, and raised her hands in mute appeal to Heaven, and then turned and glided into her own room. It was a quiet, neat apartment, on the same floor with her mistress. There was the pleasant sunny window, where she had often sat singing at her sewing; there a little case of books and various little fancy articles, ranged by them, the gifts of Christmas holidays; there was her simple wardrobe in the closet and in the drawers:—here was, in short, her home; and, on the whole, a happy one it had been to her. But there, on the bed, lay her slumbering boy, his long curls falling negligently around his unconscious face, his rosy mouth half open, his little fat hands thrown out over the bedclothes, and a smile spread like a sunbeam over his whole face.

"Poor boy! poor fellow!" said Eliza, "they have sold you! but your mother will save you yet!"

No tear dropped over that pillow; in such straits as these, the heart has no tears to give,—it drops only blood, bleeding itself away in silence. She took a piece of paper and pencil, and wrote, hastily,

"O, Missis! dear Missis! don't think me ungrateful,—don't think hard of me, any way,—I heard all you and master said to-night. I am going to try to save my boy—you will not blame me! God bless and reward you for all your kindness!"

Hastily folding and directing this, she went to a drawer and made up a little package of clothing for her boy, which she tied with a handkerchief firmly round her waist; and, so fond is a mother's remembrance that, even in the terrors of that hour, she did not forget to put in the little package one or two of his favorite toys, reserving a gayly painted parrot to amuse him, when she should be called on to awaken him. It was some trouble to arouse the little sleeper; but, after some effort, he sat up, and was playing with his bird, while his mother was putting on her bonnet and shawl.

"Where are you going, mother?" said he, as she drew near the bed, with his little coat and cap.

His mother drew near and looked so earnestly into his eyes that he at once divined that something unusual was the matter.

"Hush, Harry," she said; "mus n't speak loud, or they will hear us. A wicked man was coming to take little Harry away from his mother and carry him 'way off in the dark; but mother won't let him—she 's going to put on her little boy's cap and coat and run off with him, so the ugly man can't catch him."

Saying these words, she had tied and buttoned on the child's simple outfit, and, taking him in her arms, she whispered to him to be very still; and, opening a door in her room which led into the outer verandah, she glided noiselessly out.

It was a sparkling, frosty, star-light night, and the mother wrapped the shawl close round her child as, perfectly quiet with vague terror, he clung round her neck.

Old Bruno, a great Newfoundland, who slept at the end of the porch, rose, with a low growl as she came near. She gently spoke his name, and the animal, an old pet and playmate of hers, instantly, wagging his tail, prepared to follow her, though apparently revolving much, in his simple dog's head, what such an indiscreet midnight promenade might mean. Some dim ideas of imprudence or impropriety in the measure seemed to embarrass him considerably; for he often stopped, as Eliza glided forward, and looked wistfully, first at her and then at the house, and then, as if reässured by reflection, he pattered along after her again. A few minutes brought them to the window of Uncle Tom's cottage, and Eliza, stopping, tapped lightly on the window-pane.

The prayer-meeting at Uncle Tom's had, in the order of hymn-singing, been protracted to a very late hour; and, as Uncle Tom had indulged himself in a few lengthy solos afterwards, the consequence was that, although it was now between twelve and one o'clock, he and his worthy helpmeet were not yet asleep.

"Good Lord! what's that?" said Aunt Chloe, starting up and hastily drawing the curtain. "My sakes alive, if it an't Lizy! Get on your clothes, old man, quick!—there 's old Bruno, too, a pawin' round; what on airth! I 'm gwine to open the door."

And, suiting the action to the word, the door flew open, and the light of the tallow candle, which Tom had hastily lighted, fell on the haggard face and dark, wild eyes of the fugitive.

"Lord bless you!—I 'm skeered to look at ye, Lizy! Are ye tuck sick, or what 's come over ye?"

"I'm running away—Uncle Tom and Aunt Chloe—carrying off my child—Master sold him!"

"Sold him?" echoed both, lifting up their hands in dismay.

"Yes, sold him!" said Eliza, firmly; "I crept into the closet by Mistress' door to-night, and I heard Master tell Missis that he had sold my Harry, and you, Uncle Tom, both, to a trader; and that he was going off this morning on his horse, and that the man was to take possession to-day."

Tom had stood, during this speech, with his hands raised, and his eyes dilated, like a man in a dream. Slowly and gradually, as its meaning came over him, he collapsed, rather than seated himself, on his old chair, and sunk his head down upon his knees.

"The good Lord have pity on us!" said Aunt Chloe. "O! it don't seem as if it was true! What has he done, that Mas'r should sell *him*?"

"He has n't done anything,—it is n't for that. Master don't want to sell; and Missis—she 's always good. I heard her plead and beg for us; but he told her 't was no use; that he was in this man's debt, and that this man had got the power over him; and that if he did n't pay him off clear, it would end in his having to sell the place and all the people, and move off. Yes, I heard him say there was no choice between selling these two and selling all, the man was driving him so hard. Master said he was sorry; but oh, Missis—you ought to have heard her talk! If she an't a Christian and an angel, there never was one. I 'm a wicked girl to leave her so; but, then, I can't help it. She said, herself, one soul was worth more than the world; and this boy has a soul, and if I let him be carried off, who knows what 'll become of it? It must be right: but, if it an't right, the Lord forgive me, for I can't help doing it!"

"Well, old man!" said Aunt Chloe, "why don't you go, too? Will you wait to be toted down river, where they kill niggers with hard work and starving? I 'd a heap rather die than go there, any day! There 's time for ye,—be off with Lizy,—you've got a pass[4] to come and go any time. Come, bustle up, and I 'll get your things together."

Tom slowly raised his head, and looked sorrowfully but quietly around, and said.

"No, no—I an't going. Let Eliza go—it 's her right! I would n't be the one to say no—'t an't in *natur* for her to stay; but you heard what she said! If I must be sold, or all the people on the place, and everything go to rack, why, let me be sold. I s'pose I can b'ar it as well as any on 'em," he added, while something like a sob and a sigh shook his broad, rough chest convulsively. "Mas'r always found me on the spot—he always will. I never have broke trust nor used my pass no ways contrary to my word, and I never will. It 's better for me alone to go, than to break up the place and sell all. Mas'r an't to blame, Chloe, and he 'll take care of you and the poor—"

Here he turned to the rough trundle-bed full of little woolly heads, and broke fairly down. He leaned over the back of the chair, and covered his face with his large hands. Sobs, heavy, hoarse and loud, shook the chair, and great tears fell through his fingers on the floor: just such tears, sir, as you dropped into the coffin where lay your first-born son; such tears, woman, as you shed when you heard the cries of your dying babe. For, sir, he was a man,—and you are but another man. And, woman, though dressed in silk and jewels, you are but a woman, and, in life's great straits and mighty griefs, ye feel but one sorrow!

"And now," said Eliza, as she stood in the door, "I saw my husband only this afternoon, and I little knew then what was to come. They have pushed him to the very last standing-place, and he told me, to-day, that he was going to run away. Do try, if you can, to get word to him. Tell him how I went, and why I went; and tell him I 'm going to try and find Canada. You must give my love to him, and tell him, if I never see him again,"—she turned away, and stood with her back to them for a moment, and then added, in a husky voice, "tell him to be as good as he can, and try and meet me in the kingdom of heaven."

"Call Bruno in there," she added. "Shut the door on him, poor beast! He must n't go with me!"

A few last words and tears, a few simple adieus and blessings, and, clasping her wondering and affrighted child in her arms, she glided noiselessly away.

[4]Slaves were restricted to their plantations. If found beyond the plantation borders without a pass written by their owner or overseer, slaves were detained and subject to punishment by civil authorities.

CHAPTER VII

THE MOTHER'S STRUGGLE

It is impossible to conceive of a human creature more wholly desolate and forlorn than Eliza, when she turned her footsteps from Uncle Tom's cabin.

Her husband's suffering and dangers, and the danger of her child, all blended in her mind, with a confused and stunning sense of the risk she was running, in leaving the only home she had ever known, and cutting loose from the protection of a friend whom she loved and revered. Then there was the parting from every familiar object,—the place where she had grown up, the trees under which she had played, the groves where she had walked many an evening in happier days, by the side of her young husband,—everything, as it lay in the clear, frosty starlight, seemed to speak reproachfully to her, and ask her whither could she go from a home like that?

But stronger than all was maternal love, wrought into a paroxysm of frenzy by the near approach of a fearful danger. Her boy was old enough to have walked by her side, and, in an indifferent case, she would only have led him by the hand; but now the bare thought of putting him out of her arms made her shudder, and she strained him to her bosom with a convulsive grasp, as she went rapidly forward.

The frosty ground creaked beneath her feet, and she trembled at the sound; every quaking leaf and fluttering shadow sent the blood backward to her heart, and quickened her footsteps. She wondered within herself at the strength that seemed to be come upon her; for she felt the weight of her boy as if it had been a feather, and every flutter of fear seemed to increase the supernatural power that bore her on, while from her pale lips burst forth, in frequent ejaculations, the prayer to a Friend above—"Lord, help! Lord, save me!"

If it were *your* Harry, mother, or your Willie, that were going to be torn from you by a brutal trader, to-morrow morning,—if you had seen the man, and heard that the papers were signed and delivered, and you had only from twelve o'clock till morning to make good your escape,—how fast could *you* walk? How many miles could you make in those few brief hours, with the darling at your bosom,—the little sleepy head on your shoulder,—the small, soft arms trustingly holding on to your neck?

For the child slept. At first, the novelty and alarm kept him waking; but his mother so hurriedly repressed every breath or sound, and so assured him that if he were only still she would certainly save him, that he clung quietly round her neck, only asking, as he found himself sinking to sleep,

"Mother, I don't need to keep awake, do I?"

"No, my darling; sleep, if you want to."

"But, mother, if I do get asleep, you won't let him get me?"

"No! so may God help me!" said his mother, with a paler cheek, and a brighter light in her large dark eyes.

"You 're *sure*, an't you, mother?"

"Yes, *sure*!" said the mother, in a voice that startled herself; for it seemed to her to come from a spirit within, that was no part of her; and the boy dropped his little weary head on her shoulder, and was soon asleep. How the touch of those warm arms, the gentle breathings that came in her neck, seemed to add fire and spirit to her movements! It seemed to her as if strength poured into her in electric streams, from every gentle touch and movement of the sleeping, confiding child. Sublime is the dominion of the mind over the body, that, for a time, can make flesh and nerve impregnable, and string the sinews like steel, so that the weak become so mighty.

The boundaries of the farm, the grove, the wood-lot, passed by her dizzily, as she walked on; and still she went, leaving one familiar object after another, slacking not, pausing not, till reddening daylight found her many a long mile from all traces of any familiar objects upon the open highway.

She had often been, with her mistress, to visit some connections, in the little village of T——, not far from the Ohio river, and knew the road well. To go thither, to escape across the Ohio river, were the first hurried outlines of her plan of escape; beyond that, she could only hope in God.

When horses and vehicles began to move along the highway, with that alert perception peculiar to a state of excitement, and which seems to be a sort of inspiration, she became aware that her headlong pace and distracted air might bring on her remark and suspicion. She therefore put the boy on the ground, and, adjusting her dress and bonnet, she walked on at as rapid a pace as she thought consistent with the preservation of appearances. In her little bundle she had provided a store of cakes and apples, which she used as expedients for quickening the speed of the child, rolling the apple some yards before them, when the boy would run with all his might after it; and this ruse, often repeated, carried them over many a half-mile.

After a while, they came to a thick patch of woodland, through which murmured a clear brook. As the child complained of hunger and thirst, she climbed over the fence with him; and, sitting down behind a large rock which concealed them from the road, she gave him a breakfast out of her little package. The boy wondered and grieved that she could not eat; and when, putting his arms round her neck, he tried to wedge some of his cake into her mouth, it seemed to her that the rising in her throat would choke her.

"No, no, Harry darling! mother can't eat till you are safe! We must go on—on—till we come to the river!" And she hurried again into the road, and again constrained herself to walk regularly and composedly forward.

She was many miles past any neighborhood where she was personally known. If she should chance to meet any who knew her, she reflected that the well-known kindness of the family would be of itself a blind to suspicion, as making it an unlikely supposition that she could be a fugitive. As she was also so white as not to be known as of colored lineage, without a critical survey, and her child was white also, it was much easier for her to pass on unsuspected.

On this presumption, she stopped at noon at a neat farm-house, to rest herself, and buy some dinner for her child and self; for, as the danger decreased with the distance, the supernatural tension of the nervous system lessened, and she found herself both weary and hungry.

The good woman, kindly and gossipping, seemed rather pleased than otherwise with having somebody come in to talk with; and accepted, without examination, Eliza's statement, that she "was going on a little piece, to spend a week with her friends,"—all which she hoped in her heart might prove strictly true.

An hour before sunset, she entered the village of T——, by the Ohio river, weary and foot-sore, but still strong in heart. Her first glance was at the river, which lay, like Jordan,[1] between her and the Canaan of liberty on the other side.

It was now early spring, and the river was swollen and turbulent; great cakes of floating ice were swinging heavily to and fro in the turbid waters. Owing to the peculiar form of the shore on the Kentucky side, the land bending far out into the water, the ice had been lodged and detained in great quantities, and the narrow channel which swept round the bend was full of ice, piled one cake over another, thus forming a temporary barrier to the descending ice, which lodged, and formed a great, undulating raft, filling up the whole river, and extending almost to the Kentucky shore.

Eliza stood, for a moment, contemplating this unfavorable aspect of things, which she saw at once must prevent the usual ferry-boat from running, and then turned into a small public house on the bank, to make a few inquiries.

The hostess, who was busy in various fizzing and stewing operations over the fire, preparatory to the evening meal, stopped, with a fork in her hand, as Eliza's sweet and plaintive voice arrested her.

"What is it?" she said.

"Is n't there any ferry or boat, that takes people over to B——, now?" she said.

"No, indeed!" said the woman; "the boats has stopped running."

Eliza's look of dismay and disappointment struck the woman, and she said, inquiringly,

"May be you 're wanting to get over?—anybody sick? Ye seem mighty anxious?"

"I 've got a child that 's very dangerous,"[2] said Eliza. "I never heard of it till last night, and I 've walked quite a piece to-day, in hopes to get to the ferry."

"Well, now, that 's onlucky," said the woman, whose motherly sympathies were much aroused; "I 'm re'lly consarned for ye. Solomon!" she called, from the window towards a small back building. A man, in leather apron and very dirty hands, appeared at the door.

"I say, Sol," said the woman, "is that ar man going to tote them bar'ls over to-night?"

"He said he should try, if 't was any way prudent," said the man.

"There 's a man a piece down here, that 's going over with some truck[3] this evening, if he durs' to; he 'll be in here to supper to-night, so you 'd better set down and wait. That 's a sweet little fellow," added the woman, offering him a cake.

But the child, wholly exhausted, cried with weariness.

[1]The story of the Israelites crossing the Jordan River, in Palestine, to reach Canaan, the promised land "flowing with milk and honey," is told in Joshua 3 and 4.

[2]I.e., dangerously ill. [3]Goods, commodities.

"Poor fellow! he is n't used to walking, and I 've hurried him on so," said Eliza.

"Well, take him into this room," said the woman, opening into a small bedroom, where stood a comfortable bed. Eliza laid the weary boy upon it, and held his hands in hers till he was fast asleep. For her there was no rest. As a fire in her bones, the thought of the pursuer urged her on; and she gazed with longing eyes on the sullen, surging waters that lay between her and liberty.

Here we must take our leave of her for the present, to follow the course of her pursuers.

Though Mrs. Shelby had promised that the dinner[4] should be hurried on table, yet it was soon seen, as the thing has often been seen before, that it required more than one to make a bargain. So, although the order was fairly given out in Haley's hearing, and carried to Aunt Chloe by at least half a dozen juvenile messengers, that dignitary only gave certain very gruff snorts, and tosses of her head, and went on with every operation in an unusually leisurely and circumstantial manner.

For some singular reason, an impression seemed to reign among the servants generally that Missis would not be particularly disobliged by delay; and it was wonderful what a number of counter accidents occurred constantly, to retard the course of things. One luckless wight[5] contrived to upset the gravy; and then gravy had to be got up *de novo*,[6] with due care and formality, Aunt Chloe watching and stirring with dogged precision, answering shortly, to all suggestions of haste, that she "warn't a going to have raw gravy on the table, to help nobody's catchings."[7] One tumbled down with the water, and had to go to the spring for more; and another precipitated the butter into the path of events; and there was from time to time giggling news brought into the kitchen that "Mas'r Haley was mighty oneasy, and that he could n't sit in his cheer no ways, but was a walkin' and stalkin' to the winders and through the porch."

"Sarves him right!" said Aunt Chloe, indignantly. "He 'll get wus nor oneasy, one of these days, if he don't mend his ways. *His* master 'll be sending for him, and then see how he 'll look!"

"He 'll go to torment, and no mistake," said little Jake.

"He desarves it!" said Aunt Chloe, grimly; "he 's broke a many, many, many hearts,—I tell ye all!" she said, stopping, with a fork uplifted in her hands; "it 's like what Mas'r George reads in Ravelations,—souls a callin' under the altar! and a callin' on the Lord for vengeance on sich!—and by and by the Lord he 'll hear 'em—so he will!"[8]

Aunt Chloe, who was much revered in the kitchen, was listened to with open mouth; and, the dinner being now fairly sent in, the whole kitchen was at leisure to gossip with her, and to listen to her remarks.

[4]The noon meal. [5]Creature. [6]Latin: anew. [7]I.e., the capture of Eliza and Harry.

[8]"I saw under the altar the souls of them that were slain for the word of God, and for the testimony which they held: And they cried with a loud voice, saying, How long, O Lord, holy and true, dost thou not judge and avenge our blood on them that dwell on the earth?" Revelation 6:9–10.

"Sich 'll be burnt up forever, and no mistake; won't ther?" said Andy.

"I 'd be glad to see it, I 'll be boun'," said little Jake.

"Chil'en!" said a voice, that made them all start. It was Uncle Tom, who had come in, and stood listening to the conversation at the door.

"Chil'en!" he said. "I 'm afeard you don't know what ye 're sayin'. Forever is a *dre'ful* word, chil'en; it 's awful to think on 't. You oughtenter wish that ar to any human crittur."

"We would n't to anybody but the soul-drivers,"[9] said Andy; "nobody can help wishing it to them, they 's so awful wicked."

"Don't natur herself kinder cry out on 'em?" said Aunt Chloe. "Don't dey tear der suckin' baby right off his mother's breast, and sell him, and der little children as is crying and holding on by her clothes,—don't dey pull 'em off and sells 'em? Don't dey tear wife and husband apart?" said Aunt Chloe, beginning to cry, "when it 's jest takin' the very life on 'em?—and all the while does they feel one bit,—don't dey drink and smoke, and take it oncommon easy? Lor, if the devil don't get them, what 's he good for?" And Aunt Chloe covered her face with her checked apron, and began to sob in good earnest.

"Pray for them that 'spitefully use you,[10] the good book says," says Tom.

"Pray for 'em!" said Aunt Chloe; "Lor, it 's too tough! I can't pray for 'em."

"It 's natur, Chloe, and natur 's strong," said Tom, "but the Lord's grace is stronger; besides, you oughter think what an awful state a poor crittur's soul 's in that 'll do them ar things,—you oughter thank God that you an't *like* him, Chloe. I 'm sure I 'd rather be sold, ten thousand times over, than to have all that ar poor crittur 's got to answer for."

"So 'd I, a heap," said Jake. "Lor, *should n't* we cotch it, Andy?"

Andy shrugged his shoulders, and gave an acquiescent whistle.

"I 'm glad Mas'r did n't go off this morning, as he looked to," said Tom; "that ar hurt me more than sellin', it did. Mebbe it might have been natural for him, but 't would have come desp't hard on me, as has known him from a baby; but I 've seen Mas'r, and I begin ter feel sort o' reconciled to the Lord's will now. Mas'r could n't help hisself; he did right, but I 'm feared things will be kinder goin' to rack, when I 'm gone. Mas'r can't be spected to be a pryin' round everywhar, as I 've done, a keepin' up all the ends. The boys all means well, but they 's powerful car'less. That ar troubles me."

The bell here rang, and Tom was summoned to the parlor.

"Tom," said his master, kindly, "I want you to notice that I give this gentleman bonds to forfeit a thousand dollars if you are not on the spot when he wants you; he 's going to-day to look after his other business, and you can have the day to yourself. Go anywhere you like, boy."

"Thank you, Mas'r," said Tom.

"And mind yerself," said the trader, "and don't come it over your master with any o' yer nigger tricks; for I 'll take every cent out of him, if you an't thar. If he 'd hear to me, he would n't trust any on ye—slippery as eels!"

"Mas'r," said Tom,—and he stood very straight,—"I was jist eight years old when ole Missis put you into my arms, and you was n't a year old. 'Thar,' says she, 'Tom, that 's to be *your* young Mas'r; take good care on him,' says she.

[9] Slave traders. [10] "Pray for them which despitefully use you." Matthew 5:44.

And now I jist ask you, Mas'r, have I ever broke word to you, or gone contrary to you, 'specially since I was a Christian?"

Mr. Shelby was fairly overcome, and the tears rose to his eyes.

"My good boy," said he, "the Lord knows you say but the truth; and if I was able to help it, all the world should n't buy you."

"And sure as I am a Christian woman," said Mrs. Shelby, "you shall be redeemed as soon as I can any way bring together means. Sir," she said to Haley, "take good account of who you sell him to, and let me know."

"Lor, yes, for that matter," said the trader, "I may bring him up in a year, not much the wuss for wear, and trade him back."

"I 'll trade with you then, and make it for your advantage," said Mrs. Shelby.

"Of course," said the trader, "all 's equal with me; lives trade 'em up as down, so I does a good business. All I want is a livin', you know, ma'am; that 's all any on us wants, I s'pose."

Mr. and Mrs. Shelby both felt annoyed and degraded by the familiar impudence of the trader, and yet both saw the absolute necessity of putting a constraint on their feelings. The more hopelessly sordid and insensible he appeared, the greater became Mrs. Shelby's dread of his succeeding in recapturing Eliza and her child, and of course the greater her motive for detaining him by every female artifice. She therefore graciously smiled, assented, chatted familiarly, and did all she could to make time pass imperceptibly.

At two o'clock Sam and Andy brought the horses up to the posts, apparently greatly refreshed and invigorated by the scamper of the morning.

Sam was there new oiled from dinner, with an abundance of zealous and ready officiousness. As Haley approached, he was boasting, in flourishing style, to Andy, of the evident and eminent success of the operation, now that he had "farly come to it."

"Your master, I s'pose, don't keep no dogs," said Haley, thoughtfully, as he prepared to mount.

"Heaps on 'em," said Sam, triumphantly; "thar's Bruno—he 's a roarer! and, besides that, 'bout every nigger of us keeps a pup of some natur or uther."

"Poh!" said Haley,—and he said something else, too, with regard to the said dogs, at which Sam muttered,

"I don't see no use cussin' on 'em, no way."

"But your master don't keep no dogs (I pretty much know he don't) for trackin' out niggers."

Sam knew exactly what he meant, but he kept on a look of earnest and desperate simplicity.

"Our dogs all smells round considable sharp. I spect they 's the kind, though they han't never had no practice. They 's *far*[11] dogs, though, at most anything, if you 'd get 'em started. Here, Bruno," he called, whistling to the lumbering Newfoundland, who came pitching tumultuously toward them.

"You go hang!" said Haley, getting up. "Come, tumble up[12] now."

Sam tumbled up accordingly, dexterously contriving to tickle Andy as he

[11]Fair, good. [12]Mount up.

did so, which occasioned Andy to split out into a laugh, greatly to Haley's indignation, who made a cut at him with his riding-whip.

"I 's 'stonished at yer, Andy," said Sam, with awful gravity. "This yer 's a seris bisness, Andy. Yer must n't be a makin' game. This yer an't no way to help Mas'r."

"I shall take the straight road to the river," said Haley, decidedly, after they had come to the boundaries of the estate. "I know the way of all of 'em,—they makes tracks for the underground."[13]

"Sartin," said Sam, "dat 's de idee. Mas'r Haley hits de thing right in de middle. Now, der 's two roads to de river,—de dirt road and der pike,[14]—which Mas'r mean to take?"

Andy looked up innocently at Sam, surprised at hearing this new geographical fact, but instantly confirmed what he said, by a vehement reiteration.

"Cause," said Sam. "I 'd rather be 'clined to 'magine that Lizy 'd take de dirt road, bein' it 's the least travelled."

Haley, notwithstanding that he was a very old bird, and naturally inclined to be suspicious of chaff, was rather brought up by this view of the case.

"If yer warn't both on yer such cussed liars, now!" he said, contemplatively, as he pondered a moment.

The pensive, reflective tone in which this was spoken appeared to amuse Andy prodigiously, and he drew a little behind, and shook so as apparently to run a great risk of falling off his horse, while Sam's face was immovably composed into the most doleful gravity.

"Course," said Sam, "Mas'r can do as he 'd ruther; go de straight road, if Mas'r thinks best,—it 's all one to us. Now, when I study 'pon it, I think de straight road de best, *decidedly*."

"She would naturally go a lonesome way," said Haley, thinking aloud, and not minding Sam's remark.

"Dar an't no sayin," said Sam; "gals is pecular; they never does nothin' ye thinks they will; mose gen'lly the contrar. Gals is nat'lly made contrary; and so, if you thinks they 've gone one road, it is sartin you 'd better go t' other, and then you 'll be sure to find 'em. Now, my private 'pinion is, Lizy took der dirt road; so I think we 'd better take de straight one."

This profound generic view of the female sex did not seem to dispose Haley particularly to the straight road; and he announced decidedly that he should go the other, and asked Sam when they should come to it.

"A little piece ahead," said Sam, giving a wink to Andy with the eye which was on Andy's side of the head; and he added, gravely, "but I 've studded on de matter, and I 'm quite clar we ought not to go dat ar way. I nebber been over it no way. It 's despit lonesome, and we might lose our way,—whar we 'd come to, de Lord only knows."

"Nevertheless," said Haley, "I shall go that way."

"Now I think on 't, I think I hearn 'em tell that dat ar road was all fenced up and down by der creek, and thar, an't it, Andy?"

[13]The "Underground Railroad," the name of the system by which Northerners and Southerners opposed to slavery sheltered and guided fugitive slaves in their escape to freedom in northern non-slavery states or Canada.

[14]A highway or toll road.

Andy was n't certain; he 'd only "hearn tell" about that road, but never been over it. In short, he was strictly noncommittal.

Haley, accustomed to strike the balance of probabilities between lies of greater or lesser magnitude, thought that it lay in favor of the dirt road aforesaid. The mention of the thing he thought he perceived was involuntary on Sam's part at first, and his confused attempts to dissuade him he set down to a desperate lying on second thoughts, as being unwilling to implicate Eliza.

When, therefore, Sam indicated the road, Haley plunged briskly into it, followed by Sam and Andy.

Now, the road, in fact, was an old one, that had formerly been a thoroughfare to the river, but abandoned for many years after the laying of the new pike. It was open for about an hour's ride, and after that it was cut across by various farms and fences. Sam knew this fact perfectly well,—indeed, the road had been so long closed up, that Andy had never heard of it. He therefore rode along with an air of dutiful submission, only groaning and vociferating occasionally that 't was "desp't rough, and bad for Jerry's foot."

"Now, I jest give yer warning," said Haley, "I know yer; yer won't get me to turn off this yer road, with all yer fussin'—so you shet up!"

"Mas'r will go his own way!" said Sam, with rueful submission, at the same time winking most portentously to Andy, whose delight was now very near the explosive point.

Sam was in wonderful spirits,—professed to keep a very brisk look-out,—at one time exclaiming that he saw "a gal's bonnet" on the top of some distant eminence, or calling to Andy "if that thar was n't 'Lizy' down in the hollow;" always making these exclamations in some rough or craggy part of the road, where the sudden quickening of speed was a special inconvenience to all parties concerned, and thus keeping Haley in a state of constant commotion.

After riding about an hour in this way, the whole party made a precipitate and tumultuous descent into a barn-yard belonging to a large farming establishment. Not a soul was in sight, all the hands being employed in the fields; but, as the barn stood conspicuously and plainly square across the road, it was evident that their journey in that direction had reached a decided finale.

"Wan't dat ar what I telled Mas'r?" said Sam, with an air of injured innocence. "How does strange gentleman spect to know more about a country dan de natives born and raised?"

"You rascal!" said Haley, "you knew all about this."

"Did n't I tell yer I *know'd,* and yer would n't believe me? I telled Mas'r 't was all shet up, and fenced up, and I did n't spect we could get through,—Andy heard me."

It was all too true to be disputed, and the unlucky man had to pocket his wrath with the best grace he was able, and all three faced to the right about, and took up their line of march for the highway.

In consequence of all the various delays, it was about three-quarters of an hour after Eliza had laid her child to sleep in the village tavern that the party came riding into the same place. Eliza was standing by the window, looking out in another direction, when Sam's quick eye caught a glimpse of her. Haley and Andy were two yards behind. At this crisis, Sam contrived to have his hat blown off, and uttered a loud and characteristic ejaculation, which startled her at once; she drew suddenly back; the whole train swept by the window, round to the front door.

A thousand lives seemed to be concentrated in that one moment to Eliza. Her room opened by a side door to the river. She caught her child, and sprang down the steps towards it. The trader caught a full glimpse of her, just as she was disappearing down the bank; and throwing himself from his horse, and calling loudly on Sam and Andy, he was after her like a hound after a deer. In that dizzy moment her feet to her scarce seemed to touch the ground, and a moment brought her to the water's edge. Right on behind they came; and, nerved with strength such as God gives only to the desperate, with one wild cry and flying leap, she vaulted sheer over the turbid current by the shore, on to the raft of ice beyond. It was a desperate leap—impossible to anything but madness and despair; and Haley, Sam, and Andy, instinctively cried out, and lifted up their hands, as she did it.

The huge green fragment of ice on which she alighted pitched and creaked as her weight came on it, but she staid there not a moment. With wild cries and desperate energy she leaped to another and still another cake;—stumbling—leaping—slipping—springing upwards again! Her shoes are gone—her stockings cut from her feet—while blood marked every step; but she saw nothing, felt nothing, till dimly, as in a dream, she saw the Ohio side, and a man helping her up the bank.

"Yer a brave gal, now, whoever ye ar!" said the man, with an oath.

Eliza recognized the voice and face of a man who owned a farm not far from her old home.

"O, Mr. Symmes!—save me—do save me—do hide me!" said Eliza.

"Why, what 's this?" said the man. "Why, if 'tan't Shelby's gal!"

"My child!—this boy!—he 'd sold him! There is his Mas'r," said she, pointing to the Kentucky shore. "O, Mr. Symmes, you 've got a little boy!"

"So I have," said the man, as he roughly, but kindly, drew her up the steep bank. "Besides, you 're a right brave gal. I like grit, wherever I see it."

When they had gained the top of the bank, the man paused.

"I 'd be glad to do something for ye," said he; "but then there 's nowhar I could take ye. The best I can do is to tell ye to go *thar*," said he, pointing to a large white house which stood by itself, off the main street of the village. "Go thar; they 're kind folks. Thar 's no kind o' danger but they 'll help you,—they 're up to all that sort o' thing."

"The Lord bless you!" said Eliza, earnestly.

"No 'casion, no 'casion in the world," said the man. "What I 've done 's of no 'count."

"And, oh, surely, sir, you won't tell any one!"

"Go to thunder, gal! What do you take a feller for? In course not," said the man. "Come, now, go along like a likely, sensible gal, as you are. You 've arnt your liberty, and you shall have it, for all me."

The woman folded her child to her bosom, and walked firmly and swiftly away. The man stood and looked after her.

"Shelby, now, mebbe won't think this yer the most neighborly thing in the world; but what 's a feller to do? If he catches one of my gals in the same fix, he 's welcome to pay back. Somehow I never could see no kind o' critter a strivin' and pantin', and trying to clar theirselves, with the dogs arter 'em, and go agin 'em. Besides, I don't see no kind of 'casion for me to be hunter and catcher for other folks, neither."

So spoke this poor, heathenish Kentuckian, who had not been instructed in his constitutional relations, and consequently was betrayed into acting in a sort of Christianized manner, which, if he had been better situated and more enlightened, he would not have been left to do.

Haley had stood a perfectly amazed spectator of the scene, till Eliza had disappeared up the bank, when he turned a blank, inquiring look on Sam and Andy.

"That ar was a tolable fair stroke of business," said Sam.

"The gal 's got seven devils in her, I believe!" said Haley. "How like a wildcat she jumped!"

"Wal, now," said Sam, scratching his head, "I hope Mas'r 'll 'scuse us tryin' dat ar road. Don't think I feel spry enough for dat ar, no way!" and Sam gave a hoarse chuckle.

"*You* laugh!" said the trader, with a growl.

"Lord bless you, Mas'r, I could n't help it, now," said Sam, giving way to the long pent-up delight of his soul. "She looked so curi's, a leapin' and springin'—ice a crackin'—and only to hear her,—plump! ker chunk! ker splash! Spring! Lord! how she goes it!" and Sam and Andy laughed till the tears rolled down their cheeks.

"I 'll make ye laugh t' other side yer mouths!" said the trader, laying about their heads with his riding-whip.

Both ducked, and ran shouting up the bank, and were on their horses before he was up.

"Good-evening, Mas'r!" said Sam, with much gravity. "I berry much spect Missis be anxious 'bout Jerry. Mas'r Haley won't want us no longer. Missis would n't hear of our ridin the critters over Lizy's bridge to-night;" and, with a facetious poke into Andy's ribs, he started off, followed by the latter, at full speed,—their shouts of laughter coming faintly on the wind.

CHAPTER XL

THE MARTYR

"Deem not the just by Heaven forgot!
 Though life its common gifts deny,—
Though, with a crushed and bleeding heart,
 And spurned of man, he goes to die!

For God hath marked each sorrowing day,
 And numbered every bitter tear;
And heaven's long years of bliss shall pay
 For all his children suffer here."

BRYANT[1]

[1]William Cullen Bryant (1794–1878). The quotation is an adaptation of the last two stanzas of his hymn "Blessed Are They that Mourn" (1820).

The longest day must have its close,—the gloomiest night will wear on to a morning. An eternal, inexorable lapse of moments is ever hurrying the day of the evil to an eternal night, and the night of the just to an eternal day. We have walked with our humble friend thus far in the valley of slavery; first through flowery fields of ease and indulgence, then through heart-breaking separations from all that man holds dear. Again, we have waited with him in a sunny island, where generous hands concealed his chains with flowers; and, lastly, we have followed him when the last ray of earthly hope went out in night, and seen how, in the blackness of earthly darkness, the firmament of the unseen has blazed with stars of new and significant lustre.

The morning-star now stands over the tops of the mountains, and gales and breezes, not of earth, show that the gates of day are unclosing.

The escape of Cassy and Emmeline irritated the before surly temper of Legree to the last degree; and his fury, as was to be expected, fell upon the defenceless head of Tom. When he hurriedly announced the tidings among his hands, there was a sudden light in Tom's eye, a sudden upraising of his hands, that did not escape him. He saw that he did not join the muster of the pursuers. He thought of forcing him to do it; but, having had, of old, experience of his inflexibility when commanded to take part in any deed of inhumanity, he would not, in his hurry, stop to enter into any conflict with him.

Tom, therefore, remained behind, with a few who had learned of him to pray, and offered up prayers for the escape of the fugitives.

When Legree returned, baffled and disappointed, all the long-working hatred of his soul towards his slave began to gather in a deadly and desperate form. Had not this man braved him,[2]—steadily, powerfully, resistlessly,—ever since he bought him? Was there not a spirit in him which, silent as it was, burned on him like the fires of perdition?

"I *hate* him!" said Legree, that night, as he sat up in his bed; "I *hate* him! And is n't he MINE? Can't I do what I like with him? Who 's to hinder, I wonder?" And Legree clenched his fist, and shook it, as if he had something in his hands that he could rend in pieces.

But, then, Tom was a faithful, valuable servant; and, although Legree hated him the more for that, yet the consideration was still somewhat of a restraint to him.

The next morning, he determined to say nothing, as yet; to assemble a party, from some neighboring plantations, with dogs and guns; to surround the swamp, and go about the hunt systematically. If it succeeded, well and good; if not, he would summon Tom before him, and—his teeth clenched and his blood boiled—*then* he would break that fellow down, or——there was a dire inward whisper, to which his soul assented.

Ye say that the *interest* of the master is a sufficient safe-guard for the slave. In the fury of man's mad will, he will wittingly, and with open eye, sell his own soul to the devil to gain his ends; and will he be more careful of his neighbor's body?

"Well," said Cassy, the next day, from the garret, as she reconnoitered through the knot-hole, "the hunt 's going to begin again, to-day!"

[2]I.e., stood up to him.

Three or four mounted horsemen were curvetting about, on the space front of the house; and one or two leashes of strange dogs were struggling with the negroes who held them, baying and barking at each other.

The men are, two of them, overseers of plantations in the vicinity; and others were some of Legree's associates at the tavern-bar of a neighboring city, who had come for the interest of the sport. A more hard-favored set, perhaps, could not be imagined. Legree was serving brandy, profusely, round among them, as also among the negroes, who had been detailed from the various plantations for this service; for it was an object to make every service of this kind, among the negroes, as much of a holiday as possible.

Cassy placed her ear at the knot-hole; and, as the morning air blew directly towards the house, she could overhear a good deal of the conversation. A grave sneer overcast the dark, severe gravity of her face, as she listened, and heard them divide out the ground, discuss the rival merits of the dogs, give orders about firing, and the treatment of each, in case of capture.

Cassy drew back; and, clasping her hands, looked upward, and said, "O, great Almighty God! we are *all* sinners; but what have *we* done, more than all the rest of the world, that we should be treated so?"

There was a terrible earnestness in her face and voice, as she spoke.

"If it was n't for *you,* child," she said, looking at Emmeline, "I 'd *go* out to them; and I 'd thank any one of them that *would* shoot me down; for what use will freedom be to me? Can it give me back my children, or make me what I used to be?"

Emmeline, in her child-like simplicity, was half afraid of the dark moods of Cassy. She looked perplexed, but made no answer. She only took her hand, with a gentle, caressing movement.

"Don't!" said Cassy, trying to draw it away; "you 'll get me to loving you; and I never mean to love anything, again!"

"Poor Cassy!" said Emmeline, "don't feel so! If the Lord gives us liberty, perhaps He 'll give you back your daughter; at any rate, I 'll be like a daughter to you. I know I 'll never see my poor old mother again! I shall love you, Cassy, whether you love me or not!"

The gentle, child-like spirit conquered. Cassy sat down by her, put her arm round her neck, stroked her soft, brown hair; and Emmeline then wondered at the beauty of her magnificent eyes, now soft with tears.

"O, Em!" said Cassy, "I've hungered for my children, and thirsted for them, and my eyes fail with longing for them! Here! here!" she said, striking her breast, "it 's all desolate, all empty! If God would give me back my children, then I could pray."

"You must trust him, Cassy," said Emmeline; "He is our Father!"

"His wrath is upon us," said Cassy; "He has turned away in anger."

"No, Cassy! He will be good to us! Let us hope in Him," said Emmeline,—"I always have had hope."

The hunt was long, animated, and thorough, but unsuccessful; and, with grave, ironic exultation, Cassy looked down on Legree, as, weary and dispirited, he alighted from his horse.

"Now, Quimbo," said Legree, as he stretched himself down in the sitting-room, "you jest go and walk that Tom up here, right away! The old cuss is at the bottom of this yer whole matter; and I 'll have it out of his old black hide, or I 'll know the reason why!"

Sambo and Quimbo, both, though hating each other, were joined in one mind by a no less cordial hatred of Tom. Legree had told them, at first, that he had bought him for a general overseer, in his absence; and this had begun an ill will, on their part, which had increased, in their debased and servile natures, as they saw him becoming obnoxious to their master's displeasure. Quimbo, therefore, departed, with a will, to execute his orders.

Tom heard the message with a forewarning heart; for he knew all the plan of the fugitives' escape, and the place of their present concealment;—he knew the deadly character of the man he had to deal with, and his despotic power. But he felt strong in God to meet death, rather than betray the helpless.

He sat his basket down by the row,[3] and, looking up, said, "Into thy hands I commend my spirit! Thou hast redeemed me, oh Lord God of truth!"[4] and then quietly yielded himself to the rough, brutal grasp with which Quimbo seized him.

"Ay, ay!" said the giant, as he dragged him along: "ye 'll cotch it, now! I 'll boun' Mas'r's back 's up *high!* No sneaking out, now! Tell ye, ye 'll get it, and no mistake! See how ye 'll look, now, helpin' Mas'r's niggers to run away! See what ye 'll get!"

The savage words none of them reached that ear!—a higher voice there was saying, "Fear not them that kill the body, and, after that, have no more that they can do."[5] Nerve and bone of that poor man's body vibrated to those words, as if touched by the finger of God; and he felt the strength of a thousand souls in one. As he passed along, the trees and bushes, the huts of his servitude, the whole scene of his degradation, seemed to whirl by him as the landscape by the rushing car.[6] His soul throbbed,—his home was in sight,—and the hour of release seemed at hand.

"Well, Tom!" said Legree, walking up, and seizing him grimly by the collar of his coat, and speaking through his teeth, in a paroxysm of determined rage, "do you know I 've made up my mind to KILL you?"

"It 's very likely, Mas'r," said Tom, calmly.

"I *have,*" said Legree, with grim, terrible calmness, "*done—just—that—thing,* Tom, unless you 'll tell me what you know about these yer gals!"

Tom stood silent.

"D' ye hear?" said Legree, stamping, with a roar like that of an incensed lion. "Speak!"

"I han't got nothing to tell, Mas'r," said Tom, with a slow, firm, deliberate utterance.

"Do you dare to tell me, ye old black Christian, ye don't *know?*" said Legree.

Tom was silent.

"Speak!" thundered Legree, striking him furiously. "Do you know anything?"

"I know, Mas'r; but I can't tell anything. *I can die!*"

[3]Row of cotton in the field. [4]An adaptation of Luke 23:46 and Psalms 31:5.
[5]An adaptation of Matthew 10:28. [6]Railroad car.

Legree drew in a long breath; and, suppressing his rage, took Tom by the arm, and, approaching his face almost to his, said, in a terrible voice, "Hark 'e, Tom!—ye think, 'cause I 've let you off before, I don't mean what I say; but, this time, I 've *made up my mind,* and counted the cost. You 've always stood it out agin' me: now, I 'll *conquer ye, or kill ye!*—one or t' other. I 'll count every drop of blood there is in you, and take 'em, one by one, till ye give up!"

Tom looked up to his master, and answered, "Mas'r, if you was sick, or in trouble, or dying, and I could save ye, I 'd *give* ye my heart's blood; and, if taking every drop of blood in this poor old body would save your precious soul, I 'd give 'em freely, as the Lord gave his for me. O, Mas'r! don't bring this great sin on your soul! It will hurt you more than 't will me! Do the worst you can, my troubles 'll be over soon; but, if ye don't repent, yours won't *never* end!"

Like a strange snatch of heavenly music, heard in the lull of a tempest, this burst of feeling made a moment's blank pause. Legree stood aghast, and looked at Tom; and there was such a silence, that the tick of the old clock could be heard, measuring, with silent touch, the last moments of mercy and probation to that hardened heart.

It was but a moment. There was one hesitating pause,—one irresolute, relenting thrill,—and the spirit of evil came back, with seven-fold vehemence; and Legree, foaming with rage, smote his victim to the ground.

Scenes of blood and cruelty are shocking to our ear and heart. What man has nerve to do, man has not nerve to hear. What brother-man and brother-Christian must suffer, cannot be told us, even in our secret chamber, it so harrows up the soul! And yet, oh my country! these things are done under the shadow of thy laws! O, Christ! thy church sees them, almost in silence!

But, of old, there was One whose suffering changed an instrument of torture, degradation and shame, into a symbol of glory, honor, and immortal life; and, where His spirit is, neither degrading stripes, nor blood, nor insults, can make the Christian's last struggle less than glorious.

Was he alone, that long night, whose brave, loving spirit was bearing up, in that old shed, against buffeting and brutal stripes?

Nay! There stood by him ONE,—seen by him alone,—"like unto the Son of God."[7]

The tempter stood by him, too,—blinded by furious, despotic will,—every moment pressing him to shun that agony by the betrayal of the innocent. But the brave, true heart was firm on the Eternal Rock. Like his Master, he knew that, if he saved others, himself he could not save; nor could utmost extremity wring from him words, save of prayer and holy trust.

"He 's most gone, Mas'r," said Sambo, touched, in spite of himself, by the patience of his victim.

"Pay away, till he gives up! Give it to him!—give it to him!" shouted Legree. "I 'll take every drop of blood he has, unless he confesses!"

Tom opened his eyes, and looked upon his master. "Ye poor miserable critter!" he said, "there an't no more ye can do! I forgive ye, with all my soul!" and he fainted entirely away.

[7]Hebrews 7:3.

"I b'lieve, my soul, he 's done for, finally," said Legree, stepping forward, to look at him. "Yes, he is! Well, his mouth 's shut up, at last,—that 's one comfort!"

Yes, Legree; but who shall shut up that voice in thy soul? that soul, past repentance, past prayer, past hope, in whom the fire that never shall be quenched is already burning!

Yet Tom was not quite gone. His wondrous words and pious prayers had struck upon the hearts of the imbruted blacks, who had been the instruments of cruelty upon him; and, the instant Legree withdrew, they took him down, and, in their ignorance, sought to call him back to life,—as if *that* were any favor to him.

"Sartin, we 's been doin' a drefful wicked thing!" said Sambo; "hopes Mas'r 'll have to 'count for it, and not we."

They washed his wounds,—they provided a rude bed, of some refuse cotton, for him to lie down on; and one of them, stealing up to the house, begged a drink of brandy of Legree, pretending that he was tired, and wanted it for himself. He brought it back, and poured it down Tom's throat.

"O, Tom!" said Quimbo, "we 's been awful wicked to ye!"

"I forgive ye, with all my heart!" said Tom, faintly.

"O, Tom! do tell us who is *Jesus*, anyhow?" said Sambo;—"Jesus, that 's been a standin' by you so, all this night!—Who is he?"

The word roused the failing, fainting spirit. He poured forth a few energetic sentences of that wondrous One,—His life, His death, His everlasting presence, and power to save.

They wept,—both the two savage men.

"Why did n't I never hear this before?" said Sambo; "but I do believe!—I can't help it! Lord Jesus, have mercy on us!"

"Poor critters!" said Tom, "I 'd be willing to bar' all I have, if it 'll only bring ye to Christ! O, Lord! give me these two more souls, I pray!"

That prayer was answered!

CHAPTER XLI

THE YOUNG MASTER

Two days after, a young man drove a light wagon up through the avenue of china-trees, and, throwing the reins hastily on the horses' neck, sprang out and inquired for the owner of the place.

It was George Shelby; and, to show how he came to be there, we must go back in our story.

The letter of Miss Ophelia to Mrs. Shelby had, by some unfortunate accident, been detained, for a month or two, at some remote post-office, before it reached its destination; and, of course, before it was received, Tom was already lost to view among the distant swamps of the Red river.

Mrs. Shelby read the intelligence with the deepest concern; but any immediate action upon it was an impossibility. She was then in attendance on the sick-bed of her husband, who lay delirious in the crisis of a fever. Master George Shelby, who, in the interval, had changed from a boy to a tall young man, was her constant and faithful assistant, and her only reliance in superintending his father's affairs. Miss Ophelia had taken the precaution to send them the name of the lawyer who did business for the St. Clares; and the most that, in the emergency, could be done, was to address a letter of inquiry to him. The sudden death of Mr. Shelby, a few days after, brought, of course, an absorbing pressure of other interests, for a season.

Mr. Shelby showed his confidence in his wife's ability, by appointing her sole executrix upon his estates; and thus immediately a large and complicated amount of business was brought upon her hands.

Mrs. Shelby, with characteristic energy, applied herself to the work of straightening the entangled web of affairs; and she and George were for some time occupied with collecting and examining accounts, selling property and settling debts; for Mrs. Shelby was determined that everything should be brought into tangible and recognizable shape, let the consequences to her prove what they might. In the mean time, they received a letter from the lawyer to whom Miss Ophelia had referred them, saying that he knew nothing of the matter; that the man was sold at a public auction, and that, beyond receiving the money, he knew nothing of the affair.

Neither George nor Mrs. Shelby could be easy at this result; and, accordingly, some six months after, the latter, having business for his mother, down the river, resolved to visit New Orleans, in person, and push his inquiries, in hopes of discovering Tom's whereabouts, and restoring him.

After some months of unsuccessful search, by the merest accident, George fell in with a man, in New Orleans, who happened to be possessed of the desired information; and with his money in his pocket, our hero took steamboat for Red river, resolving to find out and re-purchase his old friend.

He was soon introduced into the house, where he found Legree in the sitting-room.

Legree received the stranger with a kind of surly hospitality.

"I understand," said the young man, "that you bought, in New Orleans, a boy, named Tom. He used to be on my father's place, and I came to see if I could n't buy him back."

Legree's brow grew dark, and he broke out, passionately. "Yes, I did buy such a fellow,—and a h—l of a bargain I had of it, too! The most rebellious, saucy, impudent dog! Set up my niggers to run away; got off two gals, worth eight hundred or a thousand dollars apiece. He owned to that, and, when I bid him tell me where they was, he up and said he knew, but he would n't tell; and stood to it, though I gave him the cussedest flogging I ever gave nigger yet. I b'lieve he 's trying to die; but I don't know as he 'll make it out."

"Where is he?" said George, impetuously. "Let me see him." The cheeks of the young man were crimson, and his eyes flashed fire; but he prudently said nothing, as yet.

"He 's in dat ar shed," said a little fellow, who stood holding George's horse.

Legree kicked the boy, and swore at him; but George, without saying another word, turned and strode to the spot.

Tom had been lying two days since the fatal night; not suffering, for every nerve of suffering was blunted and destroyed. He lay, for the most part, in a quiet stupor; for the laws of a powerful and well-knit frame would not at once release the imprisoned spirit. By stealth, there had been there, in the darkness of the night, poor desolated creatures, who stole from their scanty hours' rest, that they might repay to him some of those ministrations of love in which he had always been so abundant. Truly, those poor disciples had little to give,—only the cup of cold water; but it was given with full hearts.

Tears had fallen on that honest, insensible face,—tears of late repentance in the poor, ignorant heathen, whom his dying love and patience had awakened to repentance, and bitter prayers, breathed over him to a late-found Saviour, of whom they scarce knew more than the name, but whom the yearning ignorant heart of man never implores in vain.

Cassy, who had glided out of her place of concealment, and, by over-hearing, learned the sacrifice that had been made for her and Emmeline, had been there, the night before, defying the danger of detection; and, moved by the few last words which the affectionate soul had yet strength to breathe, the long winter of despair, the ice of years, had given way, and the dark, despairing woman had wept and prayed.

When George entered the shed, he felt his head giddy and his heart sick.

"Is it possible,—is it possible?" said he, kneeling down by him. "Uncle Tom, my poor, poor old friend!"

Something in the voice penetrated to the ear of the dying. He moved his head gently, smiled, and said,

"Jesus can make a dying-bed
Feel soft as downy pillows are."

Tears which did honor to his manly heart fell from the young man's eyes, as he bent over his poor friend.

"O, dear Uncle Tom! do wake,—do speak once more! Look up! Here 's Mas'r George,—your own little Mas'r George. Don't you know me?"

"Mas'r George!" said Tom, opening his eyes, and speaking in a feeble voice; "Mas'r George!" He looked bewildered.

Slowly the idea seemed to fill his soul; and the vacant eye became fixed and brightened, the whole face lighted up, the hard hands clasped, and tears ran down the cheeks.

"Bless the Lord! it is,—it is,—it 's all I wanted! They have n't forgot me. It warms my soul; it does my old heart good! Now I shall die content! Bless the Lord, oh my soul!"

"You shan't die! you *must n't* die, nor think of it! I 've come to buy you, and take you home," said George, with impetuous vehemence.

"O, Mas'r George, ye 're too late. The Lord 's bought me, and is going to take me home,—and I long to go. Heaven is better than Kintuck."

"O, don't die! It 'll kill me!—it 'll break my heart to think what you 've suffered,—and lying in this old shed, here! Poor, poor fellow!"

"Don't call me poor fellow!" said Tom, solemnly. "I *have* been poor fellow; but that 's all past and gone, now. I 'm right in the door, going into glory! O, Mas'r George! *Heaven has come!* I 've got the victory!—the Lord Jesus has given it to me! Glory be to His name!"

George was awe-struck at the force, the vehemence, the power, with which these broken sentences were uttered. He sat gazing in silence.

Tom grasped his hand, and continued,—"Ye must n't, now, tell Chloe, poor soul! how ye found me;—'t would be so drefful to her. Only tell her ye found me going into glory; and that I could n't stay for no one. And tell her the Lord 's stood by me everywhere and al'ays, and made everything light and easy. And oh, the poor chil'en, and the baby!—my old heart 's been most broke for 'em, time and agin! Tell 'em all to follow me—follow me! Give my love to Mas'r, and dear good Missis, and everybody in the place! Ye don't know! 'Pears like I loves 'em all! I loves every creatur' everywhar!—it 's nothing *but* love! O, Mas'r George! what a thing 't is to be a Christian!"

At this moment, Legree sauntered up to the door of the shed, looked in, with a dogged air of affected carelessness, and turned away.

"The old satan!" said George, in his indignation. "It 's a comfort to think the devil will pay *him* for this, some of these days!"

"O, don't!—oh, ye must n't!" said Tom, grasping his hand; "he 's a poor mis'able critter! it 's awful to think on 't! O, if he only could repent, the Lord would forgive him now; but I 'm 'feared he never will!"

"I hope he won't!" said George; "I never want to see *him* in heaven!"

"Hush, Mas'r George!—it worries me! Don't feel so! He an't done me no real harm,—only opened the gate of the kingdom for me; that 's all!"

At this moment, the sudden flush of strength which the joy of meeting his young master had infused into the dying man gave way. A sudden sinking fell upon him; he closed his eyes; and that mysterious and sublime change passed over his face, that told the approach of other worlds.

He began to draw his breath with long, deep inspirations; and his broad chest rose and fell, heavily. The expression of his face was that of a conqueror.

"Who,—who,—who shall separate us from the love of Christ?"[1] he said, in a voice that contended with mortal weakness; and, with a smile, he fell asleep.

George sat fixed with solemn awe. It seemed to him that the place was holy; and, as he closed the lifeless eyes, and rose up from the dead, only one thought possessed him,—that expressed by his simple old friend,— "What a thing it is to be a Christian!"

He turned. Legree was standing, sullenly, behind him.

Something in that dying scene had checked the natural fierceness of youthful passion. The presence of the man was simply loathsome to George; and he felt only an impulse to get away from him, with as few words as possible.

Fixing his keen dark eyes on Legree, he simply said, pointing to the dead, "You have got all you ever can of him. What shall I pay you for the body? I will take it away, and bury it decently."

"I don't sell dead niggers," said Legree, doggedly. "You are welcome to bury him where and when you like."

"Boys," said George, in an authoritative tone, to two or three negroes, who were looking at the body, "help me lift him up, and carry him to my wagon; and get me a spade."

One of them ran for a spade; the other two assisted George to carry the body to the wagon.

George neither spoke to nor looked at Legree, who did not countermand his orders, but stood, whistling, with an air of forced unconcern. He sulkily followed them to where the wagon stood at the door.

George spread his cloak in the wagon, and had the body carefully disposed of in it,—moving the seat, so as to give it room. Then he turned, fixed his eyes on Legree, and said, with forced composure,

"I have not, as yet, said to you what I think of this most atrocious affair;—this is not the time and place. But, sir, this innocent blood shall have justice.

[1]Hebrews 7:3.

I will proclaim this murder. I will go to the very first magistrate, and expose you."

"Do!" said Legree, snapping his fingers, scornfully. "I 'd like to see you doing it. Where you going to get witnesses?—how you going to prove it?—Come, now!"

George saw, at once, the force of this defiance. There was not a white person on the place; and, in all southern courts, the testimony of colored blood is nothing. He felt, at that moment, as if he could have rent the heavens with his heart's indignant cry for justice; but in vain.

"After all, what a fuss, for a dead nigger!" said Legree.

The word was as a spark to a powder magazine. Prudence was never a cardinal virtue of the Kentucky boy. George turned, and, with one indignant blow, knocked Legree flat upon his face; and, as he stood over him, blazing with wrath and defiance, he would have formed no bad personification of his great namesake triumphing over the dragon.

Some men, however, are decidedly bettered by being knocked down. If a man lays them fairly flat in the dust, they seem immediately to conceive a respect for him; and Legree was one of this sort. As he rose, therefore, and brushed the dust from his clothes, he eyed the slowly-retreating wagon with some evident consideration; nor did he open his mouth till it was out of sight.

Beyond the boundaries of the plantation, George had noticed a dry, sandy knoll, shaded by a few trees: there they made the grave.

"Shall we take off the cloak, Mas'r?" said the negroes, when the grave was ready.

"No, no,—bury it with him! It 's all I can give you, now, poor Tom, and you shall have it."

They laid him in; and the men shovelled away, silently. They banked it up, and laid green turf over it.

"You may go, boys," said George, slipping a quarter into the hand of each. They lingered about, however.

"If young Mas'r would please buy us—" said one.

"We 'd serve him so faithful!" said the other.

"Hard times here, Mas'r!" said the first. "Do, Mas'r, buy us, please!"

"I can't!—I can't!" said George, with difficulty, motioning them off; "it 's impossible!"

The poor fellows looked dejected, and walked off in silence.

"Witness, eternal God!" said George, kneeling on the grave of his poor friend; "oh, witness, that, from this hour, I will do *what one man can* to drive out this curse of slavery from my land!"

There is no monument to mark the last resting-place of our friend. He needs none! His Lord knows where he lies, and will raise him up, immortal, to appear with Him when He shall appear in his glory.

Pity him not! Such a life and death is not for pity! Not in the riches of omnipotence is the chief glory of God; but in self-denying, suffering love! And blessed are the men whom He calls to fellowship with Him, bearing their cross after Him with patience. Of such it is written, "Blessed are they that mourn, for they shall be comforted."[2]

1852

[2]Matthew 5:4.

Frederick Douglass 1818–1895

"I was born in Tuckahoe, near Hillsborough, and about twelve miles from Easton, in Talbot County, Maryland. I have no accurate knowledge of my age. . . . I do not remember to have ever met a slave who could tell of his birthday." Although Frederick Douglass never learned the exact date of his birth, he clearly remembered the details of his early life as a slave on a Maryland plantation. When he was around nine years old, he was sent to Baltimore, where he became a house servant and was taught to read by his mistress. At fifteen he was returned to work on a plantation, but he proved so rebellious that he was sent to a "slave-breaker" for a year to have his spirit tamed. Six years later, in 1838, he escaped to Massachusetts.

In 1841 Douglass attended an abolitionist meeting in Nantucket, and when invited to speak, he was so eloquent that he was hired by the Massachusetts Anti-Slavery Society as a lecturer. For the next four years he toured the North, speaking in favor of abolition. In 1845 he published his Narrative of the Life of Frederick Douglass, *and for the next two years he toured Great Britain, lecturing on the evils of American slavery. In 1847, after his freedom had been purchased, he returned to America, where he continued to lecture and wrote magazine articles and newspaper editorials. He founded and edited antislavery journals—the* North Star *and* Douglass' Monthly*—and twice revised and expanded his autobiography, first as* My Bondage and My Freedom *(1855) and later as* The Life and Times of Frederick Douglass *(1881, 1892). During the Civil War he helped recruit troops for the Union army, and following the war he was appointed to political office in the District of Columbia. Later he became United States minister to Haiti.*

Douglass's autobiography stands as one of the most notable examples of the fugitive slave narratives that appeared in the North (and were banned in the South) before the Civil War, eloquent stories of runaways to freedom that exposed both the terrors of Southern slavery and the cruelties of Northern discrimination. Douglass's revelations supplied such antislavery writers as Harriet Beecher Stowe with details of slave life for books that indicted slavery with increasing effectiveness as the Civil War approached. His writing, his oratory, and the example of his life were effective instruments in battling the myth that portrayed blacks as a subhuman species, members of a "knee-bending" race, bereft of intellect and fit only to labor for the white man.

Douglass was one of the nineteenth century's foremost spokesmen for the American Negro and for equal rights, a writer and orator of international fame. His autobiography was one of the few slave narratives wholly written by a former slave himself. Its ironies and burning indignation, its penetrating characterizations, and its portrayal of brutalizing slavery retain their power after more than a century.

FURTHER READING: B. Quarles, *Frederick Douglass,* 1948; *The Life and Writings of Frederick Douglass,* 4 vols., ed. P. Foner, 1950–1955; A. Bontemps, *Free at Last, The Life of Frederick Douglass,* 1971; N. Huggins, *Slave and Citizen,* 1980; *The Frederick Douglass Papers, Series One,* Vols. I–II, ed. J. Blassingame, 1980, 1982; W. Martin, *The Mind of Frederick Douglass,* 1985; *Frederick Douglass, New Literary and Historical Essays,* ed. E. Sundquist, 1990; W. McFeely, *Frederick Douglass,* 1991; *Critical Essays on Frederick Douglass,* ed. W. Andrews, 1991; D. Cheesebrough, *Frederick Douglass, Oratory from Slavery,* 1998; G. Lampe, *Frederick Douglass, Freedom's Voice,* 1998; *Liberation Sojourn, Frederick Douglass and Transatlantic Reform,* ed. A. Rice and M. Crawford, 1999; *The World of Frederick Douglass,* ed. P. Finkelman, 2005; R. Davis, *Frederick Douglass, A Precursor of Liberation Theology,* 2005.

TEXT: *The Life and Times of Frederick Douglass,* 1892.

from *THE LIFE AND TIMES OF FREDERICK DOUGLASS*

Chapter 15

COVEY, THE NEGRO BREAKER

The morning of January 1, 1834, with its chilling wind and pinching frost, quite in harmony with the winter in my own mind, found me, with my little bundle of clothing on the end of a stick swung across my shoulder, on the main road bending my way towards Covey's, whither I had been imperiously ordered by Master Thomas. He had been as good as his word, and had committed me without reserve to the mastery of that hard man. Eight or ten years had now passed since I had been taken from my grandmother's cabin in Tuckahoe, and these years, for the most part, I had spent in Baltimore, where, as the reader has already seen, I was treated with comparative tenderness. I was now about to sound profounder depths in slave life. My new master was notorious for his fierce and savage disposition, and my only consolation in going to live with him was the certainty of finding him precisely as represented by common fame. There was neither joy in my heart nor elasticity in my frame as I started for the tyrant's home. Starvation made me glad to leave Thomas Aud's, and the cruel lash made me dread to go to Covey's. Escape, however, was impossible; so, heavy and sad, I paced the seven miles which lay between his house and St. Michaels, thinking much by the solitary way of my adverse condition. But *thinking* was all I could do. Like a fish in a net, allowed to play for a time, I was not drawn rapidly to the shore and secured at all points. "I am," thought I, "but the sport of a power which makes no account either of my welfare or of my happiness. By a law which I can comprehend, but cannot evade or resist, I am ruthlessly snatched from the hearth of a fond grandmother and hurried away to the home of a mysterious old master; again I am removed from there to a master in Baltimore; thence am I snatched away to the Eastern Shore[1] to be valued with the beasts of the field, and with them divided and set apart for a possessor; then I am sent back to Baltimore, and by the time I have formed new attachments and have begun to hope that no more rude shocks shall touch me, a difference arises between brothers, and I am again broken up and sent to St. Michaels; and now from the latter place I am footing my way to the home of another master, where, I am given to understand, like a wild young working animal I am to be broken to the yoke of a bitter and lifelong bondage." With thoughts and reflections like these I came in sight of a small wood-colored building, about a mile from the main road, and which, from the description I had received at starting, I easily recognized as my new home. The Chesapeake Bay, upon the jutting banks of which the little wood-colored house was standing, white with foam raised by the heavy northwest wind; Poplar Island, covered with a thick black pine forest, standing out amid this half ocean; and Keat Point, stretching its sandy, desert-like shores out into the foam-crested bay, were all in sight, and served to deepen the wild and desolate scene.

The good clothes I had brought with me from Baltimore were now worn thin, and had not been replaced, for Master Thomas was as little careful to provide against cold as against hunger. Met here by a north wind sweeping

[1]Of Chesapeake Bay.

through an open space of forty miles, I was glad to make any port, and, therefore, I speedily pressed on to the wood-colored house. The family consisted of Mr. and Mrs. Covey, Mrs. Kemp (a broken-backed woman), sister to Mrs. Covey, William Hughes, a cousin to Mr. Covey, Caroline, the cook, Bill Smith, a hired man, and myself. Bill Smith, Bill Hughes and myself were the working force of the farm, which comprised three or four hundred acres. I was now for the first time in my life to be a fieldhand, and in my new employment I found myself even more awkward than a green country boy may be supposed to be upon his first entrance into the bewildering scenes of city life. My awkwardness gave me much trouble.

Strange and unnatural as it may seem, I had been in my new home but three days before Mr. Covey (my brother in the Methodist church) gave me a bitter foretaste of what was in reserve for me. I presume he thought that, since he had but a single year in which to complete his work, the sooner he began the better. Perhaps he thought that by coming to blows at once we should mutually better understand our relations to each other. But to whatever motive, direct or indirect, the cause may be referred, I had not been in his possession three whole days before he subjected me to a most brutal chastisement. Under his heavy blows blood flowed freely, and wales were left on my back as large as my little finger. The sores from this flogging continued for weeks, for they were kept open by the rough and coarse cloth which I wore for shirting. The occasion and details of this first chapter of my experience as a fieldhand must be told, that the reader may see how unreasonable, as well as how cruel, my new Master Covey was. The whole thing I found to be characteristic of the man, and I was probably treated no worse by him than had been scores of lads previously committed to him for reasons similar to those which induced my master to place me with him. But here are the facts connected with the affair, precisely as they occurred.

On one of the coldest mornings of the whole month of January, 1834, I was ordered at daybreak to get a load of wood, from a forest about two miles from the house. In order to perform this work, Mr. Covey gave me a pair of unbroken oxen, for it seemed that his breaking abilities had not been turned in that direction. In due form, and with all proper ceremony, I was introduced to his huge yoke of unbroken oxen, and was carefully made to understand which was "Buck," and which was "Darby,"—which was the "in hand" ox, and which was the "off hand." The master of this important ceremony was not less a person than Mr. Covey himself, and the introduction was the first of the kind I had ever had.

My life, hitherto, had been quite away from horned cattle, and I had no knowledge of the art of managing them. What was meant by the "in ox," as against the "off ox," when both were equally fastened to one cart, and under one yoke, I could not very easily divine, and the difference implied by the names, and the peculiar duties of each, were alike Greek to me. Why was not the "off ox" called the "in ox"? Where and what is the reason for this distinction in names, when there is none in the things themselves? After initiating me into the use of the "whoa," "back," "gee," "hither,"—the entire language spoken between oxen and driver—Mr. Covey took a rope about ten feet long and one inch thick, and placed one end of it around the horns of the "in hand ox," and gave the other end to me, telling me that if the oxen started to run away (as the scamp knew they would), I must hold on to the rope and stop them. I need not tell any one who is acquainted with either the strength or the disposition of an untamed ox, that this order was about as unreasonable as a command to shoulder a mad bull. I had never before driven oxen and I was as awkward a driver as it is possible to conceive. I could not plead my ignorance to Mr. Covey. There was that in his manner which forbade any reply. Cold, distant, morose, with a face wearing all the marks of captious pride and malicious sternness, he repelled all advances. He was not a large man—not more than five feet ten inches in height, I should think—short-necked, round-shouldered, of quick and wiry motion, of thin and wolfish visage, with a pair of small, greenish-gray eyes, set well back under a forehead without dignity, and which were constantly in motion, expressing his passions rather than his thoughts, in sight, but denying them utterance in words. The creature presented an appearance altogether ferocious and sinister, disagreeable and forbidding, in the extreme. When he spoke, it was from the corner of his mouth, and in a sort of light growl like that of a dog when an attempt is made to take a bone from him. I already believed him a worse fellow than he had been represented to be. With his directions, and without stopping to question, I started for the woods, quite anxious to perform in a creditable manner my first exploit in driving. The distance from the house to the wood's gate—a full mile, I should think—was passed over with little difficulty, for, although the animals ran, I was fleet enough in the open field to keep pace with them, especially as they pulled me along at the end of the rope; but on reaching the woods, I was speedily thrown into a distressing plight. The animals took fright, and started off ferociously into the woods, carrying the cart full tilt against trees, over stumps, and dashing from side to side in a manner altogether frightful. As I held the rope I expected every moment to be crushed between the cart and the huge trees, among which they were so furiously dashing. After running thus for several minutes, my oxen were finally brought to a stand, by a tree, against which they dashed themselves with great violence, upsetting the cart, and entangling themselves among sundry young saplings. By the shock the body of the cart was flung in one direction and the wheels and tongue in another, and all in the greatest confusion. There I was, all alone in a thick wood to which I was a stranger, my cart upset and shattered, my oxen, wild and enraged, were entangled, and I, poor soul, was but a green hand to set all this disorder right. I knew no more of oxen than the oxdriver is supposed to know of wisdom.

After standing a few minutes, surveying the damage, and not without a presentiment that this trouble would draw after it others, even more distressing, I took one end of the cart-body and, by an extra outlay of strength, I lifted it toward the axle-tree, from which it had been violently flung. After much pulling and straining, I succeeded in getting the body of the cart in its place. This was an important step out of the difficulty, and its performance increased my courage for the work which remained to be done. The cart was provided with an ax, a tool with which I had become pretty well acquainted in the shipyard in Baltimore. With this I cut down the saplings by which my oxen were entangled, and again pursued my journey, with my heart in my mouth, lest the oxen should again take it into their senseless heads to cut up a caper. But their spree was over for the present, and the rascals now moved off as soberly as though their behavior had been natural and exemplary. On reaching the part of the forest where I had, the day before, been chopping wood, I filled the cart with a heavy load, as a security against another runaway. But the neck of an ox is equal in strength to iron. It defies ordinary burdens. Tame and docile to a proverb, when well trained, when but half broken to the yoke the ox is the most sullen and intractable of animals. I saw in my own situation several points of similarity with that of the oxen. They were property; so was I. Covey was to break me—I was to break them. Break and be broken was the order.

Half of the day was already gone and I had not yet turned my face homeward. It required only two days' experience and observation to teach me that no such apparent waste of time would be lightly overlooked by Covey. I therefore hurried toward home, but in reaching the lane gate I met the crowning disaster of the day. This gate was a fair specimen of southern handicraft. There were two huge posts eighteen inches in diameter, rough hewed and square, and the heavy gate was so hung on one of these that it opened only about half the proper distance. On arriving here it was necessary for me to let go the end of the rope on the horns of the "in-hand ox," and as soon as the gate was open and I let go of it to get the rope again, off went my oxen, full tilt, making nothing of their load, as, catching the huge gate between the wheel and the cart-body, they literally crushed it to splinters and came within only a few inches of subjecting me to a similar catastrophe, for I was just in advance of the wheel when it struck the left gatepost. With these two hair-breadth escapes I thought I could successfully explain to Mr. Covey the delay and avert punishment—I was not without a faint hope of being commended for the stern resolution which I had displayed in accomplishing the difficult task—a task which I afterwards learned even Covey himself would not have undertaken without first driving the oxen for some time in the open field, preparatory to their going to the woods. But in this hope I was disappointed. On coming to him his countenance assumed an aspect of rigid displeasure, and as I gave him a history of the casualties of my trip, his wolfish face, with his greenish eyes, became intensely ferocious. "Go back to the woods again," he said, muttering something else about wasting time. I hastily obeyed, but I had not gone far on my way when I saw him coming after me. My oxen now behaved themselves with singular propriety, contrasting their present conduct to my representation of their former antics. I almost wished, now that Covey was coming, they *would* do something in keeping with the character I had given them; but no, they had already had their spree, and they could afford now to be extra good, readily obeying orders, and seeming to understand them quite as well as I did myself.

On reaching the woods, my tormentor, who seemed all the time to be remarking to himself upon the good behavior of the oxen, came up to me and ordered me to stop the cart, accompanying the same with the threat that he would now teach me how to break gates and idle away my time when he sent me to the woods. Suiting the action to the words, Covey paced off, in his own wiry fashion, to a large black gum tree, the young shoots of which are generally used for ox-goads, they being exceedingly tough. Three of these goads, from four to six feet long, he cut off and trimmed up with his large jackknife. This done, he ordered me to take off my clothes. To this unreasonable order I made no reply, but in my apparent unconsciousness and inattention to this command I indicated very plainly a stern determination to do no such thing. "If you will beat me," thought I, "you shall do so over my clothes." After many threats, which made no impression upon me, he rushed at me with something of the savage fierceness of a wolf, tore off the few and thinly worn clothes I had on, and proceeded to wear out on my back the heavy goads which he had cut from the gum tree. This flogging was the first of a series of floggings, and though very severe, it was less so than many which came after it, and these for offences far lighter than the gate-breaking.

I remained with Mr. Covey one year (I cannot say I lived with him), and during the first six months that I was there I was whipped, either with sticks or cowskins, every week. Aching bones and a sore back were my constant companions. Frequently as the lash was used, Mr. Covey thought less of it as a means of breaking down my spirit than that of hard and continued labor. He worked me steadily up to the point of my powers of endurance. From the dawn of day in the morning till the darkness was complete in the evening, I was kept hard at work in the field or the woods. At certain seasons of the year we were all kept in the field till eleven and twelve o'clock at night. At these times Covey would attend us in the field and urge us on with words or blows, as it seemed best to him. He had in his life been an overseer, and he well understood the business of slave-driving. There was no deceiving him. He knew just what a man or boy could do, and he held both to strict account. When he pleased he would work himself like a very Turk, making everything fly before him. It was, however, scarcely necessary for Mr. Covey to be really present in the field to have his work go on industriously. He had the faculty of making us feel that he was always present. By a series of adroitly managed surprises which he practiced, I was prepared to expect him at any moment. His plan was never to approach in an open, manly, and direct manner the spot where his hands were at work. No thief was ever more artful in his devices than this man Covey. He would creep and crawl in ditches and gullies, hide behind stumps and bushes, and practice so much of the cunning of the serpent, that Bill Smith and I, between ourselves, never called him by any other name than "the snake." We fancied that in his eyes and his gait we could see the snakish resemblance. One-half of his proficiency in the art of Negro-breaking consisted, I should think in this species of cunning. We were never secure. He could see or hear us nearly all the time. He was, to us, behind every stump, tree, bush, and fence on the plantation. He carried this kind of trickery so far that he would sometimes mount his horse and make believe he was going to St. Michaels, and in thirty minutes afterwards you might find his horse tied in the woods, and the snake-like Covey lying flat in the ditch with his head lifted above its edge, or in a fence-corner, watching every movement of the slaves. I have known him walk up to us and give us special orders as to our work in advance, as if he were leaving home with a view to being absent several days, and before he got half way to the house he would avail himself of our inattention to his movements to turn short on his heel, conceal himself behind a fence-corner or a tree, and watch us until the going down of the sun. Mean and contemptible as is all this, it is in keeping with the character which the life of a slaveholder was calculated to produce. There was no earthly inducement in the slave's condition to incite him to labor faithfully. The fear of punishment was the sole motive of any sort of industry with him. Knowing this fact as the slaveholder did, and judging the slave by himself, he naturally concluded that the slave would be idle whenever the cause for this fear was absent. Hence all sorts of petty deceptions were practiced to inspire fear.

But with Mr. Covey trickery was natural. Everything in the shape of learning or religion which he possessed was made to conform to this semi-lying propensity. He did not seem conscious that the practice had anything unmanly, base, or contemptible about it. It was with him a part of an important system essential to the relation of master and slave. I thought I saw, in his very religious devotions, this controlling element of his character. A long prayer at night made up for a short prayer in the morning, and few men could seem more devotional than he when he had nothing else to do.

Mr. Covey was not content with the cold style of family worship adopted in the cold latitudes, which begin and end with a simple prayer. No! the voice of praise as well as of prayer must be heard in his house night and morning. At first I was called upon to bear some part in the exercises, but the repeated floggings given me turned the whole thing into mockery. He was a poor singer and relied mainly upon me for raising the hymn for the family, and when I failed to do so he was thrown into much confusion. I do not think he ever abused me on account of these vexations. His religion was a thing altogether apart from his worldly concerns. He knew nothing of it as a holy principle directing and controlling his daily life and making the latter conform to the requirements of the gospel. One or two facts will illustrate his character better than a volume of generalities.

I have already implied that Mr. Edward Covey was a poor man. He was, in fact, just commencing to lay the foundation of his fortune, as fortune was regarded in a slave state. The first condition of wealth and respectability there being the ownership of human property, every nerve was strained by the poor man to obtain it, with little regard sometimes as to the means. In pursuit of this object, pious as Mr. Covey was, he proved himself as unscrupulous and base as the worst of his neighbors. In the beginning he was only able—as he said—"to buy one slave"; and scandalous and shocking as is the fact, he boasted that he bought her simply "as a breeder." But the worst of this is not told in this naked statement. This young woman (Caroline was her name) was virtually compelled by Covey to abandon herself to the object for which he had purchased her, and the result was the birth of twins at the end of the year. At this addition to his human stock Covey and his wife were ecstatic with joy. No one dreamed of reproaching the woman or of finding fault with the hired man, Bill Smith, the father of the children, for Mr. Covey had locked the two up together every night, thus inviting the result.

But I will pursue this revolting subject no farther. No better illustration of the unchaste, demoralizing, and debasing character of slavery can be found, than is furnished in the fact that this professedly Christian slaveholder, amidst all his prayers and hymns, was shamelessly and boastfully encouraging and actually compelling, in his own house, undisguised and unmitigated fornication, as a means of increasing his stock. It was the *system* of slavery which made this allowable, and which no more condemned the slaveholder for buying a slave woman and devoting her to this life, than for buying a cow and raising stock from her, and the same rules were observed, with a view to increasing the number and quality of the one, as of the other.

If at any one time of my life, more than another, I was made to drink the bitterest dregs of slavery, that time was during the first six months of my stay with this man Covey. We worked all weathers. It was never too hot, or too cold; it could never rain, blow, snow, or hail too hard for us to work in the field. Work, work, work, was scarcely more the order of the day than of the night. The longest days were too short for him, and the shortest nights were too long for him. I was somewhat unmanageable at the first, but a few months of this discipline tamed me. Mr. Covey succeeded in *breaking* me—in body, soul, and spirit. My natural elasticity was crushed; my intellect languished; the disposition to read departed, the cheerful spark that lingered about my eye died out; the dark night of slavery closed in upon me, and behold a man transformed to a brute!

Sunday was my only leisure time. I spent this under some large tree, in a sort of beast-like stupor between sleeping and waking. At times I would rise up and a flash of energetic freedom would dart through my soul, accompanied with a faint beam of hope that flickered for a moment, and then vanished. I sank down again, mourning over my wretched condition. I was sometimes tempted to take my life and that of Covey, but was prevented by a combination of hope and fear. My sufferings, as I remember them now, seem like a dream rather than like a stern reality.

Our house stood within a few rods of the Chesapeake Bay, whose broad bosom was ever white with sails from every quarter of the habitable globe. Those beautiful vessels, robed in white, and so delightful to the eyes of freemen, were to me so many shrouded ghosts, to terrify and torment me with thoughts of my wretched condition. I have often, in the deep stillness of a summer's Sabbath, stood all alone upon the banks of that noble bay, and traced, with saddened heart and tearful eye, the countless number of sails moving off to the mighty ocean. The sight of these always affected me powerfully. My thoughts would compel utterance, and there, with no audience but the Almighty, I would pour out my soul's complaint in my rude way with an apostrophe to the moving multitude of ships.

"You are loosed from your moorings, and free. I am fast in my chains, and am a slave! You move merrily before the gentle gale, and I sadly before the bloody whip. You are freedom's swift-winged angels, that fly around the world; I am confined in bonds of iron. O, that I were free! O, that I were on one of your gallant decks, and under your protecting wing! Alas! betwixt me and you the turbid waters roll. Go on, go on; O, why was I born a man, of whom to make a brute! The glad ship is gone—she hides in the dim distance. I am left in the hell of unending slavery. O, God, save me! God, deliver me! Let me be free! Is there any God? Why am I a slave? I will run away. I will not stand it. Get caught or get clear, I'll try it. I had as well die with ague as with fever. I have only one life to lose. I had as well be killed running as die standing. Only think of it: one hundred miles north, and I am free! Try it? Yes! God helping me, I will. It cannot be that I shall live and die a slave. I will take to the water. This very bay shall yet bear me into freedom. The steamboats steer in a north-east course from North Point; I will do the same, and when I get to the head of the bay, I will turn my canoe adrift, and walk straight through Delaware into Pennsylvania. When I get there I shall not be required to have a pass; I will travel there without being disturbed. Let but the first opportunity offer, and come what will, I am off. Meanwhile I will try to bear the yoke. I am not the only slave in the world. Why should I fret? I can bear as much as any of them. Besides I am but a boy yet, and all boys are bound out to some one. It may be that my misery in slavery will only increase my happiness when I get free. There is a better day coming."

I shall never be able to narrate half the mental experience through which it was my lot to pass, during my stay at Covey's. I was completely wrecked, changed, and bewildered, goaded almost to madness at one time, and at another reconciling myself to my wretched condition. All the kindness I had received at Baltimore, all my former hopes and aspirations for usefulness in the world, and even the happy moments spent in the exercises of religion, contrasted with my then present lot, served but to increase my anguish.

I suffered bodily as well as mentally. I had neither sufficient time in which to eat, or to sleep, except on Sundays. The overwork, and the brutal chastisements of which I was the victim, combined with that ever-gnawing and soul-devouring thought—"*I am a slave—a slave for life—a slave with no rational ground to hope for freedom*"—rendered me a living embodiment of mental and physical wretchedness.

Chapter 16
ANOTHER PRESSURE OF THE TYRANT'S VISE

The reader has but to repeat, in his mind, once a week the scene in the woods, where Covey subjected me to his merciless lash, to have a true idea of my bitter experience during the first six months of the breaking process through which he carried me. I have no heart to repeat each separate transaction. Such a narration would fill a volume much larger than the present one. I aim only to give the reader a truthful impression of my slave-life, without unnecessarily affecting him with harrowing details.

As I have intimated that my hardships were much greater during the first six months of my stay at Covey's than during the remainder of the year, and as the change in my condition was owing to causes which may help the reader to a better understanding of human nature, when subjected to the terrible extremities of slavery, I will narrate the circumstances of this change, although I may seem thereby to applaud my own courage.

You have, dear reader, seen me humbled, degraded, broken down, enslaved, and brutalized, and you understand how it was done; now let us see the converse of all this, and how it was brought about; and this will take us through the year 1834.

On one of the hottest days of the month of August of the year just mentioned, had the reader been passing through Covey's farm, he might have seen me at work in what was called the "treading-yard"—a yard upon which wheat was trodden out from the straw by the horses' feet. I was there at work feeding the "fan,"[1] or rather bringing wheat to the fan, while Bill Smith was feeding. Our force consisted of Bill Hughes, Bill Smith, and a slave by the name of Eli, the latter having been hired for the occasion. The work was simple, and required strength and activity, rather than any skill or intelligence, and yet to one entirely unused to such work, it came very hard. The heat was intense and overpowering, and there was much hurry to get the wheat trodden out that day through the fan, since if that work was done an hour before sundown, the hands would have, according to a promise of Covey, that hour added to their night's rest. I was not behind any of them in the wish to complete the day's work before sundown, and hence I struggled with all my

[1]Device for winnowing grain.

might to get it forward. The promise of one hour's repose on a week day was sufficient to quicken my pace, and to spur me on to extra endeavor. Besides, we had all planned to go fishing, and I certainly wished to have a hand in that. But I was disappointed, and the day turned out to be one of the bitterest I ever experienced.

About three o'clock, while the sun was pouring down his burning rays, and not a breeze was stirring, I broke down; my strength failed me; I was seized with a violent aching of the head, attended with extreme dizziness, and trembling in every limb. Finding what was coming, and feeling that it would never do to stop work, I nerved myself up and staggered on, until I fell by the side of the wheat fan, with a feeling that the earth had fallen in upon me. This brought the entire work to a dead stand. There was work for four: each one had his part to perform, and each part depended on the other, so that when one stopped, all were compelled to stop. Covey, who had become my dread, was at the house, about a hundred yards from where I was fanning, and instantly, upon hearing the fan stop, he came down to the treading-yard to inquire into the cause of the interruption. Bill Smith told him that I was sick and unable longer to bring wheat to the fan.

I had by this time crawled away in the shade, under the side of a post-and-rail fence, and was exceedingly ill. The intense heat of the sun, the heavy dust rising from the fan, and the stopping to take up the wheat from the yard, together with the hurrying to get through, had caused a rush of blood to my head. In this condition Covey, finding out where I was, came to me, and after standing over me a while asked what the matter was. I told him as well as I could, for it was with difficulty that I could speak. He gave me a savage kick in the side which jarred my whole frame, and commanded me to get up. The monster had obtained complete control over me, and if he had commanded me to do any possible thing I should, in my then state of mind, have endeavored to comply. I made an effort to rise, but fell back in the attempt before gaining my feet. He gave me another heavy kick, and again told me to rise. I again tried, and succeeded in standing up, but upon stooping to get the tub with which I was feeding the fan I again staggered and fell to the ground. I must have so fallen had I been sure that a hundred bullets would have pierced me through as the consequence. While down in this sad condition, and perfectly helpless, the merciless Negro-breaker took up the hickory slab with which Hughes had been striking off the wheat to a level with the sides of the half-bushel measure (a very hard weapon), and, with the edge of it, he dealt me a heavy blow on my head which made a large gash, and caused the blood to run freely, saying at the same time, "If you have got the headache, I'll cure you." This done, he ordered me again to rise, but I made no effort to do so, for I had now made up my mind that it was useless and that the heartless villain might do his worst. He could but kill me and that might put me out of my misery. Finding me unable to rise, or rather despairing of my doing so, Covey left me, with a view to getting on with the work without me. I was bleeding very freely, and my face was soon covered with my warm blood. Cruel and merciless as was the motive that dealt that blow, the wound was a fortunate one for me. Bleeding was never more efficacious. The pain in my head speedily abated, and I was soon able to rise. Covey had, as I have said, left me to my fate, and the question was, shall I return to my work, or shall I find my way to St. Michaels and make Capt. Auld acquainted with the atrocious cruelty of his brother Covey, and beseech him to get me another master? Remembering the object he had in view in placing me under the management of Covey, and further, his cruel treatment of my poor crippled cousin Henny, and his meanness in the matter of feeding and clothing his slaves, there was little ground to hope for a favorable reception at the hands of Capt. Thomas Auld. Nevertheless, I resolved to go straight to him, thinking that, if not animated by motives of humanity, he might be induced to interfere on my behalf from selfish considerations. "He cannot," I thought, "allow his property to be thus bruised and battered, marred and defaced, and I will go to him about the matter."

In order to get to St. Michaels by the most favorable and direct road I must walk seven miles, and this, in my sad condition, was no easy performance. I had already lost much blood, I was exhausted by over-exertion, my sides were sore from the heavy blows planted there by the stout boots of Mr. Covey, and I was in every way in an unfavorable plight for the journey. I however watched my chance while the cruel and cunning Covey was looking in an opposite direction, and started off across the field for St. Michaels. This was a daring step. If it failed it would only exasperate Covey and increase, during the remainder of my term of service under him, the rigors of my bondage. But the step was taken and I must go forward. I succeeded in getting nearly half way across the broad field toward the woods, when Covey observed me. I was still bleeding and the exertion of running had started the blood afresh. "Come back! Come back!" he vociferated, with threats of what he would do if I did not instantly return. But, disregarding his calls and threats, I pressed on toward the woods as fast as my feeble state would allow. Seeing no signs of my stopping, he caused his horse to be brought out and saddled, as if he intended to pursue me. The race was now to be an unequal one, and thinking I might be overhauled by him if I kept the main road, I walked nearly the whole distance in the woods, keeping far enough from the road to avoid detection and pursuit. But I had not gone far before my little strength again failed me, and I was obliged to lie down. The blood was still oozing from the wound in my head, and for a time I suffered more than I can describe. There I was in the deep woods, sick and emaciated, bleeding and almost bloodless, and pursued by a wretch whose character for revolting cruelty beggars all opprobrious speech. I was not without the fear of bleeding to death. The thought of dying all alone in the woods, and of being torn in pieces by the buzzards, had not yet been rendered tolerable by my many troubles and hardships, and I was glad when the shade of the trees and the cool evening breeze combined with my matted hair to stop the flow of blood. After lying there about three-quarters of an hour, brooding over the singular and mournful lot to which I was doomed, my mind passing over the whole scale or circle of belief and unbelief, from faith in the overruling Providence of God, to the blackest atheism, I again took up my journey toward St. Michaels, more weary and sad than on the morning when I left Thomas Auld's for the home of Covey. I was barefooted, bareheaded, and in my shirt-sleeves. The way was through briers and bogs, and I tore my feet often during the journey. I was full five hours in going the seven or eight miles, partly because of the difficulties of the way, and partly because of the feebleness induced by my illness, bruises, and loss of blood.

On gaining my master's store, I presented an appearance of wretchedness and woe calculated to move any but a heart of stone. From the crown of my head to the sole of my feet, there were marks of blood. My hair was all clotted with dust and blood, and the back of my shirt was literally stiff with the same. Briers and thorns had scarred and torn my feet and legs. Had I escaped from a den of tigers, I could not have looked worse. In this plight I appeared before my professedly *Christian* master, humble to invoke the interposition of his power and authority to protect me from further abuse and violence. During the latter part of my tedious journey I had begun to hope my master would not show himself in a nobler light than I had before seen him. But I was disappointed. I had jumped from a sinking ship into the sea. I had fled from a tiger to something worse. I told him as well as I could, all the circumstances: how I was endeavoring to please Covey; how hard I was at work in the present instance; how unwillingly I sank down under the heat, toil, and pain; the brutal manner in which Covey had kicked me in the side, the gash cut in my head; my hesitation about troubling him (Capt. Auld) with complaints, but that now I felt it would not be best longer to conceal from him the outrages committed from time to time upon me. At first Master Thomas seemed somewhat affected by the story of my wrongs, but he soon repressed whatever feeling he may have had, and became as cold and hard as iron. It was impossible, at first, as I stood before him, to seem indifferent. I distinctly saw his human nature asserting its conviction against the slave system, which made cases like mine possible; but, as I have said, humanity fell before the systematic tyranny of slavery. He first walked the floor, apparently much agitated by my story, and the spectacle I presented, but soon it was his turn to talk. He began moderately by finding excuses for Covey, and ended with a full justification of him, and a passionate condemnation of me. He had no doubt I deserved the flogging. He did not believe I was sick—I was only endeavoring to get rid of work. My dizziness was laziness, and Covey did right to flog me as he had done. After thus fairly annihilating me, and arousing himself by his eloquence, he fiercely demanded what I wished him to do in the case! With such a knockdown to all my hopes, and feeling as I did my entire subjection to his power, I had very little heart to reply. I must not assert my innocence of the allegations he had piled up against me, for that would be impudence. The guilt of a slave was always and everywhere presumed, and the innocence of the slaveholder, or employer, was always asserted. The word of the slave against this presumption was generally treated as impudence, worthy of punishment. "Do you dare to contradict me, you rascal?" was a final silencer of counter-statements from the lips of a slave. Calming down a little, in view of my silence and hesitation, and perhaps a little touched at my forlorn and miserable appearance, he inquired again, what I wanted him to do? Thus invited a second time, I told him I wished him to allow me to get a new home, and to find a new master; that as sure as I went back to live again with Mr. Covey, I should be killed by him; that he would never forgive my coming home with complaints; that since I had lived with him he had almost crushed my spirit, and I believed he would ruin me for future service and that my life was not safe in his hands. This Master Thomas (*my brother in the church*) regarded as "nonsense." There was no danger that Mr. Covey would kill me; he was a good man, industrious and religious, and he would not think of removing me from that home; "besides," said he—and this I found was the most distressing thought of all to him—"if you should leave Covey now that your year is but half expired, I should lose your wages for the entire year. You belong to Mr. Covey for one year, and you *must go back* to him, come what will, and you must not trouble me with any more stories; and if you don't go immediately home, I'll get hold of you myself." This was just what I expected when I found he had prejudged the case against me. "But, sir," I said, "I am sick and tired, and I cannot get home tonight." At this he somewhat relented, and finally allowed me to stay the night, but said I must be off early in the morning, and concluded his directions by making me swallow a huge dose of Epsom salts, which was about the only medicine ever administered to slaves.

It was quite natural for Master Thomas to presume I was feigning sickness to escape work, for he probably thought that were he in the place of a slave, with no wages for his work, no praise for well-doing, no motive for toil but the lash, he would try every possible scheme by which to escape labor. I say I have no doubt of this; the reason is, that there were not, under the whole heavens, a set of men who cultivated such a dread of labor as did the slaveholders. The charge of laziness against the slaves was ever on their lips and was the standing apology for every species of cruelty and brutality. These men did indeed literally "bind heavy burdens, grievous to be borne, and laid them upon men's shoulders, but they themselves would not move them with one of their fingers."[2]

Chapter 17
The Last Flogging

Sleep does not always come to the relief of the weary in body, and broken in spirit; especially is it so when past troubles only foreshadow coming disasters. My last hope had been extinguished. My master who I did not venture to hope would protect me *as a man*, had now refused to protect me *as his property*, and had cast me back, covered with reproaches and bruises, into the hands of one who was a stranger to that mercy which is the soul of the religion he professed. May the reader never know what it is to spend such a night as to me was that which heralded my return to the den of horrors from which I had made a temporary escape.

I remained—sleep I did not—all night at St. Michaels, and in the morning (Saturday) I started off, obedient to the order of Master Thomas, feeling that I had no friend on earth, and doubting if I had one in heaven. I reached Covey's about nine o'clock, and just as I stepped into the field, before I had reached the house, true to his snakish habits, Covey darted out at me from a fence-corner, in which he had secreted himself for the purpose of securing me. He was provided with a cowskin and a rope, and he evidently intended to tie me up, and wreak his vengeance on me to the fullest extent. I should have been an easy prey had he succeeded in getting his hands upon me, for I had taken no refreshment since noon on Friday, and this, with the other trying circumstances, had greatly reduced my strength. I, however, darted back into the woods before the ferocious hound could reach me, and buried myself in a thicket, where he lost sight of me. The cornfield afforded me shelter in getting to the woods. But for the tall corn, Covey would have overtaken me, and made me his captive. He was much chagrined that he did not, and

[2]Matthew 23:4.

gave up the chase very reluctantly, as I could see by his angry movements, as he returned to the house.

For a little time I was clear of Covey and his lash. I was in the wood, buried in its somber gloom and hushed in its solemn silence, hidden from all human eyes, shut in with nature and with nature's God, and absent from all human contrivances. Here was a good place to pray, to pray for help, for deliverance—a prayer I had often made before. But how could I pray? Covey could pray—Capt. Auld could pray. I would fain pray; but doubts arising, partly from my neglect of the means of grace and partly from the sham religion which everywhere prevailed there was awakened in my mind a distrust of all religion and the conviction that prayers were unavailing and delusive.

Life in itself had almost become burdensome to me. All my outward relations were against me. I must stay here and starve, or go home to Covey's and have my flesh torn to pieces and my spirit humbled under his cruel lash. These were the alternatives before me. The day was long and irksome. I was weak from the toils of the previous day and from want of food and sleep, and I had been so little concerned about my appearance that I had not yet washed the blood from my garments. I was an object of horror, even to myself. Life in Baltimore, when most oppressive, was a paradise to this. What had I done, what had my parents done, that such a life as this should be mine? That day, in the woods, I would have exchanged my manhood for the brutehood of an ox.

Night came. I was still in the woods, and still unresolved what to do. Hunger had not yet pinched me to the point of going home, and I laid myself down in the leaves to rest, for I had been watching for hunters all day, but not being molested by them during the day, I expected no disturbance from them during the night. I had come to the conclusion that Covey relied upon hunger to drive me home, and in this I was quite correct, for he made no effort to catch me after the morning.

During the night I heard the step of a man in the woods. He was coming toward the place where I lay. A person lying still in the woods in the daytime has the advantage over one walking, and this advantage is much greater at night. I was not able to engage in a physical struggle, and I had recourse to the common resort of the weak. I hid myself in the leaves to prevent discovery. But as the night rambler in the woods drew nearer I found him to be a friend, not an enemy, a slave of Mrs. William Groomes of Easton, and kind-hearted fellow named "Sandy." Sandy lived that year with Mr. Kemp, about four miles from St. Michaels. He, like myself, had been hired out, but unlike myself had not been hired out to be broken. He was the husband of a free woman who lived in the lower part of Poppie Neck, and he was now on his way through the woods to see her and to spend the Sabbath with her.

As soon as I had ascertained that the disturber of my solitude was not an enemy, but the good-hearted Sandy,—a man as famous among the slaves of the neighborhood for his own good nature as for his good sense—I came out from my hiding-place and made myself known to him. I explained the circumstances of the past two days, which had driven me to the woods, and he deeply compassionated my distress. It was a bold thing for him to shelter me, and I could not ask him to do so, for had I been found in his hut he would have suffered the penalty of thirty-nine lashes on his bare back, if not something worse. But Sandy was too generous to permit the fear of punishment to prevent his relieving a brother bondman from hunger and exposure, and therefore, on his own motion, I accompanied him home to his wife—for the house and lot were hers, as she was a free woman. It was about midnight, but his wife was called up, a fire was made, some Indian meal was soon mixed with salt and water, and an ash cake was baked in a hurry, to relieve my hunger. Sandy's wife was not behind him in kindness; both seemed to esteem it a privilege to succor me, for although I was hated by Covey and by my master, I was loved by the colored people, because they thought I was hated for my knowledge, and persecuted because I was feared. I was the only slave in that region who could read or write. There had been one other man, belonging to Mr. Hugh Hamilton, who could read, but he, poor fellow, had, shortly after coming into the neighborhood, been sold off to the far south. I saw him in the cart, to be carried to Easton for sale, ironed and pinioned like a yearling for the slaughter. My knowledge was now the pride of my brother slaves, and no doubt Sandy felt on that account something of the general interest in me. The supper was soon ready, and though over the sea I have since feasted with honorables, lord mayors and aldermen, my supper on ash cake and cold water, with Sandy, was the meal of all my life most sweet to my taste and now most vivid to my memory.

Supper over, Sandy and I went into a discussion of what was possible for me, under the perils and hardships which overshadowed my path. The question was, must I go back to Covey, or must I attempt to run away? Upon a careful survey the latter was found to be impossible, for I was on a narrow neck of land, every avenue from which would bring me in sight of pursuers. There was Chesapeake Bay to the right, and "Pot-pie" River to the left, and St. Michaels and its neighborhood occupied the only space through which there was any retreat.

I found Sandy an odd adviser. He was not only a religious man, but he professed to believe in a system for which I have no name. He was a genuine African, and had inherited some of the so-called magical powers said to be possessed by the eastern nations. He told me that he could help me, that in those very woods there was an herb which in the morning might be found, possessing all the powers required for my protection (I put his words in my own language), and that if I would take his advice he would procure me the root of the herb of which he spoke. He told me, further, that if I would take that root and wear it on my right side it would be impossible for Covey to strike me a blow, and that, with this root about my person, no white man could whip me. He said he had carried it for years, and that he had fully tested its virtues. He had never received a blow from a slaveholder since he carried it, and he never expected to receive one, for he meant always to carry that root for protection. He knew Covey well, for Mrs. Covey was the daughter of Mrs. Kemp, and he (Sandy) had heard of the barbarous treatment to which I had been subjected, and he wanted to do something for me.

Now all this talk about the root was to me very absurd and ridiculous, if not positively sinful. I at first rejected the idea that the simple carrying of a root on my right side (a root, by the way, over which I walked every time I went into the woods) could possess any such magic power as he ascribed to it, and I was, therefore, not disposed to cumber my pocket with it. I had a positive aversion to all pretenders to "divination." It was beneath one of my intelligence to countenance such dealings with the devil as this power implied. But with all my learning—it was really precious little—Sandy was more than a match for me. "My book-learning," he said, "had not kept Covey off me" (a powerful argument just then), and he entreated me, with flashing eyes, to try this. If it did me no good it could do me no harm, and it would cost me nothing any way. Sandy was so earnest and so confident of the good qualities of this weed that, to please him, I was induced to take it. He had been to me the good Samaritan, and had, almost providentially, found me and helped me when I could not help myself; how did I know but that the hand of the Lord was in it? With thoughts of this sort I took the roots from Sandy and put them in my right-hand pocket.

This was of course Sunday morning. Sandy now urged me to go home with all speed, and to walk up bravely to the house, as though nothing had happened. I saw in Sandy, with all his superstition, too deep an insight into human nature not to have some respect for his advice, and perhaps, too, a slight gleam or shadow of his superstition had fallen on me. At any rate, I started off toward Covey's, as directed. Having, the previous night, poured my griefs into Sandy's ears and enlisted him in my behalf, having made his wife a sharer in my sorrows, and having also become well refreshed by sleep and food, I moved off quite courageously toward the dreaded Covey's. Singularly enough, just as I entered the yard-gate I met him and his wife on their way to church, dressed in their Sunday best, and looking as smiling as angels. His manner perfectly astonished me. There was something really benignant in his countenance. He spoke to me as never before, told me that the pigs had got into the lot and he wished me to go to drive them out, inquired how I was, and seemed an altered man. This extraordinary conduct really made me begin to think that Sandy's herb had more virtue in it than I, in my pride, had been willing to allow, and, had the day been other than Sunday, I should have attributed Covey's altered manner solely to the power of the root. I suspected, however, that the Sabbath, not the root, was the real explanation of the change. His religion hindered him from breaking the Sabbath, but not from breaking my skin on any other day than Sunday. He had more respect for the day than for the man for whom the day was mercifully given, for while he would cut and slash my body during the week, he would on Sunday teach me the value of my soul, and the way of life and salvation by Jesus Christ.

All went well with me till Monday morning, and then, whether the root had lost its virtue, or whether my tormentor had gone deeper into the black art than I had (as was sometimes said of him), or whether he had obtained a special indulgence for his faithful Sunday's worship, it is not necessary for me to know or to inform the reader; but this much I may say, the pious and benignant smile which graced the face of Covey on Sunday wholly disappeared on Monday.

Long before daylight I was called up to go feed, rub, and curry the horses. I obeyed the call, as I should have done had it been made at an earlier hour, for I had brought to my mind a firm resolve during that Sunday's reflection to obey every order, however unreasonable, if it were possible, and if Mr. Covey should then undertake to beat me to defend and protect myself to the best of my ability. My religious views on the subject of resisting my master has suffered a serious shock by the savage persecution to which I had been subjected, and my hands were no longer tied by my religion. Master Thomas's indifference had severed the last link. I had backslidden from this point in the slaves' religious creed, and I soon had occasion to make my fallen state known to my Sunday-pious brother, Covey.

While I was obeying his order to feed and get the horses ready for the field, and when I was in the act of going up the stable-loft, for the purpose of throwing down some blades, Covey sneaked into the stable, in his peculiar way, and seizing me suddenly by the leg, he brought me to the stable-floor, giving my newly-mended body a terrible jar. I now forgot all about my roots, and remembered my pledge to stand up in my own defense. The brute was skillfully endeavoring to get a slipknot on my legs, before I could draw up my feet. As soon as I found what he was up to, I gave a sudden spring (my two days' rest had been of much service to me) and by that means, no doubt, he was able to bring me to the floor so heavily. He was defeated in his plan of tying me. While down, he seemed to think that he had me very securely in his power. He little thought he was—as the rowdies say—in for a rough and tumble fight, but such was the fact. Whence came the daring spirit necessary to grapple with a man who, eight-and-forty hours before, could, with his slightest word, have made me tremble like a leaf in a storm, I do not know; at any rate, I was resolved to fight, and what was better still, I actually was hard at it. The fighting madness had come upon me, and I found my strong fingers firmly attached to the throat of the tyrant, as heedless of consequences, at the moment, as if we stood as equals before the law. The very color of the man was forgotten. I felt supple as a cat, and was ready for him at every turn. Every blow of his was parried, though I dealt no blows in return. I was strictly on the defensive, preventing him from injuring me, rather than trying to injure him. I flung him on the ground several times when he meant to have hurled me there. I held him so firmly by the throat that his blood followed my nails. He held me and I held him.

All was fair thus far, and the contest was about equal. My resistance was entirely unexpected and Covey was taken all aback by it. He trembled in every limb. "Are you going to resist, you scoundrel?" said he. To which I returned a polite "Yes, sir," steadily gazing my interrogator in the eye, to meet the first approach or dawning of the blow which I expected my answer would call forth. But the conflict did not long remain equal. Covey soon cried lustily for help, not that I was obtaining any marked advantage over him, or was injuring him, but because he was gaining none over me, and was not able, single-handed, to conquer me. He called for his cousin Hughes to come to his assistance, and now the scene was changed. I was compelled to give blows, as well as to parry them, and since I was in any case to suffer for resistance, I felt (as the musty proverb goes) that I might as well be hanged for an old sheep as a lamb. I was still defensive toward Covey, but aggressive toward Hughes, on whom, at first approach, I dealt a blow which fairly sickened him. He went off, bending over with pain, and manifesting no disposition to come again within my reach. The poor fellow was in the act of trying to catch and tie my right hand, and while flattering himself with success, I gave him the kick which sent him staggering away in pain, at the same time that I held Covey with a firm hand.

Taken completely by surprise, Covey seemed to have lost his usual strength and coolness. He was frightened, and stood puffing and blowing, seemingly unable to command words or blows. When he saw that Hughes was standing half bent with pain, his courage quite gone, the cowardly tyrant asked if I meant to persist in my resistance. I told him I did mean to resist, come what might, that I had been treated like a brute during the last six months, and that I should stand it no longer. With that he gave me a shake, and attempted to drag me toward a stick of wood that was lying just outside the stable-door. He meant to knock me down with it, but, just as he leaned over to get the stick, I seized him with both hands, by the collar, and with a vigorous and sudden snatch brought my assailant harmlessly, his full length, on the not over-clean ground, for we were now in the cowyard. He had selected the place for the fight, and it was but right that he should have all the advantages of his own selection.

By this time Bill, the hired man, came home. He had been to Mr. Helmsley's to spend Sunday with his nominal wife. Covey and I had been skirmishing from before daybreak till now. The sun was shooting his beams almost over the eastern woods, and we were still at it. I could not see where the matter was to terminate. He evidently was afraid to let me go, lest I should again make off to the woods, otherwise he would probably have obtained arms from the house to frighten me. Holding me, he called upon Bill to assist him. The scene had something comic about it. Bill, who knew precisely what Covey wished him to do, affected ignorance, and pretended he did not know what to do. "What shall I do, Master Covey?" said Bill. "Take hold of him! Take hold of him!" cried Covey. With a toss of his head, peculiar to Bill, he said: "Indeed, Master Covey, I want to go to work." "This is your work," said Covey, "take hold of him." Bill replied, with spirit, "My master hired me here to work, and not to help you whip Frederick." It was my turn to speak. "Bill," said I, "don't put your hands on me." To which he replied, "My God, Frederick, I ain't goin' to tech ye"; and Bill walked off, leaving Covey and myself to settle our differences as best we might.

But my present advantage was threatened when I saw Caroline (the slave woman of Covey) coming to the cowyard to milk, for she was a powerful woman, and could have mastered me easily, exhausted as I was.

As soon as she came near, Covey attempted to rally her to his aid. Strangely and fortunately, Caroline was in no humor to take a hand in any such sport. We were all in open rebellion that morning. Caroline answered the command of her master to "take hold of me," precisely as Bill had done, but in her it was at far greater peril, for she was the slave of Covey, and he could do what he pleased with her. It was not so with Bill, and Bill knew it. Samuel Harris, to whom Bill belonged, did not allow his slaves to be beaten unless they were guilty of some crime which the law would punish. But poor Caroline, like myself, was at the mercy of the merciless Covey, nor did she escape the dire effects of her refusal: he gave her several sharp blows.

At length (two hours had elapsed) the contest was given over. Letting go of me, puffing and blowing at a great rate, Covey said, "Now, you scoundrel, go to your work; I would not have whipped you half so hard if you had not resisted." The fact was, he had not whipped me at all. He had not, in all the scuffle, drawn a single drop of blood from me. I had drawn blood from him, and should even without this satisfaction have been victorious, because my aim had not been to injure him, but to prevent his injuring me.

During the whole six months that I lived with Covey after this transaction, he never again laid the weight of his finger on me in anger. He would occasionally say he did not want to have to get hold of me again—a declaration which I had no difficulty in believing—and I had a secret feeling which answered, "You had better not wish to get hold of me again, for you will be likely to come off worse in a second fight than you did in the first."

This battle with Mr. Covey, undignified as it was and as I fear my narration of it is, was the turning-point in my "life as a slave." It rekindled in my breast the smouldering embers of liberty. It brought up my Baltimore dreams and revived a sense of my own manhood. I was a changed being after that fight. I was nothing before—I was a man now. It recalled to life my crushed self-respect, and my self-confidence, and inspired me with a renewed determination to be a free man. A man without force is without the essential dignity of humanity. Human nature is so constituted, that it cannot honor a helpless man, though it can pity him, and even this it cannot do long if signs of power do not arise.

He only can understand the effect of this combat on my spirit, who has himself incurred something, or hazarded something, in repelling the unjust and cruel aggressions of a tyrant. Covey was a tyrant and a cowardly one withal. After resisting him, I felt as I had never felt before. It was a resurrection from the dark and pestiferous tomb of slavery, to the heaven of comparative freedom. I was no longer a servile coward, trembling under the frown of a brother worm of the dust, but my long-cowed spirit was roused to an attitude of independence. I had reached the point at which I was *not afraid to die.* This spirit made me a freeman in *fact*, though I still remained a slave in *form.* When a slave cannot be flogged, he is more than half free. He has a domain as broad as his own manly heart to defend, and he is really "a power on earth." From this time until my escape from slavery, I was never fairly whipped. Several attempts were made, but they were always unsuccessful. Bruised I did get, but the instance I have described was the end of the brutification to which slavery had subjected me.

The reader may like to know why, after I had so grievously offended Mr. Covey, he did not have me taken in hand by the authorities; indeed, why the law of Maryland, which assigned hanging to the slave who resisted his master, was not put in force against me; at any rate why I was not taken up, as was usual in such cases, and publicly whipped as an example to other slaves, and as a means of deterring me from again committing the same offence. I confess that the easy manner in which I got off was always a surprise to me, and even now I cannot fully explain the cause, though the probability is that Covey was ashamed to have it known that he had been mastered by a boy of sixteen. He enjoyed the unbounded and very valuable reputation of being a first-rate overseer and Negro-breaker, and by means of his reputation he was able to procure his hands at very trifling compensation and with very great ease. His interest and his pride would mutually suggest the wisdom of passing the matter by in silence. The story that he had undertaken to whip a lad and had been resisted would of itself be damaging to him in the estimation of slaveholders.

It is perhaps not altogether creditable to my natural temper that after the conflict with Mr. Covey I did, at times, purposely aim to provoke him to an attack, by refusing to keep with the other hands in the field, but I could never bully him to another battle. I was determined on doing him serious damage if he ever again attempted to lay violent hands on me.

> Hereditary bondmen, know ye not
> Who would be free, themselves must strike the blow?[1]

1892

[1]From *Childe Harold's Pilgrimage* (Canto II, line 76), 1812–1818, by the English poet George Gordon, Lord Byron (1788–1824).

Harriet Ann Jacobs 1813–1897

I was born a slave; but I never knew it till six years of happy childhood had passed away.

So begins Harriet Jacobs's narrative of her life as a slave in North Carolina, of her rebellion against a cruel and debauched master, and of her eventual escape to the free states of the North. In the first years of her childhood she lived with her parents, but when she was six her mother died, and Harriet was taken from her home and sent to work in the household of the white family that had owned her mother.

Harriet's new mistress treated her well, taught her to read and spell, and trained her to be a seamstress. But six years later her mistress died, and twelve-year-old Harriet was willed to the young daughter of a local physician. It was there, in the house of the man she called Dr. Flint in her narrative, that the terrifying experiences began that almost overwhelmed her. With daily threats and entreaties, her new master sought to seduce her, to establish her in a separate house, away from the eyes of his jealous wife, where Harriet would attend him as his mistress, his concubine.

She was a slave, the daughter of slaves, with almost no legal rights. She was protected neither by the social customs of the slave society in which she lived nor by a system of laws that considered her to be not a human being with inalienable rights but a piece of property. No law protected her from her master's fury. No appeal to decency could subdue his lust. She had little to rely upon but her own guile and determination.

Because she was forbidden to marry, and to thwart her white master's continual attempts to subdue her, Harriet Jacobs became the mistress of another white man, a respected citizen of the town, and by him had two children. And she began to plot her own escape. In 1835 she went into hiding, in the attic of her grandmother's house. According to her narrative she remained there for seven years, until 1842, when local friends and anti-slavery organizations in the North helped her escape to the free states and establish herself in New York City. She became a children's nurse, but she continued to be harried by slavecatchers sent to the North by Dr. Flint and his family to recover their valuable piece of escaped property.

Early in her escape her owners had published an announcement offering a reward for her capture and her return. She was described as "a light mulatto" who

> *speaks easily and fluently, and has an agreeable carriage and address. Being a good seamstress, she had been accustomed to dress well, has a variety of very fine clothes, made in the prevailing fashion, and will probably appear, if abroad, tricked out in gay and fashionable finery.*

After Harriet Jacobs had lived for a decade in New York City, where she was reunited with her children, her employer bought her from her former owners and set her free. The following year she began to write her narrative, and in 1861 it was published as Incidents in the Life of a Slave Girl: Written by Herself.

Harriet Jacobs's story of her life as a slave and of her escape to freedom was one of many slave narratives published in the years preceding the American Civil War. But unlike many others, it was not a tale of brutal physical tortures, of agonizing labors, of whippings and starvation. Instead she emphasized the psychological torments suffered by slaves, the moral degradation suffered by slave women who could be sexually exploited by their white masters, and the jealous fury of white mistresses who saw and could not obstruct the attention paid to slave women by white husbands and sons.

When Incidents in the Life of a Slave Girl *was first published, many readers expressed doubts about its authenticity. It seemed the product of a formally educated mind. Some of its details—such as her claim that she had spent seven years hiding in the small attic of her grandmother's home—seemed dubious. And to protect those she had left behind, she had used false names for all her characters—there was no actual escaped slave named Linda Brent, no Dr. Flint her tormentor, no Mrs. Bruce her savior. But later scholarship has shown that events Harriet Jacobs described and characters she portrayed were real.*

The publication of Harriet Jacobs's book was overshadowed by the onset of the Civil War. By 1897, when she died, her narrative had almost been forgotten. But with the rise of movements for civil rights and women's rights in the late twentieth century, her story has received renewed interest. Her book has been republished and selections from it appear in public schoolbooks and readers. And scholars have begun to illuminate her life and the lives of other slaves, many of them women like Harriet Jacobs, who rose from the terrors of slavery and found the freedom that stirred them to sing out the famous lines:

Free at last, free at last.
Thank God almighty I am free at last.

FURTHER READING: *The Slave's Narrative,* ed. C. Davis and H. Gates, 1985; W. Andrews, *To Tell a Free Story, The First Century of Afro-American Autobiography, 1760–1865,* 1986; H. Carby, *Reconstructing Womanhood,* 1987; V. Smith, *Self-Discovery and Authority in Afro-American Narrative,* 1988; *Harriet Jacobs, New Critical Essays,* ed. D. Garfield and R. Zafar, 1995; *Harriet Jacobs and Incidents in the Life of a Slave Girl,* ed. R. Zarfar and D. Garfield, 1996; Y. Johnson, *The Voices of African-American Women,* 1999; F. Yellin, *Harriet Jacobs, A Life,* 2003, 2005.

TEXT: *Incidents in the Life of a Slave Girl: Written by Herself,* 1861. Some punctuation and spelling have been changed to conform more nearly to modern practice.

from *INCIDENTS IN THE LIFE OF A SLAVE GIRL*

I
CHILDHOOD

I was born a slave; but I never knew it till six years of happy childhood had passed away. My father was a carpenter, and considered so intelligent and skilful in his trade, that, when buildings out of the common line were to be erected, he was sent for from long distances, to be head workman. On condition of paying his mistress two hundred dollars a year, and supporting himself, he was allowed to work at his trade and manage his own affairs. His strongest wish was to purchase his children; but, though he several times offered his hard earnings for that purpose, he never succeeded. In complexion my parents were a light shade of brownish yellow, and were termed mulattoes. They lived together in a comfortable home; and, though we were all slaves, I was so fondly shielded that I never dreamed I was a piece of merchandise, trusted to them for safe keeping, and liable to be demanded of them at any moment. I had one brother, William, who was two years younger than myself—a bright, affectionate child. I had also a great treasure in my maternal grandmother, who was a remarkable woman in many respects. She was the daughter of a planter in South Carolina, who, at his death, left her mother and his three children free, with money to go to St. Augustine, where they had relatives. It was during the Revolutionary War; and they were captured on their passage, carried back, and sold to different purchasers. Such was the story my grandmother used to tell me; but I do not remember all the particulars. She was a little girl when she was captured and sold to the keeper of a large hotel. I have often heard her tell how hard she fared during childhood. But as she grew older she evinced so much intelligence, and was so faithful, that her master and mistress could not help seeing it was for their interest to take care of such a valuable piece of property. She became an indispensable personage in the household, officiating in all capacities, from cook and wet nurse[1] to seamstress. She was much praised for her cooking; and her nice crackers became so famous in the neighborhood that many people were desirous of obtaining them. In consequence of numerous requests of this kind, she asked permission of her mistress to bake crackers at night, after all the household work was done; and she obtained leave to do it, provided she would clothe herself and her children from the profits. Upon these terms, after working hard all day for her mistress, she began her midnight bakings, assisted by her two oldest children. The business proved profitable; and each year she laid by a little which was saved for a fund to purchase her children. Her master died, and the property was divided among his heirs. The widow had her dower[2] in the hotel, which she continued to keep open. My grandmother remained in her service as a slave; but her children were divided among her master's children. As she had five, Benjamin, the youngest one, was sold, in order that each heir might have an equal portion of dollars and cents. There was so little difference in our ages that he seemed more like my brother than my uncle. He was a bright, handsome lad, nearly white; for he inherited the complexion my grandmother had derived from Anglo-Saxon ancestors. Though [he was] only ten years old, seven hundred and twenty dollars were paid for him. His sale was a terrible blow to my grandmother; but she was naturally hopeful, and she went to work with renewed energy, trusting in time to be able to purchase some of her children. She had laid up three hundred dollars, which her mistress one day begged as a loan, promising to pay her soon. The reader probably knows that no promise or writing given to a slave is legally binding; for, according to Southern laws, a slave, *being* property, can *hold* no property. When my grandmother lent her hard earnings to her mistress, she trusted solely to her honor. The honor of a slaveholder to a slave!

To this good grandmother I was indebted for many comforts. My brother Willie and I often received portions of the crackers, cakes, and preserves, she made to sell; and after we ceased to be children we were indebted to her for many more important services.

Such were the unusually fortunate circumstances of my early childhood. When I was six years old, my mother died; and then, for the first time, I learned, by the talk around me, that I was a slave. My mother's mistress was

[1]A woman who suckles the children of other women.
[2]The portion of a dead man's estate that is required by law to be given to his widow.

the daughter of my grandmother's mistress. She was the foster sister of my mother; they were both nourished at my grandmother's breast. In fact, my mother had been weaned at three months old, that the babe of the mistress might obtain sufficient food. They played together as children; and, when they became women, my mother was a most faithful servant to her whiter foster sister. On her death-bed her mistress promised that her children should never suffer for any thing; and during her lifetime she kept her word. They all spoke kindly of my dead mother, who had been a slave merely in name, but in nature was noble and womanly. I grieved for her, and my young mind was troubled with the thought who would now take care of me and my little brother. I was told that my home was now to be with her mistress; and I found it a happy one. No toilsome or disagreeable duties were imposed upon me. My mistress was so kind to me that I was always glad to do her bidding and proud to labor for her as much as my young years would permit. I would sit by her side for hours, sewing diligently, with a heart as free from care as that of any free-born white child. When she thought I was tired, she would send me out to run and jump; and away I bounded, to gather berries or flowers to decorate her room. Those were happy days—too happy to last. The slave child had no thought for the morrow; but there came that blight, which too surely waits on every human being born to be a chattel.

When I was nearly twelve years old, my kind mistress sickened and died. As I saw the cheek grow paler, and the eye more glassy, how earnestly I prayed in my heart that she might live! I loved her; for she had been almost like a mother to me. My prayers were not answered. She died, and they buried her in the little churchyard, where, day after day, my tears fell upon her grave.

I was sent to spend a week with my grandmother.[3] I was now old enough to begin to think of the future; and again and again I asked myself what they would do with me. I felt sure I should never find another mistress so kind as the one who was gone. She had promised my dying mother that her children should never suffer for any thing; and when I remembered that, and recalled her many proofs of attachment to me, I could not help having some hopes that she had left me free. My friends were almost certain it would be so. They thought she would be sure to do it, on account of my mother's love and faithful service. But, alas! we all know that the memory of a faithful slave does not avail much to save her children from the auction block.

After a brief period of suspense, the will of my mistress was read, and we learned that she had bequeathed me to her sister's daughter, a child of five years old. So vanished our hopes. My mistress had taught me the precepts of God's Word: "Thou shalt love thy neighbor as thyself."[4] "Whatsoever ye would that men should do unto you, do ye even so unto them."[5] But I was her slave, and I suppose she did not recognize me as her neighbor. I would give much to blot out from my memory that one great wrong. As a child, I loved my mistress; and, looking back on the happy days I spent with her, I try to think with less bitterness of this act of injustice. While I was with her, she taught me to read and spell; and for this privilege, which so rarely falls to the lot of a slave, I bless her memory.

[3]Linda Brent's grandmother, formerly a slave, had been granted her freedom.
[4]Mark 12:31. [5]Matthew 7:12.

She possessed but few slaves; and at her death those were all distributed among her relatives. Five of them were my grandmother's children, and had shared the same milk that nourished her mother's children. Notwithstanding my grandmother's long and faithful service to her owners, not one of her children escaped the auction block. These God-breathing machines are no more, in the sight of their masters, than the cotton they plant, or the horses they tend.

V
THE TRIALS OF GIRLHOOD

During the first years of my service in Dr. Flint's family,[1] I was accustomed to share some indulgences with the children of my mistress. Though this seemed to me no more than right, I was grateful for it and tried to merit the kindness by the faithful discharge of my duties. But I now entered on my fifteenth year—a sad epoch in the life of a slave girl. My master began to whisper foul words in my ear. Young as I was, I could not remain ignorant of their import. I tried to treat them with indifference or contempt. The master's age, my extreme youth, and the fear that his conduct would be reported to my grandmother, made him bear this treatment for many months. He was a crafty man and resorted to many means to accomplish his purposes. Sometimes he had stormy, terrific ways that made his victims tremble; sometimes he assumed a gentleness that he thought must surely subdue. Of the two, I preferred his stormy moods, although they left me trembling. He tried his utmost to corrupt the pure principles my grandmother had instilled. He peopled my young mind with unclean images, such as only a vile monster could think of. I turned from him with disgust and hatred. But he was my master. I was compelled to live under the same roof with him—where I saw a man forty years my senior daily violating the most sacred commandments of nature. He told me I was his property; that I must be subject to his will in all things. My soul revolted against the mean tyranny. But where could I turn for protection? No matter whether the slave girl be as black as ebony or as fair as her mistress. In either case, there is no shadow of law to protect her from insult, from violence, or even from death; all these are inflicted by fiends who bear the shape of men. The mistress, who ought to protect the helpless victim, has no other feelings towards her but those of jealousy and rage. The degradation, the wrongs, the vices, that grow out of slavery, are more than I can describe. They are greater than you would willingly believe. Surely, if you credited one half the truths that are told you concerning the helpless millions suffering in this cruel bondage, you at the North would not help to tighten the yoke. You surely would refuse to do for the master, on your own soil, the mean and cruel work which trained bloodhounds and the lowest class of whites do for him at the South.[2]

[1]Linda Brent was bequeathed by her mistress to the niece of her mistress, the daughter of Dr. John Flint, who lived nearby.

[2]The Fugitive Slave Law of 1850 gave slaveholders the right to recapture escaped slaves in northern free states and return them to the South. Public officials of free states were required to assist slavecatchers in their pursuit of fugitive slaves. Officials and citizens who refused to give assistance were legally subject to fines and imprisonment.

Everywhere the years bring to all enough of sin and sorrow; but in slavery the very dawn of life is darkened by these shadows. Even the little child, who is accustomed to wait on her mistress and her children, will learn, before she is twelve years old, why it is that her mistress hates such and such a one among the slaves. Perhaps the child's own mother is among those hated ones. She listens to violent outbreaks of jealous passion and cannot help understanding what is the cause. She will become prematurely knowing in evil things. Soon she will learn to tremble when she hears her master's footfall. She will be compelled to realize that she is no longer a child. If God has bestowed beauty upon her, it will prove her greatest curse. That which commands admiration in the white woman only hastens the degradation of the female slave. I know that some are too much brutalized by slavery to feel the humiliation of their position; but many slaves feel it most acutely and shrink from the memory of it. I cannot tell how much I suffered in the presence of these wrongs nor how I am still pained by the retrospect. My master met me at every turn, reminding me that I belonged to him and swearing by heaven and earth that he would compel me to submit to him. If I went out for a breath of fresh air, after a day of unwearied toil, his footsteps dogged me. If I knelt by my mother's grave, his dark shadow fell on me even there. The light heart which nature had given me became heavy with sad forebodings. The other slaves in my master's house noticed the change. Many of them pitied me; but none dared to ask the cause. They had no need to inquire. They knew too well the guilty practices under that roof; and they were aware that to speak of them was an offence that never went unpunished.

I longed for some one to confide in. I would have given the world to have laid my head on my grandmother's faithful bosom, and told her all my troubles. But Dr. Flint swore he would kill me, if I was not as silent as the grave. Then, although my grandmother was all in all to me, I feared her as well as loved her. I had been accustomed to look up to her with a respect bordering upon awe. I was very young, and felt shamefaced about telling her such impure things, especially as I knew her to be very strict on such subjects. Moreover, she was a woman of a high spirit. She was usually very quiet in her demeanor; but if her indignation was once roused, it was not very easily quelled. I had been told that she once chased a white gentleman with a loaded pistol because he insulted one of her daughters. I dreaded the consequences of a violent outbreak; and both pride and fear kept me silent. But though I did not confide in my grandmother, and even evaded her vigilant watchfulness and inquiry, her presence in the neighborhood was some protection to me. Though she had been a slave, Dr. Flint was afraid of her. He dreaded her scorching rebukes. Moreover, she was known and patronized by many people; and he did not wish to have his villainy made public. It was lucky for me that I did not live on a distant plantation but in a town not so large that the inhabitants were ignorant of each other's affairs. Bad as are the laws and customs in a slaveholding community, the doctor, as a professional man, deemed it prudent to keep up some outward show of decency.

O, what days and nights of fear and sorrow that man caused me! Reader, it is not to awaken sympathy for myself that I am telling you truthfully what I suffered in slavery. I do it to kindle a flame of compassion in your hearts for my sisters who are still in bondage, suffering as I once suffered.

I once saw two beautiful children playing together. One was a fair white child; the other was her slave and also her sister. When I saw them embracing each other and heard their joyous laughter, I turned sadly away from the lovely sight. I foresaw the inevitable blight that would fall on the little slave's heart. I knew how soon her laughter would be changed to sighs. The fair child grew up to be a still fairer woman. From childhood to womanhood her pathway was blooming with flowers and overarched by a sunny sky. Scarcely one day of her life had been clouded when the sun rose on her happy bridal morning.

How had those years dealt with her slave sister, the little playmate of her childhood? She, also, was very beautiful; but the flowers and sunshine of love were not for her. She drank the cup of sin, and shame, and misery, whereof her persecuted race are compelled to drink.

In view of these things, why are ye silent, ye free men and women of the North? Why do your tongues falter in maintenance of the right? Would that I had more ability! But my heart is so full, and my pen is so weak! There are noble men and women who plead for us, striving to help those who cannot help themselves. God bless them! God give them strength and courage to go on! God bless those, everywhere, who are laboring to advance the cause of humanity!

VI
THE JEALOUS MISTRESS

I would ten thousand times rather that my children should be the half-starved paupers of Ireland than to be the most pampered among the slaves of America.[1] I would rather drudge out my life on a cotton plantation, till the grave opened to give me rest, than to live with an unprincipled master and a jealous mistress. The felon's home in a penitentiary is preferable. He may repent, and turn from the error of his ways, and so find peace; but it is not so with a favorite slave. She is not allowed to have any pride of character. It is deemed a crime in her to wish to be virtuous.

Mrs. Flint possessed the key to her husband's character before I was born. She might have used this knowledge to counsel and to screen the young and the innocent among her slaves; but for them she had no sympathy. They were the objects of her constant suspicion and malevolence. She watched her husband with unceasing vigilance; but he was well practised in means to evade it. What he could not find opportunity to say in words he manifested in signs. He invented more than were ever thought of in a deaf and dumb asylum. I let them pass, as if I did not understand what he meant; and many were the curses and threats bestowed on me for my stupidity. One day he caught me teaching myself to write. He frowned, as if he was not well pleased; but I suppose he came to the conclusion that such an accomplishment might help to advance his favorite scheme. Before long, notes were often slipped into my hand. I would return them, saying "I can't read them,

[1]The sufferings of the Irish during the potato famines of the nineteenth century were widely publicized in the United States.

sir." "Can't you?" he replied; "then I must read them to you." He always finished the reading by asking, "Do you understand?" Sometimes he would complain of the heat of the tea room and order his supper to be placed on a small table in the piazza. He would seat himself there with a well-satisfied smile and tell me to stand by and brush away the flies. He would eat very slowly, pausing between the mouthfuls. These intervals were employed in describing the happiness I was so foolishly throwing away and in threatening me with the penalty that finally awaited my stubborn disobedience. He boasted much of the forbearance he had exercised towards me and reminded me that there was a limit to his patience. When I succeeded in avoiding opportunities for him to talk to me at home, I was ordered to come to his office, to do some errand. When there, I was obliged to stand and listen to such language as he saw fit to address to me. Sometimes I so openly expressed my contempt for him that he would become violently enraged, and I wondered why he did not strike me. Circumstanced as he was, he probably thought it was better policy to be forbearing. But the state of things grew worse and worse daily. In desperation I told him that I must and would apply to my grandmother for protection. He threatened me with death, and worse than death, if I made any complaint to her. Strange to say, I did not despair. I was naturally of a buoyant disposition, and always I had a hope of somehow getting out of his clutches. Like many a poor, simple slave before me, I trusted that some threads of joy would yet be woven into my dark destiny.

I had entered my sixteenth year, and every day it became more apparent that my presence was intolerable to Mrs. Flint. Angry words frequently passed between her and her husband. He had never punished me himself, and he would not allow anybody else to punish me. In that respect, she was never satisfied; but, in her angry moods, no terms were too vile for her to bestow upon me. Yet I, whom she detested so bitterly, had far more pity for her than he had, whose duty it was to make her life happy. I never wronged her or wished to wrong her; and one word of kindness from her would have brought me to her feet.

After repeated quarrels between the doctor and his wife, he announced his intention to take his youngest daughter, then four years old, to sleep in his apartment.[2] It was necessary that a servant should sleep in the same room, to be on hand if the child stirred. I was selected for that office and informed for what purpose that arrangement had been made. By managing to keep within sight of people, as much as possible, during the day time, I had hitherto succeeded in eluding my master, though a razor was often held to my throat to force me to change this line of policy. At night I slept by the side of my great aunt, where I felt safe. He was too prudent to come into her room. She was an old woman and had been in the family many years. Moreover, as a married man, and a professional man, he deemed it necessary to save appearances in some degree. But he resolved to remove the obstacle in the way of his scheme; and he thought he had planned it so that he should evade suspicion. He was well aware how much I prized my refuge by the side of my old aunt, and he determined to dispossess me of it. The first night the doctor had the little child in his room alone. The next morning, I was ordered to

[2]I.e., his separate, private rooms in the house.

take my station as nurse the following night. A kind Providence interposed in my favor. During the day Mrs. Flint heard of this new arrangement, and a storm followed. I rejoiced to hear it rage.

After a while my mistress sent for me to come to her room. Her first question was, "Did you know you were to sleep in the doctor's room?"

"Yes, ma'am."

"Who told you?"

"My master."

"Will you answer truly all the questions I ask?"

"Yes, ma'am."

"Tell me, then, as you hope to be forgiven, are you innocent of what I have accused you?"

"I am."

She handed me a Bible, and said, "Lay your hand on your heart, kiss this holy book, and swear before God that you tell me the truth."

I took the oath she required, and I did it with a clear conscience.

"You have taken God's holy word to testify your innocence," said she. "If you have deceived me, beware! Now take this stool, sit down, look me directly in the face, and tell me all that has passed between your master and you."

I did as she ordered. As I went on with my account her color changed frequently, she wept and sometimes groaned. She spoke in tones so sad that I was touched by her grief. The tears came to my eyes; but I was soon convinced that her emotions arose from anger and wounded pride. She felt that her marriage vows were desecrated, her dignity insulted; but she had no compassion for the poor victim of her husband's perfidy. She pitied herself as a martyr; but she was incapable of feeling for the condition of shame and misery in which her unfortunate, helpless slave was placed.

Yet perhaps she had some touch of feeling for me; for when the conference was ended, she spoke kindly and promised to protect me. I should have been much comforted by this assurance if I could have had confidence in it; but my experiences in slavery had filled me with distrust. She was not a very refined woman and had not much control over her passions. I was an object of her jealousy and, consequently, of her hatred; and I knew I could not expect kindness or confidence from her under the circumstances in which I was placed. I could not blame her. Slaveholders' wives feel as other women would under similar circumstances. The fire of her temper kindled from small sparks, and now the flame became so intense that the doctor was obliged to give up his intended arrangement.

I knew I had ignited the torch, and I expected to suffer for it afterwards; but I felt too thankful to my mistress for the timely aid she rendered me to care much about that. She now took me to sleep in a room adjoining her own. There I was an object of her especial care, though not of her especial comfort, for she spent many a sleepless night to watch over me. Sometimes I woke up, and found her bending over me. At other times she whispered in my ear, as though it was her husband who was speaking to me, and listened to hear what I would answer. If she startled me, on such occasions, she would glide stealthily away; and the next morning she would tell me I had been talking in my sleep and ask who I was talking to. At last, I began to be fearful for my life. It had been often threatened; and you can imagine, better than I can describe, what an unpleasant sensation it must produce to wake up in the dead of night and find a jealous woman bending over you. Terrible as this experience was, I had fears that it would give place to one more terrible.

My mistress grew weary of her vigils; they did not prove satisfactory. She changed her tactics. She now tried the trick of accusing my master of crime, in my presence, and gave my name as the author of the accusation. To my utter astonishment, he replied, "I don't believe it: but if she did acknowledge it, you tortured her into exposing me." Tortured into exposing him! Truly, Satan had no difficulty in distinguishing the color of his soul! I understood his object in making this false representation. It was to show me that I gained nothing by seeking the protection of my mistress, that the power was still all in his own hands. I pitied Mrs. Flint. She was a second wife, many years the junior of her husband; and the hoary-headed[3] miscreant was enough to try the patience of a wiser and better woman. She was completely foiled and knew not how to proceed. She would gladly have had me flogged for my supposed false oath; but, as I have already stated, the doctor never allowed anyone to whip me. The old sinner was politic. The application of the lash might have led to remarks that would have exposed him in the eyes of his children and grandchildren. How often did I rejoice that I lived in a town where all the inhabitants knew each other! If I had been on a remote plantation, or lost among the multitude of a crowded city, I should not be a living woman at this day.

The secrets of slavery are concealed like those of the Inquisition.[4] My master was, to my knowledge, the father of eleven slaves. But did the mothers dare to tell who was the father of their children? Did the other slaves dare to allude to it, except in whispers among themselves? No, indeed! They knew too well the terrible consequences.

My grandmother could not avoid seeing things which excited her suspicions. She was uneasy about me, and tried various ways to buy me; but the never changing answer was always repeated: "Linda does not belong to *me.* She is my daughter's property, and I have no legal right to sell her." The conscientious man! He was too scrupulous to *sell* me; but he had no scruples whatever about committing a much greater wrong against the helpless young girl placed under his guardianship, as his daughter's property. Sometimes my persecutor would ask me whether I would like to be sold. I told him I would rather be sold to anybody than to lead such a life as I did. On such occasions he would assume the air of a very injured individual and reproach me for my ingratitude. "Did I not take you into the house and make you the companion of my own children?" he would say. "Have I ever treated you like a negro? I have never allowed you to be punished, not even to please your mistress. And this is the recompense I get, you ungrateful girl!" I answered that he had reasons of his own for screening me from punishment and that the course he pursued made my mistress hate me and persecute me. If I wept, he would say, "Poor child! Don't cry! Don't cry! I will make peace for you with your mistress. Only let me arrange matters in my own way. Poor, foolish girl! you don't know what is for your own good. I would cherish you. I would make a lady of you. Now go, and think of all I have promised you."

I did think of it.

[3]White-haired, old.

[4]Tribunals established in the Roman Catholic church to inquire into and punish heresy.

Reader, I draw no imaginary pictures of Southern homes. I am telling you the plain truth. Yet when victims make their escape from this wild beast of Slavery, Northerners consent to act the part of bloodhounds and hunt the poor fugitive back into his den, "full of dead men's bones, and of all uncleanness."[5] Nay, more, they are not only willing, but proud, to give their daughters in marriage to slaveholders. The poor girls have romantic notions of a sunny clime and of the flowering vines that all the year round shade a happy home. To what disappointments are they destined! The young wife soon learns that the husband in whose hands she has placed her happiness pays no regard to his marriage vows. Children of every shade of complexion play with her own fair babies, and too well she knows that they are born unto him of his own household. Jealousy and hatred enter the flowery home, and it is ravaged of its loveliness.

Southern women often marry a man knowing that he is the father of many little slaves. They do not trouble themselves about it. They regard such children as property, as marketable as the pigs on the plantation; and it is seldom that they do not make them aware of this by passing them into the slave-trader's hands as soon as possible and thus getting them out of their sight. I am glad to say there are some honorable exceptions.

I have myself known two Southern wives who exhorted their husbands to free those slaves towards whom they stood in a "parental relation," and their request was granted. These husbands blushed before the superior nobleness of their wives' natures. Though they had only counselled them to do that which it was their duty to do, it commanded their respect and rendered their conduct more exemplary. Concealment was at an end, and confidence took the place of distrust.

Though this bad institution deadens the moral sense, even in white women, to a fearful extent, it is not altogether extinct. I have heard Southern ladies say of Mr. Such a one, "He not only thinks it no disgrace to be the father of those little niggers, but he is not ashamed to call himself their master. I declare, such things ought not to be tolerated in any decent society!"

X
A PERILOUS PASSAGE IN THE SLAVE GIRL'S LIFE

After my lover went away,[1] Dr. Flint contrived a new plan. He seemed to have an idea that my fear of my mistress was his greatest obstacle. In the blandest tones, he told me that he was going to build a small house for me, in a secluded place, four miles away from the town. I shuddered; but I was constrained to listen, while he talked of his intention to give me a home of my

[5]Matthew 23:27.

[1]A free black man proposed to buy Linda Brent and marry her. Dr. Flint refused to sell her and forbade their marriage. She therefore encouraged her lover to leave the South and seek a new life in one of the free states of the North.

own and to make a lady of me. Hitherto, I had escaped my dreaded fate, by being in the midst of people. My grandmother had already had high words with my master about me. She had told him pretty plainly what she thought of his character, and there was considerable gossip in the neighborhood about our affairs, to which the open-mouthed jealousy of Mrs. Flint contributed not a little. When my master said he was going to build a house for me, and that he could do it with little trouble and expense, I was in hopes something would happen to frustrate his scheme; but I soon heard that the house was actually begun. I vowed before my Maker that I would never enter it. I had rather toil on the plantation from dawn till dark; I had rather live and die in jail, than drag on, from day to day, through such a living death. I was determined that the master, whom I so hated and loathed, who had blighted the prospects of my youth and made my life a desert, should not, after my long struggle with him, succeed at last in trampling his victim under his feet. I would do anything, everything, for the sake of defeating him. What *could* I do? I thought and thought, till I became desperate and made a plunge into the abyss.

And now, reader, I come to a period in my unhappy life which I would gladly forget if I could. The remembrance fills me with sorrow and shame. It pains me to tell you of it; but I have promised to tell you the truth, and I will do it honestly, let it cost me what it may. I will not try to screen myself behind the plea of compulsion from a master; for it was not so. Neither can I plead ignorance or thoughtlessness. For years, my master had done his utmost to pollute my mind with foul images, and to destroy the pure principles inculcated by my grandmother, and the good mistress of my childhood. The influences of slavery had had the same effect on me that they had on other young girls; they had made me prematurely knowing, concerning the evil ways of the world. I knew what I did, and I did it with deliberate calculation.

But, O, ye happy women, whose purity has been sheltered from childhood, who have been free to choose the objects of your affection, whose homes are protected by law, do not judge the poor desolate slave girl too severely! If slavery had been abolished, I, also, could have married the man of my choice; I could have had a home shielded by the laws; and I should have been spared the painful task of confessing what I am now about to relate; but all my prospects had been blighted by slavery. I wanted to keep myself pure; and, under the most adverse circumstances, I tried hard to preserve my self-respect; but I was struggling alone in the powerful grasp of the demon Slavery; and the monster proved too strong for me. I felt as if I was forsaken by God and man, as if all my efforts must be frustrated; and I became reckless in my despair.

I have told you that Dr. Flint's persecutions and his wife's jealousy had given rise to some gossip in the neighborhood. Among others, it chanced that a white unmarried gentleman had obtained some knowledge of the circumstances in which I was placed. He knew my grandmother and often spoke to me in the street. He became interested for me and asked questions about my master, which I answered in part. He expressed a great deal of sympathy and a wish to aid me. He constantly sought opportunities to see me and wrote to me frequently. I was a poor slave girl, only fifteen years old.

So much attention from a superior person was, of course, flattering; for human nature is the same in all. I also felt grateful for his sympathy and encouraged by his kind words. It seemed to me a great thing to have such a friend. By degrees, a more tender feeling crept into my heart. He was an educated and eloquent gentleman, too eloquent, alas, for the poor slave girl who trusted in him. Of course I saw whither all this was tending. I knew the impassable gulf between us; but to be an object of interest to a man who is not married and who is not her master, is agreeable to the pride and feelings of a slave, if her miserable situation has left her any pride or sentiment. It seems less degrading to give one's self, than to submit to compulsion. There is something akin to freedom in having a lover who has no control over you except that which he gains by kindness and attachment. A master may treat you as rudely as he pleases, and you dare not speak; moreover, the wrong does not seem so great with an unmarried man, as with one who has a wife to be made unhappy. There may be sophistry[2] in all this; but the condition of a slave confuses all principles of morality and, in fact, renders the practice of them impossible.

When I found that my master had actually begun to build the lonely cottage, other feelings mixed with those I have described. Revenge and calculations of interest were added to flattered vanity and sincere gratitude for kindness. I knew nothing would enrage Dr. Flint so much as to know that I favored another, and it was something to triumph over my tyrant even in that small way. I thought he would revenge himself by selling me, and I was sure my friend, Mr. Sands, would buy me. He was a man of more generosity and feeling than my master, and I thought my freedom could be easily obtained from him. The crisis of my fate now came so near that I was desperate. I shuddered to think of being the mother of children that should be owned by my old tyrant. I knew that as soon as a new fancy took him, his victims were sold far off to get rid of them, especially if they had children. I had seen several women sold, with his babies at the breast. He never allowed his offspring by slaves to remain long in sight of himself and his wife. Of a man who was not my master I could ask to have my children well supported; and in this case, I felt confident I should obtain the boon.[3] I also felt quite sure that they would be made free. With all these thoughts revolving in my mind, and seeing no other way of escaping the doom I so much dreaded, I made a headlong plunge. Pity me, and pardon me, O virtuous reader! You never knew what it is to be a slave; to be entirely unprotected by law or custom; to have the laws reduce you to the condition of a chattel, entirely subject to the will of another. You never exhausted your ingenuity in avoiding the snares and eluding the power of a hated tyrant; you never shuddered at the sound of his footsteps and trembled within hearing of his voice. I know I did wrong. No one can feel it more sensibly than I do. The painful and humiliating memory will haunt me to my dying day. Still, in looking back, calmly, on the events of my life, I feel that the slave woman ought not to be judged by the same standard as others.

The months passed on. I had many unhappy hours. I secretly mourned over the sorrow I was bringing on my grandmother, who had so tried to shield me from harm. I knew that I was the greatest comfort of her old age and that it was a source of pride to her that I had not degraded myself, like

[2]False, self-serving reasoning. [3]Favor, benefit.

most of the slaves. I wanted to confess to her that I was no longer worthy of her love; but I could not utter the dreaded words.

As for Dr. Flint, I had a feeling of satisfaction and triumph in the thought of telling *him*. From time to time he told me of his intended arrangements, and I was silent. At last, he came and told me the cottage was completed and ordered me to go to it. I told him I would never enter it. He said, "I have heard enough of such talk as that. You shall go, if you are carried by force; and you shall remain there."

I replied, "I will never go there. In a few months I shall be a mother."

He stood and looked at me in dumb amazement and left the house without a word. I thought I should be happy in my triumph over him. But now that the truth was out, and my relatives would hear of it, I felt wretched. Humble as were their circumstances, they had pride in my good character. Now, how could I look them in the face? My self-respect was gone! I had resolved that I would be virtuous, though I was a slave. I had said, "Let the storm beat! I will brave it till I die." And now, how humiliated I felt!

I went to my grandmother. My lips moved to make confession, but the words stuck in my throat. I sat down in the shade of a tree at her door and began to sew. I think she saw something unusual was the matter with me. The mother of slaves is very watchful. She knows there is no security for her children. After they have entered their teens she lives in daily expectation of trouble. This leads to many questions. If the girl is of a sensitive nature, timidity keeps her from answering truthfully, and this well-meant course has a tendency to drive her from maternal counsels. Presently, in came my mistress, like a mad woman, and accused me concerning her husband. My grandmother, whose suspicions had been previously awakened, believed what she said. She exclaimed, "O Linda! has it come to this? I had rather see you dead than to see you as you now are. You are a disgrace to your dead mother." She tore from my fingers my mother's wedding ring and her silver thimble. "Go away!" she exclaimed, "and never come to my house, again." Her reproaches fell so hot and heavy that they left me no chance to answer. Bitter tears, such as the eyes never shed but once, were my only answer. I rose from my seat, but fell back again, sobbing. She did not speak to me; but the tears were running down her furrowed cheeks, and they scorched me like fire. She had always been so kind to me! *So* kind! How I longed to throw myself at her feet and tell her all the truth! But she had ordered me to go and never to come there again. After a few minutes, I mustered strength, and started to obey her. With what feelings did I now close that little gate which I used to open with such an eager hand in my childhood! It closed upon me with a sound I never heard before.

Where could I go? I was afraid to return to my master's. I walked on recklessly, not caring where I went or what would become of me. When I had gone four or five miles, fatigue compelled me to stop. I sat down on the stump of an old tree. The stars were shining through the boughs above me. How they mocked me, with their bright, calm light! The hours passed by, and as I sat there alone a chilliness and deadly sickness came over me. I sank on the ground. My mind was full of horrid thoughts. I prayed to die; but the prayer was not answered. At last, with great effort I roused myself and walked some distance further, to the house of a woman who had been a friend of my mother. When I told her why I was there, she spoke soothingly to me; but I could not be comforted. I thought I could bear my shame if I could only be reconciled to my grandmother. I longed to open my heart to her. I thought if she could know the real state of the case, and all I had been bearing for years, she would perhaps judge me less harshly. My friend advised me to send for her. I did so; but days of agonizing suspense passed before she came. Had she utterly forsaken me? No. She came at last. I knelt before her and told her the things that had poisoned my life; how long I had been persecuted; that I saw no way of escape; and in an hour of extremity I had become desperate. She listened in silence. I told her I would bear anything and do anything, if in time I had hopes of obtaining her forgiveness. I begged of her to pity me for my dead mother's sake. And she did pity me. She did not say, "I forgive you," but she looked at me lovingly, with her eyes full of tears. She laid her old hand gently on my head and murmured, "Poor child! Poor child!"

XVI
SCENES AT THE PLANTATION[1]

Early the next morning I left my grandmother's with my youngest child.[2] My boy was ill, and I left him behind. I had many sad thoughts as the old wagon jolted on. Hitherto, I had suffered alone; now, my little one was to be treated as a slave. As we drew near the great house, I thought of the time when I was formerly sent there out of revenge. I wondered for what purpose I was now sent. I could not tell. I resolved to obey orders so far as duty required; but within myself, I determined to make my stay as short as possible. Mr. Flint[3] was waiting to receive us and told me to follow him up stairs to receive orders for the day. My little Ellen was left below in the kitchen. It was a change for her, who had always been so carefully tended. My young master said she might amuse herself in the yard. This was kind of him, since the child was hateful to his sight. My task was to fit up the house for the reception of the bride. In the midst of sheets, tablecloths, towels, drapery, and carpeting, my head was as busy planning as were my fingers with the needle. At noon I was allowed to go to Ellen. She had sobbed herself to sleep. I heard Mr. Flint say to a neighbor, "I've got her down here, and I'll soon take the town notions out of her head. My father is partly to blame for her nonsense. He ought to have broke her in long ago." The remark was made within my hearing, and it would have been quite as manly to have made it to my face. He *had* said things to my face which might, or might not, have surprised his neighbor if he had known of them. He was "a chip off the old block."

I resolved to give him no cause to accuse me of being too much of a lady, so far as work was concerned. I worked day and night, with wretchedness before me. When I lay down beside my child, I felt how much easier it would be to see her die than to see her master beat her about, as I daily saw him beat

[1]As punishment for her refusal to submit to him, Dr. Flint ordered that Linda Brent and her children be sent to work at the nearby plantation managed by his son, who was soon to be married.

[2]Her daughter Ellen. [3]The son of Dr. Flint.

other little ones. The spirit of the mothers was so crushed by the lash, that they stood by, without courage to remonstrate. How much more must I suffer before I should be "broke in" to that degree?

I wished to appear as contented as possible. Sometimes I had an opportunity to send a few lines home; and this brought up recollections that made it difficult, for a time, to seem calm and indifferent to my lot. Notwithstanding my efforts, I saw that Mr. Flint regarded me with a suspicious eye. Ellen broke down under the trials of her new life. Separated from me, with no one to look after her, she wandered about, and in a few days cried herself sick. One day, she sat under the window where I was at work, crying that weary cry which makes a mother's heart bleed. I was obliged to steel myself to bear it. After a while it ceased. I looked out, and she was gone. As it was near noon, I ventured to go down in search of her. The great house was raised two feet above the ground. I looked under it and saw her about midway, fast asleep. I crept under and drew her out. As I held her in my arms, I thought how well it would be for her if she never waked up; and I uttered my thought aloud. I was startled to hear some one say, "Did you speak to me?" I looked up, and saw Mr. Flint standing beside me. He said nothing further but turned, frowning, away. That night he sent Ellen a biscuit and a cup of sweetened milk. This generosity surprised me. I learned afterwards, that in the afternoon he had killed a large snake, which crept from under the house; and I supposed that incident had prompted his unusual kindness.

The next morning the old cart was loaded with shingles for town. I put Ellen into it and sent her to her grandmother. Mr. Flint said I ought to have asked his permission. I told him the child was sick and required attention which I had no time to give. He let it pass; for he was aware that I had accomplished much work in a little time.

I had been three weeks on the plantation, when I planned a visit home. It must be at night, after everybody was in bed. I was six miles from town, and the road was very dreary. I was to go with a young man who, I knew, often stole to town to see his mother. One night, when all was quiet, we started. Fear gave speed to our steps, and we were not long in performing the journey. I arrived at my grandmother's. Her bedroom was on the first floor, and the window was open, the weather being warm. I spoke to her and she awoke. She let me in and closed the window, lest some late passerby should see me. A light was brought, and the whole household gathered round me, some smiling and some crying. I went to look at my children and thanked God for their happy sleep. The tears fell as I leaned over them. As I moved to leave, Benny stirred. I turned back and whispered, "Mother is here." After digging at his eyes with his little fist, they opened, and he sat up in bed, looking at me curiously. Having satisfied himself that it was I, he exclaimed, "O mother! you ain't dead, are you? They didn't cut off your head at the plantation, did they?"

My time was up too soon, and my guide was waiting for me. I laid Benny back in his bed and dried his tears by a promise to come again soon. Rapidly we retraced our steps back to the plantation. About half way we were met by a company of four patrols.[4] Luckily we heard their horses' hoofs before they

[4]Mounted patrols of white citizens policed the countryside. Slaves found outside the boundaries of their plantations without a pass signed by their owner or overseer could be punished and their owner admonished or even fined for careless supervision of his property.

came in sight, and we had time to hide behind a large tree. They passed, hallooing and shouting in a manner that indicated a recent carousel. How thankful we were that they had not their dogs with them! We hastened our footsteps, and when we arrived on the plantation we heard the sound of the hand-mill. The slaves were grinding their corn. We were safely in the house before the horn summoned them to their labor. I divided my little parcel of food with my guide, knowing that he had lost the chance of grinding his corn and must toil all day in the field.

Mr. Flint often took an inspection of the house, to see that no one was idle. The entire management of the work was trusted to me, because he knew nothing about it; and rather than hire a superintendent he contented himself with my arrangements. He had often urged upon his father the necessity of having me at the plantation to take charge of his affairs and make clothes for the slaves; but the old man knew him too well to consent to that arrangement.

When I had been working a month at the plantation, the great aunt of Mr. Flint came to make him a visit. This was the good old lady who paid fifty dollars for my grandmother, for the purpose of making her free, when she stood on the auction block. My grandmother loved this old lady, whom we all called Miss Fanny. She often came to take tea with us. On such occasions the table was spread with a snow-white cloth, and the china cups and silver spoons were taken from the old-fashioned buffet. There were hot muffins, tea rusks, and delicious sweetmeats. My grandmother kept two cows, and the fresh cream was Miss Fanny's delight. She invariably declared that it was the best in town. The old ladies had cosey times together. They would work and chat, and sometimes, while talking over old times, their spectacles would get dim with tears and would have to be taken off and wiped. When Miss Fanny bade us good-by, her bag was filled with grandmother's best cakes, and she was urged to come again soon.

There had been a time when Dr. Flint's wife came to take tea with us and when her children were also sent to have a feast of "Aunt Marthy's" nice cooking. But after I became an object of her jealousy and spite, she was angry with grandmother for giving a shelter to me and my children. She would not even speak to her in the street. This wounded my grandmother's feelings, for she could not retain ill will against the woman whom she had nourished with her milk when a babe. The doctor's wife would gladly have prevented our intercourse with Miss Fanny if she could have done it, but fortunately she was not dependent on the bounty of the Flints. She had enough to be independent; and that is more than can ever be gained from charity, however lavish it may be.

Miss Fanny was endeared to me by many recollections, and I was rejoiced to see her at the plantation. The warmth of her large, loyal heart made the house seem pleasanter while she was in it. She staid a week, and I had many talks with her. She said her principal object in coming was to see how I was treated and whether any thing could be done for me. She inquired whether she could help me in any way. I told her I believed not. She condoled with me in her own peculiar way, saying she wished that I and all my grandmother's family were at rest in our graves, for not until then should she feel any peace about us. The good old soul did not dream that I was planning to bestow peace upon her, with regard to myself and my children, not by death but by securing our freedom.

Again and again I had traversed those dreary twelve miles, to and from the town; and all the way, I was meditating upon some means of escape for myself and my children. My friends had made every effort that ingenuity could devise to effect our purchase, but all their plans had proved abortive. Dr. Flint was suspicious and determined not to loosen his grasp upon us. I could have made my escape alone; but it was more for my helpless children than for myself that I longed for freedom. Though the boon would have been precious to me, above all price, I would not have taken it at the expense of leaving them in slavery. Every trial I endured, every sacrifice I made for their sakes, drew them closer to my heart and gave me fresh courage to beat back the dark waves that rolled and rolled over me in a seemingly endless night of storms.

The six weeks were nearly completed when Mr. Flint's bride was expected to take possession of her new home. The arrangements were all completed, and Mr. Flint said I had done well. He expected to leave home on Saturday and return with his bride the following Wednesday. After receiving various orders from him, I ventured to ask permission to spend Sunday in town. It was granted, for which favor I was thankful. It was the first I had ever asked of him, and I intended it should be the last. It needed more than one night to accomplish the project I had in view; but the whole of Sunday would give me an opportunity. I spent the Sabbath with my grandmother. A calmer, more beautiful day never came down out of heaven. To me it was a day of conflicting emotions. Perhaps it was the last day I should ever spend under that dear, old, sheltering roof! Perhaps these were the last talks I should ever have with the faithful old friend of my whole life! Perhaps it was the last time I and my children should be together! Well, better so, I thought, than that they should be slaves. I knew the doom that awaited my fair baby in slavery, and I determined to save her from it or perish in the attempt. I went to make this vow at the graves of my poor parents, in the burying-ground of the slaves. "There the wicked cease from troubling, and there the weary be at rest. There the prisoners rest together; they hear not the voice of the oppressor; the servant is free from his master."[5] I knelt by the graves of my parents and thanked God, as I had often done before, that they had not lived to witness my trials or to mourn over my sins. I had received my mother's blessing when she died; and in many an hour of tribulation I had seemed to hear her voice, sometimes chiding me, sometimes whispering loving words into my wounded heart. I have shed many and bitter tears to think that when I am gone from my children they cannot remember me with such entire satisfaction as I remembered my mother.

The graveyard was in the woods, and twilight was coming on. Nothing broke the death-like stillness except the occasional twitter of a bird. My spirit was overawed by the solemnity of the scene. For more than ten years I had frequented this spot, but never had it seemed to me so sacred as now. A black stump, at the head of my mother's grave, was all that remained of a tree my father had planted. His grave was marked by a small wooden board, bearing his name, the letters of which were nearly obliterated. I knelt down and kissed them and poured forth a prayer to God for guidance and support in

[5]Job 3:17–19.

the perilous step I was about to take. As I passed the wreck of the old meeting house, where, before Nat Turner's time,[6] the slaves had been allowed to meet for worship, I seemed to hear my father's voice come from it, bidding me not to tarry till I reached freedom or the grave. I rushed on with renovated hopes. My trust in God had been strengthened by that prayer among the graves.

My plan was to conceal myself at the house of a friend and remain there a few weeks till the search was over. My hope was that the doctor would get discouraged, and, for fear of losing my value, and also of subsequently finding my children among the missing, he would consent to sell us; and I knew somebody would buy us. I had done all in my power to make my children comfortable during the time I expected to be separated from them. I was packing my things, when grandmother came into the room and asked what I was doing. "I am putting my things in order," I replied. I tried to look and speak cheerfully, but her watchful eye detected something beneath the surface. She drew me towards her and asked me to sit down. She looked earnestly at me, and said, "Linda, do you want to kill your old grandmother? Do you mean to leave your little, helpless children? I am old now and cannot do for your babies as I once did for you."

I replied that if I went away, perhaps their father would be able to secure their freedom.

"Ah, my child," said she, "don't trust too much to him. Stand by your own children, and suffer with them till death. Nobody respects a mother who forsakes her children; and if you leave them, you will never have a happy moment. If you go, you will make me miserable the short time I have to live. You would be taken and brought back, and your sufferings would be dreadful . . . Do give it up, Linda. Try to bear a little longer. Things may turn out better than we expect."

My courage failed me, in view of the sorrow I should bring on that faithful, loving old heart. I promised that I would try longer and that I would take nothing out of her house without her knowledge.

Whenever the children climbed on my knee or laid their heads on my lap, she would say, "Poor little souls! what would you do without a mother? She don't love you as I do." And she would hug them to her own bosom, as if to reproach me for my want of affection; but she knew all the while that I loved them better than my life. I slept with her that night, and it was the last time. The memory of it haunted me for many a year.

On Monday I returned to the plantation and busied myself with preparations for the important day. Wednesday came.[7] It was a beautiful day, and the faces of the slaves were as bright as the sunshine. The poor creatures were merry. They were expecting little presents from the bride and hoping for better times under her administration. I had no such hopes for them. I knew that the young wives of slaveholders often thought their authority and

[6]American slave (1800–1831) who led a slave uprising in Virginia in 1831. More than fifty whites were killed before Turner and sixteen of his followers were captured and executed. To forestall further slave uprisings, severe new laws, further restricting the lives of slaves, were enacted throughout the South.

[7]Flint's wedding day.

importance would be best established and maintained by cruelty; and what I had heard of young Mrs. Flint gave me no reason to expect that her rule over them would be less severe than that of the master and overseer. Truly, the colored race are the most cheerful and forgiving people on the face of the earth. That their masters sleep in safety is owing to their superabundance of heart; and yet they look upon their sufferings with less pity than they would bestow on those of a horse or a dog.

I stood at the door with others to receive the bridegroom and bride. She was a handsome, delicate-looking girl, and her face flushed with emotion at sight of her new home. I thought it likely that visions of a happy future were rising before her. It made me sad; for I knew how soon clouds would come over her sunshine. She examined every part of the house and told me she was delighted with the arrangements I had made. I was afraid old Mrs. Flint had tried to prejudice her against me, and I did my best to please her.

All passed off smoothly for me until dinner time arrived. I did not mind the embarrassment of waiting on a dinner party, for the first time in my life, half so much as I did the meeting with Dr. Flint and his wife, who would be among the guests. It was a mystery to me why Mrs. Flint had not made her appearance at the plantation during all the time I was putting the house in order. I had not met her, face to face, for five years, and I had no wish to see her now. She was a praying woman and, doubtless, considered my present position a special answer to her prayers. Nothing could please her better than to see me humbled and trampled upon. I was just where she would have me—in the power of a hard, unprincipled master. She did not speak to me when she took her seat at table; but her satisfied, triumphant smile, when I handed her plate, was more eloquent than words. The old doctor was not so quiet in his demonstrations. He ordered me here and there, and spoke with peculiar emphasis when he said "your *mistress.*" I was drilled like a disgraced soldier. When all was over, and the last key turned, I sought my pillow, thankful that God had appointed a season of rest for the weary.

The next day my new mistress began her housekeeping. I was not exactly appointed maid of all work; but I was to do whatever I was told. Monday evening came. It was always a busy time. On that night the slaves received their weekly allowance of food. Three pounds of meat, a peck of corn, and perhaps a dozen herring were allowed to each man. Women received a pound and a half of meat, a peck of corn, and the same number of herring. Children over twelve years old had half the allowance of the women. The meat was cut and weighed by the foreman of the field hands and piled on planks before the meat house. Then the second foreman went behind the building, and when the first foreman called out, "Who takes this piece of meat?" he answered by calling somebody's name. This method was resorted to as means of preventing partiality in distributing the meat. The young mistress came out to see how things were done on her plantation, and she soon gave a specimen of her character. Among those in waiting for their allowance was a very old slave who had faithfully served the Flint family through three generations. When he hobbled up to get his bit of meat, the mistress said he was too old to have any allowance, that when niggers were too old to work, they ought to be fed on grass. Poor old man! He suffered much before he found rest in the grave.

My mistress and I got along very well together. At the end of a week, old Mrs. Flint made us another visit and was closeted a long time with her daughter-in-law. I had my suspicions what was the subject of the conference. The old doctor's wife had been informed that I could leave the plantation on one condition,[8] and she was very desirous to keep me there. If she had trusted me, as I deserved to be trusted by her, she would have had no fears of my accepting that condition. When she entered her carriage to return home, she said to young Mrs. Flint, "Don't neglect to send for them as quick as possible." My heart was on the watch all the time, and I at once concluded that she spoke of my children. The doctor came the next day, and as I entered the room to spread the tea table, I heard him say, "Don't wait any longer. Send for them tomorrow." I saw through the plan. They thought my children's being there would fetter me to the spot and that it was a good place to break us all in to abject submission to our lot as slaves. After the doctor left, a gentleman called, who had always manifested friendly feelings towards my grandmother and her family. Mr. Flint carried him over the plantation to show him the results of labor performed by men and women who were unpaid, miserably clothed, and half famished. The cotton crop was all they thought of. It was duly admired, and the gentleman returned with specimens to show his friends. I was ordered to carry water to wash his hands. As I did so, he said, "Linda, how do you like your new home?" I told him I liked it as well as I expected. He replied, "They don't think you are contented, and tomorrow they are going to bring your children to be with you. I am sorry for you, Linda. I hope they will treat you kindly." I hurried from the room, unable to thank him. My suspicions were correct. My children were to be brought to the plantation to be "broke in."

To this day I feel grateful to the gentleman who gave me this timely information. It nerved me to immediate action.

XXI
THE LOOPHOLE OF RETREAT[1]

A small shed had been added to my grandmother's house years ago. Some boards were laid across the joists at the top, and between these boards and the roof was a very small garret, never occupied by any thing but rats and mice. It was a pent roof,[2] covered with nothing but shingles, according to the Southern custom for such buildings. The garret was only nine feet long and seven wide. The highest part was three feet high and sloped down abruptly to the loose board floor. There was no admission for either light or air. My uncle Philip, who was a carpenter, had very skilfully made a concealed trapdoor, which communicated with the storeroom . . . The storeroom opened upon a piazza. To this hole I was conveyed as soon as I entered the house.

[8]I.e., that she submit to the will of Dr. Flint.

[1]A quotation adapted from the poem "The Task" (1785) by the English poet William Cowper (1731–1800): "'Tis pleasant, through the loopholes of retreat,/ To peep at such a world; to see the stir/ Of the great Babel, and not feel the crowd;/ To hear the roar she sends through all her gates/ At a safe distance. . . . " (Book IV, lines 89–92).

[2]A shed roof, having a single slope.

The air was stifling, the darkness total. A bed had been spread on the floor. I could sleep quite comfortably on one side; but the slope was so sudden that I could not turn on the other without hitting the roof. The rats and mice ran over my bed; but I was weary, and I slept such sleep as the wretched may, when a tempest has passed over them. Morning came. I knew it only by the noises I heard, for in my small den day and night were all the same. I suffered for air even more than for light. But I was not comfortless. I heard the voices of my children. There was joy and there was sadness in the sound. It made my tears flow. How I longed to speak to them! I was eager to look on their faces; but there was no hole, no crack, through which I could peep. This continued darkness was oppressive. It seemed horrible to sit or lie in a cramped position day after day, without one gleam of light. Yet I would have chosen this rather than my lot as a slave, though white people considered it an easy one; and it was so compared with the fate of others. I was never cruelly over-worked; I was never lacerated with the whip from head to foot; I was never so beaten and bruised that I could not turn from one side to the other; I never had my heel-strings[3] cut to prevent my running away; I was never chained to a log and forced to drag it about, while I toiled in the fields from morning till night; I was never branded with hot iron or torn by bloodhounds. On the contrary, I had always been kindly treated and tenderly cared for, until I came into the hands of Dr. Flint. I had never wished for freedom till then. But though my life in slavery was comparatively devoid of hardships, God pity the woman who is compelled to lead such a life!

My food was passed up to me through the trap-door my uncle had contrived; and my grandmother, my uncle Philip, and aunt Nancy would seize such opportunities as they could, to mount up there and chat with me at the opening. But of course this was not safe in the daytime. It must all be done in darkness. It was impossible for me to move in an erect position, but I crawled about my den for exercise. One day I hit my head against something, and found it was a gimlet.[4] My uncle had left it sticking there when he made the trap-door. I was as rejoiced as Robinson Crusoe could have been at finding such a treasure.[5] It put a lucky thought into my head. I said to myself, "Now I will have some light. Now I will see my children." I did not dare to begin my work during the daytime for fear of attracting attention. But I groped round; and having found the side next to the street, where I could frequently see my children, I stuck the gimlet in and waited for evening. I bored three rows of holes, one above another; then I bored out the interstices between. I thus succeeded in making one hole about an inch long and an inch broad. I sat by it till late into the night, to enjoy the little whiff of air that floated in. In the morning I watched for my children. The first person I saw in the street was Dr. Flint. I had a shuddering, superstitious feeling that it was a bad omen. Several familiar faces passed by. At last I heard the merry laugh of children, and presently two sweet little faces were looking up at me, as though they knew I was there and were conscious of the joy they imparted. How I longed to *tell* them I was there!

[3]Achilles tendons. [4]A small, pointed tool for boring holes in wood.

[5]In *Robinson Crusoe* (1719), by the English novelist Daniel Defoe (1660–1731), the hero is shipwrecked, loses most of his possessions, but manages to survive on a small island until rescued.

My condition was now a little improved. But for weeks I was tormented by hundreds of little red insects, fine as a needle's point, that pierced through my skin and produced an intolerable burning. The good grandmother gave me herb teas and cooling medicines, and finally I got rid of them. The heat of my den was intense, for nothing but thin shingles protected me from the scorching summer's sun. But I had my consolations. Through my peeping-hole I could watch the children, and when they were near enough, I could hear their talk. Aunt Nancy brought me all the news she could hear at Dr. Flint's. From her I learned that the doctor had written to New York to a colored woman, who had been born and raised in our neighborhood and had breathed his contaminating atmosphere. He offered her a reward if she could find out any thing about me. I know not what was the nature of her reply; but he soon after started for New York in haste, saying to his family that he had business of importance to transact. I peeped at him as he passed on his way to the steamboat. It was a satisfaction to have miles of land and water between us, even for a little while; and it was still greater satisfaction to know that he believed me to be in the Free States. My little den seemed less dreary than it had done. He returned . . . without obtaining any satisfactory information. When he passed our house next morning, Benny was standing at the gate. He had heard them say that he had gone to find me, and he called out, "Dr. Flint, did you bring my mother home? I want to see her." The doctor stamped his foot at him in a rage, and exclaimed, "Get out of the way, you little damned rascal! If you don't, I'll cut off your head."

Benny ran terrified into the house, saying "You can't put me in jail again. I don't belong to you now." It was well that the wind carried the words away from the doctor's ear. I told my grandmother of it, when we had our next conference at the trap-door, and begged of her not to allow the children to be impertinent to the irascible old man.

Autumn came, with a pleasant abatement of heat. My eyes had become accustomed to the dim light, and by holding my book or work in a certain position near the aperture I contrived to read and sew. That was a great relief to the tedious monotony of my life. But when winter came, the cold penetrated through the thin shingle roof, and I was dreadfully chilled. The winters there are not so long, or so severe as in northern latitudes; but the houses are not built to shelter from cold, and my little den was peculiarly comfortless. The kind grandmother brought me bed-clothes and warm drinks. Often I was obliged to lie in bed all day to keep comfortable; but with all my precautions, my shoulders and feet were frostbitten. O, those long, gloomy days, with no object for my eye to rest upon and no thoughts to occupy my mind except the dreary past and the uncertain future! I was thankful when there came a day sufficiently mild for me to wrap myself up and sit at the loophole to watch the passers by. Southerners have the habit of stopping and talking in the streets, and I heard many conversations not intended to meet my ears. I heard slave-hunters planning how to catch some poor fugitive. Several times I heard allusions to Dr. Flint, myself, and the history of my children, who, perhaps, were playing near the gate.[6] One would say, "I wouldn't move my little finger to catch her, as old Flint's property." Another would say, "I'll catch

[6]Soon after she began hiding, Harriet Jacob's children were bought by their father and sent to live with their grandmother.

any nigger for the reward. A man ought to have what belongs to him, if he *is* a damned brute." The opinion was often expressed that I was in the Free States. Very rarely did any one suggest that I might be in the vicinity. Had the least suspicion rested on my grandmother's house, it would have been burned to the ground. But it was the last place they thought of. Yet there was no place, where slavery existed, that could have afforded me so good a place of concealment.

Dr. Flint and his family repeatedly tried to coax and bribe my children to tell something they had heard said about me. One day the doctor took them into a shop and offered them some bright little silver pieces and gay handkerchiefs if they would tell where their mother was. Ellen shrank away from him and would not speak; but Benny spoke up and said, "Dr. Flint, I don't know where my mother is. I guess she's in New York; and when you go there again, I wish you'd ask her to come home, for I want to see her; but if you put her in jail or tell her you'll cut her head off, I'll tell her to go right back."

XLI
FREE AT LAST[1]

Mrs. Bruce[2] and every member of her family were exceedingly kind to me. I was thankful for the blessings of my lot, yet I could not always wear a cheerful countenance. I was doing harm to no one; on the contrary, I was doing all the good I could in my small way; yet I could never go out to breathe God's free air without trepidation at my heart. This seemed hard; and I could not think it was a right state of things for any civilized country.

From time to time I received news from my good old grandmother. She could not write; but she employed others to write for her. The following is an extract from one of her last letters:—

> "Dear Daughter: I cannot hope to see you again on earth; but I pray to God to unite us above, where pain will no more rack this feeble body of mine; where sorrow and parting from my children will be no more.[3] God has promised these things if we are faithful unto the end. My age and feeble health deprive me of going to church now; but God is with me here at home. Thank your brother for his kindness. Give much love to him, and tell him to remember the Creator in the days of his youth, and strive to meet me in the Father's kingdom.[4] Love to Ellen and Benjamin. Don't neglect him. Tell him for me, to be a good boy. Strive, my child, to train them for God's children. May he protect and provide for you, is the prayer of your loving old mother."

These letters both cheered and saddened me. I was always glad to have tidings from the kind, faithful old friend of my unhappy youth; but her

[1]A quotation from the lines of a traditional spiritual song: "Free at last, free at last,/ thank God almighty I am free at last."

[2]In 1842, after seven years in hiding, Linda Brent escaped to the North. In New York City she found employment as nurse to the infant child of a couple she identified as Mrs. and Mrs. Bruce.

[3]Adapted from Revelation 21:4. [4]Adapted from Ecclesiastes 12:1.

messages of love made my heart yearn to see her before she died, and I mourned over the fact that it was impossible. Some months after I returned from my flight to New England,[5] I received a letter from her, in which she wrote, "Dr. Flint is dead. He has left a distressed family. Poor old man! I hope he made his peace with God."

I remembered how he had defrauded my grandmother of the hard earnings she had loaned, how he had tried to cheat her out of the freedom her mistress had promised her, and how he had persecuted her children; and I thought to myself that she was a better Christian than I was, if she could entirely forgive him. I cannot say, with truth, that the news of my old master's death softened my feelings towards him. There are wrongs which even the grave does not bury. The man was odious to me while he lived, and his memory is odious now.

His departure from this world did not diminish my danger. He had threatened my grandmother that his heirs should hold me in slavery after he was gone, that I never should be free so long as a child of his survived. As for Mrs. Flint, I had seen her in deeper afflictions than I supposed the loss of her husband would be, for she had buried several children; yet I never saw any signs of softening in her heart. The doctor had died in embarrassed circumstances and had little to will to his heirs, except such property as he was unable to grasp. I was well aware what I had to expect from the family of Flints; and my fears were confirmed by a letter from the South, warning me to be on my guard, because Mrs. Flint openly declared that her daughter could not afford to lose so valuable a slave as I was.

I kept close watch of the newspapers for arrivals;[6] but one Saturday night, being much occupied, I forgot to examine the Evening Express as usual. I went down into the parlor for it, early in the morning, and found the boy about to kindle a fire with it. I took it from him and examined the list of arrivals. Reader, if you have never been a slave, you cannot imagine the acute sensation of suffering at my heart, when I read the names of Mrs. and Mrs. Dodge, at a hotel in Courtland Street. It was a third-rate hotel, and that circumstance convinced me of the truth of what I had heard, that they were short of funds and had need of my value, as *they* valued me; and that was by dollars and cents. I hastened with the paper to Mrs. Bruce. Her heart and hand were always open to everyone in distress, and she always warmly sympathized with mine. It was impossible to tell how near the enemy was. He might have passed and repassed the house while we were sleeping. He might at that moment be waiting to pounce upon me if I ventured out of doors. I had never seen the husband of my young mistress, and therefore I could not distinguish him from any other stranger. A carriage was hastily ordered; and, closely veiled, I followed Mrs. Bruce, taking the baby again with me into exile.[7] After various turnings and crossings, and returnings, the carriage stopped at the house of one of Mrs. Bruce's friends, where I was kindly

[5]Linda Brent had temporarily left New York City to avoid slavecatchers.

[6]Nineteenth-century newspapers traditionally reported the arrival of visitors newly registered at city hotels.

[7]On a previous occasion, when Linda Brent was forced to leave the Bruce household to avoid slavecatchers, Mrs. Bruce had deliberately sent her own baby with Linda Brent, knowing that if the two were seized, the authorities would be obliged to return the baby to the Bruces and thus reveal that her nurse had been captured and was in danger of being returned to the South.

received. Mrs. Bruce returned immediately, to instruct the domestics what to say if any one came to inquire for me.

It was lucky for me that the evening paper was not burned up before I had a chance to examine the list of arrivals. It was not long after Mrs. Bruce's return to her house, before several people came to inquire for me. One inquired for me, another asked for my daughter Ellen, and another said he had a letter from my grandmother, which he was requested to deliver in person.

They were told, "She *has* lived here, but she has left."

"How long ago?"

"I don't know, sir."

"Do you know where she went?"

"I do not, sir." And the door was closed.

This Mr. Dodge, who claimed me as his property, was originally a Yankee pedler in the South; then he became a merchant and finally a slaveholder. He managed to get introduced into what was called the first society and married Miss Emily Flint.[8] A quarrel arose between him and her brother, and the brother cowhided him. This led to a family feud, and he proposed to remove to Virginia. Dr. Flint left him no property, and his own means had become circumscribed, while a wife and children depended upon him for support. Under these circumstances, it was very natural that he should make an effort to put me into his pocket.

I had a colored friend, a man from my native place, in whom I had the most implicit confidence. I sent for him and told him that Mr. and Mrs. Dodge had arrived in New York. I proposed that he should call upon them to make inquiries about his friends at the South, with whom Dr. Flint's family were well acquainted. He thought there was no impropriety in his doing so, and he consented. He went to the hotel and knocked at the door of Mr. Dodge's room, which was opened by the gentleman himself, who gruffly inquired, "What brought you here? How came you to know I was in the city?"

"Your arrival was published in the evening papers, sir; and I called to ask Mrs. Dodge about my friends at home. I didn't suppose it would give any offence."

"Where's that negro girl, that belongs to my wife?"

"What girl, sir?"

"You know well enough. I mean Linda, that ran away from Dr. Flint's plantation, some years ago. I dare say you've seen her, and know where she is."

"Yes sir, I've seen her, and know where she is. She is out of your reach, sir."

"Tell me where she is, or bring her to me, and I will give her a chance to buy her freedom."

"I don't think it would be of any use, sir. I have heard her say she would go to the ends of the earth rather than pay any man or woman for her freedom, because she thinks she has a right to it. Besides, she couldn't do it, if she would, for she has spent her earnings to educate her children."

This made Mr. Dodge very angry, and some high words passed between them. My friend was afraid to come where I was; but in the course of the day I received a note from him. I supposed they had not come from the South, in

[8]The daughter of Dr. Flint.

the winter, for a pleasure excursion; and now the nature of their business was very plain.

Mrs. Bruce came to me and entreated me to leave the city the next morning. She said her house was watched, and it was possible that some clew to me might be obtained. I refused to take her advice. She pleaded with an earnest tenderness, that ought to have moved me; but I was in a bitter, disheartened mood. I was weary of flying from pillar to post. I had been chased during half my life, and it seemed as if the chase was never to end. There I sat, in that great city, guiltless of crime yet not daring to worship God in any of the churches. I heard the bells ringing for afternoon service, and, with contemptuous sarcasm, I said, "Will the preachers take for their text, 'Proclaim liberty to the captive, and the opening of prison doors to them that are bound'?[9] or will they preach from the text, 'Do unto others as ye would they should do unto you'?"[10] Oppressed Poles and Hungarians could find a safe refuge in that city; John Mitchell[11] was free to proclaim in the City Hall his desire for "a plantation well stocked with slaves," but there I sat, an oppressed American, not daring to show my face. God forgive the black and bitter thoughts I indulged on that Sabbath day! The Scripture says, "Oppression makes even a wise man mad,"[12] and I was not wise.

I had been told that Mr. Dodge said his wife had never signed away her right to my children, and if he could not get me, he would take them. This it was, more than anything else, that roused such a tempest in my soul. Benjamin was with his uncle William in California, but my innocent young daughter had come to spend a vacation with me. I thought of what I had suffered in slavery at her age, and my heart was like a tiger's when a hunter tries to seize her young.

Dear Mrs. Bruce! I seem to see the expression of her face, as she turned away discouraged by my obstinate mood. Finding her expostulations unavailing, she sent Ellen to entreat me. When ten o'clock in the evening arrived and Ellen had not returned, this watchful and unwearied friend became anxious. She came to us in a carriage, bringing a well-filled trunk for my journey—trusting that by this time I would listen to reason. I yielded to her, as I ought to have done before.

The next day, baby and I set out in a heavy snow storm, bound for New England again. I received letters from the City of Iniquity, addressed to me under an assumed name. In a few days one came from Mrs. Bruce, informing me that my new master was still searching for me and that she intended to put an end to this persecution by buying my freedom. I felt grateful for the kindness that prompted this offer, but the idea was not so pleasant to me as might have been expected. The more my mind had become enlightened, the more difficult it was for me to consider myself an article of property; and to pay money to those who had so grievously oppressed me seemed like taking from my sufferings the glory of triumph. I wrote to Mrs. Bruce, thanking her, but saying that being sold from one owner to another seemed too much like slavery, that such a great obligation could not be easily cancelled and that I preferred to go to my brother in California.

[9]Adapted from Isaiah 61:1. [10]Adapted from Matthew 7:12.

[11]Irish-American (1815–1875), owner of *The Citizen*, a proslavery newspaper. His comment was published in 1854.

[12]Adapted from Ecclesiastes 7:7.

Without my knowledge, Mrs. Bruce employed a gentleman in New York to enter into negotiations with Mr. Dodge. He proposed to pay three hundred dollars down, if Mr. Dodge would sell me, and enter into obligations to relinquish all claim to me or my children forever after. He who called himself my master said he scorned so small an offer for such a valuable servant. The gentleman replied, "You can do as you choose, sir. If you reject this offer you will never get anything; for the woman has friends who will convey her and her children out of the country."

Mr. Dodge concluded that "half a loaf was better than no bread," and he agreed to the proffered terms. By the next mail I received this brief letter from Mrs. Bruce: "I am rejoiced to tell you that the money for your freedom has been paid to Mr. Dodge. Come home to-morrow. I long to see you and my sweet babe."

My brain reeled as I read these lines. A gentleman near me said, "It's true; I have seen the bill of sale." "The bill of sale!" Those words struck me like a blow. So I was *sold* at last! A human being *sold* in the free city of New York! The bill of sale is on record, and future generations will learn from it that women were articles of traffic in New York, late in the nineteenth century of the Christian religion. It may hereafter prove a useful document to antiquaries, who are seeking to measure the progress of civilization in the United States. I well know the value of that bit of paper; but much as I love freedom, I do not like to look upon it. I am deeply grateful to the generous friend who procured it, but I despise the miscreant who demanded payment for what never rightfully belonged to him or his.

I had objected to having my freedom bought, yet I must confess that when it was done I felt as if a heavy load had been lifted from my weary shoulders. When I rode home in the cars[13] I was no longer afraid to unveil my face and look at people as they passed. I should have been glad to have met Daniel Dodge himself, to have had him see me and know me, that he might have mourned over the untoward circumstances which compelled him to sell me for three hundred dollars.

When I reached home, the arms of my benefactress were thrown round me, and our tears mingled. As soon as she could speak, she said, "O Linda, I'm *so* glad it's all over! You wrote to me as if you thought you were going to be transferred from one owner to another. But I did not buy you for your services. I should have done just the same if you had been going to sail for California tomorrow. I should, at least, have the satisfaction of knowing that you left me a free woman."

My heart was exceedingly full. I remembered how my poor father had tried to buy me, when I was a small child, and how he had been disappointed. I hoped his spirit was rejoicing over me now. I remembered how my good old grandmother had laid up her earnings to purchase me in later years and how often her plans had been frustrated. How that faithful, loving old heart would leap for joy, if she could look on me and my children now that we were free! My relatives had been foiled in all their efforts, but God had raised me up a friend among strangers, who had bestowed on me the precious, long-desired boon. Friend! It is a common word, often lightly used.

[13]Railroad cars.

Like other good and beautiful things, it may be tarnished by careless handling; but when I speak of Mrs. Bruce as my friend, the word is sacred.

My grandmother lived to rejoice in my freedom; but not long after, a letter came with a black seal. She had gone "where the wicked cease from troubling, and the weary are at rest."[14]

Time passed on, and a paper came to me from the South, containing an obituary notice of my uncle Phillip. It was the only case I ever knew of such an honor conferred upon a colored person. It was written by one of his friends and contained these words: "Now that death has laid him low, they call him a good man and a useful citizen; but what are eulogies to the black man, when the world has faded from his vision? It does not require man's praise to obtain rest in God's kingdom." So they called a colored man a *citizen*! Strange words to be uttered in that region!

Reader, my story ends with freedom, not in the usual way, with marriage. I and my children are now free! We are as free from the power of slaveholders as are the white people of the North; and though that, according to my ideas, is not saying a great deal, it is a vast improvement in *my* condition. The dream of my life is not yet realized. I do not sit with my children in a home of my own. I still long for a hearthstone of my own, however humble. I wish it for my children's sake far more than for my own. But God so orders circumstances as to keep me with my friend Mrs. Bruce. Love, duty, gratitude, also bind me to her side. It is a privilege to serve her who pities my oppressed people and who has bestowed the inestimable boon of freedom on me and my children.

It has been painful to me, in many ways, to recall the dreary years I passed in bondage. I would gladly forget them if I could. Yet the retrospection is not altogether without solace; for with those gloomy recollections come tender memories of my good old grandmother, like light, fleecy clouds floating over a dark and troubled sea.

1853–1858 1861

Abraham Lincoln 1809–1865

Abraham Lincoln has been idolized and mythologized beyond all other Americans, and to most of his countrymen he has become a national saint. His origins were lowly. He was born in a Kentucky log cabin to parents who were uneducated—almost illiterate. He grew up on a raw western frontier that was barren of culture, a land that was alive, as he later recalled, "with many bears and other wild animals still in the woods." When Lincoln was seven, his family moved from Kentucky to southern Indiana, where his brief formal schooling was largely at the hands of frontier schoolmasters who were themselves barely educated. Lincoln learned to write and to "cipher." To satisfy his hunger for self-improvement, he read avidly the few books he could obtain: the Bible, American history, poetry, and the biographies of great men.

[14]Adapted from Job 3:17.

In 1830, when he was twenty-one, Lincoln's family moved to Illinois, where he worked as a farmhand and a rail-splitter. He clerked in a store, managed a mill, and rose to become a village postmaster. During the Black Hawk Indian War (1831–1832) he was made the captain of a company of volunteers. Upon his return from soldiering, he ran for the Illinois legislature and was defeated, but two years later he was elected to the first of four terms (1834–1842). While in the state legislature, he began the study of law, and in 1837, when he was twenty-eight and at the midpoint of his life, he was admitted to the bar and began to practice law in Springfield, Illinois.

Lincoln was an adroit politician and an effective stump speaker. As a circuit-riding lawyer, ranging the Illinois countryside to argue before small-town courts, he built up a political following. In 1846 Illinois sent him to the U.S. Congress. There his opposition to the extension of slavery cost him the support of his constituency, and after two years in office he failed in his bid for a second term. Returning to his law practice in Springfield, he joined the newly formed Republican party, and in 1858 he was chosen as the Republican candidate for the Senate to run against Stephen A. Douglas.

The campaign that followed and the seven Lincoln-Douglas Debates on the moral issue of slavery attracted nationwide attention. Lincoln was narrowly defeated, but the campaign had brought his name before the entire nation, and in 1860 he was nominated for president by the Republican party. Although he failed to receive the majority of the popular vote, Lincoln was elected the sixteenth president of the United States, but before he could be inaugurated, the secession of Southern states had begun, the Confederate government had been formed, and the nation had been swept irresistibly toward the Civil War.

Lincoln's conduct of the war against the Confederacy and his efforts to preserve the Union were among the great achievements in American history. In 1864, after four years of bitter strife, he was reelected president, but little more than a month after his second inaugural, where he spoke of "malice toward none" and "charity for all," and only five days after the surrender of the Southern forces under General Robert E. Lee, Lincoln was assassinated by John Wilkes Booth on Good Friday, April 14, 1865.

As an orator and as a writer of prose, Lincoln had been shaped by his frontier origins and by his political ambitions. He saw the conflict of the Civil War in biblical terms and expressed himself in scriptural phrases drawn from the Bible, the book he knew best and quoted most. His enemies saw him as a crude provincial lawyer, a gawky and ungainly giant. They referred to him as a "baboon," and they laughed at his social crudities and his "lack of taste" in language. They preferred the refinements and elegancies of the ornamented political oratory of the nineteenth century. But Lincoln was an artist of the plain style. His speeches were attempts to reach the widest possible audience, and the poetic cadences and balanced rhythms of his words touched the common man and firmly molded American opinion. His inaugural addresses were both state papers and elegies that displayed the potency of simple eloquence, and in his Gettysburg Address of only ten sentences and 272 words, he created one of the most celebrated speeches in the history of the world.

FURTHER READING: J. Nicolay and J. Hay, *Abraham Lincoln, A History,* 1890; L. Robinson, *Abraham Lincoln as a Man of Letters,* 1918; D. Dodge, *Abraham Lincoln, Master of Words,* 1924; C. Sandburg, *Abraham Lincoln, The Prairie Years,* 2 vols., 1926; C. Sandburg, *Abraham Lincoln, The War Years,* 4 vols., 1939; J. Randall, *Lincoln the President,* 4 vols., 1945–1955; *Abraham Lincoln, His Speeches and Writings,* 10 vols., ed. R. Basler, 1946; B. Thomas, *Abraham Lincoln,* 1952; D. Anderson, *Abraham Lincoln,* 1970; S. Oates, *With Malice Toward None, The Life of Abraham Lincoln,* 1977; D. Anderson, *Abraham Lincoln, The Quest for Immortality,* 1982; H. Holzer, *The Lincoln Image,*

1984; R. Bruns, *Abraham Lincoln,* 1986; G. Wills, *Lincoln at Gettysburg: The Words that Remade America,* 1992; M. Neely, *The Last Best Hope of Earth, Abraham Lincoln and the Promise of America,* 1993; W. Gienapp, *Abraham Lincoln and the Civil War,* 2002; R. White, *The Eloquent President,* 2005.

TEXT: *The Collected Works of Abraham Lincoln,* 10 vols., ed. R. Basler, 1953–1955.

TO HORACE GREELEY[1]

Hon. Horace Greeley: Executive Mansion,
Dear Sir Washington, August 22, 1862.

I have just read yours of the 19th, addressed to myself through the New-York Tribune. If there be in it any statements, or assumptions of fact, which I may know to be erroneous, I do not, now and here, controvert them. If there be in it any inferences which I may believe to be falsely drawn, I do not now and here, argue against them. If there be perceptable in it an impatient and dictatorial tone, I waive it in deference to an old friend, whose heart I have always supposed to be right.

As to the policy I "seem to be pursuing" as you say, I have not meant to leave any one in doubt.

I would save the Union. I would save it the shortest way under the Constitution. The sooner the national authority can be restored; the nearer the Union will be "the Union as it was." If there be those who would not save the Union, unless they could at the same time *save* slavery, I do not agree with them. If there be those who would not save the Union unless they could at the same time *destroy* slavery, I do not agree with them. My paramount object in this struggle *is* to save the Union, and is *not* either to save or to destroy slavery. If I could save the Union without freeing *any* slave I would do it, and if I could save it by freeing *all* the slaves I would do it; and if I could save it by freeing some and leaving others alone I would also do that. What I do about slavery, and the colored race, I do because I believe it helps to save the Union; and what I forbear, I forbear because I do *not* believe it would help to save the Union. I shall do *less* whenever I shall believe what I am doing hurts the cause, and I shall do *more* whenever I shall believe doing more will help the cause. I shall try to correct errors when shown to be errors; and I shall adopt new views so fast as they shall appear to be true views.

I have here stated my purpose according to my view of *official* duty; and I intend no modification of my oft-expressed *personal* wish that all men every where could be free. Yours,

A. LINCOLN

[1]In August 1862, Horace Greeley (1811–1872), editor of the *New York Tribune,* published an editorial criticizing Lincoln's policies and urging the emancipation of slaves. The "Emancipation Proclamation," which provided that all slaves would be declared free in states still in rebellion on January 1, 1863, had already been drafted, but it was not issued until the following month, September 22, 1862.

GETTYSBURG ADDRESS

Address Delivered at the Dedication of the Cemetery at Gettysburg

Four score and seven years ago our fathers brought forth on this continent, a new nation, conceived in Liberty, and dedicated to the proposition that all men are created equal.

Now we are engaged in a great civil war, testing whether that nation, or any nation so conceived and so dedicated, can long endure. We are met on a great battle-field of that war. We have come to dedicate a portion of that field, as a final resting place for those who here gave their lives that that nation might live. It is altogether fitting and proper that we should do this.

But, in a larger sense, we can not dedicate—we can not consecrate—we can not hallow—this ground. The brave men, living and dead, who struggled here, have consecrated it, far above our poor power to add or detract. The world will little note, nor long remember what we say here, but it can never forget what they did here. It is for us the living, rather, to be dedicated here to the unfinished work which they who fought here have thus far so nobly advanced. It is rather for us to be here dedicated to the great task remaining before us—that from these honored dead we take increased devotion to that cause for which they gave the last full measure of devotion—that we here highly resolve that these dead shall not have died in vain—that this nation, under God, shall have a new birth of freedom—and that government of the people, by the people, for the people, shall not perish from the earth.

ABRAHAM LINCOLN
November 19, 1863

SECOND INAUGURAL ADDRESS

Fellow Countrymen:

At this second appearing to take the oath of the presidential office, there is less occasion for an extended address than there was at the first. Then a statement, somewhat in detail, of a course to be pursued, seemed fitting and proper. Now, at the expiration of four years, during which public declarations have been constantly called forth on every point and phase of the great contest which still absorbs the attention, and engrosses the energies of the nation, little that is new could be presented. The progress of our arms, upon which all else chiefly depends, is as well known to the public as to myself; and it is, I trust, reasonably satisfactory and encouraging to all. With high hope for the future, no prediction in regard to it is ventured.

On the occasion corresponding to this four years ago, all thoughts were anxiously directed to an impending civil-war. All dreaded it—all sought to avert it. While the inaugural address was being delivered from this place, devoted altogether to *saving* the Union without war, insurgent agents were in the city seeking to *destroy* it without war—seeking to dissol[v]e the Union, and divide effects, by negotiation. Both parties deprecated war; but one of them would *make* war rather than let the nation survive; and others would *accept* war rather than let it perish. And the war came.

One eighth of the whole population were colored slaves, not distributed generally over the Union, but localized in the Southern part of it. These slaves constituted a peculiar and powerful interest. All knew that this interest was, somehow, the cause of the war. To strengthen, perpetuate, and extend this interest was the object for which the insurgents would rend the Union, even by war; while the government claimed no right to do more than to restrict the territorial enlargement of it. Neither party expected for the war, the magnitude, or the duration, which it has already attained. Neither anticipated that the *cause* of the conflict might cease with, or even before, the conflict itself should cease. Each looked for an easier triumph, and a result less fundamental and astounding. Both read the same Bible, and pray to the same God; and each invokes His aid against the other. It may seem strange that any men should dare ask a just God's assistance in wringing their bread from the sweat of other men's faces; but let us judge not that we will be not judged.[1] The prayers of both could not be answered; that of neither has been answered fully. The Almighty has His own purposes. "Woe unto the world because of offences! for it must needs be that offences come; but woe to that man by whom the offence cometh!"[2] If we shall suppose that American Slavery is one of those offences which, in the providence of God, must needs come, but which, having continued through His appointed time, He now wills to remove, and that He gives to both North and South, this terrible war, as the woe due to those by whom the offence came, shall we discern therein any departure from those divine attributes which the believers in a Living God always ascribe to Him? Fondly do we hope—fervently do we pray—that this mighty scourge of war may speedily pass away. Yet, if God wills that it continue, until all the wealth piled by the bond-man's two hundred and fifty years of unrequited toil shall be sunk, and until every drop of blood drawn with the lash, shall be paid by another drawn with the sword, as was said three thousand years ago, so still it must be said "the judgments of the Lord, are true and righteous altogether."[3]

With malice toward none; with charity for all; with firmness in the right, as God gives us to see the right, let us strive on to finish the work we are in; to bind up the nation's wounds; to care for him who shall have borne the battle, and for his widow, and his orphan—to do all which may achieve and cherish a just, and a lasting peace, among ourselves, and with all nations.

March 4, 1865

Walt Whitman 1819–1892

In 1855, after first reading Leaves of Grass, *Ralph Waldo Emerson wrote to Walt Whitman, "I am not blind to the worth of the wonderful gift of* Leaves of Grass. *I find it the most extraordinary piece of wit and wisdom that America has yet contributed. . . . I greet you at the beginning of a great career, which yet must have had a long foreground somewhere, for such a start."*

Whitman was thirty-six years old, and nothing in his "long foreground" suggested that he would write the greatest single book of poetry in America's literary history. He had been born in 1819 in a rural village on Long Island, New York. His parents were semiliterate and could give him little more than a sympathy for political liberalism and a deistic faith shaped by the teachings of Quakerism. He had only five or six years of formal schooling, but he was a voracious reader of nineteenth-century novels, English romantic poetry, the "classics" of European literature, and the New Testament. His teachers characterized him as a "dreamy and impractical youth," and he drifted through a series of jobs as an office boy, a printer, and a country schoolteacher. He had a natural talent for journalism. For a short time he edited a Long Island weekly newspaper, and when he was twenty-two and attracted to the Bohemian life of Manhattan he went to New York City.

In New York, Whitman worked as a printer, as an editor, and as a freelance journalist contributing essays, short stories, and poems to the popular newspapers and magazines of the 1840s. When he was twenty-seven he became editor of the Brooklyn Daily Eagle, *but after only two years he was dismissed because of his radically liberal political views. He next made a brief visit to New Orleans, but he soon returned to New York City, where he opened a printing office and stationery store and began to write his greatest poetry.*

In 1855 he published the first edition of Leaves of Grass. *It contained twelve poems which Whitman himself reportedly had set in type and printed at his own expense. Few copies of his slim book of poetry were sold, yet those who read it were rarely indifferent. His apparently formless free-verse departures from poetic convention, his incantations and boasts, his sexuality (often homoerotic), and his exotic and vulgar language caused critics steeped in the gentilities of the nineteenth century to label his work a "poetry of barbarism" and warn that it was "not to be read aloud to a mixed audience." At best, the reviewers judged the poems "gross yet elevated," "superficial yet profound," a "mixture of Yankee transcendentalism and New York rowdyism." At worst, Whitman's "leaves" were called "noxious weeds," "spasmodic idiocy," "a mass of stupid filth." Emerson found the poetry "extraordinary"; Whittier judged it "loose, lurid, and impious" and threw his gift-copy into the fireplace.*

From 1857 to 1859 Whitman edited the Brooklyn Times, *and, undaunted by the critical response to the first edition, he reworked* Leaves of Grass, *publishing expanded second and third editions in 1856 and 1860. When the Civil War began, he traveled south to Washington, D.C., where he obtained an appointment as a government clerk and worked as a volunteer nurse, a "wound-dresser," in nearby military hospitals. While living in Washington he published* Drum-Taps *(1865), Civil War poems that he gathered into the fourth edition of* Leaves of Grass *(1867).*

By the appearance of the fifth edition (1871), Whitman's poetry had begun to receive increasing critical recognition in England and America. He had come to see his work as a single "poem" to be revised and improved through a lifetime, but in 1873, when he was fifty-four, he suffered a paralytic stroke. He moved from Washington, D.C., to his brother's home in Camden, New Jersey, and there, declining in his poetic abilities and cared for by a small group of devoted friends, Whitman spent most of the remaining nineteen years of his life revising successive editions of Leaves of Grass *until the final version was published shortly before his death in 1892.*

The more than four hundred poems that had appeared in the nine editions of Leaves of Grass *printed in Whitman's lifetime were unprecedented in American literature. They were a compound of commonplaces, of disorganized and raw experience, of sentimentalism, and of true poetic inspiration. They were filled with "barbaric yawps." They had ecstatic perceptions of humans and nature, united and divine. Whitman had an expansive oceanic vision, an urgent desire to incorporate the entire American experience into his life and into poetry. He aspired to be a cosmic consciousness, to experience and glorify all humanity and all human qualities, including "sex, womanhood, maternity, lusty animations, organs, acts."*

He had yearned to be the "bard of democracy," a public poet celebrated by democratic men and women "en-masse," but while he lived, the bulk of his poetry was read only by literary enthusiasts and intellectuals. In his final years, Whitman's devoted followers solemnized him as "The Good Gray Poet." He became a national figure, America's whiskery sage, but the wide popularity he had yearned to have nonetheless escaped him. He was defeated in his greatest literary ambitions, yet his poems came to exert more influence on modern American poetry than the work of any other writer. Whitman had been a radically new poet, had made his own rhythms, created his own mythic world, and in writing his sprawling epic of American democracy he helped make possible the free-verse unorthodoxies and the private literary intensities of a modern world that would one day come to honor him as one of the great poets of all time.

FURTHER READING: *The Complete Writings of Walt Whitman,* ed. R. Bucke, T. Harned, and H. Traubel, 10 vols., 1902; J. Miller, *A Critical Guide to "Leaves of Grass,"* 1957; R. Asselineau, *The Evolution of Walt Whitman,* 2 vols., 1960, 1962; *The Collected Writings of Walt Whitman,* 22 vols., ed. G. Allen et al., 1961– ; E. Miller, *Walt Whitman's Poetry,* 1968, 1969; *A Century of Whitman Criticism,* ed. E. Miller, 1969; G. Allen, *A Reader's Guide to Walt Whitman,* 1970; J. Rubin, *The Historic Whitman,* 1973; F. Stovall, *The Foreground of Leaves of Grass,* 1974; S. Black, *Whitman's Journey into Chaos,* 1975; G. Allen, *The New Walt Whitman Handbook,* 1975; J. Kaplan, *Walt Whitman, A Life,* 1980; S. Giantvalley, *Walt Whitman, 1838–1939, A Reference Guide,* 1981; P. Zweig, *Walt Whitman, The Making of the Poet,* 1984; G. Hutchinson, *The Ecstatic Whitman,* 1986; T. Wynn, *The Lunar Light of Whitman's Poetry,* 1987; K. Larson, *Whitman's Drama of Consensus,* 1988; B. Erkkila, *Whitman the Political Poet,* 1989; K. Price, *Whitman and Tradition,* 1990; E. Greenspan, *Walt Whitman and the American Reader,* 1990; M. Moon, *Disseminating Whitman,* 1991; M. Bauerlein, *Whitman and the American Idiom,* 1991; B. Fone, *Masculine Landscapes, Walt Whitman and the Homoerotic Text,* 1992; T. Nathanson, *Whitman's Presence: Body, Voice, and Writing in* Leaves of Grass, 1992; *The Continuing Presence of Walt Whitman,* ed. R. Martin, 1992; *Selected Letters of Walt Whitman,* ed. E. Miller, 1995; D. Reynolds, *Walt Whitman's America, A Cultural Biography,* 1995; E. Greenspan, *Cambridge Companion to Walt Whitman,* 1995; *Walt Whitman and the World,* ed. E. Folsom and G. Allen, 1995; E. Ingvar, *Whitman between Impressionism and Expressionism,* 1995; *Walt Whitman, the Contemparary Reviews,* ed. K. Price, 1996; B. Erkkila and J. Grossman, *Breaking Ground,* 1996; J. Krieg, *A Whitman Chronology,* 1998; *Walt Whitman, An Encyclopedia,* ed. J. LeMaster and D. Kummings, 1998; J. Loving, *Walt Whitman, Song of Himself,* 1999; S. Mack, *The Pragmatic Whitman,* 2002.

TEXTS: *The Collected Writings of Walt Whitman: The Early Poems and the Fiction,* Vol. II, ed. F. Stovall, 1964; *Leaves of Grass, Comprehensive Reader's Edition,* ed. H. Blodgett and S. Bradley, 1965.

PREFACE TO THE 1855 EDITION OF *LEAVES OF GRASS*[1]

America does not repel the past or what it has produced under its forms or amid other politics or the idea of castes or the old religions. . . . accepts the lesson with calmness . . . is not so impatient as has been supposed that the slough[2] still sticks to opinions and manners and literature while the life which served its requirements has passed into the new life of the new forms . . . perceives that the corpse is slowly borne from the eating and sleeping rooms of the house . . . perceives that it waits a little while in the door . . . that it was fittest for its days . . . that its action has descended to the stalwart and wellshaped heir who approaches . . . and that he shall be fittest for his days.

The Americans of all nations at any time upon the earth have probably the fullest poetical nature. The United States themselves are essentially the greatest poem. In the history of the earth hitherto the largest and most stirring appear tame and orderly to their ampler largeness and stir. Here at last is something in the doings of man that corresponds with the broadcast doings of the day and night. Here is not merely a nation but a teeming nation of nations. Here is action untied from strings necessarily blind to particulars and details magnificently moving in vast masses. Here is the hospitality which forever indicates heroes. . . . Here are the roughs and beards and space and ruggedness and nonchalance that the soul loves. Here the performance disdaining the trivial unapproached in the tremendous audacity of its crowds and groupings and the push of its perspective spreads with crampless and flowing breath and showers its prolific and splendid extravagance. One sees it must indeed own the riches of the summer and winter, and need never be bankrupt while corn grows from the ground or the orchards drop apples or the bays contain fish or men beget children upon women.

Other states indicate themselves in their deputies. . . . but the genius of the United States is not best or most in its executives or legislatures, nor in its ambassadors or authors or colleges or churches or parlors, nor even in its newspapers or inventors . . . but always most in the common people. Their manners speech dress friendships—the freshness and candor of their physiognomy—the picturesque looseness of their carriage . . . their deathless attachment to freedom—their aversion to anything indecorous or soft or mean—the practical acknowledgment of the citizens of one state by the citizens of all other states—the fierceness of their roused resentment—their curiosity and welcome of novelty—their self-esteem and wonderful sympathy—their susceptibility to a slight—the air they have of persons who never knew how it felt to stand in the presence of superiors—the fluency of their speech—their delight in music, the sure symptom of manly tenderness and native elegance of soul . . . their good temper and openhandedness—the

[1]The first (1855) edition of *Leaves of Grass* contained a dozen poems and a preface in which Whitman declared his literary philosophy. Later editions omitted the 1855 Preface, but portions were incorporated in poems subsequently added to the text. The marks of ellipsis (. . .) are Whitman's, as are the eccentric spellings.

[2]Dead tissue, such as the cast-off skin of a snake.

terrible significance of their elections—the President's taking off his hat to them not they to him—these too are unrhymed poetry. It awaits the gigantic and generous treatment worthy of it.

The largeness of nature or the nation were monstrous without a corresponding largeness and generosity of the spirit of the citizen. Not nature nor swarming states nor streets and steamships nor prosperous business nor farms nor capital nor learning may suffice for the ideal of man . . . nor suffice the poet. No reminiscences may suffice either. A live nation can always cut a deep mark and can have the best authority the cheapest . . . namely from its own soul. This is the sum of the profitable uses of individuals or states and of present action and grandeur and of the subjects of poets.—As if it were necessary to trot back generation after generation to the eastern records! As if the beauty and sacredness of the demonstrable must fall behind that of the mythical! As if men do not make their mark out of any times! As if the opening of the western continent by discovery and what has transpired since in North and South America were less than the small theatre of the antique or the aimless sleepwalking of the middle ages! The pride of the United States leaves the wealth and finesse of the cities and all returns of commerce and agriculture and all the magnitude of geography or shows of exterior victory to enjoy the breed of fullsized men or one fullsized man unconquerable and simple.

The American poets are to enclose old and new for America is the race of races. Of them a bard[3] is to be commensurate with a people. To him the other continents arrive as contributions . . . he gives them reception for their sake and his own sake. His spirit responds to his country's spirit. . . . he incarnates its geography and natural life and rivers and lakes. Mississippi with annual freshets and changing chutes, Missouri and Columbia and Ohio and Saint Lawrence with the falls and beautiful masculine Hudson, do not embouchure[4] where they spend themselves more than they embouchure into him. The blue breadth over the inland sea of Virginia and Maryland and the sea off Massachusetts and Maine and over Manhattan bay and over Champlain and Erie and over Ontario and Huron and Michigan and Superior, and over the Texan and Mexican and Floridian and Cuban seas and over the seas off California and Oregon, is not tallied by the blue breadth of the waters below more than the breadth of above and below is tallied by him. When the long Atlantic coast stretches longer and the Pacific coast stretches longer he easily stretches with them north or south. He spans between them also from east to west and reflects what is between them. On him rise solid growths that offset the growths of pine and cedar and hemlock and liveoak and locust and chestnut and hickory and limetree and cottonwood and tuliptree and cactus and wildvine and tamarind and persimmon. . . . and tangles as tangled as any canebrake or swamp. . . . and forests coated with transparent ice and icicles hanging from the boughs and crackling in the wind. . . . and sides and peaks of mountains. . . . and pasturage sweet and free as savannah or upland or prairie. . . . with flights and songs and screams that answer those of the wildpigeon and highhold[5] and orchard oriole and coot and surf-duck and redshouldered-hawk and fish-hawk and white-ibis and indian-hen and cat-owl and water-pheasant and qua-bird and pied-sheldrake and blackbird

[3]The poet-singer of a tribe or nation. [4]Pour out, as from a river mouth. [5]Woodpecker.

and mockingbird and buzzard and condor and night-heron and eagle. To him the hereditary countenance descends both mother's and father's. To him enter the essences of the real things and past and present events—of the enormous diversity of temperature and agriculture and mines—the tribes of red aborigines—the weatherbeaten vessels entering new ports or making landings on rocky coasts—the first settlements north or south—the rapid stature and muscle—the haughty defiance of '76,[6] and the war and peace and formation of the constitution. . . . the union always surrounded by blatherers and always calm and impregnable—the perpetual coming of immigrants—the wharf hem'd cities and superior marine—the unsurveyed interior—the loghouses and clearings and wild animals and hunters and trappers. . . . the free commerce—the fisheries and whaling and golddigging—the endless gestation of new states—the convening of Congress every December,[7] the members duly coming up from all climates and the uttermost parts. . . . the noble character of the young mechanics[8] and of all free American workmen and workwomen. . . . the general ardor and friendliness and enterprise—the perfect equality of the female with the male. . . . the large amativeness[9]— the fluid movement of the population—the factories and mercantile life and laborsaving machinery—the Yankee swap[10]—the New-York firemen and the target excursion[11]—the southern plantation life—the character of the northeast and of the northwest and southwest—slavery and the tremulous spreading of hands to protect it, and the stern opposition to it which shall never cease till it ceases or the speaking of tongues and the moving of lips cease. For such the expression of the American poet is to be transcendent and new. It is to be indirect and not direct or descriptive or epic. Its quality goes through these to much more. Let the age and wars of other nations be chanted and their eras and characters be illustrated and that finish the verse. Not so the great psalm of the republic. Here the theme is creative and has vista. Here comes one among the wellbeloved stonecutters and plans with decision and science and sees the solid and beautiful forms of the future where there are now no solid forms.

Of all nations the United States with veins full of poetical stuff most need poets and will doubtless have the greatest and use them the greatest. Their Presidents shall not be their common referee so much as their poets shall. Of all mankind the great poet is the equable man. Not in him but off from him things are grotesque or eccentric or fail of their sanity. Nothing out of its place is good and nothing in its place is bad. He bestows on every object or quality its fit proportions neither more nor less. He is the arbiter of the diverse and he is the key. He is the equalizer of his age and land. . . . he supplies what wants supplying and checks what wants checking. If peace is the routine out of him speaks the spirit of peace, large, rich, thrifty, building vast and populous cities, encouraging agriculture and the arts and commerce—lighting the study of man, the soul, immortality—federal, state or municipal government, marriage, health, freetrade, intertravel by land and sea. . . . nothing too close, nothing too far off . . . the stars not too far off. In war he

[6]The Declaration of Independence.
[7]In the nineteenth century the Congress of the United States convened in December.
[8]Manual workers, artisans. [9]Phrenological term signifying a capacity for loving others.
[10]Bargain. [11]Trip to a shooting meet.

is the most deadly force of the war. Who recruits him recruits horse and foot[12] . . . he fetches parks[13] of artillery the best that engineer ever knew. If the time becomes slothful and heavy he knows how to arouse it . . . he can make every word he speaks draw blood. Whatever stagnates in the flat[14] of custom or obedience or legislation he never stagnates. Obedience does not master him, he masters it. High up out of reach he stands turning a concentrated light . . . he turns the pivot with his finger . . . he baffles the swiftest runners as he stands and easily overtakes and envelopes them. The time straying toward infidelity and confections and persiflage he withholds by his steady faith . . . he spreads out his dishes . . . he offers the sweet firm-fibred meat that grows men and women. His brain is the ultimate brain. He is no arguer . . . he is judgment. He judges not as the judge judges but as the sun falling around a helpless thing. As he sees the farthest he has the most faith. His thoughts are the hymns of the praise of things. In the talk on the soul and eternity and God off of his equal plane he is silent. He sees eternity less like a play with a prologue and denouement. . . . he sees eternity in men and women . . . he does not see men and women as dreams or dots. Faith is the antiseptic of the soul . . . it pervades the common people and preserves them . . . they never give up believing and expecting and trusting. There is that indescribable freshness and unconsciousness about an illiterate person that humbles and mocks the power of the noblest expressive genius. The poet sees for a certainty how one not a great artist may be just as sacred and perfect as the greatest artist. . . . . The power to destroy or remould is freely used by him but never the power of attack. What is past is past. If he does not expose superior models and prove himself by every step he takes he is not what is wanted. The presence of the greatest poet conquers . . . not parleying or struggling or any prepared attempts. Now he has passed that way see after him! there is not left any vestige of despair or misanthropy or cunning or exclusiveness or the ignominy of a nativity or color or delusion of hell or the necessity of hell. . . . . and no man thenceforward shall be degraded for ignorance or weakness or sin.

The greatest poet hardly knows pettiness or triviality. If he breathes into any thing that was before thought small it dilates with the grandeur and life of the universe. He is a seer. . . . he is individual . . . he is complete in himself. . . . the others are as good as he, only he sees it and they do not. He is not one of the chorus. . . . he does not stop for any regulation . . . he is the president of regulation. What the eyesight does to the rest he does to the rest. Who knows the curious mystery of the eyesight? The other senses corroborate themselves, but this is removed from any proof but its own and foreruns the identities of the spiritual world. A single glance of it mocks all the investigations of man and all the instruments and books of the earth and all reasoning. What is marvellous? what is unlikely? what is impossible or baseless or vague? after you have once just opened the space of a peachpit and given audience to far and near to the sunset and had all things enter with electric swiftness softly and duly without confusion or jostling or jam.

The land and sea, the animals fishes and birds, the sky of heaven and the orbs, the forests mountains and rivers, are not small themes . . . but folks

[12]Horse soldiers (cavalry) and foot soldiers (infantry).
[13]Depots, assembly areas. [14]Shoal, marsh.

expect of the poet to indicate more than the beauty and dignity which always attach to dumb real objects . . . . they expect him to indicate the path between reality and their souls. Men and women perceive the beauty well enough . . probably as well as he. The passionate tenacity of hunters, woodmen, early risers, cultivators of gardens and orchards and fields, the love of healthy women for the manly form, seafaring persons, drivers of horses, the passion for light and the open air, all is an old varied sign of the unfailing perception of beauty and of a residence of the poetic in outdoor people. They can never be assisted by poets to perceive . . . some may but they never can. The poetic quality is not marshalled in rhyme or uniformity or abstract addresses to things nor in melancholy complaints or good precepts, but is the life of these and much else and is in the soul. The profit of rhyme is that it drops seeds of a sweeter and more luxuriant rhyme, and of uniformity that it conveys itself into its own roots in the ground out of sight. The rhyme and uniformity of perfect poems show the free growth of metrical laws and bud from them as unerringly and loosely as lilacs or roses on a bush, and take shapes as compact as the shapes of chestnuts and oranges and melons and pears, and shed the perfume impalpable to form. The fluency and ornaments of the finest poems or music or orations or recitations are not independent but dependent. All beauty comes from beautiful blood and a beautiful brain. If the greatnesses are in conjunction in a man or woman it is enough. . . . the fact will prevail through the universe. . . . but the gaggery[15] and gilt of a million years will not prevail. Who troubles himself about his ornaments or fluency is lost. This is what you shall do: Love the earth and sun and the animals, despise riches, give alms to every one that asks, stand up for the stupid and crazy, devote your income and labor to others, hate tyrants, argue not concerning God, have patience and indulgence toward the people, take off your hat to nothing known or unknown or to any man or number of men, go freely with powerful uneducated persons and with the young and with the mothers of families, read these leaves in the open air every season of every year of your life, re-examine all you have been told at school or church or in any book, dismiss whatever insults your own soul, and your very flesh shall be a great poem and have the richest fluency not only in its words but in the silent lines of its lips and face and between the lashes of your eyes and in every motion and joint of your body. . . . . . . The poet shall not spend his time in unneeded work. He shall know that the ground is always ready ploughed and manured. . . . others may not know it but he shall. He shall go directly to the creation. His trust shall master the trust of everything he touches. . . . and shall master all attachment.

The known universe has one complete lover and that is the greatest poet. He consumes an eternal passion and is indifferent which chance happens and which possible contingency of fortune or misfortune and persuades daily and hourly his delicious pay. What balks or breaks others is fuel for his burning progress to contact and amorous joy. Other proportions of the reception of pleasure dwindle to nothing to his proportions. All expected from heaven or from the highest he is rapport with in the sight of the daybreak or a scene of the winter woods or the presence of children playing or with his arm round the neck of a man or woman. His love above all love has leisure and

[15]Sham.

expanse. . . . he leaves room ahead of himself. He is no irresolute or suspicious lover . . . he is sure . . . he scorns intervals. His experience and the showers and thrills are not for nothing. Nothing can jar him. . . . suffering and darkness cannot—death and fear cannot. To him complaint and jealousy and envy are corpses buried and rotten in the earth. . . . he saw them buried. The sea is not surer of the shore or the shore of the sea than he is of the fruition of his love and of all perfection and beauty.

The fruition of beauty is no chance of hit or miss . . . it is inevitable as life. . . . it is exact and plumb as gravitation. From the eyesight proceeds another eyesight and from the hearing proceeds another hearing and from the voice proceeds another voice eternally curious of the harmony of things with man. To these respond perfections not only in the committees that were supposed to stand for the rest but in the rest themselves just the same. These understand the law of perfection in masses and floods . . . that its finish is to each for itself and onward from itself . . . that it is profuse and impartial . . . that there is not a minute of the light or dark nor an acre of the earth or sea without it—nor any direction of the sky nor any trade or employment nor any turn of events. This is the reason that about the proper expression of beauty there is precision and balance . . . one part does not need to be thrust above another. The best singer is not the one who has the most lithe and powerful organ . . . the pleasure of poems is not in them that take the handsomest measure and similes and sound.

Without effort and without exposing in the least how it is done the greatest poet brings the spirit of any or all events and passions and scenes and persons some more and some less to bear on your individual character as you hear or read. To do this well is to compete with the laws that pursue and follow time. What is the purpose must surely be there and the clue of it must be there. . . . and the faintest indication is the indication of the best and then becomes the clearest indication. Past and present and future are not disjoined but joined. The greatest poet forms the consistence of what is to be from what has been and is. He drags the dead out of their coffins and stands them again on their feet. . . . he says to the past, Rise and walk before me that I may realize you. He learns the lesson. . . . he places himself where the future becomes present. The greatest poet does not only dazzle his rays over character and scenes and passions . . . he finally ascends and finishes all . . . he exhibits the pinnacles that no man can tell what they are for or what is beyond. . . . he glows a moment on the extremest verge. He is most wonderful in his last half-hidden smile or frown . . . by that flash of the moment of parting the one that sees it shall be encouraged or terrified afterward for many years. The greatest poet does not moralize or make applications of morals . . . he knows the soul. The soul has that measureless pride which consists in never acknowledging any lessons but its own. But it has sympathy as measureless as its pride and the one balances the other and neither can stretch too far while it stretches in company with the other. The inmost secrets of art sleep with the twain. The greatest poet has lain close betwixt both and they are vital in his style and thoughts.

The art of art, the glory of expression and the sunshine of the light of letters is simplicity. Nothing is better than simplicity . . . nothing can make up for excess or for the lack of definiteness. To carry on the heave of impulse and pierce intellectual depths and give all subjects their articulations are powers neither common nor very uncommon. But to speak in literature with the perfect rectitude and insousiance[16] of the movements of animals and the unimpeachableness of the sentiment of trees in the woods and grass by the roadside is the flawless triumph of art. If you have looked on him who has achieved it you have looked on one of the masters of the artists of all nations and times. You shall not contemplate the flight of the graygull over the bay or the mettlesome action of the blood horse or the tall leaning of sunflowers on their stalk or the appearance of the sun journeying through heaven or the appearance of the moon afterward with any more satisfaction than you shall contemplate him. The greatest poet has less a marked style and is more the channel of thoughts and things without increase or diminution, and is the free channel of himself. He swears to his art, I will not be meddlesome, I will not have in my writing any elegance or effort or originality to hang in the way between me and the rest like curtains. I will have nothing hang in the way, not the richest curtains. What I tell I tell for precisely what it is. Let who may exalt or startle or fascinate or sooth[17] I will have purposes as health or heat or snow has and be as regardless of observation. What I experience or portray shall go from my composition without a shred of my composition. You shall stand by my side and look in the mirror with me.

The old red blood and stainless gentility of great poets will be proved by their unconstraint. A heroic person walks at his ease through and out of that custom or precedent or authority that suits him not. Of the traits of the brotherhood of writers savans[18] musicians inventors and artists nothing is finer than silent defiance advancing from new free forms. In the need of poems philosophy politics mechanism science behaviour, the craft of art, an appropriate native grand-opera, shipcraft, or any craft, he is greatest forever and forever who contributes the greatest original practical example. The cleanest expression is that which finds no sphere worthy of itself and makes one.

The messages of great poets to each man and woman are, Come to us on equal terms, Only then can you understand us, We are no better than you, What we enclose you enclose, What we enjoy you may enjoy. Did you suppose there could be only one Supreme? We affirm there can be unnumbered Supremes, and that one does not countervail another any more than one eyesight countervails another . . . and that men can be good or grand only of the consciousness of their supremacy within them. What do you think is the grandeur of storms and dismemberments and the deadliest battles and wrecks and the wildest fury of the elements and the power of the sea and the motion of nature and of the throes of human desires and dignity and hate and love? It is that something in the soul which says, Rage on, Whirl on, I tread master here and everywhere, Master of the spasms of the sky and of the shatter of the sea, Master of nature and passion and death, And of all terror and all pain.

The American bards shall be marked for generosity and affection and for encouraging competitors . . They shall be kosmos[19] . . without monopoly or secresy[20] . . glad to pass any thing to any one . . hungry for equals night and day. They shall not be careful of riches and privilege . . . . they shall be riches and privilege. . . . they shall perceive who the most affluent man is.

[16]Insouciance, lack of concern. [17]Changed to "soothe" in later texts.
[18]Savants, sages. [19]Cosmos. [20]Changed to "secrecy" in later texts.

The most affluent man is he that confronts all the shows he sees by equivalents out of the stronger wealth of himself. The American bard shall delineate no class of persons nor one or two out of the strata of interests nor love most nor truth most nor the soul most nor the body most. . . . and not be for the eastern states more than the western or the northern states more than the southern.

Exact science and its practical movements are no checks on the greatest poet but always his encouragement and support. The outset and remembrance are there . . . there the arms that lifted him first and brace[21] him best. . . . there he returns after all his goings and comings. The sailor and traveler . . the anatomist, chemist, astronomer, geologist, phrenologist, spiritualist, mathematician, historian and lexicographer are not poets, but they are the lawgivers of poets and their construction underlies the structure of every perfect poem. No matter what rises or is uttered they sent the seed of the conception of it . . . of them and by them stand the visible proofs of souls . . . . . always of their fatherstuff[22] must be begotten the sinewy races of bards. If there shall be love and content between the father and the son and if the greatness of the son is the exuding of the greatness of the father there shall be love between the poet and the man of demonstrable science. In the beauty of poems are the tuft and final applause of science.

Great is the faith of the flush of knowledge and of the investigation of the depths of qualities and things. Cleaving and circling here swells the soul of the poet yet it[23] president of itself always. The depths are fathomless and therefore calm. The innocence and nakedness are resumed . . . they are neither modest nor immodest. The whole theory of the special and supernatural and all that was twined with it or educed[24] out of it departs as a dream. What has ever happened . . . . what happens and whatever may or shall happen, the vital laws enclose all . . . . they are sufficent[25] for any case and for all cases . . . none to be hurried or retarded . . . . any miracle of affairs or persons inadmissible in the vast clear scheme where every motion and every spear of grass and the frames and spirits of men and women and all that concerns them are unspeakably perfect miracles all referring to all and each distinct and in its place. It is also not consistent with the reality of the soul to admit that there is anything in the known universe more divine than men and women.

Men and women and the earth and all upon it are simply to be taken as they are, and the investigation of their past and present and future shall be unintermitted and shall be done with perfect candor. Upon this basis philosophy speculates ever looking toward the poet, ever regarding the eternal tendencies of all toward happiness never inconsistent with what is clear to the senses and to the soul. For the eternal tendencies of all toward happiness make the only point of sane philosophy. Whatever comprehends less than that . . . whatever is less than the laws of light and of astronomical motion . . . or less than the laws that follow the thief the liar the glutton and the drunkard through this life and doubtless afterward. . . . . . or less than vast stretches of time or the slow formation of density or the patient upheaving of strata—is of no account. Whatever would put God in a poem or system of

[21]Changed to "braced" in later texts. [22]Seminal fluid. [23]Corrected to "is" in later texts.
[24]Brought. [25]Changed to "sufficient" in later texts.

philosophy as contending against some being or influence is also of no account. Sanity and ensemble characterise the great master . . . spoilt in one principle all is spoilt. The great master has nothing to do with miracles. He sees health for himself in being one of the mass . . . . he sees the hiatus in singular eminence. To the perfect shape comes common ground. To be under the general law is great for that is to correspond with it. The master knows that he is unspeakably great and that all are unspeakably great . . . . that nothing for instance is greater than to conceive children and bring them up well . . . that to be is just as great as to perceive or tell.

In the make of the great masters the idea of political liberty is indispensible. Liberty takes the adherence of heroes wherever men and women exist. . . . but never takes any adherence or welcome from the rest more than from poets. They are the voice and exposition of liberty. They out of ages are worthy the grand idea . . . . to them it is confided and they must sustain it. Nothing has precedence of it and nothing can warp or degrade it. The attitude of great poets is to cheer up slaves and horrify despots. The turn of their necks, the sound of their feet, the motions of their wrists, are full of hazard to the one and hope to the other. Come nigh them awhile and though they neither speak or advise you shall learn the faithful American lesson. Liberty is poorly served by men whose good intent is quelled from one failure or two failures or any number of failures, or from the casual indifference or ingratitude of the people, or from the sharp show of the tushes[26] of power, or the bringing to bear soldiers and cannon or any penal statutes. Liberty relies upon itself, invites no one, promises nothing, sits in calmness and light, is positive and composed, and knows no discouragement. The battle rages with many a loud alarm and frequent advance and retreat . . . . the enemy triumphs . . . . the prison, the handcuffs, the iron necklace and anklet, the scaffold, garrote and leadballs do their work . . . . the cause is asleep . . . . the strong throats are choked with their own blood . . . . the young men drop their eyelashes toward the ground when they pass each other . . . . and is liberty gone out of that place? No never. When liberty goes it is not the first to go nor the second or third to go . . it waits for all the rest to go . . it is the last . . . When the memories of the old martyrs are faded utterly away . . . . when the large names of patriots are laughed at in the public halls from the lips of the orators . . . . when the boys are no more christened after the same but christened after tyrants and traitors instead . . . . when the laws of the free are grudgingly permitted and laws for informers and bloodmoney are sweet to the taste of the people . . . . when I and you walk abroad upon the earth stung with compassion at the sight of numberless brothers answering our equal friendship and calling no man master—and when we are elated with noble joy at the sight of slaves . . . . when the soul retires in the cool communion of the night and surveys its experience and has much extasy over the word and deed that put back a helpless innocent person into the gripe of the gripers or into any cruel inferiority . . . when those in all parts of these states who could easier realize the true American character but do not yet—when the swarms of cringers, suckers,[27] doughfaces,[28] lice of politics, planners of sly involutions for their own preferment to

[26]Tusks, teeth. [27]Blackmailing politicians. [28]Pliable, unprincipled men.

city offices or state legislatures or the judiciary or congress or the presidency, obtain a response of love and natural deference from the people whether they get the offices or no . . . . when it is better to be a bound booby[29] and rogue in office at a high salary than the poorest free mechanic or farmer with his hat unmoved from his head and firm eyes and a candid and generous heart . . . . and when servility by town or state or the federal government or any oppression on a large scale or small scale can be tried on without its own punishment following duly after in exact proportion against the smallest chance of escape . . . . or rather when all life and all the souls of men and women are discharged from any part of the earth—then only shall the instinct of liberty be discharged from that part of the earth.

As the attributes of the poets of the kosmos concentre in the real body and soul and in the pleasure of things they possess the superiority of genuineness over all fiction and romance. As they emit themselves facts are showered over with light . . . . the daylight is lit with more volatile light . . . . also the deep between the setting and rising sun goes deeper many fold. Each precise object or condition or combination or process exhibits a beauty . . . . the multiplication table its—old age its—the carpenter's trade its—the grand-opera its . . . . the hugehulled cleanshaped New-York clipper at sea under steam or full sail gleams with unmatched beauty . . . . the American circles and large harmonies of government gleam with theirs . . . . and the commonest definite intentions and actions with theirs. The poets of the kosmos advance through all interpositions and coverings and turmoils and strategems to first principles. They are of use . . . . they dissolve poverty from its need and riches from its conceit. You large proprietor they say shall not realize or perceive more than any one else. The owner of the library is not he who holds a legal title to it having bought and paid for it. Any one and every one is owner of the library who can read the same through all the varieties of tongues and subjects and styles, and in whom they enter with ease and take residence and force toward paternity and maternity, and make supple and powerful and rich and large. . . . . These American states strong and healthy and accomplished shall receive no pleasure from violations of natural models and must not permit them. In paintings or mouldings or carvings in mineral or wood, or in the illustrations of books or newspapers, or in any comic or tragic prints, or in the patterns of woven stuffs or any thing to beautify rooms or furniture or costumes, or to put upon cornices or monuments or on the prows or sterns of ships, or to put anywhere before the human eye indoors or out, that which distorts honest shapes or which creates unearthly beings or places or contingencies is a nuisance and revolt. Of the human form especially it is so great it must never be made ridiculous. Of ornaments to a work nothing outre[30] can be allowed . . but those ornaments can be allowed that conform to the perfect facts of the open air and that flow out of the nature of the work and come irrepressibly from it and are necessary to the completion of the work. Most works are most beautiful without ornament . . . Exaggerations will be revenged in human physiology. Clean and vigorous children are jetted[31] and conceived only in those communities where the models of natural forms are public

[29]A political hack controlled by special interests. [30]Extravagant.
[31]I.e., produced by a jet of seminal fluid.

every day. . . . . Great genius and the people of these states must never be demeaned to romances. As soon as histories are properly told there is no more need of romances.

The great poets are also to be known by the absence in them of tricks and by the justification of perfect personal candor. Then folks echo a new cheap joy and a divine voice leaping from their brains: How beautiful is candor! All faults may be forgiven of him who has perfect candor. Henceforth let no man of us lie, for we have seen that openness wins the inner and outer world and that there is no single exception, and that never since our earth gathered itself in a mass have deceit or subterfuge or prevarication attracted its smallest particle or the faintest tinge of a shade—and that through the enveloping wealth and rank of a state or the whole republic of states a sneak or sly person shall be discovered and despised . . . . and that the soul has never been once fooled and never can be fooled . . . . and thrift without the loving nod of the soul is only a fœtid puff . . . . and there never grew up in any of the continents of the globe nor upon any planet or satellite or star, nor upon the asteroids, under the fluid wet of the sea, nor in that condition which precedes nor in any part of the ethereal space, nor in the midst of density, nor the birth of babes, nor at any time during the changes of life, nor in that condition that follows what we term death, nor in any stretch of abeyance or action afterward of vitality, nor in any process of formation or reformation anywhere, a being whose instinct hated the truth.

Extreme caution or prudence, the soundest organic health, large hope and comparison and fondness for women and children, large alimentiveness and destructiveness and causality,[32] with a perfect sense of the oneness of nature and the propriety of the same spirit applied to human affairs . . these are called up of the float[33] of the brain of the world to be parts of the greatest poet from his birth out of his mother's womb and from her birth out of her mother's. Caution seldom goes far enough. It has been thought that the prudent citizen was the citizen who applied himself to solid gains and did well for himself and his family and completed a lawful life without debt or crime. The greatest poet sees and admits these economies as he sees the economies of food and sleep, but has higher notions of prudence than to think he gives much when he gives a few slight attentions at the latch of the gate. The premises of the prudence of life are not the hospitality of it or the ripeness and harvest of it. Beyond the independence of a little sum laid aside for burial-money, and of a few clapboards around the shingles overhead on a lot[34] of American soil owned, and the easy dollars that supply the year's plain clothing and meals, the melancholy prudence of the abandonment of such a great being as a man is to the toss and pallor of years of moneymaking with all their scorching days and icy nights and all their stifling deceits and underhanded dodgings, or infinitessimals of parlors, or shameless stuffing while others starve . . and all the loss of the bloom and odor of the earth and of the flowers and atmosphere and of the sea and of the true taste of the women and men you pass or have to do with in youth or middle age, and the issuing sickness and desperate revolt at the close of a life without elevation or

[32]Phrenological terms meaning an appetite for food, an interest in destruction, and a tendency to trace effects to their causes.

[33]Flow or fluid. [34]Small plot of land.

naivete, and the ghastly chatter of a death without serenity or majesty, is the great fraud upon modern civilization and forethought, blotching the surface and system which civilization undeniably drafts, and moistening with tears the immense features it spreads and spreads with such velocity before the reached kisses of the soul . . . Still the right explanation remains to be made about prudence. The prudence of the mere wealth and respectability of the most esteemed life appears too faint for the eye to observe at all when little and large alike drop quietly aside at the thought of the prudence suitable for immortality. What is wisdom that fills the thinness of a year or seventy or eighty years to wisdom spaced out by ages and coming back at a certain time with strong reinforcements and rich presents and the clear faces of wedding-guests as far as you can look in every direction running gaily toward you? Only the soul is of itself . . . . all else has reference to what ensues. All that a person does or thinks is of consequence. Not a move can a man or woman make that affects him or her in a day or a month or any part of the direct lifetime or the hour of death but the same affects him or her onward afterward through the indirect lifetime. The indirect is always as great and real as the direct. The spirit receives from the body just as much as it gives to the body. Not one name of word or deed . . not of venereal sores or discolorations . . not the privacy of the onanist[35] . . not of the putrid veins of gluttons or rumdrinkers . . . not peculation[36] or cunning or betrayal or murder . . no serpentine poison of those that seduce women . . not the foolish yielding of women . . not prostitution . . not of any depravity of young men . . not of the attainment of gain by discreditable means . . not any nastiness of appetite . . not any harshness of officers to men or judges to prisoners or fathers to sons or sons to fathers or of husbands to wives or bosses to their boys . . not of greedy looks or malignant wishes . . . nor any of the wiles practised by people upon themselves . . . ever is or ever can be stamped on the programme but it is duly realized and returned, and that returned in further performances . . . and they returned again. Nor can the push of charity or personal force ever be any thing else than the profoundest reason, whether it bring arguments to hand or no. No specification is necessary . . to add or subtract or divide is in vain. Little or big, learned or unlearned, white or black, legal or illegal, sick or well, from the first inspiration down the windpipe to the last expiration out of it, all that a male or female does that is vigorous and benevolent and clean is so much sure profit to him or her in the unshakable order of the universe and through the whole scope of it forever. If the savage or felon is wise it is well . . . . if the greatest poet or savan is wise it is simply the same . . . if the President or chief justice is wise it is the same . . . if the young mechanic or farmer is wise it is no more or less . . if the prostitute is wise it is no more nor less. The interest will come round . . all will come round. All the best actions of war and peace . . . all help given to relatives and strangers and the poor and old and sorrowful and young children and widows and the sick, and to all shunned persons . . all furtherance of fugitives and of the escape of

[35]In the nineteenth century, the sin for which the Lord slew Onan (Genesis 38:9) was thought to have been masturbation.
[36]Embezzlement.

slaves . . all the self-denial that stood steady and aloof on wrecks and saw others take the seats of the boats . . . all offering of substance or life for the good old cause, or for a friend's sake or opinion's sake . . . all pains of enthusiasts scoffed at by their neighbors . . all the vast sweet love and precious suffering of mothers . . all honest men baffled in strifes recorded or unrecorded . . . . all the grandeur and good of the few ancient nations whose fragments of annals we inherit . . and all the good of the hundreds of far mightier and more ancient nations unknown to us by name or date or location . . . . all that was ever manfully begun, whether it succeeded or no . . . . all that has at any time been well suggested out of the divine heart of man or by the divinity of his mouth or by the shaping of his great hands . . and all that is well thought or done this day on any part of the surface of the globe . . or on any of the wandering stars or fixed stars by those there as we are here . . or that is henceforth to be well thought or done by you whoever you are, or by any one—these singly and wholly inured at their time and inure now and will inure always to the identities from which they sprung or shall spring . . . Did you guess any of them lived only its moment? The world does not so exist . . no parts palpable or impalpable so exist . . . no result exists now without being from its long antecedent result, and that from its antecedent, and so backward without the farthest mention-able spot coming a bit nearer the beginning than any other spot. . . . Whatever satisfies the soul is truth. The prudence of the greatest poet answers at last the craving and glut of the soul, is not contemptuous of less ways of prudence if they conform to its ways, puts off nothing, permits no let-up for its own case or any case, has no particular sabbath or judgment-day, divides not the living from the dead or the righteous from the unrighteous, is satisfied with the present, matches every thought or act by its correlative, knows no possible forgiveness or deputed atonement . . knows that the young man who composedly periled his life and lost it has done exceeding well for himself, while the man who has not periled his life and retains it to old age in riches and ease has perhaps achieved nothing for himself worth mentioning . . and that only that person has no great prudence to learn who has learnt to prefer real longlived things, and favors body and soul the same, and perceives the indirect assuredly following the direct, and what evil or good he does leaping onward and waiting to meet him again—and who in his spirit in any emergency whatever neither hurries or avoids death.

The direct trial of him who would be the greatest poet is today. If he does not flood himself with the immediate age as with vast oceanic tides . . . . . and if he does not attract his own land body and soul to himself and hang on its neck with incomparable love and plunge his semitic[37] muscle into its merits and demerits . . . and if he be not himself the age transfigured . . . . and if to him is not opened the eternity which gives similitude to all periods and locations and processes and animate and inanimate forms, and which is the bond of time, and rises up from its inconceivable vagueness and infiniteness in the swimming shape of today, and is held by the ductile anchors of life, and makes the present spot the passage from what was to what shall be,

[37]Seminal.

and commits itself to the representation of this wave of an hour and this one of the sixty beautiful children of the wave—let him merge in the general run and wait his development. . . . . Still the final test of poems or any character or work remains. The prescient poet projects himself centuries ahead and judges performer or performance after the changes of time. Does it live through them? Does it still hold on untired? Will the same style and the direction of genius to similar points be satisfactory now? Has no new discovery in science or arrival at superior planes of thought and judgment and behavior fixed him or his so that either can be looked down upon? Have the marches of tens and hundreds and thousands of years made willing detours to the right hand and the left hand for his sake? Is he beloved long and long after he is buried? Does the young man think often of him? and the young woman think often of him? and do the middleaged and the old think of him?

A great poem is for ages and ages in common and for all degrees and complexions and all departments and sects and for a woman as much as a man and a man as much as a woman. A great poem is no finish to a man or woman but rather a beginning. Has any one fancied he could sit at last under some due authority and rest satisfied with explanations and realize and be content and full? To no such terminus does the greatest poet bring . . . he brings neither cessation or sheltered fatness and ease. The touch of him tells in action. Whom he takes he takes with firm sure grasp into live regions previously unattained . . . . thenceforward is no rest . . . . they see the space and ineffable sheen that turn the old spots and lights into dead vacuums. The companion of him beholds the birth and progress of stars and learns one of the meanings. Now there shall be a man cohered out of a tumult and chaos . . . . the elder encourages the younger and shows him how . . . they two shall launch off fearlessly together till the new world fits an orbit for itself and looks unabashed on the lesser orbits of the stars and sweeps through the ceaseless rings and shall never be quiet again.

There will soon be no more priests. Their work is done. They may wait awhile . . perhaps a generation or two . . dropping off by degrees. A superior breed shall take their place . . . . the gangs of kosmos and prophets en masse shall take their place. A new order shall arise and they shall be the priests of man, and every man shall be his own priest. The churches built under their umbrage[38] shall be the churches of men and women. Through the divinity of themselves shall the kosmos and the new breed of poets be interpreters of men and women and of all events and things. They shall find their inspiration in real objects today, symptoms of the past and future. . . . They shall not deign to defend immortality or God or the perfection of things or liberty or the exquisite beauty and reality of the soul. They shall arise in America and be responded to from the remainder of the earth.

The English language befriends the grand American expression. . . . it is brawny enough and limber and full enough. On the tough stock of a race who through all change of circumstance was never without the idea of political liberty, which is the animus of all liberty, it has attracted the terms of daintier and gayer and subtler and more elegant tongues. It is the powerful

[38]Shadow.

language of resistance . . . it is the dialect of common sense. It is the speech of the proud and melancholy races and of all who aspire. It is the chosen tongue to express growth faith self-esteem freedom justice equality friendliness amplitude prudence decision and courage. It is the medium that shall well nigh express the inexpressible.

No great literature nor any like style of behaviour or oratory or social intercourse or household arrangements or public institutions or the treatment by bosses of employed people, nor executive detail or detail of the army or navy, nor spirit of legislation or courts or police or tuition or architecture or songs or amusements or the costumes of young men, can long elude the jealous and passionate instinct of American standards. Whether or no the sign appears from the mouths of the people, it throbs a live interrogation in every freeman's and freewoman's heart after that which passes by, or this built to remain. Is it uniform with my country? Are its disposals without ignominious distinctions? Is it for the evergrowing communes of brothers and lovers, large, well-united, proud beyond the old models, generous beyond all models? Is it something grown fresh out of the fields or drawn from the sea for use to me today here? I know that what answers for me an American must answer for any individual or nation that serves for a part of my materials. Does this answer? or is it without reference to universal needs? or sprung of the needs of the less developed society of special ranks? or old needs of pleasure overlaid by modern science and forms? Does this acknowledge liberty with audible and absolute acknowledgment, and set slavery at nought for life and death? Will it help breed one goodshaped and wellhung man, and a woman to be his perfect and independent mate? Does it improve manners? Is it for the nursing of the young of the republic? Does it solve[39] readily with the sweet milk of the nipples of the breasts of the mother of many children? Has it too the old ever-fresh forbearance and impartiality? Does it look with the same love on the last born and on those hardening toward stature, and on the errant, and on those who disdain all strength of assault outside of their own?

The poems distilled from other poems will probably pass away. The coward will surely pass away. The expectation of the vital and great can only be satisfied by the demeanor of the vital and great. The swarms of the polished deprecating and reflectors and the polite float off and leave no remembrance. America prepares with composure and goodwill for the visitors that have sent word. It is not intellect that is to be their warrant and welcome. The talented, the artist, the ingenious, the editor, the statesman, the erudite . . they are not unappreciated . . they fall in their place and do their work. The soul of the nation also does its work. No disguse can pass on it . . no disguse can conceal from it. It rejects none, it permits all. Only toward as good as itself and toward the like of itself will it advance half-way. An individual is as superb as a nation when he has the qualities which make a superb nation. The soul of the largest and wealthiest and proudest nation may well go half-way to meet that of its poets. The signs are effectual. There is no fear of mistake. If the one is true the other is true. The proof of a poet is that his country absorbs him as affectionately as he has absorbed it.

1855

[39]Dissolve.

from *INSCRIPTIONS*

ONE'S-SELF I SING

One's-Self I sing, a simple separate person,
Yet utter the word Democratic, the word En-Masse.

Of physiology from top to toe I sing,
Not physiognomy[1] alone nor brain alone is worthy for the Muse, I
 say the Form complete is worthier far,
The Female equally with the Male I sing.

Of Life immense in passion, pulse, and power,
Cheerful, for freest action form'd under the laws divine,
The Modern Man I sing.

1867, 1871[2]

WHEN I READ THE BOOK

When I read the book, the biography famous,
And is this then (said I) what the author calls a man's life?
And so will some one when I am dead and gone write my life?
(As if any man really knew aught of my life,
Why even I myself I often think know little or nothing of my real life,
Only a few hints, a few diffused faint clews and indirections
I seek for my own use to trace out here.)

1867, 1871

SONG OF MYSELF

1

I celebrate myself, and sing myself,
And what I assume you shall assume,
For every atom belonging to me as good belongs to you.

I loafe and invite my soul,
I lean and loafe at my ease observing a spear of summer grass.

My tongue, every atom of my blood, form'd from this soil, this air,
Born here of parents born here from parents the same, and their
 parents the same,

[1]Facial features, as indications of character.
[2]The first date following each of Whitman's poems indicates its first appearance in print. The second, publication in its final form.

I, now thirty-seven years old in perfect health begin,
Hoping to cease not till death.

Creeds and schools in abeyance,
Retiring back a while sufficed at what they are, but never forgotten,
I harbor for good or bad, I permit to speak at every hazard,
Nature without check with original energy.

2

Houses and rooms are full of perfumes, the shelves are crowded with perfumes,
I breathe the fragrance myself and know it and like it,
The distillation would intoxicate me also, but I shall not let it.

The atmosphere is not a perfume, it has no taste of the distillation, it is odorless,
It is for my mouth forever, I am in love with it,
I will go to the bank by the wood and become undisguised and naked,
I am mad for it to be in contact with me.
The smoke of my own breath,
Echoes, ripples, buzz'd whispers, love-root, silk-thread, crotch and vine,
My respiration and inspiration, the beating of my heart, the passing of blood and air through my lungs,
The sniff of green leaves and dry leaves, and of the shore and dark color'd sea-rocks, and of hay in the barn,
The sound of the belch'd words of my voice loos'd to the eddies of the wind,
A few light kisses, a few embraces, a reaching around of arms,
The play of shine and shade on the trees as the supple boughs wag,
The delight alone or in the rush of the streets, or along the fields and hill-sides.
The feeling of health, the full-noon trill, the song of me rising from bed and meeting the sun.

Have you reckon'd a thousand acres much? have you reckon'd the earth much?
Have you practis'd so long to learn to read?
Have you felt so proud to get at the meaning of poems?

Stop this day and night with me and you shall possess the origin of all poems,
You shall possess the good of the earth and sun, (there are millions of suns left,)
You shall no longer take things at second or third hand, nor look through the eyes of the dead, nor feed on the spectres in books,
You shall not look through my eyes either, nor take things from me,
You shall listen to all sides and filter them from your self.

3

I have heard what the talkers were talking, the talk of the beginning
and the end,
But I do not talk of the beginning or the end.

There was never any more inception than there is now,
Nor any more youth or age than there is now,
And will never be any more perfection than there is now,
Nor any more heaven or hell than there is now.

Urge and urge and urge,
Always the procreant urge of the world.

Out of the dimness opposite equals advance, always substance
and increase, always sex,
Always a knit of identity, always distinction, always a breed of life.

To elaborate is no avail, learn'd and unlearn'd feel that it is so.

Sure as the most certain sure, plumb in the uprights, well entretied,[1]
braced in the beams,
Stout as a horse, affectionate, haughty, electrical,
I and this mystery here we stand.

Clear and sweet is my soul, and clear and sweet is all that is not
my soul.

Lack one lacks both, and the unseen is proved by the seen,
Till that becomes unseen and receives proof in its turn.

Showing the best and dividing it from the worst age vexes age,
Knowing the perfect fitness and equanimity of things, while they
discuss I am silent, and go bathe and admire myself.

Welcome is every organ and attribute of me, and of any man
hearty and clean,
Not an inch nor a particle of an inch is vile, and none shall be less familiar
than the rest.

I am satisfied—I see, dance, laugh, sing;
As the hugging and loving bed-fellow[2] sleeps at my side through
the night, and withdraws at the peep of the day with stealthy tread,
Leaving me baskets cover'd with white towels swelling the house
with their plenty,
Shall I postpone my acceptation and realization and scream at
my eyes,
That they turn from gazing after and down the road,
And forthwith cipher[3] and show me to a cent,
Exactly the value of one and exactly the value of two, and which
is ahead?

[1]A carpenter's term meaning supported, braced.
[2]In the 1855 edition the "bed-fellow" is identified as God. [3]Calculate.

4

Trippers and askers[4] surround me,
People I meet, the effect upon me of my early life or the ward
  and city I live in, or the nation,
The latest dates, discoveries, inventions, societies, authors old
  and new,
My dinner, dress, associates, looks, compliments, dues,
The real or fancied indifference of some man or woman I love,
The sickness of one of my folks or of myself, or ill-doing or loss
  or lack of money, or depressions or exaltations,
Battles, the horrors of fratricidal[5] war, the fever of doubtful
  news, the fitful events;
These come to me days and nights and go from me again,
But they are not the Me myself.

Apart from the pulling and hauling stands what I am,
Stands amused, complacent, compassionating, idle, unitary,
Looks down, is erect, or bends an arm on an impalpable certain rest,
Looking with side-curved head curious what will come next,
Both in and out of the game and watching and wondering at it.

Backward I see in my own days where I sweated through fog
  with linguists and contenders,
I have no mockings or arguments, I witness and wait.

5

I believe in you my soul, the other I am must not abase itself to you,
And you must not be abased to the other.

Loafe with me on the grass, loose the stop from your throat,
Not words, not music or rhyme I want, not custom or lecture,
  not even the best,
Only the lull I like, the hum of your valvèd voice.

I mind how once we lay such a transparent summer morning,
How you settled your head athwart my hips and gently turn'd
  over upon me,
And parted the shirt from my bosom-bone, and plunged your
  tongue to my bare-stript heart,
And reach'd till you felt my beard, and reach'd till you held my feet.

Swiftly arose and spread around me the peace and knowledge
  that pass all the argument of the earth,
And I know that the hand of God is the promise of my own,
And I know that the spirit of God is the brother of my own,
And that all the men ever born are also my brothers, and the
  women my sisters and lovers,
And that a kelson[6] of the creation is love,

[4]I.e., travelers and beggars. [5]Brother killing brother.
[6]Keelson, ship timbers that brace the keel.

And limitless are leaves stiff or drooping in the fields,
And brown ants in the little wells beneath them,
And mossy scabs of the worm fence,[7] heap'd stones, elder,
  mullein and poke-weed.

6

A child said *What is the grass?* fetching it to me with full hands;
How could I answer the child? I do not know what it is any more
  than he.

I guess it must be the flag of my disposition, out of hopeful
  green stuff woven.

Or I guess it is the handkerchief of the Lord,
A scented gift and remembrancer designedly dropt,
Bearing the owner's name someway in the corners, that we may
  see and remark, and say *Whose?*

Or I guess the grass is itself a child, the produced babe of the
  vegetation.

Or I guess it is a uniform hieroglyphic,
And it means, Sprouting alike in broad zones and narrow zones,
Growing among black folks as among white,
Kanuck, Tuckahoe, Congressman, Cuff,[8] I give them the same, I
  receive them the same.

And now it seems to me the beautiful uncut hair of graves.

Tenderly will I use you curling grass,
It may be you transpire from the breasts of young men,
It may be if I had known them I would have loved them.
It may be you are from old people, or from offspring taken soon
  out of their mothers' laps,
And here you are the mothers' laps.

This grass is very dark to be from the white heads of old mothers.
Darker than the colorless beards of old men,
Dark to come from under the faint red roofs of mouths.

O I perceive after all so many uttering tongues,
And I perceive they do not come from the roofs of mouths for
  nothing.

I wish I could translate the hints about the dead young men and
  women,
And the hints about old men and mothers, and the offspring
  taken soon out of their laps.

[7]A zigzag rail fence.
[8]Canuck: a French-Canadian; Tuckahoe: a Virginian of the coastal lowlands; Cuff: a Negro.

What do you think has become of the young and old men?
And what do you think has become of the women and children?

They are alive and well somewhere,
The smallest sprout shows there is really no death,
And if ever there was it led forward life, and does not wait at
 the end to arrest it,
And ceas'd the moment life appear'd.

All goes onward and outward, nothing collapses,
And to die is different from what any one supposed, and luckier.

7

Has any one supposed it lucky to be born?
I hasten to inform him or her it is just as lucky to die, and I
 know it.

I pass death with the dying and birth with the new-wash'd babe,
 and am not contain'd between my hat and boots,
And peruse manifold objects, no two alike and every one good,
The earth good and the stars good, and their adjuncts all good.

I am not an earth nor an adjunct of an earth,
I am the mate and companion of people, all just as immortal and
 fathomless as myself,
(They do not know how immortal, but I know.)

Every kind for itself and its own, for me mine male and female,
For me those that have been boys and that love women,
For me the man that is proud and feels how it stings to be slighted,
For me the sweet-heart and the old maid, for me mothers and
 the mothers of mothers,
For me lips that have smiled, eyes that have shed tears,
For me children and the begetters of children.

Undrape! you are not guilty to me, nor stale nor discarded,
I see through the broadcloth and gingham whether or no,
And am around, tenacious, acquisitive, tireless, and cannot be
 shaken away.

8

The little one sleeps in its cradle,
I lift the gauze and look a long time, and silently brush away flies
 with my hand.

The youngster and the red-faced girl turn aside up the bushy hill,
I peeringly, view them from the top.

The suicide sprawls on the bloody floor of the bedroom,
I witness the corpse with its dabbled hair, I note where the pistol
has fallen.

The blab of the pave,[9] tires of carts, sluff[10] of boot-soles, talk of
the promenaders,
The heavy omnibus,[11] the driver with his interrogating thumb, the
clank of the shod horses on the granite floor,
The snow-sleighs, clinking, shouted jokes, pelts of snow-balls,
The hurrahs for popular favorites, the fury of rous'd mobs,
The flap of the curtain'd litter,[12] a sick man inside borne to the
hospital,
The meeting of enemies, the sudden oath, the blows and fall,
The excited crowd, the policeman with his star quickly working
his passage to the centre of the crowd,
The impassive stones that receive and return so many echoes,
What groans of over-fed or half-starv'd who fall sunstruck or in fits,
What exclamations of women taken suddenly who hurry home
and give birth to babes,
What living and buried speech is always vibrating here, what
howls restrain'd by decorum,
Arrests of criminals, slights, adulterous offers made, acceptances,
rejections with convex lips,
I mind them or the show or resonance of them—I come and I
depart.

9

The big doors of the country barn stand open and ready,
The dried grass of the harvest-time loads the slow-drawn wagon,
The clear light plays on the brown gray and green intertinged,
The armfuls are pack'd to the sagging mow.

I am there, I help, I came stretch'd atop of the load,
I felt its soft jolts, one leg reclined on the other,
I jump from the cross-beams and seize the clover and timothy,[13]
And roll head over heels and tangle my hair full of wisps.

10

Alone far in the wilds and mountains I hunt,
Wandering amazed at my own lightness and glee,
In the late afternoon choosing a safe spot to pass the night,
Kindling a fire and broiling the fresh-kill'd game,
Falling asleep on the gather'd leaves with my dog and gun by my side.

[9]The talk of the streets. [10]Shuffling sound.
[11]A large, passenger-carrying vehicle, a bus; horse-drawn in Whitman's day.
[12]A curtained vehicle, equipped with a litter (stretcher), for transporting the sick or wounded.
[13]A coarse grass, used for fodder.

The Yankee clipper[14] is under her sky-sails,[15] she cuts the sparkle and
scud,[16]
My eyes settle the land, I bend at her prow or shout joyously
from the deck.

The boatman and clam-diggers arose early and stopt for me,
I tuck'd my trowser-ends in my boots and went and had a good time;
You should have been with us that day round the chowder-kettle.

I saw the marriage of the trapper in the open air in the far west,
the bride was a red girl,
Her father and his friends sat near cross-legged and dumbly
smoking, they had moccasins to their feet and large thick
blankets hanging from their shoulders,
On a bank lounged the trapper, he was drest mostly in skins, his
luxuriant beard and curls protected his neck, he held his bride
by the hand,
She had long eyelashes, her head was bare, her coarse straight
locks descended upon her voluptuous limbs and reach'd to her
feet.

The runaway slave came to my house and stopt outside,
I heard his motions crackling the twigs of the woodpile,
Through the swung half-door of the kitchen I saw him limpsy[17]
and weak,
And went where he sat on a log and led him in and assured him,
And brought water and fill'd a tub for his sweated body and
bruis'd feet,
And gave him a room that enter'd from my own, and gave him
some coarse clean clothes,
And remember perfectly well his revolving eyes and his
awkwardness,
And remember putting plasters on the galls of his neck and ankles;
He staid with me a week before he was recuperated and pass'd
north,
I had him sit next me at table, my fire-lock[18] lean'd in the corner.

11

Twenty-eight young men bathe by the shore,
Twenty-eight young men and all so friendly;
Twenty-eight years of womanly life and all so lonesome.

She owns the fine house by the rise of the bank,
She hides handsome and richly drest aft the blinds of the window.

Which of the young men does she like the best?
Ah the homeliest of them is beautiful to her.

[14]Swift sailing vessel. [15]Upper sails. [16]Sea foam. [17]Limp. [18]Gun.

Where are you off to, lady? for I see you,
You splash in the water there, yet stay stock still in your room.

Dancing and laughing along the beach came the twenty-ninth
  bather,
The rest did not see her, but she saw them and loved them.

The beards of the young men glisten'd with wet, it ran from
  their long hair,
Little streams pass'd all over their bodies.

An unseen hand also pass'd over their bodies,
It descended tremblingly from their temples and ribs.

The young men float on their backs, their white bellies bulge to
  the sun, they do not ask who seizes fast to them,
They do not know who puffs and declines with pendant and
  bending arch,
They do not think whom they souse with spray.

12

The butcher-boy puts off his killing-clothes, or sharpens his knife
  at the stall in the market,
I loiter enjoying his repartee and his shuffle and break-down.[19]

Blacksmiths with grimed and hairy chests environ the anvil,
Each has his main-sledge, they are all out, there is a great heat
  in the fire.

From the cinder-strew'd threshold I follow their movement,
The lithe sheer[20] of their waists plays even with their massive arms,
Overhand the hammers swing, overhand so slow, overhand so sure,
They do not hasten, each man hits in his place.

13

The negro holds firmly the reins of his four horses, the block
  swags[21] underneath on its tied-over-chain,
The negro that drives the long dray[22] of the stone-yard, steady
  and tall he stands pois'd on one leg on the string-piece,[23]
His blue shirt exposes his ample neck and breast and loosens
  over his hip-band,
His glance is calm and commanding, he tosses the slouch of his
  hat away from his forehead,
The sun falls on his crispy hair and mustache, falls on the black
  of his polish'd and perfect limbs.

I behold the picturesque giant and love him, and I do not stop there,
I go with the team also.

[19]Popular dance steps. [20]Curve. [21]Sways, sags heavily.
[22]A sledge or wagon used for hauling heavy loads. [23]A long, support timber.

In me the caresser of life wherever moving, backward as well as
forward sluing,[24]
To niches aside and junior[25] bending, not a person or object missing,
Absorbing all to myself and for this song.

Oxen that rattle the yoke and chains or halt in the leafy shade,
what is that you express in your eyes?
It seems to me more than all the print I have read in my life.

My tread scares the wood-drake and wood-duck on my distant
and day-long ramble,
They rise together, they slowly circle around.

I believe in those wing'd purposes,
And acknowledge red, yellow, white, playing within me,
And consider green and violet and the tufted crown[26] intentional,
And do not call the tortoise unworthy because she is not
something else,
And the jay in the woods never studied the gamut,[27] yet trills
pretty well to me,
And the look of the bay mare shames silliness out of me.

14

The wild gander leads his flock through the cold night,
Ya-honk he says, and sounds it down to me like an invitation,
The pert[28] may suppose it meaningless, but I listening close,
Find its purpose and place up there toward the wintry sky.

The sharp-hoof'd moose of the north, the cat on the house-sill,
the chickadee, the prairie-dog,
The litter of the grunting sow as they tug at her teats,
The brood of the turkey-hen and she with her half-spread wings,
I see in them and myself the same old law.

The press of my foot to the earth springs a hundred affections,
They scorn the best I can do to relate them.

I am enamour'd of growing out-doors,
Of men that live among cattle or taste of the ocean or woods,
Of the builders and steerers of ships and the wielders of axes
and mauls, and the drivers of horses,
I can eat and sleep with them week in and week out.

What is commonest, cheapest, nearest, easiest is Me,
Me going in for my chances, spending for vast returns,
Adorning myself to bestow myself on the first that will take me,
Not asking the sky to come down to my good will,
Scattering it freely forever.

[24]Turning, twisting. [25]Smaller. [26]Of the drake.
[27]Musical scale. [28]Self-assured, cocky.

15

The pure contralto sings in the organ loft,
The carpenter dresses his plank, the tongue of his foreplane
    whistles its wild ascending lisp,
The married and unmarried children ride home to their
    Thanksgiving dinner,
The pilot seizes the king-pin,[29] he heaves down with a strong arm,
The mate stands braced in the whale-boat, lance and harpoon
    are ready,
The duck-shooter walks by silent and cautious stretches,
The deacons are ordain'd with cross'd hands at the altar,
The spinning-girl retreats and advances to the hum of the big wheel,
The farmer stops by the bars[30] as he walks on a First-day loafe[31]
    and looks at the oats and rye,
The lunatic is carried at last to the asylum a confirm'd case,
(He will never sleep any more as he did in the cot in his mother's
    bed-room;)
The jour[32] printer with gray head and gaunt jaws works at his
    case,[33]
He turns his quid of tobacco while his eyes blurr with the manuscript;
The malform'd limbs are tied to the surgeon's table,
What is removed drops horribly in a pail;
The quadroon[34] girl is sold at the auction-stand, the drunkard
    nods by the bar-room stove,
The machinist rolls up his sleeves, the policeman travels his beat,
    the gate-keeper marks who pass,
The young fellow drives the express-wagon, (I love him, though,
    I do not know him;)
The half-breed straps on his light boots to compete in the race,
The western turkey-shooting draws old and young, some lean on
    their rifles, some sit on logs,
Out from the crowd steps the marksman, takes his position,
    levels his piece;
The groups of newly-come immigrants cover the wharf or levee,
As the wooly-pates[35] hoe in the sugar-field, the overseer views
    them from his saddle,
The bugle calls in the ball-room, the gentlemen run for their
    partners, the dancers bow to each other,
The youth lies awake in the cedar-roof'd garret and harks to the
    musical rain,
The Wolverine[36] sets traps on the creek that helps fill the Huron,[37]
The squaw wrapt in her yellow-hemm'd cloth is offering
    moccasins and bead-bags for sale,
The connoisseur peers along the exhibition-gallery with half-shut
    eyes bent sideways,

[29]An extended spoke on a ship's pilot wheel. [30]Fence rails.
[31]A Sunday (from Quaker terminology) time of ease. [32]Journeyman, trained.
[33]Type case. [34]Of one-quarter black ancestry. [35]Blacks. [36]Inhabitant of Michigan.
[37]Lake Huron.

As the deck-hands make fast the steamboat the plank is thrown for
the shore-going passengers,
The young sister holds out the skein while the elder sister winds it
off in a ball, and stops now and then for the knots,
The one-year wife is recovering and happy having a week ago
borne her first child,
The clean-hair'd Yankee girl works with her sewing machine or in
the factory or mill,
The paving-man[38] leans on his two-handed rammer, the reporter's
lead flies swiftly over the note-book, the sign-painter is lettering
with blue and gold,
The canal boy trots on the tow-path,[39] the book-keeper counts at
his desk, the shoemaker waxes his thread,
The conductor beats time for the band and all the performers
follow him,
The child is baptized, the convert is making his first professions,
The regatta is spread on the bay, the race is begun, (how the white
sails sparkle!)
The drover[40] watches his drove sings out to them that would stray,
The pedler sweats with his pack on his back, (the purchaser
higgling[41] about the odd cent;)
The bride unrumples her white dress, the minute-hand of the
clock moves slowly,
The opium-eater reclines with rigid head and just-open'd lips,
The prostitute draggles her shawl, her bonnet bobs on her tipsy
and pimpled neck,
The crowd laugh at her blackguard[42] oaths, the men jeer and
wink to each other,
(Miserable! I do not laugh at your oaths nor jeer you;)
The President holding a cabinet council is surrounded by the
great Secretaries,
On the piazza walk three matrons stately and friendly with
twined arms,
The crew of the fish-smack pack repeated layers of halibut in the
hold,
The Missourian crosses the plains toting his wares and his cattle,
As the fare-collector goes through the train he gives notice by
the jingling of loose change,
The floor-men are laying the floor, the tinners are tinning[43] the
roof, the masons are calling for mortar,
In single file each shouldering his hod pass onward the laborers;
Seasons pursuing each other the indescribable crowd is gather'd,
it is the fourth of Seventh-month,[44] (what salutes of cannon
and small arms!)
Seasons pursuing each other the plougher ploughs, the mower
mows, and the winter-grain falls in the ground;

[38]Street-repair man. [39]Canal-side path for the draft animals that tow canal barges.
[40]One who drives herds of animals. [41]Bargaining. [42]Rude, abusive.
[43]I.e., tinsmiths are sealing the sheet-metal roof. [44]Quaker term for July.

Off on the lakes the pike-fisher watches and waits by the hole in the frozen surface,
The stumps stand thick round the clearing, the squatter strikes deep with his axe,
Flatboatmen make fast towards dusk near the cotton-wood or pecan-trees,
Coon-seekers[45] go through the regions of the Red river[46] or through those drain'd by the Tennessee, or through those of the Arkansas,
Torches shine in the dark that hangs on the Chattahooche or Altamahaw,[47]
Patriarchs sit at supper with sons and grandsons and great-grandsons around them,
In walls of adobie, in canvas tents, rest hunters and trappers after their day's sport,
The city sleeps and the country sleeps,
The living sleep for their time, the dead sleep for their time,
The old husband sleeps by his wife and the young husband sleeps by his wife;
And these tend inward to me, and I tend outward to them,
And such as it is to be of these more or less I am,
And of these one and all I weave the song of myself.

16

I am of old and young, of the foolish as much as the wise,
Regardless of others, ever regardful of others,
Maternal as well as paternal, a child as well as a man,
Stuff'd with the stuff that is coarse and stuff'd with the stuff that is fine,
One of the Nation of many nations, the smallest the same and the largest the same,
A Southerner soon as a Northerner, a planter nonchalant and hospitable down by the Oconee[48] I live,
A Yankee bound my own way ready for trade, my joints the limberest joints on earth and the sternest joints on earth,
A Kentuckian walking the vale of the Elkhorn[49] in my deer-skin leggings, a Louisianian or Georgian,
A boatman over lakes or bays or along coasts, a Hoosier, Badger, Buckeye[50]
At home on Kanadian[51] snow-shoes or up in the bush, or with fishermen off Newfoundland,
At home in the fleet of ice-boats, sailing with the rest and tacking,
At home on the hills of Vermont or in the woods of Maine, or the Texas ranch,
Comrade of Californians, comrade of free North-Westerners, (loving their big proportions,)

[45]Raccoon hunters. [46]Along the Oklahoma-Texas border. [47]Rivers in Georgia.
[48]River in Georgia. [49]River in Nebraska.
[50]An inhabitant of Indiana, of Wisconsin, of Ohio, respectively.
[51]Whitman's spelling of "Canadian."

Comrade of raftsmen and coalmen, comrade of all who shake
hands and welcome to drink and meat,
A learner with the simplest, a teacher of the thoughtfullest,
A novice beginning yet experient of[52] myriads of seasons,
Of every hue and caste am I, of every rank and religion,
A farmer, mechanic, artist, gentleman, sailor, quaker,
Prisoner, fancy-man,[53] rowdy, lawyer, physician, priest.

I resist any thing better than my own diversity,
Breathe the air but leave plenty after me,
And am not stuck up, and am in my place.

(The moth and the fish-eggs are in their place,
The bright suns I see and the dark suns I cannot see are in their
place,
The palpable is in its place and the impalpable is in its place.)

17

These are really the thoughts of all men in all ages and lands,
they are not original with me,
If they are not yours as much as mine they are nothing, or next
to nothing,
If they are not the riddle and the untying of the riddle they are
nothing,
If they are not just as close as they are distant they are nothing.

This is the grass that grows wherever the land is and the water is,
This the common air that bathes the globe.

18

With music strong I come, with my cornets and my drums,
I play not marches for accepted victors only, I play marches for
conquer'd and slain persons.

Have you heard that it was good to gain the day?
I also say it is good to fall, battles are lost in the same spirit in
which they are won.

I beat and pound for the dead,
I blow through my embouchures[54] my loudest and gayest for them.

Vivas[55] to those who have fail'd!
And to those whose war-vessels sank in the sea!
And to those themselves who sank in the sea!
And to all generals that lost engagements, and all overcome heroes!
And the numberless unknown heroes equal to the greatest
heroes known!

[52]I.e., one who has experienced. [53]A whore's pimp.
[54]Mouthpieces of musical instruments. [55]Salutes.

19

This is the meal equally set, this the meat for natural hunger,
It is for the wicked just the same as the righteous, I make
appointments with all,
I will not have a single person slighted or left away,
The kept-woman, sponger, thief, are hereby invited,
The heavy-lipp'd slave is invited, the venerealee[56] is invited;
There shall be no difference between them and the rest.

This is the press of a bashful hand, this the float and odor of hair,
This the touch of my lips to yours, this the murmur of yearning,
This the far-off depth and height reflecting my own face,
This the thoughtful merge[57] of myself, and the outlet again.

Do you guess I have some intricate purpose?
Well I have, for the Fourth-month[58] showers have, and the mica
on the side of a rock has.

Do you take it I would astonish?
Does the daylight astonish? does the early redstart twittering
through the woods?
Do I astonish more than they?

This hour I tell things in confidence,
I might not tell everybody, but I will tell you.

20

Who goes there? hankering, gross, mystical, nude,
How is it I extract strength from the beef I eat?

What is a man anyhow? what am I? what are you?

All I mark as my own you shall offset it with your own,
Else it were lost listening to me.

I do not snivel that snivel the world over,
That months are vacuums and the ground but wallow and filth.

Whimpering and truckling fold with powders for invalids,[59]
conformity goes to the fourth-remov'd,[60]
I wear my hat as I please indoors or out.

Why should I pray? why should I venerate and be ceremonious?

[56]One crazed by sexual desire or disease. [57]Union, convergence. [58]April.
[59]I.e., whimpering and knuckling under are suited to combine with medicines for invalids.
[60]Those distantly separated, far removed from others.

Having pried through the strata, analyzed to a hair, counsel'd
with doctors and calculated close,
I find no sweeter fat than sticks to my own bones.

In all people I see myself, none more and not one a barley-corn less,
And the good or bad I say of myself I say of them.

I know I am solid and sound,
To me the converging objects of the universe perpetually flow,
All are written to me, and I must get what the writing means.

I know I am deathless,
I know this orbit of mine cannot be swept by a carpenter's compass,
I know I shall not pass like a child's carlacue cut with a burnt stick
at night.[61]

I know I am august,
I do not trouble my spirit to vindicate itself or be understood,
I see that the elementary laws never apologize,
(I reckon I behave no prouder than the level[62] I plant my house
by, after all.)

I exist as I am, that is enough,
If no other in the world be aware I sit content,
And if each and all be aware I sit content.

One world is aware and by far the largest to me, and that is myself,
And whether I come to my own to-day or in ten thousand or ten
million years,
I can cheerfully take it now, or with equal cheerfulness I can wait.

My foothold is tenon'd and mortis'd[63] in granite,
I laugh at what you call dissolution,
And I know the amplitude of time.

21

I am the poet of the Body and I am the poet of the Soul,
The pleasures of heaven are with me the pains of hell are with me,
The first I graft and increase upon myself, the latter I translate
into a new tongue.

I am the poet of the woman the same as the man,
And I say it is as great to be a woman as to be a man,
And I say there is nothing greater than the mother of men.

[61]A momentary pattern (a curlicue) made in the dark by waving a glowing stick or ember.
[62]Carpenter's level.
[63]Carpenter's term meaning fastened together by a strong, interlocked joint.

I chant the chant of dilation or pride,
We have had ducking and deprecating about enough,
I show that size is only development.

Have you outstript the rest? are you the President?
It is a trifle, they will more than arrive there every one, and still
  pass on.

I am he that walks with the tender and growing night,
I call to the earth and sea half-held by the night.

Press close bare-bosom'd night—press close magnetic nourishing
  night!
Night of south winds—night of the large few stars!
Still nodding night—mad naked summer night.

Smile O voluptuous cool-breath'd earth!
Earth of the slumbering and liquid trees!
Earth of departed sunset—earth of the mountains misty-topt!
Earth of the vitreous[64] pour of the full moon just tinged with blue!
Earth of shine and dark mottling the tide of the river!
Earth of the limpid gray of clouds brighter and clearer for my sake!
Far-swooping elbow'd earth—rich apple-blossom'd earth!
Smile, for your lover comes.

Prodigal, you have given me love—therefore I to you give love!
O unspeakable passionate love.

22

You sea! I resign myself to you also—I guess what you mean,
I behold from the beach your crooked inviting fingers,
I believe you refuse to go back without feeling of me,
We must have a turn together, I undress, hurry me out of sight
  of the land,
Cushion me soft, rock me in billowy drowse,
Dash me with amorous wet, I can repay you.

Sea of stretch'd ground-swells,
Sea breathing broad and convulsive breaths,
Sea of the brine of life and of unshovell'd yet always-ready graves,
Howler and scooper of storms, capricious and dainty sea,
I am integral with you, I too am of one phase and of all phases.

Partaker of influx and efflux I, extoller of hate and conciliation,
Extoller of amies[65] and those that sleep in each others' arms.

I am he attesting sympathy,
(Shall I make my list of things in the house and skip the house
  that supports them?)

[64]Glassy. [65]French: friends, lovers.

I am not the poet of goodness only, I do not decline to be the
poet of wickedness also.

What blurt is this about virtue and about vice?
Evil propels me and reform of evil propels me, I stand indifferent,
My gait is no fault-finder's or rejecter's gait,
I moisten the roots of all that has grown.

Did you fear some scrofula[66] out of the unflagging pregnancy?
Did you guess the celestial laws are yet to be work'd over and
rectified?

I find one side a balance and the antipodal side a balance,
Soft doctrine as steady help as stable doctrine,
Thoughts and deeds of the present our rouse and early start.

This minute that comes to me over the past decillions,[67]
There is no better than it and now.

What behaved well in the past or behaves well to-day is not such a
wonder,
The wonder is always and always how there can be a mean man or
infidel.

23

Endless unfolding of words of ages!
And mine a word of the modern, the word En-Masse.[68]

A word of the faith that never balks,
Here or henceforward it is all the same to me, I accept Time
absolutely.

It alone is without flaw, it alone rounds and completes all,
That mystic baffling wonder alone completes all.

I accept Reality and dare not question it,
Materialism first and last imbuing.

Hurrah for positive science! long live exact demonstration!
Fetch stonecrop[69] mixt with cedar and branches of lilac,
This is the lexicographer, this the chemist, this made a grammar[70]
of the old cartouches,[71]
These mariners put the ship through dangerous unknown seas,
This is the geologist, this works with the scalpel, and this is a
mathematician.

[66]A disease of the lungs and lymph glands. [67]The number 1 followed by thirty-two zeros.
[68]French: All together, in a mass. [69]An herb used in folk medicine. [70]I.e., deciphered.
[71]Oval borders within which Egyptian hieroglyphs were inscribed.

Gentlemen, to you the first honors always!
Your facts are useful, and yet they are not my dwelling,
I but enter by them to an area of my dwelling.

Less the reminders of properties told my words,
And more the reminders they of life untold, and of freedom and
 extrication,
And make short account of neuters and geldings, and favor men
 and women fully equipt,
And beat the gong of revolt, and stop with fugitives and them
 that plot and conspire.

24

Walt Whitman, a kosmos,[72] of Manhattan the son,
Turbulent, fleshy, sensual, eating, drinking and breeding,
No sentimentalist, no stander above men and women or apart
 from them,
No more modest than immodest.

Unscrew the locks from the doors!
Unscrew the doors themselves from their jambs!

Whoever degrades another degrades me,
And whatever is done or said returns at last to me.

Through me the afflatus[73] surging and surging, through me the
 current and index.

I speak the pass-word primeval, I give the sign of democracy,
By God! I will accept nothing which all cannot have their
 counterpart of on the same terms.

Through me many long dumb voices,
Voices of the interminable generations of prisoners and slaves,
Voices of the diseas'd and despairing and of thieves and dwarfs,
Voices of cycles of preparation and accretion,
And of the threads that connect the stars, and of wombs and of
 the father-stuff,[74]
And of the rights of them the others are down upon,
Of the deform'd, trivial, flat, foolish, despised,
Fog in the air, beetles rolling balls of dung.

Through me forbidden voices,
Voices of sexes and lusts, voices veil'd and I remove the veil,
Voices indecent by me clarified and transfigur'd.

I do not press my fingers across my mouth,
I keep as delicate around the bowels as around the head and heart,
Copulation is no more rank to me than death is.

[72]Cosmos, universe. [73]Divine spirit, poetic inspiration. [74]Semen.

I believe in the flesh and the appetites,
Seeing, hearing, feeling, are miracles, and each part and tag of
me is a miracle.

Divine am I inside and out, and I make holy whatever I touch or
am touch'd from,
The scent of these arm-pits aroma finer than prayer,
This head more than churches, bibles, and all the creeds.

If I worship one thing more than another it shall be the spread of
my own body, or any part of it,
Translucent mould of me it shall be you!
Shaded ledges and rests it shall be you!
Firm masculine colter[75] it shall be you!
Whatever goes to the tilth[76] of me it shall be you!
You my rich blood! your milky stream pale strippings of my life!
Breast that presses against other breasts it shall be you!
My brain it shall be your occult convolutions!
Root of wash'd sweet-flag![77] timorous pond-snipe! nest of guarded
duplicate eggs! it shall be you!
Mix'd tussled hay of head, beard, brawn, it shall be you!
Trickling sap of maple, fibre of manly wheat, it shall be you!
Sun so generous it shall be you!
Vapors lighting and shading my face it shall be you!
You sweaty brooks and dews it shall be you!
Winds whose soft-tickling genitals rub against me it shall be you!
Broad muscular fields, branches of live oak, loving lounger in
my winding paths, it shall be you!
Hands I have taken, face I have kiss'd, mortal I have ever
touch'd, it shall be you.

I dote on myself, there is that lot of me and all so luscious,
Each moment and whatever happens thrills me with you,
I cannot tell how my ankles bend, nor whence the cause of my
faintest wish,
Nor the cause of the friendship I emit, nor the cause of the
friendship I take again.

That I walk up my stoop, I pause to consider if it really be,
A morning-glory at my window satisfies me more than the
metaphysics of books.

To behold the day-break!
The little light fades the immense and diaphanous shadows,
The air tastes good to my palate.

[75]Iron blade at the front of a plow. [76]Cultivation.
[77]The calamus, a plant with green flowers and aromatic roots.

Hefts[78] of the moving world at innocent gambols silently rising,
 freshly exuding,
Scooting obliquely high and low.

Something I cannot see puts upward libidinous prongs,
Seas of bright juice suffuse heaven.

The earth by the sky staid with, the daily close of their junction,
The heav'd challenge from the east that moment over my head,
The mocking taunt, See then whether you shall be master!

25

Dazzling and tremendous how quick the sun-rise would kill me,
If I could not now and always send sun-rise out of me.

We also ascend dazzling and tremendous as the sun,
We found our own O my soul in the calm and cool of the day-break.

My voice goes after what my eyes cannot reach,
With the twirl of my tongue I encompass worlds and volumes of
 worlds.
Speech is the twin of my vision, it is unequal to measure itself,
It provokes me forever, it says sarcastically,
Walt you contain enough, why don't you let it out then?

Come now I will not be tantalized, you conceive too much of
 articulation,
Do you not know O speech how the buds beneath you are folded?
Waiting in gloom, protected by frost,
The dirt receding before my prophetical screams,
I underlying causes to balance them at last,
My knowledge my live parts, it keeping tally with the meaning of
 all things,
Happiness, (which whoever hears me let him or her set out in
 search of this day.)

My final merit I refuse you, I refuse putting from me what I
 really am,
Encompass worlds, but never try to encompass me,
I crowd your sleekest and best by simply looking toward you.

Writing and talk do not prove me,
I carry the plenum[79] of proof and every thing else in my face,
With the hush of my lips I wholly confound the skeptic.

[78]Mass, main parts. [79]Fullness.

26

Now I will do nothing but listen,
To accrue what I hear into this song, to let sounds contribute
toward it.

I hear bravuras of birds, bustle of growing wheat, gossip of flames,
clack of sticks cooking my meals,
I hear the sound I love, the sound of the human voice,
I hear all sounds running together, combined, fused or following,
Sounds of the city and sounds out of the city, sounds of the day
and night,
Talkative young ones to those that like them, the loud laugh of
work-people at their meals,
The angry base[80] of disjointed friendship, the faint tones of the sick,
The judge with hands tight to the desk, his pallid lips pronouncing
a death-sentence,
The heave'e'yo of stevedores unlading ships by the wharves, the
refrain of the anchor-lifters,
The ring of alarm-bells, the cry of fire, the whirr of swift-
streaking engines and hose-carts with premonitory tinkles and
color'd lights,
The steam-whistle, the solid roll of the train of approaching cars,
The slow march play'd at the head of the association marching
two and two,
(They go to guard some corpse, the flag-tops are draped with
black muslin.)

I hear the violoncello, ('tis the young man's heart's complaint,)
I hear the key'd cornet, it glides quickly in through my ears,
It shakes mad-sweet pangs through my belly and breast.

I hear the chorus, it is a grand opera,
Ah this indeed is music—this suits me.

A tenor large and fresh as the creation fills me,
The orbic flex of his mouth is pouring and filling me full.

I hear the train'd soprano (what work with hers is this?)
The orchestra whirls me wider than Uranus[81] flies,
It wrenches such ardors from me I did not know I possess'd them,
It sails me, I dab with bare feet, they are lick'd by the indolent
waves,
I am cut by bitter and angry hail, I lose my breath,
Steep'd amid honey'd morphine, my windpipe throttled in
fakes[82] of death,
At length let up again to feel the puzzle of puzzles,
And that we call Being.

[80]Bass. [81]Planet with a large orbit. [82]Rope coils.

27

To be in any form, what is that?
(Round and round we go, all of us, and ever come back thither,)
If nothing lay more develop'd the quahaug[83] in its callous shell
were enough.

Mine is no callous shell,
I have instant conductors all over me whether I pass or stop,
They seize every object and lead it harmlessly through me.

I merely stir, press, feel with my fingers, and am happy,
To touch my person to some one else's is about as much as I can stand.

28

Is this then a touch? quivering me to a new identity,
Flames and ether making a rush for my veins,
Treacherous tip of me reaching and crowding to help them,
My flesh and blood playing out lightning to strike what is hardly different
from myself,
On all sides prurient provokers stiffening my limbs,
Straining the udder of my heart for its withheld drip,
Behaving licentious toward me, taking no denial,
Depriving me of my best as for a purpose,
Unbuttoning my clothes, holding me by the bare waist,
Deluding my confusion with the calm of the sunlight and
pasture-fields,
Immodestly sliding the fellow-senses away,
They bribed to swap off with touch and go and graze at the
edges of me,
No consideration, no regard for my draining strength or my anger,
Fetching the rest of the herd around to enjoy them for a while,
Then all uniting to stand on a headland and worry me.

The sentries desert every other part of me,
They have left me helpless to a red marauder,
They all come to the headland to witness and assist against me.

I am given up by traitors,
I talk wildly, I have lost my wits, I and nobody else am the
greatest traitor,
I went myself first to the headland, my own hands carried me there.

You villain touch! what are you doing? my breath is tight in its
throat,
Unclench your floodgates, you are too much for me.

29

Blind loving wrestling touch, sheath'd hooded sharp-tooth'd touch!
Did it make you ache so, leaving me?

[83]An Atlantic clam.

Parting track'd by arriving, perpetual payment of perpetual loan,
Rich showering rain, and recompense richer afterward.

Sprouts take and accumulate, stand by the curb profile and vital,
Landscapes projected masculine, full-sized and golden.

30

All truths wait in all things,
They neither hasten their own delivery nor resist it,
They do not need the obstetric forceps of the surgeon,
The insignificant is as big to me as any,
(What is less or more than a touch?)

Logic and sermons never convince,
The damp of the night drives deeper into my soul.

(Only what proves itself to every man and woman is so,
Only what nobody denies is so.)

A minute and a drop of me settle my brain,
I believe the soggy clods shall become lovers and lamps,
And a compend[84] of compends is the meat of a man or woman,
And a summit and flower there is the feeling they have for each
other,
And they are to branch boundlessly out of that lesson until it
becomes omnific,[85]
And until one and all shall delight us, and we them.

31

I believe a leaf of grass is no less than the journey-work of the stars,
And the pismire[86] is equally perfect, and a grain of sand, and the
egg of the wren,
And the tree-toad is a chef-d'oeuvre[87] for the highest,
And the running blackberry would adorn the parlors of heaven,
And the narrowest hinge in my hand puts to scorn all machinery,
And the cow crunching with depress'd head surpasses any statue,
And a mouse is miracle enough to stagger sextillions[88] of infidels.

I find I incorporate gneiss,[89] coal, long-threaded moss, fruits,
grains, esculent roots,
And am stucco'd with quadrupeds and birds all over,
And have distanced what is behind me for good reasons,
But call any thing back again when I desire it.

[84]Compendium, epitome. [85]All-creating, all-inclusive. [86]Ant. [87]French: masterpiece.
[88]The number 1 followed by twenty-one zeros.
[89]Coarse-grained rock with light and dark mineral layers, found in the United States from New England to the Rocky Mountains.

In vain the speeding or shyness,
In vain the plutonic rocks[90] send their old heat against my approach,
In vain the mastodon retreats beneath its own powder'd bones,
In vain objects stand leagues off and assume manifold shapes,
In vain the ocean settling in hollows and the great monsters
lying low,
In vain the buzzard houses herself with the sky,
In vain the snake slides through the creepers and logs,
In vain the elk takes to the inner passes of the woods,
In vain the razor-bill'd auk sails far north to Labrador,
I follow quickly, I ascend to the nest in the fissure of the cliff.

32

I think I could turn and live with animals, they are so placid and
self-contain'd,
I stand and look at them long and long.

They do not sweat and whine about their condition,
They do not lie awake in the dark and weep for their sins,
They do not make me sick discussing their duty to God,
Not one is dissatisfied, not one is demented with the mania of
owning things,
Not one kneels to another, nor to his kind that lived thousands
of years ago,
Not one is respectable or unhappy over the whole earth.

So they show their relations to me and I accept them,
They bring me tokens of myself, they evince them plainly in
their possession.

I wonder where they get those tokens,
Did I pass that way huge times ago and negligently drop them?

Myself moving forward then and now and forever,
Gathering and showing more always and with velocity,
Infinite and omnigenous,[91] and the like of these among them,
Not too exclusive toward the reachers of my remembrancers,
Picking out here one that I love, and now go with him on
brotherly terms.

A gigantic beauty of a stallion, fresh and responsive to my caresses,
Head high in the forehead, wide between the ears,
Limbs glossy and supple, tail dusting the ground,
Eyes full of sparkling wickedness, ears finely cut, flexibly moving.

His nostrils dilate as my heels embrace him,
His well-built limbs tremble with pleasure as we race around and
return.

[90]Once-molten rock formed deep within the earth. [91]Of all kinds.

I but use you a minute, then I resign you, stallion,
Why do I need your paces when I myself out-gallop them?
Even as I stand or sit passing faster than you.

33

Space and Time! now I see it is true, what I guess'd at,
What I guess'd when I loaf'd on the grass,
What I guess'd while I lay alone in my bed,
And again as I walk'd the beach under the paling stars of the morning.

My ties and ballasts[92] leave me, my elbows rest in sea-gaps,[93]
I skirt sierras, my palms cover continents,
I am afoot with my vision.

By the city's quadrangular houses—in log huts, camping with lumbermen,
Along the ruts of the turnpike, along the dry gulch and rivulet bed,
Weeding my onion-patch or hoeing rows of carrots and parsnips, crossing savannas,[94] trailing in forests,
Prospecting, gold-digging, girdling[95] the trees of a new purchase,
Scorch'd ankle-deep by the hot sand, hauling by boat down the shallow river,
Where the panther walks to and fro on a limb overhead, where the buck turns furiously at the hunter,
Where the rattlesnake suns his flabby length on a rock, where the otter is feeding on fish,
Where the alligator in his tough pimples sleeps by the bayou,
Where the black bear is searching for roots or honey, where the beaver pats the mud with his paddle-shaped tail;
Over the growing sugar, over the yellow-flower'd cotton plant, over the rice in its low moist field,
Over the sharp-peak'd farm house, with its scallop'd scum and slender shoots from the gutters,[96]
Over the western persimmon, over the long-leav'd corn, over the delicate blue-flower flax,
Over the white and brown buckwheat, a hummer and buzzer[97] there with the rest,
Over the dusky green of the rye as it ripples and shades in the breeze;
Scaling mountains, pulling myself cautiously up, holding on by low scragged[98] limbs,

[92]The ropes and heavy weights that limit the ascent of a passenger balloon.
[93]Inlets, bays. [94]Flat, tropical grasslands.
[95]Killing a tree by cutting a deep ring around the trunk.
[96]Pointed roof with sediment washed into patterns by the rain and with grass sprouting from soil deposited in the roof gutters.
[97]Hummingbird and bee. [98]Stunted.

Walking the path worn in the grass and beat through the leaves of the brush,
Where the quail is whistling betwixt the woods and the wheat-lot,
Where the bat flies in the Seventh-month eve, where the great goldbug[99] drops through the dark,
Where the brook puts out of the roots of the old tree and flows to the meadow,
Where cattle stand and shake away flies with the tremulous shuddering of their hides,
Where the cheese-cloth hangs in the kitchen, where andirons straddle the hearth-slab, where cobwebs fall in festoons from the rafters;
Where trip-hammers crash, where the press is whirling its cylinders,
Wherever the human heart beats with terrible throes under its ribs,
Where the pear-shaped balloon is floating aloft, (floating in it myself and looking composedly down,)
Where the life-car[100] is drawn on the slip-noose, where the heat hatches pale-green eggs in the dented sand,
Where the she-whale swims with her calf and never forsakes it,
Where the steam-ship trails hind-ways its long pennant of smoke,
Where the fin of the shark cuts like a black chip out of the water,
Where the half-burn'd brig[101] is riding on unknown currents,
Where shells grow to her slimy deck, where the dead are corrupting below;
Where the dense-starr'd flag is borne at the head of the regiments,
Approaching Manhattan up by the long-stretching island,
Under Niagara, the cataract falling like a veil over my countenance,
Upon a door-step, upon the horse-block[102] of hard wood outside,
Upon the race-course, or enjoying picnics or jigs or a wood game of base-ball,
At he-festivals, with blackguard gibes, ironical license, bull-dances,[103] drinking, laughter,
At the cider-mill tasting the sweets of the brown mash, sucking the juice through a straw,
At apple-peelings wanting kisses for all the red fruit I find,
At musters,[104] beach-parties, friendly bees,[105] huskings, house-raisings;
Where the mocking-bird sounds his delicious gurgles, cackles, screams, weeps,
Where the hay-rick stands in the barn-yard, where the dry-stalks are scatter'd, where the brood-cow waits in the hovel,
Where the bull advances to do his masculine work, where the stud to the mare, where the cock is treading the hen,
Where the heifers browse, where geese nip their food with short jerks,
Where sun-down shadows lengthen over the limitless and lonesome prairie,

[99]A beetle. [100]Watertight rescue vessel pulled by rope from ship to shore.
[101]Sailing ship. [102]Mounting step.
[103]Dances where men, lacking female partners, dance with each other.
[104]Gatherings. [105]Parties where friends gather to work, like bees.

Where herds of buffalo make a crawling spread of the square
 miles far and near,
Where the humming-bird shimmers, where the neck of the
 long-lived swan is curving and winding,
Where the laughing-gull scoots by the shore, where she laughs
 her near-human laugh,
Where bee-hives range on a gray bench in the garden half hid
 by the high weeds,
Where band-neck'd partridges roost in a ring on the ground
 with their heads out,
Where burial coaches enter the arch'd gates of a cemetery,
Where winter wolves bark amid wastes of snow and icicled trees,
Where the yellow-crown'd heron comes to the edge of the marsh
 at night and feeds upon small crabs,
Where the splash of swimmers and divers cools the warm noon,
Where the katy-did works her chromatic reed[106] on the walnut-
 tree over the well,
Through patches of citrons[107] and cucumbers with silver-wired leaves,
Through the salt-lick or orange glade, or under conical firs,
Through the gymnasium, through the curtain'd saloon, through
 the office or public hall;
Pleas'd with the native and pleas'd with the foreign, pleas'd with
 the new and old,
Pleas'd with the homely woman as well as the handsome,
Pleas'd with the quakeress as she puts off her bonnet and talks
 melodiously,
Pleas'd with the tune of the choir of the whitewash'd church,
Pleas'd with the earnest words of the sweating Methodist
 preacher, impress'd seriously at the camp-meeting;
Looking in at the shop-windows of Broadway the whole
 forenoon, flatting the flesh of my nose on the thick plate glass,
Wandering the same afternoon with my face turn'd up to the
 clouds, or down a lane or along the beach,
My right and left arms round the sides of two friends, and I in
 the middle;
Coming home with the silent and dark-cheek'd bush-boy,[108]
 (behind me he rides at the drape,[109] of the day,)
Far from the settlements studying the print of animals' feet, or the
 moccasin print,
By the cot in the hospital reaching lemonade to a feverish patient,
Nigh the coffin'd corpse when all is still, examining with a candle;
Voyaging to every port to dicker and adventure,
Hurrying with the modern crowd as eager and fickle as any,
Hot toward one I hate, ready in my madness to knife him,
Solitary at midnight in my back yard, my thoughts gone from me a
 long while,

[106]I.e., sounds colorful harmonies in her throat. [107]A variety of watermelon.
[108]Wilderness boy. [109]Close.

Walking the old hills of Judæa with the beautiful gentle God by my side,
Speeding through space, speeding through heaven and the stars,
Speeding amid the seven satellites and the broad ring,[110] and the diameter of eighty thousand miles,
Speeding with tail'd meteors, throwing fire-balls like the rest,
Carrying the crescent child[111] that carries its own full mother in its belly,
Storming, enjoying, planning, loving, cautioning,
Backing and filling, appearing and disappearing,
I tread day and night such roads.

I visit the orchards of spheres and look at the product,
And look at quintillions[112] ripen'd and look at quintillions green.

I fly those flights of a fluid and swallowing soul,
My course runs below the soundings of plummets.

I help myself to material and immaterial,
No guard can shut me off, no law prevent me.

I anchor my ship for a little while only,
My messengers continually cruise away or bring their returns to me.

I go hunting polar furs and the seal, leaping chasms with a pike-pointed staff, clinging to topples[113] of brittle and blue.

I ascend to the foretruck,[114]
I take my place late at night in the crow's nest,
We sail the arctic sea, it is plenty light enough,
Through the clear atmosphere I stretch around on the wonderful beauty,
The enormous masses of ice pass me and I pass them, the scenery is plain in all directions,
The white-topt mountains show in the distance, I fling out my fancies toward them,
We are approaching some great battle-field in which we are soon to be engaged,
We pass the colossal outposts of the encampment, we pass with still feet and caution,
Or we are entering by the suburbs some vast and ruin'd city,
The blocks and fallen architecture more than all the living cities of the globe.

[110]The eight major planets, including Saturn with its minute surrounding particles that appear as a broad ring.
[111]The bright, crescent portion of a new moon partially lighted by the setting sun.
[112]The number 1 followed by eighteen zeros. [113]Fallen ice.
[114]Platform near the top of a foremast.

I am a free companion, I bivouac by invading watchfires,
I turn the bridegroom out of bed and stay with the bride myself,
I tighten her all night to my thighs and lips.

My voice is the wife's voice, the screech by the rail of the stairs,
They fetch my man's body up dripping and drown'd.

I understand the large hearts of heroes,
The courage of present times and all times,
How the skipper saw the crowded and rudderless wreck of the steam-ship, and Death chasing it up and down the storm,
How he knuckled tight and gave not back an inch, and was faithful of days and faithful of nights,
And chalk'd in large letters on a board, *Be of good cheer, we will not desert you;*
How he follow'd with them and tack'd with them three days and would not give it up,
How he saved the drifting company at last,
How the lank loose-gown'd women look'd when boated from the side of their prepared graves,
How the silent old-faced infants and the lifted sick, and the sharp-lipp'd unshaved men;
All this I swallow, it tastes good, I like it well, it becomes mine,
I am the man, I suffer'd, I was there.[115]

The disdain and calmness of martyrs,
The mother of old, condemn'd for a witch, burnt with dry wood, her children gazing on,
The hounded slave that flags in the race, leans by the fence, blowing, cover'd with sweat,
The twinges that sting like needles his legs and neck, the murderous buckshot and the bullets,
All these I feel or am.

I am the hounded slave, I wince at the bite of the dogs,
Hell and despair are upon me, crack and again crack the marksmen,
I clutch the rails of the fence, my gore dribs, thinn'd with the ooze of my skin,[116]
I fall on the weeds and stones,
The riders spur their unwilling horses, haul close,
Taunt my dizzy ears and beat me violently over the head with whipstocks.

Agonies are one of my changes of garments,
I do not ask the wounded person how he feels, I myself become the wounded person,
My hurts turn livid upon me as I lean on a cane and observe,

[115]The shipwreck episode is based on an actual sea disaster reported in newspapers in January 1854.
[116]I.e., my blood drips, thinned with sweat.

I am the mash'd fireman with breast-bone broken,
Tumbling walls buried me in their debris,
Heat and smoke I inspired,[117] I heard the yelling shouts of my comrades,
I heard the distant click of their picks and shovels,
They have clear'd the beams away, they tenderly lift me forth.

I lie in the night air in my red shirt, the pervading hush is for my sake,
Painless after all I lie exhausted but not so unhappy,
White and beautiful are the faces around me, the heads are bared of their fire-caps,
The kneeling crowd fades with the light of the torches.

Distant and dead resuscitate,
They show as the dial or move as the hands of me, I am the clock myself.

I am an old artillerist, I tell of my fort's bombardment,
I am there again.

Again the long roll of the drummers,
Again the attacking cannon, mortars,
Again to my listening ears the cannon responsive.

I take part, I see and hear the whole,
The cries, curses, roar, the plaudits for well-aim'd shots,
The ambulanza[118] slowly passing trailing its red drip,
Workmen searching after damages, making indispensable repairs,
The fall of grenades through the rent roof, the fan-shaped explosion,
The whizz of limbs, heads, stone, wood, iron, high in the air.

Again gurgles the mouth of my dying general, he furiously waves with his hand,
He gasps through the clot *Mind not me—mind—the entrenchments.*

34

Now I tell what I knew in Texas in my early youth,[119]
(I tell not the fall of Alamo,
Not one escaped to tell the fall of Alamo,
The hundred and fifty are dumb yet at Alamo,)
'Tis the tale of the murder in cold blood of four hundred and twelve young men.

[117]Inhaled. [118]Military ambulance.

[119]Whitman was never in Texas. The episode described below was drawn from reports of a massacre of Texans by Mexicans in the Revolution of 1836, shortly after the fall of the Alamo.

Retreating they had form'd in a hollow square with their baggage
  for breastworks,
Nine hundred lives out of the surrounding enemy's, nine times
  their number, was the price they took in advance,
Their colonel was wounded and their ammunition gone,
They treated[120] for an honorable capitulation, receiv'd writing and
  seal, gave up their arms and march'd back prisoners of war.
They were the glory of the race of rangers,
Matchless with horse, rifle, song, supper, courtship,
Large, turbulent, generous, handsome, proud, and affectionate,
Bearded, sunburnt, drest in the free costume of hunters,
Not a single one over thirty years of age.

The second First-day morning they were brought out in squads
  and massacred, it was beautiful early summer,
The work commenced about five o'clock and was over by eight.

None obey'd the command to kneel,
Some made a mad and helpless rush, some stood stark and straight,
A few fell at once, shot in the temple or heart, the living and
  dead lay together,
The maim'd and mangled dug in the dirt, the new-comers saw
  them there,
Some half-kill'd attempted to crawl away,
These were despatch'd with bayonets or batter'd with blunts of
  muskets,
A youth not seventeen years old seiz'd his assassin till two more
  came to release him,
The three were all torn and cover'd with the boy's blood.

At eleven o'clock began the burning of the bodies;
That is the tale of the murder of the four hundred and twelve
  young men.

35

Would you hear of an old-time sea-fight?
Would you learn who won by the light of the moon and stars?
List to the yarn,[121] as my grandmother's father the sailor told it to me.

Our foe was no skulk in his ship I tell you, (said he,)
His was the surly English pluck, and there is no tougher or
  truer, and never was, and never will be;
Along the lower'd eve he came horribly raking[122] us.

[120]Negotiated.

[121]Whitman's description is based on a letter from John Paul Jones to Benjamin Franklin (September 1779) telling of the sea battle (1779) between the British ship *Serapis* and the American ship *Bonhomme Richard* commanded by John Paul Jones, whose words "I have not yet begun to fight" are paraphrased in line 916.

[122]Sweeping the length of the ship with gunfire.

We closed with him, the yards entangled, the cannon touch'd,
My captain lash'd fast[123] with his own hands.

We had receiv'd some eighteen pound shots under the water,
On our lower-gun-deck two large pieces had burst at the first fire,
 killing all around and blowing up overhead.

Fighting at sun-down, fighting at dark,
Ten o'clock at night, the full moon well up, our leaks on the gain,
 and five feet of water reported,[124]
The master-at-arms loosing the prisoners confined in the after-hold
 to give them a chance for themselves.

The transit to and from the magazine[125] is now stopt by the
 sentinels,
They see so many strange faces they do not know whom to trust.

Our frigate takes fire,
The other asks if we demand quarter?[126]
If our colors are struck[127] and the fighting done?

Now I laugh content, for I hear the voice of my little captain,
We have not struck, he composedly cries, *we have just begun our
 part of the fighting.*

Only three guns are in use,
One is directed by the captain himself against the enemy's mainmast,
Two well serv'd with grape and canister[128] silence his musketry
 and clear his decks.

The tops[129] alone second the fire of this little battery, especially
 the main-top,
They hold out bravely during the whole of the action.

Not a moment's cease,
The leaks gain fast on the pumps, the fire eats toward the
 powder-magazine.

One of the pumps has been shot away, it is generally thought we
 are sinking.

[123]Jones reported that he "made both ships fast" when they came together.

[124]Jones reported that during the battle, the destructive fire from the British *Serapis* caused the *Bonhomme Richard* to take "five feet of water in the hold."

[125]Gunpowder storage room.

[126]Ask for clemency.

[127]During the battle, the flag of the *Bonhomme Richard* was shot away, causing the British to think the flag had been lowered as a sign of surrender.

[128]Charges of large (grape) or small (canister) iron balls.

[129]The platforms on the mastheads from which sharpshooters fired onto the enemy's deck below.

Serene stands the little captain,
He is not hurried, his voice is neither high nor low,
His eyes give more light to us than our battle-lanterns.

Toward twelve there in the beams of the moon they surrender
 to us.

36

Stretch'd and still lies the midnight,
Two great hulls motionless on the breast of the darkness,
Our vessel riddled and slowly sinking, preparations to pass to the
 one we have conquer'd,
The captain on the quarter-deck coldly giving his orders through
 a countenance white as a sheet,
Near by the corpse of the child that serv'd in the cabin,
The dead face of an old salt with long white hair and carefully
 curl'd whiskers,
The flames spite of all that can be done flickering aloft and below,
The husky voices of the two or three officers yet fit for duty,
Formless stacks of bodies and bodies by themselves, dabs of flesh
 upon the masts and spars,
Cut of cordage, dangle of rigging, slight shock of the soothe of
 waves,
Black and impassive guns, litter of powder-parcels, strong scent,
A few large stars overhead, silent and mournful shining,
Delicate sniffs of sea-breeze, smells of sedgy grass and fields by
 the shore, death-messages given in charge to survivors,
The hiss of the surgeon's knife, the gnawing teeth of his saw,
Wheeze, cluck, swash of falling blood, short wild scream, and
 long, dull, tapering groan,
These so, these irretrievable.

37

You laggards there on guard! look to your arms!
In at the conquer'd doors they crowd! I am possess'd!
Embody all presences outlaw'd or suffering,
See myself in prison shaped like another man,
And feel the dull unintermitted pain.

For me the keepers of convicts shoulder their carbines and keep
 watch,
It is I let out in the morning and barr'd at night.

Not a mutineer walks handcuff'd to jail but I am handcuff'd to him
 and walk by his side,
(I am less the jolly one there, and more the silent one with sweat on
 my twitching lips.)

Not a youngster is taken for larceny but I go up too, and am tried and sentenced.

Not a cholera patient lies at the last gasp but I also lie at the last gasp,
My face is ash-color'd, my sinews gnarl, away from me people retreat.

Askers embody themselves in me and I am embodied in them,
I project[130] my hat, sit shame-faced, and beg.

38

Enough! enough! enough!
Somehow I have been stunn'd. Stand back!
Give me a little time beyond[131] my cuff'd[132] head, slumbers, dreams, gaping.
I discover myself on the verge of a usual mistake.

That I could forget the mockers and insults!
That I could forget the trickling tears and the blows of the bludgeons and hammers!
That I could look with a separate look on my own crucifixion and bloody crowning.

I remember now,
I resume the overstaid fraction,[133]
The grave of rock multiplies what has been confided to it, or to any graves,
Corpses rise, gashes heal, fastenings roll from me.

I troop forth replenish'd with supreme power, one of an average unending procession,
Inland and sea-coast we go, and pass all boundary lines,
Our swift ordinances on their way over the whole earth,
The blossoms we wear in our hats the growth of thousands of years.

Eleves,[134] I salute you! come forward!
Continue your annotations, continue your questionings.

39

The friendly and flowing savage, who is he?
Is he waiting for civilization, or past it and mastering it?

Is he some Southwesterner rais'd out-doors? is he Kanadian?
Is he from the Mississippi country? Iowa, Oregon, California?
The mountains? prairie-life, bush-life? or sailor from the sea?

[130]Hold forth. [131]I.e., time to get over, recover from.
[132]Befuddled. [133]Recalculate. [134]French: students.

Wherever he goes men and women accept and desire him,
They desire he should like them, touch them, speak to them,
  stay with them.

Behavior lawless as snow-flakes, words simple as grass, uncomb'd
  head, laughter, and naiveté,
Slow-stepping feet, common features, common modes and
  emanations,
They descend in new forms from the tips of his fingers,
They are wafted with the odor of his body or breath, they fly
  out of the glance of his eyes.

40

Flaunt of the sunshine I need not your bask—lie over!
You light surfaces only, I force surfaces and depths also.

Earth! you seem to look for something at my hands,
Say, old top-knot,[135] what do you want?

Man or woman, I might tell how I like you, but cannot,
And might tell what it is in me and what it is in you, but cannot,
And might tell that pining I have, that pulse of my nights and days.

Behold, I do not give lectures or a little charity,
When I give I give myself.

You there, impotent, loose in the knees,
Open your scarf'd chops[136] till I blow grit[137] within you,
Spread your palms and lift the flaps of your pockets,
I am not to be denied, I compel, I have stores plenty and to spare,
And any thing I have I bestow.

I do not ask who you are, that is not important to me,
You can do nothing and be nothing but what I will infold you.

To cotton-field drudge or cleaner of privies I lean,
On his right cheek I put the family kiss,
And in my soul I swear I never will deny him.

On women fit for conception I start bigger and nimbler babes,
(This day I am jetting the stuff of far more arrogant republics.)

To any one dying, thither I speed and twist the knob of the door,
Turn the bed-clothes toward the foot of the bed,
Let the physician and the priest go home.

[135]Indian, from the tuft of hair used to ornament the head.
[136]Lined and wrinkled cheeks, jaws. [137]Strength of spirit, courage.

I seize the descending man and raise him with resistless will,
O despairer, here is my neck,
By God, you shall not go down! hang your whole weight upon me.

I dilate[138] you with tremendous breath, I buoy you up,
Every room of the house do I fill with an arm'd force,
Lovers of me, bafflers of graves.

Sleep—I and they keep guard all night,
Not doubt, not decease shall dare to lay finger upon you,
I have embraced you, and henceforth possess you to myself,
And when you rise in the morning you will find what I tell you
is so.

41

I am he bringing help for the sick as they pant on their backs,
And for strong upright men I bring yet more needed help.

I heard what was said of the universe,
Heard it and heard it of several thousand years;
It is middling well as far as it goes—but is that all?

Magnifying and applying come I,
Outbidding at the start the old cautious hucksters,[139]
Taking myself the exact dimensions of Jehovah,
Lithographing Kronos, Zeus his son, and Hercules his grandson,
Buying drafts of Osiris, Isis, Belus, Brahma, Buddha,
In my portfolio placing Manito loose, Allah on a leaf, the crucifix
engraved,
With Odin and the hideous-faced Mexitli[140] and every idol and
image,
Taking them all for what they are worth and not a cent more,
Admitting they were alive and did the work of their days,
(They bore mites as for unfledg'd birds who have now to rise
and fly and sing for themselves,)
Accepting the rough deific[141] sketches to fill out better in myself,
bestowing them freely on each man and woman I see,
Discovering as much or more in a framer framing a house,
Putting higher claims for him there with his roll'd-up sleeves
driving the mallet and chisel,
Not objecting to special revelations, considering a curl of smoke
or a hair on the back of my hand just as curious as any revelation,
Lads ahold of fire-engines and hook-and-ladder ropes no less to
me than the gods of the antique wars,
Minding their voices peal through the crash of destruction,

[138]Inflate, expand. [139]Peddlers.

[140]Whitman's list of gods includes those from Greek, Egyptian, Babylonian, and Norse mythology and from Judaism, Christianity, Hinduism, Buddhism, and Islam. Manito was a nature god of the Algonquian Indians; Mexitli, an Aztec god of war.

[141]Divine.

Their brawny limbs passing safe over charr'd laths, their white
foreheads whole and unhurt out of the flames;
By the mechanic's wife with her babe at her nipple interceding
for every person born,
Three scythes at harvest whizzing in a row from three lusty
angels with shirts bagg'd out at their waists,
The snag-tooth'd hostler[142] with red hair redeeming sins past and
to come,
Selling all he possesses, traveling on foot to fee lawyers for his
brother and sit by him while he is tried for forgery;
What was strewn in the amplest strewing the square rod about
me, and not filling the square rod then,
The bull and the bug never worshipp'd half enough,
Dung and dirt more admirable than was dream'd,
The supernatural of no account, myself waiting my time to be
one of the supremes,
The day getting ready for me when I shall do as much good as
the best, and be as prodigious;
By my life-lumps![143] becoming already a creator,
Putting myself here and now to the ambush'd womb of the shadows.

42

A call in the midst of the crowd,
My own voice, orotund sweeping and final.

Come my children,
Come my boys and girls, my women, household and intimates,
Now the performer launches his nerve, he has pass'd his prelude
on the reeds within.

Easily written loose-finger'd chords—I feel the thrum of your
climax and close.

My head slues round on my neck,
Music rolls, but not from the organ,
Folks are around me, but they are no household of mine.

Ever the hard unsunk ground,
Ever the eaters and drinkers, ever the upward and downward
sun, ever the air and the ceaseless tides,
Ever myself and my neighbors, refreshing, wicked, real,
Ever the old inexplicable query, ever that thorn'd thumb, that
breath of itches and thirsts,
Ever the vexer's *hoot! hoot!* till we find where the sly one hides
and bring him forth,
Ever love, ever the sobbing liquid of life,
Ever the bandage under the chin, ever the trestles[144] of death.

[142]Stableman. [143]Testicles. [144]Supports for coffins.

Here and there with dimes on the eyes[145] walking,
To feed the greed of the belly the brains liberally spooning,
Tickets buying, taking, selling, but in to the feast never once going,
Many sweating, ploughing, thrashing, and then the chaff for
payment receiving,
A few idly owning, and they the wheat continually claiming.

This is the city and I am one of the citizens,
Whatever interests the rest interests me, politics, wars, markets,
newspapers, schools,
The mayor and councils, banks, tariffs, steamships, factories,
stocks, stores, real estate and personal estate.

The little plentiful manikins skipping around in collars and tail'd coats,
I am aware who they are, (they are positively not worms or fleas,)
I acknowledge the duplicates of myself, the weakest and shallowest
is deathless with me,
What I do and say the same waits for them,
Every thought that flounders in me the same flounders in them.

I know perfectly well my own egotism,
Know my omnivorous lines and must not write any less,
And would fetch you whoever you are flush with myself.

Not words of routine this song of mine,
But abruptly to question, to leap beyond yet nearer bring;
This printed and bound book—but the printer and the printing-
office boy?

The well-taken photographs—but your wife or friend close and
solid in your arms?
The black ship mail'd with iron, her mighty guns in her turrets—
but the pluck of the captain and engineers?
In the houses the dishes and fare and furniture—but the host
and hostess, and the look out of their eyes?
The sky up there—yet here or next door, or across the way?
The saints and sages in history—but you yourself?
Sermons, creeds, theology—but the fathomless human brain,
And what is reason? and what is love? and what is life?

43

I do not despise you priests, all time, the world over,
My faith is the greatest of faiths and the least of faiths,
Enclosing worship ancient and modern and all between ancient
and modern,
Believing I shall come again upon the earth after five thousand
years,
Waiting responses from oracles, honoring the gods, saluting the sun,
Making a fetich[146] of the first rock or stump, powowing with
sticks in the circle of obis,[147]

[145]Whitman refers both to the dead (whose eyelids are held shut by coins) and to the greedy.
[146]Fetish, an object of worship. [147]Magic charms.

Helping the llama or brahmin[148] as he trims the lamps of the idols,
Dancing yet through the streets in a phallic procession, rapt and
austere in the woods a gymnosophist,[149]
Drinking mead from the skull-cup, to Shastas and Vedas[150]
admirant,[151] minding the Koran,
Walking the teokallis,[152] spotted with gore from the stone and
knife, beating the serpent-skin drum,
Accepting the Gospels, accepting him that was crucified, knowing
assuredly that he is divine,
To the mass kneeling or the puritan's prayer rising, or sitting
patiently in a pew,
Ranting and frothing in my insane crisis, or waiting dead-like till
my spirit arouses me,
Looking forth on pavement and land, or outside of pavement
and land,
Belonging to the winders of the circuit of circuits.

One of that centripetal and centrifugal gang I turn and talk like
a man leaving charges before a journey.

Down-hearted doubters dull and excluded,
Frivolous, sullen, moping, angry, affected, dishearten'd, atheistical,
I know every one of you, I know the sea of torment, doubt,
despair and unbelief.

How the flukes[153] splash!
How they contort rapid as lightning, with spasms and spouts of
blood!

Be at peace bloody flukes of doubters and sullen mopers,
I take my place among you as much as among any,
The past is the push of you, me, all, precisely the same,
And what is yet untried and afterward is for you, me, all,
precisely the same.

I do not know what is untried and afterward,
But I know it will in its turn prove sufficient, and cannot fail.

Each who passes is consider'd, each who stops is consider'd, not
a single one can it fail.

It cannot fail the young man who died and was buried,
Nor the young woman who died and was put by his side,
Nor the little child that peep'd in at the door, and then drew
back and was never seen again,

[148]Lama, a Tibetan high priest; Brahmin, a Hindu high priest.
[149]A Hindu ascetic. [150]Hindu religious writings. [151]French: admiring.
[152]Aztec temple with sacrificial altar. [153]The tail of a whale.

Nor the old man who has lived without purpose, and feels it
with bitterness worse than gall,
Nor him in the poor house tubercled by rum and the bad
disorder,[154]
Nor the numberless slaughter'd and wreck'd, nor the brutish
koboo[155] call'd the ordure[156] of humanity,
Nor the sacs[157] merely floating with open mouths for food to slip in,
Nor any thing in the earth, or down in the oldest graves of the earth,
Nor any thing in the myriads of spheres, nor the myriads of
myriads that inhabit them,
Nor the present, nor the least wisp that is known.

44

It is time to explain myself—let us stand up.

What is known I strip away,
I launch all men and women forward with me into the Unknown.

The clock indicates the moment—but what does eternity indicate?

We have thus far exhausted trillions of winters and summers,
There are trillions ahead, and trillions ahead of them.

Births have brought us richness and variety,
And other births will bring us richness and variety.

I do not call one greater and one smaller,
That which fills its period and place is equal to any.

Were mankind murderous or jealous upon you, my brother, my
sister?
I am sorry for you, they are not murderous or jealous upon me,
All has been gentle with me, I keep no account with lamentation,
(What have I to do with lamentation?)

I am an acme of things accomplish'd, and I an encloser of things to
be.

My feet strike an apex of the apices[158] of the stairs,
On every step bunches of ages, and larger bunches between the
steps,
All below duly travel'd, and still I mount and mount.

Rise after rise bow the phantoms behind me,
Afar down I see the huge first Nothing, I know I was even there,

[154]I.e., marked by tubercles (lesions and swellings) caused by rum and syphilis.
[155]Primitive native of Sumatra. [156]Filth, excrement. [157]Primitive aquatic animals.
[158]Plural of "apex," the highest point.

I waited unseen and always, and slept through the lethargic mist,
And took my time, and took no hurt from the fetid carbon.

Long I was hugg'd close—long and long.

Immense have been the preparations for me,
Faithful and friendly the arms that have help'd me.

Cycles ferried my cradle, rowing and rowing like cheerful boatmen,
For room to me stars kept aside in their own rings,
They sent influences to look after what was to hold me.

Before I was born out of my mother generations guided me,
My embryo has never been torpid, nothing could overlay[159] it.

For it the nebula cohered to an orb,
The long slow strata piled to rest it on,
Vast vegetables gave it sustenance,
Monstrous sauroids[160] transported it in their mouths and
deposited it with care.

All forces have been steadily employ'd to complete and delight me,
Now on this spot I stand with my robust soul.

45

O span of youth! ever-push'd elasticity!
O manhood, balanced, florid and full.

My lovers suffocate me,
Crowding my lips, thick in the pores of my skin,
Jostling me through streets and public halls, coming naked to me
at night,
Crying by day *Ahoy!* from the rocks of the river, swinging and
chirping over my head,

Calling my name from flower-beds, vines, tangled underbrush,
Lighting on every moment of my life,
Bussing[161] my body with soft balsamic[162] busses,
Noiselessly passing handfuls out of their hearts and giving them to
be mine.

Old age superbly rising! O welcome, ineffable grace of dying days!

Every condition promulges[163] not only itself, it promulges what
grows after and out of itself,
And the dark hush promulges as much as any.

[159]Oppress, smother. [160]Prehistoric reptiles. [161]Kissing.
[162]Fragrant with the aroma of balsam. [163]Generates.

I open my scuttle[164] at night and see the far-sprinkled systems,
And all I see multiplied as high as I can cipher edge but the rim
of the farther systems.

Wider and wider they spread, expanding always expanding,
Outward and outward and forever outward.

My sun has his sun and round him obediently wheels,
He joins with his partners a group of superior circuit,
And greater sets follow, making specks of the greatest inside them.

There is no stoppage and never can be stoppage,
If I, you, and the worlds, and all beneath or upon their surfaces,
were this moment reduced back to a pallid float,[165] it would
not avail in the long run,
We should surely bring up again where we now stand,
And surely go as much farther, and then farther and farther.

A few quadrillions of eras, a few octillions[166] of cubic leagues, do
not hazard the span or make it impatient,
They are but parts, any thing is but a part.

See ever so far, there is limitless space outside of that,
Count ever so much, there is limitless time around that.

My rendezvous is appointed, it is certain,
The Lord will be there and wait till I come on perfect terms,
The great Camerado,[167] the lover true for whom I pine will be there.

46

I know I have the best time and space, and was never
measured and never will be measured.

I tramp a perpetual journey, (come listen all!)
My signs are a rain-proof coat, good shoes, and a staff cut from
the woods,
No friend of mine takes his ease in my chair,
I have no chair, no church, no philosophy,
I lead no man to a dinner-table, library, exchange,[168]
But each man and each woman of you I lead upon a knoll,
My left hand hooking you round the waist,
My right hand pointing to landscapes of continents and the
public road.

Not I, not any one else can travel that road for you,
You must travel it for yourself.

[164]An opening in a house roof.
[165]I.e., returned to a primordial state where all life is suspended as particles in water.
[166]The number 1 followed by twenty-seven zeros. [167]Comrade. [168]Stock exchange.

It is not far, it is within reach,
Perhaps you have been on it since you were born and did not know,
Perhaps it is everywhere on water and on land.

Shoulder your duds dear son, and I will mine, and let us hasten forth,
Wonderful cities and free nations we shall fetch[169] as we go.

If you tire, give me both burdens, and rest the chuff[170] of your hand on my hip,
And in due time you shall repay the same service to me,
For after we start we never lie by again.

This day before dawn I ascended a hill and look'd at the crowded heaven.
And I said to my spirit *When we become the enfolders of those orbs, and the pleasure and knowledge of every thing in them, shall we be fill'd and satisfied then?*
And my spirit said, *No, we but level that lift[171] to pass and continue beyond.*

You are also asking me questions and I hear you,
I answer that I cannot answer, you must find out for yourself.

Sit a while dear son,
Here are biscuits to eat and here is milk to drink,
But as soon as you sleep and renew yourself in sweet clothes, I kiss you with a good-by kiss and open the gate for your egress[172] hence.

Long enough have you dream'd contemptible dreams,
Now I wash the gum from your eyes,
You must habit yourself to the dazzle of the light and of every moment of your life.

Long have you timidly waded holding a plank by the shore,
Now I will you to be a bold swimmer,
To jump off in the midst of the sea, rise again, nod to me, shout, and laughingly dash with your hair.

47

I am the teacher of athletes,
He that by me spreads a wider breast than my own proves the width of my own,
He most honors my style who learns under it to destroy the teacher.

The boy I love, the same becomes a man, not through derived power, but in his own right,

[169]Reach. [170]Heel. [171]Rising ground. [172]Exit.

Wicked rather than virtuous out of conformity or fear,
Fond of his sweetheart, relishing well his steak,
Unrequited love or a slight cutting him worse than sharp steel cuts,
First-rate to ride, to fight, to hit the bull's eye, to sail a skiff, to
 sing a song or play on the banjo,
Preferring scars and the beard and faces pitted with small-pox
 over all latherers,[173]
And those well-tann'd to those that keep out of the sun.

I teach straying from me, yet who can stray from me?
I follow you whoever you are from the present hour,
My words itch at your ears till you understand them.

I do not say these things for a dollar or to fill up the time while
 I wait for a boat,
(It is you talking just as much as myself, I act as the tongue of you,
Tied in your mouth, in mine it begins to be loosen'd.)

I swear I will never again mention love or death inside a house,
And I swear I will never translate myself at all, only to him or
 her who privately stays with me in the open air.

If you would understand me go to the heights or water-shore,
The nearest gnat is an explanation, and a drop or motion of
 waves a key,
The maul, the oar, the hand-saw, second my words.

No shutter'd room or school can commune with me,
But roughs and little children better than they.

The young mechanic is closest to me, he knows me well,
The woodman that takes his axe and jug with him shall take me
 with him all day,
The farm-boy ploughing in the field feels good at the sound of
 my voice,
In vessels that sail my words sail, I go with fishermen and
 seamen and love them.

The soldier camp'd or upon the march is mine,
On the night ere the pending battle many seek me, and I do not
 fail them,
On that solemn night (it may be their last) those that know me
 seek me.

My face rubs to the hunter's face when he lies down alone in his
 blanket,
The driver thinking of me does not mind the jolt of his wagon,
The young mother and old mother comprehend me,

[173]Those who are clean-shaven.

The girl and the wife rest the needle a moment and forget where they are,
They and all would resume what I have told them.

48

I have said that the soul is not more than the body,
And I have said that the body is not more than the soul,
And nothing, not God, is greater to one than one's self is,
And whoever walks a furlong without sympathy walks to his own funeral drest in his shroud,
And I or you pocketless of a dime may purchase the pick of the earth,
And to glance with an eye or show a bean in its pod confounds the learning of all times,
And there is no trade or employment but the young man following it may become a hero,
And there is no object so soft but it makes a hub for the wheel'd universe,
And I say to any man or woman, Let your soul stand cool and composed before a million universes.

And I say to mankind, Be not curious about God,
For I who am curious about each am not curious about God,
(No array of terms can say how much I am at peace about God and about death.)

I hear and behold God in every object, yet understand God not in the least,
Nor do I understand who there can be more wonderful than myself.

Why should I wish to see God better than this day?
I see something of God each hour of the twenty-four, and each moment then,
In the faces of men and women I see God, and in my own face in the glass,
I find letters from God dropt in the street, and every one is sign'd by God's name.
And I leave them where they are, for I know that wheresoe'er I go,
Others will punctually come for ever and ever.

49

And as to you Death, and you bitter hug of mortality, it is idle to try to alarm me.

To his work without flinching the accoucheur[174] comes,
I see the elder-hand[175] pressing receiving supporting,
I recline by the sills of the exquisite flexible doors,
And mark the outlet, and mark the relief and escape.

[174]Midwife, obstetrician. [175]Left hand.

And as to you Corpse I think you are good manure, but that does not offend me,
I smell the white roses sweet-scented and growing,
I reach to the leafy lips, I reach to the polish'd breasts of melons.

And as to you Life I reckon you are the leavings of many deaths,
(No doubt I have died myself ten thousand times before.)

I hear you whispering there O stars of heaven,
O suns—O grass of graves—O perpetual transfers and promotions,
If you do not say any thing how can I say any thing?

Of the turbid pool that lies in the autumn forest,
Of the moon that descends the steeps of the soughing[176] twilight,
Toss, sparkles of day and dusk—toss on the black stems that decay in the muck,
Toss to the moaning gibberish of the dry limbs.

I ascend from the moon, I ascend from the night,
I perceive that the ghastly glimmer is noonday sunbeams reflected,
And debouch[177] to the steady and central from the offspring great or small.

50

There is that in me—I do not know what it is—but I know it is in me.

Wrench'd and sweaty—calm and cool then my body becomes,
I sleep—I sleep long.

I do not know it—it is without name—it is a word unsaid,
It is not in any dictionary, utterance, symbol.

Something it swings on more than the earth I swing on,
To it the creation is the friend whose embracing awakes me.

Perhaps I might tell more. Outlines! I plead for my brothers and sisters.

Do you see O my brothers and sisters?
It is not chaos or death—it is form, union, plan—it is eternal life—it is Happiness.

51

The past and present wilt—I have fill'd them, emptied them,
And proceed to fill my next fold of the future.

Listener up there! what have you to confide to me?
Look in my face while I snuff[178] the sidle[179] of evening,
(Talk honestly, no one else hears you, and I stay only a minute longer.)

[176]Sighing, moaning. [177]Emerge. [178]Extinguish. [179]Fading light.

Do I contradict myself?
Very well then I contradict myself,
(I am large, I contain multitudes.)

I concentrate toward them that are nigh, I wait on the door-slab.

Who has done his day's work? who will soonest be through with his supper?
Who wishes to walk with me?

Will you speak before I am gone? will you prove already too late?

52

The spotted hawk swoops by and accuses me, he complains of my gab and my loitering.

I too am not a bit tamed, I too am untranslatable,
I sound my barbaric yawp[180] over the roofs of the world.

The last scud[181] of day holds back for me,
It flings my likeness after the rest and true as any on the shadow'd wilds,
It coaxes me to the vapor and the dusk.

I depart as air, I shake my white locks at the runaway sun,
I effuse[182] my flesh in eddies, and drift it in lacy jags.

I bequeath myself to the dirt to grow from the grass I love,
If you want me again look for me under your boot-soles.

You will hardly know who I am or what I mean,
But I shall be good health to you nevertheless,
And filter and fibre your blood.

Failing to fetch me at first keep encouraged,
Missing me one place search another,
I stop somewhere waiting for you.

1855, 1881

from *CHILDREN OF ADAM*

OUT OF THE ROLLING OCEAN THE CROWD

Out of the rolling ocean the crowd came a drop gently to me,
Whispering *I love you, before long I die,*
I have travel'd a long way merely to look on you to touch you,
For I could not die till I once look'd on you,
For I fear'd I might afterward lose you.

[180]Loud cry, yell. [181]Wind-driven clouds or mist. [182]Pour out.

Now we have met, we have look'd, we are safe,
Return in peace to the ocean my love,
I too am part of the ocean my love, we are not so much separated,
Behold the great rondure,[1] the cohesion of all, how perfect!
But as for me, for you, the irresistible sea is to separate us,
As for an hour carrying us diverse, yet cannot carry us diverse forever;
Be not impatient—a little space—know you I salute the air, the
 ocean and the land,
Every day at sundown for your dear sake my love.

1865, 1881

ONCE I PASS'D THROUGH A POPULOUS CITY

Once I pass'd through a populous city imprinting my brain for
 future use with its shows, architecture, customs, traditions,
Yet now of all that city I remember only a woman I casually met
 there who detain'd me for love of me,
Day by day and night by night we were together—all else has long
 been forgotten by me,
I remember I say only that woman who passionately clung to me,
Again we wander, we love, we separate again,
Again she holds me by the hand, I must not go,
I see her close beside me with silent lips sad and tremulous.

1860, 1867

FACING WEST FROM CALIFORNIA'S SHORES

Facing west from California's shores,
Inquiring, tireless, seeking what is yet unfound,
I, a child, very old, over waves, towards the house of maternity,[1]
 the land of migrations, look afar,
Look off the shores of my Western sea, the circle almost circled;
For starting westward from Hindustan,[2] from the Vales of
 Kashmere,[3]
From Asia, from the north, from the God, the sage, and the hero,
From the south, from the flowery peninsulas and the spice islands,[4]
Long having wander'd since, round the earth having wander'd,
Now I face home again, very pleas'd and joyous,
(But where is what I started for so long ago?
And why is it yet unfound?)

1860, 1867

[1]Gracefully rounded curve.

[1]I.e., Asia, then thought to be the place of man's origin.

[2]India.

[3]Mountain region of northern India.

[4]The islands of Indonesia.

from *CALAMUS*[1]

I SAW IN LOUISIANA A LIVE-OAK GROWING

I saw in Louisiana a live-oak growing,
All alone stood it and the moss hung down from the branches,
Without any companion it grew there uttering joyous leaves of dark green,
And its look, rude, unbending, lusty, made me think of myself,
But I wonder'd how it could utter joyous leaves standing alone there without its friend near, for I knew I could not,
And I broke off a twig with a certain number of leaves upon it, and twined around it a little moss,
And brought it away, and I have placed it in sight in my room,
It is not needed to remind me as of my own dear friends,
(For I believe lately I think of little else than of them,)
Yet it remains to me a curious token, it makes me think of manly love;
For all that, and though the live-oak glistens there in Louisiana solitary in a wide flat space,
Uttering joyous leaves all its life without a friend a lover near,
I know very well I could not.

1860, 1867

I HEAR IT WAS CHARGED AGAINST ME

I hear it was charged against me that I sought to destroy institutions,
But really I am neither for nor against institutions,
(What indeed have I in common with them? or what with the destruction of them?)
Only I will establish in the Mannahatta[1] and in every city of these States inland and seaboard,
And in the fields and woods, and above every keel little or large that dents the water,
Without edifices or rules or trustees or any argument,
The institution of the dear love of comrades.

1860, 1867

[1]Whitman wrote that Calamus "is the very large and aromatic grass, or rush, growing about water-ponds . . . spears about three feet high."

[1]Indian word from which "Manhattan" was derived.

CROSSING BROOKLYN FERRY[1]

1

Flood-tide below me! I see you face to face!
Clouds of the west—sun there half an hour high—I see you also face to face.

Crowds of men and women attired in the usual costumes, how curious you are to me!
On the ferry-boats the hundreds and hundreds that cross, returning home, are more curious to me than you suppose,
And you that shall cross from shore to shore years hence are more to me, and more in my meditations, than you might suppose.

2

The impalpable sustenance of me from all things at all hours of the day,
The simple, compact, well-join'd scheme, myself disintegrated, every one disintegrated yet part of the scheme,
The similitudes[2] of the past and those of the future,
The glories strung like beads on my smallest sighs and hearings, on the walk in the street and the passage over the river,
The current rushing so swiftly and swimming with me far away,
The others that are to follow me, the ties between me and them,
The certainty of others, the life, love, sight, hearing of others.

Others will enter the gates of the ferry and cross from shore to shore,
Others will watch the run of the flood-tide,
Others will see the shipping of Manhattan north and west, and the heights of Brooklyn to the south and east,
Others will see the islands large and small;
Fifty years hence, others will see them as they cross, the sun half an hour high,
A hundred years hence, or ever so many hundred years hence, others will see them,
Will enjoy the sunset, the pouring-in of the flood-tide, the falling-back to the sea of the ebb-tide.

3

It avails not, time nor place—distance avails not,
I am with you, you men and women of a generation, or ever so many generations hence,
Just as you feel when you look on the river and sky, so I felt,
Just as any of you is one of a living crowd, I was one of a crowd,
Just as you are refresh'd by the gladness of the river and the bright flow, I was refresh'd,

[1]Originally titled "Sun-Down Poem." [2]Similarities.

Just as you stand and lean on the rail, yet hurry with the swift
current, I stood yet was hurried,
Just as you look on the numberless masts of ships and the thick-
stemm'd pipes of steamboats, I look'd.

I too many and many a time cross'd the river of old,
Watched the Twelfth-month[3] sea-gulls, saw them high in the air
floating with motionless wings, oscillating their bodies,
Saw how the glistening yellow lit up parts of their bodies and left
the rest in strong shadow,
Saw the slow-wheeling circles and the gradual edging toward the south,
Saw the reflection of the summer sky in the water,
Had my eyes dazzled by the shimmering track of beams,
Look'd at the fine centrifugal spokes of light round the shape of
my head in the sunlit water,
Look'd on the haze on the hills southward and south-westward,
Look'd on the vapor as it flew in fleeces tinged with violet,
Look'd toward the lower bay to notice the vessels arriving,
Saw their approach, saw aboard those that were near me,
Saw the white sails of schooners and sloops, saw the ships at anchor,
The sailors at work in the rigging or out astride the spars,
The round masts, the swinging motion of the hulls, the slender
serpentine pennants,
The large and small steamers in motion, the pilots in their pilot-
houses,
The white wake left by the passage, the quick tremulous whirl of
the wheels,
The flags of all nations, the falling of them at sunset,
The scallop-edged waves in the twilight, the ladled cups, the
frolicsome crests and glistening,
The stretch afar flowing dimmer and dimmer, the gray walls of
the granite storehouses by the docks,
On the river the shadowy group, the big steam-tug closely
flank'd on each side by the barges, the hay-boat, the belated
lighter,[4]
On the neighboring shore the fires from the foundry chimneys
burning high and glaringly into the night,
Casting their flicker of black contrasted with wild red and yellow
light over the tops of houses, and down into the clefts of streets.

4

These and all else were to me the same as they are to you,
I loved well those cities, loved well the stately and rapid river,
The men and women I saw were all near to me,
Others the same—others who look back on me because I look'd
forward to them,
(The time will come, though I stop here to-day and to-night.)

[3]December. [4]Barge used in loading and unloading cargo ships.

5

What is it then between us?
What is the count of the scores or hundreds of years between us?

Whatever it is, it avails not—distance avails not, and place avails not,
I too lived, Brooklyn of ample hills was mine,
I too walk'd the streets of Manhattan island, and bathed in the
  waters around it,
I too felt the curious abrupt questionings stir within me,
In the day among crowds of people sometimes they came upon me,
In my walks home late at night or as I lay in my bed they came
  upon me,
I too had been struck from the float forever held in solution,
I too had receiv'd identity by my body,
That I was I knew was of my body, and what I should be I knew
  I should be of my body.

6

It is not upon you alone the dark patches fall,
The dark threw its patches down upon me also,
The best I had done seem'd to me blank and suspicious,
My great thoughts as I supposed them, were they not in reality
  meagre?
Nor is it you alone who know what it is to be evil,
I am he who knew what it was to be evil,
I too knitted the old knot of contrariety,
Blabb'd, blush'd, resented, lied, stole, grudg'd,
Had guile, anger, lust, hot wishes I dared not speak,
Was wayward, vain, greedy, shallow, sly, cowardly, malignant,
The wolf, the snake, the hog, not wanting[5] in me,
The cheating look, the frivolous word, the adulterous wish, not
  wanting,
Refusals, hates, postponements, meanness, laziness, none of these
  wanting,
Was one with the rest, the days and haps[6] of the rest,
Was call'd by my nighest[7] name by clear loud voices of young
  men as they saw me approaching or passing,
Felt their arms on my neck as I stood, or the negligent leaning
  of their flesh against me as I sat,
Saw many I loved in the street or ferry-boat or public assembly,
  yet never told them a word,
Lived the same life with the rest, the same old laughing, gnawing,
  sleeping,
Play'd the part that still looks back on the actor or actress,
The same old role, the role that is what we make it, as great as
  we like,
Or as small as we like, or both great and small.

[5]Lacking. [6]Chance events. [7]Shortest or most familiar.

7

Closer yet I approach you,
What thought you have of me now, I had as much of you—I
laid in my stores in advance,
I consider'd long and seriously of you before you were born.

Who was to know what should come home to me?
Who knows but I am enjoying this?
Who knows, for all the distance, but I am as good as looking at
you now, for all you cannot see me?

8

Ah, what can ever be more stately and admirable to me than
mast-hemm'd Manhattan?
River and sunset and scallop-edg'd waves of flood-tide?
The sea-gulls oscillating their bodies, the hay-boat in the twilight,
and the belated lighter?
What gods can exceed these that clasp me by the hand, and with
voices I love call me promptly and loudly by my nighest name
as I approach?
What is more subtle than this which ties me to the woman or
man that looks in my face?
Which fuses me into you now, and pours my meaning into you?

We understand then do we not?
What I promis'd without mentioning it, have you not accepted?
What the study could not teach—what the preaching could not
accomplish is accomplish'd, is it not?

9

Flow on, river! flow with the flood-tide, and ebb with the ebb-tide!
Frolic on, crested and scallop-edg'd waves!
Gorgeous clouds of the sunset! drench with your splendor me, or
the men and women generations after me!
Cross from shore to shore, countless crowds of passengers!
Stand up, tall masts of Mannahatta! stand up, beautiful hills of
Brooklyn!
Throb, baffled and curious brain! throw our questions and answers!
Suspend here and everywhere, eternal float of solution!
Gaze, loving and thirsting eyes, in the house or street or public
assembly!
Sound out, voices of young men! loudly and musically call me by my
nighest name!
Live, old life! play the part that looks back on the actor or actress!
Play the old role, the role that is great or small according as one
makes it!
Consider, you who peruse me, whether I may not in unknown ways
be looking upon you;
Be firm, rail over the river, to support those who lean idly, yet haste
with the hasting current;

Fly on, sea-birds! fly sideways, or wheel in large circles high in
the air;
Receive the summer sky, you water, and faithfully hold it till all
downcast eyes have time to take it from you!
Diverge, fine spokes of light, from the shape of my head, or any
one's head, in the sunlit water!
Come on, ships from the lower bay! pass up or down, white-sail'd
schooners, sloops, lighters!
Flaunt away, flags of all nations! be duly lower'd at sunset!
Burn high your fires, foundry chimneys! cast black shadows at
nightfall! cast red and yellow light over the tops of the houses!
Appearances, now or henceforth, indicate what you are,
You necessary film, continue to envelop the soul,
About my body for me, and your body for you, be hung our divinest
aromas,
Thrive, cities—bring your freight, bring your shows, ample and
sufficient rivers,
Expand, being than which none else is perhaps more spiritual,
Keep your places, objects than which none else is more lasting.

You have waited, you always wait, you dumb, beautiful ministers,
We receive you with free sense at last, and are insatiate
henceforward,
Not you any more shall be able to foil us, or withhold yourselves
from us,
We use you, and do not cast you aside—we plant you permanently
within us,
We fathom you not—we love you—there is perfection in you also,
You furnish your parts toward eternity,
Great or small, you furnish your parts toward the soul.

1856, 1881

from *SEA-DRIFT*

OUT OF THE CRADLE ENDLESSLY ROCKING

Out of the cradle endlessly rocking,
Out of the mocking-bird's throat, the musical shuttle,
Out of the Ninth-month[1] midnight,
Over the sterile sands and the fields beyond, where the child leaving
his bed wander'd alone, bareheaded, barefoot,
Down from the shower'd halo,
Up from the mystic play of shadows twining and twisting as if they
were alive,
Out from the patches of briers and blackberries,
From the memories of the bird that chanted to me,

[1]September.

From your memories sad brother, from the fitful risings and fallings I heard,
From under that yellow half-moon late-risen and swollen as if with tears,
From those beginning notes of yearning and love there in the mist,
From the thousand responses of my heart never to cease,
From the myriad thence-arous'd words,
From the word stronger and more delicious than any,
From such as now they start the scene revisiting,
As a flock, twittering, rising, or overhead passing,
Borne hither, ere all eludes me, hurriedly,
A man, yet by these tears a little boy again,
Throwing myself on the sand, confronting the waves,
I, chanter of pains and joys, uniter of here and hereafter,
Taking all hints to use them, but swiftly leaping beyond them,
A reminiscence sing.

Once Paumanok,[2]
When the lilac-scent was in the air and Fifth-month[3] grass was growing,
Up this seashore in some briers,
Two feather'd guests from Alabama, two together,
And their nest, and four light-green eggs spotted with brown,
And every day the he-bird to and fro near at hand,
And every day the she-bird crouch'd on her nest, silent, with bright eyes,
And every day I, a curious boy, never too close, never disturbing them,
Cautiously peering, absorbing, translating.

Shine! shine! shine!
Pour down your warmth, great sun!
While we bask, we two together.

Two together!
Winds blow south, or winds blow north,
Day come white, or night come black,
Home, or rivers and mountains from home,
Singing all time, minding no time,
While we two keep together.

Till of a sudden,
May-be kill'd, unknown to her mate,
One forenoon the she-bird crouch'd not on the nest,
Nor return'd that afternoon, nor the next,
Nor ever appear'd again.

[2]Indian name for Long Island, New York. [3]May.

And thenceforward all summer in the sound of the sea,
And at night under the full of the moon in calmer weather,
Over the hoarse surging of the sea,
Or flitting from brier to brier by day,
I saw, I heard at intervals the remaining one, the he-bird,
The solitary guest from Alabama.

Blow! blow! blow!
Blow up sea-winds along Paumanok's shore;
I wait and I wait till you blow my mate to me.

Yes, when the stars glisten'd,
All night long on the prong of a moss-scallop'd stake,
Down almost amid the slapping waves,
Sat the lone singer wonderful causing tears.

He call'd on his mate,
He pour'd forth the meanings which I of all men know.

Yes my brother I know,
The rest might not, but I have treasur'd every note,
For more than once dimly down to the beach gliding,
Silent, avoiding the moonbeams, blending myself with the shadows,
Recalling now the obscure shapes, the echoes, the sounds and sights
after their sorts,
The white arms out in the breakers tirelessly tossing,
I, with bare feet, a child, the wind wafting my hair,
Listen'd long and long.

Listen'd to keep, to sing, now translating the notes,
Following you my brother.

Soothe! soothe! soothe!
Close on its wave soothes the wave behind,
And again another behind embracing and lapping, every one close,
But my love soothes not me, not me.

Low hangs the moon, it rose late,
It is lagging—O I think it is heavy with love, with love.

O madly the sea pushes upon the land,
With love, with love.

O night! do I not see my love fluttering out among the breakers?
What is that little black thing I see there in the white?

Loud! loud! loud!
Loud I call to you, my love!
High and clear I shoot my voice over the waves,
Surely you must know who is here, is here,
You must know who I am, my love.

Low-hanging moon!
What is that dusky spot in your brown yellow?
O it is the shape, the shape of my mate!
O moon do not keep her from me any longer.

Land! land! O land!
Whichever way I turn, O I think you could give me my mate back again if you only would,
For I am almost sure I see her dimly whichever way I look.

O rising stars!
Perhaps the one I want so much will rise, will rise with some of you.

O throat! O trembling throat!
Sound clearer through the atmosphere!
Pierce the woods, the earth,
Somewhere listening to catch you must be the one I want.

Shake out carols!
Solitary here, the night's carols!
Carols of lonesome love! death's carols!
Carols under that lagging, yellow, waning moon!
O under that moon where she droops almost down into the sea!
O reckless despairing carols.

But soft! sink low!
Soft! let me just murmur,
And do you wait a moment you husky-nois'd sea,
For somewhere I believe I heard my mate responding to me,
So faint, I must be still, be still to listen,
But not altogether still, for then she might not come immediately to me.

Hither my love!
Here I am! here!
With this just-sustain'd note I announce myself to you,
This gentle call is for you my love, for you.

Do not be decoy'd elsewhere,
That is the whistle of the wind, it is not my voice,
That is the fluttering, the fluttering of the spray,
Those are the shadows of leaves.

O darkness! O in vain!
O I am very sick and sorrowful.

O brown halo in the sky near the moon, drooping upon the sea!
O troubled reflection in the sea!
O throat! O throbbing heart!
And I singing uselessly, uselessly all the night.

O past! O happy life! O songs of joy!
In the air, in the woods, over fields,
Loved! loved! loved! loved! loved!
But my mate no more, no more with me!
We two together no more.

The aria sinking,
All else continuing, the stars shining,
The winds blowing, the notes of the bird continuous echoing,
With angry moans the fierce old mother incessantly moaning,
On the sands of Paumanok's shore gray and rustling,
The yellow half-moon enlarged, sagging down, drooping, the face of the sea almost touching,
The boy ecstatic, with his bare feet the waves, with his hair the atmosphere dallying,
The love in the heart long pent, now loose, now at last tumultuously bursting,
The aria's meaning, the ears, the soul, swiftly depositing,
The strange tears down the cheeks coursing,
The colloquy there, the trio, each uttering,
The undertone, the savage old mother incessantly crying.
To the boy's soul's questions sullenly timing, some drown'd secret hissing.
To the outsetting bard.

Demon or bird! (said the boy's soul,)
Is it indeed toward your mate you sing? or is it really to me?
For I, that was a child, my tongue's use sleeping, now I have heard you,
Now in a moment I know what I am for, I awake,
And already a thousand singers, a thousand songs, clearer, louder and more sorrowful than yours,
A thousand warbling echoes have started to life within me, never to die.

O you singer solitary, singing by yourself, projecting me,
O solitary me listening, never more shall I cease perpetuating you,
Never more shall I escape, never more the reverberations,
Never more the cries of unsatisfied love be absent from me,
Never again leave me to be the peaceful child I was before what there in the night,
By the sea under the yellow and sagging moon,
The messenger there arous'd, the fire, the sweet hell within,
The unknown want, the destiny of me.

O give me the clew![4] (it lurks in the night here somewhere,)
O if I am to have so much, let me have more!
A word then, (for I will conquer it,)

[4]Clue.

The word final, superior to all,
Subtle, sent up—what is it?—I listen:
Are you whispering it, and have been all the time, you sea-waves?
Is that it from your liquid rims and wet sands?

Whereto answering, the sea,
Delaying not, hurrying not,
Whisper'd me through the night, and very plainly before daybreak,
Lisp'd to me the low and delicious word death,
And again, death, death, death, death,
Hissing melodious, neither like the bird nor like my arous'd child's
heart,
But edging near as privately for me rustling at my feet,
Creeping thence steadily up to my ears and laving me softly all over,
Death, death, death, death, death.

Which I do not forget,
But fuse the song of my dusky demon and brother,
That he sang to me in the moonlight on Paumanok's gray beach,
With the thousand responsive songs at random,
My own songs awaked from that hour,
And with them the key, the word up from the waves,
The word of the sweetest song and all songs,
That strong and delicious word which, creeping to my feet,
(Or like some old crone rocking the cradle, swathed in sweet
garments, bending aside,)
The sea whisper'd me.

1859, 1881

from *BY THE ROADSIDE*

WHEN I HEARD THE LEARN'D ASTRONOMER

When I heard the learn'd astronomer,
When the proofs, the figures, were ranged in columns before me,
When I was shown the charts and diagrams, to add, divide, and
measure them,
When I sitting heard the astronomer where he lectured with much
applause in the lecture-room,
How soon unaccountable I became tired and sick,
Till rising and gliding out I wander'd off by myself,
In the mystical moist night-air, and from time to time,
Look'd up in perfect silence at the stars.

1865, 1865

THE DALLIANCE[1] OF THE EAGLES

Skirting the river road, (my forenoon walk, my rest,)
Skyward in air a sudden muffled sound, the dalliance of the eagles,
The rushing amorous contact high in space together,
The clinching interlocking claws, a living, fierce, gyrating wheel,
Four beating wings, two beaks, a swirling mass tight grappling,
In tumbling turning clustering loops, straight downward falling,
Till o'er the river pois'd, the twain yet one, a moment's lull,
A motionless still balance in the air, then parting, talons loosing,
Upward again on slow-firm pinions, slanting, their separate diverse flight,
She hers, he his, pursuing.

1880, 1881

from *DRUM-TAPS*

BEAT! BEAT! DRUMS!

Beat! beat! drums!—blow! bugles! blow!
Through the windows—through doors—burst like a ruthless force,
Into the solemn church, and scatter the congregation,
Into the school where the scholar is studying;
Leave not the bridegroom quiet—no happiness must he have now with his bride,
Nor the peaceful farmer any peace, ploughing his field or gathering his grain,
So fierce you whirr and pound you drums—so shrill you bugles blow.

Beat! beat! drums!—blow! bugles! blow!
Over the traffic of cities—over the rumble of wheels in the streets;
Are beds prepared for sleepers at night in the houses? no sleepers must sleep in those beds,
No bargainers' bargains by day—no brokers or speculators—would they continue?
Would the talkers be talking? would the singer attempt to sing?
Would the lawyer rise in the court to state his case before the judge?
Then rattle quicker, heavier drums—you bugles wilder blow.

[1]In the sense of amorous play and mating.

Beat! beat! drums!—blow! bugles! blow!
Make no parley—stop for no expostulation,
Mind not the timid—mind not the weeper or prayer,
Mind not the old man beseeching the young man,
Let not the child's voice be heard, nor the mother's entreaties,
Make even the trestles to shake the dead where they lie awaiting the
hearses,
So strong you thump O terrible drums—so loud you bugles blow.

1861, 1867

CAVALRY CROSSING A FORD

A line in long array where they wind betwixt green islands,
They take a serpentine course, their arms flash in the sun—hark to
the musical clank,
Behold the silvery river, in it the splashing horses loitering stop to
drink,
Behold the brown-faced men, each group, each person a picture, the
negligent rest on the saddles,
Some emerge on the opposite bank, others are just entering the
ford—while,
Scarlet and blue and snowy white,
The guidon flags[1] flutter gayly in the wind.

1865, 1871

BIVOUAC ON A MOUNTAIN SIDE

I see before me now a traveling army halting,
Below a fertile valley spread, with barns and the orchards of
summer,
Behind, the terraced sides of a mountain, abrupt, in places rising
high,
Broken, with rocks, with clinging cedars, with tall shapes dingily
seen,
The numerous camp-fires scatter'd near and far, some away up on
the mountain,
The shadowy forms of men and horses, looming, large-sized,
flickering,
And over all the sky—the sky! far, far out of reach, studded,
breaking out, the eternal stars.

1865, 1871

[1]Military flags or pennants.

VIGIL STRANGE I KEPT ON THE FIELD ONE NIGHT

Vigil strange I kept on the field one night;
When you my son and my comrade dropt at my side that day,
One look I but gave which your dear eyes return'd with a look I shall never forget,
One touch of your hand to mine O boy, reach'd up as you lay on the ground,
Then onward I sped in the battle, the even-contested battle,
Till late in the night reliev'd to the place at last again I made my way,
Found you in death so cold dear comrade, found your body son of responding kisses, (never again on earth responding,)
Bared your face in the starlight, curious the scene, cool blew the moderate night-wind,
Long there and then in vigil I stood, dimly around me the battle-field spreading,
Vigil wondrous and vigil sweet there in the fragrant silent night,
But not a tear fell, not even a long-drawn sigh, long long I gazed,
Then on the earth partially reclining sat by your side leaning my chin in my hands,
Passing sweet hours, immortal and mystic hours with you dearest comrade—not a tear, not a word,
Vigil of silence, love and death, vigil for you my son and my soldier,
As onward silently stars aloft, eastward new ones upward stole,
Vigil final for you brave boy, (I could not save you, swift was your death,
I faithfully loved you and cared for you living, I think we shall surely meet again,)
Till at latest lingering of the night, indeed just as the dawn appear'd,
My comrade I wrapt in his blanket, envelop'd well his form,
Folded the blanket well, tucking it carefully over head and carefully under feet,
And there and then and bathed by the rising sun, my son in his grave, in his rude-dug grave I deposited,
Ending my vigil strange with that, vigil of night and battle-field dim,
Vigil for boy of responding kisses, (never again on earth responding,)
Vigil for comrade swiftly slain, vigil I never forget, how as day brighten'd,
I rose from the chill ground and folded my soldier well in his blanket,
And buried him where he fell.

1865, 1867

A MARCH IN THE RANKS HARD-PREST, AND THE ROAD UNKNOWN

A march in the ranks hard-prest, and the road unknown,
A route through a heavy wood with muffled steps in the darkness,
Our army foil'd with loss severe, and the sullen remnant retreating,
Till after midnight glimmer upon us the lights of a dim-lighted building,
We come to an open space in the woods, and halt by the dim-lighted building,
'Tis a large old church at the crossing roads, now an impromptu hospital,
Entering but for a minute I see a sight beyond all the pictures and poems ever made,
Shadows of deepest, deepest black, just lit by moving candles and lamps,
And by one great pitchy torch stationary with wild red flame and clouds of smoke,
By these, crowds, groups of forms vaguely I see on the floor, some in the pews laid down,
At my feet more distinctly a soldier, a mere lad, in danger of bleeding to death, (he is shot in the abdomen,)
I stanch the blood temporarily, (the youngster's face is white as a lily,)
Then before I depart I sweep my eyes o'er the scene fain[1] to absorb it all,
Faces, varieties, postures beyond description, most in obscurity, some of them dead,
Surgeons operating, attendants holding lights, the smell of ether, the odor of blood,
The crowd, O the crowd of the bloody forms, the yard outside also fill'd,
Some on the bare ground, some on planks or stretchers, some in the death-spasm sweating,
An occasional scream or cry, the doctor's shouted orders or calls,
The glisten of the little steel instruments catching the glint of the torches,
These I resume as I chant, I see again the forms, I smell the odor,
Then hear outside the orders given, *Fall in, my men, fall in;*
But first I bend to the dying lad, his eyes open, a half-smile gives he me,
Then the eyes close, calmly close, and I speed forth to the darkness,
Resuming, marching, ever in darkness marching, on in the ranks,
The unknown road still marching.

1865, 1867

[1]Eager, desirous.

A SIGHT IN CAMP IN THE DAYBREAK GRAY AND DIM

A sight in camp in the daybreak gray and dim,
As from my tent I emerge so early sleepless,
As slow I walk in the cool fresh air the path near by the hospital tent,
Three forms I see on stretchers lying, brought out there untended lying,
Over each the blanket spread, ample brownish woolen blanket,
Gray and heavy blanket, folding, covering all.

Curious I halt and silent stand,
Then with light fingers I from the face of the nearest the first just lift the blanket;
Who are you elderly man so gaunt and grim, with well-gray'd hair, and flesh all sunken about the eyes?
Who are you my dear comrade?

Then to the second I step—and who are you my child and darling?
Who are you sweet boy with cheeks yet blooming?

Then to the third—a face nor child nor old, very calm, as of beautiful yellow-white ivory;
Young man I think I know you—I think this face is the face of the Christ himself,
Dead and divine and brother of all, and here again he lies.

1865, 1867

THE WOUND-DRESSER

1

An old man bending I come among new faces,
Years looking backward resuming in answer to children,
Come tell us old man, as from young men and maidens that love me,
(Arous'd and angry, I'd thought to beat the alarum, and urge relentless war,
But soon my fingers fail'd me, my face droop'd and I resign'd myself,
To sit by the wounded and soothe them, or silently watch the dead;)
Years hence of these scenes, of these furious passions, these chances,
Of unsurpass'd heroes, (was one side so brave? the other was equally brave;)
Now be witness again, paint the mightiest armies of earth,
Of those armies so rapid so wondrous what saw you to tell us?
What stays with you latest and deepest? of curious panics,
Of hard-fought engagements or sieges tremendous what deepest remains?

2

O maidens and young men I love and that love me,
What you ask of my days those the strangest and sudden your
talking recalls,
Soldier alert I arrive after a long march cover'd with sweat and dust,
In the nick of time I come, plunge in the fight, loudly shout in the
rush of successful charge,
Enter the captur'd works[1]—yet lo, like a swift-running river they
fade,
Pass and are gone they fade—I dwell not on soldiers' perils or
soldiers' joys,
(Both I remember well—many the hardships, few the joys, yet I was
content.)

But in silence, in dreams' projections,
While the world of gain and appearance and mirth goes on,
So soon what is over forgotten, and waves wash the imprints off the
sand,
With hinged knees returning I enter the doors, (while for you up
there,
Whoever you are, follow without noise and be of strong heart.)

Bearing the bandages, water and sponge,
Straight and swift to my wounded I go,
Where they lie on the ground after the battle brought in,
Where their priceless blood reddens the grass the ground,
Or to the rows of the hospital tent, or under the roof'd hospital,
To the long rows of cots up and down each side I return,
To each and all one after another I draw near, not one do I miss,
An attendant follows holding a tray, he carries a refuse pail,
Soon to be fill'd with clotted rags and blood, emptied, and fill'd
again.

I onward go, I stop,
With hinged knees and steady hand to dress wounds,
I am firm with each, the pangs are sharp yet unavoidable,
One turns to me his appealing eyes—poor boy! I never knew you,
Yet I think I could not refuse this moment to die for you, if that
would save you.

3

On, on I go, (open doors of time! open hospital doors!)
The crush'd head I dress, (poor crazed hand tear not the bandage
away,)
The neck of the calvalry-man with the bullet through and through I
examine,

[1]Fortifications.

Hard the breathing rattles, quite glazed already the eye, yet life struggles
hard,
(Come sweet death! be persuaded O beautiful death!
In mercy come quickly.)

From the stump of the arm, the amputated hand,
I undo the clotted lint, remove the slough, wash off the matter and
blood,
Back on his pillow the soldier bends with curv'd neck and side-falling
head,
His eyes are closed, his face is pale, he dares not look on the bloody
stump,
And has not yet look'd on it.

I dress a wound in the side, deep, deep,
But a day or two more, for see the frame all wasted and sinking,
And the yellow-blue countenance see.

I dress the perforated shoulder, the foot with the bullet-wound,
Cleanse the one with a gnawing and putrid gangrene, so sickening,
so offensive,
While the attendant stands behind aside me holding the tray and pail.

I am faithful, I do not give out,
The fractur'd thigh, the knee, the wound in the abdomen,
These and more I dress with impassive hand, (yet deep in my breast
a fire, a burning flame.)

4

Thus in silence in dreams' projections,
Returning, resuming, I thread my way through the hospitals,
The hurt and wounded I pacify with soothing hand,
I sit by the restless all the dark night, some are so young,
Some suffer so much, I recall the experience sweet and sad,
(Many a soldier's loving arms about this neck have cross'd and rested,
Many a soldier's kiss dwells on these bearded lips.)

1865, 1881

from *MEMORIES OF PRESIDENT LINCOLN*

WHEN LILACS LAST IN THE DOORYARD BLOOM'D

1

When lilacs last in the dooryard bloom'd,
And the great star[1] early droop'd in the western sky in the night,
I mourn'd, and yet shall mourn with ever-returning spring.

[1]Venus.

Ever-returning spring, trinity sure to me you bring,
Lilac blooming perennial and drooping star in the west,
And thought of him I love.

2

O powerful western fallen star!
O shades of night—O moody, tearful night!
O great star disappear'd—O the black murk that hides the star!
O cruel hands that hold me powerless—O helpless soul of me!
O harsh surrounding cloud that will not free my soul.

3

In the dooryard fronting an old farm-house near the white-wash'd
palings,
Stands the lilac-bush tall-growing with heart-shaped leaves of rich
green,
With many a pointed blossom rising delicate, with the perfume
strong I love,
With every leaf a miracle—and from this bush in the dooryard,
With delicate-color'd blossoms and heart-shaped leaves of rich green,
A sprig with its flower I break.

4

In the swamp in secluded recesses,
A shy and hidden bird is warbling a song.

Solitary the thrush,
The hermit withdrawn to himself, avoiding the settlements,
Sings by himself a song.

Song of the bleeding throat,
Death's outlet song of life, (for well dear brother I know,
If thou wast not granted to sing thou would'st surely die.)

5

Over the breast of the spring, the land, amid cities,
Amid lanes and through old woods, where lately the violets peep'd
from the ground, spotting the gray debris,
Amid the grass in the fields each side of the lanes, passing the
endless grass,
Passing the yellow-spear'd wheat, every grain from its shroud in the
dark-brown fields uprisen,
Passing the apple-tree blows[2] of white and pink in the orchards,
Carrying a corpse to where it shall rest in the grave,
Night and day journeys a coffin.[3]

[2]Blossoms.

[3]Following Lincoln's assassination in April 1865, his body was carried on a funeral train from Washington, D.C., to Springfield, Illinois, for burial.

6

Coffin that passes through lanes and streets,
Through day and night with the great cloud darkening the land,
With the pomp of the inloop'd flags with the cities draped in black,
With the show of the States themselves as of crape-veil'd women standing,
With processions long and winding and the flambeaus[4] of the night,
With the countless torches lit, with the silent sea of faces and the unbared heads,
With the waiting depot, the arriving coffin, and the sombre faces,
With dirges through the night, with the thousand voices rising strong and solemn,
With all the mournful voices of the dirges pour'd around the coffin,
The dim-lit churches and the shuddering organs—where amid these you journey,
With the tolling tolling bells' perpetual clang,
Here, coffin that slowly passes,
I give you my sprig of lilac.

7

(Not for you, for one alone,
Blossoms and branches green to coffins all I bring,
For fresh as the morning, thus would I chant a song for you O sane and sacred death.

All over bouquets of roses,
O death, I cover you over with roses and early lilies,
But mostly and now the lilac that blooms the first,
Copious I break, I break the sprigs from the bushes,
With loaded arms I come, pouring for you,
For you and the coffins all of you O death.)

8

O western orb sailing the heaven,
Now I know what you must have meant as a month since I walk'd,
As I walk'd in silence the transparent shadowy night,
As I saw you had something to tell as you bent to me night after night,
As you droop'd from the sky low down as if to my side, (while the other stars all look'd on,)
As we wander'd together the solemn night, (for something I know not what kept me from sleep,)
As the night advanced, and I saw on the rim of the west how full you were of woe,
As I stood on the rising ground in the breeze in the cool transparent night,

[4]Burning torches.

As I watch'd where you pass'd and was lost in the netherward black
of the night,
As my soul in its trouble dissatisfied sank, as where you sad orb,
Concluded, dropt in the night, and was gone.

9

Sing on there in the swamp,
O singer bashful and tender, I hear your notes, I hear your call,
I hear, I come presently, I understand you,
But a moment I linger, for the lustrous star has detain'd me,
The star my departing comrade holds and detains me.

10

O how shall I warble myself for the dead one there I love?
And how shall I deck my song for the large sweet soul that has
gone?
And what shall my perfume be for the grave of him I love?

Sea-winds blown from east and west,
Blown from the Eastern sea and blown from the Western sea, till
there on the prairies meeting,
These and with these and the breath of my chant,
I'll perfume the grave of him I love.

11

O what shall I hang on the chamber walls?
And what shall the pictures be that I hang on the walls,
To adorn the burial-house of him I love?

Pictures of growing spring and farms and homes,
With the Fourth-month[5] eve at sundown, and the gray smoke lucid
and bright,
With floods of the yellow gold of the gorgeous, indolent, sinking sun,
burning, expanding the air,
With the fresh sweet herbage under foot, and the pale green leaves
of the trees prolific,
In the distance the flowing glaze, the breast of the river, with a wind-
dapple here and there,
With ranging hills on the banks, with many a line against the sky,
and shadows,
And the city at hand with dwellings so dense, and stacks of chimneys,
And all the scenes of life and the workshops, and the workmen
homeward returning.

[5]April.

12

Lo, body and soul—this land,
My own Manhattan with spires, and the sparkling and hurrying tides, and ships,
The varied and ample land, the South and the North in the light, Ohio's shores and flashing Missouri,
And ever the far-spreading prairies cover'd with grass and corn.

Lo, the most excellent sun so calm and haughty,
The violet and purple morn with just-felt breezes,
The gentle soft-born measureless light,
The miracle spreading bathing all, the fulfill'd noon,
The coming eve delicious, the welcome night and the stars,
Over my cities shining all, enveloping man and land.

13

Sing on, sing on you gray-brown bird,
Sing from the swamps, the recesses, pour your chant from the bushes,
Limitless out of the dusk, out of the cedars and pines.

Sing on dearest brother, warble your reedy song,
Loud human song, with voice of uttermost woe.

O liquid and free and tender!
O wild and loose to my soul—O wondrous singer!
You only I hear—yet the star holds me, (but will soon depart,)
Yet the lilac with mastering odor holds me.

14

Now while I sat in the day and look'd forth,
In the close of the day with its light and the fields of spring, and the farmers preparing their crops,
In the large unconscious scenery of my land with its lakes and forests,
In the heavenly aerial beauty, (after the perturb'd winds and the storms,)
Under the arching heavens of the afternoon swift passing, and the voices of children and women,
The many-moving sea-tides, and I saw the ships how they sail'd,
And the summer approaching with richness, and the fields all busy with labor,
And the infinite separate houses, how they all went on, each with its meals and minutia of daily usages,
And the streets how their throbbings throbb'd, and the cities pent—lo, then and there,
Falling upon them all and among them all, enveloping me with the rest,

Appear'd the cloud, appear'd the long black trail,
And I knew death, its thought, and the sacred knowledge of death.

Then with the knowledge of death as walking one side of me,
And the thought of death close-walking the other side of me,
And I in the middle as with companions, and as holding the hands of
 companions,
I fled forth to the hiding receiving night that talks not,
Down to the shores of the water, the path by the swamp in the dimness,
To the solemn shadowy cedars and ghostly pines so still.

And the singer so shy to the rest receiv'd me,
The gray-brown bird I know receiv'd us comrades three,
And he sang the carol of death, and a verse for him I love.

From deep secluded recesses,
From the fragrant cedars and the ghostly pines so still,
Came the carol of the bird.

And the charm of the carol rapt me,
As I held as if by their hands my comrades in the night,
And the voice of my spirit tallied the song of the bird.

Come lovely and soothing death,
Undulate round the world, serenely arriving, arriving,
In the day, in the night, to all, to each,
Sooner or later delicate death.

Prais'd be the fathomless universe,
For life and joy, and for objects and knowledge curious,
And for love, sweet love—but praise! praise! praise!
For the sure-enwinding arms of cool-enfolding death.

Dark mother always gliding near with soft feet,
Have none chanted for thee a chant of fullest welcome?
Then I chant it for thee, I glorify thee above all,
I bring thee a song that when thou must indeed come, come unfalteringly.

Approach strong deliveress,
When it is so, when thou hast taken them I joyously sing the dead,
Lost in the loving floating ocean of thee,
Laved in the flood of thy bliss O death.

From me to thee glad serenades,
Dances for thee I propose saluting thee, adornments and feastings for thee,
And the sights of the open landscape and the high-spread sky are fitting,
And life and the fields, and the huge and thoughtful night.

The night in silence under many a star,
The ocean shore and the husky whispering wave whose voice I know,
And the soul turning to thee O vast and well-veil'd death,
And the body gratefully nestling close to thee.

Over the tree-tops I float thee a song,
Over the rising and sinking waves, over the myriad fields and the prairies wide,
Over the dense-pack'd cities all and the teeming wharves and ways,
I float this carol with joy, with joy to thee O death.

15

To the tally of my soul,
Loud and strong kept up the gray-brown bird,
With pure deliberate notes spreading filling the night.

Loud in the pines and cedars dim,
Clear in the freshness moist and the swamp-perfume,
And I with my comrades there in the night.

While my sight that was bound in my eyes unclosed,
As to long panoramas of visions.

And I saw askant[6] the armies,
I saw as in noiseless dreams hundreds of battle-flags,
Borne through the smoke of the battles and pierc'd with missiles I saw them,
And carried hither and yon through the smoke, and torn and bloody,
And at last but a few shreds left on the staffs, (and all in silence,)
And the staffs all splinter'd and broken.

I saw battle-corpses, myriads of them,
And the white skeletons of young men, I saw them,
I saw the debris and debris of all the slain soldiers of the war,
But I saw they were not as was thought,
They themselves were fully at rest, they suffer'd not,
The living remain'd and suffer'd, the mother suffer'd,
And the wife and the child and the musing comrade suffer'd,
And the armies that remain'd suffer'd.

16

Passing the visions, passing the night,
Passing, unloosing the hold of my comrades' hands,
Passing the song of the hermit bird and the tallying song of my soul,
Victorious song, death's outlet song, yet varying ever-altering song,
As low and wailing, yet clear the notes, rising and falling, flooding the night,

[6]Sideways, out of the corner of the eye, with mistrust.

Sadly sinking and fainting, as warning and warning, and yet again
bursting with joy,
Covering the earth and filling the spread of the heaven,
As that powerful psalm in the night I heard from recesses,
Passing, I leave thee lilac with heart-shaped leaves,
I leave thee there in the dooryard, blooming, returning with spring.

I cease from my song for thee,
From my gaze on thee in the west, fronting the west,
communing with thee,
O comrade lustrous with silver face in the night.

Yet each to keep and all, retrievements out of the night,
The song, the wondrous chant of the gray-brown bird,
And the tallying chant, the echo arous'd in my soul,
With the lustrous and drooping star with the countenance full of
woe,
With the holders holding my hand nearing the call of the bird,
Comrades mine and I in the midst, and their memory ever to keep,
for the dead I loved so well,
For the sweetest, wisest soul of all my days and lands—and this for
his dear sake,
Lilac and star and bird twined with the chant of my soul,
There in the fragrant pines and the cedars dusk and dim.

1865–1866, 1881

from *AUTUMN RIVULETS*

THERE WAS A CHILD WENT FORTH

There was a child went forth every day,
And the first object he look'd upon, that object he became,
And that object became part of him for the day or a certain part of
the day,
Or for many years or stretching cycles of years.

The early lilacs became part of this child,
And grass and white and red morning-glories, and white and red
clover, and the song of the phœbe-bird,
And the Third-month lambs and the sow's pink-faint litter,
and the mare's foal and the cow's calf,
And the noisy brood of the barnyard or by the mire of the pond-side,
And the fish suspending themselves so curiously below there, and
the beautiful curious liquid,
And the water-plants with their graceful flat heads, all became part
of him.

The field-sprouts of Fourth-month and Fifth-month became part of him,
Winter-grain sprouts and those of the light-yellow corn, and the esculent roots of the garden,
And the apple-trees cover'd with blossoms and the fruit afterward, and wood-berries, and the commonest weeds by the road,
And the old drunkard staggering home from the outhouse of the tavern whence he had lately risen,
And the schoolmistress that pass'd on her way to the school,
And the friendly boys that pass'd, and the quarrelsome boys,
And the tidy and fresh-cheek'd girls, and the barefoot negro boy and girl,
And all the changes of city and country wherever he went.
His own parents, he that had father'd him and she that had conceiv'd him in her womb and birth'd him,
They gave this child more of themselves than that,
They gave him afterward every day, they became part of him.

The mother at home quietly placing the dishes on the supper-table,
The mother with mild words, clean her cap and gown, a wholesome odor falling off her person and clothes as she walks by,
The father, strong, self-sufficient, manly, mean, anger'd, unjust,
The blow, the quick loud word, the tight bargain, the crafty lure,
The family usages, the language, the company, the furniture, the yearning and swelling heart,
Affection that will not be gainsay'd, the sense of what is real, the thought if after all it should prove unreal,
The doubts of day-time and the doubts of night-time, the curious whether and how,
Whether that which appears so is so, or is it all flashes and specks?
Men and women crowding fast in the streets, if they are not flashes and specks what are they?
The streets themselves and the façades of houses, and goods in the windows,
Vehicles, teams, the heavy-plank'd wharves, the huge crossing at the ferries,
The village on the highland seen from afar at sunset, the river between,
Shadows, aureola and mist, the light falling on roofs and gables of white or brown two miles off,
The schooner near by sleepily drooping down the tide, the little boat slack-tow'd astern,
The hurrying tumbling waves, quick-broken crests, slapping,
The strata of color'd clouds, the long bar of maroon-tint away solitary by itself, the spread of purity it lies motionless in,
The horizon's edge, the flying sea-crow, the fragrance of salt marsh and shore mud,
These became part of that child who went forth every day, and who now goes, and will always go forth every day.

1855, 1871

PASSAGE TO INDIA

1

Singing my days,
Singing the great achievements of the present,
Singing the strong light works of engineers,
Our modern wonders, (the antique ponderous Seven[1] outvied),
In the Old World the east the Suez canal[2]
The New by its mighty railroad spann'd,[3]
The seas inlaid with eloquent gentle wires,[4]
Yet first to sound, and ever sound, the cry with thee O soul,
The Past! the Past! the Past!

The Past—the dark unfathom'd retrospect!
The teeming gulf—the sleepers and the shadows!
The past—the infinite greatness of the past!
For what is the present after all but a growth out of the past?
(As a projectile form'd, impell'd, passing a certain line, still
keeps on,
So the present, utterly form'd, impell'd by the past.)

2

Passage O soul to India!
Eclaircise[5] the myths Asiatic, the primitive fables.

Not you alone proud truths of the world,
Not you alone ye facts of modern science,
But myths and fables of eld,[6] Asia's, Africa's fables,
The far-darting beams of the spirit, the unloos'd dreams,
The deep diving bibles and legends,
The daring plots of the poets, the elder religions;
O you temples fairer than lilies pour'd over by the rising sun!
O you fables spurning the known, eluding the hold of the known,
mounting to heaven!
You lofty and dazzling towers, pinnacled, red as roses, burnish'd
with gold!
Towers of fables immortal fashion'd from mortal dreams!
You too I welcome and fully the same as the rest!
You too with joy I sing.

[1]The Seven Wonders of the Ancient World.
[2]Completed in 1867, formally opened in 1869.
[3]The transcontinental railroad was completed at Promontory, Utah, in 1869.
[4]A transatlantic cable was laid in 1866.
[5]Clarify, explain.
[6]Antiquity.

Passage to India!
Lo, soul, seest thou not God's purpose from the first?
The earth to be spann'd, connected by network,
The races, neighbors, to marry and be given in marriage,
The oceans to be cross'd, the distant brought near,
The lands to be welded together.

A worship new I sing,
You captain, voyagers, explorers, yours,
You engineers, you architects, machinists, yours,
You, not for trade or transportation only,
But in God's name, and for thy sake O soul.

3

Passage to India!
Lo soul for thee of tableaus twain,
I see in one the Suez canal initiated, open'd,
I see the procession of steamships, the Empress Eugenie's[7] leading the van,
I mark from on deck the strange landscape, the pure sky, the level sand in the distance,
I pass swiftly the picturesque groups, the workmen gather'd,
The gigantic dredging machines.

In one again, different, (yet thine, all thine, O soul, the same,)
I see over my own continent the Pacific railroad[8] surmounting every barrier,
I see continual trains of cars winding along the Platte carrying freight and passengers,
I hear the locomotives rushing and roaring, and the shrill steamwhistle,
I hear the echoes reverberate through the grandest scenery in the world,
I cross the Laramie plains, I note the rocks in grotesque shapes, the buttes,
I see the plentiful larkspur and wild onions, the barren, colorless, sage-deserts,
I see in glimpses afar or towering immediately above me the great mountains, I see the Wind river and the Wahsatch mountains,
I see the Monument mountain the Eagle's Nest, I pass the Promontory, I ascend the Nevadas,
I scan the noble Elk mountain and wind around its base,
I see the Humboldt range, I thread the valley and cross the river,
I see the clear waters of Lake Tahoe, I see forests of majestic pines,
Or crossing the great desert, the alkaline plains, I behold enchanting mirages of waters and meadows,

[7]Empress of France, wife of Napoleon III. She was aboard the ship leading the procession at the formal opening of the Suez Canal.

[8]The transcontinental railroad linked the Atlantic and the Pacific oceans in 1869. In the remainder of the stanza, Whitman lists sites, from Nebraska to California, along the route of the railroad.

Marking through these and after all, in duplicate slender lines,
Bridging the three or four thousand miles of land travel,
Tying the Eastern to the Western sea,
The road between Europe and Asia.

(Ah Genoese[9] thy dream! thy dream!
Centuries after thou art laid in thy grave,
The shore thou foundest verifies thy dream.)

4

Passage to India!
Struggles of many a captain, tales of many a sailor dead,
Over my mood stealing and spreading they come,
Like clouds and cloudlets in the unreach'd sky.

Along all history, down the slopes,
As a rivulet running, sinking now, and now again to the surface
rising,
A ceaseless thought, a varied train—lo, soul, to thee, thy sight, they
rise,
The plans, the voyages again, the expeditions;
Again Vasco de Gama[10] sails forth,
Again the knowledge gain'd, the mariner's compass,
Lands found and nations born, thou born America,
For purpose vast, man's long probation fill'd,
Thou rondure[11] of the world at last accomplish'd,

5

O vast Rondure, swimming in space,
Cover'd all over with visible power and beauty,
Alternate light and day and the teeming spiritual darkness,
Unspeakable high processions of sun and moon and countless stars
above,
Below the manifold grass and waters, animals, mountains, trees,
With inscrutable purpose, some hidden prophetic intention,
Now first it seems my thought begins to span thee.

Down from the gardens of Asia descending radiating,
Adam and Eve appear, then their myriad progeny after them,
Wandering, yearning, curious, with restless explorations,
With questionings, baffled, formless, feverish, with never-happy
hearts,
With that sad incessant refrain, *Wherefore unsatisfied soul?* and
Whither O mocking life?

[9]Christopher Columbus, born in Genoa, Italy.
[10]Vasco da Gama. Portuguese navigator, the first European to sail from Europe, around Africa's Cape of Good Hope, to India (1497–1498).
[11]Encirclement, circumnavigation.

Ah who shall soothe these feverish children?
Who justify these restless explorations?
Who speak the secret of impassive earth?
Who bind it to us? what is this separate Nature so unnatural?
What is this earth to our affections? (unloving earth, without a throb to answer ours,
Cold earth, the place of graves.)

Yet soul be sure the first intent remains, and shall be carried out,
Perhaps even now the time has arrived.

After the seas are all cross'd, (as they seem already cross'd,)
After the great captains and engineers have accomplish'd their work,
After the noble inventors, after the scientists, the chemist, the geologist, ethnologist,
Finally shall come the poet worthy that name,
The true son of God shall come singing his songs.

Then not your deeds only O voyagers, O scientists and inventors, shall be justified,
All these hearts as of fretted children shall be sooth'd,
All affection shall be fully responded to, the secret shall be told,
All these separations and gaps shall be taken up and hook'd and link'd together,
The whole earth, this cold, impassive, voiceless earth, shall be completely justified,
Trinitas[12] divine shall be gloriously accomplish'd and compacted by the true son of God, the poet,
(He shall indeed pass the straits and conquer the mountains,
He shall double the cape of Good Hope to some purpose,)
Nature and Man shall be disjoin'd and diffused no more,
The true son of God shall absolutely fuse them.

6

Year at whose wide-flung door I sing!
Year of the purpose accomplish'd!
Year of the marriage of continents, climates and oceans!
(No mere doge of Venice now wedding the Adriatic,)[13]
I see O year in you the vast terraqueous globe given and giving all,
Europe to Asia, Africa join'd, and they to the New World,
The lands, geographies, dancing before you, holding a festival garland,
As brides and bridegrooms hand in hand.

Passage to India!
Cooling airs from Caucasus[14] far, soothing cradle of man,
The river Euphrates[15] flowing, the past lit up again.

[12]Whitman's approximate Spanish for "the Holy Trinity."
[13]The Doge (chief magistrate of the city-state of Venice, 697–1797) symbolized the union of Venice and the sea by annually casting a gold ring into the Adriatic.
[14]Mountainous area in Russia between the Black and Caspian seas.
[15]River flowing from Turkey to the Persian Gulf.

Lo soul, the retrospect brought forward,
The old, most populous, wealthiest of earth's lands,
The streams of the Indus and the Ganges[16] and their many affluents,
(I my shores of America walking to-day behold, resuming all,)
The tale of Alexander[17] on his warlike marches suddenly dying,
On one side China and on the other side Persia and Arabia,
To the south the great seas and the bay of Bengal,
The flowing literatures, tremendous epics, religions, castes,
Old occult Brahma interminably far back, the tender and junior
Buddha,
Central and southern empires and all their belongings, possessors,
The wars of Tamerlane,[18] the reign of Aurungzebe,[19]
The traders, rulers, explorers, Moslems, Venetians, Byzantium, the Arabs,
Portuguese,

The first travelers famous yet, Marco Polo,[20] Batouta the Moor,[21]
Doubts to be solv'd, the map incognita,[22] blanks to be fill'd,
The foot of man unstay'd, the hands never at rest,
Thyself O soul that will not brook a challenge.

The mediæval navigators rise before me,
The world of 1492, with its awaken'd enterprise,
Something swelling in humanity now like the sap of the earth in spring,
The sunset splendor of chivalry declining.

And who art thou sad shade?
Gigantic, visionary, thyself a visionary,
With majestic limbs and pious beaming eyes,
Spreading around with every look of thine a golden world,
Enhuing it with gorgeous hues.

As the chief histrion,[23]
Down to the footlights walks in some great scena,[24]
Dominating the rest I see the Admiral[25] himself,
(History's type[26] of courage, action, faith,)
Behold him sail from Palos[27] leading his little fleet,
His voyage behold, his return, his great fame,
His misfortunes, calumniators, behold him a prisoner, chain'd,
Behold his dejection, poverty, death.

(Curious in time I stand, noting the efforts of heroes,
Is the deferment long? bitter the slander, poverty, death?
Lies the seed unreck'd[28] for centuries in the ground? lo, to God's
due occasion,
Uprising in the night, it sprouts, blooms,
And fills the earth with use and beauty.)

[16]Rivers in India. [17]Alexander the Great (356–323 B.C.).
[18]Mongol conqueror (1336?–1405). [19]Emperor of Hindustan (1618–1707).
[20]Venetian (1254–1324), early traveler to China. [21]Explorer of Africa and Asia (1303–1377).
[22]Unknown. [23]Actor. [24]Scene. [25]Columbus. [26]Symbol, model.
[27]Spanish seaport from which Columbus sailed, August 1492. [28]Unnoticed.

7

Passage indeed O soul to primal thought,
Not lands and seas alone, thy own clear freshness,
The young maturity of brood and bloom,
To realms of budding bibles.

O soul, repressless, I with thee and thou with me,
Thy circumnavigation of the world begin,
Of man, the voyage of his mind's return,
To reason's early paradise,
Back, back to wisdom's birth, to innocent intuitions,
Again with fair creation.

8

O we can wait no longer,
We too take ship O soul,
Joyous we too launch out on trackless seas,
Fearless for unknown shores on waves of ecstasy to sail,
Amid the wafting winds, (thou pressing me to thee, I thee to me, O soul,)
Caroling free, singing our song of God,
Chanting our chant of pleasant exploration.

With laugh and many a kiss,
(Let others deprecate, let others weep for sin, remorse, humiliation,)
O soul thou pleasest me, I thee.

Ah more than any priest O soul we too believe in God,
But with the mystery of God we dare not dally.

O soul thou pleasest me, I thee,
Sailing these seas or on the hills, or waking in the night,
Thoughts, silent thoughts, of Time and Space and Death, like waters flowing,
Bear me indeed as through the regions infinite,
Whose air I breathe, whose ripples hear, lave me all over,
Bathe me O God in thee, mounting to thee,
I and my soul to range of thee.

O Thou transcendent,
Nameless, the fibre and the breath,
Light of the light, shedding forth universes, thou centre of them,
Thou mightier centre of the true, the good, the loving,
Thou moral, spiritual fountain—affection's source—thou reservoir,
(O pensive soul of me—O thirst unsatisfied—waitest not there?
Waitest not haply for us somewhere there the Comrade perfect?)
Thou pulse—thou motive of the stars, suns, systems,
That, circling, move in order, safe, harmonious,
Athwart the shapeless vastnesses of space,

How should I think, how breathe a single breath, how speak, if, out of myself,
I could not launch, to those, superior universes?

Swiftly I shrivel at the thought of God,
At Nature and its wonders, Time and Space and Death,
But that, I, turning, call to thee O soul, thou actual Me,
And lo, thou gently masterest the orbs,
Thou matest Time, smilest content at Death,
And fillest, swellest full the vastnesses of Space.

Greater than stars or suns,
Bounding O soul thou journeyest forth;
What love than thine and ours could wider amplify?
What aspirations, wishes, outvie thine and ours O soul?
What dreams of the ideal? what plans of purity, perfection, strength?
What cheerful willingness for others' sake to give up all?
For others' sake to suffer all?

Reckoning ahead O soul, when thou, the time achiev'd,
The seas all cross'd, weather'd the capes, the voyage done,
Surrounded, copest, frontest God, yieldest, the aim attain'd,
As fill'd with friendship, love complete, the Elder Brother found,
The Younger melts in fondness in his arms.

9

Passage to more than India!
Are thy wings plumed indeed for such far flights?
O soul, voyagest thou indeed on voyages like those?
Disportest thou on waters such as those?
Soundest below the Sanscrit and the Vedas?[29]
Then have thy bent[30] unleash'd.

Passage to you, your shores, ye aged fierce enigmas!
Passage to you, to mastership of you, ye strangling problems!
You, strew'd with the wrecks of skeletons, that, living, never reach'd you.

Passage to more than India!
O secret of the earth and sky!
Of you O waters of the sea! O winding creeks and rivers!
Of you O woods and fields! of you strong mountains of my land!
Of you O prairies! of you gray rocks!
O morning red! O clouds! O rain and snows!
O day and night, passage to you!

O sun and moon and all you stars! Sirius and Jupiter![31]
Passage to you!

[29]Hindu scriptures, written in Sanskrit.
[30]Force, energy.
[31]Sirius: the brightest star in the sky. Jupiter: the largest planet.

Passage, immediate passage! the blood burns in my veins!
Away O soul! hoist instantly the anchor!
Cut the hawser—haul out—shake out every sail!
Have we not stood here like trees in the ground long enough?
Have we not grovel'd here long enough, eating and drinking like
mere brutes?
Have we not darken'd and dazed ourselves with books long enough?

Sail forth—steer for the deep waters only,
Reckless O soul, exploring, I with thee, and thou with me,
For we are bound where mariner has not yet dared to go,
And we will risk the ship, ourselves and all.

O my brave soul!
O farther farther sail!
O daring joy, but safe! are they not all the seas of God?
O farther, farther, farther sail!

1871, 1881

THE SLEEPERS

1

I wander all night in my vision,
Stepping with light feet, swiftly and noiselessly stepping and
stopping,
Bending with open eyes over the shut eyes of sleepers,
Wandering and confused, lost to myself, ill-assorted, contradictory,
Pausing, gazing, bending, and stopping,

How solemn they look there, stretch'd and still,
How quiet they breathe, the little children in their cradles.

The wretched features of ennuyés,[1] the white features of corpses, the
livid faces of drunkards, the sick-gray faces of onanists,
The gash'd bodies on battle-fields, the insane in their strong-door'd
rooms, the sacred idiots, the new-born emerging from gates, and
the dying emerging from gates,
The night pervades them and infolds them.

The married couple sleep calmly in their bed, he with his palm on
the hip of the wife, and she with her palm on the hip of the
husband,
The sisters sleep lovingly side by side in their bed,
The men sleep lovingly side by side in theirs,
And the mother sleeps with her little child carefully wrapt.

[1]French: bored, vexed people.

The blind sleep, and the deaf and dumb sleep,
The prisoner sleeps well in the prison, the runaway son sleeps,
The murderer that is to be hung next day, how does he sleep?
And the murder'd person, how does he sleep?

The female that loves unrequited sleeps,
And the male that loves unrequited sleeps,
The head of the money-maker that plotted all day sleeps,
And the enraged and treacherous dispositions, all, all sleep.

I stand in the dark with drooping eyes by the worst-suffering and the most restless,
I pass my hands soothingly to and fro a few inches from them,
The restless sink in their beds, they fitfully sleep.

Now I pierce the darkness, new beings appear,
The earth recedes from me into the night,
I saw that it was beautiful, and I see that what is not the earth is beautiful.

I go from bedside to bedside, I sleep close with the other sleepers each in turn,
I dream in my dream all the dreams of the other dreamers,
And I become the other dreamers.

I am a dance—play up there! the fit is whirling me fast!

I am the ever-laughing—it is new moon and twilight,
I see the hiding of douceurs,[2] I see nimble ghosts whichever way I look,
Cache[3] and cache again deep in the ground and sea, and where it is neither ground nor sea.

Well do they do their jobs those journeymen divine,
Only from me can they hide nothing, and would not if they could,
I reckon I am their boss and they make me a pet besides,
And surround me and lead me and run ahead when I walk,
To lift their cunning covers to signify[4] me with stretch'd arms, and resume the way;
Onward we move, a gay gang of blackguards! with mirth-shouting music and wild-flapping pennants of joy!

I am the actor, the actress, the voter, the politician,
The emigrant and the exile, the criminal that stood in the box,[5]
He who has been famous and he who shall be famous after to-day,
The stammerer, the well-form'd person, the waster or feeble person.

[2]Delights, pleasures.
[3]Hide. [4]Signal.
[5]Courtroom dock, where the accused stands during a criminal trial.

I am she who adorn'd herself and folded her hair expectantly,
My truant lover has come, and it is dark.

Double yourself and receive me darkness,
Receive me and my lover too, he will not let me go without him.

I roll myself upon you as upon a bed, I resign myself to the dusk.

He whom I call answers me and takes the place of my lover,
He rises with me silently from the bed.

Darkness, you are gentler than my lover, his flesh was sweaty and panting,
I feel the hot moisture yet that he left me.

My hands are spread forth, I pass them in all directions,
I would sound up the shadowy shore to which you are journeying.

Be careful darkness! already what was it touch'd me?
I thought my lover had gone, else darkness and he are one,
I hear the heart-beat, I follow, I fade away.

2

I descend my western course,[6] my sinews are flaccid,
Perfume and youth course through me and I am their wake.

It is my face yellow and wrinkled instead of the old woman's,
I sit low in a straw-bottom chair and carefully darn my grandson's stockings.

It is I too, the sleepless widow looking out on the winter midnight,
I see the sparkles of starshine on the icy and pallid earth.

A shroud I see and I am the shroud, I wrap a body and lie in the coffin,
It is dark here under ground, it is not evil or pain here, it is blank here, for reasons.

(It seems to me that every thing in the light and air ought to be happy,
Whoever is not in his coffin and the dark grave let him know he has enough.)

3

I see a beautiful gigantic swimmer swimming naked through the eddies of the sea,
His brown hair lies close and even to his head, he strikes out with courageous arms, he urges himself with his legs,

[6] I.e., grow old.

I see his white body, I see his undaunted eyes,
I hate the swift-running eddies that would dash him head-foremost on the rocks.

What are you doing you ruffianly red-trickled waves?
Will you kill the courageous giant? will you kill him in the prime of his middle age?

Steady and long he struggles,
He is baffled, bang'd, bruis'd, he holds out while his strength holds out,
The slapping eddies are spotted with his blood, they bear him away, they roll him, swing him, turn him,
His beautiful body is borne in the circling eddies, it is continually bruis'd on rocks,
Swiftly and out of sight is borne the brave corpse.

4

I turn but do not extricate myself,
Confused, a past-reading, another, but with darkness yet.

The beach is cut by the razory ice-wind, the wreck-guns[7] sound,
The tempest lulls, the moon comes floundering through the drifts.

I look where the ship helplessly heads end on, I hear the burst as she strikes, I hear the howls of dismay, they grow fainter and fainter.

I cannot aid with my wringing fingers,
I can but rush to the surf and let it drench me and freeze upon me.

I search with the crowd, not one of the company is wash'd to us alive,
In the morning I help pick up the dead and lay them in rows in a barn.

5

Now of the older war-days, the defeat at Brooklyn,[8]
Washington stands inside the lines, he stands on the intrench'd hills amid a crowd of officers,
His face is cold and damp, he cannot repress the weeping drops,
He lifts the glass perpetually to his eyes, the color is blanch'd from his cheeks,
He sees the slaughter of the southern braves[9] confided to him by their parents.

[7]Guns that fire a lifeline to wrecked ships.
[8]British victory over American forces at the Battle of Brooklyn Heights, August 1776.
[9]Revolutionary soldiers from the southern colonies.

The same at last and at last when peace is declared,
He stands in the room of the old tavern,[10] the well-belov'd soldiers all pass through,
The officers speechless and slow draw near in their turns,
The chief encircles their necks with his arm and kisses them on the cheek,
He kisses lightly the wet cheeks one after another, he shakes hands and bids good-by to the army.

6

Now what my mother told me one day as we sat at dinner together,
Of when she was a nearly grown girl living home with her parents on the old homestead.

A red squaw came one breakfast-time to the old homestead,
On her back she carried a bundle of rushes for rush-bottoming chairs,
Her hair, straight, shiny, coarse, black, profuse, half-envelop'd her face,
Her step was free and elastic, and her voice sounded exquisitely as she spoke.

My mother look'd in delight and amazement at the stranger,
She look'd at the freshness of her tall-borne face and full and pliant limbs,
The more she look'd upon her she loved her,
Never before had she seen such wonderful beauty and purity,
She made her sit on a bench by the jamb of the fireplace, she cook'd food for her,
She had no work to give her, but she gave her remembrance and fondness.

The red squaw staid all the forenoon, and toward the middle of the afternoon she went away,
O my mother was loth[11] to have her go away,
All the week she thought of her, she watch'd for her many a month,
She remember'd her many a winter and many a summer,
But the red squaw never came nor was heard of there again.

7

A show of the summer softness—a contact of something unseen—an amour of the light and air,
I am jealous and overwhelm'd with friendliness,
And will go gallivant with the light and air myself.

O love and summer, you are in the dreams and in me,
Autumn and winter are in the dreams, the farmer goes with his thrift,
The droves[12] and crops increase, the barns are well-fill'd.

[10]Fraunces Tavern, New York City, where Washington bid farewell to his troops, in 1783.
[11]Reluctant. [12]Herds of animals.

Elements merge in the night, ships make tacks in the dreams,
The sailor sails, the exile returns home,
The fugitive returns unharm'd, the immigrant is back beyond
  months and years,
The poor Irishman lives in the simple house of his childhood with
  the well-known neighbors and faces,
They warmly welcome him, he is barefoot again, he forgets he is well
  off,
The Dutchman voyages home, and the Scotchman and Welshman
  voyage home, and the native of the Mediterranean voyages home,
To every port of England, France, Spain, enter well-fill'd ships,
The Swiss foots it towards his hills, the Prussian goes his way, the
  Hungarian his way, and the Pole his way,
The Swede returns, and the Dane and Norwegian return.

The homeward bound and the outward bound,
The beautiful lost swimmer, the ennuyé, the onanist, the female that
  loves unrequited, the money-maker,
The actor and actress, those through with their parts and those
  waiting to commence,
The affectionate boy, the husband and wife, the voter, the nominee
  that is chosen and the nominee that has fail'd,
The great already known and the great any time after to-day,
The stammerer, the sick, the perfect-form'd, the homely,
The criminal that stood in the box, the judge that sat and sentenced
  him, the fluent lawyers, the jury, the audience,
The laugher and weeper, the dancer, the midnight widow, the red
  squaw,
The consumptive, the erysipalite,[13] the idiot, he that is wrong'd,
The antipodes,[14] and every one between this and them in the dark,
I swear they are averaged now—one is no better than the other,
The night and sleep have liken'd them and restored them.

I swear they are all beautiful,
Every one that sleeps is beautiful, every thing in the dim light is
  beautiful,
The wildest and bloodiest is over, and all is peace.

Peace is always beautiful,
The myth of heaven indicates peace and night.

The myth of heaven indicates the soul,
The soul is always beautiful, it appears more or it appears less, it
  comes or it lags behind,
It comes from its embower'd garden and looks pleasantly on itself
  and encloses the world,
Perfect and clean the genitals previously jetting, and perfect and
  clean the womb cohering,

[13]One suffering from erysipelas, infected and inflamed skin.
[14]Those living on the opposite side of the earth.

The head well-grown proportion'd and plumb, and the bowels and
joints proportion'd and plumb.

The soul is always beautiful,
The universe is duly in order, every thing is in its place,
What has arrived is in its place and what waits shall be in its place,
The twisted skull waits, the watery or rotten blood waits,
The child of the glutton or venerealee waits long, and the child of
the drunkard waits long, and the drunkard himself waits long,
The sleepers that lived and died wait, the far advanced are to go on
in their turns, and the far behind are to come on in their turns,
The diverse shall be no less diverse, but they shall flow and unite—
they unite now.

8

The sleepers are very beautiful as they lie unclothed,
They flow hand in hand over the whole earth from east to west as
they lie unclothed,
The Asiatic and African are hand in hand, the European and
American are hand in hand,
Learn'd and unlearn'd are hand in hand, and male and female are
hand in hand,
The bare arm of the girl crosses the bare breast of her lover, they
press close without lust, his lips press her neck,
The father holds his grown or ungrown son in his arms with
measureless love, and the son holds the father in his arms with
measureless love,
The white hair of the mother shines on the white wrist of the
daughter,
The breath of the boy goes with the breath of the man, friend is
inarm'd by friend,
The scholar kisses the teacher and the teacher kisses the scholar, the
wrong'd is made right,
The call of the slave is one with the master's call, and the master
salutes the slave,
The felon steps forth from the prison, the insane become sane, the
suffering of sick persons is reliev'd,
The sweatings and fevers stop, the throat that was unsound is sound,
the lungs of the consumptive are resumed, the poor distress'd
head is free,
The joints of the rheumatic move as smoothly as ever, and smoother
than ever,
Stiflings and passages open, the paralyzed become supple,
The swell'd and convuls'd and congested awake to themselves in
condition,
They pass the invigoration of the night and the chemistry of the
night, and awake.

I too pass from the night,
I stay a while away O night, but I return to you again and love you.

Why should I be afraid to trust myself to you?
I am not afraid, I have been well brought forward by you,
I love the rich running day, but I do not desert her in whom I
lay so long,
I know not how I came of you and I know not where I go with you,
but I know I came well and shall go well.

I will stop only a time with the night, and rise betimes,
I will duly pass the day O my mother, and duly return to you.

1855, 1881

from *WHISPERS OF HEAVENLY DEATH*

A NOISELESS PATIENT SPIDER

A noiseless patient spider,
I mark'd where on a little promontory it stood isolated,
Mark'd how to explore the vacant vast surrounding,
It launch'd forth filament, filament, filament, out of itself,
Ever unreeling them, ever tirelessly speeding them.

And you O my soul where you stand,
Surrounded, detached, in measureless oceans of space,
Ceaselessly musing, venturing, throwing, seeking the spheres to
connect them,
Till the bridge you will need be form'd, till the ductile anchor hold,
Till the gossamer thread you fling catch somewhere, O my soul.

1868, 1881

from *FROM NOON TO STARRY NIGHT*

TO A LOCOMOTIVE IN WINTER

Thee for my recitative,[1]
Thee in the driving storm even as now, the snow, the winter-day
declining,
Thee in thy panoply,[2] thy measur'd dual throbbing and thy beat
convulsive,
Thy black cylindric body, golden brass and silvery steel,
Thy ponderous side-bars, parallel and connecting rods, gyrating,
shuttling at thy sides,
Thy metrical, now swelling pant and roar, now tapering in the
distance,
Thy great protruding head-light fix'd in front,
Thy long, pale, floating vapor-pennants, tinged with delicate purple,

[1]A rhythmically free, vocal narration, a recitation. [2]Suit of armor.

Thy dense and murky clouds out-belching from thy smoke-stack,
Thy knitted frame, thy springs and valves, the tremulous twinkle of
thy wheels,
Thy train of cars behind, obedient, merrily following,
Through gale or calm, now swift, now slack, yet steadily careering;[3]
Type of the modern—emblem of motion and power—pulse of the
continent,
For once come serve the Muse and merge in verse, even as here I
see thee,
With storm and buffeting gusts of winds and falling snow,
By day the warning ringing bell to sound its notes,

By night thy silent signal lamps to swing.
Fierce-throated beauty!
Roll through my chant with all thy lawless music, thy swinging lamps
at night,
Thy madly-whistled laughter, echoing, rumbling like an earthquake,
rousing all,
Law of thyself complete, thine own track firmly holding,
(No sweetness debonair of tearful harp or glib piano thine,)
Thy trills of shrieks by rocks and hills return'd,
Launch'd o'er the prairies wide, across the lakes,
To the free skies unpent and glad and strong.

1876, 1881

from *GOOD-BYE MY FANCY*

L. OF G.'S PURPORT

Not to exclude or demarcate, or pick out evils from their formidable
masses (even to expose them,)
But add, fuse, complete, extend—and celebrate the immortal and the
good.

Haughty this song, its word and scope,
To span vast realms of space and time,
Evolution—the cumulative—growths and generations.

Begun in ripen'd youth and steadily pursued,
Wandering, peering, dallying with all—war, peace, day, and night,
absorbing,
Never even for one brief hour abandoning my task,
I end it here in sickness, poverty, and old age.

I sing of life, yet mind me well of death:
To-day shadowy Death dogs my steps, my seated shape, and has for
years—
Draws sometimes close to me, as face to face.

1891, 1891–1892

[3]Speeding.

Emily Dickinson 1830–1886

One day in April 1862, Thomas Wentworth Higginson, a poetry critic for The Atlantic Monthly, *received a letter from Emily Dickinson of Amherst, Massachusetts, asking, "Are you too deeply occupied to say if my verse is alive?" The four poems she enclosed provoked an immediate response and began a correspondence that lasted twenty-two years. Although Emily Dickinson thanked her "preceptor" Higginson for the "surgery" he performed on her poetry, she wanted his encouragement more than his advice, and she politely ignored his suggestions for regularizing her rough rhythms and imperfect rhymes and for correcting her spelling and grammar. Recognizing Emily Dickinson's poetic genius, despite her violations of poetic convention, Higginson remained her friend and adviser throughout her life, and after her death he assisted in gathering her poems for publication.*

Only eight of Emily Dickinson's poems were published while she lived, and it was not until the appearance of Poems by Emily Dickinson *(1890), four years after her death, that her work became available to the general reading public for the first time. The early critical estimates were mixed. Some reviewers found the poetry "balderdash" suffering from lack of rhyme, faulty grammar, and incomprehensible metaphors, a "farrago of illiterate and uneducated sentiment." But other readers found them remarkably pointed and evocative. As the years passed and as more poems were published, critical estimates grew more favorable until, with the publication of all her known poetry, in* The Poems of Emily Dickinson *(1955), the shy, reclusive poet had come to be regarded, with Whitman and Poe, as one of America's greatest lyric poets.*

The range of Emily Dickinson's worldly experience was small by any standard. Her entire life, except for brief visits to nearby Boston and to Washington, D.C., was spent in and around her birthplace, Amherst. The Dickinsons of Amherst were prominent. Her grandfather was a founder of Amherst College; for seventy years her father and then her brother, both lawyers, served as College Treasurer and Trustee. Her mother claimed Emily's affection, but not her wholehearted respect: "Mother does not care for thought," she wrote to Higginson.

As Emily Dickinson grew older, she increasingly withdrew from society, seldom leaving her garden and her large family house. There she wrote poems and letters to her friends and watched the life of the town from her upstairs bedroom window. Her friends, she said, were her "estate," and among them were men, other than Higginson, her father, and her brother, who profoundly affected her creative and emotional life. One of them was her second "preceptor," the Reverend Charles Wadsworth, whom she met in Philadelphia in the mid-1850s. The facts of their relationship are obscure, but there is little doubt about her love for him and for his "kindly spiritual counsel," although they seldom met, and he was a married man with a family. His departure to California perhaps caused the emotional crisis she experienced in 1862, provoking a great creative outburst, for in that single year she wrote the astonishing total of 366 poems.

Emily Dickinson lived a more intense and passionate life than was thought by neighbors and acquaintances who saw her only as an eccentric maiden lady, the "moth" of Amherst, dressed only in white, who flitted almost ghostlike through her house and garden. Not even those closest to her knew fully the depth and extent of her emotions or that the nearly 1,800 poems, tied neatly in packets found after her death, would reveal an immensely complex and passionate sensibility.

Her subjects were love, death, nature, immortality, beauty. Written largely in meters common to Protestant hymn books, her poems employed irregular rhythms, off- or slant-rhymes, paradox, and a careful balancing of abstract Latinate and concrete Anglo-Saxon words. Her lines were gnomic and her images kinesthetic, highly concentrated, and intensely charged with feeling. Her greatest lyrics concentrated on the theme of death, which she typically personified as a monarch, a lord, or a kindly but irresistible lover, yet her moods varied widely, from melancholy to exuberance, grief to joy, leaden despair to spiritual intoxication.

Emily Dickinson's poetry at times descended to coyness and sentimentality. She had no firsthand contact with contemporary writers or with discerning critics. Her favorite authors included Shakespeare, Keats, the Brownings, Ruskin, and Sir Thomas Browne, whose uneasy balance of faith and skepticism she shared. Early in life she rebelled against the Calvinism of the Amherst Congregational Church, yet she retained the Calvinist tendency to look inwardly, and she had a Calvinist sense of both the inherent beauty and the frightening coldness of the world. With her fellow New Englanders Jonathan Edwards and Emerson, she perceived beauty in the wholeness and harmonious relationships of nature, and like Edwards and Emerson she has come to stand as a dominant figure in her nation's literary history, a poet whose work reflects a spiritual unrest and a sense of the human predicament that defy all easy categories.

FURTHER READING: T. Johnson, *Emily Dickinson,* 1955, 1960; *The Letters of Emily Dickinson,* 3 vols., ed. T. Johnson, 1958; J. Leyda, *The Years and Hours of Emily Dickinson,* 2 vols., 1960; *The Complete Poems of Emily Dickinson,* ed. T. Johnson, 1960, 1976; R. Sewall, *The Life of Emily Dickinson,* 1974; J. Loving, *Emily Dickinson, The Poet of the Second Story,* 1987; *New Poems of Emily Dickinson,* ed. W. Shurr, 1993; M. Werner, *Emily Dickinson's Open Folios,* 1995; E. Petrino, *Emily Dickinson and Her Contemporaries,* 1998; R. Lundin, *Emily Dickinson and the Art of Belief,* 1998; *An Emily Dickinson Encyclopedia,* ed. J. Donahue, 1998; J. Guthrie, *Emily Dickinson's Vision,* 1998; *The Emily Dickinson Handbook,* ed. G. Grabber, 1998; *Emily Dickinson,* ed. Graham Clarke, 2000; A. Habeggar, *My Life Is Laid Away in Books,* 2001; D. Mitchell, *Emily Dickinson, Monarch of Perception,* 2001; *The Cambridge Companion to Emily Dickinson,* ed. W. Martin, 2002; R. Brantley, *Experience and Faith, The Late-Romantic Imagination of Emily Dickinson,* 2004; *The Emily Dickinson Handbook,* ed. G. Grabber, C. Miller, and R. Hagenbuchle, 2005; A. Borus, *A Student's Guide to Emily Dickinson,* 2005.

TEXT: *Poems, First Series,* 1890; *Poems, Second Series,* 1891; *Poems, Third Series,* 1896; *The Single Hound,* 1914. Some spelling and punctuation have been changed in accordance with modern editorial principles.

49[1]

I never lost as much but twice,
And that was in the sod.
Twice have I stood a beggar
Before the door of God!

Angels—twice descending
Reimbursed my store—
Burglar! Banker—Father!
I am poor once more!
1858? 1890

[1]Few of Emily Dickinson's poems were given titles. The numbers used here were introduced by later editors.

67

Success is counted sweetest
By those who ne'er succeed.
To comprehend a nectar
Requires sorest need.

Not one of all the purple Host
Who took the Flag today
Can tell the definition
So clear of Victory

As he defeated—dying—
On whose forbidden ear
The distant strains of triumph
Burst agonized and clear!
1859 1878

125

For each ecstatic instant
We must an anguish pay
In keen and quivering ratio
To the ecstasy.

For each beloved hour
Sharp pittances of years—
Bitter contested farthings[1]—
And Coffers heaped with Tears!
1859? 1891

130

These are the days when Birds come back—
A very few—a Bird or two—
To take a backward look.

These are the days when skies resume
The old—old sophistries[1] of June—
A blue and gold mistake.

Oh fraud that cannot cheat the Bee—
Almost the plausibility
Induces my belief.

Till ranks of seeds their witness bear—
And softly thro' the altered air
Hurries a timid leaf.

[1]Coins of little value.
[1]Subtle, deceptive reasoning.

Oh Sacrament of summer days,
Oh Last Communion[2] in the Haze—
Permit a child to join.

Thy sacred emblems to partake—
Thy consecrated bread to take
And thine immortal wine!
1859? 1890

165

A *Wounded* Deer—leaps highest—
I've heard the Hunter tell—
'Tis but the Ecstasy of *death*—
And then the Brake is still!

The *Smitten* Rock that gushes!
The *trampled* Steel that springs!
A Cheek is always redder
Just where the Hectic stings!

Mirth is the Mail of Anguish—
In which it Cautious Arm,
Lest anybody spy the blood
And "you're hurt" exclaim!
1860? 1890

185

"Faith" is a fine invention
When Gentlemen can *see*—
But Microscopes are prudent
In an Emergency.
1860? 1891

210

The thought beneath so slight a film—
Is more distinctly seen—
As laces just reveal the surge—
Or Mists—the Appenine—
1860? 1891

214

I taste a liquor never brewed—
From Tankards scooped in Pearl—
Not all the Frankfort Berries[1]
Yield such an Alcohol!

[2]In the Christian sacrament of Communion, believers are united with Christ through partaking of consecrated bread and wine.

[1]Grapes grown in the region of Frankfurt am Main, Germany, and used in making a fine Rhine wine. Another version of this line reads, "Not all the Vats upon the Rhine."

Inebriate of Air—am I—
And Debauchee of Dew—
Reeling—thro endless summer days—
From inns of Molten Blue—

When "Landlords" turn the drunken Bee
Out of the Foxglove's door—
When Butterflies—renounce their "drams"—
I shall but drink the more!

Till Seraphs[2] swing their snowy Hats—
And Saints—to windows run—
To see the little Tippler
From Manzanilla[3] come![4]
1860? 1861, 1890

216

Safe in their Alabaster Chambers—
Untouched by Morning—
And untouched by Noon—
Lie the meek members of the Resurrection—
Rafter of Satin—and Roof of Stone!

Grand go the Years—in the Crescent—above them—
Worlds scoop their Arcs—
And Firmaments—row—
Diadems—drop—and Doges[1]—surrender—
Soundless as dots—on a Disc of Snow—
1861 1890

241

I like a look of Agony,
Because I know it's true—
Men do not sham Convulsion,
Nor simulate, a Throe[1]—

The Eyes glaze once—and that is Death—
Impossible to feign
The Beads upon the Forehead
By homely Anguish strung.
1861? 1890

[2]The highest ranking of the nine orders of angels.
[3]A sherry wine exported from Manzanilla, Spain.
[4]Two other versions of the final line exist:
"Come staggering toward the Sun."
"Leaning against the—Sun—"
[1]The chief magistrates of Venice (697–1797).
[1]A spasm.

249

Wild Nights—Wild Nights!
Were I with thee
Wild Nights should be
Our luxury!

Futile—the Winds—
To a Heart in port—
Done with the Compass—
Done with the Chart!

Rowing in Eden—
Ah, the Sea!
Might I but moor—Tonight—
In Thee!

1861? 1891

258

There's a certain Slant of light,
Winter Afternoons—
That oppresses, like the Heft[1]
Of Cathedral Tunes—

Heavenly Hurt, it gives us—
We can find no scar,
But internal difference,
Where the Meanings, are—

None may teach it—Any—
'Tis the Seal Despair—
An imperial affliction
Sent us of the Air—

When it comes, the Landscape listens—
Shadows—hold their breath—
When it goes, 'tis like the Distance
On the look of Death—

1861? 1890

280

I felt a Funeral, in my Brain,
And Mourners to and fro
Kept treading—treading—till it seemed
That Sense was breaking through—

And when they all were seated,
A Service, like a Drum—
Kept beating—beating—till I thought
My Mind was going numb—

[1]Weight.

And then I heard them lift a Box
And creak across my Soul
With those same Boots of Lead, again,
Then Space—began to toll,

As all the Heavens were a Bell,
And Being, but an Ear,
And I, and Silence, some strange Race
Wrecked, solitary, here—

And then a Plank in Reason, broke,
And I dropped down, and down—
And hit a World, at every plunge,
And Finished knowing—then—
1861? 1896

301

I reason, Earth is short—
And Anguish—absolute—
And many hurt—
But, what of that?

I reason, we could die—
The best Vitality
Cannot excel Decay,
But, what of that?

I reason, that in Heaven—
Somehow, it will be even—
Some new Equation, given—
But, what of that?
1862? 1890

303

The Soul selects her own Society—
Then—shuts the Door—
To her divine Majority—
Present no more—

Unmoved—she notes the Chariots—pausing—
At her low Gate—
Unmoved—an Emperor be kneeling
Upon her Mat—

I've known her—from an ample nation—
Choose One—
Then—close the Valves of her attention—
Like Stone—
1862? 1890

328

A Bird came down the Walk—
He did not know I saw—
He bit an Angleworm in halves
And ate the fellow, raw,

And then he drank a Dew
From a convenient Grass—
And then hopped sidewise to the Wall
To let a Beetle pass—

He glanced with rapid eyes
That hurried all around—
They looked like frightened Beads, I thought—
He stirred his Velvet Head

Like one in danger, Cautious,
I offered him a Crumb
And he unrolled his feathers
And rowed him softer home—

Than Oars divide the Ocean,
Too silver for a seam—
Or Butterflies, off Banks of Noon
Leap, plashless[1] as they swim.
1862 1891

338

I know that He exists.
Somewhere—in Silence—
He has hid his rare life
From our gross eyes.

'Tis an instant's play.
'Tis a fond Ambush—
Just to make Bliss
Earn her own surprise!

But—should the play
Prove piercing earnest—
Should the glee—glaze—
In Death's—stiff—stare—

Would not the fun
Look too expensive!
Would not the jest—
Have crawled too far!
1862 1891

[1]Splashless.

401

What Soft—Cherubic Creatures—
These Gentlewomen are—
One would as soon assault a Plush[1]—
Or violate a Star—

Such Dimity[2] Convictions—
A Horror so refined
Of freckled Human Nature—
Of Deity—ashamed[3]—

It's such a common—Glory—
A Fisherman's—Degree—
Redemption—Brittle Lady—
Be so—ashamed of Thee—
1862? 1896

435

Much Madness is divinest Sense—
To a discerning Eye—
Much Sense—the starkest Madness—
'Tis the Majority
In this, as All, prevail—
Assent—and you are sane—
Demur—you're straightway dangerous—
And handled with a Chain—
1862? 1890

441

This is my letter to the World
That never wrote to Me—
The simple News that Nature told—
With tender Majesty
Her Message is committed
To Hands I cannot see—
For love of Her—Sweet—countrymen—
Judge tenderly—of Me
1862 1890

449

I died for Beauty—but was scarce
Adjusted in the Tomb
When One who died for Truth, was lain
In an adjoining Room—

[1] Cloth with a long, soft pile.
[2] Cotton fabric, delicate and sheer.
[3] "For whosoever shall be ashamed of me and of my words, of him shall the Son of man be ashamed, when he shall come in his own glory . . ." Luke 9:26.

He questioned softly "Why I failed"?
"For Beauty," I replied—
"And I—for Truth—Themself are One—
We Bretheren, are," He said—

And so, as Kinsmen, met a Night—
We talked between the Rooms—
Until the Moss had reached our lips—
And covered up—our names—
1862? 1890

465

I heard a Fly buzz—when I died—
The Stillness in the Room
Was like the Stillness in the Air—
Between the Heaves of Storm—

The Eyes around—had wrung them dry—
And Breaths were gathering firm
For that last Onset—when the King
Be witnessed—in the Room—

I willed my Keepsakes—Signed away
What portion of me be
Assignable—and then it was
There interposed a Fly—

With Blue—uncertain stumbling Buzz—
Between the light—and me—
And then the Windows failed—and then
I could not see to see—
1862? 1896

510

It was not Death, for I stood up,
And all the Dead, lie down—
It was not Night, for all the Bells
Put out their Tongues, for Noon.

It was not Frost, for on my Flesh
I felt Siroccos[1]—crawl—
Nor Fire—for just my Marble feet
Could keep a Chancel,[2] cool—

And yet, it tasted, like them all,
The Figures I have seen
Set orderly, for Burial,
Reminded me, of mine—

[1]Hot, Mediterranean winds that originate in the Libyan deserts.
[2]Area of a church where the altar is placed.

As if my life were shaven,
And fitted to a frame,
And could not breathe without a key,
and 'twas like Midnight, some—

When everything that ticked—has stopped—
And Space stares all around—
Or Grisly frosts—first Autumn morns,
Repeal the Beating Ground—

But, most, like Chaos—Stopless—cool—
Without a Chance, or Spar—
Or even a Report of Land—
To justify—Despair.
1862 1891

536

The Heart asks Pleasure—first—
And then—Excuse from Pain—
And then—those little Anodynes
That deaden suffering—

And then—to go to sleep—
And then—if it should be
The will of its Inquisitor
The privilege to die—
1862? 1890

585

I like to see it lap the Miles—
And lick the Valleys up—
And stop to feed itself at Tanks
And then—prodigious step

Around a Pile of Mountains—
And supercilious peer
In Shanties—by the sides of Roads—
And then a Quarry pare

To fit its sides
And crawl between
Complaining all the while
In horrid—hooting stanza—
Then chase itself down Hill—

And neigh like Boanerges[1]—
Then—prompter than a Star
Stop—docile and omnipotent
At its own stable door—
1862? 1891

[1]Hebrew: Sons of Thunder, a term used to describe loud-voiced preachers and orators.

640

I cannot live with You—
It would be Life—
And Life is over there—
Behind the Shelf—

The Sexton[1] keeps the Key to—
Putting up
Our Life—His Porcelain—
Like a Cup—

Discarded of the Housewife—
Quaint—or Broke—
A newer Sevres[2] pleases—
Old Ones crack—

I could not die—with You—
For One must wait
To shut the Other's Gaze down—
You—could not—

And I—Could I stand by
And see You—freeze—
Without my Right of Frost—
Death's privilege?

Nor could I rise—with you—
Because Your Face
Would put out Jesus'—
That new Grace

Glow plain—and foreign
On my homesick Eye—
Except that You than He
Shone closer by—

They'd judge Us—How—
For You—served Heaven—You know,
Or sought to—
I could not—

Because You saturated Sight—
And I had no more Eyes
For sordid excellence
As Paradise.

[1]Church official in charge of a church building and its grounds.
[2]Fine porcelain made in Sèvres, France.

And were You lost, I would be—
Though My Name
Rang loudest
On the Heavenly fame—

And were You—saved—
And I—condemned to be
Where You were not—
That self—were Hell to Me—

So We must meet apart—
You there—I—here—
With just the Door ajar
That Oceans are—and Prayer—
And that White Sustenance—
Despair—
1862? 1890

650

Pain—has an Element of Blank—
It cannot recollect
When it begun—or if there were
A time when it was not—

It has no Future—but itself—
Its Infinite contain
Its Past—enlightened to perceive
New Periods—of Pain.
1862? 1890

670

One need not be a Chamber—to be Haunted—
One need not be a House—
The Brain has Corridors—surpassing
Material Place—

Far safer, of a Midnight Meeting
External Ghost
Than its interior Confronting—
That Cooler Host.

Far safer, through an Abbey gallop,
The Stones a'chase[1]—
Than Unarmed, one's a'self[2] encounter—
In lonesome Place—

[1]I.e., in pursuit.
[2]I.e., own self.

Ourself behind ourself, concealed—
Should startle most—
Assassin hid in our Apartment
Be Horror's least.

The Body—borrows a Revolver—
He bolts the Door—
O'erlooking a superior spectre—
Or More—
1863? 1891

675

Essential Oils—are wrung—
The Attar from the Rose
Be not expressed by Suns—alone—
It is the gift of Screws—

The General Rose—decay—
But this—in Lady's Drawer
Make Summer—When the Lady lie
In Ceaseless Rosemary—
1863? 1891

712

Because I could not stop for Death—
He kindly stopped for me—
The Carriage held but just Ourselves—
And Immortality.

We slowly drove—He knew no haste
And I had put away
My labor and my leisure too,
For His Civility—

We passed the School, where Children strove
At Recess—in the Ring—
We passed the Fields of Gazing Grain—
We passed the Setting Sun—

Or rather—He passed Us—
The Dews drew quivering and chill—
For only Gossamer, my Gown—
My Tippet[1] —only Tulle[2]

[1]A cape or scarf.
[2]Thin, net fabric.

We paused before a House that seemed
A Swelling of the Ground—
The Roof was scarcely visible—
The Cornice—in the Ground—

Since then—'tis Centuries—and yet
Feels shorter than the Day
I first surmised the Horses' Heads
Were toward Eternity—
1863? 1890

764

Presentiment—is that long Shadow—on the Lawn—
Indicative that Suns go down—

The Notice to the startled Grass
That Darkness—is about to pass—
1862? 1890

976

Death is a Dialogue between
The Spirit and the Dust.
"Dissolve" says Death—The Spirit "Sir
I have another Trust"—

Death doubts it—Argues from the Ground—
The Spirit turns away
Just laying off for evidence
An Overcoat of Clay.
1864? 1890

986

A narrow Fellow in the Grass
Occasionally rides—
You may have met Him—did you not
His notice sudden is—

The Grass divides as with a Comb—
A spotted shaft is seen—
And then it closes at your feet
And opens further on—

He likes a Boggy Acre
A Floor too cool for corn—
Yet when a Boy, and Barefoot—
I more than once at Noon
Have passed, I thought, a Whip lash
Unbraiding in the Sun

When stooping to secure it
It wrinkled, and was gone—

Several of Nature's People
I know, and they know me—
I feel for them a transport
Of cordiality—

But never met this Fellow
Attended, or alone
Without a tighter breathing
And Zero at the Bone—
1865 1866, 1891

1052

I never saw a Moor—
I never saw the Sea—
Yet know I how the Heather looks
And what a Billow be.

I never spoke with God
Nor visited in Heaven—
Yet certain am I of the spot
As if the Checks[1] were given—
1865? 1890

1078

The Bustle in a House
The Morning after Death
Is solemnest of industries
Enacted upon Earth—

The Sweeping up the Heart
And putting Love away
We shall not want to use again
Until Eternity.
1866? 1890

[1]Tokens of verification, tickets.

1207

He preached upon "Breadth" till it argued him narrow—
The Broad are too broad to define
And of "Truth" until it proclaimed him a Liar—
The Truth never flaunted a Sign—

Simplicity fled from his counterfeit presence
As Gold the Pyrites[1] would shun—
What confusion would cover the innocent Jesus
To meet so enabled a Man!
1872? 1891

1463

A Route of Evanescence
With a revolving Wheel—
A Resonance of Emerald—
A Rush of Cochineal[1]—
And every Blossom on the Bush
Adjusts its tumbled Head—
The mail from Tunis,[2] probably,
An easy Morning's Ride—
1879? 1891

1624

Apparently with no surprise
To any happy Flower
The Frost beheads it at its play—
In accidental power—
The blonde Assassin passes on—
That Sun proceeds unmoved
To measure off another Day
For an Approving God.
1884? 1890

[1]Iron or copper pyrites, called "fool's gold" because they resemble gold.
[1]A red dye.
[2]City in North Africa.

1732

My life closed twice before its close;
It yet remains to see
If immortality unveil
A third event to me,

So huge, so hopeless to conceive
As these that twice befell.
Parting is all we know of heaven,
And all we need of hell.

1896

1755

To make a prairie it takes a clover and one bee,
One clover, and a bee,
And revery.
The revery alone will do,
If bees are few.

1896

The Age of Realism

By the end of the Civil War (1861–1865), powerful forces had emerged that would dominate life in twentieth-century America. The industrial North had triumphed over the agrarian South, and from that victory came a society based on mass labor and mass consumption. Steam power began to replace water power, and machines driven by steam engines supplanted traditional hand labor in factories and on farms. In the 1770s, Thomas Jefferson had voiced the hope that the majority of Americans would never be "occupied at a work bench, for those who labor in the earth are the chosen people of God." But after 1865, the United States ceased to be the simple agrarian democracy that Jefferson had cherished. It became instead the most heavily industrialized nation in the world, and its people in ever greater numbers ceased to "labor in the earth" and moved to towns and cities to labor on the machines of new industries.

Industrialization and Its Consequences

As industrialism spread, the nature of labor changed. Machines displaced most of the hand labor previously required in manufacturing. Independent, skilled handcraftsmen became obsolete, unable to compete with machines operated by semiskilled laborers twenty-four hours a day, seven days a week. And the machines, with their great cost and high efficiency, came to be seen by mill owners and factory managers as far more valuable and useful than the workers who ran them. As a result, traditional relationships between employers and craftsmen weakened, grew more impersonal. In giant corporations that employed hundreds, even thousands, the workers no longer knew their customers, no longer even saw their employers. Nonetheless, great numbers of men, women, and children—native-born and foreign—flocked to American cities, drawn by hopes for steady factory work and high factory pay.

In the cities—swollen with growing numbers of the poor, the ignorant, and the unskilled—great political change was taking place. As more people of the urban underclasses sought, and found, power at the polls, the centers of political power shifted. Traditional political alliances weakened, and new political groups emerged, taking their power from, and proclaiming their devotion to, the laboring classes.

Amid the upheavals of the time, political patronage and graft rose to new heights in the United States, causing the first grand age of American civic corruption. Confused and ignorant voters elected big-city bosses and their henchmen who flourished on kickbacks and fraud, boldly collected their boodle, and scoffed at the law. In six years, during the 1860s and 1870s, New York's "Boss" William Tweed and his "Tweed Ring" of municipal crooks cost the city of New York an estimated two hundred million dollars, equal to more than two billion dollars in 2005. And during Ulysses S. Grant's presidency (1869–1877) the crimes of high federal officials were exposed in scandals unequaled in the history of the United States. The actions of Grant in protecting his political cronies and ignoring their blatant misdeeds led many Americans to conclude that the president of the United States was himself a common thief. Never before had American government, at all levels, seemed so overrun with rascals. Never before had civic virtue seemed to have fallen so low.

During the Civil War the power of the national government dramatically expanded. For the first time federal authority intruded directly into the lives of the majority of the people. The war brought the first national conscription laws; the first federal income taxes were levied, and the first national currency was issued—paper money backed by the federal government rather than by individual states and local banks. Rapid growth of federal power brought benefits and troubles: In 1865 the first official step toward nationwide racial equality was made when the Thirteenth Amendment to the Constitution was adopted, abolishing slavery within the United States. And the federal government used its powers to encourage business growth and the exploitation of natural resources, creating vast new wealth.

But great riches and economic power were increasingly concentrated in the hands of the few: bankers and industrialists who touted the glories of "business and bustle," business luminaries who revered the virtues of self-help. The laudatory term "Captain of Industry" was coined in the 1880s as business and financial tycoons came for the first time to be celebrated as national heroes, as models for young men who hoped to rise in the world through luck and pluck. It was the beginning of what Mark Twain called "The Gilded Age," an age of extremes: of decline and progress, of poverty and dazzling wealth, of gloom and bouyant hope—for the downtrodden it was a time of ever greater deprivation, but for the rich and the rising middle class it was an age of such conspicuous abundance and gluttony that one historian labeled it "The Great Barbecue."

In the last half of the nineteenth century, Americans ceased to be isolated from the world and from each other. Coast-to-coast overland mail service began in 1858—a letter could be sent from St. Louis to San Francisco in as little as four weeks. In 1860 the Pony Express cut that time to ten and a half days. And within a year a message could be sent from New York to San Francisco in seconds, on the new telegraph line that spanned the nation in 1861. A transatlantic telegraph cable joined America and Europe in 1866. Ten years later, Alexander Graham Bell patented his invention of the telephone. By 1900 the United States had 1,356,000 telephones—twice as many as all Europe.

If the telegraph and the telephone helped to bring Americans closer together, the United States were finally "united" by the railroads. The first railroad, the Baltimore and Ohio, began operation in 1830 with thirteen miles of track. In 1869 the first transcontinental railroad was completed, linking the Atlantic and the Pacific. Five years later railroad mileage exceeded 74,000 miles, and the United States had the most extensive railroad system in the world. By 1889, the trip across the continent that had taken as much as five months by wagon during the Gold Rush of 1849 could now be made in trains (with Pullman sleepers and dining cars) in 108 hours—little more than four days.

With the building of the railroads came rapid commercial development. Vast new lands reached by rail lines were put under the plow, bringing enormous increases in farm products. The production of livestock and wheat doubled, tripled, and even quadrupled. New Yorkers could now eat beef shipped in newly invented refrigerator cars all the way from the slaughterhouses of Chicago; Floridians could buy inexpensive flour from mills in Minneapolis.

Enterprising merchants like Richard Sears and Montgomery Ward created nationwide retail organizations that could undersell local shopkeepers. The clothing, household goods, and farm equipment once made locally by costly handwork were replaced by inexpensive, mass-produced goods made from standardized patterns in centralized factories. The nation was becoming a single giant marketplace, and retail stores that sold ready-made clothes and prepackaged foods began to resemble the stores of modern America, where the same goods are to be seen from one end of the land to the other.

The coming of the railroads changed how Americans worked, where they lived, how they ate, how they dressed. In 1883 the railroads even changed the way Americans kept time when the more than fifty-six time zones in the United States were reduced to four, to promote greater efficiency and safety in scheduling railroad traffic.

The Ending of the Frontier

As transportation became better and cheaper, the nation's people became increasingly mobile. In the last surge of westward expansion, Americans and immigrant Europeans, lured by the promise of free land, settled the Great Plains and the mountain states. The United States now extended from the Atlantic to the Pacific. Vast areas were no longer unknown, unexplored; by 1890 the frontier—the westward-moving line of settlement begun three hundred years before on the Atlantic Coast—ceased to exist, although its influence would long remain, shaping the life of the nation and inspiring the legends, novels, and western movies by which the world would come to know America.

Westward settlement brought great benefits but at great cost. Following the American Civil War the unique culture of America's nomadic plains Indians had reached its zenith, partly because they made use of the white man's horses, guns, and metal tools. But with the end of the 1880s, that unique Native-American culture had been ruined by the destruction of the buffalo and by the white man's land hunger, his gold fever, and his whiskey and diseases. The plains Indians were killed and displaced as other Native Americans had been before them. The surviving tribes became wards of the federal government, confined to reservations, where their life of forced dependency has continued into the twenty-first century. Their lost world now largely survives only in popular distortions of romantic legend and myth.

The age that saw the final subjugation of the Indians and the ending of the frontier was also an age of steel and steam, electricity and oil. From the Civil War to World War I, steel production in the United States increased more than six hundred times, and steelmaking became the nation's dominant industry. Alternating electrical current was introduced in 1886. Incandescent lamps illuminated the cities with electricity provided by giant, steam-driven dynamos. The tallow candles and whale-oil lamps of rural America were replaced by lanterns filled with inexpensive kerosene made from crude oil. The American petroleum industry began, and with it came the age of the automobile.

The Growth of Population and Riches

From 1870 to 1890 the total population of the United States doubled. Villages became towns, towns became cities, and cities grew to a size and with a speed that would have astonished the Founding Fathers. From 1860 to 1910 the population of Philadelphia tripled; that of New York City more than quadrupled, while the population of Chicago increased twenty times to two million, making it the nation's second largest city.

As the population doubled, the national income quadrupled, and by the mid-1890s the United States could boast 4,000 millionaires. The rich prospered mightily, and prodigious fortunes were piled up by industrial and banking magnates such as John D. Rockefeller, Andrew Carnegie, and J. Pierpont Morgan. The growth of big business and big industry also widened further the gulf between the rich and the poor, giving rise to reform movements and labor unions that voiced the grievances of debt-ridden farmers and immigrant workers who lived in city slums and labored in giant, impersonal factories. Yet it was also an age of optimism; little heed was given to such gloomy skeptics as Henry Adams, who saw America as a land of unbridled power and flamboyant greed. It was a time of glowing visions, a time of radiant prospects, when ministers preached (and congregations believed) a gospel of wealth, suggesting that riches were at last in league with virtue, that an age of unlimited progress had finally dawned.

But progress had not reached all levels of American society. In 1867, two years after the Civil War, the U.S. Congress passed a stringent series of Reconstruction Acts to force its will upon the South and to protect black freedmen. Voting rights were established for blacks, along with the right to testify in courts, to serve on juries, to own property, and to hold public office. But in 1877, when Reconstruction ended and the last of the federal troops occupying the South were withdrawn, most of the newly won rights for blacks began to erode. Well before the end of the century, poll taxes and literacy tests were legalized and used to disqualify black voters. Separate and unequal schools and public facilities were created; legal rights were denied in both the North and the South. The great hope for liberty and justice for all began to fade. White supremacy was firmly re-established, and blacks were segregated to lives of poverty and indignity that did not begin to change significantly for more than three-quarters of a century, until the passage of the Civil Rights Act of 1964.

Immigration dropped sharply during the Civil War, but after the 1880s a rising tide of foreigners, beckoned by the American promise of jobs and political freedom, came to the New World at such a rate that by 1910 more than a third of the population of America's largest cities was foreign-born. Large-scale immigration and technical advancements in industry and agriculture increased the need for literacy, creating a demand for widespread public education. In the fifty years following the Civil War, the number of high schools in the United States increased thirty-five times. Colleges were established for women: Vassar in 1861, Wellesley in 1870, Smith in 1871. Higher education ceased to be a privilege limited to children of the well-to-do. Under the Morrill Act of 1862, millions of acres of federal land were given to the states for the establishment of public "land-grant" universities for "the liberal and practical education of the industrial classes."

New Cultural and Artistic Ideals

Increased wealth and the desire for its conspicuous display gave rise to a gingerbread era of American design whose prime function was to attract attention. American millionaires built Gothic and Romanesque mansions, decorating them with towers, domes, columns, stained-glass windows, and ornamental gimcracks of wood and iron. Their rooms were filled with art imported from Europe, as were most symbols of culture. Well-to-do Americans adopted European dress styles and manners, sent their sons to Europe for an education, and eagerly married off their daughters to European noblemen, many of them impoverished, some of them bogus.

America remained culturally dependent on Europe for drama and music. Touring English actors, playing in tents and "opera houses" throughout America, presented European plays and dramatizations of popular European novels. Symphony orchestras, which had begun to appear in the United States after mid-century, limited their repertoires almost wholly to European music. The nation lacked first-rate composers of serious music until the 1900s. And even in the twenty-first century, America's greatest contributions to the world of music has remained its folk songs, its Negro spirituals, and the jazz music that spread from New Orleans around the world after World War I.

After 1865, a strong native tradition in painting began to develop, apparent in the work of such artists as Thomas Eakins, who realistically portrayed the America he saw around him and who urged his students "to remain in America, to peer deeper into the heart of American life." But numerous artists saw opportunity elsewhere and preferred to lead expatriate lives in Europe. Among them were the most renowned American painters of the period: James McNeill Whistler and John Singer Sargent. In a land of triumphant materialism, high culture had little impact on the mass of the people, who sought and found their entertainment in circuses, in vaudeville shows, in the new professional sports, and, after the 1890s, in motion-picture theaters named "nickelodeons" after their five-cent admission fee.

New Writers, New Writing

In the latter half of the nineteenth century, women became the nation's dominant cultural force, a position they have never relinquished. Ladies' journalism began to flourish. In 1891, *The Ladies Home Journal* became the first American magazine with a circulation exceeding half a million; by 1905 its circulation had reached a full million. A new generation of women authors appeared whose poetry and fiction enlivened the pages of popular ten-cent monthly and weekly magazines. The greatest woman writer of the age, Emily Dickinson, was almost completely unknown; her first collection of poetry was not published until 1890, four years after her death. But Harriet Beecher Stowe, the author of *Uncle Tom's Cabin* (1852), had become an American institution and the most famous literary woman in the world. The American public's appetite for sentiment and sensation was constantly fed by writers who seemed to be inexhaustible, spilling forth novels seething with romantic extravagance: ancestral curses, sudden passions, villains blasted, and heroes triumphant. Sales of such "molasses fiction" far exceeded the sales of works by such highly regarded writers as William Dean Howells, Edith Wharton, Henry James, and Mark Twain.

Americans continued to read the works of Irving, Cooper, Hawthorne, and Poe, but the great age of American romanticism had ended. By the 1870s the New England Renaissance had waned. Hawthorne and Thoreau were dead; Emerson, Lowell, Longfellow, Holmes, and Whittier had passed their literary zeniths. Melville, living in obscurity, had ceased to publish his fiction. Only Whitman continued to offer a new literary vision to the world, issuing a fifth edition of *Leaves of Grass* in 1870 and publishing *Democratic Vistas* in 1871. As

New England's cultural dominance waned, New York replaced Boston as the nation's literary center, drawing writers from New England, the South, and the West to the publishing houses and periodicals of the nation's largest city.

Technical improvements in printing, lower costs for paper, and the rise of national corporations that could pour money into newspaper and magazine advertisements caused the growth of a great variety of low-cost, general-interest publications. From 1865 to 1905 the total number of periodicals published in the United States increased from about seven hundred to more than six thousand, all trying to satisfy the appetites of a vast new reading audience that was hungry for news articles, essays, fiction, and poems.

Literary Realism and Naturalism

A host of new writers appeared, among them Bret Harte, William Dean Howells, and Mark Twain, whose background and training, unlike those of the older generation they displaced, were middle-class and journalistic rather than genteel or academic. Influenced by such Europeans as Zola, Flaubert, Balzac, Dostoyevsky, and Tolstoy, America's most noteworthy new authors established a literature of realism. They sought to portray American life as it really was, insisting that the ordinary and the local were just as suitable for artistic portrayal as the magnificent and the remote.

As in most literary rebellions, the new literature rose out of the authors' desire to renovate the literary theories of a previous age. Realists had grown scornful of artistic ideals that had been trivialized, worn thin by derivative writers eager to supply the "great popular want" for sentiment, adventure, and "tingling excitement." In contrast, the realists had what Henry James called "a powerful impulse to mirror the unmitigated realities of life." Earlier in the nineteenth century, James Fenimore Cooper had insisted on the author's right to avoid representations of "squalid misery" and to present instead an idealized and "poetic" portrait of life. But by the end of the nineteenth century the realists, and the literary naturalists who followed them, had turned away from the portrayal of idealized characters and events. Instead, they sought to describe the wide range of American experience and to present the subtleties of human personality, to portray characters who were not simply all good or all bad.

Realism had originated in France as *réalisme*, a literary doctrine that called for "reality and truth" in the depiction of ordinary life. Realism first appeared in America in the literature of local color, an amalgam of romantic plots and realistic descriptions of things immediately observable: the dialects, customs, sights, and sounds of regional America. Bret Harte in the 1860s was the first American writer of local color to achieve wide popularity. He presented stories about western mining towns populated by colorful gamblers, outlaws, and scandalous women. Thereafter editors—ever sensitive to public taste—demanded, and writers such as Harte, Harriet Beecher Stowe, Kate Chopin, Joel Chandler Harris, and Mark Twain provided, regional stories and tales of the life of America's Westerners, Southerners, and Easterners. Local-color fiction reached its peak of popularity in the 1880s, but by the turn of the century it had begun to decline as its limited resources were exhausted and its most popular writers grew tediously repetitious or turned to other literary modes.

The arbiter of nineteenth-century literary realism in America was William Dean Howells. He defined realism as "nothing more and nothing less than the truthful treatment of material," and he best exemplified his theories in such novels as *A Modern Instance* (1882), *The Rise of Silas Lapham* (1885), and *A Hazard of New Fortunes* (1890). Howells spoke for a generation of writers who attempted to sustain an objective point of view and who found their subject matter in the experiences of the American middle class, describing their houses, families, and jobs, their social customs, achievements, and failures. The bulk of America's literary realism was limited to optimistic treatment of the surface of life. Yet the greatest of America's realists, Henry James and Mark Twain, moved well beyond a surface portrayal of nineteenth-century America. James probed deeply into the individual psychology of his characters, writing in a rich and intricate style that supported his intense scrutiny of complex human experience. Twain, breaking out of the narrow limits of local-color fiction, described the breadth of American experience as no one had ever done before, or since, and he created, in *Huckleberry Finn* (1884), a masterpiece of American realism that is one of the great books of world literature.

In the 1880s, Howells spoke out against the writing of a bleak fiction of failure and despair. He called for the treatment of the "smiling aspects of life" as being the more "American," insisting that America was truly a land of hope and of possibility that should be reflected in its literature. But at the end of the century came a generation of writers whose ideas of the workings of the universe and whose perception of society's disorders led them to naturalism, a new and harsher realism. America's literary naturalists scorned the idea that literature should present comforting moral truths. Instead, naturalist writers attempted to achieve extreme objectivity and frankness, presenting characters of low social and economic classes who were dominated by their environment and heredity. In presenting the extremes of life, the naturalists sometimes displayed an affinity to the sensationalism of early romanticism, but unlike their romantic predecessors, the naturalists emphasized that the world was amoral, that men and women had no free will, that their lives were controlled by heredity and the environment, that religious "truths" were illusory, and that the destiny of humanity was misery in life and oblivion in death.

Naturalism, like realism, had come from Europe. In America it had been shaped by the Civil War, by the social upheavals that undermined the comforting faith of an earlier age, and by the teachings of Charles Darwin. Darwinism seemed to stress the animality of humans, to suggest that people are dominated by the irresistible forces of evolution. The pessimism and deterministic ideas of naturalism pervaded the works of such writers as Stephen Crane, Frank Norris, Jack London, Henry Adams, and Theodore Dreiser. They wrote detailed descriptions of the lives of the downtrodden and of the abnormal; they offered frank treatment of human passion and sexuality; they portrayed men and women overwhelmed by the blind forces of nature; and the works of such literary naturalists still exert a powerful influence on modern writers.

Although realism and naturalism were products of the nineteenth century, their final triumph came in the twentieth century, with the popular and critical successes of such writers as Edwin Arlington Robinson, Willa Cather, Sherwood Anderson, Robert Frost, and William Faulkner. The triumph of realism did not bring an end to romanticism, for romanticism in all its varieties still abounds in popular novels, movies, and television shows with heroes and heroines of unspotted virtue and dazzling accomplishments. Nonetheless, realism in all of its forms permanently transformed American culture by depicting a "real" America, by commemorating the lives of ordinary men and women, and by celebrating the commonplace truths of a new land and a new people.

Mark Twain 1835–1910

Mark Twain's rise to fame began with the publication in 1865 of "Jim Smiley and His Jumping Frog," a comic western tale (he later called it a "villainous backwoods sketch") that he heard in a mining camp not far from his cabin on Jackass Hill in the California gold country. By the time of his death, forty-five years later, Twain's popularity as an author and lecturer was worldwide, and he had become one of the most celebrated Americans of his day.

"The Notorious Jumping Frog of Calaveras County," as his frog story was later titled, was one of the many tall tales Twain heard in the western mining camps where he had gone in 1861 when he was twenty-five. His adventurous boyhood had been spent in Hannibal, Missouri, on the Mississippi River. After his father's death in 1847, Twain had left school to be apprenticed to a printer. He developed a talent for writing, and at the age of sixteen he had his first piece published in a Boston magazine. For four years he worked as a journeyman printer, and then he set out to fulfill his childhood ambition to be a Mississippi River steamboat pilot. After a long apprenticeship as a cub pilot, he succeeded, but his glorious career on the river ended abruptly when the Mississippi was blockaded at the beginning of the Civil War. He joined a Confederate volunteer unit, but after a short term of soldiering he abandoned the war and went to Nevada, hoping to strike it rich in the silver fields. When his mining schemes failed, he joined the staff of the Virginia City, Nevada Territorial Enterprise, *exchanged his real name, Samuel L. Clemens, for a pseudonym, "Mark Twain," and began his career as a frontier humorist.*

In 1866, after six years as a miner, newspaper reporter, and lecturer in California, Nevada, and Hawaii, Twain went east, responding, he said, to "a 'call' to literature, of a low order—i.e., humorous." He took with him a reputation as "the wild humorist of the Pacific Slope" and a lively imagination that had led him to turn many of his newspaper "reports" into burlesques and comic sketches.

While in New York, Twain was commissioned by a San Francisco paper to sail on a five-month voyage with a group of American tourists and to report their confrontations with the cultural and religious shrines of Europe and the Holy Land. Upon his return to America, Twain gathered his newspaper articles, revised them, and published them as Innocents Abroad *(1869). Next came* Roughing It *(1872), a narrative of his original journey west to Nevada. His first attempt at novel writing was* The Gilded Age *(1873), on which he collaborated with the journalist and essayist Charles Dudley Warner (1829–1900). The novel was a muddled failure, but it gave its name to the boom times, the post-Civil War age of unbridled individualism and speculation, which it satirized.*

Twain's nostalgic recollections of his early boyhood in Hannibal stirred him to write his "boys' book," Tom Sawyer *(1876) and its sequel,* Huckleberry Finn *(1884). His memories of his three years as a "cub" and master pilot on the Mississippi inspired* Life on the Mississippi *(1883). By the time he came to write* A Connecticut Yankee in King Arthur's Court *(1889), with its angry satire on royalty, religion, and the chivalric ideals of Arthurian England, his work had become more serious and critical. By the 1890s the amused tolerance that had once typified his writing had been displaced by increasingly bitter attacks on the injustices of society and the folly of man. In* Pudd'nhead Wilson *(1894) the humor was slight and the attacks on bigotry furious. By the turn of the century, with the publication of "The Man That Corrupted Hadleyburg" (1900), "To the Person Sitting in Darkness" (1901), and "The Mysterious Stranger" (1916), his obsessive vision of man as a greedy numbskull, oafish, hypocritical, cruel, and predatory, was wholly apparent. By the end of his life, moved by his fears, guilt, and incandescent rages, Twain had come to detest even the readers and audiences who had given him fame and prosperity.*

Although traces of Twain's later pessimism are evident in his earliest works, his change from jovial humorist to despairing determinist has been explained as the result of a series of personal catastrophes. The deaths of his wife and two daughters left him embittered and lonely. The failure of his publishing firm and a series of bad financial investments brought him humiliation and bankruptcy, leading him to travel throughout the world on a lecture series to pay off his debts, a long and exhausting experience he recorded with barely disguised weariness in Following the Equator *(1897). In 1906 he began to record the details of much of the best and the worst of his life, portions of which appeared as his* Autobiography *(1924), published posthumously, as was the collection entitled* Letters from the Earth *(1962), which contained the most despairing of his pronouncements and his last raging volleys at the "damned human race."*

Much of Twain's writing was uneven hack work and vastly exaggerated lampoon marred by flippancy and misdirected bitterness. As a satirist he employed his common, lowly characters as vernacular spokesman to deflate the values of the official culture of his day and what he saw as the rattle-brained folly of U.S. politics and imperialism. He was a bitter and withering foe who never forgot insults, real or imagined, whether from friends or enemies, living or, as in the case of James Fenimore Cooper, dead. Though his best work was weakened by the sound of his fury, epic despair, and irrational quirks, he had achieved not only burlesque and bitter comedy but also high art. He wrote his masterpiece, Huckleberry Finn, *at a time when the lighthearted qualities of his earlier days were in balance with his later skepticism, and the novel has come to be recognized as one of the great works of American literature. It displayed the major achievements of his art: the carefully controlled point of view with its implicit ironies expressed through the voice of a semiliterate boy, the masterful use of dialects, the felicitous balancing of nostalgic romanticism and realism, humor and pathos, innocence and evil, all united for a journey down the river that serves as the mythic center of the novel. Originally judged to be simply another "boys' book" like* Tom Sawyer, *the story of Huck and Jim and the great river was roundly condemned as too indecent for innocent young eyes, but its inherent appeal, and its scandalous reputation, ensured its success, and it has become one of the most popular books of all times, selling millions of copies in editions printed throughout the world.*

Through such works as Huckleberry Finn *and* Life on the Mississippi *Twain shaped the world's view of America and had a profound impact on the development of American writing. His presentation of native American material, his use of the vernacular idiom, his departures from the traditions of nineteenth-century gentility, and his sense of alienation influenced numerous American writers of the twentieth century, among them Ernest Hemingway, who acknowledged their common debt by writing, "All modern American literature comes from one book by Mark Twain called* Huckleberry Finn . . . *it's the best book we've had. . . . There was nothing before. There has been nothing so good since."*

FURTHER READING: E. Wagenknecht, *Mark Twain, The Man and His Work,* 1935, 1961, 1967; J. Kaplan, *Mr. Clemens and Mark Twain,* 1966; J. Seelye, *The True Adventures of Huckleberry Finn,* 1970; *The Works of Mark Twain,* ed. J. Gerber, 1972–; H. Hill, *Mark Twain, God's Fool,* 1973, 1975; J. Wilson, *A Reader's Guide to the Short Stories of Mark Twain,* 1987; *Satire or Evasion? Black Perspectives on Huckleberry Finn,* ed. J. Leonard, T. Tenney, and T. Davis, 1992; *The Mark Twain Encyclopedia,* ed. J. LeMaster and J. Wilson, 1993; *The Cambridge Companion to Mark Twain,* ed. F. Robinson, 1995; *The Oxford Mark Twain,* 29 vols., ed. S. Fishkin, 1996; T. Quirk, *Mark Twain: A Study of the Short Fiction,* 1997; J. Chadwick-Joshua, *The Jim Dilemma, Reading Race in Huckleberry Finn,* 1998; *A Historical Guide to Mark Twain,* ed. S. Fishkin, 2002; *Constructing Mark Twain,* ed. L. Skandera-Trombley and M. Kiskis, 2002; G. Camfield, *The Oxford Reader's Companion to Mark Twain,* 2003; F. Kaplan,

The Singular Mark Twain, 2003; L. Ziff, *Mark Twain,* 2004; R. Powers, *Mark Twain, A Life,* 2005; K. Rasmussen, *Mark Twain A to Z,* 2005.

TEXTS: "The Dandy Frightening the Squatter," *Carpet-Bag,* May 1, 1852; "The Notorious Jumping Frog of Calaveras County," *Mark Twain's Sketches, New and Old,* 1875; "Whittier Birthday Dinner Speech," *Harvard Library Bulletin,* Spring 1955; *Adventures of Huckleberry Finn,* 1885.

THE DANDY FRIGHTENING THE SQUATTER[1]

BY S. L. C.

About thirteen years ago, when the now flourishing young city of Hannibal, on the Mississippi River, was but a "wood-yard," surrounded by a few huts, belonging to some hardy *"squatters,"* and such a thing as a steamboat was considered quite a sight, the following incident occurred:

A tall, brawny woodsman stood leaning against a tree which stood upon the bank of the river, gazing at some approaching object, which our readers would easily have discovered to be a steamboat.

About half an hour elapsed, and the boat was moored, and the hands busily engaged in taking on wood.

Now among the many passengers on this boat, both male and female, was a spruce young dandy, with a killing moustache, &c., who seemed bent on making an impression upon the hearts of the young ladies on board, and to do this, he thought he must perform some heroic deed. Observing our squatter friend, he imagined this to be a fine opportunity to bring himself into notice; so, stepping into the cabin,[2] he said:

"Ladies, if you wish to enjoy a good laugh, step out on the guards.[3] I intend to frighten that gentleman into fits who stands on the bank."

The ladies complied with the request, and our dandy drew from his bosom a formidable looking bowie-knife,[4] and thrust it into his belt; then, taking a large horse-pistol[5] in each hand, he seemed satisfied that all was right. Thus equipped, he strode on shore, with an air which seemed to say—"The hopes of a nation depend on me." Marching up to the woodsman, he exclaimed:

"Found you at last, have I? You are the very man I've been looking for these three weeks! Say your prayers!" he continued, presenting his pistols, "you'll make a capital barn door, and I shall drill the key-hole myself!"

The squatter calmly surveyed him a moment, and then, drawing back a step, he planted his huge fist directly between the eyes of his astonished antagonist, who, in a moment, was floundering in the turbid waters of the Mississippi.

Every passenger on the boat had by this time collected on the guards, and the shout that now went up from the crowd speedily restored the crest-fallen

[1]Published in the Boston *Carpet-Bag,* May 1, 1852, when Twain was sixteen years old. It was his first tale to be published and, with the exception of short contributions he may have made to the Hannibal papers, his first appearance in print.

[2]A large public room for the use of a ship's passengers.

[3]Sections of the deck that extend out from a ship's side.

[4]Hunting knife with a large blade, said to be named after Indian-fighter Jim Bowie.

[5]A large pistol usually carried in a holster attached to a horse saddle.

hero to his senses, and, as he was sneaking off towards the boat, was thus accosted by his conquerer:

"I say, yeou, next time yeou come around drillin' key-holes, don't forget yer old acquaintances!"

The ladies unanimously voted the knife and pistols to the victor.

1852

THE NOTORIOUS JUMPING FROG OF CALAVERAS[1] COUNTY

In compliance with the request of a friend of mine, who wrote me from the East, I called on good-natured, garrulous old Simon Wheeler, and inquired after my friend's friend, Leonidas W. Smiley, as requested to do, and I hereunto append the result. I have a lurking suspicion that *Leonidas W.* Smiley is a myth; that my friend never knew such a personage; and that he only conjectured that if I asked old Wheeler about him, it would remind him of his infamous *Jim* Smiley, and he would go to work and bore me to death with some exasperating reminiscence of him as long and as tedious as it should be useless to me. If that was the design, it succeeded.

I found Simon Wheeler dozing comfortably by the bar-room stove of the dilapidated tavern in the decayed mining camp of Angel's,[2] and I noticed that he was fat and bald-headed, and had an expression of winning gentleness and simplicity upon his tranquil countenance. He roused up, and gave me good day. I told him that a friend of mine had commissioned me to make some inquiries about a cherished companion of his boyhood named *Leonidas W.* Smiley—*Rev. Leonidas W.* Smiley, a young minister of the Gospel, who he had heard was at one time a resident of Angel's Camp. I added that if Mr. Wheeler could tell me anything about this Rev. Leonidas W. Smiley, I would feel under many obligations to him.

Simon Wheeler backed me into a corner and blockaded me there with his chair, and then sat down and reeled off the monotonous narrative which follows this paragraph. He never smiled, he never frowned, he never changed his voice from the gentle-flowing key to which he tuned his initial sentence, he never betrayed the slightest suspicion of enthusiasm; but all through the interminable narrative there ran a vein of impressive earnestness and sincerity, which showed me plainly that, so far from his imagining that there was anything ridiculous or funny about his story, he regarded it as a really important matter, and admired its two heroes as men of transcendent genius in *finesse.* I let him go on in his own way, and never interrupted him once.

"Rev. Leonidas W. H'm, Reverend Le—well, there was a feller here once by the name of *Jim* Smiley, in the winter of '49—or maybe it was the spring of '50—I don't recollect exactly, somehow, though what makes me think it was one or the other is because I remember the big flume[3] warn't finished when

[1]"Pronounced Cal-e-*va*-ras."—Twain's note. First published as "Jim Smiley and His Jumping Frog," in 1865. Later versions were titled "The Celebrated . . ." or, as here, "The Notorious Jumping Frog of Calaveras County."

[2]Angel's Camp, a mining settlement in Calaveras County, California.

[3]An inclined waterway, usually made of wood, through which water is carried for use in hydraulic mining.

he first come to the camp; but anyway, he was the curiousest man about always betting on anything that turned up you ever see, if he could get anybody to bet on the other side; and if he couldn't he'd change sides. Any way that suited the other man would suit *him*—any way just so's he got a bet, *he* was satisfied. But still he was lucky, uncommon lucky; he most always come out winner. He was always ready and laying for a chance; there couldn't be no solit'ry thing mentioned but that feller'd offer to bet on it, and take ary side you please, as I was just telling you. If there was a horse-race, you'd find him flush or you'd find him busted at the end of it; if there was a dog-fight, he'd bet on it; if there was a cat-fight, he'd bet on it; if there was a chicken-fight, he'd bet on it; why, if there was two birds setting on a fence, he would bet you which one would fly first; or if there was a camp-meeting, he would be there reg'lar to bet on Parson Walker, which he judged to be the best exhorter about here, and so he was too, and a good man. If he even see a straddle-bug[4] start to go anywheres, he would bet you how long it would take him to get to—to wherever he was going to, and if you took him up, he would foller that straddle-bug to Mexico but what he would find out where he was bound for and how long he was on the road. Lots of the boys here has seen that Smiley, and can tell you about him. Why, it never made no difference to *him*—he'd bet on *any* thing—the dangdest feller. Parson Walker's wife laid very sick once for a good while, and it seemed as if they warn't going to save her; but one morning he come in, and Smiley up and asked him how she was, and he said she was considerable better—thank the Lord for his inf'nite mercy—and coming on so smart that with the blessing of Prov'dence she'd get well yet; and Smiley, before he thought, says, 'Well, I'll resk two-and-a-half she don't anyway.'

"Thish-yer Smiley had a mare—the boys called her the fifteen-minute nag, but that was only in fun, you know, because of course she was faster than that—and he used to win money on that horse, for all she was so slow and always had the asthma, or the distemper, or the consumption, or something of that kind. They used to give her two or three hundred yards' start, and then pass her under way; but always at the fag end of the race she'd get excited and desperate like, and come cavorting and straddling up, and scattering her legs around limber, sometimes in the air, and sometimes out to one side among the fences, and kicking up m-o-r-e dust and raising m-o-r-e racket with her coughing and sneezing and blowing her nose—and *always* fetch up at the stand just about a neck ahead, as near as you could cipher it down.

"And he had a little small bull-pup, that to look at him you'd think he warn't worth a cent but to set around and look ornery and lay for a chance to steal something. But as soon as money was up on him he was a different dog; his under-jaw'd begin to stick out like the fo'castle of a steamboat, and his teeth would uncover and shine like the furnaces. And a dog might tackle him and bully-rag him, and bite him, and throw him over his shoulder two or three times, and Andrew Jackson—which was the name of the pup—Andrew Jackson would never let on but what *he* was satisfied, and hadn't expected nothing else—and the bets being doubled and doubled on the other side all the time, till the money was all up; and then all of a sudden he would grab that other dog jest by the j'int of his hind leg and freeze to it—not chaw, you understand, but only just grip and hang on till they throwed up the sponge, if it was a year.

[4]A beetle with long legs, a tumble-bug.

Smiley always come out winner on that pup, till he harnessed a dog once that didn't have no hind legs, because they'd been sawed off in a circular saw, and when the thing had gone along far enough, and the money was all up, and he come to make a snatch for his pet holt, he see in a minute how he'd been imposed on, and how the other dog had him in the door, so to speak, and he 'peared surprised, and then he looked sorter discouraged-like, and didn't try no more to win the fight, and so he got shucked out bad. He give Smiley a look, as much as to say his heart was broke, and it was *his* fault, for putting up a dog that hadn't no hind legs for him to take holt of, which was his main dependence in a fight, and then he limped off a piece and laid down and died. It was a good pup, was that Andrew Jackson, and would have made a name for hisself if he'd lived, for the stuff was in him and he had genius—I know it, because he hadn't no opportunities to speak of, and it don't stand to reason that a dog could make such a fight as he could under them circumstances if he hadn't no talent. It always makes me feel sorry when I think of that last fight of his'n, and the way it turned out.

"Well, thish-yer Smiley had rat-tarriers, and chicken cocks, and tomcats and all them kind of things, till you couldn't rest, and you couldn't fetch nothing for him to bet on but he'd match you. He ketched a frog one day, and took him home, and said he cal'lated to educate him; and so he never done nothing for three months but set in his back yard and learn that frog to jump. And you bet you he *did* learn him, too. He'd give him a little punch behind, and the next minute you'd see that frog whirling in the air like a doughnut—see him turn one summerset,[5] or maybe a couple, if he got a good start, and come down flat-footed and all right, like a cat. He got him up so in the matter of ketching flies, and kep' him in practice so constant, that he'd nail a fly every time as fur as he could see him. Smiley said all a frog wanted was education, and he could do 'most anything—and I believe him. Why, I've seen him set Dan'l Webster down here on this floor—Dan'l Webster was the name of the frog—and sing out, "Flies, Dan'l, flies!" and quicker'n you could wink he'd spring straight up and snake a fly off'n the counter there, and flop down on the floor ag'in as solid as a gob of mud, and fall to scratching the side of his head with his hind foot as indifferent as if he hadn't no idea he'd been doin' any more'n any frog might do. You never see a frog so modest and straightfor'ard as he was, for all he was so gifted. And when it come to fair and square jumping on a dead level, he could get over more ground at one straddle than any animal of his breed you ever see. Jumping on a dead level was his strong suit, you understand; and when it come to that, Smiley would ante up money on him as long as he had a red.[6] Smiley was monstrous proud of his frog, and well he might be, for fellers that had traveled and been everywheres all said he laid over any frog that ever *they* see.

"Well, Smiley kep' the beast in a little lattice box, and he used to fetch him down-town sometimes and lay for a bet. One day a feller—a stranger in the camp, he was—come acrost him with his box, and says:

"'What might it be that you've got in the box?'

"And Smiley says, sorter indifferent-like, 'It might be a parrot, or it might be a canary, maybe, but it ain't—it's only just a frog.'

[5]Somersault.

[6]A "red cent," a copper penny.

"And the feller took it, and looked at it careful, and turned it round this way and that, and says, 'H'm—so 'tis. Well, what's *he* good for?'

"'Well,' Smiley says, easy and careless, 'he's good enough for *one* thing, I should judge—he can outjump any frog in Calaveras County.'

"The feller took the box again, and took another long, particular look, and give it back to Smiley, and says, very deliberate, 'Well,' he says, 'I don't see no p'ints about that frog that's any better'n any other frog.'

"'Maybe you don't,' Smiley says. 'Maybe you understand frogs and maybe you don't understand 'em; maybe you've had experience, and maybe you ain't only a amature, as it were. Anyways, I've got *my* opinion, and I'll resk forty dollars that he can outjump any frog in Calaveras County.'

"And the feller studied a minute, and then says, kinder sad-like, 'Well, I'm only a stranger here, and I ain't got no frog; but if I had a frog, I'd bet you.'

"And then Smiley says, 'That's all right—that's all right—if you'll hold my box a minute, I'll go and get you a frog.' And so the feller took the box, and put up his forty dollars along with Smiley's, and set down to wait.

"So he set there a good while thinking and thinking to himself, and then he got the frog out and prized his mouth open and took a teaspoon and filled him full of quail-shot—filled him pretty near up to his chin—and set him on the floor. Smiley he went to the swamp and slopped around in the mud for a long time, and finally he ketched a frog, and fetched him in, and give him to this feller, and says:

"Now, if you're ready, set him alongside of Dan'l, with his fore paws just even with Dan'l's, and I'll give the word.' Then he says, 'One—two—three *git!*' and him and the feller touched up the frogs from behind, and the new frog hopped off lively, but Dan'l give a heave, and hysted up his shoulders—so—like a Frenchman, but it warn't no use—he couldn't budge; he was planted as solid as a church, and he couldn't no more stir than if he was anchored out. Smiley was a good deal surprised, and he was disgusted too, but he didn't have no idea what the matter was, of course.

"The feller took the money and started away; and when he was going out at the door, he sorter jerked his thumb over his shoulder—so—at Dan'l, and says again, very deliberate, 'Well,' he says, '*I* don't see no p'ints about that frog that's any better'n any other frog.'

"Smiley he stood scratching his head and looking down at Dan'l a long time, and at last he says, 'I do wonder what in the nation[7] that frog throw'd off for—I wonder if there ain't something the matter with him—he 'pears to look mighty baggy, somehow.' And he ketched Dan'l by the nap of the neck, and hefted him, and says, "Why blame my cats if he don't weigh five pound!" and turned him upside down and he belched out a double handful of shot. And then he see how it was, and he was the maddest man—he set the frog down and took out after that feller, but he never ketched him. And—"

[Here Simon Wheeler heard his name called from the front yard, and got up to see what was wanted.] And turning to me as he moved away, he said: "Just set where you are, stranger, and rest easy—I ain't going to be gone a second."

But, by your leave, I did not think that a continuation of the history of the enterprising vagabond *Jim* Smiley would be likely to afford me much information concerning the Rev. *Leonidas W.* Smiley, and so I started away.

At the door I met the sociable Wheeler returning, and he button-holed me and recommenced:

[7]Euphemism for "damnation."

"Well, thish-yer Smiley had a yaller one-eyed cow that didn't have no tail, only just a short stump like a bannanner, and—"

However, lacking both time and inclination, I did not wait to hear about the afflicted cow, but took my leave.

1865

WHITTIER BIRTHDAY DINNER SPEECH[1]

Mr. Chairman—This is an occasion peculiarly meet for the digging up of pleasant reminiscences concerning literary folk; therefore I will drop lightly into history myself. Standing here on the shore of the Atlantic & contemplating certain of its biggest literary billows, I am reminded of a thing which happened to me fifteen years ago, when I had just succeeded in stirring up a little Nevadian literary ocean-puddle myself, whose spume-flakes were beginning to blow thinly California-wards. I started on an inspection-tramp through the Southern mines of California. I was callow & conceited, & I resolved to try the virtue of my nom de plume. I very soon had an opportunity. I knocked at a miner's lonely log cabin in the foothills of the Sierras just at nightfall. It was snowing at the time. A jaded, melancholy man of fifty, barefooted, opened to me. When he heard my nom de plume, he looked more dejected than before. He let me in—pretty reluctantly, I thought—& after the customary bacon & beans, black coffee & a hot whiskey, I took a pipe. This sorrowful man had not said three words up to this time. Now he spoke up & said in the voice of one who is secretly suffering, "You're the fourth—I'm a-going to move." "The fourth what?" said I. "The fourth littery man that's been here in twenty-four hours—I'm a-going to move." "You don't tell me!" said I; "Who were the others?" "Mr. Longfellow, Mr. Emerson, & Mr. Oliver Wendell Holmes—dad fetch the lot!"

THE MINER'S STORY

You can easily believe I was interested.—I supplicated—three hot whiskies did the rest—& finally the melancholy miner began. Said he—

They came here just at dark yesterday evening, & I let them in, of course. Said they were going to Yo Semite.[2] They were a rough lot—but that's nothing—everybody looks rough that travels afoot. Mr. Emerson was a seedy little bit of a chap—red headed. Mr. Holmes was as fat as a balloon—he weighed as much as three hundred, & had double chins all the way down to his stomach. Mr. Longfellow was built like a prize fighter. His head was cropped & bristly—like as if he had a wig made of hair-brushes. His nose lay straight down his face, like a finger, with the end-joint tilted up. They had been drinking—I could see that.

And what queer talk they used! Mr. Holmes inspected this cabin, then he took me by the button-hole, & says he—

"Through the deep caves of thought
I hear a voice that sings:

[1]On December 17, 1877, Twain spoke at a dinner in Boston commemorating the seventieth birthday of John Greenleaf Whittier. Twain intended his speech to be a triumph of humor. But the effect of his irreverent words on the august audience, which included Longfellow, Emerson, and Holmes, created what Twain later described as "a sort of black frost."

[2]Yosemite Valley, in California.

Build thee more stately mansions,
O my Soul!"[3]

Says I, "I can't afford it, Mr. Holmes, & moreover I don't want to." Blamed if I liked it pretty well, either, coming from a stranger, that way! However, I started to get out my bacon & beans, when Mr. Emerson came & looked on a while, & then *he* takes me aside by the button-hole & says—

"Give me agates for my meat;
Give me cantharides[4] to eat;
From air & ocean bring me foods,
From all zones & altitudes."[5]

Says I, "Mr. Emerson, if you'll excuse me, this ain't no hotel." You see it sort of riled me—I warn't used to the ways of littery swells. But I went on a-sweating over my work, & next comes Mr. Longfellow & button-holes me, & interrupts me. Says he—

"Honor be to Mudjekeewis!
You shall hear how Pau-Puk-Kee-wis—"[6]

But I broke in, & says I, "Begging your pardon, Mr. Longfellow, if you'll be so kind as to hold your yawp for about five minutes, & let me get this grub ready, you'll do me proud." Well, sir, after they'd filled up, I set out the jug. Mr. Holmes looks at it, & then he fires up all of a sudden & yells—

"Flash out a stream of blood-red wine!—
For I would drink to other days."[7]

By George, I was getting kind of worked up. I don't deny it, I was getting kind of worked up. I turns to Mr. Holmes, & says I, "Looky-here, my fat friend, I'm a-running this shanty, & if the court knows herself, you'll take whiskey-straight or you'll go dry!" Them's the very words I said to him. Now I didn't want to sass such famous littery people, but you see they kind of forced me. There ain't nothing onreasonable, 'bout me; I don't mind a passel of guests a-tread'n on my tail three or four times, but when it comes to *standing* on it, it's different. Well, between drinks they'd swell around the cabin & strike attitudes & spout. Says Mr. Longfellow—

"This is the forest primeval."[8]

Says Mr. Emerson—

"Here once the embattled farmers stood,
And fired the shot heard round the world."[9]

Says I, "O, blackguard the premises as much as you want to—it don't cost you a cent." Well they went on drinking, & pretty soon they got out a greasy old deck & went to playing cut-throat euchre at ten cents a corner—on trust. I begun to notice some pretty suspicious things. Mr. Emerson dealt, looked at his hand, shook his head, says—

"I am the doubter & the doubt—"

[3]From "The Chambered Nautilus," by Oliver Wendell Holmes. Twain has altered several of the following quotations for burlesque effect.
[4]An aphrodisiac, commonly called Spanish fly. [5]Emerson, "Mithridates."
[6]Longfellow, "Hiawatha." [7]Holmes, "Mare Rubrum." [8]Longfellow, "Evangeline."
[9]Emerson, "Concord Hymn."

—& calmly bunched the hands & went to shuffling for a new layout. Says he—

"They reckon ill who leave me out;
They know not well the subtle ways
I keep.———— I pass, & deal *again!*"[10]

Hang'd if he didn't go ahead & do it, too! O, he was a cool one! Well, in about a minute, things were running pretty tight, but all of a sudden I see by Mr. Emerson's eye that he judged he had 'em. He had already corralled two tricks, & each of the others one. So now he kinds of lifts a little, in his chair, & says—

"I tire of globes & aces!—
Too long the game is played!"[11]

—and down he fetches a right bower. Mr. Longfellow smiles as sweet as pie, & says—:

"Thanks, thanks to thee, my worthy friend,
For the lesson thou hast taught!"[12]

—and dog my cats if he didn't down with *another* right bower! Well, sir, up jumps Holmes, a war-whooping, as usual, & says—

"God help them if the tempest swings
The pine against the palm!"[13]

—and I wish I may go to grass if he didn't swoop down with *another* right bower! Emerson claps his hand on his bowie, Longfellow claps his on his revolver, & I went under a bunk. There was going to be trouble; but that monstrous Holmes rose up, wobbling his double chins, & says he, "Order, gentlemen; the first man that draws, I'll lay down on him & smother him!" All quiet on the Potomac, you bet you! They were pretty how-come-you-so, now, & they begun to blow. Emerson says, "The bulliest thing I ever wrote, was Barbara Frietchie."[14] Says Longfellow, "It don't begin with my Biglow Papers."[15] Says Holmes, "My Thanatopsis[16] lays over 'em both." They mighty near ended in a fight. Then they wished they had some more company—& Mr. Emerson pointed at me & says—

Is yonder squalid peasant all
That this proud nursery could breed?"[17]

He was a-whetting his bowie on his boot—so I let it pass. Well, sir, next they took it into their heads that they would like some music; so they made me stand up & sing "When Johnny Comes Marching Home" till I dropped—at thirteen minutes past four this morning. That's what I've been through, my friend. When I woke at seven, they were leaving, thank goodness, & Mr. Longfellow had my only boots on, & his own under his arm. Says I, "Hold on, there, Evangeline, what you going to do with *them?*"—He says: "Going to make tracks with 'em; because—

[10]Emerson, "Brahma." [11]Emerson, "Song of Nature." [12]Longfellow, "The Village Blacksmith."
[13]Holmes, "A Voice of the Loyal North." [14]Barbara Frietchie," by John Greenleaf Whittier.
[15]"The Biglow Papers," by James Russell Lowell. [16]"Thanatopsis," by William Cullen Bryant.
[17]Emerson, "Monadnoc."

'Lives of great men all remind us
We can make our lives sublime;
And departing, leave behind us
Footprints on the sands of Time.' "[18]

[As I said, Mr. Twain, you are the fourth in twenty-four hours—and I'm going to move; I ain't suited to a][19] littery atmosphere.

I said to the miner, "Why my dear sir, *these* were not the gracious singers to whom we & the world pay loving reverence & homage: these were imposters." The miner investigated me with a calm eye for a while, then said he, "Ah—imposters, were they? are *you?*" I did—not pursue the subject; and since then I haven't traveled on my nom de plume enough to hurt. Such is the reminiscence I was moved to contribute, Mr. Chairman. In my enthusiasm I may have exaggerated the details a little, but you will easily forgive me that fault since I believe it is the first time I have ever deflected from perpendicular fact on an occasion like this.

1877

ADVENTURES OF HUCKLEBERRY FINN[1]

(Tom Sawyer's Comrade)

Scene: The Mississippi

Time: Forty to Fifty Years Ago[2]

NOTICE

Persons attempting to find a motive in this narrative will be prosecuted; persons attempting to find a moral in it will be banished; persons attempting to find a plot in it will be shot.

BY ORDER OF THE AUTHOR
PER G.G.,[1] CHIEF OF ORDNANCE.

EXPLANATORY

In this book a number of dialects are used, to wit: the Missouri negro dialect; the extremest form of the backwoods South-Western dialect; the ordinary "Pike-County"[1] dialect; and four modified varieties of this last. The shadings have not been done in a haphazard fashion, or by guess-work; but painstakingly, and with the trustworthy guidance and support of personal familiarity with these several forms of speech.

I make this explanation for the reason that without it many readers would suppose that all these characters were trying to talk alike and not succeeding.

THE AUTHOR

[18]Longfellow, "A Psalm of Life."

[19]A portion of the manuscript is missing here. The bracketed insertion is taken from the version of the speech Twain included in his Autobiographical Dictation.

[1]The text is taken from the first American edition (1885). A small number of typographical errors have been silently corrected. [2]1845–1835.

[1]Twain probably refers to General Ulysses S. Grant (1822–1885). [1]In Missouri.

CHAPTER I

You don't know about me, without you have read a book by the name of "The Adventures of Tom Sawyer,"[1] but that ain't no matter. That book was made by Mr. Mark Twain, and he told the truth, mainly. There was things which he stretched, but mainly he told the truth. That is nothing. I never seen anybody but lied, one time or another, without it was Aunt Polly, or the widow, or maybe Mary.[2] Aunt Polly—Tom's Aunt Polly, she is—and Mary, and the Widow Douglas, is all told about in that book—which is mostly a true book; with some stretchers, as I said before.

Now the way that the book winds up, is this: Tom and me found the money that the robbers hid in the cave, and it made us rich. We got six thousand dollars apiece—all gold. It was an awful sight of money when it was piled up. Well, Judge Thatcher, he took it and put it out at interest, and it fetched us a dollar a day apiece, all the year round—more than a body could tell what to do with. The Widow Douglas, she took me for her son, and allowed she would sivilize me; but it was rough living in the house all the time, considering how dismal regular and decent the widow was in all her ways; and so when I couldn't stand it no longer, I lit out. I got into my old rags, and my sugar-hogshead[3] again, and was free and satisfied. But Tom Sawyer, he hunted me up and said he was going to start a band of robbers, and I might join if I would go back to the widow and be respectable. So I went back.

The widow she cried over me, and called me a poor lost lamb, and she called me a lot of other names, too, but she never meant no harm by it. She put me in them new clothes again, and I couldn't do nothing but sweat and sweat, and feel all cramped up. Well, then, the old thing commenced again. The widow rung a bell for supper, and you had to come to time. When you got to the table you couldn't go right to eating, but you had to wait for the widow to tuck down her head and grumble a little over the victuals, though there warn't really anything the matter with them. That is, nothing only everything was cooked by itself. In a barrel of odds and ends it is different; things get mixed up, and the juice kind of swaps around, and the things go better.

After supper she got out her book and learned me about Moses and the Bulrushers;[4] and I was in a sweat to find out all about him; but by-and-by she let it out that Moses had been dead a considerable long time; so then I didn't care no more about him; because I don't take no stock in dead people.

Pretty soon I wanted to smoke, and asked the widow to let me. But she wouldn't. She said it was a mean practice and wasn't clean, and I must try to not do it any more. That is just the way with some people. They get down on a thing when they don't know nothing about it. Here she was a bothering about Moses, which was no kin to her, and no use to anybody, being gone, you see, yet finding a power of fault with me for doing a thing that had some good in it. And she took snuff too; of course that was all right, because she done it herself.

[1]Published in 1876.
[2]Tom Sawyer's cousin.
[3]A large barrel.
[4]The daughter of Pharaoh found the infant Moses in a basket made of bulrushes (Exodus 2:1–10).

Her sister, Miss Watson, a tolerable slim old maid, with goggles on, had just come to live with her, and took a set at me now, with a spelling-book. She worked me middling hard for about an hour, and then the widow made her ease up. I couldn't stood it much longer. Then for an hour it was deadly dull, and I was fidgety. Miss Watson would say, "Don't put your feet up there, Huckleberry;" and "don't scrunch up like that, Huckleberry—set up straight;" and pretty soon she would say, "Don't gap[5] and stretch like that, Huckleberry—why don't you try to behave?" Then she told me all about the bad place, and I said I wished I was there. She got mad, then, but I didn't mean no harm. All I wanted was to go somewheres; all I wanted was a change, I warn't particular. She said it was wicked to say what I said; said she wouldn't say it for the whole world; *she* was going to live so as to go to the good place. Well, I couldn't see no advantage in going where she was going, so I made up my mind I wouldn't try for it. But I never said so, because it would only make trouble, and wouldn't do no good.

Now she had got a start, and she went on and told me all about the good place. She said all a body would have to do there was to go around all day long with a harp and sing, forever and ever. So I didn't think much of it. But I never said so. I asked her if she reckoned Tom Sawyer would go there, and, she said, not by a considerable sight. I was glad about that, because I wanted him and me to be together.

Miss Watson she kept pecking at me, and it got tiresome and lonesome. By-and-by they fetched the niggers[6] in and had prayers, and then everybody was off to bed. I went up to my room with a piece of candle and put it on the table. Then I set down in a chair by the window and tried to think of something cheerful, but it warn't no use. I felt so lonesome I most wished I was dead. The stars was shining, and the leaves rustled in the woods ever so mournful; and I heard an owl, away off, who-whooing about somebody that was dead, and a whippowill and a dog crying about somebody that was going to die; and the wind was trying to whisper something to me and I couldn't make out what it was, and so it made the cold shivers run over me. Then away out in the woods I heard that kind of a sound that a ghost makes when it wants to tell about something that's on its mind and can't make itself understood, and so can't rest easy in its grave and has to go about that way every night grieving. I got so down-hearted and scared, I did wish I had some company. Pretty soon a spider went crawling up my shoulder, and I flipped it off and it lit in the candle; and before I could budge it was all shriveled up. I didn't need anybody to tell me that that was an awful bad sign and would fetch me some bad luck, so I was scared and most shook the clothes off of me. I got up and turned around in my tracks three times and crossed my breast every time; and then I tied up a little lock of my hair with a thread to keep witches away. But I hadn't no confidence. You do that when you've lost a horseshoe that you've found, instead of nailing it up over the

[5]Yawn.

[6]I.e., slaves. "Nigger" (a corruption of "Negro") is considered abusive today. In pre–Civil War America it was widely used merely as a synonym for "slave." The presence of the term throughout the novel is not a sign of intolerance on the part of Twain, as has sometimes been charged, but of his effort to reproduce accurately the common speech of mid-nineteenth-century Americans, both black and white.

door, but I hadn't ever heard anybody say it was any way to keep off bad luck when you'd killed a spider.

I set down again, a shaking all over, and got out my pipe for a smoke; for the house was all as still as death, now, and so the widow wouldn't know. Well, after a long time I heard the clock away off in the town go boom—boom—boom—twelve licks—and all still again—stiller than ever. Pretty soon I heard a twig snap, down in the dark amongst the trees—something was a stirring. I set still and listened. Directly I could just barely hear a *"me-yow me-yow!"* down there. That was good Says I, *"me-yow me-yow"* as soft as I could, and then I put out the light and scrambled out of the window onto the shed. Then I slipped down to the ground and crawled in amongst the trees, and sure enough there was Tom Sawyer waiting for me.

CHAPTER II

We went tip-toeing along a path amongst the trees back towards the end of the widow's garden, stooping down so as the branches wouldn't scrape our heads. When we was passing by the kitchen I fell over a root and made a noise. We scrouched down and laid still. Miss Watson's big nigger, named Jim, was setting in the kitchen door; we could see him pretty clear, because there was a light behind him. He got up and stretched his neck out about a minute, listening. Then he says,

"Who dah?"

He listened some more; then he come tip-toeing down and stood right between us; we could a touched him, nearly. Well, likely it was minutes and minutes that there warn't a sound, and we all there so close together. There was a place on my ankle that got to itching; but I dasn't scratch it; and then my ear begun to itch; and next my back, right between my shoulders. Seemed like I'd die if I couldn't scratch. Well, I've noticed that thing plenty of times since. If you are with the quality,[1] or at a funeral, or trying to go to sleep when you ain't sleepy—if you are anywheres where it won't do for you to scratch, why you will itch all over in upwards of a thousand places. Pretty soon Jim says:

"Say—who is you? Whar is you? Dog my cats ef I didn't hear sumf'n. Well, I knows what I's gwyne to do. I's gwyne to set down here and listen tell I hears it agin."

So he set down on the ground betwixt me and Tom. He leaned his back up against a tree, and stretched his legs out till one of them most touched one of mine. My nose begun to itch. It itched till the tears come into my eyes. But I dasn't scratch. Then it begun to itch on the inside. Next I got to itching underneath. I didn't know how I was going to set still. This miserableness went on as much as six or seven minutes; but it seemed a sight longer than that. I was itching in eleven different places now. I reckoned I couldn't stand it more'n a minute longer, but I set my teeth hard and got ready to try. Just then Jim begun to breathe heavy; next he begun to snore—and then I was pretty soon comfortable agin.

[1]I.e., quality people, the upper classes.

Tom he made a sign to me—kind of a little noise with his mouth—and we went creeping away on our hands and knees. When we was ten foot off, Tom whispered to me and wanted to tie Jim to the tree for fun; but I said no; he might wake and make a disturbance, and then they'd find out I warn't in. Then Tom said he hadn't got candles enough, and he would slip in the kitchen and get some more. I didn't want him to try. I said Jim might wake up and come. But Tom wanted to resk it; so we slid in there and got three candles, and Tom laid five cents on the table for pay. Then we got out, and I was in a sweat to get away; but nothing would do Tom but he must crawl to where Jim was, on his hands and knees, and play something on him. I waited, and it seemed a good while, everything was so still and lonesome.

As soon as Tom was back, we cut along the path, around the garden fence, and by-and-by fetched up on the steep top of the hill the other side of the house. Tom said he slipped Jim's hat off of his head and hung it on a limb right over him, and Jim stirred a little, but he didn't wake. Afterwards Jim said the witches bewitched him and put him in a trance, and rode him all over the State, and then set him under the trees again and hung his hat on a limb to show who done it. And next time Jim told it he said they rode him down to New Orleans: and after that, every time he told it he spread it more and more, till by-and-by he said they rode him all over the world, and tired him most to death, and his back was all over saddle-boils. Jim was monstrous proud about it, and he got so he wouldn't hardly notice the other niggers. Niggers would come miles to hear Jim tell about it, and he was more looked up to than any nigger in that country. Strange niggers would stand with their mouths open and look him all over, same as if he was a wonder. Niggers is always talking about witches in the dark by the kitchen fire; but whenever one was talking and letting on to know all about such things, Jim would happen in and say, "H'm! What you know 'bout witches?" and that nigger was corked up and had to take a back seat. Jim always kept that five-center piece around his neck with a string and said it was a charm the devil give to him with his own hands and told him he could cure anybody with it and fetch witches whenever he wanted to, just by saying something to it; but he never told what it was he said to it. Niggers would come from all around there and give Jim anything they had, just for a sight of that five-center piece; but they wouldn't touch it, because the devil had had his hands on it. Jim was most ruined, for a servant, because he got so stuck up on account of having seen the devil and been rode by witches.

Well, when Tom and me got to the edge of the hill-top, we looked away down into the village and could see three or four lights twinkling, where there was sick folks, may be; and the stars over us was sparkling ever so fine; and down by the village was the river, a whole mile broad, and awful still and grand. We went down the hill and found Jo Harper, and Ben Rogers, and two or three more of the boys, hid in the old tanyard. So we unhitched a skiff[2] and pulled down the river two mile and a half, to the big scar on the hillside, and went ashore.

We went to a clump of bushes, and Tom made everybody swear to keep the secret, and then showed them a hole in the hill, right in the thickest part of

[2]A flat-bottomed rowboat.

the bushes. Then we lit the candles and crawled in on our hands and knees. We went about two hundred yards, and then the cave opened up. Tom poked about amongst the passages and pretty soon ducked under a wall where you wouldn't a noticed that there was a hole. We went along a narrow place and got into a kind of room, all damp and sweaty and cold, and there we stopped. Tom says:

"Now we'll start this band of robbers and call it Tom Sawyer's Gang. Everybody that wants to join has got to take an oath, and write his name in blood."

Everybody was willing. So Tom got out a sheet of paper that he had wrote the oath on, and read it. It swore every boy to stick to the band, and never tell any of the secrets; and if anybody done anything to any boy in the band, whichever boy was ordered to kill that person and his family must do it, and he mustn't eat and he mustn't sleep till he had killed them and hacked a cross in their breasts, which was the sign of the band. And nobody that didn't belong to the band could use that mark, and if he did he must be sued; and if he done it again he must be killed. And if anybody that belonged to the band told the secrets, he must have his throat cut, and then have his carcass burnt up and the ashes scattered all around, and his name blotted off the list with blood and never mentioned again by the gang, but have a curse put on it and be forgot, forever.

Everybody said it was a real beautiful oath, and asked Tom if he got it out of his own head. He said, some of it, but the rest was out of pirate books, and robber books, and every gang that was hightoned had it.

Some thought it would be good to kill the *families* of boys that told the secrets. Tom said it was a good idea, so he took a pencil and wrote it in. Then Ben Rogers says:

"Here's Huck Finn, he hain't got no family—what you going to do 'bout him?"

"Well, hain't he got a father?" says Tom Sawyer.

"Yes, he's got a father, but you can't never find him, these days. He used to lay drunk with the hogs in the tanyard, but he hain't been seen in these parts for a year or more."

They talked it over, and they was going to rule me out, because they said every boy must have a family or somebody to kill, or else it wouldn't be fair and square for the others. Well, nobody could think of anything to do—everybody was stumped, and set still. I was most ready to cry; but all at once I thought of a way, and so I offered them Miss Watson—they could kill her. Everybody said:

"Oh, she'll do, she'll do. That's all right. Huck can come in."

Then they all stuck a pin in their fingers to get blood to sign with, and I made my mark on the paper.

"Now," says Ben Rogers, "what's the line of business of this Gang?"

"Nothing only robbery and murder," Tom said.

"But who are we going to rob? houses—or cattle—or——"

"Stuff! stealing cattle and such things ain't robbery, it's burglary," says Tom Sawyer. "We ain't burglars. That ain't no sort of style. We are highwaymen. We stop stages and carriages on the road, with masks on, and kill the people and take their watches and money."

"Must we always kill the people?"

"Oh, certainly. It's best. Some authorities think different, but mostly it's considered best to kill them. Except some that you bring to the cave here and keep them till they're ransomed."

"Ransomed? What's that?"

"I don't know. But that's what they do. I've seen it in books; and so of course that's what we've got to do."

"But how can we do it if we don't know what it is?"

"Why blame[3] it all, we've *got* to do it. Don't I tell you it's in the books? Do you want to go to doing different from what's in the books, and get things all muddled up?"

"Oh, that's all very fine to *say,* Tom Sawyer, but how in the nation[4] are these fellows going to be ransomed if we don't know how to do it to them? that's the thing *I* want to get at. Now what do you *reckon* it is?"

"Well, I don't know. But per'aps if we keep them till they're ransomed, it means that we keep them till they're dead."

"Now, that's something *like.* That'll answer. Why couldn't you said that before? We'll keep them till they ransomed to death—and a bothersome lot they'll be, too, eating up everything and always trying to get loose."

"How you talk, Ben Rogers. How can they get loose when there's a guard over them, ready to shoot them down if they move a peg?"

"A guard. Well that *is* good. So somebody's got to set up all night and never get any sleep, just so as to watch them. I think that's foolishness. Why can't a body take a club and ransom them as soon as they get here?"

"Because it ain't in the books so—that's why. Now Ben Rogers, do you want to do things regular, or don't you?—that's the idea. Don't you reckon that the people that made the books knows what's the correct thing to do? Do you reckon *you* can learn 'em anything? Not by a good deal. No, sir, we'll just go on and ransom them in the regular way."

"All right. I don't mind; but I say it's a fool way, anyhow. Say—do we kill the women, too?"

"Well, Ben Rogers, if I was as ignorant as you I wouldn't let on. Kill the women? No—nobody ever saw anything in the books like that. You fetch them to the cave, and you're always as polite as pie to them; and by-and-by they fall in love with you and never want to go home any more."

"Well, if that's the way, I'm agreed, but I don't take no stock in it. Mighty soon we'll have the cave so cluttered up with women, and fellows waiting to be ransomed, that there won't be no place for the robbers. But go ahead, I ain't got nothing to say."

Little Tommy Barnes was asleep, now, and when they waked him up he was scared, and cried, and said he wanted to go home to his ma, and didn't want to be a robber any more.

So they all made fun of him, and called him cry-baby, and that made him mad, and he said he would go straight and tell all the secrets. But Tom give him five cents to keep quiet, and said we would all go home and meet next week and rob somebody and kill some people.

Ben Rogers said he couldn't get out much, only Sundays, and so he wanted to begin next Sunday; but all the boys said it would be wicked to do it on Sunday, and that settled the thing. They agreed to get together and fix a day

[3]Euphemism for "damn." [4]Euphemism for "damnation."

as soon as they could, and then we elected Tom Sawyer first captain and Jo Harper second captain of the Gang, and so started home.

I clumb up the shed and crept into my window just before day was breaking. My new clothes was all greased up and clayey, and I was dog-tired.

CHAPTER III

Well, I got a good going-over in the morning, from old Miss Watson, on account of my clothes; but the widow she didn't scold, but only cleaned off the grease and clay and looked so sorry that I thought I would behave a while if I could. Then Miss Watson she took me in the closet[1] and prayed, but nothing come of it. She told me to pray every day, and whatever I asked for I would get it. But it warn't so. I tried it. Once I got a fish-line, but no hooks. It warn't any good to me without hooks. I tried for the hooks three or four times, but somehow I couldn't make it work. By-and-by, one day, I asked Miss Watson to try for me, but she said I was a fool. She never told me why, and I couldn't make it out no way.

I set down, one time, back in the woods, and had a long think about it. I says to myself, if a body can get anything they pray for, why don't Deacon Winn get back the money he lost on pork? Why can't the widow get back her silver snuff-box that was stole? Why can't Miss Watson fat up? No, says I to myself, there ain't nothing in it. I went and told the widow about it, and she said the thing a body could get by praying for it was "spiritual gifts." This was too many for me, but she told me what she meant—I must help other people, and do everything I could for other people, and look out for them all the time, and never think about myself. This was including Miss Watson, as I took it. I went out in the woods and turned it over in my mind a long time, but I couldn't see no advantage about it—except for the other people—so at last I reckoned I wouldn't worry about it any more, but just let it go. Sometimes the widow would take me one side and talk about Providence in a way to make a body's mouth water; but maybe next day Miss Watson would take hold and knock it all down again. I judged I could see that there was two Providences, and a poor chap would stand considerable show with the widow's Providence, but if Miss Watson's got him there warn't no help for him any more. I thought it all out, and reckoned I would belong to the widow's, if he wanted me, though I couldn't make out how he was agoing to be any better off then than what he was before, seeing I was so ignorant and so kind of low-down and ornery.

Pap he hadn't been seen for more than a year, and that was comfortable for me; I didn't want to see him no more. He used to always whale me when he was sober and could get his hands on me; though I used to take to the woods most of the time when he was around. Well, about this time he was found in the river drowned, about twelve mile above town, so people said. They judged it was him, anyway; said this drowned man was just his size, and was ragged, and had uncommon long hair—which was all like pap—but they couldn't make nothing out of the face, because it had been in the water so long it warn't much like a face at all. They said he was floating on his back

[1]"When thou prayest, enter into thy closet. . . ." (Matthew 6:6).

in the water. They took him and buried him on the bank. But I warn't comfortable long, because I happened to think of something. I knowed mighty well that a drownded man don't float on his back, but on his face. So I knowed then, that this warn't pap, but a woman dressed up in a man's clothes. So I was uncomfortable again. I judged the old man would turn up again by-and-by, though I wished he wouldn't.

We played robber now and then about a month, and then I resigned. All the boys did. We hadn't robbed nobody, we hadn't killed any people, but only just pretended. We used to hop out of the woods and go charging down on hogdrovers and women in carts taking garden stuff to market, but we never hived[2] any of them. Tom Sawyer called the hogs "ingots," and he called the turnips and stuff "julery" and we would go to the cave and pow-wow[3] over what we had done and how many people we had killed and marked. But I couldn't see no profit in it. One time Tom sent a boy to run about town with a blazing stick, which he called a slogan (which was the sign for the Gang to get together), and then he said he had got secret news by his spies that next day a whole parcel of Spanish merchants and rich A-rabs was going to camp in Cave Hollow with two hundred elephants, and six hundred camels, and over a thousand "sumter" mules,[4] all loaded down with di'monds, and they didn't have only a guard of four hundred soldiers, and so we would lay in ambuscade, as he called it, and kill the lot and scoop the things. He said we must slick up our swords and guns, and get ready. He never could go after even a turnip-cart but he must have the swords and guns all scoured up for it; though they was only lath and broom-sticks, and you might scour at them till you rotted and then they warn't worth a mouthful of ashes more than what they was before. I didn't believe we could lick such a crowd of Spaniards and A-rabs, but I wanted to see the camels and elephants, so I was on hand next day, Saturday, in the ambuscade; and when we got the word, we rushed out of the woods and down the hill. But there warn't no Spaniards and A-rabs, and there warn't no camels nor no elephants. It warn't anything but a Sunday-school picnic, and only a primer-class[5] at that. We busted it up, and chased the children up the hollow; but we never got anything but some doughnuts and jam, though Ben Rogers got a rag doll, and Jo Harper got a hymn-book and a tract; and then the teacher charged in and made us drop everything and cut. I didn't see no di'monds, and I told Tom Sawyer so. He said there was loads of them there, anyway; and he said there was A-rabs there, too, and elephants and things. I said, why couldn't we see them, then? He said if I warn't so ignorant, but had read a book called "Don Quixote,"[6] I would know without asking. He said it was all done by enchantment. He said there was hundreds of soldiers there, and elephants and treasure, and so on, but we had enemies which he called magicians, and they had turned the whole thing into an infant Sunday School, just out of spite. I said, all right, then the thing for us to do was to go for the magicians. Tom Sawyer said I was a numskull.

[2]Got, captured. [3]Talk. [4]Pack mules. [5]First grade.

[6]Cervantes' novel, published in 1605. In the novel, Don Quixote attacks a flock of sheep, later explaining that the sheep were actually an army of knights who had been transformed by a magician.

"Why," says he, "a magician could call up a lot of genies, and they would hash you up like nothing before you could say Jack Robinson. They are as tall as a tree and as big around as a church."

"Well," I says, "s'pose we got some genies to help *us*—can't we lick the other crowd then?"

"How you going to get them?"

"I don't know. How do *they* get them?"

"Why they rub an old tin lamp or an iron ring, and then the genies come tearing in, with the thunder and lightning a-ripping around and the smoke a-rolling, and everything they're told to do they up and do it. They don't think nothing of pulling a shot tower[7] up by the roots, and belting a Sunday-school superintendent over the head with it—or any other man."

"Who makes them tear around so?"

"Why, whoever rubs the lamp or the ring. They belong to whoever rubs the lamp or the ring, and they've got to do whatever he says. If he tells them to build a palace forty miles long, out of di'monds, and fill it full of chewing gum, or whatever you want, and fetch an emperor's daughter from China for you to marry, they've got to do it—and they've got to do it before sun-up next morning, too. And more—they've got to waltz that palace around over the country wherever you want it, you understand."

"Well," says I, "I think they are a pack of flatheads for not keeping the palace themselves 'stead of fooling them away like that. And what's more—if I was one of them I would see a man in Jericho before I would drop my business and come to him for the rubbing of an old tin lamp."

"How you talk, Huck Finn. Why, you'd *have* to come when he rubbed it, whether you wanted to or not."

"What, and I as high as a tree and as big as a church? All right, then; I *would* come; but I lay I'd make that man climb the highest tree there was in the country."

"Shucks, it ain't no use to talk to you, Huck Finn. You don't seem to know anything, somehow—perfect sap-head."

I thought all this over for two or three days, and then I reckoned I would see if there was anything in it. I got an old tin lamp and an iron ring and went out in the woods and rubbed and rubbed till I sweat like an Injun, calculating to build a palace and sell it; but it warn't no use, none of the genies come. So then I judged that all that stuff was only just one of Tom Sawyer's lies. I reckoned he believed in the A-rabs and the elephants, but as for me I think different. It had all the marks of a Sunday school.

CHAPTER IV

Well, three or four months run along, and it was well into the winter, now. I had been to school most all the time, and could spell, and read, and write just a little, and could say the multiplication table up to six times seven is thirty-five, and I don't reckon I could ever get any further than that if I was to live forever. I don't take no stock in mathematics, anyway.

[7]A tower in which pellets are made by pouring molten lead from the top of the tower, through a sieve, into a tank of water.

At first I hated the school, but by-and-by I got so I could stand it. Whenever I got uncommon tired I played hookey, and the hiding I got next day done me good and cheered me up. So the longer I went to school the easier it got to be. I was getting sort of used to the widow's ways, too, and they warn't so raspy on me. Living in a house, and sleeping in a bed, pulled on me pretty tight, mostly, but before the cold weather I used to slide out and sleep in the woods, sometimes, and so that was a rest to me. I liked the old ways best, but I was getting so I liked the new ones, too, a little bit. The widow said I was coming along slow but sure, and doing very satisfactory. She said she warn't ashamed of me.

One morning I happened to turn over the salt-cellar at breakfast. I reached for some of it as quick as I could, to throw over my left shoulder and keep off the bad luck, but Miss Watson was in ahead of me, and crossed me off. She says, "Take your hands away, Huckleberry—what a mess you are always making." The widow put in a good word for me, but that warn't going to keep off the bad luck, I knowed that well enough. I started out, after breakfast, feeling worried and shaky, and wondering where it was going to fall on me, and what it was going to be. There is ways to keep off some kinds of bad luck, but this wasn't one of them kind; so I never tried to do anything, but just poked along low-spirited and on the watchout.

I went down the front garden and clumb over the stile,[1] where you go through the high board fence. There was an inch of new snow on the ground, and I seen somebody's tracks. They had come up from the quarry and stood around the stile a while, and then went on around the garden fence. It was funny they hadn't come in, after standing around so. I couldn't make it out. It was very curious, somehow. I was going to follow around, but I stooped down to look at the tracks first. I didn't notice anything at first, but next I did. There was a cross in the left boot-heel made with big nails, to keep off the devil.

I was up in a second and shinning down the hill. I looked over my shoulder every now and then, but I didn't see nobody. I was at Judge Thatcher's as quick as I could get there. He said:

"Why, my boy, you are all out of breath. Did you come for your interest?"

"No sir," I says; "is there some for me?"

"Oh, yes, a half-yearly is in, last night. Over a hundred and fifty dollars. Quite a fortune for you. You better let me invest it along with your six thousand, because if you take it you'll spend it."

"No, sir," I says, "I don't want to spend it. I don't want it at all—nor the six thousand, nuther. I want you to take it; I want to give it to you—the six thousand and all."

He looked surprised. He couldn't seem to make it out. He says:

"Why, what can you mean, my boy?"

I says, "Don't you ask me no questions about it, please. You'll take it—won't you?"

He says:

"Well I'm puzzled. Is something the matter?"

"Please take it," says I, "and don't ask me nothing—then I won't have to tell no lies."

[1]A set of steps up and over a fence.

He studied a while, and then he says:

"Oho-o. I think I see. You want to *sell* all your property to me—not give it. That's the correct idea."

Then he wrote something on a paper and read it over and says:

"There—you see it says 'for a consideration.' That means I have bought it of you and paid you for it. Here's a dollar for you. Now, you sign it."

So I signed it, and left.

Miss Watson's nigger, Jim, had a hair-ball as big as your fist, which had been took out of the fourth stomach of an ox, and he used to do magic with it. He said there was a spirit inside of it, and it knowed everything. So I went to him that night and told him pap was here again, for I found his tracks in the snow. What I wanted to know, was, what he was going to do, and was he going to stay? Jim got out his hair-ball, and said something over it, and then he held it up and dropped it on the floor. It fell pretty solid, and only rolled about an inch. Jim tried it again, and then another time, and it acted just the same. Jim got down on his knees and put his ear against it and listened. But it warn't no use; he said it wouldn't talk. He said sometimes it wouldn't talk without money. I told him I had an old slick counterfeit quarter that warn't no good because the brass showed through the silver a little, and it wouldn't pass nohow, even if the brass didn't show, because it was so slick it felt greasy, and so that would tell on it every time. (I reckoned I wouldn't say nothing about the dollar I got from the judge.) I said it was pretty bad money, but maybe the hair-ball would take it, because maybe it wouldn't know the difference. Jim smelt it, and bit it, and rubbed it, and said he would manage so the hair-ball would think it was good. He said he would split open a raw Irish potato and stick the quarter in between and keep it there all night, and next morning you couldn't see no brass, and it wouldn't feel greasy no more, and so anybody in town would take it in a minute, let alone a hair-ball. Well, I knowed a potato would do that, before, but I had forgot it.

Jim put the quarter under the hair-ball and got down and listened again. This time he said the hair-ball was all right. He said it would tell my whole fortune if I wanted it to. I says, go on. So the hair-ball talked to Jim, and Jim told it to me. He says:

"Yo' ole father doan' know, yit, what he's a-gwyne to do. Sometimes he spec he'll go 'way, en den agin he spec he'll stay. De bes' way is to res' easy en let de ole man take his own way. Dey's two angels hoverin' roun' 'bout him. One uv 'em is white en shiny, en t'other one is black. De white one gits him to go right, a little while, den de black one sail in en bust it all up. A body can't tell, yit, which one gwyne to fetch him at de las'. But you is all right. You gwyne to have considable trouble in yo' life, en considable joy. Sometimes you gwyne to git hurt, en sometimes you gwyne to git sick; but every time you's gwyne to git well agin. Dey's two gals flying' 'bout you in yo' life. One uv 'em's light en t'other one is dark. One is rich en t'other is po'. You's gwyne to marry de po' one fust en de rich one by-en-by. You wants to keep 'way fum de water as much as you kin, en don't run no resk, 'kase it's down in de bills[2] dat you's gwyne to git hung."

[2]I.e., decreed, predestined.

When I lit my candle and went up to my room that night, there set pap, his own self!

CHAPTER V

I had shut the door to. Then I turned around, and there he was. I used to be scared of him all the time, he tanned me so much. I reckoned I was scared now, too; but in a minute I see I was mistaken. That is, after the first jolt, as you may say, when my breath sort of hitched—he being so unexpected; but right away after, I see I warn't scared of him worth bothering about.

He was most fifty, and he looked it. His hair was long and tangled and greasy, and hung down, and you could see his eyes shining through like he was behind vines. It was all black, no gray; so was his long, mixed-up whiskers. There warn't no color in his face, where his face showed; it was white; not like another man's white, but a white to make a body sick, a white to make a body's flesh crawl—a tree-toad white, a fish-belly white. As for his clothes—just rags, that was all. He had one ankle resting on t'other knee; the boot on that foot was busted, and two of his toes stuck through, and he worked them now and then. His hat was laying on the floor; an old black slouch[1] with the top caved in, like a lid.

I stood a-looking at him; he set there a-looking at me, with his chair tilted back a little. I set the candle down. I noticed the window was up; so he had clumb in by the shed. He kept a-looking me all over. By-and-by he says:

"Starchy clothes—very. You think you're a good deal of a big-bug, *don't* you?"

"Maybe I am, maybe I ain't," I says.

"Don't you give me none o' your lip," says he. "You've put on considerable many frills since I been away. I'll take you down a peg before I get done with you. You're educated, too, they say; can read and write. You think you're better'n your father, now, don't you, because he can't? *I*'ll take it out of you. Who told you you might meddle with such hifalut'n foolishness, hey?—who told you you could?"

"The widow. She told me."

"The widow, hey?—and who told the widow she could put in her shovel about a thing that ain't none of her business?"

"Nobody never told her."

"Well, I'll learn her how to meddle. An looky here—you drop that school, you hear? I'll learn people to bring up a boy to put on airs over his own father and let on to be better'n what *he* is. You lemme catch you fooling around that school again, you hear? Your mother couldn't read, and she couldn't write, nuther, before she died. None of the family couldn't, before *they* died. *I* can't; and here you're a-swelling yourself up like this. I ain't the man to stand it—you hear? Say—lemme hear you read."

I took up a book and begun something about General Washington and the wars. When I'd read about a half a minute, he fetched the book a whack with his hand and knocked it across the house. He says:

[1]A felt hat with a wide brim.

"It's so. You can do it. I had my doubts when you told me. Now looky here; you stop that putting on frills. I won't have it. I'll lay[2] for you, my smarty; and if I catch you about that school I'll tan you good. First you know you'll get religion, too. I never see such a son."

He took up a little blue and yaller picture of some cows and a boy, and says:

"What's this?"

"It's something they give me for learning my lessons good."

He tore it up, and says—

"I'll give you something better—I'll give you a cowhide."[3]

He set there a-mumbling and a-growling a minute, and then he says—

"*Ain't* you a sweet-scented dandy, though? A bed; and bedclothes; and a look'n glass; and a piece of carpet on the floor—and your own father got to sleep with the hogs in the tanyard. I never see such a son. I bet I'll take some o'these frills out o' you before I'm done with you. Why there ain't no end to your airs—they say you're rich. Hey?—how's that?"

"I hain't got no money."

"It's a lie. Judge Thatcher's got it. You git it. I want it."

"They lie—that's how."

"Looky here—mind how you talk to me; I'm a-standing about all I can stand, now—so don't gimme no sass. I've been in town two days, and I hain't heard nothing but about you bein' rich. I heard about it away down the river, too. That's why I come. You git me that money to-morrow—I want it."

"I hain't got no money, I tell you. You ask Judge Thatcher; he'll tell you the same."

"All right. I'll ask him; and I'll make him pungle,[4] too, or I'll know the reason why. Say—how much you got in your pocket? I want it."

"I hain't got only a dollar, and I want that to—"

"It don't make no difference what you want it for—you just shell it out."

He took it and bit it to see if it was good, and then he said he was going down town to get some whiskey; said he hadn't had a drink all day. When he had got out on the shed, he put his head in again, and cussed me for putting on frills and trying to be better than him; and when I reckoned he was gone, he come back and put his head in again, and told me to mind about that school, because he was going to lay for me and lick me if I didn't drop that.

Next day he was drunk, and he went to Judge Thatcher's and bullyragged[5] him and tried to make him give up the money, but he couldn't, and then he swore he'd make the law force him.

The judge and the widow went to law to get the court to take me away from him and let one of them be my guardian; but it was a new judge that had just come, and he didn't know the old man; so he said courts mustn't interfere and separate families if they could help it; said he'd druther not take a child away from its father. So Judge Thatcher and the widow had to quit on the business.

That pleased the old man till he couldn't rest. He said he'd cowhide me till I was black and blue if I didn't raise some money for him. I borrowed three dollars from Judge Thatcher, and pap took it and got drunk and went a-blowing around and cussing and whooping and carrying on; and he kept it

[2]Lie in wait. [3]A whipping with a cowhide strap. [4]Pay. [5]Scolded.

up all over town, with a tin pan, till most midnight; then they jailed him, and next day they had him before court, and jailed him again for a week. But he said *he* was satisfied; said he was boss of his son, and he'd make it warm for *him.*

When he got out the new judge said he was agoing to make a man of him. So he took him to his own house, and dressed him up clean and nice, and had him to breakfast and dinner and supper with the family, and was just old pie to him, so to speak. And after supper he talked to him about temperance and such things till the old man cried, and said he'd been a fool, and fooled away his life; but now he was agoing to turn over a new leaf and be a man nobody wouldn't be ashamed of, and he hoped the judge would help him and not look down on him. The judge said he could hug him for them words; so *he* cried, and his wife she cried again; pap said he'd been a man that had always been misunderstood before, and the judge said he believed it. The old man said that what a man wanted that was down, was sympathy; and the judge said it was so; so they cried again. And when it was bedtime, the old man rose up and held out his hand, and says:

"Look at it gentlemen, and ladies all; take ahold of it; shake it. There's a hand that was the hand of a hog; but it ain't so no more; it's the hand of a man that's started in on a new life, and 'll die before he'll go back. You mark them words—don't forget I said them. It's a clean hand now; shake it—don't be afeard."

So they shook it, one after the other, all around, and cried. The judge's wife she kissed it. Then the old man he signed a pledge—made his mark.[6] The judge said it was the holiest time on record, or something like that. Then they tucked the old man into a beautiful room, which was the spare room, and in the night sometime he got powerful thirsty and clumb out onto the porch-roof and slid down a stanchion and traded his new coat for a jug of forty-rod,[7] and clumb back again and hada good old time; and towards daylight he crawled out again, drunk as a fiddler, and rolled off the porch and broke his left arm in two places and was most froze to death when somebody found him after sun-up. And when they come to look at that spare room, they had to take soundings[8] before they could navigate it.

The judge he felt kind of sore. He said he reckoned a body could reform the ole man with a shot-gun, maybe, but he didn't know no other way.

CHAPTER VI

Well, pretty soon the old man was up and around again, and then he went for Judge Thatcher in the courts to make him give up that money, and he went for me, too, for not stopping school. He catched me a couple of times and thrashed me, but I went to school just the same, and dodged him or outrun him most of the time. I didn't want to go to school much, before, but I reckoned I'd go now to spite pap. That law trial was a slow business; appeared like they warn't ever going to get started on it; so every now and then

[6] I.e., signed, by making his mark, a written pledge to abstain from alcohol.

[7] Rotgut whiskey judged powerful enough to knock a man 40 rods, or 660 feet.

[8] Measure depths, go carefully.

I'd borrow two or three dollars off of the judge for him, to keep from getting a cowhiding. Every time he got money he was drunk; and every time he got drunk he raised Cain around town; and every time he raised Cain he got jailed. He was just suited—this kind of thing was right in his line.

He got to hanging around the widow's too much, and so she told him at last, that if he didn't quit using[1] around there she would make trouble for him. Well, *wasn't* he mad? He said he would show who was Huck Finn's boss. So he watched out for me one day in the spring, and catched me, and took me up the river about three mile, in a skiff, and crossed over to the Illinois shore where it was woody and there warn't no houses but an old log hut in a place where the timber was so thick you couldn't find it if you didn't know where it was.

He kept me with him all the time, and I never got a chance to run off. We lived in that old cabin, and he always locked the door and put the key under his head, nights. He had a gun which he had stole, I reckon, and we fished and hunted, and that was what we lived on. Every little while he locked me in and went down to the store, three miles to the ferry, and traded fish and game for whisky and fetched it home and got drunk and had a good time, and licked me. The widow she found out where I was, by-and-by, and she sent a man over to try to get hold of me, but pap drove him off with the gun, and it warn't long after that till I was used to being where I was, and liked it, all but the cowhide part.

It was kind of lazy and jolly, laying off comfortable all day, smoking and fishing, and no books nor study. Two months or more ran along, and my clothes got to be all rags and dirt, and I didn't see how I'd ever got to like it so well at the widow's, where you had to wash, and eat on a plate, and comb up, and go to bed and get up regular, and be forever bothering over a book and have old Miss Watson pecking at you all the time. I didn't want to go back no more. I had stopped cussing, because the widow didn't like it; but now I took to it again because pap hadn't no objections. It was pretty good times up in the woods there, take it all around.

But by-and-by pap got too handy with his hick'ry, and I couldn't stand it. I was all over welts. He got to going away so much, too, and locking me in. Once he locked me in and was gone three days. It was dreadful lonesome. I judged he had got drowned and I wasn't ever going to get out any more. I was scared. I made up my mind I would fix up some way to leave there. I had tried to get out of that cabin many a time, but I couldn't find no way. There warn't a window to it big enough for a dog to get through. I couldn't get up the chimbly, it was too narrow. The door was thick solid oak slabs. Pap was pretty careful not to leave a knife or anything in the cabin when he was away; I reckon I had hunted the place over as much as a hundred times; well, I was 'most all the time at it, because it was about the only way to put in the time. But this time I found something at last; I found an old rusty wood-saw without any handle; it was laid in between a rafter and the clapboards of the roof. I greased it up and went to work. There was an old horse-blanket nailed against the logs at the far end of the cabin behind the table, to keep the wind from blowing through the chinks and putting the candle out. I got under the table and raised the blanket and went to work to saw a section of

[1]Loitering.

the big bottom log out, big enough to let me through. Well, it was a good long job, but I was getting towards the end of it when I heard pap's gun in the woods. I got rid of the signs of my work, and dropped the blanket and hid my saw, and pretty soon pap come in.

Pap warn't in a good humor—so he was his natural self. He said he was down to town, and everything was going wrong. His lawyer said he reckoned he would win his lawsuit and get the money, if they ever got started on the trial; but then there was ways to put it off a long time, and Judge Thatcher knowed how to do it. And he said people allowed there'd be another trial to get me away from him and give me to the widow for my guardian, and they guessed it would win, this time. This shook me up considerable, because I didn't want to go back to the widow's any more and be so cramped up and sivilized, as they called it. Then the old man got to cussing, and cussed everything and everybody he could think of, and then cussed them all over again to make sure he hadn't skipped any, and after that he polished off with a kind of a general cuss all around, including a considerable parcel of people which he didn't know the names of, and so called them what's-his-name, when he got to them, and went right along with his cussing.

He said he would like to see the widow get me. He said he would watch out, and if they tried to come any such game on him he knowed of a place six or seven mile off, to stow me in, where they might hunt till they dropped and they couldn't find me. That made me pretty uneasy again, but only for a minute; I reckoned I wouldn't stay on hand till he got that chance.

The old man made me go to the skiff and fetch the things he had got. There was a fifty-pound sack of corn meal, and a side of bacon, ammunition, and a four-gallon jug of whisky, and an old book and two newspapers for wadding,[2] besides some tow.[3] I toted up a load, and went back and set down on the bow of the skiff to rest. I thought it all over, and I reckoned I would walk off with the gun and some lines, and take to the woods when I run away. I guessed I wouldn't stay in one place, but just tramp right across the country, mostly night times, and hunt and fish to keep alive, and so get so far away that the old man nor the widow couldn't ever find me any more. I judged I would saw out and leave that night if pap got drunk enough, and I reckoned he would. I got so full of it I didn't notice how long I was staying, till the old man hollered and asked me whether I was asleep or drownded.

I got the things all up to the cabin, and then it was about dark. When I was cooking supper the old man took a swig or two and got sort of warmed up, and went to ripping again. He had been drunk over in town, and laid in the gutter all night, and he was a sight to look at. A body would a thought he was Adam, he was just all mud.[4] Whenever his liquor begun to work, he most always went for the govment. This time he says:

"Call this a govment! why, just look at it and see what it's like. Here's the law a-standing ready to take a man's son away from him—a man's own son, which he has had all the trouble and all the anxiety and all the expense of raising. Yes, just as that man has got that son raised at last, and ready to go to

[2]The material used to make the plugs inserted to retain the powder charge in a muzzle-loading gun.

[3]Short fibers of flax or hemp.

[4]"And the Lord God formed man of the dust of the ground" (Genesis 2:7).

work and begin to do suthin' for *him* and give him a rest, the law up and goes for him. And they call *that* govment! That ain't all, nuther. The law backs that old Judge Thatcher up and helps him to keep me out o' my property. Here's what the law does. The law takes a man worth six thousand dollars and upards, and jams him into an old trap of a cabin like this, and lets him go round in clothes that ain't fitten for a hog. They calls that govment! A man can't get his rights in a govment like this. Sometimes I've a mighty notion to just leave the country for good and all. Yes, and I *told* 'em so; I told old Thatcher so to his face. Lots of 'em heard me, and can tell what I said. Says I, for two cents I'd leave the blamed country and never come anear it agin. Them's the very words. I says, look at my hat—if you call it a hat—but the lid raises up and the rest of it goes down till it's below my chin, and then it ain't rightly a hat at all, but more like my head was shoved up through a jint o' stove-pipe. Look at it, says I—such a hat for me to wear—one of the wealthiest men in this town, if I could git my rights.

"Oh, yes, this is a wonderful govment, wonderful. Why, looky here. There was a free nigger there, from Ohio;[5] a mulatter,[6] most as white as a white man. He had the whitest shirt on you ever see, too, and the shiniest hat; and there ain't a man in that town that's got as fine clothes as what he had; and he had a gold watch and chain, and a silver-headed cane—the awfulest old gray-headed nabob[7] in the State. And what do you think? they said he was a p'fessor in a college, and could talk all kinds of languages, and knowed everything. And that ain't the wust. They said he could *vote,* when he was at home. Well, that let me out. Thinks I, what is the country a-coming to? It was 'lection day, and I was just about to go and vote, myself, if I warn't too drunk to get there; but when they told me there was a State in this country where they'd let a nigger vote, I drawed out. I says I'll never vote again. Them's the very words I said; they all heard me; and the country may rot for all me—I'll never vote agin as long as I live. And to see the cool way of that nigger—why, he wouldn't a give me the road if I hadn't shoved him out o' the way. I says to the people, why ain't this nigger put up at auction and sold?—that's what I want to know. And what do you reckon they said? Why, they said he couldn't be sold till he's been in the State six months,[8] and he hadn't been there that long yet. There, now—that's a specimen. They call that a govment that can't sell a free nigger till he's been in the State six months. Here's a govment that calls itself a govment, and lets on to be a govment, and thinks it is a govment, and yet's got to set stock-still for six whole months before it can take ahold of a prowling, thieving, infernal, white-shirted free nigger, and—"

Pap was agoing on so, he never noticed where his old limber legs was taking him to, so he went head over heels over the tub of salt pork, and barked both shins, and the rest of his speech was all the hottest kind of language—mostly hove at the nigger and the govment, though he give the tub some, too, all along, here and there. He hopped around the cabin considerable, first on one leg and then on the other, holding first one shin and then the other one, and at last he let out with his left foot all of a sudden and fetched the tub a rattling kick. But it warn't good judgment, because that was the

5. Ohio had no slavery. 6. Mulatto, of mixed black and white ancestry.
7. Man of prominence, a "swell."
8. A reference to the fact that in some circumstances a free Negro could be legally re-enslaved.

boot that had a couple of his toes leaking out of the front end of it; so now he raised a howl that fairly made a body's hair raise, and down he went in the dirt, and rolled there, and held his toes; and the cussing he done then laid over anything he had ever done previous. He said so his own self, afterwards. He had heard old Sowberry Hagan in his best days, and he said it laid over him, too; but I reckon that was sort of piling it on, maybe.

After supper pap took the jug, and said he had enough whisky there for two drunks and one delirium tremens. That was always his word. I judged he would be blind drunk in about an hour, and then I would steal the key, or saw myself out, one or t'other. He drank, and drank, and tumbled down on his blankets, by-and-by; but luck didn't run my way. He didn't go sound asleep, but was uneasy. He groaned, and moaned, and thrashed around this way and that, for a long time. At last I got so sleepy I couldn't keep my eyes open, all I could do, and so before I knowed what I was about I was sound asleep, and the candle burning.

I don't know how long I was asleep, but all of a sudden there was an awful scream and I was up. There was pap, looking wild and skipping around every which way and yelling about snakes. He said they was crawling up his leg; and then he would give a jump and scream, and say one had bit him on the cheek—but I couldn't see no snakes. He started and run round and round the cabin, hollering "take him off! take him off! he's biting me on the neck!" I never see a man look so wild in the eyes. Pretty soon he was all fagged out, and fell down panting; then he rolled over and over, wonderful fast, kicking things every which way, and striking and grabbing at the air with his hands, and screaming, and saying there was devils ahold of him. He wore out, by-and-by, and laid still a while, moaning. Then he laid stiller, and didn't make a sound. I could hear the owls and the wolves, away off in the woods, and it seemed terrible still. He was laying over by the corner. By-and-by he raised up, part way, and listened, with his head to one side. He says very low:

"Tramp—tramp—tramp; that's the dead; tramp—tramp—tramp; they're coming after me; but I won't go—Oh, they're here! don't touch me—don't! hands off!—they're cold; let go—Oh, let a poor devil alone!"

Then he went down on all fours and crawled off begging them to let him alone, and he rolled himself up in his blanket and wallowed in under the old pine table, still a-begging; and then he went to crying. I could hear him through the blanket.

By-and-by he rolled out and jumped up on his feet looking wild, and he see me and went for me. He chased me round and round the place, with a clasp-knife,[9] calling me the Angel of Death[10] and saying he would kill me and then I couldn't come for him no more. I begged, and told him I was only Huck, but he laughed *such* a screechy laugh, and roared and cussed, and kept on chasing me up. Once when I turned short and dodged under his arm he made a grab and got me by the jacket between my shoulders, and I thought I was gone; but I slid out of the jacket quick as lightning, and saved myself. Pretty soon he was all tired out, and dropped down with his back against the door, and said he would rest a minute and then kill me. He put

[9]A knife with a blade that folds into the clasp (handle).
[10]In folklore, the Angel of Death confronts those who are to die.

his knife under him, and said he would sleep and get strong, and then he would see who was who.

So he dozed off, pretty soon. By-and-by I got the old split-bottom[11] chair and clumb up, as easy as I could, not to make any noise, and got down the gun. I slipped the ramrod down it to make sure it was loaded, and then I laid it across the turnip barrel, pointing towards pap, and set down behind it to wait for him to stir. And how slow and still the time did drag along.

CHAPTER VII

"Git up! what you 'bout!"

I opened my eyes and looked around, trying to make out where I was. It was after sun-up, and I had been sound asleep. Pap was standing over me, looking sour—and sick, too. He says—

"What you doin' with this gun?"

I judged he didn't know nothing about what he had been doing, so I says: "Somebody tried to get in, so I was laying for him."

"Why didn't you roust me out?"

"Well, I tried to, but I couldn't; I couldn't budge you."

"Well, all right. Don't stand there palavering[1] all day, but out with you and see if there's a fish on the lines for breakfast. I'll be along in a minute."

He unlocked the door and I cleared out, up the river bank. I noticed some pieces of limbs and such things floating down, and a sprinkling of bark; so I know the river had begun to rise. I reckoned I would have great times, now, if I was over at the town. The June rise used to be always luck for me; because as soon as that rise begins, here comes cord-wood[2] floating down, and pieces of log rafts—sometimes a dozen logs together; so all you have to do is to catch them and sell them to the wood yards and the sawmill.

I went along up the bank with one eye out for pap and t'other one out for what the rise might fetch along. Well, all at once, here comes a canoe; just a beauty, too, about thirteen or fourteen foot long, riding high like a duck. I shot head first off of the bank, like a frog, clothes and all on, and struck out for the canoe. I just expected there'd be somebody laying down in it, because people often done that to fool folks, and when a chap had pulled a skiff out most to it they'd raise up and laugh at him. But it warn't so this time. It was a drift-canoe, sure enough, and I clumb in and paddled her ashore. Thinks I the old man will be glad when he sees this—she's worth ten dollars. But when I got to shore pap wasn't in sight yet, and as I was running her into a little creek like a gully, all hung over with vines and willows, I struck another idea; I judged I'd hide her good, and then, stead of taking to the woods when I run off, I'd go down the river about fifty mile and camp in one place for good, and not have such a rough time tramping on foot.

It was pretty close to the shanty, and I thought I heard the old man coming, all the time; but I got her hid; and then I out and looked around a bunch of willows, and there was the old man down the path a piece just drawing a bead on a bird with his gun. So he hadn't seen anything.

[11] I.e., with a seat of interwoven wood strips.

[1] Talking idly, jabbering. [2] Wood cut in four-foot lengths.

When he got along, I was hard at it taking up a "trot" line.[3] He abused me a little for being so slow, but I told him I fell in the river and that was what made me so long. I knowed he would see I was wet, and then he would be asking questions. We got five catfish off the lines and went home.

While we laid off, after breakfast, to sleep up, both of us being about wore out, I got to thinking that if I could fix up some way to keep pap and the widow from trying to follow me, it would be a certainer thing than trusting to luck to get far enough off before they missed me; you see, all kinds of things might happen. Well, I didn't see no way for a while, but by-and-by pap raised up a minute, to drink another barrel of water, and he says:

"Another time a man comes a-prowling round here, you roust me out, you hear? That man warn't here for no good. I'd a shot him. Next time, you roust me out, you hear?"

Then he dropped down and went to sleep again—but what he had been saying give me the very idea I wanted. I says to myself, I can fix it now so nobody won't think of following me.

About twelve o'clock we turned out and went along up the bank. The river was coming up pretty fast, and lots of drift-wood going by on the rise. By-and-by, along comes part of a log raft—nine logs fast together. We went out with the skiff and towed it ashore. Then we had dinner. Anybody but pap would a waited and see the day through, so as to catch more stuff; but that warn't pap's style. Nine logs was enough for one time; he must shove right over to town and sell. So he locked me in and took the skiff and started off towing the raft about half-past three. I judged he wouldn't come back that night. I waited till I reckoned he had got a good start, then I out with my saw and went to work on that log again. Before he was t'other side of the river I was out of the hole; him and his raft was just a speck on the water away off yonder.

I took the sack of corn meal and took it to where the canoe was hid, and shoved the vines and branches apart and put it in; then I done the same with the side of bacon; then the whisky jug; I took all the coffee and sugar there was, and all the ammunition; I took the wadding; I took the bucket and gourd, I took a dipper and a tin cup, and my old saw and two blankets, and the skillet and the coffee-pot. I took fish-lines and matches and other things—everything that was worth a cent. I cleaned out the place. I wanted an ax, but there wasn't any, only the one out at the wood pile, and I knowed why I was going to leave that. I fetched out the gun, and now I was done.

I had wore the ground a good deal, crawling out of the hole and dragging out so many things. So I fixed that as good as I could from the outside by scattering dust on the place, which covered up the smoothness and the sawdust. Then I fixed the piece of log back into its place, and put two rocks under it and one against it to hold it there,—for it was bent up at that place, and didn't quite touch ground. If you stood four or five foot away and didn't know it was sawed, you wouldn't even notice it; and besides, this was the back of the cabin and it warn't likely anybody would go fooling around there.

It was all grass clear to the canoe; so I hadn't left a track. I followed around to see. I stood on the bank and looked out over the river. All safe. So I took

[3]A long fishing line (usually set in a stream or river) from which hooks are suspended at intervals.

the gun and went up a piece into the woods and was hunting around for some birds, when I see a wild pig; hogs soon went wild in them bottoms after they had got away from the prairie farms. I shot this fellow and took him into camp.

I took the ax and smashed in the door—I beat it and hacked it considerable, a-doing it. I fetched the pig in and took him back nearly to the table and hacked into his throat with the ax, and laid him down on the ground to bleed—I say ground, because it *was* ground—hard packed, and no boards. Well, next I took an old sack and put a lot of big rocks in it,—all I could drag—and I started it from the pig and dragged it to the door and through the woods down to the river and dumped it in, and down it sunk, out of sight. You could easy see that something had been dragged over the ground. I did wish Tom Sawyer was there, I know he would take an interest in this kind of business, and throw in the fancy touches. Nobody could spread himself like Tom Sawyer in such a thing as that.

Well, last I pulled out some of my hair, and bloodied the ax good, and stuck it on the back side, and slung the ax in the corner. Then I took up the pig and held him to my breast with my jacket (so he couldn't drip) till I got a good piece below the house and then dumped him into the river. Now I thought of something else. So I went and got the bag of meal and my old saw out of the canoe and fetched them to the house. I took the bag to where it used to stand, and ripped a hole in the bottom of it with the saw, for there warn't no knives and forks on the place—pap done everything with his clasp-knife, about the cooking. Then I carried the sack about a hundred yards across the grass and through the willows east of the house, to a shallow lake that was five mile wide and full of rushes—and ducks too, you might say, in the season. There was a slough or a creek leading out of it on the other side, that went miles away, I don't know where, but it didn't go to the river. The meal sifted out and made a little track all the way to the lake. I dropped pap's whetstone there too, so as to look like it had been done by accident. Then I tied up the rip in the meal sack with a string, so it wouldn't leak no more, and took it and my saw to the canoe again.

It was about dark, now; so I dropped the canoe down the river under some willows that hung over the bank, and waited for the moon to rise. I made fast to a willow; then I took a bite to eat, and by-and-by laid down in the canoe to smoke a pipe and lay out a plan. I says to myself, they'll follow the track of that sackful of rocks to the shore and then drag the river for me. And they'll follow that meal track to the lake and go browsing down the creek that leads out of it to find the robbers that killed me and took the things. They won't ever hunt the river for anything but my dead carcass. They'll soon get tired of that, and won't bother no more about me. All right; I can stop anywhere I want to. Jackson's Island is good enough for me; I know that island pretty well, and nobody ever comes there. And then I can paddle over to town, nights, and slink around and pick up things I want. Jackson's Island's the place.

I was pretty tired, and the first thing I knowed, I was asleep. When I woke up I didn't know where I was, for a minute. I set up and looked around, a little scared. Then I remembered. The river looked miles and miles across. The moon was so bright I could a counted the drift logs that went a slipping along, black and still, hundreds of yards out from shore. Everything was dead quiet, and it looked late, and *smelt* late. You know what I mean—I don't know the words to put it in.

I took a good gap and a stretch, and was just going to unhitch and start, when I heard a sound away over the water. I listened. Pretty soon I made it out. It was that dull kind of a regular sound that comes from oars working in rowlocks when it's a still night. I peeped out through the willow branches, and there it was—a skiff, away across the water. I couldn't tell how many was in it. It kept a-coming, and when it was abreast of me I see there warn't but one man in it. Thinks I, maybe it's pap, though I warn't expecting him. He dropped below me, with the current, and by-and-by he come a-swinging up shore in the easy water,[4] and he went by so close I could a reached out the gun and touched him. Well it *was* pap, sure enough—and sober, too, by the way he laid to his oars.

I didn't lose no time. The next minute I was a-spinning down stream soft but quick in the shade of the bank. I made two mile and a half, and then struck out a quarter of a mile or more towards the middle of the river, because pretty soon I would be passing the ferry landing and people might see me and hail me. I got out amongst the drift-wood and then laid down in the bottom of the canoe and let her float. I laid there and had a good rest and a smoke out of my pipe, looking away into the sky, not a cloud in it. The sky looks ever so deep when you lay down on your back in the moonshine; I never knowed it before. And how far a body can hear on the water such nights! I heard people talking at the ferry landing. I heard what they said, too, every word of it. One man said it was getting towards the long days and the short nights, now. T'other one said *this* warn't one of the short ones, he reckoned—and then they laughed, and he said it over again and they laughed again; then they waked up another fellow and told him, and laughed, but he didn't laugh; he ripped out something brisk and said let him alone. The first fellow said he 'lowed to tell it to his old woman—she would think it was pretty good; but he said that warn't nothing to some things he had said in his time. I heard one man say it was nearly three o'clock, and he hoped daylight wouldn't wait more than about a week longer. After that, the talk got further and further away, and I couldn't make out the words any more, but I could hear the mumble; and now and then a laugh, too, but it seemed a long ways off.

I was away below the ferry now. I rise up and there was Jackson's Island, about two mile and a half down stream, heavy-timbered and standing up out of the middle of the river, big and dark and solid, like a steamboat without any lights. There warn't any signs of the bar at the head—it was all under water, now.

It didn't take me long to get there. I shot past the head at a ripping rate, the current was so swift, and then I got into the dead water[5] and landed on the side towards the Illinois shore. I run the canoe into a deep dent in the bank that I knowed about; I had to part the willow branches to get in; and when I made fast nobody could a seen the canoe from the outside.

I went up and set down on a log at the head of the island and looked out on the big river and the black driftwood, and away over to the town, three mile away, where there was three or four lights twinkling. A monstrous big

[4]Where the current is slight. [5]I.e., without current.

lumber raft was about a mile up stream, coming along down, with a lantern in the middle of it. I watched it come creeping down, and when it was most abreast of where I stood I heard a man say, "Stern oars, there! heave her head to stabboard!"[6] I heard that just as plain as if the man was by my side.

There was a little gray in the sky, now; so I stepped into the woods and laid down for a nap before breakfast.

CHAPTER VIII

The sun was up so high when I waked, that I judged it was after eight o'clock. I laid there in the grass and the cool shade, thinking about things and feeling rested and ruther comfortable and satisfied. I could see the sun out at one or two holes, but mostly it was big trees all about, and gloomy in there amongst them. There was freckled places on the ground where the light sifted down through the leaves, and the freckled places swapped about a little, showing there was a little breeze up there. A couple of squirrels set on a limb and jabbered at me very friendly.

I was powerful lazy and comfortable—didn't want to get up and cook breakfast. Well, I was dozing off again, when I thinks I hears a deep sound of "boom!" away up the river. I rouses up and rests on my elbow and listens; pretty soon I hears it again. I hopped up and went and looked out at a hole in the leaves, and I see a bunch of smoke laying on the water a long ways up—about abreast the ferry. And there was the ferry-boat full of people, floating along down. I knowed what was the matter, now. "Boom!" I see the white smoke squirt out of the ferry-boat's side. You see, they was firing cannon over the water, trying to make my carcass come to the top.

I was pretty hungry, but it warn't going to do for me to start a fire, because they might see the smoke. So I set there and watched the cannon-smoke and listened to the boom. The river was a mile wide, there, and it always looks pretty on a summer morning—so I was having a good enough time seeing them hunt for my remainders, if I only had a bite to eat. Well, then I happened to think how they always put quicksilver in loaves of bread and float them off because they always go right to the drownded carcass and stop there. So says I, I'll keep a lookout, and if any of them's floating around after me, I'll give them a show. I changed to the Illinois edge of the island to see what luck I could have, and I warn't disappointed. A big double loaf come along, and I most got it, with a long stick, but my foot slipped and she floated out further. Of course I was where the current set in the closest to the shore—I knowed enough for that. But by-and-by along comes another one, and this time I won. I took out the plug and shook out the little dab of quicksilver, and set my teeth in. It was "baker's bread"[1]—what the quality eat—none of your low-down corn-pone.[2]

I got a good place amongst the leaves, and set there on a log, munching the bread and watching the ferry-boat, and very well satisfied. And then something struck me. I says, now I reckon the widow or the parson or somebody

[6]Starboard, the right-hand side of a ship viewed by an observer looking forward. Larboard, "labboard," the left-hand side.

[1]White bread, made from wheat flour, a luxury. [2]Corn bread.

prayed that this bread would find me, and here it has gone and done it. So there ain't no doubt but there is something in that thing. That is, there's something in it when a body like the widow or the parson prays, but it don't work for me, and I reckon it don't work for only just the right kind.

I lit a pipe and had a good long smoke and went on watching. The ferry-boat was floating with the current, and I allowed I'd have a chance to see who was aboard when she come along, because she would come in close, where the bread did. When she'd got pretty well along down towards me, I put out my pipe and went to where I fished out the bread, and laid down behind a log on the bank in a little open place. Where the log forked I could peep through.

By-and-by she come along, and she drifted in so close that they could a run out a plank and walked ashore. Most everybody was on the boat. Pap, and Judge Thatcher, and Becky Thatcher, and Jo Harper, and Tom Sawyer, and his old Aunt Polly, and Sid and Mary, and plenty more. Everybody was talking about the murder, but the captain broke in and says:

"Look sharp, now; the current sets in the closest here, and maybe he's washed ashore and got tangled amongst the brush at the water's edge. I hope so, anyway."

I didn't hope so. They all crowded up and leaned over the rails, nearly in my face, and kept still, watching with all their might. I could see them first-rate, but they couldn't see me. Then the captain sung out:

"Stand away!" and the cannon let off such a blast right before me that it made me deef with the noise and pretty near blind with the smoke, and I judged I was gone. If they'd a had some bullets in, I reckon they'd a got the corpse they was after. Well, I see I warn't hurt, thanks to goodness. The boat floated on and went out of sight around the shoulder of the island. I could hear the booming, now and then, further and further off, and by-and-by after an hour, I didn't hear it no more. The island was three mile long. I judged they had got to the foot, and was giving it up. But they didn't yet a while. They turned around the foot of the island and started up the channel on the Missouri side, under steam, and booming once in a while as they went. I crossed over to that side and watched them. When they got abreast the head of the island they quit shooting and dropped over to the Missouri shore and went home to the town.

I knowed I was all right now. Nobody else would come a-hunting after me. I got my traps[3] out of the canoe and made me a nice camp in the thick woods. I made a kind of a tent out of my blankets to put my things under so the rain wouldn't get at them. I catched a cat-fish and haggled him open with my saw, and towards sundown I started my camp fire and had supper. Then I set out a line to catch some fish for breakfast.

When it was dark I set by my camp fire smoking, and feeling pretty satisfied; but by-and-by it got sort of lonesome, and so I went and set on the bank and listened to the currents washing along, and counted the stars and drift-logs and rafts that come down, and then went to bed; there ain't no better way to put in time when you are lonesome; you can't stay so, you soon get over it.

[3]Gear, belongings.

And so for three days and nights. No difference—just the same thing. But the next day I went exploring around down through the island. I was boss of it; it all belonged to me, so to say, and I wanted to know all about it; but mainly I wanted to put in the time. I found plenty strawberries, ripe and prime; and green summer-grapes, and green razberries; and the green blackberries was just beginning to show. They would all come handy by-and-by, I judged.

Well, I went fooling along in the deep woods till I judged I warn't far from the foot of the island. I had my gun along, but I hadn't shot nothing; it was for protection; thought I would kill some game nigh home. About this time I mighty near stepped on a good sized snake, and it went sliding off through the grass and flowers, and I after it, trying to get a shot at it. I clipped along, and all of a sudden I bounded right on to the ashes of a camp fire that was still smoking.

My heart jumped up amongst my lungs. I never waited for to look further, but uncocked my gun and went sneaking back on my tiptoes as fast as ever I could. Every now and then I stopped a second, amongst the thick leaves, and listened; but my breath come so hard I couldn't hear nothing else. I slunk along another piece further, then listened again; and so on, and so on; if I see a stump, I took it for a man; if I trod on a stick and broke it, it made me feel like a person had cut one of my breaths in two and I only got half, and the short half, too.

When I got to camp I warn't feeling very brash, there warn't much sand in my craw;[4] but I says, this ain't no time to be fooling around. So I got all my traps into my canoe again so as to have them out of sight, and I put out the fire and scattered the ashes around to look like an old last year's camp, and then clumb a tree.

I reckon I was up in the tree two hours; but I didn't see nothing, I didn't hear nothing—I only *thought* I heard and seen as much as a thousand things. Well, I couldn't stay up there forever; so at last I got down, but I kept in the thick woods and on the lookout all the time. All I could get to eat was berries and what was left over from breakfast.

By the time it was night I was pretty hungry. So when it was good and dark, I slid out from shore before moonrise and paddled over to the Illinois bank—about a quarter of a mile. I went out in the woods and cooked a supper, and I had about made up my mind I would stay there all night, when I hear a *plunkety-plunk, plunkety-plunk,* and says to myself, horses coming; and next I heard people's voices. I got everything into the canoe as quick as I could, and then went creeping through the woods to see what I could find out. I hadn't got far when I hear a man say:

"We better camp here, if we can find a good place; the horses is about beat out. Let's look around."

I didn't wait, but shoved out and paddled away easy. I tied up in the old place, and reckoned I would sleep in the canoe.

I didn't sleep much. I couldn't, somehow, for thinking. And every time I waked up I thought somebody had me by the neck. So the sleep didn't do me no good. By-and-by I says to myself, I can't live this way; I'm agoing to

[4]I.e., courage in my heart.

find out who it is that's here on the island with me; I'll find it out or bust. Well, I felt better, right off.

So I took my paddle and slid out from shore just a step or two, and then let the canoe drop along down amongst the shadows. The moon was shining, and outside of the shadows it made it most as light as day. I poked along well onto an hour, everything still as rocks and sound asleep. Well by this time I was most down to the foot of the island. A little ripply, cool breeze begun to blow, and that was as good as saying the night was about done. I give her a turn with the paddle and brung her nose to shore; then I got my gun and slipped out and into the edge of the woods. I set down there on a log and looked out through the leaves. I see the moon go off watch and the darkness begin to blanket the river. But in a little while I see a pale streak over the tree-tops, and knowed the day was coming. So I took my gun and slipped off towards where I had run across that camp fire, stopping every minute or two to listen. But I hadn't no luck, somehow! I couldn't seem to find the place. But by-and-by, sure enough, I catched a glimpse of fire, away through the trees. I went for it, cautious and slow. By-and-by I was close enough to have a look, and there laid a man on the ground. It most give me the fan-tods.[5] He had a blanket around his head, and his head was nearly in the fire. I set there behind a clump of bushes, in about six foot of him, and kept my eyes on him steady. It was getting gray daylight, now. Pretty soon he gapped, and stretched himself, and hove off the blanket, and it was Miss Watson's Jim! I bet I was glad to see him. I says:

"Hello, Jim!" and skipped out.

He bounced up and stared at me wild. Then he drops down on his knees, and puts his hands together and says:

"Doan' hurt me—don't! I hain't ever done no harm to a ghos'. I awluz liked dead people, en done all I could for 'em. You go en git in de river agin, whah you b'longs, en doan' do nuffin to Ole Jim, 'at 'uz awluz yo' fren'."

Well, I warn't long making him understand I warn't dead. I was ever so glad to see Jim. I warn't lonesome now. I told him I warn't afraid of *him* telling the people where I was. I talked along, but he only set there and looked at me; never said nothing. Then I says:

"It's good daylight. Le's get breakfast. Make up your camp fire good."

"What's de use er makin' up de camp fire to cook strawbries en sich truck?[6] But you got a gun, hain't you? Den we kin git sumfn better den strawbries."

"Strawberries and such truck," I says. "Is that what you live on?"

"I couldn' git nuffn else," he says.

"Why, how long you been on the island, Jim?"

"I come heah de night arter you's killed."

"What, all that time?"

"Yes-indeedy."

"And ain't you had nothing but that kind of rubbage to eat?"

"No, sah—nuffn else."

"Well, you must be most starved, ain't you?"

"I reck'n I could eat a hoss. I think I could. How long you ben on de islan'?"

[5]Fidgets. [6]Things, produce.

"Since the night I got killed."

"No! W'y, what has you lived on? But you got a gun. Oh, yes, you got a gun. Dat's good. Now you kill sumfn en I'll make up de fire."

So we went over to where the canoe was, and while he built a fire in a grassy open place amongst the trees, I fetched meal and bacon and coffee, and coffee-pot and frying-pan, and sugar and tin cups, and the nigger was set back considerable, because he reckoned it was all done with witchcraft. I catched a good big cat-fish, too, and Jim cleaned him with his knife, and fried him.

When breakfast was ready, we lolled on the grass and eat it smoking hot. Jim laid it in with all his might, for he was most about starved. Then when we had got pretty well stuffed, we laid off and lazied.

By-and-by Jim says:

"But looky here, Huck, who wuz it dat 'uz killed in dat shanty, ef it warn't you?"

Then I told him the whole thing, and he said it was smart. He said Tom Sawyer couldn't get up no better plan than what I had. Then I says:

"How do you come to be here, Jim, and how'd you get here?"

He looked pretty uneasy, and didn't say nothing for a minute. Then he says:

"Maybe I better not tell."

"Why, Jim?"

"Well, dey's reasons. But you wouldn't tell on me ef I 'uz to tell you, would you, Huck?"

"Blamed if I would, Jim."

"Well, I b'lieve you, Huck. I—I *run off.*"

"Jim!"

"But mind, you said you wouldn't tell—you know you said you wouldn't tell, Huck."

"Well, I did. I said I wouldn't, and I'll stick to it. Honest *injun* I will. People would call me a low down Ab'litionist[7] and despise me for keeping mum—but don't make no difference. I ain't agoing to tell, and I ain't agoing back there anyways. So now, le's know all about it."

"Well, you see, it 'uz dis way. Ole Missus—dat's Miss Watson—she pecks on me all de time, en treats me pooty rough, but she awluz said she wouldn't sell me down to Orleans. But I noticed dey wuz a nigger trader roun' de place considable, lately, en I begin to git oneasy. Well, one night I creeps to de do', pooty late, en de do' warn't quite shet, en I hear ole missus tell de widder she gwyne to sell me down to Orleans[8] but she didn't want to, but she could git eight hund'd dollars for me, en it 'uz sich a big stack o'money she couldn' resis'. De widder she try to git her to say she wouldn' do it, but I never waited to hear de res'. I lit out mighty quick, I tell you.

"I tuck out en shin down de hill en 'spec to steal a skift 'long de sho' som'ers 'bove de town, but dey wuz people a-stirring' yit, so I hid in de ole tumble-down cooper shop[9] on de bank to wait for everybody to go 'way. Well, I wuz dah all night. Dey wuz somebody roun' all de time. 'Long 'bout six in

[7]One devoted to the abolition of slavery.

[8]I.e., be "sold down the river" to work as a field hand on a large plantation.

[9]A barrel-maker's shop.

de mawnin', skifts begin to go by, en 'bout eight er nine every skift dat went 'long wuz talkin' 'bout how yo' pap come over to de town en say you's killed. Dese las' skifts wuz full o' ladies en genlmen agoin' over for to see de place. Sometimes dey'd pull up at de sho' en take a res' b'fo' dey started acrost, so by de talk I got to know all 'bout de killin'. I 'uz powerful sorry you's killed, Huck, but I ain't no mo', now.

"I laid dah under de shavins all day. I 'uz hungry, but I warn't afeared; bekase I knowed ole missus en de widder wuz goin' to start to de camp-meetn'[10] right arter breakfas' en be gone all day, en dey knows I goes off wid de cattle 'bout daylight, so dey wouldn't 'spec to see me roun' de place, en so dey wouldn' miss me tell arter dark in de evenin'. De yuther servants wouldn' miss me, kase dey'd shin out en take holiday, soon as de ole folks 'uz out'n de way.

"Well, when it come dark I tuck out up de river road, en went 'bout two mile er more to whah dey warn't no houses. I'd made up my mine 'bout what I's agwyne to do. You see ef I kep' on tryin' to git away afoot, de dogs 'ud track me; ef I stole a skift to cross over, dey'd miss dat skift, you see, en dey'd know 'bout whah I'd lan' on de yuther side en whah to pick up my track. So I says, a raff is what I's arter; it doan' *make* no track.

"I see a light a-comin' roun' de p'int, bymeby, so I wade' in en shove' a log ahead o' me, en swum more'n half-way acrost de river, en got in 'mongst de drift-wood, en kep' my head down low, en kinder swum agin de current tell de raff come along. Den I swum to de stern uv it, en tuck aholt. It clouded up en 'uz pooty dark for a little while. So I clumb up en laid down on de planks. De men 'uz all 'way yonder in de middle, whah de lantern wuz. De river wuz arisin' en dey wuz a good current; so I reck'n'd 'at by fo' in de mawnin' I'd be twenty-five mile down de river, en den I'd slip in, jis' b'fo' daylight, en swim asho' en take to de woods on de Illinois side.[11]

"But I didn't have no luck. When we 'uz mos' down to de head er de islan', a man begin to come aft wid de lantern. I see it warn't no use fer to wait, so I slid overboad, en struck out fer de islan'. Well, I had a notion I could lan' mos' anywhers, but I couldn't—bank too bluff. I 'uz mos' to de foot er de islan' b'fo' I foun' a good place. I went into de woods en jedged I wouldn' fool wid raffs no mo', long as dey move de lantern roun' so. I had my pipe en a plug er dog-leg,[12] en some matches in my cap, en dey warn't wet, so I 'uz all right."

"And so you ain't had no meat nor bread to eat all this time? Why didn't you get mud-turkles?"

"How you gwyne to git'm? You can't slip up on um en grab um; en how's a body gwyne to hit um wid a rock? How could a body do it in de night? en I warn't gwyne to show myself on de bank in de daytime."

[10]Evangelistic religious meetings held in rural areas and attended by enthusiasts who camp nearby.

[11]In Illinois, although it was a free state, runaway slaves lacking free papers were subject to arrest and a term of indentured labor. Jim's best chance for escape was to continue down river to the confluence of the Mississippi and Ohio rivers and thence up the Ohio to a northern state. There proslavery forces were less numerous than in southern Illinois, and Jim could hope to escape to Canada through the Underground Railway.

[12]A plug of cheap leaf tobacco, twisted and bent into the shape of a dog's hind leg.

"Well, that's so. You've had to keep in the woods all the time, of course. Did you hear 'em shooting the cannon?"

"Oh, yes. I knowed dey was arter you. I see um go by heah; watched um thoo de bushes."

Some young birds come along, flying a yard or two at a time and lighting. Jim said it was a sign it was going to rain. He said it was a sign when young chickens flew that way, and so he reckoned it was the same way when young birds done it. I was going to catch some of them, but Jim wouldn't let me. He said it was death. He said his father laid mighty sick once, and some of them catched a bird, and his old granny said his father would die, and he did.

And Jim said you mustn't count the things you are going to cook for dinner, because that would bring bad luck. The same if you shook the table-cloth after sundown. And he said if a man owned a bee-hive, and that man died, the bees must be told about it before sun-up next morning, or else the bees would all weaken down and quit work and die. Jim said bees wouldn't sting idiots; but I didn't believe that, because I had tried them lots of times myself, and they wouldn't sting me.

I had heard about some of these things before, but not all of them. Jim knowed all kinds of signs. He said he knowed most everything. I said it looked to me like all the signs was about bad luck, and so I asked him if there warn't any good-luck signs. He says:

"Mighty few—an' *dey* ain' no use to a body. What you want to know when good luck's a-comin' for? want to keep it off?" And he said: "Ef you's got hairy arms en a hairy breas', it's a sign dat you's agwyne to be rich. Well, dey's some use in a sign like dat, 'kase it's so fur ahead. You see, maybe you's got to be po' a long time fust, en so you might git discourage' en kill yo'self 'f you didn' know by de sign dat you gwyne to be rich bymeby."

"Have you got hairy arms and hairy breast, Jim?"

"What's de use to ax dat question? don' you see I has?"

"Well, are you rich?"

"No, but I ben rich wunst, and gwyne to be rich agin. Wunst I had foteen dollars, but I tuck to specalat'n', en got busted out."

"What did you speculate in, Jim?"

"Well, fust I tackled stock."

"What kind of stock?"

"Why, live stock. Cattle, you know. I put ten dollars in a cow. But I ain't gwyne to resk no mo' money in stock. De cow up 'n' died on my han's."

"So you lost the ten dollars."

"No, I didn't lose it all. I on'y los' 'bout nine of it. I sole de hide en taller[13] for a dollar en ten cents."

"You had five dollars and ten cents left. Did you speculate any more?"

"Yes. You know dat one-laigged nigger dat b'longs to ole Misto Bradish? well, he sot up a bank, en say anybody dat put in a dollar git fo' dollars mo' at de en' er de year. Well, all de niggers went in, but dey didn' have much. I wuz de on'y one dat had much. So I stuck out for mo' dan fo' dollars, en I said 'f I didn' git it I'd start a bank mysef. Well o' course dat nigger want' to keep me out er de business, bekase he say dey warn't business 'nough for two

[13]Tallow.

banks, so he say I could put in my five dollars en he pay me thirty-five at de en' er de year.

"So I done it. Den I reck'n'd I'd inves' de thirty-five dollars right off en keep things a-movin'. Dey wuz a nigger name' Bob, dat had ketched a wood-flat,[14] en his marster didn' know it;[15] en I bought it off'n him en told him to take de thirty-five dollars when de en' er de year come; but somebody stole de wood-flat dat night, en nex' day de one-laigged nigger say de bank's busted. So dey didn' none uv us git no money."

"What did you do with the ten cents, Jim?"

"Well, I 'uz gwyne to spen' it, but I had a dream, en de dream tole me to give it to a nigger name' Balum—Balum's Ass[16] dey call him for short, he's one er dem chuckle-heads, you know. But he's lucky, dey say, en I see I warn't lucky. De dream say let Balum inves' de ten cents en he'd make a raise for me. Well, Balum he tuck de money, en when he wuz in church he hear de preacher say dat whoever give to de po' len' to de Lord, en boun' to git his money back a hund'd times. So Balum he tuck en give de ten cents to de po', en laid low to see what wuz gwyne to come of it."

"Well, what did come of it, Jim?"

"Nuffn' never come of it. I couldn' manage to k'leck dat money no way; en Balum he couldn'. I ain' gwyne to len' no mo' money 'dout I see de security. Boun' to git yo' money back a hund'd times, de preacher say! Ef I could git de ten *cents* back, I'd call it squah, en be glad er de chanst."

"Well, it's all right, anyway, Jim, long as you're going to be rich again some time or other."

"Yes—en I's rich now, come to look at it. I owns mysef, en I's wuth eight hund'd dollars. I wisht I had de money, I wouldn' want no mo'."

CHAPTER IX

I wanted to go and look at a place right about the middle of the island, that I'd found when I was exploring; so we started, and soon got to it, because the island was only three miles long and a quarter of a mile wide.

This place was a tolerable long steep hill or ridge, about forty foot high. We had a rough time getting to the top, the sides were so steep and the bushes so thick. We tramped and clumb around all over it, and by-and-by found a good big cavern in the rock, most up to the top of the side toward Illinois. The cavern was as big as two or three rooms bunched together, and Jim could stand up straight in it. It was cool in there. Jim was for putting our traps in there, right away, but I said we didn't want to be climbing up and down there all the time.

Jim said if we had the canoe hid in a good place, and had all the traps in the cavern, we could rush there if anybody was to come to the island, and they would never find us without dogs. And besides, he said them little birds had said it was going to rain, and did I want the things to get wet?

[14]Flat-bottomed boat for carrying wood.

[15]Possessions of a slave were, by law, the property of the slave's owner.

[16]A pun on the Biblical story of Balaam who, blind to the truth, was saved from death by the ass upon which he rode (Numbers 22:21–34).

So we went back and got the canoe and paddled up abreast the cavern, and lugged all the traps up there. Then we hunted up a place close by to hide the canoe in, amongst the thick willows. We took some fish off of the lines and set them again, and begun to get ready for dinner.

The door of the cavern was big enough to roll a hogshead in, and on one side of the door the floor stuck out a little bit and was flat and a good place to build a fire on. So we built it there and cooked dinner.

We spread the blankets inside for a carpet, and eat our dinner in there. We put all the other things handy at the back of the cavern. Pretty soon it darkened up and begun to thunder and lighten; so the birds was right about it. Directly it begun to rain, and it rained like all fury, too, and I never see the wind blow so. It was one of these regular summer storms. It would get so dark that it looked all blue-black outside, and lovely; and the rain would thrash along by so thick that the trees off a little ways looked dim and spider-webby; and here would come a blast of wind that would bend the trees down and turn up the pale underside of the leaves; and then a perfect ripper of a gust would follow along and set the branches to tossing their arms as if they were just wild; and next, when it was just about the bluest and blackest—*fst!* it was as bright as glory and you'd have a little glimpse of tree-tops a-plunging about, away off yonder in the storm, hundreds of yards further than you could see before; dark as sin again in a second, and now you'd hear the thunder let go with an awful crash and then go rumbling, grumbling, tumbling down the sky towards the under side of the world, like rolling empty barrels down stairs, where it's long stairs and they bounce a good deal, you know.

"Jim, this is nice," I says. "I wouldn't want to be nowhere else but here. Pass me along another hunk of fish and some hot corn-bread."

"Well, you wouldn't a ben here, 'f it hadn't a ben for Jim. You'd a ben down dah in de woods widout any dinner, en gittn' mos' drownded, too, dat you would, honey. Chickens knows when it's gwyne to rain, en so do de birds, chile."

The river went on raising and raising for ten or twelve days, till at last it was over the banks. The water was three or four foot deep on the island in the low places and on the Illinois bottom. On that side it was a good many miles wide; but on the Missouri side it was the same old distance across—a half a mile—because the Missouri shore was just a wall of high bluffs.

Daytimes we paddled all over the island in the canoe. It was mighty cool and shady in the deep woods even if the sun was blazing outside. We went winding in and out amongst the trees; and sometimes the vines hung so thick we had to back away and go some other way. Well, on every old broken-down tree, you could see rabbits, and snakes, and such things; and when the island had been overflowed a day or two, they got so tame, on account of being hungry, that you could paddle right up and put your hand on them if you wanted to; but not the snakes and turtles—they would slide off in the water. The ridge our cavern was in, was full of them. We could a had pets enough if we'd wanted them.

One night we catched a little section of a lumber raft—nice pine planks. It was twelve foot wide and about fifteen or sixteen foot long, and the top stood above water six or seven inches, a solid level floor. We could see saw-logs[1] go

[1]Split, in preparation for sawing.

by in the daylight, sometimes, but we let them go; we didn't show ourselves in daylight.

Another night, when we was up at the head of the island, just before daylight, here comes a frame house down, on the west side. She was a two-story, and tilted over, considerable. We paddled out and got aboard—clumb in at an up-stairs window. But it was too dark to see yet, so we made the canoe fast and set in her to wait for daylight.

The light begun to come before we got to the foot of the island. Then we looked in at the window. We could make out a bed, and a table, and two old chairs, and lots of things around about on the floor; and there was clothes hanging against the wall. There was something laying on the floor in the far corner that looked like a man. So Jim says:

"Hello, you!"

But it didn't budge. So I hollered again, and then Jim says:

"De man ain't asleep—he's dead. You hold still—I go en see."

He went and bent down and looked, and says:

"It's a dead man. Yes, indeedy; naked, too. He's ben shot in de back. I reck'n he's ben dead two er three days. Come in, Huck, but doan' look at his face—it's too gashly."

I didn't look at him at all. Jim throwed some old rags over him, but he needn't done it; I didn't want to see him. There was heaps of old greasy cards scattered around over the floor, and old whisky bottles, and a couple of masks made out of black cloth; and all over the walls was the ignorantest kind of words and pictures, made with charcoal. There was two old dirty calico[2] dresses, and a sun-bonnet, and some women's under-clothes, hanging against the wall, and some men's clothing, too. We put the lot into the canoe; it might come good. There was a boy's old speckled straw hat on the floor; I took that too. And there was a bottle that had had milk in it; and it had a rag stopper for a baby to suck. We would a took the bottle, but it was broke. There was a seedy old chest, and an old hair trunk[3] with the hinges broke. They stood open, but there warn't nothing left in them that was any account. The way things was scattered about, we reckoned the people left in a hurry and warn't fixed so as to carry off most of their stuff.

We got an old tin lantern, and a butcher knife without any handle, and a bran-new Barlow knife[4] worth two bits in any store, and a lot of tallow candles, and a tin candlestick, and a gourd, and a tin cup, and a ratty old bedquilt off the bed, and reticule[5] with needles and pins and beeswax and buttons and thread and all such truck in it, and a hatchet and some nails, and a fish-line as thick as my little finger, with some monstrous hooks on it, and a roll of buckskin, and a leather dog-collar, and a horse-shoe, and some vials of medicine that didn't have no label on them; and just as we was leaving I found a tolerable good curry-comb,[6] and Jim he found a ratty old fiddle-bow, and a wooden leg. The straps was broke off of it, but barring that, it was a good enough leg, though it was too long for me and not long enough for Jim, and we couldn't find the other one, though we hunted all around.

[2]Colorful, printed cotton cloth.

[3]A trunk covered with cowhide from which the hair has not been removed.

[4]A pocketknife.

[5]Small bag, a purse.

[6]Metal comb used for grooming (currying) horses.

And so, take it all around, we made a good haul. When we was ready to shove off, we was a quarter of a mile below the island, and it was pretty broad day; so I made Jim lay down in the canoe and cover up with the quilt, because if he set up, people could tell he was a nigger a good ways off. I paddled over to the Illinois shore, and drifted most a half a mile doing it. I crept up the dead water under the bank, and hadn't no accidents and didn't see nobody. We got home all safe.

CHAPTER X

After breakfast I wanted to talk about the dead man and guess out how he come to be killed, but Jim didn't want to. He said it would fetch bad luck; and besides, he said, he might come and ha'nt us; he said a man that warn't buried was more likely to go a-ha'nting around than one that was planted and comfortable. That sounded pretty reasonable, so I didn't say no more; but I couldn't keep from studying over it and wishing I knowed who shot the man, and what they done it for.

We rummaged the clothes we'd got, and found eight dollars in silver sewed up in the lining of an old blanket overcoat. Jim said he reckoned the people in that house stole the coat, because if they'd a knowed the money was there they wouldn't a left it. I said I reckoned they killed him, too; but Jim didn't want to talk about that. I says:

"Now you think it's bad luck; but what did you say when I fetched in the snake-skin that I found on the top of the ridge day before yesterday? You said it was the worst bad luck in the world to touch a snake-skin with my hands. Well, here's your bad luck! We've raked in all this truck and eight dollars besides. I wish we could have some bad luck like this every day, Jim."

"Never you mind, honey, never you mind. Don't you git too peart.[1] It's a-comin'. Mind I tell you, it's a-comin'."

It did come, too. It was a Tuesday that we had that talk. Well, after dinner Friday, we was laying around in the grass at the upper end of the ridge, and got out of tobacco. I went to the cavern to get some, and found a rattlesnake in there. I killed him, and curled him up on the foot of Jim's blanket, ever so natural, thinking there'd be some fun when Jim found him there. Well, by night I forgot all about the snake, and when Jim flung himself down on the blanket while I struck a light, the snake's mate was there, and bit him.

He jumped up yelling, and the first thing the light showed was the varmint curled up and ready for another spring. I laid him out in a second with a stick, and Jim grabbed pap's whisky jug and begun to pour it down.

He was barefooted, and the snake bit him right on the heel. That all comes of being such a fool as to not remember that wherever you leave a dead snake its mate always comes there and curls around it. Jim told me to chop off the snake's head and throw it away, and then skin the body and roast a piece of it. I done it, and he eat it and said it would help cure him. He made me take off the rattles and tie them around his wrist, too. He said that that would help. Then I slid out quiet and throwed the snakes clear away amongst the bushes; for I warn't going to let Jim find out it was all my fault, not if I could help it.

[1] Smart.

Jim sucked and sucked at the jug, and now and then he got out of his head and pitched around and yelled; but every time he come to himself he went to sucking at the jug again. His foot swelled up pretty big, and so did his leg; but by-an-by the drunk begun to come, and so I judge he was all right; but I'd druther been bit with a snake than pap's whisky.

Jim was laid up for four days and nights. Then the swelling was all gone and he was around again. I made up my mind I wouldn't ever take aholt of a snake-skin again with my hands, now that I see what had come of it. Jim said he reckoned I would believe him next time. And he said that handling a snake-skin was such awful bad luck that maybe we hadn't got to the end of it yet. He said he druther see the new moon over his left shoulder as much as a thousand times than take up a snake-skin in his hand. Well, I was getting to feel that way myself, though I've always reckoned that looking at the new moon over your left shoulder is one of the carelessest and foolishest things a body can do. Old Hank Bunker done it once, and bragged about it; and in less than two years he got drunk and fell off of the shot tower and spread himself out so that he was just a kind of a layer, as you may say; and they slid him edgeways between two barn doors for a coffin, and buried him so, so they say, but I didn't see it. Pap told me. But anyway, it all come of looking at the moon that way, like a fool.

Well, the days went along, and the river went down between its banks again; and about the first thing we done was to bait one of the big hooks with a skinned rabbit and set it and catch a cat-fish that was as big as a man, being six foot two inches long, and weighed over two hundred pounds. We couldn't handle him, of course; he would a flung us into Illinois. We just set there and watched him rip and tear around till he drownded. We found a brass button in his stomach, and a round ball, and lots of rubbage. We split the ball open with the hatchet, and there was a spool in it. Jim said he'd had it there a long time, to coat it over so and make a ball of it. It was as big a fish as was ever catched in the Mississippi, I reckon. Jim said he hadn't ever seen a bigger one. He would a been worth a good deal over at the village. They peddle out such a fish as that by the pound in the market house there; everybody buys some of him; his meat's as white as snow and makes a good fry.

Next morning I said it was getting slow and dull and I wanted to get a stirring up, some way. I said I reckoned I would slip over the river and find out what was going on. Jim liked that notion; but he said I must go in the dark and look sharp. Then he studied it over and said, couldn't I put on some of them old things and dress up like a girl? That was a good notion, too. So we shortened up one of the calico gowns and I turned up my trowser-legs to my knees and got into it. Jim hitched it behind with the hooks, and it was a fair fit. I put on the sun-bonnet and tied it under my chin, and then for a body to look in and see my face was like looking down a joint of stove-pipe. Jim said nobody would know me, even in the daytime hardly. I practiced around all day to get the hang of the things, and by-and-by I could do pretty well in them, only Jim said I didn't walk like a girl; and he said I must quit pulling up my gown to get at my britches pocket. I took notice, and done better.

I started up the Illinois shore in the canoe just after dark.

I started across to the town from a little below the ferry landing, and the drift of the current fetched me in at the bottom of the town. I tied up and started along the bank. There was a light burning in a little shanty that hadn't been lived in for a long time, and I wondered who had took up quarters there. I slipped up and peeped in at the window. There was a woman about forty year old in there, knitting by a candle that was on a pine table. I didn't know her face; she was a stranger, for you couldn't start[2] a face in that town that I didn't know. Now this was lucky, because I was weakening; I was getting afraid I had come; people might know my voice and find me out. But if this woman had been in such a little town two days she could tell me all I wanted to know; so I knocked at the door, and made up my mind I wouldn't forget I was a girl.

CHAPTER XI

"Come in," says the woman, and I did. She says:

"Take a cheer."

I done it. She looked me all over with her little shiny eyes, and says: "What might your name be?"

"Sarah Williams."

"Where 'bouts do you live? In this neighborhood?"

"No'm. In Hookerville, seven mile below. I've walked all the way and I'm all tired out."

"Hungry, too, I reckon. I'll find you something."

"No'm, I ain't hungry. I was so hungry I had to stop two miles below here at a farm; so I ain't hungry no more. It's what makes me so late. My mother's down sick, and out of money and everything, and I come to tell my uncle Abner Moore. He lives at the upper end of the town, she says, I hain't ever been here before. Do you know him?"

"No; but I don't know everybody yet. I haven't lived here quite two weeks. It's a considerable ways to the upper end of the town. You better stay here all night. Take off your bonnet."

"No," I says, "I'll rest a while, I reckon, and go on. I ain't afeard of the dark."

She said she wouldn't let me go by myself, but her husband would be in by-and-by, maybe in a hour and a half, and she'd send him along with me. Then she got to talking about her husband, and about her relations up the river, and her relations down the river, and about how much better off they used to was, and how they didn't know but they'd made a mistake coming to our town, instead of letting well alone—and so on and so on, till I was afeard *I* had made a mistake coming to her to find out what was going on in the town; but by-and-by she dropped onto pap and the murder, and then I was pretty willing to let her clatter right along. She told about me and Tom Sawyer finding the six thousand dollars[1] (only she got it ten) and all about pap and what a hard lot he was, and what a hard lot I was, and at last she got down to where I was murdered. I says:

"Who done it? We've heard considerable about these goings on, down in Hookerville, but we don't know who 'twas that killed Huck Finn."

[2]Find, discover.

[1]The sum found by Huck and Tom, as described in *Tom Sawyer,* actually totaled $12,000.

"Well, I reckon there's a right smart chance[2] of people *here* that'd like to know who killed him. Some thinks old Finn done it himself."

"No—is that so?"

"Most everybody thought it at first. He'll never know how nigh he come to getting lynched. But before night they changed around and judged it was done by a runaway nigger named Jim."

"Why *he*——"

I stopped. I reckoned I better keep still. She run on, and never noticed I had put in at all.

"The nigger run off the very night Huck Finn was killed. So there's a reward out for him—three hundred dollars. And there's a reward out for old Finn too—two hundred dollars. You see, he come to town the morning after the murder, and told about it, and was out with 'em on the ferry-boat hunt, and right away after he up and left. Before night they wanted to lynch him, but he was gone, you see. Well, next day they found out the nigger was gone; they found out he hadn't ben seen sence ten o'clock the night the murder was done. So then they put it on him, you see, and while they was full of it, next day back comes old Finn and went boo-hooing to Judge Thatcher to get money to hunt for the nigger all over Illinois with. The judge give him some, and that evening he got drunk and was around till after midnight with a couple of mighty hard looking strangers, and then went off with them. Well, he hain't come back sence, and they ain't looking for him back till this thing blows over a little, for people thinks now that he killed his boy and fixed things so folks would think robbers done it, and then he'd get Huck's money without having to bother a long time with a lawsuit. People do say he warn't any too good to do it. Oh, he's sly, I reckon. If he don't come back for a year, he'll be all right. You can't prove anything on him, you know; everything will be quieted down then, and he'll walk into Huck's money as easy as nothing."

"Yes, I reckon so, 'm. I don't see nothing in the way of it. Has everybody quit thinking the nigger done it?"

"Oh, no, not everybody. A good many thinks he done it. But they'll get the nigger pretty soon, now, and maybe they can scare it out of him."

"Why, are they after him yet?"

"Well, you're innocent, ain't you! Does three hundred dollars lay round every day for people to pick up? Some folks thinks the nigger ain't far from here. I'm one of them—but I hain't talked it around. A few days ago I was talking with an old couple that lives next door in the log shanty, and they happened to say hardly anybody ever goes to that island over yonder that they call Jackson's Island. Don't anybody live there? says I. No, nobody, says they. I didn't say any more, but I done some thinking. I was pretty near certain I'd seen smoke over there, about the head of the island, a day or two before that, so I says to myself, like as not that nigger's hiding over there; anyway, says I, it's worth the trouble to give the place a hunt. I hain't seen any smoke sence, so I reckon maybe he's gone, if it was him; but husband's going over to see—him and another man. He was gone up the river; but he got back to-day and I told him as soon as he got here two hours ago."

I had got so uneasy I couldn't set still. I had to do something with my hands; so I took up a needle off of the table and went to threading it. My

[2]Southern dialect: a large number.

hands shook, and I was making a bad job of it. When the woman stopped talking, I looked up, and she was looking at me pretty curious, and smiling a little. I put down the needle and thread and let on to be interested—and I was, too—and says:

"Three hundred dollars is a power of money. I wish my mother could get it. Is your husband going over there to-night?"

"Oh, yes. He went up town with the man I was telling you of, to get a boat and see if they could borrow another gun. They'll go over after midnight."

"Couldn't they see better if they was to wait till daytime?"

"Yes. And couldn't the nigger see better, too? After midnight he'll likely be asleep, and they can slip around through the woods and hunt up his camp fire all the better for the dark, if he's got one."

"I didn't think of that."

The woman kept looking at me pretty curious, and I didn't feel a bit comfortable. Pretty soon she says:

"What did you say your name was, honey?"

"M—Mary Williams."

Somehow it didn't seem to me that I said it was Mary before, so I didn't look up; seemed to me I said it was Sarah; so I felt sort of cornered, and was afeared maybe I was looking it, too. I wished the woman would say something more; the longer she set still, the uneasier I was. But now she says:

"Honey, I thought you said it was Sarah when you first come in?"

"Oh, yes'm, I did. Sarah Mary Williams. Sarah's my first name. Some calls me Sarah, some calls me Mary."

"Oh, that's the way of it?"

"Yes'm."

I was feeling better, then, but I wished I was out of there, anyway. I couldn't look up yet.

Well, the woman fell to talking about how hard times was, and how poor they had to live, and how the rats was as free as if they owned the place, and so forth, and so on, and then I got easy again. She was right about the rats. You'd see one stick his nose out of a hole in the corner every little while. She said she had to have things handy to throw at them when she was alone, or they wouldn't give her no peace. She showed me a bar of lead, twisted up into a knot, and said she was a good shot with it generly, but she'd wrenched her arm a day or two ago, and didn't know whether she could throw true, now. But she watched for a chance, and directly she banged away at a rat, but she missed him wide, and said "Ouch!" it hurt her arm so. Then she told me to try for the next one. I wanted to be getting away before the old man got back, but of course I didn't let on. I got the thing, and the first rat that showed his nose I let drive, and if he'd a stayed where he was he'd a been a tolerable sick rat. She said that that was first-rate, and she reckoned I would hive the next one. She went and got the lump of lead and fetched it back and brought along a hank of yarn, which she wanted me to help her with. I held up my two hands and she put the hank over them and went on talking about her and her husband's matters. But she broke off to say:

"Keep your eye on the rats. You better have the lead in your lap, handy."

So she dropped the lump into my lap, just at that moment, and I clapped my legs together on it and she went on talking. But only about a minute.

Then she took off the hank and looked me straight in the face, but very pleasant, and says:

"Come, now—what's your real name?"

"Wh-what, mum?"

"What's your real name? Is it Bill, or Tom, or Bob?—or what is it?"

I reckon I shook like a leaf, and I didn't know hardly what to do. But I says:

"Please to don't poke fun at a poor girl like me, mum. If I'm in the way, here, I'll——"

"No, you won't. Set down and stay where you are. I ain't going to hurt you, and I ain't going to tell on you, nuther. You just tell me your secret, and trust me. I'll keep it; and what's more, I'll help you. So'll my old man, if you want him to. You see, you're a runaway 'prentice—that's all. It ain't anything. There ain't any harm in it. You've been treated bad, and you made up your mind to cut. Bless you, child, I wouldn't tell on you. Tell me all about it, now—that's a good boy."

So I said it wouldn't be no use to try to play it any longer, and I would just make a clean breast and tell her everything, but she mustn't go back on her promise. Then I told her my father and mother was dead, and the law had bound me[3] out to a mean old farmer in the country thirty mile back from the river, and he treated me so bad I couldn't stand it no longer; he went away to be gone a couple of days, and so I took my chance and stole some of his daughter's old clothes, and cleared out, and I had been three nights coming the thirty miles; I traveled nights, and hid day-times and slept, and the bag of bread and meat I carried from home lasted me all the way and I had a plenty. I said I believed my uncle Abner Moore would take care of me, and so that was why I struck out for this town of Goshen.

"Goshen, child? This ain't Goshen. This is St. Petersburg.[4] Goshen's ten mile further up the river. Who told you this was Goshen?"

"Why, a man I met at day-break this morning, just as I was going to turn into the woods for my regular sleep. He told me when the roads forked I must take the right hand, and five mile would fetch me to Goshen."

"He was drunk I reckon. He told you just exactly wrong."

"Well, he did act like he was drunk, but it ain't no matter now. I got to be moving along. I'll fetch Goshen before day-light."

"Hold on a minute. I'll put you up a snack to eat. You might want it."

So she put me up a snack, and says:

"Say—when a cow's laying down, which end of her gets up first? Answer up prompt, now—don't stop to study over it. Which end gets up first?"

"The hind end, mum."

"Well, then, a horse?"

"The for'rard end, mum."

"Which side of a tree does the most moss grow on?"

"North side."

"If fifteen cows is browsing on a hillside, how many of them eats with their heads pointed the same direction?"

"The whole fifteen, mum."

[3]Assigned, as a ward of the court.

[4]Twain's fictional name for Hannibal, Missouri, his boyhood home.

"Well, I reckon you *have* lived in the country. I thought maybe you was trying to hocus[5] me again. What's your real name, now?"

"George Peters, mum."

"Well, try to remember it, George. Don't forget and tell me it's Elexander before you go, and then get out by saying it's George-Elexander when I catch you. And don't go about women in that old calico. You do a girl tolerable poor, but you might fool men, maybe. Bless you, child, when you set out to thread a needle, don't hold the thread still and fetch the needle up to it; hold the needle still and poke the thread at it—that's the way a woman most always does; but a man always does t'other way. And when you throw at a rat or anything, hitch yourself up a tip-toe, and fetch your hand up over your head as awkward as you can, and miss your rat about six or seven foot. Throw stiff-armed from the shoulder, like there was a pivot there for it to turn on—like a girl; not from the wrist and elbow, with your arm out to one side, like a boy. And mind you, when a girl tries to catch anything in her lap, she throws her knees apart; she don't clap them together, the way you did when you catched the lump of lead. Why, I spotted you for a boy when you was threading the needle; and I contrived the other things just to make certain. Now trot along to your uncle, Sarah Mary Williams George Elexander Peters, and if you get into trouble you send word to Mrs. Judith Loftus, which is me, and I'll do what I can to get you out of it. Keep the river road, all the way, and next time you tramp, take shoes and socks with you. The river road's a rocky one, and your feet'll be in a condition when you get to Goshen, I reckon."

I went up the bank about fifty yards, and then I doubled on my tracks and slipped back to where my canoe was, a good piece below the house. I jumped in and was off in a hurry. I went up stream far enough to make the head of the island, and then started across. I took off the sun-bonnet, for I didn't want no blinders[6] on, then. When I was about the middle, I hear the clock begin to strike; so I stops and listens; the sound come faint over the water, but clear—eleven. When I struck the head of the island I never waited to blow, though I was most winded, but I shoved right into the timber where my old camp used to be, and started a good fire there on a high-and-dry spot.

Then I jumped in the canoe and dug out for our place a mile and a half below, as hard as I could go. I landed, and slopped through the timber and up the ridge and into the cavern. There Jim laid, sound asleep on the ground. I roused him out and says:

"Git up and hump yourself, Jim! There ain't a minute to lose. They're after us!"

Jim never asked no questions, he never said a word; but the way he worked for the next half an hour showed about how he was scared. By that time everything we had in the world was on our raft and she was ready to be shoved out from the willow cove where she was hid. We put out the camp fire at the cavern the first thing, and didn't show a candle outside after that.

I took the canoe out from shore a little piece and took a look, but if there was a boat around I couldn't see it, for stars and shadows ain't good to see by. Then we got out the raft and slipped along down in the shade, past the foot of the island dead still, never saying a word.

[5]Trick. [6]Attachments on a horse's bridle, to restrict vision

CHAPTER XII

It must a been close onto one o'clock when we got below the island at last, and the raft did seem to go mighty slow. If a boat was to come along, we was going to take to the canoe and break for the Illinois shore; and it was well a boat didn't come, for we hadn't ever thought to put the gun into the canoe, or a fishing-line or anything to eat. We was in ruther too much of a sweat to think of so many things. It warn't good judgment to put *everything* on the raft.

If the men went to the island, I just expect they found the camp fire I built, and watched it all night for Jim to come. Anyways, they stayed away from us, and if my building the fire never fooled them it warn't no fault of mine. I played it as low-down on them as I could.

When the first streak of day begun to show, we tied up to a tow-head in a big bend on the Illinois side, and hacked off cotton-wood branches with the hatchet and covered up the raft with them so she looked like there had been a cave-in in the bank there. A tow-head is a sand-bar that has cotton-woods on it as thick as harrow-teeth.[1]

We had mountains on the Missouri shore and heavy timber on the Illinois side, and the channel was down the Missouri shore at that place, so we warn't afraid of anybody running across us. We laid there all day and watched the rafts and steamboats spin down the Missouri shore, and up-bound steamboats[2] fight the big river in the middle. I told Jim all about the time I had jabbering with that woman; and Jim said she was a smart one, and if she was to start after us herself *she* wouldn't set down and watch a camp fire—no, sir, she'd fetch a dog. Well, then, I said, why couldn't she tell her husband to fetch a dog? Jim said he bet she did think of it by the time the men was ready to start, and he believed they must a gone up town to get a dog and so they lost all that time, or else we wouldn't be here on a tow-head sixteen or seventeen mile below the village—no, indeedy, we would be in that same old town again. So I said I didn't care what was the reason they didn't get us, as long as they didn't.

When it was beginning to come on dark, we poked our heads out of the cottonwood thicket and looked up, and down, and across; nothing in sight; so Jim took up some of the top planks of the raft and built a snug wigwam to get under in blazing weather and rainy, and to keep the things dry. Jim made a floor for the wigwam, and raised it a foot or more above the level of the raft, so now the blankets and all the traps was out of the reach of steamboat waves. Right in the middle of the wigwam we made a layer of dirt about five or six inches deep with a frame around it for to hold it to its place; this was to build a fire on in sloppy weather or chilly; the wigwam would keep it from being seen. We made an extra steering oar, too, because one of the others might get broke, on a snag or something. We fixed up a short forked stick to hang the old lantern on; because we must always light the lantern whenever we see a steamboat coming down stream, to keep from getting run over; but we wouldn't have to light it for upstream boats unless we see we was in what they call a "crossing"; for the river was pretty high yet, very low banks being still a little under water; so up-bound boats didn't always run the channel, but hunted easy water.

[1]As numerous as teeth on a harrow, a rake. [2]Steamboats going upriver, against the current.

This second night we run between seven and eight hours, with a current that was making over four miles an hour. We catched fish, and talked, and we took a swim now and then to keep off sleepiness. It was kind of solemn, drifting down the big still river, laying on our backs looking up at the stars, and we didn't ever feel like talking loud, and it warn't often that we laughed, only a little kind of a low chuckle. We had mighty good weather, as a general thing, and nothing ever happened to us at all, that night, nor the next, nor the next.

Every night we passed towns, some of them away up on black hillsides, nothing but just a shiny bed of lights, not a house could you see. The fifth night we passed St. Louis, and it was like the whole world lit up. In St. Petersburg they used to say there was twenty or thirty thousand people in St. Louis, but I never believed it till I see that wonderful spread of lights at two o'clock that still night. There warn't a sound there; everybody was asleep.

Every night, now, I used to slip ashore, towards ten o'clock, at some little village, and buy ten or fifteen cents' worth of meal or bacon or other stuff to eat; and sometimes I lifted a chicken that warn't roosting comfortable, and took him along. Pap always said, take a chicken when you get a chance, because if you don't want him yourself you can easy find somebody that does, and a good deed ain't ever forgot. I never see pap when he didn't want the chicken himself, but that is what he used to say, anyway.

Mornings, before daylight, I slipped into corn fields and borrowed a watermelon, or a mushmelon, or a punkin, or some new corn, or things of that kind. Pap always said it warn't no harm to borrow things, if you was meaning to pay them back, sometime; but the widow said it warn't anything but a soft name for stealing, and no decent body would do it. Jim said he reckoned the widow was partly right and pap was partly right; so the best way would be for us to pick out two or three things from the list and say we wouldn't borrow them any more—then he reckoned it wouldn't be no harm to borrow the others. So we talked it over all one night, drifting along down the river, trying to make up our minds whether to drop the watermelons, or the cantelopes, or the mushmelons, or what. But towards daylight we got it all settled satisfactory, and concluded to drop crabapples and p'simmons. We warn't feeling just right, before that, but it was all comfortable now. I was glad the way it come out, too, because crabapples ain't ever good, and the p'simmons wouldn't be ripe for two or three months yet.

We shot a water-fowl, now and then, that got up too early in the morning or didn't go to bed early enough in the evening. Take it all around, we lived pretty high.

The fifth night below St. Louis we had a big storm after midnight, with a power of thunder and lightning, and the rain poured down in a solid sheet. We stayed in the wigwam and let the raft take care of itself. When the lightning glared out we could see a big straight river ahead, and high rocky bluffs on both sides. By-and-by says I, "Hel-*lo,* Jim, looky yonder!" It was a steamboat that had killed herself on a rock. We was drifting straight down for her. The lightning showed her very distinct. She was leaning over, with part of her upper deck above water, and you could see every little chimblyguy[3] clean and

[3]Wires that brace (guy) the smoke stacks.

clear, and a chair by the big bell, with an old slouch hat hanging on the back of it when the flashes come.

Well, it being away in the night, and stormy, and all so mysterious-like, I felt just the way any other boy would a felt when I see that wreck laying there so mournful and lonesome in the middle of the river. I wanted to get aboard of her and slink around a little, and see what there was there. So I says:

"Le's land on her, Jim."

But Jim was dead against it, at first. He says:

"I doan' want to go fool'n 'long er no wrack. We's doin' blame' well, en we better let blame' well alone, as de good book says. Like as not dey's a watchman on dat wrack."

"Watchman your grandmother," I says; "there ain't nothing to watch but the texas[4] and the pilot-house; and do you reckon anybody's going to resk his life for a texas and a pilot-house such a night as this, when it's likely to break up and wash off down the river any minute?" Jim couldn't say nothing to that, so he didn't try. "And besides," I says, "we might borrow something worth having, out of the captain's stateroom.[5] Seegars, *I* bet you—and cost five cents apiece, solid cash. Steamboat captains is always rich, and get sixty dollars a month, and *they* don't care a cent what a thing costs, you know, long as they want it. Stick a candle in your pocket; I can't rest, Jim, till we give her a rummaging. Do you reckon Tom Sawyer would ever go by this thing? Not for pie, he wouldn't. He'd call it an adventure—that's what he'd call it; and he'd land on that wreck if it was his last act. And wouldn't he throw style into it?—wouldn't he spread himself, nor nothing? Why, you'd think it was Christopher C'lumbus discovering Kingdom-Come. I wish Tom Sawyer *was* here."

Jim he grumbled a little, but give in. He said we mustn't talk any more than we could help, and then talk mighty low. The lightning showed us the wreck again, just in time, and we fetched the starboard derrick,[6] and made fast there.

The deck was high out, here. We went sneaking down the slope of it to labboard,[7] in the dark, towards the texas, feeling our way slow with our feet, and spreading our hands out to fend off the guys, for it was so dark we couldn't see no sign of them. Pretty soon we struck the forward end of the skylight, and clumb onto it; and the next step fetched us in front of the captain's door, which was open, and by Jimminy, away down through the texas-hall we see a light! and all in the same second we seem to hear low voices in yonder!

Jim whispered and said he was feeling powerful sick, and told me to come along. I says, all right; and was going to start for the raft; but just then I heard a voice wail out and say:

"Oh, please don't, boys; I swear I won't ever tell!"

Another voice said, pretty loud:

"It's a lie, Jim Turner. You've acted this way before. You always want more'n your share of the truck, and you've always got it, too, because you've swore 't if you didn't you'd tell. But this time you've said it jest one time too many. You're the meanest, treacherousest hound in this country."

[4]Structure on the upper deck of a steamboat, with the biggest (hence "texas") cabins.
[5]Sleeping quarters. [6]Cargo boom for loading and unloading the ship.
[7]Left (port) side of a ship, looking forward.

By this time Jim was gone for the raft. I was just a-biling with curiosity; and I says to myself, Tom Sawyer wouldn't back out now, and so I won't either; I'm agoing to see what's going on here. So I dropped on my hands and knees, in the little passage, and crept aft in the dark, till there warn't but about one stateroom betwixt me and the cross-hall of the texas. Then, in there I see a man stretched on the floor and tied hand and foot, and two men standing over him, and one of them had a dim lantern in his hand, and the other one had a pistol. This one kept pointing the pistol at the man's head on the floor and saying—

"I'd *like* to! And I orter, too, a mean skunk!"

The man on the floor would shrivel up, and say: "Oh, please don't, Bill—I hain't ever goin' to tell."

And every time he said that, the man with the lantern would laugh, and say:

" 'Deed you *aint!* You never said no truer thing 'n that, you bet you." And once he said: "Hear him beg! and yit if we hadn't got the best of him and tied him, he'd a killed us both. And what *for?* Jist for noth'n. Jist because we stood on our *rights*—that's what for. But I lay you ain't agoin' to threaten nobody any more, Jim Turner. Put *up* that pistol, Bill."

Bill says:

"I don't want to, Jake Packard. I'm for killin' him—and didn't he kill old Hatfield jist the same way—and don't he deserve it?"

"But I don't *want* him killed, and I've got my reasons for it."

"Bless yo' heart for them words, Jake Packard! I'll never forgit you, long's I live!" says the man on the floor, sort of blubbering.

Packard didn't take no notice of that, but hung up his lantern on a nail, and started towards where I was, there in the dark, and motioned Bill to come. I crawfished[8] as fast as I could, about two yards, but the boat slanted so that I couldn't make very good time; so to keep from getting run over and catched I crawled into a stateroom on the upper side. The man come a-pawing along in the dark, and when Packard got to my stateroom, he says:

"Here—come in here."

And in he come, and Bill after him. But before they got in, I was up in the upper berth, cornered, and sorry I come. Then they stood there, with their hands on the ledge of the berth, and talked. I couldn't see them, but I could tell where they was, by the whisky they'd been having. I was glad I didn't drink whisky; but it wouldn't made much difference, anyway, because most of the time they couldn't a treed me because I didn't breathe. I was too scared. And besides, a body *couldn't* breathe, and hear such talk. They talked low and earnest. Bill wanted to kill Turner. He says:

"He's said he'll tell, and he will. If we was to give both our shares to him *now,* it wouldn't make no difference after the row, and the way we've served him. Shore's you're born, he'll turn State's evidence, now you hear *me.* I'm for putting him out of his troubles."

"So'm I," says Packard, very quiet.

"Blame it, I'd sorter begun to think you wasn't. Well, then, that's all right. Les' go and do it."

[8]Crawled backward.

"Hold on a minute; I hain't had my say yit. You listen to me. Shooting's good, but there's quieter ways if the thing's *got* to be done. But what *I* say, is this; it ain't good sense to go court'n around after a halter,[9] if you git at what you're up to in some way that's jist as good and at the same time don't bring you into no resks. Ain't that so?"

"You bet it is. But how you goin' to manage it this time?"

"Well, my idea is this: we'll rustle around and gether up whatever pickins we've overlooked in the staterooms, and shove for shore and hide the truck. Then we'll wait. Now I say it ain't agoin' to be more 'n two hours befo' this wrack breaks up and washes off down the river. See? He'll be drownded, and won't have nobody to blame for it but his own self. I reckon that's a considerable sight better'n killin' of him. I'm unfavorable to killin' a man as long as you can git around it; it ain't good sense, it ain't good morals. Ain't I right?"

"Yes—I reck'n you are. But s'pose she *don't* break up and wash off?"

"Well, we can wait the two hours, anyway, and see, can't we?"

"All right, then; come along."

So they started, and I lit out, all in a cold sweat, and scrambled forward. It was dark as pitch there; but I said in a kind of a coarse whisper,"Jim!" and he answered up, right at my elbow, with a sort of a moan, and I says:

"Quick, Jim, it ain't no time for fooling around and moaning; there's a gang of murderers in yonder, and if we don't hunt up their boat and set her drifting down the river so these fellows can't get away from the wreck, there's one of 'em going to be in a bad fix. But if we find their boat we can put *all* of 'em in a bad fix—for the Sheriff 'll get 'em. Quick—hurry! I'll hunt the labboard side, you hunt the stabboard. You start at the raft, and—"

"Oh, my lordy, lordy! *Raf'?* Dey ain' no raf' no mo', she done broke loose en gone!—'en here we is!"

CHAPTER XIII

Well, I catched my breath and most fainted. Shut up on a wreck with such a gang as that! But it warn't no time to be sentimentering. We'd *got* to find that boat, now—had to have it for ourselves. So we went a-quaking and shaking down the stabboard side, and slow work it was, too—seemed a week before we got to the stern. No sign of a boat. Jim said he didn't believe he could go any further—so scared he hadn't hardly any strength left, he said. But I said come on, if we get left on this wreck, we are in a fix, sure. So on we prowled, again. We struck for the stern of the texas, and found it, and then scrabbled along forwards on the skylight, hanging on from shutter to shutter, for the edge of the skylight was in the water. When we got pretty close to the cross-hall door, there was the skiff, sure enough! I could just barely see her. I felt ever so thankful. In another second I would a been aboard of her; but just then the door opened. One of the men stuck his head out, only about a couple of foot from me, and I thought I was gone; but he jerked it in again, and says,

"Heave that blame lantern out o' sight, Bill!"

[9]Hangman's noose.

He flung a bag of something into the boat, and then got in himself, and set down. It was Packard. Then Bill *he* come out and got in. Packard says, in a low voice:

"All ready—shove off!"

I couldn't hardly hang onto the shutters, I was so weak. But Bill says:

"Hold on—'d you go through him?"

"No. Didn't you?"

"No. So he's got his share o' the cash, yet."

"Well, then, come along—no use to take truck and leave money."

"Say—won't he suspicion what we're up to?"

"Maybe he won't. But we got to have it anyway. Come along."

So they got out and went in.

The door slammed to, because it was on the careened side; and in a half second I was in the boat, and Jim come a tumbling after me. I out with my knife and cut the rope, and away we went!

We didn't touch an oar, and we didn't speak nor whisper, nor hardly even breathe. We went gliding swift along, dead silent, past the tip of the paddle-box, and past the stern; then in a second or two more we was a hundred yards below the wreck, and the darkness soaked her up, every last sign of her, and we was safe, and knowed it.

When we was three or four hundred yards down stream, we see the lantern show like a little spark at the texas door, for a second, and we knowed by that that the rascals had missed their boat, and was beginning to understand that they was in just as much trouble, now, as Jim Turner was.

Then Jim manned the oars, and we took out after our raft. Now was the first time that I begun to worry about the men—I reckon I hadn't had time to before. I begun to think how dreadful it was, even for murderers, to be in such a fix. I says to myself, there ain't no telling but I might come to be a murderer myself, yet, and then how would *I* like it? So says I to Jim:

"The first light we see, we'll land a hundred yards below it or above it, in a place where it's a good hiding-place for you and the skiff, and then I'll go and fix up some kind of a yarn, and get somebody to go for that gang and get them out of their scrape, so they can be hung when their time comes."

But that idea was a failure; for pretty soon it begun to storm again, and this time worse than ever. The rain poured down, and never a light showed; everybody in bed, I reckon. We boomed along down the river, watching for lights and watching for our raft. After a long time the rain let up, but the clouds staid, and the lightning kept whimpering, and by-and-by a flash showed us a black thing ahead, floating, and we made for it.

It was the raft, and mighty glad was we to get aboard of it again. We seen a light, now, away down to the right, on shore. So I said I would go for it. The skiff was half full of plunder which that gang had stole, there on the wreck. We hustled it onto the raft in a pile, and I told Jim to float along down, and show a light when he judged he had gone about two mile, and keep it burning till I come; then I manned my oars and shoved for the light. As I got down towards it, three or four more showed—up on a hillside. It was a village. I closed in above the shore-light, and laid on my oars and floated. As I went by, I see it was a lantern hanging on the jackstaff[1] of a double-hull

[1]Short pole from which a flag or light can be hung.

ferry-boat. I skimmed around for the watchman, a-wondering whereabouts he slept; and by-and-by I found him roosting on the bitts,[2] forward, with his head down between his knees. I give his shoulder two or three little shoves, and begun to cry.

He stirred up, in a kind of a startlish way; but when he see it was only me, he took a good gap and stretch, and then he says:

"Hello, what's up? Don't cry, bub. What's the trouble?"

I says:

"Pap, and mam, and sis, and—"

Then I broke down. He says:

"Oh, dang it, now, *don't* take on so, we all has to have our troubles and this'n 'll come out all right. What's the matter with 'em?

"They're—they're—are you the watchman of the boat?"

"Yes," he says, kind of pretty-well-satisfied like. "I'm the captain and the owner, and the mate, and the pilot, and watchman, and head deck-hand; and sometimes I'm the freight and passengers. I ain't as rich as old Jim Hornback, and I can't be so blame' generous and good to Tom, Dick and Harry as what he is, and slam around money the way he does; but I've told him a many a time 't I wouldn't trade places with him; for, says I, a sailor's life's the life for me, and I'm derned if *I'd* live two mile out o' town, where there ain't nothing ever goin' on, not for all his spondulicks[3] and as much more on top of it. Says I——"

I broke in and says:

"They're in an awful peck of trouble, and——"

"*Who* is?"

"Why, pap, and mam, and sis, and Miss Hooker; and if you'd take your ferry-boat and go up there——"

"Up where? Where are they?"

"On the wreck."

"What wreck?"

"Why, there ain't but one."

"What, you don't mean the *Walter Scott?*"

"Yes."

"Good land! what are they doin' *there,* for gracious sakes?"

"Well, they didn't go there a-purpose."

"I bet they didn't! Why, great goodness, there ain't no chance for 'em if they don't git off mighty quick! Why, how in the nation did they ever git into such a scrape?"

"Easy enough. Miss Hooker was a-visiting, up there to the town——"

"Yes, Booth's Landing— go on."

"She was a-visiting, there at Booth's Landing, and just in the edge of the evening she started over with her nigger woman in the horseferry,[4] to stay all night at her friend's house, Miss What-you-may-call-her, I disremember her name, and they lost their steering-oar, and swung around and went a-floating down, stern-first, about two mile, and saddle-baggsed on[5] the wreck, and the ferry man and the nigger woman and the horses was all lost, but Miss Hooker she made a grab and got aboard the wreck. Well, about an hour after dark,

[2]Posts fixed on the deck, to which lines can be fastened. [3]Riches.
[4]Ferry large enough to carry horses. [5]Wrapped around.

we come along down in our trading-scow,[6] and it was so dark we didn't notice the wreck till we was right on it; and so *we* saddlebaggsed; but all of us was saved but Bill Whipple—and oh, he *was* the best cretur!—I most wish't it had been me, I do."

"My George! It's the beatenest thing I ever struck. And *then* what did you all do?"

"Well, we hollered and took on, but it's so wide there, we couldn't make nobody hear. So pap said somebody got to get ashore and get help somehow. I was the only one that could swim, so I made a dash for it, and Miss Hooker she said if I didn't strike help sooner, come here and hunt up her uncle, and he'd fix the thing. I made the land about a mile below, and been fooling along ever since, trying to get people to do something, but they said, 'What, in such a night and such a current? there ain't no sense in it; go for the steam-ferry.' Now if you'll go, and——"

"By Jackson, I'd *like* to, and blame it I don't know but I will; but who in the dingnation's agoin' to *pay* for it? Do you reckon your pap——"

"Why *that's* all right. Miss Hooker she told me, *particular,* that her uncle Hornback——"

"Great guns! is *he* her uncle? Looky here, you break for that light over yonder-way, and turn out west when you git there, and about a quarter of a mile out you'll come to the tavern; tell 'em to dart you out to Jim Hornback's and he'll foot the bill. And don't you fool around any, because he'll want to know the news. Tell him I'll have his niece all safe before he can get to town. Hump yourself, now; I'm agoing up around the corner here, to roust out my engineer."

I struck for the light, but as soon as he turned the corner I went back and got into my skiff and bailed her out and then pulled up shore in the easy water about six hundred yards, and tucked myself in among some woodboats; for I couldn't rest easy till I could see the ferry-boat start. But take it all around, I was feeling ruther comfortable on accounts of taking all this trouble for that gang, for not many would a done it. I wished the widow knowed about it. I judged she would be proud of me for helping these rapscallions, because rapscallions and dead beats is the kind the widow and good people takes the most interest in.

Well, before long, here comes the wreck, dim and dusky, sliding along down! A kind of cold shiver went through me, and then I struck out for her. She was very deep, and I see in a minute there warn't much chance for anybody being alive in her. I pulled all around her and hollered a little, but there wasn't any answer; all dead still. I felt a little bit heavy-hearted about the gang, but not much, for I reckoned if they could stand it, I could.

Then here comes the ferry-boat; so I shoved for the middle of the river on a long down-stream slant; and when I judged I was out of eye-reach, I laid on my oars, and looked back and see her go and smell around the wreck for Miss Hooker's remainders, because the captain would know her uncle Hornback would want them; and then pretty soon the ferry-boat give it up and went for shore, and I laid into my work and went a-booming down the river.

It did seem a powerful long time before Jim's light showed up; and when it did show, it looked like it was a thousand mile off. By the time I got there

[6]Flat-bottomed cargo boat.

the sky was beginning to get a little gray in the east; so we struck for an island, and hid the raft, and sunk the skiff, and turned in and slept like dead people.

CHAPTER XIV

By-and-by, when we got up, we turned over the truck the gang had stole off of the wreck, and found boots, and blankets, and clothes, and all sorts of other things, and a lot of books, and a spy-glass, and three boxes of seegars. We hadn't ever been this rich before, in neither of our lives. The seegars was prime. We laid off all the afternoon in the woods talking, and me reading the books, and having a general good time. I told Jim all about what happened inside the wreck, and at the ferry-boat; and I said these kinds of things was adventures; but he said he didn't want no more adventures. He said that when I went in the texas and he crawled back to get on the raft and found her gone, he nearly died; because he judged it was all up with *him*, anyway it could be fixed; for if he didn't get saved he would get drownded; and if he did get saved, whoever saved him would send him back home so as to get the reward, and then Miss Watson would see him South, sure. Well, he was right; he was most always right; he had an uncommon level head, for a nigger.

I read considerable to Jim about kings, and dukes, and earls, and such, and how gaudy they dressed, and how much style they put on, and called each other your majesty, and your grace, and your lordship, and so on, 'stead of mister; and Jim's eyes bugged out, and he was interested. He says:

"I didn' know dey was so many un um. I hain't heard 'bout none un um, skasely, but ole King Sollermun, onless you counts dem kings dat's in a pack er k'yards. How much do a king git?"

"Get?" I says; "why, they get a thousand dollars a month if they want it; they can have just as much as they want; everything belongs to them."

"*Ain'* dat gay? En what dey got to do, Huck?"

"*They* don't do nothing! Why how you talk. They just set around."

"No—is dat so?"

"Of course it is. They just set around. Except maybe when there's a war; then they go to the war. But other times they just lazy around; or go hawking—just hawking and sp—Sh!—d' you hear a noise?"

We skipped out and looked; but it warn't nothing but the flutter of a steamboat's wheel, away down coming around the point; so we come back.

"Yes," says I, "and other times, when things is dull, they fuss with the parlyment; and if everybody don't go just so he whacks their heads off. But mostly they hang around the harem."

"Round' de which?"

"Harem."

"What's de harem?"

"The place where he keep his wives. Don't you know about the harem? Solomon had one; he had about a million wives."

"Why, yes, dat's so; I—I'd done forgot it. A harem's a bo'd'n-house, I reck'n. Mos' likely dey has rackety times in de nussery. En I reck'n de wives quarrels considable; en dat 'crease de racket. Yit dey say Sollermun de wises' man dat ever live'. I doan' take no stock in dat. Bekase why: would a wise man want to live in de mids' er sich a blimblammin' all de time? No—'deed he wouldn't. A wise man 'ud take en buil' a biler-factry; en den he could shet *down* de biler-factry when he want to res'."

"Well, but he *was* the wisest man, anyway; because the widow she told me so, her own self."

"I doan k'yer what de widder say, he *warn't* no wise man, nuther. He had some er de dad-fetchedes' ways I ever see. Does you know 'bout dat chile dat he 'uz gwyne to chop in two?"[1]

"Yes, the widow told me all about it."

"*Well*, den! Warn' dat de beatenes' notion in de worl'? You jes' take en look at it a minute. Dah's de stump, dah—dat's one er de women; heah's you—dat's de yuther one; I's Sollermun; en dish-yer dollar bill's de chile. Bofe un you claims it. What does I do? Does I shin aroun' mongs' de neighbors en fine out which un you de bill *do* b'long to, en han' it over to de right one, all safe en soun', de way dat anybody dat had any gumption would? No—I take en whack de bill in *two*, en give half un it to you, en de yuther half to de yuther woman. Dat's de way Sollermun was gwyne to do wid de chile. Now I want to ast you: what's de use er dat half a bill?—can't buy noth'n wid it. En what use is a half a chile? I would'n give a dern for a million un um."

"But hang it, Jim, you've clean missed the point—blame it, you've missed it a thousand mile."

"Who? Me? Go 'long. Doan' talk to *me* 'bout yo' pints. I reck'n I knows sense when I sees it; en dey ain' no sense in sich doin's as dat. De 'spute warn't 'bout a half a chile, de 'spute was 'bout a whole chile; en de man dat think he kin settle a 'spute 'bout a whole chile wid a half a chile, doan' know enough to come in out'n de rain. Doan' talk to me 'bout Sollermun, Huck, I knows him by de back."

"But I tell you you don't get the point."

"Blame de pint! I reck'n I knows what I knows. En mine you, de *real* pint is down furder—it's down deeper. It lays in de way Sollermun was raised. You take a man dat's got on'y one er two chillen; is dat man gwyne to be waseful o' chillen? No, he ain't; he can't 'ford it. *He* know how to value 'em. But you take a man dat's got 'bout five million chillen runnin' roun' de house, en it's diffunt. *He* as soon chop a chile in two as a cat. Dey's plenty mo'. A chile er two, mo'er less, warn't no consekens to Sollermun, dad fetch him!"

I never see such a nigger. If he got a notion in his head once, there warn't no getting it out again. He was the most down on Solomon of any nigger I ever see. So I went to talking about other kings, and let Solomon slide. I told about Louis Sixteenth that got his head cut off in France long time ago; and about his little boy the dolphin,[2] that would a been a king, but they took and shut him up in jail, and some say he died there.

[1]To halt a dispute about the parentage of a child, Solomon threatened to divide it in two, expecting the real parent to make strenuous objections (I Kings 3:16–28).

[2]The dauphin, then eldest living son of the king of France. Louis Charles (1785–1795?), son of Louis XVI, survived his father's execution during the French Revolution but died in prison. According to legend, he escaped, and numerous imposters thereafter claimed to be the dauphin and thus Louis XVII.

"Po' little chap."

"But some says he got out and got away, and come to America."

"Dat's good! But he'll be pooty lonesome—dey ain' no kings here, is dey, Huck?"

"No."

"Den, he cain't git no situation. What he gwyne to do?"

"Well, I don't know. Some of them gets on the police, and some of them learns people how to talk French."

"Why, Huck, doan' de French people talk de same way we does?"

"*No,* Jim; you couldn't understand a word they said—not a single word."

"Well, now, I be ding-busted! How do dat come?"

"*I* don't know; but it's so. I got some of their jabber out of a book. Spose a man was to come to you and say *Polly-voo-franzy*[3]—what would you think?"

"I wouldn' think nuff'n; I'd take en bust him over de head. Dat is, if he warn't white. I wouldn't 'low no nigger to call me dat."

"Shucks, it ain't calling you anything. It's only saying do you know how to talk French."

"Well, den, why couldn't he *say* it?"

"Why, he *is* a-saying it. That's a Frenchman's *way* of saying it."

"Well, it's a blame' ridicklous way, en I doan' want to hear no mo' 'bout it. Dey ain' no sense in it."

"Looky here, Jim; does a cat talk like we do?"

"No, a cat don't."

"Well, does a cow?"

"No, a cow don't, nuther."

"Does a cat talk like a cow, or a cow talk like a cat?"

"No, dey don't."

"It's natural and right for 'em to talk different from each other, ain't it?"

" 'Course."

"And ain't it natural and right for a cat and a cow to talk different from *us?*"

"Why, mos' sholy it is."

"Well, then, why ain't it natural and right for a *Frenchman* to talk different from us? You answer me that."

"Is a cat a man, Huck?"

"No."

"Well, den, dey ain't no sense in a cat talkin' like a man. Is a cow a man?—er is a cow a cat?"

"No, she ain't either of them."

"Well, den, she ain't got no business to talk like either one er the yuther of 'em. Is a Frenchman a man?"

"Yes."

"*Well,* den! Dad blame it, why doan' he *talk* like a man? You answer me *dat!*"

I see it warn't no use wasting words—you can't learn a nigger to argue. So I quit.

[3]Huck's version of French: Parlez-vous français? (Do you speak French?)

CHAPTER XV

We judged that three nights more would fetch us to Cairo,[1] at the bottom of Illinois, where the Ohio River comes in, and that was what we was after. We would sell the raft and get on a steamboat and go way up the Ohio amongst the free States, and then be out of trouble.

Well, the second night a fog begun to come on, and we made for a tow-head to tie to, for it wouldn't do to try to run in fog; but when I paddled ahead in the canoe, with the line, to make fast, there warn't anything but little saplings to tie to. I passed the line around one of them right on the edge of the cut bank,[2] but there was a stiff current, and the raft come booming down so lively she tore it out by the roots and away she went. I see the fog closing down, and it made me so sick and scared I couldn't budge for most a half a minute it seemed to me—and then there warn't no raft in sight; you couldn't see twenty yards. I jumped into the canoe and run back to the stern and grabbed the paddle and set her back a stroke. But she didn't come. I was in such a hurry I hadn't untied her. I got up and tried to untie her, but I was so excited my hands shook so I couldn't hardly do anything with them.

As soon as I got started I took out after the raft, hot and heavy, right down the tow-head. That was all right as far as it went, but the tow-head warn't sixty yards long, and the minute I flew by the foot of it I shoot out into the solid white fog, and hadn't no more idea which way I was going than a dead man.

Thinks I, it won't do to paddle; first I know I'll run into the bank or a tow-head or something; I got to set still and float, and yet it's mighty fidgety business to have to hold your hands still at such a time. I whooped and listened. Away down there, somewhere, I hears a small whoop, and up comes my spirits. I went tearing after it, listening sharp to hear it again. The next time it come. I see I warn't heading for it but heading away to the right of it. And the next time, I was heading away to the left of it—and not gaining on it much, either, for I was flying around, this way and that and t'other, but it was going straight ahead all the time.

I did wish the fool would think to beat a tin pan, and beat it all the time, but he never did, and it was the still places between the whoops that was making the trouble for me. Well, I fought along, and directly I hears the whoop *behind* me. I was tangled good, now. That was somebody else's whoop, or else I was turned around.

I throwed the paddle down. I heard the whoop again; it was behind me yet, but in a different place; it kept coming, and kept changing its place, and I kept answering, till by-and-by it was in front of me again and I knowed the current had swung the canoe's head down stream and I was all right, if that was Jim and not some other raftsman hollering. I couldn't tell nothing about voices in a fog, for nothing don't look natural nor sound natural in a fog.

The whooping went on, and in about a minute I come a booming down on a cut bank with smoky ghosts of big trees on it, and the current throwed me off to the left and shot by, amongst a lot of snags that fairly roared, the current was tearing by them so swift.

[1]Pronounced KAY-roh. [2]Steep bank formed by the cutting force of the river's current.

In another second or two it was solid white and still again. I set perfectly still, then, listening to my heart thump, and I reckon I didn't draw a breath while it thumped a hundred.

I just give up, then. I knowed what the matter was. That cut bank was an island, and Jim had gone down t'other side of it. It warn't no tow-head, that you could float by in ten minutes. It had the big timber of a regular island; it might be five or six mile long and more than a half a mile wide.

I kept quiet, with my ears cocked, about fifteen minutes, I reckon. I was floating along, of course, four or five mile an hour; yet you don't ever think of that. No, you *feel* like you are laying dead still on the water; and if a little glimpse of snag slips by, you don't think to yourself how fast *you're* going, but you catch your breath and think, my! how that snag's tearing along. If you think it ain't dismal and lonesome out in a fog that way, by yourself, in the night, you try it once—you'll see.

Next, for about a half an hour, I whoops now and then; at last I hears the answer a long ways off, and tries to follow it, but I couldn't do it, and directly I judged I'd got into a nest of tow-heads, for I had little dim glimpses of them on both sides of me, sometimes just a narrow channel between; and some that I couldn't see, I knowed was there, because I'd hear the wash of the current against the old dead brush and trash that hung over the banks. Well, I warn't long losing the whoops, down amongst the tow-heads; and I only tried to chase them a little while, anyway, because it was worse than chasing a Jack-o-lantern.[3] You never knowed a sound dodge around so, and swap places so quick and so much.

I had to claw away from the bank pretty lively, four or five times, to keep from knocking the islands out of the river; and so I judged the raft must be butting into the bank every now and then, or else it would get further ahead and clear out of hearing—it was floating a little faster than what I was.

Well, I seemed to be in the open river again, by-and-by, but I couldn't hear no sign of a whoop nowheres. I reckoned Jim had fetched up on a snag, maybe, and it was all up with him. I was good and tired, so I laid down in the canoe and said I wouldn't bother no more. I didn't want to go to sleep, of course; but I was so sleepy I couldn't help it; so I thought I would take just one little cat-nap.

But I reckon it was more than a cat-nap, for when I waked up the stars was shining bright, the fog was all gone, and I was spinning down a big bend stern first. First I didn't know where I was; I thought I was dreaming; and when things begun to come back to me, they seemed to come up dim out of last week.

It was a monstrous big river here, with the tallest and the thickest kind of timber on both banks; just a solid wall, as well as I could see, by the stars. I looked away down stream, and seen a black speck on the water. I took out after it, but when I got to it it warn't nothing but a couple of saw-logs made fast together. Then I see another speck, and chased that; then, another, and this time I was right. It was the raft.

When I got to it Jim was setting there with his head down between his knees, asleep, with his right arm hanging over the steering oar. The other oar was smashed off, and the raft was littered up with leaves and branches and dirt. So she'd had a rough time.

[3]A will-o'-the-wisp, an elusive light.

I made fast and laid down under Jim's nose on the raft, and begun to gap, and stretch my fists out against Jim, and says:

"Hello, Jim, have I been asleep? Why didn't you stir me up?"

"Goodness gracious, is dat you, Huck? En you ain' dead—you ain' drownded—you's back agin? It's too good for true, honey, it's too good for true. Lemme look at you, chile, lemme feel o' you. No, you ain' dead! you's back agin, 'live en soun', jis de same ole Huck—de same ole Huck, thanks to goodness!"

"What's the matter with you, Jim? You been a drinking?"

"Drinkin'? Has I ben a drinkin'? Has I had a chance to be a drinkin'?"

"Well, then, what makes you talk so wild?"

"How does I talk wild?"

"*How?* why, hain't you been talking about my coming back, and all that stuff, as if I'd been gone away?"

"Huck—Huck Finn, you look me in de eye; look me in de eye. *Hain't* you been gone away?"

"Gone away? Why, what in the nation do you mean? *I* hain't been gone anywheres. Where would I go to?"

"Well, looky here, boss, dey's sumf'n wrong, dey is. Is I *me,* or who *is* I? Is I heah, or whah *is* I? Now dat's what I wants to know."

"Well, I think you're here, plain enough, but I think you're a tangle-headed old fool, Jim."

"I is, is I? Well you answer me dis. Didn't you tote out de line in de canoe, fer to make fas' to de tow-head?"

"No, I didn't. What tow-head? I hain't seen no tow-head."

"You hain't seen no tow-head? Looky here—didn't de line pull loose en de raf' go a hummin' down de river, en leave you en de canoe behine in de fog?"

"What fog?"

"Why *de* fog. De fog dat's ben aroun' all night. En didn't you whoop, en didn't I whoop, tell we got mix' up in de islands en one un us got los' en t'other one was jis' as good as los', 'kase he didn't know whah he wuz? En didn't I bust up agin a lot er dem islands en have a turrible time en mos' git drowned? Now ain' dat so, boss—ain't it so? You answer me dat."

"Well, this is too many for me, Jim. I hain't seen no fog, nor no islands, nor no troubles, nor nothing. I been setting here talking with you all night till you went to sleep about ten minutes ago, and I reckon I done the same. You couldn't a got drunk in that time, so of course you've been dreaming."

"Dad fetch it, how is I gwyne to dream all dat in ten minutes?"

"Well, hang it all, you did dream it, because there didn't any of it happen."

"But Huck, it's all jis' as plain to me as——"

"It don't make no difference how plain it is, there ain't nothing in it. I know, because I've been here all the time."

Jim didn't say nothing for about five minutes, but set there studying over it. Then he says:

"Well, den, I reck'n I did dream it, Huck; but dog my cats ef it ain't de powerfullest dream I ever see. En I hain't ever had no dream b'fo' dat's tired me like dis one."

"Oh, well, that's all right, because a dream does tire a body like everything, sometimes. But this one was a staving[4] dream—tell me all about it, Jim."

[4]Smashing.

So Jim went to work and told me the whole thing right through, just as it happened, only he painted it up considerable. Then he said he must start in and "'terpret" it, because it was sent for a warning. He said the first tow-head stood for a man that would try to do us some good, but the current was another man that would get us away from him. The whoops was warnings that would come to us every now and then, and if we didn't try hard to make out to understand them they'd just take us into bad luck, 'stead of keeping us out of it. The lot of tow-heads was troubles we was going to get into with quarrelsome people and all kinds of mean folks, but if we minded our business and didn't talk back and aggravate them, we would pull through and get out of the fog and into the big clear river,[5] which was the free States, and wouldn't have no more trouble.

It had clouded up pretty dark just after I got onto the raft, but it was clearing up again, now.

"Oh, well, that's all interpreted well enough, as far as it goes, Jim," I says; "but what does *these* things stand for?"

It was the leaves and rubbish on the raft, and the smashed oar. You could see them first rate, now.

Jim looked at the trash, and then looked at me, and back at the trash again. He had got the dream fixed so strong in his head that he couldn't seem to shake it loose and get the facts back into its place again, right away. But when he did get the thing straightened around, he looked at me steady, without ever smiling, and says:

"What do dey stan' for? I's gwyne to tell you. When I got all wore out wid work, en wid de callin' for you, en went to sleep, my heart wuz mos' broke bekase you wuz los', en I didn' k'yer no mo' what become er me en de raf'. En when I wake up en fine you back agin', all safe en soun', de tears come en I could a got down on my knees en kiss' yo' foot I's so thankful. En all you wuz thinkin 'bout wuz how you could make a fool uv ole Jim wid a lie. Dat truck dah is *trash;* en trash is what people is dat puts dirt on de head[6] er dey fren's en makes 'em ashamed."

Then he got up slow, and walked to the wigwam, and went in there, without saying anything but that. But that was enough. It made me feel so mean I could almost kissed *his* foot to get him to take it back.

It was fifteen minutes before I could work myself up to go and humble myself to a nigger—but I done it, and I warn't ever sorry for it afterwards, neither. I didn't do him no more mean tricks, and I wouldn't done that one if I'd a knowed it would make him feel that way.

CHAPTER XVI

We slept most all day, and started out at night, a little ways behind a monstrous long raft that was as long going by as a procession. She had four long sweeps[1] at each end, so we judged she carried as many as thirty men, likely.

[5]The Ohio River.

[6]A reference to various Old Testament figures who "cast up dust upon their heads" in a gesture of submission and humiliation, as in Ezekiel 27:30.

[1]Long oars used for steering.

She had five big wigwams aboard, wide apart, and an open camp fire in the middle, and a tall flag-pole at each end. There was a power of style about her. It *amounted* to something being a raftsman on such a craft as that.

We went drifting down into a big bend, and the night clouded up and got hot. The river was very wide, and was walled with solid timber on both sides; you couldn't see a break in it hardly ever, or a light. We talked about Cairo, and wondered whether we would know it when we got to it. I said likely we wouldn't, because I had heard say there warn't but about a dozen houses there, and if they didn't happen to have them lit up, how was we going to know we was passing a town? Jim said if the two big rivers joined together there, that would show. But I said maybe we might think we was passing the foot of an island and coming into the same old river again. That disturbed Jim—and me too. So the question was, what to do? I said, paddle ashore the first time a light showed, and tell them pap was behind, coming along with a trading-scow, and was a green hand at the business, and wanted to know how far it was to Cairo. Jim thought it was a good idea, so we took a smoke on it and waited.

There warn't nothing to do, now, but to look out sharp for the town, and not pass it without seeing it. He said he'd be mighty sure to see it, because he'd be a free man the minute he seen it, but if he missed it he'd be in the slave country again and no more show[2] for freedom. Every little while he jumps up and says:

"Dah she is!"

But it warn't. It was Jack-o-lanterns, or lightning-bugs; so he set down again, and went to watching, same as before. Jim said it made him all over trembly and feverish to be so close to freedom. Well, I can tell you it made me all over trembly and feverish, too, to hear him, because I begun to get it through my head that he *was* most free—and who was to blame for it? Why, *me.* I couldn't get that out of my conscience, no how nor no way. It got to troubling me so I couldn't rest; I couldn't stay still in one place. It hadn't ever come to me before, what this thing was that I was doing. But now it did; and it staid with me, and scorched me more and more. I tried to make out to myself that *I* warn't to blame, because *I* didn't run Jim off from his rightful owner; but it warn't no use, conscience up and says, every time, "But you knowed he was running for his freedom, and you could a paddled ashore and told somebody." That was so—I couldn't get around that, noway. That was where it pinched. Conscience says to me, "What had poor Miss Watson done to you, that you could see her nigger go off right under your eyes and never say one single word? What did that poor old woman do to you, that you could treat her so mean? Why, she tried to learn you your book, she tried to learn you your manners, she tried to be good to you every way she knowed how. *That's* what she done."

I got to feeling so mean and so miserable I most wished I was dead. I fidgeted up and down the raft, abusing myself to myself, and Jim was fidgeted up and down past me. We neither of us could keep still. Every time he danced around and says, "Dah's Cairo!" it went through me like a shot, and I thought if it *was* Cairo I reckoned I would die of miserableness.

[2]Chance.

Jim talked out loud all the time while I was talking to myself. He was saying how the first thing he would do when he got to a free State he would go to saving up money and never spend a single cent, and when he got enough he would buy his wife, which was owned on a farm close to where Miss Watson lived; and then they would both work to buy the two children, and if their master wouldn't sell them, they'd get an Ab'litionist to go and steal them.

It most froze me to hear such talk. He wouldn't ever dared to talk such talk in his life before. Just see what a difference it made in him the minute he judged he was about free. It was according to the old saying, "give a nigger an inch and he'll take an ell." Thinks I, this is what comes of my not thinking. Here was this nigger which I had as good as helped to run away, coming right out flat-footed and saying he would steal his children—children that belonged to a man I didn't even know; a man that hadn't ever done me no harm.

I was sorry to hear Jim say that, it was such a lowering of him. My conscience got to stirring me up hotter than ever, until at last I says to it, "Let up on me—it ain't too late, yet—I'll paddle ashore at the first light, and tell." I felt easy, and happy, and light as a feather, right off. All my troubles was gone. I went to looking out sharp for a light, and sort of singing to myself. By-and-by one showed. Jim sings out:

"We's safe. Huck, we's safe! Jump up and crack yo' heels, dat's de good ole Cairo at las', I jis knows it!"

I says:

"I'll take the canoe and go see, Jim. It mightn't be, you know."

He jumped and got the canoe ready, and put his old coat in the bottom for me to set on, and give me the paddle; and as I shoved off, he says:

"Pooty soon I'll be a-shout'n for joy, en I'll say, it's all on accounts o'Huck; I's a free man, en I couldn't ever ben free ef it hadn' ben for Huck; Huck done it. Jim won't ever forgit you, Huck; you's de bes' fren' Jim's ever had; en you's de *only* fren' ole Jim's got now."

I was paddling off, all in a sweat to tell on him; but when he says this, it seemed to kind of take the tuck all out of me. I went along slow then, and I warn't right down certain whether I was glad I started or whether I warn't. When I was fifty yards off, Jim says:

"Dah you goes, de ole true Huck; de on'y white genlman dat ever kep' his promise to ole Jim."

Well, I just felt sick. But I says, I *got* to do it—I can't get *out* of it. Right then, along comes a skiff with two men in it, with guns, and they stopped and I stopped. One of they says:

"What's that, yonder?"

"A piece of a raft," I says.

"Do you belong on it?"

"Yes, sir."

"Any men on it?"

"Only one, sir."

"Well, there's five niggers run off to-night, up yonder above the head of the bend. Is your man white or black?"

I didn't answer up prompt. I tried to, but the words wouldn't come. I tried, for a second or two, to brace up and out with it, but I warn't man enough—

hadn't the spunk of a rabbit. I see I was weakening; so I just give up trying, and up and says—

"He's white."

"I reckon we'll go and see for ourselves."

"I wish you would," says I, "because it's pap that's there, and maybe you'd help me tow the raft ashore where the light is. He's sick—and so is mam and Mary Ann."

"Oh, the devil! we're in a hurry, boy. But I s'pose we've got to. Come—buckle to your paddle, and let's get along."

I buckled to my paddle and they laid to their oars. When we had made a stroke or two, I says:

"Pap'll be mighty much obleeged to you, I can tell you. Everybody goes away when I want them to help me tow the raft ashore, and I can't do it by myself."

"Well, that's infernal mean. Odd, too. Say, boy, what's the matter with your father?"

"It's the—a—the—well, it ain't anything, much."

They stopped pulling. It warn't but a mighty little ways to the raft, now. One says:

"Boy, that's a lie. What *is* the matter with your pap? Answer up square, now, and it'll be the better for you."

"I will, sir, I will, honest—but don't leave us, please. It's the—the—gentlemen, if you'll only pull ahead, and let me heave you the head-line,[3] you won't have to come a-near the raft—please do."

"Set her back, John, set her back!" says one. They backed water. "Keep away, boy—keep to looard.[4] Confound it, I just expect the wind has blowed it to us. Your pap's got the small-pox, and you know it precious well. Why didn't you come out and say so? Do you want to spread it all over?"

"Well," says I, a-blubbering, "I've told everybody before, and then they just went away and left us."

"Poor devil, there's something in that. We are right down sorry for you, but we—well, hang it, we don't want the small-pox, you see. Look here, I'll tell you what to do. Don't you try to land by yourself, or you'll smash everything to pieces. You float along down about twenty miles and you'll come to a town on the left-hand side of the river. It will be long after sun-up, then, and when you ask for help, you tell them your folks are all down with chills and fever. Don't be a fool again, and let people guess what is the matter. Now we're trying to do you a kindness; so you just put twenty miles between us, that's a good boy. It wouldn't do any good to land yonder where the light is—it's only a wood-yard.[5] Say—I reckon your father's poor, and I'm bound to say he's in pretty hard luck. Here—I'll put a twenty dollar gold piece on this board, and you get it when it floats by. I feel mighty mean to leave you, but my kingdom! it won't do to fool with small-pox, don't you see?"

"Hold on, Parker," says the other man, "here's a twenty to put on the board for me. Good-bye, boy, you do as Mr. Parker told you, and you'll be all right."

[3]Line attached to the prow of a boat. [4]Leeward, downwind.
[5]Refueling station for wood-burning steamboats.

"That's so, my boy—good-bye, good-bye. If you see any runaway niggers, you get help and nab them, and you can make some money by it."

"Good-bye, sir," says I, "I won't let no runaway niggers get by me if I can help it."

They went off, and I got aboard the raft, feeling bad and low, because I knowed very well I had done wrong, and I see it warn't no use for me to try to learn to do right; a body that don't get *started* right when he's little, ain't got no show—when the pinch comes there ain't nothing to back him up and keep him to his work, and so he gets beat. Then I thought a minute, and says to myself, hold on,—spose you'd a done right and give Jim up; would you felt better than what you do now? No, says I, I'd feel bad—I'd feel just the same way I do now. Well, then, says I, what's the use you learning to do right, when it's troublesome to do right and ain't no trouble to do wrong, and the wages is just the same? I was stuck. I couldn't answer that. So I reckoned I wouldn't bother no more about it, but after this always do whichever come handiest at the time.

I went into the wigwam; Jim warn't there. I looked all around; he warn't anywhere. I says:

"Jim!"

"Here I is, Huck, Is dey out o' sight yit? Don't talk loud."

He was in the river, under the stern oar, with just his nose out. I told him they was out of sight, so he come aboard. He says:

"I was a-listenin' to all de talk, en I slips into de river en was gwyne to shove for sho' if dey come aboard. Den I was gwyne to swim to de raf' agin when dey was gone. But lawsy, how you did fool 'em, Huck! Dat *wuz* de smartes' dodge! I tell you, chile, I 'speck it save' ole Jim—old Jim ain't gwyne to forgit you for dat, honey."

Then we talked about the money. It was a pretty good raise, twenty dollars apiece. Jim said we could take deck passage[6] on a steamboat now, and the money would last us as far as we wanted to go in the free States. He said twenty mile more warn't far for the raft to go, but he wished we was already there.

Towards daybreak we tied up, and Jim was mighty particular about hiding the raft good. Then he worked all day fixing things in bundles, and getting all ready to quit rafting.

That night about ten we hove in sight of the lights of a town away down in a left-hand bend.

I went off in the canoe, to ask about it. Pretty soon I found a man out in the river with a skiff, setting a trot-line. I ranged up and says:

"Mister, is that town Cairo?"

"Cairo? no. You must be a blame' fool."

"What town is it, mister?"

"If you want to know, go and find out. If you stay here botherin' around me for about a half a minute longer, you'll get something you won't want."

I paddled to the raft. Jim was awful disappointed, but I said never mind, Cairo would be the next place, I reckoned.

We passed another town before daylight, and I was going out again; but it was high ground, so I didn't go. No high ground about Cairo, Jim said. I had

[6]Without a private cabin, the cheapest passage.

forgot it. We laid up for the day, on a tow-head tolerable close to the left-bank. I begun to suspicion something. So did Jim. I says:

"Maybe we went by Cairo in the fog that night."

He says:

"Doan' less talk about it, Huck. Po' niggers can't have no luck. I awluz 'spected dat rattle-snake skin warn't done wid its work."

"I wish I'd never seen that snake-skin, Jim—I do wish I'd never laid eyes on it."

"It ain't yo' fault, Huck; you didn' know. Don't you blame yo'self 'bout it."

When it was daylight, here was the clear Ohio water in shore, sure enough, and outside was the old regular Muddy! So it was all up with Cairo.[7]

We talked it all over. It wouldn't do to take to the shore; we couldn't take the raft up the stream, of course. There warn't no way but to wait for dark, and start back in the canoe and take the chances. So we slept all day amongst the cotton-wood thicket, so as to be fresh for the work, and when we went back to the raft about dark the canoe was gone!

We didn't say a word for a good while. There warn't anything to say. We both knowed well enough it was some more work of the rattle-snake skin; so what was the use to talk about it? It would only look like we was finding fault, and that would be bound to fetch more bad luck—and keep on fetching it, too, till we knowed enough to keep still.

By-and-by we talked about what we better do, and found there warn't no way but just to go along down with the raft till we got a chance to buy a canoe to go back in. We warn't going to borrow it when there warn't anybody around, the way pap would do, for that might set people after us.

So we shoved out, after dark, on the raft.

Anybody that don't believe yet, that it's foolishness to handle a snake-skin, after all that that snake-skin done for us, will believe it now, if they read on and see what more it done for us.

The place to buy canoes is off of rafts laying up at shore. But we didn't see no rafts laying up; so we went along during three hours and more. Well, the night got gray, and ruther thick, which is the next meanest thing to fog. You can't tell the shape of the river, and you can't see no distance. It got to be very late and still, and then along comes a steamboat up the river. We lit the lantern, and judged she would see it. Up-stream boats didn't generly come close to us; they go out and follow the bars and hunt for easy water under the reefs; but nights like this they bull right up the channel against the whole river.

We could hear her pounding along, but we didn't see her good till she was close. She aimed right for us. Often they do that and try to see how close they can come without touching; sometimes the wheel bites off a sweep, and then the pilot sticks his head out and laughs, and thinks he's mighty smart. Well, here she comes, and we said she was going to try to shave us; but she didn't seem to be sheering off a bit. She was a big one, and she was coming in a hurry, too, looking like a black cloud with rows of glow-worms around it; but all of a sudden she bulged out, big and scary, with a

[7]When Huck sees the clearer waters of the Ohio flowing in the Mississippi, he knows he and Jim have passed beyond the confluence of the two rivers at Cairo, where they had hoped to go up the Ohio River.

long row of wide-open furnace doors shining like red-hot teeth, and her monstrous bows and guards hanging right over us. There was a yell at us, and a jingling of bells to stop the engines, a pow-wow of cussing, and whistling of steam—and as Jim went overboard on one side and I on the other, she come smashing straight through the raft.

I dived—and I aimed to find the bottom, too, for a thirty-foot wheel had got to go over me, and I wanted it to have plenty of room. I could always stay under water a minute; this time I reckon I staid under water a minute and a half. Then I bounced for the top in a hurry, for I was nearly busting. I popped out to my arm-pits and blowed the water out of my nose, and puffed a bit. Of course there was a booming current; and of course that boat started her engines again ten seconds after she stopped them, for they never cared much for raftsmen; so now she was churning along up the river, out of sight in the thick weather, though I could hear her.

I sung out for Jim, about a dozen times, but I didn't get any answer; so I grabbed a plank that touched me while I was "treading water," and struck out for shore, shoving it ahead of me. But I made out to see that the drift of the current was towards the left-hand shore, which meant that I was in a crossing;[8] so I changed off and went that way.

It was one of these long, slanting, two-mile crossings; so I was a good long time in getting over. I made a safe landing, and clum up the bank. I couldn't see but a little ways, but I went poking along over rough ground for a quarter of a mile or more, and then I run across a big old-fashioned double log house[9] before I noticed it. I was going to rush by and get away, but a lot of dogs jumped out and went to howling and barking at me, and I knowed better than to move another peg.

CHAPTER XVII

In about half a minute somebody spoke out a window, without putting his head out, and says:

"Be done, boys! Who's there?"

I says:

"It's me."

"Who's me?"

"George Jackson, sir."

"What do you want?"

"I don't want nothing, sir. I only want to go along by, but the dogs won't let me."

"What are you prowling around here this time of night, for—hey?"

"I warn't prowling around, sir; I fell overboard off of the steamboat."

"Oh, you did, did you? Strike a light there, somebody. What did you say your name was?"

"George Jackson, sir. I'm only a boy."

[8]Where the swiftest river current (the "big water") shifts from one side of the river to another, in this case toward the Kentucky shore.

[9]A two-room log house, under a single roof and with an open passageway separating the two rooms.

"Look here; if you're telling the truth, you needn't be afraid—nobody 'll hurt you. But don't try to budge; stand right where you are. Rouse out Bob and Tom, some of you, and fetch the guns. George Jackson, is there anybody with you?"

"No, sir, nobody."

I heard the people stirring around in the house, now, and see a light. The man sung out:

"Snatch that light away, Betsy, you old fool—ain't you got any sense? Put it on the floor behind the front door. Bob, if you and Tom are ready, take your places."

"All ready."

"Now, George Jackson, do you know the Shepherdsons?"

"No, sir—I never heard of them."

"Well, that may be so, and it mayn't. Now, all ready, Step forward, George Jackson. And mind, don't you hurry—come mighty slow. If there's anybody with you, let him keep back—if he shows himself he'll be shot. Come along, now. Come slow; push the door open, yourself—just enough to squeeze in, d' you hear?"

I didn't hurry, I couldn't if I'd a wanted to. I took one slow step at a time, and there warn't a sound, only I thought I could hear my heart. The dogs were as still as the humans, but they followed a little behind me. When I got to the three log door-steps, I heard them unlocking and unbarring and unbolting. I put my hand on the door and pushed it a little and a little more, till somebody said, "There, that's enough—put your head in." I done it, but I judged they would take it off.

The candle was on the floor, and there they all was, looking at me, and me at them, for about a quarter of a minute. Three big men with guns pointed at me, which made me wince, I tell you; the oldest, gray and about sixty, the other two thirty or more—all of them fine and handsome—and the sweetest old grayheaded lady, and back of her two young women which I couldn't see right well. The old gentleman says:

"There—I reckon it's all right. Come in."

As soon as I was in, the old gentleman he locked the door and barred it and bolted it, and told the young men to come in with their guns, and they all went in a big parlor that had a new rag carpet on the floor, and got together in a corner that was out of range of the front windows—there warn't none on the side. They held the candle, and took a good look at me, and all said, "Why *he* ain't a Shepherdson—no, there ain't any Shepherdson about him." Then the old man said he hoped I wouldn't mind being searched for arms, because he didn't mean no harm by it—it was only to make sure. So he didn't pry into my pockets, but only felt outside with his hands, and said it was all right. He told me to make myself easy and at home, and tell all about myself; but the old lady says:

"Why bless you, Saul, the poor thing's as wet as he can be; and don't you reckon it may be he's hungry?"

"True for you, Rachel—I forgot."

So the old lady says:

"Betsy" (this was a nigger woman), "you fly around and get him something to eat, as quick as you can, poor thing; and one of you girls go and wake up

Buck and tell him—Oh, here he is himself. Buck, take this little stranger and get the wet clothes off from him and dress him up in some of yours that's dry."

Buck looked about as old as me—thirteen or fourteen[1] or along there, though he was a little bigger than me. He hadn't on anything but a shirt, and he was very frowsy-headed. He come in gaping and digging one fist into his eyes, and he was dragging a gun along with the other one. He says:

"Ain't they no Shepherdsons around?"

They said, no, 'twas a false alarm.

"Well," he says, "if they'd a ben some, I reckon I'd a got one."

They all laughed, and Bob says:

"Why, Buck, they might have scalped us all, you've been so slow in coming."

"Well, nobody come after me, and it ain't right. I'm always kep' down; I don't get no show."

"Never mind, Buck, my boy," says the old man, "you'll have show enough, all in good time, don't you fret about that. Go 'long with you now, and do as your mother told you."

When we got up stairs to his room, he got me a coarse shirt and a roundabout[2] and pants of his, and I put them on. While I was at it he asked me what my name was, but before I could tell him, he started to telling me about a blue jay and a young rabbit he had catched in the woods day before yesterday, and he asked me where Moses was when the candle went out. I said I didn't know; I hadn't heard about it before, no way.

"Well, guess," he says.

"How'm I going to guess," says I, "when I never heard tell about it before?"

"But you can guess, can't you? It's just as easy."

"*Which* candle?" I says.

"Why, any candle," he says.

"I don't know where he was," says I; "where was he?"

"Why he was in the *dark!* That's where he was!"

"Well, if you knowed where he was, what did you ask me for?"

"Why, blame it, it's a riddle, don't you see? Say, how long are you going to stay here? You got to stay always. We can just have booming times—they don't have no school now. Do you own a dog? I've got a dog—and he'll go in the river and bring out chips that you throw in. Do you like to comb up, Sundays, and all that kind of foolishness? You bet I don't, but ma she makes me. Confound these ole britches, I reckon I'd better put 'em on, but I'd ruther not, it's so warm. Are you all ready? All right—come along, old hoss."

Cold corn-pone, cold corn-beef, butter and butter-milk—that is what they had for me down there, and there ain't nothing better that ever I've come across yet. Buck and his ma and all of them smoked cob pipes, except the nigger woman, which was gone, and the two young women. They all smoked and talked, and I eat and talked. The young women had quilts around them, and their hair down their backs. They all asked me questions, and I told them how pap and me and all the family was living on a little farm down at the bottom of Arkansaw, and my sister Mary Ann run off and got married and never was heard of no more, and Bill went to hunt them and he warn't

[1]Elsewhere Twain wrote that Huck was fourteen. [2]A jacket.

heard of no more, and Tom and Mort died, and then there warn't nobody but just me and pap left, and he was just trimmed down to nothing, on account of his troubles; so when he died I took what was left, because the farm didn't belong to us, and started up the river, deck passage, and fell overboard; and that was how I come to be here. So they said I could have a home there as long as I wanted it. Then it was most daylight, and everybody went to bed, and I went to bed with Buck, and when I waked up in the morning, drat it all, I had forgot what my name was. So I laid there about an hour trying to think, and when Buck waked up, I says:

"Can you spell, Buck?"

"Yes," he says.

"I bet you can't spell my name," says I.

"I bet you what you dare I can," says he.

"All right," says I, "go ahead."

"G-o-r-g-e J-a-x-o-n—there now," he says.

"Well," says I, "you done it, but I didn't think you could. It ain't no slouch of a name to spell—right off without studying."

I set it down, private, because somebody might want *me* to spell it, next, and so I wanted to be handy with it and rattle it off like I was used to it.

It was a mighty nice family, and a mighty nice house, too. I hadn't seen no house out in the country before that was so nice and had so much style. It didn't have an iron latch on the front door, nor a wooden one with a buckskin string, but a brass knob to turn, the same as houses in a town. There warn't no bed in the parlor, not a sign of a bed; but heaps of parlors in towns has beds in them. There was a big fireplace that was bricked on the bottom, and the bricks was kept clean and red by pouring water on them and scrubbing them with another brick; sometimes they washed them over with red water-paint that they call Spanish-brown, same as they do in town. They had big brass dog-irons[3] that could hold up a saw-log.[4] There was a clock on the middle of the mantel-piece, with a picture of a town painted on the bottom half of the glass front, and a round place in the middle of it for the sun, and you could see the pendulum swing behind it. It was beautiful to hear that clock tick; and sometimes when one of these peddlers had been along and scoured her up and got her in good shape, she would start in and strike a hundred and fifty before she got tuckered out. They wouldn't took any money for her.

Well, there was a big outlandish parrot on each side of the clock, made out of something like chalk, and painted up gaudy. By one of the parrots was a cat made of crockery, and a crockery dog by the other; and when you pressed down on them they squeaked, but didn't open their mouths nor look different nor interested. They squeaked through underneath. There was a couple of big wild-turkey-wing fans spread out behind those things. On a table in the middle of the room was a kind of a lovely crockery basket that had apples and oranges and peaches and grapes piled up in it which was much redder and yellower and prettier than real ones is, but they warn't real because you could see where pieces had got chipped off and showed the white chalk or whatever it was, underneath.

This table had a cover made out of beautiful oil-cloth, with a red and blue spread-eagle painted on it, and a painted border all around. It come all the

[3]Andirons. [4]A log long and large enough to saw into timbers and beams.

way from Philadelphia, they said. There was some books too, piled up perfectly exact, on each corner of the table. One was a big family Bible, full of pictures. One was "Pilgrim's Progress,"[5] about a man that left his family, it didn't say why. I read considerable in it now and then. The statements was interesting, but tough. Another was "Friendship's Offering,"[6] full of beautiful stuff and poetry; but I didn't read the poetry. Another was Henry Clay's[7] Speeches, and another was Dr. Gunn's Family Medicine,[8] which told you all about what to do if a body was sick or dead. There was a Hymn Book, and a lot of other books. And there was nice split-bottom chairs, and perfectly sound, too—not bagged down in the middle and busted, like an old basket.

They had pictures hung on the walls—mainly Washingtons and Lafayettes, and battles, and Highland Marys,[9] and one called "Signing the Declaration." There was some that they called crayons, which one of the daughters which was dead made her own self when she was only fifteen years old. They was different from any pictures I ever see before; blacker, mostly, than is common. One was a woman in a slim black dress, belted small under the arm-pits, with bulges like a cabbage in the middle of the sleeves, and a large black scoop-shovel bonnet with a black veil, and white slim ankles crossed about with black tape, and very wee black slippers, like a chisel, and she was leaning pensive on a tombstone on her right elbow, under a weeping willow, and her other hand hanging down her side holding a white handkerchief and a reticule, and underneath the picture it said "Shall I Never See Thee More Alas." Another one was a young lady with her hair all combed up straight to the top of her head, and knotted there in front of a comb like a chair-back, and she was crying into a handkerchief and had a dead bird laying on its back in her other hand with its heels up, and underneath the picture it said "I Shall Never Hear Thy Sweet Chirrup More Alas." There was one where a young lady was at a window looking up at the moon, and tears running down her cheeks; and she had an open letter in one hand with black sealing-wax showing on one edge of it, and she was mashing a locket with a chain to it against her mouth, and underneath the picture it said "And Art Thou Gone Yes Thou Art Gone Alas." These was all nice pictures, I reckon, but I didn't somehow seem to take to them, because if ever I was down a little, they always give me the fan-tods. Everybody was sorry she died, because she had laid out a lot more of these pictures to do, and a body could see by what she had done what they had lost. But I reckoned, that with her disposition, she was having a better time in the graveyard. She was at work on what they said was her greatest picture when she took sick, and every day and every night it was her prayer to be allowed to live till she got it done, but she never got the chance. It was a picture of a young woman in a long white gown, standing on the rail of a bridge all ready to jump off, with her hair all down her back, and looking up to the moon, with the tears running down her face, and she had two arms folded across her breast, and two arms stretched out in front, and two more reaching up towards the moon—and the idea was, to see which pair

[5]A Christian allegory by the English Puritan John Bunyan (1628–1688).
[6]A gift-book collection of sentimental prose and poetry.
[7]Political leader and orator from Kentucky (1777–1852).
[8]A medical guide first published in 1830 and still used in 1855.
[9]Mary Campbell, the subject of several elegies by the Scottish poet Robert Burns (1759–1796). She was portrayed in numerous sentimental illustrations.

would look best and then scratch out all the other arms; but, as I was saying, she died before she got her mind made up, and now they kept this picture over the head of the bed in her room, and every time her birthday come they hung flowers on it. Other times it was hid with a little curtain. The young woman in the picture had a kind of a nice sweet face, but there was so many arms it made her look too spidery, seemed to me.

This young girl kept a scrap-book when she was alive, and used to paste obituaries and accidents and cases of patient suffering in it out of the *Presbyterian Observer,* and write poetry after them out of her own head. It was very good poetry. This is what she wrote about a boy by the name of Stephen Dowling Bots that fell down a well and was drownded:

ODE TO STEPHEN DOWLING BOTS, DEC'D.[10]

And did young Stephen sicken,
  And did young Stephen die?
And did the sad hearts thicken,
  And did the mourners cry?

No; such was not the fate of
  Young Stephen Dowling Bots;
Though sad hearts round him thickened,
  'Twas not from sickness' shots.

No whooping-cough did rack his frame,
  Nor measles drear, with spots;
Not these impaired the sacred name
  Of Stephen Dowling Bots.

Despised love struck not with woe
  That head of curly knots,
Nor stomach troubles laid him low,
  Young Stephen Dowling Bots.

O no. Then list with tearful eye,
  Whilst I his fate do tell.
His soul did from this cold world fly,
  By falling down a well.

They got him out and emptied him;
  Alas it was too late;
His spirit was gone for to sport aloft
  In the realm of the good and great.

If Emmeline Grangerford could make poetry like that before she was fourteen, there ain't no telling what she could a done by-and-by. Buck said she could rattle off poetry like nothing. She didn't ever have to stop to think. He said she would slap down a line, and if she couldn't find anything to rhyme

[10]Deceased.

with it she would just scratch it out and slap down another one, and go ahead. She warn't particular, she could write about anything you choose to give her to write about, just so it was sadful. Every time a man died, or a woman died, or a child died, she would be on hand with her "tribute" before he was cold. She called them tributes. The neighbors said it was the doctor first, then Emmeline, then the undertaker—the undertaker never got in ahead of Emmeline but once, and then she hung fire on a rhyme for the dead person's name, which was Whistler. She warn't ever the same, after that; she never complained, but she kind of pined away and did not live long. Poor thing, many's the time I made myself go up to the little room that used to be hers and get out her poor old scrap-book and read in it when her pictures had been aggravating me and I had soured on her a little. I liked all that family, dead ones and all, and warn't going to let anything come between us. Poor Emmeline made poetry about all the dead people when she was alive, and it didn't seem right that there warn't nobody to make some about her, now she was gone; so I tried to sweat out a verse or two myself, but I couldn't seem to make it go, somehow. They kept Emmeline's room trim and nice and all the things fixed in it just the way she liked to have them when she was alive, and nobody ever slept there. The old lady took care of the room herself, though there was plenty of niggers, and she sewed there a good deal and read her Bible there, mostly.

Well, as I was saying about the parlor, there was beautiful curtains on the windows; white, with pictures painted on them, of castles with vines all down the walls, and cattle coming down to drink. There was a little old piano, too, that had tin pans[11] in it, I reckon, and nothing was ever so lovely as to hear the young ladies sing, "The Last Link is Broken"[12] and play "The Battle of Prague"[13] on it. The walls of all the rooms was plastered, and most had carpets on the floors, and the whole house was whitewashed on the outside.

It was a double house, and the big open place betwixt them was roofed and floored, and sometimes the table was there in the middle of the day, and it was a cool, comfortable place. Nothing couldn't be better. And warn't the cooking good, and just bushels of it too!

CHAPTER XVIII

Col. Grangerford was a gentleman, you see. He was a gentleman all over; and so was his family. He was well born, as the saying is, and that's worth as much in a man as it is in a horse, so the Widow Douglas said, and nobody ever denied that she was of the first aristocracy in our town; and pap he always said it, too, though he warn't no more quality than a mud-cat,[1] himself. Col. Grangerford was very tall and very slim, and had a darkish-paly complexion, not a sign of red in it anywheres; he was clean-shaved every morning, all over his thin face, and he had the thinnest kind of lips, and the thinnest kind of

[11]Pianos in the nineteenth century were sometimes built with cymbals and bells that could be sounded by striking keys and foot pedals.

[12]A popular, sentimental song published in 1840.

[13]A piece of ranting, bombastic program music (1788) that attempted to recreate the sounds of the battle of Prague (1756), between the armies of Prussia and Austria.

[1]Catfish.

nostrils, and a high nose, and heavy eyebrows, and the blackest kind of eyes, sunk so deep back that they seemed like they was looking out of caverns at you, as you may say. His forehead was high, and his hair was black and straight, and hung to his shoulders. His hands was long and thin, and every day of his life he put on a clean shirt and a full suit from head to foot made out of linen so white it hurt your eyes to look at it; and on Sundays he wore a blue tail-coat with brass buttons on it. He carried a mahogany cane with a silver head to it. There warn't no frivolishness about him, not a bit, and he warn't ever loud. He was as kind as he could be—you could feel that, you know, and so you had confidence. Sometimes he smiled, and it was good to see; but when he straightened himself up like a liberty-pole,[2] and the lightning began to flicker out from under his eyebrows you wanted to climb a tree first, and find out what the matter was afterwards. He didn't ever have to tell anybody to mind their manners—everybody was always good mannered where he was. Everybody loved to have him around, too; he was sunshine most always—I mean he made it seem like good weather. When he turned into a cloud-bank it was awful dark for a half minute and that was enough; there wouldn't nothing go wrong again for a week.

When him and the old lady come down in the morning, all the family got up out of their chairs and give them good-day, and didn't set down again till they had set down. Then Tom and Bob went to the sideboard where the decanters was, and mixed a glass of bitters and handed it to him, and he held it in his hand and waited till Tom's and Bob's was mixed, and then they bowed and said "Our duty to you, sir, madam;" and *they* bowed the least bit in the world and said thank you, and so they drank, all three, and Bob and Tom poured a spoonful of water on the sugar and the mite of whisky or apple brandy in the bottom of their tumblers, and give it to me and Buck, and we drank to the old people too.

Bob was the oldest, and Tom next. Tall, beautiful men with very broad shoulders and brown faces, and long black hair and black eyes. They dressed in white linen from head to foot, like the old gentleman, and wore broad Panama hats.

Then there was Miss Charlotte, she was twenty-five, and tall and proud and grand, but as good as she could be, when she warn't stirred up; but when she was, she had a look that would make you wilt in your tracks, like her father. She was beautiful.

So was her sister, Miss Sophia, but it was a different kind. She was gentle and sweet, like a dove, and she was only twenty.

Each person had their own nigger to wait on them—Buck, too. My nigger had a monstrous easy time, because I warn't used to having anybody do anything for me, but Buck's was on the jump most of the time.

This was all there was of the family, now; but there used to be more—three sons; they got killed; and Emmeline that died.

The old gentleman owned a lot of farms, and over a hundred niggers. Sometimes a stack of people would come there, horseback, from ten to fifteen mile around, and stay five or six days, and have such junketings round about and on the river, and dances and picnics in the woods, day-times, and balls at the house, nights. These people was mostly kin-folks of the family.

[2]A tall pole, often topped with a flag, used as a symbol of liberty.

The men brought their guns with them. It was a handsome lot of quality, I tell you.

There was another clan of aristocracy around there—five or six families—mostly of the name of Shepherdson. They was as high-toned, and well born, and rich and grand, as the tribe of Grangerfords. The Shepherdsons and the Grangerfords used the same steamboat landing, which was about two mile above our house; so sometimes when I went up there with a lot of our folks I used to see a lot of Shepherdsons there, on their fine horses.

One day Buck and me was away out in the woods, hunting, and heard a horse coming. We was crossing the road. Buck says:

"Quick! Jump for the woods!"

We done it, and then peeped down the woods through the leaves. Pretty soon a splendid young man come galloping down the road, setting his horse easy and looking like a soldier. He had his gun across his pommel. I had seen him before. It was young Harney Shepherdson. I heard Buck's gun go off at my ear, and Harney's hat tumbled off from his head. He grabbed his gun and rode straight to the place where we was hid. But we didn't wait. We started through the woods on a run. The woods warn't thick, so I looked over my shoulder, to dodge the bullet, and twice I seen Harney cover Buck with his gun; and then he rode away the way he come—to get his hat, I reckon, but I couldn't see. We never stopped running till we got home. The old gentleman's eyes blazed a minute—'twas pleasure, mainly, I judged—then his face sort of smoothed down, and he says, kind of gentle:

"I don't like that shooting from behind a bush. Why didn't you step into the road, my boy?"

"The Shepherdsons don't, father. They always take advantage."

Miss Charlotte she held her head up like a queen while Buck was telling his tale, and her nostrils spread and her eyes snapped. The two young men looked dark, but never said nothing. Miss Sophia she turned pale, but the color came back when she found the man warn't hurt.

Soon as I could get Buck down by the corn-cribs[3] under the trees by ourselves, I says:

"Did you want to kill him, Buck?"

"Well, I bet I did."

"What did he do to you?"

"Him? He never done nothing to me."

"Well, then, what did you want to kill him for?"

"Why nothing—only it's on account of the feud."

"What's a feud?"

"Why, where was you raised? Don't you know what a feud is?"

"Never heard of it before—tell me about it."

"Well," says Buck, "a feud is this way. A man has a quarrel with another man, and kills him; then that other man's brother kills *him;* then the other brothers on both sides, goes for one another; then the *cousins* chip in—and by-and-by everybody's killed off, and there ain't no more feud. But it's kind of slow, and takes a long time."

"Has this one been going on long, Buck?"

[3]Wooden-frame structures used for drying corn.

"Well I should *reckon!* it started thirty year ago, or som'ers along there. There was trouble 'bout something and then a lawsuit to settle it; and the suit went agin one of the men, and so he up and shot the man that won the suit—which he would naturally do, of course. Anybody would."

"What was the trouble about, Buck?—land?"

"I reckon maybe—I don't know."

"Well, who done the shooting?—was it a Grangerford or a Shepherdson?"

"Laws, how do *I* know? It was so long ago."

"Don't anybody know?"

"Oh, yes, pa knows, I reckon, and some of the other old folks; but they don't know, now, what the row was about in the first place."

"Has there been many killed, Buck?"

"Yes—right smart chance of funerals. But they don't always kill. Pa's got a few buck-shot in him; but he don't mind it 'cuz he don't weigh much any- way. Bob's been carved up some with a bowie, and Tom's been hurt once or twice."

"Has anybody been killed this year, Buck?"

"Yes, we got one and they got one. 'Bout three months ago, my cousin Bud, fourteen year old, was riding through the woods, on t'other side of the river, and didn't have no weapon with him, which was blame' foolishness, and in a lonesome place he hears a horse a-coming behind him, and see old Baldy Shepherdson a-linkin' after him with his gun in his hand and his white hair a-flying in the wind; and 'stead of jumping off and taking to the brush, Bud 'lowed he could outrun him; so they had it, nip and tuck, for five mile or more, the old man a-gaining all the time; so at last Bud seen it warn't any use, so he stopped and faced around so as to have the bullet holes in front, you know, and the old man he rode up and shot him down. But he didn't git much chance to enjoy his luck, for inside of a week, our folks laid *him* out."

"I reckon that old man was a coward, Buck."

"I reckon he *warn't* a coward. Not by a blame' sight. There ain't a coward amongst them Shepherdsons—not a one. And there ain't no cowards amongst the Grangerfords, either. Why, that old man kep' up his end in a fight one day, for a half an hour, against three Grangerfords, and come out winner. They was all a-horseback; he lit off of his horse and got behind a little wood-pile, and kep' his horse before him to stop the bullets; but the Grangerfords staid on their horses and capered around the old man, and peppered away at him, and he peppered away at them. Him and his horse both went home pretty leady and crippled, but the Grangerfords had to be *fetched* home—and one of 'em was dead, and another died the next day. No, sir, if a body's out hunting for cowards, he don't want to fool away any time amongst them Shepherdsons, becuz they don't breed any of that *kind*."

Next Sunday we all went to church, about three mile, everybody a-horse-back. The men took their guns along, so did Buck, and kept them between their knees or stood them handy against the wall. The Shepherdsons done the same. It was pretty ornery preaching—all about brotherly love, and such-like tiresomeness; but everybody said it was a good sermon, and they all talked it over going home, and had such a powerful lot to say about faith, and good works, and free grace,[4] and preforeordestination,[5] and I don't

[4]God's grace—election for heaven, given free, without regard for human efforts.
[5]Huck combines the religious doctrines of predestination and foreordination.

know what all, that it did seem to me to be one of the roughest Sundays I had run across yet.

About an hour after dinner everybody was dozing around, some in their chairs and some in their rooms, and it got to be pretty dull. Buck and a dog was stretched out on the grass in the sun, sound sleep. I went up to our room, and judged I would take a nap myself. I found that sweet Miss Sophia standing in her door, which was next to ours, and she took me in her room and shut the door very soft, and asked me if I liked her, and I said I did; and she asked me if I would do something for her and not tell anybody, and I said I would. Then she said she'd forgot her Testament, and left it in the seat at church, between two other books and would I slip out quiet and go there and fetch it to her, and not say nothing to nobody. I said I would. So I slid out and slipped off up the road, and there warn't anybody at the church, except maybe a hog or two, for there warn't any lock on the door, and hogs like a puncheon floor[6] in summertime because it's cool. If you notice, most folks don't go to church only when they've got to; but a hog is different.

Says I to myself something's up—it ain't natural for a girl to be in such a sweat about a Testament; so I give it a shake, and out drops a little piece of paper with "*Half-past two*" wrote on it with a pencil. I ransacked it, but couldn't find anything else. I couldn't make anything out of that, so I put the paper in the book again, and when I got home and up stairs, there was Miss Sophia in her door waiting for me. She pulled me in and shut the door; then she looked in the Testament till she found the paper, and as soon as she read it she looked glad; and before a body could think, she grabbed me and give me a squeeze, and said I was the best boy in the world, and not to tell anybody. She was mighty red in the face, for a minute, and her eyes lighted up and it made her powerful pretty. I was a good deal astonished, but when I got my breath I asked her what the paper was about, and she asked me if I had read it, and I said no, and she asked me if I could read writing, and I told her "no, only coarse-hand,"[7] and then she said the paper warn't anything but a book-mark to keep her place, and I might go and play now.

I went off down to the river, studying over this thing, and pretty soon I noticed that my nigger was following along behind. When we was out of sight of the house, he looked back and around a second, and then comes a-running, and says:

"Mars Jawge, if you'll come down into de swamp, I'll show you a whole stack o' water-moccasins."[8]

Thinks I, that's mighty curious; he said that yesterday. He oughter know a body don't love water-moccasins enough to go around hunting for them. What is he up to anyway? So I says—

"All right, trot ahead."

I followed a half a mile, then he struck out over the swamp and waded ankle deep as much as another half mile. We come to a little flat piece of land which was dry and very thick with trees and bushes and vines, and he says—

"You shove right in dah, jist a few steps, Mars Jawge, dah's whah dey is. I's seed 'm befo', I don't k'yer to see 'em no mo'."

[6] A floor of rough, wooden slabs. [7] Large, rough printing by hand.
[8] A species of poisonous snakes.

Then he slopped right along and went away, and pretty soon the trees hid him. I poked into the place a-ways, and come to a little open patch as big as a bedroom, all hung around with vines, and found a man laying there asleep—and by jings it was my old Jim!

I waked him up, and I reckoned it was going to be a grand surprise to him to see me again, but it warn't. He nearly cried, he was so glad, but he warn't surprised. Said he swum along behind me, that night, and heard me yell every time, but dasn't answer, because he didn't want nobody to pick *him* up, and take him into slavery again. Says he—

"I got hurt a little, en couldn't swim fas', so I wuz a considable ways behine you, towards de las'; when you landed I reck'ned I could ketch up wid you on de lan' 'dout havin' to shout at you, but when I see dat house I begin to go slow. I 'uz off too far to hear what they dey say to you—I wuz 'fraid o' de dogs—but when it 'uz all quiet agin, I knowed you's in de house, so I struck out fer de woods to wait for day. Early in de mawnin' some er de niggers come along, gwyne to de fields, en dey tuck me en showed me dis place, whah de dogs can't track me on accounts o' de water, en dey brings me truck to eat every night, en tells me how you's a gitt'n along."

"Why didn't you tell my Jack to fetch me here sooner, Jim?"

"Well, 'twarn't no use to 'sturb you, Huck, tell we could do sumfin—but we's all right, now. I ben a-buyin' pots en pans en vittles, as I got a chanst, en a patchin' up de raf', nights when——"

"*What* raft, Jim?"

"Our ole raf'."

"You mean to say our old raft warn't smashed all to flinders?"

"No, she warn't. She was tore up a good deal—one en' of her was—but dey warn't no great harm done, on'y our traps was mos' all los'. Ef we hadn' dive' so deep en swum so fur under water, en de night hadn' ben so dark, en we warn't so sk'yerd, en ben sich punkin-heads, as de sayin' is, we'd a seed de raf'. But it's jis' as well as we didn't, 'kase now she's all fixed up agin mos' as good as new, en we's got a new lot o' stuff, too, in de place o' what 'uz los'."

"Why, how did you get hold of the raft again, Jim—did you catch her?"

"How I gwyne to ketch her, en I out in de woods? No, some er de niggers foun' her ketched on a snag, along heah in de ben', en dey hid her in a crick, 'mongst de willows, en dey wuz so much jawin' 'bout which un 'um she b'long to de mos', dat I come to heah 'bout it pooty soon, so I ups en settles de trouble by tellin' 'um she don't b'long to none uv um, but to you en me; en I ast 'm if dey gwyne to grab a young white genlman's propaty, en git a hid'n for it? Den I gin 'm ten cents apiece, en dey 'uz mighty well satisfied, en wisht some mo' raf's 'ud come along en make 'm rich agin. Dey's mighty good to me, dese niggers is, en whatever I wants 'm to do fur me, I don't have to ast 'm twice, honey. Dat Jack's a good nigger, en pooty smart."

"Yes, he is. He ain't ever told me you was here; told me to come, and he'd show me a lot of water-moccasins. If anything happens, *he* ain't mixed up in it. He can say he never seen us together, and it'll be the truth."

I don't want to talk much about the next day. I reckon I'll cut it pretty short. I waked up about dawn, and was agoing to turn over and go to sleep again, when I noticed how still it was—didn't seem to be anybody stirring. That warn't usual. Next I noticed that Buck was up and gone. Well, I gets up, a-wondering, and goes down stairs—nobody around; everything as still as a mouse. Just the same outside; thinks I, what does it mean? Down by the wood-pile I comes across my Jack, and says:

"What's it all about?"

Says he:

"Don't you know, Mars Jawge?"

"No," says I, "I don't."

"Well, den, Miss Sophia's run off! 'deed she has. She run off in de night, sometime—nobody don't know jis' when—run off to git married to dat young Harney Shepherdson, you know—leastways, so dey 'spec. De fambly foun' it out, 'bout half an hour ago—maybe a little mo'—en I *tell* you dey warn't no time los. Sich another hurryin' up guns en hosses *you* never see! De women folks has gone for to stir up de relations, en ole Mars Saul en de boys tuck dey guns en rode up de river road for to try to ketch dat young man en kill him 'fo' he kin git acrost de river wid Miss Sophia. I reck'n dey's gwyne to be mighty rough times."

"Buck went off 'thout waking me up."

"Well I reck'n he *did!* Dey warn't gwyne to mix you up in it. Mars Buck he loaded up his gun en 'lowed he's gwyne to fetch home a Shepherdson or bust. Well, dey'll be plenty un 'm dah, I reck'n, en you bet you he'll fetch one ef he gits a chanst."

I took up the river road as hard as I could put. By-and-by I begin to hear guns a good ways off. When I come in sight of the log store and the wood-pile where the steamboat lands, I worked along under the trees and brush till I got to a good place, and then I clumb up into the forks of a cotton-wood that was out of reach, and watched. There was a wood-rank[9] four foot high, a little ways in front of the tree, and first I was going to hide behind that; but maybe it was luckier I didn't.

There was four or five men cavorting around on their horses in the open place before the log store, cussing and yelling, and trying to get at a couple of young chaps that was behind the wood-rank alongside of the steamboat landing—but they couldn't come it. Every time one of them showed himself on the river side of the wood-pile he got shot at. The two boys was squatting back to back behind the pile, so they could watch both ways.

By-and-by the men stopped cavorting around and yelling. They started riding towards the store; then up gets one of the boys, draws a steady bead over the wood-rank, and drops one of them out of his saddle. All the men jumped off of their horses and grabbed the hurt one and started to carry him to the store; and that minute the two boys started on the run. They got half-way to the tree I was in before the men noticed. Then the men see them, and jumped on their horses and took out after them. They gained on the boys, but it didn't do no good, the boys had too good a start; they got to the wood-pile that was in front of my tree, and slipped in behind it, and so they had the bulge[10] on the men again. One of the boys was Buck, and the other was a slim young chap about nineteen years old.

The men ripped around awhile, and then rode away. As soon as they was out of sight, I sung out to Buck and told him. He didn't know what to make of my voice coming out of the tree, at first. He was awful surprised. He told me to watch out sharp and let him know when the men come in sight again;

[9]Stack. [10]Advantage.

said they was up to some devilment or other—wouldn't be gone long. I wished I was out of that tree, but I dasn't come down. Buck begun to cry and rip, and 'lowed that him and his cousin Joe (that was the other young chap) would make up for this day, yet. He said his father and his two brothers was killed, and two or three of the enemy. Said the Shepherdsons laid for them, in ambush. Buck said his father and brothers ought to waited for their relations—the Shepherdsons was too strong for them. I asked him what was become of young Harney and Miss Sophia. He said they'd got across the river and was safe. I was glad of that; but the way Buck did take on because he didn't manage to kill Harney that day he shot at him—I hain't ever heard anything like it.

All of a sudden, bang! bang! bang! goes three or four guns—the men had slipped around through the woods and come in from behind without their horses! The boys jumped for the river—both of them hurt—and as they swum down the current the men run along the bank shooting at them and singing out, "Kill them, kill them!" It made me so sick I most fell out of the tree. I ain't agoing to tell *all* that happened—it would make me sick again if I was to do that. I wished I hadn't ever come ashore that night, to see such things. I ain't ever going to get shut of them—lots of times I dream about them.

I staid in the tree till it begun to get dark, afraid to come down. Sometimes I heard guns away off in the woods; and twice I seen little gangs of men gallop past the log store with guns; so I reckoned the trouble was still agoing on. I was mighty down-hearted; so I made up my mind I wouldn't ever go anear that house again, because I reckoned I was to blame, somehow. I judged that that piece of paper meant that Miss Sophia was to meet Harney somewheres at half-past two and run off; and I judged I ought to told her father about that paper and the curious way she acted, and then maybe he would a locked her up and this awful mess wouldn't ever happened.

When I got down out of the tree, I crept along down the river bank a piece, and found the two bodies laying in the edge of the water, and tugged at them till I got them ashore; then I covered up their faces, and got away as quick as I could. I cried a little when I was covering up Buck's face, for he was mighty good to me.

It was just dark, now. I never went near the house, but struck through the woods and made for the swamp. Jim warn't on his island, so I tramped off in a hurry for the crick, and crowded through the willows, red-hot to jump aboard and get out of that awful country—the raft was gone! My souls, but I was scared! I couldn't get my breath for most a minute. Then I raised a yell. A voice not twenty-five foot from me, says—

"Good lan'! is dat you, honey? Doan' make no noise."

It was Jim's voice—nothing ever sounded so good before. I run along the bank a piece and got aboard, and Jim he grabbed me and hugged me, he was so glad to see me. He says—

"Laws bless you, chile, I 'uz right down sho' you'd dead agin. Jack's been heah, he say he reck'n you's ben shot, kase you didn' come home no mo'; so I's jes' dis minute a startin' de raf' down towards de mouf er de crick, so's to be all ready for to shove out en leave soon as Jack comes agin en tells me for certain you *is* dead. Lawsy, I's mighty glad to get you back agin, honey."

I says—

"All right—that's mighty good; they won't find me, and they'll think I've been killed, and floated down the river—there's something up there that'll help them to think so—so don't you lose no time, Jim, but just shove off for the big water[11] as fast as ever you can."

I never felt easy till the raft was two mile below there and out in the middle of the Mississippi. Then we hung up our signal lantern, and judged that we was free and safe once more. I hadn't had a bite to eat since yesterday; so Jim he got out some corn-dodgers[12] and buttermilk, and pork and cabbage, and greens—there ain't nothing in the world so good, when it's cooked right—and whilst I eat my supper we talked, and had a good time. I was powerful glad to get away from the feuds, and so was Jim to get away from the swamp. We said there warn't no home like a raft, after all. Other places do seem so cramped up and smothery, but a raft don't. You feel mighty free and easy and comfortable on a raft.

CHAPTER XIX

Two or three days and nights went by; I reckon I might say they swum by, they slid along so quiet and smooth and lovely. Here is the way we put in the time. It was a monstrous big river down there—sometimes a mile and a half wide; we run nights, and laid up and hid day-times; soon as night was most gone, we stopped navigating and tied up—nearly always in the dead water under a tow-head; and then cut young cotton-woods and willows and hid the raft with them. Then we set out the lines. Next we slid into the river and had a swim, so as to freshen up and cool off; then we set down on the sandy bottom where the water was about knee deep, and watched the daylight come. Not a sound, anywheres—perfectly still—just like the whole world was asleep, only sometimes the bull-frogs a-cluttering, maybe. The first thing to see, looking away over the water, was a kind of dull line—that was the woods on t'other side—you couldn't make nothing else out; then a pale place in the sky; then more paleness, spreading around; then the river softened up away off, and warn't black any more, but gray; you could see little dark spots drifting along, ever so far away—trading scows, and such things; and long black streaks—rafts; sometimes you could hear a sweep screaking; or jumbled up voices, it was so still, and sound come so far; and by-and-by you could see a streak on the water which you know by the look of the streak that there's a snag there in a swift current which breaks on it and makes that streak look that way; and you see the mist curl up off of the water, and the east reddens up, and the river, and you make out a log cabin in the edge of the woods, away on the bank on t'other side of the river, being a wood-yard, likely, and piled by them cheats so you can throw a dog through it anywheres;[1] then the nice breeze springs up, and comes fanning you from over there, so cool and fresh, and sweet to smell, on account of the woods and the flowers; but sometimes not that way, because they've left

[11]The main channel of the Mississippi River. [12]Hard-baked cornmeal cakes.

[1]Woodcutters sold wood by volume to passing steamboats. By stacking their wood loosely, with large gaps, the unscrupulous tried to sell less wood for more money.

dead fish laying around, gars,[2] and such, and they do get pretty rank; and next you've got the full day, and everything smiling in the sun, and the song-birds just going it!

A little smoke couldn't be noticed, now, so we would take some fish off of the lines, and cook up a hot breakfast. And afterwards we would watch the lonesomeness of the river, and kind of lazy along, and by-and-by lazy off to sleep. Wake up, by-and-by, and look to see what done it, and maybe see a steamboat, coughing along up stream, so far off towards the other side you couldn't tell nothing about her only whether she was stern-wheel or side-wheel; then for about an hour there wouldn't be nothing to hear nor nothing to see—just solid lonesomeness. Next you'd see a raft sliding by, away off yonder, and maybe a galoot[3] on it chopping, because they're most always doing it on a raft; you'd see the ax flash, and come down—you don't hear nothing; you see that ax go up again, and by the time it's above the man's head, then you hear the *k'chunk!*—it had took all that time to come over the water. So we would put in the day, lazying around, listening to the stillness. Once there was a thick fog, and the rafts and things that went by was beating tin pans so the steamboats wouldn't run over them. A scow or a raft went by so close we could hear them talking and cussing and laughing—heard them plain; but we couldn't see no sign of them; it made you feel crawly, it was like spirits carrying on that way in the air. Jim said he believed it was spirits; but I says:

"No, spirits wouldn't say, 'dern the dern fog.'"

Soon as it was night, out we shoved; when we got her out to about the middle, we let her alone, and let her float wherever the current wanted her to; then we lit the pipes, and dangled our legs in the water and talked about all kinds of things—we was always naked, day and night, whenever the mosquitoes would let us—the new clothes Buck's folks made for me was too good to be comfortable, and besides I didn't go much on clothes, nohow.

Sometimes we'd have that whole river all to ourselves for the longest time. Yonder was the banks and the islands, across the water; and maybe a spark—which was a candle in a cabin window—and sometimes on the water you could see a spark or two—on a raft or a scow, you know; and maybe you could hear a fiddle or a song coming over from one of them crafts. It's lovely to live on a raft. We had the sky, up there, all speckled with stars, and we used to lay on our backs and look up at them, and discuss about whether they was made, or only just happened—Jim he allowed they was made, but I allowed they happened; I judged it would have took too long to *make* so many. Jim said the moon could a *laid* them; well, that looked kind of reasonable, so I didn't say nothing against it, because I've seen a frog lay most as many, so of course it could be done. We used to watch the stars that fell, too, and see them streak down. Jim allowed they'd got spoiled and was hove out of the nest.

Once or twice of a night we would see a steamboat slipping along in the dark, and now and then she would belch a whole world of sparks up out of her chimbleys, and they would rain down in the river and look awful pretty;

[2] A tough, inedible fish, a variety of pike. [3] Fellow.

then she would turn a corner and her lights would wink out and her pow-wow[4] shut off and leave the river still again; and by-and-by her waves would get to us, a long time after she was gone, and joggle the raft a bit, and after that you wouldn't hear nothing for you couldn't tell how long, except maybe frogs or something.

After midnight the people on shore went to bed, and then for two or three hours the shores was black—no more sparks in the cabin windows. These sparks was our clock—the first one that showed again meant morning was coming, so we hunted a place to hide and tie up, right away.

One morning about day-break, I found a canoe and crossed over a chute[5] to the main shore—it was only two hundred yards—and paddled about a mile up a crick amongst the cypress woods, to see if I couldn't get some berries. Just as I was passing a place where a kind of a cow-path crossed the crick, here comes a couple of men tearing up the path as tight as they could foot it. I thought I was a goner, for whenever anybody was after anybody I judged it was *me*—or maybe Jim. I was about to dig out from there in a hurry, but they was pretty close to me then, and sung out and begged me to save their lives—said they hadn't been doing nothing, and was being chased for it—said there was men and dogs a-coming. They wanted to jump right in, but I says—

"Don't you do it. I don't hear the dogs and horses yet; you've got time to crowd through the brush and get up the crick a little ways; then you take to the water and wade down to me and get in—that'll throw the dogs off the scent."

They done it, and soon as they was aboard I lit out for our towhead and in about five or ten minutes we heard the dogs and the men away off, shouting. We heard them come along towards the crick, but couldn't see them; they seemed to stop and fool around a while; then as we got further and further away all the time, we couldn't hardly hear them at all; by the time we had left a mile of woods behind us and struck the river, everything was quiet, and we paddled over to the tow-head and hid in the cotton-woods and was safe.

One of these fellows was about seventy, or upwards, and had a bald head and very gray whiskers. He had an old battered-up slouch hat on, and a greasy blue woolen shirt, and ragged old blue jeans britches stuffed into his boot tops, and home-knit galluses[6]—no, he only had one. He had an old long-tailed blue jeans coat with slick brass buttons, flung over his arm, and both of them had big fat ratty-looking carpet-bags.[7]

The other fellow was about thirty and dressed about as ornery. After breakfast we all laid off and talked, and the first thing that come out was that these chaps didn't know one another.

"What got you into trouble?" says the baldhead to t'other chap.

"Well, I'd been selling an article to take the tartar off the teeth—and it does take it off, too, and generly the enamel along with it—but I staid about one night longer than I ought to, and was just in the act of sliding out when I ran across you on the trail this side of town, and you told me they were coming, and begged me to help you to get off. So I told you I was expecting

[4]Engine noise. [5]A narrow channel with a swift current.
[6]Suspenders. [7]Cheap suitcases made out of carpet remnants.

trouble myself and would scatter out *with* you. That's the whole yarn—what's yourn?"

"Well, I'd ben a-runnin' a little temperance revival thar, 'bout a week, and was the pet of the women-folks, big and little, for I was makin' it mighty warm for the rummies, I *tell* you, and takin' as much as five or six dollars a night—ten cents a head, children and niggers free—and business a growin' all the time; when somehow or another a little report got around, last night, that I had a way of puttin' in my time with a private jug, on the sly. A nigger rousted me out this mornin', and told me the people was getherin' on the quiet, with their dogs and horses, and they'd be along pretty soon and give me 'bout half an hour's start, and then run me down, if they could; and if they got me they'd tar and feather me and ride me on a rail, sure. I didn't wait for no breakfast—I warn't hungry."

"Old man," says the young one, "I reckon we might double-team[8] it together; what do you think?"

"I ain't undisposed. What's your line—mainly?"

"Jour[9] printer, by trade; do a little in patent medicines; theatre-actor—tragedy, you know; take a turn at mesmerism[10] and phrenology[11] when there's a chance; teach singing-geography school for a change; sling a lecture, sometimes—oh, I do lots of things—most anything that comes handy, so it ain't work. What's your lay?"[12]

"I've done considerble in the doctoring way in my time. Layin' on o' hands[13] is my best holt—for cancer, and paralysis, and sich things; and I k'n tell a fortune pretty good, when I've got somebody along to find out the facts for me. Preachin's my line, too; and workin' camp-meetin's; and missionaryin' around."

Nobody never said anything for a while; then the young man hove a sigh and says—

"Alas!"

"What're you alassin' about?" says the baldhead.

"To think I should have lived to be leading such a life, and be degraded down into such company." And he begun to wipe the corner of his eye with a rag.

"Dern your skin, ain't the company good enough for you?" says the baldhead, pretty pert and uppish.

"Yes, it *is* good enough for me; it's as good as I deserve; for who fetched me so low, when I was so high? *I* did myself. I don't blame *you,* gentlemen—far from it; I don't blame anybody. I deserve it all. Let the cold world do its worst; one thing I know—there's a grave somewhere for me. The world may go on just as it's always done, and take everything from me—loved ones, property, everything—but it can't take that. Some day I'll lie down in it and forget it all, and my poor broken heart will be at rest." He went on a-wiping.

"Drot your pore broken heart," says the baldhead; "what are you heaving your pore broken heart at *us* f'r? *We* hain't done nothing."

[8]Work together, like a team of horses. [9]Journeyman, i.e., trained. [10]Hypnotism.
[11]Presuming to read human character from the shape of the head.
[12]Trade, profession. [13]Faith healing.

"No, I know you haven't. I ain't blaming you, gentlemen. I brought myself down—yes, I did it myself. It's right I should suffer—perfectly right—I don't make any moan."

"Brought you down from whar? Whar was you brought down from?"

"Ah, you would not believe me; the world never believes—let it pass—'tis no matter. The secret of my birth——"

"The secret of your birth? Do you mean to say——"

"Gentlemen," says the young man, very solemn, "I will reveal it to you, for I feel I may have confidence in you. By rights I am a duke!"

Jim's eyes bugged out when he heard that; and I reckon mine did, too. Then the baldhead says: "No! you can't mean it?"

"Yes. My great-grandfather, eldest son of the Duke of Bridgewater, fled to this country about the end of the last century, to breathe the pure air of freedom; married here, and died, leaving a son, his own father dying about the same time. The second son of the late duke seized the title and estates—the infant real duke was ignored. I am the lineal descendant of that infant—I am the rightful Duke of Bridgewater; and here am I, forlorn, torn from my high estate, hunted of men, despised by the cold world, ragged, worn, heart-broken, and degraded to the companionship of felons on a raft!"

Jim pitied him ever so much and so did I. We tried to comfort him, but he said it warn't much use, he couldn't be much comforted; said if we was a mind to acknowledge him, that would do him more good than most anything else; so we said we would, if he would tell us how. He said we ought to bow, when we spoke to him, and say "Your Grace," or "My Lord," or "Your Lordship"—and he wouldn't mind it if we called him plain "Bridgewater," which he said was a title, anyway, and not a name; and one of us ought to wait on him at dinner, and do any little thing for him he wanted done.

Well, that was all easy, so we done it. All through dinner Jim stood around and waited on him, and says, "Will yo' Grace have some o' dis, or some o' dat?" and so on, and a body could see it was mighty pleasing to him.

But the old man got pretty silent, by-and-by—didn't have much to say, and didn't look pretty comfortable over all that petting that was going on around that duke. He seemed to have something on his mind. So, along in the afternoon, he says:

"Looky here, Bilgewater," he says, "I'm nation sorry for you, but you ain't the only person that's had troubles like that."

"No?"

"No, you ain't. You ain't the only person that's ben snaked[14] down wrongfully out'n a high place."

"Alas!"

"No, you ain't the only person that's had a secret of his birth." And by jings, *he* begins to cry.

"Hold! What do you mean?"

"Bilgewater, kin I trust you?" says the old man, still sort of sobbing.

"To the bitter death!" He took the old man by the hand and squeezed it, and says, "The secret of your being: speak!"

"Bilgewater, I am the late Dauphin!"

[14]Brought, pulled.

You bet you Jim and me started, this time. Then the duke says:

"You are what?"

"Yes, my friend, it is too true—your eyes is lookin' at this very moment on the pore disappeared Dauphin, Looy the Seventeen, son of Looy the Sixteen and Marry Antonette."

"You! At your age![15] No! You mean you're the late Charlemagne;[16] you must be six or seven hundred years old, at the very least."

"Trouble has done it, Bilgewater, trouble has done it; trouble has brung these gray hairs and this premature balditude. Yes, gentlemen, you see before you, in blue jeans and misery, the wanderin', exiled, trampled-on and sufferin' rightful King of France."

Well, he cried and took on so, that me and Jim didn't know hardly what to do, we was so sorry—and so glad and proud we'd got him with us, too. So we set in, like we done before with the duke, and tried to comfort *him*. But he said it warn't no use, nothing but to be dead and done with it all could do him any good; though he said it often made him feel easier and better for a while if people treated him according to his rights, and got down on one knee to speak to him, and always called him "Your Majesty," and waited on him first at meals, and didn't set down in his presence till he asked them. So Jim and me set to majestying him, and doing this and that and t'other for him, and standing up till he told us we might set down. This done him heaps of good, and so he got cheerful and comfortable. But the duke kind of soured on him, and didn't look a bit satisfied with the way things was going; still, the king acted real friendly towards him, and said the duke's great-grandfather and all the other Dukes of Bilgewater was a good deal thought of by *his* father and was allowed to come to the palace considerable; but the duke staid huffy a good while, till by-and-by the king says:

"Like as not we got to be together a blamed long time, on this h-yer raft, Bilgewater, and so what's the use o' your bein' sour? It'll only make things oncomfortable. It ain't my fault I warn't born a duke, it ain't your fault you warn't born a king—so what's the use to worry? Make the best o' things the way you find 'em, says I—that's my motto. This ain't no bad thing that we've struck here—plenty grub and an easy life—come, give us your hand, Duke, and less all be friends."

The duke done it, and Jim and me was pretty glad to see it. It took away all the uncomfortableness, and we felt mighty good over it, because it would a been a miserable business to have any unfriendliness on the raft; for what you want, above all things, on a raft, is for everybody to be satisfied, and feel right and kind towards the others.

It didn't take me long to make up my mind that these liars warn't no kings nor dukes, at all, but just low-down humbugs and frauds. But I never said nothing, never let on; kept it to myself; it's the best way; then you don't have no quarrels, and don't get into no trouble. If they wanted us to call them kings and dukes, I hadn't no objections, 'long as it would keep peace in the family; and it warn't no use to tell Jim, so I didn't tell him. If I never learnt nothing else out of pap, I learnt that the best way to get along with his kind of people is to let them have their own way.

[15]Had he lived, the lost dauphin would have been in his fifties.
[16]The Holy Roman Emperor Charles the Great (742–814).

CHAPTER XX

They asked us considerable many questions; wanted to know what we covered up the raft that way for, and laid by in the daytime instead of running—was Jim a runaway nigger? Says I—

"Goodness sakes, would a runaway nigger run *south?*"

No, they allowed he wouldn't. I had to account for things some way, so I says:

"My folks was living in Pike County, in Missouri, where I was born, and they all died off but me and pa and my brother Ike. Pa, he 'lowed he'd break up and go down and live with Uncle Ben, who's got a little one-horse place on the river, forty-four mile below Orleans. Pa was pretty poor, and had some debts; so when he'd squared up there warn't nothing left but sixteen dollars and our nigger, Jim. That warn't enough to take us fourteen hundred mile, deck passage nor no other way. Well, when the river rose, pa had a streak of luck one day; he ketched this piece of a raft; so we reckoned we'd go down to Orleans on it. Pa's luck didn't hold out; a steamboat run over the forrard corner of the raft, one night, and we all went overboard and dove under the wheel; Jim and me come up, all right, but pa was drunk, and Ike was only four years old, so they never come up no more. Well, for the next day or two we had considerable trouble, because people was always coming out in skiffs and trying to take Jim away from me, saying they believed he was a runaway nigger. We don't run day-times no more, now; nights they don't bother us."

The duke says—

"Leave me alone to cipher out a way so we can run in the daytime if we want to. I'll think the thing over—I'll invent a plan that'll fix it. We'll let it alone for to-day, because of course we don't want to go by that town yonder in daylight—it mightn't be healthy."

Towards night it begun to darken up and look like rain; the heat lightning was squirting around, low down in the sky, and the leaves was beginning to shiver—it was going to be pretty ugly, it was easy to see that. So the duke and the king went to overhauling our wigwam, to see what the beds was like. My bed was a straw tick[1]—better than Jim's, which was a corn-shuck tick; there's always cobs around about in a shuck tick, and they poke into you and hurt; and when you roll over, the dry shucks sound like you was rolling over in a pile of dead leaves; it makes such a rustling that you wake up. Well, the duke allowed he would take my bed; but the king allowed he wouldn't. He says—

"I should a reckoned the difference in rank would a sejested to you that a corn-shuck bed warn't just fitten for me to sleep on. Your Grace'll take the shuck bed yourself."

Jim and me was in a sweat again, for a minute, being afraid there was going to be some more trouble amongst them; so we was pretty glad when the duke says—

"'Tis my fate to be always ground into the mire under the iron heel of oppression. Misfortune has broken my once haughty spirit; I yield, I submit; 'tis my fate. I am alone in the world—let me suffer; I can bear it."

We got away as soon as it was good and dark. The king told us to stand well out towards the middle of the river, and not show a light till we got a long

[1]Mattress.

ways below the town. We come in sight of the little bunch of lights by-and-by—that was the town, you know—and slid by, about a half a mile out, all right. When we was three-quarters of a mile below, we hoisted up our signal lantern; and about ten o'clock it come on to rain and blow and thunder and lighten like everything; so the king told us to both stay on watch till the weather got better; then him and the duke crawled into the wigwam and turned in for the night. It was my watch below, till twelve,[2] but I wouldn't a turned in, anyway, if I'd had a bed; because a body don't see such a storm as that every day in the week, not by a long sight. My souls, how the wind did scream along! And every second or two there'd come a glare that lit up the white-caps for a half a mile around, and you'd see the islands looking dusty through the rain, and the trees thrashing around in the wind; then comes a *h-wack!*—bum! bum! bumble-umble-um-bum-bum-bum-bum—and the thunder would go rumbling and grumbling away, and quit—and then *rip* comes another flash and another sockdolager.[3] The waves most washed me off the raft, sometimes, but I hadn't any clothes on, and didn't mind. We didn't have no trouble about snags; the lightning was glaring and flittering around so constant that we could see them plenty soon enough to throw her head this way or that and miss them.

I had the middle watch, you know, but I was pretty sleepy by that time, so Jim he said he would stand the first half of it for me; he was always mighty good, that way, Jim was. I crawled into the wigwam, but the king and the duke had their legs sprawled around so there warn't no show for me; so I laid outside—I didn't mind the rain, because it was warm, and the waves warn't running so high, now. About two they come up again, though, and Jim was going to call me, but he changed his mind because he reckoned they warn't high enough yet to do any harm; but he was mistaken about that, for pretty soon all of a sudden along comes a regular ripper, and washed me overboard. It most killed Jim a-laughing. He was the easiest nigger to laugh that ever was, anyway.

I took the watch, and Jim he laid down and snored away; and by-and-by the storm let up for good and all; and the first cabin-light that showed, I rousted him out and we slid the raft into hiding-quarters for the day.

The king got out an old ratty deck of cards, after breakfast, and him and the duke played seven-up[4] a while, five cents a game. Then they got tired of it, and allowed they would "lay out a campaign," as they called it. The duke went down into his carpet-bag and fetched up a lot of little printed bills, and read them out loud. One bill said, "The celebrated Dr. Armand de Montalban of Paris," would "lecture on the Science of Phrenology" at such and such a place, on the blank day of blank, at ten cents admission, and "furnish charts of character at twenty-five cents apiece." The duke said that was *him.* In another bill he was the "world renowned Shakesperean tragedian, Garrick the Younger,[5] of Drury Lane, London." In other bills he had a lot of other

[2]I.e., Huck is off duty ("below") until the middle watch, midnight to 4 A.M.

[3]Tremendous crash, from "doxology," a hymn in praise of God and traditionally the loudest part of a church service.

[4]A card game in which the winner must score seven points.

[5]David Garrick (1717–1779), British actor, had died the previous century. There was no Garrick the Younger.

names and done other wonderful things, like finding water and gold with a "divining rod,"[6] "dissipating witchspells," and so on. By-and-by he says—

"But the histrionic muse is the darling. Have you ever trod the boards,[7] Royalty?"

"No," says the king.

"You shall then, before you're three days older, Fallen Grandeur," says the duke. "The first good town we come to, we'll hire a hall and do the sword-fight in Richard III, and the balcony scene in Romeo and Juliet. How does that strike you?"

"I'm in, up to the hub, for anything that will pay, Bilgewater, but you see I don't know nothing about play-actin', and hain't ever seen much of it. I was too small when pap used to have 'em at the palace. Do you reckon you can learn me?"

"Easy!"

"All right. I'm jist a-freezn' for something fresh, anyway. Less commence, right away."

So the duke he told him all about who Romeo was, and who Juliet was, and said he was used to being Romeo, so the king could be Juliet.

"But if Juliet's such a young gal, Duke, my peeled head and my white whiskers is goin' to look oncommon odd on her, maybe."

"No, don't you worry—these country jakes won't ever think of that. Besides, you know, you'll be in costume, and that makes all the difference in the world; Juliet's in a balcony, enjoying the moonlight before she goes to bed, and she's got on her night-gown and her ruffled night-cap. Here are the costumes for the parts."

He got out two or three curtain-calico suits, which he said was meedyevil armor for Richard III. and t'other chap,[8] and a long white cotton night-shirt and a ruffled night-cap to match. The king was satisfied; so the duke got out his book and read the parts over in the most splendid spread-eagle[9] way, prancing around and acting at the same time, to show how it had got to be done; then he give the book to the king and told him to get his part by heart.

There was a little one-horse town about three mile down the bend, and after dinner the duke said he had ciphered out his idea about how to run in daylight without it being dangersome for Jim; so he allowed he would go down to the town and fix that thing. The king allowed he would go too, and see if he couldn't strike something. We was out of coffee, so Jim said I better go along with them in the canoe and get some.

When we got there, there warn't nobody stirring; streets empty, and perfectly dead and still, like Sunday. We found a sick nigger sunning himself in a back yard, and he said everybody that warn't too young or too sick or too old, was gone to camp-meeting, about two mile back in the woods. The king got the directions, and allowed he'd go and work that camp-meeting for all it was worth, and I might go, too.

The duke said what he was after was a printing office. We found it; a little bit of a concern, up over a carpenter shop—carpenters and printers all gone to the meeting, and no doors locked. It was a dirty, littered-up place, and had ink marks, and handbills with pictures of horses and runaway niggers on

[6]A forked rod or stick believed to point magically toward water or buried treasure.
[7]Acted on the stage. [8]The Earl of Richmond. [9]Ornate, exaggerated.

them, all over the walls. The duke shed his coat and said he was all right, now. So me and the king lit out for the camp-meeting.

We got there in about a half an hour, fairly dripping, for it was a most awful hot day. There was as much as a thousand people there, from twenty mile around. The woods was full of teams and wagons, hitched everywheres, feeding out of the wagon troughs and stomping to keep off the flies. There was sheds made out of poles and roofed over with branches, where they had lemonade and gingerbread to sell, and piles of watermelons and green corn and such-like truck.

The preaching was going on under the same kinds of sheds, only they was bigger and held crowds of people. The benches was made out of outside slabs of logs, with holes bored in the round side to drive sticks into for legs. They didn't have no backs. The preachers had high platforms to stand on, at one end of the sheds. The women had on sun-bonnets; and some had linsey-woolsey[10] frocks, some gingham ones, and a few of the young ones had on calico. Some of the young men was barefooted, and some of the children didn't have on any clothes but just a tow-linen[11] shirt. Some of the old women was knitting, and some of the young folks was courting on the sly.

The first shed we come to, the preacher was lining out a hymn.[12] He lined out two lines, everybody sung it, and it was kind of grand to hear it, there was so many of them and they done it in such a rousing way; then he lined out two more for them to sing—and so on. The people woke up more and more, and sung louder and louder; and towards the end, some begun to groan, and some begun to shout. Then the preacher begun to preach; and begun in earnest, too; and went weaving first to one side of the platform and then the other, and then a leaning down over the front of it, with his arms and his body going all the time, and shouting his words out with all his might; and every now and then he would hold up his Bible and spread it open, and kind of pass it around this way and that, shouting, "It's the brazen serpent in the wilderness! Look upon it and live!" And people would shout out, "Glory!—A-a-*men!*" And so he went on, and the people groaning and crying and saying amen:

"Oh, come to the mourners' bench![13] come, black with sin! (*amen!*) come, sick and sore! (*amen!*) come, lame and halt, and blind! (*amen!*) come, pore and needy, sunk in shame! (*a-a-amen!*) come all that's worn, and soiled, and suffering!—come with a broken spirit! come with a contrite heart! come in your rags and sin and dirt! the waters that cleanse is free, the door of heaven stands open—oh, enter in and be at rest! (*a-a-men! glory, glory hallelujah!*)"

And so on. You couldn't make out what the preacher said, any more, on account of the shouting and crying. Folks got up, everywheres in the crowd, and worked their way, just by main strength, to the mourners' bench, with the tears running down their faces; and when all the mourners had got up there to the front benches in a crowd, they sung and shouted, and flung themselves down on the straw, just crazy and wild.

Well, the first I knowed, the king got agoing; and you could hear him over everybody; and next he went a-charging up on the platform and the

[10]Coarse cloth of linen or cotton and wool. [11]Rough linen.
[12]Speaking out the words so the congregation, lacking hymnbooks, could follow in song.
[13]Front seats, near the pulpit, for those who mourn their sins and want to repent.

preacher he begged him to speak to the people, and he done it. He told them he was a pirate—been a pirate for thirty years, out in the Indian Ocean, and his crew was thinned out considerable, last spring, in a fight, and he was home now, to take out some fresh men, and thanks to goodness he'd been robbed last night, and put ashore off a steamboat without a cent, and he was glad of it, it was the blessedest thing that ever happened to him, because he was a changed man now, and happy for the first time in his life; and poor as he was, he was going to start right off and work his way back to the Indian Ocean and put in the rest of his life trying to turn the pirates into the true path; for he could do it better than anybody else, being acquainted with all the pirate crews in that ocean; and though it would take him a long time to get there, without money, he would get there anyway, and every time he convinced a pirate he would say to him, "Don't you thank me, don't you give me no credit, it all belongs to them dear people in Pokeville camp-meeting, natural brothers and benefactors of the race—and that dear preacher there, the truest friend a pirate ever had!"

And then he busted into tears, and so did everybody. Then somebody sings out, "Take up a collection for him, take up a collection!" Well, a half a dozen made a jump to do it, but somebody sings out, "Let *him* pass the hat around!" Then everybody said it, the preacher too.

So the king went all through the crowd with his hat, swabbing his eyes, and blessing the people and praising them and thanking them for being so good to the poor pirates away off there; and every little while the prettiest kind of girls, with the tears running down their cheeks, would up and ask him would he let them kiss him, for to remember him by; and he always done it; and some of them he hugged and kissed as many as five or six times—and he was invited to stay a week; and everybody wanted him to live in their houses, and said they'd think it was an honor; but he said as this was the last day of the camp-meeting he couldn't do no good, and besides he was in a sweat to get to the Indian Ocean right off and go to work on the pirates.

When we got back to the raft and he come to count up, he found he had collected eighty-seven dollars and seventy-five cents. And then he had fetched away a three-gallon jug of whisky, too, that he found under a wagon when we was starting home through the woods. The king said, take it all around, it laid over any day he'd ever put in the missionarying line. He said it warn't no use talking, heathens don't amount to shucks, alongside of pirates, to work a camp-meeting with.

The duke was thinking *he'd* been doing pretty well, till the king come to show up, but after that he didn't think so so much. He had set up and printed off two little jobs for farmers, in that printing office—horse bills—and took the money, four dollars. And he had got in ten dollars' worth of advertisements for the paper, which he said he would put in for four dollars if they would pay in advance—so they done it. The price of the paper was two dollars a year, but he took in three subscriptions for half a dollar apiece on condition of them paying him in advance; they were going to pay in cordwood and onions, as usual, but he said he had just bought the concern and knocked down the price as low as he could afford it, and was going to run it for cash. He set up a little piece of poetry, which he made, himself, out of his own head—three verses—kind of sweet and saddish—the name of it was,

"Yes, crush, cold world, this breaking heart"—and he left that all set up and ready to print in the paper and didn't charge nothing for it. Well, he took in nine dollars and a half, and said he'd done a pretty square day's work for it.

Then he showed us another little job he'd printed and hadn't charged for, because it was for us. It had a picture of a runaway nigger, with a bundle on a stick, over his shoulder, and "$200 reward" under it. The reading was all about Jim, and just described him to a dot. It said he run away from St. Jacques' plantation, forty mile below New Orleans, last winter, and likely went north, and whoever would catch him and send him back, he could have the reward and expenses.

"Now," says duke, "after to-night we can run in the day-time if we want to. Whenever we see anybody coming, we can tie Jim hand and foot with a rope, and lay him in the wigwam and show this handbill and say we captured him up the river, and were too poor to travel on a steamboat, so we got this little raft on credit from our friends and are going down to get the reward. Handcuffs and chains would look better on Jim, but it wouldn't go well with the story of us being so poor. Too much like jewelry. Ropes are the correct thing—we must preserve the unities,[14] as we say on the boards."

We all said the duke was pretty smart, and there couldn't be no trouble about running day-times. We judged we could make miles enough that night to get out of the reach of the pow-wow we reckoned the duke's work in the printing office was going to make in that little town—then we could boom right along, if we wanted to.

We laid low and kept still, and never shoved out till nearly ten o'clock; then we slid by, pretty wide away from the town, and didn't hoist our lantern till we was clear out of sight of it.

When Jim called me to take the watch at four in the morning, he says—

"Huck, does you reck'n we gwyne to run acrost any mo' kings on dis trip?"

"No," I says, "I reckon not."

"Well," says he, "dat's all right, den. I doan' mine one er two kings, but dat's enough. Dis one's powerful drunk, en de duke ain' much better."

I found Jim had been trying to get him to talk French, so he could hear what it was like; but he said he had been in this country so long, and had so much trouble, he'd forgot it.

CHAPTER XXI

It was after sun-up, now, but we went right on, and didn't tie up. The king and the duke turned out, by-and-by, looking pretty rusty; but after they'd jumped overboard and took a swim, it chippered them up a good deal. After breakfast the king he took a seat on a corner of the raft, and pulled off his boots and rolled up his britches, and let his legs dangle in the water, so as to be comfortable, and lit his pipe, and went to getting his Romeo and Juliet by heart. When he had got it pretty good, him and the duke begun to practice it together. The duke had to learn him over and over again, how to say every speech; and he made him sigh, and put his hand on his heart, and after

[14]The dramatic unities of time, place, and action of the neoclassic French theater.

while he said he done it pretty well; "only," he says, "you mustn't bellow out *Romeo!* that way, like a bull—you must say it soft, and sick, and languishy, so—R-o-o-meo! that is the idea; for Juliet's a dear sweet mere child of a girl, you know, and she don't bray like a jackass."

Well, next they got out a couple of long swords that the duke made out of oak laths, and begun to practice the sword-fight—the duke called himself Richard III.; and the way they laid on, and pranced around the raft was grand to see. But by-and-by the king tripped and fell overboard, and after that they took a rest, and had a talk about all kinds of adventures they'd had in other times along the river.

After dinner, the duke says:

"Well, Capet,[1] we'll want to make this a first-class show, you know, so I guess we'll add a little more to it. We want a little something to answer encores with, anyway."

"What's onkores, Bilgewater?"

The duke told him, and then says:

"I'll answer by doing the Highland fling or the sailor's hornpipe;[2] and you—well, let me see—oh, I've got it—you can do Hamlet's soliloquy."

"Hamlet's which?"

"Hamlet's soliloquy, you know; the most celebrated thing in Shakespeare. Ah, it's sublime, sublime! Always fetches the house. I haven't got it in the book—I've only got one volume—but I reckon I can piece it out from memory. I'll just walk up and down a minute, and see if I can call it back from recollection's vaults."

So he went to marching up and down, thinking, and frowning horrible every now and then; then he would hoist up his eyebrows; next he would squeeze his hand on his forehead and stagger back and kind of moan; next he would sigh, and next he'd let on to drop a tear. It was beautiful to see him. By-and-by he got it. He told us to give attention. Then he strikes a most noble attitude, with one leg shoved forwards, and his arms stretched away up, and his head tilted back, looking up at the sky; and then he begins to rip and rave and grit his teeth; and after that, all through his speech he howled, and spread around, and swelled up his chest, and just knocked the spots out of any acting ever *I* see before. This is the speech—I learned it, easy enough, while he was learning it to the king:

To be, or not to be; that is the bare bodkin
That makes calamity of so long life;
For who would fardels bear, till Birnam Wood do come
  to Dunsinane,
But that the fear of something after death
Murders the innocent sleep,
Great nature's second course,
And makes us rather sling the arrows of outrageous fortune
Than fly to others that we know not of.
There's the respect must give us pause:

[1]Family name of Louis XVI.

[2]Highland fling: a lively Scottish dance. Sailor's hornpipe: a dance in which the performer, accompanied by a hornpipe, acts out the tasks of a sailor.

Wake Duncan with thy knocking! I would thou couldst;
For who would bear the whips and scorns of time,
The oppressor's wrong, the proud man's contumely,
The law's delay, and the quietus which his pangs might
take,
In the dead waste and middle of the night, when church-
yards yawn
In customary suits of solemn black,
But that the undiscovered country from whose bourne no
traveler returns,
Breathes forth contagion on the world,
And thus the native hue of resolution, like the poor cat
i' the adage,
Is sicklied o'er with care.
And all the clouds that lowered o'er our housetops,
With this regard their currents turn awry,
And lose the name of action.
'Tis a consummation devoutly to be wished. But soft you,
the fair Ophelia:
Ope not thy ponderous and marble jaws,
But get thee to a nunnery—go![3]

Well, the old man he liked that speech, and he mighty soon got it so he could do it first rate. It seemed like he was just born for it; and when he had his hand in and was excited, it was perfectly lovely the way he would rip and tear and rair up behind when he was getting it off.

The first chance we got, the duke he had some show bills printed; and after that, for two or three days as we floated along, the raft was a most uncommon lively place, for there warn't nothing but sword-fighting and rehearsing—as the duke called it—going on all the time. One morning, when we was pretty well down the State of Arkansaw, we come in sight of a little one-horse town in a big bend; so we tied up about three-quarters of a mile above it, in the mouth of a crick which was shut in like a tunnel by the cypress trees, and all of us but Jim took the canoe and went down there to see if there was any chance in that place for our show.

We struck it mighty lucky; there was going to be a circus there that afternoon, and the country people was already beginning to come in, in all kinds of old shackly wagons, and on horses. The circus would leave before night, so our show would have a pretty good chance. The duke he hired the court house, and we went around and stuck up our bills. They read like this:

Shaksperean Revival! ! !
Wonderful Attraction!
For One Night Only!
The world renowned tragedians,
David Garrick, the younger, of Drury Lane Theatre, London,
and

[3]The Duke's soliloquy is a hodgepodge of Shakespeare quotations from *Hamlet, Macbeth,* and *Richard III.*

Edmund Kean the elder,[4] of the Royal Haymarket Theatre, White-
chapel, Pudding Lane, Piccadilly, London, and the
Royal Continental Theatres, in their sublime
Shaksperean Spectacle entitled
The Balcony Scene
in
Romeo and Juliet! ! !
Romeo.......................................Mr. Garrick.
Juliet..Mr. Kean.
Assisted by the whole strength of the company
New costumes, new scenery, new appointments!
Also:
The thrilling, masterly, and blood-curdling
Broad-sword conflict
In Richard III.! ! !
Richard III...............................Mr. Garrick.
Richmond.............................Mr. Kean.
also:
(by special request,)
Hamlet's Immortal Soliloquy!
By the Illustrious Kean!
Done by him 300 consecutive nights in Paris!
For One Night Only,
On account of imperative European engagements!
Admission 25 cents; children and servants, 10 cents.

Then we went loafing around the town. The stores and houses was most all old shackly dried-up frame concerns that hadn't even been painted; they was set up three or four foot above ground on stilts, so as to be out of reach of the water when the river was overflowed. The houses had little gardens around them, but they didn't seem to raise hardly anything in them but jimpson weeds, and sunflowers, and ash-piles, and old curled-up boots and shoes, and pieces of bottles, and rags, and played-out tin-ware. The fences was made of different kinds of boards, nailed on at different times; and they leaned every which-way, and had gates that didn't generly have but one hinge—a leather one. Some of the fences had been whitewashed, some time or another, but the duke said it was in Clumbus's time, like enough. There was generly hogs in the garden, and people driving them out.

All the stores was along one street. They had white-domestic[5] awnings in front, and the country people hitched their horses to the awning-posts. There was empty dry-goods boxes under the awnings, and loafers roosting on them all day long, whittling them with their Barlow knives; and chawing tobacco, and gaping and yawning and stretching—a mighty ornery lot. They generly had on yellow straw hats most as wide as an umbrella, but didn't wear no coats nor waistcoats; they called one another Bill, and Buck, and Hank, and Joe, and Andy, and talked lazy and drawly, and used considerable many cusswords. There was as many as one loafer leaning up against every awning-post, and he most always had his hands in his britches pockets, except when he fetches them out to lend a chaw of tobacco or scratch. What a body was hearing amongst them, all the time was—

"Gimme a chaw'v tobacker, Hank."

[4]British actor (1787?–1833). [5]Crude canvas.

"Cain't—I hain't got but one chaw left. Ask Bill."

Maybe Bill he gives him a chaw; maybe he lies and says he ain't got none. Some of them kinds of loafers never has a cent in the world, nor a chaw of tobacco of their own. They get all their chawing by borrowing—they say to a fellow, "I wisht you'd len' me a chaw, Jack, I jist this minute give Ben Thompson the last chaw I had"—which is a lie, pretty much every time; it don't fool nobody but a stranger; but Jack ain't no stranger, so he says—

"*You* give him a chaw, did you? so did your sister's cat's grandmother. You pay me back the chaws you've awready borry'd off'n me, Lafe Buckner, then I'll loan you one or two ton of it, and won't charge you no back intrust, nuther."

"Well, I *did* pay you back some of it wunst."

"Yes, you did—'bout six chaws. You borry'd store tobacker and paid back nigger-head."[6]

Store tobacco is flat black plug, but these fellow mostly chaws the natural leaf twisted. When they borrow a chaw, they don't generly cut it off with a knife, but they set the plug in between their teeth, and gnaw with their teeth and tug at the plug with their hands till they get it in two—then sometimes the one that owns the tobacco looks mournful at it when it's handed back, and says, sarcastic—

"Here, gimme the *chaw,* and you take the *plug.*"

All the streets and lanes was just mud, they warn't nothing else *but* mud—mud as black as tar, and nigh about a foot deep in some places; and two or three inches deep in *all* the places. The hogs loafed and grunted around, everywheres. You'd see a muddy sow and a litter of pigs come lazying along the street and whollop herself right down in the way, where folks had to walk around her, and she'd stretch out, and shut her eyes, and wave her ears, whilst the pigs was milking her, and look as happy as if she was on salary. And pretty soon you'd hear a loafer sing out, "Hi! *so* boy! sick him, Tige!" and away the sow would go, squealing most horrible, with a dog or two swinging to each ear, and three or four dozen more a-coming; and then you would see all the loafers get up and watch the thing out of sight, and laugh at the fun and look grateful for the noise. Then they'd settle back again till there was a dog-fight. There couldn't anything wake them up all over, and make them happy all over, like a dog-fight—unless it might be putting turpentine on a stray dog and setting fire to him, or tying a tin pan to his tail and see him run himself to death.

On the river front some of the houses was sticking out over the bank, and they was bowed and bent, and about ready to tumble in. The people had moved out of them. The bank was caved away under once corner of some others, and that corner was hanging over. People lived in them yet, but it was dangersome, because sometimes a strip of land as wide as a house caves in at a time. Sometimes a belt of land a quarter of a mile deep will start in and cave along and cave along till it all caves into the river in one summer. Such a town as that has to be always moving back, and back, and back, because the river's always gnawing at it.

The nearer it got to the noon that day, the thicker and thicker was the wagons and horses in the streets, and more coming all the time. Families fetched

[6]Cheap, leaf tobacco.

their dinners with them, from the country, and eat them in the wagons. There was considerable whisky drinking going on, and I seen three fights. By-and-by somebody sings out—

"Here comes old Boggs!—in from the country for his little old monthly drunk—here he comes, boys!"

All the loafers looked glad—I reckoned they was used to having fun out of Boggs. One of them says—

"Wonder who he's a gwyne to chaw up this time. If he'd a chawed up all the men he's ben a gwyne to chaw up in the last twenty year, he'd have considerable ruputation, now."

Another one says, "I wisht old Boggs'd threaten me, 'cuz then I'd know I warn't gwyne to die for a thousan' year."

Boggs comes a-tearing along on his horse, whooping and yelling like an Injun, and singing out—

"Cler the track, thar. I'm on the waw-path, and the price uv coffins is a gwyne to raise."

He was drunk, and weaving about in his saddle; he was over fifty year old, and had a very red face. Everybody yelled at him, and laughed at him, and sassed him, and he sassed back, and said he'd attend to them and lay them out in their regular turns, but he couldn't wait now, because he'd come to town to kill old Colonel Sherburn, and his motto was, "meat first, and spoon vittles to top off on."

He see me, and rode up and says—

"Whar'd you come f'm, boy? You prepared to die?"

Then he rode on. I was scared; but a man says—

"He don't mean nothing; he's always a carryin' on like that, when he's drunk. He's the best-naturedness old fool in Arkansaw—never hurt nobody, drunk nor sober."

Boggs rode up before the biggest store in town and bent his head down so he could see under the curtain of the awning, and yells—

"Come out here, Sherburn! Come out and meet the man you've swindled. You're the houn' I'm after, and I'm a gwyne to have you, too!"

And so he went on, calling Sherburn everything he could lay his tongue to, and the whole street packed with people listening and laughing and going on. By-and-by a proud-looking man about fifty-five—and he was a heap the best dressed man in that town, too—steps out of the store, and the crowd drops back on each side to let him come. He says to Boggs, mighty ca'm and slow—he says:

"I'm tired of this; but I'll endure it till one o'clock. Till one o'clock, mind—no longer. If you open your mouth against me once, after that time, you can't travel so far but I will find you."

Then he turns and goes in. The crowd looked mighty sober; nobody stirred, and there warn't no more laughing. Boggs rode off blackguarding Sherburn as loud as he could yell, all down the street; and pretty soon back he comes and stops before the store, still keeping it up. Some men crowded around him and tried to get him to shut up, but he wouldn't; they told him it would be one o'clock in about fifteen minutes, and so he *must* go home—he must go right away. But it didn't do no good. He cussed away, with all his might, and throwed his hat down in the mud and rode over it, and pretty soon away he went a-raging down the street again, with his gray hair a-flying.

Everybody that could get a chance at him tried their best to coax him off of his horse so they could lock him up and get him sober; but it warn't no use—up the street he would tear again, and give Sherburn another cussing. By-and-by somebody says—

"Go for his daughter!—quick, go for his daughter; sometimes he'll listen to her. If anybody can persuade him, she can."

So somebody started on a run. I walked down street a ways, and stopped. In about five or ten minutes, here comes Boggs again—but not on his horse. He was a-reeling across the street towards me, bareheaded, with a friend on both sides of him aloft of this arms and hurrying him along. He was quiet, and looked uneasy; and he warn't hanging back any, but was doing some of the hurrying himself. Somebody sings out—

"Boggs!"

I looked over there to see who said it, and it was that Colonel Sherburn. He was standing perfectly still, in the street, and had a pistol raised in his right hand—not aiming it, but holding it out with the barrel tilted up towards the sky. The same second I see a young girl coming on the run, and two men with her. Boggs and the men turned round, to see who called him, and when they see the pistol the men jumped to one side, and the pistol barrel come down slow and steady to a level—both barrels cocked. Boggs throws up both of his hands, and says, "O Lord, don't shoot!" Bang! goes the first shot, and he staggers back clawing at the air—bang! goes the second one, and he tumbles backwards onto the ground, heavy and solid, with his arms spread out. The young girl screamed out, and comes rushing, and down she throws herself on her father, crying, and saying. "Oh, he's killed him, he's killed him!" The crowd closed up around them, and shouldered and jammed one another, with their necks stretched, trying to see, and people on the inside trying to shove them back, and shouting, "Back, back! give him air, give him air!"

Colonel Sherburn he tossed his pistol onto the ground, and turned around on his heels and walked off.

They took Boggs to a little drug store, the crowd pressing around, just the same, and the whole town following, and I rushed and got a good place at the window, where I was close to him and could see in. They laid him on the floor, and put one large Bible under his head, and opened another one and spread it on his breast—but they tore open his shirt first, and I seen where one of the bullets went in. He made about a dozen long gasps, his breast lifting the Bible up when he drawed in his breath, and letting it down again when he breathed it out—and after that he laid still; he was dead.[7] Then they pulled his daughter away from him, screaming and crying, and took her off. She was about sixteen, and very sweet and gentle-looking, but awful pale and scared.

Well, pretty soon the whole town was there, squirming and scrouging and pushing and shoving to get at the window and have a look, but people that had the places wouldn't give them up, and folks behind them was saying all the time, "Say, now, you've looked enough, you fellows; 'taint right and 'taint

[7]Twain's description of the death of Boggs closely follows the details of a murder that occurred in Hannibal in 1845. Twain's father served as judge at the subsequent trial. The defendant was acquitted.

fair, for you to stay thar all the time, and never give nobody a chance; other folks has their rights as well as you."

There was considerable jawing back, so I slid out, thinking maybe there was going to be trouble. The streets was full, and everybody was excited. Everybody that seen the shooting was telling how it happened, and there was a big crowd packed around each one of these fellows, stretching their necks and listening. One long lanky man, with long hair and a big white fur stove-pipe hat on the back of his head, and a crooked-handled cane, marked out the places on the ground where Boggs stood, and where Sherburn stood, and the people following him around from one place to t'other and watching everything he done, and bobbing their heads to show they understood, and stooping a little and resting their hands on their thighs to watch him mark the places on the ground with his cane; and then he stood up straight and stiff where Sherburn had stood, frowning and having his hat-brim down over his eyes, and sung out, "Boggs!" and then fetched his cane down slow to a level, and says "Bang!" staggered backwards, says "Bang!" again, and fell down flat on his back. The people that had seen the thing said he done it perfect; said it was just exactly the way it all happened. Then as much as a dozen people got out their bottles and treated him.

Well, by-and-by somebody said Sherburn ought to be lynched. In about a minute everybody was saying it; so away they went, mad and yelling, and snatching down every clothes-line they come to, to do the hanging with.

CHAPTER XXII

They swarmed up the street towards Sherburn's house, a-whooping and yelling and raging like Injuns, and everything had to clear the way or get run over and tromped to mush, and it was awful to see. Children was heeling it ahead of the mob, screaming and trying to get out of the way; and every window along the road was full of women's heads, and there was nigger boys in every tree, and bucks and wenches[1] looking over every fence; and as soon as the mob would get nearly to them they would break and skaddle back out of reach. Lots of the women and girls was crying and taking on, scared most to death.

They swarmed up in front of Sherburn's palings as thick as they could jam together, and you couldn't hear yourself think for the noise. It was a little twenty-foot yard. Some sung out "Tear down the fence! tear down the fence!" Then there was a racket of ripping and tearing and smashing, and down she goes, and the front wall of the crowd begins to roll in like a wave.

Just then Sherburn steps out on the roof of his little front porch, with a double-barrel gun in his hand, and takes his stand, perfectly ca'm and deliberate, not saying a word. The racket stopped, and the wave sucked back.

Sherburn never said a word—just stood there, looking down. The stillness was awful creepy and uncomfortable. Sherburn run his eye slow along the crowd; and wherever it struck, the people tried a little to outgaze him, but they couldn't; they dropped their eyes and looked sneaky. Then pretty soon

[1]Young male and female slaves.

Sherburn sort of laughed; not the pleasant kind, but the kind that makes you feel like when you are eating bread that's got sand in it.

Then he says, slow and scornful:

"The idea of *you* lynching anybody! It's amusing. The idea of you thinking you had pluck enough to lynch a *man!* Because you're brave enough to tar and feather poor friendless cast-out women that come along here, did that make you think you had grit enough to lay your hands on a *man?* Why a *man's* safe in the hands of ten thousand of your kind—as long as it's day-time and you're not behind him.

"Do I know you? I know you clear through. I was born and raised in the South, and I've lived in the North; so I know the average all around. The average man's a coward. In the North he lets anybody walk over him that wants to, and goes home and prays for a humble spirit to bear it. In the South one man, all by himself, has stopped a stage full of men, in the day-time, and robbed the lot. Your newspapers call you a brave people so much that you think you *are* braver than any other people—whereas you're just *as* brave, and no braver. Why don't your juries hang murderers? Because they're afraid the man's friends will shoot them in the back, in the dark—and it's just what they *would* do.

"So they always acquit; and then a *man* goes in the night, with a hundred masked cowards at his back, and lynches the rascal. Your mistake is, that you didn't bring a man with you; that's one mistake, and the other is that you didn't come in the dark, and fetch your masks. You brought *part* of a man—Buck Harkness, there—and if you hadn't had him to start you, you'd a taken it out in blowing.

"You didn't want to come. The average man don't like trouble and danger. *You* don't like trouble and danger. But if only *half* a man—like Buck Harkness, there—shouts 'Lynch him, lynch him!' you're afraid to back down—afraid you'll be found out to be what you are—*cowards*—and so you raise a yell, and hang yourselves onto that half-a-man's coat tail, and come raging up here, swearing what big things you're going to do. The pitifulest thing out is a mob; that's what an army is—a mob; they don't fight with courage that's born in them, but with courage that's borrowed from their mass, and from their officers. But a mob without any *man* at the head of it, is *beneath* pitifulness. Now the thing for *you* to do, is to droop your tails and go home and crawl in a hole. If any real lynching's going to be done, it will be done in the dark, Southern fashion; and when they come they'll bring their masks, and fetch a *man* along. Now *leave*—and take your half-a-man with you"—tossing his gun up across his left arm and cocking it, when he says this.

The crowd washed back sudden, and then broke all apart and went tearing off every which way, and Buck Harkness he heeled it after them, looking tolerable cheap. I could a staid, if I'd a wanted to, but I didn't want to.

I went to the circus, and loafed around the back side till the watchman went by, and then dived in under the tent. I had my twenty-dollar gold piece and some other money, but I reckoned I better save it, because there ain't no telling how soon you are going to need it, away from home and amongst strangers, that way. You can't be too careful. I ain't opposed to spending money on circuses, when there ain't no other way, but there ain't no use in *wasting* it on them.

It was a real bully circus. It was the splendidest sight that ever was, when they all come riding in, two and two, a gentleman and lady, side by side, the men just in their drawers and under-shirts, and no shoes nor stirrups, and resting their hands on their thighs, easy and comfortable—there must a been twenty of them—and every lady with a lovely complexion, and perfectly beautiful, and looking just like a gang of real sure-enough queens, and dressed in clothes that cost millions of dollars, and just littered with diamonds. It was a powerful fine sight; I never see anything so lovely. And then one by one they got up and stood, and went a-weaving around the ring so gentle and wavy and graceful, the men looking ever so tall and airy and straight, with their heads bobbing and skimming along, away up there under the tent-roof, and every lady's rose-leafy dress flapping soft and silky around her hips, and she looking like the most loveliest parasol.

And then faster and faster they went, all of them dancing, first one foot stuck out in the air and then the other, the horses leaning more and more, and the ring-master going round and round the centre-pole, cracking his whip and shouting "hi!—hi!" and the clown cracking jokes behind him; and by-and-by all hands dropped the reins, and every lady put her knuckles on her hips and every gentleman folded his arms, and then how the horses did lean over and hump themselves! And so, one after the other they all skipped off into the ring, and made the sweetest bow I ever see, and then scampered out, and everybody clapped their hands and went just about wild.

Well, all through the circus they done the most astonishing things; and all the time that clown carried on so it most killed the people. The ring-master couldn't ever say a word to him but he was back at him quick as a wink with the funniest things a body ever said; and how he ever *could* think of so many of them, and so sudden and so pat, was what I couldn't noway understand. Why, I couldn't a thought of them in a year. And by-and-by a drunk man tried to get into the ring—said he wanted to ride; said he could ride as well as anybody that ever was. They argued and tried to keep him out, but he wouldn't listen, and the whole show come to a standstill. Then the people begun to holler at him and make fun of him, and that made him mad, and he begun to rip and tear; so that stirred up the people, and a lot of men begun to pile down off of the benches and swarm towards the ring, saying, "Knock him down! throw him out!" and one or two women begun to scream. So, then, the ringmaster he made a little speech, and said he hoped there wouldn't be no disturbance, and if the man would promise he wouldn't make no more trouble, he would let him ride, if he thought he could stay on the horse. So everybody laughed and said all right, and the man got on. The minute he was on, the horse begun to rip and tear and jump and cavort around, with two circus men hanging onto his bridle trying to hold him, and the drunk man hanging onto his neck, and his heels flying in the air every jump, and the whole crowd of people standing up and shouting and laughing till the tears rolled down. And at last, sure enough, all the circus men could do, the horse broke loose, and away he went like the very nation, round and round the ring, with that sot laying down on him and hanging to his neck, with first one leg hanging most to the ground on one side, and then t'other one on t'other side, and the people just crazy. It warn't funny to me, though; I was all of a tremble to see his danger. But pretty soon he struggled up astraddle and grabbed the bridle, a-reeling this way and that; and the next minute he sprung up and dropped the bridle and stood! and the horse agoing like a house afire too. He just stood up there, a-sailing around as easy and comfortable as if he warn't ever drunk in his life—and then he begun to pull off his clothes and sling them. He shed them so thick they kind of clogged up the air, and altogether he shed seventeen suits. And then, there he was, slim and handsome, and dressed the gaudiest and prettiest you ever saw, and he lit into that horse with his whip and made him fairly hum—and finally skipped off to the dressing-room, and everybody just a-howling with pleasure and astonishment.

Then the ring-master he see how he had been fooled, and he *was* the sickest ring-master you ever see, I reckon. Why, it was one of his own men! He had got up that joke all out of his own head, and never let on to nobody. Well, I felt sheepish enough, to be took in so, but I wouldn't a been in that ring-master's place, not for a thousand dollars. I don't know; there may be bullier circuses than what that one was, but I never struck them yet. Anyways it was plenty good enough for *me*; and wherever I run across it, it can have all of *my* custom, every time.

Well, that night we had *our* show; but there warn't only about twelve people there, just enough to pay expenses. And they laughed all the time, and that made the duke mad; and everybody left, anyway, before the show was over, but one boy which was asleep. So the duke said these Arkansaw lunkheads couldn't come up to Shakspeare; what they wanted was low comedy—and may be something ruther worse than low comedy, he reckoned. He said he could size their style. So next morning he got some big sheets of wrapping-paper and some black paint, and drawed off some handbills and stuck them up all over the village. The bills said:

AT THE COURT HOUSE!
FOR 3 NIGHTS ONLY!
The World-Renowned Tragedians
DAVID GARRICK THE YOUNGER!
AND
EDMUND KEAN THE ELDER!
Of the London and Continental
Theatres,
In their Thrilling Tragedy of
THE KING'S CAMELOPARD[2]
OR
THE ROYAL NONESUCH! ! !
Admission 50 cents.

Then at the bottom was the biggest line of all—which said:

LADIES AND CHILDREN NOT ADMITTED.

"There," says he, "if that line don't fetch them, I don't know Arkansaw!"

[2]A giraffe.

CHAPTER XXIII

Well, all day him and the king was hard at it, rigging up a stage, and a curtain, and a row of candles for footlights; and that night the house was jam full of men in no time. When the place couldn't hold no more, the duke he quit tending door and went around the back way and come onto the stage and stood up before the curtain, and made a little speech, and praised up this tragedy, and said it was the most thrillingest one that ever was; and so he went on a-bragging about the tragedy and about Edmund Kean the Elder, which was to play the main principal part in it; and at last when he'd got everybody's expectations up high enough, he rolled up the curtain, and the next minute the king come a-prancing out on all fours, naked; and he was painted all over, ring-streaked-and-striped, all sorts of colors, as splendid as a rainbow. And—but never mind the rest of his outfit, it was just wild, but it was awful funny. The people most killed themselves laughing; and when the king got done capering, and capered off behind the scenes, they roared and clapped and stormed and haw-hawed till he come back and done it over again; and after that, they made him do it another time. Well, it would a made a cow laugh to see the shines that old idiot cut.

Then the duke he lets the curtain down, and bows to the people and says the great tragedy will be performed only two nights more, on accounts of pressing London engagements, where the seats is all sold already for it in Drury Lane; and then he makes them another bow, and says if he has succeeded in pleasing them and instructing them, he will be deeply obleeged if they will mention it to their friends and get them to come and see it.

Twenty people sings out:

"What, is it over? Is that *all?*"

The duke says yes. Then there was a fine time. Everybody sings out "sold,"[1] and rose up mad, and was agoing for that stage and them tragedians. But a big fine-looking man jumps up on a bench, and shouts:

"Hold on! Just a word, gentlemen." They stopped to listen. "We are sold—mighty badly sold. But we don't want to be the laughing-stock of this whole town, I reckon, and never hear the last of this thing as long as we live. *No.* What we want, is to go out of here quiet, and talk this show up, and sell the *rest* of the town! Then we'll all be in the same boat. Ain't that sensible?" ("You bet it is!—the jedge is right!" everybody sings out.) "All right, then—not a word about any sell. Go along home, and advise everybody to come and see the tragedy."

Next day you couldn't hear nothing around that town but how splendid that show was. House was jammed again, that night, and we sold this crowd the same way. When me and the king and the duke got home to the raft, we all had a supper; and by-and-by, about midnight, they made Jim and me back her out and float her down the middle of the river and fetch her in and hide her about two mile below town.

The third night the house was crammed again—and they warn't new-comers, this time, but people that was at the show the other two nights. I stood by the duke at the door, and I see that every man that went in had his pockets bulging, or something muffled up under his coat—and I see it warn't no

[1]"Cheated."

perfumery neither, not by a long sight. I smelt sickly eggs by the barrel, and rotten cabbages, and such things; and if I know the signs of a dead cat being around, and I bet I do, there was sixty-four of them went in. I shoved in there for a minute, but it was too various[2] for me, I couldn't stand it. Well, when the place couldn't hold no more people, the duke he give a fellow a quarter and told him to tend door for him a minute, and then he started around for the stage door, I after him; but the minute we turned the corner and was in the dark, he says:

"Walk fast, now, till you get away from the houses, and then shin for the raft like the dickens was after you!"

I done it, and he done the same. We struck the raft at the same time, and in less than two seconds we was gliding down stream, all dark and still, and edging towards the middle of the river, nobody saying a word. I reckoned the poor king was in for a gaudy time of it with the audience; but nothing of the sort; pretty soon he crawls out from under the wigwam, and says:

"Well, how'd the old thing pan out this time, Duke?"

He hadn't been up town at all.

We never showed a light till we was about ten mile below that village. Then we lit up and had a supper, and the king and the duke fairly laughed their bones loose over the way they'd served them people. The duke says:

"Greenhorns, flatheads! *I* knew the first house would keep mum and let the rest of the town get roped in; and I knew they'd lay for us the third night, and consider it was *their* turn now. Well, it *is* their turn, and I'd give something to know how much they'd take for it. I *would* just like to know how they're putting in their opportunity. They can turn it into a picnic, if they want to—they brought plenty provisions."

Them rapscallions took in four hundred and sixty-five dollars in that three nights. I never see money hauled in by the wagon-load like that, before.

By-and-by, when they was asleep and snoring, Jim says:

"Don't it 'spise you, de way dem kings carries on, Huck?"

"No," I says, "it don't."

"Why don't it, Huck?"

"Well, it don't, because it's in the breed. I reckon they're all alike."

"But, Huck, dese kings o' ourn is regular rapscallions; dat's jist what dey is; dey's regular rapscallions."

"Well, that's what I'm a-saying; all kings is mostly rapscallions, as fur as I can make out."

"Is dat so?"

"You read about them once—you'll see. Look at Henry the Eight; this'n's a Sunday-School Superintendent to *him*. And look at Charles Second, and Louis Fourteen, and Louis Fifteen, and James Second, and Edward Second, and Richard Third, and forty more; beside all them Saxon heptarchies[3] that used to rip around so in old times and raise Cain. My, you ought to seen old Henry the Eight when he was in bloom. He *was* a blossom. He used to marry a new wife every day, and chop off her head next morning. And he would do it just as indifferent as if he was ordering up eggs. 'Fetch up Nell Gwynn,' he

[2]I.e., it was too much.

[3]The seven Anglo-Saxon kingdoms of England (Northumbria, Mercia, East Anglia, Essex, Kent, Sussex, and Wessex), and their period of dominance, from the sixth to the ninth century.

says. They fetch her up. Next morning, 'Chop off her head!' And they chop it off. 'Fetch up Jane Shore,' he says; and up she comes. Next morning, 'Chop off her head'—'Ring up Fair Rosamun.'[4] Fair Rosamun answers the bell. Next morning, 'Chop off her head.' And he made every one of them tell him a tale every night; and he kept that up till he had hogged a thousand and one tales that way, and then he put them all in a book, and called it Domesday Book—which was a good name and stated the case.[5] You don't know kings, Jim, but I know them; and this old rip of ourn is one of the cleanest I've struck in history. Well, Henry he takes a notion he wants to get up some trouble with this country. How does he got at it—give notice?—give the country a show? No. All of a sudden he heaves all the tea in Boston Harbor overboard, and whacks out a declaration of independence, and dares them to come on. That was *his* style—he never give anybody a chance. He had suspicions of his father, the Duke of Wellington. Well, what did he do?—ask him to show up? No—drownded him in a butt of mamsey, like a cat. Spose people left money laying around where he was—what did he do? He collared it. Spose he contracted to do a thing; and you paid him, and didn't set down there and see he done it—what did he do? He always done the other thing. Spose he opened his mouth—what then? If he didn't shut it up powerful quick, he'd lose a lie, every time. That's the kind of a bug Henry was; and if we'd a had him along 'stead of our kings, he'd a fooled that town a heap worse than ourn done. I don't say that ourn is lambs, because they ain't, when you come right down to the cold facts; but they ain't nothing to *that* old ram, anyway. All I say is, kings is kings, and you got to make allowances. Take them all around, they're a mighty ornery lot. It's the way they're raised."

"But dis one do *smell* so like de nation, Huck."

"Well, they all do, Jim. *We* can't help the way a king smells; history don't tell no way."

"Now de duke, he's a tolerble likely man, in some ways."

"Yes, a duke's different. But not very different. This one's a middling hard lot, for a duke. When he's drunk, there ain't no nearsighted man could tell him from a king."

"Well, anyways, I doan' hanker for no mo' un um, Huck. Dese is all I kin stan'."

"It's the way I feel, too, Jim. But we've got them on our hands, and we got to remember what they are, and make allowances. Sometimes I wish we could hear of a country that's out of kings."

What was the use to tell Jim these warn't real kings and dukes? It wouldn't a done no good; and besides, it was just as I said; you couldn't tell them from the real kind.

I went to sleep, and Jim didn't call me when it was my turn. He often done that. When I waked up, just at day-break, he was setting there with his head down betwixt his knees, moaning and mourning to himself. I didn't take notice, nor let on. I knowed what it was about. He was thinking about his wife and his children, away up yonder, and he was low and homesick; because he

[4]Women who were mistresses of English kings of the twelfth, fifteenth, and seventeenth centuries. None was married to King Henry VIII.

[5]Here as elsewhere, Huck mixes the events and characters of history and fiction.

hadn't ever been away from home before in his life; and I do believe he cared just as much for his people as white folks does for theirn. It don't seem natural, but I reckon it's so. He was often moaning and mourning that way, nights, when he judged I was asleep, and saying, "Po' little 'Lizabeth! po' little Johnny! it's mighty hard; I spec' I ain't ever gwyne to see you no mo', no mo'!" He was a mighty good nigger, Jim was.

But this time I somehow got to talking to him about his wife and young ones; and by-and-by he says:

"What makes me feel so bad dis time, uz bekase I hear sumpn over yonder on de bank like a whack, er a slam, while ago, en it mine me er de time I treat my little 'Lizabeth so ornery. She warn't on'y 'bout fo' year ole, en she tuck de sk'yarlet-fever, an had a powful rough spell; but she got well, en one day she was a-stannin' aroun', en I says to her, I says:

"Shet de do'."

"She never done it; jis' stood dah, kiner smilin' up at me. It make me mad; en I says agin, mighty loud, I says:

" 'Doan' you hear me?—shet de do'!'

"She jis' stood de same way, kiner smilin' up. I was a-bilin'! I says: " 'I lay I *make* you mine!'

"En wid dat I fetch' her a slap side de head dat sont her a-sprawlin'. Den I went into de yuther room, en 'uz gone 'bout ten minutes; en when I come back, dah was dat do' a-stannin' open *yit,* en dat chile stannin' mos' right in it, a-lookin' down and mournin', en de tears runnin' down. My, but I *wuz* mad, I was agwyne for de chile, but jis' den—it was a do' dat open innerds—jis' den, 'long come de wind en slam it to, behind de chile, ker-*blam!*—en my lan', de chile never move'! My breff mos' hop outer me; en I feel so—so—I doan' know *how* I feel, I crope out, all a-tremblin', en crope aroun' en open de do' easy en slow, en poke my head in behine de chile, sof' en still, en all uv a sudden, I says *pow!* jis' as loud as I could yell. *She never budge!* Oh, Huck, I bust out a-cryin' en grab her up in my arms, en say, 'Oh, de po' little thing! de Lord God Amighty fogive po' ole Jim, kaze he never gwyne to fogive hisself as long's he live!' Oh, she was plumb deef en dumb, Huck, plumb deef en dumb—en I'd ben a-treat'n her so!"

CHAPTER XXIV

Next day, towards night, we laid up under a little willow towhead out in the middle; where there was a village on each side of the river, and the duke and the king begun to lay out a plan for working them towns. Jim he spoke to the duke, and said he hoped it wouldn't take but a few hours, because it got mighty heavy and tiresome to him when he had to lay all day in the wigwam tied with the rope. You see, when we left him all alone we had to tie him, because if anybody happened on him all by himself and not tied, it wouldn't look much like he was a runaway nigger, you know. So the duke said it *was* kind of hard to have to lay roped all day, and he'd cipher out some way to get around it.

He was uncommon bright, the duke was, and he soon struck it. He dressed Jim up in King Lear's outfit—it was a long curtain-calico gown, and a white horse-hair wig and whiskers; and then he took his theatre-paint and painted

Jim's face and hands and ears and neck all over a dead dull solid blue, like a man that's been drownded nine days. Blamed if he warn't the horriblest looking outrage I ever see. Then the duke took and wrote out a sign on a shingle so—

Sick Arab—but harmless when not out of his head.

And he nailed that shingle to a lath, and stood the lath up four or five foot in front of the wigwam. Jim was satisfied. He said it was a sight better than laying tied a couple of years every day and trembling all over every time there was a sound. The duke told him to make himself free and easy, and if anybody ever come meddling around, he must hop out of the wigwam, and carry on a little, and fetch a howl or two like a wild beast, and he reckoned they would light out and leave him alone. Which was sound enough judgment; but you take the average man, and he wouldn't wait for him to howl. Why, he didn't only look like he was dead, he looked considerable more than that.

These rapscallions wanted to try the Nonesuch again, because there was so much money in it, but they judged it wouldn't be safe, because maybe the news might a worked along down by this time. They couldn't hit no project that suited, exactly; so at last the duke said he reckoned he'd lay off and work his brains an hour or two and see if he couldn't put up something on the Arkansaw village; and the king he allowed he would drop over to t'other village, without any plan, but just trust in Providence to lead him the profitable way—meaning the devil, I reckon. We had all bought store clothes where we stopped last; and now the king put his'n on, and he told me to put mine on. I done it, of course. The king's duds was all black, and he did look real swell and starchy. I never knowed how clothes could change a body before. Why, before, he looked like the orneriest old rip that ever was; but now, when he'd take off his new white beaver[1] and make a bow and do a smile, he looked that grand and good and pious that you'd say he had walked right out of the ark, and maybe was old Leviticus[2] himself. Jim cleaned up the canoe, and I got my paddle ready. There was a big steamboat laying at the shore away up under the point, about three mile above town—been there a couple of hours, taking on freight. Says the king:

"Seein' how I'm dressed, I reckon maybe I better arrive down from St. Louis or Cincinnati, or some other big place. Go for the steamboat, Huckleberry; we'll come down to the village on her."

I didn't have to be ordered twice, to go and take a steamboat ride. I fetched the store a half a mile above the village, and then went scooting along the bluff bank in the easy water. Pretty soon we come to a nice innocent-looking young country jake setting on a log swabbing the sweat off of his face, for it was powerful warm weather; and he had a couple of big carpet-bags by him.

"Run her nose in shore," says the king. I done it. "Wher' you bound for, young man?"

"For the steamboat; going to Orleans."

[1]Hat.

[2]Huck confuses Leviticus, a book of the Old Testament, with Noah, who built the ark and survived the flood.

"Git aboard," says the king. "Hold on a minute, my servant'll he'p you with them bags. Jump out and he'p the gentleman Adolphus"—meaning me, I see.

I done so, and then we all three started on again. The young chap was mighty thankful; said it was tough work toting his baggage in such weather. He asked the king where he was going, and the king told him he'd come down the river and landed at the other village this morning, and now he was going up a few miles to see an old friend on a farm up there. The young fellow says:

"When I first see you, I says to myself, 'It's Mr. Wilks, sure, and he come mighty near getting here in time.' But then I says again, 'No, I reckon it ain't him, or else he wouldn't be paddling up the river.' You *ain't* him, are you?"

"No, my name's Blodgett—Elexander Blodgett—*Reverend* Elexander Blodgett, I spose I must say, as I'm one o' the Lord's poor servants. But still I'm jist as able to be sorry for Mr. Wilks for not arriving in time, all the same, if he's missed anything by it—which I hope he hasn't."

"Well, he don't miss any property by it, because he'll get that all right; but he's missed seeing his brother Peter die—which he mayn't mind, nobody can tell as to that—but his brother would a give anything in this world to see *him* before he died; never talked about nothing else all these three weeks; hadn't seen him since they was boys together—and hadn't ever seen his brother William at all—that's the deef and dumb one—William ain't more than thirty or thirty-five. Peter and George was the only ones that come out here; George was the married brother; him and his wife both died last year. Harvey and William's the only ones that's left now; and, as I was saying, they haven't got here in time."

"Did anybody send 'em word?"

"Oh, yes; a month or two ago, when Peter was first took; because Peter said then that he sorter felt like he warn't going to get well this time. You see, he was pretty old, and George's g'yirls was too young to be much company for him, except Mary Jane the redheaded one; and so he was kinder lonesome after George and his wife died, and didn't seem to care much to live. He most desperately wanted to see Harvey—and William too, for that matter—because he was one of them kind that can't bear to make a will. He left a letter behind for Harvey, and said he'd told in it where his money was hid, and how he wanted the rest of the property divided up so George's g'yirls would be all right—for George didn't leave nothing. And that letter was all they could get him to put a pen to."

"Why do you reckon Harvey don't come? Wher' does he live?"

"Oh, he lives in England—Sheffield—preaches there—hasn't ever been in this country. He hasn't had any too much time—and besides he mightn't a got the letter at all, you know."

"Too bad, too bad he couldn't a lived to see his brothers, poor soul. You going to Orleans, you say?"

"Yes, but that ain't only a part of it. I'm going in a ship, next Wednesday, for Ryo Janeero,[3] where my uncle lives."

"It's a pretty long journey. But it'll be lovely; I wisht I was agoing. Is Mary Jane the oldest? How old is the others?"

[3]Rio de Janeiro, Brazil.

"Mary Jane's nineteen, Susan's fifteen, and Joann's about fourteen—that's the one that gives herself to good works and has a hare-lip."

"Poor things! to be left alone in the cold world so."

"Well, they could be worse off. Old Peter had friends, and they ain't going to let them come to no harm. There's Hobson, the Babtis' preacher; and Deacon Lot Hovey, and Ben Rucker, and Abner Shackleford, and Levi Bell, the lawyer; and Dr. Robinson, and their wives, and the widow Bartley, and—well, there's a lot of them; but these are the ones that Peter was thickest with, and used to write about sometimes, when he wrote home; so Harvey 'll know where to look for friends when he gets here."

Well, the old man he went on asking questions till he just fairly emptied that young fellow. Blamed if he didn't inquire about everybody and everything in that blessed town, and all about all the Wilkses; and about Peter's business—which was a tanner; and about George's—which was a carpenter; and about Harvey's—which was a dissentering minister;[4] and so on, and so on. Then he says:

"What did you want to walk all the way up to the steamboat for?"

"Because she's a big Orleans boat, and I was afeared she mightn't stop there. When they're deep they won't stop for a hail. A Cincinnati boat will, but this is a St. Louis one."

"Was Peter Wilks well off?"

"Oh, yes, pretty well off. He had houses and land, and it's reckoned he left three or four thousand in cash hid up som'ers."

"When did you say he died?"

"I didn't say, but it was last night."

"Funeral to-morrow, likely?"

"Yes, 'bout the middle of the day."

"Well, it's all terrible sad; but we've all got to go, one time or another. So what we want to do is to be prepared; then we're all right."

"Yes, sir, it's the best way. Ma used to always say that."

When we struck the boat, she was about done loading, and pretty soon she got off. The king never said nothing about going aboard so I lost my ride, after all. When the boat was gone, the king made me paddle up another mile to a lonesome place, and then he got ashore, and says:

"Now, hustle back, right off, and fetch the duke up here, and the new carpetbags. And if he's gone over to t'other side, go over there and git him. And tell him to git himself up regardless. Shove along, now."

I see what *he* was up to; but I never said nothing, of course. When I got back with the duke, we hid the canoe and then they set down on a log, and the king told him everything, just like the young fellow had said it—every last word of it. And all the time he was a doing it, he tried to talk like an Englishman; and he done it pretty well too, for a slouch. I can't imitate him, and so I ain't agoing to try to; but he really done it pretty good. Then he says:

"How are you on the deef and dumb, Bilgewater?"

The duke said, leave him alone for that; said he had played a deef and dumb person on the histrionic boards. So then they waited for a steamboat.

[4]Dissenting minister, one who rejects the traditional doctrines of an established church, a nonconformist.

About the middle of the afternoon a couple of little boats come along, but they didn't come from high enough up the river; but a last there was a big one, and they hailed her. She sent out her yawl, and we went aboard, and she was from Cincinnati; and when they found we only wanted to go four or five mile, they was booming mad, and give us a cussing, and said they wouldn't land us. But the king was ca'm. He says:

"If gentlemen kin afford to pay a dollar a mile apiece, to be took on and put off in a yawl, a steamboat kin afford to carry 'em, can't it?"

So they softened down and said it was all right; and when we got to the village, they yawled us ashore. About two dozen men flocked down, when they see the yawl a coming; and when the king says—

"Kin any of you gentlemen tell me wher' Mr. Peter Wilks lives?" they give a glance at one another, and nodded their heads, as much as to say, "What d' I tell you?" Then one of them says, kind of soft and gentle:

"I'm sorry, sir, but the best we can do is tell you where he *did* live yesterday evening."

Sudden as winking, the ornery old cretur went all to smash, and fell up against the man, and put his chin on his shoulder, and cried down his back, and says:

"Alas, alas, our poor brother—gone, and we never got to see him; oh, it's too, *too* hard!"

Then he turns around, blubbering, and makes a lot of idiotic signs to the duke on his hands, and blamed if *he* didn't drop a carpet-bag and bust out a-crying. If they warn't the beatenest lot, them two frauds, that ever I struck.

Well, the men gethered around, and sympathized with them, and said all sorts of kind things to them, and carried their carpet-bags up the hill for them, and let them lean on them and cry, and told the king all about his brother's last moments, and the king he told it all over again on his hands to the duke, and both of them took on about that dead tanner like they'd lost the twelve disciples. Well, if ever I struck anything like it, I'm a nigger. It was enough to make a body ashamed of the human race.

CHAPTER XXV

The news was all over town in two minutes, and you could see the people tearing down on the run, from every which way, some of them putting on their coats as they come. Pretty soon we was in the middle of a crowd, and the noise of the tramping was like a soldier-march. The windows and dooryards was full; and every minute somebody would say, over a fence:

"Is it *them?*"

And somebody trotting along with the gang would answer back and say, "You bet it is."

When we got to the house, the street in front of it was packed, and the three girls was standing in the door. Mary Jane *was* red-headed, but that don't make no difference, she was most awful beautiful, and her face and her eyes was all lit up like glory, she was so glad her uncles was come. The king he spread his arms, and Mary Jane she jumped for them, and the hare-lip jumped for the duke, and there they *had* it! Everybody most, leastways women, cried for joy to see them meet at last and have such good times.

Then the king he hunched the duke, private—I see him do it—and then he looked around and see the coffin, over in the corner on two chairs; so then, him and the duke, with a hand across each other's shoulder, and t'other hand to their eyes, walked slow and solemn over there, everybody dropping back to give them room, and all the talk and noise stopping, people saying "Sh!" and all the men taking their hats off and drooping their heads, so you could a heard a pin fall. And when they got there, they bent over and looked in the coffin, and took one sight, and then they bust out a crying so you could a heard them to Orleans, most; and then they put their arms around each other's necks, and hung their chins over each other's shoulders; and then for three minutes, or maybe four, I never see two men leak the way they done. And mind you, everybody was doing the same; and the place was that damp I never see anything like it. Then one of them got on one side of the coffin, and t'other on t'other side, and they kneeled down and rested their foreheads on the coffin, and let on to pray all to theirselves. Well, when it come to that, it worked the crowd like you never see anything like it, and so everybody broke down and went to sobbing right out loud—the poor girls, too; and every woman, nearly, went up to the girls, without saying a word, and kissed them, solemn, on the forehead, and then put their hand on their head, and looked up towards the sky, with the tears running down, and then busted out and went off sobbing and swabbing, and give the next woman a show. I never see anything so disgusting.

Well, by-and-by the king he gets up and comes forward a little, and works himself up and slobbers out a speech, all full of tears and flapdoodle about its being a sore trial for him and his poor brother to lose the diseased and to miss seeing diseased alive, after the long journey of four thousand mile, but it's a trial that's sweetened and sanctified to us by this dear sympathy and these holy tears, and so he thanks them out of his heart and out of his brother's heart, because out of their mouths they can't, words being too weak and cold, and all that kind of rot and slush, till it was just sickening; and then he blubbers out a pious goody-goody Amen, and turns himself loose and goes to crying fit to bust.

And the minute the words was out of his mouth somebody over in the crowd struck up the doxolojer,[1] and everybody joined in with all their might, and it just warmed you up and made you feel as good as church letting out. Music *is* a good thing; and after all that soul-butter and hogwash, I never see it freshen up things so, and sound so honest and bully.

Then the king begins to work his jaws again, and says how him and his nieces would be glad if a few of the main principal friends of the family would take supper here with them this evening, and help set up with the ashes of the diseased; and says if his poor brother laying yonder could speak, he knows who he would name, for they was names that was very dear to him, and mentioned often in his letters; and so he will name the same, to-wit, as follows, vizz:—Rev. Mr. Hobson, and Deacon Lot Hovey, and Mr. Ben Rucker, and Abner Shackleford, and Levi Bell, and Dr. Robinson, and their wives, and the widow Bartley.

[1]Doxology, a hymn in praise of God.

Rev. Hobson and Dr. Robinson was down to the end of the town, a-hunting together; that is, I mean the doctor was shipping a sick man to t'other world, and the preacher was pinting him right. Lawyer Bell was away up to Louisville on some business. But the rest was on hand, and so they all come and shook hands with the king and thanked him and talked to him; and then they shook hands with the duke, and didn't say nothing but just kept a-smiling and bobbing their heads like a passel of sapheads whilst he made all sorts of signs with his hands and said "Goo-goo—goo-goo-goo," all the time, like a baby that can't talk.

So the king he blatted along, and managed to inquire about pretty much everybody and dog in town, by his name, and mentioned all sorts of little things that happened one time or another in the town, or to George's family, or to Peter; and he always let on that Peter wrote him the things, but that was a lie, he got every blessed one of them out of that young flathead that we canoed up to the steamboat.

Then Mary Jane she fetched the letter her uncle left behind, and the king he read it out loud and cried over it. It give the dwelling-house and three thousand dollars, gold, to the girls; and it give the tanyard (which was doing a good business), along with some other houses and land (worth about seven thousand), and three thousand dollars in gold to Harvey and William, and told where the six thousand cash was hid, down cellar. So these two frauds said they'd go and fetch it up, and have everything square and above-board; and told me to come with a candle. We shut the cellar door behind us, and when they found the bag they spilt it out on the floor, and it was a lovely sight, all of them yaller-boys.[2] My, the way the king's eyes did shine! He slaps the duke on the shoulder, and says:

"Oh, *this* ain't bully, nor noth'n! Oh, no, I reckon not! Why, Biljy, it beats the Nonesuch, *don't* it!"

The duke allowed it did. They pawed the yaller-boys, and sifted them through their fingers and let them jingle down on the floor; and the king says:

"It ain't no use talkin'; bein' brothers to a rich dead man, and representatives of furrin heirs that's got left, is the line for you and me, Bilge. Thish-yer comes of trust'n to Providence. It's the best way, in the long run. I've tried 'em all, and ther' ain't no better way."

Most everybody would a been satisfied with the pile, and took it on trust; but no, they must count it. So they counts it, and it comes out four hundred and fifteen dollars short. Says the King:

"Dern him, I wonder what he done with that four hundred and fifteen dollars?"

They worried over that a while, and ransacked all around for it. Then the duke says:

"Well, he was a pretty sick man, and likely he made a mistake—I reckon that's the way of it. The best way's to let it go, and keep still about it. We can spare it."

"Oh, shucks, yes, we can *spare* it. I don't k'yer noth'n 'bout that—it's the *count* I'm thinkin' about. We want to be awful square and open and above-board, here, you know. We want to lug this h-yer money up stairs and count it

[2]Gold coins.

before everybody—then ther' ain't noth'n suspicious. But when the dead man says ther's six thous'n dollars, you know, we don't want to—"

"Hold on," says the duke. "Less make up the deffsit"—and he begun to haul out yaller-boys out of his pocket.

"It's a most amaz'n' good idea, duke—you *have* got a rattlin' clever head on you," says the king. "Blest if the old Nonesuch ain't a heppin' us out agin"—and *he* begun to haul out yaller-jackets and stack them up.

It most busted them, but they made up the six thousand clean and clear.

"Say," says the duke, "I got another idea. Le's go up stairs and count this money, and then take and *give it to the girls.*"

"Good land, duke, lemme hug you! It's the most dazzling idea 'at ever a man struck. You have cert'nly got the most astonishin' head I ever see. Oh, this is the boss dodge,[3] ther' ain't no mistake 'bout it. Let 'em fetch along their suspicions now, if they want to—this'll lay 'em out."

When we got up stairs, everybody gethered around the table, and the king he counted it and stacked it up, three hundred dollars in a pile—twenty elegant little piles. Everybody looked hungry at it, and licked their chops. Then they raked it into the bag again, and I see the king begin to swell himself up for another speech. He says:

"Friends all, my poor brother that lays yonder, has done generous by them that's left behind in the vale of sorrers. He has done generous by these-yer poor little lambs that he loved and sheltered, and that's left fatherless and motherless. Yes, and we that knowed him, knows that he would a done *more* generous by 'em if he hadn't ben afeard o' woundin' his dear William and me. Now, *wouldn't* he? Ther' ain't no question 'bout it, in *my* mind. Well, then—what kind o' brothers would it be, that 'd stand in his way at sech a time? And what kind o' uncles would it be that'd rob—yes, *rob*—sech poor sweet lambs as these 'at he loved so, at sech a time? If I know William—and I *think* I do—he—well, I'll jest ask him." He turns around and begins to make a lot of signs to the duke with his hands; and the duke he looks at him stupid and leather-headed a while, then all of a sudden he seems to catch his meaning, and jumps for the king, goo-gooing with all his might for joy, and hugs him about fifteen times before he lets up. Then the king says, "I knowed it; I reckon *that*'ll convince anybody the way *he* feels about it. Here, Mary Jane, Susan, Joanner, take the money—take it *all.* It's the gift of him that lays yonder, cold but joyful."

Mary Jane she went for him, Susan and the hare-lip went for the duke, and then such another hugging and kissing I never see yet. And everybody crowded up with the tears in their eyes, and most shook the hands off of them frauds, saying all the time:

"You *dear* good souls!—how *lovely!*—how *could* you!"

Well, then, pretty soon all hands got to talking about the diseased again, and how good he was, and what a loss he was, and all that; and before long a big iron-jawed man worked himself in there from outside, and stood a listening and looking, and not saying anything; and nobody saying anything to him either, because the king was talking and they was all busy listening. The king was saying—in the middle of something he's started in on—

[3]Best scam.

"—they bein' partickler friends o' the diseased. That's why they're invited here this evenin'; but to-morrow we want *all* to come—everybody; for he respected everybody, he liked everybody, and so it's fitten that his funeral orgies sh'd be public."

And so he went a-mooning on and on, liking to hear himself talk, and every little while he fetched in his funeral orgies again, till the duke he couldn't stand it no more; so he writes on a little scrap of paper, "*obsequies,* you old fool," and folds it up and goes to goo-gooing and reaching it over people's heads to him. The king he reads it, and puts it in his pocket, and says:

"Poor William, afflicted as he is, his *heart's* aluz right. Asks me to invite everybody to come to the funeral—wants me to make 'em all welcome. But he needn't a worried—it was jest what I was at."

Then he weaves along again, perfectly ca'm, and goes to dropping in his funeral orgies again every now and then, just like he done before. And when he done it the third time, he says:

"I say orgies, not because it's the common term, because it ain't—obsequies bein' the common term—but because orgies is the right term. Obsequies ain't used in England no more, now—it's gone out. We say orgies now, in England. Orgies is better, because it means the thing you're after, more exact. It's a word that's made up out'n the Greek *orgo,* outside, open, abroad; and the Hebrew *jeesum,* to plant, cover up; hence in*ter.* So, you see, funeral orgies is an open er public funeral."

He was the *worst* I ever struck. Well, the iron-jawed man he laughed right in his face. Everybody was shocked. Everybody says, "Why *doctor!*" and Abner Shackleford says:

"Why, Robinson, hain't you heard the news? This is Harvey Wilks."

The king he smiled eager, and shoved out his flapper, and says:

"*Is* it my poor brother's dear good friend and physician? I——"

"Keep your hands off of me!" says the doctor. "*You* talk like an Englishman—*don't* you? It's the worst imitation I ever heard. *You* Peter Wilks's brother. You're a fraud, that's what you are!"

Well, how they all took on! They crowded around the doctor, and tried to quiet him down, and tried to explain to him, and tell him how Harvey'd showed in forty ways that he *was* Harvey, and knowed everybody by name, and the names of the very dogs, and begged and *begged* him not to hurt Harvey's feelings and the poor girls' feelings, and all that; but it warn't no use, he stormed right along, and said any man that pretended to be an Englishman and couldn't imitate the lingo no better than what he did, was a fraud and a liar. The poor girls was hanging to the king and crying; and all of a sudden the doctor ups and turns on *them.* He says:

"I was your father's friend, and I'm your friend; and I warn you *as* a friend, and an honest one, that wants to protect you and keep you out of harm and trouble, to turn your backs on that scoundrel, and have nothing to do with him, the ignorant tramp, with his idiotic Greek and Hebrew as he calls it. He is the thinnest kind of an imposter—has come here with a lot of empty names and facts which he has picked up somewheres, and you take them for *proofs,* and are helped to fool yourselves by these foolish friends here, who ought to know better. Mary Jane Wilks, you know me for your friend, and for your unselfish friend, too. Now listen to me; turn this pitiful rascal out—I *beg* you to do it. Will you?"

Mary Jane straightened herself up, and my, but she was handsome! she says:

"*Here* is my answer." She hove up the bag of money and put it in the king's hands, and says, "Take this six thousand dollars, and invest it for me and my sisters any way you want to, and don't give us no receipt for it."

Then she put her arm around the king on one side, and Susan and the hare-lip done the same on the other. Everybody clapped their hands and stomped on the floor like a perfect storm, whilst the king held up his head and smiled proud. The doctor says:

"All right, I wash *my* hands of the matter. But I warn you all that a time's coming when you're going to feel sick whenever you think of this day"—and away he went.

"All right, doctor," says the king, kinder mocking him, "we'll try and get 'em to send for you"—which made them all laugh, and they said it was a prime good hit.

CHAPTER XXVI

Well when they was all gone, the king asks Mary Jane how they was off for spare rooms, and she said she had one spare room, which would do for Uncle William, and she'd give her own room to Uncle Harvey, which was a little bigger, and she would turn into the room with her sisters and sleep on a cot; and up garret was a little cubby, with a pallet in it. The king said the cubby would do for his valley—meaning me.

So Mary Jane took us up, and she showed them their rooms, which was plain but nice. She said she'd have her frocks and a lot of other traps took out of her room if they was in Uncle Harvey's way, but he said they warn't. The frocks was hung along the wall, and before them was a curtain made out of calico that hung down to the floor. There was an old hair trunk in one corner, and a guitar box in another, and all sorts of little knick-knacks and jimcracks around, like girls brisken up a room with. The king said it was all the more homely and more pleasanter for these fixings, and so don't disturb them. The duke's room was pretty small, but plenty good enough, and so was my cubby.

That night they had a big supper, and all them men and women was there, and I stood behind the king and the duke's chairs and waited on them, and the niggers waited on the rest. Mary Jane she set at the head of the table with Susan along side of her, and said how bad the biscuits was, and how mean the preserves was, and how ornery and tough the fried chicken was—and all that kind of rot, the way women always do to force out compliments; and the people all knowed everything was tip-top, and said so—said "How *do* you get biscuits to brown so nice?" and "Where, for the land's sake *did* you get these amaz'n pickles?" and all that kind of humbug talky-talk, just the way people always does at a supper, you know.

And when it was all done, me and the hare-lip had supper in the kitchen off of the leavings, whilst the others was helping the niggers clean up the things. The hare-lip she got to pumping me about England, and blest if I didn't think the ice was getting mighty thin, sometimes. She says:

"Did you ever see the king?"

"Who? William Fourth?[1] Well, I bet I have—he goes to our church." I knowed he was dead years ago, but I never let on. So when I says he goes to our church, she says:

"What—regular?"

"Yes—regular. His pew's right over opposite ourn—on t'other side the pulpit."

"I thought he lived in London?"

"Well, he does. Where *would* he live?"

"But I thought *you* lived in Sheffield?"[2]

I see I was up a stump. I had to let on to get choked with a chicken bone, so as to get time to think how to get down again. Then I says:

"I mean he goes to our church regular when he's in Sheffield. That's only in the summer-time, when he comes there to take the sea baths."

"Why, how you talk—Sheffield ain't on the sea."

"Well, who said it was?"

"Why, you did."

"I *didn't* nuther."

"You did!"

"I didn't."

"You did."

"I never said nothing of the kind."

"Well, what *did* you say, then?"

"Said he come to take the sea *baths*—that's what I said."

"Well, then! how's he going to take the sea baths if it ain't on the sea?"

"Looky here," I says; "did you ever see any Congress water?"[3]

"Yes."

"Well, did you have to go to Congress to get it?"

"Why, no."

"Well, neither does William Fourth have to go to the sea to get a sea bath."

"How does he get it, then?"

"Gets it the way people down here gets Congress-water—in barrels. There in the palace at Sheffield they've got furnaces, and he wants his water hot. They can't bile that amount of water away off there at the sea. They haven't got no conveniences for it."

"Oh, I see, now. You might a said that in the first place and saved time."

When she said that, I see I was out of the woods again, and so I was comfortable and glad. Next she says:

"Do you go to church, too?"

"Yes—regular."

"Where do you set?"

"Why, in our pew."

"*Whose* pew?"

"Why, *ourn*—your Uncle Harvey's."

"His'n? What does *he* want with a pew?"

"Wants it to set in. What did you *reckon* he wanted with it?"

"Why, I thought he'd be in the pulpit."

[1]King of England, 1830–1837. [2]English city north of London.
[3]Mineral water from the Congress Spring, Saratoga, New York.

Rot him, I forgot he was a preacher. I see I was up a stump again, so I played another chicken bone and got another think. Then I says:

"Blame it, do you suppose there ain't but one preacher to a church?"

"Why, what do they want with more?"

"What!—to preach before a king? I never see such a girl as you. They don't have no less than seventeen."

"Seventeen! My land! Why, I wouldn't set out such a string as that, not if I *never* got to glory. It must take 'em a week."

"Shucks, they don't *all* of 'em preach the same day—only *one* of 'em."

"Well, then, what does the rest of 'em do?"

"Oh, nothing much. Loll around, pass the plate—and one thing or another. But mainly they don't do nothing."

"Well, then, what are they *for?*"

"Why, they're for *style.* Don't you know nothing?"

"Well, I don't *want* to know no such foolishness as that. How is servants treated in England? Do they treat 'em better 'n we treat our niggers?"

"*No!* A servant ain't nobody there. They treat them worse than dogs."

"Don't they give 'em holidays, the way we do, Christmas and New Year's week, and Fourth of July?"

"Oh, just listen! A body could tell *you* hain't ever been to England, by that. Why, Hare-l—why, Joanna, they never see a holiday from year's end to year's end; never go to the circus, nor theatre, nor nigger shows,[4] nor nowheres."

"Nor church?"

"Nor church."

"But *you* always went to church."

Well, I was gone up again. I forgot I was the old man's servant. But next minute I whirled in on a kind of an explanation how a valley was different from a common servant, and *had* to go to church whether he wanted to or not, and set with the family, on account of it's being the law. But I didn't do it pretty good, and when I got done I see she warn't satisfied. She says:

"Honest injun, now, hain't you been telling me a lot of lies?"

"Honest injun," says I.

"None of it at all?"

"None of it at all. Not a lie in it," says I.

"Lay your hand on this book and say it."

I see it warn't nothing but a dictionary, so I laid my hand on it and said it. So then she looked a little better satisfied, and says:

"Well, then, I'll believe some of it; but I hope to gracious if I'll believe the rest."

"What is it you won't believe, Joe?" says Mary Jane, stepping in with Susan behind her. "It ain't right nor kind for you to talk so to him, and him a stranger and so far from his people. How would you like to be treated so?"

"That's always your way, Maim—always sailing in to help somebody before they're hurt. I hain't done nothing to him. He's told some stretchers, I reckon; and I said I wouldn't swallow it all; and that's every bit and grain I *did* say. I reckon he can stand a little thing like that, can't he?"

"I don't care whether 'twas little or whether 'twas big, he's here in our house and a stranger, and it wasn't good of you to say it. If you was in his

[4]Minstrel shows.

place, it would make you feel ashamed; and so you oughtn't to say a thing to another person that will make *them* feel ashamed."

"Why, Maim, he said——"

"It don't make no difference what he *said*—that ain't the thing. The thing is for you to treat him *kind*, and not be saying things to make him remember he ain't in his own country and amongst his own folks."

I says to myself, *this* is a girl that I'm letting that old reptile rob her of her money!

Then Susan *she* waltzed in; and if you'll believe me, she did give Hare-lip hark from the tomb![5]

Says I to myself, And this is *another* one that I'm letting him rob her of her money!

Then Mary Jane she took another inning, and went in sweet and lovely again—which was her way—but when she got done there warn't hardly anything left o' poor Hare-lip. So she hollered.

"All right, then," says the other girls, "you just ask his pardon."

She done it, too. And she done it beautiful. She done it so beautiful it was good to hear; and I wished I could tell her a thousand lies, so she could do it again.

I says to myself, this is *another* one that I'm letting him rob her of her money. And when she got through, they all jest laid theirselves out to make me feel at home and know I was amongst friends. I felt so ornery and low down and mean, that I says to myself, My mind's made up; I'll hive[6] that money for them or bust.

So then I lit out—for bed, I said, meaning some time or another. When I got by myself, I went to thinking the thing over. I says to myself, shall I go to that doctor, private, and blow on these frauds? No—that won't do. He might tell who told him; then the king and the duke would make it warm for me. Shall I go, private, and tell Mary Jane? No—I dasn't do it. Her face would give them a hint, sure; they've got the money, and they'd slide right out and get away with it. If she was to fetch in help, I'd get mixed up in the business, before it was done with, I judge. No, there ain't no good way but one. I got to steal that money, somehow; and I got to steal it some way that they won't suspicion that I done it. They've got a good thing, here; and they ain't agoing to leave till they've played this family and this town for all they're worth, so I'll find a chance time enough. I'll steal it, and hide it; and by-and-by, when I'm away down the river, I'll write a letter and tell Mary Jane where it's hid. But I better hive it to-night, if I can, because the doctor maybe hasn't let up as much as he lets on he has; he might scare them out of here, yet.

So, thinks I, I'll go and search them rooms. Up stairs the hall was dark, but I found the duke's room, and started to paw around it with my hands; but I recollected it wouldn't be much like the king to let anybody else take care of that money but his own self; so then I went to his room and begun to paw around there. But I see I couldn't do nothing without a candle, and I dasn't light one, of course. So I judged I'd got to do the other thing—lay for them, and eavesdrop. About that time, I hears their footsteps coming, and was going to skip

[5]A scolding—derived from "Hark! from the tombs a doleful sound. . . ," a line from the hymn "A Funeral Thought," by Isaac Watts (1674–1748), English hymnist.

[6]Secure.

under the bed; I reached for it, but it wasn't where I thought it would be; but I touched the curtain that hid Mary Jane's frocks, so I jumped in behind that and snuggled in amongst the gowns, and stood there perfectly still.

They come in and shut the door; and the first thing the duke done was to get down and look under the bed. Then I was glad I hadn't found the bed when I wanted it. And yet, you know, it's kind of natural to hide under the bed when you are up to anything private. They sets down, then, and the king says:

"Well, what is it? and cut it middlin' short, because it's better for us to be down there a whoopin'-up the mournin' than up here givin' 'em a chance to talk us over."

"Well, this is it, Capet. I ain't easy; I ain't comfortable. That doctor lays on my mind. I wanted to know your plans. I've got a notion, and I think it's a sound one."

"What is it, duke?"

"That we better glide out of this, before three in the morning, and clip it down the river with what we've got. Specially, seeing we got it so easy—*given* back to us, flung at our heads, as you may say, when of course we allowed to have to steal it back. I'm for knocking off and lighting out."

That made me feel pretty bad. About an hour or two ago, it would a been a little different, but now it made me feel bad and disappointed. The king rips out and says:

"What! And not sell out the rest o' the property? March off like a passel o' fools and leave eight or nine thous'n' dollars' worth o' property layin' around jest sufferin' to be scooped in?—and all good salable stuff, too."

The duke he grumbled; said the bag of gold was enough, and he didn't want to go no deeper—didn't want to rob a lot of orphans of *everything* they had.

"Why, how you talk!" says the king. "We shan't rob 'em of nothing at all but jest this money. The people that *buys* the property is the suff'rers; because as soon's it's found out 'at we didn't own it—which won't be long after we've slid—the sale won't be valid, and it'll all go back to the estate. These-yer orphans 'll git their house back agin, and that's enough for *them;* they're young and spry, and k'n easy earn a livin'. *They* ain't agoing to suffer. Why, jest think—there's thous'n's and thous'n's that ain't nigh so well off. Bless you, *they* ain't got noth'n to complain of."

Well, the king he talked him blind; so at last he give in, and said all right, but said he believed it was blame foolishness to stay, and that doctor hanging over them. But the king says:

"Cuss the doctor! What do we k'yer for *him?* Hain't we got all the fools in town on our side? and ain't that a big enough majority in any town?"

So they got ready to go down stairs again. The duke says:

"I don't think we put that money in a good place."

That cheered me up. I'd begun to think I warn't going to get a hint of no kind to help me. The king says:

"Why?"

"Because Mary Jane'll be in mourning from this out; and first you know the nigger that does up the rooms will get an order to box these duds up and put 'em away; and do you reckon a nigger can run across money and not borrow some of it?"

"Your head's level, agin, duke," says the king; and he come a fumbling under the curtain two or three foot from where I was. I stuck tight to the wall, and kept mighty still, though quivery; and I wondered what them fellows would say to me if they catched me; and I tried to think what I'd better do if they did catch me. But the king he got the bag before I could think more than about a half a thought, and he never suspicioned I was around. They took and shoved the bag through a rip in the straw tick that was under the feather bed, and crammed it in a foot or two amongst the straw and said it was all right, now, because a nigger only make up the feather bed, and don't turn over the straw tick only about twice a year, and so it warn't in no danger of getting stole, now.

But I knowed better. I had it out of there before they was half-way down stairs. I groped along up to my cubby, and hid it there till I could get a chance to do better. I judged I better hide it outside of the house somewheres, because if they missed it they would give the house a good ransacking. I knowed that very well. Then I turned in, with my clothes all on; but I couldn't a gone to sleep, if I wanted to, I was in such a sweat to get through with the business. By-and-by I heard the king and the duke come up; so I rolled off of my pallet and laid with my chin at the top of my ladder and waited to see if anything was going to happen. But nothing did.

So I held on till all the late sounds had quit and the early ones hadn't begun, yet; and then I slipped down the ladder.

CHAPTER XXVII

I crept to their doors and listened; they was snoring, so I tip-toed along, and got down stairs all right. There warn't a sound anywheres. I peeped through a crack of the dining-room door, and see the men that was watching the corpse all sound asleep on their chairs. The door was open into the parlor, where the corpse was laying, and there was a candle in both rooms. I passed along, and the parlor door was open; but I see there warn't nobody in there but the remainders of Peter; so I shoved on by; but the front door was locked, and the key wasn't there. Just then I heard somebody coming down the stairs, back behind me. I run in the parlor, and took a swift look around, and the only place I see to hide the bag was in the coffin. The lid was shoved along about a foot, showing the dead man's face down in there, with a wet cloth over it, and his shroud on. I tucked the moneybag in under the lid, just down beyond where his hands was crossed, which made me creep, they was so cold, and then I run back across the room and in behind the door.

The person coming was Mary Jane. She went to the coffin, very soft, and kneeled down and looked in; then she put up her handkerchief and I see she begun to cry, though I couldn't hear her, and her back was to me. I slid out, and as I passed the dining-room I thought I'd make sure them watchers hadn't seen me; so I looked through the crack and everything was all right. They hadn't stirred.

I slipped up to bed, feeling ruther blue, on accounts of the thing playing out that way after I had took so much trouble and run so much resk about it. Says I, if it could stay where it is, all right; because when we get down the river a hundred mile or two, I could write back to Mary Jane, and she could dig him up again and get it; but that ain't the thing that's going to happen; the thing that's going to happen is, the money'll be found when they come to screw on the lid. Then the king 'll get it again, and it 'll be a long day before he gives anybody another chance to smouch[1] it from him. Of course I *wanted* to slide down and get it out of there, but I dasn't try it. Every minute it was getting earlier, now, and pretty soon some of them watchers would begin to stir, and I might get catched—catched with six thousand dollars in my hands that nobody hadn't hired me to take care of. I don't wish to be mixed up in no such business as that, I says to myself.

When I got down stairs in the morning, the parlor was shut up, and the watchers was gone. There warn't nobody around but the family and the widow Bartley and our tribe. I watched their faces to see if anything had been happening, but I couldn't tell.

Towards the middle of the day the undertaker come, with his man, and they set the coffin in the middle of the room on a couple of chairs, and then set all our chairs in rows, and borrowed more from the neighbors till the hall and the parlor and the dining-room was full. I see the coffin lid was the way it was before, but I dasn't go to look in under it, with folks around.

Then the people begun to flock in, and the beats[2] and the girls took seats in the front row at the head of the coffin, and for half an hour the people filed around slow, in single rank, and looked down at the dead man's face a minute, and some dropped in a tear, and it was all very still and solemn, only the girls and the beats holding handkerchiefs to their eyes and keeping their heads bent, and sobbing a little. There warn't no other sound but the scraping of the feet on the floor, and blowing noses—because people always blows them more at a funeral than they do at other places except church.

When the place was packed full, the undertaker he slid around in his black gloves with his softy soothering ways, putting on the last touches, and getting people and things all shipshape and comfortable, and making no more sound than a cat. He never spoke; he moved people around, he squeezed in late ones, he opened up passage-ways, and done it all with nods, and signs with his hands. Then he took his place over against the wall. He was the softest, glidingest, stealthiest man I ever see; and there warn't no more smile to him than there is to a ham.

They had borrowed a melodeum[3]—a sick one; and when everything was ready, a young woman set down and worked it, and it was pretty skreeky and colicky, and everybody joined in and sung, and Peter was the only one that had a good thing, according to my notion. Then the Reverend Hobson opened up, slow and solemn, and begun to talk; and straight off the most outrageous row busted out in the cellar a body ever heard; it was only one dog, but he made a most powerful racket, and he kept it up, right along; the parson he had to stand there, over the coffin, and wait—you couldn't hear yourself think. It was right down awkward, and nobody didn't seem to know what to do. But pretty soon they see that long-legged undertaker make a sign to the preacher as much to say, "Don't you worry—just depend on me." Then he stooped down and begun to glide along the wall, just his shoulders showing

[1]Steal. [2]Deadbeats, i.e., the Duke and the Dauphin. [3]A small, reed organ.

over the people's heads. So he glided along, and the pow-wow and racket getting more and more outrageous all the time; and at last, when he had gone around two sides of the room, he disappears down cellar. Then, in about two seconds we heard a whack, and the dog he finished up with a most amazing howl or two, and then everything was dead still, and the parson begun his solemn talk where he left off. In a minute or two here comes this undertaker's back and shoulders gliding along the wall again, and so he glided, and glided, around three sides of the room, and then rose up, and shaded his mouth with his hands, and stretched his neck out towards the preacher over the people's heads, and says, in a kind of a coarse whisper, *"He had a rat!"* Then he drooped down and glided along the wall again to his place. You could see it was a great satisfaction to the people, because naturally they wanted to know. A little thing like that don't cost nothing, and it's just the little things that makes a man to be looked up to and liked. There warn't no more popular man in town than what that undertaker was.

Well, the funeral sermon was very good, but pison long and tiresome; and then the king he shoved in and got off some of his usual rubbage, and at last the job was through, and the undertaker begun to sneak up on the coffin with his screw-driver. I was in a sweat then, and watched him pretty keen. But he never meddled at all; just slid the lid along, as soft as mush, and screwed it down tight and fast. So there I was! I didn't know whether the money was in there, or not. So, says I, spose somebody has hogged that bag on the sly?—now how do *I* know whether to write to Mary Jane or not? 'Spose she dug him up and didn't find nothing—what would she think of me? Blame it, I says, I might get hunted up and jailed; I'd better lay low and keep dark, and not write at all; the thing's awful mixed, now; trying to better it, I've worsened it a hundred times, and I wish to goodness I'd just let it alone, dad fetch the whole business!

They buried him, and we come back home, and I went to watching faces again—I couldn't help it, and I couldn't rest easy. But nothing come of it; the faces didn't tell me nothing.

The king he visited around, in the evening, and sweetened everybody up, and made himself ever so friendly; and he give out the idea that his congregation over in England would be in a sweat about him, so he must hurry and settle up the estate right away, and leave for home. He was very sorry he was so pushed, and so was everybody; they wished he could stay longer, but they said they could see it couldn't be done. And he said of course him and William would take the girls home with him; and that pleased everybody too, because then the girls would be well fixed, and amongst their own relations; and it pleased the girls, too—tickled them so they clean forgot they ever had a trouble in the world; and told him to sell out as quick as he wanted to, they would be ready. Them poor things was that glad and happy it made my heart ache to see them getting fooled and lied to so, but I didn't see no safe way for me to chip in and change the general tune.

Well, blamed if the king didn't bill[4] the house and the niggers and all the property for auction straight off—sale two days after the funeral; but anybody could buy private beforehand if they wanted to.

[4]Advertise.

So the next day after the funeral, along about noontime, the girl's joy got the first jolt; a couple of nigger traders come along, and the king sold them the niggers reasonable, for three-day drafts[5] as they called it, and away they went, the two sons up the river to Memphis, and their mother down the river to Orleans. I thought them poor girls and them niggers would break their hearts for grief; they cried around each other, and took on so it most made me down sick to see it. The girls said they hadn't ever dreamed of seeing the family separated or sold away from the town. I can't ever get it out of my memory, the sight of them poor miserable girls and niggers hanging around each other's necks and crying; and I reckon I couldn't a stood it all but would a had to bust out and tell on our gang if I hadn't knowed the sale warn't no account and the niggers would be back home in a week or two.

The thing made a big stir in the town, too, and a good many come out flat-footed and said it was scandalous to separate the mother and the children that way. It injured the frauds some; but the old fool he bulled right along, spite of all the duke could say or do, and I tell you the duke was powerful uneasy.

Next day was auction day. About broad-day in the morning, the king and the duke come up in the garret and woke me up, and I see by their look that there was trouble. The king says:

"Was you in my room night before last?"

"No, your majesty"—which was the way I always called him when nobody but our gang warn't around.

"Was you in there yisterday er last night?"

"No, your majesty."

"Honor bright, now—no lies."

"Honor bright, your majesty, I'm telling you the truth. I hain't been near your room since Miss Mary Jane took you and the duke and showed it to you."

The duke says:

"Have you seen anybody else go in there?"

"No, your grace, not as I remember, I believe."

"Stop and think."

I studied a while, and see my chance, then I says:

"Well, I see the niggers go in there several times."

Both of them give a little jump; and looked like they hadn't ever expected it, and then like they *had*. Then the duke says:

"What, *all* of them?"

"No—leastways not all at once. That is, I don't think I ever see them all come *out* at once but just one time."

"Hello—when was that?"

"It was the day we had the funeral. In the morning. It warn't early, because I overslept. I was just starting down the ladder, and I see them."

"Well, go on, *go* on—what did they do? How'd they act?"

"They didn't do nothing. And they didn't act anyway, much, as fur as I see. They tip-toed away; so I seen, easy enough, that they'd shoved in there to do up your majesty's room, or something, sposing you was up; and found you

[5]Bank drafts (checks) that can be cashed after three days.

warn't up, and so they was hoping to slide out of the way of trouble without waking you up, if they hadn't already waked you up."

"Great guns, *this* is a go!" says the king; and both of them looked pretty sick, and tolerable silly. They stood there a thinking and scratching their heads, a minute, and then the duke he burst into a kind of a little raspy chuckle, and says:

"It does beat all, how neat the niggers played their hand. They let on to be *sorry* they was going out of this region! and I believed they *was* sorry. And so did you, and so did everybody. Don't ever tell *me* any more that a nigger ain't got any histrionic talent. Why, the way they played that thing, it would fool *anybody.* In my opinion, there's a fortune in 'em. If I had capital and a theatre, I wouldn't want a better lay out than that—and here we've gone and sold 'em for a song. Yes, and ain't privileged to sing the song, yet. Say, where *is* that song?—that draft."

"In the bank for to be collected. Where *would* it be?"

"Well, *that's* all right then, thank goodness."

Says I, kind of timid-like:

"Is something gone wrong?"

The king whirls on me and rips out:

"None o' your business! You keep your head shet, and mind y'r own affairs—if you got any. Long as you're in this town, don't you forgit *that,* you hear?" Then he says to the duke, "We got to jest swaller it, and say noth'n: mum's the word for *us.*"

As they was starting down the ladder, the duke he chuckles again, and says:

"Quick sales *and* small profits! It's a good business—yes."

The king snarls around on him and says,

"I was trying to do for the best, in sellin' 'm out so quick. If the profits has turned out to be none, lackin' considable, an none to carry, is it my fault any more'n it's yourn?"

"Well, *they'd* be in this house yet, and we *wouldn't* if I could a got my advice listened to."

The king sassed back, as much as was safe for him, and then swapped around and lit into *me* again. He give me down the banks[6] for not coming and *telling* him I see the niggers come out of his room acting that way—said any fool would a *knowed* something was up. And then waltzed in and cussed *himself* a while; and said it all come of him not laying late and taking his natural rest that morning, and he'd be blamed if he'd ever do it again. So they went off a jawing; and I felt dreadful glad I'd worked it all off onto the niggers and yet hadn't done the niggers no harm by it.

CHAPTER XXVIII

By-and-by it was getting-up time; so I come down the ladder and started for down stairs, but as I come to the girls' room, the door was open, and I see Mary Jane setting by her old hair trunk, which was open and she'd been packing things in it—getting ready to go to England. But she had stopped now, with a folded gown in her lap, and had her face in her

[6] A tongue-lashing.

hands, crying. I felt awful bad to see it; of course anybody would. I went in there, and says:

"Miss Mary Jane, you can't abear to see people in trouble, and *I* can't—most always. Tell me about it."

So she done it. And it was the niggers—I just expected it. She said the beautiful trip to England was most about spoiled for her; and she didn't know *how* she was ever going to be happy there, knowing the mother and the children warn't ever going to see each other no more—and then busted out bitterer than ever, and flung up her hands, and says:

"Oh, dear, dear, to think they ain't *ever* going to see each other any more!"

"But they *will*—and inside of two weeks—and I *know* it!" says I.

Laws, it was out before I could think!—and before I could budge, she throws her arms arond my neck, and told me to say it *again,* say it *again,* say it *again!*

I see I had spoke too sudden, and said too much, and was in a close place. I asked her to let me think a minute; and she set there, very impatient and excited, and handsome, but looking kind of happy and eased-up, like a person that's had a tooth pulled out. So I went to studying it out. I says to myself, I reckon a body that ups and tells the truth when he is in a tight place, is taking considerable many resks, though I ain't had no experience, and can't say for certain; but it looks so to me, anyway; and yet here's a case where I'm blest if it don't look to me like the truth is better, and actuly *safer,* than a lie. I must lay it by in my mind, and think it over some time or other, it's so kind of strange and unregular. I never see nothing like it. Well, I says to myself at last, I'm agoing to chance it; I'll up and tell the truth this time, though it does seem most like setting down on a kag of powder and touching it off just to see where you'll go to. Then I says:

"Miss Mary Jane, is there any place out of town a little ways, where you could go and stay three or four days?"

"Yes—Mr. Lothrop's. Why?"

"Never mind why, yet. If I'll tell you how I know the niggers will see each other again—inside of two weeks—here in this house—and *prove* how I know it—will you go to Mr. Lothrop's and stay four days?"

"Four days!" she says; "I'll stay a year!"

"All right," I says, "I don't want nothing more out of *you* than just your word—I druther have it than another man's kiss-the-Bible."[1] She smiled, and reddened up very sweet, and I says, "If you don't mind it, I'll shut the door—and bolt it."

Then I come back and set down again, and says:

"Don't you holler. Just set still, and take it like a man. I got to tell the truth, and you want to brace up, Miss Mary, because it's a bad kind, and going to be hard to take, but there ain't no help for it. These uncles of yourn ain't no uncles at all—they're a couple of frauds—regular dead beats. There, now we're over the worst of it—you can stand the rest middling easy."

It jolted her up like everything, of course; but I was over the shoal water[2] now, so I went right along, her eyes a blazing higher and higher all the time, and told her every blame thing, from where we first struck that young fool

[1]Oath sworn on the Bible. [2]Past the most dangerous water, "over the worst of it."

going up to the steamboat, clear through to where she flung herself onto the king's breast at the front door and he kissed her sixteen or seventeen times—and then up she jumps, with her face afire like sunset, and says:

"The brute! Come—don't waste a minute—not a *second*—we'll have them tarred and feathered, and flung in the river!"

Says I:

"Cert'nly. But do you mean, *before* you go to Mr. Lothrop's, or——"

"Oh," she says, "what am I *thinking* about!" she says, and set right down again. "Don't mind what I said—please don't—you *won't* now, *will* you?" Laying her silky hand on mine in that kind of a way that I said I would die first. "I never thought, I was so stirred up," she says; "now go on, and I won't do so any more. You tell me what to do, and whatever you say, I'll do it."

"Well," I says, "it's a rough gang, them two frauds, and I'm fixed so I got to travel with them a while longer, whether I want to or not—I druther not tell you why—and if you was to blow on them this town would get me out of their claws, and *I*'d be all right, but there'd be another person that you don't know about who'd be in big trouble. Well, we got to save *him,* hain't we? Of course. Well, then, we won't blow on them."

Saying them words put a good idea in my head. I see how maybe I could get me and Jim rid of the frauds; get them jailed here, and then leave. But I didn't want to run the raft in day-time, without anybody aboard to answer questions but me; so I didn't want the plan to begin working till pretty late to-night. I says:

"Miss Mary Jane, I'll tell you what we'll do—and you won't have to stay at Mr. Lothrop's so long, nuther. How fur is it?"

"A little short of four miles—right out in the country, back here."

"Well, that'll answer. Now you go along out there, and lay low till nine or half-past, to-night, and then get them to fetch you home again—tell them you've thought of something. If you get here before eleven, put a candle in this window, and if I don't turn up, wait *till* eleven, and *then* if I don't turn up it means I'm gone, and out of the way, and safe. Then you come out and spread the news around, and get these beats jailed."

"Good," she says, "I'll do it."

"And if it just happens so that I don't get away, but get took up along with them, you must up and say I told you the whole thing beforehand, and you must stand by me all you can."

"Stand by you, indeed I will. They sha'n't touch a hair of your head!" she says, and I see her nostrils spread and her eyes snap when she said it, too.

"If I get away, I sha'n't be here," I says, "to prove these rapscallions ain't your uncles, and I couldn't do it if I *was* here. I could swear they was beats and bummers, that's all; though that's worth something. Well, there's others can do that better than what I can—and they're people that ain't going to be doubted as quick as I'd be. I'll tell you how to find them. Gimme a pencil and a piece of paper. There—*'Royal Nonesuch, Bricksville.'* Put it away, and don't lose it. When the court wants to find out something about these two, let them send up to Bricksville and say they've got the men that played the Royal Nonesuch, and ask for some witnesses—why, you'll have that entire town down here before you can hardly wink, Miss Mary. And they'll come a-biling, too."

I judged we had got everything fixed about right, now. So I says:

"Just let the auction go right along, and don't worry. Nobody don't have to pay for the things, and they ain't going out of this till they get that money—and the way we've fixed it the sale ain't going to count, and they ain't going to *get* no money. It's just like the way it was with the niggers—it warn't no sale, and the niggers will be back before long. Why, they can't collect the money for the *niggers,* yet—they're in the worst kind of a fix, Miss Mary."

"Well," she says. "I'll run down to breakfast now, and then I'll start straight for Mr. Lothrop's."

"'Deed, *that* ain't the ticket, Miss Mary Jane." I says, "by no manner of means; go *before* breakfast."

"Why?"

"What did you reckon I wanted you to go at all for, Miss Mary?"

"Well, I never thought—and come to think, I don't know. What was it?"

"Why, it's because you ain't one of these leather-face people. I don't want no better book than what your face is. A body can set down and read it off like coarse print. Do you reckon you can go and face your uncles, when they come to kiss you good-morning, and never—"

"There, there, don't! Yes, I'll go before breakfast—I'll be glad to. And leave my sisters with them?"

"Yes—never mind about them. They've got to stand it yet a while. They might suspicion something if all of you was to go. I don't want you to see them, nor your sisters, nor nobody in this town—if a neighbor was to ask how is your uncles this morning, your face would tell something. No, you go right along, Miss Mary Jane, and I'll fix it with all of them. I'll tell Miss Susan to give your love to your uncles and say you've went away for a few hours for to get a little rest and change, or to see a friend, and you'll be back to-night or early in the morning."

"Gone to see a friend is all right, but I won't have my love given to them."

"Well, then, it sha'n't be." It was well enough to tell *her* so—no harm in it. It was only a little thing to do, and no trouble; and it's the little things that smooths people's roads and most, down here below; it would make Mary Jane comfortable, and it wouldn't cost nothing. Then I says: "There's one more thing—that bag of money."

"Well, they've got that; and it makes me feel pretty silly to think *how* they got it."

"No, you're out, there. They hain't got it."

"Why, who's got it?"

"I wish I knowed, but I don't. I *had* it, because I stole it from them: and I stole it to give to you; and I know where I hid it, but I'm afraid it ain't there no more. I'm awful sorry, Miss Mary Jane, I'm just as sorry as I can be; but I done the best I could; I did, honest. I come nigh getting caught, and I had to shove it into the first place I come to, and run—and it warn't a good place."

"Oh, stop blaming yourself—it's too bad to do it, and I won't allow it—you couldn't help it; it wasn't your fault. Where did you hide it?"

I didn't want to set her to thinking about her troubles again; I couldn't seem to get my mouth to tell her what would make her see that corpse layin' in the coffin with that bag of money on his stomach. So for a minute I didn't say nothing—then I says:

"I'd druther not *tell* you where I put it, Miss Mary Jane, if you don't mind letting me off; but I'll write it for you on a piece of paper, and you can read it along the road to Mr. Lothrop's, if you want to. Do you reckon that'll do?"

"Oh, yes."

So I wrote: "I put it in the coffin. It was in there when you was crying there, away in the night. I was behind the door, and I was mighty sorry for you, Miss Mary Jane."

It made my eyes water a little, to remember her crying there all by herself in the night, and them devils laying there right under her own roof, shaming her and robbing her; and when I folded it up and give it to her, I see the water come into her eyes, too; and she shook me by the hand, hard, and says:

"*Good*-bye—I'm going to do everything just as you've told me; and if I don't ever see you again, I sha'n't ever forget you, and I'll think of you a many and a many a time, and I'll *pray* for you, too!"—and she was gone.

Pray for me! I reckoned if she knowed me she'd take a job that was more nearer her size. But I bet she done it, just the same—she was just that kind. She had the grit to pray for Judus if she took the notion—there warn't no back-down to her, I judge. You may say what you want to, but in my opinion she had more sand[3] in her than any girl I ever see; in my opinion she was just full of sand. It sounds like flattery, but it ain't no flattery. And when it comes to beauty—and goodness too—she lays over them all. I hain't ever seen her since that time that I see her go out of that door; no, I hain't ever seen her since, but I reckon I've thought of her a many and a many a million times, and of her saying she would pray for me; and if ever I'd a thought it would do any good for me to pray for *her*, blamed if I wouldn't a done it or bust.

Well, Mary Jane she lit out the back way, I reckon; because nobody see her go. When I struck Susan and the hare-lip, I says:

"What's the name of them people over on t'other side of the river that you all goes to see sometimes?"

They says:

"There's several; but it's the Proctors, mainly."

"That's the name," I says; "I most forgot it. Well, Miss Mary Jane she told me to tell you she's gone over there in a dreadful hurry—one of them's sick."

"Which one?"

"I don't know; leastways I kinder forget; but I think it's——"

"Sakes alive, I hope it ain't *Hanner*?"

"I'm sorry to say it," I says, "but Hanner's the very one."

"My goodness—and she so well only last week! Is she took bad?"

"It ain't no name for it. They set up with her all night, Miss Mary Jane said, and they don't think she'll last many hours."

"Only think of that, now! What's the matter with her!"

I couldn't think of anything reasonable, right off that way, so I says:

"Mumps."

"Mumps your granny! They don't set up with people that's got the mumps."

"They don't, don't they? You better bet they do with *these* mumps. These mumps is different. It's a new kind, Miss Mary Jane said."

"How's it a new kind?"

"Because it's mixed up with other things."

"What other things?"

[3] Grit, courage.

"Well, measles, and whooping-cough, and erysiplas,[4] and consumption,[5] and yaller jaunders,[6] and brain fever, and I don't know what all."

"My land! And they call it the *mumps?*"

"That's what Miss Mary Jane said."

"Well, what in the nation do they call it the *mumps* for?"

"Why, because it *is* the mumps. That's what it starts with."

"Well, ther' ain't no sense in it. A body might stump his toe, and take pison, and fall down the well, and break his neck, and bust his brains out, and somebody come along and ask what killed him, and some numskull up and say, 'Why, he stumped his *toe.*' Would ther' be any sense in that? No. And ther' ain't no sense in *this,* nuther. Is it ketching?"

"Is it *ketching?* Why, how you talk. Is a *harrow* catching?—in the dark? If you don't hitch onto one tooth, you're bound to on another, ain't you? And you can't get away with that tooth without fetching the whole harrow along, can you? Well, these kind of mumps is a kind of a harrow, as you may say—and it ain't no slouch of a harrow, nuther, you come to get it hitched on good."

"Well, it's awful, I think," says the hare-lip. "I'll go to Uncle Harvey and——"

"Oh, yes," I says, "I *would.* Of *course* I would. I wouldn't lose no time."

"Well, why wouldn't you?"

"Just look at it a minute, and maybe you can see. Hain't your uncles obleeged to get along home to England as fast as they can? And do you reckon they'd be mean enough to go off and leave you to go all that journey by yourselves? *You* know they'll wait for you. So fur, so good. Your uncle Harvey's a preacher, ain't he? Very well, then; is a *preacher* going to deceive a steamboat clerk? is he going to deceive a *ship clerk?*—so as to get them to let Miss Mary Jane go aboard? Now *you* know he ain't. What *will* he do, then? Why, he'll say, 'It's a great pity, but my church matters has got to get along the best way they can; for my niece has been exposed to the dreadful pluribus-unum[7] mumps, and so it's my bounden duty to set down here and wait the three months it takes to show on her if she's got it.' But never mind, if you think it's best to tell your uncle Harvey——"

"Shucks, and stay fooling around here when we could all be having good times in England whilst we was waiting to find out whether Mary Jane's got it or not? Why, you talk like a muggins."[8]

"Well, anyway, maybe you better tell some of the neighbors."

"Listen at that, now. You do beat all, for natural stupidness. Can't you *see* that *they'd* go and tell? Ther' ain't no way but just to not tell anybody at *all.*"

"Well, maybe you're right—yes, I judge you *are* right."

"But I reckon we ought to tell Uncle Harvey she's gone out a while, anyway, so he won't be uneasy about her."

"Yes, Miss Mary Jane she wanted you to do that. She says, 'Tell them to give Uncle Harvey and William my love and a kiss, and say I've run over the river to see Mr.—Mr.—what *is* the name of that rich family your uncle Peter used to think so much of?—I mean the one that——"

[4]A skin disease. [5]Tuberculosis. [6]Yellow jaundice.

[7]High-sounding Latin, taken from the United States motto that is stamped on coins: "E Pluribus Unum," One Out of Many.

[8]Fool.

"Why, you must mean the Apthorps, ain't it?"

"Of course; bother them kind of names, a body can't ever seem to remember them, half the time, somehow. Yes, she said, say she has run over for to ask the Apthorps to be sure and come to the auction and buy this house, because she allowed her uncle Peter would rather they had it than anybody else; and she's going to stick to them till they say they'll come, and then, if she ain't too tired, she's coming home; and if she is, she'll be home in the morning anyway. She said, don't say nothing about the Proctors, but only about the Apthorps—which'll be perfectly true, because she *is* going there to speak about their buying the house; I know it, because she told me so, herself."

"All right," she said, and cleared out to lay for her uncles, and give them the love and the kisses, and tell them the message.

Everything was all right now. The girls wouldn't say nothing because they wanted to go to England; and the king and the duke would ruther Mary Jane was off working for the auction than around in reach of Doctor Robinson. I felt very good; I judged I had done it pretty neat—I reckoned Tom Sawyer couldn't a done it no neater himself. Of course he would a throwed more style into it, but I can't do that very handy, not being brung up to it.

Well, they held the auction in the public square, along towards the end of the afternoon, and it strung along, and strung along, and the old man he was on hand and looking his level piousest, up there longside of the auctioneer, and chipping in a little Scripture, now and then, or a little goody-goody saying, of some kind, and the duke he was around goo-gooing for sympathy all he knowed how, and just spreading himself generly.

But by-and-by the thing dragged through, and everything was sold. Everything but a little old trifling lot in the graveyard. So they'd got to work *that* off—I never see such a girafft as the king was for wanting to swallow *everything.* Well, whilst they was at it, a steamboat landed, and in about two minutes up comes a crowd a whooping and yelling and laughing and carrying on, and singing out:

"*Here's* your opposition line! here's your two sets o' heirs to old Peter Wilks—and you pays your money and you takes your choice!"

CHAPTER XXIX

They was fetching a very nice looking old gentleman along, and a nice looking younger one, with his right arm in a sling. And my souls, how the people yelled, and laughed, and kept it up. But I didn't see no joke about it, and I judged it would strain the duke and the king some to see any. I reckoned they'd turn pale. But no, nary a pale did *they* turn. The duke he never let on he suspicioned what was up, but just went a goo-gooing around, happy and satisfied, like a jug that's googling out buttermilk; and as for the king, he just gazed and gazed down sorrowful on them new-comers like it give him the stomach-ache in his very heart to think there could be such frauds and rascals in the world. Oh, he done it admirable. Lots of the principal people gethered around the king, to let him see they was on his side. That old gentleman that had just come looked all puzzled to death. Pretty soon he began to speak, and I see, straight off, he pronounced *like* an Englishman, not the king's way, though the king's *was* pretty good, for an imitation. I can't give the old gent's words, nor I can't imitate him; but he turned around to the crowd, and says, about like this:

"This is a surprise to me which I wasn't looking for; and I'll acknowledge, candid and frank, I ain't very well fixed to meet it and answer it; for my brother and me has had misfortunes, he's broke his arm, and our baggage got put off at a town above here, last night in the night by a mistake. I am Peter Wilks's brother Harvey, and this is his brother William, which can't hear nor speak—and can't even make signs to amount to much, now 't he's only got one hand to work them with. We are who we say we are; and in a day or two, when I get the baggage, I can prove it. But, up till then, I won't say nothing more, but go to the hotel and wait."

So him and the new dummy[1] started off; and the king he laughs, and blethers out:

"Broke his arm—*very* likely *ain't* it?—and very convenient, too, for a fraud that's got to make signs, and hain't learnt how. Lost their baggage! That's *mighty* good!—and mighty ingenious—under the *circumstances!*"

So he laughed again; and so did everybody else, except three or four, or maybe half a dozen. One of these was that doctor; another one was a sharp looking gentleman, with a carpet-bag of the old-fashioned kind made out of carpet-stuff, that had just come off the steamboat and was talking to him in a low voice, and glancing towards the king now and then and nodding their heads—it was Levi Bell, the lawyer that was gone up to Louisville; and another one was a big rough husky that come along and listened to all the old gentleman said, and was listening to the king now. And when the king got done, this husky up and says:

"Say, looky here; if you are Harvey Wilks, when'd you come to this town?"

"The day before the funeral, friend," says the king.

"But what time o' day?"

"In the evenin'—'bout an hour er two before sundown."

"*How'd* you come?"

"I come down on the *Susan Powell,* from Cincinnati."

"Well, then, how'd you come to be up the Pint in the *mornin'*—in a canoe?"

"I warn't up at the Pint in the mornin'."

"It's a lie."

Several of them jumped for him and begged him not to talk that way to an old man and preacher.

"Preacher be hanged, he's a fraud and a liar. He was up at the Pint that mornin'. I live up there, don't I? Well, I was up there, and he was up there. I *see* him there. He come in a canoe, along with Tim Collins and a boy."

The doctor he up and says:

"Would you know the boy again if you was to see him, Hines?"

"I reckon I would, but I don't know. Why, yonder he is, now. I know him perfectly easy."

It was me he pointed at. The doctor says:

"Neighbors, I don't know whether the new couple is frauds or not; but if *these* two ain't frauds, I am an idiot, that's all. I think it's our duty to see that

[1]Deaf mute.

they don't get away from here till we've looked into this thing. Come along, Hines; come along, the rest of you. We'll take these fellows to the tavern and affront them with t'other couple, and I reckon we'll find out *something* before we get through."

It was nuts for the crowd, though maybe not for the king's friends; so we all started. It was about sundown. The doctor he led me along by the hand, and was plenty kind enough, but he never let *go* my hand.

We all got in a big room in the hotel, and lit up some candles, and fetched in the new couple. First, the doctor says:

"I don't wish to be too hard on these two men, but *I* think they're frauds, and they may have complices that we don't know nothing about. If they have, won't the complices get away with that bag of gold Peter Wilks left? It ain't unlikely. If these men ain't frauds, they won't object to sending for that money and letting us keep it till they prove they're all right—ain't that so?"

Everybody agreed to that. So I judged they had our gang in a pretty tight place, right at the outstart. But the king he only looked sorrowful, and says:

"Gentlemen, I wish the money was there, for I ain't got no disposition to throw anything in the way of a fair, open, out-and-out investigation o' this misable business; but alas, the money ain't there; you k'n send and see, if you want to."

"Where is it, then?"

"Well, when my niece give it to me to keep for her, I took and hid it inside o' the straw tick o' my bed, not wishin' to bank it for the few days we'd be here, and considerin' the bed a safe place, we not bein' used to niggers, and suppos'n' 'em honest, like servants in England. The niggers stole it the very next mornin' after I had went down stairs; and when I sold 'em, I hadn't missed the money yit, so they got clean away with it. My servant here k'n tell you 'bout it, gentlemen."

The doctor and several said "Shucks!" and I see nobody didn't altogether believe him. One man asked me if I see the niggers steal it. I said no, but I see them sneaking out of the room and hustling away, and I never thought nothing, only I reckoned they was afraid they had waked up my master and was trying to get away before he made trouble with them. That was all they asked me. Then the doctor whirls on me and says:

"Are *you* English too?"

I says yes; and him and some others laughed, and said, "Stuff!"

Well, then they sailed in on the general investigation, and there we had it, up and down, hour in, hour out, and nobody never said a word about supper, nor ever seemed to think about it—and so they kept it up, and kept it up; and it *was* the worst mixed-up thing you ever see. They made the king tell his yarn, and they made the old gentleman tell his'n; and anybody but a lot of prejudiced chuckleheads would a *seen* that the old gentleman was spinning truth and t'other one lies. And by-and-by they had me up to tell what I knowed. The king he give me a left-handed look out of the corner of his eye, and so I knowed enough to talk on the right side. I begun to tell about Sheffield, and how we lived there, and all about the English Wilkses, and so on; but I didn't get pretty fur till the doctor begun to laugh; and Levi Bell, the lawyer, says:

"Set down, my boy, I wouldn't strain myself, if I was you. I reckon you ain't used to lying, it don't seem to come handy; what you want is practice. You do it pretty awkward."

I didn't care nothing for the compliment, but I was glad to be let off, anyway.

The doctor he started to say something, and turns and says:

"If you'd been in town at first, Levi Bell——"

The king broke in and reached out his hand, and says:

"Why, is this my poor dead brother's old friend that he's wrote so often about?"

The lawyer and him shook hands, and the lawyer smiled and looked pleased, and they talked right along a while, and then got to one side and talked low; and at last the lawyer speaks up and says:

"That'll fix it. I'll take the order and send it, along with your brother's, and then they'll know it's all right."

So they got some paper and a pen, and the king he set down and twisted his head to one side, and chawed his tongue, and scrawled off something; and then they give the pen to the duke—and then for the first time, the duke looked sick. But he took the pen and wrote. So then the lawyer turns to the new old gentleman and says:

"You and your brother please write a line or two and sign your names."

The old gentleman wrote, but nobody couldn't read it. The lawyer looked powerful astonished, and says:

"Well, it beats *me*"—and snaked a lot of old letters out of his pocket, and examined them, and then examined the old man's writing, and then *them* again; and then says: "These old letters is from Harvey Wilks; and here's *these* two's handwritings, and anybody can see *they* didn't write them" (the king and the duke looked sold and foolish, I tell you, to see how the lawyer had took them in), "and here's *this* old gentleman's handwriting, and anybody can tell, easy enough, *he* didn't write them—fact is, the scratches he makes ain't properly *writing,* at all. Now here's some letters from——"

The new old gentleman says:

"If you please, let me explain. Nobody can read my hand but my brother there—so he copies for me. It's *his* hand you've got there, not mine."

"Well!" says the lawyer, "this *is* a state of things. I've got some of William's letters too; so if you'll get him to write a line or so we can com—"

"He *can't* write with his left hand," says the old gentleman. "If he could use his right hand, you would see that he wrote his own letters and mine too. Look at both, please—they're by the same hand."

The lawyer done it, and says:

"I believe it's so—and if it ain't so, there's a heap stronger resemblance than I'd noticed before, anyway. Well, well, well! I thought we was right on the track of a solution, but it's gone to grass, partly. But anyway, *one* thing is proved—*these* two ain't either of 'em Wilkses"—and he wagged his head towards the king and the duke.

Well, what do you think?—that muleheaded old fool wouldn't give in *then!* Indeed he wouldn't. Said it warn't no fair test. Said his brother William was the cussedest joker in the world, and hadn't *tried* to write—*he* see William was going to play one of his jokes the minute he put the pen to paper. And so he warmed up and went warbling and warbling right along, till he was actuly beginning to believe what he was saying, *himself*—but pretty soon the new old gentleman broke in, and says:

"I've thought of something. Is there anybody here that helped to lay out my br—helped to lay out the late Peter Wilks for burying?"

"Yes," says somebody, "me and Ab Turner done it. We're both here."

Then the old man turns towards the king, and says:

"Peraps this gentleman can tell me what was tatooed on his breast?"

Blamed if the king didn't have to brace up mighty quick, or he'd a squshed down like a bluff bank that the river has cut under, it took him so sudden—and mind you, it was a thing that was calculated to make most *anybody* sqush to get fetched such a solid one as that without any notice—because how was *he* going to know what was tatooed on the man? He whitened a little; he couldn't help it; and it was mighty still in there, and everybody bending a little forwards and gazing at him. Says I to myself, *Now* he'll throw up the sponge—there ain't no more use. Well, did he? A body can't hardly believe it, but he didn't. I reckon he thought he'd keep the thing up till he tired them people out, so they'd thin out, and him and the duke could break loose and get away. Anyway, he set there, and pretty soon he begun to smile, and says:

"Mf! It's a *very* tough question, *ain't* it! *Yes,* sir, I k'n tell you what's tatooed on his breast. It's jest a small, thin, blue arrow—that's what it is; and if you don't look clost, you can't see it. *Now* what do you say—hey?"

Well, *I* never see anything like that old blister for clean out-and-out cheek.

The new old gentleman turns brisk towards Ab Turner and his pard, and his eye lights up like he judged he'd got the king *this* time, and says:

"There—you've heard what he said! Was there any such mark on Peter Wilks's breast?"

Both of them spoke up and says:

"We didn't see no such mark."

"Good!" says the old gentleman. "Now, what you *did* see on his breast was a small dim P, and a B (which is an initial he dropped when he was young), and a W, with dashes between them, so: P—B—W"—and he marked them that way on a piece of paper. "Come—ain't that what you saw?"

Both of them spoke up again, and says:

"No, we *didn't.* We never seen any marks at all."

Well, everybody *was* in a state of mind, now; and they sings out:

"The whole *bilin'* of 'm's frauds! Le's duck 'em! le's drown 'em! le's ride 'em on a rail!" and everybody was whooping at once, and there was a rattling pow-wow. But the lawyer he jumps on the table and yells, and says:

"Gentlemen—gentle*men!* Hear me just a word—just a *single* word—if you PLEASE! There's one way yet—let's go and dig up the corpse and look."

That took them.

"Hooray!" they all shouted, and was starting right off; but the lawyer and the doctor sung out:

"Hold on, hold on! Collar all these four men and the boy, and fetch *them* along, too!"

"We'll do it!" they all shouted; "and if we don't find them marks we'll lynch the whole gang!"

I *was* scared, now, I tell you. But there warn't no getting away, you know. They gripped us all, and marched us right along, straight for the graveyard, which was a mile and a half down the river, and the whole town at our heels, for we made noise enough, and it was only nine in the evening.

As we went by our house I wished I hadn't sent Mary Jane out of town; because now if I could tip her the wink, she'd light out and save me, and blow on our dead-beats.

Well, we swarmed along down the river road, just carrying on like wild-cats; and to make it more scary, the sky was darking up, and the lightning beginning to wink and flitter, and the wind to shiver amongst the leaves. This was the most awful trouble and most dangersome I ever was in; and I was kinder stunned; everything was going so different from what I had allowed for; stead of being fixed so I could take my own time, if I wanted to, and see all the fun, and have Mary Jane at my back to save me and set me free when the close-fit come, here was nothing in the world betwixt me and sudden death but just them tatoo-marks. If they didn't find them—

I couldn't bear to think about it; and yet, somehow, I couldn't think about nothing else. It got darker and darker, and it was a beautiful time to give the crowd the slip; but that big husky had me by the wrist—Hines—and a body might as well try to give Goliar[2] the slip. He dragged me right along, he was so excited; and I had to run to keep up.

When they got there they swarmed into the graveyard and washed over it like an overflow. And when they got to the grave, they found they had about a hundred times as many shovels as they wanted, but nobody hadn't thought to fetch a lantern. But they sailed into digging, anyway, by the flicker of the lightning, and sent a man to the nearest house a half a mile off, to borrow one.

So they dug and dug, like everything; and it got awful dark, and the rain started, and the wind swished and swushed along, and the lightning come brisker and brisker, and the thunder boomed; but them people never took no notice of it, they was so full of this business; and one minute you could see everything and every face in that big crowd, and the shovelfuls of dirt sailing up out of the grave, and the next second the dark wiped it all out, and you couldn't see nothing at all.

At last they got out the coffin, and begun to unscrew the lid, and then such another crowding, and shouldering, and shoving as there was, to scrouge in and get a sight, you never see; and in the dark, that way, it was awful. Hines he hurt my wrist dreadful, pulling and tugging so, and I reckon he clean forgot I was in the world, he was so excited and panting.

All of a sudden the lightning let go a perfect sluice of white glare, and somebody sings out:

"By the living jingo, here's the bag of gold on his breast!"

Hines let out a whoop, like everybody else, and dropped my wrist and give a big surge to burst his way in and get a look, and the way I lit out and shinned for the road in the dark, there ain't nobody can tell.

I had the road all to myself, and I fairly flew—leastways I had it all to myself except the solid dark, and the now-and-then glares, and the buzzing of the rain, and the thrashing of the wind, and the splitting of the thunder; and sure as you are born I did clip it along!

When I struck the town, I see there warn't nobody out in the storm, so I never hunted for no back streets, but humped it straight through the main one; and when I begun to get towards our house I aimed my eye and set it.

[2]Goliath.

No light there; the house all dark—which made me feel sorry and disappointed, I didn't know why. But at last, just as I was sailing by, *flash* comes the light in Mary Jane's window! and my heart swelled up sudden, like to burst; and the same second the house and all was behind me in the dark, and wasn't ever going to be before me no more in this world. She *was* the best girl I ever see, and had the most sand.

The minute I was far enough above the town to see I could make the tow-head, I begun to look sharp for a boat to borrow; and the first time the lightning showed me one that wasn't chained, I snatched it and shoved. It was a canoe, and warn't fastened with nothing but a rope. The tow-head was a rattling big distance off, away out there in the middle of the river, but I didn't lose no time; and when I struck the raft at last, I was so fagged I would a just laid down to blow and gasp if I could afforded it. But I didn't. As I sprung aboard I sung out:

"Out with you, Jim, and set her loose! Glory be to goodness, we're shut of them!"

Jim lit out, and was a coming for me with both arms spread, he was so full of joy; but when I glimpsed him in the lightning, my heart shot up in my mouth, and I went overboard backwards; for I forgot he was old King Lear and a drownded A-rab all in one, and it most scared the livers and lights[3] out of me. But Jim fished me out, and was going to hug me and bless me, and so on, he was so glad I was back and we was shut of the king and the duke, but I says:

"Not now—have it for breakfast,[4] have it for breakfast! Cut loose and let her slide!"

So, in two seconds, away we went, a sliding down the river, and it *did* seem so good to be free again and all by ourselves on the big river and nobody to bother us. I had to skip around a bit, and jump up and crack my heels a few times, I couldn't help it; but about the third crack, I noticed a sound that I knowed mighty well—and held my breath and listened and waited—and sure enough, when the next flash busted out over the water, here they come!—and just a laying to their oars and making their skiff hum! It was the king and the duke. So I wilted right down onto the planks, then, and give up; and it was all I could do to keep from crying.

CHAPTER XXX

When they got aboard, the king went for me, and shook me by the collar, and says:

"Tryin' to give us the slip, was ye, you pup! Tired of our company—hey?"

I says:

"No, your majesty, we warn't—*please* don't, your majesty!"

"Quick, then, and tell us what *was* your idea, or I'll shake the insides out o' you!"

"Honest, I'll tell you everything, just as it happened, your majesty. The man that had aholt of me was very good to me, and kept saying he had a boy about as big as me that died last year, and he was sorry to see a boy in such a

[3]I.e., "livers and lungs," hence "guts." [4]Save it for later.

dangerous fix; and when they was all took by surprise by finding the gold, and made a rush for the coffin, he lets go of me and whispers, 'Heel it, now, or they'll hang ye, sure!' and I lit out. It didn't seem no good for *me* to stay—*I* couldn't do nothing, and I didn't want to be hung if I could get away. So I never stopped running till I found the canoe; and when I got here I told Jim to hurry, or they'd catch me and hang me yet, and said I was afeard you and the duke wasn't alive, now, and I was awful sorry, and so was Jim, and was awful glad when we see you coming, you may ask Jim if I didn't."

Jim said it was so; and the king told him to shut up, and said, "Oh, yes, it's *mighty* likely!" and shook me up again, and said he reckoned he'd drownd me. But the duke says:

"Leggo the boy, you old idiot! Would *you* a done any different? Did you inquire around for *him,* when you got loose? *I* don't remember it."

So the king let go of me, and begun to cuss that town and everybody in it. But the duke says:

"You better a blame sight give *yourself* a good cussing, for you're the one that's entitled to it most. You hain't done a thing, from the start, that had any sense in it, except coming out so cool and cheeky with that imaginary blue-arrow mark. That *was* bright—it was right down bully; and it was the thing that saved us. For if it hadn't been for that, they'd a jailed us till them Englishmen's baggage come—and then—the penitentiary, you bet! But that trick took 'em to the graveyard, and the gold done us a still bigger kindness; for if the excited fools hadn't let go all holts and made that rush to get a look, we'd a slept in our cravats[1] to-night—cravats warranted to *wear,* too—longer than *we'd* need 'em."

They was still a minute—thinking—then the king says, kind of absent-minded like:

"Mf! And we reckoned the *niggers* stole it!"

That made me squirm!

"Yes," says the duke, kinder slow, and deliberate, and sarcastic, "*We* did."

After about a half a minute, the king drawls out:

"Leastways—*I* did."

The duke says, the same way:

"On the contrary—*I* did."

The king kind of ruffles up, and says:

"Looky here, Bilgewater, what'r you referrin' to?"

The duke says, pretty brisk:

"When it comes to that, maybe you'll let me ask, what was *you* referring to?"

"Shucks!" says the king, very sarcastic; "but *I* don't know—maybe you was asleep, and didn't know what you was about."

The duke bristles right up, now, and says:

"Oh, let *up* on this cussed nonsense—do you take me for a blame' fool? Don't you reckon *I* know who hid that money in that coffin?"

"*Yes,* sir! I know you *do* know—because you done it yourself!"

"It's a lie!"—and the duke went for him. The king sings out:

[1]I.e., hangman's nooses.

"Take y'r hands off!—leggo my throat!—I take it all back!"

The duke says:

"Well, you just own up, first, that you *did* hide that money there, intending to give me the slip one of these days, and come back and dig it up, and have it all to yourself."

"Wait jest a minute, duke—answer me this one question, honest and fair; if you didn't put the money there, say it, and I'll b'lieve you, and take back everything I said."

"You old scoundrel, I didn't, and you know I didn't. There, now!"

"Well, then, I b'lieve you. But answer me only jest this one more—now *don't* git mad; didn't you have it in your *mind* to hook the money and hide it?"

The duke never said nothing for a little bit; then he says:

"Well—I don't care if I *did,* I didn't *do* it, anyway. But you not only had it in mind to do it, but you *done* it."

"I wisht I may never die if I done it, duke, and that's honest. I won't say I warn't *goin'* to do it, because I *was;* but you—I mean somebody—got in ahead o' me."

"It's a lie! You done it, and you got to *say* you done it, or——"

The king begun to gurgle, and then he gasps out:

"'Nough!—*I own up!*"

I was very glad to hear him say that, it made me feel much more easier than what I was feeling before. So the duke took his hands off, and says:

"If you ever deny it again, I'll drown you. It's *well* for you to set there and blubber like a baby—it's fitten for you, after the way you've acted. I never see such an old ostrich for wanting to gobble everything—and I a trusting you all the time, like you was my own father. You ought to been ashamed of yourself to stand by and hear it saddled onto a lot of poor niggers and you never say a word for 'em. It makes me feel ridiculous to think I was soft enough to *believe* that rubbage. Cuss you, I can see, now, why you was so anxious to make up the deffersit—you wanted to get what money I'd got out of the Nonesuch and one thing or another, and scoop it *all!*"

The king says, timid, and still a snuffling:

"Why, duke, it was you that said make up the deffersit, it warn't me."

"Dry up! I don't want to hear no more *out* of you!" says the duke. "And *now* you see what you *got* by it. They've got all their own money back, and all of *ourn* but a shekel[2] or two, *besides.* G'long to bed—and don't you deffersit *me* no more deffersits, long 's *you* live!"

So the king sneaked into the wigwam, and took to his bottle for comfort; and before long the duke tackled *his* bottle; and so in about a half an hour they was as thick as thieves again, and the tighter they got, the lovinger they got; and went off a snoring in each other's arms. They both got powerful mellow, but I noticed the king didn't get mellow enough to forget to remember to not deny about hiding the money-bag again. That made me feel easy and satisfied. Of course when they got to snoring, we had a long gabble, and I told Jim everything.

[2]An ancient coin of the Near East; here the term is used to mean any coin that does not have high monetary value.

CHAPTER XXXI

We dasn't stop again at any town, for days and days; kept right along down the river. We was down south in the warm weather, now, and a mighty long ways from home. We begun to come to trees with Spanish moss on them, hanging down from the limbs like long gray beards. It was the first I ever see it growing, and it made the woods look solemn and dismal. So now the frauds reckoned they was out of danger, and they begun to work the villages again.

First they done a lecture on temperance; but they didn't make enough for them both to get drunk on. Then in another village they started a dancing school; but they didn't know no more how to dance than a kangaroo does; so the first prance they made, the general public jumped in and pranced them out of town. Another time they tried a go at yellocution; but they didn't yellocute long till the audience got up and give them a solid good cussing and made them skip out. They tackled missionarying, and mesmerizering, and doctoring, and telling fortunes, and a little of everything; but they couldn't seem to have no luck. So at last they got just about dead broke, and laid around the raft, as she floated along, thinking, and thinking, and never saying nothing, by the half a day at a time, and dreadful blue and desperate.

And at last they took a change, and begun to lay their heads together in the wigwam and talk low and confidential two or three hours at a time. Jim and me got uneasy. We didn't like the look of it. We judged they was studying up some kind of worse deviltry than ever. We turned it over and over, and at last we made up our minds they was going to break into somebody's house or store, or was going into the counterfeit-money business, or something. So then we was pretty scared, and made up an agreement that we wouldn't have nothing in the world to do with such actions, and if we ever got the least show we would give them the cold shake, and clear out and leave them behind. Well, early one morning we hid the raft in a good safe place about two mile below a little bit of a shabby village, named Pikesville, and the king he went ashore, and told us all to stay hid whilst he went up to town and smelt around to see if anybody had got any wind of the Royal Nonesuch there yet. ("House to rob, you *mean,*" says I to myself; "and when you get through robbing it you'll come back here and wonder what's become of me and Jim and the raft—and you'll have to take it out in wondering.") And he said if he warn't back by mid-day, the duke and me would know it was all right, and we was to come along.

So we staid where we was. The duke he fretted and sweated around, and was in a mighty sour way. He scolded us for everything, and we couldn't seem to do nothing right; he found fault with every little thing. Something was a-brewing, sure. I was good and glad when midday come and no king; we could have a change, anyway—and maybe a chance for *the* change, on top of it. So me and the duke went up to the village, and hunted around there for the king, and by-and-by we found him in the back room of a little low doggery,[1] very tight, and a lot of loafers bullyragging him for sport, and he a cussing and threatening with all his might, and so tight he couldn't walk, and couldn't do nothing to them. The duke he begun to abuse him for

[1]Saloon.

an old fool, and the king begun to sass back; and the minute they was fairly at it, I lit out, and shook the reefs out of[2] my hind legs, and spun down the river road like a deer—for I see our chance; and I made up my mind that it would be a long day before they ever see me and Jim again. I got down there all out of breath but loaded up with joy, and sung out—

"Set her loose, Jim, we're all right now!"

But there warn't no answer, and nobody come out of the wigwam. Jim was gone! I set up a shout—and then another—and then another one; and run this way and that in the woods, whooping and screeching; but it warn't no use—old Jim was gone. Then I set down and cried; I couldn't help it. But I couldn't set still long. Pretty soon I went out on the road, trying to think what I better do, and I run across a boy walking, and asked him if he'd seen a strange nigger, dressed so and so, and he says:

"Yes."

"Whereabouts?" says I.

"Down to Silas Phelps's place, two mile below here. He's a runaway nigger, and they've got him. Was you looking for him?"

"You bet I ain't! I run across him in the woods about an hour or two ago, and he said if I hollered he'd cut my livers out—and told me to lay down and stay where I was; and I done it. Been there ever since; afeard to come out."

"Well," he says, "you needn't be afeard no more, becuz they've got him. He run off f'm down South, som'ers."

"It's a good job they got him."

"Well, I *reckon!* There's two hundred dollars reward on him. It's like picking up money out'n the road."

"Yes, it is—and *I* could a had it if I'd been big enough; I see him *first.* Who nailed him?"

"It was an old fellow—a stranger—and he sold out his chance in him for forty dollars, becuz he's got to go up the river and can't wait. Think o' that, now! You bet *I'd* wait, if it was seven year."

"That's me, every time," says I. "But maybe his chance ain't worth no more than that, if he'll sell it so cheap. Maybe there's something ain't straight about it."

"But it *is,* though—straight as a string. I see the handbill myself. It tells all about him, to a dot—paints him like a picture, and tells the plantation he's frum, below Newr*leans.* No-sirree-*bob,* they ain't no trouble 'bout *that* speculation, you bet you. Say, gimme a chaw tobacker, won't ye?"

I didn't have none, so he left. I went to the raft, and set down in the wigwam to think. But I couldn't come to nothing. I thought till I wore my head sore, but I couldn't see no way out of the trouble. After all this long journey, and after all we'd done for them scoundrels, here was it all come to nothing, everything all busted up and ruined, because they could have the heart to serve Jim such a trick as that, and make him a slave again all his life, and amongst strangers, too, for forty dirty dollars.

Once I said to myself it would be a thousand times better for Jim to be a slave at home where his family was, as long as he'd *got* to be a slave, and so I'd better write a letter to Tom Sawyer and tell him to tell Miss Watson where he

[2]Stretched out.

was. But I soon give up that notion, for two things: she'd be mad and disgusted at his rascality and ungratefulness for leaving her, and so she'd sell him straight down the river again; and if she didn't everybody naturally despises an ungrateful nigger, and they'd make Jim feel it all the time, and so he'd feel ornery and disgraced. And then think of *me!* It would get all around, that Huck Finn helped a nigger to get his freedom; and if I was to ever see anybody from that town again, I'd be ready to get down and lick his boots for shame. That's just the way: a person does a low-down thing, and then he don't want to take no consequences of it. Thinks as long as he can hide it, it ain't no disgrace. That was my fix exactly. The more I studied about this, the more my conscience went to grinding me, and the more wicked and low-down and ornery I got to feeling. And at last, when it hit me all of a sudden that here was the plain hand of Providence slapping me in the face and letting me know my wickedness was being watched all the time from up there in heaven, whilst I was stealing a poor old woman's nigger that hadn't ever done me no harm, and now was showing me there's One that's always on the lookout, and ain't agoing to allow no such miserable doings to go only just so fur and no further, I most dropped in my tracks I was so scared. Well, I tried the best I could to kinder soften it up somehow for myself, by saying I was brung up wicked, and so I warn't so much to blame; but something inside of me kept saying, "There was the Sunday school, you could a gone to it; and if you'd a done it they'd a learnt you, there, that people that acts as I'd been acting about that nigger goes to everlasting fire."

It made me shiver. And I about made up my mind to pray; and see if I couldn't try to quit being the kind of a boy I was, and be better. So I kneeled down. But the words wouldn't come. Why wouldn't they? It warn't no use to try and hide it from Him. Nor from *me,* neither. I knowed very well why they wouldn't come. It was because my heart warn't right; it was because I warn't square; it was because I was playing double. I was letting *on* to give up sin, but away inside of me I was holding to the biggest one of all. I was trying to make my mouth *say* I would do the right thing and the clean thing, and go and write to that nigger's owner and tell where he was; but deep down in me I knowed it was a lie—and He knowed it. You can't pray a lie—I found that out.

So I was full of trouble, full as I could be; and didn't know what to do. At last I had an idea; and I says, I'll go and write the letter—and *then* see if I can pray. Why, it was astonishing, the way I felt as light as a feather, right straight off, and my troubles all gone. So I got a piece of paper and a pencil, all glad and excited, and set down and wrote:

> Miss Watson your runaway nigger Jim is down here two mile below Pikesville and Mr. Phelps has got him and he will give him up for the reward if you send.
>
> HUCK FINN.

I felt good and all washed clean of sin for the first time I had ever felt so in my life, and I knowed I could pray now. But I didn't do it straight off, but laid the paper down and set there thinking—thinking how good it was all this happened so, and how near I come to being lost and going to hell. And went on thinking. And got to thinking over our trip down the river; and I see Jim before me, all the time, in the day, and in the night-time, sometimes moonlight, sometimes storms, and we a floating along, talking, and singing, and laughing. But somehow I couldn't seem to strike no places to harden me against him, but only the other kind. I'd see him standing my watch on top of his'n, stead of calling me, so I could go on sleeping; and see him how glad he was when I come back out of the fog; and when I come to him again in the swamp, up there where the feud was; and such-like times; and would always call me honey, and pet me, and do everything he could think of for me, and how good he always was; and at last I struck the time I saved him by telling the men we had small-pox aboard, and he was so grateful, and said I was the best friend ole Jim ever had in the world, and the *only* one he's got now; and then I happened to look around, and see that paper.

It was a close place. I took it up, and held it in my hand. I was a trembling, because I'd got to decide, forever, betwixt two things, and I knowed it. I studied a minute, sort of holding my breath, and then says to myself:

"All right, then, I'll *go* to hell"—and tore it up.

It was awful thoughts, and awful words, but they was said. And I let them stay said; and never thought no more about reforming. I shoved the whole thing out of my head; and said I would take up wickedness again, which was in my line, being brung up to it, and the other warn't. And for a starter, I would go to work and steal Jim out of slavery again; and if I could think up anything worse, I would do that, too; because as long as I was in, and in for good, I might as well go the whole hog.

Then I set to thinking over how to get at it, and turned over considerable many things in my mind; and at last fixed up a plan that suited me. So then I took the bearings of a woody island that was down the river a piece, and as soon as it was fairly dark I crept out with my raft and went for it, and hid it there, and then turned in. I slept the night through, and got up before it was light, and had my breakfast, and put on my store clothes, and tied up some others and one thing or another in a bundle, and took the canoe and cleared for shore. I landed below where I judged was Phelps's place, and hid my bundle in the woods, and then filled up the canoe with water, and loaded rocks into her and sunk her where I could find her again when I wanted her, about a quarter of a mile below a little steam sawmill that was on the bank.

Then I struck up the road, and when I passed the mill I see a sign on it, "Phelps's Sawmill," and when I come to the farm-houses, two or three hundred yards further along, I kept my eyes peeled, but didn't see nobody around, though it was good daylight, now. But I didn't mind, because I didn't want to see nobody just yet—I only wanted to get the lay of the land. According to my plan, I was going to turn up there from the village, not from below. So I just took a look, and shoved along, straight for town. Well, the very first man I see, when I got there, was the duke. He was sticking up a bill for the Royal Nonesuch—three-night performance—like that other time. *They* had the cheek, them frauds! I was right on him, before I could shirk. He looked astonished, and says:

"Hel-*lo!* Where'd *you* come from?" Then he says, kind of glad and eager, "Where's the raft?—got her in a good place?"

I says:

"Why, that's just what I was agoing to ask your grace."

Then he didn't look so joyful—and says:

"What was your idea for asking *me?*" he says.

"Well," I says, "when I see the king in that doggery yesterday, I says to myself, we can't get him home for hours, till he's soberer; so I went a loafing around town to put in the time, and wait. A man up and offered me ten cents to help him pull a skiff over the river and back to fetch a sheep, and so I went along; but when we was dragging him to the boat, and the man left me aholt of the rope and went behind him to shove him along, he was too strong for me, and jerked loose and run, and we after him. We didn't have no dog, and so we had to chase him all over the country till we tired him out. We never got him till dark, then we fetched him over, and I started down for the raft. When I got there and see it was gone, I says to myself, 'they've got into trouble and had to leave; and they've took my nigger, which is the only nigger I've got in the world, and now I'm in a strange country, and ain't got no property no more, nor nothing, and no way to make my living;' so I set down and cried. I slept in the woods all night. But what *did* become of the raft then?—and Jim, poor Jim!"

"Blamed if *I* know—that is, what's become of the raft. That old fool had made a trade and got forty dollars, and when we found him in the doggery the loafers had matched half dollars with him and got every cent but what he'd spent for whisky; and when I got him home late last night and found the raft gone, we said, 'That little rascal has stole our raft and shook us, and run off down the river.' "

"I wouldn't shake my *nigger,* would I?—the only nigger I had in the world, and the only property."

"We never thought of that. Fact is, I reckon we'd come to consider him *our* nigger; yes, we did consider him so—goodness knows we had trouble enough for him. So when we see the raft was gone, and we flat broke, there warn't anything for it but to try the Royal Nonesuch another shake. And I've pegged along ever since, dry as a powder-horn. Where's that ten cents? Give it here."

I had considerable money, so I give him ten cents, but begged him to spend it for something to eat, and give me some, because it was all the money I had, and I hadn't had nothing to eat since yesterday. He never said nothing. The next minute he whirls on me and says:

"Do you reckon that nigger would blow on us? We'd skin him if he done that!"

"How can he blow? Hain't he run off?"

"No! That old fool sold him, and never divided with me, and the money's gone."

"*Sold* him?" I says, and begun to cry; "why, he was *my* nigger, and that was my money. Where is he?—I want my nigger."

"Well, you can't *get* your nigger, that's all—so dry up your blubbering. Looky here—do you think *you'd* venture to blow on us? Blamed if I think I'd trust you. Why, if you *was* to blow on us——"

He stopped, but I never see the duke look so ugly out of his eyes before. I went on a-whimpering, and says:

"I don't want to blow on nobody; and I ain't got no time to blow, nohow. I got to turn out and find my nigger."

He looked kinder bothered, and stood there with his bills fluttering on his arm, thinking, and wrinkling up his forehead. At last he says:

"I'll tell you something. We got to be here three days. If you'll promise you won't blow, and won't let the nigger blow, I'll tell you where to find him."

So I promised, and he says:

"A farmer by the name of Silas Ph——" and then he stopped. You see he started to tell me the truth; but when he stopped, that way, and begun to study and think again, I reckoned he was changing his mind. And so he was. He wouldn't trust me; he wanted to make sure of having me out of the way the whole three days. So pretty soon he says: "The man that bought him is named Abram Foster—Abram G. Foster—and he lives forty mile back here in the country, on the road to Lafayette."

"All right," I says, "I can walk it in three days. And I'll start this very afternoon."

"No you won't, you'll start *now;* and don't you lose any time about it, neither, nor do any gabbling by the way. Just keep a tight tongue in your head and move right along, and then you won't get into trouble with *us,* d'ye hear?"

That was the order I wanted, and that was the one I played for. I wanted to be left free to work my plans.

"So clear out," he says; "and you can tell Mr. Foster whatever you want to. Maybe you can get him to believe that Jim *is* your nigger—some idiots don't require documents—leastways I've heard there's such down South here. And when you tell him the handbill and the reward's bogus, maybe he'll believe you when you explain to him what the idea was for getting 'em out. Go 'long, now, and tell him anything you want to; but mind you don't work your jaw any *between* here and there."

So I left, and struck for the back country. I didn't look around, but I kinder felt like he was watching me. But I knowed I could tire him out at that. I went straight out in the country as much as a mile, before I stopped; then I doubled back through the woods towards Phelps's. I reckoned I better start in on my plan straight off, without fooling around, because I wanted to stop Jim's mouth till these fellows could get away. I didn't want no trouble with their kind. I'd seen all I wanted to of them, and wanted to get entirely shut of them.

CHAPTER XXXII

When I got there it was still and Sunday-like, and hot and sunshiny—the hands was gone to the fields; and there was them kind of faint dronings of bugs and flies in the air that makes it seem so lonesome and like everybody's dead and gone; and if a breeze fans along and quivers the leaves, it makes you feel mournful, because you feel like it's spirits whispering—spirits that's been dead ever so many years—and you always think they're talking about *you.* As a general thing it makes a body wish *he* was dead, too, and done with it all.

Phelps's was one of these little one-horse cotton plantations; and they all look alike. A rail fence round a two-acre yard; a stile, made out of logs sawed off and up-ended, in steps, like barrels of a different length, to climb over the fence with, and for the women to stand on when they are going to jump onto a horse; some sickly grass-patches in the big yard, but mostly it was bare and smooth, like an old hat with the nap rubbed off; big double log house for the white folks—hewed logs, with the chinks stopped up with mud or mortar, and these mud-stripes been whitewashed some time or another; round-log kitchen, with a big broad, open but roofed passage joining it to the house; log smoke-house back of the kitchen; three little log nigger-cabins in a row t'other side the smoke-house; one little hut all by itself away down against the back fence, and some out-buildings down a piece the other side; ash-hopper,[1] and big kettle to bile soap in, by the little hut; bench by the kitchen door, with bucket of water and a gourd; hound asleep there, in the sun; more hounds asleep, round about; about three shade-trees away off in a corner; some currant bushes and gooseberry bushes in one place by the fence; outside of the fence a garden and a water-melon patch; then the cotton fields begins; and after the fields, the woods.

I went around and clumb over the back stile by the ash-hopper, and started for the kitchen. When I got a little ways, I heard the dim hum of a spinning-wheel wailing along up and sinking along down again; and then I knowed for certain I wished I was dead—for that *is* the lonesomest sound in the whole world.

I went right along, not fixing up any particular plan, but just trusting to Providence to put the right words in my mouth when the time come; for I'd noticed that Providence always did put the right words in my mouth, if I left it alone.

When I got half-way, first one hound and then another got up and went for me, and of course I stopped and faced them, and kept still. And such another pow-wow as they made! In a quarter of a minute I was a kind of a hub of a wheel, as you may say—spokes made out of dogs—circle of fifteen of them packed together around me, with their necks and noses stretched up towards me, a barking and howling; and more a coming; you see them sailing over fences and around corners from everywheres.

A nigger woman come tearing out of the kitchen with a rolling-pin in her hand, singing out, "Begone! *you* Tige! you Spot! begon sah!" and she fetched first one and then another of them a clip and sent him howling, and then the rest followed; and the next second, half of them come back, wagging their tails around me and making friends with me. There ain't no harm in a hound, nohow.

And behind the woman comes a little nigger girl and two little nigger boys, without anything on but tow-linen shirts, and they hung onto their mother's gown, and peeped out from behind her at me, bashful, the way they always do. And here comes the white woman running from the house, about forty-five or fifty year old, bareheaded, and her spinning-stick in her hand; and behind her comes her little white children, acting the same way the little niggers was doing. She was smiling all over so she could hardly stand—and says: "It's *you,* at last!—*ain't* it?"

I out with a "Yes'm," before I thought.

She grabbed me and hugged me tight; and then gripped me by both hands and shook and shook; and the tears come in her eyes, and run down over; and she couldn't seem to hug and shake enough, and kept saying, "You

[1]A bin for the fireplace ashes from which lye was extracted for use in making soap.

don't look as much like your mother as I reckoned you would, but law sakes, I don't care for that, I'm *so* glad to see you! Dear, dear, it does seem like I could eat you up! Children, it's your cousin Tom!—tell him howdy."

But they ducked their heads, and put their fingers in their mouths, and hid behind her. So she run on:

"Lize, hurry up and get him a hot breakfast, right away—or did you get your breakfast on the boat?"

I said I had got it on the boat. So then she started for the house, leading me by the hand, and the children tagging after. When we got there, she set me down in a split-bottomed chair, and set herself down on a little low stool in front of me, holding both of my hands, and says:

"Now I can have a *good* look at you; and laws-a-me, I've been hungry for it a many and a many a time, all these long years, and it's come at last! We been expecting you a couple of days and more. What's kep' you?—boat get aground?"

"Yes'm—she——"

"Don't say yes'm—say Aunt Sally. Where'd she get aground?"

I didn't rightly know what to say, because I didn't know whether the boat would be coming up the river or down. But I go a good deal on instinct; and my instinct said she would be coming up—from down towards Orleans. That didn't help me much, though; for I didn't know the names of bars down that way. I see I'd got to invent a bar, or forget the name of the one we got aground on—or—Now I struck an idea, and fetched it out:

"It warn't the grounding—that didn't keep us back but a little. We blowed out a cylinder-head."

"Good gracious! anybody hurt?"

"No'm. Killed a nigger."

"Well, it's lucky; because sometimes people do get hurt. Two years ago last Christmas, your uncle Silas was coming up from Newrleans on the old *Lally Rook,*[2] and she blowed out a cylinder-head and crippled a man. And I think he died afterwards. He was a Babtist. Your uncle Silas knowed a family in Baton Rouge that knowed his people very well. Yes, I remember, now he *did* die. Mortification[3] set in, and they had to amputate him. But it didn't save him. Yes, it was mortification—that was it. He turned blue all over, and died in the hope of a glorious resurrection. They say he was a sight to look at. Your uncle's been up to the town every day to fetch you. And he's gone again, not more'n an hour ago; he'll be back any minute, now. You must a met him on the road, didn't you?—oldish man, with a——"

"No, I didn't see nobody, Aunt Sally. The boat landed just at daylight, and I left my baggage on the wharf-boat[4] and went looking around the town and out a piece in the country, to put in the time and not get here too soon; and so I come down the back way."

"Who'd you give the baggage to?"

"Nobody."

"Why, child, it'll be stole!"

"Not where *I* hid it I reckon it won't," I says.

[2]Named for the beautiful princess in *Lalla Rookh* (1817), a series of Oriental tales by the English poet Thomas Moore (1779–1852).

[3]Gangrene. [4]A floating dock or landing platform.

"How'd you get your breakfast so early on the boat?"

It was kinder thin ice, but I says:

"The captain see me standing around, and told me I better have something to eat before I went ashore; so he took me in the texas to the officers' lunch,[5] and give me all I wanted."

I was getting so uneasy I couldn't listen good. I had my mind on the children all the time; I wanted to get them out to one side, and pump them a little, and find out who I was. But I couldn't get no show, Mrs. Phelps kept it up and run on so. Pretty soon she made the cold chills streak all down my back, because she says:

"But here we're a running on this way, and you hain't told me a word about Sis, nor any of them. Now I'll rest my works a little, and you start up yourn; just tell me *everything*—tell me all about 'm all—every one of 'm; and how they are, and what they're doing, and what they told you to tell me; and every last thing you can think of."

Well, I see I was up a stump—and up it good. Providence had stood by me this fur, all right, but I was hard and tight aground, now. I see it warn't a bit of use to try to go ahead—I'd *got* to throw up my hand. So I says to myself, here's another place where I got to resk the truth. I opened my mouth to begin; but she grabbed me and hustled me in behind the bed, and says:

"Here he comes! stick your head down lower—there, that'll do; you can't be seen, now. Don't you let on you're here. I'll play a joke on him. Children, don't you say a word."

I see I was in a fix, now. But it warn't no use to worry; there warn't nothing to do but just hold still, and try and be ready to stand from under when the lightning struck.

I had just one little glimpse of the old gentleman when he come in, then the bed hid him. Mrs. Phelps she jumps for him and says:

"Has he come?"

"No," says her husband.

"Good-*ness* gracious!" she says, "what in the world *can* have become of him?"

"I can't imagine," says the old gentleman; "and I must say, it makes me dreadful uneasy."

"Uneasy!" she says, "I'm ready to go distracted! He *must* a come; and you've missed him along the road. I *know* it's so—something *tells* me so."

"Why Sally, I *couldn't* miss him along the road—*you* know that."

"But oh, dear, dear, what *will* Sis say! He must a come! You must a missed him. He—"

"Oh, don't distress me any more'n I'm already distressed. I don't know what in the world to make of it. I'm at my wit's end, and I don't mind acknowledging 't I'm right down scared. But there's no hope that he's come; for he *couldn't* come and me miss him. Sally, it's terrible—just terrible—something's happened to the boat, sure!"

"Why, Silas! Look yonder!—up the road!—ain't that somebody coming?"

He sprung to the window at the head of the bed, and that give Mrs. Phelps the chance she wanted. She stooped down quick, at the foot of the bed, and give me a pull, and out I come; and when he turned back from the window,

[5] Mess, eating room.

there she stood, a-beaming and a-smiling like a house afire, and I standing pretty meek and sweaty alongside. The old gentleman stared, and says:

"Why, who's that?"

"Who do you reckon 't is?"

"I hain't no idea. Who *is* it?"

"It's *Tom Sawyer!*"

By jings, I most slumped through the floor. But there warn't no time to swap knives;[6] the old man grabbed me by the hand and shook, and kept on shaking; and all the time, how the woman did dance around and laugh and cry; and then how they both did fire off questions about Sid, Mary, and the rest of the tribe.

But if they was joyful, it warn't nothing to what I was; for it was like being born again, I was so glad to find out who I was. Well, they froze to me for two hours; and at last when my chin was so tired it couldn't hardly go, any more, I had told them more about my family—I mean the Sawyer family—than ever happened to any six Sawyer families. And I explained all about how we blowed out a cylinder-head at the mouth of White River and it took us three days to fix it. Which was all right, and worked first rate; because *they* didn't know but what it would take three days to fix it. If I'd a called it a bolt-head it would a done just as well.

Now I was feeling pretty comfortable all down one side, and pretty uncomfortable all up the other. Being Tom Sawyer was easy and comfortable; and it stayed easy and comfortable till by-and-by I hear a steamboat coughing along down the river—then I says to myself, spose Tom Sawyer come down on that boat?—and spose he steps in here, any minute, and sings out my name before I can throw him a wink to keep quiet? Well, I couldn't *have* it that way—it wouldn't do at all. I must go up the road and waylay him. So I told the folks I reckoned I would go up to the town and fetch down my baggage. The old gentleman was for going along with me, but I said no, I could drive the horse myself, and I druther he wouldn't take no trouble about me.

CHAPTER XXXIII

So I started for town, in the wagon, and when I was half-way I see a wagon coming, and sure enough it was Tom Sawyer, and I stopped and waited till he come along. I says "Hold on!" and it stopped alongside, and his mouth opened up like a trunk, and staid so; and he swallowed two or three times like a person that's got a dry throat, and then says:

"I hain't ever done you no harm. You know that. So then, what you want to come back and ha'nt *me* for?"

I says:

"I hain't come back—I hain't *gone*."

When he heard my voice, it righted him up some, but he warn't quite satisfied yet. He says:

"Don't you play nothing on me, because I wouldn't on you. Honest injun, now, you ain't a ghost?"

"Honest injun, I ain't," I says.

[6] I.e., to change plans.

"Well—I—I—well, that ought to settle it, of course; but I can't somehow seem to understand it, no way. Looky here, warn't you ever murdered at *all?*"

"No. I warn't ever murdered at all—I played it on them. You come in here and feel of me if you don't believe me."

So he done it; and it satisfied him; and he was that glad to see me again, he didn't know what to do. And he wanted to know all about it right off; because it was a grand adventure, and mysterious, and so it hit him where he lived. But I said, leave it alone till by-and-by; and told his driver to wait, and we drove off a little piece, and I told him the kind of a fix I was in, and what did he reckon we better do? He said, let him alone a minute, and don't disturb him. So he thought and thought, and pretty soon he says:

"It's all right, I've got it. Take my trunk in your wagon, and let on it's your'n; and you turn back and fool along slow, so as to get to the house about the time you ought to; and I'll go towards town a piece, and take a fresh start, and get there a quarter or a half an hour after you; and you needn't let on to know me, at first."

I says:

"All right; but wait a minute. There's one more thing—a thing that *nobody* don't know but me. And that is, there's a nigger here that I'm a trying to steal out of slavery—and his name is *Jim*—old Miss Watson's Jim."

He says:

"What! Why Jim is——"

He stopped and went to studying. I says:

"*I* know what you'll say. You'll say it's dirty low-down business; but what if it is?—*I*'m low down; and I'm agoing to steal him, and I want you to keep mum and not let on. Will you?"

His eye lit up, and he says:

"I'll *help* you steal him!"

Well, I let go all holts then, like I was shot. It was the most astonishing speech I ever heard—and I'm bound to say Tom Sawyer fell, considerable, in my estimation. Only I couldn't believe it. Tom Sawyer a *nigger stealer!*

"Oh, shucks," I says, "you're joking."

"I ain't joking, either."

"Well, then," I says, "joking or no joking, if you hear anything said about a runaway nigger, don't forget to remember that *you* don't know nothing about him, and *I* don't know nothing about him."

Then we took the trunk and put it in my wagon, and he drove off his way, and I drove mine. But of course I forgot all about driving slow, on accounts of being glad and full of thinking; so I got home a heap too quick for that length of a trip. The old gentleman was at the door, and he says:

"Why, this is wonderful. Who ever would a thought it was in that mare to do it. I wish we'd a timed her. And she hain't sweated a hair—not a hair. It's wonderful. Why, I wouldn't take a hundred dollars for that horse now; I wouldn't, honest; and yet I'd a sold her for fifteen before, and thought 'twas all she was worth."

That's all he said. He was the innocentest, best old soul I ever see. But it warn't surprising; because he warn't only just a farmer, he was a preacher, too, and had a little one-horse log church down back of the plantation, which he built it himself at his own expense, for a church and school-house, and never charged nothing for his preaching, and it was worth it, too. There was plenty other farmer-preachers like that, and done the same way, down South.

In about half an hour Tom's wagon drove up to the front stile, and Aunt Sally she see it through the window because it was only about fifty yards, and says:

"Why, there's somebody come! I wonder who 'tis? Why, I do believe it's a stranger. Jimmy" (that's one of the children), "run and tell Lize to put on another plate for dinner."

Everybody made a rush for the front door, because, of course, a stranger don't come *every* year, and so he lays over the yaller fever, for interest, when he does come. Tom was over the stile and starting for the house; the wagon was spinning up the road for the village, and we was all bunched in the front door. Tom had his store clothes on, and an audience—and that was always nuts for Tom Sawyer. In them circumstances it warn't no trouble to him to throw in an amount of style that was suitable. He warn't a boy to meeky[1] along up that yard like a sheep; no, he come ca'm and important, like the ram. When he got afront of us, he lifts his hat ever so gracious and dainty, like it was the lid of a box that had butterflies asleep in it and he didn't want to disturb them, and says:

"Mr. Archibald Nichols, I presume?"

"No, my boy," says the old gentleman, "I'm sorry to say't your driver has deceived you; Nichols's place is down a matter of three mile more. Come in, come in."

Tom he took a look back over his shoulder, and says, "Too late—he's out of sight."

"Yes, he's gone, my son, and you must come in and eat your dinner with us; and then we'll hitch up and take you down to Nichols's."

"Oh, I *can't* make you so much trouble; I couldn't think of it. I'll walk—I don't mind the distance."

"But we won't *let* you walk—it wouldn't be Southern hospitality to do it. Come right in."

"Oh, *do*," says Aunt Sally; "it ain't a bit of trouble to us, not a bit in the world. You *must* stay. It's a long, dusty three mile, and we *can't* let you walk. And besides, I've already told 'em to put on another plate, when I see you coming; so you mustn't disappoint us. Come right in, and make yourself at home."

So Tom he thanked them very hearty and handsome, and let himself be persuaded, and come in; and when he was in, he said he was a stranger from Hicksville, Ohio, and his name was William Thompson—and he made another bow.

Well, he run on, and on, and on, making up stuff about Hicksville and everybody in it he could invent, and I getting a little nervous, and wondering how this was going to help me out of my scrape: and at last, still talking along, he reached over and kissed Aunt Sally right on the mouth, and then settled back again in his chair, comfortable, and was going on talking; but she jumped up and wiped it off with the back of her hand, and says:

"You owdacious puppy!"

He looked kind of hurt, and says:

[1]Come meekly.

"I'm surprised at you, m'am."

"You're s'rp— Why, what do you reckin *I* am? I've a good notion to take and—say, what do you mean by kissing me?"

He looked kind of humble, and says:

"I didn't mean nothing, m'am. I didn't mean no harm. I—I—thought you'd like it."

"Why, you born fool!" She took up the spinning-stick, and it looked like it was all she could do to keep from giving him a crack with it. "What made you think I'd like it?"

"Well, I don't know. Only, they—they—told me you would."

"*They* told you I would. Whoever told you's *another* lunatic. I never heard the beat of it. Who's *they?*"

"Why—everybody. They all said so, m'am."

It was all she could do to hold in; and her eyes snapped, and her fingers worked like she wanted to scratch him; and she says:

"Who's 'everybody?' Out with their names—or ther'll be an idiot short."

He got up and looked distressed, and fumbled his hat, and says:

"I'm sorry, and I warn't expecting it. They told me to. They all told me to. They all said kiss her; and said she'll like it. They all said it—every one of them. But I'm sorry, m'am, and I won't do it no more—I won't, honest."

"You won't, won't you? Well, I sh'd *reckon* you won't!"

"No'm, I'm honest about it; I won't ever do it again. Till you ask me."

"Till I *ask* you! Well, I never see the beat of it in my born days! I lay you'll be the Methusalem-numskull[2] of creation before ever *I* ask you—or the likes of you."

"Well," he says "it does surprise me so. I can't make it out, somehow. They said you would, and I thought you would. But—" He stopped and looked around slow, like he wished he could run across a friendly eye, somewhere's; and fetched up on the old gentleman's, and says, "Didn't *you* think she'd like me to kiss her, sir?"

"Why, no, I—I—well, no, I b'lieve I didn't."

Then he looks on around, the same way, to me—and says:

"Tom, didn't *you* think Aunt Sally 'd open out her arms and say, 'Sid Sawyer——'"

"My land!" she says, breaking in and jumping for him, "you impudent young rascal, to fool a body so—" and was going to hug him, but he fended her off, and says:

"No, not till you've asked me, first."

So she didn't lose no time, but asked him; and hugged him and kissed him, over and over again, and then turned him over to the old man, and he took what was left. And after they got a little quiet again, she says:

"Why, dear me, I never see such a surprise. We warn't looking for *you,* at all, but only Tom. Sis never wrote to me about anybody coming but him."

"It's because it warn't *intended* for any of us to come but Tom," he says; "but I begged and begged, and at the last minute she let me come, too; so coming down the river, me and Tom thought it would be a first-rate surprise for him to come here to the house first, and for me to by-and-by tag along and drop

[2]I.e., a numbskull as old as Methuselah, the Biblical patriarch said to have lived 969 years (Genesis 5:27).

in and let on to be a stranger. But it was a mistake, Aunt Sally. This ain't no healthy place for a stranger to come."

"No—not impudent whelps, Sid. You ought to had your jaws boxed; I hain't been so put out since I don't know when. But I don't care, I don't mind the terms—I'd be willing to stand a thousand such jokes to have you here. Well, to think of that performance! I don't deny it, I was most putrified[3] with astonishment when you give me that smack."

We had dinner out in that broad open passage betwixt the house and the kitchen; and there was things enough on that table for seven families—and all hot, too; none of your flabby tough meat that's laid in a cupboard in a damp cellar all night and tastes like a hunk of old cold cannibal in the morning. Uncle Silas he asked a pretty long blessing over it, but it was worth it; and it didn't cool it a bit, neither, the way I've seen them kind of interruptions do, lots of times.

There was a considerable good deal of talk, all the afternoon, and me and Tom was on the lookout all the time, but it warn't no use, they didn't happen to say nothing about any runaway nigger, and we was afraid to try to work up to it. But at supper, at night, one of the little boys says:

"Pa, mayn't Tom and Sid and me go to the show?"

"No," says the old man, "I reckon there ain't going to be any; and you couldn't go if there was; because the runaway nigger told Burton and me all about that scandalous show, and Burton said he would tell the people; so I reckon they've drove the owdacious loafers out of town before this time."

So there it was!—but *I* couldn't help it. Tom and me was to sleep in the same room and bed; so, being tired, we bid good-night and went up to bed, right after supper, and clumb out of the window and down the lightning-rod, and shoved for the town; for I didn't believe anybody was going to give the king and the duke a hint, and so, if I didn't hurry up and give them one they'd get into trouble sure.

On the road Tom he told me all about how it was reckoned I was murdered, and how pap disappeared, pretty soon, and didn't come back no more, and what a stir there was when Jim run away; and I told Tom all about our Royal Nonesuch rapscallions, and as much of the raft-voyage as I had time to; and as we struck into the town and up through the middle of it—it was as much as half-after eight, then—here comes a raging rush of people, with torches, and an awful whooping and yelling, and banging tin pans and blowing horns; and we jumped to one side to let them go by; and as they went by, I see they had the king and the duke astraddle of a rail—that is, I knowed it *was* the king and the duke, though they was all over tar and feathers, and didn't look like nothing in the world that was human—just looked like a couple of monstrous big soldier-plumes.[4] Well, it made me sick to see it; and I was sorry for them poor pitiful rascals, it seemed like I couldn't ever feel any hardness against them any more in the world. It was a dreadful thing to see. Human beings *can* be awful cruel to one another.

We see we was too late—couldn't do no good. We asked some straggler about it, and they said everybody went to the show looking very innocent; and laid low and kept dark till the poor old king was in the middle of his

[3]Petrified, turned to stone. [4]The decorative feathered crests on military headgear.

cavortings on the stage; then somebody give a signal, and the house rose up and went for them.

So we poked along back home, and I warn't feeling so brash as I was before, but kind of ornery, and humble, and to blame, somehow—though *I* hadn't done nothing. But that's always the way; it don't make no difference whether you do right or wrong, a person's conscience ain't got no sense, and just goes for him *anyway*. If I had a yaller dog that didn't know no more than a person's conscience does, I would pison him. It takes up more room than all the rest of a person's insides, and yet ain't no good, nohow. Tom Sawyer he says the same.

CHAPTER XXXIV

We stopped talking, and got to thinking. By-and-by Tom says:

"Looky here, Huck, what fools we are, to not think of it before! I bet I know where Jim is."

"No! Where?"

"In that hut down by the ash-hopper. Why, looky here. When we was at dinner, didn't you see a nigger man go in there with some vittles?"

"Yes."

"What did you think the vittles was for?"

"For a dog."

"So'd I. Well, it wasn't for a dog."

"Why?"

"Because part of it was watermelon."

"So it was—I noticed it. Well, it does beat all, that I never thought about a dog not eating watermelon. It shows how a body can see and don't see at the same time."

"Well, the nigger unlocked the padlock when he went in, and he locked it again when he come out. He fetched uncle a key, about the time we got up from table—same key, I bet. Watermelon shows man, lock shows prisoner; and it ain't likely there's two prisoners on such a little plantation, and where the people's all so kind and good. Jim's the prisoner. All right—I'm glad we found it out detective fashion; I wouldn't give shucks for any other way. Now you work your mind and study out a plan to steal Jim, and I will study out one, too; and we'll take the one we like the best."

What a head for just a boy to have! If I had Tom Sawyer's head, I wouldn't trade it off to be a duke, nor mate of a steamboat, nor clown in a circus, nor nothing I can think of. I went to thinking out a plan, but only just to be doing something; I knowed very well where the right plan was going to come from. Pretty soon, Tom says:

"Ready?"

"Yes," I says.

"All right—bring it out."

"My plan is this," I says. "We can easy find out if it's Jim in there. Then get up my canoe to-morrow night, and fetch my raft over from the island. Then the first dark night that comes, steal the key out of the old man's britches, after he goes to bed, and shove off down the river on the raft, with Jim, hiding day-times and running nights, the way me and Jim used to do before. Wouldn't that plan work?"

"*Work?* Why cert'nly, it would work, like rats a fighting. But it's too blame' simple; there ain't nothing *to* it. What's the good of a plan that ain't no more trouble than that? It's as mild as goosemilk. Why, Huck, it wouldn't make no more talk than breaking into a soap factory."

I never said nothing, because I warn't expecting nothing different; but I knowed mighty well that whenever he got *his* plan ready it wouldn't have none of them objections to it.

And it didn't. He told me what it was, and I see in a minute it was worth fifteen of mine, for style, and would make Jim just as free a man as mine would, and maybe get us all killed besides. So I was satisfied, and said we would waltz in on it. I needn't tell what it was, here, because I knowed it wouldn't stay the way it was. I knowed he would be changing it around, every which way, as we went along, and heaving in new bullinesses wherever he got a chance. And that is what he done.

Well, one thing was dead sure; and that was, that Tom Sawyer was in earnest and was actuly going to help steal that nigger out of slavery. That was the thing that was too many for me. Here was a boy that was respectable, and well brung up; and had a character to lose; and folks at home that had characters; and he was bright and not leather-headed; and knowing and not ignorant; and not mean but kind; and yet here he was, without any more pride, or rightness or feeling, than to stoop to this business, and make himself a shame and his family a shame, before everybody. I *couldn't* understand it no way at all. It was outrageous, and I knowed I ought to just up and tell him so; and so be his true friend, and let him quit the thing right where he was, and save himself. And I *did* start to tell him; but he shut me up, and says:

"Don't you reckon I know what I'm about? Don't I generly know what I'm about?"

"Yes."

"Didn't I *say* I was going to help steal the nigger?"

"Yes."

"*Well* then."

That's all he said, and that's all I said. It warn't no use to say any more; because when he said he'd do a thing, he always done it. But *I* couldn't make out how he was willing to go into this thing; so I just let it go, and never bothered no more about it. If he was bound to have it so, *I* couldn't help it.

When we got home, the house was all dark and still; so we went on down to the hut by the ash-hopper, for to examine it. We went through the yard, so as to see what the hounds would do. They knowed us, and didn't make no more noise than country dogs is always doing when anything comes by in the night. When we got to the cabin, we took a look at the front and the two sides; and on the side I warn't acquainted with—which was the north side—we found a square window-hole, up tolerable high, with just one stout board nailed across it. I says:

"Here's the ticket. This hole's big enough for Jim to get through, if we wrench off the board."

Tom says:

"It's as simple as tit-tat-toe, three-in-a-row, and as easy as playing hooky. I should *hope* we can find a way that's a little more complicated than *that,* Huck Finn."

"Well, then," I says, "how'll it do to saw him out, the way I done before I was murdered, that time?"

"That's more *like,*" he says. "It's real mysterious, and troublesome, and good," he says; "but I bet we can find a way that's twice as long. There ain't no hurry; le's keep on looking around."

Betwixt the hut and the fence, on the back side, was a lean-to, that joined the hut at the eaves, and was made out of plank. It was as long as the hut, but narrow—only about six foot wide. The door to it was at the south end, and was padlocked. Tom he went to the soap kettle, and searched around and fetched back the iron thing they lift the lid with; so he took it and prized out one of the staples. The chain fell down, and we opened the door and went in, and shut it, and struck a match, and see the shed was only built against the cabin and hadn't no connection with it; and there warn't no floor to the shed, nor nothing in it but some old rusty played-out hoes, and spades, and picks, and a crippled plow. The match went out, and so did we, and shoved in the staple again, and the door was locked as good as ever. Tom was joyful. He says:

"Now we're all right. We'll *dig* him out. It'll take about a week!"

Then we started for the house, and I went in the back door—you only have to pull a buckskin latch-string, they don't fasten the doors—but that warn't romantical enough for Tom Sawyer: no way would do him but he must climb up the lightning-rod. But after he got up half-way about three times, and missed fire and fell every time, and the last time most busted his brains out, he thought he'd got to give it up; but after he was rested, he allowed he would give her one more turn for luck, and this time he made the trip.

In the morning we was up at break of day, and down to the nigger cabins to pet the dogs and make friends with the nigger that fed Jim—if it *was* Jim that was being fed. The niggers was just getting through breakfast and starting for the fields; and Jim's nigger was piling up a tin pan with bread and meat and things; and whilst the others was leaving, the key come from the house.

This nigger had a good-natured, chuckle-headed face, and his wool was all tied up in little bunches with thread. That was to keep witches off. He said the witches was pestering him awful, these nights, and making him see all kinds of strange things, and hear all kinds of strange words and noises, and he didn't believe he was ever witched so long, before, in his life. He got so worked up, and got to running on so about his troubles, he forgot all about what he'd been agoing to do. So Tom says:

"What's the vittles for? Going to feed the dogs?"

The nigger kind of smiled around graduly over his face, like when you heave a brickbat[1] in a mud puddle, and he says:

"Yes, Mars Sid, *a* dog. Cur'us dog, too. Does you want to go en look at 'im?"

"Yes."

I hunched Tom, and whispers:

"You going, right here in the day-break? *That* warn't the plan."

"No, it warn't—but it's the plan *now.*"

[1]A piece of brick.

So, drat him, we went along, but I didn't like it much. When we got in, we couldn't hardly see anything, it was so dark; but Jim was there, sure enough, and could see us; and he sings out:

"Why, *Huck!* En good *lan'!* ain' dat Misto Tom?"

I just knowed how it would be; I just expected it. *I* didn't know nothing to do; and if I had, I couldn't a done it; because that nigger busted in and says:

"Why, de gracious sakes! do he know you genlmen?"

We could see pretty well, now. Tom he looked at the nigger, steady and kind of wondering, and says:

"Does *who* know us?"

"Why, dish-yer runaway nigger."

"I don't reckon he does; but what put that into your head?"

"What *put* it dar? Didn' he jis' dis minute sing out like he knowed you?"

Tom says, in a puzzle-up kind of way:

"Well, that's mighty curious. *Who* sung out? *When* did he sing out? *What* did he sing out?" And turns to me, perfectly ca'm, and says, "Did *you* hear anybody sing out?"

Of course there warn't nothing to be said but the one thing; so I says:

"No; *I* ain't heard nobody say nothing."

Then he turns to Jim, and looks him over like he never see him before; and says:

"Did you sing out?"

"No, sah," says Jim; "*I* hain't said nothing, sah."

"Not a word?"

"No, sah, I hain't said a word."

"Did you ever see us before?"

"No, sah; not as *I* knows on."

So Tom turns to the nigger, which was looking wild and distressed, and says, kind of severe:

"What do you reckon's the matter with you, anyway? What made you think somebody sung out?"

"Oh, it's de dad-blame' witches, sah, en I wisht I was dead, I do. Dey's awluz at it, sah, en dey do mos' kill me, dey sk'yers me so. Please to don't tell nobody 'bout it sah, er ole Mars Silas he'll scole me; 'kase he say dey *ain't* no witches. I jis' wish to goodness he was heah now—*den* what would he say! I jis' bet he couldn't fine no way to git aroun' it *dis* time. But it's awluz jis' so; people dat's *sot,* stays sot; dey won't look into nothn' en fine it out f'r dey-selves, en when *you* fine it out en tell um 'bout it, dey doan' b'lieve you."

Tom give him a dime, and said we wouldn't tell nobody; and told him to buy some more thread to tie up his wool with; and then looks at Jim, and says:

"I wonder if Uncle Silas is going to hang this nigger. If I was to catch a nigger that was ungrateful enough to run away, *I* wouldn't give him up, I'd hang him:" And whilst the nigger stepped to the door to look at the dime and bite it to see if it was good, he whispers to Jim, and says:

"Don't ever let on to know us. And if you hear any digging going on nights, it's us: we're going to set you free."

Jim only had time to grab us by the hand and squeeze it, then the nigger come back, and we said we'd come again some time if the nigger wanted us to; and he said he would, more particular if it was dark, because the witches went for him mostly in the dark, and it was good to have folks around then.

CHAPTER XXXV

It would be most an hour yet till breakfast, so we left, and struck down into the wood; because Tom said we got to have *some* light to see how to dig by, and a lantern makes too much, and might get us into trouble; what we must have was a lot of them rotten chunks that's called fox-fire[1] and just makes a soft kind of a glow when you lay them in a dark place. We fetched an armful and hid it in the weeds, and set down to rest, and Tom says, kind of dissatisfied:

"Blame it, this whole thing is just as easy and awkard as it can be. And so it makes it so rotten difficult to get up a difficult plan. There ain't no watchman to be drugged—now there *ought* to be a watchman. There ain't even a dog to give a sleeping-mixture to. And there's Jim chained by one leg, with a ten-foot chain, to the leg of his bed: why, all you got to do is to lift up the bedstead and slip off the chain. And Uncle Silas he trusts everybody; sends the key to the punkin-headed nigger, and don't send nobody to watch the nigger. Jim could a got out of that window hole before this, only there wouldn't be no use trying to travel with a ten-foot chain on his leg. Why, drat it, Huck, it's the stupidest arrangement I ever see. You got to invent *all* the difficulties. Well, we can't help it, we got to do the best we can with the materials we've got. Anyhow, there's one thing—there's more honor in getting him out through a lot of difficulties and dangers, where there warn't one of them furnished to you by the people who it was their duty to furnish them, and you had to contrive them all out of your own head. Now look at just that one thing of the lantern. When you come down to the cold facts, we simply got to *let on* that a lantern's resky. Why, we could work with a torchlight procession if we wanted to, I believe. Now, whilst I think of it, we got to hunt up something to make a saw out of, the first chance we get."

"What do we want of a saw?"

"What do we *want* of it? Hain't we got to saw the leg of Jim's bed off, so as to get the chain loose?"

"Why, you just said a body cold lift up the bedstead and slip the chain off."

"Well, if that ain't just like you, Huck Finn. You *can* get up the infant-schooliest[2] ways of going at a thing. Why, hain't you ever read any books at all?—Baron Trenck, nor Casanova, nor Benvenuto Chelleeny, nor Henri IV,[3] nor none of them heroes? Whoever heard of getting a prisoner loose in such an old-maidy way as that? No; the way all the best authorities does, is to saw the bed-leg in two, and leave it just so, and swallow the sawdust, so it can't be found, and put some dirt and grease around the sawed place so the very keenest seneskal[4] can't see no sign of it's being sawed, and thinks the bed-leg

[1]Luminous glow of fungi on rotting wood. [2]"Nursery-schooliest."

[3]Baron Friedrich von Trenck (1726–1794), Giovanni Giacomo Casanova (1725–1798), Benvenuto Cellini (1500–1571), Henry IV, King of France (1589–1610). All were adventurers who attempted daring escapes.

[4]Seneschal, an official in a medieval household, a steward.

is perfectly sound. Then, the night you're ready, fetch the leg a kick, down she goes; slip off your chain, and there you are. Nothing to do but hitch your rope-ladder to the battlements, shin down it, break your leg in the moat—because a rope-ladder is nineteen foot too short, you know—and there's your horses and your trusty vassles, and they scoop you up and fling you across a saddle and away you go, to your native Langudoc, or Navarre,[5] or wherever it is. It's gaudy, Huck. I wish there was a moat to this cabin. If we get time, the night of the escape, we'll dig one."

I says:

"What do we want of a moat, when we're going to snake him out from under the cabin?"

But he never heard me. He had forgot me and everything else. He had his chin in his hand, thinking. Pretty soon, he sighs, and shakes his head; then sighs again, and says:

"No, it wouldn't do—there ain't necessity enough for it."

"For what?" I says.

"Why, to saw Jim's leg off," he says.

"Good land!" I says, "why, there ain't *no* necessity for it. And what would you want to saw his leg off for, anyway?"

"Well, some of the best authorities has done it. They couldn't get the chain off, so they just cut their hand off, and shoved. And a leg would be better still. But we got to let that go. There ain't necessity enough in this case; and besides, Jim's a nigger and wouldn't understand the reasons for it, and how it's the custom in Europe; so we'll let it go. But there's one thing—he can have a rope-ladder; we can tear up our sheets and make him a rope-ladder easy enough. And we can send it to him in a pie; it's mostly done that way. And I've et worse pies."

"Why, Tom Sawyer, how you talk," I says; "Jim ain't got no use for a rope-ladder."

"He *has* got use for it. How *you* talk, you better say; you don't know nothing about it. He's *got* to have a rope-ladder; they all do."

"What in the nation can he *do* with it?"

"*Do* with it? He can hide it in his bed, can't he? That's what they all do; and *he's* got to, too. Huck, you don't ever seem to want to do anything that's regular; you want to be starting something fresh all the time. Spose he *don't* do nothing with it? ain't it there in his bed, for a clew, after he's gone? and don't you reckon they'll want clews? Of course they will. And you wouldn't leave them any? That would be a *pretty* howdy-do, *wouldn't* it! I never heard of such a thing."

"Well," I says, "if it's in the regulations, and he's got to have it, all right, let him have it; because I don't wish to go back on no regulations; but there's one thing, Tom Sawyer—if we go to tearing up our sheets to make Jim a rope-ladder, we're going to get into trouble with Aunt Sally, just as sure as you're born. Now, the way I look at it, a hickry-bark ladder don't cost nothing, and don't waste nothing, and is just as good to load up a pie with, and hide in a straw tick, as any rag ladder you can start; and as for Jim, he ain't had no experience, and so *he* don't care what kind of a——"

[5]Languedoc, a medieval province of southern France. Navarre, an ancient kingdom in the Pyrenees between France and Spain.

"Oh, shucks, Huck Finn, if I was as ignorant as you, I'd keep still—that's what *I'd* do. Who ever heard of a state prisoner escaping by a hickry-bark ladder? Why, it's perfectly ridiculous."

"Well, all right, Tom, fix it your own way; but if you'll take my advice, you'll let me borrow a sheet off of the clothes-line."

He said that would do. And that give him another idea, and he says:

"Borrow a shirt, too."

"What do we want of a shirt, Tom?"

"Want it for Jim to keep a journal on."

"Journal your granny—*Jim* can't write."

"Spose he *can't* write—he can make marks on the shirt, can't he, if we make him a pen out of an old pewter spoon or a piece of an old iron barrel-hoop?"

"Why, Tom, we can pull a feather out of a goose and make him a better one; and quicker, too."

"*Prisoners* don't have geese running around the donjon-keep to pull pens out of, you muggins. They *always* make their pens out of the hardest, toughest, troublesome piece of old brass candlestick or something like that they can get their hands on; and it takes them weeks and weeks, and months and months to file it out, too, because they've got to do it by rubbing it on the wall. *They* wouldn't use a goose-quill if they had it. It ain't regular."

"Well, then, what'll we make him the ink out of?"

"Many makes it out of iron-rust and tears; but that's the common sort and women; the best authorities uses their own blood. Jim can do that; and when he wants to send any little common ordinary mysterious message to let the world know where he's captivated, he can write it on the bottom of a tin plate with a fork and throw it out of the window. The Iron Mask[6] always done that, and it's a blame' good way, too."

"Jim ain't got no tin plates. They feed him in a pan."

"That ain't anything; we can get him some."

"Can't nobody *read* his plates."

"That ain't got nothing to *do* with it, Huck Finn. All *he's* got to do is write on the plate and throw it out. You don't *have* to be able to read it. Why, half the time you can't read anything a prisoner writes on a tin plate, or anywhere else."

"Well, then what's the sense in wasting the plates?"

"Why, blame it all, it ain't the *prisoner's* plates."

"But it's *somebody's* plates, ain't it?"

"Well, spos'n it is? What does the *prisoner* care whose——"

He broke off there, because we heard the breakfast-horn blowing. So we cleared out for the house.

Along during the morning I borrowed a sheet and a white shirt off of the clothes-line; and I found an old sack and put them in it, and we went down and got the fox-fire, and put that in too. I called it borrowing, because that was what pap always called it; but Tom said it warn't borrowing, it was stealing. He said we was representing prisoners; and prisoners don't care how

[6]The legendary masked prisoner in the Bastille who was a character in the romantic novel *Le Vicomte de Bragelonne* (1848–1850) by Alexandre Dumas (1802–1870). Portions of the novel were translated into English in the 1850s.

they get a thing so they get it, and nobody don't blame them for it, either. It ain't no crime in a prisoner to steal the thing he needs to get away with, Tom said; it's his right; and so, as long as we was representing a prisoner, we had a perfect right to steal anything on this place we had the least use for, to get ourselves out of prison with. He said if we warn't prisoners it would be a very different thing, and nobody but a mean ornery person would steal when he warn't a prisoner. So we allowed we would steal everything there was that come handy. And yet he made a mighty fuss, one day, after that, when I stole a watermelon out of the nigger patch[7] and eat it; and he made me go and give the niggers a dime, without telling them what it was for. Tom said that what he meant was, we could steal anything we *needed*. Well, I says, I needed the watermelon. But he said I didn't need it to get out of prison with, there's where the difference was. He said if I'd a wanted it to hide a knife in, and smuggle it to Jim to kill the seneskal with, it would a been all right. So I let it go at that, though I couldn't see no advantage in my representing a prisoner, if I got to set down and chaw over a lot of gold-leaf[8] distinctions like that, every time I see a chance to hog a watermelon.

Well, as I was saying, we waited that morning till everybody was settled down to business, and nobody in sight around the yard; then Tom he carried the sack into the lean-to whilst I stood off a piece to keep watch. By-and-by he come out, and we went and set down on the wood-pile, to talk. He says:

"Everything's all right, now, except tools; and that's easy fixed."

"Tools?" I says.

"Yes."

"Tools for what?"

"Why, to dig with. We ain't agoing to *gnaw* him out, are we?"

"Ain't them old crippled picks and things in there good enough to dig a nigger out with?" I says.

He turns on me looking pitying enough to make a body cry, and says:

"Huck Finn, did you *ever* hear of a prisoner having picks and shovels, and all the modern conveniences in his wardrobe to dig himself out with? Now I want to ask you—if you got any reasonableness in you at all—what kind of a show would *that* give him to be a hero? Why, they might as well lend him the key, and done with it. Picks and shovels—why they wouldn't furnish 'em to a king."

"Well, then," I says, "if we don't want the picks and shovels, what do we want?"

"A couple of case-knives."[9]

"To dig the foundations out from under that cabin with?"

"Yes."

"Confound it, it's foolish, Tom."

"It didn't make no difference how foolish it is, it's the *right* way—and it's the regular way. And there ain't no *other* way, that ever *I* heard of, and I've read all the books that gives any information about these things. They always dig out with a case-knife—and not through dirt, mind you; generly it's through solid rock. And it takes them weeks and weeks and weeks, and for ever and ever. Why, look at one of them prisoners in the bottom dungeon of

[7]Slaves' garden. [8]Thin, superficial. [9]Kitchen knives, kept in a case.

the Castle Deef,[10] in the harbor of Marseilles, that dug himself out that way; how long was *he* at it, you reckon?"

"I don't know."

"Well, guess."

"I don't know. A month and a half?"

"*Thirty-seven year*—and he come out in China. *That's* the kind. I wish the bottom of *this* fortress was solid rock."

"*Jim* don't know nobody in China."

"What's *that* got to do with it? Neither did that other fellow. But you're always a-wandering off on a side issue. Why can't you stick to the main point?"

"All right—*I* don't care where he comes out, so he *comes* out; and Jim don't, either, I reckon. But there's one thing, anyway—Jim's too old to be dug out with a case-knife. He won't last."

"Yes he will *last,* too. You don't reckon it's going to take thirty-seven years to dig out through a *dirt* foundation, do you?"

"How long will it take, Tom?"

"Well, we can't resk being as long as we ought to, because it mayn't take very long for Uncle Silas to hear from down there by New Orleans. He'll hear Jim ain't from there. Then his next move will be to advertise Jim, or something like that. So we can't resk being as long digging him out as we ought to. By rights I reckon we ought to be a couple of years; but we can't. Things being so uncertain, what I recommend is this: that we really dig right in, as quick as we can; and after that, we can *let on,* to ourselves, that we was at it thirty-seven years. Then we can snatch him out and rush him away the first time there's an alarm. Yes, I reckon that'll be the best way."

"Now, there's *sense* in that," I says. "Letting on don't cost nothing; letting on ain't no trouble; and if it's any object, I don't mind letting on we was at it a hundred and fifty year. It wouldn't strain me none, after I got my hand in. So I'll mosey along now, and smouch[11] a couple of case-knives."

"Smouch three," he says; "we want one to make a saw out of."

"Tom, if it ain't unregular and irreligious to sejest it," I says, "there's an old rusty saw-blade around yonder sticking under the weatherboarding behind the smoke-house."

He looked kind of weary and discouraged-like, and says:

"It ain't no use to try to learn you nothing, Huck. Run along and smouch the knives—three of them." So I done it.

CHAPTER XXXVI

As soon as we reckoned everybody was asleep, that night, we went down the lightning-rod, and shut ourselves up in the lean-to, and got out our pile of fox-fire, and went to work. We cleared everything out of the way, about four or five foot along the middle of the bottom log. Tom said he was right behind Jim's bed now, and we'd dig in under it, and when we got through there couldn't nobody in the cabin ever know there was any hole there, because

[10] The Chateau d'If, a prison in *The Count of Monte Cristo* (1845) by Alexandre Dumas.

[11] Steal.

Jim's counterpin[1] hung down most to the ground, and you'd have to raise it up and look under to see the hole. So we dug and dug, with the case-knives, till most midnight; and then we was dog-tired, and our hands was blistered, and yet you couldn't see we'd done anything, hardly. At last I says:

"This ain't no thirty-seven year job, this is a thirty-eight year job, Tom Sawyer."

He never said nothing. But he sighed, and pretty soon he stopped digging, and then for a good little while I knowed he was thinking. Then he says:

"It ain't no use, Huck, it ain't agoing to work. If we was prisoners it would, because then we'd have as many years as we wanted, and no hurry; and we wouldn't get but a few minutes to dig, every day, while they was changing watches, and so our hands wouldn't get blistered, and we could keep it up right along, year in and year out, and do it right; and the way it ought to be done. But *we* can't fool along, we got to rush; we ain't got no time to spare. If we was to put in another night this way, we'd have to knock off for a week to let our hands get well—couldn't touch a case-knife with them sooner."

"Well, then, what we going to do, Tom?"

"I'll tell you. It ain't right, and it ain't moral, and I wouldn't like it to get out—but there ain't only just the one way; we got to dig him out with the picks, and *let on* it's case-knives."

"*Now* you're *talking!*" I says; "your head gets leveler and leveler all the time, Tom Sawyer," I says. "Picks is the thing, moral or no moral; and as for me, I don't care shucks for the morality of it, nohow. When I start in to steal a nigger, or a watermelon, or a Sunday-school book, I ain't no ways particular how it's done so it's done. What I want is my nigger; or what I want is my watermelon; or what I want is my Sunday-school book; and if a pick's the handiest thing, that's the thing I'm agoing to dig that nigger or that watermelon or that Sunday-school book out with; and I don't give a dead rat what the authorities thinks about it nuther."

"Well," he says, "there's excuse for picks and letting-on in a case like this; if it warn't so, I wouldn't approve of it, nor I wouldn't stand by and see the rules broke—because right is right, and wrong is wrong, and a body ain't got no business doing wrong when he ain't ignorant and knows better. It might answer for *you* to dig Jim out with a pick, *without* any letting-on, because you don't know no better; but it wouldn't for me, because I do know better. Gimme a case-knife."

He had his own by him, but I handed him mine. He flung it down, and says:

"Gimme a *case-knife*."

I didn't know just what to do—but then I thought. I scratched around amongst the old tools, and got a pick-ax and give it to him, and he took it and went to work, and never said a word.

He was always just that particular. Full of principle.

So then I got a shovel, and then we picked and shoveled, turn about, and made the fur fly. We stuck to it about a half an hour, which was as long as we could stand up; but we had a good deal of a hole to show for it. When I got up stairs, I looked out at the window and see Tom doing his level best with

[1]Counterpane, bedspread.

the lightning-rod, but he couldn't come it, his hands was so sore. At last he says:

"It ain't no use, it can't be done. What you reckon I better do? Can't you think up no way?"

"Yes," I says, "but I reckon it ain't regular. Come up the stairs, and let on it's a lightning-rod."

So he done it.

Next day Tom stole a pewter spoon and a brass candlestick in the house, for to make some pens for Jim out of, and six tallow candles; and I hung around the nigger cabins, and laid for a chance, and stole three tin plates. Tom said it wasn't enough; but I said nobody wouldn't ever see the plates that Jim throwed out, because they'd fall in the dog-fennel and jimpson weeds under the window-hole—then we could tote them back and he could use them over again. So Tom was satisfied. Then he says:

"Now, the thing to study out is, how to get the things to Jim."

"Take them in through the hole," I says, "when we get it done."

He only just looked scornful, and said something about nobody ever heard of such an idiotic idea, and then he went to studying. By-and-by he said he had ciphered out two or three ways, but there warn't no need to decide on any of them yet. Said we'd got to post Jim first.

That night we went down the lightning-rod a little after ten, and took one of the candles along, and listened under the window-hole, and heard Jim snoring; so we pitched it in, and it didn't wake him. Then we whirled in with the pick and shovel, and in about two hours and a half the job was done. We crept in under Jim's bed and into the cabin, and pawed around and found the candle and lit it, and stood over Jim a while, and found him looking hearty and healthy, and then we woke him up gentle and gradual. He was so glad to see us he most cried; and called us honey, and all the pet names he could think of; and was for having us hunt up a cold chisel to cut the chain off of his leg with, right away, and clearing out without losing any time. But Tom he showed him how unregular it would be, and set down and told him all about our plans, and how we could alter them in a minute any time there was an alarm; and not to be the least afraid, because we would see he got away, *sure.* So Jim he said it was all right, and we set there and talked over old times a while, and then Tom asked a lot of questions, and when Jim told him Uncle Silas come in every day or two to pray with him, and Aunt Sally come in to see if he was comfortable and had plenty to eat, and both of them was kind as they could be, Tom says:

"*Now* I know how to fix it. We'll send you some things by them."

I said, "Don't do nothing of the kind; it's one of the most jackass ideas I ever struck;" but he never paid no attention to me; went right on. It was his way when he'd got his plans set.

So he told Jim how we'd have to smuggle in the rope-ladder pie, and other large things, by Nat, the nigger that fed him, and he must be on the lookout, and not be surprised, and not let Nat see him open them; and we would put small things in uncle's coat pockets and he must steal them out; and we would tie things to aunt's apron strings or put them in her apron pocket, if we got a chance; and told him what they would be and what they was for. And told him how to keep a journal on the shirt with his blood, and all that. He told him everything. Jim he couldn't see no sense in the most of it, but he allowed we was white folks and knowed better than him; so he was satisfied, and said he would do it all just as Tom said.

Jim had plenty corn-cob pipes and tobacco; so we had a right down good sociable time; then we crawled out through the hole, and so home to bed, with hands that looked like they'd been chawed. Tom was in high spirits. He said it was the best fun he ever had in his life, and the most intellectural; and said if he could see his way to it we would keep it up all the rest of our lives and leave Jim to our children to get out; for he believed Jim would come to like it better and better the more he got used to it. He said that in that way it could be strung out to as much as eighty year, and would be the best time on record. And he said it would make us all celebrated that had a hand in it.

In the morning we went out to the wood-pile and chopped up the brass candlestick into handy sizes, and Tom put them and the pewter spoon in his pocket. Then we went to the nigger cabins, and while I got Nat's notice off, Tom shoved a piece of candlestick into the middle of a corn-pone that was in Jim's pan, and we went along with Nat to see how it would work, and it just worked noble; when Jim bit into it it most mashed all his teeth out; and there warn't ever anything could a worked better. Tom said so himself. Jim he never let on but what it was only just a piece of rock or something like that that's always getting into bread, you know; but after that he never bit into nothing but what he jabbed his fork into it three or four places, first.

And whilst we was a standing there in the dimmish light, here comes a couple of the hounds bulging in, from under Jim's bed; and they kept on piling in till there was eleven of them, and there warn't hardly room in there to get your breath. By jings, we forgot to fasten that lean-to door. The nigger Nat he only just hollered "witches!" once, and keeled over onto the floor amongst the dogs, and begun to groan like he was dying. Tom jerked the door open and flung out a slab of Jim's meat, and the dogs went for it, and in two seconds he was out himself and back again and shut the door, and I knowed he'd fixed the other door too. Then he went to work on the nigger, coaxing him and petting him, and asking him it he'd been imagining he saw something again. He raised up, and blinked his eyes around, and says:

"Mars Sid, you'll say I's a fool, but if I didn't b'lieve I see most a million dogs, er devils, er some'n, I wisht I may die right heah in dese tracks. I did, mos' sholy. Mars Sid, I *felt* um—I *felt* um, sah; dey was all over me. Dad fetch it, I jis' wisht I could get my han's on one er dem witches jis' wunst—on'y jis' wunst—it's all I'd ast. But mos'ly I wisht dey'd leme 'lone, I does."

Tom says:

"Well, I tell you what *I* think. What makes them come here just at this runaway nigger's breakfast-time? It's because they're hungry; that's the reason. You make them a witch pie; that's the thing for *you* to do."

"But my lan', Mars Sid, how's *I* gwyne to make 'm a witch pie? I doan' know how to make it. I hain't ever hearn er sich a thing b'fo'."

"Well, then, I'll have to make it myself."

"Will you do it, honey?—will you? I'll wusshup de groun' und' yo' foot, I will!"

"All right, I'll do it, seeing it's you, and you've been good to us and showed us the runaway nigger. But you got to be mighty careful. When we come around, you turn your back; and then whatever we've put in the pan, don't you let on you see it at all. And don't you look, when Jim unloads the pan—something might happen, I don't know what. And above all, don't you *handle* the witch-things."

"*Hannel* 'm Mars Sid? What *is* you talkin' 'bout? I wouldn't lay de weight er my fingers on um, not f'r ten hund'd thous'n' billion dollars, I wouldn't."

CHAPTER XXXVII

That was all fixed. So then we went away and went to the rubbage-pile in the back yard where they keep the old boots, and rags, and pieces of bottles, and wore-out tin things, and all such truck, and scratched around and found an old tin washpan and stopped up the holes as well as we could, to bake the pie in, and took it down cellar and stole it full of flour, and started for breakfast and found a couple of shingle-nails that Tom said would be handy for a prisoner to scrabble his name and sorrows on the dungeon walls with, and dropped one of them in Aunt Sally's apron pocket which was hanging on a chair, and t'other we stuck in the band of Uncle Silas's hat, which was on the bureau, because we heard the children say their pa and ma was going to the runaway nigger's house this morning, and then went to breakfast, and Tom dropped the pewter spoon in Uncle Silas's coat pocket, and Aunt Sally wasn't come yet, so we had to wait a little while.

And when she come she was hot, and red, and cross, and couldn't hardly wait for the blessing; and then she went to sluicing out coffee with one hand and cracking the handiest child's head with her thimble with the other, and says:

"I've hunted high, and I've hunted low, and it does beat all, what *has* become of your other shirt."

My heart fell down amongst my lungs and livers and things, and a hard piece of corn-crust started down my throat after it and got met on the road with a cough and was shot across the table and took one of the children in the eye and curled him up like a fishing-worm, and let a cry out of him the size of a war-whoop, and Tom he turned kinder blue around the gills, and it all amounted to a considerable state of things for about a quarter of a minute or as much as that, and I would a sold out for half price if there was a bidder. But after that we was all right again—it was the sudden surprise of it that knocked us so kind of cold. Uncle Silas he says:

"It's most uncommon curious, I can't understand it. I know perfectly well I took it *off,* because——"

"Because you hain't got but one *on.* Just *listen* at the man! *I* know you took it off, and know it by a better way than your wool gethering memory, too, because it was on the clo'es-line yesterday—I see it there myself. But it's gone—that's the long and the short of it, and you'll just have to change to a red flann'l one till I can get time to make a new one. And it'll be the third I've made in two years; it just keep a body on the jump to keep you in shirts; and whatever you do manage to *do* with 'm all, is more'n *I* can make out. A body'd think you *would* learn to take some sort of care of 'em, at your time of life."

"I know it, Sally, and I do try all I can. But it oughtn't to be altogether my fault, because you know I don't see them nor have nothing to do with them except when they're on me; and I don't believe I've ever lost one of them *off* of me."

"Well, it ain't *your* fault if you haven't, Silas—you'd a done it if you could, I reckon. And the shirt ain't all that's gone, nuther. Ther's a spoon gone; and *that* ain't all. There was ten, and now ther's only nine. The calf got the shirt I reckon, but the calf never took the spoon, *that's* certain."

"Why, what else is gone, Sally?"

"Ther's six *candles* gone—that's what. The rats could a got the candles, and I reckon they did; I wonder they don't walk off with the whole place, the way you're always going to stop their holes and don't do it; and if they warn't fools they'd sleep in your hair, Silas—*you'd* never find it out; but you can't lay the *spoon* on the rats, and that I *know.*"

"Well, Sally, I'm in fault, and I acknowledge it; I've been remiss; but I won't let to-morrow go by without stopping up them holes."

"Oh, I wouldn't hurry, next year'll do. Matilda Angelina Araminta *Phelps!*"

Whack comes the thimble, and the child snatches her claws out of the sugar-bowl without fooling around any. Just then, the nigger woman steps onto the passage, and says:

"Missus, dey's a sheet gone."

"A *sheet* gone! Well, for the land's sake!"

"I'll stop up them holes *to-day,*" says Uncle Silas, looking sorrowful.

"Oh, *do* shet up!—spose the rats took the *sheet? Where's* it gone, Lize?"

"Clah to goodness I hain't no notion, Miss Sally. She wuz on de clo's-line yistiddy, but she doen gone; she ain' dah no mo', now."

"I reckon the world *is* coming to an end. I *never* see the beat of it, in all my born days. A shirt, and a sheet, and a spoon, and six can——"

"Missus," comes a young yaller wench, "dey's a brass cannelstick miss'n."

"Cler out from here, you hussy, er I'll take a skillet to ye!"

Well, she was just a biling. I begun to lay for a chance; I reckoned I would sneak out and go for the woods till the weather moderated. She kept a raging right along, running her insurrection all by herself, and everybody else mighty meek and quiet; and at last Uncle Silas, looking kind of foolish, fishes up that spoon out of his pocket. She stopped, with her mouth open and her hands up; and as for me, I wished I was in Jeruslem or somewheres. But not long; because she says:

"It's *just* as I expected. So you had it in your pocket all the time; and like as not you've got the other things there, too. How'd it get there?"

"I reely don't know, Sally," he says, kind of apologizing, "or you know I would tell. I was a-studying over my text in Acts Seventeen,[1] before breakfast, and I reckon it put it in there not noticing, meaning to put my Testament in, and it must be so, because my Testament ain't in, but I'll go and see, and if the Testament is where I had it, I'll know I didn't put it in, and that will show that I laid the Testament down and took up the spoon, and——"

"Oh, for the land's sake! Give a body a rest! Go 'long now, the hole kit and biling of ye; and don't come nigh me again till I've got back my peace of mind."

[1]Acts 17, in the New Testament, which describes the experiences of the biblical Silas.

I'd a heard her, if she'd a said it to herself, let alone speaking it out; and I'd a got up and obeyed her, if I'd a been dead. As we was passing through the setting-room, the old man he took up his hat, and the shingle-nail fell out on the floor, and he just merely picked it up and laid it on the mantel-shelf, and never said nothing, and went out. Tom see him do it, and remembered about the spoon, and says:

"Well, it ain't no use to send things by *him* no more, he ain't reliable." Then he says: "But he done us a good turn with the spoon, anyway, without knowing it, and so we'll go and do him one without *him* knowing it—stop up his rat-holes."

There was a noble good lot of them, down cellar, and it took us a whole hour, but we done the job tight and good, and ship-shape. Then we heard steps on the stairs, and blowed out our light, and hid; and here comes the old man, with a candle in one hand and a bundle of stuff in t'other, looking as absent-minded as year before last. He went a mooning around, first to one rat-hole and then another, till he'd been to them all. Then he stood about five minutes, picking tallow-drip off of his candle and thinking. Then he turns off slow and dreamy towards the stairs, saying:

"Well, for the life of me I can't remember when I done it. I could show her now that I warn't to blame on account of the rats. But never mind—let it go. I reckon it wouldn't do no good."

And so he went on a mumbling up stairs, and then we left. He was a mighty nice old man. And always is.

Tom was a good deal bothered about what to do for a spoon, but he said we'd got to have it; so he took a think. When he had ciphered it out, he told me how we was to do; then we went and waited around the spoon-basket till we see Aunt Sally coming, and then Tom went to counting the spoons and laying them out to one side, and I slid one of them up my sleeve, and Tom says:

"Why, Aunt Sally, there ain't but nine spoons, *yet.*"

She says:

"Go 'long to your play, and don't bother me. I know better, I counted 'm myself."

"Well, I've counted them twice, Aunty, and *I* can't make but nine."

She looked out of all patience, but of course she come to count—anybody would.

"I declare to gracious ther' *ain't* but nine!" she says. "Why, what in the world—plague *take* the things, I'll count 'm again."

So I slipped back the one I had, and when she got done counting, she says: "Hang the troublesome rubbage, ther's *ten,* now!" and she looked huffy and bothered both. But Tom says:

"Why, Aunty, *I* don't think there's ten."

"You numskull, didn't you see me *count* im?"

"I know, but——"

"Well, I'll count 'm *again.*"

So I smouched one, and they come out nine same as the other time. Well, she *was* in a tearing way—just a trembling all over, she was so mad. But she counted and counted, till she got that addled she'd start to count-in the *basket* for a spoon, sometimes; and so, three times they come out right, and three times they come out wrong. Then she grabbed up the basket and slammed it across the house and knocked the cat galley-west;[2] and she said cle'r out and let her have some peace, and if we come bothering around her again betwixt that and dinner, she'd skin us. So we had the odd spoon; and dropped it in her apron pocket whilst she was a giving us our sailing-orders, and Jim got it all right, along with her shingle-nail, before noon. We was very well satisfied with this business, and Tom allowed it was worth twice the trouble it took, because he said *now* she couldn't even count them spoons twice alike again to save her life; and wouldn't believe she'd counted them right, if she *did;* and said that after she'd about counted her head off, for the next three days, he judged she'd give it up and offer to kill anybody that wanted her to ever count them any more.

So we put the sheet back on the line, that night, and stole one out of her closet; and kept on putting it back and stealing it again, for a couple of days, till she didn't know how many sheets she had, any more, and said she didn't *care,* and warn't agoing to bullyrag[3] the rest of her soul out about it, and wouldn't count them again not to save her life, she druther die first.

So we was all right now, as to the shirt and the sheet and the spoon and the candles, by the help of the calf and the rats and the mixed-up counting; and as to the candlestick, it warn't no consequence, it would blow over by-and-by.

But that pie was a job; we had no end of trouble with that pie. We fixed it up away down in the woods, and cooked it there; and we got it done at last, and very satisfactory, too; but not all in one day; and we had to use up three washpans full of flour, before we got through, and we got burnt pretty much all over, in places, and eyes put out with the smoke; because, you see, we didn't want nothing but a crust, and we couldn't prop it up right, and she would always cave in. But of course we thought of the right way at last; which was to cook the ladder, too, in the pie. So then we laid in with Jim, the second night, and tore up the sheet all in little strings, and twisted them together, and long before daylight we had a lovely rope, that you could a hung a person with. We let on it took nine months to make it.

And in the forenoon we took it down to the woods, but it wouldn't go in the pie. Being made of a whole sheet, that way, there was rope enough for forty pies, if we'd a wanted them, and plenty left over for soup, or sausage, or anything you choose. We could a had a whole dinner.

But we didn't need it. All we needed was just enough for the pie, and so we throwed the rest away. We didn't cook none of the pies in the washpan, afraid the solder would melt; but Uncle Silas he had a noble brass warming-pan[4] which he thought considerable of, because it belonged to one of his ancesters with a long wooden handle that come over from England with William the Conqueror in the *Mayflower*[5] or one of them early ships and was hid away up garret with a lot of other old pots and things that was valuable, not on account of being any account because they warn't, but on account of them being relicts, you know, and we snaked her out, private, and took her down there, but she failed on the first pies, because we didn't know how, but she come up smiling on the last one. We took and lined her with dough, and

[2]For a loop. [3]Mistreat, punish.

[4]Long-handled pan, filled with hot coals and used to warm a bed.

[5]William the Conquerer lived 1027–1087. The *Mayflower* carried the Pilgrims to America in 1620.

set her in the coals, and loaded her up with rag-rope, and put on a dough roof, and shut down the lid, and put hot embers on top, and stood off five foot, with the long handle, cool and comfortable, and in fifteen minutes she turned out a pie that was a satisfaction to look at. But the person that et it would want to fetch a couple of kags of toothpicks along, for if that rope-ladder wouldn't cramp him down to business, I don't know nothing what I'm talking about, and lay him in enough stomach-ache to last him till next time, too.

Nat didn't look, when we put the witch-pie in Jim's pan; and we put the three tin plates in the bottom of the pan under the vittles; and so Jim got everything all right, and as soon as he was by himself he busted into the pie and hid the rope-ladder inside of his straw-tick, and scratched some marks on a tin plate and throwed it out of the window-hole.

CHAPTER XXXVIII

Making them pens was a distressid-tough job, and so was the saw; and Jim allowed the inscription was going to be the toughest of all. That's the one which the prisoner has to scrabble on the wall. But we had to have it; Tom said we'd *got* to; there warn't no case of a state prisoner not scrabbling his inscription to leave behind, and his coat of arms.

"Look at Lady Jane Grey," he says; "look at Gilford Dudley; look at old Northumberland![1] Why, Huck, spose it *is* considerble trouble?—what you going to do?—how you going to get around it? Jim's *got* to do his inscription and coat of arms. They all do."

Jim says:

"Why, Mars Tom, I hain't got no coat o' arms; I hain't got nuffn but dishyer ole shirt, en you knows I got to keep de journal on dat."

"Oh, you don't understand, Jim; a coat of arms is very different."

"Well," I says, "Jim's right, anyway, when he says he hain't got no coat of arms, because he hain't."

"I reckon *I* knowed that," Tom says, "but you bet he'll have one before he goes out of this—because he's going out *right,* and there ain't going to be no flaws in his record."

So whilst me and Jim filed away at the pens on a brickbat apiece, Jim a making his'n out of the brass and I making mine out of the spoon, Tom set to work to think out the coat of arms. By-and-by he said he'd struck so many good ones he didn't hardly know which to take, but there was one which he reckoned he'd decide on. He says:

"On the scutcheon[2] we'll have a bend *or* in the dexter base, a saltire *murrey* in the fess, with a dog, couchant, for common charge, and under his foot a chain embattled, for slavery, with a chevron *vert* in a chief engrailed, and

[1]In 1553, the Duke of Northumberland attempted to make his daughter-in-law, Lady Jane Grey, Queen of England. Subsequently, Northumberland, Lady Jane Grey, and Guilford Dudley, her husband, were first imprisoned and then executed.

[2]An armorial shield. The jumble of technical heraldic terms that follows describes a coat-of-arms made up of a shield decorated with a slanted band of speckled gold, vertical bands of red, a purple cross in the center, a lying dog at the bottom, and a green chevron at the top, all surmounted by the figure of a runaway slave.

three invected lines on a field *azure,* with the nombril points rampant on a dancette indented; crest, a runaway nigger, *sable,* with his bundle over his shoulder on a bar sinister: and a couple of gules for supporters, which is you and me; motto, *Maggiore fretta, minore atto.* Got it out of a book—means, the more haste, the less speed."[3]

"Geewhillikins," I says, "but what does the rest of it mean?"

"We ain't got no time to bother over that," he says, "we got to dig in like all git-out."

"Well, anyway," I says, "what's *some* of it? What's a fess?"

"A fess—a fess is—*you* don't need to know what a fess is. I'll show him how to make it when he gets to it."

"Shucks, Tom," I says, "I think you might tell a person. What's a bar sinister?"

"Oh, *I* don't know. But he's got to have it. All the nobility does."

That was just his way. If it didn't suit him to explain a thing to you, he wouldn't do it. You might pump at him a week, it wouldn't make no difference.

He'd got all that coat of arms business fixed, so now he started in to finish up the rest of that part of work, which was to plan out a mournful inscription—said Jim got to have one, like they all done. He made up a lot, and wrote them out on a paper, and read them off, so:

1. *Here a captive heart busted.*
2. *Here a poor prisoner, forsook by the world and friends, fretted out his sorrowful life.*
3. *Here a lonely heart broke, and a worn spirit went to its rest, after thirty-seven years of solitary captivity.*
4. *Here, homeless and friendless, after thirty-seven years of bitter captivity, perished a noble stranger, natural son of Louis XIV.*

Tom's voice trembled, whilst he was reading them, and he most broke down. When he got done, he couldn't no way make up his mind which one for Jim to scrabble onto the wall, they was all so good; but at last he allowed he would let him scrabble them all on. Jim said it would take him a year to scrabble such a lot of truck onto the logs with a nail, and he didn't know how to make letters, besides; but Tom said he would block them out for him, and then he wouldn't have nothing to do but just follow the lines. Then pretty soon he says:

"Come to think, the logs ain't agoing to do; they don't have log walls in a dungeon: we got to dig the inscriptions into a rock. We'll fetch a rock."

Jim said the rock was worse than the logs; he said it would take him such a pison long time to dig them into a rock, he wouldn't ever get out. But Tom said he would let me help him do it. Then he took a look to see how me and Jim was getting along with the pens. It was most pesky tedious hard work and slow, and didn't give my hands no show to get well of the sores, and we didn't seem to make no headway, hardly. So Tom says:

"I know how to fix it. We got to have a rock for the coat of arms and mournful inscriptions, and we can kill two birds with that same rock. There's

[3]Actually, "The more fretting, the less action."

a gaudy big grindstone down at the mill, and we'll smouch it, and carve the things on it, and file out the pens and the saw on it, too."

It warn't no slouch of an idea; and it warn't no slouch of a grindstone nuther; but we allowed we'd tackle it. It warn't quite midnight, yet, so we cleared out for the mill, leaving Jim at work. We smouched the grindstone, and set out to roll her home, but it was a most nation tough job. Sometimes, do what we could, we couldn't keep her from falling over, and she come mighty near mashing us, every time. Tom said she was going to get one of us, sure, before we got through. We got her half way; and then we was plumb played out, and most drownded with sweat. We see it warn't no use, we got to go and fetch Jim, so he raised up his bed and slid the chain off the bed-leg, and wrapt it round and round his neck, and we crawled out through our hole and down there, and Jim and me laid into that grindstone and walked her along like nothing; and Tom superintended. He could out-superintend any boy I ever see. He knowed how to do everything.

Our hole was pretty big, but it warn't big enough to get the grindstone through; but Jim he took the pick and soon made it big enough. Then Tom marked out them things on it with the nail, and set Jim to work on them, with the nail for a chisel and an iron bolt from the rubbage in the lean-to for a hammer, and told him to work till the rest of his candle quit on him, and then he could go to bed, and hide the grindstone under his straw tick and sleep on it. Then we helped him fix his chain back on the bed-leg, and was ready for bed ourselves. But Tom thought of something, and says:

"You got any spiders in here, Jim?"

"No, sah, thanks to goodness I hain't, Mars Tom."

"All right, we'll get you some."

"But bless you, honey, I doan' *want* none. I's afeard un um. I jis' 's soon have rattlesnakes aroun'."

Tom thought a minute or two, and says:

"It's a good idea. And I reckon it's been done. It *must* a been done; it stands to reason. Yes, it's a prime good idea. Where could you keep it?"

"Keep what, Mars Tom?"

"Why, a rattlesnake."

"De goodness gracious alive, Mars Tom! Why, if dey was a rattlesnake to come in heah, I'd take en bust right out thoo dat log wall, I would, wid my head."

"Why, Jim, you wouldn't be afraid of it, after a little. You could tame it."

"*Tame* it!"

"Yes—easy enough. Every animal is grateful for kindness and petting, and they wouldn't *think* of hurting a person that pets them. Any book will tell you that. You try—that's all I ask; just try for two or three days. Why, you can get him so, in a little while, that he'll love you; and sleep with you; and won't stay away from you a minute; and will let you wrap him round your neck and put his head in your mouth."

"*Please,* Mars Tom—doan' talk so! I can't *stan'* it. He'd *let* me shove his head in my mouf—fer a favor, hain't it? I lay he'd wait a pow'ful long time 'fo' I *ast* him. En mo' en dat, I doan' *want* him to sleep wid me."

"Jim, don't act so foolish. A prisoner's *got* to have some kind of a dumb pet, and if a rattlesnake hain't ever been tried, why, there's more glory to be gained in your being the first to ever try it than any other way you could ever think of to save your life."

"Why, Mars Tom, I doan' *want* no sich glory. Snake take 'n bite Jim's chin off, den *whah* is de glory? No, sah, I doan' want no sich doin's."

"Blame it, can't you *try?* I only want you to try—you needn't keep it up if it don't work."

"But de trouble all *done,* ef de snake bit me while's I's a tryin' him. Mars Tom, I's willin' to tackle mos' anything 'at ain't onreasonable, but ef you en Huck fetches a rattlesnake in heah for me to tame, I's gwyne to *leave,* dat's *shore.*"

"Well, then, let it go, let it go, if you're so bullheaded about it. We can get you some garter-snakes and you can tie some buttons on their tails, and let on they're rattlesnakes, and I reckon that'll have to do."

"I k'n stan' *dem,* Mars Tom, but blame' 'f I couldn't get along widout um, I tell you dat. I never knowed b'fo', 't was so much bother and trouble to be a prisoner."

"Well, it *always* is, when it's done right. You got any rats around here?"

"No, sah, I hain't seed none."

"Well, we'll get you some rats."

"Well, Mars Tom, I doan' *want* no rats. Dey's de dad-blamedest creturs to 'sturb a body, en rustle roun' over 'im, en bite his feet, when he's trying' to sleep, I ever see. No, sah, gimme g'yarter-snakes, 'f I's got to have 'm, but doan' gimme no rats. I ain' got no use f'r um, skasely."

"But Jim, you *got* to have 'em—they all do. So don't make no more fuss about it. Prisoners ain't ever without rats. There ain't no instance of it. And they train them, and pet them, and learn them tricks, and they get to be as sociable as flies. But you got to play music to them. You got anything to play music on?"

"I ain't got nuffn but a coase comb en a piece o' paper, en a juice-harp; but I reck'n dey wouldn' take no stock in a juice-harp."

"Yes they would. *They* don't care what kind of music 'tis. A jews-harp's plenty good enough for a rat. All animals likes music—in a prison they dote on it. Specially, painful music; and you can't get no other kind out of a jews-harp. It always interests them; they come out to see what's the matter with you. Yes, you're all right; you're fixed very well. You want to set on your bed, nights, before you go to sleep, and early in the mornings, and play your jews-harp; play The Last Link Is Broken—that's the thing that'll scoop a rat, quicker'n anything else: and when you've played about two minutes, you'll see all the rats, and the snakes, and spiders, and things begin to feel worried about you, and come. And they'll just fairly swarm over you, and have a noble good time."

"Yes, *dey* will, I reck'n, Mars Tom, but what kine er time is *Jim* havin'? Blest if I kin see de pint. But I'll do it ef I got to. I reck'n I better keep de animals satisfied, en not have no trouble in de house."

Tom waited to think over, and see if there wasn't nothing else; and pretty soon he says:

"Oh—there's one thing I forgot. Could you raise a flower here, do you reckon?"

"I doan' know but maybe I could, Mars Tom; but it's tolable dark in heah, en I ain' got no use f'r no flower, no how, en she'd be a pow'ful sight o' trouble."

"Well, you try it, anyway. Some other prisoners has done it."

"One er dem big cat-tail-lookin' mullen-stalks would grow in heah, Mars Tom, I reck'n, but she wouldn' be wuth half de trouble she'd coss."

"Don't you believe it. We'll fetch you a little one, and you plant it in the corner, over there, and raise it. And don't call it mullen, call it Pitchiola[4]—that's its right name, when it's in a prison. And you want to water it with your tears."

"Why, I got plenty spring water, Mars Tom."

"You don't *want* spring water; you want to water it with your tears. It's the way they always do."

"Why, Mars Tom, I lay I kin raise one er dem mullen-stalks twyste wid spring water whiles another man's a *start'n* one wid tears."

"That ain't the idea. You *got* to do it with tears."

"She'll die on my han's, Mars Tom, she sholy will; kase I doan' skasely ever cry."

So Tom was stumped. But he studied it over, and then said Jim would have to worry along the best he could with an onion. He promised he would go to the nigger cabins and drop one, private, in Jim's coffee-pot, in the morning. Jim said he would "jis' 's soon have tobacker in his coffee"; and found so much fault with it, and with the work and bother of raising the mullen, and jews-harping the rats, and petting and flattering up the snakes and spiders and things, on top of all the other work he had to do on pens, and inscriptions, and journals, and things, which made it more trouble and worry and responsibility to be a prisoner than anything he ever undertook, that Tom most lost all patience with him; and said he was just loadened down with more gaudier chances than a prisoner ever had in the world to make a name for himself, and yet he didn't know enough to appreciate them, and they was just about wasted on him. So Jim he was sorry, and said he wouldn't behave so no more, and then me and Tom shoved for bed.

CHAPTER XXXIX

In the morning we went up to the village and bought a wire rat trap and fetched it down, and unstopped the best rat hole, and in about an hour we had fifteen of the bulliest kind of ones; and then we took it and put it in a safe place under Aunt Sally's bed. But while we was gone for spiders, little Thomas Franklin Benjamin Jefferson Elexander Phelps found it there, and opened the door of it to see if the rats would come out, and they did; and Aunt Sally she come in, and when we got back she was a standing on top of the bed raising Cain, and the rats was doing what they could to keep off the dull times for her. So she took and dusted us both with the hickry, and we was as much as two hours catching another fifteen or sixteen, drat that meddlesome cub, and they warn't the likeliest, nuther, because the first haul was the pick of the flock. I never see a likelier lot of rats than what that first haul was.

[4]In the romantic novel *Picciola* (1836) by Joseph Boniface (1798–1865), a prisoner is kept alive by a plant growing in his cell.

We got a splendid stock of sorted spiders, and bugs, and frogs, and caterpillars, and one thing or another; and we like-to got a hornet's nest, but we didn't. The family was at home. We didn't give it right up, but staid with them as long as we could; because we allowed we'd tire them out or they'd got to tire us out, and they done it. Then we got allycumpain[1] and rubbed on the places, and was pretty near all right again, but couldn't set down convenient. And so we went for the snakes, and grabbed a couple of dozen garters and house-snakes, and put them in a bag, and put it in our room, and by that time it was supper time, and a rattling good honest day's work; and hungry?—oh, no, I reckon not! And there warn't a blessed snake up there, when we went back—we didn't half tie the sack, and they worked out, somehow, and left. But it didn't matter much, because they was still on the premises somewhere. So we judged we could get some of them again. No, there warn't no real scarcity of snakes about the house for a considerable spell. You'd see them dripping from the rafters and places, every now and then; and they generly landed in your plate, or down the back of your neck, and most of the time where you didn't want them. Well, they was handsome, and striped, and there warn't no harm in a million of them; but that never made no difference to Aunt Sally, she despised snakes, be the breed what they might, and she couldn't stand them no way you could fix it; and every time one of them flopped down on her, it didn't make no difference what she was doing, she would just lay that work down and light out. I never see such a woman. And you could hear her whoop to Jericho. You couldn't get her to take aholt of one of them with the tongs. And if she turned over and found one in bed, she would scramble out and lift a howl that you would think the house was afire. She disturbed the old man so, that he said he could most wish there hadn't ever been no snakes created. Why, after every last snake had been gone clear out of the house for as much as a week, Aunt Sally warn't over it yet; she warn't near over it; when she was setting thinking about something, you could touch her on the back of her neck with a feather and she would jump right out of her stockings. It was very curious. But Tom said all women was just so. He said they was made that way; for some reason or other.

We got a licking every time one of our snakes come in her way; and she allowed these lickings warn't nothing to what she would do if we ever loaded up the place again with them. I didn't mind the lickings, because they didn't amount to nothing; but I minded the trouble we had, to lay in another lot. But we got them laid in, and all the other things; and you never see a cabin as blithesome as Jim's was when they'd all swarm out for music and go for him. Jim didn't like the spiders, and the spiders didn't like Jim; and so they'd lay for him and make it mighty warm for him. And he said that between the rats, and the snakes, and the grindstone, there warn't no room in bed for him skasely; and when there was, a body couldn't sleep, it was so lively, and it was always lively, he said, because *they* never all slept at one time, but took turn about, so when the snakes was asleep the rats was on deck, and when the rats turned in the snakes come on watch, so he always had one gang under him, in his way, and t'other gang having a circus over him, and if he got up to hunt a new place, the spiders would take a chance at him as he crossed

[1]Elecampane, a medicinal herb.

over. He said if he ever got out, this time, he wouldn't ever be a prisoner again, not for a salary.

Well, by the end of three weeks, everything was in pretty good shape. The shirt was sent in early, in a pie, and every time a rat bit Jim he would get up and write a little in his journal whilst the ink was fresh; the pens was made, the inscriptions and so on was all carved on the grindstone; the bed-leg was sawed in two, and we had et up the sawdust, and it give us a most amazing stomach-ache. We reckoned we was all going to die, but didn't. It was the most undigestible sawdust I ever see; and Tom said the same. But as I was saying, we'd got all the work done, now, at last; and we was all pretty much fagged out, too, but mainly Jim. The old man had wrote a couple of times to the plantation below Orleans to come and get their runaway nigger, but hadn't got no answer, because there warn't no such plantation; so he allowed he would advertise Jim in the St. Louis and New Orleans papers; and when he mentioned the St. Louis ones, it give me the cold shivers, and I see we hadn't no time to lose. So Tom said, now for the nonnamous letters.

"What's them?" I says.

"Warnings to the people that something is up. Sometimes it's done one way, sometimes another. But there's always somebody spying around, that gives notice to the governor of the castle. When Louis XVI was going to light out of the Tooleries, a servant girl done it.[2] It's a very good way, and so is the nonnamous letters. We'll use them both. And it's usual for the prisoner's mother to change clothes with him, and she stays in, and he slides out in her clothes. We'll do that too."

"But looky here, Tom, what do we want to *warn* anybody for, that something's up? Let them find it out for themselves—it's their lookout."

"Yes, I know; but you can't depend on them. It's the way they've acted from the very start—left us to do *everything*. They're so confiding and mullet-headed[3] they don't take notice of nothing at all. So if we don't *give* them notice, there won't be nobody nor nothing to interfere with us, and so after all our hard work and trouble this escape 'll go off perfectly flat: won't amount to nothing—won't be nothing *to* it."

"Well, as for me, Tom, that's the way I'd like."

"Shucks," he says, and looked disgusted. So I says:

"But I ain't going to make no complaint. Anyway that suits you suits me. What you going to do about the servant-girl?"

"You'll be her. You slide in, in the middle of the night, and hook that yaller girl's frock."

"Why, Tom, that'll make trouble next morning; because of course she prob'bly hain't got any but that one."

"I know; but you don't want it but fifteen minutes, to carry the nonnamous letter and shove it under the front door."

"All right, then, I'll do it; but I could carry it just as handly in my own togs."

"You wouldn't look like a servant-girl *then*, would you?"

[2]The Tuileries, royal residence in Paris, France (1564–1871). Following the French Revolution, King Louis XVI's plans to escape his imprisonment were said to have been revealed to the authorities by a chambermaid.

[3]Stupid.

"No, but there won't be nobody to see what I look like, *anyway.*"

"That ain't got nothing to do with it. The thing for us to do, is just to do our *duty,* and not worry about whether anybody *sees* us do it or not. Hain't you got no principle at all?"

"All right, I ain't saying nothing; I'm the servant-girl. Who's Jim's mother?"

"I'm his mother. I'll hook a gown from Aunt Sally."

"Well, then, you'll have to stay in the cabin when me and Jim leaves."

"Not much. I'll stuff Jim's clothes full of straw and lay it on his bed to represent his mother in disguise, and Jim 'll take the nigger woman's gown[4] off of me and wear it, and we'll all evade together. When a prisoner of style escapes, it's called an evasion. It's always called so when a king escapes, f'rinstance. And the same with a king's son; it don't make no difference whether he's a natural one or an unnatural one."

So Tom he wrote the nonnamous letter, and I smouched the yaller wench's frock, that night, and put it on, and shoved it under the front door, the way Tom told me to. It said:

Beware. Trouble is brewing. Keep a sharp lookout.
UNKNOWN FRIEND.

Next night we stuck a picture which Tom drawed in blood, of a skull and crossbones, on the front door; and next night another one of a coffin, on the back door. I never see a family in such a sweat. They couldn't been worse scared if the place had a been full of ghosts laying for them behind everything and under the beds and shivering through the air. If a door banged, Aunt Sally she jumped, and said "ouch!" if anything fell, she jumped and said "ouch!" if you happened to touch her, when she warn't noticing, she done the same; she couldn't face noway and be satisfied, because she allowed there was something behind her every time—so she was always a whirling around, sudden, and saying "ouch," and before she'd get two-thirds around, she'd whirl back again, and say it again; and she was afraid to go to bed, but she dasn't set up. So the thing was working very well, Tom said; he said he never see a thing work more satisfactory. He said it showed it was done right.

So he said, now for the grand bulge! So the very next morning at the streak of dawn we got another letter ready, and was wondering what we better do with it, because we heard them say at supper they was going to have a nigger on watch at both doors all night. Tom he went down the lightning-rod to spy around; and the nigger at the back door was asleep, and he stuck it in the back of his neck and come back. This letter said:

Don't betray me, I wish to be your friend. There is a desprate gang of cutthroats from over in the Ingean Territory[5] going to steal your runaway nigger to-night, and they have been trying to scare you so as you will stay in the house and not bother them. I am one of the gang, but have got religgion and wish to quit it and lead a honest life again, and will betray the helish design. They will sneak down from northards, along the fence, at midnight exact, with a false key, and go in the nigger's cabin to get him. I am to be off a piece and blow a tin horn if I see any danger;

[4]Some of Twain's editors have considered this an error in consistency and have corrected the text to read "Aunt Sally's gown."

[5]From 1834 to 1890, present-day Oklahoma was designated Indian Territory. During those years it was frequently used by outlaws as a refuge from state and federal authorities.

but stead of that, I will BA *like a sheep soon as they get in and not blow at all; then whilst they are getting his chains loose, you slip there and lock them in, and can kill them at your leasure. Don't do anything but just the way I am telling you, if you do they will suspicion something and raise whoopjamboreehoo. I do not wish any reward but to know I have done the right thing.*

UNKNOWN FRIEND.

CHAPTER XL

We was feeling pretty good, after breakfast, and took my canoe and went over the river a fishing, with a lunch, and had a good time, and took a look at the raft and found her all right, and got home late to supper, and found them in such a sweat and worry they didn't know which end they was standing on, and made us go right off to bed the minute we was done supper, and wouldn't tell us what the trouble was, and never let on a word about the new letter, but didn't need to, because we knowed as much about it as anybody did, and as soon as we was half up stairs and her back was turned, we slid for the cellar cubboard and loaded up a good lunch and took it up to our room and went to bed, and got up about half-past eleven, and Tom put on Aunt Sally's dress that he stole and was going to start with the lunch, but says:

"Where's the butter?"

"I laid out a hunk of it," I says, "on a piece of a corn-pone."

"Well, you *left* it laid out, then—it ain't here."

"We can get along without it," I says.

"We can get along *with* it, too," he says; "just you slide down cellar and fetch it. And then mosey right down the lightning-rod and come along. I'll go and stuff the straw into Jim's clothes to represent his mother in disguise, and be ready to *ba* like a sheep and shove soon as you get there."

So out he went, and down cellar went I. The hunk of butter, big as a person's fist, was where I had left it, so I took up the slab of corn-pone with it on, and blowed out my light, and started up stairs, very stealthy, and got up to the main floor all right, but here comes Aunt Sally with a candle, and I clapped the truck in my hat, and clapped my hat on my head, and the next second she see me; and she says:

"You been down cellar?"

"Yes'm."

"What you been doing down there?"

"Noth'n."

"Noth'n!"

"No'm."

"Well, then, what possessed you to go down there, this time of night?"

"I don't know'm."

"You don't *know?* Don't answer me that way, Tom, I want to know what you been *doing* down there?"

"I hain't been doing a single thing, Aunt Sally, I hope to gracious if I have."

I reckoned she'd let me go, now, and as a generl thing she would; but I spose there was so many strange things going on she was just in a sweat about every little thing that warn't yard-stick straight; so she says, very decided:

"You just march into that setting-room and stay there till I come. You been up to something you no business to, and I lay I'll find out what it is before *I'm* done with you."

So she went away as I opened the door and walked into the setting-room. My, but there was a crowd there! Fifteen farmers, and every one of them had a gun. I was most powerful sick, and slunk to a chair and set down. They was setting around, some of them talking a little, in a low voice, and all of them fidgety and uneasy, but trying to look like they warn't; but I knowed they was, because they was always taking off their hats, and putting them on, and scratching their heads, and changing their seats, and fumbling with their buttons. I warn't easy myself, but I didn't take my hat off, all the same.

I did wish Aunt Sally would come, and get done with me, and lick me, if she wanted to, and let me get away and tell Tom how we'd overdone this thing, and what a thundering hornet's nest we'd got ourselves into, so we could stop fooling around, straight-off, and clear out with Jim before these rips got out of patience and come for us.

At last she come, and begun to ask me questions, but I *couldn't* answer them straight, I didn't know which end of me was up; because these men was in such a fidget now, that some was wanting to start right *now* and lay for them desperadoes, and saying it warn't but a few minutes to midnight; and others was trying to get them to hold on and wait for the sheep-signal; and here was aunty pegging away at the questions, and me a shaking all over and ready to sink down in my tracks I was that scared; and the place getting hotter and hotter, and the butter beginning to melt and run down my neck and behind my ears; and pretty soon, when one of them says, "*I'm* for going and getting in the cabin *first,* and right *now,* and catching them when they come," I most dropped; and a streak of butter come a trickling down my forehead, and Aunt Sally she see it, and turns white as a sheet, and says:

"For the land's sake what *is* the matter with the child!—he's got the brain fever as shore as you're born, and they're oozing out!"

And everybody runs to see, and she snatches off my hat, and out comes the bread, and what was left of the butter, and she grabbed me, and hugged me, and says:

"Oh, what a turn you did give me! and how glad and grateful I am it ain't no worse; for luck's against us, and it never rains but it pours, and when I see that truck I thought we'd lost you, for I knowed by the color and all, it was just like your brains would be if—Dear, dear, whyd'nt you *tell* me that was what you'd been down there for, *I* wouldn't a cared. Now cler out to bed, and don't lemme see no more of you till morning!"

I was up stairs in a second, and down the lightning-rod in another one, and shinning through the dark for the lean-to. I couldn't hardly get my words out, I was so anxious; but I told Tom as quick as I could, we must jump for it, now, and not a minute to lose—the house full of men, yonder, with guns!

His eyes just blazed; and he says:

"No!—is that so? *Ain't* it bully! Why, Huck, if it was to do over again, I bet I could fetch two hundred! If we could put it off till——"

"Hurry! *hurry!*" I says, "Where's Jim?"

"Right at your elbow; if you reach out your arm you can touch him. He's dressed, and everything's ready. Now we'll slide out and give the sheep-signal."

But then we heard the tramp of men coming to the door, and heard them begin to fumble with the padlock; and heard a man say:

"I *told* you we'd be too soon; they haven't come—the door is locked. Here, I'll lock some of you in the cabin and you lay for 'em in the dark and kill 'em when they come; and the rest scatter around a piece, and listen if you can hear 'em coming."

So in they come, but couldn't see us in the dark, and most trod on us whilst we was hustling to get under the bed. But we got under all right, and out through the hole, swift but soft—Jim first, me next, and Tom last, which was according to Tom's orders. Now we was in the lean-to, and heard trampings close by outside. So we crept to the door, and Tom stopped us there and put his eye to the crack, but couldn't make out nothing, it was so dark; and whispered and said he would listen for the steps to get further, and when he nudged us Jim must glide out first, and him last. So he set his ear to the crack and listened, and listened, and listened, and the steps a scraping around, out there, all the time; and at last he nudged us, and we slid out, and stooped down, not breathing, and not making the least noise, and slipped stealthy towards the fence, in Injun file,[1] and got to it, all right, and me and Jim over it; but Tom's britches catched fast on a splinter on the top rail, and then he hear the steps coming, so he had to pull loose, which snapped the splinter and made a noise; and as he dropped in our tracks and started, somebody sings out:

"Who's that? Answer, or I'll shoot!"

But we didn't answer; we just unfurled our heels and shoved. Then there was a rush, and a *bang, bang, bang!* and the bullets fairly whizzed around us! We heard them sing out:

"Here they are! They've broke for the river! after 'em boys! And turn loose the dogs!"

So here they come, full tilt. We could hear them, because they wore boots, and yelled, but we didn't wear no boots, and didn't yell. We was in the path to the mill; and when they got pretty close onto us, we dodged in the bush and let them go by, and then dropped in behind them. They'd had all the dogs shut up, so they wouldn't scare off the robbers; but by this time somebody had let them loose, and here they come, making pow-wow enough for a million; but they was our dogs; so we stopped in our tracks till they catch up; and when they see it warn't nobody but us, and no excitement to offer them, they only just said howdy, and tore right ahead towards the shouting and clattering; and then we up stream again and whizzed along after them till we was nearly to the mill, and then struck up through the bush to where my canoe was tied, and hopped in and pulled for dear life towards the middle of the river, but didn't make no more noise than we was obleeged to. Then we struck out, easy and comfortable, for the island where my raft was; and we could hear them yelling and barking at each other all up and down the bank, till we was so far away the sounds got dim and died out. And when we stepped onto the raft, I says:

"*Now,* old Jim, you're a free man *again,* and I bet you won't ever be a slave nomore."

[1]Single file.

"En a mighty good job it wuz, too. Huck. It 'uz planned beautiful, en it 'uz *done* beautiful; en dey ain't *nobody* kin git up a plan dat's mo' mixed-up en splendid den what dat one wuz."

We was all as glad as we could be, but Tom was the gladdest of all, because he had a bullet in the calf of his leg.

When me and Jim heard that, we didn't feel so brash as what we did before. It was hurting him considerable, and bleeding; so we laid him in the wigwam and tore up one of the duke's shirts for to bandage him, but he says:

"Gimme the rags, I can do it myself. Don't stop, now; don't fool around here, and the evasion booming along so handsome; man the sweeps, and set her loose! Boys, we done it elegant—'deed we did. I wish *we'd* a had the handling of Louis XVI., there wouldn't a been no "Son of Saint Louis, ascend to heaven!"[2] wrote down in *his* biography: no, sir, we'd a whooped him over the *border*—that's what we'd a done with *him*—and done it just as slick as nothing at all, too. Man the sweeps—man the sweeps!"

But me and Jim was consulting—and thinking. And after we'd thought a minute, I says:

"Say it, Jim."

So he says:

"Well, den, dis is de way it look to me, Huck. Ef it wuz *him* dat 'uz bein' sot free, en one er de boys wuz to git shot, would he say, 'Go on en save me, nemmine 'bout a doctor f'r to save dis one? Is dat like Mars Tom Sawyer? Would he say dat? You *bet* he wouldn't! *Well,* den, is *Jim* gwyne to say it? No, sah—I doan' budge a step out'n dis place, 'dout a *doctor;* not if it's forty year!"

I knowed he was white inside, and I reckoned he'd say what he did say—so it was all right, now, and I told Tom I was agoing for a doctor. He raised considerble row about it, but me and Jim stuck to it and wouldn't budge; so he was for crawling out and setting the raft loose himself; but we wouldn't let him. Then he give us a piece of his mind—but it didn't do no good.

So when he see me getting the canoe ready, he says:

"Well, then, if you're bound to go, I'll tell you the way to do, when you get to the village. Shut the door, and blindfold the doctor tight and fast, and make him swear to be silent as the grave, and put a purse full of gold in his hand, and then take and lead him all around the back alleys and everywheres, in the dark, and then fetch him here in the canoe, in a roundabout way amongst the islands, and search him and take his chalk away from him, and don't give it back to him till you get him back to the village, or else he will chalk this raft so he can find it again. It's the way they all do."

So I said I would, and left, and Jim was to hide in the woods when he see the doctor coming, till he was gone again.

CHAPTER XLI

The doctor was an old man; a very nice, kind-looking old man, when I got him up. I told him me and my brother was over on Spanish Island hunting, yesterday afternoon, and camped on a piece of a raft we found, and about

[2]A quotation from *The French Revolution* (1837) by Scottish historian Thomas Carlyle (1795–1881).

midnight he must a kicked his gun in his dreams, for it went off and shot him in the leg, and we wanted him to go over there and fix it and not say nothing about it, nor let anybody know, because we wanted to come home this evening, and surprise the folks.

"Who is your folks?" he says.

"The Phelpses, down yonder."

"Oh," he says. And after a minute, he says: "How'd you say he got shot?"

"He had a dream," I says, "and it shot him."

"Singular dream," he says.

So he lit up his lantern, and got his saddle-bags, and we started. But when he see the canoe, he didn't like the look of her—said she was big enough for one, but didn't look pretty safe for two. I says:

"Oh, you needn't be afeard, sir, she carried the three of us, easy enough."

"What three?"

"Why, me and Sid, and—and—and *the guns;* that's what I mean."

"Oh," he says.

But he put his foot on the gunnel, and rocked her; and shook his head, and said he reckoned he'd look around for a bigger one. But they was all locked and chained; so he took my canoe, and said for me to wait till he come back, or I could hunt around further, or maybe I better go down home and get them ready for the surprise, if I wanted to. But I said I didn't; so I told him just how to find the raft, and then he started.

I struck an idea, pretty soon. I says to myself, spos'n he can't fix that leg just in three shakes of a sheep's tail, as the saying is? spos'n it takes him three or four days? What are we going to do?—lay around there till he lets the cat out of the bag? No, sir, I know what *I'll* do. I'll wait, and when he comes back, if he says he's got to go any more, I'll get down there, too, if I swim; and we'll take and tie him, and keep him, and shove out down the river; and when Tom's done with him, we'll give him what it's worth, or all we got, and then let him get ashore.

So then I crept into a lumber pile to get some sleep; and next time I waked up the sun was away up over my head! I shot out and went for the doctor's house, but they told me he'd gone away in the night, some time or other, and warn't back yet. Well, thinks I, that looks powerful bad for Tom, and I'll dig out for the island, right off. So away I shoved, and turned the corner, and nearly rammed my head into Uncle Silas's stomach! He says:

"Why, *Tom!* Where you been all this time, you rascal?"

"I hain't been nowheres," I says, "only just hunting for the runaway nigger—me and Sid."

"Why, where ever did you go?" he says. "Your aunt's been mighty un-easy."

"She needn't," I says, "because we was all right. We followed the men and the dogs, but they out-run us, and we lost them; but we thought we heard them on the water, so we got a canoe and took out after them, and crossed over but couldn't find nothing of them; so we cruised along up-shore till we got kind of tired and beat out; and tied up the canoe and went to sleep, and never waked up till about an hour ago, then we paddled over here to hear the news, and Sid's at the post-office to see what he can hear, and I'm branching out to get something to eat for us, and then we're going home."

So then we went to the post-office to get "Sid"; but just as I suspicioned, he warn't there; so the old man he got a letter out of the office, and we waited a while longer but Sid didn't come; so the old man said come along, let Sid foot it home, or canoe-it, when he got done fooling around—but we would ride. I couldn't get him to let me stay and wait for Sid; and he said there warn't no use in it, and I must come along, and let Aunt Sally see we was all right.

When we got home, Aunt Sally was that glad to see me she laughed and cried both, and hugged me, and give me one of them lickings of hern that don't amount to shucks, and said she serve Sid the same when he come.

And the place was plumb full of farmers and farmers' wives, to dinner; and such another clack a body never heard. Old Mrs. Hotchkiss was the worst; her tongue was agoing all the time. She says:

"Well, Sister Phelps, I've ransacked that-air cabin over an' I b'lieve the nigger was crazy. I says so to Sister Damrell—didn't I, Sister Damrell?—s'I, he's crazy, s'I—them's the very words I said. You all hearn me: he's crazy, s'I; everything shows it, s'I. Look as that-air grindstone, s'I; want to tell *me*'t any cretur 'ts in his right mind's agoin' to scrabble all them crazy things onto a grindstone, s'I? Here sich 'n' sich a person busted his heart; 'n' here so 'n' so pegged along for thirty-seven year, 'n' all that—natcherl son o' Louis somebody, 'n' sich everlast'n rubbage. He's plumb crazy, s'I; it's what I says in the fust place, it's what I says in the middle, 'n' it's what I says last 'n' all the time—the nigger's crazy—crazy's Nebokoodneezer,[1] s'I."

"An' look at that air-ladder made out'n rags, Sister Hotchkiss," says old Mrs. Damrell, "what in the name o' goodness *could* he ever want of——"

"The very words I was a-sayin' no longer ago th'n this minute to Sister Utterback, 'n' she'll tell you so herself. Sh-she, look at that-air rag ladder, sh-she; 'n' s'I, yes, *look* at it, s'I—what *could* he a wanted of it, s'I. Sh-she, Sister Hotchkiss, sh-she——"

"But how in the nation'd they ever *git* that grindstone *in* there, *anyway?* 'n' who dug that-air *hole?* 'n' who——"

"My very *words,* Brer Penrod! I was a-sayin'—pass that-air sasser o' m'lasses, won't ye?—I was a-sayin' to Sister Dunlap, jist this minute, how *did* they git that grindstone in there, s'I. Without *help,* mind you—'thout *help! Thar's* wher' tis. Don't tell *me,* s'I; there *wuz* help, s'I; 'n' ther' wuz a *plenty* help, too, s'I; ther's ben a *dozen* a-helpin' that nigger, 'n' I lay I'd skin every last nigger on this place, but *I'd* find out who done it, s'I; 'n' moreover, s'I——"

"A *dozen* says you!—*forty* couldn't a done everything that's been done. Look at them case-knife saws and things, how tedious they've been made; look at that bed-leg sawed off with 'm, a week's work for six men; look at that nigger made out'n straw on the bed; and look at——"

"You may *well* say it, Brer Hightower! It's jist as I was a-sayin' to Brer Phelps, his own self. S'e, what do *you* think of it, Sister Hotchkiss, s'e? think o' what, Brer Phelps, s'I? think o' that bed-leg sawed off that a way, s'e? *think* of it, s'I? I lay it never sawed *itself* off, s'I—somebody *sawed* it, s'I; that's my opinion, take it or leave it, it mayn't be no 'count, s'I, but sich as 'tis, it's my opinion,

[1]Nebuchadnezzar, King of Babylon, was deprived of his reason for failure to honor the Lord (Daniel 4:29–37).

s'I, 'n' if anybody k'n start a better one, s'I, let him *do* it, s'I, that's all. I says to Sister Dunlap, s'I——"

"Why, dog my cats, they must a ben a house-ful o'niggers in there every night for four weeks, to a done all that work, Sister Phelps. Look at that shirt—every last inch of it kivered over with secret African writ'n done with blood! Must a ben a raft uv'm at it right along, all the time, almost. Why, I'd give two dollars to have it read to me; 'n' as for the niggers that wrote it, I 'low I'd take 'n' lash 'm t'll——"

"People to *help* him, Brother Marples! Well, I reckon you'd *think* so, if you'd a been in this house for a while back. Why, they've stole everything they could lay their hands on—and we a watching, all the time, mind you. They stole that shirt right off o' the line! and as for that sheet they made the rag ladder out of ther' ain't no telling how many times they *didn't* steal that; and flour, and candles, and candlesticks, and spoons, and the old warming-pan, and most a thousand things that I disremember, now, and my new calico dress; and me, and Silas, and my Sid and Tom on the constant watch day *and* night, as I was'a telling you, and not a one of us could catch hide nor hair, nor sight nor sound of them; and here at the last minute, lo and behold you, they slides right in under our noses, and fools us, and not only fools *us* but the Injun Territory robbers too, and actuly gets *away* with that nigger, safe and sound, and that with sixteen men and twenty-two dogs right on their very heels at that very time! I tell you, it just bangs anything I ever *heard* of. Why, *sperits* couldn't a done better, and been no smarter. And I reckon they must a *been* sperits—because, *you* know our dogs, and ther' ain't no better; well, them dogs never even got on the *track* of'm, once! You explain *that* to me, if you can!—*any* of you!"

"Well, it does beat——"

"Laws alive, I never——"

"So help me, I wouldn't a be——"

"*House* thieves as well as——"

"Goodnessgracioussakes, I'd a ben afeard to *live* in sich a——"

"'Fraid to *live!*—why, I was that scared I dasn't hardly go to bed, or get up, or lay down, or *set* down, Sister Ridgeway. Why, they'd steal the very—why, goodness sakes, you can guess what kind of a fluster *I* was in by the time midnight come, last night. I hope to gracious if I warn't afraid they'd steal some o'the family! I was just to that pass, I didn't have no reasoning faculties no more. It looks foolish enough, *now,* in the day-time; but I says to myself, there's my two poor boys asleep, 'way up stairs in that lonesome room, and I declare to goodness I was that uneasy 't I crep' up there and locked 'em in! I *did.* And anybody would. Because, you know, when you get scared, that way, and it keeps running on, and getting worse and worse, all the time, and your wits gets to addling, and you get to doing all sorts o' wild things, and by-and-by you think to yourself, spos'n *I* was a boy, and was away up there, and the door ain't locked, and you—" She stopped, looking kind of wondering, and then she turned her head around slow, and when her eye lit on me—I got up and took a walk.

Says I to myself, I can explain better how we come to not be in that room this morning, if I go out to one side and study over it a little. So I done it. But I dasn't go fur, or she'd a sent for me. And when it was late in the day, the people all went, and then I come in and told her the noise and shooting waked up me and "Sid," and the door was locked, and we wanted to see the fun, so we went down the lightning-rod, and both of us got hurt a little, and we didn't never want to try *that* no more. And then I went on and told her all what I told Uncle Silas before; and then she said she'd forgive us, and maybe it was all right enough anyway, and about what a body might expect of boys, for all boys was a pretty harum-scarum lot, as fur as she could see; and so, as long as no harm hadn't come of it, she judged she better put in her time being grateful we was alive and well and she had us still, stead of fretting over what was past and done. So then she kissed me, and patted me on the head, and dropped into a kind of a brown study; and pretty soon jumps up, and says:

"Why, lawsamercy, it's most night, and Sid not come yet! What *has* become of that boy?"

I see my chance; so I skips and says:

"I'll run right up to town and get him," I says.

"No you won't," she says. "You'll stay right wher' you are; *one's* enough to be lost at a time. If he ain't here to supper, your uncle'll go."

Well, he warn't there to supper; so right after supper uncle went.

He come back about ten, a little bit uneasy; hadn't run across Tom's track. Aunt Sally was a good *deal* uneasy; but Uncle Silas he said there warn't no occasion to be—boys will be boys, he said, and you'll see this one turn up in the morning, all sound and right. So she had to be satisfied. But she said she'd set up for him a while, anyway, and keep a light burning, so he could see it.

And then when I went up to bed she come up with me and fetched her candle, and tucked me in, and mothered me so good I felt mean, and like I couldn't look her in the face; and she sat down on the bed and talked with me a long time, and said what a splendid boy Sid was, and didn't seem to want to ever stop talking about him; and kept asking me every now and then, if I reckoned he could a got lost, or hurt, or maybe drownded, and might be laying at this minute, somewheres, suffering or dead, and she not by him to help him, and so the tears would drip down, silent, and I would tell her that Sid was all right, and would be home in the morning, sure; and she would squeeze my hand, or maybe kiss me, and tell me to say it again, and keep on saying it, because it done her good, and she was in so much trouble. And when she was going away, she looked down in my eyes, so steady and gentle, and says:

"The door ain't going to be locked, Tom; and there's the window and the rod; but you'll be good, *won't* you? And you won't go? For *my* sake."

Laws knows I *wanted* to go, bad enough, to see about Tom, and was all intending to go; but after that, I wouldn't a went, not for kingdoms.

But she was on my mind, and Tom was on my mind; so I slept very restless. And twice I went down the rod, away in the night, and slipped around front, and see her setting there by her candle in the window with her eyes towards the road and the tears in them; and I wished I could do something for her, but I couldn't, only to swear that I wouldn't never do nothing to grieve her any more. And the third time, I waked up at dawn, and slid down, and she was there yet, and her candle was most out, and her old gray head was resting on her hand, and she was asleep.

CHAPTER XLII

The old man was up town again, before breakfast, but couldn't get no track of Tom; and both of them set at the table, thinking, and not saying nothing, and looking mournful, and their coffee getting cold, and not eating anything. And by-and-by the old man says:

"Did I give you the letter?"

"What letter?"

"The one I got yesterday out of the post-office."

"No, you didn't give me no letter."

"Well, I must a forgot it."

So he rummaged his pockets, and then went off somewheres where he had laid it down, and fetched it, and give it to her. She says:

"Why, it's from St. Petersburg—it's from Sis."

I allowed another walk would do me good; but I couldn't stir. But before she could break it open, she dropped and run—for she see something. And so did I. It was Tom Sawyer on a mattress; and that old doctor; and Jim, in *her* calico dress, with his hands tied behind him; and a lot of people. I hid the letter behind the first thing that come handy, and rushed. She flung herself at Tom, crying, and says:

"Oh, he's dead, he's dead, I know he's dead!"

And Tom he turned his head a little, and muttered something or other, which showed he warn't in his right mind; then she flung up her hands, and says:

"He's alive, thank God! And that's enough!" she snatched a kiss of him, and flew for the house to get the bed ready, and scattering orders right and left at the niggers and everybody else, as fast as her tongue could go, every jump of the way.

I followed the men to see what they was going to do with Jim; and the old doctor and Uncle Silas followed after Tom into the house. The men was very huffy, and some of them wanted to hang Jim, for an example to all the other niggers around there, so they wouldn't be trying to run away, like Jim done, and making such a raft of trouble, and keeping a whole family scared most to death for days and nights. But the others said, don't do it, it wouldn't answer at all, he ain't our nigger, and his owner would turn up and make us pay for him, sure. So that cooled them down a little, because the people that's always the most anxious for to hang a nigger that hain't done just right, is always the very ones that ain't the most anxious to pay for him when they've got their satisfaction out of him.

They cussed Jim considerable, though, and give him a cuff or two, side the head, once in a while, but Jim never said nothing, and he never let on to know me, and they took him to the same cabin, and put his own clothes on him, and chained him again, and not to no bed-leg, this time, but to a big staple drove into the bottom log, and chained his hands, too, and both legs, and said he warn't to have nothing but bread and water to eat, after this, till his owner come or he was sold at auction, because he didn't come in a certain length of time, and filled up our hole, and said a couple of farmers with guns must stand watch around about the cabin every night, and bull-dog tied to the door in the day-time; and about this time they was through with the job and was tapering off with a kind of generl good-bye cussing, and then the old doctor comes and takes a look, and says:

"Don't be no rougher on him than you're obleeged to, because he ain't a bad nigger. When I got to where I found the boy, I see I couldn't cut the bullet out without some help, and he warn't in no condition for me to leave, to go and get help; and he got a little worse and a little worse, and after a long time he went out of his head, and wouldn't let me come anigh him, any more, and said if I chalked his raft he'd kill me, and no end of wild foolishness like that, and I see I couldn't do anything at all with him; so I says, I got to have *help,* somehow; and the minute I says it, out crawls this nigger from somewheres, and says he'll help, and he done it, too, and done it very well. Of course I judged he must be a runaway nigger, and there I *was!* and there I had to stick, right straight along all the rest of the days, and all night. It was a fix, I tell you! I had a couple of patients with the chills, and of course I'd of liked to run up to town and see them, but I dasn't because the nigger might get away, and then I'd be to blame; and yet never a skiff come close enough for me to hail. So there I had to stick, plumb till daylight this morning' and I never see a nigger that was a better nuss or faithfuller, and yet he was resking his freedom to do it, and was all tired out, too, and I see plain enough he'd been worked main hard, lately, I liked the nigger for that; I tell you, gentlemen, a nigger like that is worth a thousand dollars—and kind treatment, too. I had everything I needed, and the boy was doing as well there as he would a done at home—better, maybe, because it was so quiet; but there I *was,* with both of 'm on my hands; and there I had to stick, till about dawn this morning; then some men in a skiff come by, and as good luck would have it, the nigger was setting by the pallet with his head propped on his knees, sound asleep; so I motioned them in, quiet, and they slipped up on him and grabbed him and tied him before he knowed what he was about, and we never had no trouble. And the boy being in a kind of a flightly sleep, too, we muffled the oars and hitched the raft on, and towed her over very nice and quiet, and the nigger never made the least row nor said a word, from the start. He ain't no bad nigger, gentlemen; that's what I think about him."

Somebody says:

"Well, it sounds very good, doctor, I'm obleeged to say."

Then the others softened up a little, too, and I was mightly thankful to that old doctor for doing Jim that good turn; and I was glad it was according to my judgment of him, too; because I thought he had a good heart in him and was a good man, the first time I see him. Then they all agreed that Jim had acted very well, and was deserving to have some notice took of it, and reward. So every one of them promised, right out and hearty, that they wouldn't cuss him no more.

Then they come out and locked him up. I hoped they was going to say he could have one or two of the chains took off, because they was rotten heavy, or could have meat and greens with his bread and water, but they didn't think of it, and I reckoned it warn't best for me to mix in, but I judged I'd get the doctor's yarn to Aunt Sally, somehow or other, as soon as I'd got through the breakers that was laying just ahead of me. Explanations, I mean, of how I forgot to mention about Sid being shot, when I was telling how him and me put in that drafted night paddling around hunting the runaway nigger.

But I had plenty time. Aunt Sally she stuck to the sick-room all day and all night; and every time I see Uncle Silas mooning around, I dodged him.

Next morning I heard Tom was a good deal better, and they said Aunt Sally was gone to get a nap. So I slips to the sick-room, and if I found him awake I reckoned we could put up a yarn for the family that would wash. But he was sleeping, and sleeping very peaceful, too; and pale, not fire-faced the way he was when he come. So I set down and laid for him to wake. In about a half an hour, Aunt Sally comes gliding in, and there I was, up a stump again! She motioned me to be still, and set down by me, and begun to whisper, and said we could all be joyful now, because all the symptoms was first rate, and he'd been sleeping like that for ever so long, and looking better and peacefuller all the time, and ten to one he'd wake up in his right mind.

So we set there watching, and by-and-by he stirs a bit, and opens his eyes very natural, and takes a look, and says:

"Hello, why I'm at *home!* How's that? Where's the raft?"

"It's all right," I says.

"And *Jim?*"

"The same," I says, but couldn't say it pretty brash. But he never noticed, but says:

"Good! Splendid! *Now* we're all right and safe! Did you tell Aunty?"

I was going to say yes; but she chipped in and says:

"About what, Sid?"

"Why, about the way the whole thing was done."

"What whole thing?"

"Why, *the* whole thing. There ain't but one; how we set the runaway nigger free—me and Tom."

"Good land! Set the run—What *is* the child talking about! Dear, dear out of his head again!"

"*No,* I ain't out of my HEAD; I know all what I'm talking about. We *did* set him free—me and Tom. We laid out to do it, and we *done* it. And we done it elegant, too." He'd got a start, and she never checked him up, just set and stared and stared, and let him clip along, and I see it warn't no use for *me* to put it. "Why, Aunty, it cost us a power of work—weeks of it—hours and hours, every night, whilst you was all asleep. And we had to steal candles, and the sheet, and the shirt, and your dress, and spoons, and tin plates, and case-knives, and the warming-pan, and the grind-stone, and flour, and just no end of things, and you can't think what work it was to make the saws and pens, and inscriptions, and one thing or another, and you can't think *half* the fun it was. And we had to make up the pictures of coffins and things, and nonnamous letters from the robbers, and get up and down the lightning-rod, and dig the hole into the cabin, and make the rope-ladder and send it in cooked up in a pie, and send in spoons and things to work with, in your apron pocket"—

"Mercy sakes!"

——"and load up the cabin with rats and snakes and so on, for company for Jim; and then you kept Tom here so long with the butter in his hat that you come near spilling the whole business, because the men come before we was out of the cabin, and we had to rush, and they heard us and let drive at us, and I got my share, and we dodged out of the path and let them go by, and when the dogs come they warn't interested in us, but went for the most noise, and we got our canoe, and made for the raft, and was all safe, and Jim was a free man, and we done it all by ourselves, and *wasn't* it bully, Aunty!"

"Well, I never heard the likes of it in all my born days! So it was *you*, you little rapscallions, that's been making all this trouble, and turned everybody's wits clean inside out and scared us all most to death. I've as good a notion as ever I had in my life, to take it out o' you this very minute. To think, here I've been, night after night, a—*you* just get well once, you young scamp, and I lay I'll tan the Old Harry[1] out o' both o' ye!"

But Tom, he *was* so proud and joyful, he just *couldn't* hold in, and his tongue just *went* it—she a-chipping in, and spitting fire all along, and both of them going it at once, like a cat-convention; and she says:

"*Well*, you get all the enjoyment you can out of it *now*, for mind I tell you if I catch you meddling with him again——"

"Meddling with *who?*" Tom says, dropping his smile and looking surprised.

"With *who?*" Why, the runaway nigger, of course. Who'd you reckon?"

Tom looks at me very grave, and says:

"Tom, didn't you just tell me he was all right? Hasn't he got away?"

"*Him?*" says Aunt Sally; "the runaway nigger? 'Deed he hasn't. They've got him back, safe and sound, and he's in that cabin again, on bread and water, and loaded down with chains, till he's claimed or sold!"

Tom rose square up in bed, with his eye hot, and his nostrils opening and shutting like gills, and sings out to me:

"They hain't no *right* to shut him up! *Shove!*—and don't you lose a minute. Turn him loose! he ain't no slave; he's as free as any cretur that walks this earth!"

"What *does* this child mean?"

"I mean every word I *say*, Aunt Sally, and if somebody don't go, *I*'ll go. I've knowed him all his life, and so has Tom, there. Old Miss Watson died two months ago, and she was ashamed she ever was going to sell him down the river, and *said* so; and she set him free in her will."

"Then what on earth did *you* want to set him free for, seeing he was already free?"

"Well, that *is* a question, I must say; and *just* like women! Why, I wanted the *adventure* of it; and I'd a waded neck-deep in blood to—goodness alive, AUNT POLLY!"

If she warn't standing right there, just inside the door, looking as sweet and contented as an angel half-full of pie, I wish I may never!

Aunt Sally jumped for her, and most hugged the head off of her, and cried over her, and I found a good enough place for me under the bed, for it was

[1]The Devil.

getting pretty sultry, for *us,* seemed to me. And I peeped out, and in a little while Tom's Aunt Polly shook herself loose and stood there looking across at Tom over her spectacles—kind of grinding him into the earth, you know. And then she says:

"Yes, you *better* turn y'r head away—I would if I was you, Tom."

"Oh, deary me!" says Aunt Sally; "*is* he changed so? Why, that ain't *Tom,* it's Sid; Tom's—Tom's—why, where is Tom? He was here a minute ago."

"You mean where's Huck *Finn*—that's what you mean! I reckon I hain't raised such a scamp as my Tom all these years, not to know him when I *see* him. That *would* be a pretty howdy-do. Come out from under that bed, Huck Finn."

So I don it. But not feeling brash.

Aunt Sally she was one of the mixed-upset looking persons I ever see; except one, and that was Uncle Silas, when he come in, and they told it all to him. It kind of made him drunk, as you may say, and he didn't know nothing at all the rest of the day, and preached a prayer-meeting sermon that night that give him a rattling ruputation, because the oldest man in the world couldn't a understood it. So Tom's Aunt Polly, she told all about who I was, and what; and I had to up and tell how I was in such a tight place that when Mrs. Phelps took me for Tom Sawyer—she chipped in and says, "Oh, go on and call me Aunt Sally, I'm used to it, now, and 'tain't no need to change"——that when Aunt Sally took me for Tom Sawyer, I had to stand it—there warn't no other way, and I knowed he wouldn't mind, because it would be nuts for him, being a mystery, and he'd make an adventure out of it and be perfectly satisfied. And so it turned out, and he let on to be Sid, and made things as soft as he could for me.

And his Aunt Polly she said Tom was right about old Miss Watson setting Jim free in her will; and so, sure enough, Tom Sawyer had gone and took all that trouble and bother to set a free nigger free! and I couldn't ever understand, before, until that minute and that talk, how he *could* help a body set a nigger free, with his bringing-up.

Well, Aunt Polly she said that when Aunt Sally wrote to her that Tom and *Sid* had come, all right and safe, she says to herself:

"Look at that, now! I might have expected it, letting him go off that way without anybody to watch him. So now I got to go and trapse all the way down the river, eleven hundred mile, and find out what the creetur's up to, *this* time; as long as I couldn't seem to get any answer out of you about it."

"Why, I never heard nothing from you," says Aunt Sally.

"Well, I wonder! Why, I wrote to you twice, to ask you what you could mean by Sid being here."

"Well, I never got 'em, Sis."

Aunt Polly, she turns around slow and severe, and says:

"You, Tom!"

"Well—*what?*" he says, kind of pettish.

"Don't you what *me,* you impudent thing—hand out them letters."

"What letters?"

"*Them* letters. I be bound, if I have to take aholt of you I'll——"

"They're in the trunk. There, now. And they're just the same as they was when I got them out of the office. I hain't looked into them, I hain't touched them. But I knowed they'd make trouble, and I thought if you warn't in no hurry, I'd——"

"Well, you *do* need skinning, there ain't no mistake about it. And I wrote another one to tell you I was coming; and I spose he——"

"No, it come yesterday; I hain't read it yet, but *it's* all right, I've got that one."

I wanted to offer to bet two dollars she hadn't, but I reckoned maybe it was just as safe to not to. So, I never said nothing.

CHAPTER THE LAST

The first time I catched Tom, private, I asked him what was his idea, time of the evasion?—what it was he'd planned to do if the evasion worked all right and he managed to set a nigger free that was already free before? And he said, what he had planned in his head, from the start, if we got Jim out all safe, was for us to run him down the river, on the raft, and have adventures plumb to the mouth of the river, and then tell him about his being free, and take him back up home on a steamboat, in style, and pay him for his lost time, and write word ahead and get out all the niggers around, and have them waltz him into town with a torchlight procession and a brass band, and then he would be a hero, and so would we. But I reckoned it was about as well the way it was.

We had Jim out of the chains in no time, and when Aunt Polly and Uncle Silas and Aunt Sally found out how good he helped the doctor nurse Tom, they made a heap of fuss over him, and fixed him up prime, and give him all he wanted to eat, and a good time, and nothing to do. And we had him up to the sick-room; and had a high talk; and Tom give Jim forty dollars for being prisoner for us so patient, and doing it up so good, and Jim was pleased most to death, and busted out, and says:

"*Dah,* now, Huck, what I tell you?—what I tell you up dah on Jackson islan'? I *tole* you I got a hairy breas', en what's de sign un it; en I *tole* you I ben rich wunst, en gwineter to be rich *agin;* en it's come true; en heah she *is! Dah,* now! doan' talk to *me*—signs is *signs,* mine I tell you; en I knowed jis' 's well 'at I 'uz gwineter be rich agin as I's a stannin' heah dis minute!"

And then Tom he talked along, and talked along, and says le's all three slide out of here, one of these nights, and get an outfit, and go for howling adventures amongst the Injuns, over in the Terrority, for a couple of weeks or two; and I says, all right, that suits me, but I ain't got no money for to buy the outfit, and I reckon I couldn't get none from home, because it's likely pap's been back before now, and got it all away from Judge Thatcher and drunk it up.

"No he hain't," Tom says; "it's all there, yet—six thousand dollars and more; and your pap hain't ever been back since. Hadn't when I come away, anyhow."

Jim says, kind of solemn:

"He ain't a comin' back no mo', Huck."

I says:

"Why, Jim?"

"Nemmine why, Huck—but he ain't comin' back no mo'."

But I kept at him; so at last he says:

"Doan' you 'member de house dat was float'n down de river, en dey wuz a man in dah, kivered up, en I went in en unkivered him and didn't let you come in? Well, den, you k'n git yo' money when you wants it; kase dat wuz him."

Tom's most well, now, and got his bullet around his neck on a watch-guard for a watch, and is always seeing what time it is, and so there ain't nothing more to write about, and I am rotten glad of it, because if I'd a knowed what a trouble it was to make a book I wouldn't a tackled it and ain't agoing to no more. But I reckon I got to light out for the Territory ahead of the rest, because Aunt Sally she's going to adopt me and sivilize me and I can't stand it. I been there before.

THE END. YOURS TRULY, HUCK FINN.

1876–1883 1884, 1885

Mary E. Wilkins Freeman 1852–1930

In the years following the Civil War, decaying villages and abandoned farms marked the landscape of rural New England. Cheap land in the West and the lure of jobs in growing industrial centers to the south drew off the stronger, younger, and more adventurous. Those who remained behind often lacked the opportunity or the will to leave. A substantial portion were unmarried women. They were so numerous that the strong-willed New England spinster, the stern old maid, became a public institution, the object of poems, jokes, songs, and newspaper cartoons. It was just such women, waiting tidily in fading New England villages, who became the subjects of Mary Wilkins Freeman's best stories.

Until her marriage in middle age to Dr. Charles Freeman of Metuchen, New Jersey, Mary Eleanor Wilkins lived in Randolph, Massachusetts, and in Brattleboro, Vermont, small towns in decline, with empty stores along the main street and silent mills along the river. She was in frail health as a girl, and in her solitude she turned naturally to reading. As a teenager she wrote and published a number of poems for children, but she decided to make writing her career when she was in her early twenties and needed a vocation to help support her family. Her love of books was equaled by a curiosity about the towns of Vermont and Massachusetts. She studied their histories, their distinctive buildings, and the dialect and character of their people.

In 1881, she received ten dollars for a poem published in a children's magazine. Her first book was a collection of children's verse, Decorative Plaques *(1883). Her first success in writing fiction for adults came in 1882 with "A Shadow Story," which won a prize of fifty dollars from a Boston weekly. Two years later, when* Harper's Bazar *accepted "Two Old Lovers" for publication, her career was launched, and her stories were soon in demand by editors of major magazines. She drew the admiration of such literary notables as James Russell Lowell and Henry James. Her stories were republished in England, and from France came requests for permission to translate her stories into French. In all she published thirty-nine volumes. Her best were* A Humble Romance and Other Stories *(1887), and* A New England Nun and Other Stories *(1891), tales of stolid village and farm people in remote New England.*

Mary Wilkins Freeman aimed "to preserve in literature" the "old and probably disappearing ways of New England character." Her stories mix elements of romance, realism, and naturalism. She wrote of strong-minded people whose individualism earns the wrath of friends and village neighbors. She depicted the pinched and stagnating lives of hesitant lovers whose endlessly prolonged courtships are destined never to conclude in marriage. Her work is frequently compared to that of Sarah Orne Jewett. Both were spinster ladies, describing the lives of the men and women of small-town New England. Both have been identified with the local color tradition in American literature—writers whose stories and sketches emphasize the character types, customs, settings, and speech of regions that in nineteenth-century America still preserved their distinct identity.

Yet Mary Freeman's writing was less concerned with locale, more concerned with character. And her writing had a sharp, ironic edge to it that Sarah Orne Jewett seldom attempted. Freeman's stories are written with greater detachment, less sympathetic musing at the dilemmas of her characters. Her view could be sharp, critical, unsparing. Lacking the lenient tenderness that Sarah Orne Jewett exhibited for the people she described, Mary Wilkins Freeman could achieve a realism that to modern eyes more clearly portrays the strength and follies of the people she lived among, a realism that justifiably brought her recognition as "the most truthful recorder in fiction of New England life."

FURTHER READING: E. Foster, *Mary E. Wilkins Freeman,* 1956; A. Hamblen, *The New England Art of Mary E. Wilkins Freeman,* 1966; P. Westbrook, *Mary Wilkins Freeman,* 1967, 1988; *Critical Essays on Mary Wilkins Freeman,* ed. S. Marchalonis, 1991; *The Uncollected Stories of Mary Wilkins Freeman,* ed. M. Reichardt, 1992; M. Reichardt, *A Web of Relationship, Women in the Short Fiction of Mary Wilkins Freeman,* 1992; L. Glasser, *In a Closet Hidden, The Life of Mary E. Wilkins Freeman,* 1996; *A Mary Wilkins Freeman Reader,* ed. M. Reichardt, 1997; M. Reichardt, *Mary Wilkins Freeman, A Study of the Short Fiction,* 1998.

TEXT: *A New England Nun and Other Stories,* 1891.

A NEW ENGLAND NUN

It was late in the afternoon, and the light was waning. There was a difference in the look of the tree shadows out in the yard. Somewhere in the distance cows were lowing and a little bell was tinkling; now and then a farm-wagon tilted by, and the dust flew; some blue-shirted laborers with shovels over their shoulders plodded past; little swarms of flies were dancing up and down before the people's faces in the soft air. There seemed to be a gentle stir arising over everything for the mere sake of subsidence—a very premonition of rest and hush and night.

This soft diurnal[1] commotion was over Louisa Ellis also. She had been peacefully sewing at her sitting-room window all the afternoon. Now she quilted her needle carefully into her work, which she folded precisely, and laid in a basket with her thimble and thread and scissors. Louisa Ellis could not remember that ever in her life she had mislaid one of these little feminine appurtenances, which had become, from long use and constant association, a very part of her personality.

Louisa tied a green apron round her waist, and got out a flat straw hat with a green ribbon. Then she went into the garden with a little blue crockery bowl, to pick some currants for her tea. After the currants were picked she sat on the back door-step and stemmed them, collecting the stems carefully in her apron, and afterwards throwing them into the hen-coop. She looked sharply at the grass beside the step to see if any had fallen there.

Louisa was slow and still in her movements; it took her a long time to prepare her tea; but when ready it was set forth, with as much grace as if she had been a veritable[2] guest to her own self. The little square table stood exactly in the centre of the kitchen, and was covered with a starched linen cloth whose border pattern of flowers glistened. Louisa had a damask[3] napkin on her tea-tray, where were arranged a cut-glass tumbler full of teaspoons, a silver cream-pitcher, a china sugar-bowl, and one pink china cup and saucer. Louisa used china every day—something which none of her neighbors did. They whispered about it among themselves. Their daily tables were laid with common crockery, their sets of best china stayed in the parlor closet, and Louisa Ellis was no richer nor better bred than they. Still she would use the china. She had for her supper a glass dish full of sugared currants, a plate of little cakes, and one of light white biscuits. Also a leaf or two of lettuce, which she cut up daintily. Louisa was very fond of lettuce, which she raised to perfection in her little garden. She ate quite heartily, though in a delicate, pecking way; it seemed almost surprising that any considerable bulk of the food should vanish.

After tea she filled a plate with nicely baked thin corncakes, and carried them out into the back-yard.

"Cæsar!" she called. "Cæsar! Cæsar!"

There was a little rush, and the clank of a chain, and a large yellow-and-white dog appeared at the door of his tiny hut, which was half hidden among the tall grasses and flowers. Louisa patted him and gave him the corn-cakes. Then she returned to the house and washed the tea-things, polishing the china carefully. The twilight had deepened; the chorus of the frogs floated in at the open window wonderfully loud and shrill, and once in a while a long sharp drone from a tree-toad pierced it. Louisa took off her green gingham apron, disclosing a shorter one of pink and white print. She lighted her lamp, and sat down again with her sewing.

In about half an hour Joe Dagget came. She heard his heavy step on the walk, and rose and took off her pink-and-white apron. Under that was still another—white linen with a little cambric edging on the bottom; that was Louisa's company apron. She never wore it without her calico sewing apron over it unless she had a guest. She had barely folded the pink and white one

[1]Daily. [2]True. [3]Elegant, richly patterned linen.

with methodical haste and laid it in a table-drawer when the door opened and Joe Dagget entered.

He seemed to fill up the whole room. A little yellow canary that had been asleep in his green cage at the south window woke up and fluttered wildly, beating his little yellow wings against the wires. He always did so when Joe Dagget came into the room.

"Good-evening," said Louisa. She extended her hand with a kind of solemn cordiality.

"Good-evening, Louisa," returned the man, in a loud voice.

She placed a chair for him, and they sat facing each other, with the table between them. He sat bolt-upright, toeing out his heavy feet squarely, glancing with a good-humored uneasiness around the room. She sat gently erect, folding her slender hands in her white-linen lap.

"Been a pleasant day," remarked Dagget.

"Real pleasant," Louisa assented, softly. "Have you been haying?" she asked, after a little while.

"Yes, I've been haying all day, down in the ten-acre lot. Pretty hot work."

"It must be."

"Yes, it's pretty hot work in the sun."

"Is your mother well to-day?"

"Yes, mother's pretty well."

"I suppose Lily Dyer's with her now?"

Dagget colored. "Yes, she's with her," he answered, slowly.

He was not very young, but there was a boyish look about his large face. Louisa was not quite as old as he, her face was fairer and smoother, but she gave people the impression of being older.

"I suppose she's a good deal of help to your mother," she said, further.

"I guess she is; I don't know how mother'd get along without her," said Dagget, with a sort of embarrassed warmth.

"She looks like a real capable girl. She's pretty-looking too," remarked Louisa.

"Yes, she is pretty fair looking."

Presently Dagget began fingering the books on the table. There was a square red autograph album, and a Young Lady's Gift-Book[4] which had belonged to Louisa's mother. He took them up one after the other and opened them; then laid them down again, the album on the Gift-Book.

Louisa kept eying them with mild uneasiness. Finally she rose and changed the position of the books, putting the album underneath. That was the way they had been arranged in the first place.

Dagget gave an awkward little laugh. "Now what difference did it make which book was on top?" said he.

Louisa looked at him with a deprecating smile. "I always keep them that way," murmured she.

"You do beat everything," said Dagget, trying to laugh again. His large face was flushed.

[4]An expensive, decorative book. Widely popular in the nineteenth century, gift-books were collections of poems, essays, and fiction of elevated sentiment. They were often set out, like modern coffee-table books, as evidence of the refined gentility of the household.

He remained about an hour longer, then rose to take leave. Going out, he stumbled over a rug, and trying to recover himself, hit Louisa's work-basket on the table, and knocked it on the floor.

He looked at Louisa, then at the rolling spools; he ducked himself awkwardly toward them, but she stopped him. "Never mind," said she; "I'll pick them up after you're gone."

She spoke with a mild stiffness. Either she was a little disturbed, or his nervousness affected her, and made her seem constrained in her effort to reassure him.

When Joe Dagget was outside he drew in the sweet evening air with a sigh, and felt much as an innocent and perfectly well-intentioned bear might after his exit from a china shop.

Louisa, on her part, felt much as the kind-hearted, long-suffering owner of the china shop might have done after the exit of the bear.

She tied on the pink, then the green apron, picked up all the scattered treasures and replaced them in her work-basket, and straightened the rug. Then she set the lamp on the floor, and began sharply examining the carpet. She even rubbed her fingers over it, and looked at them.

"He's tracked in a good deal of dust," she murmured. "I thought he must have."

Louisa got a dust-pan and brush, and swept Joe Dagget's track carefully.

If he could have known it, it would have increased his perplexity and uneasiness, although it would not have disturbed his loyalty in the least. He came twice a week to see Louisa Ellis, and every time, sitting there in her delicately sweet room, he felt as if surrounded by a hedge of lace. He was afraid to stir lest he should put a clumsy foot or hand through the fairy web, and he had always the consciousness that Louisa was watching fearfully lest he should.

Still the lace and Louisa commanded perforce his perfect respect and patience and loyalty. They were to be married in a month, after a singular courtship which had lasted for a matter of fifteen years. For fourteen out of the fifteen years the two had not once seen each other, and they had seldom exchanged letters. Joe had been all those years in Australia, where he had gone to make his fortune, and where he had stayed until he made it. He would have stayed fifty years if it had taken so long, and come home feeble and tottering, or never come home at all, to marry Louisa.

But the fortune had been made in the fourteen years, and he had come home now to marry the woman who had been patiently and unquestioningly waiting for him all that time.

Shortly after they were engaged he had announced to Louisa his determination to strike out into new fields, and secure a competency before they should be married. She had listened and assented with the sweet serenity which never failed her, not even when her lover set forth on that long and uncertain journey. Joe, buoyed up as he was by his sturdy determination, broke down a little at the last, but Louisa kissed him with a mild blush, and said good-by.

"It won't be for long," poor Joe had said, huskily; but it was for fourteen years.

In that length of time much had happened. Louisa's mother and brother had died, and she was all alone in the world. But greatest happening of all—

a subtle happening which both were too simple to understand—Louisa's feet had turned into a path, smooth maybe under a calm, serene sky, but so straight and unswerving that it could only meet a check at her grave, and so narrow that there was no room for any one at her side.

Louisa's first emotion when Joe Dagget came home (he had not apprised her of his coming) was consternation, although she would not admit it to herself, and he never dreamed of it. Fifteen years ago she had been in love with him—at least she considered herself to be. Just at that time, gently acquiescing with and falling into the natural drift of girlhood, she had seen marriage ahead as a reasonable feature and a probable desirability of life. She had listened with calm docility to her mother's views upon the subject. Her mother was remarkable for her cool sense and sweet, even temperament. She talked wisely to her daughter when Joe Dagget presented himself, and Louisa accepted him with no hesitation. He was the first lover she had ever had.

She had been faithful to him all these years. She had never dreamed of the possibility of marrying any one else. Her life, especially for the last seven years, had been full of a pleasant peace, she had never felt discontented nor impatient over her lover's absence; still she had always looked forward to his return and their marriage as the inevitable conclusion of things. However, she had fallen into a way of placing it so far in the future that it was almost equal to placing it over the boundaries of another life.

When Joe came she had been expecting him, and expecting to be married for fourteen years, but she was much surprised and taken aback as if she had never thought of it.

Joe's consternation came later. He eyed Louisa with an instant confirmation of his old admiration. She had changed but little. She still kept her pretty manner and soft grace, and was, he considered, every whit as attractive as ever. As for himself, his stent[5] was done; he had turned his face away from fortune-seeking, and the old winds of romance whistled as loud and sweet as ever through his ears. All the song which he had been wont to hear in them was Louisa; he had for a long time a loyal belief that he heard it still, but finally it seemed to him that although the winds sang always that one song, it had another name. But for Louisa the wind had never more than murmured; now it had gone down, and everything was still. She listened for a little while with half-wistful attention; then she turned quietly away and went to work on her wedding clothes.

Joe had made some extensive and quite magnificent alterations in his house. It was the old homestead; the newly-married couple would live there, for Joe could not desert his mother, who refused to leave her old home. So Louisa must leave hers. Every morning, rising and going about among her neat maidenly possessions, she felt as one looking her last upon the faces of dear friends. It was true that in a measure she could take them with her, but, robbed of their old environments, they would appear in such new guises that they would almost cease to be themselves. Then there were some peculiar features of her happy solitary life which she would probably be obliged to relinquish altogether. Sterner tasks than these graceful but half-needless ones would probably devolve upon her. There would be a large house to care for;

[5]Stint: task, time of service.

there would be company to entertain; there would be Joe's rigorous and feeble old mother to wait upon; and it would be contrary to all thrifty village traditions for her to keep more than one servant. Louisa had a little still, and she used to occupy herself pleasantly in summer weather with distilling the sweet and aromatic essences from roses and peppermint and spearmint. By-and-by her still must be laid away. Her store of essences was already considerable, and there would be no time for her to distil for the mere pleasure of it. Then Joe's mother would think it foolishness; she had already hinted her opinion in the matter. Louisa dearly loved to sew a linen seam, not always for use, but for the simple, mild pleasure which she took in it. She would have been loath to confess how more than once she had ripped a seam for the mere delight of sewing it together again. Sitting at her window during long sweet afternoons, drawing her needle gently through the dainty fabric, she was peace itself. But there was a small chance of such foolish comfort in the future. Joe's mother, domineering, shrewd old matron that she was even in her old age, and very likely even Joe himself, with his honest masculine rudeness, would laugh and frown down all these pretty but senseless old maiden ways.

Louisa had almost the enthusiasm of an artist over the mere order and cleanliness of her solitary home. She had throbs of genuine triumph at the sight of the window-panes which she had polished until they shone like jewels. She gloated gently over her orderly bureau-drawers, with their exquisitely folded contents redolent with lavender and sweet clover and very purity. Could she be sure of the endurance of even this? She had visions, so startling that she half repudiated them as indelicate, of coarse masculine belongings strewn about in endless litter; of dust and disorder arising necessarily from a coarse masculine presence in the midst of all this delicate harmony.

Among her forebodings of disturbance, not the least was with regard to Cæsar. Cæsar was a veritable hermit of a dog. For the greater part of his life he had dwelt in his secluded hut, shut out from the society of his kind and all innocent canine joys. Never had Cæsar since his early youth watched at a woodchuck's hole; never had he known the delights of a stray bone at a neighbor's kitchen door. And it was all on account of a sin committed when hardly out of his puppyhood. No one knew the possible depth of remorse of which this mild-visaged, altogether innocent-looking old dog might be capable; but whether or not he had encountered remorse, he had encountered a full measure of righteous retribution. Old Cæsar seldom lifted up his voice in a growl or a bark; he was fat and sleepy; there were yellow rings which looked like spectacles around his dim old eyes; but there was a neighbor who bore on his hand the imprint of several of Cæsar's sharp white youthful teeth, and for that he had lived at the end of a chain, all alone in a little hut, for fourteen years. The neighbor, who was choleric and smarting with the pain of his wound, had demanded either Cæsar's death or complete ostracism. So Louisa's brother, to whom the dog had belonged, had built him his little kennel and tied him up. It was now fourteen years since, in a flood of youthful spirits, he had inflicted that memorable bite, and with the exception of short excursions, always at the end of the chain, under the strict guardianship of his master or Louisa, the old dog had remained a close prisoner. It is doubtful if, with his limited ambition, he took much pride in the fact, but it is certain that he was possessed of considerable cheap fame. He was regarded by all the children in the village and by many adults as a very monster of ferocity. St. George's dragon[6] could hardly have surpassed in evil repute Louisa Ellis's old yellow dog. Mothers charged their children with solemn emphasis not to go too near to him, and the children listened and believed greedily, with a fascinated appetite for terror, and ran by Louisa's house stealthily, with many sidelong and backward glances at the terrible dog. If perchance he sounded a hoarse bark, there was a panic. Wayfarers chancing into Louisa's yard eyed him with respect, and inquired if the chain were stout. Cæsar at large might have seemed a very ordinary dog, and excited no comment whatever; chained, his reputation overshadowed him, so that he lost his own proper outlines and looked darkly vague and enormous. Joe Dagget, however, with his good-humored sense and shrewdness, saw him as he was. He strode valiantly up to him and patted him on the head, in spite of Louisa's soft clamor of warning, and even attempted to set him loose. Louisa grew so alarmed that he desisted, but kept announcing his opinion in the matter quite forcibly at intervals. "There ain't a better-natured dog in town," he would say, "and it's down-right cruel to keep him tied up there. Some day I'm going to take him out."

Louisa had very little hope that he would not, one of these days, when their interests and possessions should be more completely fused in one. She pictured to herself Cæsar on the rampage through the quiet and unguarded village. She saw innocent children bleeding in his path. She was herself very fond of the old dog, because he had belonged to her dead brother and he was always very gentle with her; still she had great faith in his ferocity. She always warned people not to go too near him. She fed him on ascetic fare of corn-mush and cakes, and never fired his dangerous temper with heating and sanguinary diet of flesh and bones. Louisa looked at the old dog munching his simple fare, and thought of her approaching marriage and trembled. Still no anticipation of disorder and confusion in lieu of sweet peace and harmony, no forebodings of Cæsar on the rampage, no wild fluttering of her little yellow canary, were sufficient to turn her a hair's-breadth. Joe Dagget had been fond of her and working for her all these years. It was not for her, whatever came to pass, to prove untrue and break his heart. She put the exquisite little stitches into her wedding-garments, and the time went on until it was only a week before her wedding-day. It was a Tuesday evening, and the wedding was to be a week from Wednesday.

There was a full moon that night. About nine o'clock Louisa strolled down the road a little way. There were harvest-fields on either hand, bordered by low stone walls. Luxuriant clumps of bushes grew beside the wall, and trees—wild cherry and old apple-trees—at intervals. Presently Louisa sat down on the wall and looked about her with mildly sorrowful reflectiveness. Tall shrubs of blueberry and meadow-sweet, all woven together and tangled with blackberry vines and horsebriers, shut her in on either side. She had a little clear space between them. Opposite her, on the other side of the road, was a spreading tree; the moon shone between its boughs, and the leaves twinkled

[6]According to medieval legend, the Christian hero Saint George slew a ferocious dragon, thus freeing an innocent maiden (the dragon's hostage) and ridding the land of terror.

like silver. The road was bespread with a beautiful shifting dapple of silver and shadow; the air was full of a mysterious sweetness. "I wonder if it's wild grapes?" murmured Louisa. She sat there some time. She was just thinking of rising, when she heard footsteps and low voices, and remained quiet. It was a lonely place, and she felt a little timid. She thought she would keep still in the shadow and let the persons, whoever they might be, pass her.

But just before they reached her the voices ceased, and the footsteps. She understood that their owners had also found seats upon the stone wall. She was wondering if she could not steal away unobserved, when the voice broke the stillness. It was Joe Dagget's. She sat still and listened.

The voice was announced by a loud sigh, which was familiar as itself. "Well," said Dagget, "you've made up your mind, then, I suppose?"

"Yes," returned another voice; "I'm going day after to-morrow."

"That's Lily Dyer," thought Louisa to herself. The voice embodied itself in her mind. She saw a girl tall and full-figured, with a firm, fair face, looking fairer and firmer in the moonlight, her strong yellow hair braided in a close knot. A girl full of a calm rustic strength and bloom, with a masterful way which might have beseemed a princess. Lily Dyer was a favorite with the village folk; she had just the qualities to arouse the admiration. She was good and handsome and smart. Louisa had often heard her praises sounded.

"Well," said Joe Dagget, "I ain't got a word to say."

"I don't know what you could say," returned Lily Dyer.

"Not a word to say," repeated Joe, drawing out the words heavily. Then there was a silence. "I ain't sorry," he began at last, "that that happened yesterday—that we kind of let on how we felt to each other. I guess it's just as well we knew. Of course I can't do anything any different. I'm going right on an' get married next week. I ain't going back on a woman that's waited for me fourteen years, an' break her heart."

"If you should jilt her to-morrow, I wouldn't have you," spoke up the girl, with sudden vehemence.

"Well, I ain't going to give you the chance," said he; "but I don't believe you would, either."

"You'd see I wouldn't. Honor's honor, an' right's right. An' I'd never think anything of any man that went against 'em for me or any other girl; you'd find that out, Joe Dagget."

"Well, you'll find out fast enough that I ain't going against 'em for you or any other girl," returned he. Their voices sounded almost as if they were angry with each other. Louisa was listening eagerly.

"I'm sorry you feel as if you must go away," said Joe, "but I don't know but it's best."

"Of course it's best. I hope you and I have got common-sense."

"Well, I suppose you're right." Suddenly Joe's voice got an undertone of tenderness. "Say, Lily," said he, "I'll get along well enough myself, but I can't bear to think—You don't suppose you're going to fret much over it?"

"I guess you'll find out I sha'n't fret much over a married man."

"Well, I hope you won't—I hope you won't, Lily. God knows I do. And—I hope—one of these days—you'll—come across somebody else—"

"I don't see any reason why I shouldn't." Suddenly her tone changed. She spoke in a sweet, clear voice, so loud that she could have been heard across the street. "No, Joe Dagget," said she, "I'll never marry any other man as long as I live. I've got good sense, an' I ain't going to break my heart nor make a fool of myself; but I'm never going to be married, you can be sure of that. I ain't that sort of a girl to feel this way twice."

Louisa heard an exclamation and a soft commotion behind the bushes; then Lily spoke again—the voice sounded as if she had risen. "This must be put a stop to," said she. "We've stayed here long enough. I'm going home."

Louisa sat there in a daze, listening to their retreating steps. After a while she got up and slunk softly home herself. The next day she did her housework methodically; that was as much a matter of course as breathing; but she did not sew on her wedding-clothes. She sat at her window and meditated. In the evening Joe came. Louisa Ellis had never known that she had any diplomacy in her, but when she came to look for it that night she found it, although meek of its kind, among her little feminine weapons. Even now she could hardly believe that she had heard aright, and that she would not do Joe a terrible injury should she break her troth-plight.[7] She wanted to sound him without betraying too soon her own inclinations in the matter. She did it successfully, and they finally came to an understanding; but it was a difficult thing, for he was as afraid of betraying himself as she.

She never mentioned Lily Dyer. She simply said that while she had no cause of complaint against him, she had lived so long in one way that she shrank from making a change.

"Well, I never shrank, Louisa," said Dagget. "I'm going to be honest enough to say that I think maybe it's better this way; but if you'd wanted to keep on, I'd have stuck to you till my dying day. I hope you know that."

"Yes, I do," said she.

That night she and Joe parted more tenderly than they had done for a long time. Standing in the door, holding each other's hands, a last great wave of regretful memory swept over them.

"Well, this ain't the way we've thought it was all going to end, is it, Louisa?" said Joe.

She shook her head. There was a little quiver on her placid face.

"You let me know if there's ever anything I can do for you," said he. "I ain't ever going to forget you, Louisa." Then he kissed her, and went down the path.

Louisa, all alone by herself that night, wept a little, she hardly knew why; but the next morning, on waking, she felt like a queen who, after fearing lest her domain be wrested away from her, sees it firmly insured in her possession.

Now the tall weeds and grasses might cluster around Cæsar's little hermit hut, the snow might fall on its roof year in and year out, but he never would go on a rampage through the unguarded village. Now the little canary might turn itself into a peaceful yellow ball night after night, and have no need to wake and flutter with wild terror against its bars. Louisa could sew linen seams, and distil roses, and dust and polish and fold away in lavender, as long as she listed. That afternoon she sat with her needle-work at the window, and felt fairly steeped in peace. Lily Dyer, tall and erect and blooming, went past;

[7]Pledge to marry.

but she felt no qualm. If Louisa Ellis had sold her birthright she did not know it, the taste of the pottage[8] was so delicious, and had been her sole satisfaction for so long. Serenity and placid narrowness had become to her as the birthright itself. She gazed ahead through a long reach of future days strung together like pearls in a rosary, every one like the others, and all smooth and flawless and innocent, and her heart went up in thankfulness. Outside was the fervid summer afternoon; the air was filled with the sounds of the busy harvest of men and birds and bees; there were halloos, metallic clatterings, sweet calls, and long hummings. Louisa sat, prayerfully numbering her days, like an uncloistered nun.

1891

Bret Harte 1836–1902

Like many other Americans who wrote about the West, Bret Harte was originally an Easterner. Born in Albany, New York, he did not go west until 1854, following his father's death and his mother's remarriage. His reports of his early life were filled with fantasy and romance. He claimed early genius, to have been reading Shakespeare at the age of six. It is certain that he taught school for a time. He may also have prospected for gold for a short period, and there is evidence that he spent a "brief, delightful hour" in 1857 riding shotgun on a stagecoach for Wells Fargo Express. The job was as dangerous as legend and the movies have represented it: Harte's predecessor as guard was wounded by bandits; his successor was shot and killed.

Harte next became a professional writer, first for a newspaper in northern California. After he imprudently denounced a mob's massacre of sixty Indians, mostly women and children, his life was threatened, and he fled to San Francisco. There, in 1868, he became the first editor of The Overland Monthly, *a magazine that was to be influential and prosperous until he left it. He had published poems and stories prior to his employment on* The Overland Monthly, *but it was while he was its editor that he wrote the works that made him famous: "The Luck of Roaring Camp" appeared in the second issue, soon followed by "The Outcasts of Poker Flat" and his most famous poem, "Plain Language from Truthful James," usually known as "The Heathen Chinee."*

The enormous success of Harte's fiction brought him wide acclaim: Charles Dickens (Harte's favorite author) praised his writing and urged Harte to come to London to work for him; publishers from the East flooded Harte with offers. His career was at its peak: He was a famous writer and editor, he had been appointed Secretary of the U.S. Mint in San Francisco and Professor of Literature at the University of California.

In 1871, Harte accepted an unprecedented contract of ten thousand dollars from The Atlantic Monthly *for twelve "poems and sketches," and he left California for*

[8]A thick soup, cooked in a pot. The reference is to the biblical Esau, who foolishly sold his birthright (inheritance) for a meal of bread and pottage (Genesis 25:29–34).

Boston, now so famous that an English newspaper issued daily accounts of his journey from coast to coast. Although he was to live nearly thirty years more, the remainder of his life was a disappointment and anticlimax. After California, his writing became self-imitative and repetitious, as he himself admitted late in his life: "I grind out the old tunes on the old organ, and gather up the coppers." Without the immediate inspiration of the West to bring energy to his stories, his sentimentality became more obvious. In his later writings, a dominant theme—moral redemption through sacrifice—was tiresomely repeated. His contract was not renewed by The Atlantic Monthly, *and, unable to make a living from his writing, he went on a series of lecture tours, served in the U.S. diplomatic corps in Germany and Scotland, and spent the last years of his life in England. His last letters are full of his worries over money, self-pitying complaints about his health, and a grieving awareness of a wasted talent.*

In fact, Harte's talent was always minor. Even the best of his stories are overly sentimental; the characters seem deadly similar from tale to poem. Cynical gamblers, gruff but ever-loyal partners, and whores "with hearts of gold" recur again and again. Nevertheless, Harte did vividly characterize a vital period in American history—the final settlement of the West. He was the first widely acclaimed, and one of the best, local color writers who emphasized American regionalism and paved the way for the coming of literary realism. Harte's writing was noteworthy, in an age of genteel evasions, for its frequent portrayal of crucial areas of human experience—sex, love, and death—directly and openly. But perhaps above all, Harte's works and his great, though short-lived, success stand as a notable expression of the world's long-lasting fascination with life on the American frontier.

FURTHER READING: *The Works of Bret Harte,* 18 vols., 1899, 1981; T. Pemberton, *The Life of Bret Harte,* 1903; H. Boynton, *Bret Harte,* 1903, 1973; G. Stewart, *Bret Harte, Argonaut and Exile,* 1931; *Bret Harte, Representative Selections,* ed., J. Harrison, 1941; M. Duckett, *Mark Twain and Bret Harte,* 1964; R. O'Connor, *Bret Harte,* 1966; P. Morrow, *Bret Harte, Literary Critic,* 1979; L. Barnett, *Bret Harte, A Reference Guide,* 1980; G. Scharnhorst, *Bret Harte,* 1992; A. Nissen, *Bret Harte, Prince and Pauper,* 2000.

TEXT: *The Writings of Bret Harte,* 20 vols. 1896–1914.

TENNESSEE'S PARTNER

I do not think that we ever knew his real name. Our ignorance of it certainly never gave us any social inconvenience, for at Sandy Bar in 1854 most men were christened anew. Sometimes these appellatives were derived from some distinctiveness of dress, as in the case of "Dungaree Jack"; or from some peculiarity of habit, as shown in "Saleratus Bill," so called from an undue proportion of that chemical[1] in his daily bread; or from some unlucky slip, as exhibited in "The Iron Pirate," a mild, inoffensive man, who earned that baleful title by his unfortunate mispronunciation of the term "iron pyrites." Perhaps this may have been the beginning of a rude heraldry; but I am constrained to think that it was because a man's real name in that day rested solely upon his own unsupported statement. "Call yourself, Clifford, do you?" said Boston, addressing a timid new-comer with infinite scorn; "hell is full of such Cliffords!" He then introduced the unfortunate man, whose

[1]Saleratus, baking soda.

name happened to be really Clifford, as "Jay-bird Charley,"—an unhallowed inspiration of the moment, that clung to him ever after.

But to return to Tennessee's Partner, whom we never knew by any other than this relative title; that he had ever existed as a separate and distinct individuality we only learned later. It seems that in 1853 he left Poker Flat to go to San Francisco, ostensibly to procure a wife. He never got any farther than Stockton. At that place he was attracted by a young person who waited upon the table at the hotel where he took his meals. One morning he said something to her which caused her to smile not unkindly, to somewhat coquettishly break a plate of toast over his upturned, serious simple face, and to retreat to the kitchen. He followed her, and emerged a few moments later, covered with more toast and victory. That day a week they were married by a Justice of the Peace, and returned to Poker Flat. I am aware that something more might be made of this episode, but I prefer to tell it as it was current at Sandy Bar,—in the gulches and barrooms,—where all sentiment was modified by a strong sense of humor.

Of their married felicity but little is known, perhaps for the reason that Tennessee, then living with his partner, one day took occasion to say something to the bride on his own account, at which, it is said, she smiled not unkindly and chastely retreated,—this time as far as Marysville, where Tennessee followed her, and where they went to housekeeping without the aid of a Justice of the Peace. Tennessee's Partner took the loss of his wife simply and seriously, as was his fashion. But to everybody's surprise, when Tennessee one day returned from Marysville, without his partner's wife,—she having smiled and retreated with somebody else,—Tennessee's Partner was the first man to shake his hand and greet him with affection. The boys who had gathered in the cañon to see the shooting were naturally indignant. Their indignation might have found vent in sarcasm but for a certain look in Tennessee's Partner's eye that indicated a lack of humorous appreciation. In fact he was a grave man, with a steady application to practical detail which was unpleasant in a difficulty.

Meanwhile a popular feeling against Tennessee had grown up on the Bar. He was known to be a gambler; he was suspected to be a thief. In these suspicions Tennessee's Partner was equally compromised; his continued intimacy with Tennessee after the affair above quoted could only be accounted for on the hypothesis of a copartnership of crime. At last Tennessee's guilt became flagrant. One day he overtook a stranger on his way to Red Dog. The stranger afterward related that Tennessee beguiled the time with interesting anecdote and reminiscence, but illogically concluded the interview in the following words: "And now, young man, I'll trouble you for your knife, your pistols, and your money. You see your weppings might get you into trouble at Red Dog, and your money's a temptation to the evilly disposed. I think you said your address was San Francisco. I shall endeavor to call." It may be stated here that Tennessee had a fine flow of humor, which no business preoccupation could wholly subdue.

This exploit was his last. Red Dog and Sandy Bar made common cause against the highwayman. Tennessee was hunted in very much the same fashion as his prototype, the grizzly. As the toils[2] closed around him, he made a

[2]Snares, traps.

desperate dash through the Bar, emptying his revolver at the crowd before the Arcade Saloon, and so on up Grizzly Cañon; but at its farther extremity he was stopped by a small man on a gray horse. The men looked at each other a moment in silence. Both were fearless, both self-possessed and independent; and both types of a civilization that in the seventeenth century would have been called heroic, but, in the nineteenth, simply "reckless." "What have you got there?—I call," said Tennessee, quietly. "Two bowers[3] and an ace," said the stranger, as quietly, showing two revolvers and a bowie-knife. "That takes me," returned Tennessee; and with this gamblers' epigram, he threw away his useless pistol, and rode back with his captor.

It was a warm night. The cool breeze which usually sprang up with the going down of the sun behind the *chaparral*-crested mountain was that evening withheld from Sandy Bar. The little cañon was stifling with heated resinous odors, and the decaying drift-wood on the Bar sent forth faint, sickening exhalations. The feverishness of day, and its fierce passions, still filled the camp. Lights moved restlessly along the bank of the river, striking no answering reflection from its tawny current. Against the blackness of the pines the windows of the old loft above the express-office stood out staringly bright; and through their curtainless panes the loungers below could see the forms of those who were even then deciding the fate of Tennessee. And above all this, etched on the dark firmament, rose the Sierra, remote and passionless, crowned with the remoter passionless stars.

The trial of Tennessee was conducted as fairly as was consistent with a judge and jury who felt themselves to some extent obliged to justify, in their verdict, the previous irregularities of arrest and indictment. The law of Sandy Bar was implacable, but not vengeful. The excitement and personal feeling of the chase were over; with Tennessee safe in their hands they were ready to listen patiently to any defence, which they were already satisfied was insufficient. There being no doubt in their own minds, they were willing to give the prisoner the benefit of any that might exist. Secure in the hypothesis that he ought to be hanged, on general principles, they indulged him with more latitude or defence than his reckless hardihood seemed to ask. The Judge appeared to be more anxious than the prisoner, who, otherwise, unconcerned, evidently took a grim pleasure in the responsibility he had created. "I don't take any hand in this yer game," had been his invariable, but good-humored reply to all questions. The Judge—who was also his captor—for a moment vaguely regretted that he had not shot him "on sight," that morning, but presently dismissed this human weakness as unworthy of the judicial mind. Nevertheless, when there was a tap at the door, and it was said that Tennessee's Partner was there on behalf of the prisoner, he was admitted at once without question. Perhaps the younger member of the jury, to whom the proceedings were becoming irksomely thoughtful, hailed him as a relief.

For he was not, certainly, an imposing figure. Short and stout, with a square face, sunburned into a preternatural redness, clad in a loose duck "jumper," and trousers streaked and splashed with red soil, his aspect under any circumstances would have been quaint, and was now even ridiculous. As he stooped to deposit at his feet a heavy carpet-bag he was carrying, it became obvious,

[3]High cards.

from partially developed legends and inscriptions, that the material with which his trousers had been patched had been originally intended for a less ambitious covering. Yet he advanced with great gravity, and after having shaken the hand of each person in the room with labored cordiality, he wiped his serious, perplexed face on a red bandanna handkerchief, a shade lighter than his complexion, laid his powerful hand upon the table to steady himself, and thus addressed the Judge:—

"I was passin' by," he began, by way of apology, "and I thought I'd just step in and see how things was gittin' on with Tennessee thar,—my pardner. It's a hot night. I disremember any sich weather before on the Bar."

He paused a moment, but nobody volunteering any other meteorological recollection, he again had recourse to his pocket-handkerchief, and for some moments mopped his face diligently.

"Have you anything to say in behalf of the prisoner?" said the Judge, finally.

"Thet's it," said Tennessee's Partner, in a tone of relief. "I come yar as Tennessee's pardner,—knowing him nigh on four year, off and on, wet and dry, in luck and out o' luck. His ways ain't allers my ways, but thar ain't any p'ints in that young man, thar ain't any liveliness as he's been up to, as I don't know. And you sez to me, sez you,—confidential-like, and between man and man,—sez you, 'Do you know anything in his behalf?' and I sez to you, sez I,—confidential-like, as between man and man,—'What should a man know of his pardner?' "

"Is this all you have to say?" asked the Judge, impatiently, feeling, perhaps, that a dangerous sympathy of humor was beginning to humanize the Court.

"Thet's so," continued Tennessee's Partner. "It ain't for me to say anything agin' him. And now, what's the case? Here's Tennessee wants money, wants it bad, and does n't like to ask it of his old pardner. Well, what does Tennessee do? He lays for a stranger, and he fetches that stranger. And you lays for *him,* and you fetches *him;* and the honors is easy.[4] And I put it to you, bein' a far-minded man, and to you, gentlemen, all, as far-minded men, ef this is n't so."

"Prisoner," said the Judge, interrupting, "have you any questions to ask this man?"

"No! no!" continued Tennessee's Partner, hastily. "I play this yer hand alone. To come down to the bed-rock, it's just this: Tennessee, thar, has played it pretty rough and expensive-like on a stranger, and on this yer camp. And now, what's the fair thing? Some would say more; some would say less. Here's seventeen hundred dollars in coarse gold and a watch,—it's about all my pile,—and call it square!" And before a hand could be raised to prevent him, he had emptied the contents of the carpet-bag upon the table.

For a moment his life was in jeopardy. One or two men sprang to their feet, several hands groped for hidden weapons, and a suggestion to "throw him from the window" was only overridden by a gesture from the Judge. Tennessee laughed. And apparently oblivious of the excitement, Tennessee's Partner improved the opportunity to mop his face again with his handkerchief.

When order was restored, and the man was made to understand, by the use of forcible figures and rhetoric, that Tennessee's offence could not be condoned by money, his face took a more serious and sanguinary hue, and

[4]I.e., honor cards are equally divided; thus, everything is equal.

those who were nearest to him noticed that his rough hand trembled slightly on the table. He hesitated a moment as he slowly returned the gold to the carpet-bag, as if he had not yet entirely caught the elevated sense of justice which swayed the tribunal, and was perplexed with the belief that he had not offered enough. Then he turned to the Judge, and saying, "This yer is a lone hand, played alone, and without my pardner," he bowed to the jury and was about to withdraw, when the Judge called him back. "If you have anything to say to Tennessee, you had better say it now." For the first time that evening the eyes of the prisoner and his stranger advocate met. Tennessee smiled, showed his white teeth, and, saying, "Euchred,[5] old man!" held out his hand. Tennessee's Partner took it in his own, and saying, "I just dropped in as I was passin' to see how things was gettin' on," let the hand passively fall, and adding that "it was a warm night," again mopped his face with his handkerchief, and without another word withdrew.

The two men never again met each other alive. For the unparalleled insult of a bribe offered to Judge Lynch—who, whether bigoted, weak, or narrow, was at least incorruptible—firmly fixed in the mind of that mythical personage any wavering determination of Tennessee's fate; and at the break of day he was marched, closely guarded, to meet it at the top of Marley's Hill.

How he met it, how cool he was, how he refused to say anything, how perfect were the arrangements of the committee, were all duly reported, with the addition of a warning moral and example to all future evil-doers, in the Red Dog Clarion, by its editor, who was present, and to whose vigorous English I cheerfully refer the reader. But the beauty of that midsummer morning, the blessed amity of earth and air and sky, the awakened life of the free woods and hills, the joyous renewal and promise of Nature, and above all, the infinite Serenity that thrilled through each, was not reported, as not being a part of the social lesson. And yet, when the weak and foolish deed was done, and a life, with its possibilities and responsibilities, had passed out of the misshapen thing that dangled between earth and sky, the birds sang, the flowers bloomed, the sun shone, as cheerily as before; and possibly the Red Dog Clarion was right.

Tennessee's Partner was not in the group that surrounded the ominous tree. But as they turned to disperse attention was drawn to the singular appearance of a motionless donkey-cart halted at the side of the road. As they approached, they at once recognized the venerable "Jenny" and the two-wheeled cart as the property of Tennessee's Partner,—used by him in carrying dirt from his claim; and a few paces distant the owner of the equipage himself, sitting under a buckeye-tree, wiping the perspiration from his glowing face. In answer to an inquiry, he said he had come for the body of the "diseased," "if it was all the same to the committee." He did n't wish to "hurry anything"; he could "wait." He was not working that day; and when the gentlemen were done with the "diseased," he would take him. "Ef thar is any present," he added, in his simple, serious way, "as would care to jine in the fun'l, they kin come." Perhaps it was from a sense of humor, which I have already intimated was a feature of Sandy Bar,—perhaps it was from something even better than that; but two thirds of the loungers accepted the invitation at once.

[5]From the card game euchre, the loser of which is "euchred."

It was noon when the body of Tennessee was delivered into the hands of his partner. As the cart drew up to the fatal tree, we noticed that it contained a rough, oblong box,—apparently made from a section of sluicing,[6]—and half filled with bark and the tassels of pine. The cart was further decorated with slips of willow, and made fragrant with buckeye-blossoms. When the body was deposited in the box, Tennessee's Partner drew over it a piece of tarred canvas, and gravely mounting the narrow seat in front, with his feet upon the shafts, urged the little donkey forward. The equipage moved slowly on, at that decorous pace which was habitual with "Jenny" even under less solemn circumstances. The men—half curiously, half jestingly, but all good-humoredly—strolled along beside the cart; some in advance, some a little in the rear of the homely catafalque.[7] But, whether from the narrowing of the road or some present sense of decorum, as the cart passed on, the company fell to the rear in couples, keeping step, and otherwise assuming the external show of a formal procession. Jack Folinsbee, who had at the outset played a funeral march in dumb show[8] upon an imaginary trombone, desisted, from a lack of sympathy and appreciation,—not having, perhaps, your true humorist's capacity to be content with the enjoyment of his own fun.

The way led through Grizzly Cañon,—by this time clothed in funeral drapery and shadows. The redwoods, burying their moccasined feet in the red soil, stood in Indian-file along the track, trailing an uncouth benediction from their bending boughs upon the passing bier. A hare, surprised into helpless inactivity, sat upright and pulsating in the ferns by the roadside, as the *cortège* went by. Squirrels hastened to gain a secure outlook from higher boughs; and the blue-jays, spreading their wings, fluttered before them like outriders, until the outskirts of Sandy Bar were reached, and the solitary cabin of Tennessee's Partner.

Viewed under more favorable circumstances, it would not have been a cheerful place. The unpicturesque site, the rude and unlovely outlines, the unsavory details, which distinguish the nestbuilding of the California miner, were all here, with the dreariness of decay superadded. A few paces from the cabin there was a rough enclosure, which, in the brief days of Tennessee's Partner's matrimonial felicity, had been used as a garden, but was now overgrown with fern. As we approached it we were surprised to find that what we had taken for a recent attempt at cultivation was the broken soil about an open grave.

The cart was halted before the enclosure; and rejecting the offers of assistance with the same air of simple self-reliance he had displayed throughout, Tennessee's Partner lifted the rough coffin on his back, and deposited it, unaided, within the shallow grave. He then nailed down the board which served as a lid; and mounting the little mound of earth beside it, took off his

[6]Long boards used in building water channels.
[7]Ornamental framework that carries a coffin.
[8]Silently.

hat, and slowly mopped his face with his handkerchief. This the crowd felt was a preliminary to speech; and they disposed themselves variously on stumps and boulders, and sat expectant.

"When a man," began Tennessee's Partner, slowly, "has been running free all day, what's the natural thing for him to do? Why, to come home. And if he ain't in a condition to go home, what can his best friend do? Why, bring him home! And here's Tennessee has been running free, and we brings him home from his wandering." He paused, and picked up a fragment of quartz, rubbed it thoughtfully on his sleeve, and went on: "It ain't the first time that I've packed him on my back, as you see'd me now. It ain't the first time that I brought him to this yer cabin when he could n't help himself; it ain't the first time that I and 'Jinny' have waited for him on yon hill, and picked him up and so fetched him home, when he could n't speak, and did n't know me. And now that it's the last time, why—" he paused, and rubbed the quartz gently on his sleeve—"you see it's sort of rough on his pardner. And now, gentlemen," he added, abruptly, picking up his long-handled shovel, "the fun'l's over; and my thanks, and Tennessee's thanks, to you for your trouble."

Resisting any proffers of assistance, he began to fill in the grave, turning his back upon the crowd, that after a few moments' hesitation gradually withdrew. As they crossed the little ridge that hid Sandy Bar from view, some, looking back, thought they could see Tennessee's Partner, his work done, sitting upon the grave, his shovel between his knees, and his face buried in his red bandanna handkerchief. But it was argued by others that you couldn't tell his face from his handkerchief at that distance; and this point remained undecided.

In the reaction that followed the feverish excitement of that day, Tennessee's Partner was not forgotten. A secret investigation had cleared him of any complicity in Tennessee's guilt, and left only a suspicion of his general sanity. Sandy Bar made a point of calling on him, and proffering various uncouth, but well-meant kindnesses. But from that day his rude health and great strength seemed visibly to decline; and when the rainy season fairly set in, and the tiny grass-blades were beginning to peep from the rocky mound above Tennessee's grave, he took to his bed.

One night, when the pines beside the cabin were swaying in the storm, and trailing their slender fingers over the roof, and the roar and rush of the swollen river were heard below, Tennessee's Partner lifted his head from the pillow, saying, "It is time to go for Tennessee; I must put 'Jinny' in the cart"; and would have risen from his bed but for the restraint. Struggling, he still pursued his singular fancy: "There, now, steady, 'Jinny,'—steady, old girl. How dark it is! Look out for the ruts,—and look out for him, too, old gal. Sometimes, you know, when he's blind drunk, he drops down right in the trail. Keep on straight up to the pine on the top of the hill. Thar—I told you so!—thar he is,—coming this way, too,—all by himself, sober, and his face a-shining. Tennessee! Pardner!"

And so they met.

1869

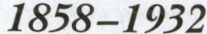

Charles Waddell Chesnutt 1858–1932

Charles Waddell Chesnutt, a black man, was born free in Ohio shortly before the Civil War. He spent much of his early life in North Carolina, first as a teacher, then as a principal of a segregated high school. But Chesnutt disliked the South; he missed "civilization and companionship," and so he moved to New York in 1883. There he worked as a stenographic reporter and as an accountant, and he began to write poetry and short fiction.

In 1885 and 1886, several of his stories and poems were published in popular magazines, but he seldom received more than five or ten dollars for each. To support his family, he studied law, and he returned to Ohio, where he was admitted to the bar in 1887, scoring the highest mark of all those who took the bar examination. Black lawyers seldom prospered in nineteenth-century America, and Chesnutt was forced to make a living as a legal stenographer. But he continued writing, and recognition came swiftly when the most prestigious magazine in America, The Atlantic Monthly, *published his story "The Goophered Grapevine" in August 1887.*

Many of Chesnutt's stories were folktales in the manner of Joel Chandler Harris, and some were without apparent racial concerns or implications. Other stories dealt with racial matters in ways generally acceptable to the prejudices of the white reading public of his time. Chesnutt's recurring subjects were "passing" (blacks passing themselves off as whites—usually with disastrous results), humorous intraracial conflicts between mulattoes and full-blooded blacks, and examples of the instinctively wise (but properly subservient) black man fooling the whites. But the stories are often highly ironic, and racial issues were presented in ways that were subtle, forceful, and well ahead of their time.

By 1900, the year of the publication of his first novel, The House Behind the Cedars, *Chesnutt's racial attitudes had become increasingly militant. He condemned and satirized the South and showed that his black heroine's attempt to pass as white was clearly misguided and so led to tragedy. Chesnutt's major criticism was reserved for his novel's protagonist, who did succeed in passing and who thereafter denied his black heritage. In subsequent novels,* The Marrow of Tradition *(1901) and* The Colonel's Dream *(1905), Chesnutt's racial statements became increasingly blunt and candid. His subjects were race riots, racial injustice, and bigotry; he relied less on veiled irony and more on direct statement, and the tone of his novels became more pessimistic. Even William Dean Howells, Chesnutt's patron, criticized the bitterness of* The Marrow of Tradition, *and others said the novel was an attempt to "humiliate the whites."*

Chesnutt had great hopes for the improvement of race relations in the United States, and his novels were conscious attempts to bring such improvement about. Perhaps disillusioned by the failure of his work to lead to any marked change in the relations between blacks and whites, Chesnutt gave up writing after 1905 and retreated to the consolations of family, travel, and work. By today's standards his attitudes seem passive and dated. But his subtlety, irony, and militancy are often unperceived and undervalued, and he remains an important and pivotal figure in the development of black literature in twentieth-century America.

FURTHER READING: H. Chesnutt, *Charles Waddell Chesnutt, Pioneer of the Color Line,* 1952; J. Heermance, *Charles W. Chesnutt,* 1974; *The Short Fiction of Charles W. Chesnutt,* ed. S. Lyons, 1974; F. Keller, *An American Crusade, The Life of Charles Waddell Chesnutt,* 1978; S. Lyons, *Charles W. Chesnutt,* 1980; W. Andrews, *The Literary Career of Charles W. Chesnutt,* 1980; S. Render, *Charles W. Chesnutt,* 1980; *The Collected Stories of Charles W. Chesnutt,* ed. W. Andrews, 1991; *The Journals of Charles W. Chesnutt,* ed. R. Brodhead, 1993; *To Be an Author, Letters of Charles Waddell Chesnutt,* ed. J. McElrath and R. Leitz,

1997; H. Wonham, *Charles Waddell Chesnutt,* 1998; *Critical Essays on Charles Chesnutt,* ed. J. McElrath, 1999; D. McWilliams, *Charles W. Chesnutt and the Fictions of Race,* 2002; M. Wilson, *Whiteness in the Novels of Charles W. Chesnutt,* 2004.

TEXT: *The Conjure Woman,* 1899.

THE GOOPHERED GRAPEVINE

Some years ago my wife was in poor health, and our family doctor, in whose skill and honesty I had implicit confidence, advised a change of climate. I shared, from an unprofessional standpoint, his opinion that the raw winds, the chill rains, and the violent changes of temperature that characterized the winters in the region of the Great Lakes tended to aggravate my wife's difficulty, and would undoubtedly shorten her life if she remained exposed to them. The doctor's advice was that we seek, not a temporary place of sojourn, but a permanent residence, in a warmer and more equable climate. I was engaged at the time in grape-culture in northern Ohio, and, as I liked the business and had given it much study, I decided to look for some other locality suitable for carrying it on. I thought of sunny France, of sleepy Spain, of Southern California, but there were objections to them all. It occurred to me that I might find what I wanted in some one of our own Southern States. It was a sufficient time after the war for conditions in the South to have become somewhat settled; and I was enough of a pioneer to start a new industry, if I could not find a place where grape-culture had been tried. I wrote to a cousin who had gone into the turpentine business in central North Carolina. He assured me, in response to my inquiries, that no better place could be found in the South than the State and neighborhood where he lived; the climate was perfect for health, and, in conjunction with the soil, ideal for grape-culture; labor was cheap, and land could be bought for a mere song. He gave us a cordial invitation to come and visit him while we looked into the matter. We accepted the invitation, and after several days of leisurely travel, the last hundred miles of which were up a river on a sidewheel steamer, we reached our destination, a quaint old town, which I shall call Patesville, because, for one reason, that is not its name. There was a red brick market-house in the public square, with a tall tower, which held a four-faced clock that struck the hours, and from which there pealed out a curfew at nine o'clock. There were two or three hotels, a court-house, a jail, stores, offices, and all the appurtenances of a county seat and a commercial emporium; for while Patesville numbered only four or five thousand inhabitants, of all shades of complexion, it was one of the principal towns in North Carolina, and had a considerable trade in cotton and naval stores.[1] This business activity was not immediately apparent to my unaccustomed eyes. Indeed, when I first saw the town, there brooded over it a calm that seemed almost sabbatic in its restfulness, though I learned later on that underneath its somnolent exterior the deeper currents of life—love and hatred, joy and despair, ambition and avarice, faith and friendship—flowed not less steadily than in livelier latitudes.

[1]Pitch, turpentine, rosin, and other supplies used in maintaining wooden sailing vessels.

We found the weather delightful at that season, the end of summer, and were hospitably entertained. Our host was a man of means and evidently regarded our visit as a pleasure, and we were therefore correspondingly at our ease, and in a position to act with the coolness of judgment desirable in making so radical a change in our lives. My cousin placed a horse and buggy at our disposal, and himself acted as our guide until I became somewhat familiar with the country.

I found that grape-culture, while it had never been carried on to any great extent, was not entirely unknown in the neighborhood. Several planters thereabouts had attempted it on a commercial scale, in former years, with greater or less success; but like most Southern industries, it had felt the blight of war and had fallen into desuetude.

I went several times to look at a place that I thought might suit me. It was a plantation of considerable extent, that had formerly belonged to a wealthy man by the name of McAdoo. The estate had been for years involved in litigation between disputing heirs, during which period shiftless cultivation had well-nigh exhausted the soil. There had been a vineyard of some extent on the place, but it had not been attended to since the war, and had lapsed into utter neglect. The vines—here partly supported by decayed and broken-down trellises, there twining themselves among the branches of the slender saplings which had sprung up among them—grew in wild and unpruned luxuriance, and the few scattered grapes they bore were the undisputed prey of the first comer. The site was admirably adapted to grape-raising; the soil, with a little attention, could not have been better; and with the native grape, the luscious scuppernong,[2] as my main reliance in the beginning, I felt sure that I could introduce and cultivate successfully a number of other varieties.

One day I went over with my wife to show her the place. We drove out of the town over a long wooden bridge that spanned a spreading mill-pond, passed the long whitewashed fence surrounding the county fair-ground, and struck into a road so sandy that the horse's feet sank to the fetlocks. Our route lay partly up hill and partly down, for we were in the sand-hill country; we drove past cultivated farms, and then by abandoned fields grown up in scrub-oak and short-leaved pine, and once or twice through the solemn aisles of the virgin forest, where the tall pines, well-nigh meeting over the narrow road, shut out the sun, and wrapped us in cloistral solitude. Once, at a cross-roads, I was in doubt as to the turn to take, and we sat there waiting ten minutes—we had already caught some of the native infection of restfulness—for some human being to come along, who could direct us on our way. At length a little negro girl appeared, walking straight as an arrow, with a piggin[3] full of water on her head. After a little patient investigation, necessary to overcome the child's shyness, we learned what we wished to know, and at the end of about five miles from the town reached our destination.

We drove between a pair of decayed gateposts—the gate itself had long since disappeared—and up a straight sandy lane, between two lines of rotting rail fence, partly concealed by jimson-weeds and briers, to the open space where a dwelling-house had once stood, evidently a spacious mansion, if we might judge from the ruined chimneys that were still standing, and the

[2]A muscadine grape. [3]Wooden pail.

brick pillars on which the sills rested. The house itself, we had been informed, had fallen a victim to the fortunes of war.

We alighted from the buggy, walked about the yard for a while, and then wandered off into the adjoining vineyard. Upon Annie's complaining of weariness I led the way back to the yard, where a pine log, lying under a spreading elm, afforded a shady though somewhat hard seat. One end of the log was already occupied by a venerable-looking colored man. He held on his knees a hat full of grapes, over which he was smacking his lips with great gusto, and a pile of grapeskins near him indicated that the performance was no new thing. We approached him at an angle from the rear, and were close to him before he perceived us. He respectfully rose as we drew near, and was moving away, when I begged him to keep his seat.

"Don't let us disturb you," I said. "There is plenty of room for us all."

He resumed his seat with somewhat of embarrassment. While he had been standing, I had observed that he was a tall man, and, though slightly bowed by the weight of years, apparently quite vigorous. He was not entirely black, and this fact, together with the quality of his hair, which was about six inches long and very bushy, except on the top of his head, where he was quite bald, suggested a slight strain of other than negro blood. There was a shrewdness in his eyes, too, which was not altogether African, and which, as we afterwards learned from experience, was indicative of a corresponding shrewdness in his character. He went on eating the grapes, but did not seem to enjoy himself quite so well as he had apparently done before he became aware of our presence.

"Do you live around here?" I asked, anxious to put him at his ease.

"Yas, sah. I lives des ober yander, behine de nex' san'-hill, on de Lumberton plank-road."

"Do you know anything about the time when this vineyard was cultivated?"

"Lawd bless you, suh, I knows all about it. Dey ain' na'er a man in dis settlement w'at won' tel you ole Julius McAdoo 'uz bawn en raise' on dis yer same plantation. Is you de Norv'n gemman w'at's gwine ter buy de ole vimya'd?"

"I am looking at it," I replied; "but I don't know that I shall care to buy unless I can be reasonably sure of making something out of it."

"Well, suh, you is a stranger ter me, en I is a stranger ter you, en we is bofe strangers ter one anudder, but 'f I 'uz in yo' place, I wouldn' buy dis vimya'd."

"Why not?" I asked.

"Well, I dunno whe'r you b'lieves in conj'in 'er not,—some er de w'ite folks don't, er says dey don't,—but de truf er de matter is dat dis yer old vimya'd is goophered."

"Is what?" I asked, not grasping the meaning of this unfamiliar word.

"Is goophered,—conju'd, bewitch'."

He imparted this information with such solemn earnestness, and with such an air of confidential mystery, that I felt somewhat interested, while Annie was evidently much impressed, and drew closer to me.

"How do you know it is bewitched?" I asked.

"I would n' spec' fer you ter b'lieve me 'less you know all 'bout de fac's. But ef you en young miss dere doan' min' lis'nin' ter a ole nigger run on a minute er two w'ile you ere restin', I kin 'splain to you how it all happen'."

We assured him that we would be glad to hear how it all happened, and he began to tell us. At first the current of his memory—or imagination—seemed somewhat sluggish; but as his embarrassment wore off, his language flowed more freely, and the story acquired perspective and coherence. As he became more and more absorbed in the narrative, his eyes assumed a dreamy expression, and he seemed to lose sight of his auditors, and to be living over again in monologue his life on the old plantation.

"Ole Mars Dugal' McAdoo," he began, "bought dis place long many years befo' de wah, en I 'member well w'en he sot out all dis yer part er de plantation in scuppernon's. De vimes growed monst'us fas', en Mars Dugal' made a thousan' gallon er scuppernon' wine eve'y year.

"Now, ef dey's an'thing a nigger lub, nex' ter 'possum, en chick'n, en watermillyums, it's scuppernon's. Dey ain' nuffin dat kin stan' up side'n de scuppernon' fer sweetness; sugar ain't a suckumstance ter scuppernon'. W'en de season is nigh 'bout ober, en de grapes begin ter swivel up des a little wid de wrinkles er ole age,—w'en de skin git sof' en brown,—den de scuppernon' make you smack yo' lip en roll yo' eye en wush fer mo'; so I reckon it ain' very stonishin' dat niggers lub scuppernon'.

"Dey wuz a sight er niggers in de naberhood er de vimya'd. Dere wuz ole Mars Henry Brayboy's niggers, en ole Mars Jeems McLean's niggers, en Mars Dugal's own niggers; den dey wuz a settlement er free niggers en po' buckrahs[4] down by de Wim'l'ton Road, en Mars Dugal' had de only vimya'd in de naberhood. I reckon it ain' so much so nowadays, but befo' de wah, in slab'ry times, a nigger did n' mine goin' fi' er ten mile in a night, w'en dey wuz sump'n good ter eat at de yuther een'.

"So atter a w'ile Mars Dugal' begin ter miss his scuppernon's. Co'se he 'cuse' de niggers er it, but dey all 'nied it ter de las'. Mars Dugal's sot spring guns[5] en steel traps, en he en de oberseah sot up nights once't er twice't, tel one night Mars Dugal'—he 'uz a monst'us keerless man—got his leg shot full er cow-peas.[6] But somehow er nudder dey couldn' nebber ketch none er de niggers. I dunner how it happen, but it happen des like I tell you, en de grapes kep' on a-goin' des de same.

"But bimbey ole Mars Dugal' fix' up a plan ter stop it. Dey wuz a conjuh 'oman livin' down 'mongs' de free niggers on de Wim'l'ton Road, en all de darkies fum Rockfish ter Beaver Crick wuz feared er her. She could wuk de mos' powerfulles' kin' er goopher,—could make people hab fits, er rheumatiz, er make 'em des dwinel away en die; en dey say she went out ridin' de niggers at night, fer she wuz a witch 'sides bein' a conjah 'oman. Mars Dugal' hearn 'bout Aun' Peggy's doins, en begun ter 'flect whe'r er no he could n' git her ter he'p him keep de niggers off'n de grapevimes. One day in spring er de year, ole miss pack' up a basket er chick'n en poun'-cake, en a bottle er scuppernon' wine, en Mars Dugal' tuk it in his buggy en driv ober ter Aun' Peggy's cabin. He tuk de basket in, en had a long talk wid Aun' Peggy.

"De nex' day Aun' Peggy come up ter de vimya'd. De niggers seed her slippin' roun', en dey soon foun' out what she 'uz doin' dere. Mars Dugal' had hi'ed her ter goopher de grapevimes. She sa'ntered 'roun' 'mongs' de vimes,

[4]Whites. [5]Guns set to fire when a trespasser trips a wire attached to the trigger.
[6]Dried peas used in place of lead buckshot in a shotgun load.

en tuk a leaf fum dis one, en a grape-hull fum dat one, en a grape-seed fum anudder one; en den a little twig fum here, en a little pinch er dirt fum dere, en put it all in a big black bottle, wid a snake's toof en a speckle' hen's gall en some ha'rs fum a black cat's tail, en den fill' de bottle wid scuppernon' wine. W'en she got de goopher all ready en fix', she tuk 'n went out in de woods en buried it under de root uv a red oak tree, en den come back en tole one er de niggers she done goopher de grapevimes, en a'er a nigger w'at eat dem grapes 'ud be sho ter die inside'n twel' mont's.

"Atter dat de niggers let de scuppernon's 'lone, en Mars Dugal' did n' hab no 'casion ter fine no mo' fault; en de season wuz mos' gone, w'en a strange gemman stop at de plantation one night ter see Mars Dugal' on some business; en his coachman, seein' de scuppernon's growin' so nice en sweet, slip 'roun' behine de smoke-house, en et all de scuppernon's he could hole. Nobody did n' notice it at de time, but dat night, on de way home, de gemman's hoss runned away en kill' de coachman. W'en we hearn de noos, Aun' Lucy, de cook, she up'n say she seed de strange nigger eat'n er de scuppernon's behine de smoke-house; en den we knowed de goopher had b'en er wukkin'. Den one er de nigger chilluns runned away fum de quarters one day, en got in de scuppernon's, en died de nex' week. W'ite folks say he die' er de fevuh, but de niggers knowed it wuz de goopher. So you k'n be sho de darkies did n' hab much ter do wid dem scuppernon' vimes.

"W'en de scuppernon' season 'uz ober fer dat year, Mars Dugal' foun' he had made fifteen hund'ed gallon er wine; en one er de niggers hearn him laffin' wid de oberseah fit ter kill, en sayin' dem fifteen hund'ed gallon er wine wuz monst'us good intrus' on de ten dollars he laid out on de vimya'd. So I 'low ez he paid Aun' Peggy ten dollars fer to goopher de grapevimes.

"De goopher did n' wuk no mo tel de nex' summer, w'en 'long to'ds de middle er de season one er de fiel' han's died; en ez dat lef' Mars Dugal' sho't er han's, he went off ter town fer ter buy anudder. He fotch de noo nigger home wid 'im. He wuz er ole nigger, er de color er a gingy-cake, en ball ez a hoss-apple on de top er his head. He wuz a peart ole nigger, do', en could do a big day's wuk.

"Now it happen dat one er de niggers on de nex' plantation, one er ole Mars Henry Brayboy's niggers, had runned away de day befo', en tuk ter de swamp, en ole Mars Dugal' en some er de yuther nabor w'ite folks had gone out wid dere guns en dere dogs fer ter he'p 'em hunt fer de nigger; en de han's on our own plantation wuz all so flusterated dat we fuhgot ter tell de noo han' 'bout de goopher on de scuppernon' vimes. Co'se he smell de grapes en see de vimes, an atter dahk de fus' thing he done wuz ter slip off ter de grapevimes 'dout sayin' nuffin ter nobody. Nex' mawnin' he tole some er de niggers 'bout de fine bait er scuppernon' he et de night befo'.

"W'en dey tole 'im 'bout de goopher on de grapevimes, he 'uz dat tarrified dat he turn pale, en look des like he gwine ter die right in his tracks. De oberseah come up en axed w'at 'uz de matter; en w'en dey tole 'im Henry be'n eatin' er de scuppernon's, en got de goopher on 'im, he gin Henry a big drink er w'iskey, en 'low dat de nex' rainy day he take 'im ober ter Aun't Peggy's, en see ef she would n' take de goopher off'n him, seein' ez he did n' know nuffin erbout it tell he done et de grapes.

"Sho nuff, it rain de nex' day, en de oberseah went over ter Aun' Peggy's wid Henry. En Aun' Peggy say dat bein' ez Henry did n' know 'bout de goopher, en et de grapes in ign'ance er de conseq'ences, she reckon she mought be able fer ter take de goopher off'n him. So she fotch out her bottle wid some conjuh medicine in it, en po'd some out in a go'd fer Henry ter drink. He manage ter git it down; he say it tas'e like whiskey wid sump'n bitter in it. She 'lowed dat 'ud keep de goopher off'n him tel de spring; but w'en de sap begin ter rise in de grapevimes he ha' ter come en see her ag'in, en she tell him w'at e's ter do.

"Nex' spring, w'en de sap commence' ter rise in de scuppernon' vime, Henry tuk a ham one night. What'd de git de ham? *I* doan know; dey wa'n't no hams on de plantation 'cep'n w'at 'uz in de smoke-house, but *I* never see Henry 'bout de smoke-house. But ez I wuz a-sayin', he tuk de ham ober ter Aun' Peggy's; en Aun' Peggy tole 'im dat w'en Mars Dugal' begin ter prune de grapevimes, he mus' go en take 'n scrape off de sap whar it ooze out'n de cut een's er de vimes, en 'n'int his ball head wid it; en ef he do dat once't a year de goopher would n' wuk agin 'im long ez he done it. En bein' ez he fotch her de ham, she fix' it so he kin eat all de scuppernon' he want.

"So Henry 'n'into his head wid de sap out'n de big grapevime des ha'f way 'twix' de quarters en de big house, en de goopher nebber wuk again him dat summer. But de beatenes' thing you eber see happen ter Henry. Up ter dat time he wuz ez ball ez a sweeten' 'tater, but des ez soon ez de young leaves begun ter come out on de grapevimes, de ha'r begun ter grow out on Henry's head, en by de middle er de summer he had de bigges' head er ha'r on de plantation. Befo' dat, Henry had tol'able good ha'r roun' de aidges, but soon ez de young grapes begun ter come, Henry's ha'r begun to quirl all up in little balls, des like dis yer reg'lar grapy ha'r, en by de time de grapes got ripe his head look des like a bunch er grapes. Combin' it did n' do no good; he wuk at it ha'f de night wid er Jim Crow,[7] en think he git it straighten' out, but in de mawnin' de grapes 'ud be dere des de same. So he gin it up, en tried ter keep de grapes down by havin' his ha'r cut sho't.

"But dat wa'n't de quares' thing 'bout de goopher. When Henry come ter de plantation, he wuz gittin' a little ole an stiff in de j'ints. But dat summer he got des ez spry en libely ez any young nigger on de plantation; fac', he got so biggity dat Mars Jackson, de oberseah, ha' ter th'eaten ter whip 'im, ef he did n' stop cuttin' up his didos en behave hisse'f. But de mos' cur'ouses' thing happen' in de fall, when de sap begin ter go down in de grapevimes. Fus', when de grapes 'uz gethered, de knots begun ter straighten out'n Henry's ha'r; en we'en de leaves begin ter fall, Henry's ha'r 'mence' ter drap out; en when de vimes 'uz bar', Henry's head wuz baller 'n it wuz in de spring, en he begin ter git ole en stiff in de j'ints ag'in, en paid no mo' 'tention ter de gals dyoin' er de whole winter. En nex' spring, w'en he rub de sap on ag'in, he got young ag'in, en so soopl en libely dat none er de young niggers on de plantation could n' jump, ner dance, ner hoe ez much cotton ez Henry. But in de fall er de year his grapes 'mence' ter

[7]"A small card, resembling a currycomb in construction, and used by negroes in the rural districts instead of a comb."—Chesnutt's note. Card: a tool with wire teeth, used for carding (combing) fibers.

straighten out, en his j'ints ter git stiff, en his ha'r drap off, en de rheumatiz begin ter wrastle wid 'im.

"Now, ef you'd 'a' knowed ole Mars Dugal' McAdoo, you'd 'a' knowed dat it ha' ter be a mighty rainy day when he could n' fine sump'n fer his niggers ter do, en it ha' ter be a mighty little hole he could n' crawl thoo, en ha' ter be a monst'us cloudy night when a dollar git by him in de dahkness; en w'en he see how Henry git young in de spring en ole in defall, he 'lowed ter hisse'f ez how he could make mo' money out'n Henry dan by wukkin' him in de cotton-fiel'. 'Long de nex' spring, atter de sap 'mence' ter rise, en Henry 'n'int 'is hed en sta'ted fer ter git young en soopl, Mars Dugal' up 'n tuk Henry ter town, en sole 'im fer fifteen hunder' dollars. Co'se de man w'at bought Henry did n' know nuffin 'bout de goopher, en Mars Dugal' did n' see no 'casion fer ter till 'im. Long to'ds de fall, w'en de sap went down, Henry begin ter git ole ag'in same ez yuzhal, en his noo marster begin ter git skeered les'n he gwine ter lose his fifteen-hunder'-dollar nigger. He sent fer a mighty fine doctor, but de med'cine did n' 'pear ter do no good; de goopher had a good holt. Henry tole de doctor 'bout de goopher, but de doctor des laff at 'im.

"One day in de winter Mars Dugal' went ter town, en wuz santerin' 'long de Main Street, when who should he meet but Henry's noo marster. Dey said 'Hoody,' en Mars Dugal' ax 'im ter hab a seegyar; en atter dey run on awhile 'bout de craps en de weather, Mars Dugal' ax 'im, sorter keerless, like ez ef he des thought of it,—

" 'How you like de nigger I sole you las' spring?'

"Henry's marster shuck his head en knock de ashes off'n his seegyar.

" 'Spec' I made a bad bahgin when I bought dat nigger. Henry done good wuk all de summer, but sence de fall set in he 'pears ter be sorter pinin' away. Dey ain' nuffin pertickler de matter wid 'im—leastways de doctor say so—'cep'n a tech er de rheumatiz; but his ha'r is all fell out, en ef he don't pick up his strenk mighty soon, I spec' I'm gwine ter lose 'im.'

"Dey smoked on awhile, en bimeby ole mars say, "Well, a bahgin's a bahgin, but you en me is good fren's, en I doan wan' ter see you lose all de money you paid fer dat nigger; en ef w'at you say is so, en I ain't 'sputin' it, he ain't wuf much now. I 'spec's you wukked him too ha'd dis summer, er e'se de swamps down here don't agree wid de san'-hill nigger. So you des lemme know, en ef he gits any wusser I'll be willin' ter gib yer five hund'ed dollars fer 'im, en take my chances on his livin'."

"Sho 'nuff, when Henry begun ter draw up wid de rheumatiz en it look like he gwine ter die fer sho, his noo marster sen' fer Mars Dugal', en Mars Dugal' gin him what he promus, en brung Henry home ag'in. He tuk good keer uv 'im dyoin' er de winter,—give 'im w'iskey ter rub his rheumatiz, en terbacker ter smoke, en all he want ter eat,—caze a nigger w'at he could make a thousan' dollars a year off'n did n' grow on eve'y huckleberry bush.

"Nex' spring, w'en de sap ris en Henry's ha'r commence' ter sprout, Mars Dugal' sole 'im ag'in, down in Robeson County dis time; en he kep' dat sellin' business up fer five year er mo'. Henry nebber say nuffin 'bout de goopher ter his noo marsters, 'caze he know he gwine ter be tuk good keer uv de nex' winter, w'en Mars Dugal' buy him back. En Mars Dugal' made 'nuff money off'n Henry ter buy anudder plantation ober on Beaver Crick.

"But 'long 'bout de een' er dat five year dey come a stranger ter stop at de plantation. De fus' day he 'uz dere he went out wid Mars Dugal' en spent all de mawnin' lookin' ober de vimya'd, en atter dinner dey spent all de evenin' playin' kya'ds. De niggers soon 'skiver' dat he wuz a Yankee, en dat he come down ter Norf C'lina fer ter l'arn de w'ite folks how to raise grapes en make wine. He promus Mars Dugal' he c'd make de grapevimes b'ar twice't ez many grapes, en dat de noo winepress he wuz a-sellin' would make mo' d'n twice't ez many gallons er wine. En ole Mars Dugal' des drunk it all in, des 'peared ter be bewitch' wid dat Yankee. W'en de darkies see dat Yankee runnin' 'roun' de vimy'd en diggin' under de grapevimes, dey shuk dere heads, en 'lowed dat dey feared Mars Dugal' losin' his min'. Mars Dugal' had all de dirt dug away fum under de roots er all de scuppernon' vimes, an' let 'em stan' dat away fer a week er mo'. Den dat Yankee made de niggers fix up a mixtry er lime en ashes en manyo,[8] en po' it 'roun' de roots er de grapevimes. Den he 'vise Mars Dugal' fer ter trim de vimes close't, en Mars Dugal' tuck 'n done eve'ything de Yankee tole him ter do. Dyoin' all er dis time, mind yer, dis yer Yankee wuz libbin' off'n de fat er de lan', at de big house, en playin' kya'ds wid Mars Dugal' eve'y night; en dey say Mars Dugal' los' mo'n a thousan' dollars dyoin's er de week dat Yankee wuz a-ruinin' de grapevimes.

"W'en de sap ris nex' spring, ole Henry 'n'inted his head ez yuzhal, en his ha'r 'mence' ter grow des de same ez it done eve'y year. De scuppernon' vimes growed monst'us fas', en de leaves wuz greener en thicker dan dey eber be'n dyoin' my rememb'ance; en Henry's ha'r growed out thicker dan eber, en he 'peared ter git younger 'n younger, en soopler 'n soopler; en seein' ez he wuz sh'ot er han's dat spring, havin' tuk in consid'able noo groun', Mars Dugal' cluded he would n' sell Henry 'tel he git de crap in en de cotton chop'. So he kep' Henry on de plantation.

"But long 'bout time fer de grapes ter come on de scuppernon' vimes, dey 'peared ter come a change ober 'em; de leaves withered en swivel' up, en de young grapes turn' yaller, en bimeby eve'ybody on de plantation could see dat de whole vimya'd wuz dyin'. Mars Dugal' tuk 'n water de vimes en done all he could, but 't wa'n' no use: dat Yankee had done bus' de watermillyum. One time de vimes picked up a bit, en Mars Dugal' 'lowed dey wuz gwine ter come out ag'in; but dat Yankee done dug too close under de roots, en prune de branches too close ter de vime, en all dat lime en ashes done burn' de life out'n de vimes, en dey des kep' a-with'in' en a-swivelin'.

"All dis time de goopher wuz a-wukken'. When de vimes sta'ted ter wither, Henry 'mence' ter complain er his rheumatiz; en when de leaves begin ter dry up, his ha'r 'mence' ter drap out. When de vimes fresh' up a bit, Henry 'd git peart ag'in, en when de vimes wither' ag'in, Henry 'd git ole ag'in, en des kep' gittin' mo' en mo' fitten fer nuffin; he des pined away, en pined away, en fine'ly tuk ter his cabin; en when de big vime whar he

[8]"Manure."

got de sap ter 'n'int his head withered en turned yaller en died, Henry died too,—des went out sorter like a cannel. Dey did n't 'pear ter be nuffin de matter wid 'im, 'cep'n' de rheumatiz, but his strenk des dwinnel' away 'tel he did n' hab ernuff lef' ter draw his bref. De goopher had got de under holt, en th'owed Henry dat time fer good en all.

"Mars Dugal' tuk on might'ly 'bout losin' his vimes en his nigger in de same year; en he swo' dat ef he could git holt er dat Yankee he'd wear 'im ter a frazzle, en den chaw up de frazzle; en he'd done it, too, for Mars Dugal' 'uz a monst'us brash man w'en he once git started. He sot de vimya'd out ober ag'in, but it wuz th'ee er fo' year befo' de vimes got ter b'arin' any scuppernon's.

"W'en de wah broke out, Maars Dugal' raise' a comp'ny, en went off ter fight de Yankees. He say he wuz mighty glad dat wah come, en he des want ter kill a Yankee fer eve'y dollar he los' 'long er dat grape-raisin' Yankee. En I 'spec' he would 'a' done it, too, ef de Yankees had n' s'picioned sump'n, en killed him fus'. Atter de s'render ole miss move' ter town, de niggers all scattered 'way fum de plantation, en de vimya'd ain' be'n culter-vated sence."

"Is that story true?" asked Annie doubtfully, but seriously, as the old man concluded his narrative.

"It's des ez true ez I'm a-settin' here, miss. Dey's a easy way ter prove it: I kin lead de way right ter Henry's grave ober yander in de plantation buryin'-groun'. En I tell yer w'at, marster, I would n' 'vise you to buy dis yer ole vimya'd, 'caze de goopher's on it yit, en dey ain' no tellin' w'en it's gwine ter crap out."

"But I thought you said all the ole vines died."

Dey did 'pear ter die, but a few un 'em come out ag'in, en is mixed in 'mongs' de yuthers. I ain' skeered ter eat de grapes, 'caze I knows de old vimes fum de noo ones; but wid strangers dey ain' no tellin' w'at mought happen. I would n' 'vise yer ter buy dis vimya'd."

I bought the vineyard, nevertheless, and it has been for a long time in a thriving condition, and is often referred to by the local press as a striking illustration of the opportunities open to Northern capital in the development of Southern industries. The luscious scuppernong holds first rank among our grapes, though we cultivate a great many other varieties, and our income from grapes packed and shipped to the Northern markets is quite considerable. I have not noticed any developments of the goopher in the vineyard, although I have a mild suspicion that our colored assistants do not suffer from want of grapes during the season.

I found, when I bought the vineyard, that Uncle Julius had occupied a cabin on the place for many years, and derived a respectable revenue from the product of the neglected grapevines. This, doubtless, accounted for his advice to me not to buy the vineyard, though whether it inspired the goopher story I am unable to state. I believe, however, that the wages I paid him for his services as coachman, for I gave him employment in that capacity, were more than an equivalent for anything he lost by the sale of the vineyard.

1887

William Dean Howells 1837–1920 

As a novelist, critic, and magazine editor, Howells was the leading spokesman of literary realism in nineteenth-century America. In an age of genteel authors, he was one of a new breed, like Twain and Hamlin Garland, raised in humble surroundings in America's midlands. Born in Ohio, the son of a printer, Howells was considered a small-town prodigy. By the age of seven he was setting type in his father's print shop, and though he had little formal education he remained throughout his life an omnivorous reader who could enjoy everything but historical novels, romantic fiction, and detective stories.

At twenty-one he became city editor of the Ohio State Journal in Columbus. In 1860, he wrote a campaign biography of Lincoln, and after Lincoln was elected President, Howells was rewarded with appointment as American Consul in Venice, Italy. His life in Italy and his reading of Italian literature sharpened his taste for realistic writing and gave him the subject matter for a series of essays on Italian poets, four novels about Americans in Italy, and three travel books, including Venetian Life (1866), a collection of sketches that was reissued more than twenty times and was his most profitable book.

With the end of the Civil War, Howells returned to America and moved to Boston, where he was appointed assistant editor and later editor-in-chief of the nation's most eminent journal, The Atlantic Monthly. He came to know the literary "gods and half gods and quarter gods of New England," among them Lowell, who was amazed that such a book of "airy elegance" as Venetian Life could have been written by a man from "the rough-and-ready West."

Howells' ten years as editor refined his critical sense, while his experiences as an outlander observing the domestic manners of the American middle class gave him the themes and events of his fiction of urban society. In 1872, he published his first novel, Their Wedding Journey, and in 1881, having written more than a dozen books, six of them novels, Howells left the Atlantic and eventually settled in New York where he continued his prolific writing. He wrote over a hundred books—novels, collections of short stories, essays, autobiographies, and verse. His finest novel, The Rise of Silas Lapham, was published in 1885. His literary doctrines were partially "summed up" in Criticism and Fiction (1891), a selection of essays he had written for his column, "The Editor's Study," which appeared in Harper's from 1886 to 1892.

Howells portrayed the American scene in mansions, summer resorts, railroad cars, and offices. He attempted to make his characters not heroic but "real," with all their virtues and all their "vacancy and tiresomeness." Much of his realism was external, characters and events viewed from without. His works rarely achieved, or sought to achieve, what modern critics think of as psychological depth. He dealt with proprieties. The evils of his characters were slight, their passions restrained, their triumphs few. He avoided the excitements and catastrophes of romanticism just as he avoided sex and sensuality and what he considered to be the sordid excesses of naturalism.

More than any other writer or critic, Howells brought the Age of Realism to America. His reviews and his personal attention had encouraged the development of Mark Twain, Stephen Crane, Hamlin Garland, and Frank Norris, and he helped introduce to America such famous writers as Ibsen, Dostoyevsky, and Tolstoy. Howells was called the literary symbol of his age; he received honorary degrees from Yale, Columbia, Princeton, and Oxford. Newspaper and magazine writers exalted him, among them Theodore Dreiser, who reported on Howells' climb up "Fame's Ladder." But by the early years of the century his "smiling" realism had been displaced by the naturalism and harsher realisms of the twentieth century; his vogue had passed, and he wrote to Henry James, "I am comparatively a dead cult with my statues cut down and the grass growing over me in the pale moonlight."

FURTHER READING: E. Carter, *Howells and the Age of Realism,* 1954; E. Cady, *The Road to Realism,* 1956, 1986; E. Cady, *The Realist at War,* 1958, 1986; V. Brooks, *Howells, His Life and World,* 1959; *The Complete Plays of W. D. Howells,* ed. W. Meserve, 1960; *A Selected Edition of W. D. Howells,* 41 vols. projected, ed. E. Cady, 1968–; K. Lynn, *William Dean Howells, An American Life,* 1971; J. Crowley, *The Black Heart's Truth, The Early Career of William Dean Howells,* 1985; E. Nettels, *Language, Race, and Social Class in Howells' America,* 1988; J. Crowley, *The Mask of Fiction, Essays on W. D. Howells,* 1989; R. Olsen, *Dancing in Chains, The Youth of William Dean Howells,* 1991; J. Crowley, *The Dean of American Letters,* 1999; P. Abeln, *William Dean Howells and the Ends of Realism,* 2005; S. Goodwin and C. Dawson, *William Dean Howells, A Writer's Life,* 2005.

TEXT: "Editha," *Between the Dark and the Daylight,* 1907.

EDITHA

The air was thick with the war feeling,[1] like the electricity of a storm which has not yet burst. Editha sat looking out into the hot spring afternoon, with her lips parted, and panting with the intensity of the question whether she could let him go. She had decided that she could not let him stay, when she saw him at the end of the still leafless avenue, making slowly up towards the house, with his head down and his figure relaxed. She ran impatiently out on the veranda, to the edge of the steps, and imperatively demanded greater haste of him with her will before she called aloud to him: "George!"

He had quickened his pace in mystical response to her mystical urgence, before he could have heard her; now he looked up and answered, "Well?"

"Oh, how united we are!" she exulted, and then she swooped down the steps to him. "What is it?" she cried.

"It's war," he said, and he pulled her up to him and kissed her.

She kissed him back intensely, but irrelevantly, as to their passion, and uttered from deep in her throat, "How glorious!"

"It's war," he repeated, without consenting to her sense of it; and she did not know just what to think at first. She never knew what to think of him; that made his mystery, his charm. All through their courtship, which was contemporaneous with the growth of the war feeling, she had been puzzled by his want of seriousness about it. He seemed to despise it even more than he abhorred it. She could have understood his abhorring any sort of bloodshed; that would have been a survival of his old life when he thought he would be a minister, and before he changed and took up the law. But making light of a cause so high and noble seemed to show a want of earnestness at the core of his being. Not but that she felt herself able to cope with a congenital defect of that sort, and make his love for her save him from himself. Now perhaps the miracle was already wrought in him. In the presence of the tremendous fact that he announced, all triviality seemed to have gone out of him; she began to feel that. He sank down on the top step, and wiped his forehead with his handkerchief, while she poured out upon him her question of the origin and authenticity of his news.

[1] I.e., the emotions roused by the coming of the Spanish-American war (1898).

All the while, in her duplex emotioning, she was aware that now at the very beginning she must put a guard upon herself against urging him, by any word or act, to take the part that her whole soul willed him to take, for the completion of her ideal of him. He was very nearly perfect as he was, and he must be allowed to perfect himself. But he was peculiar, and he might very well be reasoned out of his peculiarity. Before her reasoning went her emotioning: her nature pulling upon his nature, her womanhood upon his manhood, without her knowing the means she was using to the end she was willing. She had always supposed that the man who won her would have done something to win her; she did not know what, but something. George Gearson had simply asked her for her love, on the way home from a concert, and she gave her love to him, without, as it were, thinking. But now, it flashed upon her, if he could do something worthy to *have* won her—be a hero, *her* hero—it would be even better than if he had done it before asking her; it would be grander. Besides, she had believed in the war from the beginning.

"But don't you see, dearest," she said, "that it wouldn't have come to this if it hadn't been in the order of Providence? And I call any war glorious that is for the liberation of people who have been struggling for years against the cruelest oppression. Don't you think so, too?"

"I suppose so," he returned languidly. "But war! Is it glorious to break the peace of the world?"

"That ignoble peace! It was no peace at all, with that crime and shame at our very gates." She was conscious of parroting the current phrases of the newspapers, but it was no time to pick and choose her words. She must sacrifice anything to the high ideal she had for him, and after a good deal of rapid argument she ended with the climax: "But now it doesn't matter about the how or why. Since the war has come, all that is gone. There are no two sides any more. There is nothing now but our country."

He sat with his eyes closed and his head leant back against the veranda, and he remarked, with a vague smile, as if musing aloud, "Our country—right or wrong."[2]

"Yes, right or wrong!" she returned, fervidly. "I'll go and get you some lemonade." She rose rustling, and whisked away; when she came back with two tall glasses of clouded liquid on a tray, and the ice clucking in them, he still sat as she had left him, and she said, as if there had been no interruption: "But there is no question of wrong in this case. I call it a sacred war. A war for liberty and humanity, if ever there was one. And I know you will see it just as I do, yet."

He took half the lemonade at a gulp, and he answered as he set the glass down: "I know you always have the highest ideal. When I differ from you I ought to doubt myself."

A generous sob rose in Editha's throat for the humility of a man, so very nearly perfect, who was willing to put himself below her.

Besides, she felt, more subliminally, that he was never so near slipping through her fingers as when he took that meek way.

"You shall not say that! Only, for once I happen to be right." She seized his hand in her two hands, and poured her soul from her eyes into his. "Don't you think so?" she entreated him.

[2]A phrase coined in 1816 by the American naval hero Stephen Decatur (1779–1820).

He released his hand and drank the rest of his lemonade, and she added, “Have mine too,” but he shook his head in answering, “I’ve no business to think so, unless I act so, too.”

Her heart stopped a beat before it pulsed on with leaps that she felt in her neck. She had noticed that strange thing in men: they seemed to feel bound to do what they believed, and not think a thing was finished when they said it, as girls did. She knew what was in his mind, but she pretended not, as she said, “Oh, I am not sure,” and then faltered.

He went on as if to himself, without apparently heeding her: “There’s only one way of proving one’s faith in a thing like this.”

She could not say that she understood, but she did understand.

He went on again. “If I believed—if I felt as you do about this war—Do you wish me to feel as you do?”

Now she was really not sure; so she said: “George, I don’t know what you mean.”

He seemed to muse away from her as before. “There is a sort of fascination in it. I suppose that at the bottom of his heart every man would like at times to have his courage tested, to see how he would act.”

“How can you talk in that ghastly way?”

“It *is* rather morbid. Still, that’s what it comes to, unless you’re swept away by ambition or driven by conviction. I haven’t the conviction or the ambition, and the other thing is what it comes to with me. I ought to have been a preacher, after all; then I couldn’t have asked it of myself, as I must, now I’m a lawyer. And you believe it’s a holy war, Editha?” he suddenly addressed her. “Oh, I know you do! But you wish me to believe so, too?”

She hardly knew whether he was mocking or not, in the ironical way he always had with her plainer mind. But the only thing was to be outspoken with him.

“George, I wish you to believe whatever you think is true, at any and every cost. If I’ve tried to talk you into anything, I take it all back.”

“Oh, I know that, Editha. I know how sincere you are, and how—I wish I had your undoubting spirit! I’ll think it over; I’d like to believe as you do. But I don’t, now; I don’t, indeed. It isn’t this war alone; though this seems peculiarly wanton and needless; but it’s every war—so stupid; it makes me sick. Why shouldn’t this thing have been settled reasonably?”

“Because,” she said, very throatily again, “God meant it to be war.”

“You think it was God? Yes, I suppose that is what people will say.”

“Do you suppose it would have been war if God hadn’t meant it?”

“I don’t know. Sometimes it seems as if God had put this world into men’s keeping to work it as they pleased.”

“Now, George, that is blasphemy.”

“Well, I won’t blaspheme. I’ll try to believe in your pocket Providence,” he said, and then he rose to go.

“Why don’t you stay to dinner?” Dinner at Balcom’s Works was at one o’clock.

“I’ll come back to supper, if you’ll let me. Perhaps I shall bring you a convert.”

“Well, you may come back, on that condition.”

“All right. If I don’t come, you’ll understand.”

He went away without kissing her, and she felt it a suspension of their engagement. It all interested her intensely; she was undergoing a tremendous experience, and she was being equal to it. While she stood looking after him, her mother came out through one of the long windows onto the veranda, with a catlike softness and vagueness.

"Why didn't he stay to dinner?"

"Because—because—war has been declared," Editha pronounced, without turning.

Her mother said, "Oh, my!" and then said nothing more until she had sat down in one of the large Shaker chairs[3] and rocked herself for some time. Then she closed whatever tacit passage of thought there had been in her mind with the spoken words: "Well, I hope *he* won't go."

"And *I* hope he *will*," the girl said, and confronted her mother with a stormy exaltation that would have frightened any creature less unimpressionable than a cat.

Her mother rocked herself again for an interval of cogitation. What she arrived at in speech was: "Well, I guess you've done a wicked thing, Editha Balcom."

The girl said, as she passed indoors through the same window her mother had come out by: "I haven't done anything—yet."

In her room, she put together all her letters and gifts from Gearson, down to the withered petals of the first flower he had offered, with that timidity of his veiled in that irony of his. In the heart of the packet she enshrined her engagement ring which she had restored to the pretty box he had brought it to her in. Then she sat down, if not calmly yet strongly, and wrote:

"GEORGE:—I understood when you left me. But I think we had better emphasize your meaning that if we cannot be one in everything we had better be one in nothing. So I am sending these things for your keeping till you have made up your mind.

"I shall always love you, and therefore I shall never marry any one else. But the man I marry must love his country first of all, and be able to say to me,

'I could not love thee, dear, so much,
Loved I not honor more.'[4]

"There is no honor above America with me. In this great hour there is no other honor.

"Your heart will make my words clear to you. I had never expected to say so much, but it has come upon me that I must say the utmost. EDITHA."

She thought she had worded her letter well, worded it in a way that could not be bettered; all had been implied and nothing expressed.

She had it ready to send with the packet she had tied with red, white, and blue ribbon, when it occurred to her that she was not just to him, that she was not giving him a fair chance. He had said he would go and think it over, and she was not waiting. She was pushing, threatening, compelling. That was not a woman's part. She must leave him free, free, free. She could not accept for her country or herself a forced sacrifice.

[3]Furniture manufactured at Shaker religious communes and characterized by elegant simplicity.
[4]From "To Lucasta, Going to the Wars," by the English poet Richard Lovelace (1618–1658).

In writing her letter she had satisfied the impulse from which it sprang; she could well afford to wait till he had thought it over. She put the packet and the letter by, and rested serene in the consciousness of having done what was laid upon her by her love itself to do, and yet used patience, mercy, justice.

She had her reward. Gearson did not come to tea, but she had given him till morning, when, late at night there came up from the village the sound of a fife and drum, with a tumult of voices, in shouting, singing, and laughing. The noise drew nearer and nearer; it reached the street end of the avenue; there it silenced itself, and one voice, the voice she knew best, rose over the silence. It fell; the air was filled with cheers; the fife and drum struck up, with the shouting, singing, and laughing again, but now retreating; and a single figure came hurrying up the avenue.

She ran down to meet her lover and clung to him. He was very gay, and he put his arm round her with a boisterous laugh. "Well, you must call me Captain now; or Cap, if you prefer; that's what the boys call me. Yes, we've had a meeting at the town-hall, and everybody has volunteered; and they selected me for captain, and I'm going to the war, the big war, the glorious war, the holy war ordained by the pocket Providence that blesses butchery. Come along; let's tell the whole family about it. Call them from their downy beds, father, mother, Aunt Hitty, and all the folks!"

But when they mounted the veranda steps he did not wait for a larger audience; he poured the story out upon Editha alone.

"There was a lot of speaking, and then some of the fools set up a shout for me. It was all going one way, and I thought it would be a good joke to sprinkle a little cold water on them. But you can't do that with a crowd that adores you. The first thing I knew I was sprinkling hell-fire on them. 'Cry havoc, and let slip the dogs of war.'[5] That was the style. Now that it had come to the fight, there were no two parties; there was one country, and the thing was to fight to a finish as quick as possible. I suggested volunteering then and there, and I wrote my name first of all on the roster. Then they elected me—that's all. I wish I had some ice-water."

She left him walking up and down the veranda, while she ran for the ice-pitcher and a goblet, and when she came back he was still walking up and down, shouting the story he had told her to her father and mother, who had come out more sketchily dressed than they commonly were by day. He drank goblet after goblet of the ice-water without noticing who was giving it, and kept on talking, and laughing through his talk wildly. "It's astonishing," he said, "how well the worse reason looks when you try to make it appear the better. Why, I believe I was the first convert to the war in that crowd to-night! I never thought I should like to kill a man; but now I shouldn't care; and the smokeless powder lets you see the man drop that you kill. It's all for the country! What a thing it is to have a country that *can't* be wrong, but if it is, is right, anyway!"

Editha had a great, vital thought, an inspiration. She set down the ice-pitcher on the veranda floor, and ran up-stairs and got the letter she had written him. When at last he noisily bade her father and mother, "Well, good-night. I forgot I woke you up; I sha'n't want any sleep myself," she followed

[5]From Shakespeare's *Julius Caesar,* Act III, Scene i, line 273.

him down the avenue to the gate. There, after the whirling words that seemed to fly away from her thoughts and refuse to serve them, she made a last effort to solemnize the moment that seemed so crazy, and pressed the letter she had written upon him.

"What's this?" he said. "Want me to mail it?"

"No, no. It's for you. I wrote it after you went this morning. Keep it—keep it—and read it sometime—" She thought, and then her inspiration came: "Read it if ever you doubt what you've done, or fear that I regret your having done it. Read it after you've started."

They strained each other in embraces that seemed as ineffective as their words, and he kissed her face with quick, hot breaths that were so unlike him, that made her feel as if she had lost her old lover and found a stranger in his place. The stranger said: "What a gorgeous flower you are, with your red hair, and your blue eyes that look black now, and your face with the color painted out by the white moonshine! Let me hold you under the chin, to see whether I love blood, you tiger-lily!" Then he laughed Gearson's laugh, and released her, scared and giddy. Within her wilfulness she had been frightened by a sense of subtler force in him, and mystically mastered as she had never been before.

She ran all the way back to the house, and mounted the steps panting. Her mother and father were talking of the great affair. Her mother said: "Wa'n't Mr. Gearson in rather of an excited state of mind? Didn't you think he acted curious?"

"Well, not for a man who'd just been elected captain and had set 'em up for the whole of Company A," her father chuckled back.

"What in the world do you mean, Mr. Balcom? Oh! There's Editha!" She offered to follow the girl indoors.

"Don't come, mother!" Editha called, vanishing.

Mrs. Balcom remained to reproach her husband. "I don't see much of anything to laugh at."

"Well, it's catching. Caught it from Gearson. I guess it won't be much of a war, and I guess Gearson don't think so, either. The other fellows will back down as soon as they see we mean it. I wouldn't lose any sleep over it. I'm going back to bed, myself."

Gearson came again next afternoon, looking pale and rather sick, but quite himself, even to his languid irony. "I guess I'd better tell you, Editha, that I consecrated myself to your god of battles last night by pouring too many libations to him down my own throat. But I'm all right now. One has to carry off the excitement, somehow."

"Promise me," she commanded, "that you'll never touch it again!"

"What! Not let the cannikin clink? Not let the soldier drink?[6] Well, I promise."

"You don't belong to yourself now; you don't even belong to *me*. You belong to your country, and you have a sacred charge to keep yourself strong and well for your country's sake. I have been thinking, thinking all night and all day long."

[6]Adapted from Shakespeare's *Othello,* Act II, Scene iii, lines 71–75.

"You look as if you had been crying a little, too," he said, with his queer smile.

"That's all past. I've been thinking, and worshipping *you.* Don't you suppose I know all that you've been through, to come to this? I've followed you every step from your old theories and opinions."

"Well, you've had a long row to hoe."

"And I know you've done this from the highest motives—"

"Oh, there won't be much pettifogging[7] to do till this cruel war is—"

"And you haven't simply done it for my sake. I couldn't respect you if you had."

"Well, then we'll say I haven't. A man that hasn't got his own respect intact wants the respect of all the other people he can corner. But we won't go into that. I'm in for the thing now, and we've got to face our future. My idea is that this isn't going to be a very protracted struggle; we shall just scare the enemy to death before it comes to a fight at all. But we must provide for contingencies, Editha. If anything happens to me—"

"Oh, George!" She clung to him, sobbing.

"I don't want you to feel foolishly bound to my memory. I should hate that, wherever I happened to be."

"I am yours, for time and eternity—time and eternity." She liked the words; they satisfied her famine for phrases.

"Well, say eternity; that's all right; but time's another thing; and I'm talking about time. But there is something! My mother! If anything happens—"

She winced, and he laughed. "You're not the bold soldier-girl of yesterday!"

Then he sobered. "If anything happens, I want you to help my mother out. She won't like my doing this thing. She brought me up to think war a fool thing as well as a bad thing. My father was in the Civil War; all through it; lost his arm in it." She thrilled with the sense of the arm round her; what if that should be lost? He laughed as if divining her: "Oh, it doesn't run in the family, as far as I know!" Then he added, gravely: "He came home with misgivings about war, and they grew on him. I guess he and mother agreed between them that I was to be brought up in his final mind about it; but that was before my time. I only knew him from my mother's report of him and his opinions; I don't know whether they were hers first; but they were hers last. This will be a blow to her. I shall have to write and tell her—"

He stopped, and she asked: "Would you like me to write, too, George?"

"I don't believe that would do. No, I'll do the writing. She'll understand a little if I say that I thought the way to minimize it was to make war on the largest possible scale at once—that I felt I must have been helping on the war somehow if I hadn't helped keep it from coming, and I knew I hadn't; when it came, I had no right to stay out of it."

Whether his sophistries satisfied him or not, they satisfied her. She clung to his breast, and whispered, with closed eyes and quivering lips: "Yes, yes, yes!"

"But if anything should happen, you might go to her and see what you could do for her. You know? It's rather far off; she can't leave her chair—"

[7]Quibbling, bickering.

"Oh, I'll go, if it's the ends of the earth! But nothing will happen! Nothing *can!* I—"

She felt herself lifted with his rising, and Gearson was saying, with his arm still round her, to her father: "Well, we're off at once, Mr. Balcom. We're to be formally accepted at the capital, and then bunched up with the rest somehow, and sent into camp somewhere, and got to the front as soon as possible. We all want to be in the van,[8] of course; we're the first company to report to the Governor. I came to tell Editha, but I hadn't got round to it."

She saw him again for a moment at the capital, in the station, just before the train started southward with his regiment. He looked well, in his uniform, and very soldierly, but somehow girlish, too, with his clean-shaven face and slim figure. The manly eyes and the strong voice satisfied her, and his preoccupation with some unexpected details of duty flattered her. Other girls were weeping and bemoaning themselves, but she felt a sort of noble distinction in the abstraction, the almost unconsciousness, with which they parted. Only at the last moment he said: "Don't forget my mother. It mayn't be such a walk-over as I supposed," and he laughed at the notion.

He waved his hand to her as the train moved off—she knew it among a score of hands that were waved to other girls from the platform of the car, for it held a letter which she knew was hers. Then he went inside the car to read it, doubtless, and she did not see him again. But she felt safe for him through the strength of what she called her love. What she called her God, always speaking the name in a deep voice and with the implication of a mutual understanding, would watch over him and keep him and bring him back to her. If with an empty sleeve, then he should have three arms instead of two, for both of hers should be his for life. She did not see, though, why she should always be thinking of the arm his father had lost.

There were not many letters from him, but they were such as she could have wished, and she put her whole strength into making hers such as she imagined he could have wished, glorifying and supporting him. She wrote to his mother glorifying him as their hero, but the brief answer she got was merely to the effect that Mrs. Gearson was not well enough to write herself, and thanking her for her letter by the hand of some one who called herself "Yrs truly, Mrs. W. J. Andrews."

Editha determined not to be hurt, but to write again quite as if the answer had been all she expected. Before it seemed as if she could have written, there came news of the first skirmish, and in the list of the killed, which was telegraphed as a trifling loss on our side, was Gearson's name. There was a frantic time of trying to make out that it might be, must be, some other Gearson; but the name and the company and the regiment and the State were too definitely given.

Then there was a lapse into depths out of which it seemed as if she never could rise again; then a lift into clouds far above all grief, black clouds, that blotted out the sun, but where she soared with him, with George—George! She had the fever that she expected of herself, but she did not die in it; she

[8]Vanguard, forefront.

was not even delirious, and it did not last long. When she was well enough to leave her bed, her one thought was of George's mother, of his strangely worded wish that she should go to her and see what she could do for her. In the exaltation of the duty laid upon her—it buoyed her up instead of burdening her—she rapidly recovered.

Her father went with her on the long railroad journey from northern New York to western Iowa; he had business out at Davenport, and he said he could just as well go then as any other time; and he went with her to the little country town where George's mother lived in a little house on the edge of the illimitable cornfields, under trees pushed to a top of the rolling prairie. George's father had settled there after the Civil War, as so many other old soldiers had done; but they were Eastern people, and Editha fancied touches of the East in the June rose overhanging the front door, and the garden with early summer flowers stretching from the gate of the paling fence.

It was very low inside the house, and so dim, with the closed blinds, that they could scarcely see one another: Editha tall and black in her crapes which filled the air with smell of their dyes; her father standing decorously apart with his hat on his forearm, as at funerals; a woman rested in a deep armchair, and the woman who had let the strangers in stood behind the chair.

The seated woman turned her head round and up, and asked the woman behind her chair: "*Who* did you say?"

Editha, if she had done what she expected of herself, would have gone down on her knees at the feet of the seated figure and said, "I am George's Editha," for answer.

But instead of her own voice she heard that other woman's voice saying: "Well, I don't know as I *did* get the name just right. I guess I'll have to make a little more light in here," and she went and pushed two of the shutters ajar.

Then Editha's father said, in his public will-now-address-a-few-remarks tone: "My name is Balcom, ma'am—Junius H. Balcom, of Balcom's Works. New York: my daughter—"

"Oh!" the seated woman broke in, with a powerful voice, the voice that always surprised Editha from Gearson's slender frame. "Let me see you. Stand round where the light can strike your face," and Editha dumbly obeyed. "So, you're Editha Balcom," she sighed.

"Yes," Editha said, more like a culprit than a comforter.

"What did you come for?" Mrs. Gearson asked.

Editha's face quivered and her knees shook. "I came—because—because George—" She could go no further.

"Yes," the mother said, "he told me he had asked you to come if he got killed. You didn't expect that, I suppose, when you sent him."

"I would rather have died myself than done it!" Editha said, with more truth in her deep voice than she ordinarily found in it. "I tried to leave him free—"

"Yes, that letter of yours, that came back with his other things, left him free."

Editha saw now where George's irony came from.

"It was not to be read before—unless—until—I told him so," she faltered.

"Of course, he wouldn't read a letter of yours, under the circumstances, till he thought you wanted him to. Been sick?" the woman abruptly demanded.

"Very sick," Editha said, with self-pity.

"Daughter's life," her father interposed, "was almost despaired of, at one time."

Mrs. Gearson gave him no heed. "I suppose you would have been glad to die, such a brave person as you! I don't believe *he* was glad to die. He was always a timid boy, that way; he was afraid of a good many things; but if he was afraid he did what he made up his mind to. I suppose he made up his mind to go, but I knew what it cost him by what it cost me when I heard of it. I had been through *one* war before. When you sent him you didn't expect he would get killed."

The voice seemed to compassionate Editha, and it was time. "No," she huskily murmured.

"No, girls don't; women don't when they give their men up to their country. They think they'll come marching back, somehow, just as gay as they went, or if it's an empty sleeve, or even an empty pantaloon, it's all the more glory, and they're so much the prouder of them, poor things!"

The tears began to run down Editha's face; she had not wept till then; but it was now such a relief to be understood that the tears came.

"No, you didn't expect him to get killed," Mrs. Gearson repeated, in a voice which was startlingly like George's again. "You just expected him to kill some one else, some of those foreigners, that weren't there because they had any say about it, but because they had to be there, poor wretches—conscripts, or whatever they call 'em. You thought it would be all right for my George, *your* George, to kill the sons of those miserable mothers and the husbands of those girls that you would never see the faces of." The woman lifted her powerful voice in a psalmlike note. "I thank my God he didn't live to do it! I thank my God they killed him first, and that he ain't livin' with their blood on his hands!" She dropped her eyes, which she had raised with her voice, and glared at Editha. "What you got that black on for?" She lifted herself by her powerful arms so high that her helpless body seemed to hang limp its full length. "Take it off, take it off, before I tear it from your back!"

The lady who was passing the summer near Balcom's Works was sketching Editha's beauty, which lent itself wonderfully to the effects of a colorist. It had come to that confidence which is rather apt to grow between artist and sitter, and Editha had told her everything.

"To think of your having such a tragedy in your life!" the lady said. She added: "I suppose there are people who feel that way about war. But when you consider the good this war has done—how much it has done for the country! I can't understand such people, for my part. And when you had come all the way out there to console her—got up out of a sick-bed! Well!"

"I think," Editha said, magnanimously, "she wasn't quite in her right mind; and so did papa."

"Yes," the lady said, looking at Editha's lips in nature and then at her lips in art, and giving an empirical touch to them in the picture. "But how dreadful of her! How perfectly—excuse me—how *vulgar!*"

A light broke upon Editha in the darkness which she felt she had been without a gleam of brightness for weeks and months. The mystery that had bewildered her was solved by the word; and from that moment she rose from grovelling in shame and self-pity, and began to live again in the ideal.

1905

Henry James 1843–1916

Like one of his own characters, Henry James was an artist reconnoitering society, a "passionate pilgrim" in search of experience. His intense perceptions of life undoubtedly owed much to his unusual upbringing. James's wealthy father provided his children with tutors and took them back and forth across the Atlantic to give them a European education and expose them to international society. As a youth, James lived in New York, Geneva, London, Paris, and Newport, Rhode Island, where he and his brother William, who later became a distinguished philosopher and psychologist, studied art and enjoyed the society of their American cousins and the children of their wealthy neighbors.

In 1862, James entered Harvard Law School but soon withdrew and embarked on a literary career. He published his first short story in 1864 at the age of twenty-one. In the next decade, spent alternately in America and Europe, he came under the influence of Flaubert, Turgenev, and Balzac.

In 1871, the Atlantic *serialized James's first novel,* Watch and Ward, *with which he hoped, but failed, to achieve fame. Years later, looking back and finding such early works "hideous," James preferred to declare that his first real novel was* Roderick Hudson *(1875). In 1876, when he was thirty-three, James settled permanently in England and, except for one long visit to the United States, remained in Europe for the rest of his life. The next decade saw the appearance of novels that brought him popular success:* The American *(1877), with its "international" theme of the traditionless American confronting the complexity of European life;* Daisy Miller *(1878), which one American critic described as "an outrage to American girlhood" but which brought James his first international fame; and* The Portrait of a Lady *(1881), the finest example of James's early work.*

The most ambitious novels of James's second period, The Bostonians *(1886),* The Princess Casamassima *(1886), and* The Tragic Muse *(1890), were failures with the public, as were his attempts, in the 1890s, to write for the stage. But James continued to write short stories and novels, and while he never recovered his early popularity, his last novels,* The Wings of the Dove *(1902),* The Ambassadors *(1903), and* The Golden Bowl *(1904), exemplify the mature and formidable style of a third literary period, which critics have come to praise as "The Major Phase."*

In 1915, James, the American expatriate, became a British subject, largely to show his support for the British cause in the First World War. His gesture was his last noteworthy symbolic achievement, for seven months later (February 1916) he died. At the time of his death, James's audience was small. Few of his works remained in print. His writing was no longer in vogue, especially in his native land where he was criticized as anti-American for portraying his fellow Americans as crass and shallow.

Readers in both England and America objected to the narrow emotional and social range of characters drawn from "the hothouse life of the leisured classes." And James was criticized, even parodied, for the obscure and costive style of his final period—a style capable of expressing great subtleties, but based on the assumption that the reader was as well-educated, as heedful of implications, and as unhurried as the author himself. James's mannered works were dismissed as "cathedrals of frosted glass," and at the end of his life James himself was forced to acknowledge that his writing had become "insurmountably unsaleable."

But unlike his contemporary Howells, James was to have his greatest influence not on his own age but on the age that followed. And since the 1930s and 1940s, his influence on writers and readers of modern fiction has grown to be immense. His twenty-two novels and over a hundred short stories, and his critical commentaries, are seen as major contributions to the art of fiction itself, helping to free the novel from its alliances with journalism and romantic storytelling. And he has come to be called the "first of the modern psychological novelists" because his novels and stories of men and women confronting complex society are chronicles of the psychological perceptions that James himself defined as the highest form of experience.

FURTHER READING: F. Mattheissen, *Henry James, The Major Phase,* 1944; *The Complete Plays of Henry James,* ed. L. Edel, 1949, 1990; F. Dupee, *Henry James,* 1951, 1956, 1965; L. Edel, *Henry James,* 5 vols., 1953–1972, 2 vols., 1977, 1 vol., 1985; *The Complete Tales of Henry James,* 12 vols., ed. L. Edel, 1962–1965; *The Letters of Henry James,* 4 vols., ed. L. Edel, 1975–1984; R. Norrman, *The Insecure World of Henry James's Fiction,* 1982; E. Wagenknecht, *The Novels of Henry James,* 1983; A. Margolis, *Henry James and the Problem of Audience,* 1985; *The Complete Notebooks of Henry James,* ed. L. Edel and L. Powers, 1987; *Critical Essays on Henry James, The Early Novels,* ed. J. Gargano, 1987; *Critical Essays on Henry James, The Late Novels,* ed. J. Gargano, 1987; D. Smit, *The Language of a Master,* 1988; S. Mizruchi, *The Power of Historical Knowledge,* 1988; R. Gale, *A Henry James Encyclopedia,* 1989; S. Cameron, *Thinking in Henry James,* 1989; R. Hocks, *Henry James,* 1990; M. Bell, *Meaning in Henry James,* 1990; P. Horne, *Henry James and Revision,* 1991; A Tinter, *The Cosmopolitan World of Henry James,* 1991; *Henry James, A Reference Guide, 1975–1987,* ed. J. Funston, 1991; J. Woolf, *Henry James, The Major Novels,* 1991; R. Posnock, *The Trial of Curiosity, Henry James, William James, and the Challenge of Modernity,* 1991; I. Bell, *Henry James and the Past,* 1991; F. Kaplan, *Henry James, The Imagination of Genius,* 1992; *A Companion to Henry James Studies,* ed. D. Fogel, 1993; R. Jolly, *Henry James, History, Narrative, Fiction,* 1993. S. Teahan, *The Rhetorical Logic of Henry James,* 1995; *Henry James, The Contemporary Reviews,* ed. K. Hayes, 1996; S. Blair, *Henry James and the Writing of Race and Nation,* 1996; J. Freedman, *The Cambridge Companion to Henry James,* 1997; L. Gordon, *A Private Life of Henry James,* 1999; J. Tambling, *Henry James,* 2000; R. Pippin, *Henry James and Modern Moral Life,* 2001; T. Hadley, *Henry James and the Imagination of Pleasure,* 2002; E. Harden, *A Henry James Chronology,* 2005.

TEXTS: *Daisy Miller, Cornhill Magazine,* June–July, 1878; "The Real Thing," *The Novels and Tales of Henry James,* New York Edition, 26 vols., 1907–1917.

DAISY MILLER: A STUDY[1]

PART I

At the little town of Vevey, in Switzerland, there is a particularly comfortable hotel. There are, indeed, many hotels; for the entertainment of tourists is the business of the place, which, as many travellers will remember, is seated upon the edge of a remarkably blue lake[2]—a lake that it behoves every tourist to visit. The shore of the lake presents an unbroken array of establishments of this order, of every category, from the "grand hotel" of the newest fashion, with a chalk-white front, a hundred balconies, and a dozen flags flying from its roof, to the little Swiss *pension*[3] of an elder day, with its name inscribed in German-looking lettering upon a pink or yellow wall, and an awkward summerhouse in the angle of the garden. One of the hotels of Vevey, however, is famous, even classical, being distinguished from many of its upstart neighbours by an air both of luxury and of maturity. In this region, in the month of June, American travellers are extremely numerous; it may be said, indeed, that Vevey assumes at this period some of the characteristics of an American watering-place. There are sights and sounds which evoke a vision, an echo, of Newport and Saratoga.[4] There is a flitting hither and thither of "stylish" young girls, a rustling of muslin flounces, a rattle of dance-music in the morning hours, a sound of high-pitched voices at all times. You receive an impression of these things at the excellent inn of the "Trois Couronnes,"[5] and are transported in fancy to the Ocean House or to Congress Hall.[6] But at the "Trois Couronnes," it must be added, there are other features that are much at variance with these suggestions: neat German waiters, who look like secretaries of legation; Russian princesses sitting in the garden; little Polish boys walking about, held by the hand, with their governors; a view of the sunny crest of the Dent du Midi[7] and the picturesque towers of the Castle of Chillon.[8]

I hardly know whether it was the analogies or the differences that were uppermost in the mind of a young American, who, two or three years ago, sat in the garden of the "Trois Couronnes," looking about him, rather idly, at some of the graceful objects I have mentioned. It was a beautiful summer morning, and in whatever fashion the young American looked at things, they must have seemed to him charming. He had come from Geneva the day before, by the little steamer, to see his aunt, who was staying at the hotel—Geneva having been for a long time his place of residence. But his aunt had a

[1]First published in *Cornhill Magazine*, June–July 1878 (the text presented here) and later revised by James in 1909 for inclusion in *The Novels and Tales of Henry James,* New York Edition, 26 vols., 1907–1909, 1917.

[2]Lake Geneva. [3]A residential hotel.

[4]Newport, Rhode Island, and Saratoga Springs, New York, fashionable nineteenth-century American summer resorts.

[5]French: "Three Crowns." [6]Resort hotels at Newport and Saratoga.

[7]Mountain peak in the Swiss Alps, south of Vevey.

[8]Thirteenth-century castle on Lake Geneva, the setting for Byron's poem "The Prisoner of Chillon" (1816).

headache—his aunt had almost always a headache—and now she was shut up in her room, smelling camphor, so that he was at liberty to wander about. He was some seven-and-twenty years of age; when his friends spoke of him, they usually said that he was at Geneva, "studying." When his enemies spoke of him they said—but, after all, he had no enemies; he was an extremely amiable fellow, and universally liked. What I should say is, simply, that when certain persons spoke of him they affirmed the reason of his spending so much time at Geneva was that he was extremely devoted to a lady who lived there—a foreign lady—a person older than himself. Very few Americans—indeed I think none—had ever seen this lady, about whom there were some singular stories. But Winterbourne had an old attachment for the little metropolis of Calvinism;[9] he had been put to school there as a boy, and he had afterwards gone to college there—circumstances which had led to his forming a great many youthful friendships. Many of these he had kept, and they were a source of great satisfaction to him.

After knocking at his aunt's door and learning that she was indisposed, he had taken a walk about the town, and then he had come in to his breakfast. He had now finished his breakfast; but he was drinking a small cup of coffee, which had been served to him on a little table in the garden by one of the waiters who looked like an *attaché*.[10] At last he finished his coffee and lit a cigarette. Presently a small boy came walking along the path—an urchin of nine or ten. The child, who was diminutive for his years, had an aged expression of countenance, a pale complexion, and sharp little features. He was dressed in knickerbockers, with red stockings, which displayed his poor little spindleshanks;[11] he also wore a brilliant red cravat. He carried in his hand a long alpenstock,[12] the sharp point of which he thrust into everything that he approached—the flower-beds, the garden-benches, the trains of the ladies' dresses. In front of Winterbourne he paused, looking at him with a pair of bright, penetrating little eyes.

"Will you give me a lump of sugar?" he asked, in a sharp, hard little voice—a voice immature, and yet, somehow, not young.

Winterbourne glanced at the small table near him, on which his coffee-service rested, and saw that several morsels of sugar remained. "Yes, you may take one," he answered; "but I don't think sugar is good for little boys."

The little boy stepped forward and carefully selected three of the coveted fragments, two of which he buried in the pocket of his knickerbockers, depositing the other as promptly in another place. He poked his alpenstock, lance-fashion, into Winterbourne's bench, and tried to crack the lump of sugar with his teeth.

"Oh, blazes; it's har-r-d!" he exclaimed, pronouncing the adjective in a peculiar manner.

Winterbourne had immediately perceived that he might have the honour of claiming him as a fellow-countryman. "Take care you don't hurt your teeth," he said, paternally.

"I haven't got any teeth to hurt. They have all come out. I have only got seven teeth. My mother counted them last night, and one came out right

[9]The Protestant reformer John Calvin (1509–1564) lived in Geneva (1541–1564).
[10]A minor diplomat, one who is "attached" to an embassy.
[11]Legs. [12]A long staff with a metal point, used in mountain climbing.

afterwards. She said she'd slap me if any more came out. I can't help it. It's this old Europe. It's the climate that makes them come out. In America they didn't come out. It's these hotels."

Winterbourne was much amused. "If you eat three lumps of sugar, your mother will certainly slap you," he said.

"She's got to give me some candy, then," rejoined his young interlocutor. "I can't get any candy here—any American candy. American candy's the best candy."

"And are American little boys the best little boys?" asked Winterbourne.

"I don't know. I'm an American boy," said the child.

"I see you are one of the best!" laughed Winterbourne.

"Are you an American man?" pursued this vivacious infant. And then, on Winterbourne's affirmative reply—"American men are the best," he declared.

His companion thanked him for the compliment; and the child, who had now got astride of his alpenstock, stood looking about him, while he attacked a second lump of sugar. Winterbourne wondered if he himself had been like this in his infancy, for he had been brought to Europe at about this age.

"Here comes my sister!" cried the child, in a moment. "She's an American girl."

Winterbourne looked along the path and saw a beautiful young lady advancing. "American girls are the best girls," he said, cheerfully, to his young companion.

"My sister ain't the best!" the child declared. "She's always blowing[13] at me."

"I imagine that is your fault, not hers," said Winterbourne. The young lady meanwhile had drawn near. She was dressed in white muslin, with a hundred frills and flounces, and knots of pale-coloured ribbon. She was bare-headed; but she balanced in her hand a large parasol, with a deep border of embroidery; and she was strikingly, admirably pretty. "How pretty they are!" thought Winterbourne, straightening himself in his seat, as if he were prepared to rise.

The young lady paused in front of his bench, near the parapet of the garden, which overlooked the lake. The little boy had now converted his alpenstock into a vaulting-pole, by the aid of which he was springing about in the gravel, and kicking it up not a little.

"Randolph," said the young lady, "what *are* you doing?"

"I'm going up the Alps," replied Randolph. "This is the way!" And he gave another little jump, scattering the pebbles about Winterbourne's ears.

"That's the way they come down," said Winterbourne.

"He's an American man!" cried Randolph, in his little hard voice.

The young lady gave no heed to this announcement, but looked straight at her brother. "Well, I guess you had better be quiet," she simply observed.

It seemed to Winterbourne that he had been in a manner presented. He got up and stepped slowly towards the young girl, throwing away his cigarette. "This little boy and I have made acquaintance," he said, with great civility. In Geneva, as he had been perfectly aware, a young man was not at liberty to speak to a young unmarried lady except under certain rarely-occurring

[13]Fussing, nagging.

conditions; but here at Vevey, what conditions could be better than these?—a pretty American girl coming and standing in front of you in a garden. This pretty American girl, however, on hearing Winterbourne's observation, simply glanced at him; she then turned her head and looked over the parapet, at the lake and the opposite mountains. He wondered whether he had gone too far; but he decided that he must advance farther, rather than retreat. While he was thinking of something else to say, the young lady turned to the little boy again.

"I should like to know where you got that pole," she said.

"I bought it!" responded Randolph.

"You don't mean to say you're going to take it to Italy."

"Yes, I am going to take it to Italy!" the child declared.

The young girl glanced over the front of her dress, and smoothed out a knot or two of ribbon. Then she rested her eyes upon the prospect again. "Well, I guess you had better leave it somewhere," she said, after a moment.

"Are you going to Italy?" Winterbourne inquired, in a tone of great respect.

The young lady glanced at him again. "Yes, sir," she replied. And she said nothing more.

"Are you—a—going over the Simplon?"[14] Winterbourne pursued, a little embarrassed.

"I don't know," she said. "I suppose it's some mountain. Randolph, what mountain are we going over?"

"Going where?" the child demanded.

"To Italy," Winterbourne explained.

"I don't know," said Randolph. "I don't want to go to Italy. I want to go to America."

"Oh, Italy is a beautiful place!" rejoined the young man.

"Can you get candy there?" Randolph loudly inquired.

"I hope not," said his sister. "I guess you have had enough candy, and mother thinks so too."

"I haven't had any for ever so long—for a hundred weeks!" cried the boy, still jumping about.

The young lady inspected her flounces and smoothed her ribbons again; and Winterbourne presently risked an observation upon the beauty of the view. He was ceasing to be embarrassed, for he had begun to perceive that she was not in the least embarrassed herself. There had not been the slightest alteration in her charming complexion; she was evidently neither offended nor fluttered. If she looked another way when he spoke to her, and seemed not particularly to hear him, this was simply her habit, her manner. Yet, as he talked a little more, and pointed out some of the objects of interest in the view, with which she appeared quite unacquainted, she gradually gave him more of the benefit of her glance; and then he saw that this glance was perfectly direct and unshrinking. It was not, however, what would have been called an immodest glance, for the young girl's eyes were singularly honest and fresh. They were wonderfully pretty eyes; and, indeed, Winterbourne had not seen for a long time anything prettier than his fair countrywoman's various features—her complexion, her nose, her ears, her teeth. He had a

[14]Mountain pass between Switzerland and Italy.

great relish for feminine beauty; he was addicted to observing and analysing it; and as regards this young lady's face he made several observations. It was not at all insipid, but it was not exactly expressive; and though it was eminently delicate Winterbourne mentally accused it—very forgivingly—of a want of finish. He thought it very possible that Master Randolph's sister was a coquette;[15] he was sure she had a spirit of her own; but in her bright, sweet, superficial little visage there was no mockery, no irony. Before long it became obvious that she was much disposed towards conversation. She told him that they were going to Rome for the winter—she and her mother and Randolph. She asked him if he was a "real American;" she shouldn't have taken him for one; he seemed more like a German—this was said after a little hesitation, especially when he spoke. Winterbourne, laughing, answered that he had met Germans who spoke like Americans; but that he had not, so far as he remembered, met an American who spoke like a German. Then he asked her if she should not be more comfortable in sitting upon the bench which he had just quitted. She answered that she liked standing up and walking about; but she presently sat down. She told him she was from New York State—"if you know where that is." Winterbourne learned more about her by catching hold of her small, slippery brother and making him stand a few minutes by his side.

"Tell me your name, my boy," he said.

"Randolph C. Miller," said the boy, sharply. "And I'll tell you her name;" and he levelled his alpenstock at his sister.

"You had better wait till you are asked!" said this young lady, calmly.

"I should like very much to know your name," said Winterbourne.

"Her name is Daisy Miller!" cried the child. "But that isn't her real name; that isn't her name on her cards."

"It's a pity you haven't got one of my cards!" said Miss Miller.

"Her real name is Annie P. Miller," the boy went on.

"Ask him *his* name," said his sister, indicating Winterbourne.

But on this point Randolph seemed perfectly indifferent; he continued to supply information with regard to his own family. "My father's name is Ezra B. Miller," he announced. "My father ain't in Europe; my father's in a better place than Europe."

Winterbourne imagined for a moment that this was the manner in which the child had been taught to intimate that Mr. Miller had been removed to the sphere of celestial rewards. But Randolph immediately added, "My father's in Schenectady. He's got a big business. My father's rich, you bet."

"Well!" ejaculated Miss Miller, lowering her parasol and looking at the embroidered border. Winterbourne presently released the child, who departed, dragging his alpenstock along the path. "He doesn't like Europe," said the young girl. "He wants to go back."

"To Schenectady, you mean?"

"Yes; he wants to go right home. He hasn't got any boys here. There is one boy here, but he always goes round with a teacher; they won't let him play."

"And your brother hasn't any teacher?" Winterbourne inquired.

"Mother thought of getting him one, to travel round with us. There was a lady told her of a very good teacher; an American lady—perhaps you know

[15]A flirtatious tease.

her—Mrs. Sanders. I think she came from Boston. She told her of this teacher, and we thought of getting him to travel round with us. But Randolph said he didn't want a teacher travelling round with us. He said he wouldn't have lessons when he was in the cars.[16] And we *are* in the cars about half the time. There was an English lady we met in the cars—I think her name was Miss Featherstone; perhaps you know her. She wanted to know why I didn't give Randolph lessons—give him "instruction," she called it. I guess he could give me more instruction than I could give him. He's very smart."

"Yes," said Winterbourne; "he seems very smart."

"Mother's going to get a teacher for him as soon as we get to Italy. Can you get good teachers in Italy?"

"Very good, I should think," said Winterbourne.

"Or else she's going to find some school. He ought to learn some more. He's only nine. He's going to college." And in this way Miss Miller continued to converse upon the affairs of her family, and upon other topics. She sat there with her extremely pretty hands, ornamented with very brilliant rings, folded in her lap, and with her pretty eyes now resting upon those of Winterbourne, now wandering over the garden, the people who passed by, and the beautiful view. She talked to Winterbourne as if she had known him a long time. He found it very pleasant. It was many years since he had heard a young girl talk so much. It might have been said of this unknown young lady, who had come and sat down beside him upon a bench, that she chattered. She was very quiet; she sat in a charming tranquil attitude, but her lips and her eyes were constantly moving. She had a soft, slender, agreeable voice, and her tone was decidedly sociable. She gave Winterbourne a history of her movements and intentions, and those of her mother and brother, in Europe, and enumerated, in particular, the various hotels at which they had stopped. "That English lady, in the cars," she said—"Miss Featherstone—asked me if we didn't all live in hotels in America. I told her I had never been in so many hotels in my life as since I came to Europe. I have never seen so many—it's nothing but hotels." But Miss Miller did not make this remark with a querulous accent; she appeared to be in the best humour with everything. She declared that the hotels were very good, when once you got used to their ways, and that Europe was perfectly sweet. She was not disappointed—not a bit. Perhaps it was because she had heard so much about it before. She had ever so many intimate friends that had been there ever so many times. And then she had had ever so many dresses and things from Paris. Whenever she put on a Paris dress she felt as if she were in Europe.

"It was a kind of a wishing-cap," said Winterbourne.

"Yes," said Miss Miller, without examining this analogy; "it always made me wish I was here. But I needn't have done that for dresses. I am sure they send all the pretty ones to America; you see the most frightful things here. The only thing I don't like," she proceeded, "is the society. There isn't any society; or, if there is, I don't know where it keeps itself. Do you? I suppose there is some society somewhere, but I haven't seen anything of it. I'm very fond of society, and I have always had a great deal of it. I don't mean only in Schenectady, but in New York. I used to go to New York every winter. In New York I had lots of society. Last winter I had seventeen dinners given me; and three

[16]Railroad cars.

of them were by gentlemen," added Daisy Miller. "I have more friends in New York than in Schenectady—more gentleman friends; and more young lady friends too," she resumed in a moment. She paused again for an instant; she was looking at Winterbourne with all her prettiness in her lively eyes and in her light, slightly monotonous smile. "I have always had," she said, "a great deal of gentlemen's society."

Poor Winterbourne was amused, perplexed, and decidedly charmed. He had never yet heard a young girl express herself in just this fashion; never, at least, save in cases where to say such things seemed a kind of demonstrative evidence of a certain laxity of deportment. And yet was he to accuse Miss Daisy Miller of actual or potential *inconduite,*[17] as they said at Geneva? He felt that he had lived at Geneva so long that he had lost a good deal; he had become dishabituated to the American tone. Never, indeed, since he had grown old enough to appreciate things, had he encountered a young American girl of so pronounced a type as this. Certainly she was very charming, but how deucedly sociable! Was she simply a pretty girl from New York State—were they all like that, the pretty girls who had a good deal of gentlemen's society? Or was she also a designing, an audacious, an unscrupulous young person? Winterbourne had lost his instinct in this matter, and his reason could not help him. Miss Daisy Miller looked extremely innocent. Some people had told him that, after all, American girls were exceedingly innocent; and others had told him that, after all, they were not. He was inclined to think Miss Daisy Miller was a flirt—a pretty American flirt. He had never, as yet, had any relations with young ladies of this category. He had known, here in Europe, two or three women—persons older than Miss Daisy Miller, and provided, for respectability's sake, with husbands—who were great coquettes—dangerous, terrible women, with whom one's relations were liable to take a serious turn. But this young girl was not a coquette in that sense; she was very unsophisticated; she was only a pretty American flirt. Winterbourne was almost grateful for having found the formula that applied to Miss Daisy Miller. He leaned back in his seat; he remarked to himself that she had the most charming nose he had ever seen; he wondered what were the regular conditions and limitations of one's intercourse with a pretty American flirt. It presently became apparent that he was on the way to learn.

"Have you been to that old castle?" asked the young girl, pointing with her parasol to the far-gleaming walls of the Château de Chillon.

"Yes, formerly, more than once," said Winterbourne. "You too, I suppose, have seen it?"

"No; we haven't been there. I want to go there dreadfully. Of course I mean to go there. I wouldn't go away from here without having seen that old castle."

"It's a very pretty excursion," said Winterbourne, "and very easy to make. You can drive, you know, or you can go by the little steamer."

"You can go in the cars," said Miss Miller.

"Yes; you can go in the cars," Winterbourne assented.

"Our courier[18] says they take you right up to the castle," the young girl continued. "We were going last week; but my mother gave out. She suffers dreadfully from dyspepsia. She said she couldn't go. Randolph wouldn't go

[17]French: misconduct. [18]A servant who accompanies travelers.

either; he says he doesn't think much of old castles. But I guess we'll go this week, if we can get Randolph."

"Your brother is not interested in ancient monuments?" Winterbourne inquired, smiling.

"He says he don't care much about old castles. He's only nine. He wants to stay at the hotel. Mother's afraid to leave him alone, and the courier won't stay with him; so we haven't been to many places. But it will be too bad if we don't go up there." And Miss Miller pointed again at the Château de Chillon.

"I should think it might be arranged," said Winterbourne. "Couldn't you get some one to stay—for the afternoon—with Randolph?"

Miss Miller looked at him a moment; and then, very placidly—"I wish *you* would stay with him!" she said.

Winterbourne hesitated a moment. "I should much rather go to Chillon with you."

"With me?" asked the young girl, with the same placidity.

She didn't rise, blushing, as a young girl at Geneva would have done; and yet Winterbourne, conscious that he had been very bold, thought it possible she was offended. "With your mother," he answered very respectfully.

But it seemed that both his audacity and his respect were lost upon Miss Daisy Miller. "I guess my mother won't go after all," she said. "She don't like to ride round in the afternoon. But did you really mean what you said just now; that you would like to go up there?"

"Most earnestly," Winterbourne declared.

"Then we may arrange it. If mother will stay with Randolph, I guess Eugenio will."

"Eugenio?" the young man inquired.

"Eugenio's our courier. He doesn't like to stay with Randolph; he's the most fastidious man I ever saw. But he's a splendid courier. I guess he'll stay at home with Randolph if mother does, and then we can go to the castle."

Winterbourne reflected for an instant as lucidly as possible—"we" could only mean Miss Daisy Miller and himself. This programme seemed almost too agreeable for credence; he felt as if he ought to kiss the young lady's hand. Possibly he would have done so—and quite spoiled the project; but at this moment another person—presumably Eugenio—appeared. A tall, handsome man, with superb whiskers, wearing a velvet morning-coat and a brilliant watch-chain, approached Miss Miller, looking sharply at her companion. "Oh, Eugenio!" said Miss Miller, with the friendliest accent.

Eugenio had looked at Winterbourne from head to foot; he now bowed gravely to the young lady. "I have the honour to inform mademoiselle that luncheon is upon the table."

Miss Miller slowly rose. "See here, Eugenio," she said. "I'm going to that old castle, any way."

"To the Château de Chillon, mademoiselle?" the courier inquired. "Mademoiselle has made arrangements?" he added, in a tone which struck Winterbourne as very impertinent.

Eugenio's tone apparently threw, even to Miss Miller's own apprehension, a slightly ironical light upon the young girl's situation. She turned to Winterbourne, blushing a little—a very little. "You won't back out?" she said.

"I shall not be happy till we go!" he protested.

"And you are staying in this hotel?" she went on. "And you are really an American?"

The courier stood looking at Winterbourne, offensively. The young man, at least, thought his manner of looking an offence to Miss Miller; it conveyed an imputation that she "picked up" acquaintances. "I shall have the honour of presenting to you a person who will tell you all about me," he said smiling, and referring to his aunt.

"Oh, well, we'll go some day," said Miss Miller. And she gave him a smile and turned away. She put up her parasol and walked back to the inn beside Eugenio. Winterbourne stood looking after her; and as she moved away, drawing her muslin furbelows over the gravel, said to himself that she had the *tourmure*[19] of a princess.

He had, however, engaged to do more than proved feasible, in promising to present his aunt, Mrs. Costello, to Miss Daisy Miller. As soon as the former lady had got better of her headache he waited upon her in her apartment; and, after the proper inquiries in regard to her health, he asked her if she had observed, in the hotel, an American family—a mamma, a daughter, and a little boy.

"And a courier?" said Mrs. Costello. "Oh, yes I have observed them. Seen them—heard them—and kept out of their way." Mrs. Costello was a widow with a fortune; a person of much distinction, who frequently intimated that, if she were not so dreadfully liable to sick-headaches, she would probably have left a deeper impress upon her time. She had a long pale face, a high nose, and a great deal of very striking white hair, which she wore in large puffs and *rouleaux*[20] over the top of her head. She had two sons married in New York, and another who was now in Europe. This young man was amusing himself at Hombourg,[21] and, though he was on his travels, was rarely perceived to visit any particular city at the moment selected by his mother for her own appearance there. Her nephew, who had come up to Vevey expressly to see her, was therefore more attentive than those who, as she said, were nearer to her. He had imbibed at Geneva the idea that one must always be attentive to one's aunt. Mrs. Costello had not seen him for many years, and she was greatly pleased with him, manifesting her approbation by initiating him into many of the secrets of that social sway which, as she gave him to understand, she exerted in the American capital.[22] She admitted that she was very exclusive; but, if he were acquainted with New York, he would see that one had to be. And her picture of the minutely hierarchical constitution of the society of that city, which she presented to him in many different lights, was, to Winterbourne's imagination, almost oppressively striking.

He immediately perceived, from her tone, that Miss Daisy Miller's place in the social scale was low. "I am afraid you don't approve of them," he said.

"They are very common," Mrs. Costello declared. "They are the sort of Americans that one does one's duty by not—not accepting."

"Ah, you don't accept them?" said the young man.

"I can't, my dear Frederick. I would if I could, but I can't."

[19]French: appearance. [20]French: rolls, coils.
[21]A German health resort. [22]America's social capital, New York City.

"The young girl is very pretty," said Winterbourne, in a moment.

"Of course she's pretty. But she is very common."

"I see what you mean of course," said Winterbourne, after another pause.

"She has that charming look that they all have," his aunt resumed. "I can't think where they pick it up; and she dressed in perfection—no, you don't know how well she dresses. I can't think where they get their taste."

"But, my dear aunt, she is not, after all, a Comanche savage."

"She is a young lady," said Mrs. Costello, "who has an intimacy with her mamma's courier."

"An intimacy with the courier?" the young man demanded.

"Oh, the mother is just as bad! They treat the courier like a familiar friend—like a gentleman. I shouldn't wonder if he dines with them. Very likely they have never seen a man with such good manners, such fine clothes, so like a gentleman. He probably corresponds to the young lady's idea of a Count. He sits with them in the garden, in the evening. I think he smokes."

Winterbourne listened with interest to these disclosures; they helped him to make up his mind about Miss Daisy. Evidently she was rather wild. "Well," he said, "I am not a courier, and yet she was very charming to me."

"You had better have said at first," said Mrs. Costello with dignity, "that you had made her acquaintance."

"We simply met in the garden and we talked a bit."

"*Tout bonnement!*[23] And pray what did you say?"

"I said I should take the liberty of introducing her to my admirable aunt."

"I am much obliged to you."

"It was to guarantee my respectability," said Winterbourne.

"And pray who is to guarantee hers?"

"Ah, you are cruel!" said the young man. "She's a very nice young girl."

"You don't say that as if you believed it," Mrs. Costello observed.

"She is completely uncultivated," Winterbourne went on. "But she is wonderfully pretty, and, in short, she is very nice. To prove that I believe it, I am going to take her to the Château de Chillon."

"You two are going off there together? I should say it proved just the contrary. How long had you known her, may I ask, when this interesting project was formed? You haven't been twenty-four hours in the house."

"I had known her half an hour!" said Winterbourne, smiling.

"Dear me!" cried Mrs. Costello. "What a dreadful girl!"

Her nephew was silent for some moments. "You really think, then," he began, earnestly, and with a desire for trustworthy information—"you really think that——" But he paused again.

"Think what, sir?" said his aunt.

"That she is the sort of young lady who expects a man—sooner or later—to carry her off?"

"I haven't the least idea what such young ladies expect a man to do. But I really think that you had better not meddle with little American girls that are uncultivated, as you call them. You have lived too long out of the country. You will be sure to make some great mistake. You are too innocent."

"My dear aunt, I am not so innocent," said Winterbourne, smiling and curling his moustache.

[23]French: "Is that so!"

"You are too guilty, then!"

Winterbourne continued to curl his moustache, meditatively. "You won't let the poor girl know you then?" he asked at last.

"Is it literally true that she is going to the Château de Chillon with you?"

"I think that she fully intends it."

"Then, my dear Frederick," said Mrs. Costello, "I must decline the honour of her acquaintance. I am an old woman, but I am not too old—thank Heaven—to be shocked!"

"But don't they all do these things—the young girls in America?" Winterbourne inquired.

Mrs. Costello stared a moment. "I should like to see my granddaughters do them!" she declared, grimly.

This seemed to throw some light upon the matter, for Winterbourne remembered to have heard that his pretty cousins in New York were "tremendous flirts." If, therefore, Miss Daisy Miller exceeded the liberal margin allowed to these young ladies, it was probable that anything might be expected of her. Winterbourne was impatient to see her again, and he was vexed with himself that, by instinct, he should not appreciate her justly.

Though he was impatient to see her, he hardly knew what he should say to her about his aunt's refusal to become acquainted with her; but he discovered, promptly enough, that with Miss Daisy Miller there was no great need of walking on tiptoe. He found her that evening in the garden, wandering about in the warm starlight, like an indolent sylph, and swinging to and fro the largest fan he had ever beheld. It was ten o'clock. He had dined with his aunt, had been sitting with her since dinner, and had just taken leave of her till the morrow. Miss Daisy Miller seemed very glad to see him; she declared it was the longest evening she had ever passed.

"Have you been all alone?" he asked.

"I have been walking round with mother. But mother gets tired walking round," she answered.

"Has she gone to bed?"

"No; she doesn't like to go to bed," said the young girl. "She doesn't sleep—not three hours. She says she doesn't know how she lives. She's dreadfully nervous. I guess she sleeps more than she thinks. She's gone somewhere after Randolph; she wants to try to get him to go to bed. He doesn't like to go to bed."

"Let us hope she will persuade him," observed Winterbourne.

"She will talk to him all she can; but he doesn't like her to talk to him," said Miss Daisy, opening her fan. "She's going to try to get Eugenio to talk to him. But he isn't afraid of Eugenio. Eugenio's a splendid courier, but he can't make much impression on Randolph! I don't believe he'll go to bed before eleven." It appears that Randolph's vigil was in fact triumphantly prolonged, for Winterbourne strolled about with the young girl for some time without meeting her mother. "I have been looking round for that lady you want to introduce me to," his companion resumed. "She's your aunt." Then, on Winterbourne's admitting the fact, and expressing some curiosity as to how she learned it, she said she heard all about Mrs. Costello from the chambermaid. She was very quiet and very *comme il faut;*[24] she wore white puffs;

[24]French: proper.

she spoke to no one, and she never dined at the *table d'hôte*.[25] Every two days she had a headache. "I think that's a lovely description, headache and all!" said Miss Daisy, chattering along in her thin, gay voice. "I want to know her ever so much. I know just what *your* aunt would be; I know I should like her. She would be very exclusive. I like a lady to be exclusive; I'm dying to be exclusive myself. Well, we *are* exclusive, mother and I. We don't speak to every one—or they don't speak to us. I suppose it's about the same thing. Any way, I shall be ever so glad to know your aunt."

Winterbourne was embarrassed. "She would be most happy," he said; "but I am afraid those headaches will interfere."

The young girl looked at him through the dusk. "But I suppose she doesn't have a headache every day," she said, sympathetically.

Winterbourne was silent a moment. "She tells me she does," he answered at last—not knowing what to say.

Miss Daisy Miller stopped and stood looking at him. Her prettiness was still visible in the darkness; she was opening and closing her enormous fan. "She doesn't want to know me!" she said, suddenly. "Why don't you say so? You needn't be afraid. I'm not afraid!" And she gave a little laugh.

Winterbourne fancied there was a tremor in her voice; he was touched, shocked, mortified by it. "My dear young lady," he protested, "she knows no one. It's her wretched health."

The young girl walked on a few steps, laughing still. "You needn't be afraid," she repeated. "Why should she want to know me?" Then she paused again; she was close to the parapet of the garden, and in front of her was the starlit lake. There was a vague sheen upon its surface, and in the distance were dimly-seen mountain forms. Daisy Miller looked out upon the mysterious prospect, and then she gave another little laugh. "Gracious! she *is* exclusive!" she said. Winterbourne wondered whether she was seriously wounded, and for a moment almost wished that her sense of injury might be such as to make it becoming in him to attempt to reassure and comfort her. He had a pleasant sense that she would be very approachable for consolatory purposes. He felt then, for the instant, quite ready to sacrifice his aunt, conversationally; to admit that she was a proud, rude woman, and to declare that they needn't mind her. But before he had time to commit himself to this perilous mixture of gallantry and impiety, the young lady, resuming her walk, gave an exclamation in quite another tone. "Well; here's mother! I guess she hasn't got Randolph to go to bed." The figure of a lady appeared, at a distance, very indistinct in the darkness, and advancing with a slow and wavering movement. Suddenly it seemed to pause.

"Are you sure it is your mother? Can you distinguish her in this thick dusk?" Winterbourne asked.

"Well!" cried Miss Daisy Miller, with a laugh, "I guess I know my own mother. And when she has got on my shawl, too! She is always wearing my things."

The lady in question, ceasing to advance, hovered vaguely about the spot at which she had checked her steps.

[25]French: ordinary public dining table.

"I am afraid your mother doesn't see you," said Winterbourne. "Or perhaps," he added—thinking, with Miss Miller, the joke permissible—"perhaps she feels guilty about your shawl."

"Oh, it's a fearful old thing!" the young girl replied, serenely. "I told her she could wear it. She won't come here, because she sees you."

"Ah, then!" said Winterbourne, "I had better leave you."

"Oh, no; come on!" urged Miss Daisy Miller.

"I'm afraid your mother doesn't approve of my walking with you."

Miss Miller gave him a serious glance. "It isn't for me; it's for you—that is, it's for *her*. Well; I don't know who it's for! But mother doesn't like any of my gentlemen friends. She's right down timid. She always makes a fuss if I introduce a gentleman. But I *do* introduce them—almost always. If I didn't introduce my gentlemen friends to mother," the young girl added, in her little soft, flat monotone, "I shouldn't think I was natural."

"To introduce me," said Winterbourne, "you must know my name." And he proceeded to pronounce it.

"Oh, dear; I can't say all that!" said his companion, with a laugh. But by this time they had come up to Mrs. Miller, who, as they drew near, walked to the parapet of the garden and leaned upon it, looking intently at the lake, and turning her back on them. "Mother!" said the young girl, in a tone of decision. Upon this the elder lady turned round. "Mr. Winterbourne," said Miss Daisy Miller, introducing the young man very frankly and prettily. "Common" she was, as Mrs. Costello had pronounced her; yet it was a wonder to Winterbourne that, with her commonness, she had a singularly delicate grace.

Her mother was a small, spare, light person, with a wandering eye, a very exiguous nose, and a large forehead, decorated with a certain amount of thin, much-frizzled hair. Like her daughter, Mrs. Miller was dressed with extreme elegance; she had enormous diamonds in her ears. So far as Winterbourne could observe, she gave him no greeting—she certainly was not looking at him. Daisy was near her, pulling her shawl straight. "What are you doing, poking round here?" this young lady inquired; but by no means with that harshness of accent which her choice of words may imply.

"I don't know," said her mother, turning towards the lake again.

"I shouldn't think you'd want that shawl!" Daisy exclaimed.

"Well—I do!" her mother answered, with a little laugh.

"Did you get Randolph to go to bed?" asked the young girl.

"No; I couldn't induce him," said Mrs. Miller, very gently. "He wants to talk to the waiter. He likes to talk to that waiter."

"I was telling Mr. Winterbourne," the young girl went on; and to the young man's ear her tone might have indicated that she had been uttering his name all her life.

"Oh, yes!" said Winterbourne; "I have the pleasure of knowing your son."

Randolph's mamma was silent; she turned her attention to the lake. But at last she spoke. "Well, I don't see how he lives!"

"Anyhow, it isn't so bad as it was at Dover," said Daisy Miller.

"And what occurred at Dover?" Winterbourne asked.

"He wouldn't go to bed at all. I guess he sat up all night—in the public parlour. He wasn't in bed at twelve o'clock: I know that."

"It was half-past twelve," declared Mrs. Miller, with mild emphasis.

"Does he sleep much during the day?" Winterbourne demanded.

"I guess he doesn't sleep much," Daisy rejoined.

"I wish he would!" said her mother. "It seems as if he couldn't."

"I think he's real tiresome," Daisy pursued.

Then, for some moments, there was silence. "Well Daisy Miller," said the elder lady, presently, "I shouldn't think you'd want to talk against your own brother!"

"Well, he *is* tiresome, mother," said Daisy, quite without the asperity of a retort.

"He's only nine," urged Mrs. Miller.

"Well, he wouldn't go to that castle," said the young girl. "I'm going there with Mr. Winterbourne."

To this announcement, very placidly made, Daisy's mamma offered no response. Winterbourne took for granted that she deeply disapproved of the projected excursion; but he said to himself that she was a simple, easily-managed person, and that a few deferential protestations would take the edge from her displeasure. "Yes," he began; "Your daughter has kindly allowed me the honour of being her guide."

Mrs. Miller's wandering eyes attached themselves, with a sort of appealing air, to Daisy, who, however, strolled a few steps farther, gently humming to herself. "I presume you will go in the cars," said her mother.

"Yes; or in the boat," said Winterbourne.

"Well, of course, I don't know," Mrs. Miller rejoined. "I have never been to that castle."

"It is a pity you shouldn't go," said Winterbourne, beginning to feel reassured as to her opposition. And yet he was quite prepared to find that, as a matter of course, she meant to accompany her daughter.

"We've been thinking ever so much about going," she pursued; "but it seems as if we couldn't. Of course Daisy—she wants to go round. But there's a lady here—I don't know her name—she says she shouldn't think we'd want to go to see castles *here;* she should think we'd want to wait till we got to Italy. It seems as if there would be so many there," continued Mrs. Miller, with an air of increasing confidence. "Of course, we only want to see the principal ones. We visited several in England," she presently added.

"Ah, yes! in England there are beautiful castles," said Winterbourne. "But Chillon, here, is very well worth seeing."

"Well, if Daisy feels up to it——," said Mrs. Miller, in a tone impregnated with a sense of the magnitude of the enterprise. "It seems as if there was nothing she wouldn't undertake."

"Oh, I think she'll enjoy it!" Winterbourne declared. And he desired more and more to make it a certainty that he was to have the privilege of a *tête-à-tête*[26] with the young lady, who was still strolling along in front of them, softly vocalising. "You are not disposed, madam," he inquired, "to undertake it yourself?"

Daisy's mother looked at him, an instant, askance, and then walked forward in silence. Then—"I guess she had better go alone," she said, simply.

Winterbourne observed to himself that this was a very different type of maternity from that of the vigilant matrons who massed themselves in the

[26]French: private talk.

forefront of social intercourse in the dark old city at the other end of the lake. But his meditations were interrupted by hearing his name very distinctly pronounced by Mrs. Miller's unprotected daughter.

"Mr. Winterbourne!" murmured Daisy.

"Mademoiselle!" said the young man.

"Don't you want to take me out in a boat?"

"At present?" he asked.

"Of course!" said Daisy.

"Well, Annie Miller!" exclaimed her mother.

"I beg you, madam, to let her go," said Winterbourne, ardently; for he had never yet enjoyed the sensation of guiding through the summer starlight a skiff freighted with a fresh and beautiful young girl.

"I shouldn't think she'd want to," said her mother. "I should think she'd rather go indoors."

"I'm sure Mr. Winterbourne wants to take me," Daisy declared. "He's so awfully devoted!"

"I will row you over to Chillon, in the starlight."

"I don't believe it!" said Daisy.

"Well!" ejaculated the elder lady again.

"You haven't spoken to me for half an hour," her daughter went on.

"I have been having some very pleasant conversation with your mother," said Winterbourne.

"Well; I want you to take me out in a boat!" Daisy repeated. They had all stopped, and she had turned round and was looking at Winterbourne. Her face wore a charming smile, her pretty eyes were gleaming, she was swinging her great fan about. No; it's impossible to be prettier than that, thought Winterbourne.

"There are half a dozen boats moored at that landing-place," he said, pointing to certain steps which descended from the garden to the lake. "If you will do me the honour to accept my arm, we will go and select one of them."

Daisy stood there smiling; she threw back her head and gave a little, light laugh. "I like a gentleman to be formal!" she declared.

"I assure you it's a formal offer."

"I was bound I would make you say something," Daisy went on.

"You see it's not very difficult," said Winterbourne. "But I am afraid you are chaffing me."

"I think not, sir," remarked Mrs. Miller, very gently.

"Do, then, let me give you a row," he said to the young girl.

"It's quite lovely, the way you say that!" cried Daisy.

"It will be still more lovely to do it."

"Yes, it would be lovely!" said Daisy. But she made no movement to accompany him; she only stood there laughing.

"I should think you had better find out what time it is," interposed her mother.

"It is eleven o'clock, madam," said a voice, with a foreign accent, out of the neighbouring darkness; and Winterbourne, turning, perceived the florid personage who was in attendance upon the two ladies. He had apparently just approached.

"Oh, Eugenio," said Daisy, "I am going out in a boat!"

Eugenio bowed. "At eleven o'clock, mademoiselle?"

"I am going with Mr. Winterbourne. This very minute."

"Do tell her she can't," said Mrs. Miller to the courier.

"I think you had better not go out in a boat, mademoiselle," Eugenio declared.

Winterbourne wished to Heaven this pretty girl were not so familiar with her courier; but he said nothing.

"I suppose you don't think it's proper!" Daisy exclaimed. "Eugenio doesn't think anything's proper."

"I am at your service," said Winterbourne.

"Does mademoiselle propose to go alone?" asked Eugenio of Mrs. Miller.

"Oh, no; with this gentleman!" answered Daisy's mamma.

The courier looked for a moment at Winterbourne—the latter thought he was smiling—and then, solemnly, with a bow, "As mademoiselle pleases!" he said.

"Oh, I hoped you would make a fuss!" said Daisy. "I don't care to go now."

"I myself shall make a fuss if you don't go," said Winterbourne.

"That's all I want—a little fuss!" And the young girl began to laugh again.

"Mr. Randolph has gone to bed!" the courier announced, frigidly.

"Oh, Daisy; now we can go!" said Mrs. Miller.

Daisy turned away from Winterbourne, looking at him, smiling, and fanning herself. "Good-night," she said; "I hope you are disappointed, or disgusted, or something!"

He looked at her, taking the hand she offered him. "I am puzzled," he answered.

"Well; I hope it won't keep you awake!" she said, very smartly; and, under the escort of the privileged Eugenio, the two ladies passed towards the house.

Winterbourne stood looking after them; he was indeed puzzled. He lingered beside the lake for a quarter of an hour; turning over the mystery of the young girl's sudden familiarities and caprices. But the only very definite conclusion he came to was that he should enjoy deucedly "going off" with her somewhere.

Two days afterwards he went off with her to the Castle of Chillon. He waited for her in the large hall of the hotel, where the couriers, the servants, the foreign tourists were lounging about and staring. It was not the place he should have chosen, but she had appointed it. She came tripping downstairs, buttoning her long gloves, squeezing her folded parasol against her pretty figure, dressed in the perfection of a soberly elegant travelling-costume. Winterbourne was a man of imagination and, as our ancestors used to say, sensibility;[27] as he looked at her dress and, on the great staircase, her little rapid, confiding step, he felt as if there were something romantic going forward. He could have believed he was going to elope with her. He passed out with her among all the idle people that were assembled there; they were all looking at her very hard; she had begun to chatter as soon as she joined him. Winterbourne's preference had been that they should be conveyed to Chillon in a carriage; but she expressed a lively wish to go in the little

[27]I.e., sensitivity.

steamer; she declared that she had a passion for steamboats. There was always such a lovely breeze upon the water, and you saw such lots of people. The sail was not long, but Winterbourne's companion found time to say a great many things. To the young man himself their little excursion was so much of an escapade—an adventure—that, even allowing for her habitual sense of freedom, he had some expectation of seeing her regard it in the same way. But it must be confessed that, in this particular, he was disappointed. Daisy Miller was extremely animated, she was in charming spirits; but she was apparently not at all excited; she was not fluttered; she avoided neither his eyes nor those of any one else; she blushed neither when she looked at him nor when she felt that people were looking at her. People continued to look at her a great deal, and Winterbourne took much satisfaction in his pretty companion's distinguished air. He had been a little afraid that she would talk loud, laugh overmuch, and even, perhaps, desire to move about the boat a good deal. But he quite forgot his fears; he sat smiling, with his eyes upon her face, while, without moving from her place, she delivered herself of a great number of original reflections. It was the most charming garrulity he had ever heard. He had assented to the idea that she was "common;" but was she so, after all, or was he simply getting used to her commonness? Her conversation was chiefly of what metaphysicians term the objective cast; but every now and then it took a subjective turn.

"What on *earth* are you so grave about?" she suddenly demanded, fixing her agreeable eyes upon Winterbourne's.

"Am I grave?" he asked. "I had an idea I was grinning from ear to ear."

"You look as if you were taking me to a funeral. If that's a grin, your ears are very near together."

"Should you like me to dance a hornpipe on the deck?"

"Pray do, and I'll carry round your hat. It will pay the expenses of our journey."

"I never was better pleased in my life," murmured Winterbourne.

She looked at him a moment, and then burst into a little laugh. "I like to make you say those things! You're a queer mixture!"

In the castle, after they had landed, the subjective element decidedly prevailed. Daisy tripped about the vaulted chambers, rustled her skirts in the corkscrew staircases, flirted back with a pretty little cry and a shudder from the edge of the *oubliettes*,[28] and turned a singularly well-shaped ear to everything that Winterbourne told her about the place. But he saw that she cared very little for feudal antiquities, and that the dusky traditions of Chillon made but a slight impression upon her. They had the good fortune to have been able to walk about without other companionship than that of the custodian; and Winterbourne arranged with this functionary that they should not be hurried—that they should linger and pause wherever they chose. The custodian interpreted the bargain generously—Winterbourne, on his side, had been generous—and ended by leaving them quite to themselves. Miss Miller's observations were not remarkable for logical consistency; for anything she wanted to say she was sure to find a pretext. She found a great many pretexts in the rugged embrasures of Chillon for asking Winterbourne

[28]French: oblivions, a term for prison cells sunk below floor level and with openings only at the top.

sudden questions about himself—his family, his previous history, his tastes, his habits, his intentions—and for supplying information upon corresponding points in her own personality. Of her own tastes, habits, and intentions Miss Miller was prepared to give the most definite, and indeed the most favourable, account.

"Well; I hope you know enough!" she said to her companion, after he had told her the history of the unhappy Bonivard.[29] "I never saw a man that knew so much!" The history of Bonivard had evidently, as they say, gone into one ear and out of the other. But Daisy went on to say that she wished Winterbourne would travel with them and "go round" with them; they might know something, in that case. "Don't you want to come and teach Randolph?" she asked. Winterbourne said that nothing could possibly please him so much; but that he had unfortunately other occupations. "Other occupations? I don't believe it!" said Miss Daisy. "What do you mean? You are not in business." The young man admitted that he was not in business; but he had engagements which, even within a day or two, would force him to go back to Geneva. "Oh, bother!" she said: "I don't believe it!" and she began to talk about something else. But a few moments later, when he was pointing out to her the pretty design of an antique fireplace, she broke out irrelevantly, "You don't mean to say you are going back to Geneva?"

"It is a melancholy fact that I shall have to return to Geneva tomorrow."

"Well, Mr. Winterbourne," said Daisy; "I think you're horrid!"

"Oh, don't say such dreadful things!" said Winterbourne—"just at the last!"

"The last!" cried the young girl; "I call it the first. I have half a mind to leave you here and go straight back to the hotel alone." And for the next ten minutes she did nothing but call him horrid. Poor Winterbourne was fairly bewildered; no young lady had as yet done him the honour to be so agitated by the announcement of his movements. His companion, after this, ceased to pay any attention to the curiosities of Chillon or the beauties of the lake; she opened fire upon the mysterious charmer in Geneva whom she appeared to have instantly taken it for granted that he was hurrying back to see. How did Miss Daisy Miller know that there was a charmer in Geneva? Winterbourne, who denied the existence of such a person, was quite unable to discover; and he was divided between amazement at the rapidity of her induction and amusement at the frankness of her *persiflage*.[30] She seemed to him, in all this, an extraordinary mixture of innocence and crudity. "Does she never allow you more than three days at a time?" asked Daisy, ironically. "Doesn't she give you a vacation in summer? There's no one so hard worked but they can get leave to go off somewhere at this season. I suppose, if you stay another day, she'll come after you in the boat. Do wait over till Friday, and I will go down to the landing to see her arrive!" Winterbourne began to think he had been wrong to feel disappointed in the temper in which the young lady had embarked. If he had missed the personal accent, the personal accent was now making its appearance. It sounded very distinctly, at last, in her telling him

[29]François de Bonnivard (1496?–1570), Swiss patriot jailed in the Castle of Chillon (1530–1536) and the hero of Byron's *The Prisoner of Chillon,* 1816.
[30]Banter.

she would stop "teasing" him if he would promise her solemnly to come down to Rome in the winter.

"That's not a difficult promise to make," said Winterbourne. "My aunt has taken an apartment in Rome for the winter, and has already asked me to come and see her."

"I don't want you to come for your aunt," said Daisy; "I want you to come for me." And this was the only allusion that the young man was ever to hear her make to his invidious kinswoman. He declared that, at any rate, he would certainly come. After this Daisy stopped teasing. Winterbourne took a carriage, and they drove back to Vevey in the dusk; the young girl was very quiet.

In the evening Winterbourne mentioned to Mrs. Costello that he had spent the afternoon at Chillon, with Miss Daisy Miller.

"The Americans—of the courier?" asked this lady.

"Ah, happily," said Winterbourne, "the courier stayed at home."

"She went with you all alone?"

"All alone."

Mrs. Costello sniffed a little at her smelling-bottle.[31] "And that," she exclaimed, "is the young person whom you wanted me to know!"

PART II

Winterbourne, who had returned to Geneva the day after his excursion to Chillon, went to Rome towards the end of January. His aunt had been established there for several weeks, and he had received a couple of letters from her. "Those people you were so devoted to last summer at Vevey have turned up here, courier and all," she wrote. "They seem to have made several acquaintances, but the courier continues to be the most *intime.*[1] The young lady, however, is also very intimate with some third-rate Italians, with whom she rackets about in a way that makes much talk. Bring me that pretty novel of Cherbuliez's—'Paule Méré'[2]—and don't come later than the 23rd."

In the natural course of events, Winterbourne, on arriving in Rome, would presently have ascertained Mrs. Miller's address at the American banker's, and have gone to pay his compliments to Miss Daisy. "After what happened at Vevey I think I may certainly call upon them," he said to Mrs. Costello.

"If, after what happens—at Vevey and everywhere—you desire to keep up the acquaintance, you are very welcome. Of course a man may know every one. Men are welcome to the privilege!"

"Pray what is it that happens—here, for instance?" Winterbourne demanded.

"The girl goes about alone with her foreigners. As to what happens further, you must apply elsewhere for information. She has picked up half-a-dozen of the regular Roman fortune-hunters, and she takes them about to people's houses. When she comes to a party she brings with her a gentleman with a good deal of manner and a wonderful moustache."

[31]A small bottle of aromatic compounds, sniffed by genteel nineteenth-century ladies as a restorative, to relieve faintness and to express disdain.

[1]French: "intimate."

[2]Charles Victor Cherbuliez (1829–1899). French novelist, author of *Paule Méré* (1868).

"And where is the mother?"

"I haven't the least idea. They are very dreadful people."

Winterbourne meditated a moment. "They are very ignorant—very innocent only. Depend upon it they are not bad."

"They are hopelessly vulgar," said Mrs. Costello. "Whether or no being hopelessly vulgar is being 'bad' is a question for the metaphysicians. They are bad enough to dislike, at any rate; and for this short life that is quite enough."

The news that Daisy Miller was surrounded by half-a-dozen wonderful moustaches checked Winterbourne's impulse to go straightway to see her. He had perhaps not definitely flattered himself that he had made an ineffaceable impression upon her heart, but he was annoyed at hearing of a state of affairs so little in harmony with an image that had lately flitted in and out of his own meditations; the image of a very pretty girl looking out of an old Roman window and asking herself urgently when Mr. Winterbourne would arrive. If, however, he determined to wait a little before reminding Miss Miller of his claims to her considerations, he went very soon to call upon two or three other friends. One of these friends was an American lady who had spent several winters at Geneva, where she had placed her children at school. She was a very accomplished woman, and she lived in the Via Gregoriana.[3] Winterbourne found her in a little crimson drawing-room, on a third floor; the room was filled with southern sunshine. He had not been there ten minutes when the servant came in, announcing "Madame Mila!" This announcement was presently followed by the entrance of little Randolph Miller, who stopped in the middle of the room and stood staring at Winterbourne. An instant later his pretty sister crossed the threshold; and then, after a considerable interval, Mrs. Miller slowly advanced.

"I know you!" said Randolph.

"I'm sure you know a great many things," exclaimed Winterbourne, taking him by the hand. "How is your education coming on?"

Daisy was exchanging greetings very prettily with her hostess; but when she heard Winterbourne's voice she quickly turned her head. "Well, I declare!" she said.

"I told you I should come, you know," Winterbourne rejoined, smiling.

"Well—I didn't believe it," said Miss Daisy.

"I am much obliged to you," laughed the young man.

"You might have come to see me!" said Daisy.

"I arrived only yesterday."

"I don't believe that!" the young girl declared.

Winterbourne turned with a protesting smile to her mother; but this lady evaded his glance, and, seating herself, fixed her eyes upon her son. "We've got a bigger place than this," said Randolph. "It's all gold on the walls."

Mrs. Miller turned uneasily in her chair. "I told you if I were to bring you, you would say something!" she murmured.

"I told *you!*" Randolph exclaimed. "I tell *you,* sir!" he added jocosely, giving Winterbourne a thump on the knee. "It *is* bigger, too!"

Daisy had entered upon a lively conversation with her hostess; Winterbourne judged it becoming to address a few words to her mother. "I hope you have been well since we parted at Vevey," he said.

[3]Fashionable street in Rome.

Mrs. Miller now certainly looked at him—at his chin. "Not very well, sir," she answered.

"She's got the dyspepsia," said Randolph. "I've got it too. Father's got it. I've got it most!"

This announcement, instead of embarrassing Mrs. Miller, seemed to relieve her. "I suffer from the liver," she said. "I think it's this climate; it's less bracing than Schenectady, especially in the winter season. I don't know whether you know we reside at Schenectady. I was saying to Daisy that I certainly hadn't found anyone like Dr. Davis, and I didn't believe I should. Oh, at Schenectady, he stands first; they think everything of him. He has so much to do, and yet there was nothing he wouldn't do for me. He said he never saw anything like my dyspepsia, but he was bound to cure it. I'm sure there was nothing he wouldn't try. He was just going to try something new when we came off. Mr. Miller wanted Daisy to see Europe for herself. But I wrote to Mr. Miller that it seems as if I couldn't get on without Dr. Davis. At Schenectady he stands at the very top; and there's a great deal of sickness there, too. It affects my sleep."

Winterbourne had a good deal of pathological gossip with Dr. Davis's patient, during which Daisy chattered unremittingly to her own companion. The young man asked Mrs. Miller how she was pleased with Rome. "Well, I must say I am disappointed," she answered. "We had heard so much about it; I suppose we had heard too much. But we couldn't help that. We had been led to expect something different."

"Ah, wait a little, and you will become very fond of it," said Winterbourne.

"I hate it worse and worse every day!" cried Randolph.

"You are like the infant Hannibal,"[4] said Winterbourne.

"No, I ain't!" Randolph declared, at a venture.

"You are not much like an infant," said his mother. "But we have seen places," she resumed, "that I should put a long way before Rome." And in reply to Winterbourne's interrogation, "There's Zurich," she concluded; "I think Zurich is lovely; and we hadn't heard half so much about it."

"The best place we've seen is the City of Richmond!" said Randolph.

"He means the ship," his mother explained. "We crossed in that ship. Randolph had a good time on the City of Richmond."

"It's the best place I've seen," the child repeated. "Only it was turned the wrong way."

"Well, we've got to turn the right way some time," said Mrs. Miller, with a little laugh. Winterbourne expressed the hope that her daughter at least found some gratification in Rome, and she declared that Daisy was quite carried away. "It's on account of the society—the society's splendid. She goes round everywhere; she has made a great number of acquaintances. Of course she goes round more than I do. I must say they have been very sociable; they have taken her right in. And then she knows a great many gentlemen. Oh, she thinks there's nothing like Rome. Of course, it's a great deal pleasanter for a young lady if she knows plenty of gentlemen."

By this time Daisy had turned her attention again to Winterbourne. "I've been telling Mrs. Walker how mean you were!" the young girl announced.

[4]Carthaginian general (247–183? B.C.) who as a youth swore eternal hatred of Rome.

"And what is the evidence you have offered?" asked Winterbourne, rather annoyed at Miss Miller's want of appreciation of the zeal of an admirer who on his way down to Rome had stopped neither at Bologna nor at Florence, simply because of a certain sentimental impatience. He remembered that a cynical compatriot had once told him that American women—the pretty ones, and this gave a largeness to the axiom—were at once the most exacting in the world and the least endowed with a sense of indebtedness.

"Why, you were awfully mean at Vevey," said Daisy. "You wouldn't do anything. You wouldn't stay there when I asked you."

"My dearest young lady," cried Winterbourne, with eloquence, "have I come all the way to Rome to encounter your reproaches?"

"Just hear him say that!" said Daisy to her hostess, giving a twist to a bow on this lady's dress. "Did you ever hear anything so quaint?"

"So quaint, my dear?" murmured Mrs. Walker, in the tone of a partisan of Winterbourne.

"Well, I don't know," said Daisy, fingering Mrs. Walker's ribbons. "Mrs. Walker, I want to tell you something."

"Motherr," interposed Randolph, with his rough ends to his words, "I tell you you've got to go. Eugenio 'll raise something!"

"I'm not afraid of Eugenio," said Daisy, with a toss of her head. "Look here, Mrs. Walker," she went on, "you know I'm coming to your party."

"I am delighted to hear it."

"I've got a lovely dress."

"I am very sure of that."

"But I want to ask a favour—permission to bring a friend."

"I shall be happy to see any of your friends," said Mrs. Walker, turning with a smile to Mrs. Miller.

"Oh, they are not my friends," answered Daisy's mamma, smiling shyly, in her own fashion. "I never spoke to them!"

"It's an intimate friend of mine—Mr. Giovanelli," said Daisy, without a tremor in her clear little voice or a shadow on her brilliant little face.

Mrs. Walker was silent a moment, she gave a rapid glance at Winterbourne. "I shall be glad to see Mr. Giovanelli," she then said.

"He's an Italian," Daisy pursued, with the prettiest serenity. "He's a great friend of mine—he's the handsomest man in the world—except Mr. Winterbourne! He knows plenty of Italians, but he wants to know some Americans. He thinks ever so much of Americans. He's tremendously clever. He's perfectly lovely!"

It was settled that this brilliant personage should be brought to Mrs. Walker's party, and then Mrs. Miller prepared to take her leave. "I guess we'll go back to the hotel," she said.

"You may go back to the hotel, mother, but I'm going to take a walk," said Daisy.

"She's going to walk with Mr. Giovanelli," Randolph proclaimed.

"I am going to the Pincio,"[5] said Daisy, smiling.

"Alone, my dear—at this hour?" Mrs. Walker asked. The afternoon was drawing to a close—it was the hour for the throng of carriages and contemplative pedestrians. "I don't think it's safe, my dear," said Mrs. Walker.

[5]One of the hills of Rome, with a panoramic view of the city.

"Neither do I," subjoined Mrs. Miller. "You'll get the fever as sure as you live. Remember what Dr. Davis told you!"

"Give her some medicine before she goes," said Randolph.

The company had risen to its feet; Daisy, still showing her pretty teeth, bent over and kissed her hostess. "Mrs. Walker, you are too perfect," she said. "I'm not going alone; I am going to meet a friend."

"Your friend won't keep you from getting the fever," Mrs. Miller observed.

"Is it Mr. Giovanelli?" asked the hostess.

Winterbourne was watching the young girl; at this question his attention quickened. She stood there smiling and smoothing her bonnet ribbons; she glanced at Winterbourne. Then, while she glanced and smiled, she answered without a shade of hesitation, "Mr. Giovanelli—the beautiful Giovanelli."

"My dear young friend," said Mrs. Walker, taking her hand, pleadingly, "don't walk off to the Pincio at this hour to meet a beautiful Italian."

"Well, he speaks English," said Mrs. Miller.

"Gracious me!" Daisy exclaimed, "I don't want to do anything improper. There's an easy way to settle it." She continued to glance at Winterbourne. "The Pincio is only a hundred yards distant, and if Mr. Winterbourne were as polite as he pretends he would offer to walk with me!"

Winterbourne's politeness hastened to affirm itself, and the young girl gave him gracious leave to accompany her. They passed downstairs before her mother, and at the door Winterbourne perceived Mrs. Miller's carriage drawn up, with the ornamental courier whose acquaintance he had made at Vevey seated within. "Good-by, Eugenio!" cried Daisy, "I'm going to take a walk." The distance from the Via Gregoriana to the beautiful garden at the other end of the Pincian Hill is, in fact, rapidly traversed. As the day was splendid, however, and the concourse of vehicles, walkers, and loungers numerous, the young Americans found this progress much delayed. This fact was highly agreeable to Winterbourne, in spite of his consciousness of his singular situation. The slow-moving, idly-gazing Roman crowd bestowed much attention upon the extremely pretty young foreign lady who was passing through it upon his arm; and he wondered what on earth had been in Daisy's mind when she proposed to expose herself, unattended, to its appreciation. His own mission, to her sense, apparently, was to consign her to the hands of Mr. Giovanelli; but Winterbourne, at once annoyed and gratified, resolved that he would do no such thing.

"Why haven't you been to see me?" asked Daisy. "You can't get out of that."

"I have had the honour of telling you that I have only just stepped out of the train."

"You must have stayed in the train a good while after it stopped!" cried the young girl, with her little laugh. "I suppose you were asleep. You have had time to go to see Mrs. Walker."

"I knew Mrs. Walker—" Winterbourne began to explain.

"I knew where you knew her. You knew her at Geneva. She told me so. Well, you knew me at Vevey. That's just as good. So you ought to have come." She asked him no other question than this; she began to prattle about her own affairs. "We've got splendid rooms at the hotel; Eugenio says they're the best rooms in Rome. We are going to stay all winter—if we don't die of the fever; and I guess we'll stay then. It's a great deal nicer than I thought; I thought it would be fearfully quiet; I was sure it would be awfully poky. I was sure we should be going round all the time with one of those dreadful old men that explain about the pictures and things. But we only had about a week of that, and now I'm enjoying myself. I know ever so many people, and they are all so charming. The society's extremely select. There are all kinds—English, and Germans, and Italians. I think I like the English best. I like their style of conversation. But there are some lovely Americans. I never saw anything so hospitable. There's something or other every day. There's not much dancing; but I must say I never thought dancing was everything. I was always fond of conversation. I guess I shall have plenty at Mrs. Walker's—her rooms are so small." When they had passed the gate of the Pincian Gardens, Miss Miller began to wonder where Mr. Giovanelli might be. "We had better go straight to that place in front," she said, "where you look at the view."

"I certainly shall not help you to find him," Winterbourne declared.

"Then I shall find him without you," said Miss Daisy.

"You certainly won't leave me!" cried Winterbourne.

She burst into her little laugh. "Are you afraid you'll get lost—or run over? But there's Giovanelli, leaning against that tree. He's staring at the woman in the carriages: did you ever see anything so cool?"

Winterbourne perceived at some distance a little man standing with folded arms, nursing his cane. He had a handsome face, an artfully poised hat, a glass in one eye and a nosegay in his buttonhole. Winterbourne looked at him a moment and then said, "Do you mean to speak to that man?"

"Do I mean to speak to him? Why, you don't suppose I mean to communicate by signs?"

"Pray understand, then," said Winterbourne, "that I intend to remain with you."

Daisy stopped and looked at him, without a sign of troubled consciousness in her face; with nothing but the presence of her charming eyes and her happy dimples. "Well, she's a cool one!" thought the young man.

"I don't like the way you say that," said Daisy. "It's too imperious."

"I beg your pardon if I say it wrong. The main point is to give you an idea of my meaning."

The young girl looked at him more gravely, but with eyes that were prettier than ever. "I have never allowed a gentleman to dictate to me, or to interfere with anything I do."

"I think you have made a mistake," said Winterbourne. "You should sometimes listen to a gentleman—the right one."

Daisy began to laugh again. "I do nothing but listen to gentlemen!" she exclaimed. "Tell me if Mr. Giovanelli is the right one?"

The gentleman with the nosegay in his bosom had now perceived our two friends, and was approaching the young girl with obsequious rapidity. He bowed to Winterbourne as well as to the latter's companion; he had a brilliant smile, an intelligent eye; Winterbourne thought him not a bad-looking fellow. But he nevertheless said to Daisy—"No, he's not the right one."

Daisy evidently had a natural talent for performing introductions; she mentioned the name of each of her companions to the other. She strolled along with one of them on each side of her; Mr. Giovanelli, who spoke English very cleverly—Winterbourne afterwards learned that he had practised the idiom upon a great many American heiresses—addressed her a great deal of very polite nonsense; he was extremely urbane, and the young

American, who said nothing, reflected upon that profundity of Italian cleverness which enables people to appear more gracious in proportion as they are more acutely disappointed. Giovanelli, of course, had counted upon something more intimate; he had not bargained for a party of three. But he kept his temper in a manner which suggested far-stretching intentions. Winterbourne flattered himself that he had taken his measure. "He is not a gentleman," said the young American; "He is only a clever imitation of one. He is a music-master, or a penny-a-liner,[6] or a third-rate artist. Damm his good looks!" Mr. Giovanelli had certainly a very pretty face; but Winterbourne felt a superior indignation at his own lovely fellow-countrywoman's not knowing the difference between a spurious gentleman and a real one. Giovanelli chattered and jested and made himself wonderfully agreeable. It was true that if he was an imitation the imitation was brilliant. "Nevertheless," Winterbourne said to himself, "a nice girl ought to know!" And then he came back to the question whether this was in fact a nice girl. Would a nice girl—even allowing for her being a little American flirt—make a rendezvous with a presumably low-lived foreigner? The rendezvous in this case, indeed, had been in broad daylight, and in the most crowded corner of Rome; but was it not impossible to regard the choice of these circumstances as a proof of extreme cynicism? Singular though it may seem, Winterbourne was vexed that the young girl, in joining her *amoroso,*[7] should not appear more impatient of his own company, and he was vexed because of his inclination. It was impossible to regard her as a perfectly well-conducted young lady; she was wanting in a certain indispensable delicacy. It would therefore simplify matters greatly to be able to treat her as the object of one of those sentiments which are called by romancers "lawless passions." That she should seem to wish to get rid of him would help him to think more lightly of her, and to be able to think more lightly of her would make her much less perplexing. But Daisy, on this occasion, continued to present herself as an inscrutable combination of audacity and innocence.

She had been walking some quarter of an hour, attended by her two cavaliers, and responding in a tone of very childish gaiety, as it seemed to Winterbourne, to the pretty speeches of Mr. Giovanelli, when a carriage that had detached itself from the revolving train drew up beside the path. At the same moment Winterbourne perceived that his friend Mrs. Walker—the lady whose house he had lately left—was seated in the vehicle and was beckoning to him. Leaving Miss Miller's side, he hastened to obey her summons. Mrs. Walker was flushed; she wore an excited air. "It is really too dreadful," she said. "That girl must not do this sort of thing. She must not walk here with you two men. Fifty people have noticed her."

Winterbourne raised his eyebrows. "I think it's a pity to make too much fuss about it."

"It's a pity to let the girl ruin herself!"

"She is very innocent," said Winterbourne.

"She's very crazy!" cried Mrs. Walker. "Did you ever see anything so imbecile as her mother? After you had all left me, just now, I could not sit still for thinking of it. It seemed too pitiful, not even to attempt to save her. I

[6]A hack writer who works for a penny a line. [7]Italian: suitor.

ordered the carriage and put on my bonnet, and came here as quickly as possible. Thank heaven, I have found you!"

"What do you propose to do with us?" asked Winterbourne, smiling.

"To ask her to get in, to drive her about here for half-an-hour, so that the world may see she is not running absolutely wild, and then to take her safely home."

"I don't think it's a very happy thought," said Winterbourne; "but you can try."

Mrs. Walker tried. The young man went in pursuit of Miss Miller, who had simply nodded and smiled at his interlocutor[8] in the carriage, and had gone her way with her companion. Daisy, on learning that Mrs. Walker wished to speak to her, retraced her steps with a perfect good grace and with Mr. Giovanelli at her side. She declared that she was delighted to have a chance to present this gentleman to Mrs. Walker. She immediately achieved the introduction, and declared that she had never in her life seen anything so lovely as Mrs. Walker's carriage-rug.

"I am glad you admire it," said this lady, smiling sweetly. "Will you get in and let me put it over you?"

"Oh, no, thank you," said Daisy. "I shall admire it much more as I see you driving round with it."

"Do get in and drive with me," said Mrs. Walker.

"That would be charming, but it's so enchanting just as I am!" and Daisy gave a brilliant glance at the gentlemen on either side of her.

"It may be enchanting, dear child, but it is not the custom here," urged Mrs. Walker, leaning forward in her victoria[9] with her hands devoutly clasped.

"Well, it ought to be, then!" said Daisy. "If I didn't walk I should expire."

"You should walk with your mother, dear," cried the lady from Geneva, losing patience.

"With my mother, dear!" exclaimed the young girl. Winterbourne saw that she scented interference. "My mother never walked ten steps in her life. And then, you know," she added with a laugh, "I am more than five years old."

"You are old enough to be more reasonable. You are old enough, dear Miss Miller, to be talked about."

Daisy looked at Mrs. Walker, smiling intensely. "Talked about? What do you mean?"

"Come into my carriage and I will tell you."

Daisy turned her quickened glance again from one of the gentlemen beside her to the other. Mr. Giovanelli was bowing to and fro, rubbing down his gloves and laughing very agreeably; Winterbourne thought it a most unpleasant scene. "I don't think I want to know what you mean," said Daisy presently. "I don't think I should like it."

Winterbourne wished that Mrs. Walker would tuck in her carriage-rug and drive away; but this lady did not enjoy being defied, as she afterwards told him. "Should you prefer being thought a very reckless girl?" she demanded.

[8]In later editions James substituted "interlocutrix," a female questioner.
[9]Horse-drawn carriage.

"Gracious!" exclaimed Daisy. She looked again at Mr. Giovanelli, then she turned to Winterbourne. There was a little pink flush in her cheek; she was tremendously pretty. "Does Mr. Winterbourne think," she asked slowly, smiling, throwing back her head and glancing at him from head to foot, "that—to save my reputation—I ought to get into the carriage?"

Winterbourne coloured; for an instant he hesitated greatly. It seemed so strange to hear her speak that way of her "reputation." But he himself, in fact, must speak in accordance with gallantry. The finest gallantry, here, was simply to tell her the truth; and the truth, for Winterbourne, as the few indications I have been able to give have made him known to the reader, was that Daisy Miller should take Mrs. Walker's advice. He looked at her exquisite prettiness; and then he said very gently, "I think you should get into the carriage."

Daisy gave a violent laugh. "I never heard anything so stiff! If this is improper, Mrs. Walker," she pursued, "then I am all improper, and you must give me up. Good-by; I hope you'll have a lovely ride!" and, with Mr. Giovanelli, who made a triumphantly obsequious salute, she turned away.

Mrs. Walker sat looking after her, and there were tears in Mrs. Walker's eyes. "Get in here, sir," she said to Winterbourne, indicating the place beside her. The young man answered that he felt bound to accompany Miss Miller; whereupon Mrs. Walker declared that if he refused her this favour she would never speak to him again. She was evidently in earnest. Winterbourne overtook Daisy and her companion and, offering the young girl his hand, told her that Mrs. Walker had made an imperious claim upon his society. He expected that in answer she would say something rather free, something to commit herself still further to that "recklessness" from which Mrs. Walker had so charitably endeavoured to dissuade her. But she only shook his hand, hardly looking at him; while Mr. Giovanelli bade him farewell with a too-emphatic flourish of the hat.

Winterbourne was not in the best possible humour as he took his seat in Mrs. Walker's victoria. "That was not clever of you," he said candidly, while the vehicle mingled again with the throng of carriages.

"In such a case," his companion answered, "I don't wish to be clever, I wish to be *earnest!*"

"Well, your earnestness has only offended her and put her off."

"It has happened very well," said Mrs. Walker. "If she is so perfectly determined to compromise herself, the sooner one knows it the better; one can act accordingly."

"I suspect she meant no harm," Winterbourne rejoined.

"So I thought a month ago. But she had been going too far."

"What has she been doing?"

"Everything that is not done here. Flirting with any man she could pick up; sitting in corners with mysterious Italians; dancing all the evening with the same partners; receiving visits at eleven o'clock at night. Her mother goes away when visitors come."

"But her brother," said Winterbourne, laughing, "sits up till midnight."

"He must be edified by what he sees. I'm told that at their hotel every one is talking about her, and that a smile goes round among all the servants when a gentleman comes and asks for Miss Miller."

"The servants be hanged!" said Winterbourne angrily. "The poor girl's fault," he presently added, "is that she is very uncultivated."

"She is naturally indelicate," Mrs. Walker declared. "Take that example this morning. How long had you known her at Vevey?"

"A couple of days."

"Fancy, then, her making it a personal matter that you should have left the place!"

Winterbourne was silent for some moments, then he said, "I suspect, Mrs. Walker, that you and I have lived too long at Geneva!" And he added a request that she should inform him with what particular design she had made him enter her carriage.

"I wished to beg you to cease your relations with Miss Miller—not to flirt with her—to give her no further opportunity to expose herself—to let her alone, in short."

"I'm afraid I can't do that," said Winterbourne. "I like her extremely."

"All the more reason that you shouldn't help her to make a scandal."

"There shall be nothing scandalous in my attentions to her."

"There certainly will be in the way she takes them. But I have said what I had on my conscience," Mrs. Walker pursued. "If you wish to rejoin the young lady I will put you down. Here, by-the-way, you have a chance."

The carriage was traversing that part of the Pincian Garden that overhangs the wall of Rome and overlooks the beautiful Villa Borghese.[10] It is bordered by a large parapet, near which there are several seats. One of the seats, at a distance, was occupied by a gentleman and a lady, towards whom Mrs. Walker gave a toss of her head. At the same moment these persons rose and walked towards the parapet. Winterbourne had asked the coachman to stop; he now descended from the carriage. His companion looked at him a moment in silence; then, while he raised his hat, she drove majestically away. Winterbourne stood there; he had turned his eyes towards Daisy and her cavalier. They evidently saw no one; they were too deeply occupied with each other. When they reached the low gardenwall they stood a moment looking off at the great flat-topped pine-clusters of the Villa Borghese; then Giovanelli seated himself, familiarly, upon the broad ledge of the wall. The western sun in the opposite sky sent out a brilliant shaft through a couple of cloud-bars, whereupon Daisy's companion took her parasol out of her hands and opened it. She came a little nearer and he held the parasol over her; then, still holding it, he let it rest upon her shoulder, so that both of their heads were hidden from Winterbourne. This young man lingered a moment, then he began to walk. But he walked—not towards the couple with the parasol; towards the residence of his aunt, Mrs. Costello.

He flattered himself on the following day that there was no smiling among the servants when he, at least, asked for Mrs. Miller at her hotel. This lady and her daughter, however, were not at home; and on the next day after, repeating his visit, Winterbourne again had the misfortune not to find them. Mrs. Walker's party took place on the evening of the third day, and in spite of the frigidity of his last interview with the hostess Winterbourne was among the guests. Mrs. Walker was one of those American ladies who, while residing abroad, make a point, in their own phrase, of studying European society; and she had on this occasion collected several specimens of her diversely-born

[10]Originally the summer palace of the Borghese family, now an art museum and its grounds a public park.

fellow-mortals to serve, as it were, as text-books. When Winterbourne arrived Daisy Miller was not there, but in a few moments he saw her mother come in alone, very shyly and ruefully. Mrs. Miller's hair above her exposed-looking temples was more frizzled than ever. As she approached Mrs. Walker, Winterbourne also drew near.

"You see I've come all alone," said poor Mrs. Miller. "I'm so frightened; I don't know what to do; it's the first time I've ever been to a party alone—especially in this country. I wanted to bring Randolph or Eugenio, or someone, but Daisy just pushed me off by myself. I ain't used to going round alone."

"And does not your daughter intend to favour us with her society?" demanded Mrs. Walker, impressively.

"Well, Daisy's all dressed," said Mrs. Miller, with that accent of the dispassionate, if not of the philosophic, historian with which she always recorded the current incidents of her daughter's career. "She got dressed on purpose before dinner. But she's got a friend of hers there; that gentleman—the Italian—that she wanted to bring. They've got going at the piano; it seems as if they couldn't leave off. Mr. Giovanelli sings splendidly. But I guess they'll come before very long," concluded Mrs. Miller hopefully.

"I'm sorry she should come—in that way," said Mrs. Walker.

"Well, I told her that there was no use in getting dressed before dinner if she was going to wait three hours," responded Daisy's mamma. "I didn't see the use of her putting on such a dress as that to sit round with Mr. Giovanelli."

"This is most horrible!" said Mrs. Walker, turning away and addressing herself to Winterbourne. *"Elle s'affiche.*[11] It's her revenge for my having ventured to remonstrate with her. When she comes I shall not speak to her."

Daisy came after eleven o'clock, but she was not, on such an occasion, a young lady to wait to be spoken to. She rustled forward in radiant loveliness, smiling and chattering, carrying a large bouquet and attended by Mr. Giovanelli. Everyone stopped talking, and turned and looked at her. She came straight to Mrs. Walker. "I'm afraid you thought I never was coming, so I sent mother off to tell you. I wanted to make Mr. Giovanelli practise some things before he came; you know he sings beautifully, and I want you to ask him to sing. This is Mr. Giovanelli; you know I introduced him to you; he's got the most lovely voice and he knows the most charming set of songs. I made him go over them this evening, on purpose; we had the greatest time at the hotel." Of all this Daisy delivered herself with the sweetest, brightest audibleness, looking now at her hostess and now round the room, while she gave a series of little pats, round her shoulders, to the edges of her dress. "Is there anyone I know?" she asked.

"I think everyone knows you!" said Mrs. Walker pregnantly, and she gave a very cursory greeting to Mr. Giovanelli. This gentleman bore himself gallantly. He smiled and bowed and showed his white teeth, he curled his moustaches and rolled his eyes, and performed all the proper functions of a handsome Italian at an evening party. He sang, very prettily, half-a-dozen songs, though Mrs. Walker afterwards declared that she had been quite unable to find out who asked him. It was apparently not Daisy who had given him his orders. Daisy sat at a distance from the piano, and though she had publicly,

[11]French: "She's making a spectacle of herself."

as it were, professed a high admiration for his singing, talked, not inaudibly, while it was going on.

"It's a pity these rooms are so small; we can't dance," she said to Winterbourne as if she had seen him five minutes before.

"I am not sorry we can't dance," Winterbourne answered; "I don't dance."

"Of course you don't dance; you're too stiff," said Miss Daisy. "I hope you enjoyed your drive with Mrs. Walker."

"No, I didn't enjoy it; I preferred walking with you."

"We paired off, that was much better," said Daisy. "But did you ever hear anything so cool as Mrs. Walker's wanting me to get into her carriage and drop poor Mr. Giovanelli, and under the pretext that it was proper? People have different ideas! It would have been most unkind; he had been talking about that walk for ten days."

"He should not have talked about it at all," said Winterbourne; "he would never have proposed to a young lady of this country to walk about the streets with him."

"About the streets?" cried Daisy, with her pretty stare. "Where then would he have proposed to her to walk? The Pincio is not the streets, either; and I, thank goodness, am not a young lady of this country. The young ladies of this country have a dreadfully poky time of it, so far as I can learn; I don't see why I should change my habits for *them*."

"I am afraid your habits are those of a flirt," said Winterbourne gravely.

"Of course they are," she cried, giving him her little smiling stare again. "I'm a fearful, frightful flirt! Did you ever hear of a nice girl that was not? But I suppose you will tell me now that I am not a nice girl."

"You're a very nice girl, but I wish you would flirt with me and me only," said Winterbourne.

"Ah! thank you, thank you very much; you are the last man I should think of flirting with. As I have had the pleasure of informing you, you are too stiff."

"You say that too often," said Winterbourne.

Daisy gave a delighted laugh. "If I could have the sweet hope of making you angry, I should say it again."

"Don't do that; when I am angry I'm stiffer than ever. But if you won't flirt with me, do cease at least to flirt with your friend at the piano; they don't understand that sort of thing here."

"I thought they understood nothing else!" exclaimed Daisy.

"Not in young unmarried women."

"It seems to me much more proper in young unmarried women than in old married ones," Daisy declared.

"Well," said Winterbourne, "when you deal with natives you must go by the custom of the place. Flirting is a purely American custom; it doesn't exist here. So when you show yourself in public with Mr. Giovanelli and without your mother——"

"Gracious! poor mother!" interposed Daisy.

"Though you may be flirting, Mr. Giovanelli is not; he means something else."

"He isn't preaching, at any rate," said Daisy with vivacity. "And if you want very much to know, we are neither of us flirting, we are too good friends for that; we are very intimate friends."

"Ah!" rejoined Winterbourne, "if you are in love with each other it is another affair."

She had allowed him up to this point to talk so frankly that he had no expectation of shocking her by this ejaculation; but she immediately got up, blushing visibly, and leaving him to exclaim mentally that little American flirts were the queerest creatures in the world. "Mr. Giovanelli, at least," she said, giving her interlocutor a single glance, "never says such very disagreeable things to me."

Winterbourne was bewildered; he stood staring. Mr. Giovanelli had finished singing; he left the piano and came over to Daisy. "Won't you come into the other room and have some tea?" he asked, bending before her with his ornamental smile.

Daisy turned to Winterbourne, beginning to smile again. He was still more perplexed, for this inconsequent smile made nothing clear, though it seemed to prove, indeed, that she had a sweetness and softness that reverted instinctively to the pardon of offences. "It has never occurred to Mr. Winterbourne to offer me any tea," she said, with her little tormenting manner.

"I have offered advice," Winterbourne rejoined.

"I prefer weak tea!" cried Daisy, and she went off with the brilliant Giovanelli. She sat with him in the adjoining room, in the embrasure of the window, for the rest of the evening. There was an interesting performance at the piano, but neither of these young people gave heed to it. When Daisy came to take leave of Mrs. Walker, this lady conscientiously repaired the weakness of which she had been guilty at the moment of the young girl's arrival. She turned her back straight upon Miss Miller and left her to depart with what grace she might. Winterbourne was standing near the door; he saw it all. Daisy turned very pale and looked at her mother, but Mrs. Miller was humbly unconscious of any violation of the usual social forms. She appeared, indeed, to have felt an incongruous impulse to draw attention to her own striking observance of them. "Good-night, Mrs. Walker," she said; "we've had a beautiful evening. You see if I let Daisy come to parties without me, I don't want her to go away without me." Daisy turned away, looking with a pale, grave face at the circle near the door; Winterbourne saw that, for the first moment, she was too much shocked and puzzled even for indignation. He on his side was greatly touched.

"That was very cruel," he said to Mrs. Walker.

"She never enters my drawing-room again," replied his hostess.

Since Winterbourne was not to meet her in Mrs. Walker's drawing-room, he went as often as possible to Mrs. Miller's hotel. The ladies were rarely at home, but when he found them the devoted Giovanelli was always present. Very often the brilliant little Roman was in the drawing-room with Daisy alone. Mrs. Miller being apparently constantly of the opinion that discretion is the better part of surveillance. Winterbourne noted, at first with surprise, that Daisy on these occasions was never embarrassed or annoyed by his own entrance; but he very presently began to feel that she had no more surprises for him; the unexpected in her behavior was the only thing to expect. She showed no displeasure at her *tête-à-tête* with Giovanelli being interrupted; she could chatter as freshly and freely with two gentlemen as with one; there was always, in her conversation, the same odd mixture of audacity and puerility. Winterbourne remarked to himself that if she was seriously interested in

Giovanelli it was very singular that she should not take more trouble to preserve the sanctity of their interviews, and he liked her the more for her innocent looking indifference and her apparently inexhaustible good humour. He could hardly have said why, but she seemed to him a girl who would never be jealous. At the risk of exciting a somewhat derisive smile on the reader's part, I may affirm that with regard to the women who had hitherto interested him, it very often seemed to Winterbourne among the possibilities that, given certain contingencies, he should be afraid—literally afraid—of these ladies; he had a pleasant sense that he should never be afraid of Daisy Miller. It must be added that this sentiment was not altogether flattering to Daisy; it was part of his conviction, or rather of his apprehension, that she would prove a very light young person.

But she was evidently very much interested in Giovanelli. She looked at him whenever he spoke; she was perpetually telling him to do this and to do that; she was constantly "chaffing" and abusing him. She appeared completely to have forgotten that Winterbourne had said anything to displease her at Mrs. Walker's little party. One Sunday afternoon, having gone to St. Peter's with his aunt, Winterbourne perceived Daisy strolling about the great church in company with the inevitable Giovanelli. Presently he pointed out the young girl and her cavalier to Mrs. Costello. This lady looked at them a moment through her eyeglass, and then she said:

"That's what makes you so pensive in these days, eh?"

"I had not the least idea I was pensive," said the young man.

"You are very much pre-occupied, you are thinking of something."

"And what is it," he asked, "that you accuse me of thinking of?"

"Of that young lady's—Miss Baker's, Miss Chandler's—what's her name? Miss Miller's intrigue with that little barber's block."[12]

"Do you call it an intrigue," Winterbourne asked—"an affair that goes on with such peculiar publicity?"

"That's their folly," said Mrs. Costello, "it's not their merit."

"No," rejoined Winterbourne, with something of that pensiveness to which his aunt had alluded. "I don't believe that there is anything to be called an intrigue."

"I have heard a dozen people speak of it; they say she is quite carried away by him."

"They are certainly very intimate," said Winterbourne.

Mrs. Costello inspected the young couple again with her optical instrument. "He is very handsome. One easily sees how it is. She thinks him the most elegant man in the world, the finest gentleman. She has never seen anything like him; he is better even than the courier. It was the courier probably who introduced him, and if he succeeds in marrying the young lady, the courier will come in for a magnificent commission."

"I don't believe she thinks of marrying him," said Winterbourne, "and I don't believe he hopes to marry her."

"You may be very sure she thinks of nothing. She goes on from day to day, from hour to hour, as they did in the Golden Age. I can imagine nothing more vulgar. And at the same time," added Mrs. Costello, "depend upon it that she may tell you any moment that she is 'engaged.'"

[12]Dandy.

"I think that is more than Giovanelli expects," said Winterbourne.

"Who is Giovanelli?"

"The little Italian. I have asked questions about him and learned something. He is apparently a perfectly respectable little man. I believe he is in a small way a *cavaliere avvocato.*[13] But he doesn't move in what are called the first circles. I think it is really not absolutely impossible that the courier introduced him. He is evidently immensely charmed with Miss Miller. If she thinks him the finest gentleman in the world, he, on his side, has never found himself in personal contact with such splendor, such opulence, such expensiveness, as this young lady's. And then she must seem to him wonderfully pretty and interesting. I rather doubt that he dreams of marrying her. That must appear to him too impossible a piece of luck. He has nothing but his handsome face to offer, and there is a substantial Mr. Miller in that mysterious land of dollars. Giovanelli knows that he hasn't a title to offer. If he were only a count or a *marchese!*[14] He must wonder at his luck at the way they have taken him up."

"He accounts for it by his handsome face, and thinks Miss Miller a young lady *qui se passe ses fantaisies!*"[15] said Mrs. Costello.

"It is very true," Winterbourne pursued, "that Daisy and her mamma have not yet risen to that stage of—what shall I call it?—of culture, at which the idea of catching a count or a *marchese* begins. I believe that they are intellectually incapable of that conception."

"Ah! but the *avvocato* can't believe it," said Mrs. Costello.

Of the observation excited by Daisy's "intrigue," Winterbourne gathered that day at St. Peter's sufficient evidence. A dozen of the American colonists in Rome came to talk with Mrs. Costello, who sat on a little portable stool at the base of one of the great pilasters. The vesper service was going forward in splendid chants and organ-tones in the adjacent choir, and meanwhile, between Mrs. Costello and her friends, there was a great deal said about poor little Miss Miller's going really "too far." Winterbourne was not pleased with what he heard; but when, coming out upon the great steps of the church, he saw Daisy, who had emerged before him, get into an open cab with her accomplice and roll away through the cynical streets of Rome, he could not deny to himself that she was going very far indeed. He felt very sorry for her—not exactly that he believed that she had completely lost her head, but because it was painful to hear so much that was pretty, and undefended, and natural, assigned to a vulgar place among the categories of disorder. He made an attempt after this to give a hint to Mrs. Miller. He met one day in the Corso[16] a friend—a tourist like himself—who had just come out of the Doria Palace,[17] where he had been walking through the beautiful gallery. His friend talked for a moment about the superb portrait of Innocent X, by Velasquez,[18] which hangs in one of the cabinets of the palace, and then said, "And in the same cabinet, by-the-way, I had the pleasure of contemplating a picture of a different kind—that pretty American girl who you pointed out to me last week." In answer to Winterbourne's inquiries, his friend narrated

[13]Italian: gentleman lawyer. [14]An Italian rank of nobility, a marquis.
[15]French: who gives in to her own whims. [16]Roman street. [17]Roman baroque palace.
[18]Diego Rodriguez de Silva y Velásquez (1599–1660), Spanish painter whose portrait of Pope Innocent X (1649) is in the Doria Gallery in Rome.

that the pretty American girl—prettier than ever—was seated with a companion in the secluded nook in which the great papal protrait was enshrined.

"Who was her companion?" asked Winterbourne.

"A little Italian with a bouquet in his button hole. The girl is delightfully pretty, but I thought I understood from you the other day that she was a young lady *du meilleur monde*."[19]

"So she is!" answered Winterbourne; and having assured himself that his informant had seen Daisy and her companion but five minutes before, he jumped into a cab and went to call on Mrs. Miller. She was at home; but she apologised to him for receiving him in Daisy's absence.

"She's gone out somewhere with Mr. Giovanelli," said Mrs. Miller. "She's always going round with Mr. Giovanelli."

"I have noticed that they are very intimate," Winterbourne observed.

"Oh! it seems as if they couldn't live without each other!" said Mrs. Miller. "Well, he's a real gentleman anyhow. I keep telling Daisy she's engaged!"

"And what does Daisy say?"

"Oh, she says she isn't engaged. But she might as well be!" this impartial parent resumed. "She goes on as if she was. But I've made Mr. Giovanelli promise to tell me, if *she* doesn't. I should want to write to Mr. Miller about it—shouldn't you?"

Winterbourne replied that he certainly should; and the state of mind of Daisy's mamma struck him as so unprecedented in the annals of parental vigilance that he gave up as utterly irrelevant the attempt to place her upon her guard.

After this Daisy was never at home, and Winterbourne ceased to meet her at the houses of their common acquaintance because, as he perceived, these shrewd people had quite made up their minds that she was going too far. They ceased to invite her, and they intimated that they desired to express to observant Europeans the great truth that, though Miss Daisy Miller was a young American lady, her behaviour was not representative—was regarded by her compatriots as abnormal. Winterbourne wondered how she felt about all the cold shoulders that were turned towards her, and sometimes it annoyed him to suspect that she did not feel at all. He said to himself that she was too light and childish, too uncultivated and unreasoning, too provincial, to have reflected upon her ostracism or even to have perceived it. Then at other moments he believed that she carried about in her elegant and irresponsible little organism a defiant, passionate, perfectly observant consciousness of the impression she produced. He asked himself whether Daisy's defiance came from the consciousness of innocence or from her being, essentially, a young person of the reckless class. It must be admitted that holding oneself to a belief in Daisy's "innocence" came to seem to Winterbourne more and more a matter of fine-spun gallantry. As I have already had occasion to relate, he was angry at finding himself reduced to chopping logic about this young lady; he was vexed at his want of instinctive certitude as to how far her eccentricities were generic, national, and how far they were personal. From either view of them he had somehow missed her, and now it was too late. She was "carried away" by Mr. Giovanelli.

[19]French: "of the best society."

A few days after his brief interview with her mother, he encountered her in that beautiful abode of flowering desolation known as the Palace of the Caesars.[20] The early Roman spring had filled the air with bloom and perfume, and the rugged surface of the Palatine was muffled with tender verdure. Daisy was strolling along the top of one of those great mounds of ruin that are embanked with mossy marble and paved with monumental inscriptions. It seemed to him that Rome had never been so lovely as just then. He stood looking off at the enchanting harmony of line and colour that remotely encircles the city, inhaling the softly humid odours and feeling the freshness of the year and the antiquity of the place reaffirm themselves in mysterious interfusion. It seemed to him also that Daisy had never looked so pretty; but this had been an observation of his whenever he met her. Giovanelli was at her side, and Giovanelli, too, wore an aspect of even unwonted brilliancy.

"Well," said Daisy, "I should think you would be lonesome!"

"Lonesome?" asked Winterbourne.

"You are always going round by yourself. Can't you get anyone to walk with you?"

"I am not so fortunate," said Winterbourne, "as your companion."

Giovanelli, from the first, had treated Winterbourne with distinguished politeness; he listened with a deferential air to his remarks; he laughed, punctiliously, at his pleasantries; he seemed disposed to testify to his belief that Winterbourne was a superior young man. He carried himself in no degree like a jealous wooer; he had obviously a great deal of tact; he had no objection to your expecting a little humility of him. It even seemed to Winterbourne at times that Giovanelli would find a certain mental relief in being able to have a private understanding with him—to say to him, as an intelligent man, that, bless you, *he* knew how extraordinary was this young lady, and didn't flatter himself with delusive—or at least *too* delusive—hopes of matrimony and dollars. On this occasion he strolled away from his companion to pluck a sprig of almond blossom, which he carefully arranged in his button hole.

"I know why you say that," said Daisy, watching Giovanelli. "Because you think I go round too much with *him!*" And she nodded at her attendant.

"Every one thinks so—if you care to know," said Winterbourne.

"Of course I care to know!" Daisy exclaimed seriously. "But I don't believe it. They are only pretending to be shocked. They don't really care a straw what I do. Besides, I don't go round so much."

"I think you will find they do care. They will show it—disagreeably."

Daisy looked at him a moment. "How—disagreeably?"

"Haven't you noticed anything?" Winterbourne asked.

"I have noticed you. But I noticed you were as stiff as an umbrella the first time I saw you."

"You will find I am not so stiff as several others," said Winterbourne, smiling.

"How shall I find it?"

"By going to see the others."

"What will they do to me?"

"They will give you the cold shoulder. Do you know what that means?"

[20]Ruins of palaces erected by the Caesars on the Palatine Hill, in Rome.

Daisy was looking at him intently; she began to colour. "Do you mean as Mrs. Walker did the other night?"

"Exactly!" said Winterbourne.

She looked away at Giovanelli, who was decorating himself with his almond-blossom. Then looking back at Winterbourne—"I shouldn't think you would let people be so unkind!" she said.

"How can I help it?" he asked.

"I should think you would say something."

"I do say something," and he paused a moment. "I say that your mother tells me she believes you are engaged."

"Well, she does," said Daisy very simply.

Winterbourne began to laugh. "And does Randolph believe it?" he asked.

"I guess Randolph doesn't believe anything," said Daisy. Randolph's scepticism excited Winterbourne to further hilarity, and he observed that Giovanelli was coming back to them. Daisy, observing it too, addressed herself again to her countryman. "Since you have mentioned it," she said, "I *am* engaged." . . . Winterbourne looked at her; he had stopped laughing. "You don't believe it!" she added.

He was silent a moment; and then, "Yes, I believe it!" he said.

"Oh, no, you don't," she answered. "Well, then—I am not!"

The young girl and her cicerone[21] were on their way to the gate of the enclosure, so that Winterbourne, who had but lately entered, presently took leave of them. A week afterwards he went to dine at a beautiful villa on the Caelian Hill,[22] and, on arriving, dismissed his hired vehicle. The evening was charming, and he promised himself the satisfaction of walking home beneath the Arch of Constantine[23] and past the vaguely-lighted monuments of the Forum.[24] There was a waning moon in the sky, and her radiance was not brilliant, but she was veiled in a thin cloud-curtain which seemed to diffuse and equalise it. When, on his return from the villa (it was eleven o'clock), Winterbourne approached the dusky circle of the Colosseum, it recurred to him, as a lover of the picturesque, that the interior, in the pale moonshine, would be well worth a glance. He turned aside and walked to one of the empty arches, near which, as he observed, an open carriage—one of the little Roman streetcabs—was stationed. Then he passed in, among the cavernous shadows of the great structure, and emerged upon the clear and silent arena. The place had never seemed to him more impressive. One-half of the gigantic circus[25] was in deep shade; the other was sleeping in the luminous dusk. As he stood there he began to murmur Byron's famous lines, out of "Manfred;"[26] but before he had finished his quotation he remembered that if nocturnal meditations in the Colosseum are recommended by the poets, they are deprecated by the doctors. The historic atmosphere was there, certainly; but the historic atmosphere, scientifically considered, was no better than a villainous miasma. Winterbourne walked to the middle of the arena, to take a more general glance, intending thereafter to make a hasty retreat.

[21]Guide. [22]One of the hills of Rome.

[23]Memorial arch built to celebrate a Roman military victory in A.D. 312.

[24]Administrative and business center of ancient Rome. [25]Arena.

[26]"I do remember me, that in my youth,/When I was wandering,—upon such a night—/I stood within the Coliseum's wall,/Midst the chief relics of almighty Rome." From Byron's verse drama "Manfred" (1817), Act III, Scene iv, lines 8–11.

The great cross in the centre was covered with shadow; it was only as he drew near it that he made it out distinctly. Then he saw that two persons were stationed upon the low steps which formed its base. One of these was a woman, seated; her companion was standing in front of her.

Presently the sound of the woman's voice came to him distinctly in the warm night-air. "Well, he looks at us as one of the old lions or tigers may have looked at the Christian martyrs!" These were the words he heard, in the familiar accent of Miss Daisy Miller.

"Let us hope he is not very hungry," responded the ingenious Giovanelli. "He will have to take me first; you will serve for dessert!"

Winterbourne stopped, with a sort of horror; and, it must be added, with a sort of relief. It was as if a sudden illumination had been flashed upon the ambiguity of Daisy's behaviour and the riddle had become easy to read. She was a young lady whom a gentleman need no longer be at pains to respect. He stood there looking at her—looking at her companion, and not reflecting that though he saw them vaguely, he himself must have been more brightly visible. He felt angry with himself that he had bothered so much about the right way of regarding Miss Daisy Miller. Then, as he was going to advance again, he checked himself; not from the fear that he was doing her injustice, but from a sense of the danger of appearing unbecomingly exhilarated by this sudden revulsion from cautious criticism. He turned away towards the entrance of the place; but as he did so he heard Daisy speak again.

"Why, it was Mr. Winterbourne! He saw me—and he cuts me!"

What a clever little reprobate she was, and how smartly she played at injured innocence! But he wouldn't cut her. Winterbourne came forward again, and went towards the great cross. Daisy had got up; Giovanelli lifted his hat. Winterbourne had not begun to think simply of the craziness, from a sanitary point of view, of a delicate young girl lounging away the evening in this nest of malaria. What if she *were* a clever little reprobate? that was no reason for her dying of the *perniciosa*.[27] "How long have you been here?" he asked, almost brutally.

Daisy, lovely in the flattering moonlight, looked at him a moment. Then—"All the evening," she answered gently. . . . "I never saw anything so pretty."

"I am afraid," said Winterbourne, "that you will not think Roman fever very pretty. This is the way people catch it. I wonder," he added, turning to Giovanelli, "that you, a native Roman, should countenance such a terrible indiscretion."

"Ah," said the handsome native, "for myself, I am not afraid."

"Neither am I—for you! I am speaking for this young lady."

Giovanelli lifted his well-shaped eyebrows and showed his brilliant teeth. But he took Winterbourne's rebuke with docility. "I told the Signorina it was a grave indiscretion; but when was the Signorina ever prudent?"

"I never was sick, and I don't mean to be!" The Signorina declared. "I don't look like much, but I'm healthy! I was bound to see the Colosseum by moonlight; I shouldn't have wanted to go home without that; and we have had the most beautiful time, haven't we, Mr. Giovanelli? If there has been any danger, Eugenio can give me some pills. He has got some splendid pills."

[27]Italian: malaria, the Roman fever.

"I should advise you," said Winterbourne, "to drive home as fast as possible and take one!"

"What you say is very wise," Giovanelli rejoined. "I will go and make sure the carriage is at hand." And he went forward rapidly.

Daisy followed with Winterbourne. He kept looking at her; she seemed not in the least embarrassed. Winterbourne said nothing; Daisy chattered about the beauty of the place. "Well, I *have* seen the Colosseum by moonlight!" she exclaimed. "That's one good thing." Then, noticing Winterbourne's silence, she asked him why he didn't speak. He made no answer; he only began to laugh. They passed under one of the dark archways; Giovanelli was in front with the carriage. Here Daisy stopped a moment, looking at the young American. "*Did* you believe I was engaged the other day?" she asked.

"It doesn't matter what I believed the other day," said Winterbourne, still laughing.

"Well, what do you believe now?"

"I believe that it makes very little difference whether you are engaged or not!"

He felt the young girl's pretty eyes fixed upon him through the thick gloom of the archway; she was apparently going to answer. But Giovanelli hurried her forward. "Quick, quick," he said; "if we get in by midnight we are quite safe."

Daisy took her seat in the carriage, and the fortunate Italian placed himself beside her. "Don't forget Eugenio's pills!" said Winterbourne, as he lifted his hat.

"I don't care," said Daisy, in a little strange tone, "Whether I have Roman fever or not!" Upon this the cab-driver cracked his whip, and they rolled away over the desultory patches of the antique pavement.

Winterbourne—to do him justice, as it were—mentioned to no one that he had encountered Miss Miller, at midnight, in the Colosseum with a gentleman; but nevertheless, a couple of days later, the fact of her having been there under these circumstances was known to every member of the little American circle, and commented accordingly. Winterbourne reflected that they had of course known it at the hotel, and that, after Daisy's return, there had been an exchange of remarks between the porter and the cab-driver. But the young man was conscious at the same moment that it had ceased to be a matter of serious regret to him that the little American flirt should be "talked about" by low-minded menials. These people, a day or two later, had serious information to give: the little American flirt was alarmingly ill. Winterbourne, when the rumor came to him, immediately went to the hotel for more news. He found that two or three charitable friends had preceded him, and that they were being entertained in Mrs. Miller's salon by Randolph.

"It's going round at night," said Randolph—"that's what made her sick. She's always going round at night. I shouldn't think she'd want to—it's so plaguey dark. You can't see anything here at night, except when there's a moon. In America there's always a moon!" Mrs. Miller was invisible; she was now, at least, giving her daughter the advantage of her society. It was evident that Daisy was dangerously ill.

Winterbourne went often to ask for news of her, and once he saw Mrs. Miller, who, though deeply alarmed, was—rather to his surprise—perfectly composed, and, as it appeared, a most efficient and judicious nurse. She talked a good deal about Dr. Davis, but Winterbourne paid her the compliment of saying to himself that she was not, after all, such a monstrous goose. "Daisy spoke of you the other day," she said to him. "Half the time she doesn't know what she's saying, but that time I think she did. She gave me a message; she told me to tell you. She told me to tell you that she never was engaged to that handsome Italian. I am sure I am very glad; Mr. Giovanelli hasn't been near us since she was taken ill. I thought he was so much a gentleman; but I don't call that very polite! A lady told me that he was afraid I was angry with him for taking Daisy round at night. Well, so I am; but I suppose he knows I'm a lady. I would scorn to scold him. Any way, she says, she's not engaged. I don't know why she wanted you to know; but she said to me three times—'Mind you tell Mr. Winterbourne.' And then she told me to ask if you remembered the time you went to that castle, in Switzerland. But I said I wouldn't give any such messages as that. Only, if she is not engaged, I'm sure I'm glad to know it."

But, as Winterbourne has said, it mattered very little. A week after this the poor girl died; it had been a terrible case of the fever. Daisy's grave was in the little Protestant cemetery, in an angle of the wall of imperial Rome, beneath the cypresses and the thick spring-flowers. Winterbourne stood there beside it, with a number of other mourners; a number larger than the scandal excited by the young lady's career would have led you to expect. Near him stood Giovanelli, who came nearer still before Winterbourne turned away. Giovanelli was very pale; on this occasion he had no flower in his buttonhole; he seemed to wish to say something. At last he said, "She was the most beautiful young lady I ever saw, and the most amiable." And then he added in a moment, "And she was the most innocent."

Winterbourne looked at him, and presently repeated his words, "And the most innocent?"

"The most innocent!"

Winterbourne felt sore and angry. "Why the devil," he asked, "did you take her to that fatal place?"

Mr. Giovanelli's urbanity was apparently imperturbable. He looked on the ground a moment, and then he said, "For myself, I had no fear; and she wanted to go."

"That was no reason!" Winterbourne declared.

The subtle Roman again dropped his eyes. "If she had lived, I should have got nothing. She would never have married me, I am sure."

"She would never have married you?"

"For a moment I hoped so. But no. I am sure."

Winterbourne listened to him; he stood staring at the raw protuberance among the April daisies. When he turned away again Mr. Giovanelli, with his light slow step, had retired.

Winterbourne almost immediately left Rome; but the following summer he again met his aunt, Mrs. Costello, at Vevey. Mrs. Costello was fond of Vevey. In the interval Winterbourne had often thought of Daisy Miller and her mystifying manners. One day he spoke of her to his aunt—said it was on his conscience he had done her injustice.

"I am sure I don't know," said Mrs. Costello. "How did your injustice affect her?"

"She sent me a message before her death which I didn't understand at the time. But I have understood it since. She would have appreciated one's esteem."

"Is that a modest way," asked Mrs. Costello, "of saying that she would have reciprocated one's affection?"

Winterbourne offered no answer to this question; but he presently said, "You were right in that remark that you made last summer. I was booked to make a mistake. I have lived too long in foreign parts."

Nevertheless, he went back to live at Geneva, whence there continue to come the most contradictory accounts of his motives of sojourn: a report that he is "studying" hard—an intimation that he is much interested in a very clever foreign lady.

1878 1878

THE REAL THING

I

When the porter's wife, who used to answer the house-bell, announced "A gentleman and a lady, sir," I had, as I often had in those days—the wish being father to the thought—an immediate vision of sitters. Sitters my visitors in this case proved to be; but not in the sense I should have preferred. There was nothing at first however to indicate that they might n't have come for a portrait. The gentleman, a man of fifty, very high and very straight, with a moustache slightly grizzled and a dark grey walking-coat admirably fitted, both of which I noted professionally—I don't mean as a barber or yet as a tailor—would have struck me as a celebrity if celebrities often were striking. It was a truth of which I had for some time been conscious that a figure with a good deal of frontage[1] was, as one might say, almost never a public institution. A glance at the lady helped to remind me of this paradoxical law: she also looked too distinguished to be a "personality." Moreover one would scarcely come across two variations together.

Neither of the pair immediately spoke—they only prolonged the preliminary gaze suggesting that each wished to give the other a chance. They were visibly shy; they stood there letting me take them in—which, as I afterwards perceived, was the most practical thing they could have done. In this way their embarrassment served their cause. I had seen people painfully reluctant to mention that they desired anything so gross as to be represented on canvas; but the scruples of my new friends appeared almost insurmountable. Yet the gentleman might have said "I should like a portrait of my wife," and the lady might have said "I should like a portrait of my husband." Perhaps they were n't husband and wife—this naturally would make the matter more delicate. Perhaps they wished to be done together—in which case they ought to have brought a third person to break the news.

"We come from Mr. Rivet," the lady finally said with a dim smile that had the effect of a moist sponge passed over a "sunk"[2] piece of painting, as well as

[1]I.e., imposing appearance. [2]Faded.

of a vague allusion to vanished beauty. She was as tall and straight, in her degree, as her companion, and with ten years less to carry. She looked as sad as a woman could look whose face was not charged with expression; that is her tinted oval mask showed waste as an exposed surface shows friction. The hand of time had played over her freely, but to an effect of elimination. She was slim and stiff, and so well-dressed, in dark blue cloth, with lappets[3] and pockets and buttons, that it was clear she employed the same tailor as her husband. The couple had an indefinable air of prosperous thrift—they evidently got a good deal of luxury for their money. If I was to be one of their luxuries it would behove me to consider my terms.

"Ah Claude Rivet recommended me?" I echoed; and I added that it was very kind of him, though I could reflect that, as he only painted landscape, this was n't a sacrifice.

The lady looked very hard at the gentleman, and the gentleman looked round the room. Then staring at the floor a moment and stroking his moustache, he rested his pleasant eyes on me with the remark: "He said you were the right one."

"I try to be, when people want to sit."

"Yes, we should like to," said the lady anxiously.

"Do you mean together?"

My visitors exchanged a glance. "If you could do anything with *me* I suppose it would be double," the gentleman stammered.

"Oh yes, there's naturally a higher charge for two figures than for one."

"We should like to make it pay," the husband confessed.

"That's very good of you," I returned, appreciating so unwonted a sympathy—for I supposed he meant pay the artist.

A sense of strangeness seemed to dawn on the lady. "We mean for the illustrations—Mr. Rivet said you might put one in."

"Put in—an illustration?" I was equally confused.

"Sketch her off, you know," said the gentleman, colouring.

It was only then that I understood the service Claude Rivet had rendered me; he had told them how I worked in black-and-white, for magazines, for storybooks, for sketches of contemporary life, and consequently had copious employment for models. These things were true, but it was not less true—I may confess it now; whether because the aspiration was to lead to everything or to nothing I leave the reader to guess—that I could n't get the honours, to say nothing of the emoluments, of a great painter of portraits out of my head. My "illustrations" were my pot-boilers; I looked to a different branch of art—far and away the most interesting it had always seemed to me—to perpetuate my fame. There was no shame in looking to it also to make my fortune; but that fortune was by so much further from being made from the moment my visitors wished to be "done" for nothing. I was disappointed; for in the pictorial sense I had immediately *seen* them. I had seized their type—I had already settled what I would do with it. Something that would n't absolutely have pleased them, I afterwards reflected.

"Ah you're—you're—a—?" I began as soon as I had mastered my surprise. I could n't bring out the dingy word "models": it seemed so little to fit the case.

[3]Folds, or flaps.

"We have n't had much practice," said the lady.

"We've got to *do* something, and we've thought that an artist in your line might perhaps make something of us," her husband threw off. He further mentioned that they did n't know many artists and that they had gone first, on the off-chance—he painted views of course, but sometimes put in figures; perhaps I remembered—to Mr. Rivet, whom they had met a few years before at a place in Norfolk where he was sketching.

"We used to sketch a little ourselves," the lady hinted.

"It's very awkward, but we absolutely *must* do something," her husband went on.

"Of course we're not so *very* young," she admitted with a wan smile.

With the remark that I might as well know something more about them the husband had handed me a card extracted from a neat new pocket-book—their appurtenances were all of the freshest—and inscribed with the words "Major Monarch." Impressive as these words were they did n't carry my knowledge much further; but my visitor presently added: "I've left the army and we've had the misfortune to lose our money. In fact our means are dreadfully small."

"It's awfully trying—a regular strain," said Mrs. Monarch.

They evidently wished to be discreet—to take care not to swagger because they were gentlefolk. I felt them willing to recognise this as something of a drawback, at the same time that I guessed at an underlying sense—their consolation in adversity—that they *had* their points. They certainly had; but these advantages struck me as preponderantly social; such for instance as would help to make a drawing-room look well. However, a drawing-room was always, or ought to be, a picture.

In consequence of his wife's allusion to their age Major Monarch observed: "Naturally it's more for the figure that we thought of going in. We can still hold ourselves up." On the instant I saw that the figure was indeed their strong point. His "naturally" did n't sound vain, but it lighted up the question. "*She* has the best one," he continued, nodding at his wife with a pleasant after-dinner absence of circumlocution. I could only reply, as if we were in fact sitting over our wine, that this did n't prevent his own from being very good; which led him in turn to make answer: "We thought that if you ever have to do people like us we might be something like it. *She* particularly—for a lady in a book, you know."

I was so amused by them that, to get more of it, I did my best to take their point of view; and though it was an embarrassment to find myself appraising physically, as if they were animals on hire or useful blacks, a pair of whom I should have expected to meet only in one of the relations in which criticism is tacit, I looked at Mrs. Monarch judicially enough to be able to exclaim after a moment with conviction: "Oh yes, a lady in a book!" She was singularly like a bad illustration.

"We'll stand up, if you like," said the Major; and he raised himself before me with a really grand air.

I could take his measure at a glance—he was six feet two and a perfect gentleman. It would have paid any club in process of formation and in want of a stamp to engage him at a salary to stand in the principal window. What struck me at once was that in coming to me they had rather missed their vocation; they could surely have been turned to better account for advertising purposes. I could n't of course see the thing in detail, but I could see them make somebody's fortune—I don't mean their own. There was something in them for a waistcoat-maker, an hotel-keeper or a soap-vendor. I could imagine "We always use it" pinned on their bosoms with the greatest effect; I had a vision of the brilliancy with which they would launch a table d'hôte.[4]

Mrs. Monarch sat still, not from pride but from shyness, and presently her husband said to her: "Get up, my dear, and show how smart you are." She obeyed, but she had no need to get up to show it. She walked to the end of the studio and then came back blushing, her fluttered eyes on the partner of her appeal. I was reminded of an incident I had accidentally had a glimpse of in Paris—being with a friend there, a dramatist about to produce a play, when an actress came to him to ask to be entrusted with a part. She went through her paces before him, walked up and down as Mrs. Monarch was doing. Mrs. Monarch did it quite as well, but I abstained from applauding. It was very odd to see such people apply for such poor pay. She looked as if she had ten thousand a year. Her husband had used the word that described her: she was in the London current jargon essentially and typically "smart." Her figure was, in the same order of ideas, conspicuously and irreproachably "good." For a woman of her age her waist was surprisingly small; her elbow moreover had the orthodox crook. She held her head at the conventional angle, but why did she come to *me?* She ought to have tried on jackets at a big shop. I feared my visitors were not only destitute but "artistic"—which would be a great complication. When she sat down again I thanked her, observing that what a draughtsman most valued in his model was the faculty of keeping quiet.

"Oh *she* can keep quiet," said Major Monarch. Then he added jocosely: "I've always kept her quiet."

"I'm not a nasty fidget, am I?" It was going to wring tears from me, I felt, the way she hid her head, ostrich-like, in the other broad bosom.

The owner of this expanse addressed his answer to me. "Perhaps it is n't out of place to mention—because we ought to be quite business-like, ought n't we?—that when I married her she was known as the Beautiful Statue."

"Oh dear!" said Mrs. Monarch ruefully.

"Of course I should want a certain amount of expression," I rejoined.

"Of *course!*"—and I had never heard such unanimity.

"And then I suppose you know that you'll get awfully tired."

"Oh, we *never* get tired!" they eagerly cried.

"Have you had any kind of practice?"

They hesitated—they looked at each other. "We've been photographed—*immensely,*" said Mrs. Monarch.

"She means the fellows have asked us themselves," added the Major.

"I see—because you're so good-looking."

"I don't know what they thought, but they were always after us."

"We always got our photographs for nothing," smiled Mrs. Monarch.

"We might have brought some, my dear," her husband remarked.

"I'm not sure we have any left. We've given quantities away," she explained to me.

[4]I.e., a restaurant.

"With our autographs and that sort of thing," said the Major.

"Are they to be got in the shops?" I enquired as a harmless pleasantry.

"Oh yes, *hers*—they used to be."

"Not now," said Mrs. Monarch with her eyes on the floor.

II

I could fancy the "sort of thing" they put on the presentation copies of their photographs, and I was sure they wrote a beautiful hand. It was odd how quickly I was sure of everything that concerned them. If they were now so poor as to have to earn shillings and pence they could never have had much of a margin. Their good looks had been their capital, and they had good-humouredly made the most of the career that this resource marked out for them. It was in their faces, the blankness, the deep intellectual repose of the twenty years of country-house visiting that had given them pleasant intonations. I could see the sunny drawing-rooms, sprinkled with periodicals she did n't read, in which Mrs. Monarch had continuously sat; I could see the wet shrubberies in which she had walked, equipped to admiration for either exercise. I could see the rich covers[1] the Major had helped to shoot and the wonderful garments in which, late at night, he repaired to the smoking-room to talk about them. I could imagine their leggings and waterproofs, their knowing tweeds and rugs, their rolls of sticks and cases of tackle and neat umbrellas; and I could evoke the exact appearance of their servants and the compact variety of their luggage on the platforms of country stations.

They gave small tips, but they were liked; they did n't do anything themselves, but they were welcome. They looked so well everywhere; they gratified the general relish for stature, complexion and "form." They knew it without fatuity or vulgarity, and they respected themselves in consequence. They were n't superficial; they were thorough and kept themselves up—it had been their line. People with such a taste for activity had to have some line. I could feel how even in a dull house they could have been counted on for the joy of life. At present something had happened—it didn't matter what, their little income had grown less, it had grown least—and they had to do something for pocket-money. Their friends could like them, I made out, without liking to support them. There was something about them that represented credit—their clothes, their manners, their type; but if credit is a large empty pocket in which an occasional chink reverberates, the chink at least must be audible. What they wanted of me was to help to make it so. Fortunately they had no children—I soon divined that. They would also perhaps wish our relations to be kept secret: this was why it was "for the figure"—the reproduction of the face would betray them.

I liked them—I felt, quite as their friends must have done—they were so simple; and I had no objection to them if they would suit. But somehow with all their perfections I did n't easily believe in them. After all they were amateurs, and the ruling passion of my life was the detestation of the amateur. Combined with this was another perversity—an innate preference for the represented subject over the real one: the defect of the real one was so apt to be a lack of representation. I liked things that appeared; then one was sure. Whether they *were* or not was a subordinate and almost always a profitless

[1]Woods and thickets from which game is driven for hunters.

question. There were other considerations, the first of which was that I already had two or three recruits in use, notably a young person with big feet, in alpaca, from Kilburn, who for a couple of years had come to me regularly for my illustrations and with whom I was still—perhaps ignobly—satisfied. I frankly explained to my visitors how the case stood, but they had taken more precautions than I supposed. They had reasoned out their opportunity, for Claude Rivet had told them of the projected *édition de luxe* of one of the writers of our day—the rarest of the novelists—who, long neglected by the multitudinous vulgar and dearly prized by the attentive (need I mention Philip Vincent?) had had the happy fortune of seeing, late in life, the dawn and then the full light of a higher criticism; an estimate in which on the part of the public there was something really of expiation. The edition preparing, planned by a publisher of taste, was practically an act of high reparation; the wood-cuts with which it was to be enriched were the homage of English art to one of the most independent representatives of English letters. Major and Mrs. Monarch confessed to me they had hoped I might be able to work *them* into my branch of the enterprise. They knew I was to do the first of the books, "Rutland Ramsay," but I had to make clear to them that my participation in the rest of the affair—this first book was to be a test—must depend on the satisfaction I should give. If this should be limited my employers would drop me with scarce common forms. It was therefore a crisis for me, and naturally I was making special preparations, looking about for new people, should they be necessary, and securing the best types. I admitted however that I should like to settle down to two or three good models who would do for everything.

"Should we have often to—a—put on special clothes?" Mrs. Monarch timidly demanded.

"Dear yes—that's half the business."

"And should we be expected to supply our own costumes?"

"Oh no; I've got a lot of things. A painter's models put on—or put off—anything he likes."

"And you mean—a—the same?"

"The same?"

Mrs. Monarch looked at her husband again.

"Oh she was just wondering," he explained, "if the costumes are in *general* use." I had to confess that they were, and I mentioned further that some of them—I had a lot of genuine greasy last-century things—had served their time, a hundred years ago, on living world-stained men and women; on figures not perhaps so far removed, in that vanished world, from *their* type, the Monarchs', *quoi!*[2] of a breeched and bewigged age. "We'll put on anything that *fits*," said the Major.

"Oh I arrange that—they fit in the pictures."

"I'm afraid I should do better for the modern books. I'd come as you like," said Mrs. Monarch.

"She has got a lot of clothes at home: they might do for contemporary life," her husband continued.

"Oh I can fancy scenes in which you'd be quite natural." And indeed I could see the slipshod rearrangements of stale properties—the stories I tried

[2]French: what!

to produce pictures for without the exasperation of reading them—whose sandy tracts the good lady might help to people. But I had to return to the fact that for this sort of work—the daily mechanical grind—I was already equipped: the people I was working with were fully adequate.

"We only thought we might be more like *some* characters," said Mrs. Monarch mildly, getting up.

Her husband also rose; he stood looking at me with a dim wistfulness that was touching in so fine a man. "Would n't it be rather a pull sometimes to have—a—to have—?" He hung fire; he wanted me to help him by phrasing what he meant. But I could n't—I did n't know. So he brought it out awkwardly: "The *real* thing; a gentleman, you know, or a lady." I was quite ready to give a general assent—I admitted that there was a great deal in that. This encouraged Major Monarch to say, following up his appeal with an unacted gulp: "It's awfully hard—we've tried everything." The gulp was communicative; it proved too much for his wife. Before I knew it Mrs. Monarch had dropped again upon a divan and burst into tears. Her husband sat down beside her, holding one of her hands; whereupon she quickly dried her eyes with the other, while I felt embarrassed as she looked up at me. "There is n't a confounded job I have n't applied for—waited for—prayed for. You can fancy we'd be pretty bad first. Secretaryships and that sort of thing? You might as well ask for a peerage. I'd be *anything*—I'm strong; a messenger or a coalheaver. I'd put on a gold-laced cap and open carriage-doors in front of the haberdasher's; I'd hang about a station to carry portmanteaux;[3] I'd be a postman. But they won't *look* at you; there are thousands as good as yourself already on the ground. *Gentlemen,* poor beggars, who've drunk their wine, who've kept their hunters!"

I was as reassuring as I knew how to be, and my visitors were presently on their feet again while, for the experiment, we agreed on an hour. We were discussing it when the door opened and Miss Churm came in with a wet umbrella. Miss Churm had to take the omnibus to Maida Vale and then walk half a mile. She looked a trifle blowsy and slightly splashed. I scarcely ever saw her come in without thinking afresh how odd it was that, being so little in herself, she should yet be so much in others. She was a meagre little Miss Churm, but was such an ample heroine of romance. She was only a freckled cockney,[4] but she could represent everything, from a fine lady to a shepherdess; she had the faculty as she might have had a fine voice or long hair. She could n't spell and she loved beer, but she had two or three "points," and practice, and a knack, and mother-wit, and a whimsical sensibility, and love of the theatre, and seven sisters, and not an ounce of respect, especially for the *h*. The first thing my visitors saw was that her umbrella was wet, and in their spotless perfection they visibly winced at it. The rain had come on since their arrival.

"I'm all in a soak; there *was* a mess of people in the 'bus. I wish you lived near a stytion," said Miss Churm. I requested her to get ready as quickly as possible, and she passed into the room in which she always changed her dress. But before going out she asked me what she was to get into this time.

[3]Large suitcases.

[4]A slum dweller in London's East End, hence a member of the lower class.

"It's the Russian princess, don't you know?" I answered; "the one with the 'golden eyes,' in black velvet, for the long thing in the *Cheapside*."[5]

"Golden eyes? I *say!*" cried Miss Churm, while my companions watched her with intensity as she withdrew. She always arranged herself, when she was late, before I could turn round; and I kept my visitors a little on purpose, so that they might get an idea, from seeing her, what would be expected of themselves. I mentioned that she was quite my notion of an excellent model—she was really very clever.

"Do you think she looks like a Russian princess?" Major Monarch asked with lurking alarm.

"When I make her, yes."

"Oh if you have to *make* her—!" he reasoned, not without point.

"That's the most you can ask. There are so many who are not makeable."

"Well now, *here's* a lady"—and with a persuasive smile he passed his arm into his wife's—"who's already made!"

"Oh I'm not a Russian princess," Mrs. Monarch protested a little coldly. I could see she had known some and did n't like them. There at once was a complication of a kind I never had to fear with Miss Churm.

This young lady came back in black velvet—the gown was rather rusty and very low on her lean shoulders—and with a Japanese fan in her red hands. I reminded her that in the scene I was doing she had to look over some one's head. "I forget whose it is; but it does n't matter. Just look over a head."

"I'd rather look over a stove," said Miss Churm; and she took her station near the fire. She fell into position, settled herself into a tall attitude, gave a certain backward inclination to her head and a certain forward droop to her fan, and looked, at least to my prejudiced sense, distinguished and charming, foreign and dangerous. We left her looking so while I went downstairs with Major and Mrs. Monarch.

"I believe I could come about as near as that," said Mrs. Monarch.

"Oh you think she's shabby, but you must allow for the alchemy of art."

However, they went off with an evident increase of comfort founded on their demonstrable advantage in being the real thing. I could fancy them shuddering over Miss Churm. She was very droll about them when I went back, for I told her what they wanted.

"Well, if *she* can sit I'll tyke to bookkeeping," said my model.

"She's very ladylike," I replied as an innocent form of aggravation.

"So much the worse for *you*. That means she can't turn round."

"She'll do for the fashionable novels."

"Oh yes, she'll *do* for them!" my model humorously declared. "Ain't they bad enough without her?" I had often sociably denounced them to Miss Churm.

III

It was for the elucidation of a mystery in one of these works that I first tried Mrs. Monarch. Her husband came with her, to be useful if necessary—it was sufficiently clear that as a general thing he would prefer to come with her. At

[5]A magazine named for a commercial street in London.

first I wondered if this were for "propriety's" sake—if he were going to be jealous and meddling. The idea was too tiresome, and if it had been confirmed it would speedily have brought our acquaintance to a close. But I soon saw there was nothing in it and that if he accompanied Mrs. Monarch it was—in addition to the chance of being wanted—simply because he had nothing else to do. When they were separate his occupation was gone and they never *had* been separate. I judged rightly that in their awkward situation their close union was their main comfort and that this union had no weak spot. It was a real marriage, an encouragement to the hesitating, a nut for pessimists to crack. Their address was humble—I remember afterwards thinking it had been the only thing about them that was really professional—and I could fancy the lamentable lodgings in which the Major would have been left alone. He could sit there more or less grimly with his wife—he could n't sit there anyhow without her.

He had too much tact to try and make himself agreeable when he could n't be useful; so when I was too absorbed in my work to talk he simply sat and waited. But I liked to hear him talk—it made my work, when not interrupting it, less mechanical, less special. To listen to him was to combine the excitement of going out with the economy of staying at home. There was only one hindrance—that I seemed not to know any of the people this brilliant couple had known. I think he wondered extremely, during the term of our intercourse, whom the deuce I *did* know. He had n't a stray sixpence of an idea to fumble for, so we did n't spin it very fine; we confined ourselves to questions of leather and even of liquor—saddlers and breeches-makers and how to get excellent claret cheap—and matters like "good trains" and the habits of small game. His lore on these last subjects was astonishing—he managed to interweave the stationmaster with the ornithologist. When he could n't talk about greater things he could talk cheerfully about smaller, and since I could n't accompany him into reminiscences of the fashionable world he could lower the conversation without a visible effort to my level.

So earnest a desire to please was touching in a man who could so easily have knocked one down. He looked after the fire and had an opinion on the draught of the stove without my asking him, and I could see that he thought many of my arrangements not half knowing. I remember telling him that if I were only rich I'd offer him a salary to come and teach me how to live. Sometimes he gave a random sigh of which the essence might have been: "Give me even such a bare old barrack as *this,* and I'd do something with it!" When I wanted to use him he came alone; which was an illustration of the superior courage of women. His wife could bear her solitary second floor, and she was in general more discreet; showing by various small reserves that she was alive to the propriety of keeping our relations markedly professional—not letting them slide into sociability. She wished it to remain clear that she and the Major were employed, not cultivated, and if she approved of me as a superior, who could be kept in his place, she never thought me quite good enough for an equal.

She sat with great intensity, giving the whole of her mind to it, and was capable of remaining for an hour almost as motionless as before a photographer's lens. I could see she had been photographed often, but somehow the very habit that made her good for that purpose unfitted her for mine. At first I was extremely pleased with her ladylike air, and it was a satisfaction, on coming to follow her lines, to see how good they were and how far they could lead the pencil. But after a little skirmishing I began to find her too insurmountably stiff; do what I would with it my drawing looked like a photograph or a copy of a photograph. Her figure had no variety of expression—she herself had no sense of variety. You may say that this was my business and was only a question of placing her. Yet I placed her in every conceivable position and she managed to obliterate their differences. She was always a lady certainly, and into the bargain was always the same lady. She was the real thing, but always the same thing. There were moments when I rather writhed under the serenity of her confidence that she *was* the real thing. All her dealings with me and all her husband's were an implication that this was lucky for *me*. Meanwhile I found myself trying to invent types that approached her own, instead of making her own transform itself—in the clever way that was not impossible for instance to poor Miss Churm. Arrange as I would and take the precautions I would, she always came out, in my pictures, too tall—landing me in the dilemma of having represented a fascinating woman as seven feet high, which (out of respect perhaps to my own very much scantier inches) was far from my idea of such a personage.

The case was worse with the Major—nothing I could do would keep *him* down, so that he became useful only for the representation of brawny giants. I adored variety and range, I cherished human accidents, the illustrative note; I wanted to characterise closely, and the thing in the world I most hated was the danger of being ridden by a type. I had quarrelled with some of my friends about it; I had parted company with them for maintaining that one *had* to be, and that if the type was beautiful—witness Raphael and Leonardo[1]—the servitude was only a gain. I was neither Leonardo nor Raphael—I might only be a presumptuous young modern searcher; but I held that everything was to be sacrificed sooner than character. When they claimed that the obsessional form could easily *be* character I retorted, perhaps superficially, "Whose?" It could n't be everybody's—it might end in being nobody's.

After I had drawn Mrs. Monarch a dozen times I felt surer even than before that the value of such a model as Miss Churm resided precisely in the fact that she had no positive stamp, combined of course with the other fact that what she did have was a curious and inexplicable talent for imitation. Her usual appearance was like a curtain which she could draw up at request for a capital performance. This performance was simply suggestive; but it was a word to the wise—it was vivid and pretty. Sometimes even I thought it, though she was plain herself, too insipidly pretty; I made it a reproach to her that the figures drawn from her were monotonously (*bêtement*,[2] as we used to say) graceful. Nothing made her more angry: it was so much her pride to feel she could sit for characters that had nothing in common with each other. She would accuse me at such moments of taking away her "reputytion."

It suffered a certain shrinkage, this queer quantity, from the repeated visits of my new friends. Miss Churm was greatly in demand, never in want of employment, so I had no scruple in putting her off occasionally, to try them

[1]Raphael Sanzio (1483–1520) and Leonardo da Vinci (1452–1519), Italian painters.
[2]French: stupidly.

more at my ease. It was certainly amusing at first to do the real thing—it was amusing to do Major Monarch's trousers. They *were* the real thing, even if he did come out colossal. It was amusing to do his wife's back hair—it was so mathematically neat—and the particular "smart" tension of her tight stays. She lent herself especially to positions in which the face was somewhat averted or blurred; she abounded in ladylike back views and *profils perdus.*[3] When she stood erect she took naturally one of the attitudes in which court-painters represent queens and princesses; so that I found myself wondering whether, to draw out this accomplishment, I could n't get the editor of the *Cheapside* to publish a really royal romance, "A Tale of Buckingham Palace." Sometimes however the real thing and the make-believe came into contact; by which I mean that Miss Churm, keeping an appointment or coming to make one on days when I had much work in hand, encountered her invidious rivals. The encounter was not on their part, for they noticed her no more than if she had been the housemaid; not from intentional loftiness, but simply because as yet, professionally, they did n't know how to fraternise, as I could imagine they would have liked—or at least that the Major would. They could n't talk about the omnibus[4]—they always walked; and they did n't know what else to try—she was n't interested in good trains or cheap claret. Besides, they must have felt—in the air—that she was amused at them, secretly derisive of their ever knowing how. She wasn't a person to conceal the limits of her faith if she had had a chance to show them. On the other hand Mrs. Monarch did n't think her tidy; for why else did she take pains to say to me—it was going out of the way, for Mrs. Monarch—that she did n't like dirty women?

One day when my young lady happened to be present with my other sitters——she even dropped in, when it was convenient, for a chat—I asked her to be so good as to lend a hand in getting tea, a service with which she was familiar and which was one of a class that, living as I did in a small way, with slender domestic resources, I often appealed to my models to render. They liked to lay hands on my property, to break the sitting, and sometimes the china—it made them feel Bohemian. The next time I saw Miss Churm after this incident she surprised me greatly by making a scene about it—she accused me of having wished to humiliate her. She had n't resented the outrage at the time, but had seemed obliging and amused, enjoying the comedy of asking Mrs. Monarch, who sat vague and silent, whether she would have cream and sugar, and putting an exaggerated simper into the question. She had tried intonations—as if she too wished to pass for the real thing—till I was afraid my other visitors would take offence.

Oh they were determined not to do this, and their touching patience was the measure of their great need. They would sit by the hour, uncomplaining, till I was ready to use them; they would come back on the chance of being wanted and would walk away cheerfully if it failed. I used to go to the door with them to see in what magnificent order they retreated. I tried to find other employment for them—I introduced them to several artists. But they didn't "take," for reasons I could appreciate, and I became rather anxiously aware that after such disappointments they fell back upon me with a heavier

[3]French: lost profiles, poses that show the back of the head more than the profile.
[4]Bus.

weight. They did me the honour to think me most *their* form. They were n't romantic enough for the painters, and in those days there were few serious workers in black-and-white. Besides, they had an eye to the great job I had mentioned to them—they had secretly set their hearts on supplying the right essence for my pictorial vindication of our fine novelist. They knew that for this undertaking I should want no costume-effects, none of the frippery of past ages—that it was a case in which everything would be contemporary and satirical and presumably genteel. If I could work them into it their future would be assured, for the labour would of course be long and the occupation steady.

One day Mrs. Monarch came without her husband—she explained his absence by his having had to go to the City.[5] While she sat there in her usual relaxed majesty there came at the door a knock which I immediately recognised as the subdued appeal of a model out of work. It was followed by the entrance of a young man whom I at once saw to be a foreigner and who proved in fact an Italian acquainted with no English word but my name, which he uttered in a way that made it seem to include all others. I had n't then visited his country, nor was I proficient in his tongue; but as he was not so meanly constituted—what Italian is?—as to depend only on that member of expression he conveyed to me, in familiar but graceful mimicry, that he was in search of exactly the employment in which the lady before me was engaged. I was not struck with him at first, and while I continued to draw I dropped few signs of interest or encouragement. He stood his ground however—not importunately, but with a dumb dog-like fidelity in his eyes that amounted to innocent impudence, the manner of a devoted servant—he might have been in the house for years—unjustly suspected. Suddenly it struck me that this very attitude and expression made a picture; whereupon I told him to sit down and wait till I should be free. There was another picture in the way he obeyed me, and I observed as I worked that there were others still in the way he looked wonderingly, with his head thrown back, about the high studio. He might have been crossing himself in Saint Peter's. Before I finished I said to myself "The fellow's a bankrupt orange-monger, but a treasure."

When Mrs. Monarch withdrew he passed across the room like a flash to open the door for her, standing there with the rapt pure gaze of the young Dante spellbound by the young Beatrice.[6] As I never insisted, in such situations, on the blankness of the British domestic, I reflected that he had the making of a servant—and I needed one, but could n't pay him to be only that—as well as of a model; in short I resolved to adopt my bright adventurer if he would agree to officiate in the double capacity. He jumped at my offer, and in the event my rashness—for I had really known nothing about him—wasn't brought home to me. He proved a sympathetic though a desultory ministrant, and had in a wonderful degree the *sentiment de la pose*.[7] It was uncultivated, instinctive, a part of the happy instinct that had guided him to my door and helped him to spell out my name on the card nailed to it. He had had no other introduction to me than a guess, from the shape of my high

[5]London's financial and commercial center.

[6]Beatrice Portinari (1266–1290), Florentine woman said to be the ideal and the inspiration of the poet Dante, who first saw her when he was nine.

[7]French: instinct for posing.

north window, seen outside, that my place was a studio and that as a studio it would contain an artist. He had wandered to England in search of fortune, like other itinerants, and had embarked, with a partner and a small green hand-cart, on the sale of penny ices. The ices had melted away and the partner had dissolved in their train. My young man wore tight yellow trousers with reddish stripes and his name was Oronte. He was sallow but fair, and when I put him into some old clothes of my own he looked like an Englishman. He was as good as Miss Churm, who could look, when requested, like an Italian.

IV

I thought Mrs. Monarch's face slightly convulsed when, on her coming back with her husband, she found Oronte installed. It was strange to have to recognise in a scrap of a lazzarone[1] a competitor to her magnificent Major. It was she who scented danger first, for the Major was anecdotically unconscious. But Oronte gave us tea, with a hundred eager confusions—he had never been concerned in so queer a process—and I think she thought better of me for having at last an "establishment." They saw a couple of drawings that I had made of the establishment, and Mrs. Monarch hinted that it never would have struck her he had sat for them. "Now the drawings you make from *us*, they look exactly like us," she reminded me, smiling in triumph; and I recognised that this was indeed just their defect. When I drew the Monarchs I could n't anyhow get away from them—get into the character I wanted to represent; and I hadn't the least desire my model should be discoverable in my picture. Miss Churm never was, and Mrs. Monarch thought I hid her, very properly, because she was vulgar; whereas if she was lost it was only as the dead who go to heaven are lost—in the gain of an angel the more.

By this time I had got a certain start with "Rutland Ramsay," the first novel in the great projected series; that is I had produced a dozen drawings, several with the help of the Major and his wife, and I had sent them in for approval. My understanding with the publishers, as I have already hinted, had been that I was to be left to do my work, in this particular case, as I liked, with the whole book committed to me; but my connexion with the rest of the series was only contingent. There were moments when, frankly, it *was* a comfort to have the real thing under one's hand; for there were characters in "Rutland Ramsay" that were very much like it. There were people presumably as erect as the Major and women of as good a fashion as Mrs. Monarch. There was a great deal of countryhouse life—treated, it is true, in a fine fanciful ironical generalised way—and there was a considerable implication of knickerbockers[2] and kilts. There were certain things I had to settle at the outset; such things for instance as the exact appearance of the hero and the particular bloom and figure of the heroine. The author of course gave me a lead, but there was a margin for interpretation. I took the Monarchs into my confidence, I told them frankly what I was about, I mentioned my embarrassments and alternatives. "Oh take *him!*" Mrs. Monarch murmured sweetly, looking at

[1]Italian: beggar. [2]Trousers gathered at the knee, knickers.

her husband; and "What could you want better than my wife?" the Major enquired with the comfortable candour that now prevailed between us.

I was n't obliged to answer these remarks—I was only obliged to place my sitters. I was n't easy in mind, and I postponed a little timidly perhaps the solving of my question. The book was a large canvas, the other figures were numerous, and I worked off at first some of the episodes in which the hero and the heroine were not concerned. When once I had set *them* up I should have to stick to them—I could n't make my young man seven feet high in one place and five feet nine in another. I inclined on the whole to the latter measurement, though the Major more than once reminded me that *he* looked about as young as any one. It was indeed quite possible to arrange him, for the figure, so that it would have been difficult to detect his age. After the spontaneous Oronte had been with me a month, and after I had given him to understand several times over that his native exuberance would presently constitute an insurmountable barrier to our further intercourse, I waked to a sense of his heroic capacity. He was only five feet seven, but the remaining inches were latent. I tried him almost secretly at first, for I was really rather afraid of the judgment my other models would pass on such a choice. If they regarded Miss Churm as little better than a snare what would they think of the representation by a person so little the real thing as an Italian street-vendor of a protagonist formed by a public school?

If I went a little in fear of them it was n't because they bullied me, because they had got an oppressive foothold, but because in their really pathetic decorum and mysteriously permanent newness they counted on me so intensely. I was therefore very glad when Jack Hawley came home: he was always of such good counsel. He painted badly himself, but there was no one like him for putting his finger on the place. He had been absent from England for a year; he had been somewhere—I don't remember where—to get a fresh eye. I was in a good deal of dread of any such organ, but we were old friends; he had been away for months and a sense of emptiness was creeping into my life. I had n't dodged a missile for a year.

He came back with a fresh eye, but with the same old black velvet blouse, and the first evening he spent in my studio we smoked cigarettes till the small hours. He had done no work himself, he had only got the eye; so the field was clear for the production of my little things. He wanted to see what I had produced for the *Cheapside*, but he was disappointed in the exhibition. That at least seemed the meaning of two or three comprehensive groans which, as he lounged on my big divan, his leg folded under him, looking at my latest drawings, issued from his lips with the smoke of the cigarette.

"What's the matter with you?" I asked.

"What's the matter with *you?*"

"Nothing save that I'm mystified."

"You are indeed. You're quite off the hinge. What's the meaning of this new fad?" And he tossed me, with visible irreverence, a drawing in which I happened to have depicted both my elegant models. I asked if he did n't think it good, and he replied that it struck him as execrable, given the sort of thing I had always represented myself to him as wishing to arrive at; but I let that pass—I was so anxious to see exactly what he meant. The two figures in the picture looked colossal, but I supposed this was *not* what he meant, inasmuch as, for aught he knew to the contrary, I might have been trying for some such effect. I maintained that I was working exactly in the same way as when he last had done me the honour to tell me I might do something some day. "Well, there's a screw loose somewhere," he answered; "wait a bit and I'll discover it." I depended upon him to do so: where else was the fresh eye? But he produced at last nothing more luminous than "I don't know—I don't like your types." This was lame for a critic who had never consented to discuss with me anything but the question of execution, the direction of strokes and the mystery of values.

"In the drawings you've been looking at I think my types are very handsome."

"Oh, they won't do!"

"I've been working with new models."

"I see you have. *They* won't do."

"Are you very sure of that?"

"Absolutely—they're stupid."

"You mean *I* am—for I ought to get around that."

"You *can't*—with such people. Who are they?"

I told him, so far as was necessary, and he concluded heartlessly: "*Ce sont des gens qu'il faut mettre à la porte.*"[3]

"You've never seen them; they're awfully good"—I flew to their defence.

"Not seen them? Why all this recent work of yours drops to pieces with them. It's all I want to see of them."

"No one else has said anything against it—the *Cheapside* people are pleased."

"Every one else is an ass, and the *Cheapside* people the biggest asses of all. Come, don't pretend at this time of day to have pretty illusions about the public, especially about publishers and editors. It's not for *such* animals you work—it's for those who know, *coloro che sanno,*"[4] so keep straight for *me* if you can't keep straight for yourself. There was a certain sort of thing you used to try for—and a very good thing is was. But this twaddle is n't *in* it." When I talked with Hawley later about "Rutland Ramsay" and its possible successors he declared that I must get back into my boat again or I should go to the bottom. His voice in short was the voice of warning.

I noted the warning, but I did n't turn my friends out of doors. They bored me a good deal; but the very fact that they bored me admonished me not to sacrifice them—if there was anything to be done with them—simply to irritation. As I look back at this phase they seem to me to have pervaded my life not a little. I have a vision of them as most of the time in my studio, seated against the wall on an old velvet bench to be out of the way, and resembling the while a pair of patient courtiers in a royal ante-chamber. I'm convinced that during the coldest weeks of the winter they held their ground because it saved them fire. Their newness was losing its gloss, and it was impossible not to feel them objects of charity. Whenever Miss Churm arrived they went away,

[3]French: "They are people one must show to the door," i.e., get rid of.

[4]Italian: those who know, a quotation from Dante's *Inferno,* Canto IV, line 131.

and after I was fairly launched in "Rutland Ramsay" Miss Churm arrived pretty often. They managed to express to me tacitly that they supposed I wanted her for the low life of the book, and I let them suppose it, since they had attempted to study the work—it was lying about the studio—without discovering that it dealt only with the highest circles. They had dipped into the most brilliant of our novelists without deciphering many passages. I still took an hour from them, now and again, in spite of Jack Hawley's warning; it would be time enough to dismiss them, if dismissal should be necessary, when the rigour of the season was over. Hawley had made their acquaintance—he had met them at my fireside—and thought them a ridiculous pair. Learning that he was a painter they tried to approach him, to show him too that they were the real thing; but he looked at them, across the big room, as if they were miles away; they were a compendium of everything he most objected to in the social system of his country. Such people as that, all convention and patent-leather, with ejaculations that stopped conversation, had no business in a studio. A studio was a place to learn to see, and how could you see through a pair of feather-beds?

The main inconvenience I suffered at their hands was that at first I was shy of letting it break upon them that my artful little servant had begun to sit to me for "Rutland Ramsay." They knew I had been odd enough—they were prepared by this time to allow oddity to artist—to pick a foreign vagabond out of the streets when I might have had a person with whiskers and credentials; but it was some time before they learned how high I rated his accomplishments. They found him in an attitude more than once, but they never doubted I was doing him as an organ-grinder. There were several things they never guessed, and one of them was that for a striking scene in the novel, in which a footman briefly figured, it occurred to me to make use of Major Monarch as the menial. I kept putting this off, I did n't like to ask him to don the livery—beside the difficulty of finding a livery to fit him. At last, one day late in the winter, when I was at work on the despised Oronte, who caught one's idea on the wing, and was in the glow of feeling myself go very straight, they came in, the Major and his wife, with their society laugh about nothing (there was less and less to laugh at); came in like country-callers—they always reminded me of that—who have walked across the park after church and are presently persuaded to stay to luncheon. Luncheon was over, but they could stay to tea—I knew they wanted it. The fit was on me, however, and I could n't let my ardour cool and my work wait, with the fading daylight, while my model prepared it. So I asked Mrs. Monarch if she would mind laying it out—a request which for an instant brought all the blood to her face. Her eyes were on her husband's for a second, and some mute telegraphy passed between them. Their folly was over the next instant; his cheerful shrewdness put an end to it. So far from pitying their wounded pride, I must add, I was moved to give it as complete a lesson as I could. They bustled about together and got out the cups and saucers and made the kettle boil. I know they felt as if they were waiting on my servant, and when the tea was prepared I said: "He'll have a cup, please—he's tired." Mrs. Monarch brought him one where he stood, and he took it from her as if he had been a gentleman at a party squeezing a crush-hat with an elbow.

Then it came over me that she had made a great effort for me—made it with a kind of nobleness—and that I owed her a compensation. Each time I saw her after this I wondered what the compensation could be. I could n't go on doing the wrong thing to oblige them. Oh it *was* the wrong thing, the stamp of the work for which they sat—Hawley was not the only person to say it now. I sent in a large number of the drawings I had made for "Rutland Ramsay," and I received a warning that was more to the point than Hawley's. The artistic adviser of the house for which I was working was of opinion that many of my illustrations were not what had been looked for. Most of these illustrations were the subjects in which the Monarchs had figured. Without giving into the question of what *had* been looked for, I had to face the fact that at this rate I should n't get the other books to do. I hurled myself in despair on Miss Churm—I put her through all her paces. I not only adopted Oronte publicly as my hero, but one morning when the Major looked in to see if I did n't require him to finish a *Cheapside* figure for which he had begun to sit the week before, I told him I had changed my mind—I'd do the drawing from my man. At this my visitor turned pale and stood looking at me. "Is *he* your idea of an English gentleman?" he asked.

I was disappointed, I was nervous, I wanted to get on with my work; so I replied with irritation: "Oh my dear Major—I can't be ruined for *you!*"

It was a horrid speech, but he stood another moment—after which, without a word, he quitted the studio. I drew a long breath, for I said to myself that I should n't see him again. I had n't told him definitely that I was in danger of having my work rejected, but I was vexed at his not having felt the catastrophe in the air, read with me the moral of our fruitless collaboration, the lesson that in the deceptive atmosphere of art even the highest respectability may fail of being plastic.

I did n't owe my friends money, but I did see them again. They reappeared together three days later, and, given all the other facts, there was something tragic in that one. It was a clear proof they could find nothing else in life to do. They had threshed the matter out in a dismal conference—they had digested the bad news that they were not in for the series. If they were n't useful to me even for the *Cheapside* their function seemed difficult to determine, and I could only judge at first that they had come, forgivingly, decorously, to take a last leave. This made me rejoice in secret that I had little leisure for a scene; for I had placed both my other models in position together and I was pegging away at a drawing from which I hoped to derive glory. It had been suggested by the passage in which Rutland Ramsay, drawing up a chair to Artemisia's piano-stool, says extraordinary things to her while she ostensibly fingers out a difficult piece of music. I had done Miss Churm at the piano before—it was an attitude in which she knew how to take on an absolutely poetic grace. I wished the two figures to "compose" together with intensity, and my little Italian had entered perfectly into my conception. The pair were vividly before me, the piano had been pulled out; it was a charming show of blended youth and murmured love, which I had only to catch and keep. My visitors stood and looked at it, and I was friendly to them over my shoulder.

They made no response, but I was used to silent company and went on with my work, only a little disconcerted—even though exhilarated by the sense that *this* was at least the ideal thing—at not having got rid of them after all. Presently I heard Mrs. Monarch's sweet voice beside or rather above me: "I wish her hair were a little better done." I looked up and she was staring with a strange fixedness at Miss Churm, whose back was turned to her. "Do you mind my just touching it?" she went on—a question which made me spring up for an instant as with the instinctive fear that she might do the young lady a harm. But she quieted me with a glance I shall never forget—I confess I should like to have been able to paint *that*—and went for a moment to my model. She spoke to her softly, laying a hand on her shoulder and bending over her; and as the girl, understanding, gratefully assented, she disposed her rough curls, with a few quick passes, in such a way as to make Miss Churm's head twice as charming. It was one of the most heroic personal services I've ever seen rendered. Then Mrs. Monarch turned away with a low sigh and, looking about her as if for something to do, stooped to the floor with a noble humility and picked up a dirty rag that had dropped out of my paint-box.

The Major meanwhile had also been looking for something to do, and, wandering to the other end of the studio, saw before him my breakfast-things neglected, unremoved. "I say, can't I be useful here?" he called out to me with an irrepressible quaver. I assented with a laugh that I fear was awkward, and for the next ten minutes, while I worked, I hear the light clatter of china and the tinkle of spoons and glass. Mrs. Monarch assisted her husband—they washed up my crockery, they put it away. They wandered off into my little scullery, and I afterwards found that they had cleaned my knives and that my slender stock of plate had an unprecedented surface. When it came over me, the latent eloquence of what they were doing, I confess that my drawing was blurred for a moment—the picture swam. They had accepted their failure, but they could n't accept their fate. They had bowed their heads in bewilderment to the perverse and cruel law in virtue of which the real thing could be so much less precious than the unreal; but they did n't want to starve. If my servants were my models, then my models might be my servants. They would reverse the parts—the others would sit for the ladies and gentlemen and *they* would do the work. They would still be in the studio—it was an intense dumb appeal to me not to turn them out. "Take us on," they wanted to say—"we'll do *anything*."

My pencil dropped from my hand; my sitting was spoiled and I got rid of my sitters, who were also evidently rather mystified and awestruck. Then, alone with the Major and his wife I had a most uncomfortable moment. He put their prayer into a single sentence: "I say, you know—just let *us* do for you, can't you?" I could n't—it was dreadful to see them emptying my slops, but I pretended I could, to oblige them, for about a week. Then I gave them a sum of money to go away, and I never saw them again. I obtained the remaining books, but my friend Hawley repeats that Major and Mrs. Monarch did me a permanent harm, got me into false ways. If it be true I'm content to have paid the price—for the memory.

1892, 1909

Ambrose Bierce 1842–1914

In 1914, when he was seventy-one, Ambrose Bierce left the United States to report on the Mexican Revolution as an observer with the rebel army of Pancho Villa. One month after he arrived he wrote to a friend, "Pray for me—real hard." Shortly afterward Bierce disappeared, never to be seen again, and his mysterious fate has fascinated his biographers and his readers almost as much as the details of his misanthropic life. Bierce was born the child of poor farmers at Horse Cave Creek, Meigs County, in southeast Ohio. When he was four his family moved to a farm in Indiana, where he went to school. His parents' religious fervor left him with a lifelong hatred of faith and piety; his unhappy childhood is partially reflected in his stories filled with deaths, maimings, and the separations of parents, children, and families.

When Bierce was fifteen he went to work as a printer's devil (apprentice) on an antislavery newspaper in Indiana. Later he attended the Kentucky Military Institute for a year. And in 1861, with the outbreak of the Civil War, he enlisted in the Union Army. Bierce served with distinction throughout the war, rising from the rank of private to lieutenant and finally to the rank of brevet major. He re-enlisted twice and fought in some of the greatest and bloodiest battles of the war: Shiloh, Chickamauga, Lookout Mountain, Missionary Ridge.

Following the war, Bierce went west, first working in the San Francisco Mint but gradually establishing a career as a journalist, polemicist, and fiction writer. He spent the years from 1872 to 1876 in London, where his slashing brand of journalism won him fame and the title "Bitter Bierce." But he returned to California to write for William Randolph Hearst's San Francisco Examiner. *Bierce's writing, especially his fiction, was sardonic and obsessed with death. It has been said that "Death" was perhaps "his only character." In fact, the idea of death was not only central to Bierce's writing, it dominated his life. His early and crucial experiences in the Civil War had brought him face to face with a horrible and futile slaughter that had destroyed his youthful, romantic optimism. And in his later life Bierce was tortured by personal and professional disasters: friends and relatives fought bitterly with him, became estranged, committed suicide, died tragically. He grew increasingly cynical and malevolent, his writing vitriolic, filled with invective.*

Excerpts from his popular Devil's Dictionary *appeared from 1881 to 1906; it was a collection of waspish, witty epigrams and definitions that reflected the tone and flavor of much of his work. He defined "bride" as "a woman with a fine prospect of happiness behind her"; "Christian" as "one who believes that the New Testament is a divinely inspired book admirably suited to the spiritual needs of his neighbor"; "birth" as "The first and direst of all disasters." From 1867 until his disappearance, Bierce was a major figure in the development of American literary realism. He wrote essays, short stories, and major journalistic pieces. He was called a "West Coast Samuel Johnson," and his cynical and scathing newspaper articles were enormously popular. But his finest achievement is found in his short stories, tales about men trapped in the labyrinths of endless struggle, blinded by folly and romantic hope, abandoned to a cold and brutal providence.*

FURTHER READING: *Collected Works of Ambrose Bierce,* 12 vols., ed. W. Neale, 1909–1912; V. Starrett, *Ambrose Bierce,* 1920; *The Letters of Ambrose Bierce,* ed. B. Pope, 1922, 1967; C. Grattan, *Bitter Bierce,* 1929; C. McWilliams, *Ambrose Bierce, A Biography,* 1929, 1967; P. Fatout, *Ambrose Bierce, The Devil's Lexicographer,* 1951; P. Fatout, *Ambrose Bierce and the Black Hills,* 1956; S. Woodruff, *The Short Stories of Ambrose Bierce,* 1964; R. O'Conner, *Ambrose Bierce, A Biography,* 1967; M. Grenander, *Ambrose Bierce,* 1971; *Ambrose Bierce,*

Skepticism and Dissent, ed. L. Berkove, 1980; *Critical Essays on Ambrose Bierce,* ed. C. Davidson, 1982; L. Berkove, *Ambrose Bierce, A Braver Man than Anybody Knew,* 1983; C. Davidson, *The Experimental Fictions of Ambrose Bierce,* 1984; R. Morris, *Ambrose Bierce, Alone in Bad Company,* 1995; L. Berkove, *The Moral Art of Ambrose Bierce,* 2002; D. Blume, *Ambrose Bierce's Civilians and Soldiers in Context,* 2004.

TEXT: *Tales of Soldiers and Civilians,* 1892.

AN OCCURRENCE AT OWL CREEK BRIDGE

I

A man stood upon a railroad bridge in northern Alabama, looking down into the swift water twenty feet below. The man's hands were behind his back, the wrists bound with a cord. A rope loosely encircled his neck. It was attached to a stout cross-timber above his head, and the slack fell to the level of his knees. Some loose boards laid upon the sleepers[1] supporting the metals of the railway supplied a footing for him and his executioners—two private soldiers of the Federal army, directed by a sergeant, who in civil life may have been a deputy sheriff. At a short remove upon the same temporary platform was an officer in the uniform of his rank, armed. He was a captain. A sentinel at each end of the bridge stood with his rifle in the position known as "support," that is to say, vertical in front of the left shoulder, the hammer resting on the forearm thrown straight across the chest—a formal and unnatural position, enforcing an erect carriage of the body. It did not appear to be the duty of these two men to know what was occurring at the center of the bridge; they merely blockaded the two ends of the foot plank which traversed it.

Beyond one of the sentinels, nobody was in sight; the railroad ran straight away into a forest for a hundred yards, then, curving, was lost to view. Doubtless there was an outpost farther along. The other bank of the stream was open ground—a gentle acclivity crowned with a stockade of vertical tree trunks, loopholed for rifles, with a single embrasure through which protruded the muzzle of a brass cannon commanding the bridge. Midway of the slope between bridge and fort were the spectators—a single company of infantry in line, at "parade rest," the butts of the rifles on the ground, the barrels inclining slightly backward against the right shoulder, the hands crossed upon the stock. A lieutenant stood at the right of the line, the point of his sword upon the ground, his left hand resting upon his right. Excepting the group of four at the center of the bridge, not a man moved. The company faced the bridge, staring stonily, motionless. The sentinels, facing the banks of the stream, might have been statues to adorn the bridge. The captain stood with folded arms, silent, observing the work of his subordinates, but making no sign. Death is a dignitary who when he comes announced is to be received with formal manifestations of respect, even by those most familiar with him. In the code of military etiquette silence and fixity are forms of deference.

[1]Ties, wooden beams to which railroad tracks are attached.

The man who was engaged in being hanged was apparently about thirty-five years of age. He was a civilian, if one might judge from his dress, which was that of a planter. His features were good—a straight nose, firm mouth, broad forehead, from which his long, dark hair was combed straight back, falling behind his ears to the collar of his well-fitting frock coat. He wore a mustache and pointed beard, but no whiskers; his eyes were large and dark gray, and had a kindly expression which one would hardly have expected in one whose neck was in the hemp. Evidently this was no vulgar assassin. The liberal military code makes provision for hanging many kinds of people, and gentlemen are not excluded.

The preparations being complete, the two private soldiers stepped aside and each drew away the plank upon which he had been standing. The sergeant turned to the captain, saluted, and placed himself immediately behind that officer, who in turn moved apart one pace. These movements left the condemned man and the sergeant standing on the two ends of the same plank, which spanned three of the crossties of the bridge. The end upon which the civilian stood almost, but not quite reached a fourth. This plank had been held in place by the weight of the captain; it was now held by that of the sergeant. At a signal from the former, the latter would step aside, the plank would tilt, and the condemned man go down between two ties. The arrangement commended itself to his judgment as simple and effective. His face had not been covered nor his eyes bandaged. He looked a moment at his "unsteadfast footing," then let his gaze wander to the swirling water of the stream racing madly beneath his feet. A piece of dancing driftwood caught his attention and his eyes followed it down the current. How slowly it appeared to move! What a sluggish stream!

He closed his eyes in order to fix his last thoughts upon his wife and children. The water, touched to gold by the early sun, the brooding mists under the banks at some distance down the stream, the fort, the soldiers, the piece of drift—all had distracted him. And now he became conscious of a new disturbance. Striking through the thought of his dear ones was a sound which he could neither ignore nor understand, a sharp, distinct, metallic percussion like the stroke of a blacksmith's hammer upon the anvil; it had the same ringing quality. He wondered what it was, and whether immeasurably distant or near by—it seemed both. Its recurrence was regular, but as slow as the tolling of a death knell. He awaited each stroke with impatience and—he knew not why—apprehension. The intervals of silence grew progressively longer; the delays became maddening. With their greater infrequency the sounds increased in strength and sharpness. They hurt his ear like the thrust of a knife; he feared he would shriek. What he heard was the ticking of his watch.

He unclosed his eyes and saw again the water below him. "If I could free my hands," he thought, "I might throw off the noose and spring into the stream. By diving I could evade the bullets, and, swimming vigorously, reach the bank, take to the woods, and get away home. My home, thank God, is as yet outside their lines; my wife and little ones are still beyond the invader's farthest advance."

As these thoughts, which have here to be set down in words, were flashed into the doomed man's brain rather than evolved from it, the captain nodded to the sergeant. The sergeant stepped aside.

II

Peyton Farquhar was a well-to-do planter of an old and highly respected Alabama family. Being a slave owner and like other slave owners a politician, he was naturally an original secessionist and ardently devoted to the Southern cause. Circumstances of an imperious nature, which it is unnecessary to relate here, had prevented him from taking service with the gallant army which had fought the disastrous campaigns ending with the fall of Corinth,[1] and he chafed under the inglorious restraint, longing for the release of his energies, the larger life of the soldier, the opportunity for distinction. That opportunity, he felt, would come, as it comes to all in war time. Meanwhile he did what he could. No service was too humble for him to perform in aid of the South, no adventure too perilous for him to undertake if consistent with the character of a civilian who was at heart a soldier, and who in good faith and without too much qualification assented to at least a part of the frankly villainous dictum that all is fair in love and war.

One evening while Farquhar and his wife were sitting on a rustic bench near the entrance to his grounds, a gray-clad[2] soldier rode up to the gate and asked for a drink of water. Mrs. Farquhar was only too happy to serve him with her own white hands. While she was gone to fetch the water, her husband approached the dusty horseman and inquired eagerly for news from the front.

"The Yanks are repairing the railroads," said the man, "and are getting ready for another advance. They have reached the Owl Creek bridge, put it in order, and built a stockade on the north bank. The commandant has issued an order, which is posted everywhere, declaring that any civilian caught interfering with the railroad, its bridges, tunnels, or trains will be summarily hanged. I saw the order."

"How far is it to the Owl Creek bridge?" Farquhar asked.

"About thirty miles."

"Is there no force on this side the creek?"

"Only a picket post half a mile out, on the railroad, and a single sentinel at this end of the bridge."

"Suppose a man—a civilian and student of hanging—should elude the picket post and perhaps get the better of the sentinel," said Farquhar, smiling, "what could he accomplish?"

The soldier reflected. "I was there a month ago," he replied. "I observed that the flood of last winter had lodged a great quantity of driftwood against the wooden pier at this end of the bridge. It is now dry and would burn like tow."

The lady had now brought the water, which the soldier drank. He thanked her ceremoniously, bowed to her husband, and rode away. An hour later, after nightfall, he repassed the plantation, going northward in the direction from which he had come. He was a Federal scout.

III

As Peyton Farquhar fell straight downward through the bridge he lost consciousness and was as one already dead. From this state he was awakened—ages later, it seemed to him—by the pain of a sharp pressure upon his throat, followed by a sense of suffocation. Keen, poignant agonies seemed to

[1]Corinth, Mississippi, occupied by Union forces in May, 1862.
[2]I.e., dressed in the gray uniform of a Confederate soldier.

shoot from his neck downward through every fiber of his body and limbs. These pains appeared to flash along well-defined lines of ramification and to beat with an inconceivably rapid periodicity. They seemed like streams of pulsating fire heating him to an intolerable temperature. As to his head, he was conscious of nothing but a feeling of fullness—of congestion. These sensations were unaccompanied by thought. The intellectual part of his nature was already effaced; he had power only to feel, and feeling was torment. He was conscious of motion. Encompassed in a luminous cloud, of which he was now merely the fiery heart, without material substance, he swung through unthinkable arcs of oscillation, like a vast pendulum. Then all at once, with terrible suddenness, the light about him shot upward with the noise of a loud plash; a frightful roaring was in his ears, and all was cold and dark. The power of thought was restored; he knew that the rope had broken and he had fallen into the stream. There was no additional strangulation; the noose about his neck was already suffocating him and kept the water from his lungs. To die of hanging at the bottom of a river!—the idea seemed to him ludicrous. He opened his eyes in the darkness and saw above him a gleam of light, but how distant, how inaccessible! He was still sinking, for the light became fainter and fainter until it was a mere glimmer. Then it began to grow and brighten, and he knew that he was rising toward the surface—knew it with reluctance, for he was now very comfortable. "To be hanged and drowned," he thought, "that is not so bad; but I do not wish to be shot." No, I will not be shot, that is not fair."

He was not conscious of an effort, but a sharp pain in his wrist apprised him that he was trying to free his hands. He gave the struggle his attention, as an idler might observe the feat of a juggler, without interest in the outcome. What splendid effort!—what magnificent, what super-human strength! Ah, that was a fine endeavor! Bravo! The cord fell away; his arms parted and floated upward, the hands dimly seen on each side in the growing light. He watched them with a new interest as first one and then the other pounced upon the noose at his neck. They tore it away and thrust it fiercely aside, its undulations resembling those of a water snake. "Put it back, put it back!" He thought he shouted these words to his hands, for the undoing of the noose had been succeeded by the direst pang that he had yet experienced. His neck ached horribly; his brain was on fire; his heart, which had been fluttering faintly, gave a great leap, trying to force itself out at his mouth. His whole body was racked and wrenched with an insupportable anguish! But his disobedient hands gave no heed to the command. They beat the water vigorously with quick, downward strokes, forcing him to the surface. He felt his head emerge; his eyes were blinded by the sunlight; his chest expanded convulsively, and with a supreme and crowning agony his lungs engulfed a great draught of air, which instantly he expelled in a shriek!

He was now in full possession of his physical senses. They were, indeed, preternaturally keen and alert. Something in the awful disturbance of his organic system had so exalted and refined them that they made record of things never before perceived. He felt the ripples upon his face and heard their separate sounds as they struck. He looked at the forest on the bank of the stream, saw the individual trees, the leaves and the veining of each leaf—saw the very insects upon them: the locusts, the brilliant-bodied flies, the gray spiders stretching their webs from twig to twig. He noted the prismatic colors in all the dewdrops upon a million blades of grass. The humming of the gnats that danced above the eddies of the stream, the beating of the dragonflies' wings, the strokes of the water spiders' legs, like oars which had lifted their boat—all these made audible music. A fish slid along beneath his eyes and he heard the rush of its body parting the water.

He had come to the surface facing down the stream; in a moment the visible world seemed to wheel slowly round, himself the pivotal point, and he saw the bridge, the fort, the soldiers upon the bridge, the captain, the sergeant, the two privates, his executioners. They were in silhouette against the blue sky. They shouted and gesticulated, pointing at him. The captain had drawn his pistol, but did not fire; the others were unarmed. Their movements were grotesque and horrible, their forms gigantic.

Suddenly he heard a sharp report and something struck the water smartly within a few inches of his head, spattering his face with spray. He heard the second report, and saw one of the sentinels with his rifle at his shoulder, a light cloud of blue smoke rising from the muzzle. The man in the water saw the eye of the man on the bridge gazing into his own through the sights of the rifle. He observed that it was a gray eye and remembered having read that gray eyes were keenest, and that all famous marksmen had them. Nevertheless, this one had missed.

A counterswirl had caught Farquhar and turned him half round; he was again looking into the forest on the bank opposite the fort. The sound of a clear, high voice in a monotonous singsong now rang out behind him and came across the water with distinctness that pierced and subdued all other sounds, even the beating of the ripples in his ears. Although no soldier, he had frequented camps enough to know the dread significance of that deliberate, drawling, aspirated chant; the lieutenant on shore was taking part in the morning's work. How coldly and pitilessly—with what an even, calm intonation, presaging and enforcing tranquillity in the men—with what accurately measured intervals fell those cruel words:

"Attention, company!. . . Shoulder arms! . . . Ready! . . . Aim! . . . Fire!"

Farquhar dived—dived as deeply as he could. The water roared in his ears like the voice of Niagara, yet he heard the dulled thunder of the volley and, rising again toward the surface, met shining bits of metal, singularly flattened, oscillating slowly downward. Some of them touched him on the face and hands, then fell away, continuing their descent. One lodged between his collar and his neck; it was uncomfortably warm and he snatched it out.

As he rose to the surface, gasping for breath, he saw that he had been a long time under water; he was perceptibly farther downstream—nearer to safety. The soldiers had almost finished reloading; the metal ramrods flashed all at once in the sunshine as they were drawn from the barrels, turned in the air, and thrust into their sockets. The two sentinels fired again, independently and ineffectually.

The hunted man saw all this over his shoulder; he was now swimming vigorously with the current. His brain was as energetic as his arms and legs; he thought with the rapidity of lightning.

"The officer," he reasoned, "will not make that martinet's error a second time. It is as easy to dodge a volley as a single shot. He has probably already given the command to fire at will. God help me, I cannot dodge them all!"

An appalling plash within two yards of him was followed by a loud, rushing sound, *diminuendo,*[3] which seemed to travel back through the air to the fort and died in an explosion which stirred the very river to its deeps! A rising sheet of water, which curved over him, fell down upon him, blinded him, strangled him! The cannon had taken a hand in the game. As he shook his head free from the commotion of the smitten water, he heard the deflected shot humming through the air ahead, and in an instant it was cracking and smashing the branches in the forest beyond.

"They will not do that again," he thought; "the next time they will use a charge of grape.[4] I must keep my eye upon the gun; the smoke will apprise me—the report arrives too late; it lags behind the missile. That is a good gun."

Suddenly he felt himself whirled round and round—spinning like a top. The water, the banks, the forests, the now distant bridge, fort, and men—all were commingled and blurred. Objects were represented by their colors only; circular horizontal streaks of color—that was all he saw. He had been caught in a vortex and was being whirled on with a velocity of advance and gyration which made him giddy and sick. In a few moments he was flung upon the gravel at the foot of the left bank of the stream—the southern bank—and behind a projecting point which concealed him from his enemies. The sudden arrest of his motion, the abrasion of one of his hands on the gravel, restored him, and he wept with delight. He dug his fingers into the sand, threw it over himself in handfuls, and audibly blessed it. It looked like gold, like diamonds, rubies, emeralds; he could think of nothing beautiful which it did not resemble. The trees upon the bank were giant garden plants; he noted a definite order in their arrangement, inhaled the fragrance of their blooms. A strange, roseate light shone through the spaces among their trunks and the wind made in their branches the music of aeolian harps.[5] He had no wish to perfect his escape—was content to remain in that enchanting spot until retaken.

A whiz and rattle of grapeshot among the branches high above his head roused him from his dream. The baffled cannoneer had fired him a random farewell. He sprang to his feet, rushed up the sloping bank, and plunged into the forest.

All that day he traveled, laying his course by the rounding sun. The forest seemed interminable; nowhere did he discover a break in it, not even a woodman's road. He had not known that he lived in so wild a region. There was something uncanny in the revelation.

By nightfall he was fatigued, footsore, famishing. The thought of his wife and children urged him on. At last he found a road which led him in what he knew to be the right direction. It was wide and straight as a city street, yet it seemed untraveled. No fields bordered it, no dwelling anywhere. Not so much as the barking of a dog suggested human habitation. The black bodies of the great trees formed a straight wall on both sides, terminating on the horizon in a point, like a diagram in a lesson in perspective. Overhead, as he

[3]Italian: diminishing in volume.

[4]Grapeshot, a cluster of iron balls fired from a cannon.

[5]Stringed instruments that sound when exposed to the wind.

looked up through this rift in the wood, shone great golden stars looking unfamiliar and grouped in strange constellations. He was sure they were arranged in some order which had a secret and malign significance. The wood on either side was full of singular noises, among which—once, twice, and again—he distinctly heard whispers in an unknown tongue.

His neck was in pain and lifting his hand to it he found it horribly swollen. He knew that it had a circle of black where the rope had bruised it. His eyes felt congested; he could no longer close them. His tongue was swollen with thirst; he relieved its fever by thrusting it forward from between his teeth into the cool air. How softly the turf had carpeted the untraveled avenue—he could no longer feel the roadway beneath his feet!

Doubtless, despite his suffering, he had fallen asleep while walking, for now he sees another scene—perhaps he has merely recovered from a delirium. He stands at the gate of his own home. All is as he left it, and all bright and beautiful in the morning sunshine. He must have traveled the entire night. As he pushes open the gate and passes up the wide white walk, he sees a flutter of female garments; his wife, looking fresh and cool and sweet, steps down from the veranda to meet him. At the bottom of the steps she stands waiting, with a smile of ineffable joy, an attitude of matchless grace and dignity. Ah, how beautiful she is! He springs forward with extended arms. As he is about to clasp her, he feels a stunning blow upon the back of the neck; a blinding white light blazes all about him with a sound like the shock of a cannon—then all is darkness and silence!

Peyton Farquhar was dead; his body, with a broken neck, swung gently from side to side beneath the timbers of the Owl Creek bridge.

1890, 1891

Charlotte Perkins Gilman 1860–1935

Like the heroine of her finest short story, "The Yellow Wall-Paper," Charlotte Perkins Gilman saw the world as a place where individual lives are often smothered by the power of convention and authority. Her own life was marred by an unhappy childhood, an ill-fated first marriage, recurring mental breakdowns, and public rejection of the social reforms for which she wrote and spoke. Yet, in the last half of the twentieth century, many of the ideals to which she devoted her life have become a part of the nation's fabric of beliefs, and she is now recognized as a vital force in the history of reform in the United States.

She was born Charlotte Perkins in Hartford, Connecticut. Among her ancestors were the renowned New England preacher Henry Ward Beecher and the most famous woman of nineteenth-century America, Harriet Beecher Stowe, the author of Uncle Tom's Cabin. *Charlotte Perkins seemed destined for a genteel and congenial New England upbringing, but shortly after her birth, her father abandoned his family, leaving his wife and children to lives strained by poverty and emotional deprivation.*

As a result, Charlotte Perkins received little formal education. But she was an avid reader of history and literature, and she had a natural talent for art. After a brief period of study at the Rhode Island School of Design, in Providence, she established herself as a designer of advertising cards for businesses. Later she worked as a children's tutor. And she began to write.

Her first publication, a poem, appeared in 1880. Three years later she published a short article in the Providence Journal. *In the following year she married a fellow artist, Charles Stetson, but the marriage was a failure almost from the start. Charlotte Perkins Stetson rejected the submissive role deemed proper for nineteenth-century married women. She refused to subside into a life solely devoted to the wifely duties of housekeeping, childrearing, and obedience to her husband. Instead, she focused her energies on painting and on writing poems, essays, and short stories.*

In 1884, the year of her marriage, her second poem was published. Entitled "In Duty Bound," it began, significantly enough, "In duty bound, a life hemmed in . . . ." And for the rest of her life, her writing reflected the belief that the patriarchal culture surrounding her was one that denigrated women, hemmed them in, thwarted their natural desires for intellectual growth and expression.

Oppressed by her unhappy marriage, she suffered periodic sieges of mental depression, and she was taken to the celebrated physician Silas Weir Mitchell, a neurologist known for his "rest-cure" for nervous disorders. The "rest-cure" prescribed for Charlotte Stetson required her isolation from just those modes of self-expression and intellectual growth that had sustained her sense of independence. She was told never again to write, never to paint, never to read for more than two hours a day.

It was the most advanced medical treatment of the age, and its ideal of the tranquilized mental patient anticipated much psychiatric therapy of the late twentieth century. But Charlotte Perkins Stetson saw that her sanity lay not in submission to her physician or her husband but in her freedom and independence. In 1888, to escape her "rest-cure" and her marriage, she moved to California, where she divorced her husband and helped support herself by running a boarding house.

Free of the constraints of marriage, she began to speak out boldly on political and social issues. She wrote and lectured on women's rights and argued for a utopian socialism that would end social injustice. Soon women's clubs and church groups began to seek her out as a lecturer. More and more magazines and newspapers published her essays and articles.

In 1900, she married George Gilman. It was a successful marriage—her new husband shared many of her social and political views—and she now wrote as Charlotte Perkins Gilman, but she continued her crusade for women's rights. From 1889 to 1891, she wrote for the Pacific Monthly, *a journal of social and political commentary published in Los Angeles. Later she edited* The Impress, *a journal of the Pacific Coast Women's Association, and from 1909 to 1916 she published and edited* The Forerunner, *a monthly magazine for which she wrote almost the entire contents—editorials, stories, articles, book reviews, poems, even the advertisements.*

For five years in the 1890s, Charlotte Perkins Gilman toured America as a lecturer, arguing that women were dominated by their fathers and husbands, that women were entrapped by their innocence and their upbringing. She insisted that home was more often a prison than a shelter, and she encouraged women to assert their rights and free themselves from unthinking devotion to cooking, cleaning, church, and children.

Censorious critics said that she "despised the home" more than any other American. They denounced her as a "man-hater" and argued that her feminism and her assaults on masculinity were revenge against the father who had abandoned her as a child. Later critics have pointed out that her sympathies were primarily for middle-class women and that she showed little concern for the destitute, for minorities, or for the millions of immigrants struggling to survive in late nineteenth-century America.

In part the criticism came because Charlotte Perkins Gilman was so effective and so untiring a worker for reform. In recent years she has been called one of the "ancestral mothers" of the modern feminist movement, but she wrote prolifically on a wide variety of political, social, and economic topics: poverty, health care, civil justice, the rights of labor. She published more than a thousand articles in addition to short stories, novels, and hundreds of poems. Her most significant book, Women and Economics *(1898), is a lengthy study of the ways in which male dominance was reinforced by the economic system of her society. A popular success, and widely influential in the 1890s, the book's arguments remain cogent today, more than a century after its publication.*

Charlotte Perkins Gilman said that she wrote not to create literature but to improve the world, and she was most effective as an ideologue and a polemicist. Much of her writing was hasty—a quick response to the questions of the day. Her fiction was often stereotyped, repetitious stories of women who take charge of their lives, break the restraints imposed by a "masculinist" society, and are thereby destined to live happily ever after.

But in "The Yellow Wall-Paper" she created a story of complex literary artistry. It has been called one of the best horror stories of the nineteenth century, and it has many of the elements of gothic horror tales: the female in distress, the isolated mansion, the locked room, the threat of masculine torment.

In writing the story, Charlotte Perkins Gilman had drawn on her experience with mental illness. "The Yellow Wall-Paper" was, in part, her retaliation for the suffering she had experienced. Her own explanation was that she wrote the story to expose the mistakes made by medical science in treating the insane. But "The Yellow Wall-Paper" is more than a frightening tale, more than an effort to redress a grievance or correct therapeutic errors. It anticipates the psychological fiction of the twentieth century in its portrayal of alienation and of misunderstood suffering in a complacent society. It foreshadows the modern world's preoccupation with psychosis, distorted perceptions, receding distinctions between reality and hallucination. It is a surrealist picture of a tormented, isolated individual, and it is a call for understanding of a woman lost in a world without comprehension or memory, writhing in the tangles of madness and dead hope.

FURTHER READING: *The Living of Charlotte Perkins Gilman, An Autobiography*, 1935; *The Charlotte Perkins Gilman Reader*, ed. A. Lane, 1980; M. Hill, *Charlotte Perkins Gilman, The Making of a Radical Feminist*, 1980; B. Winkler, *Victorian Daughters*, 1980; G. Scharnhorst, *Charlotte Perkins Gilman*, 1985; P. Allen, *Building Domestic Liberty, Charlotte Perkins Gilman's Architectural Feminism*, 1988; A. Lane, *To Herland and Beyond, The Life and Work of Charlotte Perkins Gilman*, 1990; *The Diaries of Charlotte Perkins Gilman*, 2 vols., ed. D. Knight, 1993; *Critical Essays on Charlotte Perkins Gilman*, ed. J. Karpinski, 1993; C. Kessler, *Charlotte Perkins Gilman, Her Progress toward Utopia*, 1995; *Charlotte Perkins Gilman and Her Contemporaries*, ed. C. Davis and J. Knight, 2004.

TEXT: "The Yellow Wall-Paper," *New England Magazine*, January 1892.

THE YELLOW WALL-PAPER[1]

It is very seldom that mere ordinary people like John and myself secure ancestral halls for the summer.

A colonial mansion, a hereditary estate, I would say a haunted house, and reach the height of romantic felicity—but that would be asking too much of fate!

Still I will proudly declare that there is something queer about it.

Else, why should it be let so cheaply? And why have stood so long untenanted?

John laughs at me, of course, but one expects that in marriage.

John is practical in the extreme. He has no patience with faith, an intense horror of superstition, and he scoffs openly at any talk of things not to be felt and seen and put down in figures.

John is a physician, and *perhaps*—(I would not say it to a living soul, of course, but this is dead paper and a great relief to my mind—) *perhaps* that is one reason I do not get well faster.

You see he does not believe I am sick!

And what can one do?

If a physician of high standing, and one's own husband, assures friends and relatives that there is really nothing the matter with one but temporary nervous depression—a slight hysterical tendency—what is one to do?

My brother is also a physician, and also of high standing, and he says the same thing.

So I take phosphates or phosphites[2]—whichever it is, and tonics, and journeys, and air, and exercise, and am absolutely forbidden to "work" until I am well again.

Personally, I disagree with their ideas.

Personally, I believe that congenial work, with excitement and change, would do me good.

But what is one to do?

I did write for a while in spite of them; but it *does* exhaust me a good deal—having to be so sly about it, or else meet with heavy opposition.

I sometimes fancy that in my condition if I had less opposition and more society and stimulus—but John says the very worst thing I can do is to think about my condition, and I confess it always makes me feel bad.

So I will let it alone and talk about the house.

The most beautiful place! It is quite alone, standing well back from the road, quite three miles from the village. It makes me think of English places that you read about, for there are hedges and walls and gates that lock, and lots of separate little houses for the gardeners and people.

There is a *delicious* garden! I never saw such a garden—large and shady, full of box-bordered[3] paths, and lined with long grape-covered arbors with seats under them.

[1]The variant spellings of "wall-paper" in the first, 1892, printing of the story are preserved here. Some typographical errors and misspellings have been silently corrected.

[2]Carbonated water and acid phosphate, flavored with a fruit syrup.

[3]I.e., with borders of box, an evergreen shrub.

There were greenhouses, too, but they are all broken now.

There was some legal trouble, I believe, something about the heirs and coheirs; anyhow, the place has been empty for years.

That spoils my ghostliness, I am afraid, but I don't care—there is something strange about the house—I can feel it.

I even said so to John one moonlight evening, but he said what I felt was a *draught,* and shut the window.

I get unreasonably angry with John sometimes. I'm sure I never used to be so sensitive. I think it is due to this nervous condition.

But John says if I feel so, I shall neglect proper self-control; so I take pains to control myself—before him, at least, and that makes me very tired.

I don't like our room a bit. I wanted one downstairs that opened on the piazza and had roses all over the window, and such pretty old-fashioned chintz hangings! but John would not hear of it.

He said there was only one window and not room for two beds, and no near room for him if he took another.

He is very careful and loving, and hardly lets me stir without special direction.

I have a schedule prescription for each hour in the day; he takes all care from me, and so I feel basely ungrateful not to value it more.

He said we came here solely on my account, that I was to have perfect rest and all the air I could get. "Your exercise depends on your strength, my dear," said he, "and your food somewhat on your appetite; but air you can absorb all the time." So we took the nursery at the top of the house.

It is a big, airy room, the whole floor nearly, with windows that look all ways, and air and sunshine galore. It was nursery first and then playroom and gymnasium, I should judge; for the windows are barred for little children, and there are rings and things in the walls.

The paint and paper look as if a boys' school had used it. It is stripped off—the paper—in great patches all around the head of my bed, about as far as I can reach, and in a great place on the other side of the room low down. I never saw a worse paper in my life.

One of those sprawling flamboyant patterns committing every artistic sin.

It is dull enough to confuse the eye in following, pronounced enough to constantly irritate and provoke study, and when you follow the lame uncertain curves for a little distance they suddenly commit suicide—plunge off at outrageous angles, destroy themselves in unheard of contradictions.

The color is repellant, almost revolting; a smouldering unclean yellow, strangely faded by the slow-turning sunlight.

It is a dull yet lurid orange in some places, a sickly sulphur tint in others.

No wonder the children hated it! I should hate it myself if I had to live in this room long.

There comes John, and I must put this away,—he hates to have me write a word.

* * * * * *

We have been here two weeks, and I haven't felt like writing before, since that first day.

I am sitting by the window now, up in this atrocious nursery, and there is nothing to hinder my writing as much as I please, save lack of strength.

John is away all day, and even some nights when his cases are serious.

I am glad my case is not serious!

But these nervous troubles are dreadfully depressing.

John does not know how much I really suffer. He knows there is no *reason* to suffer, and that satisfies him.

Of course it is only nervousness. It does weigh on me so not to do my duty in any way!

I meant to be such a help to John, such a real rest and comfort, and here I am a comparative burden already!

Nobody would believe what an effort it is to do what little I am able,—to dress and entertain, and order things.

It is fortunate Mary is so good with the baby. Such a dear baby!

And yet I *cannot* be with him, it makes me so nervous.

I suppose John never was nervous in his life. He laughs at me so about this wall-paper!

At first he meant to repaper the room, but afterwards he said that I was letting it get the better of me, and that nothing was worse for a nervous patient than to give way to such fancies.

He said that after the wall-paper was changed it would be the heavy bedstead, and then the barred windows, and then that gate at the head of the stairs, and so on.

"You know the place is doing you good," he said, "and really, dear, I don't care to renovate the house just for a three months' rental."

"Then do let us go downstairs," I said, "there are such pretty rooms there."

Then he took me in his arms and called me a blessed little goose, and said he would go down cellar, if I wished, and have it whitewashed into the bargain.

But he is right enough about the beds and windows and things.

It is an airy and comfortable room as any one need wish, and, of course, I would not be so silly as to make him uncomfortable just for a whim.

I'm really getting quite fond of the big room, all but that horrid paper.

Out of one window I can see the garden, those mysterious deep-shaded arbors, the riotous old-fashioned flowers, and bushes and gnarly trees.

Out of another I get a lovely view of the bay and a little private wharf belonging to the estate. There is a beautiful shaded lane that runs down there from the house. I always fancy I see people walking in these numerous paths and arbors, but John has cautioned me not to give way to fancy in the least. He says that with my imaginative power and habit of story-making, a nervous weakness like mine is sure to lead to all manner of excited fancies, and that I ought to use my will and good sense to check the tendency. So I try.

I think sometimes that if I were only well enough to write a little it would relieve the press of ideas and rest me.

But I find I get pretty tired when I try.

It is so discouraging not to have any advice and companionship about my work. When I get really well, John says we will ask Cousin Henry and Julia down for a long visit; but he says he would as soon put fireworks in my pillow-case as to let me have those stimulating people about now.

I wish I could get well faster.

But I must not think about that. This paper looks to me as if it *knew* what a vicious influence it had!

There is a recurrent spot where the pattern lolls like a broken neck and two bulbous eyes stare at you upside down.

I get positively angry with the impertinence of it and the everlastingness. Up and down and sideways they crawl, and those absurd, unblinking eyes are everywhere. There is one place where two breadths didn't match, and the eyes go all up and down the line, one a little higher than the other.

I never saw so much expression in an inanimate thing before, and we all know how much expression they have! I used to lie awake as a child and get more entertainment and terror out of blank walls and plain furniture than most children could find in a toy-store.

I remember what a kindly wink the knobs of our big, old bureau used to have, and there was one chair that always seemed like a strong friend.

I used to feel that if any of the other things looked too fierce I could always hop into that chair and be safe.

The furniture in this room is no worse than inharmonious, however, for we had to bring it all from downstairs. I suppose when this was used as a playroom they had to take the nursery things out, and no wonder! I never saw such ravages as the children have made here.

The wall-paper, as I said before, is torn off in spots, and it sticketh closer than a brother[4]—they must have had perseverance as well as hatred.

Then the floor is scratched and gouged and splintered, the plaster itself is dug out here and there, and this great heavy bed which is all we found in the room, looks as if it had been through the wars.

But I don't mind it a bit—only the paper.

There comes John's sister. Such a dear girl as she is, and so careful of me! I must not let her find me writing.

She is a perfect and enthusiastic housekeeper, and hopes for no better profession. I verily believe she thinks it is the writing which made me sick!

But I can write when she is out, and see her a long way off from these windows.

There is one that commands the road, a lovely shaded winding road, and one that just looks off over the country. A lovely country, too, full of great elms and velvet meadows.

This wallpaper has a kind of subpattern in a different shade, a particularly irritating one, for you can only see it in certain lights, and not clearly then.

But in the places where it isn't faded and where the sun is just so—I can see a strange, provoking, formless sort of figure, that seems to skulk about behind that silly and conspicuous front design.

There's sister on the stairs!

* * * * * *

Well, the Fourth of July is over! The people are all gone and I am tired out. John thought it might do me good to see a little company, so we just had mother and Nellie and the children down for a week.

Of course I didn't do a thing. Jennie sees to everything now.

But it tired me all the same.

[4] "There is a friend that sticketh closer than a brother" (Proverbs 18:24).

John says if I don't pick up faster he shall send me to Weir Mitchell[5] in the fall.

But I don't want to go there at all. I had a friend who was in his hands once, and she says he is just like John and my brother, only more so!

Besides, it is such an undertaking to go so far.

I don't feel as if it was worth while to turn my hand over for anything, and I'm getting dreadfully fretful and querulous.

I cry at nothing, and cry most of the time.

Of course I don't when John is here, or anybody else, but when I am alone.

And I am alone a good deal just now. John is kept in town very often by serious cases, and Jennie is good and lets me alone when I want her to.

So I walk a little in the garden or down that lovely lane, sit on the porch under the roses, and lie down up here a good deal.

I'm getting really fond of the room in spite of the wallpaper. Perhaps *because* of the wallpaper.

It dwells in my mind so!

I lie here on this great immovable bed—it is nailed down, I believe—and follow that pattern about by the hour. It is as good as gymnastics, I assure you. I start, we'll say, at the bottom, down in the corner over there where it has not been touched, and I determine for the thousandth time that I *will* follow that pointless pattern to some sort of a conclusion.

I know a little of the principle of design, and I know this thing was not arranged on any laws of radiation, or alternation, or repetition, or symmetry, or anything else that I ever heard of.

It is repeated, of course, by the breadths, but not otherwise.

Looked at in one way each breadth stands alone, the bloated curves and flourishes—a kind of "debased Romanesque"[6] with *delirium tremens*[7]—go waddling up and down in isolated columns of fatuity.

But, on the other hand, they connect diagonally, and the sprawling outlines run off in great slanting waves of optic horror, like a lot of wallowing seaweeds in full chase.

The whole thing goes horizontally, too, at least it seems so, and I exhaust myself in trying to distinguish the order of its going in that direction.

They have used a horizontal breadth for a frieze, and that adds wonderfully to the confusion.

There is one end of the room where it is almost intact, and there, when the crosslights fade and the low sun shines directly upon it, I can almost fancy radiation after all,—the interminable grotesque seem to form around a common center and rush off in headlong plunges of equal distraction.

It makes me tired to follow it. I will take a nap I guess.

* * * * * *

I don't know why I should write this.

I don't want to.

[5]Silas Weir Mitchell (1829–1914), American physician known for his "rest-cure" treatment of "nervous disorders."

[6]Ornate style of architecture marked by curves and rounded arches.

[7]A violent mental disturbance accompanied by hallucinations, caused by alcoholism.

I don't feel able.

And I know John would think it absurd. But I *must* say what I feel and think in some way—it is such a relief!

But the effort is getting to be greater than the relief.

Half the time now I am awfully lazy, and lie down ever so much.

John says I mustn't lose my strength, and has me take cod liver oil and lots of tonics and things, to say nothing of ale and wine and rare meat.

Dear John! He loves me very dearly, and hates to have me sick. I tried to have a real earnest reasonable talk with him the other day, and tell him how I wish he would let me go and make a visit to Cousin Henry and Julia.

But he said I wasn't able to go, nor able to stand it after I got there; and I did not make out a very good case for myself, for I was crying before I had finished.

It is getting to be a great effort for me to think straight. Just this nervous weakness I suppose.

And dear John gathered me up in his arms, and just carried me upstairs and laid me on the bed, and sat by me and read to me till it tired my head.

He said I was his darling and his comfort and all he had, and that I must take care of myself for his sake, and keep well.

He says no one but myself can help me out of it, that I must use my will and self-control and not let any silly fancies run away with me.

There's one comfort, the baby is well and happy, and does not have to occupy this nursery with the horrid wallpaper.

If we had not used it, that blessed child would have! What a fortunate escape! Why, I wouldn't have a child of mine, an impressionable little thing, live in such a room for worlds.

I never thought of it before, but it is lucky that John kept me here after all, I can stand it so much easier than a baby, you see.

Of course I never mention it to them any more—I am too wise,—but I keep watch of it all the same.

There are things in that paper that nobody knows but me, or ever will.

Behind that outside pattern the dim shapes get clearer every day.

It is always the same shape, only very numerous.

And it is like a woman stooping down and creeping about behind that pattern. I don't like it a bit. I wonder—I begin to think—I wish John would take me away from here!

* * * * * *

It is so hard to talk with John about my case, because he is so wise, and because he loves me so.

But I tried it last night.

It was moonlight. The moon shines in all around just as the sun does.

I hate to see it sometimes, it creeps so slowly, and always comes in by one window or another.

John was asleep and I hated to waken him, so I kept still and watched the moonlight on that undulating wallpaper till I felt creepy.

The faint figure behind seemed to shake the pattern, just as if she wanted to get out.

I got up softly and went to feel and see if the paper *did* move, and when I came back John was awake.

"What is it, little girl?" he said. "Don't go walking about like that—you'll get cold."

I thought it was a good time to talk, so I told him that I really was not gaining here, and that I wished he would take me away.

"Why, darling!" said he, "our lease will be up in three weeks, and I can't see how to leave before.

"The repairs are not done at home, and I cannot possibly leave town just now. Of course if you were in any danger, I could and would, but you really are better, dear, whether you can see it or not. I am a doctor, dear, and I know. You are gaining flesh and color, your appetite is better, I feel really much easier about you."

"I don't weigh a bit more," said I, "nor as much; and my appetite may be better in the evening when you are here, but it is worse in the morning when you are away?"

"Bless her little heart!" said he with a big hug, "she shall be as sick as she pleases! But now let's improve the shining hours[8] by going to sleep, and talk about it in the morning!"

"And you won't go away?" I asked gloomily.

"Why, how can I dear? It is only three weeks more and then we will take a nice little trip of a few days while Jennie is getting the house ready. Really dear you are better!"

"Better in body perhaps—" I began, and stopped short, for he sat up straight and looked at me with such a stern, reproachful look that I could not say another word.

"My darling," said he, "I beg of you, for my sake and for our child's sake, as well as for your own, that you will never for one instant let that idea enter your mind! There is nothing so dangerous, so fascinating, to a temperament like yours. It is a false and foolish fancy. Can you not trust me as a physician when I tell you so?"

So of course I said no more on that score, and we went to sleep before long. He thought I was asleep first, but I wasn't, and lay there for hours trying to decide whether that front pattern and the back pattern really did move together or separately.

* * * * * *

On a pattern like this, by daylight, there is a lack of sequence, a defiance of law, that is a constant irritant to a normal mind.

The color is hideous enough, and unreliable enough, and infuriating enough, but the pattern is torturing.

You think you have mastered it, but just as you get well underway in following, it turns a back-somersault and there you are. It slaps you in the face, knocks you down, and tramples upon you. It is like a bad dream.

[8]An adaptation of "Song XX" from *The Divine Songs* of Isaac Watts (1674–1748), English hymnist:

How doth the little busy bee
Improve each shining hour,
And gather honey all the day
From every opening flower.

The outside pattern is a florid arabesque, reminding one of a fungus. If you can imagine a toadstool in joints, an interminable string of toadstools, budding and sprouting in endless convolutions—why, that is something like it.

That is, sometimes!

There is one marked peculiarity about this paper, a thing nobody seems to notice but myself, and that is that it changes as the light changes.

When the sun shoots in through the east window—I always watch for that first long, straight ray—it changes so quickly that I never can quite believe it.

That is why I watch it always.

By moonlight—the moon shines in all night when there is a moon—I wouldn't know it was the same paper.

At night in any kind of light, in twilight, candlelight, lamplight, and worst of all by moonlight, it becomes bars! The outside pattern I mean, and the woman behind it is as plain as can be.

I didn't realize for a long time what the thing was that showed behind, that dim sub-pattern, but now I am quite sure it is a woman.

By daylight she is subdued, quiet. I fancy it is the pattern that keeps her so still. It is so puzzling. It keeps me quiet by the hour.

I lie down ever so much now. John says it is good for me, and to sleep all I can.

Indeed he started the habit by making me lie down for an hour after each meal.

It is a very bad habit I am convinced, for you see I don't sleep.

And that cultivates deceit, for I don't tell them I'm awake—O no!

The fact is I am getting a little afraid of John.

He seems very queer sometimes, and even Jennie has an inexplicable look.

It strikes me occasionally, just as a scientific hypothesis,—that perhaps it is the paper!

I have watched John when he did not know I was looking, and come into the room suddenly on the most innocent excuses, and I've caught him several times *looking at the paper!* And Jennie too. I caught Jennie with her hand on it once.

She didn't know I was in the room, and when I asked her in a quiet, a very quiet voice, with the most restrained manner possible, what she was doing with the paper—she turned around as if she had been caught stealing, and looked quite angry—asked me why I should frighten her so!

Then she said that the paper stained everything it touched, that she had found yellow smooches[9] on all my clothes and John's, and she wished we would be more careful!

Did not that sound innocent? But I know she was studying that pattern, and I am determined that nobody shall find it out but myself.

* * * * * *

Life is very much more exciting now than it used to be. You see I have something more to expect, to look forward to, to watch. I really do eat better, and am more quiet than I was.

John is so pleased to see me improve! He laughed a little the other day, and said I seemed to be flourishing in spite of my wall-paper.

[9]Smudges, smears.

I turned it off with a laugh. I had no intention of telling him it was *because* of the wall-paper—he would make fun of me. He might even want to take me away.

I don't want to leave now until I have found it out. There is a week more, and I think that will be enough.

* * * * * *

I'm feeling ever so much better! I don't sleep much at night, for it is so interesting to watch developments; but I sleep a good deal in the daytime.

In the daytime it is tiresome and perplexing.

There are always new shoots on the fungus, and new shades of yellow all over it. I cannot keep count of them, though I have tried conscientiously.

It is the strangest yellow, that wall-paper! It makes me think of all the yellow things I every saw—not beautiful ones like buttercups, but old foul, bad yellow things.

But there is something else about that paper—the smell! I noticed it the moment we came into the room, but with so much air and sun it was not bad. Now we have had a week of fog and rain, and whether the windows are open or not, the smell is here.

It creeps all over the house.

I find it hovering in the dining-room, skulking in the parlor, hiding in the hall, lying in wait for me on the stairs.

It gets into my hair.

Even when I go to ride, if I turn my head suddenly and surprise it—there is that smell!

Such a peculiar odor, too! I have spent hours in trying to analyze it, to find what it smelled like.

It is not bad—at first, and very gentle, but quite the subtlest, most enduring odor I ever met.

In this damp weather it is awful, I wake up in the night and find it hanging over me.

It used to disturb me at first. I thought seriously of burning the house—to reach the smell.

But now I am used to it. The only thing I can think of that it is like is the *color* of the paper! A yellow smell.

There is a very funny mark on this wall, low down, near the mopboard. A streak that runs round the room. It goes behind every piece of furniture, except the bed, a long straight, even *smooch,* as if it had been rubbed over and over.

I wonder how it was done and who did it, and what they did it for. Round and round and round—round and round and round—it makes me dizzy!

* * * * * *

I really have discovered something at last.

Through watching so much at night, when it changes so, I have finally found out.

The front pattern *does* move—and no wonder! The woman behind shakes it!

Sometimes I think there are a great many women behind, and sometimes only one, and she crawls around fast, and her crawling shakes it all over.

Then in the very bright spots she keeps still, and in the very shady spots she just takes hold of the bars and shakes them hard.

And she is all the time trying to climb through. But nobody could climb through that pattern—it strangles so; I think that is why it has so many heads.

They get through, and then the pattern strangles them off and turns them upside down, and makes their eyes white!

If those heads were covered or taken off it would not be half so bad.

* * * * * *

I think that woman gets out in the daytime!

And I'll tell you why—privately—I've seen her!

I can see her out of every one of my windows!

It is the same woman, I know, for she is always creeping, and most women do not creep by daylight.

I see her in that long shaded lane, creeping up and down. I see her in those dark grape arbors, creeping all around the garden.

I see her on that long road under the trees creeping along, and when a carriage comes she hides under the blackberry vines.

I don't blame her a bit. It must be very humiliating to be caught creeping by daylight!

I always lock the door when I creep by daylight. I can't do it at night, for I know John would suspect something at once.

And John is so queer now, that I don't want to irritate him. I wish he would take another room! Besides, I don't want anybody to get that woman out at night but myself.

I often wonder if I could see her out of all the windows at once.

But, turn as fast as I can, I can only see out of one at one time.

And though I always see her, she *may* be able to creep faster than I can turn!

I have watched her sometimes away off in the open country, creeping as fast as a cloud shadow in a high wind.

* * * * * *

If only that top pattern could be gotten off from the under one! I mean to try it, little by little.

I have found out another funny thing, but I shan't tell it this time! It does not do to trust people too much.

There are only two more days to get this paper off, and I believe John is beginning to notice. I don't like the look in his eyes.

And I heard him ask Jennie a lot of professional questions about me. She had a very good report to give.

She said I slept a good deal in the daytime.

John knows I don't sleep very well at night, for all I'm so quiet!

He asked me all sorts of questions, too, and pretended to be very loving and kind.

As if I couldn't see through him!

Still, I don't wonder he acts so, sleeping under this paper for three months.

It only interests me, but I feel sure John and Jennie are secretly affected by it.

* * * * * *

Hurrah! This is the last day, but it is enough. John to stay in town over night, and won't be out until this evening.

Jennie wanted to sleep with me—the sly thing! But I told her I should undoubtedly rest better for a night all alone.

That was clever, for really I wasn't alone a bit! As soon as it was moonlight and that poor thing began to crawl and shake the pattern, I got up and ran to help her.

I pulled and she shook, I shook and she pulled, and before morning we had peeled off yards of that paper.

A strip about as high as my head and half around the room.

And then when the sun came and that awful pattern began to laugh at me, I declared I would finish it to-day!

We go away to-morrow, and they are moving all my furniture down again to leave things as they were before.

Jennie looked at the wall in amazement, but I told her merrily that I did it out of pure spite at the vicious thing.

She laughed and said she wouldn't mind doing it herself, but I must not get tired.

How she betrayed herself that time!

But I am here, and no person touches this paper but me,—not *alive!*

She tried to get me out of the room—it was too patent! But I said it was so quiet and empty and clean now that I believed I would lie down again and sleep all I could; and not to wake me even for dinner—I would call when I woke.

So now she is gone, and the servants are gone, and the things are gone, and there is nothing left but that great bedstead nailed down, with the canvas mattress we found on it.

We shall sleep downstairs to-night, and take the boat home to-morrow.

I quite enjoy the room, now it is bare again.

How those children did tear about here!

This bedstead is fairly gnawed!

But I must get to work.

I have locked the door and thrown the key down into the front path.

I don't want to go out, and I don't want to have anybody come in, till John comes.

I want to astonish him.

I've got a rope up here that even Jennie did not find. If that woman does get out, and tries to get away, I can tie her!

But I forgot I could not reach far without anything to stand on!

This bed will *not* move!

I tried to lift and push it until I was lame, and then I got so angry I bit off a little piece at one corner—but it hurt my teeth.

Then I peeled off all the paper I could reach standing on the floor. It sticks horribly and the pattern just enjoys it! All those strangled heads and bulbous eyes and waddling fungus growths just shriek with derision!

I am getting angry enough to do something desperate. To jump out of the window would be admirable exercise, but the bars are too strong even to try.

Besides I wouldn't do it. Of course not. I know well enough that a step like that is improper and might be misconstrued.

I don't like to *look* out of the windows even—there are so many of those creeping women, and they creep so fast.

I wonder if they all come out of that wall-paper as I did?

But I am securely fastened now by my well-hidden rope—you don't get *me* out in the road there!

I suppose I shall have to get back behind the pattern when it comes night, and that is hard!

It is so pleasant to be out in this great room and creep around as I please!

I don't want to go outside. I won't, even if Jennie asks me to.

For outside you have to creep on the ground, and everything is green instead of yellow.

But here I can creep smoothly on the floor, and my shoulder just fits in that long smooch around the wall, so I cannot lose my way.

Why there's John at the door!

It is no use, young man, you can't open it!

How he does call and pound!

Now he's crying for an axe.

It would be a shame to break down that beautiful door!

"John dear!" said I in the gentlest voice, "the key is down by the front steps, under a plantain leaf!"

That silenced him for a few moments.

Then he said—very quietly indeed, "Open the door, my darling!"

"I can't," said I. "The key is down by the front door under a plantain leaf!

And then I said it again, several times, very gently and slowly, and said it so often that he had to go and see, and he got it of course, and came in. He stopped short by the door.

"What is the matter?" he cried. "For God's sake, what are you doing!"

I kept on creeping just the same, but I looked at him over my shoulder.

"I've got out at last," said I, "in spite of you and Jane? And I've pulled off most of the paper, so you can't put me back!"

Now why should that man have fainted? But he did, and right across my path by the wall, so that I had to creep over him every time!

Kate Chopin 1851–1904

Although she became famous for her Louisiana dialect stories, Kate Chopin was born and lived most of her life in St. Louis, Missouri. As the daughter of Eliza and Thomas O'Flaherty, an Irish immigrant who had become a rich merchant in St. Louis, she was educated in a Roman Catholic convent school, learned fluent French, and became "one of the acknowledged belles" of society. At the age of nineteen she married Oscar Chopin (the name was pronounced in the French manner), and went to live in New Orleans, the picturesque and cosmopolitan city dominated by French Creole culture.

In 1879, after a decade in New Orleans, Oscar Chopin's business failed, and he moved his family to central Louisiana, where he managed plantations and ran a village store. In 1882 he died of swamp fever, and two years later Kate Chopin returned with her six children to St. Louis. Financially independent, bored with life as a society matron, she began to write poetry, sketches, and fiction dealing with Louisiana Creoles (descendants of early French and Spanish colonists), Cajuns (whose French ancestors had been exiled to Louisiana from Acadia in Canada in the eighteenth century), and the blacks and mixed-race Indians of the cities and back country.

In 1889 she began a novel, At Fault *(1890), a conventional, sentimental story set on a Louisiana plantation. The novel was a failure, but soon Kate Chopin had begun to sell her local-color stories to newspapers and such national magazines as the* Century *and* Vogue. *By 1898 she had written three novels (one of which she left unpublished and later destroyed) and nearly a hundred stories. Collections of her local-color tales of Creoles and Cajuns had been published in* Bayou Folk *(1894) and* A Night in Acadie *(1897).*

In 1899 she published her third novel, The Awakening, *later described as the story of "a sensuous woman who follows her inclinations." It was her masterpiece, but its theme of infidelity and the passions of its heroine brought condemnation from critics.* The Awakening *was judged "too strong drink for moral babes," a book that "should be labeled poison." Struck by the chorus of harsh criticism that followed the publication of her novel, Kate Chopin withdrew and ceased to write almost entirely. Five years later she died. Her shocking novel fell into obscurity; she was remembered only as one of the local-color writers who exploited the idioms and idiosyncrasies of the exotic provinces of America. Not until the 1950s did critical reevaluation begin to emphasize her subtle power to go beyond the conventions of popular "ladies fiction" and to portray the problems of race and the anguish of men and women stripped of their complacent illusions.*

FURTHER READING: D. Rankin, *Kate Chopin, and Her Creole Stories,* 1932; *The Complete Works of Kate Chopin,* 2 vols., ed. P. Seyersted, 1969; P. Seyersted, *Kate Chopin,* 1969, 1980; P. Skaggs, *Kate Chopin,* 1985; B. Ewell, *Kate Chopin,* 1986; E. Toth, *Kate Chopin,* 1990; *Perspectives on Kate Chopin,* ed. G. Ballenger, 1992; *Kate Chopin Reconsidered,* ed. L. Boren and S. Davis, 1992; *Critical Essays on Kate Chopin,* ed. A. Petry, 1996; E. Toth, *Unveiling Kate Chopin,* 1999; R. Evans, *Kate Chopin's Short Fiction,* 2001; N. Walker, *Kate Chopin, A Literary Life,* 2001; A. Stein, *Women and Autonomy in Kate Chopin's Short Fiction,* 2004.

TEXT: *Nég Créol,* 1897.

NÉG CRÉOL[1]

At the remote period of his birth he had been named César François Xavier, but no one ever thought of calling him anything but Chicot,[2] or Nég, or Maringouin.[3] Down at the French market, where he worked among the fishmongers, they called him Chicot, when they were not calling him names that are written less freely than they are spoken. But one felt privileged to call him almost anything, he was so black, lean, lame, and shriveled. He wore a headkerchief, and whatever other rags the fishermen and their wives chose to bestow upon him. Throughout one whole winter he wore a woman's discarded jacket with puffed sleeves.

[1]"Creole," meaning "native," a term used to describe both native-born Negroes and southern whites of Spanish or French ancestry. It is also the name of the dialectal French spoken in Louisiana. "Nég" is a dialectal variant of the French word "Nègre," meaning "Negro."

[2]French: stub, stump. [3]French: mosquito, fly.

Among some startling beliefs entertained by Chicot was one that "Michié[4] St. Pierre et Michié St. Paul" had created him. Of "Michié bon Dieu"[5] he held his own private opinion, and not a too flattering one at that. This fantastic notion concerning the origin of his being he owed to the early teaching of his young master, a lax believer, and a great *farceur*[6] in his day. Chicot had once been thrashed by a robust young Irish priest for expressing his religious views, and at another time knifed by a Sicilian. So he had come to hold his peace upon that subject.

Upon another theme he talked freely and harped continuously. For years he had tried to convince his associates that his master had left a progeny, rich, cultured, powerful, and numerous beyond belief. This prosperous race of beings inhabited the most imposing mansions in the city of New Orleans. Men of note and position, whose names were familiar to the public, he swore were grandchildren, great-grandchildren, or, less frequently, distant relatives of his master, long deceased. Ladies who came to the market in carriages, or whose elegance of attire attracted the attention and admiration of the fishwomen, were all *des 'tites cousines*[7] to his former master, Jean Boisduré. He never looked for recognition from any of these superior beings, but delighted to discourse by the hour upon their dignity and pride of birth and wealth.

Chicot always carried an old gunny-sack, and into this went his earnings. He cleaned stalls at the market, scaled fish, and did many odd offices for the itinerant merchants, who usually paid in trade for his service. Occasionally he saw the color of silver and got his clutch upon a coin, but he accepted anything, and seldom made terms. He was glad to get a handkerchief from the Hebrew, and grateful if the Choctaws would trade him a bottle of *filé*[8] for it. The butcher flung him a soup bone, and the fishmonger a few crabs or a paper bag of shrimps. It was the big *mulatresse, vendeuse de café,*[9] who cared for his inner man.

Once Chicot was accused by a shoe-vender of attempting to steal a pair of ladies' shoes. He declared he was only examining them. The clamor raised in the market was terrific. Young Dagoes assembled and squealed like rats; a couple of Gascon butchers bellowed like bulls. Matteo's wife shook her fist in the accuser's face and called him incomprehensible names. The Choctaw women, where they squatted, turned their slow eyes in the direction of the fray, taking no further notice; while a policeman jerked Chicot around by the puffed sleeve and brandished a club. It was a narrow escape.

Nobody knew where Chicot lived. A man—even a nég créol—who lives among the reeds and willows of Bayou St. John, in a deserted chicken-coop constructed chiefly of tarred paper, is not going to boast of his habitation or to invite attention to his domestic appointments. When, after market hours, he vanished in the direction of St. Philip street, limping, seemingly bent under the weight of his gunny-bag, it was like the disappearance from the stage of some petty actor whom the audience does not follow in imagination beyond the wings, or think of till his return in another scene.

[4]Creole French: "Great," "Master." [5]French: "God Almighty."
[6]French: practical joker. [7]French: distant cousins.
[8]Creole French: powdered sassafras leaves, traditionally gathered and ground by Choctaw Indians, used in Creole cooking to add a pungent flavor to soups and gumbos.
[9]French: mulatto woman, seller of coffee.

There was one to whom Chicot's coming or going meant more than this. In *la maison grise*[10] they called her La Chouette,[11] for no earthly reason unless that she perched high under the roof of the old rookery and scoulded in shrill sudden outbursts. Forty or fifty years before, when for a little while she acted minor parts with a company of French players (an escapade that had brought her grandmother to the grave), she was known as Mademoiselle de Montallaine. Seventy-five years before she had been christened Aglaé Boisduré.

No matter at what hour the old negro appeared at her threshold, Mamzelle Aglaé always kept him waiting till she finished her prayers. She opened the door for him and silently motioned him to a seat, returning to prostrate herself upon her knees before a crucifix, and a shell filled with holy water that stood on a small table; it represented in her imagination an altar. Chicot knew that she did it to aggravate him; he was convinced that she timed her devotions to begin when she heard his footsteps on the stairs. He would sit with sullen eyes contemplating her long, spare, poorly clad figure as she knelt and read from her book or finished her prayers. Bitter was the religious warfare that had raged for years between them, and Mamzelle Aglaé had grown, on her side, as intolerant as Chicot. She had come to hold St. Peter and St. Paul in such utter detestation that she had cut their pictures out of her prayer-book.

Then Mamzelle Aglaé pretended not to care what Chicot had in his bag. He drew forth a small hunk of beef and laid it in her basket that stood on the bare floor. She looked from the corner of her eye, and went on dusting the table. He brought out a handful of potatoes, some pieces of sliced fish, a few herbs, a yard of calico, and a small pat of butter wrapped in lettuce leaves. He was proud of the butter, and wanted her to notice it. He held it out and asked her for something to put it on. She handed him a saucer, and looked indifferent and resigned, with lifted eyebrows.

"Pas d'sucre,[12] Nég?"

Chicot shook his head and scratched it, and looked like a black picture of distress and mortification. No sugar! But tomorrow he would get a pinch here and a pinch there, and would bring as much as a cupful.

Mamzelle Aglaé then sat down, and talked to Chicot uninterruptedly and confidentially. She complained bitterly, and it was all about a pain that lodged in her leg; that crept and acted like a live, stinging serpent, twining about her waist and up her spine, and coiling round the shoulder-blade. And then *les rheumatismes* in her fingers! He could see for himself how they were knotted. She could not bend them; she could hold nothing in her hands; and had let a saucer fall that morning and broken it in pieces. And if she were to tell him that she had slept a wink through the night, she would be a liar, deserving of perdition. She had sat at the window *la nuit blanche,*[13] hearing the hours strike and the market-wagons rumble. Chicot nodded, and kept up a running fire of sympathetic comment and suggestive remedies for rheumatism and insomnia: herbs, or *tisanes,*[14] or *grigris,*[15] or all three. As if he knew! There was Purgatory Mary, a perambulating soul whose office in life

[10]French: the gray house.
[11]French: The Screech-owl. [12]French: "No sugar?"
[13]French: the whole night. [14]French: potions, medicines.
[15]West African word meaning amulets, charms.

was to pray for the shades in purgatory,—she had brought Mamzelle Aglaé a bottle of *eau de Lourdes,*[16] but so little of it! She might have kept her water of Lourdes, for all the good it did,—a drop! Not so much as would cure a fly or a mosquito! Mamzelle Aglaé was going to show Purgatory Mary the door when she came again, not only because of her avarice with the Lourdes water, but, beside that, she brought in on her feet dirt that could only be removed with a shovel after she left.

And Mamzelle Aglaé wanted to inform Chicot that there would be slaughter and bloodshed in *la maison grise* if the people below stairs did not mend their ways. She was convinced that they lived for no other purpose than to torture and molest her. The woman kept a bucket of dirty water constantly on the landing with the hope of Mamzelle Aglaé falling over it or into it. And she knew that the children were instructed to gather in the hall and on the stairway, and scream and make a noise and jump up and down like galloping horses, with the intention of driving her to suicide. Chicot should notify the policeman on the beat, and have them arrested, if possible, and thrust into the parish prison, where they belonged.

Chicot would have been extremely alarmed if he had ever chanced to find Mamzelle Aglaé in an uncomplaining mood. It never occurred to him that she might be otherwise. He felt that she had a right to quarrel with fate, if ever mortal had. Her poverty was a disgrace, and he hung his head before it and felt ashamed.

One day he found Mamzelle Aglaé stretched on the bed, with her head tied up in a handkerchief. Her sole complaint that day was, "Aïe—aïe—aïe! Aïe—aïe—aïe! uttered with every breath. He had seen her so before, especially when the weather was damp.

"Vous pas bézouin tisane, Mamzelle Aglaé? Vous pas veux mo cri gagni docteur?"[17]

She desired nothing. "Aïe—aïe—aïe!"

He emptied his bag very quietly, so as not to disturb her; and he wanted to stay there with her and lie down on the floor in case she needed him, but the woman from below had come up. She was an Irishwoman with rolled sleeves.

"It's a shtout shtick I'm afther giving her, Nég, and she do but knock on the flure it's me or Janie or wan of us that'll be hearing her."

"You too good, Brigitte. Aïe—aïe—aïe! Une goutte d'eau sucré,[18] Neg! That Purg'tory Marie,—you see hair, ma bonne Brigitte, you tell hair go say li'le prayér là-bas au Cathédral.[19] Aïe—aïe—aïe!"

Nég could hear her lamentation as he descended the stairs. It followed him as he limped his way through the city streets, and seemed part of the city's noise; he could hear it in the rumble of wheels and jangle of car-bells, and in the voices of those passing by.

He stopped at Mimotte the Voudou's shanty and bought a *grigri*—a cheap one for fifteen cents. Mimotte held her charms at all prices. This he intended to introduce next day into Mamzelle Aglaé's room—somewhere

[16]Water from the religious shrine at Lourdes, France, thought to have miraculous healing power.

[17]French: "Don't you want your medicine, Mademoiselle Aglaé? Don't you want me to call a doctor?"

[18]French: "A drop of sugar-water." [19]French: "down at the Cathedral."

about the altar,—to the confusion and discomfort of "Michié bon Dieu," who persistently declined to concern himself with the welfare of a Boisduré.

At night, among the reeds on the bayou, Chicot could still hear the woman's wail, mingled now with the croaking of the frogs. If he could have been convinced that giving up his life down there in the water would in any way have bettered her condition, he would not have hesitated to sacrifice the remnant of his existence that was wholly devoted to her. He lived but to serve her. He did not know it himself; but Chicot knew so little, and that little in such a distorted way! He could scarcely have been expected, even in his most lucid moments, to give himself over to self-analysis.

Chicot gathered an uncommon amount of dainties at market the following day. He had to work hard, and scheme and whine a little; but he got hold of an orange and a lump of ice and a *chou-fleur.*[20] He did not drink his cup of *café au lait,*[21] but asked Mimi Lambeau to put it in the little new tin pail that the Hebrew notion-vender had just given him in exchange for a mess of shrimps. This time, however, Chicot had his trouble for nothing. When he reached the upper room of *la maison grise,* it was to find that Mamzelle Aglaé had died during the night. He set his bag down in the middle of the floor, and stood shaking, and whined low like a dog in pain.

Everything had been done. The Irishwoman had gone for the doctor, and Purgatory Mary had summoned a priest. Furthermore, the woman had arranged Mamzelle Aglaé decently. She had covered the table with a white cloth, and had placed it at the head of the bed, with the crucifix and two lighted candles in silver candlesticks upon it; the little bit of ornamentation brightened and embellished the poor room. Purgatory Mary, dressed in shabby black, fat and breathing hard, sat reading half audibly from a prayer-book. She was watching the dead and the silver candlesticks, which she had borrowed from a benevolent society, and for which she held herself responsible. A young man was just leaving,—a reporter snuffing the air for items, who had scented one up there in the top room of *la maison grise.*

All the morning Janie had been escorting a procession of street Arabs up and down the stairs to view the remains. One of them—a little girl, who had had her face washed and had made a species of toilet for the occasion—refused to be dragged away. She stayed seated as if at an entertainment, fascinated alternately by the long, still figure of Mamzelle Aglaé, the mumbling lips of Purgatory Mary, and the silver candlesticks.

"Will ye get down on yer knees, man, and say a prayer for the dead!" commanded the woman.

But Chicot only shook his head, and refused to obey. He approached the bed, and laid a little black paw for a moment on the stiffened body of Mamzelle Aglaé. There was nothing for him to do here. He picked up his old ragged hat and his bag and went away.

"The black h'athen!" the woman muttered. "Shut the dure, child."

The little girl slid down from her chair, and went on tiptoe to shut the door which Chicot had left open. Having resumed her seat, she fastened her eyes upon Purgatory Mary's heaving chest.

"You, Chicot!" cried Matteo's wife the next morning. "My man, he read in paper 'bout woman name' Boisduré, use' b'long to big-a famny. She die

[20]French: cauliflower. [21]French: coffee with milk.

roun' on St. Philip—po', same-a like church rat. It's any them Boisdurés you alla talk 'bout?"

Chicot shook his head in slow but emphatic denial. No, indeed, the woman was not of kin to his Boisdurés. He surely had told Matteo's wife often—how many times did he have to repeat it!—Of their wealth, their social standing. It was doubtless now some Boisduré of *les attakapas.*[22] It was none of his.

The next day there was a small funeral procession passing a little distance away,—a hearse and a carriage or two. There was the priest who had attended Mamzelle Aglaé, and a benevolent Creole gentleman whose father had known the Boisdurés in his youth. There was a couple of player-folk, who, having got wind of the story, had thrust their hands into their pockets.

"Look, Chicot!" cried Matteo's wife. "Yonda go the fune'al. Mus-a be that-a Boisduré woman we talken 'bout yesaday."

But Chicot paid no heed. What was to him the funeral of a woman who had died in St. Philip street? He did not even turn his head in the direction of the moving procession. He went on scaling his red-snapper.

1896, 1897

Stephen Crane 1871–1900

Stephen Crane's father was a Methodist preacher in Newark, New Jersey, Crane's birthplace. His mother was a social leader and temperance crusader. Both parents exhibited a characteristic nineteenth-century faith in the benevolence of God, in the existence of free will, and in the significance of man in the universe—ideas that their son, in the course of his short and tempestuous life, would attack with humor and savage irony.

Crane had originally hoped to be a soldier, but in 1890, after two and a half years at a military prep school in New York, he entered Lafayette College to study mining-engineering. After one term he left Lafayette and transferred to Syracuse University. There he devoted most of his efforts to playing varsity baseball, working as a local correspondent for the New York Tribune, *and writing his first short stories. After less than a year at Syracuse, Crane withdrew and moved to New York City. There he mingled with Bohemian art students living in tenements, and he struggled to earn his way as a freelance journalist contributing items to New York newspapers.*

Crane's observation of life on New York's Bowery and his reading of exposés of New York slum life provided him with much of the background material for his first novel, Maggie, A Girl of the Streets *(1893). It was the first naturalistic novel written by an American, and its stark description of squalor and immorality was so shocking for its time that Crane, unable to find an interested publisher, was obliged to publish the novel at his own expense. In 1895, he published his first book of poems,* The Black Riders, *short, caustic, free-verse parables of the absurdity of the human condition. In the same year* The Red Badge of Courage *was published in book form, bringing Crane international acclaim.*

[22]District of southern Louisiana, west of New Orleans.

His travels as a reporter for a newspaper syndicate took him through the American West, to Mexico, and to Florida where he joined in the unsuccessful gun-running expedition to Cuba that led to his most famous short story, "The Open Boat." In 1897, Crane settled in England, became friends with Joseph Conrad and Henry James, and labored mightily at writing fiction and doing editorial hackwork in an effort to pay for his extravagant style of living. The next year, in spite of ill health, Crane went to Cuba as a war correspondent reporting on the Spanish-American War for the New York World. *When he returned to England early in 1899 he was suffering from tuberculosis, and in June 1900, after traveling to a German sanitorium to seek a cure, Crane died. He was twenty-eight.*

His early writing had been burlesques and satires, expressions of ironic detachment. Crane had announced that his ambition as a writer was to achieve personal honesty—to deflate romantic idealism, and portray men battered and alone in a hostile world. He has been viewed as an uncompromising determinist, a literary naturalist who saw human beings as wholly controlled by their environment and their heredity. At the same time he has been seen as a Christian symbolist expressing faith in the ultimate understanding and redemption of people. Crane was a pioneer of a new literary realism that was impressionistic in its vivid imagery, in its characterizations, and in its narrative style. And he was a master of irony, scrutinizing the persistent illusions of people and the disparity between their buoyant expectations and their doom.

FURTHER READING: *The Works of Stephen Crane,* 10 vols., ed. F. Bowers, 1969–1975; B. Knapp, *Stephen Crane,* 1987; *The Correspondence of Stephen Crane,* 2 vols., ed. S. Wertheim and P. Sorrentino, 1988; C. Wolford, *Stephen Crane, A Study of the Short Fiction,* 1989; D. Halliburton, *The Color of the Sky, A Study of Stephen Crane,* 1989; C. Benfey, *The Double Life of Stephen Crane,* 1992; S. Wertheim and P. Sorrentino, *The Crane Log, A Documentary Life of Stephen Crane,* 1993; M. Robertson, *Stephen Crane, Journalism, and the Making of Modern American Literature,* 1997; L. Davis, *Badge of Courage, The Life of Stephen Crane,* 1998; R. Morris, *Stephen Crane, A Biography,* 2005.

TEXTS: *The Poems of Stephen Crane,* ed. J. Katz, 1966; "The Open Boat," *The Works of Stephen Crane,* Vol. V, *Tales of Adventure,* ed. F. Bowers, intr. J. Levenson, 1970.

BLACK RIDERS CAME FROM THE SEA[1]

Black riders came from the sea.
There was clang and clang of spear and shield,
And clash and clash of hoof and heel,
Wild shouts and the wave of hair
In the rush upon the wind:
Thus the ride of Sin.
1894 1895

[1]Crane's poems were published without titles. The titles used here were supplied by the editor.

IN THE DESERT

In the desert
I saw a creature, naked, bestial,
Who, squatting upon the ground,
Held his heart in his hands,
And ate of it.
I said: "Is it good, friend?"
"It is bitter—bitter," he answered;
"But I like it
Because it is bitter,
And because it is my heart."
1894 1895

A GOD IN WRATH

A god in wrath
Was beating a man;
He cuffed him loudly
With thunderous blows
That rang and rolled over the earth.
All people came running.
The man screamed and struggled,
And bit madly at the feet of the god.
The people cried:
"Ah, what a wicked man!"
And—
"Ah, what a redoubtable god!"
1894 1895

I SAW A MAN PURSUING THE HORIZON

I saw a man pursuing the horizon;
Round and round they sped.
I was disturbed at this;
I accosted the man.
"It is futile," I said,
"You can never—"

"You lie," he cried,
And ran on.
1894 1895

DO NOT WEEP, MAIDEN, FOR WAR IS KIND

Do not weep, maiden, for war is kind.
Because your lover threw wild hands toward the sky
And the affrighted steed ran on alone,
Do not weep.
War is kind.

Hoarse, booming drums of the regiment,
Little souls who thirst for fight,
These men were born to drill and die.
The unexplained glory flies above them,
Great is the Battle-God, great, and his Kingdom—
A field where a thousand corpses lie.

Do not weep, babe, for war is kind.
Because your father tumbled in the yellow trenches,
Raged at his breast, gulped and died,
Do not weep.
War is kind.

Swift blazing flag of the regiment,
Eagle with crest of red and gold,
These men were born to drill and die.
Point for them the virtue of slaughter,
Make plain to them the excellence of killing
And a field where a thousand corpses lie.

Mother whose heart hung humble as a button
On the bright splendid shroud of your son,
Do not weep.
War is kind.
1895 1896, 1899

A MAN SAID TO THE UNIVERSE

A man said to the universe:
"Sir, I exist!"
"However," replied the universe,
"The fact has not created in me
A sense of obligation."
1894 1899

A MAN ADRIFT ON A SLIM SPAR

A man adrift on a slim spar
A horizon smaller than the rim of a bottle
Tented waves rearing lashy dark points
The near whine of froth in circles.
God is cold.

The incessant raise and swing of the sea
And growl after growl of crest
The sinkings, green, seething, endless
The upheaval half-completed.
God is cold.

The seas are in the hollow of The Hand;
Oceans may be turned to a spray
Raining down through the stars
Because of a gesture of pity toward a babe.
Oceans may become grey ashes,
Die with a long moan and a roar
Amid the tumult of the fishes
And the cries of the ships,
Because The Hand beckons the mice.

A horizon smaller than a doomed assassin's cap,
Inky, surging tumults
A reeling, drunken sky and no sky
A pale hand sliding from a polished spar.
God is cold.

The puff of a coat imprisoning air.
A face kissing the water-death
A weary slow sway of a lost hand
And the sea, the moving sea, the sea.
God is cold.

1897 1929

THE OPEN BOAT

A TALE INTENDED TO BE AFTER THE FACT. BEING THE EXPERIENCE OF FOUR MEN FROM THE SUNK STEAMER COMMODORE[1]

I

None of them knew the color of the sky. Their eyes glanced level, and were fastened upon the waves that swept toward them. These waves were of the hue of slate, save for the tops, which were of foaming white, and all of the men knew the colors of the sea. The horizon narrowed and widened, and

[1]On his way to report on the Cuban Revolution, Crane was aboard the tug *Commodore,* bound for Cuba with a cargo of arms for the revolutionaries, when it sank off the coast of Florida, January 2, 1897. After almost thirty hours at sea in a small dinghy, Crane landed at Daytona, Florida. Soon thereafter he shaped the details of his experience into a short story.

dipped and rose, and at all times its edge was jagged with waves that seemed thrust up in points like rocks.

Many a man ought to have a bath-tub larger than the boat which here rode upon the sea. These waves were most wrongfully and barbarously abrupt and tall, and each froth-top was a problem in small boat navigation.

The cook squatted in the bottom and looked with both eyes at the six inches of gunwale[2] which separated him from the ocean. His sleeves were rolled over his fat forearms, and the two flaps of his unbuttoned vest dangled as he bent to bail out the boat. Often he said: "gawd! That was a narrow clip." As he remarked it he invariably gazed eastward over the broken sea.

The oiler,[3] steering with one of the two oars in the boat, sometimes raised himself suddenly to keep clear of water that swirled in over the stern. It was a thin little oar and it seemed often ready to snap.

The correspondent, pulling at the other oar, watched the waves and wondered why he was there.

The injured captain, lying in the bow, was at this time buried in that profound dejection and indifference which comes, temporarily at least, to even the bravest and most enduring when, willy nilly, the firm fails, the army loses, the ship goes down. The mind of the master of a vessel is rooted deep in the timbers of her, though he command for a day or a decade, and this captain had on him the stern impression of a scene in the grays of dawn of seven turned faces, and later a stump of a top-mast with a white ball on it that slashed to and fro at the waves, went low and lower, and down. Thereafter there was something strange in his voice. Although steady, it was deep with mourning, and of a quality beyond oration or tears.

"Keep 'er a little more south, Billie," said he.

"'A little more south,' sir," said the oiler in the stern.

A seat in this boat was not unlike a seat upon a bucking broncho, and, by the same token, a broncho is not much smaller. The craft pranced and reared, and plunged like an animal. As each wave came, and she rose for it, she seemed like a horse making at a fence outrageously high. The manner of her scramble over these walls of water is a mystic thing, and, moreover, at the top of them were ordinarily these problems in white water, the foam racing down from the summit of each wave, requiring a new leap, and a leap from the air. Then, after scornfully bumping a crest, she would slide, and race, and splash down a long incline and arrive bobbing and nodding in front of the next menace.

A singular disadvantage of the sea lies in the fact that after successfully surmounting one wave you discover that there is another behind it just as important and just as nervously anxious to do something effective in the way of swamping boats. In a ten-foot dingey one can get an idea of the resources of the sea in the line of waves that is not probable to the average experience, which is never at sea in a dingey. As each salty wall of water approached, it shut all else from the view of the men in the boat, and it was the final outburst of the ocean, the last effort of the grim water. There was a terrible grace in the move of the waves, and they came in silence, save for the snarling of the crests.

[2]The upper sides of a boat. [3]A crew member who oils machinery in a ship's engine room.

In the wan light, the faces of the men must have been gray. Their eyes must have glinted in strange ways as they gazed steadily astern. Viewed from a balcony, the whole thing would doubtlessly have been weirdly picturesque. But the men in the boat had no time to see it, and if they had had leisure there were other things to occupy their minds. The sun swung steadily up the sky, and they knew it was broad day because the color of the sea changed from slate to emerald-green, streaked with amber lights, and the foam was like tumbling snow. The process of the breaking day was unknown to them. They were aware only of this effect upon the color of the waves that rolled toward them.

In disjointed sentences the cook and the correspondent argued as to the difference between a life-saving station and a house of refuge. The cook had said: "There's a house of refuge just north of the Mosquito Inlet Light, and as soon as they see us, they'll come off in their boat and pick us up."

"As soon as who see us?" said the correspondent.

"The crew," said the cook.

"Houses of refuge don't have crews," said the correspondent. "As I understand them, they are only places where clothes and grub are stored for the benefit of shipwrecked people. They don't carry crews."

"Oh, yes, they do," said the cook.

"No, they don't," said the correspondent.

"Well, we're not there yet, anyhow," said the oiler, in the stern.

"Well," said the cook, "perhaps it's not a house of refuge that I'm thinking of as being near Mosquito Inlet Light. Perhaps it's a life-saving station."

"We're not there yet," said the oiler, in the stern.

II

As the boat bounced from the top of each wave, the wind tore through the hair of the hatless men, and as the craft plopped her stern down again the spray slashed past them. The crest of each of these waves was a hill, from the top of which the men surveyed, for a moment, a broad tumultuous expanse, shining and wind-riven. It was probably splendid. It was probably glorious, this play of the free sea, wild with lights of emerald and white and amber.

"Bully good thing it's an on-shore wind," said the cook. "If not, where would we be? Wouldn't have a show."

"That's right," said the correspondent.

The busy oiler nodded his assent.

Then the captain, in the bow, chuckled in a way that expressed humor, contempt, tragedy, all in one. "Do you think we've got much of a show, now, boys?" said he.

Whereupon the three were silent, save for a trifle of hemming and hawing. To express any particular optimism at this time they felt to be childish and stupid, but they all doubtless possessed this sense of the situation in their mind. A young man thinks doggedly at such times. On the other hand, the ethics of their condition was decidedly against any open suggestion of hopelessness. So they were silent.

"Oh, well," said the captain, soothing his children, "we'll get ashore all right."

But there was that in his tone which made them think, so the oiler quoth: "Yes! If this wind holds!"

The cook was bailing. "Yes! If we don't catch hell in the surf."

Canton flannel[1] gulls flew near and far. Sometimes they sat down on the sea, near patches of brown sea-weed that rolled over the waves with a movement like carpets on a line in a gale. The birds sat comfortably in groups, and they were envied by some in the dingey, for the wrath of the sea was no more to them than it was to a covey of prairie chickens a thousand miles inland. Often they came very close and stared at the men with black bead-like eyes. At these times they were uncanny and sinister in their unblinking scrutiny, and the men hooted angrily at them, telling them to be gone. One came, and evidently decided to alight on the top of the captain's head. The bird flew parallel to the boat and did not circle, but made short sidelong jumps in the air in chicken-fashion. His black eyes were wistfully fixed upon the captain's head. "Ugly brute," said the oiler to the bird. "You look as if you were made with a jack-knife." The cook and the correspondent swore darkly at the creature. The captain naturally wished to knock it away with the end of the heavy painter,[2] but he did not dare do it, because anything resembling an emphatic gesture would have capsized this freighted boat, and so with his open hand, the captain gently and carefully waved the gull away. After it had been discouraged from the pursuit the captain breathed easier on account of his hair, and others breathed easier because the bird struck their minds at this time as being somehow gruesome and ominous.

In the meantime the oiler and the correspondent rowed. And also they rowed.

They sat together in the same seat, and each rowed an oar. Then the oiler took both oars; then the correspondent took both oars; then the oiler; then the correspondent. They rowed and they rowed. The very ticklish part of the business was when the time came for the reclining one in the stern to take his turn at the oars. By the very last star of truth, it is easier to steal eggs from under a hen than it was to change seats in the dingey. First the man in the stern slid his hand along the thwart[3] and moved with care, as if he were of Sèvres.[4] Then the man in the rowing seat slid his hand along the other thwart. It was all done with the most extraordinary care. As the two sidled past each other, the whole party kept watchful eyes on the coming wave, and the captain cried: "Look out now! Steady there!"

The brown mats of sea-weed that appeared from time to time were like islands, bits of earth. They were travelling, apparently, neither one way nor the other. They were, to all intents, stationary. They informed the men in the boat that it was making progress slowly toward the land.

The captain, rearing cautiously in the bow, after the dingey soared on a great swell, said that he had seen the light-house at Mosquito Inlet. Presently the cook remarked that he had seen it. The correspondent was at the oars, then, and for some reason he too wished to look at the light-house, but his back was toward the far shore and the waves were important, and for some time he could not seize an opportunity to turn his head. But at last there came a wave more gentle than the others, and when at the crest of it he swiftly scoured the western horizon.

[1]Cotton flannel. [2]Rope for tying the boat to a wharf.
[3]A rower's seat built into the boat crosswise (athwart) to the keel.
[4]Delicate china made in Sèvres, France.

"See it?" said the captain.

"No," said the correspondent, slowly, "I didn't see anything."

"Look again," said the captain. He pointed. "It's exactly in that direction."

At the top of another wave, the correspondent did as he was bid, and this time his eyes chanced on a small still thing on the edge of the swaying horizon. It was precisely like the point of a pin. It took an anxious eye to find a light-house so tiny.

"Think we'll make it, Captain?"

"If this wind holds and the boat don't swamp, we can't do much else," said the captain.

The little boat, lifted by each towering sea, and splashed viciously by the crests, made progress that in the absence of sea-weed was not apparent to those in her. She seemed just a wee thing wallowing, miraculously, top-up, at the mercy of five oceans. Occasionally, a great spread of water, like white flames, swarmed into her.

"Bail her, cook," said the captain, serenely.

"All right, Captain," said the cheerful cook.

III

It would be difficult to describe the subtle brotherhood of men that was here established on the seas. No one said that it was so. No one mentioned it, but it dwelt in the boat, and each man felt it warm him. They were a captain, an oiler, a cook, and a correspondent, and they were friends, friends in a more curiously ironbound degree than may be common. The hurt captain, lying against the water-jar in the bow, spoke always in a low voice and calmly but he could never command a more ready and swiftly obedient crew than the motley three of the dingey. It was more than a mere recognition of what was best for the common safety. There was surely in it a quality that was personal and heartfelt. And after this devotion to the commander of the boat there was this comradeship that the correspondent, for instance, who had been taught to be cynical of men, knew even at the time was the best experience of his life. But no one said that it was so. No one mentioned it.

"I wish we had a sail," remarked the captain. "We might try my overcoat on the end of an oar and give you two boys a chance to rest." So the cook and the correspondent held the mast and spread wide the overcoat, the oiler steered, and the little boat made good way with her new rig. Sometimes the oiler had to scull sharply to keep a sea from breaking into the boat, but otherwise sailing was a success.

Meanwhile the light-house had been growing slowly larger. It had now almost assumed color, and appeared like a little gray shadow on the sky. The man at the oars could not be prevented from turning his head rather often to try for a glimpse of this little gray shadow.

At last, from the top of each wave the men in the tossing boat could see land. Even as the light-house was an upright shadow on the sky, this land seemed but a long black shadow on the sea. It certainly was thinner than paper. "We must be about opposite New Smyrna," said the cook, who had coasted this shore often in schooners. "Captain, by the way, I believe they abandoned that life-saving station there about a year ago."

"Did they?" said the captain.

The wind slowly died away. The cook and the correspondent were not now obliged to slave in order to hold high the oar. But the waves continued their old impetuous swooping at the dingey, and the little craft, no longer under way, struggled woundily over them. The oiler or the correspondent took the oars again.

Shipwrecks are *apropos* of nothing. If men could only train for them and have them occur when the men had reached pink condition, there would be less drowning at sea. Of the four in the dingey none had slept any time worth mentioning for two days and two nights previous to embarking in the dingey, and in the excitement of clambering about the deck of a foundering ship they had also forgotten to eat heartily.

For these reasons, and for others, neither the oiler nor the correspondent was fond of rowing at this time. The correspondent wondered ingenuously how in the name of all that was sane could there be people who thought it amusing to row a boat. It was not an amusement; it was a diabolical punishment, and even a genius of mental aberrations could never conclude that it was anything but a horror to the muscles and a crime against the back. He mentioned to the boat in general how the amusement of rowing struck him, and the weary-faced oiler smiled in full sympathy. Previously to the foundering, by the way, the oiler had worked double-watch in the engine-room of the ship.

"Take her easy, now, boys," said the captain. "Don't spend yourselves. If we have to run a surf you'll need all your strength, because we'll sure have to swim for it. Take your time."

Slowly the land arose from the sea. From a black line it became a line of black and a line of white—trees and sand. Finally, the captain said that he could make out a house on the shore. "That's the house of refuge, sure," said the cook. "They'll see us before long, and come out after us."

The distant light-house reared high. "The keeper ought to be able to make us out now, if he's looking through a glass," said the captain. "He'll notify the life-saving people."

"None of those other boats could have got ashore to give word of the wreck," said the oiler, in a low voice. "Else the life-boat would be out hunting us."

Slowly and beautifully the land loomed out of the sea. The wind came again. It had veered from the northeast to the southeast. Finally, a new sound struck the ears of the men in the boat. It was the low thunder of the surf on the shore. "We'll never be able to make the light-house now," said the captain. "Swing her head a little more north, Billie."

"'A little more north,' sir," said the oiler.

Whereupon the little boat turned her nose once more down the wind, and all but the oarsman watched the shore grow. Under the influence of this expansion doubt and direful apprehension were leaving the minds of the men. The management of the boat was still most absorbing, but it could not prevent a quiet cheerfulness. In an hour, perhaps, they would be ashore.

Their back-bones had become thoroughly used to balancing in the boat and they now rode this wild colt of a dingey like circus men. The correspondent thought that he had been drenched to the skin, but happening to feel in the top pocket of his coat, he found therein eight cigars. Four of them were soaked with seawater; four were perfectly scatheless. After a search, somebody produced three dry matches, and thereupon the four waifs rode impudently in their little boat, and with an assurance of an impending rescue shining in their eyes, puffed at the big cigars and judged well and ill of all men. Everybody took a drink of water.

IV

"Cook," remarked the captain, "there don't seem to be any signs of life about your house of refuge."

"No," replied the cook. "Funny they don't see us!"

A broad stretch of lowly coast lay before the eyes of the men. It was dunes topped with dark vegetation. The roar of the surf was plain, and sometimes they could see the white lip of a wave as it spun up the beach. A tiny house was blocked out black upon the sky. Southward, the slim light-house lifted its little gray length.

Tide, wind, and waves were swinging the dingey northward. "Funny they don't see us," said the men.

The surf's roar was here dulled, but its tone was, nevertheless, thunderous and mighty. As the boat swam over the great rollers, the men sat listening to this roar. "We'll swamp sure," said everybody.

It is fair to say here that there was not a life-saving station within twenty miles in either direction, but the men did not know this fact and in consequence they made dark and opprobrious remarks concerning the eyesight of the nation's life-savers. Four scowling men sat in the dingey and surpassed records in the invention of epithets.

"Funny they don't see us."

The light-heartedness of a former time had completely faded. To their sharpened minds it was easy to conjure pictures of all kinds of incompetency and blindness and indeed, cowardice. There was the shore of the populous land, and it was bitter and bitter to them that from it came no sign.

"Well," said the captain, ultimately, "I suppose we'll have to make a try for ourselves. If we stay out here too long, we'll none of us have strength left to swim after the boat swamps."

And so the oiler, who was at the oars, turned the boat straight for the shore. There was a sudden tightening of muscles. There was some thinking.

"If we don't all get ashore—" said the captain. "If we don't all get ashore, I suppose you fellows know where to send news of my finish?"

They then briefly exchanged some addresses and admonitions. As for the reflections of the men, there was a great deal of rage in them. Perchance they might be formulated thus: "If I am going to be drowned—if I am going to be drowned—if I am going to be drowned, why, in the name of the seven mad gods who rule the sea, was I allowed to come thus far and contemplate sand and trees? Was I brought here merely to have my nose dragged away as I was about to nibble the sacred cheese of life? It is preposterous. If this old ninny-woman, Fate, cannot do better than this, she should be deprived of the management of men's fortunes. She is an old hen who knows not her intention. If she has decided to drown me, why did she not do it in the beginning and save me all this trouble. The whole affair is absurd. . . . But, no, she cannot mean to drown me. She dare not drown me. She cannot drown me. Not after all this work." Afterward the man might have had an impulse to shake his fist at the clouds. "Just you drown me, now, and then hear what I call you!"

The billows that came at this time were more formidable. They seemed always just about to break and roll over the little boat in a turmoil of foam. There was a preparatory and long growl in the speech of them. No mind unused to the sea would have concluded that the dingey could ascend these sheer heights in time. The shore was still afar. The oiler was a wily surfman. "Boys," he said, swiftly, "she won't live three minutes more and we're too far out to swim. Shall I take her to sea again, Captain?"

"Yes! Go ahead!" said the captain.

This oiler, by a series of quick miracles, and fast and steady oarsmanship, turned the boat in the middle of the surf and took her safely to sea again.

There was a considerable silence as the boat bumped over the furrowed sea to deeper water. Then somebody in gloom spoke. "Well, anyhow, they must have seen us from the shore by now."

The gulls went in slanting flight up the wind toward the gray desolate east. A squall, marked by dingy clouds, and clouds brick-red, like smoke from a burning building, appeared from the southeast.

"What do you think of those life-saving people? Ain't they peaches?"

"Funny they haven't seen us."

"Maybe they think we're out here for sport! Maybe they think we're fishin'. Maybe they think we're damned fools."

It was a long afternoon. A changed tide tried to force them southward, but wind and wave said northward. Far ahead, where coastline, sea, and sky formed their mighty angle, there were little dots which seemed to indicate a city on the shore.

"St. Augustine?"

The captain shook his head. "Too near Mosquito Inlet."

And the oiler rowed, and then the correspondent rowed. Then the oiler rowed. It was a weary business. The human back can become the seat of more aches and pains than are registered in books for the composite anatomy of a regiment. It is a limited area, but it can become the theatre of innumerable muscular conflicts, tangles, wrenches, knots, and other comforts.

"Did you ever like to row, Billie?" asked the correspondent.

"No," said the oiler. "Hang it."

When one exchanged the rowing-seat for a place in the bottom of the boat, he suffered a bodily depression that caused him to be careless of everything save an obligation to wiggle one finger. There was cold sea-water swashing to and fro in the boat, and he lay in it. His head, pillowed on a thwart, was within an inch of the swirl of a wave crest, and sometimes a particularly obstreperous sea came in-board and drenched him once more. But these matters did not annoy him. It is almost certain that if the boat had capsized he would have tumbled comfortably out upon the ocean as if he felt sure that it was a great soft mattress.

"Look! There's a man on the shore!"

"Where?"

"There! See 'im? See 'im?"

"Yes, sure! He's walking along."

"Now he's stopping. Look! He's facing us!"

"He's waving at us!"

"So he is! By thunder!"

"Ah, now, we're all right! Now we're all right! There'll be a boat out here for us in half an hour."

"He's going on. He's running. He's going up to that house there."

The remote beach seemed lower than the sea, and it required a searching glance to discern the little black figure. The captain saw a floating stick and they rowed to it. A bath-towel was by some weird chance in the boat, and, tying this on the stick, the captain waved it. The oarsman did not dare turn his head, so he was obliged to ask questions.

"What's he doing now?"

"He's standing still again. He's looking, I think . . . There he goes again. Toward the house. . . . Now he's stopped again."

"Is he waving at us?"

"No, not now; he was, though."

"Look! There comes another man!"

"He's running."

"Look at him go, would you."

"Why, he's on a bicycle. Now he's met the other man. They're both waving at us. Look!"

"There comes something up the beach."

"What the devil is that thing?"

"Why, it looks like a boat."

"Why, certainly it's a boat."

"No, it's on wheels."

"Yes, so it is. Well, that must be the life-boat. They drag them along shore on a wagon."

"That's the life-boat, sure."

"No, by——, it's—it's an omnibus."

"I tell you it's a life-boat."

"It is not! It's an omnibus. I can see it plain. See? One of those big hotel omnibuses."

"By thunder, you're right. It's an omnibus, sure as fate. What do you suppose they are doing with an omnibus? Maybe they are going around collecting the life-crew, hey?"

"That's it, likely. Look! There's a fellow waving a little black flag. He's standing on the steps of the omnibus. There come those other two fellows. Now they're all talking together. Look at the fellow with the flag. Maybe he ain't waving it!"

"That ain't a flag, is it? That's his coat. Why, certainly, that's his coat."

"So it is. It's his coat. He's taken it off and is waving it around his head. But would you look at him swing it!"

"Oh, say, there isn't any life-saving station here. That's just a winter resort hotel omnibus that has brought over some of the boarders to see us drown."

"What's that idiot with the coat mean? What's he signaling, anyhow?"

"It looks as if he were trying to tell us to go north. There must be a life-saving station up there."

"No! He thinks we're fishing. Just giving us a merry hand. See? Ah, there, Willie."

"Well, I wish I could make something out of those signals. What do you suppose he means?"

"He don't mean anything. He's just playing."

"Well, if he'd just signal us to try the surf again, or to go to sea and wait, or go north, or go south, or go to hell—there would be some reason in it. But look at him. He just stands there and keeps his coat revolving like a wheel. The ass!"

"There come more people."

"Now there's quite a mob. Look! Isn't that a boat?"

"Where? Oh, I see where you mean. No, that's no boat."

"That fellow is still waving his coat."

"He must think we like to see him do that. Why don't he quit it. It don't mean anything."

"I don't know. I think he is trying to make us go north. It must be that there's a life-saving station there somewhere."

"Say, he ain't tired yet. Look at 'im wave."

"Wonder how long he can keep that up. He's been revolving his coat ever since he caught sight of us. He's an idiot. Why aren't they getting men to bring a boat out. A fishing boat—one of those big yawls—could come out here all right. Why don't he do something?"

"Oh, it's all right, now."

"They'll have a boat out here for us in less than no time, now that they've seen us."

A faint yellow tone came into the sky over the low land. The shadows on the sea slowly deepened. The wind bore coldness with it, and the men began to shiver.

"Holy smoke!" said one, allowing his voice to express his impious mood, "if we keep on monkeying out here! If we've got to flounder out here all night!"

"Oh, we'll never have to stay here all night! don't you worry. They've seen us now, and it won't be long before they'll come chasing out after us."

The shore grew dusky. The man waving a coat blended gradually into the gloom, and it swallowed in the same manner the omnibus and the group of people. The spray, when it dashed uproariously over the side, made the voyagers shrink and swear like men who were being branded.

"I'd like to catch the chump who waved the coat. I feel like soaking him one, just for luck."

"Why? What did he do?"

"Oh, nothing, but then he seemed so damned cheerful."

In the meantime the oiler rowed, and then the correspondent rowed, and then the oiler rowed. Gray-faced and bowed forward, they mechanically, turn by turn, plied the leaden oars. The form of the light-house had vanished from the southern horizon, but finally a pale star appeared, just lifting from the sea. The streaked saffron in the west passed before the all-merging darkness, and the sea to the east was black. The land had vanished, and was expressed only by the low and drear thunder of the surf.

"If I am going to be drowned—if I am going to be drowned—if I am going to be drowned, why, in the name of the seven mad gods who rule the sea, was I allowed to come thus far and contemplate sand and trees? Was I brought here merely to have my nose dragged away as I was about to nibble the sacred cheese of life?"

The patient captain, drooped over the water-jar, was sometimes obliged to speak to the oarsman.

"Keep her head up! Keep her head up!"

" 'Keep her head up,' sir." The voices were weary and low.

This was surely a quiet evening. All save the oarsman lay heavily and listlessly in the boat's bottom. As for him, his eyes were just capable of noting the tall black waves that swept forward in a most sinister silence, save for an occasional subdued growl of a crest.

The cook's head was on a thwart, and he looked without interest at the water under his nose. He was deep in other scenes. Finally he spoke. "Billie," he murmured, dreamfully, "what kind of pie do you like best?"

V

"Pie," said the oiler and the correspondent, agitatedly. "Don't talk about those things, blast you!"

"Well," said the cook, "I was just thinking about ham sandwiches, and—"

A night on the sea in an open boat is a long night. As darkness settled finally, the shine of the light, lifting from the sea in the south, changed to full gold. On the northern horizon a new light appeared, a small bluish gleam on the edge of the waters. These two lights were the furniture of the world. Otherwise there was nothing but waves.

Two men huddled in the stern, and distances were so magnificent in the dingey that the rower was enabled to keep his feet partly warmed by thrusting them under his companions. Their legs indeed extended far under the rowing-seat until they touched the feet of the captain forward. Sometimes, despite the efforts of the tired oarsman, a wave came piling into the boat, an icy wave of the night, and the chilling water soaked them anew. They would twist their bodies for a moment and groan, and sleep the dead sleep once more, while the water in the boat gurgled about them as the craft rocked.

The plan of the oiler and the correspondent was for one to row until he lost the ability, and then arouse the other from his sea-water couch in the bottom of the boat.

The oiler plied the oars until his head drooped forward, and the overpowering sleep blinded him. And he rowed yet afterward. Then he touched a man in the bottom of the boat, and called his name. "Will you spell for me a little while?" he said, meekly.

"Sure, Billie," said the correspondent, awakening and dragging himself to a sitting position. They exchanged places carefully, and the oiler, cuddling down in the sea-water at the cook's side, seemed to go to sleep instantly.

The particular violence of the sea had ceased. The waves came without snarling. The obligation of the man at the oars was to keep the boat headed so that the tilt of the rollers would not capsize her, and to preserve her from filling when the crests rushed past. The black waves were silent and hard to be seen in the darkness. Often one was almost upon the boat before the oarsman was aware.

In a low voice the correspondent addressed the captain. He was not sure that the captain was awake, although this iron man seemed to be always awake. "Captain, shall I keep her making for that light north, sir?"

The same steady voice answered him. "Yes. Keep it about two points off the port bow."

The cook had tied a life-belt around himself in order to get even the warmth which this clumsy cork contrivance could donate, and he seemed almost stove-like when a rower, whose teeth invariably chattered wildly as soon as he ceased his labor, drooped down to sleep.

The correspondent, as he rowed, looked down at the two men sleeping under foot. The cook's arm was around the oiler's shoulders, and, with their fragmentary clothing and haggard faces, they were the babes of the sea, a grotesque rendering of the old babes in the wood.

Later he must have grown stupid at his work, for suddenly there was a growling of water, and a crest came with a roar and a swash into the boat, and it was a wonder that it did not set the cook afloat in his life-belt. The cook continued to sleep, but the oiler sat up, blinking his eyes and shaking with the new cold.

"Oh, I'm awful sorry, Billie," said the correspondent, contritely.

"That's all right, old boy," said the oiler, and lay down again and was asleep.

Presently it seemed that even the captain dozed, and the correspondent thought that he was the one man afloat on all the oceans. The wind had a voice as it came over the waves, and it was sadder than the end.

There was a long, loud swishing astern of the boat, and a gleaming trail of phosphorescence, like blue flame, was furrowed on the black waters. It might have been made by a monstrous knife.

Then there came a stillness, while the correspondent breathed with the open mouth and looked at the sea.

Suddenly there was another swish and another long flash of bluish light, and this time it was alongside the boat, and might almost have been reached with an oar. The correspondent saw an enormous fin speed like a shadow through the water, hurling the crystalline spray and leaving the long glowing trail.

The correspondent looked over his shoulder at the captain. His face was hidden, and he seemed to be asleep. He looked at the babes of the sea. They certainly were asleep. So, being bereft of sympathy, he leaned a little way to one side and swore softly into the sea.

But the thing did not then leave the vicinity of the boat. Ahead or astern, on one side or the other, at intervals long or short, fled the long sparkling streak, and there was to be heard the whiroo of the dark fin. The speed and power of the thing was greatly to be admired. It cut the water like a gigantic and keen projectile.

The presence of this biding thing did not affect the man with the same horror that it would if he had been a picknicker. He simply looked at the sea dully and swore in an undertone.

Nevertheless, it is true that he did not wish to be alone with the thing. He wished one of his companions to awaken by chance and keep him company with it. But the captain hung motionless over the water-jar and the oiler and the cook in the bottom of the boat were plunged in slumber.

VI

"If I am going to be drowned—if I am going to be drowned—if I am going to be drowned, why, in the name of the seven mad gods who rule the sea, was I allowed to come thus far and contemplate sand and trees?"

During this dismal night, it may be remarked that a man would conclude that it was really the intention of the seven mad gods to drown him, despite the abominable injustice of it. For it was certainly an abominable injustice to drown a man who had worked so hard, so hard. The man felt it would be a crime most unnatural. Other people had drowned at sea since galleys swarmed with painted sails, but still——

When it occurs to a man that nature does not regard him as important, and that she feels she would not maim the universe by disposing of him, he at first wishes to throw bricks at the temple, and he hates deeply the fact that there are no bricks and no temples. Any visible expression of nature would surely be pelleted with his jeers.

Then, if there be no tangible thing to hoot, he feels, perhaps, the desire to confront a personification and indulge in pleas, bowed to one knee, and with hands supplicant, saying: "Yes, but I love myself."

A high cold star on a winter's night is the word he feels that she says to him. Thereafter he knows the pathos of his situation.

The men in the dingey had not discussed these matters, but each had, no doubt, reflected upon them in silence and according to his mind. There was seldom any expression upon their faces save the general one of complete weariness. Speech was devoted to the business of the boat.

To chime the notes of his emotion, a verse mysteriously entered the correspondent's head. He had even forgotten that he had forgotten this verse, but it suddenly was in his mind.

> A soldier of the Legion lay dying in Algiers,
> There was lack of woman's nursing, there was dearth
> of woman's tears;
> But a comrade stood beside him, and he took that
> comrade's hand,
> And he said: "I never more shall see my own, my
> native land."[1]

In his childhood, the correspondent had been made acquainted with the fact that a soldier of the legion lay dying in Algiers, but he had never regarded it as important. Myriads of his school-fellows had informed him of the soldier's plight, but the dinning had naturally ended by making him perfectly indifferent. He had never considered it his affair that a soldier of the Legion lay dying in Algiers, nor had it appeared to him as a matter for sorrow. It was less to him than the breaking of a pencil's point.

Now, however, it quaintly came to him as a human, living thing. It was no longer merely a picture of a few throes in the breast of a poet, meanwhile drinking tea and warming his feet at the grate; it was an actuality—stern, mournful, and fine.

[1]A condensed version of the sentimental poem "Bingen on the Rhine" (1883) by Caroline E. S. Norton (1808–1877).

The correspondent plainly saw the soldier. He lay on the sand with his feet out straight and still. While his pale left hand was upon his chest in an attempt to thwart the going of his life, the blood came between his fingers. In the far Algerian distance, a city of low square forms was set against a sky that was faint with the last sunset hues. The correspondent, plying the oars and dreaming of the slow and slower movements of the soldier, was moved by a profound and perfectly impersonal comprehension. He was sorry for the soldier of the Legion who lay dying in Algiers.

The thing which had followed the boat and waited had evidently grown bored at the delay. There was no longer to be heard the slash of the cut-water, and there was no longer the flame of the long trail. The light in the north still glimmered, but it was apparently no nearer to the boat. Sometimes the boom of the surf rang in the correspondent's ears, and he turned the craft seaward then and rowed harder. Southward, some one had evidently built a watch-fire on the beach. It was too low and too far to be seen, but it made a shimmering, roseate reflection upon the bluff back of it, and this could be discerned from the boat. The wind came stronger, and sometimes a wave suddenly raged out like a mountain-cat and there was to be seen the sheen and sparkle of a broken crest.

The captain, in the bow, moved on his water-jar and sat erect. "Pretty long night," he observed to the correspondent. He looked at the shore. "Those life-saving people take their time."

"Did you see that shark playing around?"

"Yes, I saw him. He was a big fellow, all right."

"Wish I had known you were awake."

Later the correspondent spoke into the bottom of the boat.

"Billie!" There was a slow and gradual disentanglement. "Billie, will you spell me?"

"Sure," said the oiler.

As soon as the correspondent touched the cold comfortable seawater in the bottom of the boat, and had huddled close to the cook's life-belt he was deep in sleep, despite the fact that his teeth played all the popular airs. This sleep was so good to him that it was but a moment before he heard a voice call his name in a tone that demonstrated the last stages of exhaustion. "Will you spell me?"

"Sure, Billie."

The light in the north had mysteriously vanished, but the correspondent took his course from the wide-awake captain.

Later in the night they took the boat farther out to sea, and the captain directed the cook to take one oar at the stern and keep the boat facing the seas. He was to call out if he should hear the thunder of the surf. This plan enabled the oiler and the correspondent to get respite together. "We'll give those boys a chance to get into shape again," said the captain. They curled down and, after a few preliminary chatterings and trembles, slept once more the dead sleep. Neither knew they had bequeathed to the cook the company of another shark, or perhaps the same shark.

As the boat caroused on the waves, spray occasionally bumped over the side and gave them a fresh soaking, but this had no power to break their repose. The ominous slash of the wind and the water affected them as it would have affected mummies.

"Boys," said the cook, with the notes of every reluctance in his voice, "she's drifted in pretty close. I guess one of you had better take her to sea again." The correspondent, aroused, heard the crash of the toppled crests.

As he was rowing, the captain gave him some whiskey and water, and this steadied the chills out of him. "If I ever get ashore and anybody shows me even a photograph of an oar——"

At last there was a short conversation.

"Billie. . . . Billie, will you spell me?"

"Sure," said the oiler.

VII

When the correspondent again opened his eyes, the sea and the sky were each of the gray hue of the dawning. Later, carmine and gold was painted upon the waters. The morning appeared finally, in its splendor, with a sky of pure blue, and the sunlight flamed on the tips of the waves.

On the distant dunes were set many little black cottages, and a tall white wind-mill reared above them. No man, nor dog, nor bicycle appeared on the beach. The cottages might have formed a deserted village.

The voyagers scanned the shore. A conference was held in the boat. "Well," said the captain, "if no help is coming, we might better try a run through the surf right away. If we stay out here much longer we will be too weak to do anything for ourselves at all." The others silently acquiesced in this reasoning. The boat was headed for the beach. The correspondent wondered if none ever ascended the tall wind-tower, and if then they never looked seaward. This tower was a giant, standing with its back to the plight of the ants. It represented in a degree, to the correspondent, the serenity of nature amid the struggles of the individual—nature in the wind, and nature in the vision of men. She did not seem cruel to him then, nor beneficent, nor treacherous, nor wise. But she was indifferent, flatly indifferent. It is, perhaps, plausible that a man in this situation, impressed with the unconcern of the universe, should see the innumerable flaws of his life and have them taste wickedly in his mind and wish for another chance. A distinction between right and wrong seems absurdly clear to him, then, in this new ignorance of the grave-edge, and he understands that if he were given another opportunity he would mend his conduct and his words, and be better and brighter during an introduction, or a tea.

"Now, boys," said the captain, "she is going to swamp sure. All we can do is to work her in as far as possible, and then when she swamps, pile out and scramble for the beach. Keep cool now, and don't jump until she swamps sure."

The oiler took the oars. Over his shoulders he scanned the surf. "Captain," he said, "I think I'd better bring her about, and keep her head-on to the seas and back her in."

"All right Billie," said the captain. "Back her in." The oiler swung the boat then and, seated in the stern, the cook and the correspondent were obliged to look over their shouders to contemplate the lonely and indifferent shore.

The monstrous inshore rollers heaved the boat high until the men were again enabled to see the white sheets of water scudding up the slanted beach. "We won't get in very close," said the captain. Each time a man could wrest his attention from the rollers, he turned his glance toward the shore, and in the expression of the eyes during this contemplation there was a singular quality. The correspondent, observing the others, knew that they were not afraid, but the full meaning of their glances was shrouded.

As for himself, he was too tired to grapple fundamentally with the fact. He tried to coerce his mind into thinking of it, but the mind was dominated at this time by the muscles, and the muscles said they did not care. It merely occurred to him that if he should drown it would be a shame.

There were no hurried words, no pallor, no plain agitation. The men simply looked at the shore. "Now, remember to get well clear of the boat when you jump," said the captain.

Seaward the crest of a roller suddenly fell with a thunderous crash, and the long white comber came roaring down upon the boat.

"Steady now," said the captain. The men were silent. They turned their eyes from the shore to the comber and waited. The boat slid up the incline, leaped at the furious top, bounced over it, and swung down the long back of the wave. Some water had been shipped and the cook bailed it out.

But the next crest crashed also. The tumbling boiling flood of white water caught the boat and whirled it almost perpendicular. Water swarmed in from all sides. The correspondent had his hands on the gunwale at this time, and when the water entered at that place he swiftly withdrew his fingers, as if he objected to wetting them.

The little boat, drunken with this weight of water, reeled and snuggled deeper into the sea.

"Bail her out, cook! Bail her out," said the captain.

"All right, Captain," said the cook.

"Now, boys, the next one will do for us, sure," said the oiler. "Mind to jump clear of the boat."

The third wave moved forward, huge, furious, implacable. It fairly swallowed the dingey, and almost simultaneously the men tumbled into the sea. A piece of life-belt had lain in the bottom of the boat, and as the correspondent went overboard he held this to his chest with his left hand.

The January water was icy, and he reflected immediately that it was colder than he had expected to find it off the coast of Florida. This appeared to his dazed mind as a fact important enough to be noted at the time. The coldness of the water was sad; it was tragic. This fact was somehow so mixed and confused with his opinion of his own situation that it seemed almost a proper reason for tears. The water was cold.

When he came to the surface he was conscious of little but the noisy water. Afterward he saw his companions in the sea. The oiler was ahead in the race. He was swimming strongly and rapidly. Off to the correspondent's left, the cook's great white and corked back bulged out of the water, and in the rear the captain was hanging with his one good hand to the keel of the overturned dingey.

There was a certain immovable quality to a shore, and the correspondent wondered at it amid the confusion of the sea.

It seemed also very attractive, but the correspondent knew that it was a long journey, and he paddled leisurely. The piece of life-preserver lay under him, and sometimes he whirled down the incline of a wave as if he were on a hand-sled.

But finally he arrived at a place in the sea where travel was beset with difficulty. He did not pause swimming to inquire what matter of current had caught him, but there his progress ceased. The shore was set before him like a bit of scenery on a stage, and he looked at it and understood with his eyes each detail of it.

As the cook passed, much farther to the left, the captain was calling to him. "Turn over on your back, cook! Turn over on your back and use the oar."

"All right, sir." The cook turned on his back, and, paddling with an oar, went ahead as if he were a canoe.

Presently the boat also passed to the left of the correspondent with the captain clinging with one hand to the keel. He would have appeared like a man raising himself to look over a board fence, if it were not for the extraordinary gymnastics of the boat. The correspondent marvelled that the captain could still hold to it.

They passed on, nearer to shore—the oiler, the cook, the captain—and following them went the water-jar, bouncing gayly over the seas.

The correspondent remained in the grip of this strange new enemy—a current. The shore, with its white slope of sand and its green bluff, topped with little silent cottages, was spread like a picture before him. It was very near to him then, but he was impressed as one who in a gallery looks at a scene from Brittany or Holland.

He thought: "Am I going to drown? Can it be possible? Can it be possible? Can it be possible?" Perhaps an individual must consider his own death to be the final phenomenon of nature.

But later a wave perhaps whirled him out of this small deadly current, for he found suddenly that he could again make progress toward the shore. Later still, he was aware that the captain, clinging with one hand to the keel of the dingey, had his face turned away from the shore and toward him, and was calling his name. "Come to the boat! Come to the boat!"

In his struggle to reach the captain and the boat, he reflected that when one gets properly wearied, drowning must really be a comfortable arrangement, a cessation of hostilities accompanied by a large degree of relief, and he was glad of it, for the main thing in his mind for some moments had been horror of the temporary agony. He did not wish to be hurt.

Presently he saw a man running along the shore. He was undressing with most remarkable speed. Coat, trousers, shirt, everything flew magically off him.

"Come to the boat," called the captain.

"All right, Captain." As the correspondent paddled, he saw the captain let himself down to bottom and leave the boat. Then the correspondent performed his one little marvel of the voyage. A large wave caught him and flung him with ease and supreme speed completely over the boat and far beyond it. It struck him even then as an event in gymnastics, and a true miracle of the sea. An overturned boat in the surf is not a plaything to a swimming man.

The correspondent arrived in water that reached only to his waist, but his condition did not enable him to stand for more than a moment. Each wave knocked him into a heap, and the under-tow pulled at him.

Then he saw the man who had been running and undressing, and undressing and running, come bounding into the water. He dragged ashore the cook, and then waded toward the captain, but the captain waved him away, and sent him to the correspondent. He was naked, naked as a tree in winter, but a halo was about his head, and he shone like a saint. He gave a strong pull, and a long drag, and a bully heave at the correspondent's hand. The correspondent, schooled in the minor formulae, said: "Thanks, old man." But suddenly the man cried: "What's that?" He pointed a swift finger. The correspondent said: "Go."

In the shallows, face downward, lay the oiler. His forehead touched sand that was periodically, between each wave, clear of the sea.

The correspondent did not know all that transpired afterward.

When he achieved safe ground he fell, striking the sand with each particular part of his body. It was as if he had dropped from a roof, but the thud was grateful to him.

It seems that instantly the beach was populated with men with blankets, clothes, and flasks, and women with coffee-pots and all the remedies sacred to their minds. The welcome of the land to the men from the sea was warm and generous, but a still and dripping shape was carried slowly up the beach, and the land's welcome for it could only be the different and sinister hospitality of the grave.

When it came night, the white waves paced to and fro in the moonlight, and the wind brought the sound of the great sea's voice to the men on shore, and they felt that they could then be interpreters.

1897 1897

Frank Norris 1870–1902

Perhaps as much as any other writer, Frank Norris, in his life and works, revealed the contradictions and paradoxes of America at the turn of the century. He was a confirmed realist who rejected the conventions of popular sentimental fiction, but, like one of his own characters, he was sometimes drawn to search for "True Romance," to "see everything through a rose-coloured mist—a mist that dulled all harsh outlines, all crude and violent colors." The principal influences on his ideas and writing came from Harvard College and from the French literary world, yet he felt that the "big American novel is going to come out of the West." His first published work, Yvernele, A Tale of Feudal France *(1891), was a lengthy romantic poem on a medieval theme, but in the work that followed he became the foremost exponent of literary naturalism in nineteenth-century America.*

Norris was born in Chicago and moved to San Francisco with his parents when he was fourteen. After prep school he studied art in London and Paris and attended the University of California, where he first read the work of Zola. He spent a year at Harvard, and there he began work on his novels McTeague *(1899) and* Vandover and the Brute *(1914). From Harvard, Norris went to South Africa to write travel sketches, but he got involved in the politics of the Boer War and was expelled from the country. Returning to San Francisco, he went to work for a magazine which published a number of his short stories, including "A Deal in Wheat," and serialized his first novel,* Moran of the Lady Letty *(1898), a wild tale of pirate adventures.*

In 1898, Norris went to Cuba to report on the Spanish-American War for McClure's *Magazine. He became an editor for the publishing firm of Doubleday, and in 1899 his novel,* McTeague, *was published, creating a literary scandal because of its sensational treatment of greed and degeneracy. In the same year Norris conceived his most ambitious work, three novels on the American West and the growth and distribution of wheat. The first book,* The Octopus, *dealing with the strangling greed of railroad owners and the growing of wheat, appeared in 1901 and was immediately successful. The second,* The Pit *(1903), dealt with the marketing of wheat. The third novel, which was to be named* The Wolf *and portray the consumption of the wheat in Europe, was never written. Norris had just completed the second volume of the trilogy when he died from a ruptured appendix in October 1902.*

Norris is often criticized for excessive sentiment in his realistic fiction, for his romantic reliance on the regenerative power of love, and for his philosophical inconsistencies. He was, in fact, less interested in literary or social theories than in achieving dramatic power in stories of individuals moved by forces of heredity and forces of history that they could not control and rarely understood. Norris believed that fiction can express the truth of life better than any other art, "better than painting, better than poetry, better than music." It was for him a means of getting at truth, of cutting through the "tissues and wrappings of flesh, down deep into the red, living heart of things."

FURTHER READING: *The Complete Edition of Frank Norris,* 10 vols., 1928 [1929]; F. Walker, *Frank Norris, A Biography,* 1932; E. Marchand, *Frank Norris, A Study,* 1942; *The Letters of Frank Norris,* ed. F. Walker, 1956; *The Literary Criticism of Frank Norris,* ed. D. Pizer, 1962; W. French, *Frank Norris,* 1962; D. Pizer, *The Novels of Frank Norris,* 1966; W. Dillingham, *Frank Norris, Instinct and Art,* 1969; D. Graham, *The Fiction of Frank Norris,* 1978; *Critical Essays on Frank Norris,* ed. D. Graham, 1980; *Frank Norris, The Critical Reception,* ed. J. McElrath, 1981; B. Hochman, *The Art of Frank Norris,* 1988; J. McElrath, *Frank Norris Revisited,* 1992; L. Hussman, *The Novels of Frank Norris,* 1999.

TEXT: *The Complete Works of Frank Norris,* 7 vols., 1903.

A DEAL IN WHEAT

I

THE BEAR[1]—WHEAT AT SIXTY-TWO

As Sam Lewiston backed the horse into the shafts of his buckboard and began hitching the tugs to the whiffletree,[2] his wife came out from the kitchen door of the house and drew near, and stood for some time at the horse's head, her arms folded and her apron rolled around them. For a long moment neither spoke. They had talked over the situation so long and so comprehensively the night before that there seemed to be nothing more to say.

[1]In the jargon of stock exchanges, "bears" are traders who profit from a falling (bear) market; "bulls" profit from a rising (bull) market.

[2]Pivoted bar to which harness lines (tugs) are fastened.

The time was late in the summer, the place a ranch in southwestern Kansas, and Lewiston and his wife were two of a vast population of farmers, wheat growers, who at that moment were passing through a crisis—a crisis that at any moment might culminate in tragedy. Wheat was down to sixty-six.

At length Emma Lewiston spoke.

"Well," she hazarded, looking vaguely out across the ranch toward the horizon, leagues distant; "well, Sam, there's always that offer of brother Joe's. We can quit—and go to Chicago—if the worst comes."

"And give up!" exclaimed Lewiston, running the lines through the torets.[3] "Leave the ranch! Give up! After all these years!"

His wife made no reply for the moment. Lewiston climbed into the buckboard and gathered up the lines. "Well, here goes for the last try, Emmie," he said. "Good-by, girl. Maybe things will look better in town to-day."

"Maybe," she said gravely. She kissed her husband good-by and stood for some time looking after the buckboard traveling toward the town in a moving pillar of dust.

"I don't know," she murmured at length; "I don't know just how we're going to make out."

When he reached town, Lewiston tied the horse to the iron railing in front of the Odd Fellows' Hall, the ground floor of which was occupied by the post-office, and went across the street and up the stairway of a building of brick and granite—quite the most pretentious structure of the town—and knocked at a door upon the first landing. The door was furnished with a pane of frosted glass, on which in gold letters, was inscribed "Bridges & Co., Grain Dealers."

Bridges himself, a middle-aged man who wore a velvet skullcap and who was smoking a Pittsburg stogie, met the farmer at the counter and the two exchanged perfunctory greetings.

"Well," said Lewiston, tentatively, after a while.

"Well, Lewiston," said the other, "I can't take that wheat of yours at any better than sixty-two."

"Sixty-*two*."

"It's the Chicago price that does it, Lewiston. Truslow is bearing the stuff for all he's worth. It's Truslow and the bear clique that stick the knife to us. The price broke again this morning. We've just got a wire."

"Good heavens," murmured Lewiston, looking vaguely from side to side. "That—that ruins me. I *can't* carry my grain any longer—what with storage charges and—and— Bridges, I don't see just how I'm going to make out. Sixty-two cents a bushel! Why, man, what with this and with that it's cost me nearly a dollar a bushel to raise that wheat, and now Truslow——"

He turned away abruptly with a quick gesture of infinite discouragement.

He went down the stairs, and making his way to where his buckboard was hitched, got in, and, with eyes vacant, the reins slipping and sliding in his limp, half-open hands, drove slowly back to the ranch. His wife had seen him coming, and met him as he drew up before the barn.

"Well?" she demanded.

[3]Harness rings.

"Emmie," he said as he got out of the buckboard, laying his arm across her shoulder, "Emmie, I guess we'll take up with Joe's offer. We'll go to Chicago. We're cleaned out!"

II

THE BULL—WHEAT AT A DOLLAR-TEN

. . .—— *and said Party of the Second Part further covenants and agrees to merchandise such wheat in foreign ports, it being understood and agreed between the Party of the First Part and the Party of the Second Part that the wheat hereinbefore mentioned is released and sold to the Party of the Second Part for export purposes only, and not for consumption or distribution within the boundaries of the United States of America or of Canada.*

"Now, Mr. Gates, if you will sign for Mr. Truslow, I guess that'll be all," remarked Hornung when he had finished reading.

Hornung affixed his signature to the two documents and passed them over to Gates, who signed for his principal client. Truslow—or, as he had been called ever since he had gone into the fight against Hornung's corner—the Great Bear. Hornung's secretary was called in and witnessed the signatures, and Gates thrust the contract into his Gladstone bag[1] and stood up, smoothing his hat.

"You will deliver the warehouse receipts for the grain," began Gates.

"I'll send a messenger to Truslow's office before noon," interrupted Hornung. "You can pay by certified check through the Illinois Trust people."

When the other had taken himself off, Hornung sat for some moments gazing abstractedly toward his office windows, thinking over the whole matter. He had just agreed to release to Truslow, at the rate of one dollar and ten cents per bushel, one hundred thousand out of the two million and odd bushels of wheat that he, Hornung, controlled, or actually owned. And for the moment he was wondering if, after all, he had done wisely in not goring the Great Bear to actual financial death. He had made him pay one hundred thousand dollars. Truslow was good for this amount. Would it not have been better to have put a prohibitive figure on the grain and forced the Bear into bankruptcy? True, Hornung would then be without his enemy's money, but Truslow would have been eliminated from the situation, and that—so Hornung told himself—was always a consummation most devoutly, strenuously and diligently to be striven for. Truslow once dead was dead, but the Bear was never more dangerous than when desperate.

"But so long as he can't get *wheat,*" muttered Hornung at the end of his reflections, "he can't hurt me. And he can't get it. That I *know.*"

For Hornung controlled the situation. So far back as the February of that year an "unknown bull" had been making his presence felt on the floor of the Board of Trade. By the middle of March the commercial reports of the daily press had begun to speak of "the powerful bull clique"; a few weeks later that legendary condition of affairs implied and epitomized in the magic words "Dollar Wheat" had been attained, and by the first of April, when the

[1]A traveling bag with a rigid frame and flexible sides, named for William Gladstone (1809–1898), British statesman.

price had been boosted to one dollar and ten cents a bushel, Hornung had disclosed his hand, and in place of mere rumors, the definite and authoritative news that May wheat had been cornered in the Chicago Pit[2] went flashing around the world from Liverpool to Odessa and from Duluth to Buenos Ayres.

It was—as the veteran operators were persuaded—Truslow himself who had made Hornung's corner possible. The Great Bear had for once overreached himself, and, believing himself all-powerful, had hammered the price just the fatal fraction too far down. Wheat had gone to sixty-two—for the time, and under the circumstances, an abnormal price. When the reaction came it was tremendous. Hornung saw his chance, seized it, and in a few months had turned the tables, had cornered the product, and virtually driven the bear clique out of the pit.

On the same day that the delivery of the hundred thousand bushels was made to Truslow, Hornung met his broker at his lunch club.

"Well," said the latter, "I see you let go that line of stuff to Truslow."

Hornung nodded; but the broker added:

"Remember, I was against it from the very beginning. I know we've cleared up over a hundred thou'. I would have fifty times preferred to have lost twice that and *smashed Truslow dead.* Bet you what you like he makes us pay for it somehow."

"Huh!" grunted his principal. "How about insurance and warehouse charges, and carrying expenses on that lot? Guess we'd have have had to pay those, too, if we'd held on."

But the other put up his chin, unwilling to be persuaded. "I won't sleep easy," he declared, "till Truslow is busted."

III

THE PIT

Just as Going mounted the steps on the edge of the pit the great gong struck, a roar of a hundred voices developed with the swiftness of successive explosions, the rush of a hundred men surging downward to the centre of the pit filled the air with the stamp and grind of feet, a hundred hands in eager strenuous gestures tossed upward from out the brown of the crowd, the official reporter in his cage on the margin of the pit leaned far forward with straining ear to catch the opening bid, and another day of battle was begun.

Since the sale of the hundred thousand bushels of wheat to Truslow the "Hornung crowd" had steadily shouldered the price higher until on this particular morning it stood at one dollar and a half. That was Hornung's price. No one else had any grain to sell.

But not ten minutes after the opening, Going was surprised out of all countenance to hear shouted from the other side of the pit these words:

"Sell May at one-fifty."

[2]Area in the exchange where actual trading is done. A speculator has "cornered" the market when he or she owns enough of a commodity to control the selling price.

Going was for the moment touching elbows with Kimbark on one side and with Merriam on the other, all three belonging to the "Hornung crowd." Their answering challenge of *"Sold"* was as the voice of one man. They did not pause to reflect upon the strangeness of the circumstance. (That was for afterward.) Their response to the offer was as unconscious as reflex action and almost as rapid, and before the pit was well aware of what had happened the transaction of one thousand bushels was down upon Going's trading-card and fifteen hundred dollars had changed hands. But here was a marvel—the whole available supply of wheat cornered, Hornung master of the situation, invincible, unassailable; yet behold a man willing to sell, a Bear bold enough to raise his head.

"That was Kennedy, wasn't it, who made that offer?" asked Kimbark, as Going noted down the trade—"Kennedy, that new man?"

"Yes; who do you suppose he's selling for; who's willing to go short at this stage of the game?"

"Maybe he ain't short."

"Short! Great heavens, man; where'd he get the stuff?"

"Blamed if I know. We can account for every handful of May. Steady! Oh, there he goes again."

"Sell a thousand May at one-fifty," vociferated the bear-broker, throwing out his hand, one finger raised to indicate the number of "contracts" offered. This time it was evident that he was attacking the Hornung crowd deliberately, for, ignoring the jam of traders that swept toward him, he looked across the pit to where Going and Kimbark were shouting *"Sold! Sold!"* and nodded his head.

A second time Going made memoranda of the trade, and either the Hornung holdings were increased by two thousand bushels of May wheat or the Hornung bank account swelled by at least three thousand dollars of some unknown short's money.

Of late—so sure was the bull crowd of its position—no one had even thought of glancing at the inspection sheet on the bulletin board. But now one of Going's messengers hurried up to him with the announcement that this sheet showed receipts at Chicago for that morning of twenty-five thousand bushels, and not credited to Hornung. Some one had got hold of a line of wheat overlooked by the "clique" and was dumping it upon them.

"Wire the Chief," said Going over his shoulder to Merriam. This one struggled out of the crowd, and on a telegraph blank scribbled:

"Strong bear movement—New man—Kennedy—Selling in lots of five contracts—Chicago receipts twenty-five thousand."

The message was despatched, and in a few moments the answer came back, laconic, of military terseness.

"Support the market."

And Going obeyed, Merriam and Kimbark following, the new broker fairly throwing the wheat at them in thousand-bushel lots.

"Sell May at 'fifty; sell May; sell May." A moment's indecision, an instant's hesitation, the first faint suggestion of weakness, and the market would have broken under them. But for the better part of four hours they stood their ground, taking all that was offered, in constant communication with the

Chief, and from time to time stimulated and steadied by his brief, unvarying command:

"Support the market."

At the close of the session they had bought in the twenty-five thousand bushels of May. Hornung's position was as stable as a rock, and the price closed even with the opening figure—one dollar and a half.

But the morning's work was the talk of all La Salle Street.[1] Who was back of the raid? What was the meaning of this unexpected selling? For weeks the Pit trading had been merely nominal. Truslow, the Great Bear, from whom the most serious attack might have been expected, had gone to his country seat at Geneva Lake, in Wisconsin, declaring himself to be out of the market entirely. He went bass fishing every day.

IV

THE BELT LINE

On a certain day toward the middle of the month, at a time when the mysterious Bear had unloaded some eighty thousand bushels upon Hornung, a conference was held in the library of Hornung's home. His broker attended it, and also a clean-faced, bright-eyed individual whose name of Cyrus Ryder might have been found upon the pay-roll of a rather well-known detective agency. For upward of half an hour after the conference began the detective spoke, the other two listening attentively, gravely.

"Then, last of all," concluded Ryder, "I made out I was a hobo, and began stealing rides on the Belt Line Railroad. Know the road? It just circles Chicago. Truslow owns it. Yes? Well, then I began to catch on. I noticed that cars of certain numbers—thirty-one naught thirty-four, thirty-two one ninety—well, the numbers don't matter, but anyhow, these cars were always switched on to the sidings by Mr. Truslow's main elevator D soon as they came in. The wheat was shunted in, and they were pulled out again. Well, I spotted one car and stole a ride on her. Say, look here, *that car went right around the city on the Belt, and came back to D again, and the same wheat in her all the time.* The grain was reinspected—it was raw, I tell you—and the warehouse receipts made out just as though the stuff had come in from Kansas or Iowa."

"The same wheat all the time!" interrupted Hornung.

"The same wheat—your wheat, that you sold to Truslow."

"Great snakes!" ejaculated Hornung's broker. "Truslow never took it abroad at all."

"Took it abroad! Say, he's just been running it around Chicago, like the supers in 'Shenandoah,'[1] round an' round, so you'd think it was a new lot, an' selling it back to you again."

"No wonder we couldn't account for so much wheat."

[1]Location of the Chicago Board of Trade.

[1]The supernumeraries, or "extras," in the cast of the Civil War play *Shenandoah* (1888) marched in a continuous circle across and behind the stage to give the impression of a vast army.

"Bought it from us at one-ten, and made us buy it back—our own wheat—at one-fifty."

Hornung and his broker looked at each other in silence for a moment. Then all at once Hornung struck the arm of his chair with his fist and exploded in a roar of laughter. The broker stared for one bewildered moment, then followed his example.

"Sold! Sold!" shouted Hornung almost gleefully. "Upon my soul it's as good as a Gilbert and Sullivan show. And we— Oh, Lord! Billy, shake on it, and hats off to my distinguished friend, Truslow. He'll be President some day. Hey! What? Prosecute him? Not I."

"He's done us out of a neat hatful of dollars for all that," observed the broker, suddenly grave.

"Billy, it's worth the price."

"We've got to make it up somehow."

"Well, tell you what. We were going to boost the price to one seventy-five next week, and make that our settlement figure."

"Can't do it now. Can't afford it."

"No. Here; we'll let out a big link; we'll put wheat at two dollars, and let it go at that."

"Two it is, then," said the broker.

V

THE BREAD LINE

The street was very dark and absolutely deserted. It was a district on the "South Side," not far from the Chicago River, given up largely to wholesale stores, and after nightfall was empty of all life. The echoes slept but lightly hereabouts, and the slightest footfall, the faintest noise, woke them upon the instant and sent them clamoring up and down the length of the pavement between the iron-shuttered fronts. The only light visible came from the side door of a certain "Vienna" bakery, where at one o'clock in the morning loaves of bread were given away to any who should ask. Every evening about nine o'clock the outcasts began to gather about the side door. The stragglers came in rapidly, and the line—the "bread line," as it was called—began to form. By midnight it was usually some hundred yards in length, stretching almost the entire length of the block.

Toward ten in the evening, his coat collar turned up against the fine drizzle that pervaded the air, his hands in his pockets, his elbows gripping his sides, Sam Lewiston came up and silently took his place at the end of the line.

Unable to conduct his farm upon a paying basis at the time when Truslow, the "Great Bear," had sent the price of grain down to sixty-two cents a bushel, Lewiston had turned over his entire property to his creditors, and, leaving Kansas for good, had abandoned farming, and had left his wife at her sister's boarding-house in Topeka with the understanding that she was to join him in Chicago so soon as he had found a steady job. Then he had come to Chicago and had turned workman. His brother Joe conducted a small hat factory on Archer Avenue, and for a time he found there a meagre employment. But difficulties had occurred, times were bad, the hat factory was involved in debts, the repealing of a certain import duty on manufactured felt overcrowded the home market with cheap Belgian and French products, and in the end his brother had assigned[1] and gone to Milwaukee.

Thrown out of work, Lewiston drifted aimlessly about Chicago, from pillar to post, working a little, earning here a dollar, there a dime, but always sinking, sinking, till at last the ooze of the lowest bottom dragged at his feet and the rush of the great ebb went over him and engulfed him and shut him out from the light, and a park bench became his home and the "bread line" his chief makeshift of subsistence.

He stood now in the infolding drizzle, sodden, stupefied with fatigue. Before and behind stretched the line. There was no talking. There was no sound. The street was empty. It was so still that the passing of a cable-car in the adjoining thoroughfare grated like prolonged rolling explosions, beginning and ending at immeasurable distances. The drizzle descended incessantly. After a long time midnight struck.

There was something ominous and gravely impressive in this interminable line of dark figures, close-pressed, soundless; a crowd, yet absolutely still; a close-packed, silent file, waiting, waiting in the vast deserted night-ridden street; waiting without a word, without a movement, there under the night and under the slow-moving mists of rain.

Few in the crowd were professional beggars. Most of them were workmen, long since out of work, forced into idleness by long-continued "hard times," by ill luck, by sickness. To them the "bread line" was a godsend. At least they could not starve. Between jobs here in the end was something to hold them up—a small platform, as it were, above the sweep of black water, where for a moment they might pause and take breath before the plunge.

The period of waiting on this night of rain seemed endless to those silent, hungry men; but at length there was a stir. The line moved. The side door opened. Ah, at last! They were going to hand out the bread.

But instead of the usual white-aproned under-cook with his crowded hampers there now appeared in the doorway a new man—a young fellow who looked like a bookkeeper's assistant. He bore in his hand a placard, which he tacked to the outside of the door. Then he disappeared within the bakery, locking the door after him.

A shudder of poignant despair, an unformed, inarticulate sense of calamity, seemed to run from end to end of the line. What had happened? Those in the rear, unable to read the placard, surged forward, a sense of bitter disappointment clutching at their hearts.

The line broke up, disintegrated into a shapeless throng—a throng that crowded forward and collected in front of the shut door whereon the placard was affixed. Lewiston, with the others, pushed forward. On the placard he read these words:

> "Owing to the fact that the price of grain has been increased to two dollars a bushel, there will be no distribution of bread from this bakery until further notice."

Lewiston turned away, dumb, bewildered. Till morning he walked the streets, going on without purpose, without direction. But now at last his luck had turned. Overnight the wheel of his fortunes had creaked and swung

[1]Turned over his remaining property to his creditors.

upon its axis, and before noon he had found a job in the street-cleaning brigade. In the course of time he rose to be first shift-boss, then deputy inspector, then inspector, promoted to the dignity of driving a red wagon with rubber tires and drawing a salary instead of mere wages. The wife was sent for and a new start made.

But Lewiston never forgot. Dimly he began to see the significance of things. Caught once in the cogs and wheels of a great and terrible engine, he had seen—none better—its workings. Of all the men who had vainly stood in the "bread line" on that rainy night in early summer, he, perhaps, had been the only one who had struggled up to the surface again. How many others had gone down in the great ebb? Grim question; he dared not think how many.

He had seen the two ends of a great wheat operation—a battle between Bear and Bull. The stories (subsequently published in the city's press) of Truslow's counter move in selling Hornung his own wheat, supplied the unseen section. The farmer—he who raised the wheat—was ruined upon one hand; the workingman—he who consumed it—was ruined upon the other. But between the two, the great operators, who never saw the wheat they traded in, bought and sold the world's food, gambled in the nourishment of entire nations, practiced their tricks, their chicanery and oblique shifty "deals," were reconciled in their differences, and went on through their appointed way, jovial, contented, enthroned, and unassailable.

1902

Jack London 1876–1916

Jack London was the illegitimate son of a father who was a wandering astrologer and a mother who was a spiritualist and medium. Born in San Francisco, London was raised in Oakland, where he roamed the waterfront and attended school only occasionally, but, as he reported in his autobiographical novel, Martin Eden *(1909), he read constantly, as much as nineteen hours a day. He "rode the rods" over the Sierras to the East, was jailed for vagrancy in Buffalo at eighteen, worked as an "oyster pirate" in San Francisco Bay, stealing from the oyster beds belonging to other fishermen. He sailed as a seaman on a sealing trip to Japan and in 1896 joined the gold rush to the Klondike, where he found no gold but gathered ample material for the brutal, vigorous life he portrayed in* The Call of the Wild *(1903) and* White Fang *(1906), novels of man and beast struggling against the tremendous forces of nature.*

From 1900 to 1916, London wrote more than fifty books, earning a million dollars, which he spent (as quickly as he earned it) in a frantic search for contentment. But London found gratification neither in his writing nor in his personal life, and his last years were marked by struggles with alcoholism and mental disintegration. He died, probably by his own hand, when he was forty.

From social Darwinism London had absorbed the idea that to survive, people must adapt to irresistible natural forces and to "the stress and strain of life, its fevers and sweats and wild indulgences." Although his writing is often categorized simply as literary naturalism, the sources of his ideas were complex. London was most deeply influenced by the seemingly irreconcilable opposites of Nietzsche and Marx. From Nietzsche he borrowed the idea of the super human beings, evident in its most destructive form in Wolf Larsen, the predatory hero of London's The Sea Wolf *(1904). From Marx he took the idea of the need for social reform and of the power of economic determinism, concepts he embodied in his socialistic treatises,* The War of the Classes *(1905) and* The Human Drift *(1907), and in his terrifying vision of the coming of totalitarianism,* The Iron Heel *(1907).*

London was a storyteller of great emotional power and excitement, a master of tempo and pace whose adventure stories continue to fascinate a large reading public. As a writer, he was bold, sensational, tragic and, like his characters, a champion and a victim of the "wild indulgences" of life and nature.

FURTHER READING: R. O'Connor, *Jack London, A Biography,* 1964; F. Walker, *Jack London and the Klondike,* 1966; E. Labor, *Jack London,* 1974; J. McClintock, *White Logic, Jack London's Short Stories,* 1975; A. Sinclair, *Jack, A Biography of Jack London,* 1977, 1983; R. Kingman, *A Pictorial Life of Jack London,* 1981; J. Perry, *Jack London, An American Myth,* 1981; J. Hedrick, *Solitary Comrade, Jack London and His Work,* 1982; C. Watson, *The Novels of Jack London,* 1983; *Critical Essays on Jack London,* ed. J. Tavernier-Courbin, 1983; J. Lundquist, *Jack London,* 1987; C. Stasz, *American Dreamers, Charmian and Jack London,* 1988; J. London, *Jack London and His Daughters,* 1991; R. Kingman, *Jack London, A Definitive Chronology,* 1992; T. Williams, *Jack London—The Movies, An Historical Survey,* 1992; *Complete Short Stories of Jack London,* ed. E. Labor, R. Leitz, and I. Shepard, 1993; J. Auerbach, *Male Call, Becoming Jack London,* 1996; *Re-reading Jack London,* ed. L. Cassuto and J. Reesman, 1996; A. Kershaw, *Jack London, A Life,* 1997.

TEXT: *Children of the Frost,* 1902.

THE LAW OF LIFE

Old Koskoosh listened greedily. Though his sight had long since faded, his hearing was still acute, and the slightest sound penetrated to the glimmering intelligence which yet abode behind the withered forehead, but which no longer gazed forth upon the things of the world. Ah! That was Sit-cum-to-ha, shrilly anathematizing the dogs as she cuffed and beat them into the harnesses. Sit-cum-to-ha was his daughter's daughter, but she was too busy to waste a thought upon her broken grandfather, sitting alone there in the snow, forlorn and helpless. Camp must be broken. The long trail waited while the short day refused to linger. Life called her, and the duties of life, not death. And he was very close to death now.

The thought made the old man panicky for the moment, and he stretched forth a palsied hand which wandered tremblingly over the small heap of dry wood beside him. Reassured that it was indeed there, his hand returned to the shelter of his mangy furs, and he again fell to listening. The sulky crackling of half-frozen hides told him that the chief's moose-skin lodge had been struck, and even then was being rammed and jammed into portable compass. The chief was his son, stalwart and strong, headman of the tribesmen, and a mighty hunter. As the women toiled with the camp luggage, his voice rose, chiding them for their slowness. Old Koskoosh strained his ears. It was the last time he would hear that voice. There went Geehow's lodge! And Tusken's! Seven, eight, nine, only the shaman's[1] could be still standing. There! They were at work upon it now. He could hear the shaman grunt as he piled it on the sled. A child whimpered, and a woman soothed it with soft, crooning gutturals. Little Koo-tee, the old man thought, a fretful child, and not overstrong. It would die soon, perhaps, and they would burn a hole through the frozen tundra and pile rocks above to keep the wolverines away. Well, what did it matter? A few years at best, and as many an empty belly as a full one. And in the end, Death waited, ever-hungry and hungriest of them all.

What was that? Oh, the men lashing the sleds and drawing tight the thongs. He listened, who would listen no more. The whiplashes snarled and bit among the dogs. Hear them whine! How they hated the work and the trail! They were off! Sled after sled churned slowly away into the silence. They were gone. They had passed out of his life, and he faced the last bitter hour alone. No. The snow crunched beneath a moccasin; a man stood beside him; upon his head a hand rested gently. His son was good to do this thing. He remembered other old men whose sons had not waited after the tribe. But his son had. He wandered away into the past, till the young man's voice brought him back.

"It is well with you?" he asked.

And the old man answered, "It is well."

"There be wood beside you," the younger man continued, "and the fire burns bright. The morning is gray, and the cold has broken. It will snow presently. Even now it is snowing."

"Aye, even now it is snowing."

"The tribesmen hurry. Their bales are heavy and their bellies flat with lack of feasting. The trail is long and they travel fast. I go now. It is well?"

"It is well. I am as a last year's leaf, clinging lightly to the stem. The first breath that blows, and I fall. My voice is become like an old woman's. My eyes no longer show me the way of my feet, and my feet are heavy, and I am tired. It is well."

He bowed his head in content till the last noise of the complaining snow had died away, and he knew his son was beyond recall. Then his hand crept out in haste to the wood. It alone stood between him and the eternity that yawned in upon him. At last the measure of his life was a handful of faggots. One by one they would go to feed the fire, and just so, step by step, death would creep upon him. When the last stick had surrendered up its heat, the frost would begin to gather strength. First his feet would yield, then his hands; and the numbness would travel, slowly, from the extremities to the body. His head would fall forward upon his knees, and he would rest. It was easy. All men must die.

He did not complain. It was the way of life, and it was just. He had been born close to the earth, close to the earth he had lived, and the law thereof was not new to him. It was the law of all flesh. Nature was not kindly to the

[1]Medicine man's.

flesh. She had no concern for that concrete thing called the individual. Her interest lay in the species, the race. This was the deepest abstraction old Koskoosh's barbaric mind was capable of, but he grasped it firmly. He saw it exemplified in all life. The rise of the sap, the bursting greenness of the willow bud, the fall of the yellow leaf—in this alone was told the whole history. But one task did Nature set the individual. Did he not perform it, he died. Did he perform it, it was all the same, he died. Nature did not care; there were plenty who were obedient, and it was only the obedience in this matter, not the obedient, which lived and lived always. The tribe of Koskoosh was very old. The old men he had known when a boy had known old men before them. Therefore it was true that the tribe lived, that it stood for the obedience of all its members, way down into the forgotten past, whose very resting places were unremembered. They did not count; they were episodes. They had passed away like clouds from a summer sky. He also was an episode and would pass away. Nature did not care. To life she set one task, gave one law. To perpetuate was the task of life, its law was death. A maiden was a good creature to look upon, full-breasted and strong, with spring to her step and light in her eyes. But her task was yet before her. The light in her eyes brightened, her step quickened, she was now bold with the young men, now timid, and she gave them of her own unrest. And ever she grew fairer and yet fairer to look upon, till some hunter, able no longer to withhold himself, took her to his lodge to cook and toil for him and to become the mother of his children. And with the coming of her offspring her looks left her. Her limbs dragged and shuffled, her eyes dimmed and bleared, and only the little children found joy against the withered cheek of the old squaw by the fire. Her task was done. But a little while, on the first pinch of famine or the first long trail, and she would be left, even as he had been left, in the snow, with a little pile of wood. Such was the law.

He placed a stick carefully upon the fire and resumed his meditations. It was the same everywhere, with all things. The mosquitoes vanished with the first frost. The little tree squirrel crawled away to die. When age settled upon the rabbit it became slow and heavy and could no longer outfoot its enemies. Even the big bald-face grew clumsy and blind and quarrelsome, in the end to be dragged down by a handful of yelping huskies. He remembered how he had abandoned his own father on an upper reach of the Klondike one winter, the winter before the missionary came with his talk books and his box of medicines. Many a time had Koskoosh smacked his lips over the recollection of that box, though now his mouth refused to moisten. The "painkiller" had been especially good. But the missionary was a bother after all, for he brought no meat into the camp, and he ate heartily, and the hunters grumbled. But he chilled his lungs on the divide by the Mayo, and the dogs afterward nosed the stones away and fought over his bones.

Koskoosh placed another stick on the fire and harked back deeper into the past. There was the time of the great famine, when the old men crouched empty-bellied to the fire, and let fall from their lips dim traditions of the ancient day when the Yukon ran wide open for three winters, and then lay frozen for three summers. He had lost his mother in that famine. In the summer the salmon run had failed, and the tribe looked forward to the winter and the coming of the caribou. Then the winter came, but with it there were no caribou. Never had the like been known, not even in the lives of the old men. But the caribou did not come, and it was the seventh year, and the rabbits had not replenished, and the dogs were naught but bundles of bones. And through the long darkness the children wailed and died, and the women, and the old men; and not one in ten of the tribe lived to meet the sun when it came back in the spring. That *was* a famine!

But he had seen times of plenty, too, when the meat spoiled on their hands, and the dogs were fat and worthless with overeating—times when they let the game go unkilled, and the women were fertile, and the lodges were cluttered with sprawling men-children and women-children. Then it was the men became high-stomached, and revived ancient quarrels, and crossed the divides to the south to kill the Pellys, and to the west that they might sit by the dead fires of the Tananas. He remembered, when a boy, during a time of plenty, when he saw a moose pulled down by the wolves. Zing-ha lay with him in the snow and watched—Zing-ha, who later became the craftiest of hunters, and who, in the end, fell through an air hole on the Yukon. They found him, a month afterward, just as he had crawled halfway out and frozen stiff to the ice.

But the moose. Zing-ha and he had gone out that day to play at hunting after the manner of their fathers. On the bed of the creek they struck the fresh track of a moose, and with it the tracks of many wolves. "An old one," Zing-ha, who was quicker at reading the sign, said, "an old one who cannot keep up with the herd. The wolves have cut him out from his brothers, and they will never leave him." And it was so. It was their way. By day and by night, never resting, snarling on his heels, snapping at his nose, they would stay by him to the end. How Zing-ha and he felt the blood lust quicken! The finish would be a sight to see!

Eager-footed, they took the trail, and even he, Koskoosh, slow of sight and an unversed tracker, could have followed it blind, it was so wide. Hot were they on the heels of the chase, reading the grim tragedy, fresh-written, at every step. Now they came to where the moose had made a stand. Thrice the length of a grown man's body, in every direction, had the snow been stamped about and uptossed. In the midst were the deep impressions of the splay-hoofed game, and all about, everywhere, were the lighter footmarks of the wolves. Some, while their brothers harried the kill, had lain to one side and rested. The full-stretched impress of their bodies in the snow was as perfect as though made the moment before. One wolf had been caught in a wild lunge of the maddened victim and trampled to death. A few bones, well picked, bore witness.

Again, they ceased the uplift of their snowshoes at a second stand. Here the great animal had fought desperately. Twice had he been dragged down, as the snow attested, and twice had he shaken his assailants clear and gained footing once more. He had done his task long since, but none the less was life dear to him. Zing-ha said it was a strange thing, a moose once down to get free again; but this one certainly had. The shaman would see signs and wonders in this when they told him.

And yet again, they came to where the moose had made to mount the bank and gain the timber. But his foes had laid on from behind, till he reared and fell back upon them, crushing two deep into the snow. It was plain the kill was at hand, for their brothers had left them untouched. Two more stands were hurried past, brief in time length and very close together. The trail was red now, and the clean stride of the great beast had grown short and slovenly. Then they heard the first sounds of the battle—not the full-throated chorus of the chase, but the short, snappy bark which spoke of close quarters and teeth to flesh. Crawling up the wind, Zing-ha bellied it through the snow, and with him crept he, Koskoosh, who was to be chief of the tribesmen in the years to come. Together they shoved aside the underbranches of a young spruce and peered forth. It was the end they saw.

The picture, like all of youth's impressions, was still strong with him, and his dim eyes watched the end played out as vividly as in that far-off time. Koskoosh marveled at this, for in the days which followed, when he was a leader of men and a head of councilors, he had done great deeds and made his name a curse in the mouths of the Pellys, to say naught of the strange white man he had killed, knife to knife, in open fight.

For long he pondered on the days of his youth, till the fire died down and the frost bit deeper. He replenished it with two sticks this time, and gauged his grip on life by what remained. If Sit-cum-to-ha had only remembered her grandfather, and gathered a larger armful, his hours would have been longer. It would have been easy. But she was ever a careless child, and honored not her ancestors from the time the Beaver, son of the son of Zing-ha, first cast eyes upon her. Well, what mattered it? Had he not done likewise in his own quick youth? For a while he listened to the silence. Perhaps the heart of his son might soften, and he would come back with the dogs to take his old father on with the tribe to where the caribou ran thick and the fat hung heavy upon them.

He strained his ears, his restless brain for the moment stilled. Not a stir, nothing. He alone took breath in the midst of the great silence. It was very lonely. Hark! What was that? A chill passed over his body. The familiar, long-drawn howl broke the void, and it was close at hand. Then on his darkened eyes was projected the vision of the moose—the old bull moose—the torn flanks and bloody sides, the riddled mane, and the great branching horns, down low and tossing to the last. He saw the flashing forms of gray, the gleaming eyes, the lolling tongues, the slavered fangs. And he saw the inexorable circle close in till it became a dark point in the midst of the stamped snow.

A cold muzzle thrust against his cheek, and at its touch his soul leaped back to the present. His hand shot into the fire and dragged out a burning faggot. Overcome for the nonce by his hereditary fear of men, the brute retreated, raising a prolonged call to his brothers; and greedily they answered, till a ring of crouching, jaw-slobbering gray was stretched round about. The old man listened to the drawing in of this circle. He waved his hand wildly, and sniffs turned to snarls; but the panting brutes refused to scatter. Now one wormed his chest forward, dragging his haunches after, now a second, now a third; but never a one drew back. Why should he cling to life? he asked, and dropped the blazing stick into the snow. It sizzled and went out. The circle grunted uneasily but held its own. Again he saw the last stand of the old bull moose, and Koskoosh dropped his head wearily upon his knees. What did it matter after all? Was it not the law of life?

1901, 1902

Edith Wharton 1862–1937

Henry James, a close friend of her later years, called Edith Wharton "an angel of devastation"; a more respectful public has come to regard her as the grande dame *of American letters. She was, like Henry James, born into a wealthy and privileged society whose character she unflinchingly recorded in her fiction. The daughter of one of New York's oldest families, she was christened Edith Newbold Jones and raised in a manner suited to her elevated class. She was educated at home by tutors and taken for extended tours abroad, where she acquired her lifelong admiration for European art and culture. From her family and their friends she absorbed the social ideals and the prejudices that characterized the genteel society into which she was born and in which she was destined to move throughout her life.*

In 1885, after her formal "coming out," Edith Jones married Edward Wharton, a decorous gentleman from a wealthy Boston family. Although Edward Wharton was thirteen years older, he was congenial and from a family as socially distinguished as her own. At first their life together appeared to be one of gratifying ease and riches. Living off generous allowances granted by their families, and Edith Wharton's inheritances, the two traveled frequently between Europe and America. They purchased homes in New York City and in fashionable Newport, Rhode Island. They visited relatives and friends in city mansions and country estates, often accompanied by a retinue of their own servants. But the marriage soon came to be described as "unfortunate." Their relationship was passionless. They had little in common beyond their upper-class backgrounds. Edith Wharton's interests were intellectual and artistic, none of which her husband shared. She became distant. He became more and more erratic, disruptive, irascible. Their separations grew more and more extended.

Edith Wharton had been fascinated by books and storytelling since her childhood. In her teens she had worked at writing a novel that she named Fast and Loose, *and in 1878, her mother paid for the private publication of* Verses, *a volume of her precocious daughter's poetry. Now faced with a disintegrating marriage and hoping to escape what she saw as a stultifying life as a society matron, Edith Wharton returned to writing. Drawing first on her interest in the decorative arts, she collaborated on a popular guide to interior decorating,* The Decoration of Houses *(1897), and she began writing short fiction for the genteel magazines of the day. In 1899, she published her first collection of stories,* The Greater Inclination. *It was a surprising success, and, as she later wrote, it "broke the chains that had held me so long in a kind of torpor."*

In her writing Edith Wharton disdained the mawkish sentiment so common to the popular fiction of her time. She had a talent for irony and satire and an acute knowledge of the American society of the rich, the pieties they preached, the intolerance they embraced, the conventions they obeyed and evaded. She worked diligently, learning the discipline and craftsmanship required for serious fiction. More stories and novels followed, and in 1905, she published The House of Mirth, *which firmly established her reputation as a writer. The book also revealed her major strengths—an intimate knowledge of upper-class society and an ability to dramatize the plight of men and women who were bound by rigid social conventions.*

In the first years of the new century, the behavior of Edith Wharton's husband had become increasingly neurotic—even violent—and in 1911 she published Ethan Frome, *a novel of spiritual isolation and despair that seemed to be inspired by her own troubled marriage and her pessimism about life and love. It was her sixteenth book in thirteen years, and it has often been judged her finest work. In 1912, she published* The Reef, *a novel that critics have described as "Jamesian" because of its similarity to the penetrating psychological analysis found in the novels of her friend Henry James. In 1913, she published* The Custom of the Country, *and in that same year she finally gained a divorce from her husband of twenty-eight years.*

Free of the burdens of marriage, Edith Wharton settled permanently in Paris, where she continued to write, now with even greater intensity. During World War I (1914–1918), she worked for the Allied cause, establishing hostels for refugees, writing stories, essays, and books about the war in France, earning the gratitude of the French government, which made her a Chevalier of the French Legion of Honor. Two years after the war she published The Age of Innocence *(1920), for which she became, in 1921, the first woman to receive a Pulitzer Prize.*

In her remaining years, Edith Wharton wrote continuously, averaging a volume a year until her death in 1937 at the age of seventy-five. In all she published more than forty books of fiction, literary criticism, poetry, autobiography, architecture and interior design, travel, and gardening. But The Age of Innocence *(1920) has remained her most popular novel and is in many ways her most characteristic work. Its setting is the world she knew well: upper-class New York in the 1870s. The novel's theme is the conflict between society's demands for social conformity and the individual's needs for personal fulfillment. Her descriptions of late-nineteenth-century upper-class life and manners are acutely perceptive and rich with implications. But she was at her best in portraying the interior lives of women, the self-delusions that imprison them, and the dilemmas that torment them in a society unyielding in its attitudes toward fidelity and sexual liberty.*

The best-known works of Edith Wharton's last years were nonfiction: a study of her craft, entitled The Writing of Fiction *(1925), and her autobiographical* A Backward Glance *(1934). With the passing of the genteel era that she had depicted so well, her fiction seemed increasingly old-fashioned, a record of a bygone and artificial world. She wrote to F. Scott Fitzgerald, "I must represent the literary equivalent of tufted furniture and chandeliers." American critics now judged her to be only a lesser Henry James, a novelist of manners who described the same social world but whose writing lacked the rich psychological insights that James had achieved in his finest works. Edith Wharton, in turn, judged twentieth-century America to be ever more crass and materialistic, marred by cultural changes that she could not admire and to which she would not adjust. In her final years she preferred to remain in Europe, where she could preserve an older way of life, associate with the literati and the well-born, and view American vulgarity from afar. After her death she was buried, as her will directed, in France.*

In the first decades after her death, Wharton was sometimes criticized as a literary elitist, disdaining ordinary men and women whose birth and ill-formed lives left them unschooled in the graces of her narrow world and unworthy as subjects for her writing. And it is true that her satire of the newly risen, her mockery of their undistinguished lineage and social blunders, often seemed to suggest that she saw the misdeeds of the upper class as somehow more becoming than those of social upstarts and the lowly.

But, a half century after her death readers have rediscovered Edith Wharton. A new generation has been attracted to her emphasis on the perceptions and experiences of women, their ruthless conflicts with one another, their struggles against social coercion, and their yearning for a life richer than one dominated by polite society and matrimonial duty. Collections of Wharton's short stories and a dozen of her novels, including her masterpieces, The House of Mirth, Ethan Frome, *and* The Age of

Innocence, *have been republished. Her life and her ideas have recently been analyzed in elaborate biographies and numerous critical studies. Her stories have been made into richly evocative films and television movies that appeal to vast audiences. And she has, in the last decade, come to be praised as one of the most important American writers of the last hundred years.*

further reading: B. Nevius, *Edith Wharton, A Study of Her Fiction,* 1953; *The Collected Short Stories of Edith Wharton,* 2 vols., ed. R. Lewis, 1968; L. Auchincloss, *Edith Wharton, A Woman in Her Time,* 1971; *Edith Wharton,* ed. H. Bloom, 1986; J. Fryer, *The Imaginative Structures of Edith Wharton and Willa Cather,* 1986; *The Letters of Edith Wharton,* ed. R. Lewis and N. Lewis, 1988; P. Vita-Finzi, *Edith Wharton and the Art of Fiction,* 1990; L. Raphael, *Edith Wharton's Prisoners of Shame,* 1991; B. White, *Edith Wharton, A Study of the Short Fiction,* 1991; C. Waid, *Edith Wharton's Letters from the Underground,* 1991; G. Erlich, *The Sexual Education of Edith Wharton,* 1992; *Edith Wharton, New Critical Essays,* ed. A. Bendixen and A. Zilversmit, 1992; K. Hadley, *Interstices of the Tale, Edith Wharton's Narrative Strategies,* 1993; S. Benstock, *No Gifts from Chance, A Biography of Edith Wharton,* 1994; E. Dwight, *Edith Wharton, An Extraordinary Life,* 1994; S. Goodman, *Edith Wharton's Inner Circle,* 1994; C. Singley, *Edith Wharton, Matters of Mind and Spirit,* 1995; *The Cambridge Companion to Edith Wharton,* ed. M. Bell, 1995; A. Price, *The End of The Age of Innocence,* 1996; H. Killoran, *Edith Wharton, Art and Illusion,* 1996; S. Wright, *Edith Wharton A to Z,* 1998; M. Montgomery, *Displaying Women,* 1998; A. Tintner, *Edith Wharton in Context,* 1999; C. Preston, *Edith Wharton's Social Register,* 2000; J. Geer, *Edith Wharton,* 2002; J. Kassanoff, *Edith Wharton and the Politics of Race,* 2004.

texts: "The Other Two," *The Descent of Man,* 1904.

THE OTHER TWO

I

Waythorn, on the drawing-room hearth, waited for his wife to come down to dinner.

It was their first night under his own roof, and he was surprised at his thrill of boyish agitation. He was not so old, to be sure—his glass[1] gave him little more than the five-and-thirty years to which his wife confessed—but he had fancied himself already in the temperate zone; yet here he was listening for her step with a tender sense of all it symbolised, with some old trail of verse about the garlanded nuptial door-posts floating through his enjoyment of the pleasant room and the good dinner just beyond it.

They had been hastily recalled from their honeymoon by the illness of Lily Haskett, the child of Mrs. Waythorn's first marriage. The little girl, at Waythorn's desire, had been transferred to his house on the day of her mother's wedding, and the doctor, on their arrival, broke the news that she was ill with typhoid, but declared that all the symptoms were favourable. Lily could show twelve years of unblemished health, and the case promised to be

[1]Mirror.

a light one. The nurse spoke as reassuringly, and after a moment of alarm Mrs. Waythorn had adjusted herself to the situation. She was very fond of Lily—her affection for the child had perhaps been her decisive charm in Waythorn's eyes—but she had the perfectly balanced nerves which her little girl had inherited, and no woman ever wasted less tissue in unproductive worry. Waythorn was therefore quite prepared to see her come in presently, a little late because of a last look at Lily, but as serene and well-appointed as if her good-night kiss had been laid on the brow of health. Her composure was restful to him; it acted as ballast to his somewhat unstable sensibilities. As he pictured her bending over the child's bed he thought how soothing her presence must be in illness: her very step would prognosticate recovery.

His own life had been a gray one, from temperament rather than circumstance, and he had been drawn to her by the unperturbed gaiety which kept her fresh and elastic at an age when most women's activities are growing either slack or febrile. He knew what was said about her; for, popular as she was, there had always been a faint undercurrent of detraction. When she had appeared in New York, nine or ten years earlier, as the pretty Mrs. Haskett whom Gus Varick had unearthed somewhere—was it in Pittsburg or Utica?—society, while promptly accepting her, had reserved the right to cast a doubt on its own indiscrimination. Enquiry, however, established her undoubted connection with a socially reigning family, and explained her recent divorce as the natural result of a runaway match at seventeen; and as nothing was known of Mr. Haskett it was easy to believe the worst of him.

Alice Haskett's remarriage with Gus Varick was a passport to the set whose recognition she coveted, and for a few years the Varicks were the most popular couple in town. Unfortunately the alliance was brief and stormy, and this time the husband had his champions. Still, even Varick's staunchest supporters admitted that he was not meant for matrimony, and Mrs. Varick's grievances were of a nature to bear the inspection of the New York courts. A New York divorce is in itself a diploma of virtue,[2] and in the semiwidowhood of this second separation Mrs. Varick took on an air of sanctity, and was allowed to confide her wrongs to some of the most scrupulous ears in town. But when it was known that she was to marry Waythorn there was a momentary reaction. Her best friends would have preferred to see her remain in the rôle of the injured wife, which was as becoming to her as crape to a rosy complexion. True, a decent time had elapsed, and it was not even suggested that Waythorn had supplanted his predecessor. People shook their heads over him, however, and one grudging friend, to whom he affirmed that he took the step with his eyes open, replied oracularly: "Yes—and with your ears shut."

Waythorn could afford to smile at these innuendoes. In the Wall Street phrase, he had "discounted" them. He knew that society has not yet adapted itself to the consequences of divorce, and that till the adaptation takes place every woman who uses the freedom the law accords her must be her own social justification. Waythorn had an amused confidence in his wife's ability to justify herself. His expectations were fulfilled, and before the wedding took place Alice Varick's group had rallied openly to her support. She took it all imperturbably: she had a way of surmounting obstacles without seeming to be aware of them, and Waythorn looked back with wonder at the trivialities

[2]In the early 1900s in New York State, adultery was the only legal basis for divorce.

over which he had worn his nerves thin. He had the sense of having found refuge in a richer, warmer nature than his own, and his satisfaction, at the moment, was humourously summed up in the thought that his wife, when she had done all she could for Lily, would not be ashamed to come down and enjoy a good dinner.

The anticipation of such enjoyment was not, however, the sentiment expressed by Mrs. Waythorn's charming face when she presently joined him. Though she had put on her most engaging teagown she had neglected to assume the smile that went with it, and Waythorn thought he had never seen her look so nearly worried.

"What is it?" he asked. "Is anything wrong with Lily?"

"No; I've just been in and she's still sleeping." Mrs. Waythorn hesitated. "But something tiresome has happened."

He had taken her two hands, and now perceived that he was crushing a paper between them.

"This letter?"

"Yes—Mr. Haskett has written—I mean his lawyer has written."

Waythorn felt himself flush uncomfortably. He dropped his wife's hands.

"What about?"

"About seeing Lily. You know the courts——"

"Yes, yes," he interrupted nervously.

Nothing was known about Haskett in New York. He was vaguely supposed to have remained in the outer darkness from which his wife had been rescued, and Waythorn was one of the few who were aware that he had given up his business in Utica and followed her to New York in order to be near his little girl. In the days of his wooing, Waythorn had often met Lily on the doorstep, rosy and smiling, on her way "to see papa."

"I am so sorry," Mrs. Waythorn murmured.

He roused himself. "What does he want?"

"He wants to see her. You know she goes to him once a week."

"Well—he doesn't expect her to go to him now, does he?"

"No—he has heard of her illness; but he expects to come here."

"Here?"

Mrs. Waythorn reddened under his gaze. They looked away from each other.

"I'm afraid he has the right. . . . You'll see. . . ." She made a proffer of the letter.

Waythorn moved away with a gesture of refusal. He stood staring about the softly lighted room, which a moment before had seemed so full of bridal intimacy.

"I'm so sorry," she repeated. "If Lily could have been moved——"

"That's out of the question," he returned impatiently.

"I suppose so."

Her lip was beginning to tremble, and he felt himself a brute.

"He must come, of course," he said. "What is—his day?"

"I'm afraid—to-morrow."

"Very well. Send a note in the morning."

The butler entered to announce dinner.

Waythorn turned to his wife. "Come—you must be tired. It's beastly, but try to forget about it," he said, drawing her hand through his arm.

"You're so good, dear. I'll try," she whispered back.

Her face cleared at once, and as she looked at him across the flowers, between the rosy candle-shades, he saw her lips waver back into a smile.

"How pretty everything is!" she sighed luxuriously.

He turned to the butler. "The champagne at once, please. Mrs. Waythorn is tired."

In a moment or two their eyes met above the sparkling glasses. Her own were quite clear and untroubled: he saw that she had obeyed his injunction and forgotten.

II

Waythorn, the next morning, went down town earlier than usual. Haskett was not likely to come till the afternoon, but the instinct of flight drove him forth. He meant to stay away all day—he had thoughts of dining at his club. As his door closed behind him he reflected that before he opened it again it would have admitted another man who had as much right to enter it as himself, and the thought filled him with a physical repugnance.

He caught the "elevated" at the employés' hour, and found himself crushed between two layers of pendulous humanity. At Eighth Street the man facing him wriggled out, and another took his place. Waythorn glanced up and saw that it was Gus Varick. The men were so close together that it was impossible to ignore the smile of recognition on Varick's handsome overblown face. And after all—why not? They had always been on good terms, and Varick had been divorced before Waythorn's attentions to his wife began. The two exchanged a word on the perennial grievance of the congested trains, and when a seat at their side was miraculously left empty the instinct of self-preservation made Waythorn slip into it after Varick.

The latter drew the stout man's breath of relief. "Lord—I was beginning to feel like a pressed flower." He leaned back, looking unconcernedly at Waythorn. "Sorry to hear that Sellers is knocked out again."

"Sellers?" echoed Waythorn, starting at his partner's name.

Varick looked surprised. "You didn't know he was laid up with the gout?"

"No. I've been away—I only got back last night." Waythorn felt himself reddening in anticipation of the other's smile.

"Ah—yes; to be sure. And Sellers's attack came on two days ago. I'm afraid he's pretty bad. Very awkward for me, as it happens, because he was just putting through a rather important thing for me."

"Ah?" Waythorn wondered vaguely since when Varick had been dealing in "important things." Hitherto he had dabbled only in the shallow pools of speculation, with which Waythorn's office did not usually concern itself.

It occurred to him that Varick might be talking at random, to relieve the strain of their propinquity. That strain was becoming momentarily more apparent to Waythorn, and when, at Cortlandt Street, he caught sight of an acquaintance and had a sudden vision of the picture he and Varick must present to an initiated eye, he jumped up with a muttered excuse.

"I hope you'll find Sellers better," said Varick civilly, and he stammered back: "If I can be of any use to you——" and let the departing crowd sweep him to the platform.

At his office he heard that Sellers was in fact ill with the gout, and would probably not be able to leave the house for some weeks.

"I'm sorry it should have happened so, Mr. Waythorn," the senior clerk said with affable significance. "Mr. Sellers was very much upset at the idea of giving you such a lot of extra work just now."

"Oh, that's no matter," said Waythorn hastily. He secretly welcomed the pressure of additional business, and was glad to think that, when the day's work was over, he would have to call at his partner's on the way home.

He was late for luncheon, and turned in at the nearest restaurant instead of going to his club. The place was full, and the waiter hurried him to the back of the room to capture the only vacant table. In the cloud of cigar-smoke Waythorn did not at once distinguish his neighbours: but presently, looking about him, he saw Varick seated a few feet off. This time, luckily, they were too far apart for conversation, and Varick, who faced another way, had probably not even seen him; but there was an irony in their renewed nearness.

Varick was said to be fond of good living, and as Waythorn sat despatching his hurried luncheon he looked across half enviously at the other's leisurely degustation of his meal. When Waythorn first saw him he had been helping himself with critical deliberation to a bit of Camembert at the ideal point of liquefaction, and now, the cheese removed, he was just pouring his *café double* from its little two-storied earthen pot. He poured slowly, his ruddy profile bent above the task, and one beringed white hand steadying the lid of the coffee-pot; then he stretched his other hand to the decanter of cognac at his elbow, filled a liqueur-glass, took a tentative sip, and poured the brandy into his coffee-cup.

Waythorn watched him in a kind of fascination. What was he thinking of—only of the flavour of the coffee and the liqueur? Had the morning's meeting left no more trace in his thoughts than on his face? Had his wife so completely passed out of his life that even this odd encounter with her present husband, within a week after her remarriage, was no more than an incident in his day? And as Waythorn mused, another idea struck him: had Haskett ever met Varick as Varick and he had just met? The recollection of Haskett perturbed him, and he rose and left the restaurant, taking a circuitous way out to escape the placid irony of Varick's nod.

It was after seven when Waythorn reached home. He thought the footman who opened the door looked at him oddly.

"How is Miss Lily?" he asked in haste.

"Doing very well, sir. A gentleman——"

"Tell Barlow to put off dinner for half an hour," Waythorn cut him off, hurrying upstairs.

He went straight to his room and dressed without seeing his wife. When he reached the drawing-room she was there, fresh and radiant. Lily's day had been good; the doctor was not coming back that evening.

At dinner Waythorn told her of Sellers's illness and of the resulting complications. She listened sympathetically, adjuring him not to let himself be overworked, and asking vague feminine questions about the routine of the office. Then she gave him the chronicle of Lily's day; quoted the nurse and doctor, and told him who had called to inquire. He had never seen her more serene and unruffled. It struck him, with a curious pang, that she was very happy in being with him, so happy that she found a childish pleasure in rehearsing the trivial incidents of her day.

After dinner they went to the library, and the servant put the coffee and liqueurs on a low table before her and left the room. She looked singularly soft and girlish in her rosy pale dress, against the dark leather of one of his bachelor armchairs. A day earlier the contrast would have charmed him.

He turned away now, choosing a cigar with affected deliberation.

"Did Haskett come?" he asked, with his back to her.

"Oh yes—he came."

"You didn't see him, of course?"

She hesitated a moment. "I let the nurse see him."

That was all. There was nothing more to ask. He swung round toward her, applying a match to his cigar. Well, the thing was over for a week, at any rate. He would try not to think of it. She looked up at him, a trifle rosier than usual, with a smile in her eyes.

"Ready for your coffee, dear?"

He leaned against the mantelpiece, watching her as she lifted the coffee-pot. The lamplight struck a gleam from her bracelets and tipped her soft hair with brightness. How light and slender she was, and how each gesture flowed into the next! She seemed a creature all compact of harmonies. As the thought of Haskett receded, Waythorn felt himself yielding again to the joy of possessorship. They were his, those white hands with their flitting motions, his the light haze of hair, the lips and eyes. . . .

She set down the coffee-pot, and reached for the decanter of cognac, measured off a liqueur-glass and poured it into his cup.

Waythorn uttered a sudden exclamation.

"What is the matter?" she said, startled.

"Nothing; only—I don't take cognac in my coffee."

"Oh, how stupid of me," she cried.

Their eyes met, and she blushed a sudden agonised red.

III

Ten days later, Mr. Sellers, still house-bound, asked Waythorn to call on his way down town.

The senior partner, with his swaddled foot propped up by the fire, greeted his associate with an air of embarrassment.

"I'm sorry, my dear fellow; I've got to ask you to do an awkward thing for me."

Waythorn waited, and the other went on, after a pause apparently given to the arrangement of his phrases: "The fact is, when I was knocked out I had just gone into a rather complicated piece of business for—Gus Varick."

"Well?" said Waythorn, with an attempt to put him at his ease.

"Well—it's this way; Varick came to me the day before my attack. He had evidently had an inside tip from somebody, and had made about a hundred thousand. He came to me for advice, and I suggested his going in with Vanderlyn."

"Oh, the deuce!" Waythorn exclaimed. He saw in a flash what had happened. The investment was an alluring one, but required negotiation. He listened quietly while Sellers put the case before him, and, the statement ended, he said: "You think I ought to see Varick?"

"I'm afraid I can't as yet. The doctor is obdurate. And this thing can't wait. I hate to ask you, but no one else in the office knows the ins and outs of it."

Waythorn stood silent. He did not care a farthing for the success of Varick's venture, but the honour of the office was to be considered, and he could hardly refuse to oblige his partner.

"Very well," he said, "I'll do it."

That afternoon, apprised by telephone, Varick called at the office. Waythorn, waiting in his private room, wondered what the others thought of it. The newspapers, at the time of Mrs. Waythorn's marriage, had acquainted their readers with every detail of her previous matrimonial ventures, and Waythorn could fancy the clerks smiling behind Varick's back as he was ushered in.

Varick bore himself admirably. He was easy without being undignified, and Waythorn was conscious of cutting a much less impressive figure. Varick had no experience of business, and the talk prolonged itself for nearly an hour while Waythorn set forth with scrupulous precision the details of the proposed transaction.

"I'm awfully obliged to you," Varick said as he rose. "The fact is I'm not used to having much money to look after, and I don't want to make an ass of myself—" He smiled, and Waythorn could not help noticing that there was something pleasant about his smile. "It feels uncommonly queer to have enough cash to pay one's bills. I'd have sold my soul for it a few years ago!"

Waythorn winced at the illusion. He had heard it rumoured that a lack of funds had been one of the determining causes of the Varick separation, but it did not occur to him that Varick's words were intentional. It seemed more likely that the desire to keep clear of embarrassing topics had fatally drawn him into one. Waythorn did not wish to be outdone in civility.

"We'll do the best we can for you," he said. "I think this is a good thing you're in."

"Oh, I'm sure it's immense. It's awfully good of you——" Varick broke off, embarrassed. "I suppose the thing's settled now—but if——"

"If anything happens before Sellers is about, I'll see you again," said Waythorn quietly. He was glad, in the end, to appear the more self-possessed of the two.

. . . .

The course of Lily's illness ran smooth, and as the days passed Waythorn grew used to the idea of Haskett's weekly visit. The first time the day came round, he stayed out late, and questioned his wife as to the visit on his return. She replied at once that Haskett had merely seen the nurse downstairs, as the doctor did not wish any one in the child's sick-room till after the crisis.

The following week Waythorn was again conscious of the recurrence of the day, but had forgotten it by the time he came home to dinner. The crisis of the disease came a few days later, with a rapid decline of fever, and the little girl was pronounced out of danger. In the rejoicing which ensued the thought of Haskett passed out of Waythorn's mind, and one afternoon, letting himself into the house with a latch-key, he went straight to his library without noticing a shabby hat and umbrella in the hall.

In the library he found a small effaced-looking man with a thinnish gray beard sitting on the edge of a chair. The stranger might have been a piano-tuner, or one of those mysteriously efficient persons who are summoned in emergencies to adjust some detail of the domestic machinery. He blinked at Waythorn through a pair of gold-rimmed spectacles and said mildly: "Mr. Waythorn, I presume? I am Lily's father."

Waythorn flushed. "Oh——" he stammered uncomfortably. He broke off, disliking to appear rude. Inwardly he was trying to adjust the actual Haskett to the image of him projected by his wife's reminiscences. Waythorn had been allowed to infer that Alice's first husband was a brute.

"I am sorry to intrude," said Haskett, with his over-the-counter politeness.

"Don't mention it," returned Waythorn, collecting himself. "I suppose the nurse has been told?"

"I presume so. I can wait," said Haskett. He had a resigned way of speaking, as though life had worn down his natural powers of resistance.

Waythorn stood on the threshold, nervously pulling off his gloves.

"I'm sorry you've been detained. I will send for the nurse," he said; and as he opened the door he added with an effort: "I'm glad we can give you a good report of Lily." He winced as the *we* slipped out, but Haskett seemed not to notice it.

"Thank you, Mr. Waythorn. It's been an anxious time for me."

"Ah, well, that's past. Soon she'll be able to go to you." Waythorn nodded and passed out. In his own room he flung himself down with a groan. He hated the womanish sensibility which made him suffer so acutely from the grotesque chances of life. He had known when he married that his wife's former husbands were both living, and that amid the multiplied contacts of modern existence there were a thousand chances to one that he would run against one or the other, yet he found himself as much disturbed by his brief encounter with Haskett as though the law had not obligingly removed all difficulties in the way of their meeting.

Waythorn sprang up and began to pace the room nervously. He had not suffered half as much from his two meetings with Varick. It was Haskett's presence in his own house that made the situation so intolerable. He stood still, hearing steps in the passage.

"This way, please," he heard the nurse say. Haskett was being taken upstairs, then: not a corner of the house but was open to him. Waythorn dropped into another chair, staring vaguely ahead of him. On his dressing-table stood a photograph of Alice, taken when he had first known her. She was Alice Varick then—how fine and exquisite he had thought her! Those were Varick's pearls about her neck. At Waythorn's instance they had been returned before her marriage. Had Haskett ever given her any trinkets—and what had become of them, Waythorn wondered? He realised suddenly that he knew very little of Haskett's past or present situation; but from the man's appearance and manner of speech he could reconstruct with curious precision the surroundings of Alice's first marriage. And it startled him to think that she had, in the background of her life, a phase of existence so different from anything with which he had connected her. Varick, whatever his faults, was a gentleman, in the conventional, traditional sense of the term: the sense which at that moment seemed, oddly enough, to have most meaning to Waythorn. He and Varick had the same social habits, spoke the same language, understood the same allusions. But this other man . . . it was grotesquely uppermost in Waythorn's mind that Haskett had worn a made-up tie attached with an elastic. Why should that ridiculous detail symbolise the whole man? Waythorn was exasperated by his own paltriness, but the fact of the tie expanded, forced itself on him, became as it were the key to Alice's past. He could see her, as Mrs. Haskett, sitting in a "front parlour" furnished in plush, with a pianola,[1] and a copy of "Ben Hur"[2] on the centre-table. He could see her going to the theatre with Haskett—or perhaps even to a "Church Sociable"—she in a "picture hat" and Haskett in a black frock-coat, a little creased, with the made-up tie on an elastic. On the way home they would stop and look at the illuminated shop-windows, lingering over the photographs of New York actresses. On Sunday afternoons Haskett would take her for a walk, pushing Lily ahead of them in a white enamelled perambulator, and Waythorn had a vision of the people they would stop and talk to. He could fancy how pretty Alice must have looked, in a dress adroitly constructed from the hints of a New York fashion-paper, and how she must have looked down on the other women, chafing at her life, and secretly feeling that she belonged in a bigger place.

For the moment his foremost thought was one of wonder at the way in which she had shed the phase of existence which her marriage with Haskett implied. It was as if her whole aspect, every gesture, every inflection, every allusion, were a studied negation of that period of her life. If she had denied being married to Haskett she could hardly have stood more convicted of duplicity than in this obliteration of the self which had been his wife.

Waythorn started up, checking himself in the analysis of her motives. What right had he to create a fantastic effigy of her and then pass judgment on it? She had spoken vaguely of her first marriage as unhappy, had hinted, with becoming reticence, that Haskett had wrought havoc among her young illusions. . . . It was a pity for Waythorn's peace of mind that Haskett's very inoffensiveness shed a new light on the nature of those illusions. A man would rather think that his wife has been brutalised by her first husband than that the process has been reversed.

IV

"Mr. Waythorn, I don't like that French governess of Lily's."

Haskett, subdued and apologetic, stood before Waythorn in the library, revolving his shabby hat in his hand.

Waythorn, surprised in his armchair over the evening paper, stared back perplexedly at his visitor.

"You'll excuse my asking to see you," Haskett continued. "But this is my last visit, and I thought if I could have a word with you it would be a better way than writing to Mrs. Waythorn's lawyer."

[1]A player piano.

[2]*Ben Hur, A Tale of the Christ* (1880), a bestselling novel by Lew Wallace (1827–1905).

Waythorn rose uneasily. He did not like the French governess either; but that was irrelevant.

"I am not so sure of that," he returned stiffly; "but since you wish it I will give your message to—my wife." He always hesitated over the possessive pronoun in addressing Haskett.

The latter sighed. "I don't know as that will help much. She didn't like it when I spoke to her."

Waythorn turned red. "When did you see her?" he asked.

"Not since the first day I came to see Lily—right after she was taken sick. I remarked to her then that I didn't like the governess."

Waythorn made no answer. He remembered distinctly that, after that first visit, he had asked his wife if she had seen Haskett. She had lied to him then, but she had respected his wishes since; and the incident cast a curious light on her character. He was sure she would not have seen Haskett that first day if she had divined that Waythorn would object, and the fact that she did not divine it was almost as disagreeable to the latter as the discovery that she had lied to him.

"I don't like the woman," Haskett was repeating with mild persistency. "She ain't straight, Mr. Waythorn—she'll teach the child to be underhand. I've noticed a change in Lily—she's too anxious to please—and she don't always tell the truth. She used to be the straightest child, Mr. Waythorn——" He broke off, his voice a little thick. "Not but what I want her to have a stylish education," he ended.

Waythorn was touched. "I'm sorry, Mr. Haskett; but frankly, I don't quite see what I can do."

Haskett hesitated. Then he laid his hat on the table, and advanced to the hearth-rug, on which Waythorn was standing. There was nothing aggressive in his manner, but he had the solemnity of a timid man resolved on a decisive measure.

"There's just one thing you can do, Mr. Waythorn," he said. "You can remind Mrs. Waythorn that, by the decree of the courts, I am entitled to have a voice in Lily's bringing up." He paused, and went on more deprecatingly: "I'm not the kind to talk about enforcing my rights, Mr. Waythorn. I don't know as I think a man is entitled to rights he hasn't known how to hold on to; but this business of the child is different. I've never let go there—and I never mean to."

. . . .

The scene left Waythorn deeply shaken. Shamefacedly, in indirect ways, he had been finding out about Haskett; and all that he had learned was favourable. The little man, in order to be near his daughter, had sold out his share in a profitable business in Utica, and accepted a modest clerkship in a New York manufacturing house. He boarded in a shabby street and had few acquaintances. His passion for Lily filled his life. Waythorn felt that this exploration of Haskett was like groping about with a dark-lantern in his wife's past; but he saw now that there were recesses his lantern had not explored. He had never enquired into the exact circumstances of his wife's first matrimonial rupture. On the surface all had been fair. It was she who had obtained the divorce, and the court had given her the child. But Waythorn knew how many ambiguities such a verdict might cover. The mere fact that

Haskett retained a right over his daughter implied an unsuspected compromise. Waythorn was an idealist. He always refused to recognise unpleasant contingencies till he found himself confronted with them, and then he saw them followed by a special train of consequences. His next days were thus haunted, and he determined to try to lay the ghosts by conjuring them up in his wife's presence.

When he repeated Haskett's request a flame of anger passed over her face; but she subdued it instantly and spoke with a slight quiver of outraged motherhood.

"It is very ungentlemanly of him," she said.

The word grated on Waythorn. "That is neither here nor there. It's a bare question of rights."

She murmured: "It is not as if he could ever be a help to Lily——"

Waythorn flushed. This was even less to his taste. "The question is," he repeated, "what authority has he over her?"

She looked downward, twisting herself a little in her seat. "I am willing to see him—I thought you objected," she faltered.

In a flash he understood that she knew the extent of Haskett's claims. Perhaps it was not the first time she had resisted them.

"My objecting has nothing to do with it," he said coldly; "if Haskett has a right to be consulted you must consult him."

She burst into tears, and he saw that she expected him to regard her as a victim.

Haskett did not abuse his rights. Waythorn had felt miserably sure that he would not. But the governess was dismissed, and from time to time the little man demanded an interview with Alice. After the first outburst she accepted the situation with her usual adaptability. Haskett had once reminded Waythorn of the piano-tuner, and Mrs. Waythorn, after a month or two, appeared to class him with that domestic familiar. Waythorn could not but respect the father's tenacity. At first he had tried to cultivate the suspicion that Haskett might be "up to" something, that he had an object in securing a foothold in the house. But in his heart Waythorn was sure of Haskett's single-mindedness; he even guessed in the latter a mild contempt for such advantages as his relation with the Waythorns might offer. Haskett's sincerity of purpose made him invulnerable, and his successor had to accept him as a lien on the property.

. . . .

Mr. Sellers was sent to Europe to recover from his gout, and Varick's affairs hung on Waythorn's hands. The negotiations were prolonged and complicated; they necessitated frequent conferences between the two men, and the interests of the firm forbade Waythorn's suggesting that his client should transfer his business to another office.

Varick appeared well in the transaction. In moments of relaxation his coarse streak appeared, and Waythorn dreaded his geniality; but in the office he was concise and clear-headed, with a flattering deference to Waythorn's judgment. Their business relations being so affably established, it would have been absurd for the two men to ignore each other in society. The first time they met in a drawing-room, Varick took up their intercourse in the same easy key, and his hostess's grateful glance obliged Waythorn to respond to it.

After that they ran across each other frequently, and one evening at a ball Waythorn, wandering through the remoter rooms, came upon Varick seated beside his wife. She coloured a little, and faltered in what she was saying; but Varick nodded to Waythorn without rising, and the latter strolled on.

In the carriage, on the way home, he broke out nervously: "I didn't know you spoke to Varick."

Her voice trembled a little. "It's the first time—he happened to be standing near me; I didn't know what to do. It's so awkward, meeting everywhere—and he said you had been very kind about some business."

"That's different," said Waythorn.

She paused a moment. "I'll do just as you wish," she returned pliantly. "I thought it would be less awkward to speak to him when we meet."

Her pliancy was beginning to sicken him. Had she really no will of her own—no theory about her relation to these men? She had accepted Haskett—did she mean to accept Varick? It was "less awkward," as she had said, and her instinct was to evade difficulties or to circumvent them. With sudden vividness Waythorn saw how the instinct had developed. She was "as easy as an old shoe"—a shoe that too many feet had worn. Her elasticity was the result of tension in too many different directions. Alice Haskett—Alice Varick—Alice Waythorn—she had been each in turn, and had left hanging to each name a little of her privacy, a little of her personality, a little of the inmost self where the unknown god abides.

"Yes—it's better to speak to Varick," said Waythorn wearily.

V

The winter wore on, and society took advantage of the Waythorns' acceptance of Varick. Harassed hostesses were grateful to them for bridging over a social difficulty, and Mrs. Waythorn was held up as a miracle of good taste. Some experimental spirits could not resist the diversion of throwing Varick and his former wife together, and there were those who thought he found a zest in the propinquity. But Mrs. Waythorn's conduct remained irreproachable. She neither avoided Varick nor sought him out. Even Waythorn could not but admit that she had discovered the solution of the newest social problem.

He had married her without giving much thought to that problem. He had fancied that a woman can shed her past like a man. But now he saw that Alice was bound to hers both by the circumstances which forced her into continued relation with it, and by the traces it had left on her nature. With grim irony Waythorn compared himself to a member of a syndicate. He held so many shares in his wife's personality and his predecessors were his partners in the business. If there had been any element of passion in the transaction he would have felt less deteriorated by it. The fact that Alice took her change of husbands like a change of weather reduced the situation to mediocrity. He could have forgiven her for blunders, for excesses; for resisting Haskett, for yielding to Varick; for anything but her acquiescence and her tact. She reminded him of a juggler tossing knives; but the knives were blunt and he knew they would never cut her.

And then, gradually, habit formed a protecting surface for his sensibilities. If he paid for each day's comfort with the small change of his illusions, he grew daily to value the comfort more and set less store upon the coin. He had drifted into a dulling propinquity with Haskett and Varick and he took refuge in the cheap revenge of satirising the situation. He even began to reckon up the advantages which accrued from it, to ask himself if it were not better to own a third of a wife who knew how to make a man happy than a whole one who had lacked opportunity to acquire the art. For it *was* an art, and made up, like all others, of concessions, eliminations and embellishments; of lights judiciously thrown and shadows skilfully softened. His wife knew exactly how to manage the lights, and he knew exactly to what training she owed her skill. He even tried to trace the source of his obligations, to discriminate between the influences which had combined to produce his domestic happiness: he perceived that Haskett's commonness had made Alice worship good breeding, while Varick's liberal construction of the marriage bond had taught her to value the conjugal virtues; so that he was directly indebted to his predecessors for the devotion which made his life easy if not inspiring.

From this phase he passed into that of complete acceptance. He ceased to satirise himself because time dulled the irony of the situation and the joke lost its humour with its sting. Even the sight of Haskett's hat on the hall table had ceased to touch the springs of epigram. The hat was often seen there now, for it had been decided that it was better for Lily's father to visit her than for the little girl to go to his boarding-house. Waythorn, having acquiesced in this arrangement, had been surprised to find how little difference it made. Haskett was never obtrusive, and the few visitors who met him on the stairs were unaware of his identity. Waythorn did not know how often he saw Alice, but with himself Haskett was seldom in contact.

One afternoon, however, he learned on entering that Lily's father was waiting to see him. In the library he found Haskett occupying a chair in his usual provisional way. Waythorn always felt grateful to him for not leaning back.

"I hope you'll excuse me, Mr. Waythorn," he said rising. "I wanted to see Mrs. Waythorn about Lily, and your man asked me to wait here till she came in."

"Of course," said Waythorn, remembering that a sudden leak had that morning given over the drawing-room to the plumbers.

He opened his cigar-case and held it out to his visitor, and Haskett's acceptance seemed to mark a fresh stage in their intercourse. The spring evening was chilly, and Waythorn invited his guest to draw up his chair to the fire. He meant to find an excuse to leave Haskett in a moment; but he was tired and cold, and after all the little man no longer jarred on him.

The two were enclosed in the intimacy of their blended cigar-smoke when the door opened and Varick walked into the room. Waythorn rose abruptly. It was the first time that Varick had come to the house, and the surprise of seeing him, combined with the singular inopportuneness of his arrival, gave a new edge to Waythorn's blunted sensibilities. He stared at his visitor without speaking.

Varick seemed too preoccupied to notice his host's embarrassment.

"My dear fellow," he exclaimed in his most expansive tone, "I must apologise for tumbling in on you in this way, but I was too late to catch you down town, and so I thought——"

He stopped short, catching sight of Haskett, and his sanguine colour deepened to a flush which spread vividly under his scant blond hair. But in a moment he recovered himself and nodded slightly. Haskett returned the bow in silence, and Waythorn was still groping for speech when the footman came in carrying a tea-table.

The intrusion offered a welcome vent to Waythorn's nerves. "What the deuce are you bringing this here for?" he said sharply.

"I beg your pardon, sir, but the plumbers are still in the drawing-room, and Mrs. Waythorn said she would have tea in the library." The footman's perfectly respectful tone implied a reflection on Waythorn's reasonableness.

"Oh, very well," said the latter resignedly, and the footman proceeded to open the folding tea-table and set out its complicated appointments. While this interminable process continued the three men stood motionless, watching it with a fascinated stare, till Waythorn, to break the silence, said to Varick: "Won't you have a cigar?"

He held out the case he had just tendered to Haskett, and Varick helped himself with a smile. Waythorn looked about for a match, and finding none, proffered a light from his own cigar. Haskett, in the background, held his ground mildly, examining his cigar-tip now and then, and stepping forward at the right moment to knock its ashes into the fire.

The footman at last withdrew, and Varick immediately began: "If I could just say half a word to you about this business——"

"Certainly," stammered Waythorn; "in the dining-room——"

But as he placed his hand on the door it opened from without, and his wife appeared on the threshold.

She came in fresh and smiling, in her street dress and hat, shedding a fragrance from the boa[1] which she loosened in advancing.

"Shall we have tea in here, dear?" she began; and then she caught sight of Varick. Her smile deepened, veiling a slight tremor of surprise.

"Why, how do you do?" she said with a distinct note of pleasure.

As she shook hands with Varick she saw Haskett standing behind him. Her smile faded for a moment, but she recalled it quickly, with a scarcely perceptible side-glance at Waythorn.

"How do you do, Mr. Haskett?" she said, and shook hands with him a shade less cordially.

The three men stood awkwardly before her, till Varick, always the most self-possessed, dashed into an explanatory phrase.

"We—I had to see Waythorn a moment on business," he stammered, brick-red from chin to nape.

Haskett stepped forward with his air of mild obstinacy. "I am sorry to intrude; but you appointed five o'clock—" he directed his resigned glance to the timepiece on the mantel.

She swept aside their embarrassment with a charming gesture of hospitality. "I'm so sorry—I'm always late; but the afternoon was so lovely." She stood drawing off her gloves, propitiatory and graceful, diffusing about her a sense of ease and familiarity in which the situation lost its grotesqueness.

[1]A long, fluffy scarf.

"But before talking business," she added brightly, "I'm sure every one wants a cup of tea."

She dropped into her low chair by the tea-table, and the two visitors, as if drawn by her smile, advanced to receive the cups she held out.

She glanced about for Waythorn, and he took the third cup with a laugh.

1904

Theodore Dreiser 1871–1945

Theodore Dreiser was America's greatest literary naturalist. One of thirteen children, he was raised in Terre Haute, Indiana, in misery and bruising poverty. His penniless German immigrant father was fiercely pious, obsessed by religion. His mother was gentle, helpless, and illiterate—Dreiser himself taught her to read and write. His wandering and shiftless brothers and sisters, with their public drunkenness, illegitimate babies, and jail terms brought him despair and constant humiliation.

At fifteen Dreiser fled from home and went to Chicago, where he washed dishes in a cheap restaurant, clerked in a store, and painted advertising signs. He read constantly and, like one of his own helpless characters, he dreamt of wealth and social success in the great metropolis. When he was eighteen, a sympathetic teacher helped him enter the University of Indiana, but Dreiser quit after a year and returned to Chicago, where he embarked on another series of menial jobs and wandered the city streets at night, storing up impressions of drunks, thieves, prostitutes, and beggars.

Finally he got a job at a newspaper and began a career that took him to St. Louis, Cleveland, Pittsburgh, and eventually New York City, where he became a freelance journalist and a magazine editor. He read widely the evolutionary theorizing of such philosophers as Thomas Huxley and Herbert Spencer, and as the last remnants of Dreiser's religious faith drained away, he was left with the deterministic belief that a human being is merely a mechanism moved by chemical and physical forces beyond his or her control.

In 1899 he began writing Sister Carrie. *When he submitted the manuscript to a publisher, it was rejected because it was thought likely to offend "the feminine readers who control the destinies of so many novels. . . ." In 1900, when the novel was finally accepted and published, only 456 copies were sold, and Dreiser earned so little in royalties ($68.40) that he came to believe the novel had been "suppressed" by censorious prudes. Not until 1907, when it was reissued, did* Sister Carrie *finally reach a sizable reading public and begin to shape the development of American literature.*

In 1911 Dreiser published Jennie Gerhardt, *whose heroine, misled and victimized by fate, was modeled after Dreiser's own sisters. In 1912 he published* The Financier, *the first of a trilogy on the ruthlessness of American capitalism that included* The Titan *(1914) and* The Stoic *(published posthumously in 1947). In 1925 he published* An American Tragedy, *his greatest work and a critical and financial success.*

Dreiser's works, like the man himself, are ponderous and sprawling. His prose is fumbling, inexact, cliché-ridden; yet its piling up of details can produce striking portrayals of human experience. Dreiser's powerful frankness widened the social and sexual range possible for literature in America. He struck at the American myth that success and fame are to be achieved by work and virtue. He was seized by a dark, chaotic view of life, yet his determinism was softened by a romantic sensibility and by a powerful sympathy for people at radical odds with society, characters Dreiser saw as "haunted by poverty," filled with "gallant dreams," but "helpless in the clutch of relentless fate."

FURTHER READING: C. Shapiro, *Theodore Dreiser, Our Bitter Patriot,* 1962; P. Gerber, *Theodore Dreiser,* 1964; W. Swanberg, *Dreiser,* 1965; J. McAleer, *Theodore Dreiser, An Introduction and Interpretation,* 1968; *Critical Essays on Theodore Dreiser,* ed. D. Pizer, 1981; L. Hussman, *Dreiser and His Fiction,* 1983; J. Griffin, *The Small Canvas, An Introduction to Dreiser's Short Stories,* 1985; R. Lingeman, *Theodore Dreiser,* 2 vols., 1986, 1990; R. Lingeman, *Theodore Dreiser, An American Journey, 1908–1945,* 1990; *Theodore Dreiser, Beyond Naturalism,* ed. M. Gogol, 1995; D. Pizer, *Literary Masters, Theodore Dreiser,* 2000; *A Theodore Dreiser Encyclopedia,* ed. K. Newlin, 2003; *The Cambridge Companion to Theodore Dreiser,* ed. L. Cassuto and C. Eby, 2004; J. Loving, *The Last Titan, A Life of Theodore Dreiser,* 2005.

TEXT: *Free and Other Stories,* 1918.

THE LOST PHOEBE

They lived together in a part of the country which was not so prosperous as it had once been, about three miles from one of those small towns that, instead of increasing in population, is steadily decreasing. The territory was not very thickly settled; perhaps a house every other mile or so, with large areas of corn- and wheat-land and fallow fields that at odd seasons had been sown to timothy and clover. Their particular house was part log and part frame, the log portion being the old original home of Henry's grandfather. The new portion, of now rain-beaten, time-worn slabs, through which the wind squeaked in the chinks at times, and which several overshadowing elms and a butternut-tree made picturesque and reminiscently pathetic, but a little damp, was erected by Henry when he was twenty-one and just married.

That was forty-eight years before. The furniture inside, like the house outside, was old and mildewy and reminiscent of a earlier day. You have seen the what-not of cherry wood, perhaps, with spiral legs and fluted top. It was there. The old-fashioned four poster bed, with its ball-like protuberances and deep curving incisions, was there also, a sadly alienated descendant of an early Jacobean ancestor. The bureau of cherry was also high and wide and solidly built, but faded-looking, and with a musty odor. The rag carpet that underlay all these sturdy examples of enduring furniture was a weak, faded, lead-and-pink colored affair woven by Phoebe Ann's own hands, when she was fifteen years younger than she was when she died. The creaky wooden loom on which it had been done now stood like a dusty, bony skeleton, along with a broken rocking-chair, a worm-eaten clothes-press—Heaven knows how old—a lime-stained bench that had once been used to keep flowers on outside the door, and other decrepit factors of household utility, in an east room that was a lean-to against this so-called main portion. All sorts of other broken-down furniture were about this place; an antiquated clothes-horse, cracked in two of its ribs; a broken mirror in an old cherry frame, which had fallen from a nail and cracked itself three days before their youngest son, Jerry, died; an extension hat-rack, which once had had porcelain knobs on the ends of its pegs; and a sewing machine, long since outdone in its clumsy mechanism by rivals of a newer generation.

The orchard to the east of the house was full of gnarled old apple-trees, worm-eaten as to trunks and branches, and fully ornamented with green and white lichens, so that it had a sad, greenish-white, silvery effect in moonlight. The low outhouses, which had once housed chickens, a horse or two, a cow, and several pigs, were covered with patches of moss as to their roof; and the sides had been free of paint for so long that they were blackish gray as to color, and a little spongy. The picket-fence in front, with its gate squeaky and askew, and the side fences of the stake-and-rider type were in an equally run-down condition. As a matter of fact, they had aged synchronously with the persons who lived here, old Henry Reifsneider and his wife Phoebe Ann.

They had lived here, these two, ever since their marriage, forty-eight years before, and Henry had lived here before that from his childhood up. His father and mother, well along in years when he was a boy, had invited him to bring his wife here when he had first fallen in love and decided to marry; and he had done so. His father and mother were the companions of himself and his wife for ten years after they were married, when both died; and then Henry and Phoebe were left with their five children growing lustily apace. But all sorts of things had happened since then. Of the seven children, all told, that had been born to them, three had died; one girl had gone to Kansas; one boy had gone to Sioux Falls, never even to be heard of after; another boy had gone to Washington; and the last girl lived five counties away in the same State, but was so burdened with cares of her own that she rarely gave them a thought. Time and a commonplace home life that had never been attractive had weaned them thoroughly, so that, wherever they were, they gave little thought as to how it might be with their father and mother.

Old Henry Reifsneider and his wife Phoebe were a loving couple. You perhaps know how it is with simple natures that fasten themselves like lichens on the stones of circumstance and weather their days to a crumbling conclusion. The great world sounds widely, but it has no call for them. They have no soaring intellect. The orchard, the meadow, the corn-field, the pig-pen, and the chicken-lot measure the range of their human activities. When the wheat is headed it is reaped and threshed; when the corn is browned and frosted it is cut and shocked; when the timothy is in full head it is cut, and the hay-cock[1] erected. After that comes winter, with the hauling of grain to market, the sawing and splitting of wood, the simple chores of fire-building, meal-getting, occasional repairing, and visiting. Beyond these and the changes of weather—the snows, the rains, and the fair days—there are no immediate, significant things. All the rest of life is a far-off, clamorous phantasmagoria, flickering like Northern lights in the night, and sounding as faintly as cow-bells tinkling in the distance.

[1]Haystack.

Old Henry and his wife Phoebe were as fond of each other as it is possible for two old people to be who have nothing else in this life to be fond of. He was a thin old man, seventy when she died, a queer, crotchety person with coarse gray-black hair and beard, quite straggly and unkempt. He looked at you out of dull, fishy, watery eyes that had deep brown crow's-feet at the sides. His clothes, like the clothes of many farmers, were aged and angular and baggy, standing out at the pockets, not fitting about the neck, protuberant and worn at elbow and knee. Phoebe Ann was thin and shapeless, a very umbrella of a woman, clad in shabby black, and with a black bonnet for her best wear. As time had passed, and they had only themselves to look after, their movements had become slower and slower, their activities fewer and fewer. The annual keep of pigs had been reduced from five to one grunting porker, and the single horse which Henry now retained was a sleepy animal, not over-nourished and not very clean. The chickens, of which formerly there was a large flock, had almost disappeared, owing to ferrets, foxes, and the lack of proper care, which produces disease. The former healthy garden was now a straggling memory of itself, and the vines and flower-beds that formerly ornamented the windows and dooryard had now become choking thickets. A will had been made which divided the small tax-eaten property equally among the remaining four, so that it was really of no interest to any of them. Yet these two lived together in peace and sympathy, only that now and then old Henry would become unduly cranky, complaining almost invariably that something had been neglected or mislaid which was of no importance at all.

"Phoebe, where's my corn-knife? You ain't never minded to let my things alone no more."

"Now you hush, Henry," his wife would caution him in a cracked and squeaky voice. "If you don't, I'll leave yuh. I'll git up and walk out of here some day, and then where would y' be? Y' ain't got anybody but me to look after yuh, so yuh just behave yourself. Your corn knife's on the mantel where it's allus been unless you've gone an' put it summers else."

Old Henry, who knew his wife would never leave him in any circumstances, used to speculate at times as to what he would do if she were to die. That was the one leaving that he really feared. As he climbed on the chair at night to wind the old, long pendulumed, double-weighted clock, or went finally to the front and back door to see that they were safely shut in, it was a comfort to know that Phoebe was there, properly ensconced on her side of the bed, and that if he stirred restlessly in the night, she would be there to ask what he wanted.

"Now, Henry, do lie still! You're as restless as a chicken."

"Well, I can't sleep, Phoebe."

"Well, yuh needn't roll so, anyhow. Yuh kin let me sleep."

This usually reduced him to a state of somnolent ease. If she wanted a pail of water, it was a grumbling pleasure for him to get it; and if she did rise first to build the fires, he saw that the wood was cut and placed within easy reach. They divided this simple world nicely between them.

As the years had gone on, however, fewer and fewer people had called. They were well-known for a distance of as much as ten square miles as old Mr. and Mrs. Reifsneider, honest, moderately Christian, but too old to be really interesting any longer. The writing of letters had become an almost impossible burden too difficult to continue to even negotiate via others, although an occasional letter still did arrive from the daughter in Pemberton County. Now and then some old friend stopped with a pie or cake or a roasted chicken or duck, or merely to see that they were well; but even these kindly minded visits were no longer frequent.

One day in the early spring of her sixty-fourth year Mrs. Reifsneider took sick, and from a low fever passed into some indefinable ailment which, because of her age, was no longer curable. Old Henry drove to Swinnerton, the neighboring town, and procured a doctor. Some friends called, and the immediate care of her was taken off his hands. Then one chill spring night she died, and old Henry, in a fog of sorrow and uncertainty, followed her body to the nearest graveyard, an unattractive space with a few pines growing in it. Although he might have gone to the daughter in Pemberton or sent for her, it was really too much trouble and he was too weary and fixed. It was suggested to him at once by one friend and another that he come to stay with them awhile, but he did not see fit. He was so old and so fixed in his notions and so accustomed to the exact surroundings he had known all his days, that he could not think of leaving. He wanted to remain near where they had put his Phoebe; and the fact that he would have to live alone did not trouble him in the least. The living children were notified and the care of him offered if he would leave, but he would not.

"I kin make a shift for myself," he continually announced to old Dr. Morrow, who had attended his wife in this case. "I kin cook a little, and, besides, it don't take much more'n coffee an' bread in the mornin's to satisfy me. I'll get along now well enough. Yuh just let me be." And after many pleadings and proffers of advice, with supplies of coffee and bacon and baked bread duly offered and accepted, he was left to himself. For a while he sat idly outside his door brooding in the spring sun. He tried to revive his interest in farming, and to keep himself busy and free from thought by looking after the fields, which of late had been much neglected. It was a gloomy thing to come in of an evening, however, or in the afternoon and find no shadow of Phoebe where everything suggested her. By degrees he put a few of her things away. At night he sat beside his lamp and read in the papers that were left for him occasionally or in a Bible that he had neglected for years, but he could get little solace from these things. Mostly he held his hand over his mouth and looked at the floor as he sat and thought of what had become of her, and how soon he himself would die. He made a great business of making his coffee in the morning and frying himself a little bacon at night; but his appetite was gone. The shell in which he had been housed so long seemed vacant, and its shadows were suggestive of immedicable griefs. So he lived quite dolefully for five long months, and then a change began.

It was one night, after he had looked after the front and the back door, wound the clock, blown out the light, and gone through all the selfsame motions that he had indulged in for years, that he went to bed not so much to sleep as to think. It was a moonlight night. The green-lichen-covered orchard just outside and to be seen from his bed where he now lay was a silvery affair, sweetly spectral. The moon shone through the east windows, throwing the pattern of the panes on the wooden floor, and making the old furniture, to which he was accustomed, stand out dimly in the room. As usual he had been thinking of Phoebe and the years when they had been young together, and of the children who had gone, and the poor shift he was making of his present days. The house was coming to be in a very bad state indeed. The bedclothes were in disorder and not clean, for he made a wretched shift of washing. It was a terror to him. The roof leaked, causing things, some of them, to remain damp for weeks at a time, but he was getting into that brooding state where he would accept anything rather than exert himself. He preferred to pace slowly to and fro or to sit and think.

By twelve o'clock of this particular night he was asleep, however, and by two had waked again. The moon by this time had shifted to a position on the western side of the house, and it now shone in through the windows of the living-room and those of the kitchen beyond. A certain combination of furniture—a chair near a table, with his coat on it, the half-open kitchen door casting a shadow, and the position of a lamp near a paper—gave him an exact representation of Phoebe leaning over the table as he had often seen her do in life. It gave him a great start. Could it be she—or her ghost? He had scarcely ever believed in spirits; and still——— He looked at her fixedly in the feeble half-light, his old hair tingling oddly at the roots, and then sat up. The figure did not move. He put his thin legs out of the bed and sat looking at her, wondering if this could really be Phoebe. They had talked of ghosts often in their lifetime, of apparitions and omens; but they had never agreed that such things could be. It had never been a part of his wife's creed that she could have a spirit that could return to walk the earth. Her after-world was quite a different affair, a vague heaven, no less, from which the righteous did not trouble to return. Yet here she was now, bending over the table in her black skirt and gray shawl, her pale profile outlined against the moonlight.

"Phoebe," he called, thrilling from head to toe and putting out one bony hand, "have yuh come back?"

The figure did not stir, and he arose and walked uncertainly to the door, looking at it fixedly the while. As he drew near, however, the apparition resolved itself into its primal content—his old coat over the high-backed chair, the lamp by the paper, the half-open door.

"Well," he said to himself, his mouth open, "I thought shore I saw her." And he ran his hand strangely and vaguely through his hair, the while his nervous tension relaxed. Vanished as it had, it gave him the idea that she might return.

Another night, because of this first illusion, and because his mind was now constantly on her and he was old, he looked out of the window that was nearest his bed and commanded a hen-coop and pig-pen and a part of the wagon-shed, and there, a faint mist exuding from the damp of the ground, he thought he saw her again. It was one of those little wisps of mist, one of those faint exhalations of the earth that rise in a cool night after a warm day, and flicker like small white cypresses of fog before they disappear. In life it had been a custom of hers to cross this lot from her kitchen to the pig-pen to throw in any scrap that was left from her cooking, and here she was again. He sat up and watched it strangely, doubtfully, because of his previous experience, but inclined, because of the nervous titillation that passed over his body, to believe that spirits really were, and that Phoebe, who would be concerned because of his lonely state, must be thinking about him, and hence returning. What other way would she have? How otherwise could she express herself? It would be within the province of her charity so to do, and like her loving interest in him. He quivered and watched it eagerly; but a faint breath of air stirring, it wound away toward the fence and disappeared.

A third night, as he was actually dreaming, some ten days later, she came to his bedside and put her hand on his head.

"Poor Henry!" she said. "It's too bad."

He roused out of his sleep, actually to see her, he thought, moving from his bed-room into the one living-room, her figure a shadowy mass of black. The weak straining of his eyes caused little points of light to flicker about the outlines of her form. He arose, greatly astonished, walked the floor in the cool room, convinced that Phoebe was coming back to him. If he only thought sufficiently, if he made it perfectly clear by his feeling that he needed her greatly, she would come back, this kindly wife, and tell him what to do. She would perhaps be with him much of the time, in the night, anyhow; and that would make him less lonely, this state more endurable.

In age and with the feeble it is not such a far cry from the subtleties of illusion to actual hallucination, and in due time this transition was made for Henry. Night after night he waited, expecting her return. Once in his weird mood he thought he saw a pale light moving about the room, and another time he thought he saw her walking in the orchard after dark. It was one morning when the details of his lonely state were virtually unendurable that he woke with the thought that she was not dead. How he had arrived at this conclusion it is hard to say. His mind had gone. In its place was a fixed illusion. He and Phoebe had had a senseless quarrel. He had reproached her for not leaving his pipe where he was accustomed to find it, and she had left. It was an aberrated fulfillment of her old jesting threat that if he did not behave himself she would leave him.

"I guess I could find yuh ag'in," he had always said. But her cackling threat had always been:

"Yuh'll not find me if I ever leave yuh. I guess I kin git some place where yuh can't find me."

This morning when he arose he did not think to build the fire in the customary way or to grind his coffee and cut his bread, as was his wont, but solely to meditate as to where he should search for her and how he should induce her to come back. Recently the one horse had been dispensed with because he found it cumbersome and beyond his needs. He took down his soft crush hat after he had dressed himself, a new glint of interest and determination in his eye, and taking his black crook cane from behind the door, where he had always placed it, started out briskly to look for her among the nearest neighbors. His old shoes clumped soundly in the dust as he walked, and his gray-black locks, now grown rather long, straggled out in a dramatic fringe or halo from under his hat. His short coat stirred busily as he walked, and his hands and face were peaked and pale.

"Why, hello, Henry! Where're yuh goin' this morning?" inquired Farmer Dodge, who, hauling a load of wheat to market, encountered him on the public road. He had not seen the aged farmer in months, not since his wife's death, and he wondered now, seeing him looking so spry.

"Yuh ain't seen Phoebe, have yuh?" inquired the old man, looking up quizzically.

"Phoebe who?" inquired Farmer Dodge, not for the moment connecting the name with Henry's dead wife.

"Why, my wife Phoebe, o' course. Who do yuh s'pose I mean?" He stared up with a pathetic sharpness of glance from under his shaggy, gray eyebrows.

"Wall, I'll swan, Henry, yuh ain't jokin', are yuh?" said the solid Dodge, a pursy man, with a smooth, hard, red face. "It can't be your wife yuh're talkin' about. She's dead."

"Dead! Shucks!" retorted the demented Reifsneider. "She left me early this mornin', while I was sleepin'. She allus got up to build the fire, but she's gone now. We had a little spat last night, an' I guess that's the reason. But I guess I kin find her. She's gone over to Matilda Race's; that's where she's gone."

He started briskly up the road, leaving the amazed Dodge to stare in wonder after him.

"Well, I'll be switched!" he said aloud to himself. He's clean out'n his head. That poor old feller's been livin' down there till he's gone outen his mind. I'll have to notify the authorities." And he flicked his whip with great enthusiasm. "Geddap!" he said, and was off.

Reifsneider met no one else in this poorly populated region until he reached the whitewashed fence of Matilda Race and her husband three miles away. He had passed several other houses en route, but these not being within the range of his illusion were not considered. His wife, who had known Matilda well, must be here. He opened the picket-gate which guarded the walk, and stamped briskly up to the door.

"Why, Mr. Reifsneider," exclaimed old Matilda herself, a stout woman, looking out of the door in answer to his knock, "what brings yuh here this mornin'?"

"Is Phoebe here?" he demanded eagerly.

"Phoebe who? What Phoebe?" replied Mrs. Race, curious as to this sudden development of energy on his part.

"Why, my Phoebe, o'course. My wife Phoebe. Who do yuh s'pose? Ain't she here now?"

"Lawsy me!" exclaimed Mrs. Race, opening her mouth. "Yuh pore man! So you're clean out'n your mind now. Yuh come right in and sit down. I'll git yuh a cup o' coffee. O' course your wife ain't here; but yuh come in an' sit down. I'll find her fer yuh after a while. I know where she is."

The old farmer's eyes softened, and he entered. He was so thin and pale a specimen, pantalooned and patriarchal, that he aroused Mrs. Race's extremest sympathy as he took off his hat and laid it on his knees quite softly and mildly.

"We had a quarrel last night, an' she left me," he volunteered.

"Laws! laws!" sighed Mrs. Race, there being no one present with whom to share her astonishment as she went to her kitchen. "The pore man! Now somebody's just got to look after him. He can't be allowed to run around the country this way lookin' for his dead wife. It's terrible."

She boiled him a cup of coffee and brought in some of her new-baked bread and fresh butter. She set out some of her best jam and put a couple of eggs to boil, lying whole-heartedly the while.

"Now yuh stay right here, Uncle Henry, till Jake comes in, and I'll send him to look for Phoebe. I think it's more'n likely she's over to Swinnerton with some o' her friends. Anyhow, we'll find out. Now yuh just drink this coffee an' eat this bread. Yuh must be tired. Yuh've had a long walk this mornin'." Her idea was to take counsel with Jake, "her man," and perhaps have him notify the authorities.

She bustled about, meditating on the uncertainties of life, while old Reifsneider thrummed on the rim of his hat with his pale fingers and later ate abstractedly of what she offered. His mind was on his wife, however, and since she was not here, or did not appear, it wandered vaguely away to a family by the name of Murray, miles away in another direction. He decided after a time that he would not wait for Jake Race to hunt his wife but would seek her for himself. He must be on, and urge her to come back.

"Well, I'll be goin'," he said, getting up and looking strangely about him. "I guess she didn't come here after all. She went over to the Murray's, I guess. I'll not wait any longer, Mis' Race. There's a lot to do over to the house today." And out he marched in the face of her protests, taking to the dusty road again in the warm spring sun, his cane striking the earth as he went.

It was two hours later that this pale figure of a man appeared in the Murrays' doorway, dusty, perspiring, eager. He had tramped all of five miles, and it was noon. An amazed husband and wife of sixty heard his strange query, and realized also that he was mad. They begged him to stay to dinner, intending to notify the authorities later and see what could be done; but though he stayed to partake of a little something, he did not stay long, and was off again to another distant farmhouse, his idea of many things to do and his need of Phoebe impelling him. So it went for that day and the next and the next, the circle of his inquiry ever widening.

The process by which a character assumes the significance of being peculiar, his antics weird, yet harmless, in such a community is often involute and pathetic. This day, as has been said, saw Reifsneider at other doors, eagerly asking his unnatural question, and leaving a trail of amazement, sympathy, and pity in his wake. Although the authorities were informed—the county sheriff, no less—it was not deemed advisable to take him into custody; for when those who knew old Henry, and had for so long, reflected on the condition of the county insane asylum, a place which, because of the poverty of the district, was of staggering aberration and sickening environment, it was decided to let him remain at large; for, strange to relate, it was found on investigation that at night he returned peaceably enough to his lonesome domicile there to discover whether his wife had returned, and to brood in loneliness until the morning. Who would lock up a thin, eager, seeking old man with iron-gray hair and an attitude of kindly, innocent inquiry, particularly when he was well known for a past of only kindly servitude and reliability? Those who had known him best rather agreed that he should be allowed to roam at large. He could do no harm. There were many who were willing to help him as to food, old clothes, the odds and ends of his daily life—at least at first. His figure after a time became not so much a commonplace as an accepted curiosity, and the replies, "Why, no, Henry; I ain't seen her," or "No, Henry; she ain't been here today," more customary.

For several years thereafter then he was an odd figure in the sun and rain, on dusty roads and muddy ones, encountered occasionally in strange and unexpected places, pursuing his endless search. Undernourishment, after a time, although the neighbors and those who knew his history gladly contributed from their store, affected his body; for he walked much and ate little. The longer he roamed the public highway in this manner, the deeper became his strange hallucination; and finding it harder and harder to return from his more and more distant pilgrimages, he finally began taking a few utensils with him from his home, making a small package of them, in order that he might not be compelled to return. In an old tin coffee-pot of large size he placed a small tin cup, a knife, fork, and spoon, some salt and pepper, and to the outside of it, by a string forced through a pierced hole, he fastened a plate, which could be released, and which was his woodland table. It was no trouble for him to secure the little food that he needed, and with a strange, almost religious dignity, he had no hesitation in asking for that much. By degrees his hair became longer and longer, his once black hat became an earthen brown, and his clothes threadbare and dusty.

For all of three years he walked, and none knew how wide were his perambulations, nor how he survived the storms and cold. They could not see him, with homely rural understanding and forethought, sheltering himself in haycocks, or by the sides of cattle, whose warm bodies protected him from the cold, and whose dull understandings were not opposed to his harmless presence. Overhanging rocks and trees kept him at times from the rain, and a friendly hay-loft or corn-crib was not above his humble consideration.

The involute progression of hallucination is strange. From asking at doors and being constantly rebuffed or denied, he finally came to the conclusion that although his Phoebe might not be in any of the houses at the doors of which he inquired, she might nevertheless be within the sound of his voice. And so, from patient inquiry, he began to call sad, occasional cries, that ever and anon waked the quiet landscapes and ragged hill regions, and set to echoing his thin "O-o-o Phoebe! O-o-o Phoebe!" It had a pathetic, albeit insane, ring, and many a farmer or plowboy came to know it even from afar and say, "There goes old Reifsneider."

Another thing that puzzled him greatly after a time and after many hundreds of inquiries was, when he no longer had any particular dooryard in view and no special inquiry to make, which way to go. These cross-roads, which occasionally led in four or even six directions, came after a time to puzzle him. But to solve this knotty problem, which became more and more of a puzzle, there came to his aid another hallucination. Phoebe's spirit or some power of the air or wind or nature would tell him. If he stood at the center of the parting of the ways, closed his eyes, turned thrice about, and called "O-o-o Phoebe!" twice, and then threw his cane straight before him, that would surely indicate which way to go for Phoebe, or one of these mystic powers would surely govern its direction and fall! In whichever direction it went, even though, as was not infrequently the case, it took him back along the path he had already come, or across fields, he was not so far gone in his mind but that he gave himself ample time to search before he called again. Also the hallucination seemed to persist that at some time he would surely find her. There were hours when his feet were sore, and his limbs weary, when he would stop in the heat to wipe his seamed brow, or in the cold to beat his arms. Sometimes, after throwing away his cane, and finding it indicating the direction from which he had just come, he would shake his head wearily and philosophically, as if contemplating the unbelievable or an untoward fate, and then start briskly off. His strange figure came finally to be known in the farthest reaches of three or four counties. Old Reifsneider was a pathetic character. His fame was wide.

Near a little town called Watersville, in Green County, perhaps four miles from that minor center of human activity, there was a place or precipice locally known as the Red Cliff, a sheer wall of red sandstone, perhaps a hundred feet high, which raised its sharp face for half a mile or more above the fruitful cornfields and orchards that lay beneath, and which was surmounted by a thick grove of trees. The slope that slowly led up to it from the opposite side was covered by a rank growth of beech, hickory, and ash, through which threaded a number of wagon-tracks crossing at various angles. In fair weather it had become old Reifsneider's habit, so inured was he by now to the open, to make his bed in some such patch of trees as this to fry his bacon or boil his eggs at the foot of some tree before laying himself down for the night. Occasionally, so light and inconsequential was his sleep, he would walk at night. More often, the moonlight or some sudden wind stirring in the trees or a reconnoitering animal arousing him, he would sit up and think, or pursue his quest in the moonlight or the dark, a strange, unnatural, half wild, half savage-looking but utterly harmless creature, calling at lonely road crossings, staring at dark and shuttered houses, and wondering where, where Phoebe could really be.

That particular lull that comes in the systole-diastole of this earthly ball at two o'clock in the morning invariably aroused him, and though he might not go any farther he would sit up and contemplate the darkness or the stars, wondering. Sometimes in the strange processes of his mind he would fancy that he saw moving among the trees the figure of his lost wife, and then he would get up to follow, taking his utensils, always on a string, and his cane. If she seemed to evade him too easily he would run, or plead, or, suddenly losing track of the fancied figure, stand awed or disappointed, grieving for the moment over the almost insurmountable difficulties of his search.

It was in the seventh year of these hopeless peregrinations, in the dawn of a similar springtime to that in which his wife had died, that he came at last one night to the vicinity of this self-same patch that crowned the rise to the Red Cliff. His far-clung cane, used as a divining-rod at the last cross-roads, had brought him hither. He had walked many, many miles. It was after ten o'clock at night, and he was very weary. Long wandering and little eating had left him but a shadow of his former self. It was a question now not so much of physical strength but of spiritual endurance which kept him up. He had scarcely eaten this day, and now exhausted he set himself down in the dark to rest and possibly to sleep.

Curiously on this occasion a strange suggestion of the presence of his wife surrounded him. It would not be long now, he counseled with himself, although the long months had brought him nothing, until he should see her, talk to her. He fell asleep after a time, his head on his knees. At midnight the moon began to rise, and at two in the morning, his wakeful hour, was a large silver disk shining through the trees to the east. He opened his eyes when the radiance became strong, making a silver pattern at his feet and lighting the woods with strange lusters and silvery, shadowy forms. As usual, his old notion that his wife must be near occurred to him on this occasion, and he looked about him with a speculative, anticipatory eye. What was it that moved in the distant shadows along the path by which he had entered—a pale, flickering will-o'-the-wisp that bobbed gracefully among the trees and riveted his expectant gaze? Moonlight and shadows combined to give it a strange form and a stranger reality, this fluttering of bogfire or dancing of wandering fire-flies. Was it truly his lost Phoebe? By a circuitous route it passed about him, and in his fevered state he fancied that he could see the very eyes of her, not as she was when he last saw her in the black dress and shawl but now a strangely younger Phoebe, gayer, sweeter, the one whom he had known years before as a girl. Old Reifsneider got up. He had been expecting and dreaming of this hour all these years, and now as he saw the feeble light dancing lightly before him he peered at it questioningly, one thin hand in his gray hair.

Of a sudden there came to him now for the first time in many years the full charm of her girlish figure as he had known it in boyhood, the pleasing, sympathetic smile, the brown hair, the blue sash she had once worn about her waist at a picnic, her gay, graceful movements. He walked around the base of the tree, straining with his eyes, forgetting for once his cane and utensils, and following eagerly after. On she moved before him, a will-o'-the-wisp of the spring, a little flame above her head, and it seemed as though among the small saplings of ash and beech and the thick trunks of hickory and elm that she signaled with a young, a lightsome hand.

"O Phoebe! Phoebe!" he called. "Have yuh really come? Have yuh really answered me?" And hurrying faster, he fell once, scrambling lamely to his feet, only to see the light in the distance dancing illusively on. On and on he hurried until he was fairly running, brushing his ragged arms against the trees, striking his hands and face against impeding twigs. His hat was gone, his lungs were breathless, his reason quite astray, when coming to the edge of the cliff he saw her below among a silvery bed of apple-trees now blooming in the spring.

"O Phoebe!" he called. "O Phoebe! O, no, don't leave me." And feeling the lure of a world where love was young and Phoebe as this vision presented her, a delightful epitome of their quondam youth, he gave a gay cry of "Oh, wait, Phoebe!" and leaped.

Some farmer boys, reconnoitering this region of bounty and prospect some few days afterward, found first the tin utensils tied together under the tree where he had left them, and then late at the foot of the cliff, pale, broken, but elate, a molded smile of peace and delight upon his lips, his body. His old hat was discovered lying under some low-growing saplings the twigs of which had held it back. No one of all the simple population knew how eagerly and joyously he had found his lost mate.

1912 1915, 1918

The Modernist Era

The United States began the twentieth century with a population of less than 76,000,000, almost two-thirds of it living on farms and in rural villages. The dominant symbol of mobility and industrialism that would soon transform American life had just begun to appear: in all the land there were only 8,000 horseless carriages and a mere 150 miles of paved country roads.

By the beginning of the twenty-first century, the population had more than tripled, rising to more than 280,000,000. Four out of every five Americans now lived in large urban centers. They owned more than 200,000,000 motor vehicles, enough to hold the entire population of Europe—in the front seats. They traveled on more than 4,000,000 miles of roads and streets; more land in the United States was paved than remained in virgin wilderness. The nation's wealth and its technological achievements on earth and in space had astonished the world.

As the twentieth century began, the American arts were poised on the brink of a turbulent modernity. In little more than two decades American painters, architects, composers, and writers would adopt a variety of avant-garde doctrines so revolutionary as to exhaust the traditional vocabulary of the arts and require the introduction of new descriptive terms: futurism, expressionism, post-impressionism, dadaism, imagism, and surrealism.

The Armory Show of 1913

The coming changes could be seen in the visual arts early in the century. The first exhibit of modern European art in the United States took place in 1908. Five years later a vast art show, held in a National Guard armory in New York City, marked a turning point in American cultural history and introduced large numbers of Americans to modern art for the first time. Of the 1,600 works in the Armory Show, many departed radically from past tradition: urban slums and human derelicts were portrayed with harsh realism by American artists of what the newspapers derisively called the "Ash Can School"; paintings by European artists were filled with the swirling lines of neo-impressionism or with the geometric fragments and shifting viewpoints of the new cubism that seemed to defy all logic. Such "artistic anarchism" stunned the public and made the Armory Show an enormous *succès de scandale.* Bewildered critics scoffed at the show's "freak art"; students of traditional art hanged radical new artists in effigy; former President Theodore Roosevelt dismissed the startling paintings and sculpture as work of "the lunatic fringe." But the Armory Show of 1913 signaled the rise of artistic ideals that would dominate American art throughout the twentieth century.

In the years preceding World War I, nineteenth-century realism and naturalism remained vital forces in American literature. Henry James, now living in England, published two of his greatest novels, *The Ambassadors*

(1903) and *The Golden Bowl* (1904). The literary naturalists Stephen Crane and Frank Norris died in the first years of the century, but Theodore Dreiser's *Sister Carrie,* a commercial and critical failure when first published in 1900, was reissued in 1907 and won high praise for its grim, naturalistic portrayal of American society. Ezra Pound and T. S. Eliot published works that would change the nature of American poetry. But the genteel tradition and popular romanticism still dominated the nation's literary tastes.

In 1900 the best-selling novel in the United States was *To Have and To Hold,* a now forgotten historical romance by Mary Johnston. In 1902, the bestseller was Owen Wister's *The Virginian,* a western that established a pattern for hundreds of cowboy adventure stories and movies that have followed (it was revived as a television series in the 1960s). Yet the most popular single work of fiction published in the entire period (by the 1990s its sales exceeded 6,000,000 copies) was a juvenile fantasy, *The Wonderful Wizard of Oz* (1900).

A New Literature Emerges

The growth of mass-circulation periodicals created a rich marketplace for popular writers. By the 1920s, general-audience magazines that had circulations in the millions were paying as much as $6,000 for a short story and $60,000 for a serial (the equivalent of almost $400,000 in modern purchasing power). During the Depression of the 1930s, the profitable mass market for literature temporarily declined, but after World War II it expanded enormously with the growth of the population, the increase of wealth and education, the expansion of mass-distribution book clubs, and the technical advances in printing that made possible the publication of vast numbers of inexpensive paperbacks.

In the early 1900s, a rising number of "little magazines" brought numerous avant-garde writers to the attention of a limited but sophisticated audience. The most influential was *Poetry: A Magazine of Verse,* founded in Chicago by Harriet Monroe in 1912. Its first issue contained two poems by Ezra Pound. In 1915 it printed T. S. Eliot's "The Love Song of J. Alfred Prufrock." Within a few years it had published works by Edwin Arlington Robinson and Robert Frost, followed soon after by Wallace Stevens and Hart Crane. Their works forced changes in the traditional relationships between poets and their audiences, requiring learned and sophisticated readers armed with modernist sympathies. The "modernism" displayed in works by writers such as T. S. Eliot, Wallace Stevens, and Ezra Pound was, like the shocking paintings and sculpture of the Armory Show, bafflingly abstract and impressionistic, offering a fractured view of the world that was far less representational than the portrayal of life found in the literary works that readers had long been accustomed to.

Although the form and direction of modern American literature had clearly begun to emerge in the first decades of the century, the First World War (1914–1918) stands as the great dividing line between the nineteenth century and contemporary America. World War I had its origins in the political turmoil of the early 1900s and in the vain rivalries of European imperial powers that had once seemed to be the glory of the age. For the United States the war began as a crusade to "Keep the Free in Freedom" and make the world safe for democracy. At the war's end, President Woodrow Wilson proclaimed that Americans had gained everything for which they had fought. But out of the war's catastrophes and appalling waste came little more than a sense of the failure of political leadership. No abiding solutions to the world's problems were found, and the years following the war saw a resurgence of nationalism and the rise of a new totalitarianism that would bring on World War II in less than a quarter of a century.

The Movements for Social Reform

During World War I, national attention was drawn away from movements for political and social reform. But with the onset of peace, reform efforts gathered new strength, especially the movements for temperance and women's rights. The Women's Christian Temperance Union and the Anti-Saloon League raised funds for speakers and propaganda pamphleteers to denounce "Demon Rum" and "John Barleycorn." "Drys" debated "Wets" at town meetings, churches, and schools. Crusading temperance groups held parades and rallies for a "blissful, bone-dry America" and made campaign contributions to political candidates who would "vote right on the liquor issue." Victory for the temperance movement came in 1919, when the Eighteenth Amendment to the Constitution was ratified, prohibiting the sale of alcoholic beverages in the United States. But the triumph of temperance was only temporary. America refused to go dry; the manufacture and sale of illegal alcohol flourished, and during the "Roaring Twenties," the drinking of alcohol by "respectable" Americans even increased. Prohibition had failed to purify America. Instead it brought many of the excesses—including the rise of organized crime and widespread disrespect for the law—that have characterized America since the 1920s. After fourteen years, the nation finally acknowledged its failure to legislate virtue and sobriety; with the ratification of the Twenty-First Amendment in 1933, prohibition was repealed.

The movement for women's suffrage had arisen in the mid-nineteenth century, but with the end of World War I, a war fought in the name of democracy and liberty, both women and men began working with renewed vigor to obtain for women the right to vote. They held protest marches, picketed government offices, purposely got themselves arrested, and went on hunger strikes while in jail, all to dramatize the need for equal rights in the polling booth. Their campaign was so successful that less than a year after the end of the war, Congress had passed, and one year later the states had ratified, the Nineteenth Amendment that declared the right to vote could no longer be denied "on account of sex." Women looked forward to "sharing the helm" of the ship of state, but their real liberation did not begin until the coming of the movement for women's rights that marked the decades of the 1960s and 1970s in the United States.

Reform victories seemed to indicate the beginning of a better age, but the writers of the first postwar era self-consciously declared that they were a "Lost Generation," devoid of faith and alienated from a civilization that was "botched," as Ezra Pound described it, "an old bitch gone in the teeth." Yet in the decade of the 1920s American literature achieved a new diversity and reached its greatest heights. The publication in 1922 of T. S. Eliot's *The*

Waste Land, the most significant American poem of the twentieth century, helped to establish a modern tradition of literature rich with learning and symbolism. In 1920 Sinclair Lewis published his memorable denunciation of American small-town provincialism in *Main Street,* and in the same year Theodore Dreiser began writing his masterpiece of naturalism, *An American Tragedy* (1925). F. Scott Fitzgerald summarized the experiences and attitudes of the decade in his short stories and in his novel *The Great Gatsby* (1926). Ernest Hemingway wrote *The Sun Also Rises* (1926) and *A Farewell to Arms* (1929), and William Faulkner published one of the most influential American novels of the age, *The Sound and the Fury* (1929).

After the First World War new American dramatists emerged, and the American theater ceased to be wholly dependent on the dramatic traditions of Europe. Experimental playwrights, hostile to outworn and timid theatrical convention, created works of tragedy, stark realism, and social protest. In the "new American theater" plots, dialogue, staging, and acting differed radically from the bland dramatic fare of an earlier day. Plays by "advanced" dramatists won large audiences and drew widespread critical acclaim. Early in the 1920s the most prominent of the new American playwrights, Eugene O'Neill, established an international reputation with such plays as *The Emperor Jones* (1920), *Anna Christie* (1921), and *The Hairy Ape* (1922).

Visual Arts, Architecture, and Music

The years between the two world wars were a time of new directions and new achievements in all the arts. New museums and galleries were established in large and small cities throughout the United States. New York's Museum of Modern Art was founded in 1929, and New York City became the center of modern art in America, attracting artists from all over America and Europe to the visual richness of towering buildings and scenes of massed humanity. The term "modern art" had been used as early as the 1890s to describe the works of artists who deliberately chose to depart from the traditional forms, techniques, and subjects of familiar European art history. By the 1920s, words such as "modernism" and "modernistic" were part of the everyday vocabulary of millions of Americans who confronted the experimentalism of twentieth-century painting and sculpture. New theories of art sprouted, justifying flat abstractions or surrealism with nightmarish representations of the unconscious. Art came to be accepted as diverse, unusual, indecipherable. Artists attempted to present meanings without depicting conventional forms or familiar things, just as modernist literature often seemed to consist of poetry and prose that was unfamiliar and inexplicable.

It was also an age of artistic grandiloquence. The American skyscraper became the preeminent achievement of twentieth-century architecture. The American motion picture industry rose to world dominance. And with the establishment of such music schools as Eastman and Julliard after World War I, American-trained musicians at last began to challenge successfully the graduates of famous European music conservatories. The jazz music of American blacks—the most influential art form ever to originate in the United States—spread throughout the world, and in 1938, when Benny Goodman led a racially mixed jazz orchestra in a concert at prestigious Carnegie Hall in New York City, it was clear that jazz had at last been accepted by even the most patrician and rarefied audiences.

From the early years of the century to World War II there was a rebirth of writing by American blacks who boldly celebrated black culture, black folklore, black language, and the homes, family life, and familiar landscapes of black men and women in large urban centers and in small towns and farming villages. Writers such as Jean Toomer, Langston Hughes, Countée Cullen, and Zora Neale Hurston created a new black literature that distinguished the Harlem Literary Renaissance of the 1920s and paved the way for a second black literary renaissance, in the last half of the twentieth century.

In 1929 the stock market crashed, and the Great Depression of the 1930s began, a cataclysmic event that shattered public complacency and transformed American society. The abrupt end of what had seemed to be permanent prosperity weakened the nation's confidence in its government, in its political leaders, and even in its fundamental democratic ideals. American artists of all kinds began to produce works of political and social criticism. Painters created harsh visions of American life on farms and in cities. Photographers recorded the miseries of poverty and want. Writers such as John Steinbeck described the sweat-drenched lives of factory workers and migrant farmers in journalistic reports, in short stories, and in such memorable novels as *Of Mice and Men* (1937) and *The Grapes of Wrath* (1939).

The social upheavals and the artistic declarations of the Great Depression years changed with the prosperity and turmoil brought by World War II (1939–1945). And after the war a new generation of American authors appeared, writing in the skeptical, ironic tradition of the earlier realists and naturalists. New writers of the 1950s used a prose style modeled on the works of Ernest Hemingway and F. Scott Fitzgerald, narrative techniques derived from William Faulkner, and psychological insights taken from the writings of Sigmund Freud and his followers. But the literature that was to emerge in the decades following 1945, while it continued many of its modernist traditions, took new direction. It turned to what has been labeled post-modernism, to new heroes (often anti-heroes, misfits, and victims), to different subjects, and to innovative experimental techniques. And it produced a literature of new diversity, evident in fiction, poetry, the dramatic theater, and evident most of all in the vast and sprawling world of the popular arts and television that has dominated American culture from the early 1950s into the twenty-first century.

W. E. B. Du Bois 1868–1963

In 1997, the July issue of The Crisis *was dedicated to a man it praised as "the premier crusading voice of civil rights"—a man who also made an indelible mark on the nineteenth and twentieth centuries as a philosopher, author, teacher, and editor. Although William Edward Burghardt Du Bois (pronounced* du-boys*) died on the eve of the Rev. Martin Luther King's famous "I Have a Dream" speech and, therefore, did not live to witness the landmark civil rights legislation that followed, he did much to help realize King's dream. During his lifetime, Du Bois wrote nineteen books, edited eighteen books, and contributed hundreds of essays and columns to leading publications throughout the world. Moreover, he was a professor of sociology, history, Latin, Greek, English, and German, as well as a co-founder and leader of the Niagara Movement, the National Negro Academy, the Pan-African Congress, and the National Association for the Advancement of Colored People (NAACP), where he worked for nearly thirty years.*

Du Bois was born in Great Barrington, Massachusetts, on February 23, 1868, five years after Lincoln signed the Emancipation Proclamation. Since blacks in Great Barrington faced relatively little discrimination, young Du Bois went to the city's public schools. In 1884, he graduated at the top of his high school class and delivered the class oration, speaking on Wendell Phillips—a famed abolitionist and Massachusetts senator whose leadership qualities Du Bois greatly admired. Du Bois later recalled, "This was my first sweet taste of the world's applause. There were flowers and upturned faces, music and marching, and there was my mother's smile." Du Bois had hoped to attend Harvard College, but he was too poor. Knowing his plight, the townspeople gave him a modest scholarship, which he used to attend Fisk University in Nashville, Tennessee.

The influence of Fisk on Du Bois proved deep and abiding. During his three years as a student at Fisk, he spent his summers teaching black children in rural schools, and there gained a life-long understanding of the strength and resiliency of southern black culture. He excelled in his classes, but all was not well. Du Bois had arrived in Tennessee in 1885, eight years after Reconstruction had ended. The progress that blacks had made with the help of the federal government under the laws of Reconstruction had long since ended. The Ku Klux Klan and other white supremacy groups had arisen to resist the effect of black emancipation after the Civil War, and Du Bois found himself living in a world wholly dominated by whites and deeply divided by race. There for the first time he met large numbers of impoverished southern blacks and saw the harsh and restricted lives they were forced to lead.

After three years at Fisk, Du Bois was admitted to Harvard College. In 1890 he received a bachelor's degree, and he received a master's degree one year later. He then went to the University of Berlin for further study, and after two years in Germany he returned to Harvard, where he became the first African American to receive a Ph.D.

Academic degrees in hand, Du Bois confidently set out, as he wrote in his journal, "to make a name in science, to make a name in art and thus to raise my race." In 1894 he began teaching at Wilberforce University in Ohio. From Wilberforce he moved to Atlanta University, where he taught from 1897 to 1910. By then he had published a biography of the abolitionist John Brown (1909), The Philadelphia Negro *(1896),* The Suppression of the African Slave Trade to the USA *(1896),* The Training of the Negro for Social Power *(1903), and his most celebrated work,* The Souls of Black Folk *(1903). It consisted of fourteen essays in which he offered a montage of philosophy, history, autobiography, fiction, sociology, and music. His overarching goal in writing the book was to tell of his own experiences and to theorize about black life in America, promoting the ideal of "human brotherhood." It made him world famous.*

Throughout his life, as he became ever more renowned, Du Bois worked for the cause of social equality, in his teaching, lecturing, and writing. For twenty-five years he served as editor of the NAACP's magazine, The Crisis, *in which he vehemently set forth his ideas on the proper ways to achieve racial equality. As editor of* The Crisis *he helped launch the careers of notable American writers, including Zora Neale Hurston, Countee Cullen, and Langston Hughes. Du Bois disagreed with other black leaders, especially the famous and highly regarded Booker T. Washington, arguing that their gradualism, their faith in measured progress toward equality, did little to better the lives of black Americans.*

In 1927 Du Bois traveled to the Soviet Union. There he was captivated by the professed ideals of communism and the illusory communist promise of a classless society and social equality. In his later years Du Bois grew increasingly disappointed and embittered over the still unfulfilled promise of full racial, political, and civil equality in the United States. Finally, in 1961, when he was ninety-three, he formally joined the Communist Party, which he saw as the only effective instrument for social progress. He then left the United States, moved to Africa, renounced his American citizenship, and became a citizen of Ghana, where he continued to write and to speak out on issues of race. In 1963, at the age of ninety-five, he died, in Accra, Ghana, having never returned to America.

Ironically, though he disavowed his native land, Du Bois and his works are celebrated and honored more in the United States than in any other nation. Editions of his works continue to be published and sold in large numbers. Thousands of students study his ideas in American universities. His alma mater, Harvard University, has established the W. E. B. Du Bois Institute for the Study of Africa and African-America, and in 2003, at a national commemoration of the one-hundredth anniversary of the publication of The Souls of Black Folk, *scholars and students from throughout the United States gathered to celebrate Du Bois as "one of the most well-regarded and most versatile intellectuals ever to emerge from the American cultural soil."*

FURTHER READING: S. G. Du Bois, *His Day Is Marching On, A Memoir of W. E. B. Du Bois,* 1971; *The Complete Published Works of W. E. B. Du Bois,* ed. Herbert Aptheker, 1973–1986; J. Moore, *W. E. B. Du Bois,* 1981; J. DeMarco, *The Social Thought of W. E. B. Du Bois,* 1983; *Critical Essays on W. E. B. Du Bois,* ed. W. Andrews, 1985; M. Marable, *W. E. B. Du Bois, Black Radical Democrat,* 1986; G. Horne, *Black and Red, W. E. B. Du Bois and the Afro-American Response to the Cold War, 1944–1963,* 1986; *Newspaper Columns 1883–1944, 1945–1961,* ed. H. Aptheker, 1986; *Against Racism, Unpublished Essays, Papers, Addresses 1887–1961,* ed. H. Aptheker, 1988; *W. E. B. Du Bois Speaks, Speeches and Addresses, 1890–1919, 1920–1963,* 2 vols., ed. P. Foner, 1988; C. West, *The American Evasion of Philosophy, A Genealogy of Pragmatism,* 1989; D. Lewis, *W. E. B. Du Bois, Biography of a Race, 1886–1919,* 1993; E. Sundquist, *To Wake the Nations, Race in the Making of American Literature,* 1993; K. Byerman, *Seizing the Word, History, Art, and Self in the Works of W. E. B. Du Bois,* 1994; S. Zamir, *Dark Voices: W. E. B. Du Bois and American Thought,* 1995; *The Correspondence of W. E. B. Du Bois,* 3 vols., ed. H. Aptheker, 1997; A. Reed, *W. E. B. Du Bois and American Political Thought,* 1997; D. Lewis, *W. E. B. Du Bois, The Fight for Equality and the American Century,* 2000; *W. E. B. Du Bois, An Encyclopedia,* ed. G. Horne and M. Young, 2001; *W. E. B. Du Bois and Race,* ed. C. Fontenot and M. Morgan, 2002; R. Randolph, *W. E. B. Du Bois, The Fight for Civil Rights,* 2005.

TEXT: *The Souls of Black Folk,* 1903.

from *THE SOULS OF BLACK FOLK*

THE FORETHOUGHT

Herein lie buried many things which if read with patience may show the strange meaning of being black here in the dawning of the Twentieth Century. This meaning is not without interest to you, Gentle Reader; for the problem of the Twentieth Century is the problem of the color-line.

I pray you, then, receive my little book in all charity, studying my words with me, forgiving mistake and foible for sake of the faith and passion that is in me, and seeking the grain of truth hidden there.

I have sought here to sketch, in vague, uncertain outline, the spiritual world in which ten thousand thousand Americans live and strive. First, in two chapters I have tried to show what Emancipation meant to them, and what was its aftermath. In a third chapter I have pointed out the slow rise of personal leadership, and criticised candidly the leader[1] who bears the chief burden of his race to-day. Then, in two other chapters I have sketched in swift outline the two worlds within and without the Veil,[2] and thus have come to the central problem of training men for life. Venturing now into deeper detail, I have in two chapters studied the struggles of the massed millions of the black peasantry, and in another have sought to make clear the present relations of the sons of master and man.

Leaving, then, the world of the white man, I have stepped within the Veil, raising it that you may view faintly its deeper recesses,—the meaning of its religion, the passion of its human sorrow, and the struggle of its greater souls. All this I have ended with a tale twice told[3] but seldom written.

Some of these thoughts of mine have seen the light before in other guise. For kindly consenting to their republication here, in altered and extended form, I must thank the publishers of *The Atlantic Monthly, The World's Work, The Dial, The New World,* and the *Annals of the American Academy of Political and Social Science.*

Before each chapter, as now printed, stands a bar of the Sorrow Songs,—some echo of haunting melody from the only American music which welled up from black souls in the dark past. And, finally, need I add that I who speak here am bone of the bone and flesh of the flesh[4] of them that live within the Veil?

W. E. B. Du B.
Atlanta, Ga., Feb. 1, 1903.

[1]A reference to Booker T. Washington (1856–1915), American black leader and educator whom Du Bois criticized as a gradualist, one who believes that social progress is best made slowly and surely.

[2]The veil that stands between two worlds and obscures one from the other is found in Hebrews 6:19. Here Du Bois uses the phrase as a metaphor for the division between the worlds of white and black America.

[3]Often told.

[4]To show identity with his fellow blacks, Du Bois quotes Adam's declaration that newly created Eve is "bone of my bones, and flesh of my flesh." Genesis 2:23.

I

OF OUR SPIRITUAL STRIVINGS

O water, voice of my heart, crying in the sand,
  All night long crying with a mournful cry,
As I lie and listen, and cannot understand
    The voice of my heart in my side or the voice of the sea,
  O water, crying for rest, is it I, is it I?
    All night long the water is crying to me.

Unresting water there shall never be rest
  Till the last moon droop and the last tide fail,
And the fire of the end begin to burn in the west;
    And the heart shall be weary and wonder and cry like the sea,
  All life long crying without avail,
    As the water all night long is crying to me.

—Arthur Symons[5]

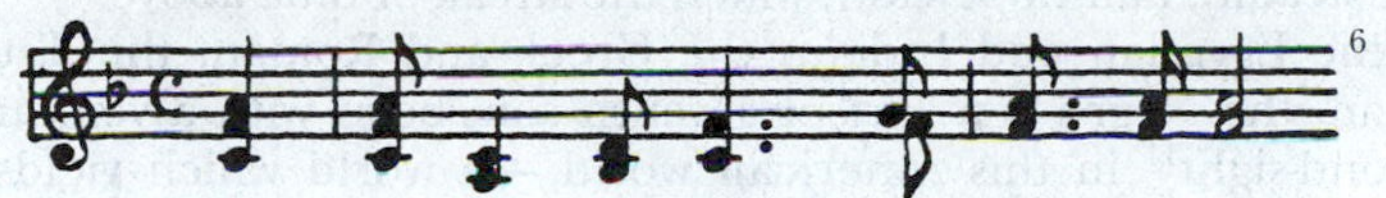
[6]

Between me and the other world there is ever an unasked question: unasked by some through feelings of delicacy; by others through the difficulty of rightly framing it. All, nevertheless, flutter round it. They approach me in a half-hesitant sort of way, eye me curiously or compassionately, and then, instead of saying directly, How does it feel to be a problem? they say, I know an excellent colored man in my town; or, I fought at Mechanicsville;[7] or, Do not these Southern outrages make your blood boil? At these I smile, or am interested, or reduce the boiling to a simmer, as the occasion may require. To the real question, How does it feel to be a problem? I answer seldom a word.

And yet, being a problem is a strange experience,—peculiar even for one who has never been anything else, save perhaps in babyhood and in Europe. It is in the early days of rollicking boyhood that the revelation first bursts upon one, all in a day, as it were. I remember well when the shadow swept across me. I was a little thing, away up in the hills of New England, where the dark Housatonic[8] winds between Hoosac and Taghkanic[9] to the sea. In a wee wooden schoolhouse, something put it into the boys' and girls' heads to buy gorgeous visiting-cards—ten cents a package—and exchange. The exchange was merry, till one girl, a tall newcomer, refused my card,—refused it peremptorily, with a glance. Then it dawned upon me with a certain

[5]Lines from *The Crying of Waters* (1903), by the English poet Arthur Symons (1865–1945).

[6]Musical notation for the first line of "Nobody Knows the Trouble I've Seen," one of the most famous of all black spirituals, religious folk songs. As part of the repertoire of the famous Fisk University Jubilee Singers, it was often performed when Du Bois was a student at Fisk.

[7]Site of a bloody Civil War battle in Virginia, June 1862.

[8]River in western Massachusetts that flows south through Connecticut to the Atlantic.

[9]Mountain ranges in western Massachusetts. Du Bois uses a variant spelling of "Taconic.".

suddenness that I was different from the others; or like, mayhap, in heart and life and longing, but shut out from their world by a vast veil. I had thereafter no desire to tear down that veil, to creep through; I held all beyond it in common contempt, and lived above it in a region of blue sky and great wandering shadows. That sky was bluest when I could beat my mates at examination-time, or beat them at a foot-race, or even beat their stringy heads. Alas, with the years all this fine contempt began to fade; for the worlds I longed for, and all their dazzling opportunities, were theirs, not mine. But they should not keep these prizes, I said; some, all, I would wrest from them. Just how I would do it I could never decide: by reading law, by healing the sick, by telling the wonderful tales that swam in my head,—some way. With other black boys the strife was not so fiercely sunny: their youth shrunk into tasteless sycophancy, or into silent hatred of the pale world about them and mocking distrust of everything white; or wasted itself in a bitter cry, Why did God make me an outcast and a stranger in mine own house? The shades of the prison-house[10] closed round about us all: walls strait and stubborn to the whitest, but relentlessly narrow, tall, and unscalable to sons of night who must plod darkly on in resignation, or beat unavailing palms against the stone, or steadily, half hopelessly, watch the streak of blue above.

After the Egyptian and Indian, the Greek and Roman, the Teuton and Mongolian, the Negro is a sort of seventh son, born with a veil, and gifted with second-sight[11] in this American world,—a world which yields him no true self-consciousness, but only lets him see himself through the revelation of the other world. It is a peculiar sensation, this double-consciousness, this sense of always looking at one's self through the eyes of others, of measuring one's soul by the tape of a world that looks on in amused contempt and pity. One ever feels his twoness,—an American, a Negro; two souls, two thoughts, two unreconciled strivings; two warring ideals in one dark body, whose dogged strength alone keeps it from being torn asunder.

The history of the American Negro is the history of this strife—this longing to attain self-conscious manhood, to merge his double self into a better and truer self. In this merging he wishes neither of the older selves to be lost. He would not Africanize America, for America has too much to teach the world and Africa. He would not bleach his Negro soul in a flood of white Americanism, for he knows that Negro blood has a message for the world. He simply wishes to make it possible for a man to be both a Negro and an American, without being cursed and spit upon by his fellows, without having the doors of Opportunity closed roughly in his face.

This, then, is the end of his striving: to be a co-worker in the kingdom of culture, to escape both death and isolation, to husband and use his best powers and his latent genius. These powers of body and mind have in the past been strangely wasted, dispersed, or forgotten. The shadow of a mighty Negro past flits through the tale of Ethiopia the Shadowy and of Egypt the Sphinx. Throughout history, the powers of single black men flash here and there like falling stars, and die sometimes before the world has rightly

[10]A quotation from "Ode: Intimations of Immortality from Recollections of Early Childhood," by the English poet William Wordsworth (1770–1850).

[11]In American folklore, seventh sons are said to have power to see beyond the present and foretell the future.

gauged their brightness. Here in America, in the few days since Emancipation,[12] the black man's turning hither and thither in hesitant and doubtful striving has often made his very strength to lose effectiveness, to seem like absence of power, like weakness. And yet it is not weakness,—it is the contradiction of double aims. The double-aimed struggle of the black artisan—on the one hand to escape white contempt for a nation of mere hewers of wood and drawers of water,[13] and on the other hand to plough and nail and dig for a poverty-stricken horde—could only result in making him a poor craftsman, for he had but half a heart in either cause. By the poverty and ignorance of his people, the Negro minister or doctor was tempted toward quackery[14] and demagogy;[15] and by the criticism of the other world, toward ideals that made him ashamed of his lowly tasks. The would-be black *savant*[16] was confronted by the paradox that the knowledge his people needed was a twice-told tale to his white neighbors, while the knowledge which would teach the white world was Greek to his own flesh and blood. The innate love of harmony and beauty that set the ruder souls of his people a-dancing and a-singing raised but confusion and doubt in the soul of the black artist; for the beauty revealed to him was the soul-beauty of a race which his larger audience despised, and he could not articulate the message of another people. This waste of double aims, this seeking to satisfy two unreconciled ideals, has wrought sad havoc with the courage and faith and deeds of ten thousand thousand people,—has sent them often wooing false gods and invoking false means of salvation, and at times has even seemed about to make them ashamed of themselves.

Away back in the days of bondage they thought to see in one divine event the end of all doubt and disappointment; few men ever worshipped Freedom with half such unquestioning faith as did the American Negro for two centuries. To him, so far as he thought and dreamed, slavery was indeed the sum of all villainies, the cause of all sorrow, the root of all prejudice; Emancipation was the key to a promised land of sweeter beauty than ever stretched before the eyes of wearied Israelites.[17] In song and exhortation swelled one refrain—Liberty; in his tears and curses the God he implored had Freedom in his right hand. At last it came,—suddenly, fearfully, like a dream. With one wild carnival of blood and passion came the message in his own plaintive cadences:—

Shout, O children!
Shout, you're free!
For God has bought your liberty![18]

[12]The Emancipation Proclamation (1863) issued by President Lincoln abolished slavery only in the rebellious Confederate states. The actual end of slavery throughout all the United States did not come until 1865 with the defeat of the Confederacy and the passage of the Thirteenth Amendment to the Constitution.

[13]Those suited only to labor, the lowly. A quotation from Joshua 9:2.

[14]Pretending to have medical skills.

[15]Demagoguery, exploiting popular prejudices and using false promises to mislead the people and gain political power.

[16]French: a learned person, a scholar.

[17]The passage of the Israelites to the land promised to them by the Lord, to which Moses led them from their bondage in Egypt, is described in Exodus and Deuteronomy 6.

[18]Lines from the spiritual "Shout, O Children."

Years have passed away since then,—ten, twenty, forty; forty years of national life, forty years of renewal and development, and yet the swarthy spectre sits in its accustomed seat at the Nation's feast. In vain do we cry to this our vastest social problem:—

> Take any shape but that, and my firm nerves
> Shall never tremble![19]

The Nation has not yet found peace from its sins; the freedman has not yet found in freedom his promised land. Whatever of good may have come in these years of change, the shadow of a deep disappointment rests upon the Negro people,—a disappointment all the more bitter because the unattained ideal was unbounded save by the simple ignorance of a lowly people.

The first decade was merely a prolongation of the vain search for freedom, the boon that seemed ever barely to elude their grasp,—like a tantalizing will-o'-the-wisp,[20] maddening and misleading the headless host. The holocaust of war, the terrors of the Ku-Klux Klan,[21] the lies of carpet-baggers,[22] the disorganization of industry, and the contradictory advice of friends and foes, left the bewildered serf with no new watch-word beyond the old cry for freedom. As the time flew, however, he began to grasp a new idea. The ideal of liberty demanded for its attainment powerful means, and these the Fifteenth Amendment[23] gave him. The ballot, which before he had looked upon as a visible sign of freedom, he now regarded as the chief means of gaining and perfecting the liberty with which war had partially endowed him. And why not? Had not votes made war and emancipated millions? Had not votes enfranchised the freedmen? Was anything impossible to a power that had done all this? A million black men started with renewed zeal to vote themselves into the kingdom. So the decade flew away, the revolution of 1876[24] came, and left the half-free serf weary, wondering, but still inspired. Slowly but steadily, in the following years, a new vision began gradually to replace the dream of political power,—a powerful movement, the rise of another ideal to guide the unguided, another pillar of fire by night[25] after a

[19]Du Bois compares the dilemma of blacks facing racism to the plight of Shakespeare's Macbeth, who is left powerless when confronted by the ghost of Banquo. *Macbeth,* III, iv, lines 103–104.

[20]A misleading hope, a false goal.

[21]A secret society of southern whites formed after the Civil War with the professed aim of protecting southern society amid the chaos that came with the defeat of the Confederacy. The Klan rapidly disintegrated into an organization devoted to white supremacy, to the intimidation of blacks, and to the suppression of black civil rights—by political coercion, threats, and violence.

[22]A term of insult used by southerners to describe northern businessmen and politicians who flocked to the South after the Civil War, carrying their belongings in cheap suitcases made of carpeting and hoping to enrich themselves amid the ruins of the defeated Confederacy.

[23]Amendment to the U.S. Constitution (1870) establishing as law that no citizen of the United States could be denied the right to vote "on account of race, color, or previous condition of servitude." To the dismay of feminists, it did not extend the right to vote to women.

[24]In the "Disputed Presidential Election of 1876," the Democratic candidate, Samuel Tilden, won the popular vote, but his Republican opponent, Rutherford B. Hayes, aided by southern political powers, won the vote in the Electoral College. Once in office, Hayes ordered the withdrawal of federal troops from the South and returned full powers of government to the southern states, thus ending Reconstruction and direct federal protection of black rights in the South.

[25]The Lord, taking the form of a "pillar of fire," guided the Israelites through the wilderness to the Promised Land. Exodus 13.

clouded day. It was the ideal of "book-learning"; the curiosity, born of compulsory ignorance, to know and test the power of the cabalistic[26] letters of the white man, the longing to know. Here at last seemed to have been discovered the mountain path to Canaan;[27] longer than the highway of Emancipation and law, steep and rugged, but straight, leading to heights high enough to overlook life.

Up the new path the advance guard toiled, slowly, heavily, doggedly; only those who have watched and guided the faltering feet, the misty minds, the dull understandings, of the dark pupils of these schools know how faithfully, how piteously, this people strove to learn. It was weary work. The cold statistician wrote down the inches of progress here and there, noted also where here and there a foot had slipped or some one had fallen. To the tired climbers, the horizon was ever dark, the mists were often cold, the Canaan was always dim and far away. If, however, the vistas disclosed as yet no goal, no resting-place, little but flattery and criticism, the journey at least gave leisure for reflection and self-examination; it changed the child of Emancipation to the youth with dawning self-consciousness, self-realization, self-respect. In those sombre forests of his striving his own soul rose before him, and he saw himself,—darkly as through a veil; and yet he saw in himself some faint revelation of his power, of his mission. He began to have a dim feeling that, to attain his place in the world, he must be himself, and not another. For the first time he sought to analyze the burden he bore upon his back, that dead-weight of social degradation partially masked behind a half-named Negro problem. He felt his poverty; without a cent, without a home, without land, tools, or savings, he had entered into competition with rich, landed, skilled neighbors. To be a poor man is hard, but to be a poor race in a land of dollars is the very bottom of hardships. He felt the weight of his ignorance,—not simply of letters, but of life, of business, of the humanities; the accumulated sloth and shirking and awkwardness of decades and centuries shackled his hands and feet. Nor was his burden all poverty and ignorance. The red stain of bastardy, which two centuries of systematic legal defilement of Negro women had stamped upon his race, meant not only the loss of ancient African chastity, but also the hereditary weight of a mass of corruption from white adulterers, threatening almost the obliteration of the Negro home.

A people thus handicapped ought not to be asked to race with the world, but rather allowed to give all its time and thought to its own social problems. But alas! while sociologists gleefully count his bastards and his prostitutes, the very soul of the toiling, sweating black man is darkened by the shadow of a vast despair. Men call the shadow prejudice, and learnedly explain it as the natural defence of culture against barbarism, learning against ignorance, purity against crime, the "higher" against the "lower" races. To which the Negro cries Amen! and swears that to so much of this strange prejudice as is founded on just homage to civilization, culture, righteousness, and progress, he humbly bows and meekly does obeisance.[28] But before that nameless prejudice that leaps beyond all this he stands helpless, dismayed, and well-nigh speechless; before that personal disrespect and

[26]Having a secret or hidden meaning.
[27]The promised land to which the Israelites came after wandering forty years in the wilderness.
[28]Shows deference, submission.

mockery, the ridicule and systematic humiliation, the distortion of fact and wanton license of fancy, the cynical ignoring of the better and the boisterous welcoming of the worse, the all-pervading desire to inculcate disdain for everything black, from Toussaint[29] to the devil,—before this there rises a sickening despair that would disarm and discourage any nation save that black host to whom "discouragement" is an unwritten word.

But the facing of so vast a prejudice could not but bring the inevitable self-questioning, self-disparagement, and lowering of ideals which ever accompany repression and breed in an atmosphere of contempt and hate. Whisperings and portents came home upon the four winds: Lo! we are diseased and dying, cried the dark hosts; we cannot write, our voting is vain; what need of education, since we must always cook and serve? And the Nation echoed and enforced this self-criticism, saying: Be content to be servants, and nothing more; what need of higher culture for half-men? Away with the black man's ballot, by force or fraud,—and behold the suicide of a race! Nevertheless, out of the evil came something of good,—the more careful adjustment of education to real life, the clearer perception of the Negroes' social responsibilities, and the sobering realization of the meaning of progress.

So dawned the time of *Sturm und Drang*:[30] storm and stress today rocks our little boat on the mad waters of the world-sea; there is within and without the sound of conflict, the burning of body and rending of soul; inspiration strives with doubt, and faith with vain questionings. The bright ideals of the past,—physical freedom, political power, the training of brains and the training of hands,—all these in turn have waxed and waned, until even the last grows dim and overcast. Are they all wrong,—all false? No, not that, but each alone was oversimple and incomplete,—the dreams of a credulous race-childhood, or the fond imaginings of the other world which does not know and does not want to know our power. To be really true, all these ideals must be melted and welded into one. The training of the schools we need to-day more than ever,—the training of deft hands, quick eyes and ears, and above all the broader, deeper, higher culture of gifted minds and pure hearts. The power of the ballot we need in sheer self-defence, else what shall save us from a second slavery? Freedom, too, the long-sought, we still seek,—the freedom of life and limb, the freedom to work and think, the freedom to love and aspire. Work, culture, liberty,—all these we need, not singly but together, not successively but together, each growing and aiding each, and all striving toward that vaster ideal that swims before the Negro people, the ideal of human brotherhood, gained through the unifying ideal of Race; the ideal of fostering and developing the traits and talents of the Negro, not in opposition to or contempt for other races, but rather in large conformity to the greater ideals of the American Republic, in order that some day on American soil two world-races may give each to each those characteristics both so sadly lack. We the darker ones come even now not altogether empty-handed: there are to-day no truer exponents of the pure human spirit of the Declaration of Independence than the American Negroes; there is no true American

[29]Toussaint L'Ouverture (1764–1803), the black leader of a slave uprising (1793–1802) that temporarily overthrew French rule in Haiti. The uprising raised fears of slave revolt throughout South America and the United States.

[30]German: storm and stress, a title often applied to nineteenth-century romantic literature that portrays the individual struggling against conventional society.

music but the wild sweet melodies of the Negro slave; the American fairy tales and folklore are Indian and African; and, all in all, we black men seem the sole oasis of simple faith and reverence in a dusty desert of dollars and smartness. Will America be poorer if she replaces her brutal dyspeptic blundering with light-hearted but determined Negro humility? or her coarse and cruel wit with loving jovial good-humor? or her vulgar music with the soul of the Sorrow Songs?

Merely a concrete test of the underlying principles of the great republic is the Negro Problem, and the spiritual striving of the freedmen's sons is the travail of souls whose burden is almost beyond the measure of their strength, but who bear it in the name of an historic race, in the name of this the land of their fathers' fathers, and in the name of human opportunity.

And now what I have briefly sketched in large outline let me on coming pages tell again in many ways, with loving emphasis and deeper detail, that men may listen to the striving in the souls of black folk.

IV

OF THE MEANING OF PROGRESS

Willst Du Deine Macht verkünden,
Wähle sie die frei von Sünden,
Steh'n in Deinem ew'gen Haus!
Deine Geister sende aus!
Die Unsterblichen, die Reinen,
Die nicht fühlen, die nicht weinen!
Nicht die zarte Jungfrau wähle,
Nicht der Hirtin weiche Seele!
—Schiller[1]

[2]

[1]Lines from *The Maid of Orleans* (1801), a verse drama by the German poet Friedrich von Schiller (1759–1805). The words are spoken by the shepherdess Joan of Arc (1412?–1431), asking God to choose someone else to lead the armies of France against the invading English.

To display your mighty power,
Choose from those around you who are free of sin.
Send forth spirits, the immortal, the pure,
Those who are unemotional, who do not weep.
Choose not the vulnerable maiden.
Choose not the tender soul of the shepherdess.

[2]Musical notation for the first two lines of the spiritual "My Way Is Cloudy":

Oh! Brethren, my way,
My way's cloudy, my way

Once upon a time I taught school[3] in the hills of Tennessee, where the broad dark vale of the Mississippi begins to roll and crumple to greet the Alleghenies.[4] I was a Fisk student then, and all Fisk men thought that Tennessee—beyond the Veil—was theirs alone, and in vacation time they sallied forth in lusty bands to meet the county school-commissioners. Young and happy, I too went, and I shall not soon forget that summer, seventeen years ago.

First, there was a Teachers' Institute[5] at the county-seat; and there distinguished guests of the superintendent taught the teachers fractions and spelling and other mysteries,—white teachers in the morning, Negroes at night. A picnic now and then, and a supper, and the rough world was softened by laughter and song. I remember how—But I wander.

There came a day when all the teachers left the Institute and began the hunt for schools. I learn from hearsay (for my mother was mortally afraid of fire-arms) that the hunting of ducks and bears and men is wonderfully interesting, but I am sure that the man who has never hunted a country school has something to learn of the pleasures of the chase. I see now the white, hot roads lazily rise and fall and wind before me under the burning July sun; I feel the deep weariness of heart and limb as ten, eight, six miles stretch relentlessly ahead; I feel my heart sink heavily as I hear again and again, "Got a teacher? Yes." So I walked on and on—horses were too expensive—until I had wandered beyond railways, beyond stage lines, to a land of "varmints" and rattlesnakes, where the coming of a stranger was an event, and men lived and died in the shadow of one blue hill.

Sprinkled over hill and dale lay cabins and farmhouses, shut out from the world by the forests and the rolling hills toward the east. There I found at last a little school. Josie told me of it; she was a thin, homely girl of twenty, with a dark-brown face and thick, hard hair. I had crossed the stream at Watertown, and rested under the great willows; then I had gone to the little cabin in the lot where Josie was resting on her way to town. The gaunt farmer made me welcome, and Josie, hearing my errand, told me anxiously that they wanted a school over the hill; that but once since the war had a teacher been there; that she herself longed to learn,—and thus she ran on, talking fast and loud, with much earnestness and energy.

Next morning I crossed the tall round hill, lingered to look at the blue and yellow mountains stretching toward the Carolinas, then plunged into the wood, and came out at Josie's home. It was a dull frame cottage with four rooms, perched just below the brow of the hill, amid peach-trees. The father was a quiet, simple soul, calmly ignorant, with no touch of vulgarity. The mother was different,—strong, bustling, and energetic, with a quick, restless tongue, and an ambition to live "like folks." There was a crowd of children. Two boys had gone away. There remained two growing girls; a shy midget of eight; John, tall, awkward, and eighteen; Jim, younger, quicker, and better looking; and two babies of indefinite age. Then there was Josie herself. She seemed to be the centre of the family: always busy at service, or at home, or berry-picking; a little nervous and inclined to scold, like her mother, yet

[3]In the summers of 1886 and 1887. [4]The mountain range in eastern Tennessee.

[5]A brief preparation course for teachers. After the institute, prospective teachers, armed with a certificate of completion, traveled the countryside to find employment.

faithful, too, like her father. She had about her a certain fineness, the shadow of an unconscious moral heroism that would willingly give all of life to make life broader, deeper, and fuller for her and hers. I saw much of this family afterwards, and grew to love them for their honest efforts to be decent and comfortable, and for their knowledge of their own ignorance. There was with them no affectation. The mother would scold the father for being so "easy"; Josie would roundly berate the boys for carelessness; and all knew that it was a hard thing to dig a living out of a rocky side-hill.

I secured the school.[6] I remember the day I rode horseback out to the commissioner's house with a pleasant young white fellow who wanted the white school. The road ran down the bed of a stream; the sun laughed and the water jingled, and we rode on. "Come in," said the commissioner,—"come in. Have a seat. Yes, that certificate will do. Stay to dinner. What do you want a month?" "Oh," thought I, "this is lucky"; but even then fell the awful shadow of the Veil, for they ate first, then I—alone.

The schoolhouse was a log hut, where Colonel Wheeler used to shelter his corn. It sat in a lot behind a rail fence and thorn bushes, near the sweetest of springs. There was an entrance where a door once was, and within, a massive rickety fireplace; great chinks between the logs served as windows. Furniture was scarce. A pale blackboard crouched in the corner. My desk was made of three boards, reinforced at critical points, and my chair, borrowed from the landlady, had to be returned every night. Seats for the children—these puzzled me much. I was haunted by a New England vision of neat little desks and chairs, but, alas! the reality was rough plank benches without backs, and at times without legs. They had the one virtue of making naps dangerous,—possibly fatal, for the floor was not to be trusted.

It was a hot morning late in July when the school opened. I trembled when I heard the patter of little feet down the dusty road, and saw the growing row of dark solemn faces and bright eager eyes facing me. First came Josie and her brothers and sisters. The longing to know, to be a student in the great school at Nashville, hovered like a star above this child-woman amid her work and worry, and she studied doggedly. There were the Dowells from their farm over toward Alexandria,—Fanny, with her smooth black face and wondering eyes; Martha, brown and dull; the pretty girl-wife of a brother, and the younger brood.

There were the Burkes,—two brown and yellow lads, and a tiny haughty-eyed girl. Fat Reuben's little chubby girl came, with golden face and old-gold hair, faithful and solemn. 'Thenie was on hand early,—a jolly, ugly, good-hearted girl, who slyly dipped snuff and looked after her little bow-legged brother. When her mother could spare her, 'Tildy came,—a midnight beauty, with starry eyes and tapering limbs; and her brother, correspondingly homely. And then the big boys,—the hulking Lawrences; the lazy Neills, unfathered sons of mother and daughter; Hickman, with a stoop in his shoulders; and the rest.

There they sat, nearly thirty of them, on the rough benches, their faces shading from a pale cream to a deep brown, the little feet bare and swinging, the eyes full of expectation, with here and there a twinkle of mischief, and

[6] I.e., got the job.

the hands grasping Webster's blue-back spelling-book.[7] I loved my school, and the fine faith the children had in the wisdom of their teacher was truly marvellous. We read and spelled together, wrote a little, picked flowers, sang, and listened to stories of the world beyond the hill. At times the school would dwindle away, and I would start out. I would visit Mun Eddings, who lived in two very dirty rooms, and ask why little Lugene, whose flaming face seemed ever ablaze with the dark-red hair uncombed, was absent all last week, or why I missed so often the inimitable rags of Mack and Ed. Then the father, who worked Colonel Wheeler's farm on shares,[8] would tell me how the crops needed the boys; and the thin, slovenly mother, whose face was pretty when washed, assured me that Lugene must mind the baby. "But we'll start them again next week." When the Lawrences stopped, I knew that the doubts of the old folks about book-learning had conquered again, and so, toiling up the hill, and getting as far into the cabin as possible, I put Cicero "pro Archia Poeta"[9] into the simplest English with local applications, and usually convinced them—for a week or so.

On Friday nights I often went home with some of the children,[10]—sometimes to Doc Burke's farm. He was a great, loud, thin Black, ever working, and trying to buy the seventy-five acres of hill and dale where he lived; but people said that he would surely fail, and the "white folks would get it all." His wife was a magnificent Amazon,[11] with saffron face and shining hair, uncorseted and barefooted, and the children were strong and beautiful. They lived in a one-and-a-half-room cabin in the hollow of the farm, near the spring. The front room was full of great fat white beds, scrupulously neat; and there were bad chromos[12] on the walls, and a tired centre-table. In the tiny back kitchen I was often invited to "take out and help" myself to fried chicken and wheat biscuit, "meat" and corn pone,[13] string-beans and berries. At first I used to be a little alarmed at the approach of bedtime in the one lone bedroom, but embarrassment was very deftly avoided. First, all the children nodded and slept, and were stowed away in one great pile of goose feathers; next, the mother and the father discreetly slipped away to the kitchen while I went to bed; then, blowing out the dim light, they retired in the dark. In the morning all were up and away before I thought of awaking. Across the road, where fat Reuben lived, they all went outdoors while the teacher retired,[14] because they did not boast the luxury of a kitchen.

[7]*The American Spelling Book*, by Noah Webster (1758–1843), American dictionary-maker. First published in 1783 as a patriotic gesture against the use of schoolbooks published in England, Webster's speller, bound in blue, became the most widely used school book in the history of the United States. Selling more than 100 million copies, it helped to standardize English usage and spelling throughout the nation.

[8]Sharecropping, a system whereby the sharecropper worked the land and paid the owner a share of the crop (usually a fourth to a half). It was a system full of abuses with one overriding virtue: even the penniless could begin farming without money, equipment, or land, and could usually make enough to survive, if eternally in debt.

[9]Oratorio Pro A. Licinius Archias Poeta," a speech by the Roman orator Cicero spoken in 62 B.C. in support of the poet Licinius Archias and of literature and the humanities. Translation of the speech was a standard schoolroom assignment for students of Latin in nineteenth-century America.

[10]In the 1900s, teachers at country schools were often paid, in part, by being fed and housed in rotation by the parents of the students.

[11]Large and powerful, like the female warriors of Greek myth.

[12]Inexpensive, bright-colored pictures printed by the process of chromolithography.

[13]A flat cake made of thick cornmeal batter, baked or cooked on a griddle.

[14]Withdrew to undress and prepare for bed.

I liked to stay with the Dowells, for they had four rooms and plenty of good country fare. Uncle Bird had a small, rough farm, all woods and hills, miles from the big road; but he was full of tales,—he preached now and then,—and with his children, berries, horses, and wheat he was happy and prosperous. Often, to keep the peace,[15] I must go where life was less lovely; for instance, 'Tildy's mother was incorrigibly dirty, Reuben's larder was limited seriously, and herds of untamed insects wandered over the Eddingses' beds. Best of all I loved to go to Josie's and sit on the porch, eating peaches, while the mother bustled and talked: how Josie had bought the sewing-machine; how Josie worked at service[16] in winter, but that four dollars a month was "mighty little" wages; how Josie longed to go away to school, but that it "looked like" they never could get far enough ahead to let her; how the crops failed and the well was yet unfinished; and, finally, how "mean" some of the white folks were.

For two summers I lived in this little world; it was dull and humdrum. The girls looked at the hill in wistful longing, and the boys fretted and haunted Alexandria. Alexandria was "town,"—a straggling, lazy village of houses, churches, and shops, and an aristocracy of Toms, Dicks, and Captains. Cuddled on the hill to the north was the village of the colored folks, who lived in three- or four-room unpainted cottages, some neat and homelike, and some dirty. The dwellings were scattered rather aimlessly, but they centered about the twin temples of the hamlet, the Methodist, and the Hard-Shell[17] Baptist churches. These, in turn, leaned gingerly on a sad-colored schoolhouse. Hither my little world wended its crooked way on Sunday to meet other worlds, and gossip, and wonder, and make the weekly sacrifice with frenzied priest[18] at the altar of the "old-time religion."[19] Then the soft melody and mighty cadences of Negro song fluttered and thundered.

I have called my tiny community a world, and so its isolation made it; and yet there was among us but a half-awakened common consciousness, sprung from common joy and grief, at burial, birth, or wedding; from a common hardship in poverty, poor land, and low wages; and, above all, from the sight of the Veil that hung between us and Opportunity. All this caused us to think some thoughts together; but these, when ripe for speech, were spoken in various languages. Those whose eyes twenty-five and more years before[20] had seen "the glory of the coming of the Lord,"[21] saw in every present hindrance or help a dark fatalism bound to bring all things right in His own good time. The mass of those to whom slavery was a dim recollection of childhood found the world a puzzling thing: it asked little of them, and they answered with little, and yet it ridiculed their offering. Such a paradox they could not understand, and therefore sank into listless indifference, or shiftlessness, or reckless bravado. There were, however, some—such as Josie, Jim, and Ben—to whom War, Hell, and Slavery were but childhood tales, whose young appetites had been whetted to an edge by school and story and half-awakened

[15]I.e., to avoid offending those whose homes he had not visited. [16]As a household servant.

[17]A term used to describe religious denominations that are rigidly fundamentalist.

[18]Volatile preachers whose gestures made them appear to be, in Abraham Lincoln's words, "fighting off a swarm of bees."

[19]A phrase from the hymn "Give Me That Old Time Religion."

[20]I.e., at the time of emancipation.

[21]"Mine eyes have seen the glory of the coming of the Lord," the first line of "The Battle Hymn of the Republic" (1862), by the American writer Julia Ward Howe (1819–1910).

thought. Ill could they be content, born without and beyond the World. And their weak wings beat against their barriers,—barriers of caste, of youth, of life; at last, in dangerous moments, against everything that opposed even a whim.

The ten years that follow youth, the years when first the realization comes that life is leading somewhere,—these were the years that passed after I left my little school. When they were past, I came by chance once more to the walls of Fisk University, to the halls of the chapel of melody.[22] As I lingered there in the joy and pain of meeting old school-friends, there swept over me a sudden longing to pass again beyond the blue hill, and to see the homes and the school of other days, and to learn how life had gone with my school-children; and I went.

Josie was dead, and the gray-haired mother said simply, "We've had a heap of trouble since you've been away." I had feared for Jim. With a cultured parentage and a social caste to uphold him, he might have made a venturesome merchant or a West Point cadet. But here he was, angry with life and reckless; and when Farmer Durham charged him with stealing wheat, the old man had to ride fast to escape the stones which the furious fool hurled after him. They told Jim to run away; but he would not run, and the constable came that afternoon. It grieved Josie, and great awkward John walked nine miles every day to see his little brother through the bars of Lebanon jail. At last the two came back together in the dark night. The mother cooked supper, and Josie emptied her purse, and the boys stole away. Josie grew thin and silent, yet worked the more. The hill became steep for the quiet old father, and with the boys away there was little to do in the valley. Josie helped them to sell the old farm, and they moved nearer town. Brother Dennis, the carpenter, built a new house with six rooms; Josie toiled a year in Nashville, and brought back ninety dollars to furnish the house and change it to a home.

When the spring came, and the birds twittered, and the stream ran proud and full, little sister Lizzie, bold and thoughtless, flushed with the passion of youth, bestowed herself on the tempter, and brought home a nameless child. Josie shivered and worked on, with the vision of schooldays all fled, with a face wan and tired,—worked until, on a summer's day, some one married another; then Josie crept to her mother like a hurt child, and slept—and sleeps.

I paused to scent the breeze as I entered the valley. The Lawrences have gone,—father and son forever,—and the other son lazily digs in the earth to live. A new young widow rents out their cabin to fat Reuben. Reuben is a Baptist preacher now, but I fear as lazy as ever, though his cabin has three rooms; and little Ella has grown into a bouncing woman, and is ploughing corn on the hot hillside. There are babies a-plenty, and one half-witted girl. Across the valley is a house I did not know before, and there I found, rocking one baby and expecting another, one of my schoolgirls, a daughter of Uncle Bird Dowell. She looked somewhat worried with her new duties, but soon bristled into pride over her neat cabin and the tale of her thrifty husband, the horse and cow, and the farm they were planning to buy.

My log schoolhouse was gone. In its place stood Progress; and Progress, I understand, is necessarily ugly. The crazy foundation stones still marked the

[22]The Fisk University chapel, where the Fisk Jubilee Singers performed.

former site of my poor little cabin, and not far away, on six weary boulders, perched a jaunty board house, perhaps twenty by thirty feet, with three windows and a door that locked. Some of the window-glass was broken, and part of an old iron stove lay mournfully under the house. I peeped through the window half reverently, and found things that were more familiar. The blackboard had grown by about two feet, and the seats were still without backs. The county owns the lot now, I hear, and every year there is a session of school. As I sat by the spring and looked on the Old and the New I felt glad, very glad, and yet—

After two long drinks I started on. There was the great double log-house on the corner. I remembered the broken, blighted family that used to live there. The strong, hard face of the mother, with its wilderness of hair, rose before me. She had driven her husband away, and while I taught school a strange man lived there, big and jovial, and people talked. I felt sure that Ben and 'Tildy would come to naught from such a home. But this is an odd world; for Ben is a busy farmer in Smith County, "doing well, too," they say, and he had cared for little 'Tildy until last spring, when a lover married her. A hard life the lad had led, toiling for meat, and laughed at because he was homely and crooked. There was Sam Carlon, an impudent old skinflint, who had definite notions about "niggers," and hired Ben a summer and would not pay him. Then the hungry boy gathered his sacks together, and in broad daylight went into Carlon's corn; and when the hard-fisted farmer set upon him, the angry boy flew at him like a beast. Doc Burke saved a murder and a lynching that day.

The story reminded me again of the Burkes, and an impatience seized me to know who won in the battle, Doc or the seventy-five acres. For it is a hard thing to make a farm out of nothing, even in fifteen years. So I hurried on, thinking of the Burkes. They used to have a certain magnificent barbarism about them that I liked. They were never vulgar, never immoral, but rather rough and primitive, with an unconventionality that spent itself in loud guffaws, slaps on the back, and naps in the corner. I hurried by the cottage of the misborn Neill boys. It was empty, and they were grown into fat, lazy farmhands. I saw the home of the Hickmans, but Albert, with his stooping shoulders, had passed from the world. Then I came to the Burkes' gate and peered through; the enclosure looked rough and untrimmed, and yet there were the same fences around the old farm save to the left, where lay twenty-five other acres. And lo! the cabin in the hollow had climbed the hill and swollen to a half-finished six-room cottage.

The Burkes held a hundred acres, but they were still in debt. Indeed, the gaunt father who toiled night and day would scarcely be happy out of debt, being so used to it. Some day he must stop, for his massive frame is showing decline. The mother wore shoes, but the lion-like physique of other days was broken. The children had grown up. Rob, the image of his father, was loud and rough with laughter. Birdie, my school baby of six, had grown to a picture of maiden beauty, tall and tawny. "Edgar is gone," said the mother, with head half bowed,—"gone to work in Nashville; he and his father couldn't agree."

Little Doc, the boy born since the time of my school, took me horseback down the creek next morning toward Farmer Dowell's. The road and the stream were battling for mastery, and the stream had the better of it. We splashed and waded, and the merry boy, perched behind me, chattered and laughed. He showed me where Simon Thompson had bought a bit of ground and a home; but his daughter Lana, a plump, brown, slow girl, was not there. She had married a man and a farm twenty miles away. We wound on down the stream till we came to a gate that I did not recognize, but the boy insisted that it was "Uncle Bird's." The farm was fat with the growing crop. In that little valley was a strange stillness as I rode up; for death and marriage had stolen youth and left age and childhood there. We sat and talked that night after the chores were done. Uncle Bird was grayer, and his eyes did not see so well, but he was still jovial. We talked of the acres bought,—one hundred and twenty-five,—of the new guest-chamber added, of Martha's marrying. Then we talked of death: Fanny and Fred were gone; a shadow hung over the other daughter, and when it lifted she was to go to Nashville to school. At last we spoke of the neighbors, and as night fell, Uncle Bird told me how, on a night like that, 'Thenie came wandering back to her home over yonder, to escape the blows of her husband. And next morning she died in the home that her little bow-legged brother, working and saving, had bought for their widowed mother.

My journey was done, and behind me lay hill and dale, and Life and Death. How shall man measure Progress there where the dark-faced Josie lies? How many heartfuls of sorrow shall balance a bushel of wheat? How hard a thing is life to the lowly, and yet how human and real! And all this life and love and strife and failure,—is it the twilight of nightfall or the flush of some faint-dawning day?

Thus sadly musing, I rode to Nashville in the Jim Crow car.[23]

THE AFTERTHOUGHT

Hear my cry, O God the Reader; vouchsafe that this my book fall not still-born into the world-wilderness. Let there spring, Gentle One, from out its leaves vigor of thought and thoughtful deed to reap the harvest wonderful. (Let the ears of a guilty people tingle with truth, and seventy millions sigh for the righteousness which exalteth nations, in this drear day when human brotherhood is mockery and a snare.) Thus in Thy good time may infinite reason turn the tangle straight, and these crooked marks on a fragile leaf be not indeed

THE END

1903

[23]Railroad car for black passengers, who were not allowed passage in cars for whites. The term "Jim Crow," an insulting nineteenth-century term for blacks, was used to describe laws that restricted the legal rights of blacks in the United States. Established in the South soon after the Civil War, Jim Crow laws remained in effect until the reforms of the Civil Rights Movement in the last half of the twentieth century.

Edwin Arlington Robinson 1869–1935

The first major poet of twentieth-century America, E. A. Robinson fit the romantic stereotype of the poet as a lonely, struggling genius. Through much of his life he experienced personal tragedy, poverty, and public disregard—all of which were reflected in his somber, often stoical poetry. He was the third son of a small-town Maine businessman and of a mother whose New England ancestors included the early colonial poet Anne Bradstreet. Except for some juvenile poems, Robinson showed little aptitude as a youth. He was an indifferent student, and after his graduation from high school, his father refused the expense of his further education. Eventually, when he was almost twenty-two, Robinson managed to enroll as a special student at Harvard, but after two years he left Harvard and returned home to Gardiner, Maine.

During the next few years he completed two books of poetry, the first of which, The Torrent and the Night Before *(1896), he published at his own expense. With the appearance of his second book,* The Children of the Night *(1897), he left home and moved to New York. Gardiner, which appeared as Tilbury Town in Robinson's poems, provided him with a colorful array of New England character types—drunkards, dreamers, and misfits with names like Richard Cory, Bewick Finzer, and Eben Flood. They embodied the spiritual drought and moral failure that Robinson made the thematic center of much of his work.*

In New York, Robinson tried his hand at journalism and later worked as a timekeeper during the construction of the New York subway system. Following the publication in 1902 of Captain Craig, *he received, with the help of President Theodore Roosevelt, a job at the New York Customs House, and in 1910 he published his fourth book of poems,* The Town Down the River. *The following year Robinson spent his first summer at the MacDowell Colony for artists in the New Hampshire countryside, where he was to return every summer for the rest of his life. There, with freedom to concentrate on his writing, he began his most productive years. The appearance of* The Man Against the Sky *(1916) marked the beginning of his reputation. The next decade saw the publication of* The Three Taverns *(1920),* Avon's Harvest *(1921), and* Dionysus in Doubt *(1925). His* Collected Poems *(1921) brought him the first of three Pulitzer Prizes, and his long narrative poem* Tristram *(1927) became a bestseller.*

Robinson was a transitional figure between the nineteenth and twentieth centuries. His life spanned the waning years of the genteel era and the rebellious period of disillusionment that followed World War I. An older generation found his poetry dangerously radical, marred by formlessness; the modernists found it tamely conservative. His deepest roots were in the Puritan ethic of his forebears. His fascination with the interior drama of human defeat earned him a reputation for pessimism, but it was a pessimism qualified by the positive values of a New England conscience—endurance, moral courage, and the conviction that, as he once put it, "There's a good deal to live for, but a man has to go through hell really to find it out."

FURTHER READING: *Selected Letters of Edwin Arlington Robinson,* ed. R. Torrence, 1940; E. Fussell, *Edwin Arlington Robinson, The Literary Background of a Traditional Poet,* 1954; *Selected Poems of Edwin Arlington Robinson,* ed. M. Zabel, 1965, 1966; W. Anderson, *Edwin Arlington Robinson,* 1967; W. Robinson, *Edwin Arlington Robinson, A Poetry of the Act,* 1967; H. Franchere, *Edwin Arlington Robinson,* 1968; L. Coxe, *Edwin Arlington Robinson, The Life of Poetry,* 1968; *Edwin Arlington Robinson, Centenary Essays,* ed. E. Barnard, 1973; R. Cary, *Early Reception of Edwin Arlington Robinson,* 1974; *Uncollected Poems and Prose of Edwin Arlington Robinson,* ed. R. Cary, 1975; C. Joyner,

Edwin Arlington Robinson, A Reference Guide, 1978; *Edwin Arlington Robinson,* ed. H. Bloom, 1988; R. Hoffpauir, *The Contemplative Poetry of Edwin Arlington Robinson, Robert Frost, and Yvor Winters,* 2002.

TEXT: *Collected Poems of Edwin Arlington Robinson,* 1937.

RICHARD CORY

Whenever Richard Cory went down town,
We people on the pavement looked at him:
He was a gentleman from sole to crown,
Clean favored, and imperially slim.

And he was always quietly arrayed,
And he was always human when he talked;
But still he fluttered pulses when he said
"Good-morning," and he glittered when he walked.

And he was rich—yes, richer than a king—
And admirably schooled in every grace:
In fine, we thought that he was everything
To make us wish that we were in his place.

So on we worked, and waited for the light,
And went without the meat, and cursed the bread;
And Richard Cory, one calm summer night,
Went home and put a bullet through his head.

1897

CLIFF KLINGENHAGEN

Cliff Klingenhagen had me in to dine
With him one day; and after soup and meat,
And all the other things there were to eat,
Cliff took two glasses and filled one with wine
And one with wormwood.[1] Then without a sign
For me to choose at all, he took the draught
Of bitterness himself, and lightly quaffed
It off, and said the other one was mine.

And when I asked him what the deuce he meant
By doing that, he only looked at me
And smiled, and said it was a way of his.
And though I know the fellow, I have spent
Long time a-wondering when I shall be
As happy as Cliff Klingenhagen is.

1897

[1]The bitter oil extracted from the wormwood plant.

MINIVER CHEEVY

Miniver Cheevy, child of scorn,
  Grew lean while he assailed the seasons;
He wept that he was ever born,
  And he had reasons.

Miniver loved the days of old
  When swords were bright and steeds were prancing;
The vision of a warrior bold
  Would set him dancing.

Miniver sighed for what was not,
  And dreamed, and rested from his labors;
He dreamed of Thebes and Camelot,[1]
  And Priam's[2] neighbors.

Miniver mourned the ripe renown
  That made so many a name so fragrant;
He mourned Romance, now on the town,
  And Art, a vagrant.

Miniver loved the Medici,[3]
  Albeit he had never seen one;
He would have sinned incessantly
  Could he have been one.

Miniver cursed the commonplace
  And eyed a khaki suit with loathing;
He missed the mediæval grace
  Of iron clothing.

Miniver scorned the gold he sought,
  But sore annoyed was he without it;
Miniver thought, and thought, and thought,
  And thought about it.

Miniver Cheevy, born too late,
  Scratched his head and kept on thinking;
Miniver coughed, and called it fate,
  And kept on drinking.

1907

[1]Thebes: name of cities in ancient Egypt and Greece; Camelot: legendary site of King Arthur's palace.

[2]Mythological king of Troy during the Trojan War.

[3]Powerful family of Renaissance Florence, Italy, with a reputation for predatory ruthlessness and sinfulness.

HOW ANNANDALE WENT OUT

"THEY called it Annandale—and I was there
To flourish, to find words, and to attend:
Liar, physician, hypocrite, and friend,
I watched him; and the sight was not so fair
As one or two that I have seen elsewhere:
An apparatus not for me to mend—
A wreck, with hell between him and the end,
Remained of Annandale; and I was there.

"I knew the ruin as I knew the man;
So put the two together, if you can,
Remembering the worst you know of me.
Now view yourself as I was, on the spot—
With a slight kind of engine. Do you see?
Like this . . . You wouldn't hang me? I thought not."

1910

EROS TURANNOS[1]

She fears him, and will always ask
  What fated her to choose him;
She meets in his engaging mask
  All reasons to refuse him;
But what she meets and what she fears
  Are less than are the downward years;
Drawn slowly to the foamless weirs[2]
  Of age, were she to lose him.

Between a blurred sagacity
  That once had power to sound him,
And Love, that will not let him be
  The Judas[3] that she found him,
Her pride assuages her almost,
As if it were alone the cost.—
He sees that he will not be lost,
  And waits and looks around him.

A sense of ocean and old trees
  Envelops and allures him;
Tradition, touching all he sees,
  Beguiles and reassures him;
And all her doubts of what he says
Are dimmed with what she knows of days—
Till even prejudice delays
  And fades, and she secures him.

[1]Greek: Love, the Tyrant. [2]A dam in a stream, used to regulate or measure water flow.
[3]Christ's disciple who betrayed Him.

The falling leaf inaugurates
  The reign of her confusion;
The pounding wave reverberates
  The dirge of her illusion;
And home, where passion lived and died,
Becomes a place where she can hide.
While all the town and harbor side
  Vibrate with her seclusion.

We tell you, tapping on our brows,
  The story as it should be,—
As if the story of a house
  Were told, or ever could be;
We'll have no kindly veil between
Her visions and those we have seen—
As if we guessed what hers have been,
  Or what they are or would be.

Meanwhile we do no harm; for they
  That with a god have striven,
Not hearing much of what we say,
  Take what the god has given;
Though like waves breaking it may be
Or like a changed familiar tree,
Or like a stairway to the sea
  Where down the blind are driven.

1914

MR. FLOOD'S PARTY

Old Eben Flood, climbing alone one night
Over the hill between the town below
And the forsaken upland hermitage
That held as much as he should ever know
On earth again of home, paused warily.
The road was his with not a native near;
And Eben, having leisure, said aloud,
For no man else in Tilbury Town to hear:

"Well, Mr. Flood, we have the harvest moon
Again, and we may not have many more;
The bird is on the wing,[1] the poet says,
And you and I have said it here before.
Drink to the bird." He raised up to the light
The jug that he had gone so far to fill,
And answered huskily: "Well, Mr. Flood,
Since you propose it, I believe I will."

[1]An allusion to a quatrain in Edward FitzGerald's *The Rubáiyát of Omar Khayyám* (1859): "Come, fill the Cup, and in the fire of Spring / Your Winter-garment of Repentance fling: / The Bird of Time has but a little way / To flutter—and the Bird is on the Wing."

Alone, as if enduring to the end
A valiant armor of scarred hopes outworn,
He stood there in the middle of the road
Like Roland's ghost winding a silent horn.[2]
Below him, in the town among the trees,
Where friends of other days had honored him,
A phantom salutation of the dead
Rang thinly till old Eben's eyes were dim.

Then, as a mother lays her sleeping child
Down tenderly, fearing it may awake,
He set the jug down slowly at his feet
With trembling care, knowing that most things break;
And only when assured that on firm earth
It stood, as the uncertain lives of men
Assuredly did not, he paced away,
And with his hand extended paused again:

"Well, Mr. Flood, we have not met like this
In a long time; and many a change has come
To both of us, I fear, since last it was
We had a drop together. Welcome home!"
Convivially returning with himself,
Again he raised the jug up to the light;
And with an acquiescent quaver said:
"Well, Mr. Flood, if you insist, I might.

"Only a very little, Mr. Flood—
For auld lang syne. No more, sir; that will do."
So, for the time, apparently it did,
And Eben evidently thought so too;
For soon amid the silver loneliness
Of night he lifted up his voice and sang,
Secure, with only two moons listening,
Until the whole harmonious landscape rang—

"For auld lang syne." The weary throat gave out,
The last word wavered, and the song was done.
He raised again the jug regretfully
And shook his head, and was again alone.
There was not much that was ahead of him,
And there was nothing in the town below
Where strangers would have shut the many doors
That many friends had opened long ago.

1920

[2]Roland, the embattled hero of the medieval French romance *Chanson de Roland*, proudly waited until he was overwhelmed before sounding his horn to summon help.

Robert Frost 1874–1963

To his rural New England neighbors, Robert Frost was an unlikely farmer who wrote poetry into the late hours and milked his cows at midnight. To much of the American public, he was a white-thatched, rustic sage, a poet of rural simplicity and public virtue. To intimate friends, he was a man frequently driven by a cantankerous desire to carry on what he called his "lover's quarrel with the world."

Although he came to be known as a poet of New England, Frost was born in San Francisco and spent his early childhood in the Far West. At the death of his father, when Frost was eleven, the family moved to Salem, New Hampshire. After graduating from high school as valedictorian and class poet in 1892, Frost entered Dartmouth College but soon left to work at odd jobs and write poetry. In 1897 he tried college again, Harvard, but he left after two years, having acquired an enduring dislike for academic convention.

For the next twelve years Frost eked out a minimal living by teaching and farming while continuing to write his poems. In 1912 he decided to venture everything on a literary career. Leaving New Hampshire, he sailed for England, where he hoped "to write poetry without further scandal to friends or family." In London, he soon found a publisher, and his first book, A Boy's Will *(1913), brought him to the attention of influential critics, among them the American expatriate Ezra Pound, who praised Frost as an authentic poet, "vurry Amur'k'n."*

Following the publication of a second volume of poems, North of Boston *(1914), Frost returned home, determined to win recognition in his native land. To support himself he taught in colleges and gave poetry readings throughout much of the United States. His fame grew with the appearance of a succession of books:* Mountain Interval *(1916),* New Hampshire *(1923),* West-Running Brook *(1928),* A Further Range *(1936),* A Witness Tree *(1942),* Steeple Bush *(1947), and* In the Clearing *(1962). By the end of his life he had become a national bard; he received honorary degrees from forty-four colleges and universities and won four Pulitzer Prizes; the United States Senate passed resolutions honoring his birthdays, and when he was eighty-seven he read his poetry at the inauguration of President John F. Kennedy.*

Frost had rejected the revolutionary poetic principles of his contemporaries, choosing instead "the old-fashioned way to be new." He employed the plain speech of rural New Englanders and preferred the short, traditional forms of lyric and narrative. As a poet of nature he had obvious affinities with romantic writers, notably Wordsworth and Emerson. He saw nature as a storehouse of analogy and symbol, announcing, "I'm always saying something that's just the edge of something more," but he had little faith in religious dogma or speculative thought. His concern with nature reflected deep moral uncertainties, and his poetry, for all its apparent simplicity, often probes mysteries of darkness and irrationality in the bleak and chaotic landscapes of an indifferent universe where men and women stand alone, forsaken and perplexed.

FURTHER READING: *Selected Letters of Robert Frost,* ed. L. Thompson, 1964; *Selected Prose of Robert Frost,* ed. H. Cox and E. Lathem, 1966; L. Thompson, *Robert Frost, The Early Years,* 1966; L. Thompson, *Robert Frost, The Years of Triumph,* 1970; *Robert Frost, Centennial Essays,* 3 vols., ed. J. Thorpe, 1974–1978; L. Thompson and R. Winnick, *Robert Frost, The Later Years,* 1976; J. Kemp, *Robert Frost and New England,* 1979; J. Potter, *Robert Frost Handbook,* 1980; T. Sharma, *Robert Frost's Poetic Style,* 1981; W. Pritchard, *Frost, A Literary Life Reconsidered,* 1984, 1993; R. Wakefield, *Robert Frost and the Opposing Lights of the Hour,* 1985; J. Walsh, *Into My Own, The English Years of Robert Frost, 1912–1915,* 1988; M. Marcus, *The Poems of Robert Frost,* 1991; J. Meyer, *Robert Frost, A Biography,* 1996; M. Richardson, *The Ordeal of Robert Frost,* 1997; *Elected Friends, Robert Frost & Edward Thomas to One Another,* ed. M. Spencer, 2003; R. Pack, *Belief and Uncertainty in the Poetry of Robert Frost,* 2003.

TEXTS: *A Boy's Will,* 1913; *North of Boston,* 1914; *Mountain Interval,* 1916, 1921; *The Poetry of Robert Frost,* ed. E. Latham, 1969.

THE TUFT OF FLOWERS

I went to turn the grass once after one
Who mowed it in the dew before the sun.

The dew was gone that made his blade so keen
Before I came to view the leveled scene.

I looked for him behind an isle of trees;
I listened for his whetstone on the breeze.

But he had gone his way, the grass all mown,
And I must be, as he had been,—alone.

'As all must be,' I said within my heart,
'Whether they work together or apart.'

But as I said it, swift there passed me by
On noiseless wing a 'wildered[1] butterfly,

Seeking with memories grown dim o'er night
Some resting flower of yesterday's delight.

And once I marked his flight go round and round,
As where some flower lay withering on the ground.

And then he flew as far as eye could see,
And then on tremulous wing came back to me.

I thought of questions that have no reply,
And would have turned to toss the grass to dry;

But he turned first, and led my eye to look
At a tall tuft of flowers beside a brook,

A leaping tongue of bloom the scythe had spared
Beside a reedy brook the scythe had bared.

I left my place to know them by their name,
Finding them butterfly weed when I came.

The mower in the dew had loved them thus,
By leaving them to flourish, not for us,

Nor yet to draw one thought of ours to him,
But from sheer morning gladness at the brim.

[1]Changed to "bewildered" in later versions of the poem.

The butterfly and I had lit upon,
Nevertheless, a message from the dawn,

That made me hear the wakening birds around,
And hear his long scythe whispering to the ground,

And feel a spirit kindred to my own;
So that henceforth I worked no more alone;

But glad with him, I worked as with his aid,
And weary, sought at noon with him the shade;

And dreaming, as it were, held brotherly speech
With one whose thought I had not hoped to reach.

'Men work together,' I told him from the heart,
'Whether they work together or apart.'

1906, 1913

MENDING WALL

Something there is that doesn't love a wall,
That sends the frozen-ground-swell under it
And spills the upper boulders in the sun,
And makes gaps even two can pass abreast.
The work of hunters is another thing:
I have come after them and made repair
Where they have left not one stone on a stone,
But they would have the rabbit out of hiding,
To please the yelping dogs. The gaps I mean,
No one has seen them made or heard them made,
But at spring mending-time we find them there.
I let my neighbor know beyond the hill;
And on a day we meet to walk the line
And set the wall between us once again.
We keep the wall between us as we go.
To each the boulders that have fallen to each.
And some are loaves and some so nearly balls
We have to use a spell to make them balance:
"Stay where you are until our backs are turned!"
We wear our fingers rough with handling them.
Oh, just another kind of outdoor game,
One on a side. It comes to little more:
There where it is we do not need the wall:
He is all pine and I am apple orchard.
My apple trees will never get across
And eat the cones under his pines, I tell him.
He only says, "Good fences make good neighbors."

Spring is the mischief in me, and I wonder
If I could put a notion in his head:
"*Why* do they make good neighbors? Isn't it
Where there are cows? But here there are no cows.
Before I built a wall I'd ask to know
What I was walling in or walling out,
And to whom I was like to give offense.
Something there is that doesn't love a wall,
That wants it down." I could say "Elves" to him,
But it's not elves exactly, and I'd rather
He said it for himself. I see him there,
Bringing a stone grasped firmly by the top
In each hand, like an old-stone savage armed.
He moves in darkness as it seems to me,
Not of woods only and the shade of trees.
He will not go behind his father's saying,
And he likes having thought of it so well
He says again, "Good fences make good neighbors."
1914

HOME BURIAL

He saw her from the bottom of the stairs
Before she saw him. She was starting down,
Looking back over her shoulder at some fear.
She took a doubtful step and then undid it
To raise herself and look again. He spoke
Advancing toward her: "What is it you see
From up there always?—for I want to know."
She turned and sank upon her skirts at that,
And her face changed from terrified to dull.
He said to gain time: "What is it you see?"
Mounting until she cowered under him.
"I will find out now—you must tell me, dear."
She, in her place, refused him any help,
With the least stiffening of her neck and silence.
She let him look, sure that he couldn't see,
Blind creature; and awhile he didn't see.
But at last he murmured, "Oh," and again, "Oh."

"What is it—what?" she said.

"Just that I see."

"You don't," she challenged. "Tell me what it is."

"The wonder is I didn't see at once.
I never noticed it from here before.

I must be wonted[1]
to it—that's the reason.
The little graveyard where my people are!
So small the window frames the whole of it.
Not so much larger than a bedroom, is it?
There are three stones of slate and one of marble,
Broad-shouldered little slabs there in the sunlight
On the sidehill. We haven't to mind *those.*
But I understand: it is not the stones,
But the child's mound——"

"Don't, don't, don't,
don't," she cried.

She withdrew, shrinking from beneath his arm
That rested on the banister, and slid downstairs;
And turned on him with such a daunting look,
He said twice over before he knew himself:
"Can't a man speak of his own child he's lost?"

"Not you!—Oh, where's my hat? Oh, I don't need it!
I must get out of here. I must get air.—
I don't know rightly whether any man can."

"Amy! Don't go to someone else this time.
Listen to me. I won't come down the stairs."
He sat and fixed his chin between his fists.
"There's something I should like to ask you, dear."

"You don't know how to ask it."

"Help me, then."

Her fingers moved the latch for all reply.

"My words are nearly always an offense.
I don't know how to speak of anything
So as to please you. But I might be taught,
I should suppose. I can't say I see how.
A man must partly give up being a man
With womenfolk. We could have some arrangement
By which I'd bind myself to keep hands off
Anything special you're a-mind to name.
Though I don't like such things 'twixt those that love.
Two that don't love can't live together without them,
But two that do can't live together with them."
She moved the latch a little. "Don't—don't go.
Don't carry it to someone else this time.

[1]Accustomed.

Tell me about it if it's something human.
Let me into your grief. I'm not so much
Unlike other folks as your standing there
Apart would make me out. Give me my chance.
I do think, though, you overdo it a little.
What was it brought you up to think it the thing
To take your mother-loss of a first child
So inconsolably—in the face of love.
You'd think his memory might be satisfied——"

"There you go sneering now!"

"I'm not, I'm not!
You make me angry. I'll come down to you.
God, what a woman! And it's come to this,
A man can't speak of his own child that's dead."

"You can't because you don't know how to speak.
If you had any feelings, you that dug
With your own hand—how could you?—his little grave;
I saw you from that very window there,
Making the gravel leap and leap in air,
Leap up, like that, like that, and land so lightly
And roll back down the mound beside the hole.
I thought, Who is that man? I didn't know you.
And I crept down the stairs and up the stairs
To look again, and still your spade kept lifting.
Then you came in. I heard your rumbling voice
Out in the kitchen, and I don't know why,
But I went near to see with my own eyes.
You could sit there with the stains on your shoes
Of the fresh earth from your own baby's grave
And talk about your everyday concerns.
You had stood the spade up against the wall
Outside there in the entry, for I saw it."

"I shall laugh the worst laugh I ever laughed.
I'm cursed. God, if I don't believe I'm cursed."

"I can repeat the very words you were saying:
'Three foggy mornings and one rainy day
Will rot the best birch fence a man can build.'
Think of it, talk like that at such a time!
What had how long it takes a birch to rot
To do with what was in the darkened parlor?
You *couldn't* care! The nearest friends can go
With anyone to death, comes so far short
They might as well not try to go at all.
No, from the time when one is sick to death,
One is alone, and he dies more alone.

Friends make pretense of following to the grave,
But before one is in it, their minds are turned
And making the best of their way back to life
And living people, and things they understand.
But the world's evil. I won't have grief so
If I can change it. Oh, I won't, I won't!"

"There, you have said it all and you feel better.
You won't go now. You're crying. Close the door.
The heart's gone out of it: why keep it up?
Amy! There's someone coming down the road!"

"*You*—oh, you think the talk is all. I must go—
Somewhere out of this house. How can I make you——"

"If—you—do!" She was opening the door wider.
"Where do you mean to go? First tell me that.
I'll follow and bring you back by force. I *will!*——"

1914

THE BLACK COTTAGE

We chanced in passing by that afternoon
To catch it in a sort of special picture
Among tar-banded ancient cherry trees,
Set well back from the road in rank lodged grass,
The little cottage we were speaking of,
A front with just a door between two windows,
Fresh painted by the shower a velvet black.
We paused, the minister and I, to look.
He made as if to hold it at arm's length
Or put the leaves aside that framed it in.
"Pretty," he said. "Come in. No one will care."
The path was a vague parting in the grass
That led us to a weathered windowsill.
We pressed our faces to the pane. "You'll see," he said,
"Everything's as she left it when she died.
Her sons won't sell the house or the things in it.
They say they mean to come and summer here
Where they were boys. They haven't come this year.
They live so far away—one is out West—
It will be hard for them to keep their word.
Anyway they won't have the place disturbed."
A buttoned haircloth lounge spread scrolling arms
Under a crayon portrait on the wall,
Done sadly from an old daguerreotype.
"That was the father as he went to war.

She always, when she talked about the war,
Sooner or later came and leaned, half knelt,
Against the lounge beside it, though I doubt
If such unlifelike lines kept power to stir
Anything in her after all the years.
He fell at Gettysburg or Fredericksburg,[1]
I ought to know—it makes a difference which:
Fredericksburg wasn't Gettysburg, of course.
But what I'm getting to is how forsaken
A little cottage this has always seemed;
Since she went, more than ever, but before—
I don't mean altogether by the lives
That had gone out of it, the father first,
Then the two sons, till she was left alone.
(Nothing could draw her after those two sons.
She valued the considerate neglect
She had at some cost taught them after years.)
I mean by the world's having passed it by—
As we almost got by this afternoon.
It always seems to me a sort of mark
To measure how far fifty years have brought us.
Why not sit down if you are in no haste?
These doorsteps seldom have a visitor.
The warping boards pull out their own old nails
With none to tread and put them in their place.
She had her own idea of things, the old lady.
And she liked talk. She had seen Garrison
And Whittier,[2] and had her story of them.
One wasn't long in learning that she thought,
Whatever else the Civil War was for,
It wasn't just to keep the states together,
Nor just to free the slaves, though it did both.
She wouldn't have believed those ends enough
To have given outright for them all she gave.
Her giving somehow touched the principle
That all men are created free and equal.[3]
And to hear her quaint phrases—so removed
From the world's view today of all those things.
That's a hard mystery of Jefferson's.
What did he mean? Of course the easy way
Is to decide it simply isn't true.
It may not be. I heard a fellow say so.
But never mind, the Welshman got it planted
Where it will trouble us a thousand years.
Each age will have to reconsider it.

[1]Battlefields of the American Civil War.

[2]The publisher William Lloyd Garrison (1805–1879) and the poet John Greenleaf Whittier (1807–1892), leaders of the American anti-slavery movement.

[3]A quotation of the words of Thomas Jefferson in the Declaration of Independence.

You couldn't tell her what the West was saying,
And what the South, to her serene belief.
She had some art of hearing and yet not
Hearing the latter wisdom of the world.
White was the only race she ever knew.
Black she had scarcely seen, and yellow never.
But how could they be made so very unlike
By the same hand working in the same stuff?
She had supposed the war decided that.
What are you going to do with such a person?
Strange how such innocence gets its own way.
I shouldn't be surprised if in this world
It were the force that would at last prevail.
Do you know but for her there was a time
When, to please the younger members of the church,
Or rather say non-members in the church,
Whom we all have to think of nowadays,
I would have changed the Creed[4] a very little?
Not that she ever had to ask me not to;
It never got so far as that; but the bare thought
Of her old tremulous bonnet in the pew,
And of her half asleep, was too much for me.
Why, I might wake her up and startle her.
It was the words 'descended into Hades'
That seemed too pagan to our liberal youth.
You know they suffered from a general onslaught.
And well, if they weren't true why keep right on
Saying them like the heathen? We could drop them.
Only—there was the bonnet in the pew.
Such a phrase couldn't have meant much to her.
But suppose she had missed it from the Creed,
As a child misses the unsaid Good-night
And falls asleep with heartache—how should I feel?
I'm just as glad she made me keep hands off,
For, dear me, why abandon a belief
Merely because it ceases to be true.
Cling to it long enough, and not a doubt
It will turn true again, for so it goes.
Most of the change we think we see in life
Is due to truths being in and out of favor.
As I sit here, and oftentimes, I wish
I could be monarch of a desert land
I could devote and dedicate forever
To the truths we keep coming back and back to.
So desert it would have to be, so walled
By mountain ranges half in summer snow,

[4]The Apostles' Creed, a formal statement of religious beliefs adopted by Protestant churches. It states that Jesus "was crucified, died, and was buried. He descended into Hades [Hell]."

No one would covet it or think it worth
The pains of conquering to force change on.
Scattered oases where men dwelt, but mostly
Sand dunes held loosely in tamarisk[5]
Blown over and over themselves in idleness.
Sand grains should sugar in the natal dew
The babe born to the desert, the sandstorm
Retard mid-waste my cowering caravans—

"There are bees in this wall." He struck the clapboards,
Fierce heads looked out; small bodies pivoted.
We rose to go. Sunset blazed on the windows.

1914

AFTER APPLE-PICKING

My long two-pointed ladder's sticking through a tree
Toward heaven still,
And there's a barrel that I didn't fill
Beside it, and there may be two or three
Apples I didn't pick upon some bough.
But I am done with apple-picking now.
Essence of winter sleep is on the night,
The scent of apples: I am drowsing off.
I cannot rub the strangeness from my sight
I got from looking through a pane of glass
I skimmed this morning from the drinking trough
And held against the world of hoary grass.
It melted, and I let it fall and break.
But I was well
Upon my way to sleep before it fell,
And I could tell
What form my dreaming was about to take.
Magnified apples appear and disappear,
Stem end and blossom end,
And every fleck of russet showing clear.
My instep arch not only keeps the ache,
It keeps the pressure of a ladder-round.
I feel the ladder sway as the boughs bend
And I keep hearing from the cellar bin
The rumbling sound
Of load on load of apples coming in.
For I have had too much
Of apple-picking: I am overtired
Of the great harvest I myself desired.

[5]A small tree shrub found in Asia and Africa.

There were ten thousand thousand fruit to touch,
Cherish in hand, lift down, and not let fall.
For all
That struck the earth,
No matter if not bruised or spiked with stubble,
Went surely to the cider-apple heap
As of no worth.
One can see what will trouble
This sleep of mine, whatever sleep it is.
Were he not gone,
The woodchuck could say whether it's like his
Long sleep, as I describe its coming on,
Or just some human sleep.

1914

THE WOOD-PILE

Out walking in the frozen swamp one gray day,
I paused and said, "I will turn back from here.
No, I will go on farther—and we shall see."
The hard snow held me, save where now and then
One foot went down.[1] The view was all in lines
Straight up and down of tall slim trees
Too much alike to mark or name a place by
So as to say for certain I was here
Or somewhere else: I was just far from home.
A small bird flew before me. He was careful
To put a tree between us when he lighted,
And say no word to tell me who he was
Who was so foolish as to think what he thought.
He thought that I was after him for a feather—
The white one in his tail; like one who takes
Everything said as personal to himself.
One flight out sideways would have undeceived him.
And then there was a pile of wood for which
I forgot him and let his little fear
Carry him off the way I might have gone,
Without so much as wishing him good-night.
He went behind it to make his last stand.
It was a cord of maple, cut and split
And piled—and measured, four by four by eight.
And not another like it could I see.
No runner tracks in this year's snow looped near it
And it was older sure than this year's cutting,
Or even last year's or the year's before.

[1]Changed to "through" in later editions.

The wood was gray and the bark warping off it
And the pile somewhat sunken. Clematis[2]
Had wound strings round and round it like a bundle.
What held it, though, on one side was a tree
Still growing, and on one a stake and prop,
These latter about to fall. I thought that only
Someone who lived in turning to fresh tasks
Could so forget his handiwork on which
He spent himself, the labor of his ax,
And leave it there far from a useful fireplace
To warm the frozen swamp as best it could
With the slow smokeless burning of decay.

1913

THE ROAD NOT TAKEN

Two roads diverged in a yellow wood,
And sorry I could not travel both
And be one traveler, long I stood
And looked down one as far as I could
To where it bent in the undergrowth;

Then took the other, as just as fair,
And having perhaps the better claim,
Because it was grassy and wanted wear;
Though as for that, the passing there
Had worn them really about the same,

And both that morning equally lay
In leaves no step had trodden black.
Oh, I kept the first for another day!
Yet knowing how way leads on to way,
I doubted if I should ever come back.

I shall be telling this with a sigh
Somewhere ages and ages hence:
Two roads diverged in a wood, and I—
I took the one less traveled by,
And that has made all the difference.

1914–1915 1915, 1916

[2]A vine-like climbing plant.

AN OLD MAN'S WINTER NIGHT

All out-of-doors looked darkly in at him
Through the thin frost, almost in separate stars,
That gathers on the pane in empty rooms.
What kept his eyes from giving back the gaze
Was the lamp tilted near them in his hand.
What kept him from remembering what it was
That brought him to that creaking room was age.
He stood with barrels round him—at a loss.
And having scared the cellar under him
In clomping here, he scared it once again
In clomping off—and scared the outer night,
Which has its sounds, familiar, like the roar
Of trees and crack of branches, common things,
But nothing so like beating on a box.
A light he was to no one but himself
Where now he sat, concerned with he knew what,
A quiet light, and then not even that.
He consigned to the moon—such as she was,
So late-arising—to the broken moon,
As better than the sun in any case
For such a charge, his snow upon the roof,
His icicles along the wall to keep;
And slept. The log that shifted with a jolt
Once in the stove, disturbed him and he shifted,
And eased his heavy breathing, but still slept.
One aged man—one man—can't keep a house,
A farm, a countryside, or if he can,
It's thus he does it of a winter night.
1906 1916

BIRCHES

When I see birches bend to left and right
Across the lines of straighter darker trees,
I like to think some boy's been swinging them.
But swinging doesn't bend them down to stay
As ice storms do. Often you must have seen them.
Loaded with ice a sunny winter morning
After a rain. They click upon themselves
As the breeze rises, and turn many-colored
As the stir cracks and crazes their enamel.
Soon the sun's warmth makes them shed crystal shells
Shattering and avalanching on the snow crust—

Such heaps of broken glass to sweep away
You'd think the inner dome of heaven had fallen.
They are dragged to the withered bracken by the load,
And they seem not to break; though once they are bowed
So low for long, they never right themselves:
You may see their trunks arching in the woods
Years afterwards, trailing their leaves on the ground
Like girls on hands and knees that throw their hair
Before them over their heads to dry in the sun.
But I was going to say when Truth broke in
With all her matter of fact about the ice storm,
I should prefer to have some boy bend them
As he went out and in to fetch the cows—
Some boy too far from town to learn baseball,
Whose only play was what he found himself,
Summer or winter, and could play alone.
One by one he subdued his father's trees
By riding them down over and over again
Until he took the stiffness out of them,
And not one but hung limp, not one was left
For him to conquer. He learned all there was
To learn about not launching out too soon
And so not carrying the tree away
Clear to the ground. He always kept his poise
To the top branches, climbing carefully
With the same pains you use to fill a cup
Up to the brim, and even above the brim.
Then he flung outward, feet first, with a swish,
Kicking his way down through the air to the ground.
So was I once myself a swinger of birches.
And so I dream of going back to be.
It's when I'm weary of considerations,
And life is too much like a pathless wood
Where your face burns and tickles with the cobwebs
Broken across it, and one eye is weeping
From a twig's having lashed across it open.
I'd like to get away from earth awhile
And then come back to it and begin over.
May no fate willfully misunderstand me
And half grant what I wish and snatch me away
Not to return. Earth's the right place for love:
I don't know where it's likely to go better.
I'd like to go by climbing a birch tree,
And climb black branches up a snow-white trunk
Toward heaven, till the tree could bear no more,
But dipped its top and set me down again.
That would be good both going and coming back.
One could do worse than be a swinger of birches.

1913–1914 1915

THE OVEN BIRD[1]

There is a singer everyone has heard,
Loud, a mid-summer and a mid-wood bird,
Who makes the solid tree trunks sound again.
He says that leaves are old and that for flowers
Mid-summer is to spring as one to ten.
He says the early petal-fall is past,
When pear and cherry bloom went down in showers
On sunny days a moment overcast;
And comes that other fall we name the fall.
He says the highway dust is over all.
The bird would cease and be as other birds
But that he knows in singing not to sing.
The question that he frames in all but words
Is what to make of a diminished thing.
1906–1907 1916

FOR ONCE, THEN, SOMETHING

Others taunt me with having knelt at well-curbs
Always wrong to the light, so never seeing
Deeper down in the well than where the water
Gives me back in a shining surface picture
Me myself in the summer heaven, godlike,
Looking out of a wreath of fern and cloud puffs.
Once, when trying with chin against a well-curb,
I discerned, as I thought, beyond the picture,
Through the picture, a something white, uncertain,
Something more of the depths—and then I lost it.
Water came to rebuke the too clear water.
One drop fell from a fern, and lo, a ripple
Shook whatever it was lay there at bottom,
Blurred it, blotted it out. What was that whiteness?
Truth? A pebble of quartz? For once, then, something.
1920

FIRE AND ICE

Some say the world will end in fire,
Some say in ice.
From what I've tasted of desire
I hold with those who favor fire.

[1]An American warbler that builds a dome-shaped nest.

But if it had to perish twice,
I think I know enough of hate
To know[1] that for destruction ice
Is also great
And would suffice.

1920

DESIGN

I found a dimpled spider, fat and white,
On a white heal-all,[1] holding up a moth
Like a white piece of rigid satin cloth—
Assorted characters of death and blight
Mixed ready to begin the morning right,
Like the ingredients of a witches' broth—
A snow-drop spider, a flower like a froth,
And dead wings carried like a paper kite.

What had that flower to do with being white,
The wayside blue and innocent heal-all?
What brought the kindred spider to that height,
Then steered the white moth thither in the night?
What but design of darkness to appall?—
If design govern in a thing so small.

1922

STOPPING BY WOODS ON A SNOWY EVENING

Whose woods these are I think I know.
His house is in the village, though;
He will not see me stopping here
To watch his woods fill up with snow.

My little horse must think it queer
To stop without a farmhouse near
Between the woods and frozen lake
The darkest evening of the year.

He gives his harness bells a shake
To ask if there is some mistake.
The only other sound's the sweep
Of easy wind and downy flake.

[1]Changed to "say" in later versions.
[1]A plant, normally with blue blossoms, reputed to have healing powers.

The woods are lovely, dark and deep,
But I have promises to keep,
And miles to go before I sleep,
And miles to go before I sleep.

1923

Willa Cather 1873–1947

In 1883, when she was nine, Willa Cather's family migrated westward from her birthplace in Virginia to the prairie lands of Nebraska. There she grew up among the pioneering European immigrants whose qualities of courage, sensitivity, and perseverance she was later to portray in her novels and short stories of rural and small-town America.

After graduating from the University of Nebraska in 1895, she returned east, to Pennsylvania, where she worked on a Pittsburgh newspaper and taught English in a high school. In 1900 she began publishing poems and short stories. Her first book, a collection of poems, April Twilights, *appeared in 1903. Following the publication of a collection of her short stories,* The Troll Garden *(1905), she moved to New York City, where she worked for six years on the editorial staff of* McClure's Magazine.

Her first novel, Alexander's Bridge *(1912), was set in England, but she soon returned to the frontier world of the prairies with* O Pioneers! *(1913). Next came* The Song of the Lark *(1915),* My Antonia *(1918), and collections of short stories:* Youth and the Bright Medusa *(1920) and* Obscure Destinies *(1932). In her later years she came to perceive the sprawling cities of the East and the joyless materialism of the twentieth century as symbolic expressions of a decline in order and meaning, and she turned to depictions of the more distant past. She wrote of the struggles of early Roman Catholic missionaries among the Indians of New Mexico in* Death Comes for the Archbishop *(1927) and of the lives of settlers in seventeenth-century Quebec in* Shadows on the Rock *(1931). Yet, like the prairie realists and the local colorists of the nineteenth century, her greatest achievement remained her portrayals, with fine simplicity and what she called "the gift of sympathy," of ordinary men and women who struggled to find meaningful lives in the midst of adversity and who stood for the noble ideals of an age that had passed.*

FURTHER READING: *The Novels and Stories of Willa Cather,* 13 vols., 1937–1941; M. Bennett, *The World of Willa Cather,* 1951, 1961, 1995; *Willa Cather's Collected Short Fiction,* ed. V. Faulkner, 1965, 1970; P. Robinson, *Willa, The Life of Willa Cather,* 1983; J. Woodress, *Willa Cather, A Literary Life,* 1987; J. Middleton, *Willa Cather's Modernism: A Study of Style and Technique,* 1990; L. Wasserman, *Willa Cather, A Study of the Short Fiction,* 1991; *A Reader's Companion to the Fiction of Willa Cather,* ed. J. March, M. Arnold, and D. Lynn, 1993; E. Wagenknecht, *Willa Cather,* 1993; G. Reynolds, *Willa Cather in Context,* 1996; J. Stout, *Willa Cather, The Writer and Her World,* 2000; H. Lee, *Willa Cather, A Life Saved Up,* 2000; *The Cambridge Companion to Willa Cather,* ed. M. Lindeman, 2004.

TEXT: *Youth and the Bright Medusa,* 1920.

PAUL'S CASE

It was Paul's afternoon to appear before the faculty of the Pittsburgh High School to account for his various misdemeanors. He had been suspended a week ago, and his father had called at the Principal's office and confessed his perplexity about his son. Paul entered the faculty room suave and smiling. His clothes were a trifle outgrown, and the tan velvet on the collar of his open overcoat was frayed and worn; but for all that there was something of a dandy about him, and he wore an opal pin in his neatly knotted black four-in-hand, and a red carnation in his buttonhole. This latter adornment the faculty somehow felt was not properly significant of the contrite spirit befitting a boy under the ban of suspension.

Paul was tall for his age and very thin, with high, cramped shoulders and a narrow chest. His eyes were remarkable for a certain hysterical brilliancy, and he continually used them in a conscious, theatrical sort of way, peculiarly offensive in a boy. The pupils were abnormally large, as though he were addicted to belladonna, but there was a glassy glitter about them which that drug does not produce.

When questioned by the Principal as to why he was there, Paul stated, politely enough, that he wanted to come back to school. This was a lie, but Paul was quite accustomed to lying; found it, indeed, indispensable for overcoming friction. His teachers were asked to state their respective charges against him, which they did with such a rancor and aggrievedness as evinced that this was not a usual case. Disorder and impertinence were among the offenses named, yet each of his instructors felt that it was scarcely possible to put into words the real cause of the trouble, which lay in a sort of hysterically defiant manner of the boy's; in the contempt which they all knew he felt for them, and which he seemingly made not the least effort to conceal. Once, when he had been making a synopsis of a paragraph at the blackboard, his English teacher had stepped to his side and attempted to guide his hand. Paul had started back with a shudder and thrust his hands violently behind him. The astonished woman could scarcely have been more hurt and embarrassed had he struck at her. The insult was so involuntary and definitely personal as to be unforgettable. In one way and another, he had made all his teachers, men and women alike, conscious of the same feeling of physical aversion. In one class he habitually sat with his hand shading his eyes; in another he always looked out of the window during the recitation; in another had made a running commentary on the lecture, with humorous intent.

His teachers felt this afternoon that his whole attitude was symbolized by his shrug and his flippantly red carnation flower, and they fell upon him without mercy, his English teacher leading the pack. He stood through it smiling, his pale lips parted over his white teeth. (His lips were continually twitching, and he had a habit of raising his eyebrows that was contemptuous and irritating to the last degree.) Older boys than Paul had broken down and shed tears under that ordeal, but his set smile did not once desert him, and his only sign of discomfort was the nervous trembling of the fingers that toyed with the buttons of his overcoat, and an occasional jerking of the other hand which held his hat. Paul was also smiling, always glancing about him, seeming to feel that people might be watching him and trying to detect something. This conscious expression, since it was as far as possible from boyish mirthfulness, was usually attributed to insolence or "smartness."

As the inquisition proceeded, one of his instructors repeated an impertinent remark of the boy's, and the Principal asked him whether he thought that a courteous speech to make to a woman. Paul shrugged his shoulders slightly and his eyebrows twitched.

"I don't know," he replied. "I didn't mean to be polite or impolite, either. I guess it's a sort of way I have, of saying things regardless."

The Principal asked him whether he didn't think that a way it would be well to get rid of. Paul grinned and said he guessed so. When he was told that he could go, he bowed gracefully and went out. His bow was like a repetition of the scandalous red carnation.

His teachers were in despair, and his drawing-master voiced the feeling of them all when he declared there was something about the boy which none of them understood. He added: "I don't really believe that smile of his comes altogether from insolence; there's something sort of haunted about it. The boy is not strong for one thing. There is something wrong about the fellow."

The drawing-master had come to realize that, in looking at Paul, one saw only his white teeth and the forced animation of his eyes. One warm afternoon the boy had gone to sleep at his drawing-board, and his master had noted with amazement what a white, blue-veined face it was; drawn and wrinkled like an old man's about the eyes, the lips twitching even in his sleep.

His teachers left the building dissatisfied and unhappy; humiliated to have felt so vindictive toward a mere boy, to have uttered this feeling in cutting terms, and to have set each other on, as it were, in the gruesome game of intemperate reproach. One of them remembered having seen a miserable street cat set at bay by a ring of tormentors.

As for Paul, he ran down the hill whistling the Soldiers' Chorus from *Faust*, looking behind him now and then to see whether some of his teachers were not there to witness his light-heartedness. As it was now late in the afternoon and Paul was on duty that evening as usher at Carnegie Hall, he decided that he would not go home to supper.

When he reached the concert hall, the doors were not yet open. It was chilly outside, and he decided to go up into the picture gallery—always deserted at this hour—where there were some of Raffelli's gay studies of Paris streets and an airy blue Venetian scene or two that always exhilarated him. He was delighted to find no one in the gallery but the old guard, who sat in the corner, a newspaper on his knee, a black patch over one eye and the other closed. Paul possessed himself of the place and walked confidently up and down, whistling under his breath. After a while he sat down before a blue Rico and lost himself. When he bethought him to look at his watch, it was after seven o'clock, and he rose with a start and ran downstairs, making a face at Augustus Caesar, peering out from the cast-room, and an evil gesture at the Venus of Milo as he passed her on the stairway.

When Paul reached the ushers' dressing-room, half a dozen boys were there already, and he began excitedly to tumble into his uniform. It was one of the few that at all approached fitting, and Paul thought it very becoming—though he knew the tight, straight coat accentuated his narrow chest, about which he was exceedingly sensitive. He was always excited while he dressed, twanging all over to the tuning of the strings and the preliminary flourishes of the horns in the music-room; but tonight he seemed quite beside himself, and he teased and plagued the boys until, telling him that he was crazy, they put him down on the floor and sat on him.

Somewhat calmed by his suppression, Paul dashed out to the front of the house to seat the early comers. He was a model usher. Gracious and smiling he ran up and down the aisles. Nothing was too much trouble for him; he carried messages and brought programs as though it were his greatest pleasure in life, and all the people in his section thought him a charming boy, feeling that he remembered and admired them. As the house filled, he grew more and more vivacious and animated, and the color came to his cheeks and lips. It was very much as though this were a great reception and Paul were the host. Just as the musicians came out to take their places, his English teacher arrived with checks for the seats which a prominent manufacturer had taken for the season. She betrayed some embarrassment when she handed Paul the tickets, and a *hauteur* which subsequently made her feel very foolish. Paul was startled for a moment, and had the feeling of wanting to put her out; what business had she here among all these fine people and gay colors? He looked her over and decided that she was not appropriately dressed and must be a fool to sit downstairs in such togs. The tickets had probably been sent her out of kindness, he reflected, as he put down a seat for her, and she had about as much right to sit there as he had.

When the symphony began, Paul sank into one of the rear seats with a long sigh of relief, and lost himself as he had done before the Rico. It was not that symphonies, as such, meant anything in particular to Paul, but the first sight of the instruments seemed to free some hilarious spirit within him; something that struggled there like the Genius in the bottle found by the Arab fisherman. He felt a sudden zest of life; the lights danced before his eyes and the concert hall blazed into unimaginable splendor. When the soprano soloist came on, Paul forgot even the nastiness of his teacher's being there, and gave himself up to the peculiar intoxication such personages always had for him. The soloist chanced to be a German woman, by no means in her first youth, and the mother of many children; but she wore a satin gown and a tiara, and she had that indefinable air of achievement, that world-shine upon her, which always blinded Paul to any possible defects.

After a concert was over, Paul was often irritable and wretched until he got to sleep—and tonight he was even more than usually restless. He had the feeling of not being able to let down; of its being impossible to give up his delicious excitement which was the only thing that could be called living at all. During the last number he withdrew and, after hastily changing his clothes in the dressing-room, slipped out to the side door where the singer's carriage stood. Here he began pacing rapidly up and down the walk, waiting to see her come out.

Over yonder the Schenley, in its vacant stretch, loomed big and square through the fine rain, the windows of its twelve stories glowing like those of a lighted cardboard house under a Christmas tree. All the actors and singers of any importance stayed there when they were in Pittsburgh, and a number of the big manufacturers of the place lived there in the winter. Paul had often hung about the hotel, watching the people go in and out, longing to enter and leave schoolmasters and dull care behind him forever.

At last the singer came out, accompanied by the conductor, who helped her into her carriage and closed the door with a cordial *auf wiedersehen*[1]—which set Paul to wondering whether she were not an old sweetheart of his. Paul followed the carriage over to the hotel, walking so rapidly as not to be far from the entrance when the singer alighted and disappeared behind the swinging glass doors which were opened by a Negro in a tall hat and a long coat. In the moment that the door was ajar, it seemed to Paul that he, too, entered. He seemed to feel himself go after her up the steps, into the warm, lighted building, into an exotic, tropical world of shiny, glistening surfaces and basking ease. He reflected upon the mysterious dishes that were brought into the dining-room, the green bottles in buckets of ice, as he had seen them in the supper-party pictures of the Sunday supplement. A quick gust of wind brought the rain down with sudden vehemence, and Paul was startled to find that he was still outside in the slush of the gravel driveway; that his boots were letting in the water and his scanty overcoat was clinging wet about him; that the lights in front of the concert hall were out, and that the rain was driving in sheets between him and the orange glow of the windows above him. There it was, what he wanted—tangibly before him, like the fairy world of a Christmas pantomime; as the rain beat in his face, Paul wondered whether he were destined always to shiver in the black night outside, looking up at it.

He turned and walked reluctantly toward the car tracks. The end had to come sometime; his father in his night-clothes at the top of the stairs, explanations that did not explain, hastily improvised fictions that were forever tripping him up, his upstairs room and its horrible yellow wallpaper, the creaking bureau with the greasy plush collar-box, and over his painted wooden bed the pictures of George Washington and John Calvin, and the framed motto. "Feed my Lambs," which had been worked in red worsted by his mother, whom Paul could not remember.

Half an hour later, Paul alighted from the Negley Avenue car and went slowly down one of the side streets off the main thoroughfare. It was a highly respectable street, where all the houses were exactly alike, and where business men of moderate means begot and reared large families of children, all of whom went to Sabbath School and learned the shorter catechism, and were interested in arithmetic; all of whom were as exactly alike as their homes, and of a piece of the monotony in which they lived. Paul never went up Cordelia Street without a shudder of loathing. His home was next to the house of the Cumberland minister. He approached it tonight with the nerveless sense of defeat, the hopeless feeling of sinking back forever into ugliness and commonness that he had always had when he came home. The moment he turned into Cordelia Street he felt the waters close above his head. After each of these orgies of living, he experienced all the physical depression which follows a debauch; the loathing of respectable beds, of common food, of a house permeated by kitchen odors; a shuddering repulsion for the flavorless, colorless mass of every-day existence; a morbid desire for cool things and soft lights and fresh flowers.

The nearer he approached the house, the more absolutely unequal Paul felt to the sight of it all: his ugly sleeping chamber; the old bathroom with

[1]German: Goodbye.

the grimy zinc tub, the cracked mirror, the dripping spigots; his father, at the top of the stairs, his hairy legs sticking out from his nightshirt, his feet thrust into carpet slippers. He was so much later than usual that there would certainly be enquiries and reproaches. Paul stopped short before the door. He felt that he could not be accosted by his father tonight; that he could not toss again on that miserable bed. He would not go in. He would tell his father that he had no carfare, and it was raining so hard he had gone home with one of the boys and stayed all night.

Meanwhile, he was wet and cold. He went around to the back of the house and tried one of the basement windows, found it open, and raised it cautiously, and scrambled down the cellar wall to the floor. There he stood, holding his breath, terrified by the noise he had made; but the floor above him was silent, and there was no creak on the stairs. He found a soap-box, and carried it over to the soft ring of light that streamed from the furnace door, and sat down. He was horribly afraid of rats, so he did not try to sleep, but sat looking distrustfully at the dark, still terrified lest he might have awakened his father. In such reactions, after one of the experiences which made days and nights out of the dreary blanks of the calendar, when his senses were deadened, Paul's head was always singularly clear. Suppose his father had heard him getting in at the window and had come down and shot him for a burglar? Then, again, suppose his father had come down, pistol in hand, and he had cried out in time to save himself, and his father had been horrified to think how nearly he had killed him? Then again, suppose a day should come when his father would remember that night, and wish there had been no warning cry to stay his hand? With this last supposition Paul entertained himself until daybreak.

The following Sunday was fine; the sodden November chill was broken by the last flash of autumnal summer. In the morning Paul had to go to church and Sabbath School, as always. On seasonable Sunday afternoons the burghers of Cordelia Street usually sat out on their front "stoops," and talked to their neighbors on the next stoop, or called to those across the street in neighborly fashion. The men sat placidly on gay cushions placed upon the steps that led down to the sidewalk, while the women, in their Sunday "waists,"[2] sat in rockers on the cramped porches, pretending to be greatly at their ease. The children played in the streets; there were so many of them that the place resembled the recreation grounds of a kindergarten. The men on the steps, all in their shirt-sleeves, their vests unbuttoned, sat with their legs well apart, their stomachs comfortably protruding, and talked of the prices of things, or told anecdotes of the sagacity of their various chiefs and overlords. They occasionally looked over the multitude of squabbling children, listened affectionately to their high-pitched, nasal voices, smiling to see their own proclivities reproduced in their offspring, and interspersed their legends of the iron kings with remarks about their sons' progress at school, their grades in arithmetic, and the amounts they had saved in their toy banks.

On this last Sunday of November, Paul sat all afternoon on the lowest step of his "stoop," staring into the street, while his sisters, in their rockers, were talking to the minister's daughters next door about how many shirtwaists

[2]A stiff, formal blouse.

they had made in the last week, and how many waffles someone had eaten at the last church supper. When the weather was warm, and his father was in a particularly jovial frame of mind, the girls made lemonade, which was always brought out in a red-glass pitcher, ornamented with forget-me-nots in blue enamel. This the girls thought very fine, and the neighbors joked about the suspicious color of the pitcher.

Today Paul's father, on the top step, was talking to a young man who shifted a restless baby from knee to knee. He happened to be the young man who was daily held up to Paul as a model, and after whom it was his father's dearest hope that he would pattern. This young man was of a ruddy complexion, with a compressed, red mouth, and faded, nearsighted eyes, over which he wore thick spectacles, with gold bows that curved about his ears. He was clerk to one of the magnates of a great steel corporation, and was looked upon in Cordelia Street as a young man with a future. There was a story that, some five years ago—he was now barely twenty-six—he had been a trifle "dissipated," but in order to curb his appetites and save the loss of time and strength that a sowing of wild oats might have entailed, he had taken his chief's advice, oft reiterated to his employees, and at twenty-one had married the first woman whom he could persuade to share his fortunes. She happened to be an angular schoolmistress, much older than he, who also wore thick glasses, and who had now borne him four children, all nearsighted like herself.

The young man was relating how his chief, now cruising in the Mediterranean, kept in touch with all the details of the business, arranging his office hours on his yacht just as though he were at home, and "knocking off work enough to keep two stenographers busy." His father told, in turn, the plan his corporation was considering, of putting in an electric railway plant at Cairo.[3] Paul snapped his teeth; he had an awful apprehension that they might spoil it all before he got there. Yet he rather liked to hear these legends of the iron kings, that were told and retold on Sundays and holidays; these stories of palaces in Venice, yachts on the Mediterranean, and high play at Monte Carlo appealed to his fancy, and he was interested in the triumphs of cash-boys who had become famous, though he had no mind for the cash-boy stage.

After supper was over, and he had helped to dry the dishes, Paul nervously asked his father whether he could go to George's to get some help in his geometry, and still more nervously asked for carfare. This latter request he had to repeat, as his father, on principle, did not like to hear requests for money, whether much or little. He asked Paul whether he could not go to some boy who lived nearer, and told him that he ought not to leave his school work until Sunday; but he gave him the dime. He was not a poor man, but he had a worthy ambition to come up in the world. His only reason for allowing Paul to usher was that he thought a boy ought to be earning a little.

Paul bounded upstairs, scrubbed the greasy odor of the dishwater from his hands with the ill-smelling soap he hated, and then shook over his fingers a few drops of violet water from the bottle he kept hidden in his drawer. He left the house with his geometry conspicuously under his arm, and the moment he got out of Cordelia Street and boarded a downtown car, he shook off the lethargy of two deadening days, and began to live again.

[3]Cairo, Illinois, on the Mississippi River, where it meets the Ohio.

The leading juvenile of the permanent stock company which played at one of the downtown theaters was an acquaintance of Paul's, and the boy had been invited to drop in at the Sunday-night rehearsals whenever he could. For more than a year Paul had spent every available moment loitering about Charley Edward's dressing-room. He had won a place among Edward's following not only because the young actor, who could not afford to employ a dresser, often found him useful, but because he recognized in Paul something akin to what churchmen term "vocation."

It was at the theater and at Carnegie Hall[4] that Paul really lived; the rest was but a sleep and a forgetting. This was Paul's fairy tale, and it had for him all the allurement of a secret love. The moment he inhaled the gassy, painty, dusty odor behind the scenes, he breathed like a prisoner set free, and felt within him the possibility of doing or saying splendid, brilliant things. The moment the cracked orchestra beat out the overture from *Martha,* or jerked at the serenade from *Rigoletto,*[5] all stupid and ugly things slid from him, and his senses were deliciously, yet delicately fired.

Perhaps it was because, in Paul's world, the natural nearly always wore the guise of ugliness, that a certain element of artificiality seemed to him necessary in beauty. Perhaps it was because his experience of life elsewhere was so full of Sabbath-School picnics, petty economies, wholesome advice as to how to succeed in life, and the unescapable odors of cooking, that he found this existence so alluring, these smartly clad men and women so attractive, that he was so moved by these starry apple orchards that bloomed perennially under the limelight.

It would be difficult to put it strongly enough how convincingly the stage entrance of the theater was for Paul the actual portal of Romance. Certainly none of the company ever suspected it, least of all Charley Edwards. It was very like the old stories that used to float about London of fabulously rich Jews, who had subterranean halls, with palms, and fountains, and soft lamps and richly appareled women who never saw the disenchanting light of London day. So, in the midst of that smoke-palled city, enamored of figures and grimy oil, Paul had his secret temple, his wishing-carpet, his bit of blue-and-white Mediterranean shore bathed in perpetual sunshine.

Several of Paul's teachers had a theory that his imagination had been perverted by garish fiction; but the truth was he scarcely ever read at all. The books at home were not such as would either tempt or corrupt a youthful mind, and as for reading the novels that some of his friends urged upon him—well, he got what he wanted much more quickly from music; any sort of music, from an orchestra to a barrel-organ. He needed only the spark, the indescribable thrill that made his imagination master of his senses, and he could make plots and pictures enough of his own. It was equally true that he was not stage-struck—not, at any rate, in the usual acceptation of the expression. He had no desire to become an actor, any more than he had to become a musician. He felt no necessity to do any of these things; what he wanted was to see, to be in the atmosphere, float on the wave of it, to be carried out, blue league after league, away from everything.

[4]Concert Hall in New York City.

[5]*Martha* (1847), opera by the German composer Friedrich von Flotow (1812–1883); *Rigoletto* (1851), opera by the Italian composer Giuseppe Verdi (1873–1901).

After a night behind the scenes, Paul found the schoolroom more than ever repulsive; the bare floors and naked walls; the prosy men who never wore frock coats, or violets in their buttonholes; the women with their dull gowns, shrill voices, and pitiful seriousness about prepositions that govern the dative. He could not bear to have the other pupils think, for a moment, that he took these people seriously; he must convey to them that he considered it all trivial, and was there only by way of a joke, anyway. He had autographed pictures of all the members of the stock company which he showed his classmates, telling them the most incredible stories of his familiarity with these people, of his acquaintance with the soloists who came to Carnegie Hall, his suppers with them and the flowers he sent them. When these stories lost their effect, and his audience grew listless, he would bid all the boys goodbye, announcing that he was going to travel for a while; going to Naples, to California, to Egypt. Then, next Monday, he would slip back, conscious and nervously smiling; his sister was ill, and he would have to defer his voyage until spring.

Matters went steadily worse with Paul at school. In the itch to let his instructors know how heartily he despised them, and how thoroughly he was appreciated elsewhere, he mentioned once or twice that he had no time to fool with theorems, adding—with a twitch of the eyebrows and a touch of that nervous bravado which so perplexed them—that he was helping the people down at the stock company; they were old friends of his.

The upshot of the matter was that the Principal went to Paul's father, and Paul was taken out of school and put to work. The manager at Carnegie Hall was told to get another usher in his stead; the doorkeeper at the theater was warned not to admit him to the house; and Charley Edwards remorsefully promised the boy's father not to see him again.

The members of the stock company were vastly amused when some of Paul's stories reached them—especially the women. They were hard-working women, most of them supporting indolent husbands or brothers, and they laughed rather bitterly at having stirred the boy to such fervid and florid inventions. They agreed with the faculty and with his father, that Paul's was a bad case.

The east-bound train was plowing through a January snowstorm; the dull dawn was beginning to show grey when the engine whistled a mile out of Newark. Paul started up from the seat where he had lain curled in uneasy slumber, rubbed the breath-misted window-glass with his hand, and peered out. The snow was whirling in curling eddies above the white bottom lands, and the drifts lay already deep in the fields and along the fences, while here and there the tall dead grass and dried weed stalks protruded black above it. Lights shone from the scattered houses, and a gang of laborers who stood beside the track waved their lanterns.

Paul had slept very little, and he felt grimy and uncomfortable. He had made the all-night journey in a day coach because he was afraid if he took a Pullman he might be seen by some Pittsburgh business man who had noticed him in Denny and Carson's office. When the whistle woke him, he clutched quickly at his breast pocket, glancing about him with an uncertain smile. But the little, clay-bespattered Italians were still sleeping, the slatternly women across the aisle were in open-mouthed oblivion, and even the crumby, crying babies were for the time stilled. Paul settled back to struggle with his impatience as best he could.

When he arrived at the Jersey City station, he hurried through his breakfast, manifestly ill at ease and keeping a sharp eye about him. After he reached the Twenty-Third Street station, he consulted a cabman, and had himself driven to a men's furnishing establishment which was just opening for the day. He spent upward of two hours there, buying with endless reconsidering and great care. His new street suit he put on in the fitting-room; the frock coat and dress clothes he had bundled into the cab with his new shirts. Then he drove to a hatter's and a shoe house. His next errand was at Tiffany's, where he selected silver-mounted brushes and a scarf-pin. He would not wait to have his silver marked, he said. Lastly, he stopped at a trunk shop on Broadway, and had his purchases packed into various traveling-bags.

It was a little after one o'clock when he drove up to the Waldorf,[6] and, after settling with the cabman, went into the office. He registered from Washington; said his mother and father had been abroad, and that he had come down to await the arrival of their steamer. He told his story plausibly and had no trouble, since he offered to pay for them in advance, in engaging his rooms; a sleeping-room, sitting-room, and bath.

Not once, but a hundred times Paul had planned his entry into New York. He had gone over every detail of it with Charley Edwards, and in his scrap-book at home there were pages of description about New York hotels, cut from the Sunday papers.

When he was shown to his sitting-room on the eighth floor, he saw at a glance that everything was as it should be; there was but one detail in his mental picture that the place did not realize, so he rang for the bell-boy and sent him down for flowers. He moved about nervously until the boy returned, putting away his new linen and fingering it delightedly as he did so. When the flowers came, he put them hastily into water, and then tumbled into a hot bath. Presently he came out of his white bathroom, resplendent in his new silk underwear, and playing with the tassels of his red robe. The snow was whirling so fiercely outside his windows that he could scarcely see across the street; but within, the air was deliciously soft and fragrant. He put the violets and jonquils on the taboret beside the couch, and threw himself down with a long sigh, covering himself with a Roman blanket. He was thoroughly tired; he had been in such haste, he had stood up to such a strain, covered so much ground in the last twenty-four hours, that he wanted to think how it had all come about. Lulled by the sound of the wind, the warm air, and the cool fragrance of the flowers, he sank into deep, drowsy retrospection.

It had been wonderfully simple; when they had shut him out of the theater and concert hall, when they had taken away his bone, the whole thing was virtually determined. The rest was a mere matter of opportunity. The only thing that at all surprised him was his own courage—for he realized well enough that he had always been tormented by fear, a sort of apprehensive dread which, of late years, as the meshes of the lies he had told closed about him, had been pulling the muscles of his body tighter and tighter. Until now, he could not remember a time when he had not been dreading something.

[6]Famous New York City hotel.

Even when he was a little boy, it was always there—behind him, or before, or on either side. There had always been the shadowed corner, the dark place into which he dared not look, but from which something seemed always to be watching him—and Paul had done things that were not pretty to watch, he knew.

But now he had a curious sense of relief, as though he had at last thrown down the gauntlet to the thing in the corner.

Yet it was but a day since he had been sulking in the traces; but yesterday afternoon that he had been sent to the bank with Denny and Carson's deposit, as usual—but this time he was instructed to leave the book to be balanced. There was above two thousand dollars in checks, and nearly a thousand in the banknotes which he had taken from the book and quietly transferred to his pocket. At the bank he had made out a new deposit slip. His nerves had been steady enough to permit of his returning to the office, where he had finished his work and asked for a full day's holiday tomorrow, Saturday, giving a perfectly reasonable pretext. The bank book, he knew, would not be returned before Monday or Tuesday, and his father would be out of town for the next week. From the time he slipped the banknotes into his pocket until he boarded the night train for New York, he had not known a moment's hesitation.

How astonishingly easy it had all been; here he was, the thing done; and this time there would be no awakening, no figure at the top of the stairs. He watched the snowflakes whirling by his window until he fell asleep.

When he awoke, it was four o'clock in the afternoon. He bounded up with a start; one of his precious days gone already! He spent nearly an hour in dressing, watching every stage of his toilet carefully in the mirror. Everything was quite perfect; he was exactly the kind of boy he had always wanted to be.

When he went downstairs, Paul took a carriage and drove up Fifth Avenue toward the Park. The snow had somewhat abated; carriages and tradesmen's wagons were hurrying soundlessly to and fro in the winter twilight; boys in woolen mufflers were shoveling off the doorsteps; the Avenue stages made fine spots of color against the white street. Here and there on the corners whole flower gardens blooming behind glass windows, against which the snowflakes stuck and melted; violets, roses, carnations, lilies-of-the-valley—somehow vastly more lovely and alluring that they blossomed thus unnaturally in the snow. The Park itself was a wonderful stage winter-piece.

When he returned, the pause of the twilight had ceased, and the tune of the streets had changed. The snow was falling faster, lights streamed from the hotels that reared their many stories fearlessly up into the storm, defying the raging Atlantic winds. A long, black stream of carriages poured down the Avenue, intersected here and there by other streams, tending horizontally. There were a score of cabs about the entrance of his hotel, and his driver had to wait. Boys in livery were running in and out of the awning stretched across the sidewalk, up and down the red velvet carpet laid from the door to the street. Above, about, within it all, was the rumble and roar, the hurry and toss of thousands of human beings as hot for pleasure as himself, and on every side of him towered the glaring affirmation of the omnipotence of wealth.

The boy set his teeth and drew his shoulders together in a spasm of realization; the plot of all dramas, the text of all romances, the nerve-stuff of all sensations was whirling about him like the snowflakes. He burnt like a fagot in a tempest.

When Paul came down to dinner, the music of the orchestra floated up the elevator shaft to greet him. As he stepped into the thronged corridor, he sank back into one of the chairs against the wall to get his breath. The lights, the chatter, the perfumes, the bewildering medley of color—he had, for a moment, the feeling of not being able to stand it. But only for a moment; these were his own people, he told himself. He went slowly about the corridors, through the writing-rooms, smoking-rooms, reception-rooms, as though he were exploring the chambers of an enchanted palace, built and peopled for him alone.

When he reached the dining-room he sat down at a table near a window. The flowers, the white linen, the many-colored wine-glasses, the gay toilettes of the women, the low popping of corks, the undulating repetitions of the *Blue Danube* from the orchestra, all flooded Paul's dream with bewildering radiance. When the roseate tinge of his champagne was added—that cold, precious, bubbling stuff that creamed and foamed in his glass—Paul wondered that there were honest men in the world at all. This was what all the world was fighting for, he reflected; this was what all the struggle was about. He doubted the reality of his past. Had he ever known a place called Cordelia Street, a place where fagged-looking business men boarded the early car? Mere rivets in a machine they seemed to Paul—sickening men, with combings of children's hair always hanging to their coats, and the smell of cooking in their clothes. Cordelia Street—Ah, that belonged to another time and country! Had he not always been thus, had he not sat here night after night, from as far back as he could remember, looking pensively over just such shimmering textures, and slowly twirling the stem of a glass like this one between his thumb and middle finger? He rather thought he had.

He was not in the least abashed or lonely. He had no especial desire to meet or to know any of these people; all he demanded was the right to look on and conjecture, to watch the pageant. The mere stage properties were all he contended for. Nor was he lonely later in the evening, in his loge at the Opera. He was entirely rid of his nervous misgivings, of his forced aggressiveness, of the imperative desire to show himself different from his surroundings. He felt now that his surroundings explained him. Nobody questioned the purple; he had only to wear it passively. He had only to glance down at his dress coat to reassure himself that here it would be impossible for anyone to humiliate him.

He found it hard to leave his beautiful sitting-room to go to bed that night, and sat long watching the raging storm from his turret window. When he went to sleep, it was with the lights turned on in his bedroom; partly because of his old timidity, and partly so that, if he should wake in the night, there would be no wretched moment of doubt, no horrible suspicion of yellow wallpaper, or of Washington and Calvin above his bed.

On Sunday morning the city was practically snowbound. Paul breakfasted late, and in the afternoon he fell in with a wild San Francisco boy, a freshman at Yale, who said he had run down for a "little flyer" over Sunday. The young man offered to show Paul the night side of the town, and the two boys went off together after dinner, not returning to the hotel until seven o'clock the next morning. They had started out in the confiding warmth of a champagne friendship, but their parting in the elevator was singularly cool. The freshman pulled himself together to make his train, and Paul went to bed. He awoke at two o'clock in the afternoon, very thirsty and dizzy, and rang for ice-water, coffee, and the Pittsburgh papers.

On the part of the hotel management, Paul excited no suspicion. There was this to be said for him, that he wore his spoils with dignity and in no way made himself conspicuous. His chief greediness lay in his ears and eyes, and his excesses were not offensive ones. His dearest pleasures were the grey winter twilights in his sitting-room; his quiet enjoyment of his flowers, his clothes, his wide divan, his cigarette, and his sense of power. He could not remember a time when he had felt so at peace with himself. The mere release from the necessity of petty lying, lying every day and every day, restored his self-respect. He had never lied for pleasure, even at school; but to make himself noticed and admired, to assert his difference from other Cordelia Street boys; and he felt a good deal more manly, more honest, even, now that he had no need for boastful pretensions, now that he could, as his actor friends used to say, "dress the part." It was characteristic that remorse did not occur to him. His golden days went by without a shadow, and he made each as perfect as he could.

On the eighth day after his arrival in New York, he found the whole affair exploited in the Pittsburgh papers, exploited with a wealth of detail which indicated that local news of a sensational nature was at a low ebb. The firm of Denny and Carson announced that the boy's father had refunded the full amount of his theft, and that they had no intention of prosecuting. The Cumberland minister had been interviewed, and expressed his hope of yet reclaiming the motherless lad, and Paul's Sabbath-School teacher declared that she would spare no effort to that end. The rumor had reached Pittsburgh that the boy had been seen in a New York hotel, and his father had gone East to find him and bring him home.

Paul had just come in to dress for dinner; he sank into the chair, weak in the knees, and clasped his head in his hands. It was to be worse than jail, even; the tepid waters of Cordelia Street were to close over him finally and forever. The grey monotony stretched before him in hopeless, unrelieved years—Sabbath School, Young People's Meeting, the yellow-papered room, the damp dish-towels; it all rushed back upon him with sickening vividness. He had the old feeling that the orchestra had suddenly stopped, the sinking sensation that the play was over. The sweat broke out on his face, and he sprang to his feet, looked about him with his white, conscious smile, and winked at himself in the mirror. With something of the childish belief in miracles with which he had so often gone to class, all his lessons unlearned, Paul dressed and dashed whistling down the corridor to the elevator.

He had no sooner entered the dining-room and caught the measure of the music than his remembrance was lightened by his old elastic power of claiming the moment, mounting with it, and finding it all-sufficient. The glare and glitter about him, the mere scenic accessories had again, and for the last time, their old potency. He would show himself that he was game, he would finish the thing splendidly. He doubted, more than ever, the existence of Cordelia Street, and for the first time he drank his wine recklessly. Was he not, after all, one of these fortunate beings? Was he not still himself, and in his own place? He drummed a nervous accompaniment to the music and looked about him, telling himself over and over that it had paid.

He reflected drowsily, to the swell of the violin and the chill sweetness of his wine, that he might have done it more wisely. He might have caught an outbound steamer and been well out of their clutches before now. But the other side of the world had seemed too far away and too uncertain then; he could not have waited for it; his need had been too sharp. If he had to choose over again, he would do the same thing tomorrow. He looked affectionately about the dining-room, now gilded with a soft mist. Ah, it had paid indeed!

Paul was awakened next morning by a painful throbbing in his head and feet. He had thrown himself across the bed without undressing, and had slept with his shoes on. His limbs and hands were lead-heavy, and his tongue and throat were parched. There came upon him one of those fateful attacks of clear-headedness that never occurred except when he was physically exhausted and his nerves hung loose. He lay still and closed his eyes and let the tide of realities wash over him.

His father was in New York, "stopping at some joint or other," he told himself. The memory of successive summers on the front stoop fell upon him like a weight of black water. He had not a hundred dollars left; and he knew now, more than ever, that money was everything, the wall that stood between all he loathed and all he wanted. The thing was winding itself up; he had thought of that on his first glorious day in New York, and had even provided a way to snap the thread. It lay on his dressing-table now; he had got it out last night when he came blindly up from dinner—but the shiny metal hurt his eyes, and he disliked the look of it, anyway.

He rose and moved about with a painful effort, succumbing now and again to attacks of nausea. It was the old depression exaggerated; all the world had become Cordelia Street. Yet somehow he was not afraid of anything, was absolutely calm; perhaps because he had looked into the dark corner at last, and knew. It was bad enough, what he saw there; but somehow not so bad as his long fear of it had been. He saw everything clearly now. He had a feeling that he had made the best of it, that he had lived the sort of life he was meant to live, and for half an hour he sat staring at the revolver. But he told himself that was not the way, so he went downstairs and took a cab to the ferry.

When Paul arrived at Newark, he got off the train and took another cab, directing the driver to follow the Pennsylvania tracks out of town. The snow lay heavy on the roadways and had drifted deep in the open fields. Only here and there the dead grass or dried weed stalks projected, singularly black, above it. Once well into the country, Paul dismissed the carriage and walked, floundering along the tracks, his mind a medley of irrelevant things. He seemed to hold in his brain an actual picture of everything he had seen that morning. He remembered every feature of both his drivers, the toothless old woman from whom he had bought the red flowers in his coat, the agent from whom he had got his ticket, and all of his fellow-passengers on the ferry. His mind, unable to cope with vital matters near at hand, worked feverishly and deftly at sorting and grouping these images. They made for him a part of the ugliness of the world, of the ache in his head, and the bitter burning on his tongue. He stooped and put a handful of snow into his mouth as he walked, but that, too, seemed hot. When he reached a little hillside, where the tracks ran through a cut some twenty feet below him, he stopped and sat down.

The carnations in his coat were drooping with cold, he noticed; their red glory over. It occurred to him that all the flowers he had seen in the show windows that first night must have gone the same way, long before this. It was only one splendid breath they had, in spite of their brave mockery at the winter outside the glass. It was a losing game in the end, it seemed, this revolt against the homilies by which the world is run. Paul took one of the blossoms carefully from his coat and scooped a little hole in the snow, where he covered it up. Then he dozed awhile, from his weak condition, seeming insensible to the cold.

The sound of an approaching train woke him and he started to his feet, remembering only his resolution, and afraid lest he should be too late. He stood watching the approaching locomotive, his teeth chattering, his lips drawn away from them in a frightened smile; once or twice he glanced nervously sidewise, as though he were being watched. When the right moment came, he jumped. As he fell, the folly of his haste occurred to him with merciless clearness, the vastness of what he had left undone. There flashed through his brain, clearer than ever before, the blue of Adriatic water, the yellow of Algerian sands.

He felt something strike his chest—his body being thrown swiftly through the air, on and on, immeasurably far and fast, while his limbs gently relaxed. Then, because the picture-making mechanism was crushed, the disturbing visions flashed into black, and Paul dropped back into the immense design of things.

1905

Gertrude Stein 1874–1946

To the world at large, Gertrude Stein and the life she led have always been more fascinating than the books she wrote or the literary theories she devised. She lived most of her life in France, where she was the confidante of celebrated artists and writers. She was the patron of Pablo Picasso and the subject of one of his most famous paintings. Writers such as Thornton Wilder, Sherwood Anderson, F. Scott Fitzgerald, and Ernest Hemingway came to her apartment in Paris to listen to her ideas on modern literature. Her association with avant-garde art and her own eccentric literary works made her a familiar symbol of modernism. Even those who have never read her books know her famous line "A rose is a rose is a rose is a rose."

Stein was born in Allegheny, Pennsylvania, and for much of her childhood she lived in Oakland, California. Her family was well-to-do and she enjoyed a privileged life, indulged by servants, governesses, and tutors. At eighteen she entered Radcliffe College, where she developed her interest in writing. Later, critics and biographers would find it significant that her professor of composition praised her "unusual power of abstract thought" but complained "Your vehemence runs away with your syntax" and gave her a C.

She also attended the classes of the famous psychologist William James, a Harvard professor and the brother of the novelist Henry James. In 1897, with James's encouragement, she entered Johns Hopkins University to study medicine and prepare for research in the psychology of perception and understanding. But she found medical school to be tedious and constricting. She was bored by her teachers and her fellow students, and they, in turn, had little patience with her imperious self-assurance. In 1901, in her last term, she made little effort to study, failed most of her courses, and left the university without an M.D. degree.

Stein then decided to move to Europe, where she could live comfortably on the inheritance she had received after the death of her father. In 1904 she settled in Paris, and with her brother Leo, a student of modern art, began to collect the paintings of Cézanne, Renoir, Matisse, and Picasso. Soon the Stein apartment became a gathering place, a salon, for avant-garde artists and writers from Europe and America. One of the regular visitors was Picasso, who in 1905 began to paint his famous portrait of her. In the same year she began writing her first book, Three Lives *(1909), stories of three women, one of them "The Gentle Lena," who submit to their fate in a world they cannot control.* Three Lives *has been called a masterpiece of realism, and it remains one of her most successful and least obscure works. Her next important book,* Tender Buttons *(1914), a collection of observations on objects and forms, departed radically from convention, stressing "the value of the individual word" so that the reader might see actual objects rather than the mere printed text that described them.*

In 1922 she published Geography and Plays, *a collection of poems, plays, and descriptions of people and places that is rich with puns, rhythmic phrases, and the word repetitions that had become characteristic of her style.* The Making of Americans, *her long and sprawling novel of an American family, was, she believed, her literary masterwork. It appeared in 1925, and that same year she was invited to lecture on her literary theories at Cambridge and Oxford Universities in England.*

Stein's theories of literary language, grammar, vocabulary, and prose form were published in 1931 in How to Write. *One of her most obscure and difficult works, it had a narrow audience. But she soon began work on a book that would bring her, for the first time, to the attention of a large reading public. It was* The Autobiography of Alice B. Toklas *(1933). Supposedly written by her longtime companion and lover, Alice B. Toklas, it was in fact Gertrude Stein's own memoirs. Her descriptions of life in Paris and the famous people she had known made the book widely popular in Europe and in the United States.*

The following year her opera Four Saints in Three Acts, *set to music by the American composer Virgil Thomson, was produced on Broadway. It battered operatic conventions with an exuberant vigor that left audiences either noisily cheering or stunned into puzzled silence. Capitalizing on her new fame and notoriety, Stein returned to America in 1934 for a lecture tour. She became a national celebrity, pictured in newspapers and quoted on the radio. American editors and book publishers who had once rejected her writing as too obscure, too exotic for their readers, now urged her to send them her essay and book manuscripts.*

She was at the peak of her fame, and in the remaining years of the 1930s and in the 1940s more than twenty volumes of her works were published. In all she wrote more than fifty books and was renowned both as a famous writer and as "The Matron Saint of Paris Art," "The Sibyl of Montparnasse." When she died in 1946, it seemed as though a cultural monument in Paris had fallen.

The renown that Gertrude Stein had achieved was, she believed, fully warranted. A self-proclaimed genius, she equated herself with Homer, and to a friend she once remarked, "Besides Shakespeare and me, who do you think there is?" She had a serene confidence in her judgments about life as well as art. She drove her car only in forward gear and refused to use road maps lest they restrict her freedom. She imperiously expected her readers to adopt her literary standards and accept her patterns of discourse. And she was unforgiving of those who disagreed with her—among them Ernest Hemingway, whom she at first admired but later criticized as "yellow," an insult he repaid with pitiless malice in A Moveable Feast *(1964).*

In her writing she often departed from conventional word order and coherence. She submerged her meaning in cryptic language and puzzling abstractions in an attempt to go beneath the surface of language to essential reality. She believed that repetition of words and phrases could erase their superficial meaning and reveal their true sense. William Carlos Williams said she was "smashing every connotation that words have ever had, in order to get them back clean." Gertrude Stein's writing was also made obscure by her use of private language and sexual coding, oblique and concealing references to her homosexuality and her erotic lesbian love affairs.

Her psychological studies had taught her that experience in life is jumbled, disorganized, and she insisted that literature should recreate that jumbled experience. Therefore traditional fiction, with clearly understandable characters and with events organized in sequential time, was false because it presented an artificial world that had never existed.

Her theories have significantly influenced critical inquiry into art and literature. Yet Gertrude Stein remains important not only as a theorist but as a literary stylist who recorded the movement of her own mind as she confronted her world and the world of women like "Gentle Lena." It was a world of profound social, cultural, and intellectual change, a world marked by economic upheavals, artistic and social revolutions, and world wars. She also knew it to be a paradoxical world of unattainable answers and unknown questions. As she lay dying in a Paris hospital, she asked, "What is the answer?" And when no one responded, she demanded, "In that case, what is the question?"

FURTHER READING: D. Sutherland, *Gertrude Stein, A Biography of Her Work,* 1951; B. Reid, *Art by Subtraction, A Dissenting Opinion on Gertrude Stein,* 1958; J. Brinnin, *The Third Rose, Gertrude Stein and Her World,* 1959; R. Bridgman, *Gertrude Stein in Pieces,* 1970; J. Mellow, *Charmed Circle, Gertrude Stein and Company,* 1974; J. Hobhouse, *Everybody Who Was Anybody, A Biography of Gertrude Stein,* 1975; R. Dubnick, *The Structure of Obscurity,* 1984; J. Walker, *The Making of a Modernist,* 1984; *Critical Essays on Gertrude Stein,* ed. M. Hoffman, 1986; *Gertrude Stein,* ed. H. Bloom, 1986; *Gertrude Stein and the Making of Literature,* ed. S. Neuman and I. Nadel, 1988; *A Gertrude Stein Companion,* ed. B. Kellner, 1988; L. Ruddick, *Reading Gertrude Stein,* 1990; J. Bowers, *They Watch Me as They Watch This,* 1991; E. Fifer, *Rescued Readings, A Reconstruction of Gertrude Stein's Difficult Texts,* 1992; E. Berry, *Curved Thought and Textual Wandering, Gertrude Stein's Postmodernism,* 1992; J. Bowers, *Gertrude Stein,* 1993; L. Wagner-Martin, *"Favored Strangers," Gertrude Stein and Her Family,* 1995; *The Critical Response to Gertrude Stein,* ed. Kirk Curnutt, 2000; J. Gill, *Detecting Gertrude Stein, and Other Suspects on the Shadow Side of Modernism,* 2003.

TEXTS: "The Gentle Lena," *Three Lives,* 1909; "Susie Asado," *Geography and Plays,* 1922; "Picasso," *Portraits and Prayers,* 1934.

from *THREE LIVES*

THE GENTLE LENA

Lena was patient, gentle, sweet and german. She had been a servant for four years and had liked it very well.

Lena had been brought from Germany to Bridgepoint by a cousin and had been in the same place there for four years.

This place Lena had found very good. There was a pleasant, unexacting mistress and her children, and they all liked Lena very well.

There was a cook there who scolded Lena a great deal but Lena's german patience held no suffering and the good incessant woman really only scolded so for Lena's good.

Lena's german voice when she knocked and called the family in the morning was as awakening, as soothing, and as appealing, as a delicate soft breeze in midday, summer. She stood in the hallway every morning a long time in her unexpectant and unsuffering german patience calling to the young ones to get up. She would call and wait a long time and then call again, always even, gentle, patient, while the young ones fell back often into that precious, tense, last bit of sleeping that gives a strength of joyous vigor in the young, over them that have come to the readiness of middle age, in their awakening.

Lena had good hard work all morning, and on the pleasant, sunny afternoons she was sent out into the park to sit and watch the little two year old girl baby of the family.

The other girls, all them that make the pleasant, lazy crowd, that watch the children in the sunny afternoons out in the park, all liked the simple, gentle, german Lena very well. They all, too, liked very well to tease her, for it was so easy to make her mixed and troubled, and all helpless, for she could never learn to know just what the other quicker girls meant by the queer things they said.

The two or three of these girls, the ones that Lena always sat with, always worked together to confuse her. Still it was pleasant, all this life for Lena.

The little girl fell down sometimes and cried, and then Lena had to soothe her. When the little girl would drop her hat, Lena had to pick it up and hold it. When the little girl was bad and threw away her playthings, Lena told her she could not have them and took them from her to hold until the little girl should need them.

It was all a peaceful life for Lena, almost as peaceful as a pleasant leisure. The other girls, of course, did tease her, but then that only made a gentle stir within her.

Lena was a brown and pleasant creature, brown as blonde races often have them brown, brown, not with the yellow or the red or the chocolate brown of sun burned countries, but brown with the clear color laid flat on the light toned skin beneath, the plain, spare brown that makes it right to have been made with hazel eyes, and not too abundant straight, brown hair, hair that only later deepens itself into brown from the straw yellow of a german childhood.

Lena had the flat chest, straight back and forward falling shoulders of the patient and enduring working woman, though her body was now still in its milder girlhood and work had not yet made these lines too clear.

The rarer feeling that there was with Lena, showed in all the even quiet of her body movements, but in all it was the strongest in the patient, old-world ignorance, and earth made pureness of her brown, flat, soft featured face. Lena had eyebrows that were a wondrous thickness. They were black, and spread, and very cool, with their dark color and their beauty, and beneath them were her hazel eyes, simple and human, with the earth patience of the working, gentle, german woman.

Yes it was all a peaceful life for Lena. The other girls, of course, did tease her, but then that only made a gentle stir within her.

"What you got on your finger Lena," Mary, one of the girls she always sat with, one day asked her. Mary was good natured, quick, intelligent and Irish.

Lena had just picked up the fancy paper made accordion that the little girl had dropped beside her, and was making it squeak sadly as she pulled it with her brown, strong, awkward finger.

"Why, what is it, Mary, paint?" said Lena, putting her finger to her mouth to taste the dirt spot.

"That's awful poison Lena, don't you know?" said Mary, "that green paint that you just tasted."

Lena had sucked a good deal of the green paint from her finger. She stopped and looked hard at the finger. She did not know just how much Mary meant by what she said.

"Ain't it poison, Nellie, that green paint, that Lena sucked just now," said Mary. "Sure it is Lena, it's real poison, I ain't foolin' this time anyhow."

Lena was a little troubled. She looked hard at her finger where the paint was, and she wondered if she had really sucked it.

It was still a little wet on the edges and she rubbed it off a long time on the inside of her dress, and in between she wondered and looked at the finger and thought, was it really poison that she had just tasted.

"Ain't it too bad, Nellie, Lena should have sucked that," Mary said.

Nellie smiled and did not answer. Nellie was dark and thin, and looked Italian. She had a big mass of black hair that she wore high up on her head, and that made her face look very fine.

Nellie always smiled and did not say much, and then she would look at Lena to perplex her.

And so they all three sat with their little charges in the pleasant sunshine a long time. And Lena would often look at her finger and wonder if it was really poison that she had just tasted and then she would rub her finger on her dress a little harder.

Mary laughed at her and teased her and Nellie smiled a little and looked queerly at her.

Then it came time, for it was growing cooler, for them to drag together the little ones, who had begun to wander, and to take each one back to its own mother. And Lena never knew for certain whether it was really poison, that green stuff that she had tasted.

During these four years of service, Lena always spent her Sundays out at the house of her aunt, who had brought her four years before to Bridgepoint.

This aunt, who had brought Lena, four years before, to Bridgepoint, was a hard, ambitious, well meaning, german woman. Her husband was a grocer in the town, and they were very well to do. Mrs. Haydon, Lena's aunt, had two daughters who were just beginning as young ladies, and she had a little boy who was not honest and who was very hard to manage.

Mrs. Haydon was a short, stout, hard built, german woman. She always hit the ground very firmly and compactly as she walked. Mrs. Haydon was all a compact and well hardened mass, even to her face, reddish and darkened from its early blonde, with its hearty, shiny cheeks, and doubled chin well covered over with the uproll from her short, square neck.

The two daughters, who were fourteen and fifteen, looked like unkneaded, unformed mounds of flesh beside her.

The elder girl, Mathilda, was blonde, and slow, and simple, and quite fat. The younger, Bertha, who was almost as tall as her sister, was dark, and quicker, and she was heavy, too, but not really fat.

These two girls the mother had brought up very firmly. They were well taught for their position. They were always both well dressed, in the same kinds of hats and dresses, as is becoming in two german sisters. The mother liked to have them dressed in red. Their best clothes were red dresses, made of good heavy cloth, and strongly trimmed with braid of a glistening black. They had stiff, red felt hats, trimmed with black velvet ribbon, and a bird. The mother dressed matronly, in a bonnet and in black, always sat between her two big daughters, firm, directing, and repressed.

The only weak spot in this good woman's conduct was the way she spoiled her boy, who was not honest and who was very hard to manage.

The father of this family was a decent, quiet, heavy, and uninterfering german man. He tried to cure the boy of his bad ways, and make him honest, but the mother could not make herself let the father manage, and so the boy was brought up very badly.

Mrs. Haydon's girls were now only just beginning as young ladies, and so to get her niece, Lena, married, was just then the most important thing that Mrs. Haydon had to do.

Mrs. Haydon had four years before gone to Germany to see her parents, and had taken the girls with her. This visit had been for Mrs. Haydon most successful, though her children had not liked it very well.

Mrs. Haydon was a good and generous woman, and she patronized her parents grandly, and all the cousins who came from all about to see her. Mrs. Haydon's people were of the middling class of farmers. They were not peasants, and they lived in a town of some pretension, but it all seemed very poor and smelly to Mrs. Haydon's american born daughters.

Mrs. Haydon liked it all. It was familiar, and then here she was so wealthy and important. She listened and decided, and advised all of her relations how to do things better. She arranged their present and their future for them, and showed them how in the past they had been wrong in all their methods.

Mrs. Haydon's only trouble was with her two daughters, whom she could not make behave well to her parents. The two girls were very nasty to all their numerous relations. Their mother could hardly make them kiss their grandparents, and every day the girls would get a scolding. But then Mrs. Haydon was so very busy that she did not have time to really manage her stubborn daughters.

These hard working, earth-rough german cousins were to these american born children, ugly and dirty and as far below them as were Italian or negro workmen, and they could not see how their mother could ever bear to touch them, and then all the women dressed so funny, and were worked all rough and different.

The two girls stuck up their noses at them all, and always talked in English to each other about how they hated all these people and how they wished their mother would not do so. The girls could talk some German, but they never chose to use it.

It was her eldest brother's family that most interested Mrs. Haydon. Here there were eight children, and out of the eight, five of them were girls.

Mrs. Haydon thought it would be a fine thing to take one of these girls back with her to Bridgepoint and get her well started. Everybody liked that she should do so, and they were all willing that it should be Lena.

Lena was the second girl in her large family. She was at this time just seventeen years old. Lena was not an important daughter in the family. She was always sort of dreamy and not there. She worked hard and went very regularly at it, but even good work never seemed to bring her near.

Lena's age just suited Mrs. Haydon's purpose. Lena could first go out to service, and learn how to do things, and then, when she was a little older, Mrs. Haydon could get her a good husband. And then Lena was so still and docile, she would never want to do things her own way. And then, too, Mrs. Haydon, with all her hardness had wisdom, and she could feel the rarer strain there was in Lena.

Lena was willing to go with Mrs. Haydon. Lena did not like her german life very well. It was not the hard work but the roughness that disturbed her. The people were not gentle, and the men when they were glad were very boisterous, and would lay hold of her and roughly tease her. They were good people enough around her, but it was all harsh and dreary for her.

Lena did not really know that she did not like it. She did not know that she was always dreamy and not there. She did not think whether it would be different for her away off there in Bridgepoint. Mrs. Haydon took her and got her different kinds of dresses, and then took her with them to the steamer. Lena did not really know what it was that had happened to her.

Mrs. Haydon, and her daughters, and Lena traveled second class on the steamer. Mrs. Haydon's daughters hated that their mother should take Lena. They hated to have a cousin, who was to them, little better than a nigger, and then everybody on the steamer there would see her. Mrs. Haydon's daughters said things like this to their mother, but she never stopped to hear them, and the girls did not dare to make their meaning very clear. And so they could only go on hating Lena hard, together. They could not stop her from going back with them to Bridgepoint.

Lena was very sick on the voyage. She thought, surely before it was over that she would die. She was so sick she could not even wish that she had not started. She could not eat, she could not moan, she was just blank and scared, and sure that every minute she would die. She could not hold herself in, nor help herself in her trouble. She just staid where she had been put, pale, and scared, and weak, and sick, and sure that she was going to die.

Mathilda and Bertha Haydon had no trouble from having Lena for a cousin on the voyage, until the last day that they were on the ship, and by that time they had made their friends and could explain.

Mrs. Haydon went down every day to Lena, gave her things to make her better, held her head when it was needful, and generally was good and did her duty by her.

Poor Lena had no power to be strong in such trouble. She did not know how to yield to her sickness nor endure. She lost all her little sense of being in her suffering. She was so scared, and then at her best, Lena, who was patient, sweet, and quiet, had not self-control, nor any active courage.

Poor Lena was so scared and weak, and every minute she was sure that she would die.

After Lena was on land again a little while, she forgot all her bad suffering. Mrs. Haydon got her the good place, with the pleasant unexacting mistress, and her children, and Lena began to learn some English and soon was very happy and content.

All her Sundays out Lena spent at Mrs. Haydon's house. Lena would have liked much better to spend her Sundays with the girls she always sat with, and who often asked her, and who teased her and made a gentle stir within her, but it never came to Lena's unexpectant and unsuffering german nature to do something different from what was expected of her, just because she would like it that way better. Mrs. Haydon had said that Lena was to come to her house every other Sunday, and so Lena always went there.

Mrs. Haydon was the only one of her family who took any interest in Lena. Mr. Haydon did not think much of her. She was his wife's cousin and he was good to her, but she was for him stupid, and a little simple, and very dull, and sure some day to need help and to be in trouble. All young poor relations, who were brought from Germany to Bridgepoint were sure, before long, to need help and to be in trouble.

The little Haydon boy was always very nasty to her. He was a hard child for any one to manage, and his mother spoiled him very badly. Mrs. Haydon's daughters as they grew older did not learn to like Lena any better. Lena never knew that she did not like them either. She did not know that she was only happy with the other quicker girls, she always sat with in the park, and who laughed at her and always teased her.

Mathilda Haydon, the simple, fat, blonde, older daughter felt very badly that she had to say that this was her cousin Lena, this Lena who was little better for her than a nigger. Mathilda was an overgrown, slow, flabby, blonde, stupid, fat girl, just beginning as a woman; thick in her speech and dull and simple in her mind, and very jealous of all her family and of other girls, and proud that she could have good dresses and new hats and learn music, and hating very badly to have a cousin who was a common servant. And then Mathilda remembered very strongly that dirty nasty place that Lena came from and that Mathilda had so turned up her nose at, and where she had been made so angry because her mother scolded her and liked all those rough, cow-smelly people.

Then, too, Mathilda would get very mad when her mother had Lena at their parties, and when she talked about how good Lena was, to certain german mothers in whose sons, perhaps, Mrs. Haydon might find Lena a good husband. All this would make the dull, blonde, fat Mathilda very angry. Sometimes she would get so angry that she would, in her thick, slow way, and with jealous anger blazing in her light blue eyes, tell her mother that she did not see how she could like that nasty Lena; and then her mother would scold Mathilda, and tell her that she knew her cousin Lena was poor and Mathilda must be good to poor people.

Mathilda Haydon did not like relations to be poor. She told all her girl friends what she thought of Lena, and so the girls would never talk to Lena at Mrs. Haydon's parties. But Lena in her unsuffering and unexpectant patience never really knew that she was slighted. When Mathilda was with her girls in the street or in the park and would see Lena, she always turned up her nose and barely nodded to her, and then she would tell her friends how funny her mother was to take care of people like that Lena, and how, back in Germany, all Lena's people lived just like pigs.

The younger daughter, the dark, large, but not fat, Bertha Haydon, who was very quick in her mind, and in her ways, and who was the favorite with her father, did not like Lena, either. She did not like her because for her Lena was a fool and so stupid, and she would let those Irish and Italian girls laugh at her and tease her, and everybody always made fun of Lena, and Lena never got mad, or even had sense enough to know that they were all making an awful fool of her.

Bertha Haydon hated people to be fools. Her father, too, thought Lena was a fool, and so neither the father nor the daughter ever paid any attention to Lena, although she came to their house every other Sunday.

Lena did not know how all the Haydons felt. She came to her aunt's house all her Sunday afternoons that she had out, because Mrs. Haydon had told her she must do so. In the same way Lena always saved all of her wages. She never thought of any way to spend it. The german cook, the good woman who always scolded Lena, helped her to put it in the bank each month, as soon as she got it. Sometimes before it got into the bank to be taken care of, somebody would ask Lena for it. The little Haydon boy sometimes asked and would get it, and sometimes some of the girls, the ones Lena always sat with, needed some more money; but the german cook, who always scolded Lena, saw to it that this did not happen very often. When it did happen she would scold Lena very sharply, and for the next few months she would not let Lena touch her wages, but put it in the bank for her on the same day that Lena got it.

So Lena always saved her wages, for she never thought to spend them, and she always went to her aunt's house for her Sundays because she did not know that she could do anything different.

Mrs. Haydon felt more and more every year that she had done right to bring Lena back with her, for it was all coming out just as she had expected. Lena was good and never wanted her own way, she was learning English, and saving all her wages, and soon Mrs. Haydon would get her a good husband.

All these four years Mrs. Haydon was busy looking around among all the german people that she knew for the right man to be Lena's husband, and now at last she was quite decided.

The man Mrs. Haydon wanted for Lena was a young german-american tailor, who worked with his father. He was good and all the family were very saving, and Mrs. Haydon was sure that this would be just right for Lena, and then too, this young tailor always did whatever his father and his mother wanted.

This old german tailor and his wife, the father and the mother of Herman Kreder, who was to marry Lena Mainz, were very thrifty, careful people. Herman was the only child they had left with them, and he always did everything they wanted. Herman was now twenty-eight years old, but he had never stopped being scolded and directed by his father and his mother. And now they wanted to see him married.

Herman Kreder did not care much to get married. He was a gentle soul and a little fearful. He had a sullen temper, too. He was obedient to his father and his mother. He always did his work well. He often went out on Saturday nights and on Sundays, with other men. He liked it with them but he never became really joyous. He liked to be with men and he hated to have women with them. He was obedient to his mother, but he did not care much to get married.

Mrs. Haydon and the elder Kreders had often talked the marriage over. They all three liked it very well. Lena would do anything that Mrs. Haydon wanted, and Herman was always obedient in everything to his father and his mother. Both Lena and Herman were saving and good workers and neither of them ever wanted their own way.

The elder Kreders, everybody knew, had saved up all their money, and they were hard, good german people, and Mrs. Haydon was sure that with these people Lena would never be in any trouble. Mr. Haydon would not say anything about it. He knew old Kreder had a lot of money and owned some good houses, and he did not care what his wife did with that simple, stupid Lena, so long as she would be sure never to need help or to be in trouble.

Lena did not care much to get married. She liked her life very well where she was working. She did not think much about Herman Kreder. She thought he was a good man and she always found him very quiet. Neither of them ever spoke much to the other. Lena did not care much just then about getting married.

Mrs. Haydon spoke to Lena about it very often. Lena never answered anything at all. Mrs. Haydon thought, perhaps Lena did not like Herman Kreder. Mrs. Haydon could not believe that any girl not even Lena, really had no feeling about getting married.

Mrs. Haydon spoke to Lena very often about Herman. Mrs. Haydon sometimes got very angry with Lena. She was afraid that Lena, for once, was going to be stubborn, now when it was all fixed right for her to be married.

"Why you stand there so stupid, why don't you answer, Lena," said Mrs. Haydon one Sunday, at the end of a long talking that she was giving Lena about Herman Kreder, and about Lena's getting married to him.

"Yes ma'am," said Lena, and then Mrs. Haydon was furious with this stupid Lena. "Why don't you answer with some sense, Lena, when I ask you if you don't like Herman Kreder. You stand there so stupid and don't answer just like you ain't heard a word what I been saying to you. I never see anybody like you, Lena. If you going to burst out at all, why don't you burst out sudden instead of standing there so silly and don't answer. And here I am so good to you, and find you a good husband so you can have a place to live in all your own. Answer me, Lena, don't you like Herman Kreder? He is a fine young fellow, almost too good for you, Lena, when you stand there so stupid and don't make no answer. There ain't many poor girls that get the chance you got now to get married."

"Why, I do anything you say, Aunt Mathilda. Yes, I like him. He don't say much to me, but I guess he is a good man, and I do anything you say for me to do."

"Well then Lena, why you stand there so silly all the time and not answer when I asked you."

"I didn't hear you say you wanted I should say anything to you. I didn't know you wanted me to say nothing. I do whatever you tell me it's right for me to do. I marry Herman Kreder, if you want me."

And so for Lena Mainz the match was made.

Old Mrs. Kreder did not discuss the matter with her Herman. She never thought that she needed to talk such things over with him. She just told him about getting married to Lena Mainz who was a good worker and very saving and never wanted her own way, and Herman made his usual little grunt in answer to her.

Mrs. Kreder and Mrs. Haydon fixed the day and made all the arrangements for the wedding and invited everybody who ought to be there to see them married.

In three months Lena Mainz and Herman Kreder were to be married.

Mrs. Haydon attended to Lena's getting all the things that she needed. Lena had to help a good deal with the sewing. Lena did not sew very well. Mrs. Haydon scolded because Lena did not do it better, but then she was very good to Lena, and she hired a girl to come and help her. Lena still stayed on with her pleasant mistress, but she spent all her evenings and her Sundays with her aunt and all the sewing.

Mrs. Haydon got Lena some nice dresses. Lena liked that very well. Lena liked having new hats even better, and Mrs. Haydon had some made for her by a real milliner who made them very pretty.

Lena was nervous these days, but she did not think much about getting married. She did not know really what it was, that, which was always coming nearer.

Lena liked the place where she was with the pleasant mistress and the good cook, who always scolded, and she liked the girls she always sat with. She did not ask if she would like being married any better. She always did whatever her aunt said and expected, but she was always nervous when she saw the Kreders with their Herman. She was excited and she liked her new hats, and everybody teased her and every day her marrying was coming nearer, and yet she did not really know what it was, this that was about to happen to her.

Herman Kreder knew more what it meant to be married and he did not like it very well. He did not like to see girls and he did not want to have to have one always near him. Herman always did everything that his father and his mother wanted and now they wanted that he should be married.

Herman had a sullen temper; he was gentle and he never said much. He liked to go out with other men, but he never wanted that there should be any women with them. The men all teased him about getting married. Herman did not mind the teasing but he did not like very well the getting married and having a girl always with him.

Three days before the wedding day, Herman went away to the country to be gone over Sunday. He and Lena were to be married Tuesday afternoon. When the day came Herman had not been seen or heard from.

The old Kreder couple had not worried much about it. Herman always did everything they wanted and he would surely come back in time to get married. But when Monday night came, and there was no Herman, they went to Mrs. Haydon to tell her what had happened.

Mrs. Haydon got very much excited. It was hard enough to work so as to get everything all ready, and then to have that silly Herman go off that way, so no one could tell what was going to happen. Here was Lena and everything all ready, and now they would have to make the wedding later so that they would know that Herman would be sure to be there.

Mrs. Haydon was very much excited, and then she could not say much to the old Kreder couple. She did not want to make them angry, for she wanted very badly now that Lena should be married to their Herman.

At last it was decided that the wedding should be put off a week longer. Old Mr. Kreder would go to New York to find Herman, for it was very likely that Herman had gone there to his married sister.

Mrs. Haydon sent word around, about waiting until a week from that Tuesday, to everybody that had been invited, and then Tuesday morning she sent for Lena to come down to see her.

Mrs. Haydon was very angry with poor Lena when she saw her. She scolded her hard because she was so foolish, and now Herman had gone off and nobody could tell where he had gone to, and all because Lena always was so dumb and silly. And Mrs. Haydon was just like a mother to her, and Lena always stood there so stupid and did not answer what anybody asked her, and Herman was so silly too, and now his father had to go and find him. Mrs. Haydon did not think that any old people should be good to their children. Their children always were so thankless, and never paid any attention, and older people were always doing things for their good. Did Lena think it gave Mrs. Haydon any pleasure, to work so hard to make Lena happy, and get her a good husband, and then Lena was so thankless and never did anything that anybody wanted. It was a lesson to poor Mrs. Haydon not to do things any more for anybody. Let everybody take care of themselves and never come to her with any troubles; she knew better now than to meddle to make other people happy. It just made trouble for her and her husband did not like it. He always said she was too good, and nobody ever thanked her for it, and there Lena was always standing stupid and not answering anything anybody wanted. Lena could always talk enough to those silly girls she liked so much, and always sat with, but who never did anything for her except to take away her money, and here was her aunt who tried so hard and was so good to her and treated her just like one of her own children and Lena stood there, and never made any answer and never tried to please her aunt, or to do anything that her aunt wanted. "No, it ain't no use your standin' there and cryin', now, Lena. It's too late now to care about that Herman. You should have cared some before, and then you wouldn't have to stand and cry now, and be a disappointment to me, and then I get scolded by my husband for taking care of everybody, and nobody ever thankful. I am glad you got the sense to feel sorry now, Lena, anyway, and I try to do what I can to help you out in your trouble, only you don't deserve to have anybody take any trouble for you. But perhaps you know better next time. You go home now and take care you don't spoil your clothes and that new hat, you had no business to be wearin' that this morning, but you ain't got no sense at all, Lena. I never in my life see anybody be so stupid."

Mrs. Haydon stopped and poor Lena stood there in her hat, all trimmed with pretty flowers, and the tears coming out of her eyes, and Lena did not know what it was that she had done, only she was not going to be married and it was a disgrace for a girl to be left by a man on the very day she was to be married.

Lena went home all alone, and cried in the street car.

Poor Lena cried very hard all alone in the street car. She almost spoiled her new hat with her hitting it against the window in her crying. Then she remembered that she must not do so.

The conductor was a kind man and he was very sorry when he saw her crying. "Don't feel so bad, you get another feller, you are such a nice girl," he said to make her cheerful. "But Aunt Mathilda said now, I never get married," poor Lena sobbed out for her answer. "Why you really got trouble like that," said the conductor, "I just said that now to josh you. I didn't ever think you really was left by a feller. He must be a stupid feller. But don't you worry, he wasn't much good if he could go away and leave you, lookin' to be such a nice girl. You just tell all your trouble to me, and I help you." The car was empty and the conductor sat down beside her to put his arm around her, and to be a comfort to her. Lena suddenly remembered where she was, and if she did things like that her aunt would scold her. She moved away from the man into the corner. He laughed, "Don't be scared," he said, "I wasn't going to hurt you. But you just keep up your spirit. You are a real nice girl, and you'll be sure to get a real good husband. Don't you let nobody fool you. You're all right and I don't want to scare you."

The conductor went back to his platform to help a passenger get on the car. All the time Lena stayed in the street car, he would come in every little while and reassure her, about her not to feel so bad about a man who hadn't no more sense than to go away and leave her. She'd be sure yet to get a good man, she needn't be so worried, he frequently assured her.

He chatted with the other passenger who had just come in, a very well dressed old man, and then with another who came in later, a good sort of a working man, and then another who came in, a nice lady, and he told them all about Lena's having trouble, and it was too bad there were men who treated a poor girl so badly. And everybody in the car was sorry for poor Lena and the workman tried to cheer her, and the old man looked sharply at her, and said she looked like a good girl, but she ought to be more careful and not to be so careless, and things like that would not happen to her, and the nice lady went and sat beside her and Lena liked it, though she shrank away from being near her.

So Lena was feeling a little better when she got off the car, and the conductor helped her, and he called out to her, "You be sure you keep up a good heart now. He wasn't no good that feller and you were lucky for to lose him. You'll get a real man yet, one that will be better for you. Don't you be worried, you're a real nice girl as I ever see in such trouble," and the conductor shook his head and went back into his car to talk it over with the other passengers he had there.

The german cook, who always scolded Lena, was very angry when she heard the story. She never did think Mrs. Haydon would do so much for Lena, though she was always talking so grand about what she could do for everybody. The good german cook always had been a little distrustful of her. People who always thought they were so much never did really do things right for anybody. Not that Mrs. Haydon wasn't a good woman. Mrs. Haydon was a real, good, german woman, and she did really mean to do well by her niece Lena. The cook knew that very well, and she had always said so, and she always had liked and respected Mrs. Haydon, who always acted very proper to her, and Lena was so backward, when there was a man to talk to, Mrs. Haydon did have hard work when she tried to marry Lena. Mrs. Haydon was a good woman, only she did talk sometimes too grand. Perhaps this trouble would make her see it wasn't always so easy to do, to make everybody do everything just like she wanted. The cook was very sorry now for Mrs. Haydon. All this must be such a disappointment, and such a worry to her, and she really had always been very good to Lena. But Lena had better go and put on her other clothes and stop with all that crying. That wouldn't do nothing now to help her, and if Lena would be a good girl, and just be real patient, her aunt would make it all come out right yet for her. "I just tell Mrs. Aldrich, Lena, you stay here yet a little longer. You know she is always so good to you, Lena, and I know she let you, and I tell her all about that stupid Herman Kreder. I got no patience, Lena, with anybody who can be so stupid. You just stop now with your crying, Lena, and take off them good clothes and put them away so you don't spoil them when you need them, and you can help me with the dishes and everything will come off better for you. You see if I ain't right by what I tell you. You just stop crying now Lena quick, or else I scold you."

Lena still choked a little and was very miserable inside her but she did everything just as the cook told her.

The girls Lena always sat with were very sorry to see her look so sad with her trouble. Mary the Irish girl sometimes got very angry with her. Mary was always very hot when she talked of Lena's aunt Mathilda, who thought she was so grand, and had such stupid, stuck up daughters. Mary wouldn't be a fat fool like that ugly tempered Mathilda Haydon, not for anything anybody could ever give her. How Lena could keep on going there so much when they all always acted as if she was just dirt to them, Mary never could see. But Lena never had any sense of how she should make people stand round for her, and that was always all the trouble with her. And poor Lena, she was so stupid to be sorry for losing that gawky fool who didn't ever know what he wanted and just said "ja" to his mamma and his papa, like a baby, and was scared to look at a girl straight, and then sneaked away the last day like as if somebody was going to do something to him. Disgrace, Lena talking about disgrace! It was a disgrace for a girl to be seen with the likes of him, let alone to be married to him. But that poor Lena, she never did know how to show herself off for what she was really. Disgrace to have him go away and leave her. Mary would just like to get a chance to show him. If Lena wasn't worth fifteen like Herman Kreder, Mary would just eat her own head all up. It was a good riddance Lena had of that Herman Kreder and his stingy, dirty parents, and if Lena didn't stop crying about it,—Mary would just naturally despise her.

Poor Lena, she knew very well how Mary meant it all, this she was always saying to her. But Lena was very miserable inside her. She felt the disgrace it was for a decent german girl that a man should go away and leave her. Lena knew very well that her aunt was right when she said the way Herman had acted to her was a disgrace to everyone that knew her. Mary and Nellie and the other girls she always sat with were always very good to Lena but that did not make her trouble any better. It was a disgrace the way Lena had been left, to any decent family, and that could never be made any different to her.

And so the slow days wore on, and Lena never saw her Aunt Mathilda. At last on Sunday she got word by a boy to go and see her aunt Mathilda. Lena's heart beat quick for she was very nervous now with all this that had happened to her. She went just as quickly as she could to see her Aunt Mathilda.

Mrs. Haydon quick, as soon as she saw Lena, began to scold her for keeping her aunt waiting so long for her, and for not coming in all the week to see her, to see if her aunt should need her, and so her aunt had to send a boy to tell her. But it was easy, even for Lena, to see that her aunt was not really angry with her. It wasn't Lena's fault, went on Mrs. Haydon, that everything was going to happen all right for her. Mrs. Haydon was very tired taking all this trouble for her, and when Lena couldn't even take trouble to come and see her aunt, to see if she needed anything to tell her. But Mrs. Haydon really never minded things like that when she could do things for anybody. She was tired now, all the trouble she had been taking to make things right for Lena, but perhaps now Lena heard it she would learn a little to be thankful to her. "You get all ready to be married Tuesday. Lena, you hear me." said Mrs. Haydon to her. "You come here Tuesday morning and I have everything all ready for you. You wear your new dress I got you, and your hat with all them flowers on it, and you be very careful coming you don't get your things all dirty, you so careless all the time, Lena, and not thinking, and you act sometimes you never got no head at all on you. You go home now, and you tell your Mrs. Aldrich that you leave her Tuesday. Don't you go forgetting now, Lena, anything I ever told you what you should do to be careful. You be a good girl, now Lena. You get married Tuesday to Herman Kreder." And that was all Lena ever knew of what had happened all this week to Herman Kreder. Lena forgot there was anything to know about it. She was really to be married Tuesday, and her Aunt Mathilda said she was a good girl, and now there was no disgrace left upon her.

Lena now fell back into the way she always had of being always dreamy and not here, the way she always had been, except for the few days she was so excited, because she had been left by a man the very day she was to have been married. Lena was a little nervous all these last days, but she did not think much about what it meant for her to be married.

Herman Kreder was not so content about it. He was quiet and was sullen and he knew he could not help it. He knew now he just had to let himself get married. It was not that Herman did not like Lena Mainz. She was as good as any other girl could be for him. She was a little better perhaps than other girls he saw, she was so very quiet, but Herman did not like to always have to have a girl around him. Herman had always done everything that his mother and his father wanted. His father had found him in New York, where Herman had gone to be with his married sister.

Herman's father when he had found him coaxed Herman a long time and went on whole days with his complaining to him, always troubled but gentle and quite patient with him, and always he was worrying to Herman about what was the right way his boy Herman should always do, always whatever it was his mother ever wanted from him, and always Herman never made him any answer.

Old Mr. Kreder kept on saying to him, he did not see how Herman could think now, it could be any different. When you make a bargain you just got to stick right to it, that was the only way old Mr. Kreder could ever see it, and saying you would get married to a girl and she got everything all ready, that was a bargain just like one you make in business and Herman he had made it, and now Herman he would just have to do it, old Mr. Kreder didn't see there was any other way a good boy like his Herman had, to do it. And then too that Lena Mainz was such a nice girl and Herman hadn't ought to really give his father so much trouble and make him pay out all that money, to come all the way to New York just to find him, and they both lose all that time from their working, when all Herman had to do was just to stand up, for an hour, and then he would be all right married, and it would be all over for him, and then everything at home would never be any different to him.

And his father went on; there was his poor mother saying always how her Herman always did everything before she ever wanted, and now just because he got notions in him, and wanted to show people how he could be stubborn, he was making all this trouble for her, and making them pay all that money just to run around and find him. "You got no idea Herman, how bad mama is feeling about the way you been acting Herman," said old Mr. Kreder to him. "She says she never can understand how you can be so thankless Herman. It hurts her very much you been so stubborn, and she find you such a nice girl for you, like Lena Mainz who is always just so quiet and always saves up all her wages, and she never wanting her own way at all like some girls are always all the time to have it, and your mama trying so hard, just so you could be comfortable Herman to be married, and then you act so stubborn Herman. You like all young people Herman, you think only about yourself, and what you are just wanting, and your mama she is thinking only what is good for you to have, for you in the future. Do you think your mama wants to have a girl around to be a bother, for herself, Herman. Its just for you Herman she is always thinking, and she talks always about how happy she will be, when she sees her Herman married to a nice girl, and then when she fixed it all up so good for you, so it never would be any bother to you, just the way she wanted you should like it, and you say yes all right, I do it, and then you go away like this and act stubborn, and make all this trouble everybody to take for you, and we spend money, and I got to travel all round to find you. You come home now with me Herman and get married, and I tell your mama she better not say anything to you about how much it cost me to come all the way to look for you—Hey Herman," said his father coaxing, "Hey, you come home now and get married. All you got to do Herman is just to stand up for an hour Herman, and then you don't never to have any more bother to it—Hey Herman!—you come home with me to-morrow and get married. Hey Herman."

Herman's married sister liked her brother Herman, and she had always tried to help him, when there was anything she knew he wanted. She liked it that he was so good and always did everything that their father and their mother wanted, but still she wished it could be that he could have more his own way, if there was anything he ever wanted.

But now she thought Herman with his girl was very funny. She wanted that Herman should be married. She thought it would do him lots of good to get married. She laughed at Herman when she heard the story. Until his father came to find him, she did not know why it was Herman had come just then to New York to see her. When she heard the story she laughed a good deal at her brother Herman and teased him a good deal about his running away, because he didn't want to have a girl to be all the time around him.

Herman's married sister liked her brother Herman, and she did not want him not to like to be with women. He was good, her brother Herman, and it would surely do him good to get married. It would make him stand up for himself stronger. Herman's sister always laughed at him and always she would try to reassure him. "Such a nice man as my brother Herman acting like as if he was afraid of women. Why the girls all like a man like you Herman, if you didn't always run away when you saw them. It do you good really Herman to get married, and then you got somebody you can boss around when you want to. It do you good Herman to get married, you see if you don't like it, when you really done it. You go along home now with papa, Herman and get married to that Lena. You don't know how nice you like it Herman when you try once how you can do it. You just don't be afraid of nothing, Herman. You good enough for any girl to marry, Herman. Any girl be glad to have a man like you to be always with them Herman. You just go along home with papa and try it what I say, Herman. Oh you so funny Herman, when you sit there, and then run away and leave your girl behind you. I know she is crying like anything Herman for to lose you. Don't be bad to her Herman. You go along home with papa now and get married Herman. I'd be awful ashamed Herman, to really have a brother didn't have spirit enough to get married, when a girl is just dying for to have him. You always like me to be with you Herman. I don't see why you say you don't want a girl to be all the time around you. You always been good to me Herman, and I know you always be good to that Lena, and you soon feel just like as if she had always been there with you. Don't act like as if you wasn't a nice strong man, Herman. Really I laugh at you Herman, but you know I like awful well to see you real happy. You go home and get married to that Lena, Herman. She is a real pretty girl and real nice and good and quiet and she make my brother Herman very happy. You just stop your fussing now with Herman, papa. He go with you to-morrow papa, and you see he like it so much to be married, he make everybody laugh just to see him be so happy. Really truly, that's the way it will be with you Herman. You just listen to me what I tell you Herman." And so his sister laughed at him and reassured him, and his father kept on telling what the mother always said about her Herman, and he coaxed him and Herman never said anything in answer, and his sister packed his things up and was very cheerful with him, and she kissed him, and then she laughed and then she kissed him, and his father went and bought the tickets for the train, and at last late on Sunday he brought Herman back to Bridgepoint with him.

It was always very hard to keep Mrs. Kreder from saying what she thought, to her Herman, but her daughter had written her a letter, so as to warn her not to say anything about what he had been doing, to him, and her husband came in with Herman and said, "Here we are come home mama, Herman and me, and we are very tired it was so crowded coming," and then he whispered to her. "You be good to Herman, mama, he didn't mean to make us so much trouble," and so old Mrs. Kreder, held in what she felt was so strong in her to say to her Herman. She just said very stiffly to him, "I'm glad to see you come home to-day, Herman." Then she went to arrange it all with Mrs. Haydon.

Herman was now again just like he always had been, sullen and very good, and very quiet, and always ready to do whatever his mother and his father wanted. Tuesday morning came, Herman got his new clothes on and went with his father and his mother to stand up for an hour and get married. Lena was there in her new dress, and her hat with all the pretty flowers, and she was very nervous for now she knew she was really very soon to be married. Mrs. Haydon had everything all ready. Everybody was there just as they should be and very soon Herman Kreder and Lena Mainz were married.

When everything was really over, they went back to the Kreder house together. They were all now to live together, Lena and Herman and the old father and the old mother, in the house where Mr. Kreder had worked so many years as a tailor, with his son Herman always there to help him.

Irish Mary had often said to Lena she never did see how Lena could ever want to have anything to do with Herman Kreder and his dirty stingy parents. The old Kreders were to an Irish nature, a stingy, dirty couple. They had not the free-hearted, thoughtless, fighting, mud bespattered, ragged, peat-smoked cabin dirt that Irish Mary knew and could forgive and love. Theirs was the german dirt of saving, of being dowdy and loose and foul in your clothes so as to save them and yourself in washing, having your hair greasy to save it in the soap and drying, having your clothes dirty, not in freedom, but because so it was cheaper, keeping the house close and smelly because so it cost less to get it heated, living so poorly not only so as to save money but so they should never even know themselves that they had it, working all the time not only because from their nature they just had to and because it made them money but also that they never could be put in any way to make them spend their money.

This was the place Lena now had for her home and to her it was very different than it could be for an Irish Mary. She too was german and was thrifty, though she was always so dreamy and not there. Lena was always careful with things and she always saved her money, for that was the only way she knew how to do it. She never had taken care of her own money and she never had thought how to use it.

Lena Mainz had been, before she was Mrs. Herman Kreder, always clean and decent in her clothes and in her person, but it was not because she ever thought about it or really needed so to have it, it was the way her people did in the german country where she came from, and her Aunt Mathilda and the good german cook who always scolded, had kept her on and made her, with their scoldings, always more careful to keep clean and to wash real often. But there was no deep need in all this for Lena and so, though Lena did not like the old Kreders, though she really did not know that, she did not think about their being stingy dirty people.

Herman Kreder was cleaner than the old people, just because it was his nature to keep cleaner, but he was used to his mother and his father, and he never thought that they should keep things cleaner. And Herman too always saved all his money, except for that little beer he drank when he went out with other men of an evening the way he always liked to do it, and he never thought of any other way to spend it. His father had always kept all the money for them and he always was doing business with it. And then too Herman really had no money, for he always had worked for his father, and his father had never thought to pay him.

And so they began all four to live in the Kreder house together, and Lena began soon with it to look careless and a little dirty, and to be more lifeless with it, and nobody ever noticed much what Lena wanted, and she never really knew herself what she needed.

The only real trouble that came to Lena with their living all four there together, was the way old Mrs. Kreder scolded. Lena had always been used to being scolded, but this scolding of old Mrs. Kreder was very different from the way she ever before had had to endure it.

Herman, now he was married to her, really liked Lena very well. He did not care very much about her but she never was a bother to him being there around him, only when his mother worried and was nasty to them because Lena was so careless, and did not know how to save things right for them with their eating, and all the other ways with money, that the old woman had to save it.

Herman Kreder had always done everything his mother and his father wanted but he did not really love his parents very deeply. With Herman it was always only that he hated to have any struggle. It was all always all right with him when he could just go along and do the same thing over every day with his working, and not to hear things, and not to have people make him listen to their anger. And now his marriage, and he just knew it would, was making trouble for him. It made him hear more what his mother was always saying, with her scolding. He had to really hear it now because Lena was there, and she was so scared and dull always when she heard it. Herman knew very well with his mother, it was all right if one ate very little and worked hard all day and did not hear her when she scolded, the way Herman always had done before they were so foolish about his getting married and having a girl there to be all the time around him, and now he had to help her so the girl could learn too, not to hear it when his mother scolded, and not to look so scared, and not to eat much, and always to be sure to save it.

Herman really did not know very well what he could do to help Lena to understand it. He could never answer his mother back to help Lena, that never would make things any better for her, and he never could feel in himself any way to comfort Lena, to make her strong not to hear his mother, in all the awful ways she always scolded. It just worried Herman to have it like that all the time around him. Herman did not know much about how a man could make a struggle with a mother, to do much to keep her quiet, and indeed Herman never knew much how to make a struggle against anyone who really wanted to have anything very badly. Herman all his life never wanted anything so badly, that he would really make a struggle against any one to get it. Herman all his life only wanted to live regular and quiet, and not talk much and to do the same way every day like every other with his working. And now his mother had made him get married to this Lena and now with his mother making all that scolding, he had all this trouble and this worry always on him.

Mrs. Haydon did not see Lena now very often. She had not lost her interest in her niece Lena, but Lena could not come much to her house to see her, it would not be right, now Lena was a married woman. And then too Mrs. Haydon had her hands full just then with her two daughters, for she was getting them ready to find them good husbands, and then too her own husband now worried her very often about her always spoiling that boy of hers, so he would be sure to turn out no good and be a disgrace to a german family, and all because his mother always spoiled him. All these things were very worrying now to Mrs. Haydon, but still she wanted to be good to Lena, though she could not see her very often. She only saw her when Mrs. Haydon went to call on Mrs. Kreder or when Mrs. Kreder came to see Mrs. Haydon, and that never could be very often. Then too these days Mrs. Haydon could not scold Lena, Mrs. Kreder was always there with her, and it would not be right to scold Lena when Mrs. Kreder was there, who had now the real right to do it. And so her aunt always said nice things now to Lena, and though Mrs. Haydon sometimes was a little worried when she saw Lena looking sad and not careful, she did not have time just then to really worry much about it.

Lena now never any more saw the girls she always used to sit with. She had no way now to see them and it was not in Lena's nature to search out ways to see them, nor did she now ever think much of the days when she had been used to see them. They never any of them had come to the Kreder house to see her. Not even Irish Mary had ever thought to come to see her. Lena had been soon forgotten by them. They had soon passed away from Lena and now Lena never thought any more that she had ever known them.

The only one of her old friends who tried to know what Lena liked and what she needed, and who always made Lena come to see her, was the good german cook who had always scolded. She now scolded Lena hard for letting herself go so, and going out when she was looking so untidy. "I know you going to have a baby Lena, but that's no way for you to be looking. I am ashamed most to see you come and sit here in my kitchen, looking so sloppy and like you never used to Lena. I never see anybody like you Lena. Herman is very good to you, you always say so, and he don't treat you bad ever though you don't deserve to have anybody good to you, you so careless all the time, Lena, letting yourself go like you never had anybody tell you what was the right way you should know how to be looking. No, Lena, I don't see no reason you should let yourself go so and look so untidy Lena, so I am ashamed to see you sit there looking so ugly, Lena. No Lena that ain't no way ever I see a woman make things come out better, letting herself go so every way and crying all the time like as if you had real trouble. I never wanted to see you marry Herman Kreder, Lena, I knew what you got to stand with that old woman always, and that old man, he is so stingy too and he don't say things out but he ain't any better in his heart than his wife with her bad ways, I know that Lena, I know they don't hardly give you enough to eat, Lena, I am real sorry for you, Lena, you know that Lena, but that ain't any way to be going round so untidy Lena, even if you have got all that trouble. You never see me do like that Lena, though sometimes I got a headache so I can't see to stand to be working hardly, and nothing comes right with all my cooking, but I always see Lena, I look decent. That's the only way a german girl can make things come out right Lena. You hear me what I am saying to you Lena. Now you eat something nice Lena, I got it all ready for you, and you wash up and be careful Lena and the baby will come all right to you, and then I make your Aunt Mathilda see that you live in a house soon all alone with Herman and your baby, and then everything go better for you. You hear me what I say to you Lena. Now don't let me ever see you come looking like this any more Lena, and you just stop with that always crying. You ain't got no reason to be sitting there now with all that crying, I never see anybody have trouble it did them any good to do the way you are doing, Lena. You hear me Lena. You go home now and you be good the way I tell you Lena, and I see what I can do. I make your Aunt Mathilda make old Mrs. Kreder let you be till you get your baby all right. Now don't you be scared and so silly Lena. I don't like to see you act so silly Lena when really you got a nice man and so many things really any girl should be grateful to be having. Now you go home Lena to-day and you do the way I say, to you, and I see what I can do to help you."

"Yes Mrs. Aldrich" said the good german woman to her mistress later, "Yes Mrs. Aldrich that's the way it is with them girls when they want so to get married. They dont know when they got it good Mrs. Aldrich. They never know what it is they're really wanting when they got it, Mrs. Aldrich. There's that poor Lena, she just been here crying and looking so careless so I scold her, but that was no good that marrying for that poor Lena, Mrs. Aldrich. She do look so pale and sad now Mrs. Aldrich, it just break my heart to see her. She was a good girl was Lena, Mrs. Aldrich, and I never had no trouble with her like I got with so many young girls nowadays, Mrs. Aldrich, and I never see any girl any better to work right than our Lena, and now she got to stand it all the time with that old woman Mrs. Kreder. My! Mrs. Aldrich, she is a bad old woman to her. I never see Mrs. Aldrich how old people can be so bad to young girls and not have no kind of patience with them. If Lena could only live with her Herman, he ain't so bad the way men are, Mrs. Aldrich, but he is just the way always his mother wants him, he ain't got no spirit in him, and so I don't really see no help for that poor Lena. I know her aunt, Mrs. Haydon, meant it all right for her Mrs. Aldrich, but poor Lena, it would be better for her if her Herman had stayed there in New York that time he went away to leave her. I don't like it the way Lena is looking now, Mrs. Aldrich. She looks like as if she don't have no life left in her hardly, Mrs. Aldrich, she just drags around and looks so dirty and after all the pains I always took to teach her and to keep her nice in her ways and looking. It don't do no good to them, for them girls to get married Mrs. Aldrich, they are much better when they only know it, to stay in a good place when they got it, and keep on regular with their working. I don't like it the way Lena looks now Mrs. Aldrich. I wish I knew some way to help that poor Lena, Mrs. Aldrich, but she is a bad old woman, that old Mrs. Kreder, Herman's mother. I speak to Mrs. Haydon real soon, Mrs. Aldrich, I see what we can do now to help that poor Lena."

These were really bad days for poor Lena. Herman always was real good to her and now he even sometimes tried to stop his mother from scolding Lena. "She ain't well now mama, you let her be now you hear me. You tell me what it is you want she should be doing, I tell her. I see she does it right just the way you want it mama. You let be, I say now mama, with that always scolding Lena. You let be, I say now, you wait till she is feeling better." Herman was getting really strong to struggle, for he could see that Lena with that baby working hard inside her, really could not stand it any longer with his mother and the awful ways she always scolded.

It was a new feeling Herman now had inside him that made him feel he was strong to make a struggle. It was new for Herman Kreder really to be wanting something, but Herman wanted strongly now to be a father, and he wanted badly that his baby should be a boy and healthy. Herman never had cared really very much about his father and his mother, though always, all his life, he had done everything just as they wanted, and he had never really cared much about his wife, Lena, though he always had been very good to her, and had always tried to keep his mother off her, with the awful way she always scolded, but to be really a father of a little baby, that feeling took hold of Herman very deeply. He was almost ready, so as to save his baby from all trouble, to really make a strong struggle with his mother and with his father, too, if he would not help him to control his mother.

Sometimes Herman even went to Mrs. Haydon to talk all this trouble over. They decided then together, it was better to wait there all four together for the baby, and Herman could make Mrs. Kreder stop a little with her scolding, and then when Lena was a little stronger, Herman should have his own house for her, next door to his father, so he could always be there to help him in his working, but so they could eat and sleep in a house where the old woman could not control them and they could not hear her awful scolding.

And so things went on, the same way, a little longer. Poor Lena was not feeling any joy to have a baby. She was scared the way she had been when she was so sick on the water. She was scared now every time when anything would hurt her. She was scared and still and lifeless, and sure that every minute she would die. Lena had no power to be strong in this kind of trouble, she could only sit still and be scared, and dull, and lifeless, and sure that every minute she would die.

Before very long, Lena had her baby. He was a good, healthy little boy, the baby. Herman cared very much to have the baby. When Lena was a little stronger he took a house next door to the old couple, so he and his own family could eat and sleep and do the way they wanted. This did not seem to make much change now for Lena. She was just the same as when she was waiting with her baby. She just dragged around and was careless with her clothes and all lifeless, and she acted always and lived on just as if she had no feeling. She always did everything regular with the work, the way she always had had to do it, but she never got back any spirit in her. Herman was always good and kind, and always helped her with her working. He did everything he knew to help her. He always did all the active new things in the house and for the baby. Lena did what she had to do the way she always had been taught it. She always just kept going now with her working, and she was always careless, and dirty, and a little dazed, and lifeless. Lena never got any better in herself of this way of being that she had had ever since she had been married.

Mrs. Haydon never saw any more of her niece, Lena. Mrs. Haydon had now so much trouble with her own house, and her daughters getting married, and her boy, who was growing up, and who always was getting so much worse to manage. She knew she had done right by Lena. Herman Kreder was a good man, she would be glad to get one so good, sometimes, for her own daughters, and now they had a home to live in together, separate from the old people, who had made their trouble for them. Mrs. Haydon felt she had done very well by her niece, Lena, and she never thought now she needed any more to go and see her. Lena would do very well now without her aunt to trouble herself any more about her.

The good german cook who had always scolded, still tried to do her duty like a mother to poor Lena. It was very hard now to do right by Lena. Lena never seemed to hear now what anyone was saying to her. Herman was always doing everything he could to help her. Herman always, when he was home, took good care of the baby. Herman loved to take care of his baby. Lena never thought to take him out or to do anything she didn't have to.

The good cook sometimes made Lena come to see her. Lena would come with her baby and sit there in the kitchen, and watch the good woman cooking, and listen to her sometimes a little, the way she used to, while the good german woman scolded her for going around looking so careless when now she had no trouble, and sitting there so dull, and always being just so thankless. Sometimes Lena would wake up a little and get back into her face her old, gentle, patient, and unsuffering sweetness, but mostly Lena did not seem to hear much when the good german woman scolded. Lena always liked it when Mrs. Aldrich her good mistress spoke to her kindly, and then Lena would seem to go back and feel herself to be like she was when she had been in service. But mostly Lena just lived along and was careless in her clothes, and dull, and lifeless.

By and by Lena had two more little babies. Lena was not so much scared now when she had the babies. She did not seem to notice very much when they hurt her, and she never seemed to feel very much now about anything that happened to her.

They were very nice babies, all these three that Lena had, and Herman took good care of them always. Herman never really cared much about his wife, Lena. The only things Herman ever really cared for were his babies. Herman always was very good to his children. He always had a gentle, tender way when he held them. He learned to be very handy with them. He spent all the time he was not working, with them. By and by he began to work all day in his own home so that he could have his children always in the same room with him.

Lena always was more and more lifeless and Herman now mostly never thought about her. He more and more took all the care of their three children. He saw to their eating right and their washing, and he dressed them every morning, and he taught them the right way to do things, and he put them to their sleeping, and he was now always every minute with them. Then there was to come to them, a fourth baby. Lena went to the hospital near by to have the baby. Lena seemed to be going to have much trouble with it. When the baby was come out at last, it was like its mother, lifeless. While it was coming, Lena had grown very pale and sicker. When it was all over Lena had died, too, and nobody knew just how it had happened to her.

The good german cook who had always scolded Lena, and had always to the last day tried to help her, was the only one who ever missed her. She remembered how nice Lena had looked all the time she was in service with her, and how her voice had been so gentle and sweet-sounding, and how she always was a good girl, and how she never had to have any trouble with her, the way she always had with all the other girls who had been taken into the house to help her. The good cook sometimes spoke so of Lena when she had time to have a talk with Mrs. Aldrich, and this was all the remembering there now ever was of Lena.

Herman Kreder now always lived very happy, very gentle, very quiet, very well content alone with his three children. He never had a woman any more to be all the time around him. He always did all his own work in his house, when he was through every day with the work he was always doing for his father. Herman always was alone, and he always worked alone, until his little ones were big enough to help him. Herman Kreder was very well content now and he always lived very regular and peaceful, and with every day just like the next one, always alone now with his three good, gentle children.

1909

SUSIE ASADO

Sweet sweet sweet sweet sweet tea.
    Susie Asado.
Sweet sweet sweet sweet sweet tea.
    Susie Asado.
Susie Asado which is a told tray sure.
A lean on the shoe this means slips slips hers.
When the ancient light grey is clean it is yellow, it
is a silver seller.
This is a please this is a please there are the saids
to jelly. These are the wets these say the sets to leave
a crown to Incy.
Incy is short for incubus.
A pot. A pot is a beginning of a rare bit of trees.
Trees tremble, the old vats are in bobbles, bobbles which
shade and shove and render clean, render clean must.
    Drink pups.
Drink pups drink pups lease a sash hold, see it shine
and a bobolink has pins. It shows a nail.
What is a nail. A nail is unison.
Sweet sweet sweet sweet sweet tea.

1922

PICASSO

One whom some were certainly following was one who was completely charming. One whom some were certainly following was one who was charming. One whom some were following was one who was completely charming.

One whom some were following was one who was certainly completely charming.

Some were certainly following and were certain that the one they were then following was one working and was one bringing out of himself then something. Some were certainly following and were certain that the one they were then following was one bringing out of himself then something that was coming to be a heavy thing, a solid thing and a complete thing.

One whom some were certainly following was one working and certainly was one bringing something out of himself then and was one who had been all his living had been one having something coming out of him.

Something had been coming out of him, certainly it had been coming out of him, certainly it was something, certainly it had been coming out of him and it had meaning, a charming meaning, a solid meaning, a struggling meaning, a clear meaning.

One whom some were certainly following and some were certainly following him, one whom some were certainly following was one certainly working.

One whom some were certainly following was one having something coming out of him something having meaning and this one was certainly working then.

This one was working and something was coming then, something was coming out of this one then. This one was one and always there was something coming out of this one and always there had been something coming out of this one. This one had never been one not having something coming out of this one. This one was one having something coming out of this one. This one had been one whom some were following. This one was one whom some were following. This one was being one whom some were following. This one was one who was working.

This one was one who was working. This one was one being one having something being coming out of him. This one was one going on having something come out of him. This one was one going on working. This one was one whom some were following. This one was one who was working.

This one always had something being coming out of this one. This one was working. This one always had been working. This one was always having something that was coming out of this one that was a solid thing, a charming thing, a lovely thing, a perplexing thing, a disconcerting thing, a simple thing, a clear thing, a complicated thing, an interesting thing, a disturbing thing, a repellant thing, a very pretty thing. This one was one certainly being one having something coming out of him. This one was one whom some were following. This one was one who was working.

This one was one who was working and certainly this one was needing to be working so as to be one being working. This one was one having something coming out of him. This one would be one all his living having something coming out of him. This one was working and then this one was working and this one was needing to be working, not to be one having something coming out of him something having meaning, but was needing to be working so as to be one working.

This one was certainly working and working was something this one was certain this one would be doing and this one was doing that thing, this one was working. This one was not one completely working. This one was not ever completely working. This one certainly was not completely working.

This one was one having always something being coming out of him, something having completely a real meaning. This one was one whom some were following. This one was one who was working. This one was one who was working and he was one needing this thing needing to be working so as to be one having some way of being one having some way of working. This one was one who was working. This one was one having something come out of him something having meaning. This one was one always having something come out of him and this thing the thing coming out of him always had real meaning. This one was one who was working. This one was one who was almost always working. This one was not one completely working. This one was one not ever completely working. This one was not one working to have anything come out of him. This one did have something having meaning that did come out of him. He always did have something come out of him. He was working, he was not ever completely working. He did have some following. They were always following him. Some were certainly following him. He was one who was working. He was one having something coming out of him something having meaning. He was not ever completely working.

1934

Sherwood Anderson 1876–1941

In his stories of rural and small-town life, Sherwood Anderson sought to portray what he called "the ugliness of life, the strange beauty of life. . . ." His sketches and tales drew upon his own experiences in the American Midwest at the end of the nineteenth century. He had grown up in the small town of Clyde, Ohio, the basis for fictional Winesburg, Ohio, which was the setting of his most notable work. When he was twenty, he left home, drawn to the metropolis of Chicago, where he took a job as a laborer. When the Spanish-American War (1898) gave him the chance to escape the dull routine of day-labor, he enlisted, serving in the army for a year. After the war he returned to Chicago, where he worked as an advertising salesman and began to write his first tales and sketches. In 1907, he moved to Elyria, Ohio, to establish a paint firm, but his literary ambitions soon came into conflict with his duties as a small-town businessman. In 1913 he abandoned his business, returned once again to Chicago, and at the age of thirty-seven began his life as a writer, asserting, "I will be a servant to words alone."

He wrote Windy McPherson's Son *(1916) and* Marching Men *(1917), novels about successful men who abandoned their own selfish aims to become populist heroes, helping the "little people." In 1919 he published* Winesburg, Ohio, *his masterpiece, a collection of tales of the "grotesque" characters he had known during his youth in Ohio. Anderson's successful volumes of short stories,* The Triumph of the Egg *(1921),* Horses and Men *(1923), and* Death in the Woods *(1933), contained work of great merit, but his later novels, among them* Many Marriages *(1923),* Dark Laughter *(1925), and* Kit Brandon *(1936), were failures and showed only flashes of the finer qualities of his earlier writing.*

Anderson was preoccupied by a desire to describe the agonies and the failures of the unsuccessful, the deprived, and the inarticulate. His range was narrow, and his idealized perceptions of innocence were sometimes shallow. Yet his sensitive depictions of poverty and eccentricity and his deceptively simple style, with its matter-of-fact midwestern sentences, opened new perspectives for twentieth-century literature. He influenced a wide range of American writers, including Hart Crane, John Steinbeck, Thomas Wolfe, Ernest Hemingway, and William Faulkner, who, in 1956, acknowledged Anderson as "the father of my generation of American writers and the tradition of American writing which our successors will carry on."

FURTHER READING: J. Schevill, *Sherwood Anderson, His Life and Work,* 1951; I. Howe, *Sherwood Anderson,* 1951, 1966; *Letters of Sherwood Anderson,* ed. H. Jones and W. Rideout, 1953; R. Burbank, *Sherwood Anderson,* 1964; *The Achievement of Sherwood Anderson, Essays in Criticism,* ed. R. White, 1966; D. Anderson, *Sherwood Anderson, An Introduction and Interpretation,* 1967; *Sherwood Anderson's Memoirs,* ed. R. White, 1969; *Sherwood Anderson, A Collection of Critical Essays,* ed. W. Rideout, 1974; *Critical Essays on Sherwood Anderson,* ed. D. Anderson, 1981; *Sherwood Anderson, Collected Letters,* ed. C. Modlin, 1983; K. Townsend, *Sherwood Anderson,* 1987; R. Papinchak, *Sherwood Anderson, A Study of the Short Stories,* 1992; J. Small, *A Reader's Guide to the Short Stories of Sherwood Anderson,* 1994; *Sherwood Anderson,* ed. H. Bloom, 2003; R. Dunne, *A New Book of the Grotesques, Contemporary Approaches to Sherwood Anderson's Early Fiction,* 2005.

TEXT: *The Triumph of the Egg,* 1921.

I WANT TO KNOW WHY

We got up at four in the morning, that first day in the east. On the evening before we had climbed off a freight train at the edge of town, and with the true instinct of Kentucky boys had found our way across town and to the racetrack and the stables at once. Then we knew we were all right. Hanley Turner right away found a nigger we knew. It was Bildad Johnson who in the winter works at Ed Becker's livery barn in our home town, Beckersville. Bildad is a good cook as almost all our niggers are and of course he, like everyone in our part of Kentucky who is anyone at all, likes the horses. In the spring Bildad begins to scratch around. A nigger from our country can flatter and wheedle anyone into letting him do most anything he wants. Bildad wheedles the stable men and the trainers from the horse farms in our country around Lexington. The trainers come into town in the evening to stand around and talk and maybe get into a poker game. Bildad gets in with them. He is always doing little favors and telling about things to eat, chicken browned in a pan, and how is the best way to cook sweet potatoes and corn bread. It makes your mouth water to hear him.

When the racing season comes on and the horses go to the races and there is all the talk on the streets in the evenings about the new colts, and everyone says when they are going over to Lexington or to the spring meeting at Churchill Downs or to Latonia,[1] and the horsemen that have been

[1]Famous race tracks in Louisville and Covington, Kentucky.

down to New Orleans or maybe at the winter meeting at Havana in Cuba come home to spend a week before they start out again, at such a time when everything talked about in Beckersville is just horses and nothing else and the outfits start out and horse racing is in every breath of air you breathe, Bildad shows up with a job as cook for some outfit. Often when I think about it, his always going all season to the races and working in the livery barn in the winter where horses are and where men like to come and talk about horses, I wish I was a nigger. It's a foolish thing to say, but that's the way I am about being around horses, just crazy. I can't help it.

Well, I must tell you about what we did and let you in on what I'm talking about. Four of us boys from Beckersville, all whites and sons of men who live in Beckersville regular, made up our minds we were going to the races, not just to Lexington or Louisville, I don't mean, but to the big eastern track we were always hearing our Beckersville men talk about, to Saratoga.[2] We were all pretty young then. I was just turned fifteen and I was the oldest of the four. It was my scheme. I admit that and I talked the others into trying it. There was Hanley Turner and Henry Rieback and Tom Tumberton and myself. I had thirty-seven dollars I had earned during the winter working nights and Saturdays in Enoch Myer's grocery. Henry Rieback had eleven dollars and the others, Hanley and Tom, had only a dollar or two each. We fixed it all up and laid low until the Kentucky spring meetings were over and some of our men, the sportiest ones, the ones we envied the most, had cut out—then we cut out too.

I won't tell you the trouble we had beating our way on freights and all. We went through Cleveland and Buffalo and other cities and saw Niagara Falls. We bought things there, souvenirs and spoons and cards and shells with pictures of the Falls on them for our sisters and mothers, but thought we had better not send any of the things home. We didn't want to put the folks on our trail and maybe be nabbed.

We got into Saratoga as I said at night and went to the track. Bildad fed us up. He showed us a place to sleep in hay over a shed and promised to keep still. Niggers are all right about things like that. They won't squeal on you. Often a white man you might meet, when you had run away from home like that, might appear to be all right and give you a quarter or a half dollar or something, and then go right and give you away. White men will do that, but not a nigger. You can trust them. They are squarer with kids. I don't know why.

At the Saratoga meeting that year there were a lot of men from home. Dave Williams and Arthur Mulford and Jerry Myers and others. Then there was a lot from Louisville and Lexington Henry Rieback knew but I didn't. They were professional gamblers and Henry Rieback's father is one too. He is what is called a sheet[3] writer and goes away most of the year to tracks. In the winter when he is home in Beckersville he don't stay there much but goes away to cities and deals faro.[4] He is a nice man and generous, is always

[2]Race track at Saratoga Springs, New York.

[3]A racing form, printed information on horses, jockeys, and races.

[4]A card game popular with gamblers in the nineteenth and early twentieth century.

sending Henry presents, a bicycle and a gold watch and a Boy Scout suit of clothes and things like that.

My own father is a lawyer. He's all right, but don't make much money and can't buy me things and anyway I'm getting so old now I don't expect it. He never said nothing to me against Henry, but Hanley Turner and Tom Tumberton's fathers did. They said to their boys that money so come by is no good and they didn't want their boys brought up to hear gamblers' talk and be thinking about such things and maybe embrace them.

That's all right and I guess the men know what they are talking about, but I don't see what it's got to do with Henry or horses either. That's what I'm writing this story about. I'm puzzled. I'm getting to be a man and want to think straight and be O.K., and there's something I saw at the race meeting at the eastern track I can't figure out.

I can't help it, I'm crazy about thoroughbred horses. I've always been that way. When I was ten years old and saw I was growing to be big and couldn't be a rider I was so sorry I nearly died. Harry Hellinfinger in Beckersville, whose father is Postmaster, is grown up and too lazy to work, but likes to stand around in the street and get up jokes on boys like sending them to a hardware store for a gimlet[5] to bore square holes and other jokes like that. He played one on me. He told me that if I would eat a half a cigar I would be stunted and not grow any more and maybe could be a rider. I did it. When father wasn't looking I took a cigar out of his pocket and gagged it down some way. It made me awful sick and the doctor had to be sent for, and then it did no good. I kept right on growing. It was a joke. When I told what I had done and why most fathers would have whipped me but mine didn't.

Well, I didn't get stunted and didn't die. It serves Harry Hellinfinger right. Then I made up my mind I would like to be a stable boy, but had to give that up too. Mostly niggers do that work and I knew father wouldn't let me go into it. No use to ask him.

If you've never been crazy about thoroughbreds it's because you've never been around where they are much and don't know any better. They're beautiful. There isn't anything so lovely and clean and full of spunk and honest and everything as some race horses. On the big horse farms that are all around our town Beckersville there are tracks and the horses run in the early morning. More than a thousand times I've got out of bed before daylight and walked two or three miles to the tracks. Mother wouldn't of let me go but father always says, "Let him alone." So I got some bread out of the bread box and some butter and jam, gobbled it and lit out.

At the tracks you sit on the fence with men, whites and niggers, and they chew tobacco and talk, and then the colts are brought out. It's early and the grass is covered with shiny dew and in another field a man is plowing and they are frying things in a shed where the track niggers sleep, and you know how a nigger can giggle and laugh and say things that make you laugh. A white man can't do it and some niggers can't but a track nigger can every time.

[5]Small hand tool with a spiral point, used for boring round holes.

And so the colts are brought out and some are just galloped by stable boys, but almost every morning on a big track owned by a rich man who lives maybe in New York, there are always, nearly every morning, a few colts and some of the old race horses and geldings[6] and mares that are cut loose.

It brings a lump up into my throat when a horse runs. I don't mean all horses but some. I can pick them nearly every time. It's in my blood like in the blood of race-track niggers and trainers. Even when they just go slop-jogging along with a little nigger on their backs I can tell a winner. If my throat hurts and it's hard for me to swallow, that's him. He'll run like Sam Hill when you let him out. If he don't win every time it'll be a wonder and because they've got him in a pocket behind another[7] or he was pulled or got off bad at the post or something. If I wanted to be a gambler like Henry Rieback's father I could get rich. I know I could and Henry says so too. All I would have to do is to wait 'til that hurt comes when I see a horse and then bet every cent. That's what I would do if I wanted to be a gambler, but I don't.

When you're at the tracks in the morning—not the race tracks but the training tracks around Beckersville—you don't see a horse, the kind I've been talking about, very often, but it's nice anyway. Any thoroughbred, that is sired right and out of a good mare and trained by a man that knows how, can run. If he couldn't what would he be there for and not pulling a plow?

Well, out of the stables they come and the boys are on their backs and it's lovely to be there. You hunch down on top of the fence and itch inside you. Over in the sheds the niggers giggle and sing. Bacon is being fried and coffee made. Everything smells lovely. Nothing smells better than coffee and manure and horses and niggers and bacon frying and pipes being smoked out of doors on a morning like that. It just gets you, that's what it does.

But about Saratoga. We was there six days and not a soul from home seen us and everything came off just as we wanted it to, fine weather and horses and races and all. We beat our way home and Bildad gave us a basket with fried chicken and bread and other eatables in, and I had eighteen dollars when we got back to Beckersville. Mother jawed and cried but Pop didn't say much. I told everything we done except one thing. I did and saw that alone. That's what I'm writing about. It got me upset. I think about it at night. Here it is.

At Saratoga we laid up nights in the hay in the shed Bildad had showed us and ate with the niggers early and at night when the race people had all gone away. The men from home stayed mostly in the grandstand and betting field, and didn't come out around the places where the horses are kept except to the paddocks[8] just before a race when the horses are saddled. At Saratoga they don't have paddocks under an open shed as at Lexington

[6]A male horse, castrated to make him gentle.
[7]I.e., Blocked by other horses, front and sides.
[8]Area where horses are saddled and paraded before a race.

and Churchill Downs and other tracks down in our country, but saddle the horses right out in an open place under trees on a lawn as smooth and nice as Banker Bohon's front yard here in Beckersville. It's lovely. The horses are sweaty and nervous and shine and the men come out and smoke cigars and look at them and the trainers are there and the owners, and your heart thumps so you can hardly breathe.

Then the bugle blows for post[9] and the boys that ride come running out with their silk clothes on and you run to get a place by the fence with the niggers.

I always am wanting to be a trainer or owner, and at the risk of being seen and caught and sent home I went to the paddocks before every race. The other boys didn't but I did.

We got to Saratoga on a Friday and on Wednesday the next week the big Mullford Handicap[10] was to be run. Middlestride was in it and Sunstreak. The weather was fine and the track fast. I couldn't sleep the night before.

What had happened was that both these horses are the kind it makes my throat hurt to see. Middlestride is long and looks awkward and is a gelding. He belongs to Joe Thompson, a little owner from home who only has a half-dozen horses. The Mullford Handicap is for a mile and Middlestride can't untrack[11] fast. He goes away slow and is always way back at the half, then he begins to run and if the race is a mile and a quarter he'll just eat up everything and get there.

Sunstreak is different. He is a stallion and nervous and belongs on the biggest farm we've got in our country, the Van Riddle place that belongs to Mr. Van Riddle of New York. Sunstreak is like a girl you think about sometimes but never see. He is hard all over and lovely too. When you look at his head you want to kiss him. He is trained by Jerry Tillford who knows me and has been good to me lots of times, lets me walk into a horse's stall to look at him close and other things. There isn't anything as sweet as that horse. He stands at the post quiet and not letting on, but he is just burning up inside. Then when the barrier goes up he is off like his name, Sunstreak. It makes you ache to see him. It hurts you. He just lays down and runs like a bird dog. There can't be anything I ever see run like him except Middlestride when he gets untracked and stretches himself.

Gee! I ached to see that race and those two horses run, ached and dreaded it too. I didn't want to see either of our horses beaten. We had never sent a pair like that to the races before. Old men in Beckersville said so and the niggers said so. It was a fact.

Before the race I went over to the paddocks to see. I looked a last look at Middlestride, who isn't such a much standing in a paddock that way, then I went to see Sunstreak.

It was his day. I knew when I seen him. I forgot all about being seen myself and walked right up. All the men from Beckersville were there and no

[9] A signal to assemble horses and riders at the starting point of the race.

[10] A race in which swifter horses and riders are assigned extra weight to carry—to equalize chances of winning.

[11] Start.

one noticed me except Jerry Tillford. He saw me and something happened. I'll tell you about that.

I was standing looking at that horse and aching. In some way, I can't tell how, I knew just how Sunstreak felt inside. He was quiet and letting the niggers rub his legs and Mr. Van Riddle himself put the saddle on, but he was just a raging torrent inside. He was like the water in the river at Niagara Falls just before it goes plunk down. That horse wasn't thinking about running. He don't have to think about that. He was just thinking about holding himself back 'til the time for the running came. I knew that. I could just in a way see right inside him. He was going to do some awful running and I knew it. He wasn't bragging or letting on much or prancing or making a fuss, but just waiting. I knew it and Jerry Tillford his trainer knew. I looked up and then that man and I looked into each other's eyes. Something happened to me. I guess I loved the man as much as I did the horse because he knew what I knew. Seemed to me there wasn't anything in the world but that man and the horse and me. I cried and Jerry Tillford had a shine in his eyes. Then I came away to the fence to wait for the race. The horse was better than me, more steadier, and now I know better than Jerry. He was the quietest and he had to do the running.

Sunstreak ran first of course and he busted the world's record for a mile. I've seen that if I never see anything more. Everything came out just as I expected. Middlestride got left at the post and was way back and closed up to be second, just as I knew he would. He'll get a world's record too some day. They can't skin the Beckersville country on horses.

I watched the race calm because I knew what would happen. I was sure. Hanley Turner and Henry Rieback and Tom Tumberton were all more excited than me.

A funny thing had happened to me. I was thinking about Jerry Tillford the trainer and how happy he was all through the race. I liked him that afternoon even more than I ever liked my own father. I almost forgot the horses thinking that way about him. It was because of what I had seen in his eyes as he stood in the paddocks beside Sunstreak before the race started. I knew he had been watching and working with Sunstreak since the horse was a baby colt, had taught him to run and be patient and when to let himself out and not to quit, never. I knew that for him it was like a mother seeing her child do something brave or wonderful. It was the first time I ever felt for a man like that.

After the race that night I cut out from Tom and Hanley and Henry. I wanted to be by myself and I wanted to be near Jerry Tillford if I could work it. Here is what happened.

The track in Saratoga is near the edge of town. It is all polished up and trees around, the evergreen kind, and grass and everything painted and nice. If you go past the track you get to a hard road made of asphalt for automobiles, and if you go along this for a few miles there is a road turns off to a little rummy-looking farmhouse set in a yard.

That night after the race I went along that road because I had seen Jerry and some other men go that way in an automobile. I didn't expect to find them. I walked for a ways and then sat down by a fence to think. It was the direction they went in. I wanted to be as near Jerry as I could. I felt close to him. Pretty soon I went up the side road—I don't know why—and came to the rummy farmhouse. I was just lonesome to see Jerry, like wanting to see your father at night when you are a young kid. Just then an automobile came along and turned in. Jerry was in it and Henry Rieback's father, and Arthur Bedford from home, and Dave Williams and two other men I didn't know. They got out of the car and went into the house, all but Henry Rieback's father who quarreled with them and said he wouldn't go. It was only about nine o'clock, but they were all drunk and the rummy-looking farmhouse was a place for bad women to stay in. That's what it was. I crept up along a fence and looked through a window and saw.

It's what give me the fantods.[12] I can't make it out. The women in the house were all ugly mean-looking women, not nice to look at or be near. They were homely too, except one who was tall and looked a little like the gelding Middlestride, but not clean like him, but with a hard ugly mouth. She had red hair. I saw everything plain. I got up by an old rosebush by an open window and looked. The women had on loose dresses and sat around in chairs. The men came in and some sat on the women's laps. The place smelled rotten and there was rotten talk, the kind a kid hears around a livery stable in a town like Beckersville in the winter but don't ever expect to hear talked when there are women around. It was rotten. A nigger wouldn't go into such a place.

I looked at Jerry Tillford. I've told you how I had been feeling about him on account of his knowing what was going on inside of Sunstreak in the minute before he went to the post for the race in which he made a world's record.

Jerry bragged in that bad-woman house as I know Sunstreak wouldn't never have bragged. He said that he made that horse, that it was him that won the race and made the record. He lied and bragged like a fool. I never heard such silly talk.

And then, what do you suppose he did! He looked at the woman in there, the one that was lean and hard-mouthed and looked a little like the gelding Middlestride, but not clean like him, and his eyes began to shine just as they did when he looked at me and at Sunstreak in the paddocks at the track in the afternoon. I stood there by the window—gee!—but I wished I hadn't gone away from the tracks, but had stayed with the boys and the niggers and the horses. The tall rotten-looking woman was between us just as Sunstreak was in the paddocks in the afternoon.

Then, all of a sudden, I began to hate that man. I wanted to scream and rush in the room and kill him. I never had such a feeling before. I was so mad clean through that I cried and my fists were doubled up so my finger-nails cut my hands.

And Jerry's eyes kept shining and he waved back and forth, and then he went and kissed that woman and I crept away and went back to the tracks

[12]High nervous tension, a fit.

and to bed and didn't sleep hardly any, and then next day I got the other kids to start home with me and never told them anything I seen.

I been thinking about it ever since. I can't make it out. Spring has come again and I'm nearly sixteen and go to the tracks mornings same as always, and I see Sunstreak and Middlestride and a new colt named Strident I'll bet will lay them all out, but no one thinks so but me and two or three niggers.

But things are different. At the tracks the air don't taste as good or smell as good. It's because a man like Jerry Tillford, who knows what he does, could see a horse like Sunstreak run, and kiss a woman like that the same day. I can't make it out. Darn him, what did he want to do like that for? I keep thinking about it and it spoils looking at horses and smelling things and hearing niggers laugh and everything. Sometimes I'm so mad about it I want to fight someone. It gives me the fantods. What did he do it for? I want to know why.

1921

Eugene O'Neill 1888–1953

Eugene O'Neill was born in a Broadway hotel and raised in the world of the American theater. His father was a famous actor, and in early childhood Eugene toured with his parents in theatrical road companies traveling throughout the United States. At the age of eighteen he entered Princeton, but at the end of his freshman year he was expelled for a drunken prank and "general hell-raising." He went to New York City, where he took a secretarial job in a business firm. When he was twenty, he sailed to Central America to prospect for gold and then signed on as an ordinary seaman on ships sailing to South America, Africa, and Europe.

After three years of wandering, he returned to New York, where he supported himself with odd jobs and lived in waterfront dives among outcasts like those he later depicted in his plays. When he was twenty-four, an attack of tuberculosis, worsened by his own rebellious dissipations, sent him to a sanitarium. During his illness he decided to become a playwright, and after his convalescence he enrolled at Harvard to study drama. In 1914 he published Thirst and Other One-Act Plays. *Two years later* Bound East for Cardiff *was staged, followed in 1917 by* The Long Voyage Home.

During the 1920s and early 1930s, O'Neill achieved a series of theatrical triumphs with the production of such plays as Beyond the Horizon *(1920)—for which he was awarded the first of four Pulitzer Prizes—*The Emperor Jones

(1920), Anna Christie *(1921),* The Hairy Ape *(1922),* Desire Under the Elms *(1924), and* Strange Interlude *(1928). In 1931 his* Mourning Becomes Electra *was widely proclaimed a dramatic masterpiece, and in 1936 he became the second American, after Sinclair Lewis, to win a Nobel Prize for Literature. O'Neill had won wealth and international renown, but in the late 1930s he withdrew into retirement and seclusion. His critical reputation declined, and his works vanished from the popular stage. In 1946 he returned to the theater with* The Iceman Cometh, *a long and notable tragedy portraying a haunted man struggling to break free of his illusions. But not until the production of* Long Day's Journey into Night *in 1956, three years after O'Neill's death, was there a lasting revival of interest in his works.*

O'Neill was a restless theatrical experimenter. His writing was shaped by European expressionistic drama and by literary naturalists such as Jack London, who portrayed people caught by overwhelming forces in a world indifferent to suffering and hope. O'Neill's plays were frequently autobiographical, pessimistic expressions of the agonies of his own life and of the degeneration he saw around him. He viewed humanity as moved by destructive passions, living in disharmony with nature, and dehumanized by a materialistic society.

O'Neill's plays are sometimes disparaged for their social pleading, their nihilism, and their occasional lapses into "overheated rhetoric." Yet his psychological probing of alienation and his depiction of the suffering of ordinary mortals made him America's most influential playwright. In little more than a decade, he transformed the American theater, changing it "utterly," in the words of Sinclair Lewis, "from a false world of neat and competent trickery into a world of splendor and fear and greatness."

FURTHER READING: S. Winther, *Eugene O'Neill, A Critical Study,* 1934, 1961; R. Skinner, *Eugene O'Neill, A Poet's Quest,* 1935, 1964; E. Engel, *The Haunted Heroes of Eugene O'Neill,* 1953; D. Falk, *Eugene O'Neill and the Tragic Tension,* 1958; *O'Neill and His Plays,* ed. O. Cargill, N. Fagin, and W. Fischer, 1961; D. Alexander, *The Tempering of Eugene O'Neill,* 1962; J. Miller, *Eugene O'Neill and the American Critic,* 1962; A. and B. Gelb, *O'Neill,* 1962, 1973; F. Carpenter, *Eugene O'Neill,* 1964, 1979; J. Raleigh, *The Plays of Eugene O'Neill,* 1965; L. Schaeffer, *O'Neill, Son and Playwright,* 1968; T. Bogard, *Contour in Time, The Plays of Eugene O'Neill,* 1972, 1988; L. Chabrowe, *Ritual and Pathos, The Theater of O'Neill,* 1976; *Eugene O'Neill, A Collection of Criticism,* ed. E. Griffin, 1976; J. Chothia, *Forging a Language, A Study of the Plays of Eugene O'Neill,* 1980; V. Floyd, *Eugene O'Neill, A World View,* 1980; C. Sinha, *Eugene O'Neill's Tragic Vision,* 1981; N. Berlin, *Eugene O'Neill,* 1982; *Eugene O'Neill's Critics,* ed. H. Frenz and S. Tuck, 1984; *Critical Essays on Eugene O'Neill,* ed. J. Martine, 1984; M. Renald, *The Eugene O'Neill Companion,* 1984; J. Barlow, *Final Acts,* 1985; V. Floyd, *The Plays of Eugene O'Neill,* 1985; *Critical Approaches to O'Neill,* ed. J. Stoupe, 1987; *Eugene O'Neill's Century,* ed. R. Moorton, 1991; K. Eisen, *The Inner Strength of Opposites, O'Neill's Novelistic Drama,* 1993; J. Pfister, *Staging Depth,* 1995; *The Cambridge Companion to Eugene O'Neill,* ed. M. Manheim, 1998; B. Voglino, *Perverse Mind, Eugene O'Neill's Struggle with Closure,* 1999; M. Miliora, *Narcissism, the Family, and Madness, A Self-Psychological Study of Eugene O'Neill and His Plays,* 2000; E. Tornqvist, *Eugene O'Neill, A Playwright's Theatre,* 2004; D. Alexander, *Eugene O'Neill's Last Plays, Separating Art from Autobiography,* 2005.

TEXT: *The Plays of Eugene O'Neill,* 3 vols., 1951.

THE HAIRY APE

CHARACTERS

ROBERT SMITH, "YANK"
PADDY
LONG
MILDRED DOUGLAS
HER AUNT
SECOND ENGINEER
A GUARD
A SECRETARY OF AN ORGANIZATION
Stokers, Ladies, Gentlemen, etc.

SCENES

Scene I: The firemen's forecastle of an ocean liner—an hour after sailing from New York.
Scene II: Section of promenade deck, two days out—morning.
Scene III: The stokehole. A few minutes later.
Scene IV: Same as Scene One. Half an hour later.
Scene V: Fifth Avenue, New York. Three weeks later.
Scene VI: An island near the city. The next night.
Scene VII: In the city. About a month later.
Scene VIII: In the city. Twilight of the next day.

SCENE ONE

The firemen's forecastle of a transatlantic liner an hour after sailing from New York for the voyage across. Tiers of narrow, steel bunks, three deep, on all sides. An entrance in rear. Benches on the floor before the bunks. The room is crowded with men, shouting, cursing, laughing, singing—a confused, inchoate uproar swelling into a sort of unity, a meaning—the bewildered, furious, baffled defiance of a beast in a cage. Nearly all of the men are drunk. Many bottles are passed from hand to hand. All are dressed in dungaree pants, heavy ugly shoes. Some wear singlets, but the majority are stripped to the waist.

The treatment of this scene, or any other scene in the play, should by no means be naturalistic. The effect sought after is a cramped space in the bowels of a ship, imprisoned by white steel. The lines of bunks, the uprights supporting them, cross each other like the steel framework of a cage. The ceiling crushes down upon the men's heads. They cannot stand upright. This accentuates the natural stooping posture which shoveling coal and the resultant overdevelopment of back and shoulder muscles have given them. The men themselves should resemble those pictures in which the appearance of Neanderthal Man is guessed at. All are hairy-chested, with long arms of tremendous power, and low, receding brows above their small, fierce, resentful eyes. All the civilized white races are represented, but except for the slight differentiation in color of hair, skin, eyes, all these men are alike.

The curtain rises on a tumult of sound. YANK *is seated in the foreground. He seems broader, fiercer, more truculent, more powerful, more sure of himself than the rest. They respect his superior strength—the grudging respect of fear. Then, too, he represents to them a self-expression, the very last word in what they are, their most highly developed individual.*

VOICES. Gif me trink dere, you!
'Ave a wet!
Salute!
Gesundheit!
Skoal!
Drunk as a lord, God stiffen you!
Here's how!
Luck!
Pass back that bottle, damn you!
Pourin' it down his neck!
Ho, Froggy! Where the devil have you been?
La Touraine,[1]
I hit him smash in yaw, py Gott!
Jenkins—the First—he's a rotten swine—
And the coppers nabbed him—and I run—
I like peer better. It don't pig head gif you.
A slut, I'm saying'! She robbed me aslape—
To hell with 'em all!
You're a bloody liar!
Say dot again! (*Commotion. Two men about to fight are pulled apart.*)
No scrappin' now!
Tonight—
See who's the best man!
Bloody Dutchman!
Tonight on the for'ard square.
I'll bet on Dutchy.
He packa da wallop. I tella you!
Shut up, Wop!
No fightin' maties. We're all chums, ain't we!
(*A voice starts bawling a song.*)

"Beer, beer, glorious beer!
Fill yourselves right up to here."

YANK. (*for the first time seeming to take notice of the uproar about him, turns around threateningly—in a tone of contemptuous authority*) Choke off dat noise! Where d'yuh get dat beer stuff? Beer, hell! Beer's for goils—and Dutchmen. Me for somep'n with a kick to it. Gimmie a drink, one of youse guys. (*Several bottles are eagerly offered. He takes a tremendous gulp at one of them; then, keeping the bottle in his hand, glares belligerently at the owner, who hastens to acquiesce in this robbery by saying*) All righto, Yank. Keep it and have another. (YANK

[1]French ocean liner.

contemptuously turns his back on the crowd again. For a second there is an embarrassed silence. Then—)

VOICES. We must be passing the Hook.[2]
She's beginning to roll to it.
Six days in hell—and then Southampton.[3]
Py Yesus, I vish somepody take my first vatch for me!
Gittin' seasick, Square-head?
Drink up and forget it!
What's in your bottle?
Gin.
Dot's nigger trink.
Absinthe? It's doped. You'll go off your chump, Froggy!
Cochon![4]
Whisky, that's the ticket!
Where's Paddy?
Going asleep
Sing up that whisky song Paddy. (*They all turn to an old, wizened Irishman who is dozing, very drunk, on the benches forward. His face is extremely monkey-like with all the sad, patient pathos of that animal in his small eyes.*)
Singa da song, Caruso Pat!
He's gettin' old. The drink is too much for him.
He's too drunk.

PADDY. (*blinking about him, starts to his feet resentfully, swaying, holding on to the edge of a bunk*) I'm never too drunk to sing. 'Tis only when I'm dead to the world I'd be wishful to sing at all. (*with a sort of sad contempt*) "Whisky Johnny," ye want? A chanty, ye want? Now that's a queer wish from the ugly like of you, God help you. But no matther. (*He starts to sing in a thin, nasal, doleful tone:*)

"Oh, whisky is the life of man!
Whisky! O Johnny! (They all join in on this.)
Oh, whisky is the life of man!
Whisky for my Johnny! (Again chorus.)
"Oh, whisky drove my old man mad!
Whisky! O Johnny!
Oh, whisky drove my old man mad!
Whisky for my Johnny!"

YANK. (*again turning around scornfully*) Aw hell! Nix on dat old sailing ship stuff! All dat bull's dead, see? And you're dead, too, yuh damned old Harp,[5] on'y yuh don't know it. Take it easy, see. Give us a rest. Nix on de loud noise. (*with a cynical grin*) Can't youse see I'm tryin' to t'ink?

ALL. (*repeating the word after him as one with the same cynical amused mockery*) Think! (*The chorused word has a brazen metallic quality as if their throats were phonograph horns. It is followed by a general uproar of hard, barking laughter.*)

VOICES. Don't be cracking your head wit ut, Yank.
You gat headache, py yingo!

[2]Sandy Hook, a peninsula at the mouth of New York Bay, leading to the open sea.
[3]In England. [4]French: Pig! [5]Slang term for Irishman.

One thing about it—it rhymes with drink!
Ha, ha, ha!
Drink, don't think!
Drink, don't think!
Drink, don't think! (*A whole chorus of voices has taken up this refrain, stamping on the floor, pounding on the benches with fists.*)

YANK. (*taking a gulp from his bottle—good-naturedly*) Aw right. Can de noise. I got yuh de foist time. (*The uproar subsides. A very drunken sentimental tenor begins to sing*):

> *"Far away in Canada,*
> *Far across the sea,*
> *There's a lass who fondly waits*
> *Making a home for me—"*

YANK. (*fiercely contemptuous*) Shut up, yuh lousy boob! Where d'yuh get dat tripe? Home? Home, hell! I'll make a home for yuh! I'll knock yuh dead. Home! T'hell wit home! Where d'yu get dat tripe? Dis is home, see? What d'yuh want with home? (*proudly*) I runned away from mine when I was a kid. On'y too glad to beat it, dat was me. Home was lickings for me, dat's all. But yuh can bet your shoit no one ain't never licked me since! Wanter try it, any of youse? Huh! I guess not. (*in a more placated but still contemptuous tone*) Goils waitin' for yuh, huh? Aw, hell! Dat's all tripe. Dey don't wait for no one. Dey'd double-cross yuh for a nickel. Dey're all tarts, get me? Treat 'em rough, dat's me. To hell wit 'em. Tarts, dat's what, de whole bunch of 'em.

LONG. (*very drunk, jumps on a bench excitedly, gesticulating with a bottle in his hand*) Listen 'ere, Comrade! Yank 'ere is right. 'E says this 'ere stinkin' ship is our 'ome. And 'e says as 'ome is 'ell. An 'e's right! This is 'ell. We lives in 'ell, Comrades—and right enough we'll die in it. (*raging*) and who's ter blame, I arsk yer? We ain't. We wasn't born this rotten way. All men is born free and ekal. That's in the bleedin' Bible, maties. But what d'they care for the Bible—them lazy, bloated swine what travels first cabin? Them's the ones. They dragged us down 'til we're on'y wage slaves in the bowels of a bloody ship, sweatin, burnin' up, eatin' coal dust! Hit's them's ter blame—the damned Capitalist class! (*There had been a gradual murmur of contemptuous resentment rising among the men until now he is interrupted by a storm of catcalls, hisses, boos, hard laughter.*)

VOICES. Turn it off!
Shut up!
Sit down!
Closa da face!
Tamn fool! (*Etc.*)

YANK. (*standing up and glaring at* LONG) Sit down before I knock yuh down! (LONG *makes haste to efface himself.* YANK *goes on contemptuously*) De Bible, huh? De Cap'tlist class, huh? Aw nix on dat Salvation Army-Socialist bull, Git a soapbox! Hire a hall! Come and be saved, huh? Jerk us to Jesus, huh? Aw g'wan! I've listened to lots of guys like you, see. Yuh're all wrong. Wanter know what I t'ink? Yuh ain't no good for no one. Yuh're de bunk. Yuh ain't go no noive, get me? Yuh're yellow, dat's what. Yellow, dat's you. Say! What's dem slobs in de foist cabin got to do wit us? We're better men dan dey are, ain't we? Sure! One of us guys could clean up de whole mob with one mit. Put one of 'em down here for one watch in de stokehole, what'd happen? Dey'd carry him off on a stretcher. Dem boids don't amount to nothin'. Dey're just baggage. Who makes dis old tub run? Ain't it us guys? Well den, we belong, don't we? We belong and dey don't. Dat's all. (*A loud chorus of approval.* YANK *goes on*) As for dis bein' hell—aw, nuts! Yuh lost your noive, dat's what. Dis is a man's job, get me? It belongs. It runs dis tub. No stiffs need apply. But yuh're a stiff, see? Yuh're yellow, dat's you.

VOICES. (*with a great hard pride in them*)
Righto!
A man's job!
Talk is cheap, Long.
He never could hold up his end.
Divil take him!
Yank's right. We make it go.
Py Gott, Yank say right ting!
We don't need no one cryin' over us.
Makin' speeches.
Throw him out!
Yellow!
Chuck him overboard!
I'll break his jaw for him!
(*They crowd around* LONG *threateningly.*)

YANK. (*half good-natured again—contemptuously*) Aw, take it easy. Leave him alone. He ain't woith a punch. Drink up. Here's how, whoever owns dis. (*He takes a long swallow from his bottle. All drink with him. In a flash all is hilarious amiability again, back-slapping, loud talk, etc.*)

PADDY. (*who has been sitting in a blinking, melancholy daze—suddenly cries out in a voice full of sorrow*) We belong to this, you're saying? We make the ship to go, you're saying? Yerra[6] then, that Almighty God have pity on us! (*His voice runs into the wail of a keen,*[7] *he rocks back and forth on his bench. The men stare at him, startled and impressed in spite of themselves*) Oh, to be back in the fine days of my youth, ochone![8] Oh, there was fine beautiful ships them days—clippers wid tall masts touching the sky—fine strong men in them—men that was sons of the sea as if 'twas the mother that bore them. Oh, the clean skins of them, and the clear eyes, the straight backs and full chests of them! Brave men they was, and bold men surely! We'd be sailing out, bound down round the Horn[9] maybe. We'd be making sail in the dawn, with a fair breeze, singing a chanty song wid no care to it. And astern the land would be sinking low and dying out, but we'd give it no heed but a laugh, and never a look behind. For the day that was, was enough, for we was free men—and I'm thinking 'tis only slaves do be giving heed to the day that's gone or the day to come—until they're old like me. (*with a sort of religious exaltation*) Oh, to be scudding south again wid the power of the Trade Wind driving her on steady through the nights and the days! Full sail on her! Nights and days! Nights when the foam of the wake would be flaming wid fire, when the sky'd be blazing and winking wid stars. Or the full of the moon maybe. Then you'd see her driving

[6]Irish: Truly. [7]A lamentation for the dead. [8]Irish: alas!
[9]Cape Horn, at the southern tip of South America.

through the gray night, her sails stretching aloft all silver and white, not a sound on the deck, the lot of us dreaming dreams, till you'd believe 'twas no real ship at all you was on but a ghost ship like the *Flying Dutchman* they say does be roaming the seas forevermore without touching a port. And there was the days, too. A warm sun on the clean decks. Sun warming the blood of you, and wind over the miles of shiny green ocean like strong drink to your lungs. Work—aye, hard work—but who'd mind that at all? Sure, you worked under the sky and 'twas work wid skill and daring to it. And wid the day done, in the dog watch, smoking me pipe at ease, the lookout would be raising land maybe, and we'd see the mountains of South Americy wid the red fire of the setting sun painting their white tops and clouds floating by them! (*His tone of exaltation ceases. He goes on mournfully*) Yerra, what's the use of talking? 'Tis a dead man's whisper. (*To* YANK *resentfully*) 'Twas them days men belonged to ships, not now. 'Twas them days a ship was part of the sea, and a man was part of a ship, and the sea joined all together and made it one. (*scornfully*) Is it one wid this you'd be, Yank—black smoke from the funnels smudging the sea, smudging the decks—the bloody engines pounding and throbbing and shaking—wid divil a sight of sun or a breath of clean air—choking our lungs wid coal dust—breaking our backs and hearts in the hell of the stokehole—feeding the bloody furnace—feeding our lives along wid the coal, I'm thinking—caged in by steel from a sight of the sky like bloody apes in the Zoo! (*with a harsh laugh*) Ho-ho, divil mend you! Is it to belong to that you're wishing? Is it a flesh and blood wheel of the engines you'd be?

YANK. (*who has been listening with a contemptuous sneer, barks out the answer*) Sure ting! Dat's me. What about it?

PADDY. (*as if to himself—with great sorrow*) Me time is past due. That a great wave wid sun in the heart of it may sweep over the side sometime I'd be dreaming of the days that's gone!

YANK. Aw, yuh crazy Mick![10] (*He springs to his feet and advances on* PADDY *threateningly—then stops, fighting some queer struggle within himself—lets his hands fall to his sides—contemptuously*) Aw, take it easy. Yuh're aw right, at dat. Yuh're bugs, dat's all—nutty as a cuckoo. All dat tripe yuh been pullin'—Aw, dat's all right. On'y it's dead, get me? Yuh don't belong no more, see. Yuh don't get de stuff. Yuh're too old. (*disgustedly*) But aw say, come up for air oncet in a while, can't yuh? See what's happened since yuh croaked. (*He suddenly bursts forth vehemently, growing more and more excited*) Say! Sure! Sure I meant it! What de hell—Say, lemme talk! Hey! Hey, you old Harp! Hey, youse guys! Say, listen to me—wait a moment—I gotter talk, see. I belong and he don't. He's dead but I'm livin'. Listen to me! Sure I'm part of de engines! Why de hell not! Dey move, don't dey? Dey're speed, ain't day? Dey smash trou, don't dey? Twenty-five knots a hour! Dat's goin' some! Dat's new stuff! Dat belongs! But him, he's too old. He gets dizzy. Say, listen. All dat crazy tripe about suns and winds, fresh air and de rest of it—Aw hell, dat's all a dope dream! Hittin' de pipe of de past, dat's what he's doin'. He's old and don't belong no more. But me, I'm young! I'm in de pink! I move wit it. It, get me! I mean de ting dat's de guts of all dis. It ploughs trou all de tripe he's been saying'. It blows dat up! It knocks dat dead! It slams dat offen de face of de oith! It, get me! De engines and de coal and de smoke and all de rest of

[10]Slang term for Irishman.

it! He can't breathe and swallow coal dust, but I kin, see? Dat's fresh air for me! Dat's food for me! I'm new, get me? Hell in de stokehole? Sure! It takes a man to work in hell. Hell, sure, dat's my fav'rite climate. I eat it up! I git fat on it! It's me makes it hot! It's me makes it roar! It's me makes it move! Sure, on'y for me everything stops. It all goes dead, get me? De noise and smoke and all de engines movin' de woild, dey stop. Dere ain't nothin' no more! Dat's what I'm sayin'. Everything else dat makes de woild move, somep'n makes it move. It can't move witout somep'n else, see? Den yuh get down to me. I'm at de bottom, get me! Dere ain't nothin' foither. I'm de end! I'm de start! I start somep'n and de woild moves! It—dat's me—de new dat's moiderin' de old! I'm de ting in coal dat makes it boin; I'm steam and oil for de engines; I'm de ting in noise dat makes yuh hear it; I'm smoke and express trains and steamers and factory whistles; I'm de ting in gold dat makes it money! And I'm what makes iron into steel! Steel, dat stands for de whole ting! And I'm steel—steel—steel! I'm de muscles in steel, de punch behind it. (*As he says this he pounds with his fist against the steel bunks. All the men, roused to a pitch of frenzied self-glorification by his speech, do likewise. There is a deafening metallic roar, through which* YANK'S *voice can be heard bellowing*) Slaves, hell! We run de whole woiks. All de rich guys dat tink dey're somep'n, dey ain't nothin'! Dey don't belong. But us guys, we're in de move, we're at de bottom, de whole ting is us! (PADDY *from the start of* YANK'S *speech has been taking one gulp after another from his bottle, at first frightenedly, as if he were afraid to listen, then desperately, as if to drown his senses, but finally has achieved complete indifferent, even amused, drunkenness.* YANK *sees his lips moving. He quells the uproar with a shout*) Hey, youse guys, take it easy! Wait a moment! De nutty Harp is sayin' somep'n.

PADDY. (*is heard now–throws his head back with a mocking burst of laughter*) Ho-ho-ho-ho-ho—

YANK. (*drawing back his fist, with a snarl*) Aw! Look out who yuh're givin' the bark!

PADDY. (*begins to sing the "Miller of Dee" with enormous good nature*)

> *"I care for nobody, no, not I,*
> *And nobody cares for me."*

YANK. (*good-natured himself in a flash, interrupts* PADDY *with a slap on the bare back like a report*) Dat's de stuff! Now you're gettin' wise to somep'n. Care for nobody, dat's de dope! To hell with 'em all! And nix on nobody else carin'. I kin care for myself, get me! (*Eight bells sound, muffled, vibrating through the steel walls as if some enormous brazen gong were imbedded in the heart of the ship. All the men jump up mechanically, file through the door silently close upon each other's heels in what is very like a prisoner's lockstep.* YANK *slaps* PADDY *on the back*) Our watch, yuh old Harp! (*mockingly*) Come on down in hell. Eat up de coal dust. Drink in de heat. It's it, see! Act like yuh liked it, yuh better—or croak yuhself.

PADDY. (*with jovial defiance*) To the devil wid it; I'll not report this watch. Let thim log[11] me and be damned. I'm no slave the like of you. I'll be sittin' here at me ease, and drinking, and thinking, and dreaming dreams.

[11]Enter charges of disobedience into the ship's log (record).

YANK. (*contemptuously*) Tinkin' and dreamin', what'll that get yuh? What's tinkin' got to do wit it? We move, don't we? Speed, ain't it? Fog, dat's all you stand for. But we drive trou dat, don't we? We split dat up and smash trou—twenty-five knots an hour! (*Turns his back on* PADDY *scornfully*) Aw, yuh make me sick! Yuh don't belong! (*He strides out the door in rear.* PADDY *hums to himself, blinking drowsily.*)

CURTAIN

SCENE TWO

Two days out. A section of the promenade deck. MILDRED DOUGLAS *and her aunt are discovered reclining in deck chairs. The former is a girl of twenty, slender, delicate, with a pale, pretty face marred by a self-conscious expression of disdainful superiority. She looks fretful, nervous and discontented, bored by her own anemia. Her aunt is a pompous and proud—and fat—old lady. She is a type even to the point of a double chin and lorgnettes.*[1] *She is dressed pretentiously, as if afraid her face alone would never indicate her position in life.* MILDRED *is dressed all in white.*

The impression to be conveyed by this scene is one of the beautiful, vivid life of the sea all about–sunshine on the deck in a great flood, the fresh sea wind blowing across it. In the midst of this, these two incongruous, artificial figures, inert and disharmonious, the elder like a gray lump of dough touched up with rouge, the younger looking as if the vitality of her stock had been sapped before she was conceived, so that she is the expression not of its life energy but merely of the artificialities that energy had won for itself in the spending.

MILDRED. (*looking up with affected dreaminess*) How the black smoke swirls back against the sky! Is it not beautiful?

AUNT. (*without looking up*) I dislike smoke of any kind.

MILDRED. My great-grandmother smoked a pipe—a clay pipe.

AUNT. (*ruffling*) Vulgar!

MILDRED. She was too distant a relative to be vulgar. Time mellows pipes.

AUNT. (*pretending boredom but irritated*) Did the sociology you took up at college teach you that—to play the ghoul on every possible occasion, excavating old bones? Why not let your great-grandmother rest in her grave?

MILDRED. (*dreamily*) With her pipe beside her—puffing in Paradise.

AUNT. (*with spite*) Yes, you are a natural born ghoul. You are even getting to look like one, my dear.

MILDRED. (*in a passionless tone*) I detest you, Aunt. (*looking at her critically*) Do you know what you remind me of? Of a cold pork pudding against a background of linoleum tablecloth in the kitchen of a—but the possibilities are wearisome. (*She closes her eyes*)

AUNT. (*with a bitter laugh*) *Merci*[2] for your candor. But since I am and must be your chaperon—in appearance, at least—let us patch up some sort of armed truce. For my part you are quite free to indulge any pose of eccentricity that beguiles you—as long as you observe the amenities—

[1]Eyeglasses with a handle. [2]French: Thanks.

MILDRED. (*drawling*) The inanities?

AUNT. (*going on as if she hadn't heard*) After exhausting the morbid thrills of social service work on New York's East Side[3]—how they must have hated you, by the way, the poor that you made so much poorer in their own eyes?—you are now bent on making your slumming international. Well, I hope Whitechapel will provide the needed nerve tonic. Do not ask me to chaperon you there, however. I told your father I would not. I loathe deformity. We will hire an army of detectives and you may investigate everything—they allow you to see.

MILDRED. (*protesting with a trace of genuine earnestness*) Please do not mock my attempts to discover how the other half lives. Give me credit for some sort of groping sincerity in that at least. I would like to help them. I would like to be some use in the world. Is it my fault I don't know how? I would like to be sincere, to touch life somewhere. (*with weary bitterness*) But I'm afraid I have neither the vitality nor integrity. All that was burnt out in our stock before I was born. Grandfather's blast furnaces, flaming to the sky, melting steel, making millions—then father keeping those home fires burning, making more millions—and little me at the tail-end of it all. I'm a waste product in the Bessemer process[4]—like the millions. Or rather, I inherit the acquired trait of the by-product, wealth, but none of the energy, none of the strength of the steel that made it. I am sired by gold and damned by it, as they say at the race track—damned in more ways than one. (*She laughs mirthlessly*).

AUNT. (*unimpressed—superciliously*) You seem to be going in for sincerity today. It isn't becoming to you, really—except as an obvious pose. Be as artificial as you are, I advise. There's a sort of sincerity in that, you know. And, after all, you must confess you like that better.

MILDRED. (*again affected and bored*) Yes, I suppose I do. Pardon me for my outburst. When a leopard complains of its spots, it must sound rather grotesque. (*in a mocking tone*) Purr, little Leopard. Purr, scratch, tear, kill, gorge yourself and be happy—only stay in the jungle where your spots are camouflaged. In a cage they make you conspicuous.

AUNT. I don't know what you are talking about.

MILDRED. It would be rude to talk about anything to you. Let's just talk. (*She looks at her wrist watch*) Well, thank goodness, it's about time for them to come for me. That ought to give me a new thrill, Aunt.

AUNT. (*affectedly troubled*) You don't mean to say you're really going? The dirt—the heat must be frightful—

MILDRED. Grandfather started as a puddler.[5] I should have inherited an immunity to heat that would make a salamander[6] shiver. It will be fun to put it to the test.

AUNT. But don't you have to have the captain's—or someone's—permission to visit the stokehole?

MILDRED. (*with a triumphant smile*) I have it—both his and the chief engineer's. Oh, they didn't want to at first, in spite of my social service credentials. They didn't seem a bit anxious that I should investigate how the other

[3]A district of tenements and slums, as is London's Whitechapel, following.
[4]A process for making steel.
[5]A steelworker.
[6]Mythical animal thought to endure fire without harm.

half lives and works on a ship. So I had to tell them that my father, the president of Nazareth Steel, chairman of the board of directors of this line, had told me it would be all right.

AUNT. He didn't.

MILDRED. How naïve age makes one! But I said he did, Aunt. I even said he had given me a letter to them—which I had lost. And they were afraid to take the chance that I might be lying. (*excitedly*) So it's ho! for the stokehole. The second engineer is to escort me. (*looking at her watch again*) It's time. And here he comes, I think. (*The* SECOND ENGINEER *enters. He is a husky, fine-looking man of thirty-five or so. He stops before the two and tips his cap, visibly embarrassed and ill-at-ease.*)

SECOND ENGINEER. Miss Douglas?

MILDRED. (*throwing off her rugs and getting to her feet*) Are we all ready to start?

SECOND ENGINEER. In just a second, ma'am. I'm waiting for the Fourth.[7] He's coming along.

MILDRED. (*with a scornful smile*) You don't care to shoulder this responsibility alone, is that it?

SECOND ENGINEER. (*forcing a smile*) Two are better than one. (*disturbed by her eyes, glances out to sea—blurts out*) A fine day we're having.

MILDRED. Is it?

SECOND ENGINEER. A nice warm breeze—

MILDRED. It feels cold to me.

SECOND ENGINEER. But it's hot enough in the sun—

MILDRED. Not hot enough for me. I don't like Nature. I was never athletic.

SECOND ENGINEER. (*forcing a smile*) Well you'll find it hot enough where you're going.

MILDRED. Do you mean hell?

SECOND ENGINEER. (*flabbergasted, decides to laugh*) Ho-ho! No, I mean the stokehole.

MILDRED. My grandfather was a puddler. He played with boiling steel.

SECOND ENGINEER. (*all at sea—uneasy*) Is that so? Hum, you'll excuse me, ma'am, but are you intending to wear that dress?

MILDRED. Why not?

SECOND ENGINEER. You'll likely rub against oil and dirt. It can't be helped.

MILDRED. It doesn't matter. I have lots of white dresses.

SECOND ENGINEER. I have an old coat you might throw over—

MILDRED. I have fifty dresses like this. I will throw this one into the sea when I come back. That ought to wash it clean, don't you think?

SECOND ENGINEER. (*doggedly*) There's ladders to climb down that are none too clean—and dark alleyways—

MILDRED. I will wear this very dress and none other.

SECOND ENGINEER. No offense meant. It's none of my business. I was only warning you—

MILDRED. Warning? That sounds thrilling.

SECOND ENGINEER. (*looking down the deck—with a sigh of relief*) There's the Fourth now. He's waiting for us. If you'll come—

[7] I.e., the fourth-ranking Engineering Officer.

MILDRED. Go on. I'll follow you. (*He goes.* MILDRED *turns a mocking smile on her aunt*) An oaf—but a handsome, virile oaf.

AUNT. (*scornfully*) Poser!

MILDRED. Take care. He said there were dark alleyways—

AUNT. (*in the same tone*) Poser!

MILDRED. (*biting her lips angrily*) You are right. But would that my millions were not so anemically chaste!

AUNT. Yes, for a fresh pose I have no doubt you would drag the name of Douglas in the gutter!

MILDRED. From which it sprang. Good-by, Aunt. Don't pray too hard that I may fall into the fiery furnace.

AUNT. Poser!

MILDRED. (*viciously*) Old hag! (*She slaps her aunt insultingly across the face and walks off, laughing gaily.*)

AUNT. (*screams after her*) I said poser!

CURTAIN

SCENE THREE

The stokehole. In the rear, the dimly-outlined bulks of the furnaces and boilers. High overhead one hanging electric bulb sheds just enough light through the murky air laden with coal dust to pile up masses of shadows everywhere. A line of men, stripped to the waist, is before the furnace doors. They bend over, looking neither to right nor left, handling their shovels as if they were part of their bodies, with a strange, awkward, swinging rhythm. They use the shovels to throw open the furnace doors. Then from these fiery round holes in the black a flood of terrific light and heat pours full upon the men who are outlined in silhouette in the crouching, inhuman attitudes of chained gorillas. The men shovel with a rhythmic motion, swinging as on a pivot from the coal which lies in heaps on the floor behind to hurl it into the flaming mouths before them. There is a tumult of noise—the brazen clang of the furnace doors as they are flung open or slammed shut, the grating, teeth-gritting grind of steel against steel, of crunching coal. This clash of sounds stuns one's ears with its rending dissonance. But there is order in it, rhythm, a mechanical regulated recurrence, a tempo. And rising above all, making the air hum with the quiver of liberated energy, the roar of leaping flames in the furnaces, the monotonous throbbing beat of the engines.

As the curtain rises, the furnace doors are shut. The men are taking a breathing spell. One or two are arranging the coal behind them, pulling it into more accessible heaps. The others can be dimly made out leaning on their shovels in relaxed attitudes of exhaustion.

PADDY. (*from somewhere in the line—plaintively*) Yerra, will this divil's own watch nivir end? Me back is broke. I'm destroyed entirely.

YANK. (*from the center of the line—with exuberant scorn*) Aw, yuh make me sick! Lie down and croak, why don't yuh? Always beefin', dat's you! Say, dis is a cinch! Dis was made for me! It's my meat, get me! (*A whistle is blown—a thin, shrill note from somewhere overhead in the darkness.* YANK *curses without resentment*) Dere's de damn engineer crackin' de whip. He tinks we're loafin'.

PADDY. (*vindictively*) God stiffen him!

YANK. (*in an exultant tone of command*) Come on, youse guys! Git into de game! She's gittin' hungry! Pile some grub in her. Trow it into her belly! Come on now, all of youse! Open her up! (*At this last all the men, who have followed his movements of getting into position, throw open their furnace doors with a deafening clang. The fiery light floods over their shoulders as they bend round for the coal. Rivulets of sooty sweat have traced maps on their backs. The enlarged muscles form bunches of high light and shadow.*)

YANK. (*chatting a count as he shovels without seeming effort*) One—two—tree—(*His voice rising exultantly in the joy of battle*) Dat's de stuff! Let her have it! All togedder now! Sling it into her! Let her ride! Shoot de piece now! Call de toin on her! Drive her into it! Feel her move! Watch her smoke! Speed, dat's her middle name! Give her coal, youse guys! Coal, dat's her booze! Drink it up, baby! Let's see yuh sprint! Dig in and gain a lap! Dere she go-o-es. (*This last in the chanting formula of the gallery gods at the six-day bike race. He slams his furnace door shut. The others do likewise with as much unison as their wearied bodies will permit. The effect is one of one fiery eye after another being blotted out with a series of accompanying bangs.*)

PADDY. (*groaning*) Me back is broke. I'm bate out—bate—(*There is a pause. Then the inexorable whistle sounds again from the dim regions above the electric light. There is a growl of cursing rage from all sides.*)

YANK. (*shaking his fist upward—contemptuously*) Take it easy dere, you! Who d'yuh tink's runnin' dis game, me or you? When I get ready, we move. Not before! When I get ready, get me!

VOICES. (*approvingly*) That's the stuff!
Yank tal him, py golly!
Yank ain't affeerd.
Goot poy, Yank!
Give him hell!
Tell 'im 'e's a bloody swine!
Bloody slave-driver!

YANK. (*contemptuously*) He ain't got no noive. He's yellow, get me? All de engineers is yellow. Dey got streaks a mile wide. Aw, to hell wit him! Let's move, youse guys. We had a rest. Come on, she needs it! Give her pep! It ain't for him. Him and his whistle, dey don't belong. But we belong, see! We gotter feed de baby! Come on! (*He turns and flings his furnace door open. They all follow his lead. At this instant the* SECOND *and* FOURTH ENGINEER *enter from darkness on the left with* MILDRED *between them. She starts, turns paler, her pose is crumbling, she shivers with fright in spite of the blazing heat, but forces herself to leave the* ENGINEERS *and take a few steps nearer the men. She is right behind* YANK. *All this happens quickly while the men have their backs turned.*)

YANK. Come on, youse guys! (*He is turning to get coal when the whistle sounds again in a peremptory, irritating note. This drives* YANK *into a sudden fury. While the other men have turned full around and stopped dumbfoundedly by the spectacle of* MILDRED *standing there in her white dress,* YANK *does not turn far enough to see her. Besides, his head is thrown back, he blinks upward through the murk trying to find the owner of the whistle, he brandishes his shovel murderously over his head in one hand, pounding on his chest, gorilla-like, with the other, shouting*) Toin off dat whistle! Come down outa dere, yuh yellow, brass-buttoned, Belfast bum, yuh! Come down and I'll knock yer brains out! Yuh lousy, stinkin', yellow mut of a Catholic-moiderin' bastard! Come down and I'll moider yuh!

Pullin dat whistle on me, huh? I'll show yuh! I'll crash yer skull in! I'll drive yer teet-down yer troat! I'll slam yer nose trou de back of yer head! I'll cut yer guts out for a nickel, yuh lousy boob, yuh dirty, crummy, muck-eatin' son of a—(*Suddenly he becomes conscious of all the other men staring at something directly behind his back. He whirls defensively with a snarling, murderous growl, crouching to spring, his lips drawn back over his teeth, his small eyes gleaming ferociously. He sees* MILDRED, *like a white apparition in the full light from the open furnace doors. He glares into her eyes, turned to stone. As for her, during his speech she has listened, paralyzed with horror, terror, her whole personality crushed, beaten in, collapsed, by the terrific impact of this unknown, abysmal brutality, naked and shameless. As she looks at his gorilla face, as his eyes bore into hers, she utters a low, choking cry and shrinks away from him, putting both hands up before her eyes to shut out the sight of his face, to protect her own. This startles* YANK *to a reaction. His mouth falls open, his eyes grow bewildered.*)

MILDRED. (*about to faint—to the* ENGINEERS, *who now have her one by each arm—whimperingly*) Take me away! Oh, the filthy beast! (*She faints. They carry her quickly back, disappearing in the darkness at the left, rear. An iron door clangs shut. Rage and bewildered fury rush back on* YANK. *He feels himself insulted in some unknown fashion in the very heart of his pride. He roars* "God damn yuh!" *and hurls his shovel after them at the door which has just closed. It hits the steel bulkhead with a clang and falls clattering on the steel floor. From overhead the whistle sounds again in a long, angry, insistent command.*)

CURTAIN

SCENE FOUR

The firemen's forecastle. YANK'S *watch has just come off duty and had dinner. Their faces and bodies shine from a soap-and-water scrubbing but around their eyes, where a hasty dousing does not touch, the coal dust sticks like black make-up, giving them a queer, sinister expression.* YANK *has not washed either face or body. He stands out in contrast to them, a blackened, brooding figure. He is seated forward on a bench in the exact attitude of Rodin's "The Thinker."*[1] *The others, most of them smoking pipes, are staring at* YANK *half-apprehensively, as if fearing an outburst; half-amusedly, as if they saw a joke somewhere that tickled them.*

VOICES. He ain't ate nothin'.
Py golly, a fallar gat to gat grub in him.
Divil a lie.
Yank feeda da fire, no feeda da face.
Ha-ha.
He ain't even washed hisself.
He's forgot.
Hey, Yank, you forgot to wash.

YANK. (*sullenly*) Forgot nothin! To hell with washin'.

VOICES. It'll stick to you.
It'll get under your skin.
Give yer the bleedin' itch, that's wot.

[1]Statue of a man sitting, with his chin on his fist, deep in thought, by Auguste Rodin (1840–1917), French sculptor.

VOICES. It'll stick to you.
It makes spots on you—like a leopard.
Like a piebald nigger, you mean.
Better wash up, Yank.
You sleep better.
Wash up, Yank!
Wash up! Wash up!

YANK. (*resentfully*) Aw say, youse guys. Lemme alone. Can't youse see I'm tryin' to tink?

ALL. (*repeating the word after him as one with cynical mockery*) Think! (*The word has a brazen, metallic quality as if their throats were phonograph horns. It is followed by a chorus of hard, barking laughter.*)

YANK. (*springing to his feet and glaring at them belligerently*) Yes, tink! Tink, dat's what I said! What about it? (*They are silent, puzzled by his sudden resentment at what used to be one of his jokes.* YANK *sits down again in the same attitude of "The Thinker."*)

VOICES. Leave him alone.
He's got a grouch on.
Why wouldn't he?

PADDY. (*with a wink at the others*) Sure I know what's the matther. 'Tis aisy to see. He's fallen in love. I'm telling you.

ALL. (*repeating the word after him as one with cynical mockery*) Love! (*The word has a brazen, metallic quality as if their throats were phonograph horns. It is followed by a chorus of hard, barking laughter.*)

YANK. (*with a contemptuous snort*) Love, Hell! Hate, dat's what. I've fallen in hate, get me?

PADDY. (*philosophically*) 'Twould take a wise man to tell one from the other. (*with a bitter, ironical scorn, increasing as he goes on*) But I'm telling you it's love that's in it. Sure what else but love for us poor bastes in the stokehole would be bringing a fine lady, dressed like a white quane, down a mile of ladders and steps to be havin' a look at us (*A growl of anger goes up from all sides.*)

LONG. (*jumping on a bench—hectically*) Hinsultin' us! Hinsultin' us, the bloody cow! And them bloody engineers! What right 'as they got to be exhibitin' us 's if we was bleedin' monkeys in a menagerie? Did we sign for hinsults to our dignity as 'onest workers? Is that in the ship's articles?[2] You kin bloody well bet it ain't! But I knows why they done it. I arsked a deck steward 'o she was and 'e told me. 'Er old man's a bleedin' millionaire, a bloody Capitalist! 'E's got enuf bloody gold to sink this bleedin' ship! 'E makes arf the bloody steel in the world! 'E owns this bloody boat! And you and me, Comrades, we're 'is slaves! and the skipper and mates and engineers, they're 'is slaves! And she's 'is bloody daughter and we're all 'er slaves, too! And she gives 'er orders as 'ow she wants to see the bloody animals below decks and down they takes 'er! (*There is a roar of rage from all sides.*)

YANK. (*blinking at him bewilderedly*) Say! Wait a moment! Is all dat straight goods?

LONG. Straight as string! The bleedin' steward as waits on 'em, 'e told me about 'er. And what're we goin' ter do, I arsks yer? 'Ave we got ter swaller 'er

[2]Employment contract.

hinsults like dogs? It ain't in the ship's articles. I tell yer we got a case. We kin go to law—

YANK. (*with abysmal contempt*) Hell! Law!

ALL. (*repeating the word after him as one with cynical mockery*) Law! (*The word has a brazen metallic quality as if their throats were phonograph horns. It is followed by a chorus of hard, barking laughter.*)

LONG. (*feeling the ground slipping from under his feet—desperately*) As voters and citizens we kin force the bloody governments—

YANK. (*with abysmal contempt*) Hell! Governments!

ALL. (*repeating the word after him as one with cynical mockery*) Governments! (*The word has a brazen metallic quality as if their throats were phonograph horns. It is followed by a chorus of hard, barking laughter.*)

LONG. (*hysterically*) We're free and equal in the sight of God—

YANK. (*with abysmal contempt*) Hell! God!

ALL. (*repeating the word after him as one with cynical mockery.*) God! (*The word has a brazen metallic quality as if their throats were phonograph horns. It is followed by a chorus of hard, barking laughter.*)

YANK. (*witheringly*) Aw, join de Salvation Army!

ALL. Sit down! Shut up! Damn fool! Sea-lawyer![3] (LONG *slinks back out of sight.*)

PADDY. (*continuing the trend of his thoughts as if he had never been interrupted—bitterly*) And there she was standing behind us, and the Second pointing at us like a man you'd hear in a circus would be saying: In this cage is a queerer kind of baboon than ever you'd find in darkest Africa. We roast them in their own sweat—and be damned if you won't hear some of them saying they like it! (*He glances scornfully at* YANK.)

YANK. (*with a bewildered uncertain growl*) Aw!

PADDY. And there was Yank roarin' curses and turning round wid his shovel to brain her—and she looked at him, and him at her—

YANK. (*slowly*) She was all white. I tought she was a ghost. Sure.

PADDY. (*with heavy, biting sarcasm*) 'Twas love at first sight, divil a doubt of it! If you'd seen the endearin' look on her pale mug when she shriviled away with her hands over her eyes to shut out the sight of him! Sure, 'twas as if she'd seen a great hairy ape escaped from the Zoo!

YANK. (*stung—with a growl of rage*) Aw!

PADDY. And the loving way Yank heaved his shovel at the skull of her, only she was out the door! (*A grin breaking over his face*) 'Twas touching, I'm telling you! It put the touch of home, swate home in the stokehole. (*There is a roar of laughter from all.*)

YANK. (*glaring at* PADDY *menacingly*) Aw, choke dat off, see!

PADDY. (*not heeding him—to the others*) And her grabbin' at the Second's arm for protection. (*With a grotesque imitation of a woman's voice*) Kiss me, Engineer dear, for it's dark down here and me old man's in Wall Street making money! Hug me tight, darlin', for I'm afeered in the dark and me mother's on deck makin' eyes at the skipper! (*another roar of laughter*)

YANK. (*threateningly*) Say! What yuh tryin' to do, kid me, yuh old Harp!

PADDY. Divil a bit! Ain't I wishin' myself you'd brained her?

[3]A complainer, troublemaker.

YANK. (*fiercely*) I'll brain her! I'll brain her yet, wait 'n' see! (*Coming over to* PADDY *slowly)* Say, is dat what she called me—a hairy ape?

PADDY. She looked it at you if she didn't say the word itself.

YANK. (*grinning horribly*) Hairy ape, huh? Sure! Dat's de way she looked at me aw right. Hairy ape! So dat's me, huh? (*bursting into rage—as if she were still in front of him*) Yuh skinny tart! Yuh white-faced bum, yuh! I'll show you who's a ape! (*turning to the others, bewilderment seizing him again*) Say, youse guys. I was bawlin' him out for pullin' de whistle on us. You heard me. And den I seen youse lookin' at somep'n and I tought he'd sneaked down to come up in back of me, and I hopped round to knock him dead wit de shovel. And dere she was wit de light on her! Christ, yuh coulda pushed me over with a finger! I was scared, get me? Sure I tought she was a ghost, see? She was all in white like dey wrap around stiffs. You seen her. Kin yuh blame me? She didn't belong, dat's what. And den when I come to and seen it was a real skoit and seen de way she was lookin' at me—like Paddy said—Christ, I was sore, get me? I don't stand for dat stuff from nobody. And I flung de shovel—on'y she'd beat it. (*furiously*) I wished it'd banged her! I wished it'd knocked her block off!

LONG. And be 'anged for murder or 'lectrocuted? She ain't bleedin' well worth it.

YANK. I don't give a damn what! I'd be square wit her, wouldn't I? Tink I wanter let her put somep'n over on me? Tink I'm goin' to let her git away wit dat stuff? Yuh don't know me! No one ain't never put nothin' over on me and got away wit it, see!—not dat kind of stuff—no guy and no skoit neither! I'll fix her! Maybe she'll come down again—

VOICE. No chance, Yank. You scared her out of a year's growth.

YANK. I scared her? Why de hell should I scare her? Who de hell is she? Ain't she de same as me? Hairy ape, huh? (*with his old confident bravado*) I'll show her I'm better'n her, if she on'y knew it. I belong and she don't, see! I move and she's dead! Twenty-five knots a hour, dat's me! Dat carries her but I make dat. She's on'y baggage. Sure! (*again bewilderedly*) But, Christ, she was funny lookin'! Did yuh pipe her hands? White and skinny. Yuh could see de bones through 'em. And her mush, dat was dead white, too. And her eyes, dey was like dey'd seen a ghost. Me, dat was! Sure! Hairy ape! Ghost, huh? Look at dat arm! (*He extends his right arm, swelling out of the great muscles*) I coulda took her wit dat, wit just my little finger even, and broke her in two. (*Again bewilderedly*) Say, who is dat skoit, huh? What is she? What's she come from? Who made her? Who give her de noive to look at me like dat? Dis ting's got my goat right. I don't get her. She's new to me. What does a skoit like her mean, huh? She don't belong, get me! I can't see her. (*with growing anger*) But one ting I'm wise to, aw right, aw right! Youse all kin bet your shoits I'll git even wit her. I'll show her if she tinks she—She grinds de organ and I'm on de string, huh? I'll fix her! Let her come down again and I'll fling her in de furnace! She'll move den! She won't shiver at nothin', den! Speed, dat'll be her! She'll belong den! (*He grins horribly*)

PADDY. She'll never come. She's had her belly-full, I'm telling you. She'll be in bed now, I'm thinking, wid ten doctors and nurses feedin' her salts[4] to clean the fear out of her.

[4]A laxative, such as Epsom salts.

YANK. (*enraged*) Yuh think I made her sick, too, do yuh? Just lookin' at me, huh? Hairy ape, huh? (*in a frenzy of rage*) I'll fix her! I'll tell her where to git off! She'll get down on her knees and take it back or I'll bust de face offen her! (*shaking one fist upward and beating on his chest with the other*) I'll find yuh! I'm comin', d'yuh hear? I'll fix yuh, God damn you! (*He makes a rush for the door.*)

VOICES. Stop him!
He'll get shot!
He'll murder her!
Trip him up!
Hold him!
Gott, he's strong!
Hold him down!
Look out for a kick!
Pin his arms!

(*They have all piled on him and, after a fierce struggle, by sheer weight of numbers have borne him to the floor just inside the door.*)

PADDY. (*who has remained detached*) Kape him down till he's cooled off. (*Scornfully*) Yerra, Yank, you're a great fool. Is it payin' attention at all you are to the like of that skinny sow widout one drop of rale blood in her?

YANK. (*frenziedly, from the bottom of the heap*) She done me doit! She done me doit, didn't she? I'll git square wit her! I'll get her some way! Git offen me, youse guys! Lemme up! I'll show her who's a ape!

CURTAIN

SCENE FIVE

Three weeks later. A corner of Fifth Avenue in the Fifties on a fine Sunday morning. A general atmosphere of clean, well-tidied, wide street; a flood of mellow, tempered sunshine; gentle, genteel breezes. In the rear, the show windows of two shops, a jewelry establishment on the corner, a furrier's next to it. Here the adornments of extreme wealth are tantalizingly displayed. The jeweler's window is gaudy with glittering diamonds, emeralds, rubies, pearls, etc., fashioned in ornate tiaras, crowns, necklaces, collars, etc. From each piece hangs an enormous tag from which a dollar sign and numerals in intermittent electric lights wink out the incredible prices. The same in the furrier's. Rich furs of all varieties hang there bathed in a downpour of artificial light. The general effect is of a background of magnificence cheapened and made grotesque by commercialism, a background in tawdry disharmony with the clear light and sunshine on the street itself.

Up the side street YANK *and* LONG *come swaggering.* LONG *is dressed in shore clothes, wears a black Windsor tie, cloth cap.* YANK *is in his dirty dungarees. A fireman's cap with black peak is cocked defiantly on the side of his head. He has not shaved for days and around his fierce, resentful eyes—as around those of* LONG *to a lesser degree—the black smudge of coal dust still sticks like make-up. They hesitate and stand together at the corner, swaggering, looking around them with a forced, defiant contempt.*

LONG. (*indicating it all with an oratorical gesture*) Well, 'ere we are. Fif' Avenoo. This 'ere's their bleedin' private lane, as yer might say. (*bitterly*) We're trespassers 'ere. Proletarians keep orf the grass!

YANK. (*dully*) I don't see no grass, yuh boob. (*staring at the sidewalk*) Clean, ain't it? Yuh could eat a fried egg offen it. The white wings[1] got some job sweepin' dis up. (*Looking up and down the avenue—surlily*) Where's all de white-collar stiffs yuh said was here—and de skoits—*her* kind?

LONG. In church, blarst 'em! Arskin' Jesus to give 'em more money.

YANK. Choich, huh? I useter go to church onct—sure—when I was a kid. Me old man and woman, dey made me. Dey never went demselves, dough. Always got too big a head on Sunday mornin', dat was dem. (*with a grin*) Dey was scrappers for fair, bot' of dem. On Satiday nights when dey bot' got a skinful dey could put up a bout oughter been staged at de Garden.[2] When dey got trough dere wasn't a chair or table with a leg under it. Or else dey bot' jumped on me for somep'n. Dat was where I loined to take punishment. (*with a grin and a swagger*) I'm a chip offen de old block, get me?

LONG. Did yer old man follow the sea?

YANK. Naw. Worked along shore. I runned away when me old lady croaked wit de tremens.[3] I helped at truckin' and in de market. Den I shipped in de stokehole. Sure. Dat belongs. De rest was nothin'. (*looking around him*) I ain't never seen dis before. De Brooklyn waterfront, dat was where I was dragged up. (*taking a deep breath*) Dis ain't so bad at dat, huh?

LONG. Not bad? Well, we pays for it wiv our bloody sweat, if yer wants to know!

YANK. (*with sudden angry disgust*) Aw, hell! I don't see no one, see—like her. All dis gives me a pain. It don't belong. Say, ain't dere a back room around dis dump? Let's go shoot a ball.[4] All dis is too clean and quiet and dolled-up, get me! It gives me a pain.

LONG. Wait and yer'll bloody well see—

YANK. I don't wait for no one. I keep on de move. Say, what yuh drag me up here for, anyway? Tryin' to kid me, yuh simp, yuh?

LONG. Yer wants to get back at 'er, don't yer? That's what yer been sayin' every bloomin' hour since she hinsulted yer.

YANK. (*vehemently*) Sure ting I do! Didn't I try to get even wit her in Southampton? Didn't I sneak on de dock and wait for her by de gangplank? I was goin' to spit in her pale mug. Sure, right in her pop-eyes! Dat woulda made me even, see? But no chanct. Dere was a whole army of plainclothes bulls around. Dey spotted me and gimme de bum's rush. I never seen her. But I'll git square wit her yet, you watch. (*Furiously*) De lousy tart! She tinks she kin get away wit moider—but not wit me! I'll fix her! I'll tink of a way!

LONG. (*as disgusted as he dares to be*) Ain't that why I brought yer up 'ere—to show yer? Yer been lookin' at this 'ere 'ole affair wrong. Yer been actin' an' talkin' 's if it was all a bleedin' personal matter between yer and that bloody cow. I wants to convince yer she was on'y a representative of 'er clarss. I wants to awaken yer bloody clarss consciousness. Then yer'll see it's 'er clarss yer've got to fight, not 'er alone. There's a ole mob of 'em like 'er, Gawd blind 'em!

YANK. (*spitting on his hands—belligerently*) De more de merrier when I gits started. Bring on de gang!

[1]White-uniformed street cleaners.
[2]Madison Square Garden in New York City, an arena sometimes used for boxing matches.
[3]Delirium tremens, a violent mental disturbance caused by alcoholism.
[4]I.e., shoot pool.

LONG. Yer'll see 'em in arf a mo', when that church lets out. (*He turns and sees the window display in the two stores for the first time*) Blimey![5] Look at that, will yer? (*They both walk back and stand looking in the jeweler's.* LONG *flies into a fury*) Just look at this 'ere bloomin' mess! Just look at it! Look at the bleedin' prices on 'em—more'n our 'ole bloody stokehole makes in ten voyages sweatin' in 'ell! And they—'er and 'er bloody clarss—buys 'em for toys to dangle on 'em! One of these 'ere would buy scoff[6] for a starvin' family for a year!

YANK. Aw, cut de sob stuff! T' hell wit de starvin' family! Yuh'll be passin' de hat to me next. (*with naïve admiration*) Say, dem tings is pretty huh? Bet yuh dey'd hock for a piece of change aw right. (*then turning away, bored*) But, aw hell, what good are dey? Let her have 'em. Dey don't belong no more'n she does. (*with a gesture of sweeping the jewelers into oblivion*) All dat don't count, get me?

LONG. (*who has moved to the furrier's—indignantly*) And I s'pose this 'ere don't count neither—skins of poor, 'armless animals slaughtered so as 'er and 'ers can keep their bleedin' noses warm!

YANK. (*who has been staring at something inside—with queer excitement*) Take a slant at dat! Git it de once-over! Monkey fur–two t'ousand bucks! (*bewilderedly*) Is dat straight goods—monkey fur! What de hell—?

LONG. (*bitterly*) It's straight enuf. (*with grim humor*) They wouldn't bloody well pay that for a 'airy ape's skin—no, nor for the 'ole livin' ape with all 'is 'ead, and a body, and soul thrown in!

YANK. (*clenching his fists, his face growing pale with rage as if the skin in the window were a personal insult*) Trowin' it up in my face! Christ! I'll fix her!

LONG. (*excitedly*) Church is out. 'Ere they come, the bleedin' swine. (*after a glance at* YANK'S *lowering face—uneasily*) Easy goes, Comrade. Keep yer bloomin' temper. Remember force defeats itself. It ain't our weapon. We must impress our demands through peaceful means—the votes of the on-marching proletarians of the bloody world!

YANK. (*with abysmal contempt*) Votes, hell! votes is a joke, see. Votes for women! Let dem do it!

LONG. (*still more uneasily*) Calm, now. Treat 'em wiv the proper contempt. Observe the bleedin' parasites but 'old yer 'orses.

YANK. (*angrily*) Git away from me! Yuh're yellow, dat's what. Force, dat's me! De punch, dat's me every time, see! (*The crowd from church enter from the right, sauntering slowly and affectedly, their heads held stiffly up, looking neither to right nor left, talking in toneless, simpering voices. The women are rouged, calcimined, dyed, overdressed to the nth degree. The men are in Prince Alberts,*[7] *high hats, spats, canes, etc. A procession of gaudy marionettes, yet with something of the relentless horror of Frankensteins in their detached, mechanical unawareness.*)

VOICES. Dear Doctor Caiphas! He is so sincere!
What was the sermon?
I dozed off.
About the radicals, my dear—and the false doctrines that are being preached.

[5] A slang contraction of "God blind me!" At the time, a strong oath.
[6] Slang: food. [7] Elegant, long-tailed suit coats.

We must organize a hundred per cent American bazaar.
And let everyone contribute one one-hundredth per cent of their income tax.
What an original idea!
We can devote the proceeds to rehabilitating the veil of the temple.[8]
But that has been done so many times.

YANK. (*glaring from one to the other of them—with an insulting snort of scorn*) Huh! Huh! (*Without seeming to see him, they make wide detours to avoid the spot where he stands in the middle of the sidewalk.*)

LONG. (*frightenedly*) Keep yer bloomin' mouth shut, I tells yer.

YANK. (*viciously*) G'wan! Tell it to Sweeney! (*He swaggers away and deliberately lurches into a top-hatted gentleman, then glares at him pugnaciously*) Say, who d'yuh tink yuh're bumpin'? Tink yuh own de oith?

GENTLEMAN. (*coldly and affectedly*) I beg your pardon. (*He has not looked at* YANK *and passes on without a glance, leaving him bewildered.*)

LONG. (*rushing up and grabbing* YANK'S *arm*) 'Ere! Come away! This wasn't what I meant. Yer'll 'ave the bloody coppers down on us.

YANK. (*savagely—giving him a push that sends him sprawling*) G'wan!

LONG. (*picks himself up—hysterically*) I'll pop orf then. This ain't what I meant. And whatever 'appens, yer can't blame me. (*He slinks off left.*)

YANK. T' hell wit youse! (*He approaches a lady—with a vicious grin and a smirking wink*) Hello, Kiddo. How's every little ting? Got anything on for tonight? I know an old boiler down to de docks we kin crawl into. (*The lady stalks by without a look, without a change of pace.* YANK *turns to others—insultingly*) Holy smokes, what a mug! Go hide yuhself before de horses shy at yuh. Gee, pipe de heine[9] on dat one! Say, youse, yuh look like de stoin[10] of a ferryboat. Paint and powder! All dolled up to kill! Yuh look like stiffs laid out for de boneyard! Aw, g'wan, de lot of youse! Yuh give me an eyeache. Yuh don't belong, get me! Look at me, why don't youse dare? I belong, dat's me! (*pointing to skyscraper across the street which is in process of construction—with bravado*) See dat building goin' up dere? See de steel work? Steel, dat's me! Youse guys live on it and tink yuh're somep'n. But I'm *in* it, see! I'm de hoistin' engine dat makes it go up! I'm it—de inside and bottom of it! Sure! I'm steel and steam and smoke and de rest of it! It moves—speed—twenty-five stories up—and me at de top and bottom—movin'! Youse simps don't move. Yuh're on'y dolls I winds up to see 'm spin. Yuh're de garbage, get me—de leavin's—de ashes we dump over de side! Now, what 'a' yuh gotta say? (*But as they seem neither to see nor hear him, he flies into a fury.*) Bums! Pigs! Tarts! Bitches! (*He turns in a rage on the men, bumping viciously into them but not jarring them the least bit. Rather it is he who recoils after each collision. He keeps growling.*) Git off de oith! G'wan, yuh bum! Look where yuh're goin', can't yuh? Git out here! Fight, why don't yuh? Put up yer mits! Don't be a dog! Fight or I'll knock yuh dead! (*But, without seeming to see him, they all answer with mechanical affected politeness* "I beg your pardon." *Then at a cry from one of the women, they all scurry to the furrier's window.*)

[8]The curtain hung before a church sanctuary, usually during Lent.
[9]I.e., look at the rump. [10]The stern, the rear end.

THE WOMAN. (*ecstatically, with a gasp of delight*) Monkey fur! (*The whole crowd of men and women chorus after her in the same tone of affected delight.* "Monkey fur!")

YANK. (*with a jerk of his head back on his shoulders, as if he had received a punch full in the face—raging*) I see yuh, all in white! I see yuh, yuh white-faced tart, yuh! Hairy ape, huh? I'll hairy ape yuh! (*He bends down and grips at the street curbing as if to pluck it out and hurl it. Foiled in this, snarling with passion, he leaps to the lamppost on the corner and tries to pull it up for a club. Just at that moment a bus is heard rumbling up. A fat, high-hatted, spatted gentleman runs out from the side street. He calls out plaintively* "Bus! Bus! Stop here!" *and runs full tilt into the bending, straining* YANK, *who is bowled off his balance.*)

YANK. (*seeing a fight—with a roar of joy as he springs to his feet*) At last! Bus, huh? I'll bust yuh! (*He lets drive a terrific swing, his fist landing full on the fat gentleman's face. But the gentleman stands unmoved as if nothing had happened.*)

GENTLEMAN. I beg your pardon. (*then irritably*) You have made me lose my bus. (*He claps his hands and begins to scream*) Officer! officer! (*Many police whistles shrill out on the instant and a whole platoon of policemen rush in on* YANK *from all sides. He tries to fight but is clubbed to the pavement and fallen upon. The crowd at the window have not moved or noticed this disturbance. The clanging gong of the patrol wagon approaches with a clamoring din.*)

CURTAIN

SCENE SIX

Night of the following day. A row of cells in the prison on Blackwell's Island.[1] *The cells extend back diagonally from right front to left rear. They do not stop, but disappear in the dark background as if they ran on, numberless, into infinity. One electric bulb from the low ceiling of the narrow corridor sheds its light through the heavy steel bars of the cell at the extreme front and reveals part of the interior.* YANK *can be seen within, crouched on the edge of his cot in the attitude of Rodin's "The Thinker." His face is spotted with black and blue bruises. A blood-stained bandage is wrapped around his head.*

YANK. (*suddenly starting as if awakening from a dream, reaches out and shakes the bars—aloud to himself, wonderingly*) Steel. Dis is de Zoo, huh? (*A burst of hard, barking laughter comes from the unseen occupants of the cells, runs back down the tier, and abruptly ceases.*)

VOICES. (*mockingly*) The Zoo? That's a new name for this coop—a damn good name!

Steel, eh? You said a mouthful. This is the old iron house.

Who is that boob talkin'?

He's the bloke they brung in out of his head. The bulls had beat him up fierce.

YANK. (*dully*) I musta been dreamin'. I thought I was in a cage at de Zoo—but de apes don't talk, do dey?

VOICES. (*with mocking laughter*) You're in a cage aw right.

A coop!

[1]Island in the East River in New York City, now called Roosevelt Island.

A pen!
A sty!
A kennel! (*hard laughter—a pause*)
Say, guy! Who are you? No, never mind lying. What are you?
Yes, tell us your sad story. What's your game?
What did they jug yuh for?

YANK. (*dully*) I was a fireman—stokin' on de liners. (*then with sudden rage, rattling his cell bars*) I'm a hairy ape, get me? And I'll bust youse all in de jaw if yuh don't lay off kiddin' me.

VOICES. Huh! You're a hard boiled duck, ain't you!
When you spit, it bounces! (*laughter*)
Aw, can it. He's a regular guy. Ain't you?
What did he say he was—a ape?

YANK. (*defiantly*) Sure ting! Ain't dat what youse all are—apes? (*a silence, then a furious rattling of bars down the corridor*).

A VOICE. (*thick with rage*) I'll show yuh who's a ape, yuh bum!

VOICES. Ssshh! Nix!
Can de noise!
Piano!
You'll have the guard down on us!

YANK. (*scornfully*) De guard? Yuh mean de keeper, don't yuh? (*angry exclamations from all the cells*)

VOICE. (*placatingly*) Aw, don't pay no attention to him. He's off his nut from the beatin'-up he got. Say, you guy! We're waitin' to hear what they landed you for—or ain't yuh tellin'?

YANK. Sure, I'll tell youse. Sure! Why de hell not? On'y—youse won't get me. Nobody gets me but me, see? I started to tell de Judge and all he says was: "Toity days to tink it over."—Tink it over! Christ, dat's all I been doin' for weeks! (*after a pause*) I was tryin' to git even wit someone, see?—someone dat done me doit.

VOICES. (*cynically*) De old stuff, I bet. Your goil, huh?
Give yuh the double-cross, huh?
That's them ever time!
Did yuh beat up de odder guy?

YANK. (*disgustedly*) Aw, yuh're all wrong! Sure dere was a skoit in it—but not what youse mean, not dat old tripe. Dis was a new kind of skoit. She was dolled up all in white—in de stokehole. I tought she was a ghost. Sure. (*A pause.*)

VOICES. (*whispering*) Gee, he's still nutty.
Let him rave. It's fun listenin'.

YANK. (*unheeding—groping in his thoughts*) Her hands—dey was skinny and white like dey wasn't real but painted on somep'n. Dere was a million miles from me to her—twenty-five knots a hour. She was like some dead ting de cat brung in. Sure, dat's what. She didn't belong. She belonged in de window of a toy store, or on de top of a garbage can, see! Sure! (*He breaks out angrily.*) But would yuh believe it, she had de noive to do me doit. She lamped[2] me like she was seein' somep'n broke loose from de menagerie. Christ, yuh'd

[2]I.e., looked at.

oughter seen her eyes! (*He rattles the bars of his cell furiously.*) But I'll get back at her yet, you watch! And if I can't find her I'll take it out on de gang she runs wit. I'm wise to where dey hangs out now. I'll show her who belongs! I'll show her who's in de move and who ain't. You watch my smoke!

VOICES. (*serious and joking*) Dat's de talkin'!
Take her for all she's got!
What was this dame, anyway? Who was she, eh?

YANK. I dunno. First cabin stiff. Her old man's a millionaire, dey says—name of Douglas.

VOICES. Douglas? That's the president of the Steel Trust, I bet.
Sure. I seen his mug in de papers.
He's filthy with dough.

VOICE. Hey, feller, take a tip from me. If you want to get back at that dame, you better join the Wobblies. You'll get some action then.

YANK. Wobblies? What de hell's dat?

VOICE. Ain't you ever heard of the I. W. W.?[3]

YANK. Naw. What is it?

VOICE. A gang of blokes—a tough gang. I been readin' about 'em today in the paper. The guard give me the *Sunday Times.* There's a long spiel about 'em. It's from a speech made in the Senate by a guy named Senator Queen. (*He is in the cell next to* YANK'S. *There is a rustling of paper*) Wait'll I see if I got light enough and I'll read you. Listen (*He reads.*) "There is a menace existing in this country today which threatens the vitals of our fair Republic—as foul a menace against the very life-blood of the American Eagle as was the foul conspiracy of Catiline[4] against the eagles of ancient Rome!"

VOICE. (*disgustedly*) Aw, hell! Tell him to salt de tail of dat eagle!

VOICE. (*reading*) "I refer to that devil's brew of rescals, jailbirds, murderers, and cutthroats who libel all honest working men by calling themselves the Industrial Workers of the World; but in the light of their nefarious plots, I call them the Industrial *Wreckers* of the World!"

YANK. (*with vengeful satisfaction*) Wreckers, dat's right dope! Dat belongs! Me for dem!

VOICE. Ssshh! (*reading*) "This fiendish organization is a foul ulcer on the fair body of our Democracy—"

VOICE. Democracy, hell! Give him the boid, fellers—the raspberry! (*They do.*)

VOICE. Ssshh! (*reading*) "Like Cato[5] I say to this Senate, the I. W. W. must be destroyed! For they represent an ever-present dagger pointed at the heart of the greatest nation the world has ever known, where all men are born free and equal, with equal opportunities to all, where the Founding Fathers have guaranteed to each one happiness, where Truth, Honor, Liberty, Justice, and the Brotherhood of Man are a religion absorbed with one's mother's milk, taught at our father's knee, sealed, signed, and stamped upon the glorious Constitution of these United States!" (*a perfect storm of hisses, catcalls, boos, and hard laughter*)

[3]Industrial Workers of the World, a radical labor organization founded in 1905. Its members were nicknamed "Wobblies."

[4]Lucius Sergius Catilina (108?–62 B.C.), Roman revolutionary conspirator.

[5]Marcus Porcius Cato (234–149 B.C.), Roman senator who urged the destruction of Carthage.

VOICES. (*scornfully*) Hurrah for de Fort' of July!
Pass de hat!
Liberty!
Justice!
Honor!
Opportunity!
Brotherhood!

ALL. (*with abysmal scorn*) Aw, hell!

VOICE. Give that Queen Senator guy the bark! All togedder now—one—two—tree—(*a terrific chorus of barking and yapping*)

GUARD. (*from a distance*) Quiet there, youse—or I'll git the hose. (*The noise subsides.*)

YANK. (*with growling rage*) I'd like to catch dat senator guy alone for a second. I'd loin him some trute!

VOICE. Ssshh! Here's where he gits down to cases on the Wobblies. (*reads*) "They plot with fire in one hand and dynamite in the other. They stop not before murder to gain their ends, nor at the outraging of defenseless womanhood. They would tear down society, put the lowest scum in the seats of the mighty, turn Almighty God's revealed plan for the world topsy-turvy, and make of our sweet and lovely civilization a shambles, a desolation where man, God's masterpiece, would soon degenerate back to the ape!"

VOICE. (*to* YANK) Hey, you guy. There's your ape stuff again.

YANK. (*with a growl of fury*) I got him. So dey blow up tings, do dey? Dey turn tings around, do dey? Hey, lend me dat paper, will yuh?

VOICE. Sure. Give it to him. On'y keep it to yourself, see. We don't wanter listen to no more of that slop.

VOICE. Here you are. Hide it under your mattress.

YANK. (*reaching out*) Tanks. I can't read much but I kin manage. (*He sits, the paper in the hand at his side, in the attitude of Rodin's "The Thinker." A pause. Several snores from down the corridor. Suddenly* YANK *jumps to his feet with a furious groan as if some appalling thought had crashed on him—bewilderedly*) Sure—her old man—president of de Steel Trust—makes half de steel in de world—steel—where I tought I belonged—drivin' trou—movin'—in dat—to make *her*—and cage me in for her to spit on! Christ! (*He shakes the bars of his cell door till the whole tier trembles. Irritated, protesting exclamations from those awakened or trying to get to sleep*) He made dis—dis cage! Steel! *It* don't belong, dat's what! Cages, cells, locks, bolts, bars—dat's what it means!—holdin' me down with him at de top! But I'll drive trou! Fire, dat melts it! I'll be fire—under de heap—fire dat never goes out—hot as hell—breakin' out in de night—(*While he has been saying this last he has shaken his cell door to a clanging accompaniment. As he comes to the "breakin' out" he seizes one bar with both hands and, putting his two feet up against the others so that his position is parallel to the floor like a monkey's, he gives a great wrench backwards. The bar bends like a licorice stick under his tremendous strength. Just at this moment the* PRISON GUARD *rushes in, dragging a hose behind him.*)

GUARD. (*angrily*) I'll loin youse bums to wake me up! (*sees* YANK) Hello, it's you, huh? Got the D. T.'s[6] hey? Well, I'll cure 'em. I'll drown your snakes for

[6]Delirium tremens.

yuh! (*noticing the bar*) Hell, look at dat bar bended! On'y a bug is strong enough for dat!

YANK. (*glaring at him*) Or a hairy ape, yuh big yellow bum! Look out! Here I come! (*He grabs another bar.*)

GUARD. (*scared now—yelling off left*) Toin de hose on, Ben!—full pressure! And call de others—and a straitjacket! (*The curtain is falling. As it hides* YANK *from view, there is a splattering smash as the stream of water hits the steel of* YANK'S *cell.*)

CURTAIN

SCENE SEVEN

Nearly a month later. An I. W. W. local near the waterfront, showing the interior of a front room on the ground floor, and the street outside. Moonlight on the narrow street, buildings massed in black shadow. The interior of the room, which is general assembly room, office, and reading room, resembles some dingy settlement boys' club. A desk and high stool are in one corner. A table with papers, stacks of pamphlets, chairs about it, is at center. The whole is decidedly cheap, banal, commonplace and unmysterious as a room could be. The SECRETARY *is perched on the stool making entries in a large ledger. An eye shade casts his face into shadows. Eight or ten men, longshoremen, iron workers, and the like, are grouped about the table. Two are playing checkers. One is writing a letter. Most of them are smoking pipes. A big signboard is on the wall at the rear, "Industrial Workers of the World—Local No. 57."*

YANK *comes down the street outside. He is dressed as in Scene Five. He moves cautiously, mysteriously. He comes to a point opposite the door; tiptoes softly up to it, listens, is impressed by the silence within, knocks carefully, as if he were guessing at the password to some secret rite. Listens. No answer. Knocks again a bit louder. No answer. Knocks impatiently, much louder.*

SECRETARY. (*turning around on his stool*) What the hell is that—someone knocking? (*shouts*) Come in, why don't you? (*All the men in the room look up.* YANK *opens the door slowly, gingerly, as if afraid of an ambush. He looks around for secret doors, mystery, is taken aback by the commonplaceness of the room and the men in it, thinks he may have gotten in the wrong place, then sees the signboard on the wall and is reassured.*)

YANK. (*blurts out*) Hello.

MEN. (*reservedly*) Hello.

YANK. (*more easily*) I thought I'd bumped into de wrong dump.

SECRETARY. (*scrutinizing him carefully*) Maybe you have. Are you a member?

YANK. Naw, not yet. Dat's what I come for—to join.

SECRETARY. That's easy. What's your job—longshore?

YANK. Naw, Fireman—stoker on de liners.

SECRETARY. (*with satisfaction*) Welcome to our city. Glad to know you people are waking up at last. We haven't got many members in your line.

YANK. Naw. Dey're all dead to de woild.

SECRETARY. Well, you can help to wake 'em. What's your name? I'll make out your card.

YANK. (*confused*) Name? Lemme tink.

SECRETARY. (*sharply*) Don't you know your own name?

YANK. Sure; but I been just Yank for so long—Bob, dat's it—Bob Smith.

SECRETARY. (*writing*) Robert Smith. (*fills out the rest of the card*) Here you are. Cost you half a dollar.

YANK. Is dat all—four bits? Dat's easy. (*gives the* SECRETARY *the money*)

SECRETARY. (*throwing it in drawer*) Thanks. Well, make yourself at home. No introductions needed. There's literature on the table. Take some of those pamphlets with you to distribute aboard ship. They may bring results. Sow the seed, only go about it right. Don't get caught and fired. We got plenty out of work. What we need is men who can hold their jobs—and work for us at the same time.

YANK. Sure. (*But he still stands, embarrassed and uneasy.*)

SECRETARY. (*looking at him—curiously*) What did you knock for? Think we had a coon in uniform to open doors?

YANK. Naw. I tought it was locked—and dat yuh'd wanter give me the once-over trou a peep-hole or somep'n to see if I was right.

SECRETARY. (*alert and suspicious but with an easy laugh*) Think we were running a crap game? That door is never locked. What put that in your nut?

YANK. (*with a knowing grin, convinced that this is all camouflage, a part of the secrecy*) Dis burg is full of bulls, ain't it?

SECRETARY. (*sharply*) What have the cops got to do with us? We're breaking no laws.

YANK. (*with a knowing wink*) Sure. Youse wouldn't for woilds. Sure. I'm wise to dat.

SECRETARY. You seem to be wise to a lot of stuff none of us knows about.

YANK. (*with another wink*) Aw, dat's aw right, see. (*then made a bit resentful by the suspicious glances from all sides*) Aw, can it! Youse needn't put me trou de toid degree. Can't youse see I belong? Sure! I'm reg'lar. I'll stick, get me? I'll shoot de woiks for youse. Dat's why I wanted to join in.

SECRETARY. (*breezily, feeling him out*) That's the right spirit. Only are you sure you understand what you've joined? It's all plain and above board; still, some guys get a wrong slant on us. (*sharply*) What's your notion of the purpose of the I. W. W.?

YANK. Aw, I know all about it.

SECRETARY. (*sarcastically*) Well, give us some of your valuable information.

YANK. (*cunningly*) I know enough not to speak outa my toin. (*then resentfully again*) Aw, say! I'm reg'lar. I'm wise to de game. I know yuh got to watch your step with a stranger. For all youse know, I might be a plain-clothes dick, or somep'n, dat's what yuh're tinkin', huh? Aw, forget it! I belong, see? Ask any guy down to de docks if I don't.

SECRETARY. Who said you didn't?

YANK. After I'm 'nitiated, I'll show yuh.

SECRETARY. (*astounded*) Initiated? There's no initiation.

YANK. (*disappointed*) Ain't there no password—no grip or nothin'?

SECRETARY. What'd you think this is—the Elks—or the Black Hand?[1]

YANK. De Elks, hell! De Black Hand, dey're a lot of yellow back-stickin' Ginees.[2] Dis is a man's gang, ain't it?

[1]Elks: an American fraternal organization. Black Hand: Italian underworld organization of the mid-nineteenth century.

[2]"Guineas," slang term for Italians.

SECRETARY. You said it! That's why we stand on our two feet in the open. We got no secrets.

YANK. (*surprised but admiringly*) Yuh mean to say yuh always run wide open—like dis?

SECRETARY. Exactly.

YANK. Den yuh sure got your noive wit youse!

SECRETARY. (*sharply*) Just what was it made you want to join us? Come out with that straight.

YANK. Yuh call me? Well, I got noive, too! Here's my hand. Yuh wanter blow tings up, don't yuh? Well, dat's me! I belong!

SECRETARY. (*with pretended carelessness*) You mean change the unequal conditions of society by legitimate direct action—or with dynamite?

YANK. Dynamite! Blow it offen de oith—steel—all de cages—all de factories, steamers, buildings, jails—de Steel Trust and all dat makes it go.

SECRETARY. So—that's your idea, eh? And did you have any special job in that line you wanted to propose to us? (*He makes a sign to the men, who get up cautiously one by one and group behind* YANK.)

YANK. (*boldly*) Sure, I'll come out wit it. I'll show youse I'm one of de gang. Dere's dat millionaire guy, Douglas—

SECRETARY. President of the Steel Trust, you mean? Do you want to assassinate him?

YANK. Naw, dat don't get yuh nothin'. I mean blow up de factory, de woiks, where he makes de steel. Dat's what I'm after—to blow up de steel, knock all de steel in de woild up to de moon. Dat'll fix things! (*eagerly, with a touch of bravado*) I'll do it by me lonesome! I'll show yuh! Tell me where his woiks is, how to git there, all de dope. Gimme de stuff, de old butter—and watch me do de rest! Watch de smoke and see it move! I don't give a damn if dey nab me—long as it's done! I'll soive life for it—and give 'em de laugh! (*half to himself*) And I'll write her a letter and tell her de hairy ape done it. Dat'll square tings.

SECRETARY. (*stepping away from* YANK) Very interesting. (*He gives a signal. The men, huskies all, throw themselves on* YANK *and before he knows it they have his legs and arms pinioned. But he is too flabbergasted to make a struggle, anyway. They feel him over for weapons.*)

MAN. No gat, no knife. Shall we give him what's what and put the boots to him?

SECRETARY. No. He isn't worth the trouble we'd get into. He's too stupid. (*He comes closer and laughs mockingly in* YANK'S *face*) Ho-ho! By God, this is the biggest joke they've put up on us yet. Hey, you Joke! Who sent you—Burns or Pinkerton?[3] No, by God, you're such a bonehead I'll bet you're in the Secret Service! Well, you dirty spy, you rotten agent provocator, you can go back and tell whatever skunk is paying you blood-money for betraying your brothers that he's wasting his coin. You couldn't catch a cold. And tell him that all he'll ever get on us, or ever has got, is just his own sneaking plots that he's framed up to put us in jail. We are what our manifesto says we are, neither more or less—and we'll give him a copy of that any time he calls. And as for you—(*He glares scornfully at* YANK, *who is sunk in an oblivious stupor*) Oh, hell, what's the use of talking? You're a brainless ape.

[3]Detective agencies.

YANK. (*aroused by the word to fierce but futile struggles*) What's dat, you Sheeny[4] bum, yuh!

SECRETARY. Throw him out, boys. (*In spite of his struggles, this is done with gusto and éclat. Propelled by several parting kicks,* YANK *lands sprawling in the middle of the narrow cobbled street. With a growl he starts to get up and storm the closed door, but stops bewildered by the confusion in his brain, pathetically impotent. He sits there, brooding, in as near to the attitude of Rodin's "The Thinker" as he can get in his position.*)

YANK. (*bitterly*) So dem boids don't tink I belong, neider. Aw, to hell wit 'em! Dey're in de wrong pew—de same old bull—soap-boxes and Salvation Army—no guts! Cut out an hour offen de job a day and make me happy! Gimme a dollar more a day and make me happy! Tree square a day, and cauliflowers in de front yard—ekal rights—a woman and kids—a lousy vote—and I'm all fixed for Jesus, huh? Aw, hell! What does dat get yuh? Dis ting's in your inside, but it ain't your belly. Feedin' your face—sinkers and coffee—dat don't touch it. It's way down—at de bottom. Yuh can't grab it, and yuh can't stop it. It moves, and everything moves. It stops and de whole woild stops. Dat's me now—I don't tick, see?—I'm a busted Ingersoll,[5] dat's what. Steel was me, and I owned de woild. Now I ain't steel, and de woild owns me. Aw, hell! I can't see—it's all dark, get me? It's all wrong! (*He turns a bitter mocking face up like an ape gibbering at the moon*) Say, youse up dere, Man in de Moon, yuh look so wise, gimme de answer, huh? Slip me de inside dope, de information right from de stable—where do I get off at, huh?

A POLICEMAN. (*who has come up the street in time to hear this last—with grim humor*) You'll get off at the station, you boob, if you don't get up out of that and keep movin'.

YANK. (*looking up at him—with a hard, bitter laugh*) Sure! Lock me up! Put me in a cage! Dat's de on'y answer yuh know. G'wan lock me up!

POLICEMAN. What you been doin'?

YANK. Enuf to gimme life for! I was born, see? Sure, dat's de charge. Write it in de blotter. I was born, get me!

POLICEMAN. (*jocosely*) God pity your old woman! (*then matter-of-factly*) But I've no time for kidding. You're soused. I'd run you in but it's too long a walk to the station. Come on now, get up, or I'll fan your ears with this club. Beat it now! (*He hauls* YANK *to his feet.*)

YANK. (*in a vague mocking tone*) Say, where do I go from here?

POLICEMAN. (*giving him a push—with a grin, indifferently*) Go to hell.

CURTAIN

SCENE EIGHT

Twilight of the next day. The monkey house at the Zoo. One spot of clear gray light falls on the front of one cage so that the interior can be seen. The other cages are vague, shrouded in shadow from which chatterings pitched in a conversational tone can be heard. On the one cage a sign from which the word "gorilla" stands out. The gigantic

[4]Slang term for Jewish. [5]A brand of inexpensive watch.

animal himself is seen squatting on his haunches on a bench in much the same attitude of Rodin's "The Thinker." YANK *enters from the left. Immediately a chorus of angry chattering and screeching breaks out. The gorilla turns his eyes but makes no sound or move.*

YANK. (*with a hard, bitter laugh*) Welcome to your city, huh? Hail, hail, de gang's all here! (*At the sound of his voice the chattering dies away into an attentive silence.* YANK *walks up to the gorilla's cage and, leaning over the railing, stares in at its occupant, who stares back at him, silent and motionless. There is a pause of dead stillness. Then* YANK *begins to talk in a friendly confidential tone, half mockingly, but with a deep undercurrent of sympathy*) Say, yuh're some hard-lookin' guy, ain't yuh? I seen lots of tough nuts dat de gang called gorillas, but yuh're the foist real one I ever seen. Some chest yuh got, and shoulders, and dem arms and mits! I bet yuh got a punch in eider fist dat'd knock 'em all silly! (*This with genuine admiration. The gorilla, as if he understood, stands upright, swelling out his chest and pounding on it with his fist.* YANK *grins sympathetically*) Sure, I get yuh. Yuh challenge de whole woild, huh? Yuh got what I was sayin' even if yuh muffed de woids. (*then bitterness creeping in*) And why wouldn't yuh get me? Ain't we both members of de same club—de Hairy Apes? (*They stare at each other—a pause—then* YANK *goes on slowly and bitterly*) So yuh're what she seen when she looked at me, de white-faced tart! I was you to her, get me? On'y outa de cage—broke out—free to moider her, see? Sure! Dat's what she tought. She wasn't wise dat I was in a cage, too—worser'n yours—sure—a damn sight—'cause you got some chanct to bust loose—but me—(*He grows confused.*) Aw, hell! It's all wrong, ain't it? (*A pause*) I s'pose yuh wanter know what I'm doin' here, huh? I been warmin' a bench down to de Battery[1]—ever since last night. Sure. I seen de sun come up. Dat was pretty, too—all red and pink and green. I was lookin' at de skyscrapers—steel—and all de ships comin' in, sailin' out, all over de oith—and dey was steel, too. De sun was warm, dey wasn't no clouds, and dere was a breeze blowin'. Sure, it was great stuff. I got it aw right—what Paddy said about dat bein' de right dope—on'y I couldn't get *in* it, see? I couldn't belong in dat. It was over my head. And I kept tinkin'—and den I beat it up here to see what youse was like. And I waited till dey was all gone to git yuh alone. Say, how d'yuh feel sittin' in dat pen all de time, havin' to stand for 'em comin' and starin' at yuh—de white-faced, skinny tarts and de boobs what marry 'em—makin' fun of yuh, laughin' at yuh, gittin' scared of yuh—damn 'em! (*He pounds on the rail with his fist. The gorilla rattles the bars of his cage and snarls. All the other monkeys set up an angry chattering in the darkness.* YANK *goes on excitedly*) Sure! Dat's de way it hits me, too. On'y yuh're lucky, see? You don't belong wit 'em and yuh know it. But me, I belong wit 'em—but I don't, see? Dey don't belong wit me, dat's what. Get me? Tinkin' is hard—(*He passes one hand across his forehead with a painful gesture. The gorilla growls impatiently.* YANK *goes on gropingly*) It's dis way, what I'm drivin' at. Youse can sit and dope dream in de past, green woods, de jungle and de rest of it. Den yuh belong and dey don't. Den yuh kin laugh at 'em, see? Yuh're de champ of de world. But me—I

[1]A park at the southern end of Manhattan Island.

ain't got no past to tink in, nor nothin' dat's comin', on'y what's now—and dat don't belong. Sure, you're de best off! You can't tink, can yuh? Yuh can't talk neider. But I kin make a bluff at talkin' and tinkin'—a'most git away wit it—a'most!—and dat's where de joker comes in. (*He laughs.*) I ain't on oith and I ain't in heaven, get me? I'm in de middle tryin' to separate 'em, takin' all de woist punches from bot' of 'em. Maybe dat's what dey call hell, huh? But you, yuh're at de bottom. You belong? Sure! Yuh're de on'y one in de woild dat does, yuh lucky stiff! (*The gorilla growls proudly.*) And dat's why dey gotter put yuh in a cage, see? (*The gorilla roars angrily.*) Sure! Yuh get me. It beats it when you try to tink it or talk it—it's way down—deep—behind—you 'n' me we feel it. Sure! Bot' members of dis club! (*he laughs—then in a savage tone*) What de hell! T'hell wit it! A little action, dat's our meat! Dat belongs! Knock 'em down and keep bustin' 'em till dey croaks yuh with a gat—wit a steel! Sure! are yuh game? Dey've looked at youse, ain't dey—in a cage? Wanter get even? Wanter wind up like a sport 'stead of croaken' slow in dere? (*The gorilla roars an emphatic affirmative.* YANK *goes on with a sort of furious exaltation.*) Sure! Yuh're reg'lar! Yuh'll stick to de finish! Me 'n' you, huh?—bot' members of dis club! We'll put up one last start bout dat'll knock 'em offen deir seats! Dey'll have to make de cages stronger after we're trou! (*The gorilla is straining at his bars, growling, hopping from one foot to the other.* YANK *takes a jimmy from under his coat and forces the lock on the cage door. He throws this open.*) Pardon from de governor! Step out and shake hands. I'll take yuh for a walk down 'Fif' Avenoo. We'll knock 'em offen de oith and croak with de band playin'. Come on, Brother. (*The gorilla scrambles gingerly out of his cage. Goes to* YANK *and stands looking at him.* YANK *keeps his mocking tone—holds out his hand*) Shake—de secret grip of our order. (*Something, the tone of mockery, perhaps, suddenly enrages the animal. With a spring he wraps his huge arms around* YANK *in a murderous hug. There is a cracking snap of crushed ribs—a gasping cry, still mocking, from* YANK.) Hey, I didn't say kiss me! (*The gorilla lets the crushed body slip to the floor; stands over it uncertainly, considering; then picks it up, throws it in the cage, shuts the door, and shuffles off menacingly into the darkness at left. A great uproar of frightened chattering and whimpering comes from the other cages. Then* YANK *moves, groaning, opening his eyes, and there is silence. He mutters painfully*) Say—dey oughter match him—with Zybszko.[2] He got me, aw right! I'm trou. Even him didn't tink I belonged. (*then, with sudden passionate despair*) Christ, where do I get off at? Where do I fit in? (*checking himself as suddenly*) Aw, what de hell! No squawkin', see! No quittin', get me! Croak wit your boots on! (*He grabs hold of the bars of the cage and hauls himself painfully to his feet—looks around him bewilderedly—forces a mocking laugh.*) In de cage, huh? (*in the strident tones of a circus barker*) Ladies and gents, step forward and take a slant at de one and only—(*his voice weakening*) one and original—Hairy Ape from de wilds of—(*He slips in a heap on the floor and dies. The monkeys set up a chattering, whimpering wail. And, perhaps, the Hairy Ape at last belongs.*)

CURTAIN

1922

[2]Stanislaus Zbyszko, a famous wrestler of the 1920s.

Ezra Pound 1885–1972

"E.P."—for two generations the mere initials have identified one of the founders of Anglo-American modernism, the first and the last of a band of revolutionists who changed the course of twentieth-century poetry. Yeats, Eliot, D. H. Lawrence, Joyce, Frost, and Williams are only a few of those who acknowledged their debt to Pound. He survived them all, and not until his death at the age of eighty-seven in Venice did it seem that a remarkable literary era had finally ended.

Pound was born in Hailey, Idaho, and raised in Pennsylvania. At fifteen he entered college already proficient in Latin, and resolved that by the age of thirty he "would know more about poetry than any man living." He attended Hamilton College and the University of Pennsylvania, where he majored in romance philology while reading his way through a large portion of classical and European literatures. At Pennsylvania, from which he received his M.A. in 1906, he associated with two other young poets—and future imagists—William Carlos Williams and Hilda Doolittle. His academic teaching career lasted four months; he was fired from his first job, at Wabash College, for having a woman in his room. The following year he sailed as a deckhand on a cattle boat for Europe and remained there for most of his life.

From Venice, where he published (and then reviewed) his first book of poems, A Lume Spento *(1908), Pound settled in London and set about to reform English letters and "To resuscitate the dead art / of poetry." The London years, between 1908 and 1920, were those in which his dictum "Make it new!" became the rallying cry of modernism, and, as London became the center of literary activity, Pound became the center of the center—discovering, coaching, promoting, and serving as a tireless gadfly to whatever new talent came his way.*

With T. E. Hulme, he started imagism, the writing of short, free-verse poems each presenting a single image; with Wyndham Lewis, he promoted vorticism, a literary version of cubism that argued for poetry of "vigorous impact" with a single image at its "vortex." He published translations of Chinese poetry and Japanese Noh drama, initiating the techniques borrowed and derived from Asian literary traditions that became a modernist vogue. As overseas editor for Harriet Monroe's Poetry Magazine, *he used its pages, along with those of other little magazines, to explain his principles of reform and to introduce such poets as Eliot and Frost to American audiences. During these years he was also writing some of his best poetry.* Personae, *which has been praised as his most important collection, first appeared in 1909 and was often reprinted with additions from subsequent major books—*Ripostes *(1912) and* Lustra *(1916). At the same time he was at work on the early sections of the* Cantos, *the projected epic poem that was to be his life's work.*

After World War I, Pound summarized his disillusionment with the war and with England in Hugh Selwyn Mauberley *(1920). He then moved to Paris for the next four years, mixing with the British and American expatriates of the "Lost Generation." During this time Pound collaborated with T. S. Eliot on the editing of Eliot's epic poem* The Waste Land. *Without Pound's contribution,* The Waste Land *would be a very different poem from the one so thoroughly canonized today.*

In 1924 Pound moved to Italy. Under the spell of Benito Mussolini and Italian fascism he became preoccupied with economic theory, issuing increasingly violent diatribes against American capitalism, usury, and Jews. His views are reflected in the Cantos *and in such prose works as* Jefferson and/or Mussolini *(1935). With the outbreak of World War II, he began broadcasting pro-Fascist propaganda to England and America. When the war ended, he was arrested, charged with treason, and held in an outdoor cage at an American prison camp near Pisa, Italy. He was returned to the United*

States for trial, but after psychiatric examination was declared insane and interned at St. Elizabeths Hospital, a mental institution near Washington, D.C. In 1948, the Pisan Cantos, *written by Pound during his imprisonment near Pisa, was awarded the Bollingen Prize by a group of distinguished literary judges. The furor that resulted from the awarding of a prize to a "traitor" divided the literary world. Eventually, through the intervention of Frost, Eliot, Hemingway, and others, Pound was released and allowed to return to Italy. The* Cantos, *now numbering over a hundred, ended in 1960, and Pound retired to silence.*

Pound's central position in the canon of modernism was established primarily on the basis of assessments (by Eliot and the many critics who followed his lead) of his formal achievements. But Pound himself would probably have been wary of such narrow evaluations. From the beginning of his work on the Cantos *in the 1910s, Pound was committed to a social and political poetry, a "poem including history." Although past critical efforts judged his poetry separately from his politics, more recent efforts assert that the two should be judged together. But the various tensions and contradictions embodied in Ezra Pound's life and work have not diminished his towering influence over twentieth-century American poetry. At the end of his life Pound acknowledged his failure as a social theorist and as a poet. He had become the lost leader for the failed ideas of a departed age. Few literary figures had stirred such hatred, but fewer still had labored so prodigiously for poetry and aroused such gratitude and admiration.*

FURTHER READING: *The Letters of Ezra Pound, 1907–1941,* ed. D. Paige, 1950; J. Cornell, *The Trial of Ezra Pound,* 1966; N. Stock, *The Life of Ezra Pound,* 1970, 1982; P. Ackroyd, *Ezra Pound and His World,* 1981; P. Nichols, *Ezra Pound, Politics, Economics, and Writing,* 1984; J. Wilhelm, *The American Roots of Ezra Pound,* 1985; K. Oderman, *Ezra Pound and the Erotic Medium,* 1986; M. Kayman, *The Modernism of Ezra Pound,* 1986; J. Tyell, *Ezra Pound,* 1987; J. Tytell, *Ezra Pound, The Solitary Volcano,* 1987; K. Lindberg, *Reading Pound Reading,* 1987; H. Carpenter, *A Serious Character, The Life of Ezra Pound,* 1988; R. Casillo, *The Genealogy of Demons, Anti-Semitism, Fascism, and the Myths of Ezra Pound,* 1988; W. Flory, *The American Ezra Pound,* 1989; J. Wilhelm, *Ezra Pound in London and Paris,* 1990; S. Rainey, *Ezra Pound and the Monument of Culture,* 1991; S. Hamilton, *Ezra Pound and the Symbolist Inheritance,* 1992; D. Davie, *Studies in Ezra Pound,* 1992; *Pound in Multiple Perspective, A Collection of Critical Essays,* ed. A. Gibson, 1993; T. Joseph, *Ezra Pound's Epic Variations, The Cantos and Major Long Poems,* 1995; M. Perloff, *The Dance of the Intellect, Studies in the Poetry of the Pound Tradition,* 1996; T. Grieve, *Ezra Pound's Early Poetry and Poetics,* 1997; *Ezra and Dorothy Pound, Letters in Captivity,* ed. O. Pound and R. Spoo, 1999; W. Baumann, *Roses from the Steel Dust, Collected Essays on Ezra Pound,* 2000; *Ezra Pound, Nature and Myth,* ed. W. Pratt, 2002; I. Nadel, *Ezra Pound, A Literary Life,* 2004.

TEXTS: *Personae,* 1949; *The Cantos of Ezra Pound,* 1970.

PORTRAIT D'UNE FEMME[1]

Your mind and you are our Sargasso Sea,[2]
London has swept about you this score[3] years
And bright ships left you this or that in fee:[4]

[1]French: Portrait of a Lady.
[2]An area of the North Atlantic Ocean, known for its entangling, floating seaweed.
[3]Twenty. [4]Payment.

Ideas, old gossip, oddments of all things,
Strange spars of knowledge and dimmed wares of price.
Great minds have sought you—lacking someone else.
You have been second always. Tragical?
No. You preferred it to the usual thing:
One dull man, dulling and uxorious,[5]
One average mind—with one thought less, each year.
Oh, you are patient, I have seen you sit
Hours, where something might have floated up.
And now you pay one. Yes, you richly pay.
You are a person of some interest, one comes to you
And takes strange gain away:
Trophies fished up; some curious suggestion;
Fact that leads nowhere; and a tale or two,
Pregnant with mandrakes,[6] or with something else
That might prove useful and yet never proves,
That never fits a corner or shows use,
Or finds its hour upon the loom of days:
The tarnished, gaudy, wonderful old work;
Idols and ambergris[7] and rare inlays,
These are your riches, your great store; and yet
For all this sea-hoard of deciduous[8] things,
Strange woods half sodden, and new brighter stuff:
In the slow float of differing light and deep,
No! there is nothing! In the whole and all,
Nothing that's quite your own.
Yet this is you.

1912, 1926

SALUTATION

O generation of the thoroughly smug
and thoroughly uncomfortable,
I have seen fishermen picnicking in the sun,
I have seen them with untidy families,
I have seen their smiles full of teeth
and heard ungainly laughter.
And I am happier than you are,
And they were happier than I am;
And the fish swim in the lake
and do not even own clothing.

1913, 1916

[5]Submissive to one's wife.
[6]An herb. Its roots were thought to have magical properties, among them the power to promote conception in women.
[7]Waxy substance, from whales, used in making perfume.
[8]Passing, impermanent.

A PACT

I make a pact with you, Walt Whitman—
I have detested you long enough.
I come to you as a grown child
Who has had a pig-headed father;
I am old enough now to make friends
It was you that broke the new wood,
Now is a time for carving.
We have one sap and one root—
Let there be commerce between us.

1913, 1916

IN A STATION OF THE METRO[1]

The apparition of these faces in the crowd;
Petals on a wet, black bough.

1913, 1916

THE RIVER-MERCHANT'S WIFE: A LETTER[1]

While my hair was still cut straight across my forehead
I played about the front gate, pulling flowers.
You came by on bamboo stilts, playing horse,
You walked about my seat, playing with blue plums.
And we went on living in the village of Chōkan:[2]
Two small people, without dislike or suspicion.

At fourteen I married My Lord you.
I never laughed, being bashful.
Lowering my head, I looked at the wall.
Called to, a thousand times, I never looked back.

At fifteen I stopped scowling,
I desired my dust to be mingled with yours
Forever and forever and forever.
Why should I climb the look out?

At sixteen you departed,
You went into far Ku-tō-yen,[3] by the river of swirling eddies,

[1]The Paris subway.
[1]Pound's translation of a poem by the Chinese poet Li Po (701–762).
[2]Near Nanjing (formerly Nanking), on the lower Yangtse River, in eastern China.
[3]Dangerous gorge and reef, on the upper Yangtse River.

And you have been gone five months.
The monkeys make sorrowful noise overhead.

You dragged your feet when you went out.
By the gate now, the moss is grown, the different mosses,
Too deep to clear them away!
The leaves fall early this autumn, in wind.
The paired butterflies are already yellow with August
Over the grass in the West garden;
They hurt me. I grow older.
If you are coming down through the narrows of the river Kiang,[4]
Please let me know beforehand,
And I will come out to meet you
As far as Chō-fū-Sa.[5]

By Rihaku[6]
1915

from *HUGH SELWYN MAUBERLEY*

(LIFE AND CONTACTS)

I

E. P. Ode Pour L'Election De Son Sepulchre[1]

For three years, out of key with his time,
He strove to resuscitate the dead art
Of poetry; to maintain "the sublime"
In the old sense. Wrong from the start—

No, hardly, but seeing he had been born
In a half savage country, out of date;
Bent resolutely on wringing lilies from the acorn;
Capaneus;[2] trout for factitious bait;

Ιδμεν γάρ τοι πάνθ', ὁσ' ἐνί Τροίη[3]
Caught in the unstopped ear;

[4]The Yangtse River. [5]A port, upstream on the Yangtse.

[6]Japanese name for the poet Li Po. In making his translation, Pound drew upon documents using Japanese versions of Chinese names and locations.

[1]French: E. P. [Ezra Pound] Ode on the Choice of His Tomb. The title is taken from "De l'élection de son sépulchre," an ode by the French poet Pierre de Ronsard (1524–1585).

[2]One of seven heroes who attacked Thebes. For his defiance of Zeus he was struck dead by a thunderbolt.

[3]Greek: For we know everything that is in Troy, from the alluring song of the Sirens (*Odyssey,* Book XII, line 189). Odysseus ordered his sailors' ears to be sealed with wax so they would not hear the Sirens' song and destroy themselves, while he had himself tied to the ship's mast so that he might listen safely with "unstopped ear."

Giving the rocks small lee-way
The chopped seas held him, therefore, that year.

His true Penelope[4] was Flaubert,[5]
He fished by obstinate isles;
Observed the elegance of Circe's[6] hair
Rather than the mottoes on sun-dials.[7]

Unaffected by "the march of events,"
He passed from men's memory in *l'an trentiesme*
De son eage;[8] the case presents
No adjunct to the Muses' diadem.

II

The age demanded an image
Of its accelerated grimace,
Something for the modern stage,
Not, at any rate, an Attic[1] grace;

Not, not certainly, the obscure reveries
Of the inward gaze;
Better mendacities
Than the classics in paraphrase!

The "age demanded" chiefly a mould in plaster,
Made with no loss of time,
A prose kinema,[2] not, not assuredly, alabaster
Or the "sculpture" of rhyme.

III

The tea-rose tea-gown, etc.
Supplants the mousseline of Cos,[1]
The pianola[2] "replaces"
Sappho's barbitos.[3]

Christ follows Dionysus,[4]
Phallic and ambrosial
Made way for macerations;[5]
Caliban casts out Ariel.[6]

[4]Odysseus's wife. [5]Gustave Flaubert (1821–1880), French novelist.

[6]The enchantress who turned Odysseus's crew into swine.

[7]Commonplace sayings, often "Time Flies."

[8]French: the thirtieth year of his life, a quotation adapted from *Le Testament* by the French poet François Villon (1431–1463?).

[1]Characteristic of ancient Attica or Athens, hence elegant.

[2]Greek: motion, whence "cinema" for "moving picture."

[1]Fine cloth from the Greek island of Cos. [2]Player piano.

[3]Sappho: sixth-century B.C. Greek poetess; barbitos: a lyre.

[4]Greek god of fertility and of wine.

[5]Extreme religious fasting that emaciates the body.

[6]Two characters in Shakespeare's *The Tempest*—Caliban: gross and bestial; Ariel: beautiful and ethereal.

All things are a flowing,
Sage Heracleitus[7] says;
But a tawdry cheapness
Shall outlast our days.

Even the Christian beauty
Defects—after Samothrace;[8]
We see *τὸ καλὸν*[9]
Decreed in the market place.

Faun's flesh is not to us,
Nor the saint's vision.
We have the press for wafer;[10]
Franchise for circumcision.

All men, in law, are equals.
Free of Pisistratus,[11]
We choose a knave or an eunuch
To rule over us.

O bright Apollo,
τίν' ἄνδρα, τίν' ἥρωα, τίνα Θεὸν,[12]
What god, man, or hero
Shall I place a tin wreath upon!

IV

These fought in any case,
and some believing,
pro domo,[1] in any case . . .[2]

Some quick to arm,
some for adventure,
some from fear of weakness,
some from fear of censure,
some for love of slaughter, in imagination,
learning later . . .
some in fear, learning love of slaughter;

[7]Greek philosopher (sixth century B.C.) who emphasized the principle of change.

[8]I.e., in the manner of Samothrace, Greek island where the statue "Winged Victory" was found and the home of a Dionysian religious cult.

[9]Greek: the beautiful. [10]Of the Christian communion service.

[11]Athenian tyrant (sixth century B.C.).

[12]Greek: what man, what hero, what god, Pound's adaptation from one of the *Olympian Odes* by the Greek lyric poet Pindar (c. 522–442 B.C.).

[1]Latin: for home, Pound's adaptation from *De Domo Sua* by the Roman statesman and orator Cicero (106–43 B.C.).

[2]Marks of ellipsis in poetry, here and below, are Pound's.

Died some, pro patria,
non "dulce" non "et decor"[3] . . .
walked eye-deep in hell
believing in old men's lies, then unbelieving
came home, home to a lie,
home to many deceits,
home to old lies and new infamy;
usury age-old and age-thick
and liars in public places.

Daring as never before, wastage as never before.
Young blood and high blood,
fair cheeks, and fine bodies;

fortitude as never before

frankness as never before,
disillusions as never told in the old days,
hysterias, trench confessions,
laughter out of dead bellies.

V

There died a myriad,
And of the best, among them,
For an old bitch gone in the teeth,
For a botched civilization,

Charm, smiling at the good mouth,
Quick eyes gone under earth's lid,

For two gross of broken statues,
For a few thousand battered books.

1920, 1926, 1949

from *THE CANTOS*

I[1]

And then went down to the ship,
Set keel to breakers, forth on the godly sea, and
We[2] set up mast and sail on that swart ship,
Bore sheep aboard her, and our bodies also

[3]Latin: for country, neither "sweet" nor "fitting." Pound ironically adapts Horace's "Dulce et decorum est pro patria mori," "It is sweet and fitting to die for one's country." (*Odes,* Book III, Ode ii, line 13).

[1]Canto I is based on Homer's *Odyssey* (Book XI) and describes the visit of Odysseus to Hades (the underworld).

[2]Odysseus and his companions.

Heavy with weeping, and winds from sternward
Bore us out onward with bellying canvas,
Circe's[3] this craft, the trim-coifed goddess,
Then sat we amidships, wind jamming the tiller,
Thus with stretched sail, we went over sea till day's end.
Sun to his slumber, shadows o'er all the ocean,
Came we then to the bounds of deepest water,
To the Kimmerian lands,[4] and peopled cities
Covered with close-webbed mist, unpierced ever
With glitter of sun-rays
Nor with stars stretched, nor looking back from heaven
Swartest night stretched over wretched men there,
The ocean flowing backward, came we then to the place
Aforesaid by Circe.
Here did they rites, Perimedes and Eurylochus,[5]
And drawing sword from my hip
I dug the ell-square pitkin;[6]
Poured we libations unto each the dead,
First mead and then sweet wine, water mixed with white flour.
Then prayed I many a prayer to the sickly death's-heads;
As set in Ithaca, sterile bulls of the best
For sacrifice, heaping the pyre with goods,
A sheep to Tiresias only, black and a bell-sheep.[7]
Dark blood flowed in the fosse,[8]
Souls out of Erebus,[9] cadaverous dead, of brides
Of youths and of the old who had borne much;
Souls stained with recent tears, girls tender,
Men many, mauled with bronze lance heads,
Battle spoil, bearing yet dreory[10] arms,
These many crowded about me; with shouting,
Pallor upon me, cried to my men for more beasts;
Slaughtered the herds, sheep slain of bronze;
Poured ointment, cried to the gods,
To Pluto[11] the strong, and praised Proserpine;
Unsheathed the narrow sword,
I sat to keep off the impetuous impotent dead,
Till I should hear Tiresias.
But first Elpenor[12] came, our friend Elpenor,
Unburied, cast on the wide earth,
Limbs that we left in the house of Circe,
Unwept, unwrapped in sepulchre, since toils urged other.

[3]The enchantress Circe instructed Odysseus how to sail to Hades, where he could learn from Theban prophet Tiresias how to return home to Ithaca.

[4]Cimmeria, a mist-shrouded land at the edge of the world, near the entrance to Hades, where Odysseus met the spirits of the dead.

[5]Two of Odysseus's companions. [6]A small pit, an arm's-length (one ell) square.

[7]The sheep, wearing a bell, that leads the flock. [8]Ditch.

[9]Place of darkness where the souls of the dead passed on their way to Hades.

[10]Anglo-Saxon: bloody.

[11]Greek god who ruled the underworld with his queen Persephone (Proserpine).

[12]One of Odysseus's companions who had died. His spirit speaks, following.

Pitiful spirit. And I cried in hurried speech:
"Elpenor, how art thou come to this dark coast?
"Cam'st thou afoot, outstripping seamen?"
And he in heavy speech:
"Ill fate and abundant wine. I slept in Circe's ingle.[13]
"Going down the long ladder unguarded,
"I fell against the buttress,
"Shattered the nape-nerve,[14] the soul sought Avernus.[15]
"But thou, O King, I bid remember me, unwept, unburied,
"Heap up mine arms, be tomb by sea-bord, and inscribed:
"*A man of no fortune, and with a name to come.*
"And set my oar up, that I swung mid fellows."

And Anticlea[16] came, whom I beat off, and then Tiresias Theban,
Holding his golden wand, knew me, and spoke first:
"A second time?[17] why? man of ill star,
"Facing the sunless dead and this joyless region?
"Stand from the fosse, leave me my bloody bever[18]
"For soothsay,"[19]
And I stepped back,
And he strong with the blood, said then: "Odysseus
"Shalt return through spiteful Neptune,[20] over dark seas,
"Lose all companions." And then Anticlea came.
Lie quiet Divus. I mean, that is Andreas Divus,[21]
In officina Wecheli, 1538,[22] out of Homer.
And he[23] sailed, by Sirens and thence outward and away
And unto Circe.
Venerandam,[24]
In the Cretan's[25] phrase, with the golden crown, Aphrodite,
Cypri munimenta sortita est,[26] mirthful, oricalchi,[27] with golden
Girdles and breast bands, thou with dark eyelids
Bearing the golden bough of Argicida.[28] So that:

1917, 1919, 1925

[13]Chimney-corner, hence house. [14]Neck-nerve.

[15]Italian lake that is, according to Virgil, the entrance to the underworld.

[16]The mother of Odysseus. She had died during his absence from Ithaca. Odysseus had been instructed by Circe to spurn his mother's spirit until Tiresias had spoken.

[17]This was their second meeting. [18]Drink.

[19]Before prophesying, Tiresias had to drink of the sacrificial blood.

[20]Roman god of the sea.

[21]Pound intrudes to address Andreas Divus, author of a Latin translation of the *Odyssey,* published in Paris in 1538, a copy of which Pound owned.

[22]Latin: at the workshop of Wechel, a phrase taken from the imprint in Pound's copy of Divus.

[23]Odysseus.

[24]Latin: Compelling admiration, a reference to Aphrodite, Greek goddess of love.

[25]The Cretan, Georgius Dartona, whose Latin translations of the Homeric hymns (including a hymn to Aphrodite) were included in the book by Divus.

[26]Latin: The fortifications of Cyprus were her chosen realm. A quotation from Dartona's hymn to Aphrodite. According to legend Aphrodite first appeared in Cyprus.

[27]Pound's spelling of Latin *orichalci,* of copper. Dartona described Aphrodite wearing copper earrings.

[28]Latin: slayer of Argos. In classical myth, Hermes slew the 100-eyed Argos. One of the 12 Olympian gods, Hermes carried a golden staff with which he conducted the souls of the dead to Hades.

II

Hang it all, Robert Browning,[1]
there can be but the one "Sordello."
But Sordello, and my Sordello?
Lo Sordels si fo di Mantovana.[2]
So-shu[3] churned in the sea.
Seal sports in the spray-whited circles of cliff-wash,
Sleek head, daughter of Lir,[4]
    eyes of Picasso[5]
Under black fur-hood, lithe daughter of Ocean;
And the wave runs in the beach-groove:
"Eleanor, ἑλέναυς and ἑλέπτολις!"[6]
    And poor old Homer blind, blind as a bat,
Ear, ear for the sea-surge, murmur of old men's voices:
"Let her go back to the ships,[7]
Back among Grecian faces, lest evil come on our own,
Evil and further evil, and a curse cursed on our children,
Moves, yes she moves like a goddess
And has the face of a god
    and the voice of Schoeney's[8] daughters,
And doom goes with her in walking,
Let her go back to the ships,
    back among Grecian voices."
And by the beach-run, Tyro,[9]
    Twisted arms of the sea-god,
Lithe sinews of water, gripping her, cross-hold,
And the blue-gray glass of the wave tents them,
Glare azure of water, cold-welter, close cover,
Quiet sun-tawny sand-stretch,

[1]English poet (1812–1889), author of the poem *Sordello* (1840). Here, Sordello refers to the title character of Browning's poem and to an actual man, a thirteenth-century Italian poet, who appeared in Dante's *Purgatorio* (VI).

[2]Provençal: Sordello was from the region around Mantua.

[3]The Japanese name for the Chinese philosopher Chuang Tzu. "Churned in the sea" is perhaps meant to echo a Chinese pronunciation of "Chuang Tzu" and to suggest "churned in the sea of experience."

[4]Celtic sea god.

[5]Pablo Picasso (1881–1973), Spanish Cubist painter. Pound suggests that the eyes of the figures in Picasso's paintings are dark, like those of the seal described here.

[6]Greek: "ship-destroying" and "town-destroying." An adaptation of a quotation from the *Agamemnon* (lines 689–690), by Aeschylus, which describes Helen of Troy as "ship-destroying, man-destroying, and town-destroying." Pound substitutes "Eleanor" for "man-destroying" (Greek "elandros"), and thereby alludes both to Helen of Troy and to Eleanor of Aquitaine (1122?–1204), who likewise brought discord among men.

[7]The quotation beginning here is from *The Iliad* (Book III, lines 158–160). The old men of Troy speak of Helen as they see Menelaus and Paris fight.

[8]Atlanta, the daughter of Schoeneus, challenged her suitors to a footrace. Those she defeated were put to death.

[9]A mortal raped by the sea-god Poseidon, who caused a great wave to curl over them for concealment.

The gulls broad out their wings,
nipping between the splay feathers;
Snipe come for their bath,
bend out their wing-joints,
Spread wet wings to the sun-film,
And by Scios,[10]
to left of the Naxos[11] passage,
Naviform[12] rock overgrown,
algae cling to its edge,
There is a wine-red glow in the shallows,
a tin flash in the sun-dazzle.

The ship landed in Scios,
men wanting spring-water,
And by the rock-pool a young boy loggy with vine-must,[13]
"To Naxos? Yes, we'll take you to Naxos,
Cum' along lad." "Not that way!"
"Aye that way is Naxos."
And I said: "It's a straight ship."
And an ex-convict out of Italy[14]
knocked me into the fore-stays,
(He was wanted for manslaughter in Tuscany)
And the whole twenty against me,
Mad for a little slave money.
And they took her out of Scios
And off her course . . .
And the boy came to, again, with the racket,
And looked out over the bows,
and to eastward, and to the Naxos passage.
God-sleight then, god-sleight:
Ship stock fast in sea-swirl,
Ivy upon the oars, King Pentheus,[15]
grapes with no seed but sea-foam,
Ivy in scupper-hole.
Aye, I, Actes, stood there,
and the god stood by me,
Water cutting under the keel,
Sea-break from stern forrards,
wake running off from the bow,

[10]Chios, Greek island near Naxos, in the Aegean Sea.

[11]Greek island known for its wine and as a center for the worship of Dionysus (Bacchus).

[12]Having the shape of a ship.

[13]Fermenting grape juice. The boy is Dionysus to whom the grape wine and ivy are sacred.

[14]In Greek myth, Dionysus, hoping to go to Naxos, took passage on a ship manned by Italian pirates. Only one member of the crew, the steersman, recognized him as a god. The others resolved to change course to Asia where they could sell their passenger as a slave. Dionysus then caused the ship to halt; ivy entangled the masts and sails, wine flowed over the deck, and wild beasts appeared to guard him. The pirates, frightened by the magic, the "god-sleight," leaped into the sea and were changed into dolphins. Only the steersman was spared.

[15]The steersman, Acoetes, is reciting the story to Pentheus of Thebes to warn him of the power of Dionysus.

And where was gunwale, there now was vine-trunk,
And tenthril were cordage had been,
grape-leaves on the rowlocks,
Heavy vine on the oarshafts,
And, out of nothing, a breathing,
hot breath on my ankles,
Beasts like shadows in glass,
a furred tail upon nothingness.
Lynx-purr, and heathery smell of beasts,
where tar smell had been,
Sniff and pad-foot of beasts,
eye-glitter out of black air.
The sky overshot, dry, with no tempest,
Sniff and pad-foot of beasts,
fur brushing my knee-skin,
Rustle of airy sheaths,
dry forms in the œ*ther.*[16]
And the ship like a keel in ship-yard,
slung like an ox in smith's sling,
Ribs stuck fast in the ways,
grape-cluster over pin-rack,
void air taking pelt.
Lifeless air become sinewed,
feline leisure of panthers,
Leopards sniffing the grape shoots by scupper-hole,
Crouched panthers by fore-hatch,
And the sea blue-deep about us,
green-ruddy in shadows,
And Lyæus:[17] "From now, Actes, my altars,
Fearing no bondage,
fearing no cat of the wood,
Safe with my lynxes,
feeding grapes to my leopards,
Olibanum[18] is my incense,
the vines grow in my homage."

The back-swell now smooth in the rudder-chains,
Black snout of a porpoise
where Lycabs[19] had been,
Fish-scales on the oarsmen.
And I worship.
I have seen what I have seen.
When they brought the boy I said:
"He has a god in him,
though I do not know which god."
And they kicked me into the fore-stays.

[16]Latin: air. [17]Another name for Dionysus.
[18]Frankincense. [19]One of the sailors who had tried to abduct Dionysus.

I have seen what I have seen:
        Medon's[20] face like the face of a dory,[21]
Arms shrunk into fins. And you, Pentheus,
Had as well listen to Tiresias, and to Cadmus,[22]
        or your luck will go out of you.
Fish-scales over groin muscles,
        lynx-purr amid sea. . .
And of a later year,
        pale in the wine-red algæ,
If you will lean over the rock,
        the coral face under wave-tinge,
Rose-paleness under water-shift,
        Ileuthyeria,[23] fair Dafne[24] of sea-bords,
The swimmer's arms turned to branches,
Who will say in what year,
        fleeing what band of tritons,
The smooth brows, seen, and half seen,
        now ivory stillness.

And So-shu churned in the sea, So-shu also,
    using the long moon for a churn-stick. . .
Lithe turning of water,
        sinews of Poseidon,
Black azure and hyaline,[25]
        glass wave over Tyro,
Close cover, unstillness,
        bright welter of wave-cords,
Then quiet water,
        quiet in the buff sands,
Sea-fowl stretching wing-joints,
        splashing in rock-hollows and sand-hollows
In the wave-runs by the half-dune;
Glass-glint of wave in the tide-rips against sunlight,
        pallor of Hesperus,[26]
Grey peak of the wave,
        wave, colour of grape's pulp,

Olive grey in the near,
        far, smoke grey of the rock-slide,
Salmon-pink wings of the fish-hawk
        cast grey shadows in water,
The tower like a one-eyed great goose
        cranes up out of the olive-grove,

[20]Another sailor. [21]A fish.
[22]Grandfather of Pentheus and founder of Thebes. With Tiresias he had urged Pentheus not to forbid the worship of Dionysus.
[23]A nymph.
[24]Daphne, a nymph who was turned into a tree to save her from her pursuer, Apollo.
[25]Clear, transparent. [26]The evening star (the planet Venus).

And we have heard the fauns chiding Proteus[27]
in the smell of hay under the olive-trees,
And the frogs singing against the fauns
in the half-light.
And. . .

1917, 1925

XLV

With *Usura*[1]
With usura hath no man a house of good stone
each block cut smooth and well fitting
that design might cover their face,
with usura
hath no man a painted paradise on his church wall
harpes et luz[2]
or where virgin receiveth message[3]
and halo projects from incision,
with usura
seeth no man Gonzaga his heirs and his concubines[4]
no picture is made to endure nor to live with
but it is made to sell and sell quickly
with usura, sin against nature,
is thy bread ever more of stale rags
is thy bread dry as paper,
with no mountain wheat, no strong flour
with usura the line grows thick[5]
with usura is no clear demarcation
and no man can find site for his dwelling.
Stone cutter is kept from his stone
weaver is kept from his loom
WITH USURA
wool comes not to market
sheep bringeth no gain with usura
Usura is a murrain,[6] usura
blunteth the needle in the maid's hand
and stoppeth the spinner's cunning. Pietro Lombardo[7]
came not by usura

[27]Greek sea god who could assume different shapes.

[1]Latin: usury, interest paid for money borrowed. Pound uses the term to refer generally to greed for money.

[2]French: harps and lutes. Quoted from François Villon's *Le Testament* (line 896): "In my parish church I see a painted paradise where there are harps and lutes."

[3]I.e., paintings of the Annunciation, the announcement to Mary, by the angel Gabriel, that she will be the mother of Jesus (Luke 1:26–38).

[4]The portraits, by Andrea Mantegna (1431–1506), of Ludovico Gonzaga (1414–1478), with members of his family and court, on the walls of the ducal palace in Mantua, Italy.

[5]Pound believed that the lines in Italian painting grew thick and coarse after the rise of usury.

[6]Plague. [7]Italian sculptor (1435–1515).

Duccio[8] came not by usura
nor Pier della Francesca; Zuan Bellin'[9] not by usura
nor was 'La Calunnia'[10] painted.
Came not by usura Angelico; came not Ambrogio Praedis,[11]
Came no church of cut stone signed: *Adamo me fecit.*[12]
Not by usura St Trophime;[13]
Not by usura Saint Hilaire,[14]
Usura rusteth the chisel
It rusteth the craft and the craftsman
It gnaweth the thread in the loom
None learneth to weave gold in her pattern;
Azure hath a canker by usura; cramoisi[15] is unbroidered
Emerald findeth no Memling[16]
Usura slayeth the child in the womb
It stayeth the young man's courting
It hath brought palsey[17] to bed, lyeth
between the young bride and her bridegroom
CONTRA NATURAM[18]
They have brought whores for Eleusis[19]
Corpses are set to banquet
at behest of usura.

1936, 1937

LXXXI

What thou lovest well remains,
the rest is dross
What thou lov'st well shall not be reft from thee
What thou lov'st well is thy true heritage
Whose world, or mine or theirs
or is it of none?
First came the seen, then thus the palpable
Elysium, though it were in the halls of hell,
What thou lovest well is thy true heritage
What thou lov'st well shall not be reft from thee.

The ant's a centaur in his dragon world.
Pull down thy vanity, it is not man
Made courage, or made order, or made grace,

[8]Duccio de Buoninsegna (1260?–1318?), the first great Sienese painter.
[9]Piero della Francesca (1420?–1492?) and Giovanni Bellini (1430?–1516), Italian painters.
[10]*La Calumnia*, a painting by the Italian Sandro Botticelli (1445?–1510).
[11]Fra Angelico (1387?–1455) and Ambrogio de Predis (1455?–1506?), Italian painters.
[12]Latin: Adam made me, Pound's recollection of an inscription carved on a stone column in the Church of San Zeno Maggiore in Verona, Italy.
[13]Church in Arles, France. [14]Church in Poitiers, France. [15]French: crimson cloth.
[16]Hans Memling (1430?–1495), Flemish painter. [17]I.e., the aged, the infirm.
[18]Latin: contrary to nature. [19]Ancient religious sanctuary near Athens, Greece.

Pull down thy vanity, I say pull down.
Learn of the green world what can be thy place
In scaled invention or true artistry,
Pull down thy vanity,
Paquin[1] pull down!
The green casque has outdone your elegance.[2]

"Master thyself, then others shall thee beare"[3]
Pull down thy vanity,
Thou art a beaten dog beneath the hail,
A swollen magpie in a fitful sun,
Half black half white
Nor knowst'ou wing from tail
Pull down thy vanity
How mean thy hates
Fostered in falsity,
Pull down thy vanity,
Rathe[4] to destroy, niggard[5] in charity,
Pull down thy vanity,
I say pull down.

But to have done instead of not doing
this is not vanity
To have, with decency, knocked
That a Blunt should open[6]
To have gathered from the air a live tradition
or from a fine old eye the unconquered flame
This is not vanity.
Here error is all in the not done,
all in the diffidence that faltered . . .[7]

1947, 1948

T. S. Eliot 1888–1965

In the period between the two world wars, poetry and criticism were largely dominated by a single figure, T. S. Eliot. Even more than Ezra Pound, he shaped the tastes and the critical vocabulary of a generation. The Waste Land, *the most startling and innovative of Eliot's poems, had the effect, as William Carlos Williams remarked, of "an atom bomb"; and in the decades that followed, Eliot became the major poet writing in English and the authoritative voice of modern criticism—esteemed, imitated, and quoted on both sides of the Atlantic.*

[1]A Parisian dress designer.
[2]I.e., the green forms of insects outdo the artificial designs of Paquin.
[3]A paraphrase of Chaucer's *Ballade of Good Counsel,* line 13. [4]Hasty, quick. [5]Stingy.
[6]A reference to Matthew 7:7, "knock, and it shall be opened unto you." Wilfred Blunt (1840–1922), English poet and political essayist who was much admired by Pound.
[7]Pound's ellipsis.

Eliot was a descendant of a prominent New England family dating from the seventeenth century. He was born in St. Louis, Missouri. In his youth he attended a Boston preparatory school and then entered Harvard, where he studied literature and philosophy. He served as editor of the Harvard Advocate, *and he developed, from reading the poetry of the French symbolists, his early poetic style. From Harvard, Eliot went to Europe to complete a doctoral dissertation on F. H. Bradley, an English philosopher from whom Eliot derived one of his pervasive themes, the "isolated consciousness."*

When World War I began, Eliot settled in London, where he worked as a bank clerk. In 1917, in the wake of a fateful meeting with Ezra Pound, Eliot published his first book of poems, Prufrock and Other Observations. *He became an editor of the* Egoist *and then founding editor of the* Criterion, *for which he wrote some of his early reviews and criticism. Then in 1922,* The Waste Land *(dedicated to its editor, Pound) became the poem that set the tone of the postwar era. Emphasizing the decay of Western culture, Eliot's poem was heralded as the major document of modern despair. Its ranging meters and fragmented style—an interweaving of reminiscences, vignettes, literary allusions, and anthropological lore—became models of modernist techniques.*

Loosely patterned on medieval Grail legend, The Waste Land *reflects the theme and direction of Eliot's own life: the quest for salvation. In the years that followed, Eliot's writing expressed a deepening conservatism in religion and politics. In 1927 he startled many admirers by announcing his adoption of British citizenship and his conversion to the Church of England. The change was paralleled by the movement of his poetry from the secular to the ascetic—from the pessimism of "Gerontion" (1919), to the religious faith of "Ash Wednesday" (1930), the "conversion" poem drawn from the Anglican service and the disciplines of Christian asceticism. Eliot's poetry culminated in the religious meditations of* Four Quartets *(1936–1943), in which the theme of spiritual quest becomes both personal and universal, presenting man's effort to transcend the force of time and to achieve the "still moment" of the eternal.*

In his later years Eliot devoted himself mainly to verse drama, a genre he had long wanted to restore to the modern stage. His first play, based upon the martyrdom of Saint Thomas Becket, Murder in the Cathedral *(1935), met with some success. The later plays, in contemporary settings, include* The Family Reunion *(1939),* The Cocktail Party *(1950),* The Confidential Clerk *(1954), and* The Elder Statesman *(1958). Although Eliot's plays are often impressive in their poetry, in general, their sophisticated moral and religious arguments have kept them from achieving wide popular appreciation.*

The antiromantic tendency of Eliot's literary criticism was evident with his first book of essays, The Sacred Wood *(1920). His focus on the English writers of the sixteenth and seventeenth centuries led to a general reassessment of poetic tradition. Most notable was his "discovery" of the Metaphysical poets, in an essay that made John Donne and his followers a contemporary vogue. In 1948 Eliot's achievements were recognized by awards of the British Order of Merit and the Nobel Prize for Literature. In the years that followed, Eliot's reputation declined, yet he continued to the end to exercise authority in the world of letters, just as his masterpiece,* The Waste Land, *has remained one of the most influential poems of the twentieth century.*

FURTHER READING: *Collected Plays,* 1962; *The Waste Land, A Facsimile and Transcript of the Original Drafts,* ed. V. Eliot, 1971; L. Gordon, *Eliot's Early Years,* Vol. I, 1977, *Eliot's New Life,* Vol. II, 1988; C. Behr, *T. S. Eliot, A Chronology of His Life and Works,* 1982; P. Ackroyd, *T. S. Eliot, A Life,* 1984; *The Letters of T. S. Eliot,* Vols. I and II, ed. V. Eliot, 1988, 1991; F. Pinion, *A T. S. Eliot Companion,* 1988; M. Scofield, *T. S. Eliot, The Poems,* 1988; C. Ricks, *Eliot and Prejudice,* 1989; E. Sigg, *The American T. S. Eliot,* 1989; J. Brooker and J. Bentley, *Reading the Waste Land,* 1990; T. Sharpe, *T. S. Eliot, A Literary Life,* 1992; *The Cambridge*

Companion to T. S. Eliot, ed. A. Moody, 1994; D. Chinitz, *T. S. Eliot and the Cultural Divide,* 2003; J. Miller, *T. S. Eliot, The Making of an American Poet,* 2005; R. Badenhausen, *T. S. Eliot and the Art of Collaboration,* 2005; L. Rainey, *Revisiting the Waste Land,* 2005.

TEXT: *Collected Poems, 1909–1962,* 1963, with corrections supplied by the editor.

THE LOVE SONG OF J. ALFRED PRUFROCK

S'io credessi che mia risposta fosse
a persona che mai tornasse al mondo,
questa fiamma staria senza più scosse.
Ma per ciò giammai di questo fondo
non tornò vivo alcun, s'i'odo il vero,
senza tema d'infamia ti rispondo.[1]

Let us go then, you and I,
When the evening is spread out against the sky
Like a patient etherised upon a table;
Let us go through certain half-deserted streets,
The muttering retreats
Of restless nights in one-night cheap hotels
And sawdust restaurants with oyster-shells:
Streets that follow like a tedious argument
Of insidious intent
To lead you to an overwhelming question. . .[2]
Oh, do not ask, "What is it?"
Let us go and make our visit.

In the room the women come and go
Talking of Michelangelo.

The yellow fog that rubs its back upon the window-panes,
The yellow smoke that rubs its muzzle on the window-panes,
Licked its tongue into the corners of the evening,
Lingered upon the pools that stand in drains,
Let fall upon its back the soot that falls from chimneys,
Slipped by the terrace, made a sudden leap,
And seeing that it was a soft October night,
Curled once about the house, and fell asleep.

And indeed there will be time
For the yellow smoke that slides along the street
Rubbing its back upon the window-panes;
There will be time, there will be time
To prepare a face to meet the faces that you meet;
There will be time to murder and create,

[1]"If I thought my reply were to one who could ever return to the world, this flame would shake no more; but since, if what I hear is true, none ever did return alive from this depth, I answer you without fear of infamy." The flame (or spirit) of Guido de Montefeltro, suffering in Hades for his sins, confesses to the poet Dante (*Inferno,* Canto XXVII, lines 61–66).

[2]Here, and throughout, the ellipsis points are Eliot's and do not indicate omissions by the editor.

And time for all the works and days[3] of hands
That lift and drop a question on your plate;
Time for you and time for me,
And time yet for a hundred indecisions,
And for a hundred visions and revisions,
Before the taking of a toast and tea.

In the room the women come and go
Talking of Michelangelo.

And indeed there will be time
To wonder, "Do I dare?" and, "Do I dare?"
Time to turn back and descend the stair,
With a bald spot in the middle of my hair—
(They will say: "How his hair is growing thin!")
My morning coat, my collar mounting firmly to the chin,
My necktie rich and modest, but asserted by a simple pin—
(They will say: "But how his arms and legs are thin!")
Do I dare
Disturb the universe?
In a minute there is time
For decisions and revisions which a minute will reverse.

For I have known them all already, known them all—
Have known the evenings, mornings, afternoons,
I have measured out my life with coffee spoons;
I know the voices dying with a dying fall
Beneath the music from a farther room.
  So how should I presume?

And I have known the eyes already, known them all—
The eyes that fix you in a formulated phrase,
And when I am formulated, sprawling on a pin,
When I am pinned and wriggling on the wall,
Then how should I begin
To spit out all the butt-ends of my days and ways?
  And how should I presume?

And I have known the arms already, known them all—
Arms that are braceleted and white and bare
(But in the lamplight, downed with light brown hair!)
Is it perfume from a dress
That makes me so digress?
Arms that lie along a table, or wrap about a shawl.
  And should I then presume?
  And how should I begin?

. . . . .

Shall I say, I have gone at dusk through narrow streets
And watched the smoke that rises from the pipes
Of lonely men in shirt-sleeves, leaning out of windows? . . .

[3]A reference to *Works and Days,* a poem, by the ancient Greek poet Hesiod, on the rural life and labors of a peasant.

I should have been a pair of ragged claws
Scuttling across the floors of silent seas.

. . . . .

And the afternoon, the evening, sleeps so peacefully!
Smoothed by long fingers,
Asleep . . . tired . . . or it malingers,
Stretched on the floor, here beside you and me.
Should I, after tea and cakes and ices,
Have the strength to force the moment to its crisis?

But though I have wept and fasted, wept and prayed,
Though I have seen my head (grown slightly bald) brought in upon a
    platter,[4]
I am no prophet—and here's no great matter;
I have seen the moment of my greatness flicker,
And I have seen the eternal Footman hold my coat, and snicker,
And in short, I was afraid.

And would it have been worth it, after all,
After the cups, the marmalade, the tea,
Among the porcelain, among some talk of you and me,
Would it have been worth while,
To have bitten off the matter with a smile,
To have squeezed the universe into a ball[5]
To roll it towards some overwhelming question,
To say: "I am Lazarus, come from the dead,[6]
Come back to tell you all, I shall tell you all"—
If one, settling a pillow by her head,
Should say: "That is not what I meant at all.
That is not it, at all."

And would it have been worth it, after all,
Would it have been worth while,
After the sunsets and the dooryards and the sprinkled streets,
After the novels, after the teacups, after the skirts that trail along
    the floor—
And this, and so much more?—
It is impossible to say just what I mean!
But as if a magic lantern threw the nerves in patterns on a screen:
Would it have been worth while
If one, settling a pillow or throwing off a shawl,

[4]The prophet John the Baptist was beheaded and his head brought on a platter to Salome, the daughter of Herodias (Matthew 14:1–11).

[5]An allusion to the poem "To His Coy Mistress," by the English poet Andrew Marvell (1621–1678): "Let us roll all our strength and all/Our sweetness up into one ball. . . ."

[6]The rich man Dives, suffering in Hell, begged that Lazarus be returned from heaven to earth to warn sinners of the torments that await them (Luke 16:19–31).

And turning toward the window, should say:
  "That is not it at all,
  That is not what I meant, at all."

  . . . . .

No! I am not Prince Hamlet, nor was meant to be;
Am an attendant lord, one that will do
To swell a progress,[7] start a scene or two,
Advise the prince: no doubt, an easy tool,
Deferential, glad to be of use,
Politic, cautious, and meticulous;
Full of high sentence,[8] but a bit obtuse;
At times, indeed, almost ridiculous—
Almost, at times, the Fool.

I grow old . . . I grow old . . .
I shall wear the bottoms of my trousers rolled.[9]
Shall I part my hair behind? Do I dare to eat a peach?
I shall wear white flannel trousers, and walk upon the beach.
I have heard the mermaids[10] singing, each to each.

I do not think that they will sing to me.

I have seen them riding seaward on the waves
Combing the white hair of the waves blown back
When the wind blows the water white and black.

We have lingered in the chambers of the sea
By sea-girls wreathed with seaweed red and brown
Till human voices wake us, and we drown.
1910–1911 1915, 1917

PRELUDES

I

The winter evening settles down
With smell of steaks in passageways.
Six o'clock.
The burnt-out ends of smoky days
And now a gusty shower wraps
The grimy scraps
Of withered leaves about your feet
And newspapers from vacant lots;
The showers beat

[7]To be part of a royal procession. [8]Judgment, pronouncement.
[9]To form fashionable cuffs. [10]Mythical alluring creatures, half woman and half fish.

On broken blinds and chimney-pots,
And at the corner of the street
A lonely cab-horse steams and stamps.
And then the lighting of the lamps.

II

The morning comes to consciousness
Of faint stale smells of beer
From the sawdust-trampled street
With all its muddy feet that press
To early coffee-stands.

With the other masquerades
That times resumes,
One thinks of all the hands
That are raising dingy shades
In a thousand furnished rooms.

III

You tossed a blanket from the bed,
You lay upon your back, and waited;
You dozed, and watched the night revealing
The thousand sordid images
Of which your soul was constituted;
They flickered against the ceiling.
And when all the world came back
And the light crept up between the shutters
And you heard the sparrows in the gutters,
You had such a vision of the street
As the street hardly understands;
Sitting along the bed's edge, where
You curled the papers from your hair,
Or clasped the yellow soles of feet
In the palms of both soiled hands.

IV

His soul stretched tight across the skies
That fade behind a city block,
Or trampled by insistent feet
At four and five and six o'clock;
And short square fingers stuffing pipes,
And evening newspapers, and eyes
Assured of certain certainties,
The conscience of a blackened street
Impatient to assume the world.

I am moved by fancies that are curled
Around these images, and cling:
The notion of some infinitely gentle
Infinitely suffering thing.

Wipe your hand across your mouth, and
 laugh;
The worlds revolve like ancient women
Gathering fuel in vacant lots.
1910–1911 1915, 1917

GERONTION[1]

Thou has nor youth nor age
But as it were an after-dinner's sleep
Dreaming on both.[2]

Here I am, an old man in a dry month
Being read to by a boy, waiting for rain.
I was neither at the hot gates[3]
Nor fought in the warm rain
Nor knee deep in the salt marsh, heaving a cutlass,
Bitten by flies, fought.
My house is a decayed house,
And the Jew squats on the window sill, the owner,
Spawned in some estaminet[4] of Antwerp,
Blistered in Brussels, patched and peeled[5] in London.
The goat coughs at night in the field overhead;
Rocks, moss, stonecrop,[6] iron, merds.[7]
The woman keeps the kitchen, makes tea,
Sneezes at evening, poking the peevish gutter.
 I an old man,
A dull head among windy spaces.

Signs are taken for wonders. "We would see a sign!"[8]
The word within a word, unable to speak a word,
Swaddled with darkness. In the juvescence[9] of the year
Came Christ the tiger

In depraved May, dogwood and chestnut, flowering judas,[10]
To be eaten, to be divided, to be drunk
Among whispers; by Mr. Silvero[11]

[1]A name derived from Greek "geron," "an old man."
[2]Shakespeare, *Measure for Measure* (Act III, Scene i, lines 32–34).
[3]At Thermopylae (Greek: hot gates) the Greeks battled the Persian invaders under Xerxes (480 B.C.).
[4]A cheap café.
[5]Medical procedures that, with blistering, were used to treat inflammation and venereal disease.
[6]A scrubby plant. [7]French: excrement.
[8]Jesus rebuked the doubting Pharisees when they said, "Master we would see a sign from thee" (Matthew 12:38–39).
[9]Juvenescence, youth. [10]The tree on which Judas was said to have hanged himself.
[11]An acquaintance (like Hakagawa, line 26) recalled by the aged Gerontion.

With caressing hands, at Limoges[12]
Who walked all night in the next room;
By Hakagawa, bowing among the Titians;[13]
By Madame de Tornquist, in the dark room
Shifting the candles; Fräulein von Kulp
Who turned in the hall, one hand on the door.
Vacant shuttles
Weave the wind. I have no ghosts,
An old man in a draughty house
Under a windy knob.

After such knowledge, what forgiveness? Think now
History has many cunning passages, contrived corridors
And issues; deceives with whispering ambitions,
Guides us by vanities. Think now
She gives when our attention is distracted,
And what she gives, gives with such supple confusions
That the giving famishes the craving. Gives too late
What's not believed in, or if still believed,
In memory only, reconsidered passion. Gives too soon
Into weak hands, what's thought can be dispensed with
Till the refusal propagates a fear. Think
Neither fear nor courage saves us. Unnatural vices
Are fathered by our heroism. Virtues
Are forced upon us by our impudent crimes.
These tears are shaken from the wrath-bearing tree.[14]

The tiger springs in the new year. Us he devours. Think at last
We have not reached conclusion, when I
Stiffen in a rented house. Think at last
I have not made this show purposelessly
And it is not by any concitation[15]
Of the backward devils.
I would meet you upon this honestly.
I that was near your heart was removed therefrom
To lose beauty in terror, terror in inquisition.
I have lost my passion: why should I need to keep it
Since what is kept must be adulterated?
I have lost my sight, smell, hearing, taste and touch:
How should I use them for your closer contact?

These with a thousand small deliberations
Protract the profit of their chilled delirium,
Excite the membrane, when the sense has cooled,
With pungent sauces, multiply variety
In a wilderness of mirrors. What will the spider do,

[12]French city noted for fine porcelain. [13]Paintings by the Italian artist Titian (1477–1576).
[14]The tree from which Adam and Eve ate the forbidden fruit (Genesis 2:16–17; 3:16–19).
[15]Agitation, excitement.

Suspend its operations, will the weevil
Delay? De Bailhache, Fresca, Mrs. Cammel,[16] whirled
Beyond the circuit of the shuddering Bear[17]
In fractured atoms. Gull against the wind, in the windy straits
Of Belle Isle,[18] or running on the Horn.[19]
White feathers in the snow, the Gulf claims,
And an old man driven by the Trades[20]
To a sleepy corner.
                                        Tenants of the house.
Thoughts of a dry brain in a dry season.
1919   1920

THE WASTE LAND[1]

"Nam Sibyllam quidem Cumis ego ipse oculis meis vidi in ampulla pendere, et cum illi pueri dicerent: Σίβυλλα τί θέλεις; *respondebat illa:* ἀποθανεῖν θέλω."[2]

For Ezra Pound
il miglior fabbro.[3]

I. THE BURIAL OF THE DEAD[4]

April is the cruellest month, breeding
Lilacs out of the dead land, mixing
Memory and desire, stirring
Dull roots with spring rain.
Winter kept us warm, covering
Earth in forgetful snow, feeding
A little life with dried tubers.
Summer surprised us, coming over the Starnbergersee[5]
With a shower of rain; we stopped in the colonnade,
And went on in sunlight, into the Hofgarten,[6]
And drank coffee, and talked for an hour.

[16]Other names recollected by Gerontion.
[17]One of constellations Ursa, the Big or Little Dipper.
[18]Straits between Labrador and Newfoundland, Canada.
[19]Cape Horn, at the southern tip of South America. [20]Trade winds.

[1]Footnotes to this poem and to Eliot's "Notes on 'The Waste Land'" are supplied by the editor.

[2]"For I myself saw with my own eyes the Sibyl of Cumae [in Italy] hanging in a bottle; and when the boys cried to her, 'Sibyl, what do you want?' she used to reply, 'I want to die.'" (Petronius, *Satyricon,* Chapter XLVIII). The Sibyl, a prophetess, had been given long life by Apollo, but she had failed to ask for eternal youth and health.

[3]"The better craftsman," a quotation from Dante's *Purgatorio* (Canto XXVI, line 117). Pound had assisted Eliot in writing "The Waste Land."

[4]The title of the services for the dead in *The Book of Common Prayer* of the Church of England.

[5]Lake near Munich, Germany. [6]Public park in Munich.

Bin gar keine Russin, stamm' aus Litauen, echt deutsch.[7]
And when we were children, staying at the archduke's,
My cousin's, he took me out on a sled,
And I was frightened. He said, Marie,
Marie, hold on tight. And down we went.
In the mountains, there you feel free.
I read, much of the night, and go south in the winter.
What are the roots that clutch, what branches grow
Out of this stony rubbish? Son of man,
You cannot say, or guess, for you know only
A heap of broken images, where the sun beats,
And the dead tree gives no shelter, the cricket no relief,
And the dry stone no sound of water. Only
There is shadow under this red rock,
(Come in under the shadow of this red rock),
And I will show you something different from either
Your shadow at morning striding behind you
Or your shadow at evening rising to meet you;
I will show you fear in a handful of dust.
Frisch weht der Wind
Der Heimat zu.
Mein Irisch Kind,
Wo weilest du?[8]
"You gave me hyacinths[9] first a year ago;
"They called me the hyacinth girl."
—Yet when we came back, late, from the hyacinth garden,
Your arms full, and your hair wet, I could not
Speak, and my eyes failed, I was neither
Living nor dead, and I knew nothing,
Looking into the heart of light, the silence.
Oed' und leer das Meer.[10]

Madame Sosostris, famous clairvoyante,
Had a bad cold, nevertheless
Is known to be the wisest woman in Europe,
With a wicked pack of cards.[11] Here, said she,
Is your card, the drowned Phoenician Sailor,
(Those are pearls that were his eyes.[12] Look!)
Here is Belladonna, the Lady of the Rocks,
The lady of situations.

[7]German: I'm not Russian; I come from Lithuania, pure German.

[8]"Fresh blows the wind / To the homeland / My Irish child; / Where are you waiting?" See Eliot's note, I, line 31.

[9]A flower named for Hyacinthus, ancient Greek fertility god. The Hyacinthia, a resurrection festival in his honor, was celebrated in July to commemorate the seasonal rebirth and growth of vegetation.

[10]"Desolate and empty the sea." See Eliot's note, I, line 42.

[11]Tarot cards, used in fortune-telling. See Eliot's note, I, line 46.

[12]From Shakespeare's *The Tempest* (Act I, Scene ii, line 398).

Here is the man with three staves, and here the Wheel,
And here is the one-eyed merchant, and this card,
Which is blank, is something he carries on his back,
Which I am forbidden to see. I do not find
The Hanged Man. Fear death by water.
I see crowds of people, walking round in a ring.
Thank you. If you see dear Mrs. Equitone,
Tell her I bring the horoscope myself:
One must be so careful these days.

Unreal City,
Under the brown fog of a winter dawn,
A crowd flowed over London Bridge, so many,
I had not thought death had undone so many.[13]
Sighs, short and infrequent, were exhaled,
And each man fixed his eyes before his feet.
Flowed up the hill and down King William Street,
To where Saint Mary Woolnoth[14] kept the hours
With a dead sound on the final stroke of nine.
There I saw one I knew, and stopped him, crying: "Stetson!
"You who were with me in the ships at Mylae![15]
"That corpse you planted last year in your garden,
"Has it begun to sprout? Will it bloom this year?
"Or has the sudden frost disturbed its bed?
"O keep the Dog far hence, that's friend to men,
"Or with his nails he'll dig it up again![16]
"You! hypocrite lecteur!—mon semblable,—mon frère!"[17]

II. A GAME OF CHESS

The Chair she sat in, like a burnished throne,
Glowed on the marble,[18] where the glass
Held up by standards wrought with fruited vines
From which a golden Cupidon[19] peeped out
(Another hid his eyes behind his wing)
Doubled the flames of sevenbranched candelabra
Reflecting light upon the table as
The glitter of her jewels rose to meet it,
From satin cases poured in rich profusion.

[13]A quotation from Dante's *Inferno.* See Eliot's note, I, line 63. [14]London church.

[15]Site of a Roman naval victory over the Carthaginians (260 B.C.).

[16]An adaptation from John Webster's *The White Devil* (1612): "But keep the wolf far thence, that's foe to men, / For with his nails he'll dig them up again." (Act V, Scene iv, lines 97–98).

[17]French: "hypocrite reader!—my likeness,—my brother!" See Eliot's note, I, line 76.

[18]An adaptation of the description of Cleopatra's barge in Shakespeare's *Antony and Cleopatra:* "The barge she sat in, like a burnish'd throne, / Burn'd on the water." (Act II, Scene ii, lines 196–197).

[19]A statue of Cupid, Roman god of love.

In vials of ivory and coloured glass
Unstoppered, lurked her strange synthetic perfumes,
Unguent, powdered, or liquid—troubled, confused
And drowned the sense in odours; stirred by the air
That freshened from the window, these ascended
In fattening the prolonged candle-flames,
Flung their smoke into the laquearia,[20]
Stirring the pattern on the coffered ceiling.
Huge sea-wood fed with copper
Burned green and orange, framed by the coloured stone,
In which sad light a carvèd dolphin swam.
Above the antique mantel was displayed
As though a window gave upon the sylvan scene[21]
The change of Philomel,[22] by the barbarous king
So rudely forced; yet there the nightingale
Filled all the desert with inviolable voice
And still she cries, and still the world pursues,
"Jug Jug"[23] to dirty ears.
And other withered stumps of time
Were told upon the walls; staring forms
Leaned out, leaning, hushing the room enclosed.
Footsteps shuffled on the stair.
Under the firelight, under the brush, her hair
Spread out in fiery points
Glowed into words, then would be savagely still.

"My nerves are bad to-night. Yes, bad. Stay with me.
"Speak to me. Why do you never speak? Speak.
"What are you thinking of? What thinking? What?
"I never know what you are thinking. Think."

I think we are in rats' alley
Where the dead men lost their bones.

"What is that noise?"
                                        The wind under the door.
"What is that noise now? What is the wind doing?"
                                        Nothing again nothing.
                                                                                "Do

"You know nothing? Do you see nothing? Do you remember
Nothing?"

[20]Fretted ceiling. See Eliot's note, II, line 92.

[21]A reference to *Paradise Lost* (Book IV, line 140) where Milton describes the Garden of Eden.

[22]In classical legend Philomel was raped by Tereus, King of Thrace. The gods then turned her into a nightingale. The story is told in Ovid's *Metamorphoses.* See Eliot's note, II, line 99.

[23]Words traditionally used in English poetry to represent the song of the nightingale.

I remember
Those are pearls that were his eyes.
"Are you alive, or not? Is there nothing in your head?"
But
O O O O that Shakespeherian Rag—
It's so elegant
So intelligent[24]

"What shall I do now? What shall I do?
"I shall rush out as I am, and walk the street
"With my hair down, so. What shall we do tomorrow?
"What shall we ever do?"
The hot water at ten.
And if it rains, a closed car at four.
And we shall play a game of chess,
Pressing lidless eyes and waiting for a knock upon the door.
When Lil's husband got demobbed,[25] I said—
I didn't mince my words, I said to her myself,
HURRY UP PLEASE IT'S TIME[26]
Now Albert's coming back, make yourself a bit smart.
He'll want to know what you done with that money he gave you
To get yourself some teeth. He did, I was there.
You have them all out, Lil, and get a nice set,
He said, I swear, I can't bear to look at you.
And no more can't I, I said, and think of poor Albert,
He's been in the army four years, he wants a good time,
And if you don't give it him, there's others will, I said.
Oh is there, she said. Something o' that, I said.
Then I'll know who to thank, she said, and give me a straight look.
HURRY UP PLEASE IT'S TIME
If you don't like it you can get on with it, I said,
Others can pick and choose if you can't.
But if Albert makes off, it won't be for lack of telling.
You ought to be ashamed, I said, to look so antique.
(And her only thirty-one.)
I can't help it, she said, pulling a long face,
It's them pills I took, to bring it off, she said
(She's had five already, and nearly died of young George.)
The chemist[27] said it would be all right, but I've never been the same.
You *are* a proper fool, I said.
Well, if Albert won't leave you alone, there it is, I said,
What you get married for if you don't want children?
HURRY UP PLEASE IT'S TIME
Well, that Sunday Albert was home, they had a hot gammon,[28]
And they asked me in to dinner, to get the beauty of it hot—

[24]Lines adapted from the lyrics of *That Shakespearian Rag*, a popular song of 1912.
[25]Demobilized from the army. [26]English pubkeeper's call to announce closing time.
[27]English pharmacist. [28]Smoked ham.

HURRY UP PLEASE IT'S TIME
HURRY UP PLEASE IT'S TIME
Goonight Bill. Goonight Lou. Goonight May. Goonight.
Ta ta. Goonight. Goonight.
Good night, ladies, good night, sweet ladies, good night, good night.[29]

III. THE FIRE SERMON

The river's tent is broken; the last fingers of leaf
Clutch and sink into the wet bank. The wind
Crosses the brown land, unheard. The nymphs are departed.
Sweet Thames, run softly, till I end my song.[30]
The river bears no empty bottles, sandwich papers,
Silk handkerchiefs, cardboard boxes, cigarette ends
Or other testimony of summer nights. The nymphs are departed.
And their friends, the loitering heirs of City directors;[31]
Departed, have left no addresses.
By the waters of Leman I sat down and wept[32] . . .
Sweet Thames, run softly till I end my song,
Sweet Thames, run softly, for I speak not loud or long.
But at my back in a cold blast I hear[33]
The rattle of the bones, and chuckle spread from ear to ear.
A rat crept softly through the vegetation
Dragging its slimy belly on the bank
While I was fishing in the dull canal
On a winter evening round behind the gashouse
Musing upon the king my brother's wreck
And on the king my father's death before him.[34]
White bodies naked on the low damp ground
And bones cast in a little low garret,
Rattled by the rat's foot only, year to year.
But at my back from time to time I hear
The sound of horns and motors, which shall bring
Sweeney to Mrs. Porter[35] in the spring.
O the moon shone bright on Mrs. Porter

[29]From the speech by Ophelia, after she has gone mad. Shakespeare, *Hamlet* (Act IV, Scene v, lines 72–74).

[30]A quotation from Edmund Spenser's "Prothalamion" (1596), which describes an elegant procession of nymphs down the river Thames.

[31]Directors of business firms in the City, the financial district of London.

[32]From the lamentations of the Jews exiled from Palestine: "By the rivers of Babylon, there we sat down, yea, we wept, when we remembered Zion" (Psalm 137). Eliot substitutes "Leman," the French name for Lake Geneva, Switzerland.

[33]Adapted from "To His Coy Mistress," by Andrew Marvell (1621–1678): "But at my back I always hear / Time's winged chariot hurrying near" (lines 21–22).

[34]Adapted from the words of Ferdinand, son of the King of Naples, in Shakespeare's *The Tempest* (Act I, Scene ii, lines 389–391): "Sitting on a bank, / Weeping against the King my father's wreck, / This music crept by me upon the waters."

[35]Here, as elsewhere in Eliot's poetry, Sweeney represents crude humankind. Mrs. Porter and her daughter were whores described in a bawdy song popular with British troops in World War I. See Eliot's note, III, line 199.

And on her daughter
They wash their feet in soda water
Et, O ces voix d'enfants chantant dans la coupole.[36]

Twit twit twit
Jug jug jug jug jug jug
So rudely forc'd.
Tereu[37]

Unreal City
Under the brown fog of a winter noon
Mr. Eugenides,[38] the Smyrna[39] merchant
Unshaven, with a pocket full of currants
C.i.f. London: documents at sight,[40]
Asked me in demotic[41] French
To luncheon at the Cannon Street Hotel
Followed by a weekend at the Metropole.
At the violet hour, when eyes and back
Turn upward from the desk, when the human engine waits
Like a taxi throbbing waiting
I Tiresias, though blind, throbbing between two lives,[42]
Old man with wrinkled female breasts, can see
At the violet hour, the evening hour that strives
Homeward, and brings the sailor home from sea,[43]
The typist home at teatime, clears her breakfast, lights
Her stove, and lays out food in tins.
Out of the window perilously spread
Her drying combinations[44] touched by the sun's last rays,
On the divan are piled (at night her bed)
Stockings, slippers, camisoles, and stays.[45]
I Tiresias, old man with wrinkled dugs[46]
Perceived the scene, and foretold the rest—
I too awaited the expected guest.
He, the young man carbuncular,[47] arrives,
A small house agent's clerk, with one bold stare,

[36]French: And, O those voices of children [choirboys] singing in the dome. From "Parsifal," a sonnet by Paul Verlaine (1844–1896).

[37]A conventional representation, with "jug, jug," of the nightingale's song and an allusion to King Tereus, the despoiler of Philomela.

[38]Greek for *wellborn.* [39]Seaport in Turkey.

[40]Business terms used in the buying and selling of commodities. See Eliot's note, III, line 210.

[41]Vulgar.

[42]Tiresias, a blind prophet in Greek myth, had been transformed into a woman for seven years. See Eliot's note, III, line 218.

[43]Eliot refers (see his note) to "Sappho's lines," probably a reference to her poem to Hesperus, the Evening Star that brings "home all things the bright morning dispersed." Eliot may also have had in mind the lines from "Requiem" by Robert Louis Stevenson (1850–1894): "Home is the sailor, home from the sea."

[44]One-piece underwear.

[45]Camisoles: short, sleeveless underwear. Stays: corset with bone stiffeners. [46]Breasts.

[47]Afflicted with carbuncles, boils.

One of the low on whom assurance sits
As a silk hat on a Bradford millionaire.[48]
The time is now propitious, as he guesses,
The meal is ended, she is bored and tired,
Endeavours to engage her in caresses
Which still are unreproved, if undesired.
Flushed and decided, he assaults at once;
Exploring hands encounter no defence;
His vanity requires no response,
And makes a welcome of indifference.
(And I Tiresias have foresuffered all
Enacted on this same divan or bed;
I who have sat by Thebes below the wall
And walked among the lowest of the dead.)[49]
Bestows one final patronising kiss,
And gropes his way, finding the stairs unlit . . .
She turns and looks a moment in the glass,
Hardly aware of her departed lover;
Her brain allows one half-formed thought to pass:
"Well now that's done: and I'm glad it's over."
When lovely woman stoops to folly and
Paces about her room again, alone,
She smoothes her hair with automatic hand,
And puts a record on the gramophone.[50]

"This music crept by me upon the waters"[51]
And along the Strand,[52] up Queen Victoria Street.
O City, City, I can sometimes hear
Beside a public bar in Lower Thames Street,
The pleasant whining of a mandoline
And a clatter and a chatter from within
Where fishmen lounge at noon: where the walls
Of Magnus Martyr[53] hold
Inexplicable splendour of Ionian white and gold.

The river sweats
Oil and tar
The barges drift
With the turning tide
Red sails
Wide
To leeward, swing on the heavy spar.

[48]One of the newly rich from the English industrial city of Bradford.

[49]Tiresias made his prophecies in Thebes, where he lived, and in Hades, the underworld, after his death.

[50]An ironic adaptation from Oliver Goldsmith's *The Vicar of Wakefield* (Chapter 24): "When lovely woman stoops to folly, / And finds too late that men betray; / What charm can soothe her melancholy? / What art can wash her guilt away?"

[51]From *The Tempest.* [52]A London street.

[53]A London church built by Sir Christopher Wren (1632–1723). See Eliot's note, III, line 264.

The barges wash
Drifting logs
Down Greenwich Reach[54]
Past the Isle of Dogs.[55]
Weialala leia
Wallala leialala[56]
Elizabeth and Leicester[57]
Beating oars
The stern was formed
A gilded shell
Red and gold
The brisk swell
Rippled both shores
Southwest wind
Carried down stream
The peal of bells
White towers
Weialala leia
Wallala leialala

"Trams[58] and dusty trees.
Highbury bore me. Richmond and Kew
Undid me.[59] By Richmond I raised my knees
Supine on the floor of a narrow canoe."

"My feet are at Moorgate,[60] and my heart
Under my feet. After the event
He wept. He promised 'a new start.'
I made no comment. What should I resent?"

"On Margate Sands.[61]
I can connect
Nothing with nothing.
The broken fingernails of dirty hands.
My people humble people who expect
Nothing."
la la

[54]The Thames River at Greenwich.

[55]A peninsula in the Thames.

[56]The refrain in the song of the Rhine-maidens from the opera *Die Götterdämmerung*, by Richard Wagner (1813–1883).

[57]Queen Elizabeth I of England and Robert Dudley, the Earl of Leicester. Their boat-ride on the Thames (see Eliot's note, III, line 279) is contrasted to the three sordid love affairs that follow (lines 292–308).

[58]Streetcars.

[59]Highbury: London suburb; Richmond and Kew: park and resort areas near London. Eliot echoes the lines from Dante, "Siena bore me; Maremma undid me," used also by Ezra Pound in one of his "Hugh Selwyn Mauberley" poems.

[60]Slum area of London.

[61]A seaside resort on the Thames.

To Carthage then I came[62]

Burning burning burning burning[63]
O Lord Thou pluckest me out[64]
O Lord Thou pluckest

burning

IV. DEATH BY WATER

Phlebas the Phoenician, a fortnight dead,
Forgot the cry of gulls, and the deep sea swell
And the profit and loss.
A current under sea
Picked his bones in whispers. As he rose and fell
He passed the stages of his age and youth
Entering the whirlpool.
Gentile or jew
O you who turn the wheel[65] and look to windward,
Consider Phlebas, who was once handsome and tall as you.

V. WHAT THE THUNDER SAID[66]

After the torch light red on sweaty faces
After the frosty silence in the gardens
After the agony in stony places
The shouting and the crying
Prison and palace and reverberation
Of thunder of spring over distant mountains
He who was living is now dead[67]
We who were living are now dying
With a little patience

Here is no water but only rock
Rock and no water and the sandy road
The road winding above among the mountains
Which are mountains of rock without water
If there were water we should stop and drink

[62]From St. Augustine's *Confessions* (Book III, Chapter i). See Eliot's note, III, line 307.

[63]From the Fire Sermon of Buddha, which calls for a life free of fiery passion. See Eliot's note, III, line 308.

[64]In his *Confessions,* St. Augustine thanks the Lord for plucking him from his broiling, unholy loves. See Eliot's note, III, line 309.

[65]The wheel of fortune or (more likely) a ship's steersman's wheel.

[66]In the Indian *Upanishads,* the Lord speaks through the thunder.

[67]Lines 322–328 refer to Christ's ordeal after The Last Supper and His martyrdom.

Amongst the rock one cannot stop or think
Sweat is dry and feet are in the sand
If there were only water amongst the rock
Dead mountain mouth of carious[68] teeth that cannot spit
Here one can neither stand nor lie nor sit
There is not even silence in the mountains
But dry sterile thunder without rain
There is not even solitude in the mountains
But red sullen faces sneer and snarl
From doors of mudcracked houses
                                        If there were water

    And no rock
    If there were rock
    And also water
    And water
    A spring
    A pool among the rock
    If there were the sound of water only
    Not the cicada
    And dry grass singing
    But sound of water over a rock
    Where the hermit-thrush sings in the pine trees
    Drip drop drip drop drop drop drop
    But there is no water

Who is the third, who walks always beside you?[69]
When I count, there are only you and I together
But when I look ahead up the white road
There is always another one walking beside you
Gliding wrapt in a brown mantle, hooded
I do not know whether a man or a woman
—But who is that on the other side of you?
What is that sound high in the air[70]
Murmur of maternal lamentation
Who are those hooded hordes swarming
Over endless plains, stumbling in cracked earth
Ringed by the flat horizon only
What is the city over the mountains
Cracks and reforms and bursts in the violet air
Falling towers
Jerusalem Athens Alexandria
Vienna London
Unreal

[68]Decayed.

[69]After His crucifixion, Christ appeared before two travelers to Emmaus (Luke 24:13–31). See also Eliot's note, V, line 360.

[70]Lines 367–377 allude to the upheavals resulting from the Russian Revolution that threatened the centers of civilization: Jerusalem, Athens, Alexandria, etc. See Eliot's note, V, lines 366–377.

A woman drew her long black hair out tight
And fiddled whisper music on those strings
And bats with baby faces in the violet light
Whistled, and beat their wings
And crawled head downward down a blackened wall
And upside down in air were towers
Tolling reminiscent bells, that kept the hours
And voices singing out of empty cisterns and exhausted wells.

In this decayed hole among the mountains
In the faint moonlight, the grass is singing
Over the tumbled graves, about the chapel
There is the empty chapel,[71] only the wind's home.
It has no windows, and the door swings,
Dry bones can harm no one.
Only a cock stood on the rooftree
Co co rico co co rico[72]
In a flash of lightning. Then a damp gust
Bringing rain

Ganga[73] was sunken, and the limp leaves
Waited for rain, while the black clouds
Gathered far distant, over Himavant.[74]
The jungle crouched, humped in silence.
Then spoke the thunder
DA
Datta:[75] what have we given?
My friend, blood shaking my heart
The awful daring of a moment's surrender
Which an age of prudence can never retract
By this, and this only, we have existed
Which is not to be found in our obituaries
Or in memories draped by the beneficent spider
Or under seals broken by the lean solicitor
In our empty rooms
DA
Dayadhvam:[76] I have heard the key
Turn in the door once and turn once only
We think of the key, each in his prison
Thinking of the key, each confirms a prison
Only at nightfall, aethereal rumours
Revive for a moment a broken Coriolanus[77]
DA

[71]The Chapel Perilous, wherein the knight was prepared for his quest for the Holy Grail.
[72]The sound of the cock's crow (French version), indicating the coming of dawn and renewal.
[73]The Ganges River. [74]The Himalaya Mountains.
[75]Sanskrit: Give. From the words of the thunder in the *Upanishads.*
[76]Sanskrit: Sympathize.
[77]Roman general and title character of Shakespeare's *Coriolanus.* He was ruined by his pride and the ingratitude of the masses.

Damyata:[78] The boat responded
Gaily, to the hand expert with sail and oar
The sea was calm, your heart would have responded
Gaily, when invited, beating obedient
To controlling hands

I sat upon the shore
Fishing,[79] with the arid plain behind me
Shall I at least set my lands in order?[80]
London Bridge is falling down falling down falling down
Poi s'ascose nel foco che gli affina[81]
Quando fiam uti chelidon[82]—O swallow swallow
Le Prince d'Aquitaine à la tour abolie[83]
These fragments I have shored against my ruins
Why then Ile fit you.[84] Hieronymo's mad againe.[85]
Datta. Dayadhvam. Damyata.

Shantih shantih shantih[86]

1914?–1922 1922

NOTES ON "THE WASTE LAND"[1]

Not only the title, but the plan and a good deal of the incidental symbolism of the poem were suggested by Miss Jessie L. Weston's book on the Grail legend: *From Ritual to Romance* (Cambridge). Indeed, so deeply am I indebted, Miss Weston's book will elucidate the difficulties of the poem much better than my notes can do; and I recommend it (apart from the great interest of the book itself) to any who think such elucidation of the poem worth the trouble. To another work of anthropology I am indebted in general, one which has influenced our generation profoundly; I mean *The Golden Bough,*[2] I

[78]Sanskrit: Control yourselves.

[79]The Fisher King, to whom Eliot alludes, is, like Christ, a symbol of resurrection. See Eliot's note, V, line 425.

[80]"Thus saith the Lord, Set thine house in order: for thou shalt die, and not live" (Isaiah 38:1).

[81]Italian: Then he hid himself in the flame that purifies them, i.e., the flame that destroys lust. Dante, *Purgatorio* (Canto XXVI, *line* 148).

[82]"When shall I be like the swallow?" From the anonymous Latin poem (fourth century?) "Pervigilium Veneris" ("The Vigil of Venus"), celebrating love and the return of spring. See Eliot's note, V, line 429.

[83]French: The Prince of Aquitaine at the ruined tower. From the sonnet "El Desdichado" by Gérard de Nerval (1808–1855).

[84]From *The Spanish Tragedy* by Thomas Kyd (1557?–1595?). The words are spoken by Hieronymo, who seeks revenge for the murder of his son.

[85]The subtitle of *The Spanish Tragedy.*

[86]Sanskrit: The Peace which passeth understanding. See Eliot's note, V, line 434.

[1]In *The Frontiers of Criticism* (1956) Eliot wrote, "When it came to print *The Waste Land* as a little book [1922]—for the poem on its first appearance in *The Dial* [1922] and in *The Criterion* [1922] had no notes whatever—it was discovered that the poem was inconveniently short, so I set to work to expand the notes, in order to provide a few more pages of printed matter. . . ."

[2]Anthropological study (1890) of myth and religion, by Sir James Frazer (1854–1941).

have used especially the two volumes *Adonis, Attis, Osiris.* Anyone who is acquainted with these works will immediately recognise in the poem certain references to vegetation ceremonies.

I. The Burial of the Dead

Line 20. Cf. Ezekiel II, i.

23. Cf. Ecclesiastes XII, v.

31. V. *Tristan und Isolde,* I, verses 5–8.

42. Id. III, verse 24.

46. I am not familiar with the exact constitution of the Tarot pack of cards, from which I have obviously departed to suit my own convenience. The Hanged Man, a member of the traditional pack, fits my purpose in two ways: because he is associated in my mind with the Hanged God of Frazer, and because I associate him with the hooded figure in the passage of the disciples to Emmaus in Part V. The Phoenician Sailor and the Merchant appear later; also the "crowds of people," and Death by Water is executed in Part IV. The Man with Three Staves (an authentic member of the Tarot pack) I associate, quite arbitrarily, with the Fisher King himself.

60. Cf. Baudelaire:
"Fourmillante cité, cité pleine de rêves,
Où le spectre en plein jour raccroche le passant."[3]

63. Cf. *Inferno,* III, 55–57:
"si lunga tratta
di gente, ch'io non avrei mai creduto
che morte tanta n'avesse disfatta."[4]

64. Cf. *Inferno,* IV, 25–27:
"Quivi, secondo che per ascoltare,
"non avea pianto, ma' che di sospiri,
"che l'aura eterna facevan tremare."[5]

68. A phenomenon which I have often noticed.

74. Cf. the Dirge in Webster's *White Devil.*

76. V. Baudelaire, Preface to *Fleurs du mal.*

II. A Game of Chess

77. Cf. *Antony and Cleopatra,* II, ii, l. 190.

92. Laquearia. V. *Aeneid,* I, 726:
dependent lychni laquearibus aureis incensi, et noctem flammis funalia vincunt.[6]

98. Sylvan scene. V. Milton, *Paradise Lost,* IV, 140.

99. V. Ovid, *Metamorphoses,* VI, Philomela.

100. Cf. Part III, l. 204.

115. Cf. Part III, l. 195.

[3]"Swarming city, city full of dreams, / Where the ghost in broad daylight accosts the passerby." From the opening lines of the poem "Les Sept Vieillards" ("The Seven Old Men"), by the French poet Charles Baudelaire (1821–1867).

[4]"So long a train of people, I should never have believed death had undone so many."

[5]"Here was no complaint, that could be heard, except of sighs, which caused the eternal air to tremble."

[6]Lighted lamps hang from the gold, fretted ceiling, and flaming torches drive out the night.

118. Cf. Webster: "Is the wind in that door still?"[7]
126. Cf. Part I, l. 37, 48.
138. Cf. the game of chess in Middleton's *Women Beware Women.*[8]

III. THE FIRE SERMON

176. V. Spenser, *Prothalamion.*
192. Cf. *The Tempest,* I, ii.
196. Cf. Marvell, *To His Coy Mistress.*
197. Cf. Day, *Parliament of Bees:*

"When of the sudden, listening, you shall hear,
"A noise of horns and hunting, which shall bring
"Actaeon to Diana in the spring,
"Where all shall see her naked skin[9]. . . ."

199. I do not know the origin of the ballad from which these lines are taken: it was reported to me from Sydney, Australia.

202. V. Verlaine, *Parsifal.*

210. The currants were quoted at a price "cost insurance and freight to London"; and the Bill of Lading, etc., were to be handed to the buyer upon payment of the sight draft.

218. Tiresias, although a mere spectator and not indeed a "character," is yet the most important personage in the poem, uniting all the rest. Just as the one-eyed merchant, seller of currants, melts into the Phoenician Sailor, and the latter is not wholly distinct from Ferdinand Prince of Naples,[10] so all the women are one woman, and the two sexes meet in Tiresias. What Tiresias *sees,* in fact, is the substance of the poem. The whole passage from Ovid is of great anthropological interest:

". . .Cum Iunone iocos et maior vestra profecto est
Quam, quae contingit maribus," dixisse, "voluptas."
Illa negat; placuit quae sit sententia docti
Quaerere Tiresiae: venus huic erat utraque nota.
Nam duo magnorum viridi coeuntia silva
Corpora serpentum baculi violaverat ictu
Deque viro factus, mirabile, femina septem
Egerat autumnos; octavo rursus eosdem
Vidit et "est vestrae si tanta potentia plagae,"
Dixit "ut auctoris sortem in contraria mutet,
Nunc quoque vos feriam!" percussis anguibus isdem
Forma prior rediit genetivaque venit imago.
Arbiter hic igitur sumptus de lite iocosa
Dicta Iovis firmat; gravius Saturnia iusto
Nec pro materia fertur doluisse suique
Iudicis aeterna damnavit lumina nocte,
At pater omnipotens (neque enim licet inrita cuiquam

[7] I.e., "Is he breathing still?" Spoken of a dying man in John Webster's *The Devil's Law-Case* (1623).

[8] In Thomas Middleton's play (1657), a young wife is seduced while her guardian is occupied with a game of chess.

[9] From "Character 3" of John Day's Elizabethan verse dialogues, *The Parliament of Bees* (1641).

[10] In Shakespeare's *The Tempest.*

Facta dei fecisse deo) pro lumine adempto
Scire futura dedit poenamque levavit honore.[11]

221. This may not appear as exact as Sappho's lines, but I had in mind the "longshore" or "dory" fisherman, who returns at nightfall.

253. V. Goldsmith, the song in *The Vicar of Wakefield.*

257. V. *The Tempest,* as above.

264. The interior of St. Magnus Martyr is to my mind one of the finest among Wren's interiors. See *The Proposed Demolition of Nineteen City Churches:* (P.S. King & Son, Ltd.).

266. The Song of the (three) Thames-daughters begins here. From line 292 to 306 inclusive they speak in turn. V. *Götterdämmerung,* III, i: the Rhine-daughters.[12]

279. V. Froude, *Elizabeth,* Vol. I, ch. iv, letter of De Quadra to Philip of Spain: "In the afternoon we were in a barge, watching the games on the river. (The queen) was alone with Lord Robert and myself on the poop, when they began to talk nonsense, and went so far that Lord Robert at last said, as I was on the spot there was no reason why they should not be married if the queen pleased."[13]

293. Cf. *Purgatorio,* V. 133:
"Ricorditi di me, che son la Pia;
"Siena mi fe', disfecemi Maremma."[14]

307. V. St. Augustine's *Confessions:* "to Carthage then I came, where a cauldron of unholy loves sang all about mine ears."

308. The complete text of the Buddha's Fire Sermon (which corresponds in importance to the Sermon on the Mount) from which these words are taken, will be found translated in the late Henry Clarke Warren's *Buddhism in Translation* (Harvard Oriental Series). Mr. Warren was one of the great pioneers of Buddhist studies in the Occident.

309. From St. Augustine's *Confessions* again. The collocation of these two representatives of eastern and western asceticism, as the culmination of this part of the poem, is not an accident.

V. What the Thunder Said

In the first part of Part V three themes are employed: the journey to Emmaus, the approach to the Chapel Perilous (see Miss Weston's book) and the present decay of eastern Europe.

[11]The Latin quotation, from Ovid's *Metamorphoses* (Book III, lines 320–338), may be summarized as: Jove and Juno once argued whether women or men received more pleasure in lovemaking. To settle the argument they agreed to ask Tiresias, who had once been transformed into a woman. Tiresias, agreeing with Jove, said that women received more pleasure. The answer so angered Juno that she blinded Tiresias. Whereupon, as compensation, Jove gave the blind Tiresias the power to know the future.

[12]Eliot compares the three modern daughters of the Thames with the three legendary Rhine-maidens in *Die Götterdämmerung*, one of the four operas in Richard Wagner's *Der Ring des Nibelungen* (1853–1870).

[13]The quotation, taken from a letter from the Spanish Ambassador (Bishop de Quadra) to his king, appeared in a biography of Queen Elizabeth I by the English historian James Anthony Froude (1818–1894).

[14]Italian: "Remember me, who am La Pia; Siena bore me, Maremma undid me." Spoken by a Sienese woman, La Pia, who was killed in Maremma.

357. This is *Turdus aonalaschkae pallasii,* the hermit-thrush which I have heard in Quebec Province. Chapman says *(Handbook of Birds of Eastern North America)* "it is most at home in secluded woodland and thickety retreats. . . . Its notes are not remarkable for variety or volume, but in purity and sweetness of tone and exquisite modulation they are unequalled." Its "water-dripping song" is justly celebrated.

360. The following lines were stimulated by the account of one of the Antarctic expeditions (I forget which, but I think one of Shackleton's): it was related that the party of explorers, at the extremity of their strength, had the constant delusion that there was *one more member* than could actually be counted.

366–77. Cf. Hermann Hesse, *Blick ins Chaos:* "Schon ist halb Europa, schon ist zumindest der halbe Osten Europas auf dem Wege zum Chaos, fährt betrunken im heiligen Wahn am Abgrund entlang und singt dazu, singt betrunken und hymnisch wie Dmitri Karamasoff sang. Ueber diese Lieder lacht der Bürger beleidigt, der Heilige und Seher hört sie mit Tränen."[15]

402. "Datta, dayadhvam, damyata" (Give, sympathise, control). The fable of the meaning of the Thunder is found in the *Brihadaranyaka—Upanishad,* 5, 1. A translation is found in Deussen's *Sechzig Upanishads des Veda,* p. 489.

408. Cf. Webster, *The White Devil,* V, vi:

"... they'll remarry
Ere the worm pierce your winding-sheet, ere the spider
Make a thin curtain for your epithaphs."

412. Cf. *Inferno,* XXXIII, 46:

"ed io sentii chiavar l'uscio di sotto
all'orrible torre."[16]

Also F. H. Bradley, *Appearance and Reality,* p. 346.

"My external sensations are no less private to myself than are my thoughts or my feelings. In either case my experience falls within my own circle, a circle closed on the outside; and, with all its elements alike, every sphere is opaque to the others which surround it . . . . In brief, regarded as an existence which appears in a soul, the whole world for each is peculiar and private to that soul."

425. V. Weston: *From Ritual to Romance;* chapter on the Fisher King.

428. V. *Purgatorio,* XXVI, 48.

" 'Ara vos prec er aquella valor
'que vos condus al som de l'escalina,
'sovegna vos a temps de ma dolor.'
Poi s'ascose nel foco che gli affina."[17]

429. V. *Pervigilium Veneris.* Cf. Philomela in Parts II and III.

430. V. Gerard de Nerval, Sonnet *El Desdichado.*

[15]"Already half of Europe, already at least half of Eastern Europe, is on the way to chaos, going drunk, in spiritual madness, along the edge of the abyss, while singing drunkenly and rapturously, as did Dimitri Karamazov [in Dostoyevsky's *The Brothers Karamazov*]. The shocked bourgeois laughs at these songs; the saint and the prophet hear them with tears." From *A Glimpse into Chaos* by Herman Hesse (1877–1962), German poet and novelist.

[16]"And below I heard the door of the horrible tower being locked."

[17]" 'Now I pray you, by the goodness that guides you to the top of this stairway [i.e., to paradise], be mindful in due season of my pain.' Then he hid himself in the flame that purifies." The words are spoken to Dante by the poet Arnaut Daniel, who is suffering for his sins of lust.

432. V. Kyd's *Spanish Tragedy.*

434. Shantih. Repeated as here, a formal ending to an Upanishad. "The Peace which passeth understanding" is our equivalent to this word.

JOURNEY OF THE MAGI[1]

'A cold coming we had of it,
Just the worst time of the year
For a journey, and such a long journey:
The ways deep and the weather sharp,
The very dead of winter.'[2]
And the camels galled,[3] sore-footed, refractory,
Lying down in the melting snow.
There were times we regretted
The summer palaces on slopes, the terraces,
And the silken girls bringing sherbet.
Then the camel men cursing and grumbling
And running away, and wanting their liquor and women,
And the night-fires going out, and the lack of shelters,
And the cities hostile and the towns unfriendly
And the villages dirty and charging high prices:
A hard time we had of it.
At the end we preferred to travel all night,
Sleeping in snatches,
With the voices singing in our ears, saying
That this was all folly.

Then at dawn we came down to a temperate valley,
Wet, below the snow line, smelling of vegetation,
With a running stream and a water-mill beating the darkness,
And three trees on the low sky.[4]
And an old white horse[5] galloped away in the meadow.
Then we came to a tavern with vine-leaves over the lintel,[6]
Six hands at an open door dicing for pieces of silver,[7]
And feet kicking the empty wine-skins.

[1]One of a series of lyrics, the "Ariel Poems," on the theme of death and rebirth. The speaker is one of the three wise men whose journey to Bethlehem, to the birth of Christ, is described in Matthew 2:1–11.

[2]The first five lines are taken from a nativity sermon by Lancelot Andrewes (1555–1626), Bishop of Winchester.

[3]Rubbed raw by their harness.

[4]A suggestion of the three crosses on Calvary and the "darkness over all the land" (Matthew 27:38, 45).

[5]"Behold a white horse; and he that sat upon him was Faithful and True" (Revelation 19:11).

[6]The Israelites marked their door lintels with sacrificial blood so that the Lord would pass over them when he smote the Egyptians (Exodus 12:7–13). Here, the vine leaves on the tavern door suggest instead the vegetation sacred to such pagan fertility gods as Dionysus, god of wine.

[7]A suggestion of the silver paid Judas for the betrayal of Christ.

But there was no information, and so we continued
And arrived at evening, not a moment too soon
Finding the place; it was (you may say) satisfactory.

All this was a long time ago, I remember,
And I would do it again, but set down
This set down
This: were we led all that way for
Birth or Death? There was a Birth, certainly,
We had evidence and no doubt. I had seen birth and death,
But had thought they were different; this Birth was
Hard and bitter agony for us, like Death, our death.
We returned to our places, these Kingdoms,
But no longer at ease here, in the old dispensation,
With an alien people clutching their gods.
I should be glad of another death.

1927

E. E. Cummings 1894–1962

From the time he left college in 1916 until his death in 1962, E. E. Cummings held only one formal job: For three months he answered letters for a mail-order firm. Later he compared those three months to his time spent in a French concentration camp during the First World War. For Cummings, life was too important to spend in pursuit of the material success desired by "most people." Instead he chose to be a dedicated, full-time artist: a painter, a novelist, a playwright, a "nonlecturer"—but most of all a poet.

Edward Estlin Cummings was born in Cambridge, Massachusetts. His father was a Harvard professor who later served as a Unitarian minister in Boston. Cummings went to Harvard, and at his graduation gave the commencement address, speaking on "The New Art." In 1917, after taking his M.A. at Harvard and suffering his brief ordeal as a mail-order letter writer, Cummings went to France to serve as a volunteer ambulance driver with the Red Cross in World War I.

Shortly after arriving in France, Cummings was imprisoned for three months in a concentration camp, partly because of the stupidity of the French military authorities and partly because of Cummings's own stubbornness (he refused to say he hated the Germans; he would only admit that he loved the French). After influential friends secured his release, Cummings was encouraged to write about his experiences. The result was The Enormous Room *(1922), a novel that was the first significant statement of his lifelong dedication to individual freedom and his opposition to the dehumanizing forces he saw in the modern world.*

After World War I, Cummings returned to Europe to study painting. He joined the artistic expatriates who flourished in Paris in the 1920s, and whose experimentation in the visual arts profoundly influenced his literary development. In 1923 his first volume of poetry, Tulips and Chimneys, *was published. The following year he returned to America, and in 1925 he published* XLI Poems. *During the remainder of his life he traveled widely and wrote expansively: plays; a book describing a journey to Russia,* Eimi *(1933); and the poems that made him famous.*

Cummings's poetry is noted for its eccentric and playful style: its unusual typography, odd spellings, and deliberate grammatical tricks. But beneath the surface of trickery and apparent formlessness, his poetry is curiously conventional. He was a love poet in the romantic tradition; he celebrated families, parents, children, fun, and old-fashioned virtues. He admired youth, spring, and all things natural. He hated automatic patriotism and deplored intellectualism—the rationality that, he believed, stifles humankind's ability to feel deeply. He fiercely condemned the inhumanity of science and technology, writing, "Never will mankind become human . . . until it rises up and smashes its machines." He found modern conveniences contemptible; he shunned electricity in his home, hated radio and television, and called packaged food "Battle Creek seaweed." Above all he loved poetry. Reading to an indifferent audience in 1950, he finally grew angry and stormed out, shouting at his apathetic listeners, "Well, write poetry, for God's sake; it's the only thing that matters."

FURTHER READING: N. Friedman, *E. E. Cummings, The Growth of a Writer,* 1964, 1980; *Selected Letters of E. E. Cummings,* ed. F. Dupee and G. Stade, 1969; *E. E. Cummings, The Critical Reception,* ed. L. Dendinger, 1979; R. Kennedy, *Dreams in the Mirror, A Biography of E. E. Cummings,* 1980; *Critical Essays on E. E. Cummings,* ed. G. Rotella, 1984; M. Cohen, *Poet and Painter, The Aesthetic of E. E. Cummings' Early Work,* 1987; R. Kennedy, *E. E. Cummings Revisited,* 1993; N. Friedman, *(Re)Valuing Cummings,* 1996; M. Heusser, *I Am My Writing, The Poetry E. E. Cummings,* 1997; *E. E. Cummings,* ed. H. Bloom, 2003; C. Sawyer-Laucanno, *E. E. Cummings, A Biography,* 2004.

TEXTS: *The Harvard Monthly,* March 1916; *The Dial,* January, May 1920; *Broom,* May 1922; *S·4·N,* December 1922; *The Complete Poems, 1904–1962,* 1999.

[All in green went my love riding][1]

All in green went my love riding
On a great horse of gold
into the silver dawn.

Four lean hounds crouched low and smiling
the merry deer ran before.

Fleeter be they than dappled dreams
the swift sweet deer
the red rare deer.

Four red roebuck at a white water
the cruel bugle sang before.

Horn at hip went my love riding
riding the echo down
into the silver dawn.

four lean hounds crouched low and smiling
the level meadows ran before.

[1]Titles in brackets are supplied by the editor.

Softer be they than slippered sleep
the lean lithe deer
the fleet flown deer.

Four fleet does at a gold valley
the famished arrow sang before.

Bow at belt went my love riding
riding the mountain down
into the silver dawn.

four lean hounds crouched low and smiling
the sheer peaks ran before.

Paler be they than daunting death
the sleek slim deer
the tall tense deer.

Four tall stags at a green mountain
the lucky hunter sang before.

All in green went my love riding
on a great horse of gold
into the silver dawn.

four lean hounds crouched low and smiling
my heart fell dead before.

1916, 1923

[when god lets my body be]

when god lets my body be

From each brave eye shall sprout a tree
fruit that dangles therefrom

the purpled world will dance upon
Between my lips which did sing

a rose shall beget the spring
that maidens whom passion wastes

will lay between their little breasts
My strong fingers beneath the snow

Into strenuous birds shall go
my love walking in the grass

their wings will touch with her face
and all the while shall my heart be

With the bulge and nuzzle of the sea

1920, 1923

[in Just—]

in Just—
spring   when the world is mud-
luscious the little
lame balloonman

whistles   far   and wee

and eddieandbill come
running from marbles and
piracies and it's
spring

when the world is puddle-wonderful

the queer
old balloonman whistles
far   and   wee
and bettyandisbel come dancing

from hopscotch and jump-rope and

it's
spring
and
    the

        goat-footed

balloonMan   whistles
far
and
wee

1920, 1923

[O sweet spontaneous][1]

O sweet spontaneous
earth how often have
the
doting

        fingers of
prurient philosophers pinched
and
poked

[1]In later editions Cummings inserted a comma before "has" in line 10 (thus: ",has"), a period before "how" in line 13 (thus: ".how"), and parenthesis marks before "but" in line 19 and after "spring" in line 27 (thus: "(but . . . spring)").

thee
has the naughty thumb
of science prodded
thy

beauty how
often have religions taken
thee upon their scraggy
knees squeezing and

buffeting thee that thou mightest conceive
gods
but
true

to the incomparable
couch of death thy
rhythmic
lover
thou answerest

them only with

spring

1920, 1923

[Buffalo Bill's[1] defunct]

Buffalo Bill's
defunct
who used to
ride a watersmooth-silver
stallion
and break onetwothreefourfive pigeonsjustlikethat
Jesus

he was a handsome man
and what i want to know is
how do you like your blueeyed boy
Mister Death

1920, 1923

[1]William F. Cody (1846–1917), American frontiersman and later a star performer in "Buffalo Bill's Wild West Show," which toured America and Europe in the 1880s and 1890s.

[the Cambridge ladies who live in furnished souls]

the Cambridge ladies who live in furnished souls
are unbeautiful and have comfortable minds
(also, with the church's protestant blessings
daughters, unscented shapeless spirited)
they believe in Christ and Longfellow, both dead,
are invariably interested in so many things—
at the present writing one still finds
delighted fingers knitting for the is it Poles?
perhaps. While permanent faces coyly bandy
scandal of Mrs. N and Professor D
. . . . the Cambridge ladies do not care, above
Cambridge if sometimes in its box of
sky lavender and cornerless, the
moon rattles like a fragment of angry candy

1922, 1923

[Poem, or beauty hurts Mr. Vinal][1]

take it from me kiddo
believe me
my country, 'tis of

you,[2] land of the Cluett
Shirt Boston Garter and Spearmint
Girl With The Wrigley Eyes (of you
land of the Arrow Ide
and Earl &
Wilson
Collars) of you i
sing: land of Abraham Lincoln and Lydia E. Pinkham,
land above all of Just Add Hot Water and Serve—
from every B.V.D.

let freedom ring

amen. i do however protest, anent the un
-spontaneous and otherwise scented merde[3] which
greets one (Everywhere Why) as divine poesy per

[1]Harold Vinal (1891–1965), editor of *Voices*, a magazine of traditional verse. From 1938 to 1954 he served as Secretary of the Poetry Society of America.

[2]Here and below Cummings creates a collage by combining references to patriotic songs and commercial slogans and advertisements, including "America" ("My country, 'tis of thee"); Cluett, Peabody Inc., makers of Arrow shirts; Boston Garters (for men); Wrigley's Spearmint chewing gum; Earl and Wilson shirt collars; Lydia E. Pinkham patent medicine (for "female disorders"); B.V.D. men's underwear (named for its manufacturers, Bradley, Voorhies, and Day); Eastman Kodak cameras; Carter's Little Liver Pills and Nujol (laxatives); Odor-o-no (a personal deodorant); and Colgate toothpaste that "comes out like a ribbon lies flat on the brush."

[3]French: excrement.

that and this radically defunct periodical.   i would
suggest that certain ideas gestures
rhymes, like Gillette Razor Blades
having been used and reused
to the mystical moment of dullness emphatically are
Not To Be Resharpened.   (Case in point

if we are to believe these gently O sweetly
melancholy trillers amid the thrillers
these crepuscular[4] violinists among my and your
skyscrapers—Helen & Cleopatra[5] were Just Too Lovely,
The Snails On The Thorn enter Morn and God's
In His andsoforth[6]

do you get me?) according
to such supposedly indigenous
throstles[7] Art is O World O Life[8]
a formula: example, Turn Your Shirttails Into
Drawers and If It Isn't An Eastman It Isn't A
Kodak therefore my friends let
us now sing each and all fortissimo A-
mer
i

ca, I
love,
You.   And there're a
hun-dred-mil-lion-oth-ers, like
all of you successfully if
delicately gelded[9] (or spaded)[10]
gentlemen (and ladies)—pretty

littleliverpill-
hearted-Nujolneeding-There's-A-Reason
americans (who tensetendoned and with
upward vacant eyes, painfully
perpetually crouched, quivering, upon the
sternly allottedsandpile
—how silently
emit a tiny violetflavoured nuisance: Odor?

ono.
comes out like a ribbon lies flat on the brush

1922, 1926

[4]Shadowy.   [5]Helen of Troy and Cleopatra, Queen of Egypt.

[6]An adaptation of "The snail's on the thorn; / God's in his heaven— / All's right with the world!" from *Pippa Passes* (1841), by the English poet Robert Browning (1812–1889).

[7]Thrushes. Their scientific name is *turdus musicus.*

[8]An adaptation of "O world! O life! O time!—the opening lines of "A Lament" (1824), by the English poet Percy Bysshe Shelley (1792–1822).

[9]Castrated.   [10]Spayed; i.e., with ovaries removed.

[my sweet old etcetera]

my sweet old etcetera
aunt lucy during the recent

war could and what
is more did tell you just
what everybody was fighting

for,
my sister

isabel created hundreds
(and
hundreds)of socks not to
mention shirts fleaproof earwarmers

etcetera wristers etcetera, my
mother hoped that

i would die etcetera
bravely of course my father used
to become hoarse talking about how it was
a privilege and if only he
could meanwhile my

self etcetera lay quietly
in the deep mud et

cetera
(dreaming,
et
    cetera, of
Your smile
eyes knees and of your Etcetera)
1926

[anyone lived in a pretty how town]

anyone lived in a pretty how town
(with up so floating many bells down)
spring summer autumn winter
he sang his didn't he danced his did.

Women and men(both little and small)
cared for anyone not at all
they sowed their isn't they reaped their same
sun moon stars rain

children guessed(but only a few
and down they forgot as up they grew
autumn winter spring summer)
that noone loved him more by more

when by now and tree by leaf
she laughed his joy she cried his grief
bird by snow and stir by still
anyone's any was all to her

someones married their everyones
laughed their cryings and did their dance
(sleep wake hope and then)they
said their nevers they slept their dream

stars rain sun moon
(and only the snow can begin to explain
how children are apt to forget to remember
with up so floating many bells down)

one day anyone died i guess
(and noone stooped to kiss his face)
busy folk buried them side by side
little by little and was by was

all by all and deep by deep
and more by more they dream their sleep
noone and anyone earth by april
wish by spirit and if by yes.

Women and men(both dong and ding)
summer autumn winter spring
reaped their sowing and went their came
sun moon stars rain

1940

Hart Crane 1899–1932

Although the quantity of his work was small (he published only two volumes of poetry in his lifetime), Hart Crane has achieved a position in the first rank of American poets. His fame rests primarily on his extraordinary and controversial poems, yet his life was so turbulent, so much the model for popular, exaggerated notions of the poet, that it, too, has been partly responsible for his renown.

Crane, an avowed homosexual, was a neurotic, self-destructive alcoholic whose life was a chaotic jumble of emotional confusion and despair. Born in Ohio in 1899, he spent much of his early life with his grandparents in refuge from the fierce wrangling of his strong-willed mother and father. His father, a successful manufacturer of candy (he invented Life Savers), tried unsuccessfully to make his son into a businessman; his mother, a domineering woman of artistic pretensions, imposed her religious enthusiasms on her son's consciousness.

Crane began to write poetry as a schoolboy. He published his first poem when he was seventeen, and in the same year he dropped out of school to begin a life of wandering and frantic excess, interrupted by periods of intense creativity. In his early twenties, he finally managed to break with his family, an event that coincided with the writing of his first major poems. He then left Ohio for New York City, where he unknowingly moved into a room once occupied by Washington Roebling, the builder of the Brooklyn Bridge. There Crane began work on the loosely unified series of poems out of which he eventually created his masterpiece, The Bridge.

In 1926, his first volume of poetry, White Buildings, *was published. But the book received mixed reviews, and Crane's life turned sour once more. After a final, bitter argument with his mother, he fled to Europe. Seven months later he returned to New York, and there, late in 1929, he finished* The Bridge. *In 1930 he went to Mexico, planning to write an epic poem on Mexican history and hoping to create a stable emotional life, but in April 1932, while returning from Mexico to New York by sea, Crane walked to the stern of his ship, leaped into the sea, and drowned. He was thirty-two.*

The Bridge *was Crane's endeavor to write a national epic, a "mythical synthesis of America" such as Walt Whitman had attempted in* Leaves of Grass. *Written partly in refutation of T. S. Eliot's* The Waste Land, *which Crane felt was too pessimistic and ignored "spiritual events and possibilities,"* The Bridge *reflected his desire to find unity in an age of disharmony and disbelief. He wanted to unite, literally and figuratively, the old and the new, east and west, human and divine. That he failed is conceded by many. He achieved poetic intensity at the expense of clarity and reason; his poetry is flawed by vague meanings and jumbled images and symbols. Nevertheless, the force of his poetic imagination and his extraordinary power to portray the human quest for unity, love, and beauty have brought him recognition as one of the finest poets of twentieth-century America, despite his tormented, brief life and the ravaging emotions that led to his destruction.*

FURTHER READING: B. Weber, *Hart Crane, A Biographical and Critical Study,* 1948, 1970; *The Letters of Hart Crane, 1916–1932,* ed. B. Weber, 1952, 1965; *Critical Essays on Hart Crane,* ed. D. Clark, 1982; *Hart Crane, A Reference Guide,* ed. J. Schwartz, 1983; E. Brunner, *Splendid Failure, Hart Crane and the Making of The Bridge,* 1985; *Hart Crane,* ed. H. Bloom, 1986; P. Giles, *Hart Crane, The Contexts of "The Bridge,"* 1986; M. Bennett, *Unfractioned Idiom, Hart Crane and Modernism,* 1987; W. Berthoff, *Hart Crane, A Re-Introduction,* 1989; P. Mariani, *The Broken Tower, A Life of Hart Crane,* 1999; R. Lewis, *The Poetry of Hart Crane,* 2000; C. Fisher, *Hart Crane, A Life,* 2002.

TEXT: *The Complete Poems and Selected Letters and Prose of Hart Crane,* ed. B. Weber, 1966.

BLACK TAMBOURINE

The interests of a black man in a cellar
Mark tardy judgment on the world's closed door.
Gnats toss in the shadow of a bottle,
And a roach spans a crevice in the floor.

Aesop,[1] driven to pondering, found
Heaven with the tortoise and the hare;
Fox brush and sow ear top his grave
And mingling incantations on the air.

The black man, forlorn in the cellar,
Wanders in some mid-kingdom, dark, that lies,
Between his tambourine, stuck on the wall,
And, in Africa, a carcass quick with flies.

1926

CHAPLINESQUE[1]

We make our meek adjustments,
Contented with such random consolations
As the wind deposits
In slithered and too ample pockets.

For we can still love the world, who find
A famished kitten on the step, and know
Recesses for it from the fury of the street,
Or warm torn elbow coverts.

We will sidestep, and to the final smirk
Dally the doom of that inevitable thumb
That slowly chafes its puckered index toward us,
Facing the dull squint with what innocence
And what surprise!

And yet these fine collapses are not lies
More than the pirouettes of any pliant cane;
Our obsequies are, in a way, no enterprise.
We can evade you, and all else but the heart:
What blame to us if the heart live on.

The game enforces smirks; but we have seen
The moon in lonely alleys make
A grail of laughter of an empty ash can,
And through all sound of gaiety and quest
Have heard a kitten in the wilderness.

1921, 1926

AT MELVILLE'S[1] TOMB

Often beneath the wave, wide from this ledge
The dice of drowned men's bones he saw bequeath
An embassy. Their numbers as he watched,
Beat on the dusty shore and were obscured.

[1]Greek storyteller (sixth century B.C.). His best known fables are "The Tortoise and the Hare" and "The Fox and the Grapes."

[1]Inspired by the comedian Charlie Chaplin, whom Crane saw in the movie *The Kid,* in 1921.

[1]Herman Melville (1819–1891). He is buried at Woodlawn Cemetery in New York City.

And wrecks passed without sound of bells,
The calyx[2] of death's bounty giving back
A scattered chapter, livid hieroglyph,
The portent wound in corridors of shells.

Then in the circuit calm of one vast coil,
Its lashings charmed and malice reconciled,
Frosted eyes there were that lifted altars;
And silent answers crept across the stars.

Compass, quadrant and sextant contrive
No farther tides . . .[3] High in the azure steeps
Monody shall not wake the mariner.
This fabulous shadow only the sea keeps.

1926

VOYAGES

I

Above the fresh ruffles of the surf
Bright striped urchins flay each other with sand.
They have contrived a conquest for shell shucks,
And their fingers crumble fragments of baked weed
Gaily digging and scattering.

And in answer to their treble interjections
The sun beats lightning on the waves,
The waves fold thunder on the sand;
And could they hear me I would tell them:

O brilliant kids, frisk with your dog,
Fondle your shells and sticks, bleached
By time and the elements; but there is a line
You must not cross nor ever trust beyond it
Spry cordage of your bodies to caresses
To lichen-faithful from too wide a breast.
The bottom of the sea is cruel.

1921–1923 1923, 1926

II

—And yet this great wink of eternity,
Of rimless floods, unfettered leewardings,
Samite[1] sheeted and processioned where
Her undinal[2] vast belly moonward bends,
Laughing the wrapt inflections of our love;

[2]"This calyx refers in a double ironic sense both to cornucopia and vortex made by a sinking vessel."—Crane's note.

[3]Here, and throughout, the ellipses are Crane's and do not indicate omissions by the editor.

[1]Heavy silk, threaded with silver and gold, used in medieval ecclesiastical robes.

[2]From Undine, a water goddess—hence, "oceanic."

Take this Sea, whose diapason[3] knells
On scrolls of silver snowy sentences,
The sceptred terror of whose sessions rends
As her demeanors motion well or ill,
All but the pieties of lovers' hands.

And onward, as bells of San Salvador[4]
Salute the crocus lustres of the stars,
In these poinsettia meadows of her tides,—
Adagios of islands, O my Prodigal,
Complete the dark confessions her veins spell.

Mark how her turning shoulders wind the hours,
And hasten while her penniless rich palms
Pass superscription of bent foam and wave,—
Hasten, while they are true,—sleep, death, desire,
Close round one instant in one floating flower.

Bind us in time, O Seasons clear, and awe.
O minstrel galleons of Carib fire,
Bequeath us to no earthly shore until
Is answered in the vortex of our grave
The seal's wide spindrift[5] gaze toward paradise.
1924 1926

III

Infinite consanguinity[1] it bears—
This tendered theme of you that light
Retrieves from sea plains where the sky
Resigns a breast that every wave enthrones;
While ribboned water lanes I wind
Are laved and scattered with no stroke
Wide from your side, whereto this hour
The sea lifts, also, reliquary hands.

And so, admitted through black swollen gates
That must arrest all distance otherwise,—
Past whirling pillars and lithe pediments,
Light wrestling there incessantly with light,
Star kissing star through wave on wave unto
Your body rocking!
and where death, if shed,

[3]Musical notes or harmony.
[4]A reference to the legendary tolling bells of a sunken city off San Salvador.
[5]Sea foam.
[1]Blood relationship.

Presumes no carnage, but this single change,—
Upon the steep floor flung from dawn to dawn
The silken skilled transmemberment of song;

Permit me voyage, love, into your hands . . .
1924 1926

from *THE BRIDGE*

TO BROOKLYN BRIDGE

How many dawns, chill from his rippling rest
The seagull's wings shall dip and pivot him,
Shedding white rings of tumult, building high
Over the chained bay waters Liberty—

Then, with inviolate curve, forsake our eyes
As apparitional as sails that cross
Some page of figures to be filed away;
—Till elevators drop us from our day . . .

I think of cinemas, panoramic sleights
With multitudes bent toward some flashing scene
Never disclosed, but hastened to again,
Foretold to other eyes on the same screen;

And Thee,[1] across the harbor, silver-paced
As though the sun took step of thee, yet left
Some motion ever unspent in thy stride,—
Implicitly thy freedom staying thee!

Out of some subway scuttle, cell or loft
A bedlamite[2] speeds to thy parapets,
Tilting there momently, shrill shirt ballooning,
A jest falls from the speechless caravan.

Down Wall,[3] from girder into street noon leaks,
A rip-tooth of the sky's acetylene;
All afternoon the cloud-flown derricks turn . . .
Thy cables breathe the North Atlantic still.

And obscure as that heaven of the Jews,
Thy guerdon[4] . . . Accolade thou dost bestow
Of anonymity time cannot raise:
Vibrant reprieve and pardon thou dost show.

[1]I.e., Brooklyn Bridge. [2]Lunatic. [3]Wall Street in New York City. [4]Reward.

O harp and altar, of the fury fused,
(How could mere toil align thy choiring strings!)
Terrific threshold of the prophet's pledge,
Prayer of pariah, and the lover's cry,—

Again the traffic lights that skim thy swift
Unfractioned idiom, immaculate sigh of stars,
Beading thy path—condense eternity:
And we have seen night lifted in thine arms.

Under thy shadow by the piers I waited;
Only in darkness is thy shadow clear.
The City's fiery parcels all undone,
Already snow submerges an iron year . . .

O Sleepless as the river under thee,
Vaulting the sea, the prairies' dreaming sod,
Unto us lowliest sometime sweep, descend
And of the curveship lend a myth to God.

1926 1927, 1930

POWHATAN'S DAUGHTER

"—Pocahuntus, a well-featured but wanton yong girle . . . of the age of eleven or twelve years, get the boyes forth with her into the market place, and make them wheele, falling on their hands, turning their heels upwards, whom she would followe, and wheele so herself, naked as she was, all the fort over."[1]

THE HARBOR DAWN

400 years and more . . . or is it from the soundless shore of sleep that time

Insistently through sleep—a tide of voices—
They meet you listening midway in your dream,
The long, tired sounds, fog-insulated noises:
Gongs in white surplices, beshrouded wails,
Far strum of fog horns . . . signals dispersed in veils.

And then a truck will lumber past the wharves
As winch engines begin throbbing on some deck;
Or a drunken stevedore's howl and thud below
Comes echoing alley-upward through dim snow.

And if they take your sleep away sometimes
They give it back again. Soft sleeves of sound

[1]From William Strachey, *Historie of Travell into Virginia Britania,* written 1609–1612, first published 1849.

Attend the darkling harbor, the pillowed bay;
Somewhere out there in blankness steam

Spills into steam, and wanders, washed away
—Flurried by keen fifings, eddied
Among distant chiming buoys—adrift. The sky,
Cool feathery fold, suspends, distills
This wavering slumber. . . . Slowly—
Immemorially the window, the half-covered chair
Ask nothing but this sheath of pallid air.

recalls you to your love, there in a waking dream to merge your seed

And you beside me, blessèd now while sirens
Sing to us, stealthily weave us into day—
Serenely now, before day claims our eyes
Your cool arms murmurously about me lay.

While myriad snowy hands are clustering at the panes—

your hands within my hands are deeds;
my tongue upon your throat—singing
arms close; eyes wide, undoubtful
dark
drink the dawn—
a forest shudders in your hair!

—with whom?

The window goes blond slowly. Frostily clears.
From Cyclopean[1] towers across Manhattan waters
—Two—three bright window-eyes aglitter, disk
The sun, released—aloft with cold gulls hither.

Who is the woman with us in the dawn? . . . whose is the flesh our feet have moved upon

The fog leans one last moment on the sill.
Under the mistletoe of dreams, a star—
As though to join us at some distant hill—
Turns in the waking west and goes to sleep.
1926 1927, 1930

VAN WINKLE

Streets spread past store and factory—sped by sunlight and her smile . . .

Macadam, gun-grey as the tunny's[1] belt,
Leaps from Far Rockaway to Golden Gate:[2]
Listen! the miles a hurdy-gurdy grinds—
Down gold arpeggios mile on mile unwinds.

Times earlier, when you hurried off to school,
—It is the same hour though a later day—
You walked with Pizarro in a copybook,

[1]Gigantic—as though built by giants.
[1]A tuna. [2]I.e., from the Atlantic to the Pacific.

—And Cortes rode up, reining tautly in—
Firmly as coffee grips the taste,—and away!

Like Memory, she is time's truant, shall take you by the hand . . .

There was Priscilla's[3] cheek close in the wind.
And Captain Smith,[4] all beard and certainty,
And Rip Van Winkle bowing by the way,—
"Is this Sleepy Hollow,[5] friend—?" And he—

And Rip forgot the office hours,
and he forgot the pay;
Van Winkle sweeps a tenement
way down on Avenue A,—

The grind-organ says . . . Remember, remember
The cinder pile at the end of the backyard
Where we stoned the family of young
Garter snakes under . . . And the monoplanes
We launched—with paper wings and twisted
Rubber bands . . . Recall—recall
the rapid tongues
That flittered from under the ash heap day
After day whenever your stick discovered
Some sunning inch of unsuspecting fibre—
It flashed back at your thrust, as clean as fire.

And Rip was slowly made aware
that he, Van Winkle, was not here
nor there. He woke and swore he'd seen Broadway
a Catskill daisy chain in May—

So memory, that strikes a rhyme out of a box,
Or splits a random smell of flowers through glass—
Is it the whip stripped from the lilac tree
One day in spring my father took to me,
Or is it the Sabbatical, unconscious smile
My mother almost brought me once from church
And once only, as I recall—?

It flickered through the snow screen, blindly
It forsook her at the doorway, it was gone
Before I had left the window. It
Did not return with the kiss in the hall.

Macadam, gun-grey as the tunny's belt,
Leaps from Far Rockaway to Golden Gate. . . .

[3]Priscilla Alden of the Pilgrim Colony at Plymouth.
[4]John Smith, English explorer said to have been rescued by Pocahontas.
[5]The setting of "The Legend of Sleepy Hollow" (1819), by Washington Irving.

Keep hold of that nickel for car-change, Rip,—
Have you got your *"Times"*[6]—?
And hurry along, Van Winkle—it's getting late!

1927, 1930

THE RIVER

. . . and past the din and slogans of the year—

Stick your patent name on a signboard
brother—all over—going west—young man[1]
Tintex—Japalac[2]—Certain-teed[3] Overalls ads
and lands sakes! under the new playbill ripped
in the guaranteed corner—see Bert Williams[4] what?
Minstrels when you steal a chicken just
save me the wing for if it isn't
Erie it ain't for miles around a
Mazda[5]—and the telegraphic night coming on Thomas

a Ediford[6]—and whistling down the tracks
a headlight rushing with the sound—can you
imagine—while an EXpress makes time like
SCIENCE—COMMERCE AND THE HOLYGHOST
RADIO ROARS IN EVERY HOME WE HAVE THE NORTHPOLE
WALLSTREET AND VIRGINBIRTH WITHOUT STONES OR
WIRES OR EVEN RUNning brooks connecting ears
and no more sermons windows flashing roar
breathtaking—as you like it . . . eh?

So the 20th Century—so
whizzed the Limited[7]—roared by and left
three men, still hungry on the tracks, ploddingly
watching the tail lights wizen and converge, slipping
gimleted and neatly out of sight

* * *

The last bear, shot drinking in the Dakotas
Loped under wires[8] that span the mountain stream.
Keen instruments, strung to a vast precision
Bind town to town and dream to ticking dream.

[6] *The New York Times.*

[1] "Go west, young man," a saying often attributed (incorrectly) to Horace Greeley, nineteenth-century newspaper publisher.

[2] Brand names for widely sold cloth dye and household paint products.

[3] Brand name for home maintenance products.

[4] Black vaudeville comedian (1877–1922).

[5] A fusion of advertisement slogans for the Erie Railroad, for Eastman cameras ("If it isn't an Eastman, it isn't a Kodak"), and for Mazda light bulbs.

[6] A pun that combines the names of the inventor Thomas A. Edison (1847–1931), the automaker Henry Ford (1863–1947), and the Archbishop of Canterbury and saint, Thomas à Becket (1118?–1170).

[7] Twentieth-Century Limited: luxurious, high-speed, passenger train.

[8] Telegraph and telephone wires.

to those whose addresses are never near

But some men take their liquor slow—and count
—Though they'll confess no rosary nor clue—
The river's minute by the far brook's year.
Under a world of whistles, wires and steam
Caboose-like they go ruminating through
Ohio, Indiana—blind baggage—
To Cheyenne tagging . . . Maybe Kalamazoo.

Time's rendings, time's blendings they construe
As final reckonings of fire and snow;
Strange bird-wit, like the elemental gist
Of unwalled winds they offer, singing low
My Old Kentucky Home and *Casey Jones,*
Some Sunny Day. I heard a road-gang chanting so.
And afterwards, who had a colt's eyes—one said,
"Jesus! Oh I remember watermelon days!" And sped
High in a cloud of merriment, recalled
"—And when my Aunt Sally Simpson smiled," he drawled—
"It was almost Louisiana, long ago."
"There's no place like Booneville though, Buddy,"
One said, excising a last burr from his vest,
"—For early trouting." Then peering in the can,
"—But I kept on the tracks." Possessed, resigned.
He trod the fire down pensively and grinned,
Spreading dry shingles of a beard. . . .

Behind
My father's cannery works I used to see
Rail-squatters ranged in nomad raillery,
The ancient men—wifeless or runaway
Hobo-trekkers that forever search
An empire wilderness of freight and rails.
Each seemed a child, like me, on a loose perch,
Holding to childhood like some termless play.
John, Jake or Charley, hopping the slow freight
—Memphis to Tallahassee—riding the rods,
Blind fists of nothing, humpty-dumpty clods.

but who have touched her, knowing her without name

Yet they touch something like a key perhaps.
From pole to pole across the hills, the states
—They know a body under the wide rain;
Youngsters with eyes like fjords, old reprobates
With racetrack jargon,—dotting immensity
They lurk across her, knowing her yonder breast
Snow-silvered, sumac-stained or smoky blue—
Is past the valley-sleepers, south or west.
—As I have trod the rumorous midnights, too,

And past the circuit of the lamp's thin flame
(O Nights that brought me to her body bare!)

Have dreamed beyond the print that bound her name.
Trains sounding the long blizzards out—I heard
Wail into distances I knew were hers.
Papooses crying on the wind's long mane
Screamed redskin dynasties that fled the brain,
—Dead echoes! But I knew her body there,
Time like a serpent down her shoulder, dark,
And space, an eaglet's wing, laid on her hair.

Under the Ozarks, domed by Iron Mountain,[9]
The old gods of the rain lie wrapped in pools
Where eyeless fish[10] curvet[11] a sunken fountain
nor the myths of her fathers. . .
And re-descend with corn from querulous crows.
Such pilferings make up their timeless eatage,
Propitiate them for their timber torn
By iron, iron—always the iron dealt cleavage!
They doze, now, below axe and powder horn.

And Pullman breakfasters glide glistening steel.
From tunnel into field—iron strides the dew—
Straddles the hill, a dance of wheel on wheel.
You have a half-hour's wait at Siskiyou,[12]
Or stay the night and take the next train through.
Southward, near Cairo[13] passing, you can see

The Ohio merging,—borne down Tennessee;
And if it's summer and the sun's in dusk
Maybe the breeze will lift the River's musk
—As though the waters breathed that you might know
Memphis Johnny, Steamboat Bill, Missouri Joe.
Oh, lean from the window, if the train slows down,
As though you touched hands with some ancient clown,
—A little while gaze absently below
And hum *Deep River* with them while they go.

Yes, turn again and sniff once more—look see,
O Sheriff, Brakeman and Authority—
Hitch up your pants and crunch another quid,[14]
For you, too, feed the River timelessly.
And few evade full measure of their fate;
Always they smile out eerily what they seem.
I could believe he joked at heaven's gate—
Dan Midland[15]—jolted from the cold brake-beam.

[9]In southeast Missouri.
[10]Blind fish that dwell in underground waters.
[11]Curve or leap about.
[12]In northern California.
[13]In southern Illinois.
[14]Wad of chewing tobacco.
[15]A legendary hobo killed while "riding the rods."

Down, down—born pioneers in time's despite,
Grimed tributaries to an ancient flow—
They win no frontier by their wayward plight,
But drift in stillness, as from Jordan's brow.[16]

You will not hear it as the sea; even stone
Is not more hushed by gravity . . . But slow,
As loth to take more tribute—sliding prone
Like one whose eyes were buried long ago

The River, spreading, flows—and spends your dream.
What are you, lost within this tideless spell?
You are your father's father, and the stream—
A liquid theme that floating niggers swell.

Damp tonnage and alluvial march of days—
Nights turbid, vascular with silted shale
And roots surrendered down of moraine clays:
The Mississippi drinks the farthest dale.

O quarrying passion, undertowed sunlight!
The basalt surface drags a jungle grace
Ochreous and lynx-barred in lengthening might;
Patience! and you shall reach the biding place!

Over De Soto's bones[17] the freighted floors
Throb past the City storied of three thrones.[18]
Down two more turns the Mississippi pours
(Anon tall ironsides up from salt lagoons)

And flows within itself, heaps itself free.
All fades but one thin skyline 'round . . . Ahead
No embrace opens but the stinging sea;
The River lifts itself from its long bed,

Poised wholly on its dream, a mustard glow
Tortured with history, its one will—flow!
—The Passion spreads in wide tongues, choked and
  slow,
Meeting the Gulf, hosannas silently below.
1926 1928, 1930

[16]The bank of the Jordan River in Palestine.
[17]The Spanish explorer Hernando de Soto (1500–1542) was buried in the Mississippi River near present-day New Orleans.
[18]New Orleans was governed alternately by the monarchies of France, Spain, and England.

THE TUNNEL

To Find the
Western path
Right thro' the
Gates of Wrath.
BLAKE[1]

Performances, assortments, résumés—
Up Times Square to Columbus Circle[2] lights
Channel the congresses, nightly sessions,
Refractions of the thousand theatres, faces—
Mysterious kitchens. . . . You shall search them all.
Someday by heart you'll learn each famous sight
And watch the curtain lift in hell's despite;
You'll find the garden in the third act dead,
Finger your knees—and wish yourself in bed
With tabloid crime-sheets perched in easy sight.

Then let you reach your hat
and go.
As usual, let you—also
walking down—exclaim
to twelve upward leaving
a subscription praise
for what time slays.

Or can't you quite make up your mind to ride;
A walk is better underneath the L[3] a brisk
Ten blocks or so before? But you find yourself
Preparing penguin flexions of the arms,—
As usual you will meet the scuttle yawn:
The subway yawns the quickest promise home.

Be minimum, then, to swim the hiving swarms
Out of the Square, the Circle burning bright—
Avoid the glass doors gyring[4] at your right,

[1]From "Morning" (lines 1–2), by William Blake (1757–1827), English poet.
[2]Along Broadway, in New York City.
[3]The elevated railway.
[4]Spinning.

Where boxed alone a second, eyes take fright
—Quite unprepared rush naked back to light:
And down beside the turnstile press the coin
Into the slot. The gongs already rattle.

And so
of cities you bespeak
subways, rivered under streets
and rivers. . . . In the car
the overtone of motion
underground, the monotone
of motion is the sound
of other faces, also underground—

"Let's have a pencil Jimmy—living now
at Floral Park
Flatbush[5]—on the fourth of July—
like a pigeon's muddy dream—potatoes
to dig in the field—travlin the town—too—
night after night—the Culver line[6]—the
girls all shaping up—it used to be—"

Our tongues recant like beaten weather vanes.
This answer lives like verdigris,[7] like hair
Beyond extinction, surcease of the bone;
And repetition freezes—"What

"what do you want? getting weak on the links?
fandaddle daddy don't ask for change—IS THIS
FOURTEENTH? it's half past six she said—if
you don't like my gate why did you
swing on it, why *didja*
swing on it
anyhow—"

And somehow anyhow swing—

[5]Section of New York City in the borough of Brooklyn.
[6]A former branch of the Brooklyn Rapid Transit system; originally elevated, later converted to a subway.
[7]A greenish-blue substance.

The phonographs of hades in the brain
Are tunnels that re-wind themselves, and love
A burnt match skating in a urinal—
Somewhere above Fourteenth TAKE THE EXPRESS
To brush some new presentiment of pain—

"But I want service in this office service
I said—after
the show she cried a little afterwards but—"

Whose head is swinging from the swollen strap?
Whose body smokes along the bitten rails,
Bursts from a smoldering bundle far behind
In back forks of the chasms of the brain,—
Puffs from a river stump far out behind
In interborough fissures of the mind . . . ?

And why do I often meet your visage[8] here,
Your eyes like agate lanterns—on and on
Below the toothpaste and the dandruff ads?
—And did their riding eyes right through your side,
And did their eyes like unwashed platters ride?
And Death, aloft,—gigantically down
Probing through you—toward me, O evermore!
And when they dragged your retching flesh,
Your trembling hands that night through Baltimore—
That last night on the ballot rounds,[9] did you
Shaking, did you deny the ticket, Poe?

For Gravesend Manor change at Chambers Street.[10]
The platform hurries along to a dead stop.

The intent escalator lifts a serenade
Stilly
Of shoes, umbrellas, each eye attending its shoe, then
Bolting outright somewhere above where streets
Burst suddenly in rain. . . . The gongs recur:
Elbows and levers, guard and hissing door.

[8]The poet addresses Edgar Allan Poe.
[9]A reference to the death of Poe in Baltimore, on Election Day, October 7, 1849.
[10]Near the southern tip of Manhattan Island.

Thunder is galvothermic[11] here below. . . . The car
Wheels off. The train rounds, bending to a scream,
Taking the final level for the dive
Under the river—
And somewhat emptier than before,
Demented, for a hitching second, humps; then
Lets go. . . . Toward corners of the floor
Newspapers wing, revolve and wing.
Blank windows gargle signals through the roar.

And does the Dæmon take you home, also,
Wop washerwoman, with the bandaged hair?
After the corridors are swept, the cuspidors—
The gaunt sky-barracks cleanly now, and bare,
O Genoese,[12] do you bring mother eyes and hands
Back home to children and to golden hair?

Dæmon, demurring and eventful yawn!
Whose hideous laughter is a bellows mirth
—Or the muffled slaughter of a day in birth—
O cruelly to inoculate the brinking dawn
With antennæ toward worlds that glow and sink;—
To spoon us out more liquid than the dim
Locution of the eldest star, and pack
The conscience navelled in the plunging wind,
Umbilical to call—and straightway die!

O caught like pennies beneath soot and steam,
Kiss of our agony thou gatherest;
Condensed, thou takest all—shrill ganglia
Impassioned with some song we fail to keep.
And yet, like Lazarus,[13] to feel the slope,
The sod and billow breaking,—lifting ground,

—A sound of waters bending astride the sky
Unceasing with some Word that will not die . . . !

* * *

A tugboat, wheezing wreaths of steam,
Lunged past, with one galvanic blare stove up the River.

[11]Galvanothermic; i.e., produces heat by electricity.
[12]Christopher Columbus.
[13]Jesus raised Lazarus from the dead (John 11:43–44).

I counted the echoes assembling, one after one,
Searching, thumbing and midnight on the piers.
Lights, coasting, left the oily tympanum of waters;
The blackness somewhere gouged glass on a sky.
And this thy harbor, O my City, I have driven under,
Tossed from the coil of ticking towers. . . . Tomorrow,
And to be. . . . Here by the River that is East—
Here at the waters' edge the hands drop memory;
Shadowless in that abyss they unaccounting lie.
How far away the star has pooled the sea—
Or shall the hands be drawn away, to die?

Kiss of our agony Thou gatherest,
O Hand of Fire
gatherest—

1926 1927, 1930

ATLANTIS

Music is then the knowledge of that which relates to love in harmony and system.

PLATO[1]

Through the bound cable strands, the arching path
Upward, veering with light, the flight of strings—
Taut miles of shuttling moonlight syncopate
The whispered rush, telepathy of wires.
Up the index of night, granite and steel—
Transparent meshes—fleckless and gleaming staves—
Sibylline voices[2] flicker, waveringly stream
As though a god were issue of the strings. . . .

And through that cordage, threading with its call
One are synoptic of all tides below—
Their labyrinthine mouths of history
Pouring reply as though all ships at sea
Complighted in one vibrant breath made cry,—
"Make thy love sure—to weave whose song we ply!"
—From black embankments, moveless soundings hailed,
So seven oceans answer from their dream.

And on, obliquely up bright carrier bars
New octaves trestle the twin monoliths
Beyond whose frosted capes the moon bequeaths
Two worlds of sleep (O arching strands of song!)—
Onward and up the crystal-flooded aisle
White tempest nets file upward, upward ring

[1]From the *Symposium*, III, 403.
[2]Voices of the Sibyls, female oracles and prophets of the ancient world.

With silver terraces the humming spars,
The loft of vision, palladium helm of stars.

Sheerly the eyes, like seagulls stung with rime[3]—
Slit and propelled by glistening fins of light—
Pick biting way up towering looms that press
Sidelong with flight of blade on tendon blade
—Tomorrows into yesteryear—and link
What cipher-script of time no traveller reads
But who, through smoking pyres of love and death,
Searches the timeless laugh of mythic spears.

Like hails, farewells—up planet-sequined heights
Some trillion whispering hammers glimmer Tyre:[4]
Serenely, sharply up the long anvil cry
Of inchling ons silence rivets Troy.[5]
And you, aloft there—Jason![6] hesting[7] shout!
Still wrapping harness to the swarming air!
Silvery the rushing wake, surpassing call,
Beams yelling Æolus![8] splintered in the straights!

From gulfs unfolding, terrible of drums,
Tall Vision-of-the-Voyage, tensely spare—
Bridge, lifting night to cycloramic crest
Of deepest day—O Choir, translating time
Into what multitudinous Verb the suns
And synergy of waters ever fuse, recast
In myriad syllables,—Psalm of Cathay![9]
O Love, thy white, pervasive Paradigm . . . !

We left the haven hanging in the night—
Sheened harbor lanterns backward fled the keel.
Pacific here at time's end, bearing corn,—
Eyes stammer through the pangs of dust and steel.
And still the circular, indubitable frieze
Of heaven's meditations, yoking wave
To kneeling wave, one song devoutly binds—
The vernal strophe chimes from deathless strings!

O Thou steeled Cognizance whose leap commits
The agile precincts of the lark's return;
Within whose lariat sweep encinctured sing
In single chrysalis the many twain,
Of stars Thou art the stitch and stallion glow
And like an organ, Thou, with sound of doom—

[3]White frost. [4]Ancient Phoenician city. [5]Scene of the Trojan War described by Homer.
[6]Greek leader in the quest for the Golden Fleece. [7]Commanding.
[8]Keeper of the winds in classical myth. [9]Ancient name for China.

Sight, sound and flesh Thou leadest from time's realm
As love strikes clear direction for the helm.

Swift peal of secular light, intrinsic Myth
Whose fell unshadow is death's utter wound,—
O River-throated—iridescently upborne
Through the bright drench and fabric of our veins;
With white escarpments swinging into light,
Sustained in tears the cities are endowed
And justified conclamant with ripe fields
Revolving through their harvests in sweet torment.

Forever Deity's glittering Pledge, O Thou
Whose canticle fresh chemistry assigns
To wrapt inception and beatitude,—
Always through blinding cables, to our joy,
Of thy white seizure springs the prophecy:
Always through spiring cordage, pyramids
Of silver sequel, Deity's young name
Kinetic of white choiring wings . . . ascends.

Migrations that must needs void memory,
Inventions that cobblestone the heart,—
Unspeakable Thou Bridge to Thee, O Love.
Thy pardon for this history, whitest Flower,
O Answerer of all,—Anemone,—
Now while thy petals spend the suns about us, hold—
(O Thou whose radiance doth inherit me)
Atlantis,—hold thy floating singer late!

So to thine Everpresence, beyond time,
Like spears ensanguined[10] of one tolling star
That bleeds infinity—the orphic[11] strings,
Sidereal phalanxes, leap and converge:
—One Song, one Bridge of Fire! Is it Cathay,
Now pity steeps the grass and rainbows ring
The serpent with the eagle in the leaves . . . ?
Whispers antiphonal[12] in azure swing.

1926 1930

[10]Made bloody.

[11]Mystic, oracular. In Greek myth the musician Orpheus could charm animals and even the gods.

[12]Like a psalm or an anthem sung in response during church service.

Wallace Stevens 1879–1955

Wallace Stevens—are we for him?
Brother, he's our father!

Theodore Roethke was speaking for the next generation when he thus paid tribute to the man who, in his final years, became one of the most noted of American poets. A reticent man who placed unusual value upon his privacy, Stevens remained during his lifetime something of a mystery. He successfully pursued two seemingly incompatible careers: business and art. His business, he said, was "insurance," and unlike his most distinguished contemporaries, Pound, Eliot, and Williams, he was rarely comfortable in the role of professional poet. He lived a quiet, secluded life, disliked giving public readings, and in his last years refused a Harvard lectureship on the grounds that acceptance would force his retirement from "the office." Yet for over forty years he was deeply dedicated to poetry, and many younger poets agreed with Roethke's assertion that they had been influenced by a master.

Stevens spent his boyhood in his birthplace, Reading, Pennsylvania, where his father was a prosperous attorney. Stevens's earliest ambition was to be a writer, and after three years at Harvard, where he published poems in the Harvard Advocate, *he went to New York in 1900 for a try at journalism. But the following year, on his father's advice, he entered New York Law School. Admitted to the bar in 1904, he worked for several law firms before marrying and moving to Connecticut, where he eventually rose to the position of vice-president of the Hartford Accident and Indemnity Company.*

During his years in New York, with the modernist movement gaining momentum, Stevens became acquainted with a number of young writers, among them the poets William Carlos Williams and Marianne Moore. He also began submitting his own poems to the little magazines and, for a time, tried writing for the experimental theater. It was not until 1923, however, that Stevens, at the age of forty-four, was finally persuaded to publish a book of poems, Harmonium. *The book's poor reception (fewer than one hundred copies were sold) and its author's growing business responsibilities almost led him to abandon poetry. For over a decade he published little, but with the reprinting of* Harmonium *(1931) and the resulting increase in critical attention, he began his years of steady publication.*

In 1935 Stevens published Ideas of Order. *Then followed* The Man with the Blue Guitar *(1937),* Parts of a World *(1942),* Transport to Summer *(1947), and* The Auroras of Autumn *(1950). These, along with a collection of his occasional lectures on poetry,* The Necessary Angel *(1951), established him as a major American poet. For the publication of his* Collected Poems *(1954) he received his second National Book Award and a Pulitzer Prize. After his death, his previously uncollected work appeared in* Opus Posthumous *(1957), and his* Letters *were published in 1966.*

From the beginning it was evident that Harmonium *was part of a revolution in American poetry. Although some of its best poems, including "Sunday Morning," are relatively traditional in form, the book baffled even the most sophisticated. Stevens had rebelled against the "stale intelligence" of the past. Setting out "to make a new intelligence prevail," he invoked the comic, the strange, the bizarre. He adopted a variety of experimental styles, creating poetic surfaces of Frenchified elegance, exotic imagery, odd sounds, curious analogies, and inscrutable titles.*

For many readers it seemed that Stevens had carried originality to the point of mere eccentricity, and he was called a "dandy," a "virtuoso of the inane," a writer of "near nonsense." But beneath his gaudiest surfaces, Stevens's abiding concerns were clearly present. He confronted the contemporary abandonment of traditional values and sought to come to terms with the confusions of his time. The problem of the relation between the ideal and the real became a constant theme in his later poetry, and he elaborated a series of oppositions between inner and outer worlds—between subject and object, perceiver and perceived, fiction and fact, or as he most often phrased it, between "imagination and reality." These contraries meet ultimately in his concept of a "supreme fiction," a modern mythology that might serve as a replacement for the mythologies of the past, a new vision with "which men could propose to themselves a fulfilment." Although he constantly dealt with the nature of poetry, in his later work Stevens became increasingly meditative and philosophical, an intellectual elitist, at times difficult and obscure, who wrote, as he admitted, "for a gallery of one's own."

FURTHER READINGS: H. Stevens, *Souvenirs and Prophecies, The Young Wallace Stevens,* 1977; P. Brazeau, *Parts of a World, Wallace Stevens Remembered,* 1983; H. Vendler, *Wallace Stevens, Words Chosen out of Desire,* 1984; M. Bates, *Wallace Stevens, A Mythology of Self,* 1985; J. Richardson, *Wallace Stevens, The Early Years,* 1986; J. Carroll, *Wallace Stevens' Supreme Fiction, A New Romanticism,* 1987; J. Leonard and C. Wharton, *The Fluent Mundo, Wallace Stevens and the Structure of Reality,* 1988; J. Richardson, *Wallace Stevens, The Later Years,* 1988; E. Cook, *Poetry, Word-Play, and Word-War in Wallace Stevens,* 1988; B. Fisher, *Wallace Stevens, The Intensest Rendezvous,* 1990; M. Halliday, *Stevens and the Interpersonal,* 1991; J. Longenbach, *Wallace Stevens, The Plain Sense of Things,* 1991; A. Filreis, *Wallace Stevens and the Actual World,* 1991; G. Lensing, *Wallace Stevens, A Poet's Growth,* 1991; T. Grey, *The Wallace Stevens Case,* 1991; B. Leggett, *Early Stevens, The Nietzschean Intertext,* 1992; D. Schwarz, *Narrative and Representation in the Poetry of Wallace Stevens,* 1993; G. MacLeod, *Wallace Stevens and Modern Art,* 1993; J. McCann, *Wallace Stevens Revisited,* 1995; A. Whiting, *The Never-Resting Mind,* 1996; G. Lensing, *Wallace Stevens and the Seasons,* 2001; B. Eeckhout, *Wallace Stevens and the Limits of Reading and Writing,* 2002; *Wallace Stevens,* ed. H. Bloom, 2003; B. Leggett, *Late Stevens: The Final Fiction,* 2005; M. Woodland, *Wallace Stevens and the Apocalyptic Mode,* 2005.

TEXT: *The Collected Poems of Wallace Stevens,* 1954.

PETER QUINCE AT THE CLAVIER[1]

I

Just as my fingers on these keys
Make music, so the selfsame sounds
On my spirit make a music, too.

[1]In Shakespeare's *A Midsummer Night's Dream,* Peter Quince (a carpenter) attempts, with little success, to direct a group in putting on a play. Clavier: the keyboard of a musical instrument, such as a harmonium (reed organ) or harpsichord.

Music is feeling, then, not sound;
And thus it is that what I feel,
Here in this room, desiring you,

Thinking of your blue-shadowed silk,
Is music. It is like the strain
Waked in the elders by Susanna.[2]

Of a green evening, clear and warm,
She bathed in her still garden, while
The red-eyed elders watching, felt

The basses of their beings throb
In witching chords, and their thin blood
Pulse pizzicati[3] of Hosanna.[4]

II

In the green water, clear and warm,
Susanna lay.
She searched
The touch of springs,
And found
Concealed imaginings.
She sighed,
For so much melody.

Upon the bank, she stood
In the cool
Of spent emotions.
She felt, among the leaves,
The dew
Of old devotions.

She walked upon the grass,
Still quavering.
The winds were like her maids,
On timid feet,
Fetching her woven scarves,
Yet wavering.

[2]A reference to the story of Daniel and Susanna in the Apocrypha of the Bible. Two elders were obsessed with lust for Susanna. When rejected by her they falsely charged her with fornication. When they were questioned by Daniel their lies were exposed, and they were put to death.

[3]Musical notes made when the strings of an instrument such as a harpsichord are plucked.

[4]A cry of adoration or praise.

A breath upon her hand
Muted the night.
She turned—
A cymbal crashed,
And roaring horns.

III

Soon, with a noise like tambourines,
Came her attendant Byzantines.[5]

They wondered why Susanna cried
Against the elders by her side;

And as they whispered, the refrain
Was like a willow swept by rain.

Anon, their lamps' uplifted flame
Revealed Susanna and her shame.

And then, the simpering Byzantines
Fled, with a noise like tambourines.

IV

Beauty is momentary in the mind—
The fitful tracing of a portal;
But in the flesh it is immortal.
The body dies; the body's beauty lives.
So evenings die, in their green going,
A wave, interminably flowing.
So gardens die, their meek breath scenting
The cowl of winter, done repenting.
So maidens die, to the auroral
Celebration of a maiden's choral.
Susanna's music touched the bawdy strings
Of those white elders; but, escaping,
Left only Death's ironic scraping.
Now, in its immortality, it plays
On the clear viol of her memory,
And makes a constant sacrament of praise.

1915, 1923

[5]Natives of the ancient city of Byzantium (present-day Istanbul, Turkey).

DISILLUSIONMENT OF TEN O'CLOCK

The houses are haunted
By white night-gowns.
None are green,
Or purple with green rings,
Or green with yellow rings,
Or yellow with blue rings.
None of them are strange,
With socks of lace
And beaded ceintures.[1]
People are not going
To dream of baboons and periwinkles.[2]
Only, here and there, an old sailor,
Drunk and asleep in his boots,
Catches tigers
In red weather.

1915, 1923

SUNDAY MORNING

I

Complacencies of the peignoir,[1] and late
Coffee and oranges in a sunny chair,
And the green freedom of a cockatoo
Upon a rug mingle to dissipate
The holy hush of ancient sacrifice.
She dreams a little, and she feels the dark
Encroachment of that old catastrophe,
As a calm darkens among water-lights.
The pungent oranges and bright, green wings
Seem things in some procession of the dead,
Winding across wide water, without sound.
The day is like wide water, without sound,
Stilled for the passing of her dreaming feet
Over the seas, to silent Palestine,
Dominion of the blood and sepulchre.

[1]Belts, sashes.
[2]A plant with blue and white flowers.
[1]A woman's negligee, a dressing gown.

II

Why should she give her bounty to the dead?
What is divinity if it can come
Only in silent shadows and in dreams?
Shall she not find in comforts of the sun,
In pungent fruit and bright, green wings, or else
In any balm or beauty of the earth,
Things to be cherished like the thought of heaven?
Divinity must live within herself:
Passions of rain, or moods in falling snow;
Grievings in loneliness, or unsubdued
Elations when the forest blooms; gusty
Emotions on wet roads on autumn nights;
All pleasures and all pains, remembering
The bough of summer and the winter branch.
These are the measures destined for her soul.

III

Jove[2] in the clouds had his inhuman birth.
No mother suckled him, no sweet land gave
Large-mannered motions to his mythy mind.
He moved among us, as a muttering king,
Magnificent, would move among his hinds,[3]
Until our blood, commingling, virginal,
With heaven, brought such requital to desire
The very hinds discerned it, in a star.
Shall our blood fail? Or shall it come to be
The blood of paradise? And shall the earth
Seem all of paradise that we shall know?
The sky will be much friendlier then than now,
A part of labor and a part of pain,
And next in glory to enduring love,
Not this dividing and indifferent blue.

IV

She says, "I am content when wakened birds,
Before they fly, test the reality
Of misty fields, by their sweet questionings;
But when the birds are gone, and their warm fields
Return no more, where, then, is paradise?"

[2]Jupiter, god of the sky and chief Roman deity.
[3]Servants, farm hands.

There is not any haunt of prophecy,
Nor any old chimera[4] of the grave,
Neither the golden underground, nor isle
Melodious, where spirits gat them home,
Nor visionary south, nor cloudy palm
Remote on heaven's hill, that has endured
As April's green endures; or will endure
Like her remembrance of awakened birds,
Or her desire for June and evening, tipped
By the consummation of the swallow's wings.

V

She says, "But in contentment I still feel
The need of some imperishable bliss."
Death is the mother of beauty; hence from her,
Alone, shall come fulfilment to our dreams
And our desires. Although she strews the leaves
Of sure obliteration on our paths,
The path sick sorrow took, the many paths
Where triumph rang its brassy phrase, or love
Whispered a little out of tenderness,
She makes the willow shiver in the sun
For maidens who were wont to sit and gaze
Upon the grass, relinquished to their feet.
She causes boys to pile new plums and pears
On disregarded plate. The maidens taste
And stray impassioned in the littering leaves.

VI

Is there no change of death in paradise?
Does ripe fruit never fall? Or do the boughs
Hang always heavy in that perfect sky,
Unchanging, yet so like our perishing earth,
With rivers like our own that seek for seas
They never find, the same receding shores
That never touch with inarticulate pang?
Why set the pear upon those river-banks
Or spice the shores with odors of the plum?
Alas, that they should wear our colors there,
The silken weavings of our afternoons,
And pick the strings of our insipid lutes!
Death is the mother of beauty, mystical,
Within whose burning bosom we devise
Our earthly mothers waiting, sleeplessly.

[4]Illusion, unattainable ideal.

VII

Supple and turbulent, a ring of men
Shall chant in orgy on a summer morn
Their boisterous devotion to the sun,
Not as a god, but as a god might be,
Naked among them, like a savage source.
Their chant shall be a chant of paradise,
Out of their blood, returning to the sky;
And in their chant shall enter, voice by voice,
The windy lake wherein their lord delights,
The trees, like serafin,[5] and echoing hills,
That choir among themselves long afterward.
They shall know well the heavenly fellowship
Of men that perish and of summer morn.
And whence they came and whither they shall go
The dew upon their feet shall manifest.

VIII

She hears, upon that water without sound,
A voice that cries, "The tomb in Palestine
Is not the porch of spirits lingering.
It is the grave of Jesus, where he lay."
We live in an old chaos of the sun,
Or old dependency of day and night,
Or island solitude, unsponsored, free,
Of that wide water, inescapable.
Deer walk upon our mountains, and the quail
Whistle about us their spontaneous cries;
Sweet berries ripen in the wilderness;
And, in the isolation of the sky,
At evening, casual flocks of pigeons make
Ambiguous undulations as they sink,
Downward to darkness, on extended wings.

1915, 1923

BANTAMS IN PINE-WOODS

Chieftain Iffucan of Azcan in caftan
Of tan with henna hackles, halt!

Damned universal cock, as if the sun
Was blackamoor to bear your blazing tail.

[5]Seraphim, heavenly beings.

Fat! Fat! Fat! Fat! I am the personal.
Your world is you. I am my world.

You ten-foot poet among inchlings. Fat!
Begone! An inchling bristles in these pines,

Bristles, and points their Appalachian tangs,
And fears not portly Azcan nor his hoos.

1922

ANECDOTE OF THE JAR

I placed a jar in Tennessee,
And round it was, upon a hill.
It made the slovenly wilderness
Surround that hill.

The wilderness rose up to it,
And sprawled around, no longer wild.
The jar was round upon the ground
And tall and of a port in air.

It took dominion everywhere.
The jar was gray and bare.
It did not give of bird or bush,
Like nothing else in Tennessee.

1919, 1923

TO THE ONE OF FICTIVE MUSIC

Sister and mother and diviner love,
And of the sisterhood of the living dead
Most near, most clear, and of the clearest bloom,
And of the fragrant mothers the most dear
And queen, and of diviner love the day
And flame and summer and sweet fire, no thread
Of cloudy silver sprinkles in your gown
Its venom of renown, and on your head
No crown is simpler than the simple hair.

Now, of the music summoned by the birth
That separates us from the wind and sea,
Yet leaves us in them, until earth becomes,
By being so much of the things we are,

Gross effigy and simulacrum, none
Gives motion to perfection more serene
Than yours, out of our imperfections wrought,
Most rare, or ever of more kindred air
In the laborious weaving that you wear.

For so retentive of themselves are men
That music is intensest which proclaims
The near, the clear, and vaunts the clearest bloom,
And of all vigils musing the obscure,
That apprehends the most which sees and names,
As in your name, an image that is sure,
Among the arrant spices of the sun,
O bough and bush and scented vine, in whom
We give ourselves our likest issuance.

Yet not too like, yet not so like to be
Too near, too clear, saving a little to endow
Our feigning with the strange unlike, whence springs
The difference that heavenly pity brings.
For this, musician, in your girdle fixed
Bear other perfumes. On your pale head wear
A band entwining, set with fatal stones.
Unreal, give back to us what once you gave:
The imagination that we spurned and crave.

1922

THE EMPEROR OF ICE-CREAM

Call the roller of big cigars,
The muscular one, and bid him whip
In kitchen cups concupiscent curds.
Let the wenches dawdle in such dress
As they are used to wear, and let the boys
Bring flowers in last month's newspapers.
Let be be finale of seem.
The only emperor is the emperor of ice-cream.

Take from the dresser of deal,[1]
Lacking the three glass knobs, that sheet
On which she embroidered fantails[2] once

[1]Made of cheap pine or fir planks.
[2]Fan-shaped designs, like the tails of birds.

And spread it so as to cover her face.
If her horny feet protrude, they come
To show how cold she is, and dumb.
Let the lamp affix its beam.
The only emperor is the emperor of ice-cream.

1922, 1923

OF MODERN POETRY

The poem of the mind in the act of finding
What will suffice. It has not always had
To find: the scene was set; it repeated what
Was in the script.
Then the theatre was changed
To something else. Its past was a souvenir.
It has to be living, to learn the speech of the place.
It has to face the men of the time and to meet
The women of the time. It has to think about war
And it has to find what will suffice. It has
To construct a new stage. It has to be on that stage
And, like an insatiable actor, slowly and
With meditation, speak words that in the ear,
In the delicatest ear of the mind, repeat,
Exactly, that which it wants to hear, at the sound
Of which, an invisible audience listens,
Not to the play, but to itself, expressed
In an emotion as of two people, as of two
Emotions becoming one. The actor is
A metaphysician in the dark, twanging
An instrument, twanging a wiry string that gives
Sounds passing through sudden rightnesses, wholly
Containing the mind, below which it cannot descend,
Beyond which it has no will to rise.
It must
Be the finding of a satisfaction, and may
Be of a man skating, a woman dancing, a woman
Combing. The poem of the act of the mind.

1940, 1942

FINAL SOLILOQUY OF THE INTERIOR PARAMOUR

Light the first light of evening, as in a room
In which we rest and, for small reason, think
The world imagined is the ultimate good.

This is, therefore, the intensest rendezvous.
It is in that thought that we collect ourselves,
Out of all the indifferences, into one thing:

Within a single thing, a single shawl
Wrapped tightly round us, since we are poor, a warmth,
A light, a power, the miraculous influence.

Here, now, we forget each other and ourselves.
We feel the obscurity of an order, a whole,
A knowledge, that which arranged the rendezvous.

Within its vital boundary, in the mind.
We say God and the imagination are one . . .
How high that highest candle lights the dark.

Out of this same light, out of the central mind,
We make a dwelling in the evening air,
In which being there together is enough.

1951, 1953

THE PLAIN SENSE OF THINGS

After the leaves have fallen, we return
To a plain sense of things. It is as if
We had come to an end of the imagination,
Inanimate in an inert savoir.

It is difficult even to choose the adjective
For this blank cold, this sadness without cause.
The great structure has become a minor house.
No turban walks across the lessened floors.

The greenhouse never so badly needed paint.
The chimney is fifty years old and slants to one side.
A fantastic effort has failed, a repetition
In a repetitiousness of men and flies.

Yet the absence of the imagination had
Itself to be imagined. The great pond,
The plain sense of it, without reflections, leaves,
Mud, water like dirty glass, expressing silence

Of a sort, silence of a rat come out to see,
The great pond and its waste of the lilies, all this
Had to be imagined as an inevitable knowledge,
Required, as a necessity requires.

1952, 1954

William Carlos Williams 1883–1963

Along with nineteenth-century Russian playwright Anton Chekhov, William Carlos Williams is one of the two most famous doctors in modern literary history. He was also perhaps the most influential source for U.S. poetry of the second half of the twentieth century. Williams was born in Rutherford, New Jersey, in 1883 and died there in 1963. Throughout his career he often emphasized things American and working class, belying his international and privileged background. His father was British and his mother was the product of Basque and European Jewish descent by way of Puerto Rico. As a child, Williams was schooled in Geneva and Paris, and he attended high school in New York City. In 1902 he was admitted to medical school at the University of Pennsylvania. He did his internship in New York City, studied pediatrics for a year in Leipzig, and then returned to Rutherford, where he practiced medicine for the rest of his career.

By the time he got to the University of Pennsylvania, Williams had developed an interest in writing poetry and was writing a lot of it, mostly in imitation of the English Romantics. While at Penn, he met the poets Ezra Pound and Hilda Doolittle (also known as H. D.). Williams's relationship with Pound was intense, lifelong, and often antagonistic; he often spoke of his life as being divided into "Before Pound" and "After Pound." After graduating from medical school, Williams continued to write poems in the moments between patients, and he published his first volume of poetry, Poems *(1909), at his own expense (at a cost of fifty dollars). It was a thin volume of imitative verse that sold only "about four copies" at thirty-five cents each, but it was the first of the more than forty volumes of stories, novels, plays, essays, and poetry that were to come. In 1913 he published a second volume of verse,* The Tempers, *followed by* Al Que Quiere! *(1917),* Kora in Hell *(1920), and* Sour Grapes *(1921). In 1923 he published* Spring and All, *which contained some of his most anthologized poems, including "Spring and All" and "The Red Wheelbarrow," poems whose spare images exemplified Williams's famous dictum, "No ideas but in things." Collected editions of his poems appeared in 1934 and 1938. His most ambitious work,* Paterson, *was an epic poem, a montage of images and themes mixed with the details of American history, published in installments: the first book in 1946, the sixth, posthumously, in 1963.*

Williams famously disagreed with some of his most famous contemporaries. He disparaged T. S. Eliot and Ezra Pound for their expatriation, their elitist allusiveness, and their preference for dead European literature rather than the material world, calling Eliot's The Waste Land *(1922) "the great catastrophe." Like the nineteenth-century U.S. poet Walt Whitman, Williams was committed to celebrating a multicultural America, and like his older contemporary Robert Frost, he remained convinced that the universal could only be found in the local. But Williams also had many things in common with the high modernists. Like Pound and Eliot, he demanded hard, clear, concrete images, and he echoed Pound when he wrote in the preface to* Kora in Hell*: "Nothing is good save the new." Like Pound and Eliot, and unlike Frost, Williams spent his poetic career trying to create a sinewy free verse. He found traditional forms to be flaccid and no longer useful, writing in "The Poem as a Field of Action": "I propose sweeping changes from top to bottom of the poetic structure . . . . I say we are through with the iambic pentameter as presently conceived . . . through with the measured quatrain, the staid concatenations of sounds in the usual stanza, the sonnet." Williams's most famous contributions to the development of twentieth-century free verse are "the variable foot," and a flexible use of three-line stanzas, both of which he uses extensively in his important late poem "Asphodel, That Greeny Flower."*

The differences between Pound and Eliot on the one side and Williams on the other have been emphasized by the many later poets who claim Williams as their dominant influence. Black Mountain poets like Charles Olson and Robert Creeley and Beat poets like Allen Ginsberg explicitly reject the dominating early twentieth-century influence of Pound and Eliot and embrace Williams as a neglected giant. They tend to emphasize Williams's localism, his concrete language, and his supple forms. These later poets' specific opposition of Williams to Pound and Eliot has tended to exaggerate their poetic differences, and has sometimes confused the literary and the political. Postwar poets may have found in Williams a poet with modernist techniques whose democratic tendencies and working class affinities were much more palatable than Pound's and Eliot's frequent fascism. Many of the literary differences among Williams and Pound and Eliot are divergences of degree rather than kind, and Williams's egalitarian outlook has often been overstated. Parts of Paterson *and a poem like "To Elsie" show the same kind of elitism that characterized most Anglo-American modernism.*

Due primarily to the critical dominance of Pound and Eliot in the first half of the twentieth century, Williams, until the last decade of his life, often saw himself as the great neglected American poet. Common readers had shunned him and erudite critics had scorned him. But since the 1950s, Williams's influence has been tremendous, and his work has drawn the serious poetic and scholarly attention that eluded him for most of his life.

FURTHER READING: *The Autobiography of William Carlos Williams,* 1951; *The Selected Letters of William Carlos Williams,* ed. J. Thirwall, 1957, 1985; A. Ostrom, *The Poetic World of William Carlos Williams,* 1966; T. Whitaker, *William Carlos Williams,* 1968; J. Guimond, *The Art of William Carlos Williams,* 1968; J. Breslin, *William Carlos Williams, An American Artist,* 1970; M. Weaver, *William Carlos Williams, The American Background,* 1971; J. Mazzaro, *William Carlos Williams, The Later Poems,* 1973; R. Coles, *William Carlos Williams, The Knack of Survival in America,* 1975; R. Doyle, *William Carlos Williams and the American Poem,* 1982; H. Sayre, *The Visual Art of William Carlos Williams,* 1983; S. Cushman, *William Carlos Williams and the Meanings of Measure,* 1985; *William Carlos Williams,* ed. H. Bloom, 1986; C. MacGowan, *William Carlos Williams's Early Poetry, The Visual Arts,* 1987; P. Schmidt, *William Carlos Williams, the Arts, and Literary Tradition,* 1988; A. Fisher-Wirth, *William Carlos Williams and Autobiography,* 1989; J. Riddell, *The Inverted Bell, Modernism and the Counter-Poetics of William Carlos Williams,* 1991; D. Markos, *Ideas in Things, The Poems of William Carlos Williams,* 1994; D. Morris, *The Writings of William Carlos Williams, Publicity for the Self,* 1995; S. Koehler, *Countries of the Mind, The Poetry of William Carlos Williams,* 1998; *William Carlos Williams and the Language of Poetry,* ed. B. Hatlen and D. Tryphonopoulos, 2002.

TEXTS: *The Collected Poems of William Carlos Williams,* Vol. I, ed. A. Litz and C. MacGowan, 1986; *The Collected Poems of William Carlos Williams,* Vol. II, ed. C. MacGowan, 1988.

CON BRIO[1]

Miserly, is the best description of that poor fool
Who holds Lancelot to have been a morose fellow,
Dolefully brooding over the events which had naturally to follow
The high time of his deed with Guinevere.[2]
He has a sick historical sight, if I judge rightly,
To believe any such thing as that ever occurred.

[1]Italian: With Vigor. [2]The wife of King Arthur; she committed adultery with Sir Lancelot.

But, by the god of blood, what else is it that has deterred
Us all from an out and out defiance of fear
But this same perdamnable miserliness,
Which cries about our necks how we shall have less and less
Than we have now if we spend too wantonly?
Bah, this sort of slither is below contempt!
In the same vein we should have apple trees exempt
From bearing anything but pink blossoms all the year,
Fixed permanent lest their bellies wax unseemly, and the dear
Innocent days of them be wasted quite.
How can we have less? Have we not the deed?
Lancelot thought little, spent his gold and rode to fight
Mounted, if God was willing, on a good steed.

1913

THE YOUNG HOUSEWIFE

At ten A.M. the young housewife
moves about in negligee behind
the wooden walls of her husband's house.
I pass solitary in my car.

Then again she comes to the curb
to call the ice-man, fish-man, and stands
shy, uncorseted, tucking in
stray ends of hair, and I compare her
to a fallen leaf.

The noiseless wheels of my car
rush with a crackling sound over
dried leaves as I bow and pass smiling.

1916

PASTORAL

When I was younger
it was plain to me
I must make something of myself.
Older now
I walk back streets
admiring the houses
of the very poor:
roof out of line with sides
the yards cluttered
with old chicken wire, ashes,
furniture gone wrong;

the fences and outhouses
built of barrel-staves
and parts of boxes, all,
if I am fortunate,
smeared a bluish green
that properly weathered
pleases me best
of all colors.
No one

will believe this
of vast import to the nation.

1917

TRACT

I will teach you my townspeople
how to perform a funeral—
for you have it over a troop
of artists—
unless one should scour the world—
you have the ground sense necessary.

See! the hearse leads.
I begin with a design for a hearse.
For Christ's sake not black—
nor white either—and not polished!
Let it be weathered—like a farm wagon—
with gilt wheels (this could be
applied fresh at small expense)
or no wheels at all:
a rough dray[1] to drag over the ground.

Knock the glass out!
My God—glass, my townspeople!
For what purpose? Is it for the dead
to look out or for us to see
how well he is housed or to see
the flowers or the lack of them—
or what?
To keep the rain and snow from him?
He will have a heavier rain soon:
pebbles and dirt and what not.

[1]A low cart, without sides or wheels, a sledge.

Let there be no glass—
and no upholstery, phew!
and no little brass rollers
and small easy wheels on the bottom—
my townspeople what are you thinking of?

A rough plain hearse then
with gilt wheels and no top at all.
On this the coffin lies
by its own weight.

No wreaths please—
especially no hot house flowers.
Some common memento is better,
something he prized and is known by:
his old clothes—a few books perhaps—
God knows what! You realize
how we are about these things
my townspeople—
something will be found—anything
even flowers if he had come to that.
So much for the hearse.

For heaven's sake though see to the driver!
Take off the silk hat; In fact
that's no place at all for him—
up there unceremoniously
dragging our friend out to his own dignity!
Bring him down—bring him down!
Low and inconspicuous! I'd not have him ride
on the wagon at all—damn him—
the undertaker's understrapper!
Let him hold the reins
and walk at the side
and inconspicuously too!

Then briefly as to yourselves:
Walk behind—as they do in France,
seventh class, or if you ride
Hell take curtains! Go with some show
of inconvenience; sit openly—
to the weather as to grief.
Or do you think you can shut grief in?
What—from us? We who have perhaps
nothing to lose? Share with us
share with us—it will be money
in your pockets.
Go now
I think you are ready.

1916, 1917

DANSE RUSSE[1]

If when my wife is sleeping
and the baby and Kathleen[2]
are sleeping
and the sun is a flame-white disc
in silken mists
above shining trees,—
if I in my north room
dance naked, grotesquely
before my mirror
waving my shirt round my head
and singing softly to myself:
"I am lonely, lonely.
I was born to be lonely,
I am best so!"
If I admire my arms, my face,
my shoulders, flanks, buttocks
against the yellow drawn shades,—

Who shall say I am not
the happy genius[3] of my household?

1916, 1917

QUEEN-ANNE'S-LACE[1]

Her body is not so white as
anemone petals nor so smooth—nor
so remote a thing. It is a field
of the wild carrot taking
the field by force; the grass
does not raise above it.
Here is no question of whiteness,
white as can be, with a purple mole
at the center of each flower.
Each flower is a hand's span
of her whiteness. Wherever
his hand has lain there is
a tiny purple blemish. Each part
is a blossom under his touch

[1]French: Russian Dance.
[2]Kathleen McBride, nursemaid for the Williams children.
[3]Distinctive local spirit.
[1]A wild carrot, which has clusters of white flowers often with a purple blossom in the center.

to which the fibres of her being
stem one by one, each to its end,
until the whole field is a
white desire, empty, a single stem,
a cluster, flower by flower,
a pious wish to whiteness gone over—
or nothing.

1920, 1921

SPRING AND ALL

By the road to the contagious hospital
under the surge of the blue
mottled clouds driven from the
northeast—a cold wind. Beyond, the
waste of broad, muddy fields
brown with dried weeds, standing and fallen

patches of standing water
the scattering of tall trees

All along the road the reddish
purplish, forked, upstanding, twiggy
stuff of bushes and small trees
with dead, brown leaves under them
leafless vines—

Lifeless in appearance, sluggish
dazed spring approaches—

They enter the new world naked,
cold, uncertain of all
save that they enter. All about them
the cold, familiar wind—

Now the grass, tomorrow
the stiff curl of wildcarrot leaf

One by one objects are defined—
It quickens: clarity, outline of leaf

But now the stark dignity of
entrance—Still, the profound change
has come upon them: rooted, they
grip down and begin to awaken

1923

TO ELSIE

The pure products of America
go crazy—
mountain folk from Kentucky

or the ribbed north end of
Jersey
with its isolate lakes and

valleys, its deaf-mutes, thieves
old names
and promiscuity between

devil-may-care men who have taken
to railroading
out of sheer lust of adventure—

and young slatterns, bathed
in filth
from Monday to Saturday

to be tricked out that night
with gauds
from imaginations which have no

peasant traditions to give them
character
but flutter and flaunt

sheer rags—succumbing without
emotion
save numbed terror

under some hedge of choke-cherry
or viburnum—
which they cannot express—

Unless it be that marriage
perhaps
with a dash of Indian blood

will throw up a girl so desolate
so hemmed round
with disease or murder

that she'll be rescued by an
agent—
reared by the state and

sent out at fifteen to work in
some hard-pressed
house in the suburbs—

some doctor's family, some Elsie—
voluptuous water
expressing with broken

brain the truth about us—
her great
ungainly hips and flopping breasts

addressed to cheap
jewelry
and rich young men with fine eyes

as if the earth under our feet
were
an excrement of some sky

and we degraded prisoners
destined
to hunger until we eat filth

while the imagination strains
after deer
going by fields of goldenrod in

the stifling heat of September
Somehow
it seems to destroy us

It is only in isolate flecks that
something
is given off

No one
to witness
and adjust, no one to drive the car

1923

THE RED WHEELBARROW

so much depends
upon

a red wheel
barrow

glazed with rain
water

beside the white
chickens

1923

AT THE BALL GAME

The crowd at the ball game
is moved uniformly

by a spirit of uselessness
which delights them—

all the exciting detail
of the chase

and the escape, the error
the flash of genius—

all to no end save beauty
the eternal—

So in detail they, the crowd,
are beautiful

for this
to be warned against

saluted and defied—
It is alive, venomous

it smiles grimly
its words cut—

The flashy female with her
mother, gets it—

The Jew gets it straight—it
is deadly, terrifying—

It is the Inquisition, the
Revolution

It is beauty itself
that lives

day by day in them
idly—

This is
the power of their faces

It is summer, it is the solstice[1]
the crowd is

cheering, the crowd is laughing
in detail

permanently, seriously
without thought

1923

BETWEEN WALLS

the back wings
of the

hospital where
nothing

will grow lie
cinders

in which shine
the broken

pieces of a green
bottle

1934

THIS IS JUST TO SAY

I have eaten
the plums
that were in
the icebox

and which
you were probably
saving
for breakfast

[1]The beginning of summer, around June 22.

Forgive me
they were delicious
so sweet
and so cold
1934

THESE

are the desolate, dark weeks
when nature in its barrenness
equals the stupidity of man.

The year plunges into night
and the heart plunges
lower than night

to an empty, windswept place
without sun, stars or moon
but a peculiar light as of thought

that spins a dark fire—
whirling upon itself until,
in the cold, it kindles

to make a man aware of nothing
that he knows, not loneliness
itself—Not a ghost but

would be embraced—emptiness,
despair—(They
whine and whistle) among

the flashes and booms of war;
houses of whose rooms
the cold is greater than can be thought,

the people gone that we loved,
the beds lying empty, the couches
damp, the chairs unused—

Hide it away somewhere
out of the mind, let it get roots
and grow, unrelated to jealous

ears and eyes—for itself
In this mine they come to dig—all.
Is this the counterfoil to sweetest

music? The source of poetry that
seeing the clock stopped, says,
The clock has stopped

that ticked yesterday so well?
and hears the sound of lakewater
splashing—that is now stone.

1938

SEAFARER

The sea will wash in
but the rocks—jagged ribs
riding the cloth of foam
or a knob or pinnacles
with gannets[1]—
are the stubborn man.

He invites the storm, he
lives by it! instinct
with fears that are not fears
but prickles of ecstasy,
a secret liquor, a fire
that inflames his blood to
coldness so that the rocks
seem rather to leap
at the sea than the sea
to envelop them. They strain
forward to grasp ships
or even the sky itself that
bends down to be torn
upon them. To which he says,
It is I! who am the rocks!
Without me nothing laughs.

1948

LANDSCAPE WITH THE FALL OF ICARUS

According to Brueghel[1]
when Icarus fell
it was spring

[1]Large seabirds.

[1]Pieter Brueghel (1525?–1569), Flemish artist whose painting "Landscape with the Fall of Icarus" (1555?) displays just such a pastoral scene as Williams describes.

a farmer was ploughing
his field
the whole pageantry

of the year was
awake tingling
near

the edge of the sea
concerned
with itself

sweating in the sun
that melted
the wings' wax

unsignificantly
off the coast
there was

a splash quite unnoticed
this was
Icarus drowning
1960, 1962

Marianne Moore 1887–1972

By the end of her life Marianne Moore was well-known as one of America's most devoted baseball fans and as one of its premier poets. Her devotion to baseball won her the honor of throwing out the first ball at the opening of the 1968 season at Yankee Stadium in New York. Her poetic descriptions of exotic animals and plants, and things as varied as steamrollers and quartz crystal clocks, won her numerous awards and the distinction of being described as "The World's Greatest Living Observer."

She spent her childhood near St. Louis, Missouri, and in Carlisle, Pennsylvania. After graduating from Bryn Mawr College in 1909, she returned to Carlisle, where she taught for four years in a U.S. government school for American Indians. In 1916, having already begun to distinguish herself as one of the nation's innovative "new poets," she moved east, eventually settling in New York City. She worked in the New York Public Library and then became editor of a literary magazine, The Dial, *all the while developing her meticulous and subtle poetic craft. Her first book,* Poems *(1921), was published in England by her friends and without her knowledge. In 1924 her prize-winning volume* Observations *appeared, followed by* The Pangolin

(1936), What Are Years *(1941), and* Nevertheless *(1944). Her* Collected Poems *were published in 1951, and in a single year (1952), she received a Bollingen Prize, a Pulitzer Prize, and a National Book Award for Poetry.*

Marianne Moore was a book reviewer, translator, and essayist, as well as poet, and her sprightly and eccentric ways were, to many, as engaging as her fresh and compact writing. She had an acute eye for detail, and her poetry is marked by movements from "imagistic" portrayals of visible objects to metaphysical reflections. She sprinkled her poetry with quotations, which she compared to "collections of flies in amber." She used near or approximate rhyme and light rhyme—in which the rhyming syllables of words are unaccented. Much of her verse was syllabic, relying on the number of syllables in a poetic line, rather than on a conventional pattern of stress accents, to produce a subdued metrical cadence. As a result, some of her poems display the rhetorical qualities of succinct prose, yet with their carefully controlled forms, their glittering surfaces, and their intellectual complexities they are expressions of an authentic poetic imagination and "lit with piercing glances into the life of things."

FURTHER READING: *The Complete Prose of Marianne Moore,* ed. P. Willis, 1986; J. Slatin, *The Savage's Romance, The Poetry of Marianne Moore,* 1986; G. Schulman, *Marianne Moore, The Poetry of Engagement,* 1986; *Marianne Moore, The Art of a Modernist,* ed. J. Parisi, 1990; C. Molesworth, *Marianne Moore, A Literary Life,* 1990; C. Miller, *Marianne Moore, Questions of Authority,* 1995; L. Leavell, *Marianne Moore and the Visual Arts,* 1995; *The Selected Letters of Marianne Moore,* ed. B. Costello, 1997; E. Joyce, *Cultural Critique and Abstraction, Marianne Moore and the Avant-Garde,* 1998; *The Critical Response to Marianne Moore,* ed. E. Gregory, 2003; *Marianne Moore,* ed. H. Bloom, 2004.

TEXTS: The text of "Poetry" is from *Collected Poems,* 1951; all other poems are from *The Complete Poems of Marianne Moore,* 1980.

TO A STEAM ROLLER

The illustration
is nothing to you without the application.
You lack half wit. You crush all the particles down
into close conformity, and then walk back and forth on them.

Sparkling chips of rock
are crushed down to the level of the parent block.
Were not "impersonal judgment in aesthetic
matters, a metaphysical impossibility," you

might fairly achieve
it. As for butterflies, I can hardly conceive
of one's attending upon you, but to question
the congruence of the complement is vain, if it exists.

1915, 1921

THE FISH

wade
through black jade.
Of the crow-blue mussel shells, one keeps
adjusting the ash heaps;
opening and shutting itself like

an
injured fan.
The barnacles which encrust the side
of the wave, cannot hide
there for the submerged shafts of the

sun,
split like spun
glass, move themselves with spotlight switfness
into the crevices—
in and out, illuminating

the
turquoise sea
of bodies. The water drives a wedge
of iron through the iron edge
of the cliff; whereupon the stars,

pink
rice-grains, ink-
bespattered jellyfish, crabs like green
lilies, and submarine
toadstools, slide each on the other.

All
external
marks of abuse are present on this
defiant edifice—
all the physical features of

ac-
cident—lack
of cornice, dynamite grooves, burns, and
hatchet strokes, these things stand
out on it; the chasm side is
dead.

Repeated
evidence has proved that it can live
on what can not revive
its youth. The sea grows old in it.

1918, 1921

POETRY[1]

I, too, dislike it: there are things that are important beyond
all this fiddle.
Reading it, however, with a perfect contempt for it, one
discovers in
it after all, a place for the genuine.
Hands that can grasp, eyes
that can dilate, hair that can rise
if it must, these things are important not because a

high-sounding interpretation can be put upon them but because they are
useful. When they become so derivative as to become
unintelligible,
the same thing may be said for all of us, that we
do not admire what
we cannot understand: the bat
holding on upside down or in quest of something to

eat, elephants pushing, a wild horse taking a roll, a tireless
wolf under
a tree, the immovable critic twitching his skin like a horse
that feels a flea, the base-
ball fan, the statistician—
nor is it valid
to discriminate against "business documents and

school-books";[2] all these phenomena are important. One
must make a distinction
however: when dragged into prominence by half poets,
the result is not poetry,
nor till the poets among us can be
"literalists of
the imagination"[3]—above
insolence and triviality and can present

[1]The text reprinted here is from *Collected Poems* (1951). In a revised version, published in *The Complete Poems* (1967), the poem was reduced to three lines: "I, too, dislike it. / Reading it, however, with a perfect contempt for it, one discovers in / it, after all, a place for the genuine."

[2]"Diary of Tolstoy, p. 84: 'Where the boundary between prose and poetry lies, I shall never be able to understand. The question is raised in manuals of style, yet the answer to it lies beyond me. Poetry is verse: prose is not verse. Or else poetry is everything with the exception of business documents and school books.' "—Moore's note. The quotation is from *The Diaries of Leo Tolstoy* (1917).

[3]"Yeats, *Ideas of Good and Evil* (A. H. Bullen, 1903), p. 182. 'The limitation of his view was from the very intensity of his vision; he was a too literal realist of imagination, as others are of nature; and because he believed that the figures seen by the mind's eye, when exalted by inspiration, were "eternal existences," symbols of divine essences, he hated every grace of style that might obscure their lineaments' "—Moore's note. The quotation is from an essay, "William Blake and His Illustrations to the *Divine Comedy*," by William Butler Yeats.

for inspection, "imaginary gardens with real toads in them,"
shall we have
it. In the meantime, if you demand on the one hand,
the raw material of poetry in
all its rawness and
that which is on the other hand
genuine, you are interested in poetry.

1919, 1935

NO SWAN SO FINE

"No water so still as the
dead fountains of Versailles,"[1] No swan,
with swart blind look askance
and gondoliering legs, so fine
as the chintz china one with fawn-
brown eyes and toothed gold
collar on to show whose bird it was.

Lodged in the Louis Fifteenth
candelabrum[2]-tree of cockscomb-
tinted buttons, dahlias, sea urchins, and everlastings,
it perches on the branching foam
of polished sculptured
flowers—at ease and tall. The king is dead.

1932, 1935

IN DISTRUST OF MERITS

Strengthened to live, strengthened to die for
medals and positioned victories?
They're fighting, fighting, fighting the blind
man who thinks he sees,—
who cannot see that the enslaver is
enslaved; the hater, harmed. O shining O
firm star, O tumultuous
ocean lashed till small things go
as they will, the mountainous
wave makes us who look, know

[1]" 'There is no water so still as in the dead fountains of Versailles.' Percy Phillip, *New York Times Magazine,* May 10, 1931."—Moore's note.

[2]"A pair of Louis XV candelabra with Dresden figures of swans belonging to Lord Balfour."—Moore's note. The age of Louis XV, King of France (1715–1774), was one of ornate and delicate art.

depth. Lost at sea before they fought! O
star of David, star of Bethlehem,
O black imperial lion
of the Lord—emblem
of a risen world—be joined at last, be
joined. There is hate's crown beneath which all is
death; there's love's without which none
is king; the blessed deeds bless
the halo. As contagion
of sickness makes sickness,

contagion of trust can make trust. They're
fighting in deserts and caves, one by
one, in battalions and squadrons;
they're fighting that I
may yet recover from the disease, My
Self; some have it lightly; some will die. "Man's
wolf to man" and we devour
ourselves. The enemy could not
have made a greater breach in our
defenses. One pilot-

ing a blind man can escape him, but
Job disheartened by false comfort knew
that nothing can be so defeating
as a blind man who
can see. O alive who are dead, who are
proud not to see, O small dust of the earth
that walks so arrogantly,
trust begets power and faith is
an affectionate thing. We
vow, we make this promise

to the fighting—it's a promise—"We'll
never hate black, white, red, yellow, Jew,
Gentile, Untouchable." We are
not competent to
make our vows. With set jaw they are fighting,
fighting, fighting,—some we love whom we know,
some we love but know not—that
hearts may feel and not be numb.
It cures me; or am I what
I can't believe in? Some

in snow, some on crags, some in quicksands,
little by little, much by much, they
are fighting fighting fighting that where
there was death there may

be life. "When a man is prey to anger,
he is moved by outside things; when he holds
his ground in patience patience
patience, that is action or
beauty," the soldier's defense
and hardest armor for

the fight. The world's an orphans' home. Shall
we never have peace without sorrow?
without pleas of the dying for
help that won't come? O
quiet form upon the dust, I cannot
look and yet I must. If these great patient
dyings—all these agonies
and wound bearings and bloodshed—
can teach us how to live, these
dyings were not wasted.

Hate-hardened heart, O heart of iron,
iron is iron till it is rust.
There never was a war that was
not inward; I must
fight till I have conquered in myself what
causes war, but I would not believe it.
I inwardly did nothing.
O Iscariot-like crime!
Beauty is everlasting
and dust is for a time.

1943 1943, 1944

Countée Cullen 1903–1946

He was born Countée Porter and raised in Baltimore and in New York City. When he was fifteen he was adopted by the Reverend Frederick Cullen, a Methodist minister in Harlem, who took his foster son on a tour of the Holy Land and to the literary shrines of Europe and strongly encouraged his academic interests. Cullen went to New York University, where he was elected to Phi Beta Kappa and won awards for his poetry. In 1925, Color, *his first book of poems, was published. By the time he was twenty-six, he had published three more volumes:* Copper Sun *(1927),* The Ballad of the Brown Girl *(1927), and* The Black Christ *(1929). He wrote a Harlem novel,* One Way to Heaven *(1932), translated Euripides's* Medea *(1935), and served as an editor for two important African-American magazines of the day:* Opportunity, Journal of Negro Life, *and* The Crisis, *an official periodical of the NAACP. But after his early, prolific years, Cullen's productivity declined, and he supported himself mainly by teaching French in the New York public schools, although he continued to write verse and in 1946 collaborated in writing a Broadway musical,* St. Louis Woman. *In 1947 his collected poems were published posthumously under the title* On These I Stand.

Cullen, a conscientious, dedicated craftsman, was one of the most notable writers of the Harlem Renaissance, a period of remarkable literary achievement by black writers in New York City during the 1920s. Cullen's techniques were conventional; his models were the romantic poets, not black poets, and he often insisted that his poems in particular and poetry in general should be free from political or racial matters. At other times he could not escape the fact of his race. His finest poem, "Heritage," is an assertion of the black American's relationship with Africa, and he came to acknowledge that "in spite of myself, I find that I am actuated by a strong sense of race consciousness. This grows upon me." Cullen was caught between his conflicting allegiances to his art, his country, and his race, but, like other black writers after him, he managed to create a body of memorable writing out of disparate loyalties and ideologies and out of his struggles in a world that made "a poet black, and bid him sing."

FURTHER READING: B. Ferguson, *Countée Cullen and the Negro Renaissance,* 1966; M. Perry, *A Bio-Biography of Countée Cullen, 1903–1946,* 1971; A. Shucard, *Countée Cullen,* 1984; *My Soul's High Song, The Collected Writings of Countée Cullen,* ed. G. Early, 1991; S. Onyeberechi, *Critical Essays, Achebe, Baldwin, Cullen, Ngugi, and Tutuola,* 1999.

TEXT: *On These I Stand,* 1947.

YET DO I MARVEL

I doubt not God is good, well-meaning, kind,
And did He stoop to quibble could tell why
The little buried mole continues blind,
Why flesh that mirrors Him must some day die,
Make plain the reason tortured Tantalus[1]
Is baited by the fickle fruit, declare
If merely brute caprice dooms Sisyphus[2]
To struggle up a never-ending stair.
Inscrutable His ways are, and immune
To catechism by a mind too strewn
With petty cares to slightly understand
What awful brain compels His awful hand.
Yet do I marvel at this curious thing:
To make a poet black, and bid him sing!

1924, 1925

[1]In Greek myth, Tantalus, for his defiance of the gods, was condemned forever to stand, "tantalized," with food and drink just beyond his grasp.

[2]A crafty deceiver in Greek myth who was condemned eternally to push a huge stone up the slope of a hill.

FOR A LADY I KNOW

She even thinks that up in heaven
Her class lies late and snores,
While poor black cherubs rise at seven
To do celestial chores.
1924, 1925

INCIDENT

(For Eric Walrond)

Once riding in old Baltimore,
Heart-filled, head-filled with glee,
I saw a Baltimorean
Keep looking straight at me.

Now I was eight and very small,
And he was no whit bigger,
And so I smiled, but he poked out
His tongue, and called me, "Nigger."

I saw the whole of Baltimore
From May until December;
Of all the things the happened there
That's all that I remember.
1924, 1924

FROM THE DARK TOWER

(To Charles S. Johnson)

We shall not always plant while others reap
The golden increment of bursting fruit,
Not always countenance, abject and mute,
That lesser men should hold their brothers cheap;
Not everlastingly while others sleep
Shall we beguile their limbs with mellow flute,
Not always bend to some more subtle brute;
We were not made eternally to weep.

The night whose sable breast relieves the stark
White stars is no less lovely being dark
And there are buds that cannot bloom at all
In light, but crumple, piteous, and fall;
So in the dark we hide the heart that bleeds,
And wait, and tend our agonizing seeds.

1924, 1927

A BROWN GIRL DEAD

With two white roses on her breasts,
  White candles at head and feet,
Dark Madonna of the grave she rests;
  Lord Death has found her sweet.

Her mother pawned her wedding ring
  To lay her out in white;
She'd be so proud she'd dance and sing
  To see herself tonight.

1925

HERITAGE

(For Harold Jackman)

What is Africa to me:
Copper sun or scarlet sea,
Jungle star or jungle track,
Strong bronzed me, or regal black
Women from whose loins I sprang
When the birds of Eden sang?
One three centuries removed
From the scenes his fathers loved,
Spicy grove, cinnamon tree,
What is Africa to me?

So I lie, who all day long
Want no sound except the song
Sung by wild barbaric birds
Goading massive jungle herds,

Juggernauts of flesh that pass
Trampling tall defiant grass
Where young forest lovers lie,
Plighting troth beneath the sky.
So I lie, who always hear,
Though I cram against my ear
Both my thumbs, and keep them there,
Great drums throbbing through the
air.
So I die, whose fount of pride,
Dear distress, and joy allied,
Is my somber flesh and skin,
With the dark blood dammed within
Like great pulsing tides of wine
That, I fear, must burst the fine
Channels of the chafing net
Where they surge and foam and fret.

Africa? A book one thumbs
Listlessly, till slumber comes.
Unremembered are her bats
Circling through the night, her cats
Crouching in the river reeds,
Stalking gentle flesh that feeds
By the river brink; no more
Does the bugle-throated roar
Cry that monarch claws have leapt
From the scabbards where they slept.
Silver snakes that once a year
Doff the lovely coats you wear,
Seek no covert in your fear
Lest a mortal eye should see;
What's your nakedness to me?
Here no leprous flowers rear
Fierce corollas[1] in the air;
Here no bodies sleek and wet,
Dripping mingled rain and sweat,
Tread the savage measures of
Jungle boys and girls in love.
What is last year's snow to me,
Last year's anything? The tree
Budding yearly must forget
How its past arose or set—
Bough and blossom, flower, fruit,

[1]Petals.

Even what shy bird with mute
Wonder at her travail there,
Meekly labored in its hair.
One three centuries removed
From the scenes his fathers loved,
Spicy grove, cinnamon tree,
What is Africa to me?

So I lie, who finds no peace
Night or day, no slight release
From the unremittant beat
Made by cruel padded feet
Walking through my body's street.
Up and down they go, and back,
Treading out a jungle track.
So I lie, who never quite
Safely sleep from rain at night—
I can never rest at all
When the rain begins to fall;
Like a soul gone mad with pain
I must match its weird refrain;
Ever must I twist and squirm,
Writhing like a baited worm,
While its primal measures drip
Through my body, crying, "Strip!
Doff this new exuberance.
Come and dance the Lover's Dance!"
In an old remembered way
Rain works on me night and day.
Quaint, outlandish heathen gods
Black men fashion out of rods,
Clay, and brittle bits of stone,
In a likeness like their own
My conversion came high-priced;
I belong to Jesus Christ,
Preacher of humility;
Heathen gods are naught to me.

Father, Son, and Holy Ghost,
So I make an idle boast;
Jesus of the twice-turned cheek,[2]
Lamb of God, although I speak
With my mouth thus, in my heart

[2]". . . whosoever shall smite thee on thy right cheek, turn to him the other also." (Matthew 5:39).

Do I play a double part.
Ever at Thy glowing altar
Must my heart grow sick and falter,
Wishing He I served were black,
Thinking then it would not lack
Precedent of pain to guide it,
Let who would or might deride it;
Surely then this flesh would know
Yours had borne a kindred woe.
Lord, I fashion dark gods, too,
Daring even to give You
Dark despairing features where,
Crowned with dark rebellious hair,
Patience wavers just so much as
Mortal grief compels, while touches
Quick and hot, of anger, rise
To smitten cheek and weary eyes.
Lord, forgive me if my need
Sometimes shapes all human creed.
All day long and all night through,
One thing only must I do:
Quench my pride and cool my blood,
Lest I perish in the flood.
Lest a hidden ember set
Timber that I thought was wet
Burning like the dryest flax,
Melting like the merest wax,
Lest the grave restore its dead.
Not yet has my heart or head
In the least way realized
They and I are civilized.

1925

Jean Toomer 1894–1967

From beginning to end, Jean Toomer's life vacillated between the white and black worlds. His father deserted his family after a year of marriage, and Toomer grew up unhappily in the home of his maternal grandfather, who had once been acting governor of Louisiana during the Reconstruction period after the Civil War. Following high school, Toomer restlessly shifted from one city and from one college to another. He studied agriculture at the University of Wisconsin and in Massachusetts; he entered a physical training program in Chicago; he studied sociology and history at colleges in New

York City, sold cars in Chicago, taught physical education in Milwaukee, worked in a shipyard in New Jersey.

After several years of wandering, Toomer returned to his grandfather's home in Washington, D.C. There he began to write, and quickly succeeded, placing poems in several avant-garde magazines. In 1921, still restless, he went to Georgia, as superintendent of a rural black school. Although he was there only four months, his stay deeply influenced him, and provided him with the material for his novel Cane *(1923).*

The book, with its mixture of poems, quasi-dramas, and short fiction, was widely acclaimed as a notable contribution to the experimental fiction of the time and as a major work in the history of black literature. Toomer became one of the leaders, along with Langston Hughes and Countée Cullen, of the Harlem Literary Renaissance of the 1920s. Following the publication of Cane, *Toomer went to France, and there he fell under the influence of Georges Gurdjieff, a Russian philosopher whose mystical system "Unitism" helped turn Toomer away from the world of daily experience and into a private world of introspection. For a time Toomer continued to write, but his work became increasingly abstract, and he published little. In his last years he became a Quaker and lectured occasionally at Quaker meetings. By the end of his life he had retreated almost completely into literary obscurity, yet in* Cane *he had created a literary monument, a testament to his perception of the distressed and uprooted lives of black men and women living in white America.*

FURTHER READING: *The Wayward and the Seeking, A Collection of the Writings of Jean Toomer,* ed. D. Turner, 1981; *The Collected Poems of Jean Toomer,* ed. R. Jones and M. Latimer, 1988; *A Jean Toomer Reader: Selected Unpublished Writings,* ed. F. Rusch, 1993; *Anger and Beyond, The Negro Writer in the United States,* ed. H. Hill, 1966; *Studies in Cane,* ed. F. Durham, 1971; B. Benson and M. Dillard, *Jean Toomer,* 1980; N. McKay, *Jean Toomer, A Study of His Literary Life and Work,* 1984; C. Kerman, *The Lives of Jean Toomer,* 1987; *Jean Toomer, A Critical Evaluation,* ed. T. O'Daniel, 1988; R. Byrd, *Jean Toomer's Years with Gurdjieff,* 1990; C. Larson, *Invisible Darkness,* 1993; J. Woodson, *To Make a New Race, Gurdjieff, Toomer, and the Harlem Renaissance,* 1999.

TEXT: *Cane,* 1923.

BLOOD-BURNING MOON

I

Up from the skeleton stone walls, up from the rotting floor boards and the solid hand-hewn beams of oak of the pre-war cotton factory, dusk came. Up from the dusk the full moon came. Glowing like a fired pine-knot, it illumined the great door and soft showered the Negro shanties aligned along the single street of factory town. The full moon in the great door was an omen. Negro women improvised songs against its spell.

Louisa sang as she came over the crest of the hill from the white folks' kitchen. Her skin was the color of oak leaves on young trees in fall. Her breasts, firm and up-pointed like ripe acorns. And her singing had the low murmur of winds in fig trees. Bob Stone, younger son of the people she worked for, loved her. By the way the world reckons things, he had won her. By measure of that warm glow which came into her mind at thought of him, he had won her. Tom Burwell, whom the whole town called Big Boy, also loved her. But working in the fields all day, and far away from her, gave him no chance to show it. Though often enough of evenings he had tried to. Somehow, he never got along. Strong as he was with hands upon the ax or plow, he found it difficult to hold her. Or so he thought. But the fact was that he held her to factory town more firmly than he thought for. His black balanced, and pulled against, the white of Stone, when she thought of them. And her mind was vaguely upon them as she came over the crest of the hill, coming from the white folks' kitchen. As she sang softly at the evil face of the full moon.

A strange stir was in her. Indolently, she tried to fix upon Bob or Tom as the cause of it. To meet Bob in the canebrake, as she was going to do an hour or so later, was nothing new. And Tom's proposal which she felt on its way to her could be indefinitely put off. Separately, there was no unusual significance to either one. But for some reason, they jumbled when her eyes gazed vacantly at the rising moon. And from the jumble came the stir that was strangely within her. Her lips trembled. The slow rhythm of her song grew agitant and restless. Rusty black and tan spotted hounds, lying in the dark corners of porches or prowling around back yards, put their noses in the air and caught its tremor. They began plaintively to yelp and howl. Chickens woke up and cackled. Intermittently, all over the countryside dogs barked and roosters crowed as if heralding a weird dawn or some ungodly awakening. The women sang lustily. Their songs were cotton-wads to stop their ears. Louisa came down into factory town and sank wearily upon the step before her home. The moon was rising towards a thick cloud-bank which soon would hide it.

Red nigger moon. Sinner!
Blood-burning moon. Sinner!
Come out that fact'ry door.

II

Up from the deep dusk of a cleared spot on the edge of the forest a mellow glow arose and spread fan-wise into the low-hanging heavens. And all around the air was heavy with the scent of boiling cane. A large pile of cane-stalks lay like ribboned shadows upon the ground. A mule, harnessed to a pole, trudged lazily round and round the pivot of the grinder. Beneath a swaying oil lamp, a Negro alternately whipped out at the mule, and fed cane-stalks to the grinder. A fat boy waddled pails of fresh ground juice between the grinder and the boiling stove. Steam came from the copper boiling pan. The scent of cane came from the copper pan and drenched the forest and the hill that sloped to factory town, beneath its fragrance. It drenched the men in circle seated around the stove. Some of them chewed at the white pulp of stalks, but there was no need for them to, if all they wanted was to taste the cane. One tasted it in factory town. And from factory town one could see the soft haze thrown by the glowing stove upon the low-hanging heavens.

Old David Georgia stirred the thickening syrup with a long ladle, and every so often drew it off. Old David Georgia tended his stove and told tales about the white folk, about moonshining and cotton picking, and about sweet nigger gals, to the men who sat there about his stove to listen to him. Tom Burwell chewed cane-stalk and laughed with the others till someone mentioned Louisa. Till some one said something about Louisa and Bob Stone, about the silk stockings she must have gotten from him. Blood ran up Tom's neck hotter than the glow that flooded from the stove. He sprang up. Glared at the men and said, "She's my gal." Will Manning laughed. Tom strode over to him. Yanked him up and knocked him to the ground. Several of Manning's friends got up to fight for him. Tom whipped out a long knife and would have cut them to shreds if they hadnt ducked into the woods. Tom had had enough. He nodded to Old David Georgia and swung down the path to factory town. Just then, the dogs started barking and the roosters began to crow. Tom felt funny. Away from the fight, away from the stove, chill got to him. He shivered. He shuddered when he saw the full moon rising towards the cloud-bank. He who didnt give a godam for the fears of old women. He forced his mind to fasten on Louisa. Bob Stone. Better not be. He turned into the street and saw Louisa sitting before her home. He went towards her, ambling, touched the brim of a marvelously shaped, spotted, felt hat, said he wanted to say something to her, and then found that he didnt know what he had to say, or if he did, that he couldnt say it. He shoved his big fists in his overalls, grinned, and started to move off.

"Youall want me, Tom?"

"Thats what us wants, sho, Louisa."

"Well, here I am—"

"An here I is, but that aint ahelpin none, all th same."

"You wanted to say something? . . ."

"I did that, sho. But words is like th spots on dice: no matter how y fumbles em, there's times when they jes wont come. I dunno why. Seems like th love I feels fo yo done stole m tongue. I got it now. Whee! Louisa, honey, I oughtnt tell y, I feel I oughtnt cause yo is young and goes t church an I has had other gals, but Louisa I sho do love y. Lil gal, Ise watched y from them first days when youall sat right here befo yo door befo th well an sang sometimes in a way that like t broke m heart. Ise carried y with me into th fields, day after day, an after that, an I sho can plow when yo is there, an I can pick cotton. Yassur! Come near beatin Barlo yesterday. I sho did. Yassur! An next year if old Stone'll trust me, I'll have a farm. My own. My bales will buy you what y gets from white folks now. Silk stockings an purple dresses—course I dont believe what some folks been whisperin as t how y gets them things now. White folks always did do for niggers what they likes. An they jes cant help alikin yo, Louisa. Bob Stone likes y. Course he does. But not th way folks is awhisperin. Does he, hon?"

"I dont know what you mean, Tom"

"Course y dont. Ise already cut two niggers. Had t hon, t tell em so. Niggers always tryin t make somethin out a nothin. And then besides, white folks aint up t them tricks so much nowadays. Godam better not be. Leastawise not with yo. Cause I wouldnt stand f it. Nassur."

"What would you do, Tom?"

"Cut him jes like I cut a nigger."

"No, Tom—"

"I said I would an there aint no mo to it. But that aint th talk f now. Sing, honey Louisa, an while I'm listenin t y I'll be makin love."

Tom took her hand in his. Against the tough thickness of his own, hers felt soft and small. His huge body slipped down to the step beside her. The full moon sank upward into the deep purple of the cloud-bank. An old woman brought a lighted lamp and hung it on the common well whose bulky shadow squatted in the middle of the road, opposite Tom and Louisa. The old woman lifted the well-lid, took hold the chain, and began drawing up the heavy bucket. As she did so, she sang. Figures shifted, restless-like, between lamp and window in the front rooms of the shanties. Shadows of the figures fought each other on the gray dust of the road. Figures raised the windows and joined the old woman in song. Louisa and Tom, the whole street, singing:

> Red nigger moon. Sinner!
> Blood-burning moon. Sinner!
> Come out that fact'ry door.

III

Bob Stone sauntered from his veranda out into the gloom of fir trees and magnolias. The clear white of his skin paled, and the flush of his cheeks turned purple. As if to balance this outer change, his mind became consciously a white man's. He passed the house with its huge open hearth which, in the days of slavery, was the plantation cookery. He saw Louisa bent over that hearth. He went in as a master should and took her. Direct, honest, bold. None of this sneaking that he had to go through now. The contrast was repulsive to him. His family had lost ground. Hell no, his family still owned the niggers, practically. Damned if they did, or he wouldnt have to duck around so. What would they think if they knew? His mother? His sister? He shouldnt mention them, shouldnt think of them in this connection. There in the dusk he blushed at doing so. Fellows about town were all right, but how about his friends up North? He could see them incredible, repulsed. They didnt know. The thought first made him laugh. Then, with their eyes still upon him, he began to feel embarrassed. He felt the need of explaining things to them. Explain hell. They wouldnt understand, and moreover, who ever heard of a Southerner getting on his knees to any Yankee, or anyone. No sir. He was going to see Louisa to-night, and love her. She was lovely—in her way. Nigger way. What way was that? Damned if he knew. Must know. He'd known her long enough to know. Was there something about niggers that you couldnt know? Listening to them at church didnt tell you anything. Looking at them didnt tell you anything. Talking to them didnt tell you anything—unless it was gossip, unless they wanted to talk. Of course, about farming, and licker, and craps—but those werent nigger. Nigger was something more. How much more? Something to be afraid of, more? Hell no. Who ever heard of being afraid of a nigger? Tom Burwell. Cartwell had told him that Tom went with Louisa after she reached home. No sir. No nigger had ever been with his girl. He'd like to see one try. Some position for him to be in. Him, Bob Stone, of the old Stone family, in a scrap with a nigger over a nigger girl. In the good old days . . . Ha! Those were the days. His family had lost ground. Not so much, though. Enough for him to have cut through old Lemon's canefield by way of the woods, that he might meet her. She was worth it. Beautiful nigger gal. Why nigger? Why not, just gal? No, it was because she was a nigger that he went to her. Sweet . . . The scent of boiling cane came to him. Then he saw the rich glow of the stove. He heard the voices of the men circled around it. He was about to skirt the clearing when he heard his own name mentioned. He stopped. Quivering. Leaning against a tree, he listened.

"Bad nigger. Yassur, he sho is one bad nigger when he gets started."

"Tom Burwell's been on th gang[1] three times fo cuttin men."

"What y think he's agwine t do t Bob Stone?"

"Dunno yet. He aint found out. When he does—Baby!"

"Aint no tellin."

"Young Stone aint no quitter an I ken tell y that. Blood of th old uns in his veins."

"Thats right. He'll scrap, sho."

"Be gettin too hot f niggers round this away."

"Shut up, nigger. Y dont know what y talkin bout."

Bob Stone's ears burned as though he had been holding them over the stove. Sizzling heat welled up within him. His feet felt as if they rested on red-hot coals. They stung him to quick movement. He circled the fringe of the

[1]I.e., sentenced to a prison chain gang.

glowing. Not a twig cracked beneath his feet. He reached the path that led to factory town. Plunged furiously down it. Halfway along, a blindness within him veered him aside. He crashed into the bordering canebrake. Cane leaves cut his face and lips. He tasted blood. He threw himself down and dug his fingers in the ground. The earth was cool. Cane-roots took the fever from his hands. After a long while, or so it seemed to him, the thought came to him that it must be time to see Louisa. He got to his feet and walked calmly to their meeting place. No Louisa. Tom Burwell had her. Veins in his forehead bulged and distended. Saliva moistened the dried blood on his lips. He bit down on his lips. He tasted blood. Not his own blood; Tom Burwell's blood. Bob drove through the cane and out again upon the road. A hound swung down the path before him towards factory town. Bob couldnt see it. The dog loped aside to let him pass. Bob's blind rushing made him stumble over it. He fell with a thud that dazed him. The hound yelped. Answering yelps came from all over the countryside. Chickens cackled. Roosters crowed, heralding the bloodshot eyes of southern awakening. Singers in the town were silenced. They shut their windows down. Palpitant between the rooster crows, a chill hush settled upon the huddled forms of Tom and Louisa. A figure rushed from the shadow and stood before them. Tom popped to his feet.

"Whats y want?"

"I'm Bob Stone."

"Yassur—an I'm Tom Burwell. Whats y want?"

Bob lunged at him. Tom side-stepped, caught him by the shoulder, and flung him to the ground. Straddled him.

"Let me up."

"Yassur—but watch yo doins, Bob Stone."

A few dark figures, drawn by the sound of scuffle, stood about them. Bob sprang to his feet.

"Fight like a man, Tom Burwell, an I'll lick y."

Again he lunged. Tom side-stepped and flung him to the ground. Straddled him.

"Get off me, you godam nigger you."

"Yo sho has started somethin now. Get up."

Tom yanked him up and began hammering at him. Each blow sounded as if it smashed into a precious, irreplaceable soft something. Beneath them, Bob staggered back. He reached in his pocket and whipped out a knife.

"Thats my game, sho."

Blue flash, a steel blade slashed across Bob Stone's throat. He had a sweetish sick feeling. Blood began to flow. Then he felt a sharp twitch of pain. He let his knife drop. He slapped one hand against his neck. He pressed the other on top of his head as if to hold it down. He groaned. He turned, and staggered towards the crest of the hill in the direction of white town. Negroes who had seen the fight slunk into their homes and blew the lamps out. Louisa, dazed, hysterical, refused to go indoors. She slipped, crumbled, her body loosely propped against the woodwork of the well. Tom Burwell leaned against it. He seemed rooted there.

Bob reached Broad Street. White men rushed up to him. He collapsed in their arms.

"Tom Burwell. . . ."

White men like ants upon a forage rushed about. Except for the taut hum of their moving, all was silent. Shotguns, revolvers, rope, kerosene, torches. Two high-powered cars with glaring search-lights. They came together. The taut hum rose to a low roar. Then nothing could be heard but the flop of their feet in the thick dust of the road. The moving body of their silence preceded over the crest of the hill into factory town. It flattened the Negroes beneath it. It rolled to the wall of the factory, where it stopped. Tom knew that they were coming. He couldnt move. And then he saw the search-lights of the two cars glaring down on him. A quick shot went through him. He stiffened. He started to run. A yell went up from the mob. Tom wheeled about and faced them. They poured down on him. They swarmed. A large man with dead-white face and flabby cheeks came to him and almost jabbed a gun-barrel through his guts.

"Hands behind y, nigger."

Tom's wrists were bound. The big man shoved him to the well. Burn him over it, and when the woodwork caved in, his body would drop to the bottom. Two deaths for a godam nigger. Louisa was driven back. The mob pushed in. Its pressure, its momentum was too great. Drag him to the factory. Wood and stakes already there. Tom moved in the direction indicated. But they had to drag him. They reached the great door. Too many to get in there. The mob divided and flowed around the walls to either sides. The big man shoved him through the door. The mob pressed in from the sides. Taut humming. No words. A stake was sunk into the ground. Rotting floor boards piled around it. Kerosene poured on the rotting floor boards. Tom bound to the stake. His breast was bare. Nail scratches let little lines of blood trickle down and mat into the hair. His face, his eyes were wet and stony. Except for irregular breathing, one would have thought him already dead. Torches were flung onto the pile. A great flare muffled in black smoke shot upward. The mob yelled. The mob was silent. Now Tom could be seen within the flames. Only his head, erect, lean, like a blackened stone. Stench of burning flesh soaked the air. Tom's eyes popped. His head settled downward. The mob yelled. Its yell echoed against the skeleton stone walls and sounded like a hundred yells. Like a hundred mobs yelling. Its yell thudded against the thick front wall and fell back. Ghost of a yell slipped through the flames and out the great door of the factory. It fluttered like a dying thing down the single street of factory town. Louisa, upon the step before her home, did not hear it, but her eyes opened slowly. They saw the full moon glowing in the great door. The full moon, an evil thing, an omen, soft showering the homes of folks she knew. Where were they, these people? She'd sing, and perhaps they'd come out and join her. Perhaps Tom Burwell would come. At any rate, the full moon in the great door was an omen which she must sing to:

Red nigger moon. Sinner!
Blood-burning moon. Sinner!
Come out that fact'ry door.

1923

Zora Neale Hurston 1891?–1960

Zora Neale Hurston was born in the small town of Notasulga, Alabama, probably in the year 1891. The date is uncertain—in later life she frequently reported her birth year as 1901 or 1903. When she was about three years old her family moved to Eatonville, Florida, the first completely black town to be incorporated in the United States. Her father was a carpenter and a Baptist preacher. He became an important figure in Eatonville and served as mayor. But it was her mother who most influenced Zora Neale Hurston's life. Her mother had been a schoolteacher before her marriage, and she encouraged her daughter to reach out in life, to "jump at the sun."

When Hurston was thirteen, her mother died. Hurston's father, unwilling or unable to care for his daughter, sent her away to live with relatives, passed her "around the family like a bad penny." Life in all-black Eatonville had been idyllic. Now, far from Eatonville, she confronted for the first time the difficulty of growing up black among whites. She attended school and did household chores for her relatives, but when her father suffered financial reverses and could no longer contribute to her care, she was returned home and left to fend for herself.

She found jobs working as a maid. Later she ran off to work as a wardrobe girl with a theatrical group touring Florida and the South. For a time she lived in Baltimore, where she supported herself by working as a waitress while she took high school classes. In 1918, hoping to prepare herself to be a writer, she moved to Washington, D.C. and entered Howard University. She enrolled in literature courses, joined the campus literary club, and published her first short story, "John Redding Goes to Sea," in the Howard University literary journal.

When another of her short stories was published in a New York City magazine, she left Washington, D.C. and moved to New York. She was a woman of high spirits, a born storyteller, and she immediately found a wide circle of friends. With their help she got a job as secretary to the best-selling novelist Fannie Hurst and won a scholarship to Barnard College, of Columbia University, graduating in 1928 with a bachelor's degree in anthropology.

Her class papers had attracted the attention of her anthropology professors, and after graduation she was awarded a fellowship to go back to the South to collect folklore. When she completed her research, she returned to New York City and began writing dramatic sketches based on the material she had collected. In 1932 she produced her own stage review, The Great Day. *The show was a critical success, but it failed to draw audiences large enough to pay its way and soon closed.*

In 1934 her first novel, Jonah's Gourd Vine, *was published. The novel, based on her experiences in Eatonville and on the folklore material she had collected, was a critical and financial success, selected as one of the offerings of the Book of the Month Club. The following year, her publishers, encouraged by the success of* Jonah's Gourd Vine, *brought out a collection of her short writings,* Mules and Men.

In 1936, now a successful writer with a growing reputation as a folklorist, Hurston received a fellowship from the Guggenheim Foundation to support her research. She went to the Caribbean to collect more black folklore, and while there she wrote her second novel, Their Eyes Were Watching God *(1937). Set in Eatonville, the novel told of a young black woman determined to find self-realization and love. It was Zora Neale Hurston's finest novel and brought her wide critical acclaim.*

At the urging of her publishers, she next wrote an autobiography, Dust Tracks on a Road *(1942). It was an award-winning success. But not all reviews were approving. Black activist critics charged that she had neglected the burning issues of racism, that she had failed to deal realistically with minority life in America, that she presented only a "white-washed" picture of American blacks. It is true that her writing did not emphasize the plight of black Americans and the bitterness of their struggle. But her aim was not to report racial tempests or to cry out for social change. She wanted to portray the culture and people of the American South that she knew, to write about human beings not about race: "My interest lies in what makes a man or woman do such-and-so regardless of his color."*

For a brief time during World War II she taught at a black college in Florida while continuing to write fiction. But the tastes of the book-reading public had begun to change, and when she submitted her next novel to her publishers it was rejected. She then changed publishers and submitted the manuscript of a different novel that was published in 1948 as Seraph on the Suwanee. *It received favorable reviews, but to the surprise of Hurston's readers, and to the dismay of her critics, the book was not about blacks but about whites.*

Her career now began its decline. Her best work and her greatest public success had come in the 1930s. Now her manuscripts were increasingly rejected by publishers, and her personal life was shattered when she became the victim of charges (later disproved) that she had molested children. Her "crime" was widely reported in lurid newspaper stories, and Zora Neale Hurston, feeling betrayed by her friends and by the system of legal justice, disappeared, later to be discovered working as a housemaid in Florida.

She continued to write magazine articles on the lives of black men and women in America, and over the years she worked on a novel of the Jews and the biblical Herod, but the manuscript was rejected by every publishing house she sent it to. In her last years she scraped out a living by working as a librarian, as a substitute teacher, and by writing articles for a local weekly newspaper. In 1960 she died, penniless, in a welfare home in Florida.

By the time of her death, Hurston's work had been forgotten; her books had long since gone out of print and could only be found on the back shelves of used book stores. But then in the late 1970s she was rediscovered. Her finest novel, Their Eyes Were Watching God, *was republished. New critical studies of her fiction and biographies appeared that praised her writing and probed the meaning of her stories and the events of her life. Her achievement had been remarkable. She had published more books than any other American black woman, receiving critical and popular acclaim from black and white readers alike. And in recording the lives and the language of black men and women in the American South, she had preserved a part of the black tradition in America that would otherwise have been lost.*

Now, in the twenty-first century, Hurston's popularity is even greater. Her work is widely studied in schools and colleges. Her novels and stories continue to be reprinted in new editions. Even the unpublished manuscripts of her writing have been searched out and printed. And her play, Polk County, *has recently been staged with great success, winning tributes as a dramatic triumph and, from one critic, praise as a playgoer's joyous feast, decorated with "more voodoo, sass, and authentic blues than a fruitcake has chewy bits."*

FURTHER READING: D. Turner, *In a Minor Chord,* 1971; R. Hemenway, *Zora Neale Hurston, A Literary Biography,* 1977; *I Love Myself When I Am Laughing . . . And Then Again When I Am Looking Mean and Impressive: A Zora Neale Hurston Reader,* ed. A. Walker, 1979; L. Howard, *Zora Neale Hurston,* 1980; K. Holloway, *The Character of the Word, The Texts of Zora Neale Hurston,* 1987; M. Awkward, *Inspiriting Influences: Tradition, Revision, and Afro-American Women's Novels,* 1989; M. Lyons, *Sorrow's Kitchen, The Life and Folklore of Zora Neale Hurston,* 1990; *Zora! Zora Neale Hurston, The Woman and Her*

Country, ed. N. Nathiri, 1991; P. Witcover, *Zora Neale Hurston,* 1991; J. Yates, *Zora Neale Hurston, A Story Teller's Life,* 1991; D. Plant, *Every Tub Must Sit on Its Own Bottom, The Philosophy and Politics of Zora Neale Hurston,* 1995; C. Wall, *Women of the Harlem Renaissance,* 1995; T. Harris, *The Power of the Porch, The Story Teller's Craft in Zora Neale Hurston,* 1996; L. Hill, *Social Rituals and the Verbal Art of Zora Neale Hurston,* 1996; *Critical Essays on Zora Neale Hurston,* ed. G. Cronin, 1998; *Zora Neale Hurston's Their Eyes Were Watching God: A Casebook,* ed. C. Wall, 2000; *Zora Neale Hurston, Every Tongue Got to Confess: Negro Folk-Tales from the Gulf States,* ed. C. Kaplan, 2001; *Zora Neale Hurston: A Life in Letters,* ed. C. Kaplan, 2001; V. Boyd, *Wrapped in Rainbows: The Life of Zora Neale Hurston,* 2002; V. Boyd, *Wrapped in Rainbows, The Life of Zora Neale Hurston,* 2003; M. West, *Zora Neale Hurston and American Literary Culture,* 2005; T. Patterson, *Zora Neale Hurston and a History of Southern Life,* 2005.

TEXT: *The Stylus,* 1921.

JOHN REDDING GOES TO SEA

The Villagers said that John Redding was a queer child. His mother thought he was too. She would shake her head sadly, and observe to John's father, "Alf, it's too bad our boy's got a spell on him." The father always met this lament with indifference, if not impatience.

"Aw, woman, stop dat talk 'bout conjure.[1] 'Taint so nohow. Ah doan want Jawn tuh git dat foolishness in him."

"Case you allus tries tuh know mo' than me, but Ah aint so ign'rant. Ah knows a heap mahseff. Many and manys the people been drove outa their senses by conjuration, or rid tuh deat' by witches."

"Ah keep on telling yur, woman, taint so. B'lieve it all you wants tuh, but dontcher tell mah son none of it."

Perhaps ten-year old John was puzzling to the simple folk there in the Florida woods, for he was an imaginative child and fond of day-dreams. The St. John river flowed a scarce three hundred feet from his back door. On its banks at this point grow numerous palms, luxuriant magnolias and bay trees with a dense undergrowth of ferns, cat-tails and rope-grass. On the bosom of the stream float millions of delicately colored hyacinths. The little brown boy loved to wander down to the water's edge and cast in dry twigs, and watch them sail away down stream to Jacksonville, the sea, and the wide world and John Redding wanted to follow them.

Sometimes in his dreams he was a prince, riding away in a gorgeous carriage. Often he was a knight bestride a fiery charger prancing down the white shellroad that led to distant lands. At other times he was a steamboat Captain piloting his craft down the St. John river to where the sky seemed to touch the water. No matter what he dreamed or whom he fancied himself to be, he always ended by riding away to the horizon, for in his childish ignorance he thought this to be farthest land.

But these twigs, which John called his ships, did not always sail away. Sometimes they would be swept in among the weeds growing in the shallow water, and be held there. One day his father came upon him scolding the weeds for stopping his sea-going vessels.

[1]Voodoo, spell casting.

"Let go mah ships! you old mean weeds, you!" John screamed and stamped impotently, "They wants tuh go 'way, you let 'em go on."

Alfred laid his hand on his son's head lovingly. "What's mattah, son?"

"Mah ships, Pa," the child answered weeping. "Ah throwed 'em in to go way off an them ole weeds won't let 'em."

"Well, well, doan cry. Ah thought youse uh grown up man. Men doan cry lak babies. You mustn't take it too hard bout yo ships. You gotter git uster things gitten tied up. They's lotsa folks that 'ud go on off too ef something didn' ketch 'em and hol' em!"

Alfred Redding's brown face grew wistful for a moment, and the child noticing it asked quickly, "Do weeds tangle up folks too, Pa?"

"Now, now chile, doan be takin' too much stock of what ah say. Ah talks in parables sometimes. Come on, le's go on tuh supper."

Alf took his son's hand, and started slowly toward the house. Soon John broke the silence.

"Pa, when ah gets as big as you ah'm goin' farther than them ships. Ah'm going to where the sky touches the ground."

"Well, son, when ah waz a boy, ah said ah wuz going too, but heah ah am. Ah hopes you have better luck than I had."

"Pa, ah betcher ah seen something in th' wood that you ain't seen."

"What?"

"See dat tallest pine tree ovah dere how it looks like a skull wid a crown on!"

"Yes, indeed," said the father looking toward the tree designated, "It do look lak a skull since you call mah 'tention to it. You 'magine lotser things nobody else evah did, son."

"Sometimes, Pa, dat ole tree waves at me just after th' sun goes down, an' makes me sad an' skeered too."

"Ah specks youse skeered of de dahk, thas all, sonny. When you gits biggah you wont think of sich."

Hand in hand these two trudged across the plowed land and up to the house—the child dreaming of the days when he should wander to far countries, and the man of the days when he might have—and thus they entered the kitchen.

Matty Redding, John's mother, was setting the table for supper. She was a small wiry woman with large eyes that might have been beautiful when she was young, but too much weeping had left them watery and weak.

"Matty," Alf began as he took his place at the table, "dontcher know our boy is different from any othah chile roun' heah. He 'lows he's goin to sea when he gits grown, and ah reckon ah'll let 'im."

The woman turned from the stove, skillet in hand. "Alf, you aint gone crazy is you? John kaint help wantin tuh stray off, cause he's got a spell on 'im, but you oughter be shamed to be encouragin' 'im."

"Aint ah done tole you forty times not tuh tawk dat low-life mess in front of mah boy?"

"Well, if taint no conjure in de world, how come Mitch Potts been layin' on his back six mont's an' de doctah kaint do 'im no good? Answer me dat. The very night John wuz bawn, Granny seed ole witch Judy Davis creepin outer dis yahd. You knows she had swore tuh fix me fuh marryin' you way from her darter Edna. She put travel dust down fuh mah chile, dats what she done, to make him walk 'way fum me. An' evah sence he's been able tuh crawl, he's been tryin' tuh go."

"Matty, a man doan need no travel dust tuh make 'im wanter hit de road. It jes comes natcheral fuh er man tuh travel. Dey all wants tuh go at some time or other but they kaint all git away. Ah wants mah John tuh go an' see, cause ah wanted to go mahself. When he comes back ah kin see them furrin places wid his eyes. He kaint help wantin tuh go cause he's a man chile."

Mrs. Redding promptly went off into a fit of weeping but the man and boy ate supper unmoved. Twelve years of married life had taught Alfred that, far from being miserable when she wept, his wife was enjoying a bit of self-pity.

Thus John Redding grew to manhood, playing, studying and dreaming. He attended the village school as did most of the youth about him, but he also went to high school at the county seat where none of the villagers went. His father shared his dreams and ambitions, but his mother could not understand why he should wish to go to strange places where neither she nor his father had been. No one of their community had ever been farther away than Jacksonville. Few, indeed, had ever been there. Their own gardens, general store, and occasional trips to the County seat—seven miles away—sufficed for all their needs. Life was simple indeed with these folk.

John was the subject of much discussion among the country folk. Why didn't he teach school instead of thinking about strange places and people? Did he think himself better than any of the belles thereabout that he would not go a courting any of them? He must be "fixed" as his mother claimed, else where did his queer notions come from? Well, he was always queer, and one could not expect the man to be different from the child. They never failed to stop work at the approach of Alfred in order to be at the fence to inquire after John's health and ask when he expected to leave.

"Oh," Alfred would answer, "yes, as soon as his ma gets reconciled to th' notion. He's a mighty dutiful boy, mah John is. He doan wanna hurt her feelings."

The boy had on several occasions attempted to reconcile his mother to the notion, but found it a difficult task. Matty always took refuge in self-pity and tears. Her son's desires were incomprehensible to her, that was all. She did not want to hurt him. It was love, mother love, that made her cling so desperately to John.

"Lawd knows," she would sigh, "Ah nevah wuz happy an' nevah specks tuh be."

"An from yo actions," put in Alfred hotly, "you's determined not to be."

"Thas right, Alfred, go on an' 'buse me. You allus does. Ah knows Ah'm ign'rant an' all dat, but dis is mah son. Ah bred an' born 'im. He kain't help from wantin' to go rovin' cause travel dust been put down fuh him. But mabbe we kin cure 'im by disincouragin' the idea."

"Well, ah wants mah son tuh go, an' he wants tuh go too. He's a man now, Matty, an' we mus let John hoe his own row. If it's travelin', 'twont be for long. He'll come back to us bettah than when he went off. Anyhow he'll learn dat folks is human all ovah de world. Dats worth a lot to know, an' it's worth going a long way tuh fin out. What do you say, son?"

"Mama," John began slowly, "It hurts me to see you so troubled over my going away, but I feel that I must go. I'm stagnating here. This indolent atmosphere will stifle every bit of ambition that's in me. Let me go, Mama, please.

What is there here for me? Give me two or three years to look around and I will be back here with you and papa, and I'll never leave you again. Mama, please let me go."

"Now, John, its bettah for you to stay heah and take over the school. Why wont you marry and settle down?"

"I'm sorry Mama that you won't consent. I am going, nevertheless."

"John, John, mah baby! You wouldn't kill yo' po' ole mama, would you? Come kiss me, Son."

The boy flung his arms about his mother and held her closely while she sobbed on his breast. To all of her pleas, however, he answered that he must go.

"I'll stay at home this year, Mama, then I'll go for a while, but it won't be long. I'll come back and make you and Papa oh so happy. Do you agree, Mama dear?"

"Ah reckon t'aint nothin' 'tall fuh me to do else."

Things went on very well around the Reddings home for some time. During the day John helped his father about the farm and read a great deal at night.

Then the unexpected happened. John married Stella Kanty, a neighbor's daughter. The courtship was brief but ardent—on John's part at least. He danced with Stella at a candy-pulling, walked with her home and in three weeks had declared himself. Mrs. Redding declared that she was happier than she had ever been in her life. She therefore indulged in a whole afternoon of weeping. John's change was occasioned possibly by the fact that Stella was really beautiful, he was young and red-blooded, and the time was spring.

Spring time in Florida is not a matter of peeping violets or bursting buds merely. It is a riot of color, in nature—glistening green leaves, pink, blue, purple, yellow blossoms that fairly stagger the visitor from the north. The miles of hyacinths are like an undulating carpet on the surface of the river and divide reluctantly when the slow-moving alligators push their way loglike across. The nights are white nights for the moon shines with dazzling splendor, or in the absence of that goddess, the soft darkness creeps down laden with innumerable scents. The heavy fragrance of magnolias mingled with the delicate sweetness of jasmine and wild roses.

If time and propinquity conquered John, what then? These forces have overcome older men.

The raptures of the first few weeks over, John began to saunter out to the gate to gaze wistfully down the white dusty road, or to wander again to the river as he had done in childhood. To be sure he did not send forth twigships any longer, but his thoughts would in spite of himself, stray down river to Jacksonville, the sea, the wide world—and poor home-tied John Redding wanted to follow them.

He grew silent and pensive. Matty accounted for this by her ever-ready explanation of conjuration. Alfred said nothing, but smoked and puttered about the barn more than ever. Stella accused her husband of indifference and pouting. At last John decided to bring matters to a head and broached the subject to his wife.

"Stella, dear, I want to go roving about the world for a spell, would you stop here with Papa and Mama and wait for me to come back?"

"John, is you crazy sho 'nuff? If you don't want me, say so, and I kin go home to mah folks."

"Stella, darling, I do want you, but I want to go away too. I can have both if you'll let me. We'll be so happy when I return."

Now, John, you cain't push me off one side like that. You didn't hafta marry me. There's a plenty others that would hev been glad enuff tuh get me. You know ah want educated befo han'."

"Don't make me too conscious of my weakness, Stella. I know I should never have married with my inclinations, but its done now. No use to talk about what is past. I love you and want to keep you, but I can't stifle that longing for the open road, rolling seas, for peoples and countries I have never seen. I'm suffering, too, Stella, I'm paying for my rashness in marrying before I was ready. I'm not trying to shirk my duty—you'll be well taken care of in the meanwhile."

"John, folks allus said you was queer and tol' me not to marry yuh, but ah jes loved yuh so ah couldn't help it, an now to think you wants tuh sneak off an' leave me."

"But I'm coming back, darling. Listen, Stella——— " But the girl would not. Matty came in and Stella fell into her arms weeping. John's mother immediately took up arms against him. The two women carried on such an effective war against him for the next few days that finally Alfred was forced to take his son's part.

"Matty, let dat boy alone ah tell yuh! Ef he wuz uh homeboddy he'd be drove 'way by you-all's racket."

"Well, Alf, dats all we po' wommen kin do. We wants our husbands an' our sons. John's got a wife now, an' he ain't got no business to be talkin' bout goin' nowhere. I 'lowed dat marryin' Stella would settle him."

"Yas, das all you wimmen study 'bout—settlin' some man. You takes all de get-up out of 'em. Jes let uh fellah mak a motion lak gettin' somewhere an' some 'oman'll begin tuh hollah 'Stop theah! Wheres you goin'? don't fuhgit you b'long tuh me!'"

"My Gawd! Alf! What you reckon Stella's gwine do? Let John walk off an leave huh?"

"Naw. Git outer huh foolishness an' go 'long wid him. He'd take huh."

"Stella ain't got no call tuh go crazy 'cause John is. She ain't no woman tuh be floppin' roun' from place tuh place lak some uh dese reps follerin' uh section gang."

The man turned abruptly from his wife and stood in the kitchen door. A blue haze hung over the river and Alfred's attention seemed fixed upon this. In reality his thoughts were turned inward. He was thinking of the numerous occasions upon which he and his son had sat on the fallen log at the edge of the water and talked of John's proposed travels. He had encouraged his son, given him every advantage his poor circumstances would permit. And now John was home-tied.

The young man suddenly turned the corner of the house and approached his father.

"Hello, Papa."

"'Lo, Son."

"Where's Mama and Stella?"

The older man merely jerked his thumb toward the interior of the house and once more gazed pensively toward the river. John entered the kitchen and kissed his mother fondly.

"Great news, Mama."

"What now."

"Got a chance to join the Navy, Mama, and go all around the world. Ain't that grand!"

"John, you shorely ain't gointer leave me and Stella, is yuh?"

"Yes, I think I am, I know how both of you feel, but I know how I feel also. You preach to me the gospel of self-sacrifice for the happiness of others, but you are unwilling to practice any of it yourself. Stella can stay here—I am going to support her and spend all the time I can with her. I am going; that's settled, but I want to go with your blessing. I want to do something worthy of a strong man. I have done nothing so far but look to you and papa for everything. Let me learn to strive and think—in short, be a man."

"Naw, John, Ah'll nevah give mah consent. I know you's hard headed jes lak you paw, but if you leave dis place ovah mah head, ah never wants you tuh come back heah no mo. Ef I wuz laid on de coolin' board, ah doan' want yuh standin' ovah me, young man. Doan never come neah mah grave, you ongrateful wretch!"

Mrs Redding arose and flung out of the room. For once, she was too incensed to cry. John stood in his tracks, his eyes dilated with terror at his mother's pronouncement. Alfred, too, was moved. Mrs. Redding banged the bed-room door violently and startled John slightly. Alfred took his son's arm saying softly, "Come, son, let's go down to the river."

At the water's edge they halted for a short space before seating themselves on the log. The sun was setting in a purple cloud. Hundreds of mosquito hawks darted here and there, catching gnats and being themselves caught by the lightning-swift bull-bats. John abstractedly snapped in two the stalk of a slender young bamboo. Taking no note of what he was doing, he broke it into short lengths and tossed them singly into the stream. The old man watched him silently for a while, but finally he said, "Oh, yes, my boy, some ships get tangled in the weeds."

"Yes, Papa, they certainly do; I guess I'm beaten—might as well surrender."

"Nevah say die. Yuh nevah kin tell what will happen."

"What can happen? I have courage enough to make things happen, but what can I do against Mama! What man wants to go on a long journey with his mother's curses ringing in his ears? She doesn't understand. I'll wait another year, but I am going because I must."

Alfred threw an arm around his son's neck and drew him nearer but quickly removed it. Both men instantly drew apart—ashamed for having been so demonstrative. The father looked off to the wood-lot and asked with a reminiscent smile, "Son, do you remember showing me the tree dat looked lak a skeleton head?"

"Yes, I do. It's there still. I look at it sometimes when things have become too painful for me at the house, and I run down here to cool off and think."

"You wuz always imaginin' things, John, things that nobody else evah thought on."

"Oh, yes, I'm a dreamer. I have such wonderfully complete dreams, Papa. They never come true. But even as my dreams fade, I have others."

The men arose without more conversation. Possibly they feared to trust themselves to speech. As they walked leisurely toward the house Alfred remarked the freshness of the breeze.

"It's about time the rains set in," added his son. "The year is wearin' on."

After a gloomy supper, John strolled out into the spacious front yard and seated himself beneath a China-berry tree. The breeze had grown a trifle stronger since sunset and continued from the southwest. Matty and Stella sat on the deep front porch, but Alfred joined John under the tree. The family was divided into two armed camps and the hostilities had reached that stage where no quarter could be asked or given.

About nine o'clock an automobile came flying down the dusty white road and halted at the gate. A white man slammed the gate and hurried up the walk towards the house, but stopped abruptly before the men beneath the China-berry tree. It was Mr. Hill, the builder of the new bridge that spanned the river.

"Howdy John, howdy Alf, I'm mighty glad I found you; I am in trouble."

"Well, now, Mist' Hill," answered Alfred slowly but pleasantly, "we'se glad you foun' us too. What trouble could you be having now?"

"It's the bridge. The weather bureau says that the rains will be upon us in forty-eight hours. If it catches the bridge as it is now, I'm afraid all my work of the past five months will be swept away, to say nothing of half a million of dollars' worth of labor and material. I've got all my men at work now and I thought to get as many extra hands as I could to help out tonight and tomorrow. We can make her weather tight in that time if I can get about twenty more."

"I'll go Mister Hill," said John with a great deal of energy. "I don't want papa out on that bridge—too dangerous."

"Good for you, John!" cried the white man. "Now if I had a few more men of your brawn, I could build an entirely new bridge in forty-eight hours. Come on and jump into the car. I am taking the men down as I find them."

"Wait a minute. I must put on my blue-jeans. I won't be long."

John arose and strode to the house. He knew that his mother and wife had overheard everything, but he paused for a moment to speak to them.

"Mama, I am going to work all night on the bridge."

There was no answer. He turned to his wife.

"Stella, don't be lonesome, I'll be home at daybreak."

His wife was as silent as his mother. John stood for a moment on the steps, then resolutely strode past the women and into the house. A few minutes later he emerged clad in his blue jeans and brogans.[2] This time he said nothing to the silent figures rocking back and forth on the porch. But when he was a few feet from the steps he called back, "Bye, Mama, bye Stella," and hurried on down the walk to where his father sat.

"So long, Papa, I'll be home around seven."

Alfred roused himself and stood. Placing both hands upon his son's broad shoulders he said softly, "Be keerful, son, don't fall or nothin'."

"I will, Papa. Don't you get into a quarrel on my account."

John hurried on to the waiting car and was whirled away.

[2]Heavy, high-topped work shoes.

Alfred sat for a long time beneath the tree where his son had left him and smoked on. The women soon went in doors. On the night breeze were borne the mingled scents of jasmine, of roses, of damp earth, of the river, of the pine forest near by. A solitary whip-poor-will sent forth his plaintive call from the nearby shrubbery. A giant owl hooted and screeched from the wood lot. The calf confined in the barn bleated and was answered by his mother's sympathetic "Moo" from the pen.

Around ten o'clock the breeze freshened, growing stiffer until midnight when it became a gale. Alfred fastened the doors and bolted the wooden shutters at the windows. The three persons sat about a round table in the kitchen upon which stood a bulky kerosene lamp, flickering and sputtering in the wind that came through the numerous cracks in the walls. The wind rushed down the chimney blowing puffs of ashes about the room. It banged the cooking utensils on the walls. The drinking gourd hanging outside the door played a weird tattoo, hollow and unearthly, against the thin wooden wall.

The man and the women sat silently. Even if there had been no storm they would not have talked. They could not go to bed because the women were afraid to retire during a storm and the man wished to stay awake and think of his son. Thus they sat: the women hot with resentment toward the man and terrified by the storm, the man hardly mindful of the tempest, but eating his heart out in pity for his boy. Time wore heavily on.

And now a new element of terror was added. A screech-owl alighted on the roof and shivered forth his doleful cry. Possibly he had been blown out of his nest by the wind. Matty started up at the sound but fell back in her chair pale as death. "My Gawd!" she gasped, "dat's a sho' sound of death."

Stella hurriedly thrust her hand into the salt jar and threw some into the chimney of the lamp. The color of the flame changed from yellow to blue-green, but this burning of salt did not have the desired effect—to drive away the bird from the roof. Matty slipped out of her blue calico wrapper and turned it wrong side out before replacing it. Even Alfred turned one sock.

"Alf," said Matty, "what do you reckon's gonna happen from this?":

"How do ah know, Matty?"

"Ah wisht John hadner went way from heah tuh night."

"Huh."

Outside the tempest raged. The palms rattled dryly, and the giant pines groaned and sighed in the grip of the wind. Flying leaves and pine-mast filled the air. Now and then a brilliant flash of lightening disclosed a bird being blown here and there with the wind. The prodigious roar of the thunder seemed to rock the earth. Black clouds hung so low that the tops of the pines among them moaned slowly before the wind and made the darkness awful. The screech-owl continued his tremulous cry.

The wind ceased and the rain commenced. Huge drops clattered down upon the shingle roof like buckshot and ran from the eaves in torrents. It entered the house through the cracks in the walls and under the doors. It was a deluge in volume and force, but subsided before morning. The sun came up brightly on the havoc of the wind and rain, calling forth millions of feathered creatures. The white sand everywhere was full of tiny cups dug out by the force of the falling rain drops. The rims of the little depressions crunched noisily underfoot.

At daybreak Mr. Redding set out for the bridge. He was uneasy. On arriving he found that the river had risen twelve feet during the cloudburst and was still rising. The slow St. John[3] was swollen far beyond its banks and rushing on to sea like a mountain stream, sweeping away houses, great blocks of earth, cattle, trees, in short, anything that came within its grasp. Even the steel framework of the new bridge was gone.

The siren of the fibre factory was tied down for half an hour, announcing the disaster to the countryside. When Alfred arrived therefore he found nearly all the men of the district there.

The river, red and swollen, was full of floating debris. Huge trees were swept along as relentlessly as chicken coops and fence rails. Some steel piles were all that was left of the bridge.

Alfred went down to a group of men who were fishing members of the ill-fated construction gang out of the water. Many were able to swim ashore unassisted. Wagons backed up and were hurriedly driven away loaded with wet, shivering men. Two men had been killed outright; others seriously wounded. Three men had been drowned. At last all had been accounted for except John Redding. His father ran here and there, asking for him or calling him. No one knew where he was. No one remembered seeing him since daybreak.

Dozens of women had arrived at the scene of the disaster by this time. Matty and Stella, wrapped in woolen shawls, were among them. They rushed to Alfred in alarm and asked where was John.

"Ah doan' know," answered Alfred impatiently, "that's what ah'm tryin' to fin' out now."

"Do you reckon he's run away?" asked Stella thoughtlessly.

"Naw," she answered sternly, "he ain't no sneak."

The father turned to Fred Mimms, one of the survivors, and asked him where John was and how had the bridge been destroyed.

"You see," said Mimms, "when dat terrible win' come up we wuz out 'bout de middle of the river. Some of us wuz on de bridge, some on de derrick. De win' blowed so hahd we could skeercely stan'; and Mist' Hill tol' us tuh set down fuh a speel. He's afraid some of us mought go over board. Den all of a sudden de lights went out—guess de wires wuz blown down. We wuz all skeered tuh move for slippin' overboard. Den dat rain commenced—and ah nevah seed such a downpour since the flood. We set dere an' someone begins tuh pray. Lawd, how we did pray tuh be spared! Den somebody raised a song and we sung, you hear me. We sung from the bottom of our hearts till daybreak. When the first light come we couldn't see nothin' but fog everywhere. You couldn't tell which wuz water an' which wuz lan'. But when de sun come up de fog began to lift, and we could see de water. Dat fog was so thick an' so heavy dat it wuz huggin' dat river lak a windin' sheet. And when it rose we saw dat de river had rose way up durin' the rain. My Gawd, Alf, it was running high—so high it nearly teched de bridge an' red as blood, so much clay, you know, from lan' she done overflowed. Coming down stream, as fast as 'press train was three big pine trees. De fust one wasn't forty feet from us and there wasn't no chance to do nothin' but pray. De fust one struck us and shock de whole works, an' befo it could stop shakin' the other two hit us an' down we went. Ah thought ah'd never see home again."

"But, Mimms, where's John?"

"Ah ain't seen him, Alf, since de logs struck us. Mebbe he's swum ashore, mebbe dey picked him up. What's dat floatin' way out dere in de water?"

[3]River in northeast Florida.

Alfred shaded his eyes with his guarded brown hand, and gazed out into the stream. Sure enough there was a man floating on a piece of timber. He lay prone upon his back. His arms were outstretched and the water washed over his brogans, but his feet were lifted out of the water whenever the timber was buoyed up by the stream. His blue overalls were nearly torn from his body. A heavy piece of steel or timber had struck him in falling, for his left side was laid open by the thrust. A great jagged hole, wherein the double fists of a man might be thrust, could plainly be seen from the shore. The man was John Redding.

Everyone seemed to see him at once. Stella fell to the wet earth in a faint. Matty clung to her husband's arm, weeping hysterically. Alfred stood very erect with his wife clinging tearfully to him, but he said nothing. A single tear hung on his lashes for a time, then trickled slowly down his wrinkled brown cheek.

"Alf! Alf!" screamed Matty, "Dere's our son. Ah knowed when ah heard dat owl las' night."

"Ah see 'im Matty," returned her husband softly.

"Why is yuh standin' heah? Go git mah boy."

The men were manning a boat to rescue the remains of John Redding when Alfred spoke again.

"Mah po boy, his dreams never come true."

"Alf," complained Matty, "why doan't-cher hurry an' git my boy. Doan't-cher see he's floatin' on off?"

Her husband paid her no attention, but addressed himself to the rescue party.

"You all stop. Leave my boy go on. Doan stop 'im. He wants tuh go. Ah'm happy 'cause dis mawnin' mah boy is going tuh sea, he's goin' tuh sea."

Out on the bosom of the river, bobbing up and down as if waving goodbye, John Redding floated away toward Jacksonville, the sea, the wide world—at last.

1921

Thomas Wolfe 1900–1938

Thomas Wolfe was born in Asheville, North Carolina, the youngest of eight children. His father was a stonecutter, fond of Shakespeare and rhetoric, and he saw to it that his precocious son, Tom, unlike the other poor children of that rural region, was educated in a private school, where his writing talent was first recognized and encouraged. Thomas Wolfe went on to the University of North Carolina and, after graduation, to Harvard, where he developed his literary talents by studying playwriting, and after two years at Harvard, received an M.A. degree.

From Harvard, Wolfe moved to New York, where he taught at New York University. But a trip to Europe begun in the fall of 1924 interrupted his teaching career and led to crucial events in his development as a writer: After a memorable year in Europe, he met on the return voyage Aline Bernstein, a married woman eighteen years older than Wolfe. She became Wolfe's confidante, editor, and inspiration. With her emotional and financial support he completed Look Homeward, Angel, *his first novel. It was submitted to Scribner's in 1929, where it was read by Maxwell Perkins, who was also the editor of Fitzgerald and Hemingway. Working closely with Perkins, Wolfe revised the manuscript, and it was published in October 1929.*

The novel, which corresponds closely to the experiences of Wolfe's first twenty years, was a critical success, and it was singled out for particular praise in 1930 by Sinclair Lewis in his Nobel Prize acceptance speech. The only people who did not like the book, it seemed, were the inhabitants of Wolfe's hometown who felt insulted by their portraits in a novel drawn so clearly from Wolfe's own background. In 1935, again with substantial help from Perkins, Wolfe published Of Time and the River, *which is in effect a sequel to his first book. It continued the story of Eugene Gant, Wolfe's own fictional equivalent. But the book met with less critical favor than* Look Homeward, Angel. *Reviewers objected to the biographical basis and the formlessness of the novel. Barnard De Voto, a noted critic of American literature, was concise: Wolfe may be a genius, but "genius is not enough." Perhaps more significant for Wolfe than the mixed reviews was the fact that he broke with his editor, Perkins, and his publisher, Scribner's.*

Fortunately for Wolfe, he soon established a similar relationship with Edward Aswell, an editor at Harper and Brothers, and in 1938 he delivered an enormous manuscript of nearly a million words. While Aswell was editing the manuscript, Wolfe went on a tour of the western United States. There he contracted pneumonia. Subsequently it was discovered that he was suffering from tuberculosis of the brain. He returned to the East, to Baltimore, where he died on September 15, 1938. He was thirty-seven.

From the mass of material Wolfe had left behind, his editor fashioned three posthumously published books: the novels The Web and the Rock (*1939*) *and* You Can't Go Home Again (*1940*), *and a compilation of sketches, fiction, and drama,* The Hills Beyond (*1941*). *Like the earlier novels they reveal Wolfe's strengths and weaknesses. His creative energy made his writing rich with vitality and human sensations; at the same time, this energy was so uncontrolled and excessive as to overwhelm his novels with undigested experiences and ill-defined ideas. In places his work shines with passion, excitement, the joys of life. In others it is dulled by insistent emotional pleading, by intensity without respite.*

He attempted a great task: He wished to discover "an entire universe" and "a complete language"; he wanted to portray the wide range of the American experience, and to that end he planned an elaborate, structured, myth-laden series of works spanning the history of America. But death came too soon, and today Thomas Wolfe is best remembered as the author of a few formless but powerful novels. Yet his work also includes essays, plays, and short stories, and it is paradoxical that in such shorter works, where the limitations of space and time impose a need for restraint and control, Wolfe achieves some of his best work, marked by vitality and power, and with clear insight into the turbulence and the breadth of American life.

FURTHER READING: *The Letters of Thomas Wolfe,* ed. E. Nowell, 1956; *The World of Thomas Wolfe,* ed. C. Holman, 1962; *The Letters of Thomas Wolfe to His Mother,* ed. C. Holman and S. Ross, 1968; *Thomas Wolfe, Three Decades of Criticism,* ed. L. Field, 1968; *The Notebooks of Thomas Wolfe,* 2 vols., ed. R. Kennedy and P. Reeves, 1970; *Thomas Wolfe, The Critical Reception,* ed. P. Reeves, 1974; *The Loneliness at the Core, Studies in Thomas Wolfe,* ed. C. Holman, 1975; L. Gurko, *Thomas Wolfe, Beyond the Romantic Ego,* 1975; E. Evans, *Thomas Wolfe,* 1984; *Critical Essays on Thomas Wolfe,* ed. S. Phillipson, 1985; D. Donald, *Look Homeward, A Life of Thomas Wolfe,* 1987; J. Idol, *A Thomas Wolfe Companion,* 1987; L. Field, *Thomas Wolfe and His Editors,* 1987; C. Johnston, *Of Time and the Artist,* 1996; S. Holliday, *Thomas Wolfe and the Politics of Modernism,* 2001; R. Ensign, *Lean Down Your Ear upon the Earth, and Listen, Thomas Wolfe's Greener Modernism,* 2003.

TEXT: *From Death to Morning,* 1935.

ONLY THE DEAD KNOW BROOKLYN

Dere's no guy livin' dat known Brooklyn t'roo an' t'roo, because it'd take a guy a lifetime just to find his way aroun' duh f—— town.

So like I say, I'm waitin' for my train t' come when I sees dis big guy standin' deh—dis is duh foist I eveh see of him. Well, he's lookin' wild, y' know, an' I can see dat he's had plenty, but still he's holdin' it; he talks good an' is walkin' straight enough. So den, dis big guy steps up to a little guy dat's standin' deh, an' says, "How d'yuh get t' eighteent' Avenoo an' Sixty-sevent' Street?" he says.

"Jesus! Yuh got me, chief," duh little guy says to him. "I ain't been heah long myself. Where is duh place?" he says. "Out in duh Flatbush section somewhere?"

"Nah," duh big guy says. "It's out in Bensonhoist. But I was neveh deh befoeh. How d'yuh get deh?"

"Jesus," duh little guy says, scratchin' his head, y'know—yuh could see duh little guy didn't know his way about—"yuh got me, chief. I neveh hoid of it. Do any of youse guys know where it is?" he says to me.

"Sure," I says. "It's out in Bensonhoist. Yuh take duh Fourt' Avenoo express, get off at Fifty-nint' Street, change to a Sea Beach local deh, get off at Eighteent' Avenoo an' Sixty-toid, an' den walk down foeh blocks. Dat's all yuh got to do," I says.

"G'wan!" some wise guy dat I neveh seen befoeh pipes up. "Whatcha talkin' about?" he says—oh, he was wise, y'know. "Duh guy is crazy! I tell yuh what yuh do," he says to duh big guy. "Yuh change to duh West End line at Toity-sixt'," he tells him. "Get off at Noo Utrecht an' Sixteent' Avenoo," he says. "Walk two blocks oveh, foeh blocks up," he says, "an' you'll be right deh." Oh, a *wise* guy, y'know.

"Oh, yeah?" I says. "Who told *you* so much?" He got me sore because he was so wise about it. "How long you been livin' heah?" I says.

"All my life," he says. "I was bawn in Williamsboig," he says. "An' I can tell you t'ings about dis town you neveh hoid of," he says.

"Yeah?" I says.

"Yeah," he says.

"Well, den, you can tell me t'ings about dis town dat nobody else has eveh hoid of, either. Maybe you make it all up yoehself at night," I says, "befoeh you go to sleep—like cuttin' out papeh dolls, or somp'n."

"Oh, yeah?" he says. "You're pretty wise, ain't yuh?"

"Oh, I don't know," I says. "Duh boids ain't usin my head for Lincoln's statue yet," I says. "But I'm wise enough to know a phony when I see one."

"Yeah?" he says. "A wise guy, huh? Well, you're so wise dat some one's goin' t'bust yuh one right on duh snoot some day," he says. "Dat's how wise *you* are."

Well, my train was comin', or I'da smacked him den and dere, but when I seen duh train was comin', all I said was, "All right, mugg! I'm sorry I can't stay to take keh of you, but I'll be seein' yuh sometime, I hope, out in duh cemetery." So den I says to duh big guy, who'd been standin' deh all duh time, "You come wit me," I says. So when we gets onto duh train I says to him, "Where yuh goin' out in Bensonhoist?" I says. "What numbeh are yuh lookin' for?" I says. *You* know—I t'ought if he told me duh address I might be able to help him out.

"Oh," he says, "I'm not lookin' for no one. I don't know no one out deh."

"Then whatcha goin' out deh for?" I says.

"Oh," duh guy says, "I'm just goin' out to see duh place," he says. "I like duh sound of duh name—Bensonhoist, y'know—so I t'ought I'd go out an' have a look at it."

"Whatcha tryin' t'hand me?" I says. "Whatcha tryin' t'do—kid me?" *You* know, I t'ought duh guy was bein' wise wit me.

"No," he says, "I'm tellin' yuh duh troot. I like to go out an' take a look at places wit nice names like dat. I like to go out an' look at all kinds of places," he says.

"How'd yuh know deh was such a place," I says, "if yuh neveh been deh befoeh?"

"Oh," he says, "I got a map."

"A *map?*" I says.

"Sure," he says, "I got a map dat ells me about all dese places. I take it wit me every time I come out heah," he says.

And Jesus! Wit dat, he pulls it out of his pocket, an' so help me, but he's *got* it—he's tellin' duh troot—a big map of duh whole f—— place with all duh different pahts mahked out. You know—Canarsie an' East Noo Yawk an' Flatbush, Bensonhoist, Sout' Brooklyn, duh Heights, Bay Ridge, Greenpernt—duh whole goddam layout, he's got it right deh on duh map.

"You been to any of dose places?" I says.

"Sure," he says, "I been to most of 'em. I was down in Red Hook just last night," he says.

"Jesus! Red Hook!" I says. "Whatcha do down deh?"

"Oh," he says, "nuttin' much. I just walked aroun'. I went into a coupla places an' had a drink," he says, "but most of the time I just walked aroun'."

"Just walked aroun'?" I says.

"Sure," he says, "just lookin' at t'ings, y'know."

"Oh," he says, "I don't know duh name of duh place, but I could find it on my map," he says. "One time I was walkin' across some big fields where deh ain't no houses," he says, "but I could see ships oveh deh all lighted up. Dey was loadin'. So I walks across duh fields," he says, "to where duh ships are."

"Sure," I says, "I know where you was. You was down to duh Erie Basin."

"Yeah," he says, "I guess dat was it. Dey had some of dose big elevators an' cranes an' dey was loadin' ships, an' I could see some ships in drydock all lighted up, so I walks across duh fields to where dey are," he says.

"Den what did yuh do?" I says.

"Oh," he says, "nuttin' much. I came on back across duh fields after a while an' went into a coupla places an' had a drink."

"Didn't nuttin' happen while yuh was in dere?" I says.

"No," he says. "Nuttin' much. A coupla guys was drunk in one of duh places an' started a fight, but dey bounced 'em out," he says, "an' den one of duh guys stahted to come back again, but duh bartender gets his baseball bat out from under duh counteh, so duh guy goes on."

"Jesus!" I said, "Red Hook!"

"Sure," he says. "Dat's where it was, all right."

"Well, you keep outa deh," I says. "You stay away from deh."

"Why?" he says. "What's wrong wit it?"

"Oh," I says, "it's a good place to stay away from, dat's all. It's a good place to keep out of."

"Why?" he says. "Why is it?"

Jesus! Whatcha gonna do wit a guy as dumb as dat? I saw it wasn't no use to try to tell him nuttin', he wouldn't know what I was talkin' about, so I just says to him, "Oh, nuttin'. Yuh might get lost down deh, dat's all."

"Lost?" he says. "No, *I* wouldn't get lost. I got a map," he says.

A map! Red Hook! Jesus!

So den duh guy begins to ast me all kinds of nutty questions: how big was Brooklyn an' could I find my way aroun' in it, an' how long would it take a guy to know duh place.

"Listen!" I says. "You get dat idea outa yoeh head right now," I says. "You ain't neveh gonna get to know Brooklyn," I says. "Not in a hunderd yeahs. I been livin' heah all my life," I says, "an' I don't even know all deh is to know about it, so how do you expect to know duh town," I says, "when you don't even live heah?"

"Yes," he says, "but I got a map to help me find my way about."

"Map or no map," I says, "yuh ain't gonna get to know Brooklyn wit no map," I says.

"Can you swim?" he says, just like dat. Jesus! By dat time, y'know, I begun to see dat guy was some kind of nut. He'd had plenty to drink, of course, but he had dat crazy look in his eye I didn't like. "Can you swim?" he says.

"Sure," I says. "Can't you?"

"No," he says. "Not more'n a stroke or two. I neveh loined good."

"Well, it's easy," I says. "All yuh need is a little confidence. Duh way I loined, me older bruddeh pitched me off duh dock one day when I was eight yeahs old, cloes an' all. 'You'll swim,' he says. 'You'll swim all right—or drown.' An', believe me, I *swam!* When yuh know yuh got to, you'll do it. Duh only t'ing yuh need is confidence. An' once you've loined," I says, "you've got nuttin' else to worry about. You'll neveh forget it. It's somp'n dat stays wit yuh as long as yuh live."

"Can you swim good?" he says.

"Like a fish," I tells him. "I'm a regulah fish in duh wateh," I says. "I loined to swim right off duh docks wit all duh oddeh kids," I says.

"What would you do if yuh saw a man drownin'?" duh guy says.

"Do? Why, I'd jump in an' pull him out," I says. "Dat's what I'd do."

"Did yuh eveh see a man drown?" he says.

"Sure," I says. "I see two guys—bot' times at Coney Island. Dey got out too far, an' neider one could swim. Dey drowned befoeh any one could get to 'em."

"What becomes of people after dey've drowned out heah?" he says.

"Drowned out where?" I says.

"Out heah in Brooklyn."

"I don't know whatcha mean," I says. "Neveh hoid of no one drownin' heah in Brooklyn, unless you mean a swimmin' pool. Yuh can't drown in Brooklyn," I says. "Yuh gotta drown somewhere else—in duh ocean, where dere's wateh."

"Drownin'," duh guy says, lookin' at his map. "Drownin'." Jesus! I could see by den he was some kind of nut, he had dat crazy expression in his eyes when he looked at you, an' I didn't know what he might do. So we was comin' to a station, an' it wasn't my stop, but I got off anyway, an' waited for duh next train.

"Drownin'," duh guy says, lookin' at his map. "Drownin'."

Jesus! I've t'ought about dat guy a t'ousand times since den an' wondered what eveh happened to 'm goin' out to look at Bensonhoist because he liked duh name! Walkin' aroun' t'roo Red Hook by himself at night an' lookin' at his map! How many people did I see get drowned out heah in Brooklyn! How long would it take a guy with a good map to know all deh was to know about Brooklyn!

Jesus! What a nut *he* was! I wondeh what eveh happened to 'im, anyway! I wondeh if some one knocked him on duh head, or if he's still wanderin' aroun' in duh subway in duh middle of duh night wit his little map! Duh poor guy! Say, I've got to laugh, at dat, when I t'ink about him! Maybe he's found out by now dat he'll neveh live long enough to know duh whole of Brooklyn. It'd take a guy a lifetime to know Brooklyn t'roo an' t'roo. An' even den, yuh wouldn't know it all.

1935

F. Scott Fitzgerald 1896–1940

In 1925 T. S. Eliot described The Great Gatsby, *written by F. Scott Fitzgerald, as "the first step that American fiction has taken since Henry James." Fitzgerald seemed destined for almost unlimited success as one of America's great writers, but only a few years later, John Dos Passos began a letter to him by calling him a "poor miserable bastard" who was spilling his talent out "in little pieces." In the early 1920s, Fitzgerald was the embodiment as well as the chronicler of the Jazz Age (a term for which he was largely responsible). He was handsome, uninhibited, and successful. He not only wrote some of the best prose, but he also drank the best wines, knew the best people, went to the best parties, and lived as though the money supply would never dry up. Even in 1931, two years after the stock market crash and well into the Great Depression, Fitzgerald's writing earned nearly $40,000. But the money supply did dry up. And the acclaim. In 1939 his royalties totaled only $33; by the following year not a single one of his books was in print. His life, which had represented the fulfillment of the American dream of wealth and achievement, seemed to end in a nightmare of squandered talent and despair.*

He was born Francis Scott Key Fitzgerald (among his forebears was the author of The Star Spangled Banner*). In his hometown of St. Paul, Minnesota, his family was considered socially prominent and genteelly poor. With the financial aid of relatives he was sent to prep school and to Princeton. In college he compiled a record of social triumphs and academic failures, and in 1917, his senior year, he left Princeton to serve in World War I. In Alabama, where he was sent for military training, he fell hopelessly in love with Zelda Sayre. She was the embodiment of all his romantic notions of a Southern belle, and when Fitzgerald was discharged from the army in 1919, he was determined to win success, fame, and Zelda. He took a job with an advertising agency and worked on short stories and a novel at night. Eventually his first novel,* This Side of Paradise, *was accepted for publication. The book appeared in March 1920. A week later Fitzgerald and Zelda were married.*

This Side of Paradise, *with its portrayal of the casual dissipations of "flaming youth," was an immediate commercial success, and Zelda and Scott Fitzgerald attempted to live up to—or even beyond—his fictional portraits of scandalous young men and women. They swam in public fountains in New York, rode to parties on the hoods of taxis, fought with waiters, and danced on dining tables. Life had become a long cocktail party, yet Fitzgerald managed somehow to continue writing. In 1922, he published his second novel,* The Beautiful and Damned, *and a collection of short stories,* Tales of the Jazz Age. *In 1923, he wrote a satirical play,* The Vegetable, Or from Postman to President. *It was a critical and financial failure, and to maintain his extravagant lifestyle, Fitzgerald ground out short stories rapidly for money, which he squandered just as rapidly. In 1925 Fitzgerald managed to complete* The Great Gatsby. *It was a critical success but a commercial disappointment; it sold only about half as many copies as either of his first two novels, and it earned little more than enough to repay debts to his publishers.*

Over the next two years Fitzgerald wrote little; it was, in his own words, a time of "1,000 parties and no work." In desperation he went to Hollywood, in 1927, for his first period of screenwriting, an occupation that was to sustain him for much of his remaining life. In 1934, Tender is the Night *was published. The year of its publication, it sold only 13,000 copies, and although it is a precise indictment of irresponsible social values of the 1930s, the critics harshly accused Fitzgerald of ignoring the Depression while writing a frivolous novel about neurotic Americans who preferred Europe over their native land.*

Battered by the illness of his wife (in the 1930s, Zelda began to suffer a series of mental breakdowns), by his own alcoholism, and by the failures of his writing, Fitzgerald now worked mainly in Hollywood. He continued to engage in periodic drinking bouts and grew seriously ill. In November 1940 he suffered a heart attack and a second one a month later. On December 21, 1940, he died. He was forty-four. His last novel, The Last Tycoon, *remained unfinished.*

At the time of his death Fitzgerald was considered (when considered at all) a failed literary hope, a writer victimized by his own indulgences. But since the 1940s his literary reputation has steadily risen. Today he is judged to be one of the major American prose writers of the twentieth century, and more copies of his works are now sold each year than were sold during his entire lifetime. In a number of his short stories, and in his finest novels, The Great Gatsby *and* Tender is the Night, *Fitzgerald had revealed, as no other American writer had, the stridency of an age of glittering innocence. In vivid and graceful prose he had, at the same time, portrayed the hollowness of the American worship of riches and the American dreams of love and splendor and gratified desire.*

FURTHER READING: A. Mizener, *The Far Side of Paradise, A Biography,* 1951, 1967; *The Letters of F. Scott Fitzgerald,* ed. A. Turnbull, 1963; A. Latham, *Crazy Sundays, F. Scott Fitzgerald in Hollywood,* 1971; S. Mayfield, *Exiles from Paradise, Zelda and Scott Fitzgerald,* 1972; *The Notebooks of F. Scott Fitzgerald,* ed. M. Bruccoli, 1980; *Correspondence of F. Scott Fitzgerald,* ed. M. Bruccoli and M. Duggan, 1980; M. Bruccoli, *Some Sort of Epic Grandeur, The Life of F. Scott Fitzgerald,* 1983; S. Donaldson, *Fool for Love, F. Scott Fitzgerald,* 1983; W. Dixon, *The Cinematic Vision of F. Scott Fitzgerald,* 1986; A. Petry, *Fitzgerald's Craft of Short Fiction, The Collected Stories 1920–1935,* 1989; J. Kuehl, *F. Scott Fitzgerald, A Study of the Short Fiction,* 1991; J. Meyers, *Scott Fitzgerald, A Biography,* 1993; *F. Scott Fitzgerald, A Life in Letters,* ed. M. Bruccoli, 1994; R. Roulston and H. Roulston, *The Winding Road to West Egg,* 1995; *New Essays on F. Scott Fitzgerald's Neglected Stories,* ed. J. Bryer, 1996; J. Baughman, *F. Scott Fitzgerald,* 2000; L. Pelzer, *Student Companion to F. Scott Fitzgerald,* 2000; M. Bruccoli, *Classes on F. Scott Fitzgerald,* 2001; *F. Scott Fitzgerald,* ed. H. Bloom, 2002; *A Historical Guide to F. Scott Fitzgerald,* ed. K. Curnutt, 2004.

TEXT: *Metropolitan Magazine,* December 1922.

WINTER DREAMS[1]

Some of the caddies were poor as sin and lived in one-room houses with a neurasthenic cow in the front yard, but Dexter Green's father owned the second best grocery store in Dillard—the best one was "The Hub," patronized by the wealthy people from Lake Erminie—and Dexter caddied only for pocket-money.

In the fall when the days became crisp and grey and the long Minnesota winter shut down like the white lid of a box, Dexter's skis moved over the snow that hid the fairways of the golf course. At these times the country gave him a feeling of profound melancholy—it offended him that the links should lie in enforced fallowness, haunted by ragged sparrows for the long season. It was dreary, too, that on the tees where the gay colors fluttered in summer there were now only the desolate sand-boxes[2] knee-deep in crusted ice. When he crossed the hills the wind blew cold as misery, and if the sun was out he tramped with his eyes squinted up against the hard dimensionless glare.

In April the winter ceased abruptly. The snow ran down into Lake Erminie scarcely tarrying for the early golfers to brave the season with red and black balls.[3] Without elation, without an interval of moist glory the cold was gone.

Dexter knew that there was something dismal about this northern spring, just as he knew there was something gorgeous about the fall. Fall made him clench his hands and tremble and repeat idiotic sentences to himself and make brisk abrupt gestures of command to imaginary audiences and armies. October filled him with hope which November raised to a sort of ecstatic

[1]The first published version of the story. Though now considered the best version and "aesthetically superior," the text was altered and shortened soon after it appeared, by editors and perhaps by Fitzgerald himself, for republication in an English magazine (1923) and in *All the Sad Young Men* (1926). Some spelling and punctuation errors have been corrected by the present editor for this edition.

[2]Receptacles for the sand formerly used to tee a golf ball.

[3]For play on snow covered ground.

triumph, and in this wood the fleeting brilliant impressions of the summer at Lake Erminie were ready grist to his will. He became a golf champion and defeated Mr. T. A. Hedrick in a marvelous match played over a hundred times in the fairways of his imagination, a match each detail of which he changed about untiringly—sometimes winning with almost laughable ease, sometimes coming up magnificently from behind. Again, stepping from a Pierce-Arrow[4] automobile, like Mr. Mortimer Jones, he strolled frigidly into the lounge of the Erminie Golf Club—or perhaps, surrounded by an admiring crowd, he gave an exhibition of fancy diving from the springboard of the Erminie Club raft . . . Among those most impressed was Mr. Mortimer Jones.

And one day it came to pass that Mr. Jones, himself and not his ghost, came up to Dexter, almost with tears in his eyes and said that Dexter was the — — best caddy in the club and wouldn't he decide not to quit if Mr. Jones made it worth his while, because every other — — caddy in the club lost one ball a hole for him—regularly———

"No, sir," said Dexter, decisively, "I don't want to caddy anymore." Then, after a pause, "I'm too old."

"You're—why, you're not more than fourteen. Why did you decide just this morning that you wanted to quit? You promised that next week you'd go over to the state tournament with me."

"I decided I was too old."

Dexter handed in his "A Class" badge,[5] collected what money was due him from the caddy master and caught the train for Dillard.

"The best — — caddy I ever saw," shouted Mr. Mortimer Jones over a drink that afternoon, "Never lost a ball! Willing! Intelligent! Quiet! Honest! Grateful!———"

The little girl who had done this was eleven—beautifully ugly as little girls are apt to be who are destined after a few years to be inexpressibly lovely and bring no end of misery to a great number of men. The spark, however, was perceptible. There was a general ungodliness in the way her lips twisted down at the corners when she smiled and in the—Heaven help us!—in the almost passionate quality of her eyes. Vitality is born early in such women. It was utterly in evidence now, shining through her thin frame in a sort of glow.

She had come eagerly out on to the course at nine o'clock with a white linen nurse and five small new golf clubs in a white canvas bag which the nurse was carrying. When Dexter first saw her she was standing by the caddy house, rather ill-at-ease and trying to conceal the fact by engaging her nurse in an obviously unnatural conversation illumined by startling and irrevelant smiles from herself.

"Well, it's certainly a nice day, Hilda," Dexter heard her say, then she drew down the corners of her mouth, smiled and glanced furtively around, her eyes in transit falling for an instant on Dexter.

Then to the nurse:

"Well, I guess there aren't very many people out here this morning, are there?"

[4]Elegant and costly American automobile produced from 1901 to 1938.
[5]Indication that he was a caddy of the highest rank.

The smile again radiant, blatantly artificial—convincing.

"I don't know what we're supposed to do now," said the nurse, looking nowhere in particular.

"Oh, that's all right"—the smile—"I'll fix it up."

Dexter stood perfectly still, his mouth faintly ajar. He knew that if he moved forward a step his stare would be in her line of vision—if he moved backward he would lose his full view of her face—For a moment he had not realized how young she was. Now he remembered having seen her several times the year before—in bloomers.

Suddenly, involuntarily, he laughed, a short abrupt laugh—then, startled by himself, he turned and began to walk quickly away.

"Boy!"

Dexter stopped.

"Boy——"

Beyond question he was addressed. Not only that, but he was treated to that absurd smile, that preposterous smile—the memory of which at least half a dozen men were to carry to the grave.

"Boy, do you know where the golf teacher is?"

"He's giving a lesson."

"Well, do you know where the caddy-master is?"

"He's not here yet this morning."

"Oh." For a moment this baffled her. She stood alternately on her right and left foot.

"We'd like to get a caddy," said the nurse, "Mrs. Mortimer Jones sent us out to play golf and we don't know how without we get a caddy."

Here she was stopped by an ominous glance from Miss Jones, followed immediately by the smile.

"There aren't any caddies here except me," said Dexter to the nurse, "And I got to stay here in charge until the caddy-master gets here."

"Oh."

Miss Jones and her retinue now withdrew and at a proper distance from Dexter became involved in a heated conversation. The conversation was concluded by Miss Jones taking one of the clubs and hitting it on the ground with violence. For further emphasis she raised it again and was about to bring it down smartly upon the nurse's bosom, when the nurse seized the club and twisted it from her hands.

"You darn *fool*!" cried Miss Jones wildly.

Another argument ensued. Realizing that the elements of the comedy were implied in the scene, Dexter several times began to smile but each time slew the smile before it reached maturity. He could not resist the monstrous conviction that the little girl was justified in beating the nurse.

The situation was resolved by the fortuitous appearance of the caddy-master who was appealed to immediately by the nurse.

"Miss Jones is to have a little caddy and this one says he can't go."

"Mr. McKenna said I was to wait here till you came," said Dexter quickly.

"Well, he's here now." Miss Jones smiled cheerfully at the caddy-master. Then she dropped her bag and set off at a haughty mince toward the first tee.

"Well?" The caddy-master turned to Dexter, "What you standing there like a dummy for? Go pick up the young lady's clubs."

"I don't think I'll go out today," said Dexter.

"You don't———"

"I think I'll quit."

The enormity of his decision frightened him. He was a favorite caddy and the thirty dollars a month he earned through the summer were not to be made elsewhere in Dillard. But he had received a strong, emotional shock and his perturbation required a violent and immediate outlet.

It is not so simple as that, either. As so frequently would be the case in the future, Dexter was unconsciously dictated to by his winter dreams.

Now, of course, the quality and the seasonability of these winter dreams varied, but the stuff of them remained. They persuaded Dexter several years later to pass up a business course at the State University—his father, prospering now, would have paid his way—for the precarious advantage of attending an older and more famous university in the East, where he was bothered by his scanty funds. But do not get the impression, because his winter dreams happened to be concerned at first with musings on the rich, that there was anything shoddy in the boy. He wanted not association with glittering things and glittering people—he wanted the glittering things themselves. Often he reached out for the best without knowing why he wanted it—and sometimes he ran up against the mysterious denials and prohibitions in which life indulges. It is with one of those denials and not with his career as a whole that this story deals.

He made money. It was rather amazing. After college he went to the city from which Lake Erminie draws its wealthy patrons. When he was only twenty-three and had been there not quite two years, there were already people who liked to say, "Now *there's* a boy—" All about him rich men's sons were peddling bonds precariously, or investing patrimonies precariously, or plodding through the two dozen volumes of canned rubbish in the "George Washington Commercial Course," but Dexter borrowed a thousand dollars on his college degree and his steady eyes, and bought a partnership in a *laundry.*

It was a small laundry when he went into it. Dexter made a specialty of learning how the English washed fine woolen golf stockings without shrinking them. Inside of a year he was catering to the trade who wore knickerbockers. Men were insisting that their Shetland hose and sweaters go to his laundry just as they had insisted on a caddy who could find golf balls. A little later he was doing their wives' lingerie as well—and running five branches in different parts of the city. Before he was twenty-seven he owned the largest string of laundries in his section of the country. It was then that he sold out and went to New York. But the part of his story that concerns us here goes back to when he was making his first big success.

When he was twenty-three Mr. W. L. Hart, one of the grey-haired men who like to say "Now there's a boy"—gave him a guest card to the Lake Erminie Club for over a week-end. So he signed his name one day on the register, and that afternoon played golf in a foursome with Mr. Hart and Mr. Sandwood and Mr. T. A. Hedrick. He did not consider it necessary to remark that he had once carried Mr. Hart's bag over this same links and that he knew every trap and gully with his eyes shut—but he found himself glancing at the four caddies who trailed them, trying to catch a gleam or gesture that would remind him of himself, that would lessen the gap which lay between his past and his future.

It was a curious day, slashed abruptly with fleeting, familiar impressions. One minute he had the sense of being a trespasser—in the next he was impressed by the tremendous superiority he felt toward Mr. T. A. Hedrick, who was a bore and not even a good golfer any more.

Then, because of a ball Mr. Hart lost near the fifteenth green an enormous thing happened. While they were searching the stiff grasses of the rough there was a clear call of "Fore!" from behind a hill in their rear. And as they all turned abruptly from their search a bright new ball sliced abruptly over the hill and caught Mr. T. A. Hedrick rather neatly in the stomach.

Mr. T. A. Hedrick grunted and cursed.

"By Gad!" cried Mr. Hedrick, "they ought to put some of these crazy women off the course. It's getting to be outrageous."

A head and a voice came up together over the hill:

"Do you mind if we go through?"

"You hit me in the stomach!" thundered Mr. Hedrick.

"Did I?" The girl approached the group of men. "I'm sorry. I yelled 'Fore!'"

Her glance fell casually on each of the men. She nodded to Sandwood and then scanned the fairway for her ball.

"Did I bounce off into the rough?"

It was impossible to determine whether this question was ingenuous or malicious. In a moment, however, she left no doubt, for as her partner came up over the hill she called cheerfully.

"Here I am! I'd have gone on the green except that I hit something."

As she took her stance for a short mashie[6] shot, Dexter looked at her closely. She wore a blue gingham dress, rimmed at throat and shoulders with a white edging that accentuated her tan. The quality of exaggeration, of thinness that had made her passionate eyes and down turning mouth absurd at eleven was gone now. She was arrestingly beautiful. The color in her cheeks was centered like the color in a picture—it was not a "high" color, but a sort of fluctuating and feverish warmth, so shaded that it seemed at any moment it would recede and disappear. This color and the mobility of her mouth gave a continual impression of flux, of intense life, of passionate vitality—balanced only partially by the sad luxury of her eyes.

She swung her mashie impatiently and without interest, pitching the ball into a sandpit on the other side of the green. With a quick insincere smile and a careless "Thank you!" she went on after it.

"That Judy Jones!" remarked Mr. Hedrick on the next tee, as they waited—some moments—for her to play on ahead, "All she needs is to be turned up and spanked for six months and then to be married off to an old-fashioned cavalry captain."

"Gosh, she's good looking!" said Mr. Sandwood, who was just over thirty.

"Good-looking!" cried Mr. Hedrick contemptuously, "she always looks as if she wanted to be kissed! Turning those big cow-eyes on every young calf in town!"

It is doubtful if Mr. Hedrick intended a reference to the maternal instinct.

"She'd play pretty good golf if she'd try," said Mr. Sandwood.

[6]Former name of the modern five iron.

"She has no form," said Mr. Hedrick solemnly.

"She has a nice figure," said Mr. Sandwood.

"Better thank the Lord she doesn't drive a swifter ball," said Mr. Hart, winking at Dexter. "Come on. Let's go."

Later in the afternoon the sun went down with a riotous swirl of gold and varying blues and scarlets, and left the dry rustling night of western summer. Dexter watched from the verandah of the Erminie Club, watched the even overlap of the waters in the little wind, silver molasses under the harvest moon. Then the moon held a finger to her lips and the lake became a clear pool, pale and quiet. Dexter put on his bathing suit and swam out to the farthest raft, where he stretched dripping on the wet canvas of the spring board.

There was a fish jumping and a star shining and the lights around the lake were gleaming. Over on a dark peninsula a piano was playing the songs of last summer and of summers before that—songs from "The Pink Lady" and "The Chocolate Soldier" and "Mlle. Modiste"[7]—and because the sound of a piano over a stretch of water had always seemed beautiful to Dexter he lay perfectly quiet and listened.

The tune the piano was playing at that moment had been gay and new five years before when Dexter was a sophomore at college. They had played it at a prom once and because he could not afford the luxury of proms in those days he had stood outside the gymnasium and listened. The sound of the tune and the splash of the fish jumping precipitated in him a sort of ecstasy and it was with that ecstasy he viewed what happened to him now. The ecstasy was a gorgeous appreciation. It was his sense that, for once, he was magnificently atune to life and that everything about him was radiating a brightness and a glamour he might never know again.

A low pale oblong detached itself suddenly from the darkness of the peninsula, spitting forth the reverberate sound of a racing motorboat. Two white streamers of cleft water rolled themselves out behind it and almost immediately the boat was beside him, drowning out the hot tinkle of the piano in the drone of its spray. Dexter raising himself on his arms was aware of a figure standing at the wheel, of two dark eyes regarding him over the lengthening space of water—then the boat had gone by and was sweeping in an immense and purposeless circle of spray round and round in the middle of the lake. With equal eccentricity one of the circles flattened out and headed back toward the raft.

"Who's that?" she called, shutting off her motor. She was so near now that Dexter could see her bathing suit, which consisted apparently of pink rompers. "Oh—you're one of the men I hit in the stomach."

The nose of the boat bumped the raft. After an inexpert struggle, Dexter managed to twist the line around a two-by-four. Then the raft tilted rakishly as she sprang on.

"Well, kiddo," she said huskily, "do you"—she broke off. She had sat herself upon the springboard, found it damp and jumped up quickly,—"do you want to go surf-board riding?"

He indicated that he would be delighted.

"The name is Judy Jones. Ghastly reputation but enormously popular." She favored him with an absurd smirk—rather, what tried to be a smirk, for, twist

[7]Popular stage musicals of the first decades of the twentieth century.

her mouth as she might, it was not grotesque, it was merely beautiful. "See that house over on the peninsula?"

"No."

"Well, there's a house there that I live in only you can't see it because it's too dark. And in that house there is a fella waiting for me. When he drove up by the door I drove out by the dock because he has watery eyes and asks me if I have an ideal."

There was a fish jumping and a star shining and the lights around the lake were gleaming. Dexter sat beside Judy Jones and she explained how her boat was driven. Then she was in the water, swimming to the floating surf-board with an exquisite crawl. Watching her was as without effort to the eye as watching a branch waving or a sea-gull flying. Her arms, burned to butternut, moved sinuously among the dull platinum ripples, elbow appearing first, casting the forearm back with a cadence of falling water, then reaching out and down stabbing a path ahead.

They moved out into the lake and, turning, Dexter saw that she was kneeling on the low rear of the now up-tilted surf-board.

"Go faster," she called, "fast as it'll go."

Obediently he jammed the lever forward and the white spray mounted at the bow. When he looked around again the girl was standing up on the rushing board, her arms spread ecstatically, her eyes lifted toward the moon.

"It's awful cold, kiddo," she shouted, "What's your name anyways."

"The name is Dexter Green. Would it amuse you to know how good you look back there?"

"Yes," she shouted, "It would amuse me. Except that I'm too cold. Come to dinner tomorrow night."

He kept thinking how glad he was that he had never caddied for this girl. The damp gingham clinging made her like a statue and turned her intense mobility to immobility at last.

"—At seven o'clock," she shouted, "Judy Jones, Girl, who hit man in stomach. Better write it down"—and then, "Faster—oh, faster!"

Had he been as calm inwardly as he was in appearance, Dexter would have had time to examine his surroundings in detail. He received, however, an enduring impression that the house was the most elaborate he had ever seen. He had known for a long time that it was the finest on Lake Erminie, with a Pompeiian swimming pool and twelve acres of lawn and garden. But what gave it an air of breathless intensity was the sense that it was inhabited by Judy Jones—that it was as casual a thing to her as the little house in the village had once been to Dexter. There was a feeling of mystery in it, of bedrooms upstairs more beautiful and strange than other bedrooms, of gay and radiant activities taking place through these deep corridors and of romances that were not musty and laid already in lavender, but were fresh and breathing and set forth in rich motor cars and in great dances whose flowers were scarcely withered. They were more real because he could feel them all about him, pervading the air with the shades and echoes of still vibrant emotion.

And so while he waited for her to appear he peopled the soft deep summer room and the sun porch that opened from it with the men who had already loved Judy Jones. He knew the sort of men they were—the men who when he first went to college had entered from the great prep schools with graceful clothes and the deep tan of healthy summer, who did nothing or anything with the same debonair ease.

Dexter had seen that, in one sense, he was better than these men. He was newer and stronger. Yet in acknowledging to himself that he wished his children to be like them he was admitting that he was but the rough, strong stuff from which this graceful aristocracy eternally sprang.

When, a year before, the time had come when he could wear good clothes, he had known who were the best tailors in America, and the best tailor in America had made him the suit he wore this evening. He had acquired that particular reserve peculiar to his university, that set it off from other universities. He recognized the value to him of such a mannerism and he had adopted it; he knew that to be careless in dress and manner required more confidence than to be careful. But carelessness was for his children. His mother's name had been Krimslich. She was a Bohemian of the peasant class and she had talked broken English to the end of her days. Her son must keep to the set patterns.

He waited for Judy Jones in her house, and he saw these other young men around him. It excited him that many men had loved her. It increased her value in his eyes.

At a little after seven Judy Jones came downstairs. She wore a blue silk afternoon dress. He was disappointed at first that she had not put on something more elaborate, and this feeling was accentuated when, after a brief greeting, she went to the door of a butler's pantry and pushing it open called: "You can serve dinner, Martha." He had rather expected that a butler would announce dinner, that there would be a cocktail perhaps. It even offended him that she should know the maid's name.

Then he put these thoughts behind him as they sat down together on a chintz-covered lounge.

"Father and mother won't be here," she said.

"Ought I to be sorry?"

"They're really quite nice," she confessed, as if it had just occurred to her. "I think my father's the best looking man of his age I've ever seen. And mother looks about thirty."

He remembered the last time he had seen her father, and found he was glad the parents were not to be here tonight. They would wonder who he was. He had been born in Keeble, a Minnesota village fifty miles father north and he always gave Keeble as his home instead of Dillard. Country towns were well enough to come from if they weren't inconveniently in sight and used as foot-stools by fashionable lakes.

Before dinner he found the conversation unsatisfactory. The beautiful Judy seemed faintly irritable—as much so as it was possible to be with a comparative stranger. They discussed Lake Erminie and its golf course, the surfboard riding of the night before and the cold she had caught, which made her voice more husky and charming than ever. They talked of his university which she had visited frequently during the past two years, and of the nearby city which supplied Lake Erminie with its patrons and whither Dexter would return next day to his prospering laundries.

During dinner she slipped into a moody depression which gave Dexter a feeling of guilt. Whatever petulance she uttered in her throaty voice worried him. Whatever she smiled at—at him, at a silver fork, at nothing—, it disturbed him that her smile could have no root in mirth, or even in amusement. When the red corners of her lips curved down, it was less a smile than an invitation to a kiss.

Then, after dinner, she led him out on the dark sun-porch and deliberately changed the atmosphere.

"Do I seem gloomy?" she demanded.

"No, but I'm afraid I'm boring you," he answered quickly.

"You're not. I like you. But I've just had an unpleasant afternoon. There was a—man I cared about. He told me out of a clear sky that he was poor as a church-mouse. He'd never even hinted it before. Does this sound horribly mundane?"

"Perhaps he was afraid to tell you."

"I suppose he was," she answered thoughtfully. "He didn't start right. You see, if I'd thought of him as poor—well, I've been mad about loads of poor men, and fully intended to marry them all. But in this case, I hadn't thought of him that way and my interest in him wasn't strong enough to survive the shock."

"I know. As if a girl calmly informed her fiancé that she was a widow. He might not object to widows, but———"

"Let's start right," she suggested suddenly. "Who are you, anyhow?"

For a moment Dexter hesitated. There were two versions of his life that he could tell. There was Dillard and his caddying and his struggle through college, or———

"I'm nobody," he announced. "My career is largely a matter of futures."

"Are you poor?"

"No," he said frankly. "I'm probably making more money than any man my age in the northwest. I know that's an obnoxious remark, but you advised me to start right."

There was a pause. She smiled, and with a touch of amusement.

"You sound like a man in a play."

"It's your fault. You tempted me into being assertive."

Suddenly she turned her dark eyes directly upon him and the corners of her mouth drooped until her face seemed to open like a flower. He dared scarcely to breathe, he had the sense that she was exerting some force upon him; making him overwhelmingly conscious of the youth and mystery that wealth imprisons and preserves, the freshness of many clothes, of cool rooms and gleaming things, safe and proud above the hot struggles of the poor.

The porch was bright with the bought luxury of starshine. The wicker of the settee squeaked fashionably when he put his arm around her, commanded by her eyes. He kissed her curious and lovely mouth and committed himself to the following of a grail.

It began like that—and continued, with varying shades of intensity, on such a note right up to the dénoument. Dexter surrendered a part of himself to the most direct and unprincipled personality with which he had ever come in contact. Whatever the beautiful Judy Jones desired, she went after with the full pressure of her charm. There was no divergence of method, no jockeying for position or premeditation of effects—there was very little mental quality in any of her affairs. She simply made men conscious to the highest degree of her physical loveliness.

Dexter had no desire to change her. Her deficiencies were knit up with a passionate energy that transcended and justified them.

When, as Judy's head lay against his shoulder that first night, she whispered:

"I don't know what's the matter with me. Last night I thought I was in love with a man and tonight I think I'm in love with you———"

It seemed to him a beautiful and romantic thing to say. It was the exquisite excitability that for the moment he controlled and owned. But a week later he was compelled to view this same quality in a different light. She took him in her roadster to a picnic supper and after supper she disappeared, likewise in her roadster, with another man. Dexter became enormously upset and was scarcely able to be decently civil to the other people present. When she assured him that she had not kissed the other man he knew she was lying—yet he was glad that she had taken the trouble to lie to him.

He was, as he found before the summer ended, one of a dozen, a varying dozen, who circulated about her. Each of them had at one time been favored above all others—about half of them still basked in the solace of occasional sentimental revivals. Whenever one showed signs of dropping out through long neglect she granted him a brief honeyed hour which encouraged him to tag along for a year or so longer. Judy made these forays upon the helpless and defeated without malice, indeed half unconscious that there was anything mischievous in what she did.

When a new man came to town everyone dropped out—dates were automatically cancelled.

The helpless part of trying to do anything about it was that she did it all herself. She was not a girl who could be "won" in the kinetic sense—she was proof against cleverness, she was proof against charm, if any of these assailed her too strongly she would immediately resolve the affair to a physical basis and under the magic of her physical splendor the strong as well as the brilliant played her game and not their own. She was entertained only by the gratification of her desires and by the direct exercise of her own charm. Perhaps from so much youthful love, so many youthful lovers she had come, in self defense, to nourish herself wholly from within.

Succeeding Dexter's first exhilaration came restlessness and dissatisfaction. The helpless ecstasy of losing himself in her charm was a powerful opiate rather than a tonic. It was fortunate for his work during the winter that those moments of ecstasy came infrequently. Early in their acquaintance it had seemed for a while that there was a deep and mutual attraction—that first August for example—three days of long evenings on her dusky verandah, of strange wan kisses through the late afternoon, in shadowy alcoves or behind the protecting trellises of the garden arbors, of mornings when she was fresh as a dream and almost shy at meeting him in the clarity of the rising day. There was all the ecstasty of an engagement about it, sharpened by his realization that there was no engagement. It was during those three days that, for the first time, he had asked her to marry him. She said, "maybe some day," she said, "kiss me," she said, "I'd like to marry you," she said, "I love you,"—she said—nothing.

The three days were interrupted by the arrival of a New York man who visited the Jones's for half September. To Dexter's agony, rumor engaged them.

The man was the son of the president of a great trust company. But at the end of a month it was reported that Judy was yawning. At a dance one night she sat all evening in a motor boat with an old beau, while the New Yorker searched the club for her frantically. She told the old beau that she was bored with her visitor and two days later he left. She was seen with him at the station and it was reported that he looked very mournful indeed.

On this note the summer ended. Dexter was twenty-four and he found himself increasingly in a position to do as he wished. He joined two clubs in the city and lived at one of them. Though he was by no means an integral part of the stag-lines at these clubs he managed to be on hand at dances where Judy Jones was likely to appear. He could have gone out socially as much as he liked—he was an eligible young man, now, and popular with downtown fathers. His confessed devotion to Judy Jones had rather solidified his position. But he had no social aspirations and rather despised the dancing men who were always on tap for the Thursday and Saturday parties and who filled in at dinners with the younger married set. Already he was playing with the idea of going East to New York. He wanted to take Judy Jones with him. No disillusion as to the world in which she had grown up could cure his illusion as to her desirability.

Remember that—for only in the light of it can what he did for her be understood.

Eighteen months after he first met Judy Jones, he became engaged to another girl. Her name was Irene Scheerer and her father was one of the men who had always believed in Dexter. Irene was light haired and sweet and honorable and a little stout and she had two beaus whom she pleasantly relinquished when Dexter formally asked her to marry him.

Summer, fall, winter, spring, another summer, another fall—so much he had given of his active life to the curved lips of Judy Jones. She had treated him with interest, with encouragement, with malice, with indifference, with contempt. She had inflicted on him the innumerable little slights and indignities possible in such a case—as if in revenge for having ever cared for him at all. She had beckoned him and yawned at him and beckoned him again and he had responded often with bitterness and narrowed eyes. She had brought him ecstatic happiness and intolerable agony of spirit. She had caused him untold inconvenience and not a little trouble. She had insulted him and she had ridden over him and she had played his interest in her against his interest in his work—for fun. She had done everything to him except to criticize him—this she had not done—it seemed to him only because it might have sullied the utter indifference she manifested and sincerely felt toward him.

When autumn had come and gone again it occurred to him that he could not have Judy Jones. He had to beat this into his mind but he convinced himself at last. He lay awake at night for a while and argued it over. He told himself the trouble and the pain she had caused him, he enumerated her glaring deficiencies as a wife. Then he said to himself that he loved her and after a while he fell asleep. For a week, lest he imagine her husky voice over the telephone or her eyes opposite him at lunch, he worked hard and late and at night he went to his office and plotted out his years.

At the end of a week he went to a dance and cut in on her once. For almost the first time since they had met he did not ask her to sit out with him or tell her that she was lovely. It hurt him that she did not miss these things—that was all. He was not jealous when he saw that there was a new man tonight. He had been hardened against jealousy long before.

He stayed late at the dance. He sat for an hour with Irene Scheerer and talked about books and about music. He knew very little about either. But he was beginning to be master of his own time now and he had a rather priggish notion that he—the young and already fabulously successful Dexter Green—should know more about such things.

That was in October when he was twenty-five. In January Dexter and Irene became engaged. It was to be announced in June and they were to be married three months later.

The Minnesota winter prolonged itself interminably and it was almost May when the winds came soft and the snow ran down into Lake Erminie at last. For the first time in over a year Dexter was enjoying a certain tranquility of spirit. Judy Jones had been in Florida and afterwards in Hot Springs[8] and somewhere she had been engaged and somewhere she had broken it off. At first, when Dexter had definitely given her up, it had made him sad that people still linked them together and asked for news of her, but when he began to be placed at dinner next to Irene Scheerer people didn't ask him about her any more—they told him about her. He ceased to be an authority on her.

May at last. Dexter walked the streets at night when the darkness was damp as rain, wondering that so soon, with so little done, so much of ecstacy had gone from him. May, one year back had been marked by Judy's poignant, unforgivable, yet forgiven turbulence—it had been one of those rare times when he fancied she had grown to care for him. That old penny's worth of happiness he had spent for this bushel of content. He knew that Irene would be no more than a curtain spread behind him, a hand moving among gleaming tea cups, a voice calling to children . . . fire and loveliness were gone, magic of night and the hushed wonder of the hours and seasons . . . slender lips, down turning, dropping to his lips like poppy petals, bearing him up into a heaven of eyes . . . a haunting gesture, light of a warm lamp on her hair. The thing was deep in him. He was too strong, to alive for it to die lightly.

In the middle of May when the weather balanced for a few days on the thin bridge that led to deep summer he turned in one night at Irene's house. Their engagement was to be announced in a week now—no one would be surprised at it. And tonight they would sit together on the lounge at the College Club and look on for an hour at the dancers. It gave him a sense of solidity to go with her——— She was so sturdily popular, so intensely a "good egg."

He mounted the steps of the brown stone house and stepped inside.

"Irene," he called.

Mrs Scheerer came out of the living room to meet him.

"Dexter," she said, "Irene's gone upstairs with a splitting headache. She wanted to go with you but I made her go to bed."

"Nothing serious I———"

"Oh, no. She's going to play golf with you in the morning. You can spare her for just one night, can't you, Dexter?"

[8]Fashionable health spa and resort in Virginia.

Her smile was kind. She and Dexter liked each other. In the living room he talked for a moment before he said goodnight.

Returning to the College Club, where he had rooms, he stood in the doorway for a moment and watched the dancers. He leaned against the door post, nodded at a man or two—yawned.

"Hello, kiddo."

The familiar voice at his elbow startled him. Judy Jones had left a man and crossed the room to him—Judy Jones, a slender enameled doll in cloth of gold, gold in a band at her head, gold in two slipper points at her dress's hem. The fragile glow of her face seemed to blossom as she smiled at him. A breeze of warmth and light blew through the room. His hands in the pockets of his dinner jacket tightened spasmodically. He was filled with a sudden excitement.

"When did you get back?" he asked casually.

"Come here and I'll tell you about it."

She turned and he followed her. She had been away—he could have wept at the wonder of her return. She had passed through enchanted streets, doing young things that were like plaintive music. All mysterious happenings, all fresh and quickening hopes, had gone away with her, come back with her now.

She turned in the doorway.

"Have you a car here? If you haven't I have."

"I have a coupe."

In then, with a rustle of golden cloth.

He slammed the door. Into so many cars she had stepped—like this—like that—her back against the leather, so—her elbow resting on the door—waiting. She would have been soiled long since had there been anything to soil her,—except herself—but these things were all her own outpouring.

With an effort he forced himself to start the car and avoiding her surprised glance backed into the street. This was nothing, he must remember. She had done this before and he had put her behind him, as he would have slashed a bad account from his books.

He drove slowly downtown and affecting a disinterested abstraction traversed the deserted streets of the business section, peopled here and there, where a movie was giving out its crowd or where consumptive or pugilistic youth lounged in front of pool halls. The clink of glasses and the slap of hands on the bars issued from saloons, cloisters of glazed glass and dirty yellow light.

She was watching him closely and the silence was embarrassing yet in this crisis he could find no casual word with which to profane the hour. At a convenient turning he began to zig-zag back toward the College Club.

"Have you missed me?" she asked suddenly.

"Everybody missed you."

He wondered if she knew of Irene Scheerer. She had been back only a day—her absence had been almost contemporaneous with his engagement.

"What a remark!" Judy laughed sadly—without sadness. She looked at him searchingly. He became absorbed for a moment in the dashboard.

"You're handsomer than you used to be," she said thoughtfully. "Dexter, you have the most rememberable eyes."

He could have laughed at this, but he did not laugh. It was the sort of thing that was said to sophomores. Yet it stabbed at him.

"I'm awfully tired of everything, kiddo." She called everyone kiddo, endowing the obsolete slang with careless, individual comradery. "I wish you'd marry me."

The directness of this confused him. He should have told her now that he was going to marry another girl but he could not tell her. He could as easily have sworn that he had never loved her.

"I think we'd get along," she continued, on the same note, "unless probably you've forgotten me and fallen love with another girl."

Her confidence was obviously enormous. She had said, in effect, that she found such a thing impossible to believe, that if it were true he had merely committed a childish indiscretion—and probably to show off. She would forgive him, because it was not a matter of any moment but rather something to be brushed aside lightly.

"Of course you could never love anybody but me," she continued, "I like the way you love me. Oh, Dexter, have you forgotten last year?"

"No, I haven't forgotten."

"Neither have I!"

Was she sincerely moved—or was she carried along by the wave of her own acting?

"I wish we could be like that again," she said, and he forced himself to answer:

"I don't think we can."

"I suppose not . . . I hear you're giving Irene Scheerer a violent rush."

There was not the faintest emphasis on the name, yet Dexter was suddenly ashamed.

"Oh, take me home," cried Judy suddenly, "I don't want to go back to that idiotic dance—with those children."

Then, as he turned up the street that led to the residence district, Judy began to cry quietly to herself. He had never seen her cry before.

The dark street lightened, the dwellings of the rich loomed up around them, he stopped his coupé in front of the great white bulk of the Mortimer Jones's house, somnolent, gorgeous, drenched with the splendor of the damp moonlight. Its solidity startled him. The strong walls, the fine steel of the girders, the breadth and beam and pomp of it were there only to bring out the contrast with the young beauty beside him.

It was sturdy to accentuate her slightness—as if to show what a breeze could be generated by a butterfly's wing.

He sat perfectly quiet, his nerves in wild clamor, afraid that if he moved he would find her irresistibly in his arms. Two tears had rolled down her wet face and trembled on her upper lip.

"I'm more beautiful than anybody else," she said brokenly, "why can't I be happy?" Her moist eyes tore at his stability—mouth turned slowly downward with an exquisite sadness. "I'd like to marry you if you'll have me, Dexter. I suppose you think I'm not worth having but I'll be so beautiful for you, Dexter."

A million phrases of anger, of pride, of passion, of hatred, of tenderness fought on his lips. Then a perfect wave of emotion washed over him, carrying off with it a sediment of wisdom, of convention, of doubt, of honor. This was his girl who was speaking, his own, his beautiful, his pride.

"Won't you come in?" he heard her draw in her breath sharply.

Waiting.

"All right," his voice was trembling, "I'll come in."

It seems strange to say that neither when it was over nor a long time afterward did he regret that night. Looking at it from the perspective of ten years, the fact that Judy's flare for him endured just one month seemed of little importance. Nor did it matter that by his yielding he subjected himself to a deeper agony in the end and gave serious hurt to Irene Scheerer and to Irene's parents who had befriended him. There was nothing sufficiently pictorial about Irene's grief to stamp itself on his mind.

Dexter was at bottom hard-minded. The attitude of the city on his action was of no importance to him, not because he was going to leave the city, but because any outside attitude on the situation seemed superficial. He was completely indifferent to popular opinion. Nor, when he had seen that it was no use, that he did not possess in himself the power to move fundamentally or to hold Judy Jones, did he bear any malice toward her. He loved her and he would love her until the day he was too old for loving—but he could not have her. So he tasted the deep pain that is reserved only for the strong, just as he had tasted for a little while the deep happiness.

Even the ultimate falsity of the grounds upon which Judy terminated the engagement—that she did not want to "take him away" from Irene, that it was on her conscience—did not revolt him. He was beyond any revulsion or any amusement.

He went east in February with the intention of selling out his laundries and settling in New York—but the war came to America in March and changed his plans. He returned to the west, handed over the management of the business to his partner and went into the first officers' training camp in late April. He was one of those young thousands who greeted the war with a certain amount of relief, welcoming the liberation from webs of tangled emotion.

This story is not his biography, remember, although things creep into it which have nothing to do with those dreams he had when he was young. We are almost done with them and with him now. There is only one more incident to be related here and it happens seven years farther on.

It took place in New York, where he had done well—so well that there were no barriers too high for him now. He was thirty-two years old, and, except for one flying trip immediately after the war, he had not been west in seven years. A man named Devlin from Detroit came into his office to see him in a business way, and then and there this incident occurred, and closed out, so to speak, this particular side of his life.

"So, you're from the middle west," said the man Devlin with careless curiosity. "That's funny—I thought men like you were probably born and raised on Wall Street. You know—wife of one of my best friends in Detroit came from your city. I was an usher at the wedding."

Dexter waited with no apprehension of what was coming. There was a magic that his city would never lose for him. Just as Judy's house had always seemed to him more mysterious and gay than other houses, so his dream of the city itself, now that he had gone from it, was pervaded with a melancholy beauty.

"Judy Simms," said Devlin with no particular interest, "Judy Jones she was once."

"Yes, I knew her." A dull impatience spread over him. He had heard, of course, that she was married,—perhaps deliberately he had heard no more.

"Awfully nice girl," brooded Devlin, meaninglessly, "I'm sort of sorry for her."

"Why?" Something in Dexter was alert, receptive, at once.

"Oh, Joe Simms has gone to pieces in a way. I don't mean he beats her, you understand, or anything like that. But he drinks and runs around———"

"Doesn't she run around?"

"No. Stays at home with her kids."

"Oh."

"She's a little too old for him," said Devlin.

"Too old!" cried Dexter, "why man, she's only twenty-seven."

He was possessed with a wild notion of rushing out into the streets and taking a train to Detroit. He rose to his feet, spasmodically, involuntarily.

"I guess you're busy," Devlin apologized quickly. "I didn't realize——"

"No, I'm not busy," said Dexter, steadying his voice, "I'm not busy at all. Not busy at all. Did you say she was—twenty-seven? No, I said she was twenty-seven."

"Yes, you did," agreed Devlin drily.

"Go on, then. Go on."

"What do you mean?"

"About Judy Jones."

Devlin looked at him helplessly.

"Well, that's—I told you all there is to it. He treats her like the devil. Oh, they're not going to get divorced or anything. When he's particularly outrageous she forgives him. In fact, I'm inclined to think she loves him. She was a pretty girl when she first came to Detroit."

A pretty girl! The phrase struck Dexter as ludicrous.

"Isn't she—a pretty girl any more?"

"Oh, she's all right."

"Look here," said Dexter, sitting down suddenly, "I don't understand. You say she was a 'pretty girl' and now you say she's 'all right.' I don't understand what you mean—Judy Jones wasn't a pretty girl, at all. She was a great beauty. Why, I knew her, I knew her. She was———"

Devlin laughed pleasantly.

"I'm not trying to start a row," he said. "I think Judy's a nice girl and I like her. I can't understand how a man like Joe Simms could fall madly in love with her, but he did." Then he added, "Most of the women like her."

Dexter looked closely at Devlin, thinking wildly that there must be a reason for this, some insensitivity in the man or some private malice.

"Lots of women fade just-like-*that*," Devlin snapped his fingers. "You must have seen it happen. Perhaps I've forgotten how pretty she was at her wedding. I've seen her so much since then, you see. She has nice eyes."

A sort of dullness settled down upon Dexter. For the first time in his life he felt like getting very drunk. He knew that he was laughing loudly at something Devlin had said but he did not know what it was or why it was funny. When Devlin went, in a few minutes, he lay down on his lounge and looked out the window at the New York skyline into which the sun was sinking in dull lovely shades of pink and gold.

He had thought that having nothing else to lose he was invulnerable at last—but he knew that he had just lost something more, as surely as if he had married Judy Jones and seen her fade away before his eyes.

The dream was gone. Something had been taken from him. In a sort of panic he pushed the palms of his hands into his eyes and tried to bring up a picture of the waters lapping at Lake Erminie and the moonlit verandah, and gingham on the golf links and the dry sun and the gold color of her neck's soft down. And her mouth damp to his kisses and her eyes plaintive with melancholy and her freshness like new fine linen in the morning. Why these things were no longer in the world. They had existed and they existed no more.

For the first time in years the tears were streaming down his face. But they were for himself now. He did not care about mouth and eyes and moving hands. He wanted to care and he could not care. For he had gone away and he could never go back any more. The gates were closed, the sun was gone down and there was no beauty but the grey beauty of steel that withstands all time. Even the grief he could have borne was left behind in the country of illusion, of youth, of the richness of life, where his winter dreams had flourished.

"Long ago," he said, "long ago, there was something in me, but now that thing is gone. I cannot cry. I cannot care. That thing will come back no more."

1922

Ernest Hemingway 1899–1961

Ernest Hemingway was born in Oak Park, Illinois, a suburb of Chicago. His father, a well-to-do physician, initiated his son into the rituals of hunting and fishing and bequeathed to him a way of life, and of death. In 1917, after graduation from high school, Hemingway went to work as a reporter for the Kansas City Star. *Rejected for army service in World War I because of poor vision, he volunteered to serve as a driver for an American ambulance unit in France. He then transferred to duty on the Italian front, where he was seriously wounded in the explosion of a mortar shell. He was the first American to be wounded and survive during World War I on the Italian front. After his recovery, and with decorations for valor which he believed he did not deserve, Hemingway returned home. He worked for the Toronto* Star, *covered the Greco-Turkish War as a foreign correspondent, and then returned to Paris, which, after World War I, was a city full of intellectual life, creativity, and genius.*

In Paris, Hemingway—along with Gertrude Stein, Ezra Pound, T. S. Eliot, and James Joyce—helped create a revolution in literary style and language. He developed a spare, tight, reportorial prose based on deceptively simple sentence structure. He used a restricted vocabulary, precise imagery, and an impersonal, dramatic tone. His first book, Three Stories and Ten Poems, *appeared in 1923. Three years later, with the publication of* The Sun Also Rises, *Hemingway became the spokesman for the men and women that Gertrude Stein had called "a lost generation."*

*His works have sometimes been read as an essentially negative commentary on a modern world filled with sterility, failure, and death. Yet that nihilistic vision is repeatedly modified by Hemingway's affirmative assertion of the possibility of living with style and courage. His primary concern was an individual's "moment of truth" (a notion derived from bullfighting), and he was fascinated by the threat of physical, emotional, or psychic death, a fascination reflected in his lifelong preoccupation with stories of war (*A Farewell to Arms, *1929, and* For Whom the Bell Tolls, *1940*), *the bullfight* (Death in the Afternoon, *1932*), *and the hunt* (Green Hills of Africa, *1935*). *To Hemingway, a person's greatest achievement is to show "grace under pressure," or what he described in* The Sun Also Rises *as holding the "purity of line through the maximum of exposure."*

Hemingway's stature as a writer was confirmed with the publication of A Farewell to Arms *in 1929. The novel portrays a farewell both to war and to love. Hemingway had rejected the romantic ideal of the ultimate union of lovers. He suggested instead that all relationships must end in destruction and in death.*

In 1937 he became a foreign correspondent covering the Spanish Civil War. Three years later he published For Whom the Bell Tolls. *Set in Spain during the Civil War, the novel restates his view of love found and lost and describes the indomitable spirit of the common people. In 1952 the same judgment was reflected in his portrayal of the old fisherman, Santiago, triumphant even in defeat, in* The Old Man and the Sea.

Hemingway received wide acclaim for his novels and for his short stories, which include some of the finest in the English language. In 1954 he was awarded a Nobel Prize for his "mastery of the art of modern narration." He became a public figure whose pronouncements and adventures were publicized and scrutinized throughout the world. Numerous parallels exist between the events of Hemingway's life and those of his characters, but few were closer than those of Richard Cantwell, the hero of Across the River and into the Trees *(1950), whose attempts at stoic control of physical and mental illness foreshadow the struggles and defeats of Hemingway's final years, which ended when he, as his father had done some thirty years before, took his own life on July 2, 1961.*

FURTHER READING: C. Baker, *Ernest Hemingway, The Writer as Artist,* 1952, 1956, 1963, 1972; C. Baker, *Ernest Hemingway, A Life Story,* 1969; *The Short Stories of Ernest Hemingway, Critical Essays,* ed. J. Benson, 1975; S. Donaldson, *By Force of Will, The Life and Art of Ernest Hemingway,* 1977; *Ernest Hemingway, The Papers of a Writer,* ed. B. Oldsey, 1981; *Ernest Hemingway, Selected Letters,* ed. C. Baker, 1981; P. Griffin, *Along with Youth, Hemingway, The Early Years,* 1985; M. Reynolds, *The Young Hemingway,* 1986; K. Lynn, *Hemingway, The Life and the Work,* 1987; P. Smith, *A Reader's Guide to the Short Stories of Ernest Hemingway,* 1989; M. Reynolds, *Hemingway, The Paris Years,* 1989; *New Critical Approaches to the Short Stories of Ernest Hemingway,* ed. J. Benson, 1990; *Hemingway, Essays of Reassessment,* ed. F. Scafella, 1991; M. Reynolds, *Hemingway, The American Homecoming,* 1992; J. Mellow, *Hemingway, A Life Without Consequences,* 1994; M. Mandel, *Reading Hemingway,* 1995; *The Cambridge Companion to Hemingway,* ed. S. Donaldson, 1996; D. Moddelmog, *Reading Desire, In Pursuit of Ernest Hemingway,* 1999; M. Bruccoli, *Classes on Ernest Hemingway,* 2002.

TEXT: *The Complete Short Stories of Ernest Hemingway,* 1987.

THE KILLERS

The door of Henry's lunch-room opened and two men came in. They sat down at the counter.

"What's yours?" George asked them.

"I don't know," one of the men said. "What do you want to eat, Al?"

"I don't know," said Al. "I don't know what I want to eat."

Outside it was getting dark. The street-light came on outside the window. The two men at the counter read the menu. From the other end of the counter Nick Adams watched them. He had been talking to George when they came in.

"I'll have a roast pork tenderloin with apple sauce and mashed potatoes," the first man said.

"It isn't ready yet."

"What the hell do you put it on the card for?"

"That's the dinner," George explained. "You can get that at six o'clock."

George looked at the clock on the wall behind the counter.

"It's five o'clock."

"The clock says twenty minutes past five," the second man said.

"It's twenty minutes fast."

"Oh, to hell with the clock," the first man said. "What have you got to eat?"

"I can give you any kind of sandwiches," George said. "You can have ham and eggs, bacon and eggs, liver and bacon, or a steak."

"Give me chicken croquettes with green peas and cream sauce and mashed potatoes."

"That's the dinner."

"Everything we want's the dinner, eh? That's the way you work it."

"I can give you ham and eggs, bacon and eggs, liver——"

"I'll take ham and eggs," the man called Al said. He wore a derby hat and a black overcoat buttoned across the chest. His face was small and white and he had tight lips. He wore a silk muffler and gloves.

"Give me bacon and eggs," said the other man. He was about the same size as Al. Their faces were different, but they were dressed like twins. Both wore overcoats too tight for them. They sat leaning forward, their elbows on the counter.

"Got anything to drink?" Al asked.

"Silver beer, bevo, ginger-ale," George said.

"I mean you got anything to *drink*?"

"Just those I said."

"This is a hot town," said the other. "What do they call it?"

"Summit."

"Ever hear of it?" Al asked his friend.

"No," said the friend.

"What do you do here nights?" Al asked.

"They eat the dinner," his friend said. "They all come here and eat the big dinner."

"That's right," George said.

"So you think that's right?" Al asked George.

"Sure."

"You're a pretty bright boy, aren't you?"

"Sure," said George.

"Well, you're not," said the other little man. "Is he, Al?"

"He's dumb," said Al. He turned to Nick. "What's your name?"

"Adams."

"Another bright boy," Al said. "Ain't he a bright boy, Max?"

"The town's full of bright boys," Max said.

George put the two platters, one of ham and eggs, the other of bacon and eggs, on the counter. He set down two side-dishes of fried potatoes and closed the wicket into the kitchen.

"Which is yours?" he asked Al.

"Don't you remember?"

"Ham and eggs."

"Just a bright boy," Max said. He leaned forward and took the ham and eggs. Both men ate with their gloves on. George watched them eat.

"What are *you* looking at?" Max looked at George.

"Nothing."

"The hell you were. You were looking at me."

"Maybe the boy meant it for a joke, Max," Al said.

George laughed.

"*You* don't have to laugh," Max said to him. "*You* don't have to laugh at all, see?"

"All right," said George.

"So he thinks it's all right." Max turned to Al. "He thinks it's all right. That's a good one."

"Oh, he's a thinker," Al said. They went on eating.

"What's the bright boy's name down the counter?" Al asked Max.

"Hey, bright boy," Max said to Nick. "You go around on the other side of the counter with your boy friend."

"What's the idea?" Nick asked.

"There isn't any idea."

"You better go around, bright boy," Al said. Nick went around behind the counter.

"What's the idea?" George asked.

"None of your damn business," Al said. "Who's out in the kitchen?"

"The nigger."

"What do you mean the nigger?"

"The nigger that cooks."

"Tell him to come in."

"Where do you think you are?"

"We know damn well where we are," the man called Max said. "Do we look silly?"

"You talk silly," Al said to him. "What the hell do you argue with this kid for? Listen," he said to George, "tell the nigger to come out here."

"What are you going to do to him?"

"Nothing. Use your head, bright boy. What would we do to a nigger?"

George opened the slip that opened back into the kitchen. "Sam," he called. "Come in here a minute."

The door to the kitchen opened and the nigger came in. "What was it?" he asked. The two men at the counter took a look at him.

"All right, nigger. You stand right there," Al said.

Sam, the nigger, standing in his apron, looked at the two men sitting at the counter. "Yes, sir," he said. Al got down from his stool.

"I'm going back to the kitchen with the nigger and bright boy," he said. "Go on back to the kitchen, nigger. You go with him, bright boy." The little man walked after Nick and Sam, the cook, back into the kitchen. The door shut after them. The man called Max sat at the counter opposite George. He didn't look at George but looked in the mirror that ran along back of the counter. Henry's had been made over from a saloon into a lunch-counter.

"Well, bright boy," Max said, looking into the mirror, "why don't you say something?"

"What's it all about?"

"Hey, Al," Max called, "bright boy wants to know what it's all about."

"Why don't you tell him?" Al's voice came from the kitchen."

"What do you think it's all about?"

"I don't know."'

"What do you think?"

Max looked into the mirror all the time he was talking.

"I wouldn't say."

"Hey, Al, bright boy says he wouldn't say what he thinks it's all about."

"I can hear you, all right," Al said from the kitchen. He had propped open the slit that dishes passed through into the kitchen with a catsup bottle. "Listen, bright boy," he said from the kitchen to George. "Stand a little further along the bar. You move a little to the left, Max." He was like a photographer arranging for a group picture.

"Talk to me, bright boy," Max said. "What do you think's going to happen?"

George did not say anything.

"I'll tell you," Max said. "We're going to kill a Swede. Do you know a big Swede named Ole Andreson?"

"Yes."

"He comes here to eat every night, don't he?"

"Sometimes he comes here."

"He comes here at six o'clock, don't he?"

"If he comes."

"We know all that, bright boy," Max said. "Talk about something else. Ever go to the movies?"

"Once in a while."

"You ought to go to the movies more. The movies are fine for a bright boy like you."

"What are you going to kill Ole Andreson for? What did he ever do to you?"

"He never had a chance to do anything to us. He never even seen us."

"And he's only going to see us once," Al said from the kitchen."

"What are you going to kill him for, then?" George asked.

"We're killing him for a friend. Just to oblige a friend, bright boy."

"Shut up," said Al from the kitchen. "You talk too goddam much."

"Well, I got to keep bright boy amused. Don't I, bright boy?"

"You talk too damn much," Al said. "The nigger and my bright boy are amused by themselves. I got them tied up like a couple of girl friends in the convent."

"I suppose you were in a convent?"

"You never know."

"You were in a kosher convent. That's where you were."

George looked up at the clock.

"If anybody comes in you tell them the cook is off, and if they keep after it, you tell them you'll go back and cook yourself. Do you get that, bright boy?"

"All right," George said. "What you going to do with us afterward?"

"That'll depend," Max said. "That's one of those things you never know at the time."

George looked up at the clock. It was a quarter past six. The door from the street opened. A street-car motorman came in.

"Hello, George," he said. "Can I get supper?"

"Sam's gone out," George said. "He'll be back in about half an hour."

"I'd better go up the street," the motorman said. George looked at the clock. It was twenty minutes past six.

"That was nice, bright boy." Max said. "You're a regular little gentleman."

"He knew I'd blow his head off," Al said from the kitchen.

"No," said Max. "It ain't that. Bright boy is nice. He's a nice boy. I like him."

At six-fifty-five George said, "He's not coming."

Two other people had been in the lunch-room. Once George had gone out to the kitchen and made a ham-and-egg sandwich "to go" that a man wanted to take with him. Inside the kitchen he saw Al, his derby hat tipped back, sitting on a stool beside the wicket with the muzzle of a sawed-off shot-gun resting on the ledge. Nick and the cook were back to back in the corner, a towel tied in each of their mouths. George had cooked the sandwich, wrapped it up in oiled paper, put it in a bag, brought it in, and the man had paid for it and gone out.

"Bright boy can do everything," Max said. "He can cook and everything. You'd make some girl a nice wife, bright boy."

"Yes?" George said. "Your friend, Ole Andreson, isn't going to come."

"We'll give him ten minutes," Max said.

Max watched the mirror and the clock. The hands of the clock marked seven o'clock, and then five minutes past seven.

"Come on, Al," said Max. "We better go. He's not coming."

"Better give him five minutes," Al said from the kitchen.

In the five minutes a man came in, and George explained that the cook was sick.

"Why the hell don't you get another cook?" the man asked. "Aren't you running a lunch-counter?" He went out.

"Come on, Al," Max said.

"What about the two bright boys and the nigger?"

"They're all right."

"You think so?"

"Sure. We're through with it."

"I don't like it," said Al. "It's sloppy. You talk too much."

"Oh, what the hell," said Max. "We got to keep amused, haven't we?"

"You talk too much, all the same," Al said. He came out from the kitchen. The cutoff barrels of the shotgun made a slight bulge under the waist of his too tight-fitting overcoat. He straightened his coat with his gloved hands.

"So long, bright boy," he said to George. "You got a lot of luck."

"That's the truth," Max said. "You ought to play the races, bright boy."

The two of them went out the door. George watched them, through the window, pass under the arc-light and cross the street. In their tight overcoats and derby hats they looked like a vaudeville team. George went back through the swinging-door into the kitchen and untied Nick and the cook.

"I don't want any more of that," said Sam, the cook. "I don't want any more of that."

Nick stood up. He had never had a towel in his mouth before.

"Say," he said. "What the hell?" He was trying to swagger it off.

"They were going to kill Ole Andreson," George said. "They were going to shoot him when he came in to eat."

"Ole Andreson?"

"Sure."

The cook felt the corners of his mouth with his thumbs.

"They all gone?" he asked.

"Yeah," said George. "They're gone now."

"I don't like it," said the cook. "I don't like any of it at all."

"Listen," George said to Nick. "You better go see Ole Andreson."

"All right."

"You better not have anything to do with it at all," Sam, the cook, said. "You better stay way out of it."

"Don't go if you don't want to," George said.

"Mixing up in this ain't going to get you anywhere," the cook said. "You stay out of it."

"I'll go see him," Nick said to George. "Where does he live?"

The cook turned away.

"Little boys always know what they want to do," he said.

"He lives up at Hirsch's rooming house," George said to Nick.

"I'll go up there."

Outside the arc-light shone through the bare branches of a tree. Nick walked up the street beside the car-tracks and turned at the next arc-light down a side-street. Three houses up the street was Hirsch's rooming-house. Nick walked up the two steps and pushed the bell. A woman came to the door.

"Is Ole Andreson here?"

"Do you want to see him?"

"Yes, if he's in."

Nick followed the woman up a flight of stairs and back to the end of a corridor. She knocked on the door.

"Who is it?"

"It's somebody to see you, Mr. Andreson," the woman said.

"It's Nick Adams."

"Come in.""

Nick opened the door and went into the room. Ole Andreson was lying on the bed with all his clothes on. He had been a heavyweight prizefighter and he was too long for the bed. He lay with his head on two pillows. He did not look at Nick.

"What was it?" he asked.

"I was up at Henry's," Nick said, "and two fellows came in and tied up me and the cook, and they said they were going to kill you."

It sounded silly when he said it. Ole Andreson said nothing.

"They put us out in the kitchen," Nick went on. "They were going to shoot you when you came in to supper."

Ole Andreson looked at the wall and did not say anything.

"George thought I better come and tell you about it."

"There isn't anything I can do about it," Ole Andreson said.

"I'll tell you what they were like."

"I don't want to know what they were like," Ole Andreson said. He looked at the wall. "Thanks for coming to tell me about it."

"That's all right."

Nick looked at the big man lying on the bed.

"Don't you want me to go and see the police?"

"No," Ole Andreson said. "That wouldn't do any good."

"Isn't there something I could do?"

"No. There ain't anything to do."

"Maybe it was just a bluff."

"No. It ain't just a bluff."

Ole Andreson rolled over toward the wall.

"The only thing is," he said, talking toward the wall, "I just can't make up my mind to go out. I been in here all day."

"Couldn't you get out of town?"

"No," Ole Andreson said. "I'm through with all that running around."

He looked at the wall.

"There ain't anything to do now."

"Couldn't you fix it up some way?"

"No. I got in wrong." He talked in the same flat voice. "There ain't anything to do. After a while I'll make up my mind to go out."

"I better go back and see George," Nick said.

"So long," said Ole Andreson. He did not look toward Nick. "Thanks for coming around."

Nick went out. As he shut the door he saw Ole Andreson with all his clothes on, lying on the bed looking at the wall.

"He's been in his room all day," the landlady said down-stairs. "I guess he don't feel well. I said to him: 'Mr. Andreson, you ought to go out and take a walk on a nice fall day like this.' But he didn't feel like it."

"He doesn't want to go out."

"I'm sorry he don't feel well," the woman said. "He's an awfully nice man. He was in the ring, you know."

"I know it."

"You'd never know it except from the way his face is," the woman said. They stood talking just inside the street door. "He's just as gentle."

"Well, good-night, Mrs. Hirsch," Nick said.

"I'm not Mrs. Hirsch," the woman said. "She owns the place. I just look after it for her. I'm Mrs. Bell."

"Well, good-night, Mrs. Bell," Nick said.

"Good-night," the woman said.

Nick walked up the dark street to the corner under the arc-light, and then along the car-tracks to Henry's eating-house. George was inside, back of the counter.

"Did you see Ole?"

"Yes," said Nick. "He's in his room and he won't go out."

The cook opened the door from the kitchen when he heard Nick's voice.

"I don't even listen to it," he said and shut the door.

"Did you tell him about it?" George asked.

"Sure. I told him but he knows what it's all about."

"What's he going to do?"

"Nothing."

"They'll kill him."

"I guess they will."

"He must have got mixed up in something in Chicago."

"I guess so," said Nick.

"It's a hell of a thing."

"It's an awful thing," Nick said.

They did not say anything. George reached down for a towel and wiped the counter.

"I wonder what he did?" Nick said.

"Double-crossed somebody. That's what they kill them for."

"I'm going to get out of this town," Nick said.

"Yes," said George. "That's a good thing to do."

"I can't stand to think about him waiting in the room and knowing he's going to get it. It's too damned awful."

"Well," said George, "you better not think about it."

1926 1927

William Faulkner 1897–1962

After he received a Nobel Prize for Literature in 1949, William Faulkner's reputation and influence spread throughout the world. But, ironically, the Nobel Prize was awarded largely for works that he had written years before and were so little recognized at the time of their publication that most of them were out of print by the 1940's. The only Faulkner novel that had come close to being a bestseller in its day was Sanctuary, *a book more famous for its shock value than for its literary quality.*

Faulkner was born William Cuthbert Falkner (the "u" he added to his last name when he began to publish) in New Albany, Mississippi. When he was four or five years old, the family moved to Oxford, Mississippi, where he resided for the rest of his life. Oxford was, with some fictional modifications, a prototype of Jefferson, in the mythical county of Yoknapatawpha, the setting of Sartoris *and most of his subsequent works. His central theme, however, was not Oxford, or Mississippi, or even America. It was, as he put it, the universal theme of "the problems of the human heart in conflict with itself."*

Faulkner began his literary career as a poet rather than a fiction writer, but his poetry was undistinguished and commercially unsuccessful. He turned to the writing of prose in 1925 after meeting Sherwood Anderson in New Orleans. With Faulkner's third published novel, Sartoris, *which he completed in 1927 and which was printed in 1929, he "discovered," as he said later, "that my own little postage stamp of native soil was worth writing about and that I would never live long enough to exhaust it, and that by sublimating the actual into the apocryphal I would have complete liberty to use whatever talent I might have to its absolute top. It opened up a gold mine of other people, so I created a cosmos of my own." Using his own cosmos to express his universal theme of "the problems of the human heart," Faulkner created the novels for which he is now best known:* The Sound and the Fury *(1929),* As I Lay Dying *(1930),* The Hamlet *(1940), and* Go Down, Moses *(1942).*

In 1948, after six years in which he published only a few short stories, he resumed his career with Intruder in the Dust. *Three years later* Requiem for a Nun, *a kind of sequel to* Sanctuary, *appeared. His most ambitious single effort was, perhaps,* A Fable *(1954), an allegorical novel, which took him at least nine years to write and which has so far proved baffling to readers and critics alike.* The Town *(1957) and* The Mansion *(1959) complete the trilogy on the Snopes family which began with* The Hamlet. *Faulkner's last novel,* The Reivers, *was published on June 4, 1962. A month later he died.*

Faulkner also published about seventy short stories, some of which were later incorporated into novels, such as "Wash" in Absalom, Absalom!, *"Spotted Horses" in* The Hamlet, *and "The Bear" (with a long section added) in* Go Down, Moses. *Collections of short stories appeared in* These 13 *(1931),* Doctor Martino and Other Stories *(1934),* Knight's Gambit *(1949),* Collected Stories of William Faulkner *(1950), and* Big Woods *(1955).*

Although his home was always Mississippi, Faulkner traveled extensively. He trained as a pilot for the Royal Canadian Flying Corps during 1918, worked in New York City in 1920 and 1921, spent most of 1925 in New Orleans and Europe, and labored off and on for several years as a script writer in Hollywood. Like many other American writers, he never graduated from college, but he read omnivorously a wide variety of literature: the Bible, Greek and Roman classics, Shakespeare, the standard English and American poets and novelists, and such modern writers as the French symbolist poets and Conrad, Joyce, and Eliot. Through the late 1920s and the 1930s, his bold experiments in the dislocation of narrative time and his use of stream-of-consciousness techniques placed him in the forefront of the avant-garde. Faulkner's verbal innovations and the labyrinthine organization of his novels make him difficult to read, but his popularity continues to grow, and today he is considered by many to have been the greatest writer of fiction that the United States has yet produced.

FURTHER READING: *Faulkner in the University,* ed. F. Gwynn and J. Blotner, 1959; J. Faulkner, *My Brother Bill,* 1963; *Essays, Speeches and Public Letters by William Faulkner,* ed. J. Meriwether, 1966; J. Blotner, *Faulkner, A Biography,* 2 vols., 1974, 1 vol., 1982; *Selected Letters of William Faulkner,* ed. J. Blotner, 1977; *Uncollected Short Stories of William Faulkner,* ed. J. Blotner, 1979; D. Minter, *William Faulkner, His Life and Work,* 1980, 1997; M. Kreisworth, *William Faulkner, The Making of a Novelist,* 1983; C. Brooks, *William Faulkner, First Encounters,* 1983; M. Putzel, *Genius of Place, William Faulkner's Triumphant Beginnings,* 1985; J. Sensibar, *The Origins of Faulkner's Art,* 1985; S. Oates, *William Faulkner, The Man and Artist,* 1987; T. Connolly, *Faulkner's World, A Directory of His People and Synopses of Actions in His Published Works,* 1988; F. Karl, *William Faulkner, American Writer,* 1989; M. Millgate, *The Achievement of William Faulkner,* 1989; Andre Bleikasten, *The Ink of Melancholy, Faulkner's Novels from 'The Sound and the Fury' to 'Light in August,'* 1991; J. Ferguson, *Faulkner's Short Fiction,* 1991; J. Williamson, *William Faulkner and Southern History,* 1993; D. Jones, *A Reader's Guide to the Short Stories of William Faulkner,* 1994; D. Roberts, *Faulkner and Southern Womanhood,* 1994; R. Gray, *The Life of William Faulkner,* 1995; *The Cambridge Companion to William Faulkner,* ed. P.

Weinstein, 1995; M. Millgate, *Faulkner's Place,* 1997; D. Singal, *William Faulkner, the Making of a Modernist,* 1997; *Readings on William Faulkner,* ed. C. Swisher, 1998; J. Watson, *William Faulkner, Self-Presentation and Performance,* 2000; *William Faulkner, Six Decades of Criticism,* ed. L. Wagner-Martin, 2002; E. Welty, *On William Faulkner,* 2003.

TEXT: *Collected Stories of William Faulkner,* 1950.

THAT EVENING SUN

I

Monday is no different from any other weekday in Jefferson now. The streets are paved now, and the telephone and electric companies are cutting down more and more of the shade trees—the water oaks, the maples and locusts and elms—to make room for iron poles bearing clusters of bloated and ghostly and bloodless grapes, and we have a city laundry which makes the rounds on Monday morning, gathering the bundles of clothes into bright-colored, specially-made motor cars: the soiled wearing of a whole week now flees apparition-like behind alert and irritable electric horns, with a long diminishing noise of rubber and asphalt like tearing silk, and even the Negro women who still take in white people's washing after the old custom, fetch and deliver it in automobiles.

But fifteen years ago, on Monday morning the quiet, dusty, shady streets would be full of Negro women with, balanced on their steady, turbaned heads, bundles of clothes tied up in sheets, almost as large as cotton bales, carried so without touch of hand between the kitchen door of the white house and the blackened washpot beside a cabin door in Negro Hollow.

Nancy would set her bundle on top of her head, then upon the bundle in turn she would set the black straw sailor hat which she wore winter and summer. She was tall, with a high, sad face sunken a little where her teeth were missing. Sometimes we would go a part of the way down the lane across the pasture with her, to watch the balanced bundle and the hat that never bobbed nor wavered, even when she walked down into the ditch and up the other side and stooped through the fence. She would go down on her hands and knees and crawl through the gap, her head rigid, uptilted, the bundle steady as a rock or a balloon, and rise to her feet again and go on.

Sometimes the husbands of the washing women would fetch and deliver the clothes, but Jesus never did that for Nancy, even before father told him to stay away from our house, even when Dilsey was sick and Nancy would come to cook for us.

And then about half the time we'd have to go down the lane to Nancy's cabin and tell her to come on and cook breakfast. We would stop at the ditch, because father told us to not have anything to do with Jesus—he was a short black man, with a razor scar down his face—and we would throw rocks at Nancy's house until she came to the door, leaning her head around it without any clothes on.

"What yawl mean, chunking my house?" Nancy said. "What you little devils mean?"

"Father says for you to come on and get breakfast," Caddy said. "Father says it's over a half an hour now, and you've got to come this minute."

"I ain't studying no breakfast," Nancy said. "I going to get my sleep out."

"I bet you're drunk," Jason said. "Father says you're drunk. Are you drunk, Nancy?"

"Who says I is?" Nancy said. "I got to get my sleep out. I ain't studying no breakfast."

So after a while we quit chunking the cabin and went back home. When she finally came, it was too late for me to go to school. So we thought it was whisky until that day they arrested her again and they were taking her to jail and they passed Mr Stovall. He was the cashier in the bank and a deacon in the Baptist church, and Nancy began to say:

"When you going to pay me, white man? When are you going to pay me, white man? It's been three times now since you paid me a cent—" Mr Stovall knocked her down, but she kept saying, "When you going to pay me, white man? It's been three times now since—" until Mr Stovall kicked her in the mouth with his heel and the marshall caught Mr Stovall back, and Nancy lying in the street, laughing. She turned her head and spat out some blood and teeth and said, "It's been three times now since he paid me a cent."

That was how she lost her teeth, and all that day they told about Nancy and Mr Stovall, and all that night the ones that passed the jail could hear Nancy singing and yelling. They could see her hands holding to the window bars, and a lot of them stopped along the fence, listening to her and to the jailer trying to make her stop. She didn't shut up until almost daylight, when the jailer began to hear a bumping and scraping upstairs and he went up there and found Nancy hanging from the window bar. He said that it was cocaine and not whisky, because no nigger would try to commit suicide unless he was full of cocaine, because a nigger full of cocaine wasn't a nigger any longer.

The jailer cut her down and revived her; then he beat her, whipped her. She had hung herself with her dress. She had fixed it all right, but when they arrested her she didn't have on anything except a dress and so she didn't have anything to tie her hands with and she couldn't make her hands let go of the window ledge. So the jailer heard the noise and ran up there and found Nancy hanging from the window, stark naked, her belly already swelling out a little, like a little balloon.

When Dilsey was sick in her cabin and Nancy was cooking for us, we could see her apron swelling out; that was before father told Jesus to stay away from the house. Jesus was in the kitchen, sitting behind the stove, with his razor scar on his black face like a piece of dirty string. He said it was a watermelon that Nancy had under her dress.

"It never come off your vine, though," Nancy said.

"Off of what vine?" Caddy said.

"I can cut down the vine it did come off of," Jesus said.

"What makes you want to talk like that before these children?" Nancy said. "Whyn't you go on to work? You done et. You want Mr Jason to catch you hanging around his kitchen, talking that way before these children?"

"Talking what way?" Caddy said. "What vine?"

"I can't hang around white man's kitchen," Jesus said. "But white man can hang around mine. White man can come in my house, but I can't stop him. When white man want to come in my house, I ain't got no house. I can't stop him, but he can't kick me outen it. He can't do that."

Dilsey was still sick in her cabin. Father told Jesus to stay off our place. Dilsey was still sick. It was a long time. We were in the library after supper.

"Isn't Nancy through in the kitchen yet?" mother said. "It seems to me that she has had plenty of time to have finished the dishes."

"Let Quentin go and see," father said. "Go and see if Nancy is through, Quentin. Tell her she can go on home."

I went to the kitchen. Nancy was through. The dishes were put away and the fire was out. Nancy was sitting in a chair, close to the cold stove. She looked at me.

"Mother wants to know if you are through," I said.

"Yes," Nancy said. She looked at me. "I done finished." She looked at me.

"What is it?" I said. "What is it?"

"I ain't nothing but a nigger," Nancy said. "It ain't none of my fault."

She looked at me, sitting in the chair before the cold stove, the sailor hat on her head. I went back to the library. It was the cold stove and all, when you think of a kitchen being warm and busy and cheerful. And with a cold stove and the dishes all put away, and nobody wanting to eat at that hour.

"Is she through?" mother said.

"Yessum," I said.

"What is she doing?" mother said.

"She's not doing anything. She's through."

"I'll go and see," father said.

"Maybe she's waiting for Jesus to come and take her home." Caddy said.

"Jesus is gone," I said. Nancy told us how one morning she woke up and Jesus was gone.

"He quit me," Nancy said. "Done gone to Memphis, I reckon. Dodging them city *po*-lice for a while, I reckon."

"And a good riddance," father said. "I hope he stays there."

"Nancy's scaired of the dark," Jason said.

"So are you," Caddy said.

"I'm not," Jason said.

"Scairy cat," Caddy said.

"I'm not," Jason said.

"You, Candace!" mother said. Father came back.

"I am going to walk down the lane with Nancy," he said. "She says that Jesus is back."

"Has she seen him?" mother said.

"No. Some Negro sent her word that he was back in town. I won't be long."

"You'll leave me alone, to take Nancy home?" mother said. "Is her safety more precious to you than mine?"

"I won't be long," father said.

"You'll leave these children unprotected, with that Negro about?"

"I'm going too," Caddy said. "Let me go, Father."

"What would he do with them, if he were unfortunate enough to have them?" father said.

"I want go to, too," Jason said.

"Jason!" mother said. She was speaking to father. You could tell that by the way she said the name. Like she believed that all day father had been trying to think of doing the thing she wouldn't like the most, and that she knew all the time that after a while he would think of it. I stayed quiet, because father and I both knew that mother would want him to make me stay with her if she just thought of it in time. So father didn't look at me. I was the oldest. I was nine and Caddy was seven and Jason was five.

"Nonsense," father said. "We won't be long."

Nancy had her hat on. We came to the lane. "Jesus always been good to me." Nancy said. "Whenever he had two dollars, one of them was mine." We walked in the lane. "If I just get through the lane," Nancy said. "I be all right then."

The lane was always dark. "This is where Jason got scared on Hallowe'en," Caddy said.

"I didn't," Jason said.

"Can't Aunt Rachel do anything with him?" father said. Aunt Rachel was old. She lived in a cabin beyond Nancy's, by herself. She had white hair and she smoked a pipe in the door, all day long; she didn't work any more. They said she was Jesus' mother. Sometimes she said she was and sometimes she said she wasn't any kin to Jesus.

"Yes, you did," Caddy said. "You were scairder than Frony. You were scairder than T.P. even. Scairder than niggers."

"Can't nobody do nothing with him," Nancy said. "He say I done woke up the devil in him and ain't but one thing going to lay it down again."

"Well, he's gone now," father said. "There's nothing for you to be afraid of now. And if you'd just let white men alone."

"Let what white men alone?" Caddy said. "How let them alone?"

"He ain't gone nowhere," Nancy said. "I can feel him. I can feel him now, in this lane. He hearing us talk, every word, hid somewhere, waiting. I ain't seen him, and I ain't going to see him again but once more, with that razor in his mouth. That razor on that string down his back, inside his shirt. And then I ain't going to be even surprised."

"I wasn't scaird," Jason said.

"If you'd behave yourself, you'd have kept out of this," father said. "But it's all right now. He's probably in St. Louis now. Probably got another wife by now and forgot all about you."

"If he has, I better not find out about it," Nancy said. "I'd stand there right over them, and every time he wropped her, I'd cut that arm off. I'd cut his head off and I'd slit her belly and I'd shove—"

"Hush," father said.

"Slit whose belly, Nancy?" Caddy said.

"I wasn't scaired," Jason said. "I'd walk right down this lane by myself."

"Yah," Caddy said. "You wouldn't dare to put your foot down in it if we were not here too."

II

Dilsey was still sick, so we took Nancy home every night until mother said, "How much longer is this going on? I to be left alone in this big house while you take home a frightened Negro?"

We fixed a pallet in the kitchen for Nancy. One night we waked up, hearing the sound. It was not singing and it was not crying, coming up the dark stairs. There was a light in mother's room and we heard father going down the hall, down the back stairs, and Caddy and I went into the hall. The floor was cold. Our toes curled away from it while we listened to the sound. It was like singing and it wasn't like singing, like the sounds that Negroes make.

Then it stopped and we heard father going down the back stairs, and we went to the head of the stairs. Then the sound began again, in the stairway, not loud, and we could see Nancy's eyes halfway up the stairs, against the wall. They looked like cat's eyes do, like a big cat against the wall, watching us. When we came down the steps to where she was, she quit making the sound again, and we stood there until father came back up from the kitchen, with his pistol in his hand. He went back down with Nancy and they came back with Nancy's pallet.

We spread the pallet in our room. After the light in mother's room went off, we could see Nancy's eyes again. "Nancy," Caddy whispered, "are you asleep, Nancy?"

Nancy whispered something. It was oh or no, I don't know which. Like nobody had made it, like it came from nowhere and went nowhere, until it was like Nancy was not there at all; that I had looked so hard at her eyes on the stairs that they had got printed on my eyeballs, like the sun does when you have closed your eyes and there is no sun. "Jesus," Nancy whispered. "Jesus."

"Was it Jesus?" Caddy said. "Did he try to come into the kitchen?"

"Jesus," Nancy said. Like this: Jeeeeeeeeeeeeeeesus, until the sound went out, like a match or a candle does.

"It's the other Jesus she means," I said.

"Can you see us, Nancy?" Caddy whispered. "Can you see our eyes too?"

"I ain't nothing but a nigger," Nancy said. "God knows. God knows."

"What did you see down there in the kitchen?" Caddy whispered. "What tried to get in?"

"God knows," Nancy said. We could see her eyes. "God knows."

Dilsey got well. She cooked dinner. "You'd bettter stay in bed a day or two longer," father said.

"What for?" Dilsey said. "If I had been a day later, this place would be to rack and ruin. Get on out of here now, and let me get my kitchen straight again."

Dilsey cooked supper too. And that night, just before dark, Nancy came into the kitchen.

"How do you know he's back?" Dilsey said. "You ain't seen him."

"Jesus is a nigger," Jason said.

"I can feel him," Nancy said. "I can feel him laying yonder in the ditch."

"Tonight?" Dilsey said. "Is he there tonight?"

"Dilsey's a nigger too," Jason said.

"You try to eat something," Dilsey said.

"I don't want nothing," Nancy said.

"I ain't a nigger," Jason said.

"Drink some coffee." Dilsey said. She poured a cup of coffee for Nancy. "Do you know he's out there tonight? How come you know it's tonight?"

"I know," Nancy said. "He's there, waiting. I know. I done lived with him too long. I know what he is fixing to do fore he know it himself."

"Drink some coffee," Dilsey said. Nancy held the cup to her mouth and blew into the cup. Her mouth pursed out like a spreading adder's, like a rubber mouth, like she had blown all the color out of her lips with blowing the coffee.

"I ain't a nigger," Jason said. "Are you a nigger, Nancy?"

"I hellborn, child," Nancy said. "I won't be nothing soon. I going back where I come from soon."

III

She began to drink the coffee. While she was drinking, holding the cup in both hands, she began to make the sound again. She made the sound into the cup and the coffee sploshed out onto her hands and her dress. Her eyes looked at us and she sat there, her elbows on her knees, holding the cup in both hands, looking at us across the wet cup, making the sound. "Look at Nancy," Jason said. "Nancy can't cook for us now. Dilsey's got well now."

"You hush up," Dilsey said. Nancy held the cup in both hands, looking at us, making the sound, like there were two of them: one looking at us and the other making the sound. "Whyn't you let Mr Jason telefoam the marshal?" Dilsey said. Nancy stopped then, holding the cup in her long brown hands. She tried to drink some coffee again, but it sploshed out of the cup, onto her hands and her dress, and she put the cup down. Jason watched her.

"I can't swallow it," Nancy said. "I swallows but it won't go down me."

"You go down to the cabin," Dilsey said. "Frony will fix you a pallet and I'll be there soon."

"Won't no nigger stop him," Nancy said.

"I ain't a nigger," Jason said. "Am I, Dilsey?"

"I reckon not," Dilsey said. She looked at Nancy. "I don't reckon so. What you going to do, then?"

Nancy looked at us. Her eyes went fast, like she was afraid there wasn't time to look, without hardly moving at all. She looked at us, at all three of us at one time. "You member that night I stayed in yawls' room?" she said. She told about how we waked up early the next morning, and played. We had to play quiet, on her pallet, until father woke up and it was time to get breakfast. "Go and ask your maw to let me stay here tonight," Nancy said. "I won't need no pallet. We can play some more."

Caddy asked mother. Jason went too. "I can't have Negroes sleeping in the bedrooms," mother said. Jason cried. He cried until mother said he couldn't have any dessert for three days if he didn't stop. Then Jason said he would stop if Dilsey would make a chocolate cake. Father was there.

"Why don't you do something about it?" mother said. "What do we have officers for?"

"Why is Nancy afraid of Jesus?" Caddy said. "Are you afraid of father, mother?"

"What could the officers do?" father said. "If Nancy hasn't seen him, how could the officers find him?"

"Then why is she afraid?" mother said.

"She says he is there. She says she knows he is there tonight."

"Yet we pay taxes," mother said. "I must wait here alone in this big house while you take a Negro woman home."

"You know that I am not lying outside with a razor," father said.

"I'll stop if Dilsey will make a chocolate cake," Jason said. Mother told us to go out and father said he didn't know if Jason would get a chocolate cake or not, but he knew what Jason was going to get in about a minute. We went back to the kitchen and told Nancy.

"Father said for you to go home and lock the door, and you'll be all right," Caddy said. "All right from what, Nancy? Is Jesus mad at you?" Nancy was holding the coffee cup in her hands again, her elbows on her knees and her hands holding the cup between her knees. She was looking into the cup. "What have you done that made Jesus mad?" Caddy said. Nancy let the cup go. It didn't break on the floor, but the coffee spilled out, and Nancy sat there with her hands still making the shape of the cup. She began to make that sound again, not loud. Not singing and not unsinging. We watched her.

"Here," Dilsey said. "You quit that, now. You get aholt of yourself. You wait here. I going to get Versh to walk home with you." Dilsey went out.

We looked at Nancy. Her shoulders kept shaking, but she quit making the sound. We watched her. "What's Jesus going to do to you?" Caddy said. "He went away."

Nancy looked at us. "We had fun that night I stayed in yawls' room, didn't we?"

"I didn't," Jason said. "I didn't have any fun."

"You were asleep in mother's room," Caddy said. "You were not there."

"Let's go down to my house and have some more fun," Nancy said.

"Mother won't let us," I said. "It's too late now."

"Don't bother her," Nancy said. "We can tell her in the morning. She won't mind."

"She wouldn't let us," I said.

"Don't ask her now," Nancy said. "Don't bother her now."

"She didn't say we couldn't go," Caddy said.

"We didn't ask," I said.

"If you go, I'll tell," Jason said.

"We'll have fun," Nancy said. "They won't mind, just to my house. I been working for yawl a long time. They won't mind."

"I'm not afraid to go." Caddy said. "Jason is the one that's afraid. He'll tell."

"I'm not," Jason said.

"Yes, you are," Caddy said. "You'll tell."

"I won't tell," Jason said. "I'm not afraid."

"Jason ain't afraid to go with me," Nancy said. "Is you, Jason?"

"Jason is going to tell," Caddy said. The lane was dark. We passed the pasture gate. "I bet if something was to jump out from behind that gate, Jason would holler."

"I wouldn't," Jason said. We walked down the lane. Nancy was talking loud.

"What are you talking so loud for, Nancy?" Caddy said.

"Who; me?" Nancy said. "Listen at Quentin and Caddy and Jason saying I'm talking loud."

"You talk like there was five of us here," Caddy said. "You talk like father was here too."

"Who; me talking loud, Mr. Jason?" Nancy said.

"Nancy called Jason 'Mister,' " Caddy said.

"Listen how Caddy and Quentin and Jason talk," Nancy said.

"We're not talking loud," Caddy said. "You're the one that's talking like father—"

"Hush," Nancy said; "hush, Mr. Jason."

"Nancy called Jason 'Mister' aguh—"

"Hush," Nancy said. She was talking loud when we crossed the ditch and stooped through the fence where she used to stoop through with the clothes on her head. Then we came to her house. We were going fast then. She opened the door. The smell of the house was like the lamp and the smell of Nancy was like the wick, like they were waiting for one another to begin to smell. She lit the lamp and closed the door and put the bar up. Then she quit talking loud, looking at us.

"What're we going to do?" Caddy said.

"What do yawl want to do?" Nancy said.

"You said we would have some fun," Caddy said.

There was something about Nancy's house; something you could smell besides Nancy and the house. Jason smelled it, even. "I don't want to stay here," he said. "I want to go home."

"Go home, then," Caddy said.

"I don't want to go by myself," Jason said.

"We're going to have some fun," Nancy said.

"How?" Caddy said.

Nancy stood by the door. She was looking at us, only it was like she had emptied her eyes, like she had quit using them. "What do you want to do?" she said.

"Tell us a story," Caddy said. "Can you tell a story?"

"Yes," Nancy said.

"Tell it," Caddy said. We looked at Nancy. "You don't know any stories."

"Yes," Nancy said. "Yes I do."

She came and sat in a chair before the hearth. There was a little fire there. Nancy built it up, when it was already hot inside. She built a good blaze. She told a story. She talked like her eyes looked, like her eyes watching us and her voice talking to us did not belong to her. Like she was living somewhere else, waiting somewhere else. She was outside the cabin. Her voice was inside and the shape of her, the Nancy that could stoop under a barbed wire fence with a bundle of clothes balanced on her head as though without weight, like a balloon, was there. But that was all. "And so this here queen come walking up to the ditch, where that bad man was hiding. She was walking up to the ditch, and she say, 'If I can just get past this here ditch,' was what she say . . ."

"What ditch?" Caddy said. "A ditch like that one there? Why did a queen want to go into a ditch?"

"To get to her house," Nancy said. She looked at us. "She had to cross the ditch to get into her house quick and bar the door."

"Why did she want to go home and bar the door?" Caddy said.

IV

Nancy looked at us. She quit talking. She looked at us. Jason's legs stuck straight out of his pants where he sat on Nancy's lap. "I don't think that's a good story," he said. "I want to go home."

"Maybe we had better," Caddy said. She got up from the floor. "I bet they are looking for us right now." She went toward the door.

"No," Nancy said. "Don't open it." She got up quick and passed Caddy. She didn't touch the door, the wooden bar.

"Why not?" Caddy said.

"Come back to the lamp," Nancy said. "We'll have fun. You don't have to go."

"We ought to go," Caddy said. "Unless we have a lot of fun." She and Nancy came back to the fire, the lamp.

"I want to go home," Jason said. "I'm going to tell."

"I know another story," Nancy said. She stood close to the lamp. She looked at Caddy, like when your eyes look up at a stick balanced on your nose. She had to look down to see Caddy, but her eyes looked like that, like when you are balancing a stick.

"I won't listen to it," Jason said. "I'll bang on the floor."

"It's a good one," Nancy said. "It's better than the other one."

"What's it about?" Caddy said. Nancy was standing by the lamp. Her hand was on the lamp, against the light, long and brown.

"Your hand is on that hot globe," Caddy said. "Don't it feel hot to your hand?"

Nancy looked at her hand on the lamp chimney. She took her hand away, slow. She stood there, looking at Caddy, wringing her long hand as though it were tied to her wrist with a string.

"Let's do something else," Caddy said.

"I want to go home," Jason said.

"I got some popcorn," Nancy said. She looked at Caddy and then at Jason and then at me and then at Caddy again. "I got some popcorn."

"I don't like popcorn," Jason said. "I'd rather have candy."

Nancy looked at Jason. "You can hold the popper." She was still wringing her hand; it was long and limp and brown.

"All right," Jason said. "I'll stay a while if I can do that. Caddy can't hold it. I'll want to go home if Caddy holds the popper."

Nancy built up the fire. "Look at Nancy putting her hands in the fire," Caddy said. "What's the matter with you, Nancy?"

"I got popcorn," Nancy said. "I got some." She took the popper from under the bed. It was broken. Jason began to cry.

"Now we can't have any popcorn," he said.

"We ought to go home, anyway," Caddy said. "Come on, Quentin."

"Wait," Nancy said; "wait. I can fix it. Don't you want to help me fix it?"

"I don't think I want any," Caddy said. "It's too late now."

"You help me, Jason," Nancy said. "Don't you want to help me?"

"No," Jason said. "I want to go home."

"Hush," Nancy said; "hush. Watch. Watch me. I can fix it so Jason can hold it and pop the corn." She got a piece of wire and fixed the popper.

"It won't hold good," Caddy said.

"Yes, it will," Nancy said. "Yawl watch. Yawl help me shell some corn."

The popcorn was under the bed too. We shelled it into the popper and Nancy helped Jason hold the popper over the fire.

"It's not popping," Jason said. "I want to go home."

"You wait," Nancy said. "It'll begin to pop. We'll have fun then." She was sitting close to the fire. The lamp was turned up so high it was beginning to smoke.

"Why don't you turn it down some?" I said.

"It's all right," Nancy said. "I'll clean it. Yawl wait. The popcorn will start in a minute."

"I don't believe it's going to start," Caddy said. "We ought to start home, anyway. They'll be worried."

"No," Nancy said. "It's going to pop. Dilsey will tell um yawl with me. I been working for yawl long time. They won't mind if yawl at my house. You wait, now. It'll start popping any minute now."

Then Jason got some smoke in his eyes and he began to cry. He dropped the popper into the fire. Nancy got a wet rag and wiped Jason's face, but he didn't stop crying.

"Hush," she said. "Hush." But he didn't hush. Caddy took the popper out of the fire.

"It's burned up," she said. "You'll have to get some more popcorn, Nancy."

"Did you put all of it in?" Nancy said.

"Yes," Caddy said. Nancy looked at Caddy. Then she took the popper and opened it and poured the cinders into her apron and began to sort the grains, her hands long and brown, and we watching her.

"Haven't you got any more?" Caddy said.

"Yes," Nancy said; "yes. Look. This here ain't burnt. All we need to do is—"

"I want to go home," Jason said. "I'm going to tell."

"Hush," Caddy said. We all listened. Nancy's head was already turned toward the barred door, her eyes filled with red lamplight. "Somebody is coming," Caddy said.

Then Nancy began to make that sound again, not loud, sitting there above the fire, her long hands dangling between her knees; all of a sudden water began to come out on her face in big drops, running down her face, carrying in each one a little turning ball of firelight like a spark until it dropped off her chin. "She's not crying," I said.

"I ain't crying," Nancy said. Her eyes were closed. "I ain't crying. Who is it?"

"I don't know," Caddy said. She went to the door and looked out. "We've got to go now," she said. "Here comes father."

"I'm going to tell," Jason said. "Yawl made me come."

The water still ran down Nancy's face. She turned in her chair. "Listen. Tell him. Tell him we going to have fun. Tell him I take good care of yawl until in the morning. Tell him to let me come home with yawl and sleep on the floor. Tell him I won't need no pallet. We'll have fun. You member last time how we had so much fun?"

"I didn't have fun," Jason said. "You hurt me. You put smoke in my eyes. I'm going to tell."

V

Father came in. He looked at us. Nancy did not get up.

"Tell him," she said.

"Caddy made us come down here," Jason said. "I didn't want to."

Father came to the fire. Nancy looked up at him. "Can't you go to Aunt Rachel's and stay?" he said. Nancy looked up at father, her hands between her knees. "He's not here," father said. "I would have seen him. There's not a soul in sight."

"He in the ditch," Nancy said. "He waiting in the ditch yonder."

"Nonsense," father said. He looked at Nancy. "Do you know he's there?"

"I got the sign," Nancy said.

"What sign?"

"I got it. It was on the table when I come in. It was a hogbone, with blood meat still on it, laying by the lamp. He's out there. When yawl walk out that door, I gone."

"Gone where, Nancy?" Caddy said.

"I'm not a tattletale," Jason said.

"Nonsense," father said.

"He out there," Nancy said. "He looking through that window this minute, waiting for yawl to go. Then I gone."

"Nonsense," father said. "Lock up your house and we'll take you on to Aunt Rachel's."

" 'Twon't do no good," Nancy said. She didn't look at father now, but he looked down at her, at her long, limp, moving hands. "Putting it off won't do no good."

"Then what do you want to do?" father said.

"I don't know," Nancy said. "I can't do nothing. Just put it off. And that don't do no good. I reckon it belong to me. I reckon what I going to get ain't no more than mine."

"Get what?" Caddy said. "What's yours?"

"Nothing," father said. "You all must get to bed."

"Caddy made me come," Jason said.

"Go on to Aunt Rachel's," father said.

"It won't do no good," Nancy said. She sat before the fire, her elbows on her knees, her long hands between her knees. "When even your own kitchen wouldn't do no good. When even if I was sleeping on the floor in the room with your children, and the next morning there I am, and blood—"

"Hush," father said. "Lock the door and put out the lamp and go to bed."

"I scared of the dark," Nancy said. "I scared for it to happen in the dark."

"You mean you're going to sit right here with the lamp lighted?" father said. Then Nancy began to make the sound again, sitting before the fire, her long hands between her knees. "Ah, damnation," father said. "Come along, chillen. It's past bedtime."

"When yawl go home, I gone," Nancy said. She talked quieter now, and her face looked quiet, like her hands. "Anyway, I got my coffin money saved up with Mr. Lovelady." Mr. Lovelady was a short, dirty man who collected the Negro insurance, coming around the the cabins or the kitchens every Saturday morning, to collect fifteen cents. He and his wife lived at the hotel. One morning his wife committed suicide. They had a child, a little girl. He and the child went away. After a week or two he came back alone. We would see him going along the lanes and the back streets on Saturday mornings.

"Nonsense," father said. "You'll be the first thing I'll see in the kitchen tomorrow morning."

"You'll see what you'll see, I reckon," Nancy said. "But it will take the Lord to say what that will be."

VI

We left her sitting before the fire.

"Come and put the bar up," father said. But she didn't move. She didn't look at us again, sitting quietly there between the lamp and the fire. From some distance down the lane we could look back and see her through the open door.

"What, Father?" Caddy said. "What's going to happen?"

"Nothing," father said. Jason was on father's back, so Jason was the tallest of all of us. We went down in to the ditch. I looked at it, quiet. I couldn't see much where the moonlight and the shadows tangled.

"If Jesus is hid here, he can see us, can't he?" Caddy said.

"He's not there," father said. "He went away a long time ago."

"You made me come," Jason said, high; against the sky it looked like father had two heads, a little one and a big one. "I didn't want to."

We went up out of the ditch. We could still see Nancy's house and the open door, but we couldn't see Nancy now, sitting before the fire with the door open, because she was tired. "I just done got tired," she said. "I just a nigger. It ain't no fault of mine."

But we could hear her, because she began just after we came up out of the ditch, the sound that was not singing and not unsinging. "Who will do our washing now, Father?" I said.

"I'm not a nigger," Jason said, high and close to father's head.

"You're worse," Caddy said, "you are a tattletale. If something was to jump out, you'd be scairder than a nigger."

"I wouldn't," Jason said.

"You'd cry," Caddy said.

"Caddy," father said.

"I wouldn't!" Jason said.

"Scairy cat," Caddy said.

"Candace!" father said.

1928? 1931

Langston Hughes 1902–1967

Although Langston Hughes became the leader of the Harlem writers who created the Black Literary Renaissance of the 1920s, he was born in Joplin, Missouri, and spent most of his youth in the American Midwest. He first came to New York in 1921 to attend Columbia University. A year later he shipped out as a seaman and cook's helper on a tramp steamer to Africa and Europe. He lived and worked in Paris and Italy and then returned to the United States, where he took a job as a busboy in a Washington, D.C., hotel. There, in 1925, he was "discovered" by the poet Vachel Lindsay, who praised Hughes's poems and advised him to devote himself to literature and to "hide and write and study and think."

But Hughes had begun writing long before. In grammar school he had been chosen class poet, and while still in high school he published two poems in national magazines.

His first books, The Weary Blues *(1926) and* Fine Clothes to the Jew *(1927), won poetry prizes and brought him wide acclaim. His first novel,* Not Without Laughter, *appeared in 1930. Hughes had a wide-ranging talent. He was a successful humorist and a historian of the lives of blacks. He wrote novels, short stories, poems, children's books, song lyrics, and operas. He translated foreign writers and wrote numerous plays, three of which were produced on Broadway.*

Much of his best writing was journalistic. In 1937 he served as a foreign correspondent covering the Spanish Civil War for the Baltimore Afro-American *newspaper. His most popular works were newspaper sketches written for the* Chicago Defender *in the 1940s. The sketches recounted the adventures and opinions of an innocent, downtrodden Negro, "Simple," whose penetrating views of blacks and whites provided Hughes with the means for making broad satirical and critical commentary on society and government.*

Hughes was a worldly cosmopolite who lived an almost nomadic life. He traveled to Mexico, Cuba, and the Caribbean, to Africa, Western Europe, the Soviet Union, China, and Japan. But he was most influenced by his American experience, by his black heritage, and by the vivid life of New York City's Harlem with its blues and jazz music that so influenced the structure and rhythm of such poems as "The Weary Blues."

Langston Hughes was the first black American to support himself as a professional writer. In all, he produced more than sixty books. He was also one of the first American writers to receive extended and serious critical attention for realistic portrayals of black Americans. Through his poetry, fiction, and essays, he became one of the dominant voices speaking out for the significance of black culture at the core of life in twentieth-century America. In the twenty-first century his work still proclaims, "I, too, am America."

FURTHER READING: *I Wonder as I Wander, An Autobiographical Journey,* 1956; *The Langston Hughes Reader,* 1958; J. Emanuel, *Langston Hughes,* 1967; M. Meltzer, *Langston Hughes, A Biography,* 1968; C. Rollins, *Black Troubadour,* 1970; F. Berry, *Langston Hughes, Before and Beyond Harlem,* 1983; A. Rampersad, *The Life of Langston Hughes,* 2 vols., 1986; S. Tracy, *Langston Hughes and the Blues,* 1988; R. Miller, *The Art and Imagination of Langston Hughes,* 1989; H. Ostrom, *Langston Hughes,* 1993; *Short Stories of Langston Hughes,* ed. A. Harper, 1997; *Langston Hughes, The Contemporary Reviews,* ed. T. Dace, 1997; *Langston Hughes,* ed. H. Bloom, 2002; *The Collected Works of Langston Hughes,* 16 vols., ed. A. Rampersad and others, 2001–2003.

TEXTS: "Dream Boogie" and "Harlem" from *Montage of a Dream Deferred,* 1951. All other poems from *Selected Poems of Langston Hughes,* 1973.

THE NEGRO SPEAKS OF RIVERS

To W. E. Du Bois[1]

I've known rivers:
I've known rivers ancient as the world and older than the
flow of human blood in human veins.

My soul has grown deep like the rivers.

[1]William Edward Du Bois (1868–1963), black American writer and civil rights leader.

I bathed in the Euphrates[2] when dawns were young.
I built my hut near the Congo and it lulled me to sleep.
I looked upon the Nile and raised the pyramids above it.
I heard the singing of the Mississippi when Abe Lincoln
went down to New Orleans, and I've seen its muddy
bosom turn all golden in the sunset.

I've known rivers:
Ancient, dusky rivers.

My soul has grown deep like the rivers.
1920 1921, 1926

YOUNG GAL'S BLUES

I'm gonna walk to the graveyard
'Hind ma friend Miss Cora Lee.
Gonna walk to the graveyard
'Hind ma dear friend Cora Lee.
Cause when I'm dead some
Body'll have to walk behind me.

I'm goin' to the po' house
To see ma old Aunt Clew.
Goin' to the po' house
To see ma old Aunt Clew.
When I'm old an' ugly
I'll want to see somebody, too.

The po' house is lonely
An' the grave is cold.
O, the po' house is lonely,
The graveyard grave is cold.
But I'd rather be dead than
To be ugly an' old.

When love is gone what
Can a young gal do?
When love is gone, O,
What can a young gal do?
Keep on a-lovin' me, daddy,
Cause I don't want to be blue.
1927

[2]Euphrates: river flowing through Turkey, Syria, and Iraq into the Persian Gulf. Congo: river flowing through west central Africa into the Atlantic. Nile: river flowing through Egypt into the Mediterranean. Each passes through lands where ancient civilizations once flourished.

I, TOO

I, too, sing America.

I am the darker brother.
They send me to eat in the kitchen
When company comes,
But I laugh,
And eat well,
And grow strong.

Tomorrow,
I'll be at the table
When company comes.
Nobody'll dare
Say to me,
"Eat in the kitchen,"
Then.

Besides,
They'll see how beautiful I am
And be ashamed—

I, too, am America.

1932

NOTE ON COMMERCIAL THEATRE

You've taken my blues and gone—
You sing 'em on Broadway
And you sing 'em in Hollywood Bowl,
And you mixed 'em up with symphonies
And you fixed 'em
So they don't sound like me.
Yep, you done taken my blues and gone.

You also took my spirituals and gone.
You put me in *Macbeth* and *Carmen Jones*
And all kinds of *Swing Mikados*[1]
And in everything but what's about me—
But someday somebody'll
Stand up and talk about me,
And write about me—
Black and beautiful—
And sing about me,
And put on plays about me!

[1]Hughes refers to three Broadway shows produced with black casts.

I reckon it'll be
Me myself!

Yes, it'll be me.

1949

DREAM BOOGIE

Good morning, daddy!
Ain't you heard
The boogie-woogie rumble
Of a dream deferred?

Listen closely:
You'll hear their feet
Beating out and beating out a——

You think
It's a happy beat?

Listen to it closely:
Ain't you heard
something underneath
like a——

What did I say?

Sure,
I'm happy!
Take it away!

Hey, pop!
Re-bop!
Mop!

Y-e-a-h!

1951

HARLEM

What happens to a dream deferred?

Does it dry up
like a raisin in the sun?
Or fester like a sore——
And then run?

Does it stink like rotten meat?
Or crust and sugar over—
like a syrupy sweet?

Maybe it just sags
like a heavy load.

Or does it explode?

1951

John Steinbeck 1902–1968

John Steinbeck was the foremost novelist of the American Depression of the 1930s. He was born in Salinas, California, the locale of much of his finest fiction. His sympathy for the migrant workers and the downtrodden, so evident in his writing, was the result of firsthand knowledge of their struggles. From his boyhood he was self-supporting; he worked as a laborer, a seaman on a cattle-boat (where he hoped and failed to become a writer), newspaper reporter, bricklayer, chemist's assistant, surveyor, and migratory fruit picker. His writing reflected his concern with the rituals of manual labor, people "doing" rather than "being," and he believed that the writer's first duty was to "set down his time as nearly as he can understand it" and serve as "the watch-dog of society . . . to satirize its silliness, to attack its injustices, to stigmatize its faults."

The publication of Tortilla Flat *(1935), the tender, sentimental portrait of the indestructibility of the California* paisanos, *brought him sudden fame. In the following year* In Dubious Battle *appeared. It was Steinbeck's most clearly "proletarian" novel of class struggle, depicting the lives of migrant workers and their resistance to exploitation by the entrenched forces of society. In* Of Mice and Men *(1937) he portrayed the friendship of two itinerant workers who yearn for a permanent home they will never find. In* The Long Valley *(1938) he described the fate of the lowly whose instinctive responses to life led only to destruction.* The Grapes of Wrath *(1939), generally regarded as his masterpiece, showed the migration of the "Okies" from the "Dust Bowls" to California, a migration that ended in broken dreams and misery but at the same time affirmed the ability of the common people to endure and prevail.*

Steinbeck's treatment of the social problems of his time, particularly the plight of the dispossessed farmer, earned him a Pulitzer Prize in 1940 and, in 1962, a Nobel Prize for Literature. At its best, Steinbeck's lyric prose vividly caught the qualities of speech, the character, the legends, and the humor of his native region. He was a superb storyteller whose reforming vision led him to contrast the conflicting moral codes of people in search of permanent ideals: "What we have always wanted," he wrote in The Sea of Cortez *(1941), "is an* unchangeable, *and we have found that only a compass point, a thought, an individual ideal, does not change."*

FURTHER READING: *Steinbeck, A Life in Letters,* ed. E. Steinbeck and R. Wallsten, 1975; N. Valjean, *John Steinbeck,* 1975; J. Benson, *The True Adventures of John Steinbeck, Writer,* 1984; L. Owens, *John Steinbeck's Re-Vision of America,* 1985; J. Timmerman, *John*

Steinbeck's Fiction, 1986; J. Hughes, *John Steinbeck, A Study of the Short Fiction,* 1989; J. Timmerman, *The Domestic Landscape of John Steinbeck's Short Stories,* 1990; *The Steinbeck Question, New Essays in Criticism,* ed. D. Noble, 1993; W. French, *John Steinbeck's Fiction Revisited,* 1994; J. Parini, *John Steinbeck, A Biography,* 1994; R. Simmond, *John Steinbeck, The War Years,* 1996; *Beyond Boundaries, Rereading John Steinbeck,* ed. S. Shillinglaw and K. Hearle, 2002; *John Steinbeck,* ed. H. Bloom, 2003; S. George, *The Moral Philosophy of John Steinbeck,* 2005; J. Schulz, *John Steinbeck A to Z,* 2005.

TEXT: *The Long Valley,* 1938.

FLIGHT

About fifteen miles below Monterey, on the wild coast, the Torres family had their farm, a few sloping acres above a cliff that dropped to the brown reefs and to the hissing white waters of the ocean. Behind the farm the stone mountains stood up against the sky. The farm buildings huddled like little clinging aphids on the mountain skirts, crouched low to the ground as though the wind might blow them into the sea. The little shack, the rattling, rotting barn were grey-bitten with sea salt, beaten by the damp wind until they had taken on the color of the granite hills. Two horses, and a red cow and a red calf, half a dozen pigs and a flock of lean, multicolored chickens stocked the place. A little corn was raised on the sterile slope, and it grew short and thick under the wind, and all the cobs formed on the landward sides of the stalks.

Mama Torres, a lean, dry woman with ancient eyes, had ruled the farm for ten years, ever since her husband tripped over a stone in the field one day and fell full length on a rattlesnake. When one is bitten on the chest there is not much that can be done.

Mama Torres had three children, two undersized black ones of twelve and fourteen, Emilio and Rosy, whom Mama kept fishing on the rocks below the farm when the sea was kind and when the truant officer was in some distant part of Monterey County. And there was Pepé the tall smiling son of nineteen, a gentle, affectionate boy, but very lazy. Pepé had a tall head, pointed at the top, and from its peak, coarse black hair grew down like a thatch all around. Over his smiling little eyes Mama cut a straight bang so he could see. Pepé had sharp Indian cheek bones and an eagle nose, but his mouth was as sweet and shapely as a girl's mouth, and his chin was fragile and chiseled. He was loose and gangling, all legs and feet and wrists, and he was very lazy. Mama thought him fine and brave, but she never told him so. She said, "Some lazy cow must have got into thy father's family, else how could I have a son like thee." And she said, "When I carried thee, a sneaking lazy coyote came out of the brush and looked at me one day. That must have made thee so."

Pepé smiled sheepishly and stabbed at the ground with his knife to keep the blade sharp and free from rust. It was his inheritance, that knife, his father's knife. The long heavy blade folded back into the black handle. There was a button on the handle. When Pepé pressed the button, the blade leaped out ready for use. The knife was with Pepé always, for it had been his father's knife.

One sunny morning when the sea below the cliff was glinting and blue and the white surf creamed on the reef, when even the stone mountains looked kindly, Mama Torres called out the door of the shack, "Pepé, I have a labor for thee."

There was no answer. Mama listened. From behind the barn she heard a burst of laughter. She lifted her full long skirt and walked in the direction of the noise.

Pepé was sitting on the ground with his back against a box. His white teeth glistened. On either side of him stood the two black ones, tense and expectant. Fifteen feet away a redwood post was set in the ground. Pepé's right hand lay limply in his lap, and in the palm the big black knife rested. The blade was closed back into the handle. Pepé looked smiling at the sky.

Suddenly Emilio cried, "Ya!"

Pepé's wrist flicked like the head of a snake. The blade seemed to fly open in mid-air, and with a thump the point dug into the redwood post, and the black handle quivered. The three burst into excited laughter. Rosy ran to the post and pulled out the knife and brought it back to Pepé. He closed the blade and settled the knife carefully in his listless palm again. He grinned self-consciously at the sky.

"Ya!"

The heavy knife lanced out and sunk into the post again. Mama moved forward like a ship and scattered the play.

"All day you do foolish things with the knife, like a toy-baby," she stormed. "Get up on thy huge feet that eat up shoes. Get up!" She took him by one loose shoulder and hoisted at him. Pepé grinned sheepishly and came half-heartedly to his feet. "Look!" Mama cried. "Big lazy, you must catch the horse and put on him thy father's saddle. You must ride to Monterey. The medicine bottle is empty. There is no salt. Go thou now, Peanut! Catch the horse."

A revolution took place in the relaxed figure of Pepé. "To Monterey, me? Alone? *Si,* Mama."

She scowled at him. "Do not think, big sheep, that you will buy candy. No, I will give you only enough for the medicine and the salt."

Pepé smiled. "Mama, you will put the hatband on the hat?"

She relented then. "Yes, Pepé. You may wear the hatband."

His voice grew insinuating. "And the green handkerchief, Mama?"

"Yes, if you go quickly and return with no trouble, the silk green handkerchief will go. If you make sure to take off the handkerchief when you eat so no spot may fall on it. . . ."

"*Si,* Mama. I will be careful. I am a man."

"Thou? A man? Thou art a peanut."

He went into the rickety barn and brought out a rope, and he walked agilely enough up the hill to catch the horse.

When he was ready and mounted before the door, mounted on his father's saddle that was so old that the oaken frame showed through torn leather in many places, then Mama brought out the round black hat with the tooled leather band, and she reached up and knotted the green silk handkerchief about his neck. Pepé's blue denim coat was much darker than his jeans, for it had been washed much less often.

Mama handed up the big medicine bottle and the silver coins. "That for the medicine," she said, "and that for the salt. That for a candle to burn for the papa. That for *dulces*[1] for the little ones. Our friend Mrs. Rodriguez will give you dinner and maybe a bed for the night. When you go to the church say only ten Paternosters and only twenty-five Ave Marias. Oh! I know, big coyote. You would sit there flapping your mouth over Aves all day while you looked at the candles and the holy pictures. That is not good devotion to stare at the pretty things."

The black hat, covering the high pointed head and black thatched hair of Pepé, gave him dignity and age. He sat the rangy horse well. Mama thought how handsome he was, dark and lean and tall. "I would not send thee now alone, thou little one, except for the medicine," she said softly. "It is not good to have no medicine, for who knows when the toothache will come, or the sadness of the stomach. These things are."

"Adios, Mama," Pepé cried. "I will come back soon. You may send me often alone. I am a man."

"Thou art a foolish chicken."

He straightened his shoulders, flipped the reins against the horse's shoulder and rode away. He turned once and saw that they still watched him, Emilio and Rosy and Mama. Pepé grinned with pride and gladness and lifted the tough buckskin horse to a trot.

When he had dropped out of sight over a little dip in the road, Mama turned to the black ones, but she spoke to herself. "He is nearly a man now," she said. "It will be a nice thing to have a man in the house again." Her eyes sharpened on the children. "Go to the rocks now. The tide is going out. There will be abalones to be found." She put the iron hooks into their hands and saw them down the steep trail to the reefs. She brought the smooth stone *metate* to the doorway and sat grinding her corn to flour and looking occasionally at the road over which Pepé had gone. The noonday came and then the afternoon, when the little ones beat the abalones on a rock to make them tender and Mama patted the tortillas to make them thin. They ate their dinner as the red sun was plunging down toward the ocean. They sat on the doorsteps and watched the big white moon come over the mountain tops.

Mama said, "He is now at the house of our friend Mrs. Rodriguez. She will give him nice things to eat and maybe a present."

Emilio said, "Some day I too will ride to Monterey for medicine. Did Pepé come to be a man today?"

Mama said wisely, "A boy gets to be a man when a man is needed. Remember this thing. I have known boys forty years old because there was no need for a man."

Soon afterwards they retired, Mama in her big oak bed on one side of the room, Emilio and Rosy in their boxes full of straw and sheepskins on the other side of the room.

The moon went over the sky and surf roared on the rocks. The roosters crowed the first call. The surf subsided to a whispering surge against the reef. The moon dropped toward the sea. The roosters crowed again.

The moon was near down to the water when Pepé rode on a winded horse to his home flat. His dog bounced out and circled the horse yelping with

[1]Spanish: sweets.

pleasure. Pepé slid off the saddle to the ground. The weathered little shack was silver in the moonlight and the square shadow of it was black to the north and east. Against the east the piling mountains were misty with light; their tops melted into the sky.

Pepé walked wearily up the three steps and into the house. It was dark inside. There was a rustle in the corner.

Mama cried out from her bed. "Who comes? Pepé, is it thou?"

"*Si,* Mama."

"Did you get the medicine?"

"*Si,* Mama."

"Well, go to sleep, then. I thought you would be sleeping at the house of Mrs. Rodriguez." Pepé stood silently in the dark room. "Why do you stand there, Pepé? Did you drink wine?"

"*Si,* Mama."

"Well, go to bed then and sleep out the wine."

His voice was tired and patient, but very firm. "Light the candle, Mama. I must go away into the mountains."

"What is this, Pepé? You are crazy." Mama struck a sulphur match and held the little blue burr until the flame spread up the stick. She set light to the candle on the floor beside her bed. "Now, Pepé, what is this you say?" She looked anxiously into his face.

He was changed. The fragile quality seemed to have gone from his chin. His mouth was less full than it had been, the lines of the lips were straighter, but in his eyes the greatest change had taken place. There was no laughter in them any more, nor any bashfulness. They were sharp and bright and purposeful.

He told her in a tired monotone, told her everything just as it had happened. A few people came into the kitchen of Mrs. Rodriguez. There was wine to drink. Pepé drank wine. The little quarrel—the man started toward Pepé and then the knife—it went almost by itself. It flew, it darted before Pepé knew it. As he talked, Mama's face grew stern, and it seemed to grow more lean. Pepé finished. "I am a man now, Mama. The man said names to me I could not allow."

Mama nodded. "Yes, thou art a man, my poor little Pepé. Thou art a man. I have seen it coming on thee. I have watched you throwing the knife into the post, and I have been afraid." For a moment her face had softened, but now it grew stern again. "Come! We must get you ready. Go. Awaken Emilio and Rosy. Go quickly."

Pepé stepped over to the corner where his brother and sister slept among the sheepskins. He leaned down and shook them gently. "Come, Rosy! Come, Emilio! The mama says you must arise."

The little black ones sat up and rubbed their eyes in the candlelight. Mama was out of bed now, her long black skirt over her nightgown. "Emilio," she cried. "Go up and catch the other horse for Pepé. Quickly, now! Quickly." Emilio put his legs in his overalls and stumbled sleepily out the door.

"You heard no one behind you on the road?" Mama demanded.

"No, Mama. I listened carefully. No one was on the road."

Mama darted like a bird about the room. From a nail on the wall she took a canvas water bag and threw it on the floor. She stripped a blanket from her bed and rolled it into a tight tube and tied the ends with string. From a box beside the stove she lifted a flour sack half full of black stringy jerky. "Your father's black coat, Pepé. Here, put it on."

Pepé stood in the middle of the floor watching her activity. She reached behind the door and brought out the rifle, a long 38-56, worn shiny the whole length of the barrel. Pepé took it from her and held it in the crook of his elbow. Mama brought a little leather bag and counted the cartridges into his hand. "Only ten left," she warned. "You must not waste them."

Emilio put his head in the door. " *'Qui 'st 'l caballo,*[2] Mama."

"Put on the saddle from the other horse. Tie on the blanket. Here, tie the jerky to the saddle horn."

Still Pepé stood silently watching his mother's frantic activity. His chin looked hard, and his sweet mouth was drawn and thin. His little eyes followed Mama about the room almost suspiciously.

Rosy asked softly, "Where goes Pepé?"

Mama's eyes were fierce. "Pepé goes on a journey. Pepé is a man now. He has a man's thing to do."

Pepé straightened his shoulders. His mouth changed until he looked very much like Mama.

At last the preparation was finished. The loaded horse stood outside the door. The water bag dripped a line of moisture down the bay shoulder.

The moonlight was being thinned by the dawn and the big white moon was near down to the sea. The family stood by the shack. Mama confronted Pepé. "Look, my son! Do not stop until it is dark again. Do not sleep even though you are tired. Take care of the horse in order that he may not stop of weariness. Remember to be careful with the bullets—there are only ten. Do not fill thy stomach with jerky or it will make thee sick. Eat a little jerky and fill thy stomach with grass. When thou comest to the high mountains, if thou seest any of the dark watching men, go not near to them nor try to speak to them. And forget not thy prayers." She put her lean hands on Pepé's shoulders, stood on her toes and kissed him formally on both cheeks, and Pepé kissed her on both cheeks. Then he went to Emilio and Rosy and kissed both of their cheeks.

Pepé turned back to Mama. He seemed to look for a little softness, a little weakness in her. His eyes were searching, but Mama's face remained fierce. "Go now," she said. "Do not wait to be caught like a chicken."

Pepé pulled himself into the saddle. "I am a man," he said.

It was the first dawn when he rode up the hill toward the little canyon which let a trail into the mountains. Moonlight and daylight fought with each other, and the two warring qualities made it difficult to see. Before Pepé had gone a hundred yards, the outlines of his figure were misty; and long before he entered the canyon, he had become a grey, indefinite shadow.

Mama stood stiffly in front of her doorstep, and on either side of her stood Emilio and Rosy. They cast furtive glances at Mama now and then.

When the grey shape of Pepé melted into the hillside and disappeared, Mama relaxed. She began the high, whining keen of the death wail. "Our

[2]Spanish: "Here's the horse."

beautiful—our brave," she cried. "Our protector, our son is gone." Emilio and Rosy moaned beside her. "Our beautiful—our brave, he is gone." It was the formal wail. It rose to a high piercing whine and subsided to a moan. Mama raised it three times and then she turned and went into the house and shut the door.

Emilio and Rosy stood wondering in the dawn. They heard Mama whimpering in the house. They went out to sit on the cliff above the ocean. They touched shoulders. "When did Pepé come to be a man?" Emilio asked.

"Last night," said Rosy. "Last night in Monterey." The ocean clouds turned red with the sun that was behind the mountains.

"We will have no breakfast," said Emilio. "Mama will not want to cook." Rosy did not answer him. "Where is Pepé gone?" he asked.

Rosy looked around at him. She drew her knowledge from the quiet air. "He has gone on a journey. He will never come back."

"Is he dead? Do you think he is dead?"

Rosy looked back at the ocean again. A little steamer, drawing a line of smoke sat on the edge of the horizon. "He is not dead," Rosy explained. "Not yet."

Pepé rested the big rifle across the saddle in front of him. He let the horse walk up the hill and he didn't look back. The stony slope took on a coat of short brush so that Pepé found the entrance to a trail and entered it.

When he came to the canyon opening, he swung once in his saddle and looked back, but the houses were swallowed in the misty light. Pepé jerked forward again. The high shoulder of the canyon closed in on him. His horse stretched out its neck and sighed and settled to the trail.

It was a well-worn path, dark soft leaf-mould earth strewn with broken pieces of sandstone. The trail rounded the shoulder of the canyon and dropped steeply into the bed of the stream. In the shallows the water ran smoothly, glinting in the first morning sun. Small round stones on the bottom were as brown as rust with sun moss. In the sand along the edges of the stream the tall, rich wild mint grew, while in the water itself the cress, old and tough, had gone to heavy seed.

The path went into the stream and emerged on the other side. The horse sloshed into the water and stopped. Pepé dropped his bridle and let the beast drink of the running water.

Soon the canyon sides became steep and the first giant sentinel redwoods guarded the trail, great round red trunks bearing foliage as green and lacy as ferns. Once Pepé was among the trees, the sun was lost. A perfumed and purple light lay in the pale green of the underbrush. Gooseberry bushes and blackberries and tall ferns lined the stream, and overhead the branches of the redwoods met and cut off the sky.

Pepé drank from the water bag, and he reached into the flour sack and brought out a black string of jerky. His white teeth gnawed at the string until the tough meat parted. He chewed slowly and drank occasionally from the water bag. His little eyes were slumberous and tired, but the muscles of his face were hard set. The earth of the trail was black now. It gave up a hollow sound under the walking hoofbeats.

The stream fell more sharply. Little waterfalls splashed on the stones. Five-fingered ferns hung over the water and dripped spray from their fingertips.

Pepé rode half over in his saddle, dangling one leg loosely. He picked a bay leaf from a tree beside the way and put it into his mouth for a moment to flavor the dry jerky. He held the gun loosely across the pommel.

Suddenly he squared in his saddle, swung the horse from the trail and kicked it hurriedly up behind a big redwood tree. He pulled up the reins tight against the bit to keep the horse from whinnying. His face was intent and his nostrils quivered a little.

A hollow pounding came down the trail, and a horseman rode by, a fat man with red cheeks and a white stubble beard. His horse put down its head and blubbered at the trail when it came to the place where Pepé had turned off. "Hold up!" said the man and he pulled up his horse's head.

When the last sound of the hoofs died away, Pepé came back into the trail again. He did not relax in the saddle any more. He lifted the big rifle and swung the lever to throw a shell into the chamber, and then he let down the hammer to half cock.

The trail grew very steep. Now the redwood trees were smaller and their tops were dead, bitten dead where the wind reached them. The horse plodded on; the sun went slowly overhead and started down toward the afternoon.

Where the stream came out of a side canyon, the trail left it. Pepé dismounted and watered his horse and filled up his water bag. As soon as the trail had parted from the stream, the trees were gone and only the thick brittle sage and manzanita and chaparral edged the trail. And the soft black earth was gone, too, leaving only the light tan broken rock for the trail bed. Lizards scampered away into the brush as the horse rattled over the little stones.

Pepé turned in his saddle and looked back. He was in the open now: he could be seen from a distance. As he ascended the trail the country grew more rough and terrible and dry. The way wound about the bases of great square rocks. Little grey rabbits skittered in the brush. A bird made a monotonous high creaking. Eastward the bare rock mountaintops were pale and powder-dry under the dropping sun. The horse plodded up and up the trail toward a little V in the ridge which was the pass.

Pepé looked suspiciously back every minute or so, and his eyes sought the tops of the ridges ahead. Once, on a white barren spur, he saw a black figure for a moment, but he looked quickly away, for it was one of the dark watchers. No one knew who the watchers were, nor where they lived, but it was better to ignore them and never to show interest in them. They did not bother one who stayed on the trail and minded his own business.

The air was parched and full of light dust blown by the breeze from the eroding mountains. Pepé drank sparingly from his bag and corked it tightly and hung it on the horn again. The trail moved up the dry shale hillside, avoiding rocks, dropping under clefts, climbing in and out of old water scars. When he arrived at the little pass he stopped and looked back for a long time. No dark watchers were to be seen now. The trail behind was empty. Only the high tops of the redwoods indicated where the stream flowed.

Pepé rode on through the pass. His little eyes were nearly closed with weariness, but his face was stern, relentless and manly. The high mountain wind coasted sighing through the pass and whistled on the edges of the big blocks of broken granite. In the air, a redtailed hawk sailed over close to the ridge and screamed angrily. Pepé went slowly through the broken jagged pass and looked down on the other side.

The trail dropped quickly, staggering among broken rock. At the bottom of the slope there was a dark crease, thick with brush, and on the other side of the crease a little flat, in which a grove of oak trees grew. A scar of green grass cut across the flat. And behind the flat another mountain rose, desolate with dead rocks and starving little black bushes. Pepé drank from the bag again for the air was so dry that it encrusted his nostrils and burned his lips. He put the horse down the trail. The hooves slipped and struggled on the steep way, starting little stones that rolled off into the brush. The sun was gone behind the westward mountain now, but still it glowed brilliantly on the oaks and on the grassy flat. The rocks and the hillsides still sent up waves of the heat they had gathered from the day's sun.

Pepé looked up to the top of the next dry withered ridge. He saw a dark form against the sky, a man's figure standing on top of a rock, and he glanced away quickly not to appear curious. When a moment later he looked up again, the figure was gone.

Downward the trail was quickly covered. Sometimes the horse floundered for footing, sometimes set his feet and slid a little way. They came at last to the bottom where the dark chaparral was higher than Pepé's head. He held up his rifle on one side and his arm on the other to shield his face from the sharp brittle fingers of the brush.

Up and out of the crease he rode, and up a little cliff. The grassy flat was before him, and the round comfortable oaks. For a moment he studied the trail down which he had come, but there was no movement and no sound from it. Finally he rode out over the flat, to the green streak, and at the upper end of the damp he found a little spring welling out of the earth and dropping into a dug basin before it seeped out over the flat.

Pepé filled his bag first, and then he let the thirsty horse drink out of the pool. He led the horse to the clump of oaks, and in the middle of the grove, fairly protected from sight on all sides, he took off the saddle and the bridle and laid them on the ground. The horse stretched his jaws sideways and yawned. Pepé knotted the lead rope about the horse's neck and tied him to a sapling among the oaks, where he could graze in a fairly large circle.

When the horse was gnawing hungrily at the dry grass, Pepé went to the saddle and took a black string of jerky from the sack and strolled to an oak tree on the edge of the grove, from under which he could watch the trail. He sat down in the crisp dry oak leaves and automatically felt for his big black knife to cut the jerky, but he had no knife. He leaned back on his elbow and gnawed at the tough strong meat. His face was blank, but it was a man's face.

The bright evening light washed the eastern ridge, but the valley was darkening. Doves flew down from the hills to the spring, and the quail came running out of the brush and joined them, calling clearly to one another.

Out of the corner of his eye Pepé saw a shadow grow out of the bushy crease. He turned his head slowly. A big spotted wildcat was creeping toward the spring, belly to the ground, moving like thought.

Pepé cocked his rifle and edged the muzzle slowly around. Then he looked apprehensively up the trail and dropped the hammer again. From the ground beside him he picked an oak twig and threw it toward the spring. The quail flew up with a roar and the doves whistled away. The big cat stood up: for a long moment he looked at Pepé with cold yellow eyes, and then fearlessly walked back into the gulch.

The dusk gathered quickly in the deep valley. Pepé muttered his prayers, put his head down on his arm and went instantly to sleep.

The moon came up and filled the valley with cold blue light, and the wind swept rustling down from the peaks. The owls worked up and down the slopes looking for rabbits. Down in the brush of the gulch a coyote gabbled. The oak trees whispered softly in the night breeze.

Pepé started up, listening. His horse had whinnied. The moon was just slipping behind the western ridge, leaving the valley in darkness behind it. Pepé sat tensely gripping his rifle. From far up the trail he heard an answering whinny and the crash of shod hooves on the broken rock. He jumped to his feet, ran to his horse and led it under the trees. He threw on the saddle and cinched it tight for the steep trail, caught the unwilling head and forced the bit into the mouth. He felt the saddle to make sure the water bag and the sack of jerky were there. Then he mounted and turned up the hill.

It was velvet dark. The horse found the entrance to the trail where it left the flat, and started up, stumbling and slipping on the rocks. Pepé's hand rose up to his head. His hat was gone. He had left it under the oak tree.

The horse had struggled far up the trail when the first exchange of dawn came into the air, a steel greyness as light mixed thoroughly with dark. Gradually the sharp snaggled edge of the ridge stood out above them, rotten granite tortured and eaten by the winds of time. Pepé had dropped his reins on the horn, leaving direction to the horse. The brush grabbed at his legs in the dark until one knee of his jeans was ripped.

Gradually the light flowed down over the ridge. The starved brush and rocks stood out in the half light, strange and lonely in high perspective. Then there came warmth into the light. Pepé drew up and looked back, but he could see nothing in the darker valley below. The sky turned blue over the coming sun. In the waste of the mountainside, the poor dry brush grew only three feet high. Here and there, big outcroppings of unrotted granite stood up like mouldering houses. Pepé relaxed a little. He drank from his water bag and bit off a piece of jerky. A single eagle flew over, high in the light.

Without warning Pepé's horse screamed and fell on its side. He was almost down before the rifle crash echoed up from the valley. From a hole behind the struggling shoulder, a stream of bright crimson blood pumped and stopped and pumped and stopped. The hooves threshed on the ground. Pepé lay half stunned beside the horse. He looked slowly down the hill. A piece of sage clipped off beside his head and another crash echoed up from side to side of the canyon. Pepé flung himself frantically behind a bush.

He crawled up the hill on his knees and one hand. His right hand held the rifle up off the ground and pushed it ahead of him. He moved with the instinctive care of an animal. Rapidly he wormed his way toward one of the big outcroppings of granite on the hill above him. Where the brush was high he doubled up and ran, but where the cover was slight he wriggled forward on his stomach, pushed the rifle ahead of him. In the last little distance there was no cover at all. Pepé poised and then he darted across the space and flashed around the corner of the rock.

He leaned panting against the stone. When his breath came easier he moved along behind the big rock until he came to a narrow slit that offered a thin section of vision down the hill. Pepé lay on his stomach and pushed the rifle barrel through the slit and waited.

The sun reddened the western ridges now. Already the buzzards were settling down toward the place where the horse lay. A small brown bird scratched in the dead sage leaves directly in front of the rifle muzzle. The coasting eagle flew back toward the rising sun.

Pepé saw a little movement in the brush far below. His grip tightened on the gun. A little brown doe stepped daintily out on the trail and crossed it and disappeared into the brush again. For a long time Pepé waited. Far below he could see the little flat and the oak trees and the slash of green. Suddenly his eyes flashed back at the trail again. A quarter of a mile down there had been a quick movement in the chaparral. The rifle swung over. The front sight nestled in the V of the rear sight. Pepé studied for a moment and then raised the rear sight a notch. The movement in the brush came again. The sight settled on it. Pepé squeezed the trigger. The explosion crashed down the mountain and up the other side, and came rattling back. The whole side of the slope grew still. No more movement. And then a white streak cut into the granite of the slit and a bullet whined away and a crash sounded up from below. Pepé felt a sharp pain in his right hand. A sliver of granite was sticking out from between his first and second knuckles and the point protruded from his palm. Carefully he pulled out the sliver of stone. The wound bled evenly and gently. No vein nor artery was cut.

Pepé looked into a little dusty cave in the rock and gathered a handful of spider web, and he pressed the mass into the cut, plastering the soft web into the blood. The flow stopped almost at once.

The rifle was on the ground. Pepé picked it up, levered a new shell into the chamber. And then he slid into the brush on his stomach. Far to the right he crawled, and then up the hill, moving slowly and carefully, crawling to cover and resting and then crawling again.

In the mountains the sun is high in its arc before it penetrates the gorges. The hot face looked over the hill and brought instant heat with it. The white light beat on the rocks and reflected from them and rose up quivering from the earth again, and the rocks and bushes seemed to quiver behind the air.

Pepé crawled in the general direction of the ridge peak, zig-zagging for cover. The deep cut between his knuckles began to throb. He crawled close to a rattlesnake before he saw it, and when it raised its dry head and made a soft beginning whirr, he backed up and took another way. The quick grey lizards flashed in front of him, raising a tiny line of dust. He found another mass of spider web and pressed it against his throbbing hand.

Pepé was pushing the rifle with his left hand now. Little drops of sweat ran to the end of his coarse black hair and rolled down his cheeks. His lips and tongue were growing thick and heavy. His lips writhed to draw saliva into his mouth. His little dark eyes were uneasy and suspicious. Once when a grey lizard paused in front of him on the parched ground and turned its head sideways he crushed it flat with a stone.

When the sun slid past noon he had not gone a mile. He crawled exhaustedly a last hundred yards to a patch of high sharp manzanita, crawled desperately, and when the patch was reached he wriggled in among the tough gnarly trunks and dropped his head on his left arm. There was little shade in the meager brush, but there was cover and safety. Pepé went to sleep as he lay and the sun beat on his back. A few little birds hopped close to him and peered and hopped away. Pepé squirmed in his sleep and he raised and dropped his wounded hand again and again.

The sun went down behind the peaks and the cool evening came, and then the dark. A coyote yelled from the hillside, Pepé started awake and looked about with misty eyes. His hand swollen and heavy; a little thread of pain ran up the inside of his arm and settled in a pocket in his armpit. He peered about and then stood up, for the mountains were black and the moon had not yet risen. Pepé stood up in the dark. The coat of his father pressed on his arm. His tongue was swollen until it nearly filled his mouth. He wriggled out of the coat and dropped it in the brush, and then he struggled up the hill, falling over rocks and tearing his way through the brush. The rifle knocked against stones as he went. Little dry avalanches of gravel and shattered stone went whispering down the hill behind him.

After a while the old moon came up and showed the jagged ridge top ahead of him. By moonlight Pepé traveled more easily. He bent forward so that his throbbing arm hung away from his body. The journey uphill was made in dashes and rests, a frantic rush up a few yards and then a rest. The wind coasted down the slope rattling the dry stems of the bushes.

The moon was at meridian when Pepé came at last to the sharp backbone of the ridge top. On the last hundred yards of the rise no soil had clung under the wearing winds. The way was on solid rock. He clambered to the top and looked down on the other side. There was a draw like the last below him, misty with moonlight, brushed with dry struggling sage and chaparral. On the other side the hill rose up sharply and at the top the jagged rotten teeth of the mountain showed against the sky. At the bottom of the cut the brush was thick and dark.

Pepé stumbled down the hill. His throat was almost closed with thirst. At first he tried to run, but immediately he fell and rolled. After that he went more carefully. The moon was just disappearing behind the mountains when he came to the bottom. He crawled into the heavy brush feeling with his fingers for water. There was no water in the bed of the stream, only damp earth. Pepé laid his gun down and scooped up a handful of mud and put it in his mouth, and then he spluttered and scraped the earth from his tongue with his finger, for the mud drew at his mouth like a poultice. He dug a hole in the stream bed with his fingers, dug a little basin to catch water; but before it was very deep his head fell forward on the damp ground and he slept.

The dawn came and the heat of the day fell on the earth, and still Pepé slept. Late in the afternoon his head jerked up. He looked slowly around. His eyes were slits of wariness. Twenty feet away in the heavy brush a big tawny mountain lion stood looking at him. Its long thick tail waved gracefully, its ears were erect with interest, not laid back dangerously. The lion squatted down on its stomach and watched him.

Pepé looked at the hole he had dug in the earth. A half inch of muddy water had collected in the bottom. He tore the sleeve from his hurt arm, with his teeth ripped out a little square, soaked it in the water and put it in his mouth. Over and over he filled the cloth and sucked it.

Still the lion sat and watched him. The evening came down but there was no movement on the hills. No birds visited the dry bottom of the cut. Pepé looked occasionally at the lion. The eyes of the yellow beast drooped as though he were about to sleep. He yawned and his long thin red tongue curled out. Suddenly his head jerked around and his nostrils quivered. His big tail lashed. He stood up and slunk like a tawny shadow into the thick brush.

A moment later Pepé heard the sound, the faint far crash of horses' hooves on gravel. And he heard something else, a high whining yelp of a dog.

Pepé took his rifle in his left hand and he glided into the brush almost as quietly as the lion had. In the darkening evening he crouched up the hill toward the next ridge. Only when the dark came did he stand up. His energy was short. Once it was dark he fell over the rocks and slipped to his knees on the steep slope, but he moved on and on up the hill, climbing and scrabbling over the broken hillside.

When he was far up toward the top, he lay down and slept for a little while. The withered moon, shining on his face, awakened him. He stood up and moved up the hill. Fifty yards away he stopped and turned back, for he had forgotten his rifle. He walked heavily down and poked about in the brush, but he could not find his gun. At last he lay down to rest. The pocket of pain in his armpit had grown more sharp. His arm seemed to swell out and fall with every heartbeat. There was no position lying down where the heavy arm did not press against his armpit.

With the effort of a hurt beast, Pepé got up and moved again toward the top of the ridge. He held his swollen arm away from his body with his left hand. Up the steep hill he dragged himself, a few steps and a rest, and a few more steps. At last he was nearing the top. The moon showed the uneven sharp back of it against the sky.

Pepé's brain spun in a big spiral up and away from him. He slumped to the ground and lay still. The rock ridge top was only a hundred feet above him.

The moon moved over the sky. Pepé half turned on his back. His tongue tried to make words, but only a thick hissing came from between his lips.

When the dawn came, Pepé pulled himself up. His eyes were sane again. He drew his great puffed arm in front of him and looked at the angry wound. The black line ran up from his wrist to his armpit. Automatically he reached in his pocket for the big black knife, but it was not there. His eyes searched the ground. He picked up a sharp blade of stone and scraped at the wound, sawed at the proud flesh and then squeezed the green juice out in big drops. Instantly he threw back his head and whined like a dog. His whole right side shuddered at the pain, but the pain cleared his head.

In the grey light he struggled up the last slope to the ridge and crawled over and lay down behind a line of rocks. Below him lay a deep canyon exactly like the last, waterless and desolate. There was no flat, no oak trees, not even heavy brush in the bottom of it. And on the other side a sharp ridge stood up, thinly brushed with starving sage, littered with broken granite. Strewn over the hill there were giant outcroppings, and on the top the granite teeth stood out against the sky.

The new day was light now. The flame of the sun came over the ridge and fell on Pepé where he lay on the ground. His coarse black hair was littered with twigs and bits of spider web. His eyes had retreated back into his head. Between his lips the tip of his black tongue showed.

He sat up and dragged his great arm into his lap and nursed it, rocking his body and moaning in his throat. He threw back his head and looked up into the pale sky. A big black bird circled nearly out of sight, and far to the left another was sailing near.

He lifted his head to listen, for a familiar sound had come to him from the valley he had climbed out of; it was the crying yelp of hounds, excited and feverish, on a trail.

Pepé bowed his head quickly. He tried to speak rapid words but only a thick hiss came from his lips. He drew a shaky cross on his breast with his left hand. It was a long struggle to get to his feet. He crawled slowly and mechanically to the top of a big rock on the ridge peak. Once there, he arose slowly, swaying to his feet, and stood erect. Far below he could see the dark brush where he had slept. He braced his feet and stood there, black against the morning sky.

There came a ripping sound at his feet. A piece of stone flew up and a bullet droned off into the next gorge. The hollow crash echoed up from below. Pepé looked down for a moment and then pulled himself straight again.

His body jarred back. His left hand fluttered helplessly toward his breast. The second crash sounded from below. Pepé swung forward and toppled from the rock. His body struck and rolled over and over, starting a little avalanche. And when at last he stopped against a bush, the avalanche slid slowly down and covered up his head.

1938

Katherine Anne Porter 1890–1980

Katherine Anne Porter published only one novel and few short stories, but she enjoyed a reputation as one of America's finest stylists. Her writing is "disciplined" (one of her own terms), ironic, concentrated, and precise. Working within a narrow range and with limited subject matter, she produced short stories of high distinction, an achievement that she suggested was the result of her dedication to art, "the substance of faith and the only reality."

Although she wrote prose of great clarity, Porter kept the details of her life obscure. She hid her poverty-stricken origins by suggesting that she came from a family of plantation aristocrats, but she was actually born in a small log house in Indian Creek, Texas, which later in life she described as a "god-forsaken wilderness." She adopted her grandmother's name and called herself Katherine Anne Porter, but she had been christened Callie Russell Porter, a name that lacked, she believed, suitable elegance. Her mother was sickly and died when Porter was two. Her father, a ne'er-do-well, failed to provide his children with a stable family life or an education.

Porter told of being educated in Catholic convents as a child, and critics have concluded that her intellectual background was Roman Catholic. In fact, as her biographer has pointed out, she had only a single year of formal education—in a school for young ladies in a small Texas town, where she was taught dancing, elocution, drama, and good manners, and was exposed to "fine" literature. At sixteen she married, hoping to escape her drab life, but the marriage was a failure.

To support herself she taught drama and elocution in small Texas towns. Having great natural beauty and a talent for theatricals, she got a job in Chicago as an extra in early motion pictures. Soon she had worked her way up from bit player to director of publicity for a movie studio. She had published some essays in regional journals, and in 1920 she was sent to Mexico to write magazine articles about the land, the people, and their customs. In Mexico she became involved in revolutionary political movements and absorbed the impressions and met the characters that were to appear in some of her best short stories. A journey from Mexico to Europe in 1931 provided the background for her long and famous novel, Ship of Fools.

Porter did her finest literary work in the 1920s and 1930s. Her first published story appeared in 1922 and her first book, Flowering Judas and Other Stories, *in 1930. A second collection of earlier stories,* Pale Horse, Pale Rider, *was published in 1939; a third collection,* The Leaning Tower and Other Stories, *appeared in 1944. In explaining why she had not written more during the twenties and thirties, Katherine Anne Porter was typically vague and cryptic: "I was not one of those who could flourish in the conditions of the past two decades." In her final years the quantity of her writing remained small. A book of her critical essays,* The Days Before, *was published in 1952;* Ship of Fools *appeared in 1962 and was later made into an award-winning motion picture. Her last work,* The Never Ending Wrong *(1977), is a memoir of events surrounding the trial and execution of Sacco and Vanzetti in the 1920s. After 1940, she spent much time lecturing and teaching at colleges and universities in the United States, taking great pleasure in being a professor at institutions she had once been unqualified to attend.*

Katherine Anne Porter has been called "a maker of darkish parables" because of her portrayal of the impoverished spirit of humankind in the modern world and because of her repeated use of the themes of isolation, guilt, and spiritual denial. Many of her most highly regarded stories are set in the South, the Southwest, or in Mexico (she called Mexico "my familiar country"). They frequently turn on the conflicts between the regions' fixed social orders and movements for change. Her works are rich (some critics say overrich) in symbolism, and she was often a harsh moralist, giving cruelly severe portrayals of the weaknesses of men and women. Yet she is now judged to have been one of the best American writers of short fiction in the twentieth century, and her finest stories, such as "María Concepción," are praised as "completely original works," for in the world of the modern short story "there is simply nothing like them."

FURTHER READING: H. Mooney, *The Fiction and Criticism of Katherine Anne Porter,* 1957, 1962; R. West, *Katherine Anne Porter,* 1963; W. Nance, *Katherine Anne Porter and the Art of Rejection,* 1964; G. Hendrick, *Katherine Anne Porter,* 1965; W. Emmons, *Katherine Anne Porter, The Regional Stories,* 1967; *Katherine Anne Porter, A Critical Symposium,* ed. L. Hartley and G. Core, 1969; *The Collected Essays and Occasional Writings of Katherine Anne Porter,* 1970; M. Liberman, *Katherine Anne Porter's Fiction,* 1971; J. Hardy, *Katherine Anne Porter,* 1973; *Katherine Anne Porter, A Collection of Critical Essays,* ed. R. Warren, 1979; E. Lopez, *Conversations with Katherine Anne Porter,* 1981; J. Givner, *Katherine Anne Porter,* 1982, 1990; D. Unrue, *Truth and Vision in Katherine Anne Porter's Fiction,* 1985; *Katherine Anne Porter, Conversations,* ed. J. Givner, 1987; D. Unrue, *Understanding Katherine Anne Porter,* 1988; *The Letters of Katherine Anne Porter,* ed. I. Bayley, 1990; R. Binkmeyer, *Katherine Anne Porter's Artistic Development,* 1993; J. Stout, *Katherine Anne Porter, A Sense of the Times,* 1995; *Critical Essays on Katharine Anne Porter,* ed. D. Harbour, 1997; *Katherine Anne Porter,* ed. H. Bloom, 2001; *From Texas to the World and Back,* ed. M. Busby and D. Heaberlin, 2001; D. Unrue, *Katherine Anne Porter, The Life of an Artist,* 2005.

TEXT: *The Century Illustrated Monthly Magazine,* December 1922.

MARÍA CONCEPCIÓN

María Concepción walked carefully, keeping to the middle of the white dusty road, where the maguey thorns and the treacherous curved spines of organ cactus had not gathered so profusely. She would have enjoyed resting for a moment in the dark shade by the roadside, but she had no time to waste drawing cactus needles from her feet. Juan and his chief would be waiting for their food in the damp trenches of the buried city.

She carried about a dozen living fowls slung over her right shoulder, their feet fastened together. Half of them fell upon the flat of her back, the balance dangled uneasily over her breast. They wriggled their benumbed and swollen legs against her neck, they twisted their stupefied eyes and peered into her face inquiringly. She did not see them or think of them. Her left arm was tired with the weight of the food basket, and she was hungry after her long morning's work.

Her straight back outlined itself strongly under her clean bright blue cotton rebozo.[1] Instinctive serenity softened her black eyes, shaped like almonds, set far apart, and tilted a bit endwise. She walked with the free, natural, guarded ease of the primitive woman carrying an unborn child. The shape of her body was easy, the swelling life was not a distortion, but the right inevitable proportions of a woman. She was entirely contented. Her husband was at work and she was on her way to market to sell her fowls.

Her small house sat half-way up a shallow hill, under a clump of peppertrees, a wall of organ cactus enclosing it on the side nearest to the road. Now she came down into the valley, divided by the narrow spring, and crossed a bridge of loose stones near the hut where María Rosa the beekeeper lived with her old godmother, Lupe the medicine woman. María Concepción had no faith in the charred owl bones, the singed rabbit fur, the cat entrails, the messes and ointments sold by Lupe to the ailing of the village. She was a good Christian, and drank simple herb teas for headache and stomachache, or bought her remedies bottled, with printed directions that she could not read, at the drugstore near the city market, where she went almost daily. But she often bought a jar of honey from young María Rosa, a pretty, shy child only fifteen years old.

María Concepción and her husband, Juan Villegas, were each a little past their eighteenth year. She had a good reputation with the neighbors as an energetic religious woman who could drive a bargain to the end. It was commonly known that if she wished to buy a new rebozo for herself or a shirt for Juan, she could bring out a sack of hard silver coins for the purpose.

She had paid for the license, nearly a year ago, the potent bit of stamped paper which permits people to be married in the church. She had given money to the priest before she and Juan walked together up to the altar the Monday after Holy Week. It had been the adventure of the villagers to go, three Sundays one after another, to hear the banns[2] called by the priest for Juan de Dios Villegas and María Concepción Manríquez, who were actually getting married in the church, instead of behind it, which was the usual custom, less expensive, and as binding as any other ceremony. But María Concepción was always as proud as if she owned a hacienda.[3]

[1]Spanish: shawl. [2]Announcement of intended marriage. [3]Large estate house.

She paused on the bridge and dabbled her feet in the water, her eyes resting themselves from the sun-rays in a fixed gaze to the far-off mountains, deeply blue under their hanging drift of clouds. It came to her that she would like a fresh crust of honey. The delicious aroma of bees, their slow thrilling hum, awakened a pleasant desire for a flake of sweetness in her mouth.

"If I do not eat it now, I shall mark my child," she thought, peering through the crevices in the thick hedge of cactus that sheered up nakedly, like bared knife blades set protectingly around the small clearing. The place was so silent she doubted if María Rosa and Lupe were at home.

The leaning jacal of dried rush-withes and corn sheaves, bound to tall saplings thrust into the earth, roofed with yellowed maguey leaves flattened and over-lapping like shingles, hunched drowsy and fragrant in the warmth of noonday. The hives, similarly made, were scattered towards the back of the clearing, like small mounds of clean vegetable refuse. Over each mound there hung a dusty golden shimmer of bees.

A light gay scream of laughter rose from behind the hut; a man's short laugh joined in. "Ah, hahahaha!" went the voices together high and low, like a song.

"So María Rosa has a man!" María Concepción stopped short, smiling, shifted her burden slightly, and bent forward shading her eyes to see more clearly through the spaces of the hedge.

María Rosa ran, dodging between beehives, parting two stunted jasmine bushes as she came, lifting her knees in swift leaps, looking over her shoulder and laughing in a quivering, excited way. A heavy jar, swung to her wrist by the handle, knocked against her thighs as she ran. Her toes pushed up sudden spurts of dust, her half-raveled braids showered around her shoulders in long crinkled wisps.

Juan Villegas ran after her, also laughing strangely, his teeth set, both rows gleaming behind the small soft black beard growing sparsely on his lips, his chin, leaving his brown cheeks girl-smooth. When he seized her, he clenched so hard her chemise gave way and ripped from her shoulder. She stopped laughing at this, pushed him away and stood silent, trying to pull up the torn sleeve with one hand. Her pointed chin and dark red mouth moved in an uncertain way, as if she wished to laugh again; her long black lashes flickered with the quick-moving lights in her hidden eyes.

María Concepción did not stir nor breathe for some seconds. Her forehead was cold, and yet boiling water seemed to be pouring slowly along her spine. An unaccountable pain was in her knees, as if they were broken. She was afraid Juan and María Rosa would feel her eyes fixed upon them and would find her there, unable to move, spying upon them. But they did not pass beyond the enclosure, nor even glance towards the gap in the wall opening upon the road.

Juan lifted one of María Rosa's loosened braids and slapped her neck with it playfully. She smiled softly, consentingly. Together they moved back through the hives of honey-comb. María Rosa balanced her jar on one hip and swung her long full petticoats with every step. Juan flourished his wide hat back and forth, walking proudly as a game-cock.

María Concepción came out of the heavy cloud which enwrapped her head and bound her throat, and found herself walking onward, keeping the road without knowing it, feeling her way delicately, her ears strumming as if all María Rosa's bees had hived in them. Her careful sense of duty kept her moving toward the buried city where Juan's chief, the American archeologist, was taking his midday rest, waiting for his food.

Juan and María Rosa! She burned all over now, as if a layer of tiny fig-cactus bristles, as cruel as spun glass, had crawled under her skin. She wished to sit down quietly and wait for her death, but not until she had cut the throats of her man and that girl who were laughing and kissing under the cornstalks. Once when she was a young girl she had come back from market to find her jacal[4] burned to a pile of ash and her few silver coins gone. A dark empty feeling had filled her; she kept moving about the place, not believing her eyes, expecting it all to take shape again before her. But it was gone, and though she knew an enemy had done it, she could not find out who it was, and could only curse and threaten the air. Now here was a worse thing, but she knew her enemy. María Rosa, that sinful girl, shameless! She heard herself saying a harsh, true word about María Rosa, saying it aloud as if she expected someone to agree with her: "Yes, she is a whore! She has no right to live."

At this moment the gray untidy head of Givens appeared over the edges of the newest trench he had caused to be dug in his field of excavations. The long deep crevasses, in which a man might stand without being seen, lay crisscrossed like orderly gashes of a giant scalpel. Nearly all of the men of the community worked for Givens, helping him to uncover the lost city of their ancestors. They worked all the year through and prospered, digging every day for those small clay heads and bits of pottery and fragments of painted walls for which there was no good use on earth, being all broken and encrusted with clay. They themselves could make better ones, perfectly stout and new, which they took to town and peddled to foreigners for real money. But the unearthly delight of the chief in finding these worn-out things was an endless puzzle. He would fairly roar for joy at times, waving a shattered pot or a human skull above his head, shouting for his photographer to come and make a picture of this!

Now he emerged, and his young enthusiast's eyes welcomed María Concepción from his old-man face, covered with hard wrinkles and burned to the color of red earth. "I hope you've brought me a nice fat one." He selected a fowl from the bunch dangling nearest him as María Concepción, wordless, leaned over the trench. "Dress it for me, there's a good girl. I'll broil it."

María Concepción took the fowl by the head, and silently, swiftly drew her knife across its throat, twisting the head off with the casual firmness she might use with the top of a beet.

"Good God, woman, you do have nerve," said Givens, watching her. "I can't do that. It gives me the creeps."

[4]Hut.

"My home country is Guadalajara,"[5] explained María Concepción, without bravado, as she picked and gutted the fowl.

She stood and regarded Givens condescendingly, that diverting white man who had no woman of his own to cook for him, and moreover appeared not to feel any loss of dignity in preparing his own food. He squatted now, eyes squinted, nose wrinkled to avoid the smoke, turning the roasting fowl busily on a stick. A mysterious man, undoubtedly rich, and Juan's chief, therefore to be respected, placated.

"The tortillas are fresh and hot, señor," she murmured gently. "With your permission I will now go to market."

"Yes, yes, run along; bring me another of these tomorrow." Givens turned his head to look at her again. Her grand manner sometimes reminded him of royalty in exile. He noticed her unnatural paleness. "The sun is too hot, eh?" he asked.

"Yes, sir. Pardon me, but Juan will be here soon?"

"He ought to be here now. Leave his food. The others will eat it."

She moved away; the blue of her rebozo became a dancing spot in the heat waves that rose from the gray-red soil. Givens liked his Indians best when he could feel a fatherly indulgence for their primitive childish ways. He told comic stories of Juan's escapades, of how often he had saved him, in the past five years, from going to jail, and even from being shot, for his varied and always unexpected misdeeds.

"I am never a minute too soon to get him out of one pickle or another," he would say. "Well, he's a good worker, and I know how to manage him."

After Juan was married, he used to twit him, with exactly the right shade of condescension, on his many infidelities to María Concepción. "She'll catch you yet, and God help you!" he was fond of saying, and Juan would laugh with immense pleasure.

It did not occur to María Concepción to tell Juan she had found him out. During the day her anger against him died, and her anger against María Rosa grew. She kept saying to herself, "When I was a young girl like María Rosa, if a man had caught hold of me so, I would have broken my jar over his head." She forgot completely that she had not resisted even so much as María Rosa, on the day that Juan had first taken hold of her. Besides she had married him afterwards in the church, and that was a very different thing.

Juan did not come home that night, but went away to war and María Rosa went with him. Juan had a rifle at his shoulder and two pistols at his belt. María Rosa wore a rifle also, slung on her back along with the blankets and the cooking pots. They joined the nearest detachment of troops in the field, and María Rosa marched ahead with the battalion of experienced women of war, which went over the crops like locusts, gathering provisions for the army. She cooked with them, and ate with them what was left after the men had eaten. After battles she went out on the field with the others to salvage clothing and ammunition and guns from the slain before they should begin to swell in the heat. Sometimes they would encounter the women from the other army, and a second battle as grim as the first would take place.

[5]City in Eastern Mexico. The surrounding countryside was renowned for its hardy people and as a place of violent insurrection and banditry.

There was no particular scandal in the village. People shrugged, grinned. It was far better that they were gone. The neighbors went around saying that María Rosa was safer in the army than she would be in the same village with María Concepción.

María Concepción did not weep when Juan left her; and when the baby was born, and died within four days, she did not weep. "She is mere stone," said old Lupe, who went over and offered charms to preserve the baby.

"May you rot in hell with your charms," said María Concepción.

If she had not gone so regularly to church, lighting candles before the saints, kneeling with her arms spread in the form of a cross for hours at a time, and receiving holy communion every month, there might have been talk of her being devil-possessed, her face was so changed and blind-looking. But this was impossible when, after all, she had been married by the priest. It must be, they reasoned, that she was being punished for her pride. They decided that this was the true cause for everything: she was altogether too proud. So they pitied her.

During the year that Juan and María Rosa were gone María Concepción sold her fowls and looked after her garden and her sack of hard coins grew. Lupe had no talent for bees, and the hives did not prosper. She began to blame María Rosa for running away, and to praise María Concepción for her behavior. She used to see María Concepción at the market or at church, and she always said that no one could tell by looking at her now that she was a woman who had such a heavy grief.

"I pray God everything goes well with María Concepción from this out," she would say, "for she has had her share of trouble."

When some idle person repeated this to the deserted woman, she went down to Lupe's house and stood within the clearing and called to the medicine woman, who sat in her doorway stirring a mess of her infallible cure for sores: "Keep your prayers to yourself, Lupe, or offer them for others who need them. I will ask God for what I want in this world."

"And will you get it, you think, María Concepción?" asked Lupe, tittering cruelly and smelling the wooden mixing spoon. "Did you pray for what you have now?"

Afterward everyone noticed that María Concepción went oftener to church, and even seldomer to the village to talk with the other women as they sat along the curb, nursing their babies and eating fruit, at the end of the market-day.

"She is wrong to take us for enemies," said old Soledad, who was a thinker and a peace-maker. "All women have these troubles. Well, we should suffer together."

But María Concepción lived alone. She was gaunt, as if something were gnawing her away inside, her eyes were sunken, and she would not speak a word if she could help it. She worked harder than ever, and her butchering knife was scarcely ever out of her hand.

Juan and María Rosa, disgusted with military life, came home one day without asking permission of anyone. The field of war had unrolled itself, a long scroll of vexations, until the end had frayed out within twenty miles of Juan's village. So he and María Rosa, now lean as a wolf, burdened with a child daily expected, set out with no farewells to the regiment and walked home.

They arrived one morning about daybreak. Juan was picked up on sight by a group of military police from the small barracks on the edge of town, and taken to prison, where the officer in charge told him with impersonal cheerfulness that he would add one to a catch of ten waiting to be shot as deserters the next morning.

María Rosa, screaming and falling on her face in the road, was taken under the armpits by two guards and helped briskly to her jacal, now sadly run down. She was received with professional importance by Lupe, who helped the baby to be born at once.

Limping with foot soreness, a layer of dust concealing his fine new clothes got mysteriously from somewhere, Juan appeared before the captain at the barracks. The captain recognized him as head digger for his good friend Givens, and dispatched a note to Givens saying: "I am holding the person of Juan Villegas awaiting your further disposition."

When Givens showed up Juan was delivered to him with the urgent request that nothing be made public about so humane and sensible an operation on the part of military authority.

Juan walked out of the rather stifling atmosphere of the drumhead court,[6] a definite air of swagger about him. His hat, of unreasonable dimensions and embroidered with silver thread, hung over one eyebrow, secured at the back by a cord of silver dripping with bright blue tassels. His shirt was of a checkerboard pattern in green and black, his white cotton trousers were bound by a belt of yellow leather tooled in red. His feet were bare, full of stone bruises, and sadly ragged as to toenails. He removed his cigarette from the corner of his full-lipped wide mouth. He removed the splendid hat. His black dusty hair, pressed moistly to his forehead, sprang up suddenly in a cloudy thatch on his crown. He bowed to the officer, who appeared to be gazing at a vacuum. He swung his arm wide in a free circle upsoaring towards the prison window, where forlorn heads poked over the window sill, hot eyes following after the lucky departing one. Two or three of the heads nodded, and a half dozen hands were flipped at him in an effort to imitate his own casual and heady manner.

Juan kept up this insufferable pantomime until they rounded the first clump of fig-cactus. Then he seized Givens' hand and burst into oratory. "Blessed be the day your servant Juan Villegas first came under your eyes. From this day my life is yours without condition, ten thousand thanks with all my heart."

"For God's sake stop playing the fool," said Givens irritably. "Some day I'm going to be five minutes too late."

"Well, it is nothing much to be shot, my chief—certainly you know I was not afraid—but to be shot in a drove of deserters, against a cold wall, just in the moment of my home-coming, by order of that . . ."

Glittering epithets tumbled over one another like explosions of a rocket. All the scandalous analogies from the animal and vegetable worlds were applied in a vivid, unique and personal way to the life, loves, and family history of the officer who had just set him free. When he had quite cursed himself

[6] A swift and decisive military court-martial, once traditionally held in the field around a drumhead.

dry, and his nerves were soothed, he added: "With your permission, my chief!"

"What will María Concepción say to all this?" asked Givens. "You are very informal, Juan, for a man who was married in the church."

Juan put on his hat.

"Oh, María Concepción! That's nothing. Look, my chief, to be married in the church is a great misfortune for a man. After that he is not himself any more. How can that woman complain when I do not drink even at fiestas enough to be really drunk? I do not beat her; never, never. We were always at peace. I say to her, Come here, and she comes straight. I say, Go there, and she goes quickly. Yet sometimes I looked at her and thought, Now I am married to that woman in the church, and I felt a sinking inside, as if something were lying heavy on my stomach. With María Rosa it is all different. She is not silent; she talks. When she talks too much, I slap her and say, Silence, thou simpleton! And she weeps. She is just a girl with whom I do as I please. You know how she used to keep those clean little bees in their hives? She is like their honey to me. I swear it. I would not harm María Concepción because I am married to her in the church; but also, my chief, I will not leave María Rosa, because she pleases me more than any other woman."

"Let me tell you, Juan, things haven't been going as well as you think. You be careful. Some day María Concepción will just take your head off with that carving knife of hers. You keep that in mind."

Juan's expression was the proper blend of masculine triumph and sentimental melancholy. It was pleasant to see himself in the rôle of hero to two such desirable women. He had just escaped from the threat of a disagreeable end. His clothes were new and handsome, and they had cost him just nothing. María Rosa had collected them for him here and there after battles. He was walking in the early sunshine, smelling the good smells of ripening cactus-figs, peaches, and melons, of pungent berries dangling from the pepper-trees, and the smoke of his cigarette under his nose. He was on his way to civilian life with his patient chief. His situation was ineffably perfect, and he swallowed it whole.

"My chief," he addressed Givens handsomely, as one man of the world to another, "women are good things, but not at this moment. With your permission, I will now go to the village and eat. My God, *how* I shall eat! Tomorrow morning very early I will come to the buried city and work like seven men. Let us forget María Concepción and María Rosa. Each one in her place. I will manage them when the time comes."

News of Juan's adventure soon got abroad, and Juan found many friends about him during the morning. They frankly commended his way of leaving the army. It was in itself the act of a hero. The new hero ate a great deal and drank somewhat, the occasion being better than a feast-day. It was almost noon before he returned to visit María Rosa.

He found her sitting on a clean, straw mat, rubbing fat on her three-hour-old son. Before this felicitous vision Juan's emotions so twisted him that he returned to the village and invited every man in the "Death and Resurrection" pulque[7] shop to drink with him.

[7]A harsh, fermented alcoholic drink made from the agave plant.

Having thus taken leave of his balance, he started back to María Rosa, and found himself unaccountably in his own house, attempting to beat María Concepción by way of reëstablishing himself in his legal household.

María Concepción, knowing all the events of that unhappy day, was not in a yielding mood, and refused to be beaten. She did not scream nor implore; she stood her ground and resisted; she even struck at him. Juan, amazed, hardly knowing what he did, stepped back and gazed at her inquiringly through a leisurely whirling film which seemed to have lodged behind his eyes. Certainly he had not even thought of touching her. Oh, well, no harm done. He gave up, turned away, half-asleep on his feet. He dropped amiably in a shadowed corner and began to snore.

María Concepción, seeing that he was quiet, began to bind the legs of her fowls. It was market-day and she was late. She fumbled and tangled the bits of cord in her haste, and set off across the plowed fields instead of taking the accustomed road. She ran with a crazy panic in her head, her stumbling legs. Now and then she would stop and look about her, trying to place herself, then go on a few steps, until she realized that she was not going towards the market.

At once she came to her senses completely, recognized the thing that troubled her so terribly, was certain of what she wanted. She sat down quietly under a sheltering thorny bush and gave herself over to her long devouring sorrow. The thing which had for so long squeezed her whole body into a tight dumb knot of suffering suddenly broke with shocking violence. She jerked with the involuntary recoil of one who receives a blow, and the sweat poured from her skin as if the wounds of her whole life were shedding their salt ichor. Drawing her rebozo over her head, she bowed her forehead upon her updrawn knees, and sat there in deadly silence and immobility. From time to time she lifted her head where the sweat formed steadily and poured down her face, drenching the front of her chemise, and her mouth had the shape of crying, but there were no tears and no sound. All her being was a dark confused memory of grief burning in her at night, of deadly baffled anger eating at her by day, until her very tongue tasted bitter, and her feet were as heavy as if she were mired in the muddy roads during the time of rains.

After a great while she stood up and threw the rebozo off her face, and set out walking again.

Juan awakened slowly, with long yawns and grumblings, alternated with short relapses into sleep full of visions and clamors. A blur of orange light seared his eyeballs when he tried to unseal his lids. There came from somewhere a low voice weeping without tears, saying meaningless phrases over and over. He began to listen. He tugged at the leash of his stupor. He strained to grasp those words which terrified him even though he could not quite hear them. Then he came awake with frightening suddenness, sitting up and staring at the long sharpened streak of light piercing the corn-husk walls from the level disappearing sun.

María Concepción stood in the doorway, looming colossally tall to his betrayed eyes. She was talking quickly, and calling his name. Then he saw her clearly.

"God's name!" said Juan, frozen to the marrow, "here I am facing my death!" for the long knife she wore habitually at her belt was in her hand. But instead, she threw it away, clear from her, and got down on her knees, crawling toward him as he had seen her crawl many times toward the shrine at Guadalupe Villa.[8] He watched her approach with such horror that the hair of his head seemed to be lifting itself away from him. Falling forward upon her face, she huddled over him, lips moving in a ghostly whisper. Her words became clear, and Juan understood them all.

For a second he could not move nor speak. Then he took her head between both his hands, and supported her in this way, saying swiftly, anxiously reassuring, almost in a babble:

"Oh, thou poor creature! Oh, madwoman! Oh, my María Concepción, unfortunate! Listen . . . Don't be afraid. Listen to me! I will hide thee away, I thy own man will protect thee! Quiet! Not a sound!"

Trying to collect himself, he held her and cursed under his breath for a few moments in the gathering darkness. María Concepción bent over, face almost on the ground, her feet folded under her, as if she would hide from him. For the first time in his life Juan was aware of danger. This was danger. María Concepción would be dragged away between two gendarmes, with him following helpless and unarmed, to spend the rest of her days in Belén Prison,[9] maybe. Danger! The night swarmed with threats. He stood up and dragged her up with him. She was silent and perfectly rigid, holding to him with resistless strength, her hands stiffened on his arms.

"Get me the knife," he told her in a whisper. She obeyed, her feet slipping along the hard earth floor, her shoulders straight, her arms close to her side. He lighted a candle. María Concepción held the knife out to him. It was stained and dark even to the handle with drying blood.

He frowned at her harshly, noting the same stains on her chemise and hands.

"Take off thy clothes and wash thy hands," he ordered. He washed the knife carefully, and threw the water wide of the doorway. She watched him and did likewise with the bowl in which she had bathed.

"Light the brasero[10] and cook food for me," he told her in the same peremptory tone. He took her garments and went out. When he returned, she was wearing an old soiled dress, and was fanning the fire in the charcoal burner. Seating himself cross-legged near her, he stared at her as at a creature unknown to him, who bewildered him utterly, for whom there was no possible explanation. She did not turn her head, but kept silent and still, except for the movements of her strong hands fanning the blaze which cast sparks and small jets of white smoke, flaring and dying rhythmically with the motion of the fan, lighting her face and darkening it by turns.

Juan's voice barely disturbed the silence: "Listen to me carefully, and tell me the truth, and when the gendarmes come here for us, thou shalt have nothing to fear. But there will be something for us to settle between us afterward."

[8]Site of the shrine, and place of pilgrimage, dedicated to the Virgin Mary.
[9]Notoriously violent prison for women in Mexico City. It was destroyed in 1935.
[10]Fireplace used for cooking.

The light from the charcoal burner shone in her eyes; a yellow phosphorescence glimmered behind the dark iris.

"For me everything is settled now," she answered, in a tone so tender, so grave, so heavy with suffering, that Juan felt his vitals contract. He wished to repent openly, not as a man, but as a very small child. He could not fathom her, nor himself, nor the mysterious fortunes of life grown so instantly confused where all had seemed so gay and simple. He felt too that she had become invaluable, a woman without equal among a million women, and he could not tell why. He drew an enormous sigh that rattled in his chest.

"Yes, yes, it is all settled. I shall not go away again. We must stay here together."

Whispering, he questioned her and she answered whispering, and he instructed her over and over until she had her lesson by heart. The hostile darkness of the night encroached upon them, flowing over the narrow threshold, invading their hearts. It brought with it sighs and murmurs, the pad of secretive feet in the near-by road, the sharp staccato whimper of wind through the cactus leaves. All these familiar, once friendly cadences were now invested with sinister terrors; a dread, formless and uncontrollable, took hold of them both.

"Light another candle," said Juan, loudly, in too resolute, too sharp a tone. "Let us eat now."

They sat facing each other and ate from the same dish, after their old habit. Neither tasted what they ate. With food half-way to his mouth, Juan listened. The sound of voices rose, spread, widened at the turn of the road along the cactus wall. A spray of lantern light shot through the hedge, a single voice slashed the blackness, ripped the fragile layer of silence suspended above the hut.

"Juan Villegas!"

"Pass, friends!" Juan roared back cheerfully.

They stood in the doorway, simple cautious gendarmes from the village, mixed-bloods themselves with Indian sympathies, well known to all the community. They flashed their lanterns almost apologetically upon the pleasant, harmless scene of a man eating supper with his wife.

"Pardon, brother," said the leader. "Someone has killed the woman María Rosa, and we must question her neighbors and friends." He paused, and added with an attempt at severity, "Naturally!"

"Naturally," agreed Juan. "You know that I was a good friend of María Rosa. This is bad news."

They all went away together, the men walking in a group, María Concepción following a few steps in the rear, near Juan. No one spoke.

The two points of candlelight at María Rosa's head fluttered uneasily; the shadows shifted and dodged on the stained darkened walls. To María Concepción everything in the smothering enclosing room shared an evil restlessness. The watchful faces of those called as witnesses, the faces of old friends, were made alien by the look of speculation in their eyes. The ridges of the rose-colored rebozo thrown over the body varied continually, as though the thing it covered was not perfectly in repose. Her eyes swerved over the body in the open painted coffin, from the candle tips at the head to the feet, jutting up thinly, the small scarred soles protruding, freshly washed, a mass of crooked, half-healed wounds, thorn-pricks and cuts of sharp stones. Her gaze went back to the candle flame, to Juan's eyes warning her, to the gendarmes talking among themselves. Her eyes would not be controlled.

With a leap that shook her her gaze settled upon the face of María Rosa. Instantly her blood ran smoothly again: there was nothing to fear. Even the restless light could not give a look of life to that fixed countenance. She was dead. María Concepción felt her muscles give way softly; her heart began beating steadily without effort. She knew no more rancor against that pitiable thing, lying indifferently in its blue coffin under the fine silk rebozo. The mouth drooped sharply at the corners in a grimace of weeping arrested half-way. The brows were distressed; the dead flesh could not cast off the shape of its last terror. It was all finished. María Rosa had eaten too much honey and had had too much love. Now she must sit in hell, crying over her sins and her hard death forever and ever.

Old Lupe's cackling voice arose. She had spent the morning helping María Rosa, and it had been hard work. The child had spat blood the moment it was born, a bad sign. She thought then that bad luck would come to the house. Well, about sunset she was in the yard at the back of the house grinding tomatoes and peppers. She had left mother and babe asleep. She heard a strange noise in the house, a choking and smothered calling, like someone wailing in sleep. Well, such a thing is only natural. But there followed a light, quick, thudding sound—

"Like the blows of a fist?" interrupted an officer.

"No, not at all like such a thing."

"How do you know?"

"I am well acquainted with that sound, friends," retorted Lupe. "This was something else."

She was at a loss to describe it exactly. A moment later, there came the sound of pebbles rolling and slipping under feet; then she knew someone had been there and was running away.

"Why did you wait so long before going to see?"

"I am old and hard in the joints," said Lupe. "I cannot run after people. I walked as fast as I could to the cactus hedge, for it is only by this way that anyone can enter. There was no one in the road, sir, no one. Three cows, with a dog driving them; nothing else. When I got to María Rosa, she was lying all tangled up, and from her neck to her middle she was full of knife-holes. It was a sight to move the Blessed Image Himself! Her eyes were—"

"Never mind. Who came oftenest to her house before she went away? Did you know her enemies?"

Lupe's face congealed, closed. Her spongy skin drew into a network of secretive wrinkles. She turned withdrawn and expressionless eyes upon the gendarmes.

"I am an old woman. I do not see well. I cannot hurry on my feet. I know no enemy of María Rosa. I did not see anyone leave the clearing."

"You did not hear splashing in the spring near the bridge?"

"No, sir."

"Why, then, do our dogs follow a scent there and lose it?"

"God only knows, my friend. I am an old wo—"

"Yes. How did the footfalls sound?"

"Like the tread of an evil spirit!" Lupe broke forth in a swelling oracular tone that startled them. The Indians stirred uneasily, glanced at the dead, then at Lupe. They half expected her to produce the evil spirit among them at once.

The gendarme began to lose his temper.

"No, poor unfortunate; I mean, were they heavy or light? The footsteps of a man or of a woman? Was the person shod or barefoot?"

A glance at the listening circle assured Lupe of their thrilled attention. She enjoyed the dangerous importance of her situation. She could have ruined that María Concepción with a word, but it was even sweeter to make fools of these gendarmes who went about spying on honest people. She raised her voice again. What she had not seen she could not describe, thank God! No one could harm her because her knees were stiff and she could not run even to seize a murderer. As for knowing the difference between footfalls, shod or bare, man or woman, nay, between devil and human, who ever heard of such madness?

"My eyes are not ears, gentlemen," she ended grandly, "but upon my heart I swear those footsteps fell as the tread of the spirit of evil!"

"Imbecile!" yapped the leader in a shrill voice. "Take her away, one of you! Now, Juan Villegas, tell me—"

Juan told his story patiently, several times over. He had returned to his wife that day. She had gone to market as usual. He had helped her prepare her fowls. She had returned about mid-afternoon, they had talked, she had cooked, they had eaten, nothing was amiss. Then the gendarmes came with the news about María Rosa. That was all. Yes, María Rosa had run away with him, but there had been no bad blood between him and his wife on this account, nor between his wife and María Rosa. Everybody knew that his wife was a quiet woman.

María Concepción heard her own voice answering without a break. It was true at first she was troubled when her husband went away, but after that she had not worried about him. It was the way of men, she believed. She was a church-married woman and knew her place. Well, he had come home at last. She had gone to market, but had come back early, because now she had her man to cook for. That was all.

Other voices broke in. A toothless old man said: "She is a woman of good reputation among us, and María Rosa was not." A smiling young mother, Anita, baby at breast, said: "If no one thinks so, how can you accuse her? It was the loss of her child and not of her husband that changed her so." Another: "María Rosa had a strange life, apart from us. How do we know who might have come from another place to do her evil?" And old Soledad spoke up boldly: "When I saw María Concepción in the market today, I said, 'Good luck to you, María Concepción, this is a happy day for you!'" and she gave María Concepción a long easy stare, and the smile of a born wise-woman.

María Concepción suddenly felt herself guarded, surrounded, upborne by her faithful friends. They were around her, speaking for her, defending her, the forces of life were ranged invincibly with her against the beaten dead.

María Rosa had thrown away her share of strength in them, she lay forfeited among them. María Concepción looked from one to the other of the circling, intent faces. Their eyes gave back reassurance, understanding, a secret and mighty sympathy.

The gendarmes were at a loss. They, too, felt that sheltering wall cast impenetrably around her. They were certain she had done it, and yet they could not accuse her. Nobody could be accused; there was not a shred of true evidence. They shrugged their shoulders and snapped their fingers and shuffled their feet. Well, then, good night to everybody. Many pardons for having intruded. Good health!

A small bundle lying against the wall at the head of the coffin squirmed like an eel. A wail, a mere sliver of sound, issued. María Concepción took the son of María Rosa in her arms.

"He is mine," she said clearly, "I will take him with me."

No one assented in words, but an approving nod, a bare breath of complete agreement, stirred among them as they made way for her.

María Concepción, carrying the child, followed Juan from the clearing. The hut was left with its lighted candles and a crowd of old women who would sit up all night, drinking coffee and smoking and telling ghost stories.

Juan's exaltation had burned out. There was not an ember of excitement left in him. He was tired. The perilous adventure was over. María Rosa had vanished, to come no more forever. Their days of marching, of eating, of quarreling and making love between battles, were all over. Tomorrow he would go back to dull and endless labor, he must descend into the trenches of the buried city as María Rosa must go into her grave. He felt his veins fill up with bitterness, with black unendurable melancholy. Oh, Jesus! what bad luck overtakes a man!

Well, there was no way out of it now. For the moment he craved only to sleep. He was so drowsy he could scarcely guide his feet. The occasional light touch of the woman at his elbow was as unreal, as ghostly as the brushing of a leaf against his face. He did not know why he had fought to save her, and now he forgot her. There was nothing in him except a vast blind hurt like a covered wound.

He entered the jacal, and without waiting to light a candle, threw off his clothing, sitting just within the door. He moved with lagging, half-awake hands, to strip his body of its heavy finery. With a long groaning sigh of relief he fell straight back on the floor, almost instantly asleep, his arms flung up and outward.

María Concepción, a small clay jar in her hand, approached the gentle little mother goat tethered to a sapling, which gave and yielded as she pulled at the rope's end after the farthest reaches of grass about her. The kid, tied up a few feet away, rose bleating, its feathery fleece shivering in the fresh wind. Sitting on her heels, holding his tether, she allowed him to suckle a few moments. Afterward—all her movements very deliberate and even—she drew a supply of milk for the child.

She sat against the wall of her house, near the doorway. The child, fed and asleep, was cradled in the hollow of her crossed legs. The silence overfilled the world, the skies flowed down evenly to the rim of the valley, the stealthy moon crept slantwise to the shelter of the mountains. She felt soft and warm all over; she dreamed that the newly born child was her own, and she was resting deliciously.

María Concepción could hear Juan's breathing. The sound vapored from the low doorway, calmly; the house seemed to be resting after a burdensome day. She breathed, too, very slowly and quietly, each inspiration saturating her with repose. The child's light, faint breath was a mere shadowy moth of sound in the silver air. The night, the earth under her, seemed to swell and recede together with a limitless, unhurried, benign breathing. She drooped and closed her eyes, feeling the slow rise and fall within her own body. She did not know what it was, but it eased her all through. Even as she was falling asleep, head bowed over the child, she was still aware of a strange, wakeful happiness.

1922

The Postmodern Era

The United States emerged from World War II as the wealthiest and most powerful nation in history. Triumphant and little damaged by the ravages of the war, America became the financial and industrial center of the world and would soon be the source of innovation that brought unprecedented technological advances: the conquest of space, the harnessing of nuclear energy, and the development of computer technology. The war had also been a catalyst for vast social change. The level of education in the United States rose dramatically as the GI Bill of Rights provided millions of veterans the chance to attend college, an opportunity they would never otherwise have had. The nation's workforce began to undergo radical transformation. Women, African Americans, minorities of all kinds, sought new opportunities for jobs. Their experience in war work and in the armed forces gave them heightened expectations for meaningful employment, and they had a new willingness to confront age-old barriers that restricted their choices in life. Rigid social limitations that once had blocked their progress now began, slowly at first, to disintegrate.

The Cold War and the End of Segregation

Although the first decades after the war were celebrated as a time of peace, they saw the beginning of the Cold War between the United States and the Soviet Union that lasted through the 1980s and seemed at times to threaten nuclear confrontation. It was a time when government publications gave instructions on how to build back-yard bomb shelters and school children were trained to huddle under their classroom desks in the event of a nuclear bomb attack.

If the decades of the Cold War were a time of fear and hostility, they also brought the beginning of the end of racial segregation in America. Landmark legal decisions and civil rights legislation that began in the 1950s and have continued into the twenty-first century declared that discrimination based on race, skin color, gender, religion, or national origin was illegal. The racial segregation of public schools was ended; citizens were guaranteed voting rights, equal opportunity for jobs, and equal pay for equal work. New rights for women, gays, and the disabled were created. Access to public facilities for everyone was now required by law; rules for fair housing were created. Legislation and court decisions also expanded the rights of those accused of crime: The 1966 "Miranda Decision" by the U.S. Supreme Court gave greater protection to the accused, especially the poor and ignorant, and restrained the conduct of police and public authorities throughout the nation, requiring a warning that soon became familiar dialogue to every reader of crime fiction, every viewer of movies and television: "You have the right to remain silent . . . You have the right to an attorney . . . If you cannot afford an attorney one will be provided to you at no cost." The years from the 1950s to the end of the century brought the greatest expansion of civil rights in the history of the nation. It came, in part, as an expression of the traditional American faith in liberty, justice, and equality, but it also came as a result of turbulence and protest that remain deeply inscribed in the national consciousness. Powerful movements attracted thousands of Americans to rally in defense of greater justice for the poor and uneducated, to demand expanded rights for women, to cry out for black power and against the seemingly endless Vietnam War that had begun in the 1960s and did not end until 1975. Militant radical groups, fiercely contentious for social change, thrust themselves into public awareness, among them the Black Panthers and the Weather Underground, whose efforts were marred by a violence that inspired retaliatory violence. The decade that began with "sit ins," nonviolent protests against racial segregation in restaurants and in public transportation, ended in destruction, as American cities like Detroit, Chicago, Newark, and Los Angeles exploded and burned with incidents of racial and civil strife. As if the domestic turbulence were not enough, the 1960s also brought the Cuban Missile Crisis, a nearly catastrophic showdown between the United States and the Soviet Union over the placement of Soviet missiles in Cuba, aimed at the United States. It seemed to be an age of unrelenting fury and demolition, exemplified ultimately by the assassinations of President John F. Kennedy, Kennedy's brother Robert (who was himself a candidate for president), civil rights leaders Medgar Evers and Martin Luther King, Jr., and Black Muslim Malcom X.

Technology and Change

In the decades that followed the 1960s, the radical impulses that inspired liberation movements and clamorous demands for social change became denatured or were exhausted by their excesses. Many of their aims had been met and many of their ideals had been absorbed into the mainstream of American political and social life. A defining event of the more peaceful 1970s was the Watergate Scandal that ended with the resignation of Richard Nixon from the presidency in 1974, but still more significant were the development of the first personal computer by Steve Wozniak and Steve Jobs (who together founded the Apple Computer company in 1976) and the deindustrialization of America. In the 1970s the United States began a radical transformation from a nation reliant on heavy industries to a nation of computers and service-based economy. By the end of the twentieth century, 80 percent of the nation's domestic product came from services. Less than 20 percent came from heavy industry, the centers of which in America's old industrial heartland came to be called, because of their abandoned mills and empty warehouses, "The Rust Belt."

The onrush of technology that made the United States a colossus of advanced applied science was not wholly beneficial. The new dominance of computer technology produced a "two-tiered" labor market and made the gap between rich and poor grow ever wider. More people were well off and fewer were living below the poverty line than ever before, but large numbers of American citizens and immigrants, uneducated and unskilled in the new technologies, were unable to compete for high-paying jobs, and thus were locked out of the general prosperity. Those at the top enjoyed high salaries and benefits, while those at the bottom were mired in what threatened to become an enduring underclass in the midst of prosperity greater than anything achieved before in the history of the world. Equally discordant and divisive was the unprecedented rise in America's prison population that began in the 1970s. Between 1975 and 2002, the number of prison inmates quadrupled, and the percentage of the American population in prisons rose to be among the highest in the world. Fervent advocates of civil liberties said it was proof of the despotic nature of the American government. Fervent advocates of law and order pointed out that as the nation's prison population rose, the rate of crime plummeted—the annual number of violent crimes dropping by more than 40 percent—and by 2005 the United States had become one of the safest of all the world's industrialized nations.

The Population Explosion

In 2005 the population of the United States reached 296 million. By the year 2025 it is projected to rise to more than 350 million, in 2050 to more than 420 million. The rapid population growth that began in the post–WWII years has been accompanied by an accelerating demographic shift. A vast road-building program after World War II had created thousands of miles of superhighways, permitting the enormous expansion of America's trucking industry and the near-extinction of its railroads. It also increased the mobility of Americans and helped create a demographic shift as families loaded their possessions into their cars and trucks, drove onto the new highways, and headed west, where new jobs were available and life was thought to be better. The large cities of the Atlantic Coast declined as the dominant cultural centers of the nation, and the West Coast became a new and imposing land of fine arts, films, music, television production, and the legitimate theater, as well as the center of the emerging world of computer technology. By the year 2000, Las Vegas, Nevada, had become the fastest-growing metropolitan area in the nation, and the population center of the United States had moved westward to central Missouri, far from the big cities of the East.

America the Superpower

With the fall of the Berlin Wall in 1989 and the collapse of the communist governments of Eastern Europe, the United States emerged as the world's single superpower. As it grew more powerful and its influence spread in the last decade of the twentieth century, it became to many ordinary men and women in foreign lands a place of great hope for political freedom and the chance to live the good life. The United States was the preferred destiny of more would-be immigrants than any other nation of the world. America had never been richer, better educated, or healthier: by the year 2000, the national income of individuals had risen to 9 trillion dollars; more than 80 percent of the population had graduated from high school (25 percent had bachelor's degrees from college), and life expectancy had risen from 66 years for men and 71 years for women in 1950 to 75 years for men, 81 years for women in 2000. Yet, in the midst of all the nation's exuberant success and self-congratulations, critics of American culture decried the fact that its citizens seemed increasingly to live in a glitz-dominated society, unwilling to face the dreary problems of unequal income distribution, a faltering national healthcare system, and runaway public and government debt.

The critics of American complacency were largely ignored, but in 2001 that national complacency was shattered as the 9/11 terrorist attacks on the World Trade Center in New York City, the Pentagon Building in Washington, D.C., and an airliner over Pennsylvania killed and injured thousands of innocent people. The nation's reaction was swift: a National Emergency was declared three days later, and a new and powerful branch of the government was created, the Department of Homeland Security. To protect against further terrorism, many freedoms that Americans took for granted now began to be curtailed. Many members of the general public were searched and interrogated; their possessions were scrutinized as they had never been before. The social and political attitudes of millions of Americans changed dramatically. Suspicion and distrust of foreigners and immigrants spread. Political attitudes shifted; it is now acknowledged by observers of American politics that the 9/11 terrorist attacks so bolstered the position of President George Bush that it insured his reelection as president in 2004. The terrorist attacks of 9/11 also helped bring about American leadership of a coalition that waged war against Iraq in 2003. The result was total victory in the war, but the United States then found itself in a forced occupancy of a bloody, strife-ridden land, a predicament that threatens to again divide the nation over the issue of lethal and costly foreign entanglements as it has not been divided since the war in Vietnam.

As America moves further into the early years of the twenty-first century, it confronts great issues that often stir poisonous debates over questions of abortion, immigration, medical care, government waste, the rising national debt, trade imbalances, and rescue of the environment. Faced with domestic problems that defy solution and with an intractable and seemingly hopeless struggle in Iraq, Americans are once again forced to consider the role they wish their nation to play in the world. In the first days of English settlement in North America, the New England Puritans declared that America had a special destiny, that it was to be "A City on a Hill," a noble and heartening example to the rest of the world. Now, again, in the twenty-first century, the people of the United States must decide whether to withdraw from direct involvement in world affairs, returning to the isolationism of bygone days, hoping for safety, prosperity, and domestic tranquility, or to accept the Utopian ideal set forth in the seventeenth century by the Puritans and restated early in the twentieth century by President Woodrow Wilson when he proclaimed that America, as a great nation, must accept its great destiny to "show the way to the nations of the world how they shall walk in liberty."

The Emergence of American Literature after World War II

At the end of World War II, a new generation of American authors appeared, writing in the skeptical, ironic tradition of the earlier realists and naturalists. The new writers of the 1950s used a prose style modeled on the works of Ernest Hemingway and F. Scott Fitzgerald, narrative techniques derived from

William Faulkner, and psychological insights taken from the writing of Sigmund Freud and his followers. Southern short story writers and novelists, among them Eudora Welty and Flannery O'Connor, were inspired by Faulkner and the regional traditions in literature to write of the grotesqueries and the menacing violence of life in small-town and rural America. Saul Bellow and Bernard Malamud portrayed the dilemmas of misfit heroes yearning for meaningful lives and moral regeneration. The anti-hero, alternately a victim, a rebel, or a bumbling failure, became a commonplace in American fiction.

Richard Wright, Ralph Ellison, James Baldwin, Alice Walker, Gloria Naylor, Toni Morrison, and other black writers created a new black literary renaissance with portrayals of the often daunting experiences of blacks in modern America. Amy Tan and Maxine Hong Kingston have written of Asian immigrants and their American-born children. Leslie Marmon Silko and Louise Erdrich have written of Native Americans living on reservations and in the cities. Raymond Carver and Bobbie Ann Mason, writing what has been called "K-mart realism," have described the everyday experiences of Americans who spend their lives in trailer parks and shopping malls.

Many American prose writers in the 1960s turned to experimental techniques, to absurd humor, and to mocking examination of the irrational and disordered. In Donald Barthelme's sardonic stories, words and ideas often lose validity and hope is shown as absurd. The characters of Don DeLillo's novels living amid ecological catastrophes and technology run wild, find comfort in the abundance of their material possessions and in the narcotizing television that surrounds them and holds off, if only briefly, the intrusion of discordant reality.

The New Popular Culture

Mass culture, especially popular music, took on new directions after mid-century. Big band jazz and swing music, popular in the late 1930s and the war years, gave way to entirely different kinds of music with far greater popular appeal. Virtuoso jazz performers like Frank Sinatra and Ella Fitzgerald continued to draw large audiences, but the dominance of jazz and swing music had ended. In its place came the music of Elvis Presley, Motown, the Beatles, Bob Dylan, Joan Baez, the Rolling Stones, Janis Joplin, and San Francisco bands like the Grateful Dead. Such musicians, and their music, in landmark performances at such places as Newport, Woodstock, and Altamont, helped define and support an emerging alternative culture. At the same time, the mass commercial packaging of rock and roll and traditional forms like rhythm and blues, with its roots deep in African-American tradition, showed how easily, and profitably, popular culture could be turned into big business and made to captivate millions.

In the midst of shifting tastes in music, traditional forms of popular literature—romance novels, adventure tales, and crime fiction—continued to thrive, despite the rise of television and the strong competition of motion pictures. But with the breakneck speed of late-twentieth-century technological innovation, the lines between high and low, popular and serious, literary and nonliterary, began to dissolve. What had previously been considered "nonliterary" cultural artifacts challenged the traditional dominance of print literature as bearer of the cultural legacy of the age. Not only television and film but also the Internet and digital technology brought forth a previously unimagined range of representational and abstract images, rearranging ideas about poetry, narrative, and the nature of art, and as the twentieth century became the twenty-first, the battle for production, control, and distribution of images was increasingly recognized as a powerful social and political determinant.

The result has been that "literature," as it has traditionally been defined, now shares the stage with a growing variety of textual productions. Some critics condemn what they view as a "decentering" of literature. Others praise the emergence of new forms as an exciting, even uproarious, development that can only broaden the impact of American art and literature, bringing us still closer to the worlds of the American present and past.

American Theater, American Poetry

Unlike the explosive growth of the popular arts in the postwar era, the traditional theater in America, centered on New York City's Broadway, declined after World War II, beset by rising costs and competition from television. Its former vitality survived primarily in off-Broadway productions, in regional theaters, and on college campuses. The works of the most notable dramatists of the period range from familiar realism to obscure psychological surrealism. From Tennessee Williams came gothic dramas of oversensitive souls stifled by fate and their own genteel illusions. Williams's plays are rich with symbols, as are those of Edward Albee, whose work is further distinguished by its ambiguities and searing dialogue.

Since World War II, more poetry has been published and read in America than in any earlier period of its history. As new poets emerged and as new audiences were created, critical values changed. Such poetic monuments of the past as T. S. Eliot and Robert Frost went temporarily out of fashion. New schools of poets, seeking guidance and inspiration, turned instead to Walt Whitman, William Carlos Williams, Wallace Stevens, Ezra Pound, and Elizabeth Bishop. One of the most visible poets of the age, Allen Ginsberg emerged out of the phenomenon of the postwar "Beat Generation." In such poems as "Howl" and in his wide-ranging public appearances, he offered Whitmanesque recitations of the contradictions and vulgarities of America, amazing and shocking audiences who had at last grown accustomed to the learned obscurities of Pound and Eliot or who were comfortable with the seemingly benign and rustic wisdom of Robert Frost.

Elizabeth Bishop, in some of the most notable poetry of the last half of the century, used a distinctive woman's voice and rich, exotic imagery to record her intense observances of life and to express her estrangement from the world through which she traveled. Robert Lowell recorded his dilemmas and suffering in a confessional mode of poetry that is intensely private and that often focuses on the catastrophes of modern existence. New women writers appeared—novelists and short-story writers such as Joyce Carol Oats, Ann Beattie, Louise Erdrich, and Tony Morrison, poets such as Sylvia Plath, Anne Sexton, Louise Glück, and Rita Dove—who brought a new perspective to American literature, spoke out on gender and race issues, and helped to define a usable feminist past and present.

The United States Begins Its Third Century

As the United States became the world's preeminent Republic of Technology, and as it became, with the collapse of the Soviet Union, the dominant political power in the world, it seemed also, in the midst of its riches, to become a nation devoted to the search for immediate gratification, a nation of instant obsolescence and constant need to recycle and replenish. Individualism seemed diluted. Americans came evermore to think alike, dress alike, and eat alike in a kingdom of bland mediocrity created and sustained by the all-powerful and inescapable force of television.

At the beginning of the twenty-first century, more than 98 percent of all households in the United States had at least one television set; the average household had 2.4 sets. The nation's most popular weekly magazine, *TV Guide*, had an annual circulation of almost 460 million copies, greater than any other magazine in history. The average American watched television more than thirty hours a week; the average high school graduating senior, who had spent 11,000 hours in the classroom, had spent 15,000 hours watching television. The national addiction to television had grown so vast, critics argued, that Americans were in danger of becoming homogenized simpletons, with goals dictated by television commercials and values drawn from the sentimental platitudes revered in television sitcoms.

Added to the athletes and movie stars in the traditional pantheon of American popular idols, there are now, because of television, new icons: fashion designers, television advice givers, high-tech tycoons—whose scientific and business accomplishments may be extraordinary but whose political pronouncements are of less-certain value. Politicians surround themselves for public display with cadres of the television glitterati. Trendies and rock stars, sometimes derided as "coming from the shallower end of the pool of intellect," are nonetheless celebrated as exemplars of the latest life style. There is a national craving for gossip and a yearning for proximity to garish opulence.

Meanwhile many other Americans addicted not to their television sets but to the Internet, obsessively attend to computer games, bloggers, and movie downloads, and seem to be endangered only by the depredations of renegade Internet hackers and by their own expanding waistlines. But to those doomsayers who condemn the Internet as an invidious source of profanity, pornography, and indecent liaisons, defenders rightly point out that it has opened new worlds to people of every class and every age; that the most popular web page, by far, is simply AOL.com; and that the most widely sold computer software, also by far, is Turbo-Tax, purchased every year by millions of Americans to help them with their income tax.

In spite of the perplexing changes it confronts, and the pop culture and technology that often distract it, the United States remains resilient and vital, in large measure because it is the nation of the greatest opportunity and social diversity in the world, where more than 34 million foreign-born men and women now live, where immigrants are admitted at the rate of one million a year, where more than 300 languages and dialects are spoken, where 250 different religious denominations coexist. And within that pluralistic society, with all its excesses and contradictions, American writers continue to explore their own lives and their own visions of the land and its people, confronting the great questions of life and forming their experiences into a new and ever-expanding world of literature.

Eudora Welty 1909–2001

Eudora Welty was born and raised in Jackson, Mississippi. She attended Mississipi State College for Women for two years and then transferred to the University of Wisconsin, graduating in 1929. The following year she entered Columbia University in New York to study advertising. Two years later she returned to Jackson, where she worked for a local radio station and wrote society news for a Memphis newspaper. She also wrote publicity for the WPA and worked for a state commission to attract tourists to Mississippi.

Welty began her first serious attempts at writing after her return to Mississippi from New York in 1931. In June of 1936 her first short story, "Death of a Traveling Salesman," was published. She wrote several novels, the last of those being Losing Battles *(1970) and* The Optimist's Daughter *(1972), and numerous short stories that have been widely anthologized, translated into various foreign languages, and dramatized on Broadway and on television.*

Welty's writing displays a strong sense of place. She insisted that successful fiction depends in large measure on the appropriate location of the appropriate action. "It seems plain," she observed, "that the art that speaks most clearly, explicitly, directly, and passionately from its place of origin will remain the longest understood." Welty evinced a strong sense of her southern heritage, yet she was capable of a sustained detachment when writing about the South. Her fiction is largely concerned with the inner life, the mysteries of human beings confronting each other. Her writing reveals the sharp eye of a painter or photographer, displaying an acute sense of light, color, and atmosphere.

As a Southerner, Eudora Welty has often been compared to William Faulkner, a fellow Mississippian, but although her writing resembles Faulkner's in its attention to metaphor and symbol and in its concern for the South and its landscape, her writing does not exhibit the tragic vision of Faulkner and his concern with the dissolution of a moribund society. And she is at her best in short stories—even her novels have the qualities of extended short tales—which present her ironic view of human beings struggling amid the follies of life and the menace of death.

FURTHER READING: *Selected Stories of Eudora Welty,* 1954; R. Vande Kieft, *Eudora Welty,* 1962, 1987; A. Appel, *A Season of Dreams, The Fiction of Eudora Welty,* 1965; J. Bryant, *Eudora Welty,* 1968; *The Eye of the Story, Selected Essays and Reviews,* 1978; *Eudora Welty, Critical Essays,* ed. P. Prenshaw, 1979; *The Collected Stories of Eudora Welty,* 1980; M. Kreyling, *Eudora Welty's Achievement of Order,* 1980; E. Evans, *Eudora Welty,* 1981; A. Devlin, *Eudora Welty's Chronicle,* 1983; *One Writer's Beginnings,* 1984; C. Manning, *Ears Opening Like Morning Glories, Eudora Welty and the Love of Story Telling,* 1985; *Eudora Welty,* ed. H. Bloom, 1986; *Welty, A Life in Literature,* ed. A. Devlin, 1987; L. Westling, *Eudora Welty,* 1989; *Critical Essays on Eudora Welty,* ed. W. Turner and L. Harding, 1989; R. MacNeil, *Seeing Black and White,* 1990; P. Schmidt, *The Heart of the Story, Eudora Welty's Fiction,* 1991; G. Mortimer, *Daughter of the Swan, Love and Knowledge in Eudora Welty's Fiction,* 1993; R. Weston, *Gothic Traditions and Narrative Techniques in the Fiction of Eudora Welty,* 1994; J. Gretlund, *Eudora Welty's Aesthetics of Place,* 1994; *More Conversations with Eudora Welty,* ed. P. Prenshaw, 1996; C. Johnston, *Eudora Welty, A Study of the Short Fiction,* 1997; A. Waldron, *Eudora, A Writer's Life,* 1998; M. Kreyling, *Understanding Eudora Welty,* 1999; S. Marrs, *One Writer's Imagination, The Fiction of Eudora Welty,* 2002.

TEXT: *The Collected Stories of Eudora Welty,* 1980.

DEATH OF A TRAVELING SALESMAN

R. J. Bowman, who for fourteen years had traveled for a shoe company through Mississippi, drove his Ford along a rutted dirt path. It was a long day! The time did not seem to clear the noon hurdle and settle into soft afternoon. The sun, keeping its strength here even in winter, stayed at the top of the sky, and every time Bowman stuck his head out of the dusty car to stare up the road, it seemed to reach a long arm down and push against the top of his head, right through his hat—like the practical joke of an old drummer, long on the road. It made him feel all the more angry and helpless. He was feverish, and he was not quite sure of the way.

This was his first day back on the road after a long siege of influenza. He had had very high fever, and dreams, and had become weakened and pale, enough to tell the difference in the mirror, and he could not think clearly. . . . All afternoon, in the midst of his anger, and for no reason, he had thought of his dead grandmother. She had been a comfortable soul. Once more Bowman wished he could fall into the big feather bed that had been in her room. . . . Then he forgot her again.

This desolate hill country! And he seemed to be going the wrong way—it was as if he were going back, far back. There was not a house in sight. . . . There was no use wishing he were back in bed, though. By paying the hotel doctor his bill he had proved his recovery. He had not even been sorry when the pretty trained nurse said good-bye. He did not like illness, he distrusted it, as he distrusted the road without signposts. It angered him. He had given the nurse a really expensive bracelet, just because she was packing up her bag and leaving.

But now—what if in fourteen years on the road he had never been ill before and never had an accident? His record was broken, and he had even begun almost to question it. . . . He had gradually put up at better hotels, in the bigger towns, but weren't they all, eternally, stuffy in summer and drafty in winter? Women? He could only remember little rooms within little rooms, like a nest of Chinese paper boxes, and if he thought of one woman he saw the worn loneliness that the furniture of that room seemed built of. And he himself—he was a man who always wore rather wide-brimmed black hats, and in the wavy hotel mirrors had looked something like a bullfighter, as he paused for that inevitable instant on the landing, walking downstairs to supper. . . . He leaned out of the car again, and once more the sun pushed at his head.

Bowman had wanted to reach Beulah by dark, to go to bed and sleep off his fatigue. As he remembered, Beulah was fifty miles away from the last town, on a graveled road. This was only a cow trail. How had he ever come to such a place? One hand wiped the sweat from his face, and he drove on.

He had made the Beulah trip before. But he had never seen this hill or this petering-out path before—or that cloud, he thought shyly, looking up and then down quickly—any more than he had seen this day before. Why did he not admit he was simply lost and had been for miles? . . . He was not in the habit of asking the way of strangers, and these people never knew where the very roads they lived on went to; but then he had not even been close enough to anyone to call out. People standing in the fields now and then, or on top of the haystacks, had been too far away, looking like leaning sticks or weeds, turning a little at the solitary rattle of his car across their countryside, watching the pale sobered winter dust where it chunked out behind like big squashes down the road. The stares of these distant people had followed him solidly like a wall, impenetrable, behind which they turned back after he had passed.

The cloud floated there to one side like the bolster on his grandmother's bed. It went over a cabin on the edge of a hill, where two bare chinaberry trees clutched at the sky. He drove through a heap of dead oak leaves, his wheels stirring their weightless sides to make a silvery melancholy whistle as the car passed through their bed. No car had been along this way ahead of him. Then he saw that he was on the edge of a ravine that fell away, a red erosion, and that this was indeed the road's end.

He pulled the brake. But it did not hold, though he put all his strength into it. The car, tipped toward the edge, rolled a little. Without doubt, it was going over the bank.

He got out quietly, as though some mischief had been done him and he had his dignity to remember. He lifted his bag and sample case out, set them down, and stood back and watched the car roll over the edge. He heard something—not the crash he was listening for, but a slow, unuproarious crackle. Rather distastefully he went to look over, and he saw that his car had fallen into a tangle of immense grapevines as thick as his arm, which caught it and held it, rocked it like a grotesque child in a dark cradle, and then, as he watched, concerned somehow that he was not still inside it, released it gently to the ground.

He sighed.

Where am I? he wondered with a shock. Why didn't I do something? All his anger seemed to have drifted away from him. There was the house, back on the hill. He took a bag in each hand and with almost childlike willingness went toward it. But his breathing came with difficulty, and he had to stop to rest.

It was a shotgun house, two rooms and an open passage between, perched on the hill. The whole cabin slanted a little under the heavy heaped-up vine that covered the roof, light and green, as though forgotten from summer. A woman stood in the passage.

He stopped still. Then all of a sudden his heart began to behave strangely. Like a rocket set off, it began to leap and expand into uneven patterns of beats which showered into his brain, and he could not think. But in scattering and falling it made no noise. It shot up with great power, almost elation, and fell gently, like acrobats into nets. It began to pound profoundly, then waited irresponsibly, hitting in some sort of inward mockery first at his ribs, then against his eyes, then under his shoulder blades, and against the roof of his mouth when he tried to say, "Good afternoon, madam." But he could not hear his heart—it was as quiet as ashes falling. This was rather comforting; still, it was shocking to Bowman to feel his heart beating at all.

Stock-still in his confusion, he dropped his bags, which seemed to drift in slow bulks gracefully through the air and to cushion themselves on the gray prostrate grass near the doorstep.

As for the woman standing there, he saw at once that she was old. Since she could not possibly hear his heart, he ignored the pounding and now looked at her carefully, and yet in his distraction dreamily, with his mouth open.

She had been cleaning the lamp, and held it, half blackened, half clear, in front of her. He saw her with the dark passage behind her. She was a big woman with a weather-beaten but unwrinkled face; her lips were held tightly together, and her eyes looked with a curious dulled brightness into his. He looked at her shoes, which were like bundles. If it were summer she would be barefoot. . . . Bowman, who automatically judged a woman's age on sight, set her age at fifty. She wore a formless garment of some gray coarse material, rough-dried from a washing, from which her arms appeared pink and unexpectedly round. When she never said a word, and sustained her quiet pose of holding the lamp, he was convinced of the strength in her body.

"Good afternoon, madam," he said.

She stared on, whether at him or at the air around him he could not tell, but after a moment she lowered her eyes to show that she would listen to whatever he had to say.

"I wonder if you would be interested—" He tried once more. "An accident—my car . . . "

Her voice emerged low and remote, like a sound across a lake. "Sonny he ain't here."

"Sonny?"

"Sonny ain't here now."

Her son—a fellow able to bring my car up, he decided in blurred relief. He pointed down the hill. "My car's in the bottom of the ditch. I'll need help."

"Sonny ain't here, but he'll be here."

She was becoming clearer to him and her voice stronger, and Bowman saw that she was stupid.

He was hardly surprised at the deepening postponement and tedium of his journey. He took a breath, and heard his voice speaking over the silent blows of his heart. "I was sick. I am not strong yet. . . . May I come in?"

He stooped and laid his big black hat over the handle on his bag. It was a humble motion, almost a bow, that instantly struck him as absurd and betraying of all his weakness. He looked up at the woman, the wind blowing his hair. He might have continued for a long time in this unfamiliar attitude; he had never been a patient man, but when he was sick he had learned to sink submissively into the pillows, to wait for his medicine. He waited on the woman.

Then she, looking at him with blue eyes, turned and held open the door, and after a moment Bowman, as if convinced in his action, stood erect and followed her in.

Inside, the darkness of the house touched him like a professional hand, the doctor's. The woman set the half-cleaned lamp on a table in the center of the room and pointed, also like a professional person, a guide, to a chair with a yellow cowhide seat. She herself crouched on the hearth, drawing her knees up under the shapeless dress.

At first he felt hopefully secure. His heart was quieter. The room was enclosed in the gloom of yellow pine boards. He could see the other room, with the foot of an iron bed showing, across the passage. The bed had been made up with a red-and-yellow pieced quilt that looked like a map or a picture, a little like his grandmother's girlhood painting of Rome burning.

He had ached for coolness, but in this room it was cold. He stared at the hearth with dead coals lying on it and iron pots in the corners. The hearth and smoked chimney were of the stone he had seen ribbing the hills, mostly slate. Why is there no fire? he wondered.

And it was so still. The silence of the fields seemed to enter and move familiarly through the house. The wind used the open hall. He felt that he was in a mysterious, quiet, cool danger. It was necessary to do what? . . . To talk.

"I have a nice line of women's low-priced shoes . . ." he said.

But the woman answered, "Sonny'll be here. He's strong. Sonny'll move your car."

"Where is he now?"

"Farms for Mr. Redmond."

Mr. Redmond. Mr. Redmond. That was someone he would never have to encounter, and he was glad. Somehow the name did not appeal to him. . . . In a flare of touchiness and anxiety, Bowman wished to avoid even mention of unknown men and their unknown farms.

"Do you two live here alone?" He was surprised to hear his old voice, chatty, confidential, inflected for selling shoes, asking a question like that—a thing he did not even want to know.

"Yes. We are alone."

He was surprised at the way she answered. She had taken a long time to say that. She had nodded her head in a deep way too. Had she wished to affect him with some sort of premonition? he wondered unhappily. Or was it only that she would not help him, after all, by talking with him? For he was not strong enough to receive the impact of unfamiliar things without a little talk to break their fall. He had lived a month in which nothing had happened except in his head and his body—an almost inaudible life of heartbeats and dreams that came back, a life of fever and privacy, a delicate life which had left him weak to the point of—what? Of begging. The pulse in his palm leapt like a trout in a brook.

He wondered over and over why the woman did not go ahead with cleaning the lamp. What prompted her to stay there across the room, silently bestowing her presence upon him? He saw that with her it was not a time for doing little tasks. Her face was grave; she was feeling how right she was. Perhaps it was only politeness. In docility he held his eyes stiffly wide; they fixed themselves on the woman's clasped hands as though she held the cord they were strung on.

Then, "Sonny's coming," she said.

He himself had not heard anything, but there came a man passing the window and then plunging in at the door, with two hounds beside him. Sonny was a big enough man, with his belt slung low about his hips. He looked at least thirty. He had a hot, red face that was yet full of silence. He wore muddy blue pants and an old military coat stained and patched. World War? Bowman wondered. Great God, it was a Confederate coat. On the back of his light hair he had a wide filthy black hat which seemed to insult Bowman's own. He pushed down the dogs from his chest. He was strong, with dignity and heaviness in his way of moving. . . . There was the resemblance to his mother.

They stood side by side. . . . He must account again for his presence here.

"Sonny, this man, he had his car to run off over the prec'pice an' wants to know if you will git it out for him," the woman said after a few minutes.

Bowman could not even state his case.

Sonny's eyes lay upon him.

He knew he should offer explanations and show money—at least appear either penitent or authoritative. But all he could do was to shrug slightly.

Sonny brushed by him going to the window, followed by the eager dogs, and looked out. There was effort even in the way he was looking, as if he could throw his sight out like a rope. Without turning Bowman felt that his own eyes could have seen nothing: it was too far.

"Got me a mule out there an' got me a block an' tackle," said Sonny meaningfully. "I *could* catch me my mule an' git me my ropes, an' before long I'd git your car out the ravine."

He looked completely around the room, as if in meditation, his eyes roving in their own distance. Then he pressed his lips firmly and yet shyly together, and with the dogs ahead of him this time, he lowered his head and strode out. The hard earth sounded, cupping to his powerful way of walking—almost a stagger.

Mischievously, at the suggestion of those sounds, Bowman's heart leapt again. It seemed to walk about inside of him.

"Sonny's goin' to do it," the woman said. She said it again, singing it almost, like a song. She was sitting in her place by the hearth.

Without looking out, he heard some shouts and the dogs barking and the pounding of hoofs in short runs on the hill. In a few minutes Sonny passed under the window with a rope, and there was a brown mule with quivering, shining, purple-looking ears. The mule actually looked in the window. Under its eyelashes it turned target-like eyes into his. Bowman averted his head and saw the woman looking serenely back at the mule, with only satisfaction in her face.

She sang a little more, under her breath. It occurred to him, and it seemed quite marvelous, that she was not really talking to him, but rather following the thing that came about with words that were unconscious and part of her looking.

So he said nothing, and this time when he did not reply he felt a curious and strong emotion, not fear, rise up in him.

This time, when his heart leapt, something—his soul—seemed to leap too, like a little colt invited out of a pen. He stared at the woman while the frantic nimbleness of his feeling made his head sway. He could not move; there was nothing he could do, unless perhaps he might embrace this woman who sat there growing old and shapeless before him.

But he wanted to leap up, to say to her, I have been sick and I found out then, only then, how lonely I am. Is it too late? My heart puts up a struggle inside me, and you may have heard it, protesting against emptiness. . . . It should be full, he would rush on to tell her, thinking of his heart now as a deep lake, it should be holding love like other hearts. It should be flooded with love. There would be a warm spring day. . . . Come and stand in my heart, whoever you are, and a whole river would cover your feet and rise higher and take your knees in whirlpools, and draw you down to itself, your whole body, your heart too.

But he moved a trembling hand across his eyes, and looked at the placid crouching woman across the room. She was still as a statue. He felt ashamed and exhausted by the thought that he might, in one more moment, have tried by simple words and embraces to communicate some strange thing—something which seemed always to have just escaped him. . . .

Sunlight touched the furthest pot on the hearth. It was late afternoon. This time tomorrow he would be somewhere on a good graveled road, driving his car past things that happened to people, quicker than their happening. Seeing ahead to the next day, he was glad, and knew that this was no time to embrace an old woman. He could feel in his pounding temples the readying of his blood for motion and for hurrying away.

"Sonny's hitched up your car by now," said the woman. "He'll git it out the ravine right shortly."

"Fine!" he cried with his customary enthusiasm.

Yet it seemed a long time that they waited. It began to get dark. Bowman was cramped in his chair. Any man should know enough to get up and walk around while he waited. There was something like guilt in such stillness and silence.

But instead of getting up, he listened. . . . His breathing restrained, his eyes powerless in the growing dark, he listened uneasily for a warning sound, forgetting in wariness what it would be. Before long he heard something—soft, continuous, insinuating.

"What's that noise?" he asked, his voice jumping into the dark. Then wildly he was afraid it would be his heart beating so plainly in the quiet room, and she would tell him so.

"You might hear the stream," she said grudgingly.

Her voice was closer. She was standing by the table. He wondered why she did not light the lamp. She stood there in the dark and did not light it.

Bowman would never speak to her now, for the time was past. I'll sleep in the dark, he thought, in his bewilderment pitying himself.

Heavily she moved on to the window. Her arm, vaguely white, rose straight from her full side and she pointed out into the darkness.

"That white speck's Sonny," she said, talking to herself.

He turned unwillingly and peered over her shoulder; he hesitated to rise and stand beside her. His eyes searched the dusky air. The white speck floated smoothly toward her finger, like a leaf on a river, growing whiter in the dark. It was as if she had shown him something secret, part of her life, but had offered no explanation. He looked away. He was moved almost to tears, feeling for no reason that she had made a silent declaration equivalent to his own. His hand waited upon his chest.

Then a step shook the house, and Sonny was in the room. Bowman felt how the woman left him there and went to the other man's side.

"I done got your car out, mister," said Sonny's voice in the dark. "She's settin' a-waitin' in the road, turned to go back where she come from."

"Fine!" said Bowman, projecting his own voice to loudness. "I'm surely much obliged—I could never have done it myself—I was sick. . . ."

"I could do it easy," said Sonny.

Bowman could feel them both waiting in the dark, and he could hear the dogs panting out in the yard, waiting to bark when he should go. He felt strangely helpless and resentful. Now that he could go, he longed to stay. Of what was he being deprived? His chest was rudely shaken by the violence of his heart. These people cherished something here that he could not see, they withheld some ancient promise of food and warmth and light. Between them they had a conspiracy. He thought of the way she had moved away from him and gone to Sonny, she had flowed toward him. He was shaking with cold, he was tired, and it was not fair. Humbly and yet angrily he stuck his hand into his pocket.

"Of course I'm going to pay you for everything—"

"We don't take money for such," said Sonny's voice belligerently.

"I want to pay. But do something more. . . . Let me stay—tonight. . . ." He took another step toward them. If only they could see him, they would know his sincerity, his real need! His voice went on, "I'm not very strong yet, I'm not able to walk far, even back to my car, maybe, I don't know—I don't know exactly where I am—"

He stopped. He felt as if he might burst into tears. What would they think of him!

Sonny came over and put his hands on him. Bowman felt them pass (they were professional too) across his chest, over his hips. He could feel Sonny's eyes upon him in the dark.

"You ain't no revenuer come sneakin' here, mister, ain't got no gun?"

To this end of nowhere! And yet *he* had come. He made a grave answer. "No."

"You can stay."

"Sonny," said the woman, "you'll have to borry some fire."

"I'll go git it from Redmond's," said Sonny.

"What?" Bowman strained to hear their words to each other.

"Our fire, it's out, and Sonny's got to borry some, because it's dark an' cold," she said.

"But matches—I have matches—"

"We don't have no need for 'em," she said proudly. "Sonny's goin' after his own fire."

"I'm goin' to Redmond's," said Sonny with an air of importance, and he went out.

After they had waited a while, Bowman looked out the window and saw a light moving over the hill. It spread itself out like a little fan. It zigzagged along the field, darting and swift, not like Sonny at all. . . . Soon enough, Sonny staggered in, holding a burning stick behind him in tongs, fire flowing in his wake, blazing light into the corners of the room.

"We'll make a fire now," the woman said, taking the brand.

When that was done she lit the lamp. It showed its dark and light. The whole room turned golden-yellow like some sort of flower, and the walls smelled of it and seemed to tremble with the quiet rushing of the fire and the waving of the burning lampwick in its funnel of light.

The woman moved among the iron pots. With the tongs she dropped hot coals on top of the iron lids. They made a set of soft vibrations, like the sound of a bell far away.

She looked up and over at Bowman, but he could not answer. He was trembling. . . .

"Have a drink, mister?" Sonny asked. He had brought in a chair from the other room and sat astride it with his folded arms across the back. Now we are all visible to one another, Bowman thought, and cried, "Yes sir, you bet, thanks!"

"Come after me and do just what I do," said Sonny.

It was another excursion into the dark. They went through the hall, out to the back of the house, past a shed and a hooded well. They came to a wilderness of thicket.

"Down on your knees," said Sonny.

"What?" Sweat broke out on his forehead.

He understood when Sonny began to crawl through a sort of tunnel that the bushes made over the ground. He followed, startled in spite of himself when a twig or a thorn touched him gently without making a sound, clinging to him and finally letting him go.

Sonny stopped crawling and, crouched on his knees, began to dig with both his hands into the dirt. Bowman shyly struck matches and made a light. In a few minutes Sonny pulled up a jug. He poured out some of the whiskey into a bottle from his coat pocket, and buried the jug again. "You never know who's liable to knock at your door," he said, and laughed. "Start back," he said, almost formally. "Ain't no need for us to drink outdoors, like hogs."

At the table by the fire, sitting opposite each other in their chairs, Sonny and Bowman took drinks out of the bottle, passing it across. The dogs slept; one of them was having a dream.

"This is good," said Bowman. "This is what I needed." It was just as though he were drinking the fire off the hearth.

"He makes it," said the woman with quiet pride.

She was pushing the coals off the pots, and the smells of corn bread and coffee circled the room. She set everything on the table before the men, with a bone-handled knife stuck into one of the potatoes, splitting out its golden fiber. Then she stood for a minute looking at them, tall and full above them where they sat. She leaned a little toward them.

"You all can eat now," she said, and suddenly smiled.

Bowman had just happened to be looking at her. He set his cup back on the table in unbelieving protest. A pain pressed at his eyes. He saw that she was not an old woman. She was young, still young. He could think of no number of years for her. She was the same age as Sonny, and she belonged to him. She stood with the deep dark corner of the room behind her, the shifting yellow light scattering over her head and her gray formless dress, trembling over her tall body when it bent over them in its sudden communication. She was young. Her teeth were shining and her eyes glowed. She turned and walked slowly and heavily out of the room, and he heard her sit down on the cot and then lie down. The pattern on the quilt moved.

"She's goin' to have a baby," said Sonny, popping a bite into his mouth.

Bowman could not speak. He was shocked with knowing what was really in this house. A marriage, a fruitful marriage. That simple thing. Anyone could have had that.

Somehow he felt unable to be indignant or protest, although some sort of joke had certainly been played upon him. There was nothing remote or mysterious here—only something private. The only secret was the ancient communication between two people. But the memory of the woman's waiting silently by the cold hearth, of the man's stubborn journey a mile away to get fire, and how they finally brought out their food and drink and filled the room proudly with all they had to show, was suddenly too clear and too enormous within him for response. . . .

"You ain't as hungry as you look," said Sonny.

The woman came out of the bedroom as soon as the men had finished, and ate her supper while her husband stared peacefully into the fire.

Then they put the dogs out, with the food that was left.

"I think I'd better sleep here by the fire, on the floor," said Bowman.

He felt that he had been cheated, and that he could afford now to be generous. Ill though he was, he was not going to ask them for their bed. He was through with asking favors in this house, now that he understood what was there.

"Sure, mister."

But he had not known yet how slowly he understood. They had not meant to give him their bed. After a little interval they both rose and looking at him gravely went into the other room.

He lay stretched by the fire until it grew low and dying. He watched every tongue of blaze lick out and vanish. "There will be special reduced prices on all footwear during the month of January," he found himself repeating quietly, and then he lay with his lips tight shut.

How many noises the night had! He heard the stream running, the fire dying, and he was sure now that he heard his heart beating, too, the sound it made under his ribs. He heard breathing, round and deep, of the man and his wife in the room across the passage. And that was all. But emotion swelled patiently within him, and he wished that the child were his.

He must get back to where he had been before. He stood weakly before the red coals and put on his overcoat. It felt too heavy on his shoulders. As he started out he looked and saw that the woman had never got through with cleaning the lamp. On some impulse he put all the money from his billfold under its fluted glass base, almost ostentatiously.

Ashamed, shrugging a little, and then shivering, he took his bags and went out. The cold of the air seemed to lift him bodily. The moon was in the sky.

On the slope he began to run, he could not help it. Just as he reached the road, where his car seemed to sit in the moonlight like a boat, his heart began to give off tremendous explosions like a rifle, bang bang bang.

He sank in fright onto the road, his bags falling about him. He felt as if all this had happened before. He covered his heart with both hands to keep anyone from hearing the noise it made.

But nobody heard it.

1936, 1941

Richard Wright 1908–1960

Richard Wright experienced a troubled and frightening Southern boyhood. His father deserted his family and left his son to be raised in an oppressive environment by his fundamentalist grandmother and stern mother. Although hindered by limited educational opportunities for blacks in the South in the 1920s, he distinguished himself in the classroom, graduating as valedictorian and having a story published while still in high school. But his talents could not find recognition in his segregated society, and, like thousands of other blacks of the time, he fled north, first to Memphis, Tennessee, and then to Chicago.

In Chicago, Wright had several menial jobs. During the Depression he became involved with the Federal Negro Theatre (a WPA project) and with the Illinois Writers' Project. At this time, he began to attend meetings of the John Reed Club, a group supported by the Communist Party. Throughout the 1930s, under the sponsorship of the John Reed Club, Wright wrote and published stories and essays. Although leaders of the Communist Party complained of his failure to follow the party line in his writing, he continued to work within the party (an affiliation that lasted until 1944), and in 1937 he moved to New York to become Harlem editor of the Daily Worker. *His first book,* Uncle Tom's Children: Four Novellas, *was published in 1938, and he subsequently won a Guggenheim Fellowship that enabled him to complete and publish* Native Son *in 1940.*

Native Son, *his dramatic and gripping story of a black man's struggle with poverty, racism, and the justice system in the 1930s, won immediate acclaim and sold a quarter of a million copies in its first month of publication. Rewritten for the stage, it was produced in 1941 and became one of the first plays by an African-American playwright to be presented on Broadway. In 1945,* Black Boy, *an autobiographical account of his youth in the South, was published, and Wright again received great popular acclaim. During this time he was also an important supporter of younger black writers, including Margaret Walker, Ralph Ellison, and James Baldwin. He had become the first black American whose work appeared on national bestseller lists, but in 1947, embittered by the racial prejudice he had encountered, he emigrated to Europe, where he was to live until his death.*

Wright published more novels, essays, and stories, but his later work never received the popular or critical acclaim of Native Son *and* Black Boy. *The work that he did after leaving the United States has generally been neglected.* American Hunger, *Wright's autobiographical sequel to* Black Boy, *never received favorable attention. And although the essays collected in* White Man, Listen! *are significant contributions to twentieth-century racial history and* The Outsider *is notable as an existentialist novel, Richard Wright's most defining work remains* Native Son. *He was at work on a novel when he died of a heart attack in France on November 28, 1960.*

FURTHER READING: *Richard Wright, Letters to Joe C. Brown,* ed. T. Knipp, 1968; C. Webb, *Richard Wright, A Biography,* 1968; D. McCall, *The Example of Richard Wright,* 1969; E. Margolies, *The Art of Richard Wright,* 1969; R. Bone, *Richard Wright,* 1969; J. Williams, *The Most Native of Sons, A Biography of Richard Wright,* 1970; R. Brignano, *Richard Wright, An Introduction to the Man and His Works,* 1970; R. Abcarian, *Richard Wright's "Native Son," A Critical Handbook,* 1970; *Richard Wright, Impressions and Perspectives,* ed. D. Ray and R. Farnsworth, 1973; K. Kinnamon, *The Emergence of Richard Wright,* 1973; *Richard Wright Reader,* ed. E. Wright and M. Fabre, 1978; M. Fabre, *The Unfinished Quest of Richard Wright,* 1979; A. Gayle, *Richard Wright, Ordeal of a Native Son,* 1980; R. Felgar, *Richard Wright,* 1980; *Critical Essays on Richard*

Wright, ed. Y. Hakutani, 1982; M. Fabre, *The World of Richard Wright,* 1985; J. Joyce, *Richard Wright's Art of Tragedy,* 1986; *Richard Wright,* ed. H. Bloom, 1987; M. Walker, *Richard Wright, Daemonic Genius,* 1988; J. Trotman, *Richard Wright, Myth and Realities,* 1989; M. Fabre, *Richard Wright, Books and Writers,* 1990; *Conversations with Richard Wright,* ed. K. Kinnamon and M. Fabre, 1993; *Richard Wright, Critical Perspectives Past and Present,* ed. H. Gates and K. Appiah, 1993; Y. Hakutani, *Richard Wright and Racial Discourse,* 1996; T. Caron, *Struggles over the World, Race and Religion in O'Connor, Faulkner, Hurston, and Wright,* 2000; R. Felgar, *Student Companion to Richard Wright,* 2000; A. Janmohamed, *The Death-Bound-Subject, Richard Wright's Archaeology of Death,* 2005.

TEXT: *Eight Men,* 1961.

from *EIGHT MEN*

THE MAN WHO WAS ALMOST A MAN

Dave struck out across the fields, looking homeward through paling light. Whut's the use talkin wid em niggers in the field? Anyhow, his mother was putting supper on the table. Them niggers can't understan nothing. One of these days he was going to get a gun and practice shooting, then they couldn't talk to him as though he were a little boy. He slowed, looking at the ground. Shucks, Ah ain scareda them even ef they are biggern me! Aw, Ah know whut Ahma do. Ahm going to ol Joe's sto n git that Sears Roebuck catlog n look at them guns. Mebbe Ma will lemme buy one when she gits mah pay from ol man Hawkins. Ahma beg her t gimme some money. Ahm ol ernough to hava gun. Ahm seventeen. Almost a man. He strode, feeling his long loose-jointed limbs. Shucks, a man oughta hava little fun aftah he done worked hard all day.

He came in sight of Joe's store. A yellow lantern glowed on the front porch. He mounted steps and went through the screen door, hearing it bang behind him. There was a strong smell of coal oil and mackerel fish. He felt very confident until he saw fat Joe walk in through the rear door, then his courage began to ooze.

"Howdy Dave! Whutcha want?"

"How yuh, Mistah Joe? Aw, Ah don wanna buy nothing. Ah just wanted to see ef yuhd lemme look at tha catlog erwhile."

"Sure! You wanna see it here?"

"Nawsuh. Ah wans t take it home wid me. Ah'll bring it back termorrow when Ah come in from the fiels."

"You plannin on buyin something?"

"Yessuh."

"Your ma letting you have your own money now?"

"Shucks. Mistah Joe, Ahm gettin t be a man like anybody else!"

Joe laughed and wiped his greasy white face with a red bandanna.

"What you plannin on buyin?"

Dave looked at the floor, scratched his head, scratched his thigh, and smiled. Then he looked up shyly.

"Ah'll tell yuh, Mistah Joe, ef yuh promise yuh won't tell."

"I promise."

"Waal, Ahma buy a gun."

"A gun? Whut you want with a gun?"

"Ah wanna keep it."

"You ain't nothing but a boy. You don't need a gun."

"Aw, lemme have the catalog. Mistah Joe. Ah'll bring it back."

Joe walked through the rear door. Dave was elated. He looked around at barrels of sugar and flour. He heard Joe coming back. He craned his neck to see if he were bringing the book. Yeah, he's got it. Gawddog, he's got it!

"Here, but be sure you bring it back. It's the only one I got."

"Sho, Mistah Joe."

"Say, if you wanna buy a gun, why don't you buy one from me? I gotta gun to sell."

"Will it shoot?"

"Sure it'll shoot."

"Whut kind is it?"

"Oh, it's kinda old . . . a left-hand Wheeler. A pistol. A big one."

"Is it got bullets in it?"

"It's loaded."

"Kin Ah see it?"

"Where's your money?"

"Whut yuh wan fer it?"

"I'll let you have it for two dollars."

"Just two dollahs? Shucks, Ah could buy that when Ah git mah pay."

"I'll have it here when you want it."

"Awright, suh. Ah be in fer it."

He went through the door, hearing it slam again behind him. Ahma git some money from Ma n buy me a gun! Only two dollahs! He tucked the thick catalogue under his arm and hurried.

"Where yuh been, boy?" His mother held a steaming dish of black-eyed peas.

"Aw, Ma, Ah just stopped down the road to talk wid the boys."

"Yuh know bettah t keep suppah waitin."

He sat down, resting the catalogue on the edge of the table.

"Yuh git up from there and git to the well n wash yosef! Ah ain feedin no hogs in mah house!"

She grabbed his shoulder and pushed him. He stumbled out of the room, then came back to get the catalogue.

"Whut this?"

"Aw, Ma, it's jusa catlog."

"Who yuh got it from?"

"From Joe, down at the sto."

"Waal thas good. We kin use it in the outhouse."

"Naw, Ma." He grabbed for it. "Gimme ma catlog, Ma."

She held onto it and glared at him.

"Quit hollerin at me! Whut's wrong wid yuh? Yuh crazy?"

"But Ma, please. It ain mine! It's Joe's! He tol me t bring it back t im termorrow."

She gave up the book. He stumbled down the back steps, hugging the thick book under his arm. When he had splashed water on his face and hands, he groped back to the kitchen and fumbled in a corner for the towel. He bumped into a chair; it clattered to the floor. The catalogue sprawled at his feet. When he had dried his eyes he snatched up the book and held it again under his arm. His mother stood watching him.

"Now, ef yuh gonna act a fool over that ol book, Ah'll take it n burn it up."

"Naw, Ma, please."

"Waal, set down n be still!"

He sat down and drew the oil lamp close. He thumbed page after page, unaware of the food his mother set on the table. His father came in. Then his small brother.

"Whutcha got there, Dave?" his father asked.

"Jusa catlog," he answered, not looking up.

"Yeah, here they is!" His eyes glowed at blue-and-black revolvers. He glanced up, feeling sudden guilt. His father was watching him. He eased the book under the table and rested it on his knees. After the blessing was asked, he ate. He scooped up peas and swallowed fat meat without chewing. Buttermilk helped to wash it down. He did not want to mention money before his father. He would do much better by cornering his mother when she was alone. He looked at his father uneasily out of the edge of his eye.

"Boy, how come yuh don quit foolin wid tha book n eat yo suppah?"

"Yessuh."

"How you n ol man Hawkins gitten erlong?"

"Suh?"

"Can't yuh hear? Why don yuh lissen? Ah ast yuh how wuz yuh n ol man Hawkins gitten erlong?"

"Oh, swell, Pa. Ah plows mo lan than anybody over there."

"Waal, yuh oughta keep you mind on whut yuh doin."

"Yessuh."

He poured his plate full of molasses and sopped it up slowly with a chunk of cornbread. When his father and brother had left the kitchen, he still sat and looked again at the guns in the catalogue, longing to muster courage enough to present his case to his mother. Lawd, ef Ah only had that pretty one! He could almost feel the slickness of the weapon with his fingers. If he had a gun like that he would polish it and keep it shining so it would never rust. N Ah'd keep it loaded, by Gawd!

"Ma?" His voice was hesitant.

"Hunh?"

"Ol man Hawkins give yuh mah money yit?"

"Yeah, but ain no usa yuh thinkin bout throwin nona it erway. Ahm keepin tha money sos yuh kin have cloes to go to school this winter."

He rose and went to her side with the open catalogue in his palms. She was washing dishes, her head bent low over a pan. Shyly he raised the book. When he spoke, his voice was husky, faint.

"Ma, Gawd knows Ah wans one of these."

"One of whut?" she asked, not raising her eyes.

"One of these," he said again, not daring even to point. She glanced up at the page, then at him with wide eyes.

"Nigger, is yuh gone plumb crazy?"

"Aw, Ma—"

"Git outta here! Don yuh talk t me bout no gun! Yuh a fool!"

"Ma, Ah kin buy one fer two dollahs."

"Not ef Ah knows it, yuh ain!"

"But yuh promised me one—"

"Ah don care what Ah promised! Yuh ain nothing but a boy yit!"

"Ma, ef yuh lemme buy one Ah'll *never* ast yuh fer nothing no mo."

"Ah tol yuh to git outta here! Yuh ain gonna toucha penny of tha money fer no gun! Thas how come Ah has Mistah Hawkins t pay yo wages to me, cause Ah knows yuh ain got no sense."

"But, Ma, we needa gun. Pa ain got no gun. We needa gun in the house. Yuh kin never tell whut might happen."

"Now don yuh try to maka fool outta me, boy! Ef we did hava gun yuh wouldn't have it!"

He laid the catalogue down and slipped his arm around her waist.

"Aw, Ma, Ah done worked hard alla summer n ain ast yuh fer nothing, is Ah, now?"

"Thas whut yuh spose t do!"

"But Ma, Ah wans a gun. Yuh kin lemme have two dollahs outta mah money. Please, Ma. I kin give it to Pa . . . Please, Ma! Ah loves yuh, Ma."

When she spoke her voice came soft and low.

"Whut yu wan wida gun, Dave? Yuh don need no gun. Yuh'll git in trouble. N ef yo pa just thought Ah let yuh have money t buy a gun he'd hava fit."

"Ah'll hide it, Ma. It ain but two dollahs."

"Lawd, chil, whut's wrong wid yuh?"

"Ain nothin wrong, Ma. Ahm almos a man now. Ah wans a gun."

"Who gonna sell yuh a gun?"

"Ol Joe at the sto."

"N it don cos but two dollahs?"

"Thas all, Ma. Jus two dollahs. Please, Ma."

She was stacking the plates away; her hands moved slowly, reflectively. Dave kept an anxious silence. Finally, she turned to him.

"Ah'll let yuh git tha gun ef yuh promise me one thing."

"Whut's tha, Ma?"

"Yuh bring it straight back t me, yuh hear? It be fer Pa."

"Yessum! Lemme go now, Ma."

She stooped, turned slightly to one side, raised the hem of her dress, rolled down the top of her stocking, and came up with a slender wad of bills. "Here," she said. "Lawd knows yuh don need no gun. But yer pa does. Yuh bring it right back t me, yuh hear? Ahma put it up. Now ef yuh don, Ahma have yuh pa lick yuh so hard yuh won fergit it."

"Yessum."

He took the money, ran down the steps, and across the yard.

"Dave! Yuuuuuh Daaaaave!"

He heard, but he was not going to stop now. "Naw, Lawd!"

The first movement he made the following morning was to reach under his pillow for the gun. In the gray light of dawn he held it loosely, feeling a sense of power. Could kill a man with a gun like this. Kill anybody, black or white. And if he were holding his gun in his hand, nobody could run over him; they would have to respect him. It was a big gun, with a long barrel and a heavy handle. He raised and lowered it in his hand, marveling at its weight.

He had not come straight home with it as his mother had asked; instead he had stayed out in the fields, holding the weapon in his hand, aiming it now and then at some imaginary foe. But he had not fired it; he had been afraid that his father might hear. Also he was not sure he knew how to fire it.

To avoid surrendering the pistol he had not come into the house until he knew that they were all asleep. When his mother had tiptoed to his bedside late that night and demanded the gun, he had first played possum; then he had told her that the gun was hidden outdoors, that he would bring it to her in the morning. Now he lay turning it slowly in his hands. He broke it, took out the cartridges, felt them, and put them back.

He slid out of bed, got a long strip of old flannel from a trunk, wrapped the gun in it, and tied it to his naked thigh while it was still loaded. He did not go in to breakfast. Even though it was not yet daylight, he started for Jim Hawkins' plantation. Just as the sun was rising he reached the barns where the mules and plows were kept.

"Hey! That you, Dave?"

He turned. Jim Hawkins stood eyeing him suspiciously.

"What're yuh doing here so early?"

"Ah didn't know Ah wuz gettin up so early, Mistah Hawkins. Ah wuz fixin t hitch up ol Jenny n taker t the fiels."

"Good. Since you're so early, how about plowing that stretch down by the woods?"

"Suits me, Mistah Hawkins."

"O.K. Go to it!"

He hitched Jenny to a plow and started across the fields. Hot dog! This was just what he wanted. If he could get down by the woods, he could shoot his gun and nobody would hear. He walked behind the plow, hearing the traces creaking, feeling the gun tied to his thigh.

When he reached the woods, he plowed two whole rows before he decided to take out the gun. Finally, he stopped, looked in all directions, then untied the gun and held it in his hand. He turned to the mule and smiled.

"Know whut this is, Jenny? Naw, yuh wouldn know! Yuhs jusa ol mule! Anyhow, this is a gun, n it kin shoot, by Gawd!"

He held the gun at arm's length. Whut t hell, Ahma shoot this thing! He looked at Jenny again.

"Lissen here, Jenny! When Ah pull this ol trigger, Ah don wan yuh t run n acka fool now!"

Jenny stood with head down, her short ears pricked straight. Dave walked off about twenty feet, held the gun far out from him at arm's length and turned his head. Hell, he told himself. Ah ain afraid. The gun felt loose in his fingers; he waved it wildly for a moment. Then he shut his eyes and tightened his forefinger. Bloom! A report half deafened him and he thought his right hand was torn from his arm. He heard Jenny whinnying and galloping over the field, and he found himself on his knees, squeezing his fingers hard between his legs. His hand was numb; he jammed it into his mouth, trying to warm it, trying to stop the pain. The gun lay at his feet. He did not quite know what had happened. He stood up and stared at the gun as though it were a living thing. He gritted his teeth and kicked the gun. Yuh almos broke mah arm! He turned to look for Jenny; she was far over the fields, tossing her head and kicking wildly.

"Hol on there, ol mule!"

When he caught up with her she stood trembling, walling her big white eyes at him. The plow was far away; the traces had broken. Then Dave stopped short, looking, not believing. Jenny was bleeding. Her left side was red and wet with blood. He went closer. Lawd, have mercy! Wondah did Ah shoot this mule? He grabbed for Jenny's mane. She flinched, snorted, whirled, tossing her head.

"Hol on now! Hol on."

Then he saw the hole in Jenny's side, right between the ribs. It was round, wet, red. A crimson stream streaked down the front leg flowing fast. Good Gawd! Ah wuzn't shootin at that mule. He felt panic. He knew he had to stop that blood, or Jenny would bleed to death. He had never seen so much blood in all his life. He chased the mule for half a mile, trying to catch her. Finally she stopped, breathing hard, stumpy tail half arched. He caught her mane and led her back to where the plow and gun lay. Then he stopped and grabbed handfuls of damp black earth and tried to plug the bullet hole. Jenny shuddered, whinnied, and broke from him.

"Hol on! Hol on now!"

He tried to plug it again, but blood came anyhow. His fingers were hot and sticky. He rubbed dirt into his palms, trying to dry them. Then again he attempted to plug the bullet hole, but Jenny shied away, kicking her heels high. He stood helpless. He had to do something. He ran at Jenny; she dodged him. He watched a red stream of blood flow down Jenny's leg and form a bright pool at her feet.

"Jenny . . . Jenny," he called weakly.

His lips trembled. She's bleeding t death! He looked in the direction of home, wanting to go back, wanting to get help. But he saw the pistol lying in the damp black clay. He had a queer feeling that if he only did something, this would not be; Jenny would not be there bleeding to death.

When he went to her this time, she did not move. She stood with sleepy, dreamy eyes; and when he touched her she gave a low-pitched whinny and knelt to the ground, her front knees slopping in blood.

"Jenny . . . Jenny . . ." he whispered.

For a long time she held her neck erect; then her head sank, slowly. Her ribs swelled with a mighty heave and she went over.

Dave's stomach felt empty, very empty. He picked up the gun and held it gingerly between his thumb and forefinger. He buried it at the foot of a tree. He took a stick and tried to cover the pool of blood with dirt—but what was the use? There was Jenny lying with her mouth open and her eyes walled and glassy. He could not tell Jim Hawkins he had shot his mule. But he had to tell something. Yeah, Ah'll tell em Jenny started gittin wil n fell on the point of the plow. . . . But that would hardly happen to a mule. He walked across the field slowly, head down.

It was sunset. Two of Jim Hawkins' men were over near the edge of the woods digging a hole in which to bury Jenny. Dave was surrounded by a knot of people, all of whom were looking down at the dead mule.

"I don't see how in the world it happened," said Jim Hawkins for the tenth time.

The crowd parted and Dave's mother, father, and small brother pushed into the center.

"Where Dave?" his mother called.

"There he is," said Jim Hawkins.

His mother grabbed him.

"What happened, Dave? Whut yuh done?"

"Nothin."

"C mon, boy, talk," his father said.

Dave took a deep breath and told the story he knew nobody believed.

"Waal," he drawled, "Ah brung ol Jenny down here sos Ah could do mah plowin. Ah plowed bout two rows, jus like yuh see." He stopped and pointed at the long rows of upturned earth. "Then somethin musta been wrong wid ol Jenny. She wouldn't ack right a-tall. She started snortin n kickin her heels. Ah tried t hol her, but she pulled erway, rearin n goin in. Then when the point of the plow was stickin up in the air, she swung erroun n twisted herself back on it . . . She stuck herself n started t bleed. N fo Ah could do anything, she wuz dead."

"Did you ever hear of anything like that in all your life?" asked Jim Hawkins.

There were white and black standing in the crowd. They murmured. Dave's mother came close to him and looked hard into his face. "Tell the truth, Dave," she said.

"Looks like a bullet hole to me," said one man.

"Dave, whut yuh do wid the gun?" his mother said.

The crowd surged in, looking at him. He jammed his hands into his pockets, shook his head slowly from left to right, and backed away. His eyes were wide and painful.

"Did he hava gun?" asked Jim Hawkins.

"By Gawd, Ah tol yuh tha wuz a gun wound," said a man, slapping his thigh.

His father caught his shoulders and shook him till his teeth rattled.

"Tell whut happened, yuh rascal! Tell whut . . ."

Dave looked at Jenny's stiff legs and began to cry.

"Whut yuh do wid tha gun?" his mother asked.

"Whut wuz he doin wida gun?" his father asked.

"Come on and tell the truth," said Hawkins. "Ain't nobody going to hurt you . . ."

His mother crowded close to him.

"Did yuh shoot tha mule, Dave?"

Dave cried, seeing blurred white and black faces.

"Ahh ddinn gggo tt sshooot hher . . . Ah ssswear ffo Gawd Ahh ddin . . . Ah wuz a-tryin t sssee ef the old gggun would sshoot—"

"Where yuh git the gun from?" his father asked.

"Ah got it from Joe, at the sto."

"Where yuh git the money?"

"Ma give it to me."

"He kept worryin me, Bob. Ah had t. Ah tol im t bring the gun right back t me . . . It was fer yuh, the gun."

"But how yuh happen to shoot that mule?" asked Jim Hawkins.

"Ah wuzn shootin at the mule, Mistah Hawkins. The gun jumped when Ah pulled the trigger . . . N fo Ah knowed anythin Jenny was there a-bleedin."

Somebody in the crowd laughed. Jim Hawkins walked close to Dave and looked into his face.

"Well, looks like you have bought you a mule, Dave."

"Ah swear fo Gawd, Ah didn go t kill the mule, Mistah Hawkins!"

"But you killed her!"

All the crowd was laughing now. They stood on tiptoe and poked heads over one another's shoulders.

"Well, boy, looks like yuh done bought a dead mule! Hahaha!"

"Ain tha ershame."

"Hohohohoho."

Dave stood, head down, twisting his feet in the dirt.

"Well, you needn't worry about it, Bob," said Jim Hawkins to Dave's father. "Just let the boy keep on working and pay me two dollars a month."

"Whut yuh wan fer yo mule, Mistah Hawkins?"

Jim Hawkins screwed up his eyes.

"Fifty dollars."

"Whut yuh do wid tha gun?" Dave's father demanded.

Dave said nothing.

"Yuh wan me t take a tree n beat yuh till yuh talk!"

" 'Nawsuh!"

"Whut yuh do wid it?"

"Ah throwed it erway."

"Where?"

"Ah . . . Ah throwed it in the creek."

"Wall, c mon home. N firs thing in the mawnin git to that creek n fin tha gun."

"Yessuh."

"Whut yuh pay fer it?"

"Two dollahs."

"Take tha gun n git yo money back n carry it t Mistah Hawkins, yuh hear? N don fergit Ahma lam you black bottom good fer this! Now march yosef on home, suh!"

Dave turned and walked slowly. He heard people laughing. Dave glared, his eyes welling with tears. Hot anger bubbled in him. Then he swallowed and stumbled on.

That night Dave did not sleep. He was glad he had gotten out of killing the mule so easily, but he was hurt. Something hot seemed to turn over inside him each time he remembered how they had laughed. He tossed on his bed, feeling his hard pillow. N Pa says he's gonna beat me . . . He remembered other beatings, and his back quivered. Naw, naw, Ah sho don wan im to beat me that way no mo. Dam em all! Nobody ever gave him anything. All he did was work. They treat me like a mule, n then they beat me. He gritted his teeth. N Ma had t tell on me.

Well, if he had to, he would take old man Hawkins that two dollars. But that meant selling the gun. And he wanted to keep that gun. Fifty dollars for a dead mule.

He turned over, thinking how he had fired the gun. He had an itch to fire it again. Ef other men kin shoota gun, by Gawd, Ah kin! He was still, listening. Mebbe they all sleepin now. The house was still. He heard the soft breathing of his brother. Yes, now! He would go down and get that gun and see if he could fire it! He eased out of bed and slipped into overalls.

The moon was bright. He ran almost all the way to the edge of the woods. He stumbled over the ground, looking for the spot where he had buried the gun. Yeah, here it is. Like a hungry dog scratching for a bone, he pawed it up. He puffed his black cheeks and blew dirt from the trigger and barrel. He broke it and found four cartridges unshot. He looked around; the fields were filled with silence and moonlight. He clutched the gun stiff and hard in his fingers. But, as soon as he wanted to pull the trigger, he shut his eyes and turned his head. Naw, Ah can't shoot wid mah eyes closed n mah head turned. With effort he held his eyes open; then he squeezed. *Blooooom!* He was stiff, not breathing. The gun was still in his hands. Dammit, he'd done it! He fired again. *Blooooom!* He smiled. *Blooooom! Blooooom! Click, click.* There! It was empty. If anybody could shoot a gun, he could. He put the gun into his hip pocket and started across the fields.

When he reached the top of a ridge he stood straight and proud in the moonlight, looking at Jim Hawkins' big white house, feeling the gun sagging in his pocket. Lawd, ef Ah had just one mo bullet Ah'd taka shot at tha house. Ah'd like to scare ol man Hawkins jusa little . . . Jusa enough t let im know Dave Saunders is a man.

To his left the road curved, running to the tracks of the Illinois Central. He jerked his head, listening. From far off came a faint *hoooof-hoooof; hoooof-hoooof; hoooof-hoooof*. . . . He stood rigid. Two dollahs a mont. Les see now . . . Tha means it'll take bout two years. Shucks! Ah'll be dam!

He started down the road, toward the tracks. Yeah, here she comes! He stood beside the track and held himself stiffly. Here she comes, erroun the ben . . . C mon, yuh slow poke! C mon! He had his hand on his gun; something quivered in his stomach. Then the train thundered past, the gray and brown box cars rumbling and clinking. He gripped the gun tightly; then he jerked his hand out of his pocket. Ah betcha Bill wouldn't do it! Ah betcha . . . The cars slid past, steel grinding upon steel. Ahm ridin yuh ternight, so help me Gawd! He was hot all over. He hesitated just a moment; then he grabbed, pulled atop a car, and lay flat. He felt his pocket; the gun was still there. Ahead the long rails were glinting in the moonlight, stretching away, away to somewhere, somewhere where he could be a man . . .

1961

Ralph Ellison 1914–1994

Ralph Ellison became one of the most important U.S. writers of the twentieth century when he published Invisible Man*—a novel that turns the odyssey of its young African-American protaganist into a deft and incisive commentary on the Western literary tradition and American history.*

Named after Ralph Waldo Emerson, the nineteenth-century essayist and poet, Ralph Waldo Ellison was born in Oklahoma in 1914. He did well in school and won a scholarship to the Tuskegee Institute in 1933, where he studied music. Before graduating he went north to Harlem to study sculpture. In New York, where he was befriended and encouraged by Richard Wright, Ellison began to write. Like many other intellectuals of the time, he became involved with the left-wing political movements of the Depression period, but Ellison's flirtation with communism was brief, and the party is bitingly satirized in Invisible Man. *In 1942 Ellison became editor of* Negro Quarterly *and, after service in the Merchant Marine in World War II, seriously began work on his novel. After the completion of* Invisible Man *Ellison held various academic positions while he continued to work on his promised second novel. A collection of his essays,* Shadow and Act, *was published in 1964.*

Despite all the acclaim it received, Invisible Man *has been criticized as insufficiently militant. In a sense, the criticism is just, for the novel is both so subtle and so complex that it lacks the immediate emotional impact of, for example, Richard Wright's novel* Native Son. *Ellison's* Invisible Man *is based on a set of symbols, on the conscious use of myth, and on historical allusions. It presents the traditional theme of the development of youth into maturity and is concerned, in Ellison's words, with "the American theme," the search for identity.* Invisible Man *is not, therefore, merely a racial protest novel. Ellison's intellect and his artistic imagination were too complex to stop at the presentation merely of anger and militancy, no matter how justified. His aim was broader. Early in life he gained, he said, "a passion to link together all I loved within the Negro community and all those things I felt in the world which lay beyond."* Invisible Man *achieves such a linking. It equates the social maturation of a young black boy with the archetypal theme of self-realization; it portrays the black man as the symbol of all men and their aspirations and frustrations, and it achieves Ellison's self-professed goal in art, the "universal."*

FURTHER READING: *Invisible Man, A Collection of Critical Essays,* ed. J. Reilly, 1970; R. O'Meally, *The Craft of Ralph Ellison,* 1980; R. List, *Dedalus in Harlem, The Joyce-Ellison Connection,* 1982; *Ralph Ellison,* ed. H. Bloom, 1986; A. Nadel, *Invisible Criticism, Ralph Ellison and the American Canon,* 1988; J. Watts, *Heroism and the Black Intellectual,* 1994; *Conversations with Ralph Ellison,* ed. M. Graham and A. Singh, 1995; *Cultural Contexts for Ralph Ellison's Invisible Man,* ed. E. Sundquist, 1995; *Trading Twelves: The Selected Letters of Ralph Ellison and Albert Murray,* ed. A. Murray and J. Callahan, 2000; *The Critical Response to Ralph Ellison,* ed. R. Butler, 2000; *Living with Music: Ralph Ellison's Jazz Writings,* ed. R. O'Meally, 2001; K. Warren, *So Black and Blue, Ralph Ellison and the Occasion of Criticism,* 2003; *A Historical Guide to Ralph Ellison,* ed. S. Tracy, 2004.

TEXT: *Invisible Man,* 1952.

from *INVISIBLE MAN*

CHAPTER I

It goes a long way back, some twenty years. All my life I had been looking for something, and everywhere I turned someone tried to tell me what it was. I accepted their answers too, though they were often in contradiction and even self-contradictory. I was naïve. I was looking for myself and asking everyone except myself questions which I, and only I, could answer. It took me a long time and much painful boomeranging of my expectations to achieve a realization everyone else appears to have been born with: That I am nobody but myself. But first I had to discover that I am an invisible man!

And yet I am no freak of nature, nor of history. I was in the cards, other things having been equal (or unequal) eighty-five years ago. I am not ashamed of my grandparents for having been slaves. I am only ashamed of myself for having at one time been ashamed. About eighty-five years ago they were told that they were free, united with others of our country in everything pertaining to the common good, and, in everything social, separate like the fingers of the hand. And they believed it. They exulted in it. They stayed in their place, worked hard, and brought up my father to do the same. But my grandfather is the one. He was an odd old guy, my grandfather, and I am told I take after him. It was he who caused the trouble. On his deathbed he called my father to him and said, "Son, after I'm gone I want you to keep up the good fight. I never told you, but our life is a war and I have been a traitor all my born days, a spy in the enemy's country ever since I give up my gun back in the Reconstruction. Live with your head in the lion's mouth. I want you to overcome 'em with yeses, undermine 'em with grins, agree 'em to death and destruction, let 'em swoller you till they vomit or bust wide open." They thought the old man had gone out of his mind. He had been the meekest of men. The younger children were rushed from the room, the shades drawn and the flame of the lamp turned so low that it sputtered on the wick like the old man's breathing. "Learn it to the younguns," he whispered fiercely; then he died.

But my folks were more alarmed over his last words than over his dying. It was as though he had not died at all, his words caused so much anxiety. I was warned emphatically to forget what he had said and, indeed, this is the first time it has been mentioned outside the family circle. It had a tremendous effect upon me, however. I could never be sure of what he meant. Grandfather had been a quiet old man who never made any trouble, yet on his deathbed he had called himself a traitor and a spy, and he had spoken of his meekness as a dangerous activity. It became a constant puzzle which lay unanswered in the back of my mind. And whenever things went well for me I remembered my grandfather and felt guilty and uncomfortable. It was as though I was carrying out his advice in spite of myself. And to make it worse, everyone loved me for it. I was praised by the most lily-white men of the town. I was considered an example of desirable conduct—just as my grandfather had been. And what puzzled me was that the old man had defined it as *treachery*. When I was praised for my conduct I felt a guilt that in some way I was doing something that was really against the wishes of the white folks, that if they had understood they would have desired me to act just the opposite, that I should have been sulky and mean, and that that really would have been what they wanted, even though they were fooled and thought they wanted me to act as I did. It made me afraid that some day they would look upon me as a traitor and I would be lost. Still I was more afraid to act any other way because they didn't like that at all. The old man's words were like a curse. On my graduation day I delivered an oration in which I showed that humility was the secret, indeed, the very essence of progress. (Not that I believed this—how could I, remembering my grandfather?—I only believed that it worked.) It was a great success. Everyone praised me and I was invited to give the speech at a gathering of the town's leading white citizens. It was a triumph for our whole community.

It was in the main ballroom of the leading hotel. When I got there I discovered that it was on the occasion of a smoker, and I was told that since I was to be there anyway I might as well take part in the battle royal to be fought by some of my schoolmates as part of the entertainment. The battle royal came first.

All of the town's big shots were there in their tuxedoes, wolfing down the buffet foods, drinking beer and whiskey and smoking black cigars. It was a large room with a high ceiling. Chairs were arranged in neat rows around three sides of a portable boxing ring. The fourth side was clear, revealing a gleaming space of polished floor. I had some misgivings over the battle royal, by the way. Not from a distaste for fighting, but because I didn't care too much for the other fellows who were to take part. They were tough guys who seemed to have no grandfather's curse worrying their minds. No one could mistake their toughness. And besides, I suspected that fighting a battle royal might detract from the dignity of my speech. In those pre-invisible days I visualized myself as a potential Booker T. Washington.[1] But the other fellows didn't care too much for me either, and there were nine of them. I felt superior to them in my way, and I didn't like the manner in which we were all crowded together into the servants' elevator. Nor did they like my being there. In fact, as the warmly lighted floors flashed past the elevator we had words over the fact that I, by taking part in the fight, had knocked one of their friends out of a night's work.

We were led out of the elevator through a rococo hall into an anteroom and told to get into our fighting togs. Each of us was issued a pair of boxing

[1]Negro educator (1856–1915), author of *Up from Slavery* (1901).

gloves and ushered out into the big mirrored hall, which we entered looking cautiously about us and whispering, lest we might accidentally be heard above the noise of the room. It was foggy with cigar smoke. And already the whiskey was taking effect. I was shocked to see some of the most important men of the town quite tipsy. They were all there—bankers, lawyers, judges, doctors, fire chiefs, teachers, merchants. Even one of the more fashionable pastors. Something we could not see was going on up front. A clarinet was vibrating sensuously and the men were standing up and moving eagerly forward. We were a small tight group, clustered together, our bare upper bodies touching and shining with anticipatory sweat; while up front the big shots were becoming increasingly excited over something we still could not see. Suddenly I heard the school superintendent, who had told me to come, yell, "Bring up the shines, gentlemen! Bring up the little shines!"

We were rushed up to the front of the ballroom, where it smelled even more strongly of tobacco and whiskey. Then we were pushed into place. I almost wet my pants. A sea of faces, some hostile, some amused, ringed around us, and in the center, facing us, stood a magnificent blonde—stark naked. There was dead silence. I felt a blast of cold air chill me. I tried to back away, but they were behind me and around me. Some of the boys stood with lowered heads, trembling. I felt a wave of irrational guilt and fear. My teeth chattered, my skin turned to goose flesh, my knees knocked. Yet I was strongly attracted and looked in spite of myself. Had the price of looking been blindness, I would have looked. The hair was yellow like that of a circus kewpie doll, the face heavily powdered and rouged, as though to form an abstract mask, the eyes hollow and smeared a cool blue, the color of a baboon's butt. I felt a desire to spit upon her as my eyes brushed slowly over her body. Her breasts were firm and round as the domes of East Indian temples, and I stood so close as to see the fine skin texture and beads of pearly perspiration glistening like dew around the pink and erected buds of her nipples. I wanted at one and the same time to run from the room, to sink through the floor, or go to her and cover her from my eyes and the eyes of the others with my body; to feel the soft thighs, to caress her and destroy her, to love her and murder her, to hide from her, and yet to stroke where below the small American flag tattooed upon her belly her thighs formed a capital V. I had a notion that of all in the room she saw only me with her impersonal eyes.

And then she began to dance, a slow sensuous movement; the smoke of a hundred cigars clinging to her like the thinnest of veils. She seemed like a fair bird-girl girdled in veils calling to me from the angry surface of some gray and threatening sea. I was transported. Then I became aware of the clarinet playing and the big shots yelling at us. Some threatened us if we looked and others if we did not. On my right I saw one boy faint. And now a man grabbed a silver pitcher from a table and stepped close as he dashed ice water upon him and stood him up and forced two of us to support him as his head hung and moans issued from his thick bluish lips. Another boy began to plead to go home. He was the largest of the group, wearing dark red fighting trunks much too small to conceal the erection which projected from him as though in answer to the insinuating low-registered moaning of the clarinet. He tried to hide himself with his boxing gloves.

And all the while the blonde continued dancing, smiling faintly at the big shots who watched her with fascination, and faintly smiling at our fear. I noticed a certain merchant who followed her hungrily, his lips loose and drooling. He was a large man who wore diamond studs in a shirtfront which swelled with the ample paunch underneath, and each time the blonde swayed her undulating hips he ran his hand through the thin hair of his bald head and, with his arms upheld, his posture clumsy like that of an intoxicated panda, wound his belly in a slow and obscene grind. This creature was completely hypnotized. The music had quickened. As the dancer flung herself about with a detached expression on her face, the men began reaching out to touch her. I could see their beefy fingers sink into the soft flesh. Some of the others tried to stop them and she began to move around the floor in graceful circles, as they gave chase, slipping and sliding over the polished floor. It was mad. Chairs went crashing, drinks were spilt, as they ran laughing and howling after her. They caught her just as she reached a door, raised her from the floor, and tossed her as college boys are tossed at a hazing, and above her red, fixed-smiling lips I saw the terror and disgust in her eyes, almost like my own terror and that which I saw in some of the other boys. As I watched, they tossed her twice and her soft breasts seemed to flatten against the air and her legs flung wildly as she spun. Some of the sober ones helped her to escape. And I started off the floor, heading for the anteroom with the rest of the boys.

Some were still crying and in hysteria. But as we tried to leave we were stopped and ordered to get into the ring. There was nothing to do but what we were told. All ten of us climbed under the ropes and allowed ourselves to be blindfolded with broad bands of white cloth. One of the men seemed to feel a bit sympathetic and tried to cheer us up as we stood with our backs against the ropes. Some of us tried to grin. “See that boy over there?” one of the men said. “I want you to run across at the bell and give it to him right in the belly. If you don’t get him, I’m going to get you. I don’t like his looks.” Each of us was told the same. The blindfolds were put on. Yet even then I had been going over my speech. In my mind each word was as bright as flame. I felt the cloth pressed into place, and frowned so that it would be loosened when I relaxed.

But now I felt a sudden fit of blind terror. I was unused to darkness. It was as though I had suddenly found myself in a dark room filled with poisonous cottonmouths. I could hear the bleary voices yelling insistently for the battle royal to begin.

“Get going in there!”

“Let me at that big nigger!”

I strained to pick up the school superintendent’s voice, as though to squeeze some security out of that slightly more familiar sound.

“Let me at those black sonsabitches!” someone yelled.

“No, Jackson, no!” another voice yelled. “Here, somebody, help me hold Jack.”

"I want to get at that ginger-colored nigger. Tear him limb from limb," the first voice yelled.

I stood against the ropes trembling. For in those days I was what they called ginger-colored, and he sounded as though he might crunch me between his teeth like a crisp ginger cookie.

Quite a struggle was going on. Chairs were being kicked about and I could hear voices grunting as with a terrific effort. I wanted to see, to see more desperately than ever before. But the blindfold was tight as a thick skin-puckering scab and when I raised my gloved hands to push the layers of white aside a voice yelled, "Oh, no you don't, black bastard! Leave that alone!"

"Ring the bell before Jackson kills him a coon!" someone boomed in the sudden silence. And I heard the bell clang and the sound of the feet scuffling forward.

A glove smacked against my head. I pivoted, striking out stiffly as someone went past, and felt the jar ripple along the length of my arm to my shoulder. Then it seemed as though all nine boys had turned upon me at once. Blows pounded me from all sides while I struck out as best I could. So many blows landed upon me that I wondered if I were not the only blindfolded fighter in the ring, or if the man called Jackson hadn't succeeded in getting me after all.

Blindfolded, I could no longer control my motions. I had no dignity. I stumbled about like a baby or a drunken man. The smoke had become thicker and with each new blow it seemed to sear and further restrict my lungs. My saliva became like hot bitter glue. A glove connected with my head, filling my mouth with warm blood. It was everywhere. I could not tell if the moisture I felt upon my body was sweat or blood. A blow landed hard against the nape of my neck. I felt myself going over, my head hitting the floor. Streaks of blue light filled the black world behind the blindfold. I lay prone, pretending that I was knocked out, but felt myself seized by hands and yanked to my feet. "Get going, black boy! Mix it up!" My arms were like lead, my head smarting from blows. I managed to feel my way to the ropes and held on, trying to catch my breath. A glove landed in my mid-section and I went over again, feeling as though the smoke had become a knife jabbed into my guts. Pushed this way and that by the legs milling around me, I finally pulled erect and discovered that I could see the black, sweat-washed forms weaving in the smoky-blue atmosphere like drunken dancers weaving to the rapid drum-like thuds of blows.

Everyone fought hysterically. It was complete anarchy. Everybody fought everybody else. No group fought together for long. Two, three, four, fought one, then turned to fight each other, were themselves attacked. Blows landed below the belt and in the kidney, with the gloves open as well as closed, and with my eye partly opened now there was not so much terror. I moved carefully, avoiding blows, although not too many to attract attention, fighting from group to group. The boys groped about like blind, cautious crabs crouching to protect their mid-sections, their heads pulled in short against their shoulders, their arms stretched nervously before them, with their fists testing the smoke-filled air like the knobbed feelers of hypersensitive snails. In one corner I glimpsed a boy violently punching the air and heard him scream in pain as he smashed his hand against a ring post. For a second I saw him bent over holding his hand, then going down as a blow caught his unprotected head. I played one group against the other, slipping in and throwing a punch then stepping out of range while pushing the others into the melee to take the blows blindly aimed at me. The smoke was agonizing and there were no rounds, no bells at three minute intervals to relieve our exhaustion. The room spun round me, a swirl of lights, smoke, sweating bodies surrounded by tense white faces. I bled from both nose and mouth, the blood spattering upon my chest.

The men kept yelling, "Slug him, black boy! Knock his guts out!"

"Uppercut him! Kill him! Kill that big boy!"

Taking a fake fall, I saw a boy going down heavily beside me as though we were felled by a single blow, saw a sneaker-clad foot shoot into his groin as the two who had knocked him down stumbled upon him. I rolled out of range, feeling a twinge of nausea.

The harder we fought the more threatening the men became. And yet, I had begun to worry about my speech again. How would it go? Would they recognize my ability? What would they give me?

I was fighting automatically when suddenly I noticed that one after another of the boys was leaving the ring. I was surprised, filled with panic, as though I had been left alone with an unknown danger. Then I understood. The boys had arranged it among themselves. It was the custom for the two men left in the ring to slug it out for the winner's prize. I discovered this too late. When the bell sounded two men in tuxedoes leaped into the ring and removed the blindfold. I found myself facing Tatlock, the biggest of the gang. I felt sick at my stomach. Hardly had the bell stopped ringing in my ears than it clanged again and I saw him moving swiftly toward me. Thinking of nothing else to do I hit him smash on the nose. He kept coming, bringing the rank sharp violence of stale sweat. His face was a black blank of a face, only his eyes alive—with hate of me and aglow with a feverish terror from what had happened to us all. I became anxious. I wanted to deliver my speech and he came at me as though he meant to beat it out of me. I smashed him again and again, taking his blows as they came. Then on a sudden impulse I struck him lightly and as we clinched, I whispered, "Fake like I knocked you out, you can have the prize."

"I'll break your behind," he whispered hoarsely.

"For *them?*"

"For *me,* sonofabitch!"

They were yelling for us to break it up and Tatlock spun me half around with a blow, and as a joggled camera sweeps in a reeling scene, I saw the howling red faces crouching tense beneath the cloud of blue-gray smoke. For a moment the world wavered, unraveled, flowed, then my head cleared and Tatlock bounced before me. The fluttering shadow before my eyes was his jabbing left hand. Then falling forward, my head against his damp shoulder, I whispered,

"I'll make it five dollars more."

"Go to hell!"

But his muscles relaxed a trifle beneath my pressure and I breathed, "Seven?"

"Give it to your ma," he said, ripping me beneath the heart.

And while I still held him I butted him and moved away. I felt myself bombarded with punches. I fought back with hopeless desperation. I wanted to deliver my speech more than anything else in the world, because I felt that only these men could judge truly my ability, and now this stupid clown was ruining my chances. I began fighting carefully now, moving in to punch him and out again with my greater speed. A lucky blow to his chin and I had him going too—until I heard a loud voice yell,"I got my money on the big boy."

Hearing this, I almost dropped my guard. I was confused: Should I try to win against the voice out there? Would not this go against my speech, and was not this a moment for humility, for nonresistance? A blow to my head as I danced about sent my right eye popping like a jack-in-the-box and settled my dilemma. The room went red as I fell. It was a dream fall, my body languid and fastidious as to where to land, until the floor became impatient and smashed up to meet me. A moment later I came to. An hypnotic voice said FIVE emphatically. And I lay there, hazily watching a dark red spot of my own blood shaping itself into a butterfly, glistening and soaking into the soiled gray world of the canvas.

When the voice drawled TEN I was lifted up and dragged to a chair. I sat dazed. My eye pained and swelled with each throb of my pounding heart and I wondered if now I would be allowed to speak. I was wringing wet, my mouth still bleeding. We were grouped along the wall now. The other boys ignored me as they congratulated Tatlock and speculated as to how much they would be paid. One boy whimpered over his smashed hand. Looking up front, I saw attendants in white jackets rolling the portable ring away and placing a small square rug in the vacant space surrounded by chairs. Perhaps, I thought, I will stand on the rug to deliver my speech.

Then the M.C. called to us, "Come on up here boys and get your money."

We ran forward to where the men laughed and talked in their chairs, waiting. Everyone seemed friendly now.

"There it is on the rug," the man said. I saw the rug covered with coins of all dimensions and a few crumpled bills. But what excited me, scattered here and there, were the gold pieces.

"Boys, it's all yours," the man said. "You get all you grab."

"That's right, Sambo," a blond man said, winking at me confidentially.

I trembled with excitement, forgetting my pain. I would get the gold and the bills, I thought. I would use both hands. I would throw my body against the boys nearest me to block them from the gold.

"Get down on the rug now," the man commanded, "and don't anyone touch it until I give the signal."

"This ought to be good," I heard.

As told, we got around the square rug on our knees. Slowly the man raised his freckled hand as we followed it upward with our eyes.

I heard, "These niggers look like they're about to pray!"

Then, "Ready," the man said, "Go!"

I lunged for a yellow coin lying on the blue design of the carpet, touching it and sending a surprised shriek to join those rising around me. I tried frantically to remove my hand but could not let go. A hot, violent force tore through my body, shaking me like a wet rat. The rug was electrified. The hair bristled up on my head as I shook myself free. My muscles jumped, my nerves jangled, writhed. But I saw that this was not stopping the other boys. Laughing in fear and embarrassment, some were holding back and scooping up the coins knocked off by the painful contortions of the others. The men roared above us as we struggled.

"Pick it up, goddamnit, pick it up!" someone called like a bass-voiced parrot. "Go on, get it!"

I crawled rapidly around the floor, picking up the coins, trying to avoid the coppers and to get greenbacks and the gold. Ignoring the shock by laughing, as I brushed the coins off quickly, I discovered that I could contain the electricity—a contradiction, but it works. Then the men began to push us onto the rug. Laughing embarrassedly, we struggled out of their hands and kept after the coins. We were all wet and slippery and hard to hold. Suddenly I saw a boy lifted into the air, glistening with sweat like a circus seal, and dropped, his wet back landing flush upon the charged rug, heard him yell and saw him literally dance upon his back, his elbows beating a frenzied tattoo upon the floor, his muscles twitching like the flesh of a horse stung by many flies. When he finally rolled off, his face was gray and no one stopped him when he ran from the floor amid booming laughter.

"Get the money," the M.C. called. "That's good hard American cash!"

And we snatched and grabbed, snatched and grabbed. I was careful not to come too close to the rug now, and when I felt the hot whiskey breath descend upon me like a cloud of foul air I reached out and grabbed the leg of a chair. It was occupied and I held on desperately.

"Leggo, nigger! Leggo!"

The huge face wavered down to mine as he tried to push me free. But my body was slippery and he was too drunk. It was Mr. Colcord, who owned a chain of movie houses and "entertainment palaces." Each time he grabbed me I slipped out of his hands. It became a real struggle. I feared the rug more than I did the drunk, so I held on, surprising myself for a moment by trying to topple *him* upon the rug. It was such an enormous idea that I found myself actually carrying it out. I tried not to be obvious, yet when I grabbed his leg, trying to tumble him out of the chair, he raised up roaring with laughter, and, looking at me with soberness dead in the eye, kicked me viciously in the chest. The chair leg flew out of my hand and I felt myself going and rolled. It was as though I had rolled through a bed of hot coals. It seemed a whole century would pass before I would roll free, a century in which I was seared through the deepest levels of my body to the fearful breath within me and the breath seared and heated to the point of explosion. It'll all be over in a flash, I thought as I rolled clear. It'll all be over in a flash.

But not yet, the men on the other side were waiting, red faces swollen as though from apoplexy as they bent forward in their chairs. Seeing their fingers coming toward me, I rolled away as a fumbled football rolls off the receiver's fingertips, back into the coals. That time I luckily sent the rug sliding out of place and heard the coins ringing against the floor and the boys scuffling to pick them up and the M.C. calling, "All right, boys that's all. Go get dressed and get your money."

I was limp as a dish rag. My back felt as though it had been beaten with wires.

When we had dressed the M.C. came in and gave us each five dollars, except Tatlock, who got ten for being last in the ring. Then he told us to leave. I was not to get a chance to deliver my speech, I thought. I was going out into the dim alley in despair when I was stopped and told to go back. I returned to the ballroom, where the men were pushing back their chairs and gathering in groups to talk.

The M.C. knocked on a table for quiet. "Gentlemen," he said, "we almost forgot about an important part of the program. A most serious part, gentlemen. This boy was brought here to deliver a speech which he made at his graduation yesterday . . ."

"Bravo!"

"I'm told that he is the smartest boy we've got out there in Greenwood. I'm told that he knows more big words than a pocket-sized dictionary."

Much applause and laughter.

"So now, gentlemen, I want you to give him your attention."

There was still laughter as I faced them, my mouth dry, my eye throbbing. I began slowly, but evidently my throat was tense, because they began shouting, "Louder! Louder!"

"We of the younger generation extol the wisdom of that great leader and educator," I shouted, "who first spoke these flaming words of wisdom: 'A ship lost at sea for many days suddenly sighted a friendly vessel. From the mast of the unfortunate vessel was seen a signal: "Water, water; we die of thirst!" The answer from the friendly vessel came back: "Cast down your bucket where you are." The captain of the distressed vessel, at last heeding the injunction, cast down his bucket, and it came up full of fresh sparkling water from the mouth of the Amazon River.' And like him I say, and in his words, 'To those of my race who depend upon bettering their condition in a foreign land, or who underestimate the importance of cultivating friendly relations with the Southern white man, who is his next-door neighbor, I would say: "Cast down your bucket where you are"—cast it down in making friends in every manly way of the people of all races by whom we are surrounded . . .' "

I spoke automatically and with such fervor that I did not realize that the men were still talking and laughing until my dry mouth, filling up with blood from the cut, almost strangled me. I coughed, wanting to stop and go to one of the tall brass, sand-filled spittoons to relieve myself, but a few of the men, especially the superintendent, were listening and I was afraid. So I gulped it down, blood, saliva and all, and continued. (What powers of endurance I had during those days! What enthusiasm! What a belief in the rightness of things!) I spoke even louder in spite of the pain. But still they talked and still they laughed, as though deaf with cotton in dirty ears. So I spoke with greater emotional emphasis. I closed my ears and swallowed blood until I was nauseated. The speech seemed a hundred times as long as before, but I could not leave out a single word. All had to be said, each memorized nuance considered, rendered. Nor was that all. Whenever I uttered a word of three syllables a group of voices would yell for me to repeat it. I used the phrase "social responsibility" and they yelled:

"What's that word you say, boy?"

"Social responsibility," I said.

"What?"

"Social . . ."

"Louder."

". . . responsibility."

"More!"

"Respon—"

"Repeat!"

"—sibility."

The room filled with the uproar of laughter until, no doubt, distracted by having to gulp down my blood, I made a mistake and yelled a phrase I had often seen denounced in newspaper editorials, heard debated in private.

"Social. . ."

"What?" they yelled.

". . . equality—"

The laughter hung smokelike in the sudden stillness. I opened my eyes, puzzled. Sounds of displeasure filled the room. The M.C. rushed forward. They shouted hostile phrases at me. But I did not understand.

A small dry mustached man in the front row blared out, "Say that slowly, son!"

"What, sir?"

"What you just said!"

"Social responsibility, sir," I said.

"You weren't being smart, were you, boy?" he said, not unkindly.

"No, sir!"

"You sure that about 'equality' was a mistake?"

"Oh, yes, sir," I said. "I was swallowing blood."

"Well, you had better speak more slowly so we can understand. We mean to do right by you, but you've got to know your place at all times. All right, now, go on with your speech."

I was afraid. I wanted to leave but I wanted also to speak and I was afraid they'd snatch me down.

"Thank you, sir," I said, beginning where I had left off, and having them ignore me as before.

Yet when I finished there was a thunderous applause. I was surprised to see the superintendent come forth with a package wrapped in white tissue paper, and, gesturing for quiet, address the men.

"Gentlemen, you see that I did not overpraise this boy. He makes a good speech and some day he'll lead his people in the proper paths. And I don't have to tell you that that is important in these days and times. This is a good, smart boy, and so to encourage him in the right direction, in the name of the Board of Education I wish to present him a prize in the form of this . . ."

He paused, removing the tissue paper and revealing a gleaming calfskin brief case.

". . . in the form of this first-class article from Shad Whitmore's shop."

"Boy," he said, addressing me, "take this prize and keep it well. Consider it a badge of office. Prize it. Keep developing as you are and some day it will be filled with important papers that will help shape the destiny of your people."

I was so moved that I could hardly express my thanks. A rope of bloody saliva forming a shape like an undiscovered continent drooled upon the leather and I wiped it quickly away. I felt an importance that I had never dreamed.

"Open it and see what's inside," I was told.

My fingers a-tremble, I complied, smelling the fresh leather and finding an official-looking document inside. It was a scholarship to the state college for Negroes. My eyes filled with tears and I ran awkwardly off the floor.

I was overjoyed; I did not even mind when I discovered that the gold pieces I had scrambled for were brass pocket tokens advertising a certain make of automobile.

When I reached home everyone was excited. Next day the neighbors came to congratulate me. I even felt safe from grandfather, whose deathbed curse usually spoiled my triumphs. I stood beneath his photograph with my brief case in hand and smiled triumphantly into his stolid black peasant's face. It was a face that fascinated me. The eyes seemed to follow everywhere I went.

That night I dreamed I was at a circus with him and that he refused to laugh at the clowns no matter what they did. Then later he told me to open my brief case and read what was inside and I did, finding an official envelope stamped with the state seal; and inside the envelope, I found another and another, endlessly, and I thought I would fall of weariness. "Them's years," he said. "Now open that one." And I did and in it I found an engraved document containing a short message in letters of gold. "Read it," my grandfather said. "Out loud!"

"To Whom It May Concern," I intoned. "Keep This Nigger-Boy Running."

I awoke with the old man's laughter ringing in my ears.

(It was a dream I was to remember and dream again for many years after. But at that time I had no insight into its meaning. First I had to attend college.)

1952

Tennessee Williams 1911–1983

Tennessee Williams achieved his first great stage success with The Glass Menagerie. *Produced in New York City in 1945, it won the New York Drama Critics' Circle Prize as the best play of the year. It portrays an American family struggling to survive physically and spiritually in the late 1930s. In writing the play, Williams drew heavily upon his own family experiences, describing the lives of his mother, his sister, and himself. He was born Thomas Lanier Williams in Columbus, Mississippi. His father, a traveling shoe-salesman, spent little time at home, and for the first years of his life, Williams and his mother lived with his mother's father, an Episcopal clergyman. In 1918, when Williams was seven, his father became a sales manager for a shoe company in St. Louis, Missouri, and seven-year-old Tom and his sister were uprooted and moved to the city. Timid and sickly, the boy found St. Louis a painful change from the happy life he had led while living in his grandfather's rectory in Mississippi. He found few friends; his mother and father quarrelled incessantly; and his father, who believed that his indulgent wife had "sissified" their son, taunted him with the name "Miss Nancy." Enveloped in an unhappy world, Williams, like his counterpart Tom Wingfield in* The Glass Menagerie, *found escape and adventure in the movies, which affected him so intensely, he later recalled, that he "used to want to climb into the screen and join the action."*

At fourteen he won first prize ($25) in an essay contest sponsored by a national magazine, The Smart Set. *When he was seventeen his first published story, a gothic tale named "The Vengeance of Nitrocris," appeared in an issue of* Weird Tales. *The next year he entered the University of Missouri, but in 1932, at his father's insistence, he withdrew from the university and took a job in the shoe factory where his father was a sales manager. After three years working in the company warehouse, a period that Williams later described as a "living death," he had a nervous breakdown. Following a year's recuperation with his grandparents in Memphis, Tennessee, he returned to college, eventually graduating from the University of Iowa with a B.A. in 1938.*

Williams had begun writing plays at the University of Missouri, and after his graduation he continued to write while supporting himself with a variety of menial jobs. By 1939, he was calling himself "Tennessee"—plain "Tom Williams" being, he thought, "rather dull." In that same year he won a national drama award for a group of plays called American Blues. *The next year his first play to be produced by a major company,* Battle of Angels, *opened in Boston and failed, closing after only one performance. Two years later he was hired as a screenwriter for Metro-Goldwyn-Mayer in Hollywood. None of his scripts was accepted, and after a few months he lost his job, but one of his rejected scripts,* The Gentleman Caller, *he later rewrote as* The Glass Menagerie.

In the decades that followed, Williams averaged a play every two years. Of his most memorable dramas, A Streetcar Named Desire *(1947) and* Cat on a Hot Tin Roof *(1955) each won a Pulitzer Prize for drama. In 1956, his controversial film* Baby Doll *was produced, and it was followed by such Broadway and motion-picture successes as* Suddenly Last Summer *(1958),* Sweet Bird of Youth *(1959), and* Night of the Iguana *(1961). In all, fifteen movies have been made from Williams's works. In addition to plays he wrote a novel,* The Roman Spring of Mrs. Stone *(1950), two volumes of poetry, and six volumes of prose, including three collections of short stories.*

Williams's plays have shocked audiences by confronting them with an array of behaviors never presented before on the American stage: murder, rape, castration, drug addiction, homosexuality, alcoholism, fetishism, nymphomania, even cannibalism. By dealing with such subjects Williams helped break taboos long imposed on the American theater, preparing the way for dramatists who would follow with even harsher depictions of violence and sexuality. In spite of, or perhaps because of, his subject matter, Williams's popularity has soared in the decades following his death.

Productions of his plays are repeatedly brought back to Broadway—in 2005, two of his plays, A Streetcar Named Desire *and* The Glass Menagerie, *ran on Broadway at the same time. And yearly, more than 900 productions of his plays are staged throughout the world.*

Williams's writing has sometimes been dismissed as willful pandering to the prurient interests of theatergoers. Yet the popular and critical acclaim that his work continues to receive has come not simply because he writes of the bizarre and fantastic but also because his plays are filled with fascinating characters and compelling dialogue. They are illuminated, even gilded, by verbal, visual, and sound symbolism that is intended to convey meanings beyond those possible in what Williams has termed "the exhausted theater of realism." He employs an array of expressionistic literary and theatrical devices: special settings, musical themes, unusual sound and lighting effects—all as a means of leading his audience to see the truths that lurk beneath life's surface.

Williams's characters and their actions are often exaggerated. They are made to resemble the characters and events of ancient myths. Certain character types recur frequently: the outsider, a man or woman who differs from the mass of humankind by seeing clearly the frightening horror of life; the physically and emotionally deformed; the neurotic and the insane; real or would-be artists; victims and victimizers; and foreigners—strangers like the gentleman caller in The Glass Menagerie*—who intrude on and disrupt the lives of others. His characters are commonly overwhelmed by one another and by a growing awareness that the universe is indifferent to their suffering.*

In Williams's view, "Whether or not we admit it to ourselves, we are all haunted by a truly awful sense of impermanence." To dramatize his dark and narrow vision of life, he wrote of faded men and women, consumed by time and decay. They attempt to escape by moving, by fleeing; they can resist time but never overcome it—for life in Williams's plays can only be attenuated, never triumphant. Yet he shows that for those who come to see clearly the frightening chaos of the world there is a kind of victory, for their vision brings release from guilt and from pointless despair. They can then achieve the kind of dignity Williams believed to be possible if one lives "steadfastly, as if he, too, like a character in a play, were immured against the corrupting rush of time."

FURTHER READING: N. Benjamin, *Tennessee Williams, The Man and His Work,* 1961; F. Donahue, *The Dramatic World of Tennessee Williams,* 1964; E. Jackson, *The Broken World of Tennessee Williams,* 1965; M. Gilbert, *Tennessee Williams and Friends,* 1965; M. Steen, *A Look at Tennessee Williams,* 1969; *The Theatre of Tennessee Williams,* 5 vols. 1972–1976; *Memoirs,* 1975; *Tennessee Williams, A Tribute,* ed. J. Tharpe, 1977; M. Yacowar, *Tennessee Williams and Film,* 1977; *The World of Tennessee Williams,* ed. R. Leavitt, 1978; *Twentieth-Century Interpretations of the Glass Menagerie,* 1983; H. Rasky, *Tennessee Williams,* 1986; *Tennessee Williams,* ed. H. Bloom, 1987; R. Bloxill, *Tennessee Williams,* 1987; *Tennessee Williams' The Glass Menagerie,* ed. H. Bloom, 1988; J. Thompson, *Tennessee Williams' Plays,* 1988; R. Hayman, *Tennessee Williams, Everyone Else Is an Audience,* 1993; L. Leverich, *Tom, The Unknown Tennessee Williams,* 1995; *The Cambridge Companion to Tennessee Williams,* ed. M. Roudané, 1997; N. Tischler, *Student Companion to Tennessee Williams,* 2000; *The Selected Letters of Tennessee Williams,* 2 vols., ed. A. Devlin, 2002, 2004; J. Thompson, *Tennessee Williams's Plays, Memory, Myth, and Symbol,* 2002; G. Heintzelmann and A. Howard, *Tennessee Williams A to Z,* 2005.

TEXT: *The Glass Menagerie,* 1945.

THE GLASS MENAGERIE

Nobody, not even the rain, has such small hands.[1]

E. E. CUMMINGS

SCENE: An Alley in St. Louis

Part I. Preparation for a Gentleman Caller.
Part II. The Gentleman calls.
Time: Now and the Past.

THE CHARACTERS

AMANDA WINGFIELD (*the mother*): A little woman of great but confused vitality clinging frantically to another time and place. Her characterization must be carefully created, not copied from type. She is not paranoiac, but her life is paranoia. There is much to admire in Amanda, and as much to love and pity as there is to laugh at. Certainly she has endurance and a kind of heroism, and though her foolishness makes her unwittingly cruel at times, there is tenderness in her slight person.

LAURA WINGFIELD (*her daughter*): Amanda, having failed to establish contact with reality, continues to live vitally in her illusions, but Laura's situation is even graver. A childhood illness has left her crippled, one leg slightly shorter than the other, and held in a brace. This defect need not be more than suggested on the stage. Stemming from this, Laura's separation increases till she is like a piece of her own glass collection, too exquisitely fragile to move from the shelf.

TOM WINGFIELD (*her son*): And the narrator of the play. A poet with a job in a warehouse. His nature is not remorseless, but to escape from a trap he has to act without pity.

JIM O'CONNOR (*the gentleman caller*): A nice, ordinary, young man.

SCENE ONE

The Wingfield apartment is in the rear of the building, one of those vast hive-like conglomerations of cellular living-units that flower as warty growths in overcrowded urban centers of lower middle-class population and are symptomatic of the impulse of this largest and fundamentally enslaved section of American society to avoid fluidity and differentiation and to exist and function as one interfused mass of automatism.

The apartment faces an alley and is entered by a fire escape, a structure whose name is a touch of accidental poetic truth, for all of these huge buildings are always burning

[1]From "[somewhere i have never travelled, gladly beyond]."

with the slow and implaccable fires of human desperation. The fire escape is part of what we see—that is, the landing of it and steps descending from it.

The scene is memory and is therefore nonrealistic. Memory takes a lot of poetic license. It omits some details; others are exaggerated, according to the emotional value of the articles it touches, for memory is seated predominantly in the heart. The interior is therefore rather dim and poetic.

At the rise of the curtain, the audience is faced with the dark, grim rear wall of the Wingfield tenement. This building is flanked on both sides by dark, narrow alleys which run into murky canyons of tangled clotheslines, garbage cans, and the sinister latticework of neighboring fire escapes. It is up and down these side alleys that exterior entrances and exits are made during the play. At the end of Tom's opening commentary, the dark tenement wall slowly becomes transparent and reveals the interior of the ground-floor Wingfield apartment.

Nearest the audience is the living room, which also serves as a sleeping room for Laura, the sofa unfolding to make her bed. Just beyond, separated from the living room by a wide arch or second proscenium with transparent faded portieres (or second curtain), is the dining room. In an old-fashioned whatnot in the living room are seen scores of transparent glass animals. A blown-up photograph of the father hangs on the wall of the living room, to the left of the archway. It is the face of a very handsome young man in a doughboy's First World War cap. He is gallantly smiling, ineluctably smiling, as if to say "I will be smiling forever."

Also hanging on the wall, near the photograph, are a typewriter keyboard chart and a Gregg shorthand diagram. An upright typewriter on a small table stands beneath the charts.

The audience hears and sees the opening scene in the dining room through both the transparent fourth wall of the building and the transparent gauze portiers of the dining-room arch. It is during this revealing scene that the fourth wall slowly ascends, out of sight. This transparent exterior wall is not brought down again until the very end of the play, during Tom's final speech.

The narrator is an undisguised convention of the play. He takes whatever license with dramatic convention is convenient to his purposes.

Tom enters, dressed as a merchant sailor, and strolls across to the fire escape. There he stops and lights a cigarette. He addresses the audience.

TOM: Yes, I have tricks in my pocket, I have things up my sleeve. But I am the opposite of a stage magician. He gives you illusion the appearance of truth. I give you truth in the pleasant disguise of illusion.
To begin with, I turn back time. I reverse it to that quaint period, the thirties, when the huge middle class of America was matriculating in a school for the blind. Their eyes had failed them, or they had failed their eyes, and so they were having their fingers pressed forcibly down on the fiery Braille alphabet of a dissolving economy.
In Spain there was a revolution. Here there was only shouting and confusion. In Spain there was Guernica.[2] Here there were disturbances of labor, sometimes pretty violent, in otherwise peaceful cities such as Chicago, Cleveland, Saint Louis . . .

[2]Town in northern Spain, bombed in April 1937 by German planes flying for the Fascists during the Spanish Civil War.

This is the social background of the play.

[*Music begins to play*]

The play is memory. Being a memory play, it is dimly lighted, it is sentimental, it is not realistic. In memory everything seems to happen to music. That explains the fiddle in the wings.

I am the narrator of the play, and also a character in it. The other characters are my mother, Amanda, my sister, Laura, and a gentleman caller who appears in the final scenes. He is the most realistic character in the play, being an emissary from a world of reality that we were somehow set apart from. But since I have a poet's weakness for symbols, I am using this character also as a symbol; he is the long-delayed but always expected something that we live for. There is a fifth character in the play who doesn't appear except in this larger-than-life-size photograph over the mantel. This is our father who left us a long time ago. He was a telephone man who fell in love with long distances; he gave up his job with the telephone company and skipped the light fantastic out of town . . .

The last we heard of him was a picture postcard from Mazatlan, on the Pacific coast of Mexico, containing a message of two words: "Hello—Goodbye!" and no address.

I think the rest of the play will explain itself. . . .

[*Amanda's voice becomes audible through the portieres.*]

[*Legend on screen:* "Ou sont les neiges d'antan?"[3]]

[*Tom divides the portieres and enters the dining room. Amanda and Laura are seated at a drop-leaf table. Eating is indicated by gestures without food or utensils. Amanda faces the audience. Tom and Laura are seated in Profile. The interior is lit up softly and through the scrim we see Amanda and Laura seated at the table.*]

AMANDA [*calling*]: Tom?

TOM: Yes, Mother.

AMANDA: We can't say grace until you come to the table!

TOM: Coming, Mother. [*He bows slightly and withdraws, reappearing a few moments later in his place at the table.*]

AMANDA [*to her son*]: Honey, don't *push* with your *fingers.* If you have to push with something, the thing to push with is a crust of bread. And chew—chew! Animals have secretions in their stomachs which enable them to digest food without mastication, but human beings are supposed to chew their food before they swallow it down. Eat food leisurely, son, and really enjoy it. A well-cooked meal has lots of delicate flavors that have to be held in the mouth for appreciation. So chew your food and give your salivary glands a chance to function!

[*Tom deliberately lays his imaginary fork down and pushes his chair back from the table.*]

TOM: I haven't enjoyed one bite of this dinner because of your constant directions on how to eat it. It's you that make me rush through meals with your hawklike attention to every bite I take. Sickening—spoils my appetite—all this discussion of—animals' secretion—salivary glands—mastication!

AMANDA [*lightly*]: Temperament like a Metropolitan star!

[3]French: "Where are the snows of bygone years?" A refrain from "Ballade of the Ladies of Bygone Times" by François Villon (1431–1463?).

[*Tom rises and walks toward the living room.*]

You're not excused from the table.

TOM: I'm getting a cigarette.

AMANDA: You smoke too much.

[*Laura rises.*]

LAURA: I'll bring in the blanc mange.

[*Tom remains standing with his cigarette by the portieres.*]

AMANDA [*rising*]: No, sister, no, sister—you be the lady this time and I'll be the darky.

LAURA: I'm already up.

AMANDA: Resume your seat, little sister— I want you to stay fresh and pretty—for gentlemen callers!

LAURA [*sitting down*]: I'm not expecting any gentlemen callers.

AMANDA [*crossing out to the kitchenette, airily*]: Sometimes they come when they are least expected! Why, I remember one Sunday afternoon in Blue Mountain—

[*She enters the kitchenette.*]

TOM: I know what's coming!

LAURA: Yes. But let her tell it.

TOM: Again?

LAURA: She loves to tell it.

[*Amanda returns with a bowl of dessert.*]

AMANDA: One Sunday afternoon in Blue Mountain—your mother received—*seventeen!*—gentlemen callers! Why, sometimes there weren't chairs enough to accommodate them all. We had to send the nigger over to bring in folding chairs from the parish house.

TOM [*remaining at the portieres*]: How did you entertain those gentlemen callers?

AMANDA: I understood the art of conversation!

TOM: I bet you could talk.

AMANDA: Girls in those days *knew* how to talk, I can tell you.

TOM: Yes?

[*Image on screen:* Amanda as a girl on a porch, greeting callers.]

AMANDA: They knew how to entertain their gentlemen callers. It wasn't enough for a girl to be possessed of a pretty face and a graceful figure—although I wasn't slighted in either respect. She also needed to have nimble wit and a tongue to meet all occasions.

TOM: What did you talk about?

AMANDA: Things of importance going on in the world! Never anything coarse or common or vulgar.

[*She addresses Tom as though he were seated in the vacant chair at the table though he remains by the portieres. He plays this scene as though reading from a script.*]

My callers were gentlemen—all! Among my callers were some of the most prominent young planters of the Mississippi Delta—planters and sons of planters!

[*Tom motions for music and a spot of light on Amanda. Her eyes lift, her face glows, her voice becomes rich and elegiac.*]

[*Screen legend:* "Ou sont les neiges d'antan?"]

There was young Champ Laughlin who later became vice-president of the Delta Planters Bank. Hadley Stevenson who was drowned in Moon Lake and left his widow one hundred and fifty thousand in Government bonds. There were the Cutrere brothers, Wesley and Bates. Bates was one of my bright particular beaux! He got in a quarrel with that wild Wainwright boy. They shot it out on the floor of Moon Lake Casino. Bates was shot through the stomach. Died in the ambulance on his way to Memphis. His widow was also well provided-for, came into eight or ten thousand acres, that's all. She married him on the rebound—never loved her—carried my picture on him the night he died! And there was that boy that every girl in the Delta had set her cap for! That beautiful, brilliant young Fitzhugh boy from Greene County!

TOM: What did he leave his widow?

AMANDA: He never married! Gracious, you talk as though all of my old admirers had turned up their toes to the daisies!

TOM: Isn't this the first you've mentioned that still survives?

AMANDA: That Fitzhugh boy went North and made a fortune—came to be known as the Wolf of Wall Street! He had the Midas touch, whatever he touched turned to gold! And I could have been Mrs. Duncan J. Fitzhugh, mind you! But—I picked your *father!*

LAURA [*rising*]: Mother, let me clear the table.

AMANDA: No, dear, you go in front and study your typewriter chart. Or practice your shorthand a little. Stay fresh and pretty!—It's almost time for our gentlemen callers to start arriving. [*She flounces girlishly toward the kitchenette*] How many do you suppose we're going to entertain this afternoon?

[*Tom throws down the paper and jumps up with a groan.*]

LAURA [*alone in the dining room*]: I don't believe we're going to receive any, Mother.

AMANDA [*reappearing, airily*]: What? No one—not one? You must be joking!

[*Laura nervously echoes her laugh. She slips in a fugitive manner through the half-open portieres and draws them gently behind her. A shaft of very clear light is thrown on her face against the faded tapestry of the curtains. Faintly the music of "The Glass Menagerie" is heard as she continues, lightly:*]

Not one gentleman caller? It can't be true! There must be a flood, there must have been a tornado!

LAURA: It isn't a flood, it's not a tornado, Mother. I'm just not popular like you were in Blue Mountain. . . .

[*Tom utters another groan. Laura glances at him with a faint, apologetic smile. Her voice catches a little:*]

Mother's afraid I'm going to be an old maid.

[*The scene dims out with the "Glass Menagerie" music.*]

SCENE TWO

On the dark stage the screen is lighted with the image of blue roses. Gradually Laura's figure becomes apparent and the screen goes out. The music subsides.

Laura is seated in the delicate ivory chair at the small claw-foot table. She wears a dress of soft violet material for a kimono—her hair is tied back from her forehead with a ribbon. She is washing and polishing her collection of glass. Amanda appears on the fire escape steps. At the sound of her ascent, Laura catches her breath, thrusts the bowl of ornaments away, and sets herself stiffly before the diagram of the typewriter keyboard as though it held her spellbound. Something has happened to Amanda. It is written in her face as she climbs to the landing: a look that is grim and hopeless and a little absurd. She has on one of those cheap or imitation velvety-looking cloth coats with imitation fur collar. Her hat is five or six years old, one of those dreadful cloche hats that were worn in the late Twenties, and she is clutching an enormous black patent-leather pocketbook with nickel clasps and initials. This is her full-dress outfit, the one she usually wears to the D.A.R.[1] *Before entering she looks through the door. She purses her lips, opens her eyes very wide, rolls them upward and shakes her head. Then she slowly lets herself in the door. Seeing her mother's expression Laura touches her lips with a nervous gesture.*

LAURA: Hello, Mother, I was— [*She makes a nervous gesture toward the chart on the wall. Amanda leans against the shut door and stares at Laura with a martyred look.*]

AMANDA: Deception? Deception? [*She slowly removes her hat and gloves, continuing the sweet suffering stare. She lets the hat and gloves fall on the floor—a bit of acting.*]

LAURA [*shakily*]: How was the D.A.R. meeting?

[*Amanda slowly opens her purse and removes a dainty white handkerchief which she shakes out delicately and delicately touches to her lips and nostrils.*]

Didn't you go to the D.A.R. meeting, Mother?

AMANDA [*faintly, almost inaudibly*]:—No.—No. [*then more forcibly:*] I did not have the strength—to go to the D.A.R. In fact, I did not have the courage! I wanted to find a hole in the ground and hide myself in it forever! [*She crosses slowly to the wall and removes the diagram of the typewriter keyboard. She holds it in front of her for a second, staring at it sweetly and sorrowfully—then bites her lips and tears it in two pieces.*]

LAURA [*faintly*]: Why did you do that, Mother?

[*Amanda repeats the same procedure with the chart of the Gregg Alphabet.*]

Why are you—

AMANDA: Why? Why? How old are you, Laura?

LAURA: Mother, you know my age.

AMANDA: I thought that you were an adult; it seems that I was mistaken. [*She crosses slowly to the sofa and sinks down and stares at Laura.*]

LAURA: Please don't stare at me, Mother.

[*Amanda closes her eyes and lowers her head. There is a ten-second pause.*]

AMANDA: What are we going to do, what is going to become of us, what is the future?

[*There is another pause.*]

LAURA: Has something happened, Mother?

[*Amanda draws a long breath, takes out the handkerchief again, goes through the dabbing process.*]

Mother, has—something happened?

AMANDA: I'll be all right in a minute, I'm just bewildered—[*She hesitates.*] —by life. . . .

LAURA: Mother, I wish that you would tell me what's happened!

[1] I.e., to a meeting of the Daughters of the American Revolution, a patriotic society dedicated to celebration of the participants of the American Revolution.

AMANDA: As you know, I was supposed to be inducted into my office at the D.A.R. this afternoon.

[*Screen image:* A swarm of typewriters.]

But I stopped off at Rubicam's Business College to speak to your teachers about your having a cold and ask them what progress they thought you were making down there.

LAURA: Oh . . . .

AMANDA: I went to the typing instructor and introduced myself as your mother. She didn't know who you were. "Wingfield," she said, "We don't have any such student enrolled at the school!"

I assured her she did, that you had been going to classes since early in January. "I wonder," she said, "If you could be talking about that terribly shy little girl who dropped out of school after only a few days' attendance?"

"No," I said, "Laura, my daughter, has been going to school every day for the past six weeks!"

"Excuse me," she said. She took the attendance book out and there was your name, unmistakably printed, and all the dates you were absent until they decided you had dropped out of school.

I still said, "No, there must have been some mistake! There must have been some mix-up in the records!"

And she said, "No—I remember her perfectly now. Her hands shook so that she couldn't hit the right keys! The first time we gave a speed test, she broke down completely—was sick at the stomach and almost had to be carried into the wash room! After that morning she never showed up any more. We phoned the house but never got any answer"—While I was working at Famous-Barr, I suppose, demonstrating those—

[*She indicates a brassiere with her hands.*]

Oh! I felt so weak I could barely keep on my feet! I had to sit down while they got me a glass of water! Fifty dollars' tuition, all of our plans—my hopes and ambitions for you—just gone up the spout, just gone up the spout like that.

[*Laura draws a long breath and gets awkwardly to her feet. She crosses to the Victrola and winds it up.*]

What are you doing?

LAURA: Oh! [*She releases the handle and returns to her seat.*]

AMANDA: Laura, where have you been going when you've gone out pretending that you were going to business college?

LAURA: I've just been going out walking.

AMANDA: That's not true.

LAURA: It is. I just went walking.

AMANDA: Walking? Walking? In winter? Deliberately courting pneumonia in that light coat? Where did you walk to, Laura?

LAURA: All sorts of places—mostly in the park.

AMANDA: Even after you'd started catching that cold?

LAURA: It was the lesser of two evils, Mother.

[*Screen image:* Winter scene in a park.]

I couldn't go back there. I—threw up—on the floor!

AMANDA: From half past seven till after five every day you mean to tell me you walked around in the park, because you wanted to make me think that you were still going to Rubicam's Business College?

LAURA: It wasn't as bad as it sounds. I went inside places to get warmed up.

AMANDA: Inside where?

LAURA: I went in the art museum and the bird houses at the Zoo. I visited the penguins every day! Sometimes I did without lunch and went to the movies. Lately I've been spending most of my afternoons in the Jewel Box, that big glass house where they raise tropical flowers.

AMANDA: You did all this to deceive me, just for deception?

[*Laura looks down.*] Why?

LAURA: Mother, when you're disappointed, you get that awful suffering look on your face, like the picture of Jesus' mother in the museum!

AMANDA: Hush!

LAURA: I couldn't face it.

[*There is a pause. A whisper of strings is heard. Legend on screen:* "The Crust of Humility."]

AMANDA [*hopelessly fingering the huge pocketbook*]: So what are we going to do the rest of our lives? Stay home and watch the parades go by? Amuse ourselves with the glass menagerie, darling? Eternally play those worn-out phonograph records your father left as a painful reminder of him? We won't have a business career—we've given that up because it gave us nervous indigestion! [*She laughs wearily.*] What is there left but dependency all our lives? I know so well what becomes of unmarried women who aren't prepared to occupy a position. I've seen such pitiful cases in the South—barely tolerated spinsters living upon the grudging patronage of sister's husband or brother's wife!—stuck away in some little mousetrap of a room—encouraged by one in-law to visit another—little birdlike women without any nest—eating the crust of humility all their life! Is that the future that we've mapped out for ourselves? I swear it's the only alternative I can think of! [*She pauses.*] It isn't a very pleasant alternative, is it? [*She pauses again.*] Of course—some girls *do marry.*

[*Laura twists her hands nervously.*]

Haven't you ever liked some boy?

LAURA: Yes. I liked one once. [*She rises.*] I came across his picture a while ago.

AMANDA [*with some interest*]: He gave you his picture?

LAURA: No, it's in the yearbook.

AMANDA [*disappointed*]: Oh—a high school boy.

[*Screen image:* Jim as the high school hero bearing a silver cup.]

LAURA: Yes. His name was Jim. [*She lifts the heavy annual from the claw-foot table.*] Here he is in *The Pirates of Penzance.*

AMANDA [*absently*]: The what?

LAURA: The operetta the senior class put on. He had a wonderful voice and we sat across the aisle from each other Mondays, Wednesdays and Fridays in the Aud. Here he is with the silver cup for debating! See his grin?

AMANDA [*absently*]: He must have had a jolly disposition.

LAURA: He used to call me—Blue Roses.

[*Screen image:* Blue roses.]

AMANDA: Why did he call you such a name as that?

LAURA: When I had that attack of pleurosis—he asked me what was the matter when I came back. I said pleurosis—he thought I said Blue Roses! So that's what he always called me after that. Whenever he saw me, he'd holler, "Hello, Blue Roses!" I didn't care for the girl that he went out with. Emily Meisenbach. Emily was the best-dressed girl at Soldan. She never struck me, though, as being sincere . . . It says in the Personal Section—they're engaged. That's—six years ago! They must be married by now.

AMANDA: Girls that aren't cut out for business careers usually wind up married to some nice man. [*She gets up with a spark of revival.*] Sister, that's what you'll do!

[*Laura utters a startled, doubtful laugh. She reaches quickly for a piece of glass.*]

LAURA: But, Mother—

AMANDA: Yes? [*She goes over to the phonograph.*]

LAURA [*in a tone of frightened apology*]: I'm—crippled!

AMANDA: Nonsense! Laura, I've told you never, never to use that word. Why, you're not crippled, you just have a little defect—hardly noticeable, even! When people have some slight disadvantage like that, they cultivate other things to make up for it—develop charm—and vivacity—and—*charm!* That's all you have to do! [*She turns again to the phonograph.*] One thing your father had *plenty of*—was *charm!*

[*The scene fades out with music.*]

SCENE THREE

Legend on screen: "After the fiasco—"

Tom speaks from the fire escape landing.

TOM: After the fiasco at Rubicam's Business College, the idea of getting a gentleman caller for Laura began to play a more and more important part in Mother's calculations. It became an obsession. Like some archetype of the universal unconscious, the image of the gentleman caller haunted our small apartment. . . .

[*Screen image:* A young man at the door of a house with flowers.]

An evening at home rarely passed without some allusion to this image, this specter, this hope. . . . Even when he wasn't mentioned, his presence hung in Mother's preoccupied look and in my sister's frightened, apologetic manner—hung like a sentence passed upon the Wingfields!

Mother was a woman of action as well as words. She began to take logical steps in the planned direction. Late that winter and in the early spring—realizing that extra money would be needed to properly feather the nest and plume the bird—she conducted a vigorous campaign on the telephone, roping in subscribers to one of those magazines for matrons called *The Homemaker's Companion,* the type of journal that features the serialized sublimations of ladies of letters who think in terms of delicate cuplike breasts, slim, tapering waists, rich, creamy thighs, eyes like wood smoke in autumn, fingers that soothe and caress like strains of music, bodies as powerful as Etruscan sculpture.

[*Screen image:* The cover of a glamor magazine.]

[*Amanda enters with the telephone on a long extension cord. She is spotlighted in the dim stage.*]

AMANDA: Ida Scott? This is Amanda Wingfield! We *missed* you at the D.A.R. last Monday! I said to myself: She's probably suffering with that sinus condition! How is that sinus condition?
Horrors! Heaven have mercy!—You're a Christian martyr, yes, that's what you are, a Christian martyr!
Well, I just now happened to notice that your subscription to the *Companion's* about to expire! Yes, it expires with the next issue, honey!—just when that wonderful new serial by Bessie Mae Hopper is getting off to such an exciting start. Oh, honey, it's something that you can't miss! You remember how *Gone with the Wind* took everybody by storm? You simply couldn't go out if you hadn't read it. All everybody *talked* was Scarlett O'Hara. Well, this is a book that critics already compare to *Gone with the Wind.* It's the *Gone with the Wind* of the post-World-War generation!—What?—Burning?—Oh, honey, don't let them burn, go take a look in the oven and I'll hold the wire! Heavens—I think she's hung up!

[*The scene dims out.*]

[*Legend on screen:* "You think I'm in love with Continental Shoemakers?]"

[*Before the lights come up again, the violent voices of Tom and Amanda are heard. They are quarrelling behind the portieres. In front of them stands Laura with clenched hands and panicky expression. A clear pool of light is on her figure throughout this scene.*]

TOM: What in Christ's name am I—

AMANDA [*shrilly*]: Don't you use that—

TOM: —supposed to do!

AMANDA: —expression! Not in my—

TOM: Ohhh!

AMANDA: —presence! Have you gone out of your senses?

TOM: I have, that's true, *driven* out!

AMANDA: What is the matter with you, you—big—big—IDIOT!

TOM: Look!—I've got *no thing,* no single thing—

AMANDA: Lower your voice!

TOM: —in my life here that I can call my OWN! Everything is—

AMANDA: Stop that shouting!

TOM: Yesterday you confiscated my books! You had the nerve to—

AMANDA: I took that horrible novel back to the library—yes! That hideous book by that insane Mr. Lawrence.

[*Tom laughs wildly,*]

I cannot control the output of diseased minds or people who cater to them—

[*Tom laughs still more wildly.*]

BUT I WON'T ALLOW SUCH FILTH BROUGHT INTO MY HOUSE! No, no, no, no, no!

TOM: House, house! Who pays rent on it, who makes a slave of himself to—

AMANDA [*fairly screeching*]: Don't you DARE to—

TOM: No, no, *I* mustn't say things! *I've* got to just—

AMANDA: Let me tell you—

TOM: I don't want to hear any more!

[*He tears the portieres open. The dining-room area is lit with a turgid smoky red glow. Now we see Amanda; her hair is in metal curlers and she is wearing a very old bathrobe, much too large for her slight figure, a relic of the faithless Mr. Wingfield.*

The upright typewriter now stands on the drop-leaf table, along with a wild disarray of manuscripts. The quarrel was probably precipitated by Amanda's interruption of Tom's creative labor. A chair lies overthrown on the floor. Their gesticulating shadows are cast on the ceiling by the fiery glow.]

AMANDA: You *will* hear more, you—

TOM: No, I won't hear more, I'm going out!

AMANDA: You come right back in—

TOM: Out, out, out! Because I'm—

AMANDA: Come back here, Tom Wingfield! I'm not through talking to you!

TOM: Oh, go—

LAURA [*desperately*]:—Tom!

AMANDA: You're going to listen, and no more insolence from you! I'm at the end of my patience!

[*He comes back toward her.*]

TOM: What do you think I'm at? Aren't I supposed to have any patience to reach the end of, Mother? I know, I know. It seems unimportant to you, what I'm *doing*—what I *want* to do—having a little *difference* between them! You don't think that—

AMANDA: I think you've been doing things that you're ashamed of. That's why you act like this. I don't believe that you go every night to the movies. Nobody goes to the movies night after night. Nobody in their right minds goes to the movies as often as you pretend to. People don't go to the movies at nearly midnight, and movies don't let out at two A.M.: Come in stumbling. Muttering to yourself like a maniac! You get three hours' sleep and then go to work. Oh, I can picture the way you're doing down there. Moping, doping, because you're in no condition.

TOM [*wildly*]: No, I'm in no condition!

AMANDA: What right have you got to jeopardize your job? Jeopardize the security of us all? How do you think we'd manage if you were—

TOM: Listen! You think I'm crazy about the *warehouse?* [*He bends fiercely toward her slight figure.*] You think I'm in love with the Continental Shoemakers? You think I want to spend fifty-five *years* down there in that—*celotex interior!* with—*fluorescent*—*tubes!* I'd rather somebody picked up a crowbar and battered out my brains—than go back mornings! I *go!* Every time you come in yelling that Goddamn *"Rise and Shine!" "Rise and Shine!"* I say to myself. "How *lucky dead* people are!" But I get up. I *go!* For sixty-five dollars a month I give up all that I dream of doing and being *ever!* And you say self—*self's* all I ever think of. Why, listen, if self is what I thought of, Mother, I'd be where he is—GONE! [*He points to his father's picture.*] As far as the system of transportation reaches! [*He starts past her. She grabs his arm.*] Don't grab at me, Mother!

AMANDA: Where are you going?

TOM: I'm going to the *movies!*

AMANDA: I don't believe that lie!

[*Tom crouches toward her, overtowering her tiny figure. She backs away, gasping.*]

TOM: I'm going to opium dens! Yes, opium dens, dens of vice and criminals' hangouts, Mother. I've joined the Hogan Gang, I'm a hired assassin, I carry a tommy gun in a violin case! I run a string of cat houses in the Valley! They call me Killer, Killer Wingfield, I'm leading a double-life, a simple, honest warehouse worker by day, by night a dynamic *czar* of the *underworld, Mother.* I go to gambling casinos, I spin away fortunes on the roulette table! I wear a patch over one eye and a false mustache, sometimes I put on green whiskers. On those occasions they call me—*El Diablo!*[1] Oh, I could tell you many things to make you sleepless! My enemies plan to dynamite this place. They're going to blow us all sky-high some night! I'll be glad, very happy, and so will you! You'll go up, up on a broomstick, over Blue Mountain with seventeen gentlemen callers! You ugly—babbling old—*witch*. . . .

[*He goes through a series of violent, clumsy movements, seizing his overcoat, lunging to the door, pulling it fiercely open. The women watch him, aghast. His arm catches in the sleeve of the coat as he struggles to pull it on. For a moment he is pinioned by the bulky garment. With an outraged groan he tears the coat off again, splitting the shoulder of it, and hurls it across the room. It strikes against the shelf of Laura's glass collection, and there is a tinkle of shattering glass. Laura cries out as if wounded.*]

[*Music.*]

[*Screen legend:* "The Glass Menagerie."]

LAURA [*shrilly*]: *My glass!*—menagerie. . . . [*She covers her face and turns away.*]

[*But Amanda is still stunned and stupefied by the "ugly witch" so that she barely notices this occurrence. Now she recovers her speech.*]

AMANDA [*in an awful voice*]: I won't speak to you—until you apologize!

[*She crosses through the portieres and draws them together behind her. Tom is left with Laura. Laura clings weakly to the mantel with her face averted. Tom stares at her stupidly for a moment. Then he crosses to the shelf. He drops awkwardly on his knees to collect the fallen glass, glancing at Laura as if he would speak but couldn't.*]

[*"The Glass Menagerie" music steals in as the scene dims out.*]

SCENE FOUR

The interior of the apartment is dark. There is a faint light in the alley. A deep-voiced bell in a church is tolling the hour of five.

Tom appears at the top of the alley. After each solemn boom of the bell in the tower, he shakes a little noisemaker or rattle as if to express the tiny spasm of man in contrast to the sustained power and dignity of the Almighty. This and the unsteadiness of his advance make it evident that he has been drinking. As he climbs the few steps to the fire escape landing light steals up inside. Laura appears in the front room in a nightdress. She notices that Tom's bed is empty. Tom fishes in his pockets for his door key, removing a motley assortment of articles in his search, including a shower of movie ticket stubs and an empty bottle. At last he finds the key, but just as he is about to insert it, it slips from his fingers. He strikes a match and crouches below the door.

TOM [*bitterly*]: One crack—and it falls through!

[*Laura opens the door.*]

LAURA: Tom! Tom, what are you doing?

TOM: Looking for a door key.

LAURA: Where have you been all this time?

[1]Spanish: The Devil!

TOM: I have been to the movies.

LAURA: All this time at the movies?

TOM: There was a very long program. There was a Garbo picture and a Mickey Mouse and a travelogue and a newsreel and a preview of coming attractions. And there was an organ solo and a collection for the Milk Fund—simultaneously—which ended up in a terrible fight between a fat lady and an usher!

LAURA [*innocently*]: Did you have to stay through everything?

TOM: Of course! And, oh, I forgot! There was a big stage show! The headliner on this stage show was Malvolio the Magician. He performed wonderful tricks, many of them, such as pouring water back and forth between pitchers. First it turned to wine and then it turned to beer and then it turned to whisky. I know it was whisky it finally turned into because he needed somebody to come up out of the audience to help him, and I came up—both shows! It was Kentucky Straight Bourbon. A very generous fellow, he gave souvenirs. [*He pulls from his back pocket a shimmering rainbow-colored scarf.*] He gave me this. This is his magic scarf. You can have it, Laura. You wave it over a canary cage and you get a bowl of goldfish. You wave it over the goldfish bowl and they fly away canaries. . . . But the wonderfullest trick of all was the coffin trick. We nailed him into a coffin and he got out of the coffin without removing one nail. [*He has come inside.*] There is a trick that would come in handy for me—get me out of this two-by-four situation! [*He flops on the bed and starts removing his shoes.*]

LAURA: Tom—shhh!

TOM: What're you shushing me for?

LAURA: You'll wake up Mother.

TOM: Goody, goody! Pay'er back for all those "Rise an' Shines." [*He lies down, groaning.*] You know it don't take much intelligence to get yourself into a nailed-up coffin, Laura. But who the hell ever got himself out of one without removing one nail?

[*As if in answer, the father's grinning photograph lights up. The scene dims out.*]

[*Immediately following, the church bell is heard striking six. At the sixth stroke the alarm clock goes off in Amanda's room, and after a few moments we hear her calling: "Rise and Shine! Rise and Shine! Laura, go tell your brother to rise and shine!"*]

TOM [*sitting up slowly*]: I'll rise—but I won't shine.

[*The light increases.*]

AMANDA: Laura, tell your brother his coffee is ready.

[*Laura slips into the front room.*]

LAURA: Tom!—It's nearly seven. Don't make Mother nervous.

[*He stares at her stupidly.*]

LAURA: [*beseechingly:*] Tom, speak to Mother this morning. Make up with her, apologize, speak to her!

TOM: She won't to me. It's her that started not speaking.

LAURA: If you just say you're sorry she'll start speaking.

TOM: Her not speaking—is that such a tragedy?

LAURA: Please—please!

AMANDA [*calling from the kitchenette*]: Laura, are you going to do what I asked you to do, or do I have to get dressed and go out myself?

LAURA: Going, going—soon as I get on my coat!

[*She pulls on a shapeless felt hat with a nervous, jerky movement, pleadingly glancing at Tom. She rushes awkwardly for her coat. The coat is one of Amanda's inaccurately made-over, the sleeves too short for Laura.*]

Butter and what else?

AMANDA [*entering from the kitchenette*]: Just butter. Tell them to charge it.

LAURA: Mother, they make such faces when I do that.

AMANDA: Sticks and stones can break our bones, but the expression on Mr. Garfinkel's face won't harm us! Tell your brother his coffee is getting cold.

LAURA [*at the door*]: Do what I asked you, will you, will you, Tom?

[*He looks sullenly away.*]

AMANDA: Laura, go now or just don't go at all!

LAURA [*rushing out*]: Going—going!

[*A second later she cries out. Tom springs up and crosses to the door. Tom opens the door.*]

TOM: Laura?

LAURA: I'm all right. I slipped, but I'm all right.

AMANDA [*peering anxiously after her*]: If anyone breaks a leg on those fire-escape steps, the landlord ought to be sued for every cent he possesses! [*She shuts the door. Now she remembers she isn't speaking to Tom and returns to the other room.*]

[*As Tom comes listlessly for his coffee, she turns her back to him and stands rigidly facing the window on the gloomy gray vault of the areaway. Its light on her face with its aged but childish features is cruelly sharp, satirical as a Daumier*[1] *print.*]

[*The music of "Ave Maria" is heard softly.*]

[*Tom glances sheepishly but sullenly at her averted figure and slumps at the table. The coffee is scalding hot; he sips it and gasps and spits it back in the cup. At his gasp, Amanda catches her breath and half turns. Then she catches herself and turns back to the window. Tom blows on his coffee, glancing sidewise at his mother. She clears her throat. Tom clears his. He starts to rise, sinks back down again, scratches his head, clears his throat again. Amanda coughs. Tom raises his cup in both hands to blow on it, his eyes staring over the rim of it at his mother for several moments. Then he slowly sets the cup down and awkwardly and hesitantly rises from the chair.*]

TOM [*hoarsely*]: Mother. I—I apologize, Mother.

[*Amanda draws a quick, shuddering breath. Her face works grotesquely. She breaks into childlike tears.*]

I'm sorry for what I said, for everything that I said, I didn't mean it.

AMANDA [*sobbingly*]: My devotion has made me a witch and so I make myself hateful to my children!

TOM: No, you *don't.*

AMANDA: I worry so much, don't sleep, it makes me nervous!

TOM [*gently*]: I understand that.

AMANDA: I've had to put up a solitary battle all these years. But you're my right-hand bower! Don't fall down, don't fail!

TOM [*gently*]: I try, Mother.

AMANDA [*with great enthusiasm*]: Try and you will *succeed!* [*The notion makes her breathless.*] Why, you—you're just *full* of natural endowments! Both of my

[1]Honoré Daumier (1808–1879), French caricaturist and painter.

children—they're *unusual* children! Don't you think I know it? I'm so—*proud!* Happy and—feel I've—so much to be thankful for but—promise me one thing, son!

TOM: What, Mother?

AMANDA: Promise, son, you'll—never be a drunkard!

TOM [*turns to her grinning*]: I will never be a drunkard, Mother.

AMANDA: That's what frightened me so, that you'd be drinking! Eat a bowl of Purina!

TOM: Just coffee, Mother.

AMANDA: Shredded wheat biscuit?

TOM: No. No, Mother, just coffee.

AMANDA: You can't put in a day's work on an empty stomach. You've got ten minutes—don't gulp! Drinking too-hot liquids makes cancer of the stomach. . . . Put cream in.

TOM: No, thank you.

AMANDA: To cool it.

TOM: No! No, thank you, I want it black.

AMANDA: I know, but it's not good for you. We have to do all that we can to build ourselves up. In these trying times we live in, all that we have to cling to is—each other. . . . That's why it's important to—Tom, I—I sent out your sister so I could discuss something with you. If you hadn't spoken I would have spoken to you. [*She sits down.*]

TOM [*gently*]: What is it, Mother, that you want to discuss?

AMANDA: *Laura!*

[*Tom puts his cup down slowly.*]

[*Legend on screen:* "Laura." *Music: "The Glass Menagerie."*]

TOM: —Oh.—Laura . . .

AMANDA [*touching his sleeve*]: You know how Laura is. So quiet but—still water runs deep! She notices things and I think she—broods about them.

[*Tom looks up.*]

A few days ago I came in and she was crying.

TOM: What about?

AMANDA: You.

TOM: Me?

AMANDA: She has an idea that you're not happy here.

TOM: What gave her that idea?

AMANDA: What gives her any idea? However, you do act strangely. I—I'm not criticizing, understand *that!* I know your ambitions do not lie in the warehouse, that like everybody in the whole wide world—you've had to—make sacrifices, but—Tom—Tom—life's not easy, it calls for—Spartan endurance! There's so many things in my heart that I cannot describe to you! I've never told you but I—*loved* your father. . . .

TOM [*gently*]: I know that, Mother.

AMANDA: And you—when I see you taking after his ways! Staying out late—and—well, you *had* been drinking the night you were in that—terrifying condition! Laura says that you hate the apartment and that you go out nights to get away from it! Is that true, Tom?

TOM: No. You say there's so much in your heart that you can't describe to me. That's true of me, too. There's so much in my heart that I can't describe to *you!* So let's respect each other's—

AMANDA: But, why—*why,* Tom—are you always so *restless?* Where do you *go* to, nights?

TOM: I—go to the movies.

AMANDA: Why do you go to the movies so much, Tom?

TOM: I go to the movies because—I like adventure. Adventure is something I don't have much of at work, so I go to the movies.

AMANDA: But, Tom, you go to the movies *entirely* too *much!*

TOM: I like a lot of adventure.

[*Amanda looks baffled, then hurt. As the familiar inquisition resumes, Tom becomes hard and impatient again. Amanda slips back into her querulous attitude toward him.*]

[*Image on screen:* A sailing vessel with Jolly Roger.]

AMANDA: Most young men find adventure in their careers.

TOM: Then most young men are not employed in a warehouse.

AMANDA: The world is full of young men employed in warehouses and offices and factories.

TOM: Do all of them find adventure in their careers?

AMANDA: They do or they do without it! Not everybody has a craze for adventure.

TOM: Man is by instinct a lover, a hunter, a fighter, and none of those instincts are given much play at the warehouse!

AMANDA: Man is by instinct! Don't quote instinct to me! Instinct is something that people have got away from! It belongs to animals! Christian adults don't want it!

TOM: What do Christian adults want, then, Mother?

AMANDA: Superior things! Things of the mind and the spirit! Only animals have to satisfy instincts! Surely your aims are somewhat higher than theirs! Than monkeys—pigs—

TOM: I reckon they're not.

AMANDA: You're joking. However, that isn't what I wanted to discuss.

TOM [*rising*]: I haven't much time.

AMANDA [*pushing his shoulders*]: Sit down.

TOM: You want me to punch in red at the warehouse, Mother?

AMANDA: You have five minutes. I want to talk about Laura.

[*Screen legend:* "Plans and Provisions."]

TOM: All right! What about Laura?

AMANDA: We have to be making some plans and provisions for her. She's older than you, two years, and nothing has happened. She just drifts along doing nothing. It frightens me terribly how she just drifts along.

TOM: I guess she's the type that people call home girls.

AMANDA: There's no such type, and if there is, it's a pity! That is unless the home is hers, with a husband!

TOM: What?

AMANDA: Oh, I can see the handwriting on the wall as plain as I see the nose in front of my face! It's terrifying! More and more you remind me of your father! He was out all hours without explanation!—Then *left! Goodbye!* And me with the bag to hold. I saw that letter you got from the Merchant Marine. I know what you're dreaming of. I'm not standing here blindfolded. [*She pauses.*] Very well, then. Then *do* it! But not till there's somebody to take your place.

TOM: What do you mean?

AMANDA: I mean that as soon as Laura has got somebody to take care of her, married, a home of her own, independent—why, then you'll be free to go wherever you please, on land, on sea, whichever way the wind blows you! But until that time you've got to look out for your sister. I don't say me because I'm old and don't matter! I say for your sister because she's young and dependent.

I put her in business college—a dismal failure! Frightened her so it made her sick at the stomach. I took her over to the Young People's League at the church. Another fiasco. She spoke to nobody, nobody spoke to her. Now all she does is fool with those pieces of glass and play those worn-out records. What kind of a life is that for a girl to lead?

TOM: What can I do about it?

AMANDA: Overcome selfishness! Self, self, self is all that you ever think of!

[*Tom springs up and crosses to get his coat. It is ugly and bulky. He pulls on a cap with earmuffs.*]

Where is your muffler? Put your wool muffler on!

[*He snatches it angrily from the closet, tosses it around his neck and pulls both ends tight.*]

Tom! I haven't said what I had in mind to ask you.

TOM: I'm too late to—

AMANDA [*catching his arm—very importunately; then shyly*]: Down at the warehouse, aren't there some—nice young men?

TOM: No!

AMANDA: There *must* be—*some* . . .

TOM: Mother—[*He gestures.*]

AMANDA: Find out one that's clean-living—doesn't drink and ask him out for sister!

TOM: What?

AMANDA: For *sister!* To *meet!* Get *acquainted!*

TOM [*stamping to the door*]: Oh, my *go-osh!*

AMANDA: Will you?

[*He opens the door. She says, imploringly:*]

Will you?

[*He starts down the fire escape.*]

Will you? *Will* you, dear?

TOM [*calling back*]: Yes!

[*Amanda closes the door hesitantly and with a troubled but faintly hopeful expression.*]

[*Screen image:* The cover of a glamor magazine.]

[*The spotlight picks up Amanda at the phone.*]

AMANDA: Ella Cartwright? This is Amanda Wingfield!

How are you, honey?

How is that kidney condition?

[*There is a five-second pause.*]

Horrors!

[*There is another pause.*]

You're a Christian martyr, yes, honey, that's what you are, a Christian martyr! Well, I just now happened to notice in my little red book that your subscription to the *Companion* has just run out! I knew that you wouldn't want to miss out on the wonderful serial starting in this new issue. It's by Bessie Mae Hopper, the first thing she's written since *Honeymoon for Three.* Wasn't that a strange and interesting story? Well, this one is even lovelier, I believe. It has a sophisticated, society background. It's all about the horsey set on Long Island!

[*The light fades out.*]

SCENE FIVE

Legend on the screen: "Annunciation."
Music is heard as the light slowly comes on.
It is early dusk of a spring evening. Supper has just been finished in the Wingfield apartment. Amanda and Laura, in light-colored dresses, are removing dishes from the table in the dining room, which is shadowy, their movements formalized almost as a dance or ritual, their moving forms as pale and silent as moths. Tom, in white shirt and trousers, rises from the table and crosses toward the fire escape.

AMANDA [*as he passes her*]: Son, will you do me a favor?

TOM: What?

AMANDA: Comb your hair! You look so pretty when your hair is combed!

[*Tom slouches on the sofa with the evening paper. Its enormous headline reads: "Franco Triumphs."*][1]

There is only one respect in which I would like you to emulate your father.

TOM: What respect is that?

AMANDA: The care he always took of his appearance. He never allowed himself to look untidy.

[*He throws down the paper and crosses to the fire escape.*]

Where are you going?

TOM: I'm going out to smoke.

AMANDA: You smoke too much. A pack a day at fifteen cents a pack. How much would that amount to in a month? Thirty times fifteen is how much Tom? Figure it out and you will be astounded at what you could save. Enough to give you a night-school course in accounting at Washington U.! Just think what a wonderful thing that would be for you, son!

[*Tom is unmoved by the thought.*]

TOM: I'd rather smoke. [*He steps out on the landing, letting the screen door slam.*]

AMANDA [*sharply*]: I know! That's the tragedy of it. . . . [*Alone, she turns to look at her husband's picture.*]

[*Dance music: "The World Is Waiting for the Sunrise!"*]

TOM [*to the audience*]: Across the alley from us was the Paradise Dance Hall. On evenings in spring the windows and doors were open and the music came outdoors. Sometimes the lights were turned out except for a large glass sphere that hung from the ceiling. It would turn slowly about and filter the dusk with delicate rainbow colors. Then the orchestra played a waltz or a

[1]A reference to a military victory of Francisco Franco, leader of the Fascist forces in the Spanish Civil War.

tango, something that had a slow and sensuous rhythm. Couples would come outside, to the relative privacy of the alley. You could see them kissing behind ash pits and telephone poles. This was the compensation for lives that passed like mine, without any change or adventure. Adventure and change were imminent in this year. They were waiting around the corner for all these kids. Suspended in the midst over Berchtesgaden, caught in the folds of Chamberlain's umbrella.[2] In Spain there was Guernica! But here there was only hot swing music and liquor, dance halls, bars, and movies, and sex that hung in the gloom like a chandelier and flooded the world with brief, deceptive rainbows. . . . All the world was waiting for bombardments!

[*Amanda turns from the picture and comes outside.*]

AMANDA [*sighing*]: A fire escape landing's a poor excuse for a porch. [*She spreads a newspaper on a step and sits down, gracefully and demurely as if she were settling into a swing on a Mississippi veranda.*] What are you looking at?

TOM: The moon.

AMANDA: Is there a moon this evening?

TOM: It's rising over Garfinkel's Delicatessen.

AMANDA: So it is! A little silver slipper of a moon. Have you made a wish on it yet?

TOM: Um-hum.

AMANDA: What did you wish for?

TOM: That's a secret.

AMANDA: A secret, huh? Well, I won't tell mine either. I will be just as mysterious as you.

TOM: I bet I can guess what yours is.

AMANDA: Is my head so transparent?

TOM: You're not a sphinx.

AMANDA: No, I don't have secrets. I'll tell you what I wished for on the moon. Success and happiness for my precious children! I wish for that whenever there's a moon, and when there isn't a moon, I wish for it, too.

TOM: I thought perhaps you wished for a gentleman caller.

AMANDA: Why do you say that?

TOM: Don't you remember asking me to fetch one?

AMANDA: I remember suggesting that it would be nice for your sister if you brought home some nice young man from the warehouse. I think that I've made that suggestion more than once.

TOM: Yes, you have made it repeatedly.

AMANDA: Well?

TOM: We are going to have one.

AMANDA: *What?*

TOM: A gentleman caller!

[*The annunciation is celebrated with music.*]

[*Amanda rises.*]

[*Image on screen:* A caller with a bouquet.]

[2]Near Berchtesgaden, Germany, Neville Chamberlain, the Prime Minister of Great Britain (1937–1940), met with Adolf Hitler in a futile effort to avoid World War II. On his return to England, he declared that he had arranged for "peace in our time." Because of his folly, Chamberlain and the umbrella that he carried subsequently became symbols of the foolish appeasement of evil.

AMANDA: You mean you have asked some nice young man to come over?

TOM: Yep. I've asked him to dinner.

AMANDA: You really did?

TOM: I did!

AMANDA: You did, and did he—*accept?*

TOM: He did!

AMANDA: Well, well—well, well! That's—lovely!

TOM: I thought that you would be pleased.

AMANDA: It's definite then?

TOM: Very definite.

AMANDA: Soon?

TOM: Very soon.

AMANDA: For heaven's sake, stop putting on and tell me some things, will you?

TOM: What things do you want me to tell you?

AMANDA: *Naturally* I would like to know when he's *coming!*

TOM: He's coming tomorrow.

AMANDA: *Tomorrow?*

TOM: Yep. Tomorrow.

AMANDA: But, Tom!

TOM: Yes, Mother?

AMANDA: Tomorrow gives me no time!

TOM: Time for what?

AMANDA: Preparations! Why didn't you phone me at once, as soon as you asked him, the minute that he accepted? Then, don't you see, I could have been getting ready!

TOM: You don't have to make any fuss.

AMANDA: Oh, Tom, Tom, Tom, of course I have to make a fuss! I want things nice, not sloppy! Not thrown together. I'll certainly have to do some fast thinking, won't I?

TOM: I don't see why you have to think at all.

AMANDA: You just don't know. We can't have a gentleman caller in a pigsty! All my wedding silver has to be polished, the monogrammed table linen ought to be laundered! The windows have to be washed and fresh curtains put up. And how about clothes? We have to *wear* something, don't we?

TOM: Mother, this boy is no one to make a fuss over!

AMANDA: Do you realize he's the first young man we've introduced to your sister? It's terrible, dreadful, disgraceful that poor little sister has never received a single gentleman caller! Tom, come inside!

[*She opens the screen door.*]

TOM: What for?

AMANDA: I want to ask you some things.

TOM: If you're going to make such a fuss, I'll call it off, I'll tell him not to come!

AMANDA: You certainly won't do anything of the kind. Nothing offends people worse than broken engagements. It simply means I'll have to work like a Turk! We won't be brilliant, but we will pass inspection. Come on inside.

[*Tom follows her inside, groaning.*]

Sit down.

TOM: Any particular place you would like me to sit?

AMANDA: Thank heavens I've got that new sofa! I'm also making payments on a floor lamp I'll have sent out! And put the chintz covers on, they'll brighten things up! Of course I'd hoped to have these walls re-papered . . . . What is the young man's name?

TOM: His name is O'Connor.

AMANDA: That, of course, means fish—tomorrow is Friday! I'll have that salmon loaf—with Durkee's dressing! What does he do? He works at the warehouse?

TOM: Of course! How else would I—

AMANDA: Tom, he—doesn't drink?

TOM: Why do you ask me that?

AMANDA: Your father *did!*

TOM: Don't get started on that!

AMANDA: He *does* drink, then?

TOM: Not that I know of!

AMANDA: Make sure, be certain! The last thing I want for my daughter's a boy who drinks!

TOM: Aren't you being a little bit premature? Mr. O'Connor has not yet appeared on the scene!

AMANDA: But will tomorrow. To meet your sister, and what do I know about his character? Nothing! Old maids are better off than wives of drunkards!

TOM: Oh, my God!

AMANDA: Be still!

TOM [*leaning forward to whisper*]: Lots of fellows meet girls whom they don't marry!

AMANDA: Oh, talk sensibly, Tom—and don't be sarcastic! [*She has gotten a hairbrush.*]

TOM: What are you doing?

AMANDA: I'm brushing that cowlick down! [*She attacks his hair with the brush.*] What is this young man's position at the warehouse?

TOM [*submitting grimly to the brush and the interrogation*]: This young man's position is that of a shipping clerk, Mother.

AMANDA: Sounds to me like a fairly responsible job, the sort of a job *you* would be in if you just had more *get-up.* What is his salary? Have you any idea?

TOM: I would judge it to be approximately eighty-five dollars a month.

AMANDA: Well—not princely, but—

TOM: Twenty more than I make.

AMANDA: Yes, how well I know! But for a family man, eighty-five dollars a month is not much more than you can just get by on. . . .

TOM: Yes, but Mr. O'Connor is not a family man.

AMANDA: He might be, mightn't he? Some time in the future?

TOM: I see. Plans and provisions.

AMANDA: You are the only young man that I know of who ignores the fact that the future becomes the present, the present the past, and the past turns into everlasting regret if you don't plan for it!

TOM: I will think that over and see what I can make of it.

AMANDA: Don't be supercilious with your mother! Tell me some more about this—what do you call him?

TOM: James D. O'Connor. The D. is for Delaney.

AMANDA: Irish on *both* sides! *Gracious!* And doesn't drink?

TOM: Shall I call him up and ask him right this minute?

AMANDA: The only way to find out about those things is to make discreet inquiries at the proper moment. When I was a girl in Blue Mountain and it was suspected that a young man drank, the girl whose attentions he had been receiving, if any girl *was,* would sometimes speak to the minister of his church, or rather her father would if her father was living, and sort of feel him out on the young man's character. That is the way such things are discreetly handled to keep a young woman from making a tragic mistake!

TOM: Then how did you happen to make a tragic mistake?

AMANDA: That innocent look of your father's had everyone fooled! He *smiled*—the world was *enchanted!* No girl can do worse than put herself at the mercy of a handsome appearance! I hope that Mr. O'Connor is not too good-looking.

TOM: No, he's not too good-looking. He's covered with freckles and hasn't too much of a nose.

AMANDA: He's not right-down homely, though?

TOM: Not right-down homely. Just medium homely, I'd say.

AMANDA: Character's what to look for in a man.

TOM: That's what I've always said, Mother.

AMANDA: You've never said anything of the kind and I suspect you would never give it a thought.

TOM: Don't be so suspicious of me.

AMANDA: At least I hope he's the type that's up and coming.

TOM: I think he really goes in for self-improvement.

AMANDA: What reason have you to think so?

TOM: He goes to night school.

AMANDA [*beaming*]: Splendid! What does he do, I mean study?

TOM: Radio engineering and public speaking!

AMANDA: Then he has visions of being advanced in the world! Any young man who studies public speaking is aiming to have an executive job some day! And radio engineering! A thing for the future! Both of these facts are very illuminating. Those are the sort of things that a mother should know concerning any young man who comes to call on her daughter. Seriously or—not.

TOM: One little warning. He doesn't know about Laura. I didn't let on that we had dark ulterior motives. I just said, why don't you come and have dinner with us? He said okay and that was the whole conversation.

AMANDA: I bet it was! You're eloquent as an oyster. However, he'll know about Laura when he gets here. When he sees how lovely and sweet and pretty she is, he'll thank his lucky stars he was asked to dinner.

TOM: Mother, you mustn't expect too much of Laura.

AMANDA: What do you mean?

TOM: Laura seems all those things to you and me because she's ours and we love her. We don't even notice she's crippled any more.

AMANDA: Don't say crippled! You know that I never allow that word to be used!

TOM: But face facts, Mother. She is and—that's not all—

AMANDA: What do you mean "not all"?

TOM: Laura is very different from other girls.

AMANDA: I think the difference is to her advantage.

TOM: Not quite all—in the eyes of others—strangers—she's terribly shy and lives in a world of her own and those things make her seem a little peculiar to people outside the house.

AMANDA: Don't say peculiar.

TOM: Face the facts. She is.

[*The dance hall music changes to a tango that has a minor and somewhat ominous tone.*]

AMANDA: In what way is she peculiar—may I ask?

TOM [*gently*]: She lives in a world of her own—a world of little glass ornaments, Mother. . . .

[*He gets up. Amanda remains holding the brush, looking at him, troubled.*]
She plays old phonograph records and—that's about all—[*He glances at himself in the mirror and crosses to the door.*]

AMANDA [*sharply*]: Where are you going?

TOM: I'm going to the movies. [*He goes out the screen door.*]

AMANDA: Not to the movies, every night to the movies! [*She follows quickly to the screen door.*] I don't believe you always go to the movies!

[*He is gone. Amanda looks worriedly after him for a moment. Then vitality and optimism return and she turns from the door, crossing the portieres.*]
Laura! Laura!

[*Laura answers from the kitchenette.*]

LAURA: Yes, Mother.

AMANDA: Let those dishes go and come in front!

[*Laura appears with a dish towel. Amanda speaks to her gaily.*]
Laura, come here and make a wish on the moon!

[*Screen image:* The Moon.]

LAURA [*entering*]: Moon—moon?

AMANDA: A little silver slipper of a moon. Look over your left shoulder, Laura, and make a wish!

[*Laura looks faintly puzzled as if called out of sleep. Amanda seizes her shoulders and turns her at an angle by the door.*]
Now! Now, darling, *wish!*

LAURA: What shall I wish for, Mother?

AMANDA [*her voice trembling and her eyes suddenly filling with tears*]: Happiness! Good fortune!

[*The sound of the violin rises and the stage dims out.*]

SCENE SIX

The light comes up on the fire escape landing. Tom is leaning against the grill, smoking.

[*Screen image:* The high school hero.]

TOM: And so the following evening I brought Jim home to dinner. I had known Jim slightly in high school. In high school Jim was a hero. He had tremendous Irish good nature and vitality with the scrubbed and polished look of white chinaware. He seemed to move in a continual spotlight. He was a star in basketball, captain of the debating club, president of the senior class and the glee club and he sang the lead in the annual light operas. He was always running or bounding, never just walking. He seemed always at the point of defeating the law of gravity. He was shooting with such velocity through his adolescence that you would logically expect him to arrive at nothing short of the White House by the time he was thirty. But Jim apparently ran into more interference after his graduation from Soldan. His speed had definitely slowed. Six years after he left high school he was holding a job that wasn't much better than mine.

[*Screen image:* The Clerk.]

He was the only one at the warehouse with whom I was on friendly terms. I was valuable to him as someone who could remember his former glory, who had seen him win basketball games and the silver cup in debating. He knew of my secret practice of retiring to a cabinet of the washroom to work on poems when business was slack in the warehouse. He called me Shakespeare. And while the other boys in the warehouse regarded me with suspicious hostility, Jim took a humorous attitude toward me. Gradually his attitude affected the others, their hostility wore off and they also began to smile at me as people smile at an oddly fashioned dog who trots across their path at some distance.

I knew that Jim and Laura had known each other at Soldan, and I had heard Laura speak admiringly of his voice. I didn't know if Jim remembered her or not. In high school Laura had been as unobtrusive as Jim had been astonishing. If he did remember Laura, it was not as my sister, for when I asked him to dinner, he grinned and said, "You know, Shakespeare, I never thought of you as having folks!"

He was about to discover that I did. . . .

[*Legend on screen:* "The accent of a coming foot."]

[*The light dims out on Tom and comes up in the Wingfield living room—a delicate lemony light. It is about five on a Friday evening of late spring which comes "scattering poems in the sky."*]

[*Amanda has worked like a Turk in preparation for the gentleman caller. The results are astonishing. The new floor lamp with its rose silk shade is in place, a colored paper lantern conceals the broken light fixture in the ceiling, new billowing white curtains are at the windows, chintz covers are on the chairs and sofa, a pair of new sofa pillows make their initial appearance. Open boxes and tissue paper are scattered on the floor.*]

[*Laura stands in the middle of the room with lifted arms while Amanda crouches before her, adjusting the hem of a new dress, devout and ritualistic. The dress is colored and designed by memory. The arrangement of Laura's hair is changed; it is softer and more becoming. A fragile, unearthly prettiness has come out in Laura: she is like a piece of translucent glass touched by light, given a momentary radiance, not actual, not lasting.*]

AMANDA [*impatiently*]: Why are you trembling?

LAURA: Mother, you've made me so nervous!

AMANDA: How have I made you nervous?

LAURA: By all this fuss! You make it seem so important!

AMANDA: I don't understand you, Laura. You couldn't be satisfied with just sitting home, and yet whenever I try to arrange something for you, you seem to resist it. [*She gets up.*] Now take a look at yourself. No, wait! Wait just a moment—I have an idea!

LAURA: What is it now?

[*Amanda produces two powder puffs which she wraps in handkerchiefs and stuffs in Laura's bosom.*]

LAURA: Mother, what are you doing?

AMANDA: They call them "Gay Deceivers"!

LAURA: I won't wear them!

AMANDA: You will!

LAURA: Why should I?

AMANDA: Because, to be painfully honest, your chest is flat.

LAURA: You make it seem like we were setting a trap.

AMANDA: All pretty girls are a trap, a pretty trap, and men expect them to be.

[*Legend on screen:* "A pretty trap."]

Now look at yourself, young lady. This is the prettiest you will ever be! [*She stands back to admire Laura.*] I've got to fix myself now! You're going to be surprised by your mother's appearance!

[*Amanda crosses through the portieres, humming gaily. Laura moves slowly to the long mirror and stares solemnly at herself. A wind blows the white curtains inward in a slow, graceful motion and with a faint, sorrowful sighing.*]

AMANDA [*from somewhere behind the portieres*]: It isn't dark enough yet.

[*Laura turns slowly before the mirror with a troubled look.*]

[*Legend on screen:* "This is my sister: Celebrate her with strings!" *Music plays.*]

AMANDA [*laughing, still not visible*]: I'm going to show you something. I'm going to make a spectacular appearance!

LAURA: What is it, Mother?

AMANDA: Possess your soul in patience—you will see! Something I've resurrected from that old trunk! Styles haven't changed so terribly much after all. . . . [*She parts the portieres.*] Now just look at your mother! [*She wears a girlish frock of yellowed voile with a blue silk sash. She carries a bunch of jonquils—the legend of her youth is nearly revived. Now she speaks feverishly:*] This is the dress in which I led the cotillion. Won the cakewalk twice at Sunset Hill, wore one Spring to the Governor's Ball in Jackson! See how I sashayed around the ballroom, Laura? [*She raises her skirt and does a mincing step around the room.*] I wore it on Sundays for my gentlemen callers! I had it on the day I met your father. . . . I had malaria fever all that Spring. The change of climate from East Tennessee to the Delta—weakened resistance. I had a little temperature all the time—not enough to be serious—just enough to make me restless and giddy! Invitations poured in—parties all over the Delta! "Stay in bed," said Mother, "you have a fever!"—but I just wouldn't. I took quinine but kept on going, going! Evenings, dances! Afternoons, long, long rides! Picnics—lovely! So lovely, that country in May—all lacy with dogwood, literally flooded with jonquils! That was the spring I had the craze for jonquils. Jonquils became an absolute obsession. Mother said, "Honey, there's no more room for jonquils." And still I kept on bringing in more jonquils. Whenever, wherever I saw them, I'd say, "Stop! Stop! I see jonquils!" I made the young men help me gather the jonquils! It was a joke, Amanda and her jonquils. Finally there were no more vases to hold them, every available space was filled with jonquils. No vases to hold them? All right, I'll hold them myself! And then I—[*She stops in front of the picture. Music plays.*] met your father! Malaria fever and jonquils and then—this—boy. . . . [*She switches on the rose-colored lamp.*] I hope they get here before it starts to rain. [*She crosses the room and places the jonquils in a bowl on the table.*] I gave your brother a little extra change so he and Mr. O'Connor could take the service car home.

LAURA [*with an altered look*]: What did you say his name was?

AMANDA: O'Connor.

LAURA: What is his first name?

AMANDA: I don't remember. Oh, yes, I do. It was—Jim!

[*Laura sways slightly and catches hold of a chair.*]

[*Legend on screen:* "Not, Jim!"]

LAURA [*faintly*]: Not—Jim!

AMANDA: Yes, that was it, it was Jim! I've never known a Jim that wasn't nice! [*The music becomes ominous.*]

LAURA: Are you sure his name is Jim O'Connor?

AMANDA: Yes. Why?

LAURA: Is he the one that Tom used to know in high school?

AMANDA: He didn't say so. I think he just got to know him at the warehouse.

LAURA: There was a Jim O'Connor we both knew in high school—[*then, with effort*] If that is the one that Tom is bringing to dinner—you'll have to excuse me, I won't come to the table.

AMANDA: What sort of nonsense is this?

LAURA: You asked me once if I'd ever liked a boy. Don't you remember I showed you this boy's picture?

AMANDA: You mean the boy you showed me in the year-book?

LAURA: Yes, that boy.

AMANDA: Laura, Laura, were you in love with that boy?

LAURA: I don't know, Mother. All I know is I couldn't sit at the table if it was him!

AMANDA: It won't be him! It isn't the least bit likely. But whether it is or not, you will come to the table. You will not be excused.

LAURA: I'll have to be, Mother.

AMANDA: I don't intend to humor your silliness, Laura. I've had too much from you and your brother, both! So just sit down and compose yourself till they come. Tom has forgotten his key so you'll have to let them in, when they arrive.

LAURA [*panicky*]: Oh, Mother—*you* answer the door!

AMANDA [*lightly*]: I'll be in the kitchen—busy!

LAURA: Oh, Mother, please answer the door, don't make me do it!

AMANDA [*crossing into the kitchenette*]: I've got to fix the dressing for the salmon. Fuss, fuss—silliness!—over a gentleman caller!

[*The door swings shut. Laura is left alone.*]

[*Legend on screen:* "Terror!"]

[*She utters a low moan and turns off the lamp—sits stiffly on the edge of the sofa, knotting her fingers together.*]

[*Legend on screen:* "The Opening of a Door!"]

[*Tom and Jim appear on the fire escape steps and climb to the landing. Hearing their approach, Laura rises with a panicky gesture. She retreats to the portieres. The doorbell rings. Laura catches her breath and touches her throat. Low drums sound.*]

AMANDA [*calling*]: Laura, sweetheart! The door!

[*Laura stares at it without moving.*]

JIM: I think we just beat the rain.

TOM: Uh-huh. [*He rings again, nervously. Jim whistles and fishes for a cigarette.*]

AMANDA [*very, very gaily*]: Laura, that is your brother and Mr. O'Connor! Will you let them in, darling!

[*Laura crosses toward the kitchenettte door.*]

LAURA [*breathlessly*]: Mother—you go to the door!

[*Amanda steps out of the kitchenette and stares furiously at Laura. She points imperiously at the door.*]

LAURA: Please, please!

AMANDA [*in fierce whisper*]: What is the matter with you, you silly thing?

LAURA [*desperately*]: Please, you answer it, *please!*

AMANDA: I told you I wasn't going to humor you, Laura. Why have you chosen this moment to lose your mind?

LAURA: Please, please, please, you go!

AMANDA: You'll have to go to the door because I can't!

LAURA [*despairingly*]: I can't either!

AMANDA: *Why?*

LAURA: I'm *sick!*

AMANDA: I'm sick, too—of your nonsense! Why can't you and your brother be normal people? Fantastic whims and behavior!

[*Tom gives a long ring.*]

Preposterous goings on! Can you give me one reason—[*She calls out lyrically.*] *Coming! Just one second!*—why should you be afraid to open a door? Now you answer it, Laura!

LAURA: Oh, oh, oh . . . [*She returns through the portieres, darts to the Victrola, winds it frantically and turns it on.*]

AMANDA: Laura Wingfield, you march right to that door!

LAURA: *Yes—yes, Mother!*

[*A faraway, scratchy rendition of "Dardanella" softens the air and gives her strength to move through it. She slips to the door and draws it cautiously open. Tom enters with the caller, Jim O'Connor.*]

TOM: Laura, this is Jim. Jim, this is my sister, Laura.

JIM [*stepping inside*]: I didn't know that Shakespeare had a sister!

LAURA [*retreating, stiff and trembling, from the door*]: How—how do you do?

JIM [*heartily, extending his hand*]: Okay!

[*Laura touches it hesitantly with hers.*]

JIM: Your hand's *cold,* Laura!

LAURA: Yes, well—I've been playing the Victrola. . . .

JIM: Must have been playing classical music on it! You ought to play a little hot swing music to warm you up!

LAURA: Excuse me—I haven't finished playing the Victrola. . . . [*She awkwardly hurries into the front room. She pauses a second by the Victrola. Then she catches her breath and darts through the portieres like a frightened deer.*]

JIM [*grinning*]: What was the matter?

TOM: Oh—with Laura? Laura is—terribly shy.

JIM: Shy, huh? It's unusual to meet a shy girl nowadays. I don't believe you ever mentioned you had a sister.

TOM: Well, now you know. I have one. Here is the *Post Dispatch*. You want a piece of it?

JIM: Uh-huh.

TOM: What piece? The comics?

JIM: Sports! [*He glances at it.*] Ole Dizzy Dean is on his bad behavior.

TOM [*uninterested*]: Yeah? [*He lights a cigarette and goes over to the fire-escape door.*]

JIM: Where are *you* going?

TOM: I'm going out on the terrace.

JIM [*going after him*]: You know, Shakespeare—I'm going to sell you a bill of goods!

TOM: What goods?

JIM: A course I'm taking.

TOM: Huh?

JIM: In public speaking! You and me, we're not the warehouse type.

TOM: Thanks—that's good news. But what has public speaking got to do with it?

JIM: It fits you for—executive positions!

TOM: Awww.

JIM: I tell you it's done a helluva lot for me.

[*Image on screen:* Executive at his desk.]

TOM: In what respect?

JIM: In every! Ask yourself what is the difference between you an' me and men in the office down front? Brains?—No!—Ability?—No! Then what? Just one little thing—

TOM: What is that one little thing?

JIM: Primarily it amounts to—social poise! Being able to square up to people and hold your own on any social level!

AMANDA [*from the kitchenette*]: Tom?

TOM: Yes, Mother?

AMANDA: Is that you and Mr. O'Connor?

TOM: Yes, Mother.

AMANDA: Well, you just make yourselves comfortable in there.

TOM: Yes, Mother.

AMANDA: Ask Mr. O'Connor if he would like to wash his hands.

JIM: Aw, no—no—thank you—I took care of that at the warehouse. Tom—

TOM: Yes?

JIM: Mr. Mendoza was speaking to me about you.

TOM: Favorably?

JIM: What do you think?

TOM: Well—

JIM: You're going to be out of a job if you don't wake up.

TOM: I am waking up—

JIM: You show no signs.

TOM: The signs are interior.

[*Image on screen:* The sailing vessel with the Jolly Roger again.]

TOM: I'm planning to change. [*He leans over the fire-escape rail, speaking with quiet exhilaration. The incandescent marquees and signs of the first-run movie houses light his face from across the alley. He looks like a voyager.*] I'm right at the point of committing myself to a future that doesn't include the warehouse and Mr. Mendoza or even a night-school course in public speaking.

JIM: What are you gassing about?

TOM: I'm tired of the movies.

JIM: Movies!

TOM: Yes, movies! Look at them—[*a wave toward the marvels of Grand Avenue*] All of those glamorous people—having adventures—hogging it all, gobbling the whole thing up! You know what happens? People go to the *movies* instead of *moving!* Hollywood characters are supposed to have all the adventures for everybody in America, while everybody in America sits in a dark room and watches them have them! Yes, until there's a war. That's when adventure becomes available to the masses! *Everyone's* dish, not only Gable's! Then the people in the dark room come out of the dark room to have some adventures themselves—goody, goody! It's our turn now, to go to the South Sea Island—to make a safari—to be exotic, far-off! But I'm not patient. I don't want to wait till then. I'm tired of the *movies* and I am *about* to *move!*

JIM [*incredulously*]: Move?

TOM: Yes.

JIM: When?

TOM: Soon!

JIM: Where? When?

[*The music seems to answer the question, while Tom thinks it over. He searches in his pockets.*]

TOM: I'm starting to boil inside. I know I seem dreamy, but inside—well, I'm boiling! Whenever I pick up a shoe, I shudder a little thinking how short life is and what I am doing! Whatever that means, I know it doesn't mean shoes—except as something to wear on a traveler's feet! [*He finds what he has been searching for in his pockets and holds out a paper to Jim.*] Look—

JIM: What?

TOM: I'm a member.

JIM [*reading*]: The Union of Merchant Seamen.

TOM: I paid my dues this month, instead of the light bill.

JIM: You will regret it when they turn the lights off.

TOM: I won't be here.

JIM: How about your mother?

TOM: I'm like my father. The bastard son of a bastard! Did you notice how he's grinning in his picture in there? And he's been absent going on sixteen years!

JIM: You're just talking, you drip. How does your mother feel about it?

TOM: Shhh! Here comes Mother! Mother is not acquainted with my plans!

AMANDA [*coming through the portieres*]: Where are you all?

TOM: On the terrace, Mother.

[*They start inside. She advances to them. Tom is distinctly shocked at her appearance. Even Jim blinks a little. He is making his first contact with girlish Southern vivacity and in spite of the night-school course in public speaking is somewhat thrown off the beam by the unexpected outlay of social charm. Certain responses are attempted by Jim but are swept aside by Amanda's gay laughter and chatter. Tom is embarrassed but after the first shock Jim reacts very warmly. He grins and chuckles, is altogether won over.*]

[*Image on screen:* Amanda as a girl.]

AMANDA [*coyly smiling, shaking her girlish ringlets*]: Well, well, well, so this is Mr. O'Connor. Introductions entirely unnecessary. I've heard so much about you from my boy. I finally said to him, Tom—good gracious!—why don't you bring this paragon to supper? I'd like to meet this nice young man at the warehouse!—instead of just hearing him sing your praises so much! I don't know why my son is so stand-offish—that's not Southern behavior!

Let's sit down and—I think we could stand a little more air in here! Tom, leave the door open. I felt a nice fresh breeze a moment ago. Where has it gone to? Mmm, so warm already! And not quite summer, even. We're going to burn up when summer really gets started. However, we're having—we're having a very light supper. I think light things are better fo' this time of year. The same as light clothes are. Light clothes an' light food are what warm weather calls fo'. You know our blood gets so thick during th' winter—it takes a while fo' us to *adjust* ou'selves—when the season changes . . . . It's come so quick this year. I wasn't prepared. All of a sudden—heavens! Already summer! I ran to the trunk an' pulled out this light dress—terribly old! Historical almost! But feels so good—so good an' co-ol, y' know. . . .

TOM: Mother—

AMANDA: Yes, honey?

TOM: How about—supper?

AMANDA: Honey, you go ask Sister if supper is ready! You know that Sister is in full charge of supper! Tell her you hungry boys are waiting for it. [*to Jim*] Have you met Laura?

JIM: She—

AMANDA: Let you in? Oh, good, you've met already! It's rare for a girl as sweet an' pretty as Laura to be domestic! But Laura is, thank heavens, not only pretty but also very domestic. I'm not at all. I never was a bit. I never could make a thing but angel-food cake. Well, in the South we had so many servants. Gone, gone, gone. All vestiges of gracious living! Gone completely! I wasn't prepared for what the future brought me. All of my gentlemen callers were sons of planters and so of course I assumed that I would be married to one and raise my family on a large piece of land with plenty of servants. But man proposes—and woman accepts the proposal! To vary that old, old saying a little bit—I married no planter! I married a man who worked for the telephone company! That gallantly smiling gentleman over there! [*She points to the picture.*] A telephone man who—fell in love with long-distance! Now he travels and I don't even know where! But what am I going on for about my—tribulations? Tell me yours—I hope you don't have any! Tom?

TOM [*returning*]: Yes, Mother?

AMANDA: Is supper nearly ready?

TOM: It looks to me like supper is on the table.

AMANDA: Let me look—[*She rises prettily and looks through the portieres.*] Oh, lovely! But where is Sister?

TOM: Laura is not feeling well and says that she thinks she'd better not come to the table.

AMANDA: What? Nonsense! Laura? Oh, Laura!

LAURA [*from the kitchenette, faintly*]: Yes, Mother.

AMANDA: You really must come to the table. We won't be seated until you come to the table! Come in, Mr. O'Connor. You sit over there, and I'll. . . . Laura? Laura Wingfield! You're keeping us waiting, honey! We can't say grace until you come to the table!

[*The kitchenette door is pushed weakly open and Laura comes in. She is obviously quite faint, her lips trembling, her eyes wide and staring. She moves unsteadily toward the table.*]

[*Screen legend:* "Terror!"]

[*Outside a summer storm is coming on abruptly. The white curtains billow inward at the windows and there is a sorrowful murmur from the deep blue dusk.*]

[*Laura suddenly stumbles; she catches at a chair with a faint moan.*]

TOM: Laura!

AMANDA: Laura!

[*There is a clap of thunder.*]

[*Screen legend:* "Ah!"]

[*despairingly*] Why, Laura, you *are* ill, darling! Tom, help your sister into the living room, dear! Sit in the living room, Laura—rest on the sofa. Well! [*to Jim as Tom helps his sister to the sofa in the living room*] Standing over the hot stove made her ill! I told her that it was just too warm this evening, but—

[*Tom comes back to the table.*]

Is Laura all right now?

TOM: Yes.

AMANDA: What *is* that? Rain? A nice cool rain has come up! [*She gives Jim a frightened look.*] I think we may—have grace—now . . .

[*Tom looks at her stupidly.*] Tom, honey—you say grace!

TOM: Oh . . . "For these and all thy mercies—"

[*They bow their heads, Amanda stealing a nervous glance at Jim. In the living room Laura, stretched on the sofa, clenches her hand to her lips, to hold back a shuddering sob.*]

God's Holy Name be praised—

[*The scene dims out.*]

SCENE SEVEN

It is half an hour later. Dinner is just being finished in the dining room. Laura is still huddled upon the sofa, her feet drawn under her, her head resting on a pale blue pillow, her eyes wide and mysteriously watchful. The new floor lamp with its shade of rose-colored silk gives a soft, becoming light to her face, bringing out the fragile, unearthly prettiness which usually escapes attention. From outside there is a steady murmur of rain, but it is slackening and soon stops; the air outside becomes pale and luminous as the moon breaks through the clouds. A moment after the curtain rises, the lights in both rooms flicker and go out.

JIM: Hey, there, Mr. Light Bulb!

[*Amanda laughs nervously.*]

[*Legend on screen:* "Suspension of public service."]

AMANDA: Where was Moses when the lights went out? Ha-ha. Do you know the answer to that one, Mr. O'Connor?

JIM: No, Ma'am, what's the answer?

AMANDA: In the dark!

[*Jim laughs appreciatively.*]

Everybody sit still. I'll light the candles. Isn't it lucky we have them on the table? Where's a match? Which of you gentlemen can provide a match?

JIM: Here.

AMANDA: Thank you, Sir.

JIM: Not at all, Ma'am!

AMANDA [*as she lights the candles*]: I guess the fuse has burnt out. Mr. O'Connor, can you tell a burnt-out fuse? I know I can't and Tom is a total loss when it comes to mechanics.

[*They rise from the table and go into the kitchenette, from where their voices are heard.*]

Oh, be careful you don't bump into something. We don't want our gentleman caller to break his neck. Now wouldn't that be a fine howdy-do?

JIM: Ha-ha! Where is the fuse-box?

AMANDA: Right here next to the stove. Can you see anything?

JIM: Just a minute.

AMANDA: Isn't electricity a mysterious thing? Wasn't it Benjamin Franklin who tied a key to a kite? We live in such a mysterious universe, don't we? Some people say that science clears up all the mysteries for us. In my opinion it only creates more! Have you found it yet?

JIM: No, Ma'am. All these fuses look okay to me.

AMANDA: Tom!

TOM: Yes, Mother?

AMANDA: That light bill I gave you several days ago. The one I told you we got the notices about?

[*Legend on screen:* "Ha!"]

TOM: Oh—yeah.

AMANDA: You didn't neglect to pay it by any chance?

TOM: Why, I—

AMANDA: Didn't! I might have known it!

JIM: Shakespeare probably wrote a poem on that light bill, Mrs. Wingfield.

AMANDA: I might have known better than to trust him with it! There's such a high price for negligence in this world!

JIM: Maybe the poem will win a ten-dollar prize!

AMANDA: We'll just have to spend the remainder of the evening in the nineteenth century, before Mr. Edison made the Mazda lamp!

JIM: Candlelight is my favorite kind of light.

AMANDA: That shows you're romantic! But that's no excuse for Tom. Well, we got through dinner. Very considerate of them to let us get through dinner before they plunged us into everlasting darkness, wasn't it, Mr. O'Connor?

JIM: Ha-ha!

AMANDA: Tom, as a penalty for your carelessness you can help me with the dishes.

JIM: Let me give you a hand.

AMANDA: Indeed you will not!

JIM: I ought to be good for something.

AMANDA: Good for something? [*Her tone is rhapsodic.*] Why, Mr. O'Connor, nobody, *nobody's* given me this much entertainment in years—as you have!

JIM: Aw, now, Mrs. Wingfield!

AMANDA: I'm not exaggerating, not one bit! But Sister is all by her lonesome. You go keep her company in the parlor! I'll give you this lovely old candelabrum that used to be on the altar at the Church of the Heavenly Rest. It was melted a little out of shape when the church burnt down. Lightning struck it one spring. Gypsy Jones was holding a revival at the time and he intimated that the church was destroyed because the Episcopalians gave card parties.

JIM: Ha-ha.

AMANDA: And how about you coaxing Sister to drink a little wine? I think it would be good for her! Can you carry both at once?

JIM: Sure. I'm Superman!

AMANDA: Now, Thomas, get into this apron!

[*Jim comes into the dining room, carrying the candelabrum, its candles lighted, in one hand and a glass of wine in the other. The door of the kitchenette swings closed on Amanda's gay laughter; the flickering light approaches the portieres. Laura sits up nervously as Jim enters. She can hardly speak from the almost intolerable strain of being alone with a stranger.*]

[*Screen legend:* "I don't suppose you remember me at all!"]

[*At first, before Jim's warmth overcomes her paralyzing shyness, Laura's voice is thin and breathless, as though she had just run up a steep flight of stairs. Jim's attitude is gently humorous. While the incident is apparently unimportant, it is to Laura the climax of her secret life.*]

JIM: Hello there, Laura.

LAURA [*faintly*]: Hello.

[*She clears her throat.*]

JIM: How are you feeling now? Better?

LAURA: Yes. Yes, thank you.

JIM: This is for you. A little dandelion wine. [*He extends the glass toward her with extravagant gallantry.*]

LAURA: Thank you.

JIM: Drink it—but don't get drunk!

[*He laughs heartily. Laura takes the glass uncertainly; she laughs shyly.*] Where shall I set the candles?

LAURA: Oh—oh, anywhere . . .

JIM: How about here on the floor? Any objections?

LAURA: No.

JIM: I'll spread a newspaper under to catch the drippings. I like to sit on the floor. Mind if I do?

LAURA: Oh, no.

JIM: Give me a pillow?

LAURA: What?

JIM: A pillow!

LAURA: Oh . . . [*She hands him one quickly.*]

JIM: How about you? Don't you like to sit on the floor?

LAURA: Oh—yes.

JIM: Why don't you, then?

LAURA: I—will.

JIM: Take a pillow!

[*Laura does. She sits on the floor on the other side of the candelabrum. Jim crosses his legs and smiles engagingly at her.*] I can't hardly see you sitting way over there.

LAURA: I can—see you.

JIM: I know, but that's not fair, I'm in the limelight.

[*Laura moves her pillow closer.*]

Good! Now I can see you! Comfortable?

LAURA: Yes.

JIM: So am I. Comfortable as a cow! Will you have some gum?

LAURA: No thank you.

JIM: I think that I will indulge, with your permission. [*He musingly unwraps a stick of gum and holds it up.*] Think of the fortune made by the guy that invented the first piece of chewing gum. Amazing, huh? The Wrigley Building is one of the sights of Chicago—I saw it when I went up to the Century of Progress. Did you take in the Century of Progress?

LAURA: No, I didn't.

JIM: Well, it was quite a wonderful exposition. What impressed me most was the Hall of Science. Gives you an idea of what the future will be in America, even more wonderful than the present time is! [*There is a pause. Jim smiles at her.*] Your brother tells me you're shy. Is that right, Laura?

LAURA: I—don't know.

JIM: I judge you to be an old-fashioned type of girl. Well, I think that's a pretty good type to be. Hope you don't think I'm being too personal—do you?

LAURA [*hastily, out of embarrassment*]: I believe I *will* take a piece of gum, if you—don't mind. [*clearing her throat*] Mr. O'Connor, have you—kept up with your singing?

JIM: Singing? Me?

LAURA: Yes. I remember what a beautiful voice you had.

JIM: When did you hear me sing?

[*Laura does not answer, and in the long pause which follows a man's voice is heard singing offstage.*]

VOICE:
O blow, ye winds, heigh-ho,
A-roving I will go!
I'm off to my love
With a boxing glove—
Ten thousand miles away!

JIM: You say you've heard me sing?

LAURA: Oh, yes! Yes, very often . . . I—don't suppose—you remember me—at all?

JIM [*smiling doubtfully*]: You know I have an idea I've seen you before. I had that idea as soon as you opened the door. It seemed almost like I was about to remember your name. But the name that I started to call you—wasn't a name! And so I stopped myself before I said it.

LAURA: Wasn't it—Blue Roses?

JIM [*springing up, grinning*]: Blue Roses! My gosh, yes—Blue Roses! That's what I had on my tongue when you opened the door! Isn't it funny what tricks your memory plays? I didn't connect you with high school somehow or other. But that's where it was; it was high school. I didn't even know you were Shakespeare's sister! Gosh, I'm sorry.

LAURA: I didn't expect you to. You—barely knew me!

JIM: But we did have a speaking acquaintance, huh?

LAURA: Yes, we—spoke to each other.

JIM: When did you recognize me?

LAURA: Oh, right away!

JIM: Soon as I came in the door?

LAURA: When I heard your name I thought it was probably you. I knew that Tom used to know you a little in high school. So when you came in the door—well, then I was—sure.

JIM: Why didn't you *say* something, then?

LAURA [*breathlessly*]: I didn't know what to say, I was—too surprised!

JIM: For goodness sakes! You know, this sure is funny!

LAURA: Yes! Yes, isn't it, though . . .

JIM: Didn't we have a class in something together?

LAURA: Yes, we did.

JIM: What class was that?

LAURA: It was—singing—chorus!

JIM: Aw!

LAURA: I sat across the aisle from you in the Aud.

JIM: Aw.

LAURA: Mondays, Wednesdays, and Fridays.

JIM: Now I remember—you always came in late.

LAURA: Yes, it was so hard for me, getting upstairs. I had that brace on my leg—it clumped so loud!

JIM: I never heard any clumping.

LAURA [*wincing at the recollection*]: To me it sounded like—thunder!

JIM: Well, well, well, I never even noticed.

LAURA: And everybody was seated before I came in. I had to walk in front of all those people. My seat was in the back row. I had to go clumping all the way up the aisle with everyone watching!

JIM: You shouldn't have been self-conscious.

LAURA: I know, but I was. It was always such a relief when the singing started.

JIM: Aw, yes, I've placed you now! I used to call you Blue Roses. How was it that I got started calling you that?

LAURA: I was out of school a little with pleurosis. When I came back you asked me what was the matter. I said I had pleurosis—you thought I said *Blue Roses*. That's what you always called me after that!

JIM: I hope you didn't mind.

LAURA: Oh, no—I liked it. You see, I wasn't acquainted with many—people. . . .

JIM: As I remember you sort of stuck by yourself.

LAURA: I—I—never have had much luck at—making friends.

JIM: I don't see why you wouldn't.

LAURA: Well, I—started out badly.

JIM: You mean being—

LAURA: Yes, it sort of—stood between me—

JIM: You shouldn't have let it!

LAURA: I know, but it did, and—

JIM: You were shy with people!

LAURA: I tried not to be but never could—

JIM: Overcome it?

LAURA: No, I—I never could!

JIM: I guess being shy is something you have to work out of kind of gradually.

LAURA [*sorrowfully*]: Yes—I guess it—

JIM: Takes time!

LAURA: Yes—

JIM: People are not so dreadful when you know them. That's what you have to remember! And everybody has problems, not just you, but practically everybody has got some problems. You think of yourself as having the only problems, as being the only one who is disappointed. But just look around you and you will see lots of people as disappointed as you are. For instance, I hoped when I was going to high school that I would be further along at this time, six years later, than I am now. You remember that wonderful write-up I had in *The Torch?*

LAURA: Yes! [*She rises and crosses to the table.*]

JIM: It said I was bound to succeed in anything I went into!

[*Laura returns with the high school yearbook.*]

Holy Jeez! *The Torch!*

[*He accepts it reverently. They smile across the book with mutual wonder. Laura crouches beside him and they begin to turn the pages. Laura's shyness is dissolving in his warmth.*]

LAURA: Here you are in *The Pirates of Penzance!*

JIM [*wistfully*]: I sang the baritone lead in that operetta.

LAURA [*raptly*]: So—*beautifully!*

JIM [*protesting*]: Aw—

LAURA: Yes, yes—beautifully—beautifully!

JIM: You heard me?

LAURA: All three times!

JIM: No!

LAURA: Yes!

JIM: All three performances?

LAURA [*looking down*]: Yes.

JIM: Why?

LAURA: I—wanted to ask you to—autograph my program.

[*She takes the program from the back of the yearbook and shows it to him.*]

JIM: Why didn't you ask me to?

LAURA: You were always surrounded by your own friends so much that I never had a chance to.

JIM: You should have just—

LAURA: Well, I—thought you might think I was—

JIM: Thought I might think you was—what?

LAURA: Oh—

JIM [*with reflective relish*]: I was beleaguered by females in those days.

LAURA: You were terribly popular!

JIM: Yeah—

LAURA: You had such a—friendly way—

JIM: I was spoiled in high school.

LAURA: Everybody—liked you!

JIM: Including you?

LAURA: I—yes, I—did, too—[*She gently closes the book in her lap.*]

JIM: Well, well, well! Give me that program, Laura.

[*She hands it to him. He signs it with a flourish.*]

There you are—better late than never!

LAURA: Oh, I—what a—surprise!

JIM: My signature isn't worth very much right now. But some day—maybe—it will increase in value! Being disappointed is one thing and being discouraged is something else. I am disappointed but I am not discouraged. I'm twenty-three years old. How old are you?

LAURA: I'll be twenty-four in June.

JIM: That's not old age!

LAURA: No, but—

JIM: You finished high school?

LAURA [*with difficulty*]: I didn't go back.

JIM: You mean you dropped out?

LAURA: I made bad grades in my final examinations. [*She rises and replaces the book and the program on the table. Her voice is strained.*] How is—Emily Meisenbach getting along?

JIM: Oh, that kraut-head!

LAURA: Why do you call her that?

JIM: That's what she was.

LAURA: You're not still—going with her?

JIM: I never see her.

LAURA: It said in the "Personal" section that you were—engaged!

JIM: I know, but I wasn't impressed by that—propaganda!

LAURA: It wasn't—the truth?

JIM: Only in Emily's optimistic opinion!

LAURA: Oh—

[*Legend:* "What have you done since high school?"]

[*Jim lights a cigarette and leans indolently back on his elbows smiling at Laura with a warmth and charm which lights her inwardly with altar candles. She remains by the table, picks up a piece from the glass menagerie collection, and turns it in her hands to cover her tumult.*]

JIM [*after several reflective puffs on his cigarette*]: What have you done since high school?

[*She seems not to hear him.*]

Huh?

[*Laura looks up.*]

I said what have you done since high school, Laura?

LAURA: Nothing much.

JIM: You must have been doing something these six long years.

LAURA: Yes.

JIM: Well, then, such as what?

LAURA: I took a business course at business college—

JIM: How did that work out?

LAURA: Well, not very—well—I had to drop out, it gave me—indigestion—[*Jim laughs gently.*]

JIM: What are you doing now?

LAURA: I don't do anything—much. Oh, please don't think I sit around doing nothing! My glass collection takes up a good deal of time. Glass is something you have to take good care of.

JIM: What did you say—about glass?

LAURA: Collection I said—I have one—[*She clears her throat and turns away again, acutely shy.*]

JIM [*abruptly*]: You know what I judge to be the trouble with you? Inferiority complex! Know what that is? That's what they call it when someone lowrates himself! I understand it because I had it, too. Although my case was not so aggravated as yours seems to be. I had it until I took up public speaking, developed my voice, and learned that I had an aptitude for science. Before that time I never thought of myself as being outstanding in any way whatsoever! Now I've never made a regular study of it, but I have a friend who says I can analyze people better than doctors that make a profession of it. I don't claim that to be necessarily true, but I can sure guess a person's psychology, Laura! [*He takes out his gum.*] Excuse me, Laura. I always take it out when the flavor is gone. I'll use this scrap of paper to wrap it in. I know how it is to get it stuck on a shoe. [*He wraps the gum in paper and puts it in his pocket.*] Yep—that's what I judge to be your principal trouble. A lack of confidence in yourself as a person. You don't have the proper amount of faith in yourself. I'm basing that fact on a number of your remarks and also on certain observations I've made. For instance that clumping you thought was so awful in high school. You say that you even dreaded to walk into class. You see what you did? You dropped out of school, you gave up an education because of a clump, which as far as I know was practically nonexistent! A little physical defect is what you have. Hardly noticeable even! Magnified thousands of times by imagination! You know what my strong advice to you is? Think of yourself as *superior* in some way!

LAURA: In what way would I think?

JIM: Why, man alive, Laura! Just look about you a little. What do you see? A world full of common people! All of 'em born and all of 'em going to die! Which of them has one-tenth of your good points! Or mine! Or anyone else's, as far as that goes—gosh! Everybody excels in some one thing. Some in many! [*He unconsciously glances at himself in the mirror.*] All you've got to do is to discover in *what!* Take me, for instance. [*He adjusts his tie at the mirror.*] My interest happens to lie in electro-dynamics. I'm taking a course in radio engineering at night school, Laura, on top of a fairly responsible job at the warehouse. I'm taking that course and studying public speaking.

LAURA: Ohhhh.

JIM: Because I believe in the future of television! [*turning his back to her.*] I wish to be ready to go up right along with it. Therefore I'm planning to get in on the ground floor. In fact I've already made the right connections and all that remains is for the industry itself to get under way! Full steam—[*His eyes are starry.*] *Knowledge*—Zzzzzp! *Money*—Zzzzzp!—*Power!* That's the cycle democracy is built on!

[*His attitude is convincingly dynamic. Laura stares at him, even her shyness eclipsed in her absolute wonder. He suddenly grins.*]

I guess you think I think a lot of myself?

LAURA: No—o-o-o, I—

JIM: Now how about you? Isn't there something you take more interest in than anything else?

LAURA: Well, I do—as I said—have my—glass collection—

[*A peal of girlish laughter rings from the kitchenette.*]

JIM: I'm not right sure I know what you're talking about. What kind of glass is it?

LAURA: Little articles of it, they're ornaments mostly! Most of them are little animals made out of glass, the tiniest little animals in the world. Mother calls them the glass menagerie! Here's an example of one, if you'd like to see it! This one is one of the oldest. It's nearly thirteen.

[*Music:* "The Glass Menagerie."]

Oh, be careful—if you breathe, it breaks!

JIM: I'd better not take it. I'm pretty clumsy with things.

LAURA: Go on, I trust you with him! [*She places the piece in his palm.*] There now—you're holding him gently! Hold him over the light, he loves the light! You see how the light shines through him?

JIM: It sure does shine!

LAURA: I shouldn't be partial, but he is my favorite one.

JIM: What kind of a thing is this one supposed to be?

LAURA: Haven't you noticed the single horn on his forehead?

JIM: A unicorn, huh?

LAURA: Mmmm-hmmm!

JIM: Unicorns—aren't they extinct in the modern world?

LAURA: I know!

JIM: Poor little fellow, he must feel sort of lonesome.

LAURA [*smiling*]: Well, if he does, he doesn't complain about it. He stays on a shelf with some horses that don't have horns and all of them seem to get along nicely together.

JIM: How do you know?

LAURA [*lightly*]: I haven't heard any arguments among them!

JIM [*grinning*]: No arguments, huh? Well, that's a pretty good sign! Where shall I set him!

LAURA: Put him on the table. They all like a change of scenery once in a while!

JIM: Well, well, well, well—[*He places the glass piece on the table, then raises his arms and stretches.*] Look how big my shadow is when I stretch!

LAURA: Oh, oh, yes—it stretches across the ceiling!

JIM [*crossing to the door*]: I think it's stopped raining. [*He opens the fire-escape door and the background music changes to a dance tune.*] Where does the music come from?

LAURA: From the Paradise Dance Hall across the alley.

JIM: How about cutting the rug a little, Miss Wingfield?

LAURA: Oh, I—

JIM: Or is your program filled up? Let me have a look at it. [*He grasps an imaginary card.*] Why, every dance is taken! I'll just have to scratch some out.

[*Waltz music:* "La Golondrina."]

Ahhh, a waltz! [*He executes some sweeping turns by himself, then holds his arms toward Laura.*]

LAURA [*breathlessly*]: I—can't dance!

JIM: There you go, that inferiority stuff!

LAURA: I've never danced in my life!

JIM: Come on, try!

LAURA: Oh, but I'd step on you!

JIM: I'm not made out of glass.

LAURA: How—how—how do we start?

JIM: Just leave it to me. You hold your arms out a little.

LAURA: Like this?

JIM [*taking her in his arms*]: A little bit higher. Right. Now don't tighten up, that's the main thing about it—relax.

LAURA [*laughing breathlessly*]: It's hard not to.

JIM: Okay.

LAURA: I'm afraid you can't budge me.

JIM: What do you bet I can't? [*He swings her into motion.*]

LAURA: Goodness, yes, you can!

JIM: Let yourself go, now, Laura, just let yourself go.

LAURA: I'm—

JIM: Come on!

LAURA: —trying!

JIM: Not so stiff—easy does it!

LAURA: I know but I'm—

JIM: Loosen th' backbone! There now, that's a lot better.

LAURA: Am I?

JIM: Lots, lots better! [*He moves her about the room in a clumsy waltz.*]

LAURA: Oh, my!

JIM: Ha-ha!

LAURA: Oh, my goodness!

JIM: Ha-ha-ha!

[*They suddenly bump into the table, and the glass piece on it falls to the floor. Jim stops the dance.*]

What did we hit on?

LAURA: Table.

JIM: Did something fall off it? I think—

LAURA: Yes.

JIM: I hope that it wasn't the little glass horse with the horn!

LAURA: Yes. [*She stoops to pick it up.*]

JIM: Aw, aw, aw. It is broken?

LAURA: Now it is just like all the other horses.

JIM: It's lost its—

LAURA: Horn! It doesn't matter. Maybe it's a blessing in disguise.

JIM: You'll never forgive me. I bet that that was your favorite piece of glass.

LAURA: I don't have favorites much. It's no tragedy, Freckles. Glass breaks so easily. No matter how careful you are. The traffic jars the shelves and things fall off them.

JIM: Still I'm awfully sorry that I was the cause.

LAURA [*smiling*]: I'll just imagine he had an operation. The horn was removed to make him feel less—freakish!

[*They both laugh.*]

Now he will feel more at home with the other horses, the ones that don't have horns.

JIM: Ha-ha, that's very funny! [*Suddenly he is serious.*] I'm glad to see that you have a sense of humor. You know—you're—well—very different! Surprisingly different from anyone else I know! [*His voice becomes soft and hesitant with a genuine feeling.*] Do you mind me telling you that?

[*Laura is abashed beyond speech.*]

I mean it in a nice way—

[*Laura nods shyly, looking away.*]

You make me feel sort of—I don't know how to put it! I'm usually pretty good at expressing things, but—this is something that I don't know how to say!

[*Laura touches her throat and clears it—turns the broken unicorn in her hands. His voice becomes softer.*]

Has anyone ever told you that you were pretty?

[*There is a pause, and the music rises slightly. Laura looks up slowly, with wonder, and shakes her head.*]

Well, you are! In a very different way from anyone else. And all the nicer because of the difference, too.

[*His voice becomes low and husky. Laura turns away, nearly faint with the novelty of her emotions.*]

I wish that you were my sister. I'd teach you to have some confidence in yourself. The different people are not like other people, but being different is nothing to be ashamed of. Because other people are not such wonderful people. They're one hundred times one thousand. You're one times one! They walk all over the earth. You just stay here. They're common as—weeds, but—you—well, you're—*Blue Roses!*

[*Image on screen:* Blue Roses.]

[*The music changes.*]

LAURA: But blue is wrong for—roses. . . .

JIM: It's right for you! You're—pretty!

LAURA: In what respect am I pretty?

JIM: In all respects—believe me! Your eyes—your hair—are pretty! Your hands are pretty! [*He catches hold of her hand.*] You think I'm making this up because I'm invited to dinner and have to be nice. Oh, I could do that! I could put on an act for you, Laura, and say lots of things without being very sincere. But this time I am. I'm talking to you sincerely. I happened to notice you had this inferiority complex that keeps you from feeling comfortable with people. Somebody needs to build your confidence up and make you proud instead of shy and turning away and—blushing. Somebody—ought to—*kiss* you, Laura!

[*His hand slips slowly up her arm to her shoulder as the music swells tumultuously. He suddenly turns her about and kisses her on the lips. When he releases her, Laura sinks on the sofa with a bright, dazed look. Jim backs away and fishes in his pocket for a cigarette.*]

[*Legend on screen:* "A souvenir."]

Stumblejohn!

[*He lights the cigarette, avoiding her look. There is a peal of girlish laughter from

Amanda in the kitchenette. Laura slowly raises and opens her hand. It still contains the little broken glass animal. She looks at it with a tender, bewildered expression.]

Stumblejohn! I shouldn't have done that—that was way off the beam. You don't smoke, do you?

[*She looks up, smiling, not hearing the question. He sits beside her rather gingerly. She looks at him speechlessly—waiting. He coughs decorously and moves a little farther aside as he considers the situation and senses her feelings, dimly, with perturbation. He speaks gently.*]

Would you—care for a—mint?

[*She doesn't seem to hear him but her look grows brighter even.*]

Peppermint? Life Saver? My pocket's a regular drugstore—wherever I go. . . . [*He pops a mint in his mouth. Then he gulps and decides to make a clean breast of it. He speaks slowly and gingerly.*] Laura, you know, if I had a sister like you, I'd do the same thing as Tom. I'd bring out fellows and—introduce her to them. The right type of boys—of a type to—appreciate her. Only—well—he made a mistake about me. Maybe I've got no call to be saying this. That may not have been the idea in having me over. But what if it was? There's nothing wrong about that. The only trouble is that in my case—I'm not in a situation to—do the right thing. I can't take down your number and say I'll phone. I can't call up next week and—ask for a date. I thought I had better explain the situation in case you—misunderstood it and—I hurt your feelings. . . .

[*There is a pause. Slowly, very slowly, Laura's look changes, her eyes returning slowly from his to the glass figure in her palm. Amanda utters another gay laugh in the kitchenette.*]

LAURA [*faintly*]: You—won't—call again?

JIM: No, Laura, I can't. [*He rises from the sofa.*] As I was just explaining, I've—got strings on me. Laura, I've—been going steady! I go out all the time with a girl named Betty. She's a home-girl like you, and Catholic, and Irish, and in a great many ways we—get along fine. I met her last summer on a moonlight boat trip up the river to Alton, on the *Majestic.* Well—right away from the start it was—love!

[*Legend:* Love!]

[*Laura sways slightly forward and grips the arm of the sofa. He fails to notice, now enrapt in his own comfortable being.*]

Being in love has made a new man of me!

[*Leaning stiffly forward, clutching the arm of the sofa, Laura struggles visibly with her storm. But Jim is oblivious; she is a long way off.*]

The power of love is really pretty tremendous! Love is something that—changes the whole world, Laura!

[*The storm abates a little and Laura leans back. He notices her again.*]

It happened that Betty's aunt took sick, she got a wire and had to go to Centralia. So Tom—when he asked me to dinner—I naturally just accepted the invitation, not knowing that you—that he—that I—[*He stops awkwardly.*] Huh—I'm a stumblejohn!

[*He flops back on the sofa. The holy candles on the altar of Laura's face have been snuffed out. There is a look of almost infinite desolation. Jim glances at her uneasily.*]

I wish that you would—say something.

[*She bites her lip which was trembling and then bravely smiles. She opens her hand again on the broken glass figure. Then she gently takes his hand and raises it level with her own. She carefully places the unicorn in the palm of his hand, then pushes his fingers closed upon it.*]

What are you—doing that for? You want me to have him? Laura?

[*She nods.*]

What for?

LAURA: A—souvenir. . . .

[*She rises unsteadily and crouches beside the Victrola to wind it up.*]

[*Legend on screen:* "Things have a way of turning out so badly!" *Or image:* "Gentleman caller waving goodbye—gaily."]

[*At this moment Amanda rushes brightly back into the living room. She bears a pitcher of fruit punch in an old-fashioned cut-glass pitcher, and a plate of macaroons. The plate has a gold border and poppies painted on it.*]

AMANDA: Well, well, well! Isn't the air delightful after the shower! I've made you children a little liquid refreshment.

[*She turns gaily to Jim.*] Jim, do you know that song about lemonade?

"Lemonade, lemonade
Made in the shade and stirred with a spade—
Good enough for any old maid!"

JIM [*uneasily*]: Ha-ha! No—I never heard it.

AMANDA: Why, Laura! You look so serious!

JIM: We were having a serious conversation.

AMANDA: Good! Now you're better acquainted!

JIM [*uncertainly*]: Ha-ha! Yes.

AMANDA: You modern young people are much more serious-minded than my generation. I was so gay as a girl!

JIM: You haven't changed, Mrs. Wingfield.

AMANDA: Tonight I'm rejuvenated! The gaiety of the occasion, Mr. O'Connor! [*She tosses her head with a peal of laughter, spilling some lemonade.*] Oooo! I'm baptizing myself!

JIM: Here—let me—

AMANDA [*setting the pitcher down*]: There now. I discovered we had some maraschino cherries. I dumped them in, juice and all!

JIM: You shouldn't have gone to that trouble, Mrs. Wingfield.

AMANDA: Trouble, trouble? Why, it was loads of fun! Didn't you hear me cutting up in the kitchen? I bet your ears were burning! I told Tom how outdone with him I was for keeping you to himself so long a time! He should have brought you over much, much sooner! Well, now that you've found your way, I want you to be a very frequent caller! Not just occasional but all the time. Oh, we're going to have a lot of gay times together! I see them coming! Mmm, just breathe that air! So fresh, and the moon's so pretty! I'll skip back out—I know where my place is when young folks are having a—serious conversation!

JIM: Oh, don't go out, Mrs. Wingfield. The fact of the matter is I've got to be going.

AMANDA: Going, now? You're joking! Why, it's only the shank of the evening, Mr. O'Connor.

JIM: Well, you know how it is.

AMANDA: You mean you're a young workingman and have to keep workingmen's hours. We'll let you off early tonight. But only on the condition that next time you stay later. What's the best night for you? Isn't Saturday night the best night for you workingmen?

JIM: I have a couple of time-clocks to punch, Mrs. Wingfield. One at morning, another one at night!

AMANDA: My, but you *are* ambitious! You work at night, too?

JIM: No, Ma'am, not work but—Betty!

[*He crosses deliberately to pick up his hat. The band at the Paradise Dance Hall goes into a tender waltz.*]

AMANDA: Betty? Betty? Who's—Betty!

[*There is an ominous cracking sound in the sky.*]

JIM: Oh, just a girl. The girl I go steady with!

[*He smiles charmingly. The sky falls.*]

[*Legend:* "The Sky Falls."]

AMANDA [*a long-drawn exhalation*]: Ohhhh . . . Is it a serious romance, Mr. O'Connor?

JIM: We're going to be married the second Sunday in June.

AMANDA: Ohhhh—how nice! Tom didn't mention that you were engaged to be married.

JIM: The cat's not out of the bag at the warehouse yet. You know how they are. They call you Romeo and stuff like that. [*He stops at the oval mirror to put on his hat. He carefully shapes the brim and the crown to give a discreetly dashing effect.*] It's been a wonderful evening, Mrs. Wingfield. I guess this is what they mean by Southern hospitality.

AMANDA: It really wasn't anything at all.

JIM: I hope it don't seem like I'm rushing off. But I promised Betty I'd pick her up at the Wabash depot, an' by the time I get my jalopy down there her train'll be in. Some women are pretty upset if you keep 'em waiting.

AMANDA: Yes, I know—the tyranny of women! [*She extends her hand.*] Goodbye, Mr. O'Connor. I wish you luck—and happiness—and success! All three of them, and so does Laura! Don't you, Laura?

LAURA: Yes!

JIM [*taking Laura's hand*]: Goodbye, Laura. I'm certainly going to treasure that souvenir. And don't you forget the good advice I gave you. [*He raises his voice to a cheery shout.*] So long, Shakespeare! Thanks again, ladies. Good night!

[*He grins and ducks jauntily out. Still barely grimacing, Amanda closes the door on the gentleman caller. Then she turns back to the room with a puzzled expression. She and Laura don't dare to face each other. Laura crouches beside the Victrola to wind it.*]

AMANDA [*faintly*]: Things have a way of turning out so badly. I don't believe that I would play the Victrola. Well, well—well! Our gentleman caller was engaged to be married! [*She raises her voice.*] Tom!

TOM [*from the kitchenette*]: Yes, Mother?

AMANDA: Come in here a minute. I want to tell you something awfully funny.

TOM [*entering with a macaroon and a glass of the lemonade*]: Has the gentleman caller gotten away already?

AMANDA: The gentleman caller has made an early departure. What a wonderful joke you played on us!

TOM: How do you mean?

AMANDA: You didn't mention that he was engaged to be married.

TOM: Jim? Engaged?

AMANDA: That's what he just informed us.

TOM: I'll be jiggered! I didn't know about that.

AMANDA: That seems very peculiar.

TOM: What's peculiar about it?

AMANDA: Didn't you call him your best friend down at the warehouse?

TOM: He is, but how did I know?

AMANDA: It seems extremely peculiar that you wouldn't know your best friend was going to be married!

TOM: The warehouse is where I work, not where I know things about people!

AMANDA: You don't know things anywhere! You live in a dream; you manufacture illusions!

[*He crosses to the door.*]

Where are you going?

TOM: I'm going to the movies.

AMANDA: That's right, now that you've had us make such fools of ourselves. The effort, the preparations, all the expense! The new floor lamp, the rug, the clothes for Laura! All for what? To entertain some other girl's fiancé! Go to the movies, go! Don't think about us, a mother deserted, an unmarried sister who's crippled and has no job! Don't let anything interfere with your selfish pleasure! Just go, go, go—to the movies!

TOM: All right, I will! The more you shout about my selfishness to me the quicker I'll go, and I won't go to the movies!

AMANDA: Go, then! Go to the moon—you selfish dreamer!

[*Tom smashes his glass on the floor. He plunges out on the fire escape, slamming the door. Laura screams in fright. The dance-hall music becomes louder. Tom stands on the fire escape, gripping the rail. The moon breaks through the storm clouds, illuminating his face.*]

[*Legend on screen:* "And so goodbye . . ."]

[*Tom's closing speech is timed with what is happening inside the house. We see, as though through soundproof glass, that Amanda appears to be making a comforting speech to Laura, who is huddled upon the sofa. Now that we cannot hear the mother's speech, her silliness is gone and she has dignity and tragic beauty. Laura's hair hides her face until, at the end of the speech, she lifts her head to smile at her mother. Amanda's gestures are slow and graceful, almost dancelike, as she comforts her daughter. At the end of her speech she glances a moment at the father's picture—then withdraws through the portieres. At the close of Tom's speech, Laura blows out the candles, ending the play.*]

TOM: I didn't go to the moon, I went much further—for time is the longest distance between two places. Not long after that I was fired for writing a poem on the lid of a shoe-box. I left Saint Louis. I descended the steps of this fire escape for a last time and followed, from then on, in my father's footsteps, attempting to find in motion what was lost in space. I traveled around a great deal. The cities swept about me like dead leaves, leaves that were brightly colored but torn away from the branches. I would have stopped, but I was pursued by something. It always came upon me unawares, taking me altogether by surprise. Perhaps it was a familiar bit of music. Perhaps it was only a piece of transparent glass. Perhaps I am walking along a street at night, in some strange city, before I have found companions. I pass the lighted window of a shop where perfume is sold. The window is filled with pieces of colored glass, tiny transparent bottles in delicate colors, like bits of a shattered rainbow. Then all at once my sister touches my shoulder. I turn around and look into her eyes. Oh, Laura, Laura, I tried to leave you behind me, but I am more faithful than I intended to be! I reach for a cigarette, I cross the street, I run into the movies or a bar, I buy a drink, I speak to the nearest stranger—anything that can blow your candles out!

[*Laura bends over the candles.*]

For nowadays the world is lit by lightning! Blow out your candles, Laura—and so goodbye . . . .

[*She blows the candles out.*]

1945

Theodore Roethke 1908–1963

Theodore Roethke died at the height of his creative powers, but fame and honor had come to him well before his death. After receiving Guggenheim Fellowships in 1946 and 1950, he was awarded a Pulitzer Prize in 1954 for The Waking: Poems, 1933–1953 *(1953).* Words for the Wind *(1958) received a Bollingen Prize in 1958 and the Edna St. Vincent Millay Prize in 1959. And acclaim for his work continued after his death:* The Far Field, *published posthumously in 1964, won the National Book Award in 1965. Since the publication of his* Collected Poems *(1966), and as critics have looked more deeply into Roethke's poems, his reputation has continued to rise.*

Roethke was born in Saginaw, Michigan, where a dingy industrial atmosphere contrasted sharply with the loveliness of nearby lakes and streams, woods and farmlands, scenes that aroused in him a mystical reverence for nature. His father was a florist, and the strange paradoxes Roethke perceived in the plant world of his father's greenhouse—where death and life mingled in a weird, grotesque kind of beauty—helped shape his poetic sensibility and provided him with a rich source of imagery.

After taking his B.A. in 1929 at the University of Michigan, Roethke began a career in college and university teaching that took him first to Lafayette College in Pennsylvania, from 1931 to 1935, then, after he completed his M.A. at Michigan in 1936, to Pennsylvania State College, where he remained until 1943. During World War II he taught at Bennington College, and in 1947 he took a position at the University of Washington, Seattle, where he remained for the rest of his life.

Roethke's development as a poet began in his early twenties, soon after he graduated from the University of Michigan, but he was well into his thirties when his first volume, Open House, *appeared in 1941. His poems may be divided broadly into two groups: first, those that are orthodox in form, rational in theme, ironic in tone; and second, poems that utilize free forms, reflecting the influence of Whitman ("Be with me, Whitman, maker of catalogues") and the romantic transcendentalism of Emerson. He shared Emerson's belief in the inherent presence of spirit in nature, but he also saw the dark side of nature that Emerson tended to explain away. The impact of T. S. Eliot on Roethke was chiefly formal and technical, evident particularly in Roethke's efforts to effect "something other than the usual in old forms." From the whimsy of Roethke's delightful "Nonsense Poems" to the irony of the pieces in* The Far Field, *his vision of life and poetic style remained uniquely his own.*

FURTHER READING: *On the Poet and His Craft, Selected Prose of Theodore Roethke,* ed. R. Mills, 1965; *Selected Letters of Theodore Roethke,* ed. R. Mills, 1968; A. Seagar, *The Glass House, The Life of Theodore Roethke,* 1968; *Straw from Fire, From the Notebooks of Theodore Roethke,* ed. D. Wagoner, 1972; G. Wolff, *Theodore Roethke,* 1981; N. Chaney, *Theodore Roethke, The Poetics of Wonder,* 1981; L. Ross-Bryant, *Theodore Roethke, Poetry of the Earth,* 1981; N. Bowers, *Theodore Roethke, The Journey from I to Otherwise,* 1982; R. Stiffler, *Theodore Roethke, The Poet and His Critics,* 1986; W. Kalaidjian, *Understanding Theodore Roethke,* 1987; *Theodore Roethke,* ed. H. Bloom, 1988; P. Balakian, *Theodore Roethke's Far Fields, The Evolution of His Poetry,* 1989. D. Bogen, *A Necessary Order, Theodore Roethke and the Writing Process,* 1991; R. Kusch, *My Toughest Mentor, Theodore Roethke and William Carlos Williams,* 1999.

TEXT: *The Collected Poems of Theodore Roethke,* 1966.

OPEN HOUSE

My secrets cry aloud.
I have no need for tongue.
My heart keeps open house,
My doors are widely swung.
An epic of the eyes
My love, with no disguise.

My truths are all foreknown,
This anguish self-revealed.
I'm naked to the bone,
With nakedness my shield.
Myself is what I wear:
I keep the spirit spare.

The anger will endure,
The deed will speak the truth
In language strict and pure.
I stop the lying mouth:
Rage warps my clearest cry
To witless agony.

1936 1936, 1941

CUTTINGS

Sticks-in-a-drowse droop over sugary loam,
Their intricate stem-fur dries;
But still the delicate slips keep coaxing up water;
The small cells bulge;

One nub of growth
Nudges a sand-crumb loose,
Pokes through a musty sheath
Its pale tendrilous horn.
1943–1944 1948

CUTTINGS (LATER)

This urge, wrestle, resurrection of dry sticks,
Cut stems struggling to put down feet,
What saint strained so much,
Rose on such lopped limbs to a new life?

I can hear, underground, that sucking and sobbing,
In my veins, in my bones I feel it,—
The small waters seeping upward,
The tight grains parting at last.
When sprouts break out,
Slippery as fish,
I quail, lean to beginnings, sheath-wet.
1943–1944 1948

ROOT CELLAR

Nothing would sleep in that cellar, dank as a ditch,
Bulbs broke out of boxes hunting for chinks in the dark,
Shoots dangled and drooped,
Lolling obscenely from mildewed crates,
Hung down long yellow evil necks, like tropical snakes.
And what a congress of stinks!—
Roots ripe as old bait,
Pulpy stems, rank, silo-rich,
Leaf-mold, manure, lime, piled against slippery planks.
Nothing would give up life:
Even the dirt kept breathing a small breath.
1943 1943, 1948

MY PAPA'S WALTZ

The whiskey on your breath
Could make a small boy dizzy;
But I hung on like death:
Such waltzing was not easy.

We romped until the pans
Slid from the kitchen shelf;
My mother's countenance
Could not unfrown itself.

The hand that held my wrist
Was battered on one knuckle;
At every step you missed
My right ear scraped a buckle.

You beat time on my head
With a palm caked hard by dirt,
Then waltzed me off to bed
Still clinging to your shirt.
1942 1942, 1948

Elizabeth Bishop 1911–1979

Elizabeth Bishop was born in Worcester, Massachusetts, and raised in Nova Scotia, Canada, and Boston, Massachusetts. She attended Vassar College, where she majored in English literature, and in her graduation year, 1934, she met Marianne Moore, whose poetry of closely observed detail was a significant influence on Bishop's work. She traveled widely in Europe and South America (from 1952 to 1969 she lived in Brazil), and some of the themes and details of her poetry are responses to her travels and to her early childhood experiences in New England and Canada.

Her first volume, North and South, *appeared in 1946. For her* Poems *(1955) she received a Pulitzer Prize. A third volume of poetry,* Questions of Travel *(1965), was followed by* The Complete Poems *(1969), which received a National Book Award. Her last book of poems was* Geography III *(1976). In her poetry, Bishop often functioned as an impersonal observer capable of detachment and understanding at the same time. She used subtle rhythms, unlikely rhymes, and the impressionist's technique of implication and suggestion. She had a painter's eye for surfaces and appearances, yet her portrayals of the stark landscapes of the matter-of-fact world frequently evolved into dreamlike sequences, contrasting the commonsense world of everyday reality and the world of impressions and the imagination.*

FURTHER READING: *Elizabeth Bishop and Her Art,* ed. L. Schwartz and S. Estes, 1983; *The Collected Prose,* 1984; T. Travisano, *Elizabeth Bishop, Her Artistic Development,* 1988; R. Parker, *The Unbeliever, The Poetry of Elizabeth Bishop,* 1988; B. Costello, *Elizabeth Bishop,*

Questions of Mastery, 1991; L. Goldensohn, *Elizabeth Bishop, The Biography of a Poetry,* 1992; C. Doreski, *Elizabeth Bishop, The Restraints of Language,* 1993; *One Art, Letters by Elizabeth Bishop,* ed. R. Giroux, 1994; G. Fountain and B. Brazeau, *Remembering Elizabeth Bishop,* 1994; S. McCabe, *Elizabeth Bishop, Her Poetics of Loss,* 1994; M. Lombardi, *The Body and the Song,* 1995; D. Kalstone, *Becoming a Poet,* 1997; B. Miller, *Elizabeth Bishop; Life and the Memory of It,* 1997; *Divisions of the Heart, Elizabeth Bishop and the Art of Memory and Place,* ed. S. Barry, G. Davies, and P. Sanger, 2001; *Elizabeth Bishop,* ed. H. Bloom, 2002; K. Fortuny, *Elizabeth Bishop, The Art of Travel,* 2003.

TEXT: *Elizabeth Bishop, The Complete Poems, 1927–1979,* 1983.

A MIRACLE FOR BREAKFAST

At six o'clock we were waiting for coffee,
waiting for coffee and the charitable crumb
that was going to be served from a certain balcony,
—like kings of old, or like a miracle.
It was still dark. One foot of the sun
steadied itself on a long ripple in the river.

The first ferry of the day had just crossed the river.
It was so cold we hoped that the coffee
would be very hot, seeing that the sun
was not going to warm us; and that the crumb
would be a loaf each, buttered, by a miracle.
At seven a man stepped out on the balcony.

He stood for a minute alone on the balcony
looking over our heads toward the river.
A servant handed him the makings of a miracle,
consisting of one lone cup of coffee
and one roll, which he proceeded to crumb,
his head, so to speak, in the clouds—along with the sun.

Was the man crazy? What under the sun
was he trying to do, up there on his balcony!
Each man received one rather hard crumb,
which some flicked scornfully into the river,
and, in a cup, one drop of the coffee.
Some of us stood around, waiting for the miracle.

I can tell what I saw next; it was not a miracle.
A beautiful villa stood in the sun
and from its doors came the smell of hot coffee.
In front, a baroque white plaster balcony
added by birds, who nest along the river,
—I saw it with one eye close to the crumb—

and galleries and marble chambers. My crumb
my mansion, made for me by a miracle,

through ages, by insects, birds, and the river
working the stone. Every day, in the sun,
at breakfast time I sit on my balcony
with my feet up, and drink gallons of coffee.

We licked up the crumb and swallowed the coffee.
A window across the river caught the sun
as if the miracle were working, on the wrong balcony.

1937, 1946

OVER 2,000 ILLUSTRATIONS AND A COMPLETE CONCORDANCE

Thus should have been our travels:
serious, engravable.
The Seven Wonders of the World are tired
and a touch familiar, but the other scenes,
innumerable, though equally sad and still,
are foreign. Often the squatting Arab,
or group of Arabs, plotting, probably,
against our Christian Empire,
while one apart, with outstretched arm and hand
points to the Tomb, the Pit, the Sepulcher.[1]
The branches of the date-palms look like files.
The cobbled courtyard, where the Well is dry,
is like a diagram, the brickwork conduits
are vast and obvious, the human figure
far gone in history or theology,
gone with its camel or its faithful horse.
Always the silence, the gesture, the specks of birds
suspended on invisible threads above the Site,
or the smoke rising solemnly, pulled by threads.
Granted a page alone or a page made up
of several scenes arranged in cattycornered rectangles
or circles set on stippled gray,
granted a grim lunette,[2]
caught in the toils of an initial letter,
when dwelt upon, they all resolve themselves.
The eye drops, weighted, through the lines
the burin[3] made, the lines that move apart
like ripples above sand,
dispersing storms, God's spreading fingerprint,
and painfully, finally, that ignite
in watery prismatic white-and-blue.
Entering the Narrows at St. Johns[4]

[1]The tomb, enclosed in the Church of the Holy Sepulcher in Jerusalem, where Jesus is said to have been buried.
[2]A crescent-shaped or semicircular form. [3]Engraver's tool.
[4]Entrance to St. John's Harbor in Newfoundland, Canada.

the touching bleat of goats reached to the ship.
We glimpsed them, reddish, leaping up the cliffs
among the fog-soaked weeds and butter-and-eggs.
And at St. Peter's[5] the wind blew and the sun shone madly.
Rapidly, purposefully, the Collegians marched in lines,
crisscrossing the great square with black,[6] like ants.
In Mexico the dead man lay
in a blue arcade; the dead volcanoes
glistened like Easter lilies.
The jukebox went on playing "Ay, Jalisco!"[7]
And at Volubilis[8] there were beautiful poppies
splitting the mosaics; the fat old guide made eyes.
In Dingle[9] harbor a golden length of evening
the rotting hulks held up their dripping plush.
The Englishwoman poured tea, informing us
that the Duchess was going to have a baby.
And in the brothels of Marrakesh[10]
the little pockmarked prostitutes
balanced their tea-trays on their heads
and did their belly-dances; flung themselves
naked and giggling against our knees,
asking for cigarettes. It was somewhere near there
I saw what frightened me most of all:
A holy grave, not looking particularly holy,
one of a group under a keyhole-arched stone baldaquin[11]
open to every wind from the pink desert.
An open, gritty, marble trough, carved solid
with exhortation, yellowed
as scattered cattle-teeth;
half-filled with dust, not even the dust
of the poor prophet paynim[12] who once lay there.
In a smart burnoose[13] Khadour looked on amused.

Everything only connected by "and" and "and."
Open the book. (The gilt rubs off the edges
of the pages and pollinates the fingertips.)
Open the heavy book. Why couldn't we have seen
this old Nativity[14] while we were at it?
—the dark ajar, the rocks breaking with light,
an undisturbed, unbreathing flame,
colorless, sparkless, freely fed on straw,
and, lulled within, a family with pets,
—and looked and looked our infant sight away.

1948, 1955

[5]Church in Rome.

[6]I.e., files of seminary students, wearing black robes, crossing St. Peter's Square from their residential colleges to their university classrooms.

[7]Jalisco: state in Mexico where mariachi music originated.

[8]Ancient Roman city in North Africa, now a ruin. [9]Town in southwest Ireland.

[10]City in Morocco. [11]Ornamental structure, resembling a canopy, built over a sacred object.

[12]A pagan, a nonbeliever—a term sometimes used by Christians to refer to a Muslim.

[13]Hooded cloak worn by Arabs. [14]The birth of Christ.

BRAZIL, JANUARY 1, 1502[1]

. . . embroidered nature . . . tapestried landscape.
—*Landscape into Art*, by SIR KENNETH CLARK[2]

Januaries, Nature greets our eyes
exactly as she must have greeted theirs:
every square inch filling in with foliage—
big leaves, little leaves, and giant leaves,
blue, blue-green, and olive,
with occasional lighter veins and edges,
or a satin underleaf turned over;
monster ferns
in silver-gray relief,
and flowers, too, like giant water lilies
up in the air—up, rather, in the leaves—
purple, yellow, two yellows, pink,
rust red and greenish white;
solid but airy; fresh as if just finished
and taken off the frame.

A blue-white sky, a simple web,
backing for feathery detail:
brief arcs, a pale-green broken wheel,
a few palms, swarthy, squat, but delicate;
and perching there in profile, beaks agape,
the big symbolic birds keep quiet,
each showing only half his puffed and padded,
pure-colored or spotted breast.
Still in the foreground there is Sin:
five sooty dragons near some massy rocks.
The rocks are worked with lichens, gray moonbursts
splattered and overlapping,
threatened from underneath by moss
in lovely hell-green flames,
attacked above
by scaling-ladder vines, oblique and neat,
"one leaf yes and one leaf no" (in Portuguese).
The lizards scarcely breathe; all eyes
are on the smaller, female one, back-to,
her wicked tail straight up and over,
red as a red-hot wire.

Just so the Christians, hard as nails,
tiny as nails, and glinting,

[1]The date on which Portuguese navigators first explored the present site of Rio de Janeiro, Brazil.

[2]A book on landscape painting, published in 1949, in which Clark asserts that medieval landscape painting showed nature, often depicted as though embroidered on a tapestry, as symbolic of "spiritual truths."

in creaking armor, came and found it all,
not unfamiliar:
no lovers' walks, no bowers,
no cherries to be picked, no lute music,
but corresponding, nevertheless,
to an old dream of wealth and luxury
already out of style when they left home—
wealth, plus a brand-new pleasure.
Directly after Mass, humming perhaps
L'Homme armé[3] or some such tune,
they ripped away into the hanging fabric,
each out to catch an Indian for himself—
those maddening little women who kept calling,
calling to each other (or had the birds waked up?)
and retreating, always retreating, behind it.

1959?, 1965

IN THE WAITING ROOM

In Worcester, Massachusetts,
I went with Aunt Consuelo
to keep her dentist's appointment
and sat and waited for her
in the dentist's waiting room.
It was winter, It got dark
early. The waiting room
was full of grown-up people,
arctics and overcoats,
lamps and magazines.
My aunt was inside
what seemed like a long time
and while I waited I read
the *National Geographic*
(I could read) and carefully
studied the photographs:
the inside of a volcano,
black, and full of ashes;
then it was spilling over
in rivulets of fire
Osa and Martin Johnson[1]
dressed in riding breeches,
laced boots, and pith helmets.
A dead man slung on a pole
—"Long Pig," the caption said.

[3]French: "The Armed Man," the name of a fifteenth-century melody often sung during a Roman Catholic mass.

[1]Husband and wife explorers and wildlife photographers, famous for their expeditions to the South Sea islands, Borneo, and Africa.

Babies with pointed heads
wound round and round with string;
black, naked women with necks
wound round and round with wire
like the necks of light bulbs.
Their breasts were horrifying.
I read it right straight through.
I was too shy to stop.
And then I looked at the cover:
the yellow margins, the date.

Suddenly, from inside,
came an *oh!* of pain
—Aunt Consuelo's voice—
not very loud or long.
I wasn't at all surprised;
even then I knew she was
a foolish, timid woman.
I might have been embarrassed,
but wasn't. What took me
completely by surprise
was that it was *me:*
my voice, in my mouth.
Without thinking at all
I was my foolish aunt,
I—we—were falling, falling,
our eyes glued to the cover
of the *National Geographic,*
February, 1918.

I said to myself: three days
and you'll be seven years old.
I was saying it to stop
the sensation of falling off
the round, turning world
into cold, blue-black space.
But I felt: you are an *I,*
you are an *Elizabeth,*
you are one of *them.*
Why should you be one, too?
I scarcely dared to look
to see what it was I was.
I gave a sidelong glance
—I couldn't look any higher—
at shadowy gray knees,
trousers and skirts and boots
and different pairs of hands
lying under the lamps.
I knew that nothing stranger
had ever happened, that nothing
stranger could ever happen.

Why should I be my aunt,
or me, or anyone?
What similarities—
boots, hands, the family voice
I felt in my throat, or even
the *National Geographic*
and those awful hanging breasts—
held us all together
or made us all just one?
How—I didn't know any
word for it—how "unlikely" . . .[2]
How had I come to be here,
like them, and overhear
a cry of pain that could have
got loud and worse but hadn't?

The waiting room was bright
and too hot. It was sliding
beneath a big black wave,
another, and another.

Then I was back in it.
The War was on. Outside,
in Worcester, Massachusetts,
were night and slush and cold,
and it was still the fifth
of February, 1918.

1971, 1976

Robert Lowell 1917–1977

Robert Lowell was descended from distinguished New England families that included statesmen, soldiers, Mayflower *colonists, and the poets James Russell Lowell and Amy Lowell. He was educated at a fashionable New England prep school, St. Mark's. For two years he attended Harvard, and then he transferred to Kenyon College in Ohio, where he studied under the distinguished poet and critic John Crowe Ransom.*

In 1940, Lowell graduated from Kenyon as valedictorian of his class. Soon after the United States entered World War II, he tried to enlist, first in the army and then in the navy, but he was rejected. Later, as the war progressed, he became so opposed to the Allies' mass bombing of enemy civilian targets that he refused to serve when he was called for the draft. As a result, in 1943 he was convicted of draft evasion and sentenced to a year and a day in a federal prison.

After serving five months of his sentence, Lowell was paroled. Shortly afterward, he published Land of Unlikeness *(1944), his first book of poems. Two years later his*

[2]The ellipsis points are Bishop's.

fame as a poet was established with the publication of Lord Weary's Castle, *for which he received a Pulitzer Prize for poetry. The volume deals with Lowell's New England background, his ancestry, and especially the moral and spiritual decline he saw in society. In both* Lord Weary's Castle *and his next book,* The Mills of the Kavanaughs *(1951), his despair is expressed in highly symbolic, richly allusive, rhetorical language.*

With the publication of Life Studies *(1959) a new direction in Lowell's poetry was confirmed. The poems are, in a painfully candid way, self-revelation. Their descriptions of personal disturbances and confinement in a hospital for the insane marked the advent of a new school of "confessional poets" who were given to intense self-examination and emotional self-exposure.* Life Studies, *Lowell's finest work and one of the most influential volumes of poetry of the age, also exhibits a less formal and less rhetorical manner than his earlier poems, for, as he said in an interview, he chose not to get his new "experience into tight metrical forms."*

*In his subsequent poetry (*For the Union Dead, *1964, is especially notable) Lowell partially moved away from personal revelation, just as he had moved away from his New England background as a subject for his writing. He also worked with a variety of literary forms, writing verse dramas and translating poems into English. As he grew older Lowell turned increasingly to political activity: In 1956, as a protest against America's foreign policy, he publicly refused to attend a White House Festival to promote the fine arts, and in 1967 he was arrested during a march on the Pentagon to protest the Vietnam War. In his final years he published* History *(1973), in which he attempted a new presentation of poems written in blank verse. His last work,* Day by Day, *was published in 1977, shortly before his death.*

Lowell's early work inspired vast and flattering praise—one fawning critic has been derisively described as falling "to his knees" in his reverent zeal to describe Lowell as the "king" of American poetry. But since his death, Lowell's glittering reputation has dimmed, yielding to the growing recognition of Sylvia Plath and Elizabeth Bishop as the finest poets of the age. Nevertheless, Lowell's work remains of great significance, in part because it embodies two of the major developments of modern poetry: the pursuit of the impersonal (the assumption of "masks," the reliance on allusion, reference, and translation) and its contrary, the open expression of self-revelation, the exposure of the "I."

Lowell's output was enormous: A recent edition of his collected poems totals almost twelve hundred pages. The poems are often dense, difficult, highly charged with "thrashing eloquence." Robert Frost judged that much of Lowell's early poetry lacked "compression," and some of his late work has been criticized as "trivia," as "organized jotting." For the demands that his writing often makes upon his readers, Lowell has been called the most "exacting poet of his time." But at its best, Lowell's work displays great technical craft and elegance. And for its descriptions of the instability of life, for its portrayals of death, sin, and furtive guilt, it stands with the finest American poetry of the twentieth century.

FURTHER READING: H. Staples, *Robert Lowell, The First Twenty Years,* 1962; C. Heymann, *American Aristocracy,* 1980; B. Raffel, *Robert Lowell,* 1981; I. Hamilton, *Robert Lowell, A Biography,* 1982; V. Bell, *Robert Lowell, Nihilist as Hero,* 1983; M. Rudman, *Robert Lowell, An Introduction to the Poetry,* 1983; N. Procopiow, *Robert Lowell, The Poet and His Critics,* 1984; J. Meyers, *Manic Power, Robert Lowell and His Circle,* 1987; *Robert Lowell,* ed. H. Bloom, 1987; *R. Lowell, Interviews and Memoirs,* ed. J. Meyers, 1988; P. Hobsbaum, *A Reader's Guide to Robert Lowell,* 1988; K. Wallingford, *Robert Lowell's Language of the Self,* 1988; *Robert Lowell, Essays on the Poetry,* ed. S. Axelrod and R. Deese, 1989; P. Mariani, *Lost Puritan, A Life of Robert Lowell,* 1994; R. Tillinghast, *Robert Lowell's Life and Work,* 1995; H. Hart, *Robert Lowell and the Sublime,* 1995; *Robert Lowell's Life and Work: Damaged Grandeur,* ed. R. Tillinghast, 1996; W. Doreski, *Robert Lowell's Shifting*

Colors, The Poetics of the Public and the Personal, 1999; *The Critical Response to Robert Lowell,* ed. S. Axelrod, 1999.

TEXT: *Robert Lowell, Collected Poems,* ed. F. Bidart and D. Gewanter, 2003.

MR. EDWARDS[1] AND THE SPIDER

I saw the spiders marching through the air,
Swimming from tree to tree that mildewed day
In latter August when the hay
Came creaking to the barn. But where
The wind is westerly,
Where gnarled November makes the spiders fly
Into the apparitions of the sky,
They purpose nothing but their ease and die
Urgently beating east to sunrise and the sea;

What are we in the hands of the great God?
It was in vain you set up thorn and briar
In battle array against the fire
And treason crackling in your blood;
For the wild thorns grow tame
And will do nothing to oppose the flame;
Your lacerations tell the losing game
You play against a sickness past your cure.
How will the hands be strong? How will the heart
endure?[2]

A very little thing, a little worm,
Or hourglass-blazoned spider,[3] it is said,
Can kill a tiger. Will the dead
Hold up his mirror and affirm
To the four winds the smell
And flash of his authority? It's well
If God who holds you to the pit of hell,
Much as one holds a spider, will destroy,
Baffle and dissipate your soul. As a small boy

On Windsor Marsh,[4] I saw the spider die
When thrown into the bowels of fierce fire:
There's no long struggle, no desire
To get up on its feet and fly—

[1]A reference to Jonathan Edwards (1703–1758), the last great defender of American Puritanism. The poem derives from Edwards' renowned essay "The Flying Spiders" and from his sermons, among them "Sinners in the Hands of an Angry God."

[2]Can thine heart endure, or can thine hands be strong, in the days that I shall deal with thee? (Ezekiel 22:14). Edwards used this text for his sermon "Sinners in the Hands of an Angry God."

[3]The venomous female black widow spider has a red hourglass design on its underside.

[4]Near East Windsor, Connecticut, Edwards' boyhood home.

It stretches out its feet
And dies. This is the sinner's last retreat;
Yes, and no strength exerted on the heat
Then sinews the abolished will, when sick
And full of burning, it will whistle on a brick.

But who can plumb the sinking of that soul?
Josiah Hawley,[5] picture yourself cast
Into a brick-kiln where the blast
Fans your quick vitals to a coal—
If measured by a glass,
How long would it seem burning! Let there pass
A minute, ten, ten trillion; but the blaze
Is infinite, eternal: this is death,
To die and know it. This is the Black Widow, death.
1946

MEMORIES OF WEST STREET AND LEPKE

Only teaching on Tuesdays, book-worming
in pajamas fresh from the washer each morning,
I hog a whole house on Boston's
"hardly passionate Marlborough Street,"[1]
where even the man
scavenging filth in the back alley trash cans,
has two children, a beach wagon, a helpmate,
and is a "young Republican."
I have a nine months' daughter,
young enough to be my granddaughter.
Like the sun she rises in her flame-flamingo infants' wear.

These are the tranquillized *Fifties,*
and I am forty. Ought I to regret my seedtime?
I was a fire-breathing Catholic C.O.,[2]
and made my manic statement,
telling off the state and president, and then
sat waiting sentence in the bull pen
beside a Negro boy with curlicues
of marijuana in his hair.

[5]A relative of Edwards and a suicide whose death Edwards attributed to the devil.

[1]A phrase by Henry James describing a street in an elegant section of Boston. Lowell lived in a house on Marlborough Street from 1955 to 1958.

[2]In 1943 Lowell, a conscientious objector ("C.O."), was convicted of violating the Selective Service Act and sentenced to prison for a year and a day. While awaiting transfer to a federal prison he was held for ten days in the West Side Jail in New York City.

Given a year,
I walked on the roof of the West Street Jail, a short
enclosure like my school soccer court,
and saw the Hudson River once a day
through sooty clothesline entanglements
and bleaching khaki tenements.
Strolling, I yammered metaphysics with Abramowitz,
a jaundice-yellow ("it's really tan")
and fly-weight pacifist,
so vegetarian,
he wore rope shoes and preferred fallen fruit.
He tried to convert Bioff and Brown,[3]
the Hollywood pimps, to his diet.
Hairy, muscular, suburban,
wearing chocolate double-breasted suits,
they blew their tops and beat him black and blue.

I was so out of things, I'd never heard
of the Jehovah's Witnesses.[4]
"Are you a C.O.?" I asked a fellow jailbird.
"No," he answered, "I'm a J.W."
He taught me the "hospital tuck,"[5]
and pointed out the T shirted back
of *Murder Incorporated's* Czar Lepke,[6]
there piling towels on a rack,
or dawdling off to his little segregated cell full
of things forbidden the common man:
a portable radio, a dresser, two toy American
flags tied together with a ribbon of Easter palm.
Flabby, bald, lobotomized,
he drifted in a sheepish calm,
where no agonizing reappraisal[7]
jarred his concentration on the electric chair—
hanging like an oasis in his air
of lost connections. . . .[8]

1958

[3]William Bioff and George Browne, officials of a theatrical union, convicted in 1943 of extortion in Hollywood. In 1922 Browne had been convicted of pandering.

[4]Religious sect in the United States whose members refuse to participate in affairs of government or bear arms in wartime.

[5]Making a bed by tucking the loose ends of the bed clothes under the mattress tautly and forming a mitred corner at the foot of the bed.

[6]Louis "Lepke" Buchalter, a notorious racketeer convicted of murder in 1941. He had been the leader of "Murder Incorporated," a criminal assassination gang whose services were for hire. He was executed by electrocution in March 1944.

[7]In a speech given December 1953, John Foster Dulles, the United States Secretary of State, called for an "agonizing reappraisal" of American foreign policy.

[8]Here, and throughout, the ellipses are Lowell's.

SKUNK HOUR

(For Elizabeth Bishop)

Nautilus Island's hermit
heiress still lives through winter in her Spartan cottage;
her sheep still graze above the sea.
Her son's a bishop. Her farmer
is first selectman[1] in our village;
she's in her dotage.[2]

Thirsting for
the hierarchic privacy
of Queen Victoria's century,
she buys up all
the eyesores facing her shore,
and lets them fall.

The season's ill—
we've lost our summer millionaire,
who seemed to leap from an L. L. Bean[3]
catalogue. His nine-knot yawl[4]
was auctioned off to lobstermen.
A red fox stain covers Blue Hill.[5]

And now our fairy
decorator brightens his shop for fall;
his fishnet's filled with orange cork,
orange, his cobbler's bench and awl;
there is no money in his work,
he'd rather marry.

One dark night,
my Tudor Ford climbed the hill's skull;
I watched for love-cars. Lights turned down,
they lay together, hull to hull,
where the graveyard shelves on the town. . . .
My mind's not right.

A car radio bleats,
"Love, O careless Love. . . ."[6] I hear
my ill-spirit sob in each blood cell,
as if my hand were at its throat. . . .
I myself am hell;[7]
nobody's here—

[1]An official elected to administer town affairs. [2]I.e., is senile.
[3]Mail-order clothing and sporting goods store in Freeport, Maine. [4]Sailboat.
[5]A hill and coastal town near Bangor, Maine.
[6]A quotation from the lyrics of the folk song, "Careless Love."
[7]An adaptation of "Which way I fly is Hell; myself am Hell," the words of Satan in *Paradise Lost* (Book IV, line 75) by John Milton.

only skunks, that search
in the moonlight for a bite to eat.
They march on their soles up Main Street:
white stripes, moonstruck eyes' red fire
under the chalk-dry and spar spire
of the Trinitarian Church.

I stand on top
of our back steps and breathe the rich air—
a mother skunk with her column of kittens swills the garbage pail.
She jabs her wedge-head in a cup
of sour cream, drops her ostrich tail,
and will not scare.
1957 1958, 1959

FOR THE UNION DEAD

"Relinquunt Omnia Servare Rem Publicam."[1]

The old South Boston Aquarium stands
in a Sahara of snow now. Its broken windows are boarded.
The bronze weathervane cod has lost half its scales.
The airy tanks are dry.

Once my nose crawled like a snail on the glass;
my hand tingled
to burst the bubbles
drifting from the noses of the cowed, compliant fish.

My hand draws back. I often sigh still
for the dark downward and vegetating kingdom
of the fish and reptile. One morning last March,
I pressed against the new barbed and galvanized

fence on the Boston Common. Behind their cage,
yellow dinosaur steamshovels were grunting
as they cropped up tons of mush and grass
to gouge their underworld garage.

Parking spaces luxuriate like civic
sandpiles in the heart of Boston.
A girdle of orange, Puritan-pumpkin colored girders
braces the tingling Statehouse,

shaking over the excavations, as it faces Colonel Shaw[2]
and his bell-cheeked Negro infantry

[1]Latin: "They give up everything to serve the republic."
[2]Colonel Robert Shaw (1837–1863), commander of a black regiment, the 54th Massachusetts, during the Civil War.

on St. Gaudens' shaking Civil War relief,[3]
propped by a plank splint against the garage's earthquake.

Two months after marching through Boston,
half the regiment was dead;
at the dedication,
William James[4] could almost hear the bronze Negroes breathe.

Their monument sticks like a fishbone
in the city's throat.
Its Colonel is as lean
as a compass-needle.

He has an angry wrenlike vigilance,
a greyhound's gentle tautness;
he seems to wince at pleasure,
and suffocate for privacy.

He is out of bounds now. He rejoices in man's lovely,
peculiar power to choose life and die—
when he leads his black soldiers to death,
he cannot bend his back.

On a thousand small town New England greens,
the old white churches hold their air
of sparse, sincere rebellion; frayed flags
quilt the graveyards of the Grand Army of the Republic.[5]

The stone statues of the abstract Union Soldier
grow slimmer and younger each year—
wasp-waisted they doze over muskets
and muse through their sideburns . . .

Shaw's father wanted no monument
except the ditch,
where his son's body was thrown
and lost with his "niggers."[6]

[3]A monument by the American sculptor Augustus Saint-Gaudens (1848–1907), on the Boston Common across from the Boston State House.

[4]American philosopher (1842–1910), brother of the novelist Henry James. In his "Oration at the Dedication of the Monument" (May 1897) William James said, "There on foot go the dark outcasts, so true to nature that one can almost hear them breathing as they march."

[5]Civil War veterans' organization of former members of the Union army and navy.

[6]The term used by a Confederate officer to describe Shaw's troops. Shaw and much of his regiment were killed in an assault on the Confederate Fort Wagner in South Carolina, 18 July 1863. They were buried in a common grave.

The ditch is nearer.
There are no statues for the last war[7] here;
on Boylston Street,[8] a commercial photograph
shows Hiroshima boiling

over a Mosler Safe, the "Rock of Ages"
that survived the blast. Space is nearer.
When I crouch to my television set,
the drained faces of Negro school-children rise like balloons.

Colonel Shaw
is riding on his bubble,
he waits
for the blessèd break.

The Aquarium is gone. Everywhere,
giant finned cars nose forward like fish;
a savage servility
slides by on grease.

1959, 1964

WILL NOT COME BACK

[VOLVERAN][1]

Dark swallows will doubtless come back killing
the injudicious nightflies with a clack of the beak;
but these that stopped full flight to see your beauty
and my good fortune . . . as if they knew our names—
they'll not come back. The thick lemony honeysuckle,
climbing from the earthroot to your window,
will open more beautiful blossoms to the evening;
but these . . . like dewdrops, trembling, shining, falling,
the tears of day—they'll not come back. . . .
Some other love will sound his fireword for you
and wake your heart, perhaps, from its cool sleep;
but silent, absorbed, and on his knees,
as men adore God at the altar, as I love you—
don't blind yourself, you'll not be loved like that.

1970, 1973

[7]World War II, 1939–1945.
[8]A street in Boston.
[1]Spanish: they will return, the title given the poem in its first version, published in 1970.

Anne Sexton 1928–1974

Anne Sexton was one of America's most notable confessional poets: "I tell so much truth in my poetry that I'm a fool if I say any more." She was born in Newton, Massachusetts, attended private and public schools, worked simultaneously as a librarian and a fashion model, and began writing poetry in 1957 when she studied at Boston University under Robert Lowell.

Her best work has the quality of a succinct short story in verse. It reads like a forced confession that is painfully direct and marked by witty irony, self-mockery, and sensitive meditation. The subject matter of her first volume, To Bedlam and Part Way Back *(1960), is apparent in the title—mental disturbance and psychic distress.* Bedlam *grew out of her own mental breakdown and her consequent commitment to an asylum, and it charts with painful honesty her journeys into madness and her visions of death. Her views of life and death were developed further in her second volume,* All My Pretty Ones *(1962), and in collections that followed:* Live or Die *(1967), which won a Pulitzer Prize,* Love Poems *(1969), and* Transformations *(1971), which offers macabre reappraisals of familiar fairy tales. In* The Book of Folly *(1972) and in works published after her death, such as* 45 Mercy Street *(1976), she continued her conversions of experience into harsh metaphors expressing an awareness of victimization, guilt, chaos. She was fascinated with death—with suicide as a rebuke of life and the living. Her later work sometimes was uneven, emotionally indulgent. Yet with its irrationalism and violence it was nonetheless compelling and piercing, just as she had wanted it to be. In an interview shortly before her death, by suicide, in 1974, she said of poetry: "I think it should be a shock to the senses. It should almost hurt."*

FURTHER READING: *Anne Sexton, A Self-Portrait in Letters,* ed. L. Sexton and L. Ames, 1977; *Anne Sexton, The Artist and Her Critics,* ed. J. McClatchy, 1978; *No Evil Star,* ed. S. Colburn, 1985; D. George, *Oedipus Anne, The Poetry of Anne Sexton,* 1987; *Original Essays on the Poetry of Anne Sexton,* ed. F. Bixler, 1988; H. Bernard-King, *Anne Sexton,* 1989; D. Middlebrook, *Anne Sexton, A Biography,* 1991; G. Swiontkowski, *Imagining Incest, Sexton, Plath, Rich, and Olds on Life with Daddy,* 2003; P. McGowan, *Anne Sexton and Middle Generation Poetry, The Geography of Grief,* 2004.

TEXT: *The Complete Poems,* ed. L. Sexton, 1981.

THE FARMER'S WIFE

From the hodge porridge
of their country lust,
their local life in Illinois,
where all their acres look
like a sprouting broom factory,
they name just ten years now
that she has been his habit;
as again tonight he'll say
honey bunch let's go
and she will not say how there
must be more to living
than this brief bright bridge
of the raucous bed or even
the slow braille touch of him

like a heavy god grown light,
that old pantomime of love
that she wants although
it leaves her still alone,
built back again at last,
mind's apart from him, living
her own self in her own words
and hating the sweat of the house
they keep when they finally lie
each in separate dreams
and then how she watches him,
still strong in the blowzy bag
of his usual sleep while
her young years bungle past
their same marriage bed
and she wishes him cripple, or poet,
or even lonely, or sometimes,
better, my lover, dead.

1960

RINGING THE BELLS

And this is the way they ring
the bells in Bedlam
and this is the bell-lady
who comes each Tuesday morning
to give us a music lesson
and because the attendants make you go
and because we mind by instinct,
like bees caught in the wrong hive,
we are the circle of the crazy ladies
who sit in the lounge of the mental house
and smile at the smiling woman
who passes us each a bell,
who points at my hand
that holds my bell, E flat,
and this is the gray dress next to me
who grumbles as if it were special
to be old, to be old,
and this is the small hunched squirrel girl
on the other side of me
who picks at the hairs over her lip,
who picks at the hairs over her lip all day,
and this is how the bells really sound,
as untroubled and clean
as a workable kitchen,

and this is always my bell responding
to my hand that responds to the lady
who points at me, E flat;
and although we are no better for it,
they tell you to go. And you do.
1960

AND ONE FOR MY DAME

A born salesman,
my father made all his dough
by selling wool to Fieldcrest, Woolrich and Faribo.

A born talker,
he could sell one hundred wet-down bales
of that white stuff. He could clock the miles and sales

and make it pay.
At home each sentence he would utter
had first pleased the buyer who'd paid him off in butter.

Each word
had been tried over and over, at any rate,
on the man who was sold by the man who filled my plate.

My father hovered
over the Yorkshire pudding and the beef:
a peddler, a hawker, a merchant and an Indian chief.

Roosevelt! Willkie! and war!
How suddenly gauche I was
with my old-maid heart and my funny teenage applause.

Each night at home
my father was in love with maps
while the radio fought its battles with Nazis and Japs.

Except when he hid
in his bedroom on a three-day drunk,
he typed out complex itineraries, packed his trunk,

his matched luggage
and pocketed a confirmed reservation,
his heart already pushing over the red routes of the nation.

I sit at my desk
each night with no place to go,
opening the wrinkled maps of Milwaukee and Buffalo,

the whole U.S.,
its cemeteries, its arbitrary time zones,
through routes like small veins, capitals like small stones.

He died on the road,
his heart pushed from neck to back,
his white hanky signaling from the window of the Cadillac.

My husband,
as blue-eyed as a picture book, sells wool:
boxes of card waste, laps and rovings he can pull

to the thread
and say *Leicester, Rambouillet, Merino,*[1]
a half-blood, it's greasy and thick, yellow as old snow.

And when you drive off, my darling,
Yes, sir! Yes, sir! It's one for my dame,
your sample cases branded with my father's name,

your itinerary open,
its tolls ticking and greedy,
its highways built up like new loves, raw and speedy.
1962 1966

THE ADDICT

Sleepmonger,
deathmonger,
with capsules in my palms each night,
eight at a time from sweet pharmaceutical bottles
I make arrangements for a pint-sized journey.
I'm the queen of this condition.
I'm an expert on making the trip
and now they say I'm an addict.
Now they ask why.
Why!

Don't they know
that I promised to die!
I'm keeping in practice.
I'm merely staying in shape.
The pills are a mother, but better,
every color and as good as sour balls.
I'm on a diet from death.

[1]Breeds of sheep.

Yes, I admit
it has gotten to be a bit of a habit—
blows eight at a time, socked in the eye,
hauled away by the pink, the orange,
the green and the white goodnights.
I'm becoming something of a chemical
mixture.
That's it!

My supply
of tablets
has got to last for years and years.
I like them more than I like me.
Stubborn as hell, they won't let go.
It's a kind of marriage.
It's a kind of war
where I plant bombs inside
of myself.

Yes
I try
to kill myself in small amounts,
an innocuous occupation.
Actually I'm hung up on it.
But remember I don't make too much noise.
And frankly no one has to lug me out
and I don't stand there in my winding sheet.
I'm a little buttercup in my yellow nightie
eating my eight loaves in a row
and in a certain order as in
the laying on of hands
or the black sacrament.

It's a ceremony
but like any other sport
its full of rules.
It's like a musical tennis match where
my mouth keeps catching the ball.
Then I lie on my altar
elevated by the eight chemical kisses.

What a lay me down this is
with two pink, two orange,
two green, two white goodnights.
Fee-fi-fo-fum—
Now I'm borrowed.
Now I'm numb.
1966

US

I was wrapped in black
fur and white fur and
you undid me and then
you placed me in gold light
and then you crowned me,
while snow fell outside
the door in diagonal darts.
While a ten-inch snow
came down like stars
in small calcium fragments,
we were in our own bodies
(that room that will bury us)
and you were in my body
(that room that will outlive us)
and at first I rubbed your
feet dry with a towel
because I was your slave
and then you called me princess.
Princess!

Oh then
I stood up in my gold skin
and I beat down the psalms
and I beat down the clothes
and you undid the bridle
and you undid the reins
and I undid the buttons,
the bones, the confusions,
the New England postcards,
the January ten o'clock night,
and we rose up like wheat,
acre after acre of gold,
and we harvested,
we harvested.

1969

ROWING

A story, a story!
(Let it go. Let it come.)
I was stamped out like a Plymouth fender
into this world.
First came the crib
with its glacial bars.

Then dolls
and the devotion to their plastic mouths.
Then there was school,
the little straight rows of chairs,
blotting my name over and over,
but undersea all the time,
a stranger whose elbows wouldn't work.
Then there was life
with its cruel houses
and people who seldom touched—
though touch is all—
but I grew,
like a pig in a trenchcoat I grew,
and then there were many strange apparitions,
the nagging rain, the sun turning into poison
and all of that, saws working through my heart,
but I grew, I grew,
and God was there like an island I had not rowed to,
still ignorant of Him, my arms and my legs worked,
and I grew, I grew,
I wore rubies and bought tomatoes
and now, in my middle age,
about nineteen in the head I'd say,
I am rowing, I am rowing
though the oarlocks stick and are rusty
and the sea blinks and rolls
like a worried eyeball,
but I am rowing, I am rowing,
though the wind pushes me back
and I know that that island will not be perfect,
it will have the flaws of life,
the absurdities of the dinner table,
but there will be a door
and I will open it
and I will get rid of the rat inside of me,
the gnawing pestilential rat.
God will take it with his two hands
and embrace it.

As the African says:
This is my tale which I have told,
if it be sweet, if it be not sweet,
take somewhere else and let some return to me.
This story ends with me still rowing.

1975

Sylvia Plath 1932–1963

The work of Sylvia Plath represents a romanticism in extremis, *intense private agonies made public with a grotesque clarity. Her poetry has been praised as a supreme example of the confessional mode in modern literature and disparaged as "the longest suicide note ever written."*

She was born in Boston, Massachusetts, the daughter of a German father and an Austrian mother whose attitudes and personalities were relentlessly exposed in their daughter's writing. As a child Plath was brilliant and erratic. At seventeen she published her first poem and her first short story. She entered Smith College on a scholarship, but she became increasingly filled with apprehensions of horror and death and obsessed with a sense of isolation and entrapment: "I've gone around for most of my life as in the rarified atmosphere under a bell jar."

Unable to reconcile her inner and outer worlds, she was briefly hospitalized and underwent intense psychiatric therapy. The events of these years she later presented in The Bell Jar, *an autobiographical novel about personality disintegration, which she published in 1963 under the pseudonym Victoria Lucas.*

In 1955 she graduated from Smith with highest honors and received a fellowship to Cambridge University, where she took her M.A. degree in 1957. In England she met and married British poet Ted Hughes in 1956. After a temporary return to America she lived in England for the remainder of her life.

Plath's first book of poetry, The Colossus, *was published in 1960 and acclaimed by critics for its range of language and stylistic brilliance. She then began work on the poems that were later to appear in* Ariel, *but instead of writing in her usual laborious manner, she wrote poems at "top speed, as one might write an urgent letter." The* Ariel *poems composed during this period reflect her renewed sense of the ungovernable chaos of human experience and her frightening visions of violence and horror. On February 11, 1963, she committed suicide.*

The Ariel *poems, published posthumously in 1965, were followed by* Uncollected Poems *(1965),* Crossing the Water *(1971), and* Winter Trees *(1972), works that reveal the painful intensity and desperation of a mind seeking to express, in hideous clarity, the visions of one trapped "in The Bell Jar" for whom "the world itself is a bad dream."*

FURTHER READING: *Letters from Home by Sylvia Plath, Correspondence 1950–1963,* ed. A. Roth, 1975; *Journals of Sylvia Plath,* ed. F. McCullough and T. Hughes, 1982; S. Bassnet, *Sylvia Plath,* 1987, 2005; L. Wagner-Martin, *Sylvia Plath,* 1987; A. Stevenson, *Bitter Flame, A Life of Sylvia Plath,* 1989; P. Alexander, *Rough Magic, A Biography of Sylvia Plath,* 1990; R. Hayman, *The Death and Life of Sylvia Plath,* 1991; N. Steiner, *A Closer Look at Ariel, A Memory of Sylvia Plath,* 1973; D. Holbrook, *Sylvia Plath, Poetry and Existence,* 1987; P. Annas, *A Disturbance in Mirrors, The Poetry of Sylvia Plath,* 1988; *Sylvia Plath,* ed. H. Bloom, 1989; S. Axelrod, *Sylvia Plath, The Wound and the Cure of Words,* 1990; J. Rose, *The Haunting of Sylvia Plath,* 1993; S. Van Dyne, *Revising Life, Sylvia Plath's Ariel Poems,* 1993; C. Hall, *Sylvia Plath,* 1998; A. Strangeways, *The Shaping of Shadows,* 1998; E. Butscher, *Sylvia Plath, Method and Madness, A Biography,* 2004; D. Middlebrook, *Her Husband, Hughes and Plath,* 2004; E. Wagner, *Ariel's Gift,* 2000; T. Brain, *The Other Sylvia Plath,* 2001; S. Blosser, *A Poetics on Edge, The Poetry and Prose of Sylvia Plath,* 2001; B. Lindberg-Seyersted, *Sylvia Plath, Studies in Her Poetry and Her Personality,* 2002; S. Bassnet, *Sylvia Plath, An Introduction to the Poetry,* 2004.

TEXT: *The Collected Poems, Sylvia Plath,* ed. T. Hughes, 1981.

TWO VIEWS OF A CADAVER ROOM

1

The day she visited the dissecting room
They had four men laid out, black as burnt turkey,
Already half unstrung. A vinegary fume
Of death vats clung to them;
The white-smocked boys started working.
The head of his cadaver had caved in,
And she could scarcely make out anything
In that rubble of skull plates and old leather.
A sallow piece of string held it together.
In their jars the snail-nosed babies moon and glow.
He hands her the cut-out heart like a cracked heirloom.

2

In Brueghel's panorama of smoke and slaughter[1]
Two people only are blind to the carrion army:
He, afloat in the sea of her blue satin
Skirts, sings in the direction
Of her bare shoulder, while she bends,
Fingering a leaflet of music, over him,
Both of them deaf to the fiddle in the hands
Of the death's-head shadowing their song.
The Flemish lovers flourish; not for long.

Yet desolation, stalled in paint, spares the little country
Foolish, delicate, in the lower right-hand corner.

1959, 1960

THE BEE MEETING

Who are these people at the bridge to meet me? They are the
villagers—
The rector, the midwife, the sexton, the agent for bees.
In my sleeveless summery dress I have no protection,
And they are all gloved and covered, why did nobody tell me?
They are smiling and taking out veils tacked to ancient hats.

I am nude as a chicken neck, does nobody love me?
Yes, here is the secretary of bees with her white shop smock,
Buttoning the cuffs at my wrists and the slit from my neck to my knees.
Now I am milkweed silk, the bees will not notice.
They will not smell my fear, my fear, my fear.

[1]*The Triumph of Death* painted (?1562) by the Flemish artist Peter Brueghel the Elder (1520?–1569) and showing the army of the dead as hordes of skeletons attacking the living.

Which is the rector now, is it that man in black?
Which is the midwife, is that her blue coat?
Everybody is nodding a square black head, they are knights in visors,
Breastplates of cheesecloth knotted under the armpits.
Their smiles and their voices are changing. I am led through a
  beanfield.

Strips of tinfoil winking like people,
Feather dusters fanning their hands in a sea of bean flowers,
Creamy bean flowers with black eyes and leaves like bored hearts.
Is it blood clots the tendrils are dragging up that string?
No, no, it is scarlet flowers that will one day be edible.

Now they are giving me a fashionable white straw Italian hat
And a black veil that molds to my face, they are making me one of them.
They are leading me to the shorn grove, the circle of hives.
Is it the hawthorn that smells so sick?
The barren body of hawthorn, etherizing its children.

Is it some operation that is taking place?
It is the surgeon my neighbors are waiting for,
This apparition in a green helmet,
Shining gloves and white suit.
Is it the butcher, the grocer, the postman, someone I know?

I cannot run, I am rooted, and the gorse hurts me
With its yellow purses, its spiky armory.
I could not run without having to run forever.
The white hive is snug as a virgin,
Sealing off her brood cells, her honey, and quietly humming.

Smoke rolls and scarves in the grove.
The mind of the hive thinks this is the end of everything.
Here they come, the outriders, on their hysterical elastics.
If I stand very still, they will think I am cow-parsley,
A gullible head untouched by their animosity,

Not even nodding, a personage in a hedgerow.
The villagers open the chambers, they are hunting the queen.
Is she hiding, is she eating honey? She is very clever.
She is old, old, old, she must live another year, and she knows it.
While in their fingerjoint cells the new virgins

Dream of a duel they will win inevitably,
A curtain of wax dividing them from the bride flight,
The upflight of the murderess into a heaven that loves her.
The villagers are moving the virgins, there will be no killing.
The old queen does not show herself, is she so ungrateful?

I am exhausted, I am exhausted——
Pillar of white in a blackout of knives.
I am the magician's girl who does not flinch.
The villagers are untying their disguises, they are shaking hands.
Whose is that long white box in the grove, what have they accomplished,
    why am I cold.

1962 1962

ARIEL[1]

Stasis in darkness.
Then the substanceless blue
Pour of tor[2] and distances.

God's lioness,
How one we grow,
Pivot of heels and knees!—The furrow

Splits and passes, sister to
The brown arc
Of the neck I cannot catch,

Nigger-eye
Berries cast dark
Hooks——

Black sweet blood mouthfuls,
Shadows.
Something else

Hauls me through air——
Thighs, hair;
Flakes from my heels.

White
Godiva[3], I unpeel—
Dead hands, dead stringencies.

And now I
Foam to wheat, a glitter of seas.
The child's cry

[1]Thc horse Sylvia Plath rode while attending riding school in England.
[2]A high hill.
[3]Lady Godiva, eleventh-century wife of an English earl, famous for her legendary ride naked through the city of Coventry, to win remission of heavy taxes on the people.

Melts in the wall.
And I
Am the arrow,

The dew that flies
Suicidal, at one with the drive
Into the red

Eye, the cauldron of morning.
1962 1963, 1965

THE APPLICANT

First, are you our sort of a person?
Do you wear
A glass eye, false teeth or a crutch,
A brace or a hook,
Rubber breasts or a rubber crotch,

Stitches to show something's missing? No, no? Then
How can we give you a thing?
Stop crying.
Open your hand.
Empty? Empty. Here is a hand

To fill it and willing
To bring teacups and roll away headaches
And do whatever you tell it.
Will you marry it?
It is guaranteed

To thumb shut your eyes at the end
And dissolve of sorrow.
We make new stock from the salt.
I notice you are stark naked.
How about this suit—

Black and stiff, but not a bad fit.
Will you marry it?
It is waterproof, shatterproof, proof
Against fire and bombs through the roof.
Believe me, they'll bury you in it.

Now your head, excuse me, is empty.
I have the ticket for that.
Come here, sweetie, out of the closet.
Well, what do you think of *that*?
Naked as paper to start

But in twenty-five years she'll be silver,
In fifty, gold.[1]
A living doll, everywhere you look.
It can sew, it can cook,
It can talk, talk, talk.

It works, there is nothing wrong with it.
You have a hole, it's a poultice.
You have an eye, it's an image.
My boy, it's your last resort.
Will you marry it, marry it, marry it.
1962 1962

DADDY

You do not do, you do not do
Any more, black shoe
In which I have lived like a foot
For thirty years, poor and white,
Barely daring to breathe or Achoo.

Daddy, I have had to kill you.
You died before I had time——
Marble-heavy, a bag full of God,
Ghastly statue with one grey toe[1]
Big as a Frisco seal

And a head in the freakish Atlantic
Where it pours bean green over blue
In the waters off beautiful Nauset.[2]
I used to pray to recover you.[3]
Ach, du.[4]

In the German tongue, in the Polish town[5]
Scraped flat by the roller
Of wars, wars, wars.
But the name of the town is common.
My Polack friend

Says there are a dozen or two.
So I never could tell where you
Put your foot, your root,
I never could talk to you.
The tongue stuck in my jaw.

[1]For the twenty-fifth (silver) and fiftieth (gold) wedding anniversaries.
[1]The toe of Plath's father was swollen and discolored from diabetic gangrene.
[2]Beach and harbor on Cape Cod. [3]Plath's father died when she was a child.
[4]German: Ah, you. [5]Plath's father was born in Poland to German parents.

It stuck in a barb wire snare.
Ich, ich, ich, ich,[6]
I could hardly speak.
I thought every German was you.
And the language obscene

An engine, an engine
Chuffing me off like a Jew.
A Jew to Dachau, Auschwitz, Belsen.[7]
I began to talk like a Jew.
I think I may well be a Jew.

The snows of the Tyrol,[8] the clear beer of Vienna
Are not very pure or true.
With my gypsy ancestress and my weird luck
And my Taroc pack[9] and my Taroc pack
I may be a bit of a Jew.

I have always been scared of *you*,
With your Luftwaffe,[10] your gobbledygoo.
And your neat moustache
And your Aryan eye, bright blue.[11]
Panzer[12] man, panzer-man, O You——

Not God but a swastika
So black no sky could squeak through.
Every woman adores a Fascist,
The boot in the face, the brute
Brute heart of a brute like you.

You stand at the blackboard, daddy,
In the picture I have of you,
A cleft in your chin instead of your foot
But no less a devil for that, no not
Any less the black man who

Bit my pretty red heart in two.
I was ten when they buried you.
At twenty I tried to die
And get back, back, back to you.
I thought even the bones would do.

But they pulled me out of the sack,
And they stuck me together with glue.[13]
And then I knew what to do.

[6]German: I, I, I, I. [7]Nazi concentration camps in Germany and Poland.
[8]Mountain region of Austria. [9]Tarot cards, used in fortune-telling.
[10]The name of the German air force in World War II.
[11]Reference to the Nazi theory of the superiority of the blond, blue-eyed Aryan race.
[12]German: armored, tank.
[13]A reference to Plath's recovery from her first suicide attempt.

I made a model of you,
A man in black with a Meinkampf[14] look

And a love of the rack and the screw.
And I said I do, I do.
So daddy, I'm finally through.
The black telephone's off at the root,
The voices just can't worm through.

If I've killed one man, I've killed two——
The vampire who said he was you
And drank my blood for a year,
Seven years, if you want to know.
Daddy, you can lie back now.

There's a stake in your fat black heart
And the villagers never liked you.
They are dancing and stamping on you.
They always *knew* it was you.
Daddy, daddy, you bastard, I'm through.
1962 1963, 1965

FEVER 103°

Pure? What does it mean?
The tongues of hell
Are dull, dull as the triple

Tongues of dull, fat Cerberus[1]
Who wheezes at the gate. Incapable
Of licking clean

The aguey tendon, the sin, the sin.
The tinder cries.
The indelible smell

Of a snuffed candle!
Love, love, the low smokes roll
From me like Isadora's scarves,[2] I'm in a fright

One scarf will catch and anchor in the wheel.
Such yellow sullen smokes
Make their own element. They will not rise,

But trundle round the globe
Choking the aged and the meek,
The weak

[14]German: My struggle, the title of Adolf Hitler's political manifesto.
[1]In classical myth, the three-headed dog that guarded the entrance to Hades.
[2]Isadora Duncan (1878–1927), American dancer who was strangled when her long scarf caught in the wheel of the car in which she rode.

Hothouse baby in its crib,
The ghastly orchid
Hanging its hanging garden in the air,

Devilish leopard!
Radiation turned it white
And killed it in an hour.

Greasing the bodies of adulterers
Like Hiroshima ash and eating in.
The sin. The sin.

Darling, all night
I have been flickering, off, on, off, on.
The sheets grow heavy as a lecher's kiss.

Three days. Three nights.
Lemon water, chicken
Water, water make me retch.

I am too pure for you or anyone.
Your body
Hurts me as the world hurts God. I am a lantern—

My head a moon
Of Japanese paper, my gold beaten skin
Infinitely delicate and infinitely expensive.

Does not my heat astound you. And my light.
All by myself I am a huge camellia
Glowing and coming and going, flush on flush.

I think I am going up,
I think I may rise—
The beads of hot metal fly, and I, love, I

Am a pure acetylene
Virgin
Attended by roses,

By kisses, by cherubim,[3]
By whatever these pink things mean.
Not you, nor him

Not him, nor him
(My selves dissolving, old whore petticoats)—
To Paradise.
1962 1965

[3]One of the orders of heavenly angels.

James Dickey 1923–1997

James Dickey was everybody's notion of the muscular poet. A football player and track star in college, he was an avid outdoorsman, archery expert, and guitarist; he served as a fighter pilot in both World War II and the Korean War, and he gave up a successful business career in advertising to write poetry. He was born in Atlanta, Georgia, on Groundhog Day, as he liked to point out, a suggestion perhaps of his affinity with the wilderness, which was to Dickey "a subject of endless interest and rejoicing."

*Dickey came to poetry, in his own words, "comparatively late": He was twenty-four before he began writing seriously, and in his late thirties before the publication of his first book of poems. Most of the poems in his first three volumes of poetry (*Into the Stone, *1960;* Drowning with Others, *1962; and* Helmets, *1964) were written mainly in short, three-beat lines; the syntax is usually clear and precise; stanzas are organized around a cluster of images. The worlds of physicality, animals, and nature are frequent subjects; the dominant themes are death and renewal and the transformation possible for all living things. Even though Dickey often described dreams, memories, or illusions—"hallucinatory" subjects, in the poet's phrase—his poetry was relatively straightforward.*

Dickey's next book, Buckdancer's Choice *(1965), marked a shift to what he called the "conclusionless" poem, which would "involve the reader in it, in all its imperfections and impurities, rather than offering him a (supposedly) perfected work for contemplation, judgment, and evaluation." The "conclusionless" poems are more narrative in form, with irregular meter and with longer lines typographically set to replace conventional punctuation and denote accents. The style is lush, sometimes even "woolly." The sense of the grotesque remains strong.*

In 1977 Dickey published The Bible: A New Vision, *a series of prose poems based on biblical texts. He also wrote literary criticism and novels,* Deliverance *(1970), which was made into a successful motion picture, and* Alnilam *(1987), which parallels, as did* Deliverance, *ancient quest myths. Dickey taught at several colleges and universities and read his poetry and lectured throughout the country, and he served as Consultant in Poetry to the Library of Congress. Poetry always remained his primary vocation, and in such volumes as* Poems 1957–1967 *(1967),* The Eye-Beaters *(1970), and* The Zodiac, *(1974), he demonstrated remarkable verbal energy, intensity, sympathy, and a sense of reconciliation unique in contemporary American poetry.*

FURTHER READING: *Babel to Byzantium,* 1968; *Self Interviews,* 1970; *Sorties, Journals and New Essays,* 1971; *Striking In, The Early Notebooks of James Dickey,* ed. G. Van Ness, 1996; *The Whole Motion, Collected Poems 1945–1992,* 1993; R. Calhoun, *James Dickey, the Expansive Imagination,* 1973; R. Calhoun and R. Hill, *James Dickey,* 1983; R. Baughman, *Understanding James Dickey,* 1985; R. Kirschsten, *James Dickey and the Gentle Ecstasy of Earth,* 1988; *The Voiced Connections of James Dickey,* ed. R. Baughman, 1989; E. Suarez, *James Dickey and the Politics of Canon,* 1993; "Struggling for Wings," *The Art of James Dickey,* ed. R. Kirschten, 1997; R. Kirschten, *James Dickey and the Gentle Ecstasy of Earth,* 1997; G. Van Ness, *The One Voice of James Dickey, His Letters and Life,* 2003; *Critical Essays on James Dickey,* ed. R. Kirschten, 1994; *James Dickey,* ed. J. Baughman, 1999.

TEXT: *Poems 1957–1967,* 1967.

THE LIFEGUARD

In a stable of boats I lie still,
From all sleeping children hidden.
The leap of fish from its shadow
Makes the whole lake instantly tremble.
With my foot on the water, I feel
The moon outside

Take on the utmost of its power.
I rise and go out through the boats.
I set my broad sole upon silver,
On the skin of the sky, on the moonlight,
Stepping outward from earth onto water
In quest of the miracle

This village of children believed
That I could perform as I dived
For one who had sunk from my sight.
I saw his cropped haircut go under.
I leapt, and my steep body flashed
Once, in the sun.

Dark drew all the light from my eyes.
Like a man who explores his death
By the pull of his slow-moving shoulders,
I hung head down in the cold,
Wide-eyed, contained, and alone
Among the weeds,

And my fingertips turned into stone
From clutching immovable blackness.
Time after time I leapt upward
Exploding in breath, and fell back
From the change in the children's faces
At my defeat.

Beneath them I swam to the boathouse
With only my life in my arms
To wait for the lake to shine back
At the risen moon with such power
That my steps on the light of the ripples
Might be sustained.

Beneath me is nothing but brightness
Like the ghost of a snowfield in summer.
As I move toward the center of the lake,
Which is also the center of the moon,
I am thinking of how I may be
The savior of one

Who has already died in my care.
The dark trees fade from around me.
The moon's dust hovers together.
I call softly out, and the child's
Voice answers through blinding water.
Patiently, slowly,

He rises, dilating to break
The surface of stone with his forehead.
He is one I do not remember
Having ever seen in his life.
The ground I stand on is trembling
Upon his smile.

I wash the black mud from my hands.
On a light given off by the grave
I kneel in the quick of the moon
At the heart of a distant forest
And hold in my arms a child
Of water, water, water.
1961 1962

REINCARNATION (I)

Still, passed through the spokes of an old wheel, on and around
The hub's furry rust in the weeds and shadows of the riverbank,
This one is feeling his life as a man move slowly away.
Fallen from that estate, he has gone down on his knees
And beyond, disappearing into the egg buried under the sand

And wakened the low world being born, consisting now
Of the wheel on its side not turning, but leaning to rot away
In the sun a few feet farther off than it is for any man.
The roots bulge directly under the earth beneath him;
With his tongue he can hear them in their concerted effort

To raise something, anything, out of the dark of the ground.
He has come by gliding, by inserting the head between stems.
Everything follows that as naturally as the creation
Of the world, leaving behind arms and legs, leaving behind
The intervals between tracks, leaving one long wavering step

In sand and none in grass: he moves through, moving nothing,
And the grass stands as never entered. It is in the new
Life of resurrection that one can come in one's own time
To a place like a rotting wheel, the white paint flaking from it,
Rust slowly emerging, and coil halfway through it, stopped

By a just administration of light and dark over the diamonds
Of the body. Here, also naturally growing, is a flat leaf
To rest the new head upon. The stem bends but knows the weight
And does not touch the ground, holding the snub, patterned face
Swaying with the roots of things. Inside the jaws, saliva

Has turned ice cold, drawn from bird eggs and thunderstruck rodents,
Dusty pine needles, blunt stones, horse dung, leaf mold,
But mainly, now, from waiting—all the time a symbol of evil—
Not for food, but for the first man to walk by the gentle river:
Minute by minute the head becomes more poisonous and poised.

Here in the wheel is the place to wait, with the eyes unclosable,
Unanswerable, the tongue occasionally listening, this time
No place in the body desiring to burn the tail away or to warn,
But only to pass on, handless, what yet may be transferred
In a sudden giving-withdrawing move, like a county judge striking
a match.
1964 1965

IN THE MOUNTAIN TENT

I am hearing the shape of the rain
Take the shape of the tent and believe it,
Laying down all around where I lie
A profound, unspeakable law.
I obey, and am free-falling slowly

Through the thought-out leaves of the wood
Into the minds of animals.
I am there in the shining of water
Like dark, like light, out of Heaven.

I am there like the dead, or the beast
Itself, which thinks of a poem—
Green, plausible, living, and holy—
And cannot speak, but hears,
Called forth from the waiting of things,

A vast, proper, reinforced crying
With the sifted, harmonious pause,
The sustained intake of all breath
Before the first word of the Bible.

At midnight water dawns
Upon the held skulls of the foxes
And weasels and tousled hares
On the eastern side of the mountain.
Their light is the image I make

As I wait as if recently killed,
Receptive, fragile, half-smiling,
My brow watermarked with the mark
On the wing of a moth

And the tent taking shape on my body
Like ill-fitting, Heavenly clothes.
From holes in the ground comes my voice
In the God-silenced tongue of the beasts.
"I shall rise from the dead," I am saying.

1962

CHERRYLOG ROAD

Off Highway 106
At Cherrylog Road I entered
The '34 Ford without wheels,
Smothered in kudzu,[1]
With a seat pulled out to run
Corn whiskey down from the hills,

And then from the other side
Crept into an Essex[2]
With a rumble seat of red leather
And then out again, aboard
A blue Chevrolet, releasing
The rust from its other color,

Reared up on three building blocks.
None had the same body heat;
I changed with them inward, toward
The weedy heart of the junkyard,
For I knew that Doris Holbrook
Would escape from her father at noon

And would come from the farm
To seek parts owned by the sun
Among the abandoned chassis,
Sitting in each in turn
As I did, leaning forward
as in a wild stock-car race

[1]A rapid-growing, spreading vine used for ground cover.
[2]American automobile of the 1920s and 1930s, as is the Pierce-Arrow (line 35).

In the parking lot of the dead.
Time after time, I climbed in
And out the other side, like
An envoy or movie star
Met at the station by crickets.
A radiator cap raised its head,

Become a real toad or a kingsnake
As I neared the hub of the yard,
Passing through many states,
Many lives, to reach
Some grandmother's long Pierce-Arrow
Sending platters of blindness forth

From its nickel hubcaps
And spilling its tender upholstery
On sleepy roaches,
The glass panel in between
Lady and colored driver
Not all the way broken out,

The back-seat phone
Still on its hook.
I got in as though to exclaim,
"Let us go to the orphan asylum,
John; I have some old toys
For children who say their prayers."

I popped with sweat as I thought
I heard Doris Holbrook scrape
Like a mouse in the southern-state sun
That was eating the paint in blisters
From a hundred car tops and hoods.
She was tapping like code,

Loosening the screws,
Carrying off headlights,
Sparkplugs, bumpers,
Cracked mirrors and gear-knobs,
Getting ready, already,
To go back with something to show

Other than her lips' new trembling
I would hold to me soon, soon,
Where I sat in the ripped back seat
Talking over the interphone,
Praying for Doris Holbrook
To come from her father's farm

And to get back there
With no trace of me on her face
To be seen by her red-haired father
Who would change, in the squalling barn,
Her back's pale skin with a strop,
Then lay for me

In a bootlegger's roasting car
With a string-triggered 12-gauge shotgun
To blast the breath from the air.
Not cut by the jagged windshields,
Through the acres of wrecks she came
With a wrench in her hand,

Through dust where the blacksnake dies
Of boredom, and the beetle knows
The compost has no more life.
Someone outside would have seen
The oldest car's door inexplicably
Close from within:

I held her and held her and held her,
Convoyed at terrific speed
By the stalled, dreaming traffic around us,
So the blacksnake, stiff
With inaction, curved back
Into life, and hunted the mouse

With deadly overexcitement,
The beetles reclaimed their field
As we clung, glued together,
With the hooks of the seat springs
Working through to catch us red-handed
Amidst the gray, breathless batting

That burst from the seat at our backs.
We left by separate doors
Into the changed, other bodies
Of cars, she down Cherrylog Road
And I to my motorcycle
Parked like the soul of the junkyard

Restored, a bicycle fleshed
With power, and tore off
Up Highway 106, continually
Drunk on the wind in my mouth,
Wringing the handlebar for speed,
Wild to be wreckage forever.

1964

THE SHARK'S PARLOR

Memory: I can take my head and strike it on a wall   on Cumberland
  Island
Where the night tide came crawling under the stairs   came up the first
Two or three steps   and the cottage stood on poles all night
With the sea-sprawled under it   as we dreamed of the great fin
  circling
Under the bedroom floor. In daylight there was my first brassy taste
  of beer
And Payton Ford and I came back from the Glynn County
  slaughterhouse
With a bucket of entrails and blood. We tied one end of a hawser
To a spindling porch pillar and rowed straight out of the house
Three hundred yards into the vast front yard of windless blue water
The rope outslithering its coil   the two-gallon jug stoppered and
  sealed
With wax   and a ten-foot chain leader   a drop-forged shark hook
  nestling.
We cast our blood on the waters   the land blood easily passing
For sea blood   and we sat in it for a moment with the stain
  spreading
Out from the boat   sat in a new radiance   in the pond of blood in
  the sea
Waiting for fins,   waiting to spill our guts also in the glowing water.
We dumped the bucket, and baited the hook with a run-over collie
  pup. The jug
Bobbed, trying to shake off the sun as a dog would shake off the sea.
We rowed to the house   feeling the same water lift the boat a new
  way,
All the time seeing where we lived rise and dip with the oars.
We tied up and sat down in rocking chairs, one eye or the other
  responding
to the blue-eye wink of the jug. Payton got us a beer and we sat
All morning sat there with blood on our minds   the red mark out
In the harbor slowly failing us   then   the house groaned   the rope
Sprang out of the water   splinters flew   we leapt from our chairs
And grabbed the rope   hauled   did nothing   the house coming
  subtly
Apart   all around us   underfoot   boards beginning to sparkle
  like sand
With the glinting of the bright hidden parts of ten-year-old nails
Pulling out   the tarred poles we slept propped-up on   leaning to sea
As in land wind   crabs scuttling from under the floor   as we took
  turns about
Two more porch pillars   and looked out and saw   something
  a fish-flash
An almighty fin in trouble   a moiling of secret forces   a false start
Of water   a round wave growing: in the whole of Cumberland
  Sound the one ripple.
Payton took off without a word   I could not hold him either

But clung to the rope anyway: it was the whole house bending
Its nails that held whatever it was coming in a little and like a fool
I took up the slack on my wrist. The rope drew gently jerked I lifted
Clean off the porch and hit the water the same water it was in
I felt in blue blazing terror at the bottom of the stairs and scrambled
Back up looking desperately into the human house as deeply as I could
Stopping my gaze before it went out the wire screen of the back door
Stopped it on the thistled rattan the rugs I lay on and read
On my mother's sewing basket with next winter's socks spilling from it
The flimsy vacation furniture a bucktoothed picture of myself.
Payton came back with three men from a filling station and glanced at me
Dripping water inexplicable then we all grabbed hold like a tug-of-war.

We were gaining a little from us a cry went up from everywhere
People came running. Behind us the house filled with men and boys.
On the third step from the sea I took my place looking down the rope.
Going into the ocean, humming and shaking off drops. A houseful
Of people put their backs into it going up the steps from me
Into the living room through the kitchen down the back stairs
Up and over a hill of sand across a dust road and onto a raised field
Of dunes we were gaining the rope in my hands began to be wet
With deeper water all other haulers retreated through the house
But Payton and I on the stairs drawing hand over hand on our blood
Drawing into existence by the nose a huge body becoming
A hammerhead rolling in beery shallows and I began to let up
But the rope still strained behind me the town had gone
Pulling-mad in our house: far away in a field of sand they struggled
They had turned their backs on the sea bent double some on their knees
The rope over their shoulders like a bag of gold they strove for the ideal
Esso station across the scorched meadow with the distant fish coming up
The front stairs the sagging boards still coming in up taking
Another step toward the empty house where the rope stood straining
By itself through the rooms in the middle of the air. "Pass the word,"
Payton said, and I screamed it: "Let up, good God, let up!" to no one there.
The shark flopped on the porch, grating with salt-sand driving back in

The nails he had pulled out   coughing chunks of his formless blood.
The screen door banged and tore off   he scrambled on his tail   slid
Curved   did a thing from another world   and was out of his
element and in
Our vacation paradise   cutting all four legs from under the dinner
table
With one deep-water move   he unwove the rugs in a moment
throwing pints
Of blood over everything we owned   knocked the buck teeth out of
my picture
His odd head full of crushed jelly-glass splinters and radio tubes
thrashing
Among the pages of fan magazines   all the movie stars drenched in
sea-blood.
Each time we thought he was dead   he struggled back and smashed
One more thing   in all coming back to die   three or four more
times after death.
At last we got him out   log-rolling him   greasing his sandpaper skin
With lard to slide him   pulling on his chained lips as the tide came
Tumbled him down the steps as the first night wave went under the
floor.
He drifted off   head back   belly white as the moon. What could I
do but buy
That house   for the one black mark still there   against death   a
forehead-
toucher in the room he circles beneath   and has been invited to
wreck?
Blood hard as iron on the wall   black with time   still bloodlike
Can be touched whenever the brow is drunk enough: all changes:
Memory:
Something like three-dimensional dancing in the limbs   with age
Feeling more in two worlds than one   in all worlds the growing
encounters.

1965

W. S. Merwin 1927–

W. S. Merwin was born in New York, the son of a clergyman. He attended Princeton University, where he studied medieval literature and romance languages. In 1948 he made his way to Europe, where he lived in France, Spain, and Portugal, worked as a tutor to the children of a Portuguese nobleman, and studied writing in Majorca under the English poet Robert Graves. Since that time, he has become a prolific writer of poems, fiction, drama, essays, travel books, and translations. Working sometimes with other translators he has translated into English twenty-one volumes of works in Spanish, French, Latin, Italian, ancient Greek, and medieval English, among them the

Spanish national epic The Poem of El Cid *(1959), the* Satires *of the Roman poet Persius (1960), and the medieval French* Song of Roland *(1963). In 1998 he published* East Windows, *translations of Asian poems and sayings, and in 2000 a translation of Dante's* Purgatorio *(2000). His prize-winning translation of the medieval English poem* Sir Gawain and the Green Knight, *a fourteenth-century tale of adventure and enchantment in King Arthur's Court, appeared in 2002.*

The range of his writing is also evident in his essays—his most recent collection, Ends of the Earth *(2004), treats subjects as varied as explorers, mountains, butterflies, and Neanderthal bones. But it is for his poetry that Merwin has received the greatest acclaim. His first volume of verse,* A Mask for Janus *(1952), won a Yale Younger Poets Award. He then published* The Dancing Bears *(1954),* The Drunk in the Furnace *(1960),* The Moving Target *(1963),* The Lice *(1967),* The Carriers of Ladders *(1970), which won a Pulitzer Prize,* The Compass Flower *(1977),* Finding the Islands *(1982),* Opening the Hand *(1983), and* Rain in the Trees *(1988). A collection of his poetry,* Selected Poems, *was published in 1988. Six more volumes of his poetry were published in the 1990s. Two more volumes,* The Pupil *and* Migration *(a collection of old and new poems) were published in 2001 and 2005.*

In his torrent of poetry (he has written a total of twenty-three volumes) Merwin has moved from the full discursiveness of his earlier poetry to an epigrammatic poetry of simple statement and "shrinking margins." Much of his poetry presents an unsentimental portrait of humankind and nature; the writing is spare, undecorated, devoid even of punctuation. Yet he draws on the rich universalities of myth, finds intricate emblems and messages in everyday objects and events. Merwin has been described as a writer of poems that are both urgent and lyrical, that attempt to evoke a mood rather than tell a direct story. And he has been described as a deeply contemplative poet, one drawn to a natural world that inspires both wishful dreams and lessons of lost hope.

FURTHER READING: *W. S. Merwin, The First Four Books of Poems,* 1975; C. Davis, *W. S. Merwin,* 1981; *Regions of Memory, Uncollected Prose, 1949–1982,* 1987; *W. S. Merwin, Essays on the Poetry,* ed. C. Nelson and E. Folsom, 1987; E. Brunner, *Poetry as Labor and Privilege, The Writings of W. S. Merwin,* 1991; *The Lost Upland, Stories of Southwest France,* 1992; *Travels,* 1993; H. Hix, *Understanding W. S. Merwin,* 1997; *W. S. Merwin,* ed. H. Bloom, 2004.

TEXTS: "Direction" is from *Opening the Hand,* 1983; all other poems are from *W. S. Merwin, Selected Poems,* 1988.

GRANDFATHER IN THE OLD MEN'S HOME

Gentle at last, and as clean as ever,
He did not even need drink any more,
And his good sons unbent and brought him
Tobacco to chew, both times when they came
To be satisfied he was well cared for.
And he smiled all the time to remember
Grandmother, his wife, wearing the true faith
Like an iron nightgown, yet brought to birth
Seven times and raising the family
Through her needle's eye while he got away
Down the green river, finding directions

For boats. And himself coming home sometimes
Well-heeled but blind drunk, to hide all the bread
And shoot holes in the bucket while he made
His daughters pump. Still smiled as kindly in
His sleep beside the other clean old men
To see Grandmother, every night the same,
Huge in her age, with her thumbed-down mouth, come
Hating the river, filling with her stare
His gliding dream, while he turned to water,
While the children they both had begotten,
With old faces now, but themselves shrunken
To child-size again, stood ranged at her side,
Beating their little Bibles till he died.

1960

THE DRUNK IN THE FURNACE

For a good decade
The furnace stood in the naked gully, fireless
And vacant as any hat. Then when it was
No more to them than a hulking black fossil
To erode unnoticed with the rest of the junk-hill
By the poisonous creek, and rapidly to be added
To their ignorance.

They were afterwards astonished
To confirm, one morning, a twist of smoke like a pale
Resurrection, staggering out of its chewed hole,
And to remark then other tokens that someone,
Cosily bolted behind the eye-holed iron
Door of the drafty burner, had there established
His bad castle.

Where he gets his spirits
It's a mystery. But the stuff keeps him musical:
Hammer-and-anvilling with poker and bottle
To his jugged bellowings, till the last groaning clang
As he collapses onto the rioting
Springs of a litter of car-seats ranged on the grates,
To sleep like an iron pig.

In their tar-paper church
On a text about stoke-holes that are sated never
Their Reverend lingers. They nod and hate trespassers.
When the furnace wakes, though, all afternoon
Their witless offspring flock like piped rats to its siren
Crescendo, and agape on the crumbling ridge
Stand in a row and learn.

1960

SEPARATION

Your absence has gone through me
Like thread through a needle.
Everything I do is stitched with its color.
1963

NOAH'S RAVEN[1]

Why should I have returned?
My knowledge would not fit into theirs.
I found untouched the desert of the unknown,
Big enough for my feet. It is my home.
It is always beyond them. The future
Splits the present with the echo of my voice.
Hoarse with fulfillment, I never made promises.
1963

THE DRY STONE MASON

The mason is dead the gentle drunk
Master of dry walls
What he made of his years crosses the slopes without wavering
Upright but nameless
Ignorant in the new winter
Rubbed by running sheep
But the age of mortar has come to him

Bottles are waiting like fallen shrines
Under different trees in the rain
And stones drip where his hands left them
Leaning slightly inwards
His thirst is past

As he had no wife
The neighbors found where he kept his suit

[1]From the Ark, Noah sent forth a dove and a raven to learn if the Flood had subsided. The dove returned. The raven did not. Genesis 8:7–9.

A man with no family they sat with him
When he was carried through them they stood by their own dead
And they have buried him among the graves of the stones

1967

FLY

I have been cruel to a fat pigeon
Because he would not fly
All he wanted was to live like a friendly old man

He had let himself become a wreck filthy and confiding
Wild for his food beating the cat off the garbage
Ignoring his mate perpetually snotty at the beak
Smelling waddling having to be
Carried up the ladder at night content

Fly I said throwing him into the air
But he would drop and run back expecting to be fed
I said it again and again throwing him up
As he got worse
He let himself be picked up every time
Until I found him in the dovecote dead
Of the needless efforts

So that is what I am

Pondering his eye that could not
Conceive that I was a creature to run from

I who have always believed too much in words

1967

STRAWBERRIES

When my father died I saw   a narrow valley

it looked as though it began   across the river
from the landing where he was born   but there was no river

I was hoeing the sand of a small vegetable plot
for my mother in deepening twilight
and looked up in time to see a farm wagon
dry and gray horse already hidden
and no driver going into the valley
carrying a casket

and another wagon
coming out of the valley behind a gray horse
with a boy driving and a high load
of two kinds of berries one of them strawberries

that night when I slept I dreamed of things
wrong in the house all of them signs
the water of the shower running brackish
and an insect of a kind I had seen him kill
climbing around the walls of his bathroom
up in the morning I stopped on the stairs
my mother was awake already and asked me
if I wanted a shower before breakfast
and for breakfast she said we have strawberries

1983

DIRECTION

All I remember of the long lecture
which is all I remember of one summer
are the veins of the old old bald head
and the loose white sleeve and bony finger pointing
beyond the listeners
over their heads

there was the dazzling wall and the empty sunlight
and reaching out of his age he told them
for the last time
what to do when they got to the world
giving them his every breath to take with them like water
as they vanished

nobody was coming back that way

1983

Louise Glück 1943–

Louise Glück has been called "a poet of a fallen world"; her poems have been described as "searing," "unforgiving," "relentless," a "succession of shocks." Her writing is stark, unconsoling; it presents dreary landscapes of pain and loss. She writes of nature, of fields and ponds and trees, but it is a hostile region, a barren world of ignoble human existence. She writes of intense human relationships, of love, but it is failed love, cankered by betrayal or withering in the aftermath of passion.

Glück began publishing her poems in her early twenties. Her first book, Firstborn *(1968), appeared when she was twenty-five and brought her wide critical attention. Its range was narrow, and its poems were brief, gnomic. They were ingrained with loneliness, abandonment, and death. They spoke of "netted fish," "refuse," "poisoned air," "paralysis preceding death," "waste," "senility." And they were filled with piercing, evocative images that stunned her readers.*

In 1975 she published The House on the Marshland, *followed by* Descending Figure *(1980), books that revealed a broadening vision, a growing interest in longer poetic forms, and a use of myth and biblical metaphor to present more universal expression of her themes than was possible in her earlier, terse and imagistic lines. With the publication of* The Triumph of Achilles *(1985), which received a National Book Critics Circle prize for poetry, she came to be recognized as one of the most notable of recent American poets. For her volume entitled* The Wild Iris *(1993), she was awarded the 1993 Pulitzer Prize for American Poetry. In 2003 she was appointed Poet Laureate of the United States.*

Her poems are usually brief, often of sonnet length and near-sonnet form. Her diction is sharp, understated, blunt. She commonly avoids the flourishes and rhetoric of regular meter and rhyme, using near rhyme, internal rhyme, alliteration, and assonance to lend her poems a strong cohesiveness. Her writing has been compared to that of the "confessional" poets Robert Lowell and Sylvia Plath, but whereas Glück's poetry has some of the revelatory quality of confessional poetry and displays a similar interest in tensions and discontent, it does not depend so heavily on autobiographical details, nor does it seethe with the mad fury or exhibit the historical themes that characterize the poetry of Plath or Lowell.

Glück writes with a detached objectivity. Her poetry is devoid of sentimentalism, devoid of nostalgic celebrations of love, motherhood, and family, devoid of the conventional poetic consolations for loss, devoid even of the romantic pleasure of despair and rage. In Meadowlands *(1996) and in* Vita Nova *(1999)—for which she won the prestigious Bollingen Prize for poetry—Glück drew upon classical myths to describe the cruelties of intimacy and the strident, barbed experiences of modern marital discord. Her recent small volume,* October *(2004), evokes not a soft world of mellow fruitfulness, rich in color, but an autumn that is dark, barren, and stark. Her poems create an austere world where hope is a delusion and love a snare, a world pitilessly revealed in sardonic images of the floating wool scarves of drowned children, of passion "flushed down the refuse," and of a slatternly mother sprawled and oblivious to the lice "rooted" in her baby's hair.*

FURTHER READING: E. Dodd, *The Veiled Mirror and the Woman Poet, H. D., Louise Bogan, Elizabeth Bishop, and Louise Glück,* 1992; L. Upton, *The Muse of Abandonment, Origin, Identity, Mastery, in Five American Poets,* 1998; L. Upton, *Defensive Measures, The Poetry of Niedecker, Bishop, Glück, and Carson,* 2005; *On Louise Glück, Change What You See,* ed. J. Diehl, 2005.

TEXTS: "Vespers" and "Field Flowers" are from *The Wild Iris,* 1993. All other poems are from *First Born,* 1968.

HESITATE TO CALL

Lived to see you throwing
Me aside. That fought
Like netted fish inside me. Saw you
  throbbing
In my syrups. Saw you sleep. And lived to see
That all that all flushed down
The refuse. Done?
It lives in me.
You live in me. Malignant.
Love, you ever want me, don't.

1966

THE CHICAGO TRAIN

Across from me the whole ride
Hardly stirred: just Mister with his barren
Skull across the arm-rest while the kid
Got his head between his mama's legs and slept. The poison
That replaces air took over.
And they sat—as though paralysis preceding death
Had nailed them there. The track bent south.
I saw her pulsing crotch . . . the lice rooted in that baby's hair.

1967

THE EDGE

Time and again, time and again I tie
My heart to that headboard
While my quilted cries
Harden against his hand. He's bored—
I see it. Don't I lick his bribes, set his bouquets
In water? Over Mother's lace I watch him drive into the gored
Roasts, deal slivers in his mercy . . . I can feel his thighs
Against me for the children's sakes. Reward?
Mornings, crippled with this house,
I see him toast his toast and test
His coffee, hedgingly. The waste's my breakfast.

1967

MY NEIGHBOR IN THE MIRROR

M. le professeur[1] in prominent senility
Across the hall tidies his collected prose
And poems. Returning from a shopping spree
Not long ago, I caught him pausing to pose
Before the landing mirror in grandiose semi-profile.
It being impossible to avoid encounter on the stairs
I thought it best to smile
Openly, as though we two held equal shares
In the indiscretion. But his performance of a nod
Was labored and the infinite *politesse*[2] of rose palm
Unfurled for salutation fraud-
ulent. At any rate, lately there's been some
Change in his schedule. He receives without zeal
Now, and judging by his refuse, eats little but oatmeal.

1967

THANKSGIVING

In every room, encircled by a name-
less Southern boy from Yale,
There was my younger sister singing a Fellini theme[1]
And making phone calls
While the rest of us kept moving her discarded boots
Or sat and drank. Outside, in twenty-
nine degrees, a stray cat
Grazed in our driveway,
Seeking waste. It scratched the pail.
There were no other sounds.
Yet on and on the preparation of that vast consoling meal
Edged toward the stove. My mother
Had the skewers in her hands.
I watched her tucking skin
As though she missed her young, while bits of onion
Misted snow over the pronged death.

1968

[1]French: Mr. professor.
[2]French: politeness.
[1]I.e., music from the soundtrack of a film by the Italian director Federico Fellini (1920–).

VESPERS

In your extended absence, you permit me
use of earth, anticipating
some return on investment. I must report
failure in my assignment, principally
regarding the tomato plants.
I think I should not be encouraged to grow
tomatoes. Or, if I am, you should withhold
the heavy rains, the cold nights that come
so often here, while other regions get
twelve weeks of summer. All this
belongs to you: on the other hand,
I planted the seeds, I watched the first shoots
like wings tearing the soil, and it was my heart
broken by the blight, the black spot so quickly
multiplying in the rows. I doubt
you have a heart, in our understanding of
that term. You who do not discriminate
between the dead and the living, who are, in consequence,
immune to foreshadowing, you may not know
how much terror we bear, the spotted leaf,
the red leaves of the maple falling
even in August, in early darkness: I am responsible
for these vines.

1991

FIELD FLOWERS

What are you saying? That you want
eternal life? Are your thoughts really
as compelling as all that? Certainly
you don't look at us, don't listen to us,
on your skin
stain of sun, dust
of yellow buttercups: I'm talking
to you, you staring through
bars of high grass shaking
your little rattle—O
the soul! the soul! Is it enough
only to look inward? Contempt
for humanity is one thing, but why
disdain the expansive
field, your gaze rising over the clear heads
of the wild buttercups into what? Your poor
idea of heaven: absence
of change. Better than earth? How
would you know, who are neither
here nor there, standing in our midst?

1993

James Baldwin 1924–1987

James Baldwin has been called the most important American black writer of the twentieth century. He was born in Harlem, the oldest of nine children. His childhood and adolescence were dominated by his father—a stern, authoritarian man who was the minister of a storefront church. When he was fourteen, Baldwin underwent a deep religious experience and began to preach in competition with his father, a conflict of personal as well as religious significance. At the same time he began writing, and after his graduation from high school he began supporting himself in a succession of menial jobs.

In the winter of 1944–1945, Baldwin met Richard Wright, who encouraged him in his literary ambitions. He was to become literally and figuratively Wright's successor—his "native son" and heir as an American black writer. Like Wright, to escape American racial injustice, Baldwin left the United States for Europe, where he lived for nine years. While he was in Europe, his books first began to be published in the United States. The novel Go Tell It on the Mountain *(1953), a thinly veiled account of his youth, is considered by many critics his best work. In 1955 he produced a collection of essays,* Notes of a Native Son, *and in 1956* Giovanni's Room, *the story of a young, white expatriate in France attempting to come to terms with his homosexuality, a frequent subject of Baldwin's work.*

In 1957 he returned to America and immediately became involved in the civil rights struggle. His essays in this period, Nobody Knows My Name, More Notes of a Native Son *(1961) and* The Fire Next Time *(1963), are written with a force and a perceptiveness that have led many to consider Baldwin one of the foremost essayists in recent American literature. His next novel,* Another Country *(1962), reflects an increasing anxiety about race relations in America, as does a subsequent collection of short stories,* Going to Meet the Man *(1965). A later novel,* Tell Me How Long the Train's Been Gone *(1968), continues his preoccupation with the subjects of homosexuality, interracial love, and racial conflict.*

In 1971 Baldwin published a collection of dialogues with the noted anthropologist Margaret Mead, under the title A Rap on Race, *and in 1972 a volume of observations,* No Name in the Street, *expressing a furious disillusionment with modern America and the world. In 1974 he published* If Beale Street Could Talk, *a bitter protest novel, and in 1979* Just Above My Head, *a long and angry novel that is set in Harlem and tells the story of a famous gospel singer. In 1985 he published a collection of his nonfiction,* The Price of a Ticket. *Although Baldwin was fiercely attacked as insufficiently militant, he was nonetheless a forceful, brilliant voice, warning white America of the explosions to come and cautioning black America against the self-destructive excesses of racial hatred. Baldwin insisted that the American "complex fate" (a phrase he took from Henry James) necessarily makes the lives and the concerns of blacks and whites inseparable in modern America.*

FURTHER READING: F. Eckman, *The Furious Passage of James Baldwin,* 1966; *James Baldwin,* ed. H. Bloom, 1986; *Critical Essays on James Baldwin,* ed. F. Standley and N. Burt, 1988; W. Weatherby, *James Baldwin, Artist on Fire,* 1989; H. Porter, *Stealing the Fire, The Art and Protest of James Baldwin,* 1989; L. Rosset, *James Baldwin,* 1990; R. Lee, *James Baldwin, Climbing to the Light,* 1991; *James Baldwin,* ed. J. Köllhofer, 1991; J. Campbell, *Talking at the Gates, A Life of James Baldwin,* 1991, 2002; D. Leeming, *James Baldwin, A Biography,* 1994; *James Baldwin Now,* ed. D. McBride, 1999; *Re-viewing James Baldwin, Things Not Seen,* ed. D. Miller, 2000; L. Scott, *Witness to the Journey, James Baldwin's Later Fiction,* 2002.

TEXT: *Going to Meet the Man,* 1965.

SONNY'S BLUES

I read about it in the paper, in the subway, on my way to work. I read it, and I couldn't believe it, and I read it again. Then perhaps I just stared at it, at the newsprint spelling out his name, spelling out the story. I stared at it in the swinging lights of the subway car, and in the faces and bodies of the people, and in my own face, trapped in the darkness which roared outside.

It was not to be believed and I kept telling myself that, as I walked from the subway station to the high school. And at the same time I couldn't doubt it. I was scared, scared for Sonny. He became real to me again. A great block of ice got settled in my belly and kept melting there slowly all day long, while I taught my classes algebra. It was a special kind of ice. It kept melting, sending trickles of ice water all up and down my veins, but it never got less. Sometimes it hardened and seemed to expand until I felt my guts were going to come spilling out or that I was going to choke or scream. This would always be at a moment when I was remembering some specific thing Sonny had once said or done.

When he was about as old as the boys in my classes his face had been bright and open, there was a lot of copper in it; and he'd had wonderfully direct brown eyes, and great gentleness and privacy. I wondered what he looked like now. He had been picked up the evening before, in a raid on an apartment downtown, for peddling and using heroin.

I couldn't believe it: but what I mean by that is that I couldn't find any room for it anywhere inside me. I had kept it outside me for a long time. I hadn't wanted to know. I had had suspicions, but I didn't name them, I kept putting them away. I told myself that Sonny was wild, but he wasn't crazy. And he'd always been a good boy, he hadn't ever turned hard or evil or disrespectful, the way kids can, so quick, especially in Harlem. I didn't want to believe that I'd ever see my brother going down, coming to nothing, all that light in his face gone out, in the condition I'd already seen so many others. Yet it had happened and here I was, talking about algebra to a lot of boys who might, every one of them for all I knew, be popping off needles every time they went to the head. Maybe it did more for them than algebra could.

I was sure that the first time Sonny had ever had horse,[1] he couldn't have been much older than these boys were now. These boys, now, were living as we'd been living then, they were growing up with a rush and their heads bumped abruptly against the low ceiling of their actual possibilities. They were filled with rage. All they really knew were two darknesses, the darkness of their lives, which was now closing in on them, and the darkness of the movies, which had blinded them to that other darkness, and in which they now, vindictively, dreamed, at once more together than they were at any other time, and more alone.

When the last bell rang, the last class ended, I let out my breath. It seemed I'd been holding it for all that time. My clothes were wet—I may

[1]Heroin.

have looked as though I'd been sitting in a steam bath, all dressed up all afternoon. I sat alone in the classroom a long time. I listened to the boys outside, downstairs, shouting and cursing and laughing. Their laughter struck me for perhaps the first time. It was not the joyous laughter which—God knows why—one associates with children. It was mocking and insular, its intent was to denigrate. It was disenchanted, and in this, also, lay the authority of their curses. Perhaps I was listening to them because I was thinking about my brother and in them I heard my brother. And myself.

One boy was whistling a tune, at once very complicated and very simple, it seemed to be pouring out of him as though he were a bird, and it sounded very cool and moving through all that harsh, bright air, only just holding its own through all those other sounds.

I stood up and walked over to the window and looked down into the courtyard. It was the beginning of the spring and the sap was rising in the boys. A teacher passed through them every now and again, quickly, as though he or she couldn't wait to get out of that courtyard, to get those boys out of their sight and off their minds. I started collecting my stuff. I thought I'd better get home and talk to Isabel.

The courtyard was almost deserted by the time I got downstairs. I saw this boy standing in the shadow of a doorway, looking just like Sonny. I almost called his name. Then I saw that it wasn't Sonny, but somebody we used to know, a boy from around our block. He'd been Sonny's friend. He'd never been mine, having been too young for me, and, anyway, I'd never liked him. And now, even though he was a grown-up man, he still hung around that block, still spent hours on the street corners, was always high and raggy. I used to run into him from time to time and he'd often work around to asking me for a quarter or fifty cents. He always had some real good excuse too, and I always gave it to him, I don't know why.

But now, abruptly I hated him. I couldn't stand the way he looked at me, partly like a dog, partly like a cunning child. I wanted to ask him what the hell he was doing in the school courtyard.

He sort of shuffled over to me, and he said, "I see you got the papers. So you already know about it."

"You mean about Sonny? Yes, I already know about it. How come they didn't get you?"

He grinned. It made him repulsive and it also brought to mind what he'd looked like as a kid. "I wasn't there. I stay away from them people."

"Good for you." I offered him a cigarette and I watched him through the smoke. "You come all the way down here just to tell me about Sonny?"

"That's right." He was sort of shaking his head and his eyes looked strange, as though they were about to cross. The bright sun deadened his damp dark brown skin and it made his eyes look yellow and showed up the dirt in his kinked hair. He smelled funky. I moved a little way away from him and I said, "Well, thanks. But I already know about it and I got to get home."

"I'll walk you a little ways," he said. We started walking. There were a couple of kids still loitering in the courtyard and one of them said goodnight to me and looked strangely at the boy beside me.

"What're you going to do?" he asked me. "I mean, about Sonny?"

"Look. I haven't seen Sonny for over a year. I'm not sure I'm going to do anything. Anyway, what the hell *can* I do?"

"That's right," he said quickly, "ain't nothing you can do. Can't much help old Sonny no more, I guess."

It was what I was thinking and so it seemed to me he had no right to say it.

"I'm surprised at Sonny, though," he went on—he had a funny way of talking, he looked straight ahead as though he were talking to himself—"I thought Sonny was a smart boy, I thought he was too smart to get hung."

"I guess he thought so too," I said sharply, "and that's how he got hung. And how about you? You're pretty goddamn smart, I bet."

Then he looked directly at me, just for a minute. "I ain't smart," he said. "If I was smart, I'd have reached for a pistol a long time ago."

"Look. Don't tell *me* your sad story, if it was up to me, I'd give you one." Then I felt guilty—guilty, probably, for never having supposed that the poor bastard *had* a story of his own, much less a sad one, and I asked, quickly, "What's going to happen to him now?"

He didn't answer this. He was off by himself some place. "Funny thing," he said, and from his tone we might have been discussing the quickest way to get to Brooklyn, "when I saw the papers this morning, the first thing I asked myself was if I had anything to do with it. I felt sort of responsible."

I began to listen more carefully. The subway station was on the corner, just before us, and I stopped. He stopped, too. We were in front of a bar and he ducked slightly, peering in, but whoever he was looking for didn't seem to be there. The juke box was blasting away with something black and bouncy and I half watched the barmaid as she danced her way from the juke box to her place behind the bar. And I watched her face as she laughingly responded to something someone said to her, still keeping time to the music. When she smiled one saw the little girl, one sensed the doomed, still struggling woman beneath the battered face of the semi-whore.

"I never *give* Sonny nothing," the boy said finally, "but a long time ago I come to school high and Sonny asked me how it felt." He paused, I couldn't bear to watch him, I watched the barmaid, and I listened to the music which seemed to be causing the pavement to shake. "I told him it felt great." The music stopped, the barmaid paused and watched the juke box until the music began again. "It did."

All this was carrying me some place I didn't want to go. I certainly didn't want to know how it felt. It filled everything, the people, the houses, the music, the dark, quicksilver barmaid, with menace, and this menace was their reality.

"What's going to happen to him now?" I asked again.

"They'll send him away some place and they'll try to cure him." He shook his head. "Maybe he'll even think he's kicked the habit. Then they'll let him loose"—he gestured, throwing his cigarette into the gutter. "That's all."

"What do you mean that's *all?*"

But I knew what he meant.

"I *mean,* that's *all.*" He turned his head and looked at me, pulling down the corners of his mouth. "Don't you know what I mean?" he asked, softly.

"How the hell *would* I know what you mean?" I almost whispered it, I don't know why.

"That's right," he said to the air, "how would *he* know what I mean?" He turned toward me again, patient and calm, and yet I somehow felt him shaking, shaking as though he were going to fall apart. I felt that ice in my guts again, the dread I'd felt all afternoon; and again I watched the barmaid, moving about the bar, washing glasses, and singing. "Listen. They'll let him out and then it'll just start all over again. That's what I mean."

"You mean—they'll let him out. And then he'll just start working his way back in again. You mean he'll never kick the habit. Is that what you mean?"

"That's right," he said cheerfully. "*You* see what I mean."

"Tell me," I said at last, "why does he want to die? He must want to die, he's killing himself, why does he want to die?"

He looked at me in surprise. He licked his lips. "He don't want to die. He wants to live. Don't nobody want to die, ever."

Then I wanted to ask him—too many things. He could not have answered, or if he had, I could not have borne the answers. I started walking. "Well, I guess it's none of my business."

"It's going to be rough on old Sonny," he said. We reached the subway station. "This is your station?" he asked. I nodded. I took one step down. "Damn!" he said suddenly. I looked up at him. He grinned again. "Damn it if I didn't leave all my money home. You ain't got a dollar on you, have you? Just for a couple of days, is all."

All at once something inside gave and threatened to come pouring out of me. I didn't hate him any more. I felt that in another moment I'd start crying like a child.

"Sure," I said. "Don't sweat." I looked in my wallet and didn't have a dollar, I only had a five. "Here." I said. "That hold you?"

He didn't look at it—he didn't want to look at it. A terrible closed look came over his face, as though he were keeping the number on the bill a secret from him and me. "Thanks," he said, and now he was dying to see me go. "Don't worry about Sonny. Maybe I'll write him or something."

"Sure," I said. "You do that. So long."

"Be seeing you," he said. I went on down the steps.

And I didn't write Sonny or send him anything for a long time. When I finally did, it was just after my little girl died, he wrote me back a letter which made me feel like a bastard.

Here's what he said:

Dear brother,

You don't know how much I needed to hear from you. I wanted to write you many a time but I dug how much I must have hurt you and so I didn't write. But now I feel like a man who's been trying to climb up out of some deep, real deep and funky hole and just saw the sun up there, outside. I got to get outside.

I can't tell you much about how I got here. I mean I don't know how to tell you. I guess I was afraid of something or I was trying to escape from something and you know I have never been very strong in the head (smile). I'm glad Mama and Daddy are dead and can't see what's happened to their son and I swear if I'd known what I was doing I would never have hurt you so, you and a lot of other fine people who were nice to me and who believed in me.

I don't want you to think it had anything to do with me being a musician. It's more than that. Or maybe less than that. I can't get anything straight in my head down here and I try not to think about what's going to happen to me when I get outside again. Sometime I think I'm going to flip and *never* get outside and sometime I think I'll come straight back. I tell you one thing, though, I'd rather blow my brains out than go through this again. But that's what they all say, so they tell me. If I tell you when I'm coming to New York and if you could meet me, I sure would appreciate it. Give my love to Isabel and the kids and I was sure sorry to hear about little Gracie. I wish I could be like Mama and say the Lord's will be done, but I don't know it seems to me that trouble is the one thing that never does get stopped and I don't know what good it does to blame it on the Lord. But maybe it does some good if you believe it.

Your brother,
Sonny

Then I kept in constant touch with him and I sent him whatever I could and I went to meet him when he came back to New York. When I saw him many things I thought I had forgotten came flooding back to me. This was because I had begun, finally, to wonder about Sonny, about the life that Sonny lived inside. This life, whatever it was, had made him older and thinner and it had deepened the distant stillness in which he had always moved. He looked very unlike my baby brother. Yet, when he smiled, when we shook hands, the baby brother I'd never known looked out from the depths of his private life, like an animal waiting to be coaxed into the light.

"How you been keeping?" he asked me.

"All right. And you?"

"Just fine." He was smiling all over his face. "It's good to see you again."

"It's good to see you."

The seven years' difference in our ages lay between us like a chasm: I wondered if these years would ever operate between us as a bridge. I was remembering, and it made it hard to catch my breath, that I had been there when he was born; and I had heard the first words he had ever spoken. When he started to walk, he walked from our mother straight to me. I caught him just before he fell when he took the first steps he ever took in this world.

"How's Isabel?"

"Just fine. She's dying to see you."

"And the boys?"

"They're fine, too. They're anxious to see their uncle."

"Oh, come on. You know they don't remember me."

"Are you kidding? Of course they remember you."

He grinned again. We got into a taxi. We had a lot to say to each other, far too much to know how to begin.

As the taxi began to move, I asked, "You still want to go to India?"

He laughed. "You still remember that. Hell, no. This place is Indian enough for me."

"It used to belong to them," I said.

And he laughed again. "They damn sure knew what they were doing when they got rid of it."

Years ago, when he was around fourteen, he'd been all hipped on the idea of going to India. He read books about people sitting on rocks, naked, in all kinds of weather, but mostly bad, naturally, and walking barefoot through hot coals and arriving at wisdom. I used to say that it sounded to me as though they were getting away from wisdom as fast as they could. I think he sort of looked down on me for that.

"Do you mind," he asked, "if we have the driver drive alongside the park? On the west side—I haven't seen the city in so long."

"Of course not," I said. I was afraid that I might sound as though I were humoring him, but I hoped he wouldn't take it that way.

So we drove along, between the green of the park and the stony, lifeless elegance of hotels and apartment buildings, toward the vivid, killing streets of our childhood. These streets hadn't changed, though housing projects jutted up out of them now like rocks in the middle of a boiling sea. Most of the houses in which we had grown up had vanished, as had the stores from which we had stolen, the basements in which we had first tried sex, the rooftops from which we had hurled tin cans and bricks. But houses exactly like the houses of our past yet dominated the landscape, boys exactly like the boys we once had been found themselves smothering in these houses, came down into the streets for light and air and found themselves encircled by disaster. Some escaped the trap, most didn't. Those who got out always left something of themselves behind, as some animals amputate a leg and leave it in the trap. It might be said, perhaps, that I had escaped, after all, I was a school teacher; or that Sonny had, he hadn't lived in Harlem for years. Yet, as the cab moved uptown through streets which seemed, with a rush, to darken with dark people, and as I covertly studied Sonny's face, it came to me that what we both were seeking through our separate cab windows was that part of ourselves which had been left behind. It's always at the hour of trouble and confrontation that the missing member aches.

We hit 110th Street and started rolling up Lenox Avenue. And I'd known this avenue all my life, but it seemed to me again, as it had seemed on the day I'd first heard about Sonny's trouble, filled with a hidden menace which was its very breath of life.

"We almost there," said Sonny.

"Almost." We were both too nervous to say anything more.

We live in a housing project. It hasn't been up long. A few days after it was up it seemed uninhabitably new, now, of course, it's already rundown. It looks like a parody of the good, clean, faceless life—God knows the people who live in it do their best to make it a parody. The beat-looking grass lying around isn't enough to make their lives green, the hedges will never hold out the streets, and they know it. The big windows fool no one, they aren't big enough to make space out of no space. They don't bother with the windows, they watch the TV screen instead. The playground is most popular with the children who don't play at jacks, or skip rope, or roller skate, or swing, and they can be found in it after dark. We moved in partly because it's not too far from where I teach, and partly for the kids; but it's really just like the houses in which Sonny and I grew up. The same things happen, they'll have the same things to remember. The moment Sonny and I started into the house I had the feeling that I was simply bringing him back into the danger he had almost died trying to escape.

Sonny has never been talkative. So I don't know why I was sure he'd be dying to talk to me when supper was over the first night. Everything went fine, the oldest boy remembered him, and the youngest boy liked him, and Sonny had remembered to bring something for each of them; and Isabel, who is really much nicer than I am, more open and giving, had gone to a lot of trouble about dinner and was genuinely glad to see him. And she's always been able to tease Sonny in a way that I haven't. It was nice to see her face so vivid again and to hear her laugh and watch her make Sonny laugh. She wasn't, or, anyway, she didn't seem to be, at all uneasy or embarrassed. She chatted as though there were no subject which had to be avoided and she got Sonny past his first, faint stiffness. And thank God she was there, for I was filled with that icy dread again. Everything I did seemed awkward to me, and everything I said sounded freighted with hidden meaning. I was trying to remember everything I'd heard about dope addiction and I couldn't help watching Sonny for signs. I wasn't doing it out of malice. I was trying to find out something about my brother. I was dying to hear him tell me he was safe.

"Safe!" my father grunted, whenever Mamma suggested trying to move to a neighborhood which might be safer for children. "Safe, hell! Ain't no place safe for kids, nor nobody."

He always went on like this, but he wasn't, ever, really as bad as he sounded, not even on weekends, when he got drunk. As a matter of fact, he was always on the lookout for "something a little better," but he died before he found it. He died suddenly, during a drunken weekend in the middle of the war, when Sonny was fifteen. He and Sonny hadn't ever got on too well. And this was partly because Sonny was the apple of his father's eye. It was because he loved Sonny so much and was frightened for him, that he was always fighting with him. It doesn't do any good to fight with Sonny. Sonny just moves back, inside himself, where he can't be reached. But the principal reason that they never hit it off is that they were so much alike. Daddy was big and rough and loud-talking, just the opposite of Sonny, but they both had—that same privacy.

Mama tried to tell me something about this, just after Daddy died. I was home on leave from the army.

This was the last time I ever saw my mother alive. Just the same, this picture gets all mixed up in my mind with pictures I had of her when she was younger. The way I always see her is the way she used to be on a Sunday afternoon, say, when the old folks were talking after the big Sunday dinner. I always see her wearing pale blue. She'd be sitting on the sofa. And my father would be sitting in the easy chair, not far from her. And the living room would be full of church folks and relatives. There they sit, in chairs all around the living room, and the night is creeping up outside, but nobody knows it yet. You can see the darkness growing against the window-panes and you hear the street noises every now and again, or maybe the jangling beat of a tambourine from one of the churches close by, but it's real quiet in the room. For a moment nobody's talking, but every face looks darkening, like the sky outside. And my mother rocks a little from the waist, and my father's eyes are closed. Everyone is looking at something a child can't see. For a minute they've forgotten the children. Maybe a kid is lying on the rug, half asleep. Maybe somebody's got a kid in his lap and is absent-mindedly stroking the kid's head. Maybe there's a kid, quiet and big-eyed, curled up in a big chair in the corner. The silence, the darkness coming, and the darkness in the faces frightens the child obscurely. He hopes that the hand which strokes his forehead will never stop—will never die. He hopes that there will never come a time when the old folks won't be sitting around the living room, talking about where they've come from, and what they've seen, and what's happened to them and their kinfolk.

But something deep and watchful in the child knows that this is bound to end, is already ending. In a moment someone will get up and turn on the light. Then the old folks will remember the children and they won't talk any more that day. And when light fills the room, the child is filled with darkness. He knows that every time this happens he's moved just a little closer to that darkness outside. The darkness outside is what the old folks have been talking about. It's what they've come from. It's what they endure. The child knows that they won't talk any more because if he knows too much about what's happening to *them,* he'll know too much too soon, about what's going to happen to *him.*

The last time I talked to my mother, I remember I was restless. I wanted to get out and see Isabel. We weren't married then and we had a lot to straighten out between us.

There Mama sat, in black, by the window. She was humming an old church song, *Lord you brought me from a long ways off.* Sonny was out somewhere. Mama kept watching the streets.

"I don't know," she said, "if I'll ever see you again, after you go off from here. But I hope you'll remember the things I tried to teach you."

"Don't talk like that," I said, and smiled. "You'll be here a long time yet."

She smiled, too, but she said nothing. She was quiet for a long time. And I said, "Mama, don't you worry about nothing. I'll be writing all the time, and you be getting the checks. . . ."

"I want to talk to you about your brother," she said, suddenly. "If anything happens to me he ain't going to have nobody to look out for him."

"Mama," I said, "ain't nothing going to happen to you *or* Sonny. Sonny's all right. He's a good boy and he's got good sense."

"It ain't a question of his being a good boy," Mama said, "nor of his having good sense. It ain't only the bad ones, nor yet the dumb ones that gets sucked under." She stopped, looking at me. "Your Daddy once had a brother," she said, and she smiled in a way that made me feel she was in pain. "You didn't never know that, did you?"

"No," I said, "I never knew that," and I watched her face.

"Oh, yes," she said, "your Daddy had a brother. She looked out of the window again. "I know you never saw your Daddy cry. But *I* did—many a time, through all these years."

I asked her, "What happened to his brother? How come nobody's ever talked about him?"

This was the first time I ever saw my mother look old.

"His brother got killed," she said, "when he was just a little younger than you are now. I knew him. He was a fine boy. He was maybe a little full of the devil, but he didn't mean nobody no harm."

Then she stopped and the room was silent, exactly as it had sometimes been on those Sunday afternoons. Mama kept looking out into the streets.

"He used to have a job in the mill," she said, "and, like all young folks, he just liked to perform on Saturday nights. Saturday nights, him and your father would drift around to different places, go to dances and things like that, or just sit around with people they knew, and your father's brother would sing, he had a fine voice, and play along with himself on his guitar. Well, this particular Saturday night, him and your father was coming home from some place, and they were both a little drunk and there was a moon that night, it was bright like day. Your father's brother was feeling kind of good, and he was whistling to himself, and he had his guitar slung over his shoulder. They was coming down a hill and beneath them was a road that turned off from the highway. Well, your father's brother, being always kind of frisky, decided to run down this hill, and he did, with that guitar banging and clanging behind him, and he ran across the road, and he was making water behind a tree. And your father was sort of amused at him and he was still coming down the hill, kind of slow. Then he heard a car motor and that same minute his brother stepped from behind the tree, into the road, in the moonlight. And he started to cross the road. And your father started to run down the hill, he says he don't know why. This car was full of white men. They was all drunk, and when they seen your father's brother they let out a great whoop and holler and they aimed the car straight at him. They was having fun, they just wanted to scare him, the way they do sometimes, you know. But they was drunk. And I guess the boy, being drunk, too, and scared, kind of lost his head. By the time he jumped it was too late. Your father says he heard his brother scream when the car rolled over him, and he heard the wood of that guitar when it give, and he heard them strings go flying, and he heard them white men shouting, and the car kept on a-going and it ain't stopped till this day. And, time your father got down the hill, his brother weren't nothing but blood and pulp."

Tears were gleaming on my mother's face. There wasn't anything I could say.

"He never mentioned it," she said, "because I never let him mention it before you children. Your Daddy was like a crazy man that night and for many a night thereafter. He says he never in his life seen anything as dark as that road after the lights of that car had gone away. Weren't nothing, weren't nobody on that road, just your Daddy and his brother and that busted guitar. Oh, yes. Your Daddy never did really get right again. Till the day he died he weren't sure but that every white man he saw was the man that killed his brother."

She stopped and took out her handkerchief and dried her eyes and looked at me.

"I ain't telling you all this," she said, "to make you scared or bitter or to make you hate nobody. I'm telling you this because you got a brother. And the world ain't changed."

I guess I didn't want to believe this. I guess she saw this in my face. She turned away from me, toward the window again, searching those streets.

"But I praise my Redeemer," she said at last, "that He called your Daddy home before me. I ain't saying it to throw no flowers at myself, but, I declare, it keeps me from feeling too cast down to know I helped your father get safely through this world. Your father always acted like he was the roughest, strongest man on earth. And everybody took him to be like that. But if he hadn't had *me* there—to see his tears!"

She was crying again. Still I couldn't move. I said, "Lord, Lord, Mama, I didn't know it was like that."

"Oh, honey," she said, "there's a lot that you don't know. But you are going to find it out." She stood up from the window and came over to me. "You got to hold on to your brother," she said, "and don't let him fall, no matter what it looks like is happening to him and no matter how evil you gets with him. You going to be evil with him many a time. But don't you forget what I told you, you hear?"

"I won't forget," I said. "Don't you worry, I won't forget. I won't let nothing happen to Sonny."

My mother smiled as though she were amused at something she saw in my face. Then, "You may not be able to stop nothing from happening. But you got to let him know you's *there*."

Two days later I was married, and then I was gone. And I had a lot of things on my mind and I pretty well forgot my promise to Mama until I got shipped home on a special furlough for her funeral.

And, after the funeral, with just Sonny and me alone in the empty kitchen, I tried to find out something about him.

"What do you want to do?" I asked him.

"I'm going to be a musician," he said.

For he had graduated, in the time I had been away, from dancing to the juke box to finding out who was playing what, and what they were doing with it, and he had bought himself a set of drums.

"You mean, you want to be a drummer?" I somehow had the feeling that being a drummer might be all right for other people but not for my brother Sonny.

"I don't think," he said, looking at me very gravely, "that I'll ever be a good drummer. But I think I can play a piano."

I frowned. I'd never played the role of the older brother quite so seriously before, had scarcely ever, in fact, *asked* Sonny a damn thing. I sensed myself in the presence of something I didn't really know how to handle, didn't understand. So I made my frown a little deeper as I asked: "What kind of musician do you want to be?"

He grinned. "How many kinds do you think there are?"

"Be *serious,*" I said.

He laughed, throwing his head back, and then looked at me. "I *am* serious."

"Well, then, for Christ's sake, stop kidding around and answer a serious question. I mean, do you want to be a concert pianist, or want to play classical music and all that, or—or what?" Long before I finished he was laughing again. "For Christ's *sake,* Sonny!"

He sobered, but with difficulty. "I'm sorry. But you sound so—*scared!*" and he was off again.

"Well, you may think it's funny now, baby, but it's not going to be so funny when you have to make your living at it, let me tell you *that.*" I was furious because I knew he was laughing at me and I didn't know why.

"No," he said, very sober now, and afraid, perhaps, that he'd hurt me, "I don't want to be a classical pianist. That isn't what interests me. I mean"—he paused, looking hard at me, as though his eyes would help me to understand, and then gestured helplessly, as though perhaps his hand would help— "I mean, I'll have a lot of studying to do, and I'll have to study *everything,* but, I mean, I want to play *with*—jazz musicians." He stopped. "I want to play jazz," he said.

Well, the word had never before sounded as heavy, as real, as it sounded that afternoon in Sonny's mouth. I just looked at him and I was probably frowning a real frown by this time. I simply couldn't see why on earth he'd want to spend his time hanging around nightclubs, clowning around on bandstands, while people pushed each other around a dance floor. It seemed —beneath him, somehow. I had never thought about it before, had never been forced to, but I suppose I had always put jazz musicians in a class with what Daddy called "good-time people."

"Are you *serious?*"

"Hell, *yes,* I'm serious."

He looked more helpless than ever, and annoyed, and deeply hurt.

I suggested helpfully: "You mean—like Louis Armstrong?"

His face closed as though I'd struck him. "No. I'm not talking about none of that old-time, down home crap."

"Well, look Sonny, I'm sorry, don't get mad. I just don't altogether get it, that's all. Name somebody—you know, a jazz musician you admire."

"Bird."

"Who?"

"Bird! Charlie Parker! Don't they teach you nothing in the god-damn army?"

I lit a cigarette. I was surprised and then a little amused to discover that I was trembling. "I've been out of touch," I said. "You'll have to be patient with me. Now. Who's this Parker character?"

"He's just one of the greatest jazz musicians alive," said Sonny, sullenly, his hands in his pockets, his back to me. "Maybe *the* greatest," he added, bitterly, "that's probably why *you* never heard of him."

"All right," I said, "I'm ignorant. I'm sorry. I'll go out and buy all the cat's records right away, all right?"

"It don't," said Sonny, with dignity, "make any difference to me. I don't care what you listen to. Don't do me no favors."

I was beginning to realize that I'd never seen him so upset before. With another part of my mind I was thinking that this would probably turn out to be one of those things kids go through and that I shouldn't make it seem important by pushing it too hard. Still, I didn't think it would do any harm to ask: "Doesn't all this take a lot of time? Can you make a living at it?"

He turned back to me and half leaned, half sat, on the kitchen table. "Everything takes time," he said, "and—well, yes, sure, I can make a living at it. But what I don't seem to be able to make you understand is that it's the only thing I want to do."

"Well, Sonny," I said gently, "you know people can't always do exactly what they *want* to do—"

"*No,* I don't know that," said Sonny, surprising me. "I think people *ought* to do what they want to do, what else are they alive for?"

"You are getting to be a big boy," I said desperately, "it's time you started thinking about your future."

"I'm thinking about my future," said Sonny, grimly. "I think about it all the time."

I gave up. I decided, if he didn't change his mind, that we could always talk about it later. "In the meantime," I said, "you got to finish school." We had already decided that he'd have to move in with Isabel and her folks. I knew this wasn't the ideal arrangement because Isabel's folks are inclined to be dicty[2] and they hadn't especially wanted Isabel to marry me. But I didn't know what else to do. "And we have to get you fixed up at Isabel's."

There was a long silence. He moved from the kitchen table to the window. "That's a terrible idea. You know it yourself."

"Do you have a *better* idea?"

He just walked up and down the kitchen for a minute. He was as tall as I was. He had started to shave. I suddenly had the feeling that I didn't know him at all.

He stopped at the kitchen table and picked up my cigarettes. Looking at me with a kind of mocking, amused defiance, he put one between his lips. "You mind?"

"You smoking already?"

He lit the cigarette and nodded, watching me through the smoke. "I just wanted to see if I'd have the courage to smoke in front of you." He grinned and blew a great cloud of smoke to the ceiling. "It was easy." He looked at my face. "Come on, now. I bet you was smoking at my age, tell the truth."

[2]Snobbish.

I didn't say anything but the truth was on my face, and he laughed. But now there was something very strained in his laugh. "Sure. And I bet that ain't all you was doing."

He was frightening me a little. "Cut the crap," I said. "We already decided that you was going to go and live at Isabel's. Now what's got into you all of a sudden?"

"*You* decided it," he pointed out. "*I* didn't decide nothing." He stopped in front of me, leaning against the stove, arms loosely folded. "Look, brother. I don't want to stay in Harlem no more, I really don't." He was very earnest. He looked at me, then over toward the kitchen window. There was something in his eyes I'd never seen before, some thoughtfulness, some worry all his own. He rubbed the muscle of one arm. "It's time I was getting out of here."

"Where do you want to *go*, Sonny?"

"I want to join the army. Or the navy, I don't care. If I say I'm old enough, they'll believe me."

Then I got mad. It was because I was so scared. "You must be crazy. You goddamn fool, what the hell do you want to go and join the *army* for?"

"I just told you. To get out of Harlem."

"Sonny, you haven't even finished *school*. And if you really want to be a musician, how do you expect to study if you're in the *army?*"

He looked at me, trapped, and in anguish. "There's ways. I might be able to work out some kind of deal. Anyway, I'll have the G.I. Bill when I come out."

"*If* you come out." We stared at each other. "Sonny, please. Be reasonable. I know the setup is far from perfect. But we got to do the best we can."

"I ain't learning nothing in school," he said. "Even when I go." He turned away from me and opened the window and threw his cigarette out into the narrow alley. I watched his back. "At least, I ain't learning nothing you'd want me to learn." He slammed the window so hard I thought the glass would fly out, and turned back to me. "And I'm sick of the stink of these garbage cans!"

"Sonny," I said, "I know how you feel, but if you don't finish school now, you're going to be sorry later that you didn't." I grabbed him by the shoulders. "And you only got another year. It ain't so bad. And I'll come back and I swear I'll help you do *whatever* you want to do. Just try to put up with it till I come back. Will you please do that? For me?"

He didn't answer and he wouldn't look at me.

"Sonny. You hear me?"

He pulled away. "I hear you. But you never hear anything *I* say."

I didn't know what to say to that. He looked out of the window and then back at me. "OK," he said, and sighed. "I'll try."

Then I said, trying to cheer him up a little, "They got a piano at Isabel's. You can practice on it."

And as a matter of fact, it did cheer him up for a minute. "That's right," he said to himself. "I forgot that." His face relaxed a little. But the worry, the thoughtfulness, played on it still, the way shadows play on a face which is staring into the fire.

But I thought I'd never hear the end of that piano. At first, Isabel would write me, saying how nice it was that Sonny was so serious about his music and how, as soon as he came in from school, or wherever he had been when he was supposed to be at school, he went straight to that piano and stayed there until suppertime. And, after supper, he went back to that piano and stayed there until everybody went to bed. He was at the piano all day Saturday and all day Sunday. Then he bought a record player and started playing records. He'd play one record over and over again, all day long sometimes, and he'd improvise along with it on the piano. Or he'd play one section of the record, one chord, one change, one progression, then he'd do it on the piano. Then back to the record. Then back to the piano.

Well, I really don't know how they stood it. Isabel finally confessed that it wasn't like living with a person at all, it was like living with sound. And the sound didn't make any sense to her, didn't make any sense to any of them—naturally. They began, in a way, to be afflicted by this presence that was living in their home. It was as though Sonny were some sort of god, or monster. He moved in an atmosphere which wasn't like theirs at all. They fed him and he ate, he washed himself, he walked in and out of their door; he certainly wasn't nasty or unpleasant or rude, Sonny isn't any of those things; but it was as though he were all wrapped up in some cloud, some fire, some vision all his own; and there wasn't any way to reach him.

At the same time, he wasn't really a man yet, he was still a child, and they had to watch out for him in all kinds of ways. They certainly couldn't throw him out. Neither did they dare to make a great scene about that piano because even they dimly sensed, as I sensed, from so many thousands of miles away, that Sonny was at that piano playing for his life.

But he hadn't been going to school. One day a letter came from the school board and Isabel's mother got it—there had, apparently, been other letters but Sonny had torn them up. This day, when Sonny came in, Isabel's mother showed him the letter and asked where he'd been spending his time. And she finally got it out of him that he'd been down in Greenwich Village, with musicians and other characters, in a white girl's apartment. And this scared her and she started to scream at him and what came up, once she began—though she denies it to this day—was what sacrifices they were making to give Sonny a decent home and how little he appreciated it.

Sonny didn't play the piano that day. By evening, Isabel's mother had calmed down but then there was the old man to deal with, and Isabel herself. Isabel says she did her best to be calm but she broke down and started crying. She says she just watched Sonny's face. She could tell, by watching him, what was happening with him. And what was happening was that they penetrated his cloud, they had reached him. Even if their fingers had been a thousand times more gentle than human fingers ever are, he could hardly help feeling that they had stripped him naked and were spitting on that nakedness. For he also had to see that his presence, that music, which was life or death to him, had been torture for them and that they had endured it, not at all for his sake, but only for mine. And Sonny couldn't take that. He can take it a little better today than he could then but he's still not very good at it and, frankly, I don't know anybody who is.

The silence of the next few days must have been louder than the sound of all the music ever played since time began. One morning, before she went to work, Isabel was in his room for something and she suddenly realized that all of his records were gone. And she knew for certain that he was gone. And he was. He went as far as the navy would carry him. He finally sent me a postcard from some place in Greece and that was the first I knew that Sonny was still alive. I didn't see him any more until we were both back in New York and the war had long been over.

He was a man by then, of course, but I wasn't willing to see it. He came by the house from time to time, but we fought almost every time we met. I didn't like the way he carried himself, loose and dreamlike all the time, and I didn't like his friends, and his music seemed to be merely an excuse for the life he led. It sounded just that weird and disordered.

Then we had a fight, a pretty awful fight, and I didn't see him for months. By and by I looked him up, where he was living, in a furnished room in the Village, and I tried to make it up. But there were lots of other people in the room and Sonny just lay on his bed, and he wouldn't come downstairs with me, and he treated these other people as though they were his family and I weren't. So I got mad and then he got mad, and then I told him that he might just as well be dead as live the way he was living. Then he stood up and he told me not to worry about him any more in life, that he *was* dead as far as I was concerned. Then he pushed me to the door and the other people looked on as though nothing were happening, and he slammed the door behind me. I stood in the hallway, staring at the door. I heard somebody laugh in the room and then the tears came to my eyes. I started down the steps, whistling to keep from crying, I kept whistling to myself, *You going to need me, baby, one of these cold, rainy days.*

I read about Sonny's trouble in the spring. Little Grace died in the fall. She was a beautiful little girl. But she only lived a little over two years. She died of polio and she suffered. She had a slight fever for a couple of days, but it didn't seem like anything and we just kept her in bed. And we would certainly have called the doctor, but the fever dropped, she seemed to be all right. So we thought it had just been a cold. Then, one day, she was up, playing, Isabel was in the kitchen fixing lunch for the two boys when they'd come in from school, and she heard Grace fall down in the living room. When you have a lot of children you don't always start running when one of them falls, unless they start screaming or something. And, this time, Grace was quiet. Yet, Isabel says that when she heard that *thump* and then that silence, something happened in her to make her afraid. And she ran to the living room and there was little Grace on the floor, all twisted up, and the reason she hadn't screamed was that she couldn't get her breath. And when she did scream, it was the worst sound, Isabel says, that she'd ever heard in all her life, and she still hears it sometimes in her dreams. Isabel will sometimes wake me up with a low, moaning, strangled sound and I have to be quick to awaken her and hold her to me and where Isabel is weeping against me seems a mortal wound.

I think I may have written Sonny the very day that little Grace was buried. I was sitting in the living room in the dark, by myself, and I suddenly thought of Sonny. My trouble made his real.

One Saturday afternoon, when Sonny had been living with us, or, anyway, been in our house, for nearly two weeks, I found myself wandering aimlessly about the living room, drinking from a can of beer, and trying to work up the courage to search Sonny's room. He was out, he was usually out whenever I was home, and Isabel had taken the children to see their grandparents. Suddenly I was standing still in front of the living room window, watching Seventh Avenue. The idea of searching Sonny's room made me still. I scarcely dared to admit to myself what I'd be searching for. I didn't know what I'd do if I found it. Or if I didn't.

On the sidewalk across from me, near the entrance to a barbecue joint, some people were holding an old-fashioned revival meeting. The barbecue cook, wearing a dirty white apron, his conked hair reddish and metallic in the pale sun, and a cigarette between his lips, stood in the doorway, watching them. Kids and older people paused in their errands and stood there, along with some older men and a couple of very tough-looking women who watched everything that happened on the avenue, as though they owned it, or were maybe owned by it. Well, they were watching this, too. The revival was being carried on by three sisters in black, and a brother. All they had were their voices and their Bibles and a tambourine. The brother was testifying and while he testified two of the sisters stood together, seeming to say, amen, and the third sister walked around with the tambourine outstretched and a couple of people dropped coins into it. Then the brother's testimony ended and the sister who had been taking up the collection dumped the coins into her palm and transferred them to the pocket of her long black robe. Then she raised both hands, striking the tambourine against the air, and then against one hand, and she started to sing. And the two other sisters and the brother joined in.

It was strange, suddenly, to watch, though I had been seeing these street meetings all my life. So, of course, had everybody else down there. Yet, they paused and watched and listened and I stood still at the window. *"Tis the old ship of Zion,"* they sang, and the sister with the tambourine kept a steady, jangling beat, *"it has rescued many a thousand!"* Not a soul under the sound of their voices was hearing this song for the first time, not one of them had been rescued. Nor had they seen much in the way of rescue work being done around them. Neither did they especially believe in the holiness of the three sisters and the brother, they knew too much about them, knew where they lived, and how. The woman with the tambourine, whose voice dominated the air, whose face was bright with joy, was divided by very little from the woman who stood watching her, a cigarette between her heavy, chapped lips, her hair a cuckoo's nest, her face scarred and swollen from many beatings, and her black eyes glittering like coal. Perhaps they both knew this, which was why, when, as rarely, they addressed each other, they addressed each other as Sister. As the singing filled the air the watching, listening faces underwent a change, the eyes focusing on something within; the music seemed to soothe a poison out of them; and time seemed, nearly, to fall away from the sullen, belligerent, battered faces, as though they were fleeing back to their first condition, while dreaming of their last. The barbecue cook half shook his head and smiled, and dropped his cigarette and disappeared into his joint. A man fumbled in his pockets for change and stood holding it in his hand impatiently, as though he had just remembered a pressing appointment further up the avenue. He looked furious. Then I saw Sonny, standing on the edge of the crowd. He was carrying a wide, flat notebook with a green cover, and it made him look, from where I was standing, almost like a schoolboy. The coppery sun brought out the copper in his skin, he was very faintly smiling, standing very still. Then the singing stopped, the tambourine turned into a collection plate again. The furious man dropped in his coins and vanished, so did a couple of the women, and Sonny dropped some change in the plate, looking directly at the woman with a little smile. He started across the avenue, toward the house. He has a slow, loping walk, something like the way Harlem hipsters walk, only he's imposed on this his own half-beat. I had never really noticed it before.

I stayed at the window, both relieved and apprehensive. As Sonny disappeared from my sight, they began singing again. And they were still singing when his key turned in the lock.

"Hey," he said.

"Hey, yourself. You want some beer?"

"No. Well, maybe." But he came up to the window and stood beside me, looking out. "What a warm voice," he said.

They were singing *If I could only hear my mother pray again!*

"Yes," I said, "and she can sure beat that tambourine."

"But what a terrible song," he said, and laughed. He dropped his notebook on the sofa and disappeared into the kitchen. "Where's Isabel and the kids?"

"I think they went to see their grandparents. You hungry?"

"No." He came back into the living room with his can of beer. "You want to come some place with me tonight?"

I sensed, I don't know how, that I couldn't possibly say no. "Sure. Where?"

He sat down on the sofa and picked up his notebook and started leafing through it. "I'm going to sit in with some fellows in a joint in the Village."

"You mean, you're going to play, tonight?"

"That's right." He took a swallow of his beer and moved back, to the window. He gave me a sidelong look. "If you can stand it."

"I'll try," I said.

He smiled to himself and we both watched as the meeting across the way broke up. The three sisters and the brother, heads bowed, were singing *God be with you till we meet again*. The faces around them were very quiet. Then the song ended. The small crowd dispersed. We watched the three women and the lone man walk slowly up the avenue.

"When she was singing before," said Sonny, abruptly, "her voice reminded me for a minute of what heroin feels like sometimes—when it's in your veins. It makes you feel sort of warm and cool at the same time. And distant. And—and sure." He sipped his beer, very deliberately not looking at me. I watched his face. "It makes you feel—in control. Sometimes you've got to have that feeling."

"Do you?" I sat down slowly in the easy chair.

"Sometimes." He went to the sofa and picked up his notebook again. "Some people do."

"In order," I asked, "to play?" And my voice was very ugly, full of contempt and anger.

"Well"—he looked at me with great, troubled eyes, as though, in fact, he hoped his eyes would tell me things he could never otherwise say—"they *think* so. And *if* they think so—!"

"And what do *you* think?" I asked.

He sat on the sofa and put his can of beer on the floor. "I don't know," he said, and I couldn't be sure if he were answering my question or pursuing his thoughts. His face didn't tell me. "It's not so much to *play*. It's to *stand* it, to be able to make it at all. On any level." He frowned and smiled: "In order to keep from shaking to pieces."

"But these friends of yours," I said, "they seem to shake themselves to pieces pretty goddamn fast."

"Maybe." He played with the notebook. And something told me that I should curb my tongue, that Sonny was doing his best to talk, that I should listen. "But of course you only know the ones that've gone to pieces. Some don't—or at least they haven't *yet* and that's just about all *any* of us can say." He paused. "And then there are some who just live, really, in hell, and they know it and they see what's happening, and they go right on. I don't know." He sighed, dropped the notebook, folded his arms. "Some guys, you can tell from the way they play, they on something *all* the time. And you can see that, well, it makes something real for them. But of course," he picked up his beer from the floor and sipped it and put the can down again, "they *want* to, too, you've got to see that. Even some of them that say they don't—*some,* not all."

"And what about you?" I asked—I couldn't help it. "What about you? Do *you* want to?"

He stood up and walked to the window and remained silent for a long time. Then he sighed. "Me," he said. Then: "While I was downstairs before, on my way here, listening to that woman sing, it struck me all of a sudden how much suffering she must have had to go through—to sing like that. It's *repulsive* to think you have to suffer that much."

I said: "But there's no way not to suffer—is there, Sonny?"

"I believe not," he said and smiled, "but that's never stopped anyone from trying." He looked at me. "Has it?" I realized, with this mocking look, that there stood between us, forever, beyond the power of time or forgiveness, the fact that I had held silence—so long!—when he had needed human speech to help him. He turned back to the window. "No, there's no way not to suffer. But you try all kinds of ways to keep from drowning in it, to keep on top of it, and to make it seem—well, like *you.* Like you did something, all right, and now you're suffering for it. You know?" I said nothing. "Well you know," he said, impatiently, "why *do* people suffer? Maybe it's better to do something to give it a reason, *any* reason."

"But we just agreed," I said, "that there's no way not to suffer. Isn't it better, then, just to—take it?"

"But nobody just takes it," Sonny cried, "that's what I'm telling you! *Everybody* tries not to. You're just hung up on the *way* some people try—it's not *your* way!"

The hair on my face began to itch, my face felt wet. "That's not true," I said, "that's not true. I don't give a damn what other people do, I don't even care how they suffer. I just care how *you* suffer." And he looked at me. "Please believe me," I said. "I don't want to see you—die—trying not to suffer."

"I won't," he said, flatly, "die trying not to suffer. At least, not any faster than anybody else."

"But there's no need," I said, trying to laugh, "is there? in killing yourself."

I wanted to say more, but I couldn't. I wanted to talk about will power and how life could be—well, beautiful. I wanted to say that it was all within; but was it? or, rather, wasn't that exactly the trouble? And I wanted to promise that I would never fail him again. But it would all have sounded—empty words and lies.

So I made the promise to myself and prayed that I would keep it.

"It's terrible sometimes, inside," he said, "that's what's the trouble. You walk these streets, black and funky and cold, and there's not really a living ass to talk to, and there's nothing shaking, and there's no way of getting it out—that storm inside. You can't talk it and you can't make love with it, and when you finally try to get with it and play it, you realize *nobody's* listening. So *you've* got to listen. You got to find a way to listen."

And then he walked away from the window and sat on the sofa again, as though all the wind had suddenly been knocked out of him. "Sometimes you'll do *anything* to play, even cut your mother's throat." He laughed and looked at me. "Or your brother's." Then he sobered. "Or your own." Then: "Don't worry. I'm all right now and I think I'll *be* all right. But I can't forget—where I've been. I don't mean just the physical place I've been, I mean where I've *been.* And *what* I've been."

"What have you been, Sonny?" I asked.

He smiled—but sat sideways on the sofa, his elbow resting on the back, his fingers playing with his mouth and chin, not looking at me. "I've been something I didn't recognize, didn't know I could be. Didn't know anybody could be." He stopped, looking inward, looking helplessly young, looking old. "I'm not talking about it now because I feel *guilty* or anything like that—maybe it would be better if I did, I don't know. Anyway, I can't really talk about it. Not to you, not to anybody," and now he turned and faced me. "Sometimes, you know and it was actually when I was most *out* of the world. I felt that I was in it, that I was *with* it, really, and I could play or I didn't really have to *play,* it just came out of me, it was there. And I don't know how I played, thinking about it now, but I know I did awful things, those times, sometimes, to people. Or it wasn't that I *did* anything to them—it was that they weren't real." He picked up the beer can; it was empty; he rolled it between his palms: "And other times—well, I needed a fix, I needed to find a place to lean, I needed to clear a space to *listen*—and I couldn't find it, and I—went crazy, I did terrible things to *me,* I was terrible *for* me." He began pressing the beer can between his hands, I watched the metal begin to give. It glittered, as he played with it, like a knife, and I was afraid he would cut himself, but I said nothing. "Oh well. I can never tell you. I was all by myself at the bottom of something, stinking and sweating and crying and shaking, and I smelled it, you know? *my* stink, and I thought I'd die if I couldn't get away from it and yet, all the same, I knew that everything I was doing was just locking me in with it. And I didn't know," he paused, still flattening the beer can, "I didn't know, I still *don't* know, something kept telling me that maybe it was good to smell your own stink, but I didn't think that *that* was what I'd been trying to do—and—who can stand it?" and he abruptly dropped the ruined beer can, looking at me with a small, still smile, and then rose, walking to the window as though it were the lodestone rock. I watched his face, he watched the avenue. "I couldn't tell you when Mama died—but the reason I wanted to leave Harlem so bad was to get away from drugs. And then, when I ran away, that's what I was running from—really. When I came back, nothing had changed, *I* hadn't changed, I was just—older." And he stopped drumming with his fingers on the windowpane. The sun had vanished, soon darkness would fall. I watched his face. "It can come again," he said, almost as though speaking to himself. Then he turned to me. "It can come again," he repeated. "I just want you to know that."

"All right," I said, at last. "So it can come again, All right."

He smiled, but the smile was sorrowful. "I had to try to tell you," he said.

"Yes," I said. "I understand that."

"You're my brother," he said, looking straight at me, and not smiling at all.

"Yes," I repeated, "yes. I understand that."

He turned back to the window, looking out. "All that hatred down there," he said, "all that hatred and misery and love. It's a wonder it doesn't blow the avenue apart."

We went to the only nightclub on a short, dark street, downtown. We squeezed through the narrow, chattering, jam-packed bar to the entrance of the big room, where the bandstand was. And we stood there for a moment, for the lights were very dim in this room and we couldn't see. Then, "Hello, boy," said a voice and an enormous black man, much older than Sonny or myself, erupted out of all that atmospheric lighting and put an arm around Sonny's shoulder. "I been sitting right here," he said, "waiting for you."

He had a big voice, too, and heads in the darkness turned toward us.

Sonny grinned and pulled a little away, and said, "Creole, this is my brother. I told you about him."

Creole shook my hand. "I'm glad to meet you, son," he said, and it was clear that he was glad to meet me *there,* for Sonny's sake. And he smiled, "You got a real musician in *your* family," and he took his arm from Sonny's shoulder and slapped him, lightly, affectionately, with the back of his hand.

"Well. Now I've heard it all," said a voice behind us. This was another musician, and a friend of Sonny's, a coal-black, cheerful-looking man, built close to the ground. He immediately began confiding to me, at the top of his lungs, the most terrible things about Sonny, his teeth gleaming like a lighthouse and his laugh coming up out of him like the beginning of an earthquake. And it turned out that everyone at the bar knew Sonny, or almost everyone; some were musicians, working there, or nearby, or not working, some were simply hangers-on, and some were there to hear Sonny play. I was introduced to all of them and they were all very polite to me. Yet, it was clear that, for them, I was only Sonny's brother. Here, I was in Sonny's world. Or, rather: his kingdom. Here, it was not even a question that his veins bore royal blood.

They were going to play soon and Creole installed me, by myself, at a table in a dark corner. Then I watched them, Creole, and the little black man, and Sonny, and the others, while they horsed around, standing just below the bandstand. The light from the bandstand spilled just a little short of them and, watching them laughing and gesturing and moving about, I had the feeling that they, nevertheless, were being most careful not to step into that circle of light too suddenly: that if they moved into the light too suddenly, without thinking, they would perish in flame. Then, while I watched, one of them, the small, black man, moved into the light and crossed the bandstand

and started fooling around with his drums. Then—being funny and being, also, extremely ceremonious—Creole took Sonny by the arm and led him to the piano. A woman's voice called Sonny's name and a few hands started clapping. And Sonny, also being funny and being ceremonious, and so touched, I think, that he could have cried, but neither hiding it nor showing it, riding it like a man, grinned, and put both hands to his heart and bowed from the waist.

Creole then went to the bass fiddle and a lean, very bright-skinned brown man jumped up on the bandstand and picked up his horn. So there they were, and the atmosphere on the bandstand and in the room began to change and tighten. Someone stepped up to the microphone and announced them. Then there were all kinds of murmurs. Some people at the bar shushed others. The waitress ran around, frantically getting in the last orders, guys and chicks got closer to each other, and the lights on the bandstand, on the quartet, turned to a kind of indigo. Then they all looked different there. Creole looked about him for the last time, as though he were making certain that all his chickens were in the coop, and then he—jumped and struck the fiddle. And there they were.

All I know about music is that not many people ever really hear it. And even then, on the rare occasions when something opens within, and the music enters, what we mainly hear, or hear corroborated, are personal, private, vanishing evocations. But the man who creates the music is hearing something else, is dealing with the roar rising from the void and imposing order on it as it hits the air. What is evoked in him, then, is of another order, more terrible because it has no words, and triumphant, too, for that same reason. And his triumph, when he triumphs, is ours. I just watched Sonny's face. His face was troubled, he was working hard, but he wasn't with it. And I had the feeling that, in a way, everyone on the bandstand was waiting for him, both waiting for him and pushing him along. But as I began to watch Creole, I realized that it was Creole who held them all back. He had them on a short rein. Up there, keeping the beat with his whole body, wailing on the fiddle, with his eyes half closed, he was listening to everything, but he was listening to Sonny. He was having a dialogue with Sonny. He wanted Sonny to leave the shoreline and strike out for the deep water. He was Sonny's witness that deep water and drowning were not the same thing—he had been there, and he knew. And he wanted Sonny to know. He was waiting for Sonny to do the things on the keys which would let Creole know that Sonny was in the water.

And, while Creole listened, Sonny moved, deep within, exactly like someone in torment. I had never before thought of how awful the relationship must be between the musician and his instrument. He has to fill it, this instrument, with the breath of life, his own. He has to make it do what he wants it to do. And a piano is just a piano. It's made out of so much wood and wires and little hammers and big ones, and ivory. While there's only so much you can do with it, the only way to find this out is to try; to try and make it do everything.

And Sonny hadn't been near a piano for over a year. And he wasn't on much better terms with his life, not the life that stretched before him now. He and the piano stammered, started one way, got scared, stopped; started another way, panicked, marked time, started again; then seemed to have found a direction, panicked again, got stuck. And the face I saw on Sonny I'd never seen before. Everything had been burned out of it, and, at the same time, things usually hidden were being burned in, by the fire and fury of the battle which was occurring in him up there.

Yet, watching Creole's face as they neared the end of the first set, I had the feeling that something had happened, something I hadn't heard. Then they finished, there was scattered applause, and then, without an instant's warning, Creole started into something else, it was almost sardonic, it was *Am I Blue*. And, as though he commanded, Sonny began to play. Something began to happen. And Creole let out the reins. The dry, low, black man said something awful on the drums, Creole answered, and the drums talked back. Then the horn insisted, sweet and high, slightly detached perhaps, and Creole listened, commenting now and then, dry, and driving, beautiful and calm and old. Then they all came together again, and Sonny was part of the family again. I could tell this from his face. He seemed to have found, right there beneath his fingers, a damn brand-new piano. It seemed that he couldn't get over it. Then, for awhile, just being happy with Sonny, they seemed to be agreeing with him that brand-new pianos certainly were a gas.

Then Creole stepped forward to remind them that what they were playing was the blues. He hit something in all of them, he hit something in me, myself, and the music tightened and deepened, apprehension began to beat the air. Creole began to tell us what the blues were all about. They were not about anything very new. He and his boys up there were keeping it new, at the risk of ruin, destruction, madness, and death, in order to find new ways to make us listen. For, while the tale of how we suffer, and how we are delighted, and how we may triumph is never new, it always must be heard. There isn't any other tale to tell, it's the only light we've got in all this darkness.

And this tale, according to that face, that body, those strong hands on those strings, has another aspect in every country, and a new depth in every generation. Listen, Creole seemed to be saying, listen. Now these are Sonny's blues. He made the little black man on the drums know it, and the bright, brown man on the horn. Creole wasn't trying any longer to get Sonny in the water. He was wishing him Godspeed. Then he stepped back, very slowly, filling the air with the immense suggestion that Sonny speak for himself.

Then they all gathered around Sonny and Sonny played. Every now and again one of them seemed to say, amen. Sonny's fingers filled the air with life, his life. But that life contained so many others. And Sonny went all the way back, he really began with the spare, flat statement of the opening phrase of the song. Then he began to make it his. It was very beautiful because it wasn't hurried and it was no longer a lament. I seemed to hear with what burning he had made it his, with what burning we had yet to make it ours, how we could cease lamenting. Freedom lurked around us and I understood, at last, that he could help us to be free if we would listen, that he would never be free until we did. Yet, there was no battle in his face now. I heard what he had gone through, and would continue to go through until he came to rest in earth. He had made it his: that long line, of which we knew only Mama and Daddy. And he was giving it back, as everything must be given back, so that, passing through death, it can live forever. I saw my mother's face again, and felt, for the first time, how the stones of the road she had walked on must have bruised her feet. I saw the moonlit road where my father's brother died. And it brought something else back to me, and carried me past it, I saw my little girl again and felt Isabel's tears again, and I felt my own tears begin to rise. And I was yet aware that this was only a moment, that the world waited outside, as hungry as a tiger, and that trouble stretched above us, longer than the sky.

Then it was over. Creole and Sonny let out their breath, both soaking wet, and grinning. There was a lot of applause and some of it was real. In the dark, the girl came by and I asked her to take drinks to the bandstand. There was a long pause, while they talked up there in the indigo light and after awhile I saw the girl put a Scotch and milk on top of the piano for Sonny. He didn't seem to notice it, but just before they started playing again he sipped from it and looked toward me, and nodded. Then he put it back on top of the piano. For me, then, as they began to play again, it glowed and shook above my brother's head like the very cup of trembling.[3]

1965

Flannery O'Connor 1925–1964

Flannery O'Connor's fiction presents what she called the "sacramental view of life," a perspective usually developed out of antitheses. Her characters confront a world of violence and unexplained evil, against which none of the traditional virtues of sincerity, hard work, and foresight avail.

Her style is noted for its simplicity, wit, and masterful reproduction of the colloquial speech of her native South. She was born in Savannah, Georgia, and grew up in the small town of Milledgeville, where she lived until she died, aged thirty-eight. She attended the Women's College of Georgia and while in college published a number of short stories. She then studied in the writer's program at the University of Iowa, receiving an M.F.A. in 1947.

O'Connor's fiction is peopled with characters who have been described as haunted and grotesque, physical and emotional freaks often embracing a single and ferocious truth. They play out their lives against the backgrounds of the deepest, darkest South, as in her novel Wise Blood *(1952), which uses the setting of rural Tennessee to examine the character of a backwoods preacher both innocent and demonic, victim and assailant, who has created a church without Christ, where violence substitutes for religious faith.*

O'Connor is best known for short stories that exhibit an ironic, unsentimental acceptance of the human condition. They are filled with wry comedy and examples of satanic evil, and they are often concerned with what she called "the redemptive act" and a pervading "sense of Mystery which cannot be accounted for by human formula."

[3]"Awake, Awake, stand up O Jerusalem, which hast drunk at the hand of the LORD the cup of his fury; thou hast drunken the dregs of the cup of trembling, and wrung them out" (Isaiah 51:17).

FURTHER READING: *Flannery O'Connor, The Complete Stories,* 1971; *The Habit of Being, Letters of Flannery O'Connor,* ed. S. Fitzgerald, 1979; E. Kessler, *Flannery O'Connor and the Language of Apocalypse,* 1986; S. Paulson, *Flannery O'Connor,* 1988; J. Baumgartner, *Flannery O'Connor, A Proper Scaring,* 1988; B. Ragen, *A Wreck on the Road to Damascus, Innocence, Guilt and Conversion in Flannery O'Connor,* 1989; R. Brinkmeyer, *The Art and Vision of Flannery O'Connor,* 1990; A. Di Renzo, *American Gargoyles, Flannery O'Connor and the Medieval Grotesque,* 1993; S. Gordon, *Flannery O'Connor, The Obedient Imagination,* 2000; G. Kilcourse, *Flannery O'Connor's Religious Imagination,* 2001; C. Seel, *Ritual Performance in the Fiction of Flannery O'Connor,* 2001; H. Edmondson, *Return to Good and Evil, Flannery O'Connor's Response to Nihilism,* 2002.

TEXT: *Flannery O'Connor, The Complete Stories,* 1971.

GOOD COUNTRY PEOPLE

Besides the neutral expression that she wore when she was alone, Mrs. Freeman had two others, forward and reverse, that she used for all her human dealings. Her forward expression was steady and driving like the advance of a heavy truck. Her eyes never swerved to left or right but turned as the story turned as if they followed a yellow line down the center of it. She seldom used the other expression because it was not often necessary for her to retract a statement, but when she did, her face came to a complete stop, there was an almost imperceptible movement of her black eyes, during which they seemed to be receding, and then the observer would see that Mrs. Freeman, though she might stand there as real as several grain sacks thrown on top of each other, was no longer there in spirit. As for getting anything across to her when this was the case, Mrs. Hopewell had given it up. She might talk her head off. Mrs. Freeman could never be brought to admit herself wrong on any point. She would stand there and if she could be brought to say anything, it was something like, "Well, I wouldn't of said it was and I wouldn't of said it wasn't," or letting her gaze range over the top kitchen shelf where there was an assortment of dusty bottles, she might remark, "I see you ain't ate many of them figs you put up last summer."

They carried on their most important business in the kitchen at breakfast. Every morning Mrs. Hopewell got up at seven o'clock and lit her gas heater and Joy's. Joy was her daughter, a large blonde girl who had an artificial leg. Mrs. Hopewell thought of her as a child though she was thirty-two years old and highly educated. Joy would get up while her mother was eating and lumber into the bathroom and slam the door, and before long, Mrs. Freeman would arrive at the back door. Joy would hear her mother call, "Come on in," and then they would talk for a while in low voices that were indistinguishable in the bathroom. By the time Joy came in, they had usually finished the weather report and were on one or the other of Mrs. Freeman's daughters, Glynese or Carramae, Joy called them Glycerin and Caramel. Glynese, a redhead, was eighteen and had many admirers; Carramae, a blonde, was only fifteen but already married and pregnant. She could not keep anything on her stomach. Every morning Mrs. Freeman told Mrs. Hopewell how many times she had vomited since the last report.

Mrs. Hopewell liked to tell people that Glynese and Carramae were two of the finest girls she knew and that Mrs. Freeman was a *lady* and that she was never ashamed to take her anywhere or introduce her to anybody they might meet. Then she would tell how she had happened to hire the Freemans in the first place and how they were a godsend to her and how she had had them four years. The reason for her keeping them so long was that they were not trash. They were good country people. She had telephoned the man whose name they had given as a reference and he had told her that Mr. Freeman was a good farmer but that his wife was the nosiest woman ever to walk the earth. "She's got to be into everything," the man said. "If she don't get there before the dust settles, you can bet she's dead, that's all. She'll want to know all your business. I can stand him real good," he had said, "but me nor my wife neither could have stood that woman one more minute on this place." That had put Mrs. Hopewell off for a few days.

She had hired them in the end because there were no other applicants but she had made up her mind beforehand exactly how she would handle the woman. Since she was the type who had to be into everything, then, Mrs. Hopewell had decided, she would not only let her be into everything, she would *see to it* that she was into everything—she would give her the responsibility of everything, she would put her in charge. Mrs. Hopewell had no bad qualities of her own but she was able to use other people's in such a constructive way that she never felt the lack. She had hired the Freemans and she had kept them four years.

Nothing is perfect. This was one of Mrs. Hopewell's favorite sayings. Another was: that is life! And still another, the most important, was: well, other people have their opinions too. She would make these statements, usually at the table, in a tone of gentle insistence as if no one held them but her, and the large hulking Joy, whose constant outrage had obliterated every expression from her face, would stare just a little to the side of her, her eyes icy blue, with the look of someone who has achieved blindness by an act of will and means to keep it.

When Mrs. Hopewell said to Mrs. Freeman that life was like that, Mrs. Freeman would say, "I always said so myself." Nothing had been arrived at by anyone that had not first been arrived at by her. She was quicker than Mr. Freeman. When Mrs. Hopewell said to her after they had been on the place a while, "You know, you're the wheel behind the wheel," and winked, Mrs. Freeman had said, "I know it. I've always been quick. It's some that are quicker than others."

"Everybody is different," Mrs. Hopewell said.

"Yes, most people is," Mrs. Freeman said.

"It takes all kinds to make the world."

"I always said it did myself."

The girl was used to this kind of dialogue for breakfast and more of it for dinner; sometimes they had it for supper too. When they had no guest they ate in the kitchen because that was easier. Mrs. Freeman always managed to arrive at some point during the meal and to watch them finish it. She would stand in the doorway if it were summer but in the winter she would stand with one elbow on top of the refrigerator and look down on them, or she would stand by the gas heater, lifting the back of her skirt slightly. Occasionally she would stand against the wall and roll her head from side to side. At no time was she in any hurry to leave. All this was very trying on Mrs. Hopewell but she was a woman of great patience. She realized that nothing is perfect and that in the Freemans she had good country people and that if, in this day and age, you get good country people, you had better hang onto them.

She had had plenty of experience with trash. Before the Freemans she had averaged one tenant family a year. The wives of these farmers were not the kind you would want to be around you for very long. Mrs. Hopewell, who had divorced her husband long ago, needed someone to walk over the fields with her; and when Joy had to be impressed for these services, her remarks were usually so ugly and her face so glum that Mrs. Hopewell would say, "If you can't come pleasantly, I don't want you at all," to which the girl, standing square and rigid-shouldered with her neck thrust slightly forward, would reply, "If you want me, here I am—LIKE I AM."

Mrs. Hopewell excused this attitude because of the leg (which had been shot off in a hunting accident when Joy was ten). It was hard for Mrs. Hopewell to realize that her child was thirty-two now and that for more than twenty years she had had only one leg. She thought of her still as a child because it tore her heart to think instead of the poor stout girl in her thirties who had never danced a step or had any *normal* good times. Her name was really Joy but as soon as she was twenty-one and away from home, she had had it legally changed. Mrs. Hopewell was certain that she had thought and thought until she had hit upon the ugliest name in any language. Then she had gone and had the beautiful name, Joy, changed without telling her mother until after she had done it. Her legal name was Hulga.

When Mrs. Hopewell thought the name, Hulga, she thought of the broad blank hull of a battleship. She would not use it. She continued to call her Joy to which the girl responded but in a purely mechanical way.

Hulga had learned to tolerate Mrs. Freeman who saved her from taking walks with her mother. Even Glynese and Carramae were useful when they occupied attention that might otherwise have been directed at her. At first she had thought she could not stand Mrs. Freeman for she had found that it was not possible to be rude to her. Mrs. Freeman would take on strange resentments and for days together she would be sullen but the source of her displeasure was always obscure; a direct attack, a positive leer, blatant ugliness to her face—these never touched her. And without warning one day, she began calling her Hulga.

She did not call her that in front of Mrs. Hopewell who would have been incensed but when she and the girl happened to be out of the house together, she would say something and add the name Hulga to the end of it, and the big spectacled Joy-Hulga would scowl and redden as if her privacy had been intruded upon. She considered the name her personal affair. She had arrived at it first purely on the basis of its ugly sound and then the full genius of its fitness had struck her. She had a vision of the name working like the ugly sweating Vulcan[1] who stayed in the furnace and to whom, presumably, the goddess had to come when called. She saw it as the name of her highest creative act. One of her major triumphs was that her mother had not been able to turn her dust into Joy, but the greater one was that she had been able to turn it

[1]God of fire and blacksmith for the gods in Roman myth. He was lame and ugly. His wife was Venus, goddess of love.

herself into Hulga. However, Mrs. Freeman's relish for using the name only irritated her. It was as if Mrs. Freeman's beady steel-pointed eyes had penetrated far enough behind her face to reach some secret fact. Something about her seemed to fascinate Mrs. Freeman and then one day Hulga realized that it was the artificial leg. Mrs. Freeman had a special fondness for the details of secret infections, hidden deformities, assaults upon children. Of diseases, she preferred the lingering or incurable. Hulga had heard Mrs. Hopewell give her the details of the hunting accident, how the leg had been literally blasted off, how she had never lost consciousness. Mrs. Freeman could listen to it any time as if it had happened an hour ago.

When Hulga stumped into the kitchen in the morning (she could walk without making the awful noise but she made it—Mrs. Hopewell was certain—because it was ugly-sounding), she glanced at them and did not speak. Mrs. Hopewell would be in her red kimono with her hair tied around her head in rags. She would be sitting at the table, finishing her breakfast and Mrs. Freeman would be hanging by her elbow outward from the refrigerator, looking down at the table. Hulga always put her eggs on the stove to boil and then stood over them with her arms folded, and Mrs. Hopewell would look at her—a kind of indirect gaze divided between her and Mrs. Freeman—and would think that if she would only keep herself up a little, she wouldn't be so bad looking. There was nothing wrong with her face that a pleasant expression wouldn't help. Mrs. Hopewell said that people who looked on the bright side of things would be beautiful even if they were not.

Whenever she looked at Joy this way, she could not help but feel that it would have been better if the child had not taken the Ph.D. It had certainly not brought her out any and now that she had it, there was no more excuse for her to go to school again. Mrs. Hopewell thought it was nice for girls to go to school to have a good time but Joy had "gone through." Anyhow, she would not have been strong enough to go again. The doctors had told Mrs. Hopewell that with the best of care, Joy might see forty-five. She had a weak heart. Joy had made it plain that if it had not been for this condition, she would be far from these red hills and good country people. She would be in a university lecturing to people who knew what she was talking about. And Mrs. Hopewell could very well picture her there, looking like a scarecrow and lecturing to more of the same. Here she went about all day in a six-year-old skirt and a yellow sweat shirt with a faded cowboy on a horse embossed on it. She thought this was funny; Mrs. Hopewell thought it was idiotic and showed simply that she was still a child. She was brilliant but she didn't have a grain of sense. It seemed to Mrs. Hopewell that every year she grew less like other people and more like herself—bloated, rude, and squint-eyed. And she said such strange things! To her own mother she had said—without warning, without excuse, standing up in the middle of a meal with her face purple and her mouth half full—"Woman! do you ever look inside? Do you ever look inside and see what you are *not*? God!" she had cried sinking down again and staring at her plate, "Malebranche[2] was right: we are not our own light. We are not our own light!" Mrs. Hopewell had no idea to this day what brought that on.

[2]Nicolas Malebranche (1638–1715), French philosopher. He argued that mere human intellect, unaided by the "light of God," cannot perceive essential truths.

She had only made the remark, hoping Joy would take it in, that a smile never hurt anyone.

The girl had taken the Ph.D. in philosophy and this left Mrs. Hopewell at a complete loss. You could say, "My daughter is a nurse," or "My daughter is a schoolteacher," or even, "My daughter is a chemical engineer." You could not say, "My daughter is a philosopher." That was something that had ended with the Greeks and Romans. All day Joy sat on her neck in a deep chair, reading. Sometimes she went for walks but she didn't like dogs or cats or birds or flowers or nature or nice young men. She looked at nice young men as if she could smell their stupidity.

One day Mrs. Hopewell had picked up one of the books the girl had just put down and opening it at random, she read, "Science, on the other hand, has to assert its soberness and seriousness afresh and declare that it is concerned solely with what-is. Nothing—how can it be for science anything but a horror and a phantasm? If science is right, then one thing stands firm: science wishes to know nothing of nothing. Such is after all the strictly scientific approach to Nothing. We know it by wishing to know nothing of Nothing." These words had been underlined with a blue pencil and they worked on Mrs. Hopewell like some evil incantation in gibberish. She shut the book quickly and went out of the room as if she were having a chill.

This morning when the girl came in, Mrs. Freeman was on Carramae. "She thrown up four times after supper," she said, "and was up twict in the night after three o'clock. Yesterday she didn't do nothing but ramble in the bureau drawer. All she did. Stand up there and see what she could run up on."

"She's got to eat," Mrs. Hopewell muttered, sipping her coffee, while she watched Joy's back at the stove. She was wondering what the child had said to the Bible salesman. She could not imagine what kind of a conversation she could possibly have had with him.

He was a tall gaunt hatless youth who had called yesterday to sell them a Bible. He had appeared at the door, carrying a large black suitcase that weighted him so heavily on one side that he had to brace himself against the door facing. He seemed on the point of collapse but he said in a cheerful voice, "Good morning, Mrs. Cedars!" and set the suitcase down on the mat. He was not a bad-looking young man though he had on a bright blue suit and yellow socks that were not pulled up far enough. He had prominent face bones and a streak of sticky-looking brown hair falling across his forehead.

"I'm Mrs. Hopewell," she said.

"Oh!" he said, pretending to look puzzled but with his eyes sparkling, "I saw it said 'The Cedars' on the mailbox so I thought you was Mrs. Cedars!" and he burst out in a pleasant laugh. He picked up the satchel and under cover of a pant, he fell forward into her hall. It was rather as if the suitcase had moved first, jerking him after it. "Mrs. Hopewell!" he said and grabbed her hand. "I hope you are well!" and he laughed again and then all at once his face sobered completely. He paused and gave her a straight earnest look and said, "Lady, I've come to speak of serious things."

"Well, come in," she muttered, none too pleased because her dinner was almost ready. He came into the parlor and sat down on the edge of a straight chair and put the suitcase between his feet and glanced around the room as if he were sizing her up by it. Her silver gleamed on the two sideboards; she decided he had never been in a room as elegant as this.

"Mrs. Hopewell," he began, using her name in a way that sounded almost intimate, "I know you believe in Chrustian service."

"Well yes," she murmured.

"I know," he said and paused, looking very wise with his head cocked on one side, "that you're a good woman. Friends have told me."

Mrs. Hopewell never liked to be taken for a fool. "What are you selling?" she asked.

"Bibles," the young man said and his eye raced around the room before he added, "I see you have no family Bible in your parlor, I see that is the one lack you got!"

Mrs. Hopewell could not say, "My daughter is an atheist and won't let me keep the Bible in the parlor." She said, stiffening slightly, "I keep my Bible by my bedside." This was not the truth. It was in the attic somewhere.

"Lady," he said, "the word of God ought to be in the parlor."

"Well, I think that's a matter of taste," she began. "I think . . ."

"Lady," he said, "for a Chrustian, the word of God ought to be in every room in the house besides in his heart. I know you're a Chrustian because I can see it in every line of your face."

She stood up and said, "Well, young man, I don't want to buy a Bible and I smell my dinner burning."

He didn't get up. He began to twist his hands and looking down at them, he said softly, "Well lady, I'll tell you the truth—not many people want to buy one nowadays and besides, I know I'm real simple. I don't know how to say a thing but to say it. I'm just a country boy." He glanced up into her unfriendly face. "People like you don't like to fool with country people like me!"

"Why!" she cried, "good country people are the salt of the earth! Besides, we all have different ways of doing, it takes all kinds to make the world go 'round. That's life!"

"You said a mouthful," he said.

"Why, I think there aren't enough good country people in the world!" she said, stirred. "I think that's what's wrong with it!"

His face had brightened. "I didn't inraduce myself," he said. "I'm Manley Pointer from out in the country around Willohobie, not even from a place, just from near a place."

"You wait a minute," she said. "I have to see about my dinner." She went out to the kitchen and found Joy standing near the door where she had been listening.

"Get rid of the salt of the earth," she said, "and let's eat."

Mrs. Hopewell gave her a pained look and turned the heat down under the vegetables. "*I* can't be rude to anybody," she murmured and went back into the parlor.

He had opened the suitcase and was sitting with a Bible on each knee.

"You might as well put those up," she told him. "I don't want one."

"I appreciate your honesty," he said. "You don't see any more real honest people unless you go way out in the country."

"I know," she said, "real genuine folks!" Through the crack in the door she heard a groan.

"I guess a lot of boys come telling you they're working their way through college," he said, "but I'm not going to tell you that. Somehow," he said, "I don't want to go to college. I want to devote my life to Chrustian service.

See," he said, lowering his voice, "I got this heart condition. I may not live long. When you know it's something wrong with you and you may not live long, well then, lady . . ." He paused, with his mouth open, and stared at her.

He and Joy had the same condition! She knew that her eyes were filling with tears but she collected herself quickly and murmured, "Won't you stay for dinner? We'd love to have you!" and was sorry the instant she heard herself say it.

"Yes mam," he said in an abashed voice, "I would sher love to do that!"

Joy had given him one look on being introduced to him and then throughout the meal had not glanced at him again. He had addressed several remarks to her, which she had pretended not to hear. Mrs. Hopewell could not understand deliberate rudeness, although she lived with it, and she felt she had always to overflow with hospitality to make up for Joy's lack of courtesy. She urged him to talk about himself and he did. He said he was the seventh child of twelve and that his father had been crushed under a tree when he himself was eight year old. He had been crushed very badly, in fact, almost cut in two and was practically not recognizable. His mother had got along the best she could by hard working and she had always seen that her children went to Sunday School and that they read the Bible every evening. He was now nineteen year old and he had been selling Bibles for four months. In that time he had sold seventy-seven Bibles and had the promise of two more sales. He wanted to become a missionary because he thought that was the way you could do most for people. "He who losest his life shall find it," he said simply and he was so sincere, so genuine and earnest that Mrs. Hopewell would not for the world have smiled. He prevented his peas from sliding onto the table by blocking them with a piece of bread which he later cleaned his plate with. She could see Joy observing sidewise how he handled his knife and fork and she saw too that every few minutes, the boy would dart a keen appraising glance at the girl as if he were trying to attract her attention.

After dinner Joy cleared the dishes off the table and disappeared and Mrs. Hopewell was left to talk with him. He told her again about his childhood and his father's accident and about various things that had happened to him. Every five minutes or so she would stifle a yawn. He sat for two hours until finally she told him she must go because she had an appointment in town. He packed his Bibles and thanked her and prepared to leave, but in the doorway he stopped and wrung her hand and said that not on any of his trips had he met a lady as nice as her and he asked if he could come again. She had said she would always be happy to see him.

Joy had been standing in the road, apparently looking at something in the distance, when he came down the steps toward her, bent to the side with his heavy valise. He stopped where she was standing and confronted her directly. Mrs. Hopewell could not hear what he said but she trembled to think what Joy would say to him. She could see that after a minute Joy said something and that then the boy began to speak again, making an excited gesture with his free hand. After a minute Joy said something else at which the boy began to speak once more. Then to her amazement, Mrs. Hopewell saw the two of them walk off together, toward the gate. Joy had walked all the way to the gate with him and Mrs. Hopewell could not imagine what they had said to each other, and she had not yet dared to ask.

Mrs. Freeman was insisting upon her attention. She had moved from the refrigerator to the heater so that Mrs. Hopewell had to turn and face her in order to seem to be listening. "Glynese gone out with Harvey Hill again last night," she said. "She had this sty."

"Hill," Mrs. Hopewell said absently, "is that the one who works in the garage?"

"Nome, he's the one that goes to chiropracter school," Mrs. Freeman said. "She had this sty. Been had it two days. So she says when he brought her in the other night he says, 'Lemme get rid of that sty for you,' and she says, 'How?' and he says, 'You just lay yourself down acrost the seat of that car and I'll show you.' So she done it and he popped her neck. Kept on a-popping it several times until she made him quit. This morning," Mrs. Freeman said, "she ain't got no sty. She ain't got no traces of a sty."

"I never heard of that before," Mrs. Hopewell said.

"He ast her to marry him before the Ordinary,"[3] Mrs. Freeman went on, "and she told him she wasn't going to be married in no *office*."

"Well, Glynese is a fine girl," Mrs. Hopewell said. "Glynese and Carramae are both fine girls."

"Carramae said when her and Lyman was married Lyman said it sure felt sacred to him. She said he said he wouldn't take five hundred dollars for being married by a preacher."

"How much would he take?" the girl asked from the stove.

"He said he wouldn't take five hundred dollars," Mrs. Freeman repeated.

"Well we all have work to do," Mrs. Hopewell said.

"Lyman said it just felt more sacred to him," Mrs. Freeman said. "The doctor wants Carramae to eat prunes. Says instead of medicine. Says them cramps is coming from pressure. You know where I think it is?"

"She'll be better in a few weeks," Mrs. Hopewell said.

"In the tube,"[4] Mrs. Freeman said. "Else she wouldn't be as sick as she is."

Hulga had cracked her two eggs into a saucer and was bringing them to the table along with a cup of coffee that she had filled too full. She sat down carefully and began to eat, meaning to keep Mrs. Freeman there by questions if for any reason she showed an inclination to leave. She could perceive her mother's eye on her. The first round-about question would be about the Bible salesman and she did not wish to bring it on. "How did he pop her neck?" she asked.

Mrs. Freeman went into a description of how he had popped her neck. She said he owned a '55 Mercury but that Glynese said she would rather marry a man with only a '36 Plymouth who would be married by a preacher. The girl asked what if he had a '32 Plymouth and Mrs. Freeman said what Glynese had said was a '36 Plymouth.

Mrs. Hopewell said there were not many girls with Glynese's common sense. She said what she admired in those girls was their common sense. She said that reminded her that they had had a nice visitor yesterday, a young man selling Bibles. "Lord," she said, "he bored me to death but he was so sincere and genuine I couldn't be rude to him. He was just good country people, you know," she said, "—just the salt of the earth."

[3]A judge, empowered to perform the marriage ceremony in his chambers (office).

[4]I.e., the fetus is developing not in the uterus but in a fallopian tube, an abnormal and life-threatening occurrence.

"I seen him walk up," Mrs. Freeman said, "and then later—I seen him walk off," and Hulga could feel the slight shift in her voice, the slight insinuation, that he had not walked off alone, had he? Her face remained expressionless but the color rose into her neck and she seemed to swallow it down with the next spoonful of egg. Mrs. Freeman was looking at her as if they had a secret together.

"Well, it takes all kinds of people to make the world go 'round," Mrs. Hopewell said. "It's very good we aren't all alike."

"Some people are more alike than others," Mrs. Freeman said.

Hulga got up and stumped, with about twice the noise that was necessary, into her room and locked the door. She was to meet the Bible salesman at ten o'clock at the gate. She had thought about it half the night. She had started thinking of it as a great joke and then she had begun to see profound implications in it. She had lain in bed imagining dialogues for them that were insane on the surface but that reached below to depths that no Bible salesman would be aware of. Their conversation yesterday had been of this kind.

He had stopped in front of her and had simply stood there. His face was bony and sweaty and bright, with a little pointed nose in the center of it, and his look was different from what it had been at the dinner table. He was gazing at her with open curiosity, with fascination, like a child watching a new fantastic animal at the zoo, and he was breathing as if he had run a great distance to reach her. His gaze seemed somehow familiar but she could not think where she had been regarded with it before. For almost a minute he didn't say anything. Then on what seemed an insuck of breath, he whispered, "You ever ate a chicken that was two days old?"

The girl looked at him stonily. He might have just put this question up for consideration at the meeting of a philosophical association. "Yes," she presently replied as if she had considered it from all angles.

"It must have been mighty small!" he said triumphantly and shook all over with little nervous giggles, getting very red in the face, and subsiding finally into his gaze of complete admiration, while the girl's expression remained exactly the same.

"How old are you?" he asked softly.

She waited some time before she answered. Then in a flat voice she said, "Seventeen."

His smiles came in succession like waves breaking on the surface of a little lake. "I see you got a wooden leg," he said. "I think you're brave. I think you're real sweet."

The girl stood blank and solid and silent.

"Walk to the gate with me," he said. "You're a brave sweet little thing and I liked you the minute I seen you walk in the door."

Hulga began to move forward.

"What's your name?" he asked, smiling down on the top of her head.

"Hulga," she said.

"Hulga," he murmured, "Hulga. Hulga. I never heard of anybody name Hulga before. You're shy, aren't you, Hulga?" he asked.

She nodded, watching his large red hand on the handle of the giant valise.

"I like girls that wear glasses," he said. "I think a lot. I'm not like these people that a serious thought don't ever enter their heads. It's because I may die."

"I may die too," she said suddenly and looked up at him. His eyes were very small and brown, glittering feverishly.

"Listen," he said, "don't you think some people was meant to meet on account of what all they got in common and all? Like they both think serious thoughts and all?" He shifted the valise to his other hand so that the hand nearest her was free. He caught hold of her elbow and shook it a little. "I don't work on Saturday," he said. "I like to walk in the woods and see what Mother Nature is wearing. O'er the hills and far away. Pic-nics and things. Couldn't we go on a pic-nic tomorrow? Say yes, Hulga," he said and gave her a dying look as if he felt his insides about to drop out of him. He had even seemed to sway slightly toward her.

During the night she had imagined that she seduced him. She imagined that the two of them walked on the place until they came to the storage barn beyond the two back fields and there, she imagined, that things came to such a pass that she very easily seduced him and that then, of course, she had to reckon with his remorse. True genius can get an idea across even to an inferior mind. She imagined that she took his remorse in hand and changed it into a deeper understanding of life. She took all his shame away and turned it into something useful.

She set off for the gate at exactly ten o'clock, escaping without drawing Mrs. Hopewell's attention. She didn't take anything to eat, forgetting that food is usually taken on a picnic. She wore a pair of slacks and a dirty white shirt, and as an afterthought, she had put some Vapex on the collar of it since she did not own any perfume. When she reached the gate no one was there.

She looked up and down the empty highway and had the furious feeling that she had been tricked, that he had only meant to make her walk to the gate after the idea of him. Then suddenly he stood up, very tall, from behind a bush on the opposite embankment. Smiling, he lifted his hat which was new and wide-brimmed. He had not worn it yesterday and she wondered if he had bought it for the occasion. It was toast-colored with a red and white band around it and was slightly too large for him. He stepped from behind the bush still carrying the black valise. He had on the same suit and the same yellow socks sucked down in his shoes from walking. He crossed the highway and said, "I knew you'd come!"

The girl wondered acidly how he had known this. She pointed to the valise and asked, "Why did you bring your Bibles?"

He took her elbow, smiling down on her as if he could not stop. "You can never tell when you'll need the word of God, Hulga," he said. She had a moment in which she doubted that this was actually happening and then they began to climb the embankment. They went down into the pasture toward the woods. The boy walked lightly by her side, bouncing on his toes. The valise did not seem to be heavy today; he even swung it. They crossed half the pasture without saying anything and then, putting his hand easily on the small of her back, he asked softly, "Where does your wooden leg join on?"

She turned an ugly red and glared at him and for an instant the boy looked abashed. "I didn't mean you no harm," he said. "I only meant you're so brave and all. I guess God takes care of you."

"No," she said, looking forward and walking fast, "I don't even believe in God."

At this he stopped and whistled. "No!" he exclaimed as if he were too astonished to say anything else.

She walked on and in a second he was bouncing at her side, fanning with his hat. "That's very unusual for a girl," he remarked, watching her out of the corner of his eye. When they reached the edge of the wood, he put his hand on her back again and drew her against him without a word and kissed her heavily.

The kiss, which had more pressure than feeling behind it, produced that extra surge of adrenalin in the girl that enables one to carry a packed trunk out of a burning house, but in her, the power went at once to the brain. Even before he released her, her mind, clear and detached and ironic anyway, was regarding him from a great distance, with amusement but with pity. She had never been kissed before and she was pleased to discover that it was an unexceptional experience and all a matter of the mind's control. Some people might enjoy drain water if they were told it was vodka. When the boy, looking expectant but uncertain, pushed her gently away, she turned and walked on, saying nothing as if such business, for her, were common enough.

He came along panting at her side, trying to help her when he saw a root that she might trip over. He caught and held back the long swaying blades of thorn vine until she had passed beyond them. She led the way and he came breathing heavily behind her. Then they came out on a sunlit hillside, sloping softly into another one a little smaller. Beyond, they could see the rusted top of the old barn where the extra hay was stored.

The hill was sprinkled with small pink weeds. "Then you ain't saved?" he asked suddenly, stopping.

The girl smiled. It was the first time she had smiled at him at all. "In my economy,"[5] she said, "I'm saved and you are damned but I told you I didn't believe in God."

Nothing seemed to destroy the boy's look of admiration. He gazed at her now as if the fantastic animal at the zoo had put its paw through the bars and given him a loving poke. She thought he looked as if he wanted to kiss her again and she walked on before he had the chance.

"Ain't there somewheres we can sit down sometime?" he murmured, his voice softening toward the end of the sentence.

"In that barn," she said.

They made for it rapidly as if it might slide away like a train. It was a large two-story barn, cool and dark inside. The boy pointed up the ladder that led into the loft and said, "It's too bad we can't go up there."

"Why can't we?" she asked.

"Yer leg," he said reverently.

The girl gave him a contemptuous look and putting both hands on the ladder, she climbed it while he stood below, apparently awestruck. She pulled herself expertly through the opening and then looked down at him and said, "Well, come on if you're coming," and he began to climb the ladder, awkwardly bringing the suitcase with him.

"We won't need the Bible," she observed.

"You never can tell," he said, panting. After he had got into the loft, he was a few seconds catching his breath. She had sat down in a pile of straw. A wide

[5]I.e., "In my view of humanity. . . ."

sheath of sunlight, filled with dust particles, slanted over her. She lay back against a bale, her face turned away, looking out the front opening of the barn where hay was thrown from a wagon into the loft. The two pink-speckled hillsides lay back against a dark ridge of woods. The sky was cloudless and cold blue. The boy dropped down by her side and put one arm under her and the other over her and began methodically kissing her face, making little noises like a fish. He did not remove his hat but it was pushed far enough back not to interfere. When her glasses got in his way, he took them off of her and slipped them into his pocket.

The girl at first did not return any of the kisses but presently she began to and after she had put several on his cheek, she reached his lips and remained there, kissing him again and again as if she were trying to draw all the breath out of him. His breath was clear and sweet like a child's and the kisses were sticky like a child's. He mumbled about loving her and about knowing when he first seen her that he loved her, but the mumbling was like the sleepy fretting of a child being put to sleep by his mother. Her mind, throughout this, never stopped or lost itself for a second to her feelings. "You ain't said you loved me none," he whispered finally, pulling back from her. "You got to say that."

She looked away from him off into the hollow sky and then down at a black ridge and then down farther into what appeared to be two green swelling lakes. She didn't realize he had taken her glasses but this landscape could not seem exceptional to her for she seldom paid any close attention to her surroundings.

"You got to say it," he repeated. "You got to say you love me."

She was always careful how she committed herself. "In a sense," she began, "if you use the word loosely, you might say that. But it's not a word I use. I don't have illusions. I'm one of those people who see *through* to nothing."

The boy was frowning. "You got to say it. I said it and you got to say it," he said.

The girl looked at him almost tenderly. "You poor baby," she murmured. "It's just as well you don't understand," and she pulled him by the neck, face-down, against her. "We are all damned," she said, "but some of us have taken off our blindfolds and see that there's nothing to see. It's a kind of salvation."

The boy's astonished eyes looked blankly through the ends of her hair. "Okay," he almost whined, "but do you love me or don'tcher?"

"Yes," she said and added, "in a sense. But I must tell you something. There mustn't be anything dishonest between us." She lifted his head and looked him in the eye. "I am thirty years old," she said. "I have a number of degrees."

The boy's look was irritated but dogged. "I don't care," he said. "I don't care a thing about what all you done. I just want to know if you love me or don'tcher?" and he caught her to him and wildly planted her face with kisses until she said, "Yes, yes."

"Okay then," he said letting her go. "Prove it."

She smiled, looking dreamily out on the shifty landscape. She had seduced him without even making up her mind to try. "How?" she asked, feeling that he should be delayed a little.

He leaned over and put his lips to her ear. "Show me where your wooden leg joins on," he whispered.

The girl uttered a sharp little cry and her face instantly drained of color. The obscenity of the suggestion was not what shocked her. As a child she had sometimes been subject to feelings of shame but education had removed the last traces of that as a good surgeon scrapes for cancer; she would no more have felt it over what he was asking than she would have believed in his Bible. But she was as sensitive about the artificial leg as a peacock about his tail. No one ever touched it but her. She took care of it as someone else would his soul, in private and almost with her own eyes turned away. "No," she said.

"I known it," he muttered, sitting up. "You're just playing me for a sucker."

"Oh no no!" she cried. "It joins on at the knee. Only at the knee. Why do you want to see it?"

The boy gave her a long penetrating look. "Because," he said, "it's what makes you different. You ain't like anybody else."

She sat staring at him. There was nothing about her face or her round freezing-blue eyes to indicate that this had moved her; but she felt as if her heart had stopped and left her mind to pump her blood. She decided that for the first time in her life she was face to face with real innocence. This boy, with an instinct that came from beyond wisdom, had touched the truth about her. When after a minute, she said in a hoarse high voice, "All right," it was like surrendering to him completely. It was like losing her own life and finding it again, miraculously, in his.

Very gently he began to roll the slack leg up. The artificial limb, in a white sock and brown flat shoe, was bound in a heavy material like canvas and ended in an ugly jointure where it was attached to the stump. The boy's face and his voice were entirely reverent as he uncovered it and said, "Now show me how to take it off and on."

She took it off for him and put it back on again and then he took it off himself, handling it as tenderly as if it were a real one. "See!" he said with a delighted child's face. "Now I can do it myself!"

"Put it back on," she said. She was thinking that she would run away with him and that every night he would take the leg off and every morning put it back on again. "Put it back on," she said.

"Not yet," he murmured, setting it on its foot out of her reach. "Leave it off for a while. You got me instead."

She gave a little cry of alarm but he pushed her down and began to kiss her again. Without the leg she felt entirely dependent on him. Her brain seemed to have stopped thinking altogether and to be about some other function that it was not very good at. Different expressions raced back and forth over her face. Every now and then the boy, his eyes like two steel spikes, would glance behind him where the leg stood. Finally she pushed him off and said, "Put it back on me now."

"Wait," he said. He leaned the other way and pulled the valise toward him and opened it. It had a pale blue spotted lining and there were only two Bibles in it. He took one of these out and opened the cover of it. It was hollow and contained a pocket flask of whiskey, a pack of cards, and a small blue box with printing on it. He laid these out in front of her one at a time in an evenly-spaced row, like one presenting offerings at the shrine of a goddess. He put the blue box in her hand. THIS PRODUCT TO BE USED ONLY FOR THE PREVENTION OF DISEASE, she read, and dropped it. The boy was unscrewing the top of the flask. He stopped and pointed, with a smile, to the deck of cards. It was not an ordinary deck but one with an obscene picture on the back of each card. "Take a swig," he said, offering her the bottle first. He held it in front of her, but like one mesmerized, she did not move.

Her voice when she spoke had an almost pleading sound. "Aren't you," she murmured, "aren't you just good country people?"

The boy cocked his head. He looked as if he were just beginning to understand that she might be trying to insult him. "Yeah," he said, curling his lip slightly, "but it ain't held me back none. I'm as good as you any day in the week."

"Give me my leg," she said.

He pushed it farther away with his foot. "Come on now, let's begin to have us a good time," he said coaxingly. "We ain't got to know one another good yet."

"Give me my leg!" she screamed and tried to lunge for it but he pushed her down easily.

"What's the matter with you all of a sudden?" he asked, frowning as he screwed the top on the flask and put it quickly back inside the Bible. "You just a while ago said you didn't believe in nothing. I thought you was some girl!"

Her face was almost purple. "You're a Christian!" she hissed. "You're a fine Christian! You're just like them all—say one thing and do another. You're a perfect Christian, you're . . ."

The boy's mouth was set angrily. "I hope you don't think," he said in a lofty indignant tone, "that I believe in that crap! I may sell Bibles but I know which end is up and I wasn't born yesterday and I know where I'm going!"

"Give me my leg!" she screeched. He jumped up so quickly that she barely saw him sweep the cards and the blue box into the Bible and throw the Bible into the valise. She saw him grab the leg and then she saw it for an instant slanted forlornly across the inside of the suitcase with a Bible at either side of its opposite ends. He slammed the lid shut and snatched up the valise and swung it down the hole and then stepped through himself.

When all of him had passed but his head, he turned and regarded her with a look that no longer had any admiration in it. "I've gotten a lot of interesting things," he said. "One time I got a woman's glass eye this way. And you needn't to think you'll catch me because Pointer ain't really my name. I use a different name at every house I call at and don't stay nowhere long. And I'll tell you another thing, Hulga," he said, using the name as if he didn't think much of it, "you ain't so smart. I been believing in nothing ever since I was born!" and then the toast-colored hat disappeared down the hole and the girl was left, sitting on the straw in the dusty sunlight. When she turned her churning face toward the opening, she saw his blue figure struggling successfully over the green speckled lake.

Mrs. Hopewell and Mrs. Freeman, who were in the back pasture, digging up onions, saw him emerge a little later from the woods and head across the meadow toward the highway. "Why, that looks like that nice dull young man that tried to sell me a Bible yesterday," Mrs. Hopewell said, squinting. "He must have been selling them to the Negroes back in there. He was so simple," he said, "but I guess the world would be better off if we were all that simple."

Mrs. Freeman's gaze drove forward and just touched him before he disappeared under the hill. Then she returned her attention to the evil-smelling onion shoot she was lifting from the ground. "Some can't be that simple," she said. "I know I never could."

1955

John Updike 1932–

John Updike was born in Shillington, Pennsylvania, the son of a junior high school mathematics teacher. Growing up in what seemed to be a world of narrow horizons, he came to an early awareness that he could escape only through his own wits. Encouraged by his ambitious mother, he wrote his first short story at the age of eight. In school he was an honor student, edited his school newspaper, and was president of his high school class. When he graduated from high school, he entered Harvard, the college selected by his mother because she believed that it nurtured writers.

Updike graduated from Harvard summa cum laude *in 1954. Later that year he sold his first short story to the* New Yorker, *the magazine in which he would establish his reputation as a writer of short fiction in the 1950s and 1960s. He spent a year on a fellowship studying art in England, and then became a staff writer for the* New Yorker, *where he turned out poems, sketches, essays, short stories, and reviews. He became known as "The Brilliant Young Writer," a title that has since stirred critics to argue that in his later work he has failed to fulfill his early promise.*

In 1957 Updike left the New Yorker, *moved to Ipswich, Massachusetts, and became an independent writer. His first book,* The Carpentered Hen, *a collection of poems, appeared the next year. His first novel,* The Poorhouse Fair, *and his first collection of short stories,* The Same Door, *were published in 1959. In the years that have followed, Updike has become one of the most prolific writers in modern American literature, publishing numerous novels, as well as an opera libretto, a play, his memoirs (*Self-Consciousness, *1989), and many volumes of poetry, short stories, and essays.*

Updike won his first widespread, popular recognition with Couples *(1968), a novel of suburban life that is filled with descriptions of compulsive adulteries. To readers hardened by the extravagant carnality of today's books and movies, the eroticism of* Couples *seems mild indeed, but to many critics and reviewers in the 1960s the novel was shocking, lurid, "unredeemed pornography" and "obsessively venereal," judgments that proved to be powerfully tempting to the book-buying public and helped to make the novel a vast commercial success. Of greater artistic significance was* Centaur *(1963), a highly symbolic and allusive novel, drawing heavily on classical myth, that won the National Book Award.*

In 1978 Updike published the novel The Coup, *a dark comedy set in modern Africa and reporting the reminiscences of a one-time dictator of a newly emerged African nation. But he most frequently has set his fiction in small-town America —rural villages and prosperous suburbia—a landscape described in many of his short stories, in four "Rabbit novels":* Rabbit Run *(1960),* Rabbit Redux *(1971),* Rabbit Is Rich *(1981),* Rabbit at Rest *(1990), and in* The Witches of Eastwick *(1984), a satirical story of witchcraft and demonic possession that was made into a comic, and lucrative, movie.* Villages *(2004), Updike's twenty-first novel, returns to the world of small-town sex, mostly clandestine, which he portrayed thirty-six years before in* Couples, *and sustains his reputation as "troubadour in the melancholy poetics of adultery."*

Updike has said that "plain realism has never seemed to me to be enough," and in order to scrutinize what he sees as the "intricacy and opacity of the real world," he often turns to fantasy and illusion. In three recent novels, he has reworked themes and re-created characters from Nathaniel Hawthorne's The Scarlet Letter, *in order to portray the loves and follies of affluent "spiritual seekers" in today's America.*

Updike's America is often a drab world of middle- and lower-class materialism, a land of trivial lives centered on TV, movies, and fan magazines for the riff raff—a brand-name America whose inhabitants are sunk in installment buying, whose stomachs are bloated with franchised food, and whose minds are dulled by soap operas and by trashy tabloids sold at checkout stands. And while Updike's characters often search for spiritual and religious meaning, they usually discover that sentimental love is a trap, that their happiness is brief, and that their lives are as dull as their prepackaged meals.

Nevertheless, Updike's finest work has always come from his exploration of ordinary America and from his use of elegant prose, rich with metaphor, to portray the public and private feelings of Americans, their daily rounds of life, their language, clothes, food, houses, cars, boyfriends, and girlfriends. And he celebrates America as a place, with all its ugliness, where people hold on—enduring, if not heroically, at least doggedly—an America he has commemorated in his poetry as a land of

> *your nothing streetcorners*
> *your ugly eateries*
> *your dear barbarities*
> *and vacant lots*
>
> . . .
>
> *Don't read your reviews,*
> A*M*E*R*I*C*A
> *You are the only land.*

FURTHER READING: A. K. Hamilton, *The Elements of John Updike,* 1970; L. Taylor, *Pastoral and Anti-Pastoral Patterns in John Updike's Fiction,* 1971; R. Burchard, *John Updike, Yea Sayings,* 1971; R. Detewiler, *John Updike,* 1972; J. Markle, *John Updike's Fiction,* 1973; S. Uphaus, *John Updike,* 1980; P. Vaughan, *John Updike's Images of America,* 1981; *Critical Essays on John Updike,* ed. W. Macnaughton, 1982; D. Greiner, *The Other John Updike,* 1982; D. Greiner, *John Updike's Novels,* 1984; *John Updike,* ed. H. Bloom, 1987; J. Newman, *John Updike,* 1988; D. Ristoff, *John Updike's America,* 1988; R. Luscher, *John Updike,* 1993; *Conversations with John Updike,* ed. J. Plath, 1994; J. Schiff, *John Updike Revisited,* 1998; W. Pritchard, *Updike, America's Man of Letters,* 2000.

TEXT: *Pigeon Feathers,* 1962.

FLIGHT

At the age of seventeen I was poorly dressed and funny-looking, and went around thinking about myself in the third person. "Allen Dow strode down the street and home." "Allen Dow smiled a thin sardonic smile."

Consciousness of a special destiny made me both arrogant and shy. Years before, when I was eleven or twelve, just on the brink of ceasing to be a little boy, my mother and I, one Sunday afternoon—my father was busy, or asleep—hiked up to the top of Shale Hill, a child's mountain that formed one side of the valley that held our town. There the town lay under us, Olinger, perhaps a thousand homes, the best and biggest of them climbing Shale Hill toward us, and beyond them the blocks of brick houses, one- and two-family, the homes of my friends, sloping down to the pale thread of the Alton Pike, which strung together the high school, the tennis courts, the movie theatre, the town's few stores and gasoline stations, the elementary school, the Lutheran church. On the other side lay more homes, including our own, a tiny white patch placed just where the land began to rise toward the opposite mountain. Cedar Top. There were rims and rims of hills beyond Cedar Top, and looking south we could see the pike dissolving in other towns and turning out of sight amid the patches of green and brown farmland, and it seemed the entire county was lying exposed under a thin veil of haze. I was old enough to feel embarrassment at standing there alone with my mother, beside a wind-stunted spruce tree, on a long spine of shade. Suddenly she dug her fingers into the hair on my head and announced, "There we all are, and there we'll all be forever." She hesitated before the word "forever," and hesitated again before adding, "Except you, Allen. You're going to fly." A few birds were hung far out over the valley, at the level of our eyes, and in her impulsive way she had just plucked the image from them, but it felt like the clue I had been waiting all my childhood for. My most secret self had been made to respond, and I was intensely embarrassed, and irritably ducked my head out from under her melodramatic hand.

She was impulsive and romantic and inconsistent. I was never able to develop this spurt of reassurance into a steady theme between us. That she continued to treat me like an ordinary child seemed a betrayal of the vision she had made me share. I was captive to a hope she had tossed off and forgotten. My shy attempts to justify irregularities in my conduct—reading late at night or not coming back from school on time—by appealing to the image of flight were received with a startled blank look, as if I were talking nonsense. It seemed outrageously unjust. Yes, but, I wanted to say, yes, but it's *your* nonsense. And of course it was just this that made my appeal ineffective: her knowing that I had not made it mine, that I cynically intended to exploit both the privileges of being extraordinary and the pleasures of being ordinary. She feared my wish to be ordinary; once she did respond to my protest that I was learning to fly, by crying with red-faced ferocity, "You'll never learn, you'll stick and die in the dirt just like I'm doing. Why should you be better than your mother?"

She had been born ten miles to the south, on a farm she and her mother had loved. Her mother, a small fierce woman who looked more like an Arab than a German, worked in the fields with the men, and drove the wagon to market ten miles away every Friday. When still a tiny girl, my mother rode with her, and my impression of those rides is of fear—the little girl's fear of the gross and beery men who grabbed and hugged her, her fear of the wagon breaking, of the produce not selling, fear of her mother's possible humiliation and of her father's condition when at nightfall they returned. Friday was his holiday, and he drank. His drinking is impossible for me to picture; for I never knew him except as an enduring, didactic, almost Biblical old man, whose one passion was reading the newspapers and whose one hatred was of the Republican Party. There was something public about him; now that he is dead I keep seeing bits of him attached to famous politicians—his watch chain and his plump square stomach in old films of Theodore Roosevelt, his high-top shoes and the tilt of his head in a photograph of Alfalfa Bill Murray.[1] Alfalfa Bill is turning his head to talk, and holds his hat by the crown, pinching it between two fingers and a thumb, a gentle and courtly grip that reminded me so keenly of my grandfather that I tore the picture out of *Life* and put it in a drawer.

Laboring in the soil had never been congenial to my grandfather, though with his wife's help he prospered by it. Then, in an era when success was hard to avoid, he began to invest in stocks. In 1922 he bought our large white home in the town—its fashionable section had not yet shifted to the Shale Hill side of the valley—and settled in to reap his dividends. He believed to his death that women were foolish, and the broken hearts of his two must have seemed specially so. The dignity of finance for the indignity of farming must have struck him as an eminently advantageous exchange. It strikes me that way, too, and how to reconcile my idea of those fear-ridden wagon rides with the grief that my mother insists she and her mother felt at being taken from the farm? Perhaps prolonged fear is a ground of love. Or perhaps, and likelier, the equation is long and complex, and the few factors I know—the middle-aged woman's mannish pride of land, the adolescent girl's pleasure in riding horses across the fields, their common feeling of rejection in Olinger—are enclosed in brackets and heightened by coefficients that I cannot see. Or perhaps it is not love of land but its absence that needs explaining, in my grandfather's fastidiousness and pride. He believed that as a boy he had been abused, and bore his father a grudge that my mother could never understand. Her grandfather to her was a saintly slender giant, over six feet tall when this was a prodigy, who knew the names of everything, like Adam in Eden. In his old age he was blind. When he came out of the house, the dogs rushed forward to lick his hands. When he lay dying, he requested a Gravenstein apple from the tree on the far edge of the meadow, and his son brought him a Krauser from the orchard near the house. The old man refused it, and my grandfather made a second trip, but in my mother's eyes the outrage had been committed, a savage insult insanely without provocation. What had his father done to him? The only specific complaint I ever heard my grandfather make was that when he was a boy and had to fetch water for the men in the fields, his father would tell him sarcastically, "Pick up your feet; they'll come down

[1]William Henry Murray (1869–1956), colorful Democratic politician, governor of Oklahoma 1931–1935. His nickname came from his success as an alfalfa farmer

themselves." How incongruous! As if each generation of parents commits atrocities against their children which by God's decree remain invisible to the rest of the world.

I remember my grandmother as a little dark-eyed woman who talked seldom and who tried to feed me too much, and then as a hook-nosed profile pink against the lemon cushions of the casket. She died when I was seven. All the rest I know about her is that she was the baby of thirteen children, that while she was alive she made our yard one of the most beautiful in town, and that I am supposed to resemble her brother Pete.

My mother was precocious; she was fourteen when they moved, and for three years had been attending the county normal school. She graduated from Lake College, near Philadelphia, when she was only twenty, a tall handsome girl with a deprecatory smile, to judge from one of the curling photographs kept in a shoebox that I was always opening as a child, as if it might contain the clue to the quarrels in my house. My mother stands at the end of our brick walk, beside the elaborately trimmed end of our privet hedge—in shape a thick square column mounted by a rough ball of leaf. The ragged arc of a lilac bush in flower cuts into the right edge of the photograph, and behind my mother I can see a vacant lot where there had been a house ever since I can remember. She poses with a kind of country grace in a long fur-trimmed coat, unbuttoned to expose her beads and a short yet somehow demure flapper dress. Her hands are in her coat pockets, a beret sits on one side of her bangs, and there is a swank about her that seemed incongruous to me, examining this picture on the stained carpet of an ill-lit old house in the evening years of the thirties and in the dark of the warring forties. The costume and the girl in it look so up-to-date, so formidable. It was my grandfather's pleasure, in his prosperity, to give her a generous clothes allowance. My father, the penniless younger son of a Presbyterian minister in Passaic, had worked his way through Lake College by waiting on tables, and still speaks with mild resentment of the beautiful clothes that Lillian Baer wore. This aspect of my mother caused me some pain in high school; she was a fabric snob, and insisted on buying my slacks and sports shirts at the best store in Alton, and since we had little money, she bought me few, when of course what I needed was what my classmates had—a wide variety of cheap clothes.

At the time the photograph was taken, my mother wanted to go to New York. What she would have done there, or exactly what she wanted to do, I don't know; but her father forbade her. "Forbid" is a husk of a word today, but at that time, in that quaint province, in the mouth of an "indulgent father," it apparently was still viable, for the great moist weight of that forbidding continued to be felt in the house for years, and when I was a child, as one of my mother's endless harangues to my grandfather screamed toward its weeping peak, I could feel it around and above me, like a huge root encountered by an earthworm.

Perhaps in a reaction of anger my mother married my father, Victor Dow, who at least took her as far away as Wilmington, where he had made a beginning with an engineering firm. But the depression hit, my father was laid off, and the couple came to the white house in Olinger, where my grandfather sat reading the newspapers that traced his stocks' cautious decline into worthlessness. I was born. My grandmother went around as a cleaning lady, and grew things in our quarter-acre yard to sell. We kept chickens, and there was a large plot of asparagus. After she had died, in a frightened way I used to seek her in the asparagus patch. By midsummer it would be a forest of dainty green trees, some as tall as I was, and in their frothy touch a spirit seemed to speak, and in the soft thick net of their intermingling branches a promise seemed to be caught, as well as a menace. The asparagus trees were frightening; in the center of the patch, far from the house and the alley, I would fall under a spell, and become tiny, and wander among the great smooth green trunks expecting to find a little house with a smoking chimney, and in it my grandmother. She herself had believed in ghosts, which made her own ghost potent. Even now, sitting alone in my own house, a board creaks in the kitchen and I look up fearing she will come through the doorway. And at night, just before I fall asleep, her voice calls my name in a penetrating whisper, or calls, "*Pete.*"

My mother went to work in an Alton department store, selling inferior fabric for $14 a week. During the daytime of my first year of life it was my father who took care of me. He has since said, flattering me as he always does, that it was having me on his hands that kept him from going insane. It may have been this that has made my affection for him so inarticulate, as if I were still a wordless infant looking up into the mothering blur of his man's face. And that same shared year helps account, perhaps, for his gentleness with me, for his willingness to praise, as if everything I do has something sad and crippled in it. He feels sorry for me; my birth coincided with the birth of a great misery, a national misery—only recently has he stopped calling me by the nickname "Young America." Around my first birthday he acquired a position teaching arithmetic and algebra in the Olinger high school, and though he was so kind and humorous he couldn't enter a classroom without creating uproarious problems of discipline, he endured it day by day and year by year, and eventually came to occupy a place in this alien town, so that I believe there are now one or two dozen ex-students, men and women nearing middle-age, who carry around with them some piece of encouragement my father gave them, or remember some sentence of his that helped shape them. Certainly there are many who remember the antics with which he burlesqued his discomfort in the classroom. He kept a confiscated cap pistol in his desk, and upon getting an especially stupid answer, he would take it out and, wearing a preoccupied, regretful expression, shoot himself in the head.

My grandfather was the last to go to work, and the most degraded by it. He was hired by the borough crew, men who went around the streets shoveling stones and spreading tar. Bulky and ominous in their overalls, wreathed in steam, and associated with dramatic and portentous equipment, these men had grandeur in the eyes of a child, and it puzzled me, as I walked to and from elementary school, that my grandfather refused to wave to me or confess his presence in any way. Curiously strong for a fastidious man, he kept at it well into his seventies, when his sight failed. It was my task then to read his beloved newspapers to him as he sat in his chair by the bay window, twiddling his high-top shoes in the sunshine. I teased him, reading too fast, then maddeningly slow, skipping from column to column to create one long chaotic story; I read him the sports page, which did not interest him, and mumbled the editorials. Only the speed of his feet's twiddling betrayed vexation. When I'd stop, he would plead mildly in his rather beautiful, old-fashioned, elocutionary voice, "Now just the obituaries, Allen. Just the names to see if anyone I know is there." I imagined, as I viciously barked at him the list of names that might contain the name of a friend, that I was avenging my mother; I believed that she hated him, and for her sake I tried to hate him also. From her incessant resurrection of mysterious grievances buried far back in the confused sunless earth of the time before I was born, I had been able to deduce only that he was an evil man, who had ruined her life, that fair creature in the beret. I did not understand. She fought with him not because she wanted to fight but because *she could not bear to leave him alone.*

Sometimes, glancing up from the sheet of print where our armies swarmed in retreat like harried insects, I would catch the old man's head in the act of lifting slightly to receive the warm sunshine on his face, a dry frail face ennobled by its thick crown of combed corn-silk hair. It would dawn on me then that his sins as a father were likely no worse than any father's. But my mother's genius was to give the people closest to her mythic immensity. I was the phoenix. My father and grandmother were legendary invader-saints, she springing out of some narrow vein of Arab blood in the German race and he crossing over from the Protestant wastes of New Jersey, both of them serving and enslaving their mates with their prodigious powers of endurance and labor. For my mother felt that she and her father alike had been destroyed by marriage, been made captive by people better yet less than they. It was true, my father had loved Mom Baer, and her death made him seem more of an alien than ever. He, and her ghost, stood to one side, in the shadows but separate from the house's dark core, the inheritance of frustration and folly that had descended from my grandfather to my mother to me, and that I, with a few beats of my grown wings, was destined to reverse and redeem.

At the age of seventeen, in the fall of my senior year, I went with three girls to debate at a high school over a hundred miles away. They were, all three, bright girls, A students; they were disfigured by A's as if by acne. Yet even so it excited me to be mounting a train with them early on a Friday morning, at an hour when our schoolmates miles away were slumping into the seats of their first class. Sunshine spread broad bars of dust down the length of the half-empty car, and through the windows Pennsylvania unravelled in a long brown scroll scribbled with industry. Black pipes raced beside the tracks for miles. At rhythmic intervals one of them looped upward, like the Greek letter Ω. "Why does it do that?" I asked. "Is it sick?"

"Condensation?" Judith Potteiger suggested in her shy, transparent voice. She loved science.

"No," I said. "It's in pain. It's writhing! It's going to grab the train! Look out!" I ducked, honestly a little scared. All the girls laughed.

Judith and Catharine Miller were in my class, and expected me to be amusing; the third girl, a plump small junior named Molly Bingaman, had not known what to expect. It was her fresh audience I was playing to. She was the best dressed of us four, and the most poised; this made me suspect that she was the least bright. She had been substituted at the last moment for a sick member of the debating team; I knew her just by seeing her in the halls and in assembly. From a distance she seemed dumpy and prematurely adult. But up close she was gently fragrant, and against the weary purple cloth of the train seats her skin seemed luminous. She had beautiful skin, heartbreaking skin a pencil dot would have marred, and large blue eyes equally clear. Except for a double chin, and a mouth too large and thick, she would have been perfectly pretty, in a little woman's compact and cocky way. She and I sat side by side, facing the two senior girls, who more and more took on the wan slyness of matchmakers. It was they who had forced the seating arrangements.

We debated in the afternoon, and won. Yes, the German Federal Republic *should* be freed of all Allied control. The school, a posh castle on the edge of a miserable coal city, was the site of a statewide cycle of debates that was to continue into Saturday. There was a dance Friday night in the gym. I danced with Molly mostly, though to my annoyance she got in with a set of Harrisburg boys while I conscientiously pushed Judith and Catharine around the floor. We were stiff dancers, the three of us; only Molly made me seem good, floating backward from my feet fearlessly as her cheek rumpled my moist shirt. The gym was hung with orange and black crepe paper in honor of Hallowe'en, and the pennants of all the competing schools were fastened to the walls, and a twelve-piece band pumped away blissfully on the year's sad tunes —"Heartaches," "Near You," "That's My Desire." A great cloud of balloons gathered in the steel girders was released. There was pink punch, and a local girl sang.

Judith and Catharine decided to leave before the dance was over, and I made Molly come too, though she was in a literal sweat of pleasure; her perfect skin in the oval above her neckline was flushed and glazed. I realized, with a little shock of possessiveness and pity, that she was unused to attention back home, in competition with the gorgeous Olinger ignorant.

We walked together to the house where the four of us had been boarded, a large white frame owned by an old couple and standing with lonely decency in a semi-slum. Judith and Catharine turned up the walk, but Molly and I, with a diffident decision that I believe came from their initiative, contined, "to walk around the block." We walked miles, stopping off after midnight at a trolley-car-shaped diner. I got a hamburger, and she impressed me by ordering coffee. We walked back to the house and let ourselves in with the key we had been given; but instead of going upstairs to our rooms we sat downstairs in the living room and talked softly for more hours.

What did we say? I talked about myself. It is hard to hear, much less remember, what we ourselves say, just as it might be hard for a movie projector, given life, to see the shadows its eye of light is casting. A transcript, could I produce it, of my monologue through the wide turning point of that night, with all its word-by-word conceit, would distort the picture: this living room miles from home, the street light piercing the chinks in the curtains and erecting on the wallpaper rods of light the size of yardsticks, our hosts and companions asleep upstairs, the incessant sigh of my voice, coffee-primed Molly on the floor beside my chair, her stockinged legs stretched out on the rug; and this odd sense in the room, a tasteless and odorless aura unfamiliar to me, as a pool of water widening.

I remember one exchange. I must have been describing the steep waves of fearing death that had come over me ever since early childhood, about one every three years, and I ended by supposing that it would take great courage to be an atheist. "But I bet you'll become one," Molly said. "Just to show yourself that you're brave enough." I felt she overestimated me, and was flattered. Within a few years, while I still remembered many of her words, I realized how touchingly gauche our assumption was that an atheist is a lonely rebel; for mobs of men are united in atheism, and oblivion—the dense lead-like sea that would occasionally sweep over me—is to them a weight as negligible as the faint pressure of their wallets in their hip pockets. This grotesque and tender misestimate of the world flares in my memory of our conversation like one of the innumerable matches we struck.

The room filled with smoke. Too weary to sit, I lay down on the floor beside her, and stroked her silver arm in silence, yet still was too timid to act on the wide and negative aura that I did not understand was of compliance. On the upstairs landing, as I went to turn into my room, Molly came forward with a prim look and kissed me. With clumsy force I entered the negative space that had been waiting. Her lipstick smeared in little unflattering flecks into the skin around her mouth; it was as if I had been given a face to eat, and the presence of bone—skull under skin, teeth behind lips—impeded me. We stood for a long time under the burning hall light, until my neck began to ache from bowing. My legs were trembling when we finally parted and sneaked into our rooms. In bed I thought, "Allen Dow tossed restlessly," and realized it was the first time that day I had thought of myself in the third person.

On Saturday morning, we lost our debate. I was sleepy and verbose and haughty, and some of the students in the audience began to boo whenever I opened my mouth. The principal came up on the stage and made a scolding speech, which finished me and my cause, untrammeled Germany. On the train back, Catharine and Judith arranged the seating so that they sat behind Molly and me, and spied on only the tops of our heads. For the first time, on that ride home, I felt what it was to bury a humiliation in the body of a woman. Nothing but the friction of my face against hers drowned out the echo of those boos. When we kissed, a red shadow would well under my lids and eclipse the hostile hooting faces of the debate audience, and when our lips parted, the bright inner sea would ebb, and there the faces would be again, more intense than ever. With a shudder of shame I'd hide my face on her shoulder and in the warm darkness there, while a frill of her prissy collar gently scratched my nose, I felt united with Hitler and all the villains, traitors, madmen, and failures who had managed to keep, up to the moment of capture or death, a woman with them. This had puzzled me. In high school females were proud and remote; in the newspapers they were fantastic monsters of submission. And now Molly administered reassurance to me with small motions and bodily adjustments that had about them a strange flavor of the practical.

Our parents met us at the station. I was startled at how tired my mother looked. There were deep blue dents on either side of her nose, and her hair seemed somehow dissociated from her head, as if it were a ragged, half-gray wig she had put on carelessly. She was a heavy woman and her weight, which she usually carried upright, like a kind of wealth, had slumped away from her ownership and seemed, in the sullen light of the railway platform, to weigh on the world. I asked, "How's Grandpa?" He had taken to bed several months before with pains in his chest.

"He still sings," she said rather sharply. For entertainment in his increasing blindness my grandfather had long ago begun to sing, and his shapely old voice would pour forth hymns, forgotten comic ballads, and camp-meeting songs at any hour. His memory seemed to improve the longer he lived.

My mother's irritability was more manifest in the private cavity of the car; her heavy silence oppressed me. "You look so tired, Mother," I said, trying to take the offensive.

"That's nothing to how you look," she answered. "What happened up there? You stoop like an old married man."

"Nothing happened," I lied. My cheeks were parched, as if her high steady anger had the power of giving sunburn.

"I remember that Bingaman girl's mother when we first moved to town. She was the smuggest little snip south of the pike. They're real old Olinger stock, you know. They have no use for hillbillies."

My father and I tried to change the subject. "Well, you won one debate, Allen, and that's more than I would have done. I don't see how you do it."

"Why, he gets it from you, Victor. I've never won a debate with you."

"He gets it from Pop Baer. If that man had gone into politics, Lillian, all the misery of his life would have been avoided."

"Dad was never a debater. He was a bully. Don't go with little women, Allen. It puts you too close to the ground."

"I'm not *going* with *anybody,* Mother. Really, you're so fanciful."

"Why, when she stepped off the train from the way her chins bounced I thought she had eaten a canary. And then making my poor son, all skin and bones, carry her bag. When she walked by me I honestly was afraid she'd spit in my eye."

"I had to carry somebody's bag. I'm sure she doesn't know who you are." Though it was true I had talked a good deal about my family the night before.

My mother turned away from me. "You see, Victor—he defends her. When I was his age that girl's mother gave me a cut I'm still bleeding from, and my own son attacks me on behalf of her fat little daughter. I wonder if her mother put her up to catching him."

"Molly's a nice girl," my father interceded. "She never gave me any trouble in class like some of those smug bastards." But he was curiously listless, for so Christian a man, in pronouncing this endorsement.

I discovered that nobody wanted me to go with Molly Bingaman. My friends—for on the strength of being funny I did have some friends, classmates whose love affairs went on over my head but whom I could accompany, as clown, on communal outings—never talked with me about Molly, and when I brought her to their parties gave the impression of ignoring her, so that I stopped taking her. Teachers at school would smile an odd tight smile when they saw us leaning by her locker or hanging around in the stairways. The eleventh-grade English instructor—one of my "boosters" on the faculty, a man who was always trying to "challenge" me, to "exploit" my "potential"—took me aside and told me how stupid she was. She just couldn't grasp the logical principles of syntax. He confided her parsing mistakes to me as if they betrayed—as indeed in a way they did—an obtuseness her social manner cleverly concealed. Even the Fabers, an ultra-Republican couple who ran a luncheonette near the high school, showed malicious delight whenever Molly and I broke up, and persistently treated my attachment as being a witty piece of play, like my pretense with Mr. Faber of being a Communist. The entire town seemed ensnarled in my mother's myth, that escape was my proper fate. It was as if I were a sport that the ghostly elders of Olinger had segregated from the rest of the livestock and agreed to donate in time to the air; this fitted with the ambiguous sensation I had always had in the town, of being simultaneously flattered and rejected.

Molly's parents disapproved because in their eyes my family was virtually white trash. It was so persistently hammered into me that I was too good for Molly that I scarcely considered the proposition that, by another scale, she was too good for me. Further, Molly herself shielded me. Only once, exasperated by some tedious, condescending confession of mine, did she state that her mother didn't like me. "Why not?" I asked, genuinely surprised. I admired Mrs. Bingaman—she was beautifully preserved—and I always felt gay in her house, with its white woodwork and matching furniture and vases of iris posing before polished mirrors.

"Oh, I don't know. She thinks you're flippant."

"But that's not true. Nobody takes himself more seriously than I do."

While Molly protected me from the Bingaman side of the ugliness, I conveyed the Dow side more or less directly to her. It infuriated me that nobody allowed me to be proud of her. I kept, in effect, asking her, Why was she stupid in English? Why didn't she get along with my friends? Why did she look so dumpy and smug?—this last despite the fact that she often, especially in intimate moments, looked beautiful to me. I was especially angry with her because this affair had brought out an ignoble, hysterical, brutal aspect of my mother that I might never have had to see otherwise. I had hoped to keep things secret from her, but even if her intuition had not been relentless, my father, at school, knew everything. Sometimes, indeed, my mother said that she didn't care if I went with Molly; it was my father who was upset. Like a frantic dog tied by one leg, she snapped in any direction, mouthing ridiculous fancies—such that Mrs. Bingaman had sicked Molly on me just to keep me from going to college and giving the Dows something to be proud of—that would make us both suddenly start laughing. Laughter in that house that winter had a guilty sound. My grandfather was dying, and lay upstairs singing and coughing and weeping as the mood came to him, and we were too poor to hire a nurse, and too kind and cowardly to send him to a "home." It was still his house, after all. Any noise he made seemed to slash my mother's heart, and she was unable to sleep upstairs near him, and waited the nights out on the sofa downstairs. In her desperate state she would say unforgivable things to me even while the tears streamed down her face. I've never seen so many tears as I saw that winter.

Every time I saw my mother cry, it seemed I had to make Molly cry. I developed a skill at it; it came naturally to an only child who had been surrounded all his life by adults ransacking each other for the truth. Even in the heart of intimacy, half-naked each of us, I would say something to humiliate her. We never made love in the final, coital sense. My reason was a mixture of idealism and superstition; I felt that if I took her virginity she would be mine forever. I depended overmuch on a technicality; she gave herself to me anyway, and I had her anyway, and have her still, for the longer I travel in a direction I could not have taken with her, the more clearly she seems the one person who loved me without advantage. I was a homely, comically ambitious hillbilly, and I even refused to tell her I loved her, to pronounce the word "love"—an icy piece of pedantry that shocks me now that I have almost forgotten the context of confusion in which it seemed wise.

In addition to my grandfather's illness, and my mother's grief, and my waiting to hear if I had won a scholarship to the one college that seemed good enough for me, I was burdened with managing too many petty affairs of my graduating class. I was in charge of the yearbook writeups, art editor of the school paper, chairman of the Class Gift Committee, director of the Senior Assembly, and teachers' workhorse. Frightened by my father's tales of nervous breakdowns he had seen, I kept listening for the sounds of my brain snapping, and the image of that gray, infinitely interconnected mass seemed to extend outward, to become my whole world, one dense organic dungeon, and I felt I had to get out; if I could just get out of this, into June, it would be blue sky, and I would be all right for life.

One Friday night in spring, after trying for over an hour to write thirty-five affectionate words for the yearbook about a null girl in the Secretarial Course I had never spoken a word to, I heard my grandfather begin coughing upstairs with a sound like dry membrane tearing, and I panicked. I called up the stairs, "Mother! I must go out."

"It's nine-thirty."

"I know, but I have to. I'm going insane."

Without waiting to hear her answer or to find a coat, I left the house and got our old car out of the garage. The weekend before, I had broken up with Molly again. All week I hadn't spoken to her, though I had seen her once in Faber's, with a boy in her class, averting her face while I, hanging by the side of the pinball machine, made wisecracks in her direction. I didn't dare go up to her door and knock so late at night; I just parked across the street and watched the lit windows of her house. Through their living-room window I could see one of Mrs. Bingaman's vases of hothouse iris standing on the white mantel, and my open car window admitted the spring air, which delicately smelled of wet ashes. Molly was probably out on a date with that moron in her class. But then the Bingaman's door opened, and her figure appeared in the rectangle of light. Her back was toward me, a coat was on her arm, and her mother seemed to be screaming. Molly closed the door and ran off the porch and across the street and quickly got into the car, her eyes downcast in their sockets of shadow. *She came.* When I have finally forgotten everything else, her powdery fragrance, her lucid cool skin, the way her lower lip was like a curved pillow of two cloths, the dusty red outer and wet pink inner, I'll still be grieved by this about Molly, that she came to me.

After I returned her to her house—she told me not to worry, her mother enjoyed shouting—I went to the all-night diner just beyond the Olinger town line and ate three hamburgers, ordering them one at a time, and drank two glasses of milk. It was close to two o'clock when I got home, but my mother was still awake. She lay on the sofa in the dark, with the radio sitting on the floor murmuring Dixieland piped up from New Orleans by way of Philadelphia. Radio music was a steady feature of her insomniac life; not only did it help drown out the noise of her father upstairs but she seemed to enjoy it in itself. She would resist my father's pleas to come to bed by saying that the New Orleans program was not over yet. The radio was an old Philco we had always had; I had once drawn a fish on the orange disc of its celluloid dial, which looked to my child's eyes like a fishbowl.

Her loneliness caught at me; I went into the living room and sat on a chair with my back to the window. For a long time she looked at me tensely out of the darkness. "Well," she said at last, "how was little hotpants?" The vulgarity this affair had brought out in her language appalled me.

"I made her cry," I told her.

"Why do you torment the girl?"

"To please you."

"It doesn't please me."

"Well, then, stop nagging me."

"I'll stop nagging you if you'll solemnly tell me you're willing to marry her."

I said nothing to this, and after waiting she went on in a different voice, "Isn't it funny, that you should show this weakness."

"Weakness is a funny way to put it when it's the only thing that gives me strength."

"Does it really, Allen? Well. It may be. I forget, you were born here."

Upstairs, close to our heads, my grandfather, in a voice frail but still melodious, began to sing, "There is a happy land, far, far away, where saints in glory stand, bright, bright as day." We listened; and his voice broke into coughing, a terrible rending cough growing in fury, struggling to escape, and loud with fear he called my mother's name. She didn't stir. His voice grew enormous, a bully's voice, as he repeated, "Lillian! Lillian!" and I saw my mother's shape quiver with the force coming down the stairs into her; she was like a dam; and then the power, as my grandfather fell momentarily silent, flowed toward me in the darkness, and I felt intensely angry, and hated that black mass of suffering, even while I realized, with a rapid, light calculation, that I was too weak to withstand it.

In a dry tone of certainty and dislike—how hard my heart had become—I told her, "All right. You'll win this one, Mother; but it'll be the last one you'll win."

My pang of fright following this unprecedentedly cold insolence seemed to blot my senses; the chair ceased to be felt under me, and the walls and furniture of the room fell away—there was only the dim orange glow of the radio dial down below. In a husky voice that seemed to come across a great distance my mother said, with typical melodrama, "Goodbye, Allen."

1959 1962

Bernard Malamud 1914–1986

Bernard Malamud was a recorder of the Jewish experience, with all its despair, possibility, and hope for redemption. He was born in Brooklyn, the son of Russian immigrant parents. After graduating from the City College of New York in 1936, he attended Columbia University, from which he received an M.A. in 1942. He taught in a high school and then at Oregon State University from 1949 to 1961. While there he published The Natural *(1952), a comic novel that ironically mythologizes the American passion for "the national pastime," baseball. In 1957 he published* The Assistant, *a tragi-comedy of a young Italian-American living in the midst of a Jewish family, which many critics consider to be his most successful novel.* The Magic Barrel *(1958), a collection of short stories for which he received a National Book Award, similarly reveals the tragedy and comedy inherent in human life. In* A New Life *(1961), one of Malamud's bestselling works, he concentrated on the spiritual rebirth of a comically suffering and despairing English teacher trapped in an academic wilderness.*

In 1963 Malamud published Idiots First, *a collection of short stories which was followed by* The Fixer *(1966), a parable of the plight of Russian Jews. In* Pictures of Fidelman *(1969), he presented a comic novel of a painter who travels to Europe and tries his hand at art criticism, imitation, forgery, and creation.* The Tenants *(1971) depicts the life of a middle-aged man living in a run-down tenement house and struggling to find mercy in a hostile world. In 1979, Malamud published his seventh and most ambitious novel,* Dubin's Lives, *a story of marriage and infidelity. The novel's hero, an aging writer, seeks rejuvenation and escape from a stale world. He finds, instead, a portion of the moral insight that can be gained from painful experience.*

Malamud's works often display the search for meaning made by a bereft, bewildered wanderer who yearns, but fails, to find the secret of life and happiness. Malamud revealed the relationships of comedy and terror, failure and success, weakness and courage; and he presented the individual as an emblem of modern humanity, confused, clinging to shattered dreams, and struggling for love and self-understanding in the midst of folly and threatening doom.

FURTHER READING: J. Helterman, *Understanding Bernard Malamud,* 1985; *Bernard Malamud,* ed. H. Bloom, 1986; *Critical Essays on Bernard Malamud,* ed. J. Salzberg, 1987; K. Ochshorn, *The Heart's Essential Landscape, Bernard Malamud's Hero,* 1990; *Conversations with Bernard Malamud,* ed. L. Lasher, 1991; E. Abramson, *Bernard Malamud Revisited,* 1993; *Talking Horse, Bernard Malamud on Life and Work,* ed. A Cheuse and N. Delbanco, 1996; *The Complete Stories,* ed. R. Giroux, 1997; B. Sío-Castiñeira, *The Short Stories of Bernard Malamud, in Search of Jewish Post-Immigrant Identity,* 1998; M. Shaw, *Ethnic Identities in Bernard Malamud's Fiction,* 2000.

TEXT: *The Magic Barrel,* 1958.

THE MAGIC BARREL

Not long ago there lived in uptown New York, in a small, almost meager room, though crowded with books, Leo Finkle, a rabbinical student in the Yeshivah University. Finkle, after six years of study, was to be ordained in June and had been advised by an acquaintance that he might find it easier to win himself a congregation if he were married. Since he had no present prospects of marriage, after two tormented days of turning it over in his mind, he called in Pinye Salzman, a marriage broker whose two-line advertisement he had read in the *Forward.*[1]

The matchmaker appeared one night out of the dark fourth-floor hallway of the graystone rooming house where Finkle lived, grasping a black, strapped portfolio that had been worn thin with use. Salzman, who had been long in the business, was of slight but dignified build, wearing an old hat, and an overcoat too short and tight for him. He smelled frankly of fish, which he loved to eat, and although he was missing a few teeth, his presence was not displeasing, because of an amiable manner curiously contrasted with mournful eyes. His voice, his lips, his wisp of beard, his bony fingers were animated, but give him a moment of repose and his mild blue eyes revealed a depth of sadness, a characteristic that put Leo a little at ease although the situation, for him, was inherently tense.

He at once informed Salzman why he had asked him to come, explaining that his home was in Cleveland, and that but for his parents, who had married comparatively late in life, he was alone in the world. He had for six years devoted himself almost entirely to his studies, as a result of which, understandably, he had found himself without time for a social life and the company of young women. Therefore he thought it the better part of trial and error—of embarrassing fumbling—to call in an experienced person to advise him on these matters. He remarked in passing that the function of the marriage broker was ancient and honorable, highly approved in the Jewish community, because it made practical the necessary without hindering joy. Moreover, his own parents had been brought together by a matchmaker. They had made, if not a financially profitable marriage—since neither had possessed any worldly goods to speak of—at least a successful one in the sense of their everlasting devotion to each other. Salzman listened in embarrassed surprise, sensing a sort of apology. Later, however, he experienced a glow of pride in his work, an emotion that had left him years ago, and he heartily approved of Finkle.

The two went to their business. Leo had led Salzman to the only clear place in the room, a table near a window that overlooked the lamp-lit city. He seated himself at the matchmaker's side but facing him, attempting by an act of will to suppress the unpleasant tickle in his throat. Salzman eagerly unstrapped his portfolio and removed a loose rubber band from a thin packet of much-handled cards. As he flipped through them, a gesture and sound that physically hurt Leo, the student pretended not to see and gazed steadfastly out the window. Although it was still February, winter was on its last legs, signs of which he had for the first time in years begun to notice. He now observed the round white moon, moving high in the sky through a cloud menagerie, and watched with half-open mouth as it penetrated a huge hen, and dropped out of her like an egg laying itself. Salzman, though pretending through eyeglasses he had just slipped on, to be engaged in scanning the writing on the cards, stole occasional glances at the young man's distinguished face, noting with pleasure the long, severe scholar's nose, brown eyes heavy with learning, sensitive yet ascetic lips, and a certain, almost hollow

[1] *The Jewish Daily Forward,* Yiddish newspaper in New York City.

quality of the dark cheeks. He gazed around at shelves upon shelves of books and let out a soft, contented sigh.

When Leo's eyes fell upon the cards, he counted six spread out in Salzman's hand.

"So few?" he asked in disappointment.

"You wouldn't believe me how much cards I got in my office," Salzman replied. "The drawers are already filled to the top, so I keep them now in a barrel, but is every girl good for a new rabbi?"

Leo blushed at this, regretting all he had revealed of himself in a curriculum vitae he had sent to Salzman. He had thought it best to acquaint him with his strict standards and specifications, but in having done so, he felt he had told the marriage broker more than was absolutely necessary.

He hesitantly inquired, "Do you keep photographs of your clients on file?"

"First comes family, amount of dowry, also what kind promises," Salzman replied, unbuttoning his tight coat and settling himself in the chair. "After comes pictures, rabbi."

"Call me Mr. Finkle. I'm not yet a rabbi."

Salzman said he would, but instead called him doctor, which he changed to rabbi when Leo was not listening too attentively.

Salzman adjusted his horn-rimmed spectacles, gently cleared his throat and read in an eager voice the contents of the top card:

"Sophie P. Twenty four years. Widow one year. No children. Educated high school and two years college. Father promises eight thousand dollars. Has wonderful wholesale business. Also real estate. On the mother's side comes teachers, also one actor. Well known on Second Avenue."

Leo gazed up in surprise. "Did you say a widow?"

"A widow don't mean spoiled, rabbi. She lived with her husband maybe four months. He was a sick boy she made a mistake to marry him."

"Marrying a widow has never entered my mind."

"This is because you have no experience. A widow, especially if she is young and healthy like this girl, is a wonderful person to marry. She will be thankful to you the rest of her life. Believe me, if I was looking now for a bride, I would marry a widow."

Leo reflected, then shook his head.

Salzman hunched his shoulders in an almost imperceptible gesture of disappointment. He placed the card down on the wooden table and began to read another:

"Lily H. High school teacher. Regular. Not a substitute. Has savings and new Dodge car. Lived in Paris one year. Father is successful dentist thirty-five years. Interested in professional man. Well Americanized family. Wonderful opportunity."

"I knew her personally," said Salzman. "I wish you could see this girl. She is a doll. Also very intelligent. All day you could talk to her about books and theyater and what not. She also knows current events."

"I don't believe you mentioned her age?"

"Her age?" Salzman said, raising his brows. "Her age is thirty-two years."

Leo said after a while, "I'm afraid that seems a little too old."

Salzman let out a laugh. "So how old are you, rabbi?"

"Twenty-seven."

"So what is the difference, tell me, between twenty-seven and thirty-two? My own wife is seven years older than me. So what did I suffer?—Nothing. If Rothschild's daughter wants to marry you, would you say on account her age, no?"

"Yes," Leo said dryly.

Salzman shook off the no in the yes. "Five years don't mean a thing. I give you my word that when you will live with her for one week you will forget her age. What does it mean five years—that she lived more and knows more than somebody who is younger? On this girl, God bless her, years are not wasted. Each one that it comes makes better the bargain."

"What subject does she teach in high school?"

"Languages. If you heard the way she speaks French, you will think it is music. I am in the business twenty-five years, and I recommend her with my whole heart. Believe me, I know what I'm talking, rabbi."

"What's on the next card?" Leo said abruptly.

Salzman reluctantly turned up the third card:

"Ruth K. Nineteen years. Honor student. Father offers thirteen thousand cash to the right bridegroom. He is a medical doctor. Stomach specialist with marvelous practice. Brother in law owns own garment business. Particular people."

Salzman looked as if he had read his trump card.

"Did you say nineteen?" Leo asked with interest.

"On the dot."

"Is she attractive?" He blushed. "Pretty?"

Salzman kissed his finger tips. "A little doll. On this I give my word. Let me call the father tonight and you will see what means pretty."

But Leo was troubled. "You're sure she's that young?"

"This I am positive. The father will show you the birth certificate."

"Are you positive there isn't something wrong with her?" Leo insisted.

"Who says there is wrong?"

"I don't understand why an American girl her age should go to a marriage broker."

A smile spread over Salzman's face.

"So for the same reason you went, she comes."

Leo flushed. "I am pressed for time."

Salzman, realizing he had been tactless, quickly explained. "The father came, not her. He wants she should have the best, so he looks around himself. When we will locate the right boy he will introduce him and encourage. This makes a better marriage than if a young girl without experience takes for herself. I don't have to tell you this."

"But don't you think this young girl believes in love?" Leo spoke uneasily.

Salzman was about to guffaw but caught himself and said soberly, "Love comes with the right person, not before."

Leo parted dry lips but did not speak. Noticing that Salzman had snatched a glance at the next card, he cleverly asked, "How is her health?"

"Perfect," Salzman said, breathing with difficulty. "Of course, she is a little lame on her right foot from an auto accident that it happened to her when she was twelve years, but nobody notices on account she is so brilliant and also beautiful."

Leo got up heavily and went to the window. He felt curiously bitter and upbraided himself for having called in the marriage broker. Finally, he shook his head.

"Why not?" Salzman persisted, the pitch of his voice rising.

"Because I detest stomach specialists."

"So what do you care what is his business? After you marry her do you need him? Who says he must come every Friday night in your house?"

Ashamed of the way the talk was going, Leo dismissed Salzman, who went home with heavy, melancholy eyes.

Though he had felt only relief at the marriage broker's departure, Leo was in low spirits the next day. He explained it as arising from Salzman's failure to produce a suitable bride for him. He did not care for his type of clientele. But when Leo found himself hesitating whether to seek out another matchmaker, one more polished than Pinye, he wondered if it could be—his protestations to the contrary, and although he honored his father and mother—that he did not, in essence, care for the match-making institution? This thought he quickly put out of mind yet found himself still upset. All day he ran around in the woods—missed an important appointment, forgot to give out his laundry, walked out of a Broadway cafeteria without paying and had to run back with the ticket in his hand; had even not recognized his landlady in the street when she passed with a friend and courteously called out, "A good evening to you, Doctor Finkle." By nightfall, however, he had regained sufficient calm to sink his nose into a book and there found peace from his thoughts.

Almost at once there came a knock on the door. Before Leo could say enter, Salzman, commercial cupid, was standing in the room. His face was gray and meager, his expression hungry, and he looked as if he would expire on his feet. Yet the marriage broker managed, by some trick of the muscles, to display a broad smile.

"So good evening. I am invited?"

Leo nodded, disturbed to see him again, yet unwilling to ask the man to leave.

Beaming still, Salzman laid his portfolio on the table. "Rabbi, I got for you tonight good news."

"I've asked you not to call me rabbi. I'm still a student."

"Your worries are finished. I have for you a first-class bride."

"Leave me in peace concerning this subject." Leo pretended lack of interest.

"The world will dance at your wedding."

"Please, Mr. Salzman, no more."

"But first must come back my strength," Salzman said weakly. He fumbled with the portfolio straps and took out of the leather case an oily paper bag, from which he extracted a hard, seeded roll and a small, smoked white fish. With a quick motion of his hand he stripped the fish out of its skin and began ravenously to chew. "All day in a rush," he muttered.

Leo watched him eat.

"A sliced tomato you have maybe?" Salzman hesitantly inquired.

"No."

The marriage broker shut his eyes and ate. When he had finished he carefully cleaned up the crumbs and rolled up the remains of the fish, in the paper bag. His spectacled eyes roamed the room until he discovered, amid some piles of books, a one-burner gas stove. Lifting his hat he humbly asked, "A glass tea you got, rabbi?"

Conscience-stricken, Leo rose and brewed the tea. He served it with a chunk of lemon and two cubes of lump sugar, delighting Salzman.

After he had drunk his tea, Salzman's strength and good spirits were restored.

"So tell me, rabbi," he said amiably, "you considered some more the three clients I mentioned yesterday?"

"There was no need to consider."

"Why not?"

"None of them suits me."

"What then suits you?"

Leo let it pass because he could give only a confused answer.

Without waiting for a reply, Salzman asked, "You remember this girl I talked to you—the high school teacher?"

"Age thirty-two?"

But, surprisingly, Salzman's face lit in a smile. "Age twenty-nine."

Leo shot him a look. "Reduced from thirty-two?"

"A mistake," Salzman avowed. "I talked today with the dentist. He took me to his safety deposit box and showed me the birth certificate. She was twenty-nine years last August. They made her a party in the mountains where she went for her vacation. When her father spoke to me the first time I forgot to write the age and I told you thirty-two, but now I remember this was a different client, a widow."

"The same one you told me about? I thought she was twenty-four?"

"A different. Am I responsible that the world is filled with widows?"

"No, but I'm not interested in them, nor for that matter, in school teachers."

Salzman pulled his clasped hands to his breast. Looking at the ceiling he devoutly exclaimed, "Yiddishe kinder,[2] what can I say to somebody that he is not interested in high school teachers? So what then you are interested?"

Leo flushed but controlled himself.

"In what else will you be interested," Salzman went on, "if you not interested in this fine girl that she speaks four languages and has personally in the bank ten thousand dollars? Also her father guarantees further twelve thousand. Also she has a new car, wonderful clothes, talks on all subjects, and she will give you a first-class home and children. How near do we come in our life to paradise?"

"If she's so wonderful, why wasn't she married ten years ago?"

"Why?" said Salzman with a heavy laugh. "—Why? Because she is *partikiler.* This is why. She wants the *best.*"

Leo was silent, amused at how he had entangled himself. But Salzman had aroused his interest in Lily H., and he began seriously to consider calling on her. When the marriage broker observed how intently Leo's mind was at work on the facts he had supplied, he felt certain they would soon come to an agreement.

[2]Yiddish: Yiddish children.

Late Saturday afternoon, conscious of Salzman, Leo Finkle walked with Lily Hirschorn along Riverside Drive. He walked briskly and erectly, wearing with distinction the black fedora that he had that morning taken with trepidation out of the dusty hat box on his closet shelf, and the heavy black Saturday coat he had thoroughly whisked clean. Leo also owned a walking stick, a present from a distant relative, but quickly put temptation aside and did not use it. Lily, petite and not unpretty, had on something signifying the approach of spring. She was au courant,[3] animatedly, with all sorts of subjects, and he weighed her words and found her surprisingly sound—score another for Salzman, whom he uneasily sensed to be somewhere around, hiding perhaps high in a tree along the street, flashing the lady signals with a pocket mirror; or perhaps a cloven-hoofed Pan, piping nuptial ditties as he danced his invisible way before them, strewing wild buds on the walk and purple grapes in their path, symbolizing fruit of a union, though there was of course still none.

Lily startled Leo by remarking, "I was thinking of Mr. Salzman, a curious figure, wouldn't you say?"

Not certain what to answer, he nodded.

She bravely went on, blushing, "I for one am grateful for his introducing us. Aren't you?"

He courteously replied, "I am."

"I mean," she said with a little laugh—and it was all in good taste, or at least gave the effect of being not in bad—"do you mind that we came together so?"

He was not displeased with her honesty, recognizing that she meant to set the relationship aright, and understanding that it took a certain amount of experience in life, and courage, to want to do it quite that way. One had to have some sort of past to make that kind of beginning.

He said that he did not mind. Salzman's function was traditional and honorable—valuable for what it might achieve, which, he pointed out, was frequently nothing.

Lily agreed with a sigh. They walked on for a while and she said after a long silence, again with a nervous laugh, "Would you mind if I asked you something a little bit personal? Frankly, I find the subject fascinating." Although Leo shrugged, she went on half embarrassedly, "How was it that you came to your calling? I mean was it a sudden passionate inspiration?"

Leo, after a time, slowly replied, "I was always interested in the Law."

"You saw revealed in it the presence of the Highest?"

He nodded and changed the subject. "I understand that you spent a little time in Paris, Miss Hirschorn?"

"Oh, did Mr. Salzman tell you, Rabbi Finkle?" Leo winced but she went on, "It was ages ago and almost forgotten. I remember I had to return for my sister's wedding."

And Lily would not be put off. "When," she asked in a trembly voice, "did you become enamored of God?"

He stared at her. Then it came to him that she was talking not about Leo Finkle, but of a total stranger, some mystical figure, perhaps even passionate prophet that Salzman had dreamed up for her—no relation to the living or

[3]Informed, up-to-date.

dead. Leo trembled with rage and weakness. The trickster had obviously sold her a bill of goods, just as he had him, who'd expected to become acquainted with a young lady of twenty-nine, only to behold, the moment he laid eyes upon her strained and anxious face, a woman past thirty-five and aging rapidly. Only his self control had kept him this long in her presence.

"I am not," he said gravely, "a talented religious person," and in seeking words to go on, found himself possessed by shame and fear. "I think," he said in a strained manner, "that I came to God not because I loved Him, but because I did not."

This confession he spoke harshly because its unexpectedness shook him.

Lily wilted. Leo saw a profusion of loaves of bread go flying like ducks high over his head, not unlike the winged loaves by which he had counted himself to sleep last night. Mercifully, then, it snowed, which he would not put past Salzman's machinations.

He was infuriated with the marriage broker and swore he would throw him out of the room the minute he reappeared. But Salzman did not come that night, and when Leo's anger had subsided, an unaccountable despair grew in its place. At first he thought this was caused by his disappointment in Lily, but before long it became evident that he had involved himself with Salzman without a true knowledge of his own intent. He gradually realized—with an emptiness that seized him with six hands—that he had called in the broker to find him a bride because he was incapable of doing it himself. This terrifying insight he had derived as a result of his meeting and conversation with Lily Hirschorn. Her probing questions had somehow irritated him into revealing—to himself more than her—the true nature of his relationship to God, and from that it had come upon him, with shocking force, that apart from his parents, he had never loved anyone. Or perhaps it went the other way, that he did not love God so well as he might, because he had not loved man. It seemed to Leo that his whole life stood starkly revealed and he saw himself for the first time as he truly was—unloved and loveless. This bitter but somehow not fully unexpected revelation brought him to a point of panic controlled only by extraordinary effort. He covered his face with his hands and cried.

The week that followed was the worst of his life. He did not eat and lost weight. His beard darkened and grew ragged. He stopped attending seminars and almost never opened a book. He seriously considered leaving the Yeshivah, although he was deeply troubled at the thought of the loss of all his years of study—saw them like pages torn from a book, strewn over the city—and at the devastating effect of this decision upon his parents. But he had lived without knowledge of himself, and never in the Five Books and all the Commentaries—mea culpa[4]—had the truth been revealed to him. He did not know where to turn, and in all this desolating loneliness there was no *to whom,* although he often thought of Lily but not once could bring himself to go downstairs and make the call. He became touchy and irritable, especially with his landlady, who asked him all manner of personal questions; on the other hand, sensing his own disagreeableness, he waylaid her on the

[4]Latin: my fault, a ritual phrase traditionally spoken by those confessing their sins.

stairs and apologized abjectly, until mortified, she ran from him. Out of this, however, he drew the consolation that he was a Jew and that a Jew suffered. But gradually, as the long and terrible week drew to a close, he regained his composure and some idea of purpose in life: to go on as planned. Although he was imperfect, the ideal was not. As for his quest of a bride, the thought of continuing afflicted him with anxiety and heartburn, yet perhaps with this new knowledge of himself he would be more successful than in the past. Perhaps love would now come to him and a bride to that love. And for this sanctified seeking who needed a Salzman?

The marriage broker, a skeleton with haunted eyes, returned that very night. He looked, withal, the picture of frustrated expectancy—as if he had steadfastly waited the week at Miss Lily Hirschorn's side for a telephone call that never came.

Casually coughing, Salzman came immediately to the point: "So how did you like her?"

Leo's anger rose and he could not refrain from chiding the matchmaker: "Why did you lie to me, Salzman?"

Salzman's pale face went dead white, the world had snowed on him.

"Did you not state that she was twenty-nine?" Leo insisted.

"I gave you my word—"

"She was thirty-five, if a day. *At least* thirty-five."

"Of this don't be too sure. Her father told me—"

"Never mind. The worst of it was that you lied to her."

"How did I lie to her, tell me?"

"You told her things about me that weren't true. You made me out to be more, consequently less than I am. She had in mind a totally different person, a sort of semimystical Wonder Rabbi."

"All I said, you was a religious man."

"I can imagine."

Salzman sighed. "This is my weakness that I have," he confessed. "My wife says to me I shouldn't be a salesman, but when I have two fine people that they would be wonderful to be married, I am so happy that I talk too much." He smiled wanly. "This is why Salzman is a poor man."

Leo's anger left him. "Well, Salzman, I'm afraid that's all."

The marriage broker fastened hungry eyes on him.

"You don't want any more a bride?"

"I do," said Leo, "but I have decided to seek her in a different way. I am no longer interested in an arranged marriage. To be frank, I now admit the necessity of premarital love. That is, I want to be in love with the one I marry."

"Love?" said Salzman, astounded. After a moment he remarked "For us, our love is our life, not for the ladies. In the ghetto they—"

"I know, I know," said Leo. "I've thought of it often. Love, I have said to myself, should be a by-product of living and worship rather than its own end. Yet for myself I find it necessary to establish the level of my need and fulfill it."

Salzman shrugged but answered, "Listen, rabbi, if you want love, this I can find for you also. I have such beautiful clients that you will love them the minute your eyes will see them."

Leo smiled unhappily. "I'm afraid you don't understand."

But Salzman hastily unstrapped his portfolio and withdrew a manila packet from it.

"Pictures," he said, quickly laying the envelope on the table.

Leo called after him to take the pictures away, but as if on the wings of the wind, Salzman had disappeared.

March came. Leo had returned to his regular routine. Although he felt not quite himself yet—lacked energy—he was making plans for a more active social life. Of course it would cost something, but he was an expert in cutting corners; and when there were no corners left he would make circles rounder. All the while Salzman's pictures had lain on the table, gathering dust. Occasionally as Leo sat studying, or enjoying a cup of tea, his eyes fell on the manila envelope, but he never opened it.

The days went by and no social life to speak of developed with a member of the opposite sex—it was difficult, given the circumstances of his situation. One morning Leo toiled up the stairs to his room and stared out the window at the city. Although the day was bright his view of it was dark. For some time he watched the people in the street below hurrying along and then turned with a heavy heart to his little room. On the table was the packet. With a sudden relentless gesture he tore it open. For a half-hour he stood by the table in a state of excitement, examining the photographs of the ladies Salzman had included. Finally, with a deep sigh he put them down. There were six, of varying degrees of attractiveness, but look at them long enough and they all became Lily Hirschorn; all past their prime, all starved behind bright smiles, not a true personality in the lot. Life, despite their frantic yoohooings, had passed them by; they were pictures in a brief case that stunk of fish. After a while, however, as Leo attempted to return the photographs into the envelope, he found in it another, a snapshot of the type taken by a machine for a quarter. He gazed at it a moment and let out a cry.

Her face deeply moved him. Why, he could at first not say. It gave him the impression of youth—spring flowers, yet age—a sense of having been used to the bone, wasted; this came from the eyes, which were hauntingly familiar, yet absolutely strange. He had a vivid impression that he had met her before, but try as he might he could not place her although he could almost recall her name, as if he had read it in her own handwriting. No, this couldn't be; he would have remembered her. It was not, he affirmed, that she had an extraordinary beauty—no, though her face was attractive enough; it was that *something* about her moved him. Feature for feature, even some of the ladies of the photographs could do better; but she leaped forth to his heart—had *lived,* or wanted to—more than just wanted, perhaps regretted how she had lived—had somehow deeply suffered: it could be seen in the depths of those reluctant eyes, and from the way the light enclosed and shone from her, and within her, opening realms of possibility: this was her own. Her he desired. His head ached and eyes narrowed with the intensity of his gazing, then as if an obscure fog had blown up in the mind, he experienced fear of her and was aware that he had received an impression, somehow, of evil. He shuddered, saying softly, it is thus with us all. Leo brewed some tea in a small pot and sat sipping it without sugar, to calm himself. But before he had finished drinking, again with excitement he examined the face and found it good: good for Leo Finkle. Only such a one could understand him and help him seek whatever he was seeking. She might, perhaps, love him. How she had happened to be among the discards in Salzman's barrel he could never guess, but he knew he must urgently go find her.

Leo rushed downstairs, grabbed up the Bronx telephone book, and searched for Salzman's home address. He was not listed, nor was his office. Neither was he in the Manhattan book. But Leo remembered having written down the address on a slip of paper after he had read Salzman's advertisement in the "personals" column of the *Forward.* He ran up to his room and tore through his papers, without luck. It was exasperating. Just when he needed the matchmaker he was nowhere to be found. Fortunately Leo remembered to look in his wallet. There on a card he found his name written and a Bronx address. No phone number was listed, the reason—Leo now recalled—he had originally communicated with Salzman by letter. He got on his coat, put a hat on over his skull cap and hurried to the subway station. All the way to the far end of the Bronx he sat on the edge of his seat. He was more than once tempted to take out the picture and see if the girl's face was as he remembered it, but he refrained, allowing the snapshot to remain in his coat pocket, content to have her so close. When the train pulled into the station he was waiting at the door and bolted out. He quickly located the street Salzman had advertised.

The building he sought was less than a block from the subway, but it was not an office building, nor even a loft, nor a store in which one could rent office space. It was a very old tenement house. Leo found Salzman's name in pencil on a soiled tag under the bell and climbed three dark flights to his apartment. When he knocked, the door was opened by a thin, asthmatic, gray-haired woman, in felt slippers.

"Yes?" she said, expecting nothing. She listened without listening. He could have sworn he had seen her, too, before but knew it was an illusion.

"Salzman—does he live here? Pinye Salzman," he said, "the matchmaker?"

She stared at him a long minute. "Of course."

He felt embarrassed. "Is he in?"

"No." Her mouth, though left open, offered nothing more.

"The matter is urgent. Can you tell me where his office is?"

"In the air." She pointed upward.

"You mean he has no office?" Leo asked.

"In his socks."

He peered into the apartment. It was sunless and dingy, one large room divided by a half-open curtain, beyond which he could see a sagging metal bed. The near side of a room was crowded with rickety chairs, old bureaus, a three-legged table, racks of cooking utensils, and all the apparatus of a kitchen. But there was no sign of Salzman or his magic barrel, probably also a figment of the imagination. An odor of frying fish made Leo weak to the knees.

"Where is he?" he insisted. "I've got to see your husband."

At length she answered, "So who knows where he is? Every time he thinks a new thought he runs to a different place. Go home, he will find you."

"Tell him Leo Finkle."

She gave no sign she had heard.

He walked downstairs, depressed.

But Salzman, breathless, stood waiting at his door.

Leo was astounded and overjoyed. "How did you get here before me?"

"I rushed."

"Come inside."

They entered. Leo fixed tea, and a sardine sandwich for Salzman. As they were drinking he reached behind him for the packet of pictures and handed them to the marriage broker.

Salzman put down his glass and said expectantly, "You found somebody you like?"

"Not among these."

The marriage broker turned away.

"Here is the one I want." Leo held forth the snapshot.

Salzman slipped on his glasses and took the picture into his trembling hand. He turned ghastly and let out a groan.

"What's the matter?" cried Leo.

"Excuse me. Was an accident this picture. She isn't for you."

Salzman frantically shoved the manila packet into his portfolio. He thrust the snapshot into his pocket and fled down the stairs.

Leo, after momentary paralysis, gave chase and cornered the marriage broker in the vestibule. The landlady made hysterical outcries but neither of them listened.

"Give me back the picture, Salzman."

"No." The pain in his eyes was terrible.

"Tell me who she is then."

"This I can't tell you. Excuse me."

He made to depart, but Leo, forgetting himself, seized the matchmaker by his tight coat and shook him frenziedly.

"Please," sighed Salzman. *"Please."*

Leo ashamedly let him go. "Tell me who she is," he begged. "It's very important for me to know."

"She is not for you. She is a wild one—wild, without shame. This is not a bride for a rabbi."

"What do you mean wild?"

"Like an animal. Like a dog. For her to be poor was a sin. This is why to me she is dead now."

"In God's name, what do you mean?"

"Her I can't introduce to you," Salzman cried.

"Why are you so excited?"

"Why, he asks," Salzman said, bursting into tears. "This is my baby, my Stella, she should burn in hell."

Leo hurried up to bed and hid under the covers. Under the covers he thought his life through. Although he soon fell asleep he could not sleep her out of his mind. He woke, beating his breast. Though he prayed to be rid of her, his prayers went unanswered. Through days of torment he endlessly struggled not to love her; fearing success, he escaped it. He then concluded to convert her to goodness, himself to God. The idea alternately nauseated and exalted him.

He perhaps did not know that he had come to a final decision until he encountered Salzman in a Broadway cafeteria. He was sitting alone at a rear table, sucking the bony remains of a fish. The marriage broker appeared haggard, and transparent to the point of vanishing.

Salzman looked up at first without recognizing him. Leo had grown a pointed beard and his eyes were weighted with wisdom.

"Salzman," he said, "love has at last come to my heart."

"Who can love from a picture?" mocked the marriage broker.

"It is not impossible."

"If you can love her, then you can love anybody. Let me show you some new clients that they just sent me their photographs. One is a little doll."

"Just her I want," Leo murmured.

"Don't be a fool, doctor. Don't bother with her."

"Put me in touch with her, Salzman," Leo said humbly. "Perhaps I can be of service."

Salzman had stopped eating and Leo understood with emotion that it was now arranged.

Leaving the cafeteria, he was, however, afflicted by a tormenting suspicion that Salzman had planned it all to happen this way.

Leo was informed by letter that she would meet him on a certain corner, and she was there one spring night, waiting under a street lamp. He appeared, carrying a small bouquet of violets and rosebuds. Stella stood by the lamp post, smoking. She wore white with red shoes, which fitted his expectations, although in a troubled moment he had imagined the dress red, and only the shoes white. She waited uneasily and shyly. From afar he saw that her eyes—clearly her father's—were filled with desperate innocence. He pictured, in her, his own redemption. Violins and lit candles revolved in the sky. Leo ran forward with flowers outthrust.

Around the corner, Salzman, leaning against a wall, chanted prayers for the dead.

1954, 1958

Amiri Baraka (LeRoi Jones) 1934–

He was born LeRoi Jones in Newark, New Jersey. In 1966, when he was thirty-two, he returned to Newark to serve as a leader, known as Imamu Amiri Baraka, of Spirit House, an African culture center. Jones had graduated from high school and attended Rutgers University in Newark. Later he transferred to Howard University, in Washington, D.C., from which he received a degree in English literature. For two years he served in the Air Force, stationed much of the time in Puerto Rico. Following his discharge he returned to the United States, to New York City, where he studied at Columbia University and at the New School for Social Research, from which he received an M.A. in German literature.

Jones taught at Columbia and at the New School, wrote newspaper and magazine articles, and in 1961 published his first collection of poems, Preface to a Twenty Volume Suicide Note. *Three years later he published his second volume of poems,* The

Dead Lecturer. *He has also written volumes of plays, fiction, and essays, including* Dutchman and The Slave *(1964);* The System of Dante's Hell *(1965), a partially autobiographical novel;* Home, Social Essays *(1966);* Tales *(1967); and two books on music:* Blues People, Negro Music in White America *(1963) and* Black Music *(1967). In 1971 he published* Raise Race Rays Raze, Essays Since 1965 *and in 1978* The Motion of History and Other Plays.

Jones's early poetry shows the influence of such poets as Ezra Pound and, especially, William Carlos Williams, whose "quantitative verse" Jones sought to duplicate. He wanted to bring his poems close to the rhythms of spoken English by relating line lengths, pauses, phrasings, and the arrangements of stanzas to the rhythms of breathing, thus giving the poet a measure of control over the voicing of verse in a manner similar to that of a director of a musical score.

Jones's growing interest in the black revolution has made his later poetry increasingly nonformal and nontraditional. He has sought to write authentically of his own experiences in a vital street style, free of orthodox diction, images, and received ideas—a rejection of what he considers to be "white" poetic tradition. His views are evident in his drama Dutchman, *a fierce portrait of racial betrayal and cynical violence. As Amiri Baraka he is both a Black Power advocate and a black visionary writer. He wants, in his words, to "reach some people, move some people"—not with mere "skin drama," the black Broadway plays that lack revolutionary ideology, but with propaganda that is art: writing that unites art and politics; literature with a "clear revolutionary edge to it."*

FURTHER READING: T. Hudson, *From LeRoi Jones to Amiri Baraka,* 1973; *The Selected Plays and Prose,* 1979; *Selected Poetry,* 1979; L. Brown, *Amiri Baraka,* 1980; *The Autobiography of LeRoi Jones,* 1984; W. Harris, *The Poetry and Poetics of Amiri Baraka,* 1985; B. Bernotas, *Amiri Baraka,* 1991; H. Elam, *Taking It to the Streets, The Social Protest Theater of Luis Valdez and Amiri Baraka,* 1997; J. Watts, *Amiri Baraka, The Politics and Art of a Black Intellectual,* 2001.

TEXTS: "In Memory of Radio," "The Bridge," and "Notes for a Speech" are from *Preface to a Twenty Volume Suicide Note,* 1961; "An Agony. As Now.," "A Poem for Democrats," and "A Poem for Speculative Hipsters" are from *The Dead Lecturer,* 1964; all other poems are from *Black Magic,* 1969.

IN MEMORY OF RADIO

Who has ever stopped to think of the divinity of Lamont Cranston?[1]
(Only Jack Kerouac, that I know of: & me.
The rest of you probably had on WCBS and Kate Smith,
Or something equally unattractive.)

What can I say?
It is better to have loved and lost
Than to put linoleum in your living rooms?

[1]The hero of the radio serial "The Shadow" (1931–1954), who had "the power to cloud men's minds" and make himself invisible.

Am I a sage or something?
Mandrake's hypnotic gesture of the week?[2]
(Remember, I do not have the healing powers of Oral
Roberts . . . [3]
I cannot, like F. J. Sheen,[4] tell you how to get saved & *rich!*
I cannot even order you to gaschamber satori[5] like Hitler or
Goody Knight[6]

& Love is an evil word.
Turn it backwards/see, see what I mean?
An evol word. & besides
who understands it?
I certainly wouldn't like to go out on that kind of limb.

Saturday mornings we listened to *Red Lantern* & his undersea folk.
At 11, *Let's Pretend*/& we did/& I, the poet, still do, Thank God!

What was it he used to say (after the transformation, when he was
safe & invisible & the unbelievers couldn't throw stones?) "Heh, heh,
heh,
Who knows what evil lurks in the hearts of men? The Shadow
knows."[7]

O, yes he does
O, yes he does.
An evil word it is,
This Love.

1961

THE BRIDGE

(# for wieners & mcclure)

I have forgotten the head
of where I am. Here at the bridge. 2
bars, down the street, seeming
to warp themselves around my fingers, the day,
screams in me; pitiful like a little girl
you sense will be dead before the winter
is over.

[2]The comic-strip hero Mandrake the Magician used magic hypnotic powers to overcome evil.

[3]Here, and throughout, the ellipsis points are Baraka's.

[4]Bishop Fulton J. Sheen (1895–1979), renowned for his radio sermons in the 1930s and 1940s.

[5]A state of sudden enlightenment in Zen Buddhism.

[6]Goodwin Knight, Governor of California (1953–1959) during controversies over the use of the gas chamber for capital punishment.

[7]Repeated signature phrase of "The Shadow."

I can't see the bridge now, I've past
it, its shadow, we drove through, headed out
along the cold insensitive roads to what
we wanted to call "ourselves."
"How does the bridge go?" Even tho
you find yourself in its length
strung out along its breadth, waiting
for the cold sun to tear out your eyes. Enamoured
of its blues, spread out in the silk clubs of
this autumn tune. The changes are difficult, when
you hear them, & know they are all in you, the chords

of your disorder meddle with your would be disguises.
Sifting in, down, upon your head, with the sun & the insects.

(Late feeling) Way down till it barely, after that rush of
wind & odor reflected from hills you have forgotten the color
when you touch the water, & it closes, slowly, around your head.

The bridge will be behind you, that music you know, that place,
you feel when you look up to say, it is me, & I have forgotten,
all the things, you told me to love, to try to understand, the
bridge will stand, high up in the clouds & the light, & you,

(when you have let the song run out) will be sliding through
unmentionable black.

1961

NOTES FOR A SPEECH

African blues
does not know me. Their steps, in sands
of their own
land. A country
in black & white, newspapers
blown down pavements
of the world. Does
not feel
what I am.
                    Strength
in the dream, an oblique
suckling of nerve, the wind
throws up sand, eyes
are something locked in
hate, of hate, of hate, to
walk abroad, they conduct
their deaths apart
from my own. Those
heads, I call
my "people."

(And who are they. People. To concern
myself, ugly man. Who
you, to concern
the white flat stomachs
of maidens, inside houses
dying. Black, Peeled moon
light on my fingers
move under
her clothes. Where
is her husband. Black
words throw up sand
to eyes, fingers of
their private dead. Whose
soul, eyes, in sand. My color
is not theirs. Lighter, white man
talk. They shy away. My own
dead souls, my, so called
people. Africa
is a foreign place. You are
as any other sad man here
american.

1961

AN AGONY, AS NOW

I am inside someone
who hates me. I look
out from his eyes. Smell
what fouled tunes come in
to his breath. Love his
wretched women.

Slits in the metal, for sun. Where
my eyes sit turning, at the cool air
the glance of light, or hard flesh
rubbed against me, a woman, a man,
without shadow, or voice, or meaning.

This is the enclosure (flesh,
where innocence is a weapon. An
abstraction. Touch. (Not mine.
Or yours, if you are the soul I had
and abandoned when I was blind and had
my enemies carry me as a dead man
(if he is beautiful, or pitied.

It can be pain. (As now, as all his
flesh hurts me.) It can be that. Or
pain. As when she ran from me into
that forest.
            Or pain, the mind
silver spiraled whirled against the
sun, higher than even old men thought
God would be. Or pain. And the other. The
yes. (Inside his books, his fingers. They
are withered yellow flowers and were never
beautiful.) The yes. You will, lost soul, say
'beauty.' Beauty, practiced, as the tree. The
slow river. A white sun in its wet sentences.

Or, the cold men in their gale. Ecstasy. Flesh
or soul. The yes. (Their robes blown. Their bowls
empty. They chant at my heels, not at yours.) Flesh
or soul, as corrupt. Where the answer moves too quickly.
Where the God is a self, after all.)

Cold air blown through narrow blind eyes. Flesh,
white hot metal. Glows as the day with its sun.
It is human love, I live inside. A bony skeleton
you recognize as words or simple feeling.

But it has no feeling. As the metal, is hot, it is not,
given to love.

It burns the thing
inside it. And that thing
screams.

1964

A POEM FOR DEMOCRATS

the city rises

                in color, our sad
ness, blanket this wood place, single drop
of rain, blue image of
someone's love.
                Net of rain. Crystal ice
glass strings, smash
(on such repertoire of memory
as:
    baskets
    the long walk up harbor
    & the insistence, rain, as they build

City, is wicked. Not
this one, where I am, where they
still move, go to, out of
(transporting your loved one
across the line is death
by drowning.

            Drowned love
hanged man, swung, cement on his feet.)
                                    But
the small filth of the small mind
short structures of
newark, baltimore, cincinnati, omaha. Distress,
europe has passed we are alone. Europe
frail woman dead, we are alone

1964

A POEM FOR SPECULATIVE HIPSTERS

He had got, finally,
to the forest
of motives. There were no
owls, or hunters. No Connie Chatterleys[1]
resting beautifully
on their backs, having casually
brought socialism
to England.
            Only ideas,
and their opposites.
                        Like,
            he was *really*
            nowhere.

1964

A POEM SOME PEOPLE WILL HAVE TO UNDERSTAND

Dull unwashed windows of eyes
and buildings of industry. What
industry do I practice? A slick
colored boy, 12 miles from his
home. I practice no industry.
I am no longer a credit
to my race. I read a little,
scratch against silence slow spring
afternoons.

[1]The heroine of D. H. Lawrence's novel *Lady Chatterley's Lover* (1928).

I had thought, before, some years ago
that I'd come to the end of my life.
Watercolor ego. Without the preciseness
a violent man could propose.
But the wheel, and the wheels,
won't let us alone. All the fantasy
and justice, and dry charcoal winters
All the pitifully intelligent citizens
I've forced myself to love.

We have awaited the coming of a natural
phenomenon. Mystics and romantics, knowledgeable
workers
of the land.

But none has come.
(*Repeat*)
but none has come.
Will the machinegunners please step forward?

1969

A POEM FOR HALF-WHITE COLLEGE STUDENTS

Who are you, listening to me, who are you
listening to yourself? Are you white or
black, or does that have anything to do
with it? Can you pop your fingers to no
music, except those wild monkies go on
in your head, can you jerk, to no melody,
except finger poppers get it together
when you turn from starchecking to checking
yourself? How do you sound, your words, are they
yours? The ghost you see in the mirror, is it really
you, can you swear you are not an imitation greyboy,
can you look right next to you in that chair, and swear,
that the sister you have your hand on is not really
so full of Elizabeth Taylor, Richard Burton is
coming out of her ears. You may even have to be Richard
with a white shirt and face, and four million negroes
think you cute, you may have to be Elizabeth Taylor, old lady,
if you want to sit up in your crazy spot dreaming about dresses,
and the sway of certain porters' hips. Check yourself, learn who it is
speaking, when you make some ultrasophisticated point, check
yourself
when you find yourself gesturing like Steve McQueen, check it out,
ask

in your black heart who it is you are, and is that image black or white,

you might be surprised right out the window, whistling dixie on the way

1969

BIOGRAPHY

Hangs.
whipped
blood
striped
meat pulled
clothes ripped
slobber
feet dangled
pointing
noised
noise
churns
face
black sky
and moon
leather night
red
bleeds
drips
ground
sucks
blood
hangs
life wetting
sticky
mud

laughs
bonnets
wolfmoon
crazyteeth

hangs

hangs

granddaddy

granddaddy, they tore

his

neck

1969

June Jordan 1936–2002

Once described as "one of the most musically and lyrically gifted poets of the late twentieth century," the African-American writer June Jordan is best known for her poetry, written in the dialect of black English, that explores such themes as race relations, love, homosexuality, children's vulnerability and loss of innocence, and domestic violence. Jordan was born in 1936, in Harlem, New York City, the only child of black Jamaican immigrants. When she was a child, she later recalled, her father "pushed upon" her the "poets of the Scriptures, Shakespeare, Edgar Allan Poe." Her parents also enrolled her in the Northfield School for Girls in Massachusetts, an elite New England preparatory school. She graduated at age sixteen and shortly afterward entered Barnard College, then the women's college of Columbia University.

After two years she chose to leave Barnard because she objected to the predominantly white environment that she found there, a decision she reports in her 1975 essay "Notes of a Barnard Dropout." In 1955 Jordan married, but the marriage later unraveled, and she found herself, at twenty-nine, a single mother. Moved by the injustices she saw in life, Jordan became interested in the Black Arts Movement and also turned more ardently to her writing. Her first book-length work, Who Look at Me, *appeared in 1969. An extended poem, it explores her frustrations with racism and her experiences as a single, working mother. Her novel* His Own Where *(1971), written in black English, portrays two teenage lovers coming of age in Harlem. Next were three poetry collections,* Some Changes *(1971),* New Days: Poems of Exile and Return *(1973), and* Things I Do in the Dark *(1977). They explore the musical potential of language and address such contemporary social and political issues as civil rights and the constraints of race, class, and gender.*

While her early works were generally praised, they were also criticized for being too strident. In 1992, undeterred by negative criticism, she wrote "A New Politics of Sexuality," an essay in which she openly celebrates her bisexuality—insisting on "the equal validity of all of the components of social/sexual complexity"—and calls for a continued struggle for justice, equality, and freedom. Although she published more than twenty-five books in her lifetime—short fiction, novels, children's books, operettas, biography, essays, and dramas—she is best known for her poetry. It often boils with rage and contempt for an America that teaches "to kill to violate to pull down destroy." Yet, ironically, it was from that very land and its people, which she so excoriated as cruelly indifferent, that she herself received the most attention and the greatest critical acclaim. Her final work, Some of Us Did Not Die, *a collection of previously published and unpublished essays, appeared in 2002, the year of her death.*

FURTHER READING: *Passion: New Poems*, 1980; D. Davenport, *Four Contemporary Black Women Poets: Lucille Clifton, June Jordan, Audre Lorde, and Sherley Anne Williams*, 1987; A. Garrett and H. McCue, *Authors and Artists for Young Adults*, 1989; *Diverse Voices: Essays on Twentieth-Century Women Writers in English*, ed. H. Jump, 1991; W. White, *Dissonant Hu(e)-Manity: Another Way to Be Differently in the Work of Audre Lorde and June Jordan*, 2001; *Still Seeking an Attitude, Critical Reflections on the Work of June Jordan*, ed. V. Kinloch and M. Grebowicz, 2004.

TEXTS: "All the World Moved," "In Memoriam: Martin Luther King, Jr.," and "Meta-Rhetoric" are from *Things I Do in the Dark: Selected Poems*, 1977; "Poem about My Rights" is from *Naming Our Own Destiny: New and Selected Poems*, 1989.

ALL THE WORLD MOVED

All the world moved next to me strange
I grew on my knees
in hats and taffeta trusting
the holy water to run
like grief from a brownstone
cradling.

Blessing a fear of the anywhere
face too pale to be family
my eyes wore ribbons
for Christ on the subway
as weekly as holiness
in Harlem.

God knew no East no West no South
no Skin nothing I learned like
traditions of sin but later
life began and strangely
I survived His innocence
without my own.

1964

IN MEMORIAM: MARTIN LUTHER KING, JR.

I

honey people murder mercy U.S.A.
the milkland turn to monsters teach
to kill to violate pull down destroy
the weakly freedom growing fruit
from being born

America

tomorrow yesterday rip rape
exacerbate despoil disfigure
crazy running threat the
deadly thrall
appall belief dispel
the wildlife burn the breast
the onward tongue
the outward hand
deform the normal rainy
riot sunshine shelter wreck
of darkness derogate
delimit blank
explode deprive
assassinate and batten up

like bullets fatten up
the raving greed
reactivate a springtime
terrorizing

death by men by more
than you or I can

STOP

II

They sleep who know a regulated place
or pulse or tide or changing sky
according to some universal
stage direction obvious
like shorewashed shells

we share an afternoon of mourning
in between no next predictable
except for wild reversal hearse rehearsal
bleach the blacklong lunging
ritual of fright insanity and more
deplorable abortion
more and
more

1968

META-RHETORIC

Homophobia
racism
self-definition
revolutionary struggle

the subject tonight for
public discussion is
our love

we sit apart
apparently at opposite ends of a line
and I feel the distance
between my eyes
between my legs
a dry
dust topography of our separation

In the meantime people
dispute the probabilities
of union

They reminisce about the chasmic histories
no ideology yet dares to surmount

I disagree with you
You disagree with me
The problem seems to be a matter of scale

Can you give me the statistical dimensions
of your mouth on my mouth
your breasts resting on my own?

I believe the agenda involves
several inches (at least)
of coincidence and endless recovery

My hope is that our lives will declare
this meeting
open

1976

POEM ABOUT MY RIGHTS

Even tonight and I need to take a walk and clear
my head about this poem about why I can't
go out without changing my clothes my shoes
my body posture my gender identity my age
my status as a woman alone in the evening/
alone on the streets / alone not being the point/
the point being that I can't do what I want
to do with my own body because I am the wrong
sex the wrong age the wrong skin and
suppose it was not here in the city but down on the beach/
or far into the woods and I wanted to go
there by myself thinking about god/or thinking
about children or thinking about the world/all of it
disclosed by the stars and the silence:
I could not go and I could not think and I could not
stay there
alone
as I need to be
alone because I can't do what I want to do with my own
body and
who in the hell set things up
like this
and in France they say if the guy penetrates
but does not ejaculate then he did not rape me
and if after stabbing him if after screams if

after begging the bastard and if even after smashing
a hammer to his head if even after that if he
and his buddies fuck me after that
then I consented and there was
no rape because finally you understand finally
they fucked me over because I was wrong I was
wrong again to be me being me where I was/wrong
to be who I am
which is exactly like South Africa
penetration into Namibia penetrating into
Angola and does that mean I mean how do you know if
Pretoria ejaculates what will the evidence look like the
proof of the monster jackboot ejaculation on Blackland
and if
after Namibia and if after Angola and if after Zimbabwe
and if after all of my kinsmen and women resist even to
self-immolation of the villages and if after that
we lose nevertheless what will the big boys say will they
claim my consent:
Do You Follow Me: We are the wrong people of
the wrong skin on the wrong continent and what
in the hell is everybody being reasonable about
and according to the *Times* this week
back in 1966 the C.I.A. decided that they had this problem
and the problem was a man named Nkrumah[1] so they
killed him and before that it was Patrice Lumumba[2]
and before that it was my father on the campus
of my Ivy League school and my father afraid
to walk into the cafeteria because he said he
was wrong the wrong age the wrong skin the wrong
gender identity and he was paying my tuition and
before that
it was my father saying I was wrong saying that
I should have been a boy because he wanted one/a
boy and that I should have been lighter skinned and
that I should have had straighter hair and that
I should not be so boy crazy but instead I should
just be one/a boy and before that
it was my mother pleading plastic surgery for
my nose and braces for my teeth and telling me
to let the books loose to let them loose in other
words
I am very familiar with the problems of the C.I.A.
and the problems of South Africa and the problems
of Exxon Corporation and the problems of white
America in general and the problems of the teachers

[1]President of Ghana from 1960 to 1966.

[2]Prime minister of the Congo from 1960 until his assassination in 1961. He was president of the Congolese National Movement against the colonial power of Belgium and is regarded as a martyr.

and the preachers and the F.B.I. and the social
workers and my particular Mom and Dad/I am very
familiar with the problems because the problems
turn out to be
me
I am the history of rape
I am the history of the rejection of who I am
I am the history of the terrorized incarceration of
my self
I am the history of battery assault and limitless
armies against whatever I want to do with my mind
and my body and my soul and
whether it's about walking out at night
or whether it's about the love that I feel or
whether it's about the sanctity of my vagina or
the sanctity of my national boundaries
of the sanctity of my leaders or the sanctity
of each and every desire
that I know from my personal and idiosyncratic
and indisputably single and singular heart
I have been raped
be-
cause I have been wrong the wrong sex the wrong age
the wrong skin the wrong nose the wrong hair the
wrong need the wrong dream the wrong geographic
the wrong sartorial I
I have been the meaning of rape
I have been the problem everyone seeks to
eliminate by forced
penetration with or without the evidence of slime and/
but let this be unmistakable this poem
is not consent I do not consent
to my mother to my father to the teachers to
the F.B.I. to South Africa to Bedford-Stuy[3]
to Park Avenue to American Airlines to the hardon
idlers on the corners to the sneaky creeps in cars
I am not wrong: Wrong is not my name
My name is my own my own my own
and I can't tell you who the hell set things up like this
but I can tell you that from now on my resistance
my simple and daily and nightly self-determination
may very well cost you your life

1980

[3]Abbreviation for the Brooklyn section Bedford Stuyvesant, the largest concentration of blacks in New York City.

Edward Albee 1928–

In 1962, responding to critical reviews linking him to the traditions of the European Theatre of the Absurd, Edward Albee remarked, "Which theatre is the absurd one?" He was pointing scornfully at the commercial Broadway theater, which had fallen on dismal days and stood in sharp contrast to the vitality of Off-Broadway theater, the milieu from which Albee himself had come and for which he has written his finest work.

Edward Franklin Albee III was a foundling, adopted in infancy by a wealthy theatrical family. Expelled from two private schools, he did better at a third, where he had the opportunity to spend many hours writing poetry and fiction. Much of his real learning, as with Eugene O'Neill, came later from odd jobs: office boy, restaurant counterman, Western Union messenger. Except for one juvenile experiment, a three-act farce composed when he was twelve, Zoo Story *was Albee's first play. Written in 1958, it was first produced in September 1959 in Berlin; the first American staging was Off-Broadway in 1960. Like most Off-Broadway plays,* Zoo Story *is short, has a small cast, and deals with human encounter and the search for communion. Its author's structural pattern is revealed: normal opening, increasing emotional tangle, peak of intensity, quick drop-off.*

Following Zoo Story *came a series of one-act plays:* The Death of Bessie Smith *(1960), a drama of social ostracism based on the life of a famous African-American jazz singer;* The Sandbox *(1960); and* The American Dream *(1961), which displayed a situation increasingly familiar in Albee's plays: the middle-class American family living on illusion and dominated by an overbearing woman.*

Albee's first full-length play, and his greatest hit, was Who's Afraid of Virginia Woolf? *(1962), which ran on Broadway for two years, won many awards, and was made into a memorable and successful film. Notable plays followed:* Tiny Alice *(1964),* A Delicate Balance *(1966), for which Albee won his first Pulitzer Prize for Drama, and* Seascape *(1975), his second Pulitzer Prize winner. Albee's work continued to appear on Broadway and continued to startle and agitate his audiences, earning him the dubious title of "Shockmeister."*

Critics of Albee's plays argued that he made dubious excursions into metaphysics. He was said to "abhor plots," to rely overmuch on the psychological games and linguistic skirmishes of his characters to carry the action. As his plays became more cerebral and less conventionally dramatic, his audience dwindled. In 1983, his play The Man Who Had 3 Arms *was savaged by the New York critics and ignored by playgoers. A financial disaster, it closed after only sixteen performances, and for more than a decade, no new Albee play was presented on Broadway; no producer was willing to risk money on a playwright who seemed to have lost touch with his audience.*

Undaunted, Albee blamed his Broadway failures on New York's super-sensitive, "skirt-hiking" critics and on theatergoers who were, he said, incapable of understanding serious drama and wanted merely a "literate middle-browism." In an interview in 1991, he pointed out that he was only one of a number of illustrious "playwrights who are not performed on Broadway now: Sophocles, Aristophanes, Shakespeare. . . ." And he continued his prolific writing of plays, averaging almost one a year. He directed productions of his works in regional theaters in the United States and began teaching drama at the University of Houston. In Europe, where his reputation as a playwright remained high, he directed productions of his plays that attracted large audiences.

Albee once proclaimed, "I am not a Broadway playwright," but in 1994 he made a triumphal return to New York with a production of Three Tall Women. *Highly autobiographical, the play is centered on his adoptive mother in her old age as she confronts her past and a menacing future. For one play, at least, Albee had turned from the concentrated abstractions that had made his work inaccessible to audiences.* Three Tall

Women *partially re-established his reputation with critics and playgoers, and it won for him his third Pulitzer Prize for Drama.*

Over the years, as public tastes and standards have altered, Albee's plays have come to seem far less licentious than they were first thought to be: In 1961 The Zoo Story *was denounced on the floor of the U.S. Senate as an example of dramatic "filth." Thirty-five years later President Clinton praised Albee for his radical dramas, saying, "In your rebellion the American theater was reborn." Nevertheless, critical reaction to Albee's work can still be sharply divided. When his* The Play About the Baby *opened in New York in 2001, it was praised as truly "accomplished" and panned as being "not merely awful, it is offal."*

Albee, now the most notable living American dramatist, continues to teach, to direct, and to take new directions in his writing. But his best work remains, as it has always been, iconoclastic and abstract—dramas of physical and psychological violence that strip men and women of their comforting illusions and repudiate cozy pieties about the modern world that is, to Albee, chaotic, brutal, and lost to hope.

FURTHER READING: *Edward Albee, An Interview and Essays,* ed. J. Wasserman, 1983; *Critical Essays on Edward Albee,* ed. P. Kolin and J. Davis, 1986; *Edward Albee,* ed. H. Bloom, 1987; G. McCarthy, *Edward Albee,* 1987; M. Roudané, *Understanding Edward Albee,* 1987; *Conversations with Edward Albee,* ed. P. Kolin, 1988; Mel Gussow, *Edward Albee, A Singular Journey,* 1999; A. Paolucci, *From Tension to Tonic, The Plays of Edward Albee,* 2000; *Edward Albee, A Casebook,* ed. B. Mann, 2003; B. Horn, *Edward Albee, A Research and Production Sourcebook,* 2003; *The Collected Plays of Edward Albee,* 2 vols., 2004, 2005; *The Cambridge Companion to Edward Albee,* ed. S. Bottom, 2005.

TEXT: *The Zoo Story,* 1960, 1999.

THE ZOO STORY[1]

CHARACTERS

PETER: *A man in his early forties, neither fat nor gaunt, neither handsome nor homely. He wears tweeds, smokes a pipe, carries hornrimmed glasses. Although he is moving into middle age, his dress and his manner would suggest a man younger.*

JERRY: *A man in his late thirties, not poorly dressed, but carelessly. What was once a trim and lightly muscled body has begun to go to fat; and while he is no longer handsome, it is evident that he once was. His fall from physical grace should not suggest debauchery; he has, to come closest to it, a great weariness.*

THE SCENE

It is Central Park; a Sunday afternoon in summer; the present. There are two park benches, one toward either side of the stage; they both face the audience. Behind them: foliage, trees, sky. At the beginning, Peter is seated on one of the benches.

As the curtain rises, PETER *is seated on the bench stage-right. He is reading a book. He stops reading, cleans his glasses, goes back to reading.* JERRY *enters.*

[1]"This edition of *The Zoo Story* contains revisions to the original text. These revisions were made by the author in 1999, during rehearsals for his production of the play at the Alley Theatre in Houston, Texas."—Albee's note.

JERRY: I've been to the zoo. [PETER *doesn't notice*] I said, I've been to the zoo. MISTER, I'VE BEEN TO THE ZOO!

PETER: Hm? . . .[2] What? . . . I'm sorry, were you talking to me?

JERRY: I went to the zoo, and then I walked until I came here. Have I been walking north?

PETER: [*Puzzled*] North? Why . . . I . . . I think so. Let me see.

JERRY: [*Pointing past the audience*] Is that Fifth Avenue?

PETER: Why yes; yes, it is.

JERRY: And what is that cross street there; that one, to the right?

PETER: That? Oh, that's Seventy-fourth Street.

JERRY: And the zoo is around Sixty-fifth Street; so I've been walking north.

PETER: [*Anxious to get back to his reading*] Yes; it would seem so.

JERRY: Good old north.

PETER: [*Lightly, by reflex*] Ha, ha.

JERRY: [*After a slight pause*] But not due north.

PETER: I . . . well, no, not due north; but, we . . . call it north. It's northerly.

JERRY: [*Watches as* PETER, *anxious to dismiss him, prepares his pipe*] Well, boy; *you're* not going to get lung cancer, are you?

PETER: [*Looks up, a little annoyed, then smiles*] No, sir. Not from this.

JERRY: No, sir. What you'll probably get is cancer of the mouth, and then you'll have to wear one of those things Freud wore after they took one whole side of his jaw away. What do they call those things?

PETER: [*Uncomfortable*] A prosthesis?

JERRY: The very thing! A prosthesis. You're an educated man, aren't you? Are you a doctor?

PETER: Oh, no; no. I read about it somewhere; *Time* magazine, I think. [*He turns to his book*]

JERRY: Well, *Time* magazine isn't for blockheads.

PETER: No, I suppose not.

JERRY: [*After a pause*] Boy, I'm glad that's Fifth Avenue there.

PETER: [*Vaguely*] Yes.

JERRY: I don't like the west side of the park much.

PETER: Oh? [*Then, slightly wary, but interested*] Why?

JERRY: [*Offhand*] I don't know.

PETER: Oh. [*He returns to his book*]

JERRY: [*He stands for a few seconds, looking at* PETER, *who finally looks up again, puzzled*] Do you mind if we talk?

PETER: [*Obviously minding*] Why . . . no, no.

JERRY: Yes you do; you do.

PETER: [*Puts his book down, his pipe out and away, smiling*] No, really; I don't mind.

JERRY: Yes you do.

PETER: [*Finally decided*] No; I don't mind at all, really.

JERRY: It's . . . it's a nice day.

PETER: [*Stares unnecessarily at the sky*] Yes. Yes, it is; lovely.

JERRY: I've been to the zoo.

PETER: Yes, I think you said so . . . didn't you?

JERRY: I bet you've got TV, huh?

[2]Here, and throughout, the ellipsis points are Albee's.

PETER: Why yes, we have two; one for the children.

JERRY: You're married!

PETER: [*With pleased emphasis*] Why, certainly.

JERRY: It isn't a law, for God's sake.

PETER: No . . . no, of course not.

JERRY: And you have a wife.

PETER: [*Bewildered by the seeming lack of communication*] Yes!

JERRY: And you have children.

PETER: Yes; two.

JERRY: Boys?

PETER: No, girls . . . both girls.

JERRY: But you wanted boys.

PETER: Well . . . naturally, every man wants a son, but . . .

JERRY: [*Lightly mocking*] But that's the way the cookie crumbles?

PETER: [*Annoyed*] I wasn't going to say that.

JERRY: And you're not going to have any more kids, are you?

PETER: [*A bit distantly*] No. No more. [*Then back, and irksome*] Why did you say that? How would you know about that?

JERRY: The way you cross your legs, perhaps; something in the voice. Or maybe I'm just guessing. Is it your wife?

PETER: [*Furious*] That's none of your business! [*A silence*] Do you understand? [JERRY *nods.* PETER *is quiet now*] Well, you're right. We'll have no more children.

JERRY: [*Softly*] That *is* the way the cookie crumbles.

PETER: [*Forgiving*] Yes . . . I guess so.

JERRY: Do you mind if I ask you questions?

PETER: Oh, not really.

JERRY: I'll tell you why I do it; I don't talk to many people—except to say like: give me a beer, or where's the john, or what time does the feature go on, or keep your hands to yourself, buddy. You know—things like that.

PETER: I must say I don't . . .

JERRY: But every once in a while I like to talk to somebody, really *talk;* like to get to know somebody, know all about him.

PETER: [*Lightly laughing, still a little uncomfortable*] And am I the guinea pig for today?

JERRY: On a sun-drenched afternoon like this? Who better than a nice married man with two daughters and . . . uh . . . a dog? [PETER *shakes his head*] No? Two dogs. [PETER *shakes his head again*] Hm. No dogs? [PETER *shakes his head, sadly*] Oh, that's a shame. But you look like an animal man. CATS? [PETER *nods his head, ruefully*] Cats! But, that can't be your idea. No, sir. Your wife and daughters? [PETER *nods his head*] Is there anything else I should know?

PETER: [*He has to clear his throat*] There are . . . there are two parakeets. One . . . uh . . . one for each of my daughters.

JERRY: Birds.

PETER: My daughters keep them in a cage in their bedroom.

JERRY: Do they carry disease? The birds?

PETER: I don't believe so.

JERRY: That's too bad. If they did you could set them loose in the house and the cats could eat them and die, maybe. [PETER *looks blank for a moment, then laughs*] And what else? What do you do to support your enormous household?

PETER: I . . . uh . . . I have an executive position with a . . . a small publishing house. We . . . uh . . . we publish textbooks.

JERRY: That sounds nice; very nice. What do you make?

PETER: [*Still cheerful*] Now look here!

JERRY: Oh, come on.

PETER: Well, I make around 200,000 a year, but I don't carry more than forty dollars at any one time . . . in case you're a . . . a holdup man . . . ha, ha, ha.

JERRY: [*Ignoring the above*] Where do you live? [PETER *is reluctant*] Oh, look; I'm not going to rob you, and I'm not going to kidnap your parakeets, your cats, or your daughters.

PETER: [*Too loud*] I live between Lexington and Third Avenue, on Seventy-fourth Street.

JERRY: That wasn't so hard, was it?

PETER: I didn't mean to seem . . . ah . . . it's that you don't really carry on a conversation; you just ask questions. And I'm . . . I'm normally . . . uh . . . reticent. Why do you just stand there?

JERRY: I'll start walking around in a little while, and maybe later I'll sit down. Say, what's the dividing line between upper-middle-class and lower-upper-middle-class?

PETER: My dear fellow, I . . .

JERRY: Don't my dear fellow me.

PETER: [*Unhappily*] Was I patronizing? I believe I was; I'm sorry. But, you see, your question about the classes bewildered me.

JERRY: And when you're bewildered you become patronizing?

PETER: I . . . I don't express myself too well, sometimes. [*He attempts a joke on himself*] I'm in publishing, not writing.

JERRY: [*Amused, but not at the humor*] So be it. The truth *is: I* was being patronizing.

PETER: Oh, now; you needn't say that. [*It is at this point that* JERRY *may begin to move about the stage with slowly increasing determination and authority, but pacing himself, so that the long speech about the dog comes at the high point of the arc*]

JERRY: All right. Who are your favorite writers? Baudelaire and Stephen King?[3]

PETER: [*Wary*] Well, I like a great many writers; I have a considerable . . . catholicity of taste, if I may say so. Those two men are fine, each in his way. [*Warming up*] Baudelaire, of course . . . uh . . . is by far the finer of the two, but Stephen King has a place . . . in our . . . uh . . . national . . .

JERRY: Skip it.

PETER: I . . . sorry.

JERRY: Do you know what I did before I went to the zoo today? I walked all the way up Fifth Avenue from Washington Square; all the way.

PETER: Oh; you live in the Village! [*This seems to enlighten* PETER]

[3]Charles Baudelaire (1821–1867), French poet. His *Les Fleurs du mal* (*The Flowers of Evil*), published in 1857, describes his sense of despair, sin, and the degradation of life. Stephen King (1947–), best-selling American writer of macabre, fantastic, and supernatural tales.

JERRY: No, I don't. I took the subway down to the Village so I could walk all the way up Fifth Avenue to the zoo. It's one of those things a person has to do; sometimes a person has to go a very long distance out of his way to come back a short distance correctly.

PETER: [*Almost pouting*] Oh, I thought you lived in Greenwich Village.

JERRY: What were you trying to do? Make sense out of things? Bring order? The old pigeonhole bit? Well, that's easy; I'll tell you. I live in a four-story brownstone rooming-house on the upper West Side between Columbus Avenue and Central Park West. I live on the top floor; rear; west. It's a laughably small room, and one of my walls is made of beaverboard; this beaverboard separates my room from another laughably small room, so I assume that the two rooms were once one room, a small room, but not necessarily laughable. The room beyond my beaverboard wall is occupied by a black queen who always keeps his door open; well, not always but *always* when he's plucking his eyebrows, which he does with Buddhist concentration. This black queen has rotten teeth, which is rare, and he has a Japanese kimono, which is also pretty rare; and he wears this kimono to and from the john in the hall, which is pretty frequent. I mean, he goes to the john a lot. He never bothers me, and he never brings anyone up to his room. All he does is pluck his eyebrows, wear his kimono and go to the john. Now, the two front rooms on my floor are a little larger, I guess; but they're pretty small, too. There's a Puerto Rican family in one of them, a husband, a wife, and some kids; I don't know how many. These people entertain a lot. And in the other front room, there's somebody living there, but I don't know who it is. I've never seen who it is. Never. Never ever.

PETER: [*Embarrassed*] Why . . . why do you live there?

JERRY: [*From a distance*] I don't know.

PETER: It doesn't sound like a very nice place . . . where you live.

JERRY: Well, no; it isn't an apartment in the East Seventies. But, then again, I don't have one wife, two daughters, two cats and two parakeets. What I do have, I have toilet articles, a few clothes, a hot plate that I'm not supposed to have, a can opener, one that works with a key, you know; a knife, two forks, and two spoons, one small, one large; three plates, a cup, a saucer, a drinking glass, two picture frames, both empty, eight or nine books, a pack of pornographic playing cards, regular deck, an old Western Union typewriter that prints nothing but capital letters, and a small strongbox without a lock which has in it . . . what? Rocks! Some rocks . . . sea-rounded rocks I picked up on the beach when I was a kid. Under which . . . weighed down . . . are some letters . . . please letters . . . please why don't you do this, and please why do you do that letters. And when letters, too. When will you write? When will you come? When? These letters are from more recent years.

PETER: [*Stares glumly at his shoes, then*] About those two empty picture frames . . . ?

JERRY: I don't see why they need any explanation at all. Isn't it clear? I don't have pictures of anyone to put in them.

PETER: Your parents . . . perhaps . . . a girl friend . . .

JERRY: You're a very sweet man, and you're possessed of a truly enviable innocence. But good old Mom and good old Pop are dead . . . you know? . . . I'm broken up about it, too . . . I mean really. BUT. That particular vaudeville act is playing the cloud circuit now, so I don't see how I can look at them, all neat and framed. Besides, or, rather, to be pointed about it, good old Mom walked out on good old Pop when I was ten and a half years old; she embarked on an adulterous turn of our southern states . . . a journey of a year's duration . . . and her most constant companion . . . among others, among many others . . . was a Mr. Barleycorn.[4] At least, that's what good old Pop told me after he went down . . . came back . . . brought her body north. We'd received the news between Christmas and New Year's, you see, that good old Mom had parted with the ghost in some dump in Alabama. And, without the ghost . . . she was less welcome. I mean, what was she? A stiff . . . a northern stiff. At any rate, good old Pop celebrated the New Year for an even two weeks and then slapped into the front of a somewhat moving city omnibus,[5] which sort of cleaned things out family-wise. Well no; then there was Mom's sister, who was given neither to sin nor the consolations of the bottle. I moved in on her, and my memory of her is slight excepting I remember still that she did all things dourly: sleeping, eating, working, praying. She dropped dead on the stairs to her apartment, my apartment then, too, on the afternoon of my high school graduation. A terribly middle-European joke, if you ask me.

PETER: Oh, my; oh, my.

JERRY: Oh, your what? But that was a long time ago, and I have no feeling about any of it that I care to admit to myself. Perhaps you can see, though, why good old Mom and good old Pop are frameless. What's your name? Your first name?

PETER: I'm Peter.

JERRY: I'd forgotten to ask you. I'm Jerry.

PETER: [*With a slight, nervous laugh*] Hello, Jerry.

JERRY: [*Nods his hello*] And let's see now; what's the point of having a girl's picture, especially in two frames? I have two picture frames, you remember. I never see the pretty little ladies more than once, and most of them wouldn't be caught in the same room with a camera. It's odd, and I wonder if it's sad.

PETER: The girls?

JERRY: No. I wonder if it's sad that I never see the little ladies more than once. I've never been able to have sex with, or, how is it put? . . . make love to anybody more than once. Once; that's it. . . . Oh, wait; for a week and a half, when I was fifteen . . . and I hang my head in shame that puberty was late . . . I was a h-o-m-o-s-e-x-u-a-l. I mean, I was queer . . . [*Very fast*] . . . queer, queer, queer . . . with bells ringing, banners snapping in the wind. And for those eleven days, I met at least twice a day with the park superintendent's son . . . a Greek boy, whose birthday was the same as mine, except he was a year older. I think I was very much in love . . . maybe just with sex. But that was the jazz of a very special hotel, wasn't it? And now; oh, do I love the little ladies; really, I love them. For about an hour.

PETER: Well, it seems perfectly simple to me. . . .

JERRY: [*Angry*] Look! Are you going to tell me to get married and have parakeets?

PETER: [*Angry himself*] Forget the parakeets! And stay single if you want to. It's no business of mine. I didn't start this conversation in the . . .

[4]I. e., John Barleycorn, a slang term for alcoholic drink.
[5]A public passenger bus.

JERRY: All right, all right. I'm sorry. All right? You're not angry?

PETER: [*Laughing*] No, I'm not angry.

JERRY: Good. Interesting that you asked me about the picture frames. I would have thought that you would have asked me about the pornographic playing cards.

PETER: [*With a knowing smile*] Oh, I've seen those cards.

JERRY: That's not the point. [*Laughs*] I suppose when you were a kid you and your pals passed them around, or you had a pack of your own.

PETER: Well, I guess a lot of us did.

JERRY: And you threw them away just before you got married.

PETER: Oh, now; look here. I didn't *need* anything like that when I got older.

JERRY: No?

PETER: [*Embarrassed*] I'd rather not talk about these things.

JERRY: So? Don't. Besides, I wasn't trying to plumb your postadolescent sexual life and hard times; what I wanted to get at is the value difference between pornographic playing cards when you're a kid, and pornographic playing cards when you're older. It's that when you're a kid you use the cards as a substitute for a real experience, and when you're older you use real experience as a substitute for the fantasy. But I imagine you'd rather hear about what happened at the zoo.

PETER: [*Enthusiastic*] Oh, yes; the zoo [*Then, awkward*] That is . . . if you. . . .

JERRY: Let me tell you about why I went . . . well, let me tell you some things. I've told you about the fourth floor of the roominghouse where I live. I think the rooms are better as you go down, floor by floor. I guess they are; I don't know. I don't know any of the people on the third and second floors. Oh, wait! I do know that there's a lady living on the third floor, in the front. I know because she cries all the time. Whenever I go out or come back in, whenever I pass her door I always hear her crying, muffled, but . . . very determined. Very determined indeed. But the one I'm getting to, and all about the dog, is the landlady. I don't like to use words that are too harsh in describing people. I don't like to. But the landlady is a fat, ugly, mean, stupid, unwashed, misanthropic, cheap, drunken bag of garbage. And you may have noticed that I very seldom use profanity, so I can't describe her as well as I might.

PETER: You describe her . . . vividly.

JERRY: Well, thanks. Anyway, she has a dog, and she and her dog are the gatekeepers of my dwelling. The woman is bad enough; she leans around in the entrance hall, spying to see that I don't bring in things or people, and when she's had her midafternoon pint of lemon-flavored gin she always stops me in the hall and grabs ahold of my coat or my arm, and she presses her disgusting body up against me to keep me in a corner so she can talk to me. The smell of her body and her breath . . . you can't imagine it . . . and somewhere, somewhere in the back of that pea-sized brain of hers, an organ developed just enough to let her eat, drink, and emit, she has some foul parody of sexual desire. And I, Peter, I am the object of her sweaty lust.

PETER: That's disgusting. That's . . . horrible.

JERRY: But I have found a way to keep her off. When she talks to me, when she presses herself to my body and mumbles about her room and how I should come there, I merely say: but, Love; wasn't yesterday enough for you, and the day before? Then she puzzles, she makes slits of her tiny eyes, she sways a little, and then, Peter . . . and it is at this moment that I think I might be doing some good in that tormented house . . . a simple-minded smile begins to form on her unthinkable face, and she giggles and groans as she thinks about yesterday and the day before; as she believes and relives what never happened. Then, she motions to that black monster of a dog she has, and she goes back to her room. And I am safe until our next meeting.

PETER: It's so . . . . I find it hard to believe that people such as that really *are.*

JERRY: [*Lightly mocking*] It's for reading about, isn't it?

PETER: [*Seriously*] Yes.

JERRY: And fact is better left to fiction. You're right, Peter. Well, what I have been meaning to tell you about is the dog; I shall, now.

PETER: [*Nervously*] Oh, yes; the dog.

JERRY: Don't go. You're not thinking of going, are you?

PETER: Well . . . no, I don't think so.

JERRY: [*As if to a child*] Because after I tell you about the dog, do you know what then? Then . . . then I'll tell you about what happened at the zoo.

PETER: [*Laughing faintly*] You're . . . you're full of stories, aren't you?

JERRY: You don't *have* to listen. Nobody is holding you here; remember that. Keep that in your mind.

PETER: [*Irritably*] I know that.

JERRY: You do? Good. [*The following long speech, it seems to me, should be done with a great deal of action, to achieve a hypnotic effect on* PETER, *and on the audience, too. Some specific actions have been suggested, but the director and the actor playing* JERRY *might best work it out for themselves*] ALL RIGHT. [*As if reading from a huge billboard*] THE STORY OF JERRY AND THE DOG! [*Natural again*] What I am going to tell you has something to do with how sometimes it's necessary to go a long distance out of the way in order to come back a short distance correctly; or, maybe I only think that it has something to do with that. But, it's why I went to the zoo today, and why I walked north . . . northerly, rather . . . until I came here. All right. The dog, I think I told you, is a black monster of a beast: an oversized head, tiny, tiny ears, and eyes . . . bloodshot, infected, maybe; and a body you can see the ribs through the skin. The dog is black, all black; all black except for the bloodshot eyes, and . . . yes . . . and open sore on its . . . *right* forepaw; that is red, too. And, oh yes; the poor monster, and I do believe it's an old dog . . . it's certainly a misused one . . . almost always has an erection . . . of sorts. That's red, too. And . . . what else? . . . oh, yes; there's a gray-yellow-white color, too, when he bares his fangs. Like this: Grrrrrrr! Which is what he did when he saw me for the first time . . . the day I moved in. I worried about that animal the very first minute I met him. Now, animals don't take to me like Saint Francis had birds hanging off him all the time. What I mean is: animals are indifferent to me . . . like people [*He smiles slightly*] . . . most of the time. But this dog wasn't indifferent. From the very beginning he'd snarl and then go for me, to get one of my legs. Not like he was rabid, you know; he was sort of a stumbly dog, but he wasn't half-assed, either. It was a good, stumbly run;

but I always got away. He got a piece of my trouser leg, look, you can see right here, where it's mended; he got that the second day I lived there; but, I kicked free and got upstairs fast, so that was that. [*Puzzles*] I still don't know to this day how the other roomers manage it, but you know what I *think:* I think it had to do only with me. Cozy. So. Anyway, this went on for over a week, whenever I came in; but never when I went out. That's funny. Or, it *was* funny. I could pack up and live in the street for all the dog cared. Well, I thought about it up in my room one day, one of the times after I'd bolted upstairs, and I made up my mind. I decided: First, I'll kill the dog with kindness, and if that doesn't work . . . I'll just kill him. [PETER *winces*] Don't react, Peter; just listen. So, the next day I went out and bought a bag of hamburgers, medium rare, no catsup, no onion; and on the way home I threw away the rolls and kept just the meat. [*Action for the following, perhaps*] When I got back to the roominghouse the dog was waiting for me. I half-opened the door that led into the entrance hall, and there he was; waiting for me. It figured. I went in, very cautiously, and I had the hamburgers, you remember; I opened the bag, and I set the meat down about twelve feet from where the dog was snarling at me. Like so! He snarled; stopped snarling; sniffed; moved slowly; then faster; then faster toward the meat. Well, when he got to it he stopped, and he looked at me. I smiled; but tentatively, you understand. He turned his face back to the hamburgers, smelled, sniffed some more, and then . . . RRRAAAAGGGGGHHHH, like that . . . he tore into them. It was as if he had never eaten anything in his life before, except like garbage. Which might very well have been the truth. I don't think the landlady ever eats anything but garbage. But. He ate all the hamburgers, almost all at once, making sounds in his throat like a woman. *Then,* when he'd finished the meat, the hamburger, and tried to eat the paper, too, he sat down and smiled. I think he smiled; I know cats do. It was a very gratifying few moments. Then, BAM, he snarled and made for me again. He didn't get me this time, either. So, I got upstairs, and I lay down on my bed and started to think about the dog again. To be truthful, I was offended, and I was damn mad, too. It was six perfectly good hamburgers with not enough pork in them to make it disgusting. I was offended. But, after a while, I decided to try it for a few more days. If you think about it, this dog had what amounted to an antipathy toward me; really. And, I wondered if I mightn't overcome this antipathy. So, I tried it for five more days, but it was always the same: snarl, sniff: move; faster; stare: gobble; RAAGGGHHH; smile; snarl; BAM. Well, now; by this time Columbus Avenue was strewn with hamburger rolls and I was less offended than disgusted. So, I decided to kill the dog. [PETER *raises a hand in protest*] Oh, don't be so alarmed, Peter; I didn't succeed. The day I tried to kill the dog I bought only one hamburger and what I thought was a murderous portion of rat poison. When I bought the hamburger I asked the man not to bother with the roll, all I wanted was the meat. I expected some reaction from him, like: we don't sell no hamburgers without rolls; or, wha' d'ya wanna do, eat it out'a ya han's? But no; he smiled benignly, wrapped up the hamburger in waxed paper, and said: A bite for ya pussy-cat? I wanted to say: No, not really; it's part of a plan to poison a dog I know. But, you can't say "a dog I know" without sounding funny; so I said, a little too loud, I'm afraid, and too formally: YES, A BITE FOR MY PUSSY-CAT. People looked up. It always happens when I try to simplify things; people look up.

But that's neither hither nor thither. So. On my way back to the rooming-house, I kneaded the hamburger and the rat poison together between my hands, at that point feeling as much sadness as disgust. I opened the door to the entrance hall, and there the monster was, waiting to take the offering and then jump me. Poor bastard; he never learned that the moment he took to smile before he went for me gave me time enough to get out of range. BUT, there he was; malevolence with an erection, waiting. I put the poison patty down, moved toward the stairs and watched. The poor animal gobbled the food down as usual, smiled, which made me almost sick, and then, BAM. But, I sprinted up the stairs, as usual, and the dog didn't get me, as usual. AND IT CAME TO PASS THAT THE BEAST WAS DEATHLY ILL. I knew this because he no longer attended me, and because the landlady sobered up. She stopped me in the hall the same evening of the attempted murder and confided the information that God had struck her puppy-dog a surely fatal blow. She had forgotten her bewildered lust, and her eyes were wide open for the first time. They looked like the dog's eyes. She sniveled and implored me to pray for the animal. I wanted to say to her: Madam, I have myself to pray for, the black queen, the Puerto Rican family, the person in the front room whom I've never seen, the woman who cries deliberately behind her closed door, and the rest of the people in all roominghouses, everywhere; besides, Madam, I don't understand how to pray. But . . . to simplify things . . . I told her I would pray. She looked up. She said that I was a liar, and that I probably wanted the dog to die. I told her, and there was so much truth here, that I didn't want the dog to die. I didn't, and not just because I'd poisoned him. I'm afraid that I must tell you I wanted the dog to live so that I could see what our new relationship might come to. [PETER *indicates his increasing displeasure and slowing growing antagonism*] Please understand, Peter; that sort of thing is important. You must believe me; it *is* important. We have to know the effect of our actions. [*Another deep sigh*] Well, anyway; the dog recovered. I have no idea why, unless he was a descendant of the puppy that guarded the gates of hell or some such resort. I'm not up on my mythology. [*He pronounces the word myth-o-logy*] Are you? [PETER *sets to thinking, but* JERRY *goes on*] At any rate, and you've missed the eight-thousand-dollar question, Peter; at any rate, the dog recovered his health and the landlady recovered her thirst, in no way altered by the bow-wow's deliverance. When I came home from a movie that was playing on Forty-second Street, a movie I'd seen, or one that was very much like one or several I'd seen, after the landlady told me puppykins was better, I was so hoping for the dog to be waiting for me. I was . . . well, how would you put it . . . enticed? . . . fascinated? . . . no, I don't think so . . . heart-shatteringly anxious, that's it; I was heart-shatteringly anxious to confront my friend again. [PETER *reacts scoffingly*] Yes, Peter; friend. That's the only word for it. I was heart-shatteringly et cetera to confront my doggy friend again. I came in the door and advanced, unafraid, to the center of the entrance hall. The beast was there . . . looking at me. And, you know, he looked better for his scrape with the nevermind. I stopped; I looked at him; he looked at me. I think . . . I think we stayed a long time that way . . . still, stone-statue . . . just looking at one another. I looked more into his face than he looked into mine. I mean, I can concentrate longer at looking into a dog's face than a dog can concentrate at looking into mine, or into anybody else's face, for that matter. But during that twenty seconds or two hours that we looked into each other's face, we made contact. Now, here is what I had wanted to happen: I loved the dog now, and I wanted him to love me. I had tried to love, and I had tried to kill, and both had been unsuccessful by themselves. I hoped . . . and I don't really know why I expected the dog to understand anything, much less my motivations . . . I hoped that the dog would understand. [PETER *seems to be hypnotized*] It's just . . . it's just that . . . [JERRY *is abnormally tense, now*] . . . it's just that if you can't deal with people, you have to make a start somewhere. WITH ANIMALS! [*Much faster now, and like a conspirator*] Don't you see? A person has to have some way of dealing with SOMETHING. If not with people . . . if not with people . . . SOMETHING. With a bed, with a cockroach, with a mirror . . . no, that's too hard, that's one of the last steps. With a cockroach, with a . . . with a . . . carpet, a roll of toilet paper . . . no, not that, either . . . that's a mirror, too; always check bleeding. You see how hard it is to find things? With a street corner, and too many lights, all colors reflecting on the oily-wet streets . . . with a wisp of smoke, a wisp . . . of smoke . . . with . . . with pornographic playing cards, with a strongbox . . . WITHOUT A LOCK . . . with love, with vomiting, with crying, with fury because the pretty little ladies aren't pretty little ladies, with making money with your body which is an act of love and I could prove it, with howling because you're alive; with God. How about that? WITH GOD WHO IS A BLACK QUEEN WHO WEARS A KIMONO AND PLUCKS HIS EYEBROWS, WHO IS A WOMAN WHO CRIES WITH DETERMINATION BEHIND HER CLOSED DOOR . . . with God who, I'm told, turned his back on the whole thing some time ago . . . with . . . some day, with people. [JERRY *sighs the next word heavily*] People. With an idea; a concept. And where better, where ever better in this humiliating excuse for a jail, where better to communicate one single, simple-minded idea than in an entrance hall? Where? It would be A START! Where better to make a beginning . . . to understand and just possibly be understood . . . a beginning of an understanding, that with . . . [*Here* JERRY *seems to fall into almost grotesque fatigue*] . . . than with A DOG. Just that; a dog. [*Here there is a silence that might be prolonged for a moment or so; then* JERRY *wearily finishes his story*] A dog. It seemed like a perfect sensible idea. Man is a dog's best friend, remember. So: the dog and I looked at each other. I longer than the dog. And what I saw then has been the same ever since. Whenever the dog and I see each other we both stop where we are. We regard each other with a mixture of sadness and suspicion, and then we feign indifference. We walk past each other safely; we have an understanding. It's very sad, but you'll have to admit that it is an understanding. We had made many attempts at contact, and we had failed. The dog has returned to garbage, and I to solitary but free passage. I have not returned. I mean to say, I have *gained* solitary free passage, if that much further loss can be said to be gain. I have learned that neither kindness nor cruelty by themselves, independent of each other, creates any effect beyond themselves; and I have learned that the two combined, together, at the same time, are the teaching emotion. And what is gained is loss. And what has been the result: the dog and I have attained a compromise; more of a bargain, really. We neither love nor hurt because we do not try to reach each other. And, *was* trying to feed the dog an act of love? And, perhaps, was the dog's attempt to bite me *not* an act of love? If we can so misunderstand, well then, why have we invented the word love in the first place? [*There is silence.*] The Story of Jerry and the Dog; the end. [PETER *is silent*] Well, Peter? [JERRY *is suddenly cheerful*] Well, Peter? Do you think I could sell that story to the *Reader's Digest* and make a couple of hundred bucks for *The Most Unforgettable Character I've Ever Met*? Huh? [JERRY *is animated, but* PETER *is disturbed*] Oh, come on now, Peter; tell me what you think.

PETER: [*Numb*] I . . . I don't understand what . . . I don't think I . . . [*Now, almost tearfully*] Why did you tell me all of this?

JERRY: Why not?

PETER: I DON'T UNDERSTAND!

JERRY: [*Furious, but whispering*] That's a lie.

PETER: No. No, it's not.

JERRY: [*Quietly*] I tried to explain it to you as I went along. I went slowly; it all has to do with . . .

PETER: I DON'T WANT TO HEAR ANY MORE. I don't understand you, or your landlady, or her dog . . .

JERRY: *Her* dog! I thought it was my . . . No. No, you're right. It *is* her dog. [*Looks at* PETER *intently, shaking his head*] I don't know what I was thinking about; of course you don't understand. [*In a monotone, wearily*] I don't live in your block; I'm not married to two parakeets, or whatever your setup is. I am a *permanent transient,* and my home is the sickening roominghouses on the West Side of New York City, which is the greatest city in the world. Amen.

PETER: I'm . . . I'm sorry; I didn't mean to . . .

JERRY: Forget it. I suppose you don't quite know what to make of me, eh?

PETER: [*A joke*] We get all kinds in publishing. [*Chuckles*]

JERRY: You're a funny man. [*He forces a laugh*] You know that? You're a very . . . a richly comic person.

PETER: [*Modestly, but amused*] Oh, now, not really. [*Still chuckling*]

JERRY: Peter, do I annoy you, or confuse you?

PETER: [*Lightly*] Well, I must confess that this wasn't the kind of afternoon I'd anticipated.

JERRY: You mean, I'm not the gentleman you were expecting.

PETER: I wasn't expecting anybody.

JERRY: No, I don't imagine you were. But I'm here, and I'm not leaving.

PETER: [*Consulting his watch*] Well, you may not be, but I must be getting home soon.

JERRY: Oh, come on; stay a while longer.

PETER: I really should get home; you see . . .

JERRY: [*Tickles* PETER'S *ribs with his fingers*] Oh, come on.

PETER: [*He is very ticklish; as* JERRY *continues to tickle him his voice becomes falsetto*] No, I . . . OHHHHH! Don't do that. Stop, Stop. Ohhh, no, no.

JERRY: Oh, come on.

PETER: [*As* JERRY *tickles*] Oh, hee, hee, hee. I must go. I . . . hee, hee, hee. After all, stop, stop, hee, hee, hee, after all, the parakeets will be getting dinner ready soon. Hee, hee. And the cats are setting the table. Stop, stop, and, and . . . [PETER *is beside himself now*] . . . and we're having . . . hee,

hee . . . uh . . . ho, ho, ho. [JERRY *stops tickling* PETER, *but the combination of the tickling and his own mad whimsy has* PETER *laughing almost hysterically. As his laughter continues, then subsides,* JERRY *watches him, with a curious fixed smile*]

JERRY: Peter?

PETER: Oh, ha, ha, ha, ha, ha. What? What?

JERRY: Listen, now.

PETER: Oh, ho, ho. What . . . what is it, Jerry? Oh, my.

JERRY: [*Mysteriously*] Peter, do you want to know what happened at the zoo?

PETER: Ah, ha, ha. The what? Oh, yes; the zoo. Oh, ho, ho. Well, I had my own zoo there for a moment with . . . hee, hee, the parakeets getting dinner ready, and the . . . ha, ha, whatever it was, the . . .

JERRY: [*Calmly*] Yes, that was very funny, Peter. I wouldn't have expected it. But do you want to hear about what happened at the zoo, or not?

PETER: Yes. Yes, by all means; tell me what happened at the zoo. Oh, my. I don't know what happened to me.

JERRY: Now I'll let you in on what happened at the zoo; but first, I should tell you why I went to the zoo. I went to the zoo to find out more about the way people exist with animals, and the way animals exist with each other, and with people too. It probably wasn't a fair test, what with everyone separated by bars from everyone else, the animals for the most part from each other, and always the people from the animals. But, if it's a zoo, that's the way it is. [*He pokes* PETER *on the arm*] Move over.

PETER: [*Friendly*] I'm sorry, haven't you enough room? [*He shifts a little*]

JERRY: [*Smiling slightly*] Well, all the animals are there, and all the people are there, and it's Sunday and all the children are there. [*He pokes* PETER *again*] Move over.

PETER: [*Patiently, still friendly*] All right. [*He moves some more, and* JERRY *has all the room he might need*]

JERRY: And it's a hot day, so all the stench is there, too, and all the balloon sellers, and all the ice cream sellers, and all the seals are barking, and all the birds are screaming. [*Pokes* PETER *harder*] Move over!

PETER: [*Beginning to be annoyed*] Look here, you have more than enough room! [*But he moves more, and is now fairly cramped at one end of the bench*]

JERRY: And I am there, and it's feeding time at the lions' house, and the lion keeper comes into the lion cage, one of the lion cages, to feed one of the lions. [*Punches* PETER *on the arm, hard*] MOVE OVER!

PETER: [*Very annoyed*] I can't move over any more, and stop hitting me. What's the matter with you?

JERRY: Do you want to hear the story? [*Punches* PETER'S *arm again*]

PETER: [*Flabbergasted*] I'm not so sure! I certainly don't want to be punched in the arm.

JERRY: [*Punches* PETER'S *arm again*] Like that?

PETER: Stop it! What's the matter with you?

JERRY: I'm crazy, you bastard.

PETER: That isn't funny.

JERRY: Listen to me, Peter. I want this bench. You go sit on the bench over there, and if you're good I'll tell you the rest of the story.

PETER: [*Flustered*] But . . . whatever for? What *is* the matter with you? Besides, I see no reason why I should give up this bench. I sit on this bench almost every Sunday afternoon, in good weather. It's secluded here; there's never anyone sitting here, so I have it all to myself.

JERRY: [*Softly*] Get off this bench, Peter; I want it.

PETER: [*Almost whining*] No.

JERRY: I said I want this bench, and I'm going to have it. Now get over there.

PETER: People can't have everything they want. You should know that; it's a rule; people can have some of the things they want, but they can't have everything.

JERRY: [*Laughs*] Imbecile! You're slow-witted!

PETER: Stop that!

JERRY: You're a vegetable! Go lie down on the ground.

PETER: [*Intense*] Now *you* listen to me. I've put up with you all afternoon.

JERRY: Not really.

PETER: LONG ENOUGH. I've put up with you long enough. I've listened to you because you seemed . . . well, because I thought you wanted to talk to somebody.

JERRY: You put things well; economically, and, yet . . . oh, what is the word I want to put justice to your . . . JESUS, you make me sick . . . get off here and give me my bench.

PETER: MY BENCH!

JERRY: [*Pushes* PETER *almost, but not quite, off the bench*] Get out of my sight.

PETER: [*Regarding his position*] God da . . . mn you. That's enough! I've had enough of you. I will not give up this bench; you can't have it, and that's that. Now, go away [JERRY *snorts but does not move*] Go away, I said. [JERRY *does not move*] Get away from here. If you don't move on . . . you're a bum . . . that's what you are. . . . If you don't move on, I'll get a policeman here and make you go. [JERRY *laughs, stays*] I warn you. I'll call a policeman.

JERRY: [*Softly*] You won't find a policeman around here; they're all over the west side of the park chasing fairies down from trees or out of the bushes. That's all they do. That's their function. So scream your head off; it won't do you any good.

PETER: POLICE! I warn you, I'll have you arrested. POLICE! [*Pause*] I said POLICE! [*Pause*] I feel ridiculous.

JERRY: You look ridiculous: a grown man screaming for the police on a bright Sunday afternoon in the park with nobody harming you. If a policeman *did* fill his quota and come sludging over this way he'd probably take you in as a nut.

PETER: [*With disgust and impotence*] Great God, I just came here to read, and now you want me to give up the bench. You're mad.

JERRY: Hey, I got news for you, as they say. I'm on your precious bench, and you're never going to have it for yourself again.

PETER: [*Furious*] Look, you; get off my bench. I don't care if it makes any sense or not. I want this bench to myself; I want you OFF IT!

JERRY: [*Mocking*] Aw . . . look who's mad.

PETER: GET OUT!

JERRY: No.

PETER: I WARN YOU!

JERRY: Do you know how ridiculous you look *now?*

PETER: [*His fury and self-consciousness have possessed him*] It doesn't matter. [*He is almost crying*] GET AWAY FROM MY BENCH!

JERRY: Why? You have everything in the world you want; you've told me about your home, and your family, and *your own* little zoo. You have everything, and now you want this bench. Are these the things men fight for? Tell me, Peter, is this bench, this iron and this wood, is this your honor? Is this the thing in the world you'd fight for? Can you think of anything more absurd?

PETER: Absurd? Look, I'm not going to talk to you about honor, or even try to explain it to you. Besides, it isn't a question of honor; but even if it were, you wouldn't understand.

JERRY: [*Contemptuously*] You don't even know what you're saying, do you? This is probably the first time in your life you've had anything more trying to face than changing your cats' toilet box. Stupid! Don't you have any idea, not even the slightest, what other people *need?*

PETER: Oh, boy, listen to you; well, you don't need this bench. That's for sure.

JERRY: Yes; yes, I do.

PETER: [*Quivering*] I've come here for years; I have hours of great pleasure, great satisfaction, right here. And that's important to a man. I'm a responsible person, and I'm a GROWNUP. This is my bench, and you have no right to take it away from me.

JERRY: Fight for it, then. Defend yourself; defend your bench.

PETER: You've *pushed* me to it. Get up and fight.

JERRY: Like a man?

PETER: [*Still angry*] Yes, like a man, if you insist on mocking me even further.

JERRY: I'll have to give you credit for one thing; you *are* a vegetable, and a slightly nearsighted one, I think . . .

PETER: THAT'S ENOUGH.

JERRY: . . . but, you know, as they say on TV all the time—you know—and I mean this, Peter, you have a certain dignity; it surprises me. . . .

PETER: STOP!

JERRY: [*Rises lazily*] Very well, Peter, we'll battle for the bench, but we're not evenly matched. [*He takes out and clicks open an ugly-looking knife*]

PETER: [*Suddenly awakening to the reality of the situation*] You *are* mad! You're stark raving mad! YOU'RE GOING TO KILL ME? [*But before* PETER *has time to think what to do,* JERRY *tosses the knife at* PETER'S *feet*]

JERRY: There you go. Pick it up. You have the knife and we'll be more evenly matched.

PETER: [*Horrified*] No!

JERRY: [*Rushes over to* PETER, *grabs him by the collar;* PETER *rises; their faces almost touch*] Now you pick up that knife and you fight with me. You fight for your self-respect; you fight for that goddamned bench.

PETER: [*Struggling*] No! Let . . . let go of me! He . . . Help!

JERRY: [*Slaps* PETER *on each "fight"*] You fight, you miserable bastard; fight for that bench; fight for your manhood, you pathetic little vegetable. [*Spits in* PETER'S *face*] You couldn't even get your wife with a male child.

PETER: [*Breaks away, enraged*] It's a matter of genetics, not manhood, you . . . you monster. [*He darts down, picks up the knife and backs off a little; he is breathing heavily*] I'll give you one last chance; get out of here and leave me alone! [*He holds the knife with a firm arm, but far in front of him, not to attack, but to defend*]

JERRY: [*Sighs heavily*] So be it! [*With a rush he charges* PETER *and impales himself on the knife. Tableau: For just a moment, complete silence,* JERRY *impaled on the knife at the end of* PETER'S *still firm arm. Then* PETER *screams, pulls away, leaving the knife in* JERRY. JERRY *is motionless, on point. Then he, too, screams, and it must be the sound of an infuriated and fatally wounded animal. With the knife in him, he stumbles back to the bench that* PETER *had vacated. He crumbles there, sitting facing* PETER, *his eyes wide in agony, his mouth open*]

PETER: [*Whispering*] Oh my God, oh my God, oh my God. . . . [*He repeats these words many times, very rapidly*]

JERRY: [JERRY *is dying; but now his expression seems to change. His features relax, and while his voice varies, sometimes wrenched with pain, for the most part he seems removed from his dying. He smiles*] Peter, thank you, Peter. I mean that, now; thank you very much. [PETER'S *mouth drops open. He cannot move; he is transfixed*] I came unto you [*He laughs, so faintly*] and you have comforted me. Dear Peter.

PETER: [*Almost fainting*] Oh my God!

JERRY: You'd better go now. Somebody might come by, and you don't want to be here when anyone comes.

PETER: [*Does not move, but begins to weep*] Oh my God, oh my God.

JERRY: And Peter, I'll tell you something now; you're not really a vegetable; it's all right, you're an animal. You're an animal, too. But you'd better hurry now, Peter. Hurry, you'd better go . . . . [JERRY *takes a handkerchief and with great effort and pain wipes the knife handle clean of finger prints*] Hurry away, Peter. [PETER *begins to stagger away*] Wait . . . wait, Peter. Take your book . . . book. Right here . . . beside me . . . on your bench . . . my bench, rather. Come . . . take your book. [PETER *starts for the book, but retreats*] Hurry . . . Peter. [PETER *rushes to the bench, grabs the book, retreats*] Very good, Peter . . . very good. Now . . . hurry away. [PETER *hesitates for a moment, then flees, stage-left*] Hurry away . . . [*His eyes are closed now.*]

PETER: OH MY GOD!

JERRY: Hurry away, your parakeets are making the dinner . . . the cats . . . are setting the table . . .

PETER: [*Off stage. A pitiful howl*] OH MY GOD!

JERRY: [*His eyes still closed, he shakes his head and speaks; a combination of scornful mimicry and supplication*] Oh . . . my . . . God. [*He is dead*]

CURTAIN

1958 1959, 1960, 1999

Saul Bellow 1915–2005

The work of Saul Bellow is dominated by the figure of the marginal man, an alienated and absurd character caught between his own inadequacies and those imposed on him by his friends and society. Bellow's major themes were evident in his first novel, Dangling Man *(1944), which was based in part on the experiences of his early life. He was born in a small town in Quebec, Canada, of Russian immigrant parents who gave him the name Solomon Bellows. Later, when he was in his twenties and had begun to publish his writing, he omitted the final "s" from his last name and changed his first name from Solomon to Saul. When he was still a child, his parents moved to the United States, to Chicago, Illinois, where he grew up in a multilingual (English, French, Yiddish, and Hebrew), Orthodox Jewish household, an environment he later recalled as deeply religious, almost superstitious. In 1937 he graduated from Northwestern University, with honors in anthropology and sociology, and entered the University of Wisconsin on a graduate scholarship, but he soon withdrew to follow his consuming interest, fiction writing. For four years he supported himself by teaching in a Chicago teachers' college; he then served briefly in the Merchant Marine in World War II and later worked on the editorial staff of* Encyclopedia Britannica.

Dangling Man *was published when he was twenty-nine. Three years later he published his second novel,* The Victim. *In 1953 his picaresque novel,* The Adventures of Augie March, *appeared. Bellow's first best-seller, it firmly established him as a writer of national significance and won the first of his three National Book Awards. Bellow's fourth novel,* Seize the Day *(1956), was followed by* Henderson the Rain King *(1958),* Herzog *(1964), and* Mr. Sammler's Planet *(1970), a grim novel of social turmoil. Bellow also wrote numerous short stories, some of which are collected in* Mosby's Memories *(1968), and a number of plays, including* The Last Analysis, *which was produced in 1964. In 1975 he published* Humboldt's Gift, *a "comedy of success and failure" that is his most humorous book. In the following year he became the seventh American to receive the Nobel Prize for Literature.*

In More Die of Heartbreak *(1987), Bellow again dealt with the dilemmas and follies of intellectuals struggling to flourish in materialist and mechanical America. In a short novel,* The Bellarosa Connection *(1989), he presented a sardonic exploration of a memory expert, a man who remembers everything but whose consciousness (Bellow's abiding subject) is too shallow to allow him to understand himself. In 1994 Bellow published* It All Adds Up, *a collection of his essays. They summarize his views on what ails America and what he sees as the causes of a deteriorating culture.*

For many years Bellow taught at the University of Chicago. In 1993 he moved to Boston University, where, though he was world famous and distinguished as a Nobel Prize winner, he sometimes taught freshman-level classes in literature. It is often thought that because he portrayed them so well, Bellow must have resembled his most memorable heroes: dreamy, bumbling, rumpled, hopelessly mired in their own problems and struggling with their "ideals." Bellow himself believed that he most resembled the hero of Henderson the Rain King, *a "quixotic violinist and pig farmer who vainly sought a higher truth and moral purpose in life." But to those around him, including his students, Bellow was a man of high intellect and wide learning, a man of certainties and often of sarcastic and withering wit. He did not suffer fools gladly, and in his last long novel,* Ravelstein *(2000), he portrayed the final days of a university professor whose aim in life was to expose the "creeping boobism and vulgarity" that surrounded him in America.*

Although he seemed to grow more irascible over the years, his outlook darker, Bellow did not abandon the hope and compassion for humankind that are fundamental to his work. The citation for Bellow's Nobel Prize praised his "exuberant ideas, flashing irony, hilarious comedy, and burning compassion." That compassion found its expression in his creation of vivid characters who, in Bellow's words, struggled against the necessity of living life "in a mass. Transformed by Science. Under organized power. Subject to tremendous controls. In a condition caused by mechanization." His vivid characters ranged from the highest intellectuals to the lowly: "the cheapies, the stingies, the hypochondriacs, the family bores, humanoids." But his greatest achievement was his depiction of the modern antihero, the contemporary man "who keeps on trying to find a foothold during his wanderings in our tottering world, one who can never relinquish his faith that the value of life depends on its dignity, not its success."

FURTHER READING: R. Kiernan, *Saul Bellow,* 1988; *Saul Bellow in the 1980s,* ed. G. Cronin and L. Goldman, 1989; M. Glenday, *Saul Bellow and the Decline of Humanism,* 1990; E. Pifer, *Saul Bellow against the Grain,* 1990; R. Miller, *Saul Bellow, A Biography of the Imagination,* 1991; *Saul Bellow at Seventy Five, A Collection of Critical Essays,* ed. G. Bach, 1991; P. Hyland, *Saul Bellow,* 1992; *Saul Bellow, A Mosaic,* ed. L. Goldman, 1992; M. Friedrich, *Character and Narration in the Short Fiction of Saul Bellow,* 1995; *Saul Bellow and the Struggle at the Center,* ed. E. Hollahan, 1996; J. Atlas, *Bellow,* 2000; *Small Planets, Saul Bellow and the Art of Short Fiction,* ed. G. Bach and G. Cronin, 2000; M. Quayum, *Saul Bellow and American Transcendentalism,* 2004.

TEXT: *Him with His Foot in His Mouth,* 1984.

A SILVER DISH

What do you do about death—in this case, the death of an old father? If you're a modern person, sixty years of age, and a man who's been around, like Woody Selbst, what do you do? Take this matter of mourning, and take it against a contemporary background. How, against a contemporary background, do you mourn an octogenarian father, nearly blind, his heart enlarged, his lungs filling with fluid, who creeps, stumbles, gives off the odors, the moldiness or gassiness, of old men. I *mean!* As Woody put it, be realistic. Think what times these are. The papers daily give it to you—the Lufthansa pilot in Aden[1] is described by the hostages on his knees, begging the Palestinian terrorists not to execute him, but they shoot him through the head. Later they themselves are killed. And still others shoot others, or shoot themselves. That's what you read in the press, see on the tube, mention at dinner. We know now what goes daily through the whole of the human community, like a global death-peristalsis.

Woody, a businessman in South Chicago, was not an ignorant person. He knew more such phrases than you would expect a tile contractor (offices, lobbies, lavatories) to know. The kind of knowledge he had was not the kind for which you get academic degrees. Although Woody had studied for two years in a seminary, preparing to be a minister. Two years of college during the Depression was more than most high-school graduates could afford. After that, in his own vital, picturesque, original way (Morris, his old man, was also, in his days of nature, vital and picturesque), Woody had read up on many subjects, subscribed to *Science* and other magazines that gave real information, and had taken night courses at De Paul and Northwestern in

[1]In October 1977, a Lufthansa airliner was hijacked by terrorists and flown to Aden, South Yemen, where the pilot was murdered. German commandos then stormed the airliner, killed the terrorists, and freed the passenger hostages.

ecology, criminology, existentialism. Also he had traveled extensively in Japan, Mexico, and Africa, and there was an African experience that was especially relevant to mourning. It was this: on a launch near the Murchison Falls in Uganda,[2] he had seen a buffalo calf seized by a crocodile from the bank of the White Nile.[3] There were giraffes along the tropical river, and hippopotamuses, and baboons, and flamingos and other brilliant birds crossing the bright air in the heat of the morning, when the calf, stepping into the river to drink, was grabbed by the hoof and dragged down. The parent buffaloes couldn't figure it out. Under the water the calf still threshed, fought, churned the mud. Woody, the robust traveler, took this in as he sailed by, and to him it looked as if the parent cattle were asking each other dumbly what had happened. He chose to assume that there was pain in this, he read brute grief into it. On the White Nile, Woody had the impression that he had gone back to the pre-Adamite past, and he brought reflections on this impression home to South Chicago. He brought also a bundle of hashish from Kampala.[4] In this he took a chance with the customs inspectors, banking perhaps on his broad build, frank face, high color. He didn't look like a wrongdoer, a bad guy; he looked like a good guy. But he liked taking chances. Risk was a wonderful stimulus. He threw down his trenchcoat on the customs counter. If the inspectors searched the pockets, he was prepared to say that the coat wasn't his. But he got away with it, and the Thanksgiving turkey was stuffed with hashish. This was much enjoyed. That was practically the last feast at which Pop, who also relished risk or defiance, was present. The hashish Woody had tried to raise in his backyard from the Africa seeds didn't take. But behind his warehouse, where the Lincoln Continental was parked, he kept a patch of marijuana. There was no harm at all in Woody, but he didn't like being entirely within the law. It was simply a question of self-respect.

After that Thanksgiving, Pop gradually sank as if he had a slow leak. This went on for some years. In and out of the hospital, he dwindled, his mind wandered, he couldn't even concentrate enough to complain, except in exceptional moments on the Sundays Woody regularly devoted to him. Morris, an amateur who once was taken seriously by Willie Hoppe, the great pro himself, couldn't execute the simplest billiard shots anymore. He could only conceive shots; he began to theorize about impossible three-cushion combinations. Halina, the Polish woman with whom Morris had lived for over forty years as man and wife, was too old herself now to run to the hospital. So Woody had to do it. There was Woody's mother, too—a Christian convert—needing care; she was over eighty and frequently hospitalized. Everybody had diabetes and pleurisy and arthritis and cataracts and cardiac pacemakers. And everybody had lived by the body, but the body was giving out.

There was Woody's two sisters as well, unmarried, in their fifties, very Christian, very straight, still living with Mama in an entirely Christian bungalow. Woody, who took full responsibility for them all, occasionally had to put one of the girls (they had become sick girls) in a mental institution. Nothing severe. The sisters were wonderful women, both of them gorgeous once, but neither of the poor things was playing with a full deck. And all the factions had to be kept separate—Mama, the Christian convert; the fundamentalist sisters; Pop, who read the Yiddish paper as long as he could still see print;

[2]Nation in east central Africa.

[3]A chief—and remote—tributary of the Nile River in Africa. [4]Capital city of Uganda.

Halina, a good Catholic. Woody, the seminary forty years behind him, described himself as an agnostic. Pop had no more religion than you could find in the Yiddish paper, but he made Woody promise to bury him among Jews, and that was where he lay now, in the Hawaiian shirt Woody had bought for him at the tilers' convention in Honolulu. Woody would allow no undertaker's assistant to dress him, but came to the parlor and buttoned the stiff into the shirt himself, and the old man went down looking like Ben-Gurion[5] in a simple wooden coffin, sure to rot fast. That was how Woody wanted it all. At the graveside, he had taken off and folded his jacket, rolled up his sleeves on thick freckled biceps, waved back the little tractor standing by, and shoveled the dirt himself. His big face, broad at the bottom, narrowed upward like a Dutch house. And, his small good lower teeth taking hold of the upper lip in his exertion, he performed the final duty of a son. He was very fit, so it must have been emotion, not the shoveling, that made him redden so. After the funeral, he went home with Halina and her son, a decent Polack like his mother, and talented, too—Mitosh played the organ at hockey and basketball games in the Stadium,[6] which took a smart man because it was a rabble-rousing kind of occupation—and they had some drinks and comforted the old girl. Halina was true blue, always one hundred percent for Morris.

Then for the rest of the week Woody was busy, had jobs to run, office responsibilities, family responsibilities. He lived alone; as did his wife; as did his mistress: everybody in a separate establishment. Since his wife, after fifteen years of separation, had not learned to take care of herself, Woody did her shopping on Fridays, filled her freezer. He had to take her this week to buy shoes. Also, Friday night he always spent with Helen—Helen was his wife de facto. Saturday he did his big weekly shopping. Saturday night he devoted to Mom and his sisters. So he was too busy to attend to his own feelings except, intermittently, to note to himself, "First Thursday in the grave." "First Friday, and fine weather." "First Saturday; he's got to be getting used to it." Under his breath he occasionally said, "Oh, Pop."

But it was Sunday that hit him, when the bells rang all over South Chicago—the Ukrainian, Roman Catholic, Greek, Russian, African Methodist churches, sounding off one after another. Woody had his offices in his warehouse, and there had built an apartment for himself, very spacious and convenient, in the top story. Because he left every Sunday morning at seven to spend the day with Pop, he had forgotten by how many churches Selbst Tile Company was surrounded. He was still in bed when he heard the bells, and all at once he knew how heartbroken he was. This sudden big heartache in a man of sixty, a practical, healthy-minded, and experienced man, was deeply unpleasant. When he had an unpleasant condition, he believed in taking something for it. So he thought: What shall I take? There was plenty of remedies available. His cellar was stocked with cases of Scotch whisky, Polish vodka, Armagnac, Moselle, Burgundy. There were also freezers with steaks and with game and with Alaskan King crab. He bought with a broad hand—by the crate and by the dozen. But in the end, when he got out of bed, he took nothing but a cup of coffee. While the kettle was heating, he put on his Japanese judo-style suit and sat down to reflect.

[5]David Ben-Gurion (1886–1973), Zionist leader and Israel's first prime minister.
[6]Chicago sports arena.

Woody was moved when things were *honest*. Bearing beams were honest, undisguised concrete pillars inside high-rise apartments were honest. It was bad to cover up anything. He hated faking. Stone was honest. Metal was honest. These Sunday bells were very straight. They broke loose, they wagged and rocked, and the vibrations and the banging did something for him—cleansed his insides, purified his blood. A bell was a one-way throat, had only one thing to tell you and simply told it. He listened.

He had had some connections with bells and churches. He was after all something of a Christian. Born a Jew, he was a Jew facially, with a hint of Iroquois or Cherokee, but his mother had been converted more than fifty years ago by her brother-in-law, the Reverend Doctor Kovner. Kovner, a rabbinical student who had left the Hebrew Union College in Cincinnati to become a minister and establish a mission, had given Woody a partly Christian upbringing. Now, Pop was on the outs with these fundamentalists. He said that the Jews came to the mission to get coffee, bacon, canned pineapple, day-old bread, and dairy products. And if they had to listen to sermons, that was okay—this was the Depression[7] and you couldn't be too particular—but he knew they sold the bacon.

The Gospels said it plainly: "Salvation is from the Jews."

Backing the Reverend Doctor were wealthy fundamentalists, mainly Swedes, eager to speed up the Second Coming by converting all Jews. The foremost of Kovner's backers was Mrs. Skoglund, who had inherited a large dairy business from her late husband. Woody was under her special protection.

Woody was fourteen years of age when Pop took off with Halina, who worked in his shop, leaving his difficult Christian wife and his converted son and his small daughters. He came to Woody in the backyard one spring day and said, "From now on you're the man of the house." Woody was practicing with a golf club, knocking off the heads of dandelions. Pop came into the yard in his good suit, which was too hot for the weather, and when he took off his fedora[8] the skin of his head was marked with a deep ring and the sweat was sprinkled over his scalp—more drops than hairs. He said, "I'm going to move out." Pop was anxious, but he was set to go—determined. "It's no use. I can't live a life like this." Envisioning the life Pop simply *had* to live, his free life, Woody was able to picture him in the billiard parlor, under the El tracks in a crap game, or playing poker at Brown and Koppel's upstairs. "You're going to be the man of the house," said Pop. "It's okay. I put you all on welfare. I just got back from Wabansia Avenue, from the relief station." Hence the suit and the hat. "They're sending out a caseworker." Then he said, "You got to lend me money to buy gasoline—the caddie money you saved."

Understanding that Pop couldn't get away without his help, Woody turned over to him all he had earned at the Sunset Ridge Club in Winnetka.[9] Pop felt that the valuable life lesson he was transmitting was worth far more than these dollars, and whenever he was conning his boy a sort of high-priest expression came down over his bent nose, his ruddy face. The children, who got their finest ideas at the movies, called him Richard Dix.[10] Later, when the comic strip came out, they said he was Dick Tracy.

[7]The Great Depression of the 1930s in the United States.

[8]A man's felt hat with the crown creased lengthwise.

[9]Upper-middle-class suburb north of Chicago, as is Evanston, mentioned later in the story.

[10]American movie actor (1894–1949) of the 1920s and 1930s, famous for his heroic roles in movie westerns.

As Woody now saw it, under the tumbling bells, he had bankrolled his own desertion. Ha ha! He found this delightful; and especially Pop's attitude of "That'll teach you to trust your father." For this was a demonstration on behalf of real life and free instincts, against religion and hypocrisy. But mainly it was aimed against being a fool, the disgrace of foolishness. Pop had it in for the Reverend Doctor Kovner, not because he was an apostate (Pop couldn't have cared less), not because the mission was a racket (he admitted that the Reverend Doctor was personally honest), but because Doctor Kovner behaved foolishly, spoke like a fool, and acted like a fiddler. He tossed his hair like a Paganini[11] (this was Woody's addition; Pop had never even heard of Paganini). Proof that he was not a spiritual leader was that he converted Jewish women by stealing their hearts. "He works up all those broads," said Pop. "He doesn't even know it himself, I swear he doesn't know how he gets them."

From the other side, Kovner often warned Woody, "Your father is a dangerous person. Of course, you love him; you should love him and forgive him, Voodrow, but you are old enough to understand he is leading a life of wice."

It was all petty stuff: Pop's sinning was on a boy level and therefore made a big impression on a boy. And on Mother. Are wives children, or what? Mother often said, "I hope you put that brute in your prayers. Look what he has done to us. But only pray for him, don't see him." But he saw him all the time. Woodrow was leading a double life, sacred and profane. He accepted Jesus Christ as his personal redeemer. Aunt Rebecca took advantage of this. She made him work. He had to work under Aunt Rebecca. He filled in for the janitor at the mission and settlement house.[12] In winter, he had to feed the coal furnace, and on some nights he slept near the furnace room, on the pool table. He also picked the lock of the storeroom. He took canned pineapple and cut bacon from the flitch[13] with his pocketknife. He crammed himself with uncooked bacon. He had a big frame to fill out.

Only now, sipping Melitta coffee, he asked himself: Had he been so hungry? No, he loved being reckless. He was fighting Aunt Rebecca Kovner when he took out his knife and got on a box to reach the bacon. She didn't know, she couldn't prove that Woody, such a frank, strong, positive boy, who looked you in the eye, so direct, was a thief also. But he was also a thief. Whenever she looked at him, he knew that she was seeing his father. In the curve of his nose, the movements of his eyes, the thickness of his body, in his healthy face, she saw that wicked savage Morris.

Morris, you see, had been a street boy in Liverpool—Woody's mother and her sister were British by birth. Morris's Polish family, on their way to America, abandoned him in Liverpool because he had an eye infection and they would all have been sent back from Ellis Island.[14] They stopped awhile in England, but his eyes kept running and they ditched him. They slipped away, and he had to make out alone in Liverpool at the age of twelve. Mother came

[11]Niccolò Paganini (1782–1840), Italian violin virtuoso whose performances were marked by his dramatic gestures.

[12]An institution established to provide community service to the poor and newly arrived immigrants.

[13]A slab or side of meat.

[14]Now a national monument in New York Bay, Ellis Island was, from 1892 to 1943, the main immigration center for immigrants entering the United States.

of better people. Pop, who slept in the cellar of her house, fell in love with her. At sixteen, scabbing during a seamen's strike, he shoveled his way[15] across the Atlantic and jumped ship in Brooklyn. He became an American, and America never knew it. He voted without papers, he drove without a license, he paid no taxes, he cut every corner. Horses, cards, billiards, and women were his lifelong interests, in ascending order. Did he love anyone (he was so busy)? Yes, he loved Halina. He loved his son. To this day, Mother believed that he had loved her most and always wanted to come back. This gave her a chance to act the queen, with her plump wrists and faded Queen Victoria face. "The girls are instructed never to admit him," she said. The Empress of India speaking.

Bell-battered Woodrow's soul was whirling this Sunday morning, indoors and out, to the past, back to this upper corner of the warehouse, laid out with such originality—the bells coming and going, metal on naked metal, until the bell circle expanded over the whole of steel-making, oil-refining, power-producing mid-autumn South Chicago, and all its Croatians, Ukrainians, Greeks, Poles, and respectable blacks heading for their churches to hear Mass or to sing hymns.

Woody himself had been a good hymn singer. He still knew the hymns. He had testified, too. He was often sent by Aunt Rebecca to get up and tell a churchful of Scandihoovians that he, a Jewish lad, accepted Jesus Christ. For this she paid him fifty cents. She made the disbursement. She was the bookkeeper, fiscal chief, general manager of the mission. The Reverend Doctor didn't know a thing about the operation. What the Doctor supplied was the fervor. He was genuine, a wonderful preacher. And what about Woody himself? He also had fervor. He was drawn to the Reverend Doctor. The Reverend Doctor taught him to lift up his eyes, gave him his higher life. Apart from this higher life, the rest was Chicago—the ways of Chicago, which came so natural that nobody thought to question them. So, for instance, in 1933 (what ancient, ancient times!), at the Century of Progress World's Fair, when Woody was a coolie and pulled a rickshaw, wearing a peaked straw hat and trotting with powerful, thick legs, while the brawny red farmers—his boozing passengers—were laughing their heads off and pestered him for whores, he, although a freshman at the seminary, saw nothing wrong, when girls asked him to steer a little business their way, in making dates and accepting tips from both sides. He necked in Grant Park with a powerful girl who had to go home quickly to nurse her baby. Smelling of milk, she rode beside him on the streetcar to the West Side, squeezing his rickshaw puller's thigh and wetting her blouse. This was the Roosevelt Road car. Then, in the apartment where she lived with her mother, he couldn't remember that there were any husbands around. What he did remember was the strong milk odor. Without inconsistency, next morning he did New Testament Greek: The light shineth in darkness—*to fos en te skotia fainei*—and the darkness comprehended it not.

And all the while he trotted between the shafts on the fairgrounds he had one idea, nothing to do with these horny giants having a big time in the city: that the goal, the project, the purpose was (and he couldn't explain why he thought so; all evidence was against it)—God's idea was that this world

[15]I.e., worked his way as a coal stoker on a transatlantic steamship.

should be a love world, that it should eventually recover and be entirely a world of love. He wouldn't have said this to a soul, for he could see himself how stupid it was—personal and stupid. Nevertheless, there it was at the center of his feelings. And at the same time, Aunt Rebecca was right when she said to him, strictly private, close to his ear even, "You're a little crook, like your father."

There was some evidence for this, or what stood for evidence to an impatient person like Rebecca. Woody matured quickly—he had to—but how could you expect a boy of seventeen, he wondered, to interpret the viewpoint, the feelings, of a middle-aged woman, and one whose breast had been removed? Morris said that if titties were not fondled and kissed, they got cancer in protest. It was a cry of the flesh. And this had seemed true to Woody. When his imagination tried the theory on the Reverend Doctor, it worked out—he couldn't see the Reverend Doctor behaving in that way to Aunt Rebecca's breasts! Morris's theory kept Woody looking from bosoms to husbands and from husbands to bosoms. He still did that. It's an exceptionally smart man who isn't marked forever by the sexual theories he hears from his father, and Woody wasn't all that smart. He knew this himself. Personally, he had gone far out of his way to do right by women in this regard. What nature demanded. He and Pop were common, thick men, but there's nobody too gross to have ideas of delicacy.

The Reverend Doctor preached, Rebecca preached, rich Mrs. Skoglund preached from Evanston, Mother preached. Pop also was on a soapbox. Everyone was doing it. Up and down Division Street, under every lamp, almost, speakers were giving out: anarchists, Socialists, Stalinists, single-taxers,[16] Zionists, Tolstoyans, vegetarians, and fundamentalist Christian preachers—you name it. A beef, a hope, a way of life or salvation, a protest. How was it that the accumulated gripes of all the ages took off so when transplanted to America?

And that fine Swedish immigrant Aase (Osie, they pronounced it), who had been the Skoglunds' cook and married the eldest son, to become his rich, religious widow—she supported the Reverend Doctor. In her time she must have been built like a chorus girl. And women seem to have lost the secret of putting up their hair in the high basketry fence of braid she wore. Aase took Woody under her special protection and paid his tuition at the seminary. And Pop said . . . But on this Sunday, at peace as soon as the bells stopped banging, this velvet autumn day when the grass was finest and thickest, silky green: before the first frost, and the blood in your lungs is redder than summer air can make it and smarts with oxygen, as if the iron in your system was hungry for it, and the chill was sticking it to you in every breath . . . Pop, six feet under, would never feel this blissful sting again. The last of the bells still had the bright air streaming with vibrations.

On weekends, the institutional vacancy of decades came back to the warehouse and crept under the door of Woody's apartment. It felt as empty on Sundays as churches were during the week. Before each business day, before the trucks and the crews got started, Woody jogged five miles in his Adidas suit. Not on this day still reserved for Pop, however. Although it was tempting to go out and run off the grief. Being alone hit Woody hard this morning. He

[16]Radical reformers who seek to replace all taxes with a single tax levied on land holdings.

thought: Me and the world; the world and me. Meaning that there always was some activity to interpose, an errand or a visit, a picture to paint (he was a creative amateur), a massage, a meal—a shield between himself and that troublesome solitude which used the world as its reservoir. But Pop! Last Tuesday, Woody had gotten into the hospital bed with Pop because he kept pulling out the intravenous needles. Nurses stuck them back, and then Woody astonished them all by climbing into bed to hold the struggling old guy in his arms. "Easy, Morris, Morris, go easy." But Pop still groped feebly for the pipes.

When the tolling stopped, Woody didn't notice that a great lake of quiet had come over his kingdom, the Selbst Tile warehouse. What he heard and saw was an old red Chicago streetcar, one of those trams the color of a stockyard steer. Cars of this type went out before Pearl Harbor—clumsy, big-bellied, with tough rattan seats and brass grips for the standing passengers. Those cars used to make four stops to the mile, and ran with a wallowing motion. They stank of carbolic or ozone and throbbed when the air compressors were being charged. The conductor had his knotted signal cord to pull, and the motorman beat the foot gong with his mad heel.

Woody recognized himself on the Western Avenue line and riding through a blizzard with his father, both in sheepskins and with hands and faces raw, the snow blowing in from the rear platform when the doors opened and getting into the longitudinal cleats of the floor. There wasn't warmth enough inside to melt it. And Western Avenue was the longest car line in the world, the boosters said, as if it was a thing to brag about. Twenty-three miles long, made by a draftsman with a T square, lined with factories, storage buildings, machine shops, used-car lots, trolley barns, gas stations, funeral parlors, six-flats, utility buildings, and junkyards, on and on from the prairies on the south to Evanston on the north. Woodrow and his father were going north to Evanston, to Howard Street, and then some, to see Mrs. Skoglund. At the end of the line they would still have about five blocks to hike. The purpose of the trip? To raise money for Pop. Pop had talked him into this. When they found out, Mother and Aunt Rebecca would be furious, and Woody was afraid, but he couldn't help it.

Morris had come and said, "Son, I'm in trouble. It's bad."

"What's bad, Pop?"

"Halina took money from her husband for me and has to put it back before old Bujak misses it. He could kill her."

"What did she do it for?"

"Son, you know how the bookies collect? They send a goon. They'll break my head open."

"Pop! You know I can't take you to Mrs. Skoglund."

"Why not? You're my kid, aren't you? The old broad wants to adopt you, doesn't she? Shouldn't I get something out of it for my trouble? What am I—outside? And what about Halina? She puts her life on the line, but my own kid says no."

"Oh, Bujak wouldn't hurt her."

"Woody, he'd beat her to death."

Bujak? Uniform in color with his dark-gray work clothes, short in the legs, his whole strength in his tool-and-die-maker's forearms and black fingers;

and beat-looking—there was Bujak for you. But, according to Pop, there was big, big violence in Bujak, a regular boiling Bessemer[17] inside his narrow chest. Woody could never see the violence in him. Bujak wanted no trouble. If anything, maybe he was afraid that Morris and Halina would gang up on him and kill him, screaming. But Pop was no desperado murderer. And Halina was a calm, serious woman. Bujak kept his savings in the cellar (banks were going out of business). The worst they did was to take some of his money, intending to put it back. As Woody saw him, Bujak was trying to be sensible. He accepted his sorrow. He set minimum requirements for Halina: cook the meals, clean the house, show respect. But at stealing Bujak might have drawn the line, for money was different, money was vital substance. If they stole his savings he might have had to take action, out of respect for the substance, for himself—self-respect. But you couldn't be sure that Pop hadn't invented the bookie, the goon, the theft—the whole thing. He was capable of it, and you'd be a fool not to suspect him. Morris knew that Mother and Aunt Rebecca had told Mrs. Skoglund how wicked he was. They had painted him for her in poster colors—purple for vice, black for his soul, red for Hell flames: a gambler, smoker, drinker, deserter, screwer of women, and atheist. So Pop was determined to reach her. It was risky for everybody. The Reverend Doctor's operating costs were met by Skoglund Dairies. The widow paid Woody's seminary tuition; she bought dresses for the little sisters.

Woody, now sixty, fleshy and big, like a figure for the victory of American materialism, sunk in his lounge chair, the leather of its armrests softer to his fingertips than a woman's skin, was puzzled and, in his depths, disturbed by certain blots within him, blots of light in his brain, a blot combining pain and amusement in his breast (how did *that* get there?). Intense thought puckered the skin between his eyes with a strain bordering on headache. Why had he let Pop have his way? Why did he agree to meet him that day, in the dim rear of the poolroom?

"But what will you tell Mrs. Skoglund?"

"The old broad? Don't worry, there's plenty to tell her, and it's all true. Ain't I trying to save my little laundry-and-cleaning shop? Isn't that bailiff coming for the fixtures next week?" And Pop rehearsed his pitch on the Western Avenue car. He counted on Woody's health and his freshness. Such a straightforward-looking body was perfect for a con.

Did they still have such winter storms in Chicago as they used to have? Now they somehow seemed less fierce. Blizzards used to come straight down from Ontario, from the Arctic, and drop five feet of snow in an afternoon. Then the rusty green platform cars, with revolving brushes at both ends, came out of the barns to sweep the tracks. Ten or twelve streetcars followed in slow processions, or waited, block after block.

There was a long delay at the gates of Riverview Park, all the amusements covered for the winter, boarded up—the dragon's-back high-rides, the Bobs, the Chute, the Tilt-a-Whirl, all the fun machinery put together by mechanics and electricians, men like Bujak the tool-and-die maker, good with engines. The blizzard was having it all its own way behind the gates, and you couldn't see far inside; only a few bulbs burned behind the palings. When Woody

[17]Large container in which iron ore is heated. When oxygen is pumped through the molten iron, steel is produced, with a shower of sparks and a blast of heat.

wiped the vapor from the glass, the wire mesh of the window guards was stuffed solid at eye level with snow. Looking higher, you saw mostly the streaked wind horizontally driving from the north. In the seat ahead, two black coal heavers, both in leather Lindbergh flying helmets, sat with shovels between their legs, returning from a job. They smelled of sweat, burlap sacking, and coal. Mostly dull with black dust, they also sparkled here and there.

There weren't many riders. People weren't leaving the house. This was a day to sit legs stuck out beside the stove, mummified by both the outdoor and the indoor forces. Only a fellow with an angle, like Pop, would go and buck such weather. A storm like this was out of the compass, and you kept the human scale by having a scheme to raise fifty bucks. Fifty soldiers! Real money in 1933.

"That woman is crazy for you," said Pop.

"She's just a good woman, sweet to all of us."

"Who knows what she's got in mind. You're a husky kid. Not such a kid, either."

"She's a religious woman. She really has religion."

"Well, your mother isn't your only parent. She and Rebecca and Kovner aren't going to fill you up with their ideas. I know your mother wants to wipe me out of your life. Unless I take a hand, you won't even understand what life is. Because they don't know—those silly Christers."

"Yes, Pop."

"The girls I can't help. They're too young. I'm sorry about them, but I can't do anything. With you it's different."

He wanted me like himself, an American.

They were stalled in the storm, while the cattle-colored car waited to have the trolley[18] reset in the crazy wind, which boomed, tingled, blasted. At Howard Street they would have to walk straight into it, due north.

"You'll do the talking at first," said Pop.

Woody had the makings of a salesman, a pitchman. He was aware of this when he got to his feet in church to testify before fifty or sixty people. Even though Aunt Rebecca made it worth his while, he moved his own heart when he spoke up about his faith. But occasionally, without notice, his heart went away as he spoke religion and he couldn't find it anywhere. In its absence, sincere behavior got him through. He had to rely for delivery on his face, his voice—on behavior. Then his eyes came closer and closer together. And in this approach of eye to eye he felt the strain of hypocrisy. The twisting of his face threatened to betray him. It took everything he had to keep looking honest. So, since he couldn't bear the cynicism of it, he fell back on mischievousness. Mischief was where Pop came in. Pop passed straight through all those divided fields, gap after gap, and arrived at his side, bent-nosed and broad-faced. In regard to Pop, you thought of neither sincerity nor insincerity. Pop was like the man in the song: He wanted what he wanted when he wanted it. Pop was physical; Pop was digestive, circulatory, sexual. If Pop got serious, he talked to you about washing under the arms or in the crotch or of

[18]Upward extending arm that conducts electricity from an overhead wire to the electric motors of a streetcar. When the trolley breaks loose from the overhead wire, the conductor must reconnect the trolley before the streetcar can move.

drying between your toes or of cooking supper, of baked beans and fried onions, of draw poker or of a certain horse in the fifth race at Arlington. Pop was elemental. That was why he gave such relief from religion and paradoxes, and things like that. Now, Mother *thought* she was spiritual, but Woody knew that she was kidding herself. Oh, yes, in the British accent she never gave up she was always talking to God or about Him—please God, God willing, praise God. But she was a big substantial bread-and-butter down-to-earth woman, with down-to-earth duties like feeding the girls, protecting, refining, keeping pure the girls. And those two protected doves grew up so overweight, heavy in the hips and thighs, that their poor heads looked long and slim. And mad. Sweet but cuckoo—Paula cheerfully cuckoo, Joanna depressed and having episodes.

"I'll do my best by you, but you have to promise, Pop, not to get me in Dutch with Mrs. Skoglund."

"You worried because I speak bad English? Embarrassed? I have a mockie accent?"

"It's not that. Kovner has a heavy accent, and she doesn't mind."

"Who the hell are those freaks to look down on me? You're practically a man and your dad has a right to expect help from you. He's in a fix. And you bring him to her house because she's bighearted, and you haven't got anybody else to go to."

"I got you, Pop."

The two coal trimmers stood up at Devon Avenue. One of them wore a woman's coat. Men wore women's clothing in those years, and women men's when there was no choice. The fur collar was spiky with the wet, and sprinkled with soot. Heavy, they dragged their shovels and got off at the front. The slow car ground on, very slow. It was after four when they reached the end of the line, and somewhere between gray and black, with snow spouting and whirling under the street lamps. In Howard Street, autos were stalled at all angles and abandoned. The sidewalks were blocked. Woody led the way into Evanston, and Pop followed him up the middle of the street in the furrows made earlier by trucks. For four blocks they bucked the wind and then Woody broke through the drifts to the snowbound mansion, where they both had to push the wrought-iron gate because of the drift behind it. Twenty rooms or more in this dignified house and nobody in them but Mrs. Skoglund and her servant Hjordis, also religious.

As Woody and Pop waited, brushing the slush from their sheepskin collars and Pop wiping his big eyebrows with the ends of his scarf, sweating and freezing, the chains began to rattle and Hjordis uncovered the air holes of the glass storm door by turning a wooden bar. Woody called her "monkfaced." You no longer see women like that, who put no female touch on the face. She came plain, as God made her. She said, "Who is it and what do you want?"

"It's Woodrow Selbst. Hjordis? It's Woody."

"You're not expected."

"No, but we're here."

"What do you want?"

"We came to see Mrs. Skoglund."

"What for do you want to see her?"

"Just tell her we're here."

"I have to tell her what you came for, without calling up first."

"Why don't you say it's Woody with his father, and we wouldn't come in a snowstorm like this if it wasn't important."

The understandable caution of women who live alone. Respectable old-time women, too. There was no such respectability now in those Evanston houses, with their big verandas and deep yards and with a servant like Hjordis, who carried at her belt keys to the pantry and to every closet and every dresser and every padlocked bin in the cellar. And in High Episcopal Christian Science Women's Temperance[19] Evanston, no tradespeople rang at the front door. Only invited guests. And here, after a ten-mile grind through the blizzard, came two tramps from the West Side. To this mansion where a Swedish immigrant lady, herself once a cook and now a philanthropic widow, dreamed, snowbound, while frozen lilac twigs clapped at her storm windows, of a new Jerusalem and a Second Coming and a Resurrection and a Last Judgment. To hasten the Second Coming, and all the rest, you had to reach the hearts of these scheming bums arriving in a snowstorm.

Sure, they let us in.

Then in the heat that swam suddenly up to their mufflered chins Pop and Woody felt the blizzard for what it was; their cheeks were frozen slabs. They stood beat, itching, trickling in the front hall that *was* a hall, with a carved newel post staircase and a big stained-glass window at the top. Picturing Jesus with the Samaritan woman. There was a kind of Gentile closeness to the air. Perhaps when he was with Pop, Woody made more Jewish observations than he would otherwise. Although Pop's most Jewish characteristic was that Yiddish was the only language he could read a paper in. Pop was with Polish Halina, and Mother was with Jesus Christ, and Woody ate uncooked bacon from the flitch. Still, now and then he had a Jewish impression.

Mrs. Skoglund was the cleanest of women—her fingernails, her white neck, her ears—and Pop's sexual hints to Woody all went wrong because she was so intensely clean, and made Woody think of a waterfall, large as she was, and grandly built. Her bust was big. Woody's imagination had investigated this. He thought she kept things tied down tight, very tight. But she lifted both arms once to a raise a window and there it was, her bust, beside him, the whole unbindable thing. Her hair was like the raffia you had to soak before you could weave with it in a basket class—pale, pale. Pop, as he took his sheepskin off, was in sweaters, no jacket. His darting looks made him seem crooked. Hardest of all for these Selbsts with their bent noses and big, apparently straightforward faces was to look honest. All the signs of dishonesty played over them. Woody had often puzzled about it. Did it go back to the muscles, was it fundamentally a jaw problem—the projecting angles of the jaws? Or was it the angling that went on in the heart? The girls called Pop Dick Tracy, but Dick Tracy was a good guy. Whom could Pop convince? Here Woody caught a possibility as it flitted by. Precisely because of the way Pop looked, a sensitive person might feel remorse for condemning unfairly or judging unkindly. Just because of a face? Some must have bent over backward. Then he had them. Not Hjordis. She would have put Pop into the street then and there, storm or no storm. Hjordis was religious but she was

[19]Women's Christian Temperance Union, an organization devoted to the prohibition of alcoholic beverages. Its headquarters is in Evanston, Illinois.

wised up, too. She hadn't come over in steerage and worked forty years in Chicago for nothing.

Mrs. Skoglund, Aase (Osie), led the visitors into the front room. This, the biggest room in the house, needed supplementary heating. Because of fifteen-foot ceilings and high windows, Hjordis had kept the parlor stove burning. It was one of those elegant parlor stoves that wore a nickel crown, or miter, and this miter, when you moved it aside, automatically raised the hinge of an iron stove lid. Into this hole you tipped the scuttle and the anthracite chestnut rattled down. It made a cake or dome of fire visible through the small isinglass frames. It was a pretty room, three-quarters paneled in wood. The stove was plugged into the flue of the marble fireplace, and there were parquet floors and Axminster carpets and cranberry colored tufted Victorian upholstery, and a kind of Chinese étagère,[20] inside a cabinet, lined with mirrors and containing silver pitchers, trophies won by Skoglund cows, fancy sugar tongs and cut-glass pitchers and goblets. There were Bibles and pictures of Jesus and the Holy Land and that faint Gentile odor, as if things had been rinsed in a weak vinegar solution.

"Mrs. Skoglund, I brought my dad to you. I don't think you ever met him," said Woody.

"Yes, Missus, that's me, Selbst."

Pop stood short but masterful in the sweaters, and his belly sticking out, not soft but hard. He was a man of the hard-bellied type. Nobody intimidated Pop. He never presented himself as a beggar. There wasn't a cringe in him anywhere. He let her see at once by the way he said "Missus" that he was independent and that he knew his way around. He communicated that he was able to handle himself with women. Handsome Mrs. Skoglund, carrying a basket woven out of her own hair, was in her fifties—eight, maybe ten years his senior.

"I asked my son to bring me because I know you do the kid a lot of good. It's natural you should know both his parents."

"Mrs. Skoglund, my dad is in a tight corner and I don't know anybody else to ask for help."

This was all the preliminary Pop wanted. He took over and told the widow his story about the laundry-and-cleaning business and payments overdue, and explained about the fixtures and attachment notice, and the bailiff's office and what they were going to do to him; and he said, "I'm a small man trying to make a living."

"You don't support your children," said Mrs. Skoglund.

"That's right," said Hjordis.

"I haven't got it. If I had it, wouldn't I give it? There's bread lines and soup lines all over town. Is it just me? What I have I divvy with. I give the kids. A bad father? You think my son would bring me if I was a bad father into your house? He loves his dad, he trusts his dad, he knows his dad is a good dad. Every time I start a little business going I get wiped out. This one is a good little business, if I could hold on to that little business. Three people work for me, I meet a payroll, and three people will be on the street, too, if I close

[20]A cabinet that holds a tier of shelves.

down. Missus, I can sign a note and pay you in two months. I'm a common man, but I'm a hard worker and a fellow you can trust."

Woody was startled when Pop used the word "trust." It was as if from all four corners a Sousa band[21] blew a blast to warn the entire world: "Crook! This is a crook!" But Mrs. Skoglund, on account of her religious preoccupations, was remote. She heard nothing. Although everybody in this part of the world, unless he was crazy, led a practical life, and you'd have nothing to say to anyone, your neighbors would have nothing to say to you, if communications were not of a practical sort, Mrs. Skoglund, with all her money, was unworldly—two-thirds out of this world.

"Give me a chance to show what's in me," said Pop, "and you'll see what I do for my kids."

So Mrs. Skoglund hesitated, and then she said she'd have to go upstairs, she'd have to go to her room and pray on it and ask for guidance—would they sit down and wait. There were two rocking chairs by the stove. Hjordis gave Pop a grim look (a dangerous person) and Woody a blaming one (he brought a dangerous stranger and disrupter to injure two kind Christian ladies). Then she went out with Mrs. Skoglund.

As soon as they left, Pop jumped up from the rocker and said in anger, "What's this with the praying? She has to ask God to lend me fifty bucks?"

Woody said, "It's not you, Pop, it's the way these religious people do."

"No," said Pop. "She'll come back and say that God wouldn't let her."

Woody didn't like that; he thought Pop was being gross and he said, "No, she's sincere. Pop, try to understand: she's emotional, nervous, and sincere, and tries to do right by everybody."

And Pop said, "That servant will talk her out of it. She's a toughie. It's all over her face that we're a couple of chiselers."

"What's the use of us arguing," said Woody. He drew the rocker closer to the stove. His shoes were wet through and would never dry. The blue flames fluttered like a school of fishes in the coal fire. But Pop went over to the Chinese-style cabinet or étagère and tried the handle, and then opened the blade of his penknife and in a second had forced the lock of the curved glass door. He took out a silver dish.

"Pop, what is this?" said Woody.

Pop, cool and level, knew exactly what this was. He relocked the étagère, crossed the carpet, listened. He stuffed the dish under his belt and pushed it down into his trousers. He put the side of his short thick finger to his mouth.

So Woody kept his voice down, but he was all shook up. He went to Pop and took him by the edge of his hand. As he looked into Pop's face, he felt his eyes growing smaller and smaller, as if something were contracting all the skin on his head. They call it hyperventilation when everything feels tight and light and close and dizzy. Hardly breathing, he said, "Put it back, Pop."

Pop said, "It's solid silver; it's worth dough."

"Pop, you said you wouldn't get me in Dutch."

"It's only insurance in case she comes back from praying and tells me no. If she says yes, I'll put it back."

[21]A band led by "The March King," John Philip Sousa (1854–1932), renowned for playing loud, military march music.

"How?"

"It'll get back. If I don't put it back, you will."

"You picked the lock. I couldn't. I don't know how."

"There's nothing to it."

"We're going to put it back now. Give it here."

"Woody, it's under my fly, inside my underpants. Don't make such a noise about nothing."

"Pop, I can't believe this."

"For cry-ninety-nine, shut your mouth. If I didn't trust you I wouldn't have let you watch me do it. You don't understand such a thing. What's with you?"

"Before they come down, Pop, will you dig that dish out of your long johns."

Pop turned stiff on him. He became absolutely military. He said, "Look, I order you!"

Before he knew it, Woody had jumped his father and begun to wrestle with him. It was outrageous to clutch your own father, to put a heel behind him, to force him to the wall. Pop was taken by surprise and said loudly, "You want Halina killed? Kill her! Go on, you be responsible." He began to resist, angry, and they turned about several times, when Woody, with a trick he had learned in a Western movie and used once on the playground, tripped him and they fell to the ground. Woody, who already outweighed the old man by twenty pounds, was on top. They landed on the floor beside the stove, which stood on a tray of decorated tin to protect the carpet. In this position, pressing Pop's hard belly, Woody recognized that to have wrestled him to the floor counted for nothing. It was impossible to thrust his hand under Pop's belt to recover the dish. And now Pop had turned furious, as a father has every right to be when his son is violent with him, and he freed his hand and hit Woody in the face. He hit him three or four times in midface. Then Woody dug his head into Pop's shoulder and held tight only to keep from being struck and began to say in his ear, "Jesus, Pop for Christ sake remember where you are. Those women will be back!" But Pop brought up his short knee and fought and butted him with his chin and rattled Woody's teeth. Woody thought the old man was about to bite him. And because he was a seminarian, he thought: Like an unclean spirit. And held tight. Gradually Pop stopped threshing and struggling. His eyes stuck out and his mouth was open, sullen. Like a stout fish. Woody released him and gave him a hand up. He was then overcome with many many bad feelings of a sort he knew the old man never suffered. Never, never. Pop never had these groveling emotions. There was his whole superiority. Pop had no such feelings. He was like a horseman from Central Asia, a bandit from China. It was Mother, from Liverpool, who had the refinement, the English manners. It was the preaching Reverend Doctor in his black suit. You have refinement, and all they do is oppress you? The hell with that.

The long door opened and Mrs. Skoglund stepped in, saying "Did I imagine, or did something shake the house?"

"I was lifting the scuttle to put coal on the fire and it fell out of my hand. I'm sorry I was so clumsy," said Woody.

Pop was too huffy to speak. With his eyes big and sore and the thin hair down over his forehead, you could see by the tightness of his belly how angrily he was fetching his breath, though his mouth was shut.

"I prayed," said Mrs. Skoglund.

"I hope it came out well," said Woody.

"Well, I don't do anything without guidance, but the answer was yes, and I feel right about it now. So if you'll wait, I'll go to my office and write a check. I asked Hjordis to bring you a cup of coffee. Coming in such a storm."

And Pop, consistently a terrible little man, as soon as she shut the door, said, "A check? Hell with a check. Get me the greenbacks."

"They don't keep money in the house. You can cash it in her bank tomorrow. But if they miss that dish, Pop, they'll stop the check, and then where are you?"

As Pop was reaching below the belt, Hjordis brought in the tray. She was very sharp with him. She said, "Is this a place to adjust clothing, Mister? A men's washroom?"

"Well, which way is the toilet, then?" said Pop.

She had served the coffee in the seamiest mugs in the pantry, and she bumped down the tray and led Pop down the corridor, standing guard at the bathroom door so that he shouldn't wander about the house.

Mrs. Skoglund called Woody to her office and after she had given him the folded check said that they should pray together for Morris. So once more he was on his knees, under rows and rows of musty marbled-cardboard files, by the glass lamp by the edge of the desk, the shade with flounced edges, like the candy dish. Mrs. Skoglund, in her Scandinavian accent—an emotional contralto—raising her voice to Jesus-uh Christ-uh, as the wind lashed the trees, kicked the side of the house, and drove the snow seething on the windowpanes, to send light-uh, give guidance-uh, put a new heart-uh in Pop's bosom. Woody asked God only to make Pop put the dish back. He kept Mrs. Skoglund on her knees as long as possible. Then he thanked her, shining with candor (as much as knew how), for her Christian generosity and he said, "I know that Hjordis has a cousin who works at the Evanston YMCA. Could she please phone him and try to get us a room tonight so that we don't have to fight the blizzard all the way back? We're almost as close to the Y as to the car line. Maybe the cars have even stopped running."

Suspicious Hjordis, coming when Mrs. Skoglund called to her, was burning now. First they barged in, made themselves at home, asked for money, had to have coffee, probably left gonorrhea on the toilet seat. Hjordis, Woody remembered, was a woman who wiped the doorknobs with rubbing alcohol after guests had left. Nevertheless, she telephoned the Y and got them a room with two cots for six bits.

Pop had plenty of time, therefore, to reopen the étagère, lined with reflecting glass or German silver (something exquisitely delicate and tricky), and as soon as the two Selbsts had said thank you and goodbye and were in midstreet again up to the knees in snow, Woody said, "Well, I covered for you. Is that thing back?"

"Of course it is," said Pop.

They fought their way to the small Y building, shut up with wire grille and resembling a police station—about the same dimensions. It was locked, but they made a racket on the grille, and a small black man let them in and shuffled them upstairs to a cement corridor with low doors. It was like the small-mammal house in Lincoln Park.[22] He said there was nothing to eat, so they

[22]Chicago park and site of the city zoo.

took off their wet pants, wrapped themselves tightly in the khaki army blankets, and passed out on their cots.

First thing in the morning, they went to the Evanston National Bank and got the fifty dollars. Not without difficulties. The teller went to call Mrs. Skoglund and was absent a long time from the wicket. "Where the hell has he gone?" said Pop.

But when the fellow came back, he said "How do you want it?"

Pop said, "Singles." He told Woody, "Bujak stashes it in one-dollar bills."

But by now Woody no longer believed Halina had stolen the old man's money.

Then they went into the street, where the snow-removal crews were at work. The sun shone broad, broad, out of the morning blue, and all Chicago would be releasing itself from the temporary beauty of those vast drifts.

"You shouldn't have jumped me last night, Sonny."

"I know, Pop, but you promised you wouldn't get me in Dutch."

"Well, it's okay. We can forget it, seeing you stood by me."

Only, Pop had taken the silver dish. Of course he had, and in a few days Mrs. Skoglund and Hjordis knew it, and later in the week they were all waiting for Woody in Kovner's office at the settlement house. The group included the Reverend Doctor Crabbie, head of the seminary, and Woody, who had been flying along, level and smooth, was shot down in flames. He told them he was innocent. Even as he was falling, he warned that they were wronging him. He denied that he or Pop had touched Mrs. Skoglund's property. The missing object—he didn't even know what it was—had probably been misplaced, and they would be very sorry on the day it turned up. After the others were done with him, Dr. Crabbie said that until he was able to tell the truth he would be suspended from the seminary, where his work had been unsatisfactory anyway. Aunt Rebecca took him aside and said to him, "You are a little crook, like your father. The door is closed to you here."

To this Pop's comment was "So what, kid?"

"Pop, you shouldn't have done it."

"No? Well, I don't give a care, if you want to know. You can have the dish if you want to go back and square yourself with all those hypocrites."

"I didn't like doing Mrs. Skoglund in the eye, she was so kind to us."

"Kind?"

"Kind."

"Kind has a price tag."

Well, there was no winning such arguments with Pop. But they debated it in various moods and from various elevations and perspectives for forty years and more, as their intimacy changed, developed, matured.

"Why did you do it, Pop? For the money? What did you do with the fifty bucks?" Woody, decades later, asked him that.

"I settled with the bookie, and the rest I put in the business."

"You tried a few more horses."

"I maybe did. But it was a double, Woody, I didn't hurt myself, and at the same time did you a favor."

"It was for me?"

"It was too strange of a life. That life wasn't *you*, Woody. All those women . . . Kovner was no man, he was an in-between. Suppose they made you a minister? Some Christian minister! First of all, you wouldn't have been able to stand it, and second, they would throw you out sooner or later."

"Maybe so."

"And you wouldn't have converted the Jews, which was the main thing they wanted."

"And what a time to bother the Jews," Woody said, "At least *I* didn't bug them."

Pop had carried him back to his side of the line, blood of his blood, the same thick body walls, the same coarse grain. Not cut out for a spiritual life. Simply not up to it.

Pop was no worse than Woody, and Woody was no better than Pop. Pop wanted no relation to theory, and yet he was always pointing Woody toward a position—a jolly, hearty, natural, likable, unprincipled position. If Woody had a weakness, it was to be unselfish. This worked to Pop's advantage, but he criticized Woody for it, nevertheless. "You take too much on yourself," Pop was always saying. And it's true that Woody gave Pop his heart because Pop was so selfish. It's usually the selfish people who are loved the most. They do what you deny yourself, and you love them for it. You give them your heart.

Remembering the pawn ticket for the silver dish, Woody startled himself with a laugh so sudden that it made him cough. Pop said to him after his expulsion from the seminary and banishment from the settlement house, "You want in again? Here's the ticket. I hocked that thing. It wasn't so valuable as I thought."

"What did they give?"

"Twelve-fifty was all I could get. But if you want it you'll have to raise the dough yourself, because I haven't got it anymore."

"You must have been sweating in the bank when the teller went to call Mrs. Skoglund about the check."

"I was a little nervous," said Pop. "But I didn't think they could miss the thing so soon."

That theft was part of Pop's war with Mother. With Mother, and Aunt Rebecca, and the Reverend Doctor. Pop took his stand on realism. Mother represented the forces of religion and hypochondria. In four decades, the fighting never stopped. In the course of time, Mother and the girls turned into welfare personalities and lost their individual outlines. Ah, the poor things, they became dependents and cranks. In the meantime, Woody, the sinful man, was their dutiful and loving son and brother. He maintained the bungalow—this took in roofing, painting, wiring, insulation, air-conditioning—and he paid for heat and light and food, and dressed them all out of Sears, Roebuck and Wieboldt's, and bought them a TV, which they watched as devoutly as they prayed. Paula took courses to learn skills like macramé-making and needlepoint, and sometimes got a little job as recreational worker in a nursing home. But she wasn't steady enough to keep it. Wicked Pop spent most of his life removing stains from people's clothing. He and Halina in the last years ran a Cleanomat in West Rogers Park—a so-so business resembling a laundromat—which gave him leisure for billiards, the horses, rummy and pinochle. Every morning he went behind the partition to check out the filters of the cleaning equipment. He found amusing things that had been thrown into the vats with the clothing—sometimes, when he got lucky, a locket chain or a brooch. And when he had fortified the cleaning fluid, pouring all that blue and pink stuff in from plastic jugs, he read the *Forward*[23] over a second cup of coffee, and went out, leaving Halina in charge. When they needed help with the rent, Woody gave it.

After the new Disney World was opened in Florida, Woody treated all his dependents to a holiday. He sent them down in separate batches, of course. Halina enjoyed this more than anybody else. She couldn't stop talking about the address given by an Abraham Lincoln automaton. "Wonderful, how he stood up and moved his hands, and his mouth. So real! And how beautiful he talked." Of them all, Halina was the soundest, the most human, the most honest. Now that Pop was gone, Woody and Halina's son, Mitosh, the organist at the Stadium, took care of her needs over and above Social Security, splitting expenses. In Pop's opinion, insurance was a racket. He left Halina nothing but some out-of-date equipment.

Woody treated himself, too. Once a year, and sometimes oftener, he left his business to run itself, arranged with the trust department at the bank to take care of his gang, and went off. He did that in style, imaginatively, expensively. In Japan, he wasted little time on Tokyo. He spent three weeks in Kyoto and stayed at the Tawaraya Inn, dating from the seventeenth century or so. There he slept on the floor, the Japanese way, and bathed in scalding water. He saw the dirtiest strip show on earth, as well as the holy places and the temple gardens. He visited also Istanbul, Jerusalem, Delphi, and went to Burma and Uganda and Kenya on safari, on democratic terms with drivers, Bedouins, bazaar merchants. Open, lavish, familiar, fleshier and fleshier but (he jogged, he lifted weights) still muscular—in his naked person beginning to resemble a Renaissance courtier in full costume—becoming ruddier every year, an outdoor type with freckles on his back and spots across the flaming forehead and the honest nose. In Addis Ababa he took an Ethiopian beauty to his room from the street and washed her, getting into the shower with her to soap her with his broad, kindly hands. In Kenya he taught certain American obscenities to a black woman so that she could shout them out during the act. On the Nile, below Murchison Falls, those fever trees rose huge from the mud, and hippos on the sandbars belched at the passing launch, hostile. One of them danced on his spit of sand, springing from the ground and coming down heavy, on all fours. There Woody saw the buffalo calf disappear, snatched by the crocodile.

Mother, soon to follow Pop, was being lightheaded these days. In company, she spoke of Woody as her boy— "What do you think of my Sonny?"—as though he was ten years old. She was silly with him, her behavior was frivolous, almost flirtatious. She just didn't seem to know the facts. And behind her all the others, like kids at the playground, were waiting their turn to go down the slide: one on each step, and moving toward the top.

Over Woody's residence and place of business there had gathered a pool of silence of the same perimeter as the church bells while they were ringing, and he mourned under it, this melancholy morning of sun and autumn. Doing a life survey, taking a deliberate look at the gross side of his case—of the

[23] *The Jewish Forward*, a Yiddish-language newspaper.

other side as well, what there was of it. But if this heartache continued, he'd go out and run it off. A three-mile job—five, if necessary. And you'd think that this jogging was an entirely physical activity, wouldn't you? But there was something else in it. Because, when he was a seminarian, between the shafts of his World's Fair rickshaw, he used to receive, pulling along (capable and stable), his religious experiences while he trotted. Maybe it was all a single experience repeated. He felt truth coming to him from the sun. He received a communication that was also light and warmth. It made him very remote from his horny Wisconsin passengers, those farmers whose whoops and whore cries he could hardly hear when he was in one of his states. And again out of the flaming of the sun would come to him a secret certainty that the goal set for this earth was that it should be filled with good, saturated with it. After everything preposterous, after dog had eaten dog, after crocodile death had pulled everyone into his mud. It wouldn't conclude as Mrs. Skoglund, bribing him to round up the Jews and hasten the Second Coming, imagined it, but in another way. This was his clumsy intuition. It went no further. Subsequently, he proceeded through life as life seemed to want him to do it.

There remained one thing more this morning, which was explicitly physical, occurring first as a sensation in his arms and against his breast and, from the pressure, passing into him and going into his breast.

It was like this: When he came into the hospital room and saw Pop with the sides of his bed raised, like a crib, and Pop, so very feeble, and writhing, and toothless, like a baby, and the dirt already cast into his face, into the wrinkles—Pop wanted to pluck out the intravenous needles and he was piping his weak death noise. The gauze patches taped over the needles were soiled with dark blood. Then Woody took off his shoes, lowered the side of the bed, and climbed in and held him in his arms to soothe and still him. As if he were Pop's father, he said to him, "Now, Pop. Pop." Then it was like the wrestle in Mrs. Skoglund's parlor, when Pop turned angry like an unclean spirit and Woody tried to appease him, and warn him, saying, "Those women will be back!" Beside the coal stove, when Pop hit Woody in the teeth with his head and then became sullen, like a stout fish. But this struggle in the hospital was weak—so weak! In his great pity, Woody held Pop, who was fluttering and shivering. From those people, Pop had told him, you'll never find out what life is, because they don't know what it is. Yes, Pop—well, what is it, Pop? Hard to comprehend that Pop, who was dug in for eighty-three years and had done all he could to stay, should now want nothing but to free himself. How could Woody allow the old man to pull the intravenous needles out? Willful Pop, he wanted what he wanted when he wanted it. But what he wanted at the very last Woody failed to follow, it was such a switch.

After a time, Pop's resistance ended. He subsided and subsided. He rested against his son, his small body curled there. Nurses came and looked. They disapproved, but Woody, who couldn't spare a hand to wave them out, motioned with his head toward the door. Pop, whom Woody thought he had stilled, only had found a better way to get around him. Loss of heat was the way he did it. His heat was leaving him. As can happen with small animals while you hold them in your hand, Woody presently felt him cooling. Then, as Woody did his best to restrain him, and thought he was succeeding, Pop divided himself. And when he was separated from his warmth, he slipped into death. And there was his elderly, large, muscular son, still holding and pressing him when there was nothing anymore to press. You could never pin down that self-willed man. When he was ready to make his move, he made it—always on his own terms. And always, always, something up his sleeve. That was how he was.

1978, 1984

Joyce Carol Oates 1938–

Joyce Carol Oates is one of the most prolific of modern American writers. Since the appearance of her first book, By the North Gate *(1963), a collection of short stories, she has published more than one hundred volumes—short stories, novels, poems, plays, and essays. She began telling stories at an early age: "Before I could write," she has said, "I drew pictures to tell my stories." Her first published fiction appeared in* Mademoiselle *magazine in 1959, when she was twenty-one. Since that time her writing has gained wide critical acclaim. She has received awards from the Guggenheim Foundation and the National Institute of Arts and Letters, and her novel* them *(1969) won a National Book Award.*

Oates has said that "all art is autobiographical," but nothing in the outward events of her own life parallels the terror-filled and violent lives that exist in her fiction. She was born in Lockport, New York, and raised in a middle-class family. She attended Syracuse University on a scholarship, and after her graduation in 1960 she received a fellowship at the University of Wisconsin. One year later she graduated with an M.A., and for the next six years she taught literature at the University of Detroit. In 1967 she moved to Canada, where she was a faculty member of the University of Windsor, in Ontario. In recent years she has been teaching at Princeton University.

As a writer Oates is praised not only for her phenomenal productivity and wide-ranging talents, but also for her power to depict the torments and frightening derangements suffered by ordinary people in the modern world. She writes of factory workers, school girls, businessmen, teachers, preachers. They live in a middle-class world centered on their houses, large and small, and on backyard barbecues, shopping centers, drive-in restaurants, automobiles, and television. Outwardly her characters seem commonplace and predictable. Inwardly they are complex, often terrorized by others, by cruel fate, or by their own corrosive fears. Her works often portray frightening violence: murder, suicide, rape, riots, arson, beatings. Her use of sudden horrors and grotesque experiences has been described as "gothic," like tales by Washington Irving, Edgar Allan Poe, and their contemporaries who wrote of graveyards, ancient ruins, and mysterious forces of demonic evil. To Oates, today's "gothic" world is not one of ghosts in ancient ruined castles but of haunted lives in modern ruined cities. To perceive our situation as fundamentally grotesque and "gothic," she has said, is nothing more than to make "a fairly realistic assessment of modern life."

Oates's writing has been compared with that of Flannery O'Connor and William Faulkner, whose characters also confront violence and enigmatic malice, yet Oates has been accused of taking excessive delight in showing only the frightening destinies that await us. For the unrelieved sense of dread that pervades much of her writing, for the gloomy view of life it expresses, she has been called "The Dark Lady of American Letters." But from the brutal eruptions that she describes there often comes an affirmation, a revelation of the world behind—or beneath—the apparent world, a redeeming insight imposed on characters and readers alike by the very nightmarish experiences that she describes.

At a time when modern literature increasingly seems to move toward antirealism, away from depiction of the world of everyday things seen and heard and felt, Joyce Carol Oates continues to write primarily in the realistic tradition, rejecting the fragmentary and surrealistic quality of much avant-garde fiction. At times she does use narrative techniques common to experimental writers, but from her early work to her most recent, the impact of her writing has depended not as much on the mode of storytelling as on her ability to reveal the extraordinary behind the façade of the ordinary and on her compelling vision of urban America as a swirling, nightmarish world of obsessions, neurotic fears, and grotesque brutality.

FURTHER READING: *Joyce Carol Oates,* ed. H. Bloom, 1987; E. Bender, *Artist in Residence, The Phenomenon of Joyce Carol Oates;* 1987; G. Johnson, *Understanding Joyce Carol Oates,* 1987; *Conversations with Joyce Carol Oates,* ed. L. Milazzo, 1989; M. Wesley, *Refusal and Transgression in Joyce Carol Oates' Fiction,* 1993; B. Daly, *Lavish Self-Divisions, The Novels of Joyce Carol Oates,* 1996; M. Loeb, *Literary Marriages, A Study of Intertextuality in a Series of Short Stories by Joyce Carol Oates,* 2001; G. Cologne-Brookes, *Dark Eyes on America, The Novels of Joyce Carol Oates,* 2004.

TEXT: *Heat,* 1991.

THE KNIFE

She was a religious woman, mildly—the aftermath of a rural Methodist upbringing. But that was some time ago and she rarely gave a thought to religion now, or to what's called God. Certainly she wasn't superstitious. If her dreams of the previous night had brought her a premonition of disaster, she didn't recall it and would have discounted it in any case; she was always edgy, though not necessarily unhappy, when her husband was away. She rather liked, she said, spending a day or two alone with her daughter. It was like old times, she said. Meaning a few years ago when Bonnie was a baby.

The night before, Bonnie had showed Harriet a glossy reproduction of a Chagall[1] painting—the one in which a startled woman is being kissed by a floating, sinuous lover, a dream transmuted into colors so audacious you couldn't help smiling as if in recognition—and when Bonnie said with her new skepticism, "Nobody can do *this,* can they!" Harriet said, "Oh, people can do anything, sometimes." The answer was meant to be fanciful: Bonnie was of an age now—eight, nearly nine—when the most subtle intonations and nuances in adults' voices registered with her, like music. Harriet sometimes wondered if she and her husband were training their daughter in the ambiguities of life and not its stark primary colorations.

[1]Marc Chagall (1887–1985) Russian-born artist noted for his dream-like, brilliantly colored expressionist paintings.

That day, a day in late spring, had been unusually warm but by evening the temperature had dropped twenty degrees. A sudden fierce wind was blowing up so Harriet went about closing windows; she was straining to close a window in the rear room—a handsome converted porch, mostly glass, her husband used as his study at home—when she saw a movement, the fleet afterimage of a movement, somewhere behind her, reflected in the glass. And she knew. She knew: the height of the figure, its peculiar swiftness, meant it wasn't Bonnie, and of course it wasn't her husband, who was away at an academic conference. She knew, she knew, yet she continued tugging at the window even as her heart beat rapidly and a wave of terror washed over her. She thought, I can get out the back door, I can run for help, but she knew she'd never leave Bonnie behind; Bonnie was upstairs in her room.

She had left a door unlocked, the door leading into the garage. She knew at once that was it. Everyone in the neighborhood kept doors unlocked during the day, children were always trailing in and out of houses, why had hers been singled out? She could have wept for the mistake she'd made she could not now undo.

She saw by the digital clock on her husband's desk that it was 7:40. She thought, I must remember that time.

She was behaving, still, as if nothing were wrong. Dreamy and shivering. Walking a little slower and more stiffly than usual. Even as she reentered the house knowing how the air was disturbed by their presence, smelling them, something acrid and sweaty and excited, sensing their very weight on the floorboards, she was consciously behaving as if nothing were wrong. As if, observing her, taking pity on her, they might yet relent and go away. She found herself staring at the dining room clock, but this time the hour didn't register.

Someone said loudly, "Lady!" and she turned to see two youngish men advancing toward her, two strangers, both in jeans, T-shirts: one of them with a flattened nose and oddly appealing eyes, the other tall, rangy, weedy, with long lank faded red hair, jutting ears, a light dusting of freckles on his face. He was the one carrying the knife.

They were high, nerved up, staring at her and grinning, both talking at once. "We're not going to hurt you, lady! Just stay cool! Stay cool!"—she would think afterward that they spoke like hoodlums on television or in the movies, for how otherwise would they speak?—"Got some cash in here? Find us some cash, lady! Where's your purse, lady? C'mon, lady, nobody's going to get hurt! Get your ass moving and nobody's going to get hurt!"

Her heartbeat was so hard and rapid she thought she was going to faint, and afterward she would realize with a stab of angry regret that had she fainted at that moment, had she simply fallen, limp and helpless, crashing to the floor, they would probably have fled the house: grabbed a few things, whatever was handy, and fled. But, no: she made an effort to keep from fainting as if out of courtesy! And it was pride too, for she thought of herself as a woman who took control of situations, a woman who was mature, responsible, not hysterical—a woman with a steady level gaze whom you could trust.

That was what she wanted the men to think, wasn't it—that they could trust her—for wasn't she cooperative, wasn't she calm and even in a way gracious, leading them into the kitchen where she'd left her purse (except it wasn't there: where was it?) and speaking quietly to them, saying, "You don't want to do this, really; my husband will be home in a few minutes—he'll be back before eight o'clock"; saying, "That knife makes me nervous, why don't you put it away, it isn't necessary, really"; not quite pleading: "My daughter is upstairs, she's only eight years old, please don't frighten her—please go away before you frighten her." But where was her purse? Why couldn't she find her purse? Her teeth had begun to chatter and her hands and knees were shaking uncontrollably.

They were her age, perhaps a year or two younger. Mature men in their early thirties, but loud, loutish, deliberately clumsy, it almost seemed, like teenagers. Scared of what they were doing but exhilarated by it too—showing off, Harriet saw, for each other's benefit. And, seeing that she was an attractive woman, a small-boned terrified woman, no match for them, perhaps for her benefit as well.

They gave her orders in high breathless voices, telling her to get some cash and where's the silverware and nobody's going to get hurt if she did what they said. "Move your ass, lady! C'mon, lady!" the man with the knife said repeatedly in a boyish sniggering tone as if Harriet were a dumb creature in need of prodding. So naturally Bonnie heard them—how could the child have failed to hear them?—and started downstairs, and Harriet, her hands shaking even more violently, pulling open a drawer to show the men her silverware in its worn chamois-lined tray—what remained of an elegant sterling set belonging to her grandmother, rarely used now and badly tarnished—thought she would never hear anything again in her life so wrenching, so unspeakably terrible, as her daughter's running footsteps on the stairs and her daughter's lifted voice, inquisitive rather than alarmed, "Mommy? Mommy?"

"Don't come in here, honey," Harriet called out. "Bonnie? Go back upstairs, please," keeping her voice level and taking pride in the fact: yes, her voice *is* level, Mommy *is* calm, Bonnie will remember when it's over.

For she was thinking, even then, even as Bonnie ran into the kitchen, that this wasn't happening to her alone, this was happening to Bonnie as well and she must behave in a way that reflected the fact. And she was thinking that the men would be yet more impressed, how could they not be impressed—a woman behaving so rationally so cooperatively you might even say so sweetly under these emergency circumstances; surely they would feel admiration for her? sympathy for her? Surely they would go away quickly with whatever she could give them and would not injure her or her daughter—wouldn't they?

Harriet saw that the men were nearly as frightened of Bonnie as Bonnie was frightened of them; they were so high, so stoned, they hadn't seemed to have counted on a child. She said calmly, "Let her go up to her room, please"—she didn't want to plead or beg, she hoped simply to sound reasonable—"she's just a little girl, let her go up to her room, please," as Bonnie, whimpering and sobbing, hid behind her, clutching at her legs. The child was small-boned like her mother, with her mother's pale silvery-blond hair, her wide-spaced brown eyes. Her cheeks were babyish, plump, streaked now with tears. How quickly, Harriet thought, children cry . . . as if the tears are always there, in readiness. "Let her go upstairs, please," Harriet told the men with as much an air of authority, maternal authority, as she could simulate. "Don't frighten her like this—have some compassion!" The man with the flattened nose seemed confused by her words and shrugged OK, but the one with the knife said no—"Hell, no, lady"—his mouth stretching like a rubber band in a fond leering smile as if he knew Harriet intended to trick him and he was too smart for her. When he smiled his cheeks dimpled.

"She'd call the police or something. You think we're assholes? She don't need to go anywhere."

They were examining the silverware, they were going to dump it into a grocery bag they'd found in one of the cupboards, but the man with the flattened nose said nervously he didn't think it looked like anything much and the man with the knife, the lanky red-haired grinning man, said in derision, "That's *tarnish*, asshole, that's how you know it's the real thing."

Harriet said desperately, "Please take it. It's good silver, really. It's worth money."

"OK, lady, and where's your purse?" the man with the knife said. "Where's your purse you said was out here?"

"I think it must be in the bedroom—"

"You said it was out here, lady."

"I don't know where it is. I don't think there's much money in it—"

"Shut up! Find it! Get a move on!"

"My husband will be home in a few minutes. He—"

"Fuck 'my husband'! Fuck that shit! Who you think you're jiving? *Get a move on!*"

He was furious suddenly, shouting in her face. Bonnie began screaming "Mommy! Mommy! Mommy!" She was pawing at Harriet as if she were crazed and Harriet had all she could do to subdue her, pinion her arms, clutch her tight. She could feel her daughter's heart beating wildly inside her small rib cage. How fragile, she thought, how easily smashed . . . . "Bonnie," she whispered, "Bonnie—it's all right, it's all right, really," saying the same words over and over like an incantation. To the men she said, "Let me put her in the bathroom, at least—there's a bathroom downstairs. Let me get her out of the way, please." She was pleading now, her voice rising: "My daughter can't help you, she has nothing to do with this—*please!*"

The man with the knife was still suspicious but his friend said, "Yeah, OK—good idea," and that seemed to be it. Bonnie was making them both very nervous. Harriet half carried her daughter to the bathroom in the hall, whispering to her to be a good girl, to be quiet, it would all be over in a few minutes, please please be quiet, could she promise? Lock the door and don't unlock it until Mommy tells her to: promise? "What if the kid climbs out the fucking window?" the man with the knife was saying in an aggrieved voice. His friend said, "She ain't going to climb out no window, it's too high. Get cool."

So Harriet hugged Bonnie a final time and shut her up in the closet-sized prettily decorated guest bathroom that always smelled of lemon-scented soap no one, even guests, ever used, and she thought, Now it will be all right, telling herself, Now it will be all right, even as she turned back to the men and saw the light around their heads blotch and darken as if it were about to go out. She was panicked, swaying, on the verge of fainting again, and again she willed herself to recover: head lowered, blood rushing into the arteries with a terrible percussive force. One of the men grabbed her by the shoulder and gave her a furious shake. "C'mon, lady! Cut that shit! *C'mon!*"

They shoved Harriet forward. They carried the silverware loose in the paper bag, and in the dining room she showed them the brass candlesticks on the mantel and they took those too, "They're expensive, they're worth money," Harriet said, and she led them into her husband's study where his newly purchased German-made camera was kept on a shelf, "There—that's worth at least a thousand dollars," she said, absurdly gratified when the man with the flattened nose snatched the camera up like a prize, though she knew it wasn't worth $1,000 or half that much. "You can sell all these things," she said. "They're worth money."

She could hear Bonnie crying in the rear of the house.

She said, still in her reasonable voice, "Why don't you leave now? If you leave now I won't call the police. You can have those things. I promise I won't call the police."

They were in the living room, which ran nearly the length of the front of the house. Its pretensions of understated taste, elegance—nubby tweed sofa, matching chairs, glass-topped coffee table, wall-to-wall beige carpeting, above all the glossy-leafed plants in their earthenware pots—struck Harriet as comical. She wondered that the men, hands on their hips, staring, assessing, did not laugh aloud.

They asked where was the TV and when Harriet said it was kept in another room one of them said, "OK, show me," and the other said derisively, "Who's going to carry a TV?" so that was dropped. They were going to go upstairs but one of them changed his mind, suddenly gripping Harriet by the back of the neck—it was this gesture that made her understand she was in trouble, seriously in trouble: the abrupt contact, the hard canny fingers closing on her flesh stopping her cold as a dog is stopped by his collar—and said in a triumphant voice, "Just a minute lady, *take that down*"—indicating of all things an oil painting, an unframed abstract canvas done by one of Harriet's friends, on the wall behind the sofa.

"Take it down? Why?"

"Let's just see what's behind it!"

"Behind it?"

Then she realized: he thought there might be a wall safe hidden behind the painting.

She said, "I'm afraid you have the wrong idea about this household," actually trying to laugh, to make a sound like laughter, faint and breathless, incredulous. She said, "Do you think we're wealthy people? This isn't a wealthy neighborhood—can't you tell?" She added, not wanting to insult them, "I'm just trying to save you time."

One of the men pushed her forward, the flat of his hand between her shoulder blades in a rude shove. "Do what I *say*, lady!" It was the young man with the knife: his dull-red hair had fallen into his face; he gave off a fierce hot odor of sweat and indignation. "Do what I *say* and you won't get hurt."

They were on the stairs when for no reason Harriet could determine the man with the flattened nose changed his mind: he was leaving.

He'd had it, he said, he was getting the hell out, and he and his friend argued briefly on the stairway landing but he had his way and ran back downstairs. He was carrying the bulky grocery bag with its mismatched rattling contents.

Harriet felt her heart clench, knowing it would be worse now.

(It would turn out that the first man to leave the house left by the front door—bold, brash, stupid, unthinking—and no one in the neighborhood saw him, or reported having seen him. The second man was to leave, a half hour later, by the door to the garage, as he'd come in.)

He was angry now, angrier, because of his "asshole" friend and Harriet "wasting his time like she was"—pushing her along the darkened hall to the bedroom where her purse had to be; it couldn't be any other place, Harriet was thinking, biting her lower lip and praying; it can't be any other place; and when she switched on the bedroom light there it was, there, on the bureau where of course she'd left it. She could have wept with gratitude.

She would have handed her purse over to the man but he snatched it up eagerly, opened it, drew out the wallet, letting the purse fall to the floor, his own hands trembling as if with a faint palsy. Harriet saw that his knuckles were oddly big-boned, scraped-looking. His fingernails were edged with dirt.

She said, apologetically, "I'm afraid there isn't much."

He was counting out bills, breathing hard. Harriet's eye darted about the bedroom hopeful of things—anything—she might offer. Her jewelry, of course, a few heirlooms but they were inexpensive; the rings she was wearing; and her watch—not really expensive items but could he tell the difference? She was thinking that the bedroom was so quietly attractive a room, neat, clean, the bed made (of course: Harriet had been trained from the age of nine to make any bed she slept in within a few seconds of rising from it), the mahogany furniture polished, lovely pale silky curtains, and the rest—the evidence of lives intelligently but not extravagantly lived. Surely the man with the knife could *see*? And would not want to hurt her, for so little reason?

(Bonnie had stopped crying. Or, more likely, Harriet couldn't hear her any longer. The house was unnaturally quiet: no radio, no television, no voices. Harriet would have liked to think that Bonnie had disobeyed her and left the bathroom—was now running, running for her life, next door to get help—but she knew this couldn't be: Bonnie would never have disobeyed her under these extreme circumstances. She would not unlock the door until Mommy gave her permission.

The man with the knife counted out 73 dollars and some change and didn't look very happy, and Harriet said quickly, "I just went shopping today, that's why there isn't—" He raised his eyes to hers: blood-threaded, glassy, the irises so dark they couldn't be distinguished from the pupils. The eyes seemed too loose in their sockets and Harriet could see, close up, scar tissue above each eye, tiny stitchlike marks in the skin.

He said, slyly, "OK, where's the rest?"

"The rest?"

"Hidden somewhere? In a drawer? Underneath something?"

"I don't have any more money," Harriet said. "This is all I have."

"Come off it!"

"Please, you promised—"

"Where's the money? Where's the *real* money?"

He was getting excited, waving the knife, gesturing with it, giving off a frantic hot scent like rancid grease. His facial skin was now the color and texture of curdled milk. The freckles stood out like dirty rain spots. "Just don't you lie to me, lady," he said, "nobody lies to me, lady." He stuffed the bills in his jeans pocket, taking no notice of the coins that fell to the floor. "Nobody lies to *me*."

Harriet said, stammering, "But we don't keep money in the house. We don't keep cash. I have a checkbook—"

"A checkbook! You going to write me a check, lady?"

"I have some jewelry—that's all I have—in this drawer here—"

He shoved her aside and yanked open the drawer, pawing through Harriet's things. She had costume jewelry mainly, dozens of pairs of earrings, glass beads, Indian necklaces, brooches she rarely wore, but in her little red jewelry box—a gift from her parents for her sixteenth birthday—there were a string of good cultured pearls and an old diamond-and-emerald bracelet of her grandmother's and several rings of varying degrees of worth, and these things the man with the knife scooped up, greedy yet embittered, as if knowing they were worth very little, really: he was being cheated.

"My watch," Harriet said, slipping it off, handing it over. "It might be worth something." He examined it skeptically (and he had a right to be skeptical; it was only a moderately priced watch classily styled, with miniature facets in the white gold framing the timepiece that winked and glittered in a simulation of diamonds). "That's all I have. I don't have anything else—please believe me," Harriet said.

He ignored her, didn't hear her, rifling through the bureau drawers in search of cash—and there was no cash—tossing clothing to the floor: Harriet's underwear, Harriet's panty hose, her husband's socks, shorts, undershirts. He found several pair of cuff links and tried to stuff them in a pocket and when they slipped through his fingers he didn't trouble to pick them up. Next he went to the clothes closet and pawed furiously through Harriet's and her husband's clothes, cursing in a loud whining voice like a small child. His breath came so harshly now Harriet could hear him across the room.

Why was he staying on so long, risking so much? He should have been eager, like his friend, to escape.

Why was he talking to himself, behaving with such self-conscious bravado? Was it for Harriet's benefit?

Her initial shock had subsided. Like a powerful shot of adrenaline, it had been; now it was gone. She was left with a chill desperate calm, thinking, I am trapped, and Bonnie is trapped, until this is over.

"My husband—" she began, and broke down.

"If you leave now—" she began.

"I don't have anything more. We don't—"

The man with the knife approached her and stood with his hands on his hips, smiling his sly little smile. "OK, lady, cut the shit," he said flatly.

Harriet didn't want to think that she knew, even before he knew, what he would do. She didn't want to think that.

She would wonder afterward when it first occurred to him: after he'd counted out the money in her wallet, seen how little there was, how little the break-in was going to net him—so much energy expended, so much risk, for so little? Or had it been when he'd first glimpsed her, downstairs, tugging at the window in her husband's study? But perhaps it had been his plan, his intention, all along, before he'd ever stepped into her house: any woman, any female, helpless, and available to him . . .?

He said, not meanly, "You think you're hot shit, don't you? People like you."

"What? Why?"

"Living up here. People like you."

"What do you mean?" Harriet asked, though she knew what he meant. Her voice sounded weak, guilty.

"What's your husband do?"

"He teaches history at the university."

He laughed to show he didn't think much of it, history at the university.

They were standing quite close together and might have been having an ordinary if rather intense conversation. Until this moment Harriet had not really looked at the knife. She had seen it, she'd known what it was but had not wanted to look. Now she saw that it was about eight inches long and there was something strange about it—a sporty, chunky look to it—a fat two-edged blade. Two edged? The handle was unnaturally long, simulated carved wood, probably plastic, black. She thought, He won't really hurt me. He doesn't intend to hurt me.

She thought, I could run.

The knife held conspicuously, he brushed his long damp hair out of his face with both hands in a deft, practiced gesture. He liked himself and he liked her watching him, and Harriet thought of a mass murderer who'd been quoted in the newspaper the previous year, a man who'd killed forty women including a twelve-year-old girl, and he'd said arrogantly, rhetorically, "Who has seen the past? Who has touched the past?" He was an intelligent man, an educated man, a lawyer in fact; he'd been eloquent enough, saying, "The past? The past is a mist. The past doesn't exist."

And a woman had consented to marry him, after his conviction: borne him a child, a little girl.

Harriet thought, These things can't be.

Harriet thought, How can God let such things happen?

The red-haired young man with the knife was pulling back the bedspread—an odd, even quaint, sense of decorum. He said, "Get down."

Harriet stood frozen. She said, "You promised you wouldn't hurt me."

"I'm not going to hurt you," he said. "Just get down."

"My daughter is downstairs—"

"C'mon. Now. Do it. Get *down.*"

"I can't," Harriet said, her voice breaking. "I can't do it." She began to cry. She said, "My husband—"

"You're somebody's wife!" the man said. He spoke with an air of angry incredulity as if Harriet were trying to trick him again. "You fuck all the time! You had a kid! What the hell! It's nothing! Don't tell *me!*"

Harriet said desperately, "No. Please. You promised. You said you wouldn't—"

"Nobody's going to hurt you, for Christ's sake," the man said. "Just get down here," he said, shoving her onto the bed, "and shut *up.*"

"My daughter—"

"You want to see her again? Your daughter? Do you? You want to see her again?" he said.

He rapped her against the mouth with his knuckles. Harriet drew breath to scream, but knew she should not scream—should not scream—not now: he was standing over her, panting, big-eyed, the knife in his hand.

She said, "You promised you wouldn't hurt me. I'm afraid of the knife."

"I'm not going to use the knife."

"Yes, but I'm afraid of it."

He was fumbling with his pants, flush-faced, excited. Harriet shut her eyes to a flurry of lights, something hot and crackling behind her eyelids; she shut her eyes and forced herself to open them again, to speak clearly, coherently, even now. "I'm afraid of the knife. Please put away the knife."

"You want to hold it? You can hold it," he said, crouching over her. "Go ahead, hold it. *Take* it." He was smiling his hard tight clenched smile. Harriet thought, He's crazy. Then she thought, He's trying to be a gentleman—is that it?

He pressed the knife into her fingers and it fell onto the bed. He picked it up and pressed it again into her fingers, closed her fingers around it. He said, "You're nice. You're pretty. You owe me money. You owe me fucking *something*, and you know it. Just lay still."

Harriet held the knife; Harriet was holding it, her arm bent awkwardly at the elbow. Her wrist was so weak it might have snapped like dried kindling.

Is this rape? she thought. *This?*—as the man pried her legs apart, poked himself against her. Rivulets of sweat ran down his face; his tongue appeared between his teeth in a parody of intense childlike concentration. Again he said he wouldn't hurt her, "This won't hurt, lady, just lay still," and Harriet was pinned beneath him rigid and disbelieving, thinking even now, This can't be happening, this can't, can't be happening—her legs spread wide, sweat-slick and clumsy, knees high as if she were on an examination table, feet caught in stirrups. The knife had slipped again from her fingers and she could not keep from crying out, a series of high little screams, she could not keep from fighting, threshing—

"Just lay still."

As a child of four Harriet had fallen from a porch on the second floor of her parents' Cape Cod summer house; she'd leaned against a railing that was badly rotted and gave way beneath her weight. Very likely she would have been killed or severely injured if it hadn't been for an overgrown evergreen shrub that broke her fall.

But she wasn't killed, wasn't even injured except for scratches and bruises and the shock of the accident. And forever afterward it was a legend of the family, one of those happy legends that spring up and thrive and are never forgotten in families, that Harriet was blessed with luck: fool's luck, perhaps, but luck nonetheless.

So now, returning to consciousness, alone in her bed, alone in her bedroom, alive, throbbing with pain but alive, she thought only, It's over.

In that first instant, before the pain really hit, and the disbelief, the loathing, the nausea—before, even, she began to call her daughter's name—she thought only, It's over. We're safe.

She telephoned the police first, and then her husband who was in Chicago, and she spoke evenly and carefully, keeping her voice low, calm, modulated; she was determined to demonstrate that she wasn't all that upset, she certainly wasn't hysterical: only a robbery after all, and they hadn't take very much.

The police arrived within minutes and questioned her for about an hour. They asked for descriptions of the men and they asked if she recognized either or both of the men and they asked were the men armed, and Harriet said hesitantly, "Well—yes. I think one of them had a knife."

Bonnie was upstairs in bed by this time, Bonnie would have no part in the interrogation, perhaps Bonnie had not even seen the knife? Harriet was saying carefully, "I think one of them had a knife he kept in his pocket, you know, sort of threatening, in his pocket—"

"A knife? Not a gun?"

"Oh, no, not a gun. A knife, I think—"

"Did you see it?"

"I think I did, yes, actually—"

"Did he threaten you with it?"

"He did, yes, in a way, but not—"

"He didn't touch you with it?"

"Oh, no. No, he didn't touch me with it," she said emphatically. "He wasn't the kind—I mean, he didn't do that."

"Did either of them touch you?"

"Yes, but not—"

"Not roughly?"

She began to speak quickly. "I don't know, really. It was all so frightening and confused and I was worried mainly about my daughter. I mean—as soon as I thought she'd be safe it was only a matter of time, giving them some money, not much but all I had: seventy-three dollars, it was, and some jewelry, and my husband's camera, and a few other things, I've forgotten exactly; we don't have much that's valuable and I offered them what we had, I didn't protest or try to resist, I didn't think it was worth it, after all—not with my daughter here."

Which was of course—wasn't it?—the wisest thing to have done.

As the police told her. And others were to tell her, admiringly: the wisest thing to have done—to save your and Bonnie's lives.

She told the police about the robbery in as much detail as she could recall—she was to remember more the next morning and more, by degrees, in the days following—but she did not tell them about the rape because perhaps it had not been a rape? She'd held the knife in her fingers, after all, and had not used it.

And he had not hurt her—much. Not so much as he might have.

I think he liked me, she thought.

He didn't really want to hurt me, she thought.

I left the door unlocked and wasn't that an invitation to—something?

And the shame. And the public humiliation.

And her husband. "I can't do that to him," she said aloud. She was angry, not despairing, as if she were arguing with someone.

The police believed her, or seemed to. Her husband believed her. Or seemed to. (But she wasn't sure. Those much-repeated questions, questions: Did they threaten you physically? Did they touch you? What kind of knife was it—how close did he come to using it on you?) The men were to be apprehended within two weeks, but it was only a few days later that Harriet was standing at a window in Bonnie's room—headachy, groggy from a powerful dose of codeine—watching steamy air rise from grass, sidewalks, the roofs of neighboring houses. It was a prematurely warm day, the sun seemed unnaturally bright though the sky was massed with rain clouds, and Harriet glanced up and saw a human figure—an angel?—contorted and struggling like a swimmer in the clouds: angular, sculpted, purely white, beautiful as living marble.

What was it? Was she going mad? She fell to her knees as her parents had done in the little Methodist church in the country long ago and she cried aloud, "God, don't let me turn into a religious lunatic!" and when she looked up again of course the figure was gone. Just oddly shaped clouds, rain-swollen, turbulent, an El Greco[2] sky.

That evening she would tell her husband about the rape. And what would happen, as a consequence, would happen.

Alice Walker 1944–

Alice Walker was born in Georgia, the eighth child of impoverished black sharecroppers. Encouraged by her mother, who supported her desire to gain an education and become a writer, Walker graduated at the top of her high school class and received a scholarship to Spelman College for women in Atlanta. After two years at Spelman, she transferred to Sarah Lawrence College in New York, graduating with a B.A. in 1965.

Returning to the South, to Mississippi, she taught writing and black literature and joined in efforts to improve welfare rights and increase voter registration among Southern blacks. Her first publication appeared in 1966, an essay on the civil rights movement. Two years later she published her first book, Once *(1968), a collection of poems. Her first collection of short fiction,* In Love and Trouble *(1973), won an award from the National Institute of Arts and Letters for its unflinching portrayals of black women who exist as the wretched victims of racial and sexual oppression. Her second volume of stories,* You Can't Keep a Good Woman Down *(1981), brought her additional recognition as a short-story writer, but her greatest recognition has come as a writer of novels.*

The Third Life of Grange Copeland *(1970), Walker's first novel, presented themes that appear in much of her writing: the dehumanizing racism and sexism that black women experience at the hands of whites and blacks alike. Her second novel,* Meridian *(1976), won praise as the finest novel of the 1960s civil rights movement. Her third novel,* The Color Purple *(1982), received worldwide acclaim. Set in the first half of the twentieth century and written in the black English of the American South, the novel covers thirty years in the life of a semiliterate, downtrodden black woman who triumphs over black male oppression and demonstrates the power of women to join together and liberate themselves from sexual abuse and violence.* The Color Purple *won for its author a Pulitzer Prize and was made into an award-winning motion picture. By 1988 the novel had been translated into twenty-two languages and had sold more than six million copies.* The Same River Twice *(1996), a compilation of passages drawn from Walker's journals and letters, describes her experiences during the writing of the novel and the production of the movie* The Color Purple *and reports the difficulties that came with the fame and riches the movie brought.*

[2]Greek-born Spanish painter (1541–1614).

Walker has dealt unflinchingly with violence and sexuality, abortion, sadism, rape, pornography, and the impact of racial and sexual stereotypes on the relations of black men and women. Some critics have objected that her stories are too often melodramatic, that her characterizations are simplistic, a repetitious portrayal of good women suffering at the hands of bad men. And Walker has acknowledged that as a black feminist (she prefers the word "womanist"), her sympathies lie almost entirely with black women.

But in her collection of essays titled Living by the Word, Selected Writings 1973–1987 *(1988), in a film documentary on her life and work,* Visions of the Spirit *(1988), and in the novels* The Temple of My Familiar *(1990),* Possessing the Secret of Joy *(1992),* By the Light of My Father's Smile *(1998), and* The Way Forward Is with a Broken Heart *(2000), Walker reveals a vision that has grown beyond black feminism to a sympathy for all living things on a planet filled with greed, ignorance, and the threat of nuclear war. Nevertheless, her greatest achievement remains her portrayal of the lives of black women, often grotesque and inarticulate, who struggle to deliver themselves from what Alice Walker has described as the black woman's demeaning life as "the mule of the world."*

FURTHER READING: *Alice Walker,* ed. H. Bloom, 1990; D. Winchell, *Alice Walker,* 1992; *Critical Essays on Alice Walker,* ed. I. Dieke, 1999; M. Lauret, *Alice Walker,* 2000; E. White, *Alice Walker, A Life,* 2004.

TEXT: *In Love and Trouble,* 1973.

EVERYDAY USE

for your grandmama

I will wait for her in the yard that Maggie and I made so clean and wavy yesterday afternoon. A yard like this is more comfortable than most people know. It is not just a yard. It is like an extended living room. When the hard clay is swept clean as a floor and the fine sand around the edges lined with tiny, irregular grooves, anyone can come and sit and look up into the elm tree and wait for the breezes that never come inside the house.

Maggie will be nervous until after her sister goes: she will stand hopelessly in corners, homely and ashamed of the burn scars down her arms and legs, eying her sister with a mixture of envy and awe. She thinks her sister has held life always in the palm of one hand, that "no" is a word the world never learned to say to her.

You've no doubt seen those TV shows where the child who has "made it" is confronted, as a surprise, by her own mother and father, tottering in weakly from backstage. (A pleasant surprise, of course: What would they do if parent and child came on the show only to curse out and insult each other?) On TV mother and child embrace and smile into each other's faces. Sometimes the mother and father weep, the child wraps them in her arms and leans across the table to tell how she would not have made it without their help. I have seen these programs.

Sometimes I dream a dream in which Dee and I are suddenly brought together on a TV program of this sort. Out of a dark and soft-seated limousine

I am ushered into a bright room filled with many people. There I meet a smiling, gray, sporty man like Johnny Carson who shakes my hand and tells me what a fine girl I have. Then we are on the stage and Dee is embracing me with tears in her eyes. She pins on my dress a large orchid, even though she has told me once that she thinks orchids are tacky flowers.

In real life I am a large, big-boned woman with rough, man-working hands. In the winter I wear flannel nightgowns to bed and overalls during the day. I can kill and clean a hog as mercilessly as a man. My fat keeps me hot in zero weather. I can work outside all day, breaking ice to get water for washing; I can eat pork liver cooked over the open fire minutes after it comes steaming from the hog. One winter I knocked a bull calf straight in the brain between the eyes with a sledge hammer and had the meat hung up to chill before nightfall. But of course all this does not show on television. I am the way my daughter would want me to be: a hundred pounds lighter, my skin like an uncooked barley pancake. My hair glistens in the hot bright lights. Johnny Carson has much to do to keep up with my quick and witty tongue.

But that is a mistake. I know even before I wake up. Who ever knew a Johnson with a quick tongue? Who can even imagine me looking a strange white man in the eye? It seems to me I have talked to them always with one foot raised in flight, with my head turned in whichever way is farthest from them. Dee, though. She would always look anyone in the eye. Hesitation was no part of her nature.

"How do I look, Mama?" Maggie says, showing just enough of her thin body enveloped in pink skirt and red blouse for me to know she's there, almost hidden by the door.

"Come out into the yard," I say.

Have you ever seen a lame animal, perhaps a dog run over by some careless person rich enough to own a car, sidle up to someone who is ignorant enough to be kind to him? That is the way my Maggie walks. She has been like this, chin on chest, eyes on ground, feet in shuffle, ever since the fire that burned the other house to the ground.

Dee is lighter than Maggie, with nicer hair and a fuller figure. She's a woman now, though sometimes I forget. How long ago was it that the other house burned? Ten, twelve years? Sometimes I can still hear the flames and feel Maggie's arms sticking to me, her hair smoking and her dress falling off her in little black papery flakes. Her eyes seemed stretched open, blazed open by the flames reflected in them. And Dee. I see her standing off under the sweet gum tree she used to dig gum out of; a look of concentration on her face as she watched the last dingy gray board of the house fall in toward the red-hot brick chimney. Why don't you do a dance around the ashes? I'd wanted to ask her. She had hated the house that much.

I used to think she hated Maggie, too. But that was before we raised the money, the church and me, to send her to Augusta to school. She used to read to us without pity; forcing words, lies, other folks' habits, whole lives upon us two, sitting trapped and ignorant underneath the sound of her voice. She washed us in a river of make-believe, burned us with a lot of knowledge we didn't necessarily need to know. Pressed us to her with the serious way she read, to shove us away at just the moment, like dimwits, we seemed about to understand.

Dee wanted nice things. A yellow organdy dress to wear to her graduation from high school; black pumps to match a green suit she'd made from an old suit somebody gave me. She was determined to stare down any disaster in her efforts. Her eyelids would not flicker for minutes at a time. Often I fought off the temptation to shake her. At sixteen she had a style of her own: and knew what style was.

I never had an education myself. After second grade the school was closed down. Don't ask me why: in 1927 colored asked fewer questions than they do now. Sometimes Maggie reads to me. She stumbles along good-naturedly but can't see well. She knows she is not bright. Like good looks and money, quickness passed her by. She will marry John Thomas (who has mossy teeth in an earnest face) and then I'll be free to sit here and I guess just sing church songs to myself. Although I never was a good singer. Never could carry a tune. I was always better at a man's job. I used to love to milk till I was hooked in the side in '49. Cows are soothing and slow and don't bother you, unless you try to milk them the wrong way.

I have deliberately turned my back on the house. It is three rooms, just like the one that burned, except the roof is tin; they don't make shingle roofs any more. There are no real windows, just some holes cut in the sides, like the portholes in a ship, but not round and not square, with rawhide holding the shutters up on the outside. This house is in a pasture, too, like the other one. No doubt when Dee sees it she will want to tear it down. She wrote me once that no matter where we "choose" to live, she will manage to come see us. But she will never bring her friends. Maggie and I thought about this and Maggie asked me, "Mama, when did Dee ever *have* any friends?"

She had a few. Furtive boys in pink shirts hanging about on washday after school. Nervous girls who never laughed. Impressed with her they worshiped the well-turned phrase, the cute shape, the scalding humor that erupted like bubbles in lye. She read to them.

When she was courting Jimmy T she didn't have much time to pay to us, but turned all her faultfinding power on him. He *flew* to marry a cheap city girl from a family of ignorant flashy people. She hardly had time to recompose herself.

When she comes I will meet—but there they are!

Maggie attempts to make a dash for the house, in her shuffling way, but I stay her with my hand. "Come back here," I say. And she stops and tries to dig a well in the sand with her toe.

It is hard to see them clearly through the strong sun. But even the first glimpse of leg out of the car tells me it is Dee. Her feet were always neat-looking, as if God himself had shaped them with a certain style. From the other side of the car comes a short, stocky man. Hair is all over his head a foot long and hanging from his chin like a kinky mule tail. I hear Maggie suck in her breath. "Uhnnnh," is what it sounds like. Like when you see the wriggling end of a snake just in front of your foot on the road. "Uhnnnh."

Dee next. A dress down to the ground, in this hot weather. A dress so loud it hurts my eyes. There are yellows and oranges enough to throw back the light of the sun. I feel my whole face warming from the heat waves it throws out. Earrings gold, too, and hanging down to her shoulders.

Bracelets dangling and making noises when she moves her arm up to shake the folds of the dress out of her armpits. The dress is loose and flows, and as she walks closer, I like it. I hear Maggie go "Uhnnnh" again. It is her sister's hair. It stands straight up like the wool on a sheep. It is black as night and around the edges are two long pigtails that rope about like small lizards disappearing behind her ears.

"Wa-su-zo-Tean-o!" she says, coming on in that gliding way the dress makes her move. The short stocky fellow with the hair to his naval is all grinning and he follows up with "Asalamalakim, my mother and sister!" He moves to hug Maggie but she falls back, right up against the back of my chair. I feel her trembling there and when I look up I see the perspiration falling off her chin.

"Don't get up," says Dee. Since I am stout it takes something of a push. You can see me trying to move a second or two before I make it. She turns, showing white heels through her sandals, and goes back to the car. Out she peeks next with a Polaroid. She stoops down quickly and lines up picture after picture of me sitting there in front of the house with Maggie cowering behind me. She never takes a shot without making sure the house is included. When a cow comes nibbling around the edge of the yard she snaps it and me and Maggie *and* the house. Then she puts the Polaroid in the back seat of the car, and comes up and kisses me on the forehead.

Meanwhile Asalamalakim is going through motions with Maggie's hand. Maggie's hand is as limp as a fish, and probably as cold, despite the sweat, and she keeps trying to pull it back. It looks like Asalamalakim wants to shake hands but wants to do it fancy. Or maybe he don't know how people shake hands. Anyhow, he soon gives up on Maggie.

"Well," I say. "Dee."

"No, Mama," she says. "Not 'Dee,' Wangero Leewanika Kemanjo!"

"What happened to 'Dee'?" I wanted to know.

"She's dead," Wangero said. "I couldn't bear it any longer, being named after the people who oppress me."

"You know as well as me you was named after your aunt Dicie," I said. Dicie is my sister. She named Dee. We called her "Big Dee" after Dee was born.

"But who was *she* named after?" asked Wangero.

"I guess after Grandma Dee," I said.

"And who was she named after?" asked Wangero.

"Her mother," I said, and saw Wangero was getting tired. "That's about as far back as I can trace it," I said. Though, in fact, I probably could have carried it back beyond the Civil War through the branches.

"Well," said Asalamalakim, "there you are."

"Uhnnnh," I heard Maggie say.

"There I was not," I said, "before 'Dicie' cropped up in our family, so why should I try to trace it that far back?"

He just stood there grinning, looking down on me like somebody inspecting a Model A car. Every once in a while he and Wangero sent eye signals over my head.

"How do you pronounce this name?" I asked.

"You don't have to call me by it if you don't want to," said Wangero.

"Why shouldn't I?" I asked. "If that's what you want us to call you, we'll call you."

"I know it might sound awkward at first," said Wangero.

"I'll get used to it," I said. "Ream it out again."

Well, soon we got the name out of the way. Asalamalakim had a name twice as long and three times as hard. After I tripped over it two or three times he told me to just call him Hakim-a-barber. I wanted to ask him was he a barber, but I didn't really think he was, so I didn't ask.

"You must belong to those beef-cattle peoples down the road," I said. They said "Asalamalakim" when they met you, too, but they didn't shake hands. Always too busy: feeding the cattle, fixing the fences, putting up salt-lick shelters, throwing down hay. When the white folks poisoned some of the herd the men stayed up all night with rifles in their hands. I walked a mile and a half just to see the sight.

Hakim-a-barber said, "I accept some of their doctrines, but farming and raising cattle is not my style." (They didn't tell me, and I didn't ask, whether Wangero (Dee) had really gone and married him.)

We sat down to eat and right away he said he didn't eat collards and pork was unclean. Wangero, though, went on through the chitlins and corn bread, the greens and everything else. She talked a blue streak over the sweet potatoes. Everything delighted her. Even the fact that we still used the benches her daddy made for the table when we couldn't afford to buy chairs.

"Oh, Mama!" she cried. Then turned to Hakim-a-barber. "I never knew how lovely these benches are. You can feel the rump prints," she said, running her hands underneath her and along the bench. Then she gave a sigh and her hand closed over Grandma Dee's butter dish. "That's it!" she said. "I knew there was something I wanted to ask you if I could have." She jumped up from the table and went over in the corner where the churn stood, the milk in it clabber by now. She looked at the churn and looked at it.

"This churn top is what I need," she said. "Didn't Uncle Buddy whittle it out of a tree you all used to have?"

"Yes," I said.

"Uh huh," she said happily. "And I want the dasher, too."

"Uncle Buddy whittle that, too?" asked the barber.

Dee (Wangero) looked up at me.

"Aunt Dee's first husband whittled the dash," said Maggie so low you almost couldn't hear her. "His name was Henry, but they called him Stash."

"Maggie's brain is like an elephant's," Wangero said, laughing. "I can use the churn top as a centerpiece for the alcove table," she said, sliding a plate over the churn, "and I'll think of something artistic to do with the dasher."

When she finished wrapping the dasher the handle stuck out. I took it for a moment in my hands. You didn't even have to look close to see where hands pushing the dasher up and down to make butter had left a kind of sink in the wood. In fact, there were a lot of small sinks; you could see where thumbs and fingers had sunk into the wood. It was beautiful light yellow wood, from a tree that grew in the yard where Big Dee and Stash had lived.

After dinner Dee (Wangero) went to the trunk at the foot of my bed and started rifling through it. Maggie hung back in the kitchen over the dishpan. Out came Wangero with two quilts. They had been pieced by Grandma Dee and then Big Dee and me had hung them on the quilt frames on the front porch and quilted them. One was in the Lone Star pattern. The other was Walk Around the Mountain. In both of them were scraps of dresses Grandma

Dee had worn fifty and more years ago. Bits and pieces of Grandpa Jarrell's Paisley shirts. And one teeny faded blue piece, about the size of a penny matchbox, that was from Great Grandpa Ezra's uniform that he wore in the Civil War.

"Mama," Wangero said sweet as a bird. "Can I have these old quilts?"

I heard something fall in the kitchen, and a minute later the kitchen door slammed.

"Why don't you take one or two of the others?" I asked. "These old things was just done by me and Big Dee from some tops your grandma pieced before she died."

"No," said Wangero. "I don't want those. They are stitched around the borders by machine."

"That'll make them last better," I said.

"That's not the point," said Wangero. "These are all pieces of dresses Grandma used to wear. She did all this stitching by hand. Imagine!" She held the quilts securely in her arms, stroking them.

"Some of the pieces, like those lavender ones, come from old clothes her mother handed down to her," I said, moving up to touch the quilts. Dee (Wangero) moved back just enough so that I couldn't reach the quilts. They already belonged to her.

"Imagine!" she breathed again, clutching them closely to her bosom.

"The truth is," I said, "I promised to give them quilts to Maggie, for when she marries John Thomas."

She gasped like a bee had stung her.

"Maggie can't appreciate these quilts!" she said. "She'd probably be backward enough to put them to everyday use."

"I reckon she would," I said. "God knows I been saving 'em for long enough with nobody using 'em. I hope she will!" I didn't want to bring up how I had offered Dee (Wangero) a quilt when she went away to college. Then she had told me they were old-fashioned, out of style.

"But they're *priceless*!" she was saying now, furiously; for she has a temper. "Maggie would put them on the bed and in five years they'd be in rags. Less than that!"

"She can always make some more," I said. "Maggie knows how to quilt."

Dee (Wangero) looked at me with hatred. "You just will not understand. The point is these quilts, *these* quilts!"

"Well," I said, stumped. "What would *you* do with them?"

"Hang them," she said. As if that was the only thing you *could* do with quilts.

Maggie by now was standing in the door. I could almost hear the sound her feet made as they scraped over each other.

"She can have them, Mama," she said, like somebody used to never winning anything, or having anything reserved for her. "I can 'member Grandma Dee without the quilts."

I looked at her hard. She had filled her bottom lip with checkerberry snuff and it gave her face a kind of dopey, hangdog look. It was Grandma Dee and Big Dee who taught her how to quilt herself. She stood there with her scarred hands hidden in the folds of her skirt. She looked at her sister with something like fear but she wasn't mad at her. This was Maggie's portion. This was the way she knew God to work.

When I looked at her like that something hit me in the top of my head and ran down to the soles of my feet. Just like when I'm in church and the spirit of God touches me and I get happy and shout. I did something I never had done before: hugged Maggie to me, then dragged her on into the room, snatched the quilts out of Miss Wangero's hands and dumped them into Maggie's lap. Maggie just sat there on my bed with her mouth open.

"Take one or two of the others," I said to Dee.

But she turned without a word and went out to Hakim-a-barber.

"You just don't understand," she said, as Maggie and I came out to the car.

"What don't I understand?" I wanted to know.

"Your heritage," she said. And then she turned to Maggie, kissed her, and said, "You ought to try to make something of yourself, too, Maggie. It's really a new day for us. But from the way you and Mama still live you'd never know it."

She put on some sunglasses that hid everything above the tip of her nose and her chin.

Maggie smiled; maybe at the sunglasses. But a real smile, not scared. After we watched the car dust settle I asked Maggie to bring me a dip of snuff. And then the two of us sat there just enjoying, until it was time to go in the house and go to bed.

1973

Amy Tan 1952–

Amy Tan's parents emigrated from China to California, where she was born and has spent most of her life. In 1973, after graduating from college, she spent three years in postgraduate study and then worked as a reporter, as an editor, and as a technical writer for computer companies.

In 1989 she published The Joy Luck Club, *a collection of interwoven stories about four Chinese women and their Chinese-American daughters. It was an immediate success and soon was followed by her second novel,* The Kitchen God's Wife *(1991), the story of her grandmother and mother and of their lives in China. In her third novel,* The Hundred Secret Senses *(1995), Tan moved from the subject of mothers and daughters to a story of two half-sisters, one American, one Chinese, who make a pilgrimage to a remote mountain village in China where the American sister grows into an understanding of the mystical and spiritual wisdom of her Chinese half-sister. Tan has also written a children's book,* The Moon Lady *(1992). In her recent novel,* The Bonesetter's Daughter *(2001), as in much of her best fiction, Tan examines layers of family relationships and the shared and often anguished experiences of mothers from an ancient civilization and their modern Chinese-American daughters living in today's America. A collection of Tan's autobiographical essays,* The Opposite of Fate, A Book of Musings, *was published in 2003.*

FURTHER READING: E. Huntley, *Amy Tan, A Critical Companion,* 1998; *Amy Tan,* ed. H. Bloom, 2000; M. Snodgrass, *Amy Tan, A Literary Companion,* 2004.
TEXT: *The Joy Luck Club,* 1989.

from *THE JOY LUCK CLUB*

HALF AND HALF

As proof of her faith, my mother used to carry a small leatherette Bible when she went to the First Chinese Baptist Church every Sunday. But later, after my mother lost her faith in God, that leatherette Bible wound up wedged under a too-short table leg, a way for her to correct the imbalances of life. It's been there for over twenty years.

My mother pretends that Bible isn't there. Whenever anyone asks her what it's doing there, she says, a little too loudly, "Oh, this? I forgot." But I know she sees it. My mother is not the best housekeeper in the world, and after all these years that Bible is still clean white.

Tonight I'm watching my mother sweep under the same kitchen table, something she does every night after dinner. She gently pokes her broom around the table leg propped up by the Bible. I watch her, sweep after sweep, waiting for the right moment to tell her about Ted and me, that we're getting divorced. When I tell her, I know she's going to say, "This cannot be."

And when I say that it is certainly true, that our marriage is over, I know what else she will say: "Then you must save it."

And even though I know it's hopeless—there's absolutely nothing left to save—I'm afraid if I tell her that, she'll still persuade me to try.

I think it's ironic that my mother wants me to fight the divorce. Seventeen years ago she was chagrined when I started dating Ted. My oldest sisters had dated only Chinese boys from church before getting married.

Ted and I met in a politics of ecology class when he leaned over and offered to pay me two dollars for the last week's notes. I refused the money and accepted a cup of coffee instead. This was during my second semester at UC Berkeley, where I had enrolled as a liberal arts major and later changed to fine arts. Ted was in his third year in pre-med, his choice, he told me, ever since he dissected a fetal pig in the sixth grade.

I have to admit that what I initially found attractive in Ted were precisely the things that made him different from my brothers and the Chinese boys I had dated; his brashness; the assuredness in which he asked for things and expected to get them; his opinionated manner; his angular face and lanky body; the thickness of his arms; the fact that his parents immigrated from Tarrytown, New York, not Tientsin, China.

My mother must have noticed these same differences after Ted picked me up one evening at my parents' house. When I returned home, my mother was still up, watching television.

"He is American," warned my mother, as if I had been too blind to notice. "A *waigoren.*"[1]

[1]Chinese: "foreigner."

"I'm American too," I said, "And it's not as if I'm going to marry him or something."

Mrs. Jordan also had a few words to say. Ted had casually invited me to a family picnic, the annual clan reunion held by the polo fields in Golden Gate Park. Although we had dated only a few times in the last month—and certainly had never slept together, since both of us lived at home—Ted introduced me to all his relatives as his girlfriend, which, until then, I didn't know I was.

Later, when Ted and his father went off to play volleyball with the others, his mother took my hand, and we started walking along the grass, away from the crowd. She squeezed my palm warmly but never seemed to look at me.

"I'm so glad to meet you *finally,*" Mrs. Jordan said. I wanted to tell her I wasn't really Ted's girlfriend, but she went on. "I think it's nice that you and Ted are having such a lot of fun together. So I hope you won't misunderstand what I have to say."

And then she spoke quietly about Ted's future, his needs to concentrate on his medical studies, why it would be years before he could even think about marriage. She assured me she had nothing whatsoever against minorities; she and her husband, who owned a chain of office-supply stores, personally knew many fine people who were Oriental, Spanish, and even black. But Ted was going to be in one of those professions where he would be judged by a different standard, by patients and other doctors who might not be as understanding as the Jordans were. She said it was so unfortunate the way the rest of the world was, how unpopular the Vietnam War was.

"Mrs. Jordan, I am not Vietnamese," I said softly, even though I was on the verge of shouting. "And I have no intention of marrying your son."

When Ted drove me home that day, I told him I couldn't see him anymore. When he asked me why, I shrugged. When he pressed me, I told him what his mother had said, verbatim, without comment.

"And you're just going to sit there! Let my mother decide what's right?" he shouted, as if I were a co-conspirator who had turned traitor. I was touched that Ted was so upset.

"What should we do?" I asked, and I had a pained feeling I thought was the beginning of love.

In those early months, we clung to each other with a rather silly desperation, because, in spite of anything my mother or Mrs. Jordan could say, there was nothing that really prevented us from seeing one another. With imagined tragedy hovering over us, we became inseparable, two halves creating the whole: yin and yang.[2] I was victim to his hero. I was always in danger and he was always rescuing me. I would fall and he would lift me up. It was exhilarating and draining. The emotional effect of saving and being saved was addicting to both of us. And that, as much as anything we ever did in bed, was how we made love to each other: conjoined where my weaknesses needed protection.

"What should we do?" I continued to ask him. And within a year of our first meeting we were living together. The month before Ted started medical school at UCSF[3] we were married in the Episcopal church, and Mrs. Jordan sat in the front pew, crying as was expected of the groom's mother. When

[2]Chinese philosophical principle of opposites, whose union and interactions shape the destiny of all things.

[3]University of California at San Francisco.

Ted finished his residency in dermatology, we bought a run-down three-story Victorian with a large garden in Ashbury Heights. Ted helped me set up a studio downstairs so I could take in work as a free-lance production assistant for graphic artists.

Over the years, Ted decided where we went on vacation. He decided what new furniture we should buy. He decided we should wait until we moved into a better neighborhood before having children. We used to discuss some of these matters, but we both knew the question would boil down to my saying, "Ted, you decide." After a while, there were no more discussions. Ted simply decided. And I never thought of objecting. I preferred to ignore the world around me, obsessing only over what was in front of me: my T-square, my X-acto knife, my blue pencil.

But last year Ted's feelings about what he called "decision and responsibility" changed. A new patient had come to him asking what she could do about the spidery veins on her cheeks. And when he told her he could suck the red veins out and make her beautiful again, she believed him. But instead, he accidentally sucked a nerve out, and the left side of her smile fell down and she sued him.

After he lost the malpractice lawsuit—his first, and a big shock to him I now realize—he started pushing me to make decisions. Did I think we should buy an American car or a Japanese car? Should we change from whole-life to term insurance? What did I think about that candidate who supported the contras? What about a family?

I thought about things, the pros and the cons. But in the end I would be so confused, because I never believed there was ever any one right answer, yet there were many wrong ones. So whenever I said, "You decide," or "I don't care," or "Either way is fine with me," Ted would say in his impatient voice, "No, *you* decide. You can't have it both ways, none of the responsibility, none of the blame."

I could feel things changing between us. A protective veil had been lifted and Ted now started pushing me about everything. He asked me to decide on the most trivial matters, as if he were baiting me. Italian food or Thai. One appetizer or two. Which appetizer. Credit card or cash. Visa or MasterCard.

Last month, when he was leaving for a two-day dermatology course in Los Angeles, he asked if I wanted to come along and then quickly, before I could say anything, he added, "Never mind, I'd rather go alone."

"More time to study," I agreed.

"No, because you can never make up your mind about anything," he said.

And I protested, "But it's only with things that aren't important."

"Nothing is important to you, then," he said in a tone of disgust.

"Ted, if you want me to go, I'll go."

And it was as if something snapped in him. "How the hell did we ever get married? Did you just say 'I do' because the minister said 'repeat after me'? What would you have done with your life if I had never married you? Did it ever occur to you?"

This was such a big leap in logic, between what I said and what he said, that I thought we were like two people standing apart on separate mountain peaks, recklessly leaning forward to throw stones at one another, unaware of the dangerous chasm that separated us.

But now I realize Ted knew what he was saying all along. He wanted to show me the rift. Because later that evening he called from Los Angeles and said he wanted a divorce.

Ever since Ted's been gone, I've been thinking. Even if I had expected it, even if I had known what I was going to do with my life, it still would have knocked the wind out of me.

When something that violent hits you, you can't help but lose your balance and fall. And after you pick yourself up, you realize you can't trust anybody to save you—not your husband, not your mother, not God. So what can you do to stop yourself from tilting and falling all over again?

My mother believed in God's will for many years. It was as if she had turned on a celestial faucet and goodness kept pouring out. She said it was faith that kept all these good things coming our way, only I thought she said "fate," because she couldn't pronounce that "th" sound in "faith."

And later, I discovered that maybe it was fate all along, that faith was just an illusion that somehow you're in control. I found out the most I could have was hope, and with that I was not denying any possibility, good or bad. I was just saying, If there is a choice, dear God or whatever you are, here's where the odds should be placed.

I remember the day I started thinking this, it was such a revelation to me. It was the day my mother lost her faith in God. She found that things of unquestioned certainty could never be trusted again.

We had gone to the beach, to a secluded spot south of the city near Devil's Slide. My father had read in *Sunset* magazine that this was a good place to catch ocean perch. And although my father was not a fisherman but a pharmacist's assistant who had once been a doctor in China, he believed in his *nengkan,* his ability to do anything he put his mind to. My mother believed she had *nengkan* to cook anything my father had a mind to catch. It was this belief in their *nengkan* that had brought my parents to America. It had enabled them to have seven children and buy a house in the Sunset district with very little money. It had given them the confidence to believe their luck would never run out, that God was on their side, that the house gods had only benevolent things to report and our ancestors were pleased, that lifetime warranties meant our lucky streak would never break, that all the elements were in balance, the right amount of wind and water.

So there we were, the nine of us: my father, my mother, my two sisters, four brothers, and myself, so confident as we walked along our first beach. We marched in single file across the cool gray sand, from oldest to youngest. I was in the middle, fourteen years old. We would have made quite a sight, if anyone else had been watching, nine pairs of bare feet trudging, nine pairs of shoes in hand, nine black-haired heads turned toward the water to watch the waves tumbling in.

The wind was whipping the cotton trousers around my legs and I looked for some place where the sand wouldn't kick into my eyes. I saw we were standing in the hollow of a cove. It was like a giant bowl, cracked in half, the other half washed out to sea. My mother walked toward the right, where the beach was clean, and we all followed. On this side, the wall of the cove curved around and protected the beach from both the rough surf and the wind. And along this wall, in its shadow, was a reef ledge that started at the edge of the beach and continued out past the cove where the waters became rough. It seemed as though a person could walk out to sea on this reef, although it looked very rocky and slippery. On the other side of the cove, the wall was more jagged, eaten away by the water. It was pitted with crevices, so when the waves crashed against the wall, the water spewed out of these holes like white gulleys.

Thinking back, I remember that this beach cove was a terrible place, full of wet shadows that chilled us and invisible specks that flew into our eyes and made it hard for us to see the dangers. We were all blind with the newness of this experience: a Chinese family trying to act like a typical American family at the beach.

My mother spread out an old striped bedspread, which flapped in the wind until nine pairs of shoes weighed it down. My father assembled his long bamboo fishing pole, a pole he had made with his own two hands, remembering its design from his childhood in China. And we children sat huddled shoulder to shoulder on the blanket, reaching into the grocery sack full of bologna sandwiches, which we hungrily ate salted with sand from our fingers.

Then my father stood up and admired his fishing pole, its grace, its strength. Satisfied, he picked up his shoes and walked to the edge of the beach and then onto the reef to the point just before it was wet. My two older sisters, Janice and Ruth, jumped up from the blanket and slapped their thighs to get the sand off. Then they slapped each other's back and raced off down the beach shrieking. I was about to get up and chase them, but my mother nodded toward my four brothers and reminded me: "*Dangsying tamende shenti,*" which means "Take care of them," or literally, "Watch out for their bodies." These bodies were the anchors of my life: Matthew, Mark, Luke, and Bing. I fell back onto the sand, groaning as my throat grew tight, as I made the same lament: "Why?" Why did I have to care for them?

And she gave me the same answer: "*Yiding.*"

I must. Because they were my brothers. My sisters had once taken care of me. How else could I learn responsibility? How else could I appreciate what my parents had done for me?

Matthew, Mark, and Luke were twelve, ten, and nine, old enough to keep themselves loudly amused. They had already buried Luke in a shallow grave of sand so that only his head stuck out. Now they were starting to pat together the outlines of a sand-castle wall on top of him.

But Bing was only four, easily excitable and easily bored and irritable. He didn't want to play with the other brothers because they had pushed him off to the side, admonishing him, "No, Bing, you'll just wreck it."

So Bing wandered down the beach, walking stiffly like an ousted emperor, picking up shards of rock and chunks of driftwood and flinging them with all his might into the surf. I trailed behind, imagining tidal waves and wondering what I would do if one appeared. I called to Bing every now and then, "Don't go too close to the water. You'll get your feet wet." And I thought how much I seemed like my mother, always worried beyond reason inside, but at the same time talking about the danger as if it were less than it really was. The worry surrounded me, like the wall of the cove, and it made me feel everything had been considered and was now safe.

My mother had a superstition, in fact, that children were predisposed to certain dangers on certain days, all depending on their Chinese birthdate. It was explained in a little Chinese book called *The Twenty-Six Malignant Gates.* There, on each page, was an illustration of some terrible danger that awaited young innocent children. In the corners was a description written in Chinese, and since I couldn't read the characters, I could only see what the picture meant.

The same little boy appeared in each picture: climbing a broken tree limb, standing by a falling gate, slipping in a wooden tub, being carried away by a snapping dog, fleeing from a bolt of lightning. And in each of these pictures stood a man who looked as if he were wearing a lizard costume. He had a big crease in his forehead, or maybe it was actually that he had two round horns. In one picture, the lizard man was standing on a curved bridge, laughing as he watched the little boy flying forward over the bridge rail, his slippered feet already in the air.

It would have been enough to think that even one of these dangers could befall a child. And even though the birthdates corresponded to only one danger, my mother worried about them all. This was because she couldn't figure out how the Chinese dates, based on the lunar calendar, translated into American dates. So by taking them all into account, she had absolute faith she could prevent every one of them.

The sun had shifted and moved over the other side of the cove wall. Everything had settled into place. My mother was busy keeping sand from blowing onto the blanket, then shaking sand out of shoes, and tacking corners of blankets back down again with the now clean shoes. My father was still standing at the end of the reef, patiently casting out, waiting for *nengkan* to manifest itself as a fish. I could see small figures farther down on the beach, and I could tell they were my sisters by their two dark heads and yellow pants. My brothers' shrieks were mixed with those of seagulls. Bing had found an empty soda bottle and was using this to dig sand next to the dark cove wall. And I sat on the sand, just where the shadows ended and the sunny part began.

Bing was pounding the soda bottle against the rock, so I called to him, "Don't dig so hard. You'll bust a hole in the wall and fall all the way to China." And I laughed when he looked at me as though he thought what I said was true. He stood up and started walking toward the water. He put one foot tentatively on the reef, and I warned him, "Bing."

"I'm gonna see Daddy," he protested.

"Stay close to the wall, then, away from the water," I said. "Stay away from the mean fish."

And I watched as he inched his way along the reef, his back hugging the bumpy cove wall. I still see him, so clearly that I almost feel I can make him stay there forever.

I see him standing by the wall, safe, calling to my father, who looks over his shoulder toward Bing. How glad I am that my father is going to watch him for a while! Bing starts to walk over and then something tugs on my father's line and he's reeling as fast as he can.

Shouts erupt. Someone has thrown sand in Luke's face and he's jumped out of his sand grave and thrown himself on top of Mark, thrashing and kicking. My mother shouts for me to stop them. And right after I pull Luke off Mark, I look up and see Bing walking alone to the edge of the reef. In the confusion of the fight, nobody notices. I am the only one who sees what Bing is doing.

Bing walks one, two, three steps. His little body is moving so quickly, as if he spotted something wonderful by the water's edge. And I think, *He's going to fall in.* I'm expecting it. And just as I think this, his feet are already in the air, in a moment of balance, before he splashes into the sea and disappears without leaving so much as a ripple in the water.

I sank to my knees watching that spot where he disappeared, not moving, not saying anything. I couldn't make sense of it. I was thinking, Should I run to the water and try to pull him out? Should I shout to my father? Can I rise on my legs fast enough? Can I take it all back and forbid Bing from joining my father on the ledge?

And then my sisters were back, and one of them said, "Where's Bing?" There was silence for a few seconds and then shouts and sand flying as everyone rushed past me toward the water's edge. I stood there unable to move as my sisters looked by the cove wall, as my brothers scrambled to see what lay behind pieces of driftwood. My mother and father were trying to part the waves with their hands.

We were there for many hours. I remember the search boats and the sunset when dusk came. I had never seen a sunset like that: a bright orange flame touching the water's edge and then fanning out, warming the sea. When it became dark, the boats turned their yellow orbs on and bounced up and down on the dark shiny water.

As I look back, it seems unnatural to think about the colors of the sunset and boats at a time like that. But we all had strange thoughts. My father was calculating minutes, estimating the temperature of the water, readjusting his estimate of when Bing fell. My sisters were calling, "Bing! Bing!" as if he were hiding in some bushes high above the beach cliffs. My brothers sat in the car, quietly reading comic books. And when the boats turned off their yellow orbs, my mother went for a swim. She had never swum a stroke in her life, but her faith in her own *nengkan* convinced her that what these Americans couldn't do, she could. She could find Bing.

And when the rescue people finally pulled her out of the water, she still had her *nengkan* intact. Her hair, her clothes, they were all heavy with the cold water, but she stood quietly, calm and regal as a mermaid queen who had just arrived out of the sea. The police called off the search, put us all in our car, and sent us home to grieve.

I had expected to be beaten to death, by my father, by my mother, by my sisters and brothers. I knew it was my fault. I hadn't watched him closely enough, and yet I saw him. But as we sat in the dark living room, I heard them, one by one whispering their regrets.

"I was selfish to want to go fishing," said my father.

"We shouldn't have gone for a walk," said Janice, while Ruth blew her nose yet another time.

"Why'd you have to throw sand in my face?" moaned Luke. "Why'd you have to make me start a fight?"

And my mother quietly admitted to me, "I told you to stop their fight. I told you to take your eyes off him."

If I had had any time at all to feel a sense of relief, it would have quickly evaporated, because my mother also said, "So now I am telling you, we must go and find him, quickly, tomorrow morning." And everybody's eyes looked down. But I saw it as my punishment: to go out with my mother, back to the beach, to help her find Bing's body.

Nothing prepared me for what my mother did the next day. When I woke up, it was still dark and she was already dressed. On the kitchen table was a thermos, a teacup, the white leatherette Bible, and the car keys.

"Is Daddy ready?" I asked.

"Daddy's not coming," she said.

"Then how will we get there? Who will drive us?"

She picked up the keys and I followed her out the door to the car. I wondered the whole time as we drove to the beach how she had learned to drive overnight. She used no map. She drove smoothly ahead, turning down Geary, then the Great Highway, signaling at all the right times, getting on the Coast Highway and easily winding the car around the sharp curves that often led inexperienced drivers off and over the cliffs.

When we arrived at the beach, she walked immediately down the dirt path and over to the end of the reef ledge, where I had seen Bing disappear. She held in her hand the white Bible. And looking out over the water, she called to God, her small voice carried up by the gulls to heaven. It began with "Dear God" and ended with "Amen," and in between she spoke in Chinese.

"I have always believed in your blessings," she praised God in that same tone she used for exaggerated Chinese compliments. "We knew they would come. We did not question them. Your decisions were our decisions. You rewarded us for our faith.

"In return we have always tried to show our deepest respect. We went to your house. We brought you money. We sang your songs. You gave us more blessings. And now we have misplaced one of them. We were careless. This is true. We had so many good things, we couldn't keep them in our mind all the time.

"So maybe you hid him from us to teach us a lesson, to be more careful with your gifts in the future. I have learned this. I have put it in my memory. And now I have come to take Bing back."

I listened quietly as my mother said these words, horrified. And I began to cry when she added, "Forgive us for his bad manners. My daughter, this one standing here, will be sure to teach him better lessons of obedience before he visits you again."

After her prayer, her faith was so great that she saw him, three times, waving to her from just beyond the first wave. "*Nale!*"—There! And she would stand straight as a sentinel, until three times her eyesight failed her and Bing turned into a dark spot of churning seaweed.

My mother did not let her chin fall down. She walked back to the beach and put the Bible down. She picked up the thermos and teacup and walked to the water's edge. Then she told me that the night before she had reached back into her life, back when she was a girl in China, and this is what she had found.

"I remember a boy who lost his hand in a firecracker accident," she said. "I saw the shreds of this boy's arm, his tears, and then I heard his mother's claim that he would grow back another hand, better than the last. This mother said she would pay back an ancestral debt ten times over. She would use a water treatment to soothe the wrath of Chu Jung, the three-eyed god of fire. And true enough, the next week this boy was riding a bicycle, both hands steering a straight course past my astonished eyes!"

And then my mother became very quiet. She spoke again in a thoughtful, respectful manner.

"An ancestor of ours once stole water from a sacred well. Now the water is trying to steal back. We must sweeten the temper of the Coiling Dragon who lives in the sea. And then we must make him loosen his coils from Bing by giving him another treasure he can hide."

My mother poured out tea sweetened with sugar into the teacup, and threw this into the sea. And then she opened her fist. In her palm was a ring of watery blue sapphire, a gift from her mother, who had died many years before. This ring, she told me, drew coveting stares from women and made them inattentive to the children they guarded so jealously. This would make the Coiling Dragon forgetful of Bing. She threw the ring into the water.

But even with this, Bing did not appear right away. For an hour or so, all we saw was seaweed drifting by. And then I saw her clasp her hands to her chest, and she said in a wondrous voice, "See, it's because we were watching the wrong direction." And I too saw Bing trudging wearily at the far end of the beach, his shoes hanging in his hand, his dark head bent over in exhaustion. I could feel what my mother felt. The hunger in our hearts was instantly filled. And then the two of us, before we could even get to our feet, saw him light a cigarette, grow tall, and become a stranger.

"Ma, let's go," I said as softly as possible.

"He's there," she said firmly. She pointed to the jagged wall across the water. "I see him. He is in a cave, sitting on a little step above the water. He is hungry and a little cold, but he has learned now not to complain too much."

And then she stood up and started walking across the sandy beach as though it were a solid paved path, and I was trying to follow behind, struggling and stumbling in the soft mounds. She marched up the steep path to where the car was parked, and she wasn't even breathing hard as she pulled a large inner tube from the trunk. To this lifesaver, she tied the fishing line from my father's bamboo pole. She walked back and threw the tube into the sea, holding onto the pole.

"This will go where Bing is. I will bring him back," she said fiercely. I had never heard so much *nengkan* in my mother's voice.

The tube followed her mind. It drifted out, toward the other side of the cove where it was caught by stronger waves. The line became taut and she strained to hold on tight. But the line snapped and then spiraled into the water.

We both climbed toward the end of the reef to watch. The tube had now reached the other side of the cove. A big wave smashed it into the wall. The bloated tube leapt up and then it was sucked in, under the wall and into a cavern. It popped out. Over and over again, it disappeared, emerged, glistening black, faithfully reporting it had seen Bing and was going back to try to pluck him from the cave. Over and over again, it dove and popped back up again, empty but still hopeful. And then, after a dozen or so times, it was sucked into the dark recess, and when it came out, it was torn and lifeless.

At that moment, and not until that moment, did she give up. My mother had a look on her face that I'll never forget. It was one of complete despair and horror, for losing Bing, for being so foolish as to think she could use faith to change fate. And it made me angry—so blindingly angry—that everything had failed us.

I know now that I had never expected to find Bing, just as I know now I will never find a way to save my marriage. My mother tells me, though, that I should still try.

"What's the point?" I say. "There's no hope. There's no reason to keep trying."

"Because you must," she says, "This is not hope. Not reason. This is your fate. This is your life, what you must do."

"So what can I do?"

And my mother says, "You must think for yourself, what you must do. If someone tells you, then you are not trying." And then she walks out of the kitchen to let me think about this.

I think about Bing, how I knew he was in danger, how I let it happen. I think about my marriage, how I had seen the signs, really I had. But I just let it happen. And I think now that fate is shaped half by expectation, half by inattention. But somehow, when you lose something you love, faith takes over. You have to pay attention to what you lost. You have to undo the expectation.

My mother, she still pays attention to it. That Bible under the table, I know she sees it. I remember seeing her write in it before she wedged it under.

I lift the table and slide the Bible out. I put the Bible on the table, flipping quickly through the pages, because I know it's there. On the page before the New Testament begins, there's a section called "Deaths," and that's where she wrote "Bing Hsu" lightly, in erasable pencil.

1989

Bobbie Ann Mason 1940–

Bobbie Ann Mason writes about blue-collar people in small-town and rural America—store clerks, waitresses, truck drivers—men and women who, she says, believe in "progress," but who "are kind of naive and optimistic, for the most part: they think better times are coming." They are, she says, a "shopping mall generation," people adrift in a high-tech world that controls their jobs and their desires, that gives them fast foods that gratify their taste and television sitcoms that fill their empty hours.

Mason came to know the lives of small-town working people and the world of mass culture while growing up in Kentucky, on a farm outside the small town of Mayfield. She spent her youth doing farm chores, reading stories of the Bobbsey Twins and the girl detective Nancy Drew, listening to rock music on the radio, and following the lives of celebrities. In the 1950s, she became the teenage president of the national fan club of a popular singing quartet, The Hilltoppers, and followed them on concert tours through midwest America.

Her youthful experiences at the edge of the world of entertainment glitz and glamour made her want to be a journalist, and when she was eighteen, she entered the University of Kentucky. Four years later she graduated and moved to New York, where she earned her living by writing articles on teen idols such as Fabian and Annette Funicello for "fan mags" like Movie Stars, Movie Life, *and* T. V. Star Parade.

But her university courses had stirred her interest in literature, and she entered the State University of New York at Binghamton, where she earned an M.A. in 1966. She then went to the University of Connecticut, where she graduated with a Ph.D. in English in 1972. She wrote her doctoral dissertation on Vladimir Nabokov, and in 1974 it was published as Nabokov's Garden. *From 1972 to 1979, she taught at Mansfield State College in Pennsylvania, and she published her second book,* The Girl Sleuth: A Feminist Guide to the Bobbsey Twins, Nancy Drew, and Their Sisters *(1975), a scholarly study of the popular books she had enjoyed when she was young.*

In her late thirties Mason began to write short stories, and she soon discovered that her best subjects for fiction were the working-class people of her native western Kentucky. Her stories began to appear in the New Yorker, Atlantic Monthly, Paris Review, Mother Jones, *and* Harper's. *In 1982 her first collection,* Shiloh and Other Stories, *appeared. Her next book was a novel,* In Country *(1985), which was made into a successful motion picture. A second collection of her short stories,* Love Life, *appeared in 1989. Her novel* Feather Crowns *(1993) sympathetically examines a pair of ordinary Americans to whom fate brings instant fame as curiosities in the carnival and freak-show world of the early twentieth century, foreboding antecedents of the grotesque simpletons who display themselves on today's TV talk shows before audiences fascinated by prurience and abnormality.* Midnight Magic, Selected Stories of Bobbie Ann Mason *appeared in 1998, and in 1999 she published* Clear Springs, A Memoir, *describing her origins in Kentucky and the stern and often numbing life on farms and in small towns that shaped her view of men and women and the lives they struggle to endure. Her most recent collection of short stories is* Zigzagging Down a Wild Trail *(2002).*

Mason's writing is peeled and terse. Her flat diction, direct sentences, and references to common, everyday things, to brand names, to the icons of pop culture, convey the sparseness and the pathos of her characters' lives. Her women shop at K mart, wear Dr. Scholl's sandals, and eat "tasty" food prepackaged for the microwave. They have frosted curls, like the heroine of "Shiloh," who works on her pectorals with dumbbells and reminds her husband of Wonder Woman. The men are vague. They sit, waiting, amid the wreckage of their lives. They have ill-fated plans for triumphs and exploits, like the hero of "Shiloh," who creates a log cabin out of Popsicle sticks and has noble dreams of building a real log cabin—from a kit. Drugged by American consumerism, they are fascinated by America's materialistic trivia and the higher sleaze exhibited by their moneyed betters, the rich and famous.

Mason's stories have been called "Grit Lit" and "Shopping Mall Realism." Her fiction is the kind, it is said, that "her own characters would never read" even if they were to "turn off the television long enough to look at a book at all." She is resolutely unsentimental, a regional writer in the tradition of William Faulkner, Flannery O'Connor, and Eudora Welty, and like them she has created characters who are recognizable anywhere in America.

FURTHER READING: A. Wilhelm, *Bobbie Ann Mason,* 1998; J. Price, *Understanding Bobbie Ann Mason,* 2000.
TEXT: *Shiloh and Other Stories,* 1982.

SHILOH

Leroy Moffitt's wife, Norma Jean, is working on her pectorals. She lifts three-pound dumbbells to warm up, then progresses to a twenty-pound barbell. Standing with her legs apart, she reminds Leroy of Wonder Woman.

"I'd give anything if I could just get these muscles to where they're real hard," says Norma Jean. "Feel this arm. It's not as hard as the other one."

"That's 'cause you're right-handed," says Leroy, dodging as she swings the barbell in an arc.

"Do you think so?"

"Sure."

Leroy is a truckdriver. He injured his leg in a highway accident four months ago, and his physical therapy, which involves weights and a pulley, prompted Norma Jean to try building herself up. Now she is attending a body-building class. Leroy has been collecting temporary disability since his tractor-trailer jackknifed in Missouri, badly twisting his left leg in its socket. He has a steel pin in his hip. He will probably not be able to drive his rig again. It sits in the backyard, like a gigantic bird that has flown home to roost. Leroy has been home in Kentucky for three months, and his leg is almost healed, but the accident frightened him and he does not want to drive any more long hauls. He is not sure what to do next. In the meantime, he makes things from craft kits. He started by building a miniature log cabin from notched Popsicle sticks. He varnished it and placed it on the TV set, where it remains. It reminds him of a rustic Nativity scene. Then he tried string art (sailing ships on black velvet), a macramé owl kit, a snap-together B-17 Flying Fortress, and a lamp made out of a model truck, with a light fixture screwed in the top of the cab. At first the kits were diversions, something to kill time, but now he is thinking about building a full-scale log house from a kit. It would be considerably cheaper than building a regular house, and besides, Leroy has grown to appreciate how things are put together. He has begun to realize that in all the years he was on the road he never took time to examine anything. He was always flying past scenery.

"They won't let you build a log cabin in any of the new subdivisions," Norma Jean tells him.

"They will if I tell them it's for you," he says, teasing her. Ever since they were married, he has promised Norma Jean he would build her a new home one day. They have always rented, and the house they live in is small and nondescript. It does not even feel like a home, Leroy realizes now.

Norma Jean works at the Rexall drugstore, and she has acquired an amazing amount of information about cosmetics. When she explains to Leroy the three stages of complexion care, involving creams, toners, and moisturizers, he thinks happily of other petroleum products—axle grease, diesel fuel. This is a connection between him and Norma Jean. Since he has been home, he has felt unusually tender about his wife and guilty over his long absences.

But he can't tell what she feels about him. Norma Jean has never complained about his traveling; she has never made hurt remarks, like calling his truck a "widow-maker." He is reasonably certain she has been faithful to him, but he wishes she would celebrate his permanent homecoming more happily. Norma Jean is often startled to find Leroy at home, and he thinks she seems a little disappointed about it. Perhaps he reminds her too much of the early days of their marriage, before he went on the road. They had a child who died as an infant, years ago. They never speak about their memories of Randy, which have almost faded, but now that Leroy is home all the time, they sometimes feel awkward around each other, and Leroy wonders if one of them should mention the child. He has the feeling that they are waking up out of a dream together—that they must create a new marriage, start afresh. They are lucky they are still married. Leroy has read that for most people losing a child destroys the marriage—or else he heard this on *Donahue.* He can't always remember where he learns things anymore.

At Christmas, Leroy bought an electric organ for Norma Jean. She used to play the piano when she was in high school. "It don't leave you," she told him once. "It's like riding a bicycle."

The new instrument had so many keys and buttons that she was bewildered by it at first. She touched the keys tentatively, pushed some buttons, then pecked out "Chopsticks." It came out in an amplified fox-trot rhythm, with marimba sounds.

"It's an orchestra!" she cried.

The organ had a pecan-look finish and eighteen preset chords, with optional flute, violin, trumpet, clarinet, and banjo accompaniments. Norma Jean mastered the organ almost immediately. At first she played Christmas songs. Then she bought *The Sixties Songbook* and learned every tune in it, adding variations to each with the rows of brightly colored buttons.

"I didn't like these old songs back then," she said. "But I have this crazy feeling I missed something."

"You didn't miss a thing," said Leroy.

Leroy likes to lie on the couch and smoke a joint and listen to Norma Jean play "Can't Take My Eyes Off You" and "I'll Be Back." He is back again. After fifteen years on the road, he is finally settling down with the woman he loves. She is still pretty. Her skin is flawless. Her frosted curls resemble pencil trimmings.

Now that Leroy has come home to stay, he notices how much the town has changed. Subdivisions are spreading across western Kentucky like an oil slick. The sign at the edge of town says "Pop: 11,500"—only seven hundred more than it said twenty years before. Leroy can't figure out who is living in all the new houses. The farmers who used to gather around the courthouse square on Saturday afternoons to play checkers and spit tobacco juice have gone. It has been years since Leroy has thought about the farmers, and they have disappeared without his noticing.

Leroy meets a kid named Stevie Hamilton in the parking lot at the new shopping center. While they pretend to be strangers meeting over a stalled car, Stevie tosses an ounce of marijuana under the front seat of Leroy's car.

Stevie is wearing orange jogging shoes and a T-shirt that says CHATTAHOOCHEE SUPER-RAT. His father is a prominent doctor who lives in one of the expensive subdivisions in a new white-columned brick house that looks like a funeral parlor. In the phone book under his name there is a separate number, with the listing "Teenagers."

"Where do you get this stuff?" asks Leroy. "From your pappy?"

"That's for me to know and you to find out," Stevie says. He is slit-eyed and skinny.

"What else you got?"

"What you interested in?"

"Nothing special. Just wondered."

Leroy used to take speed on the road. Now he has to go slowly. He needs to be mellow. He leans back against the car and says, "I'm aiming to build me a log house, soon as I get time. My wife, though, I don't think she likes the idea."

"Well, let me know when you want me again," Stevie says. He has a cigarette in his cupped palm, as though sheltering it from the wind. He takes a long drag, then stomps it on the asphalt and slouches away.

Stevie's father was two years ahead of Leroy in high school. Leroy is thirty-four. He married Norma Jean when they were both eighteen, and their child Randy was born a few months later, but he died at the age of four months and three days. He would be about Stevie's age now. Norma Jean and Leroy were at the drive-in, watching a double feature (*Dr. Strangelove* and *Lover Come Back*), and the baby was sleeping in the back seat. When the first movie ended, the baby was dead. It was the sudden infant death syndrome. Leroy remembers handing Randy to a nurse at the emergency room, as though he were offering her a large doll as a present. A dead baby feels like a sack of flour. "It just happens sometimes," said the doctor, in what Leroy always recalls as a nonchalant tone. Leroy can hardly remember the child anymore, but he still sees vividly a scene from *Dr. Strangelove* in which the President of the United States was talking in a folksy voice on the hot line to the Soviet premier about the bomber accidentally headed toward Russia. He was in the War Room, and the world map was lit up. Leroy remembers Norma Jean standing catatonically beside him in the hospital and himself thinking: Who is this strange girl? He had forgotten who she was. Now scientists are saying that crib death is caused by a virus. Nobody knows anything, Leroy thinks. The answers are always changing.

When Leroy gets home from the shopping center, Norma Jean's mother, Mabel Beasley, is there. Until this year, Leroy has not realized how much time she spends with Norma Jean. When she visits, she inspects the closets and then the plants, informing Norma Jean when a plant is droopy or yellow. Mabel calls the plants "flowers," although there are never any blooms. She always notices if Norma Jean's laundry is piling up. Mabel is a short, overweight woman whose tight, brown-dyed curls look more like a wig than the actual wig she sometimes wears. Today she has brought Norma Jean an off-white dust ruffle she made for the bed; Mabel works in a custom-upholstery shop.

"This is the tenth one I made this year," Mabel says. "I got started and couldn't stop."

"It's real pretty," says Norma Jean.

"Now we can hide things under the bed," says Leroy, who gets along with his mother-in-law primarily by joking with her. Mabel has never really forgiven him for disgracing her by getting Norma Jean pregnant. When the baby died, she said that fate was mocking her.

"What's that thing?" Mabel says to Leroy in a loud voice, pointing to a tangle of yarn on a piece of canvas.

Leroy holds it up for Mabel to see. "It's my needlepoint," he explains. "This is a *Star Trek* pillow cover."

"That's what a woman would do," says Mabel. "Great day in the morning!"

"All the big football players on TV do it," he says.

"Why, Leroy, you're always trying to fool me. I don't believe you for one minute. You don't know what to do with yourself—that's the whole trouble. Sewing!"

"I'm aiming to build us a log house," says Leroy. "Soon as my plans come."

"Like *heck* you are," says Norma Jean. She takes Leroy's needlepoint and shoves it into a drawer. "You have to find a job first. Nobody can afford to build now anyway."

Mabel straightens her girdle and says, "I still think before you get tied down y'all ought to take a little run to Shiloh."

"One of these days, Mama," Norma Jean says impatiently.

Mabel is talking about Shiloh, Tennessee. For the past few years, she has been urging Leroy and Norma Jean to visit the Civil War battleground there. Mabel went there on her honeymoon—the only real trip she ever took. Her husband died of a perforated ulcer when Norma Jean was ten, but Mabel, who was accepted into the United Daughters of the Confederacy in 1975, is still preoccupied with going back to Shiloh.

"I've been to kingdom come and back in that truck out yonder," Leroy says to Mabel, "but we never yet set foot in that battleground. Ain't that something? How did I miss it?"

"It's not even that far," Mabel says.

After Mabel leaves, Norma Jean reads to Leroy from a list she has made. "Things you could do," she announces. "You could get a job as a guard at Union Carbide, where they'd let you set on a stool. You could get on at the lumberyard. You could do a little carpenter work, if you want to build so bad. You could—"

"I can't do something where I'd have to stand up all day."

"You ought to try standing up all day behind a cosmetics counter. It's amazing that I have strong feet, coming from two parents that never had strong feet at all." At the moment Norma Jean is holding on to the kitchen counter, raising her knees one at a time as she talks. She is wearing two-pound ankle weights.

"Don't worry," says Leroy. "I'll do something."

"You could truck calves to slaughter for somebody. You wouldn't have to drive any big old truck for that."

"I'm going to build you this house," says Leroy. "I want to make you a real home."

"I don't want to live in any log cabin."

"It's not a cabin. It's a house."

"I don't care. It looks like a cabin."

"You and me together could lift those logs. It's just like lifting weights."

Norma Jean doesn't answer. Under her breath, she is counting. Now she is marching through the kitchen. She is doing goose steps.

Before his accident, when Leroy came home he used to stay in the house with Norma Jean, watching TV in bed and playing cards. She would cook fried chicken, picnic ham, chocolate pie—all his favorites. Now he is home alone much of the time. In the mornings, Norma Jean disappears, leaving a cooling place in the bed. She eats a cereal called Body Buddies, and she leaves the bowl on the table, with the soggy tan balls floating in a milk puddle. He sees things about Norma Jean that he never realized before. When she chops onions, she stares off into a corner, as if she can't bear to look. She puts on her house slippers almost precisely at nine o'clock every evening and nudges her jogging shoes under the couch. She saves bread heels for the birds. Leroy watches the birds at the feeder. He notices the peculiar way goldfinches fly past the window. They close their wings, then fall, then spread their wings to catch and lift themselves. He wonders if they close their eyes when they fall. Norma Jean closes her eyes when they are in bed. She wants the lights turned out. Even then, he is sure she closes her eyes.

He goes for long drives around town. He tends to drive a car rather carelessly. Power steering and an automatic shift make a car feel so small and inconsequential that his body is hardly involved in the driving process. His injured leg stretches out comfortably. Once or twice he has almost hit something, but even the prospect of an accident seems minor in a car. He cruises the new subdivisions, feeling like a criminal rehearsing for a robbery. Norma Jean is probably right about a log house being inappropriate here in the new subdivisions. All the houses look grand and complicated. They depress him.

One day when Leroy comes home from a drive he finds Norma Jean in tears. She is in the kitchen making a potato and mushroom-soup casserole, with grated-cheese topping. She is crying because her mother caught her smoking.

"I didn't hear her coming. I was standing here puffing away pretty as you please," Norma Jean says, wiping her eyes.

"I knew it would happen sooner or later," says Leroy, putting his arm around her.

"She don't know the meaning of the word 'knock,'" says Norma Jean. "It's a wonder she hadn't caught me years ago."

"Think of it this way," Leroy says. "What if she caught me with a joint?"

"You better not let her!" Norma Jean shrieks. "I'm warning you, Leroy Moffitt!"

"I'm just kidding. Here, play me a tune. That'll help you relax."

Norma Jean puts the casserole in the oven and sets the timer. Then she plays a ragtime tune, with horns and banjo, as Leroy lights up a joint and lies on the couch, laughing to himself about Mabel's catching him at it. He thinks of Stevie Hamilton—a doctor's son pushing grass. Everything is funny. The whole town seems crazy and small. He is reminded of Virgil Mathis, a boastful policeman Leroy used to shoot pool with. Virgil recently led a drug bust in a back room at a bowling alley, where he seized ten thousand dollars' worth of marijuana. The newspaper had a picture of him holding up the bags of grass and grinning widely. Right now, Leroy can imagine Virgil breaking down the door and arresting him with a lungful of smoke. Virgil would probably have been alerted to the scene because of all the racket Norma Jean is making. Now she sounds like a hard-rock band. Norma Jean is terrific. When she switches to a Latin-rhythm version of "Sunshine Superman," Leroy hums along. Norma Jean's foot goes up and down, up and down.

"Well, what do you think?" Leroy says, when Norma Jean pauses to search through her music.

"What do I think about what?"

His mind has gone blank. Then he says, "I'll sell my rig and build us a house." That wasn't what he wanted to say. He wanted to know what she thought—what she *really* thought—about them.

"Don't start in on that again," says Norma Jean. She begins playing "Who'll Be the Next in Line?"

Leroy used to tell hitchhikers his whole life story—about his travels, his hometown, the baby. He would end with a question: "Well, what do you think?" It was just a rhetorical question. In time, he had the feeling that he'd been telling the same story over and over to the same hitchhikers. He quit talking to hitchhikers when he realized how his voice sounded—whining and self-pitying, like some teenage-tragedy song. Now Leroy has the sudden impulse to tell Norma Jean about himself, as if he had just met her. They have known each other so long they have forgotten a lot about each other. They could become reacquainted. But when the oven timer goes off and she runs to the kitchen, he forgets why he wants to do this.

The next day, Mabel drops by. It is Saturday and Norma Jean is cleaning. Leroy is studying the plans of his log house, which have finally come in the mail. He has them spread out on the table—big sheets of stiff blue paper, with diagrams and numbers printed in white. While Norma Jean runs the vacuum, Mabel drinks coffee. She sets her coffee cup on a blueprint.

"I'm just waiting for time to pass," she says to Leroy, drumming her fingers on the table.

As soon as Norma Jean switches off the vacuum, Mabel says in a loud voice, "Did you hear about the datsun dog that killed the baby?"

Norma Jean says, "The word is 'dachshund.'"

"They put the dog on trial. It chewed the baby's legs off. The mother was in the next room all the time." She raises her voice. "They thought it was neglect."

Norma Jean is holding her ears. Leroy manages to open the refrigerator and get some Diet Pepsi to offer Mabel. Mabel still has some coffee and she waves away the Pepsi.

"Datsuns are like that," Mabel says. "They're jealous dogs. They'll tear a place to pieces if you don't keep an eye on them."

"You better watch out what you're saying, Mabel," says Leroy.

"Well, facts is facts."

Leroy looks out the window at his rig. It is like a huge piece of furniture gathering dust in the backyard. Pretty soon it will be an antique. He hears the vacuum cleaner. Norma Jean seems to be cleaning the living room rug again.

Later, she says to Leroy, "She just said that about the baby because she caught me smoking. She's trying to pay me back."

"What are you talking about?" Leroy says, nervously shuffling blueprints.

"You know good and well," Norma Jean says. She is sitting in a kitchen chair with her feet up and her arms wrapped around her knees. She looks small and helpless. She says, "The very idea, her bringing up a subject like that! Saying it was neglect."

"She didn't mean that," Leroy says.

"She might not have *thought* she meant it. She always says things like that. You don't know how she goes on."

"But she didn't really mean it. She was just talking."

Leroy opens a king-sized bottle of beer and pours it into two glasses, dividing it carefully. He hands a glass to Norma Jean and she takes it from him mechanically. For a long time, they sit by the kitchen window watching the birds at the feeder.

Something is happening. Norma Jean is going to night school. She has graduated from her six-week body-building course and now she is taking an adult-education course in composition at Paducah Community College. She spends her evenings outlining paragraphs.

"First you have a topic sentence," she explains to Leroy. "Then you divide it up. Your secondary topic has to be connected to your primary topic."

To Leroy, this sounds intimidating. "I never was any good in English," he says.

"It makes a lot of sense."

"What are you doing this for, anyhow?"

She shrugs. "It's something to do." She stands up and lifts her dumbbells a few times.

"Driving a rig, nobody cared about my English."

"I'm not criticizing your English."

Norma Jean used to say, "If I lose ten minutes' sleep, I just drag all day." Now she stays up late, writing compositions. She got a B on her first paper—a how-to theme on soup-based casseroles. Recently Norma Jean has been cooking unusual foods—tacos, lasagna, Bombay chicken. She doesn't play the organ anymore, though her second paper was called "Why Music Is Important to Me." She sits at the kitchen table, concentrating on her outlines, while Leroy plays with his log house plans, practicing with a set of Lincoln Logs. The thought of getting a truckload of notched, numbered logs scares him, and he wants to be prepared. As he and Norma Jean work together at the kitchen table, Leroy has the hopeful thought that they are sharing something, but he knows he is a fool to think this. Norma Jean is miles away. He knows he is going to lose her. Like Mabel, he is just waiting for time to pass.

One day, Mabel is there before Norma Jean gets home from work, and Leroy finds himself confiding in her. Mabel, he realizes, must know Norma Jean better than he does.

"I don't know what's got into that girl," Mabel says. "She used to go to bed with the chickens. Now you say she's up all hours. Plus her a-smoking. I like to died."

"I want to make her this beautiful home," Leroy says, indicating the Lincoln Logs. "I don't think she even wants it. Maybe she was happier with me gone."

"She don't know what to make of you, coming home like this."

"Is that it?"

Mabel takes the roof off his Lincoln Log cabin. "You couldn't get *me* in a log cabin," she says. "I was raised in one. It's no picnic, let me tell you."

"They're different now," says Leroy.

"I tell you what," Mabel says, smiling oddly at Leroy.

"What?"

"Take her on down to Shiloh. Y'all need to get out together, stir a little. Her brain's all balled up over them books."

Leroy can see traces of Norma Jean's features in her mother's face. Mabel's worn face has the texture of crinkled cotton, but suddenly she looks pretty. It occurs to Leroy that Mabel has been hinting all along that she wants them to take her with them to Shiloh.

"Let's all go to Shiloh," he says. "You and me and her. Come Sunday."

Mabel throws up her hands in protest. "Oh, no, not me. Young folks want to be by theirselves."

When Norma Jean comes in with groceries, Leroy says excitedly, "Your mama here's been dying to go to Shiloh for thirty-five years. It's about time we went, don't you think?"

"I'm not going to butt in on anybody's second honeymoon," Mabel says.

"Who's going on a honeymoon, for Christ's sake?" Norma Jean says loudly.

"I never raised no daughter of mine to talk that-a-way," Mabel says.

"You ain't seen nothing yet," says Norma Jean. She starts putting away boxes and cans, slamming cabinet doors.

"There's a log cabin at Shiloh," Mabel says. "It was there during the battle. There's bullet holes in it."

"When are you going to *shut up* about Shiloh, Mama?" asks Norma Jean.

"I always thought Shiloh was the prettiest place, so full of history," Mabel goes on. "I just hoped y'all could see it once before I die, so you could tell me about it." Later, she whispers to Leroy, "You do what I said. A little change is what she needs."

"Your name means 'the king,'" Norma Jean says to Leroy that evening. He is trying to get her to go to Shiloh, and she is reading a book about another century.

"Well, I reckon I ought to be right proud."

"I guess so."

"Am I still king around here?"

Norma Jean flexes her biceps and feels them for hardness. "I'm not fooling around with anybody, if that's what you mean," she says.

"Would you tell me if you were?"

"I don't know."

"What does *your* name mean?"

"It was Marilyn Monroe's real name."

"No kidding!"

"Norma comes from the Normans. They were invaders," she says. She closes her book and looks hard at Leroy. "I'll go to Shiloh with you if you'll stop staring at me."

On Sunday, Norma Jean packs a picnic and they go to Shiloh. To Leroy's relief, Mabel says she does not want to come with them. Norma Jean drives, and Leroy, sitting beside her, feels like some boring hitchhiker she has picked up. He tries some conversation, but she answers him in monosyllables. At Shiloh, she drives aimlessly through the park, past bluffs and trails and steep ravines. Shiloh is an immense place, and Leroy cannot see it as a battleground. It is not what he expected. He thought it would look like a golf course. Monuments are everywhere, showing through the thick clusters of trees. Norma Jean passes the log cabin Mabel mentioned. It is surrounded by tourists looking for bullet holes.

"That's not the kind of log house I've got in mind," says Leroy apologetically.

"I know *that*."

"This is a pretty place. Your Mama was right."

"It's O.K.," says Norma Jean. "Well, we've seen it. I hope she's satisfied."

They burst out laughing together.

At the park museum, a movie on Shiloh is shown every half hour, but they decide that they don't want to see it. They buy a souvenir Confederate flag for Mabel, and then they find a picnic spot near the cemetery. Norma Jean has brought a picnic cooler, with pimiento sandwiches, soft drinks, and Yodels. Leroy eats a sandwich and then smokes a joint, hiding it behind the picnic cooler. Norma Jean has quit smoking altogether. She is picking cake crumbs from the cellophane wrapper, like a fussy bird.

Leroy says, "So the boys in gray ended up in Corinth. The Union soldiers zapped 'em finally. April 7, 1862."

They both know that he doesn't know any history. He is just talking about some of the historical plaques they have read. He feels awkward, like a boy on a date with an older girl. They are still just making conversation.

"Corinth is where Mama eloped to," says Norma Jean.

They sit in silence and stare at the cemetery for the Union dead and, beyond, at a tall cluster of trees. Campers are parked nearby, bumper to bumper, and small children in bright clothing are cavorting and squealing. Norma Jean wads up the cake wrapper and squeezes it tightly in her hand. Without looking at Leroy, she says, "I want to leave you."

Leroy takes a bottle of Coke out of the cooler and flips off the cap. He holds the bottle poised near his mouth but cannot remember to take a drink. Finally he says, "No, you don't."

"Yes, I do."

"I won't let you."

"You can't stop me."

"Don't do me that way."

Leroy knows Norma Jean will have her own way. "Didn't I promise to be home from now on?" he says.

"In some ways, a woman prefers a man who wanders," says Norma Jean. "That sounds crazy, I know."

"You're not crazy."

Leroy remembers to drink from his Coke. Then he says, "Yes, you *are* crazy. You and me could start all over again. Right back at the beginning."

"We *have* started all over again," says Norma Jean. "And this is how it turned out."

"What did I do wrong?"

"Nothing."

"Is this one of those women's lib things?" Leroy asks.

"Don't be funny."

The cemetery, a green slope dotted with white markers, looks like a subdivision site. Leroy is trying to comprehend that his marriage is breaking up, but for some reason he is wondering about white slabs in a graveyard.

"Everything was fine till Mama caught me smoking," says Norma Jean, standing up. "That set something off."

"What are you talking about?"

"She won't leave me alone—*you* won't leave me alone." Norma Jean seems to be crying, but she is looking away from him. "I feel eighteen again. I can't face that all over again." She starts walking away. "No, it *wasn't* fine. I don't know what I'm saying. Forget it."

Leroy takes a lungful of smoke and closes his eyes as Norma Jean's words sink in. He tries to focus on the fact that thirty-five hundred soldiers died on the grounds around him. He can only think of that war as a board game with plastic soldiers. Leroy almost smiles, as he compares the Confederates' daring attack on the Union camps and Virgil Mathis's raid on the bowling alley. General Grant, drunk and furious, shoved the Southerners back to Corinth, where Mabel and Jet Beasley were married years later, when Mabel was still thin and good-looking. The next day, Mabel and Jet visited the battleground, and then Norma Jean was born, and then she married Leroy and they had a baby, which they lost, and now Leroy and Norma Jean are here at the same battleground. Leroy knows he is leaving out a lot. He is leaving out the insides of history. History was always just names and dates to him. It occurs to him that building a house out of logs is similarly empty—too simple. And the real inner workings of a marriage, like most of history, have escaped him. Now he sees that building a log house is the dumbest idea he could have had. It was clumsy of him to think Norma Jean would want a log house. It was a crazy idea. He'll have to think of something else, quickly. He will wad the blueprints into tight balls and fling them into the lake. Then he'll get moving again. He opens his eyes. Norma Jean has moved away and is walking through the cemetery, following a serpentine brick path.

Leroy gets up to follow his wife, but his good leg is asleep and his bad leg still hurts him. Norma Jean is far away, walking rapidly toward the bluff by the river, and he tries to hobble toward her. Some children run past him, screaming noisily. Norma Jean has reached the bluff, and she is looking out over the Tennessee River. Now she turns toward Leroy and waves her arms. Is she beckoning to him? She seems to be doing an exercise for her chest muscles. The sky is unusually pale—the color of the dust ruffle Mabel made for their bed.

1980, 1982

Gloria Naylor 1950–

Gloria Naylor has won wide recognition for her portrayal of the world of black women. She knows the lives of black women in both the urban North and the rural South. She was born and grew up in New York City, but from her late teens to her mid-twenties she served as a missionary for the Jehovah's Witnesses in North Carolina and Florida. She then returned to New York, where she worked her way through Brooklyn College as a telephone operator in a New York City hotel. After graduation, in 1981, she entered Yale University, from which she received an M.A. in 1983.

She has written five novels, The Women of Brewster Place *(1982),* Linden Hills *(1985),* Mama Day *(1988),* Bailey's Cafe *(1992), and* The Men of Brewster Place *(1998). They explore the experience of black women and men in America as they themselves see it. Naylor shows their experiences of oppression, their strength of spirit, their sense of communion, and their awareness of the riches of their culture.*

The Women of Brewster Place *won the American Book Award as the year's best first novel, and in 1989 it was made into a motion picture. In seven chapters, one of them "Lucielia Louise Turner," it presents a panorama of the lives of seven different women who live on a dead-end street, Brewster Place. It is Naylor's attempt to present a revealing "microcosm" of the life of black women in the United States, showing their independence, their resilience, their sexuality, and the strategies they "have employed historically for their psychic health and survival."* Linden Hills *and* Mama Day *continue the same themes and with some of the same characters, showing the dangers of middle-class life in the suburbs, where black men and women are separated from their unique culture and their sense of identity. In* The Men of Brewster Place *Naylor returns to the inner-city neighborhood but now writes from the viewpoint of husbands and sons.*

Gloria Naylor has taught at Princeton, George Washington University, New York University, and Boston University; and she has lectured in India as a part of a cultural exchange program sponsored by the U.S. government. Yet she has retained a strong sense of her origins and an appreciation of the unique richness those origins have brought to her work. She argues that writers cannot escape their heritage, cannot escape the fact that the material of literature must be "filtered through the mind of the writer . . . and that filter can only be what he or she is." What the writer produces, she says, "is always rooted in a specific body politic, both personal and historical."

FURTHER READING: *Gloria Naylor, Critical Perspectives Past and Present,* ed. H. Gates and K. Appiah, 1993; V. Fowler, *Gloria Naylor, In Search of Sanctuary,* 1996; *The Critical Response to Gloria Naylor,* ed. S. Felton and M. Loris, 1997; *Gloria Naylor's Early Novels,* ed. M. Kelley, 1999; M. Whitt, *Understanding Gloria Naylor,* 1999; C. Wilson, *Gloria Naylor, A Critical Companion,* 2001; *Gloria Naylor, Strategy and Technique, Magic and Myth,* ed. S. Stave, 2001; *Conversations with Gloria Naylor,* ed. M. Montgomery, 2004.

TEXT: *The Women of Brewster Place,* 1982.

from *THE WOMEN OF BREWSTER PLACE*

LUCIELIA LOUISE TURNER

The sunlight was still watery as Ben trudged into Brewster Place, and the street had just begun to yawn and stretch itself. He eased himself onto his garbage can, which was pushed against the sagging brick wall that turned

Brewster into a dead-end street. The metallic cold of the can's lid seeped into the bottom of his thin trousers. Sucking on a piece of breakfast sausage caught in his back teeth, he began to muse. Mightly cold, these spring mornings. The old days you could build a good trash fire in one of them barrels to keep warm. Well, don't want no summons now, and can't freeze to death. Yup, can't freeze to death.

His daily soliloquy completed, he reached into his coat pocket and pulled out a crumpled brown bag that contained his morning sun. The cheap red liquid moved slowly down his throat, providing immediate justification as the blood began to warm in his body. In the hazy light a lean dark figure began to make its way slowly up the block. It hesitated in front of the stoop at 316, but looking around and seeing Ben, it hurried over.

"Yo, Ben."

"Hey, Eugene, I thought that was you. Ain't seen ya round for a coupla days."

"Yeah." The young man put his hands in his pockets, frowned into the ground, and kicked the edge of Ben's can. "The funeral's today, ya know."

"Yeah."

"You going?" He looked up into Ben's face.

"Naw, I ain't got no clothes for them things. Can't abide 'em no way—too sad—it being a baby and all."

"Yeah. I was going myself, people expect it, ya know?"

"Yeah."

"But, man, the way Ciel's friends look at me and all—like I was filth or something. Hey, I even tried to go see Ciel in the hospital, heard she was freaked out and all."

"Yeah, she took it real bad."

"Yeah, well, damn, I took it bad. It was my kid, too, ya know. But Mattie, that fat, black bitch, just standin' in the hospital hall sayin' to me—to me, now, 'Whatcha want?' Like I was a fuckin' germ or something. Man, I just turned and left. You gotta be treated with respect, ya know?"

"Yeah."

"I mean, I should be there today with my woman in the limo and all, sittin' up there, doin' it right. But how you gonna be a man with them ball-busters tellin' everybody it was my fault and I should be the one dead? Damn!"

"Yeah, a man's gotta be a man." Ben felt the need to wet his reply with another sip. "Have some?"

"Naw, I'm gonna be heading on—Ciel don't need me today. I bet that frig, Mattie, rides in the head limo, wearing the pants. Shit—let 'em." He looked up again. "Ya know?"

"Yup."

"Take it easy, Ben." He turned to go.

"You too, Eugene."

"Hey, you going?"

"Naw."

"Me neither. Later."

"Later, Eugene."

Funny, Ben thought, Eugene ain't stopped to chat like that for a long time—near on a year, yup, a good year. He took another swallow to help him bring back the year-old conversation, but it didn't work; the second and third one didn't either. But he did remember that it had been an early spring morning like this one, and Eugene had been wearing those same tight jeans. He had hestitated outside of 316 then, too. But that time he went in . . .

Lucielia had just run water into the tea kettle and was putting it on the burner when she heard the cylinder turn. He didn't have to knock on the door; his key still fit the lock. Her thin knuckles gripped the handle of the kettle, but she didn't turn around. She knew. The last eleven months of her life hung compressed in the air between the click of the lock and his "Yo, baby."

The vibrations from those words rode like parasites on the air waves and came rushing into her kitchen, smashing the compression into indistinguishable days and hours that swirled dizzily before her. It was all there: the frustration of being left alone, sick, with a month-old baby; her humiliation reflected in the caseworker's blue eyes for the unanswerable "you can find him to have it, but can't find him to take care of it" smile; the raw urges that crept, uninvited, between her thighs on countless nights; the eternal whys all meshed with the explainable hate and unexplainable love. They kept circling in such a confusing pattern before her that she couldn't seem to grab even one to answer him with. So there was nothing in Lucielia's face when she turned it toward Eugene, standing in her kitchen door holding a ridiculously pink Easter bunny, nothing but sheer relief. . . .

"So he's back." Mattie sat at Lucielia's kitchen table, playing with Serena. It was rare that Mattie ever spoke more than two sentences to anybody about anything. She didn't have to. She chose her words with the grinding precision of a diamond cutter's drill.

"You think I'm a fool, don't you?"

"I ain't said that."

"You didn't have to," Ciel snapped.

"Why you mad at me, Ciel? It's your life, honey."

"Oh, Mattie, you don't understand. He's really straightened up this time. He's got a new job on the docks that pays real good, and he was just so depressed before with the new baby and no work. You'll see. He's even gone out now to buy paint and stuff to fix up the apartment. And, and Serena needs a daddy."

"You ain't gotta convince me, Ciel."

No, she wasn't talking to Mattie, she was talking to herself. She was convincing herself it was the new job and the paint and Serena that let him back into her life. Yet, the real truth went beyond her scope of understanding. When she laid her head in the hollow of his neck there was a deep musky scent to his body that brought back the ghosts of the Tennessee soil of her childhood. It reached up and lined the inside of her nostrils so that she inhaled his presence almost every minute of her life. The feel of his sooty flesh penetrated the skin of her fingers and coursed through her blood and became one, somewhere, wherever it was, with her actual being. But how do you tell yourself, let alone this practical old woman who loves you, that he was back because of that. So you don't.

You get up and fix you both another cup of coffee, calm the fretting baby on your lap with her pacifier, and you pray silently—very silently—behind veiled eyes that the man will stay.

Ciel was trying to remember exactly when it had started to go wrong again. Her mind sought for the slender threads of a clue that she could trace back to—perhaps—something she had said or done. Her brow was set tightly in concentration as she folded towels and smoothed the wrinkles over and over, as if the answer lay concealed in the stubborn creases of the terry cloth.

The months since Eugene's return began to tick off slowly before her, and she examined each one to pinpoint when the nagging whispers of trouble had begun in her brain. The friction on the towels increased when she came to the month that she had gotten pregnant again, but it couldn't be that. Things were different now. She wasn't sick as she had been with Serena, he was still working—no it wasn't the baby. It's not the baby, it's not the baby—the rhythm of those words sped up the motion of her hands, and she had almost yanked and folded and pressed them into a reality when, bewildered, she realized that she had run out of towels.

Ciel jumped when the front door slammed shut. She waited tensely for the metallic bang of his keys on the coffee table and the blast of the stereo. Lately that was how Eugene announced his presence home. Ciel walked into the living room with the motion of a swimmer entering a cold lake.

"Eugene, you're home early, huh?"

"You see anybody else sittin' here?" He spoke without looking at her and rose to turn up the stereo.

He wants to pick a fight, she thought, confused and hurt. He knows Serena's taking her nap, and now I'm supposed to say, Eugene, the baby's asleep, please cut the music down. Then he's going to say, you mean a man can't even relax in his own home without being picked on? I'm not picking on you, but you're going to wake up the baby. Which is always supposed to lead to: You don't give a damn about me. Everybody's more important than me—that kid, your friends, everybody. I'm just chickenshit around here, huh?

All this went through Ciel's head as she watched him leave the stereo and drop defiantly back down on the couch. Without saying a word, she turned and went into the bedroom. She looked down on the peaceful face of her daughter and softly caressed her small cheek. Her heart became full as she realized, this is the only thing I have ever loved without pain. She pulled the sheet gently over the tiny shoulders and firmly closed the door, protecting her from the music. She then went into the kitchen and began washing the rice for their dinner.

Eugene, seeing that he had been left alone, turned off the stereo and came and stood in the kitchen door.

"I lost my job today," he shot at her, as if she had been the cause.

The water was turning cloudy in the rice pot, and the force of the stream from the faucet caused scummy bubbles to rise to the surface. These broke and sprayed tiny starchy particles onto the dirty surface. Each bubble that broke seemed to increase the volume of the dogged whispers she had been ignoring for the last few months. She poured the dirty water off the rice to destroy and silence them, then watched with a malicious joy as they disappeared down the drain.

"So now, how in the hell I'm gonna make it with no money, huh? And another brat comin' here, huh?"

The second change of the water was slightly clearer, but the starch-speckled bubbles were still there, and this time there was no way to pretend deafness to their message. She had stood at that sink countless times before, washing rice, and she knew the water was never going to be totally clear. She couldn't stand there forever—her fingers were getting cold, and the rest of the dinner had to be fixed, and Serena would be waking up soon and wanting attention. Feverishly she poured the water off and tried again.

"I'm fuckin' sick of never getting ahead. Babies and bills, that's all you good for."

The bubbles were almost transparent now, but when they broke they left light trails of starch on top of the water that curled around her fingers. She knew it would be useless to try again. Defeated, Ciel placed the wet pot on the burner, and the flames leaped up bright red and orange, turning the water droplets clinging on the outside into steam.

Turning to him, she silently acquiesced. "All right, Eugene, what do you want me to do?"

He wasn't going to let her off so easily. "Hey, baby, look, I don't care what you do. I just can't have all these hassles on me right now, ya know?"

"I'll get a job. I don't mind, but I've got no one to keep Serena, and you don't want Mattie watching her."

"Mattie—no way. That fat bitch'll turn the kid against me. She hates my ass, and you know it."

"No, she doesn't, Eugene." Ciel remembered throwing that at Mattie once. "You hate him, don't you?" "Naw, honey," and she had cupped both hands on Ciel's face. "Maybe I just loves you too much."

"I don't give a damn what you say—she ain't minding my kid."

"Well, look, after the baby comes, they can tie my tubes—I don't care." She swallowed hard to keep down the lie.

"And what the hell we gonna feed it when it gets here, huh—air? With two kids and you on my back, I ain't never gonna have nothin'." He came and grabbed her by the shoulders and was shouting into her face. "Nothin', do you hear me, nothin'!"

"Nothing to it, Mrs. Turner." The face over hers was as calm and antiseptic as the room she lay in. "Please, relax. I'm going to give you a local anesthetic and then perform a simple D & C, or what you'd call a scraping to clean out the uterus. Then you'll rest here for about an hour and be on your way. There won't even be much bleeding." The voice droned on in its practiced monologue, peppered with sterile kindness.

Ciel was not listening. It was important that she keep herself completely isolated from these surroundings. All the activities of the past week of her life were balled up and jammed on the right side of her brain, as if belonging to some other woman. And when she had endured this one last thing for her, she would push it up there, too, and then one day give it all to her—Ciel wanted no part of it.

The next few days Ciel found it difficult to connect herself up again with her own world. Everything seemed to have taken on new textures and colors. When she washed the dishes, the plates felt peculiar in her hands, and she was more conscious of their smoothness and the heat of the water. There was a disturbing split second between someone talking to her and the words penetrating sufficiently to elicit a response. Her neighbors left her presence with slight frowns of puzzlement, and Eugene could be heard mumbling, "Moody bitch."

She became terribly possessive of Serena. She refused to leave her alone, even with Eugene. The little girl went everywhere with Ciel, toddling along on plump uncertain legs. When someone asked to hold or play with her, Ciel sat nearby, watching every move. She found herself walking into the bedroom several times when the child napped to see if she was still breathing. Each time she chided herself for this unreasonable foolishness, but within the next few minutes some strange force still drove her back.

Spring was slowly beginning to announce itself at Brewster Place. The arthritic cold was seeping out of the worn gray bricks, and the tenants with apartment windows facing the street were awakened by six o'clock sunlight. The music no longer blasted inside of 3C, and Ciel grew strong with the peacefulness of her household. The playful laughter of her daughter, heard more often now, brought a sort of redemption with it.

"Isn't she marvelous, Mattie? You know she's even trying to make whole sentences. Come on, baby, talk for Auntie Mattie."

Serena, totally uninterested in living up to her mother's proud claims, was trying to tear a gold-toned button off the bosom of Mattie's dress.

"It's so cute. She even knows her father's name. She says, my da da is Gene."

"Better teach her your name," Mattie said, while playing with the baby's hand. "She'll be using it more."

Ciel's mouth flew open to ask her what she meant by that, but she checked herself. It was useless to argue with Mattie. You could take her words however you wanted. The burden of their truth lay with you, not her.

Eugene came through the front door and stopped short when he saw Mattie. He avoided being around her as much as possible. She was always polite to him, but he sensed a silent condemnation behind even her most innocent words. He constantly felt the need to prove himself in front of her. These frustrations often took the form of unwarranted rudeness on his part.

Serena struggled out of Mattie's lap and went toward her father and tugged on his legs to be picked up. Ignoring the child and cutting short the greetings of the two women, he said coldly, "Ciel, I wanna talk to you."

Sensing trouble, Mattie rose to go. "Ciel, why don't you let me take Serena downstairs for a while. I got some ice cream for her."

"She can stay right here," Eugene broke in. "If she needs ice cream, I can buy it for her."

Hastening to soften his abruptness, Ciel said, "That's okay, Mattie, it's almost time for her nap. I'll bring her later—after dinner."

"All right. Now you all keep good." Her voice was warm. "You too, Eugene," she called back from the front door.

The click of the lock restored his balance to him. "Why in the hell is she always up here?"

"You just had your chance—why didn't you ask her yourself? If you don't want her here, tell her to stay out," Ciel snapped back confidently, knowing he never would.

"Look, I ain't got time to argue with you about that old hag. I got big doings in the making, and I need you to help me pack." Without waiting for a response, he hurried into the bedroom and pulled his old leather suitcase from under the bed.

A tight, icy knot formed in the center of Ciel's stomach and began to melt rapidly, watering the blood in her legs so that they almost refused to support her weight. She pulled Serena back from following Eugene and sat her in the middle of the living room floor.

"Here, honey, play with the blocks for Mommy—she has to talk to Daddy." She piled a few plastic alphabet blocks in front of the child, and on her way out of the room, she glanced around quickly and removed the glass ashtrays off the coffee table and put them on a shelf over the stereo.

Then, taking a deep breath to calm her racing heart, she started toward the bedroom.

Serena loved the light colorful cubes and would sometimes sit for an entire half-hour, repeatedly stacking them up and kicking them over with her feet. The hollow sound of their falling fascinated her, and she would often bang two of them together to re-create the magical noise. She was sitting, contentedly engaged in this particular activity, when a slow dark movement along the baseboard caught her eye.

A round black roach was making its way from behind the couch toward the kitchen. Serena threw one of her blocks at the insect, and, feeling the vibrations of the wall above it, the roach sped around the door into the kitchen. Finding a totally new game to amuse herself, Serena took off behind the insect with a block in each hand. Seeing her moving toy trying to bury itself under the linoleum by the garbage pail she threw another block, and the frantic roach now raced along the wall and found security in the electric wall socket under the kitchen table.

Angry at losing her plaything, she banged the block against the socket, attempting to get it to come back out. When that failed, she unsuccessfully tried to poke her chubby finger into the thin horizontal slit. Frustrated, tiring of the game, she sat under the table and realized she had found an entirely new place in the house to play. The shiny chrome of the table and chair legs drew her attention, and she experimented with the sound of the block against their smooth surfaces.

This would have entertained her until Ciel came, but the roach, thinking itself safe, ventured outside of the socket. Serena gave a cry of delight and attempted to catch her lost playmate, but it was too quick and darted back into the wall. She tried once again to poke her finger into the slit. Then a bright slender object, lying dropped and forgotten, came into her view. Picking up the fork, Serena finally managed to fit the thin flattened prongs into the electric socket.

Eugene was avoiding Ciel's eyes as he packed. "You know, baby, this is really a good deal after me bein' out of work for so long." He moved around her still figure to open the drawer that held his T-shirts and shorts. "And hell, Maine ain't far. Once I get settled on the docks up there, I'll be able to come home all the time."

"Why can't you take us with you?" She followed each of his movements with her eyes and saw herself being buried in the case under the growing pile of clothes.

"'Cause I gotta check out what's happening before I drag you and the kid up there."

"I don't mind. We'll make do. I've learned to live on very little."

"No, it just won't work right now. I gotta see my way clear first."

"Eugene, please." She listened with growing horror to herself quietly begging.

"No, and that's it!" He flung his shoes into the suitcase.

"Well, how far is it? Where did you say you were going?" She moved toward the suitcase.

"I told ya—the docks in Newport."

"That's not in Maine. You said you were going to Maine."

"Well, I made a mistake."

"How could you know about a place so far up? Who got you the job?"

"A friend."

"Who?"

"None of your damned business!" His eyes were flashing with the anger of a caged animal. He slammed down the top of the suitcase and yanked it off the bed.

"You're lying, aren't you? You don't have a job, do you? Do you?"

"Look, Ciel, believe whatever the fuck you want to. I gotta go." He tried to push past her.

She grabbed the handle of the case. "No, you can't go."

"Why?"

Her eyes widened slowly. She realized that to answer that would require that she uncurl that week of her life, pushed safely up into her head, when she had done all those terrible things for that other woman who had wanted an abortion. She and she alone would have to take responsibility for them now. He must understand what those actions had meant to her, but somehow, he had meant even more. She sought desperately for the right words, but it all came out as—

"Because I love you."

"Well, that ain't good enough."

Ciel had let the suitcase go before he jerked it away. She looked at Eugene, and the poison of reality began to spread through her body like gangrene. It drew his scent out of her nostrils and scraped the veil from her eyes, and he stood before her just as he really was—a tall, skinny black man with arrogance and selfishness twisting his mouth into a strange shape. And, she thought, I don't feel anything now. But soon, very soon, I will start to hate you. I promise—I will hate you. And I'll never forgive myself for not having done it sooner—soon enough to have saved my baby. Oh, dear God, my baby.

Eugene thought the tears that began to crowd into her eyes were for him. But she was allowing herself this one last luxury of brief mourning for the loss of something denied to her. It troubled her that she wasn't sure exactly what that something was, or which one of them was to blame for taking it away. Ciel began to feel the overpowering need to be near someone who loved her. I'll get Serena and we'll go visit Mattie now, she thought in a daze.

Then they heard the scream from the kitchen.

The church was small and dark. The air hung about them like a stale blanket. Ciel looked straight ahead, oblivious to the seats filling up behind her. She didn't feel the damp pressure of Mattie's heavy arm or the doubt that invaded the air over Eugene's absence. The plaintive Merciful Jesuses, lightly sprinkled with sobs, were lost on her ears. Her dry eyes were locked on the tiny pearl-gray casket, flanked with oversized arrangements of red-carnationed bleeding hearts and white-lilied eternal circles. The sagging chords that came loping out of the huge organ and mixed with the droning voice of the black-robed old man behind the coffin were also unable to penetrate her.

Ciel's whole universe existed in the seven feet of space between herself and her child's narrow coffin. There was not even room for this comforting God whose melodious virtues floated around her sphere, attempting to get in. Obviously, He had deserted or damned her, it didn't matter which. All Ciel knew was that her prayers had gone unheeded—that afternoon she had lifted her daughter's body off the kitchen floor, those blank days in the hospital, and now. So she was left to do what God had chosen not to.

People had mistaken it for shock when she refused to cry. They thought it some special sort of grief when she stopped eating and even drinking water unless forced to; her hair went uncombed and her body unbathed. But Ciel was not grieving for Serena. She was simply tired of hurting. And she was forced to slowly give up the life that God had refused to take from her.

After the funeral the well-meaning came to console and offer their dog-eared faith in the form of coconut cakes, potato pies, fried chicken, and tears. Ciel sat in the bed with her back resting against the headboard; her long thin fingers, still as midnight frost on a frozen pond, lay on the covers. She acknowledged their kindnesses with nods of her head and slight lip movements, but no sound. It was as if her voice was too tired to make the journey from the diaphragm through the larynx to the mouth.

Her visitors' impotent words flew against the steel edge of her pain, bled slowly, and returned to die in the senders' throats. No one came too near. They stood around the door and the dressing table, or sat on the edges of the two worn chairs that needed upholstering, but they unconsciously pushed themselves back against the wall as if her hurt was contagious.

A neighbor woman entered in studied certainty and stood in the middle of the room. "Child, I know how you feel, but don't do this to yourself. I lost one, too. The Lord will . . ." And she choked, because the words were jammed down into her throat by the naked force of Ciel's eyes. Ciel had opened them fully now to look at the woman, but raw fires had eaten them worse than lifeless—worse than death. The woman saw in that mute appeal for silence the ragings of a personal hell flowing through Ciel's eyes. And just as she went to reach for the girl's hand, she stopped as if a muscle spasm had overtaken her body and, cowardly, shrank back. Reminiscences of old, dried-over pains were no consolation in the face of this. They had the effect of cold beads of water on a hot iron—they danced and fizzled up while the room stank from their steam.

Mattie stood in the doorway, and an involuntary shudder went through her when she saw Ciel's eyes. Dear God, she thought, she's dying, and right in front of our faces.

"Merciful Father, no!" she bellowed. There was no prayer, no bended knee or sackcloth supplication in those words, but a blasphemous fireball that shot forth and went smashing against the gates of heaven, raging and kicking, demanding to be heard.

"No! No! No!" Like a black Brahman cow, desperate to protect her young, she surged into the room, pushing the neighbor woman and the others out of her way. She approached the bed with her lips clamped shut in such force that the muscles in her jaw and the back of her neck began to ache.

She sat on the edge of the bed and enfolded the tissue-thin body in her huge ebony arms. And she rocked. Ciel's body was so hot it burned Mattie when she first touched her, but she held on and rocked. Back and forth, back and forth—she held Ciel so tightly she could feel her young breasts flatten against the buttons of her dress. The black mammoth gripped so firmly that the slightest increase of pressure would have cracked the girl's spine. But she rocked.

And somewhere from the bowels of her being came a moan from Ciel, so high at first it couldn't be heard by anyone there, but the yard dogs began an unholy howling. And Mattie rocked. And then, agonizingly slow, it broke its way through the parched lips in a spaghetti-thin column of air that could be faintly heard in the frozen room.

Ciel moaned. Mattie rocked. Propelled by the sound, Mattie rocked her out of that bed, out of that room, into a blue vastness just underneath the sun and above time. She rocked her over Aegean seas so clean they shone like crystal, so clear the fresh blood of sacrificed babies torn from their mother's arms and given to Neptune could be seen like pink froth on the water. She rocked her on and on, past Dachau, where soul-gutted Jewish mothers swept their children's entrails off laboratory floors. They flew past the spilled brains of Senegalese infants whose mothers had dashed them on the wooden sides of slave ships. And she rocked on.

She rocked her into her childhood and let her see murdered dreams. And she rocked her back, back into the womb, to the nadir of her hurt, and they found it—a slight silver splinter, embedded just below the surface of the skin. And Mattie rocked and pulled—and the splinter gave way, but its roots were deep, gigantic, ragged, and they tore up flesh with bits of fat and muscle tissue clinging to them. They left a huge hole, which was already starting to pus over, but Mattie was satisfied. It would heal.

The bile that had formed a tight knot in Ciel's stomach began to rise and gagged her just as it passed her throat. Mattie put her hand over the girl's mouth and rushed her out the now-empty room to the toilet. Ciel retched yellowish-green phlegm, and she brought up white lumps of slime that hit the seat of the toilet and rolled off, splattering onto the tiles. After a while she heaved only air, but the body did not seem to want to stop. It was exorcising the evilness of pain.

Mattie cupped her hands under the faucet and motioned for Ciel to drink and clean her mouth. When the water left Ciel's mouth, it tasted as if she had been rinsing with a mild acid. Mattie drew a tub of hot water and undressed Ciel. She let the nightgown fall off the narrow shoulders, over the pitifully thin breasts and jutting hipbones. She slowly helped her into the water, and it was like a dried brown autumn leaf hitting the surface of a puddle.

And slowly she bathed her. She took the soap, and, using only her hands, she washed Ciel's hair and the back of her neck. She raised her arms and cleaned the armpits, soaping well the downy brown hair there. She let the soap slip between the girl's breasts, and she washed each one separately, cupping it in her hands. She took each leg and even cleaned under the toenails. Making Ciel rise and kneel in the tub, she cleaned the crack in her behind, soaped her pubic hair, and gently washed the creases in her vagina—slowly, reverently, as if handling a newborn.

She took her from the tub and toweled her in the same manner she had been bathed—as if too much friction would break the skin tissue. All of this had been done without either woman saying a word. Ciel stood there, naked, and felt the cool air play against the clean surface of her skin. She had the sensation of fresh mint coursing through her pores. She closed her eyes and the fire was gone. Her tears no longer fried within her, killing her internal organs with their steam. So Ciel began to cry—there, naked, in the center of the bathroom floor.

Mattie emptied the tub and rinsed it. She led the still-naked Ciel to a chair in the bedroom. The tears were flowing so freely now Ciel couldn't see, and she allowed herself to be led as if blind. She sat on the chair and cried—head erect. Since she made no effort to wipe them away, the tears dripped down her chin and landed on her chest and rolled down to her stomach and onto her dark pubic hair. Ignoring Ciel, Mattie took away the crumpled linen and made the bed, stretching the sheets tight and fresh. She beat the pillows into a virgin plumpness and dressed them in white cases.

And Ciel sat. And cried. The unmolested tears had rolled down her parted thighs and were beginning to wet the chair. But they were cold and good. She put out her tongue and began to drink in their saltiness, feeding on them. The first tears were gone. Her thin shoulders began to quiver, and spasms circled her body as new tears came—this time, hot and stinging. And she sobbed, the first sound she'd made since the moaning.

Mattie took the edges of the dirty sheet she'd pulled off the bed and wiped the mucus that had been running out of Ciel's nose. She then led her freshly wet, glistening body, baptized now, to the bed. She covered her with one sheet and laid a towel across the pillow—it would help for a while.

And Ciel lay down and cried. But Mattie knew the tears would end. And she would sleep. And morning would come.

1980, 1982

Raymond Carver 1938–1988

"A long time ago," Raymond Carver once recalled, "my wife and I and our two baby children moved from Yakima, Washington, to a little town outside of Chico, California. There we found an old house and paid twenty-five dollars a month rent. In order to finance this move, I'd had to borrow a hundred and twenty-five dollars from a druggist I'd delivered prescriptions for. . . ." They were "stone broke," he added, but he had wanted to be a writer as long as he could remember, and he knew that he needed an education.

He enrolled at Chico State College and signed up for "Creative Writing 101," a course taught by John Gardner, who was soon to become famous as a novelist. Gardner encouraged Carver, introduced him to the works of major writers such as Flaubert, James Joyce, and Isak Dinesen. Gardner also introduced Carver to the small literary magazines that published the best fiction and poetry in the United States—a "revelation" to Carver, whose reading and aspirations as a writer had been confined to such publications as Sports Afield, True, Argosy, *and* Rogue. *Gardner advised Carver to "Read all the Faulkner you can get your hands on, and then read all of Hemingway to clean Faulkner out of your system."*

The influence of Hemingway is evident in the undecorated prose and the conversational tone of Carver's fiction, but Carver drew the events and characters for his stories from his own working-class background. He was born in Clatskanie, Oregon, and grew up in Yakima, Washington, where his father worked in a sawmill. At the age of eighteen Carver married and was forced to work, he later reported, at "some crap job or other" to support his family. Like many of his characters, he and his family seemed condemned to live a life of bare subsistence, but he managed to graduate from college in 1963 and to continue studying writing at the University of Iowa and at Stanford.

Carver's first published works were volumes of poems, and he published poetry and essays all his life, but his reputation rests on his short fiction. In 1967, one of his stories, "Will You Please Be Quiet, Please?" was included in Best American Short Stories, *and it provided the title for a collection of his stories published in 1976. Three other collections,* What We Talk about When We Talk about Love *(1981),* Cathedral *(1983), and* Where I'm Calling from *(1988) have been received enthusiastically not only by critics but by numerous writers who have been strongly influenced by his work.*

Carver has been called a "minimalist" for his flat diction, his spare plots, his faceless characters. He often writes of men and women who are culturally impoverished, small-town people who are physical and spiritual cripples, alcoholics, insomniacs, men without jobs, couples in failed marriages—people who dwell in trailer camps and spend their evenings in laundromats. Carver said, "I admit I hold to the dark view of things," and the meager lives of his characters seem to be wholly vacuous, barren of hope, yet they are portrayed by a narrative voice that speaks with profound compassion for ordinary men and women even while showing their flaws with a relentless force.

FURTHER READING: *All of Us, The Collected Poems,* 1998; A. Saltzman, *Understanding Raymond Carver,* 1988; *Conversations with Raymond Carver,* ed. M. Gentry and W. Stull, 1990; *Carver Country,* ed. T. Gallagher, 1990; P. Runyon, *Reading Raymond Carver,* 1992; E. Campbell, *Raymond Carver, A Study of the Short Fiction,* 1992; S. Halpert, *Raymond Carver, An Oral Biography,* 1993, 1995; A. Meyer, *Raymond Carver,* 1995; K. Nesset, *The Stories of Raymond Carver,* 1995; A. Bethea, *Techniques and Sensibility in the Fiction and Poetry of Raymond Carver,* 2001; H. Bloom, *Raymond Carver, Comprehensive Research and Study Guide,* 2002; G. Lainsbury, *The Carver Chronotope,* 2003; M. Carver, *What It Used to Be Like,* 2005.

TEXT: *Cathedral,* 1983.

CATHEDRAL

This blind man, an old friend of my wife's, he was on his way to spend the night. His wife had died. So he was visiting the dead wife's relatives in Connecticut. He called my wife from his in-laws'. Arrangements were made. He would come by train, a five-hour trip, and my wife would meet him at the station. She hadn't seen him since she worked for him one summer in Seattle ten years ago. But she and the blind man had kept in touch. They made tapes and mailed them back and forth. I wasn't enthusiastic about his visit. He was no one I knew. And his being blind bothered me. My idea of blindness came from the movies. In the movies, the blind moved slowly and never laughed. Sometimes they were led by seeing-eye dogs. A blind man in my house was not something I looked forward to.

That summer in Seattle she had needed a job. She didn't have any money. The man she was going to marry at the end of the summer was in officers' training school. He didn't have any money, either. But she was in love with the guy, and he was in love with her, etc. She'd seen something in the paper: HELP WANTED—*Reading to Blind Man,* and a telephone number. She phoned and went over, was hired on the spot. She'd worked with this blind man all summer. She read stuff to him, case studies, reports, that sort of thing. She helped him organize his little office in the county social-service department. They'd become good friends, my wife and the blind man. How do I know these things? She told me. And she told me something else. On her last day in the office, the blind man asked if he could touch her face. She agreed to this. She told me he touched his fingers to every part of her face, her nose—even her neck! She never forgot it. She even tried to write a poem about it. She was always trying to write a poem. She wrote a poem or two every year, usually after something really important had happened to her.

When we first started going out together, she showed me the poem. In the poem, she recalled his fingers and the way they had moved around over her face. In the poem, she talked about what she had felt at the time, about what went through her mind when the blind man touched her nose and lips. I can remember I didn't think much of the poem. Of course, I didn't tell her that. Maybe I just don't understand poetry. I admit it's not the first thing I reach for when I pick up something to read.

Anyway, this man who'd first enjoyed her favors, the officer-to-be, he'd been her childhood sweetheart. So okay. I'm saying that at the end of the summer she let the blind man run his hands over her face, said goodbye to him, married her childhood etc., who was now a commissioned officer, and she moved away from Seattle. But they'd kept in touch, she and the blind man. She made the first contact after a year or so. She called him up one night from an Air Force base in Alabama. She wanted to talk. They talked. He asked her to send him a tape and tell him about her life. She did this. She sent the tape. On the tape, she told the blind man about her husband and about their life together in the military. She told the blind man she loved her husband but she didn't like it where they lived and she didn't like it that he was a part of the military-industrial thing. She told the blind man she'd written a poem and he was in it. She told him that she was writing a poem about what it was like to be an Air Force officer's wife. The poem wasn't finished yet. She was still writing it. The blind man made a tape. He sent her the tape. She made a tape. This went on for years. My wife's officer was posted to one base and then another. She sent tapes from Moody AFB, McGuire, McConnell, and finally Travis, near Sacramento, where one night she got to feeling lonely and cut off from people she kept losing in that moving-around life. She got to feeling she couldn't go it another step. She went in and swallowed all the pills and capsules in the medicine chest and washed them down with a bottle of gin. Then she got into a hot bath and passed out.

But instead of dying, she got sick. She threw up. Her officer—why should he have a name? he was the childhood sweetheart, and what more does he want?—came home from somewhere, found her, and called the ambulance. In time, she put it all on a tape and sent the tape to the blind man. Over the years, she put all kinds of stuff on tapes and sent the tapes off lickety-split. Next to writing a poem every year, I think it was her chief means of recreation. On one tape, she told the blind man she'd decided to live away from her officer for a time. On another tape, she told him about her divorce. She and I began going out, and of course she told her blind man about it. She told him everything, or so it seemed to me. Once she asked me if I'd like to hear the latest tape from the blind man. This was a year ago. I was on the tape, she said. So I said okay, I'd listen to it. I got us drinks and we settled down in the living room. We made ready to listen. First she inserted the tape into the player and adjusted a couple of dials. Then she pushed a lever. The tape squeaked and someone began to talk in this loud voice. She lowered the volume. After a few minutes of harmless chitchat, I heard my own name in the mouth of this stranger, this blind man I didn't even know! And then this: "From all you've said about him, I can only conclude—" But we were interrupted, a knock at the door, something, and we didn't ever get back to the tape. Maybe it was just as well. I'd heard all I wanted to.

Now this same blind man was coming to sleep in my house.

"Maybe I could take him bowling," I said to my wife. She was at the draining board doing scalloped potatoes. She put down the knife she was using and turned around.

"If you love me," she said, "you can do this for me. If you don't love me, okay. But if you had a friend, any friend, and the friend came to visit, I'd make him feel comfortable." She wiped her hands with the dish towel.

"I don't have any blind friends," I said.

"You don't have *any* friends," she said. "Period. Besides," she said, "goddamn it, his wife's just died! Don't you understand that? The man's lost his wife!"

I didn't answer. She'd told me a little about the blind man's wife. Her name was Beulah. Beulah! That's a name for a colored woman.

"Was his wife a Negro?" I asked.

"Are you crazy?" my wife said. "Have you just flipped or something?" She picked up a potato. I saw it hit the floor, then roll under the stove. "What's wrong with you?" she said. "Are you drunk?"

"I'm just asking," I said.

Right then my wife filled me in with more detail than I cared to know. I made a drink and sat at the kitchen table to listen. Pieces of the story began to fall into place.

Beulah had gone to work for the blind man the summer after my wife had stopped working for him. Pretty soon Beulah and the blind man had themselves a church wedding. It was a little wedding—who'd want to go to such a wedding in the first place?—just the two of them, plus the minister and the minister's wife. But it was a church wedding just the same. It was what Beulah had wanted, he'd said. But even then Beulah must have been carrying the cancer in her glands. After they had been inseparable for eight years—my wife's word, *inseparable*—Beulah's health went into a rapid decline. She died in a Seattle hospital room, the blind man sitting beside the bed and holding on to her hand. They'd married, lived and worked together, slept together—had sex, sure—and then the blind man had to bury her. All this without his having ever seen what the goddamned woman looked like. It was beyond my understanding. Hearing this, I felt sorry for the blind man for a little bit. And then I found myself thinking what a pitiful life this woman must have led. Imagine a woman who could never see herself as she was seen in the eyes of her loved one. A woman who could go on day after day and never receive the smallest compliment from her beloved. A woman whose husband could never read the expression on her face, be it misery or something better. Someone who could wear makeup or not—what difference to him? She could, if she wanted, wear green eye-shadow around one eye, a straight pin in her nostril, yellow slacks and purple shoes, no matter. And then to slip off into death, the blind man's hand on her hand, his blind eyes streaming tears—I'm imagining now—her last thought maybe this: that he never even knew what she looked like, and she on an express to the grave. Robert was left with a small insurance policy and half of a twenty-peso Mexican coin. The other half of the coin went into the box with her. Pathetic.

So when the time rolled around, my wife went to the depot to pick him up. With nothing to do but wait—sure, I blamed him for that—I was having a drink and watching the TV when I heard the car pull into the drive. I got up from the sofa with my drink and went to the window to have a look.

I saw my wife laughing as she parked the car. I saw her get out of the car and shut the door. She was still wearing a smile. Just amazing. She went around to the other side of the car to where the blind man was already starting to get out. This blind man, feature this, he was wearing a full beard! A beard on a blind man! Too much, I say. The blind man reached into the back seat and dragged out a suitcase. My wife took his arm, shut the car door, and, talking all the way, moved him down the drive and then up the steps to the front porch. I turned off the TV. I finished my drink, rinsed the glass, dried my hands. Then I went to the door.

My wife said, "I want you to meet Robert. Robert, this is my husband. I've told you all about him." She was beaming. She had this blind man by his coat sleeve.

The blind man let go of his suitcase and up came his hand.

I took it. He squeezed hard, held my hand, and then he let it go.

"I feel like we've already met," he boomed.

"Likewise," I said. I didn't know what else to say. Then I said, "Welcome. I've heard a lot about you." We began to move then, a little group, from the porch into the living room, my wife guiding him by the arm. The blind man was carrying his suitcase in his other hand. My wife said things like, "To your left here, Robert. That's right. Now watch it, there's a chair. That's it. Sit down right here. This is the sofa. We just bought this sofa two weeks ago."

I started to say something about the old sofa. I'd liked that old sofa. But I didn't say anything. Then I wanted to say something else, small-talk, about the scenic ride along the Hudson. How going *to* New York, you should sit on the right-hand side of the train, and coming *from* New York, the left-hand side.

"Did you have a good train ride?" I said. "Which side of the train did you sit on, by the way?"

"What a question, which side!" my wife said. "What's it matter which side?" she said.

"I just asked," I said.

"Right side," the blind man said. "I hadn't been on a train in nearly forty years. Not since I was a kid. With my folks. That's been a long time. I'd nearly forgotten the sensation. I have winter in my beard now," he said. "So I've been told, anyway. Do I look distinguished, my dear?" the blind man said to my wife.

"You look distinguished, Robert," she said. "Robert," she said. "Robert, it's just so good to see you."

My wife finally took her eyes off the blind man and looked at me. I had the feeling she didn't like what she saw. I shrugged.

I've never met, or personally known, anyone who was blind. This blind man was late forties, a heavy-set, balding man with stooped shoulders, as if he carried a great weight there. He wore brown slacks, brown shoes, a light-brown shirt, a tie, a sports coat. Spiffy. He also had this full beard. But he didn't use a cane and he didn't wear dark glasses. I'd always thought dark glasses were a must for the blind. Fact was, I wished he had a pair. At first glance, his eyes looked like anyone else's eyes. But if you looked close, there was something different about them. Too much white in the iris, for one thing, and the pupils seemed to move around in the sockets without his knowing it or being able to stop it. Creepy. As I stared at his face, I saw the left pupil turn in toward his nose while the other made an effort to keep in one place. But it was only an effort, for that eye was on the roam without his knowing it or wanting it to be.

I said, "Let me get you a drink. What's your pleasure? We have a little of everything. It's one of our pastimes."

"Bub, I'm a Scotch man myself," he said fast enough in this big voice.

"Right," I said. Bub! "Sure you are. I knew it."

He let his fingers touch his suitcase, which was sitting alongside the sofa. He was taking his bearings. I didn't blame him for that.

"I'll move that up to your room," my wife said.

"No, that's fine," the blind man said loudly. "It can go up when I go up."

"A little water with the Scotch?" I said.

"Very little," he said.

"I knew it," I said.

He said, "Just a tad. The Irish actor, Barry Fitzgerald? I'm like that fellow. When I drink water, Fitzgerald said, I drink water. When I drink whiskey, I drink whiskey."[1] My wife laughed. The blind man brought his hand up under his beard. He lifted his beard slowly and let it drop.

I did the drinks, three big glasses of Scotch with a splash of water in each. Then we made ourselves comfortable and talked about Robert's travels. First the long flight from the West Coast to Connecticut, we covered that. Then from Connecticut up here by train. We had another drink concerning that leg of the trip.

I remembered having read somewhere that the blind didn't smoke because, as speculation had it, they couldn't see the smoke they exhaled. I

[1]An approximation of words spoken by the Irish actor Barry Fitzgerald in the motion picture *The Quiet Man* (1952).

thought I knew that much and that much only about blind people. But this blind man smoked his cigarette down to the nubbin and then lit another one. This blind man filled his ashtray and my wife emptied it.

When we sat down at the table for dinner, we had another drink. My wife heaped Robert's plate with cube steak, scalloped potatoes, green beans. I buttered him up two slices of bread. I said, "Here's bread and butter for you." I swallowed some of my drink. "Now let us pray," I said, and the blind man lowered his head. My wife looked at me, her mouth agape. "Pray the phone won't ring and the food doesn't get cold," I said.

We dug in. We ate everything there was to eat on the table. We ate like there was no tomorrow. We didn't talk. We ate. We scarfed. We grazed that table. We were into serious eating. The blind man had right away located his foods, he knew just where everything was on his plate. I watched with admiration as he used his knife and fork on the meat. He'd cut two pieces of meat, fork the meat into his mouth, and then go all out for the scalloped potatoes, the beans next, and then he'd tear off a hunk of buttered bread and eat that. He'd follow this up with a big drink of milk. It didn't seem to bother him to use his fingers once in a while, either.

We finished everything, including half a strawberry pie. For a few moments, we sat as if stunned. Sweat beaded on our faces. Finally, we got up from the table and left the dirty plates. We didn't look back. We took ourselves into the living room and sank into our places again. Robert and my wife sat on the sofa. I took the big chair. We had us two or three more drinks while they talked about the major things that had come to pass for them in the past ten years. For the most part, I just listened. Now and then I joined in. I didn't want him to think I'd left the room, and I didn't want her to think I was feeling left out. They talked of things that had happened to them—to them!—these past ten years. I waited in vain to hear my name on my wife's sweet lips: "And then my dear husband came into my life"—something like that. But I heard nothing of the sort. More talk of Robert. Robert had done a little of everything, it seemed, a regular blind jack-of-all-trades. But most recently he and his wife had had an Amway distributorship, from which, I gathered, they'd earned their living, such as it was. The blind man was also a ham radio operator. He talked in his loud voice about conversations he'd had with fellow operators in Guam, in the Philippines, in Alaska, and even in Tahiti. He said he'd have a lot of friends there if he ever wanted to go visit those places. From time to time, he'd turn his blind face toward me, put his hand under his beard, ask me something. How long had I been in my present position? (Three years.) Did I like my work? (I didn't.) Was I going to stay with it? (What were the options?) Finally, when I thought he was beginning to run down, I got up and turned on the TV.

My wife looked at me with irritation. She was heading toward a boil. Then she looked at the blind man and said, "Robert, do you have a TV?"

The blind man said, "My dear, I have two TVs. I have a color set and a black-and-white thing, an old relic. It's funny, but if I turn the TV on, and I'm always turning it on, I turn on the color set. It's funny, don't you think?"

I didn't know what to say to that. I had absolutely nothing to say to that. No opinion. So I watched the news program and tried to listen to what the announcer was saying.

"This is a color TV," the blind man said. "Don't ask me how, but I can tell."

"We traded up a while ago," I said.

The blind man had another taste of his drink. He lifted his beard, sniffed it, and let it fall. He leaned forward on the sofa. He positioned his ashtray on the coffee table, then put the lighter to his cigarette. He leaned back on the sofa and crossed his legs at the ankles.

My wife covered her mouth, and then she yawned. She stretched. She said, "I think I'll go upstairs and put on my robe. I think I'll change into something else. Robert, you make yourself comfortable," she said.

"I'm comfortable," the blind man said.

"I want you to feel comfortable in this house," she said.

"I am comfortable," the blind man said.

After she'd left the room, he and I listened to the weather report and then to the sports roundup. By that time, she'd been gone so long I didn't know if she was going to come back. I thought she might have gone to bed. I wished she'd come back downstairs. I didn't want to be left alone with a blind man. I asked him if he wanted another drink, and he said sure. Then I asked if he wanted to smoke some dope with me. I said I'd just rolled a number. I hadn't, but I planned to do so in about two shakes.

"I'll try some with you," he said.

"Damn right," I said. "That's the stuff."

I got our drinks and sat down on the sofa with him. Then I rolled us two fat numbers. I lit one and passed it. I brought it to his fingers. He took it and inhaled.

"Hold it as long as you can," I said. I could tell he didn't know the first thing.

My wife came back downstairs wearing her pink robe and her pink slippers.

"What do I smell?" she said.

"We thought we'd have us some cannabis," I said.

My wife gave me a savage look. Then she looked at the blind man and said, "Robert, I didn't know you smoked."

He said, "I do now, my dear. There's a first time for everything. But I don't feel anything yet."

"This stuff is pretty mellow," I said. "This stuff is mild. It's dope you can reason with," I said. "It doesn't mess you up."

"Not much it doesn't, bub," he said, and laughed.

My wife sat on the sofa between the blind man and me. I passed her the number. She took it and toked and then passed it back to me. "Which way is this going?" she said. Then she said, "I shouldn't be smoking this. I can hardly keep my eyes open as it is. That dinner did me in. I shouldn't have eaten so much."

"It was the strawberry pie," the blind man said. "That's what did it," he said, and he laughed his big laugh. Then he shook his head.

"There's more strawberry pie," I said.

"Do you want some more, Robert?" my wife said.

"Maybe in a little while," he said.

We gave our attention to the TV. My wife yawned again. She said, "Your bed is made up when you feel like going to bed, Robert. I know you must have had a long day. When you're ready to go to bed, say so." She pulled his arm. "Robert?"

He came to and said, "I've had a real nice time. This beats tapes, doesn't it?"

I said, "Coming at you," and I put the number between his fingers. He inhaled, held the smoke, and then let it go. It was like he'd been doing it since he was nine years old.

"Thanks, bub," he said. "But I think this is all for me. I think I'm beginning to feel it," he said. He held the burning roach out for my wife.

"Same here," she said. "Ditto. Me, too." She took the roach and passed it to me. "I may just sit here for a while between you two guys with my eyes closed. But don't let me bother you, okay? Either one of you. If it bothers you, say so. Otherwise, I may just sit here with my eyes closed until you're ready to go to bed," she said. "Your bed's made up, Robert, when you're ready. It's right next to our room at the top of the stairs. We'll show you up when you're ready. You wake me up now, you guys, if I fall asleep." She said that and then she closed her eyes and went to sleep.

The news program ended. I got up and changed the channel. I sat back down on the sofa. I wished my wife hadn't pooped out. Her head lay across the back of the sofa, her mouth open. She'd turned so that her robe had slipped away from her legs, exposing a juicy thigh. I reached to draw her robe back over her, and it was then that I glanced at the blind man. What the hell! I flipped the robe open again.

"You say when you want some strawberry pie," I said.

"I will," he said.

I said, "Are you tired? Do you want me to take you up to your bed? Are you ready to hit the hay?"

"Not yet," he said. "No, I'll stay up with you, bub. If that's all right. I'll stay up until you're ready to turn in. We haven't had a chance to talk. Know what I mean? I feel like me and her monopolized the evening." He lifted his beard and he let it fall. He picked up his cigarettes and his lighter.

"That's all right," I said. Then I said, "I'm glad for the company."

And I guess I was. Every night I smoked dope and stayed up as long as I could before I fell asleep. My wife and I hardly ever went to bed at the same time. When I did go to sleep, I had these dreams. Sometimes I'd wake up from one of them, my heart going crazy.

Something about the church and the Middle Ages was on the TV. Not your run-of-the-mill TV fare. I wanted to watch something else. I turned to the other channels. But there was nothing on them, either. So I turned back to the first channel and apologized.

"Bub, it's all right," the blind man said. "It's fine with me. Whatever you want to watch is okay. I'm always learning something. Learning never ends. It won't hurt me to learn something tonight. I got ears," he said.

We didn't say anything for a time. He was leaning forward with his head turned at me, his right ear aimed in the direction of the set. Very disconcerting. Now and then his eyelids drooped and then they snapped open again. Now and then he put his fingers into his beard and tugged, like he was thinking about something he was hearing on the television.

On the screen, a group of men wearing cowls was being set upon and tormented by men dressed in skeleton costumes and men dressed as devils. The men dressed as devils wore devil masks, horns, and long tails. This pageant was part of a procession. The Englishman who was narrating the thing said it took place in Spain once a year. I tried to explain to the blind man what was happening.

"Skeletons," he said. "I know about skeletons," he said, and he nodded.

The TV showed this one cathedral. Then there was a long, slow look at another one. Finally, the picture switched to the famous one in Paris, with its flying buttresses, and its spires reaching up to the clouds. The camera pulled away to show the whole of the cathedral rising above the skyline.

There were times when the Englishman who was telling the thing would shut up, would simply let the camera move around over the cathedrals. Or else the camera would tour the countryside, men in fields walking behind oxen. I waited as long as I could. Then I felt I had to say something. I said, "They're showing the outside of this cathedral now. Gargoyles. Little statues carved to look like monsters. Now I guess they're in Italy. Yeah, they're in Italy. There's paintings on the walls of this one church."

"Are those fresco paintings, bub?" he asked, and he sipped from his drink.

I reached for my glass. But it was empty. I tried to remember what I could remember. "You're asking me are those frescoes?" I said. "That's a good question. I don't know."

The camera moved to a cathedral outside Lisbon. The differences in the Portuguese cathedral compared with the French and Italian were not that great. But they were there. Mostly the interior stuff. Then something occurred to me, and I said, "Something has occurred to me. Do you have any idea what a cathedral is? What they look like, that is? Do you follow me? If somebody says cathedral to you, do you have any notion what they're talking about? Do you know the difference between that and a Baptist church, say?"

He let the smoke dribble from his mouth. "I know they took hundreds of workers fifty or a hundred years to build," he said. "I just heard the man say that, of course. I know generations of the same families worked on a cathedral. I heard him say that, too. The men who began their life's work on them, they never lived to see the completion of their work. In that wise, bub, they're no different from the rest of us, right?" He laughed. Then his eyelids drooped again. His head nodded. He seemed to be snoozing. Maybe he was imagining himself in Portugal. The TV was showing another cathedral now. This one was in Germany. The Englishman's voice droned on. "Cathedrals," the blind man said. He sat up and rolled his head back and forth. "If you want the truth, bub, that's about all I know. What I just said. What I heard him say. But maybe you could describe one to me? I wish you'd do it. I'd like that. If you want to know, I really don't have a good idea."

I stared hard at the shot of the cathedral on the TV. How could I even begin to describe it? But say my life depended on it. Say my life was being threatened by an insane guy who said I had to do it or else.

I stared some more at the cathedral before the picture flipped off into the countryside. There was no use. I turned to the blind man and said, "To begin with, they're very tall." I was looking around the room for clues. "They reach way up. Up and up. Toward the sky. They're so big, some of them, they have to have these supports. To help hold them up, so to speak. These supports are called buttresses. They remind me of viaducts, for some reason. But maybe you don't know viaducts, either? Sometimes the cathedrals have devils and such carved into the front. Sometimes lords and ladies. Don't ask me why this is," I said.

He was nodding. The whole upper part of his body seemed to be moving back and forth.

"I'm not doing so good, am I?" I said.

He stopped nodding and leaned forward on the edge of the sofa. As he listened to me, he was running his fingers through his beard. I wasn't getting through to him, I could see that. But he waited for me to go on just the same. He nodded, like he was trying to encourage me. I tried to think what else to say. "They're really big," I said. "They're massive. They're built of stone. Marble, too, sometimes. In those olden days, when they built cathedrals, men wanted to be close to God. In those olden days, God was an important part of everyone's life. You could tell this from their cathedral-building. I'm sorry," I said, "but it looks like that's the best I can do for you. I'm just no good at it."

"That's all right, bub," the blind man said. "Hey, listen. I hope you don't mind my asking you. Can I ask you something? Let me ask you a simple question, yes or no. I'm just curious and there's no offense. You're my host. But let me ask if you are in any way religious? You don't mind my asking?"

I shook my head. He couldn't see that, though. A wink is the same as a nod to a blind man. "I guess I don't believe in it. In anything. Sometimes it's hard. You know what I'm saying?"

"Sure, I do," he said.

"Right," I said.

The Englishman was still holding forth. My wife sighed in her sleep. She drew a long breath and went on with her sleeping.

"You'll have to forgive me," I said. "But I can't tell you what a cathedral looks like. It just isn't in me to do it. I can't do any more than I've done."

The blind man sat very still, his head down, as he listened to me.

I said, "The truth is, cathedrals don't mean anything special to me. Nothing. Cathedrals. They're something to look at on late-night TV. That's all they are."

It was then that the blind man cleared his throat. He brought something up. He took a handkerchief from his back pocket. Then he said, "I get it, bub. It's okay. It happens. Don't worry about it," he said. "Hey, listen to me. Will you do me a favor? I got an idea. Why don't you find us some heavy paper? And a pen. We'll do something. We'll draw one together. Get us a pen and some heavy paper. Go on, bub, get the stuff," he said.

So I went upstairs. My legs felt like they didn't have any strength in them. They felt like they did after I'd done some running. In my wife's room, I looked around. I found some ballpoints in a little basket on her table. And then I tried to think where to look for the kind of paper he was talking about.

Downstairs, in the kitchen, I found a shopping bag with onion skins in the bottom of the bag. I emptied the bag and shook it. I brought it into the living room and sat down with it near his legs. I moved some things, smoothed the wrinkles from the bag, spread it out on the coffee table.

The blind man got down from the sofa and sat next to me on the carpet.

He ran his fingers over the paper. He was blind. He went up and down the sides of the paper. The edges, even the edges. He fingered the corners.

"All right," he said. "All right, let's do her."

He found my hand, the hand with the pen. He closed his hand over my hand. "Go ahead, bub, draw," he said. "Draw. You'll see. I'll follow along with you. It'll be okay. Just begin now like I'm telling you. You'll see. Draw," the blind man said.

So I began. First I drew a box that looked like a house. It could have been the house I lived in. Then I put a roof on it. At either end of the roof, I drew spires. Crazy.

"Swell," he said. "Terrific. You're doing fine," he said. "Never thought anything like this could happen in your lifetime, did you, bub? Well, it's a strange life, we all know that. Go on now. Keep it up."

I put in windows with arches. I drew flying buttresses. I hung great doors. I couldn't stop. The TV station went off the air. I put down the pen and closed and opened my fingers. The blind man felt around over the paper. He moved the tips of his fingers over the paper, all over what I had drawn, and he nodded.

"Doing fine," the blind man said.

I took up the pen again, and he found my hand. I kept at it. I'm no artist. But I kept drawing just the same.

My wife opened up her eyes and gazed at us. She sat up on the sofa, her robe hanging open. She said, "What are you doing? Tell me, I want to know."

I didn't answer her.

The blind man said, "We're drawing a cathedral. Me and him are working on it. Press hard," he said to me. "That's right. That's good," he said. "Sure. You got it, bub. I can tell. You didn't think you could. But you can, can't you? You're cooking with gas now. You know what I'm saying? We're going to really have us something here in a minute. How's the old arm?" he said. "Put some people in there now. What's a cathedral without people?"

My wife said, "What's going on? Robert, what are you doing? What's going on?"

"It's all right," he said to her. "Close your eyes now," the blind man said to me.

I did it. I closed them just like he said.

"Are they closed?" he said. "Don't fudge."

"They're closed," I said.

"Keep them that way," he said. He said, "Don't stop now. Draw."

So we kept on with it. His fingers rode my fingers as my hand went over the paper. It was like nothing else in my life up to now.

Then he said, "I think that's it. I think you got it," he said. "Take a look. What do you think?"

But I had my eyes closed. I thought I'd keep them that way for a little longer. I thought it was something I ought to do.

"Well?" he said. "Are you looking?"

My eyes were still closed. I was in my house. I knew that. But I didn't feel like I was inside anything.

"It's really something," I said.

1981, 1983

Sandra Cisneros 1954–

Sandra Cisneros was born and raised in a Mexican-American family living in the Latino neighborhoods of Chicago. She grew up in three worlds: the Latino world of her Chicago home; the Mexican world of her father's family in Mexico City, with whom she spent long visits; and the Anglo world of the American Middle West.

As the only daughter in a family with six sons, she was the focus of her parents' attention. Her mother encouraged her daughter's rich imaginings and obtained for her a library card even before she learned to read. In primary school Cisneros began writing poetry, and her interest in writing continued to develop through her school years. After high school she entered Loyola University of Chicago and graduated with a B.A. in English. She then entered the writer's program at Iowa State University, graduating with a Master of Fine Arts degree in 1978.

By the late 1970s, Cisneros was writing short stories and sketches, but her first published book, Bad Boys *(1980), was a collection of poems. In 1987 she published her second book of poems,* My Wicked Wicked Ways, *a revised and expanded version of her master's thesis. The poems in the two volumes re-created the scenes and events she had experienced during her childhood in the Latino neighborhoods of Chicago. She described her working-class life as a "Daughter/of a daddy with a hammer and blistered feet." And she wrote of what others had judged to be her "wicked wicked ways" because she had rejected the traditional life of women in her bicultural world and spoken out against the idea that women's choice in life must typically be "rolling pin or factory."*

In 1994 Cisneros published a third book of poems, Loose Woman, *and a children's book,* Hairs = Pelitos, *but her greatest recognition has come from her two collections of short fiction and sketches,* The House on Mango Street *(1983) and* Woman Hollering Creek and Other Stories *(1991). Cisneros has stated: "All fiction is non-fiction. Every piece of fiction is based on something that really happened," and her stories are largely autobiographical, recollecting her life in the Mexican-American world of her childhood and early adulthood.*

The House on Mango Street *presents forty-four interrelated, autobiographical sketches and tales, narrated by a young girl who grows toward maturity while recording the struggles of her family in the tragicomic world of a Latino barrio. The stories of* Woman Hollering Creek *are set in the bicultural borderland of northern Mexico and the southwestern United States. Both books are marked by their use of the realistic details of the everyday life, language, and ideas of people who are both Hispanic and Anglo—and at the same time neither one nor the other. More recently, her novel* Caramelo *(2002) has been described as "a joyful, fizzy American novel," but "deliciously subversive" in the way it redefines "American" to include much more than the middle-class European culture found in much of modern-day America.*

FURTHER READING: *Vintage Cisneros,* 2004; C. Mirriam-Goldberg, *Sandra Cisneros, Latina Writer and Activist,* 1998.

TEXT: *Woman Hollering Creek and Other Stories,* 1991.

MERICANS

We're waiting for the awful grandmother who is inside dropping pesos into *la ofrenda*[1] box before the altar to La Divina Providencia.[2] Lighting votive candles and genuflecting. Blessing herself and kissing her thumb. Running a crystal rosary between her fingers. Mumbling, mumbling, mumbling.

There are so many prayers and promises and thanks-be-to-God to be given in the name of the husband and the sons and the only daughter who never attend mass. It doesn't matter. Like La Virgen de Guadalupe,[3] the awful grandmother intercedes on their behalf. For the grandfather who hasn't believed in anything since the first PRI[4] elections. For my father, El Periquin,[5] so skinny he needs his sleep. For Auntie Light-skin, who only a few hours before was breakfasting on brain and goat tacos after dancing all night in the pink zone.[6] For Uncle Fat-face, the blackest of the black sheep—*Always remember your Uncle Fat-face in your prayers.* And Uncle Baby—*You go for me, Mamá—God listens to you.*

The awful grandmother has been gone a long time. She disappeared behind the heavy leather outer curtain and the dusty velvet inner.[7] We must stay near the church entrance. We must not wander over to the balloon and punch-ball vendors. We cannot spend our allowance on fried cookies or Familia Burron comic books or those clear cone-shaped suckers that make everything look like a rainbow when you look through them. We cannot run off and have our picture taken on the wooden ponies. We must not climb the steps up the hill behind the church and chase each other through the cemetery. We have promised to stay right where the awful grandmother left us until she returns.

There are those walking to church on their knees. Some with fat rags tied around their legs and others with pillows, one to kneel on, and one to flop ahead. There are women with black shawls crossing and uncrossing themselves. There are armies of penitents carrying banners and flowered arches while musicians play tinny trumpets and tinny drums.

La Virgen de Guadalupe is waiting inside behind a plate of thick glass. There's also a gold crucifix bent crooked as a mesquite tree when someone once threw a bomb. La Virgen de Guadalupe on the main alter because she's a big miracle, the crooked crucifix on a side altar because that's a little miracle.

But we're outside in the sun. My big brother Junior hunkered against the wall with his eyes shut. My little brother Keeks running around in circles.

Maybe and most probably my little brother is imagining he's a flying feather dancer,[8] like the ones we saw swinging high up from a pole on the Virgin's birthday. I want to be a flying feather dancer too, but when he circles past me he shouts, "I'm a B-Fifty-two bomber, you're a German," and shoots

[1]Spanish: the offering. [2]Spanish: The Divine Providence.

[3]Spanish: The Virgin of Guadalupe. Her shrine in Mexico City is a famous destination for religious pilgrims, some of whom approach the shrine on their knees as an act of penance and devotion.

[4]Mexico's longtime ruling political party. Founded as the National Revolutionary Party (PNR) in 1929, its name was changed to the Institutional Revolutionary Party (PRI) in 1946.

[5]Spanish: The Little Parakeet.

[6]The Zona Rosa in Mexico City, a district of tourist hotels, bars, and shops.

[7]Curtains hung at the church entrance to protect against the weather when the outer church doors are open.

[8]Acrobat dressed in feathered costume who performs while suspended in the air by ropes attached to a tall pole or shaft.

me with an invisible machine gun. I'd rather play flying feather dancers, but if I tell my brother this, he might not play with me at all.

"*Girl.* We can't play with a *girl.*" Girl. It's my brothers' favorite insult now instead of "sissy." "You *girl,*" they yell at each other. "You throw that ball like a *girl.*"

I've already made up my mind to be a German when Keeks swoops past again, this time yelling, "I'm Flash Gordon. You're Ming the Merciless and the Mud People." I don't mind being Ming the Merciless, but I don't like being the Mud People. Something wants to come out of the corners of my eyes, but I don't let it. Crying is what *girls* do.

I leave Keeks running around in circles—"I'm the Lone Ranger, you're Tonto." I leave Junior squatting on his ankles and go look for the awful grandmother.

Why do churches smell like the inside of an ear? Like incense and the dark and candles in blue glass? And why does holy water smell of tears? The awful grandmother makes me kneel and fold my hands. The ceiling high and everyone's prayers bumping up there like balloons.

If I stare at the eyes of the saints long enough, they move and wink at me, which makes me a sort of saint too. When I get tired of winking saints, I count the awful grandmother's mustache hairs while she prays for Uncle Old, sick from the worm,[9] and Auntie Cuca, suffering from a life of troubles that left half her face crooked and the other half sad.

There must be a long, long list of relatives who haven't gone to church. The awful grandmother knits the names of the dead and the living into one long prayer fringed with the grandchildren born in that barbaric country with its barbarian ways.

I put my weight on one knee, then the other, and when they both grow fat as a mattress of pins, I slap them each awake. *Micaela, you may wait outside with Alfredito and Enrique.* The awful grandmother says it all in Spanish, which I understand when I'm paying attention. "What?" I say, though it's neither proper nor polite. "What?" which the awful grandmother hears as "*¿Güat?*" But she only gives me a look and shoves me toward the door.

After all that dust and dark, the light from the plaza makes me squinch my eyes like if I just came out of the movies. My brother Keeks is drawing squiggly lines on the concrete with a wedge of glass and the heel of his shoe. My brother Junior squatting against the entrance, talking to a lady and man.

They're not from here. Ladies don't come to church dressed in pants. And everybody knows men aren't supposed to wear shorts.

"*¿Quieres chicle?*"[10] the lady asks in a spanish too big for her mouth. "*Gracias.*" The lady gives him a whole handful of gum for free, little cellophane cubes of Chiclets, cinnamon and aqua and the white ones that don't taste like anything but are good for pretend buck teeth.

"*Por favor,*" says the lady. "*¿Un foto?*" pointing to her camera.

"*Sí.*"

She's so busy taking Junior's picture, she doesn't notice me and Keeks.

"Hey, Michele, Keeks. You guys want gum?"

"But you speak English!"

"Yeah," my brother says, "we're Mericans."

We're Mericans, we're Mericans, and inside the awful grandmother prays.

1991

[9]A common name for such ailments as acute mental depression and spiritual despair.
[10]Spanish: "Do you want chewing gum?"

Louise Erdrich 1954–

Louise Erdrich has received wide critical acclaim for her novels portraying the lives of Indians and whites living in North Dakota over the past century. The first novel, Love Medicine *(1984, 1993), a series of interconnected stories, follows members of two Chippewa families living on the Turtle Mountain Reservation in North Dakota from the 1930s to the 1980s. A great critical success, the novel was translated into eighteen languages and became an international bestseller. The next in the series,* The Beet Queen *(1986), deals with Native Americans only indirectly while concentrating on the lives of Americans of Polish and German descent living in the small-town world of North Dakota. In her third novel,* Tracks *(1988), set at the turn of the century, and her fourth novel,* The Bingo Palace *(1994), set in the present day, Erdrich returns to the Indian characters introduced in* Love Medicine*, completing her account of the lives of small-town whites and three generations of Native Americans.*

Erdrich's narratives exist both as independent short stories and as extended tales in a loosely connected fictional cycle, a form that is traditional in Indian storytelling. Erdrich, of Chippewa descent, describes herself as "half German-American and half French-Indian," but insists that her stories are not simply autobiographical. Rather, her work has developed out of the narrative traditions and storytelling cycles of the Native American people with whom she was raised. She was born in Little Falls, Minnesota, and spent her childhood in the small town of Wahpeton, North Dakota. Her mother and father were teachers in an Indian school run by the U.S. Bureau of Indian Affairs. They told her stories of the Indian and white communities of which she was a part and encouraged her to read and to write her own stories. She often visited her maternal grandparents on the Turtle Mountain Reservation in North Dakota, and she later acknowledged that "the people in our families made everything into a story. They love to tell a good story. . . . people just sit and the stories start coming, one after another."

When she was eighteen Erdrich won a scholarship to Dartmouth College, which had just instituted a new program in Native American studies. At Dartmouth she won prizes for her short stories and poetry and saw her writing published for the first time, in college literary magazines. After graduation she worked as a school teacher, waitress, short-order cook, even as a flagger on a construction site, absorbing the experiences that would later appear as illuminating details in her fiction. In 1979 she entered the creative writing program at Johns Hopkins University, graduating with a master's degree in 1980. She then worked as an editor of an Indian council newspaper in Boston, and in 1981 was appointed writer-in-residence at Dartmouth. In that same year she married Michael Dorris, an anthropologist and writer who was a professor of Native American studies at Dartmouth. Until his death, the couple worked in a collaboration that resulted in the publication of more than twenty volumes.

Erdrich's novel Tales of Burning Love *(1996) revisits the people and the scenes of middle-western America that she portrayed in her most noted work of fiction,* Love Medicine. *Her sixth novel,* The Antelope Wife *(1998), portrays the agonies and complexities of life for Native Americans living in the foreign world of Big City America. One of Erdrich's most recent works,* The Last Report on the Miracles at Little No Horse *(2001)—a tale about a woman who lives most of her life as a Catholic mission priest—is again set in the same fictional town as* Love Medicine. *One of the most prolific of American writers, Erdrich has published three additional novels since 2001:* The Master Butcher's Singing Club *(2003),* Four Souls *(2004), and* The Painted Drum *(2005). Recently, in addition to fiction, she has published* The Blue Jay's Dance, A Birth Year *(1995), a yearlong journal mixed with nature essays and meditations on motherhood, and several volumes of poetry, including*

Jacklight *(1984),* Baptism of Desire *(1998), and* Original Fire, Selected and New Poems *(2003).*

Erdrich has acknowledged a desire to "undermine" the stereotypical images of the Indian so strongly embedded in American popular culture: the oversimplified visions of Native Americans as picture-gallery oddities and exotics, the noble savages, dying braves, and love-torn Indian maidens of romantic novels, motion pictures, and television. She attempts to portray the strengths and weaknesses of Native American culture as it exists on reservations where the intrusion of the non-Indian world creates cross-cultural confusions and controversies. Her characters show all the strengths and the weaknesses of Native Americans living in complex relationships with each other and with an outside world of sometimes overwhelming dimensions.

Erdrich has been criticized for lacking "political commitment" and for failing to use her writing to advance constantly the cause of Indian rights in the United States. Her response is that she has no desire to be "polemical" in her fiction, that she is not solely an "ethnic writer," and does not write exclusively about American Indians, adding, "I really consider myself a writer first. Then an Indian, or a woman, or a mother." Nonetheless, her greatest achievement has been to convey, with noteworthy humor and stylistic grace, the excitements and the bleak sadness of a people who must live in an uncertain world of shifting traditions, a people who are being altered by the urbanizing force of American industrial society but are at the same time sustaining a vital resistance to that external world, which with all its electronic and cultural potency has not yet silenced the many voices of native America.

FURTHER READING: J. Fleischner, *A Reader's Guide to the Fiction of Louise Erdrich,* 1994; P. Beidler and G. Barton, *A Reader's Guide to the Novels of Louise Erdrich,* 1999; *The Chippewa Landscape of Louise Erdrich,* ed. A. Chavkin, 1999; L. Stookey, *Louise Erdrich, A Critical Companion,* 1999; H. Wong, *Louise Erdrich's Love Medicine, A Casebook,* 2000; C. Jacobs, *The Novels of Louise Erdrich, Stories of Her People,* 2001; P. Hafen, *Reading Louise Erdrich's Love Medicine,* 2003.

TEXT: *Love Medicine,* 1993.

from *LOVE MEDICINE*

THE RED CONVERTIBLE (1974)

LYMAN LAMARTINE

I was the first one to drive a convertible on my reservation. And of course it was red, a red Olds. I owned that car along with my brother Henry Junior. We owned it together until his boots filled with water on a windy night and he bought out my share. Now Henry owns the whole car, and his younger brother Lyman (that's myself), Lyman walks everywhere he goes.

How did I earn enough money to buy my share in the first place? My one talent was I could always make money. I had a touch for it, unusual in a Chippewa. From the first I was different that way, and everyone recognized it. I was the only kid they let in the American Legion Hall to shine shoes, for example, and one Christmas I sold spiritual bouquets for the mission door to door. The nuns let me keep a percentage. Once I started, it seemed the more money I made the easier the money came. Everyone encouraged it. When I was fifteen I got a job washing dishes at the Joliet Café, and that was where my first big break happened.

It wasn't long before I was promoted to busing tables, and then the short-order cook quit and I was hired to take her place. No sooner than you know it I was managing the Joliet. The rest is history. I went on managing. I soon became part owner, and of course there was no stopping me then. It wasn't long before the whole thing was mine.

After I'd owned the Joliet for one year, it blew over in the worst tornado ever seen around here. The whole operation was smashed to bits. A total loss. The fryalator was up in a tree, the grill torn in half like it was paper. I was only sixteen. I had it all in my mother's name, and I lost it quick, but before I lost it I had every one of my relatives, and their relatives, to dinner, and I also bought that red Olds I mentioned, along with Henry.

The first time we saw it! I'll tell you when we first saw it. We had gotten a ride up to Winnipeg, and both of us had money. Don't ask me why, because we never mentioned a car or anything, we just had all our money. Mine was cash, a big bankroll from the Joliet's insurance. Henry had two checks—a week's extra pay for being laid off, and his regular check from the Jewel Bearing Plant.

We were walking down Portage anyway, seeing the sights, when we saw it. There it was, parked, large as life. Really as *if* it was alive. I thought of the word *repose,* because the car wasn't simply stopped, parked, or whatever. That car reposed, calm and gleaming, a FOR SALE sign in its left front window. Then, before we had thought it over at all, the car belonged to us and our pockets were empty. We had just enough money for gas back home.

We went places in that car, me and Henry. We took off driving all one whole summer. We started off toward the Little Knife River and Mandaree in Fort Berthold and then we found ourselves down in Wakpala somehow, and then suddenly we were over in Montana on the Rocky Boy, and yet the summer was not even half over. Some people hang on to details when they travel, but we didn't let them bother us and just lived our everyday lives here to there.

I do remember this one place with willows. I remember I laid under those trees and it was comfortable. So comfortable. The branches bent down all around me like a tent or a stable. And quiet, it was quiet, even though there was a powwow close enough so I could see it going on. The air was not too still, not too windy either. When the dust rises up and hangs in the air around the dancers like that, I feel good. Henry was asleep with his arms thrown wide. Later on, he woke up and we started driving again. We were somewhere in Montana, or maybe on the Blood Reserve—it could have been anywhere. Anyway it was where we met the girl.

All her hair was in buns around her ears, that's the first thing I noticed about her. She was posed alongside the road with her arm out, so we stopped. That girl was short, so short her lumber shirt looked comical on her, like a nightgown. She had jeans on and fancy moccasins and she carried a little suitcase.

"Hop on in," says Henry. So she climbs in between us.

"We'll take you home," I says. "Where do you live?"

"Chicken," she says.

"Where the hell's that?" I ask her.

"Alaska."

"Okay," says Henry, and we drive.

We got up there and never wanted to leave. The sun doesn't truly set there in summer, and the night is more a soft dusk. You might doze off, sometimes, but before you know it you're up again, like an animal in nature. You never feel like you have to sleep hard or put away the world. And things would grow up there. One day just dirt or moss, the next day flowers and long grass. The girl's name was Susy. Her family really took to us. They fed us and put us up. We had our own tent to live in by their house, and the kids would be in and out of there all day and night. They couldn't get over me and Henry being brothers, we looked so different. We told them we knew we had the same mother, anyway.

One night Susy came in to visit us. We sat around in the tent talking of this and that. The season was changing. It was getting darker by that time, and the cold was even getting just a little mean. I told her it was time for us to go. She stood up on a chair.

"You never seen my hair," Susy said.

That was true. She was standing on a chair, but still, when she unclipped her buns the hair reached all the way to the ground. Our eyes opened. You couldn't tell how much hair she had when it was rolled up so neatly. Then my brother Henry did something funny. He went up to the chair and said, "Jump on my shoulders." So she did that, and her hair reached down past his waist, and he started twirling, this way and that, so her hair was flung out from side to side.

"I always wondered what it was like to have long pretty hair," Henry says. Well we laughed. It was a funny sight, the way he did it. The next morning we got up and took leave of those people.

On to greener pastures, as they say. It was down through Spokane and across Idaho then Montana and very soon we were racing the weather right along under the Canadian border through Columbus, Des Lacs, and then we were in Bottineau County and soon home. We'd made most of the trip, that summer, without putting up the car hood at all. We got home just in time, it turned out, for the army to remember Henry had signed up to join it.

I don't wonder that the army was so glad to get my brother that they turned him into a Marine. He was built like a brick outhouse anyway. We liked to tease him that they really wanted him for his Indian nose. He had a nose big and sharp as a hatchet, like the nose on Red Tomahawk, the Indian who killed Sitting Bull, whose profile is on signs all along the North Dakota highways. Henry went off to training camp, came home once during Christmas, then the next thing you know we got an overseas letter from him. It was 1970, and he said he was stationed up in the northern hill country. Whereabouts I did not know. He wasn't such a hot letter writer, and only got off two before the enemy caught him. I could never keep it straight, which direction those good Vietnam soldiers were from.

I wrote him back several times, even though I didn't know if those letters would get through. I kept him informed all about the car. Most of the time I had it up on blocks in the yard or half taken apart, because that long trip did a hard job on it under the hood.

I always had good luck with numbers, and never worried about the draft myself. I never even had to think about what my number was. But Henry was never lucky in the same way as me. It was at least three years before Henry came home. By then I guess the whole war was solved in the government's mind, but for him it would keep on going. In those years I'd put his car into almost perfect shape. I always thought of it as his car while he was gone, even though when he left he said, "Now it's yours," and threw me his key.

"Thanks for the extra key," I'd said. "I'll put it up in your drawer just in case I need it." He laughed.

When he came home, though, Henry was very different, and I'll say this: the change was no good. You could hardly expect him to change for the better, I know. But he was quiet, so quiet, and never comfortable sitting still anywhere but always up and moving around. I thought back to times we'd sat still for whole afternoons, never moving a muscle, just shifting our weight along the ground, talking to whoever sat with us, watching things. He'd always had a joke, then, too, and now you couldn't get him to laugh, or when he did it was more the sound of a man choking, a sound that stopped up the throats of other people around him. They got to leaving him alone most of the time, and I didn't blame them. It was a fact: Henry was jumpy and mean.

I'd bought a color TV set for my mom and the rest of us while Henry was away. Money still came very easy. I was sorry I'd ever bought it though, because of Henry. I was also sorry I'd bought color, because with black-and-white the pictures seem older and farther away. But what are you going to do? He sat in front of it, watching it, and that was the only time he was completely still. But it was the kind of stillness that you see in a rabbit when it freezes and before it will bolt. He was not easy. He sat in his chair gripping the armrests with all his might, as if the chair itself was moving at a high speed and if he let go at all he would rocket forward and maybe crash right through the set.

Once I was in the room watching TV with Henry and I heard his teeth click at something. I looked over, and he'd bitten through his lip. Blood was going down his chin. I tell you right then I wanted to smash that tube to pieces. I went over to it but Henry must have known what I was up to. He rushed from his chair and shoved me out of the way, against the wall. I told myself he didn't know what he was doing.

My mom came in, turned the set off real quiet, and told us she had made something for supper. So we went and sat down. There was still blood going down Henry's chin, but he didn't notice it and no one said anything, even though every time he took a bite of his bread his blood fell onto it until he was eating his own blood mixed in with the food.

While Henry was not around we talked about what was going to happen to him. There were no Indian doctors on the reservation, and my mom couldn't come around to trusting the old man, Moses Pillager, because he courted her long ago and was jealous of her husbands. He might take revenge through her son. We were afraid that if we brought Henry to a regular hospital they would keep him.

"They don't fix them in those places," Mom said; "they just give them drugs."

"We wouldn't get him there in the first place," I agreed, "so let's just forget about it."

Then I thought about the car.

Henry had not even looked at the car since he'd gotten home, though like I said, it was in tip-top condition and ready to drive. I thought the car might bring the old Henry back somehow. So I bided my time and waited for my chance to interest him in the vehicle.

One night Henry was off somewhere. I took myself a hammer. I went out to that car and I did a number on its underside. Whacked it up. Bent the tail pipe double. Ripped the muffler loose. By the time I was done with the car it looked worse than any typical Indian car that has been driven all its life on reservation roads, which they always say are like government promises—full of holes. It just about hurt me, I'll tell you that! I threw dirt in the carburetor and I ripped all the electric tape off the seats. I made it look just as beat up as I could. Then I sat back and waited for Henry to find it.

Still, it took him over a month. That was all right, because it was just getting warm enough, not melting, but warm enough to work outside.

"Lyman," he says, walking in one day, "that red car looks like shit."

"Well it's old," I says. "You got to expect that."

"No way!" says Henry. "That car's a classic! But you went and ran the piss right out of it, Lyman, and you know it don't deserve that. I kept that car in A-one shape. You don't remember. You're too young. But when I left, that car was running like a watch. Now I don't even know if I can get it to start again, let alone get it anywhere near its old condition."

"Well you try," I said, like I was getting mad, "but I say it's a piece of junk."

Then I walked out before he could realize I knew he'd strung together more than six words at once.

After that I thought he'd freeze himself to death working on that car. He was out there all day, and at night he rigged up a little lamp, ran a cord out the window, and had himself some light to see by while he worked. He was better than he had been before, but that's still not saying much. It was easier for him to do the things the rest of us did. He ate more slowly and didn't jump up and down during the meal to get this or that or look out the window. I put my hand in the back of the TV set, I admit, and fiddled around with it good, so that it was almost impossible now to get a clear picture. He didn't look at it very often anyway. He was always out with that car or going off to get parts for it. By the time it was really melting outside, he had it fixed.

I had been feeling down in the dumps about Henry around this time. We had always been together before. Henry and Lyman. But he was such a loner now that I didn't know how to take it. So I jumped at the chance one day when Henry seemed friendly. It's not that he smiled or anything. He just said, "Let's take that old shitbox for a spin." Just the way he said it made me think he could be coming around.

We went out to the car. It was spring. The sun was shining very bright. My only sister, Bonita, who was just eleven years old, came out and made us stand together for a picture. Henry leaned his elbow on the red car's windshield, and he took his other arm and put it over my shoulder, very carefully, as though it was heavy for him to lift and he didn't want to bring the weight down all at once.

"Smile," Bonita said, and he did.

That picture. I never look at it anymore. A few months ago, I don't know why, I got his picture out and tacked it on the wall. I felt good about Henry at the time, close to him. I felt good having his picture on the wall, until one night when I was looking at television. I was a little drunk and stoned. I looked up at the wall and Henry was staring at me. I don't know what it was, but his smile had changed, or maybe it was gone. All I know is I couldn't stay in the same room with that picture. I was shaking. I got up, closed the door, and went into the kitchen. A little later my friend Ray came over and we both went back into that room. We put the picture in a brown bag, folded the bag over and over tightly, then put it way back in a closet.

I still see that picture now, as if it tugs at me, whenever I pass that closet door. The picture is very clear in my mind. It was so sunny that day Henry had to squint against the glare. Or maybe the camera Bonita held flashed like a mirror, blinding him, before she snapped the picture. My face is right out in the sun, big and round. But he might have drawn back, because the shadows on his face are deep as holes. There are two shadows curved like little hooks around the ends of his smile, as if to frame it and try to keep it there—that one, first smile that looked like it might have hurt his face. He has his field jacket on and the worn-in clothes he'd come back in and kept wearing ever since. After Bonita took the picture, she went into the house and we got into the car. There was a full cooler in the trunk. We started off, east, toward Pembina and the Red River because Henry said he wanted to see the high water.

The trip over there was beautiful. When everything starts changing, drying up, clearing off, you feel like your whole life is starting. Henry felt it, too. The top was down and the car hummed like a top. He'd really put it back in shape, even the tape on the seats was very carefully put down and glued back in layers. It's not that he smiled again or even joked, but his face looked to me as if it was clear, more peaceful. It looked as though he wasn't thinking of anything in particular except the bare fields and windbreaks and houses we were passing.

The river was high and full of winter trash when we got there. The sun was still out, but it was colder by the river. There were still little clumps of dirty snow here and there on the banks. The water hadn't gone over the banks yet, but it would, you could tell. It was just at its limit, hard swollen, glossy like an old gray scar. We made ourselves a fire, and we sat down and watched the current go. As I watched it I felt something squeezing inside me and tightening and trying to let go all at the same time. I knew I was not just feeling it myself; I knew I was feeling what Henry was going through at that moment. Except that I couldn't stand it, the closing and opening. I jumped to my feet. I took Henry by the shoulders and I started shaking him. "Wake up," I says, "wake up, wake up, wake up!" I didn't know what had come over me. I sat down beside him again.

His face was totally white and hard. Then it broke, like stones break all of a sudden when water boils up inside them.

"I know it," he says. "I know it. I can't help it. It's no use."

We start talking. He said he knew what I'd done with the car. It was obvious it had been whacked out of shape and not just neglected. He said he wanted to give the car to me for good now, it was no use. He said he'd fixed it just to give it back and I should take it.

"No way," I says. "I don't want it."

"That's okay," he says, "you take it."

"I don't want it, though," I says back to him, and then to emphasize, just to emphasize, you understand, I touch his shoulder. He slaps my hand off.

"Take that car," he says.

"No," I say. "Make me," I say, and then he grabs my jacket and rips the arm loose. That jacket is a class act, suede with tags and zippers. I push Henry backwards, off the log. He jumps up and bowls me over. We go down in a clinch and come up swinging hard, for all we're worth, with our fists. He socks my jaw so hard I feel like it swings loose. Then I'm at his rib cage and land a good one under his chin so his head snaps back. He's dazzled. He looks at me and I look at him and then his eyes are full of tears and blood and at first I think he's crying. But no, he's laughing. "Ha! Ha!" he says. "Ha! Ha! Take good care of it."

"Okay," I says. "Okay, no problem. Ha! Ha!"

I can't help it, and I start laughing, too. My face feels fat and strange, and after a while I get a beer from the cooler in the trunk, and when I hand it to Henry he takes his shirt and wipes my germs off. "Hoof-and-mouth disease," he says. For some reason this cracks me up, and so we're really laughing for a while, and then we drink all the rest of the beers one by one and throw them in the river and see how far, how fast, the current takes them before they fill up and sink.

"You want to go on back?" I ask after a while. "Maybe we could snag a couple of nice Kashpaw girls."

He says nothing. But I can tell his mood is turning again.

"They're all crazy, the girls up here, every damn one of them."

"You're crazy too," I say, to jolly him up. "Crazy Lamartine boys!"

He looks as though he will take this wrong at first. His face twists, then clears, and he jumps up on his feet. "That's right!" he says. "Crazier 'n hell. Crazy Indians!"

I think it's the old Henry again. He throws off his jacket and starts springing his legs up from the knees like a fancy dancer. He's down doing something between a grass dance and a bunny hop, no kind of dance I ever saw before, but neither has anyone else on all this green growing earth. He's wild. He wants to pitch whoopee! He's up and at me and all over. All this time I'm laughing so hard, so hard my belly is getting tied up in a knot.

"Got to cool me off!" he shouts all of a sudden. Then he runs over to the river and jumps in.

There's boards and other things in the current. It's so high. No sound comes from the river after the splash he makes, so I run right over. I look around. It's getting dark. I see he's halfway across the water already, and I know he didn't swim there but the current took him. It's far. I hear his voice, though, very clearly across it.

"My boots are filling," he says.

He says this in a normal voice, like he just noticed and he doesn't know what to think of it. Then he's gone. A branch comes by. Another branch. And I go in.

By the time I get out of the river, off the snag I pulled myself onto, the sun is down. I walk back to the car, turn on the high beams, and drive it up the bank. I put it in first gear and then I take my foot off the clutch. I get out, close the door, and watch it plow softly into the water. The headlights reach in as they go down, searching, still lighted even after the water swirls over the back end. I wait. The wires short out. It is all finally dark. And then there is only the water, the sound of it going and running and going and running and running.

1984 1993

Tina Howe 1937–

Tina Howe's plays are recurrently autobiographical, which she has acknowledged with the cryptic observation, "All of the events are true, but none of them happened." Painting Churches, *her most autobiographical play, and her best, has characters and events that reflect her own experiences, but they are not simply replicas of the characters and experiences of her actual life. Her father, Quincy Howe, was not a famous poet, like the aging parent Gardner Church in* Painting Churches, *but a nationally famous journalist and radio and TV news analyst of the 1940s and 1950s. And her mother's eccentricities, noteworthy as they may have been (she decorated the family home with the skeletons of small animals), are reflected in her daughter's plays only in their vehemence.*

Howe's childhood was steeped in discussions of intellectual issues, books, writing, and politics. She was led to an interest in the stage because she was, in her own words, "tall and goofy-looking as a child" and became a mimic as "the ultimate defense: Get them to laugh with *you before they laugh* at *you. So all through school and college I was the class clown." She went to private schools and to Sarah Lawrence College in New York. There she studied the writing of fiction, and when she had difficulty in writing a short story, she turned instead to writing a short play,* Closing Time. *Its subject was the end of the world, and its diversity of actors played the roles of kings, queens, and talking pigeons. The success of her play, when it was first staged at the college, caused the audience to break into applause at the final curtain and to shout, "Author, author!" The response to her work astonished her, and once she heard it, she later acknowledged, "I was hooked."*

After graduating from college, she taught English in high schools and worked as a drama coach. And she began the struggle to establish herself as a serious playwright. She first wrote two strongly feminist plays about the life of women: The Nest *(1969) and* Birth and After Birth *(1977). The reviews of* The Nest *were so harshly critical that the play closed after only a single performance.* Birth and After Birth *presented such unrelenting details of women giving birth and in language so explicit that no producer has ever been willing to bring it to the stage.*

Her next play, Museum *(1976), had a lighter touch and received more complimentary reviews. It was a satirical examination of the products of modern art seen through the eyes and described in the conversations of visitors to exhibits of modern art. Next came* The Art of Dining *(1979). It was about the complexities of life revealed in the way men and women eat, and it was marked by an on-stage food fight, perhaps the first ever seen on the legitimate stage in America.* Appearances *and* Painting Churches *followed in 1982 and 1983. Her next play,* Coastal Disturbances *(1986), presented the love stories of several couples whose passions and recriminations were sounded out from the sand dunes in which they lay under a summer sun on a New England beach, which required, for its recreation on a theater stage, the importation of twenty tons of sand. Other works include* Approaching Zanzibar *(1989),* One Shoe Off *(1993),* Pride's Crossing *(1997),* Women in Flames *(1999),* Rembrandt's Gift *(1999),* Agog in the Galapagos *(2002), and* Water Music *(2003).*

Howe has said, "I am motivated very strongly by esthetics," and in Painting Churches, *as in a number of her plays, she has a character of artistic temperament confronting a world of conventionality and encountering the subtle complexities amid which one must live and die. Howe's plays also express a feminist viewpoint, although she argues that her work challenges the conformist ideal of a single, unitary feminist point of view in art or in life: "We all have our own pasts, and we all have our own points of view, and our own intentions. . . . I don't think there's such a thing as a woman's voice. I think there are women's voices and that all our voices are very distinct from each other."*

FURTHER READING: *Feminine Focus, The New Women Playwrights,* ed. E. Brater, 1989; *A Search for a Postmodern Theater, Interviews with Contemporary Playwrights,* ed. J. DiGaetani, 1991; *Speaking on Stage, Interviews with Contemporary American Playwrights,* ed. C. Kullman, 1996; C. Bigsby, *Contemporary American Playwrights,* 2000.

TEXT: *Painting Churches* from *Contemporary Plays by Women,* ed. E. Kilgore, 1991.

PAINTING CHURCHES

CHARACTERS

FANNY SEDGWICK CHURCH, a Bostonian from a fine old family, in her sixties.
GARDNER CHURCH, her husband, an eminent New England poet from a finer family, in his seventies.
MARGARET CHURCH (MAGS), their daughter, a painter, in her early thirties.

TIME: Several years ago.

PLACE: Boston, Massachusetts.

ACT I

SCENE ONE

The living room of the Churches' townhouse on Beacon Hill one week before everything will be moved to Cape Cod. Empty packing cartons line the room and all the furniture has been tagged with brightly colored markers. At first glance it looks like any discreet Boston interior, but on closer scrutiny one notices a certain flamboyance. Oddities from secondhand stores are mixed in with the fine old furniture, and exotic handmade curios vie with tasteful family objets d'art. What makes the room remarkable, though, is the play of light that pours through three soaring arched windows. At one hour it's hard edged and brilliant; the next, it's dappled and yielding. It transforms whatever it touches, giving the room a distinct feeling of unreality. It's several years ago, a bright spring morning.

FANNY is sitting on the sofa, wrapping a valuable old silver coffee service. She's wearing a worn bathrobe and fashionable hat. As she works, she makes a list of everything on a yellow legal pad. GARDNER can be heard typing in his study down the hall.

FANNY *(Picks up a coffee pot):* God, this is good-looking! I'd forgotten how handsome Mama's old silver was! It's probably worth a fortune. It certainly weighs enough! (*Calling*) GARRRRRRRRRRRRRRRRRDNERRRRRRRRRRRR? . . . Well, it should bring us a pretty penny, that's for sure: *(Wraps it, places it in a carton, and then picks up the tray that goes with it. She holds it up like a mirror and adjusts her hat. Louder in another register)* OH, GARRRRRRRRRRRRRRRRRDNERRRRR? (GARDNER *continues typing. She then reaches for a small box and opens it with reverence)* Grandma's Paul Revere teaspoons![1] . . . *(She takes out several and fondles them)* I don't care how desperate things get, these will never go! One has to maintain some standards! *(She writes on her list)* Grandma's Paul Revere teaspoons, Cotuit![2] WASN'T IT THE AMERICAN WING OF THE METROPOLITAN MUSEUM OF ART[3] THAT WANTED GRANDMA'S PAUL REVERE TEASPOONS SO BADLY? . . . *(She looks at her reflection in the tray again)* This is a very good-looking hat, if I do say so. I was awfully smart to grab it up. *(Silence)* DON'T YOU REMEMBER A DISTINGUISHED-LOOKING MAN COMING TO THE HOUSE AND OFFERING US FIFTY THOUSAND DOLLARS FOR GRANDMA'S PAUL REVERE TEASPOONS? . . . HE HAD ON THESE MARVELOUS SHOES! THEY WERE SO POINTED AT THE ENDS WE COULDN'T IMAGINE HOW HE EVER GOT THEM ON AND THEY WERE SHINED TO WITHIN AN INCH OF THEIR LIVES AND I REMEMBER HIM SAYING HE CAME FROM THE . . . AMERICAN WING OF THE METROPOLITAN MUSEUM OF ART! . . . HELLO? . . . GARDNER? . . . ARE YOU THERE! *(The typing stops)* YOO-HOOOOOOO . . . *(Like a foghorn)* GARRRRRRRRRRDNERRRRRR?

GARDNER (*Offstage; from his study*): YES, DEAR . . . IS THAT YOU?

FANNY: OF COURSE IT'S ME! WHO ELSE COULD IT POSSIBLY BE? . . . DARLING, PLEASE COME HERE FOR A MINUTE. (*The typing resumes*) FOR GOD'S SAKE, WILL YOU STOP THAT DREADFUL TYPING BEFORE YOU SEND ME STRAIGHT TO THE NUT HOUSE? . . . (*In a new register*) GARRRRRRRRRRRRRDNERRRRR?

[*He stops.*]

GARDNER (*Offstage*): WHAT'S THAT? MAGS IS BACK FROM THE NUT HOUSE?

FANNY: I SAID . . . Lord, I hate this yelling. . . . PLEASE . . . COME . . . HERE!

[*Brief silence.*]

GARDNER (*Offstage*): I'LL BE WITH YOU IN A MOMENT, I DIDN'T HEAR HER RING. (*Starts singing*) "Nothing could be finer than to be in Carolina."

FANNY: It's a wonder I'm not in a straight-jacket already. Actually, it might be rather nice for a change . . . peaceful. DARLING . . . I WANT TO SHOW YOU MY NEW HAT!

[*Silence.* GARDNER *enters, still singing. He's wearing mismatched tweeds and is holding a stack of papers which keep drifting to the floor.*]

GARDNER: Oh, don't you look nice! Very attractive, very attractive!

FANNY: But I'm still in my bathrobe.

[1]Because of his fame as an American Revolutionary War hero, the silverware of the Boston silversmith Paul Revere (1735–1818) is highly prized and valuable.

[2]Seaside village, on the Cape Cod Peninsula, sixty miles southeast of Boston.

[3]Museum in New York City. Its American Wing houses a collection of American art from colonial times to the present.

GARDNER (*Looking around the room, leaking more papers*): Well, where's Mags?

FANNY: Darling, you're dropping your papers all over the floor.

GARDNER (*Spies the silver tray*): I remember this! Aunt Alice gave it to us, didn't she? (*He picks it up*) Good Lord, it's heavy. What's it made of? Lead?!

FANNY: No, Aunt Alice did *not* give it to us. It was Mama's.

GARDNER: Oh, yes . . . (*He starts to exit with it*)

FANNY: Could I have it back, please?

GARDNER (*Hands it to her, dropping more papers*): Oh, sure thing. . . . Where's Mags? I thought you said she was here.

FANNY: I didn't say Mags was here, I asked *you* to come here.

GARDNER (*Papers spilling*): Damned papers keep falling . . .

FANNY: I wanted to show you my new hat. I bought it in honor of Mags' visit. Isn't it marvelous?

GARDNER (*Picking up the papers as more drop*): Yes, yes, very nice . . .

FANNY: Gardner, you're not even looking at it!

GARDNER: Very becoming . . .

FANNY: You don't think it's too bright, do you? I don't want to look like a traffic light. Guess how much it cost?

GARDNER (*A whole sheaf of papers slides to the floor; he dives for them*): OH, SHIT!

FANNY (*Gets to them first*): It's all right, I've got them, I've got them. (*She hands them to him*)

GARDNER: You'd think they had wings on them . . .

FANNY: Here you go . . .	GARDNER: . . . damned things won't hold still!

FANNY: Gar . . . ?

GARDNER (*Engrossed in one of the pages*): Mmmmm?

FANNY: HELLO?

GARDNER (*Startled*): What's that?

FANNY (*In a whisper*): My hat. Guess how much it cost.

GARDNER: Oh, yes. Let's see . . . ten dollars?

FANNY: Ten dollars . . . IS THAT ALL?

GARDNER: Twenty?

FANNY: GARDNER, THIS HAPPENS TO BE A DESIGNER HAT! DESIGNER HATS START AT FIFTY DOLLARS . . . SEVENTY-FIVE!

GARDNER (*Jumps*): Was that the door bell?

FANNY: No, it wasn't the door bell. Though it's high time Mags were here. She was probably in a train wreck!

GARDNER (*Looking through his papers*): I'm beginning to get fond of Wallace Stevens[4] again.

FANNY: This damned move is going to kill me! Send me straight to my grave!

GARDNER (*Reading from a page*):

> "The mules that angels ride come slowly down
> The blazing passes, from beyond the sun.
> Descensions of their tinkling bells arrive.
> These muleteers are dainty of their way . . ."

[4]Wallace Stevens (1879–1955), American poet. The following quotation is from his poem "Le Monocle de Mon Oncle."

(*Pause*) Don't you love that! "These muleteers are *dainty* of their way"!?

FANNY: Gar, the hat. How much? (GARDNER *sighs*) Darling . . . ?

GARDNER: Oh, yes. Let's see . . . fifty dollars? Seventy-five?

FANNY: It's French.

GARDNER: Three hundred!

FANNY (*Triumphant*): No, eighty-five cents.

GARDNER: Eighty-five cents! . . . I thought you said . . .

FANNY: That's right . . . eighty . . . five . . . *cents*!

GARDNER: Well, you sure had me fooled!

FANNY: I found it at the thrift shop.

GARDNER: I thought it cost at least fifty dollars or seventy-five. You know, designer hats are very expensive!

FANNY: It was on the markdown table. (*She takes it off and shows him the label*) See that? Lily Daché![5] When I saw that label, I nearly keeled over right into the fur coats!

GARDNER (*Handling it*): Well, what do you know, that's the same label that's in my bathrobe.

FANNY: Darling, Lily Daché designed hats, not men's bathrobes!

GARDNER: Yup . . . Lily Daché . . . same name . . .

FANNY: If you look again, I'm sure you'll see . . .

GARDNER: . . . same script, same color, same size. I'll show you. (*He exits*)

FANNY: Poor lamb can't keep anything straight anymore. (*Looks at herself in the tray again*) God, this is a good-looking hat!

GARDNER (*Returns with a nondescript plaid bathrobe. He points to the label*): See that? . . . What does it say?

FANNY (*Refusing to look at it*): Lily Daché was a *hat* designer! She designed ladies' *hats*!

GARDNER: What . . . does . . . it . . . say?

FANNY: Gardner, you're being ridiculous.

GARDNER (*Forcing it on her*): Read . . . the label!

FANNY: Lily Daché did *not* design this bathrobe, I don't care what the label says!

GARDNER: READ! (FANNY *reads it*) ALL RIGHT, NOW WHAT DOES IT SAY!

FANNY (*Chagrined*): Lily Daché.

GARDNER: I told you!

FANNY: Wait a minute, let me look at that again. (*She does; then throws the robe at him in disgust*) Gar, Lily Daché never designed a bathrobe in her life! Someone obviously ripped the label off one of her hats and then sewed it into the robe.

GARDNER (*Puts it on over his jacket*): It's damned good-looking. I've always loved this robe. I think you gave it to me. . . . Well, I've got to get back to work. (*He abruptly exits*)

FANNY: Where did you get that robe anyway? . . . I didn't give it to you, did I . . . ?

[*Silence.* GARDNER *resumes typing.*]

FANNY (*Holding the tray up again and admiring herself*): You know, I think I *did* give it to him. I remember how excited I was when I found it at the thrift

[5]Renowned American fashion designer (1892–1989).

shop . . . fifty cents and never worn! *I* couldn't have sewn that label in to impress him, could I? . . . I can't be that far gone! . . . The poor lamb wouldn't even notice it, let alone understand its cachet.[6] . . . Uuuuuuh, this damned tray is even heavier than the coffee pot. They must have been amazons in the old days! (*Writes on her pad*) "Empire tray, Parke-Bernet Galleries," and good riddance! (*She wraps it and drops it into the carton with the coffee pot*) Where *is* that wretched Mags? It would be just like her to get into a train wreck! She was supposed to be here hours ago. Well, if she doesn't show up soon, I'm going to drop dead of exhaustion. God, wouldn't that be wonderful? . . . Then they could just cart me off into storage with all the old chandeliers and china . . .

[*The doorbell rings.*]

FANNY: It's Mags, it's Mags! (*A pause. Dashing out of the room, colliding into* GARDNER) Good god, look at me! I'm still in my bathrobe!

GARDNER (*Offstage*): Coming, coming . . . I've got it . . . coming! (*Dashing into the room, colliding into* FANNY) I've got it . . . hold on . . . coming . . . coming . . .

FANNY (*Offstage*): Mags is here! It's Mags . . . she's finally here!

[*GARDNER exits to open the front door. MAGS comes staggering in carrying a suitcase and an enormous duffel bag. She wears wonderfully distinctive clothes and has very much her own look. She's extremely out of breath and too wrought up to drop her heavy bags.*]

MAGS: I'm sorry. . . . I'm sorry I'm so late. . . . Everything went wrong! A passenger had a heart attack outside of New London[7] and we had to stop. . . . It was terrifying! All these medics and policemen came swarming onto the train and the conductor kept running up and down the aisles telling everyone not to leave their seats under any circumstances. . . . Then the New London fire department came screeching down to the tracks, sirens blaring, lights whirling, and all these men in black rubber suits started pouring through the doors. . . . *That* took two hours . . .

FANNY (*Offstage*): Darling . . . darling . . . where are you?

MAGS: *Then,* I couldn't get a cab at the station. There just weren't any! I must have circled the block fifteen times. Finally I just stepped out into the traffic with my thumb out, but no one would pick me up . . . so I walked . . .

FANNY (*Offstage*): Damned zipper's stuck . . .

GARDNER: You walked all the way from the South Station?[8]

MAGS: Well actually, I ran . . .

GARDNER: You had poor Mum scared to death.

MAGS (*Finally puts the bags down with a deep sigh*): I'm sorry. . . . I'm really sorry. It was a nightmare.

[6] Prestigious, esteemed quality.
[7] City in southeast Connecticut, on the rail line between New York City and Boston.
[8] Boston railroad station.

[*FANNY reenters the room, her dress over her head. The zipper's stuck; she staggers around blindly.*]

FANNY: Damned zipper! Gar, will you please help me with this?

MAGS: I sprinted all the way up Beacon Hill.

GARDNER (*Opening his arms wide*): Well come here and let's get a look at you. (*He hugs her*) Mags!

MAGS (*Squeezing him tight*): Oh, Daddy . . . Daddy!

GARDNER: My Mags!

MAGS: I never thought I'd get here! . . . Oh, you look wonderful!

GARDNER: Well, you don't look so bad yourself!

MAGS: I love your hair. It's gotten so . . . white!

FANNY (*Still lost in her dress, struggling with the zipper*): This is *so* typical . . . just as Mags arrives, my zipper has to break! (*She grunts and struggles*)

MAGS (*Waves at her*): Hi, Mum . . .

FANNY: Just a minute, dear, my zipper's . . .

GARDNER (*Picks up* MAGS' *bags*): Well, sit down and take a load off your feet . . .

MAGS: I was so afraid I'd never make it . . .

GARDNER (*Staggering under the weight of the bags*): What have you got in here? Lead weights?

MAGS: I can't believe you're finally letting me do you.

[*FANNY flings her arms around MAGS, practically knocking her over.*]

FANNY: Oh, darling . . . my precious Mags, you're here at last.

GARDNER (*Lurching around in circles*): Now let's see . . . where should I put these . . . ?

FANNY: I was sure your train had derailed and you were lying dead in some ditch!

MAGS (*Pulls away from* FANNY *to come to* GARDNER'S *rescue*): Daddy, please, let me . . . these are much too heavy.

FANNY (*Finally noticing* MAGS): GOOD LORD, WHAT HAVE YOU DONE TO YOUR HAIR?!

MAGS (*Struggling to take the bags from* GARDNER): Come on, give them to me . . . please? (*She sets them down by the sofa*)

FANNY (*As her dress starts to slide off one shoulder*): Oh, not again! . . . Gar, would you give me a hand and see what's wrong with this zipper. One minute it's stuck, the next it's falling to pieces.

[*GARDNER goes to her and starts fussing with it.*]

MAGS (*Pacing*): I don't know, it's been crazy all week. Monday, I forgot to keep an appointment I'd made with a new model. . . . Tuesday, I overslept and stood up my advanced painting students. . . . Wednesday, the day of my meeting with Max Zoll, I forgot to put on my underpants . . .

FANNY: GODDAMMIT, GAR, CAN'T YOU DO ANYTHING ABOUT THIS ZIPPER?!

MAGS: I mean, there I was, racing down Broome Street in this gauzy Tibetan skirt when I tripped and fell right at his feet . . . SPLATTT! My skirt goes flying over my head and there I am . . . everything staring him in the face . . .

FANNY: COME ON GAR, USE A LITTLE MUSCLE!

MAGS (*Laughing*): Oh, well, all that matters is that I finally got here. . . . I mean . . . there you are . . .

GARDNER (*Struggling with the zipper*): I can't see it, it's too small!

FANNY (*Whirls away from* GARDNER, *pulling her dress off altogether*): OH, FORGET IT! JUST FORGET IT! The trolley's[9] probably missing half its teeth, just like someone else I know. (*To* MAGS) I grind my teeth in my sleep now, I've worn them all down to stubs. Look at that! (*She flings open her mouth and points*) Nothing left but the gums!

GARDNER: I never hear you grind your teeth . . .

FANNY: That's because I'm snoring so loud. How could you hear anything through all that racket? It even wakes me up. It's no wonder poor Daddy has to sleep downstairs.

MAGS (*Looking around*): Jeez, look at the place! So, you're finally doing it . . . selling the house and moving to Cotuit year round. I don't believe it. I just don't believe it!

GARDNER: Well, how about a drink to celebrate Mags' arrival?

MAGS: You've been here so long. Why move now?

FANNY: Gardner, what are you wearing that bathrobe for?

MAGS: You can't move. I won't let you!

FANNY (*Softly to* GARDNER): Really, darling, you ought to pay more attention to your appearance.

MAGS: You love this house. *I* love this house . . . the room . . . the light.

GARDNER: So, Mags, how about a little . . . (*He drinks from an imaginary glass*) to wet your whistle?

FANNY: We can't start drinking now, it isn't even noon yet!

MAGS: I'm starving. I've got to get something to eat before I collapse! (*She exits toward the kitchen*)

FANNY: What *have* you done to your hair, dear? The color's so queer and all your nice curl is gone.

GARDNER: It looks to me as if she dyed it.

FANNY: Yes, that's it. You're absolutely right! It's a completely different color. She dyed it bright red!

[*MAGS can be heard thumping and thudding through the icebox.*]

FANNY: NOW, MAGS, I DON'T WANT YOU FILLING UP ON SNACKS. . . . I'VE MADE A PERFECTLY BEAUTIFUL LEG OF LAMB FOR LUNCH! . . . HELLO? . . . DO YOU HEAR ME? . . . (*To* GARDNER) No one in our family has *ever* had red hair, it's so common looking.

GARDNER: I like it. It brings out her eyes.

FANNY: WHY ON EARTH DID YOU DYE YOUR HAIR *RED*, OF ALL COLORS?!

MAGS (*Returns, eating Saltines out of the box*): I didn't dye my hair, I just added some highlight.

FANNY: I suppose that's what your arty friends in New York do . . . dye their hair all the colors of the rainbow!

GARDNER: Well, it's damned attractive if you asked me . . . damned attractive!

[9]Zipper track.

[*MAGS unzips her duffel bag and rummages around in it while eating the Saltines.*]

FANNY: Darling, I told you not to bring a lot of stuff with you. We're trying to get rid of things.

MAGS (*Pulls out a folding easel and starts setting it up*): AAAAAHHHHHH, here it is. Isn't it a beauty? I bought it just for you!

FANNY: Please don't get crumbs all over the floor. Crystal was just here yesterday. It was her last time before we move.

MAGS (*At her easel*): God, I can hardly wait! I can't believe you're finally letting me do you.

FANNY: *Do* us? . . . What *are* you talking about?

GARDNER (*Reaching for the Saltines*): Hey, Mags, could I have a couple of those?

MAGS (*Tosses him the box*): Sure! (*To* FANNY) Your portrait.

GARDNER: Thanks. (*He starts munching on a handful*)

FANNY: You're planning to paint our portrait now? While we're trying to move . . . ?

GARDNER (*Sputtering Saltines*): Mmmmm, I'd forgotten just how delicious Saltines are!

MAGS: It's a perfect opportunity. There'll be no distractions; you'll be completely at my mercy. Also, you promised.

FANNY: I did?

MAGS: Yes, you did.

FANNY: Well, I must have been off my rocker.

MAGS: No, you said, "You can paint us, you can dip us in concrete, you can do anything you want with us just so long as you help us get out of here!"

GARDNER (*Offering the box of Saltines to* FANNY): You really ought to try some of these, Fan, they're absolutely delicious!

FANNY (*Taking a few*): Why, thank you.

MAGS: I figure we'll pack in the morning and you'll pose in the afternoons. It'll be a nice diversion.

FANNY: These *are* good!

GARDNER: Here, dig in . . . take some more.

MAGS: I have some wonderful news . . . amazing news! I wanted to wait till I got here to tell you.

[*GARDNER and FANNY eat their Saltines, passing the box back and forth as MAGS speaks.*]

MAGS: You'll die! Just fall over into the packing cartons and die! Are you ready? . . . BRACE YOURSELVES . . . OKAY, HERE GOES. . . . I'm being given a one-woman show at one of the most important galleries in New York this fall. Me, Margaret Church, exhibited at Castelli's, 420 West Broadway. . . . Can you believe it?! . . . MY PORTRAITS HANGING IN THE SAME ROOMS THAT HAVE SHOWN RAUSCHENBERG, JOHNS, WARHOL, KELLY, LICHTENSTEIN, STELLA, SERRA, ALL THE HEAVIES.[10] . . . It's incredible, beyond belief . . . I mean, at my age. . . . Do you know how good you have to be to get in there? It's a miracle . . . an honest-to-God, star-spangled miracle!

[10]Famous twentieth-century painters of abstract, experimental, and "Pop" art.

[*Pause.*]

FANNY (*Mouth full*): Oh, darling, that's wonderful. We're so happy for you!

GARDNER (*Mouth full*): No one deserves it more, no one deserves it more!

MAGS: Through some fluke, some of Castelli's people showed up at our last faculty show at Pratt[11] and were knocked out . . .

FANNY (*Reaching for the box of Saltines*): More, more . . .

MAGS: They said they hadn't seen anyone handle light like me since the French Impressionists. They said I was this weird blend of Pierre Bonnard, Mary Cassatt and David Hockney . . .[12]

GARDNER (*Swallowing his mouthful*): I told you they were good.

MAGS: Also, no one's doing portraits these days. They're considered passé. I'm so out of it, I'm in.

GARDNER: Well, you're loaded with talent and always have been.

FANNY: She gets it all from Mama, you know. Her miniature of Henry James is still one of the main attractions at the Atheneum.[13] Of course no woman of breeding could be a professional artist in her day. It simply wasn't done. But talk about talent . . . that woman had talent to burn!

MAGS: I want to do one of you for the show.

FANNY: Oh, do Daddy, he's the famous one.

MAGS: No, I want to do you both. I've always wanted to do you and now I've finally got a good excuse.

FANNY: It's high time somebody painted Daddy again! I'm sick to death of that dreadful portrait of him in the National Gallery[14] they keep reproducing. He looks like an undertaker!

GARDNER: Well, I think you should just do Mum. She's never looked handsomer.

FANNY: Oh, come on, I'm a perfect fright and you know it.

MAGS: I want to do you both. Side by side. In this room. Something really classy. You look so great. Mum with her crazy hats and everything and you with that face. If I could just get you to hold still long enough and actually pose.

GARDNER (*Walking around, distracted*): Where are those papers I just had? Goddammit, Fanny . . .

MAGS: I have the feeling it's either now or never.

GARDNER: I can't hold on to anything around here. (*He exits to his study*)

MAGS: I've always wanted to do you. It would be such a challenge.

FANNY (*Pulling* MAGS *onto the sofa next to her*): I'm so glad you're finally here, Mags. I'm very worried about Daddy.

MAGS: Mummy, please. I just got here.

FANNY: He's getting quite gaga.

MAGS: Mummy . . . !

[11]School in Brooklyn, New York, for training in professions and the arts.

[12]David Hockney (1937–), British "Pop" artist; Pierre Bonnard (1867–1947), French Neo-Impressionist and Expressionist painter; Mary Cassatt (1844–1926), Impressionist American painter.

[13]Private library founded in Boston in 1807.

[14]National Gallery of Art, in Washington, D.C., a branch of the Smithsonian Institution.

FANNY: You haven't seen him in almost a year. Two weeks ago he walked through the front door of the Codman's house, kissed Emily on the cheek and settled down in the maid's room, thinking he was home!

MAGS: Oh, come on, you're exaggerating.

FANNY: He's as mad as a hatter and getting worse every day! It's this damned new book of his. He works on it around the clock. I've read some of it, and it doesn't make one word of sense, it's all at sixes and sevens . . .

GARDNER (*Pokes his head back in the room, spies some of his papers on a table and grabs them*): Ahhh, here they are. (*He exits*)

FANNY (*Voice lowered*): Ever since this dry spell with his poetry, he's been frantic, absolutely . . . frantic!

MAGS: I hate it when you do this.

FANNY: I'm just trying to get you to face the facts around here.

MAGS: There's nothing wrong with him! He's just as sane as the next man. Even saner, if you ask me.

FANNY: You know what he's doing now? You couldn't guess in a million years! . . . He's writing criticism! Daddy! (*She laughs*) Can you believe it? The man doesn't have one analytic bone in his body. His mind is a complete jumble and always has been!

[*There's a loud crash from* GARDNER*'s study.*]

GARDNER (*Offstage*): SHIT!

MAGS: He's abstracted. . . . That's the way he is.

FANNY: He doesn't spend any time with me anymore. He just holes up in that filthy study with Toots. God, I hate that bird! Though actually they're quite cunning together. Daddy's teaching him Gray's *Elegy*. You ought to see them in there, Toots perched on top of Daddy's head, spouting out verse after verse . . . Daddy, tap-tap-tapping away on his typewriter. They're quite a pair.

GARDNER (*Pokes his head back in*): Have you seen that Stevens' poem I was reading before?

FANNY (*Long-suffering*): NO, I HAVEN'T SEEN THAT STEVENS' POEM YOU WERE READING BEFORE! . . . Things are getting very tight around here, in case you haven't noticed. Daddy's last Pulitzer[15] didn't even cover our real estate tax, and now that he's too doddery to give readings anymore, that income is gone . . . (*Suddenly handing* MAGS *the sugar bowl she'd been wrapping*) Mags, *do* take this sugar bowl. You can use it to serve tea to your students at that wretched art school of yours . . .

MAGS: It's called Pratt! The Pratt Institute.

FANNY: Pratt, Splatt, whatever . . .

MAGS: And I don't serve tea to my students, I teach them how to paint.

FANNY: Well, I'm sure none of them has ever seen a sugar bowl as handsome as this before.

GARDNER (*Reappearing again*): You're sure you haven't seen it?

FANNY (*Loud and angry*): YES, I'M SURE I HAVEN'T SEEN IT! I JUST TOLD YOU I HAVEN'T SEEN IT!

GARDNER (*Retreating*): Right you are, right you are. (*He exits*)

[15]Pulitzer Prize, one of the annual awards for achievements in American journalism and in prose and poetry.

FANNY: God!

[*Silence.*]

MAGS: What do you have to yell at him like that for?

FANNY: Because the poor thing's as deaf as an adder![16]

[*MAGS sighs deeply; silence. FANNY, suddenly exuberant, leads her over to a lamp.*]

FANNY: Come, I want to show you something.

MAGS (*Looking at it*): What is it?

FANNY: Something I made. (MAGS *is about to turn it on*) WAIT, DON'T TURN IT ON YET! It's got to be dark to get the full effect. (*She rushes to the windows and pulls down the shades*)

MAGS: What *are* you doing?

FANNY: Hold your horses a minute. You'll see . . . (*As the room gets darker and darker*) Poor me, you wouldn't believe the lengths I go to to amuse myself these days . . .

MAGS (*Touching the lampshade*): What is this? It looks like a scene of some sort.

FANNY: It's an invention I made . . . a kind of magic lantern.

MAGS: Gee . . . it's amazing . . .

FANNY: What I did was buy an old engraving of the Grand Canal . . .[17]

MAGS: You *made* this?

FANNY: . . . and then color it in with crayons. Next, I got out my sewing scissors and cut out all the street lamps and windows . . . anything that light would shine through. Then I pasted it over a plain lampshade, put the shade on this old horror of a lamp, turned on the switch and . . . (*She turns it on*) VOILA . . . VENICE TWINKLING AT DUSK! It's quite effective, don't you think . . . ?

MAGS (*Walking around it*): Jeez . . .

FANNY: And see, I poked out all the little lights on the gondolas with a straight pin.

MAGS: Where on earth did you get the idea?

FANNY: Well you know, idle minds . . . (*She spins the shade, making the lights whirl*)

MAGS: It's really amazing. I mean, you could sell this in a store!

GARDNER (*Enters*): Here it is. It was right on top of my desk the whole time. (*He crashes into a table*) OOOOOWWWWW!

FANNY: LOOK OUT, LOOK OUT!

MAGS (*Rushes over to* GARDNER): Oh, Daddy, are you all right?

FANNY: Watch where you're going, watch where you're going!

GARDNER (*Hopping up and down on one leg*): GODDAMMIT! . . . I HIT MY SHIN.

FANNY: I was just showing Mags my lamp . . .

[16]According to ancient proverbial belief, the adder (a venomous snake) cannot hear.
[17]Largest of the canals in the city of Venice, Italy.

GARDNER (*Limping over to it*): Oh, yes, isn't that something? Mum is awfully clever with that kind of thing. . . . It was all her idea. Buying the engraving, coloring it in, cutting out all those little dots.

FANNY: Not "dots" . . . lights and windows, lights and windows!

GARDNER: Right, right . . . lights and windows.

FANNY: Well, we'd better get some light back in here before someone breaks their neck. (*She zaps the shades back up*)

GARDNER (*Puts his arm around* MAGS): Gee, it's good to have you back.

MAGS: It's good to be back.

GARDNER: And I like that new red hair of yours. It's very becoming.

MAGS: But I told you, I hardly touched it . . .

GARDNER: Well, something's different. You've got a glow. So . . . how do you want us to pose for this grand portrait of yours . . . ? (*He poses self-consciously*)

MAGS: Oh, Daddy, setting up a portrait takes a lot of time and thought. You've got to figure out the background, the lighting, what to wear, the sort of mood you want to—

FANNY: OOOOH, LET'S DRESS UP, LET'S DRESS UP! (*She grabs a packing blanket, drapes it around herself and links arms with* GARDNER, *striking an elegant pose*) This *is* going to be fun. She was absolutely right! Come on, Gar, look distinguished!

MAGS: Mummy, please, it's not a game!

FANNY (*More and more excited*): You still have your tuxedo, don't you? And I'll wear my marvelous long black dress that makes me look like that fascinating woman in the Sargent painting![18] (*She strikes the famous profile pose*)

MAGS: MUMMY?!

FANNY: I'm sorry, we'll behave, just tell us what to do.

[*FANNY and GARDNER settle down next to each other.*]

GARDNER: That's right, you're the boss.

FANNY: Yes, you're the boss.

MAGS: But I'm not ready yet; I haven't set anything up.

FANNY: Relax, darling, we just want to get the hang of it . . .

[*FANNY and GARDNER stare straight ahead, trying to look like suitable subjects, but they can't hold still. They keep making faces, lifting an eyebrow, wriggling a nose, twitching a lip. Nothing big and grotesque, just flickering changes; a half-smile here, a self-important frown there. They steal glances at each other every so often.*]

GARDNER: How am I doing, Fan?

FANNY: Brilliantly, absolutely brilliantly!

MAGS: But you're making faces.

FANNY: *I'm* not making faces. (*Turning to* GARDNER *and making a face*) Are *you* making faces, Gar?

GARDNER (*Instantly making one*): Certainly not! I'm the picture of restraint!

[18]The portrait entitled "Madame X" (now in the Metropolitan Museum of Art) by the American painter John Singer Sargent (1856–1925) shows a beautiful woman dressed in a long black gown and posed as a symbol of fashionable elegance and high social status.

[*Without meaning to,* FANNY *and* GARDNER *get sillier and sillier. They start giggling, then laughing.*]

MAGS (*Can't help but join in*): You two are impossible . . . completely impossible! I was crazy to think I could ever pull this off! (*Laughing away*) Look at you . . . just . . . look at you!

[*Blackout.*]

SCENE 2

Two days later, around five in the afternoon. Half of the Church household has been dragged into the living room for packing. Overflowing cartons are everywhere. They're filled with pots and pans, dishes and glasses, and the entire contents of two linen closets. MAGS *has placed a stepladder under one of the windows. A pile of tablecloths and curtains is flung beneath it. Two side chairs are in readiness for the eventual pose.*

MAGS *has just pulled a large crimson tablecloth out of a carton. She unfurls it with one shimmering toss.*

MAGS: PERFECT . . . PERFECT!

FANNY (*Seated on the sofa, clutches an old pair of galoshes to her chest*): Look at these old horrors; half the rubber is rotted away and the fasteners are falling to pieces. . . . GARDNER? . . . OH, GARRRRRRRRRRDNERRRRR?

MAGS (*Rippling out the tablecloth with shorter snapping motions*): Have you ever seen such a color?

FANNY: I've found your old sledding galoshes in with the pots and pans. Do you still want them?

MAGS: It's like something out of a Rubens![1]

[MAGS *slings the tablecloth over a chair and then sits on a footstool to finish the Sara Lee banana cake she started. As she eats, she looks at the tablecloth, making happy grunting sounds.* FANNY *lovingly puts the galoshes on over her shoes and wiggles her feet.*]

FANNY: God, these bring back memories! There were real snowstorms in the old days. Not these pathetic little two-inch droppings we have now. After a particularly heavy one, Daddy and I used to go sledding on the Common.[2] This was way before you were born. . . . God, it was a hundred years ago! . . . Daddy would stop writing early, put on these galoshes and come looking for me, jingling the fasteners like castanets. It was a kind of mating call, almost . . . (*She jingles them*) The Common was always deserted after a storm; we had the whole place to ourselves. It was so romantic. . . . We'd haul the sled up Beacon Street, stop under the State House,[3] and aim it straight down to the Park Street Church, which was much further away in those days. . . . Then Daddy would lie down on the sled, I'd lower myself on top of him, we'd rock back and forth a few times to gain momentum and then . . .

[1]I.e., like the richly ornate scenes painted by the Flemish artist Peter Paul Rubens (1577–1640).
[2]Public park in central Boston.
[3]The Massachusetts State House, seat of the state legislature, adjacent to the Boston Common.

WHOOOOOOOOSSSSSSHHHHH . . . down we'd plunge like a pair of eagles locked in a spasm of lovemaking. God, it was wonderful! . . . The city whizzing past us at ninety miles an hour . . . the cold . . . the darkness . . . Daddy's hair in my mouth . . . GAR . . . REMEMBER HOW WE USED TO GO SLEDDING IN THE OLD DAYS? . . . Sometimes he'd lie on top of me. That was fun. I liked that even more. (*In her foghorn voice*) GARRRRRRRRRDNERRRRR?

MAGS: Didn't he say he was going out this afternoon?

FANNY: Why, so he did! I completely forgot. (*She takes off the galoshes*) I'm getting just as bad as him. (*She drops them into a different carton—wistful*) Gar's galoshes, Cotuit.

[*A pause.* MAGS *picks up the tablecloth again, holds it high over her head.*]

MAGS: Isn't this fabulous? . . . (*She then wraps* FANNY *in it*) It's the perfect backdrop. Look what it does to your skin.

FANNY: Mags, what *are* you doing?

MAGS: It makes you glow like a pomegranate . . . (*She whips it off her*) Now all I need is a hammer and nails . . . (*She finds them*) YES! (*She climbs up the stepladder and starts hammering a corner of the cloth into the molding of one of the windows*) This is going to look so great! . . . I've never seen such color!

FANNY: Darling, what is going on . . . ?

MAGS: Rembrandt, eat your heart out! You seventeenth-century Dutch has-been, you. (*She hammers more furiously*)

FANNY: MARGARET, THIS IS NOT A CONSTRUCTION SITE. . . . PLEASE . . . STOP IT . . . YOO-HOOOOO . . . DO YOU HEAR ME?

[GARDNER *suddenly appears, dressed in a raincoat.*]

GARDNER: Yes, dear, here I am. I just stepped out for a walk down Chestnut Street. Beautiful afternoon, absolutely beautiful! . . . Why, that looks very nice, Mags, very nice indeed . . .

FANNY (*To* MAGS): You're going to ruin the walls to say nothing of mama's best tablecloth. . . . Mags, do you hear me? . . . yoo-hoo! . . . darling, I must insist you stop that dreadful . . .

MAGS (*Steps down; stands back and looks at the tablecloth*): That's it. That's IT!

FANNY (*To* GARDNER, *worried*): Where have *you* been?

[MAGS *kisses her fingers at the backdrop and settles back into her banana cake.*]

GARDNER (*To* FANNY): You'll never guess who I ran into on Chestnut Street . . . Pate Baldwin!

[GARDNER *takes his coat off and drops it on the floor. He sits in one of the posing chairs.*]

MAGS (*Mouth full of cake*): Oh, Daddy, I'm nowhere near ready for you yet.

FANNY (*Picks up* GARDNER'S *coat and hands it to him*): Darling, coats do *not* go on the floor.

GARDNER (*Rises, but forgets where he's supposed to go*): He was in terrible shape. I hardly recognized him. Well, it's the Parkinson's disease . . .

FANNY: You mean, Hodgkin's disease . . .

GARDNER: Hodgkin's disease . . . ?

MAGS (*Leaves her cake and returns to the tablecloth*): Now to figure out exactly how to use this gorgeous light . . .

FANNY: Yes, Pate has Hodgkin's disease, not Parkinson's disease. Sammy Bishop has Parkinson's disease. In the closet . . . your coat goes . . . in the closet!

GARDNER: You're absolutely right! Pate has Hodgkin's disease. (*He stands motionless, the coat over his arm*)

FANNY: And Goat Davis has Addison's disease.

GARDNER: I always get them confused.

FANNY (*Pointing towards the closet*): That way . . .

[*GARDNER exits to the closet; FANNY calls after him.*]

FANNY: Grace Phelps has it too, I think. Or, it might be Hodgkin's, like Pate. I can't remember.

GARDNER (*Returns with a hanger*): Doesn't The Goat have Parkinson's disease?

FANNY: No, that's Sammy Bishop.

GARDNER: God, I haven't seen The Goat in ages! (*The coat still over his arm, he hands* FANNY *the hanger*)

FANNY: He hasn't been well.

GARDNER: Didn't Heppy . . . *die*?!

FANNY: What are you giving me this for? . . . Oh, Heppy's been dead for years. She died on the same day as Luster Bright, don't you remember?

GARDNER: I always liked her.

FANNY (*Gives* GARDNER *back the hanger*): Here, I don't want this.

GARDNER: She was awfully attractive.

FANNY: Who?

GARDNER: Heppy!

FANNY: Oh, yes, Heppy had real charm.

MAGS (*Keeps adjusting the tablecloth*): Better . . . better . . .

GARDNER: Which is something The Goat is short on, if you ask me. He has Hodgkin's disease, doesn't he? (*Puts his raincoat back on and sits down*)

FANNY: Darling, what *are* you doing? I thought you wanted to hang up your coat!

GARDNER (*After a pause*): OH, YES, THAT'S RIGHT!

[*GARDNER goes back to the closet; a pause.*]

FANNY: Where were we?

GARDNER (*Returns with yet another hanger*): Let's see . . .

FANNY (*Takes both hangers from him*): FOR GOD'S SAKE, GAR, PAY ATTENTION!

GARDNER: It was something about The Goat . . .

FANNY (*Takes the coat from* GARDNER): HERE, LET ME DO IT! . . . (*Under her breath to* MAGS) See what I mean about him? You don't know the half of it!

[*FANNY hangs the raincoat up in the closet.*]

FANNY: Not the half.

MAGS (*Still tinkering with the backdrop*): Almost . . . almost . . .

GARDNER (*Sitting back down in one of the posing chairs*): Oh, Fan, did I tell you, I ran into Pate Baldwin just now. I'm afraid he's not long for this world.

FANNY (*Returning*): Well, it's that Hodgkin's disease . . . (*She sits on the posing chair next to him*)

GARDNER: God, I'd hate to see him go. He's one of the great editors of our times. I couldn't have done it without him. He gave me everything, everything!

MAGS (*Makes a final adjustment*): Yes, that's it! (*She stands back and gazes at them*) You look wonderful!

FANNY: Isn't it getting to be . . . (*She taps at an imaginary watch on her wrist and drains an imaginary glass*) cocktail time?!

GARDNER (*Looks at his watch*): On the button, on the button! (*He rises*)

FANNY: I'll have the usual, please. Do join us, Mags! Daddy bought some Dubonnet[4] especially for you!

MAGS: Hey. I was just getting some ideas.

GARDNER (*To* MAGS, *as he exits for the bar*): How about a little . . . Dubonnet to wet your whistle?

FANNY: Oh, Mags, it's like old times having you back with us like this!

GARDNER (*Offstage*): THE USUAL FOR YOU, FAN?

FANNY: I wish we saw more of you. . . . PLEASE! . . . Isn't he darling? Have you ever known anyone more darling than Daddy?

GARDNER (*Offstage; hums Jolson's "You Made Me Love You"*)[5]: MAGS, HOW ABOUT YOU? . . . A LITTLE . . . DUBONNET?

FANNY: Oh, *do* join us!

MAGS (*To* GARDNER): No, nothing, thanks.

FANNY: Well, what do you think of your aged parents picking up and moving to Cotuit year round? Pretty crazy, eh what? . . . Nothing but the gulls, oysters and us!

GARDNER (*Returns with* FANNY's *drink*): Here you go . . .

FANNY: Why thank you, Gar. (*To* MAGS) You sure you won't join us?

GARDNER (*Lifts his glass towards* FANNY *and* MAGS): Cheers!

[*GARDNER and FANNY take that first lifesaving gulp.*]

FANNY: Aaaaahhhhh!

GARDNER: Hits the spot, hits the spot!

MAGS: Well, I certainly can't do you like that!

FANNY: Why not? I think we look very . . . *comme il faut!*

[*FANNY slouches into a rummy pose; GARDNER joins her.*]

FANNY: WAIT . . . I'VE GOT IT! I'VE GOT IT! (*She whispers excitedly to* GARDNER)

[4]Brand of alcoholic drink, taken as an appetizer before meals.

[5]Al Jolson (1888–1950), American musical theater and movie star. He first sang "You Made Me Love You" in the Broadway musical *Honeymoon Express* (1913). Interest in Jolson and his rendition of the song was revived in the 1940s with the production of the motion picture *The Jolson Story* (1945).

MAGS: Come on, let's not start this again!

GARDNER: What's that? . . . Oh, yes . . . yes, yes . . . I know the one you mean. Yes, right, right . . . of course.

[*A pause.*]

FANNY: How's . . . *this*?!

[*FANNY grabs a large serving fork and she and GARDNER fly into an imitation of Grant Wood's American Gothic.*][6]

MAGS: And I wonder why it's taken me all these years to get you to pose for me. You just don't take me seriously! Poor old Mags and her ridiculous portraits . . .

FANNY: Oh, darling, your portraits aren't *ridiculous!* They may not be all that one *hopes* for, but they're certainly not—

MAGS: Remember how you behaved at my first group show in Soho? . . . Oh, come on, you remember. It was a real circus! Think back. . . . It was about six years ago. . . . Daddy had just been awarded some presidential medal of achievement and you insisted he wear it around his neck on a bright red ribbon, and you wore this . . . *huge* feathered hat to match! I'll never forget it! It was the size of a giant pizza with twenty-inch red turkey feathers shooting straight up into the air. . . . Oh, come on, you remember, don't you?

FANNY (*Leaping to her feet*): HOLD EVERYTHING! THIS IS IT! THIS IS REALLY IT! Forgive me for interrupting, Mags darling, it'll just take a minute. (*She whispers excitedly to* GARDNER)

MAGS: I had about eight portraits in the show, mostly of friends of mine, except for this old one I'd done of Mrs. Crowninshield.

GARDNER: All right, all right . . . let's give it a whirl.

[*A pause; then they mime Michelangelo's* Pietà[7] *with GARDNER lying across FANNY's lap as the dead Christ.*]

MAGS (*Depressed*): The *Pietà*. Terrific!

FANNY (*Jabbing* GARDNER *in the ribs*): Hey, we're getting good at this.

GARDNER: Of course it would help if we didn't have all these modern clothes on.

MAGS: AS I WAS SAYING . . .

FANNY: Sorry, Mags . . . sorry . . .

[*Huffing and creaking with the physical exertion of it all, FANNY and GARDNER return to their seats.*]

MAGS: As soon as you stepped foot in the gallery you spotted it and cried out, "MY GOD, WHAT'S MILLICENT CROWNINSHIELD DOING HERE?" Everyone looked

[6]Title of a painting by Grant Wood (1892–1942), American artist. One of the most recognizable pieces of American art ever created, it shows a stern-faced woman and man standing before a framed house built in American gothic style, the man holding a pitchfork upright.

[7]Statue of the Virgin Mary holding the body of the dead Jesus, created by the Italian artist Michelangelo Buonarroti (1475–1561).

up, what with Daddy's clanking medal and your amazing hat which I was sure would take off and start flying around the room. A crowd gathered. . . . Through some utter fluke, you latched on to *the* most important critic in the city, I mean . . . Mr. Modern Art himself, and you hauled him over to the painting, trumpeting out for all to hear, "THAT'S MILLICENT CROWNINSHIELD! I GREW UP WITH HER. SHE LIVES RIGHT DOWN THE STREET FROM US IN BOSTON. BUT IT'S A VERY POOR LIKENESS, IF YOU ASK ME! HER NOSE ISN'T NEARLY THAT LARGE AND SHE DOESN'T HAVE SOMETHING QUEER GROWING OUT OF HER CHIN! THE CROWNINSHIELDS ARE REALLY QUITE GOOD-LOOKING, STUFFY, BUT GOOD-LOOKING NONETHELESS!"

GARDNER (*Suddenly jumps up, ablaze*): WAIT, WAIT . . . IF IT'S MICHELANGELO YOU WANT . . . I'm sorry, Mags. . . . One more . . . just one more . . . please?

MAGS: Sure, why not? Be my guest.

GARDNER: Fanny, prepare yourself!

[*More whispering.*]

FANNY: But I think *you* should be God.

GARDNER: Me? . . . Really?

FANNY: Yes, it's much more appropriate.

GARDNER: Well, if you say so . . .

[*FANNY and GARDNER ease down to the floor with some difficulty and lie on their sides, FANNY as Adam, GARDNER as God, their fingers inching closer and closer in the attitude of Michelangelo's The Creation.*[8] *Finally they touch. MAGS cheers, whistles, applauds.*]

MAGS: THREE CHEERS . . . VERY GOOD . . . NICELY DONE, NICELY DONE!

[*FANNY and GARDNER hold the pose a moment more, flushed with pleasure; then rise, dust themselves off and grope back to their chairs.*]

MAGS: So, there we were . . .

FANNY: Yes, *do* go on!

MAGS: . . . huddled around Millicent Crowninshield, when you whipped into your pocketbook and suddenly announced, "HOLD EVERYTHING! I'VE GOT A PHOTOGRAPH OF HER RIGHT HERE, THEN YOU CAN SEE WHAT SHE REALLY LOOKS LIKE!" . . . You then proceeded to crouch down to the floor and dump everything out of your bag, and I mean . . . *everything!* . . . leaking packets of sequins and gummed stars, seashells, odd pieces of fur, crochet hooks, a monarch butterfly embedded in plastic, dental floss, antique glass buttons, small jingling bells, lace . . . I thought I'd die! Just sink to the floor and quietly die! . . . You couldn't find it, you see. I mean, you spent the rest of the afternoon on your hands and knees crawling through this ocean of junk, muttering, "It's *got* to be here somewhere; I know I had it with me!" . . . Then Daddy pulled me into the thick of it all and said, "By the way, have you met our daughter Mags yet? She's the one who did all these pictures . . .

[8]The name given a section of Michelangelo's painting on the ceiling of the Sistine Chapel in the Vatican. It shows the finger of God reaching out to touch and give life to Adam.

paintings . . . portraits . . . whatever you call them." (*She drops to her hands and knees and begins crawling out of the room*) By this time, Mum had somehow crawled out of the gallery and was lost on another floor. She began calling for me . . . "YOO-HOO, MAGS . . . WHERE ARE YOU? . . . OH, MAGS, DARLING . . . HELLO? . . . ARE YOU THERE?" (*She reenters and faces them*) This was at my *first* show.

[*Blackout.*]

SCENE 3

Twenty-four hours later. The impact of the impending move has struck with hurricane force. FANNY has lugged all their clothing into the room and dumped it in various cartons. There are coats, jackets, shoes, skirts, suits, hats, sweaters, dresses, the works. She and GARDNER are seated on the sofa, going through it all. FANNY, wearing a different hat and dress, holds up a ratty overcoat.

FANNY: What about this gruesome old thing?

[*GARDNER is wearing several sweaters and vests, a Hawaiian holiday shirt, and a variety of scarves and ties around his neck. He holds up a pair of shoes.*]

GARDNER: God . . . remember these shoes? Pound[1] gave them to me when he came back from Italy. I remember it vividly.

FANNY: *Do* let me give it to the thrift shop! (*She stuffs the coat into the appropriate carton*)

GARDNER: He bought them for me in Rome. Said he couldn't resist; bought himself a pair too since we both wore the same size. God, I miss him! (*Pause*) HEY, WHAT ARE YOU DOING WITH MY OVERCOAT?!

FANNY: Darling, it's threadbare!

GARDNER: But that's my overcoat! (*He grabs it out of the carton*) I've been wearing it every day for the past thirty-five years!

FANNY: That's just my point: it's had it.

GARDNER (*Puts it on over everything else*): There's nothing wrong with this coat!

FANNY: I trust you remember that the cottage is an eighth the size of this place and you simply won't have room for half this stuff! (*She holds up a sports jacket*) This dreary old jacket, for instance. You've had it since Hector was a pup!

GARDNER (*Grabs the jacket and puts it on over his coat*): Oh, no, you don't . . .

FANNY: And this God-awful hat . . .

GARDNER: Let me see that.

[*GARDNER stands next to FANNY and they fall into a lovely tableau. MAGS suddenly pops out from behind a wardrobe carton with a flash camera and takes a picture of them.*]

MAGS: PERFECT!

[1]Ezra Pound (1885–1972), American poet.

Fanny (*Hands flying to her face*): GOOD GOD, WHAT WAS THAT . . . ?

Gardner (*Hands flying to his heart*): JESUS CHRIST, I'VE BEEN SHOT!

Mags (*Walks to the center of the room, advancing the film*): That was terrific. See if you can do it again.

Fanny: What *are* you doing . . . ?

Gardner (*Feeling his chest*): Is there blood?

Fanny: I see lace everywhere . . .

Mags: It's all right, I was just taking a picture of you. I often use a Polaroid at this stage.

Fanny (*Rubbing her eyes*): Really, Mags, you might have given us some warning!

Mags: But that's the whole point: to catch you unawares!

Gardner (*Rubbing his eyes*): It's the damndest thing . . . I see lace everywhere.

Fanny: Yes, so do I . . .

Gardner: It's rather nice, actually. It looks as if you're wearing a veil.

Fanny: I *am* wearing a veil!

[*The camera spits out the photograph.*]

Mags: OH GOODY, HERE COMES THE PICTURE!

Fanny (*Grabs the partially developed print out of her hands*): Let me see, let me see . . .

Gardner: Yes, let's have a look.

[*Gardner and Fanny have another quiet moment together looking at the photograph. Mags tiptoes away from them and takes another picture.*]

Mags: YES!

Fanny: NOT AGAIN! PLEASE, DARLING!

Gardner: WHAT WAS THAT? . . . WHAT HAPPENED?

[*Fanny and Gardner stagger towards each other.*]

Mags: I'm sorry, I just couldn't resist. You looked so—

Fanny: WHAT ARE YOU TRYING TO DO . . . *BLIND* US?!

Gardner: Really, Mags, enough is enough . . .

[*Gardner and Fanny keep stumbling about kiddingly.*]

Fanny: Are you still there, Gar?

Gardner: Right as rain, right as rain!

Mags: I'm sorry; I didn't mean to scare you. It's just a photograph can show you things you weren't aware of. Here, have a look. (*She gives them to* Fanny) Well, I'm going out to the kitchen to get something to eat. Anybody want anything? (*She exits*)

Fanny (*Looking at the photos, half-amused, half-horrified*): Oh, Gardner, have you ever . . . ?

Gardner (*Looks at the photos and laughs*): Good grief . . .

Mags (*Offstage; from the kitchen*): IS IT ALL RIGHT IF I TAKE THE REST OF THIS TAPIOCA FROM LAST NIGHT?

FANNY: IT'S ALL RIGHT WITH ME. How about you, Gar?

GARDNER: Sure, go right ahead. I've never been that crazy about tapioca.

FANNY: What are you talking about, tapioca is one of your favorites.

MAGS (*Enters, slurping from a large bowl*):
Mmmmmmmm . . .

FANNY: Really, Mags, I've never seen anyone eat as much as you.

MAGS (*Takes the photos back*): It's strange. I only do this when I come home.

FANNY: What's the matter, don't I feed you enough?

GARDNER: Gee, it's hot in here! (*Starts taking off his coat*)

FANNY: God knows, you didn't eat anything as a child! I've never seen such a fussy eater. Gar, what *are* you doing?

GARDNER (*Shedding clothes to the floor*): Taking off some of these clothes. It's hotter than Tophet[2] in here!

MAGS (*Looking at her photos*): Yes, I like you looking at each other like that . . .

FANNY (*To* GARDNER): Please watch where you're dropping things; I'm trying to keep some order around here.

GARDNER (*Picks up what he dropped, dropping even more in the process*): Right, right . . .

MAGS: Now all I've got to do is figure out what you should wear.

FANNY: Well, I'm going to wear my long black dress, and you'd be a fool not to do Daddy in his tuxedo. He looks so distinguished in it, just like a banker!

MAGS: I haven't really decided yet.

FANNY: Just because you walk around looking like something the cat dragged in, doesn't mean Daddy and I want to, do we Gar?

[*GARDNER is making a worse and worse tangle of his clothes.*]

FANNY: HELLO . . . ?

GARDNER (*Looks up at* FANNY): Oh, yes, awfully attractive, awfully attractive!

FANNY (*To* MAGS): If you don't mind me saying so, I've never seen you looking so forlorn. You'll never catch a husband looking that way. Those peculiar clothes, that God-awful hair . . . really, Mags, it's very distressing!

MAGS: I don't think my hair's so bad, not that it's terrific or anything . . .

FANNY: Well, I don't see other girls walking around like you. I mean, girls from your background. What would Lyman Wigglesworth think if he saw you in the street?

MAGS: Lyman Wigglesworth?! . . .
Uuuuuuughhhhhh! (*She shudders*)

FANNY: All right then, that brilliant Cabot boy . . . what *is* his name?

GARDNER: Sammy.

FANNY: No, not Sammy . . .

GARDNER: Stephen . . . Stanley . . . Stuart . . . Sheldon . . . Sherlock . . . Sherlock! It's *Sherlock!*

MAGS: Spence!

FANNY: SPENCE, THAT'S IT! HIS NAME IS SPENCE!

GARDNER: THAT'S IT . . . SPENCE! SPENCE CABOT!

FANNY: Spence Cabot was first in his class at Harvard.

[2]In the Bible, a place for the punishment of the wicked after death.

MAGS: Mum, he has no facial hair.

FANNY: He has his own law firm on Arlington Street.

MAGS: Spence Cabot has six fingers on his right hand!

FANNY: So, he isn't the best-looking thing in the world. Looks isn't everything. He can't help it if he has extra fingers. Have a little sympathy!

MAGS: But the extra one has this weird nail on it that looks like a talon . . . It's long and black and . . . (*She shudders*)

FANNY: No one's perfect, darling. He has lovely handwriting and an absolutely saintly mother. Also, he's as rich as Croesus![3] He's a lot more promising than some of those creatures you've dragged home. What was the name of that dreadful Frenchman who smelled like sweaty socks? . . . Jean Duke of Scripto?

MAGS: (*Laughing*): Jean-Luc Zichot!

FANNY: And that peculiar little Oriental fellow with all the teeth! Really, Mags, he could have been put on display at the circus!

MAGS: Oh, yes, Tsu Chin. He was strange, but very sexy . . .

FANNY: (*Shudders*) He had such tiny . . . feet! Really, Mags, you've got to bear down. You're not getting any younger. Before you know it, all the nice young men will be taken and then where will you be? . . . All by yourself in that grim little apartment of yours with those peculiar clothes and that bright red hair . . .

MAGS: MY HAIR IS NOT BRIGHT RED!

FANNY: I only want what's best for you, you know that. You seem to go out of your way to look wanting. I don't understand it. . . . Gar, what *are* you putting your coat on for? . . . You look like some derelict out on the street. We don't wear coats in the house. (*She helps him out of it*) That's the way. . . . I'll just put this in the carton along with everything else . . . (*She drops it into the carton, then pauses*) Isn't it about time for . . . *cocktails!*

GARDNER: What's that?

[*FANNY taps her wrist and mimes drinking.*]

GARDNER (*Looks at his watch*): Right you are, right you are! (*Exits to the bar*) THE USUAL . . .?

FANNY: *Please!*

GARDNER (*Offstage*): HOW ABOUT SOMETHING FOR YOU MAGS?

MAGS: SURE, WHY NOT? . . . LET'ER RIP!

GARDNER (*Offstage*): WHAT'S THAT . . .?

FANNY: SHE SAID YES. SHE SAID YES!

MAGS: I'LL HAVE SOME DUBONNET! YES!

GARDNER (*Poking his head back in*): How about a little Dubonnet?

FANNY: That's just what she said. . . . She'd like some . . . Dubonnet!

GARDNER (*Goes back to the bar and hums another Jolson tune*): GEE, IT'S GREAT HAVING YOU BACK LIKE THIS, MAGS . . . IT'S JUST GREAT! (*More singing*)

FANNY (*Leaning closer to* MAGS): You have such *potential*, darling! It breaks my heart to see how you've let yourself go. If Lyman Wigglesworth . . .

MAGS: Amazing as it may seem, I don't *care* about Lyman Wigglesworth!

[3] Ancient king of Lydia (560–546 B.C.), noted for his immense wealth.

FANNY: From what I've heard, he's quite a lady killer!

MAGS: But with whom? . . . Don't think I haven't heard about his fling with . . . Hopie Stonewall!

FANNY (*Begins to laugh*): Oh, God, let's not get started on Hopie Stonewall again . . . ten feet tall with spots on her neck . . . (*To* GARDNER) OH, DARLING, DO HURRY BACK! WE'RE TALKING ABOUT PATHETIC HOPIE STONEWALL!

MAGS: It's not so much her incredible height and spotted skin; it's those tiny pointed teeth and the size eleven shoes!

FANNY: I love it when you're like this!

[*MAGS starts clomping around the room making tiny pointed-teeth nibbling sounds.*]

FANNY: GARDNER . . . YOU'RE MISSING EVERYTHING! (*Still laughing*) Why is it Boston girls are always so . . . tall?

MAGS: Hopie Stonewall isn't a Boston girl; she's a giraffe. (*She prances around the room with an imaginary dwarf-sized Lyman*) She's perfect for Lyman Wigglesworth!

GARDNER (*Returns with* FANNY'S *drink, which he hands her*): Now, where were we . . . ?

FANNY (*Trying not to laugh*): HOPIE STONEWALL . . . !

GARDNER: Oh, yes, she's the very tall one, isn't she?

[*FANNY and MAGS burst into gales.*]

MAGS: The only hope for us . . . "Boston girls" is to get as far away from our kind as possible.

FANNY: She always asks after you, darling. She's very fond of you, you know.

MAGS: Please, I don't want to hear!

FANNY: Your old friends are *always* asking after you.

MAGS: It's not so much how creepy they all are, as how much they remind me of myself!

FANNY: But you're not "creepy," darling . . . just . . . shabby!

MAGS: I mean, give me a few more inches and some brown splotches here and there, and Hopie and I could be sisters!

FANNY (*In a whisper to* GARDNER): Don't you love it when Mags is like this? I could listen to her forever!

MAGS: I mean . . . look at me!

FANNY (*Gasping*): Don't stop, don't stop!

MAGS: Awkward . . . plain . . . I don't know how to dress, I don't know how to talk. When people find out Daddy's my father, they're always amazed. . . . "Gardner Church is YOUR father?! Aw, come on, you're kidding?!"

FANNY (*In a whisper*): Isn't she divine . . . ?

MAGS: Sometimes I don't even tell them. I pretend I grew up in the Midwest somewhere . . . farming people . . . we work with our hands.

GARDNER (*To* MAGS): Well, how about a little refill . . . ?

MAGS: No, no more thanks.

[*Pause.*]

FANNY: What did you have to go and interrupt her for? She was just getting up a head of steam . . .

MAGS (*Walking over to her easel*): The great thing about being a portrait painter, you see, is it's the *other* guy that's exposed; you're safely hidden behind the canvas and easel. (*Standing behind it*) You can be as plain as a pitchfork, as inarticulate as mud, but it doesn't matter because you're completely concealed: your body, your face, your intentions. Just as you make your most intimate move, throw open your soul . . . they stretch and yawn, remembering the dog has to be let out at five. . . . To be so invisible while so enthralled . . . it takes your breath away!

GARDNER: Well put, Mags. Awfully well put!

MAGS: That's why I've always wanted to paint you, to see if I'm up to it. It's quite a risk. Remember what I went through as a child with my great masterpiece . . . ?

FANNY: You painted a masterpiece when you were a child . . . ?

MAGS: Well, it was a masterpiece to me.

FANNY: I had no idea you were precocious as a child. Gardner, do you remember Mags painting a masterpiece as a child?

MAGS: I didn't paint it. It was something I made!

FANNY: Well, this is all news to me! Gar, *do* get me another drink! I haven't had this much fun in years! (*She hands him her glass and reaches for* MAGS'S) Come on, darling, join me . . .

MAGS: No, no more, thanks. I don't really like the taste.

FANNY: Oh, come on, kick up your heels for once!

MAGS: No, nothing . . . really.

FANNY: Please? Pretty please? . . . To keep me company?!

MAGS (*Hands* GARDNER *her glass*): Oh, all right, what the hell . . .

FANNY: That's a good girl!

GARDNER (*Exiting*): Coming right up, coming right up!

FANNY (*Yelling after* GARDNER): DON'T GIVE ME TOO MUCH NOW. THE LAST ONE WAS AWFULLY STRONG . . . AND HURRY BACK SO YOU DON'T MISS ANYTHING! . . . Daddy's so cunning, I don't know what I'd do without him. If anything should happen to him, I'd just . . .

MAGS: Mummy, nothing's going to happen to him . . . !

FANNY: Well, wait till you're our age, it's no garden party. Now . . . where were we . . . ?

MAGS: My first masterpiece . . .

FANNY: Oh, yes, but *do* wait till Daddy gets back so he can hear it too: . . . YOO-HOO . . . GARRRRRRDNERRRRRR? . . . ARE YOU COMING? (*Silence*) Go and check on him will you?

[*GARDNER enters with both drinks. He's very shaken.*]

GARDNER: I couldn't find the ice.

FANNY: Well, *finally!*

GARDNER: It just up and disappeared . . . (*Hands* FANNY *her drink*) There you go. (FANNY *kisses her fingers and takes a hefty swig*) Mags. (*He hands* MAGS *her drink*)

MAGS: Thanks, Daddy.

GARDNER: Sorry about the ice.

MAGS: No problem, no problem.

[*GARDNER sits down; silence.*]

FANNY (*To* MAGS): Well, drink up, drink up! (MAGS *downs it in one gulp*) GOOD-GIRL! . . . Now, what's all this about a masterpiece . . . ?

MAGS: I did it during that winter you sent me away from the dinner table. I was about nine years old.

FANNY: We sent you from the dinner table?

MAGS: I was banished for six months.

FANNY: You *were*? . . . How extraordinary!

MAGS: Yes, it *was* rather extraordinary!

FANNY: But why?

MAGS: Because I played with my food.

FANNY: You did?

MAGS: I used to squirt it out between my front teeth.

FANNY: Oh, I remember that! God, it used to drive me crazy, absolutely . . . crazy! (*Pause*) "MARGARET, STOP THAT OOZING RIGHT THIS MINUTE, YOU ARE NOT A TUBE OF TOOTHPASTE!"

GARDNER: Oh, yes . . .

FANNY: It was perfectly disgusting!

GARDNER: I remember. She used to lean over her plate and squirt it out in long runny ribbons . . .

FANNY: That's enough, dear.

GARDNER: They were quite colorful, actually; decorative almost. She made the most intricate designs. They looked rather like small, moist Oriental rugs . . .

FANNY (*To* MAGS): But why, darling? What on earth possessed you to do it?

MAGS: I couldn't swallow anything. My throat just closed up. I don't know, I must have been afraid of choking or something.

GARDNER: I remember one in particular. We'd had chicken fricassee and spinach. . . . She made the most extraordinary—

FANNY (*To* GARDNER): WILL YOU PLEASE SHUT UP?! (*Pause*) Mags, what *are* you talking about? You never choked in your entire life! This is the most distressing conversation I've ever had. Don't you think it's distressing, Gar?

GARDNER: Well, that's not quite the word I'd use.

FANNY: What word *would* you use, then?

GARDNER: I don't know right off the bat, I'd have to think about it.

FANNY: THEN, THINK ABOUT IT!

[*Silence.*]

MAGS: I guess I was afraid of making a mess. I don't know; you were awfully strict about table manners. I was always afraid of losing control. What if I started to choke and began spitting up over everything . . . ?

FANNY: All right, dear, that's enough.

MAGS: No, I was really terrified about making a mess; you always got so mad whenever I spilled. If I just got rid of everything in neat little curlicues beforehand, you see . . .

FANNY: I SAID: THAT'S ENOUGH!

[*Silence.*]

MAGS: I thought it was quite ingenious, but you didn't see it that way. You finally sent me from the table with, "When you're ready to eat like a human being, you can come back and join us!" . . . So, it was off to my room with a tray. But I couldn't seem to eat there either. I mean, it was so strange settling down to dinner in my *bedroom*. . . . So I just flushed everything down the toilet and sat on my bed listening to you: clinkity-clink, clatter clatter, slurp, slurp . . . but that got pretty boring after a while, so I looked around for something to do. It was wintertime, because I noticed I'd left some crayons on top of my radiator and they'd melted down into these beautiful shimmering globs, like spilled jello, trembling and pulsing . . .

GARDNER (*Overlapping; eyes closed*):
"This luscious and impeccable fruit of life
Falls, it appears, of its own weight to earth . . ."

MAGS: Naturally, I wanted to try it myself, so I grabbed a red one and pressed it down against the hissing lid. It oozed and bubbled like raspberry jam!

GARDNER:
"When you were Eve, its acrid juice was sweet,
Untasted, in its heavenly, orchard air . . ."

MAGS: I mean, that radiator was really hot! It took incredible will power not to let go, but I held on, whispering, "Mags, if you let go of this crayon, you'll be run over by a truck on Newberry Street, so help you God!" . . . So I pressed down harder, my fingers steaming and blistering . . .

FANNY: I had no idea about any of this, did you, Gar?

MAGS: Once I'd melted one, I was hooked! I finished off my entire supply in one night, mixing color over color until my head swam! . . . The heat, the smell, the brilliance that sank and rose . . . I'd never felt such exhilaration! . . . Every week I spent my allowance on crayons. I must have cleared out every box of Crayolas in the city!

GARDNER (*Gazing at* MAGS): You know, I don't think I've ever seen you looking prettier! You're awfully attractive when you get going!

FANNY: Why, what a lovely thing to say.

MAGS: AFTER THREE MONTHS THAT RADIATOR WAS . . . SPECTACULAR! I MEAN, IT LOOKED LIKE SOME COLOSSAL FRUITCAKE, FIVE FEET TALL . . . !

FANNY: It sounds perfectly hideous.

MAGS: It was a knockout; shimmering with pinks and blues, lavenders, and maroons, turquoise and golds, oranges and creams. . . . For every color, I imagined a taste . . . YELLOW: lemon curls dipped in sugar . . . RED: glazed cherries laced with rum . . . GREEN: tiny peppermint leaves veined with chocolate . . . PURPLE:—

FANNY: That's quite enough!

MAGS: And then the frosting . . . ahhhh, the frosting! A satiny mix of white and silver . . . I kept it hidden under blankets during the day. . . . My huge . . . (*She starts laughing*) looming . . . teetering sweet—

FANNY: I ASKED YOU TO STOP! GARDNER, WILL YOU PLEASE GET HER TO STOP!

GARDNER: See here, Mags, Mum asked you to—

MAGS: I was so . . . *hungry* . . . losing weight every week. I looked like a scarecrow what with the bags under my eyes and bits of crayon wrapper leaking out of my clothes. It's a wonder you didn't notice. But finally you came to my rescue . . . if you could call what happened rescue. It was more like a rout!

FANNY: Darling . . . *please!* GARDNER: Now, look, young lady—

MAGS: The winter was almost over . . . It was very late at night. . . . I must have been having a nightmare because suddenly you and Daddy were at my bed, shaking me. . . . I quickly glanced towards the radiator to see if it was covered. . . . *It wasn't!* It glittered and towered in the moonlight like some . . . gigantic Viennese pastry! You followed my gaze and saw it. Mummy screamed . . . "WHAT HAVE YOU GOT IN HERE? . . . MAGS, WHAT HAVE YOU BEEN DOING?" . . . She crept forward and touched it, and then jumped back. "IT'S FOOD!" she cried . . . "IT'S ALL THE FOOD SHE'S BEEN SPITTING OUT! OH, GARDNER, ITS A MOUNTAIN OF ROTTING GARBAGE!"

FANNY (*Softly*): Yes . . . it's coming back . . . it's coming back . . .

MAGS: Daddy exited as usual; left the premises. He fainted, just keeled over onto the floor . . .

GARDNER: Gosh, I don't remember any of this . . .

MAGS: My heart stopped! I mean, I knew it was all over. My lovely creation didn't have a chance. Sure enough . . . out came the blowtorch. Well, it couldn't have *really* been a blowtorch, I mean, where would you have ever gotten a blowtorch? . . . I just have this very strong memory of you standing over my bed, your hair streaming around your face, aiming this . . . flamethrower at my confection . . . my cake . . . my tart . . . my strudel. . . . "IT'S GOT TO BE DESTROYED IMMEDIATELY! THE THING'S ALIVE WITH VERMIN! . . . JUST LOOK AT IT! . . . IT'S PRACTICALLY CRAWLING ACROSS THE ROOM!" . . . Of course in a sense you were right. It *was* a monument of my castoff dinners, only I hadn't built it with food. . . . I found my own materials. I was languishing with hunger, but oh, dear Mother . . . I FOUND MY OWN MATERIALS . . . !

FANNY: Darling . . . *please?!*

MAGS: I tried to stop you, but you wouldn't listen. . . . OUT SHOT THE FLAME! . . . I remember these waves of wax rolling across the room and Daddy coming to, wondering what on earth was going on. . . . Well, what did you know about my abilities? . . . You see, I had . . . I mean, I *have* abilities . . . (*Struggling to say it*) I have abilities. I have . . . strong abilities. I have . . . very strong abilities. They are very strong . . . very, very strong . . .

[*MAGS rises and runs out of the room overcome as FANNY and GARDNER watch, speechless. The curtain falls.*]

ACT II

SCENE 1

Three days later. Miracles have been accomplished. Almost all of the Churches' furniture has been moved out, and the cartons of dishes and clothing are gone. All that remains are odds and ends. MAGS'S tableau looms, impregnable. FANNY and GARDNER are dressed in their formal evening clothes, frozen in their pose. They hold absolutely still. MAGS stands at her easel, her hands covering her eyes.

FANNY: All right, you can look now.

MAGS (*Removes her hands*): Yes! . . . I told you you could trust me on the pose.

FANNY: Well, thank God you let us dress up. It makes all the difference. Now we really look like something.

MAGS (*Starts to sketch them*): I'll say . . .

[*A silence as she sketches.*]

GARDNER (*Recites Yeats's "The Song of Wandering Aengus"*[1] *in a wonderfully resonant voice as they pose*):

"I went out to the hazel wood,
Because a fire was in my head,
And cut and peeled a hazel wand,
And hooked a berry to a thread;
And when white moths were on the wing,
And moth-like stars were flickering out,
I dropped the berry in a stream
And caught a little silver trout.

When I had laid it on the floor
I went to blow the fire a-flame,
But something rustled on the floor,
And someone called me by my name:
It had become a glimmering girl
With apple blossoms in her hair
Who called me by my name and ran
And faded through the brightening air.

Though I am old with wandering
Through hollow lands and hilly lands,
I will find out where she has gone,
And kiss her lips and take her hands;
And walk among long dappled grass,
And pluck till time and times are done,
The silver apples of the moon,
The golden apples of the sun."

FANNY: That's lovely, dear. Just lovely. Is it one of yours?

GARDNER: No, no, it's Yeats. I'm using it in my book.

FANNY: Well, you recited it beautifully, but then you've always recited beautifully. That's how you wooed me, in case you've forgotten. . . . You must have memorized every love poem in the English language! There was no stopping you when you got going . . . your Shakespeare, Byron, and Shelley . . . you were shameless . . . *shameless!*

GARDNER (*Eyes closed*):

"I will find out where she has gone,
And kiss her lips and take her hands . . ."

[1]Gardner quotes the complete text of "The Song of the Wandering Aengus" by the Irish poet William Butler Yeats (1865–1939).

FANNY: And then there was your own poetry to do battle with; your sonnets and quatrains. When you got going with them, there was nothing left of me! You could have had your pick of any girl in Boston! Why you chose me, I'll never understand. I had no looks to speak of and nothing much in the brains department. . . . Well, what did you know about women and the world? . . . What did any of us know . . . ?

[*Silence.*]

FANNY: GOD, MAGS, HOW LONG ARE WE SUPPOSED TO SIT LIKE THIS? . . . IT'S AGONY!

MAGS (*Working away*): You're doing fine . . . just fine . . .

FANNY (*Breaking her pose*): It's so . . . boring!

MAGS: Come on, don't move. You can have a break soon.

FANNY: I had no idea it would be so boring!

GARDNER: Gee, I'm enjoying it.

FANNY: You would . . . !

[*A pause.*]

GARDNER (*Begins reciting more Yeats, almost singing it*):

> "He stood among a crowd at Drumahair;
> His heart hung all upon a silken dress,
> And he had known at last some tenderness,
> Before earth made of him her sleepy care;
> But when a man poured fish into a pile,
> It seemed they raised their little silver heads . . ."[2]

FANNY: Gar . . . PLEASE! (*She lurches out of her seat*) God, I can't take this anymore!

MAGS (*Keeps sketching* GARDNER): I know it's tedious at first, but it gets easier . . .

FANNY: It's like a Chinese water torture! (*Crosses to* MAGS *and looks at* GARDNER *posing*) Oh, darling, you look marvelous, absolutely marvelous! Why don't you just do Daddy!?

MAGS: Because you look marvelous too. I want to do you both!

FANNY: Please! . . . I have one foot in the grave and you know it! Also, we're way behind in our packing. There's still one room left which everyone seems to have forgotten about!

GARDNER: Which one is that?

FANNY: You know perfectly well which one it is!

GARDNER: I do . . . ?

FANNY: Yes, you do!

GARDNER: Well, it's news to me.

FANNY: I'll give you a hint. It's in . . . *that* direction. (*She points*)

GARDNER: The dining room?

[2] A quotation from Yeats's "The Man Who Dreamed of Faeryland."

FANNY: No.

GARDNER: The bedroom?

FANNY: No.

GARDNER: Mags' room?

FANNY: No.

GARDNER: The kitchen?

FANNY: *Gar?!*

GARDNER: The guest room?

FANNY: Your God-awful study!

GARDNER: Oh, shit!

FANNY: That's right, "Oh, shit!" It's books and papers up to the ceiling! If you ask me, we should just forget it's there and quietly tiptoe away . . .

GARDNER: My study . . . !

FANNY: Let the new owners dispose of everything . . .

GARDNER (*Gets out of his posing chair*): Now, just one minute . . .

FANNY: You never look at half the stuff in there!

GARDNER: I don't want you touching those books! They're mine!

FANNY: Darling, we're moving to a cottage the size of a handkerchief! Where, pray tell, is there room for all your books?

GARDNER: I don't know. We'll just have to make room!

MAGS (*Sketching away*): RATS!

FANNY: I don't know what we're doing fooling around with Mags like this when there's still so much to do . . .

GARDNER (*Sits back down, overwhelmed*): My study . . . !

FANNY: You can stay with her if you'd like, but one of us has got to tackle those books! (*She exits to his study*)

GARDNER: I'm not up to this.

MAGS: Oh, good, you're staying!

GARDNER: There's a lifetime of work in there . . .

MAGS: Don't worry, I'll help. Mum and I will be able to pack everything up in no time.

GARDNER: God . . .

MAGS: It won't be so bad . . .

GARDNER: I'm just not up to it.

MAGS: We'll all pitch in . . .

[*GARDNER sighs, speechless. A silence as FANNY comes staggering in with an armload of books, which she drops to the floor with a crash.*]

GARDNER: WHAT WAS THAT?! MAGS: GOOD GRIEF!

FANNY (*Sheepish*): Sorry, sorry . . . (*She exits for more*)

GARDNER: I don't know if I can take this . . .

MAGS: Moving is awful . . . I know . . .

GARDNER (*Settling back into his pose*): Ever since Mum began tearing the house apart, I've been having these dreams. . . . I'm a child again back at 16 Louisberg Square[3] . . . and this stream of moving men is carrying furniture into our house . . . van after van of tables and chairs, sofas and love

[3]Louisberg Square, elegant residential district in Boston.

seats, desks and bureaus . . . rugs, bathtubs, mirrors, chiming clocks, pianos, iceboxes, china cabinets . . . but what's amazing is that all of it is familiar . . .

[*FANNY comes in with another load, which she drops on the floor. She exits for more.*]

GARDNER: No matter how many items appear, I've seen every one of them before. Since my mother is standing in the midst of it directing traffic, I ask her where it's all coming from, but she doesn't hear me because of the racket . . . so finally I just scream out . . . "WHERE IS ALL THIS FURNITURE COMING FROM?" . . . Just as a moving man is carrying Toots into the room, she looks at me and says, "Why, from the land of Skye!" . . . The next thing I know, *people* are being carried in along with it . . .

[*FANNY enters with her next load; drops it and exits.*]

GARDNER: People I've never seen before are sitting around our dining-room table. A group of foreigners is going through my books, chattering in a language I've never heard before. A man is playing a Chopin polonaise on Aunt Alice's piano. Several children are taking baths in our tubs from Cotuit . . .

MAGS: It sounds marvelous.

GARDNER: Well, it isn't marvelous at all because all of these perfect strangers have taken over our things . . .

[*FANNY enters, hurls down another load and exits.*]

MAGS: How odd . . .

GARDNER: Well, it *is* odd, but then something even odder happens . . .

MAGS: (*Sketching away*): Tell me, tell me!

GARDNER: Well, our beds are carried in. They're all made up with sheets and everything, but instead of all these strange people in them, *we're* in them . . . !

MAGS: What's so odd about that?

GARDNER: Well, you and Mum are brought in, both sleeping like angels . . . Mum snoring away to beat the band . . .

MAGS: Yes . . .

[*FANNY enters with another load, lets it fall.*]

GARDNER: But there's no one in mine. It's completely empty, never even been slept in! It's as if I were dead or had never even existed . . .

[*FANNY exits.*]

GARDNER: "HEY . . . WAIT UP!" I yell to the moving men . . . "THAT'S MY BED YOU'VE GOT THERE!" But they don't stop; they don't even acknowledge me. . . . "HEY, COME BACK HERE . . . I WANT TO GET INTO MY BED!" I cry again and I start running after them . . . down the hall, through the dining room, past the library. . . . Finally I catch up to them and hurl myself right into the center of the pillow. Just as I'm about to land, the bed suddenly vanishes and I go crashing down to the floor like some insect that's been hit by a fly swatter!

[*FANNY staggers in with her final load; she drops it with a crash and then collapses in her posing chair.*]

FANNY: THAT'S IT FOR ME! I'M DEAD!

[*Silence.*]

FANNY: Come on, Mags, how about you doing a little work around here.

MAGS: That's all I've been doing! This is the first free moment you've given me!

FANNY: You should see all the books in there . . . and papers! There are enough loose papers to sink a ship!

GARDNER: Why is it we're moving, again . . . ?

FANNY: Because life is getting too complicated here.

GARDNER: (*Remembering*): Oh, yes . . .

FANNY: And we can't afford it anymore.

GARDNER: That's right, that's right . . .

FANNY: We don't have the . . . *income* we used to!

GARDNER: Oh, yes . . . *income!*

FANNY (*Assuming her pose again*): Of course, we have our savings and various trust funds, but I wouldn't dream of touching those!

GARDNER: No, no, you must never dip into capital!

FANNY: I told Daddy I'd be perfectly happy to buy a gun and put a bullet through our heads so we could avoid all this, but he wouldn't hear of it!

MAGS (*Sketching away*): No, I shouldn't think so.

[*Pause.*]

FANNY: I've always admired people who kill themselves when they get to our stage of life. Well, no one can touch my Uncle Edmond in that department . . .

MAGS: I know, I know . . .

FANNY: The day before his seventieth birthday he climbed to the top of the Old North Church and hurled himself face down into Salem Street! They had to scrape him up with a spatula! God, he was a remarkable man . . . state senator, president of Harvard . . .

GARDNER (*Rises and wanders over to his books*): Well, I guess I'm going to have to do something about all of these . . .

FANNY: Come on Mags, help Daddy! Why don't you start bringing in his papers . . .

[*GARDNER sits on the floor; he picks up a book and soon is engrossed in it. MAGS keeps sketching, oblivious. Silence.*]

FANNY (*To* MAGS): Darling? . . . HELLO? . . . God, you two are impossible! Just look at you . . . heads in the clouds! No one would ever know we've got to be out of here in two days. If it weren't for me, nothing would get done around here . . . (*She starts stacking* GARDNER'S *books into piles*) There! That's all the maroon ones!

GARDNER (*Looks up*): What do you mean, *maroon* ones?!

FANNY: All your books that are maroon are in *this* pile . . . and your books that are green in *that* pile! . . . I'm trying to bring some order into your life for once. This will make unpacking so much easier.

GARDNER: But, my dear Fanny, it's not the color of a book that distinguishes it, but what's *inside* it!

FANNY: This will be a great help, you'll see. Now what about this awful striped thing? (*She picks up a slim, aged volume*) Can't it go . . . ?

GARDNER: No!

FANNY: But it's as queer as Dick's hatband! There are no others like it.

GARDNER: Open it and read. Go on . . . open it!

FANNY: We'll get nowhere at this rate.

GARDNER: I said . . . READ!

FANNY: Really, Gar, I—

GARDNER: Read the dedication!

FANNY (*Opens and reads*): "To Gardner Church, you led the way. With gratitude and affection, Robert Frost.[4] (*She closes it and hands it to him*)

GARDNER: It was published the same year as my *Salem Gardens.*

FANNY (*Picking up a very worn book*): Well, what about this dreadful thing? It's filthy. (*She blows off a cloud of dust*)

GARDNER: Please . . . *please?!*

FANNY (*Looking through it*): It's all in French.

GARDNER (*Snatching it away from her*): André Malraux[5] gave me that . . . !

FANNY: I'm just trying to help.

GARDNER: It's a first edition of Baudelaire's *Fleurs du mal.*[6]

FANNY (*Giving it back*): Well, pardon me for living!

GARDNER: Why do you have to drag everything in here in the first place . . . ?

FANNY: Because there's no room in your study. You ought to see the mess in there! . . . WAKE UP, MAGS, ARE YOU GOING TO PITCH IN OR NOT?!

GARDNER: I'm not up to this.

FANNY: Well, you'd better be unless you want to be left behind!

MAGS (*Stops her sketching*): All right, all right . . . I just hope you'll give me some more time later this evening.

FANNY (*To* MAGS): Since you're young and in the best shape, why don't you bring in the books and I'll cope with the papers. (*She exits to the study*)

GARDNER: Now just a minute . . .

FANNY (*Offstage*): WE NEED A STEAM SHOVEL FOR THIS!

MAGS: Okay, what do you want me to do?

GARDNER: Look, I don't want you messing around with my—

[*FANNY enters with an armful of papers, which she drops into an empty carton.*]

GARDNER: HEY, WHAT'S GOING ON HERE?!

[4]Robert Frost (1874–1963), American poet.

[5]André Malraux (1901–1976), French literary and political figure.

[6]Charles Baudelaire (1821–1867). His collected poems were published as *Les Fleurs du mal* (*The Flowers of Evil*) in 1857.

FANNY: I'm packing up your papers. COME ON, MAGS, LET'S GET CRACKING! (*She exits for more papers*)

GARDNER (*Plucks several papers out of the carton*): What is this . . . ?

MAGS (*Exits into his study*): GOOD LORD, WHAT HAVE YOU DONE IN HERE?!

GARDNER (*Reading*): This is my manuscript.

[*FANNY enters with another batch, which she tosses on top of the others.*]

GARDNER: What *are* you doing?!

FANNY: Packing, darling . . . PACKING! (*She exits for more*)

GARDNER: SEE HERE, YOU CAN'T MANHANDLE MY THINGS THIS WAY!

[*MAGS enters, staggering under a load of books, which she sets down on the floor.*]

GARDNER: *I* PACK MY MANUSCRIPT! I KNOW WHERE EVERYTHING IS!

FANNY (*Offstage*): IF IT WERE UP TO YOU, WE'D NEVER GET OUT OF HERE! WE'RE UNDER A TIME LIMIT, GARDNER. KITTY'S PICKING US UP IN TWO DAYS . . . TWO . . . DAYS! (*She enters with a larger batch of papers and heads for the carton*)

GARDNER (*Grabbing* FANNY'S *wrist*): NOW, HOLD IT! . . . JUST . . . HOLD IT RIGHT THERE!

FANNY: OOOOOWWWWWWWW!

GARDNER: *I* PACK MY THINGS!

FANNY: LET GO, YOU'RE HURTING ME!

GARDNER: THAT'S MY MANUSCRIPT! GIVE IT TO ME!

FANNY (*Lifting the papers high over her head*): I'M IN CHARGE OF THIS MOVE, GARDNER! WE'VE GOT TO GET CRACKING!

GARDNER: I said . . . GIVE IT TO ME!

MAGS: Come on, Mum, let him have it.

[*FANNY and GARDNER struggle.*]

GARDNER (*Finally wrenches the pages from* FANNY): LET . . . ME . . . HAVE IT! . . . THAT'S MORE LIKE IT!

FANNY (*Soft and weepy*): You see what he's like? . . . I try and help with his packing and what does he do . . . ?

GARDNER (*Rescues the rest of his papers from the carton*): YOU DON'T JUST THROW EVERYTHING INTO A BOX LIKE A PILE OF GARBAGE! THIS IS A BOOK, FANNY. SOMETHING I'VE BEEN WORKING ON FOR TWO YEARS! (*Trying to assemble his papers, but only making things worse, dropping them all over the place*) You show a little respect for my things. . . . You don't just throw them around every which way. . . . It's tricky trying to make sense of poetry; it's much easier to write the stuff . . . that is, if you've still got it in you . . .

MAGS: Here, let me help . . . (*Taking some of the papers*)

GARDNER: Criticism is tough sledding. You can't just dash off a few images here, a few rhymes there . . .

MAGS: Do you have these pages numbered in any way?

FANNY (*Returning to her posing chair*): HA!

GARDNER: This is just the introduction.

MAGS: I don't see any numbers on these.

GARDNER (*Exiting to his study*): The important stuff is in my study . . .

FANNY (*To* MAGS): You don't know the half of it . . . *not the half* . . . !

GARDNER (*Offstage; thumping around*): HAVE YOU SEEN THOSE YEATS POEMS I JUST HAD . . . ?

MAGS (*Reading over several pages*): What is this? . . . It doesn't make sense. It's just fragments . . . pieces of poems.

FANNY: That's it, honey! That's his book. His great critical study! Now that he can't write his own poetry, he's trying to explain other people's. The only problem is, he can't get beyond typing them out. The poor lamb doesn't have the stamina to get beyond the opening stanzas, let alone trying to make sense of them.

GARDNER (*Thundering back with more papers, which keep falling*): GODDAMMIT, FANNY, WHAT DID YOU DO IN THERE? I CAN'T FIND ANYTHING!

FANNY: I just took the papers that were on your desk.

GARDNER: Well, the entire beginning is gone. (*He exits*)

FANNY: I'M TRYING TO HELP YOU, DARLING!

GARDNER (*Returns with another armload*): SEE THAT? . . . NO SIGN OF CHAPTER ONE OR TWO . . . (*He flings it all down to the floor*)

FANNY: Gardner . . . PLEASE?!

GARDNER (*Kicking through the mess*): I TURN MY BACK FOR ONE MINUTE AND WHAT HAPPENS? . . . MY ENTIRE STUDY IS TORN APART! (*He exits*)

MAGS: Oh, Daddy . . . don't . . . please . . . Daddy . . . *please?!*

GARDNER (*Returns with a new batch of papers, which he tosses up into the air*): THROWN OUT! . . . THE BEST PART IS THROWN OUT! . . . lost . . . (*He starts to exit again*)

MAGS (*Reads one of the fragments to steady herself*):

> "I have known the inexorable sadness of pencils,
> Neat in their boxes, dolor of pad and paperweight,
> All the misery of manila folders and mucilage . . ."[7]

They're beautiful . . . just beautiful.

GARDNER (*Stops*): Hey, what's that you've got there?

FANNY: It's your manuscript, darling. You see, it's right where you left it.

GARDNER (*To* MAGS): Read that again.

MAGS:

> "I have known the inexorable sadness of pencils,
> Neat in their boxes, dolor of pad and paperweight,
> All the misery of manila folders and mucilage . . ."

GARDNER: Well, well, what do you know . . .

FANNY (*Hands him several random papers*): You see . . . no one lost anything. Everything's here, still intact.

GARDNER (*Reads*):

> "I knew a woman, lovely in her bones,
> When small birds sighed, she would sigh back at them;

[7]From the poem "Dolor" by the American poet Theodore Roethke (1908–1963). Among the following quotations are selections from the poetry of Roethke, Robert Frost, James Dickey, and Emily Dickinson.

Ah, when she moved, she moved more ways than one:
The shapes a bright container can contain! . . ."

FANNY (*Hands him another*): And . . .
GARDNER (*Reads*): Ahh . . . Frost . . .

"Some say the world will end in fire,
Some say in ice.
From what I've tasted of desire
I hold with those who favor fire."

FANNY (*Under her breath to* MAGS): He can't give up the words. It's the best he can do. (*Handing him another*) Here you go, here's more.

GARDNER:

"Farm boys wild to couple
With anything   with soft-wooded trees
With mounds of earth   mounds
Of pinestraw   will keep themselves off
Animals by legends of their own . . ."

MAGS (*Eyes shut*): Oh, Daddy, I can't bear it . . . I . . .
FANNY: Of course no one will ever publish this.
GARDNER: Oh, here's a marvelous one. Listen to this!

"There came a Wind like a Bugle—
It quivered through the Grass
And a Green Chill upon the Heat
So ominous did pass
We barred the Windows and the Doors
As from an Emerald Ghost—
The Doom's electric Moccasin . . ."

SHIT, WHERE DID THE REST OF IT GO . . . ?

FANNY: Well, don't ask *me*.
GARDNER: It just stopped in mid-air!
FANNY: Then go look for the original.
GARDNER: Good idea, good idea! (*He exits to his study*)
FANNY (*To* MAGS): He's incontinent now, too. He wets his pants, in case you haven't noticed. (*She starts laughing*) You're not laughing. Don't you think it's funny? Daddy needs diapers. . . . I don't know about you, but I could use a drink! GAR . . . WILL YOU GET ME A SPLASH WHILE YOU'RE OUT THERE . . . ?
MAGS: STOP IT!
FANNY: It means we can't go out anymore. I mean, what would people say . . . ?
MAGS: Stop it. Just stop it.
FANNY: My poet laureate can't hold it in! (*She laughs harder*)
MAGS: That's enough . . . STOP IT . . . Mummy . . . I beg of you . . . *please stop it!*

[GARDNER *enters with a book and indeed a large stain has blossomed on his trousers. He plucks it away from his leg.*]

GARDNER: Here we go . . . I found it . . .

FANNY (*Pointing at it*): See that? See? . . . He just did it again! (*Goes off into a shower of laughter*)

MAGS: (*Looks, turns away*): SHUT . . . UP! . . . (*Building to a howl*) WILL YOU PLEASE JUST . . . SHUT . . . UP!

FANNY (*To* GARDNER): Hey, what about that drink?

FANNY: Never mind, I'll get it, I'll get it.

[*FANNY exits, convulsed. Silence.*]

GARDNER: Well, where were we?

MAGS (*Near tears*): Your poem.

GARDNER: Oh yes . . . the Dickinson. (*He shuts his eyes, reciting from memory, holding the book against his chest*)

"There came a Wind like a Bugle—
It quivered through the Grass
And a Green Chill upon the Heat
So ominous did pass
We barred the Windows and the Doors
As from an Emerald Ghost—"

(*Opens the book and starts riffling through it*) Let's see now, where's the rest? . . . (*He finally finds it*) Ahhh, here we go . . . !

FANNY (*Reenters, drink in hand*): I'm back! (*Takes one look at* GARDNER *and bursts out laughing again*)

MAGS: I don't believe you! How you can laugh at him?!

[*They all speak simultaneously as MAGS gets angrier and angrier.*]

FANNY: I'm sorry, I wish I could stop, but there's really nothing else to do. Look at him . . . just . . . look at him . . . !

MAGS: It's so cruel . . . You're so . . . incredibly cruel to him . . . I mean, YOUR DISDAIN REALLY TAKES MY BREATH AWAY! YOU'RE IN A CLASS BY YOURSELF WHEN IT COMES TO HUMILIATION!

GARDNER (*Reading*):

"The Doom's electric Moccasin
That very instant passed—
On a strange Mob of panting Trees
And Fences fled away
And Rivers where the Houses ran
Those looked that lived—that Day—
The Bell within the steeple wild
The flying tidings told—

How much can come
And much can go,
And yet abide the World!"

(*He shuts the book with a bang, pauses and looks around the room, confused*) Now, where was I . . . ?

FANNY: Safe and sound in the middle of the living room with Mags and me.

GARDNER: But I was looking for something, wasn't I . . . ?

FANNY: Your manuscript.

GARDNER: THAT'S RIGHT! MY MANUSCRIPT! My manuscript!

FANNY: And here it is all over the floor. See, you're standing on it.

GARDNER (*Picks up a few pages and looks at them*): Why so I am . . .

FANNY: Now all we have to do is get it up off the floor and packed neatly into these cartons!

GARDNER: Yes, yes, that's right. Into the cartons!

FANNY (*Kicks a carton over to him*): Here, you use this one and I'll start over here . . . (*She starts dropping papers into a carton nearby*) BOMBS AWAY! . . . Hey . . . this is fun!

GARDNER (*Picks up his own pile, lifts it high over his head and flings it down into the carton*): BOMBS AWAY . . . This is fun!

FANNY: I told you! The whole thing is to figure out a system!

GARDNER: I don't know what I'd do without you, Fan. I thought I'd lost everything.

FANNY (*Makes dive-bomber noises and machine-gun explosions as she wheels more and more papers into the carton*): TAKE THAT AND THAT AND THAT!

GARDNER (*Joins in the fun, outdoing her with dips, dives, and blastings of his own*): BLAM BLAM BLAM BLAM! . . . ZZZZZZZZRAAAAAAFOOM! . . . BLATTY-DE-BLATTY-DE-BLATTY-DE-KABOOOOOOOOOM! . . .
WHAAAAAAA . . . DA-DAT-DAT-DAT-DAT-DAT . . .
WHEEEEEEEE AAAAAAAAAAAAA . . . FOOOOOO . . .

[*They get louder and louder as papers fly every which way.*]

FANNY (*Mimes getting hit with a bomb*): AEEEEEEEIIIIIIIIIIIII! YOU GOT ME RIGHT IN THE GIZZARD! (*She collapses on the floor and starts going through death throes, having an absolute ball*)

GARDNER: TAKE THAT AND THAT AND THAT AND THAT . . . (*A series of explosions follow*)

MAGS (*Furious*): This is how you help him? . . . THIS IS HOW YOU PACK HIS THINGS?

FANNY: I keep him company. I get involved . . . which is a hell of a lot more than you do!

MAGS (*Wild with rage*): BUT YOU'RE MAKING A MOCKERY OF HIM. . . . YOU TREAT HIM LIKE A CHILD OR SOME DIMWITTED SERVING BOY. HE'S JUST AN AMUSEMENT TO YOU!

FANNY (*Fatigue has finally overtaken her. She's calm, almost serene*): And to you who see him once a year, if that . . . what is he to *you?* . . . I mean, what do you give him from yourself that costs you something? . . . Hmmmmmmm? . . . (*Imitating* MAGS) "Oh, hi Daddy, it's great to see you again. How have you been? . . . Gee, I love your hair. It's gotten so . . . *white!*" . . . What color do you expect it to get when he's this age? . . . I mean, if you care so much how he looks, why don't you come and see him once in a while? . . . But oh, no . . . you have your paintings to do and your shows to put on. You just come and see us when the whim strikes. (*Imitating* MAGS) "Hey, you know what would be really great? . . . To do a portrait of you! I've always wanted to paint you, you're such great subjects!" . . . *Paint* us?! . . . What about opening your eyes and really *seeing* us? . . . Noticing what's going on around here for a change! It's all over for Daddy and me. This is it! "Finita la commedia!" . . . All I'm trying to do is exit with a little flourish; have some fun. . . . What's so terrible about that? . . . It can get pretty grim around here, in case you haven't noticed . . . Daddy, tap-tap-tapping out his nonsense all day; me traipsing around to the thrift shops trying to amuse myself. . . He never keeps me company anymore; never takes me out anywhere. . . . I'd put a bullet through my head in a minute, but then who'd look after him? . . . What do you think we're moving to the cottage for? . . So I can watch him like a hawk and make sure he doesn't get lost. Do you think that's anything to look forward to? . . . Being Daddy's nursemaid out in the middle of nowhere? I'd much rather stay here in Boston with the few friends I have left, but you can't always do what you want in this world! "L'homme propose, Dieu dispose!"[8] . . . If you want to paint us so badly, you ought to paint us as we really are. There's your picture."

[*FANNY points to GARDNER, who's quietly playing with a paper glider.*]

FANNY: Daddy spread out on the floor with all his toys and me hovering over him to make sure he doesn't hurt himself! (*She goes over to him*) YOO-HOO . . . GAR? . . . HELLO?

GARDNER (*Looks up at her*): Oh, hi there, Fan. What's up?

FANNY: How's the packing coming . . . ?

GARDNER: Packing . . . ?

FANNY: Yes, you were packing your manuscript, remember? (*She lifts up a page and lets it fall into a carton*)

GARDNER: Oh, yes . . .

FANNY: Here's your picture, Mags. Face over this way . . . turn your easel over here . . . (*She lets a few more papers fall*) Up, up . . . and away . . .

[*Blackout.*]

SCENE 2

The last day. All the books and boxes are gone. The room is completely empty except for MAGS*'s backdrop. Late afternoon light dapples the walls; it changes from pale peach to deeper violet. The finished portrait sits on the easel, covered with a cloth.* MAGS *is taking down the backdrop.*

FANNY (*Offstage to* GARDNER): DON'T FORGET TOOTS!

GARDNER (*Offstage; from another part of the house*): WHAT'S THAT?

[8]French: Man proposes, God disposes.

FANNY (*Offstage*): I SAID: DON'T FORGET TOOTS! HIS CAGE IS SITTING IN THE MIDDLE OF YOUR STUDY!

[*Silence.*]

FANNY (*Offstage*): HELLO? . . . ARE YOU THERE?

GARDNER (*Offstage*): I'LL BE RIGHT WITH YOU; I'M JUST GETTING TOOTS!

GARDNER (*Offstage*): WHAT'S THAT? I CAN'T HEAR YOU?

FANNY (*Offstage*): I'M GOING THROUGH THE ROOMS ONE MORE TIME TO MAKE SURE WE DIDN'T FORGET ANYTHING . . . KITTY'S PICKING US UP IN FIFTEEN MINUTES, SO PLEASE BE READY. . . . SHE'S DROPPING MAGS OFF AT THE STATION AND THEN IT'S OUT TO ROUTE 3 AND THE CAPE HIGHWAY . . .

GARDNER (*Enters, carrying* TOOTS *in his cage*): Well, this is it. The big moment has finally come, eh what, Toots? (*He sees* MAGS) Oh, hi there, Mags, I didn't see you . . .

MAGS: Oh, hi, Daddy, I'm just taking this down . . . (*She does and walks over to* TOOTS) Oh, Toots, I'll miss you. (*She makes little chattering noises into his cage*)

GARDNER: Come on, recite a little Gray's *Elegy* for Mags before we go.

MAGS: Yes, Mum said he was really good at it now.

GARDNER: Well, the whole thing is to keep at it every day. (*Slowly to* TOOTS)

> "The curfew tolls the knell of parting day,
> The lowing herd wind slowly o'er the lea . . ."[1]

Come on, show Mags your stuff! (*Slower*)

> "The curfew tolls the knell of parting day,
> The lowing herd wind slowly o'er the lea . . ."

[*Silence;* GARDNER *makes little chattering sounds.*]

GARDNER: Come on, Toots, old boy . . .

MAGS: How does it go?

GARDNER (*To* MAGS):

> "The curfew tolls the knell of parting day,
> The lowing herd wind slowly o'er the lea . . ."

MAGS (*Slowly to* TOOTS):

> The curfew tolls for you and me,
> As quietly the herd winds down . . .

GARDNER: No, no, it's "The curfew tolls the knell of parting *day* . . ."!

MAGS (*Repeating after him*): "The curfew tolls the knell of parting day . . ."

GARDNER: "The lowing herd wind slowly o'er the lea . . ."

MAGS (*With a deep breath*):

> The curfew tolls at parting day,
> The herd low slowly down the lea . . . no, *knell!*
> They come winding down the *knell!*

[1]The opening lines from "Elegy in a Country Churchyard" (1751) by the English poet Thomas Gray (1716–1771).

GARDNER: Listen, Mags . . . *listen!*

[*A pause.*]

TOOTS (*Loud and clear with* GARDNER'S *inflection*):

"The curfew tolls the knell of parting day,
The lowing herd wind slowly o'er the lea,
The ploughman homeward plods his weary way,
And leaves the world to darkness and to me."

MAGS: HE SAID IT. . . . HE SAID IT! . . . AND IN YOUR VOICE . . . OH, DADDY, THAT'S AMAZING!

GARDNER: Well, Toots is very smart, which is more than I can say for a lot of people I know . . .

MAGS (*To* TOOTS): Polly want a cracker? Polly want a cracker?

GARDNER: You can teach a parakeet to say anything; all you need is patience . . .

MAGS: But *poetry* . . . that's so hard . . .

[*FANNY enters carrying a suitcase and GARDNER'S typewriter in its case. She's dressed in her traveling suit, wearing a hat to match.*]

FANNY: WELL, THERE YOU ARE! I THOUGHT YOU'D DIED!

MAGS (*To* FANNY): HE SAID IT! I FINALLY HEARD TOOTS RECITE GRAY'S *ELEGY.* (*She makes silly clucking sounds into the cage*)

FANNY: Isn't it uncanny how much he sounds like Daddy? Sometimes when I'm alone here with him, I've actually thought he *was* Daddy and started talking to him. Oh, yes, Toots and I have had quite a few meaty conversations together!

[*FANNY wolf-whistles into the cage; then draws back. GARDNER covers the cage with a traveling cloth. Silence.*]

FANNY (*Looking around the room*): God, the place looks so bare.

MAGS: I still can't believe it . . . Cotuit, year round. I wonder if there'll be any phosphorus when you get there?

FANNY: What on earth are you talking about? (*She carries the discarded backdrop out into the hall*)

MAGS: Remember that summer when the ocean was full of phosphorus?

GARDNER (*Taking* TOOTS *out into the hall*): Oh, yes . . .

MAGS: It was a great mystery where it came from or why it settled in Cotuit. But one evening when Daddy and I were taking a swim, suddenly it was there!

GARDNER (*Returns*): I remember.

MAGS: I don't know where Mum was . . .

FANNY (*Reentering*): Probably doing the dishes!

MAGS (*To* GARDNER): As you dove into the water, this shower of silvery green sparks erupted all around you. It was incredible! I thought you were turning into a saint or something; but then you told me to jump in too and the same thing happened to me . . .

GARDNER: Oh, yes, I remember that . . . the water smelled all queer.

MAGS: What *is* phosphorus, anyway?

GARDNER: Chemicals, chemicals . . .

FANNY: No, it isn't. Phosphorus is a green liquid inside insects. Fireflies have it. When you see sparks in the water it means insects are swimming around . . .

GARDNER: Where on earth did you get that idea . . . ?

FANNY: If you're bitten by one of them, it's fatal!

MAGS: And the next morning it was still there . . .

GARDNER: It was the damndest stuff to get off! We'd have to stay in the shower a good ten minutes. It comes from chemical waste, you see . . .

MAGS: Our bodies looked like mercury as we swam around . . .

GARDNER: It stained all the towels a strange yellow green.

MAGS: I was in heaven, and so were you for that matter. You'd finished your day's poetry and would turn somersaults like some happy dolphin . . .

FANNY: Damned dishes . . . why didn't I see any of this?!

MAGS: I remember one night in particular. . . . We sensed the phosphorus was about to desert us; blow off to another town. We were chasing each other under water. At one point I lost you, the brilliance was so intense . . . but finally your foot appeared . . . then your leg. I grabbed it! . . . I remember wishing the moment would hold forever; that we could just be fixed there, laughing and iridescent. . . . Then I began to get panicky because I knew it would pass; it was passing already. You were slipping from my grasp. The summer was almost over. I'd be going back to art school; you'd be going back to Boston. . . . Even as I was reaching for you, you were gone. We'd never be like that again.

[*Silence. FANNY spies MAGS's portrait covered on the easel.*]

FANNY: What's that over there? Don't tell me we forgot something!

MAGS: It's your portrait. I finished it.

FANNY: You finished it? How on earth did you manage that?

MAGS: I stayed up all night.

FANNY: You did? . . . *I* didn't hear you, did you hear her, Gar . . . ?

GARDNER: Not a peep, not a peep!

MAGS: Well, I wanted to get it done before you left. You know, see what you thought. It's not bad, considering . . . I mean, I did it almost completely from memory. The light was terrible and I was trying to be quiet so I wouldn't wake you. It was hardly an ideal situation. . . . I mean, you weren't the most cooperative models . . . (*She suddenly panics and snatches the painting off the easel. She hugs it to her chest and starts dancing around the room with it*) Oh, God, you're going to hate it! You're going to hate it! How did I ever get into this? . . . Listen, you don't really want to see it . . . it's nothing . . . just a few dabs here and there. . . . It was awfully late when I finished it. The light was really impossible and my eyes were hurting like crazy. . . . Look, why don't we just go out to the sidewalk and wait for Kitty so she doesn't have to honk—

GARDNER (*Snatches the painting out from under her grasp*): WOULD YOU JUST SHUT UP A MINUTE AND LET US SEE IT?

Mags (*Laughing and crying*): But it's nothing, Daddy . . . *really*! . . . I've done better with my eyes closed! It was so late I could hardly see anything and then I spilled a whole bottle of thinner into my palette . . .

Gardner (*Sets the portrait down on the easel and stands back to look at it*): THERE!

Mags (*Dancing around them in a panic*): Listen, it's just a quick sketch. . . . It's still wet. . . . I didn't have enough time. . . . It takes at least forty hours to do a decent portrait . . .

[*Suddenly it's very quiet as Fanny and Gardner stand back to look at the painting. More and more beside herself, Mags keeps leaping around the room wrapping her arms around herself, making little whimpering sounds.*]

Mags: Please don't . . . no . . . don't . . . oh, please! . . . Come on, don't look. . . . Oh, God, don't . . . please . . .

[*An eternity passes as Fanny and Gardner gaze at their portrait.*]

Gardner: Well . . .

Fanny: Well . . .

[*More silence.*]

Fanny: I think it's perfectly dreadful!

Gardner: Awfully clever, awfully clever!

Fanny: What on earth did you do to my face . . . ?

Gardner: I particularly like Mum!

Fanny: Since when do I have purple skin?!

Mags: I told you it was nothing, just a silly—

Gardner: She looks like a million dollars!

Fanny: AND WILL YOU LOOK AT MY HAIR . . . IT'S BRIGHT ORANGE!

Gardner (*Views the painting from another angle*): It's really very good!

Fanny (*Pointing*): That doesn't look anything like me!

Gardner: First-rate!

Fanny: Since when do I have purple skin and bright orange hair?

Mags (*Trying to snatch the painting off the easel*): Listen, you don't have to worry about my feelings . . . really . . . I—

Gardner (*Blocking her way*): NOT SO FAST . . .

Fanny: And look at how I'm sitting! I've never sat like that in my life!

Gardner (*Moving closer to the painting*): Yes, yes, it's awfully clever . .

Fanny: I HAVE NO FEET!

Gardner: The whole thing is quite remarkable!

Fanny: And what happened to my legs, pray tell? . . . They just vanish below the knees! . . . At least my dress is presentable. I've always loved that dress.

Gardner: It sparkles somehow . . .

Fanny (*To* Gardner): Don't you think it's becoming?

Gardner: Yes, very becoming, awfully becoming . . .

Fanny (*Examining it at closer range*): Yes, she got the dress very well, how it shows off what's left of my figure . . . My smile is nice too.

Gardner: Good and wide . . .

FANNY: I love how the corners of my mouth turn up . . .
GARDNER: It's very clever . . .
FANNY: They're almost quivering . . .
GARDNER: Good lighting effects!
FANNY: Actually, I look quite . . . *young*, don't you think?
GARDNER (*To* MAGS): You're awfully good with those highlights.
FANNY (*Looking at it from different angles*): And you look darling . . . !
GARDNER: Well, I don't know about that . . .
FANNY: No, you look absolutely darling. Good enough to eat.
MAGS (*In a whisper*): They like it. . . . They like it!

[*A silence as FANNY and GARDNER keep gazing at their portrait.*]

FANNY: You know what it is? The wispy brush stroke makes us look like a couple in a French Impressionist painting.
GARDNER: Yes, I see what you mean . . .
FANNY: A Manet or Renoir[2] . . .
GARDNER: It's very evocative.
FANNY: There's something about the light . . .

[*They back up to survey the picture from a distance.*]

FANNY: You know those Renoir café scenes . . . ?
GARDNER: She doesn't lay on the paint with a trowel; it's just touches here and there . . .
MAGS: They *like* it . . . !
FANNY: You know the one with the couple dancing? . . . Not that we're dancing. There's just something similar in the mood . . . a kind of gaiety, almost. . . . The man has his back to you and he's swinging the woman around. . . . OH, GAR, YOU'VE SEEN IT A MILLION TIMES! IT'S HANGING IN THE MUSEUM OF FINE ARTS! . . . They're dancing like this . . .

[*FANNY goes up to GARDNER and puts an arm on his shoulders.*]

MAGS: They like it. . . . They like it!
FANNY: She's got on this wonderful flowered dress with ruffles at the neck and he's holding her like this. . . . That's right . . . and she's got the most rhapsodic expression on her face . . .

[*Getting into the spirit of it, GARDNER takes FANNY in his arms and slowly begins to dance around the room.*]

GARDNER: Oh, yes . . . I know the one you mean. . . . They're in a sort of haze . . . and isn't there a little band playing off to one side . . . ?
FANNY: Yes, that's it!

[*KITTY'S horn honks outside. MAGS is the only one who hears it.*]

MAGS: There's Kitty! (*She's torn and keeps looking towards the door, but finally gives in to their stolen moment*)

[2]Edouard Manet (1832–1883) and Pierre August Renoir (1841–1919), French Impressionist painters.

FANNY: And there's a man in a dark suit playing the violin and someone's conducting, I think. . . . And aren't Japanese lanterns strung up . . . ?

[*FANNY and GARDNER pick up speed, dipping and whirling around the room. Strains of a faraway Chopin waltz are heard.*]

GARDNER: Oh, yes! There are all these little lights twinkling in the trees . . .
FANNY: And doesn't the woman have a hat on? . . . A big red hat . . . ?
GARDNER: . . . and lights all over the dancers, too. Everything shimmers with this marvelous glow. Yes, yes . . . I can see it perfectly! The whole thing is absolutely extraordinary!

[*The lights become dreamy and dappled as FANNY and GARDNER dance around the room. MAGS watches them, moved to tears as slowly the curtain falls.*]

END

Toni Morrison 1931–

Through her fiction and her essays, Toni Morrison has become a powerful force speaking out on issues of race and gender in modern America. Born in Lorain, Ohio, as Chloe Anthony Wofford, she was an honor student in high school and attended Howard University, graduating in 1953. She enrolled in graduate school at Cornell University, and in 1955 received an M.A. in English, writing her master's thesis on modern writers, including novelist William Faulkner, whose rhythmic prose she admires and sometimes emulates. Morrison has also expressed her admiration for the characterizations achieved by Faulkner, who "seemed to me the only writer who took black people seriously." After graduation from Cornell, Morrison began a teaching career, first at Texas Southern University and then at Howard. During that time she married Harold Morrison and had two children. From 1965 to 1984, she worked as an editor for Random House, and continued teaching: at Yale, Bard, SUNY–Albany, and, since 1989, at Princeton. In recent years, she has also traveled extensively and has given readings of her work, sometimes in joint recitals where her reading is interpreted on the stage by the choreographer and dancer Bill Jones to the rhythmic accompaniment of jazz drummer Max Roach.

Morrison published her first novel, The Bluest Eye, *in 1970. It was followed by* Sula *in 1974. Her third novel,* Song of Solomon *(1977), won the Fiction Award of the National Book Critics Circle. It was followed by her fourth novel,* Tar Baby *(1981), and by her highly successful fifth novel,* Beloved *(1987), which won a Pulitzer Prize for Fiction and was produced as a movie in 1998. In 1992 a collection of lectures she gave at Harvard on racism in literature was published under the title* Playing in the Dark, Whiteness and the Literary Imagination, *and in the same year her sixth novel,* Jazz, *appeared. Her novel* Paradise *(1998) was criticized for being "heavy-handed" and lacking in "novelistic magic." Nevertheless, Morrison has been hailed as "the best writer in America," and her works are read throughout the world. Her greatest single distinction came in 1993 when she became the first African American and the eighth woman to win a Nobel Prize for Literature. In 2003 she published her eighth novel,* Love.

Morrison stands prominently in the line of black writers that includes Douglass, Toomer, Cullen, Hughes, Wright, and Ellison. She directly confronts issues of race and oppression, especially the oppression of women. She rarely focuses on male characters; Song of Solomon *is her only novel with a male protagonist. From the beginning of her career she has written about the crushing effect of racism on "the most vulnerable unit in society—a black female and a child." Morrison's writing is strewn with descriptions of sexual violence against women, and her novels are alive with characters who are victims and scapegoats, made grotesque and stunted by racism and poverty. Her characters experience rejection and degradation that cause them to turn on themselves with self-loathing, and Morrison does not flinch from showing lives of stunning brutality. In* Beloved, *an escaped slave mother kills her baby daughter to keep her from the clutches of slave catchers; in* Jazz *a middle-aged, married man heedlessly murders his teenage lover, and at her funeral his rejected wife attempts to disfigure the girl's corpse with a kitchen knife. In* Paradise, *a careless mother leaves her infant twins to die of heat in a Cadillac that has its windows closed. Pain and the anguish of loneliness dominate the lives of her characters, yet she also writes of their love and endurance, in a contrasting prose that is measured and smooth flowing.*

Morrison upbraids blacks who abandon their black heritage for the alluring materialism of the United States, a nation that she has described as "Star spangled. Race strangled." Of Morrison it has been said that "There is not an angrier writer in the United States today. . . . She has unleashed a firestorm of vituperation against white America for the ongoing suffering of black slaves and their descendants." It has also been said that Morrison is "a great novelist and the closest thing the country has to a national writer. The fact that she speaks as a woman and a black only enhances her ability to speak as an American." Morrison herself says that her fictions are meant to show all readers "how to survive whole in a world where we are all of us, in some measure, victims of something." Morrison's fiction shows not only how people can survive, but also how they can, through their suffering and resistance to repression, move toward a redeeming understanding of their true selves.

FURTHER READING: K. Carmean, *Toni Morrison's World of Fiction,* 1993; *Toni Morrison, Critical Perspectives Past and Present,* ed. H. Gates and K. Appiah, 1994; *Conversations with Toni Morrison,* ed. D. Taylor-Guthrie, 1994; L. Peach, *Toni Morrison,* 1995; J. Furman, *Toni Morrison's Fiction,* 1996; *Toni Morrison's Fiction,* ed. D. Middleton, 1997; *Toni Morrison, Critical and Theoretical Approaches,* ed. N. Peterson, 1997; A. Mori, *Toni Morrison and Womanist Discourse,* 1999; J. Duvall, *The Identifying Fictions of Toni Morrison, Modernist Authenticity and Postmodern Blackness,* 2000; T. Higgins, *Religiosity, Cosmology, and Folklore, the African Influence in the Novels of Toni Morrison,* 2002; L. Fulti, *Toni Morrison, Playing with Difference,* 2003; *The Toni Morrison Encyclopedia,* ed. E. Beaulieu, 2003.

TEXT: *Sula,* 1974.

from *SULA*

1922

It was too cool for ice cream. A hill wind was blowing dust and empty Camels wrappers about their ankles. It pushed their dresses into the creases of their behinds, then lifted the hems to peek at their cotton underwear. They were on their way to Edna Finch's Mellow House, an ice-cream parlor catering to nice folks—where even children would feel comfortable, you know, even though it was right next to Reba's Grill and just one block down from the Time and a Half Pool Hall. It sat in the curve of Carpenter's Road, which, in four blocks, made up all the sporting life available in the Bottom. Old men and young ones draped themselves in front of the Elmira Theater, Irene's Palace of Cosmetology, the pool hall, the grill and the other sagging business enterprises that lined the street. On sills, on stoops, on crates and broken chairs they sat tasting their teeth and waiting for something to distract them. Every passerby, every motorcar, every alteration in stance caught their attention and was commented on. Particularly they watched women. When a woman approached, the older men tipped their hats; the younger ones opened and closed their thighs. But all of them, whatever their age, watched her retreating view with interest.

Nel and Sula walked through this valley of eyes chilled by the wind and heated by the embarrassment of appraising stares. The old men looked at their stalklike legs, dwelled on the cords in the backs of their knees and remembered old dance steps they had not done in twenty years. In their lust, which age had turned to kindness, they moved their lips as though to stir up the taste of young sweat on tight skin.

Pig meat. The words were in all their minds. And one of them, one of the young ones, said it aloud. Softly but definitively and there was no mistaking the compliment. His name was Ajax, a twenty-one-year-old pool haunt of sinister beauty. Graceful and economical in every movement, he held a place of envy with men of all ages for his magnificently foul mouth. In fact he seldom cursed, and the epithets he chose were dull, even harmless. His reputation was derived from the way he handled the words. When he said "hell" he hit the *h* with his lungs and the impact was greater than the achievement of the most imaginative foul mouth in the town. He could say "shit" with a nastiness impossible to imitate. So, when he said "pig meat" as Nel and Sula passed, they guarded their eyes lest someone see their delight.

It was not really Edna Finch's ice cream that made them brave the stretch of those panther eyes. Years later their own eyes would glaze as they cupped their chins in remembrance of the inchworm smiles, the squatting haunches, the track-rail legs straddling broken chairs. The cream-colored trousers marking with a mere seam the place where the mystery curled. Those smooth vanilla crotches invited them; those lemon-yellow gabardines beckoned to them.

They moved toward the ice-cream parlor like tightrope walkers, as thrilled by the possibility of a slip as by the maintenance of tension and balance. The least sideways glance, the merest toe stub, could pitch them into those creamy haunches spread wide with welcome. Somewhere beneath all of that daintiness, chambered in all that neatness, lay the thing that clotted their dreams.

Which was only fitting, for it was in dreams that the two girls had first met. Long before Edna Finch's Mellow House opened, even before they marched through the chocolate halls of Garfield Primary School out onto the playground and stood facing each other through the ropes of the one vacant swing ("Go on." "No. You go."), they had already made each other's acquaintance in the delirium of their noon dreams. They were solitary little girls whose loneliness was so profound it intoxicated them and sent them stumbling into Technicolored visions that always included a presence, a someone, who, quite like the dreamer, shared the delight of the dream. When Nel, an only child, sat on the steps of her back porch surrounded by the high silence of her mother's incredibly orderly house, feeling the neatness pointing at her back, she studied the poplars and fell easily into a picture of herself lying on a flowered bed, tangled in her own hair, waiting for some fiery prince. He approached but never quite arrived. But always, watching the dream along with her, were some smiling sympathetic eyes. Someone as interested as she herself in the flow of her imagined hair, the thickness of the mattress of flowers, the voile sleeves that closed below her elbows in gold-threaded cuffs.

Similarly, Sula, also an only child, but wedged into a household of throbbing disorder constantly awry with things, people, voices and the slamming of doors, spent hours in the attic behind a roll of linoleum galloping through her own mind on a gray-and-white horse tasting sugar and smelling roses in full view of a someone who shared both the taste and the speed.

So when they met, first in those chocolate halls and next through the ropes of the swing, they felt the ease and comfort of old friends. Because each had discovered years before that they were neither white nor male, and that all freedom and triumph was forbidden to them, they had set about creating something else to be. Their meeting was fortunate, for it let them use each other to grow on. Daughters of distant mothers and incomprehensible fathers (Sula's because he was dead; Nel's because he wasn't), they found in each other's eyes the intimacy they were looking for.

Nel Wright and Sula Peace were both twelve in 1922, wishbone thin and easy-assed. Nel was the color of wet sandpaper—just dark enough to escape the blows of the pitch-black truebloods and the contempt of old women who worried about such things as bad blood mixtures and knew that the origins of a mule and a mulatto were one and the same. Had she been any lighter-skinned she would have needed either her mother's protection on the way to school or a streak of mean to defend herself. Sula was a heavy brown with large quiet eyes, one of which featured a birthmark that spread from the middle of the lid toward the eyebrow, shaped something like a stemmed rose. It gave her otherwise plain face a broken excitement and blue-blade threat like the keloid[1] scar of the razored man who sometimes played checkers with her grandmother. The birthmark was to grow darker as the years passed, but now it was the same shade as her gold-flecked eyes, which, to the end, were as steady and clean as rain.

Their friendship was as intense as it was sudden. They found relief in each other's personality. Although both were unshaped, formless things, Nel seemed stronger and more consistent than Sula, who could hardly be counted on to sustain any emotion for more than three minutes. Yet there was one time when that was not true, when she held on to a mood for weeks, but even that was in defense of Nel.

Four white boys in their early teens, sons of some newly arrived Irish people, occasionally entertained themselves in the afternoon by harassing black

[1]Thick, fibrous.

schoolchildren. With shoes that pinched and woolen knickers that made red rings on their calves, they had come to this valley with their parents believing as they did that it was a promised land—green and shimmering with welcome. What they found was a strange accent, a pervasive fear of their religion and firm resistance to their attempts to find work. With one exception the older residents of Medallion scorned them. The one exception was the black community. Although some of the Negroes had been in Medallion before the Civil War (the town didn't even have a name then), if they had any hatred for these newcomers it didn't matter because it didn't show. As a matter of fact, baiting them was the one activity that the white Protestant residents concurred in. In part their place in this world was secured only when they echoed the old residents' attitude toward blacks.

These particular boys caught Nel once, and pushed her from hand to hand until they grew tired of the frightened helpless face. Because of that incident, Nel's route home from school became elaborate. She, and then Sula, managed to duck them for weeks until a chilly day in November when Sula said, "Let's us go on home the shortest way."

Nel blinked, but acquiesced. They walked up the street until they got to the bend of Carpenter's Road where the boys lounged on a disused well. Spotting their prey, the boys sauntered forward as though there were nothing in the world on their minds but the gray sky. Hardly able to control their grins, they stood like a gate blocking the path. When the girls were three feet in front of the boys, Sula reached into her coat pocket and pulled out Eva's paring knife. The boys stopped short, exchanged looks and dropped all pretense of innocence. This was going to be better than they thought. They were going to try and fight back, and with a knife. Maybe they could get an arm around one of their waists, or tear . . .

Sula squatted down in the dirt road and put everything down on the ground: her lunchpail, her reader, her mittens, her slate. Holding the knife in her right hand, she pulled the slate toward her and pressed her left forefinger down hard on its edge. Her aim was determined but inaccurate. She slashed off only the tip of her finger. The four boys stared open-mouthed at the wound and the scrap of flesh, like a button mushroom, curling in the cherry blood that ran into the corners of the slate.

Sula raised her eyes to them. Her voice was quiet. "If I can do that to myself, what you suppose I'll do to you?"

The shifting dirt was the only way Nel knew that they were moving away; she was looking at Sula's face, which seemed miles and miles away.

But toughness was not their quality—adventuresomeness was—and a mean determination to explore everything that interested them, from one-eyed chickens high-stepping in their penned yards to Mr. Buckland Reed's gold teeth, from the sound of sheets flapping in the wind to the labels on Tar Baby's wine bottles. And they had no priorities. They could be distracted from watching a fight with mean razors by the glorious smell of hot tar being poured by roadmen two hundred yards away.

In the safe harbor of each other's company they could afford to abandon the ways of other people and concentrate on their own perceptions of things. When Mrs. Wright reminded Nel to pull her nose, she would do it enthusiastically but without the least hope in the world.

"While you sittin' there, honey, go 'head and pull your nose."

"It hurts, Mamma."

"Don't you want a nice nose when you grow up?"

After she met Sula, Nel slid the clothespin under the blanket as soon as she got in the bed. And although there was still the hateful hot comb to suffer through each Saturday evening, its consequences—smooth hair—no longer interested her.

Joined in mutual admiration they watched each day as though it were a movie arranged for their amusement. The new theme they were now discovering was men. So they met regularly, without even planning it, to walk down the road to Edna Finch's Mellow House, even though it was too cool for ice cream.

Then summer came. A summer limp with the weight of blossomed things. Heavy sunflowers weeping over fences; iris curling and browning at the edges far away from their purple hearts; ears of corn letting their auburn hair wind down to their stalks. And the boys. The beautiful, beautiful boys who dotted the landscape like jewels, split the air with their shouts in the field, and thickened the river with their shining wet backs. Even their footsteps left a smell of smoke behind.

It was in that summer, the summer of their twelfth year, the summer of the beautiful black boys, that they became skittish, frightened and bold—all at the same time.

In that mercury mood in July, Sula and Nel wandered about the Bottom barefoot looking for mischief. They decided to go down by the river where the boys sometimes swam. Nel waited on the porch of 7 Carpenter's Road while Sula ran into the house to go to the toilet. On the way up the stairs, she passed the kitchen where Hannah sat with two friends, Patsy and Valentine. The two women were fanning themselves and watching Hannah put down some dough, all talking casually about one thing and another, and had gotten around, when Sula passed by, to the problems of child rearing.

"They a pain."

"Yeh. Wish I'd listened to mamma. She told me not to have 'em too soon."

"Any time atall is too soon for me."

"Oh, I don't know. My Rudy minds his daddy. He just wild with me. Be glad when he growed and gone."

Hannah smiled and said, "Shut your mouth. You love the ground he pee on."

"Sure I do. But he still a pain. Can't help loving your own child. No matter what they do."

"Well, Hester grown now and I can't say love is exactly what I feel."

"Sure you do. You love her, like I love Sula. I just don't like her. That's the difference."

"Guess so. Likin' them is another thing."

"Sure. They different people, you know . . ."

She only heard Hannah's words, and the pronouncement sent her flying up the stairs. In bewilderment, she stood at the window fingering the curtain edge, aware of a sting in her eye. Nel's call floated up and into the window, pulling her away from dark thoughts back into the bright, hot daylight.

They ran most of the way.

Heading toward the wide part of the river where trees grouped themselves in families darkening the earth below. They passed some boys swimming and clowning in the water, shrouding their words in laughter.

They ran in the sunlight, creating their own breeze, which pressed their dresses into their damp skin. Reaching a kind of square of four leaf-locked trees which promised cooling, they flung themselves into the four-cornered shade to taste their lip sweat and contemplate the wildness that had come upon them so suddenly. They lay in the grass, their foreheads almost touching, their bodies stretched away from each other at a 180-degree angle. Sula's head rested on her arm, an undone braid coiled around her wrist. Nel leaned on her elbows and worried long blades of grass with her fingers. Underneath their dresses flesh tightened and shivered in the high coolness, their small breasts just now beginning to create some pleasant discomfort when they were lying on their stomachs.

Sula lifted her head and joined Nel in the grass play. In concert, without ever meeting each other's eyes, they stroked the blades up and down, up and down. Nel found a thick twig and, with her thumbnail, pulled away its bark until it was stripped to a smooth, creamy innocence. Sula looked about and found one too. When both twigs were undressed Nel moved easily to the next stage and began tearing up rooted grass to make a bare spot of earth. When a generous clearing was made, Sula traced intricate patterns in it with her twig. At first Nel was content to do the same. But soon she grew impatient and poked her twig rhythmically and intensely into the earth, making a small neat hole that grew deeper and wider with the least manipulation of her twig. Sula copied her, and soon each had a hole the size of a cup. Nel began a more strenuous digging and, rising to her knee, was careful to scoop out the dirt as she made her hole deeper. Together they worked until the two holes were one and the same. When the depression was the size of a small dishpan, Nel's twig broke. With a gesture of disgust she threw the pieces into the hole they had made. Sula threw hers in too. Nel saw a bottle cap and tossed it in as well. Each then looked around for more debris to throw into the hole: paper, bits of glass, butts of cigarettes, until all of the small defiling things they could find were collected there. Carefully they replaced the soil and covered the entire grave with uprooted grass.

Neither one had spoken a word.

They stood up, stretched, then gazed out over the swift dull water as an unspeakable restlessness and agitation held them. At the same instant each girl heard footsteps in the grass. A little boy in too big knickers was coming up from the lower bank of the river. He stopped when he saw them and picked his nose.

"Your mamma tole you to stop eatin' snot, Chicken," Nel hollered at him through cupped hands.

"Shut up," he said, still picking.

"Come up here and say that."

"Leave him 'lone, Nel. Come here, Chicken. Lemme show you something."

"Naw."

"You scared we gone take your bugger away?"

"Leave him 'lone, I said. Come on, Chicken. Look. I'll help you climb a tree."

Chicken looked at the tree Sula was pointing to—a big double beech with low branches and lots of bends for sitting.

He moved slowly toward her.

"Come on, Chicken, I'll help you up."

Still picking his nose, his eyes wide, he came to where they were standing. Sula took him by the hand and coaxed him along. When they reached the base of the beech, she lifted him to the first branch saying, "Go on. Go on. I got you." She followed the boy, steadying him, when he needed it, with her hand and her reassuring voice. When they were as high as they could go, Sula pointed to the far side of the river.

"See? Bet you never saw that far before, did you?"

"Uh uh."

"Now look down there." They both leaned a little and peered through the leaves at Nel standing below, squinting up at them. From their height she looked small and fore-shortened.

Chicken Little laughed.

"Y'all better come on down before you break your neck," Nel hollered.

"I ain't never coming down," the boy hollered back.

"Yeah. We better. Come on, Chicken."

"Naw. Lemme go."

"Yeah, Chicken. Come on, now."

Sula pulled his leg gently.

"Lemme go."

"OK, I'm leavin' you." She started on.

"Wait!" he screamed.

Sula stopped and together they slowly worked their way down.

Chicken was still elated. "I was way up there, wasn't I? Wasn't I? I'm a tell my brovver."

Sula and Nel began to mimic him: "I'm a tell my brovver; I'm a tell my brovver."

Sula picked him up by his hands and swung him outward then around and around. His knickers ballooned and his shrieks of frightened joy startled the birds and the fat grasshoppers. When he slipped from her hands and sailed away out over the water they could still hear his bubbly laughter.

The water darkened and closed quickly over the place where Chicken Little sank. The pressure of his hard and tight little fingers was still in Sula's palms as she stood looking at the closed place in the water. They expected him to come back up, laughing. Both girls stared at the water.

Nel spoke first. "Somebody saw." A figure appeared briefly on the opposite shore.

The only house over there was Shadrack's. Sula glanced at Nel. Terror widened her nostrils. Had he seen?

The water was so peaceful now. There was nothing but the baking sun and something newly missing. Sula cupped her face for an instant, then turned and ran up to the little plank bridge that crossed the river to Shadrack's house. There was no path. It was as though neither Shadrack nor anyone else ever came this way.

Her running was swift and determined, but when she was close to the three little steps that led to his porch, fear crawled into her stomach and only the something newly missing back there in the river made it possible for her to walk up the three steps and knock at the door.

No one answered. She started back, but thought again of the peace of the river. Shadrack would be inside, just behind the door ready to pounce on her. Still she could not go back. Ever so gently she pushed the door with the tips of her fingers and heard only the hinges weep. More. And then she was inside. Alone. The neatness, the order startled her, but more surprising was the restfulness. Everything was so tiny, so common, so unthreatening. Perhaps this was not the house of the Shad. The terrible Shad who walked about with his penis out, who peed in front of ladies and girl-children, the only black who could curse white people and get away with it, who drank in the road from the mouth of the bottle, who shouted and shook in the streets. This cottage? This sweet old cottage? With its made-up bed? With its rag rug and wooden table? Sula stood in the middle of the little room and in her wonder forgot what she had come for until a sound at the door made her jump. He was there in the doorway looking at her. She had not heard his coming and now he was looking at her.

More in embarrassment than terror she averted her glance. When she called up enough courage to look back at him, she saw his hand resting upon the door frame. His fingers, barely touching the wood, were arranged in a graceful arc. Relieved and encouraged (no one with hands like that, no one with fingers that curved around wood so tenderly could kill her), she walked past him out of the door, feeling his gaze turning, turning with her.

At the edge of the porch, gathering the wisps of courage that were fast leaving her, she turned once more to look at him, to ask him . . . had he . . . ?

He was smiling, a great smile, heavy with lust and time to come. He nodded his head as though answering a question, and said, in a pleasant conversational tone, a tone of cooled butter, "Always."

Sula fled down the steps, and shot through the greenness and the baking sun back to Nel and the dark closed place in the water. There she collapsed in tears.

Nel quieted her. "Sh, sh. Don't, don't. You didn't mean it. It ain't your fault. Sh. Sh. Come on, le's go, Sula. Come on, now. Was he there? Did he see? Where's the belt to your dress?"

Sula shook her head while she searched her waist for the belt.

Finally she stood up and allowed Nel to lead her away. "He said, 'Always. Always.' "

"What?"

Sula covered her mouth as they walked down the hill. Always. He had answered a question she had not asked, and its promise licked at her feet.

A bargeman, poling away from the shore, found Chicken late that afternoon stuck in some rocks and weeds, his knickers ballooning about his legs. He would have left him there but noticed that it was a child, not an old black man, as it first appeared, and he prodded the body loose, netted it and hauled it aboard. He shook his head in disgust at the kind of parents who would drown their own children. When, he wondered, will those people ever be anything but animals, fit for nothing but substitutes for mules, only mules didn't kill each other the way niggers did. He dumped Chicken Little into a burlap sack and tossed him next to some egg crates and boxes of wool cloth. Later, sitting down to smoke on an empty lard tin, still bemused by God's curse and the terrible burden his own kind had of elevating Ham's[2] sons, he suddenly became alarmed by the thought that the corpse in this heat would have a terrible odor, which might get into the fabric of his woolen cloth. He dragged the sack away and hooked it over the side, so that the Chicken's body was half in and half out of the water.

Wiping the sweat from his neck, he reported his find to the sheriff at Porter's Landing, who said they didn't have no niggers in their county, but that some lived in those hills 'cross the river, up above Medallion. The bargeman said he couldn't go all the way back there, it was every bit of two miles. The sheriff said whyn't he throw it on back into the water. The bargeman said he never shoulda taken it out in the first place. Finally they got the man who ran the ferry twice a day to agree to take it over in the morning.

That was why Chicken Little was missing for three days and didn't get to the embalmer's until the fourth day, by which time he was unrecognizable to almost everybody who once knew him, and even his mother wasn't deep down sure, except that it just had to be him since nobody could find him. When she saw his clothes lying on the table in the basement of the mortuary, her mouth snapped shut, and when she saw his body her mouth flew wide open again and it was seven hours before she was able to close it and make the first sound.

So the coffin was closed.

The Junior Choir, dressed in white, sang "Nearer My God to Thee" and "Precious Memories," their eyes fastened on the songbooks they did not need, for this was the first time their voices had presided at a real-life event.

Nel and Sula did not touch hands or look at each other during the funeral. There was a space, a separateness, between them. Nel's legs had turned to granite and she expected the sheriff or Reverend Deal's pointing finger at any moment. Although she knew she had "done nothing," she felt convicted and hanged right there in the pew—two rows down from her parents in the children's section.

Sula simply cried. Soundlessly and with no heaving and gasping for breath, she let the tears roll into her mouth and slide down her chin to dot the front of her dress.

As Reverend Deal moved into his sermon, the hands of the women unfolded like pairs of raven's wings and flew high above their hats in the air. They did not hear all of what he said; they heard the one word, or phrase, or inflection that was for them the connection between the event and themselves. For some it was the term "Sweet Jesus." And they saw the Lamb's eye and the truly innocent victim: themselves. They acknowledged the innocent child hiding in the corner of their hearts, holding a sugar-and-butter sandwich. That one. The one who lodged deep in their fat, thin, old, young skin, and was the one the world had hurt. Or they thought of their son newly

[2]The second son of the biblical Noah, and said to be the forefather of the dark races of humankind.

killed and remembered his legs in short pants and wondered where the bullet went in. Or they remembered how dirty the room looked when their father left home and wondered if that is the way the slim, young Jew felt, he who for them was both son and lover and in whose downy face they could see the sugar-and-butter sandwiches and feel the oldest and most devastating pain there is: not the pain of childhood, but the remembrance of it.

Then they left their pews. For with some emotions one has to stand. They spoke, for they were full and needed to say. They swayed, for the rivulets of grief or of ecstasy must be rocked. And when they thought of all that life and death locked into that little closed coffin they danced and screamed, not to protest God's will but to acknowledge it and confirm once more their conviction that the only way to avoid the Hand of God is to get in it.

In the colored part of the cemetery, they sank Chicken Little in between his grandfather and an aunt. Butterflies flew in and out of the bunches of field flowers now loosened from the top of the bier and lying in a small heap at the edge of the grave. The heat had gone, but there was still no breeze to lift the hair of the willows.

Nel and Sula stood some distance away from the grave, the space that had sat between them in the pews had dissolved. They held hands and knew that only the coffin would lie in the earth; the bubbly laughter and the press of fingers in the palm would stay aboveground forever. At first, as they stood there, their hands were clenched together. They relaxed slowly until during the walk back home their fingers were laced in as gentle a clasp as that of any two young girlfriends trotting up the road on a summer day wondering what happened to butterflies in the winter.

1974

David Mamet 1947–

David Mamet is reported to have once proclaimed, "If I hadn't been a playwright I'd have lived the life of a criminal." He has not made so dire a choice, but in his work he has displayed a fascination with violence and outlawry that has attracted audiences to his plays, movies, and television dramas throughout the world. In contrast to his preoccupations and his choice of dramatic subjects, he was born into an affluent and comfortable middle-class world in suburban Chicago. His father was a successful lawyer, his mother a schoolteacher. His interest in the theater emerged in high school, where he took drama classes and acted in student plays. During vacations he worked backstage in community theaters and at Second City, the famous Chicago theater of satirical revues.

After high school Mamet enrolled in Vermont's Goddard College, where he took courses in drama. He spent his required work-study junior year in New York City, studying acting at the Neighborhood Playhouse. During one college vacation he worked as a seaman on a Great Lakes merchant ship (an experience he drew on when writing his play Lakeboat, *1980). For his college thesis he wrote a dramatic revue,* Camel, *in the fashion of the satiric revues of Second City. And after college he worked as an actor and a stagehand for a small professional company in Montreal, Canada.*

Mamet returned to Chicago, where he drove a taxi and worked in a children's theater company and in dinner theaters in Chicago and its suburbs. He served for a brief time as an office manager for a real estate firm—where he saw the strident moral decay that later formed the core of his Broadway hit Glengarry Glen Ross *(1983), which won a Pulitzer Prize and was later made into a highly-praised movie (1992).*

In 1972 Mamet's play The Duck Variations *was performed in a "store-front" theater in Chicago. Two years later his play* Sexual Perversity in Chicago *was staged. It shocked theatergoers with its obscene language and seamy portrayal of sexual perversity, but the play won for Mamet an award (the first of many), as the best play of the Chicago 1974 season. In 1975* American Buffalo, *his first hit play, was staged in Chicago. Two years later it was produced on Broadway in New York City, where it won the New York Drama Critics Award for best play of the year. Then, after a series of theatrical successes in the United States and Europe in the 1970s and 1980s, he turned to screen writing.*

Working by himself or in collaboration with others, Mamet has produced a flood of screenplays, often adaptations of his own dramas: The Postman Always Rings Twice *(1981),* The Verdict *(1982), which brought Mamet a nomination for an Academy Award,* The Untouchables *(1985),* House of Games *(1987), which Mamet both wrote and directed,* Oleanna *(1994),* Wag the Dog *(1997),* The Spanish Prisoner *(1997),* Ronin *(1998),* The Winslow Boy *(1999),* State and Main *(2000),* Heist *(2001), and* Spartan *(2004).*

While Mamet's dramatic works deal with moral issues, he does not use his work as a platform for moral or political preachment; he has dismissed the world of political action and of politics as "the last refuge of the unimaginative." His dramatic language no longer shocks audiences, who have become accustomed to representation on television and in movies of the repetitive commonplaces of obscene English. But his audiences continue to be fascinated by the moral decadence of his characters and by his sometimes convoluted plots. Like his audiences, he is fascinated by cheaters, treachery, deceit, and dishonesty, by characters betrayed by their own innocence, made gullible by inherent greed and criminality, men and women lost in illusory worlds of facades and uncertainties that are as confusing to them as they often are to the audiences before which they are portrayed.

By any standard, Mamet's output as a writer has been enormous. In addition to his stage plays and movie and television dramas, Mamet has published novels, books of poetry, children's fiction, five volumes of essays, including Writing in Restaurants *(1986) and* Jafsie and John Henry *(1999), and books on acting and directing, among them* On Directing Film *(1992) and* True and False, Heresy and Common Sense for the Actor *(1999). Recently he has even begun contributing cartoons to a Boston Magazine.*

FURTHER READING: C. Bigsby, *David Mamet,* 1985; D. Carroll, *David Mamet,* 1987; A. Dean, *David Mamet,* 1990; G. Brewer, *David Mamet and Film,* 1993; L. Kane, *Weasels and Wisemen,* 1999; J. Heilpern, *How Good Is David Mamet, Anyway,* 1999; *Gender and Genre, Essays on David Mamet,* ed. C. Hudgins and L. Kane, 2001; *The Cambridge Companion to David Mamet,* ed. C. Bigsby, 2004; *David Mamet,* ed. H. Bloom, 2004.
TEXT: *House of Games,* 1985, 1987.

HOUSE OF GAMES

THE CAST

MARGARET FORD	Lindsay Crouse
MIKE	Joe Mantegna
JOEY	Mike Nussbaum
DR. LITTAUER	Lilia Skala
THE BUSINESSMAN	J. T. Walsh
GIRL WITH BOOK	Willo Hausman
PRISON WARD PATIENT	Karen Kohlhaas
BILLY HAHN	Steve Goldstein
BARTENDER/HOUSE OF GAMES	Jack Wallace
GEORGE/VEGAS MAN	Ricky Jay
POKER PLAYERS	G. Roy Levin
	Bob Lumbra
	Andy Potok
	Allen Soule
BARTENDER/CHARLIE'S TAVERN	Ben Blakeman
WESTERN UNION CLERK	Scott Zigler
SGT. MORAN	W. H. Macy
HOTEL DESK CLERK	John Pritchett
MR. DEAN	Meshach Taylor
HOTEL DOORMAN	Sugarbear Willis
GARAGE ATTENDANT	Josh Conescu
LATE STUDENT	Julie Mendenhall
STUDENT	Rachel Cline
PATIENT/FORD'S OFFICE	Patricia Wolff
MAN IN RESTAURANT	Paul Walsh
RESTAURANT HOSTESS	Roberta Maguire
WOMAN WITH LIGHTER	Jacqueline de la Chaume

THE CREDITS

Produced by	Michael Hausman
Directed by	David Mamet
Screenplay by	David Mamet
Story by	Jonathan Katz and David Mamet
Director of Photography	Juan Ruiz Anchia
Music by	Alaric Jans
Edited by	Trudy Ship
Production Designer	Michael Merritt
Costume Designer	Nan Cibula
Unit Production Manager	Lee R. Mayes
First Assistant Director	Ned Dowd
Second Assistant Director	Michael Hausman
Location Manager	Ron Lynch
Script Supervisor	Christine Wilson
Casting by	Cyrena Hausman
Production Office Coordinators	Deborah Pritchett and Cathy Sarkowsky
Assistant to the Producer	Rachel Cline
Key Production Assistant	Lynn Wegenka
First Assistant Camera	George Mooradian
Second Assistant Camera	Henry Cline

Gaffer	Michael Barrow
Best Boy	John Merriman
Key Dolly Grip	Chris Centrella
Best Boy	Hugh McCallum
Sound Mixer	John Pritchett
Boom Man	Douglas Axtell
Set Decorator	Derek Hill
Lead Man	Grey Smith
Set Dresser	Jeff Soderberg
Property Master	Samara Schaffer

MUSIC

Fugue from the Toccata in C Minor by Johann Sebastian Bach (BWV 911)
Performed by Warren Bernhardt, piano

"This True Love Stopped for You (But Not for Me)" by Rokko Jans
Sung by June Shellene

Fade In: Exterior: Office Building Plaza—Day

People hurrying to work across a crowded plaza. Camera moves forward toward a coffee cart in the background.

A young woman walks into the frame in the foreground. She takes a book out of her purse, looks down at the book.

Camera moves in on the book. The cover reads:

Driven:
Compulsion and Obsession
in Everyday Life
by
Margaret Ford, M.D.

The book is turned over to show photo of Dr. Ford on the back cover.

Angle. The coffee cart, the young woman with the book in the background. Dr. Ford, taking a cup of coffee from the cart, moves toward the camera. The young woman hurries after her.

YOUNG WOMAN: Excuse me . . . Excuse me . . .

Ford stops, the young woman comes up to her.

YOUNG WOMAN: Are you Dr. Margaret Ford . . . ?
FORD: Yes.
YOUNG WOMAN: Could I ask you, would you sign my book . . . ?
FORD: Of course.

The young woman hands the book and a pen to FORD, *who signs the book.*

YOUNG WOMAN: I recognized you from your picture.
FORD: Uh huh.
YOUNG WOMAN: It's the second one I've bought.
FORD: Then I am doubly pleased. Thank you for buying it.

(FORD *hands the signed book back, starts to turn away.*)

YOUNG WOMAN: You've helped me very much.
FORD: I'm glad I have. (*Beat.*) Thank you. (*Beat.*) Goodbye.

FORD *walks away, through the crowded plaza.*

Interior: Hospital Cell—Day

Insert—Ford's hand, writing on a pad.

WOMAN PATIENT (*voice over*): . . . and he said that we all try to run from experience. From Experience. Do you understand me . . . but that it will seek us out. Do you think that you're exempt . . . ?

Angle—Close-up. The woman patient. Dressed in a hospital gown.

WOMAN PATIENT: I'm *talking* to you. Do you think that you're exempt?

Angle. FORD *and the woman patient, sitting across from each other in front of a white background.* FORD *looks up from her writing.*

FORD: Do I think that I'm exempt . . . that I'm exempt from what . . . ?
WOMAN PATIENT: *Experience.*
FORD: No. I don't think I'm exempt.
WOMAN PATIENT: Well, you'd better be assured you're not.
FORD: What is the animal?
WOMAN PATIENT: The animal?
FORD: You said in your dream you saw an animal. (*Beat.* FORD *glances at her watch.*)
WOMAN PATIENT: It's . . .

Angle—Insert. FORD *writing on the pad.*

WOMAN PATIENT (*voice over*): It's . . . I . . . I want to say . . . I don't know how to say it . . .

Interior: Greenhousey Restaurant—Day

DR. MARIA LITTAUER, *a woman in her sixties, sitting alone at a table.* FORD *hurries in. Sits.*

FORD: I'm so sorry I'm late.
MARIA: Oh. It's alright.

FORD *sits, opens her notebook, reads.*

FORD: Listen to this: in her dream: she saw a foreign animal. What is the animal? She cannot think of the name. It's saying, the animal is saying "I am only trying to do good." I say, "What name comes up when you think of this animal?" She says it is a "lurg," it is called a "lurg." So if we invert "Lurg," a "lurg" is a "girl," and *she* is the animal, and *she* is saying "I am only trying to do good."

MARIA: And now someone has heard her. Good, Maggie, good for you. And now what are you going to eat?

MARIA *hands* FORD *a menu,* FORD *puts it down.*

FORD: I don't have time. (FORD *takes out a pack of cigarettes. Picks up a lighter from the table in front of* MARIA.)

Angle—Insert. FORD, *holding the gold lighter, lights her cigarette.*

FORD (*voice over*): It's so beautiful. It's old and it's heavy, and it looks like someone gave it to you. Sometimes I think the only pressures in my life . . .

Angle. MARIA.

MARIA: The only . . . ?

Angle.

FORD: I'm sorry . . . ?

MARIA: You said the only "pressures . . ."

FORD: "Pleasures." I said "pleasures."

MARIA: No, what you said was "pressures," you see? And this is what I'm telling you. Your book is a best seller, your income jumps up, people look at you differently, perhaps. This is confusing. Listen to me: Slow Down. Give *yourself* all those rewards you would like to have. You see a beautiful gold lighter, *buy* one for yourself. Your friend asks you to lunch, go and *eat* lunch with her.

Beast.

FORD: Do you forgive me . . . ?

MARIA (*smiles*): No. Go. Work.

FORD *smiles at* MARIA, *gets up from the table.*

Interior: FORD*'s Office—Day*

Insert. FORD*'s hand holding a pen. Poised to write.*

MAN'S (BILLY HAHN'S) VOICE (*voice over*): a uh . . . a . . . a . . . I don't know . . .

The hand relaxes.

Angle. FORD*'s office. She is seated across from a young man of about thirty* (BILLY HAHN).

FORD (*pause*): A what?

BILLY (*sighs*): A feeling of . . . of . . . of . . . of *nothingness.*

FORD: What does that make you think of?

BILLY (*standing, shouting*): Will you leave me *alone* . . . for *chrissake* . . . what does it matter? What does it *mean*? You understand? It's in my head or *not* . . . it doesn't make . . . it . . .

FORD: Billy . . .

BILLY: What? Are you going to tell me I'm "entitled to my feelings . . ."? What does it . . . what. the. hell. does. it. *matter*? (*Pause.*)

FORD: It matters if you're going to cure yourself.

BILLY: If I'm going to cure myself. And what do I do now?

FORD: What do you do now? You . . .

BILLY: No, no, what do I do today? What do I do *tomorrow*?

FORD: Today and tomorrow you say this: "I am a compulsive gambler. The reasons for this . . ."

BILLY: Oh, maan . . . oh, maan . . . *I* don't know . . . what am I *doing* here . . . ? What am I *doing* here . . . ?

FORD: You're here to take control of your life.

BILLY: I lost, what do *you* care maan, you're rich, you're comfortable, you got your goddamn *book* you wrote, you don't do *dick*, you don't do *nothing*, maan, it's all a con game, you do nothing. You say you want to help? You want to *help* . . . ? help me with *this*. (*He produces a small, nickeled automatic pistol.*) Help me with this, if you can, cause if not I got to use it.

FORD: To use it for what . . . ?

Beat.

BILLY: Aren't you going to ask me is it loaded?

FORD: To use it for what?

BILLY: To use it to *kill* myself, or, *you* know, *I* don't know, to . . .

FORD: Why would you want to kill yourself?

BILLY: What do you think this is? Some "dream"? Maan, *you're* living in the dream, your "questions," 'cause there. is. a. real. world. (*Pause.*)

FORD: And what happened to you in that world? (*Pause.*) What happened to you?

BILLY: What difference does it make? You say you "want to help." You *can't* help, 'cause, babe, you don't know what trouble *is*.

FORD: Give me the gun and I will help you. (*Pause.*) Billy. (*Pause.*) I swear to you. (*Pause.*) You give me the gun and I will help you.

He hands her the gun.

BILLY: I just lost twenty-five thousand dollars. That I do not have. And if I do not pay it by tomorrow they are going to kill me. Now: what kind of help is your damn promise now?

Interior: FORD*'s Office—Later—Night*

Insert. FORD *writing on a sheet of paper: "Compulsive succeeds in establishing a situation where he is out of control."*

Angle. FORD, *alone at her desk, with a cup of coffee. Smoking. Writing (pause), she sighs. Looks up, takes off her glasses. Shakes her head from side to side. She picks up off her desk* BILLY*'s nickeled automatic pistol.*

Angle—Insert. The pistol in her hand. She lays it on the desk. Camera follows her hands. She picks up a sheaf of notes, shuffles through the notes. Brings up a sheet from the bottom. On it is written: ". . . The character of MIKE*—the 'Unbeatable Gambler.' Seen as omniscient, who 'doles out punishment' . . .* HOUSE OF GAMES."

Interior: Rundown Commercial Building—Night

A dark, dirty corridor in an old building. A woman in jeans and a leather bomber jacket walks into the frame. We see her from the back as she starts down the corridor. At the end of the corridor, she stops before a door. Looks up at the sign over the door.

Angle. It is FORD*, looking at the sign. We see the sign reads:*

The House of Games
Backgammon, Chess, Ping-Pong, Pool

She looks down, opens the door. She walks through the door. Camera follows her into a large hall. There are two Ping-Pong tables. A pool table. Along the side of the hall various small card tables. At one table two old men are playing gin. A Ping-Pong game is in progress. A man sits behind the cash desk. Looks at FORD. FORD *takes out a cigarette. Puts it in her mouth.*

MAN: N'I help you?
FORD: Yeah. I need a match.

He hands her a match. She lights her cigarette. BOB *gestures at the game area.*

BOB: You lookin' f'ra *partner.* To *play* something?
FORD: I'm looking for *Mike.*
BOB: Who's Mike?
FORD: Would you get him for me?
BOB: I don't think that Mike's here.
FORD: Why don't you take a look?

(Pause.) BOB *shrugs. Gets up off his stool, walks to a door behind him, opens it. We hear sounds of a card game in the room behind.*

Angle—Point of view. BOB *beckons a man over to him. They talk in the doorway.* BOB *gestures at* FORD. *The man looks at her, starts over to her.*

*Angle. The other man (*MIKE*) walks over to* FORD.

MIKE: What the fuck is it?
FORD: I'm looking for Mike.
MIKE: Mike isn't here. What do you want? (*Pause.*)
FORD: A *friend* of mine . . .
MIKE: Cut to the chase, I'm very busy, what do you want with *Mike* . . .
FORD: I'm *telling* you, and *you're* Mike, and I want you to *listen* to this, 'cause you threatened to kill a *friend* of mine . . .
MIKE: Is that what I did?

FORD: Yes. That's *exactly* what you did. And I'm putting you on notice, "Mike," that that behavior doesn't go. Whether you mean it or *not*, and, it's irrelevant to *me*, because you aren't going to *do* it. Now: this is a sick kid. He's a compulsive gambler, and he hasn't got . . .

MIKE: . . . wait wait wait. What is this, what are you going to *do* to me, what are you "fronting *off*" about? And if I'm this bad dude whyn't I just take out some gun, blow you to a billion parts?

FORD: I'll tell you why. Because I think you're just a bully . . .

MIKE: Just a "bully." What, and you're not going to let me carry your *books*? Aren't *you* a caution . . .

FORD: Let's talk turkey, Pal. One: You threatened to kill my friend. You aren't going to *do* that because if you do you're going away for Life. Two is the *money*.

MIKE: Money.

FORD: Now: he doesn't *have* it, but we can . . .

MIKE: Who *is* this friend?

FORD: Billy Hahn.

MIKE: Billy Hahn. And he lost how much to me?

FORD: Come on, come on: twenty-five thousand dollars.

MIKE: Twenty-five thousand dollars Billy Hahn lost to me. Excuse me one moment, will you . . . ?

MIKE *walks back into the back room.*

(Off camera; sotto:) Deal me out. I'll be right back . . .

MIKE *comes back into the room with a small briefcase, opens it up, takes out a pocket notebook.*

I'm showing you this because I *like* you, okay? 'Cause you got blond hair.

He opens book. Turns to a page.

Angle—Insert. The page. The name "BILLY HAHN," *with various figures in hundreds added to, subtracted from, crossed out, the final figure is "$800.00."*

Angle. FORD *holding the book.*

MIKE: Okay? Billy Hahn owes me eight hundred bucks.

A CARD PLAYER (*voice over*): In or Out?

MIKE (*to card player*): Out. (*To* FORD:) How come you *made* me so quick, I'm not a hard[1] guy? How did you size me up so quick?

FORD: I, *I* don't know . . . in my work . . .

MIKE: What work is *that*?

FORD: Well, it's none of your *business* . . .

MIKE: Stand *corrected.* Here's the thing. Listen: I want something from you.

FORD: What do you want?

MIKE: I want you to do me a favor. And if you do I'll wipe out the eight hundred your friend owes me.

FORD: What do you want?

[1]Rough looking, sinister.

MIKE *draws her aside.*
MIKE: Do you know what a "tell" is?
FORD: A "tell"?

He takes a coin out of his pocket.

MIKE: Here: do this:

He puts the coin in his hands, puts his hands behind his back, brings the hands in front of him.

You have to choose a hand . . . (*He hands her the coin.*) You do it to me. Do it.

She does it, brings the two hands, one of which hides the coin, in front of her. He taps one of her hands.

Angle. She opens the hand he has tapped. It holds the coin.

Angle. MIKE *and* FORD.

Do it again.

She does it again, the hand he taps holds the coin.

Okay, now I can do that all day. How? You got a "tell." You're "telling" me the hand that has the coin.
FORD: I *am*?
MIKE: Yes.
FORD: How?
MIKE: It's not important. Ah, okay—you're doing it with your nose. You're pointing your nose slightly at the hand that has the coin. Okay? That's a "tell." Now: the guy from *Vegas* (*he points at the back room*) has got a shitload of my money. *He's* got a "tell." Okay? When he's *bluffing*, okay, he plays with his little gold ring. Now: I *caught* him doing it. N'he knows I did, so he *stopped.* He's conscious of himself. I want you to do me this *favor.* I want you to be my "girlfriend" for a while, come in the game, you stand *behind* me, watch me *play.* We get in a big *hand*, okay? I, uh, I go to go "pee" you *watch* this guy, and *tell* me, does he play with his gold ring. I know he's *bluffing*, I win the big hand. I'll forget the eight hundred dollars your friend owes.
FORD: If you're such a hot gambler, how'd you fall into this bind?
MIKE: Who told you I was a good gambler? I'm not a gambler, this is a *sickness* . . .
FORD: You're *not* a gambler.
MIKE: No.
FORD: Well . . . what *are* you, then?
MIKE: Aha.

Interior: Back Room—Night

Five men playing cards.

VEGAS MAN: Up two hundred.

ANDY: Your two and five more.

MIKE: I'm out.

He throws in his cards. The game continues. He leans back to talk to FORD.

MIKE: Guy's got a full house, you got two pair, it puts you in a philosophically indefensible position.

AL: New Hand.

MIKE: Well, it's good that I can *joke* about it, isn't it . . . ?

VEGAS MAN: Full house. (*He lays down his cards.*)

MIKE: What did you do, "win" again . . . ?

VEGAS MAN: That's right. You want to win the hand, you have to stay in 'til the end.

MIKE: Thank you.

Angle—Close-up. MIKE *and* FORD.

MIKE (*sotto*): You going to back me up here?

FORD (*sotto*): Yes.

MIKE (*sotto*): You keep looking for the tell, I'm going to *gut* that sonofabitch . . .

Angle. Interior cardroom. Later.

MIKE: I bet the fifty.

AL: Your fifty, and one fifty back.

VEGAS MAN: Two hundred. I call it.

ANDY (*dealer*): Cards to the players. Two good players. Mike?

MIKE: One card.

A card is dealt to MIKE.

Angle—Insert. He takes the card, puts it in his hand, he holds three aces.

ANDY (*voice over*): Al . . . ?

AL (*voice over*): Two cards.

VEGAS MAN (*voice over*): One card.

Angle: The card table.

MIKE: I pass.

AL: Wha's the pot? Two, four, five, *eight* hundred dollars. That's my bet.

VEGAS MAN: I call.

MIKE: You "call . . ." you only "call . . ."? Well, let's go visit Mr. More.[2] Your eight, and I raise you twenty-five hundred dollars.

AL (*throwing in his hand*): I can't stand it. South.

VEGAS MAN: South Street Seaport the man says. He Can't Stand the Heat. He can't stand it.

MIKE: You want to play cards? The bet is two and a half thou.

VEGAS MAN: The bet? *I'll* tell you what the bet is. Your twenty-five, and I raise you six thousand bucks.

[2]I.e., raise the bet.

MIKE *pushes his chair back from the table, gets up.*

MIKE: You sonofabitch, you've been steamrolling over me all night, what are you trying to tell me, one card, you caught a flush, a boat, what? I think you're bluffing pal, I think you're trying to *buy* it.

VEGAS MAN: Then you're going to have to give me some respect, or give me some Money.

ANDY: The bet is six thousand dollars.

MIKE: I know what the goddamn bet is. I'm going to pee. (*To* FORD, *as he exits:*) I thought that you were going to bring me luck.

VEGAS MAN: Make your own luck.

MIKE *exits. Beat.*

ANDY: Yes, yes, yes. Some people say *one* thing, some people say something *else.*

VEGAS MAN: The man can't *play,* he should stay *away.*

AL: His money's as good as yours is.

VEGAS MAN: His money is, and now we're going to see about his cards. That's right, Miss, isn't it?

From the back of the room, JOEY, *a man in his sixties, dressed like a college professor, comes forward.*

JOEY: Leave the woman alone.

VEGAS MAN: I'm just making conversation. That's right, isn't it? How's he doing, Miss, you bringing him "good fortune"?

FORD: Excuse me?

VEGAS MAN: Who do you *like* here, your friend or me?

FORD: Well, I've seen his hand, but I haven't seen yours.

VEGAS MAN: That's right. That's absolutely right.

The VEGAS MAN *starts playing with his little gold ring.*

Angle. FORD *looking at him.*

Angle—Point of view. The VEGAS MAN *turning his gold ring.*

Angle. FORD, *as she watches the* VEGAS MAN *playing with his ring. She looks around as* MIKE *comes back into the room.*

MIKE (*voice over*): Okay.

Angle. He slides back into his seat.

Let's play some fucken *cards* . . . Now: the bet is *what* . . . ?

ANDY: You're raised six thousand dollars, Mike.

FORD: How you doing? You ready to take this guy's money . . . ?

She takes his head in her hands as if to kiss him.

Angle—Close-up. The two of them, heads together. She whispers to him.

FORD: He's bluffing.

MIKE: You saw him?
FORD: He did exactly what you said. He played with his ring, and . . .
MIKE: He did . . . ?
FORD: He's bluffing.
MIKE: Well, he *better* be, 'cause my problem is that I don't have the six. If I *lose,* I can't . . .
FORD: You aren't *going* to. He played with his ring. Call the bet.

He pulls back and looks at her a moment. He nods.

MIKE (*to Vegas man*): Six thousand dollars? (*Pause.*) I think you're *bluffing.*
VEGAS MAN: What are you, Joe *Hep*? Raise, call, or fold . . .
MIKE: I should raise your ass, but I'm just going to call. (*Generally: to the table:*) My marker's good for a moment?
VEGAS MAN: What is this "marker"?[3] Where are you "from"?
MIKE: Where am I "from"? I'm from the United States of kiss my *ass.* My marker's *good.*
VEGAS MAN: Fuck *you.* And get the money up, or fold the goddamn *hand.*
JOEY: Look, mister: this man is a man of his word. He's a *regular* in the games—and if he says . . .
VEGAS MAN: Where I come from, the rule is if you can't call the bet you're out of the hand.
FORD: I'll call the bet.
VEGAS MAN: With what . . . ?
FORD: I said I'll back it up. If he loses I'll write you a check.
VEGAS MAN (*pause; generally*): Who is this broad?
JOEY: She's a friend of Mike's, she's alright. Your bet is called.
MIKE: Trip[4] tens. *Beat* 'em, my friend.

The VEGAS MAN *turns over his cards.*

Angle—Insert. The VEGAS MAN *has a club Flush.*[5] *Pause.*

Angle. The table full of men, looking at the hand.

VEGAS MAN: All blue. (*To Ford:*) You owe me six thousand dollars. (*He stands and starts raking in his chips.*) Thank you very *much,* next case.

The VEGAS MAN *and the others move away.*

ANDY (*over his shoulder*): Tough beat, Mike . . .

MIKE *and* FORD *are left alone at the table.*

MIKE: Huh. (MIKE *gets up, stunned; takes* FORD *over in the corner.*) Huh. (*Pause.*)
JOEY: Tough beat, Mike.
MIKE: I, uh . . . (*He shakes his head.*) He didn't do the thing with his ring.
FORD (*nods head*): No, he *did* it.
MIKE: He *did,* n'a-*fuck* is he doing with a Flush . . . ? (*To* VEGAS MAN*:*) What the *fuck* are you doing with a *Flush*?

[3]IOU. [4]Triple. [5]A poker hand with all cards of the same suit.

VEGAS MAN: Does that beat trips in Chicago? (*Pause.*) Well, then. Gimme the goddamn money.

MIKE (*to* FORD): We lost.

FORD: I have gathered that.

VEGAS MAN: And if you think I'm leaving here without that check, you're out of your motherfucking mind.

MIKE: *Okay. Okay,* hey, don't get Pushy.

VEGAS MAN: Pushy, Jim . . . ? Pushy . . . ? You don't know what pushy *is.*

He takes a large pistol out of his back pocket, puts it on the table.

Now give me my six thousand dollars.

Beat.

MIKE (*to* FORD): Uh, look, I'm going to have to ask you for that money.

FORD: That's right.

MIKE: I can't tell you how *sorry* I am . . .

FORD: No, no, *please*: let's just complete this transaction, and . . .

She starts writing check.

MIKE: I think that's probably wise . . .

VEGAS MAN: . . . and this check had better be like gold, or I'm coming back here, because I *won* this money.

MIKE: Okay, okay. You're going to get your money . . .

Angle—Insert. FORD*'s hand writing the check, beyond it, the revolver of the* VEGAS MAN.

Angle—Close-up. FORD, *looking intently at something.*

Angle—Point of view. Very tight on the revolver, the muzzle end is leaking little drops of water.

Angle. FORD, *surrounded by the men at the table. She stops writing.*

FORD: You know what? I don't think I'm going to pay you.

JOEY: *Don't* get the guy mad . . . for *heaven's* sake: *don't* get the guy *mad* . . .

MIKE: *Pay* the man.

VEGAS MAN: You crazy bitch. Pay me what you *owe* . . .

He picks up the revolver. The other men retreat.

FORD: No. I don't think I will (*she folds up the check and drops it in her purse*), and I will *tell* you why not: it is that *you cannot threaten someone with a Squirtgun*!

VEGAS MAN: You crazy bitch, I can threaten you with anything I goddamn want.

MIKE: George.

VEGAS MAN: Shuddup.

MIKE: George.
VEGAS MAN: What?
MIKE: I think it's Olley Olley In Free.
VEGAS MAN: No, I'm doing fine.
JOEY: No, George, you've blown the Gaff.[6]
VEGAS MAN: I have?
MIKE: Yes.
VEGAS MAN: I told you a squirtgun wouldn't work.
MIKE: A squirtgun would've worked. You didn't have to *fill* it.
VEGAS MAN: What, am I going to threaten someone with an empty gun . . . ?
MIKE: No, George, you're right, of course.
FORD: You guys are fantastic. What do you, do this for a living . . . ?
VEGAS MAN: Ask her is she mad.
MIKE: You aren't miffed with us, are you, I mean, nothing personal.
FORD: You were going to con me out of my money.
MIKE: It was only business.
FORD: It was only business, huh?
JOEY: It's the American Way. I don't know about the rest of you, but I'm starved. Anyone care for a snack . . . ?

JOEY *leaves the room, followed by the* VEGAS MAN.

VEGAS MAN: I told you a damn squirtgun wouldn't work.
JOEY: (*sotto*): One-eyed Jacks, Man with the Ax, suicide King.[7]
Beat. FORD *is alone with* MIKE.

MIKE: Well, there you have it.
FORD: A sucker born every minute, huh?
MIKE: And two to take him. Play past it. Here: (*He picks up a House of Games chip.*) A souvenir of your close escape from con men.

Beat. FORD *laughs, takes the chip.*

Exterior: House of Games—Night

FORD, VEGAS MAN, MIKE *and* JOEY, *lounging around, eating hot-dogs, at an open-air market, across from the House of Games.*

MIKE (*to* JOEY): Oh! Tell her the Mitt.[8]
JOEY: Na, they're still *using* the Mitt today, show her something historical . . .
VEGAS MAN: Show her the Tap.[9]
MIKE: What, they aren't doing the Tap. It's like a *kid's* game.
JOEY (*to* FORD): Okay. You run a candy store. Miss, excuse me, please, I'd like that Spearmint Gum. (*He digs for a bill; hands it to her.*) You say, "Don't you have anything smaller?"

[6]I.e., ruined the scam.
[7]Poker players' terms for the Jack of Hearts, the Jack of Spades, the King of Diamonds, and the King of Hearts.
[8]A confidence game in which a thief uses his quickness with his "mitt" (his sleight-of-hand) to confuse and steal from his victim.
[9]One of various confidence games in which the victim is "tapped" (swindled) for a small sum of money.

FORD: Don't you have anything smaller.

JOEY: No, I'm *sorry* . . . you make change . . . give me the change . . .

MIKE: *George,* what the *hell* are you doing out of the office . . . ?

JOEY: . . . I . . . (*To* FORD*:*) Okay? I pick up the ten bucks change. I leave the ten. I leave the gum. (*To* MIKE*:*) I'm on my lunch hour.

MIKE: I'm gonna have your job, you *know* that? I'm going to *Anderson* . . .

JOEY (*to* FORD): Oh. I found a nickel . . . I'm sorry . . . I hand you the nickel and I take back the ten and the gum. Timing, timing, it's all timing!

MIKE: Gum is not a nickel anymore.

JOEY: Shows you how long since I did the . . .

VEGAS MAN: Here's your cab.

MIKE *gets up, starts to walk her to the cab.*

FORD: Gentlemen, good evening.

Camera follows them as they walk. She turns back.

My friend's square with you. On the eight hundred dollars.

MIKE: Well, I *thought* you'd probably say that.

FORD: We struck the bargain. You said, "Watch for the tell and you'd cancel his debt." A man of your word?

MIKE: Alright. He's square.

FORD: May I have the I.O.U.?

MIKE: Hey, you're right—what's right is right. (*He hands her the I.O.U.*) Come back again and I'll show you some other Jolly Pranks.

FORD: Thank you.

Camera follows them to the cab. The cab is waiting at the curb. MIKE *knocks on the window, the cabbie opens the door.*

(*To* FORD*:*) Who are you, by the way?

FORD: Thank you for a lovely evening.

MIKE: You're a lovely woman. Come back any time you'd enjoy some more excitement.

She gets in the cab. Cab starts to drive away.

Angle. MIKE *watching the cab drive away. He reaches in his pocket, takes out a coin.*

Angle—Insert. MIKE *manipulating the coin. A half dollar. He puts the coin in one palm, rubs his hands together, opens one hand at a time, the coin is gone.*

Angle. MIKE, *still watching the cab. He puts his hand to his mouth, coughs. Opens his hand, which now holds the coin, flips the coin into the air. Looks at the departing cab.*

Angle—Point of view. The cab turning a corner down the street. It is gone.

Angle. MIKE. *Flips the coin up again. Catches it, puts it in his pocket, turns and starts back into the building.*

Interior: FORD*'s Apartment—Night*

A picture window, Lake Michigan beyond it. Curtains blowing. Classical music playing. FORD, *dressed in a chaste flannel nightgown, carrying a cup of tea, walks into the frame, closes the window. Camera follows her around the apartment. Obviously the abode of a single woman. Small, neat, modern, non-personal. She goes into the kitchen. Finishes her tea, puts the cup in the sink. Turns off the radio. Turns off the lights in the living room. She goes into the bedroom, turns down the covers on her bed. Gets into the bed. Pause. Picks up the House of Games chip from the bedside table, looks at it. She gives a big belly laugh, laughs for a moment. Turns out the lights, snuggles down into the bed.*

Interior: Hospital—Day

A window. A hospital-gowned woman patient, smoking a cigarette, walks into the frame.

WOMAN PATIENT: He said, "I can make any woman a whore in fifteen minutes."

FORD (*off camera*): . . . and what did you say to that?

WOMAN PATIENT: I said he couldn't make anybody a whore that was not a whore to start out with.

The woman nods, as if agreeing with herself.

Angle. The hospital room. The woman patient packing. FORD, *seated, talking to her.*

He said, "I been reading your mail, and you *are* that whore." And . . . (*pause*) *later* you see . . . (*Pause.*) When . . . then . . . then . . . 'cause he didn't realize what he had done.

FORD: And what *had* he done . . . ?

WOMAN PATIENT: You know, I know there are people who are normal . . .

FORD: *Are* there?

WOMAN PATIENT: Yes, there are. But . . .

FORD: But what?

WOMAN PATIENT: But I don't know what those people *do* . . .

Pause. The woman starts to cry. Pause. FORD *goes over to her.*

It's alright, darling . . .

WOMAN PATIENT: No. It's not alright. It never was alright. How can you live, when you've done something . . . when . . . ?

Interior: Hospital Corridor, Prison Ward—Day

FORD *walking down the corridor, escorted by a policeman. He escorts her through a locked door.*

MARIA *comes around the corner.*

FORD (*to* MARIA): I have to talk to you.

Exterior: Hospital—Day

FORD *and* MARIA *sitting on a bench, the hospital in the background.*

FORD: Why do we listen to their troubles when we can't help them?

MARIA: Oh. You have been talking to your murderess again.

FORD: I know why she is in the hospital, she's sick. The question is what am *I* doing there. It's a sham, it's a con game. There's nothing I can do to help her, and there's nothing I can learn from her to help others avoid her mistakes. That poor girl, all her life my father tells her she's a whore, so all her life she seeks out . . .

MARIA: "My father . . ."?

FORD: I'm sorry?

MARIA: You said, "*My* father says that she's a whore."

FORD: *My* father . . . ? (*Beat.*) I said, "*My*" father . . . ?

MARIA: Take your own prescription. If you're driven to do a thing you don't like, do something *else.* What gives you satisfaction? (*Pause.*) Maggie: what gives you satisfaction, what do you always enjoy?

FORD: I . . . I don't know . . . I enjoyed writing my *book* . . .

MARIA: So write another book. And in the short term, you come to my house for dinner tonight, will you do that?

FORD *takes out her appointment book. Beat.*

FORD: I'm sorry, I can't come tonight.

MARIA: Tonight, excuse me for asking, you have something to do that brings you joy?

FORD: Yes. I think I do.

Beat.

MARIA: Good. That's good.

MARIA *gets up, leaving* FORD *alone on the bench.* FORD *looks at her appointment book.*

Angle—Point of view. The check made out for six thousand dollars, clipped into the book.

Exterior: House of Games—Night

FORD, *dressed in casual clothes, walking across the street to the House of Games. She passes* BOB, *the proprietor.*

BOB: You come back to play some pool?

FORD: I'm looking for Mike.

BOB: Mike ain't here, try down at Charlie's.

FORD: Thanks.

Angle. FORD *walking across the street, takes out a cigarette, lights it. Camera follows her around the corner. In the middle of the block is a "lounge" with a large neon sign "Charlie's."* FORD *brushes back her hair, flicks away her cigarette, walks into the lounge.*

Interior: Charlie's—Night

A dark lounge. Men and a couple of women at the bar watching a sports event on television. FORD *is walking slowly past the bar, looking around.*

BARTENDER: . . . help you?

She shakes her head "no." Looks around again.

. . . drinking?
FORD: Scotch and water.

She points to an empty booth. The bartender nods. FORD *goes over to the booth and slides in. Looks around again. She lights another cigarette. Beat.*

A waiter, seen only from the waist down, napkin over his arm, comes into the frame.

WAITER: Scotch and water.
FORD (*without looking up*): Thank you.
WAITER: You pay now.
FORD (*opens her purse*): How much is it?
WAITER: How much have you got?
FORD *looks up.*

Angle. The waiter is MIKE, *dressed in a good suit, who has just draped a napkin over his arm.* MIKE *slides into the booth.*

MIKE: Oldest trick in the book. Never fails. Not *good* for much of anything, but still of great historical interest. Hiya.
FORD: Hi.
MIKE: Did I ever tell you my name? My name is Mike.
FORD: Glad to meet you. I've got a *proposition* for you.
MIKE: And what's "your" name?
FORD: Listen to this: how would you feel if someone were to do a *study* of . . . a study of . . . the *confidence* game . . . and someone were to *talk* to you, and learn your views and watch the way you operate. (*Pause.*)
MIKE: "A study of." (*Pause.*)
FORD: Yes.
MIKE: For what?
FORD: For my own reasons.
MIKE: And that's why you came back here?
FORD: Yes . . . how would you feel about that?
MIKE: Is that what you want? To see how a true bad man plies his trade . . . ?
FORD: Yes. (*Beat.*)
MIKE: Alright. (*He gets up and extends his hand to her.*)

Exterior: City Street—Night

FORD *and* MIKE *walking.*

MIKE: The basic idea is this: it's called a "*confidence*" game. Why? Because you give me your confidence? No. Because I give you *mine.* So what we have here, in addition to "Adventures in Human Misery," is a short course in psychology.

How do you get money when you *have* no money? (*He indicates with his head that they are to enter a building.*) This is called "Short Con." Watch closely.

Angle—Point of view. They are entering an all-night Western Union office.

Interior: Western Union Office—Night

FORD *and* MIKE *sitting in the empty office, reading old magazines. Pause. A young man enters the office. As he does so* MIKE *gets up and goes over to the cashier's window.*

MIKE (*to cashier*): Would you please check *again,* please. *Howard.* Martin *Howard* . . . money order for three hundred . . .

CLERK: It hasn't come *in* yet. As I told you, sir, the moment . . .

MIKE: . . . it was supposed to have been here this aft . . .

CLERK: . . . the *moment* it . . .

MIKE: . . . alright. Alright. Thank you.

MIKE *goes back and sits down. The young man goes up to the window.*

YOUNG MAN (*to cashier*): I'm expecting some money? John *Moran* . . . ?

CASHIER: One moment. (*He checks.*) *Moran* . . . ?

YOUNG MAN: Yessir.

CASHIER: No, I'm sorry. It hasn't . . .

YOUNG MAN: They told me definite by nine o' . . .

CASHIER: If you'll have a seat I'll tell you the *moment* . . .

YOUNG MAN: Thank you.

He sits down, across from FORD *and* MIKE. *Pause.* MIKE *sighs.*

MIKE: Can you beat that? (*Pause.*) Can you beat this? I've been waiting here since . . . (*To* FORD:) Honey . . . ? (*To young man:*) Since three o'clock this afternoon.

YOUNG MAN: No.

MIKE: Three o'clock this afternoon. I got my *car* stolen, my *wallet* . . . kid in a hotel, he hasn't *eaten* since . . .

YOUNG MAN: They told me they'd have my money by *nine,* and . . .

MIKE: I swear to god . . .

YOUNG MAN: . . . and I've got to get a *bus* ticket before . . .

MIKE: . . . when does the bus leave?

YOUNG MAN: . . . not til six. But it's selling out, and I've got to pick the ticket up by . . .

MIKE: . . . where you going?

YOUNG MAN: . . . back to Camp.

MIKE: . . . where is that?

YOUNG MAN: Pendleton.

MIKE: You're in the Corps? *I* was in the Corps.

YOUNG MAN: When were you in?

MIKE: '69, '70—yeah, *I* was there . . .

YOUNG MAN (*extending his hand*): John Moran.

MIKE: John. Marty Howard. (*Shakes hand. Pause.*) *Okay.* Look. What do you need for the bus?

YOUNG MAN: Forty.

MIKE: When my money comes in I'll give you the forty. Go back to the . . .

YOUNG MAN: No, I couldn't take it.

MIKE: The *Hell.* What are you going to? Miss your Formation? I'll lend you the forty. When you get back to Pendleton, send it back. (*Pause.*)

YOUNG MAN: Um.

MIKE: No. You get on that bus.

YOUNG MAN: *Thank* you.

MIKE: Nothing to it.

YOUNG MAN: If *mine* comes in first . . .

MIKE: No, *we'll* be alright . . .

YOUNG MAN: Uh uh. No. If *mine* comes in first *you* take . . .

MIKE: No. I couldn't do that . . .

CASHIER: *Moran* . . . ?

The YOUNG MAN *goes over to the window.*

Could I see some I.D., please . . . ?

YOUNG MAN (*to* MIKE): Now: you've got to take . . . what do you need?

MIKE: No. *We'll* get by . . .

YOUNG MAN (*turns around with money in his hands*): No. You tell me: what do you need . . . ?

MIKE *gestures to the soldier with the money in his hand.*

MIKE: (*to* FORD): What's more fun than human nature!? (*He takes* FORD *by the hand and starts out the door. To the soldier:*) Save your money, Pally. *Semper Fi*[10] . . .

Exterior: Western Union Office—Night

FORD *and* MIKE *exiting the office.*

FORD: Well. You learn something new every day.

MIKE: Innit the truth? You impressed?

FORD: So "you can't cheat an Honest Man."

MIKE: That's probably true. But what we have just seen is the operation of a slightly different philosophic principle.

FORD: Which is?

MIKE: "Don't Trust Nobody." Also this: everybody gets something out of every transaction. What that nice kid gets is the opportunity to feel like a good man. (*Pause.*) Now: what do *you* get out of *this* transaction?

FORD: I told you, I . . .

MIKE: Be *real,* Babe. Let's up the ante here. (*He stops.*) Do you want to make love to me . . . ?

FORD: *Excuse* me . . . ?

MIKE: Because you're blushing. *That's* a tell. The things we want, we can do them or not do them, but we can't hide them.

FORD: And *what* is it you think I want?

MIKE: I'll tell you: someone to come along, to take you into a new thing. Do you want that? Would you like that?

[10]Traditional greeting used by those who have served in the U.S. Marine Corps, from the Marine Corps motto *Semper fidelis* (Latin: Always faithful).

Beat.

FORD (*softly*): Yes.
MIKE: *What* is it . . . ?
FORD: Yes.
MIKE: That's good.

Interior: Hotel Lobby—Night

FORD *and* MIKE *walking through the lobby of a very fine hotel. Many people in the lobby. Camera follows them up to the check-in desk.*

MIKE (*to clerk*): A room.
CLERK (*checking files*): Your name, sir?
MIKE (*as he takes out some cash*): Douglas Johnson.
CLERK (*checking files*): I'm . . . you have a reservation . . . ?
MIKE: No, I . . .
CLERK: Oh, I'm *so* sorry, Mr. Johnson, we're *completely* booked up with the Apparel Show . . .
As the CLERK *talks, a well-built black man in a tuxedo drops his key off on the desk.*
WELL-BUILT BLACK MAN: Goodnight.
CLERK (*to black man*): Goodnight, Mr. Dean.
MIKE: Well . . .
CLERK (*to Mike*): I'm very sorry, sir . . .
MIKE (*pointing, behind desk*): Who's that man? Is that the manager?
The clerk turns to see who MIKE *is pointing at.*

Angle. MIKE*'s hand on the counter. Picks up the key that* MR. DEAN *has just left off.*

CLERK (*voice over*): No, sir, the manager is on a call at the moment.

Angle. MIKE *and the* CLERK, FORD *standing behind* MIKE.

CLERK: But, I assure you, we have *no* . . .
MIKE (*turning away from the desk*): That's alright. Thank you . . .
CLERK: I'm *very* sorry, sir . . . if . . .
MIKE (*walks away from the desk with* FORD): That's alright. (*To* FORD*; sotto:*) Did you see what I just did?
FORD: Yes.
MIKE *nods.*
Interior: Elevator—Night
FORD *and* MIKE.
FORD: What if he comes back?
MIKE: He had on a tuxedo. We would believe he's going out for the evening.
FORD: What if he does?

They get off the elevator.

Interior: Hotel Corridor—Night

FORD *and* MIKE *stepping off the elevator.*

MIKE: If he does, we deal with *that* thing *then.* (*He holds up the room key.*) In or out . . . ?

FORD *takes the key. He pulls her to him and kisses her passionately.*

Interior: Hotel Room—Night

FORD *and* MIKE *getting dressed.*

MIKE: We should be leaving.

FORD: You said he wasn't coming back.

MIKE: Probably not, but why should we wait for him.

FORD: Some people would say you're an interesting man.

MIKE: I'm a con man, I'm a criminal. You don't have to delude yourself. You can call things what they are. You can call yourself what you are.

FORD: What am I?

MIKE: Listen to me, because there's lots of things in the world, and there's many sides to each of us: good blood, bad blood, and somehow all those parts have got to speak. The burden of responsibility's just become too great. It's true, isn't it . . . ?

FORD: Yes. It is.

MIKE: I know it is. I read this somewhere: if you're fired from your job, take something, take a pencil, something, to assert yourself, take something from life. And I think what draws you to me is this: I'm not afraid to stand up and assert myself, and I think *you* aren't, either.

FORD: Do you really think so . . . ?

MIKE: Yes. That's *exactly* what I think. I'm going to wash up, and then let's get out of this guy's room. (*Mike leaves the room.*)

Pause. FORD *sighs, goes over to the dresser, picks up a comb, starts combing her hair, looks down at the dresser.*

Angle—Point of view. Personal effects on the dresser. A pile of change, a small antique silver pocketknife. Some cigars.

Angle. FORD *picks up the pocketknife. Looks at it. Takes it over to her pile of clothes and slips it into her pants pocket.*

Interior: Hotel Lobby—Night

FORD *and* MIKE *walking out of the hotel lobby. Camera follows them out onto the street.*

DOORMAN: Taxi . . . ?

MIKE (*to* FORD*; leans over and kisses her*): You gonna take a taxi home?

FORD: Where are you going?

MIKE: I've actually, got to be right *here* in . . . (*Checks his watch.*) Oh, *Christ* . . .

FORD: What *is* it?

MIKE (*quickly, worried*): Look, look, you remember Joey from last night? The . . .

FORD: Your friend . . .
MIKE: *Slowly* . . . look around, and tell me if you see him.

FORD *looks around.*

Angle—Point of view. Across the street JOEY *and a businessman are walking down the street, slowly, conversing, as after a good meal.*

Angle. FORD *and* MIKE.

FORD: Uh, *yes* . . . he's just crossing the . . . I don't under . . .
MIKE: Look . . . oh, Christ . . . (*He looks around.*)
FORD: What is it?
MIKE: There's a *bit* that I'm supposed to do here.
FORD: I'll do it with you.
MIKE: No. This is not "games," this is . . .
FORD: I'll do it with you. Just tell me what to . . .
MIKE *looks around.*
MIKE: Aw, *hell* . . . Babe, you're fucken up my timing . . . (*Decides, he takes her arm. They start to walk toward the corner.*) *Come* on. You're my *wife.* You follow my cue. Whatever I do. Don't volunteer *anything.* However strange things seem, KEEP YOUR MOUTH SHUT. And the only one you know is *me.*

Angle. FORD *and* MIKE *walking toward the street corner.* JOEY *and the* BUSINESSMAN *are approaching the same corner from the other side of the street. Both pairs arrive at the street corner at the same time. Also, another man, carrying a small suitcase, arrives at the corner, and hails a cab. This is the* VEGAS MAN *from the card game at the House of Games. The* VEGAS MAN *hails a cab, and we hear him say, "Airport, in a hurry" to the cab driver, as he gets in the cab. The cab drives away. But the* VEGAS MAN *has forgotten his suitcase, which is left standing on the curb, just as the two pairs of people,* MIKE *and* FORD *and* JOEY *and the* BUSINESSMAN, *converge next to it, waiting for the traffic light to change. Pause.*

JOEY (*to the group*): Ha. Fellow left his suitcase.
MIKE: I'm sorry . . . ?
JOEY: Fellow left his suitcase.
MIKE: Well, he probably came from the hotel. Let's, uh . . . let's take it back, and . . .

MIKE *leans down to pick up the suitcase. As he picks it up, the suitcase falls open revealing its contents to* MIKE *and* FORD. FORD *gasps. Pause.*

(*Softly:*) Holy Christ . . .

Angle—Point of view. The interior of the suitcase. It is full of stacks of hundred dollar bills.

Angle. The group. The BUSINESSMAN *and* JOEY *have crowded around, they are all looking awestruck at the case. Pause.*

MIKE: Um . . . (*Pause.*) I think we should . . .

He starts to walk back to the hotel with the case.

JOEY: No, hold on, wherever you're going, *I'm* going *with* you . . .
BUSINESSMAN: That's for *goddamn* sure.

Interior: BUSINESSMAN*'s Hotel Room—Night*

The BUSINESSMAN *is in his shirtsleeves, smoking. The suitcase is on the bed.*

BUSINESSMAN: Now: look: look: look; this has *got* to be stolen money . . .

MIKE: How do we know that?

JOEY: What are you, fucking *nuts?* There's eighty thousand *dollars* in the goddamn bag. Who's going to be . . .

BUSINESSMAN: . . . that's right . . .

JOEY: . . . carrying that kind of money in a "bag" the middle of the *night* . . .

BUSINESSMAN: That's absolutely right . . .

JOEY: . . . and . . .

BUSINESSMAN: And there's no *goddamned* way I'm turning that money over . . .

JOEY: . . . why should we? So some "cops" can split it?

BUSINESSMAN: . . . that's absolutely right . . .

JOEY: I'm not going to do it, and I'm not going to let *you* do it.

BUSINESSMAN: Now, let's just stop fucking around here: this money fell into our *laps*—there's no way to give it *back* . . . and all of us *know* what we're going to do, so let's just face the goddamn *facts*, 'cause we're going to *split* the *money*. So let's just *do* it. (*Pause.*)

MIKE: I . . . uh . . . now . . . um . . . look. I . . . I . . . I work in a *bank* . . .

JOEY: I don't want to know your personal . . .

MIKE: Will you just shut up for a second. Listen to what I'm going to tell you: I work in a bank. *If* this money is clean . . . *If* it's clean, *if* it's not counterfeit . . . I say this: I say we *split* it. (*Pause.*) And we split it down the middle, and we walk away and this never happened.

BUSINESSMAN: . . . that's what *I* say.

MIKE: I . . . here's what I think we should do: I say that . . . we're going home tomorrow. I'll take the money to the bank, and . . .

JOEY (*laughs*): Are you *nuts* . . . do you think that we're *insane* . . . ?

MIKE: Listen to what I'm going to say: we keep it *intact* . . . we don't *touch* it. I check it out. *If* it's hot, we . . . we *sit* on it. For six months, a year . . .

JOEY: . . . and you have the money all this time.

MIKE: Listen to what I'm going to tell you . . . I'll . . . alright: I'll go to . . . I can go to a bank tomorrow morning. *Here.* In *Chicago* . . . and . . . I can get . . . I can get ten, twenty thousand dollars. Clean money. *My* money . . . I'll write a draft . . . you *keep* the money . . .

JOEY: . . . we keep *your* money . . . ?

MIKE: . . . yes . . .

BUSINESSMAN: *Wait* a second . . . wait a second . . . *back* up . . . back up: *I'll* go to a bank. Alright? *I'll* . . . (*To Joey:*) Eh?

JOEY *shrugs.*

I'll give *you thirty* thousand dollars . . . and *I'll* get the thing checked out. I'll give you my money, and *I'll* keep the suitcase, you sonofabitch . . .

Angle—Close-up. MIKE *and* FORD. MIKE *turns to* FORD, *nods slightly, sadly, meaning you see what human nature is?*

Interior: Hotel Room—Day

Angle—Insert. MIKE*'s hand holding his own wristwatch. It reads 8:30.*

Angle. The hotel room. The suitcase is still on the bed. MIKE *is holding his wristwatch; he rubs his wrist and puts his watch back down on the bureau.* FORD, JOEY, *and the* BUSINESSMAN, *also, seated around the room.*

BUSINESSMAN (*sighs*): I'm going to wash up, and then we'll go.

MIKE *nods.*

JOEY (*to* BUSINESSMAN): Go. I'll keep a watch on the suitcase.

The BUSINESSMAN *goes into the bathroom. We hear running water. Pause.*

MIKE (*to* FORD*; sotto*): You got a little bit more than you *bargained* for, hey?

FORD (*waking up*): Hmmm. (*Beat.*) What's happening?

MIKE: Yeah.

FORD: I don't understand how this thing works.

MIKE: Well, alright, I'm going to tell you.

JOEY: Don't include the broad in it, Mike, for chrissakes, you had to drag her along, she don't have to know how we do this.

MIKE: Cool it, Joe, it's going good.

JOEY: Don't mouth it, it's going how it's going. You were a fool to've brought the broad.

MIKE: Be that as it may. (*To* FORD*:*) The mark gets dressed, we take him to the bank, he gets to ship the suitcase to himself in . . . where's he from . . . ?

JOEY: Baltimore.

MIKE: Baltimore. Before we let him do that, he gives up thirty thousand dollars. Before we ship it, we switch the suitcases on him, and we've got his thirty thousand dollars.

FORD: I don't get it, if it's phony money in the case, why do you have to switch it?

MIKE: Who said it was phony money? It's real. That's the beauty of the thing. We're showing the guy eighty thousand real dollars. We borrowed the money from the mob for one night, tonight we've got to pay it back.

JOEY: Okay, he's finishing up, let's take it to the Bank.

MIKE (*to* FORD): I hope you've enjoyed yourself. You have seen sights that few have seen.

JOEY: You were a fool to have brought the broad.

MIKE: It's *over*, Joe. (*To* FORD*:*) You did real good. (FORD *smiles.*) You better get your coat.

FORD *nods, starts for the coat closet. Looks back at the* BUSINESSMAN *in the bathroom. Reflected in the door mirror she sees he is wearing a gun in a holster. He closes the door.*

FORD *walks to the door. Camera follows. Through the door she hears:*

BUSINESSMAN (*voice over*)*:* Coming out in about five minutes. Not as far as I can determine, negative, none of them are armed, we'll act as if they were in any case. When you come in . . . have the female officer go for the woman, get her down on the ground and *frisk her good.* I don't trust her. I'll take the young guy, and you take the old. The signal is I clear my throat. (*Pause.*) Say again . . . ? (*Holds the earpiece closer to his ears.*) Yes. At the bank.

Angle—Close-up. FORD *moves her head back, terrified.*

Angle. FORD *comes back to* JOEY *and* MIKE.

FORD (*sotto*): He's a cop.
MIKE: What?
FORD: He's a cop. I . . . he's . . . I heard him on the walkie-talkie.
MIKE *stands.*
MIKE: Get out of here . . . you got to get *out* of here . . . get *clear.*
FORD (*terrified*): I . . . *Yes.* I *have* to . . . I. . .
MIKE: *Come* on . . .

He starts moving her toward the door. Camera pans to show MIKE *and* FORD *moving toward the door to the hall. As they do so, the* BUSINESSMAN *comes out of the bathroom and blocks their way.*

BUSINESSMAN: Where you going . . . ?
MIKE: Well, it's just my *wife* . . . she's got to call the . . .
MIKE *starts opening the door.*
BUSINESSMAN: No, no, no, hold *on* . . .
MIKE: *We're* going to stay with you, *she* . . .
The BUSINESSMAN *blocks the door.*
BUSINESSMAN: Nobody goes anyw . . .
MIKE (*starts to shove him aside*): She's very *ill* . . . she . . .
MIKE *shoulders the door open,* FORD *starts to squeeze through. The* BUSINESSMAN *draws a gun. Also pulls out his badge case and flips it open.*
BUSINESSMAN: Police! *Don't move.* Get back or I'll blow your goddamned . . .

FORD *and* MIKE *are still trying to get through the door, all pushing the* BUSINESSMAN. *There is a shot. The* BUSINESSMAN *throws* MIKE *out of the way and tries to prevent* FORD *from exiting the door. Pause.* FORD *and* MIKE *step back. Pause. The* BUSINESSMAN *falls to the floor, splattered by blood. Pause.* MIKE *kneels over him.*

JOEY: How is . . .
MIKE: Yeah. He's dead . . . let's get the hell *out* of . . .
FORD: Oh, my god . . .
JOEY: Why did you have to kill him, are you out of your mind?

They all stand. JOEY *starts looking around the room, picking up any stuff he may have left.*

MIKE: We've got about seconds to get out of here . . .

MIKE *holds open the door,* FORD *and* JOEY *go through the room.*

Interior: Staircase, Hotel—Day

In a succession of shots, we follow FORD, MIKE, *and* JOEY *down the staircase, out into a service corridor on the ground floor.*

MIKE *motions the others back, leans around a corner.*

Angle—Point of view. A policeman, standing guard out on the street.

Angle. FORD, MIKE, *and* JOEY, *in an alcove off the hotel garage.*

MIKE: They're out there.
JOEY: She's killed us, man, the bitch has killed us dead.

In the background, the garage elevator opens, a vintage red Cadillac inside. MIKE *looks at the car.*

MIKE (*to* FORD): Steal the car.
FORD: I can't do that.

JOEY *grabs* FORD *and hits her viciously in the face.*

JOEY: Do you want to spend the rest of your life in jail, or do you want the steal the car?
MIKE (*to* FORD): They don't know you. We need you to steal the car.

Beat. FORD *walks across to the car. Camera follows.*

Angle. FORD *getting into the car. She starts the car. Pulls over to the two men. They get in the car, crouching in the backseat.*

Angle. FORD *driving the car out of the garage, past the policeman.*

Exterior: Desolated Area—Day

A deserted industrial area on a canal. The red Cadillac, JOEY *wiping down the interior with a rag.* FORD *and* MIKE *in the background.*

JOEY: All my life, Mike, all my life I never had a moment's violence. Never had a moment's violence.
MIKE: Forget it. Wipe it down and let's get out of here.
JOEY: And then you had to bring your squarejohn broad into it. You had to bring your trick into the game.

JOEY *takes the keys from the car and throws them into the canal.*

MIKE: I brought the broad? What about the cop, where'd you get the cop?

JOEY: I found him at the apparel show, he looked like a businessman, he looked . . .

MIKE: Okay, okay, okay. Wipe it down. Let's get out of here.

Angle. FORD *and* MIKE.

MIKE: In a couple of minutes we're out of here, it's over, nobody even knows your name. We give the money back to the mob . . .

Pause. MIKE *turns to* JOEY.

Angle. JOEY, MIKE *and* FORD, JOEY *standing, fixed, looking inside the car.*

MIKE (*to* JOEY): Where's the briefcase . . . ? You had it, you had it at the hotel.

Beat.

JOEY: It's not here.

MIKE: Where *is* it, Joe . . . ?

FORD: What does it mean?

MIKE: Where *is* it, Joe . . . ?

JOEY: I'm sorry, Mike, I was scared.

MIKE: You were scared? You sonofabitch, you've *killed* us . . .

JOEY: I'm sorry, Mike, when we were at the Hotel.

MIKE: SHUT UP. Let me think for a second . . .

FORD: WHAT DOES THIS MEAN?

MIKE: It means we lost eighty thousand dollars, and if we can't give it back tonight to the Mob, they'll turn us over for that cop we killed. (*To* JOEY*:*) You got senile, old man . . .

FORD: I can give you the money.

MIKE: I need eighty thousand dollars by this evening.

FORD: I'll get it, I'll give it to you.

Beat.

MIKE: You have that kind of money?

FORD: I can get it.

Beat.

MIKE: Then, for god's sake, *get* it.

Interior: Taxicab—Day

MIKE *and* JOEY *in the backseat.*

MIKE: Funny how things happen sometime.

JOEY *turns to look out of the window.*

Angle—Point of view. FORD *coming out of a bank, carrying a large bag under her arm.*

Angle. Interior, the cab, JOEY *gets out, takes the bag,* FORD *gets in.*

JOEY: I'll tell them . . .

MIKE: They know what happened, you don't have to tell them a goddamned thing. (*To driver:*) Start for the airport.

The car starts. MIKE *and* FORD *hold a whispered conversation in close-up.*

FORD: What happens now?

MIKE: Joey gives the money back to the mob, and then he goes away. I'm going to go away. You're going to stay here because you have a life here. Listen to me: You're going to get a strong urge to confess. To thievery, to murder, you're going to want to confess. Don't do it. What happened was an accident. The fact you were there was an accident. So you go and forget it. I just wish . . .

He kisses her.

(*To driver:*) Stop the cab.

Angle. Exterior of the cab. The cab pulled over on the shoulder of a throughway on ramp. FORD *gets out of the cab. The cab pulls into traffic.*

Angle—Close-up. FORD *watching the cab pull away.*

Interior: College Hallway—Day

MARIA, *lecturing to a group of students. We hear nothing.*

Angle. FORD, *outside the lecture room, looking in. A late student moves past* FORD *to open the door. We hear* MARIA *lecturing as the door opens.*

MARIA: Compression, inversion, elaboration, are devices for transforming the latent into the manifest. In the dream, and also, in the . . . ? In the *Joke*!

As she makes her point she points her finger at the class, as if she held a gun. We hear a gunshot.

Angle—Close-up. FORD, *recoiling.*

Angle. The BUSINESSMAN*'s face.*

Angle. FORD*'s hand, turning the pages of her notebook, to the page which reads "House of Games."*

Angle. The BUSINESSMAN *sliding down the wall. A loud bell rings.*

Angle. FORD *in the hall, stunned. The bell stops. We hear* MARIA *calling* "Maggie . . . Maggie, What is it . . . ?"

Angle. The hall. The students, changing classes. MARIA, *in the classroom door, calling to* FORD.

FORD: I have to . . . I have to talk to you.
MARIA: What. *Anything.* (*Pause.*) What *is* it . . . ? (*Pause.*)
FORD: You know . . . you know the dream where . . . you've done something terrible . . . some . . . some . . . and you're . . . going to . . . *die,* or . . . you've *killed* someone . . . and you say: you say: "If Only This Was a Dream . . ." I've had dreams like this. What would I not give if this was a dream, and . . .
MARIA: Maggie. Darling. Come upstairs. Sit down and tell me. (*Takes her arm.*)
FORD *breaks free.*
FORD: No! Listen to me. No. What do you do? What do you do when . . . when . . . And if you reveal yourself you betray someone else, and . . .
MARIA: When you've done something "unforgivable." When you've done something unforgivable, you *forgive* yourself. Now, come upstairs and . . .
FORD: No.
MARIA: My God! Maggie, what's the trouble! My poor child. *Whatever* it is . . . there's nothing that doesn't have a second ch . . .
FORD: "It isn't as if I've *killed* someone . . . "

A student comes over and pulls MARIA *aside to ask a question. As she does so* FORD *pulls away. Walks out the door.*

Interior: FORD*'s Office—Vestibule—Day*

FORD, *still clothed in the clothes of the night before, walks into her vestibule. A young woman patient rises from one of the chairs.*

YOUNG WOMAN PATIENT: Dr. Ford . . . do I have the wrong day, am I . . . ?
FORD (*moving past her, opens the door to her inner office*): I'm very sorry. I'm very sorry. I'm quite ill. I'll have to . . .
YOUNG WOMAN PATIENT: . . . are you *alright* . . . ?
FORD *brushes past her.*
FORD: Didn't I just tell you. What did I just say . . . ?

FORD *goes into the inner office. Camera follows. She closes the door behind her. Moves to the window shades. Draws them. Goes over and sits in her chair. Picks up the telephone.*

(*On phone:*) No calls through . . . on any circumstances. Call my appointments for today and cancel them.

She hangs up the phone, she rubs her face. She takes out a cigarette and lights it. She shakes her head, closes her eyes. Starts to cry. She reaches down to her desktop.

Angle—Insert. FORD *is picking up a copy of her book* Driven.

Angle. She takes the book. Pause. She hurls it across the room.

Angle. The book hits a large framed diploma on the other side of the room. The glass shatters.

Angle. FORD *walks over to the diploma, a medical degree in her name. She reaches through the fragments of glass and takes out the diploma. Crumples it. She looks down at her hand.*

Angle—Point of view. Her hand is bleeding badly.

Angle. She goes to her desk. Opens the desk drawer. Looks down.

Angle—Point of view. Various objects in the desk drawer. A small package of Band-aids. She is bleeding all over the desk drawer. Trying to put on the Band-aid. She does so. Her hand stops.

Angle. FORD *looking down in horror at something in the desk drawer. She picks it up.*

Angle—Point of view. FORD *holding the now-bloody pocketknife which she took from the black man's hotel room.*

Angle. FORD *holding the bloody pocketknife. Frightened. Throws it in her wastebasket. Thinks.*

FORD *takes all the artifacts, throws them in the wastebasket. She leans back, unbuttons her jacket, sighs. She looks down; her shirt, inside her jacket, is spattered with blood. She rips off her bloody shirt, throws it in the wastebasket.*

Camera follows her across the room to a gymbag. She takes out a sweatshirt, puts it on. We hear a knock on the door.

Angle—Close-up. FORD *turns to look at the door. The knock is repeated.*

BILLY HAHN (*voice over*): Dr. Ford? Dr. Ford, it's Bill Hahn.

Angle: At the door. She opens it, to reveal BILLY *beyond.*

FORD: What do you want?
BILLY: I called up to cancel. Your office said that you weren't taking any calls. I have to be away for a few days.
FORD: Yes. I think it's best if we suspended treatment for a while.

Beat.

BILLY: Are you alright?
FORD: Yes. Thank you.

Beat. FORD *closes the door. Camera follows her to the wastebasket. She picks it up, starts out of the room.*

Pause. She thinks of something. She hurries back to her desk. Takes her purse, rummages through it, takes out the datebook, takes out a folded piece of paper.

Angle—Insert. It is the check for six thousand dollars she wrote when she went to the House of Games the first time. Her fumbling hands put the check in an ashtray and set fire to it.

Angle. FORD *watching the check burn. Pause. She rummages through her desk, pulls out a file.*

Angle—Point of view. The file reads "Billy Hahn." FORD *flips through the pages.*

We see the page we have seen previously, which reads: "Compulsive succeeds in establishing a situation where he is out of control." And below it, written "The character of MIKE, *the 'Unbeatable Gambler.' Seen as omniscient, who 'doles out punishment'. . .* HOUSE OF GAMES.*"*

Her hands lay these pages aside. She digs deeper in the file, takes out the small nickeled automatic pistol she had taken from BILLY. *She pulls out another sheet. It is* BILLY*'s I.O.U.*

Exterior: FORD*'s office building—Day*

FORD *comes out of the service door, carrying her wastebasket. She walks toward a dumpster. As she walks she sees something.*

Angle—Point of view. BILLY HAHN, *hanging up a payphone across the street.* BILLY *continues walking down the street. As he turns the corner we see the vintage red Cadillac.* BILLY *gets into the car.*

Angle. FORD *at the dumpster, looking at* BILLY *getting into the car.*

Exterior: Charlie's Tavern—Night

The red Cadillac parked.

Angle. FORD, *across the street, camera follows her across toward the tavern, and into the back door.*

Interior: Charlie's—Night

FORD*'s moving point of view. A well-built black man, his back to camera, talking on the payphone in the back of the tavern.*

Angle. FORD, *sneaking into Charlie's through the back.*

Angle—Point of view. In the front of the tavern, BILLY HAHN *having a drink with the* VEGAS MAN. *Behind* FORD *the black man brushes past, and announces to a table:* "I just won five thousand dollars in a baseball game." FORD *turns to look at him.*

Angle—Point of view. It is MR. DEAN. *As he slides into a booth, the* BUSINESSMAN/POLICEMAN *gets out.*

BUSINESSMAN: Whyn't you let me have a taste?

MR. DEAN: I'd let you have a taste, you weren't so goddamn *cheap* all the time.

BUSINESSMAN: How come I always got to play the straight guy . . . ?

MR. DEAN: *Think* about it.

MIKE (*voice over*): Who filled the goddamn water pistol . . . ?

JOEY (*voice over*): I did.

MIKE (*voice over*): Goddamn water pistol made a puddle big enough to swim in.

Angle. FORD, *walking over toward their booth, shielded by a stack of beer cases.*

*Angle—*FORD*'s point of view.* JOEY, MIKE, MR. DEAN, *the* BUSINESSMAN, *seated at the booth.*

BUSINESSMAN: Well, it's what you pay for, it's realism.

The VEGAS MAN *comes over to the booth.*

JOEY: Well, is she going to stand up?

VEGAS MAN: Well, like he said, she's On Tilt, but he thinks she'll stand up.

MIKE: Pay the kid off.

JOEY *takes some bills from* FORD*'s bank bag, hands them to the* VEGAS MAN.

MIKE: Keep him a little scared.

VEGAS MAN (*takes the bills, starts off*): *Oh* yeah.

MR. DEAN: Mike: How'd you know she was going to go for it?

MIKE: Go for it, the broad's an *addict* . . .

JOEY: Oh. This is great. This is fantastic. Listen to this: we're dressing up the hotel room . . .

MR. DEAN: "My" hotel room . . . ?

MIKE: Yeah. We put some stuff, we put forty, fifty bucks up on the bureau . . .

MR. DEAN: Uh huh . . .

MIKE: Yeah, so it looks like somebody's in the room. Now: the broad steals my pocketknife.

BUSINESSMAN: No.

MIKE: My hand to God. She boosts my Lucky Pocketknife.

JOEY: The bitch is a booster.

MIKE: The bitch is a born thief, man, "Show me some con men . . ."

BUSINESSMAN: Well, we showed her some con men.

MIKE: We showed her some *Old* style . . .

MR. DEAN: Yessir . . .

MIKE: Some *Dinosaur* con men. Years from now, they'll have to go to a *museum*, see a frame like this.

MR. DEAN: Took her money, and screwed her, too.

MIKE: A small price to pay.

Angle—Close-up. FORD*, recoiling. She leans back against the wall, her back to the booth.*

BUSINESSMAN (*voice over*): Mike, you are the Ring-Tailed Rounder, you are King Kong.

MIKE (*voice over*): One Riot, one Ranger.

MR. DEAN (*voice over*): What's next?

MIKE (*voice over*): For me, a rest. I'm going to Vegas tonight on the ten o'-clock. You want to come?

MR. DEAN (*voice over*): Nah, this time I'm quitting winners.

MIKE (*voice over*): Missing you. What did I say? We got the two hotel rooms. Speaking of which, three hundred dollars for a hotel room?

MR. DEAN (*voice over*): Always show a little front, Mike, you taught me that yourself.

MIKE (*voice over*): Oh, you're such a flatterer. Fifty-two ninety for the two policemen's uniforms, two hundred dollars that we gave the kid . . .

Interior: Airport—Night

A departures announcement TV screen. Announces three flights left, the final one is for Las Vegas, departing 10:00 p.m. The Las Vegas entry is joined by a blinking "Now Boarding" sign.

Angle. FORD*, dressed for traveling, looking up at the screen. Checks her watch.*

Angle—Insert. The watch reads 9:42.

Angle. FORD *looking at her watch. Sees something.*

Angle—Point of view. MIKE*, carrying a small suitcase, coming in from the street.*

Angle. FORD *takes a deep breath, moves toward him on an oblique angle. He sees her, stops, she "sees" him. She walks over to him.*

FORD (*softly*): Mike . . . Mike . . . what are you . . . what are you here . . . ? We can't be here . . .

MIKE: What are you doing here . . . ?

Angle—Close-up.

FORD (*sotto*): Listen . . . listen . . . they're *following* me . . . they're *following* me . . .

MIKE (*sotto*): . . . they are?

FORD: Come on . . . we . . . we . . . we . . . we must keep moving . . .

She leads him outside. They come out of the building.

Angle. FORD *and* MIKE.

MIKE: Look: we can't be seen together.
FORD: No. We must. Don't leave me . . .
MIKE: You're in no danger . . .
FORD (*simultaneous with "danger"*): I *told* you. They're *waiting* for me . . . there were *men* there. (*Pause.*) What are you doing here? I thought you . . . I thought you . . .
MIKE: I couldn't get on the right flight. Now: Look: If they haven't followed you here, then you have some time. We have to split up.
FORD: No. I can't . . .
MIKE: *Yes.*
FORD: No. I can't . . . how can I do it without *you*, we, this is a *godsend* that . . .
MIKE: I'm going to tell you where I'm going. Alright. Yes. We'll . . . you're right. We're going to take separate flights.
FORD: No. No. No. I'm so frightened. And . . . Mike: Mike: I . . . I took all my money. I took all my money out of the bank. I'm . . . and you'll help us disappear. We'll disappear together. Mike: I've got a quarter of a million dollars. We can live . . . we . . . I can't believe I'm seeing you . . .

Interior: Airport, Lower Floor

MIKE *and* FORD *by a bank of lockers.* FORD *opens a locker, takes out a small Gladstone bag.*

MIKE: Do you think that you were followed?
FORD: I don't know. I'm frightened all the time.
MIKE: Yes.

He looks around, leads her down a corridor, camera follows.

FORD: I bought my ticket in another name.
MIKE: I think that's wise.
FORD: My real name is Margaret.
MIKE: Margaret. (*Beat.*) We're going to get you out of here. I promise you. We need a plan.

They stop outside a door to the baggage area. MIKE *tries the door, it is open. Camera follows them into the deserted baggage area.* MIKE *leads* FORD *over to an unused conveyor belt. They sit.*

FORD: It was fate I found you.
MIKE: Yes. It was.
FORD: Because, *together* . . .
MIKE: . . . Yes. We *can.*

FORD: And when I saw them . . . when I saw that they came *after* me . . .

MIKE: It's alright now. You're safe.

FORD: . . . I *knew.* That I was being *punished.*

MIKE: No. It was an *accident* . . . No . . .

FORD: No. I knew. That I was bad. Do you know why? Do you know when I knew? Because I took that knife.

MIKE: What knife?

FORD: Your pocket knife. From that hotel room. And I said, "That's why it happened. That's why it all . . . " Yes. Because I'm bad. (*Pause.*) Because I'm a *thief.* Because I'm . . . It's because I'm . . .

She sees something in him.

*Angle—*FORD*'s point of view.* MIKE.

(*Voice over:*) What is it . . . ?

Angle. MIKE *and* FORD.

Mike, Mike: what is it?

MIKE *gets up, starts checking the baggage area slowly.*

MIKE: Oh. You're a bad pony. N'I'm not going to *bet* on you. (*Pause.*)

FORD: I . . . ?

MIKE: You see: The thing of it is: You just said "*my* pocketknife." (*Pause.*)

He continues checking out the baggage area.

FORD: I . . . I don't underst . . .

MIKE: You said you took "My" pocketknife out of the hotel room.

FORD: I . . . ?

MIKE: You see, in my trade this is called, what you did, you "cracked-out-of-turn." Eh? You see? You crumbed the play. (*Pause.*) What do you want? (*Pause.*) What do you fucken *want* from me . . . ? You want your eighty *grand* back, I can't *give* it back. I split it up. What do you want? Revenge?

He sits down. Pause.

FORD: I gave you my trust.

MIKE (*laughs*): Of *course,* you gave me your trust. That's . . . you asked me what I *did* for a living . . . this is it. Look, look, I'm *sorry.* I'm sorry I "hurt" you. Really. You're a good kid, now, whatever it is that you feel that you have to do . . .

He starts for the door.

FORD: Sit down, please.

MIKE: I'd love to, but I . . .

FORD: I said to Sit Down.

MIKE: Whaddaya gonna do, go to the *Cops*?

FORD: I may.

MIKE: And tell them *what*? Whattayagonna tell 'em, Stud? That the author of the best-selling *Driven*, "A Guide to Compulsive Behavior," gave her cash away to some con man? (*Pause.*) You see my point? (*He starts to leave the baggage area.*) But we've had fun! You must say that.

FORD: I said sit *down*.

She takes the nickeled automatic pistol out of her pocket. MIKE *reaches for the doorknob.*

If you walk out that door I'm going to kill you.

MIKE: I don't believe you.

FORD: What is life without adventure? (*She chambers a round and points the pistol at him. Pause.*)

MIKE *lets go of the doorknob. He sits down. Pause. He shrugs.*

MIKE: What . . . ? (*Pause.*) What do you want?

FORD: You took my money.

MIKE: How naughty of me.

FORD: You raped me.

MIKE: Is that what I did . . . ?

FORD: You took me under false pretenses.

MIKE: Golly. Margaret. Well, that's just what "happened," then, *isn't* it? *Okay*: Look: You got "Stung," and you're "Hurt." I can understand that. You're *stuck* 'n you're steaming . . .

FORD: I want to know how you could do what you did to me.

MIKE: It wasn't *personal*. Okay? And, really, funny as that sounds, I'm sorry that it happened. But it *did*, and we've all got to live in an imperfect world. (*He gets up.*)

FORD: You used me.

MIKE: I "used" you. I did. I'm *sorry*. And you learned some *things* about yourself that you'd rather not know. I'm sorry for that, too. You say I Acted Atrociously. Yes. I did. I do it for a living. (*He gives her a salute and starts for the door.*)

FORD: You sit down.

MIKE: I'd love to, but I've got some things to do.

She cocks the gun.

(*Of gun:*) You can't bluff someone who's not paying attention.

FORD *shoots him. He falls.*

Are you *nuts*? What are you . . . *nuts* . . . ?

FORD: I want you to beg me.

MIKE: Fuck *you*. I'm not going to beg you for a goddamn *thing*.

FORD: Beg me.

MIKE: S's a goddamn bluff. You're *all* bluff. Whataya, gonna *kill* me? and then go to Jail? Give up that good *shit* that you have that "Doctor" stuff, that "money," your "car" . . .

FORD: It's not my pistol, I was never here. (*She shoots him again.*) Beg for your life. Or I'm going to kill you.

MIKE: Hey, no.

FORD: I can't help it—"I'm out of control."

MIKE: Hey, no. Oh . . . I . . . .

FORD: Beg me for your life.

MIKE (*coughing*): Hey, fuck *you.* This is what you always *wanted*—you crooked bitch . . . you *thief* . . . this is what you always . . . (*He starts to cough blood.*) You always need to get caught—'cause you know you're bad . . . live with *this. I* never hurt anybody. *I* Never shot anybody . . . you're gonna . . . you're gonna . . . you're gonna . . . you sought this out . . .

We hear a jet revving up and starting its take-off.

This is what you always wanted. I knew it the first time you came in. You're worthless, you know it. You're a whore. I knew you the first time you came in. You came back like a dog to its own vomit. You sought it out.

FORD *shoots him again.*

"Thank you, sir, may I have another?"

FORD *shoots him three times. As a jet thunders by overhead.* FORD *walks slowly to retrieve her bag, leaves the room. Pause. Silence.*

Interior: Restaurant—Day

An open greenhousey restaurant. FORD, *tanned, dressed lightly, at the bar, holding a drink. She looks around. A man accosts her.*

MAN: Are you Dr. Margaret Ford? (*Pause.*) Are you Dr. Margaret Ford?

FORD: Yes. I am.

MAN: Would you sign my book . . . ?

The man produces a copy of the book, hands it over to FORD. FORD *takes it, takes a pen, begins to write.*

Angle—Insert. FORD *writing on the title page:* "Forgive yourself." *As she finishes writing, we hear someone calling her* "Maggie."

Angle. FORD *finishes with the book. The call is repeated. She looks for the source.*

Angle—Point of view. MARIA *standing in the restaurant doorway beckoning to* FORD.

Angle. FORD *goes over to* MARIA. *They embrace.*

MARIA: Oh, darling. I've missed you. How are you?

FORD: I'm fine. Really fine.

MARIA: Are you?
FORD: Yes. I absolutely am.

Camera follows them to a table in the dining room. They sit.

MARIA: Do you know how frightened I was for you? Before your trip?
FORD: . . . it was just the strain . . . what with the book coming out . . .
MARIA: No, no, I know. But there was something . . . something . . . Something on your mind . . .
FORD: That's right—and you said, when you've done something unforgivable, forgive yourself, and that's what I've done, and it's done.
MARIA: Good. What are we going to eat? What did you eat down there?
A waitress comes to the table.
WAITRESS: Dr. Littauer?
MARIA: Yes?
WAITRESS: You're wanted on the phone.
MARIA *sighs. Gets up.*
MARIA (*over her shoulder*): I'm sorry, darling. Order for me.

FORD *is left alone at the table. She looks around the restaurant. The woman at the table backing up theirs is lighting a cigarette with a gold lighter. She and* FORD *nod slightly at each other. Pause.*

The woman replaces the gold lighter in her purse. FORD *looks down at the menu, puts the menu down.*

FORD *turns to the woman.*

FORD: Excuse me . . . ?
WOMAN WITH LIGHTER: Yes?
FORD: Could you tell me what that is on the buffet?

The woman turns to look at the buffet. As she does so, FORD *reaches across toward her purse.*

Angle—Insert. FORD*'s hand taking the gold lighter out of the woman's purse.*

Angle. The woman, turning back, FORD*, sitting at her table.*

WOMAN: A Waldorf salad.
FORD: Thank you.

Angle. FORD*'s hands under the table, holding the lighter.*

Angle. FORD *at the table, her hands come up with the lighter, she lights a cigarette, and then holds the lighter covered in her hands. She smiles.*

1985

Judy Budnitz 1973–

Judy Budnitz is called a "fabulist," a writer, like others who are taking American literature in a new direction, whose stories make wild flights of departure from the limits of realism and the possible events of common life. Her modern-day fables, unlike those of ancient fabulists, do not have animals that speak and act like human beings, nor does she depict the exploits of gods and legendary heroes. But like her ancient predecessors, she writes cautionary tales, narratives that are ironic, edifying, moralizing, often weighted with fear, unkindness, confusion, and social catastrophe.

She grew up in Atlanta, Georgia, and began writing stories early in life: "I just started doing it. It's never been a question of wanting to do it, I just do it." She attended Harvard, graduating in 1995. She next entered the creative writing program at New York University and in 1998 graduated with an MFA. Her own life has lacked the grotesque, off-the-wall, wacky experiences she portrays in her stories: She has worked for a publishing house, as a lifeguard, as a free-lance illustrator, and has taught creative writing workshops. The weird, and often hilarious, experiences of her characters, she says, simply "bubble up" from her unconscious.

Her stories have appeared in numerous magazines, in the New Yorker, Harper's, *the* Paris Review. *Her first collection of stories,* Flying Leap, *published in 1998, demonstrated her ability to master the unexpected in short fiction and keep her readers off base. The next year she published an experimental novel,* If I Told You Once, *which presents the experiences of four generations of Jewish immigrant women who move from Russia of a century ago to modern-day New York. Told from varying points of view, and narrated by different characters with different assessments of events, the novel tests the reader's ability to determine what was real and what was imaginary.*

Budnitz says that she likes to start her stories with attention-catching first lines— "There was a woman who had seven sons and was happy"—and she insists that she has "no idea what is going to happen next"; the story "usually writes itself." She often sets her stories in unnamed countries with nameless characters who live in unidentified places. Budnitz wants her characters to escape identification with specific lands because that "limits the stories" and confines the characters to national stereotypes.

She has said, "I like exploring human behavior, trying to suss out why people treat each other as they do. I am not offering any grand global salvation." Yet much of her writing has a political overtone, expresses annoyance at the disparity between pious, self-congratulating declarations and bleak political reality. Her work is called "dystopian" because it often deals with difficulties, oppression, bruising deprivation. It shows the influence of Franz Kafka's portrayals of impossible events occurring in the everyday world. And it is also mordantly funny with characters and events like the heroine of "Where We Come From," who will stop at nothing, or will stop nature itself, to insure that her baby is born in America, and finds that in its first words it demonstrates its true American identity with what Budnitz sees as a national incantation: "Give me, I want, I need, I deserve, I have earned . . . ."

TEXT: *Nice Big American Baby*, 2005.

from *NICE BIG AMERICAN BABY*

WHERE WE COME FROM

1. BEFORE

There was a woman who had seven sons and was happy. Then she had a daughter.

She loved her sons with a furious devotion. But she did not want the daughter, even before she knew it was a daughter. She could feel the baby sitting low in her belly and did not want it.

Another burden on my back, the woman thought, another mouth to feed.

From the moment the girl was born she was frail and sickly; she greeted the world with a sneeze. The mother heard the sneeze and felt a heaviness descend upon her heart. Even with the best coddling and foreign medicine, the girl would probably die within the month. Three years at the most. A waste. It would be better, she thought, if the girl died now and got it over with. There were many ways a baby could die. Infant death was common in that part of the world; no one would notice one baby more or less.

Then she looked at the tiny wrinkled face and felt ashamed. She resolved to love her daughter as she did her sons.

She named the girl Precious, to remind herself.

She made a promise to her daughter, but her seven sons were a delight and a distraction and if she did not break that promise she did bend it to its limits, like a young tree in a windstorm. Precious learned to make no demands on her mother. She took the food from the bottom of the bowl at meals and kept her feet clean so she would not leave footprints behind her.

The woman was happy. Her sons grew tall. People told her how lucky she was: eight children, all of them still living.

But I have seven children, she would say. And then: Oh. Yes.

One year the rains came doubly hard, the roads became rivers of mud, and the fruit rotted on the vine. The next year the rains did not come at all. Surely, people said, the third year will be a good year. But they were wrong.

It had never happened before—two years without rain. Even those people who considered themselves modern began to pray again and to hang charms at their doors.

The underground stream that fed the electric pump in the village dried up. The woman's sons went searching for water. They were tall and thin and knew how to travel in the heat of day. They ran and rested, ran and rested. Each time they paused they arranged themselves in a descending line so that all but the oldest could rest in a brother's shadow.

They had taken buckets and jars to carry water back to their mother. And to Precious. Precious: always remembered, but always as an afterthought.

They found a wire fence. The top of the fence was lined with prickly wire like a thornbush. They tore their hands on it, climbing over. Far in the distance they could see a dark smudge bleeding into the sky. They ran closer. It was the largest building they had ever seen, massive and gray and faceless, with three tall chimneys like fingers pointing to the sky. The black smoke that poured from them was like nothing they had ever seen before. It hung in the sky without dissipating, it was dense and heavy, like rain clouds about to burst.

The oldest said it was a rain factory. He said he remembered hearing people talk about it. He was sure.

Yes, said another, I heard that too. It's true.

Beyond the building they saw a pool, almost a lake. It was perfectly shaped and perfectly still, and the water was the strangest color they had ever seen—bright, bright blue and iridescent, with pearly rainbows on its surface. They agreed that the color must mean it was very pure.

The first one to taste the water became very sick. His brothers watched him twisting and retching, his arms folded in on themselves like wings. A thick white gravy came out of his mouth and nose. They heard a roaring in the stillness and looked up to see two trucks speeding toward them trailing clouds of dust. They lifted their brother and ran.

They knew their brother could not climb the fence, so they hid among the rocks where they knew the trucks could not follow, and they waited for dark. They dug beneath the fence with their hands. It took them most of the night. They knotted their shirts into a sling and headed home, carrying their brother between them.

The woman was waiting on her doorstep for her sons to return. In the red light of dawn she saw their silhouettes approaching. She counted only six bobbing heads and began to keen in her throat.

Her son did not die. Eventually his hands uncoiled and he was able to walk again. But he was not the same as he was before. His face had hardened into a new expression that made him look like a suspicious stranger.

She knew that was not the end of it. The poisoned water was the beginning, a portent of what was to come. She was not surprised when, soon after, her sons began to disappear one by one.

The rains still did not fall. Everyone was hungry. The earth was cracked and barren. There was no work to be done, and anger and discontent began to ferment in the hearts of the people. Some complained against the government, though many had never seen the slightest evidence of any government and did not believe it existed. There was talk of electing leaders, building an army, an army for the people. The woman listened but did not understand how an army could bring the rains.

The woman's eldest son came to her and said he was going to become a soldier.

But you're just a child, she said.

The army has a whole division just for children, he said. I'm already too old for it. I will have to join the men.

She saw his thin chest surge with pride as he said this, and her heart ached.

So he left and she knew she would not see him again. Soon another son left to join his brother. It was the one who had drunk the tainted water; he waved as he walked up the dusty road and she could see he was trying to smile for her, but his facial muscles were frozen in a sneer.

One of the younger boys announced that he was going to join the children's army. She forbade it. He ran away in the night.

She heard rumors of fighting, the people's army fighting the government's, factions of the people's army fighting each other. There was an outbreak of fever in the village and many people died, including her youngest son.

So she had three sons left. Then two more went off to fight. They went together; that, at least, was a comfort.

Don't become a soldier, she told her last remaining son.

I don't want to, he said, but they will force me to if I stay.

She knew. She had seen boys being dragged down the street, people averting their eyes. But she did not want him to leave.

He told her he wanted to go to the capital. He asked for money to get there. She would not give it to him, but he stole it and left while she slept. He was a hundred miles from home when the bus skidded off the road and rolled over.

Now the daughter she didn't want was all she had. The woman was not so much bitter as resigned to her fate; she suspected she was being punished for her thoughts at the girl's birth. All the furious love the woman had lavished on her sons she now poured on her daughter, and for the first time Precious's name seemed justified.

The daughter cowered under the assault, after the years in her brothers' shadows. She had been accustomed to being invisible. Her mother's attention now seemed like a burden; she missed the airy feeling of being disposable, inconsequential.

The woman did not speak of her sons at home. To the others in the village she bemoaned her losses. But you are lucky, people said. You still have a child. Still alive. Many of us have none left. You are one of the lucky ones.

Yes, she said, I suppose I am.

The woman who had never been afraid now began to fear that her one last child would be taken from her. She tried to hide her daughter, disguise her value, shield her from anyone who might take her away.

She stopped calling her daughter by her name and instead used "Sister."

Precious did not mind. Her mother seemed determined to name her exactly what she was not.

The woman closed her doors and kept her happiness close and hidden, a miser with her hoard.

. . .

The soldier appeared at the door, and before Precious could say a word he cried out how he'd missed her and hugged her to him. He smelled like a week's worth of sweat, and when he smiled his cheeks stretched into taut creases that looked like they might split at any moment. Don't you remember me? he said. Of course she didn't. She'd never seen him before.

He did the same to her mother, embracing her before she could resist. Precious saw her mother's face, propped on the man's shoulder, the eyes closed, and for just a moment her mother looked blissful. Then the eyes opened and her mother's face hardened again.

It's good to be home, he said.

He's lying, Precious said sullenly.

Her mother knew it too. And yet she cooked him a meal and allowed him to stay the night. She kept closing her eyes for a few seconds at a time; Precious knew she was imagining that it was true, that one of her sons really had come home.

In the dark of early morning Precious heard a creak and felt a breath on her shoulder. A finger found its way beneath her blanket; it pointed and beckoned. She turned over. And then everything happened fast, before she could say a word, like a gourd cracked open and the pulp scooped out, to be replaced by something else.

In the morning the woman arose to find her imposter son gone and her daughter too. One of them had taken all the money she had.

This is the story the daughter tells to her unseen audience, the listener swaying in a travel hammock made of her own flesh. She tells the story over and over, the rhythm of her voice matching the rocking rhythm of her legs, hoping he will understand.

2. DURING

"If you're an illegal," the man says, "the only absolutely sure-fire way to get into America is to stow away inside a woman's belly."

She asks him what he means. He tells her that anyone born on American soil is automatically a citizen. "Doesn't matter who or what the parents are."

"But what happens to the baby's mother? She's the mother of a citizen now."

"Doesn't matter," he says. "Anyone without papers, if they catch you they'll deport you. And they *will* catch you. Probably take your baby away."

Her hands slide down the front of her dress.

He narrows his eyes. "You seem determined." She nods. "Do you know how to swim? Ever been chased by dogs? Can you run fast on those pretty legs?" She nods; she has never done the first two, but surely they are instinctive. Surely, under duress, her body will know what to do.

"Will you still be able to run fast in a month? Two?" he says and with a sudden brisk movement cups his hand against her stomach.

"Yes," she says, trying not to flinch.

"I might just be able to help you," he says. "How much money do you have?"

. . .

She wants to go to America. She's heard they give you a free dishwasher the minute you cross the border. In American stores there is always a hundred of everything, food as far as the eye can see, more food than you could eat in a lifetime. There is plenty of work for anyone who wants it, because the Americans are the laziest people on earth and will do nothing they can pay someone else to do for them.

Once you get there, everyone agrees, the rest is easy. Soon you'll be a lazy American yourself, having fat children and buying furniture. Furniture? Yes, a woman tells her, in America if you want furniture, a refrigerator, even a car, you can pay a tenth of the price and take the things home; the Americans will trust you to pay the rest later. They are as trusting and gullible as children.

The visions of abundance keep her up at night. It's not for herself that she wants these things. It's for her baby. She knows he is a son, riding high inside her; with every breath she feels his heels crowding against her lungs.

Months earlier, when she told her cousin she was pregnant, her cousin hugged her and said, "Don't worry. We'll take care of it. I know two good ways. One hurts less but takes longer. The other hurts a lot but is over quick. Which do you want?"

"No!" she cried. "Neither," she said, pushing her cousin away.

She cannot even contemplate getting rid of the baby. She loves him already, has begun crooning to him and addressing conversations to her belly long before she starts to show. But as her son pushes out the front of her dress farther and farther, she begins to wonder. Does she want to raise her son in a country where half the babies die before they are a year old? A country where a woman could have eight children and consider herself lucky if one survives to adulthood?

She begins collecting stories of America. She builds a house in her mind, furnishes it, plants trees outside. She imagines her son, fat and white, playing on a vast expanse of immaculate carpet. She sees him as a boy, big and healthy and strong, wearing stiff brand-new clothes, pushing the other boys so they fall down. She pictures him when he's her age—by American standards, still a child, he'll be going to school, playing with his friends, whistling at girls, and trying to put his hand up their short American skirts.

For some reason, whenever she pictures her son he is bald, his head white and oversized and glowing slightly, like an enormous lightbulb. She puts a baseball cap on him. Better.

"You're crazy," her cousin says. "They'll take your baby away and give him to some American parents. They'll snatch him away the minute you get there and send you back. Americans love foreign babies."

"Love to *eat* them," the cousin's friend says. "At least that's what I've heard."

"Do you want your baby taken away and raised by foreigners?" her cousin says.

Of course not, she says, and suddenly realizes she does.

. . .

She sees the strange man again and asks if he can help her.

"You want to cross over," he says. She gives him half a nod.

"You're in luck. It's a side business of mine, arranging these things."

She looks around to see if anyone is listening.

"Just remember," he says, "there are no guarantees. If they catch you and deport you, I don't give you your money back. If they catch you, I don't know you. I've never seen you before in my life."

She nods. The first time she met him he was wearing a flowered shirt and a baseball cap like the one her son wears in her daydreams. Today he is wearing a cowboy hat and a nice-looking suit. When he turns to go she sees that it is all crumpled in the back, riding up into his armpits.

She tries, and fails, to remember his eyes. She thinks he has a mustache.

. . .

They meet again so she can give him the money, and he asks for her name.

"Precious," she says, and looks away. She does not like to reveal her name; she senses it is dangerous for anyone to know her true worth. Precious is the name of someone treasured, adored. It means there are people somewhere who would gladly pay ransom for her, rescue her from a tower, lay down their lives for her. This is not true, but it is what people assume. She's afraid he'll raise his price.

But he grins a wide face-creasing grin. He thinks they're playing a game, giving themselves nicknames. "Then call me Hopper," he says. "First name Border. And what about"—he nods at the front of her dress—"what about Junior there?"

She stares back at him stonily refusing to acknowledge anything.

"You know," he says softly, "they don't like it. They don't like this kind of thing."

"What thing?"

"What you're trying to do. They see it as an abuse of the system. They'll try to stop you."

"I don't care."

"Good!" he says, breaking into a smile again. Today he is wearing grease-stained coveralls such as a car mechanic would wear and, beneath it, incongruously, a spotless white dress shirt. In a brisk businesslike voice, he says, "We here at Hopper and Associates have many options to offer the busy traveler. Would you prefer plane, train, boat, or automobile? Business class or coach? Smoking or nonsmoking?"

She turns the choices over in her mind. "I've never been on a boat."

"I'm joking, sweetie."

"Yes," she says. "I knew that."

. . .

She sees the border in her dreams: an orange stripe, wide as a road, dividing a desert from horizon to horizon. The border is hot; people run across it screaming in pain, their shoes smoking. The border guards are lined up in pairs on the other side, each pair with a swatch of black rubbery webbing stretched between them. The moment someone reaches their side of the border, two guards snag him and slingshot him back to the other side. The guards are neat and precise; nobody gets through. The people pick themselves up and try again, running across the scalding line. Again and again they are repulsed. Some are flung through the air; some are sent skidding across the border on their faces. The people tire, they are staggering, crawling, propping each other up. The guards continue their work mechanically, occasionally pausing to take a man's wallet or fondle a woman's breast before sending them back over. There is something about the guards' alert, smooth movements that seems familiar, as if she's seen all this before.

. . .

She must work out the timing of the crossing as precisely as possible. If she goes too soon, it will mean spending more time, pregnant and waiting, on the other side. The longer she's there, the greater the chances the deportation people will catch her and send her back before her son is even born.

But if she waits too long he'll be born outside the border, on un-American soil, and will never get his baseball cap, his citizenship.

She has told her son about America, told him about her plans. Told him the story of a woman and her seven stolen sons. That's what you can look forward to, she told him, if we stay. She hopes she can count on his cooperation.

. . .

The man, Hopper, doesn't care about her plans. "You'll go when I tell you to go," he says. "You can't control these things. You have to seize opportunities as they arise."

She waits and waits. Apparently the opportunities are slow to bubble up. She's in her ninth month when the time comes. She rides a bus to a border town, arrives at the meeting place.

She and six others cram into a secret space behind a false panel in the back of a delivery truck. There are a few nail holes for air. They are afraid to talk; when one makes the slightest noise the others pinch him, roll their eyes. They are all strangers to one another. Their initial excessive courtesy dissipates with the rising heat. The metal walls are like an oven. One man insists on smoking. The two people on either side of Precious accuse her of taking up too much room.

There are delays; the truck stops and starts, the back door opens and closes. At first they all freeze expectantly every time this happens. But the stops continue. Precious begins to wonder if the driver has forgotten about them and is going about his usual deliveries.

Night falls, they know this when dots of light in the nail holes go out and they are in total blackness. No one lets them out.

The second day is more of the same. One man wants to bang on the walls; they've forgotten us, he says. The others restrain him. The heat rises and they squabble silently over the last plastic jug of water.

On the third day they all fall into a stupor, frozen in positions of cramped despair. The only one stirring is Precious's son, kicking impatiently. On the evening of the third day they cross the border without knowing it.

It is dark again when the truck stops, footsteps approach, the metal door is wrenched back. They blink in the glare of a flashlight as the driver helps them out. He tries to make them hurry but they cannot unfold themselves. He carries them out one by one, like statues in tortured poses, and places them on the ground, where they lie unmoving for a long time and then begin to uncurl as slowly as new leaves unfurling.

They lie on hard earth surrounded by trees. The truck disappears down a dirt track leading back to the highway. They begin to groan and creak and stretch themselves—small things first, fingers and toes. Precious stands up and leans against a tree. She tries walking a few steps. The movement makes something shift within her, then shift again, sinking lower, like the tumblers of a lock falling into place. Good, she thinks. Right on time.

She heads down the track toward the highway. The others call after her, warnings, halfhearted offers of help. She knows they're glad to be rid of her. She's a burden, a liability.

She walks along the highway. So far America is a disappointment, bare and empty. It'll get better, she tells herself. Americans, she knows, are optimistic. She thinks of big white gleaming American hospitals.

She waves at the occasional cars zooming past. She can't see the drivers' faces. If she were in their place she wouldn't stop either, she thinks. Who wants a strange woman having a baby all over your nice clean American car?

But within minutes a car pulls over to the shoulder ahead of her. She clutches her son, tries to walk more quickly. Americans really are friendly after all.

The car is a dull gray, dirty, unremarkable, and she's close before she notices the heavy wire mesh separating the backseat from the front. The driver has already stepped out of the car and has his hand on her arm before she can think of running.

He helps her into the backseat and drives on. He doesn't seem surprised to see her, seems to know exactly who she is and what she's doing. He's driving in the same direction she'd been heading. At first she thinks he's going to help her after all; then she realizes that they are heading back to the border, that she'd been pointed in the wrong direction.

She's still hopeful. Everyone says even when you get caught, they make you stay in a detention center for weeks while they ask you questions and write words on pieces of paper. She'll have her baby and then go home.

But that's not allowed to happen. She's rushed through a series of gates and hallways and waiting rooms, and people ask her questions and eye her belly and hustle her along. Before she knows it she's sitting in a van with other defeated-looking people who don't meet her eyes. She recognizes two of the people who shared her secret place in the delivery truck but pretends not to.

This time she can see the boarder as they cross it. It's not how she pictured it. Just a fence, a checkpoint on the road. She holds her belly. Her son is shifting around. Not yet, she thinks fiercely. Not yet.

. . .

She looks for the Hopper man. She assumes he would have disappeared by now, but no, there he is. "Don't be mad, little mama," he says. "I told you there were no guarantees."

She stamps her foot. The pressure inside her is unbelievable. But she wills her body to hold itself together.

"Tell you what," he says. "How about I set up another trip for you? Free of charge? Because I'm such a nice guy?"

"Not the truck. The driver was bad. I think he told the border police where to find us."

"That's terrible," the man says. "You just can't trust anyone, can you? I won't use him again."

. . .

The second time is on a boat, a huge boat, a cargo ship. She doesn't know what it's carrying; the cargo could be anything; it's packed into truck-sized metal rectangles, stacked up in anonymous piles.

She and twelve others hide in the hold. It's dank, dark, cramped, but the gentle motion of the boat soothes her; this is what it must feel like for her son, she thinks.

Her son is very still. She worries that he is dead, but she tells herself that it's only because he's grown too big, has no room to move. Just a little longer, she thinks, and then you can come out and begin your new life. Some people told her America's territory extends from its coastline, fifty miles into the ocean. Others have said five miles. She wants to wait for solid land to be absolutely sure.

But they're stopped almost immediately. She and the others are sought out with flashlights, led up to the deck, and lowered into a smaller boat that speeds them back to the harbor. She would have tried to run, to hide, if not for her son. Any violent motion, she fears, will bring him tumbling out. If she jumped in the water, he might swim right out of her to play in the familiar element.

. . .

"My goodness," the Hopper man says when he sees her. "Are you having twins?"

"Your boat people are bad," she says furiously. "They told the border people we were there."

"You don't say! I certainly won't be using their services anymore."

"I think the border people pay them money to turn us in. A price for each person."

"What makes you think that?"

She has heard people arguing, pointing at her and arguing over whether she should bring the price of one or two.

"We'll get you over there," the man says. "I give you my promise. Three's the charm."

. . .

The next time, she rides in a hiding place built between the backseat and trunk of a small car. They have trouble shutting her in; her belly gets in the way. It seems luxurious, after the first two trips. She has the space to herself. A man and woman sit in the front. On the backseat, inches from her, a baby coos in a car seat. She doesn't know if it's their baby or someone else's, a borrowed prop. Her son shifts irritably, probably sensing the other baby, probably thinking, Now *that's* the way to travel.

At the border they're stopped, the trunk is opened. The panel is ripped away, and for the third time she's blinking in bright light. She imagines her son beating his fists against the sides of her womb.

Not yet, she thinks, not yet, my son. Just a little longer.

. . .

She's now nearing the end of her tenth month. Her belly is strained to the breaking point, her back aches, her knees buckle. But she's more determined than ever. And her son seems to be as stubborn as he is.

"Now it looks like quadruplets," Hopper says.

"He's going to be an American baby," she says, through gritted teeth. "Babies are bigger there. A nice big healthy American baby."

"Is that what he told you?"

"He's not going to come out until we get there," she says.

"I'll do what I can," he says. "No guarantees."

She's been told there are places where you can climb over the fence. There are places where there is no fence, only guards in towers who sometimes look the other way. She's going to take her chances on her own. Enough of his gambles.

"I wish you the best," he says, tipping his fishing hat.

. . .

She can barely walk; she stumbles, lurching and weaving. Other people look at her and say, "There's no way. It's impossible." She ignores them.

She walks, through scrub brush and rocks and burning sand and stagnant, stinking water. She walks and walks, thinking: American baby. Nice big American baby.

She hears a sound echoing from far away: dogs yelping, frenzied. She can almost hear them calling to one another: *There she is, there she is, get her.*

They burst over a rise and she can see them, a mob of dark insects growing rapidly bigger, a man with a gun trailing far behind. Has she crossed the border already? It's impossible to tell.

The first dog runs straight at her. She stands still and waits. It seems nearly as big as she is, a small horse. At the last minute it veers away and circles. All the dogs swarm around her. But they do not touch her. They keep their heads lowered abjectly to the ground. They seem in awe of her big belly.

The fat sweating guard who comes puffing up behind them is not impressed. Soon she's sitting in a familiar van, heading back.

. . .

She's been carrying her son for over a year now, with no intention of letting him go.

"Now, that can't possibly be good for him, little mama," Hopper says. "You should let the little feller out."

"He's going to be an *American* baby," she says slowly, as if talking to a child.

"Let me help you," he says. "I know a man—"

"No," she says.

"We'll try another way. I can get you a fake passport."

"No," she says. She hobbles back to the border, is stopped by a fence, and begins tunneling under it, clawing the dirt with her fingernails. She's crawling through, nearly breaking the surface on the other side, when her son shifts, or perhaps instantaneously grows a fraction of an inch, and suddenly she's stuck. Border guards come and drag her out by her heels. They don't seem surprised, they seem as if they've been expecting her. They look bored, almost disappointed, as if they'd expected her to have a little more originality.

. . .

"Why won't you let me help you?" Hopper says.

She doesn't answer.

"Free of charge."

"Why are you being so generous?"

"I don't know. Out of the goodness of my heart?"

Today he's wearing a bolo tie, a snakeskin vest. He is wearing rings on every finger, like a king, like a pirate. Like a pirate king.

"Please," he says. "I *want* to. I insist."

She realizes something she should have seen months ago. He's been tipping off the border guards. He takes money from people for helping them cross; then he takes money from the guards for telling them when and where to expect visitors. She's been making money for him with each of her trips.

"You are a bad man," she says.

"Oh, come now," he says. "You can't blame me. It's a game of chance."

"An evil man. When my son gets big he'll come back and kill you."

"Your son's already big," he says. "And I don't see him doing anything."

. . .

She is determined. She flings herself at the border again and again. She travels in cars, trucks, buses. She walks on blistered feet. She travels in a fishing boat, an inflatable raft. She wears disguises, buys false papers. Each time the border repulses her, spits her back.

Big American baby, she tells herself. She sees his size as proof of his American-ness. Only American babies could be so big, so healthy. She has convinced herself that he has always been American, that she is merely a vehicle, a shell, a seed casing meant to protect him until he can be planted in his rightful home.

She carries him for two years. She constructs a sort of sling for herself, with shoulder straps and a strip of webbing, to balance the weight. She uses a cane. She looks like a spider, round fat body, limbs like sticks.

Her son is alive; she can feel the pulse of his heartbeat, feel the pressure as he strains to stretch a finger, an eyelid.

She thinks she can see a dark shadow through the taut translucent skin of her belly. She can see his hair growing long and black.

Her body is adaptable. Her skin stretches, her bones shift, her blood feeds him. When people see her they are amazed, but she is not; she has seen it before, the lengths the body will go to to preserve itself, to cling to life.

Big American baby, she thinks. Nice big American baby. It is her mantra.

She carries him for three years. Three and a half. She becomes a legend, then a joke, with the border guards. They wave to her as she creeps past, cheer her on, drag her back at the last minute.

Don't you think he wants to come out by now? people at home say to her.

He's safer living in my belly than in this wretched country, she says, though she has been so single-mindedly set on her mission that she has taken no notice of external events. War, famine, peace, prosperity: it is all the same to her. America is the only option, the only ray of hope.

She carries him for four years.

Big American baby. Nice big American baby.

She has in her mind pictures of hot-air balloons attached to bicycles, fanciful flying machines. Some days she imagines she will simply lift off the ground and float over, suspended by the power of her will alone. Hers and her son's. Or she imagines that she is invisible, intangible; she breezes across the border. The air, it seems, is the only thing that crosses freely.

Her son is so big, she imagines he fills her completely, his arms fill her arms, his legs fill her legs. She is a mere skin covering him, like an insect's carapace, soon to be flaked off and shucked away.

She's too tired to speak now, just pants and whistles through her teeth. The words rattle in her head.

Nice big American baby, someone chants. Not her. Him. The voice of her son gurgling up from her belly. Muffled and airless but undeniable.

My son's first words, she thinks, smiling proudly at a shriveled bush. You hear that? No baby-talk preliminaries, no babbling or lisping. My son; so precocious, so American.

One day, as she is panting out her mantra and picking her way across the sand, a border guard appears: suddenly, as if he sprang up out of the ground. He carries the usual gun, wears the usual impenetrable sunglasses, has the regulation sweat stains blooming from his armpits. He takes her arm. She obediently turns around and begins walking back. She does not want him to start pushing her, getting rough; the baby might come out.

But to her surprise she finds him pulling her forward, forward across the magic invisible line. Forward, toward the magnificent city that hovers like a mirage in the distance.

"Come on, little mama," he says. "You've had enough."

.

When she closes her eyes she sees the hospital of her dreams, a white sparkling grand hotel. When she opens them she sees speckled ceiling tiles, masked alien faces. She can't feel a thing; she's a floating head. It's finally happened, then: her stubborn impatient head has taken off and left the slow body behind somewhere to gestate, egg and nest all in one.

"My son," she says.

"He's coming," they tell her. They have to operate. "There's no way he's fitting through the usual door," they tell her.

She sees a foot kicking. It's as long as her hand. She hears a stupendous, deafening roar. The foot catches one of the masked doctors on the chin and sends him flying backward into the spattered arms of another masked figure.

Her balloon head is bobbing near the ceiling now, borne on the baby's howls, but she'd swear she can hear, interspersed with the empty cries, bellowed words. I want, the baby demands. Give me, I want, I need, I deserve, I have *earned* . . .

She sees rising up out of her tired body a sodden mop of long black hair. She sees grasping fists.

She hears—and surely she must be dreaming now—she hears the scrape of a rubber-gloved hand rubbing a sore chin and a doctor's voice saying, "Now *that's* what I call a nice big American baby."

. . .

Empty, deflated, she sits alone in the back of the van. She hears weeping somewhere, mingled with the sounds of tires on asphalt. It must be the driver. It can't be her. Can it? Impossible. There's nothing inside her to come out, not a drop. She's hollow, she's still floating, they forgot to reattach her head to those rags and remnants that were her body.

"But it's what you wanted, isn't it? Wasn't that the whole plan, give birth and leave him here with a new set of folks?"

"I never even got a chance to hold him."

"He's too big for holding already. He could hold you."

"I had things to say. Stories to tell him."

"He heard them. He was listening, all those years when you talked to him. He'll remember."

It's the voice of the Hopper man; she's not sure if he's the man driving the van or if the voice is inside her head. It doesn't matter.

"I want to stay," she whispers. "He's mine."

"You can always have another."

3. AFTER

The prospective parents had applied for a newborn baby, so they did not know what to make of the walking, talking child they visited at the temporary foster home. The adoption agent assured them he had been born only a few days earlier. "I have his birth certificate right here," she said.

Maybe children these days grow up faster than they used to, the hopeful parents told themselves. We should have studied the child development book more carefully, they thought.

They did not voice their doubts, fearing they'd reveal their inexperience, their ignorance. One slip of the tongue and their application would be rejected.

They felt intimidated by the adoption agent, who handled babies as carelessly as basketballs, and also by the foster mother, who had eight children in her charge.

The prospective mother had been looking forward to the cuddling, burping, nurturing years; she'd been gearing herself up for sleepless nights of colic and lullabies and martyrdom. The child before them, calmly regarding them with large brown eyes, was already far beyond that stage. Yet there was something so appealing, so desirable, so eminently *wantable* about him that both prospective parents found themselves smitten. They *had* to have him. He sat on the carpet knocking one block against another, seemingly bored, covertly watchful. They both felt a quickening in their hearts: the anxiety of bargain hunting—the sensation that if they did not get him immediately, someone else would come along, perceive his value, and snatch him up.

When they brought him home he ran through the house pointing at things, wanting to learn their names. "Microwave," they said. "Piano." "Baby monitor." "Treadmill." "Shoe tree." "Television."

They were charmed by his curiosity. Privately they fretted over the way he stiffened whenever they touched him. He was remote, as patiently tolerant as a teenager suffering the whims of unhip parents.

He just needs time, they thought, to get used to us.

What does bonding mean, *exactly?* the new mother wondered. She thought of the unknown woman, the biological mother who'd carried the boy inside her body for nine whole months, and realized she was jealous.

The boy was too well-behaved, too precocious, too perfect. It made them nervous. His perfection made him seem vulnerable, ripe for spoiling. Doesn't it seem like the perfect, angelic little boys are always the ones to get cancer, get hit by cars? the mother thought.

He never made any mistakes. If there were mistakes to be made, they'd be made by the parents. So they washed everything twice, planned educational vacations. The pressure was excruciating.

He'd been their son for over a year when he told them about the face.

He appeared at their bedside in the middle of the night, white and glowing in his astronaut pajamas. "Can I come in?" he said.

They relished the moment, kissing him, tickling him, tucking him in between them.

"Did you have a bad dream?" the mother said.

"There was a face in the window," the boy said, and described glittering eyes and shining teeth and a wiry net of hair, long fingers scrabbling at the sill and warm breath that seeped into the room. A sad face. It watched him for a long time, he said, not moving.

"It isn't real," the father said. "It's only a dream."

The mother thought of goblins, gypsies, pirates, a hundred fairy tales of stolen children. She tightened her grip. "We'll protect you," she whispered fervently. "We'll never let anyone take you away."

"Take me away?" the boy said. The father groaned softly.

She realized she'd made a blunder, planting a new fear in his head that had not been there before.

The next day the father made a great show of testing the locks on the boy's bedroom window. He pointed out the tree branches that moved in the wind like hair. He talked about the damp smells rising up from the basement, the stink and scrabbling of skunks digging through the garbage cans. The boy listened impassively.

For the next few nights the boy slept peacefully. The parents did not.

And then he was back, glowing in the dark, his feet padding across the floor. "It's back," he said calmly. They lifted their covers for him, pleased that he was finally having the normal problems of a normal child.

The face came back periodically. Not often, but every few weeks. The parents tried to dispel the son's fears, but with less and less enthusiasm as time went on. They worried that if the nightmares stopped, the tenuous intimacy with their son would be gone forever. The mother, in her heart of hearts, secretly made contingency plans—if his nightmares stopped, she'd simulate them (a Halloween mask dangled from the roof, say).

If she left the imprint of a finger in his sandwich, her son would eat around it and leave the little island on his plate. He continued to flinch at the touch of her hand. Still, she sometimes wondered if he was secretly starved for affection, if he'd fabricated the face story as an excuse.

Or maybe, she thought, he'd invented the face as a way of comforting *them.* She wouldn't put it past him, her wise little son.

In the night she stroked her son's shoulders and kissed the top of his head. She wrapped her arms around him and pretended he was inside her.

The next morning she went into his room to make the bed and found the window open and the curtains frothing in the wind. She felt a momentary panic—danger! falling baby!—but the window guard was still in place. She closed the window and locked it. As she was turning away she noticed fingerprints spotting the glass. She must have done that herself, just now. How careless. I'll clean it later, she thought, and bent to the bed, brushing away a few of her son's long black hairs.

To her surprise, she found the bottom sheet damp. Never before had her son wet the bed. She dipped her fingers in the wet spot, feeling fascinated, amazed, intensely maternal. My son, she thought proudly, wets the bed. She imagined telling a friend about it. *Oh, yes, like any normal child, he wets the bed occasionally. When he has a nightmare. What can you do? No, of course we're not worried about it. He'll outgrow it eventually.*

But still there was something strange about it . . . The stain was perfectly clear; it looked like water. And rather than one spot it was composed of many, a string of drops.

She glanced around furtively to make sure she was alone, then raised her wet fingers to her nose. She smelled nothing. She put her fingers to her tongue. The wetness tasted like tears.

2005

Reference Works, Bibliographies

Abrahams, Roger, and Szwed, John. *Afro-American Folk Culture,* 1978.

Alexander, Harriet. *American and British Poetry: A Guide to the Criticism, 1979–1990,* 1996.

Andrews, William L., and others, eds. *The Oxford Companion to African American Literature,* 1997.

Atlick, Richard D., and Wright, Andrew. *Selective Bibliography for the Study of English and American Literature,* 6th edition, 1979.

Bain, Robert, and Flora, Joseph M. *Fifty Southern Writers Before 1900,* 1987.

———. *Fifty Southern Writers After 1900,* 1987.

Beidler, Peter G., and Egge, Marion F. *The American Indian in Short Fiction: An Annotated Bibliography,* 1979.

Bercovitch, Sacvan, ed. *The Cambridge History of American Literature,* 2 vols., 1994.

Benardete, Jane, ed. *American Realism,* 1972.

Biblowitz, Iris, ed. *Women and Literature: An Annotated Bibliography of Women Writers,* 3rd edition, 1976.

Blanck, Jacob. *Bibliography of American Literature,* Vols. I–, 1955–.

Bordman, Gerald. *The Oxford Companion to American Theatre,* 1984.

Brown, Julie, ed. *American Short Story Writers,* 1995.

Bryer, J. R., ed. *Sixteen Modern American Authors: A Survey of Research and Criticism,* 1973.

Burke, W. J., and Howe, W. D. *American Authors and Books,* revised by Irving Weiss, 1962.

Charters, Ann, ed. *The Beats: Literary Bohemians in Postwar America,* 2 parts, 1983.

Clark, H. H. *American Literature: Poe Through Garland,* 1971.

Colonnese, Tom, and Owens, Louise, eds. *American Indian Novelists: An Annotated Critical Bibliography,* 1985.

Davidson, Cathy, and others, eds. *The Oxford Companion to Women's Writing in the United States,* 1995.

Davis, R. B. *American Literature Through Bryant,* 1969.

Davis, Thadious M., and Harris, Trudier, eds. *Afro-American Fiction Writers after 1955,* 1984.

———. *Afro-American Writers after 1955: Dramatists and Prose Writers,* 1985.

Duke, Maurice, and others, eds. *American Women Writers: Bibliographical Essays,* 1983.

Erisman, Fred, and Etulain, Richard, eds. *Fifty Western Writers: A Bio-Bibliographical Sourcebook,* 1982.

Etheridge, James M., and Kapala, Barbara, eds. *Contemporary Authors: A Bio-Bibliographical Guide . . .,* 1962– (a continuing series).

Etulain, Richard. *A Bibliographical Guide to the Study of Western American Literature,* 1982.

Fabre, Genevieve. *Afro-American Poetry and Drama, 1760–1975,* 1979.
Flora, Joseph M. and Bain, Robert. *Contemporary Fiction Writers of the South: A Bio-Bibliographical Sourcebook,* 1993.
French, William P., ed. *Afro-American Poetry and Drama, 1760–1975,* 1979.
Frye, Northrop, and others, eds. *The Harper Handbook to Literature,* 2nd edition, 1997.
Gerstenberger, Donna, and Hendrick, George. *The American Novel: A Checklist of Twentieth-Century Criticism on Novels Written Since 1789,* 2 vols., 1961, 1970.
Gohdes, Clarence. *Literature and Theater in the States and Regions of the U.S.A.: An Historical Bibliography,* 1967.
Gohdes, Clarence, and Marovitz, Sanford. *Bibliographical Guide to the Study of the Literature of the U.S.A.,* 5th edition, 1983.
Gossin, Pamela. *Encyclopedia of Literature and Science,* 2002.
Greiner, Donald J., ed. *American Poets Since World War II,* 2 parts, 1980.
Gwynn, R. S., ed. *American Poets Since World War II,* Second Series, 1991.
Handlin, Oscar, and others. *Harvard Guide to American History,* 1954.
Hanna, Archibald. *A Mirror for the Nation: An Annotated Bibliography of American Social Fiction, 1901–1950,* 1985.
Harnes, James. *Literary Research Guide: An Annotated Listing of Reference Sources in English Literary Studies,* 4th edition, 2002.
Harold, Jan. *American Folklore: An Encyclopedia,* 1996.
Harris, Trudier, and Davis, Thadious M., eds. *Afro-American Poets Since 1955,* 1985.
Harris, Trudier, ed. *Afro-American Writers Before the Harlem Renaissance,* 1986.
———. *Afro-American Writers from the Harlem Renaissance to 1940,* 1987.
Hart, J. D., and Leininger, Philip. *The Oxford Companion to American Literature,* 6th edition, 1995.
Hatch, James V., and Abdullah, Omanii. *Black Playwrights, 1823–1977,* 1977.
Havelice, Patricia. *Index to American Author Bibliographies,* 1971.
Hawkins-Dady, Mark. *Reader's Guide to Literature in English,* 1996.
Helterman, Jeffrey, and Layman, Richard, eds. *American Novelists Since World War II,* 1978.
Herzberg, M. J., and others. *The Reader's Encyclopedia of American Literature,* 1961.
Hoffman, Daniel, ed. *Harvard Guide to Contemporary American Writing,* 1979.
Holman, C. H. *The American Novel Through Henry James,* 1966.
Holman, C. H., and Harmon, William, eds. *A Handbook to Literature,* 6th edition, 1992.
Howard, Sharon M. *African American Women Fiction Writers, 1859–1986,* 1989.
Inge, M. Thomas, and others, eds. *Black American Writers,* 2 vols., 1978.
Jackson, Blyden, and Rubin, Louis D., Jr., eds. *Black Poetry in America,* 1974.
Jehlen, Myra, and Warner, Michael, eds. *The English Literatures of America, 1500–1800,* 1997.
Jones, H. M., and Ludwig, R. M. *Guide to American Literature and Its Backgrounds Since 1890,* 4th edition, 1972.
Jordan, Casper LeRoy. *Bibliographical Guide to African-American Women Writers,* 1993.
Kanellos, Nicolás. *Biographical Dictionary of Hispanic Literature in the United States,* 1989.

Kibler, James E., Jr., ed. *American Novelists Since World War II,* Second Series, 1980.

Kimbel, Bobby Ellen, ed. *American Short-Story Writers Before 1880,* 1988.

———. *American Short-Story Writers, 1880–1910,* 1988.

———. *American Short-Story Writers, 1910–1945,* Second Series, 1991.

Kolb, Harold. *A Field Guide to the Study of American Literature,* 1976.

Koster, Donald. *American Literature and Language: A Guide to Information Sources,* 1974.

Kunitz, S. J., and Haycraft, Howard, eds. *American Authors, 1600–1900,* 1944.

———. *Twentieth Century Authors,* 1942. 1st supplement, 1955.

Kuntz, Joseph. *Poetry Explication,* 1953. Revised 1962.

———. *American Literature: A Study and Research Guide,* 1976.

Larchman, Marvin. *A Reader's Guide to the American Novel of Detection,* 1993.

Leary, Lewis. *Articles on American Literature, 1900–1950,* 1954.

———. *Articles on American Literature, 1950–1967,* 1970.

———. *Articles on American Literature, 1968–1975,* 1979.

Littlefield, Daniel L., ed. *A Biobibliography of Native American Writers, 1771–1924,* 1981.

———. *A Biobibliography of Native American Writers, 1772–1924: A Supplement,* 1985.

Lomeli, Francisco A. and Shirley, Carl R., eds. *Chicano Writers,* First Series, 1989.

Long, E. H. *American Drama from Its Beginning to the Present,* 1970.

Ludwig, Richard M., ed. *Bibliographical Supplement, Literary History of the United States,* 4th edition, revised, 1974.

Ludwig, Richard M., and Nault, Clifford A., Jr. *Annals of American Literature, 1602–1983,* 1986.

MacNicholas, John, ed. *Twentieth-Century American Dramatists,* 2 parts, 1981.

Mainiero, Lina. *American Women Writers: A Critical Reference Guide from Colonial Times to the Present,* 4 vols., 1979–1982.

Malkoff, Karl. *Crowell's Handbook of Contemporary American Poetry,* 1973.

Margolies, Edward, and Bakish, David. *Afro-American Fiction, 1853–1976,* 1979.

Martine, James J., ed. *American Novelists,* 1910–1945, 3 parts, 1981.

Martinez, Julio A., and Lomeli, Francisco A., eds. *Chicano Literature, A Reference Guide,* 1985.

Millet, F. B. *Contemporary American Authors: A Critical Survey and 219 Biographies,* 1940.

Morris, R. B., ed. *Encyclopedia of American History,* 1953.

Myerson, Joel, ed. *The American Renaissance in New England,* 1978.

Myerson, Joel, and Helterman, J., eds. *Dictionary of Literary Biography,* 9 vols., 1978–1983.

Nadel, I. B. *Jewish Writers of North America: A Guide to Information Sources,* 1981.

Nevius, Blake. *The American Novel: Sinclair Lewis to the Present,* 1970.

Nilon, Charles. *Bibliography of Bibliographies of American Literature,* 1970.

Page, James, and Min Roh, Joe. *Selected Black American, African, and Caribbean Authors: A Bio-Bibliography,* 1985.

Palmer, Helen, and Dyson, Jane. *American Drama Criticism,* 1967. Supplement 1970.

Parini, Jay, ed. *The Columbia History of American Poetry,* 1993.
Parker, Patricia. *Early American Fiction: A Reference Guide,* 1984.
Perkins, George, and others, eds. *Benét's Reader's Encyclopedia of American Literature,* 1991.
Perry, Margaret. *The Harlem Renaissance: An Annotated Bibliography,* 1982.
Pizer, Donald, ed. *Documents of American Realism and Naturalism,* 1998.
Pizer, Donald, ed. *The Cambridge Companion to American Realism and Naturalism, Howells to London,* 1995.
Pizer, Donald, and Harbert, Earl N., eds. *American Realists and Naturalists,* 1982.
Quartermain, Peter, ed. *American Poets, 1880–1945,* First Series, 1986.
———. *American Poets, 1880–1945,* Second Series, 1986.
———. *American Poets, 1880–1945,* Third Series, 1987.
Rawlings, Peter, ed. *Americans on Fiction, 1776–1900,* 3 vols., 2002.
Reardon, Joan, and Thorsen, Kristine A. *Poetry by American Women, 1900–1975,* 1979.
Rees, Robert, and Harbert, Earl, eds. *Fifteen American Authors Before 1900,* 1984.
Rock, Roger. *The Native American in American Literature: A Selectively Annotated Bibliography,* 1985.
Rogal, Samuel. *A Chronological Outline of American Literature,* 1987.
Rood, Karen L., and others, eds. *Dictionary of Literary Biography Yearbook: 1980,* 1981– (a continuing annual series).
Rubin, Louis, ed. *A Bibliographical Guide to the Study of Southern Literature,* 1969.
Ruoff, A. LaVonne Brown. *American Indian Literatures: An Introduction, Bibliographic Review, and Selected Bibliography,* 1990.
Rush, T. G., and others, eds. *Black American Writers Past and Present: A Biographical and Bibliographical Dictionary,* 1975.
Sabin, Joseph, and others. *A Dictionary of Books Relating to America from Its Discovery to the Present Time,* 29 vols., 1868–1936.
Salzman, Jack, ed. *Cambridge Handbook of American Literature,* 1986.
Schweik, Robert, and Riesner, Dieter. *Reference Sources in English and American Literature,* 1977.
Sternlicht, Sanford. *A Reader's Guide to Modern American Drama,* 2002.
Stringer, Jenny, ed. *Oxford Companion to Twentieth-Century Literature in English,* 1996.
Thurston, Jarvis, and others. *Short Fiction Criticism,* 1960.
Tompkins, Jane. *Sensational Designs: The Cultural Work of American Fiction, 1790–1860,* 1985.
Trachtenberg, Stanley, ed. *American Humorists, 1800–1950,* 2 parts, 1982.
Turner, Darwin. *Afro-American Writers,* 1970.
Tyler, Gary. *Drama Criticism,* 1966.
Ungar, Leonard. *American Writers: A Collection of Literary Biographies,* 8 vols., 1974–1981.
Vinson, James, ed. *Contemporary Dramatists,* 2nd edition, 1977.
———. *Contemporary Novelists,* 3rd edition, 1980.
———. *Contemporary Poets,* 3rd edition, 1980.
Vinson, James, and Kirkpatrick, D. L. *Twentieth-Century Western Writers,* 1982.
Vrana, Stan. *Interviews and Conversations with Twentieth-Century Authors Writing in English: An Index,* 1982.

Walker, Warren, *Twentieth-Century Short Story Explication,* 3rd edition, 1977; Supplement I, 1980; Supplement II, 1983.
Weixlmann, Joe. *American Short-Fiction Criticism and Scholarship, 1959–1977,* 1982.
White, Barbara A. *American Women Writers: An Annotated Bibliography of Criticism,* 1977.
William, Jerry. *Southern Literature, 1968–1975: A Checklist of Scholarship,* 1978.
Wilmeth, Don B., and Miller, Tice, eds. *Cambridge Guide to American Theatre,* 1993.
Wolfreys, Julian, and others. *The Continuum Encyclopedia of Modern Criticism and Theory,* 2002.
Woodress, James. *Dissertations in American Literature, 1891–1966,* 1968.
———, ed. *Eight American Authors: A Review of Research and Criticism,* revised edition, 1971.
Woodress, James, and others, eds. *American Literary Scholarship: An Annual,* 1965–.
Wright, Lyle. *American Fiction, 1774–1850,* 1948. 2nd edition, 1969.
———. *American Fiction, 1851–1875,* 1957.
———. *American Fiction, 1876–1900,* 1966.

Criticism, Literary and Cultural History

Aaron, Daniel. *Writers on the Left: Episodes in American Literary Communism,* 1961.

———. *The Unwritten War: American Writers and the Civil War,* 1973.

Ahnebrink, Lars. *The Beginnings of Naturalism in American Fiction,* 1961.

Aldridge, John. *After the Lost Generation: A Critical Study of the Writers of Two Wars,* 1951.

Aldridge, Owen. *Early American Literature: A Comparatist Approach,* 1983.

Allen, G. W. *American Prosody,* 1935.

Altieri, Charles. *Enlarging the Temple: New Directions in American Poetry During the 1960s,* 1979.

Anderson, Quentin. *The Imperial Self,* 1971.

Auchincloss, Louis. *Pioneers and Caretakers: A Study of Nine American Women Novelists,* 1965.

Baumbach, Jonathan. *The Landscape of Nightmare: Studies in the Contemporary American Novel,* 1965.

Baym, Nina. *American Women Writers and the Work of History,* 1995.

Beach, J. W. *American Fiction: 1920–1940,* 1941.

Bell, Bernard W. *The Afro-American Novel and Its Tradition,* 1988.

Bercovitch, Sacvan, ed. *The Revaluation of Puritanism,* 1974.

———. *The Puritan Origins of the American Self,* 1975.

Berthoff, Warner. *The Ferment of Realism: American Literature, 1884–1919,* 1965.

———. *A Literature Without Qualities: American Writing Since 1945,* 1979.

Bewley, Marius. *The Complex Fate,* 1954.

———. *The Eccentric Design,* 1959.

Bigsby, C. W. E. *A Critical Introduction to Twentieth-Century American Drama,* Vol. I, 1900–1940, 1982.

Blair, Walter, ed. *Native American Humor,* 2nd edition, 1960.

Bogan, Louise. *Achievement in American Poetry, 1900–1950,* 1951.

Bone, R. A. *The Negro Novel in America,* revised edition, 1965.

Bradbury, John. *Renaissance in the South,* 1963.

Bradbury, Malcolm. *The Modern American Novel,* 1983.

Breslin, James. *From Modern to Contemporary American Poetry, 1945–1965,* 1984.

Bridgman, Richard. *The Colloquial Style in America,* 1966.

Brooks, Peter. *Reading for the Plot: Design and Intention in Narrative,* 1985.

Brooks, Van Wyck. *The Flowering of New England, 1815–1865,* 1937.

———. *New England: Indian Summer, 1865–1915,* 1940.

———. *The Times of Melville and Whitman,* 1947.

———. *The Confident Years: 1885–1915,* 1955.

Brown, H. R. *The Sentimental Novel in America, 1789–1860,* 1940.

Brown, Sterling. *Negro Poetry and Drama,* 1937.

Buell, Lawrence. *Literary Transcendentalism,* 1973.

———. *New England Literary Culture,* 1986.

Byerman, Keith. *Fingering the Jagged Grain: Tradition and Form in Recent Black Fiction,* 1985.
Cady, E. H. *The Light of Common Day: Realism in American Fiction,* 1971.
Canby, H. S. *Classic Americans,* 1958.
Cargill, Oscar. *Intellectual America: Ideas on the March,* 1941.
Carter, Everett. *The American Idea,* 1977.
Cassuto, Leonard. *The Inhuman Race: The Racial Grotesque in American Literature,* 1996.
Chase, Richard. *The American Novel and Its Tradition,* 1957.
Clark, H. H., ed. *Transitions in American Literary History,* 1954.
Commager, H. S. *The American Mind,* 1950.
Cowie, Alexander. *The Rise of the American Novel,* 1948.
Cowley, Malcolm. *After the Genteel Tradition: American Writers, 1910–1930,* revised edition, 1964.
———. *A Second Flowering: Works and Days of the Lost Generation,* 1973.
Cunliffe, Marcus. *The Literature of the United States,* 1967, 1984.
Curti, Merle. *The Growth of American Thought,* 3rd edition, 1964.
Davidson, Cathy. *Revolution and the Word: The Rise of the Novel in America,* 1986; 2nd edition, 2004.
Davis, Richard. *Intellectual Life in the Colonial South, 1585–1763,* 1977.
Davis, Thadious, and Harris, Trudier. *Afro-American Literary Critics: An Introduction,* 1984.
Dekker, George. *The American Historical Romance,* 1988.
Dembo, L. S. *Conceptions of Reality in Modern American Poetry,* 1966.
Drake, William. *The First Wave: Women Poets in America, 1915–1945,* 1987.
Edel, Leon. *The Psychological Novel, 1900–1950,* 1955.
Eisdein, Gregory, *Literature and Humanitarian Reform in the Civil War Era,* 1996.
Eisinger, Chester. *Fiction of the Forties,* 1963.
Elder, John. *Imagining the Earth: Poetry and the Vision of Nature,* 1985.
Elliott, Emory. *American Colonial Writers, 1735–1781,* 1984.
———. *American Writers of the Early Republic,* 1984.
———. *Colonial Writers, 1606–1734,* 1984.
———. *The Columbia History of the American Novel: New Views,* 1991.
———. *The Cambridge Introduction to Early American Literature,* 2002.
Elliott, Emory, and others, eds. *Columbia Literary History of the United States,* 1988.
Emerson, Everett, ed. *Major Writers of Early American Literature,* 1972.
———. ed. *American Literature, 1764–1789: The Revolutionary Years,* 1977.
———. *Puritanism in America, 1620–1750,* 1977.
Fabre, Genevieve. *Afro-American Poetry and Drama,* 1760–1975, 1979.
Falk, Robert. *The Victorian Mode in American Fiction, 1865–1885,* 1965.
Feidelson, Charles. *Symbolism and American Literature,* 1959.
Feller, Daniel. *The Jacksonian Promise: America 1815–1840,* 1995.
Felperin, Howard. *Beyond Deconstruction: The Uses and Abuses of Literary Theory,* 1985.
Ferguson, Robert. *Reading the Early Republic,* 2004.
Fiedler, Leslie. *Love and Death in the American Novel,* 1960.
Fisher, Philip. *Hard Facts: Setting and Form in the American Novel,* 1985.
Fishkin, Shelley Fisher. *From Fact to Fiction: Journalism and Imaginative Writing in America,* 1985.

Fletcher, Angus. *A New Theory for American Poetry: Democracy, the Environment, and the Future of the Imagination,* 2004.

French, Warren. *The Social Novel at the End of an Era,* 1966.

Frohock, W. M. *The Novel of Violence in America,* revised edition, 1957.

Fryer, Judith. *The Faces of Eve: Women in the Nineteenth-Century American Novel,* 1976.

Fussell, Edwin. *Frontier: American Literature and the American West,* 1965.

Galloway, David. *The Absurd Hero in American Fiction,* 1966.

Gates, Henry Louis. *Figures in Black: Words, Signs, and the Racial Self,* 1987.

———. *The Signifying Monkey: A Theory of African-American Literary Criticism,* 1989.

Geismar, Maxwell. *Writers in Crisis: The American Novel Between Two Wars,* 1942.

———. *The Last of the Provincials: The American Novel, 1915–1925,* 1947.

———. *Rebels and Ancestors: The American Novel, 1890–1915,* 1953.

———. *American Moderns: From Rebellion to Conformity,* 1958.

Gelpi, Albert. *The Tenth Muse: The Psyche of the American Poet,* 1975.

Gould, Jean. *American Women Poets: Pioneers of Modern Poetry,* 1980.

Gould, Philip. *Covenant and Republic: Historical Romance and the Politics of Puritanism,* 1996.

Gray, Richard. *The Literature of Memory: Modern Writers of the American South,* 1977.

———. *Writing the South,* 1986, 1998.

Gregory, Horace, and Zaturenska, Marya. *A History of American Poetry, 1900–1940,* 1946, 1969.

Gross, S. L., and Hardy, J. E., eds. *Images of the Negro in American Literature,* 1966.

Hart, J. D. *The Popular Book: A History of America's Literary Taste,* 1950.

Hassan, Ihab. *Radical Innocence, Studies in the Contemporary American Novel,* 1961.

———. *Contemporary American Literature, 1945–1972,* 1973.

Hoffman, Daniel. *Form and Fable in American Fiction,* 1961.

———. *Harvard Guide to American Writing,* 1979.

Hoffman, Frederick. *The Twenties: American Writing in the Postwar Decade,* 1955.

———. *The Art of Southern Fiction,* 1967.

Horton, R. W., and Edwards, Herbert. *Backgrounds of American Literary Thought,* 1952.

Howard, Leon. *Literature and the American Tradition,* 1960.

Hubbell, Jay B. *The South in American Literature, 1607–1900,* 1954.

Huggins, R. I. *Harlem Renaissance,* 1971.

Jackson, Blyden. *A History of African American Literature,* Volume I, 1989.

Jameson, Fredric. *Postmodernism, or, The Cultural Logic of Late Capitalism,* 1991.

Jaskoski, Helen. *Early Native American Writing,* 1996.

Jones, Howard Mumford. *O Strange New World: American Culture, The Formative Years,* 1964.

———. *The Theory of American Literature,* 2nd edition, 1965.

———. *The Age of Energy: Varieties of American Experience, 1865–1915,* 1971.

Kammer, Michael. *A Season of Youth,* 1978.

Kartiganer, Donald M., and Griffith, Malcolm A. *Theories of American Literature,* 1972.

Kaul, A. N. *The American Vision: Actual and Ideal Society in Nineteenth-Century Fiction,* 1963.

Kazin, Alfred. *On Native Grounds: An Interpretation of Modern American Prose Literature,* 1942.

———. *Bright Book of Life: American Novelists and Storytellers from Hemingway to Mailer,* 1973.

Kenner, Hugh. *A Homemade World: The American Modernist Writers,* 1975.

Kermode, Frank. *The Uses of Error,* 1991.

Klein, Marcus. *After Alienation: American Novels in Mid-Century,* 1964.

Knight, Grant. *The Critical Period in American Literature, 1890–1900,* 1951.

———. *The Strenuous Age in American Literature, 1900–1910,* 1954.

Kolb, Harold. *The Illusion of Life: American Realism as a Literary Form,* 1970.

Kramer, Dale. *Chicago Renaissance: The Literary Life in the Midwest, 1900–1930,* 1966.

Krutch, J. W. *The American Drama Since 1918,* 1939.

Kupperman, Karen, ed. *America in European Consciousness,* 1995.

Lawrence, D. H. *Studies in Classic American Literature,* 1923.

Lee, Robert Edson. *From West to East: Studies in the Literature of the American West,* 1966.

Leisy, E. E. *The American Historical Novel,* 1950.

Levin, David. *In Defense of Historical Literature,* 1967.

Levin, Harry. *The Power of Blackness: Hawthorne, Poe, Melville,* 1958.

Lewis, R. W. B. *The American Adam; Innocence, Tragedy, and Tradition in the Nineteenth Century,* 1955.

Lively, Robert. *Fiction Fights the Civil War,* 1956.

Long, Eugene Hudson. *American Drama from Its Beginnings to the Present,* 1970.

Loving, Jerome. *Lost in the Customhouse: Authorship in the American Renaissance,* 1993.

Lynen, J. F. *The Design of the Present: Essays on Time and Form in American Literature,* 1969.

Lynn, Kenneth S. *The Dream of Success: A Study of the Modern American Imagination,* 1955.

McGiffert, Michael. *Puritanism and the American Experience,* 1969.

Malin, Irving. *New American Gothic,* 1962.

Margolies, Edward. *Native Sons: A Critical Study of Twentieth-Century Negro American Authors,* 1968.

Martin, Jay. *Harvests of Change: American Literature, 1865–1914,* 1967.

Marx, Leo. *The Machine in the Garden: Technology and the Pastoral Ideal in America,* 1964.

Matthiessen, F. O. *American Renaissance: Art and Expression in the Age of Emerson and Whitman,* 1941.

May, Henry. *The End of American Innocence: The First Years of Our Own Time, 1912–1917,* 1959.

———. *The Enlightenment in America,* 1976.

Mazzaro, Jerome. *Postmodern American Poetry,* 1980.

McWilliams, John. *New England's Crises and Cultural Memory: Literature, Politics, History, Religion, 1620–1860,* 2004.

Menand, Louis. *The Metaphysical Club: A Story of Ideas in America,* 2001.

Mencken, H. L. *The American Language: An Inquiry into the Development of English in the United States,* revised edition, 1936. Supplement I, 1945; Supplement II, 1948.

Meserve, Walter. *An Emerging Entertainment: The Drama of the American People from the Beginnings to 1828,* 1977.

Miller, Jordan, and Frazer, Winifred. *American Drama Between the Wars,* 1991.

Miller, Perry. *The New England Mind: The Seventeenth Century,* 1939.

———. *The New England Mind: From Colony to Province,* 1953.

———. *The Raven and the Whale: The War of Words and Wits in the Era of Poe and Melville,* 1956.

Miller, Ruth. *Backgrounds to Black American Literature,* 1971.

Millgate, Michael. *American Social Fiction,* 1967.

Moers, Ellen. *Literary Women,* 1976.

Moffitt, John, and Sebastián, Santiago. *O Brave New People: The European Invention of the American Indian,* 1996.

Mordden, Ethan. *The American Theatre,* 1981.

Morgan, E. S. *Visible Saints: The History of a Puritan Idea,* 1963.

Morison, S. E. *The Intellectual Life of Colonial New England,* 1956.

Mott, F. L. *Golden Multitudes: The Story of Best Sellers in the United States,* 1947.

———. *American Journalism: A History of Newspapers in the United States Through 250 Years, 1690 to 1940,* 1941, revised 1951.

———. *A History of American Magazines,* 4 vols., 1938–1957.

Mumford, Lewis. *The Golden Day,* 1926.

Murdock, K. B. *Literature and Theology in Colonial New England,* 1949.

Myerson, Joel, ed. *The Transcendentalists: A Review of Research and Criticism,* 1984.

Newman, Charles. *The Post-Modern Aura: The Act of Fiction in an Age of Inflation,* 1985.

Nye, Russel. *The Cultural Life of the New Nation,* 1960.

Olderman, Raymond. *Beyond the Wasteland: The American Novel in the 1960s,* 1972.

Parrington, V. L. *Main Currents in American Thought: An Interpretation of American Literature from the Beginnings to 1920,* 3 vols., 1927–1930.

Pattee, F. L. *A History of American Literature Since 1870,* 1915, 1968.

———. *The Development of the American Short Story,* 1923, 1966.

Pearce, R. H. *The Continuity of American Poetry,* 1961.

Peden, William. *The American Short Story: Continuity and Change, 1940–1975,* 2nd edition, 1975.

Perkins, David. *A History of Modern Poetry,* 2 vols., 1976, 1987.

Person, Stow. *American Minds: A History of Ideas,* 1958.

Phillips, Robert. *The Confessional Poets,* 1963.

Pinsky, Robert. *The Situation of Poetry: Contemporary Poetry and Its Traditions,* 1977.

Pizer, Donald. *Realism and Naturalism in Nineteenth-Century American Literature,* 1966.

———, and Harbert, Earl. *American Realists and Naturalists,* 1982.

Poirier, Richard. *A World Elsewhere: The Place of Style in American Literature,* 1966.

———. *Poetry and Pragmatism,* 1991.

Porte, Joel. *The Romance in America,* 1969.

Quinn, A. H. *A History of the American Drama from the Civil War to the Present Day,* revised edition, 1936.

———. *American Fiction: An Historical and Critical Survey,* 1936.

———. *A History of the American Drama from the Beginning to the Civil War,* revised edition, 1943.
———, and others. *The Literature of the American People,* 1951.
Quinones, Ricardo. *Mapping Literary Modernism: Time and Development,* 1985.
Reising, Russell. *The Unusable Past: Theory and Study of American Literature,* 1986.
Rideout, Walter. *The Radical Novel in the United States, 1900–1954,* 1956.
Ridgely, J. V. *Nineteenth-Century Southern Literature,* 1980.
Riley, I. W. *American Thought from Puritanism to Pragmatism and Beyond,* 1923, 1959.
Rosenblatt, Roger. *Black Fiction,* 1974.
Rourke, Constance. *American Humor: A Study of the National Character,* 1931.
Rubin, Louis. *The Faraway Country: Writers of the Modern South,* 1963.
———, ed. *The History of Southern Literature,* 1985.
Ruland, Richard. *The Rediscovery of American Literature: Premises of Critical Taste, 1900–1940,* 1967.
———, ed. *The Native Muse: Theories of American Literature,* Vol. I, 1972.
———, ed. *A Storied Land: Theories of American Literature.* Vol. II, 1976.
Ruland, Richard, and Bradbury, Malcolm. *From Puritanism to Modernism, A History of American Literature,* 1991.
Ruoff, LaVonne Brown, and Ward, Jerry W., eds. *Redefining American Literary History,* 1990.
Samuels, Shirley. *Romances of the Republic,* 1996.
Schneider, H. W. *The Puritan Mind,* 1930, 1958.
Shafer, Yvonne. *American Women Playwrights: 1900–1950,* 1996.
Seed, Patricia. *Ceremonies of Possession in Europe's Conquest of the New World,* 1996.
Seelye, John. *Prophetic Waters: The River in Early American Life and Literature,* 1977.
Silverman, Kenneth. *A Cultural History of the American Revolution,* 1976.
Slotkin, Richard. *Regeneration Through Violence: The Mythology of the American Frontier, 1600–1860,* 1973.
Smith, H. N. *Virgin Land: The American West as Symbol and Myth,* 1950.
———. *Democracy and The Novel,* 1979.
Spencer, Benjamin. *The Quest for Nationality: An American Literary Campaign,* 1957.
Spengermann, William C. *The Adventurous Muse: The Poetics of American Fiction: 1789–1900,* 1977.
Spiller, R. E. *The Cycle of American Literature,* 1951, 1967.
———, and others. *Literary History of the United States,* 4th edition, revised, 1974.
Stepanchev, Stephen. *American Poetry Since 1945,* 1965.
Stewart, Randall. *American Literature and the Christian Tradition,* 1958.
Stipes, Emily. *The Poetry of American Women from 1632 to 1945,* 1977.
Straumann, Heinrich. *American Literature in the Twentieth Century,* 1965.
Sundquist, Eric. *To Wake the Nations: Race in the Making of American Literature,* 1993.
Tanner, Tony. *The Reign of Wonder,* 1965.
Taubmann, Howard. *The Making of the American Theatre,* 1965.
Tompkins, Jane. *Sensational Designs: The Cultural Work of American Fiction, 1790–1860,* 1985.

Trachtenberg, Stanley. *American Humorists, 1800–1950,* 1982.
———. *Colonial Writers, 1606–1734,* 1984.
Trent, W. P., and others. *Cambridge History of American Literature,* 4 vols., 1917–1933.
Tuttleton, James W. *The Novel of Manners in America,* 1972.
Tyler, M. C. *A History of American Literature, 1607–1765,* 2 vols., 1878.
Van Doren, Carl. *The American Novel, 1789–1939,* 1940.
Vendler, Helen. *Part of Nature, Part of Us: Modern American Poets,* 1980.
Vogel, Dan. *The Three Masks of American Tragedy,* 1976.
von Hallberg, Robert. *American Poetry and Culture, 1945–1980,* 1985.
Wagenknecht, Edward. *Cavalcade of the American Novel,* 1952.
Waggoner, H. H. *American Poets: From the Puritans to the Present Day,* 1968.
Walcutt, C. C. *American Literary Nationalism, A Divided Stream,* 1956.
Weales, Gerald. *American Drama Since World War II,* 1962.
———. *The Jumping-Off Place: American Drama in the 1960s,* 1969.
Weaver, Gordon, ed. *The American Short Story, 1945–1980: A Critical History,* 1983.
West, Ray. *The Short Story in America, 1900–1950,* 1952.
White, Peter, ed. *Puritan Poets and Poetics: Seventeenth-Century Poetry in Theory and Practice,* 1985.
Wiget, Andrew. *Native American Literature,* 1985.
Williams, S. T. *The Spanish Background of American Literature,* 1955.
Wilson, Edmund. *Patriotic Gore: Studies in the Literature of the American Civil War,* 1962.
Wood, James. *Magazines in the United States,* 2nd edition, 1956.
Ziff, Larzer. *The American 1890's,* 1966.
———. *Puritanism in America: New Culture in a New World,* 1973.

Chronology

1600

International Affairs, Exploration, Settlement, and Science

1600 Spaniards explore American Southwest

1603–1613 Champlain explores Saint Lawrence River. Founds Quebec

1607 Jamestown settlers arrive in Virginia in April. First permanent British settlement in North America

1609–1610 Henry Hudson discovers Hudson River and Hudson Bay

1611 First Virginia tobacco crop

1620 Pilgrims found Plymouth

1621 Dutch found New Amsterdam

1622 Indians massacre Jamestown settlers

1624 Dutch settle Manhattan

1628 Fifty Puritans led by John Endicott settle at Salem

1630–1643 "Great Migration" of the Puritans to Massachusetts

1633 Maryland founded

1636 Roger Williams founds Providence

1639 First colonial printing press established at Cambridge, Massachusetts

1640 Colonial population of British North America c. 28,000

1650

1656 First Quakers arrive in Massachusetts

Politics and Government

1558–1603 Elizabeth I reigns in England

1603–1625 James I reigns in Engla

1619 America's first legislature cc venes in Virginia

1621 William Bradford succeeds John Carver as governor of Plymouth Colony

1624 Virginia becomes Royal Co

1625–1649 Charles I reigns in E land

1625 Colonial office established London

1628 Charles I dissolves Parliame

1637 Pequot War

1637 Anne Hutchinson banishe from Massachusetts Bay Colony

1642–1646 English Civil War

1642–1684 New England Confederation

1649 Charles I executed

1653–1658 Oliver Cromwell ru England as Lord Protector

ociety and Culture

508 John Smith publishes *A True Relation,* earliest firsthand account of Virginia settlement

516 John Smith publishes *A Description of New England*

519 African Negroes first sold as slaves, in Virginia

21 First Thanksgiving at Plymouth

24 John Smith publishes *General History of Virginia*

30–1649 John Winthrop writes his *Journal*

30–1651 William Bradford writes *History of Plymouth Plantation*

35 Boston Latin School established. First American public school

36 Harvard College founded

37 Thomas Morton publishes *The New English Canan*

39 First printing press established n Massachusetts

0 Colonial population estimated t 28,000

3 Roger Williams publishes *A Key nto the Language of America*

0 Anne Bradstreet's book of oems *The Tenth Muse* published in ondon

Lives of Authors

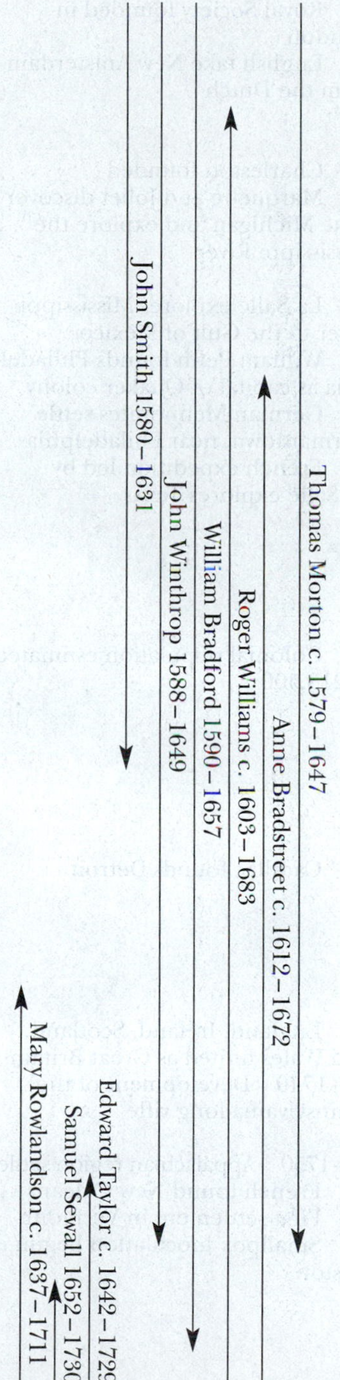

International Affairs, Exploration, Settlement, and Science

1662 Royal Society founded in London
1664 English take New Amsterdam from the Dutch

1670 Charleston founded
1673 Marquette and Joliet discover Lake Michigan and explore the Mississippi River

1682 La Salle explores Mississippi River to the Gulf of Mexico
1682 William Penn founds Philadelphia as capital of Quaker colony
1683 German Mennonites settle Germantown, near Philadelphia
1685 French expedition led by La Salle explores Texas

1690 Colonial population estimated at 213,500

1700

1701 Cadillac founds Detroit

1707 England, Ireland, Scotland, and Wales united as Great Britain
1710–1740 Development of the Pennsylvania long rifle

1716–1750 Appalachian region settled
1718 French found New Orleans
1720 First settlement in Vermont
1721 Smallpox inoculation begun in Boston

Politics and Government

1675–1678 King Philip's War in N
England
1680 New Hampshire made a roy
colony, separate from Massachu

1684 Massachusetts charter revok
1685–1688 James II reigns in Eng

1688 "Glorious Revolution" ends
reign of James II. William and M
begin reign as king and queen
England
1689 Boston colonists rebel agai
Governor Andros

1691 Massachusetts receives a ne
charter and a royal governor. T
Plymouth Colony is absorbed b
Massachusetts

1702 New Jersey becomes a roya
colony

1713 Carolina divided into Nor
and South Carolina

1729 North and South Carolin
come separate royal colonies

ociety and Culture

Lives of Authors

662 Michael Wigglesworth's *Day of Doom* published

569 Nathaniel Morton publishes *New England's Memorial*

578 Anne Bradstreet publishes *Poems*

582 Mary Rowlandson publishes her *Narrative of Captivity*

1683 *New England Primer* published

587 First Church of England service held in Boston

590 First newspaper published, in Boston

592 Salem witch trials

593 College of William and Mary founded in Virginia

)1 Yale College founded

)2 Cotton Mather's *Magnalia Christi Americana* published

)4 First weekly newspaper, *Boston News-Letter*

4 First organ built, in Philadelphia

9–1712 William Byrd writes his *Secret Diary*

4 Tea is introduced into the colonies

2 Benjamin Franklin publishes "Dogood Papers"

5–1756 Great Awakening. Religious revivalism throughout the colonies

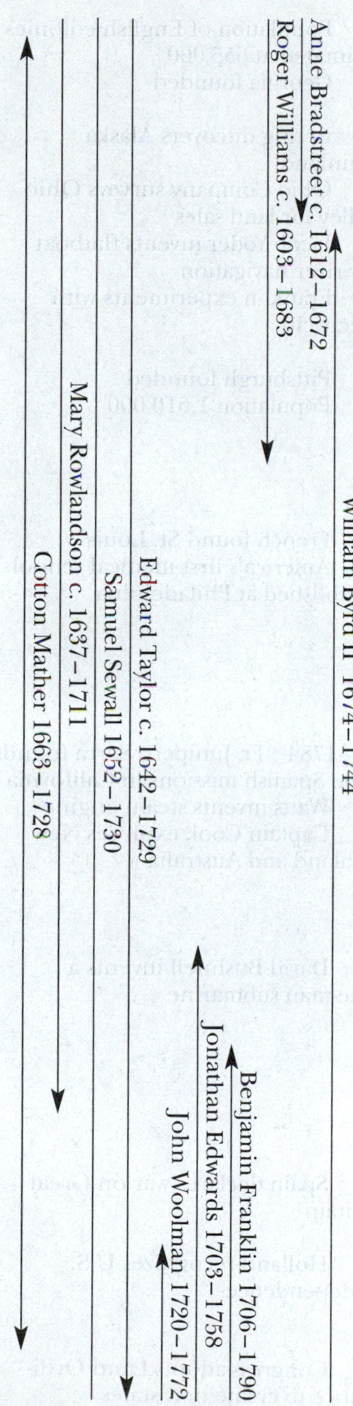

International Affairs, Exploration, Settlement, and Science

1730 Population of English colonies estimated at 655,000

1733 Georgia founded

1741 Bering discovers Alaska mainland

1749 Ohio Company surveys Ohio Valley for land sales

1750

1750 Jacob Yoder invents flatboat for river navigation

1752 Franklin experiments with electricity

1758 Pittsburgh founded

1760 Population 1,610,000

1764 French found St. Louis

1765 America's first medical school established at Philadelphia

1769–1784 Fr. Junipero Serra founds nine Spanish missions in California

1769 Watts invents steam engine

1770 Captain Cook explores New Zealand and Australia

1775 David Bushnell invents a one-man submarine

1779 Spain declares war on Great Britain

1782 Holland recognizes U.S. independence

1784 Congress adopts Land Ordinance to create new states

Politics and Government

1745 New Englanders capture French fortress at Louisburg, Ca Breton Island, Canada

1754–1763 French and Indian W Victorious British gain all Frenc Canada

1763–1767 Mason-Dixon Line su veyed

1764 Sugar Act, Currency Act

1765 Stamp Act, Sons of Liberty formed

1766 Repeal of Stamp Act

1767 Townshend Acts tax tea, pa etc.

1768 British troops land in Bost

1770 Boston Massacre

1773 Boston Tea Party

1774 First Continental Congres meets in Philadelphia

1775–1781 War for American Independence

1775 Battles at Lexington, Conc Ticonderoga, Bunker Hill

1775 Britain hires German mercenaries to fight in Americ

1776 France sends aid to Ameri revolutionaries

1781 Cornwallis surrenders at Yorktown

1783 Treat of Paris formally en American Revolution

ociety and Culture

730 First art exhibition, in Boston
732–1757 Benjamin Franklin publishes *Poor Richard's Almanack*
738 Painters John Singleton Copley and Benjamin West born

749 First drama company established, at Philadelphia

752 First general hospital, Philadelphia
'54 Franklin publishes first American political cartoon, calling for action against the French

61 First musical society founded in Charleston, South Carolina

67 Jefferson builds Monticello
67 First American play professionally produced: Thomas Godfrey's *The Prince of Parthia*
69 American Philosophical Society founded

71–1790 Benjamin Franklin writes his *Autobiography*
74–1781 Crèvecoeur writes *Letters from an American Farmer*
5 Quakers establish first antislavery society
5 "Yankee Doodle" written

6 Tom Paine publishes *Common ense* and *The American Crisis I*

2–1783 Jefferson writes *Notes on e State of Virginia*
3 Noah Webster publishes *The merican Spelling Book*

Lives of Authors

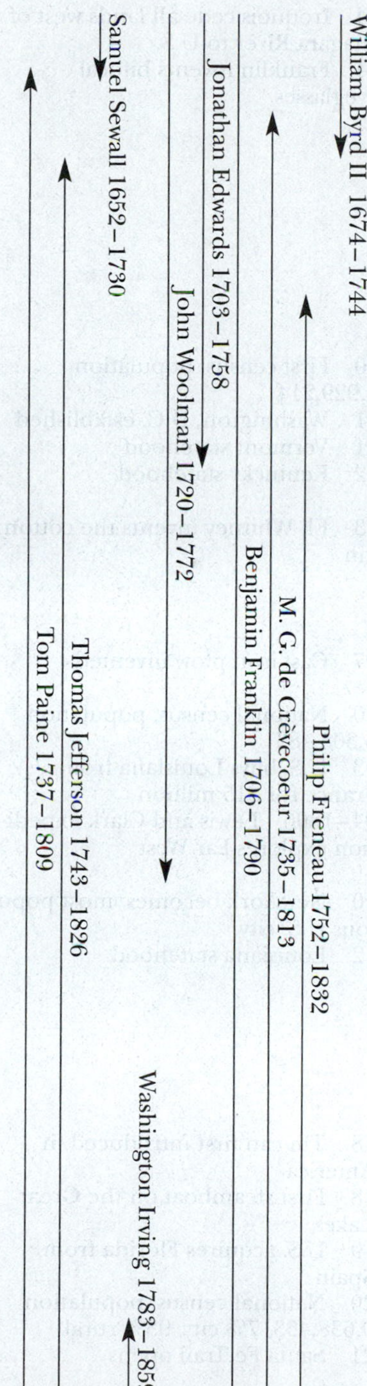

International Affairs, Exploration, Settlement, and Science

1784 Iroquois cede all lands west of Niagara River to U.S.
1784 Franklin invents bifocal eyeglasses

1790 First census: population 3,929,214
1791 Washington, D.C. established
1791 Vermont statehood
1792 Kentucky statehood

1793 Eli Whitney invents the cotton gin

1797 Cast-iron plow invented

1800

1800 National census: population 5,308,483
1803 U.S. buys Louisiana from France for $15 million
1804–1806 Lewis and Clark expedition explores Far West

1810 New York becomes most populous U.S. city
1812 Louisiana statehood

1818 Tin can first introduced in America
1818 First steamboat on the Great Lakes
1819 U.S. acquires Florida from Spain
1820 National census: population 9,638,453, 7% city, 93% rural
1821 Santa Fe Trail opens

Politics and Government

1786–1787 Shays's Rebellion

1787 Constitutional Convention meets in Philadelphia

1789 Constitution ratified by stat[e]
Washington elected first Preside[nt]
1789 French Revolution begins

1791 Bill of Rights adopted
1792 Congress establishes decim[al] system of coinage. Washington reelected for second term
1793 Construction of U.S. Capit[ol] Building started

1796 Washington's Farewell Add[ress]
John Adams elected President

1799 Death of Washington
1800 Thomas Jefferson elected President. Reelected 1804

1808 James Madison elected Pre[si]dent. Reelected 1812

1812–1815 War with Great Brit[ain]
1814 Washington, D.C. burned [by] British troops
1815 Battle of New Orleans, An[drew] Jackson defeats British troops
1816 James Monroe elected Pres[ident]

1820 Missouri Compromise

1823 Monroe Doctrine procla[imed]

Society and Culture

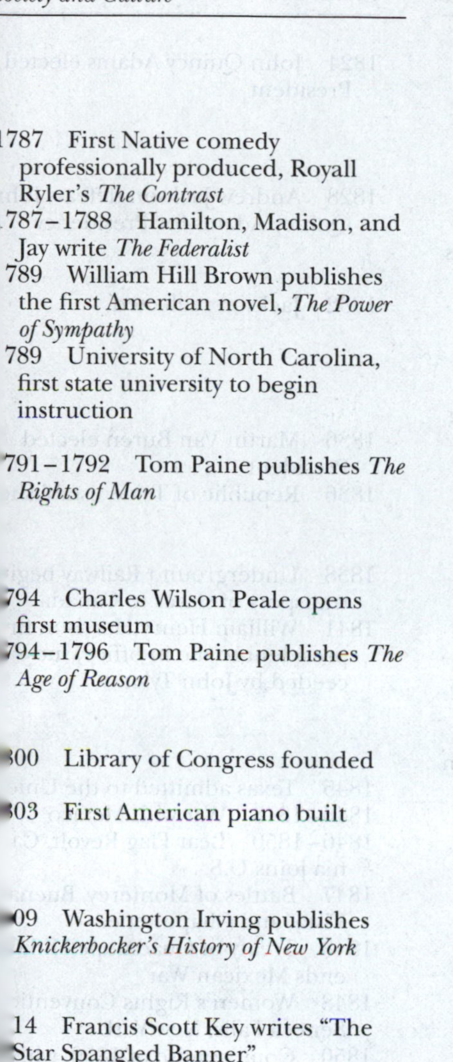

1787 First Native comedy professionally produced, Royall Ryler's *The Contrast*

.787–1788 Hamilton, Madison, and Jay write *The Federalist*

789 William Hill Brown publishes the first American novel, *The Power of Sympathy*

789 University of North Carolina, first state university to begin instruction

791–1792 Tom Paine publishes *The Rights of Man*

794 Charles Wilson Peale opens first museum

794–1796 Tom Paine publishes *The Age of Reason*

300 Library of Congress founded

303 First American piano built

09 Washington Irving publishes *Knickerbocker's History of New York*

14 Francis Scott Key writes "The Star Spangled Banner"

17 William Cullen Bryant publishes "Thanatopsis"

.9–1820 Irving publishes *The Sketch Book*

3 James Fenimore Cooper begins "The Leatherstocking Tales"

Lives of Authors

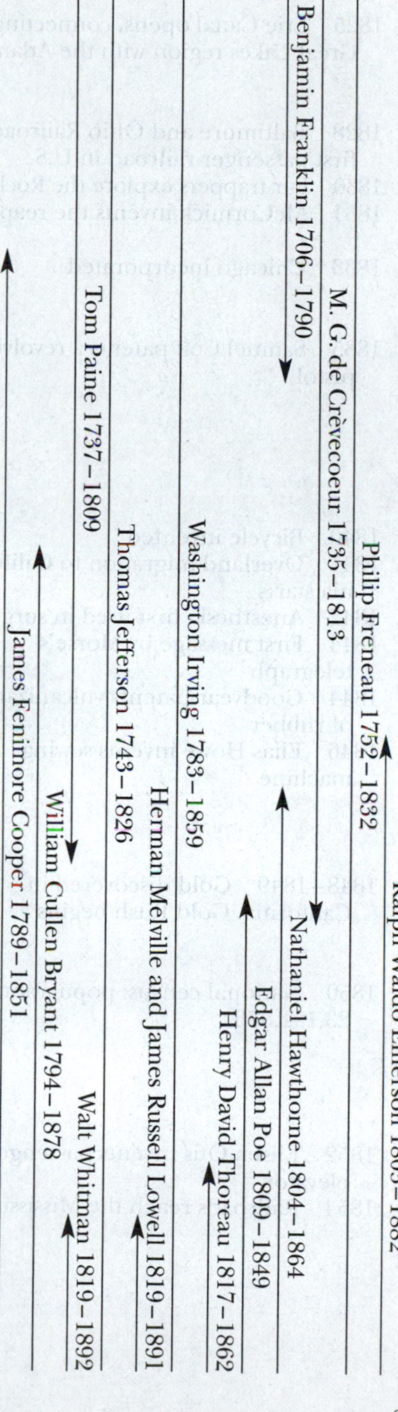

International Affairs, Exploration, Settlement, and Science

1825 Erie Canal opens, connecting Great Lakes region with the Atlantic

1828 Baltimore and Ohio Railroad, first passenger railroad in U.S.

1830 Fur trappers explore the Rockies

1831 McCormick invents the reaper

1833 Chicago incorporated

1835 Samuel Colt patents a revolving pistol

1840 Bicycle invented

1841 Overland migration to California starts

1842 Anesthesia first used in surgery

1844 First message by Morse's telegraph

1844 Goodyear patents vulcanization of rubber

1846 Elias Howe invents sewing machine

1848–1849 Gold discovered in California. Gold Rush begins

1850

1850 National census: population 23,191,876

1852 Elisha Otis invents passenger elevator

1854 Railroads reach the Mississippi

Politics and Government

1824 John Quincy Adams elected President

1828 Andrew Jackson defeats John Quincy Adams for Presidency

1832 Jackson reelected

1836 Martin Van Buren elected President

1836 Republic of Texas establishe

1838 Underground Railway begi transport of slaves to Canada

1841 William Henry Harrison fir president to die in office, succeeded by John Tyler

1845 Texas admitted to the Unic

1846–1848 War with Mexico

1846–1850 Bear Flag Revolt, Ca nia joins U.S.

1847 Battles of Monterey, Buena Vista, and Chapultepec

1848 Treaty of Guadalupe Hidal ends Mexican War

1848 Women's Rights Conventic Seneca Falls, New York

1850 Compromise of 1850, with Fugitive Slave Act, passed by Congress

1852 Democrat Franklin Pierce elected President

1854 Republican Party formed

1857 Supreme Court makes Dr Scott decision

ciety and Culture

825 Thomas Cole begins the Hudson River School of painting
827 John James Audubon publishes his *Birds of America*
828 Noah Webster publishes *An American Dictionary of the English Language*

833 American Anti-Slavery society formed
833 Oberlin College founded, first coeducational college
36 American Temperance Union established
36 Ralph Waldo Emerson publishes *Nature*
37 Mount Holyoke, first women's college, established
41–1847 Brook Farm

44 Poe publishes "The Raven"

45 Thoreau moves to Walden Pond
46 Congress founds the Smithsonan Institution

8 Stephen Foster's "Oh! Susanna" becomes a popular song

0 *Harper's Magazine* founded
0 Hawthorne publishes *The Scart Letter*
1 *The New York Times* established
1 Herman Melville publishes *loby Dick*
2 Harriet Beecher Stow pubshes *Uncle Tom's Cabin*

5 Walt Whitman publishes *Leaves Grass*
5 First U.S. kindergarten opens Wisconsin
7 *Atlantic Monthly* magazine egins publication

Lives of Authors

Philip Freneau 1752–1832
Ralph Waldo Emerson 1803–1882
Henry James 1843–1916
Mark Twain 1835–1910
Nathaniel Hawthorne 1804–1864
Edgar Allan Poe 1809–1849
Henry David Thoreau 1817–1862
Washington Irving 1783–1859
Herman Melville and James Russell Lowell 1819–1891
Thomas Jefferson 1743–1826
Walt Whitman 1819–1892
William Cullen Bryant 1794–1878
James Fenimore Cooper 1789–1851
Emily Dickinson 1830–1886

International Affairs, Exploration, Settlement, and Science

1858 Transatlantic telegraph cable

1858 President Buchanan and Queen Victoria of England communicate over first transatlantic cable

1858 First stagecoach line from Missouri to Pacific coast

1859 Edwin Drake drills successful oil well at Titusville, Pennsylvania; American oil industry begins

1859 Charles Darwin publishes *On The Origin of Species*

1859 Oregon statehood

1859 Gold discovered in Colorado and Nevada

1860 Pony Express runs from Missouri to California

1860 Oliver Winchester develops the repeating rifle

1861 Telegraph links east and west coasts

1862 Richard Gatling perfects the revolving machine gun

1864 First Pullman sleeper railroad car built

1867 Typewriter invented

1867 U.S. buys Alaska from Russia for $7.2 million

1867 British establish The Dominion of Canada. Alfred Nobel patents dynamite

1868 First commercial typewriter patented

Politics and Government

1858 Lincoln-Douglas Debates du ing Illinois senatorial race

1859 John Brown raids Harpers Fe

1860 Southern states assert right secede

1860 Abraham Lincoln elected President

1860 South Carolina secedes fro the Union

1861 Mississippi, Florida, Alabam Georgia, Louisiana, Virginia, Arkansas, Tennessee, North Carolina, and Texas secede

1861 West Virginia separates fro Virginia, remains loyal to the U

1861–1865 American Civil War

1862 First Federal income tax

1862 Lincoln issues Emancipatic Proclamation

1863 Lincoln delivers Gettysbur Address

1864 Lincoln reelected

1865 Lee surrenders at Appoma

1865 Lincoln assassinated. Andr Johnson becomes President

1865 13th Amendment abolishe slavery

1867 U.S. buys Alaska for $7,20

1867 Reconstruction begins in American South

1868 Congress approves 8-hour for federal employees

1868 14th Amendment grants Negroes citizenship

1868 U.S. Grant elected Preside Reelected 1872

ciety and Culture

|58 Longfellow publishes *The Courtship of Miles Standish*

59 Harriet Beecher Stowe publishes *The Minister's Wooing*

60 Hawthorne publishes *The Marble Faun*

60 First Beadle dime novel published

2 Julia Ward Howe publishes "The Battle Hymn of the Republic"

3 Lincoln's "Gettysburg Address"

5 Mark Twain publishes "The Celebrated Jumping Frog of Calaveras County"

6 Whittier publishes *Snow-Bound*

8 Louisa May Alcott publishes *Little Women*

Lives of Authors

Ralph Waldo Emerson 1803–1882

Henry James 1843–1916

Mark Twain 1835–1910

Nathaniel Hawthorne 1804–1864

Henry David Thoreau 1817–1862

Washington Irving 1783–1859

Herman Melville and James Russell Lowell 1819–1891

Walt Whitman 1819–1892

William Cullen Bryant 1794–1878

Emily Dickinson 1830–1886

International Affairs, Exploration, Settlement, and Science	*Politics and Government*
1869 Vacuum cleaner invented 1869 Transcontinental railroad completed	1869 Wyoming passes first U.S. woman-suffrage law
1870 National census: population 39,818,494 1871 Charles Darwin publishes *The Descent of Man* 1876 General Custer and 265 men killed at Little Bighorn, Montana 1876 Alexander Graham Bell patents the telephone	1870 Virginia, Mississippi, Texas, and Georgia readmitted to the Union
	1877 Reconstruction ends. All fe eral troops withdrawn from the South 1877 Chief Joseph leads Nez Per Indians in battles with U.S. Arm
1878 Bicycles first manufactured in U.S. 1878 Edison patents phonograph 1879 Edison invents workable incandescent lightbulb 1880 First important gold strike in Alaska	1880 Chinese Treaty (limiting in gration) signed
1881 First electric light power plant built, in New York 1882 Indian chief Geronimo captured; Plains Indian warfare ends 1883 Brooklyn Bridge completed	1881 President Garfield assassin Chester Arther becomes Presid 1883 Standard time zones estab lished in U.S.
1884 Hiram Maxim invents machine gun 1884 Steam turbine invented 1885 Automobile invented	1884–1888 Woman Suffragettes Equal Rights party, nominate woman candidate for Presiden
1887 First true golf course built 1888 First successful electric trolley line opened. First Kodak hand camera developed	1888 Department of Labor esta lished 1889 Indian Territory (Oklaho opened to white settlement
1890 As settlement expands, American frontier disappears. National census: 62,947,714	1890 Sherman Anti-Trust Act p

ociety and Culture

869 Mark Twain publishes *Innocents Abroad*

869 First professional baseball team, Cincinnati Red Stockings, established

869 First intercollegiate football game. Rutgers defeats Princeton

872 Mark Twain publishes *Roughing It*

876 National Baseball League founded

876 Mark Twain publishes *Tom Sawyer*

877 American Museum of Natural History opens in New York City

877 Philadelphia Conservatory of Music founded

878 Henry James publishes *Daisy Miller*

79 Henry George publishes *Progress and Poverty*

80 Salvation Army established in U.S.

80 Metropolitan Museum of New York City opens

80 Joel Chandler Harris publishes *Uncle Remus*

81 American Red Cross formed

81 Boston Symphony founded

83 New York Metropolitan Opera House opens

84 Mark Twain publishes *Huckleberry Finn*

85 First "skyscraper" built, in Chicago

86 Statue of Liberty dedicated

86 American Federation of Labor formed

89 First All-American football team selected

1 James Naismith invents basketball

Lives of Authors

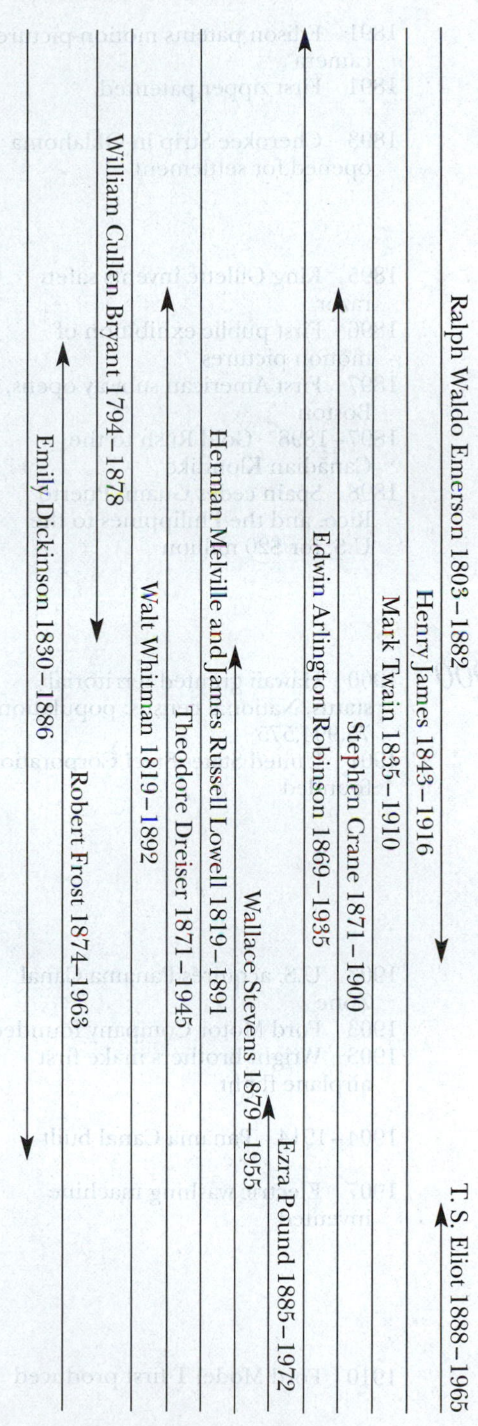

International Affairs, Exploration, Settlement, and Science

1891 Edison patents motion-picture camera

1891 First zipper patented

1893 Cherokee Strip in Oklahoma opened for settlement

1895 King Gillette invents safety razor

1896 First public exhibition of motion pictures

1897 First American subway opens, Boston

1897–1898 Gold Rush to the Canadian Klondike

1898 Spain cedes Guam, Puerto Rico, and the Philippines to the U.S. for $20 million

1900

1900 Hawaii granted territorial status, National census: population 75,994,575

1901 United States Steel Corporation founded

1903 U.S. acquires Panama Canal Zone

1903 Ford Motor Company founded

1903 Wright brothers make first airplane flight

1904–1914 Panama Canal built

1907 Electric washing machine invented

1910 Ford Model T first produced

Politics and Government

1892 Grover Cleveland elected Pr dent

1894 Coxey's Army of protesters marches on Washington, D.C.

1894 U.S. recognizes Republic of Hawaii

1896 Rural free delivery of U.S. n begins

1898 U.S. Battleship *Maine* blows in Havana, Cuba harbor

1898–1899 Spanish-American wa

1900 Socialist Party formed

1901 Anti-saloon leader Carrie N tion makes first raid on a saloor Wichita, Kansas

1901 President McKinley assassinated. Theodore Roosevelt becomes President

1901 Socialist Party of America formed

1904 Theodore Roosevelt electe President

1906 Federal Pure Food and Dr Act passed

1907–1909 Georgia, Oklahoma Mississippi, North Carolina, Te nessee, Alabama enact "dry" la

ociety and Culture

891 International Copyright Law established

893 Chicago World's Columbian Exposition

894 Labor Day declared legal holiday

895 Stephen Crane publishes *The Red Badge of Courage*

897 Library of Congress completed

898 First show of American Impressionist painters

99 Scott Joplin introduces ragtime to white Americans

99 Coca-Cola first bottled

99 Sigmund Freud publishes *The Interpretation of Dreams*

00 Theodore Dreiser publishes *Sister Carrie*

00–1920 Most American workers have sixty-hour, six-day work week.

01 Connecticut passes first law regulating auto speed

)2 First Rose Bowl football game

)3 *The Great Train Robbery* exhibited, first film telling a story

)3 Henry James publishes *The Ambassadors*

7 First Mother's Day celebration

7 Henry Adams publishes *The Education of Henry Adams*

8 Works by American Ash Can chool of painters exhibited

9 National Associated for the dvancement of Colored People ounded

0 Boy Scouts of America founded

Lives of Authors

Walt Whitman 1819–1892

Herman Melville and James Russell Lowell 1819–1891

Stephen Crane 1871–1900

Robert Frost 1874–1963

Ernest Hemingway 1898–1961

F. Scott Fitzgerald 1896–1940

Theodore Dreiser 1871–1945

William Faulkner 1897–1962

Wallace Stevens 1879–1955

Ezra Pound 1885–1972

Edwin Arlington Robinson 1869–1935

Mark Twain 1835–1910

Henry James 1843–1916

T. S. Eliot 1888–1965

International Affairs, Exploration, Settlement, and Science

1912 First neon sign created

1913 First assembly line begins to operate at Ford

1913 Niels Bohr develops theory of atomic structure

1914 Robert Goddard gets first U.S. patent for multistage rockets

1914–1918 World War I

1917 U.S. buys Virgin Islands from Denmark

1918 Armistice, World War I ends

1918–1919 World-wide influenza epidemic kills millions; 500,000 die in U.S.

1919–1921 Civil war in Russia

1920 National census: population 105,710,620. Urban population exceeds rural population for the first time

1920 League of Nations organized. U.S. Senate refuses to vote for membership

1921 Albert Einstein wins Nobel Prize for physics

1922 Mussolini forms Fascist government in Italy

1922 Union of Soviet Socialist Republics established

1924 Adolf Hitler writes *Mein Kampf*

1926 Hirohito becomes emperor of Japan

1927 Charles Lindbergh flies the Atlantic alone

1928 Television tube developed

Politics and Government

1912–1946 Progressive party established

1912 Woodrow Wilson elected President. Reelected 1916

1913 Federal Reserve Bank and Department of Labor established

1917 U.S. declares war on Germa[ny]. First U.S. troops land in France

1919 U.S. Senate fails to approve Versailles Treaty ending World War I

1919 Communist party, American Legion, and RCA established in [U.S.]

1920 Prohibition (18th) Amendm[ent] goes into effect

1920 Transcontinental airmail begins. 19th Amendment gives women the vote

1920 Warren G. Harding elected President

1920–1933 Sale of intoxicating beverages prohibited in U.S.

1923–1924 Teapot Dome scanda[l:] corrupt Harding administration exposed

1923 Harding dies. Calvin Cooli[dge] becomes president

1924 Calvin Coolidge elected President

1927–1933 U.S. Marines occupy Nicaragua

1928 Congress appropriates $32,000,000 to enforce Prohibi[tion] laws

ciety and Culture

11 Irving Berlin publishes "Alexander's Ragtime Band"

13 Armory Show opens in New York. First large exhibit of modern art in America

13 Mack Sennett begins making movie comedies

17 Pulitzer Prize awards inaugurated. First jazz band recording made

18 Theatre Guild established

9–1926 Jack Dempsey heavyweight boxing champion of the world

0 Sinclair Lewis publishes *Main Street*. F. Scott Fitzgerald publishes is first novel, *This Side of Paradise*

0 KDKA, Cincinnati transmits irst regular radio broadcasts in U.S.

2 Lincoln Memorial dedicated in Washington, D.C.

2 T.S. Eliot publishes *The Waste and*

2 *Reader's Digest* founded

2 First radio commercial broadast

3 Five-day, forty-hour work week troduced by steel industry

4 Premiere of "Rhapsody in lue" by George Gershwin

5 F. Scott Fitzgerald publishes *he Great Gatsby*

5 Ernest Hemingway publishes *he Sun Also Rises*

The Jazz Singer, first full-length und movie

First Mickey Mouse cartoon

Lives of Authors

Henry James 1843–1916
T. S. Eliot 1888–1965
Robert Lowell 1917–1978
Saul Bellow 1915–2005
Edwin Arlington Robinson 1869–1935
Ezra Pound 1885–1972
Wallace Stevens 1879–1955
William Faulkner 1897–1962
Theodore Dreiser 1871–1945
F. Scott Fitzgerald 1896–1940
Ernest Hemingway 1898–1961
Robert Frost 1874–1963
James Baldwin 1924–1987
Flannery O'Connor 1925–1964
Edward Albee 1928–

International Affairs, Exploration, Settlement, and Science

1929 First auto radios installed

1930 Jet propulsion engine-developed

1931 Japanese invade Manchuria

1933 Hitler voted into power in Germany

1934 *S.S. Normandie*, French ocean liner, crosses Atlantic in 107 hours

1935 Anti-Semitic laws passed in Germany

1935–1936 Italy invades Ethiopia

1936 King Edward VIII of Great Britain abdicates

1936–1939 Spanish Civil War

1938 Germany absorbs Austria

1939 Scientists inform President Roosevelt of the possibility of making an atomic bomb

1939 Russia invades Finland

1939 Germany invades Poland in September. World War II begins

1940 German "blitzkrieg" conquers Norway, Denmark, Low Countries, and France

1941 Dec., Japan bombs Pearl Harbor. U.S. declares war on Japan, Germany, and Italy

1942 Atomic Age begins with first self-sustaining nuclear chain reaction

1944 June, D-Day; Allies invade France

1945 May, Germany surrenders

1945 Aug., Atomic bombs dropped on Hiroshima and Nagasaki. Japan surrenders

1948 Transistor invented

1948 Israel gains independence

1949 Chinese communists proclaim People's Republic of China

1950

1950 National Census: population 150,697,361

Politics and Government

1928 Herbert Hoover defeats Al Smith for the Presidency

1929 Stock market crash. The Gr Depression begins

1932 Franklin Roosevelt elected President. Reelected 1936, 1940, 1944

1933–1936 Severe drought. Plain states become "Dust Bowl"

1933 Twenty-first Amendment repeals Prohibition

1935 W.P.A. established

1939–1945 World War II brings nomic boom to U.S.

1940 Alien Registration Act

1941 Selective Service System extends draftees' service to 18 m

1944 FDR reelected President f fourth term

1945 FDR dies. Harry S. Truma becomes President

1945 Rationing of shoes, butter, tires ends

1946 Inflation rate rises to 18.2 pe

1950 Senator Joseph McCarthy gins his attacks on Communis government *iety and Culture*

'9 William Faulkner publishes *The Sound and the Fury*

·0 Sinclair Lewis, first American ɔ win the Nobel Prize for literature

3 Film *King Kong* released

5 Premiere of George Gershwin's *'orgy and Bess*

6 Eugene O'Neill receives Nobel rize for literature

6 Margaret Mitchell publishes *'one with the Wind*

) John Steinbeck publishes *The rapes of Wrath*

) Ernest Hemingway publishes *r Whom the Bell Tolls*

Color television first shown

Orson Wells directs and stars in e film *Citizen Kane*

First television commercial own

Jitterbug dancing becomes pular

Rogers and Hammerstein's *'klahoma!* opens

Tennessee Williams' *The Glass enagerie* opens in New York City

Kinsey report *Sexual Behavior in Human Male* published

T.S. Eliot wins Nobel Prize for erature. Ezra Pound publishes *e Pisan Cantos*

William Faulkner wins Nobel ze for literature

Lives of Authors

T. S. Eliot 1888–1965

LeRoi Jones (Amiri Baraka) 1934–

Robert Lowell 1917–1978

Saul Bellow 1915–2005

Edwin Arlington Robinson 1869–1935

Joyce Carol Oates 1938–

Ezra Pound 1885–1972

Wallace Stevens 1879–1955

William Faulkner 1897–1962

Theodore Dreiser 1871–1945

F. Scott Fitzgerald 1896–1940

Ernest Hemingway 1898–1961

Robert Frost 1874–1963

James Baldwin 1924–1987

Flannery O'Connor 1925–1964

Edward Albee 1928–

Toni Morrison 1931–

International Affairs, Exploration, Settlement, and Science

1950–1953 Korean War

1953 Mount Everest climbed

1955 First microwave oven for consumer public produced

1956 First contraceptive pill marketed

1956–1959 Cuban civil war. Victory for Castro forces

1957 Russia successfully launches "Sputnik," first man-made satellite

1961 Berlin Wall seals Iron Curtain

1961 Soviet cosmonaut first man to orbit earth

1962 Russian missiles withdrawn from Cuba after America threatens action

1967 Six-Day War between Israel and Arab nations

1967 Christiaan Bernard performs first human heart transplant

1968 *Apollo 8* orbits the moon

1969 World population estimated at 3.5 billion

1969 U.S. astronauts land on the moon

1970 U.S. population 203,211,926

1971 *Mariner 9* photographs Mars

1973 Gene-splicing first achieved

1973 OPEC quintuples oil prices

Politics and Government

1952 Eisenhower elected presider Reelected 1956

1953 Department of Health, Educ tion and Welfare established

1954 U.S. Supreme Court rules school segregation unconstitutio

1957 Civil Rights Act

1958–1959 Alaska and Hawaii become states

1960 John F. Kennedy elected President

1963 John F. Kennedy assassinate Lyndon B. Johnson becomes President

1965–1979 Annual inflation rate rises from 2% to 13%

1968 Robert Kennedy and Rev. Martin Luther King assassinatec

1968 Richard M. Nixon elected President. Reelected 1972

1969 First U.S. troops withdrawn from Vietnam. Anti-Vietnam-W demonstrations increase

1969–1979 Average annual hou hold income rises from $8,000 $16,000

1971 26th Amendment gives 18- olds the vote

1971–1979 Price of gold rises fr $40 to $340 per ounce

1971 Supreme Court upholds decision requiring the busing c schoolchildren for racial balan

1972 Watergate scandal emerge

1972 U.S. military conscription

1973 Spiro Agnew resigns as Vic President

ciety and Culture	*Lives of Authors*

51 Carson McCullers publishes *Ballad of the Sad Café*

54 Elvis Presley releases first record on Sun label. Rock music begins

54 Ernest Hemingway wins Nobel Prize for literature

56 Rev. Martin Luther King leads Montgomery, Alabama, bus boycott

56 Grace Metalious publishes *Peyton Place*

60 Presidential debates appear on TV

2 John Steinbeck wins Nobel Prize for literature

4 Beatles and Rolling Stones release their first albums

5 Hippie phenomenon begins in an Francisco

8 78 million TV sets in the U.S.

9 Pants suits become stylish for omen

9 The Woodstock Festival

Fiddler on the Roof becomes ngest-running musical in Broad-ay history

First issue of *Ms* magazine pubhed

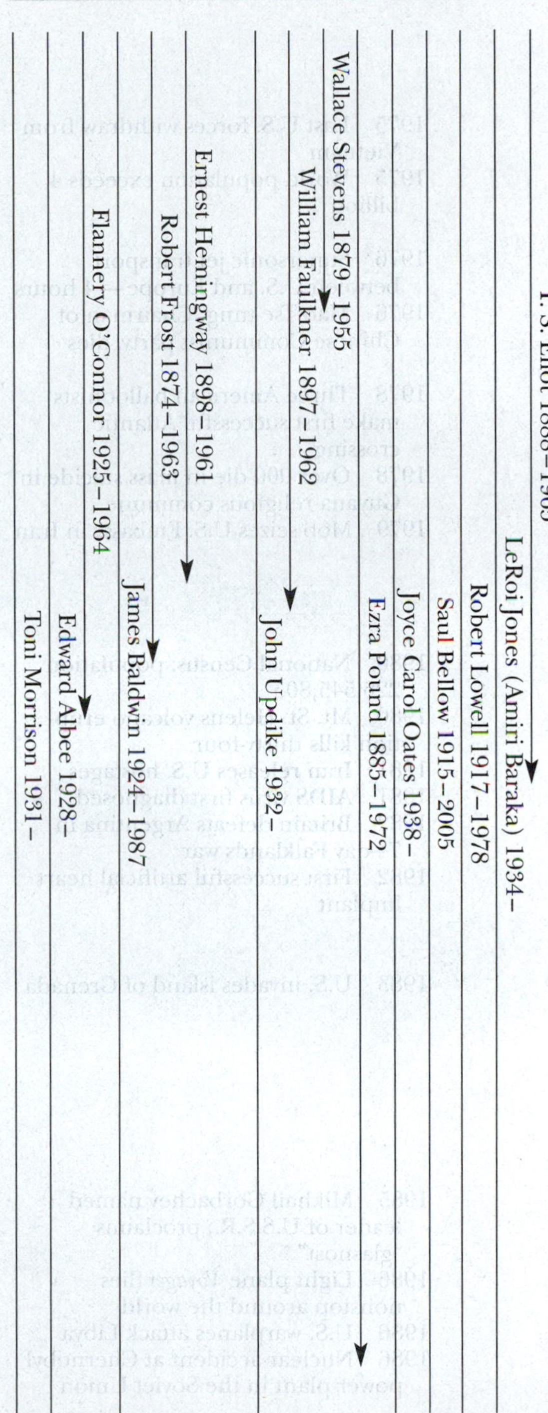

International Affairs, Exploration, Settlement, and Science

1975 Last U.S. forces withdraw from Vietnam

1975 World population exceeds 4 billion

1976 Supersonic jet transport between U.S. and Europe—4 hours

1976 Mao Tse-tung, Chairman of Chinese Communist party, dies

1978 Three American balloonists make first successful Atlantic crossing

1978 Over 900 die in mass suicide in Guyana religious commune

1979 Mob seizes U.S. Embassy in Iran

1980 National Census: population 226,545,805

1980 Mt. St. Helens volcano eruption kills thirty-four

1981 Iran releases U.S. hostages

1981 AIDS virus first diagnosed

1982 Britain defeats Argentina in 74-day Falklands war

1982 First successful artificial heart implant

1983 U.S. invades island of Grenada

1985 Mikhail Gorbachev named leader of U.S.S.R.; proclaims "glasnost"

1986 Light plane *Voyager* flies nonstop around the world

1986 U.S. warplanes attack Libya

1986 Nuclear accident at Chernobyl power plant in the Soviet Union

Politics and Government

1974 July, U.S. House of Represe atives recommends impeachme of President Nixon. August, Nix resigns

1976 Jimmy Carter elected Presic

1977 President Carter pardons d resisters

1978 Panama Canal Treaty gives trol of canal to Panama in 1999

1979 U.S. and China establish fu diplomatic relations

1979 OPEC nations continue to raise oil prices. Gas shortage an flation strike U.S.

1980 Ronald Reagan elected Pre dent. Reelected 1984

1981 Sandra Day O'Connor ma first woman Justice of U.S. Sup Court

1983 U.S. Supreme Court decla antiabortion laws unconstitutic

1984 President Reagan propose budget with record deficit of $ billion

1984 Geraldine Ferraro nomin by Democrats to run for Vice F dency

1985 U.S. becomes debtor nati

1986 Ivan Boesky fined $100 m for insider trading on Wall Str

1987 U.S. celebrates 200-year a niversary of the Constitution

1987 President Reagan submits U.S. trillion-dollar budget

ciety and Culture

76 Saul Bellow wins Nobel Prize
or literature
76 U.S. celebrates Bicentennial

77 *Star Wars* becomes biggest box
office draw to date
78 Isaac Bashevi Singer wins
Nobel Prize for literature
78 Life expectancy in U.S. reaches
9.6 years for men, 77.2 years for
women

0 TV show *Dallas* claims
00,000,000 viewers worldwide

1 Median U.S. family income
22,388
2–1983 U.S. households average
hours 55 minutes TV watching a
ay
2 Michael Jackson's *Thriller*
ecomes best-selling music album
history
3 Last episode of M*A*S*H on
BS draws 121,624,000 viewers
3 Tennessee Williams dies

The New Yorker magazine sold
r $142 million
Crack cocaine first appears in
S.

TV evangelists' sex and money
ndals exposed

Lives of Authors

Robert Lowell 1917–1978

LeRoi Jones (Amiri Baraka) 1934–

Saul Bellow 1915–2005

Joyce Carol Oates 1938–

John Updike 1932–

James Baldwin 1924–1987

Edward Albee 1928–

Toni Morrison 1931–

International Affairs, Exploration, Settlement, and Science	*Politics and Government*
	1988 George Bush elected Presid
	1988 U.S. Supreme Court rules c sorship of student publications school officials is legal
1989 Chinese army crushes student rally in Bejiing's Tiananmen Square	
1989 Popular uprisings overthrow iron-curtain governments; Cold War ends	
1989 U.S. invades Panama	
1990 U.S. population 249,632,692	1990 U.S. Supreme Court uphol right to burn U.S. flag
1991 U.S.S.R. collapses into Commonwealth of Independent States	1991 $78 billion for S&L bailout approved
1991 UN forces attack Iraq, liberate Kuwait	
1992 Earth Summit, environmental conference, meets in Rio de Janeiro, Brazil	1992 U.S. National debt exceed $3 trillion
1992 U.S. sends peacekeeping troops to Somalia	
1993 Medical research identifies genes linked to lethal diseases	1993 Federal forces besiege Bra Davidian religious cult in Texas 72 die
1993 U.S. and Russia sign treaty to reduce nuclear arms	
1995–1996 U.S. sends peacekeeping troops to Yugoslavia	1995 Republicans gain control Congress, promise to "downsiz government
	1995 Federal budget bill fails to U.S. government temporarily s down
	1996 President signs into law sv ing new telecommunications b
1997 British Colony of Hong Kong returned to Chinese rule	
1997 First mammal (Dolly, a sheep) successfully cloned	
1998 Emission limits set at Global Warming summit	1998 U.S. House of Representa impeaches President Clinton "high crimes and misdemeanc
1999 U.S. transfers full control of Panama Canal to Panama	1999 Following trial by U.S. Se President Clinton is acquitted
1999 Estimated world population 6 billion	

ociety and Culture

)89 *E.T.*, all-time top money-making movie, earns $228,618,939

)89–1990 Honda Accord is best-selling car in U.S.

'90 *Chorus Line*, longest-running Broadway show, closes after 6,317 performances

92 U.S. households with TVs, 98.2%; with refrigerators, 97.2%

92 Riots in Los Angeles, 52 dead, damage exceeds $1 billion

)93 Toni Morrison wins Nobel Prize for Literature

)3 Average salary for major-league baseball player rises to $1,076,089

)5 O.J. Simpson found not guilty n news media "Trial of the Century"

)5 Terrorists blow up Federal Building in Oklahoma City. 169 killed

8 Median age of Americans rises to 35 years, highest ever

8 Median U.S. family income, 44,568

8 Baseball star Mark McGuire its a record 70 homeruns

) Mexican drug traffic declared orst criminal threat to U.S. in last alf century

) Stock market reaches all-time igh. Dow Jones average exceeds 1,000

) Harry Potter novels become most opular children's books in history

Lives of Authors

LeRoi Jones (Amiri Baraka) 1934–

Saul Bellow 1915–2005

Joyce Carol Oates 1938–

John Updike 1932–

Edward Albee 1928–

Toni Morrison 1931–

2000

International Affairs, Exploration, Settlement, and Science

2000 Genome Project unlocks the mystery of the human blueprint

2000 Dot.com companies collapse, stock market tumbles

2000 First successful gene therapy saves infants from severe immune disorder

2001 Slobodan Milosevic, former Yugoslav President, becomes first head of state to be tried as war criminal in an international court

2001 Terrorists kill thousands in attack on New York City's World Trade Center, the Pentagon, and U.S. passenger airliner. Largest single-day loss of life through violence in U.S. history.

2002 Euro banknote becomes official currency for 12 European nations

2003 U.S. Shuttle disaster kills all crew members

2003 U.S. invades Iraq

2004 Spacecraft transmits photos of Saturn's rings

2004 U.S. death toll in Iraq exceeds 1000

2004 Human stem cells cloned for first time

2004 Price of oil rises above $50 a barrel

2004 Crimes of violence in U.S. fall to lowest level in 30 years

2005 Steve Fossett makes first solo flight, non-stop, around the earth

2005 Pope John Paul II dies.

Politics and Government

2000 George W. Bush elected 43rd U.S. President

2001 President Bush proposes anti- missile defense system to protec the U.S.

2001 U.S. Supreme Court disbars f mer President Clinton from pra ing law, for law violations, giving false testimony under oath.

2002 Enron scandal exposes corpo rate corruption.

2003 U.S. Supreme Court rules in of affirmative action at universiti

2004 CEO's of giant U.S. corporat indicted, convicted, sentenced fraud and obstruction of justice

2004 George W. Bush elected Pre dent for second term

2004 New immigration laws prop U.S. begins fingerprinting fore visitors.

2004 Proposed constitutional ban gay marriage fails to pass in U.S Senate

2005 President Bush nominates f head of new Department of H land Security

2005 Federal deficit for 2005 estimated to be $368 billion

00 Vermont becomes first state to recognize same-sex civil unions

01 AOL-Time Warner merger creates world's largest media business

01 San Francisco Giant Barry Bonds hits record 73 home runs

)2 Denzel Washington and Halle Berry win Oscars as best actors—the first time two African-Americans win in the same year

)2 Movies set U.S. box office record sales of $8.35 billion

)3 U.S. prison population increases o 2.2 million

)3 Attack by virus "Blaster Worm" disables 500,000 computers

)4 Picasso painting sells for record $104.1 million

)4 Lance Armstrong wins record-breaking 6th consecutive Tour de France bicycle race

)4 Marriage of gay couples begins n San Francisco

)4 Steroids scandals rock U.S. pro sports

)4 Former President Clinton's memoirs, *My Life*, break sales record, 500,000 sold on first day

)5 Spam intrusions and internet fraud rise to record high levels

)5 Nobel Prize winner Saul Bellow dies

Toni Morrison 1931–

Edward Albee 1928–

John Updike 1932–

Joyce Carol Oates 1938–

Saul Bellow 1915–2005

LeRoi Jones (Amiri Baraka) 1934–

Acknowledgments

CHRISTOPHER COLUMBUS, text excerpted from pages 57–59, 62–68, 73–77 from *Diario of Christopher Columbus's First Voyage to America, 1492–1493*, ed. Oliver C. Dunn and James E. Kelley, Jr. Copyright © 1988 by the University of Oklahoma Press. Reprinted by permission of the publisher.

PHILLIS WHEATLEY, "On Virtue," "To the University of Cambridge, in New England," "On Being Brought from Africa to America," "On Imagination," "To S. M. A Young African Painter, On Seeing His Works," "Recollection," "To His Excellency General Washington" from *The Trials of Phillis Wheatley*, ed. Julian Mason. Published by University of North Carolina Press.

EMILY DICKINSON, poems from *The Poems of Emily Dickinson*, ed. Thomas H. Johnson. Copyright 1951, © 1955, 1979, 1983 by the President and Fellows of Harvard College. (The Belknap Press of Harvard University Press.) Reprinted by permission of the publishers and the Trustees of Amherst College.

ROBERT FROST, "Stopping by Woods on a Snowy Evening" from *The Poetry of Robert Frost*, ed. Edward Connery Lethem. Copyright 1923, 1969 by Henry Holt and Company. Copyright 1951 by Robert Frost. Reprinted by permission of Henry Holt and Company, LLC.

EZRA POUND, "Canto I," "Canto II," "Canto XLV," and "Canto LXXXI" from *The Cantos of Ezra Pound*. Copyright 1934, 1937, 1940, 1948, © 1956, 1959, 1962, 1963, 1966, and 1968 by Ezra Pound. Reprinted by permission of New Directions Publishing Corp. "A Pact," "Hugh Selwyn Mauberley (1–V)," "In a Station of the Metro," "Portrait d'une Femme," "Salutation," and "The River-Merchant's Wife: A Letter" from *Personae* by Ezra Pound. Copyright 1926 by Ezra Pound. Reprinted by permission of New Directions Publishing Corp.

T. S. ELIOT, "The Love Song of J. Alfred Prufrock," "Preludes I–IV," "Gerontion," "The Waste Land" and "Journey of the Magi" from *Collected Poems 1909–1962* by T. S. Eliot. Copyright 1936 by Harcourt Brace & Company. Copyright 1936, © 1964 by T. S. Eliot. Reprinted by permission of Harcourt Brace & Company and Faber & Faber Ltd. "The Waste Land" and "Journey of the Magi" from *Collected Poems 1909–1962* by T. S. Eliot. Copyright 1936 by Harcourt Brace & Company. Copyright © 1963, 1964 by T. S. Eliot. Reprinted by permission of the publisher.

E. E. CUMMINGS, "All in green went my love riding" from *The Harvard Monthly*, March 1916. "in Just" from *The Dial Magazine*, January 1920.

"when god lets my body be" from *The Dial Magazine*, January 1920. "O sweet spontaneous" and "Buffalo Bill's defunct" from *The Dial Magazine*, May 1920. "the Cambridge ladies who live in furnished souls" from *Broom*, May 1922. "Poem, or beauty hurts Mr. Vinal" from *S · 4 · N*, December 1922. "my sweet old etcetera" and "anyone lived in a pretty how town" from *Complete Poems: 1904–1962* by E. E. Cummings, ed. George J. Firmage. Copyright 1940, © 1968, 1991 by the Trustees for the E. E. Cummings Trust. Copyright 1923, 1925, 1926, 1931, 1935, 1938, 1939, 1940, 1944, 1945, 1946, 1947, 1948, 1949, 1950, 1951, 1952, 1953, 1954, © 1955, 1956, 1957, 1958, 1959, 1960, 1961, 1961, 1962, 1963, 1966, 1967, 1968, 1972, 1973, 1974, 1975, 1976, 1977, 1978, 1979, 1980, 1981, 1982, 1983, 1984, 1985, 1986, 1987, 1988. 1989, 1990, 1991 by the Trustees for the E. E. Cummings Trust. Copyright © 1973, 1976, 1978, 1979, 1981, 1983, 1985, 1991 by George James Firmage. Used by permission of Liveright Publishing Corporation.

WALLACE STEVENS, "Peter Quince at the Clavier," 1915; "Disillusionment of Ten O'Clock," 1917; "Sunday Morning," 1917; "Bantams in Pine-Woods," 1922; "Anecdote of the Jar," 1919; "To the One of Fictive Music," 1922, "The Emperor of Ice-Cream," 1922. "Of Modern Poetry," "Final Soliloquy of the Interior Paramour," and "The Plain Sense of Things" from *The Collected Poems of Wallace Stevens* by Wallace Stevens. Copyright 1954 by Wallace Stevens, renewed 1982 by Holly Stevens. Used by permission of Alfred A. Knopf, a division of Random House, Inc.

WILLIAM CARLOS WILLIAMS, "At the Ball Game," "Between Walls," "Con Brio," "Danse Russe," "Pastoral," "Queen-Anne's-Lace," "Spring and All, Section I," "The Red Wheelbarrow," "The Young Housewife," "These," "This Is Just to Say," "To Elsie," and "Tract" from *Collected Poems: 1909–1939*, Volume I, by William Carlos Williams. Copyright 1938 by New Directions Publishing Corp. "Seafarer" from *Collected Poems 1939–1962*, Volume II, by William Carlos Williams. Copyright 1948 by William Carlos Williams. "Landscape with the Fall of Icarus" from *Collected Poems 1939–1962*, Volume II, by William Carlos Williams. Copyright 1953 by William Carlos Williams. Reprinted by Permission of New Directions Publishing Corp.

MARIANNE MOORE, "To a Steam Roller," "The Fish," "Poetry," and "No Swan So Fine" from *The Collected Poems of Marianne Moore* by Marianne Moore. Copyright 1935 by Marianne Moore. Renewed 1963 by Marianne Moore and T. S. Eliot. "In Distrust of Merits" from *The Collected Poems of Marianne Moore* by Marianne Moore. Copyright 1944, renewed 1972 by Marianne Moore. Reprinted by permission of Scribner, an imprint of Simon & Schuster Adult Publishing Group.

COUNTEE CULLEN, "Yet Do I Marvel," "For a Lady I Know," "Incident," "A Brown Girl Dead," and "Heritage" from *Color* by Countee Cullen. Copyright 1925 by Harper & Brothers. Renewed 1952 by Ida Cullen. "From a Dark Tower" from *Copper Sun* by Countee Cullen. Copyright 1927 by Harper & Brothers. Renewed 1954 by Ida Cullen. All reprinted by permission. Copyrights held by the Amistad Research Center, administered by Thompson and Thompson, New York, NY.

JEAN TOOMER, "Blood-Burning Moon" from *Cane* by Jean Toomer. Copyright 1923 by Boni & Liveright, renewed 1951 by Jean Toomer. Reprinted by permission of Liveright Publishing Corp.

THOMAS WOLFE, "Only the Dead Know Brooklyn" (pages 91–97) from *From Death to Morning* by Thomas Wolfe. Copyright 1935 by Charles Scribner's Sons. Copyright renewed 1963 by Paul Gitlin, Administrator C.T.A. Reprinted with the permission of Scribner, an imprint of Simon & Schuster Adult Publishing Group.

ERNEST HEMINGWAY, "The Killers" from *The Complete Short Stories of Ernest Hemingway.* Copyright 1927 by Charles Scribner's Sons. Copyright renewed 1955 by Ernest Hemingway. Reprinted with the permission of Scribner, an imprint of Simon & Schuster Adult Publishing Group.

WILLIAM FAULKNER, "That Evening Sun" from *Collected Stories of William Faulkner* by William Faulkner. Copyright 1931, renewed 1959 by William Faulkner. Reprinted by permission of Random House, Inc.

LANGSTON HUGHES, "The Negro Speaks of Rivers," 1921; "I, Too," "Young Gal's Blues," "Note on Commercial Theatre," "Dream Boogie," "Dream Deferred (Harlem)" from *The Colleted Poems of Langston Hughes* by Langston Hughes. Copyright © 1994 by The Estate of Langston Hughes. Used by permission of Alfred A. Knopf, a division of Random House, Inc.

JOHN STEINBECK, "Flight" from *The Long Valley* by John Steinbeck. Copyright 1938, renewed 1966 by John Steinbeck. Reprinted by permission of Viking Penguin, a division of Penguin Group (USA) Inc.

KATHERINE ANNE PORTER, "María Concepción" from *Flowering Judas and Other Stories* by Katherine Anne Porter, 1922.

EUDORA WELTY, "Death of a Traveling Salesman" from *A Curtain of Green and Other Stories* by Eudora Welty. Copyright 1941, renewed 1969 by Eudora Welty. Reprinted by permission of Harcourt, Inc.

RICHARD WRIGHT, "The Man Who Was Almost a Man" from *Eight Men* by Richard Wright. Copyright 1940, © 1961 by Richard Wright. Renewed 1989 by Ellen Wright. Introduction copyright © 1996 by Paul Gilroy. Reprinted by permission of HarperCollins Publishers, Inc.

RALPH ELLISON, "Battle Royal" from *Invisible Man* by Ralph Ellison. Copyright 1948 by Ralph Ellison. Reprinted by permission of Random House, Inc.

TENNESSEE WILLIAMS, *The Glass Menagerie* by Tennessee Williams. Copyright 1945 by The University of The South. Reprinted by permission of Georges Borchardt, Inc. for the Tennessee Williams Estate.

THEODORE ROETHKE, "Open House," copyright 1941 by Theodore Roethke; "Cuttings," copyright 1948 by Theodore Roethke; "Cuttings (Later)," copyright 1948 by Theodore Roethke; "Root Cellar," copyright 1943 by Modern Poetry Association, Inc.; "My Papa's Waltz," copyright 1942 by Hearst Magazines, Inc. from *Collected Poems of Theodore Roethke* by Theodore Roethke. Used by permission of Doubleday, a division of Random House, Inc.

ELIZABETH BISHOP, "A Miracle for Breakfast," "Brazil, January 1, 1502," "In the Waiting Room," and "Over 2,000 Illustrations and a Complete Concordance" from *The Complete Poems: 1927–1979* by Elizabeth Bishop. Copyright © 1979, 1984 by Alice Helen Methfessel. Reprinted by permission of Farrar, Straus and Giroux, LLC.

ROBERT LOWELL, "For the Union Dead," "Memories of West Street and Lepke," "Skunk Hour," and "Will Not Come Back" from *Collected Poems* by Robert Lowell. Copyright © 2003 by Harriet Lowell and Sheridan Lowell. Reprinted by permission of Farrar, Straus and Giroux, LLC. "Mr. Edwards and the Spider" from *Lord Weary's Castle* by Robert Lowell. Copyright 1946, renewed 1974 by Robert Lowell. Reprinted by permission of Harcourt, Inc.

ANNE SEXTON, "The Farmer's Wife" and "Ringing the Bells" from *To Bedlam and Part Way Back* by Anne Sexton. Copyright © 1960 by Anne Sexton. Renewed 1988 by Linda G. Sexton. "And One for My Dame" and "The Addict" from *Live or Die* by Anne Sexton. Copyright © 1996 by Anne Sexton. "Us" from *Love Poems* by Anne Sexton. Copyright © 1967, 1968, 1969 by Anne Sexton. "Rowing" from *The Awful Rowing Toward God* by Anne Sexton. Copyright © 1975 by Loring Conant, Jr., Executor of the Estate of Anne Sexton. All reprinted by permission of Houghton Mifflin Company. All rights reserved.

SYLVIA PLATH, "Two Views of a Cadaver Room" from *The Colossus and Other Poems* by Sylvia Plath. Copyright © 1962 by Sylvia Plath. Reprinted by permission of Alfred A. Knopf, a division of Random House, Inc. and Faber and Faber Ltd. "Ariel," "The Applicant," "Fever 103°," "Daddy," and "The Bee Meeting" from *Ariel* by Sylvia Plath. Copyright © 1965 by Ted Hughes. Renewed 1991 by Ted Hughes. Reprinted by permission of HarperCollins Publishers, Inc. and Faber and Faber Ltd. "Ariel," "The Applicant," "Fever 103°," "Daddy" and "The Bee Meeting" from *Ariel* by Sylvia Plath. Copyright © 1963, renewed 1991 by Ted Hughes. Reprinted by permission of HarperCollins Publishers, Inc. and Faber and Faber Ltd.

JAMES DICKEY, "The Lifeguard," "Reincarnation (1)," "In the Mountain Tent," "Cherrylog Road," and "The Shark's Parlor" from *The Whole Motion: Collected Poems* by James Dickey. Copyright © 1992 by James Dickey. Reprinted by permission of Wesleyan University Press.

W. S. MERWIN, "Grandfather in the Old Men's Home" and "The Drunk in the Furnace" from *The Drunk in the Furnace* by W. S. Merwin. Copyright ©

1956, 1957, 1958, 1959, 1960 by W. S. Merwin. "Noah's Raven" and "Separation" from *The Moving Target* by W. S. Merwin. Copyright © 1960, 1961, 1962, 1963 by W. S. Merwin. "The Dry Stone Mason" and "Fly" from *The Lice* by W. S. Merwin. Copyright © 1963, 1964, 1965, 1966, 1967 by W. S. Merwin. "Strawberries" and "Direction" from *Opening the Hand* by W. S. Merwin. Copyright © 1983 by W. S. Merwin. All reprinted by permission of The Wylie Agency.

LOUISE GLÜCK, "Vespers" and "Field Flowers" from *Wild Iris* by Louise Glück. Copyright © 1993 by Louise Glück. Reprinted by permission of HarperCollins Publishers. "Hesitate to Call," "The Chicago Train," "The Edge," "My Neighbor in the Mirror," and "Thanksgiving" from *Firstborn* by Louise Glück. Copyright © 1968, 1971, 1972, 1973, 1974, 1975, 1976, 1977, 1978, 1979, 1980, 1985 by Louise Glück. Reprinted by permission of HarperCollins Publishers.

JAMES BALDWIN, "Sonny's Blues," copyright © 1957 by James Baldwin was originally published in *Partisan Review*. Copyright renewed. Collected in *Going to Meet the Man*, published by Vintage Books. Used by arrangement with the James Baldwin Estate.

FLANNERY O'CONNOR, "Good Country People" from *A Good Man Is Hard to Find and Other Stories* by Flannery O'Connor. Copyright © 1955 by Flannery O'Connor, renewed 1983 by Regina O'Connor. Reprinted by permission of Harcourt, Inc.

JOHN UPDIKE, "Flight" from *Pigeon Feathers and Other Stories* by John Updike. Copyright © 1962, renewed 1990 by John Updike. Reprinted by permission of Alfred A. Knopf, a division of Random House, Inc.

BERNARD MALAMUD, "The Magic Barrel" from *The Magic Barrel* by Bernard Malamud. Copyright 195–0, © 1958, renewed 1978, 1986 by Bernard Malamud. Reprinted by permission of Farrar, Straus and Giroux, LLC.

AMIRI BARAKA, "In Memory of Radio," "The Bridge," and "Notes for a Speech" from *Preface to a Twenty-Volume Suicide Note* by Amiri Baraka. Copyright © 1961 by Amiri Baraka. "An Agony, As Now," "A Poem for Democrats," and "A Poem for Speculative Hipsters" from *The Dead Lecturer* by Amiri Baraka. Copyright © 1964 by Amiri Baraka. "A Poem Some People Will Have to Understand," "A Poem for Half-White College Students," and "Biography" from *Black Magic* by Amiri Baraka. Copyright © 1969 by Amiri Baraka. All reprinted with the permission of the Sterling Lord Literistic, Inc.

JUNE JORDAN, "All the World Moved," "In Memoriam: Martin Luther King, Jr.," and "Meta-Rhetoric" from *Things I Do in the Dark* by June Jordan. Copyright © 1977. Reprinted by permission of the Estate of June Jordan and the Watkins/Loomis Agency. "Poem About My Rights" from *Naming*

Our Destiny: New and Selected Poems by June Jordan. Copyright © 1989 by June Jordan. Appears by permission of the publisher, Carroll and Graff, a division of Avalon Publishing Group.

EDWARD ALBEE, *The Zoo Story* by Edward Albee. Copyright © 1959, renewed 1987 by Edward Albee. Reprinted by permission of William Morris Agency, LLC on behalf of Edward Albee.

SAUL BELLOW, "A Silver Dish" from *Him with His Foot in His Mouth and Other Stories* by Saul Bellow. Copyright © 1974, 1978, 1982, 1984 by Saul Bellow Ltd. Reprinted by permission of HarperCollins Publishers.

JOYCE CAROL OATES, "The Knife" from *Heat and Other Stories* by Joyce Carol Oates. Copyright © 1991 by The Ontario Review. Reprinted by permission of John Hawkins & Associates, Inc.

ALICE WALKER, "Everyday Use" from *In Love & Trouble: Stories of Black Women* by Alice Walker. Copyright © 1973 by Alice Walker. Reprinted by permission of Harcourt, Inc.

AMY TAN, "Half and Half" from *The Joy Luck Club* by Amy Tan. Copyright © 1989 by Amy Tan. Used by permission of G. P. Putnam's Sons, a division of Penguin Group (USA) Inc.

BOBBIE ANN MASON, "Shiloh" from *Shiloh and Other Stories* by Bobbie Ann Mason. Copyright © 1982 by Bobbie Ann Mason. Reprinted by permission of International Creative Manangement, Inc.

GLORIA NAYLOR, "Lucielia Louise Turner" from *The Women of Brewster Place* by Gloria Naylor. Copyright © 1980, 1982 by Gloria Naylor. Reprinted by permission of Viking Penguin, a division of Penguin Group (USA) Inc.

RAYMOND CARVER, "Cathedral" from *Cathedral* by Raymond Carver. Copyright © 1983 by Raymond Carver. Reprinted by permission of Alfred A. Knopf, a division of Random House, Inc.

SANDRA CISNEROS, "Mericans" from *Woman Hollering Creek and Other Stories* by Sandra Cisneros. Copyright © 1991 by Sandra Cisneros. Published by Vintage Books, a division of Random House, Inc., and originally in hardcover by Random House, Inc. Reprinted by permission of Susan Bergholz Literary Services, New York. All rights reserved.

LOUISE ERDRICH, "The Red Convertible" from *Love Medicine, New and Revised Edition* by Louise Erdrich. Copyright © 1983, 1993 by Louise Erdrich. Reprinted by permission of Henry Holt and Company, LLC.

TINA HOWE, "Painting Churches" from *Coastal Disturbances: Four Plays* by Tina Howe. Copyright © 1982 by Tina Howe. Reprinted by permission of Theatre Communications Group.

TONI MORRISON, "1922" from *Sula* by Toni Morrison. Copyright © 1974 by Toni Morrison. Reprinted by permission of International Creative Management, Inc.

DAVID MAMET, *House of Games* by David Mamet. Copyright © 1985, 1987 by David Mamet. Reprinted by permission of Grove/Atlantic, Inc.

JUDY BUTNITZ, "Where We Come From," excerpted from pages 3–28 from *Nice Big American Baby* by Judy Butnitz. Copyright © 2005 by Judy Budnitz. Used by permission of Alfred A. Knopf, a division of Random House, Inc.

Index to Authors, Titles, and First Lines

Note: First lines are set in roman type; all titles are italicized except titles of short works when listed under the main title of the works or under authors' names.

B

D

G

H

I

J

K

L

O

P

Q

R

S

T

Y

Z